D0935706

OFFICIAL USGA® RECORD BOOK 1895 - 1990

USGA CHAMPIONSHIPS AND INTERNATIONAL EVENTS

United States Golf Association®

Triumph Books, Inc.
Chicago

Library of Congress Catalog #92-64444

International Standard Book Number: 1-880141-39-6

For more information on the USGA®, contact:
United States Golf Association®
Golf House
Far Hills, New Jersey 07931

Triumph Books, Inc.
644 S. Clark Street Suite 2000
Chicago, Illinois 60605
312/939-3330

OFFICIAL USGA RECORD BOOK
TABLE OF CONTENTS

PART TWO: 1960 - 1980

PART THREE: 1981 - 1990

Part One

1895 - 1959

OPEN CHAMPIONS

ROBERT T. JONES, JR.
1923-26-29-30
Amateur Champion
1924-25-27-28-30

WILLIE ANDERSON
1901-03-04-05

JACK W. NICKLAUS
1962-67-72-80
Amateur Champion
1959-61

BEN HOGAN
1948-50-51-53

OPEN CHAMPIONSHIP

CHAMPIONSHIP CUP

Presented in 1895 by the

UNITED STATES GOLF ASSOCIATION

Original trophy destroyed by fire September, 1946.

Replaced by the Association in 1947.

HISTORY

1895–The first United States Open Championship conducted by the USGA was held on the nine-hole course of the Newport (R.I.) Golf Club on October 4, 1895, during the same week and on the same course as the first United States Amateur Championship. They had been scheduled for September and postponed because of a conflict with the America's Cup yacht races. Ten professionals and one amateur started the 36-hole, one-day competition. The winner, scoring 91-82–173 with the gutta percha ball, was Horace Rawlins, an English professional who had come over in January to be assistant at Newport. He was 21. There were five money prizes: $150, $100, $50, $25 and $10. Rawlins also won a $50 gold medal and, for his club, the Open Championship Cup, presented by the USGA.

1896–The second Open went to the 18-hole course of the Shinnecock Hills Golf Club, Southampton, N.Y., in July. Like the first, it was a side-show to the Amateur. However, there were 35 entrants and 28 finished the 36 holes. The course measured only 4,423 yards, and Jim Foulis, a Scottish professional representing the Chicago Golf Club, won with 78-74–152. The 74 set a record which was not broken until seven years later, after the rubber-core ball had come into use. Rawlins was runner-up, three strokes back.

1897–Chicago Golf Club entertained the 1897 men's championships on its 18-hole course in September. Having successfully bid for the competitions, the West also bid strongly for the titles, but Joe Lloyd, an English professional who worked at the Essex County Club, Manchester, Mass., in the summer and at Pau, France, in the winter, returned the Open to the East, scoring 83-79–162 to lead a field of 35. Willie Anderson, who was later to win four times, played for the first time and finished second, a stroke back.

1898–The British Open had been extended to 72 holes seven years earlier. The USGA decided to do the same in 1898. It also separated the Amateur and the Open Championships. The Open was played in June at the Myopia Hunt Club, South Hamilton, Mass., on a nine-hole course which required the competitors to go around eight times in the two allotted days. Fred Herd, a Scottish professional at the Washington Park course, Chicago, did the rounds in 84-85-75-84–328 to win. Alex Smith was second; he was later to win twice.

1899–Willie Smith, of the Carnoustie golfing family, had recently arrived to take a position as professional at the Midlothian Country Club, near Chicago, and he kept the title in Chicago by winning with 77-82-79-77–315 at the Baltimore Country Club, Roland Park Course in September. His margin of eleven strokes has never since been equalled. The first prize remained $150 and a gold medal, but the total purse for the first eight professionals, instead of five, was raised to $650.

1900–The Open title went abroad for the first time in 1900. Harry Vardon spent most of the year in the United States on an exhibition tour, and he was joined in October at the Chicago Golf Club by J. H. Taylor, another great of British golf. The two English professionals dominated the Championship, finishing first and second. Vardon's score was 79-78-76-80–313, two lower than Taylor's. It included a "whiff" on the final green, where he stabbed carelessly at a very short putt and missed the ball altogether.

1901–Willie Anderson, the dour, business-like Scottish professional who had missed tying Lloyd by a stroke in 1897, came through as a representative of the Pittsfield (Mass.) Country Club at the Myopia Hunt Club in June. His 84-83-83-81–331 created the first tie in the Championship, and he defeated Alex Smith in the playoff, 85 to 86. The 72-hole score remains the highest made by a winner, but more was to be heard from Anderson.

1902–Laurie Auchterlonie, representing the Chicago Golf Club, won at the Garden City (N.Y.) Golf Club, in October. For the first time in the Championship, 80 was broken in all four rounds as the Scot from St. Andrews posted 78-78-74-77–307. The introduction of the Haskell rubber-core ball in this Open was at least partly responsible for the lower scoring. Walter J. Travis, who had twice won the Amateur, tied for second. The entry of 90 was a new high, and there were now ten prizes totaling $970, the first of $200 and a gold medal.

1903–Willie Anderson, now playing from the Apawamis Club, Rye, N.Y., came back to win a second time at the Baltusrol Golf Club, Springfield, N.J., in June. In order to become the first repeat winner, he had to survive a second playoff. He tied David Brown by scoring 73-76-76-82–307 and then beat him, 82 to 84. The 73 was a new low.

1904–Willie Anderson won his third Open and his second in succession in July, this time at the scheduled distance. His score of 75-78-78-72–303 was best by five strokes at the Glen View Club, Golf,

Ill. The 72 again lowered the record for a single round. Gil Nicholls was second.

1905–Willie Anderson accomplished a feat at the Myopia Hunt Club in Septmeber which only the great were to approach. He won for the fourth time, the third in succession. Twenty-five years were to elapse before Bob Jones would win his fourth Open. Forty-eight years were to pass before Ben Hogan would win his fourth Open. Anderson's score was 81-80-76-77–314. He played from the Apawamis Club in winning the last three of his four championships.

1906–Alex Smith, of the Nassau Country Club, Glen Cove, N.Y., another Scot as congenial as Anderson was dour, ended Anderson's reign at the Onwentsia Club, Lake Forest, Ill., in June. Smith scored 73-74-73-75–295 to crack 300 for the first time and lead his brother Willie, the 1899 Champion now representing Mexico, by seven strokes. The 295 was the lowest score to have won either the British or United States Opens to that date. Jack White had set the British record of 296 in the 1904 British Open at the Royal St. Georges Golf Club, Sandwich, England. Anderson finished fifth. The purse was $900, to be divided among the first ten professionals, but the first prize was raised to $300 and a gold medal.

1907–Alex Ross, of another family of golfing brothers from Scotland, went down from the Brae Burn Country Club, near Boston, to win at the old St. Martin's course of the Philadelphia Cricket Club in June. His score was 76-74-76-76–302. Gil Nicholls was second for the second time.

1908–The smallest man to win, Fred McLeod, of the Midlothian Country Club, was the 1908 Champion. The Scot weighed only 108 pounds, but he played the Myopia Hunt Club course in 82-82-81-77–322 to tie with Willie Smith, of Mexico, and won the playoff, 77 to 83. It marked the fourth and last time Myopia entertained the Championship.

1909–Homebreds had appeared to be simply building character in the early years, but the character they built came to light at the Englewood (N.J.) Golf Club in June. Tom McNamara, representing the Wollaston Golf Club, near Boston, scored 69 in the second round to lead the field through the first day with 142, and his fine play forced George Sargent, an English professional from Hyde Manor, Vt., to set a new record of 75-72-72-71–290 to win. McNamara was second, four strokes back, and the era of the homebreds was dawning. Seventy was broken for the first time in this Championship. The first to do it was Dave Hunter, who made a 68 in the first round but took 84 in the second round and finished far back at 313.

1910–Alex Smith, now playing from the Wykagyl Country Club, New Rochelle, N.Y., won his second Open, and the third for his family, at the St. Martin's course of the Philadelphia Cricket Club in June. There occurred the first three-way playoff in which Alex scored 71, homebred Johnny McDermott made 75 and Alex' brother Macdonald took 77. Alex' score for the original 72 holes was 73-73-79-73–298.

1911–Johnny McDermott, of the Atlantic City (N.J.) Country Club, became the first homebred Champion at the Chicago Golf Club in June. He was a self-assured, determined alumnus of the Philadelphia caddie sheds and feared no one on a golf course. In this Championship he shot 81-72-75-79–307 to play himself into a second three-way tie, with Mike Brady and George Simpson. Then he played himself out of it with an 80 to Brady's 82 and Simpson's 85. The day of complete British supremacy had ended.

1912–To prove the point, Johnny McDermott won his second consecutive Open at the Country Club of Buffalo, N.Y., in August, and immediately behind him was that other homebred, Tom McNamara. McDermott's score was 74-75-74-71–294, and he needed it to stave off McNamara, who closed with another 69 to trail by only two strokes. The rise of the homebreds stimulated such interest that it lifted the entry to 131, another record. McDermott's total of 294 was two below par. He is now credited as being the first man to break par for 72 holes. The use of "par" came into official national usage in 1911 when the USGA defined it as "perfect play without flukes and under ordinary weather conditions, always allowing two strokes on each putting green."

1913–The homebred groundswell reached a climax at The Country Club, Brookline, Mass., in September. Francis Ouimet, of the Woodland (Mass.) Golf Club, who had learned the game as a Brookline caddie and continued to play as an amateur, won at the age of 20 and in his first try over the veteran British professionals, Harry Vardon and Ted Ray. The first amateur to win, his victory caught the fancy of the multitude and contributed largely to the popularity of the game. Ouimet finished late, in the rain, with a birdie and a par to complete a 77-74-74-79 and tie Vardon and Ray at 304, 20 over par. In the third three-way playoff, he made a 72 to Vardon's 77 and Ray's 78. McDermott finished eighth. Another new record of 165 entrants was established, which required the first qualifying round in the history of the Championship. Half the field played two rounds on Tuesday and the other half two on Wednesday, the low 32 and ties each day making up the field for the Championship proper on Thursday and Friday.

1914–The homebreds now popped up like spring flowers. A Country Club of Rochester, N.Y., professional named Walter Hagen, who in his first appearance had finished fourth at Brookline, came on to win in August at the Midlothian Country Club. He led every round and equalled George Sargent's mark with 68-74-75-73–290, two over par, yet he had only a stroke over a homebred amateur, Charles Evans, Jr. Evans needed a 2 to tie on the last hole, and his pitch hit the cup and bounced out. As Hagen came onto the scene, McDermott faded off; it was his last Championship.

1915–Jerome D. Travers, an amateur from the Upper Montclair (N.J.) Country Club, followed the trail which Ouimet had blazed. Travers already had won the Amateur four times, and he achieved his ambition in the Open by playing the last six holes in one under par to beat Tom McNamara by a stroke. The Championship was at the Baltusrol (N.J.) Golf

Club in June and Travers' score was 76-72-73-76–297, nine over par.

1916–The amateurs underscored their mastery at the Minikahda Club, Minneapolis, Minn., in June. Charles Evans, Jr., of the Edgewater Golf Club, Chicago, the third amateur winner in four years, not only won but broke par over four rounds for the second time and lowered the record by four strokes. His score was 70-69-74-73–286, two under par and a mark that was to stand for 20 years. Jock Hutchison closed with a 68 and also bettered the old record, but he was two strokes shy of a tie. Travers did not defend. The purse was increased this year to $1,200, with $500 and a gold medal for the leading professional, but there were still only 10 money places. Evans won the Amateur three months later and was the first to win both in the same year.

1917-1918–There were no Open Championships during World War I, but the USGA conducted a similar tournament for the benefit of the Red Cross at the Whitemarsh Valley Country Club, Chestnut Hill, Pa., in June, 1917. Jock Hutchison won with 292 and Tom McNamara was second with 299.

1919–When the Open was resumed in June at the Brae Burn Country Club, West Newton, Mass., Walter Hagen, now playing from the Oakland Hills Country Club, near Detroit, restored the prestige of the professionals. He played the last six holes in one under fours to overhaul Mike Brady with a 75 in the last round and then won a playoff marked by several controversies over the Rules, 77 to 78. Hagen's first four rounds were 78-73-75-75 for 301, seventeen over par. Meanwhile, Willie Chisholm took 18 on the 185-yard eighth hole in the first round. The purse was increased again, to $1,745; first professional prize remained $500, but other prizes were increased and eleventh and twelfth places were added. For the first time, play was extended to three days, with one round on each of the first two days and two rounds on the third.

1920–The Open Championship went abroad for the second time in August. Ted Ray and Harry Vardon came over from England again to play at the Inverness Club, Toledo, Ohio. With seven holes to go, Vardon was leading by five strokes, but a gale came up and Vardon, who was 50 years old, played the last seven holes in even 5s. Ray was the winner, with 74-73-73-75–295, seven over par, and Vardon finished in a four-way tie for second, one stroke back, with Leo Diegel, Jock Hutchison and Jack Burke. Ray was 43 years old and remains the oldest winner. An amateur named Bob Jones played for the first time, and finished in a tie for eighth at 299; he was 18 years old. The entry rose to another new high of 265. The two-day format for the Championship proper was restored.

1921–Jim Barnes, an Englishman representing the Pelham (N.Y.) Country Club, won the 25th Championship with remarkable ease over a strong, international field in July, 1921, at the Columbia Country Club, Chevy Chase, Md. His 69-75-73-72–289, nine over par, enabled him to lead after every round and win by nine strokes over Walter Hagen and Fred McLeod. Bob Jones tied for fifth at 303. Warren G. Harding, President of the United States, presented the trophy to Barnes.

1922–Gene Sarazen, 20 years old, burst onto the scene at the Skokie Country Club, Glencoe, Ill., in July. Representing the Highland Country Club, Pittsburgh, he scored 72-73-75 to stand four strokes behind Bob Jones and Bill Mehlhorn going into the last round, then finished with a 68, including a birdie on the last hole, to win by a stroke with 288–eight over par. Bob Jones and John Black, who was 43 and a grandfather, tied for second. It was the best finishing round so far, and an omen of Sarazen's future. The entry set another record of 323, and the qualifying at the scene of the Championship had to be extended to three days. Spectators were charged admission fees for the first time.

1923–Bob Jones' era really opened at the Inwood (N.Y.) Country Club in July, 1923. The amateur from the East Lake course in Atlanta, Ga., was leading after three rounds of 71-73-76 but finished with a two-over-par 6 on the last hole and a 76 for 296, eight over par. Bobby Cruickshank, playing behind him, birdied that last hole, and the two entered a playoff. They were even again going up the last fairway, but Cruickshank had pulled his tee shot and had to play his second short of the lagoon guarding the green. Jones hit a No. 2 iron shot nearly 200 yards from the rough over the lagoon to the green to make his 4 and win 76 to 78. It was his first major Championship. The entry of 360 set still another record, and qualifying at the scene of the Championship required four days. Since the Championship proper took two more days and the playoff another day, a full week was needed to determine the Champion.

1924–Cyril Walker, an Englishman almost as little as Fred McLeod, won at the Oakland Hills Country Club in June. Representing the Englewood (N.J.) Golf Club, he scored a deliberate 74-74-74-75–297, nine over par. Jones, who had finished earlier with a birdie 4 against the wind on the long finishing hole for 300, led until Walker completed his round. Jones finished second. The first elements of sectional qualifying were introduced; eastern and western elimination rounds were held in May at Worcester, Mass., and Oak Park, Ill., and the low 40 and ties at each place qualified for the Championship proper. Use of the steel-shafted putter was permitted for the first time.

1925–Willie Macfarlane tied Bob Jones at 291–seven over par–and they had to play off twice before Macfarlane won at the Worcester (Mass.) Country Club in June. In the first playoff, both scored 75s, marking the first time a playoff, too, had ended in a tie. Jones went four strokes ahead on the first nine of the second playoff, but Macfarlane caught him with a 72 to Jones' 73. The Scot, who wore glasses and represented the Oak Ridge Golf Club, Tuckahoe, N.Y., had scored 74-67-72-78 in the Championship proper, and had been one of five, including Francis Ouimet, Johnny Farrell, Leo Diegel and Walter Hagen, to come to the final hole with a chance to win or tie. His 67 was a new low. Preliminary elimination rounds were held at three points: Long Beach, N.Y., Lake Forest, Ill., and San

Francisco, Calif., and the entry record jumped again to 445. The Championship proper was the last condensed into two days.

1926–Bob Jones had won his first British Open during a spring tour of the British Isles and took his second United States Open at the Scioto Country Club, Columbus, Ohio, in July. It was the first time a player had won both in the same year. Despite a depressing second round in which he called a penalty on himself when his ball turned over as he was addressing a putt, he came from behind with a birdie 4 on the last hole to complete a 70-79-71-73–293, five over par, and beat Joe Turnesa by a stroke. The Championship was again extended to three days, with one round each of the first two days and two on the third day. There were 17 sectional qualifying rounds and the system was well established. So was the popularity of the Open; the entry rose to another new high of 694. The purse was increased, too, to $2,145 by the addition of eight places so that the first 20 professionals were rewarded in cash, although first prize remained $500.

1927–Tommy Armour, a Scot who had recently turned professional, holed a 10-footer for a birdie on the last green to tie Harry Cooper at the Oakmont (Pa.) Country Club in June. Cooper had three-putted the 71st green but still had seemed a winner. Their scores of 301 were 13 over par and the highest of modern times, in testimony to the terrors of the course. Armour, representing the Congressional Country Club, near Washington, D.C., won the playoff, 76 to 79; his first four rounds were 78-71-76-76. Jones made his poorest showing, with a 309 that left him tied for eleventh. Again the entry rose, this time to 898. The professional competition for the Ryder Cup was played in this country for the first time, at Worcester, and the British team participated in this Championship, Archie Compston made the best showing, tying for seventh with 308.

1928–Johnny Farrell, of the Quaker Ridge Golf Club, Scarsdale, N.Y., and Bob Jones played to another tie, with 294s, 10 over par, at the Olympia Fields Country Club, Matteson, Ill., in June. The playoff distance had been increased to 36 holes, and Farrell won it with a 70-73–143 to Jones' 73-71–144. Farrell's Championship rounds had been 77-74-71-72. The entry rose above 1,000 for the first time, as 1,064 attempted to qualify.

1929–Bob Jones took two 7s on his final round and had to hole a 12-foot putt on the last green to tie Al Espinosa at the West Course of the Winged Foot Golf Club, Mamaroneck, N.Y., in June. Jones' score was 69-75-71-79–294–six over par. In his fourth playoff, however, he was invincible; his 72-69–141 was 23 strokes better than Espinosa's 84-80–164. The purse now was $5,000. First professional prize was $1,000, instead of $500, and the rewards for the other leaders also were substantially increased, although none after those tied for 20th place was rewarded.

1930–The third trick of Bob Jones' Grand Slam was played at the Interlachen Country Club, Minneapolis, Minn., in July. He had won the British Amateur and the British Open. After three rounds he had a five-stroke lead in the United States Open, thanks in part to a half-topped spoon shot which skipped across the lake to set up a birdie 4 at the ninth hole in the second round. His 68 in the third round also contributed heavily. It was his lowest round ever in the Open. Yet he had to make three birdies on the last five holes and hole a 40-footer on the last green to win by two strokes over Macdonald Smith. His score of 71-73-68-75–287, one under par, was his best in eleven Opens, and it marked the third time par over four rounds was broken. After completing the Grand Slam by winning the Amateur, he retired at the age of 28. The entry rose to 1,177, another new record. This Open was the last for the ball no smaller than 1.62 inches in diameter and no heavier than 1.62 ounces.

1931–When Bob Jones retired, a wide-open and keen struggle was anticipated, but not such a lengthy struggle as was waged at the Inverness Club, Toledo, Ohio, in July. George Von Elm made a birdie 3 on the last hole to tie Billy Burke, of the Round Hill Club, Greenwich, Conn., at 292, eight over par, and 72 additional holes were required to determine the winner. Burke won by a stroke. Burke's score in the Championship proper was 73-72-74-73. In the first 36-hole playoff, Burke did 73-76–149 but Von Elm again birdied the last hole to tie with 75-74–149. In the second 36-hole playoff, Burke made 77-71–148 to Von Elm's 76-73–149. The margin between them thus was one stroke, acquired five holes from the finish, in 144 holes of golf, the most ever required to determine a Champion. The so-called "balloon" ball, no smaller than 1.68 inches in diameter and no heavier than 1.55 ounces, which had been used experimentally and optionally in the previous two years, was standard this year.

1932–Gene Sarazen won the British Open and came home in June to play the last 28 holes in 100 strokes and win the United States Open, too, at the old Fresh Meadow Country Club, Flushing, N.Y. He was seven strokes behind as he came to the ninth tee on the morning of the final day, and he decided to throw caution to the winds. A birdie 2 on that hole and a 32 on the second nine gave him a 70 and left him only one stroke off the pace. The final 18 he played in 66, the lowest round in the Championship to that date, to win by three strokes. He was representing the Lakeville Golf and Country Club, Great Neck, N.Y., and his full score of 74-76-70-66–286, six over par, tied the mark Evans had set 16 years earlier. The victory made him the second man, after Jones, who did it twice, to win the British and United States Opens in the same year. The present ball, no smaller than 1.68 inches in diameter and no heavier than 1.62 ounces, replaced the "balloon" ball.

1933–Johnny Goodman, an amateur, played away to one of the Open's longest leads, then turned conservative and won by only a stroke at the North Shore Golf Club, Glen View, Ill., in June. Goodman started with a 75 and a 66 to lead at the halfway mark, extended his lead to six strokes with a 70 in the third round and started his last round 4-3-2, three less than par. Yet he fell away to a 76 for 287, one under par, and Ralph Guldahl would have tied him if his iron shot to the last green had been true for a 4, instead of fading into a bunker for a 5. Goodman, the fourth man to break par in the Open, played from the Omaha (Neb.) Field Club and was the fifth and last amateur to win: like Ouimet, Evans and Jones, he was not to win his Amateur Championship until later, four years later in his case.

1934—Olin Dutra, of the Brentwood Country Club, Los Angeles, Calif., reversed Goodman's procedure in winning at the East course of the Merion Cricket Club, in Ardmore, Pa., in June. His 76-74 in the first two rounds left him eight strokes back starting the final 36 holes. Among the 17 men ahead of him were nearly all the great professionals of the times. On top of this, he was seriously upset by a stomach ailment. Yet his strokes on the last day were true as a surveyor's measure through all of Merion's hazards, and he caught and passed the pack with rounds of 71 and 72 for 293, −13 over par—to lead Gene Sarazen by one. That deficit of eight strokes was the largest a winner has made up over the final 36 holes in modern times. Arnold Palmer matched it in 1960.

1935—Sam Parks, of Pittsburgh, used his knowledge of the Oakmont (Pa.) Country Club to win in June. Although a comparatively recent convert from college and amateur ranks and little known nationally, Parks, professional at the nearby South Hills Country Club, was the only player to negotiate Oakmont's furrowed bunkers and shaved greens in less than 300. He won by posting a 77-73-73-76—299, eleven over par. Jimmy Thomson, who had been tied with him for the lead going into the final round, fell two strokes behind in his attempt to match or beat that figure. It was a heart-breaking Championship for many; none of the 20 leaders was able to break 75 in the last round.

1936—Tony Manero, of the Sedgefield Club, Greensboro, N.C., lifted himself from comparative obscurity with a final-round of 67 for 282, six under par, to break the record by four strokes over the Upper Course of the Baltusrol Golf Club, Springfield, N.J. Harry Cooper's 284 already had broken by two strokes Evans' and Sarazen's record which had stood for 20 years and all the principal challengers appeared to have foundered when Manero played out his brilliant finish, posting 73-69-73-67. Manero was six under, Cooper was four under and Clarence Clark was one under. As the scores went down, the entry went up, and the 1,277 who competed in sectional qualifying set another high mark. Among them was a young professional named Ben Hogan, who got to Baltusrol but failed to qualify for the last 36 holes.

1937—Ralph Guldahl, an unattached professional from Chicago, who had just missed four years earlier, made short work of Manero's record at the Oakland Hills Country Club. With another great finish, he completed a score of 71-69-72-69—281, seven under par. He beat Sam Snead, playing in his first Open, by two strokes. In all, five players were under par for the four rounds. The entry increased again to a new high of 1,402.

1938—Ralph Guldahl became the fourth player, after Willie Anderson, Johnny McDermott and Bob Jones, to win in successive years, and he did it easily. With a score of 74-70-71-69—284, even par, he built a lead of six strokes over Dick Metz at the Cherry Hills Country Club, Denver, Colo. This Championship also was distinguished by a new record for strokes taken on a single hole; Ray Ainsley took 19 on the par-4 16th hole in the second round, most of them in trying to extricate his ball from a brook. Prize money was increased to $6,000 by the addition of awards to those finishing from 21st to 30th; first prize remained $1,000.

1939—Byron Nelson, of the Reading (Pa.) Country Club, made up five strokes in his last round and posted 72-73-71-68—284, eight over par over the Spring Mill Course of the Philadelphia Country Club. Sam Snead came to the last hole needing a par 5 to win, took 8 and finished fifth. Craig Wood came along later needing a birdie 4 to tie and made it. Denny Shute came up last needing two pars to win but lost a stroke on the 17th hole and created the fourth three-way tie. In the first playoff, Wood appeared to have the Championship in hand, but Nelson birdied the last hole and they tied again at 68; Shute had 76 and was eliminated. In the second playoff, Nelson was in such form that he holed a full No. 1 iron shot for an eagle 2 at the fourth hole, and he won with a 70 to Wood's 73. Marvin H. Ward, who was to win the Amateur later in the season, finished fourth, one stroke out of the triple tie.

1940—Lawson Little placed a 72-69-73-73—287, one under par, on the scoreboard and then stood by while Gene Sarazen finished with three pars to tie. Little played superb golf to win the playoff, 70 to 73, at the Canterbury Golf Club, near Cleveland, Ohio. Little was playing from Bretton Woods, N.H., and had turned professional after winning the USGA and the British Amateur Championships in 1934 and 1935. He was the sixth man to win both Amateur and Open Championships. Sarazen was 38 years old and was making his bid eighteen years after he had won his first Open. Six players were disqualified for starting their last rounds ahead of schedule, with a storm brewing; they played out the round provisionally and one of them, Ed Oliver, made an unofficial 287.

1941—Craig Wood, of the Winged Foot Golf Club, Mamaroneck, N.Y., shared or held the lead after each of the last three rounds and won with 73-71-70-70—284, four over par, at the Colonial Club, Fort Worth, Texas. Wood was in pain throughout the Championship because of a back injury, and he wore a corset for support. He considered withdrawing before the Open began. He won by three strokes over Denny Shute. Rain was so heavy and lightning so severe during the second round that twice play was stopped. The Colonial course was comparatively new, having been opened in 1936.

1942-1945—Open Championships were suspended again during World War II. Instead of the competition which had been scheduled for the Interlachen Country Club, Minneapolis, a Hale America National Open was conducted in June, 1942, at the Ridgemoor Country Club, Chicago, in cooperation with the Chicago District Golf Association and the Professional Golfers' Association of America. Ben Hogan, of the Hershey (Pa.) Country Club, won with a score of 72-62-69-68—271, 17 under par. His remarkable score was three strokes lower than those of Mike Turnesa and Jimmy Demaret. Bob Jones, then a captain in the Army, came out of retirement to play and scored 290. The competition was played for the benefit of the United Service Organizations and the Navy Relief Society, which divided $25,745.27. Prizes distributed were in the form of defense bonds.

1946–When the Open was resumed at the Canterbury Golf Club, Cleveland, it was won, appropriately, by Lloyd Mangrum, of Los Angeles, an ex-soldier who had fought and earned the Purple Heart overseas. On the last day of the Championship proper, which was attended by the largest crowds to that time, Vic Ghezzi set the stage by posting a 284, four under par. Mangrum and Byron Nelson, playing together behind him, remained in the contention. Nelson had incurred a penalty stroke in the third round when his caddie had accidentally kicked his ball, but he could still win by two strokes if he finished with three pars. Mangrum was only a stroke behind him. Nelson three-putted the next-to-last green and took a 5 on the last hole to tie Ghezzi. Mangrum held steady and made it the fifth three-way tie. Ben Hogan and Herman Barron, each needed three pars to win, but they failed by a stroke of even tying. These five and four others all were under par for four rounds, the most ever. In the first playoff, Mangrum once had a lead of four strokes, but at the end all three were tied again with 72s. In the second playoff, Mangrum was three strokes behind Ghezzi and two behind Nelson with six holes to play. He birdied three of them, survived a sharp thunderstorm and won in rain under darkening skies with another 72, to 73s by Nelson and Ghezzi. Mangrum's original four rounds were 74-70-68-72. The purse was increased to $8,000, and the first professional prize was increased to $1,500.

1947–Lew Worsham, of the Oakmont (Pa.) Country Club, scored 70-70-71-71–282, two under par, and defeated Sam Snead in a playoff, 69 to 70, at the St. Louis (Mo.) Country Club. They finished 72 holes three strokes ahead of the field. A dramatic moment occurred when Snead came to the last hole needing a birdie 3 to tie; he made it with an 18-foot putt. Snead had less fortune on the last green of the playoff, he missed a putt of less than a yard after being interrupted by Worsham who asked for a measurement as Snead was about to putt. If he had made the putt, Worsham would have had to make his slightly shorter putt to tie. As it was, Worsham made his putt and won. James B. McHale, Jr., an amateur, set a new 18-hole record when he played the course in 30-35–65 in the third round. The purse was increased again, the total to $10,000 for the first 30 professionals and first prize to $2,000; and the competition was for a new cup, the original having been destroyed in a fire at the Tam O'Shanter Country Club during the winter. This Championship was the first to be televised locally.

1948–Ben Hogan, of the Hershey (Pa.) Country Club, was again a favorite, as he had been for some years, and this time he won exactly as expected at the Riviera Country Club, Los Angeles. His score of 67-72-68-69–276 was five below Ralph Guldahl's record for the Championship and eight below par, another record in itself. Jimmy Demaret, with 278, and Jim Turnesa, with 280, also were under the old Championship record in finishing two-three, and altogether five players were under par. The entry record rose again to 1,411.

1949–Dr. Cary Middlecoff, a dentist who had left the amateur ranks two years previously, and Clayton Heafner came down the stretch together, matching shot for shot. Middlecoff went ahead with a par on the 15th hole and completed 75-67-69-75–286, two over par, while Heafner missed a putt for a birdie on the last green and trailed by a stroke. Sam Snead, playing later, needed 33 on the last nine to tie but lost a stroke at the par-3 17th hole, where he needed three strokes to get down from just off the green. He tied for second place with Heafner. Play was over the No. 3 course of the Medinah (Ill.) Country Club. Hogan had been severely injured in an automobile accident in February and could not compete.

1950–Ben Hogan achieved the miracle victory in the 50th Open Championship over the East course of the Merion Golf Club. Sixteen months after a nearly fatal automobile crash in Texas, Hogan was still walking in some discomfort, but he played an exacting course in 72-69-72-74–287, seven over par, and tied Lloyd Mangrum and George Fazio. The final 36 holes marked the first time Hogan had attempted two rounds in a single day since his injury. He lost strokes to par on the 15th and 17th holes of the last round when he seemed to have the Championship won. It was the 18th tie, and the sixth three-way tie, in fifty Championships, and as in all but four of the previous deadlocks, it was settled in one round. Hogan came back to play a flawless 69 which won over Mangrum's 73 and Fazio's 75. Mangrum trailed by only a stroke with three holes to play but thoughtlessly picked up his ball to blow off an insect at the 16th green and incurred a two-stroke penalty. The record for a single round fell when Lee Mackey, Jr., opened with a 33-31–64; but he finished in a tie for 25th at 297. Prize money was increased again to approximately $15,000; the first professional now received $4,000 and every professional who returned a 72-hole score was assured of at least $100.

1951–Ben Hogan, still representing the Hershey (Pa.) Country Club, rose to more great heights at the Oakland Hills Country Club. The revamped course was perhaps as difficult as any on which the Open had been played. Hogan already had won in both of his last two tries. Despite Willie Anderson's record in the early days, the law of averages seemed against him. His first two rounds left him five strokes off the pace. Yet Hogan tamed course, fellow-competitors and the law of averages with 76-73-71-67–287, seven over par, to lead Clayton Heafner by two strokes. The 67 he considered his greatest single round to that time, and he made it by playing the last nine in 32. The only other sub-par round of the Championship was Heafner's closing 69. From the standpoint of attendance, this was the most successful in the series, and the entry, too, rose to a new high of 1,511.

1952–Julius Boros, of the Mid Pines Club, N.C., who had been a professional only two and a half years, interrupted the spell Hogan was casting over the Championship. An early starter in the final two rounds, he completed a 71-71-68-71–281, one over par, at the Northwood Club, Dallas, Texas. Hogan started with two 69s to tie the 36-hole record of 138, but he closed with two 74s on a very hot day. On the last green, Hogan's playing companion, Ed Oliver, holed a 50-putt for a birdie to finish second at 285 and Hogan had to be content with third place at 286. The entry of 1,688 set still another new high.

1953–Ben Hogan came back to win his fourth Open Championship and match the record of Willie Anderson and Bob Jones. He won in convincing fashion, too, over the testing course of the Oakmont Country Club, Oakmont, Pa., by leading at the end of every round. His scores were 67-72-73-71–283. A 3-3-3 finish, a par and two birdies, put him five strokes under par and gave him a margin of six strokes over Sam Snead, who was runnerup for the fourth time. Hogan was the first to hold the lead throughout the Championship since 1921, and the margin was the widest since 1938. A revised form was tested in this Championship and subsequently abandoned. After the sectional qualifying rounds, 299 qualifiers and exempt players competed in a second qualifying round over two courses to determine the 150 starters in the Championship proper. Jimmy Clark led these rounds with a 72 at Pittsburgh Field Club and a 66 at Oakmont for 138, and the low 150 and ties, actually 157, thereby became eligible to join Julius Boros in the Championship proper. Prize money was increased by approximately $5,000 to $20,400. The winner received $5,000.

1954–Ed Furgol, 37, of the Westwood Country Club, St. Louis, Mo., won a particularly significant victory over the Lower Course of the Baltusrol Golf Club, Springfield, N.J. He had shattered his left elbow in childhood and his left arm was withered and crooked at the elbow. He scored 71-70-71-72–284, four over par, to finish one stroke ahead of Gene Littler, 23, the 1953 Amateur Champion who had turned professional and who led after 36 holes. There was a moment of drama on the last hole when Furgol pulled his drive deep into woods, pitched out onto the 18th fairway of the Upper Course and made his par 5. Littler later missed an eight-foot putt to tie. Ben Hogan, seeking his fifth Open victory, was tied for second with Furgol going into the final day, but he took 76 for his third round and finished in a tie for sixth at 289. Billy Joe Patton, of Morganton, N.C., an amateur, led on the first day with a 69, remained a threat throughout and also finished in the tie for sixth. The event was a record-breaker: the entry reached 1,928, the gallery was 39,600, the largest ever, the play was televised nationally for the first time, every fairway was completely roped from tee to green for the first time in a USGA Championship, and prize money, increased by a 20 per cent bonus, totalled $23,280, with the first professional prize $6,000.

1955–Jack Fleck, 32, a municipal-course professional in Davenport, Iowa, playing his first full year on the tournament tour, made two birdies on the last four holes to tie Ben Hogan and then beat him in a playoff at the Lake Course of the Olympic Country Club, San Francisco. Hogan, 43, appeared to have won his fifth Open when he finished with 287, but he never was ahead in the playoff and trailed by three strokes after ten holes. However, he was only one stroke behind as they went to the 18th tee, but there his foot slipped and he drove his ball into very deep rough far to the left. It took him three strokes to move it back to the fairway. Fleck scored 69, Hogan 72. Fleck's first four rounds were 76-69-75-67–287; there were only seven rounds below the par of 70 in the Championship, and he made three of them. Exemptions from sectional qualifying were reduced; of the former Champions, only the last five individuals to win remained eligible to play at San Francisco, and of the leaders in the previous year only the first ten, other than former Champions, remained exempt.

1956–Cary Middlecoff, 35, representing the Riverlake Country Club, Dallas, Texas, won his second Open Championship with a score of 71-70-70-70–281, one over par, over the East Course of the Oak Hill Country Club, Rochester, N.Y. After an opening day devoted to a series of unusual questions on the Rules of Golf, the event developed into a drama on the final day as Ben Hogan, Julius Boros and Ted Kroll successively moved into striking positions after Middlecoff had posted his score. First, Hogan came to the 70th needing three pars to tie. He missed by a stroke when a putt of 30 inches on the 71st failed to drop, and he finished with 282. Then Boros needed one birdie in the last three to tie. His birdie putt on the last hole hit the hole but spun out. He had to be content with three straight pars and a second-place tie with Hogan at 282. Finally, Kroll, needing four pars to win, went 4-7-5-4 against par of 3-4-4-4. A hooked drive under a tree on No. 70 contributed to his undoing. He finished in a tie for fourth with Ed Furgol and Peter Thomson, the British Open Champion, at 285. Ken Venturi, of San Francisco, Calif., finished strongly to place eighth at 289 and lead the amateurs. Jack Fleck, of Davenport, Iowa, the defending Champion, scored 150 for the first two rounds and failed by one shot to qualify for the final 36 holes.

1957–Dick Mayer, 32, of St. Petersburg, Fla., scored 70-68-74-70–282, two over par, was tied by Cary Middlecoff, the defending Champion, and won in a playoff, 72 to 79, at the Inverness Club, Toledo, Ohio. Jimmy Demaret, 47, of Kiamesha Lake, N.Y., finished one stroke behind. Demaret had shared the lead at 18 holes with 68 and had led Mayer by a stroke at 54 holes with 211. Mayer and Billy Joe Patton, an amateur, had shared the lead at 36 holes with scores of 138, equalling the record. Middlecoff's 68-68 finish equalled the record of 136 for the last 36 holes; Gene Sarazen did 70-66–136 in 1932. Patton finished in a tie for eighth at 290 and was low amateur for the second time. Ben Hogan, of Fort Worth, Texas, was unable to try for a fifth victory. Pleurisy of the chest wall caused him such pain that he had to withdraw from the first round after his starting time had been postponed an hour to give him an opportunity for medical treatment. A storm near noon on the first day brought not only rain, but winds of nearly 60 miles per hour. Play was suspended for 1 hour, 10 minutes, and five groups were unable to finish until the morning of the second day. The third day's gallery was estimated at 16,527, and the three-day gallery at 39,696, USGA Championship records for one and three days. The first and second-day attendances were 11,035 and 12,134, slightly under the 1954 figures which represented the previous high. Each professional prize was again increased by 20 per cent, and the total reached a new peak of nearly $30,000. The winner's purse was $7,200. The event was televised nationally for two hours on the last day and for the last half-hour during the playoff.

1958–Tommy Bolt, 39, a native Oklahoman, led after every round with 71-71-69-72–283, three over par, and won by four strokes over Gary Player, 22, of Johannesburg, South Africa, at Southern Hills Country Club, Tulsa, Okla. Ben Hogan, injured his left wrist in practice and finished in a tie for tenth at 294. Charles R. Coe, of Oklahoma City, tied for thirteenth at 295 to be leading amateur and later in the season won the Amateur Championship. Sam Snead failed to qualify for the last 36 holes, his first such failure in 18 Opens. The entry of 2,132 set another record. Galleries of 34,500 for the three days approached record proportions in spite of heat and strong winds. The purse was increased to approximately $35,000, a new high, and first prize was raised to $8,000.

1959–Bill Casper, Jr., 27, of San Diego, Calif., won the Championship with 71-68-69-74–282 at Winged Foot Golf Club, Mamaroneck, N.Y. The 212-pound Champion was one stroke better than Robert R. Rosburg and two strokes better than Mike Souchak and Claude Harmon, the host professional. Casper took the lead in the second round and held it thereafter. A series of thunderstorms struck on the third day and the final round was postponed until the following day for the first time in Open history. The fourth round thereby was played Sunday in chilly, gusty weather. The players cooperated wonderfully with some not starting until nearly 5 P.M. James R. English, of Denver, was low amateur with 299. Defending Champion Tommy Bolt took 301. Attendance of approximately 43,377 set a record for the three regularly scheduled days. Prize money was increased 20 per cent and totaled $49,200 for the Championship proper, plus $1,300 for 13 Sectional Qualifying Championships. Casper's first prize was $12,000. The entry of 2,385 was a record and for the first time double qualifying was held. Fifty-seven districts held first local qualifying rounds and 13 sections held the final qualifying, all at 36 holes.

OPEN CHAMPIONSHIP

DATE	WINNER, RUNNER-UP	SCORE	SITE	ENTRY
1895 (Oct.)	Horace Rawlins	173	Newport G.C.,	11
	Willie Dunn	175	Newport, R.I.	
1896 (July)	James Foulis	†152	Shinnecock Hills G.C.,	28
	Horace Rawlins	155	Southampton, N.Y.	
1897 (Sept.)	Joe Lloyd	162	Chicago G.C.,	35
	Willie Anderson	163	Wheaton, Ill.	
1898 (June)	Fred Herd	328	Myopia Hunt C.,	49
	Alex Smith	335	South Hamilton, Mass.	
1899 (Sept.)	Willie Smith	315	Baltimore C.C.	81
	George Low	326	Baltimore, Md.	
	Val Fitzjohn	326		
	W. H. Way	326		
1900 (Oct.)	Harry Vardon	313	Chicago G.C.,	60
	J. H. Taylor	315	Wheaton, Ill.	
1901 (June)	Willie Anderson	331-85	Myopia Hunt C.,	60
	Alex Smith	331-86	South Hamilton, Mass.	
1902 (Oct.)	Lawrence Auchterlonie	307	Garden City G.C.,	90
	Stewart Gardner	313	Garden City, N.Y.	
	*Walter J. Travis	313		
1903 (June)	Willie Anderson	307-82	Baltusrol G.C.,	89
	David Brown	307-84	Springfield, N.J.	
1904 (July)	Willie Anderson	303	Glen View C.,	71
	Gilbert Nicholls	308	Golf, Ill.	
1905 (Sept.)	Willie Anderson	314	Myopia Hunt C.,	83
	Alex Smith	316	South Hamilton, Mass.	
1906 (June)	Alex Smith	295	Onwentsia C.,	68
	William Smith	302	Lake Forest, Ill.	
1907 (June)	Alex Ross	302	Philadelphia Cricket C.,	82
	Gilbert Nicholls	304	Philadelphia, Pa.	
1908 (Aug.)	Fred McLeod	322-77	Myopia Hunt C.,	88
	Willie Smith	322-83	South Hamilton, Mass.	
1909 (June)	George Sargent	290	Englewood G.C.,	84
	Tom McNamara	294	Englewood, N.J.	
1910 (June)	Alex Smith	298-71	Philadelphia Cricket C.,	75
	John J. McDermott	298-75	St. Martins, Pa.	
	Macdonald Smith	298-77		
1911 (June)	John J. McDermott	307-80	Chicago G.C.,	79
	Michael J. Brady	307-82	Wheaton, Ill.	
	George O. Simpson	307-85		
1912 (Aug.)	John J. McDermott	294	C. C. of Buffalo,	131
	Tom McNamara	296	Buffalo, N.Y.	
1913 (Sept.)	*Francis Ouimet	304-72	The Country Club,	165
	Harry Vardon	304-77	Brookline, Mass.	
	Edward Ray	304-78		
1914 (Aug.)	Walter Hagen	290	Midlothian C.C.,	129
	*Charles Evans, Jr.	291	Blue Island, Ill.	
1915 (June)	*Jerome D. Travers	297	Baltusrol G.C.,	141
	Tom McNamara	298	Springfield, N.J.	
1916 (June)	*Charles Evans, Jr.	286	Minikahda Club,	94
	Jock Hutchison	288	Minneapolis, Minn.	
1917-18 – No Championships: World War I				
1919 (June)	Walter Hagen	301-77	Brae Burn C.C.	142
	Michael J. Brady	301-78	West Newton, Mass.	
1920 (Aug.)	Edward Ray	295	Inverness Club,	265
	Harry Vardon	296	Toledo, Ohio	
	Jack Burke	296		
	Leo Diegel	296		
	Jock Hutchison	296		
1921 (July)	James M. Barnes	289	Columbia C.C.,	262
	Walter Hagen	298	Chevy Chase, Md.	
	Fred McLeod	298		

*Denotes Amateur.
†Record score.

Open Championship (Continued)

DATE	WINNER, RUNNER-UP	SCORE	SITE	ENTRY
1922 (July)	Gene Sarazen *Robert T. Jones, Jr. John L. Black	288 289 289	Skokie C.C., Glencoe, Ill.	323
1923 (July)	*Robert T. Jones, Jr. Robert A. Cruickshank	296-76 296-78	Inwood C.C., Inwood, N.Y.	360
1924 (June)	Cyril Walker *Robert T. Jones, Jr.	297 300	Oakland Hills C.C., Birmingham, Mich.	319
1925 (June)	William Macfarlane *Robert T. Jones, Jr.	291-75-72 291-75-73	Worcester C.C., Worcester, Mass.	445
1926 (July)	*Robert T. Jones, Jr. Joe Turnesa	293 294	Scioto C.C., Columbus, Ohio	694
1927 (June)	Tommy Armour Harry Cooper	301-76 301-79	Oakmont C.C., Oakmont, Pa.	898
1928 (June)	Johnny Farrell *Robert T. Jones, Jr.	294-143 294-144	Olympia Fields C.C., Mateson, Ill.	1,064
1929 (June)	*Robert T. Jones, Jr. Al Espinosa	294-141 294-164	Winged Foot G.C., Mamaroneck, N.Y.	1,000
1930 (July)	*Robert T. Jones, Jr. Macdonald Smith	287 289	Interlachen C.C., Minneapolis, Minn.	1,177
1931 (July)	Billy Burke George Von Elm	292-149-148 292-149-149	Inverness Club, Toledo, Ohio	1,141
1932 (June)	Gene Sarazen Robert A. Cruickshank T. Philip Perkins	286 289 289	Fresh Meadow C.C., Flushing, N.Y.	1,011
1933 (June)	*John G. Goodman Ralph Guldahl	287 288	North Shore G.C., Glen View, Ill.	915
1934 (June)	Olin Dutra Gene Sarazen	293 294	Merion Cricket C., (East Course) Ardmore, Pa.	1,063
1935 (June)	Sam Parks, Jr. Jimmy Thomson	299 301	Oakmont C.C., Oakmont, Pa.	1,125
1936 (June)	Tony Manero Harry E. Cooper	282 284	Baltusrol G.C., (Upper Course), Springfield, N.J.	1,277
1937 (June)	Ralph Guldahl Sam Snead	281 283	Oakland Hills C.C., Birmingham, Mich.	1,402
1938 (June)	Ralph Guldahl Dick Metz	284 290	Cherry Hills Club, Denver, Colo.	1,223
1939 (June)	Byron Nelson Craig Wood Denny Shute	284-68-70 284-68-73 284-76	Philadelphia Country C., (Spring Mill Course) West Conshohocken, Pa.	1,193
1940 (June)	Lawson Little Gene Sarazen	287-70 287-73	Canterbury G.C., Cleveland, Ohio	1,161
1941 (June)	Craig Wood Denny Shute	284 287	Colonial Club, Fort Worth, Texas	1,048
1942-45 – No Championships: World War II				
1946 (June)	Lloyd Mangrum Byron Nelson Victor Ghezzi	284-72-72 284-72-73 284-72-73	Canterbury G.C., Cleveland, Ohio	1,175
1947 (June)	Lew Worsham Sam Snead	282-69 282-70	St. Louis C.C., Clayton, Mo.	1,356
1948 (June)	Ben Hogan Jimmy Demaret	276 278	Riviera C.C., Los Angeles, Calif.	1,411

*Denotes Amateur

Open Championship (Continued)

DATE	WINNER, RUNNER-UP	SCORE	SITE	ENTRY
1949 (June)	Cary Middlecoff Sam Snead Clayton Heafner	286 287 287	Medinah C.C., (No. 3 Course) Medinah, Ill.	1,348
1950 (June)	Ben Hogan Lloyd Mangrum George Fazio	287-69 287-73 287-75	Merion G.C., (East Course) Ardmore, Pa.	1,379
1951 (June)	Ben Hogan Clayton Heafner	287 289	Oakland Hills C.C., Birmingham, Mich.	1,511
1952 (June)	Julius Boros Edward S. Oliver, Jr.	281 285	Northwood C., Dallas, Texas	1,688
1953 (June)	Ben Hogan Sam Snead	283 289	Oakmont C.C., Oakmont, Pa.	1,669
1954 (June)	Ed Furgol Gene Littler	284 285	Baltusrol G.C., (Lower Course), Springfield, N.J.	1,928
1955 (June)	Jack Fleck Ben Hogan	287-69 287-72	Olympic C.C., (Lake Course)	1,522
1956 (June)	Cary Middlecoff Julius Boros Ben Hogan	281 282 282	Oak Hill C.C., (East Course) Rochester, N.Y.	1,921
1957 (June)	Dick Mayer Cary Middlecoff	282-72 282-79	Inverness Club, Toledo, Ohio	1,907
1958 (June)	Tommy Bolt Gary Player	283 287	Southern Hills C.C., Tulsa, Okla.	2,132
1959 (June)	Bill Casper, Jr. Robert R. Rosburg	282 283	Winged Foot G.C., Mamaroneck, N.Y.	2,385

1917—An Open Patriotic Tournament was conducted for the benefit of the American Red Cross at the Whitemarsh Valley Country Club, Philadelphia, Pa., June 20-22. Winner: Jock Hutchison, 292; runner-up: Tom McNamara, 299.

1942—A Hale America Tournament was conducted for the benefit of the Navy Relief Society and the United Service Organization at Ridgemoor Country Club, Chicago, Ill., June 18-21. Winner: Ben Hogan, 271; runners-up: Jimmy Demaret and Mike Turnesa, 274.

* Denotes Amateur.

1895
FIRST OPEN CHAMPIONSHIP

Held at Newport Golf Club, Newport, R.I., October 4.
11 Entries.

					Score
Horace Rawlins, Newport	45	46	41	41	173
Willie Dunn, Shinnecock Hills	43	46	44	42	175
James Foulis, Chicago	46	43	44	43	176
*A. W. Smith, Toronto	47	43	44	42	176
W. F. Davis, Newport	45	49	42	42	178
W. Campbell, Brookline	41	48	42	48	179
John Patrick, Tuxedo	46	48	46	43	183
John Harland, Western	45	48	43	47	183
Samuel Tucker, St. Andrews	49	48	45	43	185
John Reid, Philadelphia	49	51	55	51	206
William Norton, Lakewood	51	58	—	—	109

*Amateur

1896
SECOND OPEN CHAMPIONSHIP

Held at the Shinnecock Hills Golf Club, Shinnecock Hills, N.Y., July 18.
35 Entries.

28 Contestants who completed 36 holes.

				Score
1	James Foulis, Chicago	78	74	152
2	Horace Rawlins, Sadaquada	79	76	155
3	G. Douglas, Brookline	79	79	158
	*A. W. Smith, Toronto	78	80	158
5	John Shippen, Shinnecock Hills	78	81	159
	*H. J. Whigham, Onwentsia	82	77	159
7	Joe Lloyd, Essex	78	82	160
	W. Tucker, St. Andrews	78	82	160
9	R. B. Wilson, Shinnecock Hills	82	80	162
10	A. Ricketts, Albany	80	83	163
11	W. H. Way, Meadowbrook	83	81	164
12	Willie Dunn, Ardsley	78	87	165
13	W. F. Davis, Newport	83	84	167
14	W. Campbell, Myopia	85	85	170
15	W. T. Hoare, Philadelphia Cricket	90	81	171
16	J. Patrick, Tuxedo	86	86	172
	John Reid, Philadelphia C.C.	88	84	172
	J. N. Mackrell, Essex	89	83	172
19	A. Patrick, Tuxedo	88	85	173
	Tom Gourley, Baltusrol	82	91	173
21	Oscar Bunn, Shinnecock Hills	89	85	174
22	G. Strath, Dyker Meadow	91	89	180
	J. I. Anson, Westbrook	88	92	180
24	John Harrison, Ridgefield	92	91	183
25	W. W. Campbell, Philadelphia	91	93	184
26	W. Norton, Lakewood	87	98	185
27	R. Anderson, Westbrook	92	95	187
28	T. Warrender, Knollwood	97	93	190

*Amateur.

1897
THIRD OPEN CHAMPIONSHIP

Held at Chicago Golf Club, Wheaton, Ill., September 17.
35 Entries.

35 Contestants who completed 36 holes.

				Score
1	Joe Lloyd, Essex	83	79	162
2	Willie Anderson, Watch Hill	79	84	163
3	James Foulis, Chicago	80	88	168
	Willie Dunn, New York	87	81	168
5	W. T. Hoare, Pittsburgh	82	87	169
6	A. Ricketts, Albany	91	81	172
	Bernard Nicholls, Lenox	87	85	172
8	Horace Rawlins, Sadaquada	91	82	173
	*H. J. Whigham, Onwentsia	87	86	173
	D. Foulis, Chicago	86	87	173
11	W. Marshall, Onwentsia	87	87	174
	R. B. Wilson, Shinnecock	83	91	174
	*Charles B. Macdonald, Chicago	85	89	174
14	H. Turpie, Washington Park	85	90	175
15	*J. A. Tyng, Morris County	86	91	177
	W. Tucker, St. Andrews	90	87	177
	R. Foulis, Onwentsia	88	89	177
	W. F. Davis, Newport	88	89	177
19	*F. S. Douglas, Fairfield	89	91	180
20	*W. G. Stewart, Seabright	91	90	181
21	G. Pearson, Rockaway	93	89	182
	R. Leslie, Washington Park	90	92	182
	R. McAndrews, Hudson	90	92	182
24	J. Harrison, Ridgefield	97	87	184
25	S. Tucker, Dyker Meadow	87	98	185
	W. H. Way, Meadowbrook	89	96	185
27	R. White, Cincinnati	89	97	186
28	*Devereux Emmet, Westbrook	98	90	188
29	*W. B. Smith, Chicago	98	91	189
30	A. L. Tollifson, Chicago	91	100	191
31	*Foxhall Keene, Oakland	93	99	192
	J. Duncan, Glenview	98	94	192
33	*J. Reid, Jr., Yale	98	96	194
	*H. R. Sweny, Albany	96	98	194
35	*S. D. Bowers, Otsego	101	98	199

*Amateur.

1898
FOURTH OPEN CHAMPIONSHIP

Held at the Myopia Hunt Club, Hamilton, Mass., June 17-18.
72 holes, 49 entries.
28 contestants who completed 72 holes.

						Score
1	Fred Herd, Washington Park	84	85	75	84	328
2	Alex. Smith, Washington Park	78	86	86	85	335
3	Willie Anderson, Baltusrol	81	82	87	86	336
4	Joe Lloyd, Essex County	87	80	86	86	339
5	Willie Smith, Shinnecock	82	91	85	82	340
6	W. V. Hoare, Dayton	84	84	87	87	342
7	Willie Dunn, New York	85	87	87	84	343
8	*H. C. Leeds, Myopia	81	84	93	89	347
	Bernard Nicholls, Lenox	86	87	88	86	347
	R. McAndrews, Cohasset	85	90	86	86	347
	J. Jones, Myopia	83	84	90	90	347
12	H. S. Turpie, Glen View	85	87	86	91	349
13	A. H. Findlay, Boston	89	88	84	89	350
14	W. Tucker, St. Andrews	90	89	87	89	355
15	*J. F. Curtis, Harvard	87	88	88	93	356
16	J. Lister, Philadelphia	92	88	91	85	356
17	J. Harland, Weston	84	93	93	87	357
18	W. F. Davis, Newport	91	88	95	85	359
19	*J.A. Tyng, Morristown	92	91	88	90	361
	Horace Rawlins, Equinox	91	90	92	88	361
21	J. Yonds, Magnolia	92	90	92	90	364
	*Q. A. Shaw, Myopia	88	85	93	98	364
23	J. H. Mercer, Larchmont	85	95	93	93	366
	Gil Nicholls, Lexington	91	92	91	92	366
24	J. D. Dunn, New York	91	88	91	97	367
25	W. Campbell, Boston	93	91	97	101	382
26	*H. R. Sweny, Albany	92	97	96	99	384
27	*W. Rutherford, Meadowbrook	100	99	98	91	388
28	W. E. Stoddard, Brookline	103	95	97	96	391

*Amateur.

1899
FIFTH OPEN CHAMPIONSHIP

Held at the Baltimore Country Club (Roland Park Course), Baltimore, Md., September 14-15.
81 Entries.
28 contestants who completed 72 holes.

						Score
1	Willie Smith, Midlothian	77	82	79	77	315
2	George Low, Dyker Meadow	82	79	89	76	326
	Val Fitzjohn, Otsego	85	80	79	82	326
	W. H. Way, Detroit	80	85	80	81	326
5	Willie Anderson, New York	77	81	85	84	327
6	J. Park, Essex County	88	80	75	85	328
7	H. Gullane, St. Davids	81	86	80	84	331
8	Alex Smith, Washington Park	82	81	82	85	330
9	Laurie Auchterlonie, Glen View	86	87	82	78	333
	P. Walker, Onwentsia	84	86	77	86	333
11	A. Findlay, Boston	88	86	79	81	334
12	Alex Campbell, Brookline	83	80	79	94	336
13	*H.M. Harriman, Meadowbrook	87	88	85	79	339
	A. Patrick, Westchester	82	83	84	90	339
15	A. Ricketts, Rochester	87	85	88	80	340
16	Bernard Nicholls, Philadelphia	86	88	85	84	343
17	Harry Turpie, Edgewater	91	88	83	83	345
	D. Foulis, Chicago	83	86	91	85	345
	James Foulis, Chicago	94	84	88	80	346
	Gil Nicholls, Boston	90	83	86	87	346
21	D. Leitch, Springfield	87	85	85	90	347
22	Ernest Way, Edgeworth	85	87	87	89	348
	W. Thompson, Huntingdon Valley	82	90	87	90	349
24	Horace Rawlins, Waumbeck	81	85	98	86	350
	Fred Herd, Washington Park	85	86	93	86	350
	John Shippen, Aronimink	86	88	88	88	350
27	R. S. Patrick, New York	85	92	88	86	351
	W. Tucker, Chevy Chase	89	91	87	84	351

*Amateur.

1900
SIXTH OPEN CHAMPIONSHIP

Held at the Chicago Golf Club, Wheaton, Ill., October 4-5.
60 Entries.
42 contestants who completed 72 holes.

						Score
1	Harry Vardon, Ganton, England	79	78	76	80	313
2	J. H. Taylor, Richmond, England	76	82	79	78	315
3	David Bell, Midlothian	78	83	83	78	322
4	Laurie Auchterlonie, Glen View	84	82	80	81	327
5	Willie Smith, Midlothian	82	83	79	83	328
6	George Low, Dyker Meadow	84	80	85	82	331
7	Tom Hutchinson, Shinnecock Hills	81	87	81	84	333
8	Henry Turpie, Edgewater	84	87	79	84	334
9	Stewart Gardner, Lenox		163	84	89	336
10	Val Fitzjohn, Sadaquada		167	89	82	338
11	Willie Anderson, Oconomowoc		171	79	89	339
	Alex Campbell, Boston		163	93	83	339
13	Alex Smith, Washington Park		174	82	84	340
14	R. Simpson, St. Louis		168	88	87	343
	James Foulis, Chicago		174	87	82	343
16	Arthur Smith, Edgewood		174	85	85	344
	W. H. Way, Detroit		173	84	87	344
	Fred Herd, Washington Park		174	84	86	344
19	Willie Norton, Seabright		174	84	87	345
	Horace Rawlins, Waumbek		170	90	85	345
21	Ernest Way, Edgeworth		181	81	84	346
22	W. B. Schlotman, Detroit		179	83	88	350
23	R. McAndrew, Dayton		180	87	84	351
24	Henry Gullane, Pittsburgh		178	92	82	352
25	John Shippen, Marine and Field		181	89	83	353
	A.C. Tolifson, Lake Geneva		181	88	84	353
27	R. Foulis, Chicago		174	90	90	354
28	*Charles B. Macdonald, Chicago		176	90	89	355
29	*Hugo R. Johnstone, Chicago		172	90	94	356
	Horace Rawlins, Waumbeck		183	88	85	356
31	J. D. Campbell, Boston		181	89	87	357
32	James Hutchinson, Philadelphia		175	87	86	358
33	David Hunter, Baltusrol		175	94	91	360
34	*William J. Holabird, Glen View		180	92	89	361
	George Turpie, Edgewater		173	91	97	361
36	*John Stuart, Washington Park		186	84	92	362
37	George Braid, Kansas City		177	90	96	363
38	David Mentiply, Onwentsia		179	94	91	364
39	Patrick Corcoran, Buffalo		191	96	90	377
40	Robert White, Cincinnati		193	93	92	378
41	*Walter E. Egan, Onwentsia		187	90	102	379
42	John Harrison, Baltimore		201	93	98	392

*Amateur.

1901
SEVENTH OPEN CHAMPIONSHIP

Held at the Myopia Hunt Club, S. Hamilton, Mass., June 14-15.
60 Entries.
39 contestants who completed 72 holes.

						Score
1	Willie Anderson. Pittsfield	84	83	83	81	331
2	Alex Smith, Washington Park	82	82	87	80	331
3	Willie Smith, Midlothian	84	86	82	81	333
4	Stewart Gardner, Garden City	86	82	81	85	334
5	Laurie Auchterlonie, Glen View	81	85	86	83	335
	Bernard Nicholls, Boston	84	85	83	83	335
7	David Brown, Crescent Athletic	86	83	83	84	336
	Alex Campbell, Brookline	86	83	83	84	336
9	John Park, Essex County		171		170	341
	George Low, Dyker Meadow		171		170	341
11	James Foulis, Chicago		173		174	347
12	John Jones, Myopia		171		177	348
	Val Fitzjchn, Mohawk		172		176	348
14	Gilbert Nicholls, Boston		174		175	349
	R. Simpson, St. Louis		175		174	349
16	Isaac S. Mackie, Fox Hills		175		175	350
17	A. H. Fenn, Poland Springs, Me.		177		174	351
	Horace Rawlins, Waumbek		174		177	351
	*A. G. Lockwood, Allston		171		180	351
20	Joseph Lloyd, Essex County, Manchester		177		175	352
21	Donald J. Ross, Oakley		180		175	355
22	Harry Turpie, Edgewater		179		178	357
	Alex Taylor, Homewood, Ill.		178		179	357
	W. C. Clark, Nassau, N.Y.		178		179	357
25	David Hunter, Baltusrol		183		176	359
	R. S. Patrick, Westchester		181		178	359
27	W. F. Davis, Apawamis		179		181	360
28	W. H. Hunter		184		177	361
	L. C. Servos, Twin Mountain, N.H.		177		184	361
	John Dingwall, Plainfield, N.J.		185		176	361
	John Harland, Fairfield		184		177	361
	E. D. Fitzjohn, Mohawk		176		185	361
33	Joe Mitchell, Cleveland		188		165	363
34	William Kirk, Knollwood, N.Y.		185		181	366
35	John Harrison, Dayton, Ohio		185		183	368
	John Hobens, Glen Ridge, N.J.		18C		188	368
37	Alec Patrick, Westchester		180		189	369
30	John I. Anson, Stamford, Conn.		194		185	379
39	C. D. Cronin, Westchester		192		192	384

*Amateur.
Playoff—June 16: Anderson, 85; Smith, 86.

1902
EIGHTH OPEN CHAMPIONSHIP

Held at The Garden City Golf Club, Garden City, N.Y., October 10-11.
90 Entries.
56 contestants who completed 72 holes.

						Score
1	Laurie Auchterlonie, Chicago	78	78	74	77	307
2	Stewart Gardner, Garden City	82	76	77	78	313
	*Walter J. Travis, Garden City	82	82	75	74	313
4	Willie Smith, Chicago	82	79	80	75	316
5	John Shippen, New York	83	81	75	79	318
	Willie Anderson, Montclair	79	82	76	81	318
7	Charles Thom, New York	80	82	80	77	319
8	Harry Turpie, Chicago	79	85	78	78	320
9	Donald J. Ross, Oakley, Mass.	80	83	78	81	322
10	Alex. Ross, Pinehurst, N.C.	83	77	84	79	323
11	Willie Norton, Deal	83	82	79	81	325
12	George Low, Brooklyn	83	84	78	81	326
	David Brown, Boston	80	88	82	76	326
14	John Hobens, Yountakah, N.J.	85	82	80	81	328
	John Campbell, Brookline, Mass.	77	87	79	85	328
16	A. S. Griffiths, Islip	79	86	82	83	330
	Horace Rawlins, Waumbek	89	83	79	79	330
18	Gilbert Nicholls, Boston	88	86	73	84	331
	Alex Smith, Nassau, L.I.	79	86	83	86	331
20	James Foulis, Chicago	81	88	82	81	332
	Alex Campbell, Brookline, Mass.	82	82	83	79	332
	John Harland, Bridgeport	82	82	83	85	332
	Willie Hunter, Northeast Harbor, Me.	82	82	81	87	332
24	Fred Herd	82	79	83	89	333
25	Jack Park, Scotland	79	89	85	81	334
26	George Braid, St. Paul	85	81	84	85	335
	James G. Campbell,Wilmington	88	84	82	81	335
28	Bernard Nicholls, Hollywood	89	84	84	79	336
29	John Mackie, Newark	88	82	84	84	338
30	R. S. Patrick, New York	85	87	84	83	339
	David Hunter, Flushing	83	81	91	84	339
	A. H. Findlay, Boston	85	81	87	86	339
33	David Ogilvie, Baltimore	86	90	83	81	340
	William A. Donovan, Kineo	88	84	83	85	340
35	*Paul Murphy, St. Paul School	86	90	83	82	341
	W. Fovargue, Philadelphia	90	86	81	84	341
37	Peter Eagan, Bellport	85	86	89	82	342
	John Young, Somerset Hills	84	86	80	92	342
39	John S. Pierson, Richmond County	87	87	85	84	343
40	*R.C. Watson, Jr. Westbrook	88	85	86	86	345
	D. Leitch, Springfield, Mass.	84	86	87	88	345
42	John Jones, Myopia, Mass.	89	88	88	82	347
43	Robert Thompson, Merion, Pa.	87	92	83	86	348
	Louis Livingston, Jr., Westbrook	90	83	87	88	348
45	David Patrick,New York	92	85	86	87	350
46	A. H. Fenn, Poland Springs, Me.	92	93	83	84	352
	Jack Jolly, Newark	84	97	95	86	352
48	*C.H. Seeley, Wee Burn	82	90	93	88	353
	John Harrison, Colonia, N.J.	91	89	85	88	353
	Robert Dow, Mount Vernon	89	92	89	83	353
52	Joseph Mitchell, Glenville, Pa.	91	84	92	89	356
	A. G. Lockwood, Allston, Mass.	96	81	87	92	356
54	*Charles B. Macdonald, Garden City	87	91	90	89	357
55	*F.H. Croker, Deal	90	88	87	95	360
56	Willie Collins, Bayside	90	90	92	89	361

First ten above were prize winners.
*Amateur.

1903
NINTH OPEN CHAMPIONSHIP

Held at the Baltusrol Golf Club, Springfield, N.J., June 26-27.
89 Entries.
59 contestants who completed 72 holes.

					Score
1	Willie Anderson, Apawamis	149	76	82	307
2	David Brown, Wollaston	156	75	76	307
3	Stewart Gardner, Garden City	154	82	79	315
4	Alex Smith, Nassau	154	81	81	316
5	Donald J. Ross, Oakley	158	78	82	318
6	Jack Campbell, Brookline	159	83	77	319
7	Laurie Auchterlonie, Glen View	154	84	83	321
8	*Findlay S. Douglas, Nassau	156	82	84	322
9	John Hobens, Yountakah	157	82	84	323
	Willie Smith, Midlothian	161	83	79	323
	Aleck Ross, Wilmington, Del.	165	78	80	323
12	Horace Rawlins, Waumbek	159	78	87	324
13	Isaac Mackie, Fox Hills	163	78	84	325
	*F.O. Reinhart, Princeton	156	89	80	325
15	Aleck Campbell, Brookline	163	80	83	326
	Gilbert Nicholls, St. Louis	168	78	80	326
	W. H. Way, Euclid Club	163	82	81	326
	*Walter J. Travis, Garden City	163	81	82	326
19	Bernard Nicholls, Hollywood	163	82	83	328
20	Will Norton, Deal	159	83	87	329
	David Ogilvie, Baltimore	167	81	81	329
22	George Cumming, Toronto	169	77	84	330
23	Harry Turpie, Auburn, Ill.	168	81	82	331
24	John Reid, Philadelphia	164	84	84	332
	Joseph Lloyd, Essex County	169	80	83	332
26	*G.T. Brokaw, Deal	160	86	87	333
	J. G. Campbell, Philadelphia	165	82	86	333
	Arthur Smith, Philadelphia	167	83	83	333
	Fred McLeod, Rockford, Ill.	163	79	91	333
30	A. H. Fenn, Poland Springs	165	83	86	334
31	David Hunter, Essex County	170	86	79	335
32	R. C. Murray, Quebec	167	84	85	336
	John Dingwell, Allegheny C.C.	171	86	79	336
34	William Braid, St. Louis	161	89	87	337
35	R. Thompson, Huntingdon Valley	165	88	85	338
36	A. H. Findlay, Boston	173	82	84	339
	John Harland, Brooklawn	164	84	91	339
38	Ernest Way, Detroit	173	80	87	340
39	T. L. McNamara, Boston	170	85	88	343
40	David Patrick, Bay Shore	172	85	88	345
	Joe Mitchell, Cleveland	169	91	85	345
42	W. H. Reynolds, Philadelphia	174	86	86	346
43	Jack Jolly, Arlington, N.J.	176	87	84	347
44	*Frank H. Croker, Deal	176	91	81	348
45	Alexander Patrick, New York	180		169	349
	J. S. Pearson, Richmond County	174		175	349
47	P. P. Burns, Morristown	177	81	94	352
48	John Brett, Tuxedo	180	87	86	353
	*W.C. Carnegie, St. Andrews	170	89	94	353
50	Robert Dow, Knollwood	177	89	90	356
	*L. L. Kellogg, Jr., Fox Hills	180	90	86	356
52	*J. S. Gillespie, Quebec	179	87	91	357
53	*C. L. Tappin, Westbrook	177	92	90	359
54	*R. C. Watson, Jr., Westbrook	179	89	92	360
55	*John M. Ward, Fox Hills	184	89	90	363
56	Robert Shiels, New Haven	186	85	94	365
57	J. C. Davidson, Washington	185	90	92	367
58	P. S. Honeyman, Champlain	185	91	94	370
59*	M. G. McDonald, Florida	191	89	92	372

First eleven were prize winners.
Playoff—June 29: Anderson, 82; Brown, 84.
*Amateur.

1904
TENTH OPEN CHAMPIONSHIP

Held at the Glen View Club, Golf, Ill., July 8-9.
71 Entries.
46 contestants who completed 72 holes.

						Score
1	Willie Anderson, Apawamis	75	78	78	72	303
2	Gilbert Nicholls, St. Louis	80	76	79	73	308
3	Fred Mackenzie, Onwentsia	76	79	74	80	309
4	Laurie Auchterlonie, Glen View	80	81	75	78	314
	Bernard Nicholls, Elyria, O.	80	77	79	78	314
6	Robert Simpson, Riverside, Ill.	82	82	76	76	316
	P. F. Barrett, Lambton, Ont.	78	79	79	80	316
	Stewart Gardner, Garden City	75	76	80	85	316
9	James Foulis, Chicago	83	74	78	82	317
10	Donald J. Ross, Oakley	80	82	78	78	318
11	C. R. Murray, Montreal		165		154	319
	Jack Hobens, Yountakah		159		160	319
13	Aleck Campbell, Brookline		168		152	320
14	Horace Rawlins, Spring Haven		155		167	322
15	G. Thomson, Lenox		165		159	324
	G. Braid, St. Paul		158		166	324
	Aleck Ross, Woodland Park		165		159	324
18	Alex Smith, Nassau		159		167	326
19	D. Robertson, Buffalo		160		168	328
20	Jack Campbell, Huntingdon Valley		168		161	329
	*H. Chandler Egan, Exmoor		163		166	329
	Harry Turpie, Auburn Park		163		166	329
23	*R. E. Hunter, Midlothian		168		163	331
	Aleck Taylor, Exmoor		168		163	331
	George Low, Baltusrol		170		161	331
26	*K. Edwards, Midlothian		167		165	332
	W. H. Way, Euclid		171		161	332
28	George Cummings, Toronto		166		167	333
29	J. Watson, Skokie		166		168	334
	P. Robertson, Buffalo		169		165	334
	T. McDeever, Bryn Mawr		163		171	334
	Fred McLeod, Rockford		174		160	334
33	Isaac Mackie, Fox Hills		170		165	335
	W. Marshall, Onwentsia		164		171	335
35	D. Foulis, Chicago		167		170	337
36	W. V. Hoare, Ridge		173		166	339
37	W. Lorimer, Racine		170		170	340
38	G. Turpie, Calumet		172		169	341
39	D. McIntosh, Westward Ho		170		173	343
40	F. Bartsch, Homewood		173		172	345
	R. G. McAndrew, Wollaston		168		177	345
42	A. Baxter, La Grange		168		178	346
43	*M. E. Phelps, Midlothian		174		174	348
	A. C. Tollifson, Lake Geneva		171		177	348
45	*G. F. Clingman, Jr., Homewood		173		176	349
46	*Walter E. Egan, Exmoor		174		189	363

First ten were prize winners.
*Amateur.

1905
ELEVENTH OPEN CHAMPIONSHIP

Held at the Myopia Hunt Club, S. Hamilton, Mass., September 21-22
83 Entries, 78 Starters.
53 contestants who completed 72 holes.

						Score
1	Willie Anderson, Apawamis	81	80	76	77	314
2	Alex Smith, Nassau	81	80	76	77	316
3	Peter Robertson, Oakmont	79	80	81	77	317
	P. F. Barrett, Canada	81	80	77	79	317
5	Stewart Gardner, Garden City	78	78	85	77	318
6	Alex Campbell, The Country Club	82	76	80	81	319
7	Gilbert Nicholls, Denver	82	76	84	79	321
8	John Hobens, Englewood	85	82	75	81	323
	George Cummings, Canada	85	82	75	81	323
10	Arthur Smith, Ohio	81	77	80	86	324
11	*A. G. Lockwood, Allston		169		156	325
	*Walter J. Travis, Garden City		161		164	325
13	Alex Ross, Brae-Burn		165		161	326
	Willie Smith, Mexico		167		159	326
15	George Low, Baltusrol		165		162	327
16	Fred Mckenzie, Onwentsia		166		162	328
	Joseph Lloyd, Essex County		161		167	328
18	Walter Clark, Springfield		167		162	329
19	Fred McLeod, Rockford, Ill.		164		166	330
20	G. C. Turnbull, Sadaquada		169		162	331
	T. L. McNamara, Boston		169		171	331
	Bernard Nicholls, Hollywood		162		169	331
	W. H. Way, Euclid Club		170		161	331
24	Laurie Auchterlonie, Glen View		167		165	332
25	Donald J. Ross, Oakley		166		167	333
26	Jack Jolly, Arlington, N.J.		165		170	335
	James Maiden, Youngstown, O.		166		169	335
28	R. B. Peebles, So. Orange, N.J.		162		174	336
29	Isaac Mackie, Fox Hills		164		173	337
	C. R. Murray, Canada		169		168	337
31	A. H. Fenn, So. Poland, Me.		165		173	338
32	Charles Rowe, Beaver Valley G.C.		165		174	339
	James Foulis, Chicago		172		167	339
	John Jones, Myopia		171		168	339
	A. G. Griffiths, Westbrook		166		173	339
	Harry Turpie, New Orleans		166		173	339
37	John Dingwall, Pittsburgh		172		168	340
	Fred Brand, Allegheny		165		175	340
	Jack Campbell, Philadelphia		169		171	340
	David Ogilvie, No. Jersey C. C.		170		170	340
	W. V. Hoare, Ellerslie		169		171	340
	Horace Rawlins, Wykagyl		174		166	340
43	David Hunter, Essex County		170		173	343
	J. Mackie, Roseville G.C.		171		172	343
	J. H. Oke, Canada		169		174	343
46	Orrin Terry, Waumbek		173		171	344
	Herbert Strong		173		171	344
48	*Fay Ingalls, Oakley		175		170	345
	*P. Gilbert, Brae Burn		168		177	345
50	George Pearson, Newark		171		179	350
	*A. L. White, Wollaston		172		178	350
	D. Robertson, Buffalo		175		175	350
53	David Brown, Boston		170		182	352

*Amateur.

1906
TWELFTH OPEN CHAMPIONSHIP

Held at the Onwentsia Club, Lake Forest, Ill., June 28–29.
68 Entries; 66 Starters.

						Score
1	Alex Smith, Nassau	73	74	73	75	295
2	William Smith, Mexico	73	81	74	74	302
3	Laurie Auchterlonie, Glen View	76	78	75	76	305
	James Maiden, Toledo	80	73	77	75	305
5	Willie Anderson, Onwentsia	73	76	74	84	307
6	Alec Ross, Brae-Burn	76	79	75	80	310
7	Stewart Gardner, Garden City	80	76	77	78	311
8	*H. Chandler Egan, Exmoor	79	78	76	80	313
	Gilbert Nicholls, Denver	76	81	77	79	313
10	John Hobens, Englewood	75	84	76	79	314
11	Bernard Nicholls, N.Y. Golf		156		160	316
	George Low, Baltusrol		161		155	316
13	Harry S. Turpie, St. Joseph Valley		160		159	319
	Walter Fovargue, Thomasville, Ga.		161		159	320
	Peter Robertson, Oakmont		157		163	320
	Jack Jolly		160		160	320
17	Alex Baxter, La Grange		164		157	321
18	Fred Brand, Allegheny		156		166	322
	George Smith, Oakland, Co.		155		167	322
	George Cumming, Toronto		155		167	322
	Aleck Campbell, The Country Club		160		162	322
22	W.R. Lovekin, Rockford, Ill.		162		162	324
	James Foulis, Calumet Country		169		155	324
	O.G. Hackbarth, Oconomowoc		164		160	324
	William Marshall, Onwentsia		162		162	324
	D. McIntosh, Westward Ho!		158		166	324
27	Ernest Way, Wheeling		164		161	325
	J.H. Watson, Skokie		156		169	325
29	David Robertson, Pittsburgh		161		165	326
	George O'Neil, Auburn		166		160	326
31	*Warren K. Wood, Homewood		163		164	327
32	C.H. Rowe, Beaver Valley		163		165	328
33	Alex Gourlay, Edgewood		163		166	329
	Percy F. Barrett, Lambton, Ont.		156		173	320
35	Fred McLeod, Midlothian		160		170	330
	Robert Taylor, Minikahda		161		169	330
37	Isaac Mackie, Fox Hills		168		163	331
	D.K. White, Algonquin		162		169	331
39	W.V. Hoare, Salt Lake		167		165	332
	*R.E. Hunter, Midlothian		162		170	332
41	Thomas O'Neil, Edgewater		166		167	333
42	A.G. Herr		167		167	334
	R. White, Ravisloe		168		166	334
44	John Reid, Toledo		168		167	335
	C.G. Horton, Evanston		163		172	335
46	James Simpson, Riverside		158		179	337
	*J.M. Sellers, Glen View		163		174	337
48	*O.W. Potter, Jr., Midlothian		165		177	342
49	Mike J. Brady, Commonwealth		168		175	343

*Amateur.

1907
THIRTEENTH OPEN CHAMPIONSHIP

Held at the Philadelphia Cricket Club, Philadelphia, Pa., June 20–21.
82 Entries: 78 Starters.

						Score
1	Aleck Ross, Brae-Burn	76	74	76	76	302
2	Gilbert Nicholls, Woodland	80	73	72	79	304
3	Aleck Campbell, The Country Club	78	74	78	75	305
4	John Hobens, Englewood G.C.	76	75	73	85	309
5	Peter Robertson, Oakmont	81	77	78	74	310
	George Low, Baltusrol	78	76	79	77	310
	Fred McLeod, Midlothian	79	77	79	75	310
8	David Brown, Boston	75	80	78	78	311
	Bernard Nicholls, Nashville	76	76	81	78	311
10	Donald J. Ross, Oakley	78	80	76	78	312
11	Laurie Auchterlonie, Glen View		154		159	313
	Fred Brand, Allegheny C.C.		158		155	313
13	David Robertson, Pittsburgh		158		156	314
14	Tom McNamara, Fall River		161		154	315
15	Willie Anderson, Onwentsia		158		158	316
16	Martin O'Loughlin, Plainfield		162		155	317
	Mike J. Brady, Commonwealth		153		164	317
	David Hunter, Essex Co. C.C.		152		165	317
14	Jack Campbell, Overbrook		157		162	319
20	G.J. Bouse, Marine & Field		156		164	320
21	Stewart Gardner, Exmoor		160		161	321
22	Walter Clark, Springfield C.C.		159		163	322
	Isaac Mackie, Fox Hills		165		157	322
	James Campbell, Mt. Airy		161		161	322
25	Jack Jolly, Arlington		164		159	323
	David Ogilvie, Baltimore C.C.		163		161	324
	W.D. Robinson, Atlantic City		166		158	324
	Horace Rawlins, Ekwanok		158		166	324
	*Jerome D. Travers, Montclair		165		159	324
30	W. Ogilvie, Philadelphia C.C.		163		162	325
	W. Gaudin, Garden City		166		159	325
32	James Thomson, Merion		162		165	327
	George Thomson, Wee Burn		169		158	327
34	*George Smith, Claremont		160		168	328
35	David Honeyman, Arsdale G.C.		161		168	329
36	W.C. Sherwood, Memphis		166		164	330
	Robert Peebles, Fairview		163		167	330
38	Herbert Strong, Apawamis		167		164	331
39	Alex Cunningham, Glen Ridge		164		168	332
	Walter Fovargue, Skokie		164		168	332
	David Foulis, Chicago G.C.		164		168	332
46	J.S. Pearson, Richmond Co. C.C.		162		172	334
	Simon Carr, Huntingdon Valley		169		165	334
44	William Byrne, Aronimink		169		166	335
	*W.T. West, Princeton G.C.		166		169	335
46	W.V. Hoare, Salt Lake		166		171	337
47	*H. M. Forrest, Philadelphia Cricket		164		174	338
48	George Pearson, Yountakah		167		174	341
49	John Burke, Delaware Co. F.C.		166		178	344
50	*B. Warren Corkran, Princeton G.C.		162		184	346

*Amateur.

1908
FOURTEENTH OPEN CHAMPIONSHIP

Held at the Myopia Hunt Club, S. Hamilton, Mass,. Aug. 27–28.
88 Entries; 85 Starters.

						Score
1	Fred McLeod, Midlothian	82	82	81	77	322
2	Willie Smith, Mexico	77	82	85	78	322
3	Alex Smith, Nassau	80	83	83	81	327
4	Willie Anderson, Onwentsia	85	86	80	79	330
5	John Jones, Myopia	81	81	87	82	331
6	Jack Hobens, Englewood	86	81	85	81	333
	Peter Robertson, Oakmont	89	84	77	83	333
8	Percy Barrett, Lambton	94	80	86	78	338
	Jock Hutchison, St. Andrews	82	84	87	85	338
10	Richard Kimball, New Bedford	84	86	83	86	339
	Tom McNamara, Wollaston		167		172	339
12	Bob Peebles, Sound Beach		170		170	340
	George Low, Baltusrol		172		168	340
	Donald Ball, Philadelphia Country		171		169	340
	Aleck Campbell, Brookline		168		172	340
16	David Hunter, Essex County		174		167	341
17	Orrin Terry, Waumbek		173		170	343
	H. H. Barker, Garden City		169		174	343
	Mike J. Brady, Commonwealth		173		170	343
20	David Robertson, Pittsburgh G.C.		172		172	344
21	Horace Rawlins, Ekwanok		174		172	346
	Laurie Auchterlonie, Glen View		168		178	346
22	*Walter J. Travis, Garden City		173		174	347
	Isaac Mackie, Fox Hills		182		165	347
	Aleck Ross, Brae-Burn		174		173	347
25	Jack Campbell, Overbrook		180		169	349
26	David Brown, Lawrence		173		177	350
	David Ogilvie, Morris County		180		170	350
28	Arthur Smith, Arlington		182		170	352
	Herbert Strong, Apawamis		180		172	352
	W.H. Way, Euclid		180		172	352
31	George Cumming, Toronto		175		179	354
32	James Maiden, Nassau		179		176	355
33	Jack Dingwell, Edgeworth		181		175	356
	J.B. Hylan, Vesper C.C.		178		178	356
	J.S. Pearson, Richmond Co.		177		179	356
	Ernest Way, Detroit G.C.		179		177	356
37	*J.G. Anderson, Woodland		178		179	357
	Walter Fovargue, Skokie		180		177	357
39	Donald J. Ross, Oakley		179		179	358
	O.G. Hackbarth, St. Louis		182		176	358
41	W.D. Robinson, Atlantic City		182		177	359
	Stewart Maiden, Wee Burn		182		177	359
	David Honeyman, Arsdale		177		182	359
44	John A. Croke, Kent County		181		179	360

*Amateur
Playoff—August 29; McLeod, 77; Smith, 83.

1909
FIFTEENTH OPEN CHAMPIONSHIP

Held at the Englewood Golf Club, Englewood, N.J., June 24–25.
84 Entries; 83 Starters.

						Score
1	George Sargent, Hyde Manor	75	72	72	71	290
2	Tom McNamara, Wollaston	73	69	75	77	294
3	Alex Smith, Wykagyl	76	73	74	72	295
4	Isaac Mackie, Fox Hills	77	75	74	73	299
	Willie Anderson, St. Louis	79	74	76	70	299
	Jack Hobens, Englewood	75	78	72	74	299
7	*Walter J. Travis, Garden City	72	78	77	73	300
	Andrew Campbell, Spring Haven	71	75	77	77	300
	Tom Anderson, Jr., Montclair	78	74	75	73	300
	Bob Peebles, St. Joseph Valley	76	73	73	78	300
	H.H. Barker, Garden City	75	79	73	73	300
12	Mike J. Brady, Commonwealth		153		149	302
13	Alec Campbell, Brookline		148		155	303
	Fred McLeod, Midlothian		154		149	303
15	*F.R. Upton, Jr., Baltusrol		151		153	304
	Orrin Terry, Canoe Brook		158		146	304
17	Gilbert Nicholls, Wilmington		148		158	306
18	Walter Fovargue, Chicago		156		151	307
	David Ogilvie, Morris County		154		153	307
20	Peter Robertson, Pittsburgh		151		157	308
	C.H. Rowe, Beaver Falls		151		157	308
22	Jack Campbell, Overbook, Pa.		153		156	309
23	*F.S. Douglas, Nassau		158		153	311
	Jock Hutchison, Pittsburgh		155		156	311
	Tom Vardon, Sandwich, England		155		156	311
	Laurie Auchterlonie, Glen View		153		158	311
28	Jack Dingwall, Edgeworth C.C.		153		159	312
	James Maiden, Nassau		154		158	312
	George Low, Baltusrol		155		157	312
31	David Hunter, Essex County		152		161	313
	C.R. Murray, Montreal		152		161	313
	Jack Burke, Aronimink		153		160	313
34	R.M. Thompson, Knollwood		161		153	314
	James Thompson, Merion		158		156	314
	George Sparling, Brooklawn		157		157	314
37	Alec Ross, Brae Burn		155		160	315
38	Herbert Strong, Apawamis		154		163	317
	Walter Clark, Springfield, Mass.		161		156	317
40	*Gilman Tiffany, Powelton		162		156	318
	F.W. Page, Rockland C.C.		159		159	318
	A.H. Murray, Montreal		160		158	318
	Joe Mitchell, Upper Montclair		161		157	318
44	George Turnbull, Columbia, G.C.		156		164	320
	Alec Cunningham, Glen Ridge		159		161	320
46	Robert Simpson, Milwaukee, Wis.		160		161	321
	Richard Kimball, New Bedford		159		162	321
	Fred Brand, Allegheny		152		169	321
49	E. Horton, Pelham Bay		164		158	322
	John J. McDermott, Merchantville, N.J.		161		161	322
	J.A. Croke, Kent Country Club		165		157	322
52	G. Gordon, Onondaga		160		163	323
53	H. Vinal, Tuxedo		160		164	324
	*W.F. Morgan, Jr., Baltusrol		162		162	324
54	*Max Behr, Morris County		164		161	325
55	W.D. Robinson, Atlantic City		165		161	326
56	L.S. Jacobs, Onondaga		157		170	327
	W. Byrne, Delaware C.C.		163		164	327
58	*Oswald Kirkby, Englewood		163		165	328
	*R.C. Watson, Westbrook		162		166	328
60	Horace Rawlins, Ekwanok		165		164	329

*Amateur

1910
SIXTEENTH OPEN CHAMPIONSHIP

Held at the Philadelphia Cricket Club, St. Martins, Pa., June 17–18.
75 Entries.

						Score
1	Alex Smith, Wykagyl	73	73	79	73	298
2	John J. McDermott, Merchantville	74	74	75	75	298
3	Macdonald Smith, Claremont	74	78	75	71	298
4	Fred McLeod, St. Louis	78	70	78	73	299
5	Tom MacNamara, Boston	73	78	73	76	300
	Gilbert Nicholls, Wilmington	73	75	77	75	300
7	John Hobens, Englewood	74	77	74	76	301
8	Tom Anderson, Jr., Inwood	72	76	81	73	302
	Jock Hutchison, Pittsburgh	77	76	75	74	302
	H.H. Barker, Garden City	75	78	77	72	302
11	Willie Anderson, Philadelphia Cricket	74	78	76	75	303
12	George Low, Baltusrol	75	77	79	74	305
	Charles D. Thom, Shinnecock	80	72	78	75	305
14	George Cummings, Toronto	78	73	79	77	307
	Tom Bonnar, Merion	78	78	71	80	307
16	Alec Campbell, The Country Club	79	76	80	74	309
	George Sargent, Chevy Chase	77	81	74	77	309
18	J.R. Thomson, Philadelphia C.C.	74	80	80	76	310
	Jack Campbell, Forest Hills	77	77	81	75	310
20	*Fred Herreshoff, Westbrook	76	77	79	79	311
21	George Smith, Claremont	76	78	79	80	313
22	Alex Ross, Brae Burn	78	84	73	79	314
23	Martin T. O'Loughlin, Plainfield	77	82	80	76	315
	Otto G. Hackbarth, Westward	79	82	78	76	315
25	*A.W. Tillinghast, Philadelphia C.C.	80	81	79	76	316
26	W.D. Robinson, Atlantic City	83	81	78	75	317
27	Jack Burke, Aronimink	81	77	77	84	319
28	Irving Stringer, St. Andrews	83	77	82	78	320
	J.A. Donaldson, Glen View	80	78	87	75	320
	David Honeyman, Sound Beach	83	79	79	79	320
31	Jack Croke, Kent	77	78	83	83	321
32	Walter Fovargue, Skokie	79	86	75	82	322
	Orrin Terry, Canoe Brook	82	84	79	77	322
	Alfred Campbell, Oak Hill	78	84	81	79	322
	Peter Robinson, Oakmont	79	81	80	82	322
36	Sam White, Philmont	82	79	82	80	323
	Isaac Mackie, Fox Hills	81	82	80	80	323
38	Bob Peebles, Dallas	83	81	80	80	324
	Willie Maguire, Wollaston	76	83	81	84	324
	Frank Pebbles, Yale	80	85	77	82	324
41	Jack Jolly, Chicago	83	80	82	80	325
42	Robert McWatt, Columbia	83	79	82	82	326
	George Griffin, Bellfield	81	81	85	79	326
44	Joe Mitchell, Upper Montclair	78	82	83	84	327
45	Karl Keffer, Albany	84	79	87	79	329
46	James Campbell, Whitemarsh	86	78	80	86	330
47	*R.C. Watson, Westbrook	86	76	86	83	331
48	Charles Burgess, Woodland	81	83	88	81	333
49	W.F. Hackney, Unattached	78	85	88	84	335

*Amateur.

Playoff, June 20—Alex Smith, 71; John J. McDermott, 75; Macdonald Smith, 77.

1911
SEVENTEENTH OPEN CHAMPIONSHIP

Held at the Chicago Golf Club, Wheaton, Ill., June 23–24.
79 Entries.

						Score
1	John J. McDermott, Atlantic City	81	72	75	79	307
2	Mike J. Brady, Wollaston	76	77	79	75	307
3	George O. Simpson, Wheaton	76	77	79	75	307
4	Fred McLeod, St. Louis	77	72	76	83	308
5	Gilbert Nicholls, Wilmington	76	78	74	81	309
	Jock Hutchison, Allegheny	80	77	73	79	309
7	George Sargent, Chevy Chase	76	77	84	74	311
	H.H. Barker, Rumson	75	81	77	78	311
9	Peter Robertson, Oakmont	79	76	78	79	312
	Alex Ross, Brae Burn	74	75	81	82	312
11	*Albert Seckel, Riverside	78	80	80	75	313
12	Alec Campbell, Brookline	81	77	72	84	314
	Harry Turpie, Edgewater	77	76	82	79	314
14	C.P. Nelson, Battle Creek	79	85	74	77	315
15	George Low, Baltusrol	80	78	82	76	316
	J.A. Donaldson, Glen View	78	81	83	74	316
17	R.L. Simpson, Kenosha	81	82	75	79	317
18	John Burke, Des Moines	79	77	78	85	319
	*D.E. Sawyer, Wheaton	84	79	77	79	319
20	George Cummings, Toronto	82	80	79	79	320
	Grange Alves, French Lick	82	80	73	85	320
	*Mason E. Phelps, Midlothian	78	78	78	86	320
23	Alex Smith, Wykagyl	76	78	82	85	321
	*Robert A. Gardner, Hinsdale	81	78	79	83	321
	*H. Chandler Egan, Exmoor	81	80	77	83	321
	*R.C. Watson, Westbrook	82	79	78	82	321
27	J.B. Simpson, Blue Mound	81	82	78	80	322
	Walter Fovargue, Skokie	83	81	80	78	322
29	Tom McNamara, Boston	77	87	79	81	324
	R.G. McDonald, Euclid	80	82	75	87	324
	Otto Hackbarth, Hinsdale	78	74	83	89	324
	T.J. Foulis, Chicago	79	80	82	83	324
33	L.M. Nelson, Highland	80	84	81	80	325
34	David Patrick, St. Louis	83	81	77	85	326
	*Knowlton L. Ames, Glen View	84	81	80	81	326
36	David Livie, Lake Geneva	82	83	77	89	327
	W.G. Mann, Northland	84	79	81	83	327
	J. Gatherum, St. Louis	80	81	82	84	327
	G.H. Rowe, Beaver Valley	83	82	83	79	327
	W. Hutchinson, Huntington Valley	82	80	81	84	327
41	Jack Hobens, Englewood	82	82	81	83	328
42	W.N. Hoare, Racine	82	82	81	84	329
	David Hunter, Essex County	79	81	82	87	329
	Alex Taylor, Losantiville	85	82	79	83	329
45	Charles Bell, Delaware	80	84	82	84	330
46	W.C. Sherwood, Memphis	79	80	87	87	333
47	J. Foulis, Jr., Calumet	83	82	85	84	334
48	Jack Dingwell, Pittsburgh	88	80	81	86	335
	R. Peebles, Wichita	84	82	85	84	335
	Jack Croke, Westward Ho	83	78	88	86	335
	Jack Jolly, Newark	80	82	84	89	335
	*J.M. Sellers, Chicago	80	81	85	89	335
53	W. Nelson, Indianapolis	82	82	80	92	336
54	Jack Morton, Peoria	81	84	84	91	340
55	*C.B. Devol, Riverside	82	81	87	91	341

*Amateur.
Playoff—June 26: John J. McDermott, 80; Mike J. Brady, 82; George O. Simpson, 85.

1912
EIGHTEENTH OPEN CHAMPIONSHIP

Held at the Country Club of Buffalo, Buffalo, N.Y., August 1–2.
131 Entries; 125 Starters.

Fifty-five Contestants who completed 72 holes.

						Score
1	John J. McDermott, Atlantic City	74	75	74	71	294
2	Tom McNamara, Boston	74	80	73	69	296
3	Alex Smith, Wykagyl	77	70	77	75	299
	Mike J. Brady, Wollaston	72	75	73	79	299
5	Alec Campbell, Brookline	74	77	80	71	302
6	George Sargent, Chevy Chase	72	78	76	77	303
7	John Dowling, Scarsdale	76	79	76	74	305
	Otto Hackbarth, Hinsdale	77	77	75	76	305
9	C.R. Murray, Royal Montreal	75	78	77	76	306
10	*Walter J. Travis, Garden City	73	79	78	77	307
	Frank Peebles, Stockbridge	73	76	83	75	307
	Tom Anderson, Jr., Oakmont	75	76	81	75	307
13	Fred McLeod, St. Louis	79	77	75	77	308
	George O. Simpson, Wheaton	79	73	77	79	308
	T.F. Barrett, Lambton	74	73	83	79	308
16	David Ogilvie, Augusta	74	83	73	80	310
	*J.G. Anderson, Brae Burn	80	79	78	73	310
18	James M. Barnes, Tacoma	77	73	79	82	311
	Willie Macfarlane, Saegkill	77	81	73	80	311
	Jack Dingwell, Pittsburgh	77	77	78	79	311
21	Tom Vardon, Onwentsia	74	83	79	76	312
	Jack Croke, Westward Ho	74	81	78	79	312
23	George Cummings, Toronto	78	79	77	79	313
	Jack Campbell, Old York Road	74	75	83	81	313
	Jock Hutchison, Allegheny	78	77	82	76	313
28	A.H. Murray, Outremont	78	79	79	78	314
29	Dave Robertson, Sunset	77	78	79	81	315
30	Peter Robertson, Fall River	80	82	77	77	316
	C.H. Rowe, Beaver Valley	77	82	81	76	316
32	David S. Livie, Lake Geneva	82	80	76	79	317
	David Black, Rivermead	78	77	78	84	317
	David Honeyman, Forest Hill	80	82	79	76	317
35	*W.H. Gardner, II, Buffalo	78	80	79	82	319
36	F.H. Belwood, Garden City	76	80	81	83	320
	J.R. Thompson, Philadelphia, C.C.	78	78	78	86	320
	John Hobens, Englewood	83	79	76	82	320
39	Tom Bonnar, Merion	76	79	81	85	321
40	T.J. Mulgrew, Cooperstown	79	85	76	84	323
	Karl Keffer, Royal Ottawa	76	76	86	85	323
42	John Harland, Buffalo	76	84	81	83	324
43	*H.B. Lee, Detroit	82	80	81	82	325
	James Dougherty, Merchantville	82	77	83	83	325
	Walter Fovargue, Skokie	81	83	78	83	325
	Ben Lord, Schenectady	80	86	88	81	325
	G.W. Singleton, Sacandaga Park	82	76	82	85	325
48	Jack Jolly, Newark	80	79	78	89	326
	J.C. Green, Virginia Hot Springs	83	81	79	83	326
	David Hunter, Essex County	80	85	77	84	326
	A. Woodward, Montreal	79	86	79	82	326
52	Thomas Edwards, Lehigh	78	87	84	80	329
53	J. Hagin, Salisbury	80	83	80	87	330
54	I. Stringer, St. Andrews	83	82	83	86	334
	William Trovinger, La Grange	77	82	86	89	334

*Amateur

1913
NINETEENTH OPEN CHAMPIONSHIP

Held at The Country Club, Brookline, Mass. September 18–19.
165 Entries; 162 Starters.

Forty-nine Contestants who completed 72 holes.

						Score
1	*Francis Ouimet, Woodland	77	74	74	79	304
2	Harry Vardon, England	75	72	78	79	304
3	Edward Ray, England	79	70	76	79	304
4	Walter Hagen, Rochester	73	78	76	80	307
	James M. Barnes, Tacoma	74	76	78	79	307
	Macdonald Smith, Wykagyl	71	79	80	77	307
	Louis Tellier, France	76	76	79	76	307
8	John J. McDermott, Atlantic City	74	79	77	78	308
9	Herbert Strong, Inwood	75	74	82	79	310
10	Patrick Doyle, Myopia	78	80	73	80	311
11	Elmer Loving, Arcola	76	80	75	81	312
	*W.C. Fownes, Jr., Oakmont	79	75	78	80	312
13	Alec Campbell, Brookline	77	80	76	80	313
14	Mike J. Brady, Wollaston	83	84	78	80	315
15	Matt Campbell, Brookline	83	80	77	76	316
16	*Fred Herreshoff, National	75	78	83	82	318
	Jock Hutchison, Allegheny	77	76	80	85	318
	Wilfrid E. Reid, England	75	72	85	86	318
	Alex Smith, Wykagyl	82	75	82	79	318
	Tom McNamara, Boston	73	86	75	84	318
21	Peter Robertson, Fall River	79	80	78	82	319
	George Sargent, Chevy Chase	75	76	79	89	319
	C.R. Murray, Royal Montreal	80	80	80	79	319
	*Robert Andrews, New Haven	83	73	83	80	319
	John Croke, Calumet	72	83	83	81	319
26	Charles Thom, Shinnecock	76	76	84	85	321
27	John Dowling, Scarsdale	77	77	82	85	322
	*Jerome D. Travers, Upper Montclair	78	78	81	85	322
	R.G. Macdonald, Hyde Park	80	79	84	79	322
30	J.H. Taylor, Lakeside	81	80	78	84	323
	Frank Belwood, Garden City	79	83	80	81	323
	James Donaldson, Glen View	79	76	85	83	323
33	Jack Hobens, Englewood	78	79	84	83	324
	A.H. Murray, Kanawaki	76	82	81	85	324
	Dave Ogilvie, Morris County	81	77	82	84	324
36	H.H. Barker, Roe Buck	80	79	85	82	326
	Alec Ross, Brae Burn	71	80	93	82	326
	Tom Anderson, Jr., Oakmont	82	85	82	80	326
39	Fred McLeod, Columbia	80	85	82	80	327
	Tom Vardon, Onwentsia	85	78	79	85	327
41	J.R. Thomson, Philadelphia C.C.	80	80	84	84	328
	John Shippen, Maidstone	81	73	87	87	328
43	Willie Maguire, Houston	85	80	82	82	329
44	Walter Fovarque, Skokie	79	83	81	87	330
45	Karl Keffer, Royal Ottawa	79	84	81	88	332
	Joe Sylvester, New York Golf	81	81	87	83	332
47	G. Cummings, Toronto	81	79	88	86	334
48	Tom Bonnar, Macklenburg	86	79	85	88	338
49	R.M. Thomson, Glen Ridge	84	79	90	87	340

*Amateur
Playoff—September 20: Ouimet, 72; Vardon, 77; Ray, 78.

1914
TWENTIETH OPEN CHAMPIONSHIP

Held at the Midlothian Country Club, Blue Island, Ill,, August 20–21.
129 Entries.
Fifty Contestants who completed 72 holes.

						Score
1	Walter C. Hagen, Rochester	68	74	75	73	290
2	*Charles Evans, Jr., Edgewater	76	74	71	70	291
3	George Sargent, Chevy Chase	74	77	74	72	297
	Fred McLeod, Columbia	78	73	75	71	297
5	*Francis Quimet, Woodland	69	76	75	78	298
	Mike J. Brady, Wollaston	78	72	74	74	298
	James A. Donaldson, Glen View	72	79	74	73	298
8	Louis Tellier, Canoe Brook	72	75	74	78	299
9	John J. McDermott, Atlantic City	77	74	74	75	300
	Arthur Smith, Arlington	79	73	76	72	300
11	*W. Rautenbusch, Chicago	76	75	75	75	301
	James Simpson, Milwaukee	76	71	77	77	301
13	J.J. O'Brien, Westbrook	74	72	77	79	302
	Joe Mitchell, Upper Montclair	77	69	77	79	302
	Bob Peebles, Topeka	78	75	74	75	302
	James Barnes, Whitemarsh	73	76	80	73	302
	Tom McNamara, Boston	72	71	76	83	302
	George Simpson, Omaha	73	76	76	77	302
	C.H. Hoffner, Atlantic City	77	76	77	72	302
20	Dan Kenny, Hamilton	76	75	76	76	303
	Tom Kerrigan, Dedham	76	73	77	77	303
22	*W.K. Wood, Homewood	77	73	77	78	305
	Alex Ross, Brae Burn	72	75	82	76	305
24	Walter Fovargue, Skokie	81	81	77	77	306
25	Jack Munro, Chicago	83	74	75	75	307
	R.M. Thompson, Glen Ridge	79	75	78	75	307
27	Otto Hackbarth, Hinsdale	82	75	77	75	309
28	C.P. Nelson, Oklahoma	77	81	77	75	310
	Jack Burke, Thunder Bay	75	77	77	81	310
	Fred Brand, Mt. Lebanon	78	74	76	82	310
31	Tom Vardon, Onwentsia	76	76	77	82	311
32	W.J. Bell, Toronto	79	79	75	79	312
33	*K.P. Edwards, Midlothian	77	76	81	78	312
	H. Lagerblade, Youngstown	75	78	75	84	312
35	Alex Taylor, Ravisloe	80	77	77	79	313
	William Kidd, Algonquin	80	77	81	75	313
37	C.W. Hall, Birmingham	76	77	81	81	315
	Jack Jolly, Newark	81	77	79	78	315
39	*Jack Neville, Claremont	78	77	80	81	316
	George Cummings	77	81	80	78	316
41	Dave McKay, Bellevue	77	82	79	79	317
	Jack Gatherum, Ridgewood	78	77	82	80	317
43	Andrew Campbell, Philadelphia	83	80	73	82	318
44	J.C. Hackbarth, Midlothian	73	84	82	80	319
45	Jack Croke, Calumet	77	83	82	78	320
	Willie Maguire, Houston	77	80	81	82	320
	A.G. Herr, Lincoln	80	78	79	83	320
48	J.C. Green, Hot Springs	80	81	79	82	322
49	J.R. Thompson, Philadelphia	81	77	84	83	325
	Frank Adams, French Lick	80	81	84	80	325

*Amateur

1915
TWENTY-FIRST OPEN CHAMPIONSHIP

Held at the Baltusrol Golf Club, Springfield, N.J., June 17–18.
141 Entries; 130 Starters.

Fifty-one Contestants who completed 72 holes.

					Score
1	*Jerome D. Travers, Upper Montclair	148	73	76	297
2	Tom McNamara, Boston	149	74	75	298
3	Robert G. MacDonald, Buffalo	149	73	78	300
4	James M. Barnes, Whitemarsh Valley	146	76	79	301
	Louis Tellier, Canoe Brook	146	76	79	301
6	Mike J. Brady, Wollaston	147	75	80	302
7	George Low, Baltusrol	152	76	75	303
8	Fred McLeod, Columbia	150	76	79	305
	Jock Hutchison, Pittsburgh	153	76	76	305
10	George Sargent, Chevy Chase	152	79	75	306
	Jack Park, Maidstone	154	75	77	306
	Emmett French, York	156	75	75	306
	Gilbert Nicholls, Wilmington	159	73	74	306
	Tom Kerrigan, Dedham	153	76	77	306
	Alex Campbell, Baltimore	151	74	81	306
	Wilfrid Reid, Seaview	155	75	76	306
	Walter C. Hagen, Rochester	151	76	79	306
18	*Charles Evans, Jr., Edgewater	152	80	75	307
19	*Maxwell R. Marston, Baltusrol	154	80	74	308
	James A. Donaldson, Glen View	162	76	70	308
21	A.J. Sanderson, Boulogne, France	153	77	79	309
22	Alex Smith, Wykagyl	154	78	79	311
	Jack Dowling, Scarsdale	154	80	77	311
24	H.H. Barker, Richmond	158	80	77	312
	C.H. Hoffner, Woodburv	158	79	75	312
26	Joe Mitchell, Ridgewood	156	74	83	313
	Herbert Strong, Inwood	159	78	76	313
28	George T. Sayers, Merion	156	81	77	314
29	Ben Sayers, North Berwick, Scotland	159	79	77	315
	David Ogilvie, Morris County	153	83	79	315
	Otto Hackbarth, Hinsdale	155	79	81	315
32	David Stevens, Mohawk	156	80	80	316
	J.J. O'Brien, Mansfield	157	80	79	316
	Elmer W. Loving, Quaker Ridge	156	75	85	316
35	William Macfarlane, Baltimore	164	75	78	317
	*Francis Quimet, Woodland	156	80	81	317
37	Tom Boyd, Fox Hills	158	79	81	318
	James R. Thompson, Philadelphia	161	78	79	318
	Tom Anderson, Montclair	158	79	81	318
	Macdonald Smith, Wykagyl	159	80	79	318
41	Jack Hobens, Englewood	159	83	78	320
	Harry Hampton, Lenox	160	78	82	320
	Bert Battell, Flushing	160	83	77	320
44	Orrin Terry, Belmont Springs	162	78	82	322
45	George McLean, Dunwoodie	165	80	78	323
	Isaac Mackie, Oakwood	160	81	82	323
47	G.O. Simpson, Oak Park	161	76	87	324
	Charles Rowe, Oakmont	163	82	79	324
49	Dan Kenny, Hamilton, Ont.	158	81	86	325
50	Joe Sylvester, West End	157	84	88	329
51	E.K. McCarthy, Jacksonville	166	81	84	331

*Amateur.

1916
TWENTY-SECOND OPEN CHAMPIONSHIP

Held at Minikahda, Minneapolis, Minn., June 29–30.
94 Entries; 81 Starters.

Fifty-six Contestants who completed 72 holes.

						Score
1	*Charles Evans, Jr., Edgewater	70	69	74	73	286
2	Jock Hutchison, Allegheny	73	75	72	68	288
3	James M. Barnes, Whitemarsh Valley	71	74	71	74	290
4	Wilfrid Reid, Wilmington	70	72	79	72	293
	Gilbert Nicholls, Great Neck	73	76	71	73	293
	George Sargent, Interlachen	75	71	72	75	293
7	Walter Hagen, Rochester	73	76	75	71	295
8	R.G. MacDonald, Buffalo	74	72	77	73	296
9	Mike J. Brady, Oakridge	75	73	75	74	297
	Tom Vardon, White Bear Yacht	76	72	75	74	297
	J.J. O'Brien, Mansfield	76	72	73	76	297
12	Jack Dowling, Scarsdale	71	76	75	76	298
13	Louis Tellier, Brookline	74	75	72	78	299
	Walter Fovargue, Skokie	76	74	74	75	299
15	Bob Peebles, Shawnee Heights	73	72	76	79	300
	H.C. Lagerblade, Youngstown	77	78	72	73	300
	Tom McNamara, Unattached	75	79	73	73	300
	J.B. Simpson, Blue Mound	75	76	76	73	300
19	Otto Hackbarth, Cincinnati	77	80	69	75	301
	George Turnbull, Midlothian	83	73	72	74	301
	George McLean, Dunwoodie	77	76	74	74	301
22	Joe Mitchell, Ridgewood	75	75	76	76	302
	J.A. Donaldson, Glen View	79	75	75	73	302
24	Fred McLeod, Columbia	74	75	77	77	303
	George Simpson, Oak Park	76	76	77	74	303
	Bert Battell, Flushing	76	75	75	77	303
	Arthur Fotheringham, Indian Hill	78	78	74	73	303
28	Alex Campbell, Baltimore	75	75	75	79	304
29	James Ferguson, Spring Lake	74	75	80	77	306
	Alex Cunningham, Wheeling	79	75	75	77	306
	Tom Kerrigan, Siwanoy	79	72	78	77	306
32	James Burke, Rockford	81	76	76	74	307
	Walter Clark, Denver	73	76	80	78	307
34	P.J. Gaudin, Onwentsia	81	77	78	72	308
	Norman Clark, Westmoreland	76	78	78	76	308
36	Herbert Strong, Inwood	78	77	77	77	309
	W.C. Sherwood, Memphis	78	76	76	79	309
	James Wilson, Chenequa	79	79	74	77	309
39	*H.G. Legg, Minikahda	76	80	76	80	312
	Tom Boyd, Fox Hills	80	78	79	75	312
41	*J.S. Worthington, Mid Surrey	77	77	79	80	313
	John Gatherum, Chicago	78	75	80	80	313
43	H.C. Fletcher, Winnepeg	76	84	74	80	314
	Alfred J. Hackbarth, Hinsdale	79	74	80	81	314
	C.W. Hackney, Atlantic City	80	77	76	81	314
	Tom Morris, Town & C.C.	78	78	82	76	314
47	Arthur Clarkson, Highland	77	81	79	78	315
	Dave Livie, Geneva	77	77	80	81	315
49	Carl H. Anderson, Unattached	81	77	80	79	317
50	Charles Morton, Unattached	83	77	80	78	318
	Jack Croke, Exmoor	77	80	84	77	318
52	Arthur Reid, Virginia	77	76	83	83	319
53	Elwood F. Queen, Interlaken	76	75	86	83	320
54	*Hugo R. Johnston, Minikahda	86	75	85	82	328
	H.L. Van Every, Lafayette	81	79	85	83	328
	Jack Jolly, Newark	78	84	82	84	328

*Amateur

1919
TWENTY-THIRD OPEN CHAMPIONSHIP

Held at the Brae Burn Country Club, West Newton, Mass., June 9–11.
142 Entries.

Fifty-six Contestants who completed 72 holes.

						Score
1	Walter Hagen, Oakland Hills	78	73	75	75	301
2	Mike J. Brady, Oakley	74	74	73	80	301
3	Jock Hutchison, Glen View	78	76	76	76	306
	Tom McNamara, New York	80	73	79	74	306
5	George McLean, Great Neck	81	75	76	76	308
	Louis Tellier, Brae Burn	73	78	82	75	308
7	John Cowan, Stockbridge	79	74	75	81	309
8	Fred McLeod, Columbia	78	77	79	78	312
9	*Charles Evans, Jr., Edgewater	77	76	82	78	313
	George Bowden, Commonwealth	73	78	75	86	313
11	Harry Hampton, Richmond, Va.	79	81	77	78	315
	James M. Barnes, Sunset Hill	77	78	79	81	315
13	Clarence Hackney, Atlantic City	83	78	81	74	316
	Charles Hoffner, Philmont	72	78	77	89	316
	Isaac Mackie, Canoe Brook	82	75	78	81	316
16	Gilbert Nicholls, Great Neck	81	78	82	77	318
	Alex Ross, Detroit	77	78	77	86	318
18	Pat Doyle, Deal	78	82	76	83	319
	*Francis Quimet, Woodland	76	79	79	85	319
	James West, Rockaway Hunt	79	82	80	78	319
21	J.D. Edgar, Druid Hills	80	78	82	80	320
	Alex Cunningham, Wheeling	79	81	79	81	320
	Wilfrid Reid, Wilmington	82	78	80	80	320
24	J. Sanderson, Sleepy Hollow	85	79	73	74	321
	*Jesse Guilford, Woodland	79	78	84	80	321
26	Herbert Lagerblade, Youngstown	79	80	82	81	322
	Tom Kerrigan, Siwanoy	80	79	82	81	322
	Otto Hackbarth, Cincinnati	77	79	82	84	322
29	George Sargent, Interlachen	84	79	82	78	323
	Bob Macdonald, Indian Hill	81	78	80	84	323
	G. Fotheringham, Glen Cove	81	82	79	81	323
32	W.D. Robinson, Philadelphia	81	78	85	80	324
	*John G. Anderson, Siwanoy	80	77	84	83	324
34	Emmet French, York	78	79	81	87	325
	John Bredemus, Unattached	83	79	86	77	325
	W.C. Sherwood, Mount Builders	80	79	83	83	325
37	W.V. Hoare, Tedesco	82	83	82	79	326
	James Macgregor, Agawam	83	78	82	83	326
	Tom Mulgrew, Hackensack	77	83	84	82	326
	Arthur Reid, Blind Brook	84	80	81	81	326
41	George Low, Baltusrol	81	81	84	81	327
	Willie Ogg, Atlanta	82	79	81	85	327
43	G.M. Gordon, Wannamoisett	83	83	80	83	329
	*D.E. Sawyer, Siwanoy	82	84	81	82	329
45	Wilbur Oaks, Bloomfield Springs	84	85	79	82	330
46	James Crossan, Wheatley Hills	81	88	83	79	331
47	Matt Campbell, Essex County	81	85	88	78	332
48	Harry Cowie, Tate Springs	85	85	80	84	334
49	*L.B. Patton, Homestead	86	79	87	83	335
50	R. Pierce, Brae Burn	83	82	89	84	338
51	Scotty Robson, Olean	83	81	92	84	340
	Alex Gerard, Hyde Park	83	84	83	90	340
	P.C. Canausa, Oak Ridge	81	82	90	87	340
	John Shea, Kernwood	83	84	84	89	340
55	Eugene McCarthy, Charlotte	82	85	90	83	345
56	R.H. Wales, Chestnut Hills	84	84	91	90	349

*Amateur.

Playoff—June 12: Hagen, 77; Brady, 78.

1920
TWENTY-FOURTH OPEN CHAMPIONSHIP

Held at Inverness Club, Toledo, Ohio, August 12–13.
265 Entries.

Sixty-seven Contestants who completed 72 holes.

						Score
1	Edward Ray, England	74	73	73	75	295
2	Harry Vardon, England	74	73	71	78	296
	Jack Burke, Town & Country	75	77	72	72	296
	Leo Diegel, Lake Shore	72	74	73	77	296
	Jock Hutchison, Glen View	69	76	74	77	296
6	*Charles Evans, Jr., Edgewater	74	76	73	75	298
	James M. Barnes, Sunset Hills	76	70	76	76	298
8	*Robert T. Jones, Jr., Atlanta	78	74	70	77	299
	Willie Macfarlane, Pt. Washington	76	75	74	74	299
10	Bob MacDonald, Bob O'Link	73	78	71	78	300
11	Walter C. Hagen, New York	74	73	77	77	301
12	Clarence Hackney, Atlantic City	78	74	74	76	302
13	Fred McLeod, Columbia	75	77	73	79	304
14	Mike Brady, Oakland Hills	77	76	74	78	305
	Frank McNamara, Cherry Valley	78	77	76	74	305
	Charles H. Rowe, Oakmont	76	78	77	74	305
17	Laurie Ayton, Evanston	75	78	76	77	306
	John Golden, Tuxedo	77	80	74	75	306
	Eddie Loos, Ravisloe	75	74	73	84	306
20	James West, Rockaway Hunt	80	77	75	75	307
	J.D. Edgar, Atlanta	73	82	74	78	307
22	Harry Hampton, Richmond	79	76	74	79	308
23	Tom Kerrigan, Siwanoy	77	81	74	77	309
	Gilbert Nicholls, New York	77	82	75	75	309
	J.J. O'Brien, Sisterville	82	77	73	77	309
	D.K. White, Toledo	78	75	79	77	309
27	William Mehlhorn, Tulsa	78	74	79	79	310
	Peter O'Hara, Shackamaxon	84	74	74	78	310
	Alexander Ross, Detroit	80	76	77	77	310
30	Gene Sarazen, Fort Wayne	79	79	76	77	311
	G.L. Bowden, Commonwealth	74	80	76	81	311
	George McLean, Great Neck	83	76	73	79	311
	Willie Kidd, Minneapolis	77	81	76	77	311
	Charles Hall, Birmingham	77	80	76	78	311
35	Fred Bell, Denver	80	79	76	77	312
	Emil Loeffler, Oakmont	76	80	77	79	312
	*W.C. Fownes, Jr., Oakmont	80	78	71	83	312
38	Wallie Hunter, Onwentsia	75	82	78	78	313
	Jack Dowling, Scarsdale	81	79	78	75	313
	Jack Gordon, Buffalo	79	77	76	81	313
	Louis Tellier, Brae Burn	78	75	77	83	313
	George Sargent, Scioto	76	81	78	78	313
43	Pat Doyle, Deal	85	76	79	74	314
	Otto Hackbarth, Cincinnati	83	78	77	76	314
45	John J. Farrell, Quaker Ridge	80	77	78	80	315
	Charles Thom, Shinnecock Hills	79	83	78	75	315
47	Rudolph E. Knepper, Cioux City	76	77	83	80	316
48	*Tommy Armour, Scotland	77	83	76	81	317
	*Harrison Johnston, Toledo	80	81	76	80	317
50	J.M. Simpson, Indianapolis	78	77	85	78	318
	Fred Brand, Allegheny	84	77	80	77	318
	Alex Cunningham, St. Joseph	79	78	80	81	318
53	Alex Ayton, Evanston	79	79	75	78	320
	Frank Adams, Winnipeg, Canada	82	84	73	81	320
	Dave Robertson, Detroit	82	77	83	78	320
56	Wilfrid Reid, Wilmington	80	85	78	78	321
	C.H. Mayo, Edgewater	77	81	83	80	321
	C.H. Lorms, Inverness	82	79	78	82	321
59	Dan Kenny, Olean, N.Y.	78	81	79	84	322
	Frank Sprogell, Montgomery, Ala.	81	82	79	80	322
	John Cowan, Oakley, Mass.	83	78	81	80	322
62	James Carberry, Lagrange, Ill.	80	81	80	83	324
63	Lloyd Gullickson, Westmoreland	80	80	76	79	325
64	*Howard Lee, Detroit	83	82	83	79	327
65	J.E. Rodgers, Parkersburg	90	82	81	76	329
66	Peter Walsh, Butler, Pa.	85	88	80	83	336
67	E.K. McCarthy, Jacksonville	76	83	87	91	337

*Amateur.

1921
TWENTY-FIFTH OPEN CHAMPIONSHIP

Held at Columbia Country Club, Chevy Chase, Md., July 21–22.
262 Entries, 258 Starters.

Sixty-four Contestants who completed 72 holes.

						Score
1	James M. Barnes, Pelham	69	75	73	72	289
2	Walter Hagen, New York	79	73	72	74	298
	Fred McLeod, Columbia	74	74	76	74	298
4	*Charles Evans, Jr., Edgewater	73	78	76	75	302
5	*Robert T. Jones, Jr., Atlanta	78	71	77	77	303
	Emmett French, Youngstown	75	77	74	77	303
	Alex Smith, Shennecossett	75	75	79	74	303
8	George Duncan, England	72	78	78	77	305
	Clarence Hackney, Atlantic City	74	76	78	77	305
10	Emil Loeffler, Oakmont, Pittsburgh	74	77	74	81	306
11	Alfred Hackbarth, Park Ridge, Ill.	80	76	82	69	307
12	Eddie Loos, Ravisloe	76	79	75	78	308
13	Cyril Walker, Englewood	78	76	76	79	309
14	Louis Tellier, Brae Burn	76	74	78	82	310
	*Jess Sweetser, Siwanoy	78	78	77	77	310
	Mike Brady, Oakland Hills, Detroit	77	80	78	75	310
17	Gene Sarazen, Titusville	83	74	77	77	311
18	Laurie Ayton, Evanston	81	74	74	83	312
	Jock Hutchison, Glen View	75	83	77	77	312
	Peter O'Hara, Shackamaxon	81	82	76	73	312
21	Charles R. Murray, Montreal	75	73	82	83	313
22	John Golden, Tuxedo	77	77	82	78	314
	Charles Mothersole, Pinehurst	81	78	79	76	314
	Harry Hampton, Brooklands	80	78	79	77	314
	Otto Hackbarth, Hamilton, Cincinnati	79	76	80	79	314
26	*Jesse Guilford, Woodland	79	75	78	83	315
	Tom Boyd, Fox Hills	81	79	79	76	315
	Robert A. Cruickshank, Essex County, N.J.	75	77	80	83	315
	Leo Diegel, Lochmoor	75	82	83	75	315
30	Pat O'Hara, Richmond County	77	78	79	82	316
	P.O. Hart, Marietta, O.	83	80	76	77	316
32	Al Watrous, Red Run	78	76	83	80	317
33	W.H. Trovinger, Bloomfield Hills	79	83	79	77	318
	Joe Kirkwood, Australia	75	81	80	82	318
35	Robert Barnett, Tredyffrin	81	81	80	77	319
	Tom Kerrigan, Siwanoy	73	81	86	79	319
37	W.M. Leach, Merchantsville, N.J.	79	83	77	81	320
38	John J. Farrell, Quaker Ridge	79	79	81	82	321
39	Jack Gordon, Buffalo	78	83	81	81	323
40	Joe Novak, Spokane	80	78	85	81	324
	*Nelson M. Whitney, Audubon	79	80	85	80	324
	Wilfred Thomson, C.C. of Virginia	79	80	82	83	324
	James West, Rockaway Hunting C.	81	81	77	85	324
44	Joe Sylvester, St. Albans	81	82	84	78	325
	Eddie Townes, Shannopin	80	77	82	86	325
46	Charles P. Betchler, Arlington, Md.	82	81	82	81	326
	Charles Thom, Shinnecock Hills	82	86	78	80	326
48	Charles Clark, Engineers	86	74	80	87	327
	George McLean, Grassy Sprain	81	79	80	87	327
50	Fred C. Canausa, West Point, N.Y.	77	85	84	82	328
51	T.J. Rajoppi, Maplewood, N.H.	84	89	77	79	329
	W. Nelson, Highlands, Indianapolis	78	82	84	85	329
53	Frank Coltart, Philadelphia, C.C.	84	82	81	83	330
	*R.L. Finkenstaedt, Columbia	82	80	85	83	330
55	Alex Campbell, Losantiville	80	86	84	81	331
	W.J. Damen, Montgomery, Ala.	81	84	79	87	331
57	J. Victor East, Australia	81	83	83	86	333
	Jack Forrester, Meadow Brook, N.Y.	78	88	89	78	333
	Jack Pirie, Woodmere, N.J.	82	80	87	84	333
60	Al Natale, Lansdowne, Pa.	88	83	73	90	334
61	James C. Ferguson, Spring Lake, N.J.	87	80	86	82	335
62	John A. Park, Maidstone	85	82	85	84	336
63	Isaac S. Mackie, Canoe Brook	81	83	84	89	337
64	Alex Cunningham, Toledo	91	81	84	82	338

*Amateur.

1922
TWENTY-SIXTH OPEN CHAMPIONSHIP

Held at Skokie Country Club, Glencoe, Illinois, July 14–15.
323 Entries, 78 Starters.

Seventy-one Contestants who completed 72 holes.

						Score
1	Gene Sarazen, Highland, Pittsburgh	72	73	75	68	288
2	John L. Black, Oakland, Calif.	71	71	75	72	289
	*Robert T. Jones, Jr., Atlanta	74	72	70	73	289
4	William E. Mehlhorn, Shreveport	73	71	72	74	290
5	Walter Hagen, New York	68	77	74	72	291
6	George Duncan, England	76	73	75	72	296
7	Leo Diegel, New Orleans	77	76	73	71	297
8	Mike Brady, Detroit	73	75	74	76	298
	John Golden, Tuxedo	73	77	77	71	298
	Jock Hutchison, Glen View	78	74	71	75	298
11	Laurie Ayton, Evanston	72	76	78	73	299
	John J. Farrell, Quaker Ridge	73	76	75	75	299
13	Bob MacDonald, Bob-O'Link	73	76	75	76	300
	Joe Kirkwood, Australia	77	74	75	74	300
15	Eddie Loos, Lake Shore	75	76	73	77	301
16	*Charles Evans, Jr., Edgewater	72	76	74	80	302
17	George W. Hackney, Atlantic City	74	78	74	77	303
	Abe Mitchell, England	79	75	76	73	303
19	*Jesse P. Guilford, Woodland	77	74	76	78	305
	Emmett French, Youngstown	76	74	77	78	305
	Willie Ogg, Worcester	79	72	78	76	305
	Charles H. Hoffner, Philmont	79	76	77	73	305
	Harry Hampton, Detroit	76	75	77	77	305
24	Cyril Hughes, Lancaster	81	74	77	74	306
	James M. Barnes, Pelham	74	75	77	80	306
	*William I. Hunter, England	75	75	76	80	306
	*Fred J. Wright, Jr., Flintridge	76	77	73	80	306
28	Jack Burke, St. Paul	76	77	81	73	307
	Lloyd Gullickson, DeKalb	77	70	83	77	307
	Robert A. Cruickshank, Shackamaxon	82	74	74	77	307
31	Alfred T. Hackbarth, Park Ridge	77	75	77	79	308
	Tom Kerrigan, Siwanoy	80	79	75	74	308
	George Bowden, Cincinnati	76	79	76	77	308
	George Kerrigan, White Beeches	76	78	78	76	308
35	*Harrison R. Johnston, St. Paul	78	75	80	76	309
	Pat O'Hara, Richmond County	79	76	76	78	309
37	Al Watrous, Detroit	73	79	79	79	310
38	Thomas J. Harmon, Hudson River	80	72	80	79	311
	Chick Fraser, St. Paul	79	76	76	80	311
40	W.M. Creavy, Kansas City	79	76	81	76	312
	P.O. Hart, Marietta	80	77	79	76	312
	Cyril Walker, Englewood	76	81	77	78	312
	Jack Turnesa, Fairview, N.Y.	75	78	81	78	312
44	George McLean, Grassy Sprain	78	78	79	78	313
	George Martin, Santa Barbara	76	80	81	76	313
	Jack Blakeslee, Delaware	80	82	76	75	313
47	John Cowan, Oakley, Mass.	74	78	84	79	315
	Otto G. Hackbarth, Cincinnati	76	81	79	79	315
	Frank Kennet, Glencoe	80	82	80	73	315
	Fred Ford, Kansas City	79	79	75	82	315
	Mortie Dutra, Del Monte	76	77	78	84	315
52	Alex Campbell, Cincinnati	78	79	78	81	316
53	Charles D. Thom, Shinnecock Hills	77	79	80	81	317
54	Tom Boyd, Fox Hills	80	81	80	78	319
55	*Frank A. Godchaux, New Orleans	79	77	80	85	321
	Harry Bolestra, Palma Ceia	76	83	82	80	321
	Dave Robertson, Grosse Pointe	76	84	77	84	321
	Charles H. Rowe, Oakmont	83	82	77	79	321
	J.E. Rogers, Dayton, O.	83	83	79	76	321
	*Dewey E. Weber, Edgewood	77	80	82	82	321
61	Bob Peebles, Louisville	84	81	80	77	322
	Edward L. Gow, Weston, Mass.	83	85	79	75	322
63	G.M. Christ, Rochester, N.Y.	77	80	81	85	323
	Frank Sprogell, Memphis	80	79	79	85	323
	F.R. Decker, Knollwood	74	76	86	87	323
	Jack Croke, Northmoor	82	85	78	78	323
67	Frank McNamara, Ortega, Fla.	77	79	87	82	325
68	Alex Guild, Exmoor	81	85	87	84	327
69	Ned McKenna, Rochester, N.Y.	78	85	84	82	329
70	Ben Lord, Glens Falls	80	83	87	86	336
71	Ira C. Couch, Glen View	86	81	86	86	339

*Amateur

1923
TWENTY-SEVENTH OPEN CHAMPIONSHIP

Held at Inwood Country Club, Inwood, N.Y., July 13–14.
Yardage—6,632. Par 72. 360 Entries; 77 Starters.

Sixty-one Contestants who completed 72 holes.

						Score
1	*Robert T. Jones, Jr., Atlanta	71	73	76	76	296
2	Robert A. Cruickshank, Shackamaxon	73	72	78	73	296
3	Jock Hutchison, Glen View	70	72	82	78	302
4	Jack Forrester, Hollywood, N.J.	75	73	77	78	303
5	John J. Farrell, Quaker Ridge	76	77	75	76	304
	Francis Gallett, Port Washington	76	72	77	79	304
	*W.M. Reekie, Upper Montclair	80	74	75	75	304
8	William E. Mehlhorn, St. Louis	73	79	75	79	306
	Leo Diegel, Friendship	77	77	76	76	306
	Al Watrous, Detroit	74	75	76	81	306
11	Cyril Hughes, Lancaster	74	76	80	77	307
12	James M. Barnes, Pelham	78	81	74	75	308
	Joe Kirkwood, New York	77	77	79	75	308
14	Joe Turnesa, Elmsford	76	81	74	78	309
	*Charles Evans, Jr., Edgewater	79	80	76	74	309
16	Charles L. Mothersole, New York	77	80	71	82	310
	Gene Sarazen, Briarcliff Lodge	79	78	73	80	310
18	Willie Ogg, Worcester	74	76	80	81	311
	Walter Hagen, New York	77	75	73	86	311
20	Mike Brady, Oakland Hills	74	81	76	81	312
	Macdonald Smith, Los Angeles	77	76	81	78	312
22	Emmett French, Youngstown	79	78	77	79	313
23	Cyril Walker, Englewood	76	78	80	80	314
24	P.O. Hart, Marietta, O.	79	80	78	78	315
	Joe Sylvester, St. Albans	77	80	79	79	315
26	John L. Black, Wichita	82	76	78	80	316
	William M. Creavy, Kansas City	73	81	77	85	316
	*Eddie Held, Algonquin	80	75	79	82	316
29	Hutt Martin, Unattached	78	78	76	85	317
	*Francis Quimet, Woodland	82	75	78	82	317
	George Sargent, Scioto	77	77	81	82	317
32	Fred Baroni, Montour Heights	80	80	78	80	318
	Bob MacDonald, Chicago	76	80	77	85	318
	Arthur Beebe, Long Branch	77	82	78	81	318
35	Abe G. Espinosa, Unattached	82	84	78	75	319
36	Dave McKay, Pittsburgh	79	82	79	80	320
	Harold A. Sampson, San Francisco	76	81	83	80	320
38	Jack Burke, St. Paul	74	78	87	82	321
39	Fred Canausa, West Point	72	82	89	79	322
40	W.L. Kline, Garden City	79	78	82	84	323
	Charles H. Rowe, Oakmont	81	78	79	85	323
	S. Sanderson, Franklin, N.H.	83	76	81	83	323
	Tom Stevens, Minikahda	77	79	82	85	323
44	Thomas J. Harmon, Jr., Hudson River	77	79	84	84	324
	Peter Harmon, Onondaga	89	77	83	75	324
46	George Bowden, Cincinnati	77	81	81	87	326
	Tom Kerrigan, Siwanoy	85	77	81	83	326
	Eugene McCarthy, Green Valley	79	75	84	88	326
49	Harry Hampton, Brooklands	78	84	84	82	328
	Arthur Reid, Arsley	80	80	80	88	328
51	Louis Chiapetta, Unattached	83	84	80	88	329
52	*Frank W. Dyer, Upper Montclair	82	85	81	83	331
	Edward H. Gow, Weston, Mass.	84	82	83	82	331
54	Harold Calloway, Rome, N.Y.	84	83	84	83	334
55	Eddie Williams, Peoria, Ill.	80	83	87	85	335
56	C.L. Booth, Putnam, L.I.	86	86	81	83	336
	Ben Parola, Linden, N.J.	86	84	82	84	336
58	Henry Ciuci, Unattached	85	82	86	85	338
59	*R.A. Walsh, Scottish-American	87	87	83	83	340
60	Dan Williams, Shackamaxon	91	82	81	87	341
61	Walter E. Ward, Woodbury, N.J.	86	89	85	85	345

*Amateur.
Playoff—July 15: Jones, 76; Cruickshank, 78.

1924
TWENTY-EIGHTH OPEN CHAMPIONSHIP

Held at Oakland Hills Country Club, Birmingham, Michigan, June 5–6.
319 Entries; 85 Starters.

57 Contestants who completed 72 holes.

						Score
1	Cyril Walker, Englewood	74	74	74	75	297
2	*Robert T. Jones, Jr., Atlanta	74	73	75	78	300
3	William E. Mehlhorn, Normandy, Mo.	72	75	76	78	301
4	Robert A. Cruickshank, Shackamaxon	77	72	76	78	303
	Walter Hagen, New York	75	75	76	77	303
	Macdonald Smith, San Francisco	78	72	77	76	303
7	Abe Espinosa, San Francisco	80	71	77	77	305
	Peter O'Hara, White Beeches	76	79	74	76	305
9	Mike Brady, Winged Foot	75	77	77	77	306
10	*Charles Evans, Jr., Edgewater	77	77	76	77	307
	Eddie Loos, Chicago	73	81	75	78	307
	Dave Robertson, Redford, Mich.	73	76	77	81	307
13	Thomas D. Armour, New York	78	76	75	80	309
	Clarence Hackney, Atlantic City	81	72	78	78	309
15	Willie Ogg, Worcester	75	80	76	79	310
	Joe Turnesa, Elmsford, N.Y.	76	78	78	78	310
17	W.R. Bourne, Westfield, N.J.	78	76	79	80	313
	Gene Sarazen, Briarcliff, N.Y.	74	80	80	79	313
19	Johnny Farrell, Quaker Ridge	79	76	77	82	314
	Tom Kerrigan, Siwanoy	77	74	89	74	314
	Jock Rogers, Dayton	82	77	77	78	314
22	Emmett French, Youngstown	79	79	78	79	315
	Joe Kirkwood, New York	77	80	80	78	315
	Jimmy West, Rockaway Hunt.	81	72	78	84	315
25	Laurie Ayton, Evanston, Ill.	77	79	84	76	316
	Leo Diegel, Friendship	78	78	82	78	316
	John Golden, Paterson, N.J.	75	83	78	80	316
	Jack Stait, Hartford, Ct.	79	77	81	79	316
29	Wiffy H. Cox, Marine & Field	82	76	81	78	317
	*Jesse P. Guilford, Woodland	80	78	79	80	317
31	Otto Hackbarth, Cincinnati	79	79	76	84	318
	Jock Hutchison, Glen View	84	79	74	81	318
33	T.J. Harmon, Jr., Hudson River	85	77	81	77	320
	P.O. Hart, Marietta, O.	81	75	80	84	320
	Charles A. Lorms, Columbus, O.	78	85	75	82	320
36	Jack Forrester, Deal, N.J.	80	82	80	79	321
37	George Aulback, Winthrop, Mass.	77	84	80	81	322
	Gunnar Nelson, Chicago	76	85	76	85	322
	Joe Novak, Berkeley, Cal.	81	80	80	81	322
40	Charles H. Hoffner, Philmont	78	76	85	84	323
	Cyril Hughes, Lancaster, Pa.	79	77	83	84	323
	Fred McLeod, Columbia	81	76	80	86	323
43	George Sargent, Scioto	79	84	77	84	324
44	Andrew Kay, Toronto	80	81	79	85	325
	R.W. Treacy, Danville, Ill.	83	79	85	78	325
46	Jock Hendry, St. Paul	79	80	83	84	326
47	R. Linares, Long Beach, Calif.	86	82	78	81	327
	Wilfrid Reid, Detroit	79	83	83	82	327
	Dave Trufelli, Wichita, Kans.	84	83	78	82	327
50	D.D. Hackney, Merrimack Valley	82	89	78	79	328
	Gene McCarthy, Memphis	81	84	80	83	328
52	Frank Sprogell, Memphis	80	83	85	81	329
53	Alex Campbell, Cincinnati	78	80	89	84	331
54	Harold Long, Pontiac, Ill.	84	81	83	85	333
55	J.B. Lord, Glens Falls, N.Y.	83	83	84	87	337
56	Joe Devaney, Grosse Isle	87	84	84	85	340
57	*Arthur B. Sweet, Chicago	81	88	87	87	343

*Amateur.

1925
TWENTY-NINTH OPEN CHAMPIONSHIP

Held at Worcester Country Club, Worcester, Mass., June 3–5.
Yardage–6,430. Par 71. 445 Entries.

Sixty-six Contestants who completed 72 holes.

						Score
1	Willie Macfarlane, Oak Ridge	74	67	72	78	291
2	*Robert T. Jones, Jr., Atlanta	77	70	70	74	291
3	Johnny Farrell, Quaker Ridge	71	74	69	78	292
	*Francis Quimet, Woodland	70	73	73	76	292
5	Gene Sarazen, Fresh Meadow	72	72	75	74	293
	Walter Hagen, Pasadena, Fla.	72	76	71	74	293
7	Mike Brady, Winged Foot	74	72	74	74	294
8	Leo Diegel, Glen Oaks, N.Y.	73	68	77	78	296
9	Laurie Ayton, Evanston	75	71	73	78	297
	Al Espinosa, Glencoe	72	71	74	80	297
11	Joe Turnesa, Fairview	76	74	71	78	299
	Macdonald Smith, Lakeville	73	79	72	75	299
13	Al Watrous, Grand Rapids	78	73	74	75	300
	Willie Hunter, Los Angeles	75	77	75	73	300
15	Bill Mehlhorn, Westmoreland	78	72	75	76	301
	Bob MacDonald, Chicago	75	77	77	72	301
17	Clarence Hackney, Atlantic City	78	72	73	79	302
18	John Golden, North Jersey	76	75	82	70	303
	Tom Kerrigan, Siwanoy	75	79	74	75	303
20	Emmett French, Youngstown	77	74	77	76	304
	Tom Boyd, Fox Hills	73	79	75	77	304
	Francis Gallett, Manitowoc	73	70	84	77	304
	Bob Shave, Cleveland	81	72	77	74	304
	Jack Forrester, Hollywood	71	76	76	81	304
	Harry Hampton, Memphis	79	75	76	74	304
26	Charles H. Mayo, Pomonock	75	74	78	78	305
27	Jock Hutchison, Glen View	78	78	79	71	306
28	Wilfrid Reid, Detroit	79	75	73	79	306
29	Jim Barnes, Temple Terrace	75	76	71	85	307
	George Heron, Westbury	75	77	77	78	307
31	George Kerrigan, Pasadena, Calif.	75	75	78	80	308
32	Arthur De Mane, Soundview	76	73	83	77	309
	Thomas J. Harmon, Jr., Hudson River	80	73	79	77	309
34	Charles Guest, Los Angeles	79	77	74	80	310
	F.W. Clarke, Asheville, N.C.	75	81	76	78	310
	Pat Doyle, Elmsford	78	77	74	81	310
37	H.C. Lagerblade, Bristol, Conn.	76	79	77	79	311
38	Fred Novak, Cohoes, N.Y.	78	77	79	79	313
	Alex Ayton, Evanston	76	80	83	74	313
	Tommy Armour, Unattached	76	84	80	73	313
	Tom Kennett, Bryn Mawr	78	77	78	80	313
	George Dernbach, Providence	75	79	81	78	313
43	G.M. Christ, Rochester, N.Y.	75	81	76	82	314
	Bill Klein, Garden City	72	81	79	82	314
45	Joe Kirkwood, Pasadena, Fla.	81	83	82	79	315
	Peter X. Harmon, Onondaga	79	77	79	80	315
47	William Creavy, Oklahoma City	83	80	73	80	316
	Jack O'Connor, West Orange	75	78	76	87	316
	Cyril Walker, Englewood	81	73	80	82	316
	Joe Novak, Berkeley, Calif.	77	85	76	78	316
51	Marty O'Loughlin, Plainfield	80	82	74	81	317
	Craig Wood, Louisville	81	78	77	81	317
53	George Stark, Indianapolis	82	78	81	77	318
54	Robert Barnett, Chevy Chase	82	81	79	77	319
	Alex Cunningham, Toledo	77	78	82	82	319
56	Eddie Murphy, Ridge	82	82	77	79	320
	George Aulbach, Arlmont	74	82	77	87	320
	Harold Long, Galesburg	77	83	76	84	320
59	Jimmy Thomson, Richmond, Va.	84	78	81	78	321
60	Capt. E.F. Carter, Brier Gate	80	77	78	87	322
	C.L. Booth, Putnam, Ct.	81	77	83	81	322
62	Ed Gayer, Los Angeles	75	81	81	86	323
	Willie Hunter, Onwentsia	77	78	86	82	323
64	J. Victor East, Longmeadow	75	81	83	85	324
65	Tom Jones, Fall River	83	79	84	81	327
66	J. C. Fee, Evanston	87	88	83	82	340

*Amateur.
Playoff, June 5; 36 holes; Macfarlane, 75–72–147; Jones, 75–73–148

1926
THIRTIETH OPEN CHAMPIONSHIP

Held at Scioto Country Club, Columbus, Ohio, July 8-10.
694 Entries, 155 Qualifiers, 147 Starters.
58 contestants who completed 72 holes.

						Score
1	*Robert T. Jones, Jr., Atlanta	70	79	71	73	293
2	Joe Turnesa, Fairview	71	74	72	77	294
3	Bill Mehlhorn, Chicago	68	75	76	78	297
	Gene Sarazen, Fresh Meadow	78	77	72	70	297
	Leo Diegel, Mountain View Farm	72	76	75	74	297
	Johnny Farrell, Quaker Ridge	76	79	69	73	297
7	Walter Hagen, Pasadena, Florida	73	77	74	74	298
8	Willie Hunter, Los Angeles	75	77	69	79	300
9	Willie Klein, Wheatley Hills	76	74	75	76	301
	Macdonald Smith, Lakeville	82	76	68	75	301
	Dan Williams, Shackamaxon	72	74	80	75	301
	Tommy Armour, Congressional	76	76	74	75	301
13	Jack Forrester, Baltusrol	76	73	77	76	302
	Al Espinosa, Glencoe	71	79	78	74	302
	*Charles Evans, Jr., Edgewater	75	75	73	79	302
16	Mike Brady, Winged Foot	77	82	76	71	306
	George McLean, Grassy Sprain	74	74	79	79	306
	Jimmy Thomson, Hermitage	77	82	73	74	306
	Laurie Ayton, Evanston	76	78	76	76	306
20	Willie Macfarlane, Oak Ridge	72	79	75	81	307
	J. E. Rogers, Shannopin	80	79	75	73	307
22	Clarence Hackney, Atlantic City	77	77	74	80	308
23	Arthur De Mane, Great Neck, N.Y.	76	80	78	75	309
	P. O. Hart, Marietta, Ohio	76	81	76	76	309
	*Harrison R. Johnston, St. Paul	79	76	77	77	309
	Tom Stevens, Culver City, Calif.	79	78	76	76	309
27	Emmett French, Southern Pines	74	79	76	81	310
	Harry Hampton, Memphis	81	75	78	76	310
	Thomas J. Harmon, Jr., Yonkers, N.Y.	73	81	76	80	310
	Bob MacDonald, Chicago	77	79	77	77	310
	Eddie Murphy, Chicago	74	77	80	79	310
32	John Golden, Paterson, N.J.	81	74	76	81	312
	Bill Leach, Overbrook, Pa.	79	74	79	80	312
34	Abe G. Espinosa, San Francisco	75	81	78	79	313
	James Gullane, Colorado Springs	73	85	76	79	313
	Alex Ross, Detroit	81	75	79	78	313
37	Charles W. Hall, Birmingham, Ala.	79	79	77	79	314
	Eddie Loos, Glencoe	78	81	76	79	314
39	Ralph Beach, Bethesda, Md.	79	80	78	78	315
	Larry Nabholtz, Wickliffe, Ohio	80	78	78	79	315
	Charles H. Rowe, Oakmont	78	78	78	81	315
	George M. Smith, St. Paul	75	79	78	83	315
43	*Denny Shute, Huntington, W. Va.	75	78	81	82	316
	L. H. Goldbeck, Philadelphia	80	78	78	80	316
	Frank T. Sprogell, Saginaw	81	75	80	80	316
	Jack Westland, Seattle	75	79	79	83	316
47	Charles H. Mayo, Flushing, N.Y.	75	83	76	83	317
	Frank Walsh, Appleton, Wis.	76	83	76	82	317
49	Bobby Cruickshank, Purchase, N.Y.	76	76	83	83	318
	John H. Junor, Portland, Ore.	70	80	84	84	318
	J. W. Kenney, Sylvania, Ohio	79	76	83	80	318
	Emil F. Loeffler, Oakmont	76	82	78	82	318
53	Pat Doyle, Elmsford, N.Y.	72	83	82	83	320
	Harold S. Long, Oklahoma City	79	79	84	78	320
55	J. E. Brennan, Ashbourne, Pa.	75	79	83	84	321
	Cyril Walker, Winter Haven, Fla.	78	81	80	82	321
57	Clarence Mainero, Greenwich, Conn.	77	79	81	85	322
	John J. O'Connor, Rye, N.Y.	74	84	87	83	328

*Amateur.
Prize money totaling $2,145 awarded to first 20 professionals.

1927
THIRTY-FIRST OPEN CHAMPIONSHIP

Held at Oakmont Country Club, Oakmont, Pa., June 14-16.
Yardage—6,965. Par 72. 898 Entries, 148 Starters.
57 contestants who completed 72 holes.

						Score
1	Tommy Armour, Congressional	78	71	76	76	301
2	Harry Cooper, El Serreno	74	76	74	77	301
3	Gene Sarazen, Fresh Meadow	74	74	80	74	302
4	Emmett French, Southern Pines	75	79	77	73	304
5	Bill Mehlhorn, New York	75	77	80	73	305
6	Walter Hagen, Pasadena, Fla.	77	73	76	81	307
7	Archie Compston, Great Britain	79	74	76	79	308
	Johnny Farrell, Quaker Ridge	81	73	78	76	308
	John Golden, Paterson, N.J.	83	77	75	73	308
	Harry Hampton, Atlantic City	73	78	80	77	308
11	Robert Cruickshank, Progress	77	78	76	78	309
	Leo Diegel, Fenimore	78	74	80	77	309
	*Robert T. Jones, Jr., Atlanta	76	77	79	77	309
	Eddie Loos, Glencoe, Ill.	78	75	79	77	309
15	Fred Baroni, Crafton, Pa.	80	72	79	79	310
	Perry Del Vecchio, Greensburg, Pa.	79	79	76	76	310
	Arthur G. Havers, Great Britain	79	77	74	80	310
18	Al Espinosa, Glencoe, Ill.	83	80	79	69	311
	Harrison R. Johnston, Minikahda	73	74	87	77	311
	Willie Macfarlane, Oak Ridge	82	76	80	73	311
	Macdonald Smith, Lakeville	78	76	81	76	311
	Al Watrous, Grand Rapids	82	74	78	77	311
22	Jock Hutchison, Golf, Ill.	80	77	77	78	312
23	Jim Barnes, New Rochelle, N.Y.	78	75	81	79	313
	P. O. Hart, Marietta, Ohio	77	77	86	73	313
	Larry Nabholtz, Sharon, Pa.	75	81	78	79	313
26	Edward Ray, Great Britain	76	83	77	78	314
	Joe Turnesa, Fairview	81	79	78	76	314
28	Tommy Harmon, Jr., Hudson River	79	77	80	79	315
	Bob MacDonald, Chicago	77	83	78	77	315
30	Aubrey Boomer, Great Britain	83	79	80	74	316
	James R. Foulis, Hinsdale, Ill.	78	84	81	73	316
	Charlie Guest, Los Angeles	78	78	81	79	316
33	*Eddie Held, Algonquin G.C.	83	79	78	77	317
	Willie Klein, Wheatley Hills	79	78	84	76	317
	Dave Sutherland, Glendale, Mo.	78	81	78	80	317
36	L. B. Schmutte, Lima, Ohio	79	80	78	81	318
37	Laurie Ayton, Evanston	80	83	80	76	319
	Jack Forrester, Baltusrol	80	81	76	82	319
	Harold S. Long, Oklahoma City	83	78	79	79	319
40	*Watts Gunn, Atlanta	78	83	81	78	320
41	Neal Christian, Milwaukee, Ore.	81	81	81	78	321
	Herbert C. Jolly, Great Britain	84	78	75	84	321
43	Willie Hunter, Brentwood, Calif.	80	79	81	82	322
	George Sargent, Scioto	80	79	80	83	322
	Horton Smith, Sedalia, Mo.	83	75	81	83	322
46	Charles H. Hoffner, Ocean City, N.J.	80	81	82	80	323
47	J. H. Jones, Glendale, Wash.	80	82	81	82	325
	Ernest Penfold, Minneapolis	79	80	82	84	325
	Wilfrid Reid, Grosse Pointe, Mich.	80	79	86	80	325
	Dave Robertson, Dearborn, Mich.	74	85	77	89	325
	*Denny Shute, Columbus, Ohio	81	81	80	83	325
52	C. W. Gamber, Detroit	81	82	79	86	328
53	Louis Chiapetta, Hartford, Conn.	84	79	85	81	329
54	George M. Christ, Rochester, N.Y.	84	78	89	81	332
	Ted Longworth, Ft. Worth, Texas	79	84	83	86	332
	George Stark, Covington, Ky.	80	79	84	89	332
57	W. W. Crowder, Shreveport	78	83	89	83	333

*Amateur.
Playoff—June 17: Armour, 76; Cooper, 79.

1928
THIRTY-SECOND OPEN CHAMPIONSHIP

Held at Olympia Fields Country Club, Matteson, Illinois, June 21–23.
1,064 Entries; 141 Starters.

Sixty-three Contestants who completed 72 holes.

						Score
1	Johnny Farrell, Quaker Ridge	77	74	71	72	294
2	*Robert T. Jones, Jr., Atlanta	73	71	73	77	294
3	Roland Hancock, Wilmington, N.C.	74	77	72	72	295
4	Walter Hagen, New York City	75	72	73	76	296
	*George Von Elm, Tam O'Shanter	74	72	76	74	296
6	Joe Turnesa, Elmsford	74	77	74	74	299
	Gene Sarazen, Fresh Meadow	78	76	73	72	299
	Henry Ciuci, Mill River, Ct.	70	77	72	80	299
	Waldo W. Crowder, Cleveland	74	74	76	75	299
	Bill Leach, Overbrook	72	74	73	80	299
	Macdonald Smith, Lakeville	75	77	75	72	299
	Denny Shute, Worthington, O.	75	73	79	72	299
	Ed Dudley, Unattached	77	79	68	75	299
14	Willie Macfarlane, Oak Ridge	73	74	73	80	300
	Al Espinosa, Illinois G.C.	74	74	77	75	300
16	Tommy Armour, Congressional	76	75	77	73	301
17	Jack Forrester, Baltusrol	77	76	75	74	302
18	Billy Burke, Blind Brook	74	79	73	77	303
	Neil Christian, Waverley, Ore.	80	78	74	71	303
	Leo Diegel, Fenimore	72	79	75	77	303
	Charles Hilgendorf, Lochmoor	76	77	79	71	303
22	Frank Ball, Atlanta	70	81	78	75	304
	Archie Compston, Great Britain	76	81	75	72	304
	*Harrison R. Johnston, White Bear Yacht	77	75	79	73	304
25	Harry Hampton, Chicago	77	76	72	80	305
	L. B. Schmutte, Lima, O.	71	81	75	78	305
27	Frank Walsh, Appleton, Wis.	74	74	80	78	306
28	Willie Hunter, Montebello, Calif.	73	83	73	78	307
	Felix Serafin, Wilkes-Barre	75	76	77	79	307
	Horton Smith, Joplin, Mo.	72	79	76	80	307
31	Jack Burke, Houston	77	73	75	83	308
	Emmett French, Southern Pines	81	73	80	74	308
	Rudolph Knepper, Onwentsia	81	74	77	76	308
	Irvin Ottman, Louisville	75	81	78	74	308
35	John Golden, Paterson, N.J.	72	78	75	84	309
36	Jim Barnes, New Rochelle, N.Y.	73	80	78	79	310
	Aubrey Boomer, France	75	77	80	78	310
	George M. Christ, Rochester, N.Y.	78	75	82	75	310
	Eddie Loos, Glencoe, Ill.	80	77	76	77	310
	J. P. Rouse, Mundelein, Ill.	78	79	78	75	310
41	Jock Hutchison, Golf, Ill.	76	81	75	79	311
	Joe Kirkwood, Albany, Ga.	80	78	77	76	311
	Anthony Manero, Elmsford, N.Y.	80	77	81	73	311
	Fred McLeod, Columbia	73	76	84	78	311
	Al Watrous, Grand Rapids	77	75	78	81	311
46	Willie Klein, Wheatley Hills	79	77	77	79	312
	Jack Tarrant, Hollywood, Calif.	76	79	84	73	312
	Craig Wood, Bloomfield, N.J.	79	70	82	81	312
49	Al Ciuci, Flushing, N.Y.	76	78	79	80	313
	William Mehlhorn, Fenimore	80	77	86	70	313
51	Charlie Guest, Detroit	80	75	79	80	314
	*Rial E. Rolfe, Ridgemoor	82	74	79	79	314
53	F. S. Gallett, Wauwatosa	78	77	78	82	315
	Johnny Jones, Seattle	73	79	82	81	315
	Ralph Kingsrud, Fargo, N.D.	77	78	80	80	315
56	Jack Gordon, E. Amherst, N.Y.	79	78	77	82	316
	P.O. Hart, Wheeling	76	80	79	81	316
	Walter Kossman, Belleville, Ill.	77	81	78	80	316
59	Fred Morrison, Monterey Park	73	82	77	86	317
	*C.L. Wolff, Sunset Hills	75	78	79	85	317
61	Chick Trout, Topeka	79	79	83	78	319
62	Chet Beer, Bakersfield, Calif.	76	82	77	90	325
63	Paul Runyan, Little Rock	78	80	88	81	327

*Amateur.
Playoff—June 24: Farrell, 70-73-143; Jones, 73-71-144.

1929
THIRTY-THIRD OPEN CHAMPIONSHIP

Held at the Winged Foot Golf Club, Mamaroneck, N.Y., June 27-30.
Yardage—6,786. Par 72. 1,000 Entries, 153 Qualifiers, 146 Starters.

63 contestants who completed 72 holes.

						Score
1	*Robert T. Jones, Atlanta	69	75	71	79	294
2	Al Espinosa, Glencoe, Ill.	70	72	77	75	294
3	Gene Sarazen, Fresh Meadow	71	71	76	78	296
	Denny Shute, Worthington, Ohio	73	71	76	76	296
5	Tommy Armour, Tam O'Shanter	74	71	76	76	297
	*George Von Elm, Tam O'Shanter	79	70	74	74	297
7	Henry Ciuci, Mill River	78	74	72	75	299
8	Leo Diegel, Mexico	74	74	76	77	301
	Peter O'Hara, Verona, Pa.	74	76	73	78	301
10	Horton Smith, Joplin	76	77	74	75	302
11	Wiffy Cox, Brooklyn	74	76	80	75	305
	J. E. Rogers, Denver	78	76	77	74	305
13	P. O. Hart, Wheeling, W. Va.	76	78	75	77	306
	Charles Hilgendorf, Grosse Pointe Shs.	72	79	75	80	306
15	Billy Burke, Westport, N.Y.	75	80	78	74	307
16	Louis Chiapetta, Hartford	78	79	72	79	308
	George B. Smith, Moorestown, N.J.	77	77	77	77	308
	Craig Wood, Bloomfield, N.J.	79	71	80	78	308
19	Walter Hagen, Unattached	76	81	74	78	309
	Joe Kirkwood, Unattached	75	82	76	76	309
21	Jim Barnes, Unattached	78	78	81	73	310
	Massie B. Miller, Norwich, Conn.	75	82	75	78	310
23	Jack Forrester, Oradell, N.J.	77	76	75	83	311
	Willie Hunter, Montebello, Calif.	76	77	76	83	311
	Ted Longworth, Fort Worth	74	82	73	82	311
	Macdonald Smith, Lakeville	77	78	80	76	311
27	Jack Burke, Houston	77	80	74	81	312
	Willie Macfarlane, Oak Ridge	79	78	76	79	312
	Leonard B. Schmutte, Lima, Ohio	73	75	89	75	312
30	Tom Boyd, Fox Hills, N.Y.	79	80	74	80	313
	Emerick Kocsis, Pontiac, Mich.	79	76	77	81	313
32	Frank Ball, Atlanta	78	81	80	75	314
	Johnny Golden, North Jersey	79	79	78	78	314
	Willie Klein, Wheatley Hills	81	78	77	78	314
	Jack Sabol, White Plains	76	78	79	81	314
	Al Watrous, Northville, Mich.	80	79	78	77	314
	Dan Williams, Shackamaxon	78	76	78	82	314
	Albert Alcroft, Youngstown	80	78	80	78	316
	James Foulis, Hinsdale	81	78	81	76	316
	Harry Hampton, Chicago	78	78	79	81	316
	Jimmie Thomson, Knoxville	77	79	79	81	316
42	Bobby Cruickshank, Purchase	75	81	83	78	317
	Thomas J. Harmon, Jr., Montclair	79	78	79	81	317
	Larry Nabholtz, Houston	74	81	76	86	317
45	*George Dawson, Glen Oak	75	80	86	77	318
	*John Goodman, Lakewood, Neb.	75	80	78	85	318
	Thomas Hughes, Unattached	80	79	77	82	318
48	Fred Baroni, Pittsburgh	77	81	84	77	319
	George M. Christ, Rochester	78	74	82	85	319
	*Roland MacKenzie, Columbia	78	79	84	78	319
51	Harry Cooper, Meadowbrook	78	81	78	83	320
	Emmett French, Southern Pines	76	78	80	86	320
	Jack Leach, Haddonfield, N.J.	79	78	83	80	320
54	Arthur H. Andrews, Davenport, Ia.	76	79	82	84	321
55	Bill Mehlhorn, Fenimore	81	77	82	82	322
	Tom Raklets, Girard, O.	83	76	83	80	322
57	Bill Leach, Overbrook	79	79	80	85	323
58	Arthur Ham, Brighton, Mich.	79	79	83	83	324
59	Clarence Gamber, Pontiac, Mich.	76	81	86	82	325
	Rocky Rich, Flushing	80	79	81	85	325
61	Neil Christian, Portland, Ore.	77	81	85	83	326
62	Charles MacAndrew, Laconia, N.H.	78	80	88	83	329
63	*Charles C. Clare, Race Brook	76	80	87	79	332

*Amateur.

PLAYOFF—Sunday, June 30th, 1929; 36 Holes:
Robert T. Jones, Jr. .... 72–69 – 141
Al Espinosa .... 84–80 – 164

Prize money totaling $5,000 awarded to professionals returning scores to 310 inclusive.

1930
THIRTY - FOURTH OPEN CHAMPIONSHIP

Held at the Interlachen Country Club, Minneapolis, Minnesota, July 10-12.
Yardage—6,609. Par 73. 1,177 Entries, 143 Starters.

66 contestants who completed 72 holes.

						Score
1	*Robert T. Jones, Jr., Atlanta	71	73	68	75	287
2	Macdonald Smith, Lakeville	70	75	74	70	289
3	Horton Smith, Cragston	72	70	76	74	292
4	Harry Cooper, Glen Elyn, Ill.	72	72	73	76	293
5	John Golden, Wee Burn	74	73	71	76	294
6	Tommy Armour, Tam O'Shanter	70	76	75	76	297
7	Charles Lacy, Pine Valley	74	70	77	77	298
8	Johnny Farrell, Quaker Ridge	74	72	73	80	299
9	William E. Mehlhorn, Pensacola	76	74	75	75	300
	Craig Wood, Forest Hill	73	75	72	80	300
11	Leo Diegel, Mexico	75	75	76	75	301
	*John Goodman, Lakewood, Neb.	74	80	72	75	301
	*Al Heron, Berkshire, Pa.	76	78	74	73	301
	Peter O'Hara, Westmoreland, Pa.	75	77	73	76	301
	George M. Smith, Onwentsia	72	81	74	74	301
	*George Von Elm, Rancho	80	74	73	74	301
17	Ed Dudley, Wilmington, Del.	74	75	78	76	303
	Mortie Dutra, Virginia, Calif.	76	80	69	78	303
	Charles Guest, Lochaven	76	73	77	77	303
	Walter Hagen, Unattached	72	75	76	80	303
	Willie Hunter, Montebello, Calif.	76	76	78	73	303
	Bob Shave, Aurora, Ohio	76	72	78	77	303
	Joe Turnesa, Elmsford	73	78	78	74	303
	Al Watrous, Oakland Hills	79	73	73	78	303
25	Olin Dutra, Brentwood, Calif.	73	79	78	75	305
	F. S. Gallett, Blue Mound, Wis.	76	75	74	80	305
	Denny Shute, Brookside, Ohio	76	78	77	74	305
28	Herman Barron, Tamarack, N.Y.	77	78	74	77	306
	Billy Burke, Round Hill	76	72	82	76	306
	Jack Forrester, Hackensack	73	75	80	78	306
	Charles Hilgendorf, Lochmoor	74	81	76	75	306
	Walter Kozak, North Hills, N.Y.	74	76	78	78	306
	Gene Sarazen, Fresh Meadow	76	78	77	75	306
	Frank Walsh, Bryn Mawr, Ill.	75	78	77	76	306
35	Wiffy Cox, Brooklyn	71	75	77	84	307
	Al Espinosa, North Brook, Ill.	76	78	77	76	307
	John E. Rogers, Denver	72	79	80	76	307
	Eddie Williams, Westwood, Ohio	73	76	78	80	307
39	Jim Barnes, Unattached	74	76	79	79	308
	Ralph Guldahl, Dallas	80	75	80	73	308
	Emerick Kocsis, Milford, Mich.	77	75	80	76	308
	Sonny Rouse, Arlington Heights, Ill.	77	77	80	74	308
43	Willie Klein, Wheatley Hills	75	77	77	80	309
	Willie Macfarlane, Oak Ridge	74	77	82	76	309
	*T. P. Perkins, Fox Hills, N.Y.	76	74	76	83	309
46	Jim Foulis, Ruth Lake, Ill.	78	78	77	77	310
47	Tom Creavy, Long Lake	81	74	79	77	311
48	George Christ, Rochester, N.Y.	75	78	79	80	312
	Arthur Ham, Charlotte, N.C.	77	79	76	80	312
50	Robert Crowley, Kenoza, Mass.	75	78	84	76	313
	Fred B. Morrison, Midwick	78	76	80	79	313
	Eddie Schultz, Troy, N.Y.	76	80	79	78	313
53	*Lester Bolstad, Golden Valley	79	75	79	81	314
54	*Charles Evans, Jr., Edgewater	81	75	81	78	315
	*Ted Luther, Corry, Pa.	76	78	82	79	315
	George J. Voigt, North Hills, N.Y.	76	79	79	81	315
57	Tom Raklets, Silver Lake, Ohio	77	77	81	81	316
58	Jack Burke, River Oak, Texas	74	80	82	81	317
	Jock Hendry, St. Paul	77	78	79	83	317
	Francis Scheider, Brook Hollow, Texas	76	77	83	81	317
	Donald Moe, Alderwood	75	81	79	82	317
62	Walter J. Bemish, Geneseo, N.Y.	80	75	82	81	318
63	Gus Novotny, Edgewood Valley	77	78	85	79	319
	Bill Tinder, Anderson, Ind.	79	77	82	81	319
65	T. J. Gibraski, Unattached	79	76	85	81	321
	Richard Martin, Briergate	78	78	82	83	321

*Amateur.

1931
THIRTY-FIFTH OPEN CHAMPIONSHIP

Held at the Inverness Club, Toledo, Ohio, July 2-4.
Yardage—6,529. Par 71. 1,141 Entries, 140 Starters.
55 contestants who completed 72 holes.

						Score	Money Prize
1	Billy Burke, Round Hill	73	72	74	73	292	$1,000.00
2	George Von Elm, Unattached	75	69	73	75	292	750.00
3	Leo Diegel, Mexico	75	73	74	72	294	650.00
4	Wiffy Cox, Brooklyn	75	74	74	72	296	450.00
	William E. Mehlhorn, Pinewald, N.J.	77	73	75	71	296	450.00
	Gene Sarazen, Lakeville	74	78	74	70	296	450.00
7	Mortie Dutra, Long Beach, Calif.	71	77	73	76	297	200.00
	Walter Hagen, Unattached	74	74	73	76	297	200.00
	*T. Philip Perkins, Fox Hills, N.Y.	78	76	73	70	297	MEDAL
10	Al Espinosa, Northbrook, Ill.	72	78	75	74	299	105.00
	Johnny Farrell, Quaker Ridge	78	70	79	72	299	105.00
	Macdonald Smith, Unattached	73	73	75	78	299	105.00
13	Guy Paulsen, Ft. Wayne, Ind.	74	72	74	80	300	77.50
	Frank Walsh, Bryn Mawr, Ill.	73	77	75	75	300	77.50
15	Herman Barron, Tamarack, N.Y.	71	75	78	77	301	57.50
	Harry Cooper, Glen Elyn, Ill.	76	75	75	75	301	57.50
	Ed Dudley, Concordville, Pa.	75	76	76	74	301	57.50
	Al Watrous, Oakland Hills	74	78	76	73	301	57.50
19	Charles Guest, Deal, N.J.	71	75	76	80	302	50.00
	Tony Manero, Unattached	74	75	80	73	302	50.00
21	Olin Dutra, Brentwood, Calif.	76	76	76	75	303	25.00
	John Kinder, Green Brook, N.J.	79	72	75	77	303	25.00
23	L. B. Ayton, New Evanston, Ill.	76	79	74	75	304	
	Willie Klein, Wheatley Hills	75	80	70	79	304	
25	Denny Shute, Lake Forest, Ohio	79	73	77	76	305	
	Eddie Williams, Westwood, Ohio	71	74	81	79	305	
27	Johnny Golden, Wee Burn	79	75	78	74	306	
	Horton Smith, Unattached	77	78	75	76	306	
29	Auguste Boyer, France	75	80	72	80	307	
	Henry Ciuci, Mill River, Conn.	73	79	81	74	307	
	W. H. Davies, Great Britain	73	83	74	77	307	
32	Tom Creavy, Albany, N.Y.	80	72	80	76	308	
	Ralph Guldahl, Highland Park, Mich.	77	80	75	76	308	
	Joe Turnesa, Unattached	73	75	79	81	308	
	Alex Watson, Hudson River, N.Y.	75	79	78	76	308	
36	Clarence Clark, Forest Hill, N.J.	76	76	77	80	309	
	Robert Cruickshank, Purchase, N.Y.	74	76	81	78	309	
	Peter O'Hara, Westmoreland, Pa.	78	76	81	74	309	
39	Walter Kozak, North Hills, N.Y.	75	77	80	78	310	
	August Nordone, Iroquois, N.Y.	83	73	78	76	310	
41	Massie B. Miller, Unattached	75	78	81	77	311	
	Francis Scheider, Brook Hollow, Texas	78	75	78	80	311	
43	C.W. Hackney, Atlantic City	80	74	82	76	312	
	Reggie Myles, Ashland, Ohio	76	76	80	80	312	
45	Lloyd Gullickson, Cleveland	75	80	82	77	314	
46	Percy Alliss, Germany	78	75	78	84	315	
	Tommy Armour, Tam O'Shanter	75	83	79	78	315	
	*Lester Bolstad, Midland Hills	80	77	78	80	315	
	Jack Cawsey, Jacksonville	80	77	79	79	315	
	George B. Smith, Moorestown, N.J.	75	78	76	86	315	
51	Jack Forrester, Hackensack	75	78	84	79	316	
52	Clark Morse, Normandie, Mo.	77	81	79	80	317	
53	Neal McIntyre, Highland, Ind.	78	78	84	79	319	
54	Nick Weber, Unattached	81	76	84	80	321	
55	Hugh C. Carpenter, Dallas, Texas	78	79	87	80	324	

*Amateur.
Playoff—July 5: Burke 73-76-149; Von Elm, 75-74-149.
Playoff—July 6: Burke 77-71-148; Von Elm, 76-73-149.

1932
THIRTY-SIXTH OPEN CHAMPIONSHIP

Held at the Fresh Meadow Country Club, Flushing, N.Y., June 23-25.
1,011 Entries, 143 Starters.
72 contestants who completed 72 holes.

						Score	Money Prize
1	Gene Sarazen, Lakeville	74	76	70	66	286	$1,000.00
2	Robert A. Cruickshank, Willowbrook, N.Y.	78	74	69	68	289	700.00
	T. Philip Perkins, Unattached	76	69	74	70	289	700.00
4	Leo Diegel, Mexico	73	74	73	74	294	500.00
5	Wiffy Cox, Brooklyn	80	73	70	72	295	450.00
6	Jose Jurado, Argentina	74	71	75	76	296	350.00
7	Billy Burke, Round Hill	75	77	74	71	297	175.00
	Harry Cooper, Glen Oak	77	73	73	74	297	175.00
	Olin Dutra, Brentwood, Calif.	69	77	75	76	297	175.00
10	Walter Hagen, Unattached	75	73	79	71	298	100.00
11	Clarence Clark, Forest Hill, N.J.	79	72	74	75	300	90.00
12	Vincent Eldred, Highland, Pa.	78	73	77	73	301	77.50
	Paul Runyan, Metropolis	79	77	69	76	301	77.50
14	Henry Ciuci, Fresh Meadow	77	74	77	74	302	63.34
	Ed Dudley, Concord, Pa.	80	74	71	77	302	63.34
	*John Goodman, Omaha Field	79	78	77	68	302	MEDAL
	Fred Morrison, Annandale, Calif.	77	80	69	76	302	63.33
	Denny Shute, Lake Forest, O.	78	76	76	72	302	63.33
	Macdonald Smith, Unattached	80	76	76	72	302	63.33
	Craig Wood, Deal	79	71	74	73	302	63.33
21	Tommy Armour, Tam O'Shanter	82	73	77	71	303	
	George B. Smith, Moorestown, N.J.	81	76	72	74	303	
23	Joe Kirkwood, Unattached	76	77	75	76	304	
	Charles Lacey, Lakeville	77	76	78	73	304	
	Mortie Dutra, Virginia, Calif.	77	77	75	75	304	
	Jack Patroni, Wykagyl	79	77	77	71	304	
27	*Johnny Fischer, Highland, Ky.	81	78	74	73	306	
	Bob MacDonald, Chicago	82	77	74	73	306	
	George Von Elm, Unattached	79	73	77	77	306	
	Al Zimmerman, Columbia. Ore.	79	77	73	77	306	
31	Herman Barron, Tamarack	78	76	79	74	307	
	Tom Creavy, Albany, N.Y.	83	71	77	76	307	
	Francis Gallett, Blue Mound	77	81	70	79	307	
	Charles Guest, Deal	77	77	72	81	307	
35	John Golden, Wee Burn	79	81	73	75	308	
	John Kinder, Green Brook, N.J.	79	77	75	77	308	
	Willie Klein, Wheatley Hills	79	72	79	78	308	
	William E. Mehlhorn, Unattached	81	76	78	73	308	
	Al Watrous, Oakland Hills	85	73	74	76	308	
40	Abe Espinosa, Medinah	83	77	81	68	309	
	Lloyd Gullickson, Willowick	75	82	82	70	309	
	Al Houghton, Kenwood, Md.	82	77	74	76	309	
	Walter Kozak, Engineers	76	78	77	78	309	
	Harold McSpaden, Victory Hills	80	74	79	76	309	
45	Victor Ghezzi, Rumson	80	74	78	78	310	
	Jock Hutchison, Glen View	81	78	74	77	310	
	Tony Manero, Unattached	81	78	75	76	310	
	Joe Turnesa, Elmsford	79	81	80	70	310	
49	Mike Brady, Winged Foot	82	78	78	73	311	
	Pat Circelli, Broadmoor, N.Y	78	82	80	71	311	
	Peter O'Hara, Westmoreland	83	76	75	77	311	
	Wilfrid Reid, Indianwood	81	79	77	74	311	
	H. J. Sanderson, Canoe Brook	77	74	82	78	311	
54	Francis Scheider, Brook Hollow	79	79	77	77	312	
55	Jim Barnes, Crescent Athletic	84	76	78	75	313	
	Dave Hackney, Vesper	76	75	79	83	313	
	Horton Smith, Oak Park	80	80	74	79	313	
58	Wilson Crain, Unattached	85	75	80	74	314	
	Leo Fraser, Saginaw	82	75	76	81	314	
	Ralph Guldahl, St. Louis	80	79	79	76	314	
61	Jack Curley, Stoney Brae	78	77	82	78	315	
	George McLean, Grassy Sprain	83	77	75	80	315	
	Phil Turnesa, Elmsford	79	81	76	79	315	
64	Leonard Schmutte, Shawnee, O.	82	76	79	79	316	
65	Ed Kirby, Fairlawn, O.	77	80	79	81	317	
66	Ted Luther, Valley Heights, Pa.	78	82	75	83	318	
	*Sam M. Parks, Jr., Uniontown, Pa.	81	78	79	80	318	
68	Frank Moore, Westborough, Mo.	78	77	76	89	320	
	Mike Turnesa, Fairview, N.Y.	79	75	82	84	320	
70	K. Schlicht, Westmoreland, Wis.	80	80	78	83	321	
71	Wm. Green, St. Davids, Pa.	80	78	84	80	322	
72	Dan Goss, Birmingham, Ala.	80	79	81	83	323	

*Amateur.

1933
THIRTY-SEVENTH OPEN CHAMPIONSHIP

Held at the North Shore Golf Club, Glen View, Illinois, June 8-10.
Yardage—6,927. Par 72. 915 Entries, 146 Starters.
65 contestants who completed 72 holes.

						Score	Money Prize
1	*Johnny Goodman, Omaha	75	66	70	76	287	MEDAL
2	Ralph Guldahl, St. Louis	76	71	70	71	288	$1,000.00
3	Craig Wood, Hollywood	73	74	71	72	290	750.00
4	Walter Hagen, Unattached	73	76	77	66	292	600.00
	Tommy Armour, Medinah	68	75	76	73	292	600.00
6	Mortie Dutra, Red Run	75	73	72	74	294	450.00
7	Olin Dutra, Brentwood	75	71	75	74	295	350.00
	*Gus Moreland, Dallas	76	76	71	72	295	MEDAL
9	Clarence Clark, Forest Hill	80	72	72	72	296	156.25
	Joe Kirkwood, Unattached	74	70	79	73	296	156.25
	Willie Goggin, San Mateo	79	73	73	71	296	156.25
	Johnny Farrell, Quaker Ridge	75	77	72	72	296	156.25
13	Herman Barron, Kings Ridge	77	77	74	69	297	85.00
	Al Watrous, Oakland Hills	74	76	77	70	297	85.00
15	Henry Ciuci, Fresh Meadow	73	79	74	72	298	72.50
	John Revolta, Menominee	73	76	75	74	298	72.50
17	*George Dawson, Glen Oak	78	74	71	76	299	MEDAL
	Leo Diegel, Unattached	78	71	75	75	299	50.00
19	*Lester Bolstad, Midland Hills	76	74	73	77	300	MEDAL
	Macdonald Smith, Unattached	77	72	77	74	300	50.00
21	Johnny Golden, Wee Burn	79	76	74	72	301	50.00
	Archie Hambrick, Zanesville	81	71	75	74	301	50.00
	Denny Shute, Llanerch	76	77	72	76	301	50.00
24	Abe Espinosa, Lemont	76	73	78	75	302	25.00
	Horton Smith, Oak Park	75	76	76	75	302	25.00
26	Bob Crowley, Norfolk	75	75	81	72	303	
	Ky Laffoon, Green Gables	74	78	79	72	303	
	Gene Sarazen, Unattached	74	77	77	75	303	
29	Harry Cooper, Glen Oak	78	76	75	75	304	
	Tony Manero, Sedgefield	79	73	77	75	304	
	Bill Schwartz, Meadow Brook	75	81	72	76	304	
	Frank Walsh, Bryn Mawr	79	73	72	80	304	
33	Billy Burke, Round Hill	79	73	76	77	305	
	Henry Kaiser, Racine	81	71	74	79	305	
	Willie Klein, Wheatley Hills	77	78	72	78	305	
	Walter Kozak, Pomonok	76	77	76	76	305	
	Phil Perkins, Kirtland	76	72	81	76	305	
	Johnny Rogers, Denver	80	74	76	75	305	
	Bob Shave, Manakiki	77	74	79	75	305	
40	Joe Belfore, C.C., Detroit	75	76	78	77	306	
	Tom Creavy, Albany	74	76	80	76	306	
	Francis Gallett, Blue Mound	77	75	77	77	306	
43	Robert Cruickshank, C.C. Virginia	75	76	79	78	308	
	*Johnny Fischer, Highland, Ky.	75	80	74	79	308	
	Charles Lacey, Lakeville	77	79	75	77	308	
46	Johnny Kinder, Jumping Brook	79	77	74	79	309	
	Charles MacAndrew, Wollaston	78	77	79	75	309	
	George M. Smith, Onwentsia	81	75	74	79	309	
	Joe Turnesa, Elmsford	79	73	80	77	309	
50	James Johnstone, Toronto	76	77	81	76	310	
	Neil White, Los Angeles	73	80	79	78	310	
52	*Pat Sawyer, Golden Valley	79	75	80	77	311	
	Ray Schwartz, St. Louis	77	79	76	79	311	
54	Leslie Madison, San Marcos, Ariz.	76	78	77	81	312	
	C. E. Manning, Shannopin	76	76	82	78	312	
	Bill Neilan, North Hills, Pa.	76	77	81	78	312	
57	Harry Hampton, Beverly	79	76	76	82	313	
58	*Don J. Armstrong, Aurora, Ill.	75	77	86	76	314	
59	Tom Carney, Northmoor, Ill.	78	77	78	82	315	
60	Tommy Harmon, Jr., Montclair	76	79	82	79	316	
	Bob MacDonald, Unattached	80	75	81	80	316	
62	Ralph Beach, Suburban, Md.	75	79	76	87	317	
63	*Wilford Wehrle, Racine	79	77	81	85	322	
	E. Loeffler, Jr., Oakmont	80	76	82	84	322	
65	Bob Randall, Spring Valley, Ohio	81	75	83	87	326	

*Amateur.

1934
THIRTY-EIGHTH OPEN CHAMPIONSHIP

Held at the Merion Cricket Club, (East Course), Ardmore, Pa., June 7-9.
Yardage—6,694. Par 70. 1,063 Entries, 149 Starters.
62 contestants who completed 72 holes.

						Score
1	Olin Dutra, Brentwood C.C., Calif.	76	74	71	72	293
2	Gene Sarazen, New York City	73	72	73	76	294
3	Wiffy Cox, Dyker Beach G.C., N.Y.	71	75	74	75	295
	Robert Cruickshank, C.C. Virginia	71	71	77	76	295
	Harry Cooper, Glen Oak C.C., Ill.	76	74	74	71	295
6	Billy Burke, C.C. of Cleveland, Ohio	76	71	77	72	296
	Macdonald Smith, Nashville, Tenn.	75	73	78	70	296
8	Ralph Guldahl, Los Angeles, Calif.	78	73	70	78	299
	Johnny Revolta, Tripoli C.C., Wis.	76	73	77	73	299
	Jimmy Hines, Timber Point Club, N.Y.	80	70	77	72	299
	Tom Creavy, Albany C.C., N.Y.	79	76	78	66	299
12	Joe Kirkwood, Chicago, Ill.	75	73	78	74	300
	Ted Luther, Valley Heights C.C., Pa.	78	71	78	73	300
14	Alvin H. Krueger, Beloit, Wis.	76	75	75	75	301
	Willie Hunter, California C.C., Calif.	75	74	80	72	301
16	Mark Fry, Oak Knoll C.C., Calif.	79	75	74	74	302
17	Leo Diegel, Philmont C.C., Pa.	76	71	78	78	303
	Johnny Golden, Wee Burn Club, Conn.	75	76	74	78	303
	Henry Ciuci, Fresh Meadow C.C., N.Y.	74	74	79	76	303
	Horton Smith, Oak Park C.C., Ill.	74	73	79	77	303
21	Al Espinosa, Portage C.C., Ohio	76	74	76	78	304
	Phil Perkins, Kirtland C.C., Ohio	78	74	79	73	304
23	Ky Laffoon, Green Gables, C.C., Colo.	76	73	80	76	305
	Herman Barron, Kings Ridge G.C., N.Y.	79	72	76	78	305
25	Orville White, Meadowbrook C.C., Mo.	76	79	76	75	306
	Eddie Loos, Lake Shore C.C., Ill.	76	75	78	77	306
	*Lawson Little, Jr., Presidio G.C., Calif.	83	72	76	75	306
28	George H. Schneiter, Ogden G. & C.C., Utah	76	76	79	76	307
	Paul Runyan, Metropolis C.C., N.Y.	74	78	79	76	307
	George Von Elm, Lido C.C., N.Y.	74	76	80	77	307
	*Rodney Bliss, Jr., Happy Hollow C., Neb.	74	73	82	78	307
	*Zell Eaton, Twin Hills G. & C.C., Okla.	76	73	78	80	307
	Bill Schwartz, Chicago, Ill.	81	74	73	79	307
	Mortie Dutra, Red Run G.C., Mich.	74	77	79	77	307
35	Jack Forrester, Hackensack G.C., N.J.	78	72	80	78	308
	Jim Foulis, Ruth Lake C.C., Ill.	79	76	82	71	308
37	William Mehlhorn, Louisville, Ky.	78	77	77	77	309
	Ed Dudley, Philadelphia Country C., Pa.	76	78	83	72	309
	Sam Parks, Jr., So. Hills C.C., Pa.	76	76	76	81	309
	Charles Lacey, Lakeville Club, N.Y.	71	78	81	79	309
41	*Jack Westland, Sunset Ridge C.C., Ill.	77	76	81	76	310
	Frank Walsh, Bryn Mawr C.C., Ill.	78	74	78	80	310
43	*Johnny Goodman, Omaha Field C., Neb.	76	77	83	75	311
	Reggie Myles, Ashland C.C., Ohio	80	75	84	72	311
	Denny Shute, Llanerch C.C., Pa.	78	73	81	79	311
	Jimmy Thomson, Los Angeles, Calif.	74	75	78	84	311
47	Al Watrous, Oakland Hills C.C., Mich.	77	78	82	76	313
	Henry G. Picard, Charleston C.C., S.C.	79	75	80	79	313
	Willie Goggin, Sharps Park G.C., Calif.	74	80	80	79	313
50	*Charles R. Yates, Atlanta A.C., Ga.	75	77	81	81	314
	Gunnard Johnson, Northwd. C.C., Minn.	76	79	80	79	314
	Clarence Ehresman, Eagles Mere, Pa.	76	77	79	82	314
	Tommy Armour, Medinah C.C., Ill.	82	72	79	81	314
	Julius Ackerbloom, Al Amin S.C.C., Ark.	80	74	79	81	314
55	*Chris Brinke, Aronimink G.C., Pa.	77	74	88	77	316
	Toney Penna, Osceola G.C., Fla.	76	76	81	83	316
57	*Gus Moreland, Dallas C.C., Texas	77	76	85	79	317
58	Johnny Farrell, Baltusrol G.C., N.J.	75	79	83	81	318
	Walter Hagen, Detroit, Mich.	76	79	83	80	318
60	*George Dawson, Glen Oak C.C., Ill.	75	79	82	83	319
	John F. Schuebel, Oak Terrace C.C., Pa.	78	77	80	84	319
62	*Rudolf Knepper, Garden City G.C., N.Y.	82	73	85	82	322

*Amateur.

1935
THIRTY-NINTH OPEN CHAMPIONSHIP

Held at the Oakmont Country Club, Oakmont, Pa., June 6–8.
Yardage–6,981. Par–72. 1,125 Entries, 159 Starters.
63 contestants who completed 72 holes.

						Score	Money Prize
1	Sam Parks, Jr., South Hills C.C., Pa.	77	73	73	76	299	$1,000.00
2	Jimmy Thomson, Lakewood G.C., Calif.	73	73	77	78	301	750.00
3	Walter Hagen, Detroit, Mich.	77	76	73	76	302	650.00
4	Denny Shute, Chicago, Ill.	78	73	76	76	303	500.00
	Ray Mangrum, Los Angeles, Calif.	76	76	72	79	303	500.00
6	Henry Picard, Hershey C.C., Pa.	79	78	70	79	306	218.75
	Gene Sarazen, Brookfield, Conn.	75	74	78	79	306	218.75
	Alvin Krueger, Beloit, Wis.	71	77	78	80	306	218.75
	Horton Smith, Oak Park C.C., Ill.	73	79	79	75	306	218.75
10	Dick Metz, Mill Road Farm, Ill.	77	76	76	78	307	95.00
	Paul Runyan, Metropolis C.C., N.Y.	76	77	79	75	307	95.00
12	Olin Dutra, Los Angeles, Calif.	77	76	78	77	308	77.50
	Vincent Eldred, Highland C.C., Pa.	75	77	77	79	308	77.50
14	Robert Cruickshank, C.C. of Virginia	78	76	77	78	309	55.00
	Ted Turner, Pine Valley G.C., N.J.	80	71	81	77	309	55.00
	Al Watrous, Oakland Hills C.C., Mich.	75	80	79	75	309	55.00
	Herman Barron, Fenimore C.C., N.Y.	73	79	78	79	309	55.00
	Macdonald Smith, Glendale, Calif.	74	82	76	77	309	55.00
	Mortie Dutra, Red Run G.C., Mich.	75	77	80	77	309	55.00
20	Victor Ghezzi, Deal G.C., N.J.	75	78	81	77	311	50.00
21	Bill Kaiser, Louisville, Ky.	78	82	78	74	312	
	Ed Dudley, Philadelphia Country, Pa.	74	83	75	80	312	
	Gene Kunes, Jeffersonville G.C., Pa.	76	79	77	80	312	
	Craig Wood, Hollywood G.C., N.J.	76	80	79	77	312	
	Sid Brews, Johannesburg, South Africa	76	81	78	77	312	
26	Ted Luther, Mahoning Valley C.C., Ohio	80	76	84	73	313	
	Frank Walsh, Bryn Mawr C.C., Ill.	76	82	82	73	313	
28	Al Espinosa, Portage C.C., Ohio	75	76	78	85	314	
	Harry Cooper, Glen Oak C.C., Ill.	77	81	79	77	314	
	Willie Hunter, Fox Hills C.C., Calif.	78	80	80	76	314	
	Ky Laffoon, Northmoor C.C., Ill.	75	83	81	75	314	
32	Jim Foulis, Ruth Lake C.C., Ill.	74	81	81	79	315	
	*Chris Brinke, Oakland Hills C.C., Mich.	80	80	81	74	315	
	Byron Nelson, Ridgewood C.C., N.J.	75	81	82	77	315	
	Billy Burke, The C.C., Cleveland, Ohio	77	84	75	79	315	
37	Phil Perkins, Kirtland C.C., Ohio	77	82	80	77	316	
	*Johnny Goodman, Omaha F.C., Neb.	77	78	83	78	316	
	John Revolta, Tripoli C.C., Wis.	80	75	82	79	316	
40	Mark Fry, Oak Knoll C.C., Calif.	80	77	80	80	317	
41	Perry Del Vecchio, Greensburg C.C., Pa.	80	81	77	80	318	
	Ralph Guldahl, Hollywood, Calif.	78	76	82	82	318	
	Tony Manero, Sedgefield C.C., N.C.	77	80	76	85	318	
	Willie Goggin, San Francisco, Calif.	77	82	82	77	318	
	Roland MacKenzie, Congressional, D.C.	72	82	80	84	318	
46	*Zell Eaton, Oklahoma City, Okla.	81	80	82	76	319	
	Cliff Spencer, Beaver Dam C.C., Md.	73	82	80	84	319	
48	Floyd Farley, Woodlawn C.C., Okla.	75	84	84	77	320	
	Willie Macfarlane, Oak Ridge, N.Y.	77	81	78	84	320	
	Al Houghton, Kenwood G. & C.C., Md.	78	82	80	80	320	
51	George Schneiter, Ogden G. & C.C., Utah	77	84	79	81	321	
	James Fogertey, Osage Hills C.C., Mo.	82	79	79	81	321	
53	Johnny Farrell, Baltusrol G.C., N.J.	77	79	84	82	322	
	Phil Turnesa, Elmsford C.C., N.Y.	77	82	82	81	322	
	*Charles R. Yates, Atlanta A.C., Ga.	77	79	84	82	322	
56	George Von Elm, Los Angeles, Calif.	81	74	83	86	324	
	*Maurice J. McCarthy, Jr., Cleveland, Ohio	79	81	81	83	324	
	Felix Serafin, C.C. of Scranton, Pa.	80	79	81	84	324	
59	Kanekichi Nakamura, Tokyo, Japan	82	79	78	86	325	
	Walter Kozak, Pomonok C.C., N.Y.	81	78	81	85	325	
61	Jack Gordon, Park C.C. of Buffalo, N.Y.	75	79	87	87	328	
62	John Golden, Wee Burn Club, Conn.	79	81	86	86	332	
63	*Earl M. Stokes, Jr., Louisville C.C., Ky.	76	80	93	85	334	

*Amateur.
Prize money awarded to professionals returning scores up to 311, inclusive.

1936
FORTIETH OPEN CHAMPIONSHIP

Held at Baltusrol Golf Club, (Upper Course), Springfield, N.J., June 4-6.
Yardage–6,866. Par 72. 1,277 Entries, 165 Starters.
76 contestants who completed 72 holes.

						Score	Money Prize
1	Tony Manero, Sedgefield C.C., N.C.	73	69	73	67	282	$1,000.00
2	Harry E. Cooper, Glen Oak C.C., Ill.	71	70	70	73	284	750.00
3	Clarence Clark, Forest Hill Field C., N.J.	69	75	71	72	287	650.00
4	Macdonald Smith, Glendale, Calif.	73	73	72	70	288	550.00
5	Henry G. Picard, Hershey C.C., Pa.	70	71	74	74	289	350.00
	Wiffy Cox, Kenwood G. & C.C., Md.	74	74	69	72	289	350.00
	Ky Laffoon, Northmoor C.C., Ill.	71	74	70	74	289	350.00
8	Ralph Guldahl, Beverly Hills, Calif.	73	70	73	74	290	137.50
	Paul Runyan, Metropolis C.C., N.Y.	69	75	73	73	290	137.50
10	Denny Shute, Brae Burn C.C., Mass.	72	69	73	77	291	100.00
11	Tom Kerrigan, Siwanoy C.C., N.Y.	70	75	72	75	292	81.66
	Ray Mangrum, MacGregor G.C., Ohio	69	71	76	76	292	81.67
	Herman Barron, Fenway G.C., N.Y.	73	74	69	76	292	81.67
14	John Revolta, Evanston G.C., Ill.	70	71	77	75	293	60.00
	*Charles Kocsis, Red Run G.C., Mich.	72	71	73	77	293	MEDAL
	Frank Moore, Scarsdale G.C., N.Y.	70	74	75	74	293	60.00
	Jimmy Thomson, Shawnee C.C., Pa.	74	73	71	75	293	60.00
18	Victor Ghezzi, Deal G.C., N.J.	70	70	73	81	294	50.00
	Harold McSpaden, Winchester C.C., Mass.	75	71	78	70	294	50.00
	Willie Goggin, El Camino Club, Calif.	73	73	72	76	294	50.00
	Billy Burke, The C.C., Cleveland, Ohio	72	76	72	74	294	50.00
22	Felix Serafin, C.C. Scranton, Pa.	72	73	74	76	295	
	Jerry Gianferante, Minute Man, Mass.	74	73	71	77	295	
	Tommy Armour, Medinah C.C., Ill.	74	76	74	71	295	
	Horton Smith, Oak Park C.C., Ill.	75	75	72	73	295	
	Johnny Farrell, Baltusrol G.C., N.J.	75	75	70	75	295	
	*Johnny Goodman, Omaha F.C., Neb.	75	73	73	74	295	
28	Al Brosch, Bethpage State Pk., N.Y.	73	75	72	76	296	
	Zell Eaton, Twin Hills G. & C.C., Okla.	72	75	72	77	296	
	*Jack Munger, Brook Hollow G.C., Texas	74	70	76	76	296	
	Gene Sarazen, Brookfield, Conn.	75	72	75	74	296	
	Dick Metz, Mill Road Farm C., Ill.	74	73	73	76	296	
33	Walter Hagen, Detroit, Mich.	74	72	73	78	297	
	Ted Longworth, Waverley C.C., Ore.	71	74	74	78	297	
	Al Watrous, Oakland Hills C.C., Mich.	76	75	74	72	297	
36	E. J. (Dutch) Harrison, Un. L. Rk., Ark.	74	75	76	73	298	
	Vincent Eldred, Highland C.C., Pa.	74	73	78	73	298	
	Willie Klein, Wheatley Hills G.C., N.Y.	75	73	75	75	298	
	Mortie Dutra, Red Run G.C., Mich.	75	75	75	73	298	
40	John Kinder, Plainfield C.C., N.J.	75	74	77	73	299	
	Jake Fassezke, Jackson C.C., Mich.	72	79	74	74	299	
	Frank Walsh, Bryn Mawr C.C., Ill	74	74	73	78	299	
	Gunnar Nelson, Rockford C.C., Ill.	74	76	74	75	299	
	Charles Lacey, Lakeville Club, N.Y.	74	74	77	74	299	
45	Seisui (Chick) Chin, Tokyo, Japan	76	71	78	75	300	
	Olin A. Dutra, Wilshire C.C., Calif.	74	77	75	74	300	
	Bruce Coltart, Woodcrest C.C., N.J.	75	76	72	77	300	
48	George Low, Jr., Plymouth C.C., Pa.	75	72	77	77	301	
	Clarence J. Doser, Lake Shore C.C., N.Y.	72	75	78	76	301	
50	Clarence Owen, Greenville C.C., S.C.	76	75	75	76	302	
	Willie Hunter, Fox Hills G.C., Calif.	73	75	77	77	302	
	Gene Kunes, Jeffersonville G.C., Pa.	73	77	75	77	302	
	*Charles Evans, Jr., Edgewater G.C., Ill.	77	74	77	74	302	
	Albert O. Huske, Butterfield C.C., Ill.	77	74	76	75	302	
55	Jack Toomer, Waynesville C.C., N.C.	74	74	78	77	303	
	*Wilford Wehrle, Racine C.C., Wis.	74	77	74	78	303	
	Leslie Madison, Hollywood C.C., Calif.	70	75	81	77	303	
	Joe Ezar, New York, N.Y.	75	75	73	80	303	
59	*Maurice J. McCarthy, Jr., Mayfield, Ohio	76	75	74	79	304	
	Ted Turner, Pine Valley G.C., N.J.	77	74	78	75	304	
	Ralph Beach, Suburban C., Md.	74	76	78	76	304	
	Ed Dudley, Philadelphia Country, Pa.	76	75	78	75	304	
63	Johnny Bulla, Woodridge, G.C., Ill.	71	78	75	81	305	
64	Albert Alcroft, Youngstown C.C., Ohio	76	75	76	79	306	
	William E. Schuchart, Highland C.C., Neb.	78	73	81	74	306	
66	Craig Wood, New York, N.Y.	71	80	78	78	307	
	Jack Isaacs, Old Dominion G.C., Va.	75	75	79	78	307	
	Pat Circelli, Rockwood Hall C.C., N.Y.	74	77	80	76	307	
	Charles Schneider, Concord C.C., Pa.	74	74	82	77	307	
70	*Chris Brinke, Oakland Hills C.C., Mich.	75	73	85	76	309	
	C. W. Hackney, C.C., Atlantic City, N.J.	77	74	76	82	309	
72	Len Gallett, North Shore C.C., Wis.	73	77	79	81	310	
73	*Morton McCarthy, Princess Anne C.C., Va.	72	76	83	80	311	
74	James D. Fogertey, Myopia Hunt, Mass.	76	74	79	83	312	
75	Al Nelson, Hopewell Valley G.C., N.J.	72	78	81	82	313	
76	Raymond Schirmer, St. Louis, Mo.	74	77	81	82	314	

*Amateur.
Prize money totaling $5,000 awarded to professionals returning scores up to 294, inclusive.

1937
FORTY-FIRST OPEN CHAMPIONSHIP

Held at Oakland Hills Country Club, Birmingham, Mich., June 10-12.
Yardage—7,037. Par 72. 1,402 Entries, 166 Starters.
65 contestants who completed 72 holes.

						Score	Money Prize
1	Ralph Guldahl, Chicago, Ill.	71	69	72	69	281	$1,000.00
2	Sam Snead, Greenbrier G. & T.C., W. Va.	69	73	70	71	283	800.00
3	Robert Cruickshank, C.C. of Virginia	73	73	67	72	285	700.00
4	Harry E. Cooper, Chicago	72	70	73	71	286	600.00
5	Ed Dudley, Philadelphia Country C., Pa.	70	70	71	76	287	450.00
6	Al Brosch, Bethpage State Park, N.Y.	74	73	68	73	288	375.00
7	Clarence Clark, Forest Hill Field C., N.J.	72	75	73	69	289	275.00
8	*Johnny Goodman, Omaha Field C., Neb.	70	73	72	75	290	MEDAL
9	*Frank Strafaci, Shore View G.C., N.Y.	70	72	77	72	291	MEDAL
10	*Charles Kocsis, University of Michigan	72	73	76	71	292	MEDAL
	Henry G. Picard, Hershey C.C., Pa.	71	75	72	74	292	175.00
	Gene Sarazen, Brookfield, Conn.	78	69	71	74	292	175.00
	Denny Shute, Brae Burn C.C., Mass.	69	76	75	72	292	175.00
14	Ray Mangrum, McGregor C.C., Ohio	75	75	71	72	293	112.50
	Paul Runyan, Metropolis C.C., N.Y.	76	72	73	72	293	112.50
16	Billy Burke, The C.C., Cleveland, Ohio	75	73	71	75	294	87.50
	Jimmy Demaret, Brae-Burn C.C., Texas	72	74	76	72	294	87.50
	Sam Parks, Jr., South Hills C.C., Pa.	74	74	72	74	294	87.50
	Pat Sawyer, Golden Valley G.C., Minn.	72	70	75	77	294	87.50
20	Victor Ghezzi, Deal G.C., N.J.	72	71	78	74	295	50.00
	Jimmy Hines, Garden City C.C., N.Y.	75	72	76	72	295	50.00
	Ky Laffoon, Northmoor C.C., Ill.	74	74	74	73	295	50.00
	Harold McSpaden, Winchester C.C., Mass.	74	75	73	73	295	50.00
	Fred Morrison, Pasadena, Calif.	71	76	74	74	295	50.00
	Byron Nelson, Reading C.C., Pa.	73	78	71	73	295	50.00
	Bob Stupple, Skokie C.C., Ill.	73	73	73	76	295	50.00
	Frank Walsh, Bryn Mawr C.C., Ill.	70	70	78	77	295	50.00
28	Leo Mallory, Wee Burn C., Conn.	73	74	76	73	296	50.00
	Toney Penna, Dayton, Ohio	76	74	75	71	296	50.00
	Johnny Revolta, Evanston G.C., Ill.	75	73	75	73	296	50.00
	Jimmy Thomson, Shawnee C.C., Pa.	74	66	78	78	296	50.00
32	E. J. (Dutch) Harrison, Riverside C.C., Ark.	74	71	74	78	297	33.37
	*Edwin C. Kingsley, Utah Copper G.C., Utah	72	76	75	74	297	MEDAL
	Mike Turnesa, Fairview C.C., N.Y.	71	74	76	76	297	33.34
	Al Watrous, Oakland Hills C.C., Mich.	77	75	75	70	297	33.34
36	Horton Smith, Oak Park C.C., Ill.	74	74	75	75	298	
	Craig Wood, Rumson C.C., N.J.	78	71	73	76	298	
39	*Bill Holt, Syracuse Yacht & C.C., N.Y.	70	79	78	72	299	
	Ralph G. Stonehouse, Northmoor G. & C.C., Ohio	75	74	74	76	299	
41	Johnny Farrell, Baltusrol G.C., N.J.	74	75	75	76	300	
	Tony Manero, Salem C.C., Mass.	76	73	77	74	300	
	Charles Lacey, Lakeville G.C., N.Y.	73	75	72	80	300	
	Felix Serafin, C.C. of Scranton, Pa.	75	74	73	78	300	
	Macdonald Smith, Glendale, Calif.	79	73	73	75	300	
46	Johnny Bulla, Woodridge G.C., Ill.	74	75	75	77	301	
	Wiffy Cox, Kenwood G. & C.C., Md.	74	74	75	78	301	
48	Willie Macfarlane, Old Oaks C.C., N.Y.	73	78	75	76	302	
	John E. Rogers, Denver, C.C., Colo.	77	72	78	75	302	
	Marvin D. Stahl, C.C. of Lansing, Mich.	72	77	78	75	302	
51	*Ted Bishop, Woodland G.C., Mass.	74	78	74	77	303	
	Bob Crowley, Norfolk G.C., Mass.	79	73	76	75	303	
	Arthur Ham, Charlotte C.C., N.C.	77	75	76	75	303	
	William Mehlhorn, Louisville, Ky.	76	76	75	76	303	
	Jim Turnesa, Louisquisset G.C., R.I.	73	78	77	75	303	
56	Olin Dutra, Los Angeles, Calif.	76	76	77	75	304	
	Jimmy Johnstone, Rosedale G.C., Toronto, Canada	75	76	81	72	304	
	Ted Longworth, Waverley C.C., Ore.	72	76	77	79	304	
59	John J. Beadle, Paxon Hollow G.C., Pa.	74	77	77	78	306	
	Orville White, Sedgefield C.C., N.C.	77	75	80	74	306	
61	Waldo Crowder, Canterbury G.C., Ohio	77	74	76	80	307	
	Ted Luther, Mahoning C.C., Ohio	75	77	80	75	307	
	Frank Moore, Quaker Ridge G.C., N.Y.	77	73	79	78	307	
64	John Malutic, Struthers, Ohio	74	78	80	77	309	
65	Ole B. Clark, Walnut Hills C.C., Mich.	74	77	82	80	313	

*Amateur.
Prize money totaling $6,000 awarded to professionals returning scores up to 297, inclusive.

1938
FORTY-SECOND OPEN CHAMPIONSHIP

Held at Cherry Hills Club, Denver, Colo., June 9-11.
Yardage—6,888. Par 71. 1,223 Entries, 165 Starters.
55 contestants who completed 72 holes.

						Score	Money Prize
1	Ralph Guldahl, Braidburn C.C., N.J.	74	70	71	69	284	$1,000.00
2	Dick Metz, Mill Road Farm C., Ill.	73	68	70	79	290	800.00
3	Harry Cooper, Chicopee, Mass.	76	69	76	71	292	650.00
	Toney Penna, Dayton, Ohio	78	72	74	68	292	650.00
5	Byron Nelson, Reading C.C., Pa.	77	71	74	72	294	412.50
	Emery Zimmerman, Columbia-Edgewater C.C., Ore.	72	71	73	78	294	412.50
7	Frank Moore, Quaker Ridge G.C., N.Y.	79	73	72	71	295	216.67
	Henry Picard, Hershey C.C., Pa.	70	70	77	78	295	216.67
	Paul Runyan, Metropolis C.C., N.Y.	78	71	72	74	295	216.66
10	Gene Sarazen, Brookfield, Conn.	74	74	75	73	296	106.25
11	Victor Ghezzi, Deal G.C., N.J.	79	71	75	72	297	106.25
	Jimmy Hines, Lakeville C., N.Y.	70	75	69	83	297	106.25
	Denny Shute, Brae Burn C.C., Mass.	77	71	72	77	297	106.25
	George Von Elm, Lakeside G.C. of Hollywood, Calif.	78	72	71	76	297	106.25
15	Willie Hunter, Riviera C.C., Calif.	73	72	78	75	298	100.00
16	Olin Dutra, Wilshire C.C., Calif.	74	71	77	77	299	50.00
	Harold McSpaden, Winchester C.C., Mass.	76	67	74	82	299	50.00
	John Revolta, Evanston G.C., Ill.	74	72	77	76	299	50.00
19	Jim Foulis, Ruth Lake C.C., Ill.	74	74	75	77	300	50.00
	Horton Smith, Oak Park C.C., Ill.	80	73	73	74	300	50.00
	Al Zimmerman, Alderwood C.C., Ore.	76	77	75	72	300	50.00
22	Charles Lacey, Hillcrest C.C., Calif.	77	75	75	75	302	50.00
23	Tommy Armour, Medinah C.C., Ill.	78	70	75	80	303	50.00
24	Al Huske, Kishwaukee C.C., Ill.	76	79	76	73	304	50.00
	John E. Rogers, Denver C.C., Colo.	71	76	73	84	304	50.00
26	Charles S. Sheppard, Oakland, Calif.	79	73	74	79	305	50.00
27	Joe Belfore, C.C. of Detroit, Mich.	75	73	80	78	306	50.00
	Stanley Kertes, Clover Field C.C., Calif.	77	72	82	75	306	50.00
	Alvin Krueger, Beloit Municipal G.C., Wis.	79	69	79	79	306	50.00
	Ray Mangrum, MacGregor G.C., Ohio	77	77	73	79	306	
31	Mike Turnesa, Fairview C.C., N.Y.	75	79	75	78	307	
32	Vernon Allen, Oak Ridge C.C., Minn.	81	74	75	78	308	
	Arthur Bell, Midwick C.C., Calif.	78	77	78	75	308	
	Neil Christian, Yakima C.C., Wash.	75	80	79	74	308	
	Willie Macfarlane, Old Oaks C.C., N.Y.	79	73	78	78	308	
	Jimmy Thomson, Shawnee C.C., Pa.	82	70	77	79	308	
	Frank Walsh, Bretton Woods, G.C., N.H.	75	77	80	76	308	
38	Lawson Little, Presidio G.C., Calif.	78	77	78	76	309	
	Levi Lynch, Cedar Crest G.C., Texas	74	74	81	80	309	
	Sam Snead, White Sulphur Springs G.C., W. Va.	77	76	76	80	309	
41	Al Brosch, Bethpage State Park, N.Y.	76	77	77	80	310	
	*Arthur L. Doering, Jr., Stanford U.G.C., Calif.	75	77	80	78	310	
	Willie Goggin, El Camino C., Calif.	79	75	78	78	310	
	Bob Stupple, Skokie C.C., Ill.	78	74	81	77	310	
45	*Wilford Wehrle, Racine C.C. of Virginia	74	76	81	80	311	
46	Robert Cruickshank, C.C. of Virginia	83	71	73	85	312	
	Alex Follmer, Los Serranos C.C., Calif.	74	76	81	81	312	
48	Tony Manero, Salem C.C., Mass.	74	80	81	78	313	
49	Mortie Dutra, Red Run G.C., Mich.	78	74	85	77	314	
50	*Richard D. Chapman, Greenwich C.C., Conn.	74	77	83	81	315	
	Ed Dudley, Philadelphia Country C., Pa.	77	77	78	83	315	
	Mike Murra, Wichita C.C., Kansas	81	71	78	85	315	
53	Herb Bowers, Cobre Valley C.C., Ariz.	77	74	80	87	318	
54	*Ted Adams, Meadow Brook C.C., Mo.	74	80	86	81	321	
55	*Robert Babbish, Brooklands G. & C.C., Mich.	78	75	86	83	322	

*Amateur.
Prize money total $6,000 awarded to professionals returning scores up to 306, inclusive.

1939
FORTY-THIRD OPEN CHAMPIONSHIP

Held at Philadelphia Country Club, (Spring Mill Course), West Conshohocken, Pa., June 8–10.
Yardage—6,786. Par 69. 1,193 Entries; 165 Starters.
64 Contestants who completed 72 holes.

						Score	Money Prize
1	Byron Nelson, Reading C.C., Pa.	72	73	71	68	284	$1,000,00
2	Craig Wood, Winged Foot G.C., N.Y.	70	71	71	72	284	800.00
3	Denny Shute, Huntington, W.Va.,	70	72	70	72	284	700.00
4	*Marvin (Bud) Ward, Spokane, C.C., Wash.	69	73	71	72	285	MEDAL
5	Sam Snead, Greenbrier, G. & T. C., W. Va.	68	71	73	74	286	600.00
6	Johnny Bulla, Chicago, Ill.	72	71	68	76	287	450.00
7	Ralph Guldahl, Braidburn C.C., N.J.	71	73	72	72	288	325.00
	Dick Metz, Mill Road Farm G.C., Ill.	76	72	71	69	288	325.00
9	Ky Laffoon, Northmoor C.C., Ill.	76	70	73	70	289	175.00
	Harold L. McSpaden, Winchester C.C., Mass.	70	73	71	75	289	175.00
	Paul Runyan, Metropolis, C.C., N.Y.	76	70	71	72	289	175.00
12	Harry E. Cooper, Shenecossett C.C., Conn.	71	72	75	72	290	108.33
	Ed Dudley, Philadelphia Country C., Pa.	76	72	73	69	290	108.34
	Henry G. Picard, Hershey C.C., Pa.	72	72	72	74	290	108.33
15	Horton Smith, Oak Park C.C., Ill.	72	68	75	76	291	100.00
16	Sam Byrd, Philadelphia Country C., Pa.	75	71	72	74	292	66.67
	Olin Dutra, Wilshire C.C., Calif.	70	74	70	78	292	66.67
	Clayton Heafner, Charlotte, N.C.	73	73	66	80	292	66.66
	*Wilford Wehrle, Racine C.C., Wis.	71	77	69	75	292	—
20	Jimmy Hines, Lakeville C., N.Y.	73	74	77	69	293	50.00
	John E. Rogers, Denver C.C., Colo.	75	70	69	79	293	50.00
22	Tommy Armour, Medinah C.C., Ill.	70	75	69	80	294	50.00
	Jimmy Demaret, Brae-Burn C.C., Texas	72	76	72	74	294	50.00
	John Revolta, Evanston G.C., Ill.	73	76	71	74	294	50.00
25	Robert A. Cruickshank, C.C., of Virginia, Va.	73	74	73	75	295	50.00
	Jim Foulis, Ruth Lake C.C., Ill.	73	75	77	70	295	50.00
	E.J. (Dutch) Harrison, Oak Park C.C., Ill.	75	72	74	74	295	50.00
	Matt Kowal, Philmont C.C., Pa.	69	76	75	75	295	50.00
29	Victor Ghezzi, Deal G.C., N.J.	73	71	76	76	296	50.00
	Edward Oliver, Hornell C.C., N.Y.	75	77	72	72	296	50.00
	Felix Serafin, C.C., of Scranton, Pa.	80	72	71	73	296	50.00
32	Al Espinosa, Portage C.C., Ohio	75	73	74	75	297	12.50
	Alvin Krueger, Beloit Municipal G.C., Wis.	71	77	73	76	297	12.50
	Ray Mangrum, Oakmont, Pa.	71	74	81	71	297	12.50
	Jim Turnesa, Louisquisset G.C., R.I.	75	74	75	73	297	12.50
36	Arthur Bell, Midwick C.C., Calif.	73	75	79	71	298	
	Leo J. Walper, Bethesda, Md.	74	75	79	70	298	
38	Terl Johnson, Plymouth C.C., Pa.	73	76	76	74	299	
	Edwin C. Kingsley, C.C., Salt Lake City, Utah	76	75	73	75	299	
	Frank Moore, Mount Washington G.C., N.H.	73	70	77	79	299	
	Sam Parks, Jr., South Hills C.C., Pa.	73	73	77	76	299	
42	Billy Burke, C.C., Cleveland Ohio	74	74	77	75	300	
	William A. Francis, Blairmont C.C., Pa.	78	74	74	74	300	
	Gene Kunes, Norristown, Pa.	76	73	75	76	300	
	Lawson Little, Bretton Woods C.C., N.H.	69	74	76	81	300	
	Frank Walsh, Rumson C.C., N.J.	74	75	76	75	300	
47	Joe Belfore, C.C. of Detroit, Mich.	76	76	68	81	301	
	*Otto P. Greiner, Rodgers Forge C., Md.	77	73	77	74	301	
	Gene Sarazen, Brookfield, Conn.	74	72	79	76	301	
	Pat Sawyer, Birmingham G.C., Mich.	75	75	77	74	301	
	*William P. Turnesa, Briar Hills G. & C.C., N.Y.	77	74	76	74	301	
52	Bruce Coltart, Woodcrest, C.C., N.J.	78	73	80	71	302	
	Tom Creavy, Albany C.C., N.Y.	72	78	77	75	302	
	Al Houghton, Georgetown Prep G.C., Md.	73	76	76	77	302	
55	Ted Luther, Churchill Valley G.C., Pa.	73	75	77	78	303	
56	Tony Manero, Salem C.C., Mass.	74	76	78	76	304	
	Lloyd Mangrum, Los Angeles, Calif.	70	74	81	79	304	
58	Ted Turner, Pine Valley G.C., N.J.	75	74	80	76	305	
59	George Von Elm, Taft, Calif.	72	77	76	81	306	
	Norman Von Nida, Sidney, Australia	79	73	72	82	306	
61	*Edward L. Meister, Jr., Canterbury G.C., Ohio	71	76	81	79	307	
62	Ben Hogan, Century C.C., N.Y.	76	74	78	80	308	
	George Slingerland, Greensboro C.C., N.C.	74	78	81	75	308	
64	Frank Gelhot, Ridgewood G.C., Ohio	74	76	78	81	309	

*Amateur.
Playoff—June 11-12: Nelson, 68–70–138; Wood, 68–73–141; Shute, 76—eliminated.

1940
FORTY-FOURTH OPEN CHAMPIONSHIP

Held at Canterbury Golf Club, Cleveland, Ohio, June 6–8.
1,161 Entries; 165 Starters.

58 Contestants who completed 72 holes.

						Score	Money Prize
1	Lawson Little, Bretton Woods, N.H.	72	69	73	73	287	$1,000.00
2	Gene Sarazen, Brookfield Center, Conn.	71	74	70	72	287	800.00
3	Horton Smith, Oak Park C.C., Ill.	69	72	78	69	288	700.00
4	Craig Wood, Winged Foot G.C., N.Y.	72	73	72	72	289	600.00
5	Ben Hogan, Century C.C., N.Y.	70	73	74	73	290	325.00
	Ralph Guldahl, Chicago, Ill.	73	71	76	70	290	325.00
	Lloyd Mangrum, Oak Park C.C., Ill.	75	70	71	74	290	325.00
	Byron Nelson, Inverness C., Ohio	72	74	70	74	290	325.00
9	Dick Metz, Oak Park C.C., Ill.	75	72	72	72	291	175.00
10	Ed Dudley, Philadelphia Country C., Pa.	73	75	71	73	292	137.50
	Frank Walsh, Rumson C.C., N.J.	73	69	71	79	292	137.50
12	Tommy Armour, Medinah C.C., Ill.	73	74	75	71	293	100.00
	Harold L. McSpaden, Winchester C.C., Mass.	74	72	70	77	293	100.00
	Henry G. Picard, Hershey C.C., Pa.	73	73	71	76	293	100.00
15	Victor Ghezzi, Deal G.C., N.J.	70	74	75	75	294	100.00
16	Jim Foulis, Ruth Lake C.C., Ill.	73	73	77	72	295	50.00
	Gene Kunes, Holmesburg, C.C., Pa.	76	72	73	74	295	50.00
	Johnny Revolta, Evanston G.C., Ill.	73	74	72	76	295	50.00
	Sam Snead, Shawnee C.C., Pa.	67	74	73	81	295	50.00
20	Andrew Gibson, Bonnie View G.C., Md.	71	75	77	73	296	50.00
	Jimmy Hines, Lakeville, C., N.Y.	73	74	77	72	296	50.00
	Felix Serafin, C.C. of Scranton, Pa.	77	74	71	74	296	50.00
23	Jock Hutchison, Jr., Forest Hills C.C., Ill.	73	72	75	77	297	50.00
	Eddie Kirk, Glen Oaks G.C., Mich.	73	77	74	73	297	50.00
	*Wilford Wehrle, Tam O'Shanter C.C., Ill.	78	73	72	74	297	–––
	Leland J. Wilcox, Sunnyside C.C., Iowa	75	73	74	75	297	50.00
27	Ray Mangrum, Oakmont, Pa.	73	78	75	72	298	50.00
28	Johnny Farrell, Baltusrol G.C., N.J.	75	77	76	71	299	50.00
29	Bruce Coltart, Seaview G.C., N.J.	80	72	74	74	300	30.00
	*Jim Ferrier, Sydney, Australia	73	74	78	75	300	–––
	Al Huske, Kishwaukee C.C., Ill.	70	80	76	74	300	30.00
	Sam Parks, Jr., South Hills C.C., Pa.	69	74	79	78	300	30.00
	Henry B. Ramson, Glen Garden G. & C.C., Texas	75	77	74	74	300	30.00
	Jack Ryan, Louisville C.C., Ky.	75	75	77	73	300	30.00
	*Andrew Szwedko, North Park G.C., Pa.	76	77	76	71	300	–––
36	*Richard D. Chapman, Aronimink G.C., Pa.	74	78	76	73	301	
	Willie Goggin, San Francisco, Calif.	78	74	75	74	301	
	Matt Kowal, Philmont C.C., Pa.	72	75	77	77	301	
	Tony Manero, Salem C.C., Mass.	75	75	77	74	301	
	Johnny Morris, C.C. of Tuscaloosa, Ala.	75	77	74	75	301	
41	Sam D. Byrd, Merion Cricket C., Pa.	72	78	79	73	302	
42	Toney Penna, Dayton, Ohio	80	73	76	74	303	
43	Leonard Dodson, Kansas City C.C., Mo.	72	72	80	81	305	
	Al Espinosa, Portage C.C., Ohio	79	71	76	79	305	
	Jim Milward, Blackhawk C.C., Wis.	74	79	76	76	305	
	John Thoren, Woodland G.C., Mass.	73	78	77	77	305	
47	Al Brosch, Bethpage State Park, N.Y.	74	73	82	77	306	
	John E. Rogers, Denver C.C., Colo.	73	76	79	78	306	
49	Paul Runyan, Metropolis C.C., N.Y.	74	79	78	76	307	
50	Jerry Gianferante, Brattleboro C.C., Vt.	76	77	81	74	308	
	Henry J. Kaiser, Meadowbrook G.C., Wis.	71	78	80	79	308	
52	*Robert N. Babbish, Brooklands G. & C.C., Mich.	71	77	80	81	309	
	Bill Barbour, Sleepy Hollow C.C., Ohio	75	78	80	76	309	
54	Mike Pavella, Washington County G. & C.C., Pa.	79	74	81	76	310	
55	Frank Commisso, Irondequoit C.C., N.Y.	73	78	80	81	312	
	Pete Webb, Cleveland Springs G.C., N.C.	77	74	83	78	312	
	Ock Willoweit, Dayton, Ohio	75	78	82	77	312	
58	*Toby Lyons, Riverside G.C., Pa.	77	76	80	80	313	

Six players were disqualified for beginning their final round ahead of their scheduled starting time because of threatening weather. Ed (Porky) Oliver was among the six, and he finished with an unofficial score of 287, which would have tied him with Little and Sarazen.

Playoff 18 holes, June 9—Little, 70; Sarazen, 73.

*Amateur. Gold medals awarded to Wilford Wehrle, Jim Ferrier and Andrew Szwedko.

Prize money totaling $6,000 awarded to professionals returning scores up to 300, inclusive.

1941
FORTY-FIFTH OPEN CHAMPIONSHIP

Held at the Colonial Club, Fort Worth, Texas, June 5–7.
Yardage–7,005. Par–70.

1,048 Entries; 163 Starters.
57 Contestants who completed 72 holes.

						Score	Money Prize
1	Craig Wood, Winged Foot G.C., N.Y.	73	71	70	70	284	$1,000,00
2	Denny Shute, Chicago, Ill.	69	75	72	71	287	800.00
3	Johnny Bulla, Chicago, Ill.	75	71	72	71	289	650.00
	Ben Hogan, Hershey C.C., Pa.	74	77	68	70	289	650.00
5	Herman Barron, Fenway G.C., N.Y.	75	71	74	71	291	412.50
	Paul Runyan, Metropolis C.C., N.Y.	73	72	71	75	291	412.50
7	E.J. (Dutch) Harrison, Chicago, Ill.	70	82	71	71	294	216.67
	Harold L. McSpaden, Winchester C.C., Mass.	71	75	74	74	294	216.67
	Gene Sarazen, Lakeview C.C., N.Y.	74	73	72	75	294	216.67
10	Ed Dudley, Broadmoor G.C., Colo.	74	74	74	73	295	125.00
	Lloyd Mangrum, Monterey Park, Calif.	73	74	72	76	295	125.00
	Dick Metz, Oak Park,C.C., Ill.	71	74	76	74	295	125.00
13	Henry Ransom, Glen Garden G. & C.C., Texas	72	74	75	75	296	100.00
	Horton Smith, Pinehurst C.C., N.C.	73	75	73	75	296	100.00
	Sam Snead, Hot Springs, Va.	76	70	77	73	296	100.00
	*Harry Todd, Lakewood C.C., Texas	72	77	76	71	296	----
17	Lawson Little, Monterey Peninsula, Calif.	71	73	79	74	297	50.00
	Byron Nelson, Inverness C., Ohio	73	73	74	77	297	50.00
19	Victor Ghezzi, Deal G.C., N.J.	70	79	77	72	298	50.00
20	Gene Kunes, Holmesbury C.C., Pa.	71	79	74	75	299	50.00
21	Ralph Guldahl, Chicago, Ill.	79	76	72	73	300	50.00
	Clayton Heafner, Linville G. & C.C., N.C.	72	72	78	78	300	50.00
	Johnny Palmer, Badin, N.C.	74	76	76	74	300	50.00
24	Jimmy Hines, Lakeville C., N.Y.	75	74	76	76	301	50.00
25	Joseph Zarhardt, Jeffersonville G.C., Pa.	74	76	77	75	302	50.00
26	Sam Byrd, Merion Cricket C., Pa.	76	78	75	74	303	50.00
	Herman Keiser, Firestone C.C., Ohio	74	77	76	76	303	50.00
	Johnny Morris, Tuscaloosa C.C., Ala.	72	73	81	77	303	50.00
	Henry G. Picard, Twin Hills G. & C.C., Okla.	77	79	72	75	303	50.00
30	Jim Ferrier, Elmhurst C.C., Ill.	77	71	81	75	304	50.00
	Jerry Gianferante, Brattleboro C.C., Vt.	76	77	74	77	304	50.00
	*Marvin H. (Bud) Ward, Spokane G.& C.C., Wash.	76	77	75	76	304	----
33	Abe G. Espinosa, C.C. of Decatur, Ill.	76	75	72	82	305	
	Sam Parks, Jr., South Hills C.C., Pa.	73	82	74	76	305	
	Toney Penna, Dayton, Ohio	75	77	76	77	305	
	Marvin D. Stahl, C.C. of Lansing, Mich.	77	76	73	79	305	
	Jimmy Turnesa, Elmsford C.C., N.Y.	74	80	77	74	305	
38	Bill Kaiser, Louisville, Ky.	72	78	80	76	306	
39	Willie Klein, Wheatley Hills G.C., N.Y.	73	80	78	76	307	
40	Bunny Torpey, Oakwood C.C., Mo.	72	79	78	79	308	
	*William P. Turnesa, Meadowbrook C.C., Mich.	75	77	75	81	308	
42	Jim Foulis, Ruth Lake C.C., Ill.	78	78	74	79	309	
	Felix Serafin, C.C. of Scranton, Pa.	76	79	78	76	309	
	Mike Turnesa, Fairview C.C., N.Y.	77	79	75	78	309	
45	Henry Castillo, L.S.U. G.C., La.	84	72	77	77	310	
	Charles B. Farlow, Piedmont, C.C., N.C.	79	77	77	77	310	
	Bob Hamilton, Helfrich Field G.C., Ind.	76	79	80	75	310	
	Jack Ryan, Louisville C.C., Ky.	71	82	80	77	310	
49	*Richard D. Chapman, Winged Foot G.C., N.Y.	76	76	80	80	312	
	Pat Wilcox, Sunnyside C.C., Iowa	80	75	79	78	312	
51	Raymond Gafford, Ridglea G.C., Texas	76	78	82	77	313	
52	Al Watrous, Oakland Hills C.C., Mich.	79	75	81	79	314	
53	Bill Nary, Rancho Santa Fe G.C., Calif.	77	76	83	79	315	
54	*John J. Jacobs, III, Cedar Rapids C.C., Iowa	74	77	82	83	316	
55	*Verne Stewart, Carrizozo C.C., N.M.	76	78	80	83	317	
56	Tom O'Connor, Yardley C.C., Pa.	73	78	79	88	318	
57	Jock Hutchison, Jr., Rockford, Ill.	78	78	83	80	319	

*Amateur.
Prize money totaling $6,000 awarded to professionals returning scores up to 304, inclusive.

1942
HALE AMERICA NATIONAL OPEN GOLF TOURNAMENT

for benefit of
Navy Relief Society and United Service Organizations
sponsored by
United States Golf Association
Chicago District Golf Association Professional Golfers' Assn. of America

Held at the Ridgemoor Country Club, Chicago, Ill., June 18 to 21, inclusive
Yardage—6,519. Par—72.

1,540 Entries, 107 Qualifiers, 96 Starters
(Local qualifying rounds, 36 holes, May 24-25 at 69 locations. Sectional qualifying rounds, 54 holes except where noted otherwise, May 26 at Toronto (36 holes); June 5 at Boston (36 holes); June 5-6 at Chicago, Kansas City, Bloomfield, N. J.; June 6-7 at Denver, Atlanta, Detroit, Minneapolis, Buffalo, Cincinnati, Tulsa, Dallas; June 8-9 at Los Angeles.)

All qualifiers eligible for all four rounds. The 62 lowest scorers:

1	Ben Hogan, Hershey C. C., Pa.	72	62	69	68	271
2	Jimmy Demaret, Plum Hollow G. C., Mich.	68	68	69	69	274
	Mike Turnesa, Elmsford C. C., N. Y.	65	66	72	71	274
4	Byron Nelson, Inverness C., Ohio	69	70	69	70	278
	Horton Smith, Pinehurst C. C., N.C.	68	67	71	72	278
	Jimmy Thomson, Del Monte G. & C. C., Cal.	73	69	70	66	278
7	Eddie Burke, Meadow Brook C. C., Conn.	71	72	69	68	280
	Lawson Little, Monterey, Cal.	67	68	71	74	280
9	Jim Ferrier, Elmhurst C. C., Ill.	69	71	68	73	281
	Lloyd Mangrum, Monterey Park, Cal.	67	72	71	71	281
	Dick Metz, Oak Park C. C., Ill.	68	70	73	70	281
12	Sam Byrd, Merion G. C., Pa.	72	68	71	72	283
	Harold McSpaden, Philadelphia Country C., Pa.	71	67	71	74	283
	Craig Wood, Winged Foot G. C., N.Y.	72	71	68	72	283
15	Herman Barron, Fenway G. C., N.Y.	68	68	76	72	284
	Buck White, Ridgeway C. C., Tenn.	70	69	71	74	284
17	Ky Laffoon, Chicago, Ill.	69	70	74	72	285
18	Al Brosch, Bethpage Park, N.Y.	67	73	70	76	286
	Toney Penna, Dayton, Ohio	71	72	70	73	286
20	Frank Commisso, Irondequoit C. C., N.Y.	69	73	71	74	287
	†John W. Dawson, Lakeside G. C. of Hollywood, Cal.	71	67	74	75	287
	Ed Dudley, Broadmoor G. C., Colo.	69	73	71	74	287
23	*Frank Connolly, Lakepointe C. C., Mich.	72	70	72	74	288
	Harry Cooper, Golden Valley G. C., Minn.	67	73	71	77	288
	*Steve Kovach, Brackenridge Heights, C. C., Pa.	71	70	73	74	288
	Ray Mangrum, New York, N.Y.	70	70	71	77	288
	Jack Mitchell, Spring Brook C. C., N.J.	70	71	74	73	288
	Paul Runyan, Metropolis C. C., N.Y.	72	71	71	74	288
29	Otey Crisman, Riverside G. C., Ala.	65	72	76	76	289
	*William Y. Dear, Jr., Essex County C. C., N.J.	72	66	76	75	289
	Joe Kirkwood, Huntingdon Valley C. C., Pa.	70	72	75	72	289
	Johnny Morris, Tuscaloosa C. C., Ala.	71	73	74	71	289
	Gene Sarazen, Brooklawn C. C., Conn.	70	72	73	74	289
	George Schneiter, Ogden G. and C. C., Utah	68	73	74	74	289
35	Willie Goggin, Century C. C., N.Y.	69	71	75	75	290
	Capt. Robert T. Jones, Jr., Atlanta A. C., Ga.	70	75	72	73	290
	Gib Sellers, Edgewood G. C., Mich.	70	70	75	75	290
	Mike Sipula, Ottawa C. C., Ill.	67	70	78	75	290
	Joe Turnesa, Rockville C. C., N.Y.	71	72	73	74	290
40	Abe G. Espinosa, Decatur C. C., Ill.	69	71	73	78	291
	Henry G. Picard, Twin Hills G. & C. C., Okla.	72	73	73	73	291
	Marvin D. Stahl, C. C. of Lansing, Mich.	69	72	73	77	291
43	*Robert Cochran, Norwood Hills C. C., Mo.	69	72	73	78	292
	Joe Coria, Phalen G. C., Minn.	70	72	76	74	292
	*Neil Croonquist, The C. C., Minneapolis, Minn.	72	70	76	74	292
	John Krutilla, Burnham Woods C. C., Ill.	72	73	72	75	292
	Denny Shute, Chicago, Ill.	69	68	80	75	292
	*Frank Stranahan, Miami Biltmore C. C., Fla.	72	71	74	75	292
	Sgt. Jim Turnesa, Fort Dix, N.J.	71	72	73	76	292
50	Dick Govern, Skaneateles C. C., N.Y.	73	72	74	74	293
	Ralph Guldahl, Chicago, Ill.	73	71	78	71	293
	Al Huske, Kishwaukee C. C., Ill.	71	74	73	75	293
53	Harry Adams, Medina C. C., Ill.	72	77	72	73	294
	John Kinder, Plainfield C. C., N.J.	72	72	74	76	294
	Herman Scharlau, Bloomington C. C., Ill.	79	70	75	70	294
56	Joe Belfore, C. C. of Detroit, Mich.	71	74	76	74	295
	Raymond Gafford, Ridglea G. C., Texas	70	74	74	77	295
	James S. Johnson, Warren Valley G. C., Mich.	71	73	76	75	295
	Frank Moore, St. Clair C. C., Ill.	71	74	74	76	295
	Tom Talbot, Columbia C. C., Mo.	71	71	79	74	295
	*Wilford Wehrle, Racine, Wis.	68	70	76	81	295
	*Neil E. White, Tamarack C. C., Conn.	72	73	76	74	295

*Amateurs. †Applicant for reinstatement to amateur classification.
Prize money totaling $6,000 awarded to professionals returning scores up to 289, inclusive; $1,200 of total in War Savings Bonds.
"Old Guard" Division—for players who competed in USGA Open Championships at least 20 years ago—won by Ed Dudley, 287. Other scores—Gene Sarazen and Joe Kirkwood, 289; Capt. Robert T. Jones, Jr., and Joe Turnesa, 290; Abe G. Espinosa, 291; Willie Hunter, 296; Tommy Armour, 301; Charles Evans, Jr., 302.

1946
FORTY-SIXTH OPEN CHAMPIONSHIP

Held at the Canterbury Golf Club, Cleveland, Ohio, June 13-16.
Yardage—6,926. Par 72.
1,175 Entries, 172 Qualifiers, 170 Starters.
62 Contestants who completed 72 holes.

						Score	Money Prize
1	†Lloyd Mangrum, Los Angeles, Calif.	74	70	68	72	284	$1,500
2	†Byron Nelson, Toledo, Ohio	71	71	69	73	284	875
	†Victor Ghezzi, Knoxville, Tenn.	71	69	72	72	284	875
4	Herman Barron, Fenway G.C., N.Y.	72	72	72	69	285	550
	Ben Hogan, Hershey C.C., Pa.	72	68	73	72	285	550
6	Jimmy Demaret, Houston, Texas	71	74	73	68	286	350
	Edward S. Oliver, Jr., Wilmington, Del.	71	71	74	70	286	350
8	Dick Metz, Arkansas City, Kansas	76	70	72	69	287	225
	Melvin R. (Chick) Harbert, Meadowbrook C.C., Mich.	72	78	67	70	287	225
10	Lawson Little, Monterey, Calif.	72	69	76	71	288	175
	E.J. (Dutch) Harrison, Chicago, Ill.	75	71	72	70	288	175
12	Clayton V. Heafner, Charlotte, N.C.	75	72	71	71	289	150
	Henry G. Picard, Canterbury G.C., Ohio	71	73	71	74	289	150
	Edward J. Furgol, Pontiac C.C., Mich.	77	69	74	69	289	150
15	Steve Kovach, Ligonier C.C., Pa.	71	72	73	75	291	125
	Claude Harmon, Winged Foot G.C., N.Y.	72	77	70	72	291	125
	Toney Penna, Cincinnati, Ohio	69	77	74	71	291	125
	Chandler Harper, Glensheallah G.C., Va.	76	74	67	74	291	125
19	Sam Snead, Cascades Club, Va.	69	75	74	74	292	100
	Gene Kunes, Homestead G.C., N.J.	74	73	73	72	292	100
21	Paul Runyan, Pasadena, Calif.	75	72	76	70	293	100
22	John G. Bulla, Little Rock, Ark.	72	74	73	75	294	100
	Henry B. Ransom, Houston,Texas	71	73	73	77	294	100
	Harry Todd, Lakewood C.C., Texas	75	73	70	76	294	100
	Lew Worsham, Congressional C.C., Md.	73	74	76	71	294	100
26	Mike Turnesa, Knollwood C.C., N.Y.	70	76	74	75	295	100
	Leland H. Gibson, Blue Hills G.C., Mo.	74	71	78	72	295	100
	Ellsworth Vines, Chicago, Ill.	73	72	75	75	295	100
	*Marvin (Bud) Ward, Spokane C.C., Wash.	74	77	72	72	295	———
	*Smiley Quick, Inglewood C.C., Calif.	75	76	72	72	295	———
31	Toby Lyons, Conewango Valley C.C., Pa.	74	73	72	77	296	100
	Harold McSpaden, Sanford, Maine	76	73	74	73	296	100
33	Raymond Gafford, Ridglea G.C., Texas	75	73	75	74	297	
	Otey Crisman, Selma, Ala.	77	72	74	74	297	
35	Johnny Palmer, Badin, N.C.	77	74	74	73	298	
	Charles Penna, Beverly C.C., Ill.	75	74	75	74	298	
37	Jimmy Hines, Lake Shore C., Ill.	77	73	75	74	299	
38	Robert Cruickshank, C.C. of Virginia, Va.	72	75	78	75	300	
	Pat Circelli, Gedney G.C., N.Y.	77	73	75	75	300	
	George Fazio, Hillcrest C.C., Calif.	77	74	76	73	300	
	Pete Cooper, Gainesville G. & C.C., Fla.	72	75	74	79	300	
	Herman Keiser, Firestone C.C., Ohio	76	75	72	77	300	
43	Al Watrous, Oakland Hills C.C., Mich.	76	75	74	76	301	
	Fred Haas, Jr., Metairie C.C., La.	74	75	77	75	301	
45	*Frank Stranahan, Inverness Club, Ohio	74	76	77	75	302	
	*Gene Dahlbender, Jr., Druid Hills G.C., Ga.	73	76	80	73	302	
	Billy Burke, The C.C., Cleveland, Ohio	76	75	76	75	302	
48	W.L. Jelliffe, Lakewood C.C., Colo.	73	74	80	76	303	
	Stewart Alexander, Lexington G.C., N.C.	71	79	76	77	303	
50	Joseph Zarhardt, Norristown, Pa.	74	76	79	75	304	
	Rod Munday, Hickory Hills C.C., Mo.	77	72	78	77	304	
	*Robert Servis, Miami Valley G.C., Ohio	76	75	77	76	304	
53	Dick Shoemaker, Alcoma G.C., Pa.	78	72	76	79	305	
	Henry Castillo, Baton Rouge C.C., La.	74	77	80	74	305	
	*A.F. Kammer, Jr., C.C. of Detroit, Mich.	75	76	74	80	305	
	Al Brosch, Bethpage Park, N.Y.	72	78	77	78	305	
57	Joe Kirkwood, Huntingdon Valley C.C., Pa.	78	73	75	81	307	
	Joe Mozel, Lloyd G.C. & D.R., Ore.	73	77	77	80	307	
59	*Otto Greiner, C.C. of Maryland, Md.	75	75	81	77	308	
	Willie Goggin, Century C.C., N.Y.	76	73	78	81	308	
	Frank Commisso, Irondequoit C.C., N.Y.	74	76	77	81	308	
62	*Ted Adams, Blue Hills Club, Mo.	73	78	75	85	311	

†Playoff: 18 holes, June 16, A.M.—Mangrum, 72; Nelson, 72; Ghezzi, 72.
18 holes, June 16, P.M.—Mangrum, 72; Nelson, 73; Ghezzi, 73.
*Amateurs. Gold medals awarded to Marvin (Bud) Ward and Smiley Quick.
Prize money totaling $8,000 awarded to professionals returning scores up to 296, inclusive.
Special playoff prize of $1,000 divided equally among Mangrum, Nelson and Ghezzi.

1947
FORTY-SEVENTH OPEN CHAMPIONSHIP

Held at the St. Louis Country Club, Clayton, Mo., June 12-15.
Yardage—6,532. Par 71.
1,356 Entries, 171 Qualifiers, 164 Starters.
67 Contestants who completed 72 holes.

						Score	Money Prize
1	†Lew Worsham, Oakmont C.C., Pa.	70	70	71	71	282	$2,000
2	†Sam Snead, Cascades G.C., Va.	72	70	70	70	282	1,500
3	A.D. (Bobby) Locke, Vereeniging, South Africa	68	74	70	73	285	900
	Edward S. Oliver, Jr., Wilmington, Del.	73	70	71	71	285	900
5	*Marvin (Bud) Ward, Spokane C.C., Wash.	69	72	73	73	287	---
6	Jim Ferrier, Chicago, Ill.	71	70	74	74	289	400
	Victor J. Ghezzi, Victory Hills C.C., Kans.	74	73	73	69	289	400
	Leland Gibson, Blue Hills C., Mo.	69	76	73	71	289	400
	Ben Hogan, Hershey C.C., Pa.	70	75	70	74	289	400
	Johnny Palmer, Badin, N.C.	72	70	75	72	289	400
	Paul Runyan, Annandale G.C., Calif.	71	74	72	72	289	400
12	M.R. (Chick) Harbert, Meadowbrook C.C., Mich.	67	72	81	70	290	200
13	Edward J. Furgol, Royal Oak, Mich.	70	75	72	74	291	140
	E.J. (Dutch) Harrison, York C.C., Pa.	76	72	70	73	291	140
	Dick Metz, Arkansas City, Kans.	69	70	78	74	291	140
	Bill Nary, Southern California G. & C.C., Calif.	77	71	70	73	291	140
	*Frank R. Stranahan, Inverness C., Ohio	73	74	72	72	291	---
	Harry Todd, Dallas, Texas	67	75	77	72	291	140
19	Claude Harmon, Winged Foot G.C., N.Y.	74	72	74	72	292	100
	Gene Kunes, Englewood G.C., N.J.	71	77	72	72	292	100
	George Payton, Hampton, Va.	71	75	75	71	292	100
	Alfred L. Smith, Danville G.C., Va.	70	73	76	73	292	100
23	Sam Byrd, Plum Hollow G.C., Mich.	72	74	70	77	293	100
	Joe Kirkwood, Huntingdon Valley C.C., Pa.	72	73	70	78	293	100
	Lloyd Mangrum, Tam O'Shanter C.C., Ill.	77	72	69	75	293	100
	*James B. McHale, Jr., Whitemarsh Valley C.C., Pa.	79	72	65	77	293	---
27	Herman Barron, Fenway G.C., N.Y.	74	71	75	74	294	100
	Billy Burke, The C.C., Cleveland, Ohio	74	75	71	74	294	100
29	Bob Hamilton, Evansville, Ind.	75	71	75	74	295	100
	Henry Ransom, Northmoor C.C., Ill.	67	74	79	75	295	100
31	Fred Haas, Jr., Metairie C.C., La.	74	73	76	73	296	75
	Bob Kepler, University G.C., Ohio	76	72	69	79	296	75
	Lawson Little, Hawthorne Valley C.C., Ohio	75	73	75	73	296	75
	Toney Penna, Cincinnati, Ohio	74	73	74	75	296	75
35	John Bulla, Phoenix, Ariz.	74	77	73	73	297	
	Pete Cooper, Ponte Vedra C.C., Fla.	76	71	72	78	297	
	Lloyd Wadkins, Odessa C.C., Texas	76	73	74	74	297	
38	Herschel Spears, C.C. of Birmingham, Ala.	73	75	75	75	298	
39	Al Brosch, Cherry Valley C., N.Y.	73	73	76	78	300	
	Jimmy Demaret, Ojai Valley, Calif.	76	69	74	81	300	
	David Douglas, Rock Manor G.C., Del.	71	80	76	73	300	
	Gene Sarazen, New York, N.Y.	72	75	74	79	300	
	Jimmy Thomson, Los Angeles, Calif.	74	75	75	76	300	
	Jim Turnesa, Metropolis C.C., N.Y.	74	74	80	72	300	
45	B. Patrick Abbott, Memphis C.C., Tenn.	75	71	80	75	301	
	Frank Moore, Meadowbrook C.C., Mo.	75	73	77	76	301	
	Harold E. West, Tualatin C.C., Ore.	77	72	75	77	301	
48	Mike DeMassey, Fairyland G.C., Tenn.	76	75	75	76	302	
	Arthur Doering, Jr., Evanston G.C., Ill.	73	76	77	76	302	
	Otto Greiner, Baltimore, Md.	69	77	77	79	302	
51	Skip Alexander, Lexington C.C., N.C.	75	76	78	74	303	
	Jack Grout, Harrisburg C.C., Pa.	71	80	78	74	303	
	*Thomas E. Sheehan, Oakland Hills C.C., Mich.	73	74	78	78	303	
	Ellsworth Vines, Los Angeles, Calif.	76	74	74	79	303	
55	Ralph Guldahl, Medinah C.C., Ill.	74	77	76	77	304	
	Toby Lyons, Conewango Valley C.C., Pa.	77	74	76	77	304	
	John J. O'Donnell, Commissioned Officers' G.C., Va.	74	74	81	75	304	
	Herman Scharlau, Bloomington C.C., Ill.	71	77	80	76	304	
59	Fred Annon, Innis Arden G.C., Conn.	77	73	80	75	305	
	George Fazio, Hillcrest C.C., Calif.	76	75	74	80	305	
	*Robert H. (Skee) Riegel, Oakmont C., Calif.	75	75	73	82	305	
	Mike Turnesa, Knollwood C.C., N.Y.	75	73	78	79	305	
63	*Jack Coyle, Illini C.C., Ill.	76	75	76	80	307	
64	*Robert E. Cochran, Meadowbrook C.C., Mo.	74	77	78	79	308	
65	*Robert W. Willits, Kansas City C.C., Mo.	75	76	79	79	309	
66	*Felice J. Torza, Wethersfield C.C., Conn.	72	78	80	80	310	
67	*Frank Strafaci, Pomonok C.C., N.Y.	72	79	81	79	311	

†Playoff: 18 holes, June 15—Worsham, 69; Snead, 70.
*Amateurs. Gold medals awarded to Marvin (Bud) Ward, Frank R. Stranahan and James B. McHale, Jr.
Prize Money totaling $10,000 awarded to professionals returning scores up to 296, inclusive.
Special playoff prize of $1,000 divided equally between Worsham and Snead.

1948
FORTY-EIGHTH OPEN CHAMPIONSHIP

Held at the Riviera Country Club, Los Angeles, Calif., June 10-12.
Yardage—7,020. Par 71.
1,411 Entries, 171 Qualifiers, 171 Starters.

Fifty-four contestants who completed 72 holes.

						Score	Money Prize
1	Ben Hogan, Hershey C.C., Pa.	67	72	68	69	276	$2,000.00
2	Jimmy Demaret, Houston, Texas	71	70	68	69	278	1,500.00
3	Jim Turnesa, Elmsford, N.Y.	71	69	70	70	280	1,000.00
4	A. D. (Bobby) Locke, Vereeniging, South Africa	70	69	73	70	282	800.00
5	Sam Snead, Greenbrier G.C., W. Va.	69	69	73	72	283	600.00
6	Lew Worsham, Oakmont C.C., Pa.	67	74	71	73	285	500.00
7	Herman Barron, Fenway G.C., N.Y.	73	70	71	72	286	400.00
8	Johnny G. Bulla, Phoenix, Ariz.	73	72	75	67	287	300.00
	Toney Penna, Cincinnati, Ohio	70	72	73	72	287	300.00
	Smiley Quick, Fox Hills G.C., Calif.	73	71	69	74	287	300.00
11	Stewart (Skip) Alexander, C.C. of Lexington, N.C.	71	73	71	73	288	200.00
12	Harold McSpaden, New York, N.Y.	74	69	69	77	289	150.00
	Charles W. Congdon, Tacoma C. & G.C., Wash.	71	70	71	77	289	150.00
14	Leland Gibson, Blue Hills G.C., Mo.	71	76	69	74	290	114.29
	George Schneiter, Ogden G. & C.C., Utah	73	68	75	74	290	114.29
	Ellsworth Vines, Finkbine G.C., Iowa	75	72	69	74	290	114.29
	Otto Greiner, Woodholme C.C., Md.	74	73	71	72	290	114.29
	Herman Keiser, Akron, Ohio	71	71	73	75	290	114.28
	Herschel Spears, Birmingham C.C., Ala.	72	71	76	71	290	114.28
	Victor J. Ghezzi, Englewood, N.J.	72	74	74	70	290	114.28
21	Alfred L. Smith, Old Town C., N.C.	73	72	77	69	291	100.00
	Cary Middlecoff, Memphis C.C., Tenn.	74	71	73	73	291	100.00
	Joe Kirkwood, Jr., Riviera C.C., Calif.	72	70	72	77	291	100.00
	Lloyd Mangrum, Tam O'Shanter C.C., Ill.	71	72	74	74	291	100.00
25	Pete Cooper, Ponte Vedra C.C., Fla.	76	72	72	72	292	100.00
	Art Bell, California G.C. of S.F., Calif.	72	75	71	74	292	100.00
	George Fazio, Los Angeles, Calif.	72	72	76	72	292	100.00
28	Frank Moore, Meadow Brook C.C., Mo.	73	75	73	72	293	75.00
	M. R. (Chick) Harbert, Meadowbrook C.C., Mich.	72	72	77	72	293	75.00
	Marty Furgol, Albuquerque, N.M.	72	74	73	74	293	75.00
	Joe Kirkwood, Sr., Huntingdon Valley C.C., Pa.	73	75	73	72	293	75.00
32	Zell Eaton, Montebello G.C., Calif.	72	74	75	73	294	
	Ralph Guldahl, Medinah C.C., Ill.	73	75	75	71	294	
34	*Ken Rogers, Oklahoma City G. & C.C., Okla.	69	76	72	78	295	
35	Johnny Palmer, Badin, N.C.	74	74	76	72	296	
	Bill Nary, Albuquerque, N.M.	73	75	75	73	296	
	E. J. (Dutch) Harrison, Albuquerque, N.M.	75	72	72	77	296	
	Jimmy Hines, North Shore C.C., Ill.	75	71	76	74	296	
	Jack Ryan, Big Spring G.C., Ky.	74	69	76	77	296	
	Jack Harden, El Paso C.C., Texas	72	73	73	78	296	
41	George Schoux, Mamaroneck, N.Y.	74	72	76	76	298	
	*John W. Dawson, Lakeside G.C., Calif.	71	72	79	76	298	
	*Frank R. Stranahan, Inverness C., Ohio	72	69	78	79	298	
	*A. Richard Mayer, Winged Foot G.C., N.Y.	75	73	78	72	298	
45	Dave Douglas, Rock Manor G.C., Del.	74	73	78	74	299	
	Jim Johnson, Glen Oaks C.C., Mich.	76	71	77	75	299	
	Ed Furgol, Royal Oak, Mich.	75	73	77	74	299	
48	Al Zimmerman, Alderwood C.C., Ore.	71	74	77	78	300	
	Jimmy Thomson, Los Angeles, Calif.	77	71	76	76	300	
50	Buck White, Battle Creek C.C., Mich.	75	73	80	73	301	
51	Iverson Martin, Graham C.C., Texas	73	73	80	76	302	
	Theodore Rhodes, Los Angeles, Calif.	70	76	77	79	302	
53	Paul Runyan, Annandale G.C., Calif.	74	73	80	76	303	
	Andrew A. Mills, Belle-Air G.C., Kansas	71	75	83	84	313	

*Amateurs. Gold medal awarded to Ken Rogers.
Prize money totaling $10,000 awarded to professionals returning scores up to 293, inclusive.

1949
FORTY-NINTH OPEN CHAMPIONSHIP

Held at the Medinah Country Club (No. 3 Course), Medinah, Ill., June 9-11.
Yardage—6,936. Par 71.
1,348 Entries, 162 Qualifiers, 162 Starters.

Forty-seven contestants who completed 72 holes.

						Score	Money Prize
1	Cary Middlecoff, Colonial C.C., Tenn.	75	67	69	75	286	$2,000.00
2	Clayton Heafner, Eastwood G.C., N.C.	72	71	71	73	287	1,250.00
	Sam Snead, Greenbrier G.C., W. Va.	73	73	71	70	287	1,250.00
4	Jim Turnesa, Briar Hall G. & C.C., N.Y.	78	69	70	72	289	700.00
	A.D. (Bobby) Locke, Vereeniging, South Africa	74	71	73	71	289	700.00
6	Buck White, Unattached, Greenwood, Miss.	74	68	70	78	290	450.00
	Dave Douglas, Newark, Del.	74	73	70	73	290	450.00
8	Johnny Palmer, Badin, N.C.	71	75	72	73	291	300.00
	Claude Harmon, Winged Foot G.C., N.Y.	71	72	74	74	291	300.00
	Pete Cooper, Ponte Vedra C., Fla.	71	73	74	73	291	300.00
11	Eric Monti, Hillcrest C.C., Calif.	75	72	70	75	292	175.00
	Herschel G. Spears, C.C. of Birmingham, Ala.	76	71	71	74	292	175.00
13	Al Brosch, Cherry Valley C., N.Y.	70	71	73	79	293	150.00
14	Harry Todd, Lakewood C.C., Texas	76	72	73	73	294	125.00
	Johnny G. Bulla, Westmoreland C.C., Pa.	73	75	72	74	294	125.00
	Lloyd Mangrum, Tam O'Shanter C.C., Ill.	74	74	70	76	294	125.00
	Ellsworth Vines, Iowa University G.C., Iowa	73	72	71	78	294	125.00
	*Robert H. (Skee) Riegel, Tulsa C.C., Okla.	72	75	73	74	294	----
19	Gene Webb, St. Louis C.C., Mo.	73	77	70	75	295	100.00
	Les Kennedy, Pawtucket G.C., R.I.	69	74	79	73	295	100.00
	Fred Haas, Jr., Metairie C.C., La.	74	73	73	75	295	100.00
22	Ralph Guldahl, Chicago, Ill.	71	75	73	77	296	100.00
23	Jack Isaacs, Langley Field G.C., Va.	73	73	74	77	297	100.00
	M.R. (Chick) Harbert, Meadowbrook C.C., Mich.	70	78	75	74	297	100.00
	Jim Ferrier, San Francisco, Calif.	74	75	74	74	297	100.00
	Horton Smith, Detroit G.C., Mich.	72	75	74	76	297	100.00
27	Craig Wood, Winged Foot G.C., N.Y.	76	73	76	73	298	71.43
	Lew Worsham, Oakmont C.C., Pa.	71	76	71	80	298	71.43
	Herman Barron, Fenway G.C., N.Y.	70	78	76	74	298	71.43
	Jack Burke, Metropolis C.C., N.Y.	74	74	75	75	298	71.43
	Charles Farlow, Starmount Forest C.C., N.C.	70	77	76	75	298	71.43
	Skip Alexander, Lexington C.C., N.C.	76	72	77	73	298	71.43
	Sam Bernardi, Old Elm C., Ill.	80	69	76	73	298	71.42
	*James B. McHale, Jr., Overbrook G.C., Pa.	72	76	74	76	298	----
35	George Fazio, Conshohocken, Pa.	73	77	70	79	299	
	Leland Gibson, Blue Hills C., Mo.	75	72	73	79	299	
37	Mike Pavella, Washington C.C., Pa.	75	75	76	74	300	
	Jimmy Thomson, New York, N.Y.	75	72	76	77	300	
	Victor Ghezzi, Deal G.C., N.J.	78	72	75	75	300	
	Sam Byrd, Detroit, Mich.	75	73	74	78	300	
41	*James Frisina, Sr., Illini C.C., Ill.	76	74	72	79	301	
42	E. E. Peelle, Victory Hills G.C., Kans.	71	79	75	77	302	
	Raymond Gafford, Ridglea G.C., Texas	76	73	78	75	302	
	Robert Cruickshank, Chartiers C.C., Pa.	71	75	79	77	302	
45	*John E. Wagner, Skokie C.C., Ill.	72	77	79	76	304	
46	Ray Hill, Unattached, Shreveport, La.	75	74	78	78	305	
47	Otto Greiner, Woodholme C.C., Md.	74	74	76	82	306	

*Amateurs. Gold medals awarded to Robert H. (Skee) Riegel and James B. McHale, Jr.
Prize money totaling $10,000 awarded to professionals returning scores up to 298, inclusive.

1950
FIFTIETH OPEN CHAMPIONSHIP

Held at the Merion Golf Club (East Course), Ardmore, Pa., June 8-11.
Yardage—6,694. Par 70.
1,379 Entries, 165 Qualifiers, 165 Starters.

Fifty-one contestants who completed 72 holes.

						Score	Money Prize
1	†Ben Hogan, Hershey C.C., Pa.	72	69	72	74	287	$4,000.00
2	†Lloyd Mangrum, Tam O'Shanter C.C., Ill.	72	70	69	76	287	2,500.00
3	†George Fazio, Woodmont C.C., Md.	73	72	72	70	287	1,000.00
4	E.J. (Dutch) Harrison, St. Andrews C.C., Ill.	72	67	73	76	288	800.00
5	Joe Kirkwood, Jr., Kirkwood G.R., Calif.	71	74	74	70	289	500.00
	Jim Ferrier, Chicago, Ill.	71	69	74	75	289	500.00
	Henry Ransom, St. Andrews C.C., Ill.	72	71	73	73	289	500.00
8	S. William Nary, Los Serranos G. & C.C., Calif.	73	70	74	73	290	350.00
9	Julius Boros, Mid Pines G.C., N.C.	68	72	77	74	291	300.00
10	Cary Middlecoff, Memphis C.C., Tenn.	71	71	71	79	292	225.00
	Johnny Palmer, Unattached, Badin, N.C.	73	70	70	79	292	225.00
12	Robert H. (Skee) Riegel, Tulsa, Okla.	73	69	79	73	294	133.34
	Sam Snead, Greenbrier C.C., W. Va.	73	75	72	74	294	133.34
	Henry G. Picard, Canterbury G.C., Ohio	71	71	79	73	294	133.33
	Dick Mayer, Old Greenwich, Conn.	73	76	73	72	294	133.33
	Johnny G. Bulla, Westmoreland C.C., Pa.	74	66	78	76	294	133.33
	Albert C. Besselink, Red Run G.C., Mich.	71	72	76	75	294	133.33
18	Skip Alexander, Deanne Hill C.C., Tenn.	68	74	77	76	295	100.00
	Fred Haas, Jr., New Orleans C.C., La.	73	74	76	72	295	100.00
20	Marty Furgol, Albuquerque C.C., N. M.	75	71	72	78	296	100.00
	Harold Williams, Meadowbrook G.C., Ala.	69	75	75	77	296	100.00
	Dick Metz, Arkansas City, Kans.	76	71	71	78	296	100.00
	Jimmy Demaret, Ojai Valley C.C., Calif.	72	77	71	76	296	100.00
	Bob Toski, Northampton C.C., Mass.	73	69	80	74	296	100.00
25	Bobby Cruickshank, Chartiers C.C., Pa.	72	77	76	72	297	100.00
	Ted Kroll, Philmont C.C., Pa.	75	72	78	72	297	100.00
	Lee Mackey, Jr., Birmingham, Ala.	64	81	75	77	297	100.00
	Paul Runyan, Annandale G.C., Calif.	76	73	73	75	297	100.00
29	Pete Cooper, Ponte Vedra G.C., Fla.	75	72	76	75	298	100.00
	Henry Williams, Jr., Tully-Secane C.C., Pa.	69	76	76	77	298	100.00
31	Denny Shute, Portage C.C., Ohio	71	73	76	79	299	100.00
	Buck White, Ormond Beach Hotel & C.C., Fla.	77	71	77	74	299	100.00
	John Barnum, Blythefield C.C., Mich.	71	75	78	75	299	100.00
34	Terl Johnson, duPont C.C., Del.	72	77	74	77	300	100.00
	Herschel G. Spears, Huntsville C.C., Ala.	75	72	75	78	300	100.00
36	Dave Douglas, Newark, Del.	72	76	79	74	301	100.00
	Walter Burkemo, Franklin Hills C.C., Mich.	72	77	74	78	301	100.00
38	Claude Harmon, Winged Foot G.C., N.Y.	71	74	77	80	302	100.00
	Jim Turnesa, Briar Hall C.C., N.Y.	74	71	78	79	302	100.00
	Gene Sarazen, Germantown, N.Y.	72	72	82	76	302	100.00
	*James B. McHale, Jr., Saucon Valley G.C., Pa.	75	73	80	74	302	----
42	Art Bell, California G.C., Calif.	72	77	78	76	303	100.00
43	B. Patrick Abbott, Memphis C.C., Tenn.	71	77	76	80	304	100.00
	Joe Thacker, Brookside C.C., Ohio	75	69	83	77	304	100.00
45	Johnny Morris, Belle Meade C.C., Tenn.	74	74	80	77	305	100.00
46	Gene Webb, St. Louis, Mo.	75	74	82	75	306	100.00
	Loddie P. Kempa, Kansas City, Mo.	71	74	78	83	306	100.00
	*Frank Stranahan, Inverness C., Ohio	79	70	79	78	306	----
49	*P. J. Boatwright, Jr., Aiken G.C., S.C.	75	74	79	79	307	----
50	George Bolesta, Danville C.C., Ill.	77	72	84	78	311	100.00
51	John J. O'Donnell, Commissioned Officers' G.C., Va.	76	72	83	85	316	100.00

†Playoff: 18 holes, June 11—Hogan, 69; Mangrum, 73; Fazio, 75.
*Amateurs. Gold medal awarded to James B. McHale, Jr.
Prize money totaling $14,900 awarded to professionals who completed 72 holes.

1951
FIFTY-FIRST OPEN CHAMPIONSHIP

Held at the Oakland Hills Country Club, Birmingham, Mich., June 14-16.
Yardage—6,927. Par 70.
1,511 Entries, 162 Qualifiers, 162 Starters.

Fifty-five contestants who completed 72 holes.

						Score	Money Prize
1	Ben Hogan, Hershey C.C., Hershey, Pa.	76	73	71	67	287	$4,000.00
2	Clayton Heafner, Eastwood G.C., Charlotte, N.C.	72	75	73	69	289	2,000.00
3	A. D. (Bobby) Locke, Ohenimuri C.C., Johannesburg, S.A.	73	71	74	73	291	1,500.00
4	Lloyd Mangrum, Tam O'Shanter C.C., Niles, Ill.	75	74	74	70	293	700.00
	Julius Boros, Mid Pines G.C., Southern Pines, N.C.	74	74	71	74	293	700.00
6	Albert C. Besselink, Hillcrest C.C., Mount Clemens, Mich.	72	77	72	73	294	387.50
	Paul Runyan, Annandale G.C., Pasadena, Calif.	73	74	72	75	294	387.50
	Fred E. Hawkins, El Paso C.C., El Paso, Texas	76	72	75	71	294	387.50
	Dave Douglas, Newark, Del.	75	70	75	74	294	387.50
10	Skee Riegel, Tulsa, Okla.	75	76	71	73	295	187.50
	Al Brosch, Cherry Valley C., Garden City, N.Y.	73	74	76	72	295	187.50
	Smiley Quick, Los Angeles, Calif.	73	76	74	72	295	187.50
	Sam Snead, Greenbrier G.&T.C., White Sulphur Spgs., W. Va.	71	78	72	74	295	187.50
14	Jimmy Demaret, Ojai Valley C.C., Ojai, Calif.	74	74	70	78	296	150.00
	Lew Worsham, Oakmont C.C., Oakmont, Pa.	76	71	76	73	296	150.00
16	*Charles Kocsis, Red Run G.C., Royal Oak, Mich.	75	74	76	72	297	----
	Buck White, Greenwood, Miss.	76	75	74	72	297	100.00
	Henry Ransom, St. Andrews G.C., St. Andrews, Ill.	74	74	76	73	297	100.00
19	Raymond Gafford, Northwood C., Dallas, Texas	76	74	74	74	298	100.00
	Johnny Revolta, Evanston G.C., Skokie, Ill.	78	72	72	76	298	100.00
21	Joe Kirkwood, Jr., Riviera C.C., Hollywood, Calif.	74	78	73	74	299	100.00
	Charles T. Bassler, Rolling Road C.C., Catonsville, Md.	79	71	74	75	299	100.00
23	Marty Furgol, Cog Hill G.C., Lemont, Ill.	78	72	74	76	300	100.00
24	Edward S. Oliver, Jr., Inglewood C.C., Kenmore, Wash.	81	71	77	72	301	100.00
	Johnny Palmer, Badin, N.C.	73	78	76	74	301	100.00
	Cary Middlecoff, Memphis C.C., Memphis, Tenn.	76	73	79	73	301	100.00
	Earl Stewart, Jr., Dallas Athletic Club C.C., Dallas, Texas	74	74	78	75	301	100.00
	Henry G. Picard, Canterbury G.C., Cleveland, Ohio	78	73	78	72	301	100.00
29	*Francis G. Wininger, Atlantic City C.C., Northfield, N.J.	75	71	77	79	302	----
	Fred Haas, Jr., Freddie Haas G.S. & D.R., New Orleans, La.	77	75	77	73	302	100.00
	Geo. Kinsman, Jr., N. Richmond G.C., New Richmond, Wis.	75	73	75	79	302	100.00
	Roberto De Vicenzo, G.C. of Arg., Buenos Aires, Argentina	75	76	74	77	302	100.00
	Tommy Bolt, Par-Way D.R., Durham, N.C.	77	72	75	78	302	100.00
	*Sam Urzetta, Irondequoit C.C., Rochester, N.Y.	78	71	78	75	302	----
35	Al Watrous, Oakland Hills C.C., Birmingham, Mich.	77	75	77	74	303	100.00
	Clarence Doser, Scarsdale G.C., Hartsdale, N.Y.	74	76	77	76	303	100.00
	Gene Sarazen, Germantown, N.Y.	74	76	76	77	303	100.00
	Charles B. Klein, Willow Springs G.C., San Antonio, Texas	73	74	81	75	303	100.00
39	*E. Harvie Ward, Jr., Highlands C.C., Fayetteville, N.C.	74	76	78	76	304	----
	Sam Bernardi, Old Elm C., Fort Sheridan, Ill.	73	76	77	78	304	100.00
41	Doug Ford, Willows C.C., Harrison, N.Y.	76	76	78	75	305	100.00
42	*Dale Morey, Martinsville C.C., Martinsville, Ind.	76	75	75	80	306	----
	*Frank Stranahan, Inverness C., Toledo, Ohio	74	77	78	77	306	----
	Bob Hamilton, Evansville, Ind.	74	77	79	76	306	100.00
	Gene Kunes, Cleveland, Ohio	77	75	77	77	306	100.00
	Jack Harden, El Paso C.C., El Paso, Texas	75	75	80	76	306	100.00
47	Craig Wood, Winged Foot G.C., Mamaroneck, N.Y.	76	72	82	77	307	100.00
	E.J. (Dutch) Harrison, Little Rock, Ark.	73	78	78	78	307	100.00
49	S. William Nary, Twin Orchard C.C., Prairie View, Ill.	77	75	77	79	308	100.00
	Gene Webb, Lakeside G.C., St. Louis, Mo.	76	74	76	82	308	100.00
	Sam Byrd, Detroit, Mich.	73	79	76	80	308	100.00
52	Johnny Bulla, Westmoreland C.C., Verona, Pa.	80	70	82	77	309	100.00
53	*James E. Funston, Plum Hollow G.C., Detroit, Mich.	76	75	84	75	310	----
54	Claude Harmon, Winged Foot G.C., Mamaroneck, N.Y.	74	75	79	83	311	100.00
	John Barnum, Blythefield C.C., Belmont, Mich.	79	73	79	80	311	100.00

*Gold medals awarded to all amateurs who completed 72 holes.
Prize money totaling $14,800 awarded to all professionals who completed 72 holes.

1952
FIFTY-SECOND OPEN CHAMPIONSHIP

Held at the Northwood Club, Dallas, Texas, June 12-14.
Yardage—6,782. Par 70.
1,688 Entries, 162 Qualifiers, 162 Starters.

Fifty-two contestants who completed 72 holes.

						Score	Money Prize
1	Julius Boros, Mid Pines C., Southern Pines, N.C.	71	71	68	71	281	$4,000.00
2	Edward S. Oliver, Jr., Cog Hill G.C., Lemont, Ill.	71	72	70	72	285	2,500.00
3	Ben Hogan, Tamarisk C.C., Palm Springs, Calif.	69	69	74	74	286	1,000.00
4	Johnny Bulla, Westmoreland C.C., Verona, Pa.	73	68	73	73	287	800.00
5	George Fazio, Pine Valley G.C., Clementon, N.J.	71	69	75	75	290	600.00
6	Dick Metz, Maple City, Kans.	70	74	76	71	291	500.00
7	Tommy Bolt, Par-Way D.R., Durham, N.C.	72	76	71	73	292	350.00
	Ted Kroll, New Hartford, N.Y.	71	75	76	70	292	350.00
	Lew Worsham, Oakmont C.C., Oakmont, Pa.	72	71	74	75	292	350.00
10	Lloyd Mangrum, Tam O'Shanter C.C., Niles, Ill.	75	74	72	72	293	200.00
	Sam Snead, Greenbrier G. & T.C., White Sulphur Spgs., W. Va.	70	75	76	72	293	200.00
	Earl Stewart, Jr., Dallas Athletic Club C.C., Dallas, Texas	76	75	70	72	293	200.00
13	Clarence Doser, Scarsdale G.C., Hartsdale, N.Y.	71	73	73	77	294	150.00
	Harry Todd, Lakewood C.C., Dallas, Texas	71	76	74	73	294	150.00
15	Al Brosch, Cherry Valley C., Garden City, N.Y.	68	79	77	71	295	112.50
	Jimmy Demaret, Concord Int'l. G.C., Kiamesha, N.Y.	74	77	73	71	295	112.50
	Milon Marusic, Herkimer, N.Y.	73	76	74	72	295	112.50
	Horton Smith, Detroit G.C., Detroit, Mich.	70	73	76	76	295	112.50
19	Doug Ford, Willows C.C., Harrison, N.Y.	74	74	74	74	296	100.00
	Bill Trombley, Brook Hollow G.C., Dallas, Texas	72	73	81	70	296	100.00
	*James G. Jackson, Greenbriar Hills C.C., Kirkwood, Mo.	74	76	75	71	296	----
22	Paul Runyan, Annandale G.C., Pasadena, Calif.	73	78	73	73	297	100.00
	Leland Gibson, Blue Hills C., Kansas City, Mo.	73	76	72	76	297	100.00
24	Francis (Bo) Wininger, Northfield, N.J.	78	72	69	79	298	100.00
	M. R. (Chick) Harbert, Meadowbrook C.C., Northville, Mich.	75	75	73	75	298	100.00
	Felice Torza, St. Charles C.C., St. Charles, Ill.	74	76	70	78	298	100.00
	Cary Middlecoff, Memphis C.C., Memphis, Tenn.	75	74	75	74	298	100.00
28	Zell Eaton, Montebello G.C., Montebello, Calif.	71	79	73	76	299	100.00
	Raymond Gafford, Northwood C., Dallas, Texas	77	74	75	73	299	100.00
	Dick Mayer, St. Petersburg, Fla.	74	77	69	79	299	100.00
	B. Patrick Abbott, Memphis C.C., Memphis, Tenn.	74	76	73	76	299	100.00
	*Stanton Mosel, North Texas State C.C., Denton, Texas	71	77	75	76	299	----
33	Gene Sarazen, Germantown, N.Y.	76	74	75	75	300	100.00
	E.J. (Dutch) Harrison, Dornick Hills C.C., Ardmore, Okla.	71	79	77	73	300	100.00
35	Charles Scally, Pittsburgh, Pa.	72	73	77	79	301	100.00
36	Henry Williams, Jr., Berkleigh C.C., Kutztown, Pa.	77	74	74	79	304	100.00
	Marty Furgol, St. Louis, Mo.	75	74	75	80	304	100.00
	Iverson Martin, Fort Worth, Texas	76	74	77	77	304	100.00
	*William J. Patton, Mimosa G.C., Morganton, N.C.	76	73	80	75	304	----
40	Johnny Revolta, Evanston G.C., Skokie, Ill.	74	75	78	78	305	100.00
41	Johnny Weitzel, Hershey C.C., Hershey, Pa.	74	74	76	82	306	100.00
	Jack Burke, Jr., Houston, Texas	74	74	78	80	306	100.00
	Chandler Harper, Elizabeth Manor C.C., Portsmouth, Va.	73	76	80	77	306	100.00
44	Herschel G. Spears, Huntsville C.C., Huntsville, Ala.	75	76	80	76	307	100.00
	Charles Farlow, Starmount Forest C.C., Greensboro, N.C.	71	80	80	76	307	100.00
	Gardner E. Dickinson, Jr., Dellwood C.C., New City, N.Y.	72	76	80	79	307	100.00
47	Art Wall, Jr., Pocono Manor G.C., Pocono Manor, Pa.	76	73	77	82	308	100.00
48	Fred Hawkins, El Paso C.C., El Paso, Texas	75	76	74	84	309	100.00
	Steve Doctor, Siwanoy C.C., Bronxville, N.Y.	75	74	78	82	309	100.00
	Max Evans, Kelly Green D.R., East Detroit, Mich.	75	73	78	83	309	100.00
51	Herman A. Coelho, Forest Hills C.C., Rockford, Ill.	76	73	77	89	315	100.00
	Charles T. Bassler, Rolling Road G.C., Catonsville, Md.	71	79	86	84	320	100.00

*Gold medals awarded to all amateurs.
Prize money totaling $14,900 awarded to professionals who completed 72 holes.

1953
FIFTY-THIRD OPEN CHAMPIONSHIP

Held at the Oakmont Country Club, Oakmont, Pa., June 11-13.
Yardage–6,916. Par 72.
1,669 Entries, 157 Qualifiers, 157 Starters.

Fifty-nine contestants who completed 72 holes.

						Score	Money Prize
1	Ben Hogan, Tamarisk C.C., Palm Springs, Calif.	67	72	73	71	283	$5,000.00
2	Sam Snead, Greenbrier G. & T.C., White Sulphur Springs, W. Va.	72	69	72	76	289	3,000.00
3	Lloyd Mangrum, Tam O'Shanter C.C., Niles, Ill.	73	70	74	75	292	1,500.00
4	Pete Cooper, Century C.C., White Plains, N.Y.	78	75	71	70	294	816.67
	George Fazio, Pine Valley G.C., Clementon, N.J.	70	71	77	76	294	816.67
	Jimmy Demaret, Concord G.C., Kiamesha Lake, N.Y.	71	76	71	76	294	816.66
	Ted Kroll, New Hartford, N.Y.	76	71	74	74	295	450.00
	Dick Metz, Maple City, Kans.	75	70	74	76	295	450.00
9	Jay Hebert, Kahkwa Club, Erie, Pa.	72	72	74	78	296	325.00
	Marty Furgol, Cog Hill G.C., Lemont, Ill.	73	74	76	73	296	325.00
	*Frank S. Souchak, Oakmont C.C., Oakmont, Pa.	70	76	76	74	296	----
12	Bill Ogden, North Shore C.C., Glenview, Ill.	71	78	75	73	297	200.00
	Fred Haas, New Orleans, La.	74	73	72	78	297	200.00
14	A. D. (Bobby) Locke, Ohenimuri C.C., Johannesburg, S.A.	78	70	74	76	298	200.00
	Jack Burke, Jr., Kiamesha Lake, N.Y.	76	73	72	77	298	200.00
	E.J. (Dutch) Harrison, Dornick Hills C.C., Ardmore, Okla.	77	75	70	76	298	200.00
17	S. William Nary, Hillcrest C.C., Kansas City, Mo.	76	74	73	76	299	200.00
	Jim Turnesa, Briar Hall G.C., Briarcliff, N.Y.	75	78	72	74	299	200.00
	Clarence Doser, Scarsdale G.C., Hartsdale, N.Y.	74	76	78	71	299	200.00
	Julius Boros, Mid Pines C., Southern Pines, N.C.	75	72	76	76	299	200.00
21	Al Mengert, Winged Foot G.C., Mamaroneck, N.Y.	75	71	78	76	300	162.50
	Robert R. Rosburg, Edgewater G.C., Chicago, Ill.	76	72	78	74	300	162.50
	Gardner Dickinson, Jr., Panama C.C., Panama City, Fla.	77	73	76	74	300	162.50
	Doug Ford, Harrison C.C., Harrison, N.Y.	74	77	74	75	300	162.50
	*Frank Stranahan, Inverness C., Toldeo, Ohio	75	75	75	75	300	----
26	Clayton V. Heafner, Eastwood G.C., Charlotte, N.C.	75	75	76	75	301	150.00
	Art Wall, Jr., Pocono Manor C.C., Pocono Manor, Pa.	80	72	77	72	301	150.00
	Peter W. Thomson, Victoria G.C., Melbourne, Australia	80	73	73	75	301	150.00
	*James B. McHale, Jr., Winged Foot G.C., Mamaroneck, N.Y.	79	74	75	73	301	----
30	Jerry Barber, La Canada, Calif.	72	75	76	79	302	150.00
	Toby Lyons, Moon Brook C.C., Jamestown, N.Y.	73	78	74	77	302	150.00
	Louis Barbaro, Hollywood G.C., Deal, N.J.	72	79	74	77	302	150.00
33	Raymond Gafford, Northwood C., Dallas, Texas	80	72	74	77	303	150.00
	Lionel P. Hebert, Westmoreland C.C., Verona, Pa.	80	71	80	72	303	150.00
	Shelley Mayfield, Rockaway Hunting C., Cedarhurst, N.Y.	76	75	75	77	303	150.00
	Johnny Bulla, Westmoreland C.C., Verona, Pa.	74	77	79	73	303	150.00
37	Felice Torza, St. Charles C.C., St. Charles, Ill.	75	74	77	78	304	150.00
	Harry Todd, Lakewood C.C., Dallas, Texas	75	76	79	74	304	150.00
	Fred Wampler, Indianapolis, Ind.	75	76	75	78	304	150.00
40	Walter Burkemo, Franklin Hills C.C., Franklin, Mich.	70	79	79	77	305	150.00
	Jackson D. Bradley, Edgewater G.C., Chicago, Ill.	78	73	76	78	305	150.00
42	M. R. (Chick) Harbert, Meadowbrook C.C., Northville, Mich.	76	76	75	79	306	150.00
	Michael Homa, Westchester C.C., Rye, N.Y.	77	76	76	77	306	150.00
	*H. H. Haverstick, Jr., Lancaster C.C., Lancaster, Pa.	73	77	79	77	306	----
45	Dennis Lavender, Charlotte C.C., Charlotte, N.C.	76	77	78	76	307	150.00
	Lawson Little, Monterey Peninsula C.C., Del Monte, Calif.	78	75	79	75	307	150.00
	Arthur L. Doering, Jr., Cincinnati C.C., Cincinnati, Ohio	73	78	77	79	307	150.00
48	Jimmy Clark, Laguna Beach C.C., Laguna Beach, Calif.	77	73	73	85	308	150.00
	Buck White, Memphis, Tenn.	77	75	78	78	308	150.00
	*Sam Urzetta, Irondequoit C.C., Rochester, N.Y.	77	74	82	75	308	----
	*Robert A. Roos, Jr., Olympic C.C., San Francisco, Calif.	75	78	78	77	308	----
52	Jack Fleck, Credit Island G.C., Davenport, Iowa	76	76	77	80	309	150.00
	John M. Garrison, Alice C.C., Alice, Texas	73	77	79	80	309	----
54	Dick Mayer, St. Petersburg, Fla.	77	76	76	82	311	150.00
	*William J. Patton, Mimosa G.C., Morganton, N.C.	80	73	77	81	311	----
56	Charles T. Bassler, Rolling Road G.C., Catonsville, Md.	78	73	83	78	312	150.00
	Errie Ball, Oak Park C.C., Oak Park, Ill.	76	74	84	79	313	150.00
58	Willie Goggin, Upper Montclair C.C., Clifton, N.J.	77	74	88	77	316	150.00
	Edward S. Oliver, Jr., El Miradora C., Palm Springs, Calif.	79	74	87	76	316	150.00

*Gold medals awarded to all amateurs who completed 72 holes.
Prize money totaling $20,400 awarded to professionals. This includes $250 awarded to Jimmy Clark as low qualifier in Championship Qualifying Rounds, with scores of 72 at the Pittsburgh Field Club and 66 at the Oakmont Country Club for total of 138.

1954
FIFTY-FOURTH OPEN CHAMPIONSHIP

Held at the Baltursol Golf Club (Lower Course), Springfield, N.J., June 17-19.
Yardage—7,027. Par 70.
1,928 Entries, 162 Qualifiers, 162 Starters.

Fifty contestants who completed 72 holes.

						Score	Money Prize
1	Ed Furgol, Westwood C.C., Clayton, Mo.	71	70	71	72	284	$6,000.00
2	Gene Littler, Thunderbird C.C., Palm Springs, Calif.	70	69	76	70	285	3,600.00
3	Dick Mayer, St. Petersburg, Fla.	72	71	70	73	286	1,500.00
	Lloyd Mangrum, Tam O'Shanter C.C., Niles, Ill.	72	71	72	71	286	1,500.00
5	A. D. (Bobby) Locke, Ohenimuri C.C., Johannesburg, S. Africa	74	70	74	70	288	960.00
6	Tommy Bolt, Memorial Park G.C., Houston, Texas	72	72	73	72	289	570.00
	Ben Hogan, Fort Worth, Texas	71	70	76	72	289	570.00
	Shelley Mayfield, Seguin, Texas	73	75	72	69	289	570.00
	Fred Haas, New Orleans, La.	73	73	71	72	289	570.00
	*William J. Patton, Mimosa G.C., Morganton, N.C.	69	76	71	73	289	----
11	Sam Snead, Greenbrier G.C., White Sulphur Springs, W. Va.	72	73	72	73	290	300.00
	Cary Middlecoff, Memphis C.C., Memphis, Tenn.	72	71	72	75	290	300.00
13	Al Mengert, Winged Foot G.C., Mamaroneck, N.Y.	71	72	73	75	291	240.00
	Rudy Horvath, Essex G.C., Windsor, Ontario, Canada	75	72	71	73	291	240.00
15	Jack Burke, Jr., Concord Int'l. G.C., Kiamesha Lake, N.Y.	73	73	72	75	293	240.00
	Claude Harmon, Winged Foot G.C., Mamaroneck, N.Y.	75	72	72	74	293	240.00
17	Jay Hebert, Woodmere C., Woodmere, N.Y.	77	70	70	77	294	240.00
18	Leland Gibson, Blue Hills C., Kansas City, Mo.	72	77	69	77	295	240.00
	Robert J. Toski, Cedar Hills C.C., Livingston, N.J.	70	74	78	73	295	240.00
	Marty Furgol, Cog Hill G.C., Lemont, Ill.	73	74	73	75	295	240.00
21	Johnny Weitzel, Hershey C.C., Hershey, Pa.	74	76	69	77	296	240.00
	*Richard D. Chapman, Pinehurst C.C., Pinehurst, N.C.	77	67	77	75	296	----
23	Lew Worsham, Oakmont C.C., Oakmont, Pa.	72	77	77	71	297	180.00
	Max Evans, Detroit, Mich.	76	74	73	74	297	180.00
	Julius Boros, Mid Pines C., Southern Pines, N.C.	78	71	78	70	297	180.00
	*William C. Campbell, Guyan G. & C.C., Huntington, W. Va.	75	73	73	76	297	----
27	Ted Kroll, New Hartford, N.Y.	70	79	73	76	298	180.00
	George Fazio, Pine Valley G.C., Clementon, N.J.	74	77	74	73	298	180.00
29	Jimmy Demaret, Concord Int'l. G.C., Kiamesha Lake, N.Y.	79	71	76	73	299	180.00
	Johnny Revolta, Evanston G.C., Skokie, Ill.	72	75	73	79	299	180.00
	Dick Metz, Newnan, Ga.	75	75	72	77	299	180.00
	Robert R. Rosburg, Edgewater G.C., Chicago, Ill.	74	77	74	74	299	180.00
33	Jim Turnesa, Briar Hall G.C., Briarcliff Manor, N.Y.	74	76	72	78	300	180.00
	Robert L. Watson, Ardsley C.C., Ardsley-on-Hudson, N.Y.	72	76	77	75	300	180.00
35	Lawson Little, Monterey Peninsula C.C., Pebble Beach, Calif.	78	73	73	77	301	180.00
	Doug Ford, Concord Int'l. G.C., Kiamesha Lake, N.Y.	75	75	75	76	301	180.00
37	Paul McGuire, MacDonald Park G.C., Wichita, Kans.	78	69	78	77	302	180.00
	George Bayer, Glen Head C.C., Glen Head, N.Y.	77	74	77	74	302	180.00
39	Lionel P. Hebert, Kahkwa C., Erie, Pa.	75	75	77	76	303	180.00
40	Raymond Gafford, Northwood C., Dallas, Texas	76	74	76	78	304	180.00
	Francis G. (Bo) Wininger, Okla. City G. & C.C., Okla. City, Okla.	74	77	76	77	304	180.00
42	Robert H. (Skee) Riegel, Radnor Valley C.C., Ithan, Pa.	75	76	77	77	305	180.00
	Toby Lyons, Moon Brook C.C., Jamestown, N.Y.	77	74	75	79	305	180.00
	Clarence J. Doser, Woodmont C.C., Rockville, Md.	76	73	78	78	305	180.00
45	Pat Abbott, Memphis C.C., Memphis, Tenn.	75	75	77	79	306	180.00
46	Bob Duden, Portland, Ore.	74	77	74	82	307	180.00
	*Gene Dahlbender, Jr., Meadowbrooks C.C., Atlanta, Ga.	77	73	77	80	307	----
48	Loddie P. Kempa, Kansas City, Mo.	75	75	85	75	310	180.00
49	Dan Herring, Lee Park G.C., Petersburg, Va.	76	75	79	84	314	180.00
50	John Bass, Clifton Park G.C., Baltimore, Md.	78	73	80	84	315	180.00

*Gold medals awarded to all amateurs.
Prize money totaling $23,280 awarded to professionals.

1955
FIFTY-FIFTH OPEN CHAMPIONSHIP

Held at the Olympic Country Club (Lake Course), San Francisco, Calif. June 16-19.
Yardage—6,700. Par 70.
1,522 Entries, 162 Qualifiers, 162 Starters.
Fifty-eight contestants who completed 72 holes.

						Score	Money Prize
1	†Jack Fleck, Davenport Municipal G.C., Davenport, Iowa	76	69	75	67	287	$6,000.00
2	†Ben Hogan, Fort Worth, Texas	72	73	72	70	287	4,000.00
3	Sam Snead, Greenbrier G. & C.C., White Sulphur Springs, W. Va.	79	69	70	74	292	1,500.00
	Tommy Bolt, Chattanooga, Tenn.	67	77	75	73	292	1,500.00
5	Julius Boros, Mid Pines C., Southern Pines, N.C.	76	69	73	77	295	870.00
	Robert R. Rosburg, Palo Alto, Calif.	78	74	67	76	295	870.00
7	Bud Holscher, Apple Valley C.C., Apple Valley, Calif.	77	75	71	73	296	540.00
	Doug Ford, Concord Int'l. G.C., Kiamesha Lake, N.Y.	74	77	74	71	296	540.00
	*E. Harvie Ward, Jr., San Francisco G.C., San Francisco, Calif.	74	70	76	76	296	----
10	Mike Souchak, Grossinger C.C., Grossinger, N.Y.	73	79	72	73	297	390.00
	Jack Burke, Jr., Concord Int'l. G.C., Kiamesha Lake, N.Y.	71	77	72	77	297	390.00
12	Frank Stranahan, Inverness C.C., Toledo, Ohio	80	71	76	71	298	226.16
	Shelley Mayfield, Meadow Brook C., Westbury, N.Y.	75	76	75	72	298	226.16
14	Walker P. Inman, Jr., Augusta C.C., Augusta, Ga.	70	75	76	78	299	226.16
15	Gene Littler, Thunderbird C.C., Palm Springs, Calif.	76	73	73	78	300	226.16
16	Al Mengert, Winged Foot G.C., Mamaroneck, N.Y.	76	76	72	77	301	226.16
	Art Wall, Jr., Pocono Manor C.C., Pocono Manor, Pa.	77	78	72	74	301	226.15
	Smiley Quick, Rio Hondo C.C., Downey, Calif.	76	74	74	77	301	226.15
19	Fred Hawkins, El Paso, Texas	73	78	75	76	302	226.15
	George Schneiter, The Country Club, Salt Lake City, Utah	78	74	77	73	302	226.15
21	Ernie Vossler, Colonial C.C., Fort Worth, Texas	77	76	76	74	303	226.15
	Arnold Palmer, Latrobe C.C., Latrobe, Pa.	77	76	74	76	303	226.15
	Cary Middlecoff, Concord Int'l. G.C., Kiamesha Lake, N.Y.	76	78	74	75	303	226.15
	Bob Harris, Edgewater C.C., Chicago, Ill.	77	71	78	77	303	226.15
25	Leland Gibson, Blue Hills C.C., Kansas City, Mo.	76	78	76	74	304	180.00
	Marty Furgol, Cog Hill G.C., Lemont, Ill.	76	77	78	73	304	180.00
27	Billy Maxwell, Odessa C.C., Odessa, Texas	77	74	75	79	305	180.00
28	Charles Rotar, Double "R" Ranch G.C., San Bernardino, Calif.	76	75	80	75	306	180.00
	Byron Nelson, Roanoke, Texas	77	74	80	75	306	180.00
	Dow H. Finsterwald, Camargo C.C., Madeira, Ohio	84	71	74	77	306	180.00
	Eric Monti, Hillcrest C.C., Los Angeles, Calif.	76	76	78	76	306	180.00
	Arthur Bell, California G.C., San Francisco, Calif.	74	76	81	75	306	180.00
	Max Evans, Sunnybrook G.C., Utica, Mich.	77	73	76	80	306	180.00
34	Errie Ball, Oak Park C.C., Oak Park, Ill.	81	74	78	74	307	180.00
	Fred Haas, New Orleans, La.	75	76	79	77	307	180.00
	Pete Cooper, Knollwood C.C., Birmingham, Mich.	75	77	81	74	307	180.00
	Johnny Palmer, Charlotte, N.C.	80	74	75	78	307	180.00
	M. R. (Chick) Harbert, Meadowbrook C.C., Northville, Mich.	77	75	80	75	307	180.00
39	Marvin (Bud) Ward, Peninsula G. & C.C., San Mateo, Calif.	76	76	80	77	309	180.00
40	Babe Lichardus, Shackamaxon C.C., Westfield, N.J.	73	80	81	76	310	180.00
	Robert (Skee) Riegel, Radnor Valley C.C., Ithan, Pa.	75	79	78	78	310	180.00
	Zell Eaton, Los Serranos C.C., Pomona, Calif.	81	74	78	77	310	180.00
43	Ted A. Neist, St. Louis C.C., Clayton, Mo.	79	75	76	81	311	180.00
	Frank W. Harned, Rock Spring C., W. Orange, N.J.	78	77	80	76	311	180.00
45	Ed Furgol, Westwood C.C., Creve Coeur, Mo.	76	79	80	77	312	180.00
	Charles Scally, Scally's D.R., Coraopolis, Pa.	77	76	79	80	312	180.00
47	Elmer W. Reed, Atlanta, Ga.	74	79	81	79	313	180.00
	Francis G. (Bo) Wininger, Oklahoma City, G. & C., Oklahoma City, Okla.	75	79	75	84	313	180.00
	Dave Douglas, Newark, Del.	79	75	76	83	313	180.00
	Ralph Blomquist, Oakmont C.C., Glendale, Calif.	79	76	79	79	313	180.00
	Ralph Evans, Clock C.C., Whittier, Calif.	76	78	78	81	313	180.00
52	Al Zimmerman, Paradise Valley C.C., Scottsdale, Ariz.	78	74	85	77	314	180.00
53	Jimmy Ukauka, Kaneohe Marine G.C., Lanikai, T.H.	76	76	82	81	315	180.00
	Jerry Kesselring, Downsview G. & C.C., Toronto, Ont., Can.	79	76	79	81	315	180.00
	George Puetz, Earlington G.C., Renton, Wash.	78	77	79	81	315	180.00
56	George Keyes, Old Elm C., Fort Sheridan, Ill.	80	75	79	82	316	180.00
57	*PFC William Thornton, Jupiter, Fla.	79	75	82	81	317	----
58	Fred Annon, Ryewood C.C., Rye, N.Y.	75	78	85	82	320	180.00

†Playoff: 18 holes, June 19—Fleck, 69; Hogan, 72.
*Gold medals awarded to all amateurs.
Prize money totaling $25,480 awarded to professionals.

1956
FIFTY-SIXTH OPEN CHAMPIONSHIP

Held at the Oak Hill Country Club (East Course), Rochester, N.Y., June 14-16.
Yardage—6,902. Par 70.
1,921 Entries, 162 Qualifiers, 162 Starters.
Fifty-one contestants who completed 72 holes.

						Score	Money Prize
1	Cary Middlecoff, Riverlake C.C., Dallas, Texas	71	70	70	70	281	$6,000.00
2	Julius Boros, Mid Pines C., Southern Pines, N.C.	71	71	71	69	282	2,650.00
	Ben Hogan, Fort Worth, Texas	72	68	72	70	282	2,650.00
4	Ed Furgol, Westwood C.C., Creve Coeur, Mo.	71	70	73	71	285	1,033.34
	Peter Thomson, Victoria G.C., Melbourne, Australia	70	69	75	71	285	1,033.33
	Ted Kroll, Fort Lauderdale, Fla.	72	70	70	73	285	1,033.33
7	Arnold Palmer, Latrobe C.C., Latrobe, Pa.	72	70	72	73	287	600.00
8	*Kenneth Venturi, California G.C., San Francisco, Calif.	77	71	68	73	289	----
9	Doug Ford, Putnam C.C., Mahopac, N.Y.	71	75	70	74	290	416.67
	Wesley Ellis, Greenwood C.C., River Vale, N.J.	71	70	71	78	290	416.67
	Jerry Barber, Wilshire C.C., Los Angeles, Calif.	72	69	74	75	290	416.66
12	Billy Maxwell, Odessa C.C., Odessa, Texas	72	71	76	72	291	300.00
13	*William J. Patton, Mimosa G.C., Morganton, N.C.	75	73	70	74	292	----
14	Bill Casper, Jr., San Diego C.C., Chula Vista, Calif.	75	71	71	76	293	300.00
	Pete Cooper, Knollwood C.C., Birmingham, Mich.	73	74	76	70	293	300.00
	Fred Haas, New Orleans, La.	72	71	72	78	293	300.00
17	E. J. (Dutch) Harrison, Old Warson C.C., St. Louis, Mo.	72	76	72	74	294	260.00
	Bill Ogden, North Shore C.C., Glenview, Ill.	76	73	76	69	294	260.00
	Jay Hebert, Mayfair Inn C.C., Sanford, Fla.	71	76	73	74	294	260.00
	Robert J. Toski, Wycoff Park C.C., Holyoke, Mass.	76	71	74	73	294	260.00
	Henry Cotton, Temple G.C., Maidenhead, England	74	72	73	75	294	260.00
22	Tommy Bolt, Memorial Park, Houston, Texas	74	71	73	77	295	225.00
	Errie Ball, Oak Park C.C., Oak Park, Ill.	71	75	73	76	295	225.00
24	Robert L. Kay, Wampanoag C.C., W. Hartford, Conn.	75	74	76	71	296	200.00
	Sam Snead, Greenbrier G.C., White Sulphur Springs, W. Va.	75	71	77	73	296	200.00
	Johnny Bulla, Syracuse, N.Y.	77	72	73	74	296	200.00
27	Roberto De Vicenzo, Club Campestre de Mexico, Mexico City, Mex.	76	69	77	75	297	200.00
	Doug Higgins, Midland C.C., Midland, Texas	74	75	72	76	297	200.00
29	Mike Dietz, Indianwood C.C., Lake Orion, Mich.	73	74	70	81	298	200.00
	Mike Souchak, Grossinger C.C., Grossinger, N.Y.	78	71	72	77	298	200.00
	Walter Burkemo, Franklin Hills C.C., Franklin, Mich.	73	74	76	75	298	200.00
	Shelley Mayfield, Meadow Brook C., Jericho, N.Y.	75	71	75	77	298	200.00
	*Dr. Frank M. Taylor, Jr., Red Hill C.C., Upland, Calif.	72	71	80	75	298	----
34	Frank Stranahan, Inverness C., Toledo, Ohio	76	71	75	77	299	200.00
	Gene Littler, Singing Hills C.C., El Cajon, Calif.	75	74	74	76	299	200.00
	Dave Douglas, Newark, Del.	72	76	78	73	299	200.00
37	*William Hyndman III, Huntingdon Valley C.C., Abington, Pa.	72	76	76	76	300	----
	Al Brosch, Woodmere Club, Woodmere, N.Y.	72	74	77	77	300	200.00
	Mickey Homa, Westchester C.C., Rye, N.Y.	74	75	79	72	300	200.00
40	Tony Holguin, Midlothian C.C., Midlothian, Ill.	74	73	78	76	301	200.00
41	Edward S. Oliver, Jr., Blue Hill C.C., Canton, Mass.	74	74	76	78	302	200.00
	Paul R. O'Leary, Bismarck, N.D.	76	73	77	76	302	200.00
	Dick Mayer, Lakewood C.C., St. Petersburg, Fla.	76	73	78	75	302	200.00
44	Buck White, Greenwood, Miss.	75	74	76	78	303	200.00
45	Walker P. Inman, Jr., Augusta, Ga.	77	72	79	76	304	200.00
	Robert R. Rosburg, Palo Alto, Calif.	68	76	79	81	304	200.00
47	*E. Harvie Ward, Jr., San Francisco G.C., San Francisco, Calif.	74	73	81	77	305	----
48	Francis G. (Bo) Wininger, Oklahoma City, Okla.	74	75	77	80	306	200.00
	Jack Isaacs, Langley A.F.B.G.C., Langley A.F.B., Va.	77	70	78	81	306	200.00
50	Tony Lema, San Francisco G.C., San Francisco, Calif.	77	71	79	81	308	200.00
51	*John Garrett, River Oaks C.C., Houston, Texas	77	72	76	84	309	----

*Gold medals awarded to all amateurs.
Prize money totaling $24,000 awarded to professionals.

1957
FIFTY-SEVENTH OPEN CHAMPIONSHIP

Held at the Inverness Club, Toledo, Ohio, June 13-15.
Yardage–6,919. Par 70.
1,907 Entries, 162 Qualifiers, 162 Starters.

Fifty-two contestants who completed 72 holes.

						Score	Money Prize
1	++Dick Mayer, St. Petersburg, Fla.	70	68	74	70	282	$7,200.00
	++Cary Middlecoff, Riverlake C.C., Dallas, Texas	71	75	68	68	282	4,200.00
3	Jimmy Demaret, Concord Int'l. G.C., Kiamesha Lake, N.Y.	68	73	70	72	283	2,160.00
4	Julius Boros, Mid Pines C., Southern Pines, N.C.	69	75	70	70	284	1,380.00
	Walter Burkemo, Franklin Hills C.C., Franklin, Mich.	74	73	72	65	284	1,380.00
6	Ken Venturi, California G.C., S. San Francisco, Calif.	69	71	75	71	286	840.00
	Fred E. Hawkins, El Paso C.C., El Paso, Texas	72	72	71	71	286	840.00
8	Sam Snead, Greenbrier G.C., White Sulphur Springs, W. Va.	74	74	69	73	290	465.00
	Roberto De Vicenzo, Club Campestre de Mexico, Mexico City, Mex.	72	70	72	76	290	465.00
	M. R. (Chick) Harbert, Meadowbrook C.C., Northville, Mich.	68	79	71	72	290	465.00
	Billy Maxwell, Odessa C.C., Odessa, Texas	70	76	72	72	290	465.00
	*William J. Patton, Mimosa Hills G.C., Morganton, N.C.	70	68	76	76	290	----
13	Michael Fetchick, Mahopac G.C., Mahopac, N.Y.	74	71	71	75	291	360.00
	Dow Finsterwald, Tequesta C.C., Tequesta, Fla.	74	72	72	73	291	360.00
	Frank Stranahan, Inverness C., Toledo, Ohio	72	76	69	74	291	360.00
	*William Hyndman, III, Huntingdon Valley C.C., Abington, Pa.	77	73	72	69	291	----
17	Don Fairfield, Casey C.C., Casey, Ill.	78	72	73	69	292	315.00
	Jim Ferree, Old Town C., Winston-Salem, N.C.	74	74	73	71	292	315.00
	Marvin (Bud) Ward, Peninsula G. & C.C., San Mateo, Calif.	70	74	70	78	292	315.00
	Doug Ford, Putnam C.C., Mahopac, N.Y.	69	71	80	72	292	315.00
21	Bo Wininger, Odessa, Texas	70	71	76	76	293	300.00
22	Edward S. Oliver, Jr., Blue Hill C.C., Canton, Mass.	74	73	73	74	294	260.00
	Peter Thomson, Victoria G.C., Melbourne, Australia	71	72	74	77	294	260.00
	George Bayer, San Gabriel, Calif.	73	77	69	75	294	260.00
	*Joe E. Campbell, Deane Hill C.C., Knoxville, Tenn.	74	72	73	75	294	----
26	Gerald Kesselring, Downsview G. & C.C., Toronto, Ont., Canada	74	71	75	75	295	240.00
	Sam Penecale, Bala G.C., Philadelphia, Pa.	71	73	73	78	295	240.00
	Jack Fleck, Rochester G. & C.C., Rochester, Mich.	72	76	73	74	295	240.00
	†E. Harvie Ward, Jr., San Francisco G. C., San Francisco, Calif.	72	75	74	74	295	----
30	Johnny Revolta, Evanston G.C., Skokie, Ill.	76	74	74	72	296	240.00
	Leo F. Biagetti, St. Paul, Minn.	73	75	72	76	296	240.00
32	Gene Littler, Singing Hills C.C., El Cajon, Calif.	73	76	73	75	297	240.00
	Stan Leonard, Lachute G.C., Lachute, Que., Canada	71	76	73	77	297	240.00
	*Charles Kocsis, Red Run G.C., Royal Oak, Mich.	76	74	74	73	297	----
35	Otto Greiner, Knickerbocker C.C., Tenafly, N.J.	76	74	75	73	298	240.00
	Jerry Barber, Wilshire C.C., Los Angeles, Calif.	75	73	73	77	298	240.00
	Fred Haas, New Orleans, La.	72	73	77	76	298	240.00
38	Lew Worsham, Jr., Oakmont C.C., Oakmont, Pa.	78	72	76	73	299	240.00
	Babe Lichardus, Hillside, N.J.	72	76	74	77	299	240.00
	Furman Hayes, Gaston C.C., Gastonia, N.C.	74	75	70	80	299	240.00
41	Johnny Pott, Shreveport C.C., Shreveport, La.	74	75	74	77	300	240.00
42	Donald E. Whitt, Alameda, Calif.	71	77	78	75	301	240.00
43	Al Brosch, Woodmere C., Woodmere, N.Y.	72	76	72	82	302	240.00
	Clarence J. Doser, Woodmont C.C., Rockville, Md.	72	78	76	76	302	240.00
45	Al Mengert, Echo Lake C.C., Westfield, N.J.	77	73	71	82	303	240.00
	Bob Gajda, Forest Lake C.C., Bloomfield Hills, Mich.	75	75	78	75	303	240.00
	Howie Johnson, Houston, Texas	72	77	77	77	303	240.00
48	Leland Gibson, Blue Hills C., Kansas City, Mo.	75	75	76	78	304	240.00
	Stan Mosel, Essex Fells C.C., Essex Fells, N.J.	74	75	77	78	304	240.00
50	*E. Fred Brown, Bel-Air C.C., Los Angeles, Calif.	74	76	79	76	305	----
51	*Rex Baxter, Jr., Amarillo C.C., Amarillo, Texas	77	73	80	78	308	----
52	*Gene R. Coulter, Forest Hills C.C., Richmond, Ind.	73	77	85	81	316	----

++Playoff: 18 holes, June 16–Mayer, 72; Middlecoff, 79.
*Gold medals awarded to all amateurs.
†Applicant for reinstatement to amateur status.
Prize money totaling $28,560 awarded to professionals.

1958
FIFTY-EIGHTH OPEN CHAMPIONSHIP

Held at the Southern Hills Country Club, Tulsa, Okla., June 12-14.
Yardage—6,907. Par 70.
2,132 Entries, 162 Qualifiers, 162 Starters.

Fifth-three contestants who completed 72 holes

						Score	Money Prize
1	Tommy Bolt, Paradise C.C., Crystal River, Fla.	71	71	69	72	283	$8,000.00
2	Gary Player, Killarney C.C., Johannesburg, South Africa	75	68	73	71	287	5,000.00
3	Julius Boros, Mid Pines C., Southern Pines, N.C.	71	75	72	71	289	3,000.00
4	Gene Littler, Singing Hills C.C., El Cajon, Calif.	74	73	67	76	290	2,000.00
5	Walter Burkemo, Franklin Hills C.C., Franklin, Mich.	75	74	70	72	291	1,625.00
	Robert R. Rosburg, Silverado G. & C.C., Napa, Calif.	75	74	72	70	291	1,625.00
7	Jay Hebert, Mayfair Inn C.C., Sanford, Fla.	77	76	71	69	293	1,016.66
	Dick Metz, Shady Oaks C.C., Fort Worth, Texas	71	78	73	71	293	1,016.67
	Don January, Eastland, Texas	79	73	68	73	293	1,016.67
10	Ben Hogan, Fort Worth, Texas	75	73	75	71	294	566.66
	Frank Stranahan, Crystal River, Fla.	72	72	75	75	294	566.67
	Tommy Jacobs, Candlewood C.C., Whittier, Calif.	76	75	71	72	294	566.67
13	Marty Furgol, Cog Hill G.C., Lemont, Ill.	75	74	74	72	295	500.00
	Bill Casper, Jr., Apple Valley C.C., Apple Valley, Calif.	79	70	75	71	295	500.00
	*Charles R. Coe, Oklahoma City G. & C.C., Oklahoma City, Okla.	75	71	75	74	295	----
16	Robert E. Goetz, Tulsa C.C., Tulsa, Okla.	75	75	77	69	296	500.00
17	Tom Nieporte, Bronxville, N.Y.	75	73	74	75	297	300.00
	*Jerry Pittman, Rolling Hills C.C., Tulsa, Okla.	75	77	71	74	297	----
19	Bruce Crampton, Beverley Park G.C., Sydney, Australia	73	75	74	76	298	300.00
	Jerry Magee, Toronto, Ont., Canada	76	77	75	70	298	300.00
	Jerry Barber, Wilshire C.C., Los Angeles, Calif.	79	73	73	73	298	300.00
	Jim Ferree, Old Town C., Winston-Salem, N.C.	76	74	73	75	298	300.00
23	Dick Mayer, St. Petersburg, Fla.	76	74	71	78	299	200.00
	Arnold Palmer, Latrobe C.C., Latrobe, Pa.	75	75	77	72	299	200.00
	Earl Stewart, Jr., Oak Cliff C.C., Dallas, Texas	75	74	77	73	299	200.00
	E. J. (Dutch) Harrison, Old Warson C.C., St. Louis, Mo.	76	76	73	74	299	200.00
27	Cary Middlecoff, Diplomat C.C., Hollywood, Fla.	75	79	75	71	300	200.00
	Billy Maxwell, Odessa, C.C., Odessa, Texas	78	76	76	70	300	200.00
	Bo Wininger, Odessa, Texas	78	74	74	74	300	200.00
	Stan Dudas, North Hills C.C., North Hills, Pa.	76	73	76	75	300	200.00
	Labron Harris, Lakeside G.C., Stillwater, Okla.	74	72	77	77	300	200.00
	Don Fairfield, Casey C.C., Casey, Ill.	78	75	72	75	300	200.00
	Michael Fetchik, Yonkers, N.Y.	78	76	73	73	300	200.00
34	Doug Ford, Paradise C.C., Crystal River, Fla.	78	75	73	75	301	200.00
35	Ken Venturi, California G.C., So. San Francisco, Calif.	79	73	75	75	302	200.00
	Buck White, Diplomat C.C., Hollywood, Fla.	76	77	71	78	302	200.00
37	Lloyd Mangrum, Apple Valley C.C., Apple Valley, Calif.	72	78	75	78	303	200.00
	Marvin (Bud) Ward, Peninsula G. & C.C., San Mateo, Calif.	78	76	74	75	303	200.00
	Paul Harney, Worcester, Mass.	77	77	72	77	303	200.00
	*E. Harvie Ward, Jr., San Francisco G. C., San Francisco, Calif.	74	80	79	70	303	----
41	Sam Penecale, Whitemarsh Valley C.C., Philadelphia, Pa.	77	77	76	74	304	200.00
	*Jack Nicklaus, Scioto C.C., Columbus, Ohio	79	75	73	77	304	----
43	Joe E. Campbell, Beaver Brook C.C., Fountain City, Tenn.	77	74	76	79	306	200.00
	Bob Crowley, Pine Brook C.C., Weston, Mass.	78	76	75	77	306	200.00
45	Lew Worsham, Jr., Oakmont C.C., Oakmont, Pa.	77	72	77	81	307	200.00
	Joe Jimenez, Manhattan C.C., Manhattan, Kans.	76	76	80	75	307	200.00
47	Babe Lichardus, Grossinger C.C., Grossinger, N.Y.	76	76	73	83	308	200.00
	Mike Pavella, Nemacolin C.C., Beallsville, Pa.	75	79	79	75	308	200.00
49	Pat Schwab, Sunningdale C.C., Toledo, Ohio	75	75	79	80	309	200.00
50	Ted Gwin, Crestview C.C., Wichita, Kans.	76	78	81	75	310	200.00
	Herman Barron, Fenway G.C., White Plains, N.Y.	78	76	79	77	310	200.00
52	M. R. (Chick) Harbert, Meadowbrook C.C., Northville, Mich.	75	78	78	80	311	200.00
	*Bobby Nichols, Midland C.C., Midland, Texas	79	75	84	73	311	----

*Gold medals awarded to all amateurs.
Prize money totaling $35,000 awarded to professionals.

1959
FIFTY-NINTH OPEN CHAMPIONSHIP

Held at the Winged Foot Golf Club, Mamaroneck, N.Y., June 11-13.
Yardage—6,873. Par 70.
2,385 Entries, 150 Qualifiers, 150 Starters.
Fifty-six contestants who completed 72 holes.

						Score	Money Prize
1	Bill Casper, Jr , Apple Valley C.C., Apple Valley, Calif.	71	68	69	74	282	$12,000.00
2	Robert R. Rosburg, Palo Alto, Calif.	75	70	67	71	283	6,600.00
3	Claude Harmon, Winged Foot G.C., Mamaroneck, N.Y.	72	71	70	71	284	3,600.00
	Mike Souchak, Grossinger G.C. Grossinger, N.Y.	71	70	72	71	284	3,600.00
5	Doug Ford, Paradise C.C., Crystal River, Fla.	72	69	72	73	286	2,100.00
	Ernie Vossler, Midland, Texas	72	70	72	72	286	2,100.00
	Arnold Palmer, Laurel Valley G.C., Ligonier, Pa.	71	69	72	74	286	2,100.00
8	Ben Hogan, Fort Worth, Texas	69	71	71	76	287	1,350.00
	Sam Snead, Greenbrier G.C., White Sulphur Springs, W. Va.	73	72	67	75	287	1,350.00
10	Dick Knight, Mission Valley C.C., San Diego, Calif.	69	75	73	73	290	900.00
11	Ted Kroll, DeSoto G. & C.C., Sarasota, Fla.	71	73	73	74	291	600.00
	Gene Littler, Singing Hills, C.C., El Cajon, Calif.	69	74	75	73	291	600.00
	Fred E. Hawkins, Coronado C.C., El Paso, Texas	76	72	69	74	291	600.00
	Dow Finsterwald, Tequesta C.C., Jupiter, Fla.	69	73	75	74	291	600.00
15	Gary Player, Killarney G.C., Johannesburg, South Africa	71	69	76	76	292	510.00
	Dave Marr, Rockaway Hunting C., Cedarhurst, N.Y.	75	73	69	75	292	510.00
17	Gardner E. Dickinson, Jr., Seminole G.C., West Palm Beach, Fla	77	70	71	75	293	420.00
	Jay Hebert, Mayfair Inn C.C., Sanford, Fla.	73	70	78	72	293	420.00
19	Don January, Pinehurst C.C., Denver, Colo.	71	73	73	77	294	300.00
	Cary Middlecoff, Diplomat C.C., Hollywood, Fla.	71	73	73	77	294	300.00
	Jack Fleck, El Caballero C.C., Los Angeles, Calif.	74	74	69	77	294	300.00
	Bo Wininger, Odessa, Texas	71	73	72	78	294	300.00
	Johnny Pott, Shreveport, La.	77	72	70	75	294	300.00
	MacGregor Hunter, Riviera C.C., Pacific Palisades, Calif.	75	74	73	72	294	300.00
25	Joe E. Campbell, Beaver Brook C.C., Knoxville, Tenn.	73	71	75	76	295	240.00
26	M. R. (Chick) Harbert, Meadowbrook C.C. Northville, Mich.	78	68	76	74	296	240.00
	Billy Maxwell, Odessa, Texas	75	75	70	76	296	240.00
28	Henry Ransom, St. Andrews G.C., St. Andrews, Ill.	72	77	71	77	297	240.00
	Fred Wampler, Selva Marina C.C., Atlantic Beach, Fla.	74	73	75	75	297	240.00
	Julius Boros, Mid Pines C., Southern Pines, N.C.	76	74	72	75	297	240.00
	Lionel P. Hebert, Oak Broune C.C., Lafayette, La.	71	74	70	82	297	240.00
32	Al Balding, Markham G. & C.C., Markham, Ont., Canada	72	74	75	78	299	240.00
	Charles Sifford, Los Angeles, Calif.	78	72	73	76	299	240.00
	*James R. English, Columbine C.C., Littleton, Colo.	74	75	77	73	299	----
35	Tommy Jacobs, Whittier, Calif.	76	71	76	77	300	240.00
	Shelley Mayfield, Meadow Brook C., Westbury, N.Y.	75	74	73	78	300	240.00
	Ewing Pomeroy, Ansley G.C., Atlanta, Ga.	72	72	76	80	300	240.00
38	Tommy Bolt, Paradise C.C., Crystal River, Fla.	75	73	77	76	301	240.00
	Vic Ghezzi, Jamaica, N.Y.	75	71	78	77	301	240.00
	Ken Venturi, Palo Alto Hills C.C., Palo Alto, Calif.	78	69	76	78	301	240.00
	Bob Goalby, St. Clair C.C., Belleville, Ill.	73	76	74	78	301	240.00
	*Charles R. Coe, Oklahoma City G. & C.C., Oklahoma City, Okla.	72	78	75	76	301	----
43	Don Fairfield, Casey C.C., Casey, Ill.	71	78	73	80	302	240.00
	Wesley Ellis, Jr., Aldecress C.C., Aldecress, N.J.	77	70	76	79	302	240.00
	Jimmy Johnson, C.C. of Harrisburg, Harrisburg, Pa.	76	74	75	77	302	240.00
46	Darrell Hickok, Edgewood Valley C.C., LaGrange, Ill.	76	72	73	82	303	240.00
	Alfred L. Smith, Danville G.C., Danville, Va.	75	75	75	78	303	240.00
	*Robert J. Batdorff II, Hershey C.C., Hershey, Pa.	73	73	78	79	303	----
49	Stan Dudas, North Hills C.C., North Hills, Pa.	75	73	75	81	304	240.00
	*Don Cherry, Wichita Falls C.C., Wichita Falls, Texas	75	75	79	75	304	----
51	Charles J. Scally, Scally's G.D.R., Coraopolis, Pa.	80	70	76	79	305	240.00
	Pvt. Rex Baxter, Jr., Amarillo C.C., Amarillo, Texas	75	72	78	80	305	240.00
	Paul Harney, Auburn, Mass.	74	76	76	79	305	240.00
54	*Richard D. Chapman, Pinehurst C.C., Pinehurst, N.C.	76	74	75	82	307	----
55	Otto Greiner, Knickerbocker C.C., Tenafly, N.J.	77	71	78	83	309	240.00
56	*Cobby Ware, Augusta C.C., Augusta, Ga.	73	75	83	80	311	----

*Gold Medals awarded to all amateurs.
Prize money totaling $49,200 awarded to professionals.

AMATEUR CHAMPIONSHIP

HAVEMEYER TROPHY

Presented in 1894 by

THEODORE A. HAVEMEYER
First President of the United States Golf Association

Original trophy destroyed by fire November, 1925. Replaced in January, 1926, by
EDWARD S. MOORE
Treasurer of the United States Golf Association, 1922-25

HISTORY

1895–The USGA, with its five charter clubs, was formed in December, 1894, and initiated its first Championship at the Newport (R.I.) Golf Club, October 1-3, 1895. Charles B. Macdonald, of the Chicago Golf Club, won handily defeating Charles E. Sands, of St. Andrews, N.Y., 12 and 11. It was entirely at match play, with no qualifying, and 32 were drawn.

1896–H.J. Whigham, of the Onwentsia Club, Lake Forest, Ill., an Oxford man and an English-trained golfer, won the qualifying honors (86-77) among a group of 58 players trying for 16 places and went on to take the Championship, defeating J.G. Thorp, 8 and 7, in the final. Whigham was Macdonald's son-in-law. The competition was held at Shinnecock Hills Golf Club, Southampton, N.Y., in July.

1897–Whigham won his second championship and Macdonald was the medalist among an entry of 58 at the Chicago Golf Club in September. Whigham defeated W.R. Betts, 8 and 6, in the final.

1898–With a field of 120 in the Championship, a new method of 36-hole qualifying for 32 places was used. Findlay S. Douglas, of the Fairfield County (Conn.) Golf Club, a native of St. Andrews, Scotland, and later president of the USGA, took the title at the Morris County Golf Club, in Morristown, N.J. in September. Douglas defeated W.B. Smith, of Chicago, 5 and 3, in the final.

1899–The Championship moved to Chicago again and was played at Onwentsia. H.M. Harriman, of Knollwood Country Club, Meadow Brook, Long Island, N.Y., defeated Findlay S. Douglas, 3 and 2, in the final. Macdonald was the medalist.

1900–Walter J. Travis of Garden City (N.Y.) Golf Club, an Australian who had come to the United States and had taken up the game at the age of 35, led a field of 120 in the qualifying with 166 and defeated Douglas, 2 up, in the final.

1901–Travis successfully defended his title at the Country Club of Atlantic City, N.J. He was low qualifier with 157, a record, and defeated Walter E. Egan, of Onwentsia, 5 and 4. He played the rubber-core ball (Haskell patent) with such success that the gutta percha ball was soon discarded by players. The final round of this Championship was postponed a week because of the death of President William McKinley.

1902–A new method was tried with 18-hole qualifying for 64 places. Louis N. James, of the home club, just squeezed in with the highest score of 94, while Travis had a 79. Travis went out in the third round and James won the Championship from Eben M. Byers, 4 and 2, in the final over the Glen View Club course, near Chicago, in July. James was 19 years and 10 months old.

1903–Travis was back again at the Nassau Country Club, Glen Cove, N.Y., in September, to win his third crown. This time the Championship Committee copied the Royal and Ancient method of allowing 128 players to compete, all at match play. Byers again lost in the final, 5 and 4.

1904–H. Chandler Egan, of the Exmoor Country Club, Chicago, was 20, and had just been graduated from Harvard when he won his first Championship the following September. The test was 54 holes qualifying (for which Egan was low with 242) for 32 places. Travis went out in the second round when George Ormiston of Oakmont holed a cleek shot for an eagle 2. Egan defeated Fred Herreshoff in the final round, 8 and 6, at the Baltusrol Golf Club, Springfield, N.J.

1905–H. Chandler Egan repeated at the Chicago Golf Club. Dr. D.P. Fredericks of Oakmont was medalist with 155. The USGA introduced the Calkins system for calculating handicaps, based on par, to provide a basis for eligibility and reverted to the 1898 system of 36 holes qualifying for 32 places. The August event produced an all-Chicago final with Egan defeating D.E. Sawyer, 6 and 5.

1906–George S. Lyon, Canadian Champion, reached the final at the Englewood (N.J.) Golf Club, in July, but Eben M. Byers, of the Allegheny Country Club, Pittsburgh, defeated him, 2 up.

1907–Jerome D. Travers, of the Montclair (N.J.) Golf Club, was just 20 when he scored the first of his four triumphs in the Amateur at the Euclid Club, Cleveland, Ohio. Charles (Chick) Evans, Jr., of Edgewater Golf Club, Chicago, made his first appearance in the Championship. Travis won the medal, with 146, for the fifth time. The tournament was held in July and Archibald Graham of Northern Jersey Country Club, was the losing finalist, 6 and 5.

1908–Travis was still in contention. He took the medal for the sixth time and won a 41-hole match from Henry Wilder, 6 and 5, of Brookline. But it was Travers' era and he repeated, this time at Garden City, where Travis had won his first title. The event was held in September and Travers defeated Max H. Behr, 8 and 7, in the final.

1909–Robert A. Gardner of the Hinsdale Golf Club, won at the age of 19 years and 5 months to become the youngest winner. H. Chandler Egan was the loser in the final by 4 and 3. Travers did not defend his title. The Championship was played at the Chicago Golf Club, in September.

1910–At The Country Club, Brookline, Mass., William C. Fownes, Jr., from Oakmont (Pa.) Country Club, was two down to Chick Evans with four to play in the semi-final round and defeated him, 1 up. He went on to win the Championship by defeating Warren K. Wood, 4 and 3, in the final. Fred Herreshoff was medalist with 152. Mr. Fownes later became President of the USGA.

1911–The title went across the seas the following September when it was won by Harold H. Hilton, 42, of Liverpool, who had been British Open Champion in 1892 and 1897, and British Amateur Champion in 1900, 1901 and 1911. He was medalist in the field of 186 entries and defeated Fred Herreshoff on the 37th hole at the Apawamis Club, Rye, N.Y. Hilton was 6 up on Herreshoff after 22 holes, but Herreshoff rallied and squared the match after 34. On the first extra hole, Hilton's approach went to the right of the green, hit a slope and rolled on. Hilton made a par 4, Herreshoff a 5, and Hilton won. Hilton's spoon shot to the 37th became legendary.

1912–Hilton was back to defend his title but did not succeed. He tied with Charles Evans, Jr., for the medal and lost the playoff. The USGA had issued the national handicap list in March, showing 471 eligible players with handicaps 0-to-6, but only 86 entered. Jerome Travers was back in form and defeated Evans 7 and 6, in the final at the Chicago Golf Club, in September.

1913–Travers, the only player listed at scratch, tied for the last place in qualifying but still was tops in match play, defeating John G. Anderson, 5 and 4, in the final, and achieved a record later surpassed only by Bob Jones, winning for the fourth time. Site: Garden City Golf Club, N.Y., in September.

1914–Francis Ouimet of the Woodland Golf Club, near Boston, who the year before had made front-page news by defeating Ray and Vardon in the Open play-off at Brookline, Mass., won the Amateur at Ekwanok Country Club, Manchester, Vt., by defeating Travers in the final, 6 and 5.

1915–Robert A. Gardner, who had won the title six years before, repeated at the Country Club of Detroit, Grosse Pointe Farms, Michigan. In the final, Gardner defeated John G. Anderson, 5 and 4. Anderson had reached the last round for the second time.

1916–Charles Evans, Jr., then 26, finally pushed through in September at Merion Cricket Club, Haverford, Pa., defeating the defending Champion, Gardner, 4 and 3, in the final. Fownes was low qualifier. Evans had won the Open in June and became the first player to win both in the same year. This was a momentous tournament in another respect; it marked the first appearance of Bob Jones in a USGA Championship. He was 14.

1917-1918–All USGA Championships were suspended because of World War I.

1919–When the Championship was revived in 1919, S. Davidson Herron, 20 years old, became one of the few to win on his home course, the Oakmont Country Club, near Pittsburgh. Herron's play was brilliant and he was four under 4s when he finished off Bob Jones, 5 and 4, in the final. The entry reached 150.

1920–The entry unexpectedly jumped to 235 in 1920, and 36-hole qualifying had to be conducted at both the Engineers Country Club, Roslyn, N.Y., site of the Championship proper, and nearby North Shore Country Club. The entry record would stand until 1931. Jones won the medal in a playoff with Fred J. Wright, Jr. Evans defeated Ouimet, 7 and 6, for the title with great iron play and putting. Cyril Tolley and several other Britishers failed to qualify.

1921–For the first time the Championship was held west of the Mississippi River, at the St. Louis Country Club, with a larger representation of associations and states than ever before, although the total entry fell off to 159 and only 132 competed in the 36-hole qualifying rounds. On a rainy September day, Jesse P. Guilford, of the Woodland (Mass.) Golf Club, defeated Gardner, 7 and 6, for the Championship. Ouimet was medalist with 144.

1922–Jess W. Sweetser, of the Siwanoy Country Club, Bronxville, N.Y., 20, defeated all the established players: defender Guilford, Bob Jones, Charles Evans, Jr., and Willie Hunter at The Country Club, Brookline, Mass. in September. He defeated Evans, 3 and 2, in the final, and in a brilliantly played semi-final match he eliminated Bob Jones, 8 and 7.

1923–Max Marston from Pine Valley Golf Club, in New Jersey, winner of the New Jersey and Pennsylvania state titles, was 31 when he beat defending Champion Sweetser at the 38th hole, after having eliminated Jones and Ouimet, at the Flossmoor Country Club in Illinois. Evans and Jones were co-medalists.

1924–Robert T. Jones, Jr., of the Atlanta Athletic Club's East Lake Course, crashed through after playing in five Championships. It was the beginning of the Jones reign. Jones crushed Ouimet, 11 and 10, in his semi-final match, and George Von Elm, 9 and 8, in the final at Merion Cricket Club's East Course in Ardmore, Pa. He was to come back there six years later to complete his Grand Slam.

1925–Jones won at Oakmont defeating Watts Gunn, his protege and friend, 8 and 7. It was the only time both finalists represented the same club, East Lake in Atlanta. A new system was tried; 16

qualified, all matches at 36 holes. It proved unpopular.

1926–Jones was not to make it three in a row. George Von Elm of the Rancho Golf Club, Los Angeles, Calif., was in good form, improving each day until he reached the final and upset Jones, the medalist (143). Entries numbered 157, and another change was tried in the form of play, reversion to the old method of 36-hole qualifying for 32 places, but the draw was seeded for eight players. There were 36-hole matches Thursday, Friday and Saturday. The Championship was played at the Baltusrol Golf Club in Springfield N.J.

1927–After a victory in the British Open, Jones won at the Minikahda Club in Minneapolis. He tied the record as medalist with 75-67–142, and defeated Charles Evans, Jr., 8 and 7, in the final round.

1928–For the first time the United States Amateur Champion confronted the British Amateur Champion in the final at Brae Burn Country Club, West Newton, Mass. It was Jones vs. T. Philip Perkins, of the British Walker Cup Team, and Jones won, 10 and 9. George Voigt was medalist.

1929–A great upset shook the tournament in the first round: Johnny Goodman, of the Omaha (Neb.) Field Club, stopped Jones, only to be stopped by a newcomer, W. Lawson Little, Jr., of the Presidio (Calif.) Golf Club, in the next at the Pebble Beach, Calif., course, the first USGA Championship on the Pacific Coast. Harrison R. (Jimmy) Johnston, of the White Bear (Minn.) Yacht Club, won the title from Dr. O.F. Willing in the final, 4 and 3. Jones and Eugene V. Homans tied for the medal.

1930–The medalists of the year before met in the final at Merion. Jones equalled his qualifying record, defeated Homans, 8 and 7, and achieved the Grand Slam by winning four major British and United States titles in one year. There were five extra-hole matches, including the longest overtime in USGA history. Maurice McCarthy defeated George Von Elm on the 28th hole, after 10 extra holes, in the second round. McCarthy had previously made a hole-in-one in the qualifying to land a place in the playoff, won the sudden death playoff while the dew was still on the grass, and then played 19 holes to defeat Watts Gunn in the first round. That September marked Jones' final appearance in a Championship.

1931–Seventeen years had passed since Francis Ouimet had won the title. He took it again at the Beverly Country Club, in Illinois, defeating Jack Westland in the final, 6 and 5. Sectional qualifying at 20 cities was tried for the first time, with success. The entry reached 583 and Sectional Qualifying was conducted at 20 locations.

1932–The cup went to Canada for the first time, C. Ross (Sandy) Somerville, of London, Ont., several times Canadian Champion, defeated Johnny Goodman in the final, 2 and 1. Johnny Fischer of the Highland (Ky.) Golf Club, equalled the qualifying record. Ouimet had 30 for nine holes in his first round against Voigt. Site: Five Farms East Course of the Baltimore Country Club.

1933–Sometimes the winner of a Championship qualifies high: George T. Dunlap, Jr., of the Pomonok Country Club of Flushing, N.Y., was in the 12 who played off for the last eight places at the Kenwood Country Club at Cincinnati and defeated ex-Champion Max Marston, 6 and 5, in the final. Somerville was knocked out by W. Lawson Little, Jr., while Johnny Fischer set a new qualifying record of 141.

1934–W. Lawson Little, Jr., then 24, came into his own. A new all-match-play program with no qualifying at the course and 36-hole final and semi-finals proved popular with players and the gallery. Little had already won the British Amateur, thus achieving a "Little Slam." Nine former Amateur Champions played, due to a new ruling that exempted former champions from qualifying sectionally. David Goldman lost in the final, 8 and 7.

1935–Little achieved a second "Little Slam," winning the British and United States Amateurs again. At the Country Club of Cleveland he was under par for his rounds and beat Walter Emery, 4 and 2, in the final. Largest entry record to date: 945 with 207 players competing, including some British.

1936–Entries were growing: 1,118 this year from 32 qualifying points, 210 in the tournament proper. Both Walker Cup teams were present. John W. Fischer, playing on the oft-tested Garden City course, was one down and three to play against visiting Walker Cupper, Scotsman Jack McLean, in the final and saved a half on the 34th only by virtue of a dead stymie against McLean. They then halved the 35th in birdie 4s, Fischer dropped a 12-foot putt for a birdie 2 to square the match on the home green and a 20-foot putt for a birdie 3 to win on the first extra hole.

1937–Johnny Goodman of Omaha, then 28, a former Open Champion, defeated Ray Billows, 2 up, in the final. For the first time since 1933 a 36-hole qualifying competition was conducted at the Championship site in addition to sectional qualifying to determine the 64 who would compete in match play at the Alderwood Country Club, Portland, Ore. This was the first time the championship had been held in the Pacific Northwest.

1938–When William P. (Willie) Turnesa won, he was reported to have been in bunkers on 13 of 29 holes of the final. Turnesa was the only Amateur in a family of seven brothers–all golfers. He defeated B. Patrick Abbott, of Altadena, Calif., 8 and 7, in the final. Abbott was a movie extra. Five of eight of the Walker Cup players were disposed of in the first two rounds. The Championship was played at the Oakmont Country Club, Oakmont, Pa.

1939–Marvin (Bud) Ward of Spokane (Wash.) Country Club, won at North Shore Country Club, Glenview, Ill., in September. He was 11 under par for 170 holes played, and in his last two matches he one-putted 29 greens. Ward defeated Ray Billows in the final, 7 and 5. A new qualifying record was set: 139 (70-69) by Thomas Sheehan, Jr.

1940–Richard D. Chapman, playing from the

Winged Foot Golf Club, Mamaroneck, N.Y., was medalist with 140 (four below par) and played 157 holes in eight under par at Winged Foot. W.B. "Duff" McCullough, whom he defeated in the final, 11 and 9, had been second low qualifier with 67-77.

1941–Marvin (Bud) Ward was playing steady golf at Omaha (Neb.) Field Club the following August. Although he had been 4 up and led only by 1 up after the 26th, he held on to defeat Pat Abbott, 1938 finalist and 1936 Public Links champion, 4 and 3. Stewart (Skip) Alexander, Jr., was medalist with 144.

1942–1945– No Championships: World War II.

1946–Interest in this Championship was high after the war. The largest galleries since 1930 were reported in September at Baltusrol Golf Club, Springfield, N.J. Robert H. (Skee) Riegel, of the Oakmont Club, Glendale, Calif., established a new qualifying record with 69-67–136. After sectional qualifying, 150 players competed for 64 places. Stanley E. (Ted) Bishop of the Norfolk (Mass.) Golf Club, had an overtime final with Smiley Quick, and won on the 37th hole.

1947–To make it possible for more to play in the Championship, qualifying at the site was abandoned, and 210 places permitted at the match play site. Robert H. (Skee) Riegel defeated Johnny Dawson at the Pebble Beach Course of the Del Monte Golf and Country Club, Pebble Beach, Calif., 2 and 1, in September.

1948–The Amateur was held at Memphis Country Club and the entry reached 1,220, the largest yet. Many younger players emerged; standard of play and keenness of competition had increased since pre-war days. But after ten years Willie Turnesa proved himself still a master, beating Ray Billows in the final, 2 and 1. It was the third time Billows had reached the final and lost, and the second time to Turnesa.

1949–Charles Coe, of the Oklahoma City Golf and Country Club, played his best game when he needed it most and dominated the field at Oak Hill Country Club, Rochester, N.Y. His biggest thrill came when he defeated E. Harvie Ward, Jr., at the 19th after being 3 down and 5 to play, and then defeated Johnny Dawson at the 21st on the same day. Coe defeated Rufus King in the final by 11 and 10, the largest winning margin ever in the final.

1950–Overtime final matches had been played before in the Amateur, but the one between Frank Stranahan and Sam Urzetta at Minneapolis Golf Club broke the record. It lasted three extra holes before Urzetta, a former caddie from the Irondequoit Country Club, East Rochester, N.Y., defeated the Toledo golfer, 1 up, at the 39th.

1951–A Texas college boy, Billy Maxwell, of the Odessa Country Club, cut through a record field of 1,416 entrants and defeated Joseph F. Gagliardi, a White Plains, N.Y., lawyer, 4 and 3, in the final at the Saucon Valley Country Club, in Bethlehem, Pa. Again the members of the successful Walker Cup Team were eliminated without regard to their prestige, and only Charles R. Coe went as far as the quarter-finals.

1952–Jack Westland, of the Everett (Wash.) Golf and Country Club, at 47 the oldest winner in the history of the Championship, climaxed a long and illustrious golfing career by defeating Al Mengert, of Spokane, Wash., 3 and 2. Westland had reached the final in 1931 and lost to Francis Ouimet. This all-Northwest final developed, appropriately enough, at the Seattle Golf Club in the Pacific Northwest. The championship was preceded by the first match for The Americas Cup, among amateur teams representing Canada, Mexico and the United States, and the United States team had won by a narrow margin.

1953–Gene Littler, of the La Jolla (Calif.) Country Club, who was serving in the United States Navy, won a victory for youth again at the Oklahoma City Golf and Country Club. He finished with a birdie to defeat Dale Morey, 1 up, after Morey had made successive birdies on the 34th and 35th holes to square the final with one hole to play. Littler was 23, and he turned professional in January, 1954.

1954–Arnold Palmer, 24, of Latrobe, Pa., defeated Robert Sweeny, 43, of New York, 1 up, in a colorful and thrilling final in the second playing at the Country Club of Detroit, Grosse Pointe Farms, Mich. Palmer was two over par for the 36 holes. He had come through what many considered the strongest quarter of the draw and defeated, among others, Frank Stranahan in the fifth round of his last Championship as an amateur. Stranahan, in turn, had defeated E. Harvie Ward, Jr., fresh from his victory the previous week in the Canadian Amateur Championship. For the first time in the event, all the fairways were roped from tee to green. Three months after the Championship, Palmer turned professional.

1955–E. Harvie Ward, Jr., 29, of the San Francisco Golf Club, originally from North Carolina, defeated William Hyndman, III, 39, of Philadelphia, 9 and 8, in the final at the James River Course of the Country Club of Virginia, Richmond. Ward had a morning round of approximately 31-35–66 and was 5 up after nine and 8 up at lunch. He had won the British Amateur in 1952 and the Canadian Amateur in 1954. There was a record entry of 1,493. Hillman Robbins, Jr., who subsequently went to the semi-finals, set a sectional qualifying record with 66-66–132 at Memphis, Tenn.

1956–E. Harvie Ward, Jr. successfully defended his Championship by defeating Charles (Chuck) Kocsis, 43, of Detroit, 5 and 4, at the Knollwood Club, Lake Forest, Ill. He was the sixth Champion to win in successive years, but it had been 21 years since Lawson Little's successive victories. One down at noon and 2 down after 19 holes in the final, Ward went five under par for the last 13 holes. He was three under for the 35 holes of the final, and 11 under for the 142 holes required to win his seven matches. Now 30, he continued to represent the San Francisco Golf Club. In the semi-finals, Joe E. Campbell, 20, Purdue University senior, played the last eight holes in five under par, including a hole-in-one on the 13th hole, and still lost to Ward, 2 and 1. Kocsis defeated Gerald J. Magee, of Toronto, Canada, 4 and 2, in the other semi-final; Magee was the second Canadian semi-finalist in four years. The entry of 1,600 set a new record.

1957—Hillman Robbins, Jr., 25, of Memphis, Tenn., a reserve lieutenant on active duty in the Air Force, won over a field which included the entire United States and British Walker Cup Teams at The Country Club, Brookline, Mass., in September. The runner-up was Dr. Frank M. Taylor, Jr., 40, of Pomona, Calif., who bowed, 5 and 4. Both Robbins and Taylor were Walker Cup Team members. Two other members of the victorious United States team, Mason Rudolph, of Clarksville, Tenn., and Rex Baxter, Jr., of Amerillo, Texas, lost in the semi-finals. Only twice before had United States Walker Cuppers filled all the semi-final positions, in 1922 and 1923. The last British survivor was Alan Thirlwell, of England, who fell in the fifth round. Reid Jack, of Scotland, the British Amateur Champion, went down in the third round. The Championship was held over a course which had been lengthened since the Amateur of 1934 by the substitution of three new holes. E. Harvie Ward, Jr., had rendered himself ineligible to try for a third successive Championship. The USGA Executive Committee had ruled in June that Ward had forfeited amateur status for accepting expenses to play in certain tournaments, but that he would be eligible for reinstatement after a probationary period of one year. Ward applied for reinstatement.

1958—Charles R. Coe, 34, of Oklahoma City, leading amateur in the 1958 Open won for the second time, defeating Thomas D. Aaron, 21, of Gainesville, Ga., 5 and 4, on the Lake Course of the Olympic Country Club, San Francisco. The field included nearly all the members of the Americas Cup teams of Canada, Mexico and the United States, and one Canadian, Eric Hanson, played in the round of 16. Lt. Hillman Robbins, Jr., of Memphis, Tenn., the defender, was off form and succumbed in the third round. Later he turned professional. E. Harvie Ward, Jr., of San Francisco, Calif., the 1955 and 1956 Champion who had been on probation as a non-amateur during 1957, returned and reached the fifth round but lost there to H. Ward Wettlaufer, 22, of Buffalo, N.Y., 3 and 2. Besides Aaron and Wettlaufer, two other college players reached the quarter-finals; they were Deane R. Beman, 20, of Bethesda, Md., and Dick Foote, 20, of Santa Ana, Calif. George Boutell, 14, of Phoenix, Ariz., made his debut at the same age as Bob Jones in 1916. Dixie Chapman, 16, of Osterville, Mass., came with his father, Richard D. Chapman, the 1940 Champion, and they were the first father-and-son pair in the Amateur field since Emerson Carey, Jr., and Emerson Carey, III, of Denver, at Minneapolis in 1950.

1959—Jack W. Nicklaus, of Columbus, Ohio, a student at Ohio State University, won the Championship by 1 up in the final over defending Champion Charles R. Coe, of Oklahoma City. The Championship was played at the Broadmoor Golf Club in Colorado Springs, Colo. The final was remarkable. Coe, 35 years old, completed the morning round in 69, two under par, and led by two holes. Nicklaus got around in 71. The match was squared early in the afternoon round, but Coe moved in front once more. Nicklaus squared the match a second time on the 12th hole and after an exchange they came to the home hole all square. Here Coe made a great effort, but a recovery shot from heavy grass behind the green failed to drop by half a turn of the ball. Nicklaus then sank an eight-foot putt for a winning birdie 3. Nicklaus, at 19 years and eight months, thus became the second youngest Amateur Champion. Robert A. Gardner, of Chicago, won in 1909 at the age of 19 years and five months. Both Coe and Nicklaus were members of the Walker Cup Team which defeated the British in May. The two other semi-finalists were Dudley Wysong, 20, of Dallas, who lost to Coe, and Gene Andrews, 46, of Los Angeles, who lost to Nicklaus. The entry reached 1,696, a record.

THE AMATEUR CHAMPIONSHIP

DATE	WINNER, RUNNER-UP	SCORE	SITE	ENTRY
1895 (Oct.)	Charles B. Macdonald d. Charles E. Sands	12 & 11	Newport G.C., Newport, R.I. All Match Play	32
1896 (July)	H. J. Whigham d. J. G. Thorp	8 & 7	Shinnecock Hills G.C., Southampton, N.Y. Medalist—163 (36): H. J. Whigham	58
1897 (Sept.)	H. J. Whigham d. W. Rossiter Betts	8 & 6	Chicago G.C., Wheaton, Ill. Medalist—174: Charles B. Macdonald	58
1898 (Sept.)	Findlay S. Douglas d. Walter B. Smith	5 & 3	Morris County G.C., Morristown, N.J. Medalist—175: J. H. Choate, Jr.	120
1899 (July)	H. M. Harriman d. Findlay S. Douglas	3 & 2	Onwentsia Club, Lake Forest, Ill. Medalist—168: Charles B. Macdonald	112
1900 (July)	Walter J. Travis d. Findlay S. Douglas	2 up	Garden City G.C., Garden City, N.Y. Medalist—166: Walter J. Travis	120
1901 (Sept.)	Walter J. Travis d. Walter E. Egan	5 & 4	C. C. of Atlantic City, Atlantic City, N.J. Medalist—157: Walter J. Travis	142
1902 (July)	Louis N. James d. Eben M. Byers	4 & 2	Glen View Club, Golf, Ill. Medalist—79 (18): Walter J. Travis	157
1903 (Sept.)	Walter J. Travis d. Eben M. Byers	5 & 4	Nassau C.C., Glen Cove, N.Y. All Match Play	140
1904 (Sept.)	H. Chandler Egan d. Fred Herreshoff	8 & 6	Baltusrol G.C., Springfield, N.J. Medalist—242 (54): H. Chandler Egan	142
1905 (Aug.)	H. Chandler Egan d. D. E. Sawyer	6 & 5	Chicago G.C., Wheaton, Ill. Medalist—155 (36): Dr. D. P. Fredericks	146
1906 (July)	Eben M. Byers d. George S. Lyon	2 up	Englewood G.C., Englewood, N.J. Medalist—152: Walter J. Travis	141
1907 (July)	Jerome D. Travers d. Archibald Graham	6 & 5	Euclid Club, Cleveland, Ohio Medalist—146: Walter J. Travis	118
1908 (Sept.)	Jerome D. Travers d. Max H. Behr	8 & 7	Garden City G.C., Garden City, N.Y. Medalist—153: Walter J. Travis	145
1909 (Sept.)	Robert A. Gardner d. H. Chandler Egan	4 & 3	Chicago G.C., Wheaton, Ill. Medalist—151: Charles Evans, Jr.	120
1910 (Sept.)	William C. Fownes, Jr. d. Warren K. Wood	4 & 3	The Country Club, Brookline, Mass. Medalist—152: Fred Herreshoff	217
1911 (Sept.)	Harold H. Hilton d. Fred Herreshoff	1 up, 37 hls.	The Apawamis Club, Rye, N.Y. Medalist—150: Harold H. Hilton	186
1912 (Sept.)	Jerome D. Travers d. Charles Evans, Jr.	7 & 6	Chicago G.C., Wheaton, Ill. Co-Medalists—152: Charles Evans, Jr. Harold H. Hilton	86
1913 (Sept.)	Jerome D. Travers d. John G. Anderson	5 & 4	Garden City G.C., Garden City, N.Y. Medalist—148: Charles Evans, Jr.	149
1914 (Aug.-Sept.)	Francis Ouimet d. Jerome D. Travers	6 & 5	Ekwanok C.C., Manchester, Vt. Co-Medalists—144: R. R. Gorton W. C. Fownes, Jr.	115
1915 (Aug.-Sept.)	Robert A. Gardner d. John G. Anderson	5 & 4	C. C. of Detroit, Grosse Pointe Farms, Mich. Medalist—152: Dudley Mudge	142
1916 (Sept.)	Charles Evans, Jr. d. Robert A. Gardner	4 & 3	Merion Cricket C. (East Course), Ardmore, Pa. Medalist—153: W. C. Fownes, Jr.	160
1917-18 — No Championships: World War I				
1919 (Aug.)	S. Davidson Herron d. Robert T. Jones, Jr.	5 & 4	Oakmont C.C., Pittsburgh, Pa. Co-Medalists—158: S. Davidson Herron J. B. Manion Paul Tewkesbury	150

THE AMATEUR CHAMPIONSHIP – Continued

DATE	WINNER, RUNNER-UP	SCORE	SITE	ENTRY
1920 (Sept.)	Charles Evans, Jr. d. Francis Ouimet	7 & 6	Engineers' C.C., Roslyn, N.Y. Medalist–154: Robert T. Jones, Jr.	235
1921 (Sept.)	Jesse P. Guilford d. Robert A. Gardner	7 & 6	St. Louis C.C., Clayton, Mo. Medalist–144: Francis Ouimet	159
1922 (Sept.)	Jess W. Sweetser d. Charles Evans, Jr.	3 & 2	The Country Club, Brookline, Mass. Medalist–144: Jesse P. Guilford	161
1923 (Sept.	Max R. Marston d. Jess W. Sweetser	1 up, 38 hls.	Flossmoor C.C., Flossmoor, Ill. Co-Medalists–149: Charles Evans, Jr. Robert T. Jones, Jr.	143
1924 (Sept.)	Robert T. Jones, Jr. d. George Von Elm	9 & 8	Merion Cricket C. (East Course), Ardmore, Pa. Medalist–142: D. Clarke Corkran	154
1925 (Aug.-Sept.)	Robert T. Jones, Jr. d. Watts Gunn	8 & 7	Oakmont C.C., Oakmont, Pa. Medalist–145: Roland R. MacKenzie	141
1926 (Sept.)	George Von Elm d. Robert T. Jones, Jr.	2 & 1	Baltusrol G.C., Springfield, N.J. Medalist–143: Robert T. Jones, Jr.	157
1927 (Aug.)	Robert T. Jones, Jr. d. Charles Evans, Jr.	8 & 7	Minikahda Club, Minneapolis, Minn. Medalist–142: Robert T. Jones, Jr.	174
1928 (Sept.)	Robert T. Jones, Jr. d. T. Phillip Perkins	10 & 9	Brae Burn C.C., West Newton, Mass. Medalist–143: George J. Voigt	158
1929 (Sept.)	Harrison R. Johnston d. Dr. O. F. Willing	4 & 3	Del Monte Golf & C.C., Pebble Beach Golf Links, Calif. Co-Medalists–145: Robert T. Jones, Jr. Eugene V. Homans	162
1930 (Sept.)	Robert T. Jones, Jr. d. Eugene V. Homans	8 & 7	Merion Cricket C. (East Course), Ardmore, Pa. Medalist–142: Robert T. Jones, Jr.	175
1931 (Sept.)	Francis Ouimet d. Jack Westland	6 & 5	Beverly C.C., Chicago, Ill. Co-Medalists–148: Arthur Yates Charles H. Seaver John E. Lehman	583
1932 (Sept.)	C. Ross Somerville d. John Goodman	2 & 1	Baltimore C.C., Five Farms Course, Timonium, Md. Medalist–142: John W. Fischer	600
1933 (Sept.)	George T. Dunlap, Jr. d. Max R. Marston	6 & 5	Kenwood C.C., Cincinnati, Ohio Medalist–141: John W. Fischer	601
1934 (Sept.)	W. Lawson Little, Jr. d. David Goldman	8 & 7	The Country Club, Brookline, Mass. All Match Play	758
1935 (Sept.)	W. Lawson Little, Jr. d. Walter Emery	4 & 2	The Country Club, Cleveland, Ohio All Match Play	945
1936 (Sept.)	John W. Fischer d. Jack McLean	1 up, 37 hls.	Garden City G.C., Garden City, N.Y. All Match Play	1,118
1937 (Aug.)	John Goodman d. Raymond E. Billows	2 up	Alderwood C.C., Portland, Ore. Medalist–142: Roger Kelly	619
1938 (Sept.)	William P. Turnesa d. B. Patrick Abbott	8 & 7	Oakmont C.C., Oakmont, Pa. Medalist–146: Gus T. Moreland	871
1939 (Sept.)	Marvin (Bud) Ward d. Raymond E. Billows	7 & 5	North Shore C.C., Glen View, Ill. Medalist–139: Thomas Sheehan	826
1940 (Sept.)	Richard D. Chapman d. W. B. McCullough, Jr.	11 & 9	Winged Foot G.C., Mamaroneck, N.Y. Medalist–140: Richard D. Chapman	755
1941 (Aug.)	Marvin (Bud) Ward d. B. Patrick Abbott	4 & 3	Omaha Field C., Omaha, Neb. Medalist–144: Stewart M. Alexander, Jr.	637

1942-45 – No Championships: World War II

THE AMATEUR CHAMPIONSHIP – Continued

DATE	WINNER, RUNNER-UP	SCORE	SITE	ENTRY
1946 (Sept.)	Stanley E. (Ted) Bishop d. Smiley L. Quick	1 up 37 hls.	Baltusrol G.C., Springfield, N.J. Medalist–†136: Robert H. (Skee) Riegel	899
		All Match Play 1947-63		
1947 (Sept.)	Robert H. (Skee) Riegel d. John W. Dawson	2 & 1	Del Monte Golf & C.C., Pebble Beach Golf Links, Calif.	1,048
1948 (Aug.-Sept.)	William P. Turnesa d. Raymond E. Billows	2 & 1	Memphis C.C., Memphis, Tenn.	1,220
1949 (Aug.-Sept.)	Charles R. Coe d. Rufus King	11 & 10	Oak Hill C.C., Rochester, N.Y.	1,060
1950 (Aug.)	Sam Urzetta d. Frank R. Stranahan	1 up, 39 hls.	Minneapolis G.C., Minneapolis, Minn.	1,025
1951 (Sept.)	Billy Maxwell d. Joseph F. Gagliardi	4 & 3	Saucon Valley C.C., Bethlehem, Pa.	1,416
1952 (Aug.)	Jack Westland d. Al Mengert	3 & 2	Seattle G.C., Seattle, Wash.	1,029
1953 (Sept.)	Gene A. Littler d. Dale Morey	1 up	Oklahoma City G. & C.C., Oklahoma City, Okla.	1,284
1954 (Aug.)	Arnold D. Palmer d. Robert J. Sweeny, Jr.	1 up	C.C. of Detroit, Grosse Pointe Farms, Mich.	1,278
1955 (Sept.)	E. Harvie Ward, Jr. d. William Hyndman, III	9 & 8	C.C. of Virginia (James River Course), Richmond, Va.	1,493
1956 (Sept.)	E. Harvie Ward, Jr. d. Charles Kocsis	5 & 4	Knollwood C., Lake Forest, Ill.	1,600
1957 (Sept.)	Hillman Robbins, Jr. d. Dr. Frank M. Taylor	5 & 4	The Country Club, Brookline, Mass.	1,578
1958 (Sept.)	Charles R. Coe d. Thomas D. Aaron	5 & 4	Olympic C.C., San Francisco, Calif.	1,472
1959 (Sept.)	Jack W. Nicklaus d. Charles R. Coe	1 up	Broadmoor G.C., (East Course), Colorado Springs, Colo.	1,696

†Record qualifying score in Championship proper. Record score in Sectional Qualifying Rounds–131 by William C. Campbell in 1961.

1895
FIRST AMATEUR CHAMPIONSHIP

Held at the Newport Golf Club, Newport, R.I., October 1-3. 32 Entries.

1st Round	2nd Round	3rd Round	Semi-Finals		Final Round
Charles B. Macdonald (Chicago)	Macdonald, 7 and 6				
H. Curtis (Brookline)		Macdonald, 8 and 6			
G. Bement (Essex)	Bement, by default				
Gould Hoyt (Tuxedo)			Macdonald, 5 and 3		
Laurence B. Stoddart (St. Andrews)	Stoddart, 6 and 5				
Q.A. Shaw (Brookline)		Rutherford, 1 up, 19 hls.			
W. Rutherford (Meadowbrook)	Rutherford, by default			Macdonald, 8 and 7	
B.S. de Garmendia (St. Andrews)					
A. Seton, Jr. (Tuxedo)	Seton, 9 and 7				
J. Moorhead (Essex)		Seton, 4 and 3			
C.S. Hanks (Essex)	Hanks, 4 and 3				
S.H. Bennett (Brookline)			Claxton, 8 and 7		Charles B. Macdonald, 12 and 11
W.H. Sands (St. Andrews)	Sands, 4 and 3				
H.G. Trevor (Shinnecock Hills)		Claxton, 4 and 3			
Dr. C. Claxton (Philadelphia)	Claxton, 2 up				
J.L. Breese (Tuxedo)					
F.I. Amory (Brookline)	Amory, 7 and 5				
R.B. Kerr (Lakewood)		Amory, 2 up			
R.J. Clark (Brookline)	Bird, 1 up, 19 hls.				
O.W. Bird (Meadowbrook)			Amory, 2 up		
A.L. Livermore (St. Andrews)	Livermore, 6 and 5				
L.A. Biddle (Philadelphia)		Rogers, 5 and 3			
Dr. E.C. Rushmore (Tuxedo)	Rogers, 3 and 2			Sands, 3 and 2	
A. Rogers (St. Andrews)					
Rev. W.S. Rainsford (St. Andrews)	Rainsford, 5 and 4				
R. Peters (Newport)		Rainsford, 4 and 3			
W. Kent (Tuxedo)	Park, 2 up				
J. Park (St. Andrews)			Sands, 4 and 3		
M.J. Henry (Brookline)	Henry,				
V. Sorchan (Newport)		Sands, 4 and 3			
G.T. Rice (Brookline)	Sands, by default				
Charles E. Sands (St. Andrews)					

1896
SECOND AMATEUR CHAMPIONSHIP

Held at the Shinnecock Hills Golf Club, Southampton, N.Y., July 14-17. 58 Entries.

Qualifying scores	1st Round	2nd Round	Semi-Finals	Final Round	
163	***H.J. Whigham (Onwentsia)**	Whigham, 2 up			
180	L.P. Bayard, Jr. (Baltusrol)		Whigham, 5 and 3		
178	W.B. Cutting, Jr. (Westbrook)	Sweny, 1 up			
176	H.R. Sweny (St. Andrews)			Whigham, 8 and 6	
170	J.A. Tyng (Morris County)	Tyng, 6 and 5			H.J. Whigham, 8 and 7
179	J.R. Chadwick (Richmond County)		Coats, 5 and 3		
173	L. Waterbury (Newport)	Coats, 5 and 3			
168	A.M. Coats (Newport)				
170	H.P. Toler (Baltusrol)	Toler, 2 up			
174	A.L. Livermore (St. Andrews)		Toler, 2 and 1		
179	E.C. Rushmore (Tuxedo)	Trevor, 2 up			
175	H.G. Trevor (Shinnecock)			Thorp, 4 and 3	
178	W.H. Sands (St. Andrews)	Sands, 2 and 1			
178	A.H. Fenn (Palmetto)		Thorp, 3 and 2		
178	Charles B. Macdonald (Chicago)	Thorp, 3 and 2			
174	J.G. Thorp (Cambridge)				

*Medalist.

1897
THIRD AMATEUR CHAMPIONSHIP

Held at the Chicago Golf Club, Wheaton, Ill., September 14-18. 58 Entries.

Qualifying scores	1st Round	2nd Round	Semi-Finals	Final Round	
177	H.J. Whigham (Onwentsia)	Whigham, 4 and 3			
191	J.A. Stillman (Newport)		Whigham, 1 up		
196	H.R. Sweny (Albany)	Coats, 3 and 2			
191	A. M. Coats (Newport)			Whigham, 6 and 5	
178	A.H. Fenn (Palmetto)	Fenn, 5 and 3			H.J. Whigham, 8 and 6
181	Devereux Emmet (Westbrook)		Douglas, 5 and 4		
185	D.R. Forgan (Onwentsia)	Douglas, 4 and 3			
182	Findlay S. Douglas (Fairfield)				
174	***Charles B. Macdonald (Chicago)**	Macdonald, 1 up			
196	John Reid, Jr. (Yale)		Macdonald, 2 up		
197	J.R. Chadwick (Richmond County)	Stewart, 3 and 2			
190	W.G. Stewart (Seabright)			Betts, 1 up	
183	H.M. Harriman (Knollwood)	Harriman, 3 and 1			
186	J.A. Tyng (Morris County)		Betts, 4 and 3		
191	G.S. Willetts (Chicago)	Betts, 1 up, 19 hls.			
185	W. Rossiter Betts (Shinnecock)				

*Medalist.

1898
FOURTH AMATEUR CHAMPIONSHIP

Held at the Morris County Golf Club, Morristown, N.J., September 12-17. 120 Entries.

Qualifying scores	1st Round	2nd Round	3rd Round	Semi-Finals		Final Round
179	Walter J. Travis (Oakland)	Travis,				
184	J.I. Blair (Morris County)	4 and 3	Travis,			
186	J.G. Thorp (Cambridge)	Thorp,	7 and 6			
179	M.R. Wright (Philadelphia)	3 and 2		Travis,		
181	Foxhall P. Keene (Newport)	Keene,		5 and 4		
181	R.E. Griscom (Philadelphia)	5 and 3	Keene,			
181	J.A. Tyng (Morris County)	Tyng,	5 and 4			
185	F.W. Menzies (St. Andrews)	6 and 5			Douglas, 8 and 6	
180	Findlay S. Douglas (Fairfield)	Douglas,				
184	James F. Curtis (Essex County)	6 and 5	Douglas,			
181	A.H. Smith (Huntingdon Valley)	Smith,	4 and 3			
178	R. Crowell (Cleveland)	2 and 1		Douglas,		
189	A. Morten (Westchester)	Morten,		9 and 8		
182	W.B. Cutting, Jr. (Westbrook)	2 and 1	Stillman,			
186	J.A. Stillman (Newport)	Stillman,	4 and 3			
188	E.C. Rushmore (Tuxedo)	6 and 4				Findlay S. Douglas, 5 and 3
178	Charles B. Macdonald (Chicago)	Macdonald,				
183	G.G. Hubbard (Cambridge)	4 and 2	Macdonald,			
188	John Reid, Jr. (St. Andrews)	Reid,	3 and 1			
186	A. De Witt Cochrane (St. Andrews)	2 and 1		Macdonald,		
180	A.M. Coats (Newport)	Coats,		9 and 7		
187	H.K. Toler (Baltusrol)	5 and 4	Coats,			
185	F.H. Bohlen (Philadelphia)	Bohlen,	8 and 7			
187	W.H. Sands (St. Andrews)	2 up				
178	Walter B. Smith (Chicago)	Smith,			Smith, 2 and 1	
175	*J.H. Choate, Jr. (Stockbridge)	8 and 7	Smith,			
185	L.P. Bayard, Jr. (Baltusrol)	Bayard,	1 up			
184	H.M. Billings (Ardsley)	by default		Smith,		
188	G.D. Fowle (Philadelphia)	Fowle,		7 and 6		
186	H.P. Toler (Baltusrol)	1 up, 37 hls.	Fowle,			
187	Jasper Lynch (Lakewood)	Lynch,	1 up, 37 hls.			
187	C.A. Lineaweaver (Philadelphia)	3 and 1				

*Medalist.

1899
FIFTH AMATEUR CHAMPIONSHIP

Held at the Onwentsia Club, Lake Forest, Ill., July 3-8. 112 Entries.

Qualifying scores	1st Round	2nd Round	3rd Round	Semi-Finals		Final Round
170	John Reid, Jr. (St. Andrews)	Reid, Jr., 7 and 6	Reid, Jr., 1 up	Travis, 2 and 1	Douglas, 2 and 1	H.M. Harriman, 3 and 2
181	Sterling Beckwith (Cleveland)					
186	R. Sykes (Overland Park)	Robbins, 1 up				
187	A.M. Robbins (St. Andrews)					
173	Walter J. Travis (Oakland)	Travis, 10 and 9	Travis, 3 and 1			
185	A.H. Smith (Huntingdon Valley)					
180	Jasper Lynch (Lakewood)	Lineaweaver, 1 up, 37 hls.				
179	C.P. Lineaweaver (Philadelphia)					
173	Findlay S. Douglas (Fairfield)	Douglas, 13 and 12	Douglas, 13 and 11	Douglas, 7 and 6		
187	William Waller (Onwentsia)					
176	H.H. Cumming (Swannanoa)	Forgan, 2 and 1				
173	D.R. Forgan (Onwentsia)					
178	G.G. Hubbard (Oakley)	Hubbard, 8 and 6	Hubbard, 5 and 4			
186	Walter E. Egan (Onwentsia)					
175	James A. Tyng (Morris County)	Tyng, 6 and 5				
180	John Stuart (Princeton)					
182	Sheldon Cary (Cleveland)	Thorp, 8 and 7	Thorp, 2 and 1	Macdonald, 3 and 2	Harriman, 6 and 5	
179	J. G. Thorp (Oakley)					
186	Herbert McBride (Cleveland)	Smith, 13 and 12				
174	Walter B. Smith (Onwentsia)					
176	W.M. McCawley (Merion)	Holabird, Jr., 6 and 5	Macdonald, 6 and 4			
179	W. Holabird, Jr. (Glen View)					
185	Stewart Stickney (St. Louis)	Macdonald, 14 and 12				
168	*Charles B. Macdonald (Chicago)					
175	Roderick Terry, Jr. (Ardsley)	Terry, Jr., 2 and 1	Harriman, 2 up	Harriman, 6 and 4		
186	Slason Thompson (Onwentsia)					
174	H.M. Harriman (Meadow Brook)	Harriman, 10 and 8				
187	W.C. Carnegie (Allegheny)					
185	Walter Fairbanks (Overland Park)	Fairbanks, 1 up, 40 hls.	Toler, 2 and 1			
185	James F. Curtis (Essex County)					
186	H.P. Toler (Baltusrol)	Toler, 4 and 3				
187	H.C. Smith (Onwentsia)					

*Medalist.

1900
SIXTH AMATEUR CHAMPIONSHIP

Held at the Garden City Golf Club, Garden City, N.Y., July 2-7. 120 Entries.

Qualifying scores	1st Round	2nd Round	3rd Round	Semi-Finals		Final Round
187	T.S. Beckwith (Cleveland)	Beckwith, 3 and 2	Travis, 8 and 7	Travis, 6 and 5	Travis, 11 and 10	Walter J. Travis, 2 up
175	J.A. Stillman (Newport)					
166	*Walter J. Travis (Garden City)	Travis, 2 and 1				
169	R.C. Watson, Jr. (Westbrook)					
184	J.A. Tyng (Morris County)	Tyng, 8 and 6	Hitchcock, 12 and 11			
183	H.P. Kneeland (Columbia)					
183	C. Hitchcock, Jr. (Pt. Judith)	Hitchcock, 5 and 3				
182	Percy Pyne, 2nd (Princeton)					
186	John Reid, Jr. (St. Andrews)	Reid, 3 and 2	Reid, 3 and 2	Lockwood, 1 up, 40 hls.		
177	C.H. Seeley (Wee Burn)					
184	T.M. Robertson (Yale)	Robertson, 7 and 6				
182	G.G. Hubbard (Harvard)					
180	A.G. Lockwood (Allston)	Lockwood, 4 and 3	Lockwood, 2 and 1			
187	A.L. Norris (Dyker Meadow)					
181	J.H. Brooks (Scranton)	Brooks, 2 and 1				
185	G.B. Tiffany (Powelton)					
184	J. Stuart (Princeton)	Stuart, 7 and 5	Stuart, 6 and 4	Douglas, 9 and 8	Douglas, 4 and 3	
181	A.M. Robbins (St. Andrews)					
185	W.M. McCawley (Merion)	McCawley, 4 and 3				
186	S. Stickney (St. Louis)					
176	Findlay S. Douglas (Fairfield)	Douglas, 5 and 4	Douglas, 10 and 9			
185	R. Brooks (Meadowbrook)					
176	Eben M. Byers (Allegheny County)	Byers, 1 up				
186	Allan Kennaday (Montclair)					
187	Q.A. Shaw (Myopia)	Shaw, 8 and 7	Hollins, 1 up	Harriman, 5 and 3		
187	R.A. Rainey (Cleveland)					
182	H.B. Hollins, Jr. (Westbrook)	Hollins, 2 up				
187	C.T. Richardson (Shinnecock)					
181	J.G. Averell (Rochester)	Averell, 3 and 1	Harriman, 4 and 2			
178	T.C. Jenkins (Baltimore)					
179	H.M. Harriman (Meadowbrook)	Harriman, 3 and 2				
183	L. Livingston (Westbrook)					

*Medalist.

1901
SEVENTH AMATEUR CHAMPIONSHIP

Held at the Country Club of Atlantic City, Atlantic City, N.J., September 9-14, 21.
Final round played September 21 instead of September 14, as scheduled, on account of the death of President William McKinley.
142 Entries.

Qualifying scores	1st Round	2nd Round	3rd Round	Semi-Finals		Final Round
171	Percy R. Pyne, 2nd (Princeton)	Pyne, 5 and 3				
170	Oliver Perin (Watch Hill)		Pyne, 3 and 2			
166	A.M. Reid (St. Andrews)	Reid, 3 and 2				
171	C.M. Hamilton (Baltusrol)			Egan, 1 up		
165	Walter E. Egan (Onwentsia)	Egan, 12 and 10				
170	John M. Ward (Fox Hills)		Egan, 4 and 3			
171	W.C. Fownes, Jr. (Highland)	Fownes, 2 and 1			Egan, 11 and 10	
161	L.P. Myers (Fox Hills)					
168	C.H. Seeley (Wee Burn)	Seeley, 4 and 3				
170	E.A. Darby (Atlantic City)		Seeley, 9 and 8			
172	H.C. Fownes (Highland)	Fownes, 2 up				
168	W.P. Smith (Huntingdon Valley)			Seeley, 2 and 1		
165	William Holabird, Jr. (Glen View)	Holabird, 12 and 10				
170	Allan Kennaday (Montclair)		Lockwood, 4 and 3			
173	A.G. Lockwood (Allston)	Lockwood, 1 up				
172	Dr. L.L. Harban (Columbia)					Walter J. Travis, 5 and 4
172	R.E. Griscom (Merion)	Griscom, 3 and 1				
173	A.D.P. Gallagher (St. David's)		Douglas, 10 and 9			
160	Findlay S. Douglas (Nassau Country)	Douglas, 1 up				
174	G.A. Ormiston (Highland)			Douglas, 4 and 3		
168	J.G. Thorp (Oakley)	Thorp, 1 up				
173	H.R. Johnstone (Chevy-Chase)		Livingston, 3 and 2			
175	L. Livingston, Jr. (Westbrook)	Livingston, 5 and 3			Travis, 1 up, 38 hls.	
171	F.O. Reinhart (Baltusrol)					
166	P.H. Jennings (Mount Anthony)	Jennings, 2 and 1				
172	Dr. D.P. Fredericks (Oil City)		Jennings, 7 and 5			
175	Eben M. Byers (Allegheny Country)	Byers, 7 and 6				
171	A.H. Smith (Huntingdon Valley)			Travis, 2 and 1		
157	***Walter J. Travis (Garden City)**	Travis, 5 and 3				
173	J.E. Porter (Edgewater)		Travis, 7 and 6			
174	Charles B. Macdonald (Chicago)	C.B. Macdonald, 1 up				
175	M.G. Macdonald (Florida Country)					

*Medalist.

1902
EIGHTH AMATEUR CHAMPIONSHIP

Held at the Glen View Club, Golf, Ill., July 15-19. 157 Entries.

Qualifying scores	1st Round	2nd Round	3rd Round	Semi-Finals		Final Round	
79	*W.J. Travis (Garden City)	Travis, 5 and 3	Travis, 7 and 6	Byers, 1 up	Byers, 3 and 2	Byers, 4 and 3	Louis N. James, 4 and 2
89	W.T.G. Bristol (Midlothian)						
86	J.C. Davidson (Columbia)	Davidson, 4 and 2					
91	Hamilton Vose (Milwaukee)						
87	J.A. Holabird (Glen View)	Holabird, 2 and 1	Byers, 1 up				
92	J.B. Rahm (Omaha)						
84	Eben M. Byers (Allegheny)	Byers, 3 and 2					
90	Howard Griffin (East Orange)						
85	W.P. Smith (Huntingdon Valley)	Bull, 2 up	L.L. Harban, 6 and 5	H.C. Egan, 6 and 5			
90	Stephen Bull (Racine)						
88	L.L. Harban (Columbia)	L.L. Harban, 4 and 2					
93	Samuel Chase (Onwentsia)						
87	Walter Fairbanks (Denver)	Daniels, 1 up, 19 hls.	H.C. Egan, 3 and 2				
92	J.C. Daniels (Midlothian)						
82	H. Chandler Egan (Exmoor)	H.C. Egan, 7 and 6					
89	W.B. Kirk (Onwentsia)						
83	Harold Weber (Toledo)	McMillan, 1 up	Pyne, 5 and 3	Leslie, 3 and 2	Fredericks, 1 up, 19 hls.		
89	Thayer McMillan (Detroit)						
87	Percy R. Pyne, 2nd (Princeton)	Pyne, 1 up, 19 hls.					
92	J.O. Hinkley (Midlothian)						
88	G.H. Leslie (Skokie)	Leslie, 6 and 4	Leslie, 3 and 2				
94	O.C. Fuller (Milwaukee)						
86	F.R. Hamlin (Chicago)	Hamlin, 3 and 2					
91	C.B. Fownes (Highland)						
84	D.P. Fredericks (Oil City)	Fredericks, 4 and 3	Fredericks, 5 and 4	Fredericks, 3 and 2			
90	W.H. Bennett (Skokie)						
88	A.G. Lockwood (Allston)	Lockwood, 6 and 4					
92	E.J. Buchan (Racine)						
87	Max Behr (Morris County)	Behr, 2 up	Poole, 2 up				
92	B.F. Cummins (Exmoor)						
80	A. Poole, Jr. (Onwentsia)	Poole, 4 and 2					
89	Charles Zeublin (Midlothian)						
82	P.B. Hoyt (Glen View)	Hoyt, 4 and 3	Hoyt, 1 up	Hoyt, 5 and 3	James, 4 and 2	James, 2 and 1	
89	R.R. Kimball (Omaha)						
87	Chisholm Beach (Cleveland)	Doran, 3 and 2					
92	M. Doran, Jr. (St. Paul)						
88	F.O. Horstman (Chevy Chase)	Tweedie, 4 and 2	Tweedie, 2 and 1				
93	H.J. Tweedie (Belmont)						
85	R.E. Hunter (Midlothian)	Hunter, 3 and 1					
90	W.S. Harban (Columbia)						
86	L.H. Conklin (Princeton)	Conklin, 2 and 1	James, 1 up	James, 6 and 5			
91	W.C. Carnegie (Allegheny)						
88	Maturin Ballou (Apawamis)	James, 6 and 5					
94	Louis N. James (Glen View)						
87	R.W. Keyes (Glen View)	Keyes, 1 up	McKittrick, 5 and 3				
92	W.A. Stickney (St. Louis)						
84	Ralph McKittrick (St. Louis)	McKittrick, 6 and 5					
90	F.D. Frazier (Glen View)						
83	Allen Hibbard (Milwaukee)	Hibbard, 4 and 2	H.C. Smith, 5 and 4	Reinhart, 5 and 3	Reinhart, 1 up		
89	R.E. James (Glen View)						
87	H.C. Smith (Onwentsia)	H.C. Smith, 6 and 4					
92	H.C. Fownes (Highland)						
88	L.T. Boyd (Milwaukee)	Boyd, 2 and 1	Reinhart, 2 and 1				
93	Charles Counselman, Jr. (Midlothian)						
86	F.O. Reinhart (Baltusrol)	Reinhart, 7 and 5					
91	O.D. Thompson (Allegheny)						
84	Walter E. Egan (Lake Geneva)	W.E. Egan, 5 and 3	W.E. Egan, 3 and 2	W.E. Egan, 2 up			
90	A.C. Brown (Springfield, Ill.)						
88	N.F. Moore (Onwentsia)	Moore, 3 and 1					
92	J.G. Thorp (Oakley)						
86	J.R. Maxwell (Des Moines)	Brokaw, 1 up	Ormiston, 2 and 1				
91	G.T. Brokaw (Princeton)						
79	G.A. Ormiston (Highland)	Ormiston, 2 and 1					
89	J.D. Cady (Rock Island)						

*Medalist.

AMATEUR CHAMPIONS

JEROME D. TRAVERS
1907-08-12-13

FRANCIS OUIMET
1914-31
Open Champion 1913

1903
NINTH AMATEUR CHAMPIONSHIP

Held at Nassau Country Club, Glen Cove, L.I., N.Y., September 1-5. 140 Entries. Championship entirely at match play.

UPPER HALF

Final Round: Walter J. Travis defeated Eben M. Byers, 5 and 4

Players						
E.W. Judd (Oil City) O.D. Thompson (Allegheny)	Judd, by default	Cooke, 2 and 1	Weber, 5 and 4	Murphy, 1 up, 19 hls.	Reinhart, 5 and 4	Travis, 5 and 4
G.J. Cooke (Philadelphia) E.A. Downey (Apawamis)	Cooke, 5 and 4					
C.B. Cory (Wollaston) A.B. Lambert (Glen Echo)	Cory, by default	Weber, 2 and 1				
H. Weber (Inverness) H.S. Naylor (Philadelphia Cricket)	Weber, 5 and 3					
P.H. Jennings (St. Andrews) P. O'Connor (Fox Hills)	Jennings, 1 up, 20 hls.	Jennings, 4 and 2	Murphy, 4 and 2			
Jerome D. Travers (Nassau) Dr. S. Carr (Huntingdon Valley)	Travers, 2 and 1					
N. Williamson (N. Brunswick) N.S. Campbell (Agawam Hunt.)	Williamson, 2 and 1	Murphy, 4 and 2				
Paul Murphy (Garden City) W.B. Wheeler (Brooklawn Country)	Murphy, by default					
C. Sawyer (Midland) Grenville Kane (Tuxedo)	Sawyer, 4 and 2	Sawyer, 5 and 4	Reinhart, 5 and 4	Reinhart, 6 and 5		
C.B. Fownes (Highland) R.H. Kennerdell (Oil City)	Fownes, by default					
T.D. Hooper (Nassau) C.H. Nattern (Oil City)	Hooper, 4 and 2	Reinhart, 4 and 2				
F.O. Reinhart (Baltusrol) T.M. Marshall, Jr. (Pittsburgh)	Reinhart, 5 and 3					
J.C. Davidson (Washington) L.H. Conklin (Princeton)	Davidson, 1 up, 19 hls.	Behr, 4 and 3	Behr, 2 up			
Max Behr (Morris County) Devereux Emmet (Garden City)	Behr, 2 and 1					
Chisholm Beach (Point Judith Country) R. Sprott (Brooklawn Country)	Beach, 5 and 3	Beach, 1 up				
D. Chauncey (Dyker Meadow) D.E. Giles (Pittsburgh)	Chauncey, by default					
A.W. Tillinghast (Philadelphia Cricket) W.L. Thompson (Huntingdon Valley)	Tillinghast, 4 and 2	**Tillinghast, 2 and 1**	Travis, 3 and 2	Travis, 5 and 4	Travis, 1 up	
Harold Wilcox (Montclair) J.H. Snowden (Oil City)	Wilcox, by default,					
J. Macy (Morris County) Price Collier (Tuxedo)	Macy, 1 up	Travis, 6 and 4				
Walter J. Travis (Garden City) W.S. Eyster (Allegheny Country)	**Travis, 8 and 7**					
W.L. Hicks (Nassau) A.L. Norris (Dyker Meadow)	Hicks, 3 and 2	Hicks, 4 and 3	Graham, 5 and 4			
W. Bergner (St. David's) W.B. Rhett (Crescent Athletic)	Bergner, 2 and 1					
W.H. Haines (Highland) Dr. A.T. Haight (Glen View)	Haines, 6 and 4	Graham, 7 and 6				
A. Graham (North Jersey Country) Louis N. James (Glen View)	Graham, 4 and 2					
G.T. Brokaw (Deal) J.M. Sellers (Glen View)	Brokaw, 6 and 4	Brokaw, 4 and 3	**Brokaw, 5 and 4**	Brokaw, 3 and 2		
Jasper Lynch (Lakewood) Matthew T. Murray (Englewood)	Lynch, 4 and 3					
Walter E. Egan (Exmoor) **J. M. Rhett** (Crescent Athletic)	**W. Egan, 2 up**	W. Egan, 1 up				
R.D. Bokum, Jr. (Glen View) J.F. Byers (Allegheny Country)	Bokum, 8 and 6					
H.C. Fownes (Highland) M.F. O'Connell (Alpine)	Fownes, 4 and 2	Fownes, 2 and 1	Fownes, 3 and 2			
J.W. Watson (St. David's) S.Y. Ramage (Oil City)	Watson, 6 and 4					
H.R. Townsend (Nassau) H.M. Day (Fairfield)	Townsend, 7 and 6	Talmadge, 2 and 1				
F.C. Talmadge (Hillside) Raymond Russel (Detroit Country)	Talmadge, by default					

LOWER HALF

Players	First Round	Second Round	Third Round	Fourth Round	Quarter-finals	Semi-finals
A. Havemeyer (Seabright) S.J. Graham (Fairfield)	Havemeyer, 2 and 1					
H.F. Whitney (Nassau) **John M. Ward (Fox Hills)**	Whitney, 2 up	Havemeyer, 1 up, 20 hls.				
H. Griffin (E. Orange) W.F. Brown (Philadelphia Cricket)	Griffin, by default					
J. Moller, Jr. (Lakewood) J.E. Porter (Allegheny Country)	Moller, 1 up	Griffin, 2 and 1	Griffin, 1 up, 21 hls.			
Roger D. Lapham (Apawamis) A.I. Sherman (E. Parkway)	Lapham, 1 up, 20 hls.					
P.H.B. Frelinghuysen (Morris County) John Reid, Jr. (St. Andrews)	Frelinghuysen, 1 up	Frelinghuysen, 4 and 3				
W.R. Tuckerman (Stockbridge) W.C. Carnegie (St. Andrews)	Tuckerman, 3 and 2					
Parke Wright (Buffalo Country) J.F. Stier (Fox Hills)	Wright, by default	Tuckerman, 1 up	Tuckerman, 2 and 1	Tuckerman, 6 and 5		
Eben M. Byers (Allegheny Country) G.C. Cassells (Crescent Athletic)	Byers, by default					
J.B.C. Tappin (Nassau) H.L. Downey (Apawamis)	Tappin, by default	Byers, 6 and 5				
R.F. Mundy (Riverside) F.H. Thomas (Morris County)	Mundy, 5 and 3					
L.L. Kellogg, Jr. (Deal) A.G. Lockwood (Allston)	Kellogg, 3 and 1	Kellogg, 5 and 3	Byers, 2 and 1			
A.F. Schwartz (Audubon) R. Carroll (Fairfield)	Schwartz, 1 up					
C.H. Seeley (Wee Burn) E.S. Knapp (Westbrook)	Seeley, 2 up	Seeley, 4 and 3				
Dr. D.P. Fredericks (Oil City) E.S. Armstrong (Deal)	Fredericks, 5 and 4					
H.W. Perrin (Philadelphia Cricket) M. Ballou (Apawamis)	Perrin, 1 up, 19 hls.	Perrin, 1 up	Perrin, 3 and 2	Byers, 5 and 3	Byers, 1 up	
W.J. Evans (Ekwanok) E.H. Brown (Euclid)	Evans, 1 up, 20 hls.					
J.A. Stillman (Garden City) T.D. Thatcher (Englewood)	Stillman, 2 and 1	Stillman, 2 and 1				
J.T. Cady (Rock Island) Frank Turner (Wyoming V.)	Cady, 2 and 1					
C.W. O'Connor (Essex County) Tracy L. Smith (New Brunswick)	Both defaulted	Cady, by default	Cady, 1 up			
F.J.O. Alsop (New Haven Country) M. Graham, Jr. (Apawamis)	Alsop, by default					
H.L. Riker (Oakland) E.A. McFall (Austin)	Riker, 5 and 3	Riker, 2 and 1				
W.S. Harban (Columbia) K.L. Ames (Glen View)	Harban, 5 and 3					
G.F. Willett (Oakley) A.M. Reid (St. Andrews)	Willet, 6 and 5	Willett, 7 and 6	Willett, 1 up	Cady, 5 and 4		
F.C. Jennings (Garden City) F.L. Hawthorne (Storm King)	Jennings, 8 and 7					
Bruce Smith (Onwentsia) Findlay S. Douglas (Nassau)	Smith, 5 and 4	Smith, 4 and 3				
G.A. Ormiston (Highland) R.S. White, 2nd (New Haven)	Ormiston, 3 and 2					
H.B. McFarland (Huntingdon Valley) W.C. Fownes, Jr. (Highland)	McFarland, 3 and 1	Ormiston, 2 up	Smith, 1 up, 19 hls.			
H. Chandler Egan (Exmoor Country) W.P. Smith (Huntingdon Valley)	H.C. Egan, 2 up					
M. McBurney (Stockbridge) H.M. Brittin (Englewood)	McBurney, 3 and 2	H.C. Egan, 5 and 4				
A.C. Williams (Philadelphia C.) W. Waller (Onwentsia)	Williams, 3 and 2					
W.P. Pickett (Crescent Athletic) R. Havemeyer (Seabright)	Pickett, 4 and 3	Williams, 4 and 3	Williams, 4 and 3	Smith, 1 up, 19 hls.	Smith, 4 and 2	Byers, 5 and 4

1904
TENTH AMATEUR CHAMPIONSHIP

Held at the Baltusrol Golf Club, Springfield, N.J., September 6-10. 142 Entries, 133 Starters.

Qualifying scores (54 holes)	1st Round	2nd Round	3rd Round	Semi-Finals		Final Round
263	M. Barnes (New Haven G.C.)	Smith,				
264	W.P. Smith (Huntingdon Valley)	2 and 1	West,			
265	B.P. McKinnie (Normandie Park)	West,	6 and 5			
264	W.T. West (Camden Co.)	3 and 2		West,		
264	R.E. Hansen **(Philadelphia C.C.)**	Graham,		2 and 1		
266	A. Graham (North Jersey C.C.)	1 up	Reid,			
260	A.M. Reid (St. Andrews)	Reid,	2 and 1			
250	W.R. Tuckerman (Chevy Chase)	1 up				
258	Walter E. Egan (Exmoor)	Byers,			Herreshoff, 6 and 5	
258	**Eben M. Byers (Allegheny)**	4 and 3	Herreshoff,			
260	**H.W. Perrin (Philadelphia C.C.)**	Herreshoff,	5 and 4			
257	Fred Herreshoff (Ekwanok)	3 and 2		Herreshoff,		
262	E.S. Knapp (Westbrook)	Ormiston,		4 and 3		
260	G.A. Ormiston (Oakmont)	1 up, 19 hls.	Ormiston,			
257	Pierre Proal (Seabright)	Travis,	3 and 1			
246	Walter J. Travis (Garden City)	6 and 5				
262	Enos Wilder (Morris Co.)	Rhett,				H. Chandler Egan, 8 and 6
262	J.M. Rhett (Crescent Athletic)	1 up	Rhett,			
262	P.H.B. Frelinghuysen (Morris Co.)	Watson,	1 up			
253	R.C. Watson, Jr. (Westbrook)	6 and 5		Fredericks,		
254	D.P. Fredericks (Oil City)	Fredericks,		1 up, 20 hls.		
249	Jerome D. Travers (Nassau)	1 up	Fredericks,			
254	Max Behr (Morris Co.)	Behr,	3 and 2			
257	F.C. Newton (Seattle)	2 up				
256	R. Abbott (Hillside)	Havemeyer,			Egan, 2 and 1	
256	A. Havemeyer (Seabright)	1 up, 19 hls.	Havemeyer,			
256	R.H. Connerly (Austin)	Brokaw,	1 up, 20 hls.			
255	G.T. Brokaw (Garden City)	3 and 2		Egan,		
254	M. McBurney (Stockbridge)	McBurney,		4 and 3		
261	**Thomas M. Sherman (Sadaquada)**	2 up	Egan,			
266	**A.W. Tillinghast (Philadelphia C.C.)**	Egan,	4 and 3			
242	***H. Chandler Egan (Exmoor)**	3 and 1				

*Medalist.

1905
ELEVENTH AMATEUR CHAMPIONSHIP

Held at the Chicago Golf Club, Wheaton, Ill., August 8-12. 146 Entries, 129 Starters.

Qualifying scores	1st Round	2nd Round	3rd Round	Semi-Finals		Final Round
172	**Percy R. Pyne, 2nd (Princeton)**	Pyne, 5 and 4				
173	A.C. Perry (Inverness)		Fownes, 4 and 3			
172	R.B. Martin (Jackson Park)	Fownes, 6 and 4				
162	W.C. Fownes, Jr. (Oakmont)			Fownes, 1 up, 19 hls.		
155	*Dr. D.P. Fredericks (Oil City)	Fredericks, 3 and 1				
169	H.C. Fownes (Oakmont)		Travis, 2 and 1			
171	H. Wilder (Elmhurst)	Travis, 6 and 5			Sawyer, 2 up	
166	Walter J. Travis (Garden City)					
163	D.E. Sawyer (Wheaton)	Sawyer, 7 and 6				
173	G.J. Cooke (Philadelphia C.C.)		Sawyer, 4 and 2			
170	F.R. Martin (Canada)	Martin, 1 up				
160	G.S. Lyon (Canada)			Sawyer, 3 and 2		
174	A.L. White (Ekwanok)	White, 5 and 4				
174	A.B. Lambert (St. Louis)		White, 3 and 2			
174	R.D. Bokum, Jr. (Glen View)	Bokum, 4 and 2				H. Chandler Egan, 6 and 5
171	C.E. Smoot (Exmoor)					
172	O.W. Potter, Jr. (Midlothian)	Potter, 1 up				
168	Thomas M. Sherman (Sadaquada)		Herreshoff, 4 and 2			
173	A.W. Mitchell (Rock Island)	Herreshoff, 3 and 2				
163	Fred Herreshoff (Ekwanok)			Egan, 2 and 1		
167	Dr. S. Carr (Huntingdon Valley)	Carr, 4 and 3				
168	W.I. Howland, Jr. (Skokie)		Egan, 3 and 2			
170	Charles B. Macdonald (Garden City)	Egan, 2 up				
162	H. Chandler Egan (Exmoor)				Egan, 7 and 5	
170	Jerome D. Travers (Nassau)	Byers, 6 and 5				
173	Eben M. Byers (Allegheny)		Byers, 3 and 2			
164	Hugh Campbell (Wheaton)	Campbell, 2 up				
174	H.J. Tweedie (Belmont)			Weber, 3 and 2		
167	R.E. Hunter (Midlothian)	Bend, 2 and 1				
173	H.P. Bend (St. Paul)		Weber, 1 up, 19 hls.			
169	H. Weber (Inverness)	Weber, 1 up, 20 hls.				
166	W.K. Wood (Homewood)					

*Medalist.

1906
TWELFTH AMATEUR CHAMPIONSHIP

Held at the Englewood Golf Club, Englewood, N.J., July 10-14. 141 Entries, 131 Starters.

Qualifying scores	1st Round	2nd Round	3rd Round	Semi-Finals	Final Round
163	Fred Herreshoff (Garden City)	Carr, 3 and 2	Johnston, 4 and 3	Knowles, 2 up	Lyon, 5 and 4
168	Dr. S. Carr (Huntingdon Valley)				
167	H.R. Johnston (Myopia)	Johnston, 5 and 3			
167	D.M. Cole (Tekoa)				
163	W.P. Smith (Huntingdon Valley)	Smith, 3 and 2	Knowles, 2 and 1		
166	Max Behr (Morris County)				
168	Ellis Knowles (Bedford)	Knowles, 4 and 3			
161	Thomas M. Sherman (Wykagyl)				
168	H. Weber (Toledo, Ohio)	Fredericks, 1 up, 19 hls.	Tiffany, 4 and 3	Lyon, 1 up	
162	D.P. Fredericks (Oil City)				
166	S.D. Bowers (Brooklawn)	Tiffany, 3 and 1			
169	G.P. Tiffany (Powelton)				
165	P.W. Wittemore (Brookline)	Egan, 6 and 5	Lyon, 1 up, 20 hls.		
159	H. Chandler Egan (Exmoor)				
165	E.M. Barnes (Englewood)	Lyon, 3 and 1			
161	G.S. Lyon (Toronto)				
166	M. Whitlatch (Montclair)	West, 3 and 2	West, 3 and 2	Byers, 5 and 4	Eben M. Byers, 2 up
169	W.T. West (Philadelphia C.C.)				
167	B.S. Evans (Brae Burn)	Bankard, 3 and 1			
158	E.H. Bankard, Jr. (Baltimore)				
166	J.G. Anderson (Woodland)	Anderson, 3 and 1	Byers, 3 and 2		
168	H. Wilcox (Montclair)				
162	Eben M. Byers (Allegheny)	Byers, 2 and 1			
162	Dwight Partridge (Bedford)				
165	A.M. Reid (St. Andrews)	Travis, 5 and 4	Travis, 5 and 4	Travis, 3 and 2	Byers, 4 and 3
152	*Walter J. Travis (Garden City)				
163	G.T. Brokaw (Garden City)	Brokaw, 3 and 2			
165	M. Olyphant, Jr. (Englewood)				
155	Jerome D. Travers (Nassau)	Travers, 7 and 5	Travers, 4 and 3		
162	Percy R. Pyne, 2nd (Princeton)				
159	C.E. Van Vleck, Jr. (Montclair)	Graham, 3 and 1			
167	Archibald Graham (North Jersey)				

*Medalist.

1907
THIRTEENTH AMATEUR CHAMPIONSHIP

Held at The Euclid Club, Cleveland, Ohio, July 9-13. 118 Entries, 102 Starters.

Qualifying scores, 36 holes.	1st Round	2nd Round	3rd Round	Semi-Finals	Final Round
162	S.G. Stickney (St. Louis Country)	Herreshoff,			
151	Fred Herreshoff (Garden City)	4 and 2	Travers,		
158	W.A. Stickney (St. Louis Country)	Travers,	3 and 2		
153	Jerome D. Travers (Montclair G.C.)	3 and 1		Travers,	
161	C.H. Stanley (Country C., Cleveland)	Behr,		1 up	
162	Max H. Behr (Morris County)	1 up	Wood,		
157	P.W. Whittemore (The Country Club)	Wood,	5 and 4		
161	Warren K. Wood (Homewood)	2 and 1			
162	Eben M. Byers (Allegheny)	Byers,			Travers, 6 and 5
155	Norman Mackbeth, Jr. (Oakmont)	2 up	Byers,		
165	H.W. Fraser (Inverness)	Fraser,	6 and 4		
151	Walter E. Egan (Exmoor)	1 up		Byers,	
158	D.E. Sawyer (Wheaton)	Sawyer,		1 up	
153	H. Chandler Egan (Exmoor)	2 and 1	Sawyer,		
160	F.R. Martin (Hamilton Golf Club)	Martin,	4 and 2		
163	J.K. Bole (Euclid)	1 up			Jerome D. Travers, 6 and 5
159	Harold Weber (Inverness)	Weber,			
159	K.P. Edwards (Midlothian)	2 and 1	West,		
164	E.M. Barnes (Englewood)	West,	1 up, 19 hls.		
147	**W.T. West (Philadelphia C.C.)**	3 and 2		Graham,	
160	G.A. Ormiston (Oakmont)	Childs,		3 and 1	
165	J.H. Childs (Allegheny)	2 up	Graham,		
163	Archibald Graham (No. Jersey Country)	Graham,	2 and 1		
159	John M. Ward (Fox Hills)	2 and 1			Graham, 4 and 3
164	Mason Phelps (Midlothian)	Fownes,			
155	W.C. Fownes, Jr. (Oakmont)	1 up, 19 hls.	Fownes,		
161	O.W. Jones (Inverness)	Reid,	3 and 2		
165	**A.M. Reid (St. Andrews)**	2 and 1		Fownes,	
160	George S. Lyon (Lambton G. & C.C.)	Lyon,		1 up, 20 hls.	
165	H.C. Fownes (Oakmont)	3 and 2	Travis,		
162	Thomas M. Sherman (Sadaquada)	Travis,	3 and 2		
146	***Walter J. Travis** (Garden City)	3 and 2			

*Medalist.

1908
FOURTEENTH AMATEUR CHAMPIONSHIP

Held at the Garden City Golf Club, Garden City, L.I., N.Y., September 14-19. 145 Entries, 132 Starters.

Qualifying scores	1st Round	2nd Round	3rd Round	Semi-Finals	Final Round
175	Mason Phelps (Midlothian)	Edwards,			
164	Kenneth Edwards (Midlothian)	1 up, 21 hls.	Travers,		
162	Jerome D. Travers (Montclair)	Travers,	9 and 8		
171	F.R. Upton, Jr. (Baltusrol)	2 and 1		Travers,	
173	W.C. Fownes, Jr. (Oakmont)	Fownes,		7 and 5	
175	B.T. Allen (Fox Hills)	5 and 4	Fownes,		
170	S.D. Bowers (Brooklawn)	Seckel,	6 and 5		Travers, 2 up
172	A. Seckel (Riverside)	1 up			
177	Thomas M. Sherman (Yahnundasis G.C.)	Sherman,			
177	Howard Gee (Arsdale)	3 and 1	Sherman,		
174	C.E. Van Vleck, Jr. (Montclair)	Van Vleck,	6 and 4		
174	L.A. Hamilton (Englewood)	3 and 2		Travis,	
170	H.B. McFarland (Huntingdon Valley)	Wilder,		8 and 7	
175	H.H. Wilder (Vesper C.C.)	1 up, 19 hls.	Travis,		
172	Chadwick Sawyer (Midland)	Travis,	1 up, 41 hls.		
153	*Walter J. Travis (Garden City)	2 up			Jerome D. Travers, 8 and 7
173	P.W. Whittemore (Brookline)	Herreshoff,			
168	Fred Herreshoff (Ekwanok)	3 and 2	Herreshoff,		
173	W.P. Smith (Philadelphia C.C.)	Smith,	12 and 10		
171	R.C. Watson (Westbrook)	2 up		Herreshoff,	
167	John M. Ward (Westbrook)	Ward,		9 and 8	
165	Findlay S. Douglas (Nassau)	1 up	Byers,		
175	Eben M. Byers (Allegheny)	Byers,	1 up, 40 hls.		
173	Ralph Peters, Jr. (Midland)	6 and 4			
174	Max Behr (Morris County)	Behr,			Behr, 1 up, 37 hls.
177	N.M. Whitney (Audubon G.C.)	2 up	Behr,		
174	H.F. Whitney (Nassau)	Whitney,	3 and 2		
175	S.J. Graham (Fairfield County)	1 up		Behr,	
170	T.M. Claflin (Weston)	Claflin,		2 and 1	
170	T.R. Fuller (Commonwealth)	7 and 6	Claflin,		
177	J.C. Parrish, Jr. (Shinnecock)	Reid,	9 and 8		
169	A.M. Reid (St. Andrews)	2 up			

*Medalist.

1909
FIFTEENTH AMATEUR CHAMPIONSHIP

Held at the Chicago Golf Club, Wheaton, Ill., September 6-11. 120 Entries, 93 Starters.

Qualifying scores	1st Round	2nd Round	3rd Round	Semi-Finals	Final Round	
152	R.E. Hunter (Midlothian)	Hunter, 3 and 2				
165	C. Waldo, Jr. (Brooklawn)		Sawyer, 6 and 4			
154	D.E. Sawyer (Wheaton)	Sawyer, 7 and 6				
164	H.R. Schollenberger (Beverly)			Egan, 1 up, 38 hls.		
163	G.T. Brokaw (Garden City)	Wood, 4 and 3				
158	W.K. Wood (Homewood)		Egan, 6 and 5			
166	C. McArthur (Homewood)	Egan, 7 and 6			Egan, 1 up	
152	H. Chandler Egan (Exmoor)					
161	A. Seckel (Riverside)	Seckel, 4 and 2				
166	B.P. Merriman (Waterbury)		Seckel, 4 and 3			
151	**Thomas M. Sherman (Yahnundasis)**	Sherman, 1 up, 19 hls.				
165	**A.W. Tillinghast (Philadelphia Cricket)**			Evans, 5 and 3		
151	***Charles Evans, Jr. (Edgewater)**	Evans, 4 and 2				
161	W.G. Pfeil (Huntingdon Valley)		Evans, 4 and 3			
161	T.M. Claflin (Wollaston)	Stillwell, 1 up, 20 hls.				
163	A. Stillwell (Midlothian)					Robert A. Gardner, 4 and 3
161	H.P. Bend (Town and Country)	Schatz, 2 up				
162	W.P. Schatz (Wheaton)		Phelps, 10 and 9			
159	A.G. Lockwood (Allston)	Phelps, 2 and 1				
160	M.E. Phelps (Midlothian)			Phelps, 2 and 1		
166	A.L. White (Brae Burn)	Weber, 2 up				
157	H. Weber (Inverness)		Hunter, 1 up			
161	W.B. Langford (Westward Ho)	Hunter, 6 and 4				
165	P. Hunter (Midlothian)				Gardner, 2 up	
156	Fred Herreshoff (Ekwanok)	Travis, 1 up, 19 hls.				
163	Walter J. Travis (Garden City)		Travis, 4 and 3			
164	R. Ainslie (Westward Ho)	Fownes, 2 and 1				
160	W.C. Fownes, Jr. (Oakmont)			Gardner, 2 and 1		
163	**H.R. Johnstone (Myopia)**	Gardner, 1 up				
151	Robert A. Gardner (Hinsdale)		Gardner, 6 and 5			
166	L.H. Reinking (Wheaton)	Reinking, 4 and 2				
166	W.C. Howland, Jr. (Glenview)					

*Medalist

1910
SIXTEENTH AMATEUR CHAMPIONSHIP

Held at The Country Club, Brookline, Mass., September 12-17. 217 Entries, 203 Starters.

Qualifying scores	1st Round	2nd Round	3rd Round	Semi-Finals	Final Round
165	Marshall Whitlach (Apawamis)	Wilder,			
162	H.H. Wilder (Vesper)	4 and 3	Wilder,		
161	W.M. Van Amringe (Commonwealth)	Brown,	4 and 2		
167	R.W. Brown (Meadow Brook)	5 and 3		Fownes,	
155	W.C. Fownes, Jr. (Oakmont)	Fownes,		4 and 3	
164	Ellis Knowles (Pensacola)	2 and 1	Fownes,		
160	A.M. Reid (St. Andrews)	Reid,	6 and 5		Fownes, 1 up
167	R. Wier (Wilmington)	5 and 4			
152	*Fred Herreshoff (Ekwanok)	Herreshoff,			
168	J.F. Shanley, Jr. (Deal)	6 and 4	Herreshoff,		
157	P.W. Whittemore (The Country Club)	Whittemore,	5 and 4		
160	Eben M. Byers (Pittsburgh)	2 and 1		Evans,	
160	Robert E. Hunter (Midlothian)	Evans,		11 and 10	
161	Charles Evans, Jr. (Edgewater)	5 and 4	Evans,		
163	D.E. Sawyer (Wheaton)	Sawyer,	2 and 1		
167	A. Seckel (Riverside)	5 and 4			W.C. Fownes, Jr., 4 and 3
163	S.D. Bowers (Brooklawn)	Wood,			
154	W.K. Wood (Homewood)	5 and 4	Wood,		
163	G.W. White (Oakland)	Gilbert,	3 and 2		
166	P. Gilbert (Brae-Burn)	2 up		Wood,	
158	John G. Anderson (Woodland)	Anderson,		2 up	
167	John M. Ward (Garden City)	1 up	Anderson,		
161	C.G. Waldo, Jr. (Brooklawn)	Travis,	5 and 3		
156	Walter J. Travis (Garden City)	7 and 6			Wood, 2 up
163	Thomas M. Sherman (Yahnundasis)	Weber,			
166	Harold Weber (Inverness)	5 and 4	Weber,		
161	Paul Hunter (Midlothian)	Gorton,	3 and 2		
166	R.R. Gorton (Brae Burn)	6 and 5		Tuckerman,	
162	W.R. Tuckerman (Stockbridge)	Tuckerman,		1 up, 37 hls.	
162	H. Schmidt (Worcester)	3 and 1	Tuckerman,		
164	G.A. Ormiston (Oakmont)	Martin,	1 up, 37 hls.		
164	F.A. Martin (Ekwanok)	3 and 2			

*Medalist.

1911
SEVENTEENTH AMATEUR CHAMPIONSHIP

Held at the Apawamis Club, Rye, N.Y., September 11-16. 186 Entries, 170 Starters.

Qualifying scores	1st Round	2nd Round	3rd Round	Semi-Finals	Final Round	
150	*Harold H. Hilton (Royal Liverpool)	Hilton, 3 and 2	Hilton, 11 and 10	Hilton, 3 and 2	Hilton, 8 and 6	Harold H. Hilton, 1 up, 37 holes
160	S.J. Graham (Greenwich)					
163	H.E. Kenworthy (Providence)	Watson, 2 and 1				
163	R.C. Watson (Westbrook)					
159	George T. Brokaw (Garden City)	Hunter, 2 and 1	Travers, 3 and 1			
153	Paul M. Hunter (Midlothian)					
159	Jerome D. Travers (Upper Montclair)	Travers, 3 and 2				
156	Walter J. Travis (Garden City)					
160	Eben M. Byers (Allegheny)	Inslee, 1 up, 19 hls.	Inslee, 1 up, 37 hls.	Inslee, 1 up		
163	C.W. Inslee (Wykagyl)					
162	F.A. Martin (Ekwanok)	Martin, 3 and 2				
160	R.F. Mundy (Ardsley)					
159	C.J. Sullivan (Baltusrol)	Bowers, 1 up, 19 hls.	Whittemore, 9 and 8			
163	S.D. Bowers (Brooklawn)					
163	A.C. Travis (Englewood)	Whittemore, 3 and 2				
162	P.W. Whittemore (The Country Club)					
161	S.G. Stickney (St. Louis)	Stickney, 1 up, 19 hls.	Herreshoff, 1 up, 37 hls.	Herreshoff, 6 and 5	Herreshoff, 3 and 2	
163	W.E. Shackleford (Atlantic City)					
157	Fred Herreshoff (Ekwanok)	Herreshoff, 5 and 4				
156	W.C. Fownes, Jr. (Oakmont)					
160	W.W. Taylor (Ardsley)	Brown, 3 and 2	Kirkby, 10 and 9			
163	J.D. Brown (Murrayfield)					
160	J.M. Rhett (Crescent A.C.)	Kirkby, 5 and 4				
155	Oswald Kirkby (Englewood)					
152	Robert A. Gardner (Midlothian)	Seckel, 4 and 3	Seckel, 5 and 4	Evans, 2 and 1		
152	Albert Seckel (Riverside)					
159	Thomas M. Sherman (Yahnundasis)	Legg, 5 and 3				
158	Harry G. Legg (Minnekada)					
155	Charles Evans, Jr. (Edgewater)	Evans, 7 and 6	Evans, 1 up, 38 hls.			
161	G. Brown (Great Barrington)					
161	A.F. Kammer (Fox Hills)	Kammer, 4 and 2				
160	Mason Phelps (Midlothian)					

*Medalist.

1912
EIGHTEENTH AMATEUR CHAMPIONSHIP

Held at the Chicago Golf Club, Wheaton, Ill., September 2-7. 86 Entries, 83 Starters.

Qualifying scores						Final Round
160	L.W. Maxwell (Exmoor)	Phelps, 10 and 9	Phelps, 6 and 5	Travers, 2 and 1	Travers, 7 and 5	Jerome D. Travers, 7 and 6
163	Mason Phelps (Midlothian)					
161	Harold Weber (Inverness)	Weber, 3 and 2				
158	Eben M. Byers (Allegheny)					
163	Sherrill Sherman (Yahnundasis)	Travers, 5 and 4	Travers, 2 and 1			
156	Jerome D. Travers (Upper Montclair)					
159	Walter J. Travis (Garden City)	Travis, 3 and 1				
157	Harry G. Legg (Minikahda)					
152	***Harold H. Hilton (Royal Liverpool)**	Waldo, 2 and 1	P. Hunter, 3 and 2	Kerr, 1 up, 37 hls.		
162	Charles G. Waldo, Jr. (Brooklawn)					
155	Paul Hunter (Midlothian)	**P. Hunter, 10 and 8**				
155	W.I. Howland, Jr. (Glenview)					
154	K.P. Edwards (Midlothian)	Kerr, 2 up	Kerr, 1 up			
154	Hamilton K. Kerr (Ekwanok)					
154	Albert Seckel (Riverside)	Seckel, 1 up, 37 hls.				
159	C.W. Inslee (Oneida Community)					
162	Oswald Kirkby (Englewood)	Lee, 4 and 3	Evans, 9 and 8	Evans, 6 and 5	Evans, 4 and 3	
156	H.B. Lee (Detroit)					
152	***Charles Evans, Jr. (Edgewater)**	Evans, 3 and 2				
163	A.W. Tillinghast (Shawnee)					
155	Robert E. Hunter (Midlothian)	**R.E. Hunter, 5 and 4**	Schmidt, 5 and 4			
155	D.E. Sawyer (Wheaton)					
163	K.L Ames (Chicago)	Schmidt, 3 and 2				
164	Heinrich Schmidt (Worcester)					
163	Addison Stillwell (Midlothian)	Smith, 9 and 8	**N.F. Hunter 4 and 3**	Wood, by default		
160	W.P. Smith (Philadelphia)					
158	Robert C. Watson (Westbrook)	**N.F. Hunter, 3 and 2**				
161	Norman F. Hunter (Edinburgh)					
156	H.A. Fleager (Skokie)	Fownes, 3 and 2	Wood, 7 and 6			
163	W.C. Fownes, Jr. (Oakmont)					
162	Warren K. Wood (Homewood)	Wood, 5 and 3				
155	C. B. Devol (Riverside)					

***Co-Medalists.**

1913
NINETEENTH AMATEUR CHAMPIONSHIP

Held at the Garden City Golf Club, Garden City, N.Y., September 1-6. 149 Entries, 141 Starters.

Qualifying scores	1st Round	2nd Round	3rd Round	Semi-Finals	Final Round	
164	John M. Ward (Garden City)	Byers, 3 and 2	**Evans, 1 up, 39 hls.**	Evans, 5 and 4	Anderson, 2 and 1	Jerome D. Travers, 5 and 4
162	Eben M. Byers (Allegheny)					
161	W.C. Fownes. Jr. (Oakmont)	Evans, 3 and 1				
148	***Charles Evans, Jr. (Edgewater)**					
165	Nelson Whitney (Audubon)	Hale, 3 and 2	**Travis, 1 up, 38 hls.**			
165	Fraser Hale (Edgewater)					
165	Hamilton K. Kerr (Ekwanok)	Travis, 6 and 5				
152	Walter J. Travis (Garden City)					
165	B.P. Merriman (Waterbury)	Merriman, 3 and 1	Sherman, 3 and 1	Anderson, 4 and 3		
165	Lee Maxwell (Scarsdale)					
157	**Thomas M. Sherman (Yahnundasis)**	Sherman, 6 and 5				
165	C.J. Sullivan (Baltusrol)					
165	B. Warren Corkran (Baltimore)	Corkran, 3 and 2	Anderson, 4 and 3			
165	H.W. Perrin (Huntingdon Valley)					
164	Samuel J. Graham (Greenwich)	Anderson, 2 and 1				
158	John G. Anderson (Brae Burn)					
155	H.J. Topping (Greenwich)	Reid, 2 up	Reid, 6 and 4	Travers, 3 and 2	Travers, 5 and 4	
162	A.M. Reid (St. Andrews)					
163	C.H. Gardner (Agawam Hunt)	Webb, 6 and 5				
154	Roy D. Webb (Englewood)					
165	Robert C. Watson (Westbrook)	Travers, 4 and 3	Travers, 3 and 2			
165	Jerome D. Travers (Upper Montclair)					
164	C.B. Buxton (Huntingdon Valley)	Ouimet, 4 and 3				
151	Francis Ouimet (Woodland)					
165	A.C. Ulmer (Florida)	**Hunter, 1 up, 23 hls.**	Herreshoff, 7 and 6	Herreshoff, 3 and 1		
162	Paul Hunter (Midlothian)					
156	Robert A. Gardner (Hinsdale)	Herreshoff, 3 and 2				
162	Fred Herreshoff (Ekwanok)					
161	P.W. Whittemore (Brookline)	Whittemore, 4 and 2	Whittemore, 6 and 5			
164	J.M. Rhett (Sleepy Hollow)					
164	Philip Carter (Nassau)	**Martin, 1 up, 19 hls.**				
162	F.A. Martin (Ekwanok)					

*Medalist.

1914
TWENTIETH AMATEUR CHAMPIONSHIP

Held at Ekwanok Country Club, Manchester, Vt., August 31-September 5. 115 Entries, 104 Starters.

Qualifying score	1st Round	2nd Round	3rd Round	Semi-Finals	Final Round
158	Walter J. Travis (Garden City)	Travis, 7 and 6	Travis, 4 and 3	Travis, 1 up, 37 hls.	Travers, 5 and 3
158	R.S. Worthington (Shawnee)				
161	H.K. Kerr (Ekwanok)	Kerr, 4 and 2			
158	Harold Weber (Toledo)				
153	J.G. Anderson (Brae Burn)	Webb, 1 up	Webb, 1 up		
155	Roy D. Webb (Englewood)				
160	Jesse P. Guilford (Intervale)	Guilford, 3 and 1			
147	**Fred Herreshoff (Ekwanok)**				
153	Eben M. Byers (Allegheny)	Byers, 1 up	Travers, 5 and 4	Travers, 6 and 5	
151	Charles Evans, Jr. (Edgewater)				
153	Jerome D. Travers (Upper Montclair)	Travers, 2 and 1			
150	J.B. Schlottman (Detroit)				
159	A.F. Kammer (Fox Hills)	Kammer, 7 and 6	Seeley, 3 and 2		Francis Ouimet, 6 and 5
161	R.W. Brown (Meadow Brook)				
161	W.P. Seeley (Brooklawn)	**Seeley, 1 up 20 hls.**			
161	W.H. Cady (Brae Burn)				
161	J.N. Stearns, 3rd (Princeton)	Stearns, 5 and 4	Gorton, 2 up		
153	Edward P. Allis, 3rd (Milwaukee)				
156	S.K. Stearne (Tatnuck)	Gorton, 1 up			
144	***R.R. Gorton (Brae Burn)**				
158	B. Warren Corkran (Baltimore)	**Lewis, 1 up, 19 hls.**	Fownes, 6 and 5	Fownes, 1 up, 37 hls.	Ouimet, 1 up
154	R.M. Lewis (Ridgefield)				
157	G.W. White (Flushing)	Fownes, 3 and 2			
144	***W.C. Fownes, Jr. (Oakmont)**				
161	Robert A. Gardner (Hinsdale)	Gardner, 4 and 3	Gardner, 4 and 2		
159	Louis Jacoby (Dallas)				
156	E.M. Barnes (Englewood)	Martin, 3 and 2			
162	**Fred Martin (Ekwanok)**				
149	D. Clarke Corkran (Baltimore)	Howland, 1 up	Ouimet, 4 and 3	Ouimet, 9 and 7	
153	W.I. Howland, Jr. (Chicago)				
145	Francis Ouimet (Woodland)	Ouimet, 1 up			
159	Max R. Marston (Baltusrol)				

*Co-Medalists.

1915
TWENTY-FIRST AMATEUR CHAMPIONSHIP

Held at the Country Club of Detroit, Grosse Pointe Farms, Mich., August 28-September 4. 142 Entries, 127 Starters.

Qualifying Score	1st Round	2nd Round	3rd Round	Semi-Finals	Final Round
154	Robert A. Gardner (Hinsdale)	Gardner, 1 up	Gardner, 2 and 1	Gardner, 7 and 6	Gardner, 1 up, 37 holes
164	L.L. Bredin (Country Club, Detroit)				
160	Thomas M. Sherman (Yahnundasis)	T.M. Sherman, 3 and 2			
168	George V. Rotan (Pine Valley)				
156	D.E. Sawyer (Wheaton)	Sawyer, 6 and 5	Sawyer, 6 and 5		
162	Charles Evans, Jr. (Edgewater)				
157	Paul Hunter (Midlothian)	White, 7 and 5			
162	Gardiner W. White (Flushing)				
162	Jerome D. Travers (Upper Montclair)	Travers, 14 and 13	Marston, 2 and 1	Marston, 1 up, 38 hls.	
167	George A. Crump (Pine Valley)				
157	Max R. Marston (Baltusrol)	Marston, 3 and 2			
160	Jesse P. Guilford (Bellevue)				
152	*Dudley Mudge (T. & C., St. Paul)	Kerr, 4 and 2	Lee, 9 and 8		
163	Hamilton K. Kerr (Ekwanok)				
162	Howard B. Lee (Country Club, Detroit)	Lee, 5 and 4			
165	Eben M. Byers (Allegheny)				
159	S. Davidson Herron (Oakmont)	Whitney, 7 and 6	Whitney, 9 and 8	Anderson, 3 and 2	Anderson, 2 and 1
157	Nelson M. Whitney (Audubon)				
163	Robert E. Hunter (Midwick)	Ulmer, 7 and 6			
165	A.C. Ulmer (Florida)				
161	John G. Anderson (Siwanoy)	Anderson, 2 and 1	Anderson, 4 and 3		
163	Reuben B. Bush (Audubon)				
161	J.B. Schlotman (Country Club, Detroit)	Schlotman, 4 and 2			
167	C.H. Gardner (Agawam)				
164	George S. Lyon (Lambton, Canada)	Stearns, 4 and 3	S. Sherman, 1 up, 37 hls.	S. Sherman, 1 up	
168	J.N. Stearns, 3rd (Williamsport)				
165	Albert Seckel (Riverside)	S. Sherman, 3 and 1			
164	Sherrill Sherman (Yahnundasis)				
166	W.C. Fownes, Jr. (Oakmont)	Standish, 1 up, 37 hls.	Standish, 5 and 4		
167	James D. Standish, Jr. (Country Club, Detroit)				
155	Francis Ouimet (Woodland)	Ouimet, 8 and 7			
166	W.H. Gardner, 2nd (Buffalo)				

Champion: Robert A. Gardner, 5 and 4

*Medalist.

1916
TWENTY-SECOND AMATEUR CHAMPIONSHIP

Held at Merion Cricket Club (East Course), Ardmore, Pa., September 4-9. 160 Entries, 157 Starters.

Qualifying score	1st Round	2nd Round	3rd Round	Semi-Finals	Final Round	
165	W.G. Pfeil (Huntingdon Valley)	Marston, 5 and 4	Gardner, 5 and 3	Gardner, 5 and 3	Gardner, 4 and 3	Charles Evans, Jr., 4 and 3
155	Max R. Marston (Baltusrol)					
163	John M. Ward (Garden City)	Gardner, 6 and 5				
160	Robert A. Gardner (Hinsdale)					
163	Robert T. Jones, Jr. (Atlanta)	Jones, 3 and 1	Jones, 4 and 2			
157	Eben M. Byers (Allegheny)					
161	F.W. Dyer (Montclair)	Dyer, 9 and 8				
158	F.R. Blossom (Exmoor)					
158	G.A. Ormiston (Oakmont)	Ormiston, 4 and 3	Guilford, 6 and 5	Guilford, 4 and 3		
166	A.Z. Huntington (Wyoming Valley)					
161	Jesse P. Guilford (Woodland)	Guilford, 10 and 9				
166	C.G. Comstock (Sleepy Hollow)					
165	G.P. Tiffany (Mohawk)	Kirkby, 8 and 6	White, 2 up			
159	Oswald Kirkby (Englewood)					
165	Gardiner W. White (Flushing)	White, 4 and 3				
165	C.E. Van Vleck, Jr. (Baltusrol)					
160	John G. Anderson (Siwanoy)	Anderson, 1 up, 37 hls.	Anderson, 6 and 5	Evans, 9 and 8	Evans, 3 and 2	
162	D.E. Sawyer (Wheaton)					
163	Meredith M. Jack (Merion Cricket)	Hunter, 5 and 3				
165	Robert E. Hunter (Midwick)					
161	H.J. Topping (Greenwich)	Smith, 1 up	Evans, 10 and 9			
159	W.P. Smith (Pine Valley)					
158	Nelson M. Whitney (Audubon)	Evans, 3 and 1				
158	Charles Evans, Jr. (Edgewater)					
162	G.W. Hoffner (Woodbury)	Corkran, 8 and 7	Corkran, 5 and 3	Corkran, 5 and 3		
164	D. Clarke Corkran (Baltimore)					
167	Perry Adair (Atlanta)	Adair, 1 up				
167	L.B. Patton (Homestead)					
165	Roger D. Lapham (San Francisco)	Small, 1 up	Buxton, 2 and 1			
166	George Small (Baltimore)					
161	C.B. Buxton (Huntingdon Valley)	Buxton, 1 up				
153	*W.C. Fownes, Jr. (Oakmont)					

*Medalist.

1919
TWENTY-THIRD AMATEUR CHAMPIONSHIP

Held at Oakmont Country Club, Pittsburgh, Pa., August 16-23. 150 Entries.

Qualifying score	1st Round	2nd Round	3rd Round	Semi-Finals	Final Round	
159	Robert T. Jones, Jr. (Atlanta)	Jones, 3 and 2	Jones, 5 and 4	Jones, 3 and 2	Jones, 5 and 3	S. Davidson Herron, 5 and 4
158	*J.B. Manion (Forest Pk., St. Louis)					
170	Max R. Marston (Baltusrol)	Gardner, 3 and 1				
164	Robert A. Gardner (Onwentsia)					
171	F.C. Newton (Brookline)	Knepper, 4 and 2	Knepper, 2 and 1			
168	R.E. Knepper (Sioux City)					
169	J.B. Crookston (Stanton Heights)	Crookston, 6 and 5				
171	R.C. Long (Stanton Heights)					
163	Gardiner W. White (Nassau)	Hoffner, 7 and 6	Hoffner, 1 up, 37 hls.	Fownes, 2 and 1		
166	George W. Hoffner (Bala)					
171	E. Hoover Bankard (Midlothian)	Peacock, 4 and 2				
166	Grant Peacock (Oakmont)					
165	Jerome D. Travers (Upper Montclair)	Waldo, 8 and 7	Fownes, 6 and 5			
171	C.G. Waldo, Jr. (Detroit)					
170	C.L. Maxwell (Trenton)	Fownes, 3 and 2				
169	W.C. Fownes, Jr. (Oakmont)					
162	Richard Woolworth (Scranton)	Whitney, 5 and 4	Thompson, 7 and 6	Herron, 8 and 7	Herron, 7 and 6	
165	Nelson Whitney (Audubon)					
166	W.J. Thompson (Mississanga)	Thompson, 1 up				
165	Louis Jacoby (Charlotte)					
172	J.N. Stearns (Nassau)	Stearns, 1 up, 37 hls.	Herron, 7 and 5			
165	R.E. Bockenkamp (Forest Pk., St. Louis)					
158	S. Davidson Herron (Oakmont)	Herron, 2 and 1				
168	W.H. Gardner (Buffalo)					
161	John G. Anderson (Siwanoy)	Platt, 4 and 3	Platt, 3 and 1	Platt, 1 up, 38 hls.		
163	J. Wood Platt (North Hills)					
170	J.S. Dean (Atlanta)	Tewkesbury, 5 and 3				
158	*Paul Tewkesbury (Aronimink)					
161	Charles Evans, Jr. (Edgewater)	Evans, 7 and 6	Ouimet, 1 up			
172	Dwight Armstrong (Oakmont)					
165	E.C. Cleary (Bala)	Ouimet, 2 and 1				
166	Francis Ouimet (Woodland)					

*Co-Medalists.

1920
TWENTY-FOURTH AMATEUR CHAMPIONSHIP

Held at the Engineers' Country Club, Roslyn, N.Y., September 6-11. 235 Entries.

Qualifying score	1st Round	2nd Round	3rd Round	Semi-Finals	Final Round	
163	F.C. Newton (Brookline)	Evans, 8 and 7				
160	Charles Evans, Jr. (Edgewater)		Evans, 1 up, 41 hls.			
161	Gardiner W. White (Nassau)	Lewis, 1 up				
162	Reginald M. Lewis (Greenwich)					
161	C.B. Grier (Royal Montreal)	Gardner, 9 and 7		Evans, 7 and 6		
159	Robert A. Gardner (Hinsdale)					
157	W.C. Fownes, Jr. (Oakmont)	Fownes, 4 and 3	Fownes, 2 and 1			
165	Harold Weber (Inverness)					
158	Robert McKee (Grand View)	Allis, 1 up			Evans, 10 and 8	
162	Edward P. Allis (Milwaukee)		Allis, 1 up, 39 hls.			
158	Oswald Kirkby (Englewood)	Kirkby, 4 and 3				
161	D. Clarke Corkran (Baltimore)			Allis, 2 and 1		
163	S. Davidson Herron (Oakmont)	Herron, 1 up, 39 hls.				
158	Peter Harmon (Scottish-American)		Platt, 2 and 1			
164	Maurice Risley (Atlantic City)	Platt, 1 up				
162	J. Wood Platt (North Hills)					Charles Evans, Jr., 7 and 6
159	Francis Ouimet (Woodland)	Ouimet, 3 and 2				
160	R.H. Hickey (Atlanta)		Ouimet, 9 and 7			
164	Meredith M. Jack (Merion)	Jack, 5 and 4				
165	Reuben B. Bush (Audubon)			Ouimet, 5 and 4		
162	Philip Carter (Shinnecock Hills)	Carter, 3 and 1				
159	Max R. Marston (Merion)		Armour, 4 and 3			
162	Thomas D. Armour (Scotland)	Armour, 1 up				
164	George W. Hoffner (Bala)				Ouimet, 6 and 5	
163	F.W. Dyer (Upper Montclair)	Dyer, 9 and 7				
162	J.B. Rose (Allegheny)		Jones, 5 and 4			
160	J. Simpson Dean (Atlanta)	Jones, 5 and 4				
154	*Robert T. Jones, Jr. (Atlanta)			Jones, 5 and 4		
164	Jess W. Sweetser (Siwanoy)	Sweetser, 7 and 6				
159	D.E. Sawyer (Siwanoy)		Wright, 2 and 1			
154	Fred J. Wright, Jr. (Albemarle)	Wright, 7 and 6				
165	Albert Seckel (Riverside)					

***Medalist.**
The 36 hole qualifying rounds were played on the Engineers' Country Club and the North Shore Country Club courses.

1921
TWENTY-FIFTH AMATEUR CHAMPIONSHIP

Held at St. Louis Country Club, Clayton, Mo., September 17-24. 159 Entries, 132 Starters.

Qualifying score	1st Round	2nd Round	3rd Round	Semi-Finals	Final Round	
154	George Von Elm (Salt Lake City)	Guilford, 5 and 4				
151	Jesse P. Guilford (Woodland)		Guilford, 3 and 2			
162	Dewey E. Weber (La Grange)	Weber, 3 and 2				
162	Roger E. Lord (St. Louis)			Guilford, 1 up		
162	Albert Seckel (Chicago)	Johnston, 2 and 1				
152	Harrison R. Johnston (St. Paul)		Johnston, 1 up			
156	Max R. Marston (Merion)	Ouimet, 2 and 1				
144	*Francis Ouimet (Woodland)				Guilford, 5 and 4	
161	R.E. Bockenkamp (St. Louis)	Bockenkamp, 4 and 2				
159	Edward Held (St. Louis)		Evans, 7 and 5			
159	C.L. Dexter, Jr. (Dallas)	Evans, 10 and 9				
158	Charles Evans, Jr. (Edgewater)			Evans, 1 up		
157	Jess W. Sweetser (Siwanoy)	Sweetser, 5 and 4				
162	John G. Anderson (Siwanoy)		Sweetser, 4 and 3			
159	A.P. Boyd (Chattanooga)	Bunning, 9 and 8				
160	L.E. Bunning (Chicago)					Jesse P. Guilford, 7 and 6
161	Lee Steil (Seattle)	Armour, 5 and 4				
155	Thomas D. Armour (Scotland)		Gardner, 4 and 3			
154	Clark Speirs (Seattle)	Gardner, 1 up				
152	Robert A. Gardner (Hinsdale)			Gardner, 4 and 3		
161	J.M. Wells (Wheeling)	Knepper, 4 and 3				
147	R.E. Knepper (Sioux City)		Knepper, 7 and 6			
162	Bon Stein (Seattle)	Stein, 6 and 5				
163	Russell Smith (Portland, Ore.)				Gardner, 6 and 5	
160	J.M. Simpson (Indianapolis)	Manion, 10 and 9				
160	James Manion (St. Louis)		Hunter, 2 and 1			
154	William I. Hunter (England)	Hunter, 7 and 5				
152	E. Hoover Bankard, Jr. (Midlothian)			Hunter, 2 and 1		
151	Robert T. Jones, Jr. (Atlanta)	Jones, 12 and 11				
159	Clarence Wolff (St. Louis)		Jones, 9 and 8			
154	Dr. O.F. Willing (Portland, Ore.)	Willing, 5 and 4				
152	Reginald M. Lewis (Greenwich)					

*Medalist.

1922
TWENTY-SIXTH AMATEUR CHAMPIONSHIP

Held at The Country Club, Brookline, Mass., September 2-9. 161 Entries, 149 Starters.

Qualifying Score	1st Round	2nd Round	3rd Round	Semi-Finals	Final Round
152	Jess W. Sweetser (Siwanoy)	Sweetser,			
162	H.E. Kenworthy (Metacomet)	10 and 9	Sweetser,		
162	William I. Hunter (England)	Hunter,	7 and 6		
159	L.M. Lloyd (Greenwich)	11 and 9		Sweetser,	
144	***Jesse P. Guilford (Woodland)**	Guilford,		4 and 3	
160	Marcus A. Greer (Llanerch)	4 and 3	Guilford,		
160	Reginald M. Lewis (Greenwich)	Lewis,	11 and 9		Sweetser, 8 and 7
161	J.A. Kennedy (Tulsa)	6 and 4			
158	William McPhail (Norfolk, Mass.)	McPhail,			
162	Carleton F. Wells (Barton Hills)	5 and 4	McPhail,		
160	Thomas D. Armour (Westchester-Bilt.)	Johnston,	4 and 3		
156	Harrison R. Johnston (St. Paul)	7 and 5		Jones,	
160	W. Parker Seeley (Brooklawn)	Gardner,		4 and 3	
151	Robert A. Gardner (Hinsdale)	5 and 4	Jones,		
160	James J. Beadle (Llanerch)	Jones,	3 and 2		
145	Robert T. Jones, Jr. (Atlanta)	3 and 1			Jess W. Sweetser, 3 and 2
160	F.A. Godchaux, Jr. (New Orleans)	Godchaux,			
160	R.S. Kampmann (Pine Valley)	9 and 7	Godchaux,		
161	W.W. Patten (Mohawk)	Rotan,	5 and 4		
160	George V. Rotan (Houston)	10 and 9		Evans,	
158	John G. Anderson (Siwanoy)	Evans,		4 and 3	
148	Charles Evans, Jr. (Edgewater)	2 and 1	Evans,		
158	W.C. Fownes, Jr. (Oakmont)	Fownes,	10 and 9		
159	Frank W. Dyer (Upper Montclair)	5 and 4			Evans, 11 and 9
148	Cyril J.H. Tolley (England)	Tolley,			
161	F.C. Newton (The Country Club)	11 and 9	Tolley,		
152	Parker W. Schofield (Albermarle)	Aulbach,	3 and 2		
159	George F. Aulbach (Scarboro)	2 and 1		Knepper,	
157	W.B. Torrance (England)	Knepper,		2 up	
150	Rudolf E. Knepper (Sioux City)	2 up	Knepper,		
155	Francis Ouimet (Woodland)	Ouimet,	4 and 2		
159	Colin C. Aylmer (England)	6 and 4			

***Medalist.**

1923
TWENTY-SEVENTH AMATEUR CHAMPIONSHIP

Held at The Flossmoor Country Club, Flossmoor, Ill., September 15-22. 143 Entries, 121 Starters.

Qualifying Score	1st Round	2nd Round	3rd Round	Semi-Finals	Final Round (36 Holes)	
158	Jesse P. Guilford (Woodland)	Guilford, 1 up				
160	Louis Jacoby (Dallas)		Guilford, 7 and 6			
157	Harold Weber (Toledo)	Cummings, 5 and 4				
157	Dexter Cummings (Onwentsia)			Sweetser, 2 and 1		
151	S. Davidson Herron (Exmoor)	Herron, 5 and 4				
161	Russell Martin (Flossmoor)		Sweetser, 4 and 3			
157	Jess W. Sweetser (Siwanoy)	Sweetser, 10 and 9				
154	Albert Seckel (Riverside)				Sweetser, 8 and 7	
158	Densmore Shute (Guyan)	Shute, 3 and 1				
161	Eddie Held (Algonquin)		Shute, 6 and 5			
158	Arthur B. Sweet (Edgewood)	Allis, 4 and 3				
160	Edward P. Allis (Milwaukee)			Gardner, 6 and 5		
159	T.J. Frainey (Edgewood)	Fownes, 3 and 2				
152	W.C. Fownes, Jr. (Oakmont)		Gardner, 2 and 1			
156	Robert A. Gardner (Onwentsia)	Gardner, 3 and 1				
155	Rudolf E. Knepper (Sioux City)					
157	Max R. Marston (Pine Valley)	Marston, 3 and 2				Max R. Marston, 1 up, 38 holes
159	John M. Simpson (Indianapolis)		Marston, 2 and 1			
161	T.B. Cochran (Wichita Falls)	Jones, 2 and 1				
149	***Robert T. Jones, Jr. (Atlanta)**			Marston, 4 and 3		
156	Joseph M. Wells (East Liverpool)	J.M. Wells, 1 up, 38 hls.				
157	Carlton F. Wells (Barton Hills)		J.M. Wells, 4 and 3			
158	H.K.B. Davis (Mount Tom)	Davis, 7 and 5				
159	George W. Blossom, Jr. (Onwentsia)				Marston, 3 and 2	
153	Francis Ouimet (Woodland)	Ouimet, 2 and 1				
159	Anthony Haines (Rockford)		Ouimet, 3 and 2			
149	***Charles Evans, Jr. (Edgewater)**	Hunter, 2 and 1				
154	William I. Hunter (Rancho)			Ouimet, 2 and 1		
158	James Manion (Midland Valley)	Manion, 3 and 2				
158	Francis R. Blossom (Indian Hill)		Von Elm, 6 and 5			
153	George Von Elm (Salt Lake City)	Von Elm, 8 and 7				
160	Capt. E.F. Carter (Flossmoor)					

*Co-Medalists.

1924
TWENTY-EIGHTH AMATEUR CHAMPIONSHIP

Held at Merion Cricket Club (East Course), Ardmore, Pa., September 20-27. 154 Entries, 147 Starters.

Qualifying score	1st Round	2nd Round	3rd Round	Semi-Finals	Final Round	
156	W.J. Thompson (Canada)	Jones, 6 and 5				
144	Robert T. Jones, Jr. (Atlanta)		Jones, 3 and 2			
142	***D. Clarke Corkran (Huntingdon Valley)**	Corkran, 4 and 2				
156	W.H. Gardner, 2nd (Buffalo)			Jones, 6 and 4		
153	Charles Evans, Jr. (Edgewater)	Knepper, 9 and 7				
158	Rudolf E. Knepper (Sioux City)		Knepper, 4 and 2			
156	Meredith M. Jack (Merion)	Augustus, 5 and 3				
150	Ellsworth Augustus (Cleveland)				Jones, 11 and 10	
149	Francis Ouimet (Woodland)	Ouimet, 2 and 1				
148	William I. Hunter (Rancho)		Ouimet, 4 and 3			
148	Eddie Held (Algonquin)	Held, 3 and 2				
150	Fred J. Wright, Jr. (Flintridge)			Ouimet, 4 and 3		
152	Jesse P. Guilford (Woodland)	Guilford, 8 and 6				
156	Robert T. Wintringer (Steubenville)		Guilford, 5 and 4			
151	Chris. J. Dunphy (Columbia)	Yates, 1 up				
153	Arthur Yates (Oak Hill)					Robert T. Jones, Jr., 9 and 8
157	Karl E. Mosser (Brae Burn)	Cummings, 10 and 8				
148	Dexter Cummings (Onwentsia)		Cummings, 7 and 5			
154	Robert A. Gardner (Hinsdale)	Hope, 1 up				
155	W.L. Hope (England)			Marston, 2 and 1		
156	J. Wood Platt (North Hills)	Platt, 3 and 2				
153	T.A. Torrance (Scotland)		Marston, 7 and 5			
149	Max R. Marston (Pine Valley)	Marston, 3 and 1				
155	Major Charles O. Hezlet (Ireland)				Von Elm, 7 and 6	
155	A.C. Ulmer (Jacksonville)	Watts, 6 and 5				
156	Lawson M. Watts (St. Louis)		Von Elm, 7 and 5			
150	George Von Elm (Rancho)	Von Elm, 1 up, 37 hls.				
153	Roland R. MacKenzie (Columbia)			Von Elm, 7 and 6		
156	H. Chandler Egan (Waverley)	Driggs, 7 and 6				
156	Edward H. Driggs, Jr. (Cherry Valley)		Driggs, 6 and 4			
156	E.E. Lowery (Norfolk)	Paul, 3 and 1				
156	Charles H. Paul (Westchester Hills)					

***Medalist.**

1925
TWENTY-NINTH AMATEUR CHAMPIONSHIP

Held at Oakmont Country Club, Oakmont, Pa., August 31-September 5. 141 Entries, 133 Starters.
[All Matches 36 holes.]

Qualifying score	1st Round	2nd Round	Semi-Finals	Final Round	
158	Jack Mackie, Jr. (Inwood)	Upson, 4 and 3			
156	Lauren Upson (Del Paso)		R.A. Jones, Jr. 2 and 1		
158	R.A. Jones, Jr. (Westchester Hills)	R.A. Jones, Jr. 2 up			
145	***Roland R. MacKenzie (Columbia)**			Gunn, 5 and 3	
158	W.C. Fownes, Jr. (Oakmont)	Sweetser, 5 and 3			
151	Jess W. Sweetser (Siwanoy)		Gunn, 10 and 9		
154	Watts Gunn (Atlanta)	Gunn, 12 and 10			
158	V.L. Bradford, Jr. (Beaver Valley)				Robert T. Jones, Jr., 8 and 7
147	Robert T. Jones, Jr. (Atlanta)	R.T. Jones, Jr., 11 and 10			
155	William M. Reekie (Upper Montclair)		R.T. Jones, Jr. 6 and 5		
157	Fred. W. Knight (Whitemarsh)	Wolff, 2 and 1			
158	Clarence L. Wolff (Sunset Hill)			R.T. Jones, Jr. 7 and 6	
154	George Von Elm (Rancho)	Von Elm, 3 and 2			
155	James S. Manion (Riverview)		Von Elm, 2 and 1		
156	Eddie Held (Algonquin)	Guilford, 7 and 5			
147	Jesse P. Guilford (Woodland)				

***Medalist.**

1926
THIRTIETH AMATEUR CHAMPIONSHIP

Held at Baltusrol Golf Club, Springfield, N.J., September 13-18. 157 Entries, 144 Starters.

Qualifying Score	1st Round (18 Holes)	2nd Round (18 Holes)	3rd Round (36 Holes)	Semi-Finals (36 Holes)	Final Round (36 Holes)
159	George Von Elm (Rancho)	Von Elm, 1 up, 19 hls.	Von Elm, 3 and 2	Von Elm, 8 and 7	Von Elm, 11 and 10
158	Ellsworth H. Augustus (Mayfield)				
160	Max R. Marston (Pine Valley)	McCarthy, 1 up, 22 hls.			
159	Maurice J. McCarthy, Jr. (Old Flatbush)				
163	Watts Gunn (Atlanta)	Gunn, 3 and 2	Gunn, 2 up		
162	Jack Westland (Seattle)				
147	Rudolf E. Knepper (Sioux City)	Knepper, 1 up			
162	Dexter Cummings (Onwentsia)				
159	Keefe Carter (Oklahoma City)	Platt, 4 and 3	Dawson, 2 and 1	Dawson, 2 and 1	
154	J. Wood Platt (Whitemarsh Valley)				
163	M.L. Massingill (Rivercrest, Ft. Worth)	Dawson, 1 up, 19 hls.			
157	**George Dawson (Glen Oak, Chicago)**				
157	Jesse P. Guilford (Woodland)	Guilford, 3 and 2	Held, 4 and 3		
160	**Eugene V. Homans (Englewood)**				
159	D. Clarke Corkran (Huntingdon Valley)	Held, 2 and 1			
163	Eddie Held (Algonquin)				
163	Francis Ouimet (Woodland)	Ouimet, 1 up	Ouimet, 2 and 1	Ouimet, 5 and 3	Jones, 5 and 4
160	Roy M. Moe (Alderwood, Portland, Ore.)				
159	Densmore Shute (Guyan)	Storey, 1 up			
154	Edward F. Storey (England)				
156	**Roland R. MacKenzie (Columbia)**	Stevinson, 2 and 1	Wright, 2 and 1		
163	M.B. Stevinson (Columbia)				
152	Lauren Upson (Englewood)	Wright, 1 up			
160	Fred J. Wright, Jr. (Albermarle)				
160	Charles Evans, Jr. (Edgewater)	Evans, 2 and 1	Evans, 2 and 1	Jones, 3 and 2	
161	**W.C. Fownes, Jr. (Oakmont)**				
159	E.M. Wild (Baltusrol)	Whittemore, 4 and 3			
161	P.W. Whittemore (The Country Club)				
143	***Robert T. Jones, Jr. (Atlanta)**	R.T. Jones, Jr. 1 up	Jones, 5 and 4		
160	R.A. Jones, Jr. (Westchester Hills)				
162	William A. Reekie (Upper Montclair)	Reekie, 1 up			
159	Paul Haviland (Brooklawn)				

Final: George Von Elm, 2 and 1

*Medalist.

1927
THIRTY-FIRST AMATEUR CHAMPIONSHIP

Held at the Minikahda Club, Minneapolis, Minn., August 22-27. 174 Entries, 160 Starters.

Qualifying Score	1st Round (18 Holes)	2nd Round (18 Holes)	3rd Round (36 Holes)	Semi-Finals (36 Holes)	Final Round (36 Holes)	
154	George Von Elm (Rancho)	Von Elm, 3 and 2				
154	**J. McKinlay, Jr. (Beverly, Chicago)**		Legg, 1 up			
156	Rudolf E. Knepper (Onwentsia)	Legg, 3 and 2				
153	Harry G. Legg (Minikahda)			MacKenzie, 1 up		
155	Roland R. MacKenzie (Columbia)	MacKenzie, 1 up, 19 hls.				
155	George Thomas (Illinois Juniors)		MacKenzie, 1 up, 19 hls.			
156	Howard R. Walton (Sunset Ridge)	Martin, 4 and 3			Evans, 1 up, 37 holes	
150	David Martin (Rio Hondo)					
150	Charles Evans, Jr. (Edgewater)	Evans, 2 and 1				
156	Ellsworth H. Augustus (Mayfield)		Evans, 3 and 1			
156	David Ward (Kent C.C., Mich.)	Moser, 1 up				
152	Allen Moser (Wilshire)			Evans, 4 and 3		
156	Eddie Held (Algonquin)	Held, 6 and 5				Robert T. Jones, Jr., 8 and 7
155	Dexter Cummings (Onwentsia)		Held, 3 and 2			
151	Paul Haviland (Brooklawn)	Yates, 1 up				
150	Arthur Yates (Oak Hill, Rochester, N.Y.)					
151	Francis Ouimet (Woodland)	Ouimet, 6 and 5				
153	Billy Sixty (Michiwaukee)		Ouimet, 3 and 2			
154	Densmore Shute (Guyan)	Marston, 4 and 2				
152	Max R. Marston (Pine Valley)			Ouimet, 5 and 3		
148	D. Clarke Corkran (Huntingdon Valley)	Corkran, 1 up				
151	George V. Rotan (Houston)		Finlay, 3 and 2			
154	Dr. O.F. Willing (Waverley)	Finlay, 4 and 3			Jones, 11 and 10	
147	Phillips Finlay (Shinnecock Hills)					
145	Harrison R. Johnston (Minikahda)	Johnston, 4 and 3				
152	R.A. Jones, Jr. (Westchester Hills)		Johnston, 2 and 1			
151	Don Carrick (Canada)	Carrick, 2 and 1				
150	Arthur B. Sweet (Ridgemoor)			Jones, 10 and 9		
142	***Robert T. Jones, Jr. (Atlanta)**	Jones, 2 up				
156	Maurice J. McCarthy, Jr. (Old Flatbush)		Jones, 3 and 2			
148	Eugene V. Homans (Englewood)	Homans, 5 and 4				
156	Frank Dolp (Alderwood)					

***Medalist.**

1928
THIRTY-SECOND AMATEUR CHAMPIONSHIP

Held at the Brae Burn Country Club, West Newton, Mass., September 10-15. 158 Entries, 143 Starters.

Qualifying Score	1st Round (18 Holes)	2nd Round (18 Holes)	3rd Round (36 Holes)	Semi-Finals (36 Holes)	Final Round (36 Holes)	
152	George Von Elm (Tam O'Shanter)	Yates,				
155	Arthur Yates (Oak Hill, Rochester)	3 and 2	Perkins,			
155	Thomas P. Perkins (Great Britain)	Perkins,	2 and 1			
149	Donald Moe (Alderwood, Ore.)	1 up, 22 hls.		Perkins,		
155	Charles Evans, Jr. (Edgewater)	Dawson,		3 and 1		
153	John Dawson (Glen Oak, Chicago)	2 and 1	Dawson,			
154	Fred J. Wright, Jr. (Albermarle)	Wright,	3 and 2			
155	Gordon Taylor (Canada)	3 and 2			Perkins, 6 and 4	
155	Watts Gunn (Atlanta)	Willing,				
155	Dr. O.F. Willing (Waverley, Ore.)	4 and 3	Willing,			
156	Edward F. Storey (Great Britain)	Storey,	6 and 4			
154	Max R. Marston (Pine Valley)	1 up		Voigt,		
155	Jess W. Sweetser (Siwanoy)	Sweetser,		4 and 3		
153	Donald J. Armstrong (Aurora, Ill.)	3 and 2	Voigt,			
157	William F. McPhail (Norfolk, Mass.)	Voigt,	3 and 2			
143	***George J. Voigt (North Hills)**	3 and 2				Robert T. Jones, Jr., 10 and 9
154	Francis Ouimet (Woodland)	Finlay,				
156	Phillips Finlay (Sandy Burr)	2 up	Finlay,			
155	John D. Ames (Glen View)	Ames,	5 and 4			
157	Maurice J. McCarthy, Jr. (Old Flatbush)	3 and 2		Finlay,		
144	Harrison R. Johnston (White Bear Yacht)	Johnston,		2 and 1		
157	T. Suffern Tailer, Jr. (Newport)	2 and 1	Johnston,			
156	George T. Dunlap, Jr. (Maplewood)	Dunlap,	3 and 2			
156	George Dawson (West.-Biltmore)	1 up			Jones, 13 and 12	
154	Frank Dolp (Alderwood, Ore.)	Somerville,				
150	C. Ross Somerville (Canada)	2 and 1	Beck,			
155	John B. Beck (Great Britain)	Beck,	1 up			
156	Rudolf E. Knepper (Onwentsia)	4 and 3		Jones,		
151	Robert T. Jones, Jr. (Atlanta)	Jones,		14 and 13		
152	J.W. Brown (Spring Lake, N.J.)	4 and 3	Jones,			
154	Robert R. Gorton (Brae Burn)	Gorton,	1 up, 19 hls.			
157	C.F. Nettelbladt (Green Hill, Wor.)	1 up				

*Medalist.

1929
THIRTY-THIRD AMATEUR CHAMPIONSHIP

Held at the Del Monte Golf and Country Club, Pebble Beach Golf Links, Calif., September 2-7. 162 Entries, 140 Starters.

Qualifying Score	1st Round (18 Holes)	2nd Round (18 Holes)	3rd Round (36 Holes)	Semi-Finals (36 Holes)	Final Round (36 Holes)	
153	Cyril J.H. Tolley (Great Britain)	Tolley, 7 and 6				
160	Eddie R. Held (Lakeville)		Tolley, 8 and 6			
154	Fay Coleman (California C.C.)	Coleman, 4 and 3				
145	***Eugene V. Homans (Englewood)**			Willing, 4 and 3		
146	Dr. O.F. Willing (Waverley, Ore.)	Willing, 2 and 1				
156	Dan H. Sangster (Potrero)		Willing, 3 and 2			
152	Chas. D. Hunter, Jr. (Tacoma)	Bourn, 1 up, 19 hls.				
157	T.A. Bourn (Great Britain)				Willing, 4 and 3	
157	Jess W. Sweetser (Siwanoy)	Sweetser, 1 up, 19 hls.				
158	Ralph F. Hoffman (Castlewood)		Sweetser, 6 and 4			
148	John E. Lehman (Gary, Ind.)	Lehman, 4 and 3				
158	John J. McHugh (Olympic Club)			Egan, 6 and 5		
157	George Von Elm (Tam O'Shanter)	Egan, 2 and 1				
152	H. Chandler Egan (Rogue Valley)		Egan, 7 and 5			
156	Rudie Wilhelm (Portland, Ore.)	Wilhelm, 1 up, 21 hls.				
155	Lee Pendergrass (Wilshire)					Harrison R. Johnston, 4 and 3
158	George J. Voigt (North Hills)	Voigt, 4 and 2				
158	Vincent Dolp (Alderwood)		Voigt, 2 and 1			
146	**Donald Moe (Alderwood)**	Moe, 3 and 1				
151	Jack Gaines (Girard)			Johnston, 1 up, 39 hls.		
149	Harrison R. Johnston (White Bear)	Johnston, 1 up				
157	John De Paolo (Stockdale)		Johnston, 5 and 3			
148	Roland MacKenzie (Columbia)	MacKenzie, 1 up, 20 hls.				
159	Edward F. Storey (Great Britain)				Johnston, 6 and 5	
154	Francis Ouimet (Woodland)	Ouimet, 4 and 2				
154	David Martin (Rio Hondo)		Ouimet, 4 and 3			
155	Clarence Hubby (Cedar Crest, Texas)	Hubby, 3 and 1				
147	Gibson Dunlap (Riviera)			Ouimet, 1 up		
145	***Robert T. Jones, Jr.** (Atlanta)	Goodman, 1 up				
157	John Goodman (Lakewood, Neb.)		Little, 2 and 1			
155	**W. Lawson Little, Jr. (Presidio)**	Little, 1 up				
157	Phillips Finlay (Redlands)					

*Co-medalists—no playoff.

1930
THIRTY-FOURTH AMATEUR CHAMPIONSHIP

Held at the Merion Cricket Club (East Course), Ardmore, Pa., September 22-27. 175 Entries, 168 Starters.

Qualifying Score	1st Round (18 Holes)	2nd Round (18 Holes)	3rd Round (36 Holes)	Semi-Finals (36 Holes)	Final Round (36 Holes)	
151	W. Lawson Little, Jr. (Presidio)	Little, 1 up, 20 hls.				
145	Dr. O.F. Willing (Waverley, Ore.)		Homans, 4 and 2			
151	Gus Novotny (Edgewood Valley, Ill.)	Homans, 1 up				
152	Eugene V. Homans (Englewood)			Homans, 8 and 7		
152	Chas. A. Reckner (Cedarbrook, Pa.)	Reckner, 3 and 2				
153	J. Wood Platt (Whitemarsh Valley)		Lehman, 6 and 5			
153	John E. Lehman (Olympia Fields)	Lehman, 3 and 1			Homans, 1 up	
148	T. Philip Perkins (Fox Hills, N.Y.)					
154	George J. Voigt (North Hills, N.Y.)	Voigt, 2 and 1				
153	Lester Bolstad (Midland Hills, Minn.)		Seaver, 2 and 1			
155	**Charles H. Seaver (Los Angeles)**	Seaver, 1 up				
154	Donald J. Armstrong (Aurora, Ill.)			Seaver, 5 and 4		
154	William F. McPhail (Norfolk, Mass.)	McPhail, 1 up, 19 hls.				Robert T. Jones, Jr., 8 and 7
147	Sidney W. Noyes, Jr. (Ardsley)		McPhail, 6 and 4			
148	Charles Kocsis (Lochaven, Mich.)	Kocsis, 3 and 2				
149	Francis Ouimet (Woodland)					
143	George Von Elm (Rancho)	Von Elm, 6 and 5				
148	Chas. D. Hunter, Jr. (Springhaven)		McCarthy, 1 up, 28 hls.			
155	Maurice J. McCarthy, Jr. (Green Meadow)	McCarthy, 1 up, 19 hls.				
155	Watts Gunn (Oakmont)			Sweetser, 5 and 4		
155	Jess W. Sweetser (Siwanoy)	Sweetser, 2 and 1				
155	Phillips Finlay (Shinnecock Hills)		Sweetser, 1 up, 19 hls.			
155	Jack A. Ahern (Wanakah)	Ahern, 3 and 1				
147	George T. Dunlap, Jr. (Garden City C.C.)				Jones, 9 and 8	
142	***Robert T. Jones, Jr. (Atlanta)**	Jones, 5 and 4				
155	C. Ross Somerville (Canada)		Jones, 5 and 4			
154	F.G. Hoblitzel (Canada)	Hoblitzel, 3 and 1				
154	Ellis Knowles (Apawamis)			Jones, 6 and 5		
155	Edmund H. Driggs, Jr. (Lakeville)	Coleman, 1 up				
145	Fay Coleman (California C.C.)		Coleman, 3 and 2			
154	John J. McHugh (Olympic Club, Calif.)	McHugh, 1 up				
149	John Goodman (Lakewood, Neb.)					

*Medalist.

1931
THIRTY-FIFTH AMATEUR CHAMPIONSHIP

Held at the Beverly Country Club, Chicago, Ill., August 31-September 5. 583 Entries, 150 Qualifiers, 139 Starters.

Qualifying Score	1st Round (18 Holes)	2nd Round (18 Holes)	3rd Round (36 Holes)	Semi-Finals (36 Holes)	Final Round (36 Holes)	
157	Owen Covey (Salt Lake City)	Covey,				
154	William Duckwall (Bradenton, Fla.)	3 and 2	Howell,			
153	Billy Howell (Hermitage)	Howell,	4 and 2			
156	John Goodman (Omaha Field)	2 and 1		Howell,		
153	Lester Bolstad (Midland Hills, Minn.)	Bolstad,		3 and 2		
154	Chris Brinke (Oakland Hills, Mich.)	3 and 2	Bolstad,			
154	Richard Martin (Briergate)	Martin,	1 up, 19 hls.		Ouimet, 2 and 1	
155	George J. Voigt (Winged Foot)	2 and 1				
154	Paul Jackson (Swope Park)	Jackson,				
148	John E. Lehman (Olympia Fields)	1 up	Jackson,			
154	Fred. J. Wright, Jr. (Albemarle)	Wright,	1 up			
152	Charles C. Clare (Race Brook)	4 and 2		Ouimet,		
152	Francis Ouimet (Woodland)	Ouimet,		7 and 6		
151	John R. Shields (Rainier)	4 and 3	Ouimet,			
155	Frank Connolly (Lake Shore, Mich.)	Connolly,	5 and 4			Francis Ouimet, 6 and 5
149	Gus Moreland (Cedar Crest, Texas)	2 and 1				
157	Carey Bellew, Jr. (Meadow Lake, Mo.)	Bellew,				
155	Ernest F. Carter (Sands Point, N.Y.)	6 and 4	Yates,			
148	*Arthur Yates (Oak Hills, N.Y.)	Yates,	6 and 4			
148	*Charles H. Seaver (Los Angeles)	1 up		Westland,		
156	Jack Westland (Sunset Ridge, Ill.)	Westland,		1 up		
149	Samuel M. Parks, Jr. (Highland, Pa.)	4 and 2	Westland,			
154	George T. Dunlap, Jr. (Garden City C.C.)	Dunlap,	3 and 2		Westland, 3 and 2	
156	Chandler Harper (Princess Anne)	3 and 2				
156	Maurice J. McCarthy, Jr. (Green Meadow)	McCarthy,				
155	Russell Martin (Flossmoor)	1 up	McCarthy,			
156	R. Emmett Spicer, Jr. (Colonial, Tenn.)	Spicer,	5 and 3			
157	J. Wolcott Brown (Spring Lake)	4 and 3		McCarthy,		
154	C. Ross Somerville (Canada)	Somerville,		6 and 5		
153	Eugene V. Homans (Englewood)	2 and 1	Coleman,			
157	Fay Coleman (California G.C.)	Coleman,	4 and 3			
157	D. Miller (G. & C.C., Des Moines)	3 and 2				

*Co-medalists—No playoff—Prize to each.

1932
THIRTY-SIXTH AMATEUR CHAMPIONSHIP

Held at the Baltimore Country Club, Five Farms Course, Timonium, Md., September 12-17. 600 Entries, 158 Qualifiers, 154 Starters.

Qualifying Score	1st Round (18 Holes)	2nd Round (18 Holes)	3rd Round (36 Holes)	Semi-Finals (36 Holes)	Final Round (36 Holes)	
150	Gene Vinson (Northwood, Miss.)	Warner, 4 and 3	Evans, 5 and 4	Guilford, 5 and 4	Somerville, 7 and 6	C. Ross Somerville, 2 and 1
151	Milton P. Warner (New Haven)					
145	Perry E. Hall (Gulph Mills)	Evans, 2 up				
149	Charles Evans, Jr. (Edgewater)					
148	Edwin A. McClure (Shreveport)	Chapin, 1 up, 19 hls.	Guilford, 4 and 3			
147	W.C. Chapin (Oak Hill, N.Y.)					
149	Eddie Held (Algonquin)	Guilford, 2 and 1				
151	Jesse P. Guilford (Woodland)					
152	John F. Brawner (Columbia)	Somerville, 5 and 3	Somerville, 3 and 2	Somerville, 6 and 5		
150	C. Ross Somerville (London, Canada)					
146	Jack Westland (Sunset Ridge)	Westland, 7 and 6				
150	John E. Lehman (Olympia Fields)					
149	W.O. Blaney (Brae Burn)	Blaney, 2 and 1	Blaney, 1 up, 22 hls.			
148	Francis I. Brown (Oahu)					
148	R.E. Spicer, Jr. (Colonial, Tenn.)	Moreland, 4 and 3				
149	Gus Moreland (Dallas)					
150	**W. Lawson Little, Jr. (Presidio)**	Fischer, 4 and 2	Fischer, 4 and 3	Ouimet, 1 up	Goodman, 4 and 2	
142*	Johnny Fischer (Highland, Ky.)					
150	Robert M. Grant (Wethersfield)	Grant, 7 and 6				
145	Wilfred Crossley (Norfolk, Mass.)					
150	Sidney W. Noyes, Jr. (Ardsley)	Noyes, 1 up	Ouimet, 1 up			
149	Chris Brinke (Aronimink)					
151	Francis Ouimet (Woodland)	Ouimet, 6 and 5				
148	**George J. Voigt (Winged Foot)**					
150	Maurice J. McCarthy, Jr. (Green Meadow)	McCarthy, 6 and 4	McCarthy, 2 and 1	Goodman, 1 up		
149	John E. Parker (Essex County)					
151	Eric A. McRuvie (Scotland)	Yates, 3 and 2				
149	Charles Yates (Atlanta)					
144	John Goodman (Omaha Field)	Goodman, 3 and 2	Goodman, 2 and 1			
150	**H. Chandler Egan (Monterey Peninsula)**					
147	Charles H. Seaver (Los Angeles)	Seaver, 6 and 4				
151	James M. Robbins (Merion)					

*Medalist.

1933
THIRTY-SEVENTH AMATEUR CHAMPIONSHIP

Held at the Kenwood Country Club, Cincinnati, Ohio, September 11-16. 601 Entries, 160 Qualifiers, 154 Starters.

Qualifying Score	1st Round (18 Holes)	2nd Round (18 Holes)	3rd Round (36 Holes)	Semi-Finals (36 Holes)	Final Round (36 Holes)	
150	Nicol Thompson, Jr. (Toronto, Can.)	Noyes,				
149	Sidney W. Noyes, Jr. (Ardsley)	3 and 1	Noyes,			
148	Eugene V. Homans (Englewood)	Fischer,	1 up			
141*	Johnny Fischer (Highland, Ky.)	3 and 2		Marston,		
150	Will Gunn, Jr. (Springhaven)	Turnesa,		1 up, 38 hls.		
148	Willie Turnesa (Fairview, N.Y.)	2 up	Marston,			
150	Max R. Marston (Gulph Mills)	Marston,	4 and 3		Marston, 6 and 5	
149	Craigie Krayenbuhl (Louisville)	6 and 4				
148	Charles R. Yates (Atlanta)	Yates,				
149	Charles H. Seaver (Los Angeles)	3 and 2	Westland,			
147	Ben H. Cowdrey (Happy Hollow, Neb.)	Westland,	3 and 2			
147	Jack Westland (Sunset Ridge)	1 up		Munger,		
150	H. Chandler Egan (Cypress Point)	Egan,		3 and 1		
145	John Goodman (Omaha Field)	2 up	Munger,			
145	Frank J. English (Cherry Hills, Colo.)	Munger,	5 and 4			George T. Dunlap, Jr., 6 and 5
148	Jack Munger (Brook Hollow)	4 and 3				
146	Ernest F. Caldwell (Hillendale, Md.)	Caldwell,				
149	Hunter Hicks (Skokie)	2 and 1	Somerville,			
150	Charles Evans, Jr. (Edgewater)	Somerville,	1 up, 20 hls.			
143	C. Ross Somerville (London, Can.)	1 up, 21 hls.		Little,		
147	Denmar Miller (Des Moines)	Little,		2 and 1		
149	W. Lawson Little, Jr. (Presidio)	4 and 3	Little,			
150	Maurice J. McCarthy, Jr. (Mayfield)	McCarthy,	2 and 1			
142	Pat Sawyer (Golden Valley)	2 and 1			Dunlap, 4 and 3	
150	Eddie Held (Forsgate)	Held,				
148	F. Paul Anderson, Jr. (Canoe Brook)	2 and 1	Held,			
146	William O. Blaney (Brae Burn)	Blaney,	1 up			
144	William R. Long, Jr. (Austin, Texas)	1 up		Dunlap,		
144	Gus Moreland (Dallas)	Moreland,		6 and 5		
144	Jim Milward (Nakoma, Wis.)	4 and 3	Dunlap,			
150	George T. Dunlap, Jr. (Pomonok)	Dunlap,	4 and 3			
149	W.B. McCullough, Jr. (Huntingdon Valley)	6 and 5				

*Medalist.

AMATEUR CHAMPIONS

LAWSON LITTLE
1934-35
Open Champion 1940

CHARLES EVANS, JR.
1916-20
Open Champion 1916

UPPER

1934
THIRTY-EIGHTH AMATEUR CHAMPIONSHIP

Held at The Country Club, Brookline, Mass., September 10-15. 758 Entries, 185 Starters.

FINAL ROUND (36 Holes)—W. Lawson Little, Jr., defeated David Goldman, 8 and 7

FIRST QUARTER

1st Round (18 Holes)	2nd Round (18 Holes)	3rd Round (18 Holes)	4th Round (18 Holes)	5th Round (18 Holes)	6th Round (18 Holes)	
Knox M. Young, Jr., Highland, Pa.	Young, 1 up					
Max R. Marston, Gulph Mills, Pa.		Haas, 2 up				
Billy Sixty, North Hills, Wis.	Haas, 1 up, 20 hls.					
Fred Haas, Jr., Colonial, La.			Haas, 4 and 2			
Verne Stewart, Stanford, Calif.	Wright, 4 and 3					
Frederick J. Wright, Jr., Trapelo, Mass.		Carr, 2 and 1				
BYE—Christopher A. Carr, Wanakah, N.Y.	Carr			Haas, 5 and 3		
Charles A. Reckner, Cedarbrook, Pa.	Reckner, 1 up					
Sayre MacLeod, Jr., Morris County, N.J.		Reckner, 6 and 5				
BYE—Spencer S. Overton, Hillendale, Md.	Overton		Reckner, 3 and 2			
Robert A. Lester, Baltusrol, N.J.	Lester, 6 and 4					
Douglas B. Lewis, Burlingame, Calif.		Hamman, 1 up			Goldman, 2 and 1	
BYE—Leland Hamman, Paris, Texas	Hamman					
Harry Root, Jr., Palma Ceia, Fla.	Tryon, 5 and 4					
Howard Tryon, Elmira, N.Y.		Goldman, 4 and 3				
BYE—David Goldman, Dallas, Texas	Goldman		Goldman, 2 and 1			
BYE—F.D. Ross, Hartford, Conn.	Ross	Riegel, 2 and 1				
Robert F. Riegel, Hermitage, Va.	Riegel, 5 and 3					
E.J. Busiere, Thorny Lea, Mass.				Goldman, 6 and 4		
BYE—John Goodman, Omaha Field, Neb.	Goodman					
BYE—Bobby Jacobson, Hollywood, N.J.	Jacobson	Jacobson, 1 up, 19 hls.	Jacobson, 1 up			
Charles Whitehead, Forsgate, N.J.	Ahern, 1 up					
Jack A. Ahern, Wanakah, N.Y.		Ahern, 4 and 3				
BYE—Francis Allan, Fox Hill, Pa.	Allan					Goldman, 2 and 1
BYE—T.A. Torrance, Scotland	Torrance	Torrance, 2 up				
Francis Brown, Waialae, Hawaii	P. Little, by default					
Philip Little, III, Woodhill, Minn.			Torrance, 4 and 3			
Brown Cannon, Lakewood, Colo.	Lehman, 2 and 1					
John E. Lehman, Olympia Fields, Ill.		Lehman, 5 and 3				
BYE—Thomas R. Hulme, Merion, Pa.	Hulme			Torrance, 2 and 1		
BYE—Jack Westland, Sunset Ridge, Ill.	Westland	Westland, 2 and 1				
BYE—Charles W. Kent, C.C. of Virginia	Kent		French, 7 and 5			
David Davis, California C.C.	Blaney, 2 and 1					
W.O. Blaney, Brae Burn, Mass.		French, 6 and 5				
BYE—J.E. French, Jr., San Francisco, Calif.	French				Driggs, 2 up	
BYE—Edmund H. Driggs, Jr., Cherry Valley, N.Y.	Driggs	Driggs, 4 and 3				
BYE—Robert Fahy, Wilshire, Calif.	Fahy		Driggs, 2 and 1			
Richard W. Ashley, Kenosha, Wis.	Cameron, 5 and 4					
J.C. Cameron, Canada		Cameron, 2 and 1				
Kenneth W. Wolcott, Trenton, N.J.	Wolcott, 2 and 1			Driggs, 7 and 6		
Nelson J. Ruddy, Maketewah, Ohio						
BYE—David Whiteside, C.C. of New Bedford, Mass.	Whiteside	Myers, 2 and 1				
BYE—Claude F. Myers, Jr., Mission Hills, Mo.	Myers		Nies, 6 and 5			
BYE—J.H. Nies, United Shoe, Mass.	**Nies**	Nies, 2 and 1				
Maurice Hankinson, Twin Hills, Okla.	Parker, 4 and 2					
John E. Parker, Jr., Essex County, N.J.						

HALF

SECOND QUARTER

	6th Round (18 Holes)	5th Round (18 Holes)	4th Round (18 Holes)	3rd Round (18 Holes)	2nd Round (18 Holes)	1st Round (18 Holes)
					Ford	BYE—Frank C. Ford, Charleston, S.C.
				Ford, 4 and 3	Dettweiler, 1 up, 21 hls.	John P. Burke, Wanumetonomy, R.I.
			Pieper, 7 and 6			W.E. Dettweiler, Jr., Congressional, Md.
					Meany, 5 and 4	William S. Meany, Jr., Tamarack, N.Y.
				Pieper, 3 and 2		Dan Dunlap, Milburn, Mo.
		Day, 1 up, 19 hls.			Pieper, 4 and 3	Ernest Pieper, Jr., San Jose, Calif.
						Charles H. Mayo, Jr., Lido, N.Y.
				Marks, 1 up	Marks, 3 and 1	W.F. Marks, Oakmont, Pa.
						James Watts, Oakwood, Va.
					Guilford, 5 and 4	**Gordon B. Taylor, Canada**
			Campbell, 1 up			**Jesse P. Guilford, Woodland, Mass.**
				Campbell, 5 and 4	Campbell	BYE—Albert Campbell, Earlington, Wash.
	Smith, 1 up 20 hls.				Hall, 4 and 2	Perry E. Hall, Gulph Mills, Pa.
						Tommy Wright, Cherokee, Tenn.
				R. Martin, 3 and 2	Grant, 4 and 3	Joseph Gagliardi, Winged Foot, N.Y.
						Robert M. Grant, Goodwin Park, Conn.
					R. Martin, 2 up	Russell W. Martin, Flossmoor, Ill.
			R. Martin, 6 and 5			Jack Mackie, Jr., Inwood, N.Y.
				Williams, 1 up	Williams	BYE—S.A. Williams, Jr., Evanston, Ill.
		Smith, 1 up, 19 hls.			Held, 3 and 1	John Jaeger, Sleepy Hollow, Ohio
						Eddie Held, Fox Hills, N.Y.
				Hoerner, 5 and 3	Hoerner, by default	Rex Hartley, Scotland
						Jack Hoerner, Stanford, Calif.
					Lardner, 1 up	John W. Grange, Merion, Pa.
						Lynford Lardner, Jr., Blue Mound, Wis.
			Hoerner, 4 and 3		Hogan	BYE—Eddie Hogan, Multnomah, Ore.
Smith, 1 up, 23 holes				Hogan, 2 and 1	Beckman	BYE—Woods Beckman, Pasadena, Fla.
					Foley	BYE—John W. Foley, Jr., Grosse Ile, Mich.
				Somerville, 2 and 1	Somerville, 2 and 1	E.P. Kirouac, Walpole, Mass.
			Somerville, 1 up			C. Ross Somerville, Canada
					McPhail	BYE—Don McPhail, Baltimore, Md.
		R. Martin, 4 and 2		Noyes, 2 up	Noyes	BYE—Sidney W. Noyes, Jr., Ardsley, N.Y.
					Howell, 2 up	William R. Howell, Hermitage, Va.
						Harry M. Eichelberger, Los Angeles, Calif.
				Smith, 1 up, 19 hls.	Smith, 1 up	Gus Fetz, Lawrence Grove, Ill.
						Reynolds Smith, Lakewood, Texas
			Smith, 1 up, 20 hls.		Knepper	BYE—Rudolf E. Knepper, Garden City Golf, N.Y.
				Caldwell, 2 and 1	Caldwell	BYE—Ernest L. Caldwell, Hillendale, Md.
	Pieper, 1 up				Jones, 1 up	Francis Ouimet, Woodland, Mass.
				Mitchell, 4 and 3		Bobby Jones, Bloomfield Hills, Mich.
					Mitchell	BYE—C. Bavard Mitchell, II, Pine Valley, N.J.
			Mitchell, 1 up		Harper, 1 up, 19 hls.	Chandler Harper, Princess Anne, Va.
				Street, 1 up		Dom Soccoli, Goodwin Park, Conn.
		Pieper, 5 and 4			Street, 4 and 2	Thad Street, Jr., Charleston, S.C.
						Joseph W. Oliver, Fox Chapel, Pa.
					Day	BYE—Winfield S. Day, Jr., Elmhurst, Ill.
				Day, 1 up, 19 hls.	Goodwin	BYE—Tommy Goodwin, Bonnie Briar, N.Y.
			Day, 4 and 3	Dexter, 3 and 2	Dexter, 5 and 4	Charles L. Dexter, Brook Hollow, Texas
						George R. Ravner, Jr., Niagara Falls, N.Y.
					Moore	BYE—Charles Moore, New Orleans, La.

SEMI-FINAL ROUND—David Goldman defeated Reynolds Smith, 4 and 2.

THIRD QUARTER

1st Round (18 Holes)	2nd Round (18 Holes)	3rd Round (18 Holes)	4th Round (18 Holes)	5th Round (18 Holes)	6th Round (18 Holes)	
BYE–Al Andereggen, Lincoln Park, Ill.	Andereggen	Andereggen, 1 up, 21 hls.				
BYE–Johnny Fischer, Highland, Ky.	Fischer		Stuart, 1 up, 19 hls.			
BYE–Dwight L. Armstrong, Lancaster, Pa.	D.L. Armstrong	Stuart, 6 and 4				
BYE–Mark J. Stuart, Fox Hills, N.Y.	Stuart			Stuart, 5 and 3		
BYE–Phil Farley, Canada	Farley	McCarthy, 4 and 3				
Maurice J. McCarthy, Jr., Mayfield, Ohio S.A. Clark, Jr., Ridgewood, N.J.	McCarthy, 1 up		McCarthy, 1 up			
BYE–Watts Gunn, Ardlsey, N.Y.	Gunn	Wilson, 6 and 5				
Dick Wilson, Gedney Farm, N.Y. W.B. Torrance, Scotland	Wilson, by default				Evans, 4 and 3	
BYE–T.L. Bright, Niagara Falls, N.Y.	Bright	Clare, 3 and 2				
Sam Perry, Birmingham, Ala. Charles C. Clare, Race Brook, Conn.	Clare, 1 up, 20 hls.		Flinn, 1 up			
BYE–George H. Flinn, Jr., Oakmont, Pa.	Flinn	Flinn, 3 and 2				
BYE–Charles Wallace, Manakiki, Ohio	Wallace			Evans, 2 up		
BYE–Ed Kingsley, Salt Lake City, Utah	Kingsley	Egan, 6 and 4				
H. Chandler Egan, Cypress Point, Calif. J. Wolcott Brown, Manasquan River, N.J.	Egan, 3 and 1		Evans, 2 and 1			
Crawford Rainwater, Atlanta A.C., Ga. Charles Evans, Jr., Edgewater, Ill.	Evans, 3 and 2	Evans, 2 and 1				
BYE–Pat Sawyer, Golden Valley, Minn.	Sawyer					Armstrong, 4 and 3
Harrison R. Johnston, Minikahda, Minn. E.S. Stimpson, Brae Burn, Mass.	Stimpson, by default	Stimpson, 2 and 1				
BYE–John S. Boyd, Portland, Me.	Boyd		Stimpson, 3 and 2			
BYE–Jack Munger, Brook Hollow, Texas	Munger	Hines, 2 up				
J. Davis Ewell, Jr., Hermitage, Va. John E. Hines, Timber Point, N.Y.	Hines, 2 and 1			Combs, 1 up		
BYE–Harold S. Cross, Jr., Huntingdon Valley, Pa.	Cross	Combs, 2 up				
Charles Becka, Calumet, Ill. Ernest F. Combs, Virginia, Calif.	Combs, 5 and 3		Combs, 2 up			
Allan V. Ellis, The Country Club, Mass. John Wagner, Kildeer, Ill.	Wagner, 1 up, 20 hls.	Wagner, 2 up				
BYE–Bobby Servis, Miami Valley, Ohio	Servis				Armstrong, 4 and 3	
BYE–T. Suffern Tailer, Jr., Newport, R.I.	Tailer	Wehrle, 1 up				
BYE–Wilford Wehrle, Racine, Wis.	Wehrle		Armstrong, 4 and 3			
Paul Jackson, Oklahoma City, Okla. Don Armstrong, Aurora, Ill.	Don Armstrong, 2 and 1	Don Armstrong, 4 and 3				
Burt Shurly, Grosse Ile, Mich. Andrew H. Kaye, Old York Road, Pa.	Kaye, 1 up, 19 hls.			Armstrong, 3 and 1		
BYE–Frank J. English, Cherry Hills, Colo.	English	English, 5 and 3				
Hal Chase, II, Wakonda, Iowa S. Davidson Herron, Oakmont, Pa.	Herron, 2 and 1		Bliss, 2 up			
M.B. Kaesche, Ridgewood, N.J. Rodney Bliss, Jr., Happy Hollow, Neb.	Bliss, 4 and 3	Bliss, 2 and 1				
BYE–Gene Vinson, Manor Club, Md.	Vinson					

CHAMPIONSHIP HALF

FOURTH QUARTER

Championship Half	6th Round (18 Holes)	5th Round (18 Holes)	4th Round (18 Holes)	3rd Round (18 Holes)	2nd Round (18 Holes)	1st Round (18 Holes)
Little, 3 and 2	Turnesa, 5 and 3	Turnesa, 4 and 2	Turnesa, 3 and 2	Turnesa, 7 and 6	Turnesa	BYE—Willie Turnesa, Fairview, N.Y.
					Taylor	BYE—Jack Taylor, Jr., Palma Ceia, Fla.
				Dunlap, 1 up	Dunlap	BYE—George T. Dunlap, Jr., Pomonok, N.Y.
					McCullough	BYE—W.B. McCullough, Jr., Huntingdon Valley, Pa.
			Nash, 1 up	Kocsis, 1 up	Conliff, 3 and 1	Bob Conliff, Jr., Oklahoma City, Okla. J.W. Hughes, Omaha Field, Neb.
					Kocsis	BYE—Charles Kocsis, Western, Mich.
				Nash, 2 and 1	Nash	BYE—John B. Nash, Canada
					Florio, 1 up	John G. Florio, Wyandot, Ohio Daniel R. Topping, Blind Brook, N.Y.
		Yates, 5 and 4	Kepler, 5 and 4	**Kepler, 1 up**	**Kepler, 2 and 1**	**Bob Kepler, Northmoor, Ohio** A.L. Miller, Bob O'Link, Ill.
					Bobel, 6 and 5	Michael J. Bobel, Metacomet, R.I. Jennings B. Gordon, Atlanta A.C., Ga.
				M.F. McCarthy, 3 and 2	M.F. McCarthy, 5 and 3	Charles B. Round, Metacomet, R.I. Martin F. McCarthy, Columbia, Md.
					Warner	BYE—Milton P. Warner, New Haven, Conn.
			Yates, 5 and 3	Yates, by default	Duvall	BYE—G.W. Duvall, Jr., Indian Hill, Mo.
					Yates, 3 and 2	Charles R. Yates, Atlanta A.C., Ga. George Berkey, Waverley, Ore.
				Dann, 2 and 1	Draper	BYE—Tom L. Draper, Jr., Normandie, Mo.
					Dann	BYE—Carl Dann, Jr., Dubsdread, Fla.
	Little, 4 and 2	Little, 4 and 3	Little, 3 and 2	L. Little, 3 and 2	L. Little	BYE—W. Lawson Little, Jr., Presidio, Calif.
					Tucker, 3 and 2	Berrien Moore, Jr., Atlanta A.C., Ga. John M. Tucker, Locust Hill, N.Y.
				Heath, 5 and 4	Heath, 1 up	Milan A. Heath, Brae Burn, Mass. M.S. Lindgrove, Baltusrol, N.J.
					Telfer, 3 and 2	Thomas Telfer, Claremont, Calif. Philip W. Simons, Longmeadow, Mass.
			O'Brien, 3 and 2	L. Martin, by default	L. Martin, by default	Robert A. Gardner, Onwentsia, Ill. Leo J. Martin, Waltham, Mass.
					Fowler	BYE—A.W. Fowler, Interlachen, Minn.
				O'Brien, 5 and 4	Beyer	BYE—H. L. Beyer, Jr., Aronimink, Pa.
					O'Brien, 1 up, 19 hls.	Chester O'Brien, Westborough, Mo. Alfred W. Breault, Grosse Ile, Mich.
		Gandy, 1 up	Givan, 3 and 2	Givan, 7 and 5	C. Little	BYE—Charles Little, Woodhill, Minn.
					Givan, 8 and 7	Lee Fowler, Forsgate, N.J. Harry L. Givan, Olympic, Wash.
				Sweetser, 3 and 1	Doyle, 1 up, 19 hls.	Francis H. Doyle, Wachusett, Mass. S.A. Carson, Jr., Kiskiminetas Springs, Pa.
					Sweetser	BYE—Jess W. Sweetser, Siwanoy, N.Y.
			Gandy, 4 and 2	Gandy, 4 and 3	Platt	BYE—J. Wood Platt, Aronimink, Pa.
					Gandy, 1 up	R.W. Brown, Jr., The Country Club, Mass. Harry Gandy, Twin Hills, Okla.
				Eaton, 4 and 3	Eaton, 4 and 3	Zell Eaton, Oklahoma City, Okla. John D. Ames, Glen View, Ill.
					Drain	BYE—James G. Drain, Washington, Va.

SEMI-FINAL ROUND—W. Lawson Little, Jr., defeated Don Armstrong, 4 and 3.

1935
THIRTY-NINTH AMATEUR CHAMPIONSHIP

Held at The Country Club (Cleveland), Chagrin Falls, Ohio, September 9-14.
945 Entries, 207 Qualifiers, 201 Starters. Championship proper entirely at match play.

FINAL ROUND (36 Holes)—W. Lawson Litter, Jr., defeated Walter Emery, 4 up and 2 to play.

FIRST QUARTER — UPPER

1st Round (18 Holes)	2nd Round (18 Holes)	3rd Round (18 Holes)	4th Round (18 Holes)	5th Round (18 Holes)	6th Round (18 Holes)	Semi-Finals
BYE—Rodney W. Bliss, Jr., Happy Hollow, Neb.	Bliss					
BYE—Horace Williams, Jr., Pasadena, Fla.	Williams	Bliss, 1 up, 19 hls.				
BYE—Edward L. Meister, Jr., Canterbury, Ohio	Meister		Meister, 3 and 1			
BYE—Johnny Banks, Big Oaks, Ill.	Banks	Meister, 5 and 4		Meister, 2 and 1		
BYE—Lewis Johnson, Jr., Charleston, S.C.	Johnson					
BYE—Warren L. Riepen, Swope Park, Mo.	Riepen	Riepen, 4 and 3				
BYE—Frederick Borsodi, C.C. Fairfield, Conn.	Borsodi		Riepen, 3 and 2			
BYE—Paul Jackson, Oklahoma City, Okla.	Jackson	Jackson, 6 and 5			Goodman, 6 and 5	
BYE—Ed White, Bonham, Texas	White					
BYE—Hunter Hicks, Bob O'Link, Ill.	Hicks	White, 4 and 3				
BYE—Fred J. Lazard, Garden City C.C., N.Y.	Lazard		White, 4 and 2			
BYE—Robert Dunkelberger, Sedgefield, N.C.	Dunkelberger	Dunkelberger, 3 and 2		Goodman, 2 and 1		
George T. Dunlap, Jr., Pomonok, N.Y. Charles S. Munson, Jr., C.C. Fairfield, Conn.	Dunlap, 2 up	Goodman, 3 and 2				
John Goodman, Omaha F.C., Neb. Richard L. Haskell, Inglewood, Wash.	Goodman, 3 and 1		Goodman, 1 up			
James A. Wright, Carnoustie, Scotland August F. Kammer, Jr., Baltusrol, N.J.	Kammer, 3 and 2	Chase, 1 up				
Craig McKee, Indian Spring, Md. Hal Chase, Wakonda, Iowa	Chase, 7 and 6					Goodman, 6 and 5
Maurice Nee, Columbia, Md. Julius Hughes, Druid Hills, Ga.	Hughes, 5 and 3	Hughes, 5 and 4				
Robert M. Monsted, New Orleans, La. Howard Tryon, Elmira, N.Y.	Tryon, 4 and 3		Smith, 3 and 2			
Charles Evans, Jr., Edgewater, Ill. Reynolds Smith, Lakewood, Texas	Smith, 8 and 7	Smith, 5 and 4		Goodwin, 2 and 1		
Carlin Short, Firestone, Ohio Glenn L. Bishop, Inverness, Ohio	Bishop, 5 and 4					
William S. Meany, Jr., Westchester, N.Y. W. F. Marks, Oakmont, Pa.	Marks, 5 and 3	Goodwin, 6 and 5				
Sam Perry, Birmingham, Ala. Tommy Goodwin, Winged Foot, N.Y.	Goodwin, 1 up		Goodwin, 7 and 5			
G. S. McCarty, Myers Park, N.C. R. A. Croslin, Oak Park, Ill.	Croslin, 5 and 3	Croslin, 3 and 2			Kocsis, 7 and 6	
Joseph Thompson, Ancaster, Canada Sidney W. Coltart, Plymouth, Pa.	Coltart, 2 up					
James Miller, Des Moines, Iowa Don Armstrong, Aurora, Ill.	Armstrong, 2 and 1	Benson, 5 and 3				
Tom Lawson Draper, Jr., Westwood, Mo. J. C. Benson, South Hills, Pa.	Benson, 5 and 4		Kocsis, 3 and 1			
Jesse Guilford, Woodland, Mass. T. Colwell Thomas, C.C. Troy, N.Y.	Thomas, by default	Kocsis, 7 and 5				
Charles Kocsis, Red Run, Mich. Page Hufty, Chevy Chase, Md.	Kocsis, 3 and 2			Kocsis, 1 up		
William T. McCallum, Kahkwa, Pa. Albert Hakes, Wanakah, N.Y.	McCallum, 2 up	McCallum, 3 and 1				
W. W. Williams, Cincinnati, Ohio Eddie Semmier, Hillendale, Md.	Williams, 2 and 1		M. J. McCarthy, 6 and 5			
Warren A. Colton, Jr., C.C. Minneapolis, Minn. E. W. Robison, Austin, Texas	Colton, 1 up, 19 hls.	M. J. McCarthy, 6 and 5				
Bernard Deering, C.C. Ithaca, N.Y. M. J. McCarthy, Jr., Mayfield, Ohio	M. J. McCarthy, 2 and 1					

HALF / **SECOND QUARTER**

6th Round (18 Holes)		5th Round (18 Holes)	4th Round (18 Holes)	3rd Round (18 Holes)	2nd Round (18 Holes)	1st Round (18 Holes)
					Becka	BYE—Charles Becka, Calumet, Ill.
				Egan, 1 up, 22 hls.	Egan	BYE—H. Chandler Egan, Cypress Point, Calif.
			Enos, 3 and 1		Allis	BYE—Ed. Allis, Jr., C.C. Little Rock, Ark.
				Enos, 3 and 2	Enos	BYE—George E. Enos, C.C. Cleveland, Ohio
		Voigt, 1 up, 19 hls.			Lenahan	BYE—J. Raymond Lenahan, Metacomet, R.I.
				Reckner, 2 and 1	Reckner	BYE—Charles A. Reckner, Cedarbrook, Pa.
			Voigt, 5 and 4		Biggs	BYE—John M. Biggs, Carolina C.C., N.C.
				Voigt, 3 and 2	Voigt	BYE—George J. Voigt, Winged Foot, N.Y.
	Voigt, 1 up				Russell	BYE—Pierre H. Russell, Jr., C.C. Troy, N.Y.
				Donovan, 1 up	Donovan	BYE—Bud Donovan, Winnepeg, Canada
			Donovan, 2 and 1		Goldman	BYE—David Goldman, Dallas, Texas
				Goldman, 3 and 2	Rainwater	BYE—Crawford Rainwater, Atlanta A.C., Ga.
		Turnesa, 2 and 1			Weppner	BYE—Fred B. Weppner, Pittsburgh F.C., Pa.
				Odom, 5 and 4	Odom, 4 and 2	Goerge Harris, Winged Foot, N.Y. Fred Odom, 2nd, New Orleans, La.
			Turnesa, 2 and 1		Yoder. 2 and 1	Levi Yoder, Indian Spring, Md. Francis Ouimet, Woodland, Mass.
				Turnesa, 3 and 2	Turnesa, 4 and 2	Willie Turnesa, Fairview, N.Y. Dick Lutz, Ashland, Ohio
Little, 4 and 3				Little, 6 and 4	Little, 3 and 1	W. Lawson Little, Jr., Presidio, Calif. Rufus King, Denver, Colo.
			Little, 6 and 5		Lain, 3 and 2	William V. V. Lain, Beverly, Ill. C. Bavard Mitchell, 2nd, Pine Valley, N.J.
				Young, 1 up	Young, 5 and 3	Knox M. Young, Jr., Shannopin, Pa. C. J. Farley, Kent, Mich.
		Little, 5 and 3			Miller, 5 and 4	Denmar Miller, Des Moines, Iowa Jack Emery, Lochmoor, Mich.
				Riegel, 3 and 1	Homans, 6 and 4	Eugene V. Homans, Englewood, N.J. Frank Aylward, Swope Park, Mo.
			Riegel, 6 and 5		Riegel, 4 and 3	Robert F. Riegel, Hermitage, Va. Bayard Storm, Myers Park, N.C.
				Friday, 1 up	Friday, by default	Bob Goldwater, Phoenix, Ariz. Rupert Friday, Pittsburgh, F.C., Pa.
	Little, 5 and 3				Harbert, 2 and 1	Lynford Lardner, Jr., Blue Mound, Wis. Melvin Harbert, Battle Creek Riverside, Mich.
				McCullough, 5 and 4	McCullough, 6 and 5	Charles H. Mayo, Jr., Lido, N.Y. W. B. McCullough, Jr., Huntingdon Valley, Pa.
			McCullough, 3 and 1		Whiteside, 4 and 3	Dave Whiteside, C.C. New Bedford, Mass. Hugh H. Clines, Audubon, Ky.
				Platt, 1 up	Platt, by default	William Notley, Honolulu, Hawaii J. Wood Platt, Whitemarsh Valley, Pa.
		McCullough, 1 up			Kowal, 1 up	Henry J. Kowal, Edison, N.Y. Christian A. Brinke, Oakland Hills, Mich.
				Bloch, 1 up	Hamman, by default	Joe Hartman, Lakewood, Colo. Leland Hamman, Paris, Texas
			Westland, 5 and 3		Bloch, 3 and 2	E. H. Molthan, Gulph Mills, Pa. T. M. Bloch, Wheeling, W. Va.
				Westland, 2 and 1	Eshelman, 6 and 5	Chris A. Carr, Wanakah, N.Y. Herbert R. Eshelman, Lancaster, Pa.
					Westland, 4 and 3	Jack Westland, Sunset Ridge, Ill. Henry W. Comstock, Wanakah, N.Y.

SEMI-FINAL ROUND—W. Lawson Little, Jr., defeated John Goodman, 4 and 3

LOWER

THIRD QUARTER

1st Round (18 Holes)	2nd Round (18 Holes)	3rd Round (18 Holes)	4th Round (18 Holes)	5th Round (18 Holes)	6th Round (18 Holes)	Semi-Finals
BYE—Arthur L. Doering, Jr., Big Oaks, Ill.	Doering					
BYE—John H. Nies, United Shoe M. A. A., Mass.	Nies	Nies, 1 up, 20 hls.				
BYE—Harry L. Givan, Inglewood, Wash.	Givan		Givan, 4 and 3			
BYE—Harry G. Pitt, Manor, Md.	Pitt	Givan, 3 and 2				
BYE—Earle E. Baruch, Merion, Pa.	Baruch			Givan, 3 and 2		
BYE—Charles A. Wallace, C.C. Cleveland, Ohio	Wallace	Wallace, 6 and 5				
BYE—Gus Fetz, Medinah, Ill.	Fetz		E. Knowles, 1 up, 20 hls.			
BYE—Ellis Knowles, Apawamis, N.Y.	E Knowles	E. Knowles, 3 and 2				
BYE—Bill Warren, Dearborn, Mich.	B. Warren				Munger, 1 up, 19 hls.	
BYE—Claude Harmon, Dubsdread, Fla.	Harmon	Harmon, 1 up				
BYE—William Chambers, Butterfield, Ill.	Chambers		Chambers, 3 and 2			
BYE—Melville F. Heath, Jr., Brae Burn, Mass.	Heath	Chambers, 1 up				
H. C. Fownes, II, Oakmont, Pa.	H. Fownes, by default					
Gerald H. Trautman, Lakeside, Calif.		Munger, 4 and 3				
Robert C. Fisher, Moon Brook, N.Y.	Munger, 2 and 1			Munger, 7 and 6		
Jack Munger, Brook Hollow, Texas			Munger, 2 and 1			
Zell Eaton, Oklahoma City, Okla.	Eaton, 6 and 4					
Frank Strafaci, Shore View, N.Y.		Mor. McCarthy, 1 up, 19 hls.				
Volney G. Burnett, Indian Spring, Md.	Mor. McCarthy, 3 and 2					W. Emery, 4 and 3
Morton McCarthy, Princess Anne, Va.						
Robert Baugh, Mayfield, Ohio	Jamison, 2 and 1					
T. S. Jamison, Jr., Oakmont, Pa.		W. Emery, 5 and 3				
Charles Whitehead, Forsgate, N.J.	W. Emery, 5 and 4					
Walter Emery, Twin Hills, Okla.			W. Emery, 1 up, 19 hls.			
C. Ross Somerville, London, Canada	Somerville, 4 and 3					
Herman Hellman, Hillcrest, Calif.		Somerville, 6 and 4				
W. D. Fondren, Biltmore Forest, N.C.	Hill, 4 and 3			W. Emery, 6 and 4		
Douglas W. Hill, Cincinnati, Ohio						
J. D. Hoblitzell, Jr., Parkersburg, W. Va.	McClure, 5 and 4					
Edwin A. McClure, Shreveport, La.		Hoerner, 1 up				
Jack Hoerner, Stanford University, Calif.	Hoerner, 1 up					
Carey Ballew, Jr., Blue Hills, Mo.			Sawyer, 3 and 2			
J. R. Ferguson, Whitemarsh Valley, Pa.	Hobart, 2 up					
John Hobart, Mauh-Nah-Tee-See, Ill.		Sawyer, 3 and 1				
Roy W. Ryden, Jr., Portage, Ohio	Sawyer, 3 and 2				W. Emery, 5 and 3	
Pat Sawyer, Golden Valley, Minn.						
Jim Milward, Nakoma, Wis.	Fischer, 3 and 2					
John W. Fischer, Highland, Ky.		Hogan, 2 and 1				
Charles Smead, Elmhurst, Ill.	Hogan, 4 and 3					
Eddie Hogan, Multnomah, Ore.			Peacock, 3 and 1			
Robert W. Knowles, Jr., C.C. Brookline, Mass.	Sweeny, 3 and 2					
Robert Sweeny, Sandwich, England		Peacock, 6 and 4		Held, 2 and 1		
Roger S. Peacock, Indian Spring, Md.	Peacock, 3 and 1					
E. Hickman Greene, Manor, Md.						
Clifton Myers, Myers Park, N.C.	Servis, 6 and 5					
Bob Servis, Miami Valley, Ohio		Held, 6 and 5				
Eddie Held, Forsgate, N.J.	Held, 2 and 1					
Wayne H. Lewis, Pine Ridge, Ohio			Held, 1 up			
Larry Trickett, Jr., Milburn, Mo.	Finger, 8 and 7					
Jack Finger, California G.C., Calif.		Campbell, 5 and 4				
S. Davidson Herron, Allegheny, Pa.	Campbell, 5 and 4					
Albert E. Campbell, Jefferson Park, Wash.						

CHAMPIONSHIP HALF

FOURTH QUARTER

Semi-final	6th Round (18 Holes)	5th Round (18 Holes)	4th Round (18 Holes)	3rd Round (18 Holes)	2nd Round (18 Holes)	1st Round (18 Holes)
					Transue	BYE—Oliver M. Transue, C.C. Cleveland, Ohio
				Transue, 1 up, 20 hls.	Andereggen	BYE—Al Andereggen, Big Oaks, Ill.
			Transue, 2 and 1		Schumacher	BYE—Don Schumacher, Glen Lakes, Texas
				Schumacher, 3 and 2	Replogle	BYE—Dee Replogle, Oklahoma City, Okla.
		Transue, 4 and 3			Tinnin	BYE—Jack Tinnin, C.C. Little Rock, Ark.
				Brumley, 2 up	Brumley	BYE—Judd L. Bruley, Cherokee, Tenn.
			Brown, 1 up, 21 hls.		Brown	BYE—Rodney W. Brown, Jr., C.C. Brookline, Mass.
				Brown, 1 up	Watts	BYE—O'Hara Watts, Dallas, Texas
	Lynch, 4 and 3				Boywid	BYE- Chick Boywid, Big Oaks, Ill.
				Boywid, 6 and 5	Ogilvie	BYE—Alex Ogilvie, Beechmont, Ohio
			Lynch, 1 up		Lynch	BYE—Joseph P. Lynch, Blue Hills, Mass.
				Lynch, 3 and 2	Grant	BYE—Robert M. Grant, Wethersfield, Conn.
		Lynch, 1 up			Torrance, 3 and 2	J. A. Fownes, Oakmont, Pa. T. A. Torrance, St. Andrews, Scotland
				Holt, 1 up, 20 hls.	Holt, 4 and 2	William E. Holt, Jr., Bellevue, N.Y. Leonard Martin, Apawamis, N.Y.
			Holt, 3 and 2		Melvin, 5 and 4	Douglas B. Lewis, Burlingame, Calif. Barrett Melvin, Wanango, Pa.
				McPhail, 3 and 1	McPhail, by default	Robert Warren, Cherry Hills, Colo. Donald McPhail, Baltimore, Md.
Lynch, 2 and 1					Yates, 3 and 2	Charles R. Yates, Atlanta A.C., Ga. Chester O'Brien, Meadow Brook, Mo.
				Yates, 3 and 1	Parco, 3 and 1	P. J. Clifford, Jr., Mexico City, Mex. Michael Parco, Cazenovia, N.Y.
			Yates, 3 and 1		Pieper, 3 and 2	Richard B. Martin, Butterfield, Ill. Ernest Pieper, Jr., San Jose, Calif.
		Nash, 3 and 2		Pieper, 5 and 4	Stuart, 3 and 2	Mark J. Stuart, Fox Hills, N.Y. Charles N. Dannals, Jr., Capital City, Ga.
				Bolesta, 1 up	Parker, 1 up, 20 hls.	Milton J. Schloss, Hillcrest, Ohio John E. Parker, Jr., Essex County, N.J.
			Nash, 5 and 4		Bolesta, 1 up	John D. Ames, Glen View, Ill. Burl Bolesta, Palma Ceia, Fla.
				Nash, 6 and 4	Nash, 2 and 1	John B. Nash, London, Canada Don Morano, Forest Hill, N.J.
	Haas, 4 and 3				Marston, 4 and 3	Fairfax H. Gouverneur, Lake Shore, N.Y. Maxwell R. Marston, Gulph Mills, Pa.
				Wagner, 6 and 5	Wagner, 3 and 2	John Wagner, Kildeer, Ill. Robert H. McCrary, Des Moines, Iowa
			Wagner, 1 up, 19 hls.		Reis, 5 and 4	Walter Acuff, Jr., Philadelphia Country, Pa. Robert S. Reis, Losantiville, Ohio
				Moreland, 1 up	Lehman, 3 and 2	John E. Lehman, Olympia Fields, Ill. Joe Feldman, Fresh Meadow, N.Y.
		Haas, 4 and 2			Moreland, 4 and 2	Gus Moreland, C.C. Peoria, Ill. Neil Ransick, Hillcrest, Ohio
				Billows, 5 and 4	R. W. Martin, 3 and 2	C. Ward Birch, Woodway, Conn. Russell W. Martin, Flossmoor, Ill.
			Haas, 1 up, 19 hls.		Billows, 6 and 4	Ray Billows, Dutchess, N.Y. K. W. Wolcott, Trenton, N.J.
				Haas, 2 and 1	Wehrle, 4 and 3	Wilford Wehrle, Racine, Wis. Richard A. Jones, Jr., Westchester Hills, N.Y.
					Haas, 6 and 5	Van Horn Ely, Jr., Gulph Mills, Pa. Fred Haas, Jr., Colonial, La.

SEMI-FINAL ROUND—Walter Emery defeated Joseph P. Lynch, 4 and 3.

The first word after the player's name is the name of the player's club, except in the case of a foreign entrant.

1936
FORTIETH AMATEUR CHAMPIONSHIP

Held at the Garden City Golf Club, Garden City, N.Y., September 14-19.
1,118 Entries, 210 Qualifiers, 208 Starters. Championship proper entirely at match play

FINAL ROUND—John W. Fischer defeated Jack McLean, 1 up, 37 holes.

UPPER

FIRST QUARTER

1st Round (18 Holes)	2nd Round (18 Holes)	3rd Round (18 Holes)	4th Round (18 Holes)	5th Round (18 Holes)	6th Round (18 Holes)	Semi-Finals
BYE—Toby Lyons, Riverside, Pa.	Lyons					
BYE—Frank Strafaci, Shore View, N.Y.	F. Strafaci	F. Strafaci, 6 and 4				
BYE—G. Alec Hill, London, England	G. Hill		F. Strafaci, 2 and 1			
BYE—C. B. Hill, Jr., Skokie, Ill.	C. Hill, Jr.	G. Hill, 3 and 2		Lloyd, 1 up		
BYE—P. T. Taylor, Guyan, W. Va.	Taylor					
BYE—Laurence M. Lloyd, Blind Brook, N.Y.	Lloyd	Lloyd, 4 and 3				
BYE—Francis Ouimet, Woodland, Mass.	Ouimet		Lloyd, 4 and 3			
BYE—John M. Biggs, Carolina, N.C.	Biggs	Ouimet, 5 and 3			Billows, 4 and 3	
BYE—Richard C. Rockwell, Albany, N.Y.	Rockwell					
BYE—James B. McHale, San Gabriel, Calif.	McHale	McHale, 7 and 6				
BYE—J. Morton Dykes, Ayrshire, Scotland	Dykes		McHale, 2 and 1			
BYE—Rudolf E. Knepper, Garden City G.C., N.Y.	Knepper	Knepper, 1 up, 19 hls.		Billows, 3 and 2		
Earle E. Baruch, Merion, Pa. Charles Whitehead, Forsgate, N.J.	Whitehead, 1 up					
Ray Billows, Dutchess, N.Y. Philip W. Simons, Longmeadow, Mass.	Billows, 4 and 2	Billows, 1 up				
Carl Dann, Jr., Dubsdread, Fla. W. B. Tomlinson, Jr., Hermitage, Va.	Dann, 1 up		Billows, 3 and 2			
Harvey Robert Dale, Coffin, Ind. Edward Down, Echo Lake, N.J.	Dale, 5 and 4	Dann, 7 and 6				Goodman, 2 and 1
Jess W. Sweetser, Siwanoy, N.Y. Tommy Wright, Cherokee, Tenn.	Sweetser, 2 and 1					
H.G. Bentley, Southport, England Walter Blevins, Swope Park, Mo.	Blevins, 1 up	Blevins, 2 and 1				
Jack Emery, Lochmoor, Mich. Robert Moffitt, Miami, Fla.	J. Emery, 4 and 2		Blevins, 3 and 2			
Bill Chambers, Kildeer, Ill. Roger Kelly, Los Angeles, Calif.	Kelly, 1 up	Kelly, 3 and 2		Goodman, 6 and 4		
Jesse P. Guilford, Woodland, Mass. Chris Brinke, Oakland Hills, Mich.	Guilford, 1 up					
Johnny Goodman, Omaha F.C., Neb. Hunter Hicks, Skokie, Ill.	Goodman, 4 and 3	Goodman, 4 and 3				
William H. Williamson, Jr., Charlotte, N.C. Rodney F. Coltart, Roxborough, Pa.	Coltart, 4 and 2		Goodman, 4 and 2			
Harry Haverstick, Jr., Meadia Heights, Pa. Lt. Col. H. A. Boyd, St. Andrews, Scotland	Haverstick, 1 up	Coltart, 3 and 1				
Joseph W. Oliver, Fox Chapel, Pa. Lieut. K. A. Rogers, San Antonio, Texas	Oliver, 3 and 2				Goodman, 5 and 3	
Thomas M. Pierce, Ekwanok, Vt. Alex Banazek, En-Joie, N.Y.	Banazek, 1 up, 19 hls.	Banazek, 2 and 1				
J. D. Langley, London, England Eugene Pittman, Kenwood, Md.	Langley, 3 and 2		Langley, 3 and 1			
Vincent Schuster, Locust Hill, N.Y. B. L. Goodes, Sedgefield, N.C.	Schuster, 4 and 3	Langley, 7 and 6				
J. Wood Platt, Whitemarsh Valley, Pa. John E. Lehman, Olympia Fields, Ill.	Lehman, 3 and 1			Langley, 2 up		
Walter C. Greiner, Rodgers Forge, Md. Tom Whiteway, Pine Ridge, Ohio	Greiner, 1 up, 19 hls.	Lehman, 1 up, 19 hls.				
Harold S. Cross, Jr., Huntingdon Valley, Pa. R. F. Glover, Jr., Brae-Burn, Texas	Cross, 1 up		Lehman, 1 up			
Andrew H. L. Anderson, Kenosha, Wis. Morton McCarthy, Princess Anne, Va.	Anderson, 2 and 1	Cross, 3 and 1				

HALF

SECOND QUARTER

6th Round (18 Holes)		5th Round (18 Holes)	4th Round (18 Holes)	3rd Round (18 Holes)	2nd Round (18 Holes)	1st Round (18 Holes)
					Tweddell	BYE–Dr. William Tweddell, Stourbridge, England
				Peacock, 1 up	Peacock	BYE–Roger S. Peacock, Congressional, Md.
			Davis, 1 up		Davis	BYE–David L. Davis, Austin, Texas
				Davis, 3 and 2	Somerville	BYE–C. Ross Somerville, London, Canada
		Davis, 5 and 4			Bellows	BYE–Frank Bellows, Waialae, Hawaii
				Harris, by default	Harris	BYE–Pete Harris, Miami, Fla.
			Cork, 2 up		T. Strafaci	BYE–Tommy Strafaci, Shore View, N.Y.
				Cork, 1 up	Cork	BYE–Harold Cork, Coffin, Ind.
	R. Martin, 3 and 2				Grange	BYE–John W. Grange, Merion, Pa.
				R. Martin, 1 up, 20 hls.	R. Martin	BYE–Russell W. Martin, Flossmoor, Ill.
			R. Martin, 3 and 2		Turnesa	BYE–Willie Turnesa, Fairview, N.Y.
				Turnesa, 1 up	Krutilla, 2 and 1	John Krutilla, Calumet, Ill. Fred G. Bannerot, Jr., Edgewood, W. Va.
		R. Martin, 3 and 2			Thomson, 7 and 6	John W. Roberts, Scioto, Ohio Hector Thomson, Glasgow, Scotland
				Kowal, 4 and 2	Kowal, 2 and 1	A. N. Anderson, Medinah, Ill. Henry J. Kowal, Seven Oaks, N.Y.
			Marston, 1 up, 20 hls.		Marston, 1 up, 19 hls.	Max R. Marston, Gulph Mills, Pa. James A. Fownes, Oakmont, Pa.
Fischer, 6 and 4				Marston, 1 up	Morris, 3 and 2	Johnny Morris, Woodward, Ala. Robert C. Fisher, Moon Brook, N.Y.
				Fischer, 5 and 4	Fischer, 6 and 5	John W. Fischer, Highland, Ky. Edward L. Meister, Jr., Canterbury, Ohio
			Fischer, 3 and 2		Short, 3 and 2	Edward E. Lowery, Charles River, Mass. Carlin Short, Firestone, Ohio
				Evans, 2 up	Bliss, 2 and 1	Edward Martin, Sandy Burr, Mass. Rodney Bliss, Jr., Happy Hollow, Neb.
		Fischer, 3 and 2			Evans, 2 and 1	F. Paul Anderson, Jr., Canoe Brook, N.J. Charles Evans, Jr., Edgewater, Ill.
				Breault, 1 up	Wright, 5 and 3	Frederick J. Wright, Jr., Trapelo, Mass. A. R. Aitken, St. Andrews, Scotland
			Breault, 3 and 2		Breault, 5 and 4	Billy Cordingley, Wakonda, Iowa A. William Breault, Grosse Ile, Mich.
				Mayo, 1 up, 19 hls.	Mayo, 1 up	Charles H. Mayo, Jr., Lido, N.Y. Fred Haas, Jr., Colonial, La.
	Fischer, 1 up				Soccoli, 1 up	Dom Soccoli, Wethersfield, Conn. Jack Munger, Brook Hollow, Texas
				Moreland, 6 and 4	Brown, 3 and 2	Bob Hamilton, French Lick Springs, Ind. Leo R. Brown, Sandy Burr, Mass.
			Moreland, 4 and 3		Moreland, 1 up	H. Law Weatherwax, Wanakah, N.Y. Gus Moreland, Peoria, Ill.
				Kaesche, 2 up	Kaesche, 3 and 2	Carl D. Cramer, Elkview, Pa. Max B. Kaesche, Ridgewood, N.J.
		Moreland, 5 and 4			Rippy 1 up, 21 hls.	Claude B. Rippy, East Potomac, D.C. Marvin (Bud) Ward, Tacoma, Wash.
				Taylor, 2 up	Taylor, 6 and 4	Alvin Duane Everett, Druid Hills, Ga. Gordon Taylor, Jr., Toronto, Canada
			Allan, 4 and 3		W. Emery, 1 up	Knox M. Young, Jr., Shannopin, Pa. Walter Emery, Twin Hills, Okla.
				Allan, 1 up, 19 hls.	Allan, 3 and 2	Tom Lawson Draper, Jr., Normandie, Mo. Francis J. Allan, Fox Hill, Pa.
					Deupree, 1 up, 21 hls.	William J. Deupree, Jr., Hyde Park, Ohio W. Y. Stembler, Miami, Fla.

SEMI-FINAL ROUND–John W. Fischer defeated John Goodman, 2 and 1

THIRD QUARTER

1st Round (18 Holes)	2nd Round (18 Holes)	3rd Round (18 Holes)	4th Round (18 Holes)	5th Round (18 Holes)	6th Round (18 Holes)	Semi-Finals
BYE—Stanley Morrison, Troon, Scotland	Morrison					
BYE—Robert Fraser, Omaha C.C., Neb.	Fraser	Fraser, 4 and 3				
BYE—Arthur L. Doering, Jr., Big Oaks, Ill.	Doering		Fraser, 2 and 1			
BYE—Charles C. Clare, Race Brook, Conn.	Clare	Clare, 2 and 1				
BYE—John Thames, Birmingham, Ala.	Thames			Fraser, 3 and 2		
BYE—G. Dudley Ward, Oak Hill, N.Y.	Ward	Ward, 4 and 3				
BYE—Gordon B. Peters, Barrhead, Scotland	Peters		Ward, 1 up			
BYE—J. D. Hoblitzell, Jr., Parkersburg, W. Va.	Hoblitzell	Hoblitzell, 1 up				
BYE—Dave Connell, Broadmoor, Colo.	Connell				Voigt, 4 and 3	
BYE—William Castleman, Jr., Louisville, Ky.	Castleman	Connell, 3 and 2				
BYE—H. C. Cook, Williams, W. Va.	Cook		Voigt, 7 and 6			
BYE—George J. Voigt, Winged Foot, N.Y.	Voigt	Voigt, 7 and 6				
Richard W. Ashley, Kenosha, Wis. Kenneth W. Wolcott, Trenton, N.J.	Wolcott, 1 up, 21 hls.	Wolcott, 1 up, 21 hls.		Voigt, 1 up		
Randall R. Ahern, Meadowbrook, Mich. E. H. Driggs, Jr., Garden City G.C., N.Y.	Driggs, 3 and 1		Crossley, 2 and 1			
Thomas Telfer, Claremont, Calif. Wilfred Crossley, Norfolk, Mass.	Crossley, 2 and 1	Crossley, 4 and 3				
William L. Maguire, Houston, Texas S. Davidson Herron, Allegheny, Pa.	W. Maguire, 5 and 3					
Seth Dekle, Palma Ceia, Fla. Jack Routh, Saucon Valley, Pa.	Routh, 2 and 1	Campbell, 8 and 7				Voigt, 4 and 3
Forrest Thompson, Beaver Dam, Md. Albert E. Campbell, Jefferson Park, Wash.	Campbell, 3 and 1		Campbell, 2 and 1			
David G. Ritchie, Brae Burn, Texas Leonard Martin, Apawamis, N.Y.	L. Martin, 3 and 1	Lucas, 2 and 1				
P. B. Lucas, London, England Hal Chase, III, Wakonda, Iowa	Lucas, 4 and 2			Campbell, 1 up		
Paul Leslie, Colonial, La. Joseph P. Lynch, Blue Hills, Mass.	Lynch, 2 and 1	Lynch, 3 and 2				
Howard A. Tryon, Elmira, N.Y. Matias Palacio, Olympic, Calif.	Palacio, 1 up, 21 hls.		Lynch, 3 and 2			
J. M. Robbins, Pine Valley, N.J. Sid Richardson, Des Moines, Iowa	Richardson, 2 and 1	Cole, 5 and 4				
Joy Cole, Oakhurst, Okla. Douglas I. Blom, Flint, Mich.	Cole, 1 up				Campbell, 3 and 2	
E. J. Rogers, Oklahoma City, Okla. Ellis Knowles, Apawamis, N.Y.	Knowles, 2 and 1	Knowles, 3 and 2				
W. B. McCullough, Jr., Pine Valley, N.J. T. A. Torrance, St. Andrews, Scotland	McCullough, 4 and 2		Knowles, 1 up, 19 hls.			
Richard Allman, Philmont, Pa. Eugene V. Homans, Knickerbocker, N.J.	Homans, 5 and 4	Homans, 1 up				
Kenneth K. Beukema, Cascade Hills, Mich. Fred Newton, South Shore, Ill.	Beukema, 4 and 3			Holt, 5 and 4		
Frank Pace, Jr., Little Rock, Ark. W. E. Holt, Jr., Bellevue, N.Y.	Holt, 7 and 6	Holt, 1 up				
Gordon Kummer, Milwaukee, Wis. Reynolds Smith, Lakewood, Texas	R. Smith, 4 and 3		Holt, 2 and 1			
F. M. Hohlfelder, Westwood, Ohio Joseph Thompson, Burlington, Canada	Thompson, 2 and 1	Thompson, 4 and 3				
C. W. Hackney, Jr., Atlantic, City, N.J. Harold Le Blond, Camargo, Ohio	Le Blond, 4 and 2					

CHAMPIONSHIP

HALF

FOURTH QUARTER

6th Round (18 Holes)		5th Round (18 Holes)	4th Round [18 Holes)	3rd Round (18 Holes)	2nd Round (18 Holes)	1st Round (18 Holes)
					Day	BYE—Winfield S. Day, Elmhurst, Ill.
				Ewing, 4 and 3	Ewing	BYE—Cecil Ewing, Ross's Point, Ireland
			Heath, 1 up		Ward	BYE—Dave Ward, Saginaw, Mich.
				Heath, 3 and 1	Heath	BYE—Melville F. Heath, Jr., Brae Burn, Mass.
		Heath, 3 and 2			Ewell	BYE—Dave Ewell, Jr., Hermitage, Va.
				Dunlap, 3 and 2	Dunlap	BYE—George T. Dunlap, Jr., Pomonok, N.Y.
			Dunlap, 7 and 5		J. McGuire	BYE—John W. McGuire, Hillcrest, Md.
				J. McGuire, by default	Bishop	BYE—Glen L. Bishop, Inverness, Ohio
	McLean, 6 and 4				Johnson	BYE—Lewis Johnson, Jr., Charleston, S.C.
				Johnson, 3 and 2	Pettigrew	BYE—Leon W. Pettigrew, Speedway, Ind.
			Pieper, 4 and 3		Pieper	BYE—Ernest Pieper, Jr., San Jose, Calif.
				Pieper, 2 and 1	Burke, 2 and 1	John P. Burke, Wanumetonomy, R.I. Tommy Goodwin, Winged Foot, N.Y.
		McLean, 1 up, 20 hls.			A. Smith, 3 and 1	Alan A. Smith, Asheville, N.C. Wally Chadwell, Hyde Park, Ohio
				Yoder, 5 and 3	Yoder, 7 and 5	C. Bayard Mitchell, Pine Valley, N.J. Levi Yoder, Kenwood, Md.
			McLean, 1 up		Longhurst, 5 and 4	Henry Longhurst, Bedford, England Kenneth Corcoran, Oyster Harbors, Mass.
				McLean, 5 and 4	McLean, 3 and 2	Jack McLean, Glasgow, Scotland Robert W. Lowe, Clarksburg, W. Va.
McLean, 3 and 1				R. Strafaci, 2 and 1	R. Strafaci, 6 and 4	Ralph T. Strafaci, Shore View, N.Y. Robert Brownell, Indian Springs, Md.
			Riddell, 1 up		Webb, 1 up, 19 hls.	Thomas D. Webb, Jr., Washington, Va. Charles Boywid, Big Oaks, Ill.
				Riddell, 1 up	Barnes, 1 up, 20 hls.	Spencer S. Overton, Rolling Road, Md. Thomas W. Barnes, Atlanta A.C., Ga.
		Riddell, 1 up, 20 hls.			Riddell, 4 and 2	J. F. Riddell, Jr., Garden City G.C., N.Y. H. E. Taylor, St. Andrews, Scotland
				Armstrong, 3 and 2	Armstrong, 2 up	John Banks, Big Oaks, Ill. Don Armstrong, Aurora, Ill.
			Armstrong, 1 up		Burnett, 2 and 1	Brown Cannon Lakewood, Colo. Volney G. Burnett, Indian Spring, Md.
				Grant, 5 and 4	Grant, 2 and 1	Robert M. Grant, Wethersfield, Conn. Lynford Lardner, Jr., Blue Mound, Wis.
					Fetz, 7 and 5	W. Edwin Wells, East Liverpool, Ohio Gus Fetz, Big Oaks, Ill.
	Riddell, 1 up, 20 hls.			Becka, 5 and 4	Becka, 5 and 3	Charles J. Becka, Jr., Ridgemoor, Ill. Richard D. Chapman, Greenwich, Conn.
			Tailer, 3 and 2		Gagliardi, 3 and 1	Joseph F. Gagliardi, Winged Foot, N.Y. Sidney W. Noyes, Jr., Ardsley, N.Y.
				Tailer, 3 and 1	Lea, 1 up	Clark Lea, Jr., C.C. Virginia, Va. Gerald R. Anderson, Wachusett, Mass.
					Tailer, 7 and 5	J. Virgil Scott, Jr., Houston, Texas T.S. Tailer, Jr., Piping Rock, N.Y.
		Tailer, 2 and 1		Cameron, 1 up, 19 hls.	Cameron, 4 and 2	Richard E. McCreary, Jr., Indianapolis, Ind. Jack A. Cameron, Flossmoor, Ill.
			Brumley, 2 and 1		Watts, 5 and 3	Gerald Shattuck, Winged Foot, N.Y. O'Hara Watts, Brook Hollow, Texas
				Brumley, 1 up, 20 hls.	Brumley, 1 up	Judd L. Brumley, Cherokee, Tenn. Edmund R. Held, Cohasse, Mass.
					Yates, 1 up, 19 hls.	Charles R. Yates, Atlanta A.C., Ga. Richard A. Jones, Jr., Westchester Hills, N.Y.

SEMI-FINAL ROUND—Jack McLean defeated George J. Voigt, 8 and 7

The first word after the player's name is the name of the player's club, except in the case of a foreign entrant.

1937
FORTY-FIRST AMATEUR CHAMPIONSHIP

Held at the Alderwood Country Club, Portland, Ore., August 23-28.
619 Entries, 180 Qualifiers, 171 Starters.
Yardage—6,601. Par 72.

Qualifying Score	1st Round (18 Holes)	2nd Round (18 Holes)	3rd Round (18 Holes)	4th Round (18 Holes)	Semi-Finals (36 Holes)	Final (36 Holes)	
151	T. Suffern Tailer, Jr., Piping Rock, N.Y.	Tailer,					
142	*Roger Kelly, Los Angeles, Calif.	1 up	Kingsley,				
148	Edwin C. Kingsley, Utah Copper, Utah	Kingsley,	2 and 1				
154	Sid Richardson, Kildeer, Ill.	7 and 6		Smith,			
150	Walter Emery, Oklahoma City, Okla.	Emery,		2 and 1			
151	Melvin Harbert, Marywood, Mich.	3 and 2	Smith,				
151	Reynolds Smith, Lakewood, Texas	Smith,	2 and 1		Billows, 2 up		
149	Eddie Hogan, Oswego, Ore.	2 up					
144	Ray Billows, Dutchess, N.Y.	Billows,					
149	Robert P. Thompson, Stanford Univ., Calif.	8 and 7	Billows,				
153	Tommy Goodwin, Winged Foot, N.Y.	Wiggins,	2 and 1				
148	Roy E. Wiggins, Oswego Lake, Ore.	1 up, 19 hls.		Billows,			
153	Charles Kocsis, Red Run, Mich.	Kocsis,		3 and 2			
153	Earl Christiansen, Miami, Fla.	4 and 3	Kocsis,				
152	Robert A. Conliff, Jr., Oklahoma City, Okla.	Conliff,	1 up			Billows, 6 and 5	
152	Harold Salvador, Columbia-Edgewater, Ore.	3 and 1					
154	George E. Victor, Glen View, Ill.	V. Dolp,					
152	Vince Dolp, Alderwood, Ore.	4 and 3	Strafaci,				
148	Walter Blevins, Swope Park, Mo.	Strafaci,	1 up				
145	Frank Strafaci, Shore View, N.Y.	4 and 3		Evans,			
154	Joseph P. Lynch, Blue Hill, Mass.	Lynch,		3 and 2			
151	Don Schumacher, Lakewood, Texas	2 up	Evans,				
152	Charles Evans, Jr., Edgewater, Ill.	Evans,	3 and 2		Fischer, 1 up		
154	Charles Finger, California, Calif.	1 up, 20 hls.					
152	Kenneth Black, Vancouver, B.C., Canada	Holt,					
150	Bill Holt, Bellevue, N.Y.	3 and 1	Holt,				
154	Richard Hale, Belle Meade, Tenn.	Doering,	4 and 3				
144	Arthur L. Doering, Jr., Big Oaks, Ill.	3 and 2		Fischer,			
150	John W. Fischer, Highland, Ky.	Fischer,		5 and 4			
149	Robert N. Babbish, Brooklands, Mich.	4 and 3	Fischer,				
153	Fred Clark, Jr., San Gabriel, Calif.	Clark,	5 and 4				John Goodman, 2 up
150	Jack Westland, Everett, Wash.	1 up					
144	Marvin (Bud) Ward, Tacoma, Wash.	Ward,					
149	Albert Campbell, Jefferson Park, Wash.	1 up	Ward,				
153	C.C. Pettijohn, Jr., Green Meadow, N.Y.	Willing,	5 and 4				
152	Dr. O.F. Willing, Waverley, Ore.	3 and 2		Ward,			
151	Leslie A. Leal, Everett, Wash.	Shea,		1 up, 21 hls.			
153	William L. Shea, Congressional, Md.	1 up, 21 hls.	Haas,				
148	C.D. Hunter, Jr., Tacoma, Wash.	Haas,	5 and 4		Ward, 1 up, 19 hls.		
149	Fred Haas, Jr., La. State Univ., La.	2 up					
149	Charles Swanston, Del Paso, Calif.	F. Dolp,					
152	Frank Dolp, San Francisco, Calif.	1 up	Day,				
154	Winfield Day, San Gabriel, Calif.	Day,	2 and 1				
153	Bobby Dunkelberger, Sedgefield, N.C.	4 and 3		Day,			
150	Matias D. Palacio, Jr., California, Calif.	Palacio,		1 up			
154	Joseph Thompson, Lakeville, N.Y.	1 up	Somerville,				
154	Bob Servis, Miami Valley, Ohio	Somerville,	3 and 1			Goodman, 1 up	
151	C. Ross Somerville, London, Ont., Canada	2 up					
149	Lieut. Ken Rogers, Waialae, Hawaii	Rogers,					
149	Paul Leslie, La. State Univ., La.	5 and 3	Rogers,				
151	Rodney Bliss, Jr., Happy Hollow, Neb.	Bliss,	1 up				
153	Donald J. Armstrong, Aurora, Ill.	2 and 1		Goodman,			
152	Jimmy McHale, San Gabriel, Calif.	McHale,		3 and 1			
145	Billy Bob Coffey, River Crest, Texas	3 and 2	Goodman,				
149	John Goodman, Omaha Field, Neb.	Goodman,	4 and 3		Goodman, 2 and 1		
152	Donald McPhail, Baltimore, Md.	7 and 6					
154	Charles R. Yates, Atlanta, Ga.	Moe,					
146	Donald Moe, Alderwood, Ore.	4 and 2	Moe,				
151	Jack Gaines, Oakmont, Calif.	Gaines,	3 and 2				
154	Glen Oatman, Swope Park, Kans.	1 up, 19 hls.		Moe,			
154	Crawford Rainwater, Druid Hills, Ga.	Cummings,		2 and 1			
154	John Cummings, Jr., Colonial, Tenn.	1 up	Givan,				
155	†T.S. Jamison, Jr., Oakmont, Pa.	Givan,	7 and 6				
147	Harry L. Givan, Inglewood, Wash.	2 and 1					

*Medalist.
†Qualified in playoff.
The first word after the player's name is the name of the player's club except in the case of a foreign entrant.

1938
FORTY-SECOND AMATEUR CHAMPIONSHIP

Held at the Oakmont Country Club, Oakmont, Pa., September 12-17.
871 Entries, 170 Qualifiers, 163 Starters.
Yardage—6,981. Par 72.

Qualifying Score	1st Round (18 Holes)	2nd Round (18 Holes)	3rd Round (18 Holes)	4th Round (18 Holes)	Semi-Finals (36 Holes)	Final (36 Holes)	
158	James M. Scott, New Albany, Ind.	Scott, 4 and 3					
154	Bud Brownell, Del Monte, Calif.		Fraser, 4 and 2				
156	Harry B. Wesbrook, Annandale, Calif.	Fraser, 1 up					
159	James E. Fraser, Seaview, N.J.			Abbott, 2 up			
157	John O. Levinson, Webhannet, Me.	Billows, 1 up, 20 hls.					
153	Ray Billows, Dutchess, N.Y.		Abbott, 2 and 1				
158	B. Patrick Abbott, Altadena, Calif.	Abbott, 4 and 3					
158	Tom Draper, Jr., Normandie, Mo.				Abbott, 1 up, 20 hls.		
157	Walter Blevins, Swope Park, Mo.	Blevins, 6 and 4					
157	Henry Castillo, L.S.U., La.		Blevins, 1 up				
158	Robert M. Grant, Wethersfield, Conn.	Krutilla, 4 and 3					
158	Johnny Krutilla, Olympia Fields, Ill.			Thompson, 1 up, 19 hls.			
154	C. Ross Somerville, London, Ont., Canada	Thompson, 1 up					
153	Joseph Thompson, Hamilton, Ont., Canada		Thompson, 1 up, 19 hls.				
153	Fred Haas, Jr., Colonial, La.	Haas, 5 and 4					
156	Edward J. Flowers, Cascade Hills, Mich.					Abbott, 5 and 4	
154	Johnny Goodman, Omaha Field, Neb.	Goodman, 4 and 3					
160	†Sid Richardson, Kildeer, Ill.		Goodman, 4 and 3				
157	Don Edwards, San Jose, Calif.	Givan, 1 up					
150	Harry L. Givan, Inglewood, Wash.			Goodman, 4 and 2			
156	J. E. French, Jr., San Francisco, Calif.	French, 6 and 4					
160	†Lloyd A. Martz, Clinton Valley, Mich.		French, 1 up, 21 hls.				
153	Roger Kelly, Los Angeles, Calif.	Kelly, 3 and 2					
158	Joe Roth, Seneca, Ky.				Chapman, 2 and 1		
152	Frank Stiedle, Colonial, Tenn.	Chapman, 4 and 3					
148	Richard D. Chapman, Greenwich, Conn.		Chapman, 5 and 4				
150	Arthur Doering, Jr., Medinah, Ill.	Doering, 3 and 1					
148	Marvin (Bud) Ward, Olympia, Wash.			Chapman, 2 and 1			
157	J. Wood Platt, Whitemarsh Valley, Pa.	Sweetser, 1 up					
156	Jess W. Sweetser, Siwanoy, N.Y.		Tailer, 1 up				
154	Earl Larson, Minneapolis, Minn.	Tailer, 2 up					
152	T. Suffern Tailer, Jr., Meadow Brook, N.Y.						Willie Turnesa, 8 and 7
157	Edwin C. Kingsley, Utah Copper, Utah	Kingsley, 1 up, 21 hls.					
151	Steve Kovach, Brackenridge Heights, Pa.		Kingsley, 2 and 1				
159	Ven Savage, Utah Copper, Utah	Yates, 3 and 2					
152	Charles R. Yates, Atlanta A.C., Ga.			Kingsley, 4 and 3			
157	Wilfred Crossley, Norfolk, Mass.	Crossley, 2 and 1					
160	†William Deupree, Jr., Hyde Park, Ohio		Crossley, 2 up				
153	Robert N. Babbish, Brooklands, Mich.	Lardner, 1 up, 19 hls.					
160	†Lynford Lardner, Jr., Blue Mound, Wis.				Kingsley, 5 and 3		
146	*Gus T. Moreland, Mt. Hawley, Ill.	Moreland, 1 up, 23 hls.					
157	Robert W. Dunkelberger, Sedgefield, N.C.		Moreland, 4 and 2				
150	Edmund R. Held, Lakewood, Colo.	Held, 3 and 2					
160	†Jack Hoerner, North Shore, Ill.			Harbert, 3 and 2			
155	William F. Reed, Jr., Highland, Ind.	Harbert, 3 and 2					
160	†Melvin Harbert, Syracuse Yacht, N.Y.		Harbert, 4 and 3				
152	Reynolds Smith, Lakewood, Texas	Brownell, 2 and 1					
151	Robert W. Brownell, Manor, Md.					Turnesa, 4 and 3	
152	Bill Holt, Syracuse Yacht, N.Y.	McCarthy, 4 and 3					
152	Maurice J. McCarthy, Jr., Wyoming, Ohio		Brinke, 2 and 1				
152	August F. Kammer, Jr., Baltusrol, N.J.	Brinke, 1 up, 20 hls.					
152	Christian A. Brinke, Oakland Hills, Mich.			Brinke, 3 and 2			
155	Frank Strafaci, Lakeville, N.Y.	Strafaci, 4 and 3					
157	Harry Todd, Lakewood, Texas		Strafaci, 1 up, 19 hls.				
158	Knox M. Young, Jr., Shannopin, Pa.	Young, 6 and 4					
159	Jimmy Walkup, Jr., Glen Garden, Texas				Turnesa, 5 and 4		
159	Carl Bowman, Yakima, Wash.	Hicks, 3 and 2					
156	Hunter Hicks, Skokie, Ill.		Fischer, 6 and 4				
155	Ted Bishop, Woodland, Mass.	Fischer, 4 and 3					
155	John W. Fischer, Fort Thomas, Ky.			Turnesa, 1 up, 20 hls.			
159	Arthur F. Lynch, Winged Foot, N.Y.	Lynch, 5 and 3					
158	Thomas M. Pierce, Rutland, Vt.		Turnesa, 4 and 3				
160	†John P. Burke, Wanumetonomy, R.I.	Turnesa, 4 and 2					
148	Willie Turnesa, Briar Hills, N.Y.						

*Medalist.
†Qualified in playoff.
The first word after the player's name is the name of the player's club, except in the case of a foreign entrant.

1939
FORTY-THIRD AMATEUR CHAMPIONSHIP

Held at the North Shore Country Club, Glen View, Ill., September 11-16.
826 Entries, 170 Qualifiers, 167 Starters.
Yardage—7,022. Par 72.

Qualifying Score	1st Round (18 Holes)	2nd Round (18 Holes)	3rd Round (18 Holes)	4th Round (18 Holes)	Semi-Finals (36 Holes)	Final (36 Holes)	
153	Fred Allen, C.C. Rochester, N.Y.	Todd, 3 and 2	Todd, 2 and 1	Givan, 2 up	Schumacher, 1 up, 19 hls.	Billows, 6 and 5	Marvin (Bud) Ward, 7 and 5
148	Harry Todd, Lakewood, Texas						
155	†Dan Carmichael, Columbus, Ohio	Carmichael, 1 up					
147	Harold H. Mandly, Jr., Wethersfield, Conn.						
153	John E. Lehman, Olympia Fields, Ill.	Haas, 4 and 3	Givan, 4 and 2				
148	Fred Haas, Jr., Metairie, La.						
150	Harry L. Givan, Inglewood, Wash.	Givan, 2 and 1					
147	Ted Adams, Blue Hills, Mo.						
151	Bruce N. McCormick, Flintridge, Calif.	Meister, 3 and 2	Meister, 5 and 4	Schumacher, 3 and 2			
153	Edward L. Meister, Jr., Canterbury, Ohio						
155	†Johnny Krutilla, Olympia Fields, Ill.	Krutilla, 1 up					
155	†Frank Stiedle, Hot Springs, Ark.						
149	Don Schumacher, Glen Lakes, Texas	Schumacher, 5 and 4	Schumacher, 1 up				
149	Bob Servis, Miami Valley, Ohio						
148	Sam Ruskin, Woodmont, Wis.	Goodman, 5 and 4					
145	John Goodman, Omaha Field, Neb.						
144	C. Ross Somerville, London, Ont., Canada	Somerville, 6 and 5	Somerville, 4 and 2	Somerville, 3 and 2	Billows, 6 and 5		
154	T.R. Johnston, Roxborough, Pa.						
154	Joseph P. Lynch, Blue Hills, Mass.	Lynch, 5 and 4					
153	Richard Allman, Philmont, Pa.						
147	Robert Fraser, Omaha, Neb.	Chapman, 6 and 4	Chapman, 4 and 2				
146	Richard D. Chapman, Greenwich, Conn.						
152	Alex Welsh, Rockford, Ill.	Overton, 5 and 4					
152	Spencer S. Overton, Rolling Road, Md.						
142	Maurice J. McCarthy, Hamilton County, Ohio	Kowal, 3 and 2	Billows, 4 and 2	Billows, 2 and 1			
153	Henry J. Kowal, Seven Oaks, N.Y.						
147	Ray Billows, Dutchess, N.Y.	Billows, 4 and 3					
152	Pat Mucci, Crestmont, N.J.						
150	Pierce H. Russell, Jr., Troy, N.Y.	Campbell, 4 and 3	Burke, 2 up				
150	Albert E. Campbell, Inglewood, Wash.						
143	B. Patrick Abbott, Flintridge, Calif.	Burke, 2 and 1					
153	John P. Burke, Green Meadow, N.Y.						
149	Willie Turnesa, Briar Hills, N.Y.	Turnesa, 5 and 3	Dawson, 2 up	Dawson, 1 up	Doering, 1 up	Ward, 2 and 1	
148	Howard Everitt, Manufacturers', Pa.						
153	George Dawson, Glen Oak, Ill.	Dawson, 4 and 3					
154	Robert E. Clark, Lakewood, Colo.						
155	†Otto Greiner, Rodgers Forge, Md.	Greiner, 2 and 1	Harbert, 2 and 1				
150	Frank Strafaci, Lido, N.Y.						
153	Melvin Harbert, Marywood, Mich.	Harbert, 5 and 3					
147	John Wagner, Kildeer, Ill.						
151	S.B. Roberts. Prestatyn, Wales	Brownell, 5 and 4	Holt, 2 and 1	Doering, 5 and 4			
151	Robert W. Brownell, Manor, Md.						
148	Bill Holt, Syracuse Yacht, N.Y.	Holt, 3 and 2					
154	Ernie F. Combs, Virginia, Calif.						
154	Arthur L. Doering, Jr., Medinah, Ill.	Doering, 5 and 4	Doering, 7 and 6				
150	Edwin A. McClure, Shreveport, La.						
152	J.E. French, Jr., San Francisco, Calif.	Haverstick, 3 and 2					
144	Harry H. Haverstick, Jr., Lancaster, Pa.						
152	Christian A. Brinke, Oakland Hills, Mich.	Brinke, 1 up	Ward, 6 and 5	Ward, 2 up	Ward, 3 and 1		
150	Burleigh Jacobs, Jr., Westmoor, Wis.						
150	Edmund R. Held, Lakewood, Colo.	Ward, 1 up, 20 hls.					
146	Marvin (Bud) Ward, Spokane, Wash.						
153	Kean Donnelly, Cedarbrook, Pa.	Donnelly, 3 and 2	Thompson, 4 and 3				
139	*Thomas Sheehan, Meadowbrook, Mich.						
154	Stewart M. Alexander, Jr., Piedmont, N.C.	Thompson, 2 up					
149	Joseph Thompson, Burlington, Ont., Canada						
150	Charles R. Yates, Atlanta A.C., Ga.	Yates, 3 and 2	Kingsley, 5 and 3	Kingsley, 2 and 1			
148	Lynford Lardner, Jr., Oconomowoc, Wis.						
150	Jack R. Munger, Brook Hollow, Texas	Kingsley, 1 up					
147	Edwin C. Kingsley, C.C., Salt Lake City, Utah						
147	John W. Fischer, Highland, Ky.	Fischer, 6 and 5	Kummer, 3 and 2				
153	W.S. Alexander, Myers Park, N.C.						
150	Gordon Kummer, Milwaukee, Wis.	Kummer, 6 and 5					
148	Jack Hoerner, North Shore, Ill.						

*Medalist.
†Qualified in playoff.
The first word after the player's name is the name of the player's club except in the case of a foreign entrant.

1940
FORTY-FOURTH AMATEUR CHAMPIONSHIP

Held at the Winged Foot Golf Club, Mamaroneck, N.Y., September 9-14.
755 Entries, 150 Qualifiers, 146 Starters.
Yardage—6,915. Par 72.

Qualifying Score	1st Round (18 Holes)	2nd Round (18 Holes)	3rd Round (18 Holes)	4th Round (18 Holes)	Semi-Finals (36 Holes)	Final (36 Holes)	
153	Skee Riegel, Oakmont, Calif.	Sheehan,					
150	Thomas Sheehan, Jr., Meadowbrook, Mich.	1 up, 20 hls.	Sheehan,				
154	Edward L. Meister, Jr., Canterbury, Ohio	Campbell,	2 up				
154	Albert E. Campbell, Rainier, Wash.	2 and 1		Wehrle,			
154	John E. Lehman, Olympia Fields, Ill.	Martin,		5 and 4			
154	Leo Martin, Trapelo, Mass.	4 and 3	Wehrle,				
155	†Toby Lyons, Riverside, Pa.	Wehrle,	2 and 1				
150	Wilford Wehrle, Tam O'Shanter, Ill.	1 up			Wehrle, 6 and 5		
146	George Dawson, Glen Oak, Ill.	Dawson,					
152	Arnold Zimmerman, Hornell, N.Y.	6 and 5	Dawson,				
150	John Krutilla, Midlothian, Ill.	Clare,	2 and 1				
155	†Charles C. Clare, Race Brook, Conn.	2 and 1		Dawson,			
150	Robert E. Clark, Lakewood, Colo.	Hoerner,		6 and 4			
151	Jack Hoerner, North Shore, Ill.	6 and 5	Greiner,				
151	Otto Greiner, Terra Mariae, Md.	Greiner,	2 up				
151	Arthur L. Doering, Jr., Medinah, Ill.	4 and 3				Chapman, 3 and 2	
149	John P. Burke, Westchester, N.Y.	Burke,					
151	Benjamin E. Skinker, Jr., Columbia, Md.	3 and 2	Burke,				
151	Christian A. Brinke, Oakland Hills, Mich.	Coffey,	5 and 4				
153	Billy Bob Coffey, River Crest, Texas	4 and 2		Burke,			
155	†Robert Dunkelberger, Sedgefield, N.C.	Cochran,		1 up			
150	Robert Cochran, Norwood Hills, Mo.	3 and 2	Strafaci,				
155	†Douglas Ford, Hickory, N.Y.	Strafaci,	1 up, 19 hls.				
147	Frank Strafaci, Sound View, N.Y.	1 up			Chapman, 6 and 5		
153	Edmund B. Overton, Pelham, N.Y.	McCarthy,					
146	Maurice J. McCarthy, Jr., Hamilton County, Ohio	2 and 1	McCarthy,				
150	John Markel, Berkshire, Pa.	Holt,	5 and 4				
148	William Holt, Jr., Syracuse Yacht, N.Y.	2 up		Chapman,			
147	Stephen Kovach, Brackenridge Heights, Pa.	Kovach,		5 and 4			
155	†Frank Toronto, Del Paso, Calif.	1 up	Chapman,				
140	*Richard D. Chapman, Winged Foot, N.Y.	Chapman,	3 and 2				Richard D. Chapman, 11 and 9
149	Neil E. White, California, Calif.	2 and 1					
148	Jess W. Sweetser, Siwanoy, N.Y.	Sweetser,					
148	Stewart M. Alexander, Jr., Piedmont, N.C.	2 and 1	Sweetser,				
153	Pat Mucci, Crestmont, N.J.	Kowal,	4 and 2				
148	Henry J. Kowal, Speedway, Ind.	4 and 3		Fischer,			
149	John W. Fischer, Highland, Ky.	Fischer,		4 and 3			
148	Dan Carmichael, Jr., Columbus, Ohio	1 up	Fischer,				
155	†Ted Bishop, Woodland, Mass.	Bishop,	1 up				
152	Ralph Bogart, Congressional, D.C.	3 and 2			McCullough, 5 and 4		
152	William P. Turnesa, Briar Hills, N.Y.	Turnesa,					
154	Bruce N. McCormick, Flintridge, Calif.	3 and 2	Turnesa,				
154	Francis J. Allan, Fox Hill, Pa.	Allan,	4 and 3				
152	Mark J. Stuart, Winged Foot, N.Y.	1 up		McCullough,			
151	Henry Pabian, Steubenville, Ohio	McCullough,		3 and 2			
145	W.B. McCullough, Jr., Huntingdon Valley, Pa.	5 and 4	McCullough,				
151	Gus T. Moreland, Mt. Hawley, Ill.	Moreland,	1 up				
154	John J. Donohue, Jr., Sioux City, Iowa	2 and 1				McCullough, 5 and 3	
154	Cary Middlecoff, Chickasaw, Tenn.	Haas,					
147	Fred Haas, Jr., Metairie, La.	3 and 1	Ward,				
145	Marvin (Bud) Ward, Spokane, Wash.	Ward,	3 and 2				
152	Ellis Knowles, Apawamis, N.Y.	6 and 5		Ward,			
152	Samuel Bates, Jr., Princess Anne, Va.	Bates,		3 and 2			
152	John Wood, Cincinnati, Ohio	2 and 1	Abbott,				
146	Thomas Whiteway, Pine Ridge, Ohio	Abbott,	1 up, 19 hls.				
152	B. Patrick Abbott, Flintridge, Calif.	2 and 1			Billows, 4 and 3		
152	William Y. Dear, Jr., Essex County, N.J.	Billows,					
152	Ray Billows, Dutchess, N.Y.	1 up, 23 hls.	Billows,				
152	Richard Allman, Philmont, Pa.	Allman,	5 and 3				
154	James Frisina, Illini, Ill.	1 up, 20 hls.		Billows,			
146	Harold H. Mandly, Jr., Avon, Conn.	Oleska,		1 up, 19 hls.			
155	†James Oleska, Shore View, N.Y.	2 and 1	Haverstick,				
151	Harry H. Haverstick, Jr., Lancaster, Pa.	Haverstick,	3 and 2				
153	Dan B. Cawley, Jr., Marietta, Ohio	2 up					

*Medalist.
†Qualified in playoff.
The first word after the player's name is the name of the player's club.

1941
FORTY-FIFTH AMATEUR CHAMPIONSHIP

Held at the Omaha Field Club, Omaha, Neb., August 25-30.
Yardage—6,745. Par 72.
637 Entries, 150 Qualifiers, 145 Starters.

Qualifying Score	1st Round (18 Holes)	2nd Round (18 Holes)	3rd Round (18 Holes)	4th Round (18 Holes)	Semi-Finals (36 Holes)	Final Round (36 Holes)	
154	Arthur L. Doering, Jr., Medinah, Ill.	Doering, 2 and 1					
155	Raymond E. Brownell, Jr., Del Monte, Calif.		McCormick, 1 up, 20 hls.				
154	Bruce N. McCormick, Oakmont, Calif.	McCormick, 4 and 3					
155	John Kraft, Lakewood, Colo.			McCormick, 3 and 2			
152	Skee Riegel, Oakmont, Calif.	S. Riegel, 3 and 1					
152	Mario Gonzalez, Sao Paolo, Brazil		S. Riegel, 6 and 5				
158	Clancy Miller, Hillcrest, Mo.	Poole, 2 and 1					
158	Grover D. Poole, Carolina, N.C.				R. Riegel, 1 up		
159†	Robert F. Riegel, Brae-Burn, Texas	R. Riegel, 1 up, 20 hls.					
148	John Goodman, Omaha Field, Neb.		R. Riegel, 1 up, 19 hls.				
152	John J. Jacobs, Cedar Rapids, Iowa	Lardner, 1 up					
150	Lynford Lardner, Jr., Oconomowoc, Wis.			R. Riegel, 4 and 3			
158	Ralph Bogart, Chevy Chase, Md.	Burkemo, 5 and 3					
156	Walter E. Burkemo, Evanston, Ill.		Burkemo, 3 and 2				
157	Pvt. Frank Strafaci, Sound View, N.Y.	Strafaci, 3 and 2					
158	Jack Hoerner, North Shore, Ill.					Ward, 9 and 8	
155	Stephen Kovach, Brackenridge Heights, Pa.	Kovach, 2 and 1					
154	Pvt. Charles R. Yates, Atlanta A.C., Ga.		Kovach, 2 and 1				
154	Harold H. Mandly, Jr., Avon, Conn.	Haas, 1 up					
156	Fred Haas, Jr., Metairie, La.			Kovach, 1 up			
144*	Stewart M. Alexander, Jr., Piedmont, N.C.	Alexander, 1 up					
151	John W. Fischer, Highland, Ky.		Haverstick, 2 and 1				
155	Benjamin Cowdery, Omaha, Neb.	Haverstick, 1 up					
157	Harry H. Haverstick, Jr., Lancaster, Pa.				Ward, 5 and 4		
152	Otto Greiner, C.C. Maryland, Md.	Greiner, 5 and 4					
155	Earl L. Christiansen, Miami-Biltmore, Fla.		Ward, 2 and 1				
156	Alex Welsh, Rockford, Ill.	Ward, 7 and 6					
148	Marvin (Bud) Ward, Spokane, Wash.			Ward, 3 and 1			
155	John Krutilla, Longwood, Ind.	Krutilla, 1 up, 19 hls.					
155	Thomas J. Goodwin, Briar Hills, N.Y.		Oatman, 5 and 4				
159†	Richard S. Durkes, Portland, Ore.	Oatman, 8 and 6					
153	Glenn Oatman, Hillcrest, Mo.						Marvin (Bud) Ward, 4 and 3
157	Hal M. Stone, Jr., Bloomington, Ill.	Stone, 3 and 2					
156	Daniel A. Carmichael, Jr., Columbus, Ohio		Stone, 2 and 1				
159†	Richard Allman, Philmont, Pa.	Stewart, 1 up, 19 hls.					
159†	Harold Stewart, Tam O'Shanter, Mich.			Bishop, 1 up			
159†	Ted Gwin, Tulsa, Okla.	Gwin, 1 up, 19 hls.					
150	Ellsworth Vines, San Gabriel, Calif.		Bishop, 1 up, 20 hls.				
149	Ted Bishop, Woodland, Mass.	Bishop, 2 and 1					
156	William M. Welch, Jr., ¤ Houston, Texas				Bishop, 5 and 3		
152	Richard D. Chapman, Winged Foot, N.Y.	Jennings, 5 and 4					
151	Louis Jennings, Portland, Ore.		Jennings, 4 and 3				
159†	Eugene Dahlbender, Jr., Atlanta A.C., Ga.	Bliss, 2 and 1					
153	Rodney Bliss, Jr., Happy Hollow, Neb.			Jennings, 1 up			
153	Jack E. Shields, Tulsa, Okla.	Shields, 1 up, 19 hls.					
156	Edwin A. McClure, Shreveport, La.		Cochran, 1 up, 19 hls.				
145	John P. Burke, Ridge, Ill.	Cochran, 1 up					
151	Robert Cochran, Norwood Hills, Mo.					Abbott, 1 up	
157	B. Patrick Abbott, Riviera, Calif.	Abbott, 2 up					
157	John S. Vavra, Cedar Rapids, Iowa		Abbott, 3 and 2				
157	Francis J. Fleming, Lincoln Park, Okla.	Wehrle, 3 and 1					
157	Wilford Wehrle, Tam O'Shanter, Ill.			Abbott, 2 up			
157	Harry Todd, Lakewood, Texas	Todd, 4 and 3					
156	James F. Lewis, Jr., Inverness, Ohio		Todd, 9 and 8				
158	Matthew Zadalis, Ralston Park, Neb.	Zadalis, 4 and 2					
158	Robert H. Busler, Mission Hills, Mo.				Abbott, 3 and 2		
156	Lloyd H. Ramsey, C.C. Lexington, Ky.	Ramsey, 3 and 2					
158	Frank Allan, Fox Hill, Pa.		Billows, 4 and 3				
158	Raymond Billows, Dutchess, N.Y.	Billows, 5 and 3					
158	Arthur K. Atkinson, Jr., Winged Foot, N.Y.			Billows, 3 and 2			
156	Dee Replogle, Oklahoma City, Okla.	Replogle, 6 and 5					
159†	Neil C. Croonquist, The C.C., Minneapolis, Minn.		White, 2 and 1				
152	Neil E. White, Tamarack, N.Y.	White, 3 and 1					
158	George W. Sharpe, Jr., Ridgewood, S.C.						

*Medalist.
†Qualified in playoff.
The first word after the player's name is the name of the player's club, except in the case of a foreign entrant or an Amateur Public Links Championship semi-finalist denoted ¤.

1946
FORTY-SIXTH AMATEUR CHAMPIONSHIP

Held at the Baltursol Golf Club, Springfield, N.J., September 9-14.
Yardage—6,686. Par 72.
899 Entries, 150 Qualifiers, 149 Starters.

Qualifying Score	1st Round (18 Holes)	2nd Round (18 Holes)	3rd Round (18 Holes)	4th Round (18 Holes)	Semi-Finals (36 Holes)	Final Round (36 Holes)	
147	Kenneth Rogers, Oklahoma City, Okal.	Ukauka, 1 up	Winter, 4 and 2	Quick, 1 up, 19 hls.	Quick, 1 up	Quick, 3 and 1	Stanley E. Bishop, 1 up, 37 holes
152†	James L. Ukauka, Honolulu, T.H.						
152†	Alpheus Winter, Jr., Brooklawn, Conn.	Winter, 2 and 1					
146	Randall R. Ahern, Meadowbrook, Mich.						
152†	Henry Martell, Edmonton, Alta., Canada	Quick, 2 up	Quick, 1 up				
141	Smiley L. Quick, ¤ Los Angeles, Calif.						
136*	Skee Riegel, Oakmont, Calif.	Riegel, 1 up					
141	Robert N. Babbish, Red Run, Mich.						
150	Otto P. Greiner, C.C. Maryland, Md.	Haskell, 2 and 1	Wall, 1 up, 20 hls.	McCarthy, 1 up, 19 hls.			
150	Gordon C. Haskell, Olympia, Wash.						
146	Arthur J. Wall, Jr., C.C. Scranton, Pa.	Wall, 4 and 3					
144	Neil E. White, Tamarack, N.Y.						
151	Thomas J. Goodwin, Westchester, N.Y.	Goodwin, 5 and 3	McCarthy, 2 and 1				
152†	Edward P. Martin, Winchester, Mass.						
146	Maurice J. McCarthy, Jr., Maketewah, Ohio	McCarthy, 1 up					
150	Richard A. Mayer, Innis Arden, Conn.						
152†	Dan Carmichael, Jr., Columbus, Ohio	Victor, 2 and 1	Torza, 1 up	Kammer, 2 and 1	Kammer, 5 and 4		
149	George E. Victor, Glen View, Ill.						
149	Ted Adams, Blue Hills, Mo.	Torza, 3 and 1					
149	Felice J. Torza, Wethersfield, Conn.						
151	Reinert M. Torgerson, Cherry Valley, N.Y.	Christiansen, 2 up	Kammer, 2 and 1				
144	Earl Christiansen, Miami, Fla.						
150	A. Frederick Kammer, Jr., C.C. Detroit, Mich.	Kammer, 8 and 7					
151	Walter Emery, Tulsa, Okla.						
145	Howard Everitt, Manufacturers, Pa.	Everitt, 5 and 4	Everitt, 2 and 1	Middlecoff, 3 and 2			
145	William P. Turnesa, Knollwood, N.Y.						
145	Thomas A. Stephenson, Blue Hills, Mo.	Dahlbender, 5 and 4					
148	Eugene Dahlbender, Jr., Druid Hills, Ga.						
151	Francis J. Allan, Fox Hill, Pa.	Allan, 1 up	Middlecoff, 3 and 2				
144	James B. McHale, Jr., Whitemarsh Valley, Pa.						
144	Capt. E. Cary Middlecoff, Memphis, Tenn.	Middlecoff, 6 and 4					
148	George Dawson, Glen Oak, Ill.						
151	Earl G. Wilde, Davenport, Iowa	Pieper, 7 and 5	Chapman, 2 and 1	Bishop, 2 and 1	Bishop, 4 and 3	Bishop, 10 and 9	
146	Ernest Pieper, Jr., San Jose, Calif.						
143	Richard D. Chapman, Winged Foot, N.Y.	Chapman, 1 up					
146	Arnold Blum, Idle Hour, Ga.						
146	Charles Kocsis, Red Run, Mich.	Kocsis, 4 and 3	Bishop, 2 up				
146	William J. Schappa, Winged Foot, N.Y.						
148	John W. Dawson, Lakeside, Calif.	Bishop, 2 and 1					
148	Stanley E. Bishop, Norfolk, Mass.						
148	Charles Lind, Lakewood, Colo.	Lind, 3 and 2	Lind, 6 and 4	Lind, 1 up			
149	Theodore D. Adams, South Shore, Mass.						
144	George S. Hamer, Jr., C.C. Columbus, Ga.	Hamer, 1 up					
143	Raymond E. Billows, Dutchess, N.Y.						
145	Frank R. Stranahan, Inverness, Ohio	Stranahan, 4 and 3	Ward, 2 and 1				
150	Bruce N. McCormick, Lakeside, Calif.						
148	John J. Sierge, Twin Brooks, N.J.	Ward, 1 up					
147	Marvin (Bud) Ward, Spokane, Wash.						
150	Robert J. Sweeny, Jr., Seminole, Fla.	Sweeny, 1 up	Sweeny, 1 up, 20 hls.	Sweeny, 1 up	Willits, 3 and 2		
151	Thomas W. Barnes, Atlanta, Ga.						
148	Robert W. Brownell, Manor, Md.	Meister, 2 and 1					
148	Edward L. Meister, Jr., Canterbury, Ohio						
151	Grover L. Dillon, Jr., Meadowbrook, Mo.	Frisina, 3 and 2	Frisina, 2 up				
150	James Frisina, Illini, Ill.						
150	Mark J. Stuart, Winged Foot, N.Y.	Stuart, 3 and 1					
151	Edmund B. Ault, Indian Spring, Md.						
149	James E. Fraser, Atlantic City, N.J.	Fraser, 4 and 3	Willits, 1 up	Willits, 4 and 3			
149	John J. Donohue, Jr., Sioux City, Iowa						
152†	Albert C. Besselink, Merchantville, N.J.	Willits, 3 and 2					
151	Robert W. Willits, Kansas City, Mo.						
150	John R. Lyons, Garden City G.C., N.Y.	Lyons, 5 and 4	Park, 1 up				
152†	Paul Dye, Jr., Urbana, Ohio						
152†	Gordon S. Park, Glen Ridge, N.J.	Park, 5 and 3					
148	James S. Oleska, Shore View, N.Y.						

*Medalist.
†Qualified in playoff.
The first word after the player's name is the name of the player's club, except in the case of a foreign entrant or an Amateur Public Links Championship semi-finalist denoted ¤.

1947
FORTY-SEVENTH AMATEUR CHAMPIONSHIP

Held at the Pebble Beach Golf Links, Del Monte Golf and Country Club, Del Monte, Calif., September 8-13.
Yardage 6,661. Par 72. 1,048 Entries, 210 Qualifiers, 200 Starters.

FINAL ROUND (36 Holes)—Robert H. (Skee) Riegel defeated John W. Dawson, 2 up and 1 to play.
Championship proper entirely at match play.

UPPER

FIRST QUARTER

1st Round (18 Holes)	2nd Round (18 Holes)	3rd Round (18 Holes)	4th Round (18 Holes)	5th Round (18 Holes)	6th Round (18 Holes)	Semi-Finals
BYE—John L. Moyer, North Hills, Pa.	Moyer					
BYE—William J. Schaller, Blue Mound, Wis.	Schaller	Moyer, 3 and 2				
BYE—Kersey C. Eldridge, III, The Oaks, Okla.	Eldridge		Coyle, 4 and 3			
BYE—Jack Coyle, Illini, Ill.	Coyle	Coyle, 1 up				
BYE—Richard D. Chapman, Winged Foot, N.Y.	Chapman			Chapman, 3 and 1		
BYE—James H. McAlvin, Knollwood, Ill.	McAlvin	Chapman, 8 and 2				
BYE—John N. C. Cameron, Baytown, Texas	Cameron		Chapman, 2 and 1			
BYE—John Daniel, Indian Canyon, Wash.	Daniel	Daniel, 2 and 1			Strafaci, 5 and 3	
BYE—Anthony J. Langan, Bellevue, N.Y.	Langan					
BYE—A. Richard Mayer, Winged Foot, N.Y.	Mayer	Mayer, 3 and 2				
BYE—Frank Strafaci, Pomonok, N.Y.	Strafaci		Strafaci, 1 up			
BYE—Thomas F. Lambie, Phoenix, Ariz.	Lambie	Strafaci, 3 and 1				
William F. Zieske, Golden Valley, Minn.				Strafaci, 3 and 2		
Dr. E. Malcolm Stokes, The Oaks, Okla.	Zieske, 5 and 4	Goodman, 4 and 3				
Herbert P. Smith, Dubsdread, Fla.						
John Goodman, Omaha Field C., Neb.	Goodman, 3 and 2		Goodman, 6 and 5			
Joe Moore, Jr., Louisiana State U., La.						
Randall R. Ahern, Meadowbrook, Mich.	Ahern, 2 and 1	Cochran, 5 and 4				
Arthur Armstrong, Waialae, Hawaii						Dawson, 6 and 5
Bob Cochran, Meadowbrook, Mo.	Cochran, 1 up, 20 hls.					
John W. Hulbert, Grays Harbor, Wash.						
Eli Bariteau, Jr., San Jose, Calif.	E. Bariteau, 4 and 3	E. Bariteau, 1 up				
James English, Jr., Happy Hollow, Neb.						
J. C. Hamilton, Jr., Twin Hills, Okla.	Hamilton, 5 and 3		E. Bariteau, 1 up			
John Wood, II, Cincinnati, Ohio						
Thomas J. Leonard, Jr., Nashua, N.H.	Leonard, 5 and 4	Leonard, 1 up		Hofmeister, 3 and 1		
Chester V. Gordon, Sand Point, Wash.						
Raymond Billows, Dutchess, N.Y.	Billows, 1 up					
John R. Lyons, Garden City G.C., N.Y.						
Charles R. Coe, Dornick Hills, Okla.	Coe, 5 and 4	Hofmeister, 4 and 3				
Otto H. Hofmeister, Lewiston, Idaho						
David Doud, Tacoma, Wash.	Hofmeister, 1 up, 19 hls.		Hofmeister, 2 and 1			
Hal M. Stone, Jr., Bloomington, Ill.						
Albert E. Campbell, Sand Point, Wash.	Stone, 1 up, 19 hls.	Stone, 4 and 3				
John J. Humm, Rockville, N.Y.					Dawson, 5 and 4	
John F. Kraft, Lakewood, Colo.	Humm, 3 and 2					
Frank R. Stranahan, Inverness, Ohio						
Douglas W. Bajus, Vancouver, Canada	Stranahan, 7 and 6	Stranahan, 6 and 4				
Lloyd D. Ribner, Fenway, N.Y.						
Walter Hagen, Jr., Hermitage, Va.	Ribner, 3 and 2		Stranahan, 5 and 4			
J. Knox Corbett, El Rio, Ariz.						
William F. Roden, Odessa, Texas	Roden, 2 and 1	Roden, 6 and 5				
A. I. Davey, Jr., Acacia, Ohio						
Kenneth Corcoran, Oyster Harbors, Mass.	Davey, 2 and 1			Dawson, 1 up, 20 hls.		
Robert E. Clark, Lakewood, Colo.						
William H. Ogden, Jr., Yolo Fliers, Calif.	Clark, 2 and 1	Haskell, 2 up				
Thomas R. Garlington, Atlanta, Ga.						
Gordon C. Haskell, Alderwood, Ore.	Haskell, 3 and 1		Dawson, 2 up			
John W. Dawson, Lakeside, Calif.						
Chester Sanok, Englewood, N.J.	Dawson, 2 and 1	Dawson, 2 and 1				
Ernest J. Gerardi, Wethersfield, Conn.						
Ken Towns, Crystal Springs, Calif.	Gerardi, 1 up, 19 hls.					

HALF

SECOND QUARTER

6th Round (18 Holes)		5th Round (18 Holes)	4th Round (18 Holes)	3rd Round (18 Holes)	2nd Round (18 Holes)	1st Round (18 Holes
					McManus	BYE—Roger T. McManus, Annandale, Calif.
				Hughes, 5 and 4	Hughes	BYE—Ben G. Hughes, Eastmoreland, Ore.
			T. Barnes, 1 up		T. Barnes	BYE—Thomas W. Barnes, Druid Hills, Ga.
				T. Barnes, 4 and 3	Hatala	BYE—Matt Hatala, Jr., Columbia-Edgewater, Ore.
		T. Barnes, 2 and 1			Stewart	BYE—Harold A. Stewart, Birmingham, Mich.
				Driver, be default	Driver	BYE—John J. Driver, Red Run, Mich.
			Clay, 3 and 1		Clay	BYE—Gordon C. Clay, Black Rock, Ga.
				Clay, 3 and 2	Nicholson	BYE—Jack Nicholson, Spokane, Wash.
	Selby, 1 up, 22 hls.				Morris	BYE—Robert L. Morris, Prince Georges, Md.
				Willits, by default	Willits	BYE—Robert W. Willits, Kansas City, Mo.
			Wild, 3 and 2		Wild	BYE—Claude Wild, Jr., Austin, Texas
				Wild, 1 up	Morey,	James W. McGonagill, Shreveport, La.
					by default	Frank Morey, Jr., San Diego, Calif.
		Selby, 3 and 2			Hickey,	Keith Welts, Seattle, Wash.
				Selby, 6 and 5	2 and 1	William J. Hickey, Jr., Town & C.C., Minn.
					Selby,	John H. Selby, Apawamis, N.Y.
			Selby, 6 and 5		2 up	Fred Wampler, Jr., Speedway, Ind.
					Roos,	Robert A. Roos, Jr., Olympic, Calif.
				Roos, 1 up	1 up, 19 hls.	Walter T. Harris, Fort Douglas, Utah
					Toronto,	Frank Toronto, Del Paso, Calif.
					1 up	Desmond Sullivan, Essex Fells, N.J.
Selby, 2 and 1					Boyd,	Bill Hoelle, Lake Merced, Calif.
				Boyd, 6 and 5	6 and 5	William S. Boyd, Jr., Burlingame, Calif.
					Marolich,	E. L. Bates, Portland, Ore.
			Hixon, 1 up		3 and 1	Frank J. Marolich, Broadmoor, Wash.
					Hixon,	James A. Wittenberg, Colonial, Tenn.
				Hixon, 2 and 1	1 up	Frank P. Hixon, San Gabriel, Calif.
					Levinson,	John S. Frey, Riverside, Ore.
		Hixon, 4 and 2			3 and 2	John O. Levinson, Webhamet, Maine
					Weston,	Fred Clark, Jr., Annandale, Calif.
				Millett, 1 up	2 up	Raymond E. Weston, Jr., Alderwood, Ore.
					Millett	Paul A. Millett, Harding Park, Calif.
			Millett, 6 and 4		3 and 2	Paul J. Bridston, Grand Forks, N.D.
					Doherty,	R. E. Talley, Jr., Greensburg, Pa.
				Doherty, 3 and 2	2 up	Ernest Doherty, Woburn, Mass.
					Oneal	Dr. William J. Oneal, Annandale, Calif.
	M. Ward, 6 and 5				4 and 2	T. J. White, Memphis, Tenn.
					Dana,	Larry Dana, Jr., Pennhills, Pa.
				M. Ward, 7 and 5	by default	Nick K. Weslock, Meadowbrook, Mich.
					M. Ward,	Marvin H. (Bud) Ward, Spokane, Wash.
			M. Ward, 3 and 2		9 and 7	W. A. Schneider, Waialae, Hawaii
					Frisina,	James L. Ukauka, Honolulu, Hawaii
				Stanovich, 5 and 3	5 and 3	James Frisina, Illini, Ill.
					Stanovich,	Martin Stanovich, Harding Park, Calif.
		M. Ward, 2 and 1			3 abd 1	Herbert A. Durham, Brook Hollow, Texas
					Paddock,	Jack Westland, Everett, Wash.
				Paddock, 1 up	3 and 2	Harold D. Paddock, Jr., Aurora, Ohio
					Andrews,	Gene Andrews, Mission Valley, Calif.
			H. M. Hunter, 3 and 1		2 and 1	Harrison R. Johnston, Minikahda, Minn.
					H. M. Hunter	H. MacGregor Hunter, Riviera, Calif.
				H. M. Hunter, 3 and 1	4 an 3	Robert K. Loane, Richmond, Calif.
					Tatum,	Ralph J. Evans, Palos Verdes, Calif.
					2 and 1	Frank D. Tatum, Jr., Stanford, Calif.

SEMI-FINAL ROUND—John W. Dawson defeated John H. Selby, 5 and 4

The first word after the player's name is the name of the player's club, except in the case of a foreign entrant.

THIRD QUARTER

1st Round (18 Holes)	2nd Round (18 Holes)	3rd Round (18 Holes)	4th Round (18 Holes)	5th Round (18 Holes)	6th Round (18 Holes)	Semi-Finals
BYE—John B. Ellis, Columbus, Ga.	Ellis					
BYE—David F. Dixon, New Orleans, La.	Dixon	Dixon, 1 up				
BYE—Robert Sweeny, Jr., Meadow Brook, N.Y.	Sweeny		Kennedy, 3 and 2			
BYE—Donald P. Kennedy, Santa Ana, Calif.	Kennedy	Kennedy, 3 and 2				
BYE—Ralph T. Strafaci, Hempstead, N.Y.	R. Strafaci			Robinson, 1 up		
BYE—Jack W. Robinson, Santa Ana, Calif.	Robinson	Robinson, by default				
BYE—Arthur C. Olfs, Jr., Oakland Hills, Mich.	Olfs		Robinson, 6 and 4			
BYE—Willis H. Blakely, Alderwood, Ore.	Blakely	Blakely, by default			H. Ward, 3 and 2	
BYE—Joey Rey, Yolo Fliers, Calif.	Rey					
BYE—Kenneth E. Sewell, Arizona, Ariz.	Sewell	Rey, 7 and 5				
BYE—Gene Dahlbender, Jr., Capital City, Ga.	Dahlbender		Dahlbender, 1 up			
BYE—George Gnau, Harding Park, Calif.	Gnau	Dahlbender, 2 up				
Frank C. McCann, Santa Ana, Calif.	McCann,			H. Ward, 1 up		
M. C. James, Jr., Cherokee, Tenn.	1 up, 19 hls.	Lance, 1 up				
Robert Goldwater, Phoenix, Ariz.	Lance,					
George Lance, Riviera, Calif.	3 and 2		H. Ward, 3 and 1			
E. Harvie Ward, Jr., Benvenue, N.C.	H.Ward,					
W. J. Berkley, Algonquin, Mo.	2 and 1	H. Ward, 3 and 1				
Arnold Goff, Fort Douglas, Utah	Goff,					Torza, 4 and 3
Richard Knight, Happy Hollow, Neb.	1 up, 20 hls.					
Charles M. Harper, Ponte Vedra, Fla.	Harper,					
Carl D. Wheeler, Reno, Nev.	5 and 3	Harper, 5 and 4				
Julius Boros, Wepawaug, Conn.	Kohlman,					
Richard F. Kohlmann, Normandie, Mo.	by default		Lind, 1 up			
Nathan T. Marshall, Los Angeles, Calif.	Marshall,					
George W. Cisar, Midlothian, Ill.	4 and 3	Lind, 1 up, 20 hls.				
Charles Lind, Lakewood, Colo.	Lind,					
J. E. Bernolfo, Jr., The C.C., Utah	3 and 2			Lind, 2 up		
Maurice J. McCarthy, Maketewah, Ohio	McCarthy,					
Paul C. Carter, Los Angeles, Calif.	3 and 2	McCarthy, 4 and 2				
Harry A. Pailer, Normandie, Mo.	Watson,					
Robert L. Watson, Wichita Falls, Texas	3 and 2		Sleppy, 3 and 2			
Ray Sleppy, Palos Verdes, Calif.	Sleppy,					
Randolph Scott, Bel-Air, Calif.	7 and 6	Sleppy, 1 up, 19 hls.				
Ernest Pieper, Jr., San Jose, Calif.	Pieper,				Torza, 2 up	
Kenneth G. Storey, Manito, Wash.	3 and 1					
George H. Rowbotham, Llanerch, Pa.	Rowbotham,					
Charles Evans, Jr., Edgewater, Ill.	5 and 4	Rowbotham, 2 and 1				
Harold Foreman, Lake Shore, Ill.	Foreman,					
Gordon Reid, Spokane, Wash..	3 and 2		Rowbotham, 1 up			
Cyril Pennell, Stanford, Calif.	Pennell,					
Silas Newton, Cherry Hills, Colo.	4 and 3	Pennell, 1 up				
William G. Ebey, Twin Hills, Okla.	Monahan,			Torza, 1 up		
Joseph W. Monahan, Jr., Winchester, Mass.	6 and 5					
Carl Vandervoort, Jr., Colonial, Texas	Meister,					
Edward L. Meister, Jr., Kirtland, Ohio	7 and 5	Meister, 1 up				
Thomas E. Sheehan, Oakland Hills, Mich.	Gardner,					
Robert Gardner, Bel-Air, Calif.	2 and 1		Torza, 4 and 3			
Ralph Wolf, California, Calif.	Torza,					
Felice J. Torza, Wethersfield, Conn.	8 and 6	Torza, 4 and 3				
Neil B. McGinnis, Phoenix, Ariz.	Paul,					
James W. Paul, Piping Rock, N.Y.	4 and 3					

CHAMPIONSHIP

HALF

FOURTH QUARTER

1st Round (18 Holes)

- BYE—Stanley E. Bishop, Norfolk, Mass.
- BYE—Henry G. Kershaw, Arizona, Ariz.
- BYE—A. W. Bijou, Sharp Park, Calif.
- BYE—James J. Molinari, Lincoln Park, Calif.
- BYE—Bruce N. McCormick, Lakeside, Calif.
- BYE—Theodore G. Roden, Odessa, Texas
- BYE—Charles Kocsis, Red Run, Mich.
- BYE—Stanley D. Moss, Riviera, Calif.
- BYE—Richard M. Bailey, Tilden Park, Calif.
- BYE—Leonard A. Holmes, Columbia-Edgewater, Ore.
- BYE—Junius J. Hebert, Louisiana State U., La.
- Rufus King, Wichita Falls, Texas / S. B. Anderson, Jr., Oklahoma City, Okla.
- Neil E. White, Tamarack, Conn. / Arnold Blum, Idle Hour, Ga.
- Arthur Langan, Bellevue, N.Y. / Jack R. Munger, Brook Hollow, Texas
- Robert R. Rosburg, Stanford, Calif. / Arthur F. Lynch, Winged Foot, N.Y.
- Franklin G. Clement, Onwentsia, Ill. / Clancy P. Miller, Swope Park, Mo.
- Guy Owen, Cut Bank, Mont. / William D. Higgins, Olympic, Calif.
- Robert H. (Skee) Riegel, Southern California, Calif. / Don Cherry, Wichita Falls, Texas
- Ted Adams, Blue Hills, Mo. / Clarke Hardwicke, Bel-Air, Calif.
- William L. Barber, Inglewood, Calif. / Adrian C. McManus, Annandale, Calif.
- James Oleska, Shore View, N.Y. / Willie I. Hunter, Jr., Riviera, Calif.
- George Treadwell, Sr., Memphis, Tenn. / Walter McAlpine, Vancouver, Canada
- William C. Campbell, Guyan, W. Va. / Clarence E. Earley, Salem, Mass.
- Luke M. Barnes, Atlanta, Ga. / Fred H. Schindler, Indian Hills, Mo.
- Harry L. Givan, Broadmoor, Wash. / Jack E. Bariteau, San Jose, Calif.
- Lloyd A. Martz, Red Run, Mich. / Smiley Quick, Inglewood, Calif.
- H. C. Dalrymple, C.C. of Lincoln, Neb. / Warren H. Berl, Lake Merced, Calif.
- Joe LaFortune, Jr., Southern Hills, Okla. / John J. Donohue, Jr., Sioux City, Iowa
- Morris Fisher, Riverside, Neb. / William H. Fortune, Alameda, Calif.
- Bernard A. Schriever, Belle Haven, Va. / Robert Cardinal, California, Calif.
- Jack Lovegren, San Jose, Calif. / Richard Irwin, Happy Hollow, Neb.
- Bud McKinney, Los Angeles, Calif. / Leonard White, Bob O'Links, Texas

2nd Round (18 Holes)

- Bishop
- Kershaw
- Bijou
- Molinari
- McCormick
- Roden
- Kocsis
- Moss
- Bailey
- Holmes
- Hebert
- King, 5 and 4
- White, 2 and 1
- Munger, 4 and 3
- Rosburg, 4 and 3
- Miller, 5 and 3
- Owen, 5 and 4
- Riegel, 2 and 1
- Hardwicke, 1 up, 19 hls.
- Barber, 3 and 1
- W. Hunter, 1 up
- Treadwell, 4 and 2
- Campbell, 3 and 2
- L. Barnes, 4 and 3
- J. Bariteau, 6 and 5
- Quick, by default
- Berl, by default
- Donohue, 3 and 2
- Fisher, 3 and 2
- Cardinal, 4 and 2
- Lovegren, 3 and 2
- McKinney, 1 up, 19 hls.

3rd Round (18 Holes)

- Bishop, by default
- Molinari, 5 and 4
- McCormick, 6 and 5
- Kocsis, 5 and 4
- Bailey, 3 and 2
- King, 1 up, 20 hls.
- Munger, 1 up
- Rosburg, 2 up
- Riegel, 5 and 4
- Hardwicke, 5 and 4
- W. Hunter, 3 and 1
- L. Barnes, 1 up, 25 hls.
- J. Bariteau, 1 up
- Berl, 4 and 3
- Cardinal, 4 and 2
- McKinney, 3 and 2

4th Round (18 Holes)

- Bishop, 3 and 1
- Kocsis, 1 up, 20 hls.
- Bailey, 3 and 2
- Rosburg, 1 up
- Riegel, 6 and 5
- L. Barnes, 4 and 3
- J. Bariteau, 5 and 4
- Cardinal, 4 and 3

5th Round (18 Holes)

- Kocsis, 2 and 1
- Rosburg, 1 up
- Riegel, 5 and 4
- J. Bariteau, 5 and 3

6th Round (18 Holes)

- Rosburg, 4 and 3
- Riegel, 3 and 1

Riegel, 2 and 1

SEMI-FINAL ROUND—Robert H. Riegel defeated Felice J. Torza, 2 and 1

1948
FORTY-EIGHTH AMATEUR CHAMPIONSHIP

Held at the Memphis Country Club, Memphis, Tenn., August 30-September 4.
Yardage—6,617. Par 70. 1,220 Entries, 210 Qualifiers, 210 Starters.
Championship entirely at match play.

FINAL ROUND (36 holes)—William P. Turnesa defeated Raymond E. Billows, 2 up and 1 to play.

UPPER

FIRST QUARTER

1st Round (18 Holes)	2nd Round (18 Holes)	3rd Round (18 Holes)	4th Round (18 Holes)	5th Round (18 Holes)	6th Round (18 Holes)	
David W. Smith, Jr., Gaston, N.C.	Jacobson,					
Robert J. Jacobson, Hollywood, N.J.	7 and 5	Kocsis,				
Glenn Oatman, Hillcrest, Mo.	Kocsis,	4 and 3				
Charles Kocsis, Red Run, Mich.	5 and 4		Kocsis,			
BYE—William C. Campbell, Guyan, W. Va.	Campbell		1 up			
		Stone,				
Hal M. Stone, Jr., Bloomington, Ill.	Stone,	2 up				
J. Pete Barnes, Atlanta, Ga.	1 up, 19 hls.			Kocsis, 6 and 5		
H.H. Pritchett, Tuscaloosa, Ala.	Pritchett,					
Robert D. Mitchell, Cedar Crest, Texas	2 up	Pritchett,				
BYE—John Griscom, Belle Meade, Tenn.	Griscom	2 up				
			Simonsen,			
Willie Barber, San Fernando Valley, Calif.	Simonsen,		4 and 3			
Adrian Simonsen, Minneapolis, Minn.	7 and 6	Simonsen,				
BYE—Gilbert Stubbs, Corsicana, Texas	Stubbs	7 and 6			Stranahan, 6 and 5	
Hiram S. Chamberlain, Fairyland, Tenn.	Dudley,					
Charles B. Dudley, Greenville, S.C.	2 and 1	Stranahan,				
Frank Strafaci, Pomonok, N.Y.	Stranahan,	1 up				
Frank R. Stranahan, Inverness, Ohio	4 and 3		Stranahan,			
BYE—Robert Lowry, Jr., Huntsville, Ala.	Lowry		3 and 2			
		Stembler,				
William Y. Stembler, Miami, Fla.	Stembler,	3 and 2		Stranahan, 3 and 1		
Frank S. Souchak, Oakmont, Pa.	1 up, 19 hls.					
Richard L. Smart, Pine Bluff, Ark.	Smart,					
Roland R. MacKenzie, Baltimore, Md.	2 up	Smart,				
BYE—Richard D. Chapman, Pinehurst, N.C.	Chapman	4 and 3				
			Smart,			
John W. Coyle, Illini, Ill.	Coyle,		1 up			
Max Felix, Hillcrest, Calif.	6 and 4	Robinson,				
Jack W. Robinson, Santa Ana, Calif.	Robinson,	4 and 2				Billows, 7 and 5
Guy Owen, Cut Bank, Mont.	1 up					
BYE—Gene Williams, Tuscaloosa, Ala.	Williams					
		Ford,				
Douglas M. Ford, Bonnie Briar, N.Y.	Ford,	6 and 5				
Gordon C. Clay, Black Rock, Ga.	4 and 3		Cestone,			
BYE—Michael Cestone, Crestmont, N.J.	Cestone		2 and 1			
		Cestone,				
James G. Jackson, Greenbriar Hills, Mo.	Jackson,	1 up				
Marcel J. Bellande, Great Southern, Miss.	6 and 4			Billows, 3 and 1		
John E. Lehman, Edgewater, Ill.	Lehman,					
Russell DeCarteret, Miami, Fla.	3 and 1	McCreary,				
BYE—Richard McCreary, Brae-Burn, Texas	McCreary	1 up				
			Billows,			
Don Schumacher, Dallas, Texas	Schumacher,		4 and 3			
Kit Carson, Miami, Fla.	4 and 2	Billows,				
Raymond E. Billows, Dutchess, N.Y.	Billows,	2 and 1				
Stanley S. Taylor, Jr., Waialae, Hawaii	6 and 5				Billows, 5 and 4	
BYE—Thomas B. Shelley, Riviera, Fla.	Shelley					
		Wright,				
Claude L. Wright, Cherry Hills, Colo.	Wright,	6 and 5				
James A. Wittenberg, Colonial, Tenn.	5 and 3		Wright,			
BYE—E.J. Rogers, Sr., Oklahoma City, Okla.	Rogers		4 and 3			
		Rogers,				
C. McVicker, Maketewah, Ohio	Sweeny,	1 up				
Robert J. Sweeny, Jr., Meadow Brook, N.Y.	4 and 3			Barrett, 1 up		
BYE—Wesley G. Brown, Chattanooga, Tenn.	Brown					
		Barrett,				
William K. Barrett, Jr., Colonial, Tenn.	Barrett,	4 and 3				
Arnold D. Palmer, Latrobe, Pa.	6 and 5		Barrett,			
BYE—Mal Galletta, North Hills, N.Y.	Galletta		4 and 3			
		Galletta,				
Sam Urzetta, Midvale, N.Y.	Houdry,	1 up, 19 hls.				
Jacques Houdry, Merion, Pa.	1 up, 20 hls.					

SEMI-FINAL ROUND (36 Holes)—Raymond E. Billows defeated Charles R. Coe, 6 up and 5 to play.

The first word after the player's name is the name of his club, except in the case of an Amateur Public Links Championship semi-finalist denoted †.

HALF | **SECOND QUARTER**

HALF	6th Round (18 Holes)	5th Round (18 Holes)	4th Round (18 Holes)	3rd Round (18 Holes)	2nd Round (18 Holes)	1st Round (18 Holes)
					Boros, 2 and 1	John A. Zoller, Ohio State, Ohio
				Boros, 1 up, 21 hls.		Julius Boros, D. Fairchild Wheeler, Conn.
					Leonard, 1 up	Daryl F. Schoonover, Shawnee, Kans.
						Thomas J. Leonard, Jr., Nashua, N.J.
			Boros, 5 and 3		Becka	BYE—Charles J. Becka, Jr., Calumet, Ill.
				Connelly, 1 up, 19 hls.	Connelly, 3 and 2	W.F. Bartels, Blue Hills, Mo.
						Harold J. Connelly, Normandie, Mo.
		Boros, 5 and 3			Sanders, 2 and 1	W.E. Sanders, Indian Hills, Mo.
				Wagner, 2 and 1		Henry A. McGrath, Jr., Winchester, Mass.
					Wagner	BYE—John E. Wagner, Skokie, Ill.
			Sloan, 2 and 1		Sloan, 2 up	William H. Zimmerman, Augusta National, Ga.
				Sloan, 3 and 2		Herbert A. Sloan, Kansas City, Mo.
					Martz	BYE—Lloyd A. Martz, Red Run, Mich.
	Coe, 4 and 3				Dana, 2 and 1	Larry Dana, Jr., Pennhills, Pa.
				Coe, 7 and 6		James E. Funston, Plum Hollow, Mich.
					Coe, 1 up	Junius J. Hebert, Louisiana State, La.
			Coe, 3 and 2			Charles R. Coe, Oklahoma City, Okla.
					Welch	BYE—Harry Welch, Salisbury, N.C.
				Key, 4 and 2	J.B. Key, 4 and 3	Jack B. Key, Jr., Columbus, Ga.
						Ralph T. Strafaci, Hempstead, N.Y.
		Coe, 6 and 4			Hardwicke, 4 and 2	B.B. Lotspeich, Miami, Fla.
				Hardwicke, 2 and 1		Clarke Hardwicke, Bel-Air, Calif.
					Andrews	BYE—Arthur H. Andrews, Jr., St. Charles, Ill.
			Hardwicke, 3 and 2		Mayer, 3 and 2	A. Richard Mayer, Winged Foot, N.Y.
				Brownell, 2 and 1		Jack Purdum, Westborough, Mo.
					Brownell, 5 and 3	Ronald Williams, Gowanie, Mich.
						Robert W. Brownell, Manor Md.
Coe, 4 and 3					Sanok	BYE—Chester Sanok, Englewood, N.J.
				Brink, 5 and 4	Brink, 1 up	Russell A. Allen, Jr., Hillcrest, Mo.
			Armstrong, 5 and 4			Harold Brink, Blythefield, Mich.
					Dickinson	BYE—Gardner E. Dickinson, Jr., La. State, La.
				Armstrong, 5 and 4	Armstrong, 3 and 2	Arthur Armstrong, Waialae, Hawaii
		Armstrong, 2 and 1				Albert E. Campbell, Sand Point, Wash.
					Bishop, 2 and 1	Stanley E. Bishop, Norfolk, Mass.
				Spomer, 1 up		Edmund K. Gravely, Benvenue, N.C.
					Spomer, 3 and 2	Don R. Spomer, Hillcrest, Neb.
			Buzick, 3 and 2			Ben Smith, Lochmoor, Mich.
					Buzick	BYE—John W. Buzick, Jr., Jonesboro, Ark.
				Buzick, 1 up	McHale, 1 up, 20 hls.	J.C. Hamilton, Jr., Twin Hills, Okla.
						James B. McHale, Jr., Saucon Valley, Pa.
	Armstrong, 3 and 2				Semple, 1 up, 19 hls.	Tom Whiteway, Canterbury, Ohio
				Fowler, 6 and 4		Harton S. Semple, Allegheny, Pa.
					Fowler	BYE—Keith Fowler, Hillcrest, Okla.
			Fowler, 2 and 1		McNair, 8 and 7	W.R. Dowtin, Myers Park, N.C.
				McNair, 1 up, 19 hls.		James M. McNair, Aiken, S.C.
					Jones	BYE—Thomas Jones, Jr., Tippecanoe, Ohio
		Levinson, 3 and 2			Levinson, 4 and 2	John O. Levinson, Webhannet, Me.
				Levinson, 1 up, 21 hls.		Edward A. Johnston, C.C. of Maryland
					Kay	BYE—Oliver Kay, †Toledo, Ohio
			Levinson, 2 and 1		Rosburg, 1 up	Raymond E. Weston, Jr., Spokane, Wash.
				Cash, 4 and 2		Robert R. Rosburg, Stanford University, Calif.
					Cash, 7 and 6	Walter Cash, Hickory Hills, Mo.
						John Schumacher, Hillcrest, Neb.

THIRD QUARTER

1st Round (18 Holes)	2nd Round (18 Holes)	3rd Round (18 Holes)	4th Round (18 Holes)	5th Round (18 Holes)	6th Round (18 Holes)	
P. James Boyle, Jr., Eveleth, Minn. •	Boyle, 6 and 5					
Robert H. Olson, Lochmoor, Mich.		Plant, 3 and 2				
John Plant, Cairo, Egypt	Plant, 8 and 7					
Charles Rosen, II, Lakewood, La.			Hamer, 8 and 6			
BYE—James Frisina, Sr., Illini, Ill.	Frisina	Hamer, 1 up				
George S. Hamer, Columbus, Ga.	Hamer, 7 and 6			Carothers, 1 up		
Cullen E. Baker, Jr., Richland, Tenn.						
Edward L. Meister, Jr., Kirtland, Ohio	H. Ward, 5 and 4					
E. Harvie Ward, Jr., Benvenue, N.C.		Carothers, 2 and 1				
BYE—Ham Carothers, Greenwood, Miss.	Carothers		Carothers, 1 up, 19 hls.			
Albert C. Besselink, Tam O'Shanter, Ill.	Besselink, 1 up, 21 hls.					
Hobart L. Manley, Jr., Savannah, Ga.		Besselink, 4 and 2				
BYE—Paul Dye, Jr., Urbana, Ohio	Dye				McGonagill, 7 and 5	
John J. Donohue, Jr., Sioux City, Iowa	Lowery, 2 and 1					
E.E. Lowery, California G.C., Calif.		Lowery, 2 and 1				
James Oleska, Shore View, N.Y.	Oleska, 1 up, 19 hls.					
Thomas W. Barnes, Druid Hills, Ga.			McGonagill, 1 up, 19 hls.			
BYE—James McGonagill, Shreveport, La.	McGonagill	McGonagill, 3 and 2				
Morris Williams, Jr., Austin, Texas	Williams, 3 and 2			McGonagill, 3 and 2		
Dr. Charles Van Epps, Phoenix, Ariz.						
Dee Replogle, Oklahoma City, Okla.	R.F. Riegel, 3 and 2					
Robert F. Riegel, Brae-Burn, Texas		R.F. Riegel, 2 and 1				
BYE—Hans Merrell, Brevard, N.C.	Merrell		R.F. Riegel, 6 and 5			
Warren Higgins, Lakewood, Texas	Taylor, 1 up					Dahlbender, 1 up, 19 holes
Perry T. Taylor, Guyan, W. Va.		Beckjord, 6 and 4				
Walter E. Beckjord, Yale, Conn.	Beckjord, 1 up					
Jack Hamilton, James River, Va.						
BYE—Edwin B. Hopkins, Jr., Austin, Texas	Hopkins	Dahlbender, 5 and 4				
Richard L. Hackett, Coosa, Ga.	Dahlbender, 5 and 4					
Eugene Dahlbender, Jr., Capital City, Ga.			Dahlbender, 3 and 1			
BYE—Robert E. Clark, Lakewood, Colo.	Clark	Skee Riegel, 1 up				
Richard Ewert, Santa Ana, Calif.	Skee Riegel, 1 up			Dahlbender, 3 and 2		
Robert H. (Skee) Riegel, Southern Cal., Calif.						
John W. Dawson, Lakeside, Calif.	Dawson, 8 and 6					
John Busemeyer, Wyoming, Ohio		Dawson, 2 and 1				
BYE—Dr. George M. Trainor, Oak Hill, N.Y.	Trainor		Harris, 4 and 2			
Harry Root, Palma Ceia, Fla.	Root, 4 and 3					
Robert F. Lewis, Ridgeway, Tenn.		Harris, 1 up, 20 hls.			Dahlbender, 6 and 4	
Robert Harris, La Rinconada, Calif.	Harris, 1 up					
Fred Wampler, Speedway, Ind.						
BYE—Hezzie Carson, San Angelo, Texas	Carson	Carson, 1 up				
Herbert P. Smith, Dubsdread, Fla.	Evans, 1 up					
Charles Evans, Jr., Edgewater, Ill.			Zachritz, 5 and 4			
BYE—Howard Zachritz, Meadow Brook, Mo.	Zachritz	Zachritz, 4 and 2				
Theodore G. Roden, Odessa, Texas	Atwood, 4 and 3			Cass, 1 up		
W.H. Atwood, Jr., Dallas, Texas						
BYE—Ben W. Thompson, Richland, Tenn.	Thompson	Childress, 4 and 3				
Henderson P. Childress, Colonial, Tenn.	Childress, 7 and 6					
Joseph C. Harris, Oak Ridge, Minn.			Cass, 1 up			
BYE—Maurice Nee, Columbia, Md.	Nee	Cass, 5 and 3				
John D. Culp, Jr., Ridge, Ill.	Cass, 3 and 2					
Louis Cass, Lakeside, Calif.						

SEMI-FINAL ROUND (36 Holes)—William P. Turnesa defeated Eugene Dahlbender, Jr., 8 up and 6 to play.

IONSHIP—Continued

HALF

FOURTH QUARTER

6th Round (18 Holes)	5th Round (18 Holes)		4th Round (18 Holes)	3rd Round (18 Holes)	2nd Round (18 Holes)	1st Round (18 Holes)
				M. Ward, 2 and 1	M. Ward, 2 and 1	Marvin (Bud) Ward, Spokane, Wash.
						James W. Key, Columbus, Ga.
					White, 1 up, 19 hls.	Benno Janssen, Jr., Farmington, Va.
			M. Ward, 3 and 2			Edward White, Houston, Texas
					Trammell	BYE—G.M. Trammell, Jr., Belle Meade, Tenn.
				Trammell, 4 and 2	Mulherin, 2 and 1	Lawrence Glosser, Twin Hills, Okla.
						Frank X. Mulherin, Jr., Augusta Natl., Ga.
		M. Ward, 2 and 1			Flenniken, 2 and 1	Arthur F. Lynch, Winged Foot, N.Y.
				A. Stone, 2 and 1		William F. Flenniken, Cherry Hills, Colo.
					Stone	BYE—Albert A. Stone, Jr., Jackson, Tenn.
			A. Stone, 3 and 2		Wild, 1 up	William Roden, Odessa, Texas
				J. Ward, 6 and 5		Claude C. Wild, Jr., Austin, Texas
	Turnesa, 3 and 1				J. Ward	BYE—James C. Ward, Belle Meade, Tenn.
					Turnesa, 1 up	Sam Kirkpatrick, Richland, Tenn.
				Turnesa, 6 and 4		William P. Turnesa, Knollwood, N.Y.
					Moore, 3 and 2	Tim Moore, La Gorce, Fla.
			Turnesa, 2 and 1			Walter Hagen, Jr., Hermitage, Va.
					Garth	BYE—C. Tyrrell Garth, Jr., Beaumont, Texas
				Garth, 5 and 3	Strange, 6 and 5	E.J. Rogers, Jr., Oklahoma City, Okla.
		Turnesa, 3 and 2				Thomas Strange, Jr., Hyde Park, Ohio
					Fottrell, 1 up, 19 hls.	Morgan M. Fottrell, Jr., Los Altos, Calif.
				Fottrell, 1 up		Louie E. Douglass, Brae-Burn, Texas
			Knowles, 5 and 4		Reynolds	BYE—Mally W. Reynolds, Dallas, Texas
					Knowles, 2 and 1	Robert W. Willits, Kansas City, Mo.
				Knowles, 1 up		Robert W. Knowles, Jr., The C.C., Mass.
					Munger, 1 up, 19 hls.	Walter Cisco, Audubon, Ky.
Turnesa, 2 and 1						Jack R. Munger, Brook Hollow, Texas
					Wood	BYE—Walter Wood, Tuscaloosa, Ala.
				Lutz, 3 and 2	Lutz, 2 and 1	J. Elmer Lutz, Jr., Reading, Pa.
			Lutz, 2 and 1			Thomas E. Walsh, Greenville, Miss.
					Penecale	BYE—Sam Penecale, Melrose, Pa.
				Penecale, 2 and 1	Sellman, 2 and 1	Jack Sellman, Golfcrest, Texas
		McCormick, 2 and 1				Norton Harris, Miami, Fla.
					Haverstick, 1 up	Robert J. Cardinal, California G.C., Calif.
				McCormick, 4 and 2		Harry H. Haverstick, Jr., Lancaster, Pa.
					McCormick, 3 and 2	Bruce N. McCormick, Lakeside, Calif.
			McCormick, 1 up, 19 hls.			Lloyd R. French, Jr., Odessa, Texas
					Seyler	BYE—Robert E. Seyler, Ashland, Ohio
	McCormick, 4 and 3			Victor, 2 and 1	Victor, 4 and 3	George E. Victor, Glen View, Ill.
						John Wood, Cincinnati, Ohio
					Lewis, 4 and 3	Paul C. Cavanagh, South Bay, N.Y.
				Lewis, 2 and 1		Norman F. Lewis, Golfcrest, Texas
					Olver	BYE—John N. Olver, Dallas, Texas
			Goodloe, 7 and 6		Goodloe, 5 and 4	Gus T. Moreland, Mt. Hawley, Ill.
				Goodloe, 2 up		W.L. Goodloe, Jr., Valdosta, Ga.
					Parent	BYE—Ervin Parent, Inglewood, Wash.
		Kraft, 1 up			Weaver, 2 up	William Ogden, Jr., Yolo Fliers, Calif.
				Kraft, 1 up		John B. Weaver, Pine Forest, Texas
					Kraft	BYE—John F. Kraft, Lakewood, Colo.
			Kraft, 2 and 1		Nelson, 5 and 4	John T. Nelson, Mission Valley, Calif.
				Russell, 1 up		Leroy MacMullin, Dallas, Texas
					Russell, 2 up	Henry H. Russell, Riviera, Fla.
						Desmond Sullivan, Essex Fells, N.J.

1949

FORTY-NINTH AMATEUR CHAMPIONSHIP

Held at the Oak Hill Country Club, Rochester, N.Y., August 29-September 3.
Yardage—6,800. Par 71. 1,060 Entries, 210 Qualifiers, 210 Starters.
Championship entirely at match play.
FINAL ROUND (36 Holes)—Charles R. Coe defeated Rufus King, 11 up and 10 to play.

UPPER

FIRST QUARTER

1st Round (18 Holes)	2nd Round (18 Holes)	3rd Round (18 Holes)	4th Round (18 Holes)	5th Round (18 Holes)	6th Round (18 Holes)	
Thomas Strafaci, Shore View, N.Y.	Paddock, 1 up					
Harold D. Paddock, Jr., Aurora, Ohio		Paddock, 2 and 1				
William L. Granberry, Belle Meade, Tenn.	Granberry, 1 up					
Royal Hogan, Colonial, Texas			Paddock, 2 and 1			
BYE—Gordon C. Peterson, Minneapolis, Minn.	Peterson					
		Connolly, 4 and 3				
Frank Connolly, Gowanie, Mich.	Connolly, 2 and 1			Paddock, 1 up, 19 hls.		
William Hyndman, III, Huntingdon Valley, Pa.						
Dow Finsterwald, Parkersburg, W. Va.	Finsterwald, 2 and 1					
Tom Henderson, Jr., Belle Meade, Tenn.		Finsterwald, 3 and 2				
BYE—Eli Bariteau, Jr., San Jose, Calif.	Bariteau					
			Rogers, 1 up			
Avery Beck, Raleigh, N.C.	Andzel, 2 up					
Walter C. Andzel, South Shore, N.Y.		Rogers, 1 up, 20 hls.				
BYE—Ken Rogers, Wilshire, Calif.	Rogers				Paddock, 2 and 1	
John B. Weaver, Brae-Burn, Texas	Weston, 6 and 5					
Ray E. Weston, Jr., Spokane, Wash.		Weston, 4 and 3				
James B. Knowles, Greenwich, Conn.	Knowles, 1 up					
Jacques Houdry, Merion, Pa.			Weston, 3 and 2			
BYE—Charles Shelden, La Gorce, Fla.	Shelden					
		Shelden, 3 and 2				
Charles J. Becka, Jr., Calumet, Ill.	Becka, 1 up, 19 hls.			Weston, 2 and 1		
James G. Jackson, Greenbriar Hills, Mo.						
Burr Melvin, James River, Va.	Moorhead, 1 up					
Harry H. Moorhead, Big Spring, Ky.		Moorhead, 8 and 6				
BYE—Harton S. Semple, Allegheny, Pa.	Semple					
			Smith, 1 up			
R.R. Ahern, Meadowbrook, Mich.	McBride, 1 up, 19 hls.					
Joseph A. McBride, Arcola, N.J.		Smith, 7 and 6				
Charles F. McKenna, Jr., Oak Hill, N.Y.	Smith, 1 up, 20 hls.					
Ben Smith, Lochmoor, Mich.						King, 1 up
BYE—Arnold Blum, Idle Hour, Ga.	Blum					
		Hunter, 5 up				
Gerald H. Micklem, Sevenoaks, Kent, England	Hunter, 5 and 3					
H. MacGregor Hunter, Riviera, Calif.			Hunter, 2 and 1			
BYE—Julian H. Roberts, Augusta C.C., Ga.	Roberts					
		Shields, 4 and 3				
John M. Garrison, McFarlin, Okla.	Shields, 3 and 2			Hunter, 1 up		
William J. Shields, Wolfert's Roost, N.Y.						
Edward P. Martin, Winchester, Mass.	Martin, 3 and 2					
William M. Cole, Mount Pleasant, Md.		Martin, 6 and 4				
BYE—Harry H. Pritchett, Tuscaloosa, Ala.	Pritchett					
			Martin, 2 and 1			
Dan Carmichael, Columbus, Ohio	Carmichael, 2 and 1					
Bob Veylupek, Broadmoor, Colo.		Carmichael, 5 and 4				
Anthony J. Langan, Syracuse Yacht, N.Y.	McCready, 4 and 2				King, 1 up	
S.M. McCready, Sunningdale, Berks, England						
BYE—Ronald J. White, Hoylake, Cheshire, England	White					
		Boatwright, 3 and 2				
P.J. Boatwright, Jr., Spartanburg, S.C.	Boatwright, 4 and 3					
Neil G. Croonquist, Minneapolis, Minn.			King, 3 and 2			
BYE—Raymond F. Allen, Jr., Rochester, N.Y.	Allen					
		King, 5 and 4				
Rufus King, Wichita Falls, Texas	King, 2 and 1			King, 3 and 1		
Robert W. Willits, Kansas City, Mo.						
BYE—F.A. Henneken, Monterey Peninsula, Calif.	Henneken					
		Lynch, 2 up				
Elbert S. Jemison, Jr., Birmingham, Ala.	Lynch, 3 and 2					
Arthur F. Lynch, Winged Foot, N.Y.			Lynch, 1 up			
BYE—Lloyd R. French, Jr., Odessa, Texas	French					
		French, 2 up				
Gay Brewer, Jr., Picadome, Ky.	Gagliardi, 2 and 1					
Joseph F. Gagliardi, Winged Foot, N.Y.						

SEMI-FINAL ROUND (36 Holes) Rufus King defeated William P. Turnesa, 2 up and 1 to play.

The first word after the player's name is the name of the player's club, except in the case of a foreign entrant.

HALF

SECOND QUARTER

6th Round (18 Holes)	5th Round (18 Holes)		4th Round (18 Holes)	3rd Round (18 Holes)	2nd Round (18 Holes)	1st Round (18 Holes)
				Garbacz, 2 up	Hewitt, 1 up	Arch M. Hewitt, Jr., Guyan, W. Va. Joseph F. Switzer, Sunset, Mo.
			Selby, 2 up		Garbacz, 1 up	B.B. Lotspeich, La Gorce, Fla. Mike Garbacz, Erskine Park Ind.
					Selby	BYE—John H. Selby, Apawamis, N.Y.
		Strafaci, 3 and 2		Selby, 2 and 1	VanNostrand, 4 and 3	Russell DeCarteret, Miami, Fla. George D. VanNostrand, Brookville, N.Y.
				Strafaci, 1 up	Hardwicke, 2 and 1	George Dawson, Glen Oak, Ill. Clarke Hardwicke, Bel-Air, Calif.
			Strafaci, 1 up		Strafaci	BYE—Frank Strafaci, Pomonok, N.Y.
				Worsham, 6 and 4	Jacobson, 7 and 6	Charles M. Sawyer, Interlachen, Minn. Robert J. Jacobson, Hollywood, N.J.
	Strafaci, 3 and 2				Worsham	BYE—Marvin C. Worsham, Bethesda, Md.
				Offutt, 2 and 1	Bogart, 5 and 4	Joseph Tereskiewicz, Race Brook, Conn. Ralph M. Bogart, Chevy Chase, Md.
			Fair, 5 and 4		Offutt, 2 and 1	Harry C. Offutt, Jr., Fort Wayne, Ind. Edward E. Lowery, California G.C., Calif.
				Fair, 5 and 3	Draper	BYE—Tom Draper, Red Run, Mich.
		Fair, 1 up			Fair, 3 and 1	Bob Fair, Scarboro, Ontario, Canada Robert A. Roos, Jr., Olympic, Calif.
				Crossley, 5 and 4	Crossley, 6 and 5	Wilfred Crossley, Norfolk Mass. H. Carl Vandervoort, Jr., Colonial, Texas
			Crossley, 2 and 1		Ragland	BYE—William E. Ragland, III, Chattanooga, Tenn.
				Hamilton, 2 up	Hamilton, 8 and 6	Tom Shelley, Riviera, Fla. J.C. Hamilton, Jr., Tulsa, Okla.
Turnesa, 3 and 2					Meister, 4 and 2	Edward L. Meister, Jr., Kirtland, Ohio Jack Munger, Brook Hollow, Texas
				Urzetta, 2 up	Moore	BYE—Bob Moore, La Gorce, Fla.
			Urzetta, 5 and 4		Urzetta, 6 and 5	Theodore G. Roden, Odessa, Texas Sam Urzetta, Midvale, N.Y.
				Dye, 1 up, 21 hls.	Dye	BYE—Paul Dye, Jr., Urbana, Ohio
		Dudley, 1 up			Bigham, 2 and 1	George F. Bigham, Jr., Swope Park, Mo. James Bruen, Jr., Little Island, Cork, Ireland
				McCormick, 7 and 5	Pierce, 4 and 3	David G. Ritchie, Brae-Burn, Texas Thomas M. Pierce, Rutland, Vt.
			Dudley, 3 and 2		McCormick, 1 up	George E. Victor, Glen View, Ill. Bruce N. McCormick, Lakeside, Calif.
				Dudley, 3 and 2	Armstrong	BYE—Arthur Armstrong, Waialae, Hawaii
	Turnesa, 3 and 2				Dudley, 4 and 2	Allan Whaling, Hyde Park, Ohio Charles B. Dudley, Greenville, S.C.
				Turnesa, 1 up	Foreman, 4 and 2	Ernest B. Millward, Parkstone, Dorset, England Harold Foreman, Jr., Lake Shore, Ill.
			Turnesa, 5 and 4		Turnesa	BYE—William P. Turnesa, Knollwood, N.Y.
				Penecale, 2 up	McCoy, 2 and 1	Alex Banazek, Westvale, N.Y. Robert E. McCoy, Druid Hills, Ga.
		Turnesa, 6 and 5			Penecale	BYE—Samuel Penecale, Melrose, Pa.
				Corcoran, 3 and 2	Palmer, 2 up	Charles Evans, Jr., Edgewater, Ill. Ray Palmer, Grosse Ile, Mich.
			Billows, 2 up		Corcoran	BYE—Kenneth F. Corcoran, Charles River, Mass.
				Billows, 1 up, 20 hls.	Bates, 1 up, 20 hls.	Eugene L. Bates, Portland, Ore. James E. Funston, Plum Hollow, Mich.
					Billows, 7 and 5	L. Welling Eisenmann, Little Rock, Ark. Ray Billows, Dutchess, N.Y.

THIRD QUARTER

1st Round (18 Holes)	2nd Round (18 Holes)	3rd Round (18 Holes)	4th Round (18 Holes)	5th Round (18 Holes)	6th Round (18 Holes)	
Arnold D. Palmer, Latrobe, Pa.	Palmer, 3 and 2					
Frederick W. Mayer, Westchester, N.Y.		Palmer, 4 and 3				
Benno Janssen, Jr., Farmington, Va.	Robinson, 4 and 2					
Charles Robinson, Belle Meade, Tenn.			Rainwater, 4 and 3			
BYE—John P. Ward, Syracuse Yacht, N.Y.	Ward					
		Rainwater, 2 and 1				
Dominick Morano, Glen Ridge, N.J.	Rainwater, 1 up			Rainwater, 1 up, 21 hls.		
Crawford Rainwater, Pensacola, Fla.						
James Frisina, Illini, Ill.	Emery, 2 and 1					
Walter Emery, Tulsa, Okla.		Emery, 5 and 4				
BYE—Warren N. Higgins, Lakewood, Texas	Higgins					
			Emery, 2 and 1			
Richard L. Spangler, Jr., Lincoln, Neb.	Spangler, 4 and 3					
Robert E. Cochoran, Meadow Brook, Mo.		Hoff, 7 and 6				
BYE—Arthur Hoff, Ruth Lake, Ill.	Hoff				Campbell, 4 and 3	
Robert A. Hill, Oak Hill, N.Y.	Campbell, 4 and 3					
William C. Campbell, Guyan, W. Va.		Campbell, 1 up, 20 hls				
W.L. Goodloe, Jr., Valdosta, Ga.	Goodloe, 3 and 2					
Edmund Janiak, Westvale, N.Y.			Campbell, 3 and 2			
BYE—Tim Moore, La Gorce, Fla.	Moore					
		Lutz, 3 and 2				
J. Elmer Lutz, Jr., Reading, Pa.	Lutz, 1 up			Campbell, 1 up		
Lionel J. Noah, Jr., Winged Foot, N.Y.						
Donald M. Bell, Lakewood, Colo.	Bell, 1 up					
Thomas J. Leonard, Jr., Nashua, N.H.		Bell, 5 and 4				
BYE—William Markham, Wethersfield, Conn.	Markham					
			Perowne, 2 and 1			
Arthur H. Perowne, Norwich, England	Perowne, 1 up					
W.Y. Stembler, Miami, Fla.		Perowne, 1 up, 19 hls.				
Edward A. Johnston, Maryland, Md.	Wall, 2 up					
Arthur J. Wall, Jr., Scranton, Pa.						Campbell, 1 up
BYE—John B. Wade, Jr., Chickasaw, Tenn.	Wade					
		Wade, 3 and 2				
Newton Burnett, Shreveport, La.	Burnett, 6 and 5					
Gage B. Fleming, Wolfert's Roost, N.Y.			Boros, 6 and 5			
BYE—Robert F. Chapman, Spartanburg, S.C.	Chapman					
		Boros, 6 and 5				
Maurice J. McCarthy, Jr., Maketewah, Ohio	Boros, 1 up, 21 hls.			Boros, 5 and 4		
Julius Boros, Rockledge, Conn.						
Marshall Trammell, Belle Meade, Tenn.	Levinson, 1 up, 19 hls.					
John O. Levinson, Tam O'Shanter, Ill.		Levinson, 5 and 4				
BYE—Adrian O. Simonsen, Minneapolis, Minn.	Simonsen					
			Levinson, 1 up			
Bud McKinney, Dallas, Texas	Cisco, 1 up					
Walter Cisco, Audubon, Ky.		Manley, 4 and 2				
Hobart L. Manley, Jr., Savannah, Ga.	Manley, 1 up				Boros, 4 and 2	
George Bruno, Jr., Tilden Park, Calif.						
BYE—James B. McHale, Jr., Saucon Valley, Pa.	McHale					
		McHale, 3 and 2				
Frank H. Hedrick, Radium, Ga.	Busemeyer, 4 and 2					
John Busemeyer, Wyoming, Ohio			McHale, 3 and 2			
BYE—Lee Markey, Transit Valley, N.Y.	Markey					
		Carr, 5 and 4				
Joseph B. Carr, Sutton, Dublin, Ireland	Carr, 3 and 2			McHale, 3 and 2		
Tony Ruddy, Inverness, Ohio						
BYE—Pat Mucci, Preakness Hills, N.J.	Mucci					
		Riegel, 6 and 5				
Robert H. (Skee) Riegel, Tulsa, Okla.	Riegel, 7 and 6					
Thomas K. Creal, II, Conewango Valley, Pa.			Riegel, 3 and 2			
BYE—Norman Mann, California, Calif.	Mann					
		Stranahan, 5 and 4				
William G. Holloway, Jr., Meadow Brook, N.Y.	Stranahan, 7 and 5					
Frank R. Stranahan, Inverness, Ohio						

SEMI-FINAL ROUND (36 Holes)—Charles R. Coe defeated William C. Campbell, 8 up and 7 to play.

1949 AMATEUR

FOURTH QUARTER

6th Round (18 Holes)	5th Round (18 Holes)	4th Round (18 Holes)	3rd Round (18 Holes)	2nd Round (18 Holes)	1st Round (18 Holes)
				Wendrow,	Louis Wendrow, Lansing, Mich.
			Wendrow,	4 and 2	Ernest J. Gerardi, Wethersfield, Conn.
			1 up	Preisler,	Edwin D. Preisler, Beechmont, Ohio
		Coe,		3 and 2	William F. Roden, Odessa, Texas
		8 and 7		Coe	BYE—Charles R. Coe, Oklahoma City, Okla.
			Coe,		
			4 and 3	Garth,	C.T. Garth, Jr., Beaumont, Texas
				3 and 1	Wilbur Bartles, Blue Hills, Mo.
		Coe, 4 and 2		Owens,	James Oleska, Shore View, N.Y.
			Sweeny,	1 up	John C. Owens, Lexington, Ky.
			5 and 3	Sweeny	BYE—Robert Sweeny, Meadow Brook N.Y.
		Sweeny,			
		4 and 3		Key,	Jack B. Key, Jr., Columbus, Ga.
			Key,	2 up	Chris Gers, Twin Hills, Okla.
			7 and 6	Moncado	BYE—Gen. Hilario C. Moncado, Riviera, Calif.
	Coe, 1 up, 19 hls.			Reed,	Ted Adams, Evanston, Ill.
			Reed,	1 up, 19 hls.	Mort Reed, Monroe, N.Y.
			2 up	Rowbotham,	George H. Rowbotham, Llanerch, Pa.
		Owen,		2 and 1	Robert E. Eckis, Jr., Park, N.Y.
		5 and 4		Kunkle	BYE—John H. Kunkle, Jr., St. Clair, Pa.
			Owen,		
			7 and 6	Owen,	Guy Owen, Cut Bank, Mont.
				4 and 3	**Bill Bobbitt, Colonial, Tenn.**
		Ward, 1 up		Kraft,	John F. Kraft, Lakewood, Colo.
			Goldwater,	3 and 2	Stanley E. Bishop, Norfolk, Mass.
			3 and 2	Goldwater	BYE—Robert Goldwater, Phoenix, Ariz.
		Ward,			
		7 and 6		Goodrich,	Clifford A. Goodrich, Brook-Lea, N.Y.
			Ward,	1 up, 19 hls.	Don Addington, Brae-Burn, Texas
Coe, 1 up, 21 hls.			2 and 1	Ward,	**E. Harvie Ward, Jr., Benvenue, N.C.**
				3 and 2	Delbert Walker, Virginia, Calif.
				Cestone	BYE—Michael Cestone, Crestmont, N.J.
			Cestone,		
			1 up	Ribner,	Henry Russell, Riviera, Fla.
		Cestone,		6 and 5	Lloyd D. Ribner, Fenway, N.Y.
		5 and 4		Patton	BYE—William J. Patton, Mimosa, N.C.
			Patton,		
			5 and 4	Morrell,	Paul Anderson, Riviera, Fla.
				1 up	John P. Morrell, Elgin, Ill.
		Kammer, 3 and 2		Spencer,	Tom Burke, Jr., Brae-Burn, Texas
			Spencer,	7 and 5	Wynsol Spencer, James River, Va.
			4 and 3	Jones,	Morton M. Jones, Mission Hills, Mo.
		Kammer,		2 and 1	John R. Lyons, Garden City G.C., N.Y.
		1 up		Towns	BYE—Kenneth J. Towns, Crystal Springs, Calif.
			Kammer,		
			2 and 1	Kammer,	Fred Kammer, Jr., Detroit, Mich.
				3 and 2	Spencer Overton, Rolling Road, Md.
	Dawson, 2 and 1			Pelnik,	Mal Galletta, North Hills, N.Y.
			Thom,	1 up	Thomas Pelnik, Binghamton, N.Y.
			9 and 7	Thom	BYE—Kenneth G. Thom, London, England
		Wampler,			
		2 up		Wampler,	Fred Wampler, Jr., Speedway, Ind.
			Wampler,	1 up, 20 hls.	Chester Sanok, Upper Montclair, N.J.
			3 and 2	Geiss	BYE—Jack Geiss, Norwood Hills, Mo.
		Dawson, 2 and 1		Dawson,	John Schumacher, Happy Hollow, Neb.
				6 and 5	John W. Dawson, Lakeside, Calif.
			Dawson,		
			4 and 2	Lucas	BYE—P.B. Lucas, Northwood, Middlesex, England
		Dawson,			
		5 and 3		Barnes,	Thomas W. Barnes, Druid Hills, Ga.
				5 and 4	Robert W. Knowles, Jr., The C.C., Mass.
			Pieper,	Pieper,	Ernest Pieper, Jr., San Jose, Calif.
			2 and 1	4 and 2	Tom Whiteway, Canterbury, Ohio

1950
FIFTIETH AMATEUR CHAMPIONSHIP

Held at the Minneapolis Golf Club, Minneapolis, Minn., August 21-26.
Yardage—6,655. Par 71. 1,025 Entries, 210 Qualifiers, 210 Starters.
Championship entirely at match play.
FINAL ROUND (36 Holes)—Sam Urzetta defeated Frank R. Stranahan, 1 up, 39 holes.

UPPER

FIRST QUARTER

1st Round (18 Holes)	2nd Round (18 Holes)	3rd Round (18 Holes)	4th Round (18 Holes)	5th Round (18 Holes)	6th Round (18 Holes)	
David Logan, Biltmore, Ill.	Logan, 1 up, 19 hls.					
Jack Anderson, Bel-Air, Calif.		Logan, 3 and 2				
Jack R. Munger, Brook Hollow, Texas	Munger, 3 and 1					
Mason Rudolph, Clarksville, Tenn.			Logan, 3 and 2			
BYE—Arnold Blum, Idle Hour, Ga.	Blum					
		Blum, 2 and 1				
Tom Strafaci, Shore View, N.Y.	Strafaci, 3 and 1					
Charles Battey, Lincoln, Neb.				Veech, 1 up		
Don Cherry, Odessa, Texas	Donohue, 3 and 2					
John J. Donohue, Jr., Sioux City, Iowa		Donohue, 5 and 3				
BYE—Henry Ernst, Univ. of Minnesota, Minn.	Ernst					
			Veech, 2 and 1			
Ward H. Marshall, Midland Hills, Minn.	Veech, 4 and 3					
Tom Veech, North Hills, Wis.		Veech, 3 and 2				
BYE—John J. Sierge, Twin Brooks, N.J.	Sierge				Veech, 2 and 1	
George L. Coleman, Jr., Southern Hills, Okla.	Coleman, 7 and 6					
Emerson Carey, Jr., Denver, Colo.		Coleman, 1 up, 19 hls.				
Marshall Trammell, Belle Meade, Tenn.	Trammell, 1 up					
Bud McKinney, Dallas, Texas			Paddock, 2 and 1			
BYE—Harold D. Paddock, Jr., Aurora, Ohio	Paddock					
		Paddock, 5 and 3				
John E. Lehman, Edgewater, Ill.	Lehman, 5 and 3			Paddock, 4 and 3		
William L. Korns, Fort Douglas, Utah						
Robert W. Goldwater, Phoenix, Ariz.	Carey, 2 and 1					
Emerson Carey, III, Denver, Colo.		Carey, 2 and 1				
BYE—George Bruno, Tilden Park, Calif.	Bruno					
			Coe, 5 and 4			
Albert Clasen, Como Park, Minn.	Clasen, 3 and 1					
Tom Martin, Jr., Mobile, Ala.		Coe, 3 and 1				
Thomas S. Jamison, Jr., Greensburg, Pa.	Coe, 5 and 4					Knowles, 3 and 2
Charles R. Coe, Oklahoma City, Okla.						
BYE—Thomas W. Barnes, Druid Hills, Ga.	Barnes					
		Barnes, 3 and 2				
Ronald C. Garretson, Miami, Fla.	Taylor, 2 and 1					
Leon C. Taylor, Corsicana, Texas			Smith, 1 up			
BYE—Walter C. Andzel, South Shore, N.Y.	Andzel					
		Smith, 2 and 1				
John W. Coyle, Illini, Ill.	Smith, 3 and 1			Knowles, 1 up		
Ben Smith, Lochmoor, Mich.						
Robert W. Knowles, Jr., The C.C., Mass.	Knowles, 4 and 3					
Mack Brothers, Jr., Belle Meade, Tenn.		Knowles, 5 and 4				
BYE—Phil Wiechman, Logan, W. Va.	Wiechman					
			Knowles, 1 up, 21 hls.			
Dr. Charles E. VanEpps, Phoenix, Ariz.	Berrien, 5 and 4					
Stephen Berrien, Upper Montclair, N.J.		Finsterwald, 5 and 4				
Dow Finsterwald, Parkersburg, W. Va.	Finsterwald, 4 and 3				Knowles, 3 and 1	
John A. Emich, Baltimore, Md.						
BYE—Paul R. Harrington, Pine Forest, Texas	Harrington					
		Rogers, 6 and 5				
P.T. Taylor, Guyan, W. Va.	Rogers, 1 up					
E.J. Rogers, Jr., Oklahoma City, Okla.			Chapman, 2 up			
BYE—Robert E. Clark, Lakewood, Colo.	Clark					
		Chapman, 1 up, 19 hls.				
Benno Janssen, Jr., Farmington, Va.	Chapman, 2 up					
Richard D. Chapman, Pinehurst, N.C.				Maxwell, 1 up		
BYE—Billy Maxwell, Odessa, Texas	Maxwell					
		Maxwell, 1 up				
Glenn Oatman, Rockwood, Mo.	Kosten, 3 and 2					
Robert T. Kosten, Blue Hills, Mo.			Maxwell, 2 and 1			
BYE—Richard L. Spangler, Jr., Lincoln, Neb.	Spangler					
		Spangler, 1 up				
Dr. E. Payne Palmer, Jr., Phoenix, Ariz.	Funston, 4 and 3					
James E. Funston, Plum Hollow, Mich.						

SEMI-FINAL ROUND (36 Holes)—Sam Urzetta defeated Robert W. Knowles, Jr., 6 up and 5 to play.

The first word after the player's name is the name of his club, except in the case of a foreign entrant.

HALF

SECOND QUARTER

6th Round (18 Holes)	5th Round (18 Holes)		4th Round (18 Holes)	3rd Round (18 Holes)	2nd Round (18 Holes)	1st Round (18 Holes)
					Simonsen, 4 and 2	Russell W. Martin, Flossmoor, Ill.
				Simonsen, 3 and 1		Adrian Simonsen, Minneapolis, Minn.
					Nauts, 1 up	Richard L. Nauts, Brae-Burn, Texas
			Urzetta, 4 and 3			Gerald F. Thompson, Fort Lauderdale, Fla.
					Urzetta	BYE—Sam Urzetta, Irondequoit, N.Y.
				Urzetta, 5 and 4	Sloan, 2 and 1	Charles Evans, Jr., Edgewater, Ill.
						Herbert A. Sloan, Kansas City, Mo.
		Urzetta, 4 and 3			Frisina, 5 and 4	James Frisina, Sr., Illini, Ill.
				Frisina, 6 and 5		Jack Purdum, Westborough, Mo.
					DiLeo	BYE—Dr. M.B. Dileo, N. Hempstead, N.Y.
			McCormick, 1 up		Malloy, 2 and 1	Jack Malloy, Oklahoma City, Okla.
				McCormick, 4 and 3		Mike A. Stolarik, Biltmore, Ill.
					McCormick	BYE—Bruce McCormick, Lakeside, Calif.
	Urzetta, 4 and 3				Mengert, 1 up, 21 hls.	Al Mengert, Spokane, Wash.
				Mengert, 4 and 3		E. E. Lowery, California, Calif.
					Schaller, 2 up	William Sixty, Jr., Blue Mound, Wis.
			Selby, 4 and 3			William J. Schaller, Blue Mound, Wis.
					Haviland	BYE—Paul Haviland, Mount Pleasant, Md.
				Selby, 4 and 3	Selby, 2 and 1	Raleigh M. Selby, Meadowbrook, Texas
						Daryl F. Schoonover, Shawnee, Kans.
		Selby, 2 and 1			Williamson, 4 and 3	Oliver S. Williamson, Theodore Wirth, Minn.
				Williamson, 2 and 1		James Wee, Grand Forks, N.D.
					Wiley	BYE—James A. Wiley, Jr., Homestead, N.J.
			Williamson, 1 up		Morey, 5 and 4	Thomas McMahon, Detroit, Mich.
				Pousette, 1 up		Dale Morey, Lakewood, Texas
					Pousette, 1 up	Howard C. Pousette, Keller, Minn.
						Jack Harris, Jr., Virginia, Va.
Urzetta, 2 up					Holscher	BYE—Frank Holscher, Riviera, Calif.
				Holscher, 3 and 2	Dudley, 6 and 5	Charles B. Dudley, Greenville, S.C.
			Holscher, 5 and 4			Joseph F. Mitchell, Wethersfield, Conn.
				Weaver, 3 and 2	Weaver	BYE—John Weaver, Brae-Burn, Texas
					Olfs, 6 and 5	Art Olfs, Jr., Oakland Hills, Mich.
		Holscher, 4 and 3				Ellis Taylor, Newark, Del.
				Cardinal, 7 and 6	Ward, 4 and 2	Dr. William Kostelecky, Fargo, N.D.
						E. Harvie Ward, Jr., Benvenue, N.C.
			Cardinal, 3 and 2		Cardinal, 5 and 3	Fred L. Gordon, Mason City, Iowa
						Robert Cardinal, California, Calif.
				Hill, 7 and 5	Jackson	BYE—James G. Jackson, Greenbriar Hills, Mo.
					Hill, 3 and 2	Robert Hill, Oak Hill, N.Y.
	Holscher, 1 up, 22 hls.					Edwin D. Preisler, Beechmont, Ohio
				Moller, 2 and 1	Moller, 1 up, 22 hls.	Larry Moller, Quincy, Ill.
						James H. Johnston, Francis A. Gross, Minn.
			Moller, 5 and 3		Hardwicke	BYE—Clarke Hardwicke, Bel-Air, Calif.
				Replogle, 2 and 1	Replogle, 5 and 3	Dee A. Replogle, Oklahoma City, Okla.
						Donald Cole, Greenville, S.C.
					Brown	BYE—Fred Brown, Bel-Air, Calif.
		Moller, 1 up, 22 hls.		Hyndman, 4 and 3	Johnston, 3 and 1	Delbert Walker, Virginia, Calif.
						Harrison R. Johnston, Woodhill, Minn.
			Watson, 1 up, 20 hls.		Hyndman	BYE—Wm. Hyndman, III, Huntingdon Valley, Pa.
				Watson, 5 and 4	Switzer, 2 up	Joseph F. Switzer, Sunset, Mo.
						Gus T. Moreland, Mt. Hawley, Ill.
					Watson, 1 up	Raymond E. Watson, Jr., Kansas City, Mo.
						Tom Strange, Jr., Hyde Park, Ohio

1950 AMATEUR CHAM

LOWER

THIRD QUARTER

1st Round (18 Holes)	2nd Round (18 Holes)	3rd Round (18 Holes)	4th Round (18 Holes)	5th Round (18 Holes)	6th Round (18 Holes)	
Valentino Chiaverini, Heather Downs, Ohio	Sawyer,					
Charles M. Sawyer, Univ. of Minnesota, Minn.	3 and 2	Sawyer,				
Carl A. Jonson, Inglewood, Wash.	Penecale,	4 and 3				
Sam Penecale, Melrose, Pa.	3 and 1		Flowers,			
BYE—Edward J. Flowers, Oakland, Mich.	Flowers		3 and 2			
		Flowers,				
Dr. Walter J. Panowski, Maryland, Md.	Panowski,	2 and 1				
T.G. Roden, Odessa, Texas	4 and 2			Ward, 2 and 1		
Raymond E. Billows, Dutchess, N.Y.	Littler,					
Gene Littler, Broadmoor, Wash.	6 and 4	Littler,				
BYE—Robert Graves, Somerset, Minn.	Graves	7 and 6				
			Ward,			
Kenneth C. Young, Interlachen, Minn.	Blair,		1 up			
James T. Blair, III, Jefferson City, Mo.	3 and 2	Ward,				
BYE—John P. Ward, Syracuse Yacht, N.Y.	Ward	2 and 1			Ward, 7 and 5	
Fred Kammer, Jr., Detroit, Mich.	Kammer,					
Dale Rose, Westbrook, Ohio	4 and 3	Weston,				
Ray E. Weston, Jr., Spokane, Wash.	Weston,	3 and 2				
Capt. Fred G. Moseley, Oak Hills, Texas	1 up		Vinson,			
BYE—Gene Vinson, Northwood, Miss.	Vinson		1 up			
		Vinson,				
Preston H. Hennies, Columbia, S.C.	Levinson,	2 and 1				
John O. Levinson, Tam O'Shanter, Ill.	6 and 5			Vinson, 1 up		
Jack J. Dreyfus, Jr., Metropolis, N.Y.	Selby,					
John H. Selby, New Orleans, La.	3 and 2	Selby,				
BYE—Karl F. Kellerman, Columbia, Md.	Kellerman	5 and 4				
			Selby,			
Stanley E. Bishop, Pine Brook, Mass.	Bishop,		1 up			
George F. Bigham, Jr., Milburn, Kans.	1 up, 19 hls.	Schumacher,				
Don Schumacher, Dallas, Texas	Schumacher,	2 up				
Harry H. Haverstick, Jr., Lancaster, Pa.	2 and 1					Ward, 2 and 1
BYE—Jimmy McGonagill, Shreveport, La.	McGonagill					
		McGonagill,				
Pat Mucci, Preakness Hills, N.J.	Mucci,	1 up				
Gerald R. Hunt, Lincoln, Neb.	4 and 2		Shields,			
BYE—I. Richard Collord, Jr., Metairie, La.	Collord		4 and 3			
		Shields,				
William Shields, Wolfert's Roost, N.Y.	Shields,	2 up				
Jerry J. Cole, Fenway, N.Y.	1 up			Shields, 2 and 1		
Robert N. Babbish, Red Run, Mich.	Kesselring,					
Gerald Kesselring, Kitchener, Ont., Canada	4 and 3	Kesselring,				
BYE—Russell Brothers, Belle Meade, Tenn.	Brothers	9 and 8				
			Kesselring,			
Harry A. Pailer, Normandie, Mo.	Pailer,		7 and 6			
Stanley Bielat, Sprain Valley, N.Y.	4 and 2	Lee,				
James M. Lee, Jr., Tallahassee, Fla.	Lee,	1 up, 19 hls.				
Richard Hessemer, Brae-Burn, Texas	7 and 5				Shields, 2 and 1	
BYE—W.L. Granberry, III, Belle Meade, Tenn.	Granberry					
		Henry,				
Richard A. Henry, Baltusrol, N.J.	Henry,	1 up				
Carling Dinkler, Jr., Capital City, Ga.	3 and 1		Castleman,			
BYE—James W. Paul, Daytona Beach, Fla.	Paul		3 and 2			
		Castleman,				
William P. Castleman, Jr., Brook Hollow, Texas	Castleman,	1 up				
William R. Keller, Miami, Fla.	1 up, 20 hls.			Hackett, 3 and 2		
BYE—R.B. Meyers, Bel-Air, Calif.	Meyers					
		Waryan,				
William Waryan, Francis A. Gross, Minn.	Waryan,	1 up				
William Markham, Wethersfield, Conn.	2 and 1		Hackett,			
BYE—William C. Fisher, Westchester, N.Y.	Fisher		4 and 3			
		Hackett,				
Thomas W. Hamper, South View, Minn.	Hackett,	1 up				
Richard L. Hackett, Coosa, Ga.	6 and 5					

SEMI-FINAL ROUND (36 Holes)—Frank R. Stranahan defeated John P. Ward, 1 up.

FOURTH QUARTER

6th Round (18 Holes)	5th Round (18 Holes)		4th Round (18 Holes)	3rd Round (18 Holes)	2nd Round (18 Holes)	1st Round (18 Holes)
					Carmichael, 1 up	Richard F. Kohlmann, Normandie, Mo.
				Wittenberg, 1 up, 19 hls.		Dan A. Carmichael, Jr., Columbus, Ohio
					Wittenberg, 5 and 4	Ray Palmer, Grosse Ile, Mich.
			Barber, 2 and 1			James A. Wittenberg, Colonial, Tenn.
					Bobbitt	BYE—O.P. Bobbitt, Colonial, Tenn.
				Barber, 6 and 4	Barber, 2 and 1	Willie Barber, San Fernando Valley, Calif.
		Barber, 4 and 3				John B. Wade, Jr., Chickasaw, Tenn.
					Sanok, 2 and 1	Chester Sanok, Upper Montclair, N.J.
				Sanok, 5 and 4		Brownie May, Lancaster, N.Y.
					Martin	BYE—Edward P. Martin, Winchester, Mass.
			Culp, 4 and 3			
					Culp, 2 and 1	Tom Draper, Red Run, Mich.
	Stranahan, 5 and 4			Culp, 8 and 7		John D. Culp, Jr., Ridge, Ill.
					Hughes	BYE—E.T. Hughes, Orangeburg, S.C.
					McFarlane, 6 and 5	Ted W. McFarlane, Meadowbrook, Minn.
				Wampler, 4 and 3		Robert Kiersky, Pittsburgh Field, Pa.
					Wampler, 4 and 3	Perry L. Byard, Birmingham, Mich.
			Wampler, 2 and 1			Fred Wampler, Speedway, Ind.
					Olson	BYE—Dr. Phil Olson, Minneapolis, Minn.
		Stranahan, 4 and 3		Adams, 4 and 3	Adams, 6 and 5	Robert Leonard, Fargo, N.D.
						Ted Adams, Evanston, Ill.
					Mawhinney, 4 and 3	Capt. John Anderson, Wright-Patterson, Ohio
				Mawhinney, 1 up		William Mawhinney, Vancouver, B.C., Canada
					Stout	BYE—Samuel C. Stout, Jr., Hinsdale, Ill.
			Stranahan, 1 up			
					Stranahan, 4 and 3	Arnold D. Palmer, Latrobe, Pa.
				Stranahan, 1 up		Frank R. Stranahan, Inverness, Ohio
					McHale, 5 and 4	James B. McHale, Jr., Saucon Valley, Pa.
Stranahan, 5 and 4						Michael V. Gallagher, Jr., Oliver Gen. Hosp., Ga.
					Knight	BYE—Richard Knight, Happy Hollow, Neb.
				Knight, 3 and 2	Jones, 8 and 7	Tom Jones, Jr., Youngstown, Ohio
			Turnesa, 1 up			Alexander P. Janssen, Farmington, Va.
					Turnesa	BYE—William P. Turnesa, Knollwood, N.Y.
				Turnesa, 3 and 2	Allman, 1 up	W.L. Goodloe, Jr., Valdosta, Ga.
		Krugel, 1 up				Richard Allman, Philmont, Pa.
					Krugel, 3 and 2	James Ferrie, Virginia, Calif.
				Krugel, 4 and 3		Loren Krugel, Mankato, Minn.
					Zieske, 1 up, 19 hls.	Joseph A. McBride, Arcola, N.J.
			Krugel, 1 up			William F. Zieske, Minnesota Valley, Minn.
					Bisplinghoff	BYE—Don Bisplinghoff, Dubsdread, Fla.
				Bisplinghoff, 1 up	Manley, 4 and 3	Ben E. Tate, Jr., Camargo, Ohio
	Kinchla, 1 up					Hobart Manley, Jr., Savannah, Ga.
					Leacox, 4 and 2	Bob Leacox, Milburn, Kans.
				Leacox, 1 up, 21 hls.		E.J. Rogers, Sr., Oklahoma City, Okla.
					Ahern	BYE—Randall R. Ahern, Meadowbrook, Mich.
			Kinchla, 4 and 3			
					Howard, 2 and 1	Alan S. Howard, Davenport, Iowa
				Kinchla, 2 and 1		Fred Brand, Jr., Pittsburgh Field, Pa.
		Kinchla, 3 and 2			Kinchla	BYE—Richard L. Kinchla, Albemarle, Mass.
					Whaling, 2 and 1	William C. Campell, Guyan, W. Va.
				Bloyer, 2 and 1		Allan Whaling, Hyde Park, Ohio
					Bloyer	BYE—John Bloyer, Como Park, Minn.
			Bernolfo, 3 and 1			
					Bernolfo, 6 and 4	J.E. Bernolfo, Jr., The C.C., Utah
				Bernolfo, 4 and 3		Arthur C. Schoen, Oahu, Hawaii
					Galletta, 1 up, 19 hls.	MacGregor Hunter, Riviera, Calif.
						Mal Galletta, North Hills, N.Y.

1951
FIFTY-FIRST AMATEUR CHAMPIONSHIP

Held at the Saucon Valley Country Club, Bethlehem, Pa., September 10-15.
Yardage–6,979. Par 71. 1,416 Entries, 200 Qualifiers, 200 Starters.
Championship entirely at match play.

FINAL ROUND (36 Holes)–Billy Maxwell defeated Joseph F. Gagliardi, 4 up and 3 to play.

UPPER

FIRST QUARTER

1st Round (18 Holes)	2nd Round (18 Holes)	3rd Round (18 Holes)	4th Round (18 Holes)	5th Round (18 Holes)	6th Round (18 Holes)	
John P. Ward, Syracuse Yacht, N.Y.	J. Ward, 2 and 1					
Edward Kringle, Sacramento, Calif.		J. Ward, 3 and 1				
Robert W. Brownell, Chevy Chase, Md.	Brownell, 2 and 1					
Edgar M. Tutwiler, Jr., White Oak, W.Va.			J. Ward, 2 and 1			
BYE–Don Cole, Greenville, S.C.	Cole					
		Wild, 7 and 5				
Claude C. Wild, Jr., Washington, Va.	Wild, 2 and 1			Picard, 2 and 1		
Emerson Carey, III, Denver, Colo.						
Curtis Person, Colonial, Tenn.	Person, 2 and 1					
Perry T. Taylor, Guyan, W. Va.		Person, 3 and 2				
BYE–Harton S. Semple, Allegheny, Pa.	Semple					
			Picard, 2 and 1			
Alan Howard, Davenport, Iowa	Picard, 4 and 3					
William H. Picard, C.C. of Charleston, S.C.		Picard, 3 and 2				
BYE–William P. Turnesa, Knollwood, N.Y.	Turnesa					
Robert Olson, Lochmoor, Mich.	Emanuelson, 5 and 4				Jacobs, 1 up	
Herbert L. Emanuelson, Jr., Race Brook, Conn.		Stanley, 7 and 5				
BYE–Dave Stanley, Montebello, Calif.	Stanley					
			Stanley, 4 and 3			
BYE–Dudley S. Humphrey, The C.C., Ohio	Humphrey					
		Humphrey, 2 up				
Ralph G. Schwab, Community, Ohio	Walker, 5 and 3			Jacobs, 1 up, 19 hls.		
Delbert Walker, Virginia, Calif.						
Frank Michalek, Mount Pleasant, Md.	Jacobs, 1 up					
K. Thomas Jacobs, Jr., Montebello, Calif.		Jacobs, 2 and 1				
BYE–Francis McArdle, Wayland, Mass.	McArdle					
			Jacobs, 1 up			
Robert F. Riegel, Beaumont, Texas	Venturi, 4 and 3					
Kenneth Venturi, Harding Park, Calif.		Venturi, 4 and 3				
W.Y. Stembler, Miami, Fla.	Manley, 3 and 1					Jacobs, 4 and 2
Hobart L. Manley, Jr., Savannah, Ga.						
BYE–John Weaver, Brae-Burn, Texas	Weaver					
		Rogers, 3 and 2				
Ken Rogers, Oklahoma City, Okla.	Rogers, 8 and 6					
Edward Ervasti, Norwood Hills, Mo.			Johnston, 1 up, 19 hls.			
BYE–Billy Sixty, Jr., Blue Mound, Wis.	Sixty					
		Johnston, 4 and 3				
Tim Holland, Rockville, N.Y.	Johnston, 5 and 4			Eckis, 2 and 1		
Edward A. Johnston, C.C. of Maryland, Md.						
Robert W. Knowles, Jr., The C.C., Mass.	Eckis, 1 up					
Robert E. Eckis, Jr., Park, N.Y.		Eckis, 1 up				
BYE–Francis J. Allan, Fox Hill, Pa.	Allan					
			Eckis, 2 and 1			
William Hyndman, III, Huntingdon Valley, Pa.	Olfs, 2 and 1					
Arthur C. Olfs, Jr., Oakland Hills, Mich.		Addington, 5 and 3				
BYE–Don Addington, Dallas Athletic C., Texas	Addington				Martin, 5 and 4	
BYE–Charles W. Harrison, Atlanta, Ga.	Harrison					
		Hoffman, 1 up, 20 hls.				
Larry Hoffman, Wanango, Pa.	Hoffman, 5 and 3					
Robert C. Harrington, Catoctin, Md.			Martin, 4 and 3			
BYE–Edward P. Martin, Winchester, Mass.	Martin					
		Martin, 2 and 1				
Robert Goldwater, Phoenix, Ariz.	Cross, 4 and 3			Martin, 2 and 1		
Harold S. Cross, Philadelphia Cricket, Pa.						
BYE–James B. McHale, Jr., Saucon Valley, Pa.	McHale					
		McHale, 1 up				
J. Wolcott Brown, Manasquan River, N.J.	Brown, 6 and 4					
Harry Welch, C.C. of Salisbury, N.C.			Patton, 1 up			
BYE–Mike Dudik, I.B.M. Johnson City, N.Y.	Dudik					
		Patton, 6 and 5				
William J. Patton, Mimosa, N.C.	Patton, 4 and 2					
Stanley E. Bishop, Pine Brook, Mass.						

SEMI-FINAL ROUND (36 Holes)–Joseph F. Gagliardi defeated K. Thomas Jacobs, Jr., 6 up and 5 to play.

The first word after the player's name is the name of his club except in the case of a foreign entrant.

HALF

SECOND QUARTER

6th Round (18 Holes)	5th Round (18 Holes)		4th Round (18 Holes)	3rd Round (18 Holes)	2nd Round (18 Holes)	1st Round (18 Holes)
Gagliardi, 2 up	Gagliardi, 3 and 1	Gagliardi, 2 and 1	Gagliardi, 2 and 1	Gagliardi, 2 and 1	Allman, 3 and 2	Richard Allman, Philmont, Pa. Richard A. Stephens, Aronimink, Pa.
					Gagliardi, 4 and 2	W.B. McCullough, Jr., Huntingdon Valley, Pa. Joseph F. Gagliardi, Winged Foot, N.Y.
				Welsh, 2 and 1	Barnes	BYE—Thomas W. Barnes, Druid Hills, Ga.
					Welsh, 4 and 3	Alex Welsh, Rockford, Ill. Ray H. Taylor, Jr., Pinehurst, N.C.
			Urzetta, 3 and 2	Urzetta, 4 and 3	Urzetta, 4 and 3	Eugene P. Zuspann, Goodland, Kans. Sam Urzetta, Irondequoit, N.Y.
					Selby	BYE—John H. Selby, Lakewood, Texas
				Stalls, 1 up	Stalls, 4 and 3	Bill Stalls, Greenville, N.C. P.J. Boatwright, Jr., C.C. of Spartanburg, S.C.
					Simonsen	BYE—Ade Simonsen, Minneapolis, Minn.
		Evans, 5 and 4	Evans, 1 up	Creason, 1 up	Creason, 2 and 1	Emerson Carey, Jr., Denver, Colo. Lynn A. Creason, Colonial, Pa.
					Leonard	BYE—Thomas J. Leonard, Jr., Nashua, N.H.
				R. Evans, 5 and 4	R. Evans	BYE—Richard E. Evans, Canterbury, Ohio
					Ozol, 2 and 1	Rudolph J. Ozol, Suburban, N.J. Joseph W. Oliver, Fox Chapel, Pa.
			Hopkins, 6 and 5	Wittenberg, 2 and 1	Panowski, 1 up, 20 hls.	Dr. Walter J. Panowski, C.C. of Maryland, Md. James T. Blair, III, Milburn, Kans.
					Wittenberg	BYE—James A. Wittenberg, Colonial, Tenn.
				Hopkins, 5 and 4	Hopkins, 6 and 5	Edwin B. Hopkins, Jr., Abilene, Texas John S. Battle, Jr., Farmington, Va.
					Morine	BYE—Kenneth H. Morine, Exmoor, Ill.
	Coe, 3 and 2	Victor, 4 and 3	Victor, 1 up, 19 hls.	Victor, 4 and 2	Lee	BYE—James M. Lee, Jr., Tallahassee Men's G.A., Fla.
					Victor, 5 and 4	George E. Victor, Glen View, Ill. Randall R. Ahern, Meadowbrook, Mich.
				Cisco, 3 and 2	Cisco	BYE—Walter Cisco, Audubon, Ky.
					Torgerson, 1 up	Michael Jaros, En-Joie, N.Y. Reinert M. Torgerson, Cherry Valley, N.Y.
			Martz, 3 and 2	Martz, 5 and 4	Morano	BYE—Dom Morano, Englewood, N.J.
					Martz, 2 up	Lloyd A. Martz, Red Run, Mich. Frank Holscher, Riviera, Calif.
				Sheehan, 4 and 2	Moynihan	BYE—John L. Moynihan, Jr., Wolfert's Roost, N.Y.
					Sheehan, 5 and 3	Royal Hogan, Colonial, Texas Thomas E. Sheehan, Oakland Hills, Mich.
		Coe, 3 and 2	Coe, 6 and 5	McCreary, 6 and 5	Price, 1 up	Charles B. Price, Kenwood, Md. Lawrence Dana, Jr., Greensburg, Pa.
					McCreary	BYE—Richard E. McCreary, Jr., Brae-Burn, Texas
				Coe, 4 and 2	Albertus, 1 up	Robert Albertus, Springhaven, Pa. Harold L. Ebbers, Clearwater, Fla.
					Coe	BYE—Charles R. Coe, Oklahoma City, Okla.
			Paul, 4 and 3	Paul, 2 up	Brownlow, 3 and 2	George W. Brownlow, Jr., Wilson, N.C. Leon Taylor, Willow Brook, Texas
					Paul	BYE—James W. Paul, Piping Rock, N.Y.
				Jamison, 1 up	Jamison, 3 and 2	Thomas S. Jamison, Jr., Greensburg, Pa. Charles Evans, Jr., Edgewater, Ill.
					McBride, 4 and 3	William J. Robinson, Whitemarsh Valley, Pa. Joseph A. McBride, Arcola, N.J.

THIRD QUARTER

1st Round (18 Holes)	2nd Round (18 Holes)	3rd Round (18 Holes)	4th Round (18 Holes)	5th Round (18 Holes)	6th Round (18 Holes)	
Richard L. Nauts, Brae-Burn, Texas	Ballard, 1 up	Ballard, 3 and 2	Ballard, 1 up	Frisina, 7 and 6	Frisina, 1 up	
Dempsey E. Ballard, Wichita Falls, Texas						
Joel M. Shepherd, Gull Lake, Mich.	Giddings, 2 and 1					
Richard J. Giddings, Del Rio, Calif.						
BYE–Robert J. Cardinal, California, Calif.	Cardinal	Cardinal, 1 up				
H. Lloyd Beyer, Jr., Aronimink, Pa.	Beyer, 1 up					
Frank S. Souchak, Jr., Oakmont, Pa.						
Robert E. Wilke, Wee Burn, Conn.	Mucci, 2 up	Munger, 1 up				
Pat Mucci, Preakness Hills, N.J.						
BYE–Jack R. Munger, Northwood, Texas	Munger		Frisina, 3 and 1			
Dr. William H. Alexander, C.C. of Petersburg, Va.	Frisina, 1 up	Frisina, 2 and 1				
James Frisina, Illini, Ill.						
BYE–William P. Lees, Portland, Ore.	Lees					
Frank R. Stranahan, Inverness, Ohio	Kuntz, 1 up, 20 hls.	Kuntz, 3 and 2				
Robert W. Kuntz, Bonnie Briar, N.Y.						
BYE–John N.C. Cameron, Houston, Texas	Cameron		Kuntz, 2 and 1	Spencer, 1 up, 19 hls.		
BYE–Frank Connolly, Gowanie, Mich.	Connolly	Connolly, 1 up				
Howard Everitt, Atlantic City, N.J.	Key, 1 up					
Billy Key, C.C. of Columbus, Ga.						
David B. Dennis, Independence, Kans.	Spencer, 2 and 1	Spencer, 5 and 3				
Wynsol K. Spencer, James River, Va.						
BYE–Arthur Peterson, Oak Hill, Mass.	Peterson		Spencer, 6 and 5			
William M. Harison, Jr., Augusta, Ga.	Owens, 5 and 4	Owens, 3 and 2				
John C. Owens, Lexington, Ky.						
William Carey, Jr., Denver, Colo.	Shelden, 4 and 3					
Charles Shelden, La Gorce, Fla.						
BYE–Charles B. Dudley, Greenville, S.C.	Dudley	Dudley, 2 and 1				Benson, 4 and 3
Chester Sanok, Upper Montclair, N.J.	Sanok, 2 up					
Keith Campbell, Logansport, Ind.			Benson, 3 and 1			
BYE–J.C. Benson, South Hills, Pa.	Benson	Benson, 3 and 2		Benson, 1 up		
Jack Malloy, Oklahoma City, Okla.	Malloy, 5 and 3					
Jack Stewart, Phoenix, Ariz.						
Glenn A. Oatman, Rock Wood, Mo.	Bisplinghoff, 2 and 1	Strack, 3 and 2				
Donald Bisplinghoff, C.C. of Orlando, Fla.						
BYE–Charles Strack, C.C. of York, Pa.	Strack		Brewer, 6 and 5			
Stanley Kowal, Wolfert's Roost, N.Y.	Brewer, 5 and 4	Brewer, 4 and 3			Benson, 1 up	
Gay Brewer, Jr., Boiling Springs, Ky.						
BYE–Cameron P. Quinn, Wannamoisett, R.I.	Quinn					
BYE–George Dawson, Winged Foot, N.Y.	G. Dawson	Rendleman, 1 up				
Richard J. Rendleman, C.C. of Salisbury, N.C.	Rendleman, 1 up					
Allan M. Loeb, Lake Shore, Ill.			Paddock, 5 and 3			
BYE–Harold D. Paddock, Jr., Aurora, Ohio	Paddock	Paddock, 4 and 3		Paddock, 1 up, 20 hls.		
David Pincus, Ashbourne, Pa.	Pincus, 3 and 1					
Walter C. Andzel, South Shore, N.Y.						
BYE–Raymond E. Weston, Jr., Spokane, Wash.	Weston	Weston, 5 and 3				
William C. Chapin, Oak Hill, N.Y.	Chapin, 8 and 7		Morey, 2 and 1			
Paul R. Harrington, Pine Forest, Texas						
BYE–Robert T. Kosten, Happy Hollow, Neb.	Kosten	Morey, 3 and 1				
Dale Morey, Martinsville, Ind.	Morey, 6 and 5					
Dow Finsterwald, Athens, Ohio						

SEMI-FINAL ROUND (36 Holes)–Billy Maxwell defeated J.C. Benson, 10 up and 9 to play.

FOURTH QUARTER

6th Round (18 Holes)	5th Round (18 Holes)	4th Round (18 Holes)	3rd Round (18 Holes)	2nd Round (18 Holes)	1st Round (18 Holes)
				Healy, 7 and 5	John J. Quinn, Baltimore, Md.
			Taylor, 3 and 2		James T. Healy, Race Brook, Conn.
				E. Taylor, 1 up, 20 hls.	George Harrington, Rogue Valley, Ore.
		Taylor, 1 up, 20 hls.			Ellis Taylor, Newark, Del.
				Pierce	BYE—Thomas M. Pierce, Rutland, Vt.
			Pierce, 2 and 1	Moseley, 7 and 6	William D. Blanton, Sedgefield, N.C.
	Taylor, 4 and 2				Capt. Frederick G. Moseley, Oak Hills, Texas
				Miller, 1 up	Louis C. Lostoski, Pequabuck, Conn.
			Babbish, 6 and 4		Clancy Miller, St. Joseph, Mo.
				Babbish	BYE—Robert N. Babbish, Detroit, Mich.
		Jackson, 2 and 1		Jackson, 2 and 1	William Shields, Albany, N.Y.
			Jackson, 1 up		James G. Jackson, Greenbriar Hills, Mo.
				Strafaci	BYE—Frank Strafaci, Garden City C.C., N.Y.
Blum, 4 and 3				Ribner, 4 and 2	William C. Campbell, Guyan, W.Va.
			Gardner, 1 up		Lloyd D. Ribner, Fenway, N.Y.
				Gardner	BYE—Robert Gardner, Bel-Air, Calif.
		Heller, 4 and 3		Kowal	BYE—Henry J. Kowal, Dutchess, N.Y.
			Heller, 1 up, 19 hls.	Heller, 1 up	Leo Heller, Chester Valley, Pa.
	Blum, 2 and 1				Frank E. O'Connor, Jr., Transit Valley, N.Y.
				Haverstick, 6 and 4	Harry H. Haverstick, Jr., Lancaster, Pa.
			Trainor, 1 up, 19 hls.		Donald R. Guariglia, Normandie, Mo.
				Trainor	BYE—Dr. George M. Trainor, Oak Hill, N.Y.
Maxwell, 1 up, 20 holes			Blum, 1 up	Blum, 1 up	L.E. Neese, Jr., Alamance, N.C.
			Blum, 2 up		Arnold Blum, Idle Hour, Ga.
				Ferrie	BYE—James Ferrie, Virginia, Calif.
			Janssen, 4 and 3	Janssen	BYE—Benno Janssen, Jr., Farmington, Va.
		Chapman, 3 and 2		Goodes, 3 and 2	Benny Goodes, Sedgefield, N.C.
					Harreld N. Kirkpatrick, Owensboro, Ky.
			Chapman, 6 and 5	Peck	BYE—Jack R. Peck, Logan, W. Va.
	Crannell, 2 and 1			Chapman, 3 and 2	Richard D. Chapman, Pinehurst, N.C.
					Robert P. Chandler, Prince Georges, Md.
			Meister, 2 and 1	Gordon, 3 and 1	Kenneth T. Gordon, Montclair, N.J.
					George Studinger, Lake Merced, Calif.
				Meister	BYE—Edward L. Meister, Jr., Kirtland, Ohio
	Maxwell, 1 up, 19 hls.	Crannell, 1 up	Crannell, 3 and 2	Crannell	BYE—L.M. Crannell, Jr., Dallas Athletic C., Texas
				Collord, 1 up	I. Richard Collord, Jr., Metairie, La.
					Richard A. Jennings, Lubbock, Texas
			Maxwell, 2 and 1	Strange, 4 and 3	Tom Strange, Jr., Hyde Park, Ohio
					John E. Wagner, Skokie, Ill.
		Maxwell, 2 up		Maxwell	BYE—Billy Maxwell, Odessa, Texas
			Wininger, 5 and 4	Wininger, 4 and 3	Walter Emery, Tulsa, Okla.
	Maxwell, 3 and 2				Francis G. Wininger, Atlantic City, N.J.
				Zinn	BYE—Jack Zinn, Red Run, Mich.
			H. Ward, 1 up	H. Ward, 3 and 2	E. Harvie Ward, Jr., Highland, N.C.
					A.D. Dorsett, Jr., C.C. of Salisbury, N.C.
		H. Ward, 3 and 2		Humm	BYE—John J. Humm, Rockville, N.Y.
			J. Dawson, 2 and 1	Calder, 1 up, 22 hls.	Stanley Calder, Montclair, N.J.
					Sanford Young, Greensboro, N.C.
				J. Dawson, 2 and 1	John W. Dawson, Lakeside, Calif.
					William C. Mawhinney, Vancouver, B.C., Canada

1952
FIFTY-SECOND AMATEUR CHAMPIONSHIP

Held at the Seattle Golf Club, Seattle, Wash., August 18-23.
Yardage—6,632. Par 71. 1,029 Entries, 200 Qualifiers, 200 Starters.
Championship entirely at match play.

FINAL ROUND (36 Holes)—Jack Westland defeated Al Mengert, 3 up and 2 to play.

FIRST QUARTER

UPPER

1st Round (18 Holes)	2nd Round (18 Holes)	3rd Round (18 Holes)	4th Round (18 Holes)	5th Round (18 Holes)	6th Round (18 Holes)	
L.M. Crannell, Jr., Dallas Athletic C., Texas	Moe, 1 up	Moe, 1 up	Billows, 2 up	Johanson, 5 and 3	Mengert, 5 and 4	Mengert, 5 and 4
Roy Moe, Jr., Spokane, Wash.						
Ben E. Tate, Jr., Camargo, Ohio	Clifford, 1 up					
Percy Clifford, Mexico City, Mexico						
BYE—Ray Billows, Dutchess, N.Y.	Billows	Billows, 1 up				
George C. Beechler, Rogue Valley, Ore.	Beechler, 3 and 2					
Cyrus W. Vaughn, Jr., Champaign County, Ill.						
Lt. Col. John W. Kline, Happy Hollow, Neb.	Johanson, 2 and 1	Johanson, 3 and 2	Johanson, 1 up			
Paul H. Johanson, Inglewood, Wash.						
BYE—Charles M. Sawyer, Univ. of Minnesota, Minn.	Sawyer					
Kenneth Venturi, Olympic, Calif.	Blum, 1 up	Blum, 3 and 1				
Arnold Blum, Idle Hour, Ga.						
BYE—Frank Hoover, Bakersfield, Calif.	Hoover					
A.E. Campbell, Sand Point, Wash.	Johnston, 1 up, 20 hls.	Johnston, 4 and 2	Mengert, 6 and 4	Mengert, 1 up		
Edward A. Johnston, C.C. of Maryland, Md.						
BYE—John R. Tate, Recreation Park, Calif.	Tate					
BYE—Ross Mitchell, Lubbock, Texas	Mitchell	Mengert, 5 and 4				
Robert A. Pancrazi, Yuma, Ariz.	Mengert, 4 and 3					
Al Mengert, Spokane, Wash.						
Donald Bisplinghoff, C.C. of Orlando, Fla.	Bisplinghoff, 5 and 4	Bisplinghoff, 4 and 3	Ribner, 2 and 1			
Dr. John J.E. Herlihy, Kanawha, W. Va.						
BYE—Anthony Perry, Lake Chabot, Calif.	Perry					
Robert A. Roos, Jr., Olympic, Calif.	Ribner, 1 up, 19 hls.	Ribner, 3 and 2				
Lloyd D. Ribner, Fenway, N.Y.						
Robert F. Vickers, Wichita, Kans.	R.F. Vickers, 3 and 2	Morey, 2 and 1	Morey, 4 and 3	McElroy, 2 up	McElroy, 3 and 2	
Fernando Gonzalez, Mexico City, Mexico						
BYE—Billy Erfurth, Oak Hills, Texas	Erfurth					
Dale Morey, Martinsville, Ind.	Morey, 1 up					
Ernie Tullis, Jr., Inglewood, Wash.						
BYE—Fred Brown, Bel-Air, Calif.	F. Brown	Manley, 1 up, 19 hls.				
Hobart L. Manley, Jr., Savannah, Ga.	Manley, 1 up					
Irving Cooper, Meadowlark, Calif.						
Frank Hardison, Oakmont, Calif.	McElroy, 4 and 3	McElroy, 5 and 3	McElroy, 2 and 1			
Walter McElroy, Vancouver, B.C., Canada						
BYE—Warren G. Campbell, Rainier, Wash.	W.G. Campbell					
Daniel J. Silvestri, Sharp Park, Calif.	Silvestri, 2 up	Silvestri, 2 and 1				
Fred Kammer, Jr., C.C. of Detroit, Mich.						
BYE—Ernie Vossler, Colonial, Texas	Vossler					
BYE—James T. Blair, III, Milburn, Kans.	Blair	Blair, 1 up	Hiskey, 1 up, 19 hls.	Hiskey, 1 up, 19 hls.		
Robert W. Knowles, Jr., Palmetto, S.C.	Knowles, 2 up					
J.D. Shriver, California, Calif.						
BYE—Chester V. Gordon, Sand Point, Wash.	Gordon	Hiskey, 2 and 1				
Sam Urzetta, Irondequoit, N.Y.	Hiskey, 1 up					
Marion P. Hiskey, Blue Lakes, Idaho						
BYE—James W. Vickers, Oklahoma City, Okla.	J. Vickers	Wiggins, 7 and 6	Trainor, 3 and 2			
Ray H. Taylor, Jr., Pinehurst, N.C.	Wiggins, 4 and 3					
Roy E. Wiggins, Oswego Lake, Ore.						
BYE—Dr. George M. Trainor, Oak Hill, N.Y.	Trainor	Trainor, 1 up				
Donald Hoenig, Wachusett, Mass.	Hoenig, 1 up					
John Berry, Jr., Tallahassee Men's, Fla.						

SEMI-FINAL ROUND (36 Holes)—Al Mengert defeated Don Cherry, 3 up and 2 to play.

The first word after the player's name is the name of his club, except in the case of a foreign entrant.

SECOND QUARTER

HALF

6th Round (18 Holes)	5th Round (18 Holes)		4th Round (18 Holes)	3rd Round (18 Holes)	2nd Round (18 Holes)	1st Round (18 Holes)
				Penrose, 4 and 2	Robbins, 2 up	Hillman Robbins, Jr., Colonial, Tenn. Roberto H. Morris, Jr., Mexico City, Mexico
			Penrose, 3 and 2		Penrose, 6 and 5	William J. Shields, Albany, N.Y. John J. Penrose, Jr., LaGorce, Fla.
				Thomas, 2 and 1	Thomas	BYE—Marion M. Thomas, Jr., Reno, Nevada
		Jackson, 3 and 2			Colm, 1 up	Richard Patton, Colonial, Texas W.F. Colm, Bakersfield, Calif.
				Jackson, 2 ans 1	Foreman, 6 and 5	Victor O. Gildemeister, Palos Verdes, Calif. Harold Foreman, Jr., Lake Shore, Ill.
			Jackson, 1 up, 19 hls.		Jackson	BYE—James G. Jackson, Greenbriar Hills, Mo.
				Molinari, 6 and 5	Molinari, 7 and 6	Harold Hall, Columbia, S.C. James J. Molinari, Harding Park, Calif.
					Kelly	BYE—Peter C. Kelly, Fredericton, N.B., Canada
	Littler, 1 up			Littler, 3 and 2	Littler, 4 and 3	Clarence R. Smith, Rainier, Wash. Gene Littler, La Jolla, Calif.
			Littler, 2 and 1		Lovegren	BYE—Carl J. Lovegren, San Jose, Calif.
				Ihlanfeldt, 3 and 2	Ihlanfeldt	BYE—Robert L. Ihlanfeldt, Rainier, Wash.
					Weston, 2 and 1	C. Harold Weston, Jr., Portland, Ore. Stephen L. Dunford, The C.C., Utah
		Littler, 4 and 2		Ward, 4 and 3	Ward, 6 and 5	E. Harvie Ward, Jr., Hilma, N.C. Danny Dell, Hyde Park, Ohio
			Ward, 2 up		Holland	BYE—Tim Holland, Rockville, N.Y.
				Parent, 3 and 2	Parent, 5 and 3	Erv Parent, Inglewood, Wash. W.L. McCrary, III, Augusta, Ga.
					Ahern	BYE—Randall R. Ahern, Meadowbrook, Mich.
Cherry, 3 and 2				Cherry, 3 and 2	Weaver	BYE—John Weaver, Brae-Burn, Texas
			Cherry, 3 and 2		Cherry, 4 and 2	Thomas Beck, Southern Hills, Okla. Don Cherry, Garden City, N.Y.
				Young, 2 and 1	Grant	BYE—Peter M. Grant, Jr., Arizona, Ariz.
					Young, 4 and 3	Carl A. Wiseman, Westbrook, Ohio Kenneth C. Young, Interlachen, Minn.
		Cherry, 3 and 1		Stranahan, 3 and 2	Stranahan	BYE—Frank Stranahan, Inverness, Ohio
			Stranahan, 5 and 4		Kocsis, 3 and 2	Charles Kocsis, Red Run, Mich. Bud McKinney, Los Angeles, Calif.
				Walker, 2 up	Makaiwa	BYE—Charles Makaiwa, Palolo, Hawaii
	Cherry, 4 and 3				Walker, 8 and 7	Del Walker, Virginia, Calif. George R. Guy, Fort Lauderdale, Fla.
				Fehr, 2 up	Fehr, 5 and 4	Jerry Kesselring, Kitchener, Ont., Canada Jerry F. Fehr, Olympic View, Wash.
			Rosburg, 1 up, 19 hls.		Zuspann	BYE—Eugene P. Zuspann, Goodland, Kans.
				Rosburg, 1 up	O'Brien, 3 and 2	Chester F. O'Brien, Normandie, Mo. Eugene J. Pidgeon, Memphis, Tenn.
					Rosburg	BYE—Robert R. Rosburg, Stanford Univ., Calif.
		Rosburg, 4 and 2		Hall, 3 and 1	Hall, 4 and 3	Don C. Taylor, Rainier, Wash. Ralph Hall, Tilden Park, Calif.
			Hall, 4 and 3		Dichter	BYE—Ralph L. Dichter, Astoria, Ore.
				Galletta, 2 and 1	Galletta, 3 and 2	Mal Galletta, North Hills, N.Y. Gene May, Spokane, Wash.
					Odell, 3 and 1	Howard Odell, Broadmoor, Wash. Alejandro Cumming, Mexico City, Mexico

THIRD QUARTER

1st Round (18 Holes)	2nd Round (18 Holes)	3rd Round (18 Holes)	4th Round (18 Holes)	5th Round (18 Holes)	6th Round (18 Holes)	
Lewis D. Bridge, Woodbridge, Calif.	Santilli, 2 and 1					
Angelo Santilli, Potowomut, R.I.		Avila, 4 and 2				
Robert McCrary, Bel-Air, Calif.	Avila, 1 up					
Reynaldo Avila, Mexico City, Mexico			Avila, 1 up			
BYE—Robert E. Eckis, Jr., Park C.C. of Buffalo, N.Y.	Eckis					
Alfred D. Gallagher, Armed Forces, Ga.	Draper, 3 and 1	Eckis, 1 up		McHale, 3 and 2		
Eddie Draper, Sand Point, Wash.						
Walter S. Cisco, Audubon, Ky.	Reed, 6 and 5					
Claude B. Reed, Jr., North Texas State, Texas		Reed, 4 and 3				
BYE—Max Wilkinson, Blue Lakes, Idaho	Wilkinson					
David M. McBeath, Bellingham, Wash.	Clogg, 2 and 1		McHale, 1 up			
Percy Clogg, Vancouver, B.C., Canada		McHale, 2 and 1				
BYE—James McHale, Winged Foot, N.Y.	McHale				McHale, 3 and 2	
MacGregor Hunter, Riviera, Calif.	Storey, 1 up					
Kenneth Storey, Wandermere, Wash.		Hyde, 2 and 1				
BYE—W.B. Hyde, Olympia, Wash.	Hyde					
BYE—Donald R. McCallister, San Gabriel, Calif.	McCallister		Hyde, 5 and 4			
Philip A. Donohue, Sioux Falls, S.D.	Donohue, 5 and 3	Donohue, 1 up				
Richard M. Bailey, Modesto, Calif.				Coe, 4 and 3		
J. Stanley Heywood, California, Calif.	R.L. Brown, 2 and 1					
Russell L. Brown, Oklahoma City, Okla.		Coe, 5 and 4				
BYE—Charles R. Coe, Oklahoma City, Okla.	Coe					
Jack R. Munger, Northwood, Texas	Munger, 3 and 2		Coe, 2 and 1			
Lynn A. Creason, Hershey, Pa.		Levinson, 1 up, 19 hls.				
Thomas A. Stephenson, Blue Hills, Mo.	Levinson, 2 and 1					Mawhinney, 1 up
John O. Levinson, Tam O'Shanter, Ill.						
BYE—William C. Campbell, Guyan, W. Va.	W.C. Campbell	Campbell, 7 and 6				
Paul A. Millett, Olympic, Calif.	Millett, 1 up					
Chuck DeVos, Inglewood, Wash.			Campbell, 2 and 1			
BYE—Harry Givan, Seattle, Wash.	Givan	Bogan, 1 up				
Omer L. Bogan, Montebello, Calif.	Bogan, 2 and 1			Campbell, 1 up		
Richard Collord, Metairie, La.						
Emerson Carey, III, Denver, Colo.	Strafaci, 5 and 4					
Frank Strafaci, Garden City, N.Y.		Strafaci, 3 and 2				
BYE—Jack M. Cunacoy, Hacienda, Calif.	Cunacoy		Albert, 1 up, 25 hls.			
Elmer Erdman, Walla Walla, Wash.	Albert, 1 up, 19 hls.					
Donald E. Albert, Alliance, Ohio		Albert, 3 and 2			Mawhinney, 3 and 2	
BYE—M. Edward Merrins, Northwood, Miss.	Merrins					
BYE—Dirk Prather, Wigwam, Ariz.	Prather	Mawhinney, 4 and 2				
Verne Perry, Jr., Columbia Edgewater, Ore.	Mawhinney, 3 and 1					
William C. Mawhinney, Vancouver, B.C., Canada			Mawhinney, 3 and 2			
BYE—Howard Johnson, Golfcrest, Texas	Johnson	McCormick, 3 and 2				
Bruce N. McCormick, Lakeside, Calif.	McCormick, 1 up, 21 hls.			Mawhinney, 6 and 4		
C. Vernon Goodwin, Claremont, Calif.						
BYE—Julie Bescos, Virginia, Calif.	Bescos	Marra, 4 and 3				
Carlos Belmont, Mexico City, Mexico	Marra, 5 and 4					
Joseph Marra, Dunwoodie, N.Y.			Wood, 2 and 1			
BYE—Joseph C. Harris, Oak Ridge, Minn.	Harris	Wood, 4 and 3				
Dick Spangler, Jr., C.C. of Lincoln, Neb.	Wood, 1 up					
John W. Wood, Sand Point, Wash.						

SEMI-FINAL ROUND (36 Holes)—Jack Westland defeated William C. Mawhinney, 5 up and 4 to play.

FOURTH QUARTER

6th Round (18 Holes)	5th Round (18 Holes)	4th Round (18 Holes)	3rd Round (18 Holes)	2nd Round (18 Holes)	1st Round (18 Holes)
Westland, 3 and 1	Westland, 4 and 2	Kuntz, 4 and 2	Smith, 2 and 1	Ellis, 4 and 2	Weslock, 2 and 1	Nick K. Weslock, Ont., Canada P.T. Taylor, Guyan, W. Va.
					Ellis, 4 and 2	Wesley Ellis, Jr., C.C. of Austin, Texas Jack G. Baty, Fircrest, Wash.
				Smith, 2 up	Smith	BYE—Talbert C. Smith, Alameda, Calif.
					Hughes, 2 and 1	Ronald W. Hughes, Western, Calif. James H. McAlvin, Knollwood, Ill.
			Kuntz, 2 up	Kuntz, 1 up	Kuntz, 4 and 3	John R. Estey, Columbia Edgewater, Ore. Robert W. Kuntz, Bonnie Briar, N.Y.
					Gagliardi	BYE—Joseph F. Gagliardi, Winged Foot, N.Y.
				Siegel, 4 and 3	Timbrook, 4 and 2	Henry Timbrook, Jr., Lake Merced, Calif. Jack P. Stewart, Phoenix, Ariz.
					Siegel	BYE—Fred Siegel, Arizona, Ariz.
		Westland, 1 up, 23 hls.	Westland, 5 and 4	Westland, 2 up	Frisina, 2 up	Frank F. Guarasci, Ohio State University, Ohio James Frisina, Sr., Illini, Ill.
					Westland	BYE—Jack Westland, Everett, Wash.
				Hanen, 2 and 1	Evans	BYE—Charles Evans, Jr., Edgewater, Ill.
					Hanen, 3 and 2	Phil S. Harison, Augusta National, Ga. Richard D. Hanen, Coos, Ore.
			Selby, 6 and 4	Marshall, 1 up, 20 hls.	Marshall, 1 up	J. Benjamin Marshall, Jr., Irem Temple, Pa. William M. Cole, Forest Park, Md.
					Norton	BYE—Richard Norton, Kent, Mich.
				Selby, 2 and 1	R.M. Selby, 4 and 3	Raleigh M. Selby, Henderson, Texas Capt. E.M. Stokes, Southern Hills, Okla.
					Ferrie	BYE—James Ferrie, Virginia, Calif.
	Yost, 2 and 1	Meister, 6 and 4	Parr, 1 up, 21 hls.	Wilbert, 2 up	Wilbert	BYE—James Wilbert, Crystal Springs, Calif.
					Foley, 2 and 1	Carlos Porraz, Mexico City, Mexico John Foley, Jefferson Park, Wash.
				Parr, 1 up	Parr	BYE—Henry Parr, IV, Green Spring Valley Hunt, Md.
					J.H. Selby, 1 up	John H. Selby, Lakewood, Texas Larry Bouchey, Inglewood, Calif.
			Meister, 1 up	Meister, 6 and 5	Bjorklund, 2 and 1	Leonard T. Bjorklund, Interlachen, Minn. Morton R. Cohn, Monroe, Mich.
					Meister	BYE—Edward L. Meister, Jr., Kirtland, Ohio
				Dawson, 6 and 5	Farley	BYE—Phil Farley, Toronto, Ont., Canada
					Dawson, 1 up	John W. Dawson, Thunderbird, Calif. Francis R. Cardi, Ohio State University, Ohio
		Yost, 2 and 1	Lumpkin, 3 and 2	Lumpkin, 3 and 2	Victor, 5 and 4	Homer O. Lichtenwalter, Jr., Baltusrol, N.J. George E. Victor, Glen View, Ill.
					Lumpkin	BYE—Jack Lumpkin, Athens, Ga.
				Dana, 4 and 2	Knutson, 1 up, 19 hls.	Michael O'Brien, Wilshire, Calif. Dr. Robert N. Knutson, California, Calif.
					Dana	BYE—Larry Dana, Jr., Greensburg, Pa.
			Yost, 4 and 2	Patton, 3 and 2	Gruber, 1 up, 21 hls.	Ira D. Gruber, Brookside, Pa. Billy J. Maxwell, Odessa, Texas
					Patton	BYE—William J. Patton, Mimosa, N.C.
				Yost, 6 and 4	Yost, 2 and 1	Dick Yost, Columbia Edgewater, Ore. Richard A. Jennings, Lubbock, Texas
					Shriver, 6 and 5	Dale Lingonbrink, Olympic View, Wash. James Shriver, Inglewood, Wash.

1953
FIFTY-THIRD AMATEUR CHAMPIONSHIP

Held at the Oklahoma City Golf and Country Club, Oklahoma City, Okla., September 14-19.
Yardage—6,852. Par 71. 1,284 Entries, 200 Qualifiers, 200 Starters.
Championship entirely at match play.

FINAL ROUND (36 Holes)—Gene A. Littler defeated Dale Morey, 1 up

UPPER

FIRST QUARTER

1st Round (18 Holes)	2nd Round (18 Holes)	3rd Round (18 Holes)	4th Round (18 Holes)	5th Round (18 Holes)	6th Round (18 Holes)
Irving A. Cooper, Meadow Lark, Calif.	Cooper, 3 and 2				
Robert Goldwater, Phoenix, Ariz.		Cooper, 3 and 2			
Robert Cochran, Meadowbrook, Mo.	Cochran, 2 and 1				
Richard D. Davies, Annandale, Calif.					
BYE—James M. Hoak, Wakonda, Iowa	Hoak		Cooper, 2 and 1		
John O. Levinson, Tam O'Shanter, Ill.	Levinson, 5 and 4	Hoak, 1 up			
Marion Hiskey, Blue Lakes, Idaho				Cooper, 3 and 2	
Hillman Robbins, Jr., Colonial, Tenn.	Robbins, 2 and 1				
Richard L. Hackett, Coosa, Ga.		Robbins, 1 up			
BYE—Lt. Col. A.A. Duncan, Bridgend, Wales	Duncan				
Jack Thompson, Jr., Tippecanoe, Ohio	Edwards, 2 and 1		Robbins, 3 and 2		
H.H. Edwards, Jr., Mohawk, Okla.		Edwards, 2 and 1			
BYE—Bill Parker, Mohawk, Okla.	Parker				Kuntz, 1 up
Glen Fowler, Lincoln Park, Okla.	Coe, 5 and 4				
Charles R. Coe, Oklahoma City, Okla.		Coe, 2 and 1			
BYE—David W. Smith, Jr., Gaston, N.C.	Smith				
BYE—William M. Brown, Jr., C.C. of Virginia, Va.	Brown		Ward, 1 up, 23 hls.		
E. Harvie Ward, Jr., Capital City, Ga.	Ward, 1 up	Ward, 6 and 5			
Ernest A. Arend, Jr., Deal, N.J.				Kuntz, 1 up	
Robert W. Kuntz, Bonnie Briar, N.Y.	Kuntz, 4 and 3				
Robert E. Clark, Lakewood, Colo.		Kuntz, 1 up, 19 hls.			
BYE—Philip A. Donohue, Minnehaha, S.D.	Donohue				
Glenn H. Johnson, Grosse Ile, Mich.	Johnson, 5 and 4		Kuntz, 3 and 2		
Jack Chambers, Brae-Burn, Texas		Johnson, 2 and 1			
L.M. Crannell, Jr., Cedar Crest, Texas	Crannell, 4 and 3				
John Sierge, Twin Brooks, N.J.					Albert, 4 and 3
BYE—Joe W. Conrad, Oak Hills, Texas	Conrad				
Raleigh M. Selby, Henderson, Texas	McGonagill, 1 up	McGonagill, 1 up			
Jimmy McGonagill, Shreveport, La.			McGonagill, 2 and 1		
BYE—Larry Dana, Jr., Greensburg, Pa.	Dana				
Mal Galletta, North Hills, N.Y.	Slattery, 1 up	Slattery, 2 and 1		Albert, 1 up, 19 hls.	
Lester Slattery, Jr., Normandie, Mo.					
Walter Emery, Tulsa, Okla.	Faulkenberry, 5 and 4				
Robert L. Faulkenberry, Jr., Lincoln Park, Okla.		Faulkenberry, 4 and 3			
BYE—Joseph Harris, Oak Ridge, Minn.	Harris				
Ralph V. Ellstrom, Dearborn, Mich.	Albert, 1 up, 19 hls.		Albert, 3 and 2		
Don Albert, Alliance, Ohio		Albert, Disqualification			
BYE—Richard H. Waters, Atlanta, Ga.	Waters				Albert, 1 up
BYE—Jack Westland, Everett, Wash.	Westland	Westland, 3 and 2			
Troye Kennon, Indian Hills, Okla.	Carey, 2 and 1				
Randy Carey, Denver, Colo.			Palmer, 1 up		
BYE—Arnold Palmer, Pine Ridge, Ohio	Palmer	Palmer, 7 and 5			
John W. Frazier, Jr., Finley, N.C.	Frazier, 4 and 3				
Louis S. Mann, C.C. of Maryland, Md.				Palmer, 2 and 1	
BYE—Arthur R. Koch, Byrnes Park, Iowa	Koch	Venturi, 3 and 2			
Ken Venturi, Olympic, Calif.	Venturi, 5 and 4				
F.B. Dickinson, Wakonda, Iowa			Venturi, 4 and 3		
BYE—Lou Wendrow, C.C. of Lansing, Mich.	Wendrow	Bernolfo, 1 up, 19 hls.			
J.E. Bernolfo, Jr., The C.C., Utah	Bernolfo, 1 up				
Les Madison, Phoenix, Ariz.					

SEMI-FINAL ROUND (36 Holes)—Dale Morey defeated Don Albert, 5 up and 4 to play.

The first word after the player's name is the name of his club, except in the case of a foreign entrant.

HALF

SECOND QUARTER

6th Round (18 Holes)	5th Round (18 Holes)	4th Round (18 Holes)	3rd Round (18 Holes)	2nd Round (18 Holes)	1st Round (18 Holes)
				McHale,	J.B. McHale, Jr., Winged Foot, N.Y.
			McHale,	5 and 4	Edmund M. Maura, Jr., Oyster Harbors, Mass.
			1 up	Ribner,	Lloyd D. Ribner, Dellwood, N.Y.
		McHale,		2 and 1	Sam Maniaci, Cedarbrook, Pa.
		7 and 6		Hardin	BYE—Hord W. Hardin, Bellerive, Mo.
			Hardwicke,		
			1 up, 19 hls.	Hardwicke,	Joseph F. Mitchell, Weathersfield, Conn.
				4 and 3	Clarke Hardwicke, Bel-Air, Calif.
		Campbell, 1 up		Campbell,	William C. Campbell, Guyan, W. Va.
			Campbell,	4 and 3	John W. Wood, Sand Point, Wash.
			4 and 3	Penrose	BYE—John J. Penrose, Jr., La Gorce, Fla.
		Campbell,			
		3 and 1		Goens,	George F. Bigham, Fort Belvoir, Va.
			Goens,	4 and 3	Orville R. Goens, Wakonda, Iowa
			1 up, 22 hls.	Hamilton	BYE—Ed Hamilton, Twin Hills, Okla.
	Morey, 1 up			Meyers,	John E. Meyers, Summit Hills, Ky.
			Morey,	4 and 3	N.C.W. Gennett, Jr., Biltmore Forest, N.C.
			4 and 3	Morey	BYE—Dale Morey, Highland, Ind.
		Morey,			
		2 and 1		Guy	BYE—George R. Guy, Fort Lauderdale, Fla.
			Key,		
			2 and 1	Key,	William T. Boutell, Interlachen, Minn.
				1 up	James W. Key, C.C. of Columbus, Ga.
		Morey, 7 and 5		Casper,	William E. Casper, Jr., Mission Valley, Calif.
			Moncrief,	4 and 3	Ted Roden, Odessa, Texas
			2 and 1	Moncrief	BYE—Robert Moncrief, River Oaks, Texas
		Trammell,			
		1 up, 19 hls.		Hogan,	Charles Evans, Jr., Edgewater, Ill.
			Trammell,	4 and 3	Royal Hogan, Colonial, Texas
			5 and 4	Trammell	BYE—Marshall Trammell, Belle Meade, Tenn.
Morey, 1 up, 20 holes				Strafaci	BYE—Frank Strafaci, Connequott, N.Y.
			Strafaci,		
			4 and 2	Stevenson,	Frank G. Stevenson, Jr., Savannah, Ga.
		Jennings,		7 and 5	Charlie Wiehrs, Jr., Palma Ceia, Fla.
		3 and 2		Molinari	BYE—James J. Molinari, Harding Park, Calif.
			Jennings,		
			3 and 2	Jennings,	Raymond B. Anderson, C.C. of Petersburg, Va.
				4 and 3	Richard A. Jennings, Lubbock, Texas
		Urzetta, 4 and 2		Urzetta	BYE—Sam Urzetta, Irondequoit, N.Y.
			Urzetta,		
			4 and 2	King,	Woodrow W. McDevitt, Brae-Burn, Texas
		Urzetta,		3 and 2	Rufus King, Wichita Falls, Texas
		3 and 2		McCormick	BYE—Bruce N. McCormick, Lakeside, Calif.
			McCormick,		
			3 and 2	Draper,	Lawrence Bouchey, Inglewood, Calif.
				5 and 4	Thomas L. Draper, Jr., Red Run, Mich.
	Santilli, 2 and 1			Santilli,	Angelo Santilli, Potowomut, R.I.
			Santilli,	8 and 7	George M. Maxwell, Augusta, Ga.
			1 up	Schoonover	BYE—Daryl F. Schoonover, Shawnee, Kans.
		Santilli,			
		1 up		Baxter,	Rex Baxter, Jr., Amarillo, Texas
			McCall,	1 up, 20 hls.	Lynn W. Burrus, Twin Hills, Okla.
			2 and 1	McCall	BYE—Robert O. McCall, Tippecanoe, Ohio
		Santilli, 3 and 1		Atkinson,	Bill R. Bobbitt, Colonial, Tenn.
			Atkinson,	1 up, 19 hls.	Robert H. Atkinson, Jr., Columbia-Edgewater, Ore.
			5 and 4	Reitz	BYE—Paul Reitz, Tulsa, Okla.
		Nieporte,			
		1 up, 19 hls.		Donohue,	John J. Donohue, Jr., Sioux City, Iowa
			Nieporte,	1 up, 21 hls.	Harry Welch, C.C. of Salisbury, N.C.
			6 and 4	Nieporte,	Fred W. Fiore, Knollwood, N.Y.
				2 up	Thomas M. Nieporte, Clovernook, Ohio

THIRD QUARTER

1st Round (18 Holes)	2nd Round (18 Holes)	3rd Round (18 Holes)	4th Round (18 Holes)	5th Round (18 Holes)	6th Round (18 Holes)	
Jerry J. Cole, Fenway, N.Y.	Cole, 2 and 1					
F. Lee Pinkston, Abilene, Texas		Cole, 1 up				
Dick Yost, Columbia-Edgewater, Ore.	Yost, 4 and 3					
W. Jack Van Rossem, Riviera, Calif.*			Draper, 1 up, 19 hls.			
BYE—Edgar Draper, Sand Point, Wash.	Draper					
John Garrett, River Oaks, Texas	Vossler, 4 and 3	Draper, 2 and 1				
Ernie O. Vossler, Colonial, Texas				Nichols, 5 and 3		
Elbert S. Jemison, Jr., C.C. of Birmingham, Ala.	Nichols, 6 and 4					
Donald C. Nichols, Shawnee, Kans.		Nichols, 1 up, 19 hls.				
BYE—Chris H. Gers, Twin Hills, Okla.	Gers					
Neil C. Croonquist, Minneapolis, Minn.	Croonquist, 2 and 1		Nichols, 5 and 4			
Ellis Taylor, Springhaven, Pa.		Hamilton, 3 and 2				
BYE—J.C. Hamilton, Jr., Tulsa, Okla.	Hamilton					
Fred Mock, Jr., Twin Hills, Okla.	Knowles, 4 and 3				Richards, 2 and 1	
Robert W. Knowles, Jr., The C.C., Mass.		Knowles, 1 up				
BYE—David P. Majors, Colonial, La.	Majors					
BYE—Rodney Bliss, Jr., Wakonda, Iowa	Bliss		Richards, 2 and 1			
Ted Richards, Jr., Rancho, Calif.	Richards, 3 and 2	Richards, 3 and 1				
William G. Holloway, Jr., Meadow Brook, N.Y.				Richards, 5 and 4		
Dan Carmichael, Columbus, Ohio	Carmichael, 1 up, 20 hls.					
William R. Watts, Jr., Riviera, Fla.		Carmichael, 1 up				
BYE—George E. Victor, Glen View, Ill.	Victor					
Walter C. Andzel, South Shore, N.Y.	Holland, 5 and 4		Wittenberg, 4 and 3			
Tim Holland, Rockville, N.Y.		Wittenberg, 3 and 2				
David A. Perkins, Harlan, Ky.	Wittenberg, 4 and 3					Littler, 4 and 3
James A. Wittenberg, Colonial, Tenn.						
BYE—Sig Harpman, Jr., Lincoln Park, Okla.	Harpman					
Fred Jones, Tippecanoe, Ohio	Jones, 2 and 1	Harpman, 4 and 3				
Phil Wiechman, C.C. of Orangeburg, S.C.			Harpman, 3 and 2			
BYE—Capt. Malcolm Stokes, Garden City, N.Y.	Stokes					
John E. Wagner, Skokie, Ill.	Wagner, 5 and 4	Wagner, 7 and 6				
C. Grant Spaeth, Stanford University, Calif.				Littler, 6 and 4		
Joseph F. Gagliardi, Winged Foot, N.Y.	Gagliardi, 2 and 1					
Ed Meyerson, Brentwood, Calif.		Dennis, 2 and 1				
BYE—David B. Dennis, Independence, Kans.	Dennis					
Thomas W. Barnes, Druid Hills, Ga.	Littler, 2 and 1		Littler, 3 and 2			
Gene A. Littler, La Jolla, Calif.		Littler, 2 up				
BYE—William E. Webb, Blue Hills, Mo.	Webb				Littler, 5 and 4	
BYE—Richard S. Norton, Kent, Mich.	Norton					
Richard L. Spangler, Jr., C.C. of Lincoln, Neb.	Spangler, 4 and 2	Norton, 1 up				
John L. Banks, Elmhurst, Ill.			Easterly, 3 and 1			
BYE—Harry Easterly, Jr., C.C. of Virginia, Va.	Easterly					
Richard E. McCreary, Jr., Conroe, Texas	McCreary, 3 and 1	Easterly, 1 up				
Grady S. Prim, Northwood, Texas				Morgan, 3 and 2		
BYE—Loy R. Martin, Southern Hills, Okla.	Martin					
Jennings Randolph, Jr., Bethesda, Md.	Randolph, 1 up	Randolph, 1 up, 20 hls.				
Peter D. Butler, Dubuque, Iowa			Morgan, 6 and 4			
BYE—John L. Morgan, Streetly, England	Morgan					
Claude Wild, Washington, Va.	Wild, 1 up	Morgan, 5 and 4				
Claude L. Wright, Cherry Hills, Colo.						

SEMI-FINAL ROUND (36 Holes)—Gene A. Littler defeated Bruce H. Cudd, 10 up and 8 to play.

IONSHIP—Continued

HALF

FOURTH QUARTER

6th Round (18 Holes)	5th Round (18 Holes)	4th Round (18 Holes)	3rd Round (18 Holes)	2nd Round (18 Holes)	1st Round (18 Holes)
				Zuspann, 1 up	Irvin Rubin, Crest Hills, Ohio
			Addington, 2 up		Eugene P. Zuspann, Cherry Hills, Colo.
				Addington, 3 and 1	Floyd W. Addington, Lakewood, Texas
		Addington, 5 and 4			James J. McCluskey, Inglewood, Calif.
				Smith	BYE—W.N. Smith, Jr., Phoenix, Ariz.
			Smith, 4 and 3	Sykes, 3 and 2	Lawrence Greenwald, Cedar Crest, Texas
	Jackson, 1 up, 22 hls.				James D. Sykes, Whitemarsh Valley, Pa.
				Taylor, 2 and 1	Ray Taylor, Greensboro, N.C.
			Jackson, 3 and 1		Gordon Stott, Nassau, N.Y.
				Jackson	BYE—James G. Jackson, Greenbriar Hills, Mo.
		Jackson, 2 and 1		Geiss, 1 up	Jack Geiss, Norwood Hills, Mo.
			Christiansen, 3 and 2		Ralph T. Strafaci, Hempstead, N.Y.
Palmer, 1 up, 19 hls.				Christiansen	BYE—Gene Christiansen, Minneapolis, Minn.
				Rogers, 3 and 2	Bill Winslow, Oaks, Okla.
			Justice, 7 and 5		E.J. Rogers, Jr., Oklahoma City, Okla.
				Justice	BYE—Donald M. Justice, Lincoln Park, Okla.
		Palmer, 3 and 1		Palmer	BYE—Raymond Palmer, Grosse Ile, Mich.
			Palmer, 3 and 2	Cragg, 1 up, 19 hls.	James P. Cragg, Rolling Road, Md.
	Palmer, 4 and 3				Norman V. Drew, Bangor, Northern Ireland
				Gordon, 5 and 3	Fred L. Gordon, Mason City, Iowa
			Logan, 1 up		Billy Erfurth, Lubbock, Texas
				Logan	BYE—David Logan, Biltmore, Ill.
		Bishop, 4 and 3		Johnson, 2 and 1	Howie Johnson, Golfcrest, Texas
			Bishop, 2 and 1		Eugene Dahlbender, Jr., Meadowbrooks, Ga.
				Bishop	BYE—Stanley E. Bishop, Pinebrook, Mass.
Cudd, 2 and 1				Cook	BYE—Archie W. Cook, Jr., Logan, W. Va.
			Kosten, 6 and 4	Kosten, 2 up	William R. Coffey, River Crest, Texas
		Kosten, 1 up			Robert T. Kosten, Wannamoisett, R.I.
				Merrins	BYE—M. Edward Merrins, Northwood, Miss.
			Merrins, 2 up	Carr, 7 and 6	Harold Foreman, Jr., Lake Shore, Ill.
	Blum, 4 and 2				Joseph B. Carr, Sutton, Ireland
				Blum, 3 and 1	Arnold S. Blum, Idle Hour, Ga.
			Blum, 6 and 5		John W. Dawson, Thunderbird, Calif.
				Bogle	BYE—William F. Bogle, Dutchess, N.Y.
		Blum, 4 and 3		Patton	BYE—Richard Patton, River Crest, Texas
			Person, 6 and 5	Person, 4 and 3	Curtis Person, Colonial, Tenn.
Cudd, 2 and 1					Don Cherry, Wichita Falls, Texas
				Brewer, 5 and 4	Gay Brewer, Jr., Boiling Springs, Ky.
			Brewer, 7 and 6		Drury W. Parks, Muskogee, Okla.
				Replogle	BYE—Dee Replogle, Oklahoma City, Okla.
		Brewer, 3 and 2		Stranahan, 4 and 3	Joe Walser, Jr., Twin Hills, Okla.
			Handt, 4 and 3		Frank Stranahan, Inverness, Ohio
				Handt	BYE—Les Handt, Palma Ceia, Fla.
	Cudd, 2 and 1			Hoenig, 1 up, 23 hls.	Joe D. Shriver, California, Calif.
			Hoenig, 1 up		Donald J. Hoenig, Wachusett, Mass.
				Young	BYE—Kenneth C. Young, Interlachen, Minn.
		Cudd, 2 and 1		Boggess, 2 up	Homer O. Lichtenwalter, Jr., Baltusrol, N.J.
			Cudd, 2 and 1		William Boggess, Swope Park, Mo.
				Cudd, 4 and 3	Bruce H. Cudd, Columbia-Edgewater, Ore.
					Robert A. Hill, Oak Hill, N.Y.

1954
FIFTY-FOURTH AMATEUR CHAMPIONSHIP

Held at the Country Club of Detroit, Grosse Pointe Farms, Mich., August 23-28.
Yardage—6,875. Par 70. 1,278 Entries, 200 Qualifiers, 200 Starters.
Championship entirely at match play.
FINAL ROUND (36 Holes)—Arnold D. Palmer defeated Robert Sweeny, 1 up.

FIRST QUARTER — UPPER

1st Round (18 Holes)	2nd Round (18 Holes)	3rd Round (18 Holes)	4th Round (18 Holes)	5th Round (18 Holes)	6th Round (18 Holes)	
Jerald R. Schenken, Omaha, Neb.	Veghte, 3 and 2					
John W. Veghte, Pine Brook, N.Y.		Palmer, 1 up				
Frank Strafaci, Garden City Country, N.Y.	Palmer, 1 up					
Arnold D. Palmer, Pine Ridge, Ohio			Palmer, 2 and 1			
BYE—Richard Price, Longview, Wash.	Price					
		Whiting, 1 up, 20 hls.				
Richard L. Whiting, Red Run, Mich.	Whiting, 3 and 2					
Hillman Robbins, Jr., Colonial, Tenn.				Palmer, 5 and 3		
Ben L. Goodes, Pennrose Park, N.C.	Goodes, 3 and 2					
George Dawson, Longmeadow, Mass.		Selby, 2 up				
BYE—John H. Selby, Apawamis, N.Y.	Selby					
			Andzel, 1 up			
E.J. Rogers, Jr., Oklahoma City, Okla.	Rogers, 2 and 1					
Ted Davies, Maketewah, Ohio		Andzel, 3 and 2				
BYE—Walter C. Andzel, South Shore, N.Y.	Andzel				Palmer, 3 and 1	
Hord W. Hardin, Bellerive, Mo.	E.H. Ward, 4 and 3					
E. Harvie Ward, Jr., San Francisco, Calif.		E.H. Ward, 2 and 1				
BYE—James W. Vickers, Wichita, Kans.	Vickers					
			Stranahan, 1 up			
BYE—Frank Stranahan, Inverness, Ohio	Stranahan					
		Stranahan, 1 up				
Ray E. Watson, Jr., Kansas City, Mo.	Watson, 2 and 1					
Thomas C. Hoak, Interlachen, Minn.				Stranahan, 4 and 3		
Harry F. Forbes, Rockford, Ill.	Sheehan, 4 and 3					
Thomas E. Sheehan, Oakland Hills, Mich.		Sheehan, 5 and 5				
BYE—Ray A. Graham, Jr., Meadow Brook, N.Y.	Graham					
			Sheehan, 4 and 3			
Roberto H. Morris, Jr., Mexico City, Mexico	Boggess, 3 and 2					
William F. Boggess, Swope Park, Mo.		Zuspann, 2 and 1				
Harold Brink, Blythefield, Mich.	Zuspann, 1 up					
Eugene P. Zuspann, Cherry Hills, Colo.						Palmer, 1 up
BYE—Thomas W. Beck, Southern Hills, Okla.	Beck					
		Bradley, Disqualification				
Foster Bradley, Griffith Park, Calif.	Bradley, 6 and 5					
Bill Webb, Blue Hills, Mo.			Tutwiler, 1 up, 19 hls.			
BYE—Edgar M. Tutwiler, Jr., Berry Hills, W. Va.	Tutwiler					
		Tutwiler, 1 up, 20 hls.				
John P. Ward, Syracuse Yacht, N.Y.	J. Ward, 7 and 6					
David M. Baldwin, Baltusrol, N.J.				McGonagill, 1 up, 21 hls.		
Charles R. Kiesling, Huntingdon Valley, Pa.	Kiesling, 5 and 4					
Dr. Paul R. Harrington, Pine Forest, Texas		McGonagill, 2 up				
BYE—Jimmy McGonagill, Shreveport, La.	McGonagill					
			McGonagill, 1 up, 21 hls.			
Ben C. Hartig, Jr., Manor, Md.	Hartig, 6 and 5					
Joseph Pasiecznik, South Shore, N.Y.		Jackson, 6 and 4				
BYE—James G. Jackson, Greenbriar Hills, Mo.	Jackson				Cherry, Default	
BYE—John F. Cree, Brookfield, N.Y.	Cree					
		Cherry, 3 and 2				
Don Cherry, Wichita Falls, Texas	Cherry, 3 and 2					
Cameron P. Quinn, West Warwick, R.I.			Cherry, 1 up			
BYE—James E. Fisher, Wykagyl, N.Y.	Fisher					
		Wright, 3 and 1				
Claude L. Wright, Cherry Hills, Colo.	Wright, 4 and 3					
Donald B. Ware, Greenville, S.C.				Cherry, 4 and 3		
BYE—Chester Sanok, Forsgate, N.J.	Sanok					
		Sanok, 3 and 1				
Paul W. Hershey, Galveston, Texas	Kirby, 3 and 2					
Wilkens J. Kirby, Jr., Newnan, Ga.			Larson, 1 up			
BYE—Earl R. Larson, Minneapolis, Minn.	Larson					
		Larson, 1 up, 19 hls.				
Stanley E. Bishop, Pine Brook, Mass.	Foutche, 2 up					
Richard Foutche, Berry Hills, W. Va.						

SEMI-FINAL ROUND (36 Holes)—Arnold D. Palmer defeated Edward L. Meister, Jr., 1 up, 39 holes.

The first word after the player's name is the name of his club, except in the case of a foreign entrant.

SECOND QUARTER

HALF 6th Round (18 Holes)	5th Round (18 Holes)		4th Round (18 Holes)	3rd Round (18 Holes)	2nd Round (18 Holes)	1st Round (18 Holes)
					Bliss, 3 and 2	Rodney Bliss, Jr., Wakonda, Iowa
				Bliss, 5 and 3		Ted Richards, Jr., Bel-Air, Calif.
					Erfurth, 3 and 1	Billy Erfurth, Lubbock, Texas
			Bliss, 4 and 3			Bernard H. Ridder, Jr., Northland, Minn.
					Bisplinghoff	BYE—Don Bisplinghoff, C.C. of Orlando, Fla.
		Meister, 1 up, 19 hls.		Owens, 2 up	Owens, 3 and 1	John C. Owens, Lexington, Ky.
						Carlos Belmont, Mexico City, Mexico
				Meister, 3 and 2	Meister, 4 and 3	Edward L. Meister, Jr., Kirtland, Ohio
						Richard Spangler, Jr., C.C. of Lincoln, Neb.
			Meister, 3 and 2		Brand	BYE—Fred Brand, Jr., Pittsburgh, Pa.
				Gray, 2 and 1	Gray, 4 and 3	William Baden, Edina, Minn.
						John D. Gray, Palos Verdes, Calif.
	Meister, 1 up				Norton	BYE—Richard Norton, Kent, Mich.
				Johnson, 2 and 1	Collord, 2 and 1	Charles R. Coe, Oklahoma City, Okla.
						Richard Collord, Jr., Metairie, La.
			Johnson, 2 and 1		Johnson	BYE—Glenn H. Johnson, Grosse Ile, Mich.
				Updegraff, 1 up	Rountree	BYE—Jack B. Rountree, Bethesda, Md.
		Johnson, 6 and 4			Updegraff, 4 and 3	Dr. Edgar R. Updegraff, Tucson, Ariz.
						R. Morgan Evans, Bloomington, Ill.
				Mann, 7 and 6	Mann, 3 and 2	George Clark, Ottumwa, Iowa
						William Mann, Highland Meadows, Ohio
			Roden, 5 and 3		Bogle	BYE—William F. Bogle, Dutchess, N.Y.
				Roden, 3 and 2	Roden, 5 and 4	Charles Evans, Jr., Edgewater, Ill.
						Lincoln Roden, III, Huntingdon Valley, Pa.
Meister, 3 and 2					Berke	BYE—Kenneth E. Berke, Brynwood, Wis.
				Campbell, 1 up, 19 hls.	Campbell	BYE—William C. Campbell, Guyan, W. Va.
			Campbell, 1 up		Coyle, 2 and 1	John W. Coyle, Illini, Ill.
						Edward Meyerson, Brentwood, Calif.
				Schwab, 4 and 2	Simonsen	BYE—Ade Simonsen, Minneapolis, Minn.
		Campbell, 1 up			Schwab 4 and 3	Thomas Jones, Jr., Youngstown, Ohio
						Pat Schwab, Community, Ohio
				Hoak, 2 and 1	Chandler	BYE—Robert P. Chandler, Congressional, D.C.
			Stevenson, 2 and 1		Hoak, 1 up	James M. Hoak, Wakonda, Iowa
						David F. Dixon, New Orleans, La.
				Stevenson, 3 and 2	Stevenson	BYE—Frank G. Stevenson, Jr., Savannah, Ga.
	Martin, 5 and 4				Victor, 3 and 2	Lawrence Murphy, Yahnundasis, N.Y.
						George E. Victor, Glen View, Ill.
				Kurz, 2 and 1	Kurz, 4 and 3	Mark G. Day, Exmoor, Ill.
						Bob Kurz, Coral Gables, Fla.
			Martin, 1 up, 20 hls.		Andrews	BYE—Gene Andrews, Rancho, Calif.
				Martin, 1 up	Martin, 3 and 1	Anthony Cullinane, Bethesda, Md.
						Edward P. Martin, Winchester, Mass.
		Martin, 6 and 5			Goodloe	BYE—W.L. Goodloe, Jr., Valdosta, Ga.
				Silverberg, 3 and 2	Draper, 3 and 1	Tom Draper, Red Run, Mich.
						Arthur C. Olfs, Jr., C.C. of Lansing, Mich.
			Silverberg, 3 and 2		Silverberg	BYE—Douglas Silverberg, Red Deer, Alberta, Canada
				Welsh, 3 and 1	Welsh, 3 and 1	Alex Welsh, Rockford, Ill.
						Fred Kammer, Jr., C.C. of Detroit, Mich.
					Yates, 2 and 1	Alan P. Yates, Atlanta, Ga.
						William Girard, Miami, Fla.

1954 AMATEUR CHAM
LOWER

THIRD QUARTER

1st Round (18 Holes)	2nd Round (18 Holes)	3rd Round (18 Holes)	4th Round (18 Holes)	5th Round (18 Holes)	6th Round (18 Holes)	
Thomas W. McMahon, C.C. of Detroit, Mich.	Love, 2 and 1					
Davis M. Love, El Dorado, Ark.		Love, 7 and 5				
Leonard A. Young, Oaks, Okla.	Young, 5 and 3					
J.W. Mowbray, C.C. of Lincoln, Neb.			Love, 5 and 4			
BYE—Bruce N. McCormick, San Gabriel, Calif.	McCormick					
Edwin C. Vare, Philadelphia Country, Pa.	Jones, 2 and 1	McCormick, 5 and 4		Love, 3 and 2		
Fletcher Jones, Bel-Air, Calif.						
Victor H. Bass, West Palm Beach, Fla.	Bass, default					
Robert Whiting, Red Run, Mich.		Addington, 4 and 3				
BYE—Floyd W. Addington, Lakewood, Texas	Addington		Addington, 2 and 1			
William S. Delk, Greenville, S.C.	Delk, 2 and 1					
Joseph May, South Shore, N.Y.		Brennan, 3 and 2			Love, 1 up, 19 hls.	
BYE—Thomas Brennan, Jr., Ozaukee, Wis.	Brennan					
N.H. Steward, III, Manufacturers', Pa.	Steward, 4 and 3					
Kenneth C. Young, Interlachen, Minn.		W. Barnes, 3 and 2				
BYE—Wilson F. Barnes, Jr., Mount Kisco, N.Y.	W. Barnes		W. Barnes, 2 up			
BYE—Walter E. Beckjord, Cincinnati, Ohio	Beckjord	Kunkle, 2 and 1				
Cy Pennel, Stanford University, Calif.	Kunkle, 1 up			Barnes, 3 and 2		
Charles Kunkle, Jr., Sunnehanna, Pa.						
Harold Tovrea, Jr., Tucson, Ariz.	Mendez, 4 and 2					
Fernando Mendez L., Monterrey, Mexico		Doe, 4 and 3				
BYE—Donald Doe, Granby, Canada	Doe		Doe, 2 up			
Sam Urzetta, Irondequoit, N.Y.	Holland, 1 up, 19 hls.					
Tim Holland, Rockville, N.Y.		Patton, 4 and 3				
Rex Baxter, Jr., Amarillo, Texas	Patton, 1 up, 19 hls.					Lenczyk, 4 and 3
William J. Patton, Mimosa, N.C.						
BYE—Wm. Hyndman, III, Huntingdon Valley, Pa.	Hyndman	Randolph, 1 up				
Jennings Randolph, Jr., Bethesda, Md.	Randolph, 6 and 5		Randolph, 3 and 2			
Raymond Palmer, Grosse Ile, Mich.						
BYE—J.E. Bernolfo, The C.C., Utah	Bernolfo	Davies, 1 up				
Herbert Klontz, Jr., Elmcrest, Iowa	Davies, 2 and 1			Culp, 5 and 3		
Richard D. Davies, Annandale, Calif.						
John Mahaffey, Jr., Oakmont, Pa.	Parent, 5 and 3					
Erv Parent, Inglewood, Wash.		Culp, 5 and 3				
BYE—John D. Culp, Jr., Kendallville, Ind.	Culp		Culp, 5 and 3			
James J. McCluskey, Inglewood, Calif.	McCluskey, 1 up, 19 hls.					
Edward G. Schultz, Chagrin Valley, Ohio		Weston, 3 and 2				
BYE—Raymond E. Weston, Jr., Spokane, Wash.	Weston				Lenczyk, 2 and 1	
BYE—Carlos Porraz, Mexico City, Mexico	Porraz	Martz, 6 and 4				
Lloyd A. Martz, Red Run, Mich.	Martz, 2 and 1					
James E. French, Jr., San Francisco, Calif.			Martz, 2 up			
BYE—Dr. Wendell R. Aldrich, Kendallville, Ind.	Aldrich	Manley, 5 and 4				
Hobart L. Manley, Jr., Savannah, Ga.	Manley, 4 and 3			Lenczyk, 1 up		
Frank M. Edens, Armed Forces, S.C.						
BYE—Dr. Ted N. Lenczyk, Indian Hill, Conn.	Lenczyk	Lenczyk, 4 and 3				
Mal Galletta, North Hills, N.Y.	Conney, 2 and 1					
Edward A. Cooney, Jr., Brae Burn, Mass.			Lenczyk, 2 and 1			
BYE—Richard L. Nauts, Brae-Burn, Texas	Nauts	Magnussen, 3 and 1				
Bernard L. Magnussen, Westmoreland, Ill.	Magnussen, 1 up					
Sandy Mosk, Jr., Riviera, Calif.						

SEMI-FINAL ROUND (36 Holes)—Robert Sweeny defeated Dr. Ted N. Lenczyk, 5 up and 4 to play.

FOURTH QUARTER

6th Round (18 Holes)	5th Round (18 Holes)		4th Round (18 Holes)	3rd Round (18 Holes)	2nd Round (18 Holes)	1st Round (18 Holes)
					Ribner, 6 and 5	Lewis E. Keller, Winged Foot, N.Y.
				Ribner, 1 up		Lloyd D. Ribner, Metropolis, N.Y.
					Mucci, 5 and 4	William R. Watts, Jr., Riviera, Fla.
			Morey, 1 up			Pat Mucci, Preakness Hills, N.J.
					Wenzler	BYE—Ronald E. Wenzler, Ridgeway, Tenn.
				Morey, 2 up	Morey, 7 and 6	Dale Morey, Highland, Ind.
						Antonio Rivas, Acapulco, Mexico
		Morey, 1 up, 19 hls.			Gonsky, 1 up, 19 hls.	Edward Gonsky, Wyoming Valley, Pa.
				Gonsky, 1 up		Eugene Dahlbender, Jr., Meadowbrook, Ga.
					Clovis	BYE—David C. Clovis, Parkersburg, W. Va.
			Garrett, 6 and 4		Garrett, 2 and 1	John Garrett, River Oaks, Texas
				Garrett, 2 and 1		Wayne Jackson, Hampton, Va.
					Veech	BYE—Thomas R. Veech, North Hills, Wis.
	Morey, 3 and 2				T. Barnes 4 and 3	Robert N. Babbish, Detroit, Mich.
				T. Barnes, 4 and 3		Thomas W. Barnes, Druid Hills, Ga.
					Giudice	BYE—Dr. Vincent W. Giudice, Hackensack, N.J.
			Taylor, 1 up		Taylor	BYE—Ray Taylor, Greensboro, N.C.
				Taylor, 7 and 6	Pyle, 6 and 5	Charles M. Pyle, Jr., The C.C., Mass.
						David Logan, Biltmore, Ill.
		Taylor, 2 and 1			Cupit, 4 and 3	Frank Hardison, Oakmont, Calif.
				Johnson, 1 up		Bobby Joe Cupit, Preston Hollow, Texas
					Johnson	BYE—Howie Johnson, Golfcrest, Texas
			Johnson, 2 and 1		Smith, 1 up	Ernie O. Vossler, Colonial, Texas
				Smith, 4 and 3		David W. Smith, Jr., Gaston, N.C.
					Turnesa	BYE—William P. Turnesa, Knollwood, N.Y.
Sweeny, 4 and 3					Conrad	BYE—Lt. Joseph W. Conrad, Oak Hills, Texas
				Moncrief, 2 and 1	Moncrief, 2 and 1	Edwin D. Preisler, Beechmont, Ohio
			Merrins, 4 and 3			Robert Moncrief, River Oaks, Texas
					Deupree	BYE—William J. Deupree, Jr., Fort Mitchell, Ky.
				Merrins, 3 and 2	Merrins, 6 and 5	M. Edward Merrins, Northwood, Miss.
						Charles M. Kittle, Memphis, Tenn.
		Merrins, 5 and 3			Wagner, 6 and 5	John McCann, Jr., Charlotte, N.C.
				Wagner, 8 and 6		John E. Wagner, Skokie, Ill.
					Ortega	BYE—Robert Ortega, University, N.M.
			Wagner, 4 and 3		Cudd	BYE—Bruce H. Cudd, Columbia-Edgewater, Ore.
				Holt, 3 and 2	Holt, 5 and 3	Beverly C. Nabers, Lakewood, Fla.
						W.E. Holt, Oakland Hills, Mich.
	Sweeny, 3 and 1				Thornton, 3 and 1	Jack Little, III, Corpus Christi, Texas
				Thornton, 2 up		George E. Thornton, Manor, Md.
					Harpman	BYE—Sig Harpman, Jr., Lincoln Park, Okla.
			Oskin, 2 and 1		Oskin, 6 and 5	James W. Brown, Jr., Manasquan River, N.J.
				Oskin, 2 and 1		Clyde Oskin, Jr., Saucon Valley, Pa.
					Dudley	BYE—Charles B. Dudley, Greenville, S.C.
		Sweeny, 1 up			Creason, 4 and 3	Glen L. Norrie, Grosse Ile, Mich.
				Brehaut, 2 and 1		Lynn A. Creason, Colonial, Pa.
					Brehaut	BYE—Gene Brehaut, Olympic, Calif.
			Sweeny, 4 and 3		Sweeny, 2 and 1	Robert Sweeny, Sands Point, N.Y.
				Sweeny, 6 and 5		Harry W. Easterly, Jr., C.C. of Virginia, Va.
					Shuler, 4 and 2	Juan Antonio Estrada, Torreon, Mexico
						Stanton Shuler, New Orleans, La.

1955
FIFTY-FIFTH AMATEUR CHAMPIONSHIP

Held at the Country Club of Virginia (James River Course), Richmond, Va., September 12-17.
Yardage—6,713. Par 70. 1,493 Entries, 200 Qualifiers, 200 Starters.
Championship entirely at match play.
FINAL ROUND (36 Holes)—E. Harvie Ward, Jr., defeated William Hyndman, III, 9 up and 8 to play.

UPPER

FIRST QUARTER

1st Round (18 Holes)	2nd Round (18 Holes)	3rd Round (18 Holes)	4th Round (18 Holes)	5th Round (18 Holes)	6th Round (18 Holes)	
James R. Hiskey, Pocatello, Idaho	Rendleman,					
William J. Rendleman, Guyan, W. Va.	2 and 1	W. Campbell, 4 and 3				
David Goldman, Lakewood, Texas	W. Campbell,					
William C. Campbell, Guyan, W. Va.	3 and 2		Meister, 4 and 3			
BYE—Edward L. Meister, Jr., Kirtland, Ohio	Meister			J. Campbell, 4 and 3		
		Meister, 4 and 3				
James W. Vickers, Wichita, Kans.	Grice,					
Keely Grice, Jr., Myers Park, N.C.	3 and 2					
William P. Haviland, Mount Pleasant, Md.	J. Campbell,					
Joe E. Campbell, Anderson, Ind.	4 and 2	J. Campbell, 3 and 1				
BYE—Eugene P. Zuspann, Cherry Hills, Colo.	Zuspann					
			J. Campbell, 2 up			
Richard D. Chapman, Pinehurst, N.C.	Hoff,					
Arthur R. Hoff, Edgewood Valley, Ill.	1 up, 20 hls.	Hoff, 4 and 3			J. Campbell, 5 and 4	
BYE—Charles R. Yates, Atlanta, Ga.	Yates					
Nelson Broach, Glenwood, Va.	Klontz,					
Herbert Klontz, Elmcrest, Iowa	2 and 1	Eley, 1 up, 21 hls.				
BYE—Cliff Eley, Naval Academy Officers, Md.	Eley					
			Eley, 4 and 2			
BYE—P.D. Yates, Jr., Atlanta, Ga.	Yates	Yates, 2 up				
Charles J. Dolan, Normandie, Mo.	LaClair,			Howard, 4 and 2		
Huston L. LaClair, C.C. of Birmingham, Ala.	1 up					
Eugene Dahlbender, Jr., Meadowbrooks, Ga.	Dahlbender,					
Edward F. Gonsky, Wyoming Valley, Pa.	3 and 2	Jackson, 1 up				
BYE—James G. Jackson, Algonquin, Mo.	Jackson					
			Howard, 3 and 2			
Jake Howard, Jr., Augusta, Ga.	Howard,					
Charles R. Coe, Oklahoma City, Okla.	2 and 1	Howard, 5 and 4				Hyndman, 2 up
Charles Evans, Jr., Edgewater, Ill.	Evans,					
John Busemeyer, Wyoming, Ohio	2 and 1					
BYE—Keith Kallio, East Potomac, D.C.	Kallio	Hyndman, 5 and 4				
Joseph F. Switzer, Old Warson, Mo.	Hyndman,					
William Hyndman, III, Huntingdon Valley, Pa.	1 up		Hyndman, 4 and 3			
BYE—Frank S. Souchak, Oakmont, Pa.	Souchak	Souchak, 1 up		Hyndman, 1 up, 19 hls.		
Donald E. Albert, Marine Corps Schools, Va.	Albert,					
Larry Dempsey, Starmount Forest, N.C.	5 and 4					
Arthur A. Ruffin, Jr., Wilson, N.C.	Humm,					
John J. Humm, Rockville, N.Y.	3 and 2	Goodes, 2 and 1				
BYE—Ben L. Goodes, Pennrose Park, N.C.	Goodes					
			Goodes, 1 up			
Alex Welsh, Rockford, Ill.	Barnes,					
Thomas W. Barnes, Druid Hills, Ga.	1 up, 19 hls.	Barnes, 2 up			Hyndman, 2 and 1	
BYE—Laurence E. Sherrill, Jr., Palma Ceia, Fla.	Sherrill					
BYE—Fordie H. Pitts, Jr., Wollaston, Mass.	Pitts	Beckjord, 1 up				
Walter E. Beckjord, Cincinnati, Ohio	Beckjord,					
Wallace I. Bradley, Pine Forest, Texas	4 and 3		Beckjord, 1 up, 20 hls.			
BYE—David F. Dixon, New Orleans, La.	Dixon	Dixon. 3 and 2				
Joel E. Spinola, Richmond, Calif.	Pott,			McHale, 4 and 2		
Johnny Pott, C.C. of Jackson, Miss.	4 and 3					
BYE—Robert Brue, Westmoor, Wis.	Brue	Brue, 5 and 3				
Richard E. McCreary, Jr., Conroe, Texas	Donohue,					
John J. Donohue, Jr., Wakonda, Iowa	2 and 1		McHale, 7 and 6			
BYE—Marvin J. Nischan, Inglewood, Calif.	Nischan	McHale, 1 up, 20 hls.				
Dr. John D. McKey, C.C. of Orlando, Fla.	McHale,					
James B. McHale, Jr., Aronimink, Pa.	3 and 2					

SEMI-FINAL ROUND (36 Holes)—William Hyndman, III., defeated Hillman Robbins, Jr., 4 up and 3 to play.

The first word after the player's name is the name of his club, except in the case of a foreign entrant.

HALF

SECOND QUARTER

6th Round (18 Holes)	5th Round (18 Holes)		4th Round (18 Holes)	3rd Round (18 Holes)	2nd Round (18 Holes)	1st Round (18 Holes)
					Sykes, 5 and 4	A. John Jordan, Chartiers, Pa.
				Redman, 1 up		James D. Sykes, Old York Road, Pa.
					Redman, 1 up	Frank P. Redman, El Paso, Texas
			Wild, 4 and 3			Dr. Ted N. Lenczyk, Indian Hill, Conn.
					Wild	BYE—Claude C. Wild, Jr., Washington, Va.
		Miles, 2 and 1		Wild, 2 and 1	Barnes, 2 and 1	Wilson F. Barnes, Jr., Mt. Kisco, N.Y.
						John F. Kraft, Lakewood, Colo.
					Gravely, 1 up, 19 hls.	Orville R. Goens, Wakonda, Iowa
				Miles, 1 up		Edmund K. Gravely, Benvenue, N.C.
					Miles	BYE—John G. Miles, Winged Foot, N.Y.
			Miles, 1 up, 19 hls.		Magnussen, 7 and 6	Bernard Magnussen, Westmoreland, Ill.
				McGonagill, 1 up, 21 hls.		Aulick Burke, C.C. of Bristol, Va.
					McGonagill	BYE—Jimmy McGonagill, Shreveport, La.
	Robbins, 2 and 1				Billows, 1 up	Donald M. Bisplinghoff, C.C. of Orlando, Fla.
				Billows, 2 and 1		Raymond Billows, Dutchess, N.Y.
					Sullivan	BYE—David B. Sullivan, Charles River, Mass.
			Billows, 3 and 1		Byrne	BYE—Charles B. Byrne, Lochmoor, Mich.
		Robbins, 9 and 7		Harpman, 2 and 1	Harpman, 3 and 2	Sig Harpman, Jr., Lincoln Park, Okla.
						Walter C. Andzel, Jr., South Shore, N.Y.
					McCallister, 1 up, 23 hls.	George L. McCallister, Wilshire, Calif.
				McCallister, 1 up		William J. Patton, Mimosa, N.C.
					Trierweiler	BYE—Louis G. Trierweiler, Kankakee, Ill.
			Robbins, 5 and 4		Harrison, 1 up	Charles W. Harrison, Atlanta, Ga.
				Robbins, 5 and 4		John W. Dawson, Silverado, Calif.
					Robbins	BYE—Hillman Robbins, Jr., Colonial, Tenn.
Robbins, 1 up					Cochran	BYE—Robert E. Cochran, Norwood Hills, Mo.
				Johnson, 2 and 1	Johnson, 3 and 2	Anthony Cullinane, Bethesda, Md.
			Wagner, 2 and 1			Glenn H. Johnson, Grosse Ile, Mich.
					Wagner	BYE—John E. Wagner, Skokie, Ill.
		Hopkins, 6 and 5		Wagner, 1 up, 20 hls.	Kraay, 5 and 4	Lawrence E. Kraay, Curtis Creek, Ind.
						Earl R. Larson, Minneapolis, Minn.
					Sterling	BYE—Robert Sterling, Deepdale, N.Y.
				Hopkins, 5 and 4	Hopkins, 1 up, 20 hls.	Edwin B. Hopkins, Jr., Abilene, Texas
			Hopkins, 1 up, 19 hls.			Fred Brand, Jr., Pittsburgh Field, Pa.
					Mucci	BYE—Pat Mucci, Preakness Hills, N.J.
	Hopkins, 3 and 1			Bogart, 1 up	Bogart, 1 up	Ralph M. Bogart, Chevy Chase, Md.
						Frank Michalek, Allview, Md.
					Magee, 2 up	G.J. Magee, Toronto, Ont., Canada
				Magee, 1 up, 20 hls.		George R. Bernardin, Andover, Mass.
					Sanders	BYE—Douglas Sanders, American Legion, Ga.
			Swift, 2 up		Rountree, 1 up	Jack B. Rountree, Bethesda, Md.
				Swift, 1 up, 19 hls.		William Cole, Mt. Pleasant, Md.
		Swift, 5 and 4			Swift	BYE—George P. Swift, Jr., C.C. of Columbus, Ga.
					Gordon, 1 up	M. Edward Merrins, Northwood, Miss.
				Gordon, 3 and 2		Fred L. Gordon, Clarmond, Iowa
					Goodwin	BYE—Thomas J. Goodwin, Westchester, N.Y.
			Gordon, 3 and 2		Penrose, 6 and 5	John J. Penrose, Jr. LaGorce, Fla.
				Penrose, 3 and 1		Peter T. Cook, Riviera, Fla.
					McFerren, 2 and 1	John D. Gray, Palos Verdes, Calif.
						Gerald T. McFerren, Manor, Md.

THIRD QUARTER

LOWER

1st Round (18 Holes)	2nd Round (18 Holes)	3rd Round (18 Holes)	4th Round (18 Holes)	5th Round (18 Holes)	6th Round (18 Holes)	
J. Elmer Lutz, Jr., Reading, Pa.	Lutz,					
Anthony Popolaski, Argyle, Md.	6 and 4	Veghte,				
Angelo Santilli, Potowomut, R.I.	Veghte,	3 and 2				
John W. Veghte, Pine Brook, N.Y.	2 and 1		Veghte,			
BYE—Richard E. Evans, Knollwood, Ill.	Evans		4 and 2			
		Evans,				
Lewis W. Oehmig, Chattanooga, Tenn.	Oehmig,	3 and 1				
Paul Stoner, Jr., North Oaks, Minn.	2 and 1			Kunkle, 2 and 1		
Cameron R. Quinn, West Warwick, R.I.	Quinn,					
James H. Kelly, Hermitage, Va.	4 and 3	Updegraff,				
BYE—Dr. Edgar R. Updegraff, Tucson, Ariz.	Updegraff	4 and 3				
			Kunkle,			
Charles W. Adams, Jr., Seattle, Wash.	Batdorff,		4 and 3			
Robert J. Batdorff, II, Berkshire, Pa.	3 and 1	Kunkle,				
BYE—Charles Kunkle, Jr., Sunnehanna, Pa.	Kunkle	4 and 3				
Beverly C. Nabers, Lakewood, Fla.	Nabers,				Kunkle, 3 and 2	
Raymond F. Roberts, Wachusett, Mass.	6 and 5	Conrad,				
BYE—Lt. Joe Conrad, Oak Hills, Texas	Conrad	4 and 3				
			Conrad,			
BYE—Bruce H. Cudd, Columbia-Edgewater, Ore.	Cudd		4 and 3			
		Vare,				
Gordon C. Clay, Capital City, Ga.	Vare,	2 and 1				
Edwin C. Vare, Point Judith, R.I.	4 and 3					
Edgar M. Tutwiler, Jr., Berry Hills, W. Va.	Tutwiler,			Conrad, 3 and 1		
Thomas W. McMahon, C.C. of Detroit, Mich.	1 up	Tutwiler,				
BYE—Lewis E. Keller, Winged Foot, N.Y.	Keller	4 and 3				
			Gardner,			
Robert Gardner, Essex County, N.J.	Gardner,		7 and 6			
Jack Nicklaus, Scioto, Ohio	1 up	Gardner,				
Arthur E. Anderson, Wilshire, Calif.	Blair,	3 and 2				
James T. Blair, III, Jefferson City, Mo.	1 up, 20 hls.					
BYE—Stanley E. (Ted) Bishop, Pine Brook, Mass.	Bishop					Booe, 1 up
		Bishop,				
Dave Dennis, Independence, Kans.	Dennis,	4 and 3				
Chris Gers, Hillcrest, Okla.	2 and 1		Waryan,			
BYE—Emil Pasnik, South Shore, N.Y.	Pasnik		1 up			
		Waryan,				
William Waryan, Midland Hills, Minn.	Waryan,	7 and 6				
Buzzy Wohl, Tam O'Shanter, Ill.	5 and 4			Waryan, 3 and 2		
Tom Draper, Red Run, Mich.	Draper,					
Robert R. Reilly, Highland, Pa.	1 up, 19 hls.	Draper,				
BYE—Lloyd D. Ribner, Metropolis, N.Y.	Ribner	4 and 3				
			Draper,			
William H. Nettle, Pine Lake, Mich.	Nettle,		2 and 1			
William H. Williamson, Charlotte, N.C.	2 up	Schwab,				
BYE—Ralph G. Schwab, Community, Ohio	Schwab	4 and 3				
BYE—Jack Muther, Hermitage, Va.	Muther				Booe, 5 and 4	
		Butler,				
		4 and 3				
Arthur F. Butler, Portsmouth, N.H.	Butler,					
Wynsol K. Spencer, Hampton, Va.	4 and 3		Butler,			
BYE—Harry W. Easterly, Jr., C.C. of Virginia, Va.	Easterly		7 and 6			
		Easterly,				
William J. Shields, Albany, N.Y.	Strange,	3 and 2				
Thomas W. Strange, Jr., Princess Anne, Va.	3 and 2					
BYE—Frank Strafaci, Great River, N.Y.	Strafaci			Booe, 5 and 4		
		Booe,				
William A. Booe, Brooklawn, Conn.	Booe,	1 up				
Harold Brink, Blythefield, Mich.	4 and 2		Booe,			
BYE—Stephen W. Pipoly, Tippecanoe, Ohio	Pipoly		5 and 4			
		Pipoly,				
		1 up, 21 hls.				
Wayne Jackson, Hampton, Va.	Webb,					
William E. Webb, Blue Hills, Mo.	3 and 1					

SEMI-FINAL ROUND (36 Holes)—E. Harvie Ward, Jr., defeated William A. Booe, 4 up and 2 to play.

CHAMPIONSHIP

HALF — **FOURTH QUARTER**

6th Round (18 Holes)	5th Round (18 Holes)		4th Round (18 Holes)	3rd Round (18 Holes)	2nd Round (18 Holes)	1st Round (18 Holes)
					Rothrock, 2 up	Robert A. Hill, Oak Hill, N.Y.
				Manning, 2 and 1		Aubrey A. Rothrock, Jr., C.C. of Spartanburg, S.C.
					Manning, 1 up	Richard L. Eichler, Lake Merced, Calif.
			Turnesa, 6 and 5			Charles E. Manning, Jr., South Hills, Pa.
					Turnesa	BYE—William P. Turnesa, Knollwood, N.Y.
				Turnesa, 1 up, 19 hls.	Sweeny, 7 and 6	Robert Sweeny, National, N.Y.
		McCall, 4 and 3				Thomas H. Prichard, Congressional, D.C.
					Girmonde, 4 and 2	Sam J. Girmonde, Wolfert's Roost, N.Y.
				McCall, 6 and 4		Robert L. Kelly, Congressional, D.C.
					McCall	BYE—Robert O. McCall, Tippecanoe, Ohio
			McCall, 6 and 4		Houdry, 2 and 1	Marvin C. Fitts, C.C. of Tuscaloosa, Ala.
				Olfs, 3 and 1		Jacques Houdry, Merion, Pa.
					Olfs	BYE—Arthur C. Olfs, Jr., C.C. of Lansing, Mich.
	Ward, 3 and 2				Wharton, 5 and 4	Frank Chilson, Brae-Burn, Texas
				Wharton, 2 up		Frank Wharton, Preston Hollow, Texas
					Corley	BYE—Dr. Robert W. Corley, C.C. of Jackson, Mich.
			Baxter, 1 up		Solinger	BYE—Raymond F. Solinger, Branch Brook, N.J.
				Baxter, 7 and 6	Baxter, 6 and 5	Rex Baxter, Jr., Amarillo, Texas
		Ward, 6 and 4				Robert A. Rankin, Zanesville, Ohio
					Stott, 2 up	Gordon Stott, Nassau, N.Y.
				Stott, 2 and 1		David W. Smith, Jr., Gaston, N.C.
					Hadley	BYE—T.A. Hadley, Meadowbrook Men's, Minn.
			Ward, 5 and 3		Palmer, 2 up	Robert W. Kuntz, Bonnie Briar, N.Y.
				Ward, 1 up, 19 hls.		Ray Palmer, Grosse Ile, Mich.
					Ward	BYE—E. Harvie Ward, Jr., San Francisco, Calif.
Ward, 6 and 4					Terry	BYE—Ray Terry, Timuquana, Fla.
				Paine, 3 and 1	Paine, 1 up, 21 hls.	Fred K. Gniadek, Berkshire Hills, Mass.
			Paine, 1 up, 19 hls.			Frederick Paine, Oakmont, Pa.
				Hall, 5 and 4	Hall	BYE—Jesse B. Hall, Jr., Hermitage, Va.
					Culley, 1 up	James Frisina, Sr., Illini, Ill.
		McCoy, 3 and 2				Lewis Culley, Jr., C.C. of Jackson, Miss.
				McCoy, 2 and 1	McCoy, 1 up, 19 hls.	James C. McCoy, West Palm Beach, Fla.
						Harry G. Silverberg, Green Gables, Colo.
					Brantly	BYE—Edward L. Brantly, Chattanooga, Tenn.
			McCoy, 2 up	Wilke, 2 and 1	Giddings	BYE—Richard J. Giddings, Del Rio, Calif.
	McCoy, 4 and 2				Wilke, 1 up	Robert E. Wilke, Lehigh, Pa.
						James D. Maver, Jr., Winged Foot, N.Y.
				Barnes, 1 up	Barnes, 2 and 1	Edward T. Barnes, Greensboro, N.C.
						James E. Funston, Plum Hollow, Mich.
			Andrews, 1 up, 19 hls.		Dudley	BYE—Charles B. Dudley, Greenville, S.C.
				Andrews, 1 up, 20 hls.	Andrews, 3 and 2	Norman F. Lewis, Brae-Burn, Texas
		Jordan, 2 and 1				Gene Andrews, Rancho, Calif.
					Chapman	BYE—Rob. H. Chapman, Jr., C.C. of Spartanburg, S.C.
				Jordan, 1 up	Jordan, 3 and 2	David B. Hatton, Laurel, Va.
						Robert J. Jordan, Starmount Forest, N.C.
			Jordan, 5 and 4		Jones	BYE—Fred Rick Jones, Tippecanoe, Ohio
				Haverstick, 1 up	Wenzler, 2 up	Ronald E. Wenzler, Ridgeway, Tenn.
						George H. Fulton, Jr., Roanoke, Va.
					Haverstick, 1 up	Robert E. Goetz, Ridglea, Texas
						Harry H. Haverstick, Jr., Lancaster, Pa.

1956
FIFTY-SIXTH AMATEUR CHAMPIONSHIP

Held at the Knollwood Club, Lake Forest, Ill., September 10-15.
Yardage—6,790. Par 71. 1,600 Entries, 200 Qualifiers, 200 Starters.
Championship entirely at match play.

FINAL ROUND (36 Holes)—E. Harvie Ward, Jr., defeated Charles Kocsis, 5 up and 4 to play.

UPPER

FIRST QUARTER

1st Round (18 Holes)	2nd Round (18 Holes)	3rd Round (18 Holes)	4th Round (18 Holes)	5th Round (18 Holes)	6th Round (18 Holes)	
Ward Wettlaufer, C.C. of Buffalo, N.Y.	Wettlaufer, 4 and 2					
Robert J. Riddle, Manasquan, N.J.		Wettlaufer, 1 up				
Robert W. Willits, Kansas City, Mo.	Katz, 1 up, 19 hls.					
Bernard Katz, Twin Orchard, Ill.			Wettlaufer, 2 up			
BYE—Louis F. Rosanova, Tam O'Shanter, Ill.	Rosanova	McBride, 6 and 5				
Lloyd Syron, Pontiac, Mich.	McBride, 3 and 2			Wettlaufer, 6 and 5		
Joseph A. McBride, Arcola, N.J.						
James T. Blair, III, Jefferson City, Mo.	Blair, 4 and 3					
Bertrand L. Kohlmann, Inwood, N.Y.		Blair, 4 and 3				
BYE—Bob Pratt, Pine Forest, Texas	Pratt		Blair, 4 and 3			
W.W. Flenniken, Cherry Hills, Colo.	McFerren, 2 up					
Gerald F. McFerren, Manor, Md.		McFerren, 3 and 2			Gleichmann, 3 and 2	
BYE—R. Morgan Evans, Bloomington, Ill.	Evans					
Charles Kunkle, Jr., Sunnehanna, Pa.	Semple, 5 and 4					
Richard H. Semple, Jr., Allegheny, Pa.		Gleichmann, 3 and 2				
BYE—Ted Gleichmann, Valley C. of Montecito, Calif.	Gleichmann		Gleichmann, 1 up			
BYE—Thomas A. Hadley, Meadowbrook Men's, Minn.	Hadley	Hadley, 2 up				
Ernest J. Gerardi, Wethersfield, Conn.	Culp, 1 up, 19 hls.			Gleichmann, 2 and 1		
John D. Culp, Jr., Kendallville, Ind.						
Robert A. Roos, Jr., Olympic, Calif.	Roos, 1 up					
Ralph L. Dichter, Astoria, Ore.		Roos, 2 up				
BYE—Frederic E. Franz, Crystal Lake, Ill.	Franz		Roos, 1 up			
Raymond Burian, Oregon, Ill.	Venturi, 5 and 4					
Kenneth Venturi, California, Calif.		Venturi, 4 and 2				
Bruce H. Cudd, Columbia-Edgewater, Ore.	Cudd, 3 and 2					Magee, 2 and 1
Philip S. Wiechman, Harlan, Ky.						
BYE—Frank Malara, Jr., Knollwood, N.Y.	Malara	Cherry, 1 up, 19 hls.				
Donald Hoenig, Wethersfield, Conn.	Cherry, 4 and 2					
Don Cherry, Wichita Falls, Texas			Cherry, 1 up			
BYE—Henry Timbrook, Jr., Lake Merced, Calif.	Timbrook	Timbrook, 4 and 2				
Joseph W. Conrad, Oak Hills, Texas	Tutwiler, 2 and 1			Magee, 3 and 2		
Edgar M. Tutwiler, Jr., Berry Hills, W. Va.						
Frank Wharton, Preston Hollow, Texas	Wharton, 1 up					
Nelson DeBardeleben, C.C. of Birmingham, Ala.		Wharton, 4 and 3				
BYE—David Adams, Jr., Idle Hour, Ga.	Adams		Magee, 1 up			
William J. Walsh, Kalamazoo, Mich.	Magee, 2 and 1					
Gerald J. Magee, Toronto, Ont., Canada		Magee, 3 and 2				
BYE—Hillman Robbins, Jr., Colonial, Tenn.	Robbins				Magee, 1 up	
BYE—Alex Welsh, Rockford, Ill.	Welsh	Croonquist, 2 and 1				
Neil Croonquist, Interlachen, Minn.	Croonquist, 1 up					
Mike A. Stolarik, Bonnie Brook, Ill.			Croonquist, 4 and 3			
BYE—Edwin D. Preisler, Beachmont, Ohio	Preisler	Preisler, 2 and 1				
Glenn H. Johnson, Grosse Ile, Mich.	Johnson, 4 and 3			Croonquist, 4 and 3		
Robert M. Beirne, Riverton, N.J.						
BYE—Ralph Ellstrom, Dearborn, Mich.	Ellstrom	Ellstrom, 5 and 3				
Donald T. Chornak, Nemacolin, Pa.	Larson, 1 up					
Earl R. Larson, Minneapolis, Minn.			Ellstrom, 2 and 1			
BYE—Chris H. Gers, Hillcrest, Okla.	Gers	Gardner, 4 and 2				
Robert F. Vickers, Wichita, Kans.	Gardner, 1 up					
Robert Gardner, Essex County, N.J.						

SEMI-FINAL ROUND (36 Holes)—Charles Kocsis defeated Gerald J. Magee, 4 up and 2 to play.

The first word after the player's name is the name of his club, except in the case of a foreign entrant.

HALF

SECOND QUARTER

6th Round (18 Holes)	5th Round (18 Holes)		4th Round (18 Holes)	3rd Round (18 Holes)	2nd Round (18 Holes)	1st Round (18 Holes)
				McCallister, 1 up	McCallister, 1 up, 19 hls.	Ronald E. Thomas, Alamance, N.C. Donald R. McCallister, San Gabriel, Calif.
			Baxter, 4 and 3		Vickers, 2 up	Nicholas Garbacz, Jr., Erskine Park, Ind. James W. Vickers, Wichita, Kans.
		Baxter, 3 and 2		Baxter, 7 and 6	Baxter	BYE–Rex Baxter, Jr., Amarillo, Texas
					Woodard, 4 and 2	Harvey E. Woodard, Lakepointe, Mich. Edward L. Hamilton, Twin Hills, Okla.
				Roden, 2 up	Roden, 3 and 2	Bill Roden, Odessa, Texas Lt. George R. Wislar, Quantico, Va.
			Updegraff, 4 and 3		Haverstick	BYE–Harry H. Haverstick, Jr., Lancaster, Pa.
	Baxter, 3 and 2			Updegraff, 1 up, 20 hls.	Updegraff, 3 and 2	Dr. Edgar R. Updegraff, Tucson, Ariz. Robert Thoren, Elgin, Ill.
					Rheams	BYE–David W. Rheams, New Orleans, La.
				Nicklaus, 5 and 3	Nicklaus, 1 up	George H. Fulton, Jr., Roanoke, Va. Jack Nicklaus, Scioto, Ohio
			Wenzler, 3 and 2		Switzer	BYE–Joseph F. Switzer, Old Warson, Mo.
				Wenzler, 1 up	Mohn	BYE–John V. Mohn, Montclair, N.J.
		Wenzler, 4 and 2			Wenzler, 3 and 2	Ronald E. Wenzler, Ridgeway, Tenn. Harold E. Pembrook, Braidburn, N.J.
				Patton, 3 and 1	Frisina, 2 and 1	James Frisina, Illini, Ill. James R. Hiskey, Pocatello, Idaho
			Patton, 4 and 3		Patton	BYE–William J. Patton, Mimosa, N.C.
				Dye, 1 up	Yost, 4 and 3	James J. McCluskey, Inglewood, Calif. Richard L. Yost, Columbia-Edgewater, Ore.
Kocsis, 3 and 2					Dye	BYE–Paul Dye, Jr., C.C. of Indianapolis, Ind.
				James, 3 and 1	Evans	BYE–Earle W. Evans, III, Wichita, Kans.
			Shave, 6 and 5		James, 4 and 3	M.C. James, Jr., Cherokee, Tenn. Wesley Steinman, White Manor, Pa.
				Shave, 3 and 2	Forbes	BYE–Harry F. Forbes, Rockford, Ill.
		Shave, 1 up, 19 hls.			Shave, 4 and 3	John J. Penrose, Jr., LaGorce, Fla. Robert Shave, Jr., Manakiki, Ohio
				Sweeny, 6 and 4	Sweeny	BYE–Robert Sweeny, National, N.Y.
			Victor, 1 up, 20 hls.		Scarbrough, 4 and 2	Wm. C. Scarbrough, Jr., U.S.N. Air Station, Fla. Kenneth E. Berke, Brynwood, Wis.
				Victor, 2 up	Victor	BYE–George E. Victor, Glen View, Ill.
	Kocsis, 2 up				Leslie, 6 and 4	Frederick V. Paine, Jr., Oakmont, Pa. Dr. J. Paul Leslie, Jefferson City, Mo.
				Kocsis, 7 and 6	Hoak, 2 and 1	R.S. Hoak, Sioux City, Iowa John C. Netcho, Race Brook, Conn.
			Kocsis, 3 and 2		Kocsis	BYE–Charles Kocsis, Red Run, Mich.
				Chapman, 1 up	Chapman, 1 up, 20 hls.	Richard D. Chapman, Oyster Harbors, Mass. Dr. Wendall R. Aldrich, Kendallville, Ind.
		Kocsis, 2 and 1			Harvey	BYE–Bill Harvey, Sedgefield, N.C.
				Morey, 5 and 3	Morey, 1 up	David Boies, Brownwood, Texas Dale Morey, Highland, Ind.
			Morey, 1 up		Coger	BYE–Henry E. Coger, Meadowlark, Calif.
				Humm, 2 up	Humm, 3 and 2	Pat Symons, Oak Hills, Texas John J. Humm, Rockville, N.Y.
					Watts, 2 and 1	James O. Watts, Jr., Boonsboro, Va. Edward F. Connell, Thorny Lea, Mass.

THIRD QUARTER

LOWER

1st Round (18 Holes)	2nd Round (18 Holes)	3rd Round (18 Holes)	4th Round (18 Holes)	5th Round (18 Holes)	6th Round (18 Holes)	
Earl R. Liff, Green Acres, Ill.	Liff, 1 up, 20 hls.					
Paul A. Tarnow, Jr., Palma Ceia, Fla.		Brue, 2 and 1				
Robert A. Brue, North Hills, Wis.	Brue, 2 and 1					
Robert L. Astleford, Field C. of Omaha, Neb.			Taylor, 1 up			
BYE—John P. Konsek, Lancaster, N.Y.	Konsek					
Wayne Jackson, James River, Va.	Taylor, 4 and 3	Taylor, 4 and 3				
Dr. Frank M. Taylor, Jr., Red Hill, Calif.				J. Campbell, 4 and 2		
Robert F. Sederberg, Sunset Valley, Ill.	Smith, 1 up					
David W. Smith, Gaston, N.C.		Smith, 3 and 2				
BYE—Eugene Francis, Shore View, N.Y.	Francis		J. Campbell, 1 up			
William Hyndman, III, Huntingdon Valley, Pa.	J. Campbell, 4 and 3					
Joe Campbell, Anderson, Ind.		J. Campbell, 2 and 1				
BYE—Robert W. Knowles, Myopia Hunt, Mass.	Knowles				J. Campbell, 4 and 3	
Keely A. Grice, Jr., Myers Park, N.C.	Grice, 4 and 2					
John Marschall, Wakonda, Iowa		Grice, 1 up				
BYE—Dr. Warren A. Colton, Jr., Arizona, Ariz.	Colton					
BYE—Robert Staats, Knollwood, N.Y.	Staats		Coe, 1 up, 19 hls.			
Charles R. Coe, Oklahoma City, Okla.	Coe, 2 up	Coe, 4 and 3				
Stephen W. Pipoly, Tippecanoe, Ohio				Coe, 5 and 4		
James W. Chestnut, Osage Hills, Okla.	Williamson, 2 and 1					
William H. Williamson, Charlotte, N.C.		McCoy, 4 and 3				
BYE—James C. McCoy, West Palm Beach, Fla.	McCoy		McCoy, 4 and 2			
Edwin B. Hopkins, Jr., Abilene, Texas	Hopkins, 1 up					
Dr. Ted N. Lenczyk, Indian Hills, Conn.		Hopkins, 3 and 2				
Kenneth G. Rodewald, Orchard Ridge, Ind.	Beman, 1 up, 20 hls.					J. Campbell, 2 and 1
Deane R. Beman, Bethesda, Md.						
BYE—Robert E. Cochran, Norwood Hills, Mo.	Cochran	Cochran, 3 and 2				
George P. Swift, Jr., C.C. of Columbus, Ga.	Gray, 2 up		Cochran, 4 and 2			
John D. Gray, Wilshire, Calif.						
BYE—Leslie R. Fowler, Boulder, Colo.	Fowler	Everitt, 2 and 1				
Frank P. Redman, Anthony, Texas	Everitt, 7 and 6					
Howard Everitt, Atlantic City, N.J.				Fontanini, 5 and 4		
Sargio M. Fontanini, Byrnes Park, Iowa	Fontanini, 2 and 1					
John W. Dawson, Silverado, Calif.		Fontanini, 3 and 2				
BYE—William G. Moody, Jr., Athens, Ga.	Moody		Fontanini, 4 and 2			
Robert P. Chandler, Congressional, D.C.	Chandler, 3 and 2	Chandler, 2 and 1				
Vernon L. Opp, Calumet, Ill.					Fontanini, 1 up, 19 hls.	
BYE—Floyd W. Addington, Lakewood, Texas	Addington					
BYE—William C. Campbell, Guyan, W. Va.	W. Campbell	W. Campbell, 4 and 3				
Ralph James, Jr., Old Town, N.C.	Lemak, 1 up		W. Campbell, 3 and 2			
Leslie L. Lemak, Lakeside, Texas						
BYE—Richard Manns, Duquesne, Pa.	Manns	Pittman, 2 and 1				
Jerry Pittman, Mohawk, Okla.	Pittman, 1 up, 21 hls.			W. Campbell, 2 and 1		
K. Thomas Jacobs, Jr., Montebello, Calif.						
BYE—Harlan Stevenson, Recreation Park Men's, Calif.	Stevenson	Jones, 2 and 1				
Fred Rick Jones, Tippecanoe, Ohio	Jones, 3 and 2		Rudolph, 5 and 4			
Bernard L. Magnussen, Westmoreland, Ill.						
BYE—Orville R. Goens, Wakonda, Iowa	Goens	Rudolph, 5 and 4				
Mason Rudolph, Clarksville, Tenn.	Rudolph, 1 up, 21 hls.					
John J. Donohue, Jr., Wakonda, Iowa						

SEMI-FINAL ROUND (36 Holes)—E. Harvie Ward, Jr., defeated Joe Campbell, 2 up and 1 to play.

CHAMPIONSHIP

HALF — **FOURTH QUARTER**

6th Round (18 Holes)	5th Round (18 Holes)		4th Round (18 Holes)	3rd Round (18 Holes)	2nd Round (18 Holes)	1st Round (18 Holes)
				Barber, 3 and 1	Baker, 3 and 2	Donald W. Baker, Santa Ana, Calif. Charles Evans, Jr., Edgewater, Ill.
			E.H. Ward, 6 and 5		Barber, 6 and 4	Miller W. Barber, Texarkana, Texas Frank D. Guernsey, Jr., Lakeside, Texas
					E.H. Ward	BYE—E. Harvie Ward, Jr., San Francisco, Calif.
		E.H. Ward, 1 up		E.H. Ward, 5 and 4	Hoff, 1 up	Arthur R. Hoff, Edgewood Valley, Ill. Robert Cardinal, California, Calif.
				Goalby, 5 and 4	Goalby, 5 and 4	John C. Owens, Lexington, Ky. Robert Goalby, St. Clair, Ill.
					Faucett	BYE—Charles W. Faucett, Jr., Norwood Hills, Mo.
			Boynton, 1 up, 20 hls.	Boynton, 4 and 3	Boynton, 1 up	Tim Holland, Rockville, N.Y. Frank E. Boynton, Dubsdread Fla.
					Taylor	BYE—Ray H. Taylor, Jr., Greensboro, N.C.
	E.H. Ward, 5 and 4			Kuntz, 3 and 2	Kuntz, 3 and 2	Robert W. Kuntz, Bonnie Briar, N.Y. Harton S. Semple, Allegheny, Pa.
					Ferguson	BYE—William Ferguson, Wakonda, Iowa
			Kuntz, 1 up		Busler	BYE—Robert H. Busler, Kansas City, Mo.
		J. Ward, 2 up		Turnesa, 1 up, 19 hls.	Turnesa, 2 and 1	Guy C. Bates, Merion, Pa. William P. Turnesa, Knollwood, N.Y.
				Wagner, 1 up, 20 hls.	Wagner, 7 and 6	Louis Wendrow, Lansing, Mich. John E. Wagner, Skokie, Ill.
					Cullinane	BYE—Anthony Cullinane, Bethesda, Md.
			J. Ward, 5 and 4		Veghte, 2 and 1	Jack Veghte, Pine Brook, N.Y. Frederick J. Wright, Oakley, Mass.
E.H. Ward, 3 and 2				J. Ward, 6 and 5	J. Ward	BYE—John P. Ward, Onondaga, N.Y.
					Holt	BYE—Frank L. Holt, II, Selma, Ala.
			Holt, 3 and 2	Holt, 1 up, 23 hls.	Jones, 1 up, 19 hls.	Charles J. Volpone, Jr., Ould Newbury, Mass. Robert T. Jones, III, C.C. of Pittsfield, Mass.
					Rubendall	BYE—Roger H. Rubendall, Freeport, Ill.
				Rubendall, 5 and 4	Berles, 5 and 4	James E. Moeller, Tulsa, Okla. Gerald J. Berles, Grand Rapids, Mich.
		Holt, 3 and 2		Souchak, 1 up	Souchak, 1 up	Hord W. Hardin, Bellerive, Mo. Frank S. Souchak, Oakmont, Pa.
					Buxbaum	BYE—James H. Buxbaum, Memphis, Tenn.
			McManus, 2 and 1	McManus, 3 and 2	McManus	BYE—Roger T. McManus, Kenwood, Ohio
	Blum, 1 up				Meade, 4 and 3	P.T. Taylor, Guyan, W. Va. Linden Leo Meade, Logan, W. Va.
				Harrison, 1 up	Harrison, 6 and 5	John Farquhar, Amarillo, Texas Charles W. Harrison, Atlanta, Ga.
					Draper	BYE—Tom Draper, Red Run, Mich.
			Harrison, 3 and 2	Reed, 6 and 4	Stroud, 3 and 1	Jack Little, III, Corpus Christi, Texas Marilynn A. Stroud, Paris Mountain, S.C.
					Reed	BYE—Thomas K. Reed, Lakewood, Colo.
		Blum, 1 up		Blum, 6 and 4	Blum, 6 and 5	Arnold Blum, Idle Hour, Ga. Paul Stoner, North Oaks, Minn.
					Zimmerman	BYE—Jack E. Zimmerman, Community, Ohio
			Blum, 3 and 2	Sanders, 1 up	Sanders, 2 up	Frank E. O'Connor, Jr., Transit Valley, N.Y. Douglas Sanders, LaGorce, Fla.
					Bliss, 2 and 1	Ade Simonsen, Minneapolis, Minn. Rodney Bliss, Jr., Wakonda, Iowa

1957
FIFTY-SEVENTH AMATEUR CHAMPIONSHIP

Held at The Country Club, Brookline, Mass., September 9-14.
Yardage—6,860, 6,825. Par 72. 1,578 Entries, 200 Qualifiers, 200 Starters.
Championship entirely at match play.

FINAL ROUND (36 Holes)—Hillman Robbins, Jr., defeated Dr. Frank M. Taylor, Jr., 5 up and 4 to play.

UPPER

FIRST QUARTER

1st Round (18 Holes)	2nd Round (18 Holes)	3rd Round (18 Holes)	4th Round (18 Holes)	5th Round (18 Holes)	6th Round (18 Holes)	
Sig Harpman, Jr., Oklahoma City, Okla.	Kufta,					
William E. Kufta, Wethersfield, Conn.	4 and 3	Steelsmith,				
Jerry Steelsmith, Oakmont, Calif.	Steelsmith,	7 and 6				
Frank Guernsey, Lakeside, Texas	6 and 5		Whiting,			
BYE—Edward L. Brantly, Signal Mountain, Tenn.	Brantly		2 and 1			
		Whiting,				
John H. Guenther, Jr., Berkshire, Pa.	Whiting,	3 and 2				
Richard L. Whiting, Red Run, Mich.	3 and 2			Blair, 5 and 4		
Edward L. Meister, Jr., Kirtland, Ohio	Blair,					
Jim Tom Blair, Greenbriar Hills, Mo.	2 and 1	Blair,				
BYE—Col John W. Kline, Zanesville, Ohio	Kline	3 and 2				
			Blair,			
Charles J. McCarthy, Jr., Salem, Mass.	Wild,		1 up			
Claude C. Wild, Jr., Burning Tree, Md.	3 and 2	Astleford,				
BYE—Bob Astleford, Field Club, Neb.	Astleford	2 and 1				
George Toms, Hope Valley, N.C.	Toms,				Taylor, 2 up	
Jerry Buchetto, Hubbard Heights, Conn.	1 up	Wolstenholme,				
BYE—Guy B. Wolstenholme, Leicester, England	Wolstenholme	2 up				
			Simon,			
BYE—Franklin Simon, Westchester, N.Y.	Simon		1 up			
		Simon,				
Donald C. Allen, C.C. of Rochester, N.Y.	Stott,	7 and 6				
Gordon Stott, Nassau, N.Y.	1 up			Taylor, 7 and 6		
Dr. Frank M. Taylor, Jr., Red Hill, Calif.	Taylor,					
Dr. Wendell R. Aldrich, Kendallville, Ind.	2 and 1	Taylor,				
BYE—Robert W. Teyro, Guyan, W. Va.	Teyro	7 and 6				
			Taylor,			
William R. Shook, Mill Valley, Calif.	Bostock,		7 and 6			
Frank B. Bostock, Arizona, Ariz.	1 up	Bostock,				
Robert O. McCall, Gary, Ind.	Bishop,	2 up				
Stanley E. Bishop, Pine Brook, Mass.	5 and 4					Taylor, 2 up
BYE—Jimmy C. McCoy, West Palm Beach, Fla.	McCoy					
		Andrews,				
James R. English, Columbine, Colo.	Andrews,	2 and 1				
Gene Andrews, Rancho, Calif.	1 up, 19 hls.		Andrews,			
BYE—Jesse P. Guilford, Woodland, Mass.	Guilford		1 up			
		Albert,				
Vernon Bell, Colonial, Tenn.	Albert,	3 and 1				
Donald E. Albert, Mount Hawley, Ill.	1 up			Andrews, 3 and 2		
Gerard J. Berles, Grand Rapids, Mich.	Diversi,					
Richard Diversi, Waterville, Maine	1 up	Diversi,				
BYE—Edwin B. Hopkins, Jr., Abilene, Texas	Hopkins	3 and 2				
			Diversi,			
William C. Campbell, Guyan, W. Va.	W. Campbell,		3 and 1			
Anthony Cullinane, Bethesda, Md.	3 and 2	W. Campbell,				
BYE—Charles B. Smith, Gaston, N.C.	Smith	3 and 2				
BYE—Arthur Barni, Fox Hill, Pa.	Barni				Andrews, 4 and 2	
		Barni,				
Richard H. Semple, Jr., Allegheny, Pa.	Semple,	6 and 5				
Francis R. Cardi, Ohio State Univ., Ohio	2 and 1		Thirlwell,			
BYE—Nick Garbacz, Erskine Park, Ind.	Garbacz		1 up			
		Thirlwell,				
Alan Thirlwell, Newcastle-on-Tyne, England	Thirlwell,	3 and 1				
William S. Terrell, Charlotte, N.C.	5 and 4			Thirlwell, 5 and 4		
BYE—Emanuele Nordone, Jr., Lafayette, N.Y.	Nordone					
		Sanok,				
Chester Sanok, Knoll, N.J.	Sanok,	4 and 3				
Kenneth C. Young, Interlachen, Minn.	6 and 4		Bussell,			
BYE—James E. Funston, Plum Hollow, Mich.	Funston		4 and 2			
		Bussell,				
Alan F. Bussell, Notts, England	Bussell,	2 and 1				
Anthony Maragno, Pine Brook, N.Y.	1 up					

SEMI-FINAL ROUND (36 Holes)—Dr. Frank M. Taylor, Jr., defeated E. Mason Rudolph, 5 up and 4 to play.

The first word after the player's name is the name of his club, except in the case of a foreign entrant.

HALF

SECOND QUARTER

6th Round (18 Holes)	5th Round (18 Holes)		4th Round (18 Holes)	3rd Round (18 Holes)	2nd Round (18 Holes)	1st Round (18 Holes)
					Beman, 5 and 4	Deane R. Beman, Bethesda, Md. John J. Donohue, Jr., Wakonda, Iowa
				Beman, 1 up, 20 hls.		
					Hoenig, 5 and 3	Joseph B. Carr, Dublin, Ireland Donald Hoenig, Wethersfield, Conn.
			Beman, 3 and 2		Grace	BYE—Joseph M. Grace, Jr., Detroit, Mich.
				Pitts, 2 and 1		
					Pitts, 1 up, 21 hls.	Fordie H. Pitts, Jr., Wollaston, Mass. George H. Fulton, Jr., Roanoke, Va.
		Rudolph, 2 and 1				
				Wagner, 2 and 1	Arend, 6 and 5	Ernest A. Arend, Jr., Deal, N.J. Lester A. Slattery, Jr., Normandie, Mo.
					Wagner	BYE—John E. Wagner, Skokie, Ill.
			Rudolph, 1 up, 19 hls.			
					Rudolph, 2 up	Charles W. Harrison, Atlanta Athletic, Ga. E. Mason Rudolph, Clarksville, Tenn.
	Rudolph, 4 and 3			Rudolph, 5 and 4		
					Siderowf	BYE—Richard L. Siderowf, Indian Hill, Conn.
				Brown, 5 and 3	Brown, 2 up	Wesley G. Brown, Chattanooga, Tenn. John D. Gray, Wilshire, Calif.
					Hannaway	BYE—Dr. Francis H. Hannaway, Tedesco, Mass.
			Beirne, 1 up, 19 hls.		Beirne	BYE—Robert M. Beirne, Riverton, N.J.
				Beirne, 5 and 4		
		Cook, 6 and 5			Sweeny, 4 and 3	Robert Sweeny, Seminole, Fla. John C. Owens, Lexington, Ky.
				Cook, 1 up, 19 hls.	Paige, 3 and 2	Thomas Wheeling, Sunnehanna, Pa. Richard L. Paige, Portage, Ohio
					Cook	BYE—Lawrence G. Cook, Pine Valley, N.C.
			Cook, 2 and 1			
				Paul, 2 up	Blum, 4 and 3	Paul E. Kelly, Sleepy Hollow, N.Y. Arnold S. Blum, Idle Hour, Ga.
					Paul	BYE—James W. Paul, Daytona Beach, Fla.
Rudolph, 1 up, 19 holes						
					Turnesa	BYE—William P. Turnesa, Knollwood, N.Y.
				Turnesa, 5 and 4		
			Turnesa, 5 and 3		T. Allen, 3 and 2	Curtis Person, Colonial, Tenn. Tracy J. Allen, Maple Bluff, Wis.
					Tarnow	BYE—Paul A. Tarnow, Jr., Palma Ceia, Fla.
		Penrose, 1 up, 24 hls.		J. Campbell, 1 up		
					J. Campbell, 3 and 2	Robert T. Jones, III, C.C. of Pittsfield, Mass. Joe E. Campbell, Deane Hill, Tenn.
					Penrose	BYE—John J. Penrose, Jr., La Gorce, Fla.
				Penrose, 2 and 1		
					Baldwin, 2 up	David M. Baldwin, Baltusrol, N.J. Leonard T. Bjorklund, Interlachen, Minn.
			Penrose, 2 and 1		Lenczyk	BYE—Dr. Ted. N. Lenczyk, Indian Hill, Conn.
				Lenczyk, 1 up		
	Yost, 1 up, 19 hls.				Veghte, 1 up	James W. Vickers, Wichita, Kans. John W. Veghte, Pine Brook, N.Y.
				S. Kocsis, 1 up	S. Kocsis, 2 and 1	Gerald H. Micklem, Kent, England Samuel D. Kocsis, Indianwood, Mich.
					Basinger	BYE—Buzzy Basinger, Myers Park, N.C.
			Nicklaus, 8 and 7			
				Nicklaus, 2 and 1	Nicklaus, 3 and 2	Robert J. Cardinal, California, Calif. Jack Nicklaus, Scioto, Ohio
					Sewell	BYE—Douglas Sewell, Surrey, England
		Yost, 3 and 2				
				Yost, 5 and 4	Yost, 5 and 3	Lewis A. McGowan, Jr., Manor, Md. Richard L. Yost, Columbia-Edgewater, Ore.
					Cupit	BYE—Jacky Cupit, Pine Forest, Texas
			Yost, 3 and 2			
				Gonsky, 3 and 2	Gonsky, 3 and 2	Edward F. Gonsky, Wyoming Valley, Pa. William G. Harding, Dedham, Mass.
					Reich, 1 up	Lawrence A. Reich, Green Acres, Ill. Keely Grice, Jr., Myers Park, N.C.

THIRD QUARTER

1st Round (18 Holes)	2nd Round (18 Holes)	3rd Round (18 Holes)	4th Round (18 Holes)	5th Round (18 Holes)	6th Round (18 Holes)	
A.D. Dorsett, Jr., C.C. of Salisbury, N.C.	Dorsett,					
William Gore, Athens, Ohio	4 and 3	Barnes,				
Wilson F. Barnes, Jr., Mount Kisco, N.Y.	Barnes,	4 and 3				
Earle W. Evans, III, Wichita, Kans.	1 up, 20 hls.		Harvey,			
BYE–E.D. Moore, C.C. of Orangeburg, S.C.	Moore		1 up			
		Harvey,				
Victor Cuiss, C.C. of Jackson, Mich.	Harvey,	4 and 3				
John V. Harvey, Winchester, Mass.	4 and 2					
Walter C. Andzel, Jr., South Shore, N.Y.	Scrutton,			Holland, 1 up, 19 hls.		
Philip F. Scrutton, Berks, England	2 and 1	Holland,				
BYE–Tim Holland, Rockville, N.Y.	Holland	2 and 1				
			Holland,			
Edward P. Martin, Winchester, Mass.	Lohren,		4 and 2			
Carl A. Lohren, Brooke Manor Farms, Md.	2 up	Lohren,				
BYE–William L. Stewart, Hickory Hills, Mo.	Stewart	1 up, 19 hls.				
Arthur R. Hoff, Edgewood Valley, Ill.	Sams,				Robbins, 1 up	
Alfred Sams, Idle Hour, Ga.	3 and 2	Sams,				
BYE–Mark H. McCormack, Shawnee, Ohio	McCormack	3 and 2				
			Sams,			
BYE–Lloyd J. Pitzer, Glen Flora, Ill.	Pitzer		3 and 2			
		C. Evans,				
Donald Dosen, Minneapolis, Minn.	C. Evans,	4 and 2				
Charles Evans, Jr., Edgewater, Ill.	4 and 3					
Larry Beck, Kinston, N.C.	Foutche,			Robbins, 1 up		
Dick Foutche, Berry Hills, W. Va.	4 and 3	Foutche,				
BYE–William F. Atkinson, Pine Forest, Texas	Atkinson	5 and 4				
			Robbins,			
Hillman Robbins, Jr., Colonial, Tenn.	Robbins,		2 and 1			
William F. Davidson, Belle Meade, Tenn.	3 and 2	Robbins,				
William Thornton, Tequesta, Fla.	Thornton,	5 and 4				
Roger H. Rubendall, Freeport, Ill.	4 and 3					
BYE–Richard D. Chapman, Oyster Harbors, Mass.	Chapman					Robbins, 3 and 1
		Chapman,				
William J. Shields, Albany, N.Y.	Shields,	5 and 4				
David W. Smith, Jr., Gaston, N.C.	4 and 3		Chapman,			
BYE–Dr. Arthur F. Butler, Portsmouth, N.H.	Butler		5 and 4			
		Butler,				
Jackie O'Neill, III, Sherwood Forest, La.	O'Neill,	5 and 4				
John H. Simmons, Sedalia, Mo.	1 up					
Ronald Royer, Crawfordsville, Ind.	Kelly,			Chapman, 2 up		
Lester R. Kelly, Druid Hills, Ga.	1 up	Wright,				
BYE–Claude L. Wright, Cherry Hills, Colo.	Wright	1 up, 20 hls.				
			Wright,			
R. Reid Jack, Dullatur, Scotland	Jack,		4 and 2			
Harry H. Haverstick, Jr., Lancaster, Pa.	2 and 1	Jack,				
BYE–Robert J. Shave, Jr., Manakiki, Ohio	Shave	1 up				
BYE–James R. Hiskey, Pocatello, Idaho	Hiskey				Chapman, 2 and 1	
		Hiskey,				
Eugene S. Pulliam, C.C. of Indianapolis, Ind.	Gardner,	6 and 5				
Robert Gardner, Essex County, N.J.	2 up		Hiskey,			
BYE–William S. Cordingley, Edina, Minn.	Cordingley		4 and 2			
		Woodard,				
Robert F. Vickers, Wichita, Kans.	Woodard,	2 and 1				
Harvey E. Woodard, Lakepointe, Mich.	3 and 2			Meyerson, 4 and 3		
BYE–Don Essig, III, Willow Brook, Ind.	Essig					
		Meyerson,				
Eddie Meyerson, Brentwood, Calif.	Meyerson,	3 and 2				
Nelson O. Occhialini, Toy Town Tavern, Mass.	4 and 3		Meyerson,			
BYE–Ward Wettlaufer, C.C. of Buffalo, N.Y.	Wettlaufer		3 and 2			
		Wettlaufer,				
Robert W. Knowles, Jr., Palmetto, S.C.	Patton,	1 up, 19 hls.				
William J. Patton, Mimosa Hills, N.C.	4 and 2					

SEMI-FINAL ROUND (36 Holes)–Hillman Robbins, Jr., defeated Rex Baxter, Jr., 2 up

CHAMPIONSHIP

FOURTH QUARTER

HALF 6th Round (18 Holes)	5th Round (18 Holes)	4th Round (18 Holes)	3rd Round (18 Holes)	2nd Round (18 Holes)	1st Round (18 Holes)
				Morey,	J.O. Harris, Jr., C.C. of Virginia, Va.
			Boies,	6 and 5	Dale Morey, Highland, Ind.
			1 up	Boies,	David Boies, Brownwood, Texas
		Boies,		3 and 2	Clyde H. Oskin, Jr., Saucon Valley, Pa.
		3 and 2		Kunkle	BYE—Charles Kunkle, Jr., Sunnehanna, Pa.
			Kunkle,		
			1 up	Beckjord,	Walter E. Beckjord, Cincinnati, Ohio
		Rodgers, 6 and 4		1 up, 19 hls.	Robert F. Sederberg, Sunset Valley, Ill.
				Roos,	Dr. Frank W. G. Deighton, Glasgow, Scotland
			Rodgers,	5 and 3	Robert A. Roos, Jr., Olympic, Calif.
			3 and 2	Rodgers	BYE—Phil Rodgers, La Jolla, Calif.
		Rodgers,			
		1 up, 20 hls.		Schmidt,	Karl H. Schmidt, Fairlawn, Ohio
			Schmidt,	2 and 1	P.J. Boatwright, Jr., Pinehurst, N.C.
			3 and 2	Dear	BYE—William Y. Dear, Jr., Morris County, N.J.
	Rodgers, 5 and 4				
				Cochran,	Joseph W. Monahan, Jr., Winchester, Mass.
			Cochran,	3 and 2	Robert E. Cochran, Norwood Hills, Mo.
			1 up	Brink	BYE—Harold Brink, Blythefield, Mich.
		C. Kocsis,			
		4 and 3		Bonallack	BYE—Michael F. Bonallack, Essex, England
			C. Kocsis,		
			1 up, 21 hls.	C. Kocsis,	Robert W. Kuntz, Bonnie Briar, N.Y.
		C. Kocsis, 3 and 2		2 and 1	Charles Kocsis, Red Run, Mich.
				Konsek,	John P. Konsek, Lancaster, N.Y.
			Konsek,	1 up, 21 hls.	Edward A. Cooney, Jr., Brae Burn, Mass.
			4 and 3	Strafaci	BYE—Frank Strafaci, Bayshore Golfers, Fla.
		Coe,			
		1 up		Randolph,	Jennings Randolph, Jr., Bethesda, Md.
			Coe,	2 and 1	Phil Donohue, Minnehaha, S.D.
			1 up, 20 hls.	Coe	BYE—Charles R. Coe, Oklahoma City, Okla.
Baxter, 1 up, 21 holes				Goodwin	BYE—Thomas J. Goodwin, Westchester, N.Y.
			Krause,		
			1 up, 22 hls.	Krause,	George B. Thurmond, Brae Burn, Mass.
		Sott,		2 and 1	Jerry Krause, Hillcrest, Mo.
		4 and 3		Wright	BYE—Frederick J. Wright, Oakley, Mass.
			Sott,		
			2 and 1	Sott,	James M. Hoak, Wakonda, Iowa
		Sott, 1 up, 19 hls.		5 and 4	Alex Sott, D. Fairchild Wheeler, Conn.
				Kohlmann,	Richard L. Kinchla, Albermarle, Mass.
			Everitt,	1 up, 19 hls.	Bertrand L. Kohlmann, Inwood, N.Y.
			6 and 4	Everitt	BYE—Howard Everitt, Atlantic City, N.J.
		Everitt,			
		3 and 2		Rose	BYE—Thomas Rose, Town & C.C., Minn.
			Kosten,		
			3 and 2	Kosten,	Ray Lovell, Birmingham, Mich.
	Baxter, 5 and 3			4 and 3	Robert T. Kosten, Wannamoisett, R.I.
				J. Kelly,	James H. Kelly, Hermitage, Va.
			Paine,	6 and 4	Marvin K. Serber, Springhaven, Pa.
			4 and 3	Paine	BYE—Frederick V. Paine, Jr., Oakmont, Pa.
		Paine,			
		2 up		McManus,	Alec E. Shepperson, Notts, England
			Thomas,	1 up	Roger T. McManus, Kenwood, Ohio
			1 up	Thomas	BYE—Ronald E. Thomas, Old Town, N.C.
		Baxter, 4 and 3			
				Baxter,	Dr. Frank Bellino, Tippecanoe, Ohio
			Baxter,	1 up	Rex Baxter, Jr., Amarillo, Texas
			7 and 6	McCue	BYE—Lawrence McCue, Torrington, Conn.
		Baxter,			
		1 up		Geiberger,	Allen L. Geiberger, Montecito, Calif.
			Geiberger,	2 and 1	Peter M. Grant, Arizona, Ariz.
			1 up	Hyndman,	William Hyndman, III, Huntingdon Valley, Pa.
				3 and 2	Tommy Bates, Atlanta Athletic, Ga.

1958
FIFTY-EIGHTH AMATEUR CHAMPIONSHIP

Held at the Olympic Country Club, San Francisco, Calif., September 8-13.
Yardage—6,680. Par 70. 1,472 Entries, 200 Qualifiers, 200 Starters.
Championship entirely at match play.

FINAL ROUND (36 Holes)—Charles R. Coe defeated Thomas D. Aaron, 5 up and 4 to play.

UPPER

FIRST QUARTER

1st Round (18 Holes)	2nd Round (18 Holes)	3rd Round (18 Holes)	4th Round (18 Holes)	5th Round (18 Holes)	6th Round (18 Holes)	
Richard L. Weyand, Birmingham, Mich.	Weyand,					
Edward Castagnetto, Lake Merced, Calif.	2 up	Williamson,				
Bobby Nichols, Midland, Texas	Williamson,	2 and 1				
William H. Williamson, Charlotte, N.C.	1 up, 20 hls.		Williamson,			
BYE—Yukio Kashiwa, Waialae, T.H.	Kashiwa		1 up			
		Castator,				
Bruce Castator, Toronto, Ont., Canada	Castator,	4 and 3				
Jerry J. Cole, Fenway, N.Y.	2 and 1					
James A. Hamilton, Jr., Pine Forest, Texas	Morgan,			Morgan, 5 and 3		
Daniel M. Morgan, Stockdale, Calif.	2 and 1	Morgan,				
BYE—Joe Hendricks, Boulder, Colo.	Hendricks	7 and 6				
			Morgan,			
Robert W. Knowles, Jr., Myopia Hunt, Mass.	Knowles,		3 and 2			
James R. Cleveland, Jr., Druid Hills, Ga.	2 and 1	B. Foote,				
BYE—Bill Foote, Jr., Santa Ana, Calif.	B. Foote	1 up, 19 hls.				
Richard L. Yost, Columbia-Edgewater, Ore.	Yost,				Coe, 1 up	
Jimmy Parks, San Jose, Fla.	2 and 1	Henrikson,				
BYE—Robert B. Henrikson, Univ. of Minnesota, Minn.	Henrikson	6 and 4				
			Gardner,			
BYE—Robert Gardner, Essex County, N.J.	Gardner		6 and 5			
		Gardner,				
Daniel J. Silvestri, Sharp Park, Calif.	Silvestri,	1 up, 19 hls.				
Robert E. Cochran, Norwood Hills, Mo.	3 and 2			Coe, 5 and 4		
Edward L. Meister, Jr., Kirtland, Ohio	Meister,					
Jose L. Ortega, Mexico City, Mexico	8 and 6	Hoff,				
BYE—Arthur R. Hoff, Edgewood Valley, Ill.	Hoff	1 up				
			Coe,			
Charles R. Coe, Oklahoma City, Okla.	Coe,		1 up			
Thomas F. Ford, Jr., Harkers Hollow, N.J.	5 and 4	Coe,				
Richard J. Giddings, Del Rio, Calif.	Giddings,	3 and 1				
Clark Espie, Hillcrest, Ind.	6 and 5					
BYE—James R. Wilbert, Sharp Park, Calif.	Wilbert					Coe, 1 up
		Griffith,				
George E. Griffith, Langley Field AFB, Va.	Griffith,	2 and 1				
Frank Wharton, Preston Hollow, Texas	4 and 3		Griffith,			
BYE—James W. Mallory, Spokane, Wash.	Mallory		1 up			
		Mallory,				
Lloyd C. Rossi, Diablo, Calif.	Simon,	3 and 2				
Franklin Simon, Westchester, N.Y.	4 and 3					
William G. Lovett, Columbia-Edgewater, Ore.	Dawson,			Dawson, 5 and 4		
John W. Dawson, Eldorado, Calif.	6 and 4	Dawson,				
BYE—James McCarthy, Joliet, Ill.	McCarthy	3 and 1				
			Dawson,			
Joe Switzer, Jr., Sunset, Mo.	Patton,		3 and 2			
William J. Patton, Mimosa Hills, N.C.	8 and 6	Patton,				
BYE—Paul Stoner, North Oaks, Minn.	Stoner	2 up				
BYE—Matthew J. Scammell, Jr., Huntingdon Valley, Pa.	Scammell				Beman, 3 and 1	
		Kline,				
Ray Lovell, Birmingham, Mich.	Kline,	2 and 1				
Col. John W. Kline, Westover, Mass.	1 up		Clites,			
BYE—James M. Hoak, Wakonda, Iowa	Hoak		2 up			
		Clites,				
Elmer L. Clites, Antioch, Calif.	Clites,	4 and 3				
Cameron P. Quinn, West Warwick, R.I.	2 and 1			Beman, 5 and 3		
BYE—William J. Deupree, Jr., Fort Mitchell, Ky.	Deupree					
		Beman,				
Deane R. Beman, Bethesda, Md.	Beman,	4 and 3				
Juan A. Estrada, Durango, Mexico	1 up		Beman,			
BYE—Edwin D. Preisler, Beechmont, Ohio	Preisler		3 and 2			
		Andrews,				
Gene Andrews, California, Calif.	Andrews,	3 and 2				
Dr. Edgar R. Updegraff, Tucson, Ariz.	3 and 1					

SEMI-FINAL ROUND (36 Holes)—Charles R. Coe defeated Roger T. McManus, 3 up and 2 to play.

The first word after the player's name is the name of his club, except in the case of a foreign entrant.

HALF

SECOND QUARTER

6th Round (18 Holes)	5th Round (18 Holes)		4th Round (18 Holes)	3rd Round (18 Holes)	2nd Round (18 Holes)	1st Round (18 Holes)
					Davidson, 3 and 2	William G. Davidson, Carlisle, Pa.
						John J. Donohue, Jr., Wakonda, Iowa
				Leider, 2 and 1	Leider, 1 up, 21 hls.	Charles Leider, Peninsula, Calif.
						Dr. Bob Knutson, California, Calif.
			Ward, 5 and 3		Ward	BYE—E. Harvie Ward, Jr., San Francisco, Calif.
				Ward, 1 up	Nicklaus, 3 and 2	Jack Nicklaus, Scioto, Ohio
						Richard B. Baird, Fort Washington, Calif.
		Ward, 3 and 1			Pittman, 6 and 4	Allen L. Geiberger, Montecito, Calif.
				Pittman, 5 and 4		Jerry W. Pittman, Rolling Hills, Okla.
					Diversi	BYE—Richard Diversi, Waterville, Maine
			Pittman, 5 and 4		Krieger, 3 and 2	Donald Krieger, Columbia-Edgewater, Ore.
				Krieger, 1 up		Rafael Quiroz, Mexicali, B.C., Mexico
					McFerren	BYE—Gerald F. McFerren, Manor, Md.
	Wettlaufer, 3 and 2				Wettlaufer, 5 and 4	H. Ward Wettlaufer, C.C. of Buffalo, N.Y.
				Wettlaufer, 5 and 4		Payne Palmer, Phoenix, Ariz.
					Magnussen	BYE—Bernard Magnussen, Westmoreland, Ill.
			Wettlaufer, 1 up		Ferrie	BYE—James A. Ferrie, Virginia, Calif.
				Wysong, 1 up, 21 hls.	Wysong, 6 and 5	John J. Penrose, Jr., La Gorce, Fla.
		Wettlaufer, 5 and 4				H. Dudley Wysong, Jr., Northwood, Texas
					Vickers, 1 up	James W. Vickers, Wichita, Kans.
				Vickers, 3 and 1		Gary Cowan, Kitchener, Ont., Canada
			Miles, 2 and 1		Fehr	BYE—Gerald F. Fehr, Inglewood, Wash.
					Miles, 6 and 5	Lt. Clifford C. Thomas, Jr., Wee Burn, Conn.
				Miles, 1 up		John G. Miles, Oakland Hills, Mich.
McManus, 1 up					Draper	BYE—Tom Draper, Red Run, Mich.
				Stimac, 2 and 1	Lucente	BYE—Louis Lucente, Hillview, Calif.
			Siderowf, 5 and 4		Stimac, 3 and 1	Stephen Stimac, Contra Costa, Calif.
						Fletcher Jones, Bel Air, Calif.
				Siderowf, 2 and 1	Ramsey	BYE—Larry Ramsey, Waveland, Iowa
		Wild, 2 and 1			Siderowf, 3 and 1	Richard L. Siderowf, Indian Hill, Conn.
						Enrique Farias, Jr., Monterrey, N.L., Mexico
				Wild, 3 and 2	Prall	BYE—Robert Prall, Eugene, Ore.
			Wild, 3 and 2		Wild, 1 up, 19 hls.	Edgar M. Tutwiler, Jr., Berry Hills, W. Va.
						Claude C. Wild, Jr., Burning Tree, Md.
				Smith, 5 and 4	Pence	BYE—Wayne A. Pence, Jr., Blue Hills, Mo.
	McManus, 3 and 1				Smith, 2 up	Edward M. Burge, Del Rio, Calif.
						James F. Smith, Jr., Amarillo, Texas
				Fowler, 1 up	Baxter, 7 and 5	George W. Boutell, Phoenix, Ariz.
						Rex Baxter, Jr., Amarillo, Texas
			McManus, 4 and 3		Fowler	BYE—Glen Fowler, Hillcrest, Okla.
				McManus, 7 and 5	Johnson, 2 up	Robert B. Johnson, Fircrest, Wash.
		McManus, 2 up				Eugene A. Howard, Jr., Glenview, Ill.
					McManus	BYE—Roger T. McManus, Kenwood, Ohio
				Eschenbrenner, 4 and 3	Kelly, 3 and 2	Art Anderson, Wilshire, Calif.
						Paul E. Kelly, Sleepy Hollow, N.Y.
			Trainor, 2 and 1		Eschenbrenner	BYE—Bill Eschenbrenner, Colonial, Texas
				Trainor, 6 and 5	Trainor, 5 and 3	Dr. George M. Trainor, Oak Hill, N.Y.
						Dale Morey, Highland, Ind.
					Paine, 6 and 5	Richard D. Chapman, Oyster Harbors, Mass.
						Frederick V. Paine, Jr., Oakmont, Pa.

THIRD QUARTER

LOWER

1st Round (18 Holes)	2nd Round (18 Holes)	3rd Round (18 Holes)	4th Round (18 Holes)	5th Round (18 Holes)	6th Round (18 Holes)	
Tim Holland, Rockville, N.Y.	T. Holland,					
John P. Konsek, Lancaster, N.Y.	2 and 1	Urdaneta,				
Mauricio Urdaneta, Mexico City, Mexico	Urdaneta,	4 and 3				
Peter V. Paxton, Riviera, Calif.	3 and 2		Lohren,			
BYE—George Dawson, Glen Oak, Ill.	Dawson		2 and 1			
		Lohren,				
Carl Lohren, Brooke Manor, Md.	Lohren,	1 up, 19 hls.				
Charles W. Mulcahy, Jr., Myopia Hunt, Mass.	4 and 2			Taylor, 5 and 3		
Robert W. Kuntz, Bonnie Briar, N.Y.	Kuntz,					
William C. Bell, Tucson, Ariz.	3 and 2	Davies,				
BYE—Richard D. Davies, Annandale, Calif.	Davies	7 and 6				
			Taylor,			
Jack Bariteau, San Jose, Calif.	Taylor,		3 and 2			
Dr. Frank M. Taylor, Jr., Red Hill, Calif.	1 up	Taylor,				
BYE—Gary A. Liotta, Mira Vista, Calif.	Liotta	3 and 2				
					Taylor, 2 up	
George O. Holland, Overlake, Wash.	G. Holland,					
Charles Kunkle, Jr., Sunnehanna, Pa.	2 and 1	McCormack,				
BYE—Mark H. McCormack, The Country C., Ohio	McCormack	3 and 2				
			Hanson,			
BYE—Jack E. Zimmerman, Dayton, Ohio	Zimmerman		2 and 1			
		Hanson,				
Eric Hanson, Toronto, Ont., Canada	Hanson,	1 up				
Thomas V. Vickers, Wichita, Kans.	4 and 3			Hanson, 1 up		
Orville R. Goens, Wakonda, Iowa	Sucher,					
Richard Sucher, Ozaukee, Wis.	1 up, 22 hls.	Korich,				
BYE—Michael P. Korich, Sierra View, Calif.	Korich	1 up, 19 hls.				
			Korich,			
Lawrence Greenwald, Dallas, Texas	Greenwald,		1 up			
John C. Doser, Woodmont, Md.	1 up	Greenwald,				
William C. Campbell, Guyan, W. Va.	Campbell,	1 up				Foote, 4 and 3
Robert McReynolds, Riverside, Ore.	4 and 2					
BYE—James M. Hawkins, Guyan, W. Va.	Hawkins					
		Bisplinghoff,				
Jack House, Milburn, Kans.	Bisplinghoff,	5 and 4				
Donald M. Bisplinghoff, La Gorce, Fla.	5 and 4		Bisplinghoff,			
BYE—William F. Bogle, Dutchess, N.Y.	Bogle		4 and 3			
		Bogle,				
Dr. Wendell R. Aldrich, Auburn, Ind.	Harrington,	3 and 2				
George E. Harrington, Arizona, Ariz.	3 and 2			Bisplinghoff, 4 and 3		
Ignacio Lopez, Jr., Guadalajara, Jal., Mexico	DiPaglia,					
Floren DiPaglia, Waveland, Iowa	1 up	Albert,				
BYE—Donald E. Albert, Brookside, Ohio	Albert	1 up, 19 hls.				
			Albert,			
Arthur Schroeder, Jr., Harding Park, Calif.	Levinson,		3 and 2			
John O. Levinson, Glen Flora, Ill.	1 up	Linhares,				
BYE—Art Linhares, Sharp Park, Calif.	Linhares	2 and 1				
					Foote, 2 and 1	
BYE—Richard Dickson, Galveston, Texas	Dickson					
		Bourne,				
C. James Bourne, Inglewood, Wash.	Bourne,	1 up, 19 hls.				
Roy Moore, Jr., Colonial, Tenn.	3 and 2		Cherry,			
BYE—Don Cherry, Wichita Falls, Texas	Cherry		3 and 1			
		Cherry,				
William Hyndman, III, Huntingdon Valley, Pa.	Hyndman,	2 and 1				
John P. Cain, Lubbock, Texas	1 up			Foote, 6 and 5		
BYE—Dick Foote, Santa Ana, Calif.	D. Foote					
David W. Smith, Jr., Gaston, N.C.	Smith,	D. Foote,				
Gerald Cundari, Portland, Ore.	4 and 2	1 up				
BYE—Eli Bariteau, Jr., Pasatiempo, Calif.	Bariteau		D. Foote,			
			2 and 1			
		Bariteau,				
George E. Stigger III, Henderson, Ky.	Stigger,	4 and 2				
Neil E. White, Virginia, Calif.	5 and 3					

SEMI-FINAL ROUND (36 Holes)—Thomas D. Aaron defeated Dick Foote, 10 up and 9 to play.

CHAMPIONSHIP

FOURTH QUARTER

HALF

6th Round (18 Holes)	5th Round (18 Holes)		4th Round (18 Holes)	3rd Round (18 Holes)	2nd Round (18 Holes)	1st Round (18 Holes)
					Keith, 9 and 8	Thomas W. Beck, Southern Hills, Okla. Dr. Don Keith, Flying Hills, Calif.
				Stanovich, 4 and 3	Stanovich, 1 up, 20 hls.	Bert Burdick, Baton Rouge, La. Martin Stanovich, Tam O'Shanter, Ill.
			Stanovich, 4 and 2		Cudd	BYE—Bruce H. Cudd, Clarksville, Tenn.
		Oskin, 1 up		Robbins, 5 and 3	Robbins, 2 up	Gordon M. Emerson, Univ. of Minn., Minn. Lt. Hillman Robbins, Jr., Colonial, Tenn.
				Oskin, 1 up, 19 hls.	Guernsey, 4 and 3	Frank Guernsey, Lakeside, Texas Joseph A. Sugar, Jr., Brookside, Ohio
					Oskin	BYE—Clyde H. Oskin, Jr., Saucon Valley, Pa.
			Oskin, 1 up, 19 hls.	Gilliam, 1 up	Gilliam, 3 and 2	Gordon Baker, Florence, S.C. Walter J. Gilliam, Jr., San Mateo, Calif.
	Kocsis, 1 up				Justa	BYE—Edwin A. Justa, Benvenue, N.C.
				Kocsis, 1 up	Kocsis, 3 and 2	Charles Kocsis, Red Run, Mich. Richard Price, Longview, Wash.
			Kocsis, 3 and 2		Ihlanfeldt	BYE—Robert L. Ihlanfeldt, Inglewood, Wash.
		Kocsis, 5 and 4		Humm, 2 and 1	Nield	BYE—Samuel Nield, Innis Arden, Conn.
					Humm, 3 and 2	James Frost, Diablo, Calif. John J. Humm, Rockville, N.Y.
				Seanor, 4 and 3	Seanor, 4 and 2	William Seanor, Stockdale, Calif. John Johnston, Vancouver, B.C., Canada
			Seanor, 4 and 2		Blum	BYE—Arnold S. Blum, Idle Hour, Ga.
				Fowler, 5 and 4	Fowler, 1 up, 19 hls.	Richard F. Kohlmann, Normandie, Mo. Leslie R. Fowler, Boulder, Colo.
Aaron, 7 and 5					Clovis	BYE—David C. Clovis, Parkersburg, W. Va.
				Evans, 3 and 2	Evans	BYE—Charles Evans, Jr., Edgewater, Ill.
			Sams, 1 up, 19 hls.		Taylor, 4 and 3	Ellis Taylor, Atlantic City, N.J. William J. Ebert, California, Calif.
		Chapman, 2 and 1		Sams, 4 and 3	Kuntz	BYE—William R. Kuntz, Bonnie Briar, N.Y.
					Sams, 1 up	Alfred Sams, Idle Hour, Ga. Hord W. Hardin, Bellerive, Mo.
				Hall, 3 and 2	Mendez, 3 and 2	Fernando Mendez, Monterrey, N.L., Mexico Robert J. Cardinal, California, Calif.
			Chapman, 3 and 2		Hall	BYE—Art Hall, Tulsa, Okla.
	Aaron, 3 and 2			Chapman, 5 and 4	Ladley	BYE—Robert Ladley, Peninsula, Calif.
					Chapman, 3 and 1	Harrison J. Neese, Sherwood Forest, La. Richard D. Chapman, Oyster Harbors, Mass.
				Aaron, 5 and 3	Aaron, 4 and 3	Dale D. Douglass, Fort Morgan, Colo. Thomas D. Aaron, Chattahoochee, Ga.
			Aaron, 2 and 1		Arreaga	BYE—Johnny R. Arreaga, Ridgewood, Texas
		Aaron, 5 and 4		Ware, 2 and 1	Ware, 2 and 1	Cobby Ware, Augusta, Ga. Leonard T. Bjorklund, Interlachen, Minn.
					Lopucki	BYE—Anthony Lopucki, Washtenaw, Mich.
				Rodgers, 4 and 3	Ball, 1 up	Gordon R. Ball, Toronto, Ont., Canada Hugh D. Thompson, Wichita Falls, Texas
			Rodgers, 1 up, 19 hls.		Rodgers	BYE—Phil Rodgers, La Jolla, Calif.
				Atkinson, 3 and 1	Atkinson, 1 up	Robert H. Atkinson, Jr., Columbia-Edgewater, Ore. Robert J. Shave, Jr., Manakiki, Ohio
					Welsh, 1 up	Sanford J. Mosk, Jr., Riviera, Calif. Alex Welsh, Rockford, Ill.

1959
FIFTY-NINTH AMATEUR CHAMPIONSHIP

Held at the Broadmoor Golf Club (East Course), Colorado Springs, Colo., September 14-19.
Yardage—7,010. Par 71. 1,696 Entries, 200 Qualifiers, 200 Starters.
Championship entirely at match play.
FINAL ROUND (36 Holes)—Jack Nicklaus defeated Charles R. Coe, 1 up

UPPER

FIRST QUARTER

1st Round (18 Holes)	2nd Round (18 Holes)	3rd Round (18 Holes)	4th Round (18 Holes)	5th Round (18 Holes)	6th Round (18 Holes)	
Gary C. Wright, Cherry Hills, Colo.	Wright, 5 and 3					
John W. Deal, Old Hickory, Tenn.		Blum, 6 and 5				
Arnold S. Blum, Idle Hour, Ga.	Blum, 6 and 5					
Francis J. Furlong, Jr., Norwood Hills, Mo.			Gleichmann, 2 and 1			
BYE—Ted V. Gleichmann, Saticoy, Calif.	Gleichmann	Gleichmann, 2 and 1				
James O. Watts, Jr., Boonsboro, Va.	Watts, 1 up			Gleichmann, 2 and 1		
Michael Cestone, Sr., Forsgate, N.J.						
Richard S. Norville, Oklahoma City, Okla.	Astleford, 4 and 2					
Robert L. Astleford, Field C. of Omaha, Neb.		Astleford, 2 and 1				
BYE—Claude C. Wild, Jr., Burning Tree, Md.	Wild		Smith, 3 and 2			
Ranson H. Bricher, Aurora, Ill.	Hudnutt, 2 and 1					
Arthur D. Hudnutt, Elyria, Ohio		Smith, 5 and 4				
BYE—Charles B. Smith, Gaston, N.C.	Smith				Coe, 4 and 3	
Robert L. Wagner, Almaden Men's, Calif.	Batdorff, 1 up, 19 hls.					
Robert Batdorff II, Hershey, Pa.		Batdorff, 7 and 6				
BYE—Louis F. Rosanova, Tam O'Shanter, Ill.	Rosanova		Coe, 3 and 1			
BYE—James W. Mallory, Spokane, Wash.	Mallory	Coe, 6 and 5				
Robert A. Meiering, N. Mex. Mil. Inst., N.M.	Coe, 7 and 6			Coe, 4 and 3		
Charles R. Coe, Oklahoma City, Okla.						
Dr. Wendell R. Aldrich, Speedway, Ind.	Vickers, 3 and 1					
James W. Vickers, Wichita, Kans.		Vickers, 8 and 6				
BYE—Norman F. Lewis, Brae Burn, Texas	Lewis		Vickers, 5 and 4			
Anthony J. Blom, Jr., Maketewah, Ohio	Bell, 5 and 3					
Alfred N. Bell, Jr., C.C. of Columbus, Ga.		Wendrow, 1 up				
Phil Donohue, Minnehaha, S.D.	Wendrow, 2 up					
Louis Wendrow, C.C. of Lansing, Mich.						Coe, 2 up
BYE—Virgil L. Parker, MacDonald Park Men's, Kans.	Parker	Kline, 5 and 4				
John W. Kline, Westover, Mass.	Kline, 3 and 1		Hyndman, 2 and 1			
Allen Geiberger, Montecito, Calif.						
BYE—Robert C. Loufek, Rock Island Arsenal, Ill.	Loufek	Hyndman, 5 and 4				
William Hyndman III, Huntingdon Valley, Pa.	Hyndman, 5 and 3			Hyndman, 1 up		
Jacky Cupit, Pine Crest, Texas						
William R. Kuntz, Bonnie Briar, N.Y.	Kuntz, 1 up, 19 hls.	Kuntz, 2 and 1				
Leonard T. Bjorklund, Interlachen, Minn.						
BYE—Walter E. Beckjord, Cincinnati, Ohio	Beckjord		Sykes, 2 and 1			
James D. Sykes, Old York Rd., Pa.	Sykes, 3 and 1	Sykes, 4 and 2				
C.E. Hendrickson, Plumbrook, Ohio					Hyndman, 1 up	
BYE—Martin Stanovich, Tam O'Shanter, Ill.	Stanovich					
BYE—Richard Davies, Annandale, Calif.	Davies	Davies, 2 up				
Jackson D. Rule, Jr., Wakonda, Iowa	Rule, 1 up		Davies, 4 and 3			
Thomas K. Reed, Lakewood, Colo.						
BYE—Wayne Jackson, James River, Va.	Jackson	Brue, 4 and 3				
Dr. Edgar R. Updegraff, Tucson, Ariz.	Brue, 2 up					
Robert A. Brue, North Hills, Wis.				Wilcox, 4 and 3		
BYE—Terry D. Wilcox, Oak Hills, Okla.	Wilcox	Wilcox, 1 up				
Carl A. Lohren, Brooke Manor Farms, Md.	Gardner, 6 and 4		Wilcox, 3 and 1			
Robert W. Gardner, Essex County, N.J.						
BYE—Edward R. Lipski, Punxsutawney, Pa.	Lipski	Lipski, 3 and 2				
William A. Wright, Fir State, Wash.	Knowles, 2 and 1					
Robert W. Knowles, Jr., Palmetto, S.C.						

SEMI-FINAL ROUND (36 Holes)—Charles R. Coe defeated H. Dudley Wysong, Jr., 6 up and 4 to play.

The first word after the player's name is the name of his club, except in the case of a foreign entrant.

HALF

SECOND QUARTER

6th Round (18 Holes)

Wysong, 3 and 1

5th Round (18 Holes)

Goldman, 3 and 1

Wysong, 1 up

Ward, 2 and 1

Goldman, 4 and 3

Draper, 4 and 3

Wysong, 1 up, 20 hls.

4th Round (18 Holes)

Person, 1 up, 22 hls.

Ward, 7 and 6

Goldman, 4 and 3

McManus, 4 and 2

Draper, 1 up

Patton, 1 up

Rodgers, 3 and 2

Wysong, 5 and 4

3rd Round (18 Holes)

Allen, 1 up, 20 hls.

Person, 5 and 4

Palmer, 4 and 3

Ward, 3 and 2

Goldman, 5 and 3

Crawford, 4 and 3

Readette, 2 and 1

McManus, 3 and 1

Draper, 4 and 2

Westland, 6 and 5

Patton, 2 and 1

Straughan, 1 up, 19 hls.

Rodgers, 1 up, 19 hls.

Bourne, 2 up

Hoenig, 7 and 6

Wysong, 2 and 1

2nd Round (18 Holes)	1st Round (18 Holes)
Allen, 4 and 2	Donald C. Allen, C.C. of Rochester, N.Y. Thomas J. Grace, Detroit, Mich.
Eichler, 7 and 6	Edward Eichler, Lake Merced, Calif. James A. Hamilton, Jr., Pine Forest, Texas
Zemljak	BYE—Edward F. Zemljak, Butte, Mont.
Person, 4 and 3	Mark H. McCormack, The C.C., Ohio Curtis Person, Colonial, Tenn.
Scammell, 4 and 3	Matthew J. Scammell, Jr., Huntingdon Valley, Pa. Ralph E. Mayerstein, Lafayette, Ind.
Palmer	BYE—Payne Palmer III, Phoenix, Ariz.
Ward, 2 and 1	E. Harvie Ward, Jr., San Francisco, Calif. James R. Cleveland, Jr., Druid Hills, Ga.
Switzer	BYE—Joseph F. Switzer, Old Warson, Mo.
Goldman, 4 and 2	Daniel W. Morgan, Jr., Sand Point, Wash. David Goldman, Sr., Brookhaven, Texas
Fish	BYE—Leslie A. Fish, Harkers Hollow, N.J.
Crawford	BYE—Richard Crawford, El Dorado, Ark.
Frederickson, 2 and 1	Daniel Frederickson, Lakeside, Calif. Mike Dull, Waveland, Iowa
Albert, 2 and 1	Ross E. Mitchell, Hillcrest, Texas Donald E. Albert, Brookside, Ohio
Readette	BYE—Gene A. Readette, Rockford, Ill.
Littler, 1 up	Robert Littler, Jr., Athens, Ohio Herbert H. Pollock, Jr., Pueblo, Colo.
McManus	BYE—Roger T. McManus, Kenwood, Ohio
Moore	BYE—Ronald L. Moore, Wellshire, Colo.
Draper, 7 and 5	Tom Draper, Red Run, Mich. Paul E. Kelly, Sleepy Hollow, N.Y.
Burdick	BYE—Albert C. Burdick III, Baton Rouge, La.
Westland, 4 and 3	Bradley Anderson, Starmount Forest, N.C. Jack Westland, Everett, Wash.
Patton	BYE—William J. Patton, Mimosa Hills, N.C.
Finke, 4 and 3	Richard A. Jennings, Lubbock, Texas Kenneth Finke, Tucson, Ariz.
Straughan	BYE—C.L. Straughan, Jr., Atlanta Athletic, Ga.
Ornstein, 5 and 4	Warren K. Ornstein, Beechmond, Ohio Joseph Raquet, Spring-Ford, Pa.
James, 4 and 3	Frank M. James, C.C. of Grinnell, Iowa Pat Mucci, Preakness Hills, N.J.
Rodgers	BYE—Pvt. Phil Rodgers, Torrey Pines Men's, Calif.
Bourne, 1 up, 23 hls.	Hord W. Hardin, Bellerive, Mo. Jim Bourne, Wayne, Wash.
Hoag	BYE—Bob Hoag, Scioto, Ohio
Hoenig, 4 and 3	Donald Hoenig, Wethersfield, Conn. Ade Simonsen, Golden Valley, Minn.
Evans	BYE—Charles Evans, Jr., Edgewater, Ill.
Campbell, 4 and 2	Henry H. Russell, Indian Creek, Fla. William C. Campbell, Guyan, W. Va.
Wysong, 5 and 4	H. Dudley Wysong, Jr., Northwood, Texas Dr. Paul E. Travis, Hacienda, Calif.

THIRD QUARTER

1st Round (18 Holes)	2nd Round (18 Holes)	3rd Round (18 Holes)	4th Round (18 Holes)	5th Round (18 Holes)	6th Round (18 Holes)	
Jim Tom Blair, Meadow Brook, Mo.	Blair, 2 and 1					
George Greenwood, Wilshire, Calif.		Blair, 4 and 2				
John O. Eisinger, Jr., Congressional, D.C.	Eisinger, 1 up					
Brian Goldsworthy, Timpanogas, Utah			Blair, 4 and 2			
BYE—Milton W. Beal, Happy Hollow, Neb.	Beal					
		Fulton, 7 and 5				
George H. Fulton, Roanoke, Va.	Fulton, 1 up					
Marshall Trammell, Belle Meade, Tenn.						
Dillard A. Traynham, Paris Mountain, S.C.	Replogle, 3 and 2					
Dee A. Replogle, Oklahoma City, Okla.		Replogle, 4 and 3		Replogle, 4 and 3		
BYE—Deane R. Beman, Bethesda, Md.	Beman					
			Replogle, 2 and 1			
Harold C. Watson, Denver, Colo.	Watson, 5 and 4					
Arthur R. Hoff, Barrington Hills, Ill.		Penrose, 2 and 1				
BYE—John J. Penrose, Jr., La Gorce, Fla.	Penrose					
John W. Wood, Sand Point, Wash.	Wood, 4 and 3				Andrews, 1 up	
Alan P. Yates, Atlanta Athletic, Ga.		Andrews, 3 and 1				
BYE—Gene Andrews, California, Calif.	Andrews					
			Andrews, 3 and 2			
BYE—Paul Spengler, Jr., Meadow, Calif.	Spengler					
		Meister, 2 up				
Clyde H. Oskin, Jr., Saucon Valley, Pa.	Meister, 3 and 1					
Edward L. Meister, Jr., Kirtland, Ohio						
John Konsek, Brookfield, N.Y.	Konsek, 7 and 6			Andrews, 6 and 5		
William K. Newcomb, Jr., Logansport, Ind.		Konsek, 2 and 1				
BYE—George P. Sarsfield, Butte, Mont.	Sarsfield					
Melvin M. Stevens, Western, Mich.	Chapman, 3 and 2		Konsek, 2 up			
Richard D. Chapman, Oyster Harbors, Mass.						
John J. Donohue, Jr., Wakonda, Iowa	Donohue, 2 and 1	Chapman, 1 up, 20 hls.				
Thomas J. Atchison, Lakeside, Texas						
BYE—Chris Blocker, Jr., Jal, N.M.	Blocker					Andrews, 1 up
Thomas C. Garrity, Hillcrest, Mo.	Dawson, 1 up, 19 hls.	Blocker, 7 and 6				
John W. Dawson, Eldorado, Calif.						
BYE—John H. Andersen, Oak Park, Ill.	Andersen		Harrison, 2 and 1			
Steve Spray, Hyperion, Iowa	Harrison, 1 up	Harrison, 5 and 3				
Charles W. Harrison, Atlanta Athletic, Ga.						
John P. Cain, Lubbock, Texas	Guenther, 2 and 1			Harrison, 5 and 4		
John H. Guenther, Jr., Hershey, Pa.						
BYE—William M. McCool, Harding Park, Calif.	McCool	Guenther, 4 and 3				
H. Ward Wettlaufer, C.C. of Buffalo, N.Y.	Allen, 2 and 1		Guenther, 3 and 1			
Robert W. Allen, Pawtucket, R.I.						
BYE—John C. Owens, Lexington, Ky.	Owens	Allen, 1 up, 19 hls.				
BYE—Neil C. Croonquist, Interlachen, Minn.	Croonquist				Harrison, 4 and 2	
		Croonquist, 4 and 3				
Thomas H. Choate, Meadow Brook, N.Y.	Oliver, 1 up					
Irl T. Oliver, Jr., Blue Hills, Mo.						
BYE—John N. Olver, Lakewood, Texas	Olver		Aaron, 6 and 4			
		Aaron, 3 and 2				
Thomas D. Aaron, Chattahoochee, Ga.	Aaron, 2 up					
Alex Welsh, Rockford, Ill.						
BYE—Ted K. Naff, Rainier, Wash.	Naff			Aaron, 1 up		
		Spangler, 6 and 5				
David N. Hall, Cincinnati, Ohio	Spangler, 3 and 1					
Richard L. Spangler, Jr., C.C. of Lincoln, Neb.						
BYE—Charles J. Volpone, Jr., Ould Newbury, Mass.	Volpone		Spangler, 3 and 2			
Robert E. Forrester, Palma Ceia, Fla.	Oppermann, 6 and 4	Volpone, 3 and 2				
Steven Oppermann, Green Hills, Calif.						

SEMI-FINAL ROUND (36 Holes)—Jack Nicklaus defeated Gene Andrews, 1 up

CHAMPIONSHIP
HALF

FOURTH QUARTER

6th Round (18 Holes)	5th Round (18 Holes)		4th Round (18 Holes)	3rd Round (18 Holes)	2nd Round (18 Holes)	1st Round (18 Holes)
				Butler, 4 and 2	Butler, 2 and 1	Philip S. Wiechman, Harlan, Ky. Dr. Arthur F. Butler, Glendora, Calif.
			Taylor, 2 up		Billows, 2 up	Harry W. Easterly, Jr. C.C. of Virginia, Va. Raymond E. Billows, Dutchess, N.Y.
				Taylor, 3 and 2	Taylor	BYE–Dr. Frank M. Taylor, Jr., Red Hill, Calif.
					Jamison, 3 and 1	Thomas S. Jamison, Jr., Oakmont, Pa. Charles Courtney, La Jolla, Calif.
		Taylor, 4 and 3		Fowler, 5 and 3	Fowler, 6 and 5	Glen Fowler, Twin Hills, Okla. Lloyd J. Pitzer, Glen Flora, Ill.
					Harvey	BYE–Ernest W. Harvey, Sedgefield, N.C.
			Fowler, 7 and 6	Hoak, 5 and 4	Johnston, 7 and 6	Bill Michaels, Detroit, Mich. Edward A. Johnston, C.C. of Maryland, Md.
					Hoak	BYE–James M. Hoak, Wakonda, Iowa
	Yost, 3 and 1			Bostwick, 7 and 5	Bostwick, 2 and 1	Charles R. Leider, Crystal Springs, Calif. G.H. Bostwick, Jr., Meadow Brook, N.Y.
					Magee	BYE–Robert W. Magee, Norfolk, Mass.
			Bostwick, 4 and 3	Farquhar, 3 and 2	House	BYE–Jack House, Milburn, Kans.
					Farquhar, 1 up	Dr. Ted N. Lenczyk, Indian Hill, Conn. John Farquhar, Amarillo, Texas
		Yost, 1 up, 22 hls.		Dye, 2 and 1	Dye, 2 and 1	James B. McHale, Jr., Aronimink, Pa. Paul Dye, Jr., C.C. of Indianapolis, Ind.
					Morrell	BYE–John P. Morrell, Glen Oak, Ill.
			Yost, 1 up	Yost, 9 and 7	Yost, 1 up, 19 hls.	Richard L. Yost, Columbia-Edgewater, Ore. William M. Ferguson, Wakonda, Iowa
					Witzel	BYE–Raymond E. Witzel, Mayfair Men's, Fla.
Nicklaus, 2 and 1				Massengale, 5 and 4	Cuffaro	BYE–Louis S. Cuffaro, Wheeling, W. Va.
			Nicklaus, 6 and 5		Massengale, 5 and 3	Don Massengale, Jacksboro, Texas James Wright, Oakwood, Okla.
				Nicklaus, 2 and 1	Williamson	BYE–William H. Williamson III, Charlotte, N.C.
		Nicklaus, 5 and 4			Nicklaus, 7 and 6	Robert T. Jones III, C.C. of Pittsfield, Mass. Jack Nicklaus, Scioto, Ohio
				Goens, 2 and 1	Dolan, 4 and 2	Richard F. Kohlmann, Normandie, Mo. James H. Dolan III, Hillcrest, Mass.
			Goens, 1 up		Goens	BYE–Orville R. Goens, Wakonda, Iowa
				Douglass, 4 and 3	Schaller	BYE–William J. Schaller, Blue Mound, Wis.
	Nicklaus, 1 up				Douglass, 5 and 4	Dale Douglass, Fort Morgan, Colo. Craig E. Vollhaber, White Bear Yacht, Minn.
				Connolly, 2 and 1	Garvin, 2 and 1	Frank J. Garvin, Cherry Hills, Colo. Paul Wise, Ardsley, N.Y.
			Smith, 2 and 1		Connolly	BYE–Frank Connolly, Gowanie, Mich.
				Smith, 5 and 4	Smith, 1 up	Don Essig III, Willow Brook, Ind. David W. Smith, Jr., Gaston, N.C.
		Smith, 2 and 1			Liechty	BYE–John H. Liechty, Finkbine, Iowa
				Bell, 5 and 3	Schubeck, 1 up, 19 hls.	Jack B. Key, Jr., C.C. of Columbus, Ga. Pvt. John Schubeck, Jr., Anderson, Ky.
			Bell, 1 up		Bell	BYE–Lawrence G. Bell, Saucon Valley, Pa.
				Carmichael, 5 and 4	Carmichael, 7 and 6	Murrell R. Tripp, Lubbock, Texas Dan Carmichael, Columbus, Ohio
					Foote, 5 and 3	Dick Foote, Santa Ana, Calif. George E. Harrington, Arizona, Ariz.

WOMEN'S AMATEUR CHAMPIONSHIP

CHAMPIONSHIP CUP

Presented in 1896 by
ROBERT COX

Gorgie Edinburg Golf Association
Golfer and Graduate of St. Andrews'

HISTORY

1895–The first USGA Women's Amateur Championship was arranged on short notice and played at the Meadow Brook Club, Hempstead, N.Y., on November 9, 1895. Thirteen ladies participated at 18 holes, stroke play, and the winner was Mrs. Charles S. Brown, of the Shinnecock Hills Golf Club, Southampton, N.Y., with 69-63–132. Miss N.C. Sargent, of the Essex County Club, Manchester, Mass., was runnerup at 134. Nine holes were played before and nine after lunch. The silver pitcher donated by Messrs. R.D. Winthrop and W.H. Sands was won outright by Mrs. Brown, and has been given to the USGA Museum by her son, A.M. Brown.

1896–The Championship was conducted at match play at the Morris County Golf Club, Morristown, N.J., in October. Twenty-nine entrants competed for eight places in the qualifying round, and the low scorer was Miss Beatrix Hoyt, 16, of the Shinnecock Hills Golf Club, with 95. She won her semi-final match by default from Miss Anna Sands and the Championship by defeating Mrs. Arthur Turnure, 2 and 1. Mrs. Brown did not defend. Miss Hoyt had not played in the first Championship. Robert Cox, M.P., of Edinburgh, Scotland, who was visiting this country, donated a permanent trophy, with the stipulation that the 1896 Championship be played at Morris County, a course he had helped to lay out in 1894. This is the trophy which is now in competition.

1897–The Essex County Club played host to 29 entrants in August. Miss Hoyt again won the medal, this time with 108, in a torrent of rain, and retained her Championship, defeating Miss Sargent in the final, 5 and 4. Eight again qualified for match play. Miss Margaret Curtis made her first appearance at 13 and carried four clubs. She qualified fourth with 122.

1898–Miss Hoyt continued to dominate, winning the medal with a 92 and her third successive title by defeating Miss Maude Wetmore in the final, 5 and 3. Miss Hoyt was the only player to break 100 in the qualifying. Increased interest in women's golf was reflected by the 61 players who competed for 16 qualifiers' places at the Ardsley Club, Ardsley-on-Hudson, N.Y., in October.

1899–Miss Ruth Underhill, of the Nassau Country Club, Glen Cove, N.Y., succeeded Miss Hoyt as Champion by beating Mrs. Caleb F. Fox, 2 and 1, in the final. Miss Hoyt had won the médal again; her 97 was the only score under 100, but she lost to Mrs. Fox in the first round, 3 and 2. Mrs. Fox was 39 and had raised a family before taking up golf. She was to become a dominant figure in woman's golf during the next three decades. The Championship was played on the Bala course of the Philadelphia Country Club in October, and attracted 78 entrants. Miss Underhill later became Mrs. Harold T. White.

1900–Miss Hoyt won the medal for the fifth year in succession with a 94 over her home course, the Shinnecock Hills Golf Club, but again lost, this time to Miss Margaret Curtis on the 20th hole in the semi-finals. Miss Frances C. Griscom, of the Merion Cricket Club, Haverford, Pa., defeated Miss Curtis in the final, 6 and 5. Miss Hoyt, now 20, thereafter gave up tournament golf.

1901–Entries rose to 84. At the Baltusrol Golf Club, Springfield, N.J. Miss Genevieve Hecker, of the Essex County Club, defeated Miss Lucy Herron, 5 and 3, in the final. The Misses Herron, Margaret Curtis, Mary B. Adams and Mrs. E.A. Manice tied for the medal at 97.

1902–Miss Hecker repeated, defeating Miss Louisa A. Wells in the final, 4 and 3. The Misses Wells and Margaret Curtis were co-medalists at 89, and were the first to break 90. The number of qualifiers' places was increased to 32, and the highest score to get in was 103. The Country Club, Brookline, Mass., entertained the Championship and the entry of 96 was a new high.

1903–The Championship moved west to the Chicago Golf Club, Wheaton, Ill. Miss Bessie Anthony, of the Glen View Club, Golf, Ill., defeated Miss J.A. Carpenter, 7 and 6, in the final. Mrs. Fox led the qualifying with a 94, and only four scores under 100 were returned. A score of 120 placed a player among the 32 qualifiers. Miss Hecker did not defend.

1904–Miss Georgianna M. Bishop, of the Brooklawn Club, Bridgeport, Conn., defeated Mrs. E.F. Sanford, 5 and 3, in the final at the Merion Cricket Club. The Misses Charlotte Dod, Louise Vanderhoef and Harriot Curtis, each with 93, were co-medalists.

1905–Miss Pauline Mackay, of the Oakley Country Club, Watertown, Mass., defeated Miss Margaret Curtis, 1 up, in the final at the Morris County Golf Club, Convent, N.J. Miss Curtis and Miss Bishop tied for the medal at 87, a new low. Earlier, the Curtis sisters, Miss Griscom, Miss Bishop, Miss Adams and Miss Ethel Burnett made the first informal visit to the British Isles to play team matches and to compete in the British Championship.

1906–Miss Harriot Curtis of the Essex County Club, Manchester, Mass., won the final from Miss Mary B. Adams, 2 and 1. Miss Mackay opened the defense of her title by winning the medal at the Brae Burn Country Club, near Boston, with another 87.

1907–The Curtis sisters took over the Championship at the Midlothian Country Club, near Chicago. Miss Margaret dethroned Miss Harriot, 7 and 6, after winning the medal with a 95. The following year Miss Margaret, with Miss Evelyn Sears, won the women's doubles championship at lawn tennis to become the only American to hold national Championships in these two sports simultaneously.

1908–Miss Kate C. Harley, of the Fall River (Mass.) Country Club, defeated Mrs. T.H. Polhemus, 6 and 5, in the final at the Chevy Chase Club, Chevy Chase, Md. Miss Harley previously had eliminated Miss Margaret Curtis in the quarter-finals. Miss Harriot Curtis' medal-winning 85 was a new low, but she lost to Mrs. Fox in the second round.

1909–The British Champion, Miss Dorothy Campbell, of North Berwick, Scotland, completed the first double in women's golf. She defeated Mrs. Ronald H. Barlow, 3 and 2, in the final at the Merion Cricket Club, Haverford, Pa. Three other British players entered, but the last of these was beaten in the quarter-finals. Mrs. Fox and the Misses Margaret Curtis and Anita Phipps tied for the medal with 86s. Miss Campbell won her first match, 10 and 8.

1910–Miss Campbell, now the Canadian Champion and playing from Hamilton, Ontario, continued her mastery over American women golfers, winning the medal with a record-equalling 85 and the all-British final from Mrs. G.M. Martin, of Tavistock, England, 2 and 1. Another Canadian representative, Miss Florence Harvey, of Hamilton, reached the semi-finals but lost to Miss Campbell. Miss Lillian B. Hyde won her first match, 10 and 8. The Championship was played at the Homewood Country Club, Flossmoor, Ill.

1911–Miss Margaret Curtis eliminated Miss Campbell in the semi-finals and won for the second time at the Baltusrol Golf Club, Springfield, N.J., defeating Miss Hyde, 5 and 3, in the title round. Miss Campbell was again the British and Canadian Champion at the time. Mrs. Barlow won the medal with an 87.

1912–Miss Margaret Curtis repeated over her home course, the Essex County Club, defeating Mrs. Barlow in the final, 3 and 2, after taking the medal with an 88. The Championship was the sixth in which she won or shared the medal.

1913–Miss Gladys Ravenscroft, of England, who had won the British Championship the year before, took the title out of the country a third time. She won the medal, with an 88, and the final from Miss Marion Hollins, 2 up, at the Wilmington (Del.) Country Club. Miss Muriel Dodd, of England, the British Champion, lost to Miss Ravenscroft in the semi-finals. Miss Ravenscroft later became Mrs. Temple Dobell.

1914–Entries rose to 93, the second highest total to that time, when the Championship was played at the Nassau Country Club. Mrs. H. Arnold Jackson, of the Oakley Country Club, who had won as Miss Kate C. Harley in 1908, became Champion again, defeating Miss Elaine V. Rosenthal in the final, 1 up. For the first time, all 32 qualifiers broke 100. Miss Bishop was medalist with 85, tying the record set by Miss Harriot Curtis and Miss Campbell. This Championship marked the first appearance of a young Georgia girl, Miss Alexa Stirling, who was to leave an indelible mark on women's golf.

1915–Entries went over 100 for the first time, and 111 played at the Onwentsia Club, near Chicago. Mrs. C.H. Vanderbeck, of the Philadelphia Cricket Club, won the medal with another record-equalling 85 and repelled another English challenger, Mrs. William A. Gavin, in the final, 3 and 2. Mrs. Vanderbeck had to survive a 22-hole match with Miss Stirling in the semi-finals. The match was the longest to that time in the Championship.

1916–Miss Alexa Stirling, of the Atlanta (Ga.) Athletic Club, won for the first time, defeating Miss Mildred Caverly, 2 and 1, in the final. Mrs. J.V. Hurd, of Pittsburgh, formerly Dorothy Campbell, was medalist with an 86. The Championship was played at the Belmont Springs Country Club, near Boston.

1917-18–No Championships: World War I

1919–Miss Stirling retained her title when play was resumed after World War I at the Shawnee Country Club, Shawnee-on-Delaware, Pa. She defeated Mrs. Gavin, now of Chicago, 6 and 5, in the final. This pair also tied for the medal at 87. Miss Glenna Collett made her first appearance in this Championship and won her first match.

1920–Miss Stirling won her third successive Championship at the Mayfield Country Club, near Cleveland. She defeated Mrs. Hurd in the final, 5 and 4. Miss Hollins lowered the qualifying record, with an 82, and only one 98 earned a place among the 32 qualifiers.

1921–Miss Marion Hollins, of the Westbrook Golf Club, Great River, N.Y., ended Miss Stirling's reign in the first 36-hole final, winning 5 and 4, at the Hollywood Golf Club, Deal, N.J., in October, 1921. Misses Cecil and Edith Leitch, of England, qualified but lost in early rounds. Mrs. F.C. Letts defeated Miss Cecil Leitch, 1 down, in a match which was the upset of the Championship since Miss Cecil was the British Champion for the second successive year. Miss Collett, who had tied with Mrs. Latham Hall at 85, won the playoff for the medal, 92 to 93. The entry climbed to 181, a new record, and 164 actually played.

1922–Miss Glenna Collett, of the Rhode Island Country Club, Nayatt, R.I., set a new qualifying record of 81 and defeated Mrs. Gavin, again representing England, 5 and 4, to win the first of her six Championships. It was the third time Mrs. Gavin had been runnerup. The 36-hole final was employed again. The Championship was held at the Greenbrier Golf Club, White Sulphur Springs, W. Va.

1923–Miss Edith Cummings, of the Onwentsia Club, Lake Forest, Ill., a sister of Dexter Cummings, the national intercollegiate champion at the time, defeated Miss Stirling, 3 and 2, in the final at Westchester-Biltmore Country Club, Rye, N.Y. Mrs. Vanderbeck upset Miss Collett in the third round, 2 and 1. Miss Stirling was medalist with an 84, and 95 was the highest score to qualify. The entry of 196 set another record, and 166 started.

1924–Mrs. Dorothy Campbell Hurd, now representing the Merion Cricket Club, won her third title, defeating Miss Mary K. Browne, 7 and 6, in the final. Miss Browne, the runnerup, had played golf but a few years, and had been national lawn tennis champion in 1912 and 1913 and a semi-finalist a month earlier in the national lawn tennis Championship. She upset Miss Collett at the 19th hole in the semi-finals. Miss Collett had set a new record in qualifying with a 79. The Championship was held at Miss Collett's home course, the Rhode Island Country Club, and the entry fell to 98 after a handicap limitation of 10 strokes was imposed.

1925–The Championship crossed the Mississippi for the first time, to the St. Louis Country Club. Miss Collett beat Mrs. W.G. Fraser, of Canada, the former Alexa Stirling, 9 and 8, in the final. Heavy rains caused a one-day postponement of the final. Mrs. Fraser lowered the qualifying record to 77. Mrs. Caleb F. Fox was playing in her 22d and last Championship. She had qualified 20 times, won 25 matches, three times reached the semi-finals and had been medalist once and co-medalist another time.

1926–Mrs. G. Henry Stetson, of the Huntingdon Valley Country Club, near Philadelphia, defeated Mrs. Wright D. Goss, Jr., in the final, 3 and 1. Mrs. Hurd and the Misses Collett and Cummings all were eliminated by the third round. Miss Collett was medalist with 81. The Championship was held at the Merion Cricket Club, and for the first time was conducted by the USGA Women's Committee, rather than by the Championship Committee.

1927–Mrs. Miriam Burns Horn, of the Milburn Country Club, Kansas City, Mo., defeated Miss Maureen Orcutt in the final, 5 and 4, at the Cherry Valley Club, Garden City, N.Y. Mrs. Horn was the first Champion from west of the Mississippi. Mlle. Simone Thion de la Chaume, the French and British Champion, was eliminated by Mrs. Fraser, 3 and 2, in the third round. Her daughter, Mlle. Catherine Lacoste, would win both the United States Women's Amateur and Open in the 1960s. The medal was won by Miss Ada Mackenzie, of Canada, with a 77, which equalled Mrs. Fraser's record.

1928–Miss Collett won her third title, defeating Miss Virginia Van Wie by 13 and 12, at the Virginia Hot Springs Golf and Tennis Club, Hot Springs, Va., a record margin that stood until 1961. Miss Orcutt was medalist, with an 80. The former Mrs. Horn, now Mrs. George W. Tyson, lost to Miss Helen Paget, of Canada, 2 and 1, in the first round.

1929–Miss Collett became the first four-time winner at the Oakland Hills Country Club, near Detroit, by defeating Mrs. Leona Pressler, 4 and 3, in the final. Previously that year Miss Collett had been runnerup in the British Championship. Miss Helen Hicks and Miss Van Wie tied for the medal, at 79, and a score of 88 or better was necessary to gain a place among the thirty-two qualifiers. Miss Collett defeated Mrs. Harley G. Higbie at the 19th hole in a quarter-final match after having been 4 down and four to play. The longest match to that time came about when Mrs. Leo Federman defeated Mrs. Stetson on the 24th hole in the first round.

1930–The Championship went to the West Coast for the first time, and the Misses Collett and Van Wie continued their rivalry in the final at the Los Angeles Country Club, Miss Collett winning, 6 and 5. This was Miss Collett's fifth title and third in succession. She had also been runnerup again this year in the British Championship. Mrs. Opal S. Hill was medalist, with 79.

1931–Miss Helen Hicks, of the Inwood (N.Y.) Country Club, dethroned Miss Collett, now Mrs. Edwin H. Vare, Jr., 2 and 1, in the final at the Country Club of Buffalo, N.Y. Miss Enid Wilson, the British Champion, was eliminated by Miss Hicks in the semi-finals, 3 and 1. Play in the qualifying round resulted in a four-way tie for the medal at 82 among Miss Orcutt, Mrs. Vare, Mrs. Hill and Mrs. Higbie.

1932–Miss Van Wie, of the Beverly Country Club, Chicago, won the first of her three successive Championships by defeating Mrs. Vare, 10 and 8, in the final at the Salem Country Club, near Boston. The margin squared an account that had been outstanding since 1928 when Mrs. Vare defeated Miss Van Wie in the final. Miss Van Wie had a 73 in the morning round. The Misses Van Wie and Orcutt tied for the medal at 77, and Miss Hicks, the defending Champion, failed to qualify. Miss Wilson, still the British Champion, again was halted, by Miss Charlotte Glutting in the quarter-finals. The competition between the United States and the British Isles, for a cup donated by the Misses Harriot and Margaret Curtis, was inaugurated this year in England.

1933–Miss Van Wie repeated, defeating Miss Hicks, 4 and 3, in the final at the Exmoor Country Club, near Chicago. Miss Wilson, the British Champion for the third year in succession, won the medal with a record 76 but lost a match of champions to Miss Van Wie, 6 and 5, in the semi-finals. One 87 was the highest score to qualify for match play and five qualifying scores were under 80.

1934–Sixty-four qualified for match play for the first time, but none could stop Miss Van Wie, who defeated Mrs. Vare in the semi-finals, 3 and 2, and Miss Dorothy Traung in the final, 2 and 1. The Championship was played at the Whitemarsh Valley Country Club, near Philadelphia. Miss Van Wie thus became the fifth three-time winner, after Miss Beatrix Hoyt, Miss Margaret Curtis, Mrs. Dorothy Campbell Hurd and Mrs. Alexa Stirling Fraser. Miss Van Wie was also the fourth to win three in succession, after Miss Hoyt, Mrs. Fraser and Mrs. Glenna Collett Vare. Mrs. Vare, of course, had won five titles. Mrs. Vare, Mrs. Leona Cheney and Miss Lucille Robinson tied for the medal with 82s. The British Curtis Cup Team participated; five of them qualified but only Miss Wanda Morgan went as far as the third round. Mrs. Opal S. Hill defeated Mrs. L.D. Cheney on the 24th hole of a quarter-final match after having been 3 down and 5 to play. It was the second 24-hole match in the history of the Championship and both were in the quarter-finals. Miss Van Wie retired from competitive golf after this victory.

1935–Mrs. Vare won her sixth Championship at the Interlachen Country Club, Minneapolis, Minn., defeating a home-town girl, Miss Patty Berg, in the final, 3 and 2. Miss Berg was 17 and playing in her first Championship. Miss Jean Bauer's 79 won the medal. The event marked Mrs. Vare's eighth and last appearance in the Championship final.

1936–The Championship trophy went overseas for the first time in 23 years. Miss Pamela Barton, a 19-year-old English girl, added the United States title to her British Championship by defeating Miss Maureen Orcutt, in the final, 4 and 3. Miss Barton played the last 24 holes in one under women's par. It was the first double since Miss Dorothy Campbell's 27 years earlier. A 78 by Mrs. Julius A. Page, Jr., won the qualifying medal at Canoe Brook Country Club, Summit, N.J. Mrs. Vare did not defend her title. The handicap limitation was reduced to six strokes.

1937–Miss Barton did not defend at the Memphis (Tenn.) Country Club. Mrs. Julius A. Page, Jr., of the Sedgefield Club, Greensboro, N.C., took the medal with a 79 and the title by defeating Miss Berg, 7 and 6, in the final.

1938–Miss Berg and Mrs. Page again met in the final at Westmoreland Country Club, near Chicago, and this time Miss Berg won, 6 and 5. Mrs. Page and Miss Dorothy Traung led the qualifying with 80s. It was the third year in succession in which Mrs. Page had won or shared the medal. Six members of the British Curtis Cup Team qualified, and Miss Clarrie Tiernan, of Ireland, who reached the third round, made the best showing. Miss Dorothy Kirby upset Mrs. Vare, 1 up, in the first round. Miss Berg won her first match, 10 and 8.

1939–The handicap limitation was increased to eight strokes, and the largest field in the history of the Championship, 201 players, entered at the Wee Burn Club, Darien, Conn., and 194 started. Miss Betty Jameson, of the San Antonio (Texas) Country Club, defeated Miss Kirby in the final, 3 and 2. Miss Barton again contributed an international filip but lost to Miss Glutting on the 19th hole in the third round. Miss Berg, the defending Champion, was unable to play because of illness. The qualifying medal went to Miss Beatrice Barrett with 74. Seven returned qualifying scores of 79 or better.

1940–Miss Jameson won again at the Pebble Beach (Calif.) Golf Links, defeating Miss Jane Cothran, 6 and 5, in the final. Miss Traung's 78 won the medal.

1941–The Country Club, Brookline, Mass., was host to the Championship, and Mrs. Elizabeth Hicks Newell, of California, defeated Miss Helen Sigel of Philadelphia, 5 and 3, in the final. Qualifiers were led by the Misses Alice Belanger, Jean Bauer, Betty Jameson and Grace Amory, all of whom had 76s. The handicap requirement was again lowered to six. Mrs. Newell turned professional after the Championship.

1942-45–No Championships: World War II.

1946–When the Championship was renewed after World War II at Southern Hills Country Club, Tulsa, Okla., Mrs. Mildred Zaharias (Babe Didrikson) of the Park Hill Country Club, Denver, Colo., defeated Mrs. Clara Callender Sherman in the final, 11 and 9. The number of qualifiers was reduced to 32, and the qualifying was extended to 36 holes for the first time. Miss Dorothy Kirby won the medal with 152. Mrs. Zaharias had won the 80-meter hurdles and the javelin throw in the 1932 Olympic Games and had been reinstated after a period as a professional golfer. She won the British Championship the following spring, the first American to do so, and then turned professional again.

1947–Miss Louise Suggs, of the Capital City Club, Atlanta, Ga., won the qualifying medal with a 78 and went on to win by defeating Miss Kirby, of the same club, 2 up, in the final. Miss Suggs played each round of the final in 74, two under par. She was 3 up at noon and was hard-pressed to hold her lead as Miss Kirby made a 72, the lowest score then recorded in the Championship, in the afternoon round. Miss Margaret Curtis played and scored a 102, which failed to qualify her, but her appearance marked her fiftieth anniversary in the Championship. The event was held at the Franklin Hills Country Club, near Detroit. Miss Suggs won the British Championship the following spring and then she turned professional.

1948–Miss Grace Lenczyk, of the Indian Hill Country Club, Newington, Conn., defeated Miss Helen Sigel in the final, 4 and 3, as the Championship returned to Pebble Beach, Calif. The only former Champions in the field were Mrs. Julius A. Page, Jr., and Mrs. Glenna Collett Vare. Miss Suggs, Mrs. Zaharias, Mrs. Newell, Miss Jameson and Miss Berg had all turned professional. Mrs. Bettye Mims White, with a 77, led the qualifying, which again was set at 18 holes. Miss Marlene Bauer reached the round of 16 at the age of 14. Miss Sigel played the first nine in 34 strokes in winning her third-round match. Miss Dorothy Kielty called a disqualification penalty on herself after inadvertently allowing an 82, instead of an 83, to be posted as her score in the qualifying round.

1949–Stroke-play qualifying at the site of the Championship was abandoned, and 171 entrants competed in 16 sectional qualifying rounds for 128 places in match play at the East Course of the Merion Golf Club. Mrs. Mark A. Porter, the former Dorothy Germain, of the Llanerch Country Club, near Philadelphia, defeated Miss Dorothy Kielty, 3 and 2, in the final. Miss Marlene Bauer reached the semi-final round at the age of 15 but lost there to Miss Kielty and later turned professional. Miss Margaret Curtis played again, losing in the first round. Merion entertained the Championship for the fourth time, more than any other club. Play had to be suspended temporarily in the first round because of rain.

1950–One hundred ten women competed in the second all-match-play Championship, without sectional qualifying at the East Lake Course of the

Atlanta (Ga.) Athletic Club. Miss Beverly Hanson, of the Fargo (N.D.) Country Club, defeated Miss Mae Murray, 6 and 4, in the final. This golden anniversary event was noteworthy for the most extra holes ever played in the Championship. Miss Murray defeated Miss Fay Crocker, of Montevideo, Uruguay, on the 27th hole in the fourth round after nine extra holes. Each player was two under par for the 27 holes. Miss Philomena Garvey went furthest of nine foreign entrants, including members of the British Curtis Cup Team, losing to Miss Hanson in the fifth round.

1951–Miss Dorothy Kirby, of the Capital City Club, Atlanta, Ga., after trying since 1934, broke through at the Town and Country Club, St. Paul, Minn., defeating Miss Claire Doran, 2 and 1, in the final. An 18-hole qualifying round was re-instituted for 64 places. The best qualifying scores were 74s by Miss Carol Diringer and Miss Barbara Romack, who equalled Miss Barrett's record of 1939. Twenty players broke 80. Vicomtesse de Saint Sauveur, the British and French Champion, qualified but lost in the second round to Miss Mary Sargent. Miss Hanson had become a professional and, therefore, could not defend her Championship.

1952–Mrs. Jacqueline Pung, of the Moanalua Golf Club, Honolulu, the first Hawaiian to win a USGA Championship, defeated Miss Shirley McFedters, a student at the University of California at Los Angeles, 2 and 1, in the final at the Waverley Country Club, Portland, Ore. Mrs. Pung was playing for only the third time and Miss McFedters for the first time. Miss McFedters qualified for one of the 64 places in match play only on the second hole of a playoff at the record low score of 88 (for 64 qualifiers). Miss Kirby won the medal with a 76, but she and the other better-known players lost in early rounds. Miss Pat Lesser, a 19 year old, went to the turn in 33 in the third round; she lost to Mrs. Pung in the semi-finals.

1953–Miss Mary Lena Faulk, of the Glen Arven Country Club, Thomasville, Ga., succeeded Mrs. Pung, who had turned professional. In sultry August heat at the Rhode Island Country Club, Miss Faulk played one of the fine rounds of the Championship, a 73, to take a six-hole lead over Miss Polly Riley in the first half of the final, and she held on to win, 3 and 2. There was no qualifying round; 149 entrants who registered were drawn for match play by a blind draw, except that 13 players of known quality were distributed among the quarters by a further draw. Miss Marlene Stewart, a Canadian who had won the British Championship earlier in the year, participated but lost her first match. Miss Wiffi Smith, a 16-year-old who represented Mexico, went to the semi-finals. Mrs. Vare was in match play for the 23d time; she had won 59 matches, six Championships, two runnerup medals, four semi-finalist medals and six qualifying medals.

1954–The longest final in point of time in the history of USGA Championships, 29 hours 15 minutes occurred at the Allegheny Country Club, Sewickley, Pa., as Miss Barbara Romack, 22, of the Del Paso Country Club, Sacramento, Calif., defeated Miss Mary K. (Mickey) Wright, 19, of San Diego, Calif., 4 and 2. The two girls were scheduled to start at 9:30 on a Saturday, but a thunder and lightning storm with heavy rain delayed them. As soon as the storm let up, the girls played away, but as they were walking after their drives on the second hole, the storm came on again and they marked their balls and retired to the clubhouse. They returned to finish the 18 holes Saturday afternoon, and the second round had to be played on Sunday afternoon. The Championship again was conducted entirely at match play. The field included all members of the British and the United States Curtis Cup Teams and the Champions of Belgium, Canada, Cuba, and Mexico and a former Champion of Argentina, but no foreigner passed the fifth round. Miss Mary Lena Faulk, the defender, reached the semi-finals, where Miss Wright stopped her with one-over-par golf. It was the best performance by a defender since Miss Betty Jameson won her second straight in 1940. Miss Faulk and Miss Wright subsequently turned professional.

1955–Miss Patricia Lesser, 22, of the Sand Point Country Club, Seattle, Wash., a senior at Seattle University, defeated Miss Jane Nelson, 27, of Indianapolis, Ind., a school teacher, 7 and 6, at the Myers Park Country Club, Charlotte, N.C. Miss Lesser, the first former Girls' Junior Champion to win the Women's Amateur Championship, approximated two over par for the 119 holes of the event, which was played entirely on bermudagrass and in high temperatures and humidity. Miss Elizabeth Price and Miss Jacqueline Gordon, of England, paid a welcome visit, but both were eliminated in the third round. Miss Barbara Romack, the defender, was eliminated in the second round. Miss Polly Riley was a semi-finalist, after having lost in the quarter-finals the previous year and in the final two years earlier; she had been a quarter-finalist on three other occasions and for nine successive years had always made at least the round of 16. The tournament was sprinkled with some remarkable young golfers, among them Miss Anne Quast, of Everett, Wash., 17, who went to the quarter-finals; Miss Margaret (Wiffi) Smith, 18, of St. Clair, Mich., who also was in the quarter-finals; and Miss Clifford Ann Creed, of Opelousas, La., 16, who was one of the last 16. The event again was conducted entirely at match play.

1956–Miss Marlene Stewart, 22, of Fonthill, Ontario, became the first Canadian winner by defeating Miss JoAnne Gunderson, 17, of Seattle, Wash., 2 and 1, at the Meridian Hills Country Club, Indianapolis, Ind. Miss Stewart thus became the second woman to win the Championships of Great Britain, Canada and the United States. The other was Mrs. Dorothy Campbell Hurd. Miss Stewart had been graduated from Rollins College in Florida the previous spring and held the United States collegiate title. Miss Gunderson had won the Girls' Junior Championship in the preceding week and, in the Women's Amateur final had been 4 up with 11 holes to play. If she had won the Women's Amateur she would have been the youngest winner since Miss Beatrix Hoyt, who was 16 when she won first in 1896. Miss Pat Lesser, the defending Champion, was eliminated by Miss Gunderson in the third round; the two were clubmates at the Sand Point Country Club. Miss Margaret (Wiffi) Smith, 19, of St. Clair, Mich., the British and French Champion, also lost in the third round, to Mrs. Ann Casey Johnstone of Iowa City, Iowa, at the 19th hole. Miss Anne Quast, of Marysville, Wash., now 19, gained the semi-finals along with Mrs. Johnstone.

There were 116 entries and 105 starters. The event again was conducted entirely at match play.

1957–Miss JoAnne Gunderson, 18, a graduate of Kirkland High School near Seattle, Wash., defeated Mrs. Ann Casey Johnstone, 34, of Mason City, Iowa, housewife and mother of a 4-year-old girl, 8 and 6, at the Del Paso Country Club, Sacramento, Calif., in August. Miss Gunderson, the 1956 Girls' Junior Champion, played 127 holes in eight over women's par. Youth dominated throughout, and three of the four semi-finalists were 21 or younger. The defending Champion, Mrs. Marlene Stewart Streit, of Toronto, Canada, reached the quarter-finals, where Miss Carole Jo Kabler, Sutherlin, Ore., the 1955 USGA Girls' Junior Champion, eliminated her with a sub-par performance. There were 102 entries and 93 starters.

1958–Miss Anne Quast, 20, of Marysville, Wash., a Stanford University senior who had been leading amateur in the Women's Open, played the last seven holes four under par to defeat Miss Barbara Romack, of Sacramento, Calif., the 1954 Champion, 3 and 2, at the Wee Burn Country Club, Darien, Conn. She became the third Champion from the Pacific Northwest in four years. Miss Romack subsequently turned professional. Miss JoAnne Gunderson, of Kirkland, Wash., the defending Champion, lost to Miss Quast in the semi-final, 1 up, after going out in 35 and being 3 up. The original entry was 195, and 189, the largest number in 19 years, were included in the draw. They included the British and United States Curtis Cup Teams, except Mrs. Frances Smith; seven former Champions; three British Champions, including the current holder Mrs. George Valentine, and Girls' Junior Champion Miss Judy Eller. Miss Polly Riley, of Fort Worth, Texas, was in the round of 16 for the twelfth straight year. Six of the eight quarter-finalists and all semi-finalists were members of the United States Curtis Cup Team.

1959–Miss Barbara McIntire, 24, from Lake Park, Fla., won the Championship by defeating Miss Joanne Goodwin, of Haverhill, Mass., 4 and 3, after leading most of the way. The champion was three down in both her quarter-final and semi-final matches. In 1956 Miss McIntire tied for the Women's Open Championship, only to lose in a playoff to Mrs. Kathy Cornelius, a professional. She was twice runnerup in the Girls' Junior Championship. The tournament was played at the Congressional Country Club near Washington, D.C. The field was limited to 128 for the all-match-play tournament. There were 150 original entrants, with a handicap maximum of six strokes; those with the highest handicaps were not accepted. Besides Miss McIntire and Miss Goodwin, semi-finalists were Mrs. Mark A. Porter, the 1949 Champion, and Mrs. Paul F. Klinefelter, Jr., both of Philadelphia. Mrs. Klinefelter was competing in her first Championship in 12 years.

WOMEN'S AMATEUR CHAMPIONSHIP

DATE	WINNER, RUNNER-UP	SCORE	SITE	ENTRY
1895 (Nov.)	Mrs. C.S. Brown d. Miss N.C. Sargent	132 134	Meadow Brook Club, Hempstead, N.Y. Championship at 18 holes, stroke play.	13
		MATCH PLAY		
1896 (Oct.)	Miss Beatrix Hoyt d. Mrs. Arthur Turnure	2 & 1	Morris County G.C., Morristown, N.J. Medalist–95: Miss Beatrix Hoyt	29
1897 (Aug.)	Miss Beatrix Hoyt d. Miss N.C. Sargent	5 & 4	Essex County Club, Manchester, Mass. Medalist–108: Miss Beatrix Hoyt	29
1898 (Oct.)	Miss Beatrix Hoyt d. Miss Maude Wetmore	5 & 3	Ardsley Club, Ardsley-on-Hudson, N.Y. Medalist–92: Miss Beatrix Hoyt	61
1899 (Oct.)	Miss Ruth Underhill d. Mrs. Caleb F. Fox	2 & 1	Philadelphia Country C., Bala, Pa. Medalist–97: Miss Beatrix Hoyt	78
1900 (Aug.-Sept.)	Miss Frances C. Griscom d. Miss Margaret Curtis	6 & 5	Shinnecock Hills G.C., Shinnecock Hills, N.Y. Medalist–94: Miss Beatrix Hoyt	62
1901 (Oct.)	Miss Genevieve Hecker d. Miss Lucy Herron	5 & 3	Baltusrol G.C., Springfield, N.J. Co-Medalists–97: Miss Margaret Curtis Miss Mary B. Adams Mrs. E. A. Manice Miss Lucy Herron	84
1902 (Sept.-Oct.)	Miss Genevieve Hecker d. Miss Louisa A. Wells	4 & 3	The Country Club, Brookline, Mass. Co-Medalists–89: Miss Louisa A. Wells Miss Margaret Curtis	96
1903 (Sept.-Oct.)	Miss Bessie Anthony d. Miss J. A. Carpenter	7 & 6	Chicago G.C., Wheaton, Ill. Medalist–94: Mrs. Caleb F. Fox	64
1904 (Oct.)	Miss Georgianna M. Bishop d. Mrs. E. F. Sanford	5 & 3	Merion Cricket C., Haverford, Pa. Co-Medalists–93: Miss Charlotte Dod Miss L. Vanderhoef Miss Harriot Curtis	86
1905 (Oct.)	Miss Pauline Mackay d. Miss Margaret Curtis	1 up	Morris County G.C., Convent, N.J. Co-Medalists–87: Miss Margaret Curtis Miss Georgianna Bishop	69
1906 (Oct.)	Miss Harriot Curtis d. Miss Mary B. Adams	2 & 1	Brae Burn C.C., West Newton, Mass. Medalist–87: Miss Pauline Mackay	75
1907 (Oct.)	Miss Margaret Curtis d. Miss Harriot Curtis	7 & 6	Midlothian C.C., Blue Island, Ill. Medalist–95: Miss Margaret Curtis	87
1908 (Oct.)	Miss Katherine C. Harley d. Mrs. T. H. Polhemus	6 & 5	Chevy Chase Club, Chevy Chase, Md. Medalist–85: Miss Harriot Curtis	41
1909 (Oct.)	Miss Dorothy I. Campbell d. Mrs. R. H. Barlow	3 & 2	Merion Cricket C., Haverford, Pa. Co-Medalists–86: Mrs. Caleb F. Fox Miss Anita Phipps Miss Margaret Curtis	70
1910 (Oct.)	Miss Dorothy I. Campbell d. Mrs. G. M. Martin	2 & 1	Homewood C.C., Flossmoor, Ill. Medalist–85: Miss Dorothy I. Campbell	57
1911 (Oct.)	Miss Margaret Curtis d. Miss Lillian B. Hyde	5 & 3	Baltusrol G.C., Springfield, N.J. Medalist–87: Mrs. R. H. Barlow	67
1912 (Sept.-Oct.)	Miss Margaret Curtis d. Mrs. R. H. Barlow	3 & 2	Essex County Club, Manchester, Mass. Medalist–88: Miss Margaret Curtis	62
1913 (Oct.)	Miss Gladys Ravenscroft d. Miss Marion Hollins	2 up	Wilmington C.C., Wilmington, Del. Medalist–88: Miss Gladys Ravenscroft	80
1914 (Sept.)	Mrs. H. Arnold Jackson (Katherine Harley) d. Miss Elaine V. Rosenthal	1 up	Nassau C.C., Glen Cove, N.Y. Medalist–85: Miss Georgianna Bishop	93
1915 (Sept.)	Mrs. C.H. Vanderbeck d. Mrs. W. A. Gavin	3 & 2	Onwentsia Club, Lake Forest, Ill. Medalist–85: Mrs. C. H. Vanderbeck	119

WOMEN'S AMATEUR CHAMPIONSHIP – Continued

DATE	WINNER, RUNNER-UP	SCORE	SITE	ENTRY
1916 (Oct.)	Miss Alexa Stirling d. Miss Mildred Caverly	2 & 1	Belmont Springs C.C., Waverley, Mass. Medalist–86: Mrs. J. V. Hurd (Dorothy Campbell)	63
1917-18 – No Championships: World War I				
1919 (Sept.-Oct.)	Miss Alexa Stirling d. Mrs. W. A. Gavin	6 & 5	Shawnee C.C., Shawnee-on-Delaware, Pa. Co-Medalists–87: Miss Alexa Stirling Mrs. W. A. Gavin	76
1920 (Oct.)	Miss Alexa Stirling d. Mrs. J. V. Hurd (Dorothy Campbell)	5 & 4	Mayfield C.C., Cleveland, Ohio Medalist–82; Miss Marion Hollins	114
1921 (Oct.)	Miss Marion Hollins d. Miss Alexa Stirling	5 & 4	Hollywood G.C., Deal, N.J. Medalist–85-92: Miss Glenna Collett Runner-up–85-93: Mrs. Latham Hall	181
1922 (Sept.)	Miss Glenna Collett d. Mrs. W. A. Gavin	5 & 4	Greenbrier G. C., White Sulphur Springs, W. Va. Medalist–81: Miss Glenna Collett	170
1923 (Oct.)	Miss Edith Cummings d. Miss Alexa Stirling	3 & 2	Westchester-Biltmore C.C., Rye, N.Y. Medalist–84: Miss Alexa Stirling	196
1924 (Sept.)	Mrs. Dorothy C. Hurd (Dorothy Campbell) d. Miss Mary K. Browne	7 & 6	Rhode Island C.C., Nyatt, R.I. Medalist–79: Miss Glenna Collett	98
1925 (Sept.-Oct.)	Miss Glenna Collett d. Mrs. W. G. Fraser (Alexa Stirling)	9 & 8	St. Louis C.C., Clayton, Mo. Medalist–77: Mrs. W. G. Fraser (Alexa Stirling)	85
1926 (Sept.-Oct.)	Mrs. G. Henry Stetson d. Mrs. W. D. Goss, Jr.	3 & 1	Merion Cricket C. (East Course), Ardmore, Pa. Medalist–81: Miss Glenna Collett	134
1927 (Sept.)	Mrs. Miriam Burns Horn d. Miss Maureen Orcutt	5 & 4	Cherry Valley Club, Garden City, N.Y. Medalist–77: Miss Ada Mackenzie	150
1928 (Sept.)	Miss Glenna Collett d. Miss Virginia Van Wie	13 & 12	Virginia Hot Springs G. & T.C., Hot Springs, Va. Medalist–80: Miss Maureen Orcutt	123
1929 (Sept.-Oct.)	Miss Glenna Collett d. Mrs. Leona Pressler	4 & 3	Oakland Hills C.C., Birmingham, Mich. Co-Medalists–79: Miss Helen Hicks Miss Virginia Van Wie	98
1930 (Oct.)	Miss Glenna Collett d. Miss Virginia Van Wie	6 & 5	Los Angeles C.C., Beverly Hills, Calif. Medalist–79: Mrs. O. S. Hill	102
1931 (Sept.)	Miss Helen Hicks d. Mrs. E. H. Vare, Jr. (Glenna Collett)	2 & 1	C. C. of Buffalo, Williamsville, N.Y. Co-Medalists–82: Miss Maureen Orcutt Mrs. Edwin H. Vare, Jr. (Glenna Collett) Mrs. Harley G. Higbie Mrs. O. S. Hill	90
1932 (Sept.-Oct.)	Miss Virginia Van Wie d. Mrs. E. H. Vare, Jr. (Glenna Collett)	10 & 8	Salem C.C., Peabody, Mass. Co-Medalists–77: Miss Maureen Orcutt Miss Virginia Van Wie	101
1933 (Aug.-Sept.)	Miss Virginia Van Wie d. Miss Helen Hicks	4 & 3	Exmoor C.C., Highland Park, Ill. Medalist–76: Miss Enid Wilson	120
1934 (Oct.)	Miss Virginia Van Wie d. Miss Dorothy Traung	2 & 1	Whitemarsh Valley C.C., Chestnut Hill, Pa. Co-Medalists–82: Mrs. L. D. Cheney Miss Lucile Robinson Mrs. Edwin H. Vare, Jr. (Glenna Collett)	157
1935 (Aug.)	Mrs. Edwin H. Vare, Jr. (Glenna Collett) d. Miss Patty Berg	3 & 2	Interlachen C.C., Hopkins, Minn. Medalist–79: Miss Jean Bauer	94
1936 (Sept.-Oct.)	Miss Pamela Barton d. Miss Maureen Orcutt	4 & 3	Canoe Brook C.C., Summit, N.J. Medalist–78: Mrs. Julius A. Page, Jr.	188
1937 (Oct.)	Mrs. Julius A. Page, Jr. d. Miss Patty Berg	7 & 6	Memphis C.C., Memphis, Tenn. Medalist–79: Mrs. Julius A. Page, Jr.	136

WOMEN'S AMATEUR CHAMPIONSHIP – Continued

DATE	WINNER, RUNNER-UP	SCORE	SITE	ENTRY
1938 (Sept.)	Miss Patty Berg d. Mrs. Julius A. Page, Jr.	6 & 5	Westmoreland C.C., Wilmette, Ill. Co-Medalists–80: Miss Dorothy Traung Mrs. Julius A. Page, Jr.	118
1939 (Aug.)	Miss Betty Jameson d. Miss Dorothy Kirby	3 & 2	Wee Burn Club, Darien, Conn. Medalist–†74: Miss Beatrice Barrett	201
1940 (Sept.)	Miss Betty Jameson d. Miss Jane S. Cothran	6 & 5	Del Monte G. & C.C., Pebble Beach Golf Links, Calif. Medalist–78: Miss Dorothy Traung	163
1941 (Sept.)	Mrs. Frank Newell (Elizabeth Hicks) d. Miss Helen Sigel	5 & 3	The Country Club, Brookline, Mass. Co-Medalists–76: Miss Grace Amory Miss Alice O. Belanger Miss Jean E. Bauer Miss Betty Jameson	124
1942-45 – No Championships: World War II				
1946 (Sept.)	Mrs. George Zaharias (Mildred Didrikson) d. Mrs. Clara Sherman	11 & 9	Southern Hills C.C., Tulsa, Okla. Medalist–152 (36): Miss Dorothy Kirby	60
1947 (Sept.)	Miss Louise Suggs d. Miss Dorothy Kirby	2 up	Franklin Hills C.C., Franklin, Mich. Medalist–78: Miss Louise Suggs	83
1948 (Sept.)	Miss Grace S. Lenczyk d. Miss Helen Sigel	4 & 3	Del Monte G. & C.C., Pebble Beach Golf Links, Calif. Medalist–77: Miss Bettye Mims White	116
1949 (Sept.)	Mrs. Mark A. Porter (Dorothy Germain) d. Miss Dorothy Kielty	3 & 2	Merion G.C. (East Course), Ardmore, Pa.	171
1950 (Sept.)	Miss Beverly Hanson d. Miss Mae Murray	6 & 4	Atlanta A. C. (East Lake), Atlanta, Ga.	110
1951 (Aug.)	Miss Dorothy Kirby d. Miss Claire Doran	2 & 1	Town & C.C., St. Paul, Minn. Co-Medalists–†74: Miss Carol Diringer Miss Barbara Romack	79
1952 (Aug.)	Mrs. Jacqueline Pung d. Miss Shirley McFedters	2 & 1	Waverley C.C., Portland, Ore. Medalist–76: Miss Dorothy Kirby	159
		All Match Play, 1953-63		
1953 (Aug.)	Miss Mary Lena Faulk d. Miss Polly Riley	3 & 2	Rhode Island C.C., West Barrington, R.I.	158
1954 (Sept.)	Miss Barbara Romack d. Miss Mary K. (Mickey) Wright	4 & 2	Allegheny C.C., Sewickley, Pa.	151
1955 (Aug.)	Miss Patricia A. Lesser d. Miss Jane Nelson	7 & 6	Myers Park C.C., Charlotte, N.C.	112
1956 (Sept.)	Miss Marlene Stewart d. Miss JoAnne Gunderson	2 & 1	Meridian Hills C.C., Indianapolis, Ind.	116
1957 (Aug.)	Miss JoAnne Gunderson d. Mrs. Anne Casey Johnstone	8 & 6	Del Paso C.C., Sacramento, Calif.	100
1958 (Aug.)	Miss Anne Quast d. Miss Barbara Romack	3 & 2	Wee Burn C.C., Darien, Conn.	195
1959 (Aug.)	Miss Barbara McIntire d. Miss Joanne Goodwin	4 & 3	Congressional C.C., Washington, D.C.	**128

** Limited entry.
* Record Qualifying score, 36 holes.
† Record Qualifying score.

1895
FIRST WOMEN'S AMATEUR CHAMPIONSHIP

Held at the Meadow Brook Club, Hempstead, N.Y., November 9. (18 holes)

Mrs. C. S. Brown (Shinnecock Hills)	132
Miss N. C. Sargent (Essex County)	134
Mrs. W. B. Thomas (Essex County)	141
Mrs. William Shippen (Morris County)	145
Miss Harrison (Shinnecock Hills)	150
Miss Anna Sands (Newport)	155
Mrs. A. Turnure (Shinnecock Hills)	155
Miss A. Howland Ford (Morris County)	161
Miss Helen Shelton (Morris County)	161
Mrs. W. Fellowes Morgan (Morris County)	164
Miss May Bird (Meadow Brook)	173

1896
SECOND WOMEN'S AMATEUR CHAMPIONSHIP

Held at the Morris County Golf Club, Morristown, N.J., October 7-9.

(Qualifying scores, 18 holes.)

Score	Player	First Round	Semi-Finals	Final
*103	Miss Anna Sands (Newport)	Miss Sands, 1 up, 19 hls.	Miss Hoyt, by default	Miss Beatrix Hoyt, 2 and 1.
102	Mrs. William Shippen (Morris County)			
*95	Miss Beatrix Hoyt (Shinnecock)	Miss Hoyt, 8 and 6		
105	Miss McLane (Baltimore)			
105	Miss C. Oliver (Albany)	Miss Oliver, 8 and 6	Mrs. Turnure, 2 up	
102	Miss Frances C. Griscom (Philadelphia)			
105	Mrs. A. Turnure (Shinnecock)	Mrs. Turnure, 3 and 2		
111	Miss Helen Shelton (Morris County)			

*Medalist.

1897
THIRD WOMEN'S AMATEUR CHAMPIONSHIP

Held at the Essex County Club, Manchester, Mass., August 24-26.

(Qualifying scores, 18 holes.)

Score	Player	First Round	Semi-Final	Final
*108	Miss Beatrix Hoyt (Shinnecock)	Miss Hoyt, 8 and 6	Miss Hoyt, 6 and 4	Miss Beatrix Hoyt, 5 and 4.
122	Miss Margaret Curtis (Essex County)			
125	Mrs. Merrill (Essex County)	Miss Longworth, 7 and 6		
123	Miss C. E. Longworth (Cincinnati)			
131	Miss Frances C. Griscom (Philadelphia)	Miss Griscom, 1 up	Miss Sargent, 3 and 2	
121	Mrs. R. C. Hooper (Essex County)			
130	Miss Lucy Herron (Cincinnati)	Miss Sargent, 5 and 3		
114	Miss N. C. Sargent (Essex County)			

*Medalist.

1898
FOURTH WOMEN'S AMATEUR CHAMPIONSHIP

Held at the Ardsley Club, Ardsley-on-Hudson, N.Y., October 11-14.

(Qualifying scores, 18 holes.) 61 Entries.

Score	Player	First Round	Second Round	Semi-Final	Final
108	Mrs. W. Fellowes Morgan (Baltusrol)	Mrs. Morgan, 5 and 4	Miss Eidlitz, 3 and 2	Miss Hoyt, 6 and 5	Miss Beatrix Hoyt, 5 and 3
109	Miss Harriot Curtis (Essex County)				
103	Miss Carol Eidlitz (Ardsley)	Miss Eidlitz, 2 and 1			
107	Miss Marion Shearson (Chicago)				
*92	Miss Beatrix Hoyt (Shinnecock)	Miss Hoyt, 4 and 3	Miss Hoyt, 6 and 5		
102	Miss Grace B. Keyes (Concord)				
100	Miss Edith D. Burt (Philadelphia)	Miss Burt, 2 up			
107	Mrs. E. A. Manice (Pittsfield)				
106	Miss Ruth Underhill (Queens County)	Miss Underhill, 1 up, 19 hls.	Miss Griscom, 6 and 4	Miss Wetmore, 4 and 3	
102	Miss Madeline Boardman (Essex County)				
107	Miss Frances C. Griscom (Merion)	Miss Griscom, 7 and 5			
103	Mrs. William Shippen (Morris County)				
109	Miss H. K. Cassatt (Philadelphia)	Miss Cassatt, 5 and 4	Miss Wetmore, 4 and 3		
106	Mrs. J. E. Griener (Baltimore)				
104	Miss Maude K. Wetmore (Newport)	Miss Wetmore, 3 and 2			
107	Miss Alice Strong (Seabright)				

*Medalist.

1899
FIFTH WOMEN'S AMATEUR CHAMPIONSHIP

Held at the Philadelphia Country Club, Bala, Pa. October 10-14. 78 Entries.

Qualifying scores, 18 holes		1st Round	2nd Round	3rd Round	Semi-Finals	Final
105	Miss Ruth Underhill (Nassau)	Miss Underhill, 3 and 2				
106	Miss Jane S. Swords (Morris County)		Miss Underhill, 3 and 2			
104	Miss Pauline Mackay (Oakley)	Miss Mackay, 3 and 2				
105	Miss Alice S. Day (Morris County)			Miss Underhill, 5 and 4		
103	Miss Elsie F. Cassatt (Merion)	Miss Cassatt, 3 and 2				
100	Miss Frances C. Griscom (Merion)		Miss Cassatt, 6 and 5		Miss Ruth Underhill, 2 and 1	
103	Mrs. A. deWitt Cochrane (Ardsley)	Mrs. Cochrane, 5 and 3				
106	Miss Georgianna Bishop (Brooklawn)					
107	Miss Marion Oliver (Albany)	Miss Oliver, 5 and 3				
107	Miss May Barron (Ardsley)		Miss Oliver, 5 and 4			
107	Mrs. J.F. McFadden (Philadelphia)	Mrs. McFadden, 1 up, 20 hls.				
105	Miss Genevieve Hecker (Wee Burn)			Mrs. Fox, 1 up, 19 hls.		
103	Mrs. Caleb F. Fox (Huntingdon Valley)	Mrs. Fox, 3 and 2				
97	*Miss Beatrix Hoyt (Shinnecock Hills)		Mrs. Fox, 1 up, 20 hls.			
101	Miss Anna Sands (Newport)	Miss Sands, 7 and 5				
107	Miss Florence McNeely (Merion)					

*Medalist.

1900
SIXTH WOMEN'S AMATEUR CHAMPIONSHIP

Held at the Shinnecock Hills Golf Club, Shinnecock Hills, L.I., N.Y. August 28-September 1. 62 Entries.

Qualifying scores, 18 holes.		1st Round	2nd Round	3rd Round	Semi-Finals	Final
104	Miss F. Ethel Wickham (Ardsley)	Miss Hecker, 4 and 2				
106	Miss Genevieve Hecker (Wee Burn)		Miss Terry, 2 and 1			
108	Miss Eunice Terry (Ardsley)	Miss Terry, 3 and 2				
110	Miss Harriot Curtis (Essex County)			Miss Griscom, 1 up, 19 hls.		
108	Mrs. N. Pendleton Rogers (Hillside)	Mrs. Rogers, 1 up				
110	Miss Ruth Underhill (Nassau Country)		Miss Griscom, 4 and 2			
109	Mrs. Edward A. Manice (Pittsfield)	Miss Griscom, 3 and 2				
96	Miss Frances C. Griscom (Merion)				Miss Frances C. Griscom, 6 and 5	
94	*Miss Beatrix Hoyt (Shinnecock)	Miss Hoyt, 7 and 6				
106	Miss H.C. Parrish (Shinnecock)		Miss Hoyt, 1 up			
109	Mrs. Caleb F. Fox (Huntingdon Valley)	Mrs. Fox, 5 and 3				
106	Miss Caroline Livingston (Westbrook)			Miss Curtis, 1 up, 20 hls.		
101	Miss Margaret Curtis (Essex County)	Miss Curtis, 7 and 6				
109	Mrs. A. deWitt Cochrane (Ardsley)		Miss Curtis, 4 and 3			
107	Mrs. H. Toulmin (Merion)	Miss Keyes, 1 up				
111	Miss Grace B. Keyes (Concord)					

*Medalist.

1901
SEVENTH WOMEN'S AMATEUR CHAMPIONSHIP

Held at the Baltusrol Golf Club, Springfield, N.J. October 8-12. 84 Entries.

Qualifying scores, 18 holes.		1st Round	2nd Round	3rd Round	Semi-Finals	Final
97	*Miss Margaret Curtis (Essex County)	Miss Curtis, 2 up				
103	Miss Pauline Mackay (Oakley)		Miss Curtis, 1 up, 19 hls.			
100	Miss Marion Oliver (Albany Country)	Miss Anthony, 5 and 4				
103	Miss Bessie Anthony (Glen View)			Miss Herron, 3 and 2		
100	Mrs. N.P. Rogers (Baltusrol)	Mrs. Rogers, 1 up				
104	Miss Harriot Curtis (Essex County)		Miss Herron, 1 up			
103	Miss Emily A. Lockwood (Lexington)	Miss Herron, 20 hls.				
97	*Miss Lucy Herron (Cincinnati)				Miss Genevieve Hecker, 5 and 3	
97	*Mrs. E.A. Manice (Lenox)	Mrs. Manice, 6 and 5				
102	Miss Louisa A. Wells (Brookline)		Mrs. Manice, 2 and 1			
104	Miss Fanny K. McLane (Baltimore)	Miss Adams, 3 and 2				
97	*Miss Mary B. Adams (Wollaston)			Miss Hecker, 2 and 1		
102	Miss Georgianna Bishop (Brooklawn)	Miss Bishop, 4 and 3				
102	Miss Elizabeth Farrington (Vespers)		Miss Hecker, 1 up, 19 hls.			
101	Miss Genevieve Hecker (Essex Co. Country)	Miss Hecker, 4 and 2				
104	Miss Grace Fargo (Seabright)					

*Co-Medalists.

1902
EIGHTH WOMEN'S AMATEUR CHAMPIONSHIP

Held at The Country Club, Brookline, Mass. September 30-October 4. 96 Entries.

Qualifying scores, 18 holes		1st Round	2nd Round	3rd Round	Semi-Finals	Final
89	*Miss Margaret Curtis (Essex County)	Miss Curtis, 5 and 3				
97	Miss Anita Phipps (Springfield)		Miss Curtis, 5 and 4			
96	Miss E.N. Lockwood (Lexington)	Miss Mackay, 3 and 2				
100	Miss Pauline Mackay (Oakley)			Mrs. Gorham, 4 and 2		
96	Miss Mollie Brownell (Agawam)	Miss Brownell, 3 and 2				
101	Miss Elsa Hurlbut (Morris County)		Mrs. Gorham, 2 up			
93	Mrs. E.A. Manice (Lenox)	Mrs. Gorham, 5 and 4				
99	Mrs. W.M. Gorham (Hunt Valley)				Miss Hecker, 4 and 2	
94	Miss Bessie Anthony (Glen View)	Miss Anthony, 1 up, 19 hls.				
99	Miss E.S. Porter (Oakley)		Miss Anthony, 4 and 3			
97	Mrs. N.P. Rogers (Baltusrol)	Mrs. Rogers, 4 and 3				
102	Miss Ruth Milne (Albany)			Miss Hecker, 2 up		
96	Miss Genevieve Hecker (Apawamis)	Miss Hecker, 3 and 2				
100	Mrs. E. Sanford (Essex County)		Miss Hecker, 4 and 3			
90	Miss Ruth Underhill (Nassau)	Miss Underhill, 1 up, 19 hls.				
98	Mrs. R.G. Brown (San Francisco)					Miss Genevieve Hecker, 4 and 3
89	*Miss Louisa A. Wells (Brookline)	Miss Wells, 6 and 4				
98	Miss Elizabeth Farrington (Vesper)		Miss Wells, 1 up			
96	Miss M.B. Adams (Wollaston)	Miss Adams, 6 and 4				
100	Miss C.G. Willis (Morris County)			Miss Wells, 6 and 5		
97	Miss M.W. Phelps (Brookline)	Miss Phelps, 5 and 3				
101	Mrs. J.B. Kinney (Baltusrol)		Miss Osgood, 1 up, 20 hls.			
93	Miss F.C. Osgood (Brookline)	Miss Osgood, 1 up, 19 hls.				
99	Miss M.K. Wetmore (Newport)				Miss Wells, 2 up	
95	Miss J.A. Carpenter (Westward Ho!)	Miss Vanderhoef, 2 up				
99	Miss E.L. Vanderhoef (Ardsley)		Miss Vanderhoef, 6 and 5			
97	Mrs. William Shippen (Morris County)	Mrs. Shippen, 2 up				
103	Mrs. J.F. Hubbard (Harbor Hill)			Mrs. Fox, 1 up		
96	Mrs. Caleb F. Fox (Philadelphia)	Mrs. Fox, 2 and 1				
101	Miss Marion Oliver (Albany)		Mrs. Fox, 2 up			
90	Miss Georgianna Bishop (Brooklawn)	Miss Bishop, 1 up, 19 hls.				
99	Miss Gertrude Fiske (Concord)					

*Co-Medalists.

1903
NINTH WOMEN'S AMATEUR CHAMPIONSHIP

Held at the Chicago Golf Club, Wheaton, Ill. September 29-October 3. 64 Entries.

Qualifying scores, 18 holes.		1st Round	2nd Round	3rd Round	Semi-Finals	Final
114	Mrs. C.L. Dering (Midlothian)	Mrs. Dering, 7 and 5				
110	Miss M. Higgins (Midlothian)		Mrs. Dering, 4 and 3			
116	Miss E. Collins (St. Louis)	Miss Collins, 2 and 1				
114	Miss Frances C. Griscom (Merion)			Miss Osgood, 9 and 7		
120	Miss E. Robertson (Glen View)	Miss Robertson, 5 and 3			Miss Anthony, 1 up	
118	Mrs. P. Manchester (Glen View)		Miss Osgood, 5 and 3			
107	Miss F.C. Osgood (Brookline)	Miss Osgood, 8 and 7				
114	Miss E. Young (Calumet)					
99	Miss Bessie Anthony (Glen View)	Miss Anthony, 6 and 4				
97	Mrs. R.H. Barlow (Merion)		Miss Anthony, 5 and 3			
94	*Mrs. Caleb F. Fox (Huntingdon Valley)	Mrs. Fox, 3 and 1				
114	Miss L. Biddle (Riverton, N.J.)			Miss Anthony, 4 and 2		
103	Miss F. Everett (Exmoor)	Miss Everett, 2 and 1				**Miss Bessie Anthony, 7 and 6**
117	Mrs. W.B. McIlvaine (Onwentsia)		Miss Everett, 1 up, 19 hls.			
108	Miss J.S. Spence (Merion)	Miss Spence, 7 and 5				
113	Miss K. Moulton (Minikahda)					
99	Miss J.A. Carpenter (Westward Ho!)	Miss Carpenter, 1 up				
109	Mrs. A.T.H. Brower (Chicago)		Miss Carpenter, 5 and 4			
101	**Miss Louisa A. Wells (Brookline)**	Miss Wells, 6 and 5				
119	Mrs. E. Rodgers (Edgeworth, Pa.)			Miss Carpenter, 1 up		
102	Miss Georgianna Bishop (Brooklawn, Conn.)	Miss Bishop, 8 and 7			Miss Carpenter, 2 and 1	
114	Mrs. L.G. McNair (St. Louis)		Miss Bishop, 8 and 7			
113	Miss M. Morris (Evanston)	Miss Morris, 4 and 2				
119	Miss A.E. Murray (Wilmington, Del.)					
114	Miss H. Bishop (St. Paul, Minn.)	Miss Bishop, 2 and 1				
120	Mrs. H.A. Beidler (Lake Geneva)		Miss Harley, 7 and 6			
107	**Miss Katherine C. Harley (Fall River)**	Miss Harley, 3 and 2				
120	Miss H. Kenny (Minikahda)			Miss Harley, 7 and 6		
117	Miss M. Anthony (Evanston)	Miss Anthony, 5 and 4				
111	Miss F. Borden (Fall River)		Mrs. Alexander, 5 and 4			
113	Mrs. W.A. Alexander (Exmoor)	Mrs. Alexander, 3 and 2				
118	Miss J. Dureil (Edgewater)					

***Medalist.**

1904
TENTH WOMEN'S AMATEUR CHAMPIONSHIP

Held at the Merion Cricket Club, Haverford, Pa. October 10-15. 86 Entries.

Qualifying scores, 18 holes.		1st Round	2nd Round	3rd Round	Semi-Finals	Final
94	Miss M.B. Adams (Wollaston)	Miss Wells, 2 up				
95	Miss L.A. Wells (The Country Club)		Miss Mackay, 3 and 2			
95	Miss Pauline Mackay (Oakley)	Miss Mackay, 2 and 1				
93	***Miss Charlotte Dod (Moreton, England)**			Miss Mackay, 1 up		
102	Miss E.S. Porter (The Country Club)	Miss Porter, 3 and 2				
106	Miss E. Terry (Ardsley)		Miss Ayres, 4 and 3			
101	Miss M.C. Dutton (The Country Club)	Miss Ayres, 3 and 1			Mrs. Sanford, 7 and 5	
106	Miss F.N. Ayres (Riverton)					
102	Miss M.K. Wetmore (Newport)	Miss Vanderhoef, 7 and 6				
93	***Miss E.L. Vanderhoef (Ardsley)**		Miss Vanderhoef, 2 up			
103	**Mrs. H. Toulmin (Merion)**	Miss Carpenter, 8 and 7				
98	Miss J.A. Carpenter (Westward Ho!)			Mrs. Sanford, 2 up		
93	***Miss Harriot Curtis (Essex County)**	Mrs. Sanford, 1 up, 19 hls.				
102	Mrs. E.F. Sanford (Essex Co. Country)		Mrs. Sanford, 1 up, 19 hls.			
102	Mrs. Caleb F. Fox (Huntingdon Valley)	Mrs. Fox, 4 and 3				
101	Miss R. Milne (Albany)					Miss Georgianna Bishop, 5 and 3
107	Miss L. Biddle (Riverton)	Miss Lockwood, 5 and 4				
104	Miss E.N. Lockwood (Lexington)		Miss Curtis, 3 and 2			
99	**Miss Margaret Curtis (Essex County)**	Miss Curtis, 8 and 6				
105	**Miss R. Badgley (Essex County)**			Miss Harley, 1 up		
100	**Miss Katherine C. Harley (Fall River)**	Miss Harley, 1 up				
95	Mrs. R.H. Barlow (Merion)		Miss Harley, 6 and 4			
97	Miss F.C. Osgood (The Country Club)	Miss Osgood, by default			Miss Bishop, 4 and 3	
106	Miss A.P. McNeely (Merion)					
107	Miss H.F. Bishop (Brooklawn)	Miss Bishop, 4 and 2				
100	Miss Georgianna Bishop (Brooklawn)		Miss Bishop, 4 and 3			
102	Miss E.W. Allen (Oakley)	Mrs. Batchelder, 2 up				
105	Mrs. F.W. Batchelder (Weston)			Miss Bishop, 4 and 3		
98	Miss M. Higgins (Midlothian)	Miss Higgins, 2 and 1				
99	Miss Anita Phipps (Springfield)		Miss Griscom, 2 and 1			
97	Miss Frances C. Griscom (Merion)	Miss Griscom, 2 and 1				
107	Miss F. McNeely (Merion)					

*Co-Medalists.

1905
ELEVENTH WOMEN'S AMATEUR CHAMPIONSHIP

Held at the Morris County Golf Club, Convent, N.J. October 9-14. 69 Entries, 66 Starters.

Qualifying Scores, 18 holes.		1st Round	2nd Round	3rd Round	Semi-Finals	Final
103	Mrs. E.F. Sanford (Essex County)	Mrs. Sanford, 1 up, 19 hls.				
104	Miss E.W. Allen (Oakley)		Miss Bishop, 5 and 3			
91	Miss E.L. Vanderhoef (Ardsley)	Miss Bishop, 3 and 2				
87	*Miss Georgianna Bishop (Brooklawn)			Miss Bishop, 5 and 4		
93	Miss E.M. Hurry (Apawamis)	Miss H. Curtis, 1 up, 19 hls.				
99	Miss Harriot Curtis (Essex County)		Miss H. Curtis, 6 and 5			
100	Mrs. S.F. Lefferts (Englewood)	Miss Ayres, 4 and 3			Miss Mackay, 3 and 1	
100	Miss F.N. Ayres (Riverton)					
92	Mrs. H. Fitzgerald (St. Davids)	Mrs. Price, 1 up				
103	Mrs. S.C. Price (Huntingdon Valley)		Mrs. Fox, 1 up			
92	Miss Louisa A. Wells (The Country Club)	Mrs. Fox, 3 and 1				
94	Mrs. Caleb F. Fox (Huntingdon Valley)			Miss Mackay, 3 and 1		
95	Miss Pauline Mackay (Oakley)	Miss Mackay, 5 and 4				
99	Miss E.S. Porter (The Country Club)		Miss Mackay, 5 and 4			
100	Miss K. North (Westchester)	Miss North, 1 up, 19 hls.				Miss Pauline Mackey, 1 up
104	Miss M.C. Dutton (Oakley)					
99	Miss C.E. Morrill (Brae Burn)	Miss Keyes, 5 and 3				
101	Miss Grace Keyes (Concord G.C.)		Miss Keyes, 1 up, 19 hls.			
103	Mrs. C.L. Dering (Midlothian)	Miss Terry, 2 and 1				
98	Miss Eunice Terry (Ardsley)			Miss Keyes, 5 and 3		
100	Miss M. Oliver (Chevy Chase)	Miss Oliver, 3 and 2				
102	Mrs. V.J. Hall (Evanston)		Miss Oliver, 1 up, 20 hls.			
104	Miss Frances C. Griscom (Merion)	Miss Adams, 3 and 1			Miss M. Curtis, 6 and 5	
101	Miss M.B. Adams (Wollaston)					
91	Miss M.W. Phelps (The Country Club)	Mrs. Stout, 3 and 2				
96	Mrs. Genevieve Hecker Stout (Apawamis)		Miss Stout, 4 and 2			
100	Miss J.R. Mix (Baltusrol)	Miss Mix, 1 up, 19 hls.				
93	Miss Katherine C. Harley (Fall River)			Miss M. Curtis, 2 and 1		
90	Miss Anita Phipps (Springfield)	Mrs. Patterson, 2 up				
103	Mrs. M.D. Paterson (Baltusrol)		Miss M. Curtis, 1 up			
87	*Miss Margaret Curtis (Essex County)	Miss M. Curtis, 7 and 5				
96	Mrs. R.H. Barlow (Merion)					

*Co-Medalists.

1906
TWELFTH WOMEN'S AMATEUR CHAMPIONSHIP

Held at the Brae Burn Country Club, West Newton, Mass. October 8-13. 75 Entries, 71 Starters.

Qualifying scores, 18 holes.		1st Round	2nd Round	3rd Round	Semi-Finals	Final
96	Miss Frances C. Griscom (Merion)	Miss Griscom, 4 and 3				
102	Mrs. M.D. Paterson (Englewood)		Miss Griscom, 8 and 7			
103	Miss E. Hurry (Englewood)	Miss Porter, 1 up, 19 hls.				
98	Miss E.S. Porter (The Country Club)			Miss Adams, 3 and 2		
102	Mrs. G.C. Dutton (Oakley)	Miss Adams, 5 and 4				
93	**Miss Mary B. Adams (Wollaston)**		Miss Adams, 4 and 3			
91	Mrs. Caleb F. Fox (Huntingdon Valley)	Mrs. Lefferts, 2 and 1				
101	Mrs. S.F. Lefferts (Englewood)				Miss Adams, 2 and 1	
97	Miss Julia Mix (Englewood)	Miss Mix, 5 and 4				
101	Miss Grace Semple (St. Louis Country)		Mrs. Barlow, 5 and 4			
99	Mrs. R.H. Barlow (Merion)	Mrs. Barlow, 4 and 2				
101	Mrs. Edwin Read (Lexington Golf)			Mrs. Barlow, 7 and 6		
99	Mrs. F.W. Batchelder (Weston)	Mrs. Batchelder, by default				
98	Miss Myra Helmer (Midlothian)		Mrs. Batchelder, 1 up			
96	Miss Georgianna Bishop (Brooklawn)	Miss Bishop, 7 and 6				
100	Miss M.C. Dutton (Oakley)					Miss Harriot Curtis, 2 and 1
89	Miss F.C. Osgood (The Country Club)	Miss Osgood, 4 and 2				
105	Miss Grace Stults (Oakley)		Miss Curtis, 8 and 6			
94	Miss Harriot Curtis (Essex County)	Miss Curtis, 4 and 2				
96	Mrs. G.W. Roope (Denver Country C.)			Miss Curtis, 6 and 4		
104	Mrs. F. Anderson (Hinsdale Golf)	Mrs. Morgan, 5 and 4				
102	Mrs. W. Fellowes Morgan (Baltusrol)		Mrs. Morgan, 2 and 1			
103	Mrs. Alex. McGregor (Oakley)	Miss Mackay, 4 and 2				
87	*Miss Pauline Mackay (Oakley)				Miss Curtis, 3 and 1	
97	Miss Phepoe (Canada)	Miss Ayres, 4 and 3				
105	Miss F.N. Ayers (Riverton)		Miss Ayres, 1 up, 20 hls.			
99	Miss Emily Lockwood (The Country Club)	Miss Harley, 5 and 3				
100	**Miss Katherine C. Harley (Fall River)**			Miss Phipps, 4 and 2		
94	Miss Anita Phipps (Springfield)	Miss Phipps, 1 up, 20 hls.				
102	Miss L.A. Wells (The Country Club)		Miss Phipps, 3 and 1			
90	Miss M.W. Phelps (Brae Burn)	Miss Phelps, 5 and 3				
102	Mrs. E.G. Fisher (Commonwealth)					

*Medalist.

1907
THIRTEENTH WOMEN'S AMATEUR CHAMPIONSHIP

Held at the Midlothian Country Club, Blue Island, Ill. October 7-12. 87 Entries, 65 Starters.

Qualifying scores, 18 holes.		1st Round	2nd Round	3rd Round	Semi-Finals	Final
105	Miss Maude Whitmore (Newport)	Miss Steele, 2 and 1	Miss M. Curtis, 9 and 7	Miss M. Curtis, 3 and 1	Miss M. Curtis, 6 and 4	Miss Margaret Curtis, 7 and 6
108	Miss R.B. Steele (Homewood)					
95	*Miss Margaret Curtis (Essex County)	**Miss M. Curtis,** 7 and 6				
108	Mrs. C.L. Dering (Midlothian)					
103	Miss E.S. Porter (The Country Club)	Miss Porter, 3 and 2	Miss Porter, 4 and 3			
101	Miss E.W. Allen (Oakley)					
108	Miss Elizabeth Young (Calumet)	Miss Young, 3 and 2				
111	Mrs. C.F. Braffette (La Grange)					
105	Miss Marjory W. Phelps (Brae Burn)	Miss Phelps, 2 up	Miss Phelps, 3 and 2	Miss Phelps, 1 up		
110	Miss F.N. Ayers (Merion)					
102	Mrs. Caleb F. Fox (Huntingdon Valley)	Miss Mackay, 2 and 1				
101	Miss Pauline Mackay (Oakley)					
111	Mrs. P. Manchester (Skokie)	Miss Painter, 1 up	Miss Adams, 7 and 5			
112	Miss C. Painter (Calumet)					
111	Mrs. W.A. Alexander (Exmoor)	Miss Adams, 6 and 4				
97	Miss Mary B. Adams (Wollaston)					
104	Miss Anita Phipps (Springfield)	Miss Phipps, 3 and 1	Miss Phipps, 4 and 2	Miss Phipps, 1 up, 21 hls.	Miss H. Curtis, 4 and 3	
110	Miss Florence Harvey (Toronto)					
111	Miss N.R. Huselton (Allegheny)	**Miss Huselton,** 1 up, 19 hls.				
112	**Miss Vida Llewellyn (La Grange)**					
111	Miss Louisa A. Wells (The Country C.)	Miss Wells, 3 and 2	Miss Ainslee, 7 and 6			
103	Miss Frances C. Griscom (Merion)					
112	Mrs. W.L. De Wolf (Onwentsia)	Miss Ainslee, 5 and 3				
98	Miss Sallie Ainslee (Westward Ho!)					
96	Miss Harriot Curtis (Essex County)	**Miss H. Curtis,** 2 up	Miss H. Curtis, 4 and 2	Miss H. Curtis, 3 and 1		
104	Miss Lillian French (Windsor)					
106	Miss Margaret Martin (Chicago)	Miss Martin, 2 and 1				
109	Miss Grace Semple (St. Louis)					
110	Mrs. R.H. Barlow (Merion)	Mrs. Barlow, 4 and 3	Mrs. Barlow, 5 and 4			
98	Miss Phepoe (Canada)					
110	Mrs. E.T. Perkins (Los Angeles)	Miss Helmer, 3 and 1				
111	Miss M.A. Helmer (Midlothian)					

*Medalist.

1908
FOURTEENTH WOMEN'S AMATEUR CHAMPIONSHIP

Held at the Chevy Chase Club, Chevy Chase, Md. October 19-24. 41 Entries, 38 Starters.

Qualifying scores, 18 holes.		1st Round	2nd Round	3rd Round	Semi-Finals	Final
93	Mrs. E.T. Perkins (Glen View)	Mrs. Perkins, 8 and 7				
103	Miss Pauline Firth (Brookline)		Mrs. McCammon, 5 and 2			
93	Miss E.W. Allen (Oakley)	Mrs. McCammon, 2 up				
94	Mrs. O. McCammon (Chevy Chase)			Miss Oliver, 7 and 6		
101	Miss Frances C. Griscom (Merion)	Miss Griscom, 9 and 8				
101	Miss M. McCain (Chevy Chase)		Miss Oliver, 1 up, 20 hls.			
96	Miss Marion Oliver (Chevy Chase)	Miss Oliver, 3 and 2			Mrs. Polhemus, 4 and 2	
100	Mrs. W. West (Woodbury C.C.)					
106	Miss E.G. Hood (Philadelphia Cricket)	Mrs. Smith, 1 up, 19 hls.				
113	Mrs. H. St. I. Smith (Portland, Me.)		Mrs. Polhemus, 1 up			
99	Mrs. T.H. Polhemus (Richmond Co.)	Mrs. Polhemus, 3 and 2				
106	Mrs. G.H. Converse (Brae Burn)			Mrs. Polhemus, 3 and 2		
102	Miss C. Shreve (Brae Burn)	Miss Shreve, 3 and 1				
110	Miss H.E. Maule (Merion)		Miss Shreve, 2 up			
108	Miss Grace Semple (St. Louis C.C.)	Miss Osgood, 7 and 6				Miss Katherine C. Harley, 6 and 5
87	Miss Fanny Osgood (Brookline)					
86	Miss Georgianna Bishop (Brooklawn)	Miss Bishop, 5 and 3				
104	Miss D. Robinson (Rochester C.C.)		Miss Bishop, 2 and 1			
99	Mrs. J.E. Kinney (Richmond County)	Miss Phelps, 4 and 3				
86	Miss M.W. Phelps (Brookline)			Mrs. Fox, 3 and 2		
89	Miss E.S. Porter (Brookline)	Mrs. Fox, 5 and 3				
91	Mrs. Caleb F. Fox (Huntingdon Valley)		Mrs. Fox, 3 and 2			
106	Mrs. M.C. Work (Huntingdon Valley)	Mrs. H. Curtis, 4 and 3			Miss Harley, 1 up	
85	*Miss Harriot Curtis (Essex County)					
88	Miss M.B. Adams (Wollaston)	Miss Adams, 4 and 3				
99	Miss Grace Keyes (Concord G.C.)		Miss Harley, 2 and 1			
104	Miss K.A. Townsend (Overbrook G.C.)	Miss Harley, 9 and 7				
95	Miss Katherine C. Harley (Fall River)			Miss Harley, 4 and 2		
88	Miss Anita Phipps (Springfield C.C.)	Miss M. Curtis, 3 and 2				
88	Miss Margaret Curtis (Essex County)		Miss M. Curtis, 2 up			
98	Miss Louisa A. Wells (Brookline)	Mrs. Barlow, 3 and 2				
91	Mrs. R.H. Barlow (Merion)					

*Medalist.

1909
FIFTEENTH WOMEN'S AMATEUR CHAMPIONSHIP

Held at the Merion Cricket Club, Haverford, Pa. October 4-9. 70 Entries, 67 Starters.

Qualifying scores, 18 holes.		1st Round	2nd Round	3rd Round	Semi-Finals	Final
96	Miss Frances C. Griscom (Merion)	Miss Griscom, 7 and 6	Mrs. Stout, 2 and 1	Miss Campbell, 2 up	Miss Campbell, 3 and 2	Miss Dorothy I. Campbell, 3 and 2
97	Mrs. H.L.C. Roome (Merion)					
86	*Miss Anita Phipps (Springfield, Mass.)	Mrs. Stout, 4 and 3				
95	Mrs. C.T. Stout (Richmond County)					
92	Mrs. E.H. Fitler (Merion)	Mrs. Fitler, 7 and 6	Miss Campbell, 2 and 1			
99	Miss Grace Semple (St. Louis)					
100	Mrs. C.W. McKelvey (Essex County)	Miss Campbell, 10 and 8				
87	Miss Dorothy I. Campbell (N. Berwick, Scotland)					
98	Miss F. Teacher (N. Berwick, Scotland)	Miss Teacher, 7 and 6	Miss Teacher, 3 and 1	Mrs. Fox, 4 and 2		
100	Miss C. Shreve (Brae Burn)					
101	Miss Georgianna Bishop (Brooklawn)	Miss Llewellyn, 2 up				
98	Miss Vida Llewellyn (La Grange, Ill.)					
94	Miss Katherine C. Harley (Fall River)	Miss Adams, 2 up	Mrs. Fox, 1 up			
91	Miss Mollie Adams (Wollaston)					
86	*Mrs. Caleb F. Fox (Huntingdon Valley)	Mrs. Fox, 2 and 1				
86	*Miss Margaret Curtis (Essex County)					
94	Miss S. Temple (Westward Ho, Eng.)	Miss Temple, 1 up	Miss Phelps, 1 up	Miss Phelps, 1 up	Mrs. Barlow, 6 and 5	
90	Mrs. E.F. Lefferts (Englewood)					
101	Mrs. F.C. Colburn (Evanston)	Miss Phelps, 7 and 6				
97	Miss M.W. Phelps (Brookline)					
102	Mrs. William West (Woodbury, N.J.)	Miss Noblit, 4 and 2	Miss Noblit, 3 and 2			
103	Miss Edith Noblit (Wilmington, Del.)					
101	Miss McCallum (Merchantville)	Mrs. Vanderbeck, 3 and 2				
101	Mrs. C.H. Vanderbeck (Phila. Country)					
94	Miss Isabel Smith (Evanston)	Miss Smith, 1 up	Miss Smith, 1 up, 19 hls.	Mrs. Barlow, 2 and 1		
97	Miss F. McNeeley (Merion)					
98	Miss E.S. Porter (Brookline)	Miss Porter, 1 up				
97	Miss Harriot Curtis (Essex County)					
101	Miss F. Dallett (St. David's)	Mrs. Barlow, 7 and 6	Mrs. Barlow, 2 up			
89	Mrs. R.H. Barlow (Merion)					
102	Miss M. McCain (Chevy Chase)	Miss Spence, 7 and 5				
96	Miss Jane Spence (Moreton, England)					

*Co-Medalists.

1910
SIXTEENTH WOMEN'S AMATEUR CHAMPIONSHIP

Held at the Homewood Country Club, Flossmoor, Ill. October 10-15. 57 Entries, 50 Starters.

Qualifying scores, 18 holes.		1st Round	2nd Round	3rd Round	Semi-Finals	Final
85	*Miss Dorothy I. Campbell (Hamilton, Ont.)	Miss Campbell, 7 and 5	Miss Campbell, 6 and 5	Miss Campbell, 4 and 3	Miss Campbell, 4 and 3	Miss Dorothy I. Campbell, 2 and 1
106	Mrs. A.E. Hedstrom (Buffalo)					
95	Miss Mary Fownes (Oakmont)	Miss Fownes, 4 and 3				
107	Miss Margaret Knapp (Skokie)					
89	Mrs. R.H. Barlow (Merion)	Mrs. Barlow, 1 up	Mrs. Barlow, 5 and 3			
98	Miss Grace Semple (St. Louis)					
99	Miss Myra Helmer (Midlothian)	Miss Helmer, 3 and 2				
97	Mrs. J.T. Harris (Westward Ho, Eng.)					
105	Mrs. L.N. Brochon (La Grange)	Mrs. Brochon, 4 and 2	Miss Layman, 5 and 4	Miss Harvey, 4 and 3		
107	Mrs. W.B. McIlvaine (Onwentsia)					
107	Miss Ruth Layman (Hinsdale)	Miss Layman, 3 and 2				
105	Miss Caroline Painter (Midlothian)					
91	Mrs. Caleb F. Fox (Huntingdon Valley)	Mrs. Fox, 8 and 7	Miss Harvey, 3 and 2			
105	Mrs. F.W. Winkler (Beverly)					
93	Miss F. Harvey (Hamilton, Ont.)	Miss Harvey, 3 and 2				
98	Mrs. Herbert Galt (Onwentsia)					
109	Miss K. Moulton (Minikahda)	Miss Moulton, 2 up	Miss Hyde, 3 and 1	Miss Hyde, 2 up	Mrs. Martin, 3 and 2	
97	Mrs. W.F. Anderson (Hinsdale)					
91	Miss L.B. Hyde (South Shore Field)	Miss Hyde, 10 and 8				
108	Mrs. C.D. Barrows (Portland)					
97	Mrs. L.M. Kennett (Evanston)	Miss Elkins, 1 up, 19 hls.	Miss Llewellyn, 1 up			
100	Miss Louise B. Elkins (Oakmont)					
95	Miss Vida Llewellyn (La Grange)	Miss Llewellyn, 4 and 2				
108	Mrs. P. Manchester (Skokie)					
93	Miss E.C. Nesbit (Woodstock, Can.)	Miss Nesbit, 6 and 5	Miss Nesbit, 2 up	Mrs. Martin, 7 and 5		
101	Mrs. E.R. Williams (Lake Geneva)					
100	Mrs. W. West (Huntingdon Valley)	Mrs. West, 3 and 1				
105	Miss Ethel Corbet (Homewood)					
90	Mrs. G.M. Martin (Tavistock, Eng.)	Mrs. Martin, 4 and 2	Mrs. Martin, 4 and 3			
104	Mrs. G.G. Carlyle (Exmoor)					
109	Miss Marion P. Warren (Skokie)	Miss Warren, 2 and 1				
107	Miss E. Chandler (Huntingdon Valley)					

*Medalist.

1911
SEVENTEENTH WOMEN'S AMATEUR CHAMPIONSHIP

Held at the Baltusrol Golf Club, Springfield, N.J. October 9-14. 67 Entries, 66 Starters.

Qualifying scores, 18 holes.		1st Round	2nd Round	3rd Round	Semi-Finals	Final
112	Miss F. McNeeley (Merion)	Miss McNeeley, 1 up, 19 hls.	Miss Allen, 1 up	Miss Allen, 2 up	Miss Hyde, 6 and 5	Miss Margaret Curtis, 5 and 3
113	Mrs. H.R. Stockton (Plainfield)					
101	Miss E.W. Allen (Oakley)	Miss Allen, 2 and 1				
112	Miss M. Wetmore (Baltusrol)					
87	*Mrs. R.H. Barlow (Merion)	Mrs. Barlow, 3 and 1	Mrs. Barlow, 6 and 4			
108	Miss Florence Harvey (Hamilton)					
99	Mrs. V.M. Earle (Deal)	Mrs. Earle, 8 and 7				
104	**Miss Edith Chesbrough (San Francisco)**					
113	Miss Frances C. Griscom (Merion)	Miss Griscom, 7 and 6	Miss Harley, 5 and 3	Miss Hyde, 1 up, 19 hls.		
113	Miss H.E. Maule (Merion)					
108	**Miss Katherine C. Harley (Fall River)**	Miss Harley, 3 and 2				
110	Miss Myra Helmer (Midlothian)					
95	Miss L.B. Hyde (South Shore)	Miss Hyde, 6 and 4	Miss Hyde, 3 and 2			
102	Miss F.H. Rosenheim (Deal)					
104	**Miss E.C. Nesbit (Toronto)**	Miss Nesbit, 4 and 3				
109	**Miss E. Noblitt (Wilmington)**					
112	**Miss Louisa A. Wells (Brookline)**	Miss Wells, 2 and 1	Miss Phipps, 7 and 6	Miss Campbell, 6 and 4	Miss Curtis, 4 and 3	
109	Mrs. W.J. Faith (Wykagyl)					
99	Miss Anita Phipps (Springfield)	Miss Phipps, 6 and 4				
96	Mrs. N.P. Rogers (Baltusrol)					
93	Miss Dorothy I. Campbell (Hamilton)	Miss Campbell, 8 and 7	Miss Campbell, 6 and 5			
111	Mrs. P. Manchester (Skokie)					
107	Miss Grace Semple (St. Louis)	Miss Semple, 4 and 3				
111	Miss E.F. Chandler (Huntingdon Valley)					
96	Miss Margaret Curtis (Essex County)	Miss Curtis, 6 and 5	Miss Curtis, 2 up	Miss Curtis, 5 and 4		
112	Mrs. C.W. Rendigs (Midland)					
104	Mrs. E.H. Fitler (Merion)	Mrs. Fitler, 6 and 4				
108	Miss M.W. Phelps (Brookline)					
104	Miss Georgianna Bishop (Brookline)	Miss Bishop, 3 and 2	Miss Porter, 3 and 2			
105	Miss Harriot Curtis (Essex County)					
102	Miss E.S. Porter (Oakley)	Miss Porter, 6 and 4				
110	Mrs. M.D. Paterson (Englewood)					

*Medalist.

1912
EIGHTEENTH WOMEN'S AMATEUR CHAMPIONSHIP

Held at the Essex County Club, Manchester, Mass., **September 30-October 5. 62 Entries, 62 Starters.**

Qualifying Score	1st Round	2nd Round	3rd Round	Semi-Finals	Final
96	Mrs. E.C. Wheeler, Jr., (Wollaston)	Mrs. Wheeler,			
92	Miss Gladys Rosenthal (Ravisloe)	4 and 3	Mrs. Wheeler,		
99	Miss Lillian B. Hyde (South Shore)	Miss Hyde,	1 up		
100	**Miss Frances C. Griscom (Merion)**	7 and 5		Miss Semple,	
105	Miss Maud K. Wetmore (Baltusrol)	**Miss H. Curtis,**		3 and 2	
97	Miss Harriot Curtis (Essex County)	4 and 2	Miss Semple,		
102	Miss Grace Semple (St. Louis)	Miss Semple,	3 and 1		Mrs. Barlow, 5 and 4
102	Miss Eleanor W. Allen (Oakley)	3 and 1			
102	Miss Ruth Chisolm (Euclid)	Mrs. Fitler,			
100	Mrs. E.H. Fitler (Merion)	4 and 3	Mrs. Fitler,		
91	**Miss Georgianna Bishop (Brooklawn)**	Miss Bishop,	8 and 6		
98	Miss Louisa A. Wells (Brookline)	4 and 3		Mrs. Barlow,	
103	Mrs. R.H. Gardner (Belmont)	Miss Osgood,		5 and 4	
102	Miss Fannie C. Osgood (Brookline)	3 and 1	Mrs. Barlow,		
99	Mrs. R.H. Barlow (Merion)	Mrs. Barlow,	4 and 2		
105	Miss H. Alexander (Tuxedo)	7 and 6			
99	Miss K.F. Duncan (Brae Burn)	Miss Mellus,			**Miss Margaret Curtis, 3 and 2**
105	Miss Katherine Mellus (Los Angeles)	3 and 1	Miss Mellus,		
104	Miss Marion Hollins (Westbrook)	Miss Hollins,	3 and 2		
104	Miss Edith Chesbrough (San Francisco)	1 up		Miss Mellus,	
99	Miss Marion L. Oliver (Chevy-Chase)	Miss Elkins,		1 up, 19 hls.	
104	Miss Louisa B. Elkins (Oakmont)	6 and 4	Miss Phelps,		
105	Miss E.S. Porter (Brookline)	Miss Phelps,	3 and 2		
99	Miss M.W. Phelps (Brookline)	2 and 1			
108	Mrs. G.W. Roope (Brae Burn)	Mrs. Roope,			Miss M. Curtis, 1 up
105	Mrs. F.W. Batchelder (Brae Burn)	6 and 5	**Miss M. Curtis,**		
107	Mrs. A.M. Perkins (Jefferson Co.)	**Miss M. Curtis,**	6 and 4		
88	*Miss Margaret Curtis (Essex County)	7 and 6		**Miss M. Curtis**	
106	Miss H. Ethel Maule (Merion)	Miss Maule,		1 up, 19 hls.	
103	Miss Edith Noblit (Wilmington)	4 and 3	Mrs. Fox,		
101	Miss Myra Helmer (Midlothian)	Mrs. Fox,	6 and 4		
97	Mrs. Caleb F. Fox (Huntingdon Valley)	5 and 3			

*Medalist.

1913
NINETEENTH WOMEN'S AMATEUR CHAMPIONSHIP

Held at the Wilmington Country Club, Wilmington, Del., October 13-18. 80 Entries, 72 Starters.

Qualifying Score	1st Round	2nd Round	3rd Round	Semi-Finals	Final
96	Miss Marion Hollins (Westbrook)	Miss Hollins, 7 and 5	Miss Hollins, 1 up	Miss Hollins, 2 up	Miss Hollins, 1 up, 20 hls.
110	Mrs. F.H. Elder (Overbrook)				
112	Miss Florence Harvey (Hamilton)	Miss Harvey, 5 and 3			
109	Miss F.B. Scott (Hamilton)				
111	Mrs. Arthur L. Cahn (Century)	Mrs. Cahn, 1 up	Mrs. Fitler, 5 and 4		
103	Miss Bertha Straton (Cranford)				
106	Miss Louise B. Elkins (Oakmont)	Mrs. Fitler, 2 and 1			
107	Mrs. E.H. Fitler (Merion)				
112	Mrs. H.R. Stockton (Plainfield)	Mrs. Stockton, 2 up	Miss Curtis, 3 and 1	Miss Curtis, 4 and 3	
94	Miss Katherine C. Harley (Fall River)				
91	Miss Harriot Curtis (Essex County)	Miss Curtis, 3 and 2			
101	Miss Eleanor W. Allen (Oakley)				
107	Miss Mabel Harrison (Ireland)	Miss Harrison, 6 and 4	Miss Harrison, 2 and 1		
111	Mrs. William Hirsh (Philmont)				
98	Miss Margaret Curtis (Essex County)	Miss Painter, 1 up			
105	Miss Caroline Painter (Midlothian)				
105	Mrs. F.S. Coburn (Glen View)	Mrs. Coburn, 3 and 2	Mrs. Vanderbeck, 4 and 3	Miss Dodd, 5 and 3	Miss Ravenscroft, 8 and 7
112	Mrs. A.L. Billstein (Bala)				
101	Mrs. C.H. Vanderbeck (Philadelphia Cricket)	Mrs. Vanderbeck, 3 and 2			
104	Mrs. A.S. Rossin (Century)				
97	Miss Lillian B. Hyde (South Shore)	Miss Pooley, 4 and 3	Miss Dodd, 4 and 3		
99	Miss Violet Pooley (Victoria)				
102	Miss Edith Noblit (Wilmington)	Miss Dodd, 5 and 3			
91	Miss Muriel Dodd (England)				
104	Mrs. Thurston Wright (Allegheny)	Miss Osgood, 5 and 3	Miss Osgood, 2 and 1	Miss Ravenscroft, 3 and 2	
95	Miss Fannie Osgood (Brookline)				
96	Miss Mildred Caverly (Philadelphia Cricket)	Miss Helmer, 2 and 1			
103	Miss Myra Helmer (Midlothian)				
111	Miss Edith Rosenthal (Ravisloe)	Miss Rosenthal, 2 and 1	Miss Ravenscroft, 6 and 5		
100	Miss Georgianna Bishop (Brooklawn)				
104	Miss Frances C. Griscom (Merion)	Miss Ravenscroft, 6 and 5			
88	*Miss Gladys Ravenscroft (England)				

Final: Miss Gladys Ravenscroft, 2 up

*Medalist.

1914
TWENTIETH WOMEN'S AMATEUR CHAMPIONSHIP

Held at the Nassau Country Club, Glen Cove, L.I., N.Y., September 14-19. 93 Entries, 92 Starters.

Qualifying Score	1st Round	2nd Round	3rd Round	Semi-Finals	Final	
94	Miss Harriot Curtis (Essex County)	Mrs. Jackson, 2 and 1				
87	Mrs. Katherine Harley Jackson (Oakley)		Mrs. Jackson, 3 and 2			
91	Miss Frances C. Grisccm (Merion)	Miss Allen, 3 and 2				
94	Miss Eleanor W. Allen (Oakley)			Mrs. Jackson, 4 and 2		
94	Mrs. Caleb F. Fox (Huntingdon Valley)	Mrs. Stockton, 1 up, 20 hls.				
95	Mrs. H.R. Stockton (Plainfield)		Miss Painter, 3 and 1		Mrs. Jackson, 2 and 1	
94	Mrs. E.H. Fitler (Merion)	Miss Painter, 1 up				
91	Miss Caroline Painter (Midlothian)					
88	Miss M.A. Irving (Richmond Co.)	Miss Campbell, 8 and 6				
95	Miss Ethel M. Campbell (Overbrook)		Miss Campbell, 2 and 1			
94	Mrs. Edwin W. Daley (Oakley)	Mrs. Daley, 4 and 2				
96	Mrs. G.M. Heckscher (Piping Rock)			Mrs. Vanderbeck, 6 and 4		
93	Mrs. Thurston Wright (Allegheny)	Miss Roberson, 1 up				
95	Miss C.C. Roberson (Bellport)		Mrs. Vanderbeck, 7 and 6			
91	Mrs. C.H. Vanderbeck (Philadelphia Cricket)	Mrs. Vanderbeck, 5 and 4				
92	Miss Fanny C. Osgood (Brookline)					Mrs. Katherine Harley Jackson, 1 up
96	Miss Elaine V. Rosenthal (Ravisloe)	Miss Rosenthal, 6 and 5				
95	Mrs. H.C. Phipps (Piping Rock)		Miss Rosenthal, 6 and 5			
85	*Miss Georgianna Bishop (Brooklawn)	Miss Bishop, 2 and 1				
93	Miss Alexa Stirling (Atlanta A.C.)			Miss Rosenthal, 1 up, 19 hls.		
92	Mrs. A.C. Sumner (Nassau)	Miss McNeely, 1 up				
96	Miss Florence McNeely (Merion)		Miss McNeely, by default		Miss Rosenthal, 1 up	
94	Miss Grace Semple (St. Louis)	Mrs. Steedman, 3 and 2				
92	Mrs. E.H. Steedman (St. Louis)					
90	Mrs. Isaac Harter (Richmond Co.)	Mrs. Harter, 1 up, 19 hls.				
90	Miss Bertha Stratton (Cranford)		Mrs. Barlow, 6 and 5			
99	Mrs. R.H. Barlow (Merion)	Mrs. Barlow, 1 up, 19 hls.				
91	Miss Margaret Curtis (Essex County)			Mrs. Barlow, 1 up		
90	Miss Marion Hollins (Westbrook)	Miss Hyde, 4 and 3				
88	Miss Lillian B. Hyde (South Shore)		Miss Hyde, 7 and 6			
91	Miss Louise Swabacker (Ravisloe)	Mrs. Davis, 2 and 1				
93	Mrs. J.E. Davis (Nassau)					

*Medalist.

1915
TWENTY-FIRST WOMEN'S AMATEUR CHAMPIONSHIP

Held at the Onwentsia Club, Lake Forest, Ill., September 6-11. 119 Entries, 111 Starters.

Qualifying Score	1st Round	2nd Round	3rd Round	Semi-Finals	Final	
96	Mrs. A.W. Gavin (Shirley Park, England)	Mrs. Gavin, 5 and 3				
100	Mrs. G.V. Henneberry (Glen View)		Mrs. Gavin, 3 and 2			
104	Mrs. Caleb F. Fox (Huntingdon Valley)	Mrs. Fox, 5 and 3				
101	Mrs. Mason Phelps (Chicago)			Mrs. Gavin, 4 and 2		
101	Mrs. L.W. Mida (Jackson Park)	Mrs. Hurd, 4 and 3				
96	Mrs. Dorothy C. Hurd (Pittsburgh)		Miss Allen, 4 and 3			
101	Mrs. A.A. Heaning (Wheaton)	Miss Allen, 5 and 3				
100	Miss Eleanor Allen (Oakley)				Mrs. Gavin, 5 and 3	
86	Miss Lillian Hyde (South Shore)	Miss Hyde, 7 and 5				
101	Mrs. A. Liveright (Philmont)		Mrs. Barlow, 1 up			
93	Miss Marion Hollins (Westbrook)	Mrs. Barlow, 1 up				
91	Mrs. R.H. Barlow (Merion Cricket)			Miss Pearce, 4 and 2		
100	Mrs. S. Widney (Beverly)	Miss Painter, 6 and 4				
99	Miss Caroline Painter (Midlothian)		Miss Pearce, 5 and 4			
102	Miss E. Pearce (Flossmoor)	Miss Pearce, 7 and 6				
101	Mrs. S. Kunstadter (Idlewild)					Mrs. C.H. Vanderbeck, 3 and 2
101	Miss F. Hadfield (Idlewild)	Miss Edwards, 3 and 2				
99	Miss M. Edwards (Midlothian)		Miss Edwards, 2 up			
102	Miss Elaine V. Rosenthal (Ravisloe)	Miss Rosenthal, 7 and 6				
97	Miss E. Chatfield (Kishwankee)			Miss Stirling, 5 and 4		
101	Mrs. H.G. Hammond (Highland)	Miss Stirling, 1 up, 19 hls.				
91	Miss Alexa Stirling (Atlanta)		Miss Stirling, 6 and 5			
97	Miss Grace Semple (St. Louis)	Miss Kaiser, 2 and 1				
96	Miss L. Kaiser (Flossmoor)				Mrs. Vanderbeck, 1 up, 22 hls.	
96	Miss E. Chandler (Huntingdon Valley)	Mrs. Vanderbeck, 7 and 6				
85	*Mrs. C.H. Vanderbeck (Philadelphia Cricket)		Mrs. Vanderbeck, 7 and 6			
102	Miss J. Jones (Sioux City)	Miss Coldham, 1 up				
98	Miss W. Coldham (Inverness)			Mrs. Vanderbeck, 3 and 1		
98	Mrs. E.L. Beifield (Ravisloe)	Mrs. Beifield, 5 and 4				
104	Miss I. Bridge (Westmoreland)		Mrs. Beifield, 4 and 3			
104	Mrs. M. Dodd (Cincinnati)	Miss Allen, 1 up				
101	Miss Elizabeth Allen (Rock Island)					

*Medalist.

1916
TWENTY-SECOND WOMEN'S AMATEUR CHAMPIONSHIP

Held at the Belmont Springs Country Club, Waverley, Mass., October 2-7. 63 Entries, 58 Starters.

Qualifying Score	1st Round	2nd Round	3rd Round	Semi-Finals	Final
99	Mrs. G.W. Roope (Brae Burn)	Miss Kaiser, 2 up	Miss Kaiser, 4 and 2	Mrs. Hucknall, 1 up	Miss Caverly, 7 and 6
96	Miss L. Kaiser (Flossmoor)				
99	Miss E.W. Allen (Oakley)	Mrs. Forrest, 2 up			
96	Mrs. T.E. Forrest (Knollwood)				
98	Miss L.G. Witherbee (Port Henry)	Miss Campbell, 3 and 2	Mrs. Hucknall, 1 up, 20 hls.		
97	Miss E.N. Campbell (Philadelphia Cricket)				
86	*Mrs. Dorothy C. Hurd (Pittsburgh)	Mrs. Hucknall, 2 up			
99	Mrs. T. Hucknall (Forest Hill)				
95	Miss F.D. McCarthy (Woodland)	Miss Caverly, 7 and 5	Miss Caverly, 1 up, 19 hls.	Miss Caverly, 3 and 1	
93	Miss Mildred Caverly (Philadelphia Cricket)				
97	Mrs. F.C. Letts (Cincinnati)	Mrs. Letts, 5 and 3			
95	Mrs. C.F. Rowley (Oakley)				
91	Mrs. Caleb F. Fox (Huntingdon Valley)	Mrs. Fox, 3 and 2	Mrs. Fox, 5 and 4		
99	Mrs. G.M. Martin (Stoke Poges)				
99	Miss A. Sargent (Brookline)	Miss Sargent, 5 and 4			
101	Miss E.B. Chandler (Huntingdon Valley)				
96	Mrs. S.A. Herzog (Fairview)	Mrs. Auchincloss, 5 and 3	Mrs. Auchincloss, 4 and 2	Mrs. Auchincloss, 2 and 1	Miss Stirling, 2 up
98	Mrs. C.C. Auchincloss (Piping Rock)				
97	Miss Mildred Smith (Evanston)	Miss Smith, 4 and 2			
102	Mrs. H.A. Knox (Oxford)				
93	Mrs. L.C. Stockton (Somerville)	Mrs. Stockton, 2 and 1	Mrs. Gavin, 4 and 2		
94	Miss Marion Hollins (Westbrook)				
90	Miss Georgianna Bishop (Brooklawn)	Mrs. Gavin, 4 and 3			
90	Mrs. W.A. Gavin (Taconic)				
92	Miss Elaine V. Rosenthal (Ravisloe)	Miss Rosenthal, 4 and 3	Miss Rosenthal, 4 and 2	Miss Stirling, 2 and 1	
99	Miss Fanny C. Osgood (Brookline)				
95	Mrs. E.W. Daly (Oakley)	Miss Chesbrough, 5 and 4			
95	Miss E. Chesbrough (Burlington)				
92	Miss Alexa Stirling (Atlanta)	Miss Stirling, 2 and 1	Miss Stirling, 5 and 4		
93	Mrs. E.H. Baker, Jr. (Bellmont Sp.)				
96	Mrs. G.H. Stetson (Huntingdon Valley)	Mrs. Stetson, 6 and 5			
90	Mrs. J.H. Lapham (San Antonio)				

Champion: Miss Alexa Stirling, 2 and 1

*Medalist.

1919
TWENTY-THIRD WOMEN'S AMATEUR CHAMPIONSHIP

Held at Shawnee Country Club, Shawnee-on-Delaware, Pa., September 29-October 4. 76 Entries.

Qualifying Score	1st Round	2nd Round	3rd Round	Semi-Finals	Final	
100	Miss M.A. Conroy (Fox Hills)	Miss Gordon, 7 and 6				
90	Miss Elizabeth Gordon (Metacomet)		Mrs. Stetson, 3 and 2			
97	Mrs. G.H. Stetson (Huntingdon Valley)	Mrs. Stetson, 1 up				
91	Miss Elaine V. Rosenthal (Ravisloe)			Miss Stirling, 3 and 2		
93	Mrs. Caleb F. Fox (Huntingdon Valley)	Miss Stirling, 3 and 1				
87	*Miss Alexa Stirling (Atlanta)		Miss Stirling, 3 and 1			
92	Miss Marion Hollins (Westbrook)	Miss Hollins, 4 and 2				
94	Miss Beatrice Lounsbery (Bedford)				Miss Stirling, 1 up	
96	Mrs. C.H. Vanderbeck (Philadelphia C.C.)	Mrs. Vanderbeck, 5 and 4				
97	Mrs. Thurston Wright (Allegheny)		Mrs. Vanderbeck, 3 and 2			
93	Miss Fanny C. Osgood (Brookline)	Mrs. Letts, 1 up				
92	Mrs. F.C. Letts, Jr. (Indian Hill)			Mrs. Vanderbeck, 1 up		
100	Mrs. Ralph Hammer (Flushing)	Mrs. Price, 5 and 4				
100	Mrs. J. Raymond Price (Shawnee)		Mrs. Barlow, 2 and 1			
89	Mrs. R.H. Barlow (Merion G.C.)	Mrs. Barlow, 5 and 4				
95	Mrs. H.G. Smith (North Hills)					Miss Alexa Stirling, 6 and 5
100	Miss Elizabeth A. Hardin (Baltusrol)	Miss Caverly, 4 and 2				
92	Miss Mildred Caverly (Phila. C.C.)		Mrs. Gavin, 1 up			
90	Miss Edith Cummings (Onwentsia)	Mrs. Gavin, 5 and 4				
87	*Mrs. W.A. Gavin (South Shore)			Mrs. Gavin, 6 and 5		
99	Mrs. A.K. Billstein (Bala)	Mrs. Byfield, 1 up				
99	Mrs. E.L. Beifield (Ravisloe)		Mrs. Byfield, 8 and 6			
95	Mrs. Katherine Harley Jackson (Onwentsia)	Mrs. Jackson, 4 and 2				
98	Miss Rosamond Sherwood (St. George's)				Mrs. Gavin, 3 and 2	
97	Miss Irene Peacock (Thousand Is.)	Miss Peacock, 2 and 1				
94	Mrs. Thomas Hucknall (Forest Hills)		Miss Peacock, 2 and 1			
101	Mrs. Stephen P. Nash (Baltusrol)	Mrs. Feitner, 8 and 6				
92	Mrs. Quentin Feitner (South Shore)			Miss Peacock, 1 up, 19 hls.		
96	Mrs. Stuart Pritchard (Midlothian)	Miss Collett, 2 and 1				
93	Miss Glenna Collett (Metacomet)		Mrs. Du Bois, 2 and 1			
98	Mrs. F.E. Du Bois (Raritan Valley)	Mrs. Du Bois, 2 up				
95	Miss Sara Fownes (Shawnee)					

*Co-Medalists.

1920
TWENTY-FOURTH WOMEN'S AMATEUR CHAMPIONSHIP

Held at Mayfield Country Club, Cleveland, Ohio, October 4-9. 114 Entries.

Qualifying Score	1st Round	2nd Round	3rd Round	Semi-Finals	Final Round (36 Holes)	
97	Mrs. J.N. Turnbull (Philadelphia)	Miss Fenn, 5 and 4				
88	Miss Bessie Fenn (Portland)		Mrs. Byfield, 3 and 1			
97	Mrs. E.T. Harwood (Chicago)	Mrs. Byfield, 5 and 4				
89	Mrs. E.L. Biefield (Ravisloe)			Mrs. Vanderbeck, 3 and 2		
97	Miss Dorothy Klotz (Chicago)	Miss Klotz, 3 and 1				
90	Mrs. A.K. Billstein (Bala)		Mrs. Vanderbeck, 5 and 4			
96	Miss Darien Kavanagh (Los Angeles)	Mrs. Vanderbeck, 4 and 3				
87	Mrs. C.H. Vanderbeck (Phila. C.C.)				Miss Stirling, 2 and 1	
92	Mrs. Thurston Wright (Allegheny)	Miss Cummings, 3 and 2				
93	Miss Edith Cummings (Onwentsia)		Miss Cummings, 3 and 2			
90	Mrs. W.A. Gavin (Belleclaire)	Mrs. Gavin, 3 and 2				
91	Mrs. Katherine Harley Jackson (Onwentsia)			Miss Stirling, 3 and 2		
94	Miss Glenna Collett (Metacomet)	Miss Rosenthal, 2 and 1				
92	Miss Elaine V. Rosenthal (Ravisloe)		Miss Stirling, 2 and 1			
85	Miss Alexa Stirling (Atlanta)	Miss Stirling, 6 and 4				
95	Miss Miriam Burns (Millburn)					Miss Alexa Stirling, 5 and 4
90	Mrs. Dorothy C. Hurd (Pittsburgh)	Mrs. Hurd, 1 up, 20 hls.				
93	Miss Sara Fownes (Shawnee)		Mrs. Hurd, 3 and 2			
93	Miss Mildred Caverly (Philadelphia C.C.)	Miss Caverly, 6 and 4				
96	Miss Frances Hadfield (Milwaukee)			Mrs. Hurd, 1 up		
97	Mrs. Eugene K. Hayes (Cleveland)	Mrs. Letts, 7 and 6				
93	Mrs. F.C. Letts, Jr. (Indian Hill)		Miss Hollins, 1 up, 20 hls.			
90	Mrs. Harold Foreman (Chicago)	Miss Hollins, 5 and 3				
82	*Miss Marion Hollins (Westbrook)				Mrs. Hurd, 2 up	
91	Mrs. Quentin Feitner (South Shore)	Mrs. Feitner, 5 and 4				
98	Mrs. H.D. Sterrett (Kansas City)		Mrs. Feitner, 7 and 5			
97	Mrs. J.M. Hodges (Memphis)	Mrs. Barlow, 3 and 1				
86	Mrs. R.H. Barlow (Merion C.C.)			Mrs. Gaut, 1 up		
89	Mrs. David C. Gaut (Memphis)	Mrs. Gaut, 2 and 1				
94	Mrs. E.H. Law (California)		Mrs. Gaut, 4 and 3			
96	Mrs. Caleb F. Fox (Huntingdon Valley)	Mrs. Fox, 7 and 5				
97	Mrs. E.M. Kunstadler (Chicago)					

*Medalist.

1921
TWENTY-FIFTH WOMEN'S AMATEUR CHAMPIONSHIP

Held at Hollywood Golf Club, Deal, N.J., October 3-8. 181 Entries, 164 Starters.

Qualifying Score	1st Round	2nd Round	3rd Round	Semi-Finals	Final Round	
85	*Miss Glenna Collett (Rhode Island C.C.)	Miss E. Leitch, 3 and 2				
95	Miss Edith Leitch (England)		Miss E. Leitch, 4 and 3			
91	Miss Bessie Fenn (Portland, Me.)	Miss Caverly, 1 up, 19 hls.				
97	Miss Mildred Caverly (Philadelphia Cricket)			Miss Rosenthal, 1 up, 19 hls.		
88	Miss Elaine V. Rosenthal (Ravisloe)	Miss Rosenthal, 3 and 2				
97	Mrs. A.S. Rossin (Hollywood)		Miss Rosenthal, 2 and 1			
94	Mrs. Alex. Smith (North Hills C.C.)	Miss Klotz, 3 and 1				
98	Miss Dorothy Klotz (Indian Hill)				Miss Hollins, 1 up, 19 hls.	
87	Miss Cecil Leitch (England)	Miss C. Leitch, 8 and 7				
96	Mrs. R.H. Hammer (Pomonok C.C.)		Mrs. Letts, 1 up			
92	Mrs. F.C. Letts, Jr. (Onwentsia)	Mrs. Letts, 5 and 4				
98	Mrs. H. Blumenthal (Fairview C.C.)			Miss Hollins, 4 and 2		
89	Miss Marion Hollins (Westbrook)	Miss Hollins, 9 and 7				
97	Mrs. M.L.R. Spaulding (Buffalo C.C.)		Miss Hollins, 4 and 2			
95	Mrs. David C. Gaut (Memphis)	Mrs. Gaut, 6 and 5				
99	Mrs. E.W. Daley (Brae Burn)					Miss Marion Hollins, 5 and 4
85	*Mrs. Latham Hall (England)	Mrs. Hall, 1 up, 20 hls.				
96	Mrs. W.A. Gavin (Belleclaire)		Mrs. Hall, 5 and 3			
92	Mrs. Melvin Jones (Olympia Fields)	Mrs. Jones, 3 and 2				
97	Miss Ernestine Pearce (Skokie)			Miss Stirling, 1 up		
89	Miss Alexa Stirling (Atlanta)	Miss Stirling, 7 and 5				
97	Miss Harrietta Shepherd (Hartford)		Miss Stirling, 5 and 4			
94	Mrs. Caleb F. Fox (Huntingdon Valley)	Mrs. Fox, 5 and 3				
99	Mrs. L.A. Wimpfheimer (Hollywood)				Miss Stirling, 1 up	
88	Mrs. T. Hucknall (Forest Hill G.C.)	Miss Bishop, 4 and 3				
96	Miss Georgianna Bishop (Brooklawn)		Miss Fownes, 2 up			
94	Miss Sara Fownes (Oakmont)	Miss Fownes, 2 and 1				
98	Mrs. L.W. Mida (Butterfield C.C.)			Mrs. Vanderbeck, 6 and 5		
90	Mrs. C.H. Vanderbeck (Philadelphia Cricket)	Mrs. Vanderbeck, 5 and 4				
97	Mrs. L.J. Grumbach (Hollywood)		Mrs. Vanderbeck, 7 and 6			
95	Miss L.H. Fordyce (Youngstown)	Miss Fordyce, 1 up				
99	Mrs. Alexander Printz (Oakwood C.)					

*Medalist playoff: Miss Collett, 92; Mrs. Hall, 93.

1922
TWENTY-SIXTH WOMEN'S AMATEUR CHAMPIONSHIP

Held at The Greenbrier Golf Club, White Sulphur Springs, West Va., September 25-30. 170 Entries, 134 Starters.

Qualifying Score	1st Round	2nd Round	3rd Round	Semi-Finals	Final Round (36 Holes)	
81	*Miss Glenna Collett (Rhode Island)	Miss Collett, 6 and 5	Miss Collett, 5 and 3	Miss Collett, 3 and 2	Miss Collett, 2 up	Miss Glenna Collett, 5 and 4
89	Mrs. H.D. Sterrett (Hutchinson)					
87	Miss E.A. Hardin (Baltusrol)	Miss Hardin, 6 and 5				
92	Miss R. Sherwood (St. George's)					
85	Mrs. Norman K. Toerge (Nassau)	Mrs. Toerge, 2 and 1	Mrs. Letts, 2 and 1			
91	Mrs. Joseph Bydolek (East Aurora)					
89	Mrs. E.C. Letts, Jr. (Onwentsia)	Mrs. Letts, 5 and 3				
93	Mrs. E.H. Fitler (Merion)					
85	Miss Louise Fordyce (Youngstown)	Miss Cummings, 3 and 2	Miss Cummings, 1 up	Miss Cummings, 5 and 4		
90	Miss Edith Cummings (Onwentsia)					
88	Mrs. David C. Gaut (Memphis)	Mrs. Gaut, 3 and 2				
93	Mrs. C.C. Russell (Milwaukee)					
86	Mrs. Norman P. Rood (Wilmington)	Mrs. Rood, 7 and 5	Mrs. Barlow, 1 up			
92	Miss Louise Elkins (Oakmont)					
89	Mrs. R.H. Barlow (Merion)	Mrs. Barlow, 6 and 4				
94	Miss Kathleen Gorman (Parkersburg)					
83	Miss Marion Hollins (Westbrook)	Mrs. Feitner, 7 and 6	Mrs. Feitner, 3 and 2	Mrs. Jackson, 5 and 4	Mrs. Gavin, 4 and 2	
89	Mrs. Quentin P. Feitner (South Shore)					
88	Mrs. Dorothy C. Hurd (Westmoreland)	Mrs. Hurd, 3 and 1				
92	Miss Audrey Faust (St. Louis)					
86	Mrs. Katherine Harley Jackson (Greenwich)	Mrs. Jackson, 4 and 3	Mrs. Jackson, 2 and 1			
91	Miss Bessie Fenn (Portland)					
89	Miss F. Halloran (Salt Lake City)	Mrs. Heckscher, 1 up				
93	Mrs. G.M. Heckscher (Piping Rock)					
85	Miss Alexa Stirling (Atlanta)	Miss Stirling, 6 and 4	Miss Stirling, 7 and 6	Mrs. Gavin, 1 up		
91	Miss E.M. Gordon (Metacomet)					
89	Mrs. Caleb F. Fox (Huntingdon Valley)	Mrs. Alexander, 2 and 1				
93	Mrs. Clifton G. Alexander (Exmoor)					
87	Mrs. William A. Gavin (England)	Mrs. Gavin, 1 up, 19 hls.	Mrs. Gavin, 7 and 6			
92	Miss M. Cameron (Annandale)					
89	Miss Frances Hadfield (Blue Mound)	Miss Hadfield, 4 and 2				
94	Miss Sara Fownes (Oakmont)					

*Medalist.

1923
TWENTY-SEVENTH WOMEN'S AMATEUR CHAMPIONSHIP

Held at Westchester-Biltmore Country Club, Rye, N.Y., October 1-6. 196 Entries, 166 Starters.

Qualifying Score	1st Round	2nd Round	3rd Round	Semi-Finals	Final Round (36 Holes)	
84	*Miss Alexa Stirling (Atlanta)	Miss Stirling, 5 and 4	Miss Stirling, 1 up	Miss Stirling, 7 and 5	Miss Stirling, 2 up	Miss Edith Cummings, 3 and 2
93	Miss Marjorie Annable (Montreal)					
95	Miss Bernice Wall (Oshkosh)	Miss Burns, 1 up				
91	Miss Miriam Burns (Milburn, Kans.)					
89	Mrs. R.H. Barlow (Merion)	Mrs. Barlow, 5 and 4	Mrs. Jones, 1 up			
94	Miss Marie Jenney (North Hempstead)					
92	Mrs. Melvin Jones (Olympia Fields)	Mrs. Jones, 2 and 1				
95	Miss Kathleen Gorman (Parkersburg)					
90	Mrs. H.C. Phipps (Piping Rock)	Miss Bishop, 1 up	Mrs. Goss, 6 and 5	Mrs. Goss, 1 up		
95	Miss Georgianna Bishop (Brooklawn)					
92	Mrs. E.A.H. Goss (Baltusrol)	Mrs. Goss, 5 and 4				
95	Miss V. Holzderber (West.-Biltmore)					
88	Mrs. J.L. Anderson (Cherry Valley)	Mrs. Toerge, 1,up	Mrs. Hurd, 8 and 7			
94	Mrs. Norman K. Toerge (Nassau)					
91	Miss Bessie Fenn (Portland, Me.)	Mrs. Hurd, 1 up, 19 hls.				
95	Mrs. Dorothy C. Hurd (Merion)					
87	Mrs. C.H. Vanderbeck (Philadelphia C.C.)	Mrs. Vanderbeck, 1 up	Mrs. Vanderbeck, 3 and 2	Mrs. Vanderbeck, 2 and 1	Miss Cummings, 1 up, 20 hls.	
93	Miss Maureen Orcutt (White Beeches)					
91	Miss R. Sherwood (St. George's)	Mrs. Renwick, 1 up				
95	Mrs. Jack Renwick (Bedford)					
89	Miss Glenna Collett (Rhode Island)	Miss Collett, 4 and 3	Miss Collett, 8 and 7			
94	Mrs. F.C. Letts (Onwentsia)					
92	Miss Dorothy Higbie (Midlothian)	Miss Higbie, 3 and 2				
95	Mrs. Lee W. Mida (Butterfield)					
91	Miss Edith Leitch (England)	Miss Leitch, 5 and 4	Miss Leitch, 7 and 5	Miss Cummings, 6 and 4		
95	Mrs. J.J. Thomson (Siwanoy)					
93	Miss F. Halloran (Salt Lake City)	Mrs. Blumenthal, 2 and 1				
95	Mrs. H. Blumenthal (Fairview, N.Y.)					
89	Miss Edith Cummings (Onwentsia)	Miss Cummings, 5 and 4	Miss Cummings, 7 and 6			
94	Mrs. Quentin F. Feitner (South Shore, N.Y.)					
91	Miss Louise Fordyce (Youngstown)	Miss Faust, 1 up				
94	Miss Audrey Faust (St. Louis)					

*Medalist.

1924
TWENTY-EIGHTH WOMEN'S AMATEUR CHAMPIONSHIP

Held at the Rhode Island Country Club, Nyatt, R.I., September 1-6. 98 Entries, 89 Starters.

Qualifying Score	1st Round	2nd Round	3rd Round	Semi-Finals	Final Round (36 Holes)	
79	***Miss Glenna Collett (Rhode Island)**	Miss Collett, 4 and 3	Miss Collett, 8 and 6	Miss Collett, 3 and 1	Miss Browne, 1 up, 19 hls.	Mrs. Dorothy Campbell Hurd, 7 and 6
92	Miss Ruth Batchelder (Weston)					
90	Mrs. F.C. Letts (Onwentsia)	Mrs. Renwick, by default				
96	Mrs. Jack Renwick (Mount Kisco)					
84	Miss Virginia Wilson (Onwentsia)	Miss Wilson, 4 and 3	Mrs. Feitner, 3 and 2			
94	Mrs. J. Bernd Rose (Allegheny)					
92	**Mrs. Quentin F. Feitner (South Shore, N.Y.)**	Mrs. Feitner, 3 and 2				
96	Mrs. Sidney R. Small (Detroit)					
81	Miss Louise Fordyce (Youngstown)	Miss Fordyce, 4 and 2	Miss Browne, 2 and 1	Miss Browne, 5 and 4		
91	Mrs. Isobel Harris (Wannamoisett)					
91	**Mrs. Katherine Harley Jackson (Greenwich)**	Miss Browne, 6 and 4				
96	Miss Mary K. Browne (Los Angeles)					
90	Miss Bernice Wall (Oshkosh)	Miss Wall, 3 and 2	Miss Wall, 1 up			
95	**Mrs. R.H. Barlow (Merion)**					
92	Mrs. H.R. Watson (Hoosick-Whisick)	Mrs. Watson, 4 and 3				
97	Miss Priscilla Maxwell (Hartford)					
80	Miss Marion Hollins (Westbrook)	Mrs. Hurd, 4 and 3	Mrs. Hurd, 6 and 4	Mrs. Hurd, 3 and 2	Mrs. Hurd, 2 and 1	
92	Mrs. Dorothy C. Hurd (Merion)					
91	Miss Maureen Orcutt (White Beeches)	Miss Orcutt, 2 up				
96	Miss Frances E. Stebbins (Brae Burn)					
85	Miss Edith Cummings (Onwentsia)	Miss Cummings, 6 and 5	Miss Burns, 1 up			
95	Mrs. E.H. Baker, Jr. (Oakley C.C.)					
92	Miss Miriam Burns (Milburn, Kans.)	Miss Burns, 3 and 1				
97	Miss Fritzi Stifel (Wheeling)					
83	**Mrs. C.H. Vanderbeck (Philadelphia C.C.)**	Mrs. Vanderbeck, 2 and 1	Mrs. Vanderbeck, 9 and 7	Mrs. Vanderbeck, 3 and 2		
94	Mrs. J.L. Anderson (Cherry Valley)					
91	Miss Mary T. Allderdice (Oakmont)	Mrs. Harwood, 4 and 3				
96	Mrs. E.E. Harwood (Olympia Fields)					
90	Miss Audrey Faust (St. Louis)	Miss Faust, 8 and 7	Miss Faust, 3 and 2			
95	Mrs. Edward F. Shay (Rhode Island)					
92	**Miss Elizabeth Gordon (Metacomet)**	Miss Gordon, 3 and 2				
97	**Miss Margaret Curtis (Essex County)**					

*Medalist.

1925
TWENTY-NINTH WOMEN'S AMATEUR CHAMPIONSHIP

Held at the St. Louis Country Club, Clayton, Mo., September 28-October 4. 85 Entries, 80 Starters.

Qualifying Score	1st Round	2nd Round	3rd Round	Semi-Finals	Final Round (36 Holes)
77	*Mrs. Alexa Stirling Fraser (Royal Ottawa)	Mrs. Fraser, 1 up	Mrs. Fraser, 2 and 1	Mrs. Fraser, 3 and 2	Mrs. Fraser, 1 up, 19 hls.
88	Miss Dorothy Klotz (Indian Hill)				
85	Miss Bernice Wall (Oshkosh)	Miss Wall, 3 and 1			
90	Mrs. Carl Liebold (Birmingham, Ala.)				
82	Miss Mary K. Browne (Brentwood)	Miss Browne, 5 and 4	Miss Browne, 1 up		
89	Mrs. H.D. Sterrett (Hutchinson)				
87	Mrs. Miriam B. Horn, Jr. (Westmoreland)	Mrs. Horn, 1 up			
92	Miss Virginia Van Wie (Beverly, Ill.)				
80	Mrs. Dorothy C. Hurd (Merion)	Mrs. Hurd, 7 and 6	Mrs. Letts, 4 and 2	Miss Fordyce, 7 and 5	
88	Mrs. Jay S. Cassriel (Aurora)				
87	Mrs. F.C. Letts (Onwentsia)	Mrs. Letts, 4 and 3			
91	Mrs. F.J. Mulqueen (Toronto, Can.)				
84	Miss Louise Fordyce (Youngstown)	Miss Fordyce, 6 and 4	Miss Fordyce, 6 and 5		
89	Miss Edith Quier (Berkshire, Pa.)				
87	Miss Helen Tillotson (Inverness)	Miss Tillotson, 2 and 1			
93	Mrs. H.A. Martelle (Hartford, Conn.)				
78	Miss Glenna Collett (Rhode Island)	Miss Collett, 7 and 5	Miss Collett, 1 up	Miss Collett, 3 and 2	Miss Collett, 1 up
88	Mrs. Caleb F. Fox (Huntingdon Valley)				
86	Miss Ada Mackenzie (Toronto, Can.)	Miss Mackenzie, 3 and 2			
91	Mrs. Lee W. Mida (Butterfield)				
82	Mrs. M.B. Wallace, Jr. (St. Louis)	Miss Wilson, 1 up, 20 hls.	Miss Stifel, 1 up		
89	Miss Virginia Wilson (Onwentsia)				
87	Mrs. Curtis Sohl (Scioto)	Miss Stifel, 2 and 1			
92	Miss Fritzi Stifel (Wheeling, W. Va.)				
80	Miss Edith Cummings (Onwentsia)	Miss Cummings, 6 and 5	Miss Cummings, 2 and 1	Miss Cummings, 4 and 3	
88	Mrs. J.W. Douglass (Barrington Hills)				
87	Mrs. David C. Gaut (Memphis)	Mrs. Gaut, 1 up, 19 hls.			
92	Mrs. Stewart Hanley (Lochmoor)				
85	Mrs. Harley G. Higbie (C.C., Detroit)	Miss Payson, 2 and 1	Mrs. Hill, 3 and 2		
90	Miss Helen Payson (Portland, Me.)				
87	Mrs. O.S. Hill (Meadow Lake, Kans.)	Mrs. Hill, 6 and 5			
93	Mrs. John Arends (Wilmette, Ill.)				

Champion: Miss Glenna Collett, 9 and 8

*Medalist.

(Final-round postponed from October 3rd to October 4th because of heavy rain.)

1926
THIRTIETH WOMEN'S AMATEUR CHAMPIONSHIP

Held at the Merion Cricket Club, Ardmore, Pa., September 27-October 2. 134 Entries, 127 Starters.

Qualifying Score	1st Round	2nd Round	3rd Round	Semi-Finals	Final Round (36 Holes)	
81	*Miss Glenna Collett (Rhode Island)	Miss Collett, 2 up				
90	Mrs. O.S. Hill (Meadow Lake, Kans.)		Miss Collett, 8 and 6			
86	Mrs. Norman P. Rood (Wilmington)	Mrs. Rood, 1 up, 20 hls.				
92	Mrs. F.C. Letts, Jr. (Onwentsia)			Miss Wilson, 2 and 1		
85	Miss Virginia Wilson (Onwentsia)	Miss Wilson, 2 and 1				
91	Mrs. J.W. Taylor (Evanston)		Miss Wilson, 4 and 3			
90	Miss Rosalie Knapp (Westbrook)	Miss Knapp, 1 up			Mrs. Stetson, 1 up, 19 hls.	
92	Mrs. J.S. Disston, Jr. (Philadelphia Cricket)					
85	Mrs. G. Henry Stetson (Huntingdon Valley)	Mrs. Stetson, 3 and 1				
91	Miss Ada Mackenzie (Toronto, Canada)		Mrs. Stetson, 6 and 5			
90	Miss Ruth Batchelder (Brae Burn)	Miss Batchelder, 4 and 3				
93	Mrs. Raymond Slotter (Philmont)			Mrs. Stetson, 6 and 5		
89	Miss Bernice Wall (Oshkosh)	Miss Wall, 6 and 5				
92	Mrs. Katherine Harley Jackson (Greenwich)		Miss Cummings, 1 up			
84	Miss Edith Cummings (Onwentsia)	Miss Cummings, 2 and 1				
90	Miss Helen Meehan (Cedarbrook)					Mrs. G. Henry Stetson, 3 and 1
82	Mrs. Wright D. Goss, Jr. (Baltusrol)	Mrs. Goss, 4 and 3				
90	Mrs. E.H. Baker, Jr. (Oakley)		Mrs. Goss, 5 and 4			
86	Mrs. E.E. Harwood (Olympia Fields)	Princess Lobkowicz, 3 and 1				
92	Princess Lobkowicz (Misquamicut)			Mrs. Goss, 2 up		
85	Mrs. Norman K. Toerge (Nassau)	Mrs. Toerge, 1 up				
91	Miss Virginia Van Wie (Beverly, Ill.)		Mrs. Toerge, 2 up			
90	Mrs. Dorothy C. Hurd (Merion)	Mrs. Cassriel, 2 and 1			Mrs. Goss, 3 and 2	
93	Mrs. J.S. Cassriel (Aurora)					
96	Mrs. Lee W. Mida (Butterfield)	Mrs. Mida, 4 and 3				
91	Miss Maureen Orcutt (White Beeches)		Mrs. Anderson, 4 and 3			
90	Mrs. J.L. Anderson (Cherry Valley)	Mrs. Anderson, 2 up				
93	Miss Jane Brooks (Rockland)			Mrs. Smith, 3 and 1		
89	Miss Helen Payson (Portland, Me.)	Miss Payson, 3 and 2				
92	Mrs. Charles E. Armstrong (Whitemarsh)		Mrs. Smith, 2 and 1			
84	Mrs. Courtland Smith (Glen Ridge)	Mrs. Smith, 1 up				
91	Mrs. Stewart Hanley (Lochmoor)					

*Medalist.

1927
THIRTY-FIRST WOMEN'S AMATEUR CHAMPIONSHIP

Held at the Cherry Valley Club, Garden City, New York, September 19-24. 150 Entries, 139 Starters.

Qualifying Score	1st Round	2nd Round	3rd Round	Semi-Finals	Final Round (36 Holes)	
77	*Miss Ada Mackenzie (Canada)	Miss Mackenzie,				
87	Mrs. E.H. Fitler (Merion)	6 and 5	Miss MacKenzie,			
85	Mrs. Gregory Lifur (California C.C.)	Miss Payson,	4 and 2			
90	Miss Helen Payson (Portland, Me.)	4 and 3		Miss MacKenzie,		
83	Miss Virginia Van Wie (Beverly C.C., Ill.)	Miss Van Wie,		1 up		
88	Mrs. Benj. F. Briggs (Pelham)	3 and 1	Miss Van Wie,			
85	Miss Edith Quier (Berkshire C.C., Pa.)	Miss Quier,	2 up		Miss Orcutt, 2 and 1	
91	Mrs. J.D. Woodfin (Brae Burn)	1 up, 20 hls.				
78	Miss Maureen Orcutt (White Beeches)	Miss Orcutt,				
88	Mrs. E.P. Harwood (Olympia Fields)	8 and 6	Miss Orcutt,			
85	Miss Peggy Wattles (Wanakah)	Miss Knapp,	5 and 4			
90	Miss Rosalie Knapp (Women's Natl.)	1 up		Miss Orcutt,		
84	Miss Marie Jenney (Hudson River)	Miss Jenney,		1 up, 20 hls.		
89	Miss Virginia Wilson (Onwentsia)	1 up	Miss Jenney,			Mrs. Miriam Burns Horn, Jr., 5 and 4
86	Miss Eileen Pattison (Bermuda)	Miss Brooks,	6 and 5			
91	Miss Jane Brooks (Englewood)	2 and 1				
78	**Mrs. Miriam B. Horn, Jr. (Milburn, Kans. C.)**	Mrs. Horn,				
87	Miss D.B. Page (Maple Bluff, Wis.)	1 up	Mrs. Horn,			
85	Miss Beatrice Gottlieb (Wolf Hollow)	Miss Wall,	5 and 4			
90	Miss Bernice Wall (Oshkosh)	5 and 3		Mrs. Horn,		
83	Mrs. Leona Pressler (San Gabriel, Calif.)	Mrs. Pressler,		2 and 1		
89	Mrs. Dorothy C. Hurd (Merion)	1 up	Mrs. Pressler,			
86	Miss Martha Kinsey (Cincinnati)	Mrs. Smith,	1 up		Mrs. Horn, 1 up	
91	Mrs. Courtland Smith (Glen Ridge)	3 and 2				
82	**Mrs. Alexa Stirling Fraser (Canada)**	Mrs. Fraser,				
88	**Mrs. Katherine Harley Jackson (Round Hill)**	6 and 5	Mrs. Fraser,			
85	Miss Glenna Collett (Greenwich)	Miss Collett,	2 and 1			
90	Mrs. J.L. Anderson (Cherry Valley)	1 up		Mrs. Fraser,		
85	Mrs. O.S. Hill (Meadow Lake, Kans.)	Mrs. Higbie,		3 and 2		
90	Mrs. Harley G. Higbie (C.C., Detroit)	1 up, 22 hls.	Mlle Chaume,			
87	Mlle. S. de la Chaume (France)	Mlle. Chaume,	1 up			
91	Mrs. Stewart Hanley (Lochmoor)	4 and 2				

*Medalist.

1928
THIRTY-SECOND WOMEN'S AMATEUR CHAMPIONSHIP

Held at the Virginia Hot Springs Golf and Tennis Club, Hot Springs, Va., **September 24-29. 123 Entries, 110 Starters.**

Qualifying Score	1st Round	2nd Round	3rd Round	Semi-Finals	Final Round (36 Holes)	
80	*Miss Maureen Orcutt (White Beeches)	Miss Orcutt, 7 and 6				
88	Mrs. Austin Pardue (Indian Hill)		Miss Orcutt, 5 and 3			
85	Miss Edith Cummings (Onwentsia)	Mrs. Higbie, 1 up, 19 hls.				
90	Mrs. Harley G. Higbie (C.C., Detroit)			Mrs. Hurd, 2 up		
84	Mrs. Dorothy C. Hurd (Merion)	Mrs. Hurd, 2 up				
89	Miss Helen Payson (Portland, Me.)		Mrs. Hurd, 2 and 1			
87	Mrs. Leona Pressler (San Gabriel, Calif.)	Mrs. Pressler, 2 and 1			Miss Van Wie, 2 up	
91	Mrs. E.H. Baker, Jr. (Oakley)					
84	Miss Virginia Van Wie (Beverly C.C., Ill.)	Miss Van Wie, 7 and 5				
90	Mrs. Stewart Hanley (Lochmoor)		Miss Van Wie, 1 up, 19 hls.			
88	Mrs. O.S. Hill (Meadow Lake, Kans.)	Miss Quier, 3 and 1				
91	Miss Edith Quier (Berkshire, Pa.)			Miss Van Wie, 1 up		
86	Miss Marion Hollins (Women's Natl.)	Miss Hollins, 7 and 6				
90	Miss Betty Guthrie (Westhampton)		Miss Hollins, 4 and 2			
83	Mrs. Lee W. Mida (Butterfield)	Miss Knapp, 2 and 1				
89	Miss Rosalie Knapp (Women's Natl.)					Miss Glenna Collett, 13 and 12
82	Miss Kathleen Wright (Flintridge)	Miss Hicks, 1 up				
89	Miss Helen Hicks (Salisbury)		Miss Virtue, 1 up, 19 hls.			
86	Miss Dora W. Virtue (Canada)	Miss Virtue, 3 and 2				
90	Mrs. L.C. Nelson (Miami Valley)			Mrs. Stetson, 1 up, 20 hls.		
84	Mrs. George W. Tyson (Milburn, Kans.)	Miss Paget, 2 and 1				
90	Miss Helen Paget (Canada)		Mrs. Stetson, 3 and 2			
87	Miss Marion Turpie (Audubon, La.)	Mrs. Stetson, 3 and 2				
91	Mrs. G.H. Stetson (Huntingdon Valley)				Miss Collett, 4 and 3	
84	Miss Glenna Collett (Rhode Island)	Miss Collett, 5 and 3				
90	Miss Beatrice Gottlieb (Olinville)		Miss Collett, 8 and 7			
88	Mrs. J.S. Disston, Jr. (Philadelphia Cricket)	Mrs. Disston, 3 and 2				
91	Mrs. C. Kyrle Bellew (Rancho)			Miss Collett, 4 and 3		
87	Mrs. J.B. Rose (Allegheny)	Mrs. Lifur, 4 and 3				
90	Mrs. G.H. Lifur (California C.C.)		Miss Wilson, 3 and 2			
89	Miss D. Page (Maple Bluff, Wis.)	Miss Wilson, 1 up, 20 hls.				
84	Miss Virginia Wilson (Onwentsia)					

*Medalist.

1929
THIRTY-THIRD WOMEN'S AMATEUR CHAMPIONSHIP

Held at the Oakland Hills Country Club, Birmingham, Mich., September 30-October 5. 98 Entries, 94 Starters.

Qualifying Score	1st Round	2nd Round	3rd Round	Semi-Finals	Final Round (36 Holes)	
79	***Miss Helen Hicks (Salisbury)**	Miss Orcutt, 3 and 2				
84	Miss Maureen Orcutt (White Beeches)		Miss Collett, 7 and 5			
82	Miss Glenna Collett (Cypress Point)	Miss Collett, 6 and 5				
87	Mrs. W.A. Johnston (St. David's)			Miss Collett, 1 up, 19 hls.		
81	Miss Edith Quier (Berkshire)	Miss Quier, 3 and 2			Miss Collett, 3 and 2	
86	Mrs. John Arends (Kildeer)		Mrs. Higbie, 1 up			
83	Mrs. Harley G. Higbie (Detroit C.C.)	Mrs. Higbie, 2 and 1				
88	Miss Helen Payson (Portland, Me.)					
80	Miss Kathleen Wright (Flintridge)	Miss Wright, 3 and 2				
85	Miss Louise Fordyce (Youngstown)		Mrs. Hill, 5 and 4			
82	Mrs. O.S. Hill (Meadow Lake, Kans.)	Mrs. Hill, 6 and 5				Miss Glenna Collett, 4 and 3
87	Miss Rosamond Vahey (Belmont Spgs.)			Mrs. Hill, 2 up		
82	Mrs. Stewart Hanley (Oakland Hills)	Mrs. Hanley, 2 and 1				
87	Miss Marjorie Kirkham (Canada)		Mrs. Hanley, 4 and 2			
84	**Mrs. Lee W. Mida (Butterfield)**	Mrs. Mida, 4 and 3				
88	Miss Helen Meehan (Whitemarsh)					
79	***Miss Virginia Van Wie (Beverly)**	Miss Van Wie, 3 and 1				
85	Miss Peggy Wattles (Wanakah)		Mrs. Federman, 2 and 1			
82	Mrs. L.G. Federman (Fresh Meadow)	Mrs. Federman, 1 up, 24 hls.				
87	Mrs. H.B. Stetson (Huntingdon Valley)			Miss Wall, 1 up		
82	Mrs. L.C. Nelson (Miami Valley)	Mrs. Nelson, 2 up				
86	Mrs. Curtis Sohl (Scioto)		Miss Wall, 5 and 3			
83	Mrs. E.H. Baker, Jr. (Oakley)	Miss Wall, 5 and 3				
88	**Miss Bernice Wall (Oshkosh)**				Mrs. Pressler, 3 and 2	
81	**Mrs. Alexa Stirling Fraser (Canada)**	Miss Hunter, 2 up				
86	Miss Anjeanette Hunter (Stanton Hts.)		Mrs. Hurd, 9 and 8			
82	Mrs. Dorothy C. Hurd (Merion)	Mrs. Hurd, 4 and 3				
88	Miss Ada Mackenzie (Canada)			Mrs. Pressler, 3 and 1		
82	Mrs. Leona Pressler (San Gabriel)	Mrs. Pressler, 2 up				
87	Mrs. Gregg Lifur (Riviera)		Mrs. Pressler, 4 and 2			
84	Miss Marion Turpie (Audubon)	Miss Turpie, 3 and 1				
88	Mrs. Melvin Jones (Lincolnshire)					

*Medalists—no playoff.

1930
THIRTY-FOURTH WOMEN'S AMATEUR CHAMPIONSHIP

Held at the Los Angeles Country Club, Beverly Hills, California, October 13-18. 102 Entries, 94 Starters.

Qualifying Score	1st Round	2nd Round	3rd Round	Semi-Finals	Final Round (36 Holes)	
79	*Mrs. O.S. Hill (Meadow Lake, Mo.)	Mrs. Hill, 4 and 3				
87	Miss Bernice Wall (Oshkosh)		Mrs. Hill, 4 and 3			
84	Miss Edith Quier (Berkshire)	Mrs. Potter, 2 up				
90	Mrs. Brent Potter (San Jose, Calif.)			Mrs. Hill, 3 and 2		
89	Mrs. George M. Lewis (Los Angeles)	Miss Orcutt, 6 and 5			Miss Van Wie, 2 and 1	
81	Miss Maureen Orcutt (White Beeches)		Miss Orcutt, 2 and 1			
91	Mrs. Russell Fowles (Virginia, Calif.)	Mrs. Hurd, 6 and 4				
85	Mrs. Dorothy C. Hurd (Merion)					
81	Miss Virginia Van Wie (Beverly)	Miss Van Wie, 3 and 2				
88	Mrs. Mark Steel (San Gabriel)		Miss Van Wie, 3 and 2			
85	Miss Marion Hollins (Women's Natl.)	Miss Hollins, 3 and 2				
91	Mrs. John W. Taylor (Evanston, Ill.)			Miss Van Wie, 7 and 5		Miss Glenna Collett, 6 and 5
83	Mrs. Gregg Lifur (Riviera)	Mrs. Lifur, 7 and 6				
90	Miss Mary Saulsberry (Santa Ana)		Mrs. Green, 6 and 4			
86	Mrs. Roy Green (California C.C.)	Mrs. Green, 4 and 3				
91	Miss Angie Pankhurst (Crystal Spgs.)					
80	Miss Helen Hicks (Inwood)	Miss Hicks, 3 and 1				
87	Miss Lucille de Long (Coronado)		Miss Hicks, 8 and 7			
84	Mrs. R.S. Edwards (California C.C.)	Miss Lee, 1 up, 19 hls.				
90	Miss Barbara Lee (Claremont)			Miss Hicks, 2 and 1		
82	Mrs. Leona Pressler (San Gabriel)	Mrs. Pressler, 6 and 5				
90	Mrs. Milton Bernard (Sequoyah)		Mrs. Pressler, 5 and 4		Miss Collett, 5 and 3	
86	Miss Hermine Wocker (Crystal Spgs.)	Miss Wocker, 1 up, 19 hls.				
91	Mrs. C.J. Woerner (Lakeside, Calif.)					
81	Miss Glenna Collett (Greenwich)	Miss Collett, 6 and 4				
89	Mrs. Harry Grossman (Hillcrest, Calif.)		Miss Collett, 5 and 3			
85	Miss Helen Lawson (Wilshire)	Miss Lawson, 2 and 1				
91	Mrs. John Hollywood (Potrero)			Miss Collett, 3 and 1		
83	Mrs. Harley G. Higbie (Detroit C.C.)	Mrs. Higbie, 4 and 3				
90	Miss Beatrice Gottlieb (Los Angeles)		Miss Wattles, 3 and 2			
87	Miss Peggy Wattles (Wanakah)	Miss Wattles, 3 and 1				
92	Mrs. R.I. Raynor (Whitemarsh Valley)					

*Medalist.

1931
THIRTY-FIFTH WOMEN'S AMATEUR CHAMPIONSHIP

Held at The Country Club of Buffalo, Williamsville, N.Y., September 21-26. 90 Entries, 85 Starters.

Qualifying Score	1st Round	2nd Round	3rd Round	Semi-Finals	Final Round (36 Holes)	
82	*Miss Maureen Orcutt (White Beeches)	Miss Orcutt, 4 and 3				
92	Miss J. Broadwell (Longmeadow, Mass.)		Miss Orcutt, 5 and 4			
87	Mrs. Gregg Lifur (Riviera)	Miss Wall, 7 and 5				
89	Miss Bernice Wall (Oshkosh)			Miss Van Wie, 2 and 1		
85	Miss Virginia Van Wie (Beverly)	Miss Van Wie, 3 and 2				
90	Mrs. Marion Turpie Lake (Old C.C.)		Miss Van Wie, 5 and 4			
87	Miss Frances Williams (Lehigh, Pa.)	Miss Williams, 5 and 3			Mrs. Vare, 2 up	
90	Miss Betty Abernethy (Oakmont, Pa.)					
82	***Mrs. Glenna Collett Vare (Philadelphia C.C.)**	Mrs. Vare, 6 and 4				
91	**Miss Jean Armstrong (Indian Hill)**		Mrs. Vare, 4 and 3			
88	**Mrs. G.S. Eddis (Rosedale, Canada)**	Mrs. Eddis, 3 and 2				
88	Mrs. Arthur Harrison (Buffalo, C.C.)			Mrs. Vare, 5 and 4		
86	Mrs. Leon Solomon (Ridgeway, Tenn.)	Mrs. Federman, 6 and 4				Miss Helen Hicks, 2 and 1
90	Mrs. L.G. Federman (Glen Oaks, N.Y.)		Mrs. Federman, 2 and 1			
87	Mrs. Henri Prunaret, Jr. (Charles River)	Mrs. Corson, 4 and 3				
89	Mrs. H.P. Corson (Plymouth, Pa.)					
86	Miss Marion Hollins (Pasatiempo)	Miss Hollins, 3 and 2				
90	**Mrs. Roy Green (California C.C.)**		Miss Hicks, 1 up, 19 hls.			
87	Miss Helen Hicks (Lido)	Miss Hicks, 6 and 5				
90	Miss Mildred Hackl (Midlothian)			Miss Hicks, 4 and 3		
88	Miss M. Parker (Westchester Hills)	Mrs. Pressler, 1 up				
88	Mrs. Leona Pressler (San Gabriel)		Mrs. Pressler, 1 up, 21 hls.			
82	*Mrs. Harley G. Higbie (C.C. Detroit)	Miss Stifel, 1 up			Miss Hicks, 2 and 1	
91	Miss Fritzi Stifel (Wheeling)					
88	Miss Enid Wilson (England)	Miss Wilson, 3 and 1				
89	Miss Martha Brewer (Weston, Mass.)		Miss Wilson, 4 and 2			
85	**Mrs. L.C. Nelson (Miami Valley)**	Mrs. Nelson, 1 up				
90	**Miss Ada Mackenzie (Ladies G.C., Toronto)**			Miss Wilson, 4 and 3		
87	Miss Marjorie Kerr (England)	Miss Kerr, 1 up, 20 hls.				
90	Miss June Beebe (Olympia Fields)		Miss Kerr, 2 and 1			
82	*Mrs. O.S. Hill (Meadow Lake, Mo.)	Miss Brooks, 2 and 1				
91	Miss Jane Brooks (Rockland, N.Y.)					

*Medalists—No playoff—Prize to each.

1932
THIRTY-SIXTH WOMEN'S AMATEUR CHAMPIONSHIP

Held at the Salem Country Club, Peabody, Mass., September 26-October 1, 101 Entries, 95 Starters.

Qualifying Score	1st Round	2nd Round	3rd Round	Semi-Finals	Final Round (36 Holes)	
77	*Miss Maureen Orcutt (White Beeches)	Miss Orcutt, 5 and 3				
88	Miss Frances Snyder (Apawamis)		Miss Orcutt, 2 and 1			
85	Mrs. Marion Turpie Lake (Old C.C.)	Mrs. Federman, 3 and 2				
85	Mrs. L.G. Federman (Glen Oaks, N.Y.)			Miss Mackenzie, 2 and 1		
83	Miss Jane Brooks (Rockland)	Miss Mackenzie, 1 up				
87	Miss Ada Mackenzie (Canada)		Miss Mackenzie, 6 and 5			
83	Miss Jean Armstrong (Indian Hill)	Miss Armstrong, 1 up, 19 hls.			Mrs. Vare, 5 and 4	
87	**Miss A. Gorczyca (Meadowbrook, Texas)**					
80	**Mrs. Glenna Collett Vare (Philadelphia C.C.)**	Mrs. Vare, 7 and 5				
88	Mrs. Karl F. Scheidt (Plymouth, Pa.)		Mrs. Vare, 7 and 5			
84	Miss Dorothy Hunter (Albemarle)	Mrs. Eddis, 2 and 1				
86	Mrs. C.S. Eddis (Rosedale, Can.)			Mrs. Vare, 2 and 1		
81	Miss Dorothy Richards (Weston)	Mrs. Eaton, 3 and 1				Miss Virginia Van Wie, 10 and 8
88	Mrs. C.F. Eaton, Jr., (Wellesley)		Miss Wattles, 4 and 3			
84	Miss Peggy Wattles (Wanakah)	Miss Wattles, 1 up, 19 hls.				
87	Mrs. Dorothy C. Hurd (Merion)					
77	*Miss Virginia Van Wie (Beverly)	Miss Van Wie, 5 and 4				
88	Mrs. Betty P. Meckley (Indian Spring)		Miss Van Wie, 4 and 3			
85	Miss Edith Quier (Berkshire, Pa.)	Miss Quier, 9 and 7				
86	Mrs. N.S. Goldberger (Norwood)			Miss Van Wie, 3 and 2		
83	Miss L. Robinson (G. & C.C., Des Moines)	Mrs. Higbie, 1 up				
87	Mrs. Harley G. Higbie (C.C., Detroit)		Miss Knapp, 1 up, 19 hls.		Miss Van Wie, 4 and 3	
83	Miss Rosalie Knapp (Women's Nat'l)	Miss Knapp, 4 and 3				
87	Mrs. Ben Fitz-Hugh (Nat'l Pk., Miss.)					
79	Miss Enid Wilson (England)	Miss Wilson, 5 and 4				
88	Miss Elizabeth Skinner (Mt. Tom)		Miss Wilson, 8 and 7			
85	Miss Grace A. English (Colonial)	Miss English, 1 up, 19 hls.				
86	**Miss Beatrice Gottlieb (Lakeville)**			Miss Glutting, 1 up		
82	Miss Mary K. Browne (Kirtland)	Miss Glutting, 1 up				
87	Miss Charlotte Glutting (Baltusrol)		Miss Glutting, 3 and 2			
84	Mrs. O.S. Hill (Meadow Lake, Mo.)	Miss Wall, 1 up, 20 hls.				
87	Miss Bernice Wall (Oshkosh)					

*Medalist—No playoff—Prize to each.

1933
THIRTY-SEVENTH WOMEN'S AMATEUR CHAMPIONSHIP

Held at the Exmoor Country Club, Highland Park, Illinois, August 28-September 2. 120 Entries, 108 Starters.

Qualifying Score	1st Round	2nd Round	3rd Round	Semi-Finals	Final Round (36 Holes)	
76	*Miss Enid Wilson (England)	Miss Wilson, 3 and 2	Miss Wilson, 4 and 3	Miss Wilson, 2 and 1	Miss Van Wie, 6 and 5	Miss Virginia Van Wie, 4 and 3
87	Mrs. Marion Turpie Lake (Old Country)					
83	Miss Rena Nelson (Exmoor)	Mrs. Higbie, 2 and 1				
83	Mrs. Harley G. Higbie (C.C., Detroit)					
82	Miss Charlotte Glutting (Rock Spring)	Miss Glutting, 5 and 3	Miss Glutting, 3 and 2			
85	Miss Helen MacMorran (Indian Hill)					
82	Miss Peggy Wattles (Wanakah)	Miss Wattles, 3 and 2				
85	Miss Ada Mackenzie (Canada)					
78	Miss Virginia Van Wie (Beverly)	Miss Van Wie, 7 and 6	Miss Van Wie, 4 and 2	Miss Van Wie, 1 up		
86	Miss Elizabeth Dunn (Highland, Ind.)					
83	Mrs. Burt Weil (Hillcrest, Ill.)	Mrs. Federman, 6 and 5				
84	Mrs. L.G. Federman (Glen Oaks, N.Y.)					
79	Mrs. L.D. Cheney (San Gabriel)	Mrs. Cheney, 6 and 5	Mrs. Cheney, 4 and 3			
85	Mrs. Mildred Green (California C.C.)					
83	Miss A. Gorczyca (River Crest, Texas)	Miss Gorczyca, 2 and 1				
84	Miss June Beebe (Olympia Fields)					
78	Miss Maureen Orcutt (White Beeches)	Miss Orcutt, 3 and 2	Miss Orcutt, 4 and 2	Miss Orcutt, 1 up	Miss Hicks, 6 and 4	
86	Mrs. Charles Dennehy (Onwentsia)					
83	Miss Helen Lawson (Wilshire)	Mrs. Newbold, 4 and 3				
83	Mrs. Charles Newbold (Wichita)					
81	Miss Frances Williams (St. Davids)	Miss Williams, 5 and 4	Mrs. Hill, 4 and 3			
85	Miss Dorothy Gustafson (Coquillard)					
82	Mrs. O.S. Hill (Blue Hill, Mo.)	Mrs. Hill, 5 and 4				
84	Miss Rosalie Knapp (Women's Nat'l.)					
78	Miss Helen Hicks (Inwood)	Miss Hicks, 4 and 3	Miss Hicks, 4 and 3	Miss Hicks, 4 and 3		
86	Miss Edith Begg (Canterbury)					
83	Mrs. Ben Fitz-Hugh (National Park)	Mrs. Fitz-Hugh, 2 up				
84	Miss Marion Miley (Miami-Biltmore)					
81	Miss Lucille Robinson (Wakonda)	Miss Robinson, 5 and 4	Miss Robinson, 5 and 4			
85	Miss Jane Brooks (Rockland)					
82	Miss Margaret Maddox (Atlanta)	Miss Maddox, 3 and 2				
84	Mrs. Austin Pardue (Indian Hill, Ill.)					

*Medalist.

1934
THIRTY-EIGHTH WOMEN'S AMATEUR CHAMPIONSHIP

Held at the Whitemarsh Valley Country Club, Chestnut Hill, Pa., October 1-6. 157 Entries, 147 Starters.

Qualifying Score	1st Round (18 Holes)	2nd Round (18 Holes)	3rd Round (18 Holes)	4th Round (18 Holes)	Semi-Finals (18 Holes)	Final Round (36 Holes)	
82*	Mrs. L. D. Cheney, San Gabriel, Calif.	Mrs. Cheney, 7 and 5					
93	Mrs. Henri F. Prunaret, Jr., Charles River, Mass.		Mrs. Cheney, 3 and 1				
90	Mrs. Wm. G. Hamilton, Jr., Huntingdon Val., Pa.	Mrs. Hamilton, 1 up					
90	Mrs. George Viebrock, Queens Valley, N.Y.			Mrs. Cheney, 3 and 1			
87	Miss Helen B. Schoff, Springhaven, Pa.	Miss Browne, 7 and 6					
91	Miss Mary K. Browne, Kirtland, Ohio		Mrs. Hurd, 1 up				
87	Miss Mary Rogers, Timuquana, Fla.	Mrs. Hurd, 4 and 3					
91	Mrs. Dorothy Campbell Hurd, Merion, Pa.				Mrs. Hill, 1 up, 24 hls.		
85	Mrs. O. S. Hill, Blue Hills, Mo.	Mrs. Hill, 5 and 4					
92	Mrs. Sylva Annenberg Federman, Lakeville, N.Y.		Mrs. Hill, 5 and 4				
89	Mrs. W. M. Ferris, Jr., Brae Burn, Mass.	Mrs. McGarry, 6 and 5					
90	Mrs. Mark McGarry, Pasadena, Fla.			Mrs. Hill, 7 and 6			
85	Miss Charlotte Glutting, Rock Spring, N.J.	Miss Glutting, 7 and 5					
92	Miss Margaret M. Maddox, Atlanta A.C., Ga.		Miss Glutting, 5 and 4				
88	Miss Marion Miley, Lexington, Ky.	Miss Miley, 2 and 1					
90	Mrs. Thomas J. O'Reilly, Knollwood, N.Y.					Miss Traung, 3 and 2	
83	Mrs. Carl H. Donner, Baltusrol, N.J.	Mrs. Donner, 2 up					
92	Miss Lily Harper, Princess Anne, Va.		Mrs. Donner, 5 and 3				
89	Miss Dorothy Hunter, Trapelo, Mass.	Miss Hunter, 2 and 1					
90	Miss Edith Begg, Canterbury, Ohio			Mrs. Donner, 1 up, 19 hls.			
86	Miss Estelle Lawson, Carolina, N.C.	Miss Lawson, 8 and 7					
91	Miss Virginia Nye, Wanakah, N.Y.		Miss Orcutt, 1 up				
88	Miss Maureen Orcutt, White Beeches, N.J.	Miss Orcutt, 4 and 2					
90	Miss Ada Mackenzie, Canada				Miss Traung, 3 and 2		
83	Miss Molly Gourlay, England	Miss Gourlay, 4 and 3					
92	Mrs. Mont Reid, Cincinnati, Ohio		Mrs. Lake, 3 and 2				
89	Miss Betty Pietsch, Tamarack, N.Y.	Mrs. Lake, 6 and 5					
90	Mrs. Marion Turpie Lake, Plandome, N.Y.			Miss Traung, 1 up, 19 hls.			
86	Miss Dorothy Traung, Olympic, Calif.	Miss Traung, 9 and 7					
91	Miss Dorothy Gardner, Williams, W. Va.		Miss Traung, 3 and 2				
88	Miss Diana Fishwick, England	Miss Fishwick, 2 up					
90	Miss Doris Chambers, England						Miss Virginia Van Wie, 2 and 1
82*	Mrs. Glenna Collett Vare, Phila. Country, Pa.	Mrs. Vare, 2 and 1					
93	Mrs. Charles Newbold, Wichita, Kans.		Mrs. Vare, 4 and 3				
89	Miss Ruth Batchelder, Brae Burn, Mass.	Mrs. Stetson, 1 up					
90	Mrs. H. B. Stetson, Huntingdon Valley, Pa.			Mrs. Vare, 8 and 6			
87	Miss Marion Fisher, Oak Ridge, N.Y.	Mrs. Dennehy, 2 and 1					
91	Mrs. Charles Dennehy, Onwentsia, Ill.		Miss Stoddard, 1 up				
87	Miss Barbara Stoddard, Women's Natl., N.Y.	Miss Stoddard, 2 up					
90	Mrs. Charles B. Harding, Rumson, N.J.				Mrs. Vare, 6 and 5		
85	Mrs. Burt Weil, Hillcrest, Ohio	Mrs. Weil, 4 and 3					
92	Mrs. Arthur Harrison, C.C. Buffalo, N.Y.		Mrs. Weil, 4 and 3				
89	Miss Bernice Wall, Glen Oak, Ill.	Miss Wall, 2 and 1					
90	Mrs. Charles Martel, Lakeville, N.Y.			Mrs. Weil, 1 up			
86	Miss Wanda Morgan, England	Miss Morgan, 6 and 5					
92	Mrs. G. E. Hackney, Nassau, N.Y.		Miss Morgan, 5 and 4				
88	Miss Jean Kyer, Barton Hills, Mich.	Miss Richards, 2 and 1					
90	Miss Dorothy Richards, Weston, Mass.					Miss Van Wie, 3 and 2	
82*	Miss Lucille Robinson, Des Moines, Iowa	Miss Quier, 3 and 2					
92	Miss Edith Quier, Berkshire, Pa.		Miss Vahey, 5 and 4				
89	Miss Rosamond Vahey, Concord, Mass.	Miss Vahey, 3 and 1					
90	Miss Hope Starr, Sunnybrook, Pa.			Miss Van Wie, 1 up, 19 hls.			
86	Miss Virginia Van Wie, Beverly, Ill.	Miss Van Wie, 3 and 1					
91	Mrs. John Lowber Welsh, Gulph Mills, Pa.		Miss Van Wie, 8 and 7				
88	Miss Betty Jameson, Lakewood, Texas	Miss Jameson, 3 and 2					
90	Miss Diana Plumpton, England				Miss Van Wie, 5 and 4		
84	Mrs. Harley G. Higbie, C.C. Detroit, Mich.	Mrs. Higbie, 6 and 5					
92	Miss Winifred Faunce, Manor, Md.		Mrs. Scheidt, 2 up				
89	Mrs. Karl F. Scheidt, Whitemarsh Valley, Pa.	Mrs. Scheidt, 2 up					
90	Mrs. E. Boyd Morrow, Elkridge, Md.			Miss Williams, 2 up			
86	Miss Frances Williams, St. Davids, Pa.	Miss Williams, 4 and 3					
92	Mrs. Leon Solomon, Oakwood, Mo.		Miss Williams, 3 and 2				
88	Mrs. Frank (A. Gorczyca) Goldthwaite, River Crest, Tx.	Mrs. Wallace, 1 up					
90	Mrs. Tom Wallace, Tulsa, Okla.						

*Medalist.

The first word after the player's name is the name of the player's club, except in the case of a foreign entrant.

1935
THIRTY-NINTH WOMEN'S AMATEUR CHAMPIONSHIP

Held at the Interlachen Country Club, Hopkins, Minn., August 26-31. 94 Entries, 80 Starters.

Qualifying Score	1st Round (18 Holes)	2nd Round (18 Holes)	3rd Round (18 Holes)	4th Round (18 Holes)	Semi-Finals (18 Holes)	Final (18 Holes)	
79*	Miss Jean Bauer, Metacomet, R.I.	Miss Bauer, 5 and 4					
92	Mrs. L. K. Zech, Calumet, Ill.		Miss Stifel, 2 and 1				
87	Miss Fritzi Stifel, Wheeling, W. Va.	Miss Stifel, 1 up, 20 hls.					
87	Miss Lucile Robinson, Des Moines, Iowa			Mrs. Vare, 4 and 3			
85	Mrs. Glenna Collett Vare, Huntingdon Valley, Pa.	Mrs. Vare, 5 and 4					
89	Miss Edith M. Begg, Canterbury, Ohio		Mrs. Vare, 4 and 3				
85	Miss Bernice Wall, Glen Oak, Ill.	Miss Wall, 8 and 6					
89	Mrs. Jonathan Thorne, Innis Arden, Conn.				Mrs. Vare, 4 and 3		
82	Miss Jean Kyer, Barton Hills, Mich.	Mrs. Selz, 1 up					
91	Mrs. Lawrence H. Selz, Northmoor, Ill.		Miss Abbott, 6 and 5				
86	Mrs. Wright D. Goss, Jr., Baltusrol, N.J.	Miss Abbott, 4 and 2					
88	Miss Elizabeth Abbott, Bel-Air, Calif.			Miss Abbott, 6 and 5			
83	Miss Lily S. Harper, Princess Anne, Va.	Miss Harper, 1 up					
91	Mrs. E. F. Cary, C.C. Minneapolis, Minn.		Mrs. Pardue, 1 up				
85	Mrs. Austin Pardue, Minikahda, Minn.	Mrs. Pardue, 3 and 2					
88	Miss Rosamond Vahey, Vesper, Mass.					Mrs. Vare, 2 and 1	
82	Mrs. Burt Weil, Hillcrest, Ohio	Mrs. Weil, 1 up					
91	Miss Edna May Johnson, Riviera, Calif.		Miss Barrett, 3 and 1				
86	Miss Betty Jameson, Lakewood, Texas	Miss Barrett, 4 and 2					
87	Miss Beatrice Barrett, Lafayette, Minn.			Miss Barrett, 2 up			
84	Mrs. Marion Turpie Lake, Plandome, N.Y.	Mrs. Lake, 4 and 2					
90	Miss Frances Hadfield, Blue Mound, Wis.		Mrs. Newbold, 2 up				
85	Miss Edith Kierland, Interlachen, Minn.	Mrs. Newbold, 7 and 6					
89	Mrs. Charles Newbold, Wichita, Kans.				Miss Barrett, 4 and 3		
82	Miss Marion McDougall, Waverley, Ore.	Miss McDougall, 4 and 2					
91	Miss Marion Leachman, Berkeley, Calif.		Miss McDougall, 1 up, 20 hls.				
86	Mrs. Timothy G. Lowry, Knollwood, Ill.	Mrs. Lowry, 2 and 1					
87	Mrs. John D. Hoblitzell, Parkersburg, W. Va.			Miss McDougall, 1 up			
84	Miss Maureen Orcutt, Miami-Biltmore, Fla.	Miss Orcutt, 5 and 4					
90	Mrs. F. Joseph Holleran, Greenwich, Conn.		Miss Orcutt, 6 and 4				
85	Mrs. Mont Reid, Camargo, Ohio	Mrs. Reid, 5 and 4					
89	Mrs. Charles J. Woerner, Los Angeles, Calif.						Mrs. Glenna Collett Vare, 3 and 2
80	Miss Charlotte Glutting, Rock Spring, N.J.	Miss Glutting, 2 and 1					
92	Mrs. Tom Wallace, Tulsa, Okla.		Miss Glutting, 3 and 2				
87	Miss Ellamae Williams, Sunset Ridge, Ill.	Miss Wattles, 1 up					
87	Miss Peggy Wattles, Wanakah, N.Y.			Miss Glutting, 3 and 1			
84	Miss Marion Miley, Lexington, Ky.	Miss Miley, 6 and 5					
90	Mrs. Marjorie Letts, Chicago G.C., Ill.		Miss Miley, 4 and 2				
85	Miss Dorothy Traung, Olympic, Calif.	Miss Hays, 3 and 2					
89	Miss Betty Hays, Interlachen, Minn.				Miss Glutting, 2 and 1		
82	Miss Phyllis Buchanan, Lakewood, Colo.	Miss Shorb, 3 and 1					
91	Miss Eva Shorb, Portage, Ohio		Mrs. Goldthwaite, 7 and 6				
86	Mrs. Frank (A. Gorczyca) Goldthwaite, River Crest, Tx.	Mrs. Goldthwaite, 6 and 5					
88	Mrs. R. S. Leachman, Berkeley, Calif.			Mrs. Hill, 2 and 1			
84	Mrs. O. S. Hill, Blue Hills, Mo.	Mrs. Hill, 7 and 6					
91	Mrs. Charles Eddis, Toronto, Canada		Mrs. Hill, 7 and 6				
86	Miss Deborah Verry, Tatnuck, Mass.	Miss Bateson, 3 and 1					
88	Miss Goldie Bateson, Westmoor, Wis.					Miss Berg, 1 up, 21 holes	
81	Miss Sylva Annenberg, Lakeville, N.Y.	Miss Bushard, 1 up					
92	Miss Margaret Bushard, California C.C., Calif.		Miss Stephenson, 3 and 2				
86	Miss Mary K. Browne, Kirtland, Ohio	Miss Stephenson, 1 up					
87	Miss Patricia Stephenson, Interlachen, Minn.			Mrs. Chandler, 2 and 1			
84	Mrs. Hayes Dansingburg, C.C. Minneapolis, Minn.	Mrs. Dansingburg, 3 and 2					
90	Miss Betty Botterill, C.C. Salt Lake City, Utah		Mrs. Chandler, 7 and 5				
85	Mrs. Dan Chandler, Brook Hollow, Texas	Mrs. Chandler, 5 and 4					
89	Mrs. D. W. Snyder, Jr., Blue Hills, Mo.				Miss Berg, 2 up		
82	Miss Ada Mackenzie, Toronto, Canada	Miss Mackenzie, 2 and 1					
91	Miss Shirley Anne Johnson, Sunset Ridge, Ill.		Miss Mackenzie, 3 and 1				
86	Mrs. Leon Solomon, Oakwood, Mo.	Mrs. Solomon, 2 and 1					
87	Miss Jean Armstrong, Indian Hill, Ill.			Miss Berg, 2 and 1			
84	Miss Betsy MacLeod, Park, N.Y.	Miss MacLeod, 3 and 2					
90	Mrs. Linton H. Fallis, Inverness, Ohio		Miss Berg, 4 and 3				
85	Miss Patty Berg, Interlachen, Minn.	Miss Berg, 3 and 2					
88	Miss Barbara Beach Thompson, Los Altos, Calif.						

*Medalist.

The first word after the player's name is the name of the player's club, except in the case of a foreign entrant.

1936

FORTIETH WOMEN'S AMATEUR CHAMPIONSHIP

Held at the Canoe Brook Country Club, Summit, N.J., September 28-October 3, 188 Entries, 174 Starters.

Qualifying Score	1st Round (18 Holes)	2nd Round (18 Holes)	3rd Round (18 Holes)	4th Round (18 Holes)	Semi-Finals (18 Holes)	Finals (36 Holes)	
78*	Mrs. Julius A. Page, Jr., Sedgefield, N.C.	Mrs. Page, 4 and 3					
91	Mrs. John J. Meenan, Nassau, N.Y.		Mrs. Page, 7 and 5				
88	Mrs. Mont Reid, Camargo, Ohio	Mrs. Holman, 1 up, 20 hls.					
88	Mrs. Russell Holman, Innis Arden, Conn.			Miss Barrett, 2 and 1			
86	Miss Beatrice Barrett, Lafayette, Minn.	Miss Barrett, 3 and 2					
90	Miss Bette Waterhouse, Warwick, R.I.		Miss Barrett, 5 and 3				
86	Miss Carol W. Smith, Hartford, Conn.	Miss Sylvester, 2 and 1					
90	Miss Katherine Sylvester, Green Meadow, N.Y.				Miss Barton, 4 and 3		
82	Miss Pamela Barton, London, England	Miss Barton 4 and 3					
91	Mrs. Leon Solomon, Oakwood, Mo.		Miss Barton, 2 and 1				
87	Miss Marian McDougall, Waverley, Ore.	Mrs. Rudel, 5 and 4					
89	Mrs. Thomas R. Rudel, Oakland, N.Y.			Miss Barton, 2 up			
84	Miss Rosamond Vahey, Vesper, Mass.	Mrs. Lack, 3 and 1					
90	Mrs. Norman M. Lack, Wilmington, Del.		Mrs. Lack, 3 and 1				
87	Mrs. George L. Austin, Hartford, Conn.	Mrs. Weil, 3 and 2					
89	Mrs. Bert Weil, Hillcrest, Ohio					Miss Barton, 3 and 1	
81	Miss Charlotte Glutting, Rock Spring, N.J.	Miss Glutting, 3 and 2					
91	Miss Jean Bauer, Metacomet, R.I.		Miss Glutting, 3 and 2				
87	Miss Elizabeth Abbott, California C.C., Calif.	Mrs. Chandler, 2 and 1					
88	Mrs. Dan Chandler, Brook Hollow, Texas			Miss Miley, 1 up, 19 hls.			
84	Miss Marion E. Miley, Lexington, Ky.	Miss Miley, 3 and 2					
90	Miss Barbara Winn, Broadmoor, Wash.		Miss Miley, 2 up				
86	Mrs. John Arends, Detroit G.C., Mich.	Miss Stephenson, 6 and 5					
89	Miss Patricia Stephenson, Interlachen, Minn.				Miss Miley, 5 and 4		
81	Miss Jane Cothran, Greenville, S.C.	Miss Cothran, 1 up					
91	Miss Mary B. Clark, Forest Hill, N.J.		Miss Cothran, 1 up, 19 hls.				
87	Mrs. Marion Turpie Lake, Plandome, N.Y.	Mrs. Lake, 1 up					
88	Mrs. Frederick Davis, Massasoit, R.I.			Mrs. Donner, 1 up, 21 hls.			
84	Mrs. Carl H. Donner, Baltusrol, N.J.	Mrs. Donner, 7 and 6					
90	Mrs. William A. Johnson, St. Davids, Pa.		Mrs. Donner, 3 and 1				
86	Mrs. William Hockenjos, Jr., Crestmont, N.J.	Mrs. Hockenjos, 7 and 6					
89	Mrs. E. F. Whalen, Westchester, N.Y.						Miss Pamela Barton, 4 and 3
80	Miss Jean Kyer, Barton Hills, Mich.	Miss Foster, 6 and 5					
91	Miss Dorothy Foster, Oak Crest, Ill.		Miss MacLeod, 4 and 3				
88	Miss Betsy MacLeod, Buffalo, N.Y.	Miss MacLeod, 4 and 2					
88	Mrs. C. R. Harbaugh, Manakiki, Ohio			Mrs. Shepherd, 3 and 2			
85	Mrs. E. Boyd Morrow, Elkridge, Md.	Mrs. Shepherd, 4 and 2					
90	Mrs. Willard E. Shepherd, Los Angeles, Calif.		Mrs. Shepherd, 1 up				
86	Miss Ada Mackenzie, Toronto, Canada	Miss Mackenzie, 5 and 3					
90	Miss Fritzi Stifel, Wheeling, W. Va.				Miss Hemphill, 1 up, 19 hls.		
82	Mrs. Gregg Lifur, Riviera, Calif.	Miss Hemphill, 3 and 1					
91	Miss Kathryn Hemphill, Forest Lake, S.C.		Miss Hemphill, 2 and 1				
87	Miss Marjorie Harrison, Indole, N.Y.	Miss Harrison, 2 and 1					
89	Miss Marion Fisher, Lakeville, N.Y.			Miss Hemphill, 2 up			
84	Miss Ruth M. Adel, Queens Valley, N.Y.	Miss Adel, 4 and 2					
90	Mrs. Karl F. Scheidt, Plymouth, Pa.		Miss Adel, 3 and 1				
87	Miss Peggy Wattles, Wanakah, N.Y.	Miss Wattles, 2 up					
89	Miss Alice Rutherford, Baltusrol, N.J.					Miss Orcutt, 4 and 2	
80	Miss Patty Berg, Interlachen, Minn.	Miss Berg, 1 up					
91	Miss Eva Shorb, Brookside, Canton, Ohio		Miss Berg, 6 and 4				
87	Mrs. Wright D. Goss, Baltusrol, N.J.	Mrs. Goss, 3 and 2					
88	Miss Dorothy Gardner, Williams, W. Va.			Mrs. Hill, 4 and 3			
85	Mrs. O. S. Hill, Blue Hills, Mo.	Mrs. Hill, 3 and 2					
90	Miss Gail Wild, Baltusrol, N.J.		Mrs. Hill, 5 and 4				
86	Mrs. Frank Goldthwaite, River Crest, Texas	Miss Browne, 3 and 1					
90	Miss Mary K. Browne, Kirtland, Ohio				Miss Orcutt, 3 and 2		
82	Miss Maureen Orcutt, Miami-Biltmore, Fla.	Miss Orcutt, 6 and 4					
91	Mrs. Henry H. Dietrich, Briar Hills, N.Y.		Miss Orcutt, 4 and 3				
87	Miss Helen Dettweiler, Congressional, Md.	Miss Dettweiler, 3 and 1					
88	Miss Helen Waterhouse, Warwick, R.I.			Miss Orcutt, 2 up			
84	Miss Dorothy Traung, Olympic, Calif.	Miss Traung, 5 and 4					
90	Mrs. Theodore W. Hawes, Canoe Brook, N.J.		Miss Traung, 1 up, 19 hls.				
86	Miss Betty Jameson, Austin, Texas	Miss Jameson, 2 and 1					
89	Miss Frances Owen, Ponte Vedra, Fla.						

*Medalist.

The first word after the player's name is the name of the player's club, except in the case of a foreign entrant.

1937
FORTY-FIRST WOMEN'S AMATEUR CHAMPIONSHIP

Held at the Memphis Country Club, Memphis, Tenn., October 4-9. 136 Entries, 119 Starters.

Qualifying Score	1st Round (18 Holes)	2nd Round (18 Holes)	3rd Round (18 Holes)	4th Round (18 Holes)	Semi-Finals (18 Holes)	Final Round (36 Holes)	
79*	Mrs. Julius A. Page, Jr., Sedgefield, N.C.	Mrs. Page, 3 and 2	Mrs. Page, 5 and 4	Mrs. Page, 5 and 3	Mrs. Page, 2 and 1.	Mrs. Page, 1 up, 19 hls.	Mrs. Julius A. Page, Jr., 7 and 6
93	Miss Marian Leachman, Berkeley, Calif.						
89	Miss Maureen Orcutt, White Beeches, N.J.	Mrs. Brantley, 1 up					
89	Mrs. George D. Brantley, Ponte Vedra, Fla.						
86	Miss Charlotte Glutting, Rock Spring, N.J.	Miss Glutting 9 and 7	Miss Bauer, 2 up				
90	Miss Betsy MacLeod, C.C. Buffalo, N.Y.						
86	Mrs. Sam Isreal, Jr., Lakewood, La.	Miss Bauer, 6 and 4					
90	Miss Jean E. Bauer, Metacomet, R.I.						
85	Mrs. Frank Goldthwaite, River Crest, Texas	Mrs. Goldthwaite, 3 and 2	Mrs. Torgerson, 1 up, 20 hls.	Mrs. Chandler, 1 up, 21 hls.			
92	Mrs. Leon Wolf, Jr., Lakewood, La.						
87	Mrs. Reinert M. Torgerson, Queens Valley, N.Y.	Mrs. Torgerson, 5 and 3					
89	Miss Mary Morse, Cypress Point, Calif.						
85	Mrs. Dan Chandler, Brook Hollow, Texas	Mrs. Chandler, 2 and 1	Mrs. Chandler, 3 and 2				
91	Mrs. David Gaut, Memphis, Tenn.						
87	Miss Dorothy Kirby, Capital City, Ga.	Miss Kirby, 8 and 6					
90	Mrs. Gaither Hatcher, Colonial, Tenn.						
83	Miss Kathryn Hemphill, Forest Lake, S.C.	Miss Hemphill, 2 and 1	Miss Hemphill, 2 and 1	Miss Hemphill, 2 up	Miss Hemphill, 4 and 3		
92	Miss Helen Sigel, Manufacturers, Pa.						
88	Miss Bernice Wall, Glen Oak, Ill.	Miss Barrett, 6 and 5					
89	Miss Beatrice Barrett, Lafayette, Minn.						
86	Mrs. Jane Cothran Jameson, Greenville, S.C.	Mrs. Jameson, 1 up, 19 hls.	Mrs. Jameson, 3 and 2				
91	Miss Jean Kyer, Barton Hills, Mich.						
87	Mrs. Donald Weiss, Flint, Mich.	Miss Jameson, 5 and 4					
90	Miss Betty Jameson, San Antonio, Texas						
84	Mrs. Charles Newbold, Wichita, Kansas	Mrs. Newbold, 6 and 5	Mrs. Newbold, 1 up	Mrs. Newbold, 2 and 1			
92	Miss Anna Bland Thompson, River Crest, Texas						
88	Miss Helen Hofmann, Fort Douglas, Utah	Miss Hofmann, 2 and 1					
89	Mrs. R. E. Winger, Colonial, Texas						
86	Mrs. Glenna Collett Vare, Jr., Philadelphia C.C., Pa.	Mrs. Vare, 2 and 1	Mrs. Vare, 1 up				
91	Miss Dorothy Traung, San Francisco, Calif.						
87	Mrs. Marion Turpie, Plandome, N.Y.	Mrs. Turpie, 1 up					
90	Mrs. James M. Robbins, Lawrence Farms, N.Y.						
82	Mrs. Gregg Lifur, Riviera, Calif.	Mrs. Lifur, 3 and 1	Mrs. Lifur, 1 up, 10 hls.	Mrs. Lifur, 2 and 1	Mrs. Lifur, 2 and 1	Miss Berg, 7 and 6	
92	Mrs. Bee Cockrell, Gadsden, Ala.						
88	Mrs. Sylva Annenberg, Fresh Meadow, N.Y.	Mrs. Annenberg, 1 up, 22 hls.					
89	Miss Hilda Livengood, Danville, Ill.						
86	Miss Lily S. Harper, Princess Anne, Va.	Miss Harper, 1 up	Miss Ransom, 2 and 1				
91	Miss Dorothy Foster, Illini, Ill.						
86	Miss Barbara Ransom, Stockton, Calif.	Miss Ransom, 1 up, 19 hls.					
90	Miss Peggy Graham, Lakeside, Calif.						
85	Mrs. William Hockenjos, Jr., Crestmont, N.J.	Miss Kuhn, 1 up	Miss Miley, 3 and 2	Mrs. Hill, 3 and 2			
92	Miss Mary Kuhn, Pittsburgh Field, Pa.						
87	Miss Marion E. Miley, Maketewah, Ohio	Miss Miley, 6 and 4					
89	Miss Virginia Fox, Hershey, Pa.						
86	Mrs. O. S. Hill, Blue Hills, Mo.	Mrs. Hill, 4 and 3	Mrs. Hill, 6 and 5				
91	Mrs. Burt Weil, Losantiville, Ohio						
87	Mrs. Wright D. Goss, Jr., Baltusrol, N.J.	Miss Hollins, 3 and 1					
90	Miss Marion Hollins, Pasatiempo, Calif.						
82	Miss Patty Berg, Interlachen, Minn.	Miss Berg, 4 and 3	Miss Berg, 3 and 2	Miss Berg, 3 and 1	Miss Berg, 2 up		
92	Mrs. Norman M. Lack, Wilmington, Del.						
88	Miss Edna Saenger, Broadmoor, La.	Miss Saenger, 5 and 4					
89	Miss Dorothy Ellis, Meridian Hills, Ind.						
86	Miss Alice Rutherfurd, Baltusrol, N.J.	Miss Rutherfurd, 6 and 5	Miss Urbantke, 1 up				
91	Mrs. Charles R. Harbaugh, Manakiki, Ohio						
87	Miss Janet Shock, Miami Valley, Ohio	Miss Urbantke, 3 and 1					
90	Miss Hilda Urbantke, Austin, Texas						
84	Miss Clarrie Tiernan, Baltray, Irish Free State	Mrs. Shepherd, 5 and 4	Mrs. Shepherd, 1 up	Mrs. Shepherd, 2 up			
92	Mrs. Willard E. Shepherd, Wilshire, Calif.						
87	Mrs. Lillian K. Zech, Tam O'Shanter, Ill.	Miss McDougall, 5 and 3					
89	Miss Marian McDougall, Waverley, Ore.						
86	Miss Clara Callender, Del Monte, Calif.	Miss Callender, 1 up, 19 hls.	Miss Callender, 5 and 4				
91	Miss Helen Dettweiler, Congressional, Md.						
87	Miss Elizabeth Falls Dunscomb, Memphis, Tenn.	Miss Dunscomb, 1 up, 20 hls.					
90	Mrs. Dewitt Untermeyer, Hollywood, N.J.						

*Medalist.

The first word after the player's name is the name of the player's club, except in the case of a foreign entrant.

1938
FORTY-SECOND WOMEN'S AMATEUR CHAMPIONSHIP

Held at the Westmoreland Country Club, Wilmette, Ill., September 19-24. 118 Entries, 107 Starters.

Qualifying Score	1st Round (18 Holes)	2nd Round (18 Holes)	3rd Round (18 Holes)	4th Round (18 Holes)	Semi-Finals (18 Holes)	Final Round (18 Holes)	
80*	Mrs. Julius A. Page, Jr., Sedgefield, N.C.	Mrs. Page, 4 and 3					
94	Mrs. Eric Phillips, Lambton Mills, Canada		Mrs. Page, 2 and 1				
90	Miss Phyllis Wade, Ferndown, England	Miss Waterhouse, 1 up					
90	Miss Helen Waterhouse, Warwick, R.I.			Mrs. Page, 4 and 2			
87	Miss Betty Jameson, San Antonio, Texas	Miss Jameson, 4 and 3					
92	Miss Shirley Ann Johnson, Sunset Ridge, Ill.		Miss Jameson, 4 and 2				
88	Mrs. J. B. Walker, Dublin, Ireland	Mrs. Walker, 7 and 5			Mrs. Page, 1 up		
92	Mrs. Tim G. Lowry, Kildeer, Ill.						
85	Miss Betsy MacLeod, C.C. Buffalo, N.Y.	Miss Dettweiler, 1 up					
93	Miss Helen Dettweiler, Congressional, D.C.		Mrs. Goldthwaite, 4 and 3				
89	Miss Dorothy L. Foster, Illini, Ill.	Mrs. Goldthwaite, 2 and 1					
91	Mrs. Frank Goldthwaite, River Crest, Texas			Mrs. Goldthwaite, 7 and 5			
85	Miss Ellamae Williams, Merdinah, Ill.	Miss Williams, 1 up, 20 hls.					
93	Mrs. Reinert M. Torgerson, Queens Valley, N.Y.		Miss Williams, 2 and 1				
89	Miss Hope Seignious, Clinton Valley, Mich.	Miss Seignious, 3 and 1				Mrs. Page, 8 and 7	
91	Mrs. William Hockenjos, Jr., Crestmont, N.J.						
84	Miss Jessie Anderson, Perth, Scotland	Miss Anderson, 5 and 4					
94	Miss Nan S. Baird, Prestwick, Scotland		Miss Graham, 2 and 1				
89	Miss Peggy Graham, Lakeside, Calif.	Miss Graham, 3 and 1					
91	Miss Janet Shock, Miami Valley, Ohio			Miss Graham, 2 and 1			
87	Mrs. Marion Turpie McNaughton, Sound View, N.Y.	Mrs. McNaughton, 3 and 1					
92	Mrs. Donald Weiss, Flint, Mich.		Mrs. McNaughton, 3 and 2				
88	Mrs. Russell C. Mann, Blue Mound, Wis.	Miss Barrett, 6 and 5			Miss Graham, 5 and 3		
92	Miss Beatrice Barrett, Lafayette, Minn.						
84	Miss Clarrie Tiernan, Baltray, Ireland	Miss Tiernan, 1 up					
94	Miss Laddie Irwin, Glen Ridge, N.J.		Miss Tiernan, 4 and 2				
89	Mrs. O. S. Hill, Blue Hills, Mo.	Mrs. Hill, 1 up, 19 hls.					
91	Mrs. Mortimer May, Inwood, N.Y.			Mrs. Hury, 2 up			
87	Miss Harriett Randall, Hillcrest, Ind.	Miss Randall, 4 and 3					
93	Mrs. C. R. Harbaugh, Manakiki, Ohio		Mrs. Hury, 5 and 3				
88	Mrs. E. R. Hury, Glen Lakes, Texas	Mrs. Hury, 4 and 2					
92	Mrs. J. D. Platt, Jr., Dayton, Ohio						Miss Patty Berg, 6 and 5
80*	Miss Dorothy Traung, San Francisco, Calif.	Miss Traung, 4 and 3					
94	Mrs. Lillian K. Zech, Tam O'Shanter, Ill.		Miss Traung, 1 up, 19 hls.				
90	Miss Jane Cothran, Greenville, S.C.	Mrs. Critchley, 3 and 2					
90	Mrs. A. C. Critchley, Wentworth, England			Miss Traung, 3 and 1			
87	Mrs. Dan Chandler, Brook Hollow, Texas	Mrs. Chandler, 1 up, 20 hls.					
92	Miss Virginia Lindblad, Lincolnshire, Ill.		Mrs. Newbold, 4 and 3				
88	Miss Virginia Guilfoil, Syracuse Yacht, N.Y.	Mrs. Newbold, 5 and 3			Miss Berg, 5 and 3		
92	Mrs. Charles Newbold, Wichita, Kansas						
85	Miss Patty Berg, Interlachen, Minn.	Miss Berg, 10 and 8					
93	Mrs. Myron Davy, Congressional, D.C.		Miss Berg, 4 and 3				
89	Miss Alice Ann Anderson, Kenosha, Wis.	Miss Bauer, 3 and 2					
91	Miss Jean E. Bauer, Metacomet, R.I.			Miss Berg, 1 up			
86	Miss Eva Shorb, Brookside, Ohio	Miss Shorb, 1 up, 19 hls.					
93	Mrs. R. E. Winger, Colonial, Texas		Miss Shorb, 4 and 3				
88	Miss Mildred O. Hackl, Midlothian, Ill.	Miss Nelson, 3 and 2				Miss Berg, 2 up	
91	Miss Rena Nelson, Exmoor, Ill.						
83	Miss Marion E. Miley, Lexington, Ky.	Miss Miley, 4 and 3					
94	Miss Dorothy Ellis, Meridian Hills, Ind.		Miss Miley, 1 up, 19 hls.				
90	Mrs. Glenna Collett Vare, Philadelphia Country, Pa.	Miss Kirby, 1 up					
90	Miss Dorothy Kirby, Capital City, Ga.			Miss Miley, 5 and 3			
87	Miss Kathryn Hemphill, Forest Lake, S.C.	Miss Hemphill, 3 and 2					
92	Mrs. Wright D. Goss, Jr., Baltusrol, N.J.		Miss Hemphill, 2 and 1				
88	Miss Charlotte Glutting, Rock Spring, N.J.	Miss Glutting, 8 and 7			Miss Miley, 4 and 3		
92	Mrs. Sam Israel, Jr., Lakewood, La.						
84	Miss Maureen Orcutt, White Beeches, N.J.	Miss Orcutt, 4 and 3					
93	Miss Bernice Wall, Glen Oak, Ill.		Miss Levengood, 2 up				
89	Miss Hilda Livengood, Danville, Ill.	Miss Livengood, 1 up					
91	Miss Virginia Ingram, Sunset Ridge, Ill.			Miss McDougall, 3 and 1			
87	Mrs. Gregg Lifur, Riviera, Calif.	Mrs. Lifur, 6 and 5					
93	Miss Marie Louise Gardner, Shoreacres, Ill.		Miss McDougall, 6 and 4				
88	Miss Marian McDougall, Waverley, Ore.	Miss McDougall, 2 and 1					
91	Miss Jean Kyer, Barton Hills, Mich.						

*Tied for medal; no playoff.
The first word after the player's name is the name of the player's club except in the case of a foreign entrant.

1939
FORTY-THIRD WOMEN'S AMATEUR CHAMPIONSHIP

Held at the Wee Burn Club, Darien, Conn., August 21-26. 201 Entries, 194 Starters.

Qualifying Score	1st Round (18 Holes)	2nd Round (18 Holes)	3rd Round (18 Holes)	4th Round (18 Holes)	Semi-Finals (18 Holes)	Final Round (36 Holes)	
74*	**Miss Beatrice Barrett, Lafayette, Minn.**	Miss Barrett, 5 and 3	Miss Kirby, 5 and 4	Miss Kirby, 4 and 3	Miss Kirby, 1 up	Miss Kirby, 1 up	Miss Betty Jameson, 3 and 2
89	Mrs. F.J. Holleran, Greenwich, Conn.						
85	Miss Deborah Verry, Kittansett, Mass.	Miss Kirby, 3 and 2					
85	Miss Dorothy Kirby, Capital City, Ga.						
82	Miss Marian McDougall, Waverley, Ore.	Miss McDougall, 1 up, 19 hls.	Miss Cothran, 3 and 1				
87	Mrs. James M. Robbins, Lawrence Farms, N.Y.						
82	Miss Jane Cothran, Greenville, S.C.	Miss Cothran, 5 and 4					
86	Mrs. Carl H. Martin, Princess Anne, Va.						
80	Miss Dorothy Traung, Olympic, Calif.	Miss Traung, 2 and 1	Miss Traung, 3 and 2	Miss Traung, 2 and 1			
89	Mrs. Warren Beard, Charles River, Mass.						
84	Mrs. Harrison F. Flippin, Huntingdon Valley, Pa.	Mrs. Flippin, 3 and 1					
86	Mrs. Reinert M. Torgerson, Lakeville, N.Y.						
80	Miss Virginia M. Guilfoil, Syracuse Yacht, N.Y.	Miss Guilfoil, 2 and 1	Mrs. Mann, 5 and 4				
89	Miss Margaret H. Nichols, Hudson River, N.Y.						
84	Mrs. Russell C. Mann, Blue Mound, Wis.	Mrs. Mann, 6 and 5					
86	Miss Janet Younker, Century, N.Y.						
78	Miss Pamela Barton, London, England	Miss Barton, 4 and 2	Miss Barton, 1 up, 19 hls.	Miss Glutting, 1 up, 19 hls.	Miss Glutting, 1 up, 19 hls.		
89	Miss Mary B. Fine, C.C. Scranton, Pa.						
84	Miss Ellamae Williams, Medinah, Ill.	Miss Williams, 3 and 1					
85	Mrs. Gregg Lifur, Riviera, Calif.						
81	Miss Charlotte Glutting, Rock Spring, N.J.	Miss Glutting, 3 and 2	Miss Glutting, 4 and 3				
88	Miss Priscilla P. Janney, Merion, Pa.						
83	**Mrs. H. Douglas McIlwraith, Ancaster, Canada**	**Mrs.** McIlwraith, 1 up, 20 hls.					
86	Miss Peggy Ann Delahant, Wolfert's Roost, N.Y.						
79	Miss Mary K. Browne, Kirtland, Ohio	Miss M.K. Browne, 1 up	Mrs. Rudel, 1 up	Miss Irwin, 3 and 2			
89	Miss Gail Wild, Baltusrol, N.J.						
84	Mrs. Thomas R. Rudel, Oakland, N.Y.	Mrs. Rudel, 1 up					
85	Mrs. Sam Israel, Jr., Lakewood, La.						
81	Miss Phyllis Buchanan, Lakewood, Colo.	Mrs. R.F. Beard, 2 up	Miss Irwin, 6 and 5				
88	Mrs. Robert F. Beard, Knollwood, N.Y.						
83	Miss Laddie Irwin, Upper Montclair, N.J.	Miss Irwin, 5 and 3					
86	Mrs. Mark McGarry, Pasadena, Fla.						
75	Mrs. Julius A. Page, Jr., Sedgefield, N.C.	Mrs. Page, 4 and 2	Mrs. Page, 2 up	Miss Orcutt, 3 and 2	Miss Hicks, 3 and 1	Miss Jameson, 3 and 1	
89	Miss Margaret M. Maddox, Atlanta A.C., Ga.						
85	Miss Nancy O. Hurst, Alderwood, Ore.	Miss Hurst, 2 up					
85	Miss Jean E. Bauer, Metacomet, R.I.						
82	Miss Maureen Orcutt, White Beeches, N.J.	Miss Orcutt, 3 and 1	Miss Orcutt, 1 up, 23 hls.				
87	Miss Jeanne Cline, Bloomington, Ill.						
82	Mrs. Glenna Collett Vare, Philadelphia Country, Pa.	Miss M.S. Brown, 2 up					
86	Miss Marion S. Brown, Manor, Md.						
79	Miss Fay Crocker, Montevideo, Uruguay	Miss Crocker, 5 and 3	Miss Crocker, 2 and 1	Miss Hicks, 1 up, 20 hls.			
89	Mrs. W.R. Kirkland, Jr., Silver Spring, Conn.						
84	Miss Kathryn Pearson, River Oaks, Texas	Miss Hemphill, 1 up					
86	Miss Kathryn Hemphill, Forest Lake, S.C.						
81	Miss Elizabeth Hicks, Virginia, Calif.	Miss Hicks, 1 up, 19 hls.	Miss Hicks, 6 and 4				
88	Mrs. Lillian K. Zech, Tam O'Shanter, Ill.						
84	Mrs. William Hockenjos, Jr., Crestmont, N.J.	Mrs. Hockenjos, 7 and 6					
86	Miss Julia C. Zima, Wethersfield, Conn.						
77	Miss Marion E. Miley, Lexington, Ky.	Miss Miley, 6 and 4	Miss Miley, 4 and 2	Miss Miley, 4 and 2	Miss Jameson, 1 up		
89	Mrs. Percy Uris, Mt. Vernon, N.Y.						
84	Miss Dorothy Germain, Llanerch, Pa.	Mrs. Chandler, 5 and 3					
85	Mrs. Dan Chandler, Brook Hollow, Texas						
82	**Miss Harriett Randall, Hillcrest, Ind.**	Miss Randall, 1 up, 19 hls.	Miss Sigel, 2 and 1				
87	Mrs. Bishop P. Hill, Chevy Chase, Md.						
83	Miss Helen Sigel, Philadelphia Country, Pa.	Miss Sigel, 1 up, 19 hls.					
86	Mrs. Henry H. Dietrich, Gedney, N.Y.						
79	Miss Betty Jameson, San Antonio, Texas	Miss Jameson, 6 and 5	Miss Jameson, 2 up	Miss Jameson, 6 and 4			
89	Miss Helen L. Waterhouse, Warwick, R.I.						
84	Miss Evelyn Marvin, Rio de Janeiro, Brazil	Miss Morrison, 1 up					
86	Miss Mary Morrison, Hershey, Pa.						
81	Miss Sheila Stroyan, Sunningdale, England	Miss Stroyan, 3 and 1	Miss Stroyan, 3 and 1				
88	Miss Marie Deasey, Llanerch, Pa.						
83	Mrs. Dewitt E. Untermeyer, Hollywood, N.J.	Mrs. Untermeyer, 2 up					
86	**Mrs. Sylva Federman Leichner, Fresh Meadow, N.Y.**						

*Medalist.
The first word after the player's name is the name of the player's club except in the case of a foreign entrant.

1940
FORTY-FOURTH WOMEN'S AMATEUR CHAMPIONSHIP

Held at the Del Monte Golf and Country Club, Pebble Beach Golf Links, Calif., September 23-28. 163 Entries, 157 Starters.

Qualifying Score	1st Round (18 Holes)	2nd Round (18 Holes)	3rd Round (18 Holes)	4th Round (18 Holes)	Semi-Finals (18 Holes)	Final Round (36 Holes)	
78*	Miss Dorothy Traung, San Francisco, Calif.	Miss Traung, 7 and 6	Miss Traung, 4 and 3	Miss Tainter, 2 and 1	Miss Cothran, 2 and 1	Miss Cothran, 2 up	Miss Betty Jameson, 6 and 5
93	Mrs. George H. Nash, San Jose, Calif.						
88	Mrs. J.K. Priebe, Sand Point, Wash.	Mrs. Smith, 2 up					
88	Mrs. C.H. Smith, San Diego, Calif.						
84	Mrs. L.J. Tescher, Berkeley, Calif.	Mrs. Pressler, 3 and 2	Miss Tainter, 2 and 1				
91	Mrs. Harry Pressler, San Gabriel, Calif.						
85	Miss Georgia Tainter, Fargo, N.D.	Miss Tainter, 6 and 5					
91	Miss Renee Lindquist, Bel-Air, Calif.						
82	Miss Helen Sigel, Philadelphia Country, Pa.	Miss Sigel, 5 and 4	Miss Barrett, 5 and 4	Miss Cothran, 4 and 2			
92	Miss Aurora Olagaray, Mexico City, Mexico						
86	Miss Beatrice Barrett, Lafayette, Minn.	Miss Barrett, 1 up					
89	Miss Jeanne Cline, Bloomington, Ill.						
83	Miss Peggy Graham, Lakeside, Calif.	Miss Graham, 8 and 7	Miss Cothran, 2 and 1				
92	Miss Margaret M. Bushard, Flintridge, Calif.						
86	Mrs. George Merriam Lewis, Los Angeles, Calif.	Miss Cothran, 2 and 1					
89	Miss Jane S. Cothran, Greenville, S.C.						
81	Miss Dorothy Kirby, Capital City, Ga.	Miss Kirby, 5 and 4	Miss Kirby, 4 and 3	Mrs. Ferrie, 2 up	Mrs. Ferrie, 5 and 3		
92	Mrs. Rod LaRocque, Wilshire, Calif.						
87	Miss Barbara Ransom, Stockton, Calif.	Miss Ransom, 5 and 4					
88	Miss Barbara Beach Thompson, Los Altos, Calif.						
84	Mrs. James Ferrie, Flintridge, Calif.	Mrs. Ferrie, 4 and 2	Mrs. Ferrie, 1 up, 19 hls.				
91	Mrs. Ethel B. Wack, Valley C. of Montecito, Calif.						
85	Miss Jean E. Bauer, Metacomet, R.I.	Miss Bauer, 4 and 3					
90	Mrs. Decker McAllister, Burlingame, Calif.						
82	Mrs. Dan Chandler, Brook Hollow, Texas	Mrs. Chandler, 4 and 2	Mrs. Goldthwaite, 1 up	Miss Morse, 1 up			
92	Mrs. Jane L. Reynolds, Wilshire, Calif.						
87	Mrs. Frank Goldthwaite, River Crest, Texas	Mrs. Goldthwaite, 4 and 2					
88	Mrs. Alan Pattee, Cypress Point, Calif.						
84	Miss Frances Glover, Sequoyah, Calif.	Miss Hurst, 2 and 1	Miss Morse, 2 and 1				
91	Miss Nancy Hurst, Alderwood, Ore.						
85	Miss Mary Morse, Cypress Point, Calif.	Miss Morse, 2 and 1					
90	Mrs. George E. Wilcox, Jr., Miami, Fla.						
79	Mrs. Frank D. Russ, Crystal Springs, Calif.	Mrs. Davy, 1 up	Miss Amory, 5 and 3	Miss Callender, 4 and 2	Miss Callender, 4 and 3	Miss Jameson, 5 and 3	
93	Mrs. Myron Davy, Congressional, D.C.						
88	Miss Grace Amory, Women's National, N.Y.	Miss Amory, 2 and 1					
88	Miss Ellamae Williams, Medinah, Ill.						
84	Miss Clara Callender, Virginia, Calif.	Miss Callender, 3 and 2	Miss Callender, 1 up				
91	Mrs. Emily Randolph, Brook Hollow, Texas						
85	Miss Catherine Shuster, Flintridge, Calif.	Miss Shuster, 5 and 4					
90	Mrs. Burton Lamfrom, Hillcrest, Calif.						
82	Mrs. Willard E. Shepherd, Los Angeles, Calif.	Mrs. Shepherd, 6 and 5	Mrs. Shepherd, 3 and 2	Mrs. Shepherd, 2 and 1			
92	Mrs. Delbert Walker, Virginia, Calif.						
87	Mrs. Robert E. Barbour, Arcola, N.J.	Mrs. Barbour, 2 up					
89	Miss Virginia Valentine, Crystal Springs, Calif.						
83	Miss Kathryn Pearson, River Oaks, Texas	Miss Pearson, 5 and 3	Mrs. MacArthur, 2 and 1				
92	Mrs. Grant Stephenson, Del Monte, Calif.						
86	Miss Elizabeth Wing, Glen View, Ill.	Mrs. MacArthur, 2 up					
89	Mrs. Arthur MacArthur, Lakeside, Calif.						
79	Miss Elizabeth Hicks, Annandale, Calif.	Miss Hicks, 5 and 4	Mrs. Wagner, 3 and 1	Miss Jameson, 5 and 4	Miss Jameson, 6 and 5		
92	Mrs. Arthur O. St. Clair, Olympic, Calif.						
87	Mrs. Ray Williams, Virginia, Calif.	Mrs. Wagner, 5 and 3					
88	Mrs. Mary Mozel Wagner, Alderwood, Ore.						
84	Miss Betty Jameson, San Antonio, Texas	Miss Jameson, 7 and 6	Miss Jameson, 1 up				
91	Mrs. Louis Lengfeld, Los Altos, Calif.						
85	Miss Louise Weyl, Riviera, Calif.	Miss Wall, 3 and 2					
90	Miss Mary Agnes Wall, Riverside, Mich.						
82	Miss Thelma Carr, Oakmont, Calif.	Miss Carr, 5 and 4	Miss Carr, 5 and 3	Mrs. Lifur, 5 and 3			
92	Mrs. Calvin Tilden, Presidio, Calif.						
87	Miss Margaret Crosbie, Alderwood, Ore.	Miss Crosbie, 7 and 6					
88	Mrs. Joseph H. Ronan, San Jose, Calif.						
84	Mrs. Gregg Lifur, Riviera, Calif.	Mrs. Lifur, 2 and 1	Mrs. Lifur, 2 up				
91	Miss Marion Hollins, Pasatiempo, Calif.						
86	Miss Marion E. Miley, Lexington, Ky.	Miss Miley, 5 and 3					
90	Miss Peggy Rutledge, Virginia, Calif.						

*Medalist.
The first word after the player's name is the name of the player's club, except in the case of a foreign entrant.

1941
FORTY-FIFTH WOMEN'S AMATEUR CHAMPIONSHIP

Held at The Country Club, Brookline, Mass., September 8-13. Yardage—6,090. Par 73. 124 Entries, 116 Starters.

Qualifying Score	1st Round (18 Holes)	2nd Round (18 Holes)	3rd Round (18 Holes)	4th Round (18 Holes)	Semi-Finals (18 Holes)	Final Round (36 Holes)	
76*	Miss Grace Amory, Cedar Creek, N.Y.	Mrs. Torgerson, 3 and 2					
84	Mrs. Reinert M. Torgerson, Lakeville, N.Y.		Mrs. Torgerson, 2 and 1				
82	Miss Margaret H. Nichols, Hudson River, N.Y.	Miss Nichols, 5 and 4					
86	Mrs. James H. Heim, Wanango, Pa.			Mrs. Torgerson, 2 and 1			
79	Miss Dorothy Kirby, Capital City, Ga.	Miss Kirby, 6 and 4					
85	Miss Cynthia Richardson, Highland, Mass.		Miss Hemphill, 5 and 4				
83	Miss Kathryn Hemphill, **Forest Lake, S.C.**	Miss Hemphill, 5 and 3					
87	Mrs. Ralph E. Seltzer, Jr., Philadelphia Country, Pa.				Miss Sigel, 1 up		
77	Miss Barbara Ransom, Stockton, Calif.	Miss Ransom, 3 and 2					
85	Miss Jane Crum, Forest Lake, S.C.		Miss Sigel, 3 and 2				
82	Miss Helen Sigel, Philadelphia Country, Pa.	Miss Sigel, 5 and 4					
87	Miss Catherine M. Fox, Glen Ridge, N.J.			Miss Sigel, 1 up, 21 hls.			
80	Miss Dorothy Germain, Llanerch, Pa.	Miss Germain, 3 and 2					
86	Mrs. T.O. McLaughlin, Western, Mich.		Miss Germain, 5 and 4				
83	Mrs. Willard E. Shepherd, Los Angeles, Calif.	Miss Schildmiller, 3 and 2					
88	Miss Dolly Schildmiller, Kenwood, Ohio					Miss Sigel, 3 and 2	
76*	Miss Alice O. Belanger, United Shoe Mach. A.A., Mass.	Mrs. Leichner, 3 and 2					
84	**Mrs. Sylva Federman Leichner, Fresh Meadow, N.Y.**		Mrs. Leichner, 2 up				
82	Miss Virginia M. Guilfoil, Syracuse Yacht, N.Y.	Miss Guilfoil, 4 and 3					
86	Mrs. John G. Capers, Merion Cricket, Pa.			Mrs. Leichner, 1 up, 20 hls.			
80	Miss Marion E. Miley, C.C. Lexington, Ky.	Miss Miley, 6 and 4					
85	Miss Peggy Rutledge, Virginia, Calif.		Miss Miley, 6 and 4				
83	Mrs. Russell C. Mann, Omaha Field, Neb.	Mrs. Mann, 4 and 2					
87	Mrs. T.E. Schluderberg, Baltimore, Md.				Mrs. Goldthwaite, 1 up, 19 hls.		
78	Mrs. James Ferrie, Virginia, Calif.	Mrs. Ferrie, 1 up, 19 hls.					
85	Mrs. Lily Harper Martin, Princess Anne, Va.		Miss Wild, 1 up, 19 hls.				
83	Miss Gail Wild, Baltusrol, N.J.	Miss Wild, 3 and 2					
87	Miss Betsy MacLeod, C.C. Buffalo, N.Y.			Mrs. Goldthwaite, 3 and 2			
81	Miss Kathleen S. Byrne, Rye, N.Y.	Miss Wilson, 1 up					
86	Miss Mary Jane Wilson, Pawtucket, R.I.		Mrs. Goldthwaite, 1 up, 22 hls.				
84	Mrs. Frank Goldthwaite, River Crest, Texas	Mrs. Goldthwaite, 5 and 4					
88	Mrs. Thomas E. Nolan, Chartiers Heights, Pa.						**Mrs. Elizabeth Hicks Newell, 5 and 3**
76*	Miss Jean E. Bauer, Metacomet, R.I.	Miss Suggs, 3 and 2					
84	Miss Louise Suggs, Capital City, Ga.		Mrs. Vare, 3 and 2				
82	Mrs. Glenna Collett Vare, Philadelphia Country, Pa.	Mrs. Vare, 5 and 4					
86	Miss Phyllis Otto, Omaha Field, Neb.			Miss Callender, 5 and 4			
80	Mrs. Frederick Davis, Rhode Island, R.I.	Miss Callender, 6 and 5					
85	Miss Clara Callender, Annandale, Calif.		Miss Callender, 6 and 4				
83	Miss Elinor Evelyn Jones, Albuquerque, N.M.	Miss Jones, 1 up					
87	Miss Shirley R. Podret, Dutchess, N.Y.				Mrs. Newell, 2 and 1		
78	Mrs. Dan Chandler, Brook Hollow, Texas	Mrs. Chandler, 7 and 6					
85	Mrs. F.J. Holleran, Round Hill, Conn.		Mrs. Beard, 1 up				
83	Mrs. H. Warren Beard, Charles River, Mass.	Mrs. Beard, 1 up					
87	Mrs. John Goodrich, The C.C., Brookline, Mass.			Mrs. Newell, 4 and 3			
81	**Mrs. Elizabeth Hicks Newell, Virginia, Calif.**	Mrs. Newell, 9 and 7					
86	Miss Mary Agnes Wall, Riverside, Mich.		Mrs. Newell, 2 up				
83	Miss Betty Jean Rucker, Spokane, Wash.	Miss Rucker, 1 up					
88	Mrs. Arthur L. Rowland, Indian Hill, Conn.					Mrs. Newell, 1 up, 19 hls.	
76*	Miss Betty Jameson, San Antonio, Texas	Miss Younker, 1 up					
84	Miss Janet Younker, Ceutury, N.Y.		Miss Younker, 2 and 1				
82	Mrs. William Hockenjos, Jr., Crestmont, N.J.	Mrs. Hockenjos, 6 and 4					
86	Miss Priscilla P. Janney, Woods Hole, Mass.			Miss Younker, 7 and 6			
80	Miss Maureen Orcutt, White Beeches, N.J.	Miss Orcutt, 5 and 4					
86	Miss Peggy Ann Delahant, Schuyler Meadows, N.Y.		Miss Orcutt, 4 and 3				
83	Mrs. Charles R. Harbaugh, Manakiki, Ohio	Mrs. Becker, 5 and 4					
88	Mrs. Albert Becker, Englewood, N.J.				Mrs. Page, 5 and 4		
78	Mrs. Julius A. Page, Jr., Sedgefield, N.C.	Mrs. Page, 1 up, 19 hls.					
85	Mrs. Raymond S. Patton, Hartford, Conn.		Mrs. Page, 4 and 2				
83	Mrs. Dewitt E. Untermeyer, Hollywood, N.J.	Miss Sears, 1 up					
87	Miss Grace M. Sears, Jefferson, Ont., Canada			Mrs. Page, 2 and 1			
81	Miss Eleanor Dudley, Ridge, Ill.	Miss Dudley, 3 and 1					
86	Miss Neoma Copic, Sylvania, Ohio		Miss Dudley, 3 and 2				
84	Mrs. Richard P. Limburg, Century, N.Y.	Mrs. Limburg, 4 and 3					
89	Miss Marjorie Harrison, Troy, N.Y.						

***Tied for medal; no playoff.**
The first word after the player's name is the name of the player's club, except in the case of a foreign entrant.

1946
FORTY-SIXTH WOMEN'S AMATEUR CHAMPIONSHIP

Held at the Southern Hills Country Club, Tulsa, Okla., September 23-28. Yardage—6,232. Par 75. 60 Entries, 58 Starters.

Qualifying Score	1st Round	2nd Round	3rd Round	Semi-Finals	Final Round (36 Holes)	
152*	Miss Dorothy Kirby, Capital City, Ga.	Miss Lenczyk, 4 and 3	Miss Sigel, 5 and 3	Miss Sigel, 6 and 5	Mrs. Zaharias, 3 and 2	Mrs. Mildred Didrikson Zaharias, 11 and 9
168	Miss Grace Lenczyk, Indian Hill, Conn.					
165	Miss Helen Sigel, Philadelphia Country, Pa.	Miss Sigel, 2 and 1				
173	Mrs. T.E. Chambers, Lakeside, Calif.					
161	Mrs. Jacqueline Pung, Honolulu, T.H.	Mrs. Goff, 2 up	Miss Gunther, 3 and 2			
171	Mrs. John Goff, Fargo, N.D.					
165	Miss Margaret Gunther, Memphis, Tenn.	Miss Gunther, 2 and 1				
175	Mrs. Fred Apostoli, Lake Merced, Calif.					
156	Mrs. Mildred Didrikson Zaharias, Park Hill, Colo.	Mrs. Zaharias, 4 and 3	Mrs. Zaharias, 4 and 3	Mrs. Zaharias, 5 and 4		
170	Miss Peggy Kirk, Findlay, Ohio					
165	Miss Betty Jean Rucker, Spokane, Wash.	Miss Rucker, 4 and 2				
174	Mrs. Frank Goldthwaite, River Crest, Texas					
163	Miss Maureen Orcutt, White Beeches, N.J.	Miss Orcutt, 2 and 1	Miss Orcutt, 4 and 3			
172	Miss Polly Riley, River Crest, Texas					
167	Miss Dorothy Kielty, Virginia, Calif.	Mrs. Williford, 3 and 1				
177	Mrs. H.T. Williford, Woodlawn, Texas					
154	Miss Louise Suggs, Capital City, Ga.	Mrs. Chandler, 1 up, 19 hls.	Mrs. Blanton, 5 and 4	Mrs. White, 3 and 1	Mrs. Sherman, 8 and 7	
169	Mrs. Dan Chandler, Brook Hollow, Texas					
165	Mrs. E.S. Blanton, Southern Hills, Okla.	Mrs. Blanton, 1 up				
173	Miss Alice Bauer, Long Beach Meadowlark, Calif.					
163	Miss Ann Casey, Mason City, Iowa	Mrs. White, 2 and 1	Mrs. White, 1 up			
172	Mrs. Bettye Mims White, Glen Lakes, Texas					
166	Miss Mary Agnes Wall, Riverside, Mich.	Miss Wall, 1 up, 19 hls.				
177	Miss Marjorie Row, Windsor, Ont., Canada					
160	Miss Jean Hopkins, Westwood, Ohio	Miss Freese, 2 and 1	Miss Hanson, 1 up, 19 hls.	Mrs. Sherman, 3 and 1		
170	Miss Carol Freese, Riverside, Ore.					
165	Miss Beverly Hanson, Fargo, N.D.	Miss Hanson, 3 and 2				
175	Miss Patricia McPhee, Peninsula, Calif.					
164	Mrs. Julius A. Page, Jr., Sedgefield, N.C.	Mrs. Page, 5 and 3	Mrs. Sherman, 1 up			
173	Miss Peggy Rutledge, Virginia, Calif.					
167	Mrs. Clara C. Sherman, Annandale, Calif.	Mrs. Sherman, 2 up				
177	Miss Ed Dell Wortz, Hardscrabble, Ark.					

*Medalist.
The first word after the player's name is the name of the player's club, except in the case of a foreign entrant.

1947
FORTY-SEVENTH WOMEN'S AMATEUR CHAMPIONSHIP

Held at the Franklin Hills Country Club, Franklin, Mich., September 22-27. Yardage—6,400. Par 76. 83 Entries, 77 Starters.

Qualifying Score	1st Round	2nd Round	3rd Round	Semi-Finals	Final Round (36 Holes)	
78*	Miss Louise Suggs, Capital City, Ga.	Miss Suggs, 6 and 4				
86	Miss Dorothy Ellis, Meridian Hills, Ind.		Miss Suggs, 2 and 1			
83	Miss Sally Sessions, Muskegon, Mich.	Miss Sessions, 4 and 2				
88	Mrs. John A. McDougald, Toronto, Canada			Miss Suggs, 1 up		
82	Miss Mary McMillin, Town & C.C., Wis.	Miss McMillin, 3 and 1				
87	Mrs. John S. Speer, Lansing, Mich.		Miss McMillin, 1 up			
85	Mrs. W.R. Kirkland, Jr., Piping Rock, N.Y.	Mrs. Kirkland, 5 and 3			Miss Suggs, 4 and 2	
89	Miss Marjorie Lindsay, Decatur, Ill.					
81	Miss Helen Sigel, Philadelphia Country, Pa.	Miss Sigel, 8 and 6				
87	Miss Margaret Russell, Oakland Hills, Mich.		Miss Lenczyk, 4 and 3			
83	Miss Grace S. Lenczyk, Indian Hill, Conn.	Miss Lenczyk, 5 and 4				
89	Mrs. Burt Weil, Losantiville, Ohio			Miss Lenczyk, 6 and 5		
82	Mrs. Eddie Bush, Western, Mich.	Mrs. Bush, 1 up				Miss Louise Suggs, 2 up
88	Miss Ruth Earle Woodward, Fall River, Mass.		Mrs. Bush, 2 and 1			
86	Miss Mary Agnes Wall, Riverside, Mich.	Miss Wall, 4 and 2				
89	Mrs. C.H. Shuttleworth, Bartonville, Canada					
81	Miss Peggy Kirk, Findlay, Ohio	Miss Kirk, 4 and 3				
87	Mrs. Harley G. Higbie, C.C. of Detroit, Mich.		Miss Riley, 4 and 3			
83	Miss Polly Riley, River Crest, Texas	Miss Riley, 2 and 1				
88	Miss Patricia O'Sullivan, Race Brook, Conn.			Miss Kirby, 3 and 2		
82	Miss Dorothy Kirby, Capital City, Ga.	Miss Kirby, 3 and 1				
88	Miss Ann J. Winslow, Cedar Lake, N.Y.		Miss Kirby, 1 up			
85	Miss Margaret Gunther, Memphis, Tenn.	Mrs. Vare, 1 up			Miss Kirby, 4 and 3	
89	Mrs. Glenna Collett Vare, Philadelphia Country, Pa.					
81	Mrs. Julius A. Page, Jr., Sedgefield, N.C.	Mrs. Page, 2 up				
87	Miss Patricia Devany, Grosse Ile, Mich.		Mrs. Page, 6 and 5			
84	Mrs. Cecil E. Gooderham, Toronto, Canada	Miss Orcutt, 2 and 1				
89	Miss Maureen Orcutt, White Beeches, N.J.			Mrs. Page, 2 up		
82	Miss Rosann Shaffer, Inverness, Ohio	Miss Irwin, 5 and 4				
88	Miss Laddie Irwin, Glen Ridge, N.J.		Miss Kielty, 1 up			
86	Miss Dorothy Kielty, Virginia, Calif.	Miss Kielty, 4 and 3				
90	Miss Jean Hopkins, Westwood, Ohio					

*Medalist.
The first word after the player's name is the name of the player's club, except in the case of a foreign entrant.

1948
FORTY-EIGHTH WOMEN'S AMATEUR CHAMPIONSHIP

Held at the Del Monte Golf and Country Club, Pebble Beach Golf Links, Calif.
September 13-18. Yardage—6,548. Par 76. 116 Entries, 108 Starters.

Qualifying Score	1st Round (18 Holes)	2nd Round (18 Holes)	3rd Round (18 Holes)	4th Round (18 Holes)	Semi-Finals (18 Holes)	Final Round (36 Holes)	
77*	Mrs. Bettye Mims White, Dallas A.C., Texas	Mrs. White, 1 up					
87	Miss Bee McWane, Mountain Brook, Ala.		Mrs. White, 1 up				
84	Miss Carol Diringer, Mohawk, Ohio	Miss Traung, 1 up					
90	Miss Dorothy Traung, Olympic, Calif.			Miss Kirby, 3 and 2			
83	Miss Dorothy Kirby, Capital City, Ga.	Miss Kirby, 4 and 3					
89	Mrs. Harry Winters, Inglewood, Calif.		Miss Kirby, 3 and 2				
85	Miss Marilynn Smith, Wichita, Kans.	Miss Smith, 3 and 2					
91	Mrs. Fred Apostoli, Lake Merced, Calif.				Miss Hanson, 1 up		
82	Miss Beverly Hanson, Fargo, N.D.	Miss Hanson, 7 and 6					
87	Miss Betty Blumenberg, San Gabriel, Calif.		Miss Hanson, 4 and 3				
85	Mrs. Joseph C. Herron, Waverley, Ore.	Mrs. Herron, 2 and 1					
90	Mrs. Frank Ingersoll, Jr., Peninsula, Calif.			Miss Hanson, 5 and 3			
84	Mrs. Willard E. Shepherd, Los Angeles, Calif.	Mrs. McCullah, 9 and 8					
89	Mrs. Ruth McCullah, Riviera, Calif.		Mrs. Lifur, 6 and 5				
86	**Mrs. Gregg H. Lifur, Riviera, Calif.**	Mrs. Lifur, 5 and 4					
92	Miss Lois M. Penn, Wakonda, Iowa					Miss Sigel, 6 and 5	
81	Miss Peggy Rutledge, Los Angeles, Calif.	Miss Rutledge, 1 up					
87	Mrs. James A. Ferrie, Virginia, Calif.		Miss Kirk, 8 and 7				
85	Miss Peggy Kirk, Findlay, Ohio	Miss Kirk, 3 and 2					
90	Mrs. William R. Millar, Los Angeles, Calif.			Miss Kirk, 1 up			
84	Miss Betty MacKinnon, Texarkana, Ark.	Miss MacKinnon, 4 and 2					
89	Miss Verna Lee Bongart, Danville, Ill.		Miss MacKinnon, 1 up, 19 hls.				
86	Mrs. Kermit A. Pearson, Peninsula, Calif.	Mrs. Pearson, 4 and 2					
91	Mrs. Roxie Setrakian, Olympic, Calif.				Miss Sigel, 5 and 3		
83	Miss Helen Sigel, Philadelphia Country, Pa.	Miss Sigel, 2 and 1					
88	Mrs. Eleanor D. Copping, Peninsula, Calif.		Miss Sigel, 2 and 1				
85	Miss Alice Bauer, California C.C., Calif.	Miss A. Bauer, 5 and 4					
90	Mrs. Arthur MacArthur, Lakeside, Calif.			Miss Sigel, 6 and 4			
84	Mrs. Julius A. Page, Jr., Sedgefield, N.C.	Mrs. Page, 6 and 5					
89	Miss Elizabeth Elliott, Claremont, Calif.		Miss McPhee, 1 up, 20 hls.				
86	Miss Marjorie Lindsay, Decatur, Ill.	Miss McPhee, 1 up					
92	Miss Patricia McPhee, Peninsula, Calif.						Miss Grace S. Lenczyk, 4 and 3
80	Miss Grace S. Lenczyk, Indian Hill, Conn.	Miss Lenczyk, 1 up, 21 hls.					
87	Miss Mary Agnes Wall, Riverside, Mich.		Miss Lenczyk, 2 and 1				
85	Miss Mary C. Sargent, Monterey Peninsula, Calif.	Miss Sargent, 2 up					
90	Miss Marilyn J. Cooper, Sacramento, Calif.			Miss Lenczyk, 6 and 5			
84	Miss Dorothy Workman, San Gabriel, Calif.	Miss Workman, 3 and 2					
89	Mrs. Charles Cary, Sequoyah, Calif.		Miss Workman, 1 up, 20 hls.				
86	Mrs. Frank Goldthwaite, River Crest, Texas	Mrs. Goldthwaite, 5 and 4					
91	Mrs. Richard Osborne, Monterey Peninsula, Calif.				Miss Lenczyk, 1 up		
83	Mrs. Maurice Glick, Woodholme, Md.	Mrs. Blanton, 3 and 2					
87	Mrs. Ernest S. Blanton, Oakwood, Okla.		Mrs. Blanton, 5 and 3				
85	Mrs. Cory Briggs, Monterey Peninsula, Calif.	Mrs. Briggs, 1 up					
90	Mrs. Paul Gardner, Los Angeles, Calif.			Miss Riley, 3 and 1			
84	Miss Polly Riley, River Crest, Texas	Miss Riley, 2 up					
89	Mrs. Floyd Ratliff, Stockdale, Calif.		Miss Riley, 7 and 6				
86	Miss Alice O'Neal, C.C. of Indianapolis, Ind.	Miss O'Neal, 2 and 1					
92	Miss Jean Hopkins, Westwood, Ohio					Miss Lenczyk, 4 and 2	
81	Mrs. Jacqueline L. Pung, Moanalua, Hawaii	Mrs. Pung, 5 and 3					
87	Mrs. George E. Wilcox, Jr., Miami, Fla.		Mrs. Pung, 1 up, 19 hls.				
85	Mrs. Glenna Collett Vare, Philadelphia C.C., Pa.	Mrs. Vare, 3 and 2					
90	Mrs. Hedley Brown, Inglewood, Calif.			Mrs. Holmes, 5 and 4			
84	Mrs. Jack Holmes, San Gabriel, Calif.	Mrs. Holmes, 3 and 2					
89	Miss Ellen Kieser, Lake Merced, Calif.		Mrs. Holmes, 7 and 5				
86	Mrs. Robert N. Palmer, Columbus, Ohio	Miss Weyl, 2 and 1					
92	Miss Louise Weyl, Riviera, Calif.				Mrs. Holmes, 2 and 1		
83	Miss Marlene Bauer, California C.C., Calif.	Miss M. Bauer, 6 and 5					
89	Mrs. Joseph H. Ronan, La Rinconada, Calif.		Miss M. Bauer, 4 and 3				
85	Miss Patricia Devany, Grosse Ile, Mich.	Miss Devany, 4 and 2					
91	Mrs. Allene G. Weissmuller, Lakeside, Calif.			Miss Gunther, 1 up			
84	Miss Margaret Gunther, Memphis, Tenn.	Miss Gunther, 2 and 1					
89	Miss Margaret Bushard, Santa Ana, Calif.		Miss Gunther, 5 and 4				
86	Mrs. M.B. Killian, San Antonio, Texas	Mrs. Killian, 6 and 5					
93	Mrs. Jean I. Anink, Alameda, Calif.						

*Medalist.
The first word after the player's name is the name of the player's club, except in the case of a foreign entrant.

1949
FORTY-NINTH WOMEN'S AMATEUR CHAMPIONSHIP

Held at the Merion Golf Club (East Course), Ardmore, Pa., September 12-17.
Yardage—6,135. Par 71. 171 Entries, 128 Qualifiers, 128 Starters.
Championship entirely at match play.
FINAL ROUND (36 Holes)—Mrs. Dorothy Germain Porter defeated Miss Dorothy Kielty, 3 and 2.

UPPER HALF

1st Round (18 Holes)	2nd Round (18 Holes)	3rd Round (18 Holes)	4th Round (18 Holes)	5th Round (18 Holes)	**Semi-Final** (18 Holes)	
Mrs. George H. Edwards, Bala, Pa. **Miss Janet Brown, Philadelphia Country C., Pa.**	Miss Brown, 1 up	Miss Brown, 1 up	Miss Brown, 4 and 3	Miss Brown, 5 and 3	Mrs. Porter, 7 and 6	Mrs. Porter, 3 and 1
Mrs. Donald F. Watkins, Birmingham, Mich. Miss Rachel C. McAvoy, Phoenixville, Pa.	Miss McAvoy, 7 and 6					
Miss Ruth Woodward, Fall River, Mass. Mrs. Thelma Richards, Maryland, Md.	Mrs. Richards, 5 and 4	Mrs. Scott, 8 and 6				
Mrs. Earl Scott, Philmont, Pa. Miss Marnie Polk, Chattanooga, Tenn.	Mrs. Scott, 3 and 2					
Mrs. Ralph I. Raynor, Old York Road, Pa. Mrs. Wm. G. Hamilton, Jr., Huntingdon Valley, Pa.	Mrs. Hamilton, 1 up, 19 hls.	Miss Orcutt, 5 and 4	Mrs. Untermeyer, 1 up			
Miss Barbara Canine, Kalamazoo, Mich. Miss Maureen Orcutt, White Beeches, N.J.	Miss Orcutt, 5 and 4					
Mrs. Betty Bush, Tam O'Shanter, Ill. Mrs. Sophie G. Untermeyer, Century, N.Y.	Mrs. Untermeyer, 2 and 1	Mrs. Untermeyer, 3 and 2				
Mrs. Jean A. Wikstrom, Colonia, N.J. Miss Mary Agnes Wall, Riverside, Mich.	Miss Wall, 8 and 6					
Mrs. T. Ellwood Webster, Merion, Pa. Miss Jane Martin, Oakmont, Pa.	Miss Martin, 4 and 2	Mrs. Parker, 5 and 3	Mrs. Porter, 8 and 7	Mrs. Porter, 1 up, 21 hls.		
Mrs. James Parker, Myopia Hunt, Mass. Mrs. Talbot Shelton, Saucon Valley, Pa.	Mrs. Parker, 5 and 4					
Mrs. William L. McGiverin, C.C. Detroit, Mich. **Mrs. Dorothy Germain Porter, Llanerch, Pa.**	Mrs. Porter, 4 and 2	Mrs. Porter, 8 and 7				
Mrs. Sylva Federman Leichner, Willow Brook, N.Y. Mrs. John Pennington, Buffalo, N.Y.	Mrs. Leichner, 2 and 1					
Mrs. Philip H. Allen, Syracuse Yacht, N.Y. Miss Mary Lena Faulk, Glen Arven, Ga.	Mrs. Allen, 3 and 2	Miss Doran, 4 and 2	Mrs. Page, 5 and 4			
Miss Claire Doran, Westwood, Ohio Mrs. Thomas Nolan, Chartiers, Pa.	Miss Doran, 1 up					
Mrs. S.R. Morgan, Jr., Gulph Mills, Pa. Miss Frances Stephens, Birkdale, England	Miss Stephens, 5 and 4	Mrs. Page, 4 and 3				
Mrs. Julius A. Page, Jr., Sedgefield, N.C. Miss Jane Thomas, Salisbury, N.C.	Mrs. Page, 4 and 2					
Miss Margaret Mackie, Inwood, N.Y. Miss Marjorie Lindsay, Decatur, Ill.	Miss Lindsay, 4 and 3	Miss Lindsay, by default	Miss Lindsay, 5 and 4	Miss Kirby, 3 and 2	Miss Kirby, 1 up, 19 hls.	
Mrs. Charles R. Harbaugh, Canterbury, Ohio Mrs. Edna Lafferty, Summit, Pa.	Mrs. Harbaugh, 2 up					
Mrs. Miriam Phipps-Lyon, Plymouth, Pa. Miss Bee McWane, Birmingham, Ala.	Miss McWane, 6 and 4	Miss McWane, 2 up				
Mrs. F. William Thacher, Jr., Riverton, N.J. Miss Betty S. Abernethy, Oakmont, Pa.	Mrs. Thacher, 2 up					
Miss Dorothy Kirby, Capital City, Ga. Mrs. Mary Longcope, Siwanoy, N.Y.	Miss Kirby, 9 and 7	Miss Kirby, 1 up	Miss Kirby, 1 up			
Miss Mary Sargent, Monterey Peninsula, Calif. Miss Rylma Strevel, Gowanie, Mich.	Miss Strevel, 5 and 4					
Miss Marjorie Burns, Starmount Forest, N.C. Mrs. Patricia A. Ficken, Tully-Secane, Pa.	Miss Burns, 2 and 1	Mrs. Tracy, 3 and 2				
Miss Grace S. Lenczyk, Indian Hill, Conn. Mrs. Joanne Barr Tracy, Dallas A.C., Texas	Mrs. Tracy, 1 up					
Mrs. James Ferrie, Virginia, Calif. Miss Peggy Kirk, Findlay, Ohio	Mrs. Ferrie, 3 and 2	Mrs. Ferrie, 1 up	Mrs. Hulteng, 3 and 1	Mrs. Hulteng, 2 up		
Miss Alice Gray, Merion, Pa. Miss Shirley G. Spork, Western, Mich.	Miss Spork, 7 and 5					
Miss Nancy Slaw, Plymouth, Pa. Mrs. John L. Hulteng, Wannamoisett, R.I.	Mrs. Hulteng, 1 up, 19 hls.	Mrs. Hulteng, 5 and 4				
Miss Barbara Dawson, Claremont, Calif. Mrs. J.B. Balding, Creek, N.Y.	Mrs. Balding, 5 and 4					
Mrs. Maurice Glick, Woodholme, Md. Miss Elinor Irving, Wilmington, Del.	Mrs. Glick, 8 and 6	Mrs. Glick, 4 and 2	Mrs. Torgerson, 2 and 1			
Mrs. James H. Bradley, Plum Hollow, Mich. Mrs. Dwight R. Anneaux, Skycrest, Ill.	Mrs. Anneaux, 4 and 2					
Miss Margaret Curtis, Essex County, Mass. Mrs. J. Albert Hayes, Phila. Country C., Pa.	Mrs. Hayes, 3 and 2	Mrs. Torgerson, 4 and 3				
Mrs. Reinert M. Torgerson, Cherry Valley, N.Y. Mrs. Maude McDougald, Long Branch, Ont., Canada	Mrs. Torgerson, 5 and 3					

The first word after the player's name is the name of the player's club, except in the case of a foreign entrant.

LOWER HALF

	Semi-Final (18 Holes)	5th Round (18 Holes)	4th Round (18 Holes)	3rd Round (18 Holes)	2nd Round (18 Holes)	1st Round (18 Holes)
Miss Kielty, 1 up	Miss Kielty, 1 up, 19 hls.	Miss Kielty, 5 and 4	Mrs. Gessler, 1 up	Mrs. Trainor, 4 and 3	Mrs. Trainor, 6 and 5	Mrs. George M. Trainor, Oak Hill, N.Y. Mrs. Joseph P. Stapchinskas, Hershey, Pa.
					Mrs. Wentz, 1 up	Mrs. Charles F. Spalding, Meadow Brook, N.Y. Mrs. Graham Wentz, Springhaven, Pa.
				Mrs. Gessler, 1 up	Mrs. Gessler, 4 and 3	Miss Helen H. Hampton, Chattanooga, Tenn. Mrs. John M. Gessler, Whitemarsh Valley, Pa.
					Mrs. Hockenjos, 1 up	Miss Mary Ann Downey, Baltimore, Md. Mrs. William Hockenjos, Jr., Baltusrol, N.J.
			Miss Kielty, 6 and 5	Miss Kielty, 5 and 4	Miss Kielty, 5 and 3	Miss Priscilla Buckley, Camden, S.C. Miss Dorothy Kielty, Virginia, Calif.
					Miss Rawls, 3 and 1	Miss Beverly Hanson, Fargo, N.D. Miss Betsy Rawls, Austin, Texas
				Miss Sigel, 4 and 3	Miss Sigel, 3 and 1	Mrs. John G. Capers, Jr., Merion, Pa. Miss Helen Sigel, Philadelphia Country Club, Pa.
					Miss Stulb, 2 and 1	Miss Patricia O'Sullivan, Race Brook, Conn. Miss Eileen Stulb, Augusta C.C., Ga.
		Miss Riley, 2 and 1	Miss Devany, 1 up	Miss McPhee, 2 and 1	Miss McPhee, 7 and 5	Miss Patricia McPhee, Peninsula, Calif. Mrs. Frank Goodyear, Gulph Mills, Pa.
					Mrs. Goldthwaite, 1 up	Mrs. Frank Goldthwaite, River Crest, Texas Miss Ann Cosgrove, Pinehurst, N.C.
				Miss Devany, 5 and 4	Mrs. Gade, 1 up	Mrs. Harold H. Gade, St. Davids, Pa. Miss Sonia E. Wise, York, Pa.
					Miss Devany, 7 and 6	Miss Patricia Devany, Grosse Ile, Mich. Mrs. Arthur Kitson, Jr., Plymouth, Pa.
			Miss Riley, 5 and 3	Miss Diringer, 1 up, 19 hls.	Miss A. Bauer, 5 and 4	**Mrs. Walter Acuff, Jr., Philadelphia Country C., Pa.** Miss Alice Bauer, California C.C., Calif.
					Miss Diringer, 4 and 3	Miss Irene Bretzlaff, Western, Mich. Miss Carol Diringer, Mohawk, Ohio
				Miss Riley, 8 and 7	Miss Riley, 6 and 5	Mrs. Cecil Gooderham, Long Branch, Ontario, Canada Miss Polly Riley, River Crest, Texas
					Miss Odom, 2 and 1	Miss Evelyn Odom, Wheatley Hills, N.Y. Mrs. Burt Weil, Losantiville, Ohio
	Miss M. Bauer, 4 and 2	Miss M. Bauer, 1 up	Miss M. Bauer, 5 and 4	Miss M. Bauer, 4 and 3	Miss M. Bauer, 6 and 4	Mrs. Harley G. Higbie, C.C. Detroit, Mich. Miss Marlene Bauer, California C.C., Calif.
					Mrs. Vare, 5 and 4	**Mrs. Glenna Collett Vare, Philadelphia Country C., Pa.** Mrs. Ralph Powers, The Country Club, Mass.
				Miss Smith, 4 and 3	Miss Smith, 4 and 3	Miss Josephine S. Smith, Merion, Pa. Mrs. J.H. McCarter, Toronto, Ontario, Canada
					Mrs. Park, 1 up	**Mrs. Marion Turpie McNaughton, N. Hempstead, N.Y.** Mrs. Catherine Fox Park, Glen Ridge, N.J.
			Miss Gunther, 3 and 2	Miss Harrington, 1 up	Miss Harrington, 3 and 1	Miss Patricia L. Harrington, Steubenville, Ohio Mrs. Henri Prunaret, Charles River, Mass.
					Mrs. May, 2 up	Mrs. H. Hoffman Dolan, Merion, Pa. Mrs. Mortimer May, Willow Brook, N.Y.
				Miss Gunther, 2 and 1	Miss Gunther, 4 and 3	Miss Margaret Gunther, Memphis, Tenn. Mrs. Clarence Cox, Wanango, Pa.
					Mrs. Bartol, 4 and 2	Mrs. Harold W. Stone, Greenville, S.C. Mrs. John H. Bartol, Greenwich, Conn.
		Miss MacKinnon, 4 and 3	Mrs. Flippin, 3 and 2	Miss Murray, 5 and 3	Mrs. Breault, 6 and 5	Miss Nancy H. Wilson, Aronimink, Pa. Mrs. H.O. Breault, Olympia Fields, Ill.
					Miss Murray, 4 and 3	Mrs. Karl F. Scheidt, Merion, Pa. Miss Mae Murray, Rutland, Vt.
				Mrs. Flippin, 3 and 1	Mrs. Flippin, 1 up, 19 hls.	Mrs. W.R. Kirkland, Jr., Piping Rock, N.Y. Mrs. Harrison Flippin, Merion, Pa.
					Miss Garber, 9 and 7	Mrs. Robert F. Beard, Merion, Pa. Miss Elizabeth L. Garber, Argyle, Md.
			Miss MacKinnon, 6 and 4	Miss Hopkins, 6 and 5	Mrs. Stetson, 1 up, 20 hls.	Mrs. J. Walker Hoopes, Wilmington, Del. Mrs. Helen B. Stetson, Huntingdon Valley, Pa.
					Miss Hopkins, 2 and 1	Miss Jean Hopkins, Westwood, Ohio Mrs. Laura C. Bostwick, Meadow Brook, N.Y.
				Miss MacKinnon, 5 and 4	Miss MacKinnon, 8 and 7	Mrs. Frederick Marshall, Jr., Gulph Mills, Pa. Miss Betty MacKinnon, Texarkana, Ark.
					Mrs. Millar, 1 up, 20 hls.	Mrs. Sam Byrd, Plum Hollow, Mich. Mrs. William Millar, Los Angeles, Calif.

1950
FIFTIETH WOMEN'S AMATEUR CHAMPIONSHIP

Held at the East Lake Course of the Atlanta Athletic Club, Atlanta, Ga., September 11-16.
Yardage–6,521. Par 74. 110 Entries, 105 Starters.
Championship entirely at match play (sectional qualifying cancelled).
FINAL ROUND (36 Holes)–Miss Beverly Hanson defeated Miss Mae Murray, 6 and 4.

UPPER HALF

1st Round (18 Holes)	2nd Round (18 Holes)	3rd Round (18 Holes)	4th Round (18 Holes)	5th Round (18 Holes)	Semi-Final (18 Holes)	
Miss Virginia Dennehy, Onwentsia, Ill.	Miss Sargent, by default					
Miss Mary Sargent, Monterey Peninsula, Calif.		Miss Sargent, 3 and 2				
Mrs. James M. Conklin, Jr., Oakwood, Ohio	Miss McKinnon, 5 and 3					
Miss Katharine McKinnon, W. Palm Beach, Fla.			Miss Thomas, 1 up			
Mrs. Catherine Fox Park, Glen Ridge, N.J.	Miss Thomas, 6 and 4					
Miss Betty Jane Thomas, Salisbury, N.C.		Miss Thomas, 2 and 1		Miss Kirby, 3 and 2		
BYE–Mrs. Frank Goldthwaite, River Crest, Texas	Mrs. Goldthwaite					
Mrs. James Parker, Myopia Hunt, Mass.	Miss Diringer, by default					
Miss Carol Diringer, Mohawk, Ohio		Miss Diringer, 1 up				
Mrs. J.A. Ochiltree, St. Charles, Ill.	Mrs. Ochiltree, 8 and 7					
Mrs. Frederick Bellinger, Atlanta A.C., Ga.			Miss Kirby, 5 and 4			
Mrs. William R. Millar, Los Angeles, Calif.	Miss Clark, 6 and 5					
Miss Carol Clark, Wyoming, Ohio		Miss Kirby, 4 and 2			Miss DeMoss, 1 up	
Mrs. Charles Dennehy, Onwentsia, Ill.	Miss Kirby, by default					
Miss Dorothy Kirby, Capital City, Ga.						
BYE–Miss Carol Gallagher, W. Palm Beach, Fla.	Miss Gallagher	Miss O'Sullivan, 7 and 6				
Miss Patricia O'Sullivan, Race Brook, Conn.	Miss O'Sullivan, 7 and 5					
Mrs. Lanier B. Yarbrough, Druid Hills, Ga.			Miss Doran, 6 and 5			
Mrs. Julius N. Boros, Pinehurst, N.C.	Miss Lenczyk, by default					
Miss Grace S. Lenczyk, Indian Hill, Conn.		Miss Doran, by default		Miss DeMoss, 2 and 1		
Miss Claire Doran, Westwood, Ohio	Miss Doran, 2 up					
Miss Elizabeth Price, Tilford, England						
BYE–Miss Barbara Blakely, Anniston, Ala.	Miss Blakely	Miss Blakely, 1 up, 20 hls.				
Mrs. Roy E. Thomas, Miami Shores, Fla.	Miss Devany, 7 and 5					
Miss Patricia Devany, Grosse Ile, Mich.			**Miss DeMoss, 6 and 5**			
Miss Grace DeMoss, Corvallis, Ore.	Miss DeMoss, 9 and 8					
Miss Frances Rich, Glen Arven, Ga.		Miss DeMoss, 2 up				
Mrs. Betty Bush, Woodmar, Ind.	Mrs. Bush, 1 up					
Mrs. George Valentine, Perth, Scotland						Miss Hanson, 1 up
BYE–Miss Marnie Polk, Chattanooga, Tenn.	Miss Polk	Miss Hanson, 6 and 5				
Mrs. Lee K. Alexander, Drumlins, N.Y.	Miss Hanson, 9 and 8					
Miss Beverly Hanson, Fargo, N.D.			Miss Hanson, 1 up			
Miss Betty MacKinnon, Dallas A.C., Texas	**Miss MacKinnon,** 1 up					
Mrs. Alexa Stirling Fraser, Ottawa, Ont., Canada		Miss MacKinnon, 5 and 3		Miss Hanson, 4 and 3		
Mrs. Calvin Tilden, San Francisco, Calif.	Miss Donald, 3 and 1					
Miss Jean Donald, North Berwick, Scotland						
BYE–Miss Mary Lou Durkin, Druid Hills, Ga.	Miss Durkin	Miss Downey, 6 and 5				
Miss Mary Ann Downey, Baltimore, Md.	Miss Downey, 3 and 2					
Miss Priscilla Buckley, Camden, S.C.			Miss Stulb, 1 up, 19 hls.		Miss Hanson, 5 and 4	
Miss Eileen Stulb, Augusta, Ga.	Miss Stulb, 7 and 5					
Mrs. Burt Weil, Losantiville, Ohio		Miss Stulb, 2 and 1				
Mrs. John Pennington, Buffalo, N.Y.	Mrs. Hampton, 3 and 1					
Miss Helen H. Hampton, Chattanooga, Tenn.						
BYE–Mrs. J. Albert Hayes, Phila. Country C., Pa.	Mrs. Hayes	Mrs. Hayes, 1 up, 19 hls.				
Mrs. Dorothy Germain Porter, Llanerch, Pa.	Mrs. Porter, 3 and 2					
Mrs. Herbert O. Breault, Olympia Fields, Ill.			Mrs. Stone, 1 up			
Miss Barbara Dawson, Orinda, Calif.	Miss Dawson, by default					
Mrs. Robert F. Sparrow, Kennett Square, Pa.		Mrs. Stone, 5 and 4				
Miss Martha Daniel, Coosa, Ga.	Mrs. Stone, 2 up					
Mrs. Harold W. Stone, Greenville, S.C.				Miss Garvey, 4 and 3		
BYE–Miss Ellen H. Gery, Berkshire, Pa.	Miss Gery	Miss Garvey, 8 and 7				
Miss Marjorie Burns, Starmount Forest, N.C.	Miss Garvey, 1 up					
Miss Philomena Garvey, Baltray, Eire			Miss Garvey, 2 and 1			
Mrs. Lyle Bowman, Riverside, Ore.	Mrs. Bowman, 5 and 4					
Mrs. William L. McGiverin, C.C. Detroit, Mich.		Mrs. Bowman, 2 and 1				
Miss Virginia M. Doyle, Toy Town Tavern, Mass.	Miss Doyle, 2 and 1					
Mrs. Sara Pierotti, Atlanta A.C., Ga.						

The first word after the player's name is the name of the player's club, except in the case of a foreign entrant.

LOWER HALF

Semi-Final (18 Holes)		5th Round (18 Holes)	4th Round (18 Holes)	3rd Round (18 Holes)	2nd Round (18 Holes)	1st Round (18 Holes)
Miss Murray, 3 and 2	Miss Murray, 1 up	Miss Kielty, 4 and 2	Miss Kirk, 4 and 2	Miss Kirk, 2 and 1	Mrs. Page, 6 and 4	Mrs. Julius A. Page, Jr., Sedgefield, N.C. Mrs. Ernest S. Blanton, Oakwood, Okla.
					Miss Kirk, 6 and 4	Mrs. Grady McDonald, Ansley Park, Ga. Miss Peggy Kirk, Findlay, Ohio
				Miss Smith, 1 up	Miss Smith, by default	Mrs. Dan Chandler, Brook Hollow, Texas Miss Josephine S. Smith, Merion, Pa.
					Mrs. Williford	BYE—Mrs. H.T. Williford, Oakwood, Okla.
			Miss Kielty, 4 and 3	Miss Kielty, 6 and 5	Miss Kielty, 5 and 4	Miss Dorothy Kielty, Virginia, Calif. Miss Mary Lena Faulk, Glen Arven, Ga.
					Miss McIntire, 3 and 1	Miss Barbara McIntire, Heather Downs, Ohio Mrs. Glenna Collett Vare, Philadelphia Country Club, Pa.
				Miss Woodward, 2 and 1	Miss Woodward, 7 and 6	Mrs. F. William Thacher, Jr., Riverton, N.J. Miss Ruth Woodward, Fall River, Mass.
					Miss Harrington, 1 up	Miss Elizabeth Jennings, Sea Island, Ga. Miss Patricia Harrington, Steubenville, Ohio
		Miss Murray, 1 up, 27 hls.	Miss Crocker, 8 and 6	Miss Garner, 5 and 3	Mrs. Allen	BYE—Mrs. Philip H. Allen, Syracuse Yacht, N.Y.
					Miss Garner, 4 and 2	Mrs. Harry G. Webb, Huntsville, Ala. Miss Pat Garner, Midland, Texas
				Miss Crocker, 7 and 5	Miss Crocker, 7 and 5	Miss Fay Crocker, Montevideo, Uruguay Capt. Patricia E. Grant, Fort McPherson, Ga.
					Mrs. Raynor, by default	Mrs. Ralph I. Raynor, Old York Road, Pa. Mrs. William E. Tracy, Glen Ridge, N.J.
			Miss Murray, 6 and 5	Miss Murray, 7 and 5	Mrs. Harbaugh	BYE—Mrs. Charles R. Harbaugh, Canterbury, Ohio
					Miss Murray, 5 and 4	Miss Mary Crawford, Americus, Ga. Miss Mae Murray, Rutland, Vt.
				Miss Maddox, 1 up, 19 hls.	Miss Maddox, by default	Miss Sydney Elliott, Farmington, Va. Miss Margaret Maddox, Atlanta A.C., Ga.
					Miss Reed, 8 and 6	Miss Sherley M. Redding, Sedgefield, N.C. Miss Nancy Reed, Richland, Tenn.
	Miss Sigel, 3 and 2	Miss Sigel, 3 and 2	Miss Sigel, 6 and 5	Miss Sigel, 3 and 2	Miss Sigel, 3 and 2	Miss Edean Anderson, Green Meadow, Mont. Miss Helen Sigel, Philadelphia Country Club, Pa.
					Miss Swift, by default	Mrs. Cecil E. Gooderham, Long Branch, Ont., Canada Miss Roslyn Swift, Glen Oaks, N.Y.
				Mrs. Wilcox, 7 and 5	Mrs. Bright	BYE—Mrs. Morton Bright, Capital City, Ga.
					Mrs. Wilcox, 2 up	Mrs. George E. Wilcox, Jr., Miami, Fla. Mrs. Robert R. Givens, Druid Hills, Ga.
			Miss Lindsay, 1 up, 19 hls.	Miss Lindsay, 4 and 3	Miss Lindsay, 5 and 4	Miss Bee McWane, Birmingham, Ala. Miss Marjorie Lindsay, Decatur, Ill.
					Mrs. Hamilton, 4 and 3	Mrs. William G. Hamilton, Jr., Huntingdon Valley, Pa. Miss Nancy Porter, Wyoming, Ohio
				Miss Keplinger, by default	Mrs. Strong, by default	Mrs. T. Ellwood Webster, Merion, Pa. Mrs. Homer Strong, Rochester, N.Y.
					Miss Keplinger	BYE—Miss Nancy Keplinger, Hempstead, N.Y.
		Miss Rawls, 1 up	Miss Riley, 1 up	Miss Bisgood, 3 and 2	Mrs. Gessler, 9 and 7	Mrs. Arthur Mims, Druid Hills, Ga. Mrs. John M. Gessler, Whitemarsh Valley, Pa.
					Miss Bisgood, 2 up	Miss Frances Stephens, Birkdale, England Miss Jeanne Bisgood, Parkstone, England
				Miss Riley, 6 and 5	Miss Wall, 8 and 6	Miss Mary Agnes Wall, Riverside, Mich. Miss Anne Twilley, Druid Hills, Ga.
					Miss Riley, 8 and 7	Miss Polly Riley, River Crest, Texas Miss Allee Chatham, Greenwood, Miss.
			Miss Rawls, 5 and 4	Miss Rawls, 2 and 1	Mrs. Torgerson	BYE—Mrs. Reinert M. Torgerson, Cherry Valley, N.Y.
					Miss Rawls, 6 and 5	Miss Betsy Rawls, Austin, Texas Miss Barbara Ransom, Stockton, Calif.
				Miss Dodd, 3 and 1	Miss Dodd, 8 and 7	Miss Elizabeth Dodd, Oak Hills, Texas Mrs. William T. Hall, Ansley Park, Ga.
					Miss Lesser, 6 and 4	Mrs. J.P. Moore, Shaker Heights, Ohio Miss Patricia Ann Lesser, Sand Point, Wash.

1951
FIFTY-FIRST WOMEN'S AMATEUR CHAMPIONSHIP

Held at the Town and Country Club, St. Paul, Minn., August 20-25. Yardage—6,210. Par 74. 79 Entries, 75 Starters.

Qualifying Score	1st Round (18 Holes)	2nd Round (18 Holes)	3rd Round (18 Holes)	4th Round (18 Holes)	Semi-Finals (18 Holes)	Final Round (36 Holes)	
74*	Miss Carol Diringer, Mohawk, Ohio	Miss Diringer, 5 and 4	Miss Diringer, 3 and 1	Miss DeMoss, 2 and 1	Miss DeMoss, 3 and 2	Miss Kirby, 6 and 5	Miss Dorothy Kirby, 2 and 1
83	Miss Mary Agnes Wall, Riverside, Mich.						
79	Miss Dorothy Kielty, Virginia, Calif.	Miss Kielty, 2 and 1					
87	Miss Beverly Gammon, University of Minnesota						
77	Miss Grace DeMoss, Corvallis, Ore.	Miss DeMoss, 4 and 3	Miss DeMoss, 2 and 1				
86	Miss Marnie Polk, Chattanooga, Tenn.						
82	Miss Marjorie Lindsay, C.C. of Decatur, Ill.	Miss Lindsay, 6 and 5					
89	Mrs. Ralph I. Raynor, Old York Road, Pa.						
76	Mrs. Maurice Glick, Woodholme, Md.	Miss Orcutt, 5 and 4	Mrs. Altmeyer, 1 up	Miss Anderson, 6 and 5			
84	Miss Maureen Orcutt, White Beeches, N.J.						
80	Miss Ruth E. Woodward, Acoaxet, Mass.	Mrs. Altmeyer, 1 up					
88	Mrs. Beatrice E. Altmeyer, Lafayette, Minn.						
78	Miss Edean Anderson, Green Meadow, Mont.	Miss Anderson, 3 and 2	Miss Anderson, 6 and 4				
87	Mrs. Calvin Tilden, San Francisco, Calif.						
83	Miss Rosalyn M. Wisen, University of Minnesota	Miss Wisen, 5 and 4					
90	Mrs. Gordon W. Mixon, Town and C.C., Minn.						
75	Miss Helen Sigel, Philadelphia Country C., Pa.	Miss Sigel, 2 and 1	Miss O'Sullivan, 1 up	Miss Kirby, 5 and 4	Miss Kirby, 5 and 3		
84	Miss Betty Rowland, Idle Hour, Ky.						
79	Miss Patricia O'Sullivan, Race Brook, Conn.	Miss O'Sullivan, 7 and 6					
88	Mrs. David Stamps, Richmond, Calif.						
78	Miss Dorothy Kirby, Capital City, Ga.	Miss Kirby, 3 and 2	Miss Kirby, 5 and 4				
86	Miss Patricia Devany, Grosse Ile, Mich.						
82	Miss Mary Lena Faulk, Glen Arven, Ga.	Miss Faulk, 7 and 6					
89	Mrs. George MacGibbon, University of Minnesota						
76	Vicomtesse de Saint-Sauveur, Oise, France	Vic. de St.-Sauveur, 1 up	Miss Sargent, 2 and 1	Miss Nelson, 2 up			
85	Miss Martha Mumby, Mission Valley, Calif.						
82	Miss Mary Sargent, Monterey Peninsula, Calif.	Miss Sargent, 7 and 6					
88	Miss Clara Jane Mosack, Plum Hollow, Mich.						
79	Mrs. Mary Jacobs, Oneida, Wis.	Mrs. Jacobs, 1 up, 19 hls.	Miss Nelson, 1 up				
87	Mrs. Harry Winters, Inglewood, Calif.						
83	Miss Jane Nelson, Highland, Ind.	Miss Nelson, 7 and 6					
90	Miss Marlene Gesell, Westfield, Minn.						
74*	Miss Barbara Romack, Del Paso, Calif.	Miss Romack, 3 and 2	Miss Dodd, 2 and 1	Miss Doran, 7 and 6	Miss Doran, 2 and 1	Miss Doran, 2 up	
83	Mrs. Harold W. Stone, Greenville, S.C.						
79	Miss Betty Dodd, Oak Hills, Texas	Miss Dodd, 1 up					
87	Miss Irene Watson, Midland Hills, Minn.						
78	Miss Claire Doran, Westwood, Ohio	Miss Doran, 4 and 2	Miss Doran, 4 and 3				
86	Mrs. George E. Wilcox, Jr., Miami, Fla.						
82	Mrs. Lyle Bowman, Richmond, Calif.	Mrs. Bowman, 1 up					
89	Mrs. Frank Goldthwaite, River Crest, Texas						
76	Miss Polly Riley, River Crest, Texas	Miss Riley, 7 and 6	Miss Riley, 3 and 2	Miss Downey, 7 and 6			
84	Mrs. Thomas J. Rurik, Town and C.C., Minn.						
81	Mrs. Harrison F. Flippin, Merion, Pa.	Miss Dawson, 4 and 3					
88	Miss Barbara Dawson, Orinda, Calif.						
78	Miss Grace S. Lenczyk, Indian Hill, Conn.	Miss Fecht, 6 and 5	Miss Downey, 1 up, 20 hls.				
87	Miss Gloria J. Fecht, Griffith Park Women's, Calif.						
83	Miss Mary Ann Downey, Baltimore, Md.	Miss Downey, 5 and 4					
90	Mrs. Peter Patch, Orinda, Calif.						
75	Mrs. Ann Casey Johnstone, Mason City, Iowa	Mrs. Johnstone, 4 and 3	Mrs. Page, 5 and 4	Mrs. Page, 5 and 4	Mrs. Page, 6 and 5		
84	Miss Nancy Reed, Richland, Tenn.						
79	Mrs. Julius A. Page, Jr., Sedgefield, N.C.	Mrs. Page, 5 and 4					
88	Miss Bee McWane, C.C. of Birmingham, Ala.						
78	Miss Mae Murray, Rutland, Vt.	Miss Murray, 7 and 5	Miss Murray, 5 and 4				
86	Mrs. John Pennington, C.C. of Buffalo, N.Y.						
82	Miss Pat Garner, Midland, Texas	Mrs. Berg, 5 and 4					
89	Mrs. Herman L. Berg, Interlachen, Minn.						
76	Miss Bonnie Randolph, Ohio State University	Miss Randolph, 2 up	Mrs. Breault, 1 up, 20 hls.	Miss Lesser, 6 and 5			
85	Miss Patricia Ann Leith, Elgin, Ill.						
82	Mrs. Richard N. Robertson, Palma Ceia, Fla.	Mrs. Breault, 2 and 1					
89	Mrs. Herbert O. Breault, Olympia Fields, Ill.						
79	Miss Patricia Ann Lesser, Sand Point, Wash.	Miss Lesser, 3 and 2	Miss Lesser, 5 and 3				
87	Miss Eileen Stulb, Athens, Ga.						
83	Miss Barbara Bruning, Whippoorwill, N.Y.	Miss Bruning, 7 and 5					
91	Miss Mary Jane Warpeha, Midland Hills, Minn.						

*Medalists.
The first word after the player's name is the name of the player's club, except in the case of a foreign entrant.

1952
FIFTY-SECOND WOMEN'S AMATEUR CHAMPIONSHIP

Held at the Waverley Country Club, Portland, Ore., August 25-30. Yardage—6,323. Par 73. 159 Entries, 147 Starters.

Qualifying Score	1st Round (18 Holes)	2nd Round (18 Holes)	3rd Round (18 Holes)	4th Round (18 Holes)	Semi-Finals (18 Holes)	Final Round (36 Holes)	
76	***Miss Dorothy Kirby, Capital City, Ga.**	Miss Kirby, 4 and 3	Miss Kirby, 1 up, 19 hls.	Miss Anderson, 4 and 3	Mrs. Pung, 2 up	Mrs. Pung, 6 and 4	Mrs. Jacqueline Pung, 2 and 1
84	Mrs. Frank T. Fisk, Alderwood, Ore.						
81	Miss Mary Agnes Wall, Riverside, Mich.	Miss Wall, 5 and 4					
87	Miss Ethel Benson, Sunnybrook, Pa.						
80	Miss Edean Anderson, Green Meadow, Mont.	Miss Anderson, 1 up, 19 hls.	Miss Anderson, 2 up				
85	Miss Mary Sargent, Memphis, Tenn.						
83	Mrs. Harrison F. Flippin, Merion, Pa.	Mrs. Flippin, 5 and 4					
88	Mrs. Merrill Rose, Rose City, Ore.						
79	Mrs. Maurice Glick, Woodholme, Md.	Mrs. Glick, 2 and 1	Miss DeMoss, 2 and 1	Mrs. Pung, 4 and 3			
85	Miss Barbara Dawson, Orinda, Calif.						
82	Miss Grace DeMoss, Corvallis, Ore.	Miss DeMoss, 6 and 5					
87	Miss Gloria J. Fecht, Thunderbird, Calif.						
80	Mrs. Jacqueline Pung, Moanalua, Hawaii	Mrs. Pung, 2 up	Mrs. Pung, 3 and 2				
86	Miss Dorothy Stamps, Richmond, Calif.						
83	Mrs. William Cunningham, Waverley, Ore.	Mrs. Cunningham, 3 and 2					
88	Mrs. William R. Millar, Los Angeles, Calif.						
79	Miss Patricia Ann Lesser, Sand Point, Wash.	Miss Lesser, 3 and 2	Miss Lesser, 6 and 5	Miss Lesser, 9 and 7	Miss Lesser, 3 and 2		
84	Miss Patricia O'Sullivan, Race Brook, Conn.						
82	Mrs. Lyle Bowman, Richmond, Calif.	Miss Quast, 1 up, 19 hls.					
87	Miss Ann Quast, Everett, Wash.						
80	Miss Mary K. Wright, La Jolla, Calif.	Miss Armstrong, 1 up, 19 hls.	Miss McWane, 3 and 1				
86	Miss Gloria Armstrong, Alameda Women's, Calif.						
83	Miss Marnie Polk, Chattanooga, Tenn.	Miss McWane, 2 and 1					
88	Miss Bee McWane, C.C. of Birmingham, Ala.						
80	Miss Barbara Romack, Del Paso, Calif.	Miss Romack, 1 up, 19 hls.	Miss Romack, 5 and 3	Miss Romack, 1 up, 20 hls.			
85	Miss Carol Diringer, Mohawk, Ohio						
83	Mrs. C.F. Spalding, Round Hill, Conn.	Mrs. Stepp, 1 up					
87	Mrs. Harry W. Stepp, Riverside, Ore.						
81	Miss Polly Riley, River Crest, Texas	Miss Riley, 4 and 3	Miss Riley, 3 and 1				
86	Miss Josephine S. Smith, Merion, Pa.						
84	Miss Ruth Jessen, Inglewood, Wash.	Miss Jessen, 1 up					
88	Mrs. J. Lewis Hedden, La Grande, Ore.						
78	Miss Pat Garner, Midland, Texas	Miss Garner, 6 and 5	Miss Garner, 4 and 2	Miss Garner, 1 up, 19 hls.	Miss Garner, 2 and 1	Miss McFedters, 1 up, 20 hls.	
84	Mrs. Harlan C. Riedel, Lakewood, Texas						
82	Miss Marjorie Lindsay, C.C. of Decatur, Ill.	Miss Lindsay, 3 and 1					
87	Miss Lois Janet Schrader, Fox Hills Men's, Calif.						
80	Mrs. George E. Wilcox, Jr., Miami, Fla.	Miss Faulk, 6 and 5	Miss Faulk, 4 and 3				
85	Miss Mary Lena Faulk, Glen Arven, Ga.						
83	Miss Betty Rowland, Idle Hour, Ky.	Mrs. Todd, 1 up					
88	Mrs. J.H. Todd, Victoria, B.C., Canada						
79	Miss Mae Murray, Rutland, Vt.	Miss Murray, 2 and 1	Miss Murray, 3 and 2	Miss Snook, 3 and 1			
85	Miss Jacqueline Yates, Mid-Pacific, Hawaii						
83	Miss Helen Sigel, Philadelphia Country C., Pa.	Miss Sigel, 4 and 2					
87	Miss Patricia Devany, Grosse Ile, Mich.						
81	Mrs. John L. Hulteng, Warwick, R.I.	Mrs. Ferrie, 1 up	Miss Snook, 1 up, 19 hls.				
86	Mrs. James Ferrie, Virginia, Calif.						
84	Miss Barbara L. Snook, Columbia-Edgewater, Ore.	Miss Snook, 3 and 1					
88	Mrs. Frank Goldthwaite, River Crest, Texas						
79	Miss Katharine McKinnon, Lake Worth, Fla.	Miss McKinnon, 2 up	Miss Lenczyk, 2 and 1	Miss Doran, 1 up	Miss McFedters, 1 up, 20 hls.		
85	Mrs. Ruth McCullah, Riviera, Calif.						
82	Miss Grace S. Lenczyk, Indian Hill, Conn.	Miss Lenczyk, 7 and 6					
87	Mrs. Naomi Kidd, Rose City, Ore.						
80	Miss Claire Doran, Westwood, Ohio	Miss Doran, 3 and 2	Miss Doran, 4 and 3				
86	Mrs. Francis Oglesby, Longview, Wash.						
83	Miss Mary Ann Downey, Baltimore, Md.	Miss Downey, 5 and 4					
88	Mrs. Harry Winters, Inglewood, Calif.						
80	Miss Bonnie Randolph, Brookside, Ohio	Miss Randolph, 3 and 2	Miss Randolph, 3 and 2	Miss McFedters, 4 and 2			
85	Mrs. Fred Apostoli, Lake Merced, Calif.						
83	Miss Barbara McIntire, Heather Downs, Ohio	Miss McIntire, 2 up					
87	Mrs. Harold W. Stone, Greenville, S.C.						
81	Miss Connie Oldershaw, Spokane, Wash.	Miss Oldershaw, 3 and 2	Miss McFedters, 4 and 2				
86	Miss Berridge Long, Guyan, W. Va.						
84	Miss Barbara Davies, Vancouver, B.C., Canada	Miss McFedters, 1 up, 19 hls.					
88	Miss Shirley McFedters, Virginia, Calif.						

*Medalist.
The first word after the player's name is the name of the player's club, except in the case of a foreign entrant.

1953

FIFTY-THIRD WOMEN'S AMATEUR CHAMPIONSHIP

Held at the Rhode Island Country Club, West Barrington, R.I., August 24-29.
Yardage—6,371. Par 74. 158 Entries, 149 Starters.
Championship entirely at match play.

FINAL ROUND (36 Holes)—Miss Mary Lena Faulk defeated Miss Polly Riley, 3 and 2.

UPPER

FIRST QUARTER

1st Round (18 Holes)	2nd Round (18 Holes)	3rd Round (18 Holes)	4th Round (18 Holes)	5th Round (18 Holes)	6th Round (18 Holes)	
Miss Patricia O'Sullivan, Race Brook, Conn.	Miss O'Sullivan, 6 and 4	Miss O'Sullivan, 3 and 2	Miss O'Sullivan, 3 and 1	Miss O'Sullivan, 3 and 2	Miss Riley, 3 and 1	Miss Riley, 3 and 2
Mrs. Chapin Fay, Hillcrest, Mass.						
Miss Barbara Dawson, Orinda, Calif.	Miss Dawson, 5 and 4					
Mrs. Joseph Malia, Portland, Me.						
Mrs. Richard E. Macdonald, Agawam Hunt, R.I.	Mrs. Gleason, 3 and 2	Miss Cranston, 3 and 2				
Mrs. Mary M. Gleason, The Country Club, Mass.						
Miss Elanne Cranston, Annandale, Calif.	Miss Cranston, 7 and 6					
Mrs. Charles Dennehy, Onwentsia, Ill.						
Mrs. Andrew A. Pierson, Edgewood, Conn.	Mrs. Parks, 4 and 3	Miss Orcutt, 7 and 6	Miss Romack, 6 and 4			
Mrs. Gordon S. Park, Glen Ridge, N.J.						
Mrs. Edward S. Schweitzer, Annandale, Calif.	Miss Orcutt, 2 and 1					
Miss Maureen Orcutt, White Beeches, N.J.						
Miss Barbara Romack, Del Paso, Calif.	Miss Romack, 8 and 7	Miss Romack, 5 and 4				
Mrs. Shirlee M. Finnegan, Wallingford, Conn.						
Miss Mary P. Janssen, Farmington, Va.	Miss Janssen, 4 and 3					
Miss Mary Ann Downey, Baltimore, Md.						
Miss Anne Quast, Everett, Wash.	Miss Quast, 4 and 3	Miss Quast, 3 and 2	Miss Quast, 2 and 1	Miss Riley, 3 and 2		
Miss Mary A. Wall, Riverside, Mich.						
Mrs. Louise deKoven Phelps, Misquamicut, R.I.	Miss O'Neil, 7 and 5					
Miss Rose M. O'Neil, Vesper, Mass.						
Miss Patty Torza, Edgewood, Conn.	Miss Frank, 6 and 5	Miss Frank, 4 and 3				
Miss Judy Frank, Aldecress, N.J.						
Mrs. Edward H. Gerry, Piping Rock, N.Y.	Miss Nelson, 5 and 4					
Miss Jane Nelson, Highland, Ind.						
Miss Dorothy Lowenstein, Fenway, N.Y.	Miss Devany, 6 and 5	Miss Devany, 5 and 4	Miss P. Riley, 5 and 3			
Miss Patricia Devany, Grosse Ile, Mich.						
Mrs. Caryl H. Sayre, The Creek, N.Y.	Miss Gaetjens, 3 and 2					
Miss Adele Gaetjens, Hackensack, N.J.						
Miss Polly Riley, River Crest, Texas	Miss P. Riley, 7 and 5	Miss P. Riley, 6 and 4				
Mrs. Charles Novotny, New Haven, Conn.						
Miss Edean Anderson, Green Meadow, Mont.	Miss Anderson, 6 and 5					
Miss Dorothy J. Sullivan, Marshfield, Mass.						
Mrs. George M. Trainor, C.C. of Rochester, N.Y.	Mrs. Trainor, 1 up, 20 hls.	Mrs. Trainor, 9 and 8	Miss Rooney, 3 and 2	Miss Kirby, 1 up	Miss Kirby, 3 and 2	
Mrs. Peg Cirino, Coral Gables Biltmore, Fla.						
Miss Priscilla L. Buckley, Argyle, Md.	Miss Gray, 2 and 1					
Miss Alice Gray, Merion, Pa.						
Mrs. Hazel Ross, Pines Ridge, N.Y.	Miss Hopkins, 8 and 6	Miss Rooney, 5 and 4				
Miss Jean Hopkins, Westwood, Ohio						
Miss Theodora C. Rooney, Charles River, Mass.	Miss Rooney, 4 and 3					
Mrs. William Tracy, Glen Ridge, N.J.						
Mrs. Thomas Findley, New Orleans, La.	Mrs. Bradley, 1 up	Miss Armstrong, 5 and 4	Miss Kirby, 8 and 7			
Mrs. James H. Bradley, Plum Hollow, Mich.						
BYE—Miss Gloria Armstrong, Alameda, Calif.	Miss Armstrong					
BYE—Miss Dorothy Kirby, Capital City, Ga.	Miss Kirby	Miss Kirby, 3 and 2				
BYE—Mrs. James J. Whelan, Springdale, N.J.	Mrs. Whelan					
BYE—Miss Molly Ann Lorms, Columbus, Ohio	Miss Lorms	Mrs. Damon, 1 up, 19 hls.	Miss M. Riley, 4 and 2	Miss Gery, 1 up		
BYE—Mrs. Joan G. Damon, Oahu, T.H.	Mrs. Damon					
BYE—Mrs. Charles E. Brainard, Hartford, Conn.	Mrs. Brainard	Miss M. Riley, 5 and 4				
BYE—Miss Maureen A. Riley, New Castle, Pa.	Miss M. Riley					
BYE—Mrs. Charles F. Bartholomew, Brae Burn, Mass.	Mrs. Bartholomew	Mrs. Bartholomew 1 up, 19 hls.	Miss Gery, 3 and 2			
BYE—Miss Ethel Benson, Sunnybrook, Pa.	Miss Benson					
BYE—Miss Jacqueline P. Yates, Waialae, T.H.	Miss Yates	Miss Gery, 1 up, 19 hls.				
BYE—Miss Ellen H. Gery, Rhode Island, R.I.	Miss Gery					

HALF

SECOND QUARTER

6th Round (18 Holes)		5th Round (18 Holes)	4th Round (18 Holes)	3rd Round (18 Holes)	2nd Round (18 Holes)	1st Round (18 Holes)
					Mrs. Capers	BYE—Mrs. John G. Capers, Jr., Merion, Pa.
				Mrs. Capers, 3 and 1	Mrs. Fischer	BYE—Mrs. William J. H. Fischer, Jr., Agawam Hunt, R.I.
			Mrs. Cudone, 1 up		Miss Blicke	BYE—Miss Judy Blicke, Brookside, Ohio
		Mrs. Cudone, 5 and 4		Mrs. Cudone, 6 and 5	Mrs. Cudone	BYE—Mrs. Philip J. Cudone, Montclair, N.J.
					Miss Venable	BYE—Miss Naomi A. Venable, Dutchess, N.Y.
				Miss McIntire, 5 and 4	Miss McIntire	BYE—Miss Barbara McIntire, Heather Downs, Ohio
			Miss McIntire, 4 and 3		Mrs. Davis	BYE—Mrs. Frederick Davis, Wannamoisett, R.I.
				Miss C. DeCozen, 1 up	Miss DeCozen	BYE—Miss Charlotte DeCozen, Montclair, N.J.
	Mrs. Cudone, 4 and 2				Miss McKay	BYE—Miss Barbara L. McKay, Thorny Lea, Mass.
				Miss Wassel, 3 and 2	Miss Wassel	BYE—Miss Joan F. Wassel, Churchill Valley, Pa.
			Miss McWane, 6 and 5		Miss McWane	BYE—Miss Bee McWane, Birmingham, Ala.
		Miss McWane, 1 up, 19 hls.		Miss McWane, 8 and 7	Miss Eames	BYE—Miss Diane E. Eames, Colonial, Tenn.
					Mrs. Raynor	BYE—Mrs. Ralph I. Raynor, Manufacturers', Pa.
				Mrs. Raynor, 7 and 6	Miss Greene	BYE—Miss Elizabeth H. Greene, Rhode Island, R.I.
			Miss Crawford, 6 and 5		Miss Crawford	BYE—Miss Mary Crawford, Americus, Ga.
Mrs. Cudone, 5 and 4				Miss Crawford, 2 and 1	Mrs. Vare	BYE—Mrs. Glenna Collett Vare, Philadelphia Country, Pa.
					Mrs. Gessler	BYE—Mrs. John M. Gessler, Whitemarsh Valley, Pa.
			Miss Diringer, 2 and 1	Mrs. Gessler, 5 and 4	Mrs. Hoopes	BYE—Mrs. J. Walker Hoopes, Wilmington, Del.
					Miss Diringer	BYE—Miss Carol Diringer, Mohawk, Ohio
		Miss Diringer, 2 and 1		Miss Diringer, 3 and 2	Miss Long	BYE—Miss Berridge Long, Guyan, W. Va.
					Mrs. Drayton	BYE—Mrs. Charles O. Drayton, Jr., Warwick, R.I.
				Miss Burns, 6 and 5	Miss Burns	BYE—Miss Marjorie Burns, Starmount Forest, N.C.
			Miss Burns, 8 and 6		Mrs. Cummings	BYE—Mrs. Mary M. Cummings, Metacomet, R.I.
	Miss Diringer, 3 and 2			Mrs. Glantz, 3 and 2	Mrs. Glantz	BYE—Mrs. Jean B. Glantz, Albuquerque, N.M.
					Mrs. Bycott	BYE—Mrs. Harold Bycott, Wheeling, W. Va.
			Mrs. Bycott, 3 and 2	Mrs. Bycott, 2 up	Miss Thomas	BYE—Miss Kathleen Thomas, C.C. of Salisbury, N.C.
					Mrs. Flippin	BYE—Mrs. Harrison F. Flippin, Merion, Pa.
		Miss Lenczyk, 1 up, 19 hls.		Mrs. Flippin, 3 and 1	Mrs. Nicolls	BYE—Mrs. Anne G. Nicolls, Weston, Mass.
					Miss Ziske	BYE—Miss Joyce Ziske, Rivermoor, Wis.
			Miss Lenczyk, 1 up, 20 hls.	Miss Ziske, 1 up, 19 hls.	Miss Stewart	BYE—Miss Marlene Stewart, Fonthill, Ont., Canada
					Mrs. Spalding	BYE—Mrs. Charles F. Spalding, Round Hill, Conn.
				Miss Lenczyk, 5 and 4	Miss Lenczyk	BYE—Miss Grace S. Lenczyk, Indian Hill, Conn.

SEMI-FINAL ROUND—Miss Polly Riley defeated Mrs. Philip J. Cudone, 1 up, 19 holes.

The first word after the player's name is the name of the player's club, except in the case of a foreign entrant.

LOWER

THIRD QUARTER

1st Round (18 Holes)	2nd Round (18 Holes)	3rd Round (18 Holes)	4th Round (18 Holes)	5th Round (18 Holes)	6th Round (18 Holes)	
BYE—Miss Patricia Ann Lesser, Sand Point, Wash.	Miss Lesser	Miss Lesser, 5 and 3				
BYE—Mrs. Donald Weiss, Flint, Mich.	Mrs. Weiss		Miss Lesser, 3 and 2			
BYE—Miss Claire Doran, Westwood, Ohio	Miss Doran	Miss Doran, 2 and 1				
BYE—Mrs. William R. Kirkland, Jr., Piping Rock, N.Y.	Mrs. Kirkland			Miss Lesser, 4 and 2		
BYE—Miss Mary E. Kerby, Fairlawn, Ohio	Miss Kerby	Miss Kerby, 6 and 5				
BYE—Mrs. Ralph A. Powers, The Country Club, Mass.	Mrs. Powers		Miss Kerby, 3 and 2			
BYE—Miss Vivian Bobinski, Edgewood, Conn.	Miss Bobinski	Miss A. Richardson, 3 and 2				
BYE—Miss Anne Richardson, Columbus, Ohio	Miss A. Richardson				Miss Lesser, 4 and 3	
BYE—Miss Jane Thomas, C.C. of Salisbury, N.C.	Miss Thomas	Miss Thomas, 3 and 1				
BYE—Mrs. Frank B. Cutts, Agawam Hunt, R.I.	Mrs. Cutts		Miss Thomas, 1 up, 21 hls.			
BYE—Mrs. George Bilowick, Butler, Pa.	Mrs. Bilowick	Dr. Rumsey, 1 up, 20 hls.				
BYE—Dr. Anne Rumsey, Brookside, Calif.	Dr. Rumsey			Mrs. H. Smith, 4 and 3		
BYE—Mrs. Marge Mason, Ridgewood, N.J.	Mrs. Mason	Mrs. Mason, 8 and 6				
BYE—Mrs. Edwin C. Wolfer, Edgewood, Conn.	Mrs. Wolfer		Mrs. H. Smith, 4 and 2			
BYE—Miss Judy Bell, Crestview, Kans.	Miss Bell	Mrs. H. Smith, 5 and 4				
BYE—Mrs. Grace DeMoss Smith, Corvallis, Ore.	Mrs. Smith					Miss M. Smith, 5 and 4
BYE—Miss Polly Martin, Belmont Hills, Ohio	Miss Martin	Miss Martin, 3 and 1				
BYE—Mrs. Edward J. Lawler, Memphis, Tenn.	Mrs. Lawler		Miss Swift, 3 and 1			
BYE—Mrs. Edward J. McAuliffe, Charles River, Mass.	Mrs. McAuliffe	Miss Swift, 4 and 3				
BYE—Miss Roslyn Swift, Glen Oaks, N.Y.	Miss Swift			Miss Swift, 6 and 5		
BYE—Mrs. Maurice Glick, Woodholme, Md.	Mrs. Glick	Mrs. Glick, 7 and 5				
BYE—Mrs. Butler Cox, C.C. of Rochester, N.Y.	Mrs. Cox		Mrs. Glick, 5 and 4			
BYE—Mrs. Reinert M. Torgerson, Cherry Valley, N.Y.	Mrs. Torgerson	Mrs. Torgerson, 5 and 3				
BYE—Miss Cynthia Richardson, Wannamoisett, R.I.	Miss C. Richardson				Miss M. Smith, 1 up	
BYE—Miss Pat Garner, Midland, Texas	Miss Garner	Miss Garner, 4 and 2				
BYE—Mrs. Raymond P. Wightman, Valley, R.I.	Mrs. Wightman		Miss Garner, 2 up			
BYE—Mrs. Carle Robbins, Hardscrabble, Ark.	Mrs. Robbins	Mrs. Robbins, 4 and 2				
BYE—Miss Josephine S. Smith, Merion, Pa.	Miss J. Smith			Miss M. Smith, 2 up		
BYE—Mrs. C. George Taylor, Sakonnet, R.I.	Mrs. Taylor	Mrs. McClusky, 7 and 5				
BYE—Mrs. Donald K. McClusky, Worcester, Mass.	Mrs. McClusky		Miss M. Smith, 1 up			
BYE—Miss Betty J. Bobel, Valley, R.I.	Miss Bobel	Miss M. Smith, 7 and 5				
BYE—Miss Margaret (Wiffi) Smith, Guadalajara, Jalisco, Mex.	Miss M. Smith					

HALF

FOURTH QUARTER

	6th Round (18 Holes)	5th Round (18 Holes)	4th Round (18 Holes)	3rd Round (18 Holes)	2nd Round (18 Holes)	1st Round (18 Holes)
					Mrs. Reeves	BYE—Mrs. Walter J. Reeves, Meridian Hills, Ind.
				Mrs. Dyson, 3 and 2	Mrs. Dyson	BYE—Mrs. John M. Dyson, Valley, Pa.
			Mrs. McMillen, 5 and 4		Miss Fecht	BYE—Miss Gloria J. Fecht, Thunderbird, Calif.
				Mrs. McMillen, 2 and 1	Mrs. McMillen	BYE—Mrs. Marjorie L. McMillen, C.C. of Decatur, Ill.
		Mrs. McMillen, 4 and 3			Miss Saper	BYE—Miss Reva Saper, Lake Merced, Calif.
				Miss Saper, 2 up	Mrs. Wilcox	BYE—Mrs. George E. Wilcox, Jr., Miami Shores, Fla.
			Miss Saper, 4 and 2		Miss Wild	BYE—Miss Gail Wild, Greenwich, Conn.
				Miss Wild, 2 and 1	Miss Toski	BYE—Miss Joan P. Toski, Forest Park, Mass.
	Mrs. Hulteng, 4 and 3				Mrs. Hayes	BYE—Mrs. J. Albert Hayes, Philadelphia Country, Pa.
				Mrs. Hayes, 1 up	Miss DeCozen	BYE—Miss Essene DeCozen, Montclair, N.J.
			Mrs. Hayes, 2 and 1		Mrs. Millar	BYE—Mrs. William R. Millar, Los Angeles, Calif.
				Mrs. Millar, 5 and 4	Mrs. Stockhausen	BYE—Mrs. William E. Stockhausen, The Creek, N.Y.
		Mrs. Hulteng, 8 and 6			Mrs. Stone	BYE—Mrs. Harold W. Stone, Greenville, S.C.
				Mrs. Stone, 4 and 2	Miss Park	BYE—Miss Betty Park, Glen Ridge, N.J.
			Mrs. Hulteng, 5 and 3		Mrs. Hulteng	BYE—Mrs. John L. Hulteng, Warwick, R.I.
				Mrs. Hulteng, 3 and 2	Miss Murray	BYE—Miss Mae Murray, Rutland, Vt.
Miss Faulk, 5 and 4					Miss Sargent	BYE—Miss Mary Sargent, Memphis, Tenn.
				Miss Sargent, 4 and 2	Mrs. Parker	BYE—Mrs. Isabel L. Parker, Myopia Hunt, Mass.
			Miss Faulk, 6 and 4		Mrs. Patton	BYE—Mrs. Raymond S. Patton, Jr., Hartford, Conn.
				Miss Faulk, 7 and 5	Miss Faulk	BYE—Miss Mary Lena Faulk, Glen Arven, Ga.
		Miss Faulk, 4 and 2			Miss Wise	BYE—Miss Sonia E. Wise, C.C. of York, Pa.
				Mrs. Marquardt, 3 and 2	Mrs. Marquardt	BYE—Mrs. H. G. Marquardt, Gowanie, Mich.
			Mrs. Porter, 3 and 2		Mrs. Porter	BYE—Mrs. Dorothy Germain Porter, Llanerch, Pa.
				Mrs. Porter, 6 and 4	Miss Moss	BYE—Miss Sheila Moss, Arrowhead, Calif.
	Miss Faulk, 6 and 5				Mrs. Brown	BYE—Mrs. Dana W. Brown, Penobscot Valley, Me.
				Mrs. Brown, 4 and 3	Miss Carroll	BYE—Miss Sally Carroll, Wheeling, W. Va.
			Mrs. Brown, 3 and 2		Miss Garber	BYE—Miss Elizabeth Garber, Argyle, Md.
				Miss Garber, 4 and 2	Miss Goss	BYE—Miss Jane Goss, Somerset Hills, N.J.
		Miss Dennehy, 4 and 3			Mrs. Slade	BYE—Mrs. George P. Slade, Agawam Hunt, R.I.
				Miss Dennehy, 1 up	Miss Dennehy	BYE—Miss Virginia Dennehy, Onwentsia, Ill.
			Miss Dennehy, 5 and 4		Mrs. Derr	BYE—Mrs. John Derr, Upper Montclair, N.J.
				Miss Cullen, 5 and 3	Miss Cullen	BYE—Miss Mary E. Cullen, Tulsa, Okla.

SEMI-FINAL ROUND—Miss Mary Lean Faulk defeated Miss Margaret (Wiffi) Smith, 3 and 2

1954
FIFTY-FOURTH WOMEN'S AMATEUR CHAMPIONSHIP

Held at the Allegheny Country Club, Sewickley, Pa., September 13-19.
Yardage—6,034. Par 73. 151 Entries, 144 Starters.
Championship entirely at match play.

FINAL ROUND (36 Holes)—Miss Barbara Romack defeated Miss Mary Kathryn (Mickey) Wright, 4 and 2.

UPPER

FIRST QUARTER

1st Round (18 Holes)	2nd Round (18 Holes)	3rd Round (18 Holes)	4th Round (18 Holes)	5th Round (18 Holes)	6th Round (18 Holes)	
Mrs. Frederic G. Wier, Shannopin, Pa.	Mrs. Weir, 2 up	Mrs. Weir, 7 and 6	Miss Bisgood, 6 and 4	Miss Stewart, 1 up, 19 hls.	Mrs. Berger, 1 up	Miss Faulk, 2 and 1
Miss Clara Jane Mosack, Detroit, Mich.						
Mrs. Charles F. Spalding, Round Hill, Conn.	Mrs. Spalding, 1 up, 19 hls.					
Mrs. Edward C. Stumpp, Wheeling, W. Va.						
Mrs. William G. Grainger, Montclair, N.J.	Miss Bisgood, 7 and 6	Miss Bisgood, 5 and 4				
Miss Jeanne Bisgood, Dorset, England						
Mrs. Marjorie A. Wyckoff, Allegheny, Pa.	Mrs. Wyckoff, 2 and 1					
Mrs. Thomas Findley, Augusta, Ga.						
Miss Marlene Stewart, Fonthill, Ont., Canada	Miss Stewart, 6 and 5	Miss Stewart, 4 and 2	Miss Stewart, 3 and 2			
Mrs. James G. Murray, Jr., Pittsburgh, Pa.						
Mrs. John G. Capers, Jr., Merion, Pa.	Mrs. Capers, 7 and 6					
Mrs. Henry J. Noerling, Columbia, N.Y.						
Mrs. Patricia S. Henry, Greensburg, Pa.	Miss Goss, 6 and 4	Miss Devany, 4 and 2				
Miss Jane Goss, Somerset Hills, N.J.						
Miss Patricia Devany, Grosse Ile, Mich.	Miss Devany, 5 and 4					
Mrs. Lee F. Mason, Edgewood, Pa.						
Mrs. Walter Acuff, Jr., Philadelphia Country, Pa.	Mrs. Acuff, 3 and 2	Mrs. Allen, 1 up, 20 hls.	Mrs. Allen, 5 and 3	Mrs. Berger, 3 and 2		
Mrs. James E. Johns, Edgewood, Pa.						
Mrs. A. H. Allen, Army Navy, Va.	Mrs. Allen, 4 and 3					
Mrs. Eric Hedstrom, C.C. of Buffalo, N.Y.						
Mrs. Samuel B. Crocker, Kenwood, Md.	Miss Carroll, 5 and 4	Miss Carroll, 6 and 4				
Miss Sally Carroll, Wheeling, W. Va.						
Miss Jeanette Myers, Suburban, Md.	Mrs. Warfield, 3 and 2					
Mrs. J. Davidge Warfield, Allegheny, Pa.						
Miss Claire Doran, Westwood, Ohio	Mrs. Glick, 4 and 3	Mrs. Berger, 2 and 1	Mrs. Berger, 5 and 4			
Mrs. Maurice Glick, Woodholme, Md.						
Miss Mary Patton Janssen, Farmington, Va.	Mrs. Berger, 3 and 2					
Mrs. Roslyn Swift Berger, Westwood, N.Y.						
Miss Barbara Little, Blue Mound, Wis.	Miss Richardson, 1 up	Miss Brooks, 3 and 2				
Miss Anne Richardson, Columbus, Ohio						
Miss Arlene Brooks, Annandale, Calif.	Miss Brooks, 4 and 3					
Mrs. Thomas E. Nolan, New Castle, Pa.						
Miss Mary E. Nelson, Llanerch, Pa.	Miss Faulk, 10 and 8	Miss Faulk, 7 and 5	Miss Faulk, 2 and 1	Miss Faulk, 1 up, 20 hls.	Miss Faulk, 5 and 4	
Miss Mary Lena Faulk, Glen Arven, Ga.						
BYE—Mrs. Sam Damon, Oahu, T. H.	Mrs. Damon					
BYE—Mrs. William Tracy, Essex Fells, N.J.	Mrs. Tracy	Miss Leone, 3 and 2				
BYE—Miss Greta Leone, St. Andrews, Ill.	Miss Leone					
BYE—Mrs. J. Stuart Brown, Allegheny, Pa.	Mrs. Brown	Miss Lenczyk, 3 and 2	Miss Lenczyk, 6 and 5			
BYE—Miss Grace S. Lenczyk, Indian Hill, Conn.	Miss Lenczyk					
BYE—Miss Betty Garber, Argyle, Md.	Miss Garber	Miss Garber, 3 and 2				
BYE—Mrs. Harrison F. Flippin, Merion, Pa.	Mrs. Flippin					
BYE—Miss Maureen Orcutt, White Beeches, N.J.	Miss Orcutt	Miss Orcutt, 4 and 2	Miss Orcutt, 3 and 2	Miss Garvey, 3 and 2		
BYE—Mrs. George Bilowick, Butler, Pa.	Mrs. Bilowick					
BYE—Miss Josephine S. Smith, Merion, Pa.	Miss J. Smith	Mrs. H. Semple, 8 and 6				
BYE—Mrs. Harton S. Semple, Allegheny, Pa.	Mrs. H. Semple					
BYE—Miss Gloria Armstrong, Alameda, Calif.	Miss Armstrong	Miss Armstrong, 3 and 2	Miss Garvey, 2 up			
BYE—Mrs. James J. Whelan, Springdale, N.J.	Mrs. Whelan					
BYE—Miss Philomena Garvey, Drogheda, Ireland	Miss Garvey	Miss Garvey, 6 and 5				
BYE—Miss Maureen A. Riley, New Castle, Pa.	Miss M. Riley					

HALF

SECOND QUARTER

6th Round (18 Holes)		5th Round (18 Holes)	4th Round (18 Holes)	3rd Round (18 Holes)	2nd Round (18 Holes)	1st Round (18 Holes)
					Mrs. Steele	BYE—Mrs. Hoyt P. Steele, Skokie, Ill.
				Mrs. Flower, 7 and 6	Mrs. Flower	BYE—Mrs. James O. Flower, Allegheny, Pa.
			Mrs. deMaglione, 7 and 5		Miss Rutherford	BYE—Miss Ann Rutherford, Carlisle, Pa.
				Mrs. deMaglione, 2 and 1	Mrs. deMaglione	BYE—Mrs. Margarita M. deMaglione, Argentina
		Mrs. deMaglione, 1 up, 19 hls.			Mrs. Peel	BYE—Mrs. Marjorie L. Peel, East Lothian, Scotland
				Mrs. Peel, 5 and 4	Miss Weeks	BYE—Miss Joan Weeks, Del Rio, Calif.
			Miss Gray, 3 and 1		Mrs. Tilden	BYE—Mrs. Calvin Tilden, San Francisco, Calif.
				Miss Gray, 1 up	Miss Gray	BYE—Miss Alice Gray, Merion, Pa.
	Miss Wright, 2 and 1				Mrs. Hayes	BYE—Mrs. J. Albert Hayes, Philadelphia Country, Pa.
				Mrs. Webster, 1 up	Mrs. Webster	BYE—Mrs. T. Ellwood Webster, Merion, Pa.
			Miss Wright, 8 and 7		Miss White	BYE—Miss Ann White, Uniontown, Pa.
		Miss Wright, 1 up		Miss Wright, 7 and 5	Miss Wright	BYE—Miss Mary Kathryn (Mickey) Wright, La Jolla, Calif.
					Mrs. McQuaide	BYE—Mrs. Henry T. McQuaide, Chartiers, Pa.
				Miss Kirby, 6 and 5	Miss Kirby	BYE—Miss Dorothy Kirby, Capital City, Ga.
			Miss Kirby, 4 and 3		Mrs. Boggs	BYE—Mrs. W. G. Boggs, Allegheny, Pa.
Miss Wright, 3 and 2				Mrs. Boggs, 1 up, 19 hls.	Mrs. Pennington	BYE—Mrs. John Pennington, C.C. of Buffalo, N.Y.
					Mrs. McAuliffe	BYE—Mrs. Edward J. McAuliffe, Charles River, Mass.
				Mrs. McAuliffe, 5 and 4	Mrs. Halpern	BYE—Mrs. Bernard M. Halpern, Westmoreland, Pa.
			Miss Riley, 3 and 1		Miss P. Riley	BYE—Miss Polly Riley, River Crest, Texas
				Miss Riley, 1 up, 19 hls.	Miss McIntire	BYE—Miss Barbara McIntire, Heather Downs, Ohio
		Miss Riley, 1 up, 20 hls.			Mrs. Paffard	BYE—Mrs. Frederic C. Paffard, Jr., Allegheny, Pa.
				Miss Downey, 6 and 5	Miss Downey	BYE—Miss Mary Ann Downey, Baltimore, Md.
			Miss Downey, 5 and 4		Miss Abernethy	BYE—Miss Betty S. Abernethy, Fox Chapel, Pa.
				Mrs. Hoopes, 2 up	Mrs. Hoopes	BYE—Mrs. J. Walker Hoopes, Wilmington, Del.
	Miss Riley, 3 and 2				Mrs. Hoke	BYE—Mrs. Elsie C. Hoke, Chartiers, Pa.
				Miss Jacquet, 6 and 5	Miss Jacquet	BYE—Miss Arlette Jacquet, Tervueren, Belgium
			Miss Robertson, 7 and 6		Miss Robertson	BYE—Miss Janette S. Robertson, Lenzie, Scotland
				Miss Robertson, 1 up	Miss Jessen	BYE—Miss Ruth Jessen, Inglewood, Wash.
		Miss Robertson, 6 and 5			Mrs. Wilson	BYE—Mrs. Helen Sigel Wilson, Philadelphia Country, Pa.
				Miss Torza, 1 up	Miss Torza	BYE—Miss Patty Torza, Rockledge, Conn.
			Miss Torza, 6 and 4		Mrs. R. Semple	BYE—Mrs. Richard H. Semple, Jr., Allegheny, Pa.
				Mrs. R. Semple, 1 up, 19 hls.	Miss Gammon	BYE—Miss Beverly A. Gammon, Univ. of Minn., Minn.

SEMI-FINAL ROUND—Miss Mary Kathryn (Mickey) Wright defeated Miss Mary Lena Faulk, 5 and 4

The first word after the player's name is the name of the player's club, except in the case of a foreign entrant.

THIRD QUARTER

LOWER

1st Round (18 Holes)	2nd Round (18 Holes)	3rd Round (18 Holes)	4th Round (18 Holes)	5th Round (18 Holes)	6th Round (18 Holes)	Semi-Finals
BYE—Miss Charlotte DeCozen, Baltusrol, N.J.	Miss DeCozen	Miss McCuskey, by default	Miss Price, 3 and 1	Miss Lesser, 5 and 4	Miss Smith, 2 up	Miss Romack, 7 and 5
BYE—Mrs. John F. McCuskey, Clarksburg, W. Va.	Mrs. McCuskey					
BYE—Miss Joan F. Wassel, Churchill Valley, Pa.	Miss Wassel	Miss Price, 2 and 1				
BYE—Miss Elizabeth Price, Surrey, England	Miss Price					
BYE—Miss Eileen Stulb, Augusta, Ga.	Miss Stulb	Miss Stulb, 3 and 2	Miss Lesser, 5 and 3			
BYE—Mrs. J. Leonard Clark, Pittsburgh, Pa.	Mrs. Clark					
BYE—Miss Patricia Ann Lesser, Sand Point, Wash.	Miss Lesser	Miss Lesser, 3 and 1				
BYE—Miss Bee McWane, C.C. of Birmingham, Ala.	Miss McWane					
BYE—Mrs. W. I. Boreman, Parkersburg, W. Va.	Mrs. Boreman	Miss Sargent, 6 and 5	Miss Smith, 5 and 4	Miss Smith, 6 and 5		
BYE—Miss Mary C. Sargent, Monterey Peninsula, Calif.	Miss Sargent					
BYE—Mrs. David Kaufmann, Jr., Suburban, Md.	Mrs. Kaufmann	Miss Smith, 7 and 6				
BYE—Miss Margaret Smith, Guadalajara, Mexico	Miss Smith					
BYE—Mrs. Mary E. Foster, Fox Chapel, Pa.	Mrs. Foster	Mrs. Foster, 3 and 2	Mrs. Summers, 8 and 6			
BYE—Mrs. George E. Wilcox, Jr., Miami Shores, Fla.	Mrs. Wilcox					
BYE—Mrs. Paul O. Summers, Parkersburg, W. Va.	Mrs. Summers	Mrs. Summers, 3 and 2				
BYE—Mrs. E. C. K. Finch, C.C. of New Canaan, Conn.	Mrs. Finch					
BYE—Miss Jo Ann Prentice, Woodward, Ala.	Miss Prentice	Miss Prentice, 2 and 1	Miss Prentice, 4 and 2	Miss Prentice, 2 up	Miss Romack, 3 and 2	
BYE—Miss Jean Hopkins, Westwood, Ohio	Miss Hopkins					
BYE—Mrs. Sarah Fownes Wedsworth, Oakmont, Pa.	Mrs. Wadsworth	Mrs. Benitoa, 1 up				
BYE—Mrs. Helen F. Benitoa, Uniontown, Pa.	Mrs. Benitoa					
BYE—Mrs. Edward C. Ferriday, Jr., Chevy Chase, Md.	Mrs. Ferriday	Mrs. Ferriday, 2 up	Mrs. Ferriday, 2 and 1			
BYE—Mrs. Daryl S. Harbaugh, Edgewood, Pa.	Mrs. Harbaugh					
BYE—Mrs. Peg Cirino, Coral Gables, Fla.	Mrs. Cirino	Miss Rich, 1 up				
BYE—Miss Frances Rich, Bainbridge, Ga.	Miss Rich					
BYE—Miss Frances Stephens, Lancashire, England	Miss Stephens	Miss Stephens, 2 and 1	Miss Dennehy, 1 up	Miss Romack, 3 and 2		
BYE—Miss Jane Martin, Oakmont, Pa.	Miss Martin					
BYE—Miss Virginia Dennehy, Onwentsia, Ill.	Miss Dennehy	Miss Dennehy, 1 up, 19 hls.				
BYE—Mrs. Marge Mason, Ridgewood, N.J.	Mrs. Mason					
BYE—Mrs. John Derr, Upper Montclair, N.J.	Mrs. Derr	Miss Romack, 8 and 7	Miss Romack, 6 and 5			
BYE—Miss Barbara Romack, Del Paso, Calif.	Miss Romack					
BYE—Mrs. Nancy B. Martin, Green Spring Valley, Md.	Mrs. Martin	Mrs. Martin, 1 up				
BYE—Mrs. James D. Berry, Jr., Wanango, Pa.	Mrs. Berry					

HALF

FOURTH QUARTER

6th Round (18 Holes)		5th Round (18 Holes)	4th Round (18 Holes)	3rd Round (18 Holes)	2nd Round (18 Holes)	1st Round (18 Holes)
					Miss Meyerson	BYE—Miss Mildred Meyerson, Brentwood, Calif.
				Mrs. Trainor, 4 and 3	Mrs. Trainor	BYE—Mrs. George M. Trainor, C.C. of Rochester, N.Y.
			Miss Frank, 4 and 3		Miss Frank	BYE—Miss Judy Frank, Aldecress, N.J.
				Miss Frank, 3 and 1	Mrs. Cooley	BYE—Mrs. E. L. Cooley, Exmoor, Ill.
		Mrs. McMillen, 1 up			Mrs. Jones	BYE—Mrs. Mae Murray Jones, Rutland, Vt.
				Mrs. Smith, 2 and 1	Mrs. Smith	BYE—Mrs. Grace De Moss Smith, Coral Gables, Fla.
			Mrs. McMillen, 7 and 6		Mrs. Valentine	BYE—Mrs. George Valentine, Perth, Scotland
				Mrs. McMillen, 2 and 1	Mrs. McMillen	BYE—Mrs. Marjorie L. McMillen, C.C. of Decatur, Ill.
	Mrs. McMillen, 6 and 4				Mrs. Nestor	BYE—Mrs. Edward P. Nestor, Duquesne, Pa.
				Mrs. Worsham, 3 and 2	Mrs. Worsham	BYE—Mrs. W. H. Worsham, Youghiogheny, Pa.
			Mrs. Cudone, 3 and 1		Miss Colby	BYE—Miss Yvonne Colby, Orange Brook, Fla.
				Mrs. Cudone, 1 up	Mrs. Cudone	BYE—Mrs. Philip J. Cudone, Montclair, N.J.
		Mrs. Cudone, 3 and 2			Mrs. Dennehy	BYE—Mrs. Charles Dennehy, Onwentsia, Ill.
				Mrs. Dennehy, 2 and 1	Mrs. Cox	BYE—Mrs. Clarence E. Cox, Wanango, Pa.
			Mrs. deConen, 5 and 4		Mrs. Lewis	BYE—Mrs. Nancy S. Lewis, Trumbull, Ohio
				Mrs. deConen, 9 and 8	Mrs. deConen	BYE—Mrs. Carmen B. C. deConen, Argentina
Mrs. McMillen, 4 and 3					Mrs. Haskell	BYE—Mrs. John S. Haskell, Wanango, Pa.
				Mrs. Haskell, 1 up	Miss Lowenstein	BYE—Miss Dorothy Lowenstein, Fenway, N.Y.
			Mrs. Ihlanfeldt, 4 and 2		Mrs. Ihlanfeldt	BYE—Mrs. Robert Ihlanfeldt, Rainier, Wash.
				Mrs. Ihlanfeldt, 1 up	Mrs. Beck	BYE—Mrs. John Beck, Berkshire, England
		Miss Yates, 1 up			Miss Yates	BYE—Miss Jacqueline P. Yates, Waialae, T.H.
				Miss Yates, 4 and 2	Miss Grinnell	BYE—Miss Helen J. Grinnell, Detroit, Mich.
			Miss Yates, 3 and 2		Mrs. Harvey	BYE—Mrs. Alexander N. Harvey, Trenton, N.J.
				Miss Burns, 7 and 6	Miss Burns	BYE—Miss Marjorie Burns, Starmount Forest, N.C.
	Miss Bruning, 6 and 5				Miss Kuhn	BYE—Miss Mary Kuhn, Pittsburgh, Pa.
				Mrs. Burress, 7 and 6	Mrs. Burress	BYE—Mrs. John C. Burress, Chartiers, Pa.
			Miss Ziske, 8 and 7		Mrs. Pardue	BYE—Mrs. Dorothy K. Pardue, Fox Chapel, Pa.
				Miss Ziske, 7 and 5	Miss Ziske	BYE—Miss Joyce Ziske, Rivermoor, Wis.
		Miss Bruning, 1 up			Mrs. McDougald	BYE—Mrs. John McDougald, Long Branch, Canada
				Mrs. McDougald, 3 and 2	Miss Cranston	BYE—Miss Lanny Cranston Annandale, Calif.
			Miss Bruning, 9 and 7		Miss Bruning	BYE—Miss Barbara Bruning, Whippoorwill, N.Y.
				Miss Bruning, 9 and 8	Mrs. Alexander	BYE—Mrs. Maitland Alexander, Jr., Allegheny, Pa.

SEMI-FINAL ROUND—Miss Barbara Romack defeated Mrs. Marjorie L. McMillen, 7 and 6.

NOTE: The final was scheduled for Saturday, September 18, but was interrupted by a thunder storm and severe rain. The last 16 holes were played on Sunday afternoon, September 19.

1955
FIFTY-FIFTH WOMEN'S AMATEUR CHAMPIONSHIP

Held at the Myers Park Country Club, Charlotte, N.C., August 22-27.

Yardage—6,413. Par 74. 112 Entries, 104 Starters.

Championship entirely at match play.

FINAL ROUND (36 Holes)—Miss Patricia Ann Lesser defeated Miss Jane Nelson, 7 and 6.

UPPER HALF

1st Round (18 Holes)	2nd Round (18 Holes)	3rd Round (18 Holes)	4th Round (18 Holes)	5th Round (18 Holes)	Semi-Final (18 Holes)	
BYE—Miss Meriam H. Bailey, Inverness, Ill.	Miss Bailey					
		Mrs. Cirino, 4 and 3				
BYE—Mrs. Peg Cirino, Locust Valley, Pa.	Mrs. Cirino					
			Miss Lenczyk, 4 and 3			
BYE—Miss Grace S. Lenczyk, Indian Hill, Conn.	Miss Lenczyk					
		Miss Lenczyk, 8 and 6				
BYE—Mrs. Veleair C. Smith, Guyan, W. Va.	Mrs. Smith					
				Mrs. Probasco, 4 and 2		
BYE—Miss Marjorie Lindsay, C.C. of Decatur, Ill.	Miss Lindsay					
		Miss Lindsay, 4 and 3				
BYE—Miss Diane Elizabeth Eames, Coral Gables, Fla.	Miss Eames					
			Mrs. Probasco, 1 up			
Miss Sally Carroll, Wheeling, W. Va.	Miss Carroll, 4 and 3					
Mrs. Charles R. Harbaugh, Canterbury, Ohio		Mrs. Probasco, 7 and 6				
Miss JoAnne Prentice, Woodward, Ala.	Mrs. Probasco, 2 and 1					
Mrs. Scott Probasco, Jr., Chattanooga, Tenn.					Mrs. Probasco, 1 up	
Miss Elizabeth Price, Tilford, Surrey, England	Miss Price, 7 and 5					
Miss Nancy Phillips, Catawba, N.C.		Miss Price, 2 up				
Mrs. Jean A. Bibby, Cumberland, Md.	Mrs. Glick, 2 and 1					
Mrs. Maurice Glick, Woodholme, Md.			Mrs. Semple, 1 up, 20 hls.			
Mrs. W.I. Boreman, Parkersburg, W. Va.	Mrs. Semple, 6 and 5					
Mrs. Harton S. Semple, Allegheny, Pa.		Mrs. Semple, 5 and 4				
Mrs. Paul O. Summers, Parkersburg, W. Va.	Miss Stulb, 3 and 1					
Miss Eileen Stulb, Augusta, Ga.						
Miss Sandra L. Clifford, Mexico City, Mexico	Miss Newton, 1 up, 23 hls.			Miss Quast, 1 up, 19 hls.		
Miss Kathleen W. Newton, Manakiki, Ohio		Miss Kerby, 6 and 5				
Miss Arlene Brooks, Annandale, Calif.	Miss Kerby, 4 and 2					
Miss Betty Kerby, Fairlawn, Ohio			Miss Quast, 1 up, 19 hls.			
Miss Carole Jo Kabler, Roseburg, Ore.	Miss Kabler, 6 and 5					
Miss Naomi A. Venable, Dutchess, N.Y.		Miss Quast, 8 and 6				
Miss Anne Quast, Everett, Wash.	Miss Quast, 3 and 1					
Mrs. Grace DeMoss Smith, Coral Gables, Fla.						Miss Nelson, 2 up
BYE—Mrs. Dorothy Germain Porter, Llanerch, Pa.	Mrs. Porter					
		Mrs. Porter, 4 and 3				
BYE—Mrs. Louis K. Faquin, C.C. of Salisbury, N.C.	Mrs. Faquin					
			Miss Nelson, 3 and 2			
BYE—Miss Glenda Felkner, Coral Gables, Fla.	Miss Felkner					
		Miss Nelson, 6 and 4		Miss Nelson, 1 up		
BYE—Miss Jane Nelson, C.C. of Indianapolis, Ind.	Miss Nelson					
BYE—Miss Jacqueline P. Yates, Waialae, T.H.	Miss Yates					
		Miss Janssen, 1 up, 19 hls.				
BYE—Miss Mary Patton Janssen, Farmington, Va.	Miss Janssen					
			Miss Creed, 2 up			
Miss Clifford Ann Creed, Indian Hill, La.	Miss Creed, 7 and 6					
Miss Jan Tarble, Bel-Air, Calif.		Miss Creed, 5 and 4				
Miss JoAnne Gunderson, Sand Point, Wash.	Miss Crawford, 3 and 2					
Miss Mary Crawford, Americus, Ga.					Miss Nelson, 5 and 3	
Miss Janice Phelps, Capital City, Ga.	Miss Phelps, 3 and 2					
Mrs. Charles M. Abrahams, Wentworth, Surrey, England		Miss Phelps, 3 and 2				
Mrs. Sam Israel, Jr., Lakewood, La.	Mrs. Israel, 3 and 2					
Mrs. Agnes Cocke, Charlotte, N.C.			Miss Phelps, 3 and 2			
Miss Charlotte DeCozen, Montclair, N.J.	Miss DeCozen, 3 and 1					
Mrs. Norma S. Shook, Mimosa, N.C.		Miss DeCozen, 7 and 6				
Mrs. James P. Lee, Coral Gables, Fla.	Mrs. Lee, 4 and 3					
Mrs. Calvin Tilden, San Francisco, Calif.				Miss McIntire, 6 and 5		
Mrs. Julius A. Page, Jr., Sedgefield, N.C.	Miss McIntire, 1 up, 20 hls.					
Miss Barbara McIntire, Heather Downs, Ohio		Miss McIntire, 6 and 4				
Mrs. Jack W. Lewis, Florence, S.C.	Mrs. Raynor, 2 and 1					
Mrs. Ralph I. Raynor, Manufacturers, Pa.			Miss McIntire, 5 and 3			
Miss Virginia Dennehy, Onwentsia, Ill.	Miss Dennehy, 6 and 5					
Miss Ann Lawson, Manufacturers, Pa.		Miss Dennehy, 2 and 1				
Miss Gloria J. Fecht, Inglewood, Calif.	Miss Fecht, 2 and 1					
Mrs. J. Albert Hayes, Philadelphia Country, Pa.						

The first word after the player's name is the name of the player's club, except in the case of a foreign entrant.

LOWER HALF

	Semi-Final (18 Holes)	5th Round (18 Holes)	4th Round (18 Holes)	3rd Round (18 Holes)	2nd Round (18 Holes)	1st Round (18 Holes)
					Miss M. Smith	BYE—Miss Margaret C. Smith, St. Clair River, Mich.
				Miss M. Smith, 7 and 6		
					Mrs. Stone	BYE—Mrs. Harold W. Stone, Greenville, S.C.
			Miss Smith, 7 and 6			
					Mrs. Tuttle	BYE—Mrs. Carl B. Tuttle, Detroit, Mich.
				Mrs. Tuttle, 1 up, 19 hls.		
					Miss Lange	BYE—Miss Jane Lange, Recreation Park, Calif.
		Miss Smith, 5 and 4				
					Mrs. Allen	BYE—Mrs. Margaret Allen, Army-Navy, Va.
				Mrs. Allen, 7 and 5		
					Miss Burns	BYE—Miss Marjorie Burns, Starmount Forest, N.C.
			Mrs. Allen, 6 and 5			
					Mrs. Hodges, 2 and 1	Miss Mary Hewitt, Florence, S.C. Mrs. W. Royce Hodges, Cumberland, Md.
				Mrs. Flippin, 5 and 3		
					Mrs. Flippin, 1 up	Mrs. Harrison F. Flippin, Merion, Pa. **Miss Marlene Stewart, Fonthill, Ont., Canada**
	Miss Riley, 1 up					
					Mrs. Cudone, 1 up, 21 hls.	Miss Wanda J. Sanches, Baton Rouge, La. Mrs. Philip J. Cudone, Montclair, N.J.
				Mrs. Cudone, 5 and 4		
					Miss Long, 2 and 1	Mrs. Richard J. Rendleman, C.C. of Salisbury, N.C. Miss Elizabeth Long, Raleigh, N.C.
			Miss P. Riley, 2 and 1			
					Miss P. Riley, 3 and 2	Miss Judy Frank, Aldecress, N.J. Miss Polly Riley, River Crest, Texas
				Miss P. Riley, 2 and 1		
					Miss Richardson, 5 and 4	Mrs. George E. Wilcox, Jr., Miami Shores, Fla. Miss Anne Richardson, Columbus, Ohio
		Miss Riley, 4 and 3				
					Miss M. Riley, 4 and 3	Miss Maureen A. Riley, New Castle, Pa. Mrs. John F. McCuskey, Clarksburg, W. Va.
				Miss Milligan, 2 up		
					Miss Milligan, 2 up	Mrs. John Pennington, C.C. of Buffalo, N.Y. Miss Rae Milligan, Jasper, Alberta, Canada
			Miss Milligan, 2 and 1			
					Miss Leone, 5 and 4	Mrs. E.R. Riccoboni, Sunset, S.C. Miss Greta Leone, St. Andrews, Ill.
				Miss Leone, 2 and 1		
					Miss Kirby, 5 and 4	Miss Annette Roddey, Sunset, S.C. Miss Dorothy Kirby, Capital City, Ga.
Miss Lesser, 6 and 5						
					Miss Thomas	BYE—Miss Jane Thomas, C.C. of Salisbury, N.C.
				Miss Gordon, 1 up		
					Miss Gordon	BYE—Miss Jacqueline Gordon, London, England
			Mrs. Covington, 3 and 2			
					Mrs. Covington	BYE—Mrs. H.S. Covington, C.C. of Orangeburg, S.C.
				Mrs. Covington, 7 and 5		
					Mrs. Barry	BYE—Mrs. Ann Trainer Barry, Manor, Md.
		Mrs. Covington, 3 and 2				
					Mrs. Findley	BYE—Mrs. Thomas Findley, Augusta, Ga.
				Mrs. Findley, 5 and 4		
					Mrs. Denham	BYE—Mrs. Ralph M. Denham, Big Springs, Ky.
			Miss Grinnell, 5 and 4			
					Miss Jessen, 1 up, 19 hls.	Miss Ruth Jessen, Inglewood, Wash. Mrs. William E. Tracy, Essex Fells, N.J.
				Miss Grinnell, 1 up		
					Miss Grinnell, 5 and 4	Miss Helen J. Grinnell, Detroit, Mich. Mrs. Wallace Palmer, C.C. of Salisbury, N.C.
	Miss Lesser, 7 and 6					
					Miss Romack, 8 and 7	Miss Constance A. Gorsuch, Starmount Forest, N.C. Miss Barbara Romack, Del Paso, Calif.
				Miss Downey, 1 up		
					Miss Downey, 5 and 4	Miss Mary Ann Downey, Baltimore, Md. Mrs. Frank Cush, Argyle, Md.
			Miss Downey, 6 and 5			
					Mrs. Burress, 9 and 7	Mrs. John C. Burress, Chartiers, Pa. Mrs. Grant Bennett, Florence, S.C.
				Mrs. Finch, 6 and 4		
					Mrs. Finch, 1 up	Mrs. Reinert M. Torgerson, Cherry Valley, N.Y. Mrs. E.C.K. Finch, C.C. of New Canaan, Conn.
		Miss Lesser, 1 up, 21 hls.				
					Miss Garner, 2 and 1	Miss Margaret H. Watkins, C.C. of Detroit, Mich. Miss Virginia M. Garner, Raleigh, N.C.
				Mrs. Brown, 4 and 3		
					Mrs. Brown, 4 and 3	Mrs. Dana W. Brown, Wright-Patterson, Ohio Miss Bee McWane, C.C. of Birmingham, Ala.
			Miss Lesser, 8 and 7			
					Miss Lesser, 7 and 5	Mrs. Charles F. Spalding, Round Hill, Conn. Miss Patricia Ann Lesser, Sand Point, Wash.
				Miss Lesser, 1 up, 19 hls.		
					Mrs. Mason, 6 and 4	Mrs. Marge Mason, Ridgewood, N.J. Miss Paula Ann West, Sacramento Women's, Calif.

1956
FIFTY-SIXTH WOMEN'S AMATEUR CHAMPIONSHIP

Held at the Meridian Hills Country Club, Indianapolis, Ind., September 17-22.

Yardage—6,340. Par 74. 116 Entries, 105 Starters.

Championship entirely at match play.

FINAL ROUND (36 Holes)—Miss Marlene Stewart defeated Miss JoAnne Gunderson, 2 and 1.

UPPER HALF

1st Round (18 Holes)	2nd Round (18 Holes)	3rd Round (18 Holes)	4th Round (18 Holes)	5th Round (18 Holes)	Semi-Final (18 Holes)	
BYE—Miss Marjorie Burns, Starmount Forest, N.C.	Miss Burns					
BYE—Mrs. Helen Sigel Wilson, Philadelphia Country, Pa.	Mrs. Wilson	Mrs. Wilson, 2 up				
BYE—Mrs. Dwight R. Anneaux, Butterfield, Ill.	Mrs. Anneaux		Mrs. Wilson, 2 and 1			
BYE—Mrs. Walter Wolfe, Naples, Fla.	Mrs. Wolfe	Mrs. Anneaux, 6 and 5		Mrs. Wilson, 1 up, 19 hls.		
BYE—Miss Dorothy Kirby, Capital City, Ga.	Miss Kirby					
Miss Nan Berry, Quincy, Ill. Mrs. George K. Conant, Jr., St. Louis, Mo.	Miss Berry, 2 up	Miss Kirby, 4 and 2				
Miss Lois Ward, C.C. of Buffalo, N.Y. Miss Margaret H. Watkins, C.C. of Detroit, Mich.	Miss Watkins, 3 and 2		Miss Kirby, 5 and 4			
Mrs. Mary Ann Reynolds, Radium, Ga. Miss E. Cynthia Howard, Brooklawn, Conn.	Mrs. Reynolds, 6 and 5	Mrs. Reynolds, 4 and 3			Miss Gunderson, 2 and 1	
Miss Meriam H. Bailey, Inverness, Ill. Mrs. Calvin Tilden, San Francisco, Calif.	Miss Bailey, 3 and 1					
Miss Betty Kerby, Fairlawn, Ohio Miss Judy Frank, Aldecress, N.J.	Miss Frank, 3 and 1	Miss Frank, 1 up				
Miss Helen J. Grinnell, Detroit, Mich. Miss Eileen Stulb, Augusta, Ga.	Miss Grinnell, 1 up		Mrs. Cudone, 2 and 1			
Mrs. Philip J. Cudone, Montclair, N.J. Mrs. Ann Gregory, Chicago Women's, Ill.	Mrs. Cudone, 2 and 1	Mrs. Cudone, 1 up				
Miss Elsie Johnson, Elkhorn, Ky. Mrs. John W. Hendricks, Meridian Hills, Ind.	Miss Johnson, 1 up			Miss Gunderson, 4 and 3		
Miss Joan Frenzel, C.C. of Indianapolis, Ind. Miss JoAnne Gunderson, Sand Point, Wash.	Miss Gunderson, 3 and 2	Miss Gunderson, 9 and 8				
Mrs. James F. Balch, Meridian Hills, Ind. Miss Judith L. Keesling, Hillcrest, Ind.	Miss Keesling, 4 and 3		Miss Gunderson, 5 and 4			Miss Gunderson, 1 up
Miss Sally Carroll, Wheeling, W. Va. Miss Patricia Ann Lesser, Sand Point, Wash.	Miss Lesser, 6 and 5	Miss Lesser, 3 and 2				
BYE—Mrs. George E. Wilcox, Jr., Miami Shores, Fla.	Mrs. Wilcox					
BYE—Miss Greta Leone, St. Andrews, Ill.	Miss Leone	Miss Leone, 5 and 4				
BYE—Mrs. Robert C. Lewis, Trumbull, Ohio	Mrs. Lewis		Miss Leone, 8 and 7			
BYE—Mrs. John B. Whitacre, Jr., Brookside, Ohio	Mrs. Whitacre	Mrs. Whitacre, 7 and 6				
BYE—Miss Margaret Smith, St. Clair River, Mich.	Miss Smith			Mrs. Johnstone, 3 and 1		
BYE—Mrs. Harrison F. Flippin, Merion, Pa.	Mrs. Flippin	Miss Smith, 1 up, 19 hls.				
Mrs. Sue Fulmer, Hillcrest, Ind. Mrs. Donald R. Ellis, C.C. of Indianapolis, Ind.	Mrs. Fulmer, 5 and 4		Mrs. Johnstone, 1 up, 19 hls.			
Mrs. Rudolph Block, Highland, Ind. Mrs. Ann Casey Johnstone, Mason City, Iowa	Mrs. Johnstone, 5 and 4	Mrs. Johnstone, 4 and 3			Mrs. Johnstone, 4 and 3	
Miss Grace S. Lenczyk, Indian Hills, Conn. Mrs. Lon C. Hall, Paintsville, Ky.	Miss Lenczyk, 6 and 5					
Mrs. John M. Dyson, Valley, Pa. Miss Virginia Dennehy, Onwentsia, Ill.	Mrs. Dyson, 2 up	Miss Lenczyk, 4 and 3				
Miss Judy Eller, Old Hickory, Tenn. Mrs. Charles Dennehy, Onwentsia, Ill.	Miss Eller, 8 and 7		Mrs. Hartson, 5 and 4			
Mrs. Ralph Denham, Big Spring, Ky. Mrs. William Hartson, San Francisco, Calif.	Mrs. Hartson, 4 and 2	Mrs. Hartson, 6 and 4		Mrs. Hartson, 1 up		
Miss Frances Rich, Glen Lakes, Texas Miss Marcia Dee Manley, Hillcrest, Ind.	Miss Manley, 2 and 1					
Miss Barbara McIntire, Heather Downs, Ohio Mrs. Charles R. Harbaugh, Canterbury, Ohio	Miss McIntire, 5 and 4	Miss McIntire, 6 and 4				
Miss Grace DeMoss, Corvallis, Ore. Miss Clifford Ann Creed, Indian Hills, La.	Miss Creed, 1 up, 20 hls.		Miss Creed, 3 and 1			
Mrs. Norman S. Woolworth, Wee Burn, Conn. Mrs. C.C. Herzer, Evansville, Ind.	Mrs. Woolworth, 8 and 6	Miss Creed, 8 and 7				

The first word after the player's name is the name of her club, except in the case of a foreign entrant.

LOWER HALF

Semi-Final (18 Holes)		5th Round (18 Holes)	4th Round (18 Holes)	3rd Round (18 Holes)	2nd Round (18 Holes)	1st Round (18 Holes)
					Mrs. Valentine	BYE—Mrs. O.G. Valentine, Cherry Hills, Colo.
				Mrs. Mason, 4 and 3	Mrs. Mason	BYE—Mrs. Marge Mason, Ridgewood, N.J.
			Miss P. Riley, 2 and 1		Miss Tully	BYE—Miss Mary E. Tully, St. Andrews, Ill.
				Miss P. Riley, 3 and 2	Miss P. Riley	BYE—Miss Polly Riley, River Crest, Texas
		Miss P. Riley, 4 and 3			Miss Wall	BYE—Miss Mary Agnes Wall, Riverside, Mich.
				Mrs. Pennington, 4 and 3	Mrs. Pennington	BYE—Mrs. John Pennington, C.C. of Buffalo, N.Y.
			Mrs. Pennington, 1 up	Miss Richardson, 3 and 1	Miss Richardson, 6 and 4	Mrs. Norma S. Shook, Mimosa, N.C. Miss Anne Richardson, Columbus, Ohio
					Miss Phelps, 1 up, 21 hls.	Miss Julie Hull, Edgewood, Ind. Miss Janice Phelps, Capital City, Ga.
	Miss Quast, 2 and 1			Miss Quast, 6 and 4	Miss Quast, 6 and 5	Miss Cynthia Sullivan, C.C. of Harrisburg, Pa. Miss Anne Quast, Everett, Wash.
			Miss Quast, 1 up, 19 hls.		Miss Downey, 7 and 5	Miss Mary Ann Downey, Baltimore, Md. Mrs. Louis Bola, Highland, Ind.
				Miss Romack, by default	Mrs. Dye, 7 and 6	Miss Betty Long, Carolina, N.C. Mrs. Paul Dye, Jr., Indianapolis, Ind.
		Miss Quast, 6 and 5			Miss Romack, 4 and 3	Miss Sandra Ann Spuzich, Speedway, Ind. Miss Barbara Romack, Del Paso, Calif.
				Miss M. Riley, 1 up, 21 hls.	Miss M. Riley, 1 up	Miss Maureen A. Riley, New Castle, Pa. Miss Berridge Long, Guyan, W. Va.
			Miss M. Riley, 4 and 3		Miss Diringer, 8 and 7	Miss Carol Diringer, Mohawk, Ohio Mrs. Ray Schwartz, Normandie, Mo.
				Mrs. Semple, 5 and 4	Mrs. Semple, 4 and 3	Mrs. Harton S. Semple, Allegheny, Pa. Mrs. Carl T. Chadsey, Jr., Round Hill, Conn.
Miss Stewart, 4 and 3					Mrs. McCarter, 1 up, 19 hls.	Mrs. John H. McCarter, Toronto, Ontario, Canada Mrs. Frank Stranahan, Inverness, Ohio
				Miss Janssen, 4 and 3	Miss Janssen	BYE—Miss Mary Patton Janssen, Farmington, Va.
			Miss Sanches, 5 and 3		Miss Lenczyk	BYE—Miss Lorraine N. Lenczyk, Indian Hill, Conn.
		Miss Sanches, 3 and 2		Miss Sanches, 5 and 3	Miss Sanches	BYE—Miss Wanda J. Sanches, Baton Rouge, La.
					Mrs. Berger	BYE—Mrs. Roslyn Swift Berger, Westwood, N.Y.
				Mrs. Tuttle, 7 and 5	Mrs. Tuttle	BYE—Mrs. Carl B. Tuttle, Detroit, Mich.
			Miss Nelson, 8 and 7		Mrs. Ray	BYE—Mrs. Charles E. Ray, Highland, Ind.
				Miss Nelson, 4 and 3	Miss Nelson, 2 and 1	Mrs. Robert J. Stancik, Westwood, Ohio Miss Jane Nelson, C.C. of Indianapolis, Ind.
	Miss Stewart, 1 up				Miss Lindsay, 3 and 1	Miss Charlotte DeCozen, Montclair, N.J. Miss Marjorie Lindsay, C.C. of Decatur, Ill.
				Mrs. Raynor, 1 up, 20 hls.	Mrs. Cain, 5 and 4	Mrs. Don J. Ahern, Lakewood, Ohio Mrs. H.D. Cain, Highland, Ind.
			Mrs. Hayes, 3 and 2		Mrs. Raynor, 1 up, 19 hls.	Mrs. Theodore W. Hawes, Baltusrol, N.J. Mrs. Ralph I. Raynor, Manufacturers, Pa.
				Mrs. Hayes, 2 and 1	Mrs. Hayes, 6 and 5	Mrs. John Angus McDougald, Todmorden, Ont., Canada Mrs. J. Albert Hayes, Philadelphia Country, Pa.
		Miss Stewart, 7 and 6			Mrs. Stumpp, 3 and 2	Mrs. Edward C. Stumpp, Wheeling, W. Va. Mrs. Stanley Emerson, Dayton, Ohio
				Miss Stewart, 6 and 5	Miss Newton, 5 and 4	Miss Kathleen Newton, Manakiki, Ohio Miss Virginia A. Ott, Williamsport, Pa.
			Miss Stewart, 2 and 1		Miss Stewart, 8 and 7	Mrs. Phebe Warren Brewster, New Haven, Conn. Miss Marlene Stewart, Fonthill, Ont., Canada
				Mrs. Barry, 3 and 2	Miss Camentz, 1 up	Miss Louise Camentz, New Albany, Ind. Mrs. Maurice Glick, Woodholme, Md.
					Mrs. Barry, 3 and 1	Mrs. Ann Trainer Barry, Columbia, Md. Mrs. J.W. Labisky, Brookside, Ohio

1957
FIFTY-SEVENTH WOMEN'S AMATEUR CHAMPIONSHIP

Held at the Del Paso Country Club, Sacramento. California, August 19-24.
Yardage—6,368. Par 74. **100 Entries,** 93 Starters.
Championship entirely at match play.
FINAL ROUND (36 Holes)—Miss JoAnne Gunderson defeated Mrs. Anne Casey Johnstone, 8 and 6.

UPPER HALF

1st Round (18 Holes)	2nd Round (18 Holes)	3rd Round (18 Holes)	4th Round (18 Holes)	5th Round (18 Holes)	Semi-Final (18 Holes)	
BYE—Miss Barbara McIntire, Heather Downs, Ohio	Miss McIntire					
BYE—Miss Jane Nelson, C.C. of Indianapolis, Ind.	Miss Nelson	Miss McIntire, 5 and 4				
BYE—Mrs. Paul Dye, Jr., C.C. of Indianapolis, Ind.	Mrs. Dye		Miss McIntire, 2 and 1			
BYE—Mrs. Ruth Stefanski, Lake Merced, Calif.	Mrs. Stefanski	Mrs. Dye, 6 and 4		Miss Richardson, 2 and 1		
BYE—Miss Anne Richardson, Columbus, Ohio	Miss Richardson					
BYE—Mrs. Clarice Richardson, Visalia, Calif.	Mrs. C. Richardson	Miss Richardson, 6 and 5				
BYE—Miss Sharon V. Johnson, Sacramento Women's, Calif....	Miss Johnson		Miss Richardson, 5 and 4			
BYE—Mrs. Robert Ives, Sierra View, Calif.	Mrs. Ives	Mrs. Ives, 1 up, 21 hls.			Miss Richardson, 1 up	
BYE—Miss Leila Fisher, La Jolla, Calif.	Miss Fisher					
Mrs. Harton S. Semple, Allegheny, Pa.	Miss De Voe, 2 and 1	Miss De Voe, 4 and 3				
Miss Sue De Voe, Rogue Valley, Ore.			Miss Quast, 4 and 3			
Miss Gail DePietro, Castlewood, Calif.	Miss Quast, 7 and 6					
Miss Anne Quast, Broadmoor, Wash.		Miss Quast, 8 and 7				
Miss Virginia Dennehy, Onwentsia, Ill.	Mrs. Weiss, 1 up, 20 hls.			Miss Quast, 6 and 4		
Mrs. Donald D. Weiss, Flint, Mich.						
Mrs. Robert Ihlanfeldt, Inglewood, Wash.	Mrs. Ihlanfeldt, 3 and 2					
Mrs. Reeves Kennedy, Riviera, Calif.		Mrs. Ihlanfeldt, 1 up				
Mrs. Henry W. Kusserow, Diablo, Calif.	Miss Williams, 4 and 3					
Miss Barbara Williams, Richmond, Calif.			Miss Bell, 1 up, 20 hls.			
Mrs. James Ferrie, Virginia, Calif.	Mrs. Ferrie, 2 and 1					
Mrs. J. Staddon Loveys, Lakeside, Calif.		Miss Bell, 2 up				Miss Gunderson, 3 and 1
Mrs. H.L. Mussels, Caughnawaga, Que., Canada	Miss Bell, 4 and 3					
Miss Judy Bell, Wichita, Kans.						
BYE—Mrs. Ruth White Miller, Santa Maria, Calif.	Mrs. Miller					
BYE—Miss Shirley Siegmund, Eugene, Ore.	Miss Siegmund	Mrs. Miller, 3 and 2				
BYE—Miss Lois Ward, Transit Valley, N.Y.	Miss Ward		Mrs. Miller, 3 and 2			
BYE—Miss Lucille E. Wardell, Silverado, Calif.	Miss Wardell	Miss Wardell, 5 and 4		Mrs. Pennington, 2 up		
BYE—Miss Elanne Cranston, Annandale, Calif.	Miss Cranston					
BYE—Mrs. John Pennington, C.C. of Buffalo, N.Y.	Mrs. Pennington	Mrs. Pennington, 1 up				
BYE—Mrs. Peter E. Patch, Orinda, Calif.	Mrs. Patch		Mrs. Pennington, 1 up			
BYE—Miss Patricia Ann Lesser, Sand Point, Wash.	Miss Lesser	Miss Lesser, by default			Miss Gunderson, 3 and 2	
Miss Rosemary Neundorf, Toronto, Ont., Canada	Miss Neundorf, 6 and 5					
Miss Sheila Moss, Arrowhead, Calif.		Mrs. Cadotte, 1 up				
Miss Angie Vote, Pasatiempo, Calif.	Mrs. Cadotte, 5 and 4					
Mrs. Jane L. Cadotte, Recreation Park, Calif.			Mrs. Cadotte, 4 and 3			
Mrs. D.A. Schaefer, Diablo, Calif.	Mrs. Wilkinson, 2 up					
Mrs. Jeanette Wilkinson, USARPAC, Hawaii		Mrs. Babson, 5 and 4				
Mrs. Aubrey E. Babson, San Jose, Calif.	Mrs. Babson, 2 and 1			Miss Gunderson, 2 and 1		
Mrs. Fulmar Keaton, Olympic, Calif.						
Mrs. Charles Cary, Sequoyah, Calif.	Miss Gunderson, 8 and 6					
Miss JoAnne Gunderson, Sand Point, Wash.		Miss Gunderson, 5 and 3				
Mrs. Clarence R. Graham, Jr., Menlo, Calif.	Miss Minch, 4 and 3					
Miss Florence M. Minch, Del Paso, Calif.			Miss Gunderson, 1 up, 20 hls.			
Miss Grace S. Lenczyk, Indian Hill, Conn.	Miss Eller, 6 and 4					
Miss Judy Eller, Old Hickory, Tenn.		Miss Eller, 2 up				
Miss Mary Patton Janssen, Farmington, Va.	Miss Janssen, 7 and 6					
Mrs. Delbert Walker, Virginia, Calif.						

The first word after the player's name is the name of her club, except in the case of a foreign entrant.

LOWER HALF

Semi-Final (18 Holes)		5th Round (18 Holes)	4th Round (18 Holes)	3rd Round (18 Holes)	2nd Round (18 Holes)	1st Round (18 Holes)
					Mrs. Hartson	BYE—Mrs. William R. Hartson, Claremont, Calif.
				Mrs. Hartson, 2 and 1	Mrs. Tilden	BYE—Mrs. Calvin Tilden, San Francisco, Calif.
			Mrs. Hartson, 4 and 3		Mrs. Marsella	BYE—Mrs. Charles E. Marsella, University-Sequoia, Calif.
				Miss Sheldon, 1 up, 20 hls.	Miss Sheldon	BYE—Miss Harriet Sheldon, Bakersfield, Calif.
		Miss Kabler, 3 and 2			Mrs. Cann	BYE—Mrs. John E. Cann, Meadow, Calif.
				Mrs. Cann, 3 and 1	Mrs. Boyd	BYE—Mrs. E.A. Boyd, Del Paso, Calif.
			Miss Kabler, 4 and 3		Miss Finkbeiner	BYE—Miss Susan Finkbeiner, Inverness, Ohio
				Miss Kabler, 8 and 7	Miss Kabler	BYE—Miss Carole Jo Kabler, Roseburg, Ore.
	Miss Kabler, 5 and 4				Mrs. Stamps	BYE—Mrs. Dorothy Stamps, Castlewood, Calif.
			Miss Riley, 4 and 3	Mrs. Stamps, 1 up	Miss Milligan, 4 and 3	Miss Rae Milligan, Calgary, Alberta, Canada Mrs. George H. Nash, Contra Costa, Calif.
					Miss Riley, 6 and 4	Miss Polly Riley, River Crest, Texas Mrs. Fred F. Patterson, Broadmoor, Wash.
				Miss Riley, 1 up	Miss DeMoss, 1 up	Mrs. Eoline Thornton, Recreation Park, Calif. Miss Grace DeMoss, Corvallis, Ore.
		Mrs. Streit, 1 up, 19 hls.			Miss Tarble, 2 and 1	Miss Jan Tarble, Bel-Air, Calif. Miss Christine DiSibio, Pittsburg, Calif.
			Mrs. Streit, 6 and 5	Mrs. Streit, 8 and 7	Mrs. Streit, 7 and 5	Miss Elizabeth S. Brand, Del Paso, Calif. Mrs. Marlene Stewart Streit, Fonthill, Ont., Canada
					Miss Bisgood, 6 and 5	Miss Jeanne Bisgood, Bournemouth, England Mrs. Harry Hamilton, Monterey Peninsula, Calif.
				Miss Bisgood, 4 and 3	Miss Sargent, 5 and 3	Miss Mary Sargent, Monterey Peninsula, Calif. Miss Judy Hoetmer, Sand Point, Wash.
Mrs. Johnstone, 7 and 6					Mrs. Johnstone	BYE—Mrs. Anne Casey Johnstone, Mason City, Iowa
				Mrs. Johnstone, 4 and 3	Miss Weeks	BYE—Miss Joan Weeks, Del Rio, Calif.
			Mrs. Johnstone, 6 and 5		Mrs. Winters	BYE—Mrs. Harry Winters, Inglewood, Calif.
				Mrs. Walshe, 4 and 3	Mrs. Walshe	BYE—Mrs. James E. Walshe, Woodbridge, Calif.
		Mrs. Johnstone, 6 and 5			Miss Stanhope	BYE—Miss Betty Stanhope, Edmonton, Alberta, Canada
				Miss Anderson, 1 up	Miss Anderson	BYE—Miss Judy Anderson, Del Paso, Calif.
			Miss Cooper, 1 up, 19 hls.		Miss Cooper	BYE—Miss Marilyn Cooper, Del Paso, Calif.
				Miss Cooper, 3 and 1	Mrs. Glick	BYE—Mrs. Maurice Glick, Woodholme, Md.
	Mrs. Johnstone, 1 up, 19 hls.				Miss Gay, 2 and 1	Miss Mary Gay, Calgary, Alberta, Canada Miss Glenda Felkner, Orangebrook, Fla.
			Miss Creed, 1 up	Mrs. Cudone, 5 and 4	Mrs. Cudone, 3 and 1	Miss Natasha Ann Matson, Rolling Hills, Kans. Mrs. Philip J. Cudone, Montclair, N.J.
					Mrs. Shook, 2 and 1	Miss Molly Murphy, Waverley, Ore. Mrs. Norma Shook, Mimosa Hills, N.C.
		Mrs. Porter, 1 up, 20 hls.		Miss Creed, 3 and 1	Miss Creed, 1 up, 20 hls.	Miss Clifford Ann Creed, Indian Hills, La. Miss Greta Leone, St. Andrews, Ill.
					Miss Long, 8 and 7	Miss Berridge Long, Guyan, W. Va. Mrs. Vera C. Polland, Annandale, Calif.
			Mrs. Porter, 7 and 6	Miss Long, 6 and 5	Mrs. Cushing, 2 and 1	Mrs. Robert O. Sproat, Reames, Ore. Mrs. Alexander Cushing, Meadow Brook, N.Y.
					Miss Porritt, 3 and 2	Miss Elaine D. Porritt, Eugene, Ore. Mrs. C.O. Danquard, Mira Vista, Calif.
				Mrs. Porter, 4 and 3	Mrs. Porter, 1 up, 20 hls.	Mrs. Barbara Romack Porter, Del Paso, Calif. Miss Harriet Glanville, Recreation Park, Calif.

1958

FIFTY-EIGHTH WOMEN'S AMATEUR CHAMPIONSHIP

Held at the Wee Burn Country Club, Darien, Conn., August 18-23.
Yardage—6,467. Par 75. 195 Entries, 189 Starters.
Championship entirely at match play.
FINAL ROUND (36 Holes)—Miss Anne Quast defeated Miss Barbara Romack, 3 and 2.

UPPER

FIRST QUARTER

1st Round (18 Holes)	2nd Round (18 Holes)	3rd Round (18 Holes)	4th Round (18 Holes)	5th Round (18 Holes)	6th Round (18 Holes)	(Final of bracket)
Mrs. John Pennington, C.C. of Buffalo, N.Y. Mrs. Sidney Frank, Sunningdale, N.Y.	Mrs. Pennington, 5 and 4					
Mrs. Donald O'Brien, C.C. of Virginia, Va. Miss Judith Ann Kier, Paradise Valley, Ariz.	Miss Kier, 1 up, 20 hls.	Mrs. Pennington, 1 up				
Miss Claudette A. LaBonte, Segregansett, Mass. Miss Dana Lombard, Weston, Mass.	Miss Lombard, 3 and 1					
Mrs. Walter M. Cooperstein, Harbor Hills, N.Y. Miss Anne Quast, Everett, Wash.	Miss Quast, 7 and 6	Miss Quast, 4 and 3	Miss Quast, 5 and 4			
Mrs. Sophie G. Untermeyer, Century, N.Y. Miss Theodora C. Rooney, Charles River, Mass.	Miss Rooney, 3 and 1					
Miss Ann Rutherford, Lebanon, Pa. Mrs. Helen Sigel Wilson, Philadelphia Country, Pa.	Mrs. Wilson, 3 and 2	Mrs. Wilson, 2 up				
Mrs. Harton S. Semple, Allegheny, Pa. Mrs. J. Harry Henderson, Jr., Alexandria, La.	Mrs. Semple, 6 and 4					
Mrs. Edwin M. Burke, Somerset Hills, N.J. Miss Patricia O'Sullivan, Race Brook, Conn.	Miss O'Sullivan, 3 and 2	Miss O'Sullivan, 5 and 3	Miss O'Sullivan, 3 and 2	Miss Quast, 1 up		
Mrs. Joseph Frelinghuysen, Somerset Hills, N.J. Mrs. John G. Capers, Jr., Merion, Pa.	Mrs. Capers, **by default**					
Mrs. William M. Doolittle, Sharon, Conn. Miss Linda Gamble, Scioto, Ohio	Miss Gamble, 2 and 1	Mrs. Capers, 6 and 5				
Mrs. William R. Hartson, Claremont, Calif. Mrs. Clarence P. Greer, Fairview, N.Y.	Mrs. Hartson, 4 and 3					
Mrs. Reinert M. Torgerson, Meadow Brook, N.Y. Mrs. Davis L. White, Toy Town Tavern, Mass.	Mrs. Torgerson, 1 up	Mrs. Torgerson, 4 and 2	Mrs. Capers, **3 and 2**			
Miss Dorothea T. Sommerville, Glasgow, Scotland Miss Evelyn A. Sawyer, Race Brook, Conn.	Miss Sawyer, 4 and 2					
Miss Constance A. Gorsuch, Roanoke, Va. Mrs. Gaines P. Wilson, Jr., Big Spring, Ky.	Mrs. Wilson, 1 up, 20 hls.	Mrs. Wilson, 2 up				
Miss Cynthia Sullivan, Florence, S.C. Mrs. Joan Kohn, Tumble Brook, Conn.	Mrs. Kohn, 2 and 1					
Mrs. H. Lindsay Mussells, Caughnawaga, Que., Canada **Mrs. George K. Conant, Jr., St. Louis, Mo.**	Mrs. Mussells, 2 and 1	Mrs. Mussells, 2 and 1	Mrs. Wilson, 1 up, 20 hls.	Mrs. Wilson, 2 up	Miss Quast, 4 and 3	
Miss Diana Hoke, Chartiers, Pa. Mrs. F.K. Thayer, Jr., Piping Rock, N.Y.	Mrs. Thayer, 1 up, 19 hls.					
Mrs. Allan A. Ryan, Creek, N.Y. Miss Carlene Hotz, Oak, Okla.	Mrs. Ryan, 5 and 4	Mrs. Ryan, 7 and 5				
Miss Margaret Watkins, C.C. of Detroit, Mich. Mrs. Marlene Stewart Streit, Fonthill, Ont., Canada	Mrs. Streit, 7 and 6					
Mrs. Calvin Tilden, San Francisco, Calif. Miss Charlotte DeCozen, Montclair, N.J.	Miss DeCozen, 5 and 4	Mrs. Streit, 8 and 6	Mrs. Streit, 3 and 2			
Mrs. Paul G. Black, Marshfield, Mass. Miss Maureen Orcutt, White Beeches, N.J.	Mrs. Black, 1 up					
Miss Elanne Cranston, Annandale, Calif. Miss Janet MacWha, St. Lambert, Que., Canada	Miss MacWha, 3 and 2	Miss MacWha, 4 and 2				
Mrs. William E. Swanson, Patterson, Conn. Miss Marjorie Burns, Starmount Forest, N.C.	Miss Burns, 4 and 3					
Mrs. John B. Kane, Jr., Whitemarsh Valley, Pa. Miss Elva Carrol, Hamilton, Ont., Canada	Mrs. Kane, 6 and 5	Miss Burns, 2 and 1	Miss Burns, 2 and 1	Mrs. Streit, 4 and 3		
Mrs. John Erickson, Belmont Hills, Ohio **Mrs. William E. Tracy, Essex Fells, N.J.**	Mrs. Erickson, 1 up, 20 hls.					
Mrs. Osmo Huoppi, Watertown, Conn. Miss Jane E. Goss, Somerset Hills, N.J.	Mrs. Huoppi, 3 and 2	Mrs. Erickson, 5 and 4				
Mrs. William G. Grainger, Somerset Hills, N.J. **Mrs. Dorothy Germain Porter, Llanerch, Pa.**	Mrs. Porter, 6 and 5					
Mrs. Harry J. Nevil, Jr., Cooperstown, N.Y. Mrs. Marge Mason, Ridgewood, N.J.	Mrs. Mason, 7 and 6	Mrs. Mason, 4 and 3	Mrs. Mason, 5 and 4			
Mrs. Jerome Miller, Rockrimmon, Conn. Miss Margaret T. Berube, Lachute, Que., Canada	Mrs. Miller, 3 and 1					
Miss Katherine Helleur, Malton, Ont., Canada Mrs. George E. Wilcox, Jr., Miami Shores, Fla.	Miss Helleur, 2 and 1	Miss Helleur, 6 and 5				
Miss Judy Bell, Wichita, Kans. Miss Elizabeth Price, Tilford, Surrey, England	Miss Bell, 2 up					
Mrs. Allison Choate, Apawamis, N.Y. Miss Mildred E. Hanisch, Metuchen, N.J.	Mrs. Choate, 2 and 1	Miss Bell, 3 and 2	Miss Helleur, 1 up	Mrs. Mason, 2 and 1	Mrs. Mason, 5 and 3	Miss Quast, 3 and 2

SEMI-FINAL ROUND (18 Holes)—Miss Anne Quast defeated Miss JoAnne Gunderson, 1 up.

The first word after the player's name is the name of her club, except in the case of a foreign entrant.

HALF

SECOND QUARTER

6th Round (18 Holes)	5th Round (18 Holes)		4th Round (18 Holes)	3rd Round (18 Holes)	2nd Round (18 Holes)	1st Round (18 Holes)
					Miss Logan, 4 and 2	Miss Terry Logan, Essex Fells, N.J. Miss Carole Pushing, Olivia, Minn.
				Mrs. Johnstone, 4 and 3	Mrs. Johnstone, 3 and 2	Mrs. Gordon S. Park, Glen Ridge, N.J. Mrs. Ann Casey Johnstone, Mason City, Iowa
			Mrs. Johnstone, 4 and 3		Mrs. Dye, 1 up	Mrs. Paul Dye, Jr., C.C. of Indianapolis, Ind. Miss Mary Ann Downey, Baltimore, Md.
		Mrs. Johnstone, 3 and 2		Mrs. Dye, 2 up	Miss DeMoss, 5 and 4	Miss Marcia Knapp, Shepard Hills, N.Y. Miss Grace DeMoss, Ponce de Leon, Fla.
					Mrs. McAuliffe, 8 and 7	Miss Joanne Winter, Encanto Women's, Ariz. Mrs. Edward J. McAuliffe, Charles River, Mass.
				Mrs. McAuliffe, 7 and 6	Miss Schiller, 4 and 3	**Miss Jane Schiller, Green Hill Yacht, Md.** Mrs. Robert Lyle, Caughnawaga, Que., Canada
			Mrs. McAuliffe, 5 and 3		Mrs. Bloch, 1 up, 19 hls.	Mrs. Edward Bloch, Fenway, N.Y. Mrs. William Greenberg, Ryewood, N.Y.
	Mrs. Johnstone, 8 and 6			Miss Tiernan, 6 and 5	Miss Tiernan, 4 and 3	Mrs. Charles F. Bartholomew, Dedham, Mass. Miss Patricia Tiernan, Wheatley Hills, N.Y.
					Mrs. Malia, 4 and 2	Mrs. Constance Malia, Portland, Maine Mrs. David Baldwin, Baltusrol, N.J.
				Miss Smith, 1 up	Miss Smith, 5 and 4	Miss Joyce Ann Smith, East Ridge, La. Mrs. Alfred P. Slaner, Old Oaks, N.Y.
			Miss Hahn, 4 and 2		Mrs. Doppelt, 2 and 1	Mrs. Manny Doppelt, Ryewood, N.Y. Miss Lida Fee Mathews, Elks, Ohio
		Mrs. Brown, 1 up, 19 hls.		Miss Hahn, 1 up, 19 hls.	Miss Hahn, 3 and 2	Mrs. W. Lincoln Boyden, Jr., Myopia Hunt, Mass. Miss Patricia Anne Hahn, DuPont, Del.
					Mrs. Brown, 4 and 3	Miss Patricia Thoreen, Wachusett, Mass. Mrs. Dana W. Brown, Antelope Valley Women's, Calif.
				Mrs. Brown, 1 up	Miss Jackson, 6 and 5	Miss Ellen H. Gerv, Berkshire, Pa. **Miss Bridget Jackson, Birmingham, England**
			Mrs. Brown, 3 and 2		Mrs. Fuld, 4 and 3	Mrs. Richard Fuld, Quaker Ridge, N.Y. Mrs. Norma S. Shook, Tam O'Shanter, Ill.
Miss Gunderson, 2 and 1				Miss Rennie, 6 and 5	Miss Rennie, 1 up	Mrs. Richard B. Hart, United Shoe Machinery, Mass. Miss Susan Rennie, Springs, Transvaal, South Africa
					Mrs. Spalding, 2 up	Mrs. Charles F. Spalding, Round Hill, Conn. Miss Shirley Woodley, Thornhill, Ont., Canada
				Mrs. Spalding, 3 and 2	Miss Weeks, 9 and 7	Miss Joan Weeks, Del Rio, Calif. Mrs. Thomas A. Burdeshaw, Griffin Ladies, Ga.
			Miss Gunderson, 1 up, 19 hls.		Miss Gunderson, 3 and 1	Miss Sherry Wheeler, Glasgow, Ky. Miss JoAnne Gunderson, Sand Point, Wash.
		Miss Gunderson, 4 and 3		Miss Gunderson, 3 and 1	Miss Lindsay, 2 and 1	Miss Marjorie Lindsay, C.C. of Decatur, Ill. Mrs. Roslyn Swift Berger, Westwood, N.Y.
					Miss Kerby, 3 and 2	Miss Betty Kerby, Fairlawn, Ohio Miss Joyce Denson, Atlanta Athletic, Ga.
				Miss Kerby, 6 and 4	Mrs. Thornton, 5 and 4	Mrs. Avery Rockefeller, Jr., Round Hill, Conn. Mrs. Eoline Thornton, Recreation Park, Calif.
			Miss Darling, 5 and 4		Mrs. Burke, 8 and 7	Mrs. John Derr, Upper Montclair, N.J. Mrs. Jane Nelson Burke, C.C. of Indianapolis, Ind.
	Miss Gunderson, 3 and 1			Miss Darling, 3 and 2	Miss Darling, 1 up	Mrs. Eric Hedstrom, Long Branch, Ont., Canada Miss Judy Darling, Hudson Heights, Que., Canada
					Mrs. Brady, 2 and 1	Mrs. George Brady, Scarsdale, N.Y. Mrs. Fred E. Wright, Winged Foot, N.Y.
				Mrs. Woolworth, 3 and 2	Mrs. Woolworth, 1 up, 20 hls.	Mrs. Norman S. Woolworth, Wee Burn, Conn. Miss Philomena Garvey, Drogheda, Ireland
			Mrs. Woolworth, 2 and 1		Mrs. Emerson, 3 and 2	Mrs. Bruce Starzenski, Whippoorwill, N.Y. Mrs. Stanley A. Emerson, Dayton, Ohio
		Miss Neundorf, 3 and 2		Miss Crawford, 1 up, 19 hls.	Miss Crawford, 1 up, 19 hls.	Miss Mary Crawford, Americus, Ga. Mrs. Frederic C. Paffard, Jr., Allegheny, Pa.
					Miss Neundorf, 7 and 6	Miss Rosemary Neundorf, Thornhill, Ont., Canada Mrs. Glenna Collett Vare, Philadelphia Country, Pa.
				Miss Neundorf, 3 and 1	Mrs. Nesbitt	BYE—Mrs. Joseph A. Nesbitt, Westchester, N.Y.
			Miss Neundorf, 6 and 4		Mrs. Freeman	BYE—Mrs. Bernard Freeman, Inwood, N.Y.
				Mrs. Freeman, 5 and 4	Mrs. Hand	BYE—Mrs. James Hand, Sleepy Hollow, N.Y.

FIFTY-EIGHTH WOMEN'S

LOWER

THIRD QUARTER

1st Round (18 Holes)	2nd Round (18 Holes)	3rd Round (18 Holes)	4th Round (18 Holes)	5th Round (18 Holes)	6th Round (18 Holes)	
BYE–Mrs. R.W. Reynolds, Radium, Ga.	Mrs. Reynolds					
BYE–Mrs. Arthur Flash, Quaker Ridge, N.Y.	Mrs. Flash	Mrs. Reynolds, 7 and 6				
BYE–Mrs. Irving Kaufmann, Century, N.Y.	Mrs. Kaufmann					
BYE–Miss Barbara Romack, Del Paso, Calif.	Miss Romack		Miss Romack, 2 and 1			
BYE–Miss Barbara Williams, Richmond, Calif.	Miss Williams	Miss Romack, 7 and 5		Miss Romack, 2 and 1		
BYE–Miss Elizabeth L. Evans, Toronto, Ont., Canada	Miss Evans					
BYE–Mrs. Frank Stranahan, Inverness, Ohio	Mrs. Stranahan	Miss Williams, 5 and 3				
BYE–Mrs. Sylva Federman Leichner, Pine Hollow, N.Y.	Mrs. Leichner		Miss Williams, 6 and 5			
BYE–Mrs. John M. Dyson, Huntingdon Valley, Pa.	Mrs. Dyson	Mrs. Stranahan, 8 and 7			Miss Romack, 4 and 3	
BYE–Miss Joanne Goodwin, Haverhill, Mass.	Miss Goodwin					
BYE–Mrs. Maurice Glick, Woodholme, Md.	Mrs. Glick	Miss Goodwin, 6 and 5				
BYE–Miss Peggie D. Cartwright, Rugby, England	Miss Cartwright		Miss Goodwin, 2 up			
BYE–Mrs. George Valentine, Perth, Scotland	Mrs. Valentine	Mrs. Glick, 5 and 3		Mrs. Valentine, 1 up		
BYE–Miss LaJunta White, Englewood, N.J.	Miss White					
BYE–Mrs. George R. Patterson, Caugnawaga, Que., Canada...	Mrs. Patterson	Mrs. Valentine, 6 and 4				
BYE–Miss Priscilla L. Buckley, Camden, S.C.	Miss Buckley		Mrs. Valentine, 7 and 6			
BYE–Mrs. Leonard A. Peto, Coral Gables Biltmore, Fla.	Mrs. Peto	Miss Buckley, 1 up, 19 hls.				Miss Romack, 6 and 4
BYE–Miss Harriet Glanville, Recreation Park, Calif.	Miss Glanville					
BYE–Miss Sue Finkbeiner, Inverness, Ohio	Miss Finkbeiner	Miss Glanville, 5 and 3				
BYE–Miss Janette S. Robertson, Lenzie, Lanarkshire, Scotland	Miss Robertson		Miss Glanville, 2 up			
BYE–Miss Mary Patton Janssen, Farmington, Va.	Miss Janssen	Miss Robertson, 3 and 1		Miss Glanville, 1 up, 21 hls.		
BYE–Mrs. George M. Trainor, C.C. of Rochester, N.Y.	Mrs. Trainor					
BYE–Miss Carol Beinbrink, St. George's, N.Y.	Miss Beinbrink	Mrs. Trainor, 1 up, 20 hls.				
BYE–Mrs. Carl T. Chadsey, Jr., Round Hill, Conn.	Mrs. Chadsey		Mrs. Trainor, 3 and 2			
BYE–Miss Kathy Fawcett, Norwood Hills, Mo.	Miss Fawcett	Miss Beinbrink, 1 up			Miss Long, 1 up	
BYE–Miss Berridge Long, Guyan, W. Va.	Miss Long					
BYE–Mrs. Angela Ward Bonallack, Sandwich, Kent, England.	Mrs. Bonallack	Miss Long, 7 and 6				
BYE–Miss Sharon Fladoos, Dubuque, Iowa	Miss Fladoos		Miss Long, 3 and 2			
BYE–Miss Sally Carroll, Wheeling, W. Va.	Miss Carroll	Mrs. Bonallack, 6 and 4		Miss Long, 3 and 1		
BYE–Mrs. O. Waring Mellick, Greenwich, Conn.	Mrs. Mellick					
BYE–Miss Dorothy Kirby, Capital City, Ga.	Miss Kirby	Miss Carroll, 5 and 4				
BYE–Miss Judy Eller, Old Hickory, Tenn.	Miss Eller	Miss Eller, 1 up, 20 hls.	Miss Eller, 2 and 1			

SEMI-FINAL ROUND (18 Holes)–Miss Barbara Romack defeated Miss Meriam H. Bailey, 4 and 2.

AMATEUR CHAMPIONSHIP—Continued

HALF

FOURTH QUARTER

6th Round (18 Holes)	5th Round (18 Holes)		4th Round (18 Holes)	3rd Round (18 Holes)	2nd Round (18 Holes)	1st Round (18 Holes)
					Miss Preuss	BYE—Miss Phyllis Preuss, Pompano Beach, Fla.
				Miss Preuss, 3 and 2	Mrs. Pyke	BYE—Mrs. Graeme Pyke, Hudson, Quebec, Canada
			Miss Bailey, 3 and 1		Miss Bailey	BYE—Miss Meriam H. Bailey, Inverness, Ill.
				Miss Bailey, 6 and 5	Miss Hoetmer	BYE—Miss Judy May Hoetmer, Sand Point, Wash.
		Miss Bailey, 3 and 1			Mrs. Marsh	BYE—Mrs. Richard B. Marsh, C.C. of Detroit, Mich.
				Mrs. Gregory, 4 and 2	Mrs. Gregory	BYE—Mrs. Anne Gregory, Chicago Women's, Ill.
			Miss Bobel, 4 and 2		Miss Stone	BYE—Miss Sandra Stone, Birmingham, N.Y.
				Miss Bobel, 1 up	Miss Bobel	BYE—Miss Betty June Bobel, Valley C.C. on Ledgemont, R.I.
	Miss Bailey, 1 up				Miss Clifford	BYE—Miss Sandra Clifford, Tlalpam, Mexico, D.F.
				Miss Clifford, 6 and 5	Dr. Rumsey	BYE—Dr. Anne Rumsey, Brookside, Calif.
			Miss Clifford, 1 up, 19 hls.		Miss Frank	BYE—Miss Judy Frank, Old Oaks, N.Y.
				Miss Frank, 4 and 3	Miss McIntire	BYE—Miss Barbara McIntire, Tequesta, Fla.
		Miss Clifford, 8 and 7			Miss Deschamps	BYE—Miss Eileen Ann Deschamps, United Shoe Machinery, Mass.
				Mrs. McCarter, 4 and 3	Mrs. McCarter	BYE—Mrs. John M. McCarter, Toronto, Ontario, Canada
			Mrs. McCarter, 3 and 2		Mrs. Hotz	BYE—Mrs. Carl Hotz, Oaks, Okla.
				Mrs. Weinsier, 3 and 1	Mrs. Weinsier	BYE—Mrs. Saul Weinsier, Fresh Meadow, N.Y.
Miss Bailey, 2 up					Mrs. Lee	BYE—Mrs. James P. Lee, Coral Gables Biltmore, Fla.
				Miss Anderson, 7 and 6	Miss Anderson	BYE—Miss Judy Anderson, Del Paso, Calif.
			Miss Anderson, 4 and 2		Miss Kimball	BYE—Miss Iris Kimball, Duquesne, Pa.
				Miss Kimball, 5 and 3	Miss Barton	BYE—Miss Margaret Barton, Scioto, Ohio
		Miss Anderson, 4 and 3			Mrs. McGhie	**BYE—Mrs. Barbara Bruning McGhie, Whippoorwill, N.Y.**
				Mrs. McGhie, 2 and 1	Miss Lindsay	BYE—Miss Shirley Lindsay, C.C. of Decatur, Ill.
			Mrs. McGhie, 2 up		Miss Richardson	BYE—Miss Anne Richardson, Columbus, Ohio
				Miss Richardson, 4 and 2	Mrs. Cralle	BYE—Mrs. Joseph B. Cralle, II, Montclair, N.J.
	Miss Riley, 1 up, 19 hls.				Mrs. Amory	BYE—Mrs. John S. Amory, Myopia Hunt, Mass.
				Mrs. Amory, 5 and 4	Miss Moro	BYE—Miss Jacqueline Moro, Burlington, Ont., Canada
			Miss Riley, 8 and 7		Miss Riley	BYE—Miss Polly Riley, River Crest, Texas.
				Miss Riley, 3 and 2	Mrs. Hayes	BYE—Mrs. J. Albert Hayes, Philadelphia Country, Pa.
		Miss Riley, 5 and 4			Miss Leone	BYE—Miss Greta Leone, Tam O'Shanter, Ill.
				Mrs. Cudone, 5 and 3	Mrs. Cudone	BYE—Mrs. Philip J. Cudone, Forest Hill Field, N.J.
			Mrs. Cudone, 3 and 1		Mrs. Cronin	**BYE—Mrs. Grace Lenczyk Cronin, Indian Hill, Conn.**
				Mrs. Manheimer, 1 up	Mrs. Manheimer	BYE—Mrs. Lawrence H. Manheimer, Metropolis, N.Y.

1959
FIFTY-NINTH WOMEN'S AMATEUR CHAMPIONSHIP

Held at the Congressional Country Club, Washington, D.C., August 24-29.
Yardage—6,457. Par 74. Entries—150 Applied, 128 Accepted, 128 Starters.
Championship entirely at match play.
FINAL ROUND (36 Holes)—Miss Barbara McIntire defeated Miss Joanne Goodwin, 4 and 3.

UPPER HALF

1st Round (18 Holes)	2nd Round (18 Holes)	3rd Round (18 Holes)	4th Round (18 Holes)	5th Round (18 Holes)	Semi-Final (18 Holes)	
Miss Helen M. Weiland, Aronimink, Pa. Miss Ann Rutherford, Lebanon, Pa.	Miss Weiland, 5 and 3					
Miss Evelyn A. Sawyer, Race Brook, Conn. Mrs. H.L. Mussells, Montreal, Que., Canada	Miss Sawyer, 3 and 2	Miss Weiland, 2 and 1				
Miss Barbara Ann Slobe, Glen Flora, Ill. Miss Josephine S. Smith, Merion, Pa.	Miss Smith, 4 and 3					
Miss Natasha Matson, Rolling Hills, Kans. Mrs. Thomas Nolan, New Castle, Pa.	Miss Matson, 1 up, 19 hls.	Miss Smith, 1 up	Miss Weiland, 1 up, 19 hls.			
Mrs. Ann Casey Johnstone, Mason City, Iowa Miss Katherine Helleur, Thornhill, Ont., Canada	Mrs. Johnstone, 4 and 2					
Mrs. Joseph A. Nesbitt, Westchester, N.Y. Mrs. James P. Lee, Huntington, N.Y.	Mrs. Lee, 1 up	Mrs. Johnstone, 2 and 1				
Miss Judy Bell, Wichita, Kans. Mrs. Allan A. Ryan, Creek, N.Y.	Miss Bell, 7 and 6					
Miss Jane Nelson, C.C. of Indianapolis, Ind. Mrs. Donald O'Brien, C.C. of Virginia, Va.	Mrs. O'Brien, 4 and 2	Miss Bell, 3 and 1	Miss Bell, 1 up	Miss Bell, 2 and 1		
Miss Patricia Anne Hahn, DuPont, Del. Miss Betty Kerby, Fairlawn, Ohio	Miss Hahn, 4 and 3					
Miss Elizabeth Price, Tilford, Surrey, England Miss Sandra Clifford, Tlalpam, Mexico, D.F.	Miss Clifford, 2 and 1	Miss Clifford, 2 and 1				
Mrs. Dwight R. Anneaux, Point O'Woods, Mich. Miss Frances Rich, Bainbridge, Ga.	Miss Rich, 3 and 2					
Mrs. William Pollard, Farmington, Va. Miss Virginia A. Ott, Williamsport, Pa.	Miss Ott, 1 up	Miss Rich, 5 and 3	Miss Clifford, 5 and 3			
Mrs. Dorothy Germain Porter, Llanerch, Pa. Miss Carol Sorenson, Janesville, Wis.	Mrs. Porter, 6 and 4					
Miss Cecilia Ann Wakin, Middlesboro, Ky. Miss Georgia Mae McKeever, Argyle, Md.	Miss Wakin, 1 up, 23 hls.	Mrs. Porter, 7 and 6				
Mrs. Barbara Bruning McGhie, Whippoorwill, N.Y. Mrs. Helen Sigel Wilson, Philadelphia Country, Pa.	Mrs. McGhie, 2 and 1					
Miss Marianne Gable, Santa Anita Women's, Calif. Mrs. Arthur Flash, Quaker Ridge, N.Y.	Miss Gable, 2 and 1	Mrs. McGhie, 4 and 3	Mrs. Porter, 2 up	Mrs. Porter, 4 and 3	Mrs. Porter, 4 and 3	
Mrs. Thaddeus C. Owings, C.C. of York, Pa. Mrs. Ann Gregory, Chicago Women's, Ill.	Mrs. Gregory, 1 up, 21 hls.					
Mrs. William Bibby, Cumberland, Md. Mrs. Curtis Jordan, Jr., C.C. of Columbus, Ga.	Mrs. Jordan, 5 and 4	Mrs. Gregory, 1 up				
Mrs. William R. Hartson, Claremont, Calif. Miss Meriam H. Bailey, Inverness, Ill.	Miss Bailey, 1 up, 20 hls.					
Mrs. Barbara Fitton, Elks, Ohio Miss Diana Hoke, Chartiers, Pa.	Miss Hoke, 1 up, 19 hls.	Miss Hoke, 3 and 2	Miss Hoke, 6 and 4			
Miss Joanne Goodwin, Haverhill, Mass. Mrs. Davis L. White, Toy Town Tavern, Mass.	Miss Goodwin, 5 and 4					
Miss Sharon Fladoos, Dubuque, Iowa Mrs. Cecil Hedstrom, Long Branch, Ont., Canada	Miss Fladoos, 6 and 4	Miss Goodwin, 6 and 4				
Miss Sandra J. Haynie, Capitol City, Texas Miss Elanne Cranston, Annandale, Calif.	Miss Haynie, 7 and 6					
Mrs. Ruth White Miller, California, Calif. Mrs. Dorothy Bloch, Fenway, N.Y.	Mrs. Miller, 7 and 6	Mrs. Miller, 4 and 2	Miss Goodwin, 4 and 3	Miss Goodwin, 1 up, 19 hls.		
Miss Judy Eller, Old Hickory, Tenn. Mrs. Maurice Glick, Woodholme, Md.	Miss Eller, 6 and 4					
Lt. Col. Patricia E. Grant, Post, Md. Miss Barbara Ann Diggs, Manor, Md.	Lt. Col. Grant, 5 and 3	Miss Eller, 3 and 2				
Miss Judy Rand, Aurora, Ohio Miss Maureen Orcutt, White Beeches, N.J.	Miss Rand, 3 and 2					
Mrs. Marlene Stewart Streit, Fonthill, Ont., Canada Miss Alice Gray, Merion, Pa.	Mrs. Streit, 5 and 3	Mrs. Streit, 3 and 2	Miss Eller, 3 and 2			
Miss Barbara Berry, Congressional, D.C. Miss Kathleen Newton, Acacia, Ohio	Miss Berry, 1 up					
Miss Mary Crawford, Americus, Ga. Miss Carol Mann, Olympia Fields, Ill.	Miss Crawford, 2 up	Miss Crawford, 6 and 5				
Miss Polly Riley, River Crest, Texas Mrs. Paul Dye, Jr., C.C. of Indianapolis, Ind.	Mrs. Dye, 1 up					
Miss Mary Ann Downey, Baltimore, Md. Miss Lois J. Drafke, St. Andrews, Ill.	Miss Downey, 1 up	Mrs. Dye, 8 and 6	Mrs. Dye, 5 and 3	Miss Eller, 2 and 1	Miss Goodwin, 1 up, 22 hls.	Miss Goodwin, 7 and 6

The first word after the player's name is the name of her club, except in the case of a foreign entrant.

LOWER HALF

	Semi-Final (18 Holes)	5th Round (18 Holes)	4th Round (18 Holes)	3rd Round (18 Holes)	2nd Round (18 Holes)	1st Round (18 Holes)
Miss McIntire, 1 up, 19 holes	Miss McIntire, 1 up, 20 hls.	Miss McIntire, 6 and 4	Miss Middlemas, 1 up	Miss Middlemas, 4 and 2	Miss Middlemas, 3 and 2	Miss Kathryn E. Diggs, Manor, Md. Miss Ann Middlemas, Panama, Fla.
					Miss Tiernan, 2 and 1	Miss Patricia Tiernan, Wheatley Hills, N.Y. Mrs. John Pennington, C.C. of Buffalo, N.Y.
				Mrs. Semple, 1 up	Mrs. Semple, 7 and 5	Mrs. Lawrence H. Manheimer, Metropolis, N.Y. Mrs. Harton S. Semple, Allegheny, Pa.
					Miss Wheeler, 8 and 7	Miss Jeanie Butler, Harlingen, Texas Miss Sherry Wheeler, Glasgow, Ky.
			Miss McIntire, 2 and 1	Miss McIntire, 6 and 5	Mrs. McDougald, 2 and 1	Mrs. John A. McDougald, Long Branch, Ont., Canada Miss Lillian R. Lea, Court House, Va.
					Miss McIntire, 6 and 5	Miss Barbara McIntire, Tequesta, Fla. Miss Donna M. O'Brien, C.C. of Virginia, Va.
				Mrs. Spearman, 4 and 3	Mrs. Spearman, 6 and 5	Miss Shirley Woodley, Thornhill, Ont., Canada Mrs. A.D. Spearman, Virginia Water, Surrey, England
					Miss Phelps, 2 and 1	Miss Janice Phelps, Capital City, Ga. Miss Jane Schiller, Green Hill Yacht, Md.
		Miss Quast, 4 and 3	Miss Quast, 5 and 3	Miss Quast, 7 and 6	Miss Painter, 1 up, 19 hls.	Mrs. Graeme Pyke, Montreal, Que., Canada Miss Martha Painter, Corpus Christi, Texas
					Miss Quast, 5 and 4	Miss Marjorie Burns, Starmount Forest, N.C. Miss Anne Quast, Everett, Wash.
				Mrs. Stranahan, 1 up, 21 hls.	Mrs. McCarter, 3 and 2	Miss Andrea Cohn, Sunnyside, Iowa Mrs. John H. McCarter, Toronto, Ont., Canada
					Mrs. Stranahan, 2 and 1	Mrs. Frank Stranahan, Inverness, Ohio Miss Doris Phillips, St. Clair, Ill.
			Miss Glanville, 4 and 3	Mrs. Cronin, 5 and 4	Mrs. Kaufmann, 3 and 2	Mrs. Irving G. Kaufmann, Century, N.Y. Miss Constance A. Gorsuch, Roanoke, Va.
					Mrs. Cronin, 2 and 1	**Mrs. Grace Lenczyk Cronin, Indian Hill, Conn.** Mrs. Edward C. Stumpp, Wheeling, W. Va.
				Miss Glanville, 1 up	Miss Glanville, 7 and 6	Miss Harriet Glanville, Recreation Park, Calif. Mrs. George M. Trainor, C.C. of Rochester, N.Y.
					Mrs. Wilson, 6 and 5	Mrs. Gaines P. Wilson, Jr., Big Spring, Ky. Mrs. Helen Konopa, Argyle, Md.
	Mrs. Klinefelter, 1 up	Mrs. Klinefelter, 1 up	Miss Gunderson, 3 and 2	Miss MacWha, by default	Miss MacWha, 5 and 4	Miss Cynthia Sullivan, Florence, S.C. Miss Janet MacWha, St. Lambert, Que., Canada
					Miss Lindsay, 2 up	Mrs. Robert Lyle, Caughnawaga, Que., Canada Miss Marjorie Lindsay, C.C. of Decatur, Ill.
				Miss Gunderson, 5 and 4	Mrs. Jewett, 2 up	Mrs. C. Lincoln Jewett, Congressional, D.C. Mrs. Robert M. Young, Tacoma, Wash.
					Miss Gunderson, 5 and 4	Mrs. George R. Patterson, Montreal, Que., Canada Miss JoAnne Gunderson, Sand Point, Wash.
			Mrs. Klinefelter, 2 and 1	Miss Darling, 6 and 5	Miss Hull, 2 and 1	Miss Julie Hull, Edgewood, Ind. Miss Ellen H. Gery, Biltmore, Fla.
					Miss Darling, 5 and 4	Miss Judy Darling, Montreal, Que., Canada Mrs. John B. Whitacre, Jr., Congress Lake, Ohio
				Mrs. Klinefelter, 2 up	Mrs. Klinefelter, 1 up	Mrs. Paul F. Klinefelter, Jr., Manufacturers, Pa. Mrs. Thelma Richards, C.C. of Maryland, Md.
					Mrs. Cudone, 4 and 3	Mrs. E.C. Kip Finch, C.C. of New Canaan, Conn. Mrs. Philip J. Cudone, Forest Hill Field, N.J.
		Miss Williams, 3 and 2	Miss Carroll, 1 up	Miss Carroll, 3 and 1	Miss Carroll, 5 and 3	Miss Louise Jane Dumler, Cincinnati, Ohio Miss Sally Carroll, Wheeling, W. Va.
					Miss Janssen, 7 and 5	Miss Mary Patton Janssen, Farmington, Va. Mrs. H. Eugene Wheeler, Aronimink, Pa.
				Miss Richardson, 3 and 2	Mrs. Capers, 6 and 5	Mrs. John G. Capers, Jr., Merion, Pa. Mrs. Susan Weinsier, Harbor Hills, N.Y.
					Miss Richardson, 3 and 2	Miss Anne Richardson, Columbus, Ohio Mrs. Pat Cici, Lido, N.Y.
			Miss Williams, 3 and 2	Miss Williams, 5 and 4	Miss Williams, 6 and 4	Mrs. W. Dale Anderson, C.C. of York, Pa. Miss Barbara Williams, Richmond, Calif.
					Mrs. Cole, 3 and 2	Mrs. Edward C. Ferriday, Chevy Chase, Md. Mrs. Gordon A. Cole, Edmonton, Alberta, Canada
				Miss Preuss, 6 and 5	Mrs. Marsh, 4 and 2	Mrs. Claire E. Castaw, Keene, N.H. Mrs. Richard B. Marsh, C.C. of Detroit, Mich.
					Miss Preuss, 1 up, 19 hls.	Miss Phyllis Preuss, Pompano Beach, Fla. Miss Rachel Milligan, Calgary, Alberta, Canada

WOMEN'S OPEN CHAMPIONSHIP

CHAMPIONSHIP TROPHY

Presented in July, 1953, by the
UNITED STATES GOLF ASSOCIATION

HISTORY

1946–The first Women's Open Championship, a match play competition, was held at the Spokane Country Club, Spokane, Wash., in 1946 and was conducted by the Women's PGA and the Spokane Athletic Round Table. Miss Patty Berg, representing Minneapolis, won the qualifying medal, with a 73-72–145, and defeated Miss Betty Jameson, of San Antonio, Texas, 5 and 4, in the final. The purse was $19,700, and Miss Berg carried away $5,600 in bonds.

1947–Miss Jameson came back to win the second Championship, at the Starmount Forest Country Club, Greensboro, N.C. The form was changed to stroke play, and she made a 72-hole score of 295. Two amateurs, the Misses Polly Riley and Sally Sessions, tied for second at 301, and Miss Sessions won the playoff by making a 4 to Miss Riley's 5 on the extra hole. Miss Jameson was believed to be the first to better 300 in a woman's 72-hole tournament. Prize money was reduced to $7,500.

1948–Mrs. George Zaharias, playing from Ferndale, N.Y., won her first Championship at the Atlantic City Country Club, Northfield, N.J., with an even 300 and led Miss Elizabeth Hicks by eight strokes. The purse was $7,500, and the competition was played in bad weather. Miss Grace Lenczyk, of Newington, Conn., with a score of 313, finished in a tie for fourth and was the leading amateur.

1949–Miss Louise Suggs, of Carrollton, Ga., succeeded Mrs. Zaharias at the Prince Georges Golf and Country Club, Landover, Md., as a second organization, the Ladies' Professional Golf Association, assumed responsibility for the competition. Miss Suggs started with a 69 and completed a then-record score of 291, which gave her a 14-stroke advantage over Mrs. Zaharias, the runnerup. The purse was $7,500. Miss Carol Diringer, of Tiffin, Ohio, finished third at 306 and was low amateur.

1950–Mrs. Zaharias came back to win her second Championship at the Rolling Hills Country Club, Wichita, Kans. In the process she matched Miss Suggs' score of 291. The runnerup was an amateur, Miss Betsy Rawls, of Austin, Texas, who scored 300. The purse was $5,000.

1951–Miss Rawls turned professional before the next Championship and succeeded Mrs. Zaharias by scoring 293 at the Druid Hills Golf Club, Atlanta, Ga. Miss Suggs was second, with 298. The purse was $7,500. Miss Patricia Lesser, of Seattle, scored 300, finished in a tie for fourth and was the best amateur.

1952–Miss Suggs won her second Championship with a record-breaking 70-69-70-75–284 at the Bala Golf Club, Philadelphia. As far as is known, her score was the lowest ever made by a woman over 72 holes in a major competition. The Misses Marlene Bauer and Betty Jameson tied for second at 291. In the second round, Miss Marilynn Smith made a single-round record of 67, and Miss Bauer matched this in the third round. The purse was $7,500. The course measured only 5,460 yards, and par was 69.

1953–The USGA assumed sponsorship at the request of the Ladies' Professional Golf Association and conducted its first Women's Open Championship, the eighth in the series, at the Country Club of Rochester, N.Y. It was an auspicious event, artistically and financially. Miss Betsy Rawls, now representing Spartanburg, S.C., tied Mrs. Jacqueline Pung, of Honolulu, T. H., with 75-78-74-75–302. They met the next day at 18 holes, and Miss Rawls won her second Championship, 71 to 77. Miss Patricia Lesser finished in a tie for sixth at 315 and was the best amateur for the second time. There were 37 entrants, including 17 professionals.

1954–Mrs. George Zaharias, representing the Tam O'Shanter Country Club, Niles, Ill., dominated the Championship at the Salem Country Club, Peabody, Mass., making an inspiring comeback after an operation for cancer in the spring of 1953. Her score of 72-71-73-75–291 was only three over par and 12 strokes ahead of the runnerup, Miss Betty Hicks. She had nothing higher than a 5 for the 72 holes. It was her third victory. Miss Mickey Wright, of La Jolla, Calif., the 1952 Girls' Junior Champion, tied for fourth at 308 and was leading amateur. The event attracted 58 entries, of whom 53 started; 21 were professionals. Prize money was $7,500, the winner receiving $2,000.

1955–Miss Fay Crocker, of Montevideo, Uruguay, who came to this country and turned professional in 1953 after winning the Uruguayan Women's Amateur 20 times, won by four strokes with 74-72-79-74–299, at the Wichita Country Club, Wichita, Kans. Her control, especially of her long irons, was decisive since play was carried on in winds that ranged up to 40 miles per hour. Miss Crocker led after every round. Mrs. George Zaharias was unable to defend because of a spinal operation just before the event.

1956–Mrs. Katherine McKinnon Cornelius, of Lake Worth, Fla., 23, mother of a baby daughter and a professional for about two years, and Miss Barbara McIntire, of Toledo, Ohio, 21 and an amateur and college student, tied with scores of 302 for 72 holes. Mrs. Cornelius won in a playoff, scoring 75 to Miss McIntire's 82, at the Northland Country Club, Duluth, Minn. Miss McIntire, finishing early on the last day, closed with a fine 71, playing the last three holes in birdie-par-eagle. Mrs. Cornelius and Mrs. Marlene Bauer Hagge, playing together behind her, fought a close duel which Mrs. Cornelius won by getting down in two on the last green to tie Miss McIntire while Mrs. Hagge was taking three from a difficult position. Mrs. Cornelius' rounds were 73-77-73-79. The entry of 46 was divided almost evenly between professionals and amateurs. Again Mrs. George Zaharias was too ill to compete. The prize money was reduced to $6,000, Mrs. Cornelius receiving $1,500.

1957–Miss Betsy Rawls won her third Women's Open on the East Course of the Winged Foot Golf Club, Mamaroneck, N.Y., after Mrs. Jacqueline Pung, of San Francisco, had returned a lower score and had been disqualified for an inadvertent error. Miss Rawls posted 74-74-75-76–299, seven over par. Mrs. Pung, behind her on the course, caught and passed her with an actual score of 78-75-73-72–298. However, the card she signed and returned, as kept by her marker and fellow-competitor, Miss Betty Jameson, showed a 5 at the fourth hole where Mrs. Pung actually had 6. The penalty for Mrs. Pung's failure to catch this error was disqualification under the Rule which makes the competitor solely responsible for the correctness of the score recorded for each hole even though Mrs. Pung's total had been correctly stated. Spontaneously, Winged Foot members, spectators and officials contributed to an unofficial purse exceeding $3,000 for Mrs. Pung to recompense her for the $1,800 first prize she had lost. The entry of 98 set a record, and of these 65 were amateurs. Best of the amateurs again was Miss Barbara McIntire, of Toledo, Ohio, who tied for eleventh at 313. The prize money was increased by 20 per cent and totaled $7,200. All competitors were requested to wear skirts, not shorts, in order to conform to a regulation of the entertaining club.

1958–Miss Mickey Wright, 23, of Chula Vista, Calif., led every round with 74-72-70-74–290, two under par, and finished five strokes ahead of Miss Louise Suggs, of Sea Island, Ga., at the Forest Lake Country Club, Bloomfield Hills, Mich. Miss Wright's score was a new record for the event under USGA sponsorship; the old USGA record of 291 had been set by Mrs. George Zaharias in 1954. The youngest player to win to date, Miss Wright had taken the Ladies PGA Championship earlier in the year. Miss Fay Crocker, the 1955 Champion, scored 68 in the second lowest 18-hole round on record to that time. Amateur honors went to Miss Anne Quast, 20, of Marysville, Wash., a Stanford University student, who tied for 11th at 307. Miss Quast went on to win the Women's Amateur Championship. The number of prize-money places was increased to 15, but the purse remained $7,200 and the winner's share $1,800.

1959–Miss Mickey Wright, of San Diego, Calif., set a scoring record for the second consecutive year, with 287. Miss Louise Suggs, of Sea Island, Ga., was second. They finished in the same order in 1958. Repeating another part of the script, Miss Anne Quast again was low amateur. Miss Wright played the Churchill Valley Country Club course near Pittsburgh two strokes better than Miss Suggs, who led the Championship after each of the first two rounds. Miss Suggs also broke the Open record of 290 set by Miss Wright in 1958. Miss Suggs closed with a 69. Miss Wright was having putting troubles and felt the need several times for advice by telephone from Paul Runyan in California. Miss Quast's 299 was the first score below 300 by an amateur in the history of the event.

WOMEN'S OPEN CHAMPIONSHIP

DATE	WINNER, RUNNER-UP	SCORE	SITE	ENTRY
	Conducted by Women's Professional Golfers' Association 1946-48			
1946	Miss Patty Berg d. Miss Betty Jameson	5 & 4	Spokane C.C., Spokane, Wash. Medalist—73-72—145: Miss Patty Berg	
1947	Miss Betty Jameson *Miss Sally Sessions *Miss Polly Riley	295 301-4 301-5	Starmount Forest C.C., Greensboro, N.C.	
1948	Mrs. George Zaharias (Mildred Didrikson) Miss Betty Hicks	300	Atlantic City C.C., Northfield, N.J.	
	Conducted by Ladies Professional Golf Association 1949-52			
1949	Miss Louise Suggs Mrs. George Zaharias (Mildred Didrikson)	291 305	Prince Georges G. & C. C., Landover, Md.	
1950	Mrs. George Zaharias (Mildred Didrikson) *Miss Betsy Rawls	291 300	Rolling Hills C.C., Wichita, Kans.	
1951	Miss Betsy Rawls Miss Louise Suggs	293 298	Druid Hills G.C., Atlanta, Ga.	
1952	Miss Louise Suggs Miss Marlene Bauer Miss Betty Jameson	†284 291 291	Bala G.C., Philadelphia, Pa.	
	Conducted by United States Golf Association as of 1953.			
1953 (June)	Miss Betsy Rawls Mrs. Jacqueline Pung	302-71 302-77	C. C. of Rochester, Rochester, N.Y.	37
1954 (July)	Mrs. George Zaharias (Mildred Didrikson) Miss Betty Hicks	291 303	Salem C.C., Peabody, Mass.	58
1955 (June-July)	Miss Fay Crocker Miss Louise Suggs Miss Mary Lena Faulk	299 303 303	Wichita C.C., Wichita, Kans.	49
1956 (July)	Mrs. Kathy Cornelius *Miss Barbara McIntire	302-75 302-82	Northland C.C., Duluth, Minn.	46
1957 (June)	Miss Betsy Rawls Miss Patty Berg	299 305	Winged Foot G.C., Mamaroneck, N.Y.	98
1958 (June)	Miss Mickey Wright Miss Louise Suggs	290 295	Forest Lake C.C., Bloomfield Hills, Mich.	57
1959 (June)	Miss Mickey Wright Miss Louise Suggs	287 289	Churchill Valley C.C., Pittsburgh, Pa.	63

*Denotes Amateur
†Record Score

1953
FIRST WOMEN'S OPEN CHAMPIONSHIP

Held at the Country Club of Rochester, Rochester, N.Y., June 25-28.
Yardage—6,417. Par 74. 37 Entries, 35 Starters.
Thirty-one contestants who completed 72 holes.

						Score	Money Prize
1†	Miss Betsy Rawls, Spartanburg C.C., Spartanburg, S.C.	75	78	74	75	302	$2,000.00
2†	Mrs. Jacqueline Pung, Glasgow C.C., Glasgow, Ky.	80	72	76	74	302	1,250.00
3	Miss Patty Berg, St. Andrews G.C., West Chicago, Ill.	71	73	80	79	303	1,000.00
4	Miss Betty Jameson, San Antonio C.C., San Antonio, Texas	79	76	77	80	312	750.00
5	Miss Marilynn Smith, Wichita C.C., Wichita, Kans.	78	74	82	79	313	600.00
6	Mrs. Betty Bush, Lakepointe G.C., Detroit, Mich.	80	78	76	81	315	450.00
	Miss Beverly Hanson, Fargo C.C., Fargo, N.D.	79	80	77	79	315	450.00
	*Miss Patricia Ann Lesser, Sand Point C.C., Seattle, Wash.	82	75	78	80	315	----
9	Mrs. Alice Bauer Hagge, Sarasota Bay C.C., Sarasota, Fla.	83	79	78	76	316	300.00
10	Miss Louise Suggs, Capital City C., Atlanta, Ga.	75	81	79	82	317	250.00
11	*Miss Mae Murray, Rutland C.C., Rutland, Vt.	79	83	78	78	318	----
12	Miss Marlene Bauer, Sarasota Bay C.C., Sarasota, Fla.	80	83	78	79	320	200.00
13	Miss Betty Hicks, Fox Hills C.C., Culver City, Calif.	81	79	84	78	322	125.00
	Miss Peggy Kirk, Ponte Vedra C., Ponte Vedra, Fla.	75	78	85	84	322	125.00
15	*Miss Patricia O'Sullivan, Race Brook C.C., Orange, Conn.	82	79	84	78	323	----
16	Miss Betty MacKinnon, Lakewood C.C., Dallas, Texas	82	82	80	81	325	
17	*Miss Polly Martin, Belmont Hills C.C., St. Clairsville, Ohio	80	79	82	86	327	
	Miss Shirley G. Spork, Ukiah G.C., Ukiah, Calif.	74	84	84	85	327	
19	Miss Bonnie Randolph, Hawthorne Valley C.C., Cleveland, Ohio	77	86	84	82	329	
20	*Miss Patricia Devany, Grosse Ile G. & C.C., Grosse Ile, Mich.	81	89	80	81	331	
21	Mrs. Herbert O. Breault, Green Diamond Fairways, Chicago, Ill.	87	79	83	85	334	
22	*Miss Shirley Anne Smith, Binghamton C.C., Johnson City, N.Y.	80	85	88	82	335	
23	*Mrs. Harrison F. Flippin, Merion G.C., Ardmore, Pa.	86	79	85	86	336	
	*Mrs. George M. Trainor, C.C. of Rochester, Rochester, N.Y.	79	89	84	84	336	
25	*Miss Ann Rutherford, Carlisle C.C., Carlisle, Pa.	84	87	82	89	342	
26	*Miss Ethel Benson, Sunnybrook G.C., Flourtown, Pa.	81	87	87	88	343	
27	*Miss Jean Hopkins, Westwood C.C., Rocky River, Ohio	85	86	84	91	346	
	*Miss Anne Richardson, Columbus C.C., Columbus, Ohio	84	88	93	81	346	
29	*Mrs. Herbert Astmann, Transit Valley C.C., East Amherst, N.Y.	80	97	89	88	354	
30	*Mrs. Charles Keating, Corning C.C., Corning, N.Y.	84	93	88	94	359	
31	*Mrs. Richard H. Guelich, Park C.C. of Buffalo, Buffalo, N.Y.	97	93	98	98	386	

†Play off: 18 holes, June 28—Miss Rawls, 71; Mrs. Pung, 77.
*Amateur.
Prize money totaling $7,500 awarded to professionals.

1954
SECOND WOMEN'S OPEN CHAMPIONSHIP

Held at the Salem Country Club, Peabody, Mass., July 1-3.
Yardage–6,393. Par 72. 58 Entries, 53 Starters.
Forty contestants who completed 72 holes.

						Score	Money Prize
1	Mrs. Mildred Didrikson Zaharias, Tam O'Shanter C.C., Niles, Ill.	72	71	73	75	291	$2,000.00
2	Miss Betty Hicks, Hillandale G.C., Durham, N.C.	75	76	75	77	303	1,250.00
3	Miss Louise Suggs, Capital City C., Atlanta, Ga.	76	77	78	76	307	1,000.00
4	Miss Betsy Rawls, Spartanburg C.C., Spartanburg, S.C.	77	73	78	80	308	750.00
	*Miss Mickey Wright, La Jolla C.C., La Jolla, Calif.	74	79	79	76	308	----
6	Mrs. Jacqueline Pung, Glasgow C.C., Glasgow, Ky.	81	77	78	73	309	600.00
7	Miss Beverly Hanson, Fargo C.C., Fargo, N.D.	77	80	78	75	310	500.00
	*Miss Patricia Ann Lesser, Sand Point G. & C.C., Seattle, Wash.	79	73	78	80	310	----
9	Mis Fay Crocker, Club de Golf del Uruguay, Montevideo, Uruguay	77	82	79	73	311	400.00
	*Miss Claire Doran, Westwood C.C., Cleveland, Ohio	72	79	80	80	311	----
11	*Mrs. Hugh B. Jones, Jr., Rutland C.C., Rutland, Vt.	79	81	74	78	312	----
12	Miss Patty Berg, St. Andrews G.C., St. Andrews, Ill.	78	76	78	81	313	300.00
13	Miss Betty Dodd, Louisville, Ky.	77	77	78	82	314	250.00
14	*Miss Mary Lena Faulk, Glen Arven C.C., Thomasville, Ga.	77	76	84	79	316	----
	Miss Bonnie Randolph, Brookside C.C., Linworth, Ohio	82	81	74	79	316	150.00
	Mrs. Betty Bush, Woodmar C.C., Hammond, Ind.	79	79	83	75	316	150.00
	Miss Betty Jameson, San Antonio C.C., San Antonio, Texas	78	78	80	80	316	150.00
18	Miss Patricia O'Sullivan, Race Brook C.C., Orange, Conn.	76	79	81	82	318	
	*Miss Joyce Ziske, Rivermoor C.C., Waterford, Wis.	78	82	78	80	318	
20	Miss Marilynn Smith, Wichita C.C., Wichita, Kans.	83	75	79	82	319	
21	Miss Betty MacKinnon, Savannah C.C., Savannah, Ga.	78	80	82	80	320	
22	*Mrs. Helen Sigel Wilson, Philadelphia Country C., Bala, Pa.	80	82	84	76	322	
23	*Miss Jean Hopkins, Westwood C.C., Cleveland, Ohio	78	79	83	86	326	
24	*Mrs. Edward J. McAuliffe, Charles River C.C., Newton Centre, Mass.	82	83	81	84	330	
25	Mrs. Bettye Mims Danoff, Lakewood C.C., Dallas, Texas	81	81	84	85	331	
26	*Miss Ellen H. Gery, Berkshire C.C., Reading, Pa.	86	80	84	85	335	
27	*Miss Virginia Dennehy, Onwentsia C., Lake Forest, Ill.	85	85	85	81	336	
	*Miss Barbara Bruning, Whippoorwill C., Armonk, N.Y.	83	84	88	81	336	
29	*Mrs. Donald K. McClusky, Worcester C.C., Worcester, Mass.	83	84	87	84	338	
30	*Miss Gloria Armstrong, Alameda Women's G.C., Alameda, Calif.	89	83	84	85	341	
31	*Miss Greta Leone, St. Andrews C.C., St. Andrews, Ill.	88	84	89	84	345	
32	*Mrs. James Parker, Myopia Hunt C., South Hamilton, Mass.	82	86	90	88	346	
33	Mrs. Frances Mahoney, Maplewood, N.J.	83	90	87	90	350	
34	*Miss Rose M. O'Neil, Vesper C.C., Lowell, Mass.	85	93	84	89	351	
35	Mrs. Herbert O. Breault, Navajo Fields C.C., Worth, Ill.	90	87	84	91	352	
	*Miss Theodora C. Rooney, Charles River C.C., Newton Centre, Mass.	87	84	87	94	352	
37	*Miss Joanne F. Goodwin, Plymouth C.C., Plymouth, Mass.	85	86	94	88	353	
38	*Miss Ann Rutherford, Carlisle C.C., Carlisle, Pa.	89	90	88	88	355	
39	*Miss Iris Kimball, Baldoc Hills C.C., Irwin, Pa.	89	88	93	91	361	
40	*Mrs. Donald D. Weiss, Flint G.C., Flint, Mich.	88	86	93	96	363	

*Amateur
Prize money totaling $7,500 awarded to professionals.

1955
THIRD WOMEN'S OPEN CHAMPIONSHIP

Held at the Wichita Country Club, Wichita, Kans., June 30-July 2.
Yardage—6,330, 6,290. Par 72, 71. 49 Entries, 46 Starters.
Thirty-eight contestants who completed 72 holes.

						Score	Money Prize
1	Miss Fay Crocker, Club de Golf del Uruguay, Montevideo, Uruguay	74	72	79	74	299	$2,000.00
2	Miss Louise Suggs, Sea Island G.C., Sea Island, Ga.	79	77	72	75	303	1,125.00
	Miss Mary Lena Faulk, Glen Arven C.C., Thomasville, Ga.	77	77	72	77	303	1,125.00
4	Mrs. Jacqueline Pung, Moanalua G.C., Honolulu, T.H.	79	76	76	75	306	750.00
5	Miss Patty Berg, St. Andrews G.C., St. Andrews, Ill.	78	80	78	71	307	600.00
6	*Miss Polly Riley, River Crest C.C., Fort Worth, Texas	80	78	74	77	309	----
	*Miss Jacqueline P. Yates, Waialae C.C., Honolulu, T. H.	76	79	76	78	309	----
8	*Miss Patricia Ann Lesser, Sand Point C.C., Seattle, Wash.	81	76	79	75	311	----
9	Miss Beverly Hanson, Fargo C.C., Fargo, N.D.	87	76	77	72	312	450.00
	Miss Betty Jameson, San Antonio C.C., San Antonio, Texas	83	77	76	76	312	450.00
11	Miss Betty Hicks, Tamarisk C.C., Palm Springs, Calif.	81	81	72	79	313	250.00
	Miss Marilynn Smith, Wichita C.C., Wichita, Kans.	80	79	79	75	313	250.00
	Miss Marlene Bauer, Sarasota Bay C.C., Sarasota, Fla.	85	75	76	77	313	250.00
14	Mrs. Peggy Kirk Bell, St. Clair River C.C., St. Clair, Mich.	84	80	75	75	314	150.00
15	Mrs. Alice Bauer Hagge, Sarasota Bay C.C., Sarasota, Fla.	81	80	74	80	315	100.00
16	Mrs. Betty Bush, Lakepointe G.C., Detroit, Mich.	87	76	78	81	322	
17	Miss Mickey Wright, La Jolla C.C., La Jolla, Calif.	86	76	78	83	323	
18	*Miss Wiffi Smith, St. Clair River C.C., St. Clair, Mich.	81	85	77	82	325	
19	*Mrs. Ann Casey Johnstone, Mason City C.C., Mason City, Iowa	81	86	76	83	326	
	Miss Betsy Rawls, Spartanburg C.C., Spartanburg, S.C.	84	81	84	77	326	
21	*Miss Virginia Dennehy, Onwentsia C., Lake Forest, Ill.	86	79	74	88	327	
22	*Miss Natasha Matson, Wichita, Kans.	84	79	82	84	329	
23	Miss Gloria Armstrong, Lake Chabot G.C., Oakland, Calif.	79	84	81	86	330	
	Mrs. Bettye Mims Danoff, Lakewood C.C., Dallas, Texas	83	81	78	88	330	
	*Miss Gloria J. Fecht, Inglewood G. & C.C., Inglewood, Calif.	86	83	77	84	330	
26	*Miss Jean Ashley, Chanute C.C., Chanute, Kans.	83	85	78	85	331	
	Miss Vonnie Colby, Hollywood Beach Hotel C.C., Hollywood, Fla.	89	83	80	79	331	
28	*Miss Ruth Jessen, Inglewood C.C., Seattle, Wash.	83	79	90	80	332	
29	Miss Betty MacKinnon, Savannah G.C., Savannah, Ga.	84	83	80	86	333	
	*Mrs. H.T. Williford, Ponca City C.C., Ponca City, Okla.	84	84	80	85	333	
31	*Miss Beverly Gammon, Univ. of Minnesota G.C., St. Paul, Minn.	84	82	88	82	336	
32	Miss Diane Garrett, Houston, Texas	88	86	78	88	340	
33	*Miss Betsy Cullen, Tulsa C.C., Tulsa, Okla.	93	83	81	84	341	
34	*Miss Jill Kreager, Southern Hills C.C., Tulsa, Okla.	87	86	79	90	342	
35	*Mrs. Russell C. Mann, Field Club of Omaha, Omaha, Neb.	90	87	86	85	348	
36	*Mrs. Harrison F. Flippin, Merion G.C., Ardmore, Pa.	88	89	86	87	350	
37	*Miss Dale Fleming, Oaks C.C., Tulsa, Okla.	93	89	86	94	362	
38	*Miss Susan Casey, Tulsa C.C., Tulsa, Okla.	93	89	93	96	371	

*Amateur.
Prize money totaling $7,500 awarded to professionals.

1956
FOURTH WOMEN'S OPEN CHAMPIONSHIP

Held at the Northland Country Club, Duluth, Minn., July 26-28.
Yardage—6,419 for first round, 6,456 for all other rounds. Par 73 for first round, 74 for all other rounds.
46 Entries, 45 Starters.
Thirty-seven contestants who completed 72 holes.

						Score	Money Prize
1†	Mrs. Kathy Cornelius, Lake Worth G.C., Lake Worth, Fla.	73	77	73	79	302	$1,500.00
2*†	Miss Barbara McIntire, Heather Downs C.C., Toledo, Ohio	75	79	77	71	302	------
3	Mrs. Marlene Bauer Hagge, No. Hills Hotel & C.C., Asheville, N.C.	74	74	75	80	303	875.00
	Miss Patty Berg, St. Andrews C.C., St. Andrews, Ill.	78	75	76	74	303	875.00
5	Miss Joyce Ziske, Rivermoor C.C., Waterford, Wis.	76	74	79	76	305	600.00
6	Miss Marilynn Smith, Forest Lake C.C., Bloomfield, Mich.	76	78	78	74	306	500.00
7	Miss Louise Suggs, Sea Island G.C., Sea Island, Ga.	76	73	80	78	307	350.00
	Miss Betty Jameson, San Antonio C.C., San Antonio, Texas	77	75	78	77	307	350.00
9	Miss Mickey Wright, San Diego C.C., San Diego, Calif.	77	80	78	73	308	250.00
10	Miss Fay Crocker, Club de Golf del Uruguay, Montevideo, Uruguay	82	80	76	71	309	200.00
	Miss Mary Lena Faulk, Glen Arven C.C., Thomasville, Ga.	75	75	81	78	309	200.00
12	Miss Beverly Hanson, Apple Valley C.C., Apple Valley, Calif.	74	77	79	80	310	150.00
13	Miss Betsy Rawls, Spartanburg C.C., Spartanburg, S.C.	82	77	78	77	314	75.00
	Mrs. Peggy Kirk Bell, Pine Needles C.C., Southern Pines, N.C.	79	78	78	79	314	75.00
15	*Miss Ruth Jessen, Inglewood C.C., Seattle, Wash.	85	77	81	74	317	----
16	*Miss Patricia Ann Lesser, Sand Point C.C., Seattle, Wash.	77	81	81	80	319	
	Miss Betty Dodd, Louisville, Ky.	80	85	76	78	319	
18	*Miss Judy Bell, Wichita C.C., Wichita, Kans.	83	77	80	80	320	
19	Miss Gloria Armstrong, Oakland, Calif.	79	81	80	82	322	
20	Miss Bonnie Randolph, Brookside C.C., Columbus, Ohio	82	77	83	81	323	
21	*Miss Wanda J. Sanches, Baton Rouge C.C., Baton Rouge, La.	80	88	76	81	325	
22	Mrs. Phyllis O. Germain, Atlantic G. & C.C., Atlantic, Iowa	83	81	84	78	326	
23	*Miss Nan Berry, Quincy C.C., Quincy, Ill.	84	80	80	83	327	
	Miss Gloria J. Fecht, Clock C.C., Whittier, Calif.	80	87	82	78	327	
25	*Miss Jacqueline P. Yates, Waialae C.C., Honolulu, T. H.	84	78	79	87	328	
	*Miss Mary Patton Janssen, Farmington C.C., Charlottesville, Va.	80	84	80	84	328	
27	*Mrs. Ann Casey Johnstone, Mason City C.C., Mason City, Iowa	82	81	85	82	330	
28	*Miss Beverly Gammon, Univ. of Minnesota G.C., St. Paul, Minn.	85	86	79	81	331	
29	Miss Vonnie Colby, Hollywood Beach Hotel C.C., Hollywood, Fla.	83	80	84	85	332	
30	*Miss Virginia Dennehy, Onwentsia C., Lake Forest, Ill.	90	83	79	87	339	
	Miss Diane Garrett, Houston, Texas	89	84	86	80	339	
32	*Miss Jean Hopkins, Westwood C.C., Cleveland, Ohio	86	82	86	89	343	
33	Miss JoAnn Prentice, Woodward G. & C.C., Birmingham, Ala.	84	90	88	83	345	
34	*Mrs. George Crane, Hillcrest C.C., St. Paul, Minn.	93	82	89	86	350	
35	*Mrs. Marlene G. Miller, Univ. of Minnesota G.C., St. Paul, Minn.	89	90	85	87	351	
36	*Miss Katherine Reichert, Rochester G. & C. C., Rochester, Minn.	87	89	85	93	354	
37	*Miss Judy Kimball, Sioux City Boat C., Sioux City, Iowa	82	98	87	90	357	

†Playoff: 18 holes, July 29—Mrs. Cornelius, 75; Miss McIntire, 82.
*Amateur.
Prize Money totaling $6,000 awarded to professionals.

1957
FIFTH WOMEN'S OPEN CHAMPIONSHIP

Held at the Winged Foot Golf Club, Mamaroneck, N.Y., July 27-29.
Yardage—6,246. Par 73. 98 Entries, 95 Starters.
Forty-one contestants who completed 72 holes.

						Score	Money Prize
1	Miss Betsy Rawls, Spartanburg C.C., Spartanburg, S.C.	74	74	75	76	299	$1,800.00
2	Miss Patty Berg, St. Andrews G.C., St. Andrews, Ill.	80	77	73	75	305	1,200.00
3	Miss Betty Hicks, Recreation Park G.C., Long Beach, Calif.	75	77	76	80	308	810.00
	Miss Louise Suggs, Sea Island G.C., Sea Island, Ga.	76	81	75	76	308	810.00
5	Miss Betty Dodd, Louisville, Ky.	74	78	76	82	310	600.00
6	Mrs. Marlene Bauer Hagge, Riverlake C.C., Dallas, Texas	72	81	81	77	311	380.00
	Miss JoAnn Prentice, Roebuck G. & C.C., Birmingham, Ala.	75	78	84	74	311	380.00
	Miss Alice Bauer, Southmoor C.C., Palos Park, Ill.	72	73	87	79	311	380.00
9	Miss Beverly Hanson, Cochran Ranch G.C., Indio, Calif.	78	76	79	79	312	240.00
	Miss Fay Crocker, Club de Golf del Uruguay, Montevideo, Uruguay	78	81	75	78	312	240.00
11	Miss Wiffi Smith, St. Clair River C.C., St. Clair, Mich.	81	76	79	77	313	180.00
	Miss Mary Lena Faulk, Glen Arven C.C., Thomasville, Ga.	76	79	83	75	313	180.00
	*Miss Barbara McIntire, Heather Downs C.C., Toledo, Ohio	78	77	82	76	313	----
14	*Mrs. Marlene Stewart Streit, Lookout Point G.C., Fonthill, Ont., Canada	79	79	75	82	315	
15	*Miss Judy Frank, Old Oaks C.C., Purchase, N.Y.	80	79	81	76	316	
	*Miss Anne Richardson, Columbus C.C., Columbus, Ohio	78	76	83	79	316	
17	Mrs. Peggy Kirk Bell, Pine Needles C.C., Southern Pines, N.C.	78	78	78	83	317	
	Miss Bonnie Randolph, Naples Beach & G.C., Naples, Fla.	78	83	75	81	317	
19	Miss Gloria Armstrong, Oakland, Calif.	73	85	84	78	320	
	Miss Marilynn Smith, Wichita C.C., Wichita, Kans.	77	80	79	84	320	
21	*Mrs. Philip J. Cudone, Montclair G.C., Montclair, N.J.	80	80	82	79	321	
22	Miss Mickey Wright, San Diego C.C., Chula Vista, Calif.	79	82	81	80	322	
	Miss Joyce Ziske, Rivermoor C.C., Waterford, Wis.	80	80	80	82	322	
24	*Miss Meriam H. Bailey, Inverness G.C., Palatine, Ill.	81	80	79	84	324	
25	Miss Ruth Jessen, Inglewood C.C., Seattle, Wash.	85	83	80	77	325	
	Miss Vonnie Colby, Normandy Shores G.C., Miami Beach, Fla.	78	86	80	81	325	
	Miss Gloria J. Fecht, Pine Needles C.C., Southern Pines, N.C.	83	81	81	80	325	
28	*Mrs. Helen Sigel Wilson, Philadelphia Country C., Spring Mill, Pa.	77	80	89	81	327	
	*Miss Mary Patton Janssen, Farmington C.C., Charlottesville, Va.	81	79	84	83	327	
30	Mrs. Kathy Cornelius, Miami Valley G.C., Dayton, Ohio	81	79	83	85	328	
31	*Mrs. Roslyn Swift Berger, Westwood C.C., Buffalo, N.Y.	83	82	84	80	329	
32	*Miss Mary Ann Downey, Baltimore C.C., Baltimore, Md.	88	80	78	84	330	
	*Mrs. Marge Mason, Ridgewood C.C., Ridgewood, N.J.	82	84	81	83	330	
34	*Mrs. Paul Dye, Jr., Indianapolis C.C., Indianapolis, Ind.	87	81	82	82	332	
35	*Miss Nan Berry, Quincy C.C., Quincy, Ill.	85	79	85	85	334	
36	*Mrs. Norman S. Woolworth, Wee Burn C.C., Darien, Conn.	83	85	85	86	339	
37	*Mrs. Charles F. Spalding, Round Hill C., Greenwich, Conn.	84	83	89	85	341	
38	*Mrs. Reinert M. Torgerson, Cherry Valley C., Garden City, N.Y.	83	82	88	90	343	
39	*Mrs. John K. Barry, Columbia C.C., Washington, D.C.	85	83	92	84	344	
40	*Miss Constance A. Gorsuch, Sedgefield C.C., Greensboro N.C.	83	85	87	90	345	
41	*Miss Terry Logan, Essex Fells C.C., Essex Fells, N.J.					350	
	†Mrs. Jacqueline Pung, San Francisco	78	75	73	disqualified)		

*Amateur.
Prize money totaling $7,200 awarded to professionals.
+See text preceding.

1958
SIXTH WOMEN'S OPEN CHAMPIONSHIP

Held at Forest Lake Country Club, Bloomfield Hills, Mich., June 26-28.
Yardage—6,240. Par 73. 57 Entries, 54 Starters.
Forty-one contestants who completed 72 holes.

						Score	Money Prize
1	Miss Mickey Wright, San Diego C.C., Chula Vista, Calif.	74	72	70	74	290	$1,800.00
2	Miss Louise Suggs, Sea Island G.C., Sea Island, Ga.	75	74	75	71	295	1,200.00
3	Miss Fay Crocker, Club de Golf del Uruguay, Montevideo, Uruguay	79	68	76	74	297	800.00
4	Miss Alice Bauer, Paradise C.C., Paradise, Fla.	76	77	75	72	300	650.00
5	Miss Betty Jameson, San Antonio C.C., San Antonio, Texas	75	80	74	74	303	500.00
6	Miss Betsy Rawls, Spartanburg C.C., Spartanburg, S.C.	79	82	73	70	304	400.00
7	Miss Wiffi Smith. St. Clair River C.C.. St. Clair. Mich.	81	76	73	75	305	325.00
	Mrs. Jacqueline Pung, San Francisco, Calif.	75	77	77	76	305	325.00
9	Miss Vonnie Colby, Normandy Shores G.C., Miami Beach, Fla.	77	76	75	78	306	250.00
	Miss Patty Berg, St. Andrews G.C., St. Andrews, Ill.	78	78	77	73	306	250.00
11	Miss Mary Lena Faulk, Glen Arven C.C., Thomasville, Ga.	79	76	79	73	307	200.00
	Miss Beverly Hanson, Cochran Ranch G.C., Indio, Calif.	79	77	75	76	307	200.00
	*Miss Anne Quast, Broadmoor G.C., Seattle, Wash.	82	73	76	76	307	----
14	Mrs. Marlene Bauer Hagge, Delray Beach, Fla.	76	79	76	77	308	100.00
15	Mrs. Kathy Cornelius, Cleveland Heights G.C., Lakeland, Fla.	80	74	77	78	309	100.00
16	Miss Joyce Ziske, Rivermoor C.C., Waterford, Wis.	78	79	76	77	310	100.00
17	*Miss Barbara McIntire, Tequesta C.C., Jupiter, Fla.	83	76	77	76	312	----
18	Mrs. Peggy Kirk Bell, Pine Needles C.C., Southern Pines, N.C.	82	79	73	79	313	
19	Miss Marilynn Smith, Wichita C.C., Wichita, Kans.	82	79	82	73	316	
20	Miss Betty Dodd, Louisville, Ky.	79	80	80	78	317	
21	Miss Bonnie Randolph, Naples Beach & G.C., Naples, Fla.	79	78	80	81	318	
22	Miss JoAnn Prentice, Birmingham, Ala.	78	82	78	81	319	
23	Miss Gloria J. Fecht, Pine Needles C.C., Southern Pines, N.C.	82	79	80	80	321	
	Miss Ruth Jessen, Inglewood C.C., Seattle, Wash.	83	81	81	76	321	
25	*Mrs. Paul Dye, Jr., C.C. of Indianapolis, Indianapolis, Ind.	84	79	79	80	322	
	Miss Murle MacKenzie, Pasadena C.C., St. Petersburg, Fla.	82	79	81	80	322	
27	Mrs. Betty Bush, Tequesta C.C., Jupiter, Fla.	86	76	80	82	324	
28	*Miss Judy Bell, Wichita C.C., Wichita, Kans.	84	76	83	82	325	
29	Miss Gloria Armstrong, Oakland, Calif.	83	81	81	81	326	
30	Miss Jon Snyder, MacDonald Park G.C., Wichita, Kans.	85	80	78	84	327	
31	Miss Pat Devany, Grosse Ile G. & C.C., Grosse Ile, Mich.	88	83	79	78	328	
32	*Miss Berridge Long, Guyan G. & C.C., Huntington, W. Va.	81	86	80	83	330	
33	*Miss Meriam H. Bailey, Inverness G.C., Palatine, Ill.	84	79	85	84	332	
34	*Mrs. Charles F. Spalding, Round Hill C., Greenwich, Conn.	84	84	85	81	334	
35	*Mrs. James P. Lee, Biltmore G.C., Coral Gables, Fla.	87	83	84	81	335	
36	Miss Wanda J. Sanches, Baton Rouge, La.	90	81	85	85	341	
	*Miss Sally Carroll, Wheeling C.C., Wheeling, W. Va.	88	86	85	82	341	
38	Miss Barbara Rotvig, Ann Arbor, Mich.	86	84	91	81	342	
39	*Miss Phyllis Preuss, Pompano Beach C.C., Pompano Beach, Fla.	84	86	89	86	345	
40	*Mrs. Frank L. Thompson, Jr., Oakland Hills C.C., Birmingham, Mich.	87	83	95	94	359	
41	*Miss Margaret Watkins, C.C. of Detroit, Grosse Pointe Farms, Mich.	88	86	105	88	367	

*Amateur.
Prize money totaling $7,200 awarded to professionals.

1959
SEVENTH WOMEN'S OPEN CHAMPIONSHIP

Held at Churchill Valley Country Club, Pittsburgh, Pa., June 25-27.
Yardage—6,104. Par 70. 63 Entries, 61 Starters.
Forty contestants who completed 72 holes.

						Score	Money Prize
1	Miss Mickey Wright, Bonita G.C., San Diego, Calif.	72	75	69	71	287	$1,800.00
2	Miss Louise Suggs, Sea Island G.C., Sea Island, Ga.	71	74	75	69	289	1,200.00
3	Miss Joyce Ziske, Rivermoor C.C., Waterford, Wis.	75	73	72	72	292	650.00
	Miss Ruth Jessen, Inglewood C.C., Seattle, Wash.	75	74	72	71	292	650.00
	Mrs. Marlene Bauer Hagge, Churchill Valley C.C., Pittsburgh, Pa.	71	76	73	72	292	650.00
6	Miss Patty Berg, St. Andrews G.C., West Chicago, Ill.	72	75	75	74	296	400.00
7	Miss Betsy Rawls, Spartanburg C.C., Spartanburg, S.C.	76	73	72	76	297	350.00
8	Miss Murle MacKenzie, Pasadena G.C., St. Petersburg, Fla.	77	75	75	71	298	300.00
9	*Miss Anne Quast, Everett G. & C.C., Everett, Wash.	75	76	75	73	299	----
10	Miss JoAnn Prentice, Birmingham, Ala.	77	74	77	74	302	250.00
11	*Miss Joanne Goodwin, Haverhill C.C., Haverhill, Mass.	80	78	72	73	303	----
	*Miss Barbara McIntire, Tequesta C.C., Jupiter, Fla.	76	77	74	76	303	----
13	Miss Mary Lena Faulk, Glen Arven C.C., Thomasville, Ga.	76	77	76	75	304	250.00
14	Miss Wanda Sanches, Baton Rouge, La.	75	73	77	80	305	200.00
15	Miss Beverly Hanson, Cochran Ranch G.C., Indio, Calif.	79	75	78	74	306	83.33
	Miss Betty Hicks, Crystaire C.C., Crystalaire, Calif.	78	76	76	76	306	83.33
	Mrs. Kathy Cornelius, Miami Valley G.C., Dayton, Ohio	75	77	76	78	306	83.34
	Miss Marilynn Smith, French Lick Sheraton C.C., French Lick, Ind.	76	74	78	78	306	83.33
	Miss Fay Crocker, Club de Golf del Uruguay, Montevideo, Uruguay	77	74	75	80	306	83.34
	Miss Betty Jameson, San Antonio C.C., San Antonio, Texas	76	75	81	74	306	83.33
21	Miss Wiffi Smith, St. Clair River C.C., St. Clair, Mich.	77	79	78	73	307	
22	Miss Gloria Armstrong, Lake Chabot G.C., Oakland, Calif.	81	76	73	81	311	
	*Miss Barbara Williams, Richmond G.C., Richmond, Calif.	76	77	80	78	311	
	Mrs. Betty Bush, Tequesta C.C., Jupiter, Fla.	77	79	79	76	311	
25	*Miss Betty Kerby, Fairlawn C.C., Akron, Ohio	75	79	80	78	312	
26	Miss Barbara Romack, Del Paso C.C., Sacramento, Calif.	81	79	75	78	313	
27	*Miss Sherry Wheeler, Glasgow C.C., Glasgow, Ky.	81	75	77	82	315	
	Mrs. Bettye Mims Danoff, Lakewood C.C., Dallas, Texas	79	77	78	81	315	
29	*Miss Phyllis Preuss, Pompano Beach C.C., Pompano Beach, Fla.	81	80	77	78	316	
	*Miss Judy Bell, Wichita C.C., Wichita, Kans.	79	81	78	78	316	
31	Miss Barbara J. Rotvig, Univ. of Michigan G.C., Ann Arbor, Mich.	83	81	76	77	317	
32	Mrs. Peggy Kirk Bell, Pine Needles C.C., Southern Pines, N.C.	77	81	80	80	318	
	Miss Kathy Whitworth, Jal C.C., Jal, N.M.	83	74	82	79	318	
34	*Miss Anne Richardson, Columbus C.C., Columbus, Ohio	83	77	79	81	320	
35	*Miss Mary Ann Downey, Baltimore C.C., Baltimore, Md.	80	80	84	78	322	
36	*Miss Cynthia Sullivan, Florence C.C., Florence, S.C.	76	84	81	83	324	
37	Miss Gloria J. Fecht, Pine Needles C.C., Southern Pines, N.C.	79	83	86	77	325	
38	*Mrs. Edward C. Stumpp, Wheeling C.C., Wheeling, W. Va.	84	79	78	85	326	
39	*Miss Meriam H. Bailey, Inverness G.C., Palatine, Ill.	84	80	79	86	329	
40	*Miss Diana Hoke, Chartiers C.C., Pittsburgh, Pa.	80	82	85	85	332	

*Amateur.
Prize money totaling $7,200 awarded to professionals.

AMATEUR PUBLIC LINKS CHAMPIONSHIP

STANDISH CUP

Presented in June, 1922, by

JAMES D. STANDISH, JR.

Chairman, United States Golf Association Public and Municipal Golf Courses Committee

WARREN G. HARDING TROPHY

Presented in June, 1923, by

HON. WARREN G. HARDING

President of the United States of America

HISTORY

1922–On February 1, 1922, James D. Standish, Jr., of Detroit, persuaded the USGA Executive Committee to establish an Amateur Public Links Championship and offered to donate a perpetual trophy. The event was awarded to the Ottawa Park Course, in Toledo, Ohio, August 28-31, 1922, at the request of Sylvanus P. Jermain, President of the Toledo District Golf Association. A USGA Committee on Public and Municipal Golf Courses, with Mr. Standish as chairman, was organized to conduct it. The Committee had no way of anticipating what to expect, and it was a matter of great satisfaction when 140 entries were received and 136 players started in the 36-hole qualifying round for 32 places in match play. The medalist by nine strokes was George Aulbach, a 19-year-old Boston University student, who scored 70-69–139. His score set a record which stood for 18 years. Scores up to 160 qualified. In the first round, R. A. Wimmer, of Toledo, defeated A. B. Hadden, also of Toledo, at the 24th hole, a distance not surpassed in 18-hole competition until a 25-hole match in 1963. The winner eventually proved to be Edmund R. Held, 19, of St. Louis, who defeated Richard J. Walsh, 18, of New York, 6 and 5, in the 36-hole final, after eliminating Aulbach on the 20th green in a semi-final. A most unusual incident occurred during match play. Two players had made their approaches on a hole near the finish when a pistol shot sounded in the rear of the gallery; a thoroughly uninterested spectator had chosen that moment to commit suicide.

1923–Prior to the second championship, at East Potomac Park, Washington, D.C., the Hon. Warren G. Harding, then President of the United States and an honorary member of the USGA Executive Committee, donated a trophy for a team competition. This second Championship was conducted on the same format as the first, except that each city area was limited to four representatives and the city team competition at stroke play was held in conjunction with the second 18 holes of qualifying. Chicago was the best of 18 teams, with a total of 311, E. B. Lloyd and Bob White scoring 76s, John W. Dawson 78, and Matt Jans 81. Ray McAuliffe, of Buffalo, led 134 starters, with 76-77–153, to win the individual qualifying medal. Richard J. Walsh, 19, of New York, the runner-up in the first Championship, defeated J. Stewart Whitham, also of New York, 6 and 5, in the final. Both finalists represented the Scottish-American Club of New York. Secretary of State Charles Evans Hughes presented the trophies. Held, the first Champion, had joined a private club and, thus, was ineligible to defend.

1924–Joseph Coble, a 27-year-old Philadelphia waiter and semi-finalist the previous year, won the third Championship at the Community Country Club, Dayton, Ohio. After being down at some point in every match, he defeated Henry Decker, of Kansas City, Mo., 2 and 1, in the final. The medalist was Earl McAleer, of Washington, who scored 150. The team competition was extended to 36 holes and Washington scored its first victory with a four-man total of 636. Walsh did not defend.

1925–Coble turned professional after his victory, and Ray McAuliffe, 30, of Buffalo, N. Y., succeeded him by defeating William F. Serrick, of New York, 6 and 5, in the final at the Salisbury Country Club, Salisbury Plains, N. Y. Nelson Davis, of Cleveland, won the medal with 73-74–147, and the qualifying deadline fell to 159. New York won the team competition with a new low of 616. Several Canadians were among the 98 starters, and Toronto placed ninth among the teams. Even with the Canadian representation, however, the entry was down to 103 and only 98 started. Both figures are the all-time lows.

1926–Lester Bolstad, a student at the University of Minnesota, defeated Carl F. Kauffmann, of

Pittsburgh, 3 and 2, in the final at Grover Cleveland Park, Buffalo. At the time of his victory, Bolstad was 18 years 3 months of age. Richard J. Walsh, the 1923 Champion, won the medal with 73-73–146, and the qualifying deadline dropped to 155. Chicago won its second team championship with another new low of 608. McAuliffe, like Coble, had turned professional and did not defend.

1927–Carl F. Kauffmann, Pittsburgh stenographer, made the big step from runnerup to Champion to inaugurate a three-year reign. He defeated William F. Serrick, of New York, on the 37th green in the first extra-hole final, at the Ridgewood Golf Links, Cleveland. Serrick, who fluffed his approach on the extra hole, had qualified in every Championship and had been runnerup in 1925. Kauffmann also led Pittsburgh to a team victory with a score of 639 in a record field of 20 teams, but individual medal honors went to 17-year-old Clarke Morse, of St. Louis, with 73-76–149. Bolstad, the defender, scored 164 in the qualifying and missed match play by two strokes.

1928–Kauffmann was the first Champion to enter match play in defense of his title, and, once in, he went on to beat Phil Ogden, of Cleveland, 8 and 7, in the final at Cobbs Creek Municipal Golf Course, Philadelphia. It was the most decisive victory scored in any final and highlighted a Pittsburgh sweep. The qualifying medal went to Sam Graham, also of Pittsburgh, on 78-74–152, as scores up to 165, the highest ever, qualified for match play. Pittsburgh also repeated in the team competition, with a four-man 36-hole total of 646, the highest ever to win, as the team entry rose again to 23. Ganson Depew, of Buffalo, replaced Mr. Standish as chairman of the USGA Public Links Committee.

1929–Kauffmann, now 30 years old, won for the third successive year at the Forest Park Municipal Golf Course, St. Louis. He tied for the medal with Milton Soncrant, of Toledo, and Patsy Tiso, of New York, at 151, and went on to beat Soncrant, 4 and 3, in the final. On the day after the final, he defeated Soncrant and Tiso in a playoff for the medal, thus becoming the first Champion to win the medal. New York and Louisville tied for the team Championship, and New York defeated Louisville in this playoff to win for the second time.

1930–At the Jacksonville (Fla.) Municipal Links, Kauffmann inadvertently disqualified himself by returning an erroneous score in the first qualifying round. This opened up the competition, and Al Quigley, of Chicago, took the medal with 145. The Championship went to Robert E. Wingate, of Jacksonville, who defeated Joseph E. Greene, of Philadelphia, 1 up, in the final. He was the first home-town player to win. Brooklyn took the team championship to the New York area for the third time with a score of 617.

1931–Charles Ferrera, a riveter from San Francisco who was accustomed to working in high places, ascended to the Championship at the Keller Golf Course, St. Paul. He defeated Joe Nichols, a 15-year-old schoolboy from Long Beach, Calif., 5 and 4, in the final. Nichols is the youngest player ever to reach the final. San Francisco also won the team competition, with a score of 620 as 28 teams took part. David A. Mitchell, of Indianapolis, prevented a San Francisco sweep by taking the medal, with 148. Both Kauffmann, the three-time winner, and Wingate, the defender, failed to qualify for match play. The entry, which had held comparatively steady through the first nine years, showed its first notable increase this year; 182 entered and 176 started. Both figures were new highs.

1932–Two Millers played in the final at the Shawnee Golf Course, Louisville, Ky., in July, 1932, but they were not related. R. L. Miller, who was 21 and insisted his initials didn't stand for anything, returned the Championship to Jacksonville, Fla., by defeating Pete Miller, of Chicago, 4 and 2. The winner had recently been reinstated to amateur status after working for a year in a professional's shop. Joe Nichols, who had been runnerup the previous year and was now 16, won the medal with 145, and five players tied for the last two places in match play at 153, a new low. One of the five was Ferrera, the defender, and he qualified the following morning on the sixth hole of the playoff. Kauffmann failed to qualify for the third successive year. Louisville set a new record of 606 in winning its first team competition by one stroke over Chicago. There were 213 individual entries and 32 team entries, both new highs.

1933–Charles Ferrera, the San Franciscan who had won in 1931, became the second Champion to repeat. He dethroned the defender, R. L. Miller, 3 and 2, in the final at the Eastmoreland Golf Course, Portland, Ore. The Championship was the first held on the West Coast, and most of the entrants were from the West. Tab Boyer, of Portland, Ore., won the medal in a playoff with Leslie Leal, of Billingham, Wash., after they had tied at 144. Boyer scored 75-70–145 to Leal's 76-81–157. Los Angeles took its first team championship with 609.

1934–David A. Mitchell, of Indianapolis, the medalist in 1931, came back to defeat Arthur Armstrong, of Honolulu, 5 and 3, in the final at the South Park Allegheny County Links, Pittsburgh. Armstrong was the first Hawaiian to reach the final of any USGA Championship. The medalist was Albert (Scotty) Campbell, of Seattle, who scored 144; and Los Angeles retained the team championship, making a new low of 603 to win over 33 other teams, a new entry record. The format of the individual Championship was changed for the first time; 64, instead of 32, qualified for match play. The first four rounds were played in two days and the semi-final round was extended to 36 holes, the same as the final. Scores up to 160 earned places in match play under the new system. Ferrera, the defender, was eliminated in the third round.

1935–The new system of play was continued at the Charles E. Coffin Course, Indianapolis, and Frank Strafaci, of Brooklyn, N. Y., won in the second extra-hole final. He defeated Joe Coria, of St. Paul, after 37 holes. Strafaci, like Held in 1922 and Walsh in 1923, was 19. Lloyd Nordstrom, of Davenport, Iowa, won the medal, with 145, and the qualifying limit fell to 159. San Antonio won its first team championship by beating Louisville in a playoff. They tied at 612, and San Antonio scored 305 in the replay. Team entries reached another new high of 45. Mitchell, the defender, lost in the third round. The entry of 198 was the second largest to that time, and 196 started.

1936–The Championship was returned to Long Island and held on the one-year-old Blue Course at Bethpage State Park, Farmingdale, N. Y. B. Patrick Abbott, of Pasadena, Calif., defeated Claude B. Rippy, of Washington, D. C., 4 and 3, in the final. Rippy had set a nine-hole record for the Championship in tying for the qualifying medal; he scored 75 in the first round and then 30-40–70 in the second, for 145. His total was matched by James B. Molinari, of San Francisco, and there was no playoff. The deadline fell to 154, another new low. Strafaci was beaten in the second round. Seattle established a new low of 599 in winning its first team Championship over 48 other teams, still another entry record. There were 223 entrants and 222 starters, both records, and they represented 58 cities. It was possible to handle the qualifying field only by using both the Blue and Red Courses at Bethpage State Park. The rule that a player could not compete in both the Amateur Public Links and Amateur Championships in the same year, except by special invitation, became effective.

1937–Bruce McCormick, 28, of Los Angeles, became Champion by defeating Don Erickson, of Alhambra, 1 up, in the first all-California final at the Harding Park Course, San Francisco. Erickson had been dormie-3 and McCormick saved the match only on the last green. Erickson had equalled the qualifying record established by George Aulbach in the first Championship in 1922 by scoring 67-72–139. His 67 was a new 18-hole record. The qualifying deadline of 152 represented another new low; although there were 64 qualifiers, it was one stroke below the old low for 32 qualifiers. Sacramento completed a California sweep by winning its first team Championship with another new low of 587. There were 190 entrants and 186 starters. Exactly half the qualifiers were Californians, and three from that state reached the semi-final round. Abbott was eliminated in the quarter-finals.

1938–Al Leach, a 26-year-old WPA worker from Cleveland, won one of the most exciting finals at the Highland Park Municipal Golf Course, in his home town, Cleveland. His opponent, Louis C. Cyr, of Portland, Ore., was six down after 23 holes but squared the match on the 34th hole. Leach pulled himself together and took the last hole. Cyr had qualified in an equally exciting playoff in which 18 players tied at 151 for the last place, still another new low; Cyr's birdie 3 on the first extra hole put him in. The medalist was Walter Burkemo, 20, of Detroit, who scored 72-69–141. Burkemo was later to win the PGA Championship in 1953. Two records were made in the team Championship; Los Angeles won for the third time with an all-time four-man, 36-hole record of 584, and 55 teams, an all-time high, participated. The winning team comprised Don Erickson, 143, and George S. Lance, Bruce McCormick and Neil Whitney, all 147. McCormick lost on the 19th hole in the first round. The entry in this second Championship at Cleveland, reached another new high of 248, and again two courses, both at Highland Park had to be used to handle the 247 starters in the qualifying round. Seventy-three communities had sent representatives, and this system was making the Championship unmanageable.

1939–Sectional qualifying rounds at 33 sites selected by the USGA were substituted for the unlimited number of city area rounds prior to the Championship at the Mount Pleasant Park Golf Course, Baltimore. These sectional rounds attracted 2,401 entrants, the largest number received to that time for any USGA Championship. Of these, 190 qualified and 178 started. The Championship proper was conducted by the same format as in previous years, and the winner was Andrew Szwedko, a 32-year-old steel worker who took the title to Pittsburgh for the fourth time and to Pennsylvania for the fifth time. He defeated Philip Gordon, of Oakland, Calif., 1 up, in the final. The qualifying round at the Championship proper developed a four-way tie at 144 among Arthur Armstrong, Honolulu, 72-72; Luke Barnes, Atlanta, 71-73; Gerry Bert, Jr., Seattle, 70-74, and Jack Taulman, Columbus, Ind., 74-70. It was the first four-way tie in any USGA Championship, and it was never played off. The team representation was reduced from four men to three, and Los Angeles again retained the team title, winning for the fourth time with a three-man, 36-hole score of 442.

1940–The sectional qualifying system had proved its worth and was continued. Thirty-eight sections were established, and the entry rose to 2,601, with 193 qualifiers and 190 starters in the Championship proper at the Rackham Golf Course, Detroit. Robert C. Clark, 31, of St. Paul, won by defeating Michael Dietz, of Detroit, 8 and 6, in the final. Clark faced a more stern challenge in the semi-final when he had to play 38 holes to eliminate Ed Furgol, of Utica, N. Y., who was to win the Open Championship in 1954. Furgol and Worth Stimits, Jr., of Colorado Springs, Colo., had tied for the medal at 138, breaking by one stroke the record which had endured for 18 years. There was no playoff. The qualifying deadline fell to 149, the all-time low. San Francisco won the team Championship with 435, a new low under the three-man, 36-hole system. Szwedko lost in the first round of match play.

1941–James C. Clark, Jr., of Long Beach, Calif., set a qualifying record of 64-71–135 to start the Championship proper at the Indian Canyon Golf Course, Spokane, Wash. His score, three strokes under the old record and seven under par, represented the lowest 18-hole and 36-hole scores made in any USGA stroke competition to that time. Clark was beaten by Jack Kerns, of Denver, in a semi-final, and Kerns, in turn, bowed to William M. Welch, Jr., of Houston, Tex., 6 and 5, in the final. Robert Clark, the defender, went down in the second round. The team Championship was won for the first time by Detroit with another 435. The entry rose to another new high of 2,816, of whom the Denver section alone contributed 516. The course measured only 6,277 yards and was one of the shortest on which the event has been played in modern times.

1942-45–No Championships: World War II

1946–The intervention of World War II did not cool Jimmy Clark. When the Championship was resumed at the 6,590-yard Wellshire Golf Course,

Denver, he bettered by a stroke his own qualifying record with 64-70–134, eight under par and again a 36-hole record for a USGA stroke competition. His play also contributed materially to Long Beach's victory in the team Championship with a record total of 431 for three men playing 18 holes; to Clark's 134 were added Marshall Holt's 143 and Oscar W. Holberg's 154. Holt eliminated Clark in the first round, Welch went down in the second round and the eventual winner was Smiley L. Quick, 37, of Los Angeles, who defeated Louis Stafford, of Portland, Ore., 3 and 2, in the final. It marked the first time since 1928 that all honors had been won by players from the same metropolitan area. Quick, who had tied for 26th place in the Open, was invited to play in the Amateur Championship of the same year and went all the way to the 37th green of the final before bowing to Ted Bishop. it was the closest approach to a double in the Amateur Public Links and Amateur Championships and the best performance in three Championships on record. The entry for this Championship was 3,586, the largest ever received for any USGA competition. The record stood until 1969. Of these 1,280 were from the Denver section, and preliminary rounds were required there. A driving contest was held prior to the Championship proper; Leo Roy Gann, of Tulsa, hit one ball 316 yards, and Einar H. Hanson, of San Francisco, averaged 286 yards with three balls.

1947–Wilfred Crossley, a 34-year-old Bostonian temporarily living in Atlanta, became the first since Kauffmann to win both the qualifying medal and the individual Championship, and he also led Atlanta to its first team Championship at the Meadowbrook Golf Course, Minneapolis. Crossley, a Harvard alumnus, scored 70-69–139 in the stroke rounds and never was down in match play. He beat Avery Beck, of Raleigh, N. C., 6 and 5, in the final. Beck had won a 38-hole semi-final against Benjamin G. Hughes, of Portland, Ore. With Crossley scoring 139, Walter R. Browne, 143, and Charles W. Barnes, 149, Atlanta tied the three-man, 36-hole record of 431 in the team competition to score the third sweep of all available honors. There were 2,633 entrants, but Quick's name was not among them. He was late in filing his entry, and it was rejected. The number of qualifiers in sectional rounds was reduced to 180, of whom 179 started. In another driving contest prior to the Championship proper, Joseph Carlone, of Cleveland, hit a ball 297 yards, 10 inches.

1948–An all-match-play Championship was instituted at the North Fulton Park Golf Course, Atlanta, Ga., the form being precisely the same as that which had been reinstituted in the Amateur Championship a year earlier. The winner after eight rounds of match play was Michael R. Ferentz, a 33-year-old Long Beach, Calif., bartender who was competing for the first time. He benefited by stymies to get a half and a win on the 34th and 35th holes and defeated Benjamin G. Hughes, of Portland, Ore., 2 and 1, in the final. Crossley gave up his title in the fifth round. Forty-four sectional qualifying rounds, a new high, were employed, and 210 players qualified out of an original entry of 2,728. The basis of the team Championship was changed again. Plav was conducted separately at only 18 holes stroke play on the Saturday prior to the start of the individual Championship, and the teams of three men represented qualifying sections rather than cities. The Raleigh, N.C., section won for the first time with a score of 223.

1949–The all-match-play form was continued, and Kenneth J. Towns, 20, won an all-San Francisco final, the second all-California final. He defeated William E. Betger, a left-hander, 5 and 4, at the Rancho Golf Course, Los Angeles. It was the third individual victory for a San Franciscan, and San Francisco also won its third team Championship with a new low of 221 for three men playing 18 holes. By sweeping all honors, San Francisco duplicated the achievements of Pittsburgh in 1928, the Los Angeles area in 1936, and Atlanta in 1947. Ferentz was stopped in the first round, and Horace Henry of Houston, Texas, defeated Gordon B. Hammond, Jr., of Rockford, Ill., at 24 holes, equalling the extra-hole record made in the 1922 Championship. The course measured 6,805 yards, the longest on which the Championship has been held.

1950–The Silver Anniversary Championship was played at the Seneca Golf Course on its return to Louisville, Ky., and Stanley Bielat, a 37-year-old truck driver from Yonkers, took the title to the metropolitan New York area for the third time. Bielat had to win four extra-hole matches to reach the final, but once there he made five birdies on the last eight holes and beat John Dobro, of Chicago, 7 and 5. Towns was eliminated in the fourth round. The Los Angeles section took the team Championship for the sixth time by scoring 217, the record for three-man, 18-hole competition. The team consisted of Stephen Z. Shaw, who scored 67, Robert Roux, 74, and James R. Griffin, 76. Thirty-eight teams participated, a record since the establishment of the event as a separate competition.

1951–Dave Stanley, a 20-year-old student at the University of California at Los Angeles, won the longest final and the third to go extra holes, at the Brown Deer Park Golf Course, Milwaukee. His par 4 on the 38th hole defeated Ralph Vranesic, of Denver. Vranesic was five down after 27 holes but one-putted five greens to square the match. Stanley had been playing golf only five years and had been crippled throughout his youth by osteomyelitis and rheumatic fever. Both finalists had had to play 37 holes to win their semi-final matches. In the Silver Anniversary of the team Championship, the Dayton, Ohio, section made a score of 234 to win for the first time. Bielat lost his title in the third round.

1952–The Championship went to a private club, the Miami Country Club, for the first time on its return to Florida, but a Californian, Omer L. (Pete) Bogan, 35, of South Gate, was the winner. He defeated Robert J. Scherer, of Decatur, Ill., 4 and 3, in the final. Like his predecessor, who was beaten by Scherer in the second round, Bogan represented the Montebello Golf Course. The team Championship was won by Chicago for the third time with a score of 227. The number of qualifiers was reduced from 210 to 200. The Championship was the first held by the

USGA under the new Rules which eliminated the stymie.

1953—For the tenth time, and the sixth time in eight years, a Californian won at the West Seattle Municipal Golf Course, Seattle, Wash. This became a certainty when Ted Richards, Jr., 30, of Santa Monica, entered the final with a fellow-Los Angelean, Irving A. Cooper, of Long Beach. Richards played level-par golf for 36 holes and was 1 up when the holes ran out. His victory was the seventh by a Los Angelean. He later went to the quarter-final round of the Amateur while Cooper went to the round of 16. A young Jacksonville, Fla., team won the team trophy by a stroke over Montebello, Calif. Honolulu would have tied for second had it not been for an inadvertent error on the score card of one of the Hawaiians which called for his automatic disqualification. Bogan was beaten in the fourth round and subsequently turned professional.

1954—Gene Andrews, of Pacific Palisades, Calif., the oldest winner to date at 40, defeated Jack E. Zimmerman, of Dayton, Ohio, 1 up, in the final at the Cedar Crest Golf Course, Dallas, Texas. Thus, Californians had won the Championship eleven times and seven times in the nine years since World War II. Andrews, playing in 108-degree heat against a 26-year-old opponent, scored 73 and 72, three over par, for his two rounds in the final. Andrews' home course was the Rancho Golf Course, in Los Angeles, where Ted Richards, Jr., the previous winner, also had played. Richards could not defend because he had become a member of a private club. Dallas won the team Championship with a score of 220.

1955—The run of California victories came to an end in the second playing of the event at the Coffin Municipal Golf Course, Indianapolis, Ind. Sam D. Kocsis, 35, of Detroit, defeated Tommy Bean, of Summerville, Ga., 2 up. The course had been considerably changed since the Amateur Public Links Championship was first played there in 1935. The key club in Kocsis' bag was his blade putter, a hand-me-down from his older brother Chuck, a member of the 1938 and 1949 Walker Cup Teams and later runnerup in the 1956 Amateur Championship. With it, Kocsis eliminated the Champion, Gene Andrews, 1 up, in the semi-final round. Andrews progressed further in defense of his title than any Champion since R. L. Miller, of Jacksonville, Fla., who won in 1932 and was runner-up 1933. The team Championship was won by Miami for the first time with a score of 224. The entry, which had been declining since World War II, turned upward once again to 2,007. Following the Championship the Amateur Public Links Committee indicated a preference for a shorter Championship, a smaller number of qualifiers and the restoration of a 36-hole qualifying round to determine 64 qualifiers for match play and the Team Championship.

1956—In response to the preference of the Public Links Committee, the field of sectional qualifiers was reduced from 200 to 150 and a 36-hole qualifying round was restored to determine 64 qualifiers and the team Championship. The Champion was exempt from sectional but not from Championship qualifying. This was substantially the form which had been used through 1947. The event attracted an entry of 1,921 and was held for the second time at the Harding Park Golf Course, in San Francisco, Calif. All honors went to Memphis, Tenn. It won the team Championship for the first time with a three-man score of 445 for 36 holes, and James H. (Junie) Buxbaum, a trucking company representative, won the individual Championship, defeating William C. Scarbrough, Jr., in the final, 3 and 2. Scarbrough, a Navy Chief Petty Officer stationed at Jacksonville, Fla., had originated in Memphis, too. Buxbaum had played as a professional from late 1947 into 1951 and been reinstated in 1953. It was his first appearance in this event. The qualifying medal was won by D.M. (Scotty) McBeath, of Palo Alto, Calif., with 69-72–141, three under par. Joe Gallardo, Jr., of Los Angeles, made a 68 in the second round, the lowest 18-hole score. Fifteen tied for the last 14 places at 155, but there was no playoff since two failed to appear and one of them was drawn into match play by lot. The scores all ran higher than in the first playing at Harding Park in 1937. Sam D. Kocsis, the defending Champion, made a 77 in the first qualifying round and then was recalled to Detroit because of the death of his father-in-law. Gene Andrews, the 1954 Champion, and 1955 semi-finalist, failed to qualify sectionally. Joe Roach, of Los Angeles, the national Negro amateur Champion, played for the first time and reached the quarter-finals.

1957—Don Essig, III, of Indianapolis, Ind., a sophomore at Louisiana State University, defeated Gene Towry, of Dallas, Texas, a graduate student at Southern Methodist University and a former professional, 6 and 5, at the Hershey Park Golf Club, Hershey, Pa. Essig, 18 years and 8 months old, was the second youngest Champion. Les Bolstad, of Minneapolis, Minn., was 18 years 3 months old when he won in 1926. Essig, defeated James H. Buxbaum, of Memphis, Tenn., the defending Champion, on the 19th hole in the quarter-finals. Bud Kivett, of High Point, N.C., a mail-carrier, won the qualifying medal with 72-69–141, one over par. Highest score to gain one of the 64 qualifying places was 153, and only five of the 10 who made 153 qualified. Honolulu won the team Championship for the first time with a three-man score of 440 for 36 holes.

1958—Daniel D. Sikes, Jr., 27, of Jacksonville, Fla., a senior at the University of Florida Law School, defeated Bob Ludlow, of Indianapolis, Ind., 3 and 2, at Silver Lake Golf Club, Orland Park, Ill. Sikes previously eliminated Don Essig, III, of Indianapolis, the defending Champion, in the third round, 5 and 4, after Essig had won the qualifying medal with 71-73–144, two under par. Essig was the first defending Champion to take the medal since Carl F. Kauffmann, of Pittsburgh, in 1929. Sikes was in the playoff for the last qualifying places at 155, and is the second Champion to have won his place in match play through a playoff. William M. Welch, Jr. did it in 1941. The sectional team Championship was won by St. Paul with a three-man score of 447 for 36 holes; it was the first victory for either of the Twin Cities. The Silver Lake Golf Club was privately owned by John R. Coghill and was the third such course to be used;

the Salisbury Plains Golf Club, on Long Island, site of the 1925 Championship, was owned by John J. Lannin, and the Ridgewood Golf Links, Cleveland, where the 1927 Championship was held, was also a privately owned fee course.

1959–William A. Wright, of Seattle, Wash., won the Championship at the Wellshire Golf Course, Denver, and thus became the first Negro to gain a national Championship conducted by the USGA. He played with two woods, nine irons and a putter. Wright defeated Frank H. Campbell, of Jacksonville, Fla., 3 and 2, in the final. Campbell was a professional for four years before turning to the insurance business. Wright attended Western Washington College of Education and said he hoped to be a school teacher. Chipping and putting were the strength of his game. Other semi-finalists were Don Essig, III, of Indianapolis, the 1957 Champion, and William H. McCool, of San Francisco. The Dallas team won the sectional team Championship and the Warren G. Harding Trophy with a record score of 425. Team members were Hal McCommas, Raymond H. Patak and Gene Towry. The entry was 2,435.

AMATEUR PUBLIC LINKS CHAMPIONSHIP

Entry figures prior to 1939 reflect only qualifiers for the championship proper.

DATE	WINNER, RUNNER-UP	SCORE	SITE	ENTRY
1922 (July)	**Edward Held** d. Richard J. Walsh	6 & 5	Ottawa Park, Toledo, Ohio Medalist—139: George F. Aulbach	140
1923 (June)	Richard J. Walsh d. J. Stewart Whitham	6 & 5	E. Potomac Park, Washington, D.C. **Medalist—153: Raymond J. McAuliffe**	142
1924 (June)	Joseph Coble d. Henry Decker	2 & 1	Community C.C., Dayton, Ohio Medalist—150: Earl McAleer	140
1925 (Aug.)	Raymond J. McAuliffe d. William F. Serrick	6 & 5	Salisbury C.C., Garden City, N.Y. Medalist—147: Nelson Davis	103
1926 (Aug.)	Lester Bolstad d. Carl F. Kauffmann	3 & 2	Grover Cleveland Park, Buffalo, N.Y. Medalist—146: Richard J. Walsh	117
1927 (Aug.)	Carl F. Kauffmann d. William F. Serrick	1 up, 37 hls.	Ridgewood, G.L., Cleveland, Ohio Medalist—149: Clarke Morse	126
1928 (July-Aug.)	Carl F. Kauffmann d. Phil Ogden	8 & 7	**Cobb's Creek Municipal G.C.,** Philadelphia, Pa. Medalist—152: Samuel Graham	134
1929 (Aug.)	Carl F. Kauffmann d. Milton Soncrant	4 & 3	**Forest Park Municipal G.C.,** St. Louis, Mo. **Medalist—151: Carl F. Kauffmann** Runners-up: Milton Soncrant, Patsy Tiso	147
1930 (Aug.)	Robert E. Wingate d. Joseph E. Greene	1 up	**Municipal G.C.,** Jacksonville, Fla. Medalist—145: Al Quigley	122
1931 (Aug.)	Charles Ferrera d. Joe Nichols	5 & 4	Keller G.C., St. Paul, Minn. Medalist—148: David A. Mitchell	182
1932 (July)	R. L. Miller d. Pete Miller	4 & 2	Shawnee G.C., Louisville, Ky. Medalist—145: Joe Nichols	213
1933 (Aug.)	Charles Ferrera d. R. L. Miller	3 & 2	Eastmoreland G.C., Portland, Ore. Medalist—144-145: Tab Boyer Runner-up—144-157: Leslie Leal	164
1934 (July-Aug.)	David A. Mitchell d. Arthur Armstrong	5 & 3	**S. Park Allegheny County Links,** Pittsburgh, Pa. **Medalist—144: Albert (Scotty) Campbell**	184
1935 (July-Aug.)	Frank Strafaci d. Joe Coria	1 up, 37 hls.	**Charles E. Coffin Course,** Indianapolis, Ind. Medalist—145: Lloyd Nordstrom	198
1936 (July)	B. Patrick Abbott d. Claude B. Rippy	4 & 3	**Bethpage State Park,** Farmingdale, N.Y. Co—Medalists—145: James J. Molinari Claude B. Rippy	223
1937 (Aug.)	Bruce N. McCormick d. Don Erickson	1 up	**Harding Park C.,** San Francisco, Calif. Medalist—139: Don Erickson	190
1938 (Aug.)	Al Leach d. Louis C. Cyr	1 up	**Highland Park G.C.,** Cleveland, Ohio Medalist—141: Walter Burkemo	248
1939 (July)	Andrew Szwedko d. Phillip Gordon	1 up	Mt. Pleasant Park G.C., Baltimore, Md. Co-Medalists—144: Luke Barnes Jack Taulman Gerry Bert, Jr. Arthur Armstrong	2,401
1940 (July)	Robert C. Clark d. Michael Dietz	8 & 6	Rackham G.C., Detroit, Mich. Co-Medalists—138: Edward J. Furgol Worth Stimits, Jr.	2,601
1941 (July)	William M. Welch, Jr. d. Jack Kerns	6 & 5	Indian Canyon G.C., Spokane, Wash. Medalist—135: James C. Clark, Jr.	2,816
1942-45 – No Championships: World War II				
1946 (July)	Smiley L. Quick d. Louis Stafford	3 & 2	Wellshire G.C., Denver, Colo. Medalist—†134: James C. Clark, Jr.	3,586

†Record qualifying score.

AMATEUR PUBLIC LINKS CHAMPIONSHIP – Continued

DATE	WINNER, RUNNER-UP	SCORE	SITE	ENTRY
1947 (July)	Wilfred Crossley d. Avery Beck	6 & 5	Meadowbrook G.C., Minneapolis, Minn. Medalist–139: Wilfred Crossley	2,633
1948 (July)	Michael R. Ferentz d. Ben G. Hughes	2 & 1	North Fulton Park G.C., Atlanta, Ga. All Match Play	2,728
1949 (July)	Kenneth J. Towns d. William E. Betger	5 & 4	Rancho G.C., Los Angeles, Calif. All Match Play	2,483
1950 (July)	Stanley Bielat d. John Dobro	7 & 5	Seneca G.C., Louisville, Ky. All Match Play	2,389
1951 (July)	Dave Stanley **d. Ralph J. Vranesic**	1 up	Brown Deer Park G.C., Milwaukee, Wis. All Match Play	2,281
1952 (July)	Omer L. Bogan d. Robert J. Scherer	4 & 3	Miami C.C., Miami, Fla. All Match Play	2,267
1953 (July)	Ted Richards, Jr. d. Irving A. Cooper	1 up	West Seattle G.C., Seattle, Wash. All Match Play	1,868
1954 (July)	Gene Andrews d. Jack E. Zimmerman	1 up	Cedar Crest G.C., Dallas, Texas All Match Play	1,854
1955 (July)	Sam D. Kocsis d. Lewis T. Bean	2 up	Coffin Municipal G.C., Indianapolis, Ind. All Match Play	2,007
1956 (July)	James H. Buxbaum d. W. C. Scarbrough, Jr.	3 & 2	Harding Park G.C., San Francisco, Calif. Medalist–141: D. M. McBeath	1,921
1957 (July-Aug.)	Don Essig, III d. Gene Towry	6 & 5	Hershey Park G.C., Hershey, Pa. Medalist–141: Bud Kivett	1,923
1958 (July)	Daniel D. Sikes, Jr. d. Bob Ludlow	3 & 2	Silver Lake G.C., Orland Park, Ill. Medalist–144: Don Essig, III	2,000
1959 (July)	William A. Wright d. Frank W. Campbell	3 & 2	Wellshire G.C., Denver, Colo. Medalist–137: Daniel D. Sikes, Jr.	2,435

AMATEUR PUBLIC LINKS TEAM CHAMPIONSHIP

DATE	WINNER	TEAM SCORE	SITE	ENTRY
1923 (June)	Chicago, Ill.	311 (18 hls., 4 men)	E. Potomac Park, Washington, D.C.	18
1924 (June)	Washington, D.C.	636 (36 hls., 4 men)	Community C.C., Dayton, Ohio	18
1925 (Aug.)	New York, N.Y.	616	Sailsbury C.C., Garden City, N.Y.	15
1926 (Aug.)	Chicago, Ill.	608	Grover Cleveland Park, Buffalo, N.Y.	18
1927 (Aug.)	Pittsburgh, Pa.	639	Ridgewood G.L., Cleveland, Ohio	20
1928 (July-Aug.)	Pittsburgh, Pa.	646	Cobb's Creek, Philadelphia, Pa.	23
1929 (Aug.)	New York, N.Y. Runner-up: Louisville, Ky.	630 630	Forest Park, St. Louis, Mo.	23
1930 (Aug.)	Brooklyn, N.Y.	617	Municipal Links, Jacksonville, Fla.	21
1931 (Aug.)	San Francisco, Calif.	620	Keller G.C., St. Paul, Minn.	28
1932 (July)	Louisville, Ky.	606	Shawnee G.C., Louisville, Ky.	32
1933 (Aug.)	Los Angeles, Calif.	609	Eastmoreland G.C., Portland, Ore.	28
1934 (July-Aug.)	Los Angeles, Calif.	603	S. Park Allegheny G.L., Pittsburgh, Pa.	34
1935 (July-Aug.)	San Antonio, Texas Runner-up: Louisville, Ky.	612-305 612	Coffin Course, Indianapolis, Ind.	45
1936 (July)	Seattle, Wash.	599	Bethpage, Farmingdale, N.Y.	49
1937 (Aug.)	Sacramento, Calif.	587	Harding Park, San Francisco, Calif.	40
1938 (Aug.)	Los Angeles, Calif.	584	Highland Park G.C., Cleveland, Ohio	55
1939 (Aug.)	Los Angeles, Calif.	442 (36 hls., 3 men)	Mt. Pleasant Park G.C., Baltimore, Md.	30
1940 (July)	San Francisco, Calif.	435	Rackham G.C., Detroit, Mich.	34
1941 (July)	Detroit, Mich.	435	Indian Canyon G.C., Spokane, Wash.	29
1942-45 – No Championships: World War II				
1946 (July)	Long Beach, Calif.	431	Wellshire G.C., Denver, Colo.	33
1947 (July)	Atlanta, Ga.	431	Meadowbrook G.C., Minneapolis, Minn.	23
1948 (July)	Raleigh, N.C.	223 (18 hls., 3 men)	N. Fulton Park G.C., Atlanta, Ga.	32
1949 (July)	San Francisco, Calif.	221	Rancho G.C., Los Angeles, Calif.	33
1950 (July)	Los Angeles, Calif.	217	Seneca G.C., Louisville, Ky.	34
1951 (July)	Dayton, Ohio	234	Brown Deer G.C., Milwaukee, Wis.	33
1952 (July)	Chicago, Ill.	227	Miami C.C., Miami, Fla.	32
1953 (July)	Jacksonville, Fla.	221	West Seattle G.C., Seattle, Wash.	26
1954 (July)	Dallas, Texas	220	Cedar Crest G.C., Dallas, Texas	30
1955 (July)	Miami, Fla.	224	Coffin Municipal G.C., Indianapolis, Ind.	32
1956 (July)	Memphis, Tenn.	445 (36 hls., 3 men)	Harding Park G.C., San Francisco, Calif.	25
1957 (July)	Honolulu, Hawaii	440	Hershey Park G.C., Hershey, Pa.	23
1958 (July)	St. Paul, Minn.	447	Silver Lake G.C., Orland Park, Ill.	25
1959 (July)	Dallas, Texas	425	Wellshire G.C., Denver, Colo.	30

1922
FIRST AMATEUR PUBLIC LINKS CHAMPIONSHIP

Held at Ottawa Park, Toledo, Ohio, July 10-15. 140 Entries, 136 Starters.

Qualifying Score	1st Round	2nd Round	3rd Round	Semi-Finals	Final Round (36 Holes)	
139*	George F. Aulbach (Boston)	Aulbach, 6 and 5				
156	Joe Kurek (Toledo)		Aulbach, 1 up			
153	Ted Lloyd (Chicago)	Lloyd, 2 up				
158	James Fee (Chicago)			Aulbach, 5 and 4		
150	Brad Smith (Chicago)	Malley, 2 and 1				
157	Thomas Malley (St. Louis)		Malley, 3 and 2			
155	Matt Jans (Chicago)	Jans, 2 up			Held, 1 up, 20 hls.	
160	Anthony Vitt (Cleveland)					
149	Edward Held (St. Louis)	Held, 3 and 2				
156	William Mudie (Detroit)		Held, 5 and 3			
154	T. K. Lomas (New York)	Lomas, 1 up				
159	Charles Agnew (Washington)			Held, 4 and 2		
151	Harry Scharff (New York)	Scharff, 6 and 5				
157	Lee M. O'Leary (Toledo)		Christie, 1 up, 20 hls.			
156	J. F. Christie (Toronto)	Christie, 3 and 2				
160	Charles Sommer (New York)					Edward Held, 6 and 5
148	Michael Tobin (Philadelphia)	Tobin, 1 up				
156	William N. Mather (Baltimore)		Quinlan, 1 up, 19 hls.			
153	William J. Quinlan (Boston)	Quinlan, 4 and 3				
158	J. F. McGuire (Toledo)			Walsh, 2 and 1		
150	Richard Walsh (New York)	Walsh, 2 and 1				
157	Francis Murphy (San Francisco)		Walsh, 2 and 1			
155	William F. Serrick (New York)	Wallace, 1 up			Walsh, 1 up	
160	William Wallace (Detroit)					
150	Joseph Ford (New York)	Ford, 3 and 1				
157	Gregg Fahey (Chicago)		Curtin, 1 up, 20 hls.			
155	Edward Curtin (Newark, N.J.)	Curtin, 3 and 2				
159	C. G. Rowe (Newark)			Decker, 2 and 1		
153	James B. Curran (St. Louis)	Decker, 3 and 2				
158	Henry Decker (Kansas City)		Decker, 6 and 5			
156	A. B. Hadden (Toledo)	Wimmer, 1 up, 24 hls.				
160	R. A. Wimmer (Toledo)					

*Medalist.

1923
SECOND AMATEUR PUBLIC LINKS CHAMPIONSHIP

Held at East Potomac Park, Washington, D.C., June 26-29.
142 Entries, 134 Starters.

Qualifying Score	1st Round	2nd Round	3rd Round	Semi-Finals		Final Round (36 holes)
153*	**Raymond J. MacAuliffe (Buffalo)**	MacAuliffe,				
161	J. C. Fraser (New York)	1 up, 19 hls.	MacAuliffe,			
163	Ed. Hayden (Milwaukee)	Lloyd,	1 up, 20 hls.			
158	E. B. Lloyd (Chicago)	1 up, 19 hls.		MacAuliffe,		
157	Frank Dolp (Portland)	Dolp,		1 up		
162	Bernard MacFarland (Pittsburgh)	5 and 4	Dolp,			
160	William F. Serrick (New York)	Curtin,	3 and 2		Whitham, 1 up, 19 hls.	
164	Ed. Curtin (Newark, N.J.)	2 up				
155	L. Gordon Haw (Seattle)	Scharff,				
161	Harry Scharff (New York)	1 up	Scharff,			
159	Walter Crowe (Chicago)	Crowe,	3 and 2			
163	Charles E. Sommer (New York)	1 up		Whitham,		Richard A. Walsh, 6 and 5
157	I. L. Thoren (New York)	Graham,		8 and 7		
163	Sam Graham (Pittsburgh)	1 up, 19 hls.	Whitham,			
160	J. Stewart Whitham (New York)	Whitham,	3 and 2			
164	Carl F. Kauffmann (Pittsburgh)	3 and 2				
154	John Dawson (Chicago)	Dawson,				
161	Joseph P. Sahre (New York)	4 and 3	MacAndrew,			
158	John MacAndrew (Boston)	MacAndrew,	8 and 6			
163	David O'Connor (Chicago)	1 up, 19 hls.		Walsh,		
157	C. Edgar Simes (Buffalo)	O'Tell,		1 up		
162	L. S. O'Tell (Baltimore)	3 and 2	Walsh,			
160	Richard A. Walsh (New York)	Walsh,	3 and 1		Walsh, 2 up	
164	Fred. Hannon (Boston)	1 up, 19 hls.				
156	J. H. Boyd (Philadelphia)	McAleer,				
162	Earl McAleer (Washington)	4 and 3	Coble,			
160	J. B. Curran, Jr. (St. Louis)	Coble,	3 and 2			
164	Joseph Coble (Philadelphia)	2 and 1		Coble,		
157	George J. Voigt (Washington)	Hamilton,		1 up		
163	R. F. Hamilton (Philadelphia)	1 up	Hamilton,			
161	G. T. Colburn (Toledo)	Mules,	2 and 1			
164	Lawrence Mules (Baltimore)	6 and 4				

*Medalist.

First Amateur Public Links Team Championship, Harding Trophy, 18 Entries, June 27.
Won by Chicago team (four-man team), 311 for 18 holes (E. B. Lloyd, 76; Bob White, 76; John Dawson, 78; Mutt Juns, 81); Second, St. Louis team, 317 (J. B. Curran, Jr., 77; Tom Malley, 78; Walter Kossman, 80; Fred Conway, 82.)

1924
THIRD AMATEUR PUBLIC LINKS CHAMPIONSHIP

Held at the Community Country Club, Dayton, Ohio, June 24-28. 140 Entries, 132 Starters.

Qualifying Score	1st Round	2nd Round	3rd Round	Semi-Finals	Final Round (36 Holes)	
150*	Earl McAleer (Washington)	McAleer,				
160	W. L. Vance (Chicago)	1 up	McAleer,			
157	Irving Peterson (Racine)	Shorey,	4 and 2			
162	James C. Shorey (Washington)	2 and 1		Decker,		
155	James Brewer (Chicago)	Brewer,		7 and 5		
161	William J. Myler (Cincinnati)	4 and 3	Decker,			
159	Henry Decker (Kansas City)	Decker,	1 up		Decker, 3 and 2	
163	Irving Ralph (Buffalo)	3 and 2				
153	Joseph Ford (New York)	Ford,				
161	Walter Delscamp (Dayton)	5 and 4	Ford,			
158	George J. Voigt (Washington)	Voigt,	2 up			
153	Raymond J. McAuliffe (Buffalo)	4 and 3		De Lury,		
155	L. J. Smith (Cincinnati)	De Lury,		1 up		
162	R. S. De Lury (Boston)	3 and 2	De Lury,			
160	A. Fons (Milwaukee)	Voisinet,	3 and 1			
163	W. E. Voisinet (Buffalo)	2 up				
151	William F. Serrick (New York)	Serrick,				
160	Russell Winters (Detroit)	6 and 4	Coble,			Joseph Coble, 2 and 1
158	William A. Sixty (Milwaukee)	Coble,	1 up			
163	Joseph Coble (Philadelphia)	4 and 3		Coble,		
155	William A. McGuire (Washington)	Behm,		3 and 2		
162	A. Behm (Cleveland)	3 and 2	Behm,			
159	Matt Jans (Chicago)	Sweitzer,	5 and 4		Coble, 6 and 5	
163	Henry Sweitzer (Cleveland)	1 up, 19 hls.				
154	Frank Dulp (Portland, Ore.)	Dolp,				
161	Samuel Graham (Pittsburgh)	5 and 4	Dolp,			
158	William Wallace (Chicago)	Wallace,	6 and 5			
163	Walter M. Pacer (Toledo)	6 and 4		Dolp,		
156	Edward Curtin (Newark, N.J.)	Sahre,		7 and 5		
162	Joseph Sahre (New York)	1 up, 21 hls.	Kauffmann,			
160	Carl F. Kauffmann (Pittsburgh)	Kauffmann,	4 and 2			
164	Walter Barrow (Chicago)	6 and 4				

*Medalist.

Second Amateur Public Links Team Championship, Harding Trophy, 18 entries, June 24-25.
Won by Washington team (four-man team), 636 for 36 holes (George J. Voigt, 158; Earl McAleer, 150; James C. Shorey, 162; Charles T. Agnew, Jr., 166). Second, New York team, 643 (William Serrick, 151; Joseph Ford, 153; Richard A. Walsh, 169; John Frauser, 170).

1925
FOURTH AMATEUR PUBLIC LINKS CHAMPIONSHIP

Held at Salisbury Country Club, Salisbury Plains, N.Y., August 4-8. 103 Entries, 98 Starters.

Qualifying Score	1st Round	2nd Round	3rd Round	Semi-Finals	Final	Final Round (36 Holes)
147*	Nelson Davies (Cleveland)	Wall, 4 and 3				
156	John J. Wall (Spokane)		Wall, 3 and 2			
153	Sam Graham (Pittsburgh)	Barth, 2 and 1				
157	William Barth (Newark, N.J.)			Serrick, 1 up		
151	Joseph P. Sahre (New York)	Bill, 1 up, 19 hls.				
157	Carmen Bill (Cleveland)		Serrick, 3 and 2			
151	**William F. Serrick (New York)**	Serrick, 4 and 3			Serrick, 7 and 6	
158	**William A. McGuire (Washington)**					
149	Walter Murray (St. Louis)	Murray, 5 and 4				
156	Lester Bolstad (Minneapolis)		Walsh, 2 and 1			
153	Eli Ross (Cleveland)	Walsh, 5 and 4				
158	Richard A. Walsh (New York)			Houghton, 1 up		
152	William Sutherland (Detroit)	Houghton, 4 and 3				
157	A. L. Houghton (Washington)		Houghton, 3 and 2			
159	Ed. L. Frost (Washington)	Albertus, 5 and 4				
159	C. Albertus (Philadelphia)					Raymond J. McAuliffe, 6 and 5
148	**Raymond J. McAuliffe (Buffalo)**	McAuliffe, 2 and 1				
156	**Henry Sweitzer (Cleveland)**		McAuliffe, 3 and 1			
153	Joseph Ford (New York)	Jans, 1 up, 19 hls.				
158	Matt Jans (Chicago)			McAuliffe, 1 up, 19 hls.		
151	A. B. Brodbeck (New York)	Wall, 2 and 1				
157	James Wall (Spokane)		Kauffmann, 3 and 2			
154	Carl Kauffmann (Pittsburgh)	Kauffmann, 5 and 4			McAuliffe, 6 and 4	
159	D. R. Napier (Richmond, Va.)					
150	C. R. Blackburn (Toronto)	Geoghegan, 5 and 4				
157	Bud Geoghegan (Hartford)		Lloyd, 3 and 1			
154	E. B. Lloyd (Chicago)	Lloyd, 3 and 2				
158	Pat McDonough (Pittsburgh)			Courtney, 3 and 2		
152	W. E. Boyne (Buffalo)	O'Tell, 3 and 2				
157	L. S. O'Tell (Baltimore)		Courtney, 5 and 4			
155	David O'Connor (Chicago)	Courtney, 2 up				
159	William Courtney (Detroit)					

*Medalist.

Third Amateur Public Links Team Championship, Harding Trophy, 15 Entries, August 4-5.
Won by New York team (four-man team), 616 for 36 holes (Richard A. Walsh, 158; Joseph Ford, 153; William F. Serrick, 154; Joseph P. Sahre, 151). Second, Cleveland team, 621 (Eddie Hasmann, 161; Nelson Davies, 147; Harry Sweitzer, 156; Carmen Bill, 157).

1926
FIFTH AMATEUR PUBLIC LINKS CHAMPIONSHIP

Held at Grover Cleveland Park, Buffalo, N.Y., August 3-7. 117 Entries, 112 Starters.

Qualifying Score	1st Round	2nd Round	3rd Round	Semi-Finals	Final Round (36 Holes)	
150	Lester Bolstad (Minneapolis)	Bolstad, 1 up				
151	Willis Owens (Jacksonville)		Bolstad, 2 and 1			
147	W.D. Martin, Jr. (Buffalo)	Martin, 2 and 1				
155	Thomas F. Cole (Baltimore)			Bolstad, 2 and 1		
151	Joe Kurek (Toledo)	Wallace, 7 and 5				
151	William Wallace (Chicago)		Wallace, 2 up			
154	William F. Serrick (New York)	Serrick, 1 up				
149	Lawrence Schuette (St. Louis)				Bolstad, 3 and 1	
154	Anthony Appice (Newark, N.J.)	Fetz, 4 and 3				
149	Gus Fetz (Chicago)		S. Ford, 2 and 1			
153	William McCrone (Hamilton, Canada)	S. Ford, 2 up				
153	Stanley Ford (Detroit)			S. Ford, 1 up		
149	Edward Curtin (Newark, N.J.)	Curtin, 4 and 3				
155	W. J. Palmer (Baltimore)		Joe Ford, 1 up, 22 hls.			
151	Joe Ford (New York)	Joe Ford, 1 up				
148	J. J. Jennings (Chicago)					Lester Bolstad, 3 and 2
152	Michael Heeney (Newark, N.J.)	Lloyd, 2 up				
154	E. B. Lloyd (Chicago)		Lloyd, 1 up			
151	Clarke Morse (St. Louis)	Morse, 4 and 3				
154	Dave O'Connor (Chicago)			Walsh, 1 up		
146*	Richard J. Walsh (New York)	Walsh, 3 and 2				
152	Jack Lord (Philadelphia)		Walsh, 4 and 3			
151	Charles Albertus (Philadelphia)	Albertus, 1 up				
149	Nicol Thompson (Hamilton, Canada)				Kauffmann, 1 up	
154	Jackson Schultz (Philadelphia)	Schultz, 3 and 2				
150	Joseph P. Sahre (New York)		Kauffmann, 6 and 4			
152	Carl F. Kauffmann (Pittsburgh)	Kauffmann, 5 and 4				
155	John D. Boger, Jr. (Washington)			Kauffmann, 3 and 1		
154	Ernest Caldwell (Baltimore)	Caldwell, 2 up				
154	Irving Dunn (Brooklyn)		D'Onofrio, 1 up			
149	Frank Brokl (St. Paul)	D'Onofrio, 2 and 1				
151	Nick D'Onofrio (New York)					

*Medalist

Fourth Amateur Public Links Team Championship, Harding Trophy, 18 entries, August 3-4.
Won by Chicago team (four-man team) 608 for 36 holes (Gus Fetz, 149; David O'Connor, 154; William Wallace, 151; E. B. Lloyd, 154). Second, New York team, 611 (William F. Serrick, 154; Joseph H. Sahre, 150; Nick D'Onofrio, 151; Joseph Merola, 156).

1927
SIXTH AMATEUR PUBLIC LINKS CHAMPIONSHIP

Held at Ridgewood Golf Links, Cleveland, Ohio, August 2-6. 126 Entries, 124 Starters.

Qualifying Score	1st Round	2nd Round	3rd Round	Semi-Finals	Final Round	
149*	Clarke Morse (St. Louis)	Palmer, 2 and 1				
159	W.J. Palmer (Baltimore)		Morrison, 1 up			
156	Kendall Morrison (St. Joseph, Mo.)	Morrison, 4 and 3				
161	R.A. Bowker (Chicago)			Morrison, 1 up		
152	Frank Brokl (St. Paul)	Brokl, 4 and 3				
160	Frank Alff (Kansas City)		Brokl, 6 and 5			
157	Tom Welsh (Boston)	Welsh, 6 and 5			Serrick, 5 and 4	
161	Walter Pacer (Toledo)					
154	Carmen Bill (Cleveland)	Walsh, 4 and 3				
159	Richard J. Walsh (New York)		Burrows, 1 up			
156	B.H. Burrows (Washington)	Burrows, 1 up, 19 hls.				
161	H.R. Wilson (Kansas City)			Serrick, 2 and 1		
155	Harry Sweitzer (Cleveland)	Serrick, 1 up, 19 hls.				Carl F. Kauffmann, 1 up, 37 holes
160	William F. Serrick (New York)		Serrick, 2 and 1			
158	Joseph P. Sahre (New York)	Sahre, 5 and 4				
161	Robert Stewart (Chicago)					
150	Carl F. Kauffmann (Pittsburgh)	Kauffmann, 6 and 4				
159	George Joyce (Philadelphia)		Kauffmann, 2 up			
156	J. J. McAuliffe (Buffalo)	Davis, 2 up				
161	Dr. I.R. Davis (St. Louis)			Kauffmann, 5 and 4		
153	John R. Miller (Washington)	Miller, 5 and 3				
160	George Thomas (Chicago)		Miller, 6 and 5			
157	Francis Clary (Chicago)	Florio, 2 and 1			Kauffmann, 3 and 1	
161	John Florio (Columbus)					
151	Robert E. Wingate (Jacksonville)	Wingate, 1 up, 19 hls.				
160	Robert B. Burton (Washington)		Wingate, 5 and 4			
156	P. J. McDonough (Pittsburgh)	McDonough, 1 up, 19 hls.				
161	Nicol Thompson (Canada)			Wingate, 1 up		
155	Edward Curtin (Newark, N.J.)	Curtin, 6 and 5				
160	Armin Mahrt (Dayton)		Curtin, 2 and 1			
159	Lester White (Erie, Pa.)	Merola, 2 and 1				
162	Joseph Merola (New York)					

Fifth Amateur Team Championship—Harding Trophy. Won by Pittsburgh Team—Total 639.
*Medalist.

1928
SEVENTH AMATEUR PUBLIC LINKS CHAMPIONSHIP

Held at Cobb's Creek Municipal Golf Course, Philadelphia, Pa., July 31-August 4. 134 Entries, 134 Starters

Qualifying Score	1st Round	2nd Round	3rd Round	Semi-Finals	Final Round	
152*	Samuel Graham (Pittsburgh)	Graham, 1 up	McAleer, 7 and 6	Kauffmann, 1 up	Kauffmann, 2 and 1	Carl F. Kauffmann, 8 and 7
161	Louis Galby (Bridgeport)					
157	Earl McAleer (Washington)	McAleer, 2 up				
163	Mike Surmiak (Philadelphia)					
156	Joe Kurek (Toledo)	Kauffmann, 9 and 7	Kauffmann, 1 up, 19 hls.			
162	Carl F. Kauffmann (Pittsburgh)					
158	H. Velotta (Cleveland)	R. Albertus, 6 and 4				
163	Robert Albertus (Philadelphia)					
160	Thomas McGrattan (Buffalo)	Invernizzi, 5 and 4	Invernizzi, 2 and 1	Morrison, 7 and 6		
164	Frank Invernizzi (Baltimore)					
161	James J. McAuliffe (Buffalo)	Toth, 8 and 7				
165	Joe Toth (Cleveland)					
161	John Cuniff (Newark, N.J.)	Cuniff, 5 and 4	Morrison, 1 up			
164	Frederick McCoy (St. Louis)					
161	John K. Reidy (Worcester)	Morrison, 1 up				
165	Kendall Morrison (St. Joseph, Mo.)					
153	Frank Brokl (Minneapolis)	Brokl, 1 up, 19 hls.	Brokl, 5 and 3	D'Onofrio, 4 and 3	Ogden, 2 and 1	
162	Elliott Martin (Jacksonville)					
157	C.J. Lunden (Pittsburgh)	Cook, 4 and 2				
163	Harold Cook (Toledo)					
156	Nicholas D'Onofrio (New York)	D'Onofrio, 5 and 4	D'Onofrio, 4 and 2			
163	Gus Fetz (Chicago)					
158	Leo Boyle (Philadelphia)	Boyle, 1 up, 20 hls.				
164	John R. Miller (Washington)					
160	Charles Albertus (Philadelphia)	Florio, 4 and 3	Lucas, 2 and 1	Ogden, 6 and 4		
164	John Florio (Columbus)					
161	Bernard Lucas (Montebello, Calif.)	Lucas, 3 and 2				
165	Harry Sweitzer (Cleveland)					
161	J.F. Conway (Detroit)	Donohue, 2 and 1	Ogden, 3 and 2			
165	Edward Donohue (St. Louis)					
161	Richard Ciuci (Bridgeport)	Ogden, 4 and 3				
165	Phil Ogden (Cleveland)					

Sixth Amateur Team Championship—Harding Trophy. Won by Pittsburgh Team—Total 646.
*Medalist.

1929
EIGHTH AMATEUR PUBLIC LINKS CHAMPIONSHIP

Held at Forest Park Municipal Golf Course, St. Louis, Mo., August 6-10. 147 Entries, 142 Starters.

Qualifying Score	1st Round	2nd Round	3rd Round	Semi-Finals	Final Round	
151*	Patsy Tiso (New York)	Tiso, 6 and 5	Hornsby, 1 up, 20 hls.	Hornsby, 3 and 1	Kauffmann, 5 and 3	Carl F. Kauffmann, 4 and 2
159	J. J. McAuliffe (Buffalo)					
152	Ernest L. Caldwell (Baltimore)	Hornsby, 1 up				
158	John Hornsby (Topeka)					
154	Dr. I.R. Davis (St. Louis)	Davis, 3 and 1	Denney, 1 up, 19 hls.			
158	Gus Fetz (Chicago)					
152	Gordon Denney (Louisville)	Denney, 2 and 1				
156	Harold Cook (Toledo)					
153	Michael Friedlein (St. Louis)	Schaber, 3 and 1	Boyd, 2 and 1	Kauffmann, 3 and 2		
156	Cooney Schaber (Louisville)					
154	John H. Boyd (Philadelphia)	Boyd, 1 up, 19 hls.				
159	Al Priebe (St. Paul)					
160	R. H. Ahlbeck (Chicago)	Kauffmann, 5 and 3	Kauffmann, 6 and 5			
151*	Carl F. Kauffmann (Pittsburgh)					
152	Henry Fabrizio (Brooklyn)	Conway, 2 and 1				
158	John F. Conway (Detroit)					
155	Sterling Dawson (Chicago)	Jaffee, 3 and 2	Jaffee, 4 and 2	Casper, 1 up	Soncrant, 1 up, 21 hls.	
159	Mortimer G. Jaffee (New York)					
160	Togo Hamamoto (St. Louis)	Hamamoto, 2 and 1				
159	Joe Tesar (Cleveland)					
155	Connell Kersey (Louisville)	Kersey, 2 and 1	Casper, 4 and 3			
158	Charles Ferrera (San Francisco)					
160	Ade Fordham (St. Paul)	Casper, 6 and 5				
152	Wesley Casper (Louisville)					
159	Jerry Stanford (St. Louis)	Merola, 3 and 1	Soncrant, 1 up	Soncrant, 5 and 3		
155	Joseph A. Merola (New York)					
151*	Milton Soncrant (Toledo)	Soncrant, 7 and 6				
155	A. J. Pardee (New Haven)					
155	Frank Connolly (Detroit)	Connolly, 1 up	Connolly, 1 up			
155	Guy McCall (Buffalo)					
153	Joseph J. Farrell (New York)	Brokl, 5 and 3				
158	Frank Brokl (St. Paul)					

Seventh Amateur Public Links Team Championship—Harding Trophy. Won by New York Team—Total 630 (**Playoff with Louisville**).

***Medalists—Playoff won by Carl F. Kauffmann.**

1930
NINTH AMATEUR PUBLIC LINKS CHAMPIONSHIP

Held at Municipal Golf Course, Jacksonville, Fla., August 5-9. 122 Entries, 116 Starters.

Qualifying Score	1st Round	2nd Round	3rd Round	Semi-Finals	Final Round	
156	James Bushong (Portland, Ore.)	Bushong,				
157	**Gordon Denney (Louisville)**	2 and 1	Wingate,			
150	Robert E. Wingate (Jacksonville)	Wingate,	1 up, 19 hls.			
157	G. W. Spencer (Sanford, Fla.)	5 and 4		Wingate,		
160	Edward J. Brown, Jr. (Baltimore)	Champi,		5 and 4		
161	Michael Champi (Brooklyn)	3 and 2	Burrows,			
157	B.H. Burrows (Washington)	Burrows,	3 and 2		Wingate, 5 and 4	
158	Albert A. Cucinell (New York)	2 and 1				
160	Dr. W.A. Norby (Portland, Ore.)	Norby,				
158	M.W. Galido (Pittsburgh)	4 and 2	Barton,			
161	Walter Barton (Akron)	Barton,	1 up			
154	Walter Thoren (Brooklyn)	1 up		O'Palka,		
161	Wesley Casper (Louisville)	Albertus,		6 and 5		
152	Charles Albertus (Philadelphia)	2 and 1	O'Palka,			
157	Larry O'Palka (Detroit)	O'Palka,	4 and 3			Robert E. Wingate, 1 up
145*	Al Quigley (Chicago)	4 and 3				
161	George Taylor (Detroit)	Fabrizio,				
150	Henry Fabrizio (Brooklyn)	1 up	Greene,			
152	Joseph S. Greene (Philadelphia)	Greene,	3 and 2			
155	Dr. I. R. Davis (St. Louis)	3 and 1		Greene,		
160	Arthur J. Pease (Portland, Ore.)	Pease,		4 and 3		
160	Joe Bommarito (Detroit)	2 and 1	Lucas,			
161	Lorraine Bradford (St. Joseph)	Lucas,	1 up, 19 hls.			
155	Barney Lucas (Los Angeles)	3 and 1			Greene, 2 and 1	
158	Thomas Mazza (Brooklyn)	Givan,				
150	Harry Givan (Seattle)	4 and 2	Fordham,			
160	C. J. Lundeen (Pittsburgh)	Fordham,	1 up			
157	A. D. Fordham (St. Paul)	4 and 3		Strafaci,		
161	Mortimer G. Jaffee (New York)	Jaffee,		1 up, 19 hls.		
161	Curtis Bryan (Jacksonville)	1 up, 19 hls.	Strafaci,			
151	Len Black (Louisville)	Strafaci,	5 and 4			
151	**Domenick Strafaci (Brooklyn)**	6 and 5				

Eighth Amateur Public Links Team Championship—Harding Trophy. Won by Brooklyn Team—Total 617.
*Medalist.

1931

TENTH AMATEUR PUBLIC LINKS CHAMPIONSHIP

Held at Keller Golf Course, St. Paul, Minn., August 4-8. 182 Entries, 176 Starters.

Qualifying Score	1st Round	2nd Round	3rd Round	Semi-Finals	Final Round	
154	James Bushong (Portland, Ore.)	Priebe, 1 up				
157	Al Priebe (St. Paul)		Priebe, 2 and 1			
154	George Bradley (Philadelphia)	Bradley, 1 up, 21 hls.				
154	M.C. Mazza (Brooklyn)			Nichols, 3 and 2		
157	**Robert J. Isherwood (St. Louis)**	Nichols, 4 and 2				
155	Joe Nichols (Long Beach, Calif.)		Nichols, 4 and 2			
153	Wesley Casper (Louisville)	Casper, 1 up				
150	A.G. Sato (San Francisco)				Nichols, 1 up	
157	Spencer Overton (Baltimore)	Overton, 3 and 2				
154	Fred Gordon (Santa Monica)		Merola, 3 and 2			
156	Joseph A. Merola (New York City)	Merola, 2 up				
156	John L. Banks (Chicago)			Greenway, 6 and 5		
155	Harry H. Ramsey (Pittsburgh)	Ramsey, 1 up				Charles Ferrera, 5 and 4
155	Ade Fordham (St. Paul)		Greenway, 3 and 1			
150	**William A. Heinlein (Indianapolis)**	Greenway, 1 up				
150	Edward Greenway (Seattle)					
156	George E. Mead (Portland, Ore.)	Albertus, 2 and 1				
149	Charles Albertus (Philadelphia)		Albertus, 2 and 1			
156	Harry Fabrizzio (Brooklyn)	Fabrizzio, 4 and 3				
155	Ray Gates (St. Louis)			Albertus, 5 and 3		
151	Edgar Bolstad (Minneapolis)	Bolstad, 2 and 1				
152	Barney Lucas (Los Angeles)		Bommarito, 2 and 1			
153	Joe Bommarito (Detroit)	Bommarito, 3 and 2			Ferrera, 3 and 1	
152	Arthur Nutting (Louisville)					
155	Horace Lacey (Little Rock)	Lacey, 5 and 4				
155	R.G. Sigler (Baltimore)		Lacey, 1 up, 19 hls.			
156	Chester Coleman (Santa Monica)	Pousette, 1 up, 19 hls.				
154	Howard Pousette (St. Paul)			Ferrera, 4 and 3		
153	Robert Gourlay (Seattle)	Gourlay, 1 up, 19 hls.				
156	Mike Surmiak (Philadelphia)		Ferrera, 1 up			
152	Charles Ferrera (San Francisco)	Ferrera, 4 and 3				
148*	David A. Mitchell (Indianapolis)					

Ninth Amateur Public Links Team Championship—Harding Trophy. Won by San Francisco Team—Total 620.
*Medalist.

1932
ELEVENTH AMATEUR PUBLIC LINKS CHAMPIONSHIP

Held at Shawnee Golf Course, Louisville, Ky., July 19-23. 213 Entries, 203 Starters.

Qualifying Score	1st Round	2nd Round	3rd Round	Semi-Finals	Final Round	
151	Ade Fordham (St. Paul)	Fordham, 4 and 3				
147	William A. Heinlein (Indianapolis)		Fordham, 2 and 1			
151	Andrew Szwedko (Pittsburgh)	Szwedko, 1 up, 19 hls.				
151	Vernon Letzler (Akron)			Boyer, 6 and 5		
150	Ed. J. Donohue (St. Louis)	Wiggins, 2 and 1				
146	Roy E. Wiggins (Oakland, Calif.)		Boyer, 1 up, 19 hls.			
151	Bob Hamilton (Evansville)	Boyer, 2 and 1				
147	Talbot Boyer (Portland, Ore.)				Pete Miller, 3 and 2	
145*	Joe Nichols (Long Beach, Calif.)	Nichols, 5 and 4				
152	Albert Wilkins (Brooklyn)		Nichols, 5 and 4			
149	Karl Karch (Brooklyn)	Karch, 1 up				
151	B.H. Burrows (Washington)			Pete Miller, 1 up		
147	Pete Miller (Chicago)	Pete Miller, 2 and 1				
152	Mike Parco (Buffalo)		Pete Miller, 1 up, 20 hls.			
146	Donald O'Bryan (Louisville)	Goddard, 5 and 4				
149	Irving Goddard (Los Angeles)					R.L. Miller, 4 and 2
150	O.C. Sleepy (Long Beach, Calif.)	Sleepy, 2 and 1				
149	Ervin Schaber (Louisville)		Sleepy, 5 and 4			
150	Hank Foley (Chicago)	Foley, 1 up				
153	Charles Ferrera (San Francisco)			R.L. Miller, 3 and 2		
150	Melvin Carpenter (Columbus)	R.L. Miller, 1 up, 19 hls.				
149	R.L. Miller (Jacksonville)		R.L. Miller, 1 up, 19 hls.			
151	Ray E. Jones (Richmond, Ind.)	Jones, 5 and 4				
146	Ralph Strafaci (Brooklyn)				R.L. Miller, 3 and 2	
151	A. Scotty Campbell (Seattle)	Campbell, 3 and 1				
150	Horace Lacey (Little Rock)		Campbell, 7 and 6			
151	Joseph A. Merola (New York)	Dale, 3 and 1				
153	Bobby Dale (Indianapolis)			Campbell, 4 and 3		
146	William Jelliffe (Los Angeles)	Bryan, 1 up				
152	Curtis Bryan (Jacksonville)		Bryan, 1 up, 19 hls.			
152	Gus Fetz (Chicago)	Fetz, 4 and 3				
152	Byron Hunt (Columbus)					

Tenth Amateur Public Links Team Championship—Harding Trophy. Won by Louisville Team—Total 606.
***Medalist.**

1933
TWELFTH AMATEUR PUBLIC LINKS CHAMPIONSHIP

Held at Eastmoreland Golf Course, Portland, Ore., August 1-5. 164 Entries, 156 Starters.

Qualifying Score	1st Round	2nd Round	3rd Round	**Semi-Finals**	Final Round (36 Holes)	
144*	Tab Boyer (Portland)	Boyer, 2 and 1	Batista, 1 up	Erickson, 2 up	Miller, 6 and 5	Charles Ferrera, 3 and 2
153	Jimmy Deeble (Minneapolis)					
148	Louis Cyr (Vancouver)	Batista, 4 and 2				
147	Henry Batista (Altadena)					
154	Lyle Decker (San Jose)	Decker, 3 and 2	Erickson, 5 and 3			
149	Merle Williams (Park Rose)					
154	Ray V. Hardin (Long Beach)	Erickson, 7 and 6				
147	Don Erickson (Los Angeles)					
147	Marvin (Bud) Ward (Olympia)	Ward, 1 up	Ward, 4 and 3	Miller, 2 and 1		
150	John Gunst (Portland)					
150	George Thomas (Chicago)	Thomas, 1 up				
150	H.J. Ingle (San Diego)					
154	D.A. Mitchell (Indianapolis)	Mitchell, 1 up	Miller, 3 and 2			
153	Bud Haskell (Olympia)					
152	M. Palacio, Jr. (San Rafael)	Miller, 2 and 1				
153	R.L. Miller (Jacksonville)					
148	**Albert (Scotty) Campbell (Seattle)**	Seymour, 2 and 1	Seymour, 3 and 2	McCormick, 2 and 1	Ferrera, 2 and 1	
153	Stanley Seymour (Los Angeles)					
154	Jack Dillon (Hollywood)	Abbott, 7 and 6				
150	B. Patrick Abbott (Altadena)					
154	Bruce McCormick (Los Angeles)	McCormick, 2 and 1	McCormick, 6 and 5			
150	Russell Meade (Portland)					
146	Joe Greene (Philadelphia)	Greene, 4 and 3				
147	Robert Tomes (Long Beach)					
146	Charles Ferrera (San Francisco)	Ferrera, 3 and 2	Ferrera, 9 and 7	Ferrera, 6 and 4		
151	William V. Brown (Seattle)					
152	Olin Cerrocki (Brooklyn)	Clarkson, 4 and 3				
149	Tad Clarkson (Beverly)					
150	Joe Coria (St. Paul)	Hofer, 4 and 2	Leal, 3 and 1			
153	Bob Hofer (Park Rose)					
152	George Hine (Santa Monica)	Leal, 1 up, 22 hls.				
144	Leslie Leal (Bellingham)					

Eleventh Amateur Public Links Team Championship—Harding Trophy: Won by Los Angeles Team — Total 609.
*Medalist.

1934

THIRTEENTH AMATEUR PUBLIC LINKS CHAMPIONSHIP

Held at the South Park Allegheny County Links, Pittsburgh, Pa., July 30-August 4. 184 Entries, 184 Starters.

Qualifying Score	1st Round (18 Holes)	2nd Round (18 Holes)	3rd Round (18 Holes)	4th Round (18 Holes)	Semi-Finals (36 Holes)	Final Round (36 Holes)	
144*	Albert (Scotty) Campbell, Seattle, Wash.	Campbell, 5 and 3	Campbell, 5 and 3	Campbell, 2 and 1	Armstrong, 1 up	Armstrong, 5 and 3	David A. Mitchell, 5 and 3
153	Mike Cestone, Newark, N.J.						
157	Byron Hunt, Columbus, Ohio	Hunt, 5 and 3					
158	Nelson Peters, Brooklyn, N.Y.						
153	John Lucas, Sharon Pa.	Lucas, 1 up	Gordon, 3 and 2				
153	Dom Soccoli, New Britain, Conn.						
157	Fred Gordon, Santa Monica, Calif.	Gordon, 2 and 1					
155	Henry Foley, Chicago, Ill.						
153	Albert Priebe, St. Paul, Minn.	Priebe, 3 and 2	Babis, 1 up	Armstrong, 6 and 5			
158	Lester Jankaski, Elizabeth, N.J.						
159	John Madara, Philadelphia	Babis, 1 up					
157	Frank Babis, Detroit						
156	Charles Amandoles, New York	Amandoles, 2 and 1	Armstrong, 3 and 2				
159	Ralph L. Kolle, Long Beach, Calif.						
153	Earl Larson, Minneapolis	Armstrong, 3 and 2					
159	Arthur Armstrong, Honolulu						
154	R.L. Miller, Jacksonville, Fla.	Jewett, 2 and 1	Jewett, 1 up	McCormick, 1 up	Young, 1 up		
155	John C. Jewett, Gary, Ind.						
157	B. Patrick Abbott, Altadena, Calif.	Abbott, 2 and 1					
155	Warren L. Riepen, St. Joseph, Mo.						
152	Frank Strafaci, Brooklyn	F. Strafaci, 6 and 5	McCormick, 1 up				
158	Bob Babbish, Detroit						
154	Lorraine Bradford, St. Joseph, Mo.	McCormick, 2 and 1					
155	Bruce McCormick, Los Angeles						
148	John M. Ross, Los Angeles	Ross, 4 and 2	Ross, 3 and 2	Young, 1 up			
160	Eric Lenaeus, Newark, N.J.						
157	William Lovebury, Columbus, Ohio	Kingsbury, 7 and 6					
156	Warren Kingsbury, Buffalo						
158	Melvin Kennedy, San Francisco	Young, 1 up	Young, 6 and 5				
157	Lorraine Young, San Antonio, Texas						
159	Willard Johnson, Moline, Ill.	Kauffmann, 5 and 4					
156	Carl F. Kauffmann, Pittsburgh						
157	Adolph Fordham, St. Paul, Minn.	Kokes, 3 and 2	Mumma, 4 and 3	Erickson, 2 and 1	Mitchell, 2 and 1	Mitchell, 2 up	
153	Wilbur Kokes, Chicago						
159	James Stevenson, Long Beach, Calif.	Mumma, 3 and 2					
153	Clyde Mumma, Dayton						
156	Michael Elko, Elizabeth, N.J.	Elko, 3 and 1	Erickson, 5 and 4				
159	Bert Bergman, St. Paul, Minn.						
158	John Mislan, Gary, Ind.	Erickson, 6 and 4					
149	Don Erickson, Los Angeles						
158	Joe Nichols, Jr., Long Beach, Calif.	Balega, 4 and 2	Balega, 1 up	Mitchell, 3 and 2			
150	Mike Balega, Minneapolis						
155	Dominick Morano, Newark, N.J.	Morano, 1 up					
158	Halbert Grumbles, San Antonio, Texas						
150	Frank Bringoli, New York	Bringoli, 1 up	Mitchell, 4 and 3				
156	Paul Segerlund, Akron						
158	David A. Mitchell, Indianapolis	Mitchell, 8 and 7					
159	Fred Gilbert, Altadena, Calif.						
150	Gordon Denney, Louisville	Denney, 2 up	Denney, 1 up	Denney, 2 and 1	Coria, 1 up, 20 hls.		
159	Larry Opalka, Detroit						
160	Dan J. Kenely, Elizabeth, N.J.	Szwedko, 1 up, 21 hls.					
155	Andrew Szwedko, Pittsburgh						
158	Ralph Strafaci, Brooklyn	R. Strafaci, 4 and 2	R. Strafaci, 1 up				
156	John Dolan, Philadelphia						
157	John Banks, Chicago	Banks, 4 and 2					
151	George S. Lance, Los Angeles						
152	John Racey, Cleveland	Coria, 3 and 2	Coria, 2 and 1	Coria, 5 and 3			
155	Joe Coria, St. Paul, Minn.						
159	George I. Phillips, Ft. Thomas, Ky.	Finlay, 3 and 2					
154	John C. Finlay, Seattle						
159	Michael Traina, New York	Traina, 5 and 4	Ferrera, 3 and 2				
158	Lester White, Erie, Pa.						
156	Mel Carpenter, Columbus, Ohio	Ferrera, 2 and 1					
159	Charles Ferrera, San Francisco						

*Medalist.

Twelfth Amateur Public Links Team Championship, Harding Trophy (34 team entries)—Won by Los Angeles team, total 603.

1935
FOURTEENTH AMATEUR PUBLIC LINKS CHAMPIONSHIP

Held at the Charles E. Coffin Course, Indianapolis, Ind., July 19-August 3. 198 Entries, 196 Starters.

Qualifying Score	1st Round (18 Holes)	2nd Round (18 Holes)	3rd Round (18 Holes)	4th Round (18 Holes)	Semi-Finals (36 Holes)	Final Round (36 Holes)	
150	John M. Ross, Los Angeles, Calif.	Rogers, 3 and 1					
148	**K.A. Rogers, San Antonio, Texas**		Rogers, 3 and 1				
157	Ade Normark, Minneapolis, Minn.	Black, 4 and 3					
156	Len Black, Louisville, Ky.			Coria, 2 and 1			
156	Warren Kingsbury, Buffalo, N.Y.	Coria, 3 and 2					
149	Joe Coria, St. Paul, Minn.		Coria, 2 up				
151	Tab Boyer, Portland, Ore.	Parco, 2 and 1					
158	Michael Parco, Buffalo, N.Y.				Coria, 5 and 3		
159	Harold Mathisen, Chicago, Ill.	Macklin, 1 up					
156	Marks Macklin, San Jose, Calif.		Casper, 4 and 3				
156	Wesley Casper, Louisville, Ky.	Casper, 1 up					
153	Larry Opalka, Detroit, Mich.			Casper, 1 up, 19 hls.			
157	Henry Foley, Chicago, Ill.	Jankoski, 5 and 4					
159	Lester Jankoski, Elizabeth, N.J.		Jankoski, 4 and 3				
159	Tom Radican, Cleveland, Ohio	Freitas, 1 up					
156	Joe Freitas, Honolulu, Hawaii					Coria, 4 and 2	
155	W.F. Lovebury, Columbus, Ohio	Russell, 4 and 2					
151	William F. Russell, Indianapolis, Ind.		Russell, 1 up, 19 hls.				
159	Byron Hunt, Columbus, Ohio	Grumbles, 1 up					
154	Halbert Grumbles, San Antonio, Texas			Russell, 1 up			
158	William J. Birofka, Elizabeth, N.J.	Peterson, 1 up					
158	Ken Peterson, Dayton, Ohio		Thomas, 1 up				
149	Louis C. Cyr, Portland, Ore.	Thomas, 3 and 2					
155	Earl Thomas, Richmond, Ind.				Russell, 5 and 3		
151	Mike Stefanchik, Gary, Ind.	Stefanchik, 2 and 1					
159	Jimmy Deeble, Minneapolis, Minn.		Stefanchik, 2 and 1				
152	John Gunst, Portland, Ore.	R. Strafaci, 6 and 5					
152	Ralph Strafaci, Brooklyn, N.Y.			Stefanchik, 4 and 2			
159	Walter Ambo, University City, Mo.	Ambo, 3 and 2					
154	George S. Lance, Los Angeles, Calif.		Rippy, 5 and 4				
148	Claude B. Rippy, Washington, D.C.	Rippy, 1 up					
146	Mike Balega, Minneapolis, Minn.						Frank Strafaci, 1 up, 37 Holes
159	George Bradley, Philadelphia, Pa.	Armstrong, 5 and 4					
157	Arthur Armstrong, Honolulu, Hawaii		Armstrong, 5 and 4				
155	Jack Dunphy, Santa Monica, Calif.	Presby, 2 up					
149	Ralph Presby, Sacramento, Calif.			Armstrong, 2 and 1			
149	Fred Gordon, Santa Monica, Calif.	Gordon, 1 up					
152	Harry Umbinetti, Seattle, Wash.		Gordon, 1 up				
159	Frank Newell, Long Beach, Calif.	Campbell, 3 and 2					
146	Albert E. Campbell, Seattle, Wash.				Tomes, 5 and 3		
145*	Lloyd Nordstrom, Davenport, Iowa	Nordstrom, 4 and 2					
154	Charles Ferrera, San Francisco, Calif.		Tomes, 1 up				
153	Robert Tomes, Long Beach, Calif.	Tomes, 3 and 2					
157	Steve Kipper, Seattle, Wash.			Tomes, 4 and 2			
156	John Lucas, Sharon, Pa.	Randall, 2 up					
157	Edward Randall, Rochester, N.Y.		Madara, 6 and 4				
157	John Jewett, Gary, Ind.	Madara, 3 and 1					
158	John Madara, Philadelphia, Pa.					F. Strafaci, 11 and 9	
157	Charles Amandoles, Staten Island, N.Y.	Amandoles, 4 and 3					
156	Ray Mitchell, Dayton, Ohio		Amandoles, 4 and 3				
157	Mike Graniteo, Cleveland, Ohio	Doll, 5 and 3					
149	Pete Doll, Louisville, Ky.			Amandoles, 2 up			
155	Ade Fordham, St. Paul, Minn.	Denney, 6 and 5					
151	Gordon Denney, Louisville, Ky.		D. Mitchell, 2 and 1				
150	David Mitchell, Indianapolis, Ind.	D. Mitchell, 7 and 6					
151	Fred Grote, St. Joseph, Mo.				F. Strafaci, 5 and 4		
158	Eddie Donohue, St. Louis, Mo.	Pettigrew, 1 up					
150	Leon Pettigrew, Anderson, Ind.		McCormick, 4 and 2				
156	Gordon Young, Dallas, Texas	McCormick, 1 up					
150	Bruce McCormick, Los Angeles, Calif.			F. Strafaci, 2 and 1			
156	Bruce Baird, Santa Monica, Calif.	Baird, 2 up					
149	**Tom Lawrence, San Antonio, Texas**		F. Strafaci, 3 and 2				
158	Frank Strafaci, Brooklyn, N.Y.	F. Strafaci, 4 and 2					
159	Frank Connolly, Detroit, Mich.						

Thirteenth Amateur Public Links Team Championship, Harding Trophy (45 Team Entries)—Won by San Antonio, Texas team (K. A. Rogers, Halbert Grumbles, Tom Lawrence, Miller Campbell), 305 in 18-hole play-off with Louisville, Ky. team (Gordon Denney, Len Black, Pete Doll, Wesley Casper), after tie at 612 for 36 holes.

*Medalist.

1936
FIFTEENTH AMATEUR PUBLIC LINKS CHAMPIONSHIP

Held at Bethpage State Park, Farmingdale, N.Y., July 20-25. 223 Entries, 222 Starters.

Qualifying Score	1st Round (18 Holes)	2nd Round (18 Holes)	3rd Round (18 Holes)	4th Round (18 Holes)	Semi-Finals (36 Holes)	Final Round (36 Holes)	
151	Andrew Szwedko, Pittsburgh, Pa.	Szwedko, 1 up	Greiner, 2 and 1	Greiner, 1 up	Greiner, 7 and 5	Rippy, 6 and 4	B. Patrick Abbott, 4 and 3
150	Mike A. Dolan, Philadelphia, Pa.						
152	Walter Greiner, Baltimore, Md.	Greiner, 3 and 1					
154	Richard Habes, Rochester, N.Y.						
147	Charles Ferrera, San Francisco, Calif.	Hromyak, 4 and 3	Hromyak, 2 and 1				
150	Vash Hromyak, Sharon, Pa.						
152	Bruce McCormick, Los Angeles, Calif.	McCormick, 3 and 2					
151	Jack Thurmond, San Antonio, Texas						
150	Harry Umbinetti, Seattle, Wash.	Umbinetti, 4 and 2	Umbinetti, 4 and 3	Umbinetti, 2 and 1			
153	Paul Telesca, Hartford, Conn.						
153	Reginald Scully, Milwaukee, Wis.	Scully, 6 and 5					
153	James Peatie, Hartford, Conn.						
153	Michael Parco, Buffalo, N.Y.	Studinger, 2 and 1	Studinger, 1 up				
153	George Studinger, Burlingame, Calif.						
149	Frank Strafaci, Brooklyn, N.Y.	F. Strafaci, 4 and 3					
154	Tab Boyer, Portland, Ore.						
145*	Claude B. Rippy, Washington, D.C.	Rippy, 5 and 4	Rippy, 5 and 3	Rippy, 2 and 1	Rippy, 4 and 2		
150	Ralph Strafaci, Brooklyn, N.Y.						
152	Louis C. Cyr, Portland, Ore.	Cyr, 2 and 1					
153	Charles Beeler, Baltimore, Md.						
152	Joseph Roth, Louisville, Ky.	Gilles, 3 and 2	Lau, 1 up				
152	Paul M. Gilles, Milwaukee, Wis.						
153	Kammy Lau, Honolulu, Hawaii	Lau, 1 up					
150	John Racey, Cleveland, Ohio						
153	Arthur Gedney, New Haven, Conn.	Lucas, 4 and 3	Lucas, 2 and 1	Lucas, 1 up			
152	John Lucas, Sharon, Pa.						
149	Walter Burkemo, Highland Park, Mich.	Sams, 1 up, 19 hls.					
153	Edward Sams, Buffalo, N.Y.						
151	Dick Covington, Long Beach, Calif.	Owen, 7 and 6	Owen, 3 and 2				
151	Arthur T. Owen, Jacksonville, Fla.						
153	Charles Amandoles, Staten Island, N.Y.	Amandoles, 2 and 1					
145*	James J. Molinari, San Francisco, Calif.						
154	John Siergej, Plainfield, N.J.	Gates, 5 and 4	Stefanchik, 2 and 1	Pardee, 1 up	Pardee, 3 and 1	Abbott, 8 and 7	
152	Ray Gates, St. Louis, Mo.						
150	Mike Stefanchik, Gary, Ind.	Stefanchik, 2 and 1					
149	Frank Connolly, Detroit, Mich.						
153	Carl F. Kauffmann, Pittsburgh, Pa.	Pardee, 1 up, 20 hls.	Pardee, 2 and 1				
153	Bruno W. Pardee, New Haven, Conn.						
154	Nelson S. Halsey, Baltimore, Md.	Halsey, 6 and 4					
153	William Fenwick, Detroit, Mich.						
153	Don Smith, St. Joseph, Mo.	Smith, 2 and 1	Sleppy, 4 and 3	Sleppy, 1 up			
151	George Bradley, Philadelphia, Pa.						
150	Paul Sleppy, Long Beach, Calif.	Sleppy, 2 up					
151	Lee Brandt, Jr., San Antonio, Texas						
153	Lionel Wendland, San Antonio, Texas	Wendland, 1 up	Wendland, 7 and 6				
151	Arloo G. Kyle, Portland, Ore.						
152	Carl A. Jonson, Seattle, Wash.	Jonson, 8 and 7					
154	R.W. Johnke, Los Angeles, Calif.						
153	Mike Balega, Minneapolis, Minn.	Balega, 2 up	Balega, 6 and 5	Erickson, 3 and 1	Abbott, 2 up		
153	Mike Pollak, Indianapolis, Ind.						
151	Al Priebe, St. Paul, Minn.	Priebe, 3 and 2					
151	Tommy Strafaci, Brooklyn, N.Y.						
149	Jack M. Evans, New Rochelle, N.Y.	Evans, 3 and 2	Erickson, 4 and 2				
149	Warren Campbell, Seattle, Wash.						
149	Don N. Erickson, Los Angeles, Calif.	Erickson, 1 up					
151	Stanley Banazek, Syracuse, N.Y.						
150	Jim Caspio, Cleveland, Ohio	Burton, 3 and 2	Soccoli, 1 up	Abbott, 5 and 4			
153	Robert B. Burton, Washington, D.C.						
150	Hack Williford, San Antonio, Texas	Soccoli, 5 and 3					
154	Dom Soccoli, New Britain, Conn.						
147	B. Patrick Abbott, Pasadena, Calif.	Abbott, 4 and 3	Abbott, 3 and 2				
148	Bill Kinkella, Seattle, Wash.						
154	Alex Banazek, Syracuse, N.Y.	A. Banazek, 3 and 2					
152	John Babis, Dearborn, Mich.						

*Tied for medal. No playoff.

Fourteenth Amateur Public Links Team Championship, Harding Trophy (49 Team Entries)—Won by Seattle, Wash., team (Bill Kinkella, 148; Warren Campbell, 149; Harry Umbinetti, 150; Carl A. Jonson, 152;) 599 for 36 holes: second, San Francisco, Calif., team (James J. Molinari, Charles Ferrera, Gordon Wayne, Paul E. Tullius). 603.

1937
SIXTEENTH AMATEUR PUBLIC LINKS CHAMPIONSHIP

Held at Harding Park Course, San Francisco, Calif., August 9-14. 190 Entries, 186 Starters.

Qualifying Score	1st Round (18 Holes)	2nd Round (18 Holes)	3rd Round (18 Holes)	4th Round (18 Holes)	Semi-Finals (36 Holes)	Final Round (36 Holes)	
151	John Louis Meier, Toledo, Ohio	Meier, 1 up					
145	Harry Umbinetti, Seattle, Wash.		McGlashan, 7 and 6				
145	Robert Abeles, Jr., Santa Monica, Calif.	McGlashan, 1 up					
147	Robert McGlashan, San Francisco, Calif.			Szwedko, 1 up, 19 hls.			
145	Lester Jankoski, Elizabeth, N.J.	Bramhall, 1 up, 21 hls.					
148	Peter Bramhall, San Mateo, Calif.		Szwedko, 5 and 4				
148	Merlin H. Luther, Buffalo, N.Y.	Szwedko, 2 up					
143	Andrew Szwedko, Pittsburgh, Pa.				Szwedko, 3 and 1		
142	Ralph Presby, Sacramento, Calif.	Abbott, 4 and 3					
141	B. Patrick Abbott, Pasadena, Calif.		Abbott, 2 and 1				
148	George Bradley, Philadelphia, Pa.	Mescall, 2 up					
146	John J. Mescall, Los Angeles, Calif.			Abbott, 3 and 2			
144	Einar Hanson, Daly City, Calif.	Hanson, 1 up					
149	Roscoe Guidero, Sacramento, Calif.		Hanson, 1 up, 20 hls.				
149	Michael P. McCarthy, Staten Island, N.Y.	McCarthy, 2 up					
150	Arloo G. Kyle, Portland, Ore.					McCormick, 5 and 4	
150	**Bruce McCormick, Los Angeles, Calif.**	McCormick, 2 and 1					
147	Bill Hoelle, San Mateo, Calif.		McCormick, 3 and 2				
150	James Johnson, Detroit, Mich.	Oliveri, 2 and 1					
152	Andrew Oliveri, Washington, D.C.			McCormick, 3 and 1			
151	Howard L. Clark, Palo Alto, Calif.	Tullius, 5 and 3					
148	Paul E. Tullius, San Francisco, Calif.		Tullius, 2 and 1				
147	Hall J. Dufour, Sacramento, Calif.	Sharpe, 1 up, 21 hls.					
152	George Sharpe, Jr., Columbia, S.C.				McCormick, 2 and 1		
146	Frank Russ, Alameda, Calif.	Russ, 4 and 2					
151	A.D. Priebe, St. Paul, Minn.		Muragin, 5 and 4				
151	Alex Muragin, Honolulu, Hawaii	Muragin, 1 up, 22 hls.					
148	Carl F. Kauffmann, Pittsburgh, Pa.			Muragin, 5 and 3			
148	Frank Babis, Dearborn, Mich.	Walters, 3 and 2					
148	E. H. Walters, San Francisco, Calif.		Genung, 2 and 1				
148	Paul Genung, Dayton, Ohio	Genung, 1 up					
148	Walter Gilliam, Jr., Burlingame, Calif.						Bruce McCormick, 1 up
150	William Fenwick, Detroit, Mich.	Fenwick, 6 and 4					
151	John Mazza, So. San Francisco, Calif.		Hoon, 2 and 1				
151	Richard Tang, Minneapolis, Minn.	Hoon, 1 up					
145	Howard Hoon, Santa Monica, Calif.			Hoon, 1 up			
151	Robert Snyder, Los Angeles, Calif.	Silvestri, 3 and 2					
147	Robert Silvestri, Daly City, Calif.		Silvestri, 3 and 1				
150	Don Winge, Minneapolis, Minn.	Williams, 5 and 4					
147	C. W. Williams, San Jose, Calif.				Erickson, 4 and 3		
148	Claude B. Rippy, Washington, D.C.	Gordon, 5 and 4					
150	Phil Gordon, Oakland, Calif.		Gordon, 3 and 2				
150	Gilbert C. Smith, Staten Island, N.Y.	Hall, 4 and 3					
148	Van Hall, Long Beach, Calif.			Erickson, 4 and 3			
147	Paul G. Jenssen, Toledo, Ohio	Erickson, 3 and 2					
139*	Don Erickson, Alhambra, Calif.		Erickson, 5 and 4				
148	Fred McLeod, Daly City, Calif.	McLeod, 4 and 3					
148	Kauila Akau, Honolulu, Hawaii					Erickson, 4 and 3	
147	Joseph Greene, Philadelphia, Pa.	Campbell, 3 and 2					
149	Warren (Bud) Campbell, Seattle, Wash.		Radican, 2 and 1				
151	Thomas J. Radican, Cleveland, Ohio	Radican, 1 up, 21 hls.					
151	Kenneth F. Long, Hawthorne, Calif.			Toronto, 7 and 5			
149	Frank Toronto, Sacramento, Calif.	Toronto, 3 and 2					
152	Henry Suico, Oakland, Calif.		Toronto, 1 up, 19 hls.				
149	Tommy Card, Raleigh, N.C.	Card, 3 and 2					
151	Jack Klein, Alameda, Calif.				Toronto, 5 and 4		
152	Vernon E. Gilstrap, Berkeley, Calif.	Gilstrap, 3 and 2					
150	Angelo Bonino, So. San Francisco, Calif.		Gilstrap, 3 and 2				
147	Wes Berner, Portland, Ore.	Walsh, 4 and 3					
149	William Walsh, Indianapolis, Ind.			Gilstrap, 3 and 2			
151	Frank Connolly, Detroit, Mich.	Clarkson, 2 and 1					
151	Tad Clarkson, Santa Monica, Calif.		Clarkson, 1 up, 23 hls.				
149	Roger Skidmore, Louisville, Ky.	Armstrong, 4 and 3					
149	Arthur Armstrong, Honolulu, Hawaii						

*Medalist.

Fifteenth Amateur Public Links Team Championship, Harding Trophy (40 team entries)—Won by Sacramento, Calif., team, 587 for 36 holes (Ralph Presby, 142; Hall J. Dufour, 147; Roscoe Guidero, 194; Frank Toronto, 149); second, Santa Monica, Calif., team, 593 (Robert Abeles, Jr., 145; Howard Hoon, 145; Ted Clarkson, 151; Fred Gordon, 152); third, San Francisco, Calif., team, 597 (Robert McGlashan, 147; Paul E. Tullius, 148; E.H. Walters, 148; C. Groswird, 154).

1938
SEVENTEENTH AMATEUR PUBLIC LINKS CHAMPIONSHIP

Held at Highland Park Municipal Golf Course, Cleveland, Ohio, August 22-27. 248 Entries, 247 Starters.

Qualifying Score	1st Round (18 Holes)	2nd Round (18 Holes)	3rd Round (18 Holes)	4th Round (18 Holes)	Semi-Finals (36 Holes)	Final Round (36 Holes)	
149	Fred H. Hill, Worcester, Mass.	Hill,					
148	Frank Metzger, East Cleveland, Ohio	4 and 3	Zadalis,				
148	Matt Zadalis, Omaha, Neb.	Zadalis,	4 and 3				
147	Ralph Bond, Cleveland, Ohio	2 and 1		Boyer,			
149	John Racey, Cleveland Heights, Ohio	Peterson,		1 up, 19 hls.			
146	Kenneth M. Peterson, Dayton, Ohio	4 and 3	Boyer,				
147	Tab Boyer, Portland, Ore.	Boyer,	2 and 1				
148	Benny Stefanik, Pittsburgh, Pa.	3 and 2					
147	Morris C. Fisher, Lincoln, Neb.	Opalka,			Cyr, 3 and 2		
150	Larry Opalka, Mt. Clemens, Mich.	3 and 2	Whitney,				
147	Neil Whitney, Los Angeles, Calif.	Whitney,	5 and 4				
150	Domenick K. Strafaci, Brooklyn, N.Y.	2 up		Cyr,			
147	Wes Berner, Portland, Ore.	Berner,		2 and 1			
150	Sadaji Kinoshita, Honolulu, Hawaii	3 and 1	Cyr,				
151	Louis C. Cyr, Portland, Ore.	Cyr,	2 and 1				
149	David A. Mitchell, Atlanta, Ga.	2 and 1					
147	Michael Cestone, Newark, N.J.	Age,				Cyr, 1 up	
147	Alton Age, Louisville, Ky.	5 and 3	Age,				
147	Loio Palenapa, Honolulu, Hawaii	Burkemo,	1 up, 19 hls.				
141*	Walter Burkemo, Detroit, Mich.	1 up		Beck,			
146	Pete Doll, Louisville, Ky.	Beck,		3 and 2			
149	Eddie Beck, Portland, Ore.	1 up	Beck,				
150	Tommy Strafaci, Brooklyn, N.Y.	T. Strafaci,	5 and 4				
150	James J. Molinari, San Francisco, Calif.	3 and 2					
148	Walter Paprock, Utica, N.Y.	Mucci,			Beck, 3 and 1		
147	Pat Mucci, Newark, N.J.	1 up	Lind,				
146	Ronald S.F. Williams, Dearborn, Mich.	Lind,	4 and 3				
146	Charles Lind, Denver, Colo.	3 and 2		Evans,			
143	Don Erickson, Los Angeles, Calif.	Hromyak,		3 and 2			
144	Vash Hromyak, Sharon, Pa.	1 up, 19 hls.	Evans,				
149	Marshall K. Hammond, Spokane, Wash.	Evans,	2 and 1				
149	Ralph J. Evans, Santa Monica, Calif.	4 and 3					
147	Frank Connolly, Dearborn, Mich.	Umbinetti,					Al Leach, 1 up
145	Harry Umbinetti, Seattle, Wash.	3 and 1	Lavender,				
145	Fred H. Gronauer, Indianapolis, Ind.	Lavender,	2 and 1				
146	Dennis Lavender, Dallas, Texas	4 and 3		Lavender,			
149	Raymond J. Ala, Highland Park, Mich.	Ala,		1 up			
147	Marshall F. Carlson, Toledo, Ohio	2 up	Young,				
147	Kenneth C. Young, Minneapolis, Minn.	Young,	5 and 3				
150	Olin Cerrocki, Brooklyn, N.Y.	1 up, 20 hls.					
143	Bart Taro, Seattle, Wash.	Taro,			Taro, 3 and 2		
148	Joseph M. Higgins, Dayton, Ohio	2 up	Taro,				
142	Edward J. Furgol, Utica, N.Y.	Fannon,	5 and 4				
147	Chase Fannon, Chicago, Ill.	4 and 2		Taro,			
144	Lloyd Nordstrom, Davenport, Iowa	Nordstrom,		4 and 3			
147	Bruce McCormick, Los Angeles, Calif.	1 up, 19 hls.	Nordstrom,				
146	Oscar Evers, Jacksonville, Fla.	Cady,	1 up				
150	William F. Cady, Santa Monica, Calif.	1 up, 19 hls.				Leach, 1 up	
144	Frank Toronto, Sacramento, Calif.	Gajda,					
149	Bob Gajda, Detroit, Mich.	2 up	Johnson,				
149	William E. Fritz, San Francisco, Calif.	Johnson,	2 and 1				
144	James Johnson, Detroit, Mich.	2 and 1		Bolt,			
146	Don Winge, Minneapolis, Minn.	Bolt,		4 and 2			
144	Tommy H. Bolt, Shreveport, La.	2 up	Bolt,				
147	George Lance, Los Angeles, Calif.	Lance,	4 and 3				
147	Alex Danko, Cleveland, Ohio	3 and 2			Leach, 2 and 1		
147	Joseph May, Buffalo, N.Y.	Szwedko,					
145	Andrew Szwedko, Pittsburgh, Pa.	2 and 1	Szwedko,				
148	Richard Habes, Rochester, N.Y.	Habes,	3 and 2				
147	Charles J. Albertus, Philadelphia, Pa.	1 up, 19 hls.		Leach,			
144	Walter Knych, Utica, N.Y.	Leach,		4 and 3			
147	Al Leach, East Cleveland, Ohio	2 up	Leach,				
149	William Birofka, Elizabeth, N.J.	Birofka,	2 and 1				
147	Carl R. Nettelbladt, Worcester, Mass.	1 up					

*Medalist.

Sixteenth Amateur Public Links Team Championship, Harding Trophy (55 team entries)—Won by Los Angeles, Calif., team, 584 for 36 holes (Don Erickson, 143; George Lance, 147; Bruce McCormick, 147; Neil Whitney, 147); second, Utica, N.Y., team, 586 (Edward Furgol, 142; Walter Knych, 144; Walter Paprock, 148; Stanley Kroll, 152); third, Detroit, Mich., team, 589 (Walter Burkemo, 141; James Johnson, 144; Bob Gajda, 149; Drew Egleston, 155).

1939
EIGHTEENTH AMATEUR PUBLIC LINKS CHAMPIONSHIP

Held at Mount Pleasant Park Golf Course, Baltimore, Md., July 24-29. 2,401 Entries, 190 Qualifiers, 178 Starters.

Qualifying Score	1st Round (18 Holes)	2nd Round (18 Holes)	3rd Round (18 Holes)	4th Round (18 Holes)	Semi-Finals (36 Holes)	Final Round (36 Holes)	
155	James Calhoun, Pittsburgh, Pa.	Alexander, 6 and 5	Peterson, 6 and 5	Gordon, 5 and 4	Gordon, 5 and 4	Gordon, 3 and 2	Andrew Szwedko, 1 up
156	Chuck Alexander, Durham, N.C.						
154	Howard Baker, Jr., Spokane, Wash.	Peterson, 3 and 2					
152	Ken Peterson, Dayton, Ohio						
155	Bobby Walker, Jacksonville, Fla.	Gordon, 3 and 2	Gordon, 1 up				
151	Phillip Gordon, Oakland, Calif.						
156	Roger Skidmore, Louisville, Ky.	Skidmore, 3 and 2					
150	Ralph A. Reed, Lincoln, Neb.						
151	Charles Amandoles, New York, N.Y.	Amandoles, 6 and 5	McCay, 1 up	Dolce, 4 and 3			
156	Telfair Ghioto, Jacksonville, Fla.						
155	William Fritz, San Francisco, Calif.	McCay, 1 up, 19 hls.					
153	Willard McCay, Long Beach, Calif.						
155	Joseph E. Goldshinsky, New Haven, Conn.	Dolce, 1 up	Dolce, 3 and 2				
156	Roy Dolce, Denver, Colo.						
155	Barker Serian, Troy, N.Y.	Knych, 2 and 1					
151	**Walter L. Knych, Utica, N.Y.**						
150	George S. Lance, Los Angeles, Calif.	Lance, 4 and 3	Krisko, 1 up	Molinari, 6 and 4	Molinari, 2 and 1		
154	Jimmy Thompson, Cleveland, Ohio						
154	Fred H. Hill, Worcester, Mass.	Krisko, 2 and 1					
155	John Krisko, Dayton, Ohio						
146	Don Erickson, Los Angeles, Calif.	Springer, 1 up, 20 hls.	Molinari, 3 and 2				
147	Marshall Springer, Chicago, Ill.						
146	Jack Colmar, Sacramento, Calif.	Molinari, 4 and 3					
150	James Molinari, San Francisco, Calif.						
154	Ted Gwin, Tulsa, Okla.	Gwin, 3 and 2	Gwin, 1 up	Furgol, 2 and 1			
144*	Luke Barnes, Atlanta, Ga.						
154	William Birofka, Summit, N.J.	Oliveri, 4 and 3					
146	Andrew Oliveri, Washington, D.C.						
147	Edward J. Furgol, Utica, N.Y.	Furgol, 3 and 2	Furgol, 3 and 2				
147	Ernest Carli, San Francisco, Calif.						
151	Stanley Kroll, Utica, N.Y.	Kroll, 4 and 3					
155	Paul Genung, Dayton, Ohio						
155	Arthur Nutting, Louisville, Ky.	Nutting, 3 and 2	Dezern, 5 and 3	Szwedko, 3 and 2	Szwedko, 3 and 2	Szwedko, 1 up	
145	Jack Brande, Los Angeles, Calif.						
150	Carl Dezern, Durham, N.C.	Dezern, 5 and 4					
155	Charles E. Harter, Indianapolis, Ind.						
156	Leo Hehir, Worcester, Mass.	Taro, 5 and 4	Szwedko, 3 and 2				
155	Bart Taro, Seattle, Wash.						
154	Ernie Tardiff, Santa Monica, Calif.	Szwedko, 2 and 1					
151	Andrew Szwedko, Pittsburgh, Pa.						
150	Ralph Presby, Sacramento, Calif.	Whitney, 1 up, 19 hls.	Bradley, 3 and 2	Cyr, 2 and 1			
149	Neil Whitney, Los Angeles, Calif.						
155	Harry Kaufman, Lincoln, Neb.	Bradley, 1 up, 21 hls.					
152	George Bradley, Philadelphia, Pa.						
154	Olin Cerrocki, New York, N.Y.	Johnston, 4 and 3	Cyr, 2 and 1				
153	Edward A. Johnston, Baltimore, Md.						
144*	Jack Taulman, Columbus, Ind.	Cyr, 2 and 1					
151	Louis C. Cyr, Vancouver, Wash.						
156	Alex Banazek, Syracuse, N.Y.	Holtz, 3 and 1	Doctor, 2 and 1	Armstrong, 5 and 4	Armstrong, 4 and 3		
154	Alex Holtz, Erie, Pa.						
154	Steve Doctor, Buffalo, N.Y.	Doctor, 4 and 3					
155	Ray Ala, Detroit, Mich.						
151	Leonard Egbert, Los Angeles, Calif.	Barrett, 1 up	Armstrong, 2 and 1				
149	Craton Barrett, Dallas, Texas						
152	Ade Fordham, St. Paul, Minn.	Armstrong, 5 and 4					
144*	Arthur Armstrong, Honolulu, Hawaii						
152	John Teal, Jacksonville, Fla.	Teal, 1 up	Berner, 3 and 1	Cestone, 4 and 3			
152	Nicholas Fabrizio, Inwood, N.Y.						
151	Wes Berner, Portland, Ore.	Berner, 2 and 1					
155	Labron Harris, Guthrie, Okla.						
144*	Gerry Bert, Jr., Seattle, Wash.	Bert, 5 and 4	Cestone, 2 and 1				
153	Robert C. Clark, St. Paul, Minn.						
155	Alex Pietrzak, Dayton, Ohio	Cestone, 3 and 2					
147	Michael Cestone, Montclair, N.J.						

*Tied for medal. No playoff.

Seventeenth Amateur Public Links Team Championship, Harding Trophy (30 team entries)—Won by Los Angeles, Calif., team, 442 for 36 holes (Jack Brande, 145; Don Erickson, 146; Leonard Egbert, 151); second, Seattle, Wash., team, 460 (Gerry Bert, Jr., 144; Bart Taro, 155; Palmer Smith, 161;) third, Jacksonville, Fla., team, 463 (John Teal, 152; Bobby Walker, 155; Telfair Ghioto, 156).

1940
NINETEENTH AMATEUR PUBLIC LINKS CHAMPIONSHIP

Held at Rackham Golf Course, Detroit, Mich., July 22-27. 2,601 Entries, 193 Qualifiers, 190 Starters.

Qualifying Score	1st Round (18 Holes)	2nd Round (18 Holes)	3rd Round (18 Holes)	4th Round (18 Holes)	Semi-Finals (36 Holes)	Final Round (36 Holes)	
145	G.W. Duvall, Jr., Kansas City, Mo.	Duvall, 2 and 1					
147	Ray Ala, Detroit, Mich.		Harris, 5 and 3				
147	Labron Harris, Guthrie, Okla.	Harris, 6 and 5					
149	Andrew Oliveri, Washington, D.C.			Harris, 4 and 3			
148	Walter Smola, Omaha, Neb.	Smola, 3 and 1					
148	Henry C. Robertson, Jr., Oklahoma City, Okla.		Smola, 4 and 3				
148	Martin Leptich, Portland, Ore.	Leptich, 3 and 1			Furgol, 4 and 3		
149	Howard Olson, Tacoma, Wash.						
149	Edward Ebel, Minneapolis, Minn.	Furgol, 3 and 2					
138*	Edward J. Furgol, Utica, N.Y.		Furgol, 2 up				
144	William Fritz, San Francisco, Calif.	Fritz, 1 up, 19 hls.					
145	Arthur Armstrong, Honolulu, Hawaii			Furgol, 3 and 2			
138*	Worth Stimits, Jr., Colorado Springs, Colo.	Stimits, 3 and 1					
144	Marshall Springer, Chicago, Ill.		Stimits, 1 up, 20 hls.			Clark, 1 up, 38 holes	
146	Carl E. Smith, Indianapolis, Ind.	Ames, 3 and 2					
148	F.E. Ames, Beaumont, Texas						
140	Adrian French, Huntington Park, Calif.	Gilliam, 2 up					
140	Walter Gilliam, San Mateo, Calif.		Lind, 1 up				
139	Charles Lind, Denver, Colo.	Lind, 1 up					
145	Roger Skidmore, Louisville, Ky.			Clark, 1 up, 19 hls.			
145	Charles E. Harter, Indianapolis, Ind.	Pollak, 1 up, 20 hls.					
145	Michael Pollak, Indianapolis, Ind.		Clark, 4 and 3				
144	Robert H. Price, Oklahoma City, Okla.	Clark, 3 and 2					
144	Robert C. Clark, St. Paul, Minn.				Clark, 1 up		
144	Einar Hanson, San Francisco, Calif.	Hanson, 1 up					
148	John Siergej, Plainfield, N.J.		Bublis, 4 and 3				
148	William Bublis, Chicago, Ill.	Bublis, 3 and 2					
147	Andrew Szwedko, Pittsburgh, Pa.			Jennings, 5 and 3			
145	Samuel Musico, Pittsburgh, Pa.	Musico, 4 and 3					
145	Fred H. Hill, Worcester, Mass.		Jennings, 3 and 2				Robert C. Clark, 8 and 6
146	William Korns, Salt Lake City, Utah	Jennings, 6 and 5					
143	Louis Jennings, Portland, Ore.						
146	Woodrow Malloy, Ann Arbor, Mich.	Bowdle, 1 up					
146	Vern Bowdle, Salt Lake City, Utah		Stefanchik, 4 and 2				
146	Michael Stefanchik, Gary, Ind.	Stefanchik, 2 and 1					
146	John Kerns, Denver, Colo.			Stefanchik, 5 and 3			
148	James C. Clark, Huntington Beach, Calif.	Pasikowski, 4 and 3					
147	John Pasikowski, Pittsburgh, Pa.		Pasikowski, 5 and 4				
147	Rollen Welch, Milwaukee, Wis.	Welch, 2 and 1			Dolce, 2 up		
147	Donald Smith, St. Joseph, Mo.						
147	Edward Castagnetto, San Francisco, Calif.	Dolce, 3 and 1					
149	Roy Dolce, Denver, Colo.		Dolce, 1 up				
148	David A. Mitchell, Atlanta, Ga.	Doll, 1 up					
146	William E. Doll, Louisville, Ky.			Dolce, 1 up, 20 hls.			
147	Edwin M. Harper, Pocatello, Idaho	Harper, 4 and 3					
145	Walter Tebaldi, Alameda, Calif.		Harper, 3 and 2				
143	Lester Jankoski, Summit, N.J.	Jankoski, 1 up				Dietz, 3 and 2	
143	Michael Szwedko, Pittsburgh, Pa.						
145	Luke Barnes, Atlanta, Ga.	Barnes, 4 and 3					
143	John A. Skinner, Cleveland, Ohio		Dietz, 3 and 2				
143	Michael Dietz, Detroit, Mich.	Dietz, 3 and 1					
145	James J. Molinari, San Francisco, Calif.			Dietz, 6 and 5			
142	James S. Johnson, Detroit, Mich.	Owen, 1 up					
149	Fred M. Owen, Atlanta, Ga.		Shock, 4 and 3				
149	Donald Shock, Dayton, Ohio	Shock, 3 and 2			Dietz, 3 and 2		
149	Stephen Doctor, Buffalo, N.Y.						
145	Carl F. Kauffmann, Pittsburgh, Pa.	Kauffmann, 4 and 2					
149	Edward Garfield, Cleveland, Ohio		LaRose, 2 and 1				
149	Barker Serian, Troy, N.Y.	LaRose, 2 and 1					
147	Jack LaRose, Detroit, Mich.			LaRose, 1 up			
146	William Szustak, Buffalo, N.Y.	Szustak, 4 and 2					
146	R.B. Kiersky, Houston, Texas		Szustak, 5 and 4				
145	Kenneth Peterson, Dayton, Ohio	Peterson, 1 up, 22 hls.					
145	Carl Nettelbladt, Worcester, Mass.						

***Tied for medal, no playoff.**

Eighteenth Amateur Public Links Team Championship, Harding Trophy (34 team entries)—Won by San Francisco, Calif., team, 435 for 36 holes (William Fritz, 144; Einar Hanson, 144; Edward Castagnetto, 147;) second, Pittsburgh, Pa., team, 437 (Michael Szwedko, 143; John Pasikowski, 147; Andrew Szwedko, 147); third, Chicago, Ill., team, 442 (Marshall Springer, 144; William Bublis, 148; John M. Hayes, 150).

1941
TWENTIETH AMATEUR PUBLIC LINKS CHAMPIONSHIP

Held at the Indian Canyon Golf Course, Spokane, Wash., July 14–19.
Yardage–6,277 Par 71. 2,816 Entries, 187 Qualifiers, 187 Starters.

Qualifying Score	1st Round (18 Holes)	2nd Round (18 Holes)	3rd Round (18 Holes)	4th Round (18 Holes)	Semi-Finals (36 Holes)	Final (36 Holes)
151	Forest M. Bishop, Spokane, Wash.	Meyer, 5 and 3	Wilson, 2 and 1	Pomy, 5 and 4	Pomy, 1 up, 19 holes	Kerns, 5 and 4
150	Charles E. Meyer, Baltimore, Md.					
151	Charles Wilson, Honolulu, Hawaii	Wilson, 3 and 1				
151	Marshall Hammond, Spokane, Wash.					
142	Arthur Pomy, Detroit, Mich.	Pomy, 5 and 4	Pomy, 1 up			
150	Earl Fry, Jr., Alameda, Calif.					
148	Robert Mort, San Francisco, Calif.	Mort, 2 and 1				
150	Lester Coleman, Inglewood, Calif.					
147	David A. Mitchell, Atlanta, Ga.	Mitchell, 2 and 1	Mitchell, 2 and 1	Daniel, 2 and 1		
151	Damon Jacobsen, Long Beach, Calif.					
147	William E. Fritz, San Francisco, Calif.	Fritz, 3 and 1				
151	Worth Stimits, Jr., Colorado Springs, Colo.					
149	Ralph Wolf, Los Angeles, Calif.	Thompson, 4 and 2	Daniel, 3 and 2			
145	James Thompson, Cleveland, Ohio					
149	Robert Daniel, San Francisco, Calif.	Daniel, 1 up				
146	James S. Johnson, Detroit, Mich.					
146	Gerald R. Anderson, Worcester, Mass.	Anderson, 1 up	Anderson, 3 and 1	J. Clark, 5 and 4	Kerns, 2 and 1	
150	Edward D. Stuckrath, Portland, Ore.					
150	David Dixon, Vancouver, B.C., Canada	Schneider, 6 and 4				
151	Ralph F. Schneider, Cleveland, Ohio					
135	*James C. Clark, Jr., Long Beach, Calif.	J. Clark, 2 and 1	J. Clark, 1 up			
148	Charles W. Barnes, Atlanta, Ga.					
150	Lawrence R. Robertson, St. Paul, Minn.	Leal, 3 and 2				
149	Leslie A. Leal, Bellingham, Wash.					
143	James. J. Molinari, San Francisco, Calif.	Molinari, 3 and 2	Hall, 2 and 1	Kerns, 4 and 3		
150	Einar Hanson, San Francisco, Calif.					
151†	Jack Brande, Inglewood, Calif.	Hall, 1 up, 21 holes				
151†	Ralph Hall, Oakland, Calif.					
150	William Cole, Baltimore, Md.	Kerns, 2 and 1	Kerns, 1 up, 21 holes			
150	Jack Kerns, Denver, Colo.					
151	Joseph May, Buffalo, N.Y.	Baird, 1 up				
147	Philip Baird, Spokane, Wash.					William M. Welch, Jr., 6 and 5
148	Raymond Wetson, Jr., Portland, Ore.	Welch, 2 up	Welch, 5 and 3	Welch, 3 and 2	Welch, 1 up	Welch, 4 and 3
151	William M. Welch, Jr., Houston, Texas					
149	Samuel Musico, Pittsburgh, Pa.	Caso, 5 and 4				
150	Moreno Caso, Seattle, Wash.					
145	Walter Tebaldi, Alameda, Calif.	Tebaldi, 2 up	Tebaldi, 2 and 1			
147	Edward Furgol, Detroit, Mich.					
151†	Angelo J. Mengali, Lancaster, Pa.	Presby, 1 up, 19 holes				
146	Ralph Presby, Sacramento, Calif.					
148	Robert C. Clark, St. Paul, Minn.	R. Clark, 4 and 2	Korns, 1 up	McReynolds, 3 and 2		
148	Alphonso Atkins, Ashland, Ky.					
148	John Sendral, Dayton, Ohio	Korns, 4 and 3				
139	William L. Korns, Salt Lake City, Utah					
144	James Tebbe, Glendale, Calif.	Tebbe, 1 up	McReynolds, 2 and 1			
147	Edward J. Axtell, St. Paul, Minn.					
147	Kenneth Peterson, Dayton, Ohio	McReynolds, 7 and 5				
143	Robert W. McReynolds, Portland, Ore.					
149	Anthony Lopucki, Detroit, Mich.	Castagnetto, 3 and 2	Genik, 1 up	Palenapa, 5 and 3	Doll, 3 and 2	
149	Edward Castagnetto, San Francisco, Calif.					
147	Fred Genick, Detroit, Mich.	Genick, 1 up, 19 holes				
147	Phillip Gordon, Oakland, Calif.					
146	Charles Ferrera, San Francisco, Calif.	Ferrera 2 and 1	Palenapa, 3 and 2			
147	John Hanley, Los Angeles, Calif.					
151	Fred Blanchard, Jr., Alameda, Calif.	Palenapa, 3 and 1				
146	Loio Palenapa, Honolulu, Hawaii					
149	Martin Leptich, Portland, Ore.	Leptich, 2 and 1	Leptich, 1 up	Doll, 6 and 5		
149	Ted Lach, Jr., New Castle, Pa.					
145	Harold Gjolme, Seattle, Wash.	Freer, 1 up, 19 holes				
149	Arthur J. Freer, Sacramento, Calif.					
149	Andrew Szwedko, Pittsburgh, Pa.	Szwedko, 6 and 5	Doll, 3 and 1			
145	Thomas Case, High Point, N.C.					
145	Alvin Puets, Seattle, Wash.	Doll, 2 and 1				
151	Pete Doll, Louisville, Ky.					

*Medalist.

Nineteenth Amateur Public Links Team Championship, Harding Trophy (29 team entries)—Won by Detroit, Mich., team, 435 for 36 holes (Arthur Pomy, 142; James S. Johnson, 146; Edward Furgol, 147); second, Long Beach, Calif., team, 439 (James C. Clark, Jr., 135; Damon Jacobsen, 151; Robert Judson, 153); third, Alameda, Calif., team, 446 (Walter Tebaldi, 145; Earl Fry, Jr., 150; Fred Blanchard, Jr., 151).

1946
TWENTY-FIRST AMATEUR PUBLIC LINKS CHAMPIONSHIP

Held at the Wellshire Golf Course, Denver, Colo., July 22-27.
Yardage—6,590. Par 71. 3,586 Entries, 193 Qualifiers, 192 Starters.

Qualifying Score	1st Round (18 Holes)	2nd Round (18 Holes)	3rd Round (18 Holes)	4th Round (18 Holes)	Semi-Finals **(36 Holes)**	Final Round **(36 Holes)**	
147	Marshall K. Hammond, Spokane, Wash.	Spisso, 2 and 1					
149	Michael D. Spisso, Plainfield, N.J.		Quick, 4 and 3				
149	John Jewett, Gary, Ind.	Quick, 3 and 2					
143	Smiley L. Quick, Los Angeles, Calif.			Quick, 3 and 2			
150	Frank J. Ogrin, Jr., Waukegan, Ill.	Lach, 3 and 2					
150	Theodore H. Lach, New Castle, Pa.		Korns, 2 up				
146	Arthur Armstrong, Honolulu, Hawaii	Korns, 1 up			Quick, 7 and 5		
150	William L. Korns, Salt Lake City, Utah						
151	Albert Clasen, St. Paul, Minn.	A. Clasen, 3 and 2					
149	William J. Moran, Baltimore, Md.		Mazur, 1 up, 20 hls.				
149	James Caspio, Cleveland, Ohio	Mazur, 3 and 1					
148	Peter J. Mazur, Jr., Buffalo, N.Y.			Mazur, 1 up			
136	Robert J. Silvestri, San Francisco, Calif.	Gunkle, 1 up, 19 hls.					
150	James Gunkle, Denver, Colo.		Brenkus, 2 and 1				
151	Charles A. Brenkus, Pittsburgh, Pa.	Brenkus, 2 and 1				Quick, 7 and 5	
148	William J. Podolski, Columbus, Ohio						
152	Bronislaus Kopra, Buffalo, N.Y.	Kopra, 1 up, 20 hls.					
148	Stanley Clasen, St. Paul, Minn.		Kopra, 2 and 1				
140	L.W. Wise, Phoenix, Ariz.	Parent, 3 and 2					
151	Erv Parent, Seattle, Wash.			Gajda, 2 up			
149	Michael Stefanchik, Gary, Ind.	Stefanchik, 5 and 4					
148	Robert C. Clark, St. Paul, Minn.		Gajda, 4 and 3				
145	Dudley Krueger, Austin, Texas	Gajda, 4 and 3			Gajda, 3 and 1		
144	Robert E. Gajda, Detroit, Mich.						
149	John F. Nowack, Cleveland, Ohio	Nowack, 1 up					
152	Stanley J. Serafin, Chicago, Ill.		Evans, 6 and 4				
151	Ralph J. Evans, Santa Monica, Calif.	Evans, 1 up					
151	Clarence Freeman, Colorado Springs, Colo.			Evans, 2 and 1			
151	Rudolph Horvath, Windsor, Ont., Canada	Horvath, 1 up					
148	Clarence E. Alexander, Raleigh, N.C.		Horvath, 2 up				
137	Leo Roy Gann, Tulsa, Okla.	Welch, 1 up, 19 hls.					
145	William M. Welch, Spokane, Wash.						Smiley L. Quick, 3 and 2
144	Arthur St. John, Tulsa, Okla.	Verge, 6 and 4					
145	John W. Verge, Pasadena, Calif.		Whitney, 2 and 1				
148	Neil Whitney, Los Angeles, Calif.	Whitney, 3 and 2					
144	Robert A. Conliff, Jr., Oklahoma City, Okla.			Whitney, 2 and 1			
150	William Ogden, Jr., Sacramento, Calif.	T. Smith, 2 and 1					
142	Talbert Smith, Alameda, Calif.		Chiaverini, 4 and 2				
152	Valentino F. Chiaverini, Toledo, Ohio	Chiaverini, 2 and 1			Stafford, 5 and 4		
148	Warren Riepen, St. Joseph, Mo.						
151	Eugene Beister, Omaha, Neb.	Daniel, 4 and 3					
146	Robert Daniel, San Francisco, Calif.		Daniel, 3 and 2				
142	Carl Dezern, Durham, N.C.	Dezern, 3 and 1					
150	Jack E. Zimmerman, Dayton, Ohio			Stafford, 2 and 1			
151	Dale Smith, Ames, Iowa	Myers, 2 up					
152	Tuffy Myers, Wichita, Kans.		Stafford, 6 and 5				
147	Louis Stafford, Portland, Ore.	Stafford, 3 and 2				Stafford, 4 and 3	
150	Thomas Reaves, Raleigh, N.C.						
151	Clarence Emery, Salt Lake City, Utah	Emery, 2 and 1					
152	Sylvester Ferrera, San Francisco, Calif.		Doll, 4 and 2				
147	William E. Doll, Louisville, Ky.	Doll, 2 and 1					
151	John Kamper, San Francisco, Calif.			Doll, 1 up, 19 hls.			
147	Robert Harris, San Jose, Calif.	Vicini, 1 up					
150	Dante C. Vicini, Ottawa, Ill.		Vicini, 2 and 1				
141	Ralph Hall, Oakland, Calif.	Koennecker, 1 up			Doll, 4 and 3		
140	Jack L. Koennecker, Denver, Colo.						
150	James Shriver, Seattle, Wash.	Vranesic, 4 and 3					
145	Ralph J. Vranesic, Denver, Colo.		Vranesic, 5 and 4				
143	Marshall Holt, Long Beach, Calif.	Holt, 2 and 1					
134*	James C. Clark, Jr., Long Beach, Calif.			Vranesic, 2 and 1			
148	Raymond F. Heins, Baltimore, Md.	Gilliam, 6 and 5					
146	Walter J. Gilliam, Jr., Burlingame, Calif.		Hanson, 1 up				
149	Einar H. Hanson, San Francisco, Calif.	Hanson, 5 and 4					
150	Ralph D. Porter, Pasadena, Calif.						

*Medalist.

Twentieth Amateur Public Links Team Championship. Harding Trophy (33 team entries)—won by Long Beach, Calif., team, 431 for 36 holes (James C. Clark, Jr., 134; Marshall Holt, 143; Oscar W. Hoberg, 154); second, Tulsa, Okla., team, 433 (Leo Roy Gann, 137; Arthur St. John, 144; Bernard Rauch, 152); third, San Francisco, Calif., team, 441 (Robert J. Silvestri, 136; Elmar R. Hanson, 149; Fred Jordan, 156).

TWENTY-SECOND AMATEUR PUBLIC LINKS CHAMPIONSHIP

Held at the Meadowbrook Golf Course, Minneapolis, Minn., July 21-26.
Yardage—6,474. Par 72. 2,633 Entries, 180 Qualifiers, 179 Starters.

Qualifying Score	1st Round (18 Holes)	2nd Round (18 Holes)	3rd Round (18 Holes)	4th Round (18 Holes)	Semi-Finals (36 Holes)	Final Round (36 Holes)	
150	Jack Kerns, Denver, Colo.	Strackbein, 6 and 4	Ervasti, 1 up, 20 hls.	Ervasti, 2 and 1	Crossley, 2 and 1	Crossley, 4 and 3	Wilfred Crossley, 6 and 5
152	Peter Strackbein, Long Beach, Calif.						
150	Edward W. Ervasti, Detroit, Mich.	Ervasti, 6 and 5					
151	Jack Gargan, Los Angeles, Calif.						
148	Rudolph Horvath, Windsor, Ont., Canada	Horvath, 6 and 4	Silvestri, 3 and 2				
151	Robert W. Lichtenwalter, Erie, Pa.						
148	Claire Emery, Salt Lake City, Utah	Silvestri, 1 up, 21 hls.					
144	Robert J. Silvestri, San Francisco, Calif.						
144	John R. Bloyer, St. Paul, Minn.	Bloyer, 4 and 3	Clasen, 2 and 1	Crossley, 2 and 1			
146	Gene Towry, Dallas, Texas						
143	Walter R. Browne, Atlanta, Ga.	Clasen, 7 and 6					
150	Albert Clasen, St. Paul, Minn.						
146	Paul Gore, Denver, Colo.	Kay, 2 and 1	Crossley, 5 and 4				
151	Robert Kay, Toledo, Ohio						
139*	Wilfred Crossley, Atlanta, Ga.	Crossley, 4 and 3					
150	Louis J. Esposito, Chicago, Ill.						
152	Ralph J. Vranesic, Denver, Colo.	Vranesic, 2 and 1	Vranesic, 3 and 2	Vranesic, 2 and 1	Dostert, 2 and 1		
150	John M. Maughan, San Francisco, Calif.						
144	Patrick J. Boyle, Eveleth, Minn.	Mikrut, 4 and 3					
145	John P. Mikrut, New York, N.Y.						
148	Robert L. Benson, St. Paul, Minn.	Benson, 2 and 1	Nounnan, 2 and 1				
148	William R. Collins, Baltimore, Md.						
146	Jack L. Nounnan, Los Angeles, Calif.	Nounnan, 1 up, 22 holes					
152	Carl I. Spain, Memphis, Tenn.						
146	Donald J. Dostert, St. Paul, Minn.	Dostert, 1 up	Dostert, 1 up	Dostert, 3 and 1			
152	Howard A. Johnson, St. Paul, Minn.						
150	Albert Nelson, Sacramento, Calif.	Major, 3 and 2					
149	Edward Major, Los Angeles, Calif.						
151	Donald Meneghin, Cleveland, Ohio	Barnes, 1 up	Barnes, 4 and 3				
149	Charles W. Barnes, Atlanta, Ga.						
151	Nathan Grimes, Denver, Colo.	Grimes, 4 and 3					
152	Howard Pousette, St. Paul, Minn.						
148	Mike Stefanchik, Gary, Ind.	Stefanchik, 6 and 5	Beck, 1 up, 19 hls.	Beck, 2 and 1	Beck, 5 and 4	Beck, 1 up, 38 hls.	
148	Frank Jurasek, Rockford, Ill.						
145	William L. Korns, Salt Lake City, Utah	Beck, 4 and 3					
143	Avery Beck, Raleigh, N.C.						
143	Thomas Suesens, Vancouver, Wash.	Caso, 2 up	Caso, 1 up				
150	Moreno C. Caso, Seattle, Wash.						
152	Arthur Jennemann, St. Louis, Mo.	Jennemann, 1 up, 19 hls.					
149	Peter Schefcick, San Francisco, Calif.						
152	Robert W. Duden, Portland, Ore.	Duden, 1 up	Gordon, 1 up	Gordon, 2 and 1			
149	Dudley Krueger, Austin, Texas						
149	Phillip Gordon, Oakland, Calif.	Gordon, 2 and 1					
150	James A. Shriver, Seattle, Wash.						
149	Jack L. Koennecker, Denver, Colo.	Koennecker, 3 and 2	Hanson, 2 and 1				
151	Dominick Morano, Belleville, N.J.						
148	Clinton Sublett, Louisville, Ky.	Hanson, 1 up					
150	Einar H. Hanson, San Francisco, Calif.						
147	Benjamin G. Hughes, Portland, Ore.	Hughes, 1 up	Hughes, 2 and 1	Hughes, 4 and 3	Hughes, 5 and 3		
150	Reinhard S. Jensen, Jr., Portland, Ore.						
144	Warren G. Campbell, Seattle, Wash.	Marlowe, 1 up, 20 hls.					
143	Thomas A. Marlowe, Portland, Ore.						
151	Clarence R. Smith, San Diego, Calif.	Richards, 2 up	Card, 2 and 1				
147	Ted Richards, Jr., Long Beach, Calif.						
151	Walter Wojda, Toledo, Ohio	Card, 1 up					
143	Thomas R. Card, Raleigh, N.C.						
149	Peter J. Mazur, Jr., Buffalo, N.Y.	Stafford, 6 and 5	McKain, 1 up, 22 hls.	Littleton, 4 and 3			
149	Louis Stafford, Portland, Ore.						
150	Charles Rishworth, Seattle, Wash.	McKain, 5 and 3					
150	Shedric E. McKain, Memphis, Tenn.						
148	Clare H. Swonson, Salt Lake City, Utah	Littleton, 1 up	Littleton, 1 up				
147	Alfred Littleton, Wichita, Kans.						
148	Andrew J. Oliveri, Washington, D.C.	Lach, 4 and 3					
151	Ted Lach, New Castle, Pa.						

*Medalist.

Twenty-First Amateur Public Links Team Championship, Harding Trophy (23 team entries)—Won by Atlanta, Ga., team, 431 for 36 holes (Wilfred Crossley, 139; Walter R. Browne, 143; Charles W. Barnes, 149); second, St. Paul, Minn., team, 440 (John R. Bloyer, 144; Donald J. Dostert, 146; Albert Clasen, 150); third, tie at 444 between San Francisco, Calif., team (Robert J. Silvestri, 144; John M. Maugham, 150; Einar H. Hanson, 150) and Seattle, Wash., team (Warren G. Campbell, 144; Moreno C. Caso, 150; Charles Rishworth, 150).

AMATEUR PUBLIC LINKS CHAMPIONS

CARL F. KAUFFMANN
1927-28-29

WILLIAM A. WRIGHT
1959

GENE ANDREWS
1954

UPPER

1948
TWENTY-THIRD AMATEUR PUBLIC LINKS CHAMPIONSHIP

Held at the North Fulton Park Golf Course, Atlanta, Ga., July 19-24.
Yardage–6,762. Par 71. 2,728 Entries, 210 Qualifiers, 210 Starters.
Championship entirely at match play.
FINAL ROUND (36 holes)–Michael R. Ferentz defeated Ben G. Hughes, 2 up and 1 to play.

FIRST QUARTER

1st Round (18 Holes)	2nd Round (18 Holes)	3rd Round (18 Holes)	4th Round (18 Holes)	5th Round (18 Holes)	6th Round (18 Holes)	
BYE–J. Cliff Leonhardt, Louisville, Ky.	Leonhardt					
BYE–Edward Hyde, Indianapolis, Ind.	Hyde	Hyde, 2 up				
BYE–Michael Graniteo, Cleveland, Ohio	Graniteo		Kay, 5 and 4			
BYE–Oliver Kay, Toledo, Ohio	Kay	Kay, 1 up				
BYE–Charles Hess, Indianapolis, Ind.	Hess			Kay, 2 and 1		
BYE–Peter P. DeCaprio, New York, N.Y.	DeCaprio	Hess, 1 up, 20 hls.				
BYE–Arnold C. Koehler, Indianapolis, Ind.	Koehler		Dennis, 2 and 1			
BYE–Dave Dennis, Independence, Kans.	Dennis	Dennis, 1 up, 20 hls.				
BYE–Herman H. Nitsch, Houston, Texas	Nitsch				Kay, 3 and 2	
BYE–James Dorr, Birmingham, Ala.	Dorr	Nitsch, 4 and 3				
BYE–James G. Iavan, Cleveland, Ohio	Iavan		Martino, 1 up, 19 hls.			
BYE–Patrick V. Martino, Washington, D.C.	Martino	Martino, 4 and 3				
Jack C. Smith, Des Moines, Iowa	Bowyer, 5 and 4			Karry, 3 and 2		
Elwin E. Bowyer, Vancouver, Wash.		Karry, 1 up				
Herman Wyman, St. Louis, Mo.	Karry, 2 up					
Rudolph L. Karry, Philadelphia, Pa.			Karry, 1 up			
Paul E. Mullins, Atlanta, Ga.	Mullins, 4 and 3					
Jakie C. Wright, Oklahoma City, Okla.		Smith, 1 up, 20 hls.				
Palmer A. Smith, Seattle, Wash.	Smith, 2 and 1					
Lawrence R. Robertson, Jacksonville, Fla.						
John Platt, Peoria, Ill.	Skowran, 3 and 2					Kay, 2 and 1
Michael Skowran, Pittsburgh, Pa.		M. Szwedko, 3 and 2				
Michael Szwedko, Sharpsburg, Pa.	M. Szwedko, 2 and 1					
Louis J. Esposito, Franklin Park, Ill.			M. Szwedko, 2 and 1			
Louis W. McLennan, Atlanta, Ga.	McLennan, 2 and 1					
Robert R. Ludlow, Indianapolis, Ind.		D. Vicini, 4 and 3				
Dante Vicini, Ottawa, Ill.	D. Vicini, 1 up			Crossley, 5 and 4		
Oliver C. Sleppy, Los Angeles, Calif.						
Wilfred Crossley, Brooklyn, N.Y.	Crossley, 4 and 3					
Alfred Serian, Troy, N.Y.		Crossley, 1 up				
James Levenhagen, West Allis, Wis.	Levenhagen, 4 and 2					
Leon Butler, Atlanta, Ga.			Crossley, 3 and 2			
Rudolph Supan, Cleveland, Ohio	Michalek, 6 and 5					
Frank Michalek, Baltimore, Md.		Michalek, 3 and 2				
John Daniel, Spokane, Wash.	Collins, 2 and 1				Schneider, 1 up	
William Collins, Baltimore, Md.						
Warren G. Campbell, Seattle, Wash.	Schneider, 4 and 2					
Ralph F. Schneider, Shaker Heights, Ohio		Schneider, 3 and 2				
Thomas Bujeker, South Bend, Ind.	Bujeker, 5 and 4					
Arnold Gray, Jackson Heights, N.Y.			Schneider, 2 and 1			
Robert W. Duden, Portland, Ore.	Foley, 1 up, 19 hls.					
John Foley, Seattle, Wash.		Foley, 2 and 1				
John M. Maughan, San Francisco, Calif.	Maughan, 1 up, 23 hls.			Schneider, 1 up		
Kermit Hagar, Oklahoma City, Okla.						
Jay Law, Detroit, Mich.	Law, 2 and 1					
Paul Gore, Denver, Colo.		Nichols, 4 and 3				
Ray Dznowski, San Diego, Calif.	Nichols, 1 up					
Clayton Nichols, Indianapolis, Ind.			Nowack, 2 and 1			
Melwyn L. Mathis, Dallas, Texas	Nowack, 4 and 3					
John F. Nowack, Cleveland, Ohio		Nowack, 2 up				
E.A. St. John, Tulsa, Okla.	St. John, 1 up, 19 hls.					
Joseph Carlone, South Euclid, Ohio						

SEMI-FINAL ROUND (36 holes)–Ben G. Hughes defeated Oliver Kay, 4 up and 3 to play.

HALF

SECOND QUARTER

6th Round (18 Holes)	5th Round (18 Holes)		4th Round (18 Holes)	3rd Round (18 Holes)	2nd Round (18 Holes)	1st Round (18 Holes)
					Gentle	BYE—Columbus Gentle, Atlanta, Ga.
				Waryan, 5 and 4	Waryan	BYE—William Waryan, Minneapolis, Minn.
			Waryan, 1 up, 19 hls.		Kile	BYE—James E. Kile, Atlanta, Ga.
				Kile, 4 and 3	Borson	BYE—Michael Borson, Anderson, Ind.
		Waryan, 4 and 2			Lyons	BYE—Robert B. Lyons, Spokane, Wash.
				Lyons, 5 and 4	Kopra	BYE—Bronislaus Kopra, Buffalo, N.Y.
			Lyons, 2 and 1		Neveraskas	BYE—Al Neveraskas, Castle Shannon, Pa.
				Neveraskas, 1 up	Byron	BYE—Thomas Byron, Cincinnati, Ohio
	Trullinger, 2 and 1				Olson	BYE—Maurice L. Olson, Chicago, Ill.
				Olson, 2 and 1	Verge	BYE—John W. Verge, Los Angeles, Calif.
			A. Clasen, 6 and 5		Beck	BYE—Avery Beck, Raleigh, N.C.
				A. Clasen, 2 and 1	Clasen, 4 and 3	Albert Clasen, St. Paul, Minn. Michael A. DiCesaro, Houston, Texas
		Trullinger, 3 and 2			Taylor, 1 up, 21 hls.	Donald C. Taylor, Seattle, Wash. Capt. Walter R. Browne, Decatur, Ga.
				Taylor, 4 and 2	Alexander, 3 and 1	Clarence Alexander, Raleigh, N.C. Andrew Monroe, Louisville, Ky.
			Trullinger, 4 and 2		Sain, 2 and 1	W. Welbourne Jameson, Jr., Chattanooga, Tenn. Robert Sain, Nashville, Tenn.
				Trullinger, 6 and 5	Trullinger, 2 and 1	Raymond B. Doyel, St. Louis, Mo. Theodore C. Trullinger, Philadelphia, Pa.
Hughes, 6 and 4					Seaholm, 5 and 4	Dan Stovall, Gainesville, Ga. George L. Seaholm, Jr., Austin, Texas
				Seaholm, 3 and 2	Carson, 1 up	James Schatz, Stillwater, Okla. John Carson, Atlanta, Ga.
			McEntire, 3 and 2		McEntire, 5 and 3	Edward Golen, Buffalo, N.Y. Clyde McEntire, Jr., Noblesville, Ind.
				McEntire, 4 and 3	Nelson, 1 up, 19 hls.	George W. Brownlow, Jr., Winston-Salem, N.C. Al Nelson, Sacramento, Calif.
		Hughes, 2 and 1			Kinoshita, 6 and 5	Wayne C. Swanfelt, Pontiac, Mich. Sadaji Kinoshita, Honolulu, Hawaii
				Kinoshita, 8 and 7	Hollingsworth 1 up, 20 hls.	Victor T. DiSantis, Erie, Pa. Oliver Hollingsworth, Indianapolis, Ind.
			Hughes, 5 and 4		Hughes, 4 and 3	Ben G. Hughes, Portland, Ore. William C. McEwen, Jacksonville, Fla.
				Hughes, 5 and 4	York, 5 and 3	James J. Brink, Jr., Kansas City, Kans. Robert York, Nashville, Tenn.
	Hughes, 2 up				Gerdes, 1 up, 20 hls.	H. R. Ozmer, Atlanta, Ga. Byron W. Gerdes, Dayton, Ohio
				Gerdes, 1 up	Chaddock, 1 up	Norando Nannini, Highwood, Ill. William Chaddock, Inglewood, Calif.
			Turrentine, 4 and 2		Turrentine, 7 and 5	Nicholas J. Dinardo, Miami, Fla. Aubrey D. Turrentine, Durham, N.C.
				Turrentine, 3 and 1	DeYoung, 2 and 1	Wesley DeYoung, Chicago, Ill. Ted Lach, New Castle, Pa.
		Turrentine, 4 and 3			Belton, 3 and 2	Joseph F. Belton, Jr., Dayton, Ohio Arthur C. Moore, Memphis, Tenn.
				Belton, 2 and 1	Evans, 2 and 1	Jack Evans, Phoenix, Ariz. Frank Jurasek, Rockford, Ill.
			Belton, 3 and 2		C. Dorr, 2 up	Harold Sewell, Tulsa, Okla. Carl H. Dorr, Birmingham, Ala.
				Taylor, 2 and 1	Taylor, 2 and 1	Percy G. Taylor, Santa Monica, Calif. Leonard Egbert, Los Angeles, Calif.

THIRD QUARTER

1st Round (18 Holes)	2nd Round (18 Holes)	3rd Round (18 Holes)	4th Round (18 Holes)	5th Round (18 Holes)	6th Round (18 Holes)	
BYE—Edson S. Cook, Memphis, Tenn.	Cook					
BYE—DeLong Rice, III, Memphis, Tenn.	Rice	Cook, 2 and 1				
BYE—Robert S. Wise, Dayton, Ohio	Wise		N. Campagni, 2 and 1			
BYE—Nello Campagni, Highwood, Ill.	Campagni	N. Campagni, 2 and 1				
BYE—Kenneth Oglesby, Tucson, Ariz.	Oglesby			Campagni, 2 and 1		
BYE—Edmund Janiak, Syracuse, N.Y.	Janiak	Oglesby, 1 up				
BYE—John Marques, Los Angeles, Calif.	Marques		Oglesby, 4 and 3			
BYE—Nicholas Garbacz, Jr., South Bend, Ind.	N. Garbacz	N. Garbacz, 2 up			North, 4 and 2	
BYE—Cotton Rockholt, Memphis, Tenn.	Rockholt					
BYE—Arthur Todd, Columbus, Ohio	Todd	Todd, 4 and 3				
BYE—Roy V. McIntire, Peoria, Ill.	McIntire		McIntire, 3 and 2			
BYE—Neil Whitney, Inglewood, Calif.	Whitney	McIntire, 1 up		North, 3 and 2		
M. Keith Downs, Phoenix, Ariz. Andrew J. Paul, Peoria, Ill.	Paul, 6 and 5	North, 1 up, 19 hls.				
James Williams, Atlanta, Ga. Louis North, Denver, Colo.	North, 3 and 1		North, 2 and 1			
M/Sgt. Charles Earle, Minneapolis, Minn. Henry Wade, Atlanta, Ga.	Wade, 3 and 2	Wade, 1 up, 19 hls.				
William E. Jones, Nashville, Tenn. **Domenic K. Strafaci, Brooklyn, N.Y.**	Jones, 4 and 3					Ferentz, 3 and 2
Lido L. Landi, Sharp Park, Calif. Harry Gurley, Denver, Colo.	Landi, 1 up, 20 hls.	Landi, 1 up, 20 hls.				
Gene F. Ring, Minneapolis, Minn. George L. Hinueber, St. Paul, Minn.	Hinueber, 7 and 5		Landi, 1 up, 19 hls.			
Peter Hahalvak, Pittsburgh, Pa. Edwin F. Bohardt, Dayton, Ohio	Bohardt, 3 and 2	Bohardt, 1 up				
John E. Blesi, Dayton, Ohio Gene Retzer, Denver, Colo.	Retzer, 3 and 2			Landi, 3 and 2		
Gerald A. Burns, Minneapolis, Minn. John Wells, Portland, Ore.	Burns, 1 up	Burns, 5 and 4				
Eugene A. Peterson, Rockford, Ill. Max Schwartz, Memphis, Tenn.	Peterson, 1 up		Burns, 5 and 4			
James R. Spencer, St. Louis, Mo. Norman S. Miller, Jacksonville, Fla.	Miller, 3 and 2	Miller, 2 and 1				
Warren L. Riepen, St. Joseph, Mo. Paul Wohlford, Milwaukee, Wis.	Riepen, 5 and 4				Ferentz, 1 up, 21 hls.	
Robert Silvestri, San Francisco, Calif. Richard Montney, Detroit, Mich.	Silvestri, 5 and 3	Silvestri, 1 up, 19 hls.				
James W. Stamps, College Park, Ga. Walter Maykut, Plymouth Meeting, Pa.	Maykut, 4 and 3		Silvestri, 2 and 1			
Stanley L. Clasen, St. Paul, Minn. Joseph Marks, Dayton, Ohio	Marks, 2 and 1	Gargan, 4 and 3				
Jack Gargan, Hollywood, Calif. Valentino Chiaverini, Walbridge, Ohio	Gargan, 1 up, 19 hls.			Ferentz, 3 and 2		
Arthur Jennemann, St. Louis, Mo. Fred Vicini, Ottawa, Ill.	F. Vicini, 1 up, 19 hls.	Ferentz, 4 and 2				
Michael R. Ferentz, Long Beach, Calif. August Tamburrino, Chicago, Ill.	Ferentz, 4 and 3		Ferentz, 2 and 1			
Julio Campagni, Highwood, Ill. Jack A. Lemcke, Milwaukee, Wis.	Campagni, 1 up	A. Szwedko, 1 up, 20 hls.				
Andrew Szwedko, Sharpsburg, Pa. Shedric McKain, Memphis, Tenn.	A. Szwedko, 2 and 1					

SEMI-FINAL ROUND (36 holes)—Michael R. Ferentz defeated Charles W. Barnes, 2 up and 1 to play.

Twenty-Second Amateur Public Links Team Championship, Harding Trophy, won by Raleigh, N.C. team, 223 for 18 holes (Clarence Alexander, 73; Aubry D. Turrentine, 74; Avery Beck, 76); second, Pittsburgh, Pa., team, 227 (Ted Lach, 74; Michael Szewedko, 75; Andrew Szwedko, 78); third, Atlanta, Ga., team, 228 (Charles W. Barnes, 73; James E. Kile, 74; James Stamps, 81).

CHAMPIONSHIP—Continued

HALF

FOURTH QUARTER

6th Round (18 Holes)	5th Round (18 Holes)		4th Round (18 Holes)	3rd Round (18 Holes)	2nd Round (18 Holes)	1st Round (18 Holes)
Barnes, 1 up	Barnes, 2 and 1	Pasikowski, 2 and 1	Pasikowski, 5 and 4	Levenhagen, 2 and 1	Levenhagen	BYE—Ted Levenhagen, Milwaukee, Wis.
					Buchen	BYE—Russell Buchen, Peoria, Ill.
				Pasikowski, 5 and 3	Pasikowski	BYE—John Pasikowski, Sharpsburg, Pa.
					Podolski	BYE—William Podolski, Columbus, Ohio
			Pollack, 6 and 4	Ickes, 1 up	Ickes	BYE—William Ickes, Detroit, Mich.
					Kamman	BYE—Joseph R. Kamman, Buffalo, N.Y.
				Pollack, 1 up	Pollack	BYE—Michael Pollack, Indianapolis, Ind.
					Andrews	BYE—John Andrews, Nashville, Tenn.
		Barnes, 2 up	Robbins, 1 up	McCool, 1 up, 19 hls.	Stafford	BYE—Louis Stafford, Portland, Ore.
					McCool	BYE—William M. McCool, San Francisco, Calif.
				Robbins, 2 and 1	Robbins	BYE—Hillman Robbins, Jr., Memphis, Tenn.
					Deverant, 3 and 2	Alexander Garbacz, South Bend, Ind. Michael Deverant, Glenside, Pa.
			Barnes, 1 up	Barnes, 3 and 2	Barnes, 7 and 5	Charles W. Barnes, Atlanta, Ga. Milton Frank, St. Louis, Mo.
					Hall, 2 and 1	Peter J. Mazur, Jr., North Tonawanda, N.Y. Ralph Hall, Oakland, Calif.
				Gustafson, 3 and 2	Gustafson, 7 and 5	John J. Biernat, Minneapolis, Minn. Alvin E. Gustafson, Spokane, Wash.
					Russell, 1 up, 19 hls.	Jack C. Russell, Jr., Memphis, Tenn. Robert C. Clark, St. Paul, Minn.
	Makaiwa, 4 and 3	Makaiwa, 3 and 2	Grassi, 4 and 3	Grassi, 4 and 3	Grassi, 1 up	Clinton Sublett, Louisville, Ky. Theodore Grassi, Erie, Pa.
					Jungen, 6 and 5	Richard Jungen, Rockford, Ill. Henry O. DeFries, Baltimore, Md.
				Finnessy, 3 and 1	Finnessy, 4 and 2	Edward Finnessy, Baltimore, Md. Robert J. McKenna, Brighton, Mass.
					McClain, 4 and 3	Walter R. McClain, Cleveland, Ohio Jack Rye, Birmingham, Ala.
			Makaiwa, 7 and 6	Kennedy, 1 up	Kennedy, 2 and 1	James Kennedy, San Francisco, Calif. Evan James Brown, St. Claire Shores, Mich.
					Cole, 4 and 3	Willard Nesmith, Houston, Texas William M. Cole, Baltimore, Md.
				Makaiwa, 8 and 7	Makaiwa, 3 and 2	Charles K. Makaiwa, Honolulu, Hawaii Earl C. Maisevich, Detroit, Mich.
					Ruck, 1 up, 19 hls.	Harold A. Saunders, Denver, Colo. Leonard Ruck, Toledo, Ohio
		Age, 2 and 1	Age, 1 up	Age, 2 and 1	Age, 2 and 1	Harry LeBeau, St. Louis, Mo. S/Sgt. Alton Age, Louisville, Ky.
					Penberthy, 2 and 1	Archie Gonzales, New Orleans, La. Jack R. Penberthy, St. Louis, Mo.
				Szustak, 3 and 2	Szustak, 3 and 2	Charles L. Sims, Kansas City, Kans. William Szustak, Buffalo, N.Y.
					Wood, 4 and 3	James E. Lemons, Chattanooga, Tenn. Seward A. Wood, Flushing, N.Y.
			Seeger, 2 and 1	Seeger, 2 up	Boyer, 5 and 3	John Garbacz, South Bend, Ind. Talbot E. Boyer, Portland, Ore.
					Seeger, 3 and 2	Robert L. Kurz, Jacksonville, Fla. Herbert Seeger, Peoria, Ill.
				O'Brien, 3 and 2	Musico, 2 and 1	Samuel Musico, Carnegie, Pa. Verne Callison, Sacramento, Calif.
					O'Brien, 2 and 1	Selden Fant, Oklahoma City, Okla. Wilford M. O'Brien, Seattle, Wash.

1949
TWENTY-FOURTH AMATEUR PUBLIC LINKS CHAMPIONSHIP

Held at the Rancho Golf Course, Los Angeles, Calif., July 11-16.
Yardage—6,805. Par 71. 2,483 Entries, 210 Qualifiers, 209 Starters.
Championship entirely at match play.

FINAL ROUND (36 Holes)—Kenneth J. Towns defeated William E. Betger, 5 up and 4 to play.

UPPER

FIRST QUARTER

1st Round (18 Holes)	2nd Round (18 Holes)	3rd Round (18 Holes)	4th Round (18 Holes)	5th Round (18 Holes)	6th Round (18 Holes)	
Columbus Gentle, Atlanta, Ga.	Bloyer,					
John R. Bloyer, St. Paul, Minn.	1 up, 19 hls.	Biernat,				
Walter Garcia, Albuquerque, N.M.	Biernat,	1 up				
John J. Biernat, Minneapolis, Minn.	2 and 1		Biernat,			
BYE—James G. Terry, Nashville, Tenn.	Terry		5 and 3			
		Barek,				
Joe Moore, Jr., San Antonio, Texas	Barck,	1 up, 20 hls.		Cooney, 2 and 1		
Norman Barck, Gardena, Calif.	5 and 4					
Richard F. Cooney, Portland, Ore.	Cooney,					
Arthur Moore, Memphis, Tenn.	2 and 1	Cooney,				
BYE—Julian G. Dowling, Jr., Jacksonville, Fla.	Dowling	5 and 4				
			Cooney,			
Richard L. Yost, Portland, Ore.	Yost,		3 and 1			
Jack R. Penberthy, St. Louis, Mo.	6 and 4	Yost,				
BYE—Libaro Giacomini, Ottawa, Ill.	Giacomini	8 and 7			Kletcke, 1 up	
Sylvester Ferrera, San Francisco, Calif.	Ferrera,					
Joseph M. Gambatese, Arlington, Va.	4 and 2	Ferrera,				
Michael DiCesaro, Houston, Texas	DiCesaro,	disqual.				
Ted Grassi, Erie, Pa.	disqual.		Ferrera,			
BYE—Hans R. Turner, Seattle, Wash.	Turner		2 and 1			
		Turner,				
James S. Rowan, Collegeville, Pa.	Verville,	3 and 2		Kletcke, 1 up, 19 hls.		
Gordon Verville, Detroit, Mich.	4 and 3					
Ted Lach, Jr., Indianapolis, Ind.	Lach,					
Bill Johnston, Salt Lake City, Utah	1 up, 20 hls.	Lach,				
BYE—Charles K. Makaiwa, Honolulu, Hawaii	Makaiwa	3 and 2				
			Kletcke,			
Eddie Kletcke, Chicago, Ill.	**Kletcke,**		3 and 2			
Sam Stassi, Porterville, Calif.	**default**	Kletcke,				
Eddie Major, Los Angeles, Calif.	Major,	5 and 4				
Howard Derrick, Chattanooga, Tenn.	1 up					
BYE—Bernard Kane, Los Angeles, Calif.	Kane					Towns, 1 up
		Maughan,				
John M. Maughan, San Francisco, Calif.	Maughan,	7 and 6				
Jack M. Lochhead, Salt Lake City, Utah	3 and 2		Maughan,			
BYE—William J. Donovan, Los Angeles, Calif.	Donovan		1 up, 20 hls.			
		Donovan,				
Dirk Prather, Phoenix, Ariz.	Prather,	3 and 2		Towns, 2 up		
Ralph Hall, Oakland, Calif.	4 and 3					
George F. Walter, Baltimore, Md.	Walter,					
Omer S. Doll, Louisville, Ky.	1 up	Caspio,				
BYE—James Caspio, Cleveland, Ohio	Caspio	1 up				
			Towns,			
James T. O'Neill, Larchmont, N.Y.	O'Neill,		3 and 2			
Eddie Wallace, San Fernando, Calif.	2 up	Towns,				
Bruce Evans, Memphis, Tenn.	Towns,	6 and 5			Towns, 6 and 5	
Kenneth J. Towns, San Francisco, Calif.	4 and 3					
BYE—Robert Geisler, Toledo, Ohio	Geisler					
		Geisler,				
Edwin Bohardt, Dayton, Ohio	Lemcke,	5 and 4				
Jack A. Lemcke, South Milwaukee, Wis.	2 and 1		Geisler,			
BYE—Percy Taylor, Santa Monica, Calif.	Taylor		1 up, 20 hls.			
		Taylor,				
Milton N. Garrett, Jr., Louisville, Ky.	Nichols,	3 and 2		Vranesic, 1 up		
Clayton Nichols, Indianapolis, Ind.	4 and 3					
BYE—Gomer Sims, Long Beach, Calif.	Sims					
		Gildemeister,				
George Puetz, Seattle, Wash.	Gildemeister,	5 and 3				
Victor O. Gildemeister, Portland, Ore.	5 and 4		Vranesic,			
BYE—Ben Trunk, Peoria, Ill.	Trunk		6 and 5			
		Vranesic,				
Jack Martin, Oklahoma City, Okla.	Vranesic,	2 and 1				
Ralph J. Vranesic, Denver, Colo.	4 and 2					

SEMI-FINAL ROUND (36 holes)—Kenneth J. Towns defeated Philip J. Kunkel, 1 up

HALF

SECOND QUARTER

6th Round (18 Holes)	5th Round (18 Holes)		4th Round (18 Holes)	3rd Round (18 Holes)	2nd Round (18 Holes)	1st Round (18 Holes)
					Baziluk, 4 and 3	Michael Baziluk, Schenectady, N.Y.
				Hubert, 3 and 2		E.A. St. John, Tulsa, Okla.
					Hubert, 6 and 5	Ralph C. Ghioto, Jacksonville, Fla.
			Hubert, 3 and 2			Ferdnand Hubert, Pekin, Ill.
					White	BYE–Vincent White, Chicago, Ill.
				White, 2 and 1	Haag, 2 and 1	Bobby Haag, Buechel, Ky.
						Carl Funseth, Spokane, Wash.
		MacDonald, 2 and 1			MacDonald, 5 and 3	Paul MacDonald, Renton, Wash.
				MacDonald, 3 and 2		Richard W. Copeland, St. Paul, Minn.
					Falls	BYE–Miles Falls, Detroit, Mich.
			MacDonald, 2 and 1		Rutkiewicz, 6 and 5	Ben G. Hughes, Portland, Ore.
				Bouchey, 1 up, 19 hls.		Frank Rutkiewicz, Honolulu, Hawaii
					Bouchey	BYE–Larry Bouchey, Los Angeles, Calif.
	MacDonald, 1 up				Hannan, 1 up, 20 hls.	Carl Hannan, Los Angeles, Calif.
				McGivern, 2 up		W. H. Steritz, Jr., Los Angeles, Calif.
					McGivern, 2 and 1	Jack McGivern, Detroit, Mich.
			McGivern, 4 and 2			Menter G. Walker, Jr., Birmingham, Ala.
					Hagen	BYE–Glenn Hagen, St. Louis, Mo.
				Alford, 6 and 5	Alford, 2 and 1	Roger T. McManus, Raleigh, N.C.
						Kyle Alford, Beaumont, Texas
		Carson, 3 and 2			Carson, 2 and 1	Allen Thum, Phoenix, Ariz.
				Carson, 3 and 2		Johnny R. Carson, Atlanta, Ga.
					San Filippo	BYE–Joseph San Filippo, Cleveland, Ohio
			Carson, 3 and 2		Bissett, 3 and 2	Robert F. Bissett, Santa Ana, Calif.
				Stanovich, 3 and 2		Jack Bielak, Milwaukee, Wis.
Kunkel, 3 and 2					Stanovich, 4 and 3	Martin Stanovich, San Francisco, Calif.
						Shedric E. McKain, Memphis, Tenn.
				Pfluger, 1 up, 20 hls.	Nelson	BYE–Albert Nelson, Sacramento, Calif.
			Gordon, 4 and 3		Pfluger, 2 up	Sukeyoshi Kushi, Honolulu, Hawaii
						Marion H. Pfluger, Austin, Texas
				Gordon, 1 up	Gordon	BYE–Philip E. Gordon, Oakland, Calif.
					Andrews, 4 and 3	John Charles Curtin, Washington, D.C.
		Gordon, 1 up, 19 hls.				John Andrews, Nashville, Tenn.
				M. Szwedko, 1 up	Spencer, 5 and 3	James R. Spencer, St. Louis, Mo.
						Donald C. Taylor, Seattle, Wash.
			Langford, 1 up, 20 hls.		M. Szwedko, 2 and 1	Michael Szwedko, Sharpsburg, Pa.
						Peter R. Flannigan, Goshen, Ind.
				Langford, 1 up, 20 hls.	Wade	BYE–Howard M. Wade, Freeport, Texas
	Kunkel, 1 up, 20 hls.				Langford, 5 and 3	Vent Langford, Stillwater, Okla.
						Rollyn O. Thomas, Burbank, Calif.
				Litzo, 3 and 1	Berry, 1 up, 19 hls.	Bernard Woody, Denver, Colo.
						Reese Berry, Indianapolis, Ind.
			Litzo, 3 and 2		Litzo	BYE–Raymond Litzo, Denver, Colo.
				Foley, 1 up	Foley, 4 and 2	John F. Foley, Seattle, Wash.
		Kunkel, 6 and 5				Leonard Egbert, Los Angeles, Calif.
					Venturi	BYE–Ken Venturi, San Francisco, Calif.
				Stone, 1 up	Stone, 1 up, 19 hls.	Arthur H. Stone, Cincinnati, Ohio
						Kenneth Kwock, Honolulu, Hawaii
			Kunkel, 3 and 2		Gargan	BYE–Jack Gargan, Los Angeles, Calif.
				Kunkel, 1 up, 22 hls.	Paul, 2 and 1	Andrew J. Paul, Peoria, Ill.
						Vincent Legler, Portland, Ore.
					Kunkel, 8 and 7	James L. Higday, Englewood, Colo.
						Philip J. Kunkel, Salt Lake City, Utah

THIRD QUARTER

1st Round (18 Holes)	2nd Round (18 Holes)	3rd Round (18 Holes)	4th Round (18 Holes)	5th Round (18 Holes)	6th Round (18 Holes)	
Thomas A. Marlow, Portland, Ore.	Marlowe, 6 and 5					
Michael R. Ferentz, Long Beach, Calif.		Gurley, 3 and 2				
Harry Gurley, Denver, Colo.	Gurley, 2 and 1					
Robert B. Lyons, Spokane, Wash.			Shock, 6 and 4			
BYE—Ronald Hughes, Lawndale, Calif.	Hughes					
Donald D. Shock, Dayton, Ohio	Shock, 4 and 3	Shock, 1 up, 19 hls.				
Stanley J. Bielat, Yonkers, N.Y.				Shock, 1 up		
Dante C. Vicini, Ottawa, Ill.	Vicini, 1 up					
Alfred N. Littleton, Wichita, Kans.						
BYE—Valentino Chiaverini, Wallbridge, Ohio	Chiaverini	Vicini, 2 up				
Robert Sain, Nashville, Tenn.	McCool, 2 and 1		Vicini, 1 up			
William M. McCool, San Francisco, Calif.						
BYE—James J. Molinari, San Francisco, Calif.	Molinari	Molinari, 1 up, 19 hls.			Shock, 3 and 1	
Howard Johnson, Houston, Texas	Ruby, 4 and 2					
Joe Ben Ruby, San Antonio, Texas						
Lido L. Landi, Sharp Park, Calif.	Draksler, 1 up	Ruby, 2 and 1				
Jay J. Draksler, Peoria, Ill.						
BYE—Wilford M. O'Brien, Seattle, Wash.	O'Brien		King, 6 and 5			
Walter King, Denver, Colo.	King, 2 and 1	King, 2 up		V. Smith, 3 and 2		
Stephen E. Milich, Portland, Ore.						
James J. McCluskey, Los Angeles, Calif.	A. Szwedko, 1 up					
Andrew Szwedko, Sharpsburg, Pa.						
BYE—Vernon Smith, Galveston, Texas	V. Smith	V. Smith, 1 up, 20 hls.				
Robert Duden, Portland, Ore.	Duden, 4 and 3		V. Smith, 1 up, 19 hls.			
Oliver C. Sleppy, Los Angeles, Calif.						
Roy Shortridge, St. Paul, Minn.	Shortridge, 4 and 3	Duden, 4 and 3				
Eldwin B. Perry, Murray, Utah						L. Barnes, 1 up
BYE—Howard C. Pousette, St. Paul, Minn.	Pousette					
Russell Rader, Indianapolis, Ind.	Rader, 5 and 4	Pousette, 3 and 2				
Raymond F. Heins, Baltimore, Md.						
BYE—Larry Tomasino, Detroit, Mich.	Tomasino		Ross, 4 and 3			
John M. Ross, Riverside, Calif.	Ross, 3 and 2	Ross, 1 up, 19 hls.				
Frank B. Jones, Raleigh, N.C.				L. Barnes, 2 up		
Neil Whitney, Los Angeles, Calif.	Whitney, 2 and 1					
Robert Buchanan, Indianapolis, Ind.						
BYE—Perrin C. Reynolds, Atlanta, Ga.	Reynolds	Reynolds, 1 up, 19 hls.				
James R. Erwin, Jacksonville, Fla.	Erwin, 3 and 2		L. Barnes, 4 and 3			
Eugene A. Peterson, Rockford, Ill.						
Stanley P. Poploski, Pittsburgh, Pa.	L. Barnes, 4 and 3	L. Barnes, 1 up, 19 hls.				
Lou Barnes, Alhambra, Calif.					L. Barnes, 1 up	
BYE—Al Mengert, Spokane, Wash.	Mengert					
Clarence R. Smith, Seattle, Wash.	C. Smith, 2 and 1	Mengert, 1 up				
Harry M. LeBeau, St. Louis, Mo.			Burton, 2 and 1			
BYE—Peter M. Grant, Jr., Phoenix, Ariz.	Grant			R. Levenhagen, 1 up, 19 holes		
Henry C. Robertson, Jr., Oklahoma City, Okla.	Burton, 2 and 1	Burton, 5 and 4				
Jesse D. Burton, Albuquerque, N.M.						
BYE—Jack C. Russell, Jr., Cordova, Tenn.	Russell					
Albert Smith, Buffalo, N.Y.	A. Smith, 1 up	A. Smith, 1 up				
Andrew Monroe, Louisville, Ky.			R. Levenhagen, 1 up, 19 hls.			
BYE—Richard Levenhagen, West Allis, Wis.	**R. Levenhagen**					
Daniel Kop, Honolulu, Hawaii	Kop, 4 and 3	R. Levenhagen, 1 up				
Robert A. Roux, Santa Ana, Calif.						

SEMI-FINAL ROUND (36 holes)—William E. Betger defeated Lou Barnes, 5 up and 4 to play.

Twenty-Third Amateur Public Links Team Championship, Harding Trophy, 32 entries.—Won by San Francisco, Calif., team, 221 (Paul A. Millett, 69; Martin Stanovich, 73; and John M. Maughan, 79).

CHAMPIONSHIP—Continued

HALF

FOURTH QUARTER

6th Round (18 Holes)	5th Round (18 Holes)		4th Round (18 Holes)	3rd Round (18 Holes)	2nd Round (18 Holes)	1st Round (18 Holes)
				Oglesby, 1 up	Oglesby, 3 and 2	Kenneth Oglesby, Tucson, Ariz. Jimmy Pickel, Nashville, Tenn.
			Caso, 3 and 2		Martino, 5 and 4	Rollin Baxter, Peoria, Ill. Patrick V. Martino, Washington, D.C.
				Caso, 3 and 2	Platt	BYE—John Platt, Peoria, Ill.
		Caso, 7 and 6			Caso, 4 and 3	Theodore Levenhagen, West Allis, Wis. Moreno Caso, Seattle, Wash.
				Santillo, 5 and 4	Santillo, 3 and 2	Paul A. Millett, San Francisco, Calif. Frank Santillo, Culver City, Calif.
			Klimecko, 5 and 4		Cooper	BYE—Irving Cooper, Long Beach, Calif.
				Klimecko, 1 up	Klimecko, 1 up	Stanley Klimecko, Niagara Falls, N.Y. Alex Garbacz, South Bend, Ind.
	Hagar, 3 and 1				Frank	BYE—Milton Frank, St. Louis, Mo.
				Hagar, 1 up	Hagar, 2 and 1	John L. Thompson, Los Angeles, Calif. Kermit Hagar, Oklahoma City, Okla.
			Hagar, 3 and 2		Frase, 2 and 1	Paul Petersen, Pasadena, Calif. Gene W. Frase, Memphis, Tenn.
				Heinlein, 1 up, 19 hls.	Heinlein	BYE—Ralph Heinlein, Indianapolis, Ind.
		Hagar, 3 and 2			Zieske, 4 and 3	Kenneth W. Carlson, South Pasadena, Calif. Robert Zieske, Cleveland, Ohio
				Chavez, 4 and 3	Chavez, 1 up	Fred F. Chavez, Albuquerque, N.M. Ray Aymami, Denver, Colo.
			Chavez, 5 and 4		Weir	BYE—Dwight Weir, San Antonio, Texas
				Williams, 4 and 3	Williams, 6 and 5	Ronald Williams, Alhambra, Calif. George Bayhi, New Orleans, La.
Betger, 5 and 4					Jennemann, 1 up	Arthur Jennemann, Jennings, Mo. Talbert Smith, Alameda, Calif.
				Wilson, 6 and 5	Spain	BYE—Carl Spain, Memphis, Tenn.
			North, 3 and 2		Wilson, 2 and 1	John Pasikowski, Sharpsburg, Pa. Charles Wilson, Honolulu, Hawaii
				North, 3 and 1	Spencer	BYE—George E. Spencer, Royal Oak, Mich.
					North, 2 and 1	Arthur J. Cumming, Minneapolis, Minn. Lewis North, Denver, Colo.
		Betger, 1 up, 19 hls.		Betger, 3 and 2	Betger, 3 and 2	Alven E. Gustafson, Spokane, Wash. William E. Betger, San Francisco, Calif.
			Betger, 1 up		Ruck, 2 and 1	Leonard Ruck, Toledo, Ohio Edward Barney, Dayton, Ohio
				Lagozzino, 7 and 5	Hart	BYE—James M. Hart, Nashville, Tenn.
					Lagozzino, 2 and 1	Charles W. Barnes, Atlanta, Ga. Joseph Lagozzino, Seattle, Wash.
	Betger, 2 and 1			Eaton, 6 and 5	Hammond, 1 up, 24 hls.	Horace Henry, Houston, Texas Gordon B. Hammond, Jr., Rockford, Ill.
			McLennan, 3 and 2		Eaton	BYE—Lee Eaton, Montebello, Calif.
				McLennan, 2 and 1	McLennan, 4 and 2	Aubrey D. Turrentine, Durham, N.C. Lewis McLennan, Atlanta, Ga.
					Mueller	BYE—Fred Mueller, Portland, Ore.
		McLennan, 1 up		Dodds, 4 and 3	Caulkins, 1 up, 21 hls.	Don Caulkins, Inglewood, Calif. William P. Lees, Portland, Ore.
			Korns, 4 and 2		Dodds	BYE—Richard A. Dodds, Abington, Pa.
				Korns, 3 and 2	Korns, 3 and 2	Robert C. Clark, St. Paul, Minn. William L. Korns, Salt Lake City, Utah
					Rahaim, 7 and 5	Dale Lambert, Phoenix, Ariz. Fred J. Rahaim, Jacksonville, Fla.

1950
TWENTY-FIFTH AMATEUR PUBLIC LINKS CHAMPIONSHIP

Held at the Seneca Golf Course, Louisville, Kentucky, July 3-8.
Yardage—6,387. Par 70. 2,389 Entries, 210 Qualifiers, 210 Starters.
Championship entirely at match play.
FINAL ROUND (36 Holes)—Stanley Bielat defeated John Dobro, 7 up and 5 to play.

UPPER

FIRST QUARTER

1st Round (18 Holes)	2nd Round (18 Holes)	3rd Round (18 Holes)	4th Round (18 Holes)	5th Round (18 Holes)	6th Round (18 Holes)	
Mike Balega, Minneapolis, Minn.	Balega, 1 up, 20 hls.					
Ted Lach, Jr., Indianapolis, Ind.						
Dirk Prather, Phoenix, Ariz.	Prather, 1 up, 20 hls.	Balega, 1 up				
Roy W. Atkins, Portland, Ore.						
BYE—Robert S. Haag, Buechel, Ky.	Haag		Silvestri, 2 and 1			
Julian M. Williams, Washington, D.C.	Silvestri, 2 and 1	Silvestri, 3 and 1				
Daniel J. (Bob) Silvestri, Daly City, Calif.						
Stanley Walker, South Milwaukee, Wis.	Walker, 5 and 4			Silvestri, 1 up		
Robert D. Robinson, West Chicago, Ill.						
BYE—Robert Lichtenwalter, Erie, Pa.	Lichtenwalter	Lichtenwalter, 3 and 1				
Ferdnand Hubert, Pekin, Ill.	Shadrach, 4 and 3		Lichtenwalter, 4 and 3			
Don Shadrach, Dayton, Ohio						
BYE—Guy G. Chancey, Miami, Fla.	Chancey	Shadrach, 2 and 1				
Lt. Walter R. Browne, Atlanta, Ga.	Browne, 2 and 1				Fiorillo, 3 and 2	
John A. LaSota, Midland Park, N.J.						
Joseph S. Pulaski, Syracuse, N.Y.	Hornbuckle, 1 up	Hornbuckle, 1 up				
William I. Hornbuckle, Jr., Kansas City, Mo.						
BYE—James Richards, Oakland, Calif.	Richards		Fiorillo, 1 up, 19 hls.			
Salvatore Fiorillo, Norristown, Pa.	Fiorillo, 2 and 1	Fiorillo, 7 and 5				
Clifford Willis, Memphis, Tenn.						
Louis J. Esposito, Franklin Park, Ill.	Bannister, 3 and 2			Fiorillo, 1 up		
Wayne C. Bannister, Donelson, Tenn.						
BYE—Pat Schwab, Dayton, Ohio	Schwab	Schwab, 6 and 4				
Harry E. Missildine, Spokane, Wash.	Carter, 3 and 2		Musico, 4 and 2			
J.D. Carter, Atlanta, Ga.						
Samuel Musico, Carnegie, Pa.	Musico, 2 and 1	Musico, 3 and 2				
John Platt, Peoria, Ill.						
BYE—Ollie V. Ellison, Birmingham, Mich.	Ellison					Fiorillo, 2 up
Doug Lund, Salt Lake City, Utah	LeBeau, 6 and 5	LaBeau, 5 and 3				
Harry LeBeau, St. Louis, Mo.						
BYE—Clarence E. Alexander, Raleigh, N.C.	Alexander		Alexander, 3 and 2			
Eddie Major, Los Angeles, Calif.	Major, 2 and 1	Alexander, 4 and 2				
John W. LaBore, St. Paul, Minn.						
Harold O'Neal, Durham, N.C.	Griffitts, 4 and 3			Alexander, 1 up		
James R. Griffitts, Arcadia, Calif.		Griffitts, 2 and 1				
BYE—Ralph Heinlein, Indianapolis, Ind.	Heinlein					
Glenn Hagan, St. Louis, Mo.	Russell, 4 and 3		Towns, 5 and 4			
Jack C. Russell, Jr., Memphis, Tenn.		Towns, 2 and 1				
Daniel D. Sikes, Jr., Jacksonville, Fla.	Towns, 5 and 3					
Kenneth J. Towns, San Francisco, Calif.						
BYE—Andy Rezak, Bridgeville, Pa.	Rezak				Sublett, 5 and 3	
Kermit C. Hager, Oklahoma City, Okla.	Kopra, 2 up	Kopra, 1 up				
Bronislaus Kopra, Buffalo, N.Y.			J. Thomas, 4 and 2			
BYE—Robert Duden, Portland, Ore.	Duden					
Frank J. Gacek, Parma, Ohio	J. Thomas, 4 and 3	J. Thomas, 2 up				
Joe Thomas, Columbus, Ohio						
BYE—Clinton Sublett, Louisville, Ky.	Sublett			Sublett, 6 and 4		
Robert Schmidt, Toledo, Ohio	Ellis, 1 up, 20 hls.	Sublett, 4 and 3				
Arthur Clyde Ellis, Jr., Albuquerque, N.M.			Sublett, 2 and 1			
BYE—Ray Sleppy, Torrance, Calif.	R. Sleppy					
Marion D. Robinson, South Bend, Ind.	Vranesic, 2 and 1	R. Sleppy, 5 and 4				
Ralph J. Vranesic, Denver, Colo.						

SEMI-FINAL ROUND (36 Holes)—John Dobro defeated Salvatore Fiorillo, 3 up and 2 to play.

HALF

SECOND QUARTER

6th Round (18 Holes)	5th Round (18 Holes)		4th Round (18 Holes)	3rd Round (18 Holes)	2nd Round (18 Holes)	1st Round (18 Holes)
				Niederhut, 2 and 1	Krueger, 1 up, 19 hls.	Dudley Krueger, Austin, Texas Clayton Johnson, St. Paul, Minn.
			Dobro, 2 and 1		Niederhut, 1 up	Wilbur Niederhut, Denver, Colo. Joseph S. Zotkiewicz, Dayton, Ohio
					Dobro	BYE—John Dobro, Chicago, Ill.
				Dobro, 2 up	Szwedko, 4 and 2	William M. McCool, San Francisco, Calif. Andrew Szwedko, Millvale, Pa.
		Dobro, 2 up			Kelly, 2 and 1	Jack McGivern, Detroit, Mich. Clyde B. Kelly, Durham, N.C.
				Kelly, 3 and 1	Wodja	BYE—Walter Wodja, Toledo, Ohio
			Caspio, 1 up		Caspio, 1 up	James Caspio, Cleveland, Ohio Andrew Holmes, Toledo, Ohio
				Caspio, 5 and 3	Seyler	BYE—Ovid S. Seyler, San Francisco, Calif.
	Dobro, 2 and 1				Weir, 2 and 1	Dwight Weir, Jr., San Antonio, Texas Robert Zieske, Cleveland, Ohio
				Weir, 2 and 1	Allen, 4 and 3	Russell A. Allen, Jr., Kansas City, Mo. Starling A. Smith, Birmingham, Ala.
			Yost, 4 and 3		Yost	BYE—Richard Yost, Portland, Ore.
				Yost, 2 and 1	Pittman, 1 up, 20 hls.	Perry P. Pittman, Hialeah, Fla. Arthur C. Moore, Memphis, Tenn.
		Campbell, 3 and 2			Campbell, 3 and 2	Warren Campbell, Seattle, Wash. James W. Martin, Milwaukee, Wis.
				Campbell, 4 and 2	Roper	BYE—Joe Roper, Nashville, Tenn.
			Campbell, 1 up		Cisowski, 2 and 1	Matt Cisowski, Harvey, Ill. Milton Frank, St. Louis, Mo.
				Zimmerman, 3 and 2	Zimmerman, 1 up, 21 hls.	James W. Hill, Memphis, Tenn. Jack Zimmerman, Dayton, Ohio
Dobro, 5 and 4					Gers	BYE—Chris Gers, Oklahoma City, Okla.
				Gers, 2 and 1	Ludlow, 2 up	Alex Garbacz, South Bend, Ind. Robert Ludlow, Indianapolis, Ind.
			Levenhagen, 2 and 1		Marcey	BYE—Earl Lee Marcey, Arlington, Va.
				Levenhagen, 3 and 2	Levenhagen, 2 and 1	James L. Manzone, New York, N.Y. James Levenhagen, Milwaukee, Wis.
		Levenhagen, 1 up, 19 hls.			Waflart, 2 and 1	Nat Waflart, Louisville, Ky. Edward Nishnick, Pittsburgh, Pa.
			Gonzales, 1 up, 21 hls.	Gonzales, 4 and 2	Gonzales, 2 and 1	Archie Gonzales, New Orleans, La. Ralph C. Ghioto, Sr., Jacksonville, Fla.
				Bruno, 6 and 5	Bruno	BYE—Frank Bruno, Los Angeles, Calif.
	Levenhagen, 1 up, 19 hls.				Durgan, 2 and 1	Edwin L. Teffeteller, Inglewood, Calif. Richard Durgan, Spokane, Wash.
				Lazarchuk, 1 up	Golen, 2 up	Edward Golen, Buffalo, N.Y. R. Brown Cullen, Jr., Louisville, Ky.
			Lazarchuk, 1 up		Lazarchuk	BYE—Stephen Lazarchuk, Ventura, Calif.
				Gunkle, 1 up, 19 hls.	Gunkle, 2 and 1	James Gunkle, Denver, Colo. H. Tommy Mathews, Atlanta, Ga.
		Kinoshita, 3 and 2			Crist	BYE—Douglas Crist, Indianapolis, Ind.
				Munsie, 2 and 1	Munsie, 2 and 1	Walter Maykut, Plymouth Meeting, Pa. Larry Munsie, Norwood, Ohio
			Kinoshita, 1 up		Mackey	BYE—Joseph P. Mackey, Chicago, Ill.
				Kinoshita, 2 up	Hooley, 2 up	George Hooley, Peoria, Ill. Jimmy Pickel, Nashville, Tenn.
					Kinoshita, 2 up	**Sadaji Kinoshita, Honolulu, Hawaii** Don Schrabulis, Kewanee, Ill.

THIRD QUARTER

1st Round (18 Holes)	2nd Round (18 Holes)	3rd Round (18 Holes)	4th Round (18 Holes)	5th Round (18 Holes)	6th Round (18 Holes)	
Bob Inman, Tulsa, Okla.	Inman, 4 and 2					
Dan Christensen, Blue Island, Ill.		Bujeker, 2 and 1				
Thomas Bujeker, South Bend, Ind.	Bujeker, 3 and 2					
Newell Beedy, Minneapolis, Minn.			Bujeker, 5 and 3			
BYE—Gordon Hall, Peoria, Ill.	Hall					
Walter R. McClain, Cleveland, Ohio	Grassi, 3 and 2	Grassi, 1 up		Faulkenberry, 4 and 3		
Ted Grassi, Erie, Pa.						
Fred Corvi, San Francisco, Calif.	Hughes, 4 and 3					
Ronnie Hughes, Lawndale, Calif.		Hughes, 2 and 1				
BYE—Truxton A. Rea, Albuquerque, N.M.	Rea		Faulkenberry, 1 up, 21 hls.			
Robert L. Faulkenberry, Jr., Oklahoma City, Okla.	Faulkenberry, 3 and 2					
Shedric E. McKain, Memphis, Tenn.		Faulkenberry, 3 and 2				
BYE—Henry Armatis, New Orleans, La.	Armatis				Bielat,1 up, 21 hls.	
R. Keith Kallio, Washington, D.C.	McLennan, 1 up					
Louis W. McLennan, Atlanta, Ga.		Bielat, 3 and 2				
Robert Togikawa, Peoria, Ill.	Bielat, 1 up, 19 hls.					
Stanley Bielat, Yonkers, N.Y.			Bielat, 1 up			
BYE—Edwin Bohardt, Dayton, Ohio	Bohardt					
Arthur Jennemann, St. Louis, Mo.	Hart, 1 up, 20 hls.	Hart, 4 and 3		Bielat, 2 up		
Edward Hart, Denver, Colo.						
Gerald Ruffo, Philadelphia, Pa.	Rice, 4 and 3					
DeLong Rice, III, Memphis, Tenn.		Rice, 2 and 1				
BYE—Joe F. Bihl, Portland, Ore.	Bihl		Waggoner, 2 up			
Joseph J. Rak, Minneapolis, Minn.	Rak, 1 up					
Fred Harvey, Jr., Miami Springs, Fla.		Waggoner, 6 and 4				
James Tefft, Spokane, Wash.	Waggoner, 5 and 4					Bielat, 1 up, 19 holes
Mel Waggoner, Janesville, Wis.						
BYE—Steve P. Lakos, Cleveland, Ohio	Lakos					
John N. Andrews, Nashville, Tenn.	E. Thomas, 3 and 1	E. Thomas, 5 and 4				
Eli Thomas, Crafton, Pa.			E. Thomas, 3 and 2			
BYE—Frank Maloney, St. Louis, Mo.	Maloney					
Joseph W. Calaban, Syracuse, N.Y.	Calaban, 6 and 5	Calaban, 4 and 3		V. Smith, 3 and 1		
Roy Teague, Durham, N.C.						
Wallace Smith, Royal Oak, Mich.	Taylor, 5 and 3					
Donald Taylor, Seattle, Wash.		V. Smith, 1 up, 20 hls.				
BYE—Vernon A. Smith, Galveston, Texas	V. Smith		V. Smith, 2 and 1			
Russell Ostrander, Toledo, Ohio	Berry, 5 and 4					
Reese Berry, Indianapolis, Ind.		Roux, 3 and 1				
Eugene Hay, Atlanta, Ga.	Roux, 1 up				Bouchey, 1 up	
Robert Roux, Santa Ana, Calif.						
BYE—Charles D. Kellar, Columbus, Ohio	Kellar					
Leonard Ruck, Toledo, Ohio	Furgerson, 7 and 6	Furgerson, 3 and 1				
Roy E. Furgerson, Kansas City, Mo.			Thum, 3 and 1			
BYE—Allen Thum, Phoenix, Ariz.	Thum					
Ralph Hall, Oakland, Calif.	Hall, 1 up	Thum, 1 up		Bouchey, 4 and 3		
Robert Crouch, Indianapolis, Ind.						
BYE—Jimmie Dezern, Durham, N.C.	Dezern					
Ralph Monroe, Louisville, Ky.	Bouchey, 6 and 5	Bouchey, 2 and 1				
Larry Bouchey, Los Angeles, Calif.			Bouchey, 2 and 1			
BYE—George L. Seaholm, Jr., Austin, Texas	Seaholm	Seaholm, 1 up				
Richard J. Walker, Jacksonville, Fla.	Walker, 1 up					
Carl Manny, Dayton, Ohio						

SEMI-FINAL ROUND (36 holes)—Stanley Bielat defeated Frank Rutkiewicz, 1 up, 37 holes.

Twenty-Fourth Amateur Public Links Team Championship, Harding Trophy, 38 Entries, July1. Won by Los Angeles, Calif., team, 217 for 18 holes (Robert Roux, 74; James R. Griffitts, 76; Stephen Z. Shaw, 67); second, tie at 223 between: New York team (Stanley Bielat, 74; John A. LaSota; 75; James L. Manzone, 74) and Oklahoma City (Kermit C. Hager, 78; Bob Inman, 67; Chris Gers 78).

CHAMPIONSHIP HALF

FOURTH QUARTER

6th Round (18 Holes)

- Rutkiewicz, 1 up, 19 hls.

5th Round (18 Holes)

- Venturi, 1 up
- Rutkiewicz, 1 up, 19 hls.

4th Round (18 Holes)

- O. Sleppy, 1 up, 20 hls.
- O. Sleppy, 3 and 1
- Grant, 3 and 2
- Parry, 1 up
- Venturi, 1 up
- Venturi, 3 and 2
- Rutkiewicz, 2 and 1
- Rutkiewicz, 6 and 5
- Maughan, 5 and 3
- Yates, 5 and 4
- Rockholt, 6 and 5
- Rockholt, 1 up, 20 hls.

3rd Round (18 Holes)

- O. Sleppy, 6 and 4
- Thornton, 1 up
- Spencer, 2 and 1
- Grant, 4 and 3
- Garcia, 1 up
- Parry 2 and 1
- Venturi, 1 up
- Gustafson, 1 up
- C. Smith, 2 and 1
- Rutkiewicz, 8 and 7
- Phillips, 3 and 2
- Maughan, 5 and 4
- Yates, 3 and 2
- Heller, 1 up
- Rockholt, 2 and 1
- Shaw, 3 and 2

2nd Round (18 Holes) / 1st Round (18 Holes)

2nd Round	1st Round
Andonian, 2 up	Mike Andonian, Pontiac, Mich.
	Sgt. Charles Earle, Minneapolis, Minn.
O. Sleppy, 5 and 4	Oliver C. Sleppy, Los Angeles, Calif.
	James D. Wallace, Peoria, Ill.
Thornton	BYE–Charles Thornton, Birmingham, Mich.
Crabb, 5 and 4	Robert Buchanan, Indianapolis, Ind.
	Robert P. Crabb, Colorado Springs, Colo.
Isbill, 1 up, 19 hls.	Russ Milne, Toledo, Ohio
	Charles A. Isbill, Miami, Fla.
Spencer	BYE–James R. Spencer, St. Louis, Mo.
Grant, 1 up	Peter M. Grant, Jr., Phoenix, Ariz.
	Lewis North, Denver, Colo.
Bednarski	BYE–Joe Bednarski, Syracuse, N.Y.
Post, 1 up	Chester Lataweic, Minneapolis, Minn.
	Howard M. Post, Miami Springs, Fla.
Garcia, 3 and 2	Walter M. Garcia, Los Alamos, N.M.
	John I. Sattler, Los Angeles, Calif.
Parry	BYE–Robert R. Parry, Portland, Ore.
Grissom, 1 up	Thomas C. Grissom, Raleigh, N.C.
	Alvin E. Seicshnaydre, New Orleans, La.
Miller, 1 up	Charles W. Lipchik, Erie, Pa.
	Norman S. Miller, Jacksonville, Fla.
Venturi	BYE–Kenneth Venturi, San Francisco, Calif.
Gustafson, 5 and 4	Herman H. Nitsch, Houston, Texas
	Alvin E. Gustafson, Spokane, Wash.
Halbach, 1 up	Joseph Smith, Albany, N.Y.
	Edward Halbach, Memphis, Tenn.
C. Smith	BYE–Clarence Smith, Seattle, Wash.
Yuska, 2 and 1	Anthony F. Yuska, Carnegie, Pa.
	Floyd Chandler, Nashville, Tenn.
Krummel	BYE–W. Paul Krummel, Cincinnati, Ohio
Rutkiewicz 5 and 4	Russ W. Stevens, Joliet, Ill.
	Frank Rutkiewicz, Honolulu, Hawaii
Phillips, 2 up	Arthur J. Wangler, Kansas City, Mo.
	John Phillips, Toledo, Ohio
McBride, 4 and 2	Robert E. McBride, Louisville, Ky.
	Joseph L. Burgdorf, Pontiac, Mich.
Collins,	BYE–William R. Collins, Baltimore, Md.
Maughan, 3 and 2	John M. Maughan, San Francisco, Calif.
	Anthony Klimecko, Niagara Falls, N.Y.
Kocak, 4 and 3	Michael Kocak, Cleveland, Ohio
	Lynn Lee, Indianapolis, Ind.
Yates	BYE–Jim Yates, Atlanta, Ga.
Heller, 2 up	Albert E. Heller, Salt Lake City, Utah
	Arthur J. Cassidy, Peoria, Ill.
Deverant	BYE–Michael Deverant, Glenside, Pa.
Curran, 3 and 2	Jack Curran, Oklahoma City, Okla.
	Alex V. Pietrzak, Dayton, Ohio
Rockholt	BYE–Cotton Rockholt, Memphis, Tenn.
Glaub, 5 and 4	Walter J. Glaub, Wauwatosa, Wis.
	Rex C. Mounger, San Antonio, Texas
Shaw, 1 up	Ralph F. Schneider, South Euclid, Ohio
	Stephen Z. Shaw, Alhambra, Calif.

1951
TWENTY-SIXTH AMATEUR PUBLIC LINKS CHAMPIONSHIP

Held at the Brown Deer Park Golf Course, Milwaukee, Wisconsin, July 9-14.

Yardage—6,573. Par 71. 2,281 Entries, 210 Qualifiers, 210 Starters.

Championship entirely at match play.

FINAL ROUND (36 Holes)—Dave Stanley defeated Ralph J. Vranesic, 1 up 38 Holes.

UPPER

FIRST QUARTER

1st Round (18 Holes)	2nd Round (18 Holes)	3rd Round (18 Holes)	4th Round (18 Holes)	5th Round (18 Holes)	6th Round (18 Holes)	
Walter Maykut, Plymouth Meeting, Pa. Erwin F. Gargen, West Allis, Wis.	Maykut, 1 up					
Paul A. Millett, San Francisco, Calif. Kenneth Lanning, Rolla, Mo.	Lanning, 6 and 5	Lanning, 2 up				
BYE—Paul Scodeller, Pekin, Ill.	Scodeller		Lanning, 2 and 1			
Stanley J. Bielat, Yonkers, N.Y. William C. Fenwick, Detroit, Mich.	Bielat, 6 and 5	Bielat, 5 and 3				
John Platt, Peoria, Ill. Fred F. Chavez, Albuquerque, N.M.	Chavez, 2 up			Lanning, 4 and 3		
BYE—Starling A. Smith, Birmingham, Ala.	Smith	Chavez, 1 up				
James C. Davey, Atlanta, Ga. George J. Baskiel, Woodhaven, N.Y.	Baskiel, 5 and 4		Baskiel, 5 and 4			
BYE—Byron W. Gerdes, Dayton, Ohio	Gerdes	Baskiel, 2 up			McClure, 3 and 2	
James Clark, Minneapolis, Minn. Sherman Conrad, Toledo, Ohio	Conrad, 1 up	Stamps, 1 up				
Karl Dosen, Minneapolis, Minn. James W. Stamps, Atlanta, Ga.	Stamps, 1 up, 19 hls.		McClure, 1 up, 19 hls.			
BYE—Jim Hoch, Oklahoma City, Okla.	Hoch					
John McClure, Wichita, Kans. Lee Fenton, Louisville, Ky.	McClure, 5 and 4	McClure, 2 and 1		McClure, 2 and 1		
Michael Sarro, Inwood, N.Y. Anthony Petric, Anderson, Ind.	Sarro, 7 and 6	Sarro, 3 and 2				
BYE—Andrew C. Sword, Dallas, Texas	Sword					
William Schwope, Detroit, Mich. Frank Romaguera, New Orleans, La.	Schwope, 6 and 4		Permenter, 2 and 1			
Joseph W. Calaban, Syracuse, N.Y. William H. Permenter, Memphis, Tenn.	Permenter, 2 and 1	Permenter, 1 up, 20 hls.				
BYE—Richard S. Ries, Los Angeles, Calif.	Ries					Stanley, 3 and 2
Capt. John F. McNeilly, Spokane, Wash. Vincent Legler, Portland, Ore.	Legler, 1 up, 19 hls.	Ries, 1 up, 19 hls.	Keith, 3 and 2			
BYE—John A. Cusano, Jr., Miami Springs, Fla.	Cusano					
Donald J. Keith, South Pasadena, Calif. Ted Levenhagen, West Allis, Wis.	Keith, 5 and 4	Keith, 6 and 5		Stanley, 5 and 4		
James Hynds, Jr., Seattle, Wash. Edwin Bohardt, Dayton, Ohio	Bohardt, 1 up	Chun, 5 and 4				
BYE—Jack S.S. Chun, Honolulu, Hawaii	Chun		Stanley, 2 and 1			
Edwin J. Lowry, Louisville, Ky. James W. Hill, Memphis, Tenn.	Hill, 5 and 4	Stanley, 4 and 2				
Albert Neveraskas, Castle Shannon, Pa. Dave Stanley, Los Angeles, Calif.	Stanley, 4 and 2				Stanley, 4 and 2	
BYE—Ollie Galen, Toledo, Ohio	Galen	Galen, 2 and 1				
Richard Copeland, St. Paul, Minn. Herbert Brandes, Kenosha, Wis.	Copeland, 9 and 7		Saunders, 4 and 3			
BYE—Harold A. Saunders, Denver, Colo.	Saunders	Saunders, 2 up				
Don Schrabulis, Kewanee, Ill. Joseph Banko, Cleveland, Ohio	Schrabulis, 7 and 5			Saunders, 4 and 3		
BYE—Matt Carvey, Harvey, Ill.	Carvey	McKevlin, 5 and 3				
Tommy Essex, Jacksonville, Fla. T. Moultrie McKevlin, Charleston, S.C.	McKevlin, 2 and 1		McKevlin, 3 and 1			
BYE—Ellsworth R. Jones, Portland, Ore.	Jones	Jones, 3 and 2				
Fred Corvi, San Francisco, Calif. Bob York, Nashville, Tenn.	York, 3 and 2					

SEMI-FINAL ROUND (36 Holes)—Dave Stanley defeated William P. Lees, 1 up, 37 .ioles.

HALF

SECOND QUARTER

6th Round (18 Holes)	5th Round (18 Holes)		4th Round (18 Holes)	3rd Round (18 Holes)	2nd Round (18 Holes)	1st Round (18 Holes)
					Goldick, 2 and 1	John J. Amanna, New York, N.Y.
				Bouchey, 2 and 1		Felix Goldick, Dayton, Ohio
					Bouchey, 3 and 2	Lawrence Bouchey, Los Angeles, Calif.
			Bouchey, 2 up			Charles Makaiwa, Honolulu, Hawaii
					Cullen	BYE—R. Brown Cullen, Jr., Louisville, Ky.
				Cullen, 6 and 4	McIntire, 2 and 1	Jack McIntire, Peoria, Ill.
		Lees, 1 up, 20 hls.				**Charles Hess, Indianapolis, Ind.**
					MacCrossen, 4 and 3	Ikey Sowell, Memphis, Tenn.
				MacCrossen, 6 and 4		Donald MacCrossen, Milwaukee, Wis.
					Hall	BYE—Gordon Hall, Peoria, Ill.
			Lees, 3 and 2		Maughan, 2 and 1	John M. Maughan, San Francisco, Calif.
				Lees, 3 and 2		Domonic Ori, Highland Park, Ill.
					Lees	BYE—William P. Lees, Portland, Ore.
	Lees, 2 and 1				Poploski, 3 and 2	Andrew J. Oliveri, Washington, D.C.
				Poploski, 1 up, 19 hls.		Stanley P. Poploski, Pittsburgh, Pa.
					Martin, 4 and 2	James W. Martin, Milwaukee, Wis.
			Wolfe, 1 up			Gene W. Frase, Sr., Memphis, Tenn.
					Wolfe	BYE—P. D. Wolfe, Jr. Terre Haute, Ind.
				Wolfe, 2 and 1	Mathews, 2 up	Albert Carson, Wichita, Kans.
		Haddock, 4 and 3				Thomas Mathews, Atlanta, Ga.
					Haddock, 4 and 3	Bernard J. Lula, Detroit, Mich.
				Haddock, 6 and 5		R. Harold Haddock, Denver, Colo.
					Halin	BYE—John T. Halin, Spokane, Wash.
			Haddock, 3 and 2		Sikes, 1 up, 19 hls.	Daniel D. Sikes, Jr., Jacksonville, Fla.
				Kurz, 1 up		James B. Proctor, Nashville, Tenn.
					Kurz, 2 up	Robert L. Benson, St. Paul, Minn.
Lees, 2 and 1						Bob Kurz, Miami Springs, Fla.
					Guthrie	BYE—James Guthrie, New Orleans, La.
				Gordon, 4 and 3	Gordon, 2 and 1	Philip E. Gordon, Oakland, Calif.
			Burns, 1 up, 19 hls.			Joseph J. Muller, New Orleans, La.
					Bendes	BYE—Ziggie Bendes, Cleveland, Ohio
				Burns, 1 up	Burns, 6 and 5	William Burns, Kirkland, Wash.
		Burns, 1 up				Walter Durdle, Peoria, Ill.
					Tate, 1 up, 20 hls.	Robert Faulkenberry, Jr., Oklahoma City, Okla.
				R. Clark, 1 up		James R. Tate, Raleigh, N.C.
					R. Clark, 1 up	Ray Kimmel, Spokane, Wash.
			Wietecha, 1 up			Robert C. Clark, St. Paul, Minn.
					Jennemann	BYE—Arthur Jennemann, St. Louis County, Mo.
				Wietecha, 3 and 2	Wietecha, 1 up	Henry Felker, Oshkosh, Wis.
	Burns, 4 and 3					Albert Wietecha, Chicago, Ill.
					Preston, 2 and 1	Richard B. Preston, Detroit, Mich.
				Chaddock, 3 and 2		Bronislaus Kopra, Buffalo, N.Y.
					Chaddock	BYE—William Chaddock, Jr., Inglewood, Calif.
			Iceberg, 2 up		Iceberg, 4 and 2	Edward H. Ebel, Minneapolis, Minn.
				Iceberg, 4 and 3		Roy A. Iceberg, Pontiac, Mich.
		H. Smith, 5 and 3			Phillips	BYE—John S. Phillips, Toledo, Ohio
					H. Smith, 6 and 4	Donald Johnson, St. Paul, Minn.
				H. Smith, 3 and 1		Harvey Smith, Philadelphia, Pa.
					Lichtenwalter	BYE—Robert Lichtenwalter, Erie, Pa.
			H. Smith, 2 up		Furgo, 2 and 1	Michael P. Furgo, Montebello, Calif.
				Krueger, 3 and 2		Bill Knick, Phoenix, Ariz.
					Krueger, 2 and 1	Dudley R. Krueger, Austin, Texas
						Arthur Todd, Columbus, Ohio

1951 AMATEUR PUBLIC LINKS
LOWER

THIRD QUARTER

1st Round (18 Holes)	2nd Round (18 Holes)	3rd Round (18 Holes)	4th Round (18 Holes)	5th Round (18 Holes)	6th Round (18 Holes)	
George Hooley, Peoria, Ill.	Vranesic,					
Ralph Vranesic, Denver, Colo.	6 and 5	Vranesic, 3 and 2				
Anton Pilney, New Orleans, La.	Williams,					
Joseph V. Williams, Nashville, Tenn.	2 and 1		Vranesic, 6 and 4			
BYE—Herman Wyman, St. Louis, Mo.	Wyman					
Norman Barck, Gardena, Calif.	Barck,	Barck, 1 up				
Alois Penzenstadler, Jr., Oshkosh, Wis.	3 and 1			Vranesic, 5 and 4		
George Smith, Jr., Dayton, Ohio	J. Levenhagen,					
James Levenhagen, West Allis, Wis.	2 and 1	J. Levenhagen, 5 and 3				
BYE—Richard F. Cooney, Portland, Ore.	Cooney		J. Levenhagen, 4 and 2			
Fred Winberg, Seattle, Wash.	Allen,					
Russell A. Allen, Kansas City, Mo.	4 and 3	Woods, 1 up, 19 hls.				
BYE—Del L. Woods, Homestead, Fla.	Woods				Vranesic, 2 up	
K. Thomas Jacobs, Jr., Montebello, Calif.	Ruck,					
Leonard Ruck, Toledo, Ohio	6 and 5	Ruck, 1 up				
Guy G. Chancey, Miami, Fla.	Reed,					
David Reed, Durham, N.C.	1 up		Alyea, 3 and 2			
BYE—Ralph F. Schneider, South Euclid, Ohio	Schneider					
Joseph Golob, Cleveland Heights, Ohio	Alyea,	Alyea, 4 and 2				
Benton E. Alyea, Santa Monica, Calif.	1 up			North, 2 and 1		
Lester Kelley, Atlanta, Ga.	North,					
Lewis North, Denver, Colo.	2 and 1	North, 4 and 3				
BYE—George J. Chikar, South Bend, Ind.	Chikar		North, 3 and 2			
Fred W. Hall, Peoria, Ill.	Hall,					
Walter Ireland, Dayton, Ohio	7 and 5	Law, 4 and 2				
Arthur C. Moore, Memphis, Tenn.	Law,					Vranesic, 5 and 4
James J. Law, Detroit, Mich.	4 and 3					
BYE—Curtis J. Reynolds, Berkley, Mich.	Reynolds	Reynolds, 2 and 1				
Albert Clasen, St. Paul, Minn.	A. Clasen,					
Clifford A. Willis, Memphis, Tenn.	6 and 5		Reynolds, 4 and 3			
BYE—Michael Skelly, Swedeland, Pa.	Skelly	Johnston, 1 up, 20 hls.				
James Johnston, Minneapolis, Minn.	Johnston,					
Ralph F. Costa, Meadville, Pa.	6 and 5			Martin, 1 up, 19 hls.		
Jack R. Martin, Oklahoma City, Okla.	Jack Martin,					
Dayton Olson, Minneapolis, Minn.	3 and 2	Jack Martin, 4 and 3				
BYE—Adolph Schweri, Louisville, Ky.	Schweri		Jack Martin, 3 and 2			
Ralph E. Heinlein, Indianapolis, Ind.	Heinlein,					
David Wilder, Pittsburgh, Pa.	6 and 5	Vicini, 3 and 2				
Aldo Galletti, Oakland, Calif.	Vicini,				Szustak, 1 up	
Dante Vicini, Ottawa, Ill.	3 and 2					
BYE—John Newmeyer, San Francisco, Calif.	Newmeyer	Szustak, 1 up				
Roger Brice, Spokane, Wash.	Szustak,					
William Szustak, Buffalo, N.Y.	5 and 4		Szustak, 3 and 1			
BYE—Stanley L. Clasen, St. Paul, Minn.	S. Clasen	S. Clasen, 1 up				
Jesse D. Burton, Albuquerque, N.M.	Burton,			Szustak, 6 and 4		
Walter Wojda, Toledo, Ohio	1 up					
BYE—Richard A. Lersch, Westfield, N.J.	Lersch	Ogrin, 5 and 4				
Frank J. Ogrin, Jr., Waukegan, Ill.	Ogrin,					
Dave Marr, Bellaire, Texas	3 and 2		Robison, 1 up, 19 hls.			
BYE—Henry L. Robison, Cottage City, Md.	Robison	Robison, 1 up, 20 hls.				
Dirk Prather, Phoenix, Ariz.	Prather,					
Warren E. Artz, Terre Haute, Ind.	1 up, 19 hls.					

SEMI-FINAL ROUND (36 Holes)—Ralph Vranesic defeated Ralph G. Schwab, 1 up, 37 holes.

Twenty-Fifth Amateur Public Links Team Championship, Harding Trophy, 33 Entries, July 7. Won by Dayton, Ohio, team 234 for 18 holes (Edwin Bohardt, 80; Byron H. Hunt, 75; Walter Ireland, 79); second, Peoria, Ill., team, 235 (Robert Togikawa, 79; Don Schrabulis, 73; Walter Durdle, 83); third, tie at 237 between Atlanta, Ga., team (Louis W. McLennan, 78; James W. Stamps, 75; Thomas Mathews, 84) and Memphis, Tenn., team (Shedric E. McKain, 79; William H. Permenter, 79; Gene W. Frase, Sr., 79).

CHAMPIONSHIP—Continued

HALF

FOURTH QUARTER

	6th Round (18 Holes)	5th Round (18 Holes)	4th Round (18 Holes)	3rd Round (18 Holes)	2nd Round (18 Holes)	1st Round (18 Holes)
					Kletcke, 3 and 2	L.O. Hatfield, Indianapolis, Ind.
				Hunt, 1 up, 19 hls.		Eddie Kletcke, Chicago, Ill.
					Hunt, 2 up	Byron H. Hunt, Columbus, Ohio
			Hunt, 1 up, 21 hls.			Fred Harvey, Jr., Miami Springs, Fla.
					Szwedko	BYE—Andrew Szwedko, Sharpsburg, Pa.
				Szwedko, 2 and 1	Lima, 6 and 4	Sam Lima, Detroit, Mich.
						Joseph Barnishin, Jr., Pittsburg, Pa.
		Schwab, 2 up			Smola, 7 and 6	Richard Beckett, Memphis, Tenn.
				Smola, 4 and 3		Walt Smola, Omaha, Neb.
					Golen	BYE—Edwin Golen, Buffalo, N.Y.
			Schwab, 3 and 2		Dobro, 1 up, 19 hls.	Peter Kramer, Manhattan Beach, Calif.
				Schwab, 4 and 3		John Dobro, Chicago, Ill.
					Schwab	BYE—Ralph G. Schwab, Dayton, Ohio
	Schwab, 6 and 5				Hart, 3 and 2	James M. Hart, Nashville, Tenn.
				W. King, 3 and 2		Donald Cantoni, Erie, Pa.
					W. King, 3 and 1	Walter King, Denver, Colo.
			Manganello, 1 up			Theodore R. King, Washington, D.C.
					LeBeau	BYE—Harry M. LeBeau, St. Louis, Mo.
				Manganello, 2 and 1	Manganello, 4 and 3	E.H. Bradham, Charleston, S.C.
						Augustine Manganello, White Plains, N.Y.
		St. John, 3 and 2			St. John, 7 and 6	John Kovach, South Bend, Ind.
				St. John 5 and 4		E.A. St. John, Tulsa, Okla.
					Oberg	BYE—Robert Oberg, Denver, Colo.
			St. John, 1 up		Togikawa, 1 up	Robert Togikawa, Peoria, Ill.
				Togikawa, 3 and 2		Roy W. Atkins, Portland, Ore.
Schwab, 1 up					Silvestri, 6 and 5	Ralph C. Ghioto, Sr., Jacksonville, Fla.
						Daniel J. Silvestri, Daly City, Calif.
					Holmes	BYE—Andy Holmes, Toledo, Ohio
				McKain, 6 and 4	McKain, 4 and 3	Shedric E. McKain, Memphis, Tenn.
			McKain, 1 up			Raymond Cane, Detroit, Mich.
					Clement	BYE—Elmer L. Clement, Redondo Beach, Calif.
				Bloyer, 1 up	Bloyer, 7 and 6	Robert Morris, Spokane, Wash.
						John R. Bloyer, St. Paul, Minn.
		Waggoner, 4 and 3			McLennan, 1 up	Bart Brown, Jr., Louisville, Ky.
				McLennan, 6 and 5		Louis W. McLennan, Atlanta, Ga.
					Kielbaso, 1 up	Salvatore Fiorillo, Norristown, Pa.
			Waggoner, 3 and 1			Ted W. Kielbaso, Dayton, Ohio
					Berry	BYE—Reese Berry, Indianapolis, Ind.
				Waggoner, 1 up, 19 hls.	Waggoner, 3 and 2	Mel Waggoner, Janesville, Wis.
						Charles A. Thornton, Birmingham, Mich.
	Waggoner, 2 and 1				Haskell, 4 and 3	Gordon E. Haskell, Seattle, Wash.
				Reif, 3 and 1		Archie Gonzales, New Orleans, La.
					Reif	BYE—John P. Reif, Madison, Wis.
			Reif, 2 and 1		Stanovich, 5 and 3	Logan Hancock, Peoria, Ill.
				Stanovich, 7 and 5		Martin Stanovich, San Francisco, Calif.
					Guinn	BYE—Mack V. Guinn, Phoenix, Ariz.
		Reif, 6 and 5		Cziok, 4 and 2	Cziok, 1 up	Lester V. Cziok, Minneapolis, Minn.
						Henry Timbrook, Jr., Houston, Texas
					Balega	BYE—Michael J. Balega, Minneapolis, Minn.
			Cziok, 6 and 5	Zieske, 2 up	Swedo, 1 up	Leo W. Swedo, Los Angeles, Calif.
						Earl Clark, Fort Lauderdale, Fla.
					Zieske, 4 and 3	Robert Huddleston, Toledo, Ohio
						Robert Zieske, Cleveland, Ohio

1952
TWENTY-SEVENTH AMATEUR PUBLIC LINKS CHAMPIONSHIP

Held at the Miami Country Club, Miami, Fla., July 7-12.
Yardage—6,411. Par 70. 2,267 Entries, 200 Qualifiers, 200 Starters.
Championship entirely at match play.

FINAL ROUND (36 Holes)—Omer L. Bogan defeated Robert J. Scherer, 4 up and 3 to play.

UPPER

FIRST QUARTER

1st Round (18 Holes)	2nd Round (18 Holes)	3rd Round (18 Holes)	4th Round (18 Holes)	5th Round (18 Holes)	6th Round (18 Holes)	
Gene Gregory, Memphis, Tenn.	Pagan,					
W.A. Pagan, Jr., West Palm Beach, Fla.	8 and 7	Pagan,				
		2 and 1				
Billy Joe Patterson, Nashville, Tenn.	Copeland,					
Richard Copeland, St. Paul, Minn.	4 and 3		Pagan,			
BYE—John J. Cusano, Jr., Miami Springs, Fla.	Cusano		3 and 1			
		Cusano,				
Anthony Petric, Anderson, Ind.	Haag,	4 and 2		Pagan, 2 and 1		
Robert S. Haag, Louisville, Ky.	2 up					
Paul B. Gehring, Baltimore, Md.	Nosewicz,					
Edward P. Nosewicz, Aurora, Colo.	7 and 5	Martin,				
BYE—James W. Martin, Milwaukee, Wis.	Martin	1 up				
			Martin,			
Harry Oates, Jr., Tonawanda, N.Y.	Oates,		1 up, 20 hls.			
Carl J. Daniels, Detroit, Mich.	1 up, 21 hls.	Poploski,				
BYE—Stanley P. Poploski, Pittsburgh, Pa.	Poploski	4 and 3			Pagan, 1 up, 19 hls.	
Chester W. Latawiec, Minneapolis, Minn.	Pilney,					
Andy Pilney, New Orleans, La.	5 and 4	Pilney,				
BYE—August Tamburrino, Chicago, Ill.	Tamburrino	8 and 7				
			Carvey,			
BYE—Howard M. Wade, Freeport, Texas	Wade		2 and 1			
		Carvey,				
Matt Carvey, Harvey, Ill.	Carvey,	3 and 2				
Samuel E. Lima, Detroit, Mich.	2 and 1					
Frank Rutkiewicz, Honolulu, Hawaii	Rutkiewicz,			Carvey, 1 up		
James T. O'Neill, Larchmont, N.Y.	2 and 1	Rutkiewicz,				
BYE—Eddie Bohardt, Dayton, Ohio	Bohardt	1 up, 21 hls.				
			Rutkiewicz,			
Ernest Althuser, Tacoma, Wash.	Hay,		1 up			
Eugene Hay, Atlanta, Ga.	3 and 2	Bielat,				
Stanley Bielat, Yonkers, N.Y.	Bielat,	1 up				
Sirio E. Startoni, Hershey, Pa.	3 and 1					Bogan, 2 and 1
BYE—Glen Fowler, Oklahoma City, Okla.	Fowler					
		Fowler,				
Bill Paul, Inspiration, Ariz.	Landi,	3 and 2				
Lido Landi, Sharp Park, Calif.	3 and 1		Fowler,			
BYE—Robert J. Sain, Nashville, Tenn.	Sain		1 up			
		Vranesic,				
Joseph W. Devlin, Philadelphia, Pa.	Vranesic,	4 and 3				
Ralph J. Vranesic, Denver, Colo.	5 and 4			T. Jenkins, 4 and 3		
Eddie Halbach, Memphis, Tenn.	Halbach,					
Walter Wodja, Toledo, Ohio	2 and 1	Halbach,				
BYE—John S. Phillips, Toledo, Ohio	Phillips	7 and 6				
			T. Jenkins,			
Ralph F. Schneider, South Euclid, Ohio	G. Smith,		4 and 3			
George A. Smith, Dayton, Ohio	3 and 2	T. Jenkins,				
BYE—Tommy Jenkins, Jacksonville, Fla.	T. Jenkins	1 up				
BYE—Omer L. Bogan, South Gate, Calif.	Bogan				Bogan, 2 and 1	
		Bogan,				
Eugene Lunini, Pekin, Ill.	Johnston,	3 and 1				
James H. Johnston, Minneapolis, Minn.	4 and 3		Bogan,			
BYE—Arlie Taylor, Dallas, Texas	Taylor		1 up			
		Taylor,				
John J. Jendrasak, Cleveland, Ohio	Ries,	4 and 2				
Richard S. Ries, Los Angeles, Calif.	1 up, 21 hls.			Bogan, 2 and 1		
BYE—Le Roy Payne, Peoria, Ill.	Payne					
		Sanders,				
W.F. Sanders, Jr., Atlanta, Ga.	Sanders,	3 and 2				
Stephen Lazarchuk, Ventura, Calif.	2 and 1		Frase,			
BYE—William K. Lanning, Rolla, Mo.	Lanning		2 and 1			
		Frase,				
Larry C. Holshouser, Charlotte, N.C.	Frase,	5 and 3				
Gene Frase, Memphis, Tenn.	4 and 2					

SEMI-FINAL ROUND (36 Holes)—Omer L. Bogan defeated Robert L. Kurz, 5 up and 4 to play.

HALF

SECOND QUARTER

6th Round (18 Holes)	5th Round (18 Holes)	4th Round (18 Holes)	3rd Round (18 Holes)	2nd Round (18 Holes)	1st Round (18 Holes)
				Gunkle, 1 up	James S. Gunkle, Denver, Colo. Bill Burns, Kirkland, Wash.
			Daniel, 1 up, 20 hls.	Daniel, 2 and 1	Robert Daniel, San Francisco, Calif. Richard B. Preston, Detroit, Mich.
		Kay, 3 and 1		Wilder	BYE—Robert E. Wilder, Phoenix, Ariz.
			Kay, 6 and 5	Kay, 1 up, 20 hls.	Robert Kay, Toledo, Ohio Dante Vicini, Ottawa, Ill.
	Kay, 2 and 1			Ori, 4 and 2	Andrew Rizak, Bridgeville, Pa. Dominic Ori, Highland Park, Ill.
			Ori, 4 and 3	Deitch	BYE—Melvin Deitch, Chattanooga, Tenn.
		Lee, 3 and 2		Baker, 3 and 2	Miles Baker, Jr., Kansas City, Kans. Logan Hancock, Peoria, Ill.
			Lee, 1 up	Lee	BYE—Lynn R. Lee, Indianapolis, Ind.
Thornton, 1 up, 19 hls.				Durgan, 2 and 1	Richard Durgan, Spokane, Wash. Edward Picquet, Charleston, S.C.
			H. Smith, 5 and 4	H. Smith	BYE—Harvey H. Smith, Philadelphia, Pa.
		E. Jenkins, 3 and 2		E. Jenkins	BYE—Edwin Jenkins, Jacksonville, Fla.
			E. Jenkins, 1 up, 21 hls.	Todd, 2 and 1	Warren Clasen, St. Paul, Minn. Arthur Todd, Columbus, Ohio
	Thornton, 3 and 1			J. Smith, 1 up	John Purvis, Memphis, Tenn. Joseph Smith, Albany, N.Y.
			J. Smith, 4 and 2	West	BYE—Edward C. West, Louisville, Ky.
		Thornton, 3 and 1		Thornton, 1 up, 20 hls.	Donald Thornton, Los Angeles, Calif. Walter H. Ireland, Dayton, Ohio
			Thornton, 2 and 1	Nicolai	BYE—Charles Nicolai, Detroit, Mich.
Kurz, 2 and 1				Faulkenberry	BYE—Robert L. Faulkenberry, Jr., Oklahoma City, Okla.
			Faulkenberry, 3 and 2	Stamps, 4 and 3	Bronislaus Kopra, Buffalo, N.Y. James W. Stamps, Atlanta, Ga.
		Faulkenberry, 2 and 1		Gillespie	BYE—James O. Gillespie, New Orleans, La.
			Balega, 2 and 1	Balega, 5 and 4	Mike Balega, Minneapolis, Minn. Edward A. Kobis, Buffalo, N.Y.
				Anteau	BYE—Robert Anteau, Toledo, Ohio
	Faulkenberry, 2 and 1		Keith, 1 up	Keith, 6 and 5	Donald J. Keith, South Pasadena, Calif. Robert Crouch, Indianapolis, Ind.
		White, 1 up, 20 hls.		White	BYE—Leonard L. White, Dallas, Texas
			White, 5 and 4	McGowan, 1 up	James T. Folden, Atlanta, Ga. James McGowan, Miami Beach, Fla.
Kurz, 1 up, 19 hls.				Atkins, 8 and 7	Jack Bielak, Milwaukee, Wis. Roy W. Atkins, Portland, Ore.
			Atkins, 6 and 5	Yearick	BYE—Charles W. Yearick, Baltimore, Md.
		Kurz, 3 and 2		Golob, 5 and 4	Bob Crenshaw, Memphis, Tenn. Joseph Golob, Cleveland, Ohio
			Kurz, 1 up, 19 hls.	Kurz	BYE—Robert L. Kurz, Miami Springs, Fla.
	Kurz, 6 and 4			Draksler, 3 and 2	Jay Draksler, Peoria, Ill. Clarence Ryder, St. Paul Minn.
			Heinlein, 3 and 2	Heinlein	BYE—Ralph Heinlein, Indianapolis, Ind.
		Thomas, 2 and 1		Thomas, 2 and 1	Eli Thomas, Pittsburgh, Pa. J. L. Blankenship, Memphis, Tenn.
			Thomas, 1 up, 19 hls.	Frank, 1 up	Milton Frank, St. Louis, Mo. Robert Togikawa, Peoria, Ill.

THIRD QUARTER

1st Round (18 Holes)	2nd Round (18 Holes)	3rd Round (18 Holes)	4th Round (18 Holes)	5th Round (18 Holes)	6th Round (18 Holes)	
Edward Vanderberg, Portland, Ore.	Szwedko, 2 and 1					
Andrew Szwedko, Sharpsburg, Pa.		Szwedko, 2 and 1				
Louis Burtner, Oklahoma City, Okla.	Ghioto, 1 up, 20 hls.					
Ralph Ghioto, Jr., Jacksonville, Fla.						
BYE—Richard Roberts, Anderson, Ind.	Roberts		Szwedko, 3 and 2			
Charles A. Owen, Jeffersonville, Ind.	Daviantis, 6 and 5	Daviantis, 2 and 1				
George J.M. Daviantis, Chicago, Ill.				Hess, 2 and 1		
Wayne Daily, Hollywood, Fla.	Daily, 1 up					
Andy Holmes, Toledo, Ohio						
BYE—Charles Hess, Indianapolis, Ind.	Hess	Hess, 7 and 5				
Les Cziok, Minneapolis, Minn.	Cziok, 2 and 1		Hess, 1 up			
Walter F. Knower, New Orleans, La.		Nahale, 3 and 2				
BYE—George Nahale, Sr., Honolulu, T.H.	Nahale				Bean, 6 and 4	
Jack Walton, Memphis, Tenn.	Walton, 8 and 6					
Joseph Wiesbrock, Wheaton, Ill.		Walton, 1 up, 19 hls.				
BYE—Dayton Olson, Minneapolis, Minn.	Olson					
BYE—Leonard Ruck, Toledo, Ohio	Ruck		Bean, 2 and 1			
Andrew Augaitis, Dayton, Ohio	Bean, 2 and 1	Bean, 7 and 5				
Tommy Bean, Trion, Ga.				Bean, 6 and 5		
Steve Trgovic, Etna, Pa.	Kocinski, 6 and 5					
Ed Kocinski, Cleveland, Ohio						
BYE—Robert J. Millar, Minneapolis, Minn.	Millar	Millar, 2 and 1				
Joseph R. Dolan, Peoria, Ill.	Olney, 5 and 3		Millar, 1 up			
George E. Olney, Wauwatosa, Wis.		V. Smith, 6 and 5				
Vernon A. Smith, Galveston, Texas	V. Smith, 4 and 3					
Alan B. Holmes, South Bend, Ind.						Scherer, 1 up
BYE—Leon J. Butler, Jr., Atlanta, Ga.	Butler					
Robert J. Scherer, Decatur, Ill.	Scherer, 1 up	Scherer, 4 and 2				
R. Brown Cullen, Jr., Louisville, Ky.			Scherer, 4 and 3			
BYE—Dave Stanley, Los Angeles, Calif.	Stanley	Stanley, 4 and 2				
George Eluck, Windsor, Ont., Canada	Eluck, 4 and 3			Scherer, 4 and 3		
James L. Basko, Phoenix, Ariz.						
Einar Hanson, San Francisco, Calif.	Paul, 3 and 1					
Andrew Paul, Peoria, Ill.		Caskey, 6 and 5				
BYE—George Caskey, Dayton, Ohio	Caskey		Caskey, 1 up, 19 hls.			
Warren A. Hawkins, Memphis, Tenn.	Brice, 6 and 5					
Roger Brice, Spokane, Wash.		Benefiel, 5 and 4				
BYE—Alvin Benefiel, Denver, Colo.	Benefiel				Scherer, 2 and 1	
BYE—Vern Olson, North Hollywood, Calif.	Olson	Lichtenwalter, 1 up				
Robert Lichtenwalter, Erie, Pa.	Lichtenwalter, 1 up		Harris, 3 and 2			
Robert Huddleston, Toledo, Ohio						
BYE—Larry Lance, Fayetteville, N.C.	Lance	Harris, 4 and 3				
Norton Harris, Key West, Fla.	Harris, 2 and 1			Sword, 1 up, 21 hls.		
James R. Hoch, Oklahoma City, Okla.						
BYE—Art Howell, Detroit, Mich.	Howell	Sword, 1 up, 22 hls.				
Frank Michalek, Baltimore, Md.	Sword, 1 up, 19 hls.		Sword, 4 and 2			
A.C. Sword, Dallas, Texas						
BYE—Robert York, Nashville, Tenn.	York	Vogt, 9 and 7				
Julius Vogt, Glendale, N.Y.	Vogt, 1 up					
W.R. Baker, Memphis, Tenn.						

SEMI-FINAL ROUND (36 Holes)—Robert J. Scherer defeated John Halin, 10 up and 8 to play.

Twenty-Sixth Amateur Public Links Team Championship, Harding Trophy, 32 Entries, July 5. Won by Chicago, Illinois, team, 227 for 18 holes (John Dobro, 77; Dante Vicini, 78; George Daviantis, 72); second, Miami, Fla., team, 228 (W. A. Pagan, Jr., 72; Guy Chancey, 72; Robert Kurz, 84); third, Atlanta, Ga., team, 231 (Eugene Hay, 79; James W. Stamps, 79; Tommy Bean, 73).

CHAMPIONSHIP—Continued

HALF

FOURTH QUARTER

6th Round (18 Holes)	5th Round (18 Holes)		4th Round (18 Holes)	3rd Round (18 Holes)	2nd Round (18 Holes)	1st Round (18 Holes)
				Woodard, 5 and 3	Donaldson, 1 up, 20 hls.	J.B. Donaldson, Memphis, Tenn. Bernard Grzegorzcwski, Toledo, Ohio
					Woodard, 1 up, 19 hls.	Harvey E. Woodard, Detroit, Mich. William Lees, Portland, Ore.
			Shaw, 3 and 1		Jensen	BYE—Paul Jensen, Englewood, Colo.
				Shaw, 5 and 4	Shaw, 1 up	Stephen Shaw, Los Angeles, Calif. Alex Brooks, Chicago, Ill.
		Vollmer, 3 and 2			Vollmer, 1 up, 19 hls.	Dennis Vollmer, Coral Gables, Fla. John T. Tighe, St. Paul, Minn.
				Vollmer, 2 up	Acosta	BYE—Mike Acosta, North Hollywood, Calif.
			Vollmer, 4 and 2		Hooley, 1 up	George Hooley, Peoria, Ill. Tex Ellison, Birmingham, Mich.
				Hart, 1 up, 19 hls.	Hart	BYE—James M. Hart, Nashville, Tenn.
	Koehler, 2 and 1				Dorr, 1 up, 22 hls.	James E. Dorr, Birmingham, Ala. **Erwin Gargen, West Allis, Wis.**
				LeBeau, 4 and 2	LeBeau	BYE—Harry M. LeBeau, St. Louis, Mo.
			LeBeau, 1 up		Lovelace	BYE—William Lovelace, Memphis, Tenn.
				Seyler, 3 and 2	Seyler, 1 up	Ovid Seyler, San Francisco, Calif. Lawrence Karkhoff, Minneapolis, Minn.
		Koehler, 4 and 2			Koehler, 1 up	Bart Pasqua, Englewood, Colo. Arnold C. Koehler, Indianapolis, Ind.
				Koehler, 7 and 6	Dombroski	BYE—John F. Dombroski, Jacksonville, Fla.
			Koehler, 4 and 3		Galbraith, 6 and 5	Walter Durdle, Peoria, Ill. Winston Galbraith, Oklahoma City, Okla.
				Galbraith, 3 and 2	Tershin	BYE—John Tershin, Seattle, Wash.
Halin, 2 and 1					Maykut	BYE—Walter Maykut, Plymouth Meeting, Pa.
				Halin, 1 up	Halin, 5 and 4	Eugene Lake, Toledo, Ohio John Halin, Spokane, Wash.
			Halin, 1 up		Christopher	BYE—Jack Christopher, Euclid, Ohio
				Chancey, 3 and 1	Chancey, 3 and 2	Guy G. Chancey, Miami, Fla. Augustine Manganello, White Plains, N.Y.
		Halin, 1 up			Kelly, 6 and 5	Robert L. Buchanan, Indianapolis, Ind. Lester Kelly, Atlanta, Ga.
				Kelly, 3 and 2	Middleton	BYE—Wayne H. Middleton, Kensington, Md.
			Muller, 5 and 4		Rizak	BYE—Frank Rizak, Bridgeville, Pa.
				Muller, 2 up	Muller, 3 and 1	Joseph J. Muller, New Orleans, La. Thomas F. Lambie, Phoenix, Ariz.
	Halin, 2 and 1				May, 4 and 2	J.D. Croxton, Atlanta, Ga. Matthew May, Lackawanna, N.Y.
				Logan, 2 and 1	Logan	BYE—Howard M. Logan, Wichita, Kans.
			Clark, 4 and 2		Dobro, 2 and 1	John C. Dobro, Chicago, Ill. Daniel D. Sikes, Jr., Jacksonville, Fla.
				Clark, 1 up, 19 hls.	Clark	BYE—James Clark, St. Paul, Minn.
		Clark, 1 up			Windahl, 2 up	Donnie Robinson, Louisville, Ky. Wayne T. Windahl, Minneapolis, Minn.
				Windahl, 1 up, 19 hls.	Kivett	BYE—James Kivett, High Point, N.C.
			Windahl, 4 and 3		Anglen, 1 up	Jack E. Zimmerman, Dayton, Ohio Marc Anglen, Dallas, Texas
				Anglen, 4 and 3	Hall, 6 and 4	Chester Filler, Pittsburgh, Pa. Robert L. Hall, Elgin, Ill.

1953
TWENTY-EIGHTH AMATEUR PUBLIC LINKS CHAMPIONSHIP

Held at the West Seattle Municipal Golf Course, Seattle, Wash., July 13-18.
Yardage—6,400. Par 71. 1,868 Entries, 200 Qualifiers, 200 Starters.
Championship entirely at match play.

FINAL ROUND (36 Holes)—Ted Richards, Jr., defeated Irving A. Cooper, 1 up.

UPPER

FIRST QUARTER

1st Round (18 Holes)	2nd Round (18 Holes)	3rd Round (18 Holes)	4th Round (18 Holes)	5th Round (18 Holes)	6th Round (18 Holes)	
Donald Nelson, Minneapolis, Minn.	Shaw,					
Stephen Z. Shaw, Monterey Park, Calif.	8 and 6					
Harry M. LeBeau, St. Louis, Mo.	LeBeau,	Le Beau, 2 up				
William Pigott, III, Seattle, Wash.	3 and 1					
BYE—Robert Korsch, Duluth, Minn.	Korsch		Le Beau, 3 and 2			
George Bayhi, New Orleans, La.	Bayhi,	Korsch, 4 and 3				
James Zoccola, Pittsburgh, Pa.	1 up, 20 hls.					
Carl Waystadt, Milwaukee, Wis.	Hanson,					
Einar H. Hanson, Daly City, Calif.	4 and 3			Le Beau, 2 and 1		
BYE—Arthur Corbin, Dallas, Texas	Corbin	Hanson, 2 and 1				
Robert Zieske, Mayfield Heights, Ohio	Kramer,		Kramer, 3 and 2			
Peter Kramer, Jr., Manhattan Beach, Calif.	4 and 2					
BYE—Louis W. McLennan, Atlanta, Ga.	McLennan	Kramer, 1 up				
Les Stephens, Portland, Ore.	Stephens,					
Ron Ault, Spokane, Wash.	5 and 4	Maidment, 1 up			Makalena, 4 and 2	
BYE—Gene Maidment, Seattle, Wash.	Maidment					
BYE—Herbert V. Seeger, Peoria, Ill.	Seeger		Miyaoka, 2 up			
Kenneth Miyaoka, Honolulu, T.H.	Miyaoka,	Miyaoka, 2 and 1				
Charles Bond, Boise, Idaho	4 and 2					
Albert L. Komp, Jr., Philadelphia, Pa.	Makalena,			Makalena, 1 up, 22 hls.		
Theodore Makalena, Honolulu, T.H.	3 and 2	Makalena, 2 up				
BYE—Robert Kay, Toledo, Ohio	Kay					
Harry R. Poland, Indianapolis, Ind.	Lukat,		Makalena, 3 and 2			
Fred E. Lukat, Washington, D.C.	3 and 2	Lukat, 5 and 3				
Chester W. Latawiec, Minneapolis, Minn.	Latawiec,					
Nelson S. Cullenward, San Francisco, Calif.	2 and 1					
BYE—Marvin C. Whitfield, Peoria, Ill.	Whitfield					
Charles Makaiwa, Honolulu, T.H.	Makaiwa,	Makaiwa, 4 and 3				Sanders, 3 and 2
Jack Christopher, Cleveland, Ohio	3 and 2		Makaiwa, 2 and 1			
BYE—Lee Eaton, Montebello, Calif.	Eaton					
Jim Peloff, Louisville, Ky.	Peloff,	Eaton, 4 and 3				
Robert T. Geisler, Toledo, Ohio	2 and 1					
Marion E. Williams, Detroit, Mich.	Foley,			Szwedko, 1 up		
John Foley, Seattle, Wash.	1 up, 19 hls.	Szwedko, 1 up, 20 hls.				
BYE—Andrew Szwedko, Pittsburgh, Pa.	Szwedko					
William Bender, Jr., Mamaroneck, N.Y.	Bender,		Szwedko, 2 and 1			
Dante Vicini, Ottawa, Ill.	7 and 5	Bender, 8 and 7				
BYE—Meredith A. Nickel, Indianapolis, Ind.	Nickel					
BYE—Douglas Sanders, Cedartown, Ga.	Sanders				Sanders, 4 and 3	
J.O. Black, Jr., Dallas, Texas	Lanning,	Sanders, 5 and 4				
William K. Lanning, Rolla, Mo.	3 and 2		Sanders, 2 and 1			
BYE—J.S. Marino, New Orleans, La.	Marino					
Frank Forst, Millbrae, Calif.	M. Holick,	M. Holick, 1 up, 19 hls.		Sanders, 4 and 3		
Mike Holick, Minneapolis, Minn.	3 and 2					
BYE—Ralph J. Vranesic, Denver, Colo.	**Vranesic**					
Rod Funseth, Spokane, Wash.	Funseth,	Vranesic, 1 up				
Hervey Thompson, Milwaukee, Wis.	4 and 3		Vranesic, 4 and 2			
BYE—Eddie Major, Burbank, Calif.	Major					
John S.S. Chun, Honolulu, T.H.	Chun,	Chun, 2 and 1				
William Szustak, Buffalo, N.Y.	2 and 1					

SEMI-FINAL ROUND (36 Holes)—Ted Richards, Jr., defeated Douglas Sanders, 5 up and 4 to play.

HALF **SECOND QUARTER**

6th Round (18 Holes)	5th Round (18 Holes)		4th Round (18 Holes)	3rd Round (18 Holes)	2nd Round (18 Holes)	1st Round (18 Holes)
				Seyler, 5 and 3	Seyler, 4 and 2	William M. Conroy, Seattle, Wash. Ovid Seyler, San Francisco, Calif.
			Seyler, 2 and 1		Olson, 4 and 3	Dayton Olson, Minneapolis, Minn. Ralph C. Emery, Salt Lake City, Utah
				Hammond, 6 and 4	Shaffer	BYE–Paschal Shaffer, Milwaukee, Wis.
		Seyler, 1 up			Hammond, 3 and 2	Thomas Fahey, Daly City, Calif. Gordon B. Hammond, Columbus, Ga.
				Gustafson, 5 and 4	Hansen, 1 up, 22 hls.	Frank O. Hansen, Downey, Calif. Don Holick, Minneapolis, Minn.
			Goetz, 1 up		Gustafson	BYE–Alvin E. Gustafson, Spokane, Wash.
				Goetz, 1 up	Goetz, 7 and 5	Bob Booth, Stillwater, Okla. Robert Goetz, Jacksonville, Fla.
	Haddock, 1 up				Dunnum	BYE–O.A. Dunnum, Oak Harbor, Wash.
				Rutkiewicz, 4 and 3	Rutkiewicz, 5 and 4	Lawrence R. Robertson, Minneapolis, Minn. Frank Rutkiewicz, Honolulu, T.H.
			Stanley, 5 and 4		Vanderberg	BYE–Ed Vanderberg, Portland, Ore.
				Stanley, 3 and 2	Carvey	BYE–Matt Carvey, Harvey, Ill.
		Haddock, 1 up, 22 hls.			Stanley, 4 and 3	David F. Stanley, Los Angeles, Calif. Jimmie Armes, Louisville, Ky.
				Friedt, 3 and 2	Friedt, 6 and 5	Eugene Friedt, Toledo, Ohio Andrew A. Jacob, McKees Rocks, Pa.
			Haddock, 3 and 2		Chmiel	BYE–John Chmiel, Buffalo, N.Y.
				Haddock, 4 and 3	Haddock, 4 and 3	Chet Baker, Indianapolis, Ind. Harold Haddock, Denver, Colo.
Richards, 5 and 4					Carlone	BYE–Joseph Carlone, South Euclid, Ohio
				Pacheco, 2 and 1	Huber	BYE–Charles H. Huber, Beverly Hills, Calif.
			Kocsis, 1 up		Pacheco, 2 up	Jim Frye, Seattle, Wash. Al Pacheco, Honolulu, T.H.
				Kocsis, 3 and 2	Jordan	BYE–Fred Jordan, San Francisco, Calif.
		Campbell, 2 and 1			Kocsis, 2 and 1	John B. Cronin, Spokane, Wash. Joe Kocsis, Pontiac, Mich.
				Campbell, 3 and 2	Campbell	BYE–Richard G. Campbell, Los Angeles, Calif.
			Campbell, 3 and 2		Won, 2 and 1	Archie Won, Honolulu, T.H. Roy Hashitana, Ontario, Ore.
				North, 4 and 3	Fair	BYE–Othello G. Fair, Daly City, Calif.
	Richards, 3 and 2				North, 6 and 5	Lewis North, Denver, Colo. William Lovelace, Birmingham, Ala.
				Richards, 4 and 3	Earnest, 5 and 3	George Earnest, Seattle, Wash. Norm Asmus, Salt Lake City, Utah
			Richards, 4 and 3		Richards	BYE–Ted Richards, Jr., Santa Monica, Calif.
				Schoux, 1 up, 20 hls.	St. John, 2 and 1	E.A. St. John, Oklahoma City, Okla. Tommy Jenkins, Jacksonville, Fla.
		Richards, 1 up, 19 hls.			Schoux	BYE–Albert Schoux, Concord, Calif.
				Karkhoff, 4 and 2	Karkhoff, 1 up	William R. Wright, Atlanta, Ga. Lawrence Karkhoff, Minneapolis, Minn.
			Pasikowski, 4 and 3		Augaitis	BYE–Andrew Augaitis, Dayton, Ohio
				Pasikowski, 2 and 1	Pasikowski, 3 and 2	John Pasikowski, Sharpsburg, Pa. Walter G. Gill, Buffalo, N.Y.
					Patterson, 1 up, 19 hls.	Harold Riach, Minneapolis, Minn. Bob Patterson, Portland, Ore.

THIRD QUARTER

1st Round (18 Holes)	2nd Round (18 Holes)	3rd Round (18 Holes)	4th Round (18 Holes)	5th Round (18 Holes)	6th Round (18 Holes)	
W.E. O'Connor, Chicago, Ill.	Eaton,					
William G. Eaton, Monterey Park, Calif.	2 up	Eaton,				
Andrew Holmes, Toledo, Ohio	Holmes,	3 and 2				
Joseph S. Lagozzino, Jr., Seattle, Wash.	3 and 2		Campagni,			
BYE—Donald Thornton, Los Angeles, Calif.	Thornton		2 and 1			
		Campagni,				
Joe Dudziak, Minneapolis, Minn.	Campagni,	4 and 3				
Nello Campagni, Highwood, Ill.	2 and 1			Lees, 3 and 1		
Bill Lees, Portland, Ore.	Lees,					
Walter L. King, Denver, Colo.	1 up, 21 hls.	Lees,				
BYE—Ed Finney, Los Angeles, Calif.	Finney	7 and 5				
			Lees,			
Walt Durdle, Peoria, Ill.	Rael,		1 up			
Jerry Rael, Los Angeles, Calif.	4 and 3	Rael,				
BYE—Bronislaus Kopra, Buffalo, N.Y.	Kopra	1 up				
Mike Rak, Minneapolis, Minn.	Zimmerman,				Lees, 4 and 3	
Jack E. Zimmerman, Dayton, Ohio	6 and 4	Zimmerman,				
BYE—Robert Swope, Nashville, Tenn.	Swope	3 and 2				
			Burns,			
BYE—Leon Radde, Minneapolis, Minn.	Radde		4 and 2			
		Burns,				
Norman Larsen, Salt Lake City, Utah	Burns,	**4 and 3**		Burns, 6 and 5		
Bill Burns, Kirkland, Wash.	3 and 2					
Kay Maruyama, Spokane, Wash.	Morrow,					
Ralph Morrow, Oklahoma City, Okla.	1 up	Sikes,				
BYE—Daniel D. Sikes, Jr., Jacksonville, Fla.	Sikes	1 up				
			Sikes,			
Ernest Althuser, Tacoma, Wash.	Hopwood,		4 and 3			
Richard H. Hopwood, Phoenix, Ariz.	3 and 2	Bielat,				
Anthony Lema, Oakland, Calif.	Bielat,	4 and 2				Hart, 1 up, 19 holes
Stanley Bielat, Yonkers, N.Y.	2 and 1					
BYE—Roy A. Iceberg, Pontiac, Mich.	Iceberg					
		Iceberg,				
Warren P. Downing, Honolulu, T.H.	MacDonald,	3 and 2				
Douglas MacDonald, Renton, Wash.	3 and 2		**R. Hughes,**			
BYE—Ronnie Hughes, Los Angeles, Calif.	**R. Hughes**		**default**			
		R. Hughes,				
Henry M. Magnaris, San Francisco, Calif.	Knick,	1 up		Zotkiewicz, 1 up, 19 hls.		
William Knick, Phoenix, Ariz.	5 and 4					
Tommy Yee, San Francisco, Calif.	Cooney,					
Richard F. Cooney, Portland, Ore.	1 up	Cooney,				
BYE—Al Wasmund, Seattle, Wash.	Wasmund	1 up				
			Zotkiewicz,			
Joe Zotkiewicz, Dayton, Ohio	Zotkiewicz,		4 and 2			
Al Neveraskas, Castle Shannon, Pa.	1 up, 20 hls.	Zotkiewicz,				
BYE—Mike Balega, Minneapolis, Minn.	Balega	1 up			Hart, 1 up	
BYE—Vincent Legler, Portland, Ore.	Legler					
		Stamps,				
James W. Stamps, Atlanta, Ga.	Stamps,	3 and 2				
Joseph Dolan, Peoria, Ill.	1 up, 19 hls.		Stamps,			
BYE—Tommy Everham, Seattle, Wash.	Everham		1 up			
		O'Brien,				
James O. Gillespie, New Orleans, La.	O'Brien,	2 up		E. Hart, 5 and 3		
Wilford M. O'Brien, Seattle, Wash.	3 and 2					
BYE—Joseph S. Evans, St. Louis, Mo.	Evans					
		Christopherson,				
Richard L. Christopherson, Los Angeles, Calif.	Christopherson,	3 and 2				
D.C. Simons, Memphis, Tenn.	6 and 5		E. Hart,			
BYE—Jack Lemcke, South Milwaukee, Wis.	Lemcke		6 and 5			
		E. Hart,				
Edward J. Hart, Denver, Colo.	E. Hart,	4 and 3				
Clarence Ryder, St. Paul, Minn.	3 and 2					

SEMI-FINAL ROUND (36 Holes)—Irving A. Cooper defeated Edward J. Hart, 12 up and 11 to play.

Twenty-Seventh Amateur Public Links Team Championship, Harding Trophy, 26 Entries, July 11—Won by Jacksonville, Florida, team, 221 for 18 holes (Tommy Jenkins, 71; Daniel D. Sikes, Jr., 74; Robert Goetz, 76); second Montebello, Calif., team, 222 (Ted Richards, Jr., 72; David F. Stanley, 73; Donald Thornton, 77); third, Dallas, Texas, team 223 (Hal McCommas, 72; Arthur Corbin, 75; Leonard L. White, 76.)

CHAMPIONSHIP—Continued

HALF

FOURTH QUARTER

6th Round (18 Holes)	5th Round (18 Holes)		4th Round (18 Holes)	3rd Round (18 Holes)	2nd Round (18 Holes)	1st Round (18 Holes)
					White, 5 and 3	Leonard L. White, Dallas, Texas
				White, 1 up, 19 hls.		Chuck Turtalk, Los Angeles, Calif.
					Hagen, 4 and 3	Norbert Anderson, St. Paul, Minn.
			Clark, 1 up			Glenn Hagen, Ferguson, Mo.
					Hutchison	BYE—Tom Hutchison, Seattle, Wash.
				Clark, 5 and 3	Clark, 2 and 1	Pat Tudor, Kansas City, Mo.
		Clark, 3 and 1				James Clark, Minneapolis, Minn.
					McCool, 2 and 1	J.L. Blankenship, Memphis, Tenn.
				McCool, 1 up, 19 hls.		William McCool, San Francisco, Calif.
			McCool, 4 and 2		Masterson	BYE—Richard Masterson, Seattle, Wash.
					Bean, 3 and 2	Warner Leppin, Phoenix, Ariz.
				Draksler, 3 and 2		Tommy Bean, Trion, Ga.
					Draksler	BYE—Jay Draksler, Peoria, Ill.
	McCommas, 3 and 2				Gjolme, 3 and 2	Harvey E. Woodard, East Detroit, Mich.
				Gjolme, 6 and 5		Harold Gjolme, Seattle, Wash.
			Bogan, 2 and 1		Makowski	BYE—Robert Makowski, West Allis, Wis.
					Brice	BYE—Roger Brice, Spokane, Wash.
				Bogan, 1 up, 20 hls.	Bogan, 1 up	LeRoy Parrish, Ontario, Ore.
		McCommas, 3 and 2				Pete Bogan, Montebello, Calif.
					Williams, 2 and 1	Julian M. Williams, Washington, D.C.
				Williams, 2 and 1		George Caskey, Dayton, Ohio
			McCommas, 4 and 3		Procup	BYE—Andrew Procup, West Mifflin, Pa.
					McCommas, 3 and 1	Hal McCommas, Dallas, Texas
				McCommas, 3 and 2		Pete Adams, Colorado Springs, Colo.
					Ries	BYE—Richard S. Ries, Los Angeles, Calif.
Cooper, 6 and 4				Cooper, 3 and 2	Jones	BYE—E.R. Jones, Portland, Ore.
					Cooper, 4 and 2	Fred T. Hall, Peoria, Ill.
			Cooper, 1 up			Irving A. Cooper, Long Beach, Calif.
				Caso, 7 and 6	Ware	BYE—James Ware, Groves, Texas
					Caso, 4 and 3	Moreno Caso, Seattle, Wash.
		Cooper, 2 and 1				Carl J. Daniels, Detroit, Mich.
					Dzierzanowski, 4 and 3	Ray Dzierzanowski, Phoenix, Ariz.
				Dzierzanowski, 3 and 1		Howard Kingsbeck, St. Paul, Minn.
			Dzierzanowski, 3 and 1		Durgan	BYE—Richard Durgan, Spokane, Wash.
				McKain, 1 up, 20 hls.	Hughes	BYE—Ben Hughes, Portland, Ore.
	Cooper, 1 up				McKain, 4 and 3	Shedrick E. McKain, Memphis, Tenn.
						Roy W. Atkins, Portland, Ore.
					Kletcke, 5 and 4	J. Paul Popovic, San Francisco, Calif.
				Kletcke, 3 and 2		Eddie Kletcke, Chicago, Ill.
			Kletcke, 1 up		Ivins	BYE—L.R. Ivins, Salt Lake City, Utah
					Shortridge, 4 and 3	David Kim, Honolulu, T.H.
		Dallas, 1 up, 22 hls.		Shortridge, 3 and 2		Roy Shortridge, St. Paul, Minn.
					Trimmell	BYE—Victor T. Trimmel, Wichita, Kans.
				Dallas, 2 and 1	Dallas, 5 and 3	Marshall Dallas, Seattle, Wash.
						James R. Griffitts, Jr., Arcadia, Calif.
			Dallas, 3 and 2		King	BYE—Theodore R. King, Washington, D.C.
					J. Hart, 2 and 1	Walter Strong, Dayton, Ohio
				Galletti, 1 up, 19 hls.		James Hart, Nashville, Tenn.
					Galletti, 6 and 5	Robert E. Schreiber, Bellevue, Wash.
						Aldo Galletti, Oakland, Calif.

1954
TWENTY-NINTH AMATEUR PUBLIC LINKS CHAMPIONSHIP

Held at the Cedar Crest Golf Course, Dallas, Texas, July 12-17.
Yardage—6,296. Par 71. 1,854 Entries, 200 Qualifiers, 200 Starters.
Championship entirely at match play.

FINAL ROUND (36 Holes)—Gene Andrews defeated Jack E. Zimmerman, 1 up.

FIRST QUARTER — UPPER

1st Round (18 Holes)	2nd Round (18 Holes)	3rd Round (18 Holes)	4th Round (18 Holes)	5th Round (18 Holes)	6th Round (18 Holes)	
Milton Frank, St. Louis, Mo.	Frank, 3 and 2					
Arthur Corbin, Dallas, Texas		Frank, 2 and 1				
John Bloyer, St. Paul, Minn.	Furukawa, 3 and 2					
Ervin K. Furukawa, Seattle, Wash.			Frank, 2 and 1			
BYE—Edmons H. Bradham, Charleston, S.C.	Bradham					
George Aubrey, Pittsburgh, Pa.	J. Martin, 3 and 2	Martin, 4 and 3		Scarbrough, 5 and 4		
Jack R. Martin, Oklahoma City, Okla.						
Thomas B. Kenney, Dayton, Ohio	Holshouser, 1 up, 19 hls.					
Larry C. Holshouser, Charlotte, N.C.		Holshouser, 2 and 1				
BYE—Harry Poland, Indianapolis, Ind.	Poland		Scarbrough, 3 and 2			
Rollin Heaton, Jr., Kewanee, Ill.	Kapu, 3 and 2					
Sam Kapu, Honolulu, T.H.		Scarbrough, 1 up, 19 hls.			Scarbrough, 4 and 2	
BYE—Wm. C. Scarbrough, Jr., Jacksonville, Fla.	Scarbrough					
Robert E. Karlin, Denver, Colo.	Wilbert, 4 and 3					
James R. Wilbert, S. San Francisco, Calif.		Wilbert, 4 and 3				
BYE—Richard A. Smith, St. Paul, Minn.	R. Smith		Preston, 1 up, 22 hls.			
BYE—Richard B. Preston, Detroit, Mich.	Preston	Preston, 1 up				
Maynard E. Garrett, New Orleans, La.	Garrett, 2 and 1			Preston, 4 and 3		
Nello Campagni, Highland, Ill.						
Jacob D. Croxton, Atlanta, Ga.	Croxton, 5 and 4					
Johnny R. Arreaga, San Antonio, Texas		Donaldson, 4 and 3				
BYE—Bill Donaldson, Memphis, Tenn.	Donaldson		Taylor, 3 and 1			
Arlie Taylor, Dallas, Texas	A. Taylor, 1 up					
Albert A. Chandler, Hawthorne, Calif.		A. Taylor, 1 up, 19 hls.				Scarbrough, 4 and 2
Albert H. Carson, Wichita, Kans.	Carson, 1 up					
Andrew J. Paul, Peoria, Ill.						
BYE—Thomas F. Lambie, Phoenix, Ariz.	Lambie	Lambie, 3 and 2				
Dr. Charles M. Taylor, Atlanta, Ga.	C. Taylor, 4 and 3					
Luke C. Kyle, Miami, Fla.			Lambie, 1 up			
BYE—Lido Landi, Sharp Park, Calif.	Landi	Landi, 5 and 4				
Chester W. Latawiec, Minneapolis, Minn.	Latawiec, 2 up			Lambie, 2 up		
William E. Archibald, Joliet, Ill.						
William O. Heyn, Roseville, Mich.	Heyn, 2 and 1					
Walter F. Knower, New Orleans, La.		Clark, 1 up, 19 hls.				
BYE—Jim Clark, Minneapolis, Minn.	J. Clark		Brown, 3 and 2			
Jouett T. Brown, Louisville, Ky.	J. Brown, 1 up					
Arthur L. Joiner, Denver, Colo.		Brown, 2 and 1				
BYE—William R. Zimmerman, Dayton, Ohio	Zimmerman				Lambie, 4 and 3	
BYE—Alvin E. Gustafson, Spokane, Wash.	Gustafson	Gustafson, 2 and 1				
Don Dorton, Salt Lake City, Utah	Ferguson, 1 up					
J. Rowland Ferguson, Dallas, Texas			Alcorn, 3 and 2			
BYE—Paul C. Sharpe, Nashville, Tenn.	Sharpe	Alcorn, 3 and 2				
Delong Rice, Memphis, Tenn.	Alcorn, 2 and 1			Alcorn, 5 and 3		
William G. Alcorn, McKeesport, Pa.						
BYE—Leonard L. White, Dallas, Texas	White	White, 3 and 2				
Charles Thurn, South Bend, Ind.	Thurn, 2 and 1					
Joseph A. Carlone, South Euclid, Ohio			White, 5 and 4			
BYE—Edward J. Korylak, North Hollywood, Calif.	Korylak	Korylak, 2 and 1				
John R. Hand, Alton, Ill.	Vanderberg, 2 up					
Edward Vanderberg, Portland, Ore.						

SEMI-FINAL ROUND (36 Holes)—Jack E. Zimmerman defeated William C. Scarbrough, Jr., 5 up and 4 to play.

HALF

SECOND QUARTER

6th Round (18 Holes) | 5th Round (18 Holes) | 4th Round (18 Holes) | 3rd Round (18 Holes) | 2nd Round (18 Holes) | 1st Round (18 Holes)

1st Round (18 Holes)

Warren J. Rebholz, St. Paul, Minn.
Jack E. Zimmerman, Dayton, Ohio
William Szustak, Buffalo, N.Y.
William T. Brown, Los Angeles, Calif.
BYE–Thomas W. O'Neill, Minneapolis, Minn.
Lawrence G. Nyberg, Peoria, Ill.
Bung Kwai Kop, Honolulu, T.H.
Thomas E. Burch, Washington, D.C.
Clayton Lindquist, West Allis, Wis.
BYE–Vard Jones, Salt Lake City, Utah
Charles A. Ribelin, Dallas, Texas
Walter Kroll, South Bend, Ind.
BYE–Shedric E. McKain, Memphis, Tenn.
John R. Trullinger, Philadelphia, Pa.
C.R. James, Jr., Dallas, Texas
BYE–Robert R. Parry, Portland, Ore.
BYE–Sherman A. Conrad, Toledo, Ohio
F.M. Wiggins, Louisville, Ky.
Hal McCommas, Dallas, Texas
Richard Hayman, Detroit, Mich.
Stanley Hobert, Phoenix, Ariz.
BYE–Howard E. Whitman, San Francisco, Calif.
Reese Berry, Indianapolis, Ind.
Richard Huff, Jr., Homestead, Fla.
BYE–Norbert Przybylski, Detroit, Mich.
BYE–Donald J. Keith, South Pasadena, Calif.
Cletus Durbin, Louisville, Ky.
Pat Rauschelbach, Dallas, Texas
BYE–Theodore R. King, Washington, D.C.
W. Morgan Barofsky, San Francisco, Calif.
Roy Iceberg, Pontiac, Mich.
BYE–Cal Burns, St. Francis, Wis.
Andy Sword, Dallas, Texas
Walker W. Hobbs, Memphis, Tenn.
BYE–T. Moultrie McKevlin, Charleston, S.C.
Andrew Szwedko, Pittsburgh, Pa.
Roland Schmidt, Toledo, Ohio
Joseph Gallardo, Jr., Los Angeles, Calif.
George D. Johnson, Atlanta, Ga.
BYE–Gus T. Moreland, Peoria, Ill.
William McGurn, Chicago, Ill.
Lawrence Robertson, Minneapolis, Minn.
BYE–Vernon Smith, Galveston, Texas
Stanley A. Klimecko, Niagara Falls, N.Y.
Miles Baker, Jr., Kansas City, Mo.
BYE–Donald A. Nelson, Minneapolis, Minn.
Auggie Navarro, Wichita, Kans.
Richard Roberts, Anderson, Ind.
Marshall Dallas, Seattle, Wash.
Paul L. Tulga, Columbus, Ohio

2nd Round (18 Holes)

Zimmerman, 4 and 3
Szustak, 3 and 1
O'Neill
Nyberg, 1 up, 19 hls.
Lindquist, default
Jones
Ribelin, 6 and 5
McKain
Trullinger, 1 up
Parry
Conrad
McCommas, 5 and 3
Hayman, 4 and 2
Whitman
Berry, 3 and 2
Przybylski
Keith
Rauschelbach, 4 and 3
King
Iceberg, 2 and 1
Burns
Sword, 4 and 2
McKevlin
Szwedko, 5 and 4
Johnson, 3 and 2
Moreland
Robertson, 4 and 3
Smith
Klimecko, 1 up, 19 hls.
Nelson
Navarro, 5 and 4
Dallas, 2 and 1

3rd Round (18 Holes)

Zimmerman, 2 and 1
Nyberg, 3 and 1
Lindquist, 2 and 1
Ribelin, 6 and 4
Parry, 6 and 5
McCommas, 5 and 4
Hayman, 3 and 1
Berry, 4 and 3
Keith, 5 and 4
King, 3 and 2
Sword, 5 and 4
McKevlin, 1 up, 19 hls.
Johnson, 1 up
Robertson, 3 and 2
Nelson, 1 up, 19 hls.
Navarro, 2 and 1

4th Round (18 Holes)

Zimmerman, 5 and 3
Ribelin, 2 and 1
McCommas, 4 and 2
Berry, 5 and 4
King, 2 up
Sword, 3 and 2
Johnson, 2 and 1
Navarro, 3 and 1

5th Round (18 Holes)

Zimmerman, 1 up
McCommas, 4 and 3
Sword, 3 and 2
Johnson, 4 and 2

6th Round (18 Holes)

Zimmerman, default
Sword, 1 up

HALF

Zimmerman, 2 up

THIRD QUARTER

1st Round (18 Holes)	2nd Round (18 Holes)	3rd Round (18 Holes)	4th Round (18 Holes)	5th Round (18 Holes)	6th Round (18 Holes)	
Lou F. Chaff, Jacksonville, Fla.	Chaff, 1 up, 19 hls.					
Homer Dunn, Englewood, Colo.		Daniel, 3 and 1				
Robert F. Daniel, San Francisco, Calif.	Daniel, 3 and 2					
D.H. Looney, Birmingham, Ala.			Andonian, 6 and 5			
BYE—Mike M. Andonian, Pontiac, Mich.	Andonian	Andonian, 3 and 2				
Clinton McHenry, Jr., New Orleans, La.	McClure, 1 up, 19 hls.			Evans, 5 and 4		
John D. McClure, Wichita, Kans.						
Bob Ludlow, Indianapolis, Ind.	Ludlow, 4 and 3					
Finley W. Brown, Peoria, Ill.		Ludlow, 3 and 1				
BYE—John Carson, Atlanta, Ga.	Carson		Evans, 7 and 6			
Robert E. Murray, Xenia, Ohio	Evans, 2 up					
Joseph S. Evans, St. Louis, Mo.		Evans, 3 and 2				
BYE—Ray Resch, St. Paul, Minn.	Resch				Evans, 2 up	
Steve P. Lakos, Cleveland, Ohio	Lakos, 4 and 3					
Don Millender, Dallas, Texas		Vicini, 7 and 5				
BYE—Dante Vicini, Ottawa, Ill.	Vicini		Vicini, 2 and 1			
BYE—Stephen Z. Shaw, Monterey Park, Calif.	Shaw	Clasen, 2 up				
Al Clasen, St. Paul, Minn.	Clasen, 3 and 2			Vicini, 2 and 1		
Ralph Emery, Salt Lake City, Utah						
James F. Stewart, Dallas, Texas	Tant, 1 up, 19 hls.					
David Tant, Nashville, Tenn.		Tant, 4 and 3				
BYE—James G. Horrês, Charleston, S.C.	Horres		Burtner, 3 and 1			
Al Neveraskas, Castle Shannon, Pa.	Burtner, 6 and 5					
Louis Burtner, Oklahoma City, Okla.		Burtner, 1 up, 19 hls.				
Harry E. Missildine, Spokane, Wash.	Bielat, 2 up					Evans, 6 and 4
Stanley Bielat, Yonkers, N.Y.						
BYE—William Kalina, Minneapolis, Minn.	Kalina	Kalina, 4 and 2				
Graydon Todd, Memphis, Tenn.	Betus, 3 and 2		Kalina, 7 and 5			
Edward Betus, Sharpsburg, Pa.						
BYE—Ellsworth R. Jones, Portland, Ore.	Jones	Jaros, 1 up, 19 hls.		Dayiantis, 2 up		
Tony Jaros, Minneapolis, Minn.	Jaros, 1 up					
William J. Podolski, Columbus, Ohio						
Thomas Bujeker, South Bend, Ind.	Dayiantis, 3 and 2					
George Dayiantis, Chicago, Ill.		Dayiantis, 5 and 3				
BYE—Tommy Williams, Ogden, Utah	Williams		Dayiantis, 2 up			
Jimmy Powell, Dallas, Texas	Powell, 2 and 1					
Harold Stevens, Nashville, Tenn.		Porter, 1 up			Funseth, 1 up, 23 hls.	
BYE—Robert Porter, Phoenix, Ariz.	Porter					
BYE—Fred E. Lukat, Washington, D.C.	Lukat	Fry, 4 and 2				
Shannon Crowell, Dallas, Texas	Fry, 2 and 1		**Smith, default**			
John Fry, Oakland, Calif.						
BYE—Wallace Smith, Royal Oak, Mich.	W. Smith	Smith, 3 and 2		Funseth, 1 up, 20 hls.		
Stephen Rowley, Shreveport, La.	Essig, 1 up					
Don Essig, III, Indianapolis, Ind.						
BYE—Frank Cain, Louisville, Ky.	Cain	Montgomery, 3 and 2	Funseth, 1 up			
Donald A. Montgomery, Long Beach, Calif.	Montgomery, 4 and 3					
Charles Afong, Honolulu, T.H.						
BYE—Donald Hess, Miami, Fla.	Hess	Funseth, 9 and 8				
Joseph Kover, Cleveland, Ohio	Funseth, 3 and 2					
Rodney Funseth, Spokane, Wash.						

SEMI-FINAL ROUND (36 Holes)—Gene Andrews defeated Joseph S. Evans, 6 up and 4 to play.

Twenty-Eighth Amateur Public Links Team Championship, Harding Trophy, 30 Entries, July 10. Won by Dallas, Texas team, 220 for 18 holes (C.R. James, Jr., 71; Andrew Sword, 73; Richard Martin, 76); second, Los Angeles, Calif., team, 225 (Gene Andrews, 72; Albert Chandler, 74; Donald J. Keith, 74); third, tie at 227 between St. Louis, Mo., and Detroit, Mich. teams.

CHAMPIONSHIP—Continued

HALF

FOURTH QUARTER

6th Round (18 Holes)	5th Round (18 Holes)		4th Round (18 Holes)	3rd Round (18 Holes)	2nd Round (18 Holes)	1st Round (18 Holes)
					Webb, 5 and 3	Rudolph Rychel, Jr., Niagara Falls, N.Y.
				Ahn, 1 up		Robbie Webb, Gulfport, Miss.
					Ahn, 3 and 2	Roy V. McIntire, Peoria, Ill.
			Ahn, 1 up			Hung Soo Ahn, Honolulu, T. H.
					Graham	BYE—William Graham, Miami, Fla.
		Masterson, 6 and 5		Lima, 2 and 1	Lima, 5 and 4	Samuel E. Lima, Detroit, Mich.
						U.C. Jones, Jr., Milwaukee, Wis.
					Masterson, 1 up	Richard P. Masterson, Seattle, Wash.
				Masterson, 4 and 3		Robert D. Mitchell, Dallas, Texas
					Green	BYE—Howard Green, Memphis, Tenn.
			Masterson, 1 up		Galantino, 3 and 2	Fred Galantino, Philadelphia, Pa.
				Todd, 6 and 4		Mike Garbacz, South Bend, Ind.
					Todd	BYE—Arthur Todd, Columbus, Ohio
	Hatch, 1 up				Hopwood, 3 and 1	Dick Hopwood, Phoenix, Ariz.
				Lee, 3 and 2		Bill Duckwall, Louisville, Ky.
					Lee	BYE—Lynn R. Lee, Indianapolis, Ind.
			Martin, 5 and 4		Martin	BYE—Richard Martin, Dallas, Texas
		Hatch, 1 up, 21 hls.		Martin, 2 up	Brotschnieder 3 and 2	Walter Brotschnieder, San Mateo, Calif.
						Bob E. Patterson, Portland, Ore.
					Gunderson, 3 and 2	Gene Friedt, Toledo, Ohio
				Hatch, 2 up		Robert J. Gunderson, Los Angeles, Calif.
					Hatch	BYE—John Hatch, Dallas, Texas
			Hatch, 3 and 2		Miracle, 5 and 4	Bob Korsch, Duluth, Minn.
				Wilson, 1 up, 19 hls.		H.C. Miracle, Washington, D.C.
					Wilson	BYE—Doug Wilson, Oak Park, Mich.
Andrews, 6 and 5					Cheslak	BYE—Joseph Cheslak, Minneapolis, Minn.
				Litzo, 1 up, 19 hls.	Litzo, 2 up	Walt Durdle, Peoria, Ill.
			Jennemann, 3 and 2			Ray Litzo, Denver, Colo.
					Kamman	BYE—Joseph R. Kamman, Tonawanda, N.Y.
		Shively, 1 up, 20 hls.		Jennemann, 2 and 1	Jennemann, 3 and 2	Arthur Jennemann, St. Louis, Mo.
						John Kurach, Detroit, Mich.
					Swedo, default	Joseph J. Muller, New Orleans, La.
				Swedo, 2 and 1		Raymond Swedo, Montebello, Calif.
					Harmon	BYE—A.T. Harmon, Atlanta, Ga.
			Shively, 2 up		Shively	BYE—E.F. Shively, Dayton, Ohio
				Shively, 1 up	King, 9 and 7	James King, Chicago, Ill.
						Edward L. Ketchum, Milwaukee, Wis.
	Andrews, 3 and 2				Jenkins, 6 and 5	Moreno Caso, Seattle, Wash.
				Jenkins, 2 and 1		Edwin H. Jenkins, Jacksonville, Fla.
					McGeehon	BYE—Ray McGeehon, Texas City, Texas
			Jenkins, 3 and 2		**Blankenship,** 4 and 3	Donald Thornton, Los Angeles, Calif.
		Andrews, 3 and 2		**Blankenship,** 5 and 4		**J.L. Blankenship, Memphis, Tenn.**
					McEwen	BYE—W.D. McEwen, Charleston, S.C.
					Apple, 2 up	Stanley P. Poploski, Pittsburgh, Pa.
				Apple, 1 up		Walter B. Apple, Dallas, Texas
					Farmer	BYE—Hubert S. Farmer, Toledo, Ohio
			Andrews, 2 and 1		Pfeiffer, 1 up, 19 hls.	V.T. Trimmell, Wichita, Kans.
				Andrews, 3 and 1		John Pfeiffer, Indianapolis, Ind.
					Andrews, 4 and 3	Gene Andrews, Pacific Palisades, Calif.
						Mike Holick, Minneapolis, Minn.

1955
THIRTIETH AMATEUR PUBLIC LINKS CHAMPIONSHIP

Held at the Coffin Municipal Golf Course, Indianapolis, Ind., July 11-16.
Yardage—6,536. Par 70. 2,007 Entries, 200 Qualifiers, 200 Starters.
Championship proper entirely at match play.
FINAL ROUND (36 Holes)—Sam D. Kocsis defeated Lewis T. Bean, 2 up.

FIRST QUARTER

UPPER

1st Round (18 Holes)	2nd Round (18 Holes)	3rd Round (18 Holes)	4th Round (18 Holes)	5th Round (18 Holes)	6th Round (18 Holes)	
Ryan Lancaster, Pekin, Ill.	Lancaster, 3 and 1					
Gary H. McKenzie, Duluth, Minn.		Kelly, 2 and 1				
Lester Kelly, Atlanta, Ga.	Kelly, 1 up, 19 hls.					
Bob Karin, Denver, Colo.			Carlson, 1 up			
BYE—Robert L. Faulkenberry, Jr., Oklahoma City, Okla.	Faulkenberry					
Robert T. Geisler, Toledo, Ohio	Carlson, 3 and 1	Carlson, 1 up, 20 hls.		Carlson, 3 and 2		
Marshall F. Carlson, Miami, Fla.						
Milton Frank, St. Louis, Mo.	Frank, 4 and 3					
William G. Alcorn, McKeesport, Pa.		Essig, 5 and 3				
BYE—Don Essig, III, Indianapolis, Ind.	Essig					
Joe Golob, Cleveland, Ohio	Chmiel, 7 and 6		Essig, 3 and 1		Scarbrough, 1 up, 19 hls.	
John Chmiel, Buffalo, N.Y.		Chmiel, 3 and 1				
BYE—Richard Hall, Indianapolis, Ind.	Hall					
William C. Scarbrough, Jr., Jacksonville, Fla.	Scarbrough, 3 and 2					
Sherry Wellons, Detroit, Mich.		Scarbrough, 1 up				
BYE—Harlan Stevenson, Long Beach, Calif.	Stevenson					
BYE—John Foley, Indianapolis, Ind.	Foley		Scarbrough, 4 and 3			
Stanley Hobert, Phoenix, Ariz.	Atkins, 4 and 3	Atkins, 4 and 3		Scarbrough, 1 up, 19 hls.		
Roy W. Atkins, Portland, Ore.						
Ron Eitel, Racine, Wis.	Todd, 3 and 2					
Arthur Todd, Columbus, Ohio		J. Kocsis, 5 and 3				
BYE—Joe Kocsis, Pontiac, Mich.	J. Kocsis					
Jack Cummings, Alameda, Calif.	Cummings, 2 and 1		J. Kocsis, 3 and 2			
Trawgott L. Schmidt, Washington, D.C.		Roddy, 1 up				
Chester W. Latawiec, Minneapolis, Minn.	Roddy, 1 up, 20 hls.					
George A. Roddy, Indianapolis, Ind.						Bean, 2 and 1
BYE—John Pasikowski, Sharpsburg, Pa.	Pasikowski	Bean, 5 and 4				
Henry Felker, Oshkosh, Wis.	Bean, 1 up, 19 hls.					
Lewis T. Bean, Summerville, Ga.			Bean, 3 and 2			
BYE—E. Imboden, St. Louis, Mo.	Imboden	Imboden, 7 and 6				
Joe San Filippo, Miami, Fla.	Gargan, 1 up, 21 hls.			Bean, 2 and 1		
Jack Gargan, Hollywood, Calif.						
Dick Martin, Dallas, Texas	Martin, 4 and 3					
Jack S.S. Chun, Honolulu, T.H.		Martin, 2 up				
BYE—Joseph P. Riordan, Phoenix, Ariz.	Riordan		Martin, 2 and 1			
Paul B. Gehring, Baltimore, Md.	Gehring, 5 and 4					
Moultrie McKevlin, Charleston, S.C.		Caspio, 4 and 3				
BYE—Jim Caspio, Cleveland, Ohio	Caspio				Bean, 5 and 4	
BYE—Art Linhares, Daly City, Calif.	Linhares	Murray, 2 and 1				
Robert E. Murray, Xenia, Ohio	Murray, 1 up					
H.A. Gilbertson, Minneapolis, Minn.			Borson, 6 and 4			
BYE—Mike Borson, Anderson, Ind.	Borson	Borson, 1 up, 22 hls.				
Arthur J. Cassidy, Peoria, Ill.	Cassidy, 3 and 2			Borson, 1 up, 19 hls.		
Gus Manganello, White Plains, N.Y.						
BYE—Richard Allison, Detroit, Mich.	Allison	Allison, 3 and 2				
Harry Oates, Tonawanda, N.Y.	Maidment, 5 and 4					
Gene Maidment, Portland, Ore.			Allison, 1 up			
BYE—Glenn Bryant, St. Paul, Minn.	Bryant	Purvis, 3 and 2				
Tom E. Black, Oklahoma City, Okla.	Purvis, 3 and 2					
John Purvis, Jr., Memphis, Tenn.						

SEMI-FINAL ROUND (36 Holes)—Lewis T. Bean defeated Ralph Allen, 1 up, 37 holes.

HALF

SECOND QUARTER

6th Round (18 Holes)	5th Round (18 Holes)		4th Round (18 Holes)	3rd Round (18 Holes)	2nd Round (18 Holes)	1st Round (18 Holes)
					Parry, 2 and 1	James R. Spencer, St. Louis, Mo. Robert Parry, Portland, Ore.
				Parry, 4 and 2		
					Glick, 1 up	Jack A. McIntire, Peoria, Ill. Harry Glick, New York, N.Y.
			Kivett, 1 up			
					Kivett	BYE—James Kivett, High Point, N.C.
				Kivett, 2 up		
		Kivett, 2 and 1			Green, 3 and 2	Eddie Kletcke, Chicago, Ill. John R. Green, Jr., Louisville, Ky.
					Ahn, 5 and 4	Earl L. Marcey, Washington, D.C. Hung Soo Ahn, Honolulu, T. H.
				Law, 5 and 3		
					Law	BYE—James Law, Harper Woods, Mich.
			Clark, 1 up			
					Clark, 3 and 1	Warren A. Hawkins, Memphis, Tenn. Milo E. Clark, Dallas, Texas
				Clark, 2 up		
	Allen, 1 up				Medina	BYE—Henry Medina, Tucson, Ariz.
					Allen, 3 and 2	Charles Lipchik, Erie, Pa. Ralph Allen, Miami Springs, Fla.
				Allen, 5 and 3		
					Quick	BYE—Marlow Quick, Salt Lake City, Utah
			Allen, 1 up, 20 hls.			
					Popovic	BYE—J. Paul Popovic, San Francisco, Calif.
				Mathews, 2 up		
					Mathews, 3 and 2	Harry T. Mathews, Atlanta, Ga. Alex Sutton, Jr., Los Angeles, Calif.
		Allen, 3 and 2			Adams, 1 up, 21 hls.	Nick Kappa, Racine, Wis. John E. Adams, Jr., Charleston, S.C.
				Stiver, 5 and 3		
					Stiver	BYE—Dale Stiver, Dayton, Ohio
			Olson, 3 and 2			
					Olson, 1 up	Russell Rader, Sr., Indianapolis, Ind. Dayton Olson, Minneapolis, Minn.
				Olson, 4 and 3		
					Shipp	BYE—James E. Shipp, Indianapolis, Ind.
Allen, 3 and 1					Ebel	BYE—Edward Ebel, Minneapolis, Minn.
				Nannini, 5 and 3		
					Nannini, 1 up	Toshio Santoki, Honolulu, T.H. Norando Nannini, Highwood, Ill.
			Nannini, 2 and 1			
					Lockie	BYE—Floyd Lockie, Jr., Spokane, Wash.
				Biernat, 1 up		
		Fry, 5 and 4			Biernat, 2 and 1	John Biernat, Minneapolis, Minn. Don Keller, Tucson, Ariz.
					Garrison	BYE—Paul B. Garrison, Palmyra, Pa.
				Fry, 4 and 2		
					Fry, 1 up, 19 hls.	Robert M. Joyce, Bayside, N.Y. John Fry, Oakland, Calif.
			Fry, 1 up			
					Kelley	BYE—Don Kelley, North Hollywood, Calif.
				Nielsen, 6 and 5		
	Turner, 3 and 2				Nielsen, 1 up, 22 hls.	Tom Nielsen, Racine, Wis. William K. Lanning, Rolla, Mo.
					Strong, 1 up	Edmons H. Bradham, Charleston, S.C. Walter Strong, Dayton, Ohio
				Strong, 3 and 2		
					Lima	BYE—Samuel E. Lima, E. Detroit, Mich.
			Lake, 1 up			
					Lake, 1 up, 19 hls.	J. Rowland Ferguson, Dallas, Texas Eugene Lake, Toledo, Ohio
				Lake, 3 and 2		
					Ellis	BYE—Alvin D. Ellis, Atlanta, Ga.
		Turner, 5 and 3			Berry, 5 and 4	Reese Berry, Indianapolis, Ind. Bill Schooley, Louisville, Ky.
				Berry, 6 and 4		
					Green	BYE—Robert M. Green, Memphis, Tenn.
			Turner, 4 and 3			
					Turner, 4 and 3	John U. Law, Detroit, Mich. Hans R. Turner, Seattle, Wash.
				Turner, 5 and 4		
					Starcevic, 1 up	Jack Simpson, Mooresville, Ind. Joe Starcevic, Peoria, Ill.

THIRD QUARTER

1st Round (18 Holes)	2nd Round (18 Holes)	3rd Round (18 Holes)	4th Round (18 Holes)	5th Round (18 Holes)	6th Round (18 Holes)	
Charles Afong, Honolulu, T.H.	Afong,					
Hans W. Schulz, Farmington, Mich.	3 and 2	Andrews,				
Wallace Smith, Pontiac, Mich.	Andrews,	6 and 5				
Gene Andrews, Pacific Palisades, Calif.	1 up, 19 hls.		Andrews,			
BYE—Foster Bradley, Los Angeles, Calif.	Bradley		5 and 3			
		Bradley,		Andrews, 4 and 3		
David Leon, Tucson, Ariz.	Leon,	4 and 3				
Norman Nelson, Dayton, Ohio	2 and 1					
Arthur H. Corbin, Dallas, Texas	Corbin,					
Bill Phillips, Louisville, Ky.	3 and 1	Corbin,				
BYE—Patsy Vivino, Philadelphia, Pa.	Vivino	4 and 3				
			O'Brien,			
Nello Campagni, Highwood, Ill.	O'Brien,		5 and 4			
Bill O'Brien, Seattle, Wash.	1 up	O'Brien,				
BYE—Pat Shanesy, Minneapolis, Minn.	Shanesy	7 and 6			Andrews, 7 and 6	
Joseph Hook, Indianapolis, Ind.	Miller,					
Robert J. Miller, Rochester, Minn.	3 and 1	Miller,				
BYE—Ray Schmidt, Spokane, Wash.	Schmidt	1 up				
			Clasen,			
BYE—Hugh E. O'Brien, Charleston, S.C.	O'Brien		3 and 2			
		Clasen,				
George Roney, Pittsburgh, Pa.	Clasen,	7 and 6				
Albert Clasen, St. Paul, Minn.	4 and 2			Robyn, 3 and 2		
Bob Funk, Indianapolis, Ind.	Funk,					
J.L. Blankenship, Memphis, Tenn.	1 up	Robyn,				
BYE—Walter Robyn, Maplewood, Mo.	Robyn	3 and 2				
			Robyn,			
Hugh Farmer, Toledo, Ohio	Farmer,		3 and 2			
Bob Reynolds, Peoria, Ill.	4 and 3	Farmer,				
Charles A. Dailey, Jr., Galveston, Texas	Douglas,	1 up, 19 hls.				Andrews, 4 and 3
Bryce Douglas, Bloomington, Ind.	7 and 6					
BYE—Richard P. Hardcastle, Jr., Dayton, Ohio	Hardcastle					
		Kapu,				
Richard Metzger, Louisville, Ky.	Kapu,	4 and 3				
Sam Kapu, Honolulu, T.H.	3 and 2		Kapu,			
BYE—Ronald E. Roach, Terre Haute, Ind.	Roach		3 and 2			
		Miller,				
Fred Hall, Peoria, Ill.	Miller,	4 and 3		Kapu, 3 and 2		
J. Eddie Miller, Los Angeles, Calif.	1 up					
Chief Henry T. Nugent, Birmingham, Ala.	Nugent,					
Louis Kaminski, Pittsburgh, Pa.	2 and 1	Clark,				
BYE—James Clark, Minneapolis, Minn.	Clark	4 and 3				
			Seyler,			
Roy Shortridge, St. Paul, Minn.	Seyler,		1 up			
Ovid Seyler, San Francisco, Calif.	5 and 4	Seyler,				
BYE—Gene Frase, Memphis, Tenn.	Frase	2 up			Gregory, 5 and 3	
BYE—Leo Kubiak, Toledo, Ohio	Kubiak					
		Kubiak,				
Ronald Jachowski, Phoenix, Ariz.	McDowell,	3 and 1				
Roy McDowell, Chicago, Ill.	2 and 1		Gregory,			
BYE—Howard Logan, Wichita, Kans.	Logan		2 and 1			
		Gregory,				
Jack H. Gregory, Detroit, Mich.	Gregory,	5 and 4		Gregory, 1 up, 21 hls.		
A. Gonzales, New Orleans, La.	2 and 1					
BYE—Billy Joe Lauer, Spokane, Wash.	Lauer					
		Lauer,				
Erv Furukawa, Seattle, Wash.	Mural,	6 and 5				
Mike Mural, Jr., Parma, Ohio	7 and 5		Lauer,			
BYE—Michael Deverant, Glenside, Pa.	Deverant		4 and 2			
		Sckrabulis,				
Don Sckrabulis, Kewanee, Ill.	Sckrabulis,	3 and 2				
Richard B. Preston, Detroit, Mich.	5 and 4					

SEMI-FINAL ROUND (36 Holes)—Sam D. Kocsis defeated Gene Andrews, 1 up.

Twenty-Ninth Amateur Public Links Team Championship, Harding Trophy, 32 Entries, July 9. Won by Miami, Fla. team, 224 for 18 holes (Joe San Filippo, 72; Marshall S. Carlson, 75; Ralph T. Allen, 77); second, Seattle, Wash., team, 225 (Bill O'Brien, 74; Erv Furukawa, 75; Hans Turner, 76); third, Indianapolis, Ind., team, 226 (George A. Roddy, 74; Bob Funk, 75; James E. Shipp, 77).

CHAMPIONSHIP—Continued

HALF

FOURTH QUARTER

6th Round (18 Holes)	5th Round (18 Holes)		4th Round (18 Holes)	3rd Round (18 Holes)	2nd Round (18 Holes)	1st Round (18 Holes)
					Korylak, 2 up	Edwin H. Jenkins, Jacksonville, Fla.
				Korylak, 1 up, 19 hls.		Edward J. Korylak, North Hollywood, Calif.
					Lindquist, 1 up, 19 hls.	Clayton Lindquist, West Allis, Wis.
			Gacek, 4 and 3			John M. Wood, Birmingham, Ala.
					Huddleston	BYE—Robert O. Huddleston, Toledo, Ohio
				Gacek, 1 up, 20 hls.	Gacek, 4 and 3	Michael Rak, Minneapolis, Minn.
		Gacek, 1 up, 19 hls.				Frank J. Gacek, Parma, Ohio
					Weishaar, 2 up	**George E. Weishaar, Spokane, Wash.**
				Weishaar, 3 and 2		Andrew Szwedko, Sharpsburg, Pa.
			Weishaar, 2 and 1		Degen	BYE—William Degen, Buffalo, N.Y.
					Hopwood, 7 and 6	Dick Hopwood, Phoenix, Ariz.
				Moreland, 1 up		George Hooley, Peoria, Ill.
					Moreland	BYE—Gus Moreland, Peoria, Ill.
	Gacek, 2 and 1				Brucker, 2 up	LaVern Grunquist, Englewood, Colo.
				Parker, 3 and 2		Jim Brucker, Indianapolis, Ind.
			Heyn, 4 and 2		Parker	BYE—Virgil Parker, Wichita, Kans.
				Heyn, 6 and 5	Barkley	**BYE—Dan Barkley, Seattle, Wash.**
					Heyn, 7 and 6	William O. Heyn, Roseville, Mich.
		Daniel, 2 and 1				Robert J. Hickey, Franklin Park, Ill.
					Nichols, 4 and 3	Newell Beedy, Minneapolis, Minn.
				Nichols, 5 and 3		Bobby Nichols, Louisville, Ky.
			Daniel, 7 and 6		Anderson	BYE—Norbert Anderson, St. Paul, Minn.
					Daniel, 5 and 4	Steve J. Bialo, Detroit, Mich.
				Daniel, 6 and 5		Bob Daniel, San Francisco, Calif.
					Garrett	BYE—M.E. Garrett, Sr., New Orleans, La.
Kocsis, 3 and 1				Lichtenwalter, 3 and 1	Lichtenwalter	BYE—Robert W. Lichtenwalter, Erie, Pa.
			Lichtenwalter, 4 and 3		Brown, 6 and 4	Jouett Brown, Louisville, Ky.
						Dexter J. Abbott, Memphis, Tenn.
				Everett, 4 and 3	Varvil	BYE—Ted Varvil, Peoria, Ill.
		Thurn, 10 and 8			Everett, 3 and 2	Leo Ken Everett, Denver, Colo.
						John Lane, San Francisco, Calif.
				Thurn, 5 and 4	Thurn, 3 and 2	Alex Solanics, Euclid, Ohio
						Charles W. Thurn, South Bend, Ind.
			Thurn, 1 up, 19 hls.		Rak	BYE—John J. Rak, Minneapolis, Minn.
				Milosch, 3 and 2	Milosch	**BYE—Bernard Milosch, Jr., South Milwaukee, Wis.**
	Kocsis, 4 and 3				Ghioto, 1 up	Jim Carrington, Wichita, Kans.
						Ralph C. Ghioto, Jr., Jacksonville, Fla.
				Cullenbine, 1 up	Sutton, 5 and 4	James D. Sutton, Atlanta, Ga.
						A. Thomas Terza, Duquesne, Pa.
			Kay, 3 and 2		Cullenbine	BYE—Roy Cullenbine, Detroit, Mich.
				Kay, 1 up	Caso, 2 and 1	Eddie Wietecha, Chicago, Ill.
						Moreno Caso, Seattle, Wash.
		Kocsis, 6 and 5			Kay	BYE—Robert Kay, Toledo, Ohio
				Kocsis, 6 and 5	Kocsis, 5 and 4	P.F. Patsue, Indianapolis, Ind.
						Sam D. Kocsis, Detroit, Mich.
			Kocsis, 6 and 5		Bujeker	BYE—Thomas Bujeker, South Bend, Ind.
				Martin, 1 up, 19 hls.	Martin, 3 and 2	Jack Martin, Oklahoma City, Okla.
						Gene Verostko, Terre Haute, Ind.
					Chandler, 4 and 2	Albert A. Chandler, Hawthorne, Calif.
						Hal Bolin, Phoenix, Ariz.

1956
THIRTY-FIRST AMATEUR PUBLIC LINKS CHAMPIONSHIP

Held at the Harding Park Golf Course, San Francisco, Calif., July 9-14.
Yardage—6,683. Par 72. 1,921 Entries, 150 Qualifiers, 150 Starters.

Qualifying Score	1st Round (18 Holes)	2nd Round (18 Holes)	3rd Round (18 Holes)	4th Round (18 Holes)	Semi-Finals (36 Holes)	Final (36 Holes)	
145	Daniel D. Sikes, Jr., Jacksonville, Fla.	Sikes, 1 up					
155	Raymond A. Morgan, Bloomington, Ill.						
154	Mike Furgo, Montebello, Calif.	Roach, 5 and 3	Roach, 3 and 1				
154	Joe Roach, Los Angeles, Calif.						
152	Stanley Hobert, Phoenix, Ariz.	Frase, 2 and 1		Roach, 1 up, 20 hls.			
153	Gene Frase, Memphis, Tenn.						
154	Mike M. Andonian, Pontiac, Mich.	Andonian, 4 and 2	Andonian, 2 and 1				
155	Lt. Isamu Murata, Honolulu, T.H.						
155	Harry Mussatto, Macomb, Ill.	DeVos, 3 and 2			Scarbrough, 3 and 2		
155	Charles F. DeVos, Lynnwood, Wash.						
151	Bobby H. Nichols, Louisville, Ky.	Nichols, 1 up	Nichols, 5 and 4				
154	Julian M. Williams, Washington, D.C.						
154	Richard Heise, Bloomington, Ill.	Langert, 7 and 6		Scarbrough, 5 and 4			
146	Eddie Langert, Memphis, Tenn.						
152	William C. Scarbrough, Jr., Jacksonville, Fla.	Scarbrough, 2 and 1	Scarbrough, 2 and 1				
155	John F. Butler, Atlanta, Ga.						
155	Norman G. Cotchonis, Los Angeles, Calif.	Olson, 3 and 2				Scarbrough, 6 and 5	
150	Craig Olson, Long Beach, Calif.						
155	Billy Joe Lauer, Spokane, Wash.	North, 1 up	North, 1 up, 20 hls.				
154	James North, North Bend, Wash.						
155	Edward Nakagaki, Honolulu, T.H.	Lane, 2 and 1		Esposito, 1 up, 19 hls.			
150	Dick Lane, Los Angeles, Calif.						
145	Fred Corvi, San Francisco, Calif.	Esposito, 2 and 1	Esposito, 3 and 2				
154	Emil Esposito, Franklin Park, Ill.						
155	John F. Fry, Oakland, Calif.	Fry, 1 up			Seyler, 3 and 2		
154	Art Linhares, Daly City, Calif.						
155	Richard G. Huff, Jr., Homestead, Fla.	Seyler, 2 and 1	Seyler, 1 up, 20 hls.				
151	Ovid Seyler, San Francisco, Calif.						
152	Dick Hermann, La Canada, Calif.	Patterson, 1 up		Seyler, 3 and 2			
153	Bob Patterson, Portland, Ore.						
151	Milo E. Clark, Dallas, Texas	DeMello, 3 and 2	DeMello, 5 and 4				
155	John A. DeMello, Honolulu, T.H.						
155	Ron Eitel, Racine, Wis.	Schefcick, 6 and 5					James H. Buxbaum, 3 and 2
150	Peter Schefcick, San Mateo, Calif.						
143	Joe Gallardo, Jr., Los Angeles, Calif.	Mural, 4 and 3	Schefcick, 2 up				
154	Mike Mural, Parma, Ohio						
152	Lee Eaton, Los Angeles, Calif.	Eaton, 5 and 3		Wilbert, 3 and 2			
150	Gerald C. Williams, Indianapolis, Ind.						
150	Phil Snouffer, Indianapolis, Ind.	Wilbert, 3 and 2	Wilbert, 4 and 3				
149	James R. Wilbert, South San Francisco, Calif.						
151	Steve P. Lakos, Cleveland, Ohio	Martin, 3 and 2			Wilbert, 4 and 3		
154	Richard Martin, Dallas, Texas						
153	George Aubrey, Moon Run, Pa.	Aubrey, 5 and 3	Aubrey, 3 and 2				
151	Shedric McKain, Memphis, Tenn.						
150	George A. Roddy, Indianapolis, Ind.	Callison, 2 and 1		Callison, 3 and 1			
142	Verne Callison, Sacramento, Calif.						
154	John Foley, Seattle, Wash.	Foley, 5 and 4	Callison, 2 and 1				
154	Gordon L. Sibley, Jr., Glencoe, Ill.						
146	James H. Buxbaum, Memphis, Tenn.	Buxbaum, 1 up				Buxbaum, 2 and 1	
149	Jouett T. Brown, Louisville, Ky.						
150	David H. Lawrence, Phoenix, Ariz.	Hart, 4 and 3	Buxbaum, 1 up				
144	Roy Hart, Daly City, Calif.						
154	Richard H. Hopwood, Phoenix, Ariz.	Hopwood, 4 and 3		Buxbaum, 2 and 1			
148	Jim Stewart, Dallas, Texas						
153	Robert Daniel, San Francisco, Calif.	Daniel, 2 and 1	Hopwood, 2 and 1				
153	John R. Hall, Atlanta, Ga.						
152	E.A. St. John, Oklahoma City, Okla.	Mazza, 2 and 1			Buxbaum, 1 up		
152	John Mazza, San Francisco, Calif.						
152	Ben G. Hughes, Portland, Ore.	Galios, 5 and 4	Galios, 1 up				
155	George Galios, Monterey, Calif.						
148	Richard A. Stearns, Portland, Ore.	Onstad, 1 up		Galios, 1 up			
151	David Onstad, Miami Springs, Fla.						
141	*D.M. McBeath, Palo Alto, Calif.	McBeath, 4 and 3	McBeath, 5 and 3				
155	Fred Hubert, Pekin, Ill.						

*Medalist.

Fifteen players tied at 155 for last fourteen places. Two players, Billy Joe Lauer and Edward Briegel failed to appear for playoff and last qualifying place was awarded to Lauer by a draw.

Thirtieth Amateur Public Links Team Championship, Harding Trophy, 25 Entries, July 9-10: Won by Memphis, Tenn. team 445 for 36 holes (James H. Buxbaum, 146; Eddie Langert, 146; Gene Frase, 153); second, tie at 453 between Dallas, Texas, team (Richard Martin, 154; Jim Stewart, 148; Milo E. Clark, 151) and Portland, Ore., team (Richard A. Sterns, 148; Ben G. Hughes, 152; Bob Patterson, 153); third, San Francisco, Calif., team, 454 (James R. Wilbert, 149; George Galios, 155; Peter Schefcick, 150).

1957
THIRTY-SECOND AMATEUR PUBLIC LINKS CHAMPIONSHIP

Held at the Hershey Park Golf Club, Hershey, Pa., July 29-August 3.
Yardage—6,055. Par 70. 1,923 Entries, 150 Qualifiers, 150 Starters.

Qualifying Score	1st Round (18 Holes)	2nd Round (18 Holes)	3rd Round (18 Holes)	4th Round (18 Holes)	Semi-Finals (36 Holes)	Final (36 Holes)
151	Gene Towry, Dallas, Texas	Towry, 1 up				
149	Marvin Hester, Jr., Birmingham, Ala.		Towry, 4 and 2			
147	Robert Daniel, San Francisco, Calif.	Daniel, 7 and 6				
144	John Clemens, Minneapolis, Minn.			Towry, 3 and 2		
145	Elmer Clites, Antioch, Calif.	Clites, 2 and 1				
149	Eugene Lunini, Pekin, Ill.		Clites, 2 up			
147	**Chester W. Latawiec, Minneapolis, Minn.**	Scarbrough, 6 and 5				
150	William C. Scarbrough, Jr., Jacksonville, Fla.				Towry, 4 and 3	
148	Arthur J. Garrison, Hershey, Pa.	Garrison, 5 and 4				
153	**Ralph Emery, Salt Lake City, Utah**		Tolf, 6 and 5			
150	Dudley Krueger, Austin, Texas	Tolf, 2 and 1				
148	Robert F. Tolf, Scarsdale, N.Y.			Kivett, 1 up, 20 hls.		
145	Stanley Hobert, Phoenix, Ariz.	Kivett, 2 and 1				
141	*Bud Kivett, High Point, N.C.		Kivett, 1 up, 19 hls.			
150	Elmer Lancie, Pittsburgh, Pa.	Pistorio, 1 up				
153	**Anthony E. Pistorio, Baltimore, Md.**					Towry, 7 and 6
151	Mike M. Andonian, Pontiac, Mich.	Patak, 1 up, 19 hls.				
149	Raymond H. Patak, Dallas, Texas		Ball, 3 and 2			
152	Woodrow W. Ball, Portland, Ore.	Ball, 4 and 3				
149	Robert E. Murray, Xenia, Ohio			Valuck, 4 and 2		
150	Phillip Cannon, Provo, Utah	Vicini, 3 and 1				
150	Dante C. Vicini, Chicago, Ill.		Valuck, 2 up			
153	John F. Butler, Atlanta, Ga.	Valuck, 4 and 3				
142	Dr. Sam W. Valuck, Denver, Colo.				Popovic, 4 and 3	
150	Traugott L. Schmidt, Upper Darby, Pa.	Schmidt, 1 up				
145	Archie Dadian, Milwaukee, Wis.		Popovic, 3 and 2			
151	Winston Galbraith, Oklahoma City, Okla.	Popovic, 2 up				
148	J. Paul Popovic, San Francisco, Calif.			Popovic, 1 up		
150	James P. King, Chicago, Ill.	King, 2 and 1				
146	Frank J. Gacek, Parma, Ohio		Chun, 1 up			
142	Jack S. S. Chun, Honolulu, Hawaii	Chun, 3 and 2				
151	Roy Shortridge, St. Paul, Minn.					Don Essig, III, 6 and 5
151	Don Sckrabulis, Kewanee, Ill.	Sckrabulis, 3 and 1				
148	Hubert S. Farmer, Toledo, Ohio		Sckrabulis, 1 up			
151	Sam Kapu, Honolulu, Hawaii	Thornton, 4 and 2				
153	**Donald L. Thornton, Los Angeles, Calif.**			Sckrabulis, 1 up		
152	Eddie Schnurr, Louisville, Ky.	Schnurr, 3 and 1				
152	William Howle, Oklahoma City, Okla.		Schnurr, 3 and 1			
150	Roger Eberhardt, Sheboygan, Wis.	Cullenbine, 2 up				
149	Roy Cullenbine, Detroit, Mich.				Sckrabulis, 2 and 1	
150	Leonard A. Pietras, Toledo, Ohio	Denton, 3 and 1				
150	Robert L. Denton, Peoria, Ill.		Denton, 4 and 3			
152	C. Allan Ducker, Charleston, S.C.	Berry, 1 up, 21 hls.				
150	Reece Berry, Indianapolis, Ind.			Gilliam, 1 up, 23 hls.		
151	Walter Gilliam, Jr., Burlingame, Calif.	Gilliam, 1 up, 19 hls.				
147	Robert C. Weathers, Miami, Fla.		Gilliam, 7 and 6			
149	**Bob Ludlow, Indianapolis, Ind.**	Conroy, 4 and 3				
153	**Bill Conroy, Seattle, Wash.**					Essig, 4 and 3
146	Mervin Isaacman, Harrisburg, Pa.	Buxbaum, 4 and 3				
142	James H. Buxbaum, Memphis, Tenn.		Buxbaum, 5 and 4			
145	Robert L. Nordstrom, Minneapolis, Minn.	Nordstrom, 1 up				
147	Eddie Kletcke, Chicago, Ill.			Buxbaum, 1 up		
151	Stanley Bielat, Yonkers, N.Y.	Sikes, 4 and 2				
152	Daniel D. Sikes, Jr., Jacksonville, Fla.		Jenkins, 1 up, 19 hls.			
147	Gerald Gallardo, Los Angeles, Calif.	Jenkins, 3 and 2				
151	Tom Jenkins, Jacksonville, Fla.				Essig, 1 up, 19 hls.	
143	Dr. Donald J. Keith, San Diego, Calif.	Roddy, 4 and 2				
146	George A. Roddy, Sr., Indianapolis, Ind.		Roddy, 5 and 4			
144	George Nahale, Sr., Honolulu, Hawaii	Nahale, 3 and 1				
152	Samuel E. Lima, E. Detroit, Mich.			Essig, 3 and 2		
146	Harry E. Langert, Minneapolis, Minn.	Essig, 5 and 4				
144	Don Essig, III, Indianapolis, Ind.		Essig, 4 and 3			
148	William Lauer, Spokane, Wash.	Lauer, 3 and 2				
152	Henry C. Barabin, Los Angeles, Calif.					

*Medalist.

Thirty-first Amateur Public Links Team Championship, Harding Trophy, 23 Entries, July 29-30: Won by Honolulu, Hawaii team, 440 for 36 holes (Edward Nakagaki, 154; George Nahale, Sr., 144; Jack S.S. Chun, 142); second, tie at 443 between San Francisco, Calif., team (Elmer Clites, 145; Robert Daniel, 147; Walter Gilliam, Jr., 151) and Indianapolis, Ind., team (Don Essig III, 144; Reece Berry, 150; Bob Ludlow, 149); third, St. Paul, Minn., team, 444 (Harry E. Langert, 146; **Chester W. Latawiec, 147; Roy Shortridge, 151).**

1958
THIRTY-THIRD AMATEUR PUBLIC LINKS CHAMPIONSHIP

Held at the Silver Lake Golf Club, Orland Park, Ill., July 7-12.

Yardage—6,866. Par 73. 2,000 Entries, 150 Qualifiers, 150 Starters.

Qualifying Score	1st Round (18 Holes)	2nd Round (18 Holes)	3rd Round (18 Holes)	4th Round (18 Holes)	Semi-Finals (36 Holes)	Final (36 Holes)	
150	Clifford Brown, Cleveland, Ohio	Ludlow, 3 and 2					
150	Bob Ludlow, Indianapolis, Ind.		Ludlow, 2 and 1				
150	Don Sckrabulis, Kewanee, Ill.	Sckrabulis, 1 up, 19 hls.					
152	Gene Towry, Dallas, Texas			Ludlow, 4 and 3			
148	Chester Kasper, Chicago Heights, Ill.	Kline, 1 up					
152	Charles V. Kline, Roswell, N.M.		Kline, 2 and 1				
153	Dr. Sam W. Valuck, Denver, Colo.	Aldred, 1 up, 19 hls.					
153	Jack Aldred, Ferndale, Mich.				Ludlow, 2 and 1		
153	Joe Gallardo, Los Angeles, Calif.	Joe Gallardo, 4 and 3					
152	James E. Everham, Seattle, Wash.		Conroy, 1 up, 19 hls.				
152	Bill Conroy, Seattle, Wash.	Conroy, 4 and 3					
147	Edward R. Petri, Austin, Texas			Luceti, 1 up, 23 hls.			
152	Ronald J. Luceti, San Francisco, Calif.	Luceti, 5 and 3					
155	**Joseph R. Harbin, Indianapolis, Ind.**		Luceti, 3 and 2				
153	Bobby Bluhm, Big Spring, Texas	Bluhm, 4 and 3					
154	Raymond Massey, Miami, Fla.					Ludlow, 1 up	
154	Rolf Deming, Minneapolis, Minn.	Strout, 3 and 1					
153	Warren E. Strout, Speedway, Ind.		Strout, 4 and 2				
154	Ralph J. Vranesic, Denver, Colo.	Latawiec, 4 and 3					
147	**Chester W. Latawiec, Minneapolis, Minn.**			Buxbaum, 3 and 2			
147	Lawrence R. Robertson, Minneapolis, Minn.	Robertson, 1 up					
152	Ray A. Borseth, Minneapolis, Minn.		Buxbaum, 2 and 1				
148	Mike Andonian, Pontiac, Mich.	Buxbaum, 5 and 4					
150	James H. Buxbaum, Memphis, Tenn.				Buxbaum, 4 and 2		
152	Emil Esposito, Franklin Park, Ill.	Bleech, 6 and 4					
150	Valray Bleech, Flint, Mich.		Bleech, 1 up, 20 hls.				
154	Robert L. Denton, Peoria, Ill.	Roach, 2 and 1					
154	Joe Roach, Los Angeles, Calif.			Faulkenberry, 2 and 1			
154	Samuel E. Lima, E. Detroit, Mich.	Faulkenberry, 2 and 1					
154	**Robert L. Faulkenberry, Jr., Oklahoma City, Okla.**		Faulkenberry, 2 and 1				
150	Fred E. Lukat, Washington, D.C.	Lukat, 4 and 3					
150	Archie Dadian, W. Allis, Wis.						Daniel D. Sikes, Jr., 3 and 2
155	**Paul Messner, Hialeah, Fla.**	Kletcke, 1 up					
149	Bob Kletcke, Chicago, Ill.		Kletcke, 5 and 4				
155	**Remo T. Crovetti, Highwood, Ill.**	Crovetti, 5 and 4					
149	Lyle Hornbacher, Moorhead, Minn.			Patterson, 1 up, 19 hls.			
154	Bob E. Patterson, Portland, Ore.	Patterson, 6 and 4					
148	James King, Macomb, Ill.		Patterson, 3 and 2				
154	Bobby Ladd, Memphis, Tenn.	Ladd, 1 up, 19 hls.					
154	Robert R. Leming, Atlanta, Ga.				Patterson, 4 and 3		
148	Harry Mussatto, Macomb, Ill.	Mussatto, 2 up					
149	Frank F. Schmidt, Dayton, Ohio		Mussatto, 2 and 1				
155	**Terry Lally, Louisville, Ky.**	Lally, 1 up					
153	**Dayton Olson** Minneapolis, Minn.			Mussatto, 5 and 4			
152	Andy Holmes, Toledo, Ohio	Holmes, 1 up, 20 hls.					
155	**Robert Turner, Cleveland, Ohio**		Hansen, 5 and 4				
153	George J. Borbely, Jr., Peekskill, N.Y.	Hansen, 2 up					
147	Gene Hansen, Minneapolis, Minn.					Sikes, 3 and 2	
155	**Albert L. Kelley, Jr., Orlando, Fla.**	Kelley, 7 and 6					
151	William C. Halvorson, Durand, Wis.		Kelley, 2 up				
151	Jack H. Omuro, Honolulu, T.H.	Omuro, 1 up, 20 hls.					
152	Moreno Caso, Seattle, Wash.			**Kelley,** 2 and 1			
154	Vard Jones, Salt Lake City, Utah	Melnikoff, 1 up					
154	Arthur Melnikoff, Chicago, Ill.		Melnikoff, 4 and 3				
153	C. Allen Ducker, Charleston, S.C.	Ducker, 1 up, 19 hls.					
147	Bill Arakawa, Honolulu, T.H.				Sikes, 3 and 1		
155	**Jerry Gallardo, Los Angeles, Calif.**	Jerry Gallardo, 2 and 1					
152	Lyle Gifford, Janesville, Wis.		Sikes, 2 and 1				
153	Leon R. Radde, Minneapolis, Minn.	Sikes, 4 and 3					
155	**Daniel D. Sikes, Jr., Jacksonville, Fla.**			Sikes, 5 and 4			
151	**William E. Krause, Palo Alto, Calif.**	Krause, 3 and 1					
155	**Robert L. Child, Jr., Springfield, Ill.**		Essig, **4 and 2**				
149	Walt Durdle, Peoria, Ill.	Essig, 4 and 3					
144	*Don Essig, III, Indianapolis, Ind.						

*Medalist.

Thirty-second Amateur Public Links Team Championship, Harding Trophy, 25 Entries, July 7-8: Won by St. Paul, Minn. team, **447 for 36 holes (Chester W. Latawiec, 147; Gene Hansen, 147; Dayton Olson, 153); second, Peoria, Ill. team, 455 (Harry Mussatto,** 148; John F. Weyl, 158; Walt Durdle, 149); third, tie at 456 between Chicago, Ill. team (Remo T. Crovetti, 155; Emil Esposito, 152; Bob Kletcke, 149) and Seattle, Wash. team (James E. Everham, 152; Bill Conroy, 152; Moreno Caso, 152).

1959
THIRTY-FOURTH AMATEUR PUBLIC LINKS CHAMPIONSHIP

Held at the Wellshire Golf Course, Denver, Colo., July 13-18.
Yardage—6,617. Par 71. 2,435 Entries, 150 Qualifiers, 150 Starters.

Qualifying Score	1st Round (18 Holes)	2nd Round (18 Holes)	3rd Round (18 Holes)	4th Round (18 Holes)	Semi-Finals (36 Holes)	Final (36 Holes)	
147	F.E. Lockie, Jr., Spokane, Wash.	Crovetti, default					
147	Remo T. Crovetti, Highwood, Ill.		McCool, 1 up				
149	William M. McCool, San Francisco, Calif.	McCool, 2 up					
144	Frank H. Huff, Tucson, Ariz.			McCool, 1 up			
149	Terry Lally, Louisville, Ky.	Dixon, 6 and 5					
141	Gene Dixon, Memphis, Tenn.		Farmer, 3 and 2				
149	Gene Hansen, Minneapolis, Minn.	Farmer, 2 up					
150	**Hugh Farmer, Toledo, Ohio**						
138	Rick Casabella, Louisville, Ky.	Denton, 1 up, 19 hls.			McCool, 2 and 1		
149	Robert Denton, Peoria, Ill.		Zimmerman, 3 and 1				
149	Dennis Tosaki, Honolulu, Hawaii	Zimmerman, 2 and 1					
150	**Jack E. Zimmerman, Dayton, Ohio**			Zimmerman, 3 and 2			
144	Gene Towry, Dallas, Texas	Towry, 5 and 4					
149	Bob Daniel, Daly City, Calif.		Towry, 2 up				
142	Donald Stickney, Columbus, Ohio	Deming, 1 up					
142	Rolf Deming, Minneapolis, Minn.						
148	Leonard Pietras, Toledo, Ohio	Pietras, 4 and 3				Campbell, 3 and 1	
148	Akira Hashimoto, Honolulu, Hawaii		Pietras, 1 up, 24 hls.				
145	Larry Lee, Spokane, Wash.	Lee, 2 up					
147	Theodore R. King, Washington, D.C.			Pietras, 2 up			
145	Marshall K. Strauss, Highland, Ill.	Strauss, 1 up, 19 hls.					
149	John J. Rak, Minneapolis, Minn.		Sikes, 2 and 1				
137	*Daniel D. Sikes, Jr., Jacksonville, Fla.	Sikes, 1 up					
142	Alvin Benefiel, Denver, Colo.						
149	Edward J. Korylak, N. Hollywood, Calif.	Brown, 3 and 2			Campbell, 3 and 1		
148	Clifford Brown, Cleveland, Ohio		Brown, 1 up				
149	Kenneth Miyaoka, Honolulu, Hawaii	Miyaoka, 5 and 4					
148	David Dixon, Memphis, Tenn.			Campbell, 1 up, 20 hls.			
147	Richard H. Hopwood, Phoenix, Ariz.	Keith, 1 up					
138	Dr. Donald J. Keith, San Diego, Calif.		Campbell, 1 up				
149	Frank W. Campbell, Jacksonville, Fla.	Campbell, 1 up, 19 hls.					
144	Ralph Johnson, Salt Lake City, Utah						
146	Lou Kane, Pittsburgh, Pa.	Ludlow, 1 up, 19 hls.					William A. Wright, 3 and 2
143	Bob Ludlow, Indianapolis, Ind.		Tindall, 2 and 1				
147	Robert Nordstrom, Minneapolis, Minn.	Tindall, 5 and 4					
145	William L. Tindall, Seattle, Wash.			Kristofitz, 3 and 1			
144	Bob E. Patterson, Portland, Ore.	Patak, 3 and 2					
142	Raymond H. Patak, Dallas, Texas		Kristofitz, 2 and 1				
146	Charles O. Griffith, Indianapolis, Ind.	Kristofitz, 3 and 2					
148	Don Kristofitz, Fargo, N.D.						
148	Max Cole, Wichita, Kans.	Kay, 5 and 4			Wright, 5 and 4		
148	Bobby Kay, Toledo, Ohio		Wright, 3 and 1				
149	William A. Wright, Seattle, Wash.	Wright, 5 and 4					
138	Pat Palacio, Jr., San Rafael, Calif.			Wright, 3 and 2			
149	Eugene A. Retzer, Denver, Colo.	Quiroz, 1 up, 19 hls.					
147	Manuel P. Quiroz, Tucson, Ariz.		Smith, 4 and 3				
147	Bob Menary, Northbrook, Ill.	Smith, 1 up, 19 hls.					
146	Wallace Smith, Pontiac, Mich.						
147	Edward R. Petri, Austin, Texas	Petri, 6 and 5				Wright, 1 up	
150	Harold Kotwitz, Janesville, Wis.		Petri, 2 and 1				
149	Jack H. Omuro, Honolulu, Hawaii	Omuro, 1 up, 19 hls.					
148	Edward Briegel, Ann Arbor, Mich.			Essig, 2 up			
141	Don Essig, III, Indianapolis, Ind.	Essig, 1 up, 20 hls.					
146	**Stephen M. Swain, Sr., Los Angeles, Calif.**		Essig, 2 up				
147	Conrad Gunther, Minneapolis, Minn.	Gunther, 1 up					
149	Gerald W. Webster, Buffalo, N.Y.						
143	Raymond Massey, Miami, Fla.	Massey, 2 up			Essig, 2 up		
144	John Newmeyer, San Francisco, Calif.		Massey, 1 up				
149	Veikko I. Juhola, Clawson, Mich.	Juhola, 3 and 2					
150	Manuel Pal[illegible], Bethlehem, Pa.			Massey, 2 up			
139	Hal McCommas, Dallas, Texas	McCommas, 5 and 4					
144	Wilbur L. Niederhut, Denver, Colo.		Dahlbender, 3 and 2				
147	Joe Cork, Speedway, Ind.	Dahlbender, 1 up					
139	Gene V. Dahlbender, Jr., Atlanta, Ga.						

*Medalist.

Thirty-third Amateur Public Links Team Championship, Harding Trophy, 30 Entries, July 13-14: Won by Dallas, Texas team, 425 for 36 holes (Gene Towry, 144; Raymond H. Patak, 142; Hal McCommas, 139); second, San Francisco, Calif. team, 431 (Bob Daniel, 149; Mat Palacio, Jr., 138; John Newmeyer, 144); third, tie at 437 between Jacksonville, Fla. team (Frank W. Campbell, 149; Thomas Jenkins, 151; Daniel D. Sikes, Jr., 137) and Louisville, Ky. team (Rick Casabella, 138; Bruce Wyatt, 150; Terry Lally, 149).

JUNIOR AMATEUR CHAMPIONS

GAY BREWER
1949

TOMMY JACOBS
1951

MASON RUDOLPH
1950

JUNIOR AMATEUR CHAMPIONSHIP

CHAMPIONSHIP TROPHY

Presented in August, 1948, by the

UNITED STATES GOLF ASSOCIATION

HISTORY

1948–On January 9, 1948, the Executive Committee decided to inaugurate a Junior Amateur Championship for boys who had not reached their 18th birthday. The first Championship was conducted by the USGA Championship Committee at the University of Michigan Golf Course, August 11-14, 1948. There were 495 entrants, of whom 128 were qualified for the Championship proper through sectional rounds at 41 locations. The lowest qualifying score was a 69 by Warren Higgins at the Dallas Country Club. This Championship, like the Amateur, was conducted entirely at match play, and Dean Lind, a 17-year-old high school graduate from Rockford, Ill., came through the seven 18-hole rounds to win. He defeated Ken Venturi, of San Francisco, 4 and 2, in the final. The youngest qualifier was Mason Rudolph, 14, of Clarksville, Tenn., who went to the quarter-final round, where he was beaten by Lind.

1949–The final of the second Championship was played between two boys who qualified together at Louisville, Ky., and roomed together at Georgetown University while play was going on at the Congressional Country Club, Washington, D.C. Gay Brewer, Jr., of Lexington, Ky., another 17-year-old high school student, defeated Mason Rudolph, now 15 years old, 6 and 4. Col. Lee S. Read, of Louisville, who had brought the boys to Washington, refereed. Brewer had been eliminated in the second round the previous year. The entry dipped to 416, and the lowest qualifying score again was a 69, by Ronnie Hughes at the Wilshire Country Club, in Los Angeles. Dean Lind was overage and could not defend his title.

1950–Young Mason Rudolph, the lad who had gone to the quarter-finals at 14 and to the final at 15, became the first 16-year-old Champion by defeating Chuck Beville, 17, of Los Angeles, 2 and 1, after twice winning on extra holes in earlier rounds. The Championship was played at the Denver Country Club. Rudolph already had qualified for the Open, and his victory in the Junior Amateur enabled him to play in the Amateur, his third USGA Championship in the same year. The first two Junior Amateur Championships had been conducted by the USGA Championship Committee, but this year a USGA Junior Championship Committee was organized to stimulate local interest, conduct sectional qualifying rounds, assist at the Championship and advise on policies regarding junior golf. Richard S. Tufts, of Pinehurst, N.C., who had conducted the first two Championships as Chairman of the Championship Committee, became Chairman of the Junior Championship Committee and continued to conduct the play. Players were housed at the University of Denver. The entry rose to 457, and Jerry Fehr led them all with a record score of 66 in the sectional round at the Olympic View Golf Club, in Seattle. Gay Brewer was over the age limit and not eligible to defend.

1951–There was a defending Champion for the first time at the University of Illinois, in July, 1951, but he lasted only four rounds. Billy Ford, of Charleston, S.C., upset Mason Rudolph by one hole. K. Tommy Jacobs, of Montebello, Calif., another 16-year-old, defeated Floyd Addington, 17, of Dallas, 4 and 2, in the final. Jacobs had lost in the third round the previous year. Entries this year rose to a new high of 596, and, as in the first year, 41 sectional qualifying rounds were held to accommodate them; Jimmy Powell's 69 at San Antonio, Texas, was the low score. The caliber of junior play was improving steadily. Twelve of the Junior qualifiers subsequently gained places in the Amateur, and Jacobs went to the semi-final round of that Championship. The new Junior Championship Committee also began to take shape and eleven members were present at the University of Illinois to assist in the conduct of play and to discuss policies at three evening meetings.

1952–Again the defender could not repeat. Don Bisplinghoff, a 17-year-old Orlando (Fla.) High School student, defeated Tommy Jacobs, 3 and 2, in a semi-final and succeeded him by beating Eddie Meyerson, also 17, of Los Angeles, 2 up, in the final. The Championship was held at the Yale Golf Course, New Haven, Conn., and attracted a record entry of 711 who took part in sectional qualifying at 42 locations. The qualifying record was equalled when Dale Lingenbrink made a 66 at the same Olympic View Golf Club, in Seattle, where Jerry Fehr had set the mark two years earlier. Bisplinghoff established another scoring record when he went to the turn in 31, three under par, in the quarter-finals. The qualifiers represented 32 states and the District of Columbia. Among them was Verner Stanley, 12, of Charlotte, N.C., the youngest ever to gain a place in match play.

1953–Rex Baxter, Jr., of Amarillo, Texas, a lean, serious boy of 17, won convincingly at the Southern Hills Country Club, Tulsa, Okla. He defeated George Warren, III, 16, of Hampton, S.C., 2 and 1, in the final. The entry list for this event closed at a new high of 713, representing 41 states, the District of Columbia, and Canada. Leo H. Jordan, Jr., technically lowered the record in sectional qualifying when he played the Santa Fe Hills Country Club course, in Kansas City, Mo., in 60, although par there was only 58. Three 13-year-olds qualified, and all advanced to the fourth round. The youngest was Jack Nicklaus, of Columbus, Ohio, who had turned 13 in January. Another was Verner Stanley, who qualified for the second time. Three Canadians also qualified, but they went out in the first round. Keith Lopp, of Long Beach, Calif., and Robert L. Prall, of Salem, Ore., went farther in the second round than any pair had gone previously in match play. Lopp finally won on the 23rd hole. Terry Thomas, of Canandaigua, N.Y., made a hole in one on the 165-yard 14th hole as he was losing in the third round. Donald Bisplinghoff was too old to defend.

1954–The Championship was held on the West Coast for the first time, and was dominated by Southern Californians. Foster (Bud) Bradley, Jr., 17, who played public links golf at the Griffith Park Course in Los Angeles, defeated Allen L. Geiberger, 16, of Santa Barbara, Calif., 3 and 1, in the final, over the North Course of the Los Angeles Country Club. The losing semi-finalists were George Warren, III, of Hampton, S.C., who had been runnerup the previous year, and Henry (Phil) Lobstein, 15, of Brownwood, Texas, the youngest to progress that far since Mason Rudolph in 1949. Rex Baxter, Jr., had passed the age limit and was ineligible to defend. The entry rose to 747.

1955–Billy John Dunn, 17, of the Elks Golf and Country Club, Duncan, Okla., defeated Billy Seanor, 17, of Bakersfield, Calif., 3 and 2, at Purdue University's South Course, West Lafayette, Ind. Dunn, a strong, raw-boned youth who stood 6 feet 5 inches, was even par for the 16 holes of the final. Californians outnumbered Dunn three to one in the semi-final round; he defeated Dick Foote, of Santa Ana, Calif., and Seanor defeated Phil Rodgers, of La Jolla, Calif. The Championship attracted another record entry of 805 players, and the 128 qualifiers represented 41 states. Foster (Bud) Bradley, Jr., of Los Angeles, was too old to defend.

1956–Harlan Stevenson, 17, of Long Beach, Calif., defeated Jack D. Rule, Jr., 17, of Waterloo, Iowa, 3 and 1, at the Taconic Golf Club of Williams College, Williamstown, Mass. Both boys were about to enter their senior years in high school, and both were public-course players. Stevenson was the third winner from California in nine years. Another record entry of 996 boys competed sectionally for 128 qualifying places. Forty-two states were represented by the qualifiers. There were four holes-in-one during the week, three in practice rounds. Virgil J. Prater, of Fountain City, Tenn., defeated Charles F. Lewis, Jr., of Little Rock, Ark., at the 24th hole in the second round. Wayne A. Pence, Jr., 17, of Kansas City, Mo., set an unofficial course record of 31-36–67; it was unofficial only because of a short concession on the fifteenth hole. In the semi-finals, Stevenson defeated Edward T. Pfister, 17, of Buffalo, N.Y., 1 up, while Rule was eliminating Jack Nicklaus, 16, of Columbus, Ohio, by the same score. Nicklaus was a qualifier for the fourth straight year and had reached the quarter-finals the previous year. Billy John Dunn was too old to defend. David Owens, of Pittsburgh, won the consolation event with a 71, at the Ekwanok Country Club, Manchester, Vt.

1957–Larry E. Beck, 17, of Kinston, N.C., a prospective freshman at Wake Forest College, defeated David C. Leon, 17, of Tucson, Ariz., a high school senior, 6 and 5, at the Manor Country Club, Rockville, Md., to win over a record entry of 1,060 boys. Jack Nicklaus, 17, of Columbus, Ohio, and John P. Konsek, 17, of Lancaster, N.Y., were qualifiers for the fifth time. Konsek defeated Gordon (Buddy) Baker, 16, of Florence, S.C., on the 24th hole in the round of sixteen, matching the overtime record for the Championship. Fred Taylor, of Portland, Ore., and Robert R. Kirouac, of Sharon, Mass., both 14, were the youngest qualifiers. Kirouac was a qualifier for the second time. Harlan Stevenson was over the age limit and ineligible to defend. Ned Johnson, of Port Arthur, Texas, won the consolation event with a one-under-par 71 at the Burning Tree Club, Bethesda, Md., where Vice President Richard M. Nixon greeted the boys during lunch. More than half the players stayed in the homes of Manor members surrounding the course, and no college or school housing was used.

1958–Gordon (Buddy) Baker, 17, a member of the Florence (S.C.) Country Club, played 17 holes in two under par to defeat R. Douglas Lindsay, 17, of Bethesda, Md., 2 and 1, at the University of Minnesota Golf Course, St. Paul, Minn. They were the survivors of another record entry of 1,117 boys. In the semi-final, Lindsay beat Billy Womack, 17, at the 19th hole to avert an all-Florence final. Womack was also a member of the Florence Country Club and a classmate of Baker. Baker, John V. Barcello, III, 17, and David B. Lawrence, Jr., 17, of New Orleans, and Marion C. (Sonny) Methvin, Jr., 17, Little Rock, Ark., all qualified for the fourth year. George Boutell, 14, of Phoenix, Ariz., was the youngest qualifier. Larry E. Beck had passed the age limit, and was ineligible to defend. Ralph Mayerstein, 17, of Lafayette, Ind., won the consolation event with a 74 at the Minneapolis Golf Club.

1959–Larry J. Lee, 17, a public course player from Spokane, Wash., won in a fine final against Michael V. McMahon, of Atlanta, 2 up. The Championship was played at Stanford University Golf Course, Palo Alto, Calif. The quarter-finals included two youngsters from Washington, two from Georgia, two from California and one each from Colorado and Florida. The final went to the last hole–a 445-yarder. Lee hit a 5-iron second shot to the center of the green, got down in two putts for a winning 4. For the 10th successive year the tournament drew a record entry. The total was 1,365. Thirty-six states were represented among the 128 players who qualified.

JUNIOR AMATEUR CHAMPIONSHIP

All Match Play 1948-1963

DATE	WINNER, RUNNER-UP	SCORE	SITE	ENTRY
1948 (Aug.)	Dean Lind d. Kenneth Venturi	4 & 2	Univ. of Michigan G.C., Ann Arbor, Mich.	495
1949 (July)	Gay Brewer, Jr d. Mason Rudolph	6 & 4	Congressional C.C., Washington, D.C.	416
1950 (July)	Mason Rudolph d. Charles Beville	2 & 1	Denver C.C., Denver, Colo.	457
1951 (July)	K. Thomas Jacobs, Jr. d. Floyd Addington	4 & 2	Univ. of Illinois G.C., Champaign, Ill.	596
1952 (July)	Donald M. Bisplinghoff d. Eddie M. Meyerson	2 up	Yale G.C., New Haven, Conn.	711
1953 (July-Aug.)	Rex Baxter, Jr. d. George Warren, III	2 & 1	Southern Hills C.C., Tulsa, Okla.	713
1954 (Aug.)	Foster Bradley, Jr. d. Allen L. Geiberger	3 & 1	Los Angeles C.C., (North Course) Los Angeles, Calif.	747
1955 (Aug.)	Billy J. Dunn d. William J. Seanor	3 & 2	Purdue University South G.C., West Lafayette, Ind.	805
1956 (Aug.)	Harlan Stevenson d. Jack D. Rule, Jr.	3 & 1	Taconic G.C., Williams College, Williamstown, Mass.	996
1957 (July)	Larry E. Beck d. David C. Leon	6 & 5	Manor C.C., Rockville, Md.	1,065
1958 (July-Aug.)	Gordon Baker d. R. Douglas Lindsay	2 & 1	Univ. of Minnesota G.C., St. Paul, Minn.	1,117
1959 (Aug.)	Larry J. Lee d. Michael V. McMahon	2 up	Stanford Univ. G.C., Stanford, Calif.	1,365

*Record qualifying score, 36 holes.

1948
FIRST JUNIOR AMATEUR CHAMPIONSHIP

Held at the University of Michigan Golf Course, Ann Arbor, Mich., August 11-14.
Yardage—6,660. Par 72. 495 Entries, 128 Qualifiers, 127 Starters.
FINAL ROUND (18 Holes)—Dean Lind defeated Kenneth Venturi, 4 up and 2 to play.

UPPER HALF

1st Round (18 Holes)	2nd Round (18 Holes)	3rd Round (18 Holes)	4th Round (18 Holes)	5th Round (18 Holes)	Semi-Final (18 Holes)	
Dennis L. Walters, Dayton, Ohio John Touchstone, Dallas, Texas	Touchstone, 4 and 3	Touchstone, 3 and 1	Touchstone, 3 and 2	Cooper, 5 and 4	Black, 4 and 2	Venturi, 3 and 1
Peter C. Burkholder, Indianapolis, Ind. Jack M. Stewart, Huntington, W. Va.	Burkholder, by default					
Norman Rackley, Salt Lake City, Utah Jack S. Radcliffe, Parkersburg, W. Va.	Radcliffe, 6 and 5	Williams, 2 and 1				
Jim Mullin, Taylorville, Ill. Gerald Williams, Indianapolis, Ind.	Williams, 1 up, 19 hls.					
Irving Cooper, Long Beach, Calif. Emmett McGoskey, Beckley, W. Va.	Cooper, 6 and 5	Cooper, 7 and 6	Cooper, 3 and 2			
Alan E. Head, Birmingham, Ala. John Foster, Lexington, Ky.	Foster, 2 and 1					
Gerry Mathison, Belmont, Mich. Welbourne Jameson, Chattanooga, Tenn.	Jameson, 1 up, 19 hls.	Wolfe, 4 and 3				
Milton Eugene Wolfe, Silver Spring, Md. Tommy Lybrand, Jr., Aiken, S.C.	Wolfe, 3 and 2					
Wayne McLaughlin, Pittsford, N.Y. Ron Guariglia, St. Louis, Mo.	R. Guariglia, 3 and 1	Moynihan, 3 and 2	Johnson, 4 and 2	Black, 6 and 5		
John Moynihan, Jr., Troy, N.Y. Lawrence A. Bentley, Plymouth, Mich.	Moynihan, 5 and 4					
Philip H. Chichester, Battle Creek, Mich. Clayton J. Johnson, St. Paul, Minn.	Johnson, 2 and 1	Johnson, 6 and 4				
Edmund J. Denburg, North Caldwell, N.J. Paul D. Kelly, Newtonville, Mass.	Kelly, 1 up					
Frank McCormick, Winchester, Ky. Arch Voris, Jr., Bedford, Ind.	Voris, 1 up	Haag, 1 up, 19 hls.	Black, 2 up			
Bobby Haag, Louisville, Ky. Robert Bowers, Cleveland, Ohio	Haag, 2 and 1					
Robert H. Black, Jenkintown, Pa. Bill Golberg, Tucson, Ariz.	Black, 3 and 2	Black, 1 up				
George M. Christ, Pittsford, N.Y. Jay Cohen, Overland, Mo.	Christ, 7 and 6					
Gene Follis, Glasgow, Ky. Jack Egnor, Huntington, W. Va.	Follis, 1 up, 19 hls.	R. Foster, 1 up	Venturi, 6 and 5	Venturi, 4 and 3	Venturi, 5 and 4	
Richard S. Foster, Chevy Chase, Md. Gray Madison, Jr., Phoenix, Ariz.	R. Foster, 5 and 4					
Don Guariglia, St. Louis, Mo. Purvis Ferree, Jr., Winston-Salem, N.C.	D. Guariglia, 3 and 1	Venturi, 6 and 5				
Don Addington, Houston, Texas Kenneth Venturi, San Francisco, Calif.	Venturi, 2 and 1					
Mitchell J. Rosenholtz, St. Paul, Minn. John Snyder, Jr., Troy, N.Y.	Rosenholtz, 4 and 3	Smith, 1 up, 19 hls.	Smith, 2 and 1			
Robert P. Smith, Hartsdale, N.Y. Torrence M. Jones, Charlotte, N.C.	Smith, 1 up					
Lincoln Roden, III, Abington, Pa. Gene P. Eyler, Olean, N.Y.	Roden, 6 and 5	Allen, 1 up				
Fred S. Allen, Jr., Elizabethtown, Ky. Paul Holmes, Jr., Tacoma, Wash.	Allen, 1 up, 20 hls.					
Miles Schlapik, Northbrook, Ill. Robert V. Wolfe, Chevy Chase, Md.	Schlapik, 3 and 2	Schlapik, 2 and 1	Schlapik 1 up	Schlapik, 1 up		
Jack Kraemer, Fort Thomas, Ky. Henry J. McFadden, Jr., Dallas, Texas	McFadden, 5 and 3					
Warren N. Higgins, Dallas, Texas Jack White, Jr., Stockbridge, Mass.	Higgins, 4 and 3	Higgins, 1 up, 19 hls.				
Robert E. Spence, Jr., Columbia, S.C. William Thomas Morrow, Shreveport, La.	Morrow, 7 and 6					
Joseph S. McVicker, Cincinnati, Ohio James H. Pollock, Columbus, Ohio	Pollock, 2 and 1	Pollock, 1 up	Key, 2 up			
Robert A. Jacobs, Bremerton, Wash. John Handley, Kansas City, Mo.	Jacobs, 5 and 4					
Donald Russell, Seattle, Wash. Richard E. Marcus, Olean, N.Y.	Marcus, 1 up, 19 hls.	Key, 4 and 3				
James W. Key, Columbus, Ga. F. Edmonds, Bremerton, Wash.	Key, 7 and 6					

LOWER HALF

Semi-Final (18 Holes)	5th Round (18 Holes)		4th Round (18 Holes)	3rd Round (18 Holes)	2nd Round (18 Holes)	1st Round (18 Holes)
				Roberts, 1 up	Picard, 1 up, 19 hls.	W.E. Leigh, Jr., Lakeland, Fla. William Picard, Cleveland, Ohio
			Roberts, 5 and 3		Roberts, 8 and 6	Thomas Roberts, Roswell, N.M. Eugene Johnson, Fargo, N.D.
				Robbins, 1 up	Robbins, 4 and 3	David A. Graham, Jr., Houston, Texas Hillman Robbins, Jr., Memphis, Tenn.
		Strange, 3 and 2			Butler, 3 and 2	Ralph W. Miller, Jr., Los Angeles, Calif. Richard W. Butler, Indianapolis, Ind.
				Godwin, 1 up	Godwin, 5 and 4	Robert Godwin, Memphis, Tenn. William L. Louth, Oakville, Ont., Canada
			Strange, 7 and 6		Hessemer, 1 up, 19 hls.	Charles Beach, Fairfax, Va. Richard Hessemer, Houston, Texas
				Strange, 2 and 1	Strange, 3 and 2	John B. Wade, Jr., Memphis, Tenn. Thomas W. Strange, Jr., Cincinnati, Ohio
	Myles, 1 up				Lund, 4 and 2	Lawrence H. Lund, Jr., Pittsburgh, Pa. William D. Wolfe, Capital View, Md.
				Myles, 4 and 2	Myles, 4 and 3	Floyd Addington, Houston, Texas Reggie Myles, Jr., East Lansing, Mich.
			Myles, 6 and 4		Meek, 5 and 4	Robert A. Meek, Tulsa, Okla. Jimmie Houghton, Concordia, Kans.
				O'Neill, 1 up	Krummel, 4 and 3	W. Paul Krummel, Cincinnati, Ohio Kenneth West, Parkersburg, W. Va.
		Myles, 2 and 1			O'Neill, 1 up	John Mahan, Indianapolis, Ind. Joseph O'Neill, Pasadena, Calif.
				R.F. Allen, 3 and 2	Blair, 5 and 4	William E. Wade, Memphis, Tenn. James T. Blair, III, Jefferson, Mo.
			Lowry, 4 and 3		Allen, 6 and 5	Fred Mitchell, Jr., Columbus, Ga. Ray F. Allen, Jr., Rochester, N.Y.
				Lowry, 5 and 3	Lowry, 7 and 6	Robert Lowry, Jr., Huntsville, Ala. Robert Bruce, Madison, Wis.
Lind, 5 and 3					Bolster, 4 and 2	Hugh Beath, La Grange, Ill. Dennis Bolster, Washington, D.C.
				Buppert, 7 and 5	Lundahl, 4 and 3	William L. Garner, III, Memphis, Tenn. John Lundahl, Logan, Utah
			Bruno, 4 and 2		Buppert, 3 and 1	William E. Ford, Florence, Ala. William I. Buppert, Towson, Md.
				Bruno, 2 and 1	Bruno, 3 and 2	Carroll Armstrong, Chattanooga, Tenn. George Bruno, Jr., Berkeley, Calif.
		Lind, 4 and 3			Brewer, 5 and 3	Gay Brewer, Jr., Lexington, Ky. Richard G. McCann, Akron, Ohio
				Lind, 3 and 2	Stanford, 2 and 1	Robert E. Lacy, Iola, Kans. Thad Stanford, Midland, Mich.
			Lind, 3 and 2		Lind, 2 and 1	Dean Lind, Rockford, Ill. Don Cheek, Memphis, Tenn.
				Evans, 2 and 1	Evans, 6 and 5	Richard E. Evans, Cleveland, Ohio Paul E. Kelly, Scarborough, N.Y.
	Lind, 5 and 3				Pitts, 3 and 2	Roswell Eldridge, Kansas City, Kans. Fordie Pitts, Wollaston, Mass.
				Laird, 5 and 4	Laird, 1 up	Keith Jorde, Thief River Falls, Minn. John D. Laird, Battle Creek, Mich.
			Gray, 7 and 6		Berling, 3 and 2	Colbert McTyler, Newport News, Va. Elmer Berling, Jr., Covington, Ky.
				Gray, 1 up	McCarty, 5 and 3	Joseph McCarty, Jr., Denver, Colo. John Muench, Louisville, Ky.
		Rudolph, 3 and 1			Gray, 7 and 6	Robert H. Nelson, Salt Lake City, Utah Robert Gray, Fort Thomas, Ky.
				Blanchard, 2 and 1	Blanchard, 8 and 6	Robert L. Blanchard, Inglewood, Calif. Joe McCarley, Camden, S.C.
			Rudolph, 1 up		Strassburger, 2 and 1	Raymond Stewart, Jr., Fairfield, Iowa Julien Strassburger, Montgomery, Ala.
				Rudolph, 7 and 6	Rudolph, 2 and 1	William L. Edwards, Hempstead, N.Y. Mason Rudolph, Clarksville, Tenn.
					Flanagan, 5 and 3	Curtis Brown, Phoenix, Ariz. Michael Flanagan, Memphis, Tenn.

1949
SECOND JUNIOR AMATEUR CHAMPIONSHIP

Held at the Congressional Country Club, Washington, D.C., July 27-30.
Yardage—6,350. Par 71. 416 Entries, 128 Qualifiers, 127 Starters.
FINAL ROUND (18 holes)—Gay Brewer, Jr., defeated Mason Rudolph, 6 up and 4 to play.

UPPER HALF

1st Round (18 Holes)	2nd Round (18 Holes)	3rd Round (18 Holes)	4th Round (18 Holes)	5th Round (18 Holes)	Semi-Final (18 Holes)	
Philip D. Jones, Westerly, R.I. Robert Meriwether, Nashville, Tenn.	Jones, 5 and 4					
William M. Parker, Charlotte, N.C. Theodore P. White, Roswell, N.M.	White, 1 up	Jones, 2 and 1				
Joseph R. Turnesa, Jr., Ferndale, N.Y. Arthur H. Wolfe, Chicago, Ill.	Turnesa, 3 and 2					
Richard S. Edwards, Atlanta, Ga. Merritt E. Marcus, Louisville, Ky.	R. Edwards, 2 and 1	Turnesa, 4 and 2	Turnesa, 1 up			
John B. Wade, Jr., Germantown, Tenn. Gene P. Eyler, Olean, N.Y.	Eyler, 2 and 1					
Richard Mulvaine, Kenton, Ohio Larry W. Harper, Ravenna, Ohio	Mulvaine, 3 and 1	Mulvaine, 3 and 2				
Florian Weinhaus, St. Paul, Minn. Edward Reihsen, Chicago, Ill.	Weinhaus, 4 and 2					
R. Aubrey Miller, Jr., Selma, Ala. Grant Spaeth, Stanford, Calif.	Miller, 1 up, 19 hls.	Weinhaus, 1 up, 19 hls.	Weinhaus, 6 and 5	Turnesa, 4 and 2		
James F. Balch, Jr., Indianapolis, Ind. Bill Barter, Topeka, Kans.	Balch, 2 and 1					
James Grady, Cincinnati, Ohio George D. Williams, Winchester, Ky.	Grady, 3 and 2	Grady, 3 and 2				
Frank X. McCoy, Baltimore, Md. Bart Brown, Jr., Louisville, Ky.	Brown, 5 and 4					
Mason Rudolph, Clarksville, Tenn. Robert Salamy, Washington, D.C.	Rudolph, 8 and 6	Rudolph, 3 and 2	Rudolph, 3 and 1			
George Williams, Monroe, Mich. Donald E. Albert, Alliance, Ohio	Albert, 1 up, 19 hls.					
Ellsworth Franklin, Jr., Dahlgren, Va. Roane Puett, Midland, Texas	Franklin, 4 and 3	Albert, 1 up				
Dilmus D. James, Abilene, Texas Harlow Lewis, Ben Avon Heights, Pa.	Lewis, by default					
Richard F. Caudill, Huntington, W. Va. Charles A. Strack, York, Pa.	Strack, 2 up	Strack, 6 and 5	Strack, 4 and 3	Rudolph, 5 and 4	Rudolph, 5 and 3	
Miles Schlapik, Chicago, Ill. Joe W. Walser, Jr., Oklahoma City, Okla.	Schlapik, 5 and 3					
James Wheeler, Olean, N.Y. Pete Beard, St. Paul, Minn.	Beard, 2 and 1	Schlapik, 5 and 3				
Donald Hinken, Cincinnati, Ohio Gene Follis, Glasgow, Ky.	Follis, 4 and 3					
Hugh M. Reed, Washington, D.C. Graham Hunt, Overland Park, Kans.	Hunt, 2 and 1	Hunt, 4 and 3	Schlapik, 1 up			
William Thomas Morrow, Shreveport, La. Kay Fletcher, Jr., Washington, D.C.	Morrow, 3 and 2					
Gerard Schultheis, Orlando, Fla. Robert C. Atwell, Indianapolis, Ind.	Atwell, 1 up	Morrow, 3 and 2				
Richard Davenport, High Falls, N.Y. Carroll Armstrong, Chattanooga, Tenn.	Armstrong, 4 and 3					
Ralph J. McNece, Inglewood, Calif. Patrick Moran, Akron, Ohio	Moran, 2 and 1	Moran, 1 up	Morrow, 4 and 3	Morrow, 4 and 3		
Stan Weislo, Lackawanna, N.Y. John Barry, Philadelphia, Pa.	Weislo, 1 up					
Billy Gooch, Huntington, W. Va. Lawrence A. Bentley, Plymouth, Mich.	Bentley, 1 up	Bentley, 3 and 2				
Richard C. Hess, Seattle, Wash. Richard Hessemer, Houston, Texas	Hessemer, 2 and 1					
Bobby Brannan, Charlotte, N.C. James Rausch, Glendale, Calif.	Brannan, 7 and 6	Hessemer, 2 up	Hessemer, 2 and 1			
Johnny Ailes, North Benton, Ohio Fred Allen, Jr., Elizabethtown, Ky.	Ailes, 2 up					
Pat Schwab, Dayton, Ohio Don Kneeter, Des Moines, Iowa	Schwab, 8 and 6	Schwab, 2 and 1				
Walter M. Baker, Atlanta, Ga. Haynes Hawkins, Mt. Vernon, Ill.	Baker, 6 and 5					
Eddie E. Merrins, Meridian, Miss. Richard O'Brien, Minneapolis, Minn.	Merrins, 3 and 2	Baker, 3 and 2	Baker, 1 up, 19 hls.	Hessemer, 4 and 2	Morrow, 1 up	Rudolph, 1 up, 19 holes

LOWER HALF

Semi-Final (18 Holes)	5th Round (18 Holes)		4th Round (18 Holes)	3rd Round (18 Holes)	2nd Round (18 Holes)	1st Round (18 Holes)
Brewer, 2 and 1	Sykes, 1 up	Sykes, 1 up, 19 hls.	Sykes, 1 up, 21 hls.	Stevens, 4 and 3	Stall, 5 and 4	Albert M. Stall, New Orleans, La. Robert Crofts, Salt Lake City, Utah
					Stevens, 2 up	Harvey M. Legg, Charleston, W. Va. Lem Stevens, Nashville, Tenn.
				Sykes, 2 up	Brown, 1 up	Roswell Eldridge, Kansas City, Mo. Fred Brown, Beverly Hills, Calif.
					Sykes, 3 and 2	James D. Sykes, Jenkintown, Pa. Richard James, Minneapolis, Minn.
			Tewart, 1 up, 21 hls.	Pinkston, 7 and 6	Pinkston, 8 and 6	Lee Pinkston, Abilene, Texas John T. Flanagan, Jr., Memphis, Tenn.
					Kiolbasa, 1 up, 19 hls.	Ronald C. Kiolbasa, Chicago, Ill. Philip Getchell, Medford, Ore.
				Tewart, 2 and 1	R. Miller, 2 up	Charles Ribelin, Dallas, Texas Ralph Miller, Los Angeles, Calif.
					Tewart, 2 and 1	Donald McLaughlin, Oklahoma City, Okla. Jim Tewart, Hamilton, Ohio
		Edwards, 3 and 2	Spilker, 5 and 3	Fayen, 3 and 2	Breckel, 5 and 3	Joseph B. Breckel, Louisville, Ky. William E. Wade, Germantown, Tenn.
					Fayen, 7 and 5	Richard A. Pedley, St. Paul, Minn. George S. Fayen, Jr., New Haven, Conn.
				Spilker, 6 and 4	Ward, 6 and 5	John Ward, Midland, Texas Nolan Wathen, Salt Lake City, Utah
					Spilker, 5 and 4	Robert E. Spence, Jr., Columbia, S.C. Eugene Spilker, Clayton, Mo.
			Edwards, 3 and 2	Nichols, 5 and 4	Nichols, 3 and 2	Charlton Yarnall, II, Haverford, Pa. Donald C. Nichols, Auburn, Kans.
					Sears, 6 and 4	Richard S. Vedder, Olean, N.Y. Donald G. Sears, Reading, Ohio
				Edwards, 1 up	Edwards, 3 and 1	Kenneth Edwards, Fort Worth, Texas James Kintz, Alliance, Ohio
					Mullin, 7 and 6	Leo R. Mullin, Brookline, Mass. Don Olsen, Minneapolis, Minn.
	Brewer, 4 and 3	Brewer, 3 and 2	Bolster, 1 up, 19 hls.	Bolster, 1 up	Bolster, 7 and 5	Dennis Bolster, Washington, D.C. William Livingston, Washington, D.C.
					Moynihan, 3 and 2	Phil Wiechman, Chapmanville, W. Va. John L. Moynihan, Troy, N.Y.
				Hughes, 5 and 4	Hughes, 2 up	Eldon Shoup, Alliance, Ohio Ronald Hughes, Lawndale, Calif.
					Derickson, 1 up, 21 hls.	Jimmy Breen, Albuquerque, N.M. Bill Derickson, Seattle, Wash.
			Brewer, 6 and 4	Brewer, 2 up	Brewer, 8 and 6	Gay Brewer, Jr., Lexington, Ky. Ronald G. Mergens, St. Paul, Minn.
					Sisk, 8 and 7	Robert Sisk, Charlotte, N.C. Edward H. Whaley, Jr., Peabody, Mass.
				Humphreys, 1 up	Humphreys, 7 and 6	Donald DeBord, Huntington, W. Va. Elmer E. Humphreys, Oklahoma City, Okla.
					Terry, 2 and 1	Ray Terry, Memphis, Tenn. Graham Mackey, Midland, Texas
		Wolfe, 5 and 4	Carey, 5 and 3	Staren, 3 and 2	Staren, 6 and 4	Edgar Staren, Congress Park, Ill. William O. Holton, Lexington, Ky.
					Brown, 2 and 1	John Y. Brown, Jr., Lexington, Ky. Hillman Robbins, Jr., Memphis, Tenn.
				Carey, 5 and 4	Burkholder, 1 up, 19 hls.	William Ball, Washington, D.C. Peter Burkholder, Indianapolis, Ind.
					Carey, 4 and 3	David Samuelsen, Jr., Salt Lake City, Utah Randolph S. Carey, Denver, Colo.
			Wolfe, 4 and 3	La Fraugh, 1 up	La Fraugh, 4 and 3	John Gleason, Kingston, N.Y. Ronald La Fraugh, Lansing, Mich.
					Fischer, 3 and 2	Robert Burch, Rochester, N.Y. George E. Fischer, Louisville, Ky.
				Wolfe, 4 and 2	Wolfe, 2 and 1	Roger J. Tuchfarber, Cincinnati, Ohio Billy D. Wolfe, Silver Spring, Md.
					Vernon, 2 and 1	John O. Eisinger, Bethesda, Md. Murray Vernon, Jr., Greenwich, Conn.

1950
THIRD JUNIOR AMATEUR CHAMPIONSHIP

Held at the Denver Country Club, Denver, Colo., July 19-22.
Yardage—6,785. Par 71. 457 Entries, 128 Qualifiers, 128 Starters.
FINAL ROUND (18 Holes) – Mason Rudolph defeated Charles Beville, 2 up and 1 to play.

UPPER HALF

1st Round (18 Holes)	2nd Round (18 Holes)	3rd Round (18 Holes)	4th Round (18 Holes)	5th Round (18 Holes)		Semi-Final (18 Holes)
Merritt E. Marcus, Louisville, Ky.	Marcus, 2 and 1					
Lloyd G. Mackey, Midland, Texas		Marcus, 1 up				
Arlyn, L. Scott, Odessa, Texas	Mobley, 4 and 2					
Wilson Mobley, Chapmanville, W. Va.			Blisplinghoff, 3 and 2			
Lem Stevens, Jr., Nashville, Tenn.	Blisplinghoff, 1 up					
Donald Blisplinghoff, Orlando, Fla.		Blisplinghoff, 6 and 5				
Jerry Edwards, Fort Worth, Texas	Edwards, 1 up					
William E. Wade, Memphis, Tenn.				Blisplinghoff, 5 and 4		
Tad Pfister, Prescott, Ariz.	Pfister, 3 and 2					
Donald Hinken, St. Bernard, Ohio		Lewis, 7 and 6				
James Lewis, Tulsa, Okla.	Lewis, 3 and 2					
John Enright, Sioux Falls, S.D.			Lewis, 4 and 3			
Eugene Brehaut, San Francisco, Calif.	Brehaut, 3 and 1					
Carl W. Boom, Jr., Denver, Colo.		Brehaut, 5 and 4				
John E. Peterson, Lincoln, Neb.	Melenson, 1 up					
James R. Melenson, Hickman Mills, Mo.					Hay, 4 and 3	
William Thomas Morrow, Shreveport, La.	Hay, 1 up					
Eugene Hay, Atlanta, Ga.		Hay, 4 and 3				
Dale Kniss, Waterloo, Iowa	Kniss, 2 and 1					
Floyd Addington, Dallas, Texas			Hay, 2 and 1			
Bennie Pell, Tulsa, Okla.	Sykes, 7 and 6					
James D. Sykes, Philadelphia, Pa.		Balch, 6 and 5				
James F. Balch, Jr., Indianapolis, Ind.	Balch, 2 and 1					
Robert Donnelly, Portland, Ore.				Hay, 1 up		
Forst E. Brown, Louisville, Ky.	Miller, 1 up					
Ralph Miller, Jr., Palos Verdes Estates, Calif.		Woelfling, 2 up				
Oliver K. Fletcher, Jr., Washington, D.C.	Woelfling, 2 and 1					
Melvin L. Woelfling, Ashland, Ohio			Woelfling, 1 up			
Michael F. Fiynn, West Peabody, Mass.	Brown, 1 up					
Neil Brown, Tucson, Ariz.		Matthews, 4 and 3				
Otis M. Matthews, Selma, Ala.	Matthews, 5 and 4					
Richard Auer, Denver, Colo.						Beville, 5 and 3
John Bryan Johnson, Oklahoma City, Okla.	Johnson, 5 and 4					
Douglas Jordal, Minneapolis, Minn.		Johnson, 2 up				
Anthony Cullinane, Bethesda, Md.	Cullinane, 3 and 1					
Don Slutes, Tucson, Ariz.			Fehr, 3 and 2			
Jerry F. Fehr, Seattle, Wash.	Fehr, 1 up					
Larry W. Harper, Ravenna, Ohio		Fehr, 2 and 1				
Phil Wiechman, Chapmanville, W. Va.	Fischer, 1 up, 20 hls.					
George E. Fischer, Louisville, Ky.				Poore, 3 and 2		
Allwyn W. Pirtle, Colorado Springs, Colo.	Pirtle, 3 and 2					
Richard O. Brune, Cincinnati, Ohio		Garner, 3 and 1				
Ronald J. Guariglia, St. Louis, Mo.	Garner, 2 and 1					
William Garner, III, Memphis, Tenn.			Poore, 2 and 1			
Elwood Poore, Jr., Frazer, Pa.	Poore, 9 and 7					
Stanford Dugdale, Butte, Mont.		Poore, 4 and 3				
Richard C. Billehus, Colorado Springs, Colo.	Billehus, 7 and 5					
Ralph W. Irick, Orangeburg, S.C.					Beville, 3 and 2	
Ronald Hickman, Nashville, Tenn.	Johnston, 1 up, 20 hls.					
Bill Johnston, Detroit, Mich.		Johnston, 8 and 6				
Nolan Wathen, Salt Lake City, Utah	Dahl, 3 and 2					
Crary Dahl, Naperville, Ill.			Kelly, 4 and 3			
Gene Follis, Glasgow, Ky.	Bolster, 2 and 1					
Dennis Bolster, Washington, D.C.		Kelly, 3 and 2				
Lester Kelly, Atlanta, Ga.	Kelly, 2 up					
Jack C. Flatt, Jr., Duluth, Minn.				Beville, 2 and 1		
Charles Beville, Los Angeles, Calif.	Beville, 6 and 4					
William B. Stevens, Jr., Loudonville, N.Y.		Beville, 8 and 7				
Raymond Leggett, Jr., Midland, Texas	Leggett, 5 and 3					
Herbert F. Mayer, Jr., Grand Island, Neb.			Beville, 1 up, 20 hls.			
Fred Brown, Los Angeles, Calif.	Brown, 7 and 6					
Edward A. Cooney, Newton Centre, Mass.		Brown, 2 and 1				
Robert F. Vickers, Wichita, Kans.	Crenshaw, 3 and 1					
William G. Crenshaw, Jr., Memphis, Tenn.						

LOWER HALF

Semi-Final (18 Holes)	5th Round (18 Holes)		4th Round (18 Holes)	3rd Round (18 Holes)	2nd Round (18 Holes)	1st Round (18 Holes)
				Strack, 2 up	D. Guariglia, 3 and 2	Donald R. Guariglia, St. Louis, Mo. Dave Samuelsen, Salt Lake City, Utah
			Rudolph, 1 up, 19 hls.		Strack, 6 and 4	Dennis Ryan, Tulsa, Okla. Charles Adam Strack, York, Pa.
				Rudolph, 5 and 4	Rudolph, 1 up, 20 hls.	Edward Meyerson, Los Angeles, Calif. Mason Rudolph, Clarksville, Tenn.
		Rudolph, 8 and 7			Manderson, 2 and 1	Webster Manderson, Tuscaloosa, Ala. Tommy Hale, Phillips, Texas
				Breen, 7 and 6	Nichols, 3 and 2	Rex Louth, Oakville, Ont., Canada Bobby Nichols, Louisville, Ky.
			Franklin, 2 and 1		Breen, 1 up	Gerald Moore, Denver, Colo. James E. Breen, Albuquerque, N.M.
				Franklin, 3 and 2	Franklin, 2 up	Robert J. Donovan, Jr., Shreveport, La. Ellsworth Franklin, Jr., Dahlgren, Va.
	Rudolph, 5 and 4				Birmingham, 1 up	Frederick R. Jones, Youngstown, Ohio Allen Birmingham, Coraopolis, Pa.
				Dyar, 2 and 1	Crowe, 3 and 2	Lonnie O'Steen, Orlando, Fla. Billy Crowe, Prescott, Ariz.
			Gillespie, 3 and 2		Dyar, 5 and 3	Robert A. Boswell, Orangeburg, S.C. Robert Dyar, Indianapolis, Ind.
				Gillespie, 2 up	Ball, 4 and 3	William R. Ball, Arlington, Va. John R. Geertsen, Jr., San Francisco, Calif.
		Winters, 1 up, 19 hls.			Gillespie, 3 and 2	Billy Gooch, Huntington, W. Va. Tom Gillespie, Cincinnati, Ohio
				Flynn, 2 and 1	Cockerell, 3 and 2	E.G. Cockerell, Abilene, Texas Thomas Shanesy, Minneapolis, Minn.
			Winters, 6 and 4		Flynn, 4 and 2	Thomas F. Flynn, Jr., Lewiston, Idaho Richard Harrison, Grand Rapids, Mich.
				Winters, 4 and 3	Baker, 3 and 1	Thomas Schwietz, St. Paul, Minn. Walter M. Baker, Atlanta, Ga.
Rudolph, 2 and 1					Winters, 2 and 1	James G. Wade, Memphis, Tenn. John O. Winters, Tulsa, Okla.
				Ginsberg, 5 and 4	Ginsberg, 2 up	Dick Jacobs, Prescott, Ariz. Joseph Ginsberg, Cheltenham, Pa.
			Ginsberg, 5 and 4		Levin, 1 up	Michael Levin, Minneapolis, Minn. William W. Wilbourne, Arlington, Va.
				Brown, 5 and 4	Brown, 4 and 3	John Y. Brown, Jr., Lexington, Ky. Rex Baxter, Amarillo, Texas
		Ginsberg, 1 up, 20 hls.			Fannin, by default	Robert Fannin, Phoenix, Ariz. Robert Godwin, Memphis, Tenn.
				Sears, 1 up, 19 hls.	Seibert, 2 and 1	Edgar W. Garbisch, Jr., Locust Valley, N.Y. Joe Seibert, Tulsa, Okla.
			Norton, 3 and 2		Sears, 1 up	Randolph Carey, Denver, Colo. Donald Sears, Cincinnati, Ohio
				Norton, 1 up	Norton, 3 and 2	Elliott Phillips, New Albany, Ind. Richard Norton, Grand Rapids, Mich.
	Wolfe, 1 up				Rutland, 5 and 4	John T. Rutland, Memphis, Tenn. Ronnie Hughes, Los Angeles, Calif.
				Jacobs, 6 and 4	Jacobs, 3 and 2	Keith Tommy Jacobs, Jr., Montebello, Calif. Tommy Beck, Tulsa, Okla.
			Merrins, 4 and 3		O'Leary, 1 up, 19 hls.	John F. O'Leary, Winchester, Mass. William D. McKillip, Riverside, Ill.
				Merrins, 6 and 5	Merrins, 1 up	Richard H. Waters, Atlanta, Ga. Martin Edward Merrins, Meridian, Miss.
		Wolfe, 2 and 1			Brennan, 5 and 4	Donald N. Matheson, Fort Worth, Texas Thomas E. Brennan, Jr., Wauwatosa, Wis.
				Mork, 2 and 1	Miller, 5 and 4	Roger Miller, Palos Verdes Estates, Calif. Thomas Humphries, Columbia, S.C.
			Wolfe, 6 and 5		Mork, 4 and 3	Earl Hansen, Jr., Seattle, Wash. Frank Mork, Golden Valley, Minn.
				Wolfe, 2 and 1	Ward, 5 and 4	Billy Strickland, Nashville, Tenn. John Ward, Midland, Texas
					Wolfe, 6 and 5	William D. Wolfe, Silver Spring, Md. Robert J. Millar, Minneapolis, Minn.

1951
FOURTH JUNIOR AMATEUR CHAMPIONSHIP

Held at the University of Illinois Golf Course, Champaign, Ill., July 25-28.
Yardage—6,678. Par 72. 596 Entries, 128 Qualifiers, 128 Starters.
FINAL ROUND (18 Holes)—K. Thomas Jacobs, Jr. defeated Floyd Addington, 4 up and 2 to play.

UPPER HALF

1st Round (18 Holes)	2nd Round (18 Holes)	3rd Round (18 Holes)	4th Round (18 Holes)	5th Round (18 Holes)		Semi-Final (18 Holes)
Maurice Chron, Memphis, Tenn.	Chron, 3 and 2	Chron, 5 and 4	Bisplinghoff, 7 and 5	Jacobs, 3 and 2	Jacobs, 2 and 1	Jacobs, 7 and 6
Kaye Walker, Spokane, Wash.						
C. W. Boom, Jr., Denver, Colo.	Boom, 1 up					
Robert Nichols, Louisville, Ky.						
John F. Gehret, Concordville, Pa.	Gehret, 2 and 1	Bisplinghoff, 2 and 1				
Steven Adams, Salt Lake City, Utah						
Joseph Campbell, Anderson, Ind.	Bisplinghoff, 3 and 2					
Donald M. Bisplinghoff, Orlando, Fla.						
Michael Chalfant, Hutchinson, Kans.	Terrell, 2 and 1	Terrell, 3 and 2	Jacobs, 5 and 4			
Carter S. Terrell, Charlotte, N.C.						
George Williams, Monroe, Mich.	Williams, 6 and 5					
Ronald E. Staley, Nashville, Tenn.						
Woody Rowe, Madeira, Ohio	Jacobs, 1 up	Jacobs, 3 and 2				
K. Thomas Jacobs, Jr., Montebello, Calif.						
John F. Sullivan, Chestnut Hill, Mass.	Rowley, 7 and 5					
Stephen J. Rowley, Shreveport, La.						
Bud Stavney, Seattle, Wash.	Howe, 1 up, 19 hls.	Howe, 3 and 2	Howe, 4 and 2	Richards, 7 and 6		
Winston Howe, Jr., San Francisco, Calif.						
Ramon L. Hamm, Crawfordville, Ind.	Stotz, 3 and 2					
David Stotz, Pittsburgh, Pa.						
Robert Milholland, Little Rock, Ark.	Williams, 4 and 2	Bolster, 5 and 4				
Pat Williams, Montgomery, Ala.						
Dennis Bolster, Bethesda, Md.	Bolster, 7 and 6					
G. Kennedy Engle, Lexington, Ky.						
Charles W. Fawcett, Normandy, Mo.	Fawcett, 3 and 2	Richards, 4 and 3	Richards, 1 up			
Thomas D. Aaron, Gainesville, Ga.						
Robert C. Richards, Lawrence, Kans.	Richards, 4 and 3					
Marcelino Moreno, Midland, Texas						
Orville Moody, Oklahoma City, Okla.	Moody, 1 up, 19 hls.	Moody, 4 and 2				
Martin Parks, Baltimore, Md.						
William Reber, St. Paul, Minn.	Antos, 3 and 2					
Thaddeus L. Antos, Hamburg, N.Y.						
Frank Holt, Jr., Selma, Ala.	Holt, 6 and 4	Holt, 3 and 2	Vare, 1 up	Vare, 6 and 5	Powell, 4 and 3	
Delano Clay, Atlanta, Ga.						
William B. Conliffe, Louisville, Ky.	Parnell, 2 and 1					
Jackson Parnell, Normandy, Mo.						
Irving Salamy, Washington, D.C.	Wyatt, 1 up, 19 hls.	Vare, 1 up, 19 hls.				
Robert Wyatt, Clarksville, Tenn.						
Edwin C. Vare, Philadelphia, Pa.	Vare, 1 up, 19 hls.					
Warner Leppin, Phoenix, Ariz.						
Larry Wayne Harper, Mogadore, Ohio	Harper, 3 and 2	Harper, 1 up	Harper, 2 and 1			
Charles Pickels, Laurel, Va.						
Larry S. Fry, Oakland, Calif.	Tatz, 3 and 1					
Charles Tatz, Belleville, N.J.						
James R. Goetcheus, Martinsville, Ind.	Goetcheus, 1 up	Kastor, 1 up				
Anthony Cullinane, Bethesda, Md.						
John Y. Brown, Jr., Lexington, Ky.	Kastor, 1 up					
Frank Kastor, Glencoe, Ill.						
Jack Norman, Bowling Green, Ky.	Melenson, 1 up	Culley 2 and 1	Howerdd, 2 and 1	Powell, 2 up		
James R. Melenson, Hickman Mills, Mo.						
Lewis L. Culley, Jr., Jackson, Miss.	Culley, 4 and 3					
Melvin Tedder, Memphis, Tenn.						
Gene Howerdd, Jr., Augusta, Ga.	Howerdd, 3 and 2	Howerdd, 2 up				
Karl J. Englert, Orchard Park, N.Y.						
Regis Sauger, Warren, Mich.	Robinson, 1 up					
Donnie Lee Robinson, Louisville, Ky.						
John B. Johnson, Jr., Oklahoma City, Okla.	Turner, 2 and 1	Turner, 2 up	Powell, 6 and 4			
Joseph Turner, Jr., Covington, Ky.						
Pete Passolt, Hopkins, Minn.	Passolt, 3 and 1					
William Garner, Memphis, Tenn.						
Peter La Riviere, Normandy, Mo.	Ginsberg, 4 and 3	Powell, 5 and 3				
James Ginsberg, Cheltenham, Pa.						
James Powell, Dallas, Texas	Powell, 3 and 2					
Ronald R. Sevier, Denver, Colo.						

LOWER HALF

Semi-Final (18 Holes)	5th Round (18 Holes)		4th Round (18 Holes)	3rd Round (18 Holes)	2nd Round (18 Holes)	1st Round (18 Holes)
Addington, 2 and 1	Parker, 5 and 4	Parker, 1 up, 22 hls.	Breckel, 6 and 4	Beck, 4 and 3	Hadley, 4 and 3	John I. Farquhar, Phillips, Texas Thomas A. Hadley, Minneapolis, Minn.
					Beck, 3 and 2	Herb Magnusson, Seattle, Wash. Thomas Beck, Tulsa, Okla.
				Breckel, 1 up	Muhlhauser, 3 and 1	Richard Muhlhauser, Denver, Colo. James Wright, Webster Groves, Mo.
					Breckel, 5 and 4	Joseph B. Breckel, Louisville, Ky. Bill Crowe, Prescott, Ariz.
			Parker, 2 and 1	Parker, 2 and 1	Parker, 1 up	Robert McCallister, San Gabriel, Calif. Bill Parker, Tulsa, Okla.
					Oman, 3 and 1	Henry S. Loeb, Highland Park, Ill. Fred Oman, Hastings-on-Hudson, N.Y.
				Kelly, 2 up	Kelly, 7 and 6	L.S. Stevens, Jr., Nashville, Tenn. Lester Kelly, Atlanta, Ga.
					Brantly, 1 up	Edward L. Brantly, Signal Mountain, Tenn. Glenn A. Mitchell, Bethesda, Md.
		Ford, 1 up	Ford, 2 and 1	Brody, 2 and 1	Brody, 3 and 2	William R. Redding, II, Logansport, Ind. Bud Brody, Daly City, Calif.
					Harrison, 6 and 4	Richard Harrison, Grand Rapids, Mich. John Wellford, Jr., Memphis, Tenn.
				Ford, 3 and 2	Sykes, 6 and 5	James D. Sykes, Philadelphia, Pa. Keith G. Swonson, Salt Lake City, Utah
					Ford, 6 and 5	William H. Ford, Charleston, S.C. Jon Robarge, Longmeadow, Mass.
			Rudolph, 7 and 6	Rudolph, 4 and 3	Beechner, 2 and 1	Eddie Kirby, Bowling Green, Ky. Richard A. Beechner, Lincoln, Neb.
					Rudolph, 4 and 3	Don W. Lundquist, Minneapolis, Minn. Mason Rudolph, Clarksville, Tenn.
				Landrey, 5 and 3	Landrey, 2 and 1	William A. Greer, St. Joseph, Mo. Richard E. Landrey, Vincennes, Ind.
					Wellman, 1 up	Ronald Wellman, Cincinnati, Ohio Ward Wettlaufer, Williamsville, N.Y.
	Addington, 1 up	Addington, 1 up	Addington, 7 and 6	Dudley, 1 up, 21 hls.	McCallum, 2 and 1	Eddie McCallum, Crawfordsville, Ind. Fred Rick Jones, Canfield, Ohio
					Dudley, 5 and 4	Fraser Lewis, Pittsburgh, Pa. Michael A. Dudley, Winchester, Ky.
				Addington, 8 and 6	Kerfoot, 3 and 1	Henry D. Kerfoot, Jr., Arlington, Va. Dean Radtke, Lexington, Ky.
					Addington, 1 up	William S. Baird, Atlanta, Ga. Floyd Addington, Dallas, Texas
			Wiechman, 3 and 2	Wiechman, 3 and 2	Morris, 2 up	Robert Morris, Spokane, Wash. Herman Krauel, Jr., Albuquerque, N.M.
					Wiechman, 3 and 2	Joseph H. Scales, Birmingham, Ala. Phil Wiechman, Chapmanville, W. Va.
				Donnelly, 1 up	Donnelly, 9 and 7	Frederick Micklow, Hillsdale, Mich. Robert Donnelly, Portland, Ore.
					Pantera, 3 and 1	Joseph Pantera, Jr., Buffalo, N.Y. James King, Niles, Ill.
		Wolfe, 2 up	Sisk, 7 and 6	Sisk, 2 and 1	Meyerson, 1 up	Earl Moeller, Jr., Normandy, Mo. Eddie Meyerson, Los Angeles, Calif.
					Sisk, 4 and 3	Robert Sisk, Charlotte, N.C. Lloyd Barnblatt, San Francisco, Calif.
				Richardson, by default	Gilmore, 2 and 1	James Mahoney, Boston, Mass. Billy C. Gilmore, Odessa, Texas
					Richardson, 1 up	James Lucius, Northfield, Minn. Joel W. Richardson, Jr., Signal Mountain, Tenn.
			Wolfe, 6 and 4	Wolfe, 6 and 4	Wolfe, 3 and 2	William D. Wolfe, Rockville, Md. Robert Prangley, Denver, Colo.
					Jones, 5 and 3	David Merle Jones, North Little Rock, Ark. Norman C. Clark, St. Joseph, Mo.
				Rench, 4 and 3	Stewart, 2 up	Bob Stewart, Fort Mitchell, Ky. John Churchman, Jr., Louisville, Ky.
					Rench, 1 up, 19 hls.	Richard Lee Rench, Jr., St. Joseph, Mo. Don Stanfill, Memphis, Tenn.

1952
FIFTH JUNIOR AMATEUR CHAMPIONSHIP

Held at the Yale Golf Course, New Haven, Conn., July 23-26.
Yardage—6,613. Par 70. 711 Entries, 128 Qualifiers, 128 Starters.
FINAL ROUND (18 Holes) — Donald M. Bisplinghoff defeated Eddie M. Meyerson, 2 up.

UPPER HALF

1st Round (18 Holes)	2nd Round (18 Holes)	3rd Round (18 Holes)	4th Round (18 Holes)	5th Round (18 Holes)		Semi-Final (18 Holes)
Richard Metzger, Louisville, Ky.	George, 7 and 6	George, 5 and 4	Stokes, 4 and 2	Hurlburt, 3 and 1	Geyer, 5 and 4	Meyerson, 4 and 2
Ernest George, San Jose, Calif.						
Fred L. Bowyer, Jr., Jackson, Tenn.	Conley, 7 and 6					
Bobby L. Conley, Chapmanville, W. Va.						
Selden C. Beebe, Long Beach, Calif.	Stokes, 6 and 5	Stokes, 1 up, 19 hls.				
Brock Stokes, Nashville, Tenn.						
Winston Howe, Jr., San Francisco, Calif.	Poore, 3 and 2					
Francis C. Poore, Chestnut Hill, Pa.						
Kent Hurlburt, Salina, Kans.	Hurlburt, 5 and 4	Hurlburt, 3 and 1	Hurlburt, 2 and 1			
Michael E. Conliffe, Louisville, Ky.						
David Boscka, Morgantown, W. Va.	Allen, 1 up, 19 hls.					
Donald C. Allen, Rochester, N.Y.						
Edward Weitz, Atlanta, Ga.	Weitz, 5 and 3	Schwister, 1 up				
Richard A. Savrann, Canton, Mass.						
Leo H. Jordan, Overland Park, Kans.	Schwister, 6 and 5					
Jerry Schwister, Fussville, Wis.						
Geoffrey Ames, Toledo, Ohio	Barteaux, 3 and 2	Cullinane, 3 and 1	Cullinane, 5 and 4	Geyer, 5 and 4		
Frank E. Barteaux, Framingham, Mass.						
Anthony Cullinane, Bethesda, Md.	Cullinane, 1 up, 19 hls.					
John Schubeck, Jr., Detroit, Mich.						
William A. Swan, Jr., Casper, Wyo.	Turbow, 2 and 1	Conway, 1 up				
Sherwyn Turbow, Santa Monica, Calif.						
Dan Conway, Seattle, Wash.	Conway, 2 and 1					
Eugene Piwowar, Lackawana, N.Y.						
Lawrence Spellman, Bethesda, Md.	Spellman, 4 and 3	Geyer, 1 up, 19 hls.	Geyer, 5 and 3			
Robert J. MacMichael, Detroit, Mich.						
Peter Weber, Wilton, Me.	Geyer, 5 and 3					
Peter Geyer, Monterey, Calif.						
William C. Cook, Nashville, Tenn.	Braun, 3 and 2	Lohr, 3 and 2				
Charles Braun, Louisville, Ky.						
G. William Lohr, Jr., East Aurora, N.Y.	Lohr, 1 up, 19 hls.					
James D. Stanfill, Memphis, Tenn.						
Ronald E. Schwarzel, Pittsburgh, Pa.	Vosburg, 1 up	T. Thomas, 2 and 1	Hadley, 8 and 6	Meyerson, 4 and 3	Meyerson, 2 and 1	
Albert C. Vosburg, Rochester, N.Y.						
Charles M. Thomas, III, Atlanta, Ga.	T. Thomas, 3 and 2					
Terry Thomas, Canandaigua, N.Y.						
Thomas Hadley, Minneapolis, Minn.	Hadley, 8 and 6	Hadley, 3 and 2				
Steve Uzelac, Detroit, Mich.						
Tom Conforti, Riverside, Ill.	Clark, 6 and 5					
John Clark, Little Rock, Ark.						
Charles G. Brennan, Scituate, Mass.	Meyerson, 4 and 3	Meyerson, 6 and 5	Meyerson, 4 and 2			
Eddie M. Meyerson, Los Angeles, Calif.						
Gerald Shore, Minneapolis, Minn.	Shore, 1 up					
Jerry Moyer, Overland Park, Kans.						
Martin L. Parks, Baltimore, Md.	Parks, 2 and 1	McLean, 7 and 5				
Joseph B. Robertson, Hilton Village, Va.						
William H. McLean, Spring Hill, Ala.	McLean, 4 and 3					
Eugene M. Howerdd, Augusta, Ga.						
Joe P. Riordan, Phoenix, Ariz.	McGuire, 3 and 1	Lingenbrink, 3 and 2	Lingenbrink, 5 and 4	Lingenbrink, 4 and 3		
Charles McGuire, Fort Dix, N.J.						
John Farquhar, Amarillo, Texas	Lingenbrink, 2 and 1					
Dale Lingenbrink, Seattle, Wash.						
Charles J. Erdman, Jr., Clarksburg, W. Va.	Erdman, 1 up, 19 hls.	Erdman, 1 up, 19 hls.				
Patrick Keenan, Rochester, N.Y.						
Abbott Baker, Watertown, Mass.	Mance, 3 and 2					
Joe Mance, Jr., Renton, Wash.						
Rex Baxter, Jr., Amarillo, Texas	Baxter, 1 up, 22 hls.	Baxter, 3 and 2	Baxter, 2 and 1			
Robert Morris, Spokane, Wash.						
Frank Cottle, III, Gladsden, Ala.	Cottle, 1 up, 19 hls.					
John C. Schwartz, Phoenix, Ariz.						
Tod O. Morrow, Butler, Pa.	Forbes, 3 and 1	Forbes, 1 up				
David H. Forbes, Monroe, Wis.						
Wendell Spragins, Memphis, Tenn.	Leggett, 5 and 4					
Raymond F. Leggett, Jr., Midland, Texas						

LOWER HALF

Semi-Final (18 Holes)	5th Round (18 Holes)		4th Round (18 Holes)	3rd Round (18 Holes)	2nd Round (18 Holes)	1st Round (18 Holes)
Bisplinghoff, 3 and 2	Jacobs, 5 and 3	Oman, 2 and 1	Oman, 3 and 1	Oman, 2 and 1	Reed, 2 and 1	Thomas K. Reed, Denver, Colo. William Cox, Pawtucket, R.I.
					Oman, 7 and 5	Max W. Culp, Huntington, W. Va. Frederick Oman, Hastings-on-Hudson, N.Y.
				Symons, 2 and 1	Ray, 3 and 1	Lewis Ray, Monticello, Ind. Gordon McCullough, New Haven, Conn.
					Symons, 1 up, 19 hls.	Jimmy Symons, San Antonio, Texas Joseph Grace, Detroit, Mich.
			Baker, 7 and 5	Baker, 2 and 1	Huetteman, 4 and 3	Joe McEwen, Jr., Nashville, Tenn. John R. Huetteman, Detroit, Mich.
					R. Baker, 2 up	Ralph Baker, Tulsa, Okla. Peter J. Diemand, Bridgeport, Conn.
				Goetcheus, 1 up	Scott, 3 and 2	L.W. Scott, Jr., Oklahoma City, Okla. Walter A. Stahl, South Euclid, Ohio
					Goetcheus, 3 and 2	James R. Goetcheus, Martinsville, Ind. James H. Kinney, Anoka, Minn.
		Jacobs, 1 up, 19 hls.	Veghte, 1 up	Veghte, 6 and 4	Hobson, 3 and 1	Daniel Hobson, Oreland, Pa. William B. Conliffe, Louisville, Ky.
					Veghte, 8 and 6	Stanley Domian, Wethersfield, Conn. John W. Veghte, Gloversville, N.Y.
				Heeseman, 3 and 2	Haddad, 1 up, 19 hls.	Ralph Haddad, Dedham, Mass. Irving Salamy, Washington, D.C.
					Heeseman, 1 up, 19 hls.	William B. Stevens, Jr., Loudonville, N.Y. Gary Heeseman, Charlotte, N.C.
			Jacobs, 3 and 2	Jacobs, 4 and 3	McDougall, 4 and 3	Richard M. Binzer, Madeira, Ohio Donald McDougall, Locust Valley, N.Y.
					Jacobs, 6 and 4	Larry Gorrell, Salina, Kans. K. Thomas Jacobs, Jr., Montebello, Calif.
				Poland, 5 and 4	Poland, 2 up	Harry Poland, Jr., Indianapolis, Ind. Vernon Stanley, Charlotte, N.C.
					Fawcett, 5 and 3	Charles W. Fawcett, Jr., Normandy, Mo. Jack Moschogianis, St. Paul, Minn.
	Bisplinghoff, 2 and 1	Bisplinghoff, 9 and 8	Jonas, 1 up, 19 hls.	Jonas, 2 up	Quick, 1 up, 19 hls.	Ronald Carmichael, Martinsville, Ind. Randy Quick, Burlington, Wis.
					Jonas, 4 and 3	Eric Jonas, Charlotte, N.C. Jimmy Russell, Amarillo, Texas
				Campbell, 2 and 1	Campbell, 2 and 1	Glenn A. Mitchell, Bethesda, Md. Joe Campbell, Anderson, Ind.
					Chapman, 2 and 1	Peter LaRiviere, Webster Groves, Mo. John D. Chapman, II, Osterville, Mass.
			Bisplinghoff, 8 and 7	Brue, 2 up	Brue, 4 and 3	Robert Brue, Milwaukee, Wis. Bobby Lemming, Atlanta, Ga.
					Thompson, 2 and 1	Robert Ornsteen, Haverhill, Mass. Josiah D. Thompson, Jr., East Liverpool, Ohio
				Bisplinghoff, 3 and 2	Bisplinghoff, 5 and 4	Donald M. Bisplinghoff, Orlando, Fla. John Churchman, Louisville, Ky.
					Rowe, 1 up	George Peters, Kansas City, Mo. W. Woodin Rowe, Madeira, Ohio
		Temple, 1 up, 19 hls.	Temple, 4 and 3	Moreno, 4 and 3	Voyda, 1 up	Jack Voyda, Hinsdale, Ill. Leo B. Werne, Jr., Normandy, Mo.
					Moreno, 4 and 3	Marcelino Moreno, Midland, Texas David Winchester, Madeira, Ohio
				Temple, 4 and 3	Beck, default	Walter S. Skinner, Wheaton, Ill. Thomas Beck, Tulsa, Okla.
					Temple, 4 and 3	Terry B. Temple, Peru, Ind. James E. Fisher, Mamaroneck, N.Y.
			Micklow, 2 up	Bradley, 2 and 1	Bradley, 1 up	Bobby G. Young, Richmond, Ky. Foster Bradley, Los Angeles, Calif.
					Cherry, 6 and 5	Ned Cherry, Jr., Maplewood, N.J. R.C. Arnett, Ashland, Ky.
				Micklow, 6 and 5	Micklow, 1 up, 19 hls.	Merle Jones, Little Rock, Ark. Frederick A. Micklow, Hillsdale, Mich.
					Wrathall, 1 up	Peter Loda, Rockville, Md. Donald Wrathall, East Aurora, N.Y.

1953
SIXTH JUNIOR AMATEUR CHAMPIONSHIP

Held at the Southern Hills Country Club, Tulsa, Okla., July 29-August 1.
Yardage—6,675. Par 71. 713 Entries, 128 Qualifiers, 128 Starters.
FINAL ROUND (18 Holes) – Rex Baxter, Jr., defeated George Warren, III, 2 up and 1 to play.

UPPER HALF

1st Round (18 Holes)	2nd Round (18 Holes)	3rd Round (18 Holes)	4th Round (18 Holes)	5th Round (18 Holes)		Semi-Final (18 Holes)
Stanley Ziobrowski, Rexford, N.Y.	Nicklaus, 6 and 5					
Jack Nicklaus, Columbus, Ohio		Nicklaus, 6 and 5				
Jerome Schwister, Menomonee Falls, Wis.	Schwister, 2 and 1					
Robert Bainbridge, Erie, Pa.			Nicklaus, 1 up			
Donald C. Kristofitz, Fargo N.D.	Nelson, 6 and 5					
William O. Nelson, Denver, Colo.		Nelson, 3 and 2				
David Boscka, Morgantown, W. Va.	Boscka, 1 up					
James Grier, Los Angeles, Calif.						
Foster Bradley, Los Angeles, Calif.	Harrell, 1 up, 19 hls.			Ruffin, 5 and 4		
John K. Harrell, II, Meridian Miss.		Schubeck, 4 and 2				
Cyrus Northrop, Owatonna, Minn.	Schubeck, 2 and 1					
John Schubeck, Jr., Grosse Pointe, Mich.			Ruffin, 2 and 1			
Gary Cross, Framingham, Mass.	Cross, 1 up					
Edward Kwasniewski, Buffalo, N.Y.		Ruffin, 6 and 4				
Robert G. Ruffin, Winston-Salem, N.C.	Ruffin, 3 and 2					
Patrick Keenan, Rochester, N.Y.						
Jimmy Russell, Amarillo, Texas	Russell, 1 up				Warren, 3 and 2	
Leo H. Jordan, Jr., Overland, Kans.		Russell, 5 and 4				
Paul Koressel, Evansville, Ind.	Sutton, 2 up					
Jimmy Sutton, Atlanta, Ga.			Warren, 6 and 5			
George Warren, III, Hampton, S.C.	Warren, 2 and 1					
Jimmy Hoe, Middlesboro, Ky.		Warren, 2 up				
Bobby Nichols, Louisville, Ky.	Nichols, 6 and 5					
Hugh Paterson, Toronto, Ont., Canada						
Francis Poore, Chestnut Hill, Pa.	Dowling, 6 and 5			Warren, 1 up, 19 hls.		
James E. Dowling, Wichita, Kans.		Austin, 3 and 2				
Ronald E. Jachowski, Phoenix, Ariz.	Austin, 3 and 2					
William G. Austin, Jr., Kansas City, Mo.			De Luca, 1 up, 21 hls.			
Art Farler, Olympia, Wash.	De Luca, 1 up, 20 hls.					
Louis DeLuca, Wilmington, Del.		De Luca, 5 and 3				
Bob Kappus, Tulsa, Okla.	Kappus, 5 and 4					
Russ Schoneberg, Normandy, Mo.						
James W. Webb, Avondale Estates, Ga.	Webb, 2 and 1					Warren, 3 and 2
Peter C. French, Columbus, Ohio		Lopp, 1 up				
Robert L. Prall, Salem, Ore.	Lopp, 1 up, 23 hls.					
Keith Lopp, Long Beach, Calif.			Campbell, 3 and 2			
Donald Torppa, Maynard, Mass.	Campbell, 4 and 3					
Joe Campbell, Anderson, Ind.		Campbell, 3 and 2				
Ward Wettlaufer, Williamsville, N.Y.	Wettlaufer, 2 up					
Douglas Rasmussen, Waukesha, Wis.						
Peter Geyer, Monterey, Calif.	Geyer, 7 and 6			Campbell, 3 and 2		
James W. Berling, Covington, Ky.		Grady, 3 and 1				
John Hyden, Tulsa, Okla.	Grady, 1 up, 19 hls.					
Richard Grady, Beverly, Mass.			Stanley, 5 and 4			
Verner Stanley, Charlotte, N.C.	Stanley, 4 and 3					
Don Essig, III, Indianapolis, Ind.		Stanley, 1 up, 21 hls.				
Anthony Morosco, Fairmont, W. Va.	Gilbert, 4 and 3					
Jimmy Gilbert, Bowling Green, Ky.						
Edward T. Pfister, Buffalo, N.Y.	McCrone, 4 and 2				Lucius, 1 up	
Charles McCrone, Dallas, Texas		Lucius, 6 and 5				
Jack Lowrey, St. Catherines, Ont., Canada	Lucius, 6 and 4					
James H. Lucius, Northfield, Minn.			Lucius, 7 and 5			
Richard Kowaleski, New Haven, Conn.	Kowaleski, 3 and 2					
Jim Haxton, St. Paul, Minn.		Kowaleski, 1 up				
Mike Conliffe, Louisville, Ky.	Riordan, 4 and 3					
Joe Riordan, Phoenix, Ariz.						
Fred L. Bowyer, Jr., Jackson, Tenn.	Bowyer, 5 and 3			Lucius, 6 and 5		
Gordon McCullough, New Haven, Conn.		Green, 6 and 5				
Billy Green, Midland, Texas	Green, 3 and 2					
Don Wilson, Kansas City, Kans.			Green, 4 and 2			
George Shorer, Aldershot, Ont., Canada	Adams, 4 and 3					
David L. Adams, Laguna Beach, Calif.		Anderson, 1 up				
Walter N. Lawson, Florence, S.C.	Anderson, 2 up					
Bob Anderson, Lincoln, Neb.						

LOWER HALF

Semi-Final (18 Holes)	5th Round (18 Holes)		4th Round (18 Holes)	3rd Round (18 Holes)	2nd Round (18 Holes)	1st Round (18 Holes)
Baxter, 8 and 7	Baxter, 3 and 2	Baxter, 7 and 5	Baxter, 4 and 2	Baxter, 1 up	Heeseman, 4 and 3	Robert Waldron, El Dorado, Ark. Gary Heeseman, Charlotte, N.C.
					Baxter, 2 up	Rex Baxter, Jr., Amarillo, Texas Pat McGonagill, Shreveport, La.
				Quick, 6 and 5	Evans, 6 and 4	Richard Metzger, Louisville, Ky. Duke Evans, Wichita, Kans.
					Quick, 2 and 1	Randolph Quick, Burlington, Wis. Denny Nead, Cincinnati, Ohio
			Konsek, 3 and 2	Konsek, 1 up	Hower, 3 and 1	Richard L. Merritt, Jr., Prescott, Ariz. Dennis Hower, Worthington, Minn.
					Konsek, 4 and 3	John W. Ramsay, Pittsburgh, Pa. John P. Konsek, III, Lancaster, N.Y.
				Moore, 2 and 1	Ball, 1 up, 19 hls.	Robert Ball, Indianapolis, Ind. Richard Bither, Hinsdale, Ill.
					Moore, 6 and 5	Jack R. Moore, Duncan, Okla. James Rowley, Erie, Pa.
		Love, 1 up	Micklow, 2 up	Thomas, 3 and 2	Thomas, 1 up	Dick N. Foote, Santa Ana, Calif. Terry Thomas, Canandaigua, N.Y.
					Boutell, 4 and 2	Wayne Pence, Jr., Kansas City, Mo. William Boutell, Minneapolis, Minn.
				Micklow, 6 and 4	Lynch, 2 and 1	David Forbes, Monroe, Wis. John Lynch, Spokane, Wash.
					Micklow, 6 and 4	Frederick Micklow, Hillsdale, Mich. Robert Holtz, Brookline, Mass.
			Love, 2 and 1	Richardson, 3 and 2	Richardson, 2 and 1	Bob Richardson, Duncan, Okla. Frank Boynton, Orlando, Fla.
					Langert, 1 up	Daniel W. Latimore, Jr., Lookout Mt., Tenn. H. Edward Langert, Huntington Beach, Calif.
				Love, 4 and 2	Joselyn, 9 and 7	Alan Morrisson, Webster Groves, Mo. Phillip Joselyn, Fort Dodge, Iowa
					Love, 3 and 2	Davis Love, El Dorado, Ark. John Dunn, Chevy Chase, Md.
	McLean, 1 up, 19 hls.	Grace, 4 and 3	Fisher, 3 and 1	Fisher, 1 up, 19 hls.	Coulson, 3 and 2	Thomas A. Coulson, Morgantown, W. Va. David Goldman, Jr., Dallas, Texas
					Fisher, 2 up	David Mahaffey, Tulsa, Okla. James E. Fisher, New Rochelle, N.Y.
				Garrity, 7 and 6	Sconiers, 6 and 5	John Mork, Worthington, Minn. Neal Sconiers, Iraan, Texas
					Garrity, 2 and 1	William E. Zimmerebuer, Little Rock, Ark. Thomas C. Garrity, Kansas City, Kans.
			Grace, 5 and 3	Carino, 7 and 6	Carino, 2 and 1	Philamon Rodgers, La Jolla, Calif. Ross Carino, Harrison, N.Y.
					Hause, 5 and 3	Jack Hause, Dayton, Ohio Lawrence W. Spellman, Bethesda, Md.
				Grace, 2 and 1	Taber, 1 up	Matt Taber, Lincoln, Neb. Thomas Hadley, Minneapolis, Minn.
					Grace, 1 up	Robert Sisk, Charlotte, N.C. Joseph M. Grace, Detroit, Mich.
		McLean, 5 and 4	McLean, 1 up, 19 hls.	McLean, 5 and 3	McLean, 5 and 4	Fred F. Brochu, Leicester, Mass. William H. McLean, Mobile, Ala.
					Voyda, 4 and 3	Robert M. Laycock, Indianapolis, Ind. John Voyda, Hinsdale, Ill.
				Muldoon, 2 and 1	Beman, 1 up	Deane R. Beman, Bethesda, Md. John Bird, Jr., Shreveport, La.
					Muldoon, 4 and 3	William Lee Hardy, Louisville, Ky. William Muldoon, Columbus, Ohio
			Puckett, 1 up, 20 hls.	Pittman, 7 and 6	Scaletty, 1 up, 20 hls.	Thomas Scaletty, Parsons, Kans. Bobby Lemming, Atlanta, Ga.
					Pittman, 1 up	Jerry Pittman, Tulsa, Okla. Tod Morrow, Butler, Pa.
				Puckett, 3 and 2	Gray, 1 up	John Gray, Milwaukee, Wis. Monte Nevis, San Francisco, Calif.
					Puckett, 7 and 6	Earl Puckett, Jr., Albuquerque, N.M. William W. Shortsleeve, Pittsford, N.Y.

1954
SEVENTH JUNIOR AMATEUR CHAMPIONSHIP

Held at the Los Angeles Country Club (North Course), Los Angeles, Calif., August 4-7.
Yardage—6,820. Par 71. 747 Entries, 128 Qualifiers, 128 Starters.
FINAL ROUND (18 Holes) — Foster Bradley, Jr., defeated Allen L. Geiberger, 3 up and 1 to play.

UPPER HALF

1st Round (18 Holes)	2nd Round (18 Holes)	3rd Round (18 Holes)	4th Round (18 Holes)	5th Round (18 Holes)		Semi-Final (18 Holes)
Edward T. Pfister, Jr., Buffalo, N.Y. James S. Burns, Honolulu, T. H.	Burns, 2 up					
Thomas L. Wulff, New Orleans, La. Gene McLaughlin, San Mateo, Calif.	McLaughlin, 1 up, 19 hls.	McLaughlin, 2 and 1				
Mack McClain, Oklahoma City, Okla. John E. Kilbride, Worthington, S.D.	Kilbride, 2 up		McLaughlin, 6 and 5			
Mark Ryan, Omaha, Neb. John Dunn, Washington, D.C.	Dunn, 8 and 7	Kilbride, 1 up				
Frank R. Lovell, Jr., Detroit, Mich. Gene Cardi, Columbus, Ohio	Lovell, 2 and 1			Stevenson, 1 up		
Paul Njaa, Spokane, Wash. Jerry Johnston, Odessa, Texas	Johnston, 4 and 2	Johnston, 5 and 3				
Edward Zemljak, Butte, Mont. Charles Honeysuckle, Little Rock, Ark.	Zemljak, 5 and 4		Stevenson, 2 and 1			
Harlan Stevenson, Long Beach, Calif. Morry Brownstein, Minneapolis, Minn.	Stevenson, 3 and 1	Stevenson, 2 and 1				
Deane R. Beman, Bethesda, Md. Donald Kristofitz, Fargo, N.D.	Kristofitz, 4 and 2				Bradley, 4 and 3	
Walter R. Shirah, Memphis, Tenn. Foster Bradley, Jr., Los Angeles, Calif.	Bradley, 6 and 5	Bradley, 5 and 4				
Jim Maschinot, Denver, Colo. Richard McNeill, Garden City, N.Y.	McNeill, 2 up		Bradley, 5 and 4			
John G. Green, Hobbs, N.M. Bryant Prentice, Green Bay, Wis.	Green, 3 and 2	McNeil, 2 and 1				
John W. F. Haner, Madison, W. Va. Jim Nelson, Norfolk, Neb.	Haner, 7 and 5			Bradley, 4 and 3		
J. J. Hagan, Portland, Ore. Thomas McGrath, Kansas City, Mo.	Hagan, 5 and 3	Haner, 1 up				
Dean O. Smith, Wichita, Kans. Edward Weitz, New Orleans, La.	Weitz, 3 and 2		Foote, 7 and 5			
Gordon Jensen, Minneapolis, Minn. Dick N. Foote, Santa Ana, Calif.	Foote, 4 and 3	Foote, 1 up, 19 hls.				Bradley, 3 and 1
Mike McCuistion, Lincoln, Neb. Don Essig, III, Indianapolis, Ind.	Essig, 1 up					
Charles Weil, Jr., Los Angeles, Calif. David K. Daniels, Columbus, Ohio	Weil, 2 and 1	Essig, 3 and 2				
Chuck Schwab, Santa Barbara, Calif. Ronald Letiecq, Newport, R.I.	Letiecq, 2 and 1		Warren, 1 up, 20 hls.			
George Warren, III, Hampton, S.C. Jimmy Bell, Little Rock, Ark.	Warren, 1 up, 19 hls.	Warren, 1 up				
Jack R. Moore, Duncan, Okla. Richard Mazzotti, Taylorville, Ill.	Moore, 3 and 2			Warren, 4 and 3		
John P. Konsek, III, Cheektowaga, N.Y. Jack Luceti, San Francisco, Calif.	Konsek, 4 and 3	Moore, 1 up				
Gerald C. Goring, Honolulu, T.H. William G. Tabb, Louisville, Ky.	Goring, 5 and 4		Goring, 4 and 3			
Joe A. Tiano, Albuquerque, N.M. John Lynch, Spokane, Wash.	Lynch, 1 up	Goring, 3 and 2			Warren, 1 up	
Roy Shreves, Sisterville, W. Va. Leslie Sladkus, Elizabeth, N.J.	Shreves, 3 and 2					
Matt Taber, Lincoln, Neb. Roger G. Byron, Waseca, Minn.	Taber, 5 and 4	Shreves, 1 up, 19 hls.				
Louis Graham, Nashville, Tenn. Andrew Clarke, Milwaukee, Wis.	Graham, 3 and 2		Reif, 6 and 5			
Ronald Reif, Lemon Grove, Calif. James T. Gilbert, Bowling Green, Ky.	Reif, 3 and 2	Reif, 4 and 2		Reif, 3 and 2		
Kent F. Frates, Oklahoma City, Okla. Thomas J. Wittenberg, New Orleans, La.	Wittenberg, 2 and 1					
Carl A. Lohren, Silver Spring, Md. Hugh Paterson, Toronto, Ont., Canada	Paterson, 1 up	Paterson, 3 and 2				
Walt Millar, Jr., Cincinnati, Ohio Tod O. Morrow, Pittsburgh, Pa.	Millar, 5 and 3		Rodgers, 3 and 1			
Wayne A. Pence, Jr., Kansas City, Mo. Phil Rodgers, San Diego Calif.	Rodgers, 5 and 4	Rodgers, 4 and 2				

LOWER HALF

Semi-Final (18 Holes)	5th Round (18 Holes)		4th Round (18 Holes)	3rd Round (18 Holes)	2nd Round (18 Holes)	1st Round (18 Holes)
				Adams, 5 and 4	Woodfin, 2 and 1	Bob Woodfin, Jr., Selma, Ala. Theodore Boots, Anderson, Ind.
					Adams, 9 and 7	Davis Adams, Jr., Macon, Ga. Robert Dice, Cincinnati, Ohio
			Hesler, 1 up	Hesler, 6 and 5	Hesler, 1 up	Howie Hesler, Kansas City, Mo. Don F. Woollard, Parkersburg, W. Va.
		Hesler, 1 up			Bono, 1 up	Richard J. Bono, Lake Charles, La. William Mott, Los Angeles, Calif.
				Hill, 1 up	Hill, 2 and 1	David Hill, Jackson, Mich. David Goldman, Jr., Dallas, Texas
			Hill, 4 and 2		Heeseman, 1 up, 20 hls.	Gary Heeseman, Charlotte, N.C. Alan Gealer, Los Angeles, Calif.
				Hoyt, 3 and 1	Hoyt, 2 and 1	Thomas Musselman, Louisville, Ky. Harvey R. Hoyt, New Rochelle, N.Y.
	Lobstein, 4 and 3				Pasnik, 1 up, 19 hls.	Arthur Pasnik, Hamburg, N.Y. Jim Hazton, St. Paul, Minn.
				H. Royer, 4 and 3	Nicklaus, 5 and 4	Jack Nicklaus, Columbus, Ohio James Noonan, Pawtucket, R.I.
			Arreaga, 4 and 3		H. Royer, 6 and 5	Ronald Gillespie, San Bernardino, Calif. Hugh Royer, Jr., Columbus, Ga.
				Arreaga, 2 and 1	Boughner, 4 and 3	Robert Boughner, Apple Valley, Calif. John R. Jackson, Jr., Hattiesburg, Miss.
		Lobstein, 2 and 1			Arreaga, 2 and 1	Johnny Arreaga, San Antonio, Texas Lee Raymond, Toledo, Ohio
				Cummings, 2 and 1	Cummings, 7 and 6	Robert E. Schneider, Louisville, Ky. Bill Cummings, Winnetka, Ill.
			Lobstein, 5 and 4		Stanley, 1 up	Louis Henderson, Little Rock, Ark. Verner E. Stanley, Charlotte, N.C.
				Lobstein, 2 and 1	R. Royer, 3 and 2	Jim Stills, Euclid, Ohio Ronald L. Royer, Crawfordsville, Ind.
Geiberger, 6 and 4					Lobstein, 1 up	Christian G. Kling, Rochester, N.Y. Henry P. Lobstein, Brownwood, Texas
				Aaron, 3 and 1	Aaron, 1 up, 19 hls.	Tommy Self, San Bernardino, Calif. Tommy Aaron, Gainesville, Ga.
			Aaron, 3 and 2		Flowers, 3 and 2	Larry Gilbert, Phoenix, Ariz. Larry Flowers, Sulphur Springs, Texas
				Conlin, 2 and 1	Simmons, 1 up	Robert B. Hardaway, Kansas City, Kans. Warren Simmons, Canandaigua, N.Y.
		Aaron, 6 and 4			Conlin, 2 up	Walter W. Conlin, III, Wethersfield, Conn. Samuel Carmichael, Martinsville, Ind.
				Bensen, 6 and 4	Bensen, 8 and 7	Kenneth Bensen, Brooklyn, N.Y. Robert J. Curley, Louisville, Ky.
			Bensen, 3 and 2		Griffith, 3 and 1	Ray Griffith, Orangeburg, S.C. Gary Vorndran, Wickliffe, Ohio
				Seanor, 3 and 1	Magnussen, 1 up	Bernard Magnussen, Winnetka, Ill. Stephen H. Miller, Jackson, Mich.
	Geiberger, 3 and 1				Seanor, 4 and 3	William Purks, Jr., Vicksburg, Miss. William Seanor, Bakersfield, Calif.
				Luceti, 4 and 3	Cook, 5 and 4	Richard J. Gilbert, Butte, Mont. William Cook, Minneapolis, Minn.
			Geiberger, 4 and 3		Luceti, 3 and 2	John Grubb, Rockville, Md. Ron Luceti, San Francisco, Calif.
				Geiberger, 5 and 4	Geiberger, 1 up	Charles F. Ankrom, Parkersburg, W. Va. Allen L. Geiberger, Santa Barbara, Calif.
		Geiberger, 6 and 5			Evans, 1 up, 19 hls.	John Clark, Little Rock, Ark. Dale Evans, III, Wichita, Kans.
				McAfee, 6 and 4	McAfee, 4 and 3	Gerald B. Muller, Bismarck, N.D. Robert M. McAfee, Chickasha, Okla.
			Joselyn, 4 and 3		Bies, 4 and 3	Donald W. Bies, Seattle, Wash. Henry Hodde, Hobbs, N.M.
				Joselyn, 5 and 3	McGuire, 5 and 4	Lee McGuire, Leavenworth, Kans. Carl F. Dahlbert, New Orleans, La.
					Joselyn, 5 and 4	Robert Epstein, Omaha, Neb. Phillip Joselyn, Fort Dodge, Iowa

1955
EIGHTH JUNIOR AMATEUR CHAMPIONSHIP

Held at the Purdue University South Golf Course, West Lafayette, Ind., August 3-6.
Yardage—6,337. Par 71. 805 Entries. 128 Qualifiers, 128 Starters.
FINAL ROUND (18 Holes) – William J. Dunn defeated William Seanor, 3 up and 2 to play.

UPPER HALF

1st Round (18 Holes)	2nd Round (18 Holes)	3rd Round (18 Holes)	4th Round (18 Holes)	5th Round (18 Holes)		Semi Final (18 Holes)
William Gore, Akron, Ohio Dale Mehaffey, Spokane, Wash.	Gore, 1 up, 20 hls.					
William Barnett, West Frankfort, Ill. Harlan Stevenson, Long Beach, Calif.	Barnett, 1 up,	Barnett, 2 up				
Harcourt Kemp, Louisville, Ky. Walter W. Conlin, III, Wethersfield, Conn.	Conlin, 2 and 1		Conlin, 3 and 1			
Don Essig, III, Indianapolis, Ind. Noel E. A. Baker, Pittsburgh, Pa.	Essig, 4 and 3	Conlin, 2 and 1				
Edward T. Pfister, Buffalo, N.Y. Robert A. Webb, Gulfport, Miss.	Webb, 4 and 3			Dunn, 6 and 5		
William J. Dunn, Duncan, Okla. Mark Rasmussen, San Jose, Calif.	Dunn, 5 and 4	Dunn, 5 and 3				
R. Paul Weyand, Jr., Detroit, Mich. Jerry Probst, Wichita, Kans.	Weyand, 2 up		Dunn, 1 up, 19 hls.			
Edward A. Menke, Waukegan, Ill. Robert Epstein, Omaha, Neb.	Menke, 6 and 4	Menke, 5 and 4				
Don Keller, Tucson, Ariz. John C. Rolston, Park Ridge, Ill.	Rolston, 1 up, 19 hls.				Dunn, 4 and 2	
Gary Wright, Denver, Colo. Gerald Zar, San Pedro, Calif.	Zar, 2 and 1	Zar, 3 and 2				
Maurice E. Teter, Jr., Dallas, Texas Murray Zaretsky, Providence, R.I.	Zaretsky, 2 and 1		Weiss, 2 and 1			
Walter E. Bailes, Vienna, W. Va. Theodore Weiss, New Orleans, La.	Weiss, 3 and 1	Weiss, 2 and 1				
George Stigger, III, Henderson, Ky. Tom Bryant, Orangeburg, S.C.	Stigger, 2 up			Nicklaus, 5 and 4		
Wayne Pence, Jr., Kansas City, Mo. Sam Carmichael, Martinsville, Ind.	Carmichael, 3 and 2	Stigger, 4 and 3				
Jack Nicklaus, Columbus, Ohio Robert E. Babcock, Duncan Okla.	Nicklaus, 4 and 2		Nicklaus, 7 and 5			
Stephen C. West, Caldwell, N.J. Bill Ford, Jr., Amarillo, Texas	Ford, 3 and 2	Nicklaus, 3 and 2				
James T. Gilbert, Bowling Green, Ky. Gustave Thurguson, Berwick, La.	Gilbert, 6 and 5					Dunn, 3 and 1
Eugene Francis, Sea Cliff, N.Y. Robert Roy, Providence, R.I.	Francis, 3 and 2	Francis, 5 and 4				
Harper Pearse, Grigham, Utah Allen L. Geiberger, Santa Barbara, Calif.	Geiberger, 4 and 3		Geiberger, 5 and 3			
Henry M. Hodde, Hobbs, N.M. Robert W. Robinson, Meridian, Miss.	Robinson, 2 and 1	Geiberger, 1 up, 20 hls.				
Carlton Sheffield, Houston, Texas Gordon B. Baker, Jr., Florence, S.C.	Baker, 6 and 4			Geiberger, 4 and 2		
Kenneth L. Bruno, Tulsa, Okla. John Ellis, Wilmette, Ill.	Bruno, 5 and 3	Baker, 2 and 1				
Thomas A. Coulson, Morgantown, W. Va. Richard D. Whipple, Jr., Phoenix, Ariz.	Coulson, 1 up, 21 hls.		Raymond, 3 and 2			
Lee Raymond, Toledo, Ohio John Hamilton, Evansville, Ind.	Raymond, 4 and 3	Raymond, 1 up, 19 hls.				
Bruce Bullis, Melrose Park, Ill. Donald C. Allen, Rochester, N.Y.	Allen, 2 and 1				Foote, 2 and 1	
Marvin Lerman, Providence. R. I. Laurence Peterson, Stow, Ohio	Peterson, 4 and 3	Allen, 7 and 5				
Jerry Camp, Jr., Spokane, Wash. Bruce Re Falo, Louisville, Ky.	Camp, 2 and 1		Allen, 3 and 2			
Russell, Hooper, Jr., Nashville, Tenn. Jim House, Wichita, Kans.	House, 4 and 2	House, 1 up				
Wally Samuels, Pittsburgh, Pa. Arnold Garfinkel, Kansas City, Mo.	Garfinkel, 5 and 3			Foote, 5 and 3		
George R. Peterson, Mankato, Minn. Robert Lerner, Chevy Chase, Md.	Lerner, 6 and 5	Garfinkel, 1 up				
Frank R. Lovell, Jr., Detroit, Mich. Bill Helfrich, Diablo, Calif.	Helfrich, 4 and 3		Foote, 6 and 4			
Dick Foote, Santa Ana, Calif. Dennis Mullins, Omaha, Neb.	Foote, 5 and 4	Foote, 3 and 2				

LOWER HALF

Semi-Final (18 Holes)	5th Round (18 Holes)		4th Round (18 Holes)	3rd Round (18 Holes)	2nd Round (18 Holes)	1st Round (18 Holes)
Seanor, 2 and 1	Rodgers, 6 and 4	Sommer, 4 and 2	Methvin, 1 up	McGuire, 3 and 2	Heeseman, 1 up, 20 hls.	Gary Heeseman, Jr., Charlotte, N.C.
						William H. Robischon, Newburgh, N.Y.
					McGuire, 3 and 2	Lee McGuire, Leavenworth, Kans.
						David Gray, Jacksonville, Texas
				Methvin, 6 and 4	Weber, 3 and 2	Fred K. Smith, Jr., Pipestone, Minn.
						Ronald M. Weber, Prineville, Ore.
					Methvin, 1 up	M.C. Methvin, Jr., Little Rock, Ark.
						Rodney G. Harris, Seattle, Wash.
			Sommer, 4 and 3	Sommer, 6 and 4	Sommer, 7 and 6	Jon Sommer, Crawfordsville, Ind.
						Michael Plitman, Minneapolis, Minn.
					Lawrence, 2 and 1	David B. Lawrence, Jr. New Orleans, La.
						William G. Tabb, Louisville, Ky.
				Beman, 2 up	Bentley, 1 up, 19 hls.	Richard Mazzoti, Taylorsville, Ill.
						J. Marvin Bentley, Macon, Ga.
					Beman, 1 up, 19 hls.	Robert Irwin, Long Beach, Calif.
						Deane R. Beman, Bethesda, Md.
		Rodgers, 1 up, 19 hls.	Rodgers, 8 and 7	Rodgers, 4 and 3	Liechty, 2 and 1	Gary A. Liotta, Albany, Calif.
						John H. Liechty, Iowa City, Iowa
					Rodgers, 5 and 4	Phil Rodgers, San Diego, Calif.
						David Vaughn, Louisville, Ky.
				Barcelo, 1 up, 19 hls.	Konsek, 4 and 3	John Konsek, Cheektowaga, N.Y.
						James M. Phillips, Kansas City, Mo.
					Barcelo, 5 and 4	Robert B. Merwin, Robbinsdale, Minn.
						Wayne Barcelo, New Orleans, La.
			Zimmerman, 4 and 3	Zimmerman, 4 and 3	Zimmerman, 2 and 1	Donovan Quam, Madison, Wis.
						Robert Zimmerman, Jackson, Mich.
					Kessler, 5 and 3	Bruce R. Kessler, Chevy Chase, Md.
						George Beach, Atlanta, Ga.
				Beacon, 7 and 5	Beacon, 3 and 2	Charles T. Whitman, Memphis, Tenn.
						Tom A. Beacon, Pittsburgh, Pa.
					Nelson, 4 and 2	Dave Hall, Cincinnati, Ohio
						Richard E. Nelson, Lewiston, Idaho
	Seanor, 1 up	Simmons, 1 up, 20 hls.	Simmons, 5 and 4	Smith, 1 up, 19 hls.	Flippen, 3 and 1	James T. Flippen, Danville, Va.
						Richard Crawford, E. Dorado, Ark.
					Smith, 4 and 3	Stephen Smith, Green Bay, Wis.
						Richard H. Harrington, Richmond, Ind.
				Simmons, 7 and 5	Simmons, 1 up	John E. Grubb, Rockville, Md.
						Warren Simmons, Canandaigua, N.Y.
					Bishop, 4 and 2	William Chilton, Memphis, Tenn.
						George Bishop, Paxinos, Pa.
			Haxton, 5 and 3	Haxton, 2 and 1	Kodelka, 1 up, 20 hls.	John J. Kodelka, Fargo, N.D.
						Wayne C. Manning, Kansas City, Mo.
					Haxton, 4 and 3	Jim Haxton, St. Paul, Minn.
						John J. Barcelo, III, New Orleans, La.
				Bell, 1 up	Bell, 6 and 5	Freddie Ganter, Jr., Glasgow, Ky.
						Alfred N. Bell, Jr., Columbus, Ga.
					Luceti, 3 and 2	Jack Luceti, San Francisco, Calif.
						Ralph Compiano, Des Moines, Iowa
		Seanor, 4 and 2	Seanor, 2 and 1	Seanor, 4 and 3	Seanor, 7 and 5	Gordon D. Onstad, Miami Springs, Fla.
						William Seanor, Bakersfield, Calif.
					Leon, 4 and 2	Wayne Timberman, Indianapolis, Ind.
						David Leon, Tucson, Ariz.
				Hecker, 3 and 2	Podolski, 6 and 5	Michael J. Podolski, Columbus, Ohio
						Henry G. Whitley, Jr., Amarillo, Texas
					Hecker, 1 up, 19 hls.	John W. Owens, St. Joseph, Mo.
						Fred Hecker, Jr., Sioux Falls, S.D.
			Conliffe, 1 up, 20 hls.	Harris, 6 and 4	Harris, 4 and 3	James L. Harris, Stillwater, Okla.
						Eugene Oeschger, Bayside, N.Y.
					Lynch, 6 and 5	Gerald E. Bailes, Vienna, W. Va.
						Terrence R. Lynch, St. Paul, Minn.
				Conliffe, 4 and 3	Conliffe, 1 up	Sammy Love, Jr., Shreveport, La.
						Mike Conliffe, Louisville, Ky.
					Mann, 3 and 2	William C. Wetzel, Bloomington, Ill.
						Don Mann, Dallas, Texas

1956
NINTH JUNIOR AMATEUR CHAMPIONSHIP

Held at the Taconic Golf Club, Williams College, Williamstown, Mass., August 8-11.
Yardage—6,475. Par 70. 996 Entries, 128 Qualifiers, 128 Starters.
FINAL ROUND (18 Holes) – Harlan Stevenson defeated Jack D. Rule, Jr., 3 up and 1 to play.

UPPER HALF

1st Round (18 Holes)	2nd Round (18 Holes)	3rd Round (18 Holes)	4th Round (18 Holes	5th Round (18 Holes)		Semi-Final (18 Holes)
Hugh Goodman, Jr., Signal Mountain, Tenn.	Warner, 2 and 1	Warner, 3 and 2	Warner, 2 and 1	Warner, 1 up, 19 hls.	Nicklaus, 3 and 1	Rule, 1 up
William Warner, Spokane, Wash.						
Charles Burda, Jr., Lincoln, Neb.	Peterson, 4 and 3					
Gary C. Peterson, Minneapolis, Minn.						
Mark Rasmussen, San Jose, Calif.	Rasmussen, 4 and 3	Rasmussen, 2 and 1				
Eddie Barrickman, Louisville, Ky.						
Robert O. Pierce, Atlanta, Ga.	Pierce, 2 and 1					
John Nichols, Downey, Calif.						
Marion C. Methvin, Jr., Little Rock, Ark.	Wilson, 1 up, 20 hls.	Moore, 3 and 1	Monroe, 4 and 2			
Tom Wilson, Grosse Pointe, Mich.						
Arthur P. Harper, Erie, Pa.	Moore, 2 and 1					
James A. Moore, Rochester, N.Y.						
Thomas D. Cunningham, Connellsville, Pa.	Cunningham, 2 and 1	Monroe, 2 and 1				
Frank Beard, Louisville, Ky.						
Lloyd S. Monroe, N. Caldwell, N.J.	Monroe, 1 up, 19 hls.					
Lawrence H. Burd, Jr., Bethesda, Md.						
Jack Nicklaus, Columbus, Ohio	Nicklaus, 5 and 3	Nicklaus, 3 and 2	Nicklaus, 5 and 4	Nicklaus, 7 and 6		
Cary Olson, Turlock, Calif.						
Fred Scrutchfield, Guthrie, Okla.	Dolan, 7 and 5					
James H. Dolan, III, Leicester, Mass.						
William F. Harris, Gillespie, Ill.	Harris, 4 and 3	Carrico, 2 and 1				
Don Achziger, Fort Morgan, Colo.						
David B. Lawrence, Jr., New Orleans, La.	Carrico, 3 and 1					
Robert R. Carrico, Fort Knox, Ky.						
Charles F. Lewis, III, Little Rock, Ark.	Lewis, 7 and 6	Prater, 1 up, 24 hls.	Prater, 1 up			
Gerald Bailes, Vienna, W. Va.						
Virgil J. Prater, Fountain City, Tenn.	Prater, 1 up 20 hls.					
Eugene Toth, Johnstown, Pa.						
Bud Williamson, Lincoln, Neb.	Williamson, 3 and 2	Grubb, 4 and 3				
James Infantino, Rochester, N.Y.						
John E. Grubb, Rockville, Md.	Grubb, 5 and 4					
Dave Mankowski, Minneapolis, Minn.						
G. Warren Schloat, III, Pleasantville, N.Y.	Fogg, 5 and 4	Fogg, 3 and 2	Cook, 3 and 1	Crawford, 4 and 3	Rule, 1 up	
Henry Fogg, Jr., Oakland, Calif.						
David Driscoll, Erie, Pa.	Siegel, 7 and 6					
Curtiss R. Siegel, Buffalo, N.Y.						
John Cook, Pittsfield, Mass.	Cook, 1 up, 20 hls.	Cook, 5 and 4				
David Owens, Pittsburgh, Pa.						
Robert Walter, Hutchinson, Kans.	Walter, 1 up					
Gary Gruenemeier, Lincoln, Neb.						
Gordon B. Baker, Florence, S.C.	Baker, 5 and 3	Baker, 5 and 4	Crawford, 4 and 3			
William Bohmer, St. Cloud, Minn.						
Terry E. Lally, Louisville, Ky.	Lally, 3 and 2					
Daniel Frederickson, Glendale, Calif.						
Richard Crawford, El Dorado, Ark.	Crawford, 6 and 5	Crawford, 1 up				
Fred W. Behymer, Jr., E. Lansing, Mich.						
Carson Herron, Minneapolis, Minn.	Patterson, 1 up					
Donald Patterson, Decatur, Ga.						
Ted W. Beal, Pipestone, Minn.	Lynch, 5 and 3	Lynch, 2 up	Lynch, 4 and 2	Rule, 1 up		
John Lynch, Spokane, Wash.						
William A. Salvatore, Watertown, Conn.	Salvatore, 1 up, 19 hls.					
Robert E. Gerring, Union, S.C.						
Michael Rombold, Chula Vista, Calif.	Kletcke, 4 and 3	Kletcke, 1 up				
Bob Kletcke, Chicago, Ill.						
Jimmy Bell, Little Rock, Ark.	Bell, 2 and 1					
Robert R. Kirovac, Sharon, Mass.						
Richard L. Weyand, Detroit, Mich.	Weyand, 7 and 6	Weyand, 7 and 5	Rule, 3 and 1			
Wayne Barcelo, New Orleans, La.						
Charles F. Holden, III, Alexandria, Va.	Lindinger, 4 and 2					
Robert C. Lindinger, Wayne, Pa.						
David MacDonald, Fargo, N.D.	MacDonald, 2 up	Rule, 5 and 4				
Edward Segal, Albany, N.Y.						
George E. Stigger, III, Henderson, Ky.	Rule, 4 and 3					
Jack D. Rule, Jr., Waterloo, Iowa						

LOWER HALF

Semi-Final (18 Holes)	5th Round (18 Holes)		4th Round (18 Holes)	3rd Round (18 Holes)	2nd Round (18 Holes)	1st Round (18 Holes)
Stevenson, 1 up	Pfister, 3 and 1	Pfister, 4 and 3	Pfister, 1 up, 19 hls.	Pfister, 2 and 1	Pfister, 5 and 4	Jerry Krause, Kansas City, Mo. Edward T. Pfister, Buffalo, N.Y.
					Pearsall, 1 up	Eddie Pearsall, Seattle, Wash. James E. Stahl, Jr., Cincinnati, Ohio
				Womack, 3 and 1	Womack, 3 and 1	William Womack, Florence, S.C. Tommy Self, San Bernardino, Calif.
					Watson, 2 and 1	Eddie Schnurr, Louisville, Ky. David S. Watson, Philadelphia, Pa.
			Hansen, 3 and 2	Cullinane, 2 and 1	Dollahan, 2 up	Craig Dollahan, Kansas City, Mo. Allen R. O'Neill, Rochester, N.Y.
					Cullinane, 4 and 3	Donn C. Kerby, North Little Rock, Ark. Eugene Cullinane, Washington, D.C.
				Hansen, 1 up	Hansen, 7 and 5	Ricky Haegele, Dwight, Ill. Gene Hansen, Minneapolis, Minn.
					Mahar, 1 up	Thomas E. Morris, Jr., Detroit, Mich. Alexander E. Mahar, Bennington, Vt.
		Webber, 3 and 1	Nix, 1 up	Cole, 1 up, 20 hls.	Cole, 2 and 1	Max Cole, Wichita, Kans. Jerry Potter, Miami, Fla.
					Minger, 5 and 3	Thomas A. Minger, Milwaukee, Ore. John D. Orr, Florence, S.C.
				Nix, 6 and 5	Smith, 3 and 1	Bobby Gaona, Tucson, Ariz. Stephen A. Smith, Green Bay, Wis.
					Nix, 2 and 1	Joseph Camillo, Port Chester, N.Y. Don Nix, Hobbs, N.M.
			Webber, 1 up	Casabella, 5 and 4	Casabella, 2 and 1	Robert A. Webb, Gulfport, Miss. Richard W. Casabella, Louisville, Ky.
					Nation, 7 and 6	Eugene Axelrod, West Lafayette, Ind. Bruce A. Nation, West Hartford, Conn.
				Webber, 5 and 3	Grace, 4 and 3	Thomas J. Grace, Detroit, Mich. Thomas Carreiro, Portsmouth, R.I.
					Webber, 4 and 3	Ronald M. Webber, Prineville, Ore. H. Dudley Wysong, McKenney, Texas
	Stevenson, 4 and 3	Stevenson, 4 and 2	Konsek, 2 up	Martindale, 1 up	Boughner, 3 and 2	Norman Vennerstrom, Fargo, N.D. Robert F. Boughner, Bell Gardens, Calif.
					Martindale, 4 and 3	Jack C. Crutcher, Louisville, Ky. Billy Martindale, Jacksonville, Texas
				Konsek, 4 and 2	Barcelo, 5 and 4	John J. Barcelo, III, New Orleans, La. Joseph Brisson, Grosse Pointe Woods, Mich.
					Konsek, 2 and 1	James Brucker, Indianapolis, Ind. John P. Konsek, Cheektowaga, N.Y.
			Stevenson, 4 and 2	Gleacher, 5 and 3	Gleacher, 4 and 3	Rick Gleacher, Fairfield, Conn. Vernon Nicholas, Mesa, Ariz.
					McKenzie, 4 and 3	Theodore R. McKenzie, Pen Mar, Pa. Bruce Larson, Fargo, N.D.
				Stevenson, 1 up	Stevenson, 1 up, 21 hls.	Harlan Stevenson, Long Beach, Calif. James H. Hooper, West Point, Va.
					Parks, 6 and 5	Jimmy Parks, Columbia, S.C. Henry Hodde, Hobbs, N.M.
		Weiss, 4 and 3	Pence, 2 and 1	Pence, 3 and 1	Pence, 5 and 3	Wayne A. Pence, Jr., Kansas City, Mo. Peter McCann, Framingham, Mass.
					Black, 1 up, 19 hls.	John T. Carmody, Jr., Bennington, Vt. Robert Black, Massillon, Ohio
				Beck, 1 up, 19 hls.	Beck, 4 and 3	Larry Beck, Kinston, N.C. Robert Gilmartin, Jr., Greenvale, N.Y.
					Essig, 4 and 3	Don Essig, III, Indianapolis, Ind. Frank J. Garvin, Englewood, Colo.
			Weiss, 2 and 1	Weiss, 2 and 1	Karl, 2 and 1	Bruce A. Dobie, Worcester, Mass. Nicholas H. Karl, Sistersville, W. Va.
					Weiss, 1 up	Peter Mitchell, Carmel, Calif. Theodore Weiss, New Orleans, La.
				Harris, 1 up, 19 hls.	Harris, 1 up	James L. Harris, Stillwater, Okla. Gerald Zar, San Pedro, Calif.
					Barnett, 3 and 1	Ben Alexander, Lamesa, Texas William E. Barnett, West Frankfort, Ill.

1957
TENTH JUNIOR AMATEUR CHAMPIONSHIP

Held at the Manor Country Club, Rockville, Md., July 17-20.
Yardage—6,455-6,465. Par 70. 1,065 Entries. 128 Qualifiers, 128 Starters.
FINAL ROUND (18 Holes) – Larry E. Beck defeated David C. Leon, 6 up and 5 to play.

UPPER HALF

1st Round (18 Holes)	2nd Round (18 Holes)	3rd Round (18 Holes)	4th Round (18 Holes)	5th Round (18 Holes)		Semi-Final (18 Holes)
Verne Burnett, Long Beach, Calif.	Burnett, 3 and 2					
Edward G. Bowers, Tacoma Park, Md.		Burnett, 5 and 4				
Dick Silverberg, Pipestone, Minn.	Silverberg, 2 and 1					
Frank Lillich, Jr., Rochester, N.Y.			Burnett, 4 and 3			
Paul Barkhouse, Lynn, Mass.	Barkhouse, 2 up					
Ben Alexander, Lamesa, Texas		Barkhouse, 1 up, 19 hls.				
John Ward, Kansas City, Kans.	Tatum, 2 and 1					
Richard Tatum, Atlanta, Ga.				Leon, 1 up, 19 hls.		
Albert Badger, Bloomfield Hills, Mich.	Leon, 3 and 2					
David C. Leon, Tucson, Ariz.		Leon, 5 and 4				
Eddie Schnurr, Louisville, Ky.	Schnurr, 3 and 1					
Gordon Aamoth, Jr., Fargo, N.D.			Leon, 6 and 4			
Robert C. Lindinger, Wayne, Pa.	Lindinger, 6 and 5					
Pat Dorgan, Stickney, Ill.		Lawrence, 2 and 1				
Gary Olson, Turlock, Calif.	Lawrence, 1 up					
David B. Lawrence, Jr., New Orleans, La.					Leon, 4 and 3	
Tom F. Dreyer, North College Hill, Ohio	Hoffman, 2 and 1					
Jon Hoffman, Windom, Minn.		Hoffman, 3 and 1				
James A. Grant, III, Wethersfield, Conn.	Haegele, 5 and 4					
John Haegele, Dwight, Ill.			Hoffman, 5 and 3			
John T. Carmody, Jr., Bennington, Vt.	Carmody, 1 up					
E. Robert Erickson, Spokane, Wash.		Carmody, 3 and 2				
Dan P. Murphy, Texarkana, Ark.	Voight, 3 and 1					
James W. Voight, Scarsdale, N.Y.				Hoffman, 3 and 2		
Daniel Morrow, Harrey, La.	Reneau, 2 and 1					
Jerry Reneau, North Hollywood, Calif.		Harris, 5 and 4				
William F. Harris, Gillespie, Ill.	Harris, 1 up, 20 hls.					
Bruce Wyatt, Louisville, Ky.			Harris, 3 and 2			
Charles Mitchell, Saginaw, Mich.	Hyndman, 4 and 2					
William Hyndman IV, Abington, Pa.		Pelts, 1 up, 22 hls.				
Don Pelts, Memphis, Tenn.	Pelts, 1 up					
Laurence Burd, Jr., Bethesda, Md.						Leon, 1 up
Thomas R. Jackson, Jr., Kennett Square, Pa.	Conley, 1 up					
Charles J. Conley, Seattle, Wash.		Conley, 2 up				
William A. Busemeyer, Cincinnati, Ohio	Agard, 1 up					
Bob Agard, Sioux City, Iowa			Weiss, 2 up			
Humphrey W. Severance, Jr., Louisville, Ky.	Kirovac, 1 up					
Robert R. Kirovac, Sharon, Mass.		Weiss, 3 and 1				
Theodore Weiss, New Orleans, La.	Weiss, 4 and 2					
Jerome L. Missel, Streator, Ill.				Finke, 2 and 1		
Don A. Heitler, Denver, Colo.	Heitler, 2 up					
Allen Carnase, Bronx, N.Y.		Finke, 7 and 5				
Kenneth Finke, Tucson, Ariz.	Finke, 2 and 1					
Dennis Murphy, Huntington Beach, Calif.			Finke, 5 and 3			
Michael Mallon, Barrington, Ill.	Cooke, 4 and 3					
Calvin W. Cooke, Dearborn, Mich.		Lubar, 1 up, 19 hls.				
Richard Staats, St. Louis, Mo.	Lubar, 3 and 1					
Charles Lubar, Washington, D.C.					Casabella, 4 and 3	
Frost Walker, Jr., Birmingham, Ala.	Walker, 4 and 3					
Dan C. Bird, Los Angeles, Calif.		Walker, 4 and 3				
Richard D. Landon, St. Joseph, Mo.	Landon, 1 up					
Michael J. Megliola, Jr., Springfield, Mass.			Walker, 1 up			
Fred Taylor, Portland, Ore.	Hellman, 2 and 1					
David Hellman, Waukegan, Ill.		Barcelo, 7 and 6				
John Walsh, Lansing, Mich.	Barcelo, 5 and 3					
John J. Barcelo III, New Orleans, La.				Casabella, 1 up, 19 hls.		
Jim Allen, Athens, Ga.	Casabella, 3 and 2					
Richard Casabella, Louisville, Ky.		Casabella, 3 and 2				
Keith Mattos, San Mateo, Calif.	Mattos, 1 up					
John C. Doser, Bethesda, Md.			Casabella, 4 and 3			
Jon M. Sheeser, Olean, N.Y.	Sheeser, 3 and 2					
Robert E. Gerring, Union, S.C.		Bratten, 4 and 3				
Jimmy Bratten, San Antonio, Texas	Bratten, 4 and 3					
David Kristofitz, Fargo, N.D.						

LOWER HALF

Semi-Final (18 Holes)	5th Round (18 Holes)		4th Round (18 Holes)	3rd Round (18 Holes)	2nd Round (18 Holes)	1st Round (18 Holes)
Beck, 6 and 5	Beck, 3 and 1	Beck, 2 and 1	Beck, 4 and 3	Nicklaus, 1 up	Nicklaus, 3 and 2	John Brim, Jr., Columbus, Ga. Jack Nicklaus, Columbus, Ohio
					Hoskins, 5 and 4	Harry Hoskins, Jr., Fort Worth, Texas James M. Shepherd, Racine, Wis.
				Beck, 2 and 1	Beck, 4 and 3	William Conway, Jr., Hamburg, N.Y. Larry E. Beck, Kinston, N.C.
					Tyler, 1 up	Charles Pessagno, Baltimore, Md. William R. Tyler, Jr., Jackson, Miss.
			Walter, 3 and 2	Shemano, 1 up	Shemano, 2 and 1	Richard Shemano, San Francisco, Calif. William E. Barnett, W. Frankfort, Ill.
					Parks, 5 and 4	Grant T. Kloppman, Shaker Heights, Ohio Jimmy Parks, Columbia, S.C.
				Walter, 1 up	Brisson, 1 up, 19 hls.	Joseph Brisson, Grosse Pointe Woods, Mich. Bill Moore, Downey, Calif.
					Walter, 3 and 2	Edward Menke, Flossmoor, Ill. Robert Walter, Hutchinson, Kans.
		Blake, 1 up	Blake, 5 and 4	Blake, 7 and 6	Lane, 1 up	Ben Lane, Jr., Amarillo, Texas Nicholas Karl, Sistersville, W. Va.
					Blake, 5 and 3	Douglas R. Hoyt, New Rochelle, N.Y. Joseph Blake, Erie, Pa.
				Vollhaber, 1 up	Vollhaber, 5 and 3	Craig Vollhaber, White Bear Lake, Minn. Curtiss R. Siegel, Buffalo, N.Y.
					Kolak, 4 and 2	Mark E. Darnell, Vandalia, Ohio Ernie Kolak, Cicero, Ill.
			Womack, 4 and 2	Bell, 5 and 4	Allers, 1 up	Harry Allers, Fort Lauderdale, Fla. Paul Quinn, Baltimore, Md.
					Bell, 3 and 2	Roger Camras, Beverly Hills, Calif. James H. Bell, Jr., Little Rock, Ark.
				Womack, 4 and 3	Grace, 4 and 3	Thomas J. Grace, Birmingham, Mich. Glen Gruenemeier, Lincoln, Neb.
					Womack, 6 and 5	Stephen Spray, Indianola, Iowa William Womack, Florence, S.C.
	Methvin, 4 and 3	Methvin, 6 and 4	Gilmartin, 2 and 1	Creagh, 3 and 1	Creagh, 1 up, 19 hls.	George Creagh, Nashville, Tenn. Jerry Johnson, Spokane, Wash.
					Mackanos, 1 up	Jack Moran, Cincinnati, Ohio M. George Mackanos III, Verona, Pa.
				Gilmartin, 1 up	Gilmartin, 5 and 3	James Fitzpatrick, Louisville, Ky. Robert Gilmartin, Greenvale, N.Y.
					DiFazio, 2 up	Charles DiFazio, Wethersfield, Conn. Jay G. Swardenski, Peoria, Ill.
			Methvin, 1 up, 19 hls.	Methvin, 1 up	Methvin, 5 and 3	Ralph E. Mayerstein, Lafayette, Ind. Marion C. Methvin, Jr., Little Rock, Ark.
					Segal, 3 and 2	James Pfleider, Anoka, Minn. Edward D. Segal, Albany, N.Y.
				Rombold, 2 up	Rombold, 5 and 3	Michael Rombold, Chula Vista, Calif. Thomas Schuchart, Omaha, Neb.
					Bowie, 3 and 2	Keith Bowie, Colmar Manor, Md. Byron R. Kantrow, Jr., Baton Rouge, La.
		Konsek, 1 up, 24 hls.	Konsek, 3 and 2	Konsek, 3 and 1	Konsek, 4 and 3	John P. Konsek, Cheektowaga, N.Y. Charles F. Holden III, Alexandria, Va.
					Hale, 3 and 2	John Wooden, Lawrence, Kans. Ted Hale, Mayfield, Ky.
				Patterson, 1 up	Patterson, 1 up, 19 hls.	Gerald Zar, San Pedro, Calif. Donald Patterson, Decatur, Ga.
					Wright, 6 and 5	Jim D. Wright, Enid, Okla. Tom Sisolak, Waukegan, Ill.
			Baker, 4 and 3	Baker, 4 and 2	Baker, 3 and 2	Gordon Baker, Florence, S.C. Ned Johnson, Port Arthur, Texas
					Green, 7 and 6	Peter Green, Franklin, Mich. Donald D. Stickney, Columbus, Ohio
				Fitta, 5 and 3	Giusti, 5 and 4	Wayne Giusti, Daly City, Calif. Robert O. Smith, Bismarck, N.D.
					Fitta, 1 up, 20 hls.	Robert Fitta, E. Providence, R.I. Max L. Cole, Wichita, Kans.

1958
ELEVENTH JUNIOR AMATEUR CHAMPIONSHIP

Held at the University of Minnesota Golf Course, St. Paul, Minn., July 30-August 2.

Yardage—6,339. Par 71. 1,117 Entries, 128 Qualifiers, 128 Starters.

FINAL ROUND (18 Holes) – Gordon Baker defeated R. Douglas Lindsay, 2 up and 1 to play.

UPPER HALF

1st Round (18 Holes)	2nd Round (18 Holes)	3rd Round (18 Holes)	4th Round (18 Holes)	5th Round (18 Holes)		Semi-Final (18 Holes)
Richard D. Landon, St. Joseph Mo.	Landon, 5 and 3	Landon, 2 and 1	Harris, 4 and 3	Harris, 6 and 5	Womack, 1 up	Lindsay, 1 up, 19 hls.
Robert L. Clark, Lakewood, Calif.						
Timothy Byrne, Mt. Kisco, N.Y.	Lubar, 3 and 2					
Charles Lubar, Washington, D.C.						
King T. Knox, Lancaster, Pa.	Harris, 1 up	Harris, 5 and 4				
Labron E. Harris, Stillwater, Okla.						
Kermit Zarley, Jr., Seattle, Wash.	Zarley, 2 and 1					
Charles T. Vance, Charlottesville, Va.						
Bruce Kronick, Minneapolis, Minn.	Pierson, 2 and 1	Pierson, 2 and 1	Boutell, 3 and 2			
Ray Pierson, Boulder, Colo.						
Rick Casabella, Louisville, Ky.	Casabella, 4 and 3					
Robert A. Morse, Lynnfield Center, Mass.						
Glenn P. Phillips, Harahan, La.	Van Dover 3 and 1	Boutell, 4 and 3				
Archie Van Dover, Jr., Poplar Bluff, Mo.						
George W. Boutell, Phoenix, Ariz.	Boutell, 4 and 2					
James M. Shepherd, Racine, Wis.						
Michael Tanzer, Redwood City, Calif.	Carello, 2 and 1	Carello, 1 up, 19 hls.	Quinn, 3 and 1	Womack, 4 and 2		
Eugene Carello, West Frankfort, Ill.						
David E. Boyd, Jacksonville, Fla.	Choate, 3 and 2					
Peter Choate, Los Angeles, Calif.						
Thomas Fuqua, Texarkana, Ark.	Fuqua, 2 and 1	Quinn, 4 and 2				
Dennis P. Golbesky, Dearborn, Mich.						
Paul W. Quinn, Baltimore, Md.	Quinn, 4 and 3					
Arthur P. Harper, Erie, Pa.						
David L. Kristofitz, Fargo, N.D.	Siegel, 6 and 5	Stevens, 1 up, 20 hls.	Womack, 3 and 2			
Curtiss Siegel, Snyder, N.Y.						
Johnny Stevens, Wichita, Kans.	Stevens, 5 and 3					
Warren B. Hughes, Washington, D.C.						
David P. Stuard, New Orleans, La.	Goldman 4 and 3	Womack, 6 and 5				
Kenny Goldman, Dallas, Texas						
Thomas Schuchart, Omaha, Neb.	Womack, 7 and 6					
William Womack, Florence, N.C.						
Edward K. Vernon, Pocatello, Idaho	Colwick, 2 up	Colwick, 2 and 1	Lindsay, 3 and 2	Lindsay, 1 up, 19 hls.	Lindsay, 3 and 2	
John Colwick, Dallas, Texas						
Paul R. Herold, Jr., Normandy, Mo.	Grace, 1 up					
Thomas Grace, Birmingham, Mich.						
R. Douglas Lindsay, Bethesda, Md.	Lindsay, 2 up	Lindsay, 5 and 4				
Joel Hirsch, Highland Park, Ill.						
Jerry Johnson, Spokane, Wash.	Johnson, 1 up, 19 hls.					
R. Edwin Alexander, Dayton, Ohio						
James A. Grant, III, Wethersfield, Conn.	Schnurr, 4 and 3	Van DeWalle, 1 up	Allen, 1 up, 19 hls.			
Eddie Schnurr, Louisville, Ky.						
Robert R. Kirovac, Sharon, Mass.	Van De Walle, 3 and 1					
John Van DeWalle, Sioux Falls, S.D.						
David R. Crowther, Villanova, Pa.	Krachmer, 5 and 4	Allen, 2 and 1				
Jay Krachmer, Cedar Rapids, Iowa						
Ralph Mayerstein, Lafayette, Ind.	Allen, 3 and 2					
Jimmy Allen, Athens, Ga.						
Charles Kohr, Decatur, Ill.	Smith, 5 and 3	Smith, 1 up, 19 hls.	Smith, 2 and 1	Smith, 1 up		
George G. Smith, Jr., New Bern, N.C.						
Peter Green, Franklin, Mich.	Green, 4 and 2					
Robert E. White, East Gadsden, Ala.						
John Massey, Cicero, Ill.	Greenbaum, 3 and 2	Barcelo, 1 up, 21 hls.				
Jerry M. Greenbaum, Atlanta, Ga.						
Dick M. Ferry, Ontario, Calif.	Barcelo, 4 and 3					
John V. Barcelo, III, New Orleans, La.						
Ted Hale, Mayfield, Ky.	Hale, 7 and 5	Folkes, 2 and 1	Folkes, 7 and 6			
Donald Shiff, Minneapolis, Minn.						
William B. Sechrest, Kansas City, Mo.	Folkes, 5 and 4					
Kenneth L. Folkes, Concord, N.C.						
David R. Thrasher, Dayton, Ohio	Creagh, 3 and 2	Creagh, 2 and 1				
George Creagh, Nashville, Tenn.						
Charles M. Keating, Corning, N.Y.	Keating, 3 and 2					
James Giffen, Stockton, Calif.						

LOWER HALF

Semi-Final (18 Holes)	5th Round (18 Holes)		4th Round (18 Holes)	3rd Round (18 Holes)	2nd Round (18 Holes)	1st Round (18 Holes)
Baker, 4 and 3	Baker, 3 and 2	Courtney, 5 and 3	Courtney, 1 up	Hoffman, 6 and 5	Hoffman, 2 and 1	Burton Page, Wakefield, Mass. Jon Hoffman, Windom, Minn.
					Kling, 5 and 3	Mike Spalding, Bowling Green, Ky. Jarrett Kling, Rochester, N.Y.
				Courtney, 7 and 6	Worsham, 3 and 1	Robert L. Worsham, Baltimore, Md. David E. Bast, New Orleans, La.
					Courtney, 2 and 1	Robert D. McLennan, Downey, Calif. Charles Courtney, La Jolla, Calif.
			McMahon, 1 up	McMahon, 1 up	McMahon, 4 and 3	Michael V. McMahon, Carrollton, Ga. Richard Earley, Erie, Pa.
					Bush, 3 and 2	Burt Mallory, Midland, Texas Joe Bush, Ephrata, Wash.
				Orr, 1 up	Orr, 4 and 3	Richard S. Griffith, Montclair, N.J. John D. Orr, Florence, S.C.
					Tullos, 5 and 4	Claude M. Tullos, Cleveland, Miss. Ronald Saffer, Omaha, Neb.
		Baker, 1 up, 19 hls.	Baker, 2 and 1	Baker, 5 and 4	Hixon, 4 and 2	Jack E. Moran, Cincinnati, Ohio George E. Hixon, Oklahoma City, Okla.
					Baker, 5 and 3	Gordon Baker, Florence, S.C. Clifford Davis, Menlo Park, Calif.
				Barnett, 1 up, 19 hls.	DiFazio, 3 and 1	James R. Miner, Louisville, Ky. Charles DiFazio, Wethersfield, Conn.
					Barnett, 5 and 4	Gerard Barnett III, Brielle, N.J. Clyde Lusk, Jr., Kenner, La.
			Badger, 2 and 1	Badger, 3 and 2	Badger, 6 and 5	Pat Dorgan, Berwyn, Ill. Albert E. Badger, Bloomfield Hills, Mich.
					Cary, 5 and 3	Richard Funk, Decatur, Ill. Stephen Cary, Tonawanda, N.Y.
				Wilkinson, 2 and 1	Ross, 5 and 4	Gerald L. Ross, Little Rock, Ark. Dudley H. Pepp, Beverly Hills, Calif.
					Wilkinson, 3 and 2	Ronald E. McLeod, Fargo, N.D. Stephan K. Wilkinson, Hagerstown, Ind.
	Finke, 3 and 2	Meerdink 1 up, 20 hls.	Meerdink, 6 and 5	Meerdink, 1 up, 19 hls.	Meerdink, 4 and 2	C. Barry Meerdink, Muscatine, Iowa Leron Blanks, Dallas, Texas
					Lovett, 3 and 1	Bill Tindall, Seattle, Wash. William G. Lovett, Portland, Ore.
				Hornbuckle, 1 up	Colbert, 3 and 2	James J. Colbert, Prairie Village, Kans. James Draskovits, South Bend, Ind.
					Hornbuckle, 1 up	Gerald Lake, Walpole, Mass. Tommy Hornbuckle, Albuquerque, N.M.
			Johnston, 6 and 5	Johnston, 2 and 1	Johnston, 4 and 3	Ralph W. Johnston, Jackson Heights, N.Y. Peter Goddard, East Rochester, N.Y.
					Pepin, 1 up	Grant T. Kloppman, Shaker Heights, Ohio Johnny Pepin, Memphis, Tenn.
				Boone, 2 and 1	Boone, 7 and 6	James W. Walters, II, Beckley, W. Va. W. Daniel Boone, Chevy Chase, Md.
					Mouw, 1 up	Garrett C. Mouw, Birmingham, Mich. Ronald Samuels, Beverly Hills, Calif.
		Finke, 4 and 2	Finke, 1 up	Griffith, 1 up	Griffith, 4 and 3	Robert Hendren, Wheaton, Ill. Charles O. Griffith, Indianapolis, Ind.
					Lotz, 2 up	John Lotz, San Lorenzo, Calif. Marion C. Methvin, Jr., Little Rock, Ark.
				Finke, 1 up	Righter, 3 and 1	Ronald A. Righter, Hyattsville, Md. David B. Lawrence, Jr., New Orleans, La.
					Finke, 5 and 3	Kenneth Finke, Tucson, Ariz. Randolph Snider, Butler, Mo.
			Littler, 6 and 4	Littler, 4 and 3	Panasiuk, 7 and 6	Paul Otto, Springfield, Mass. Robert Panasiuk, Sandwich East, Ont., Canada
					Littler, 6 and 5	Robert Littler, Jr., Athens, Ohio Michael L. Price, New Albany, Ind.
				Korniak, 5 and 3	Paulson, 3 and 1	David Kraus, Erie, Pa. John T. Paulson, Detroit Lakes, Minn.
					Korniak, 2 and 1	Norman Korniak, Schenectady, N.Y. Ronald Johnson, Duluth, Minn.

1959
TWELFTH JUNIOR AMATEUR CHAMPIONSHIP

Held at the Stanford Golf Course, Stanford University, Calif., August 5-8.
Yardage—6,665. Par 71. 1,365 Entries. 128 Qualifiers, 128 Starters.
FINAL ROUND (18 Holes) – Larry J. Lee defeated Michael V. McMahon, 2 up.

UPPER HALF

1st Round (18 Holes)	2nd Round (18 Holes)	3rd Round (18 Holes)	4th Round (18 Holes)	5th Round (18 Holes)		Semi-Final (18 Holes)
Elliot C. Pachter, Kansas City, Mo. Michael L. Price, New Albany, Ind.	Pachter, 1 up					
Robert Carson, Whitehall, Ohio Fred Taylor, Portland, Ore.	Taylor, 2 and 1	Pachter, 2 and 1				
Michael Dawes, Greenville, S.C. Gary Polumbus, Denver, Colo.	Polumbus, 7 and 5					
Ray Barnhart, Downers Grove, Ill. Ralph Johnston, Jackson Heights, N.Y.	Barnhart, 3 and 1	Polumbus, 3 and 2	Polumbus, 4 and 3			
Ron Frantz, Indianapolis, Ind. Garrett Mouw, Birmingham, Mich.	Mouw, 5 and 3					
Roger Garrett, Tucson, Ariz. Paul Tuttle, San Diego, Calif.	Tuttle, 5 and 4	Mouw, 2 and 1				
Richard M. Lotz, San Lorenzo, Calif. Tom Hornbuckle, Albuquerque, N.M.	Lotz, 5 and 3					
Robert S. Thomas, Fredericksburg, Va. James. A. Grant, III, Wethersfield, Conn.	Grant, 6 and 4	Grant, 1 up	Grant, 5 and 4	Polumbus, 4 and 3		
John H. Foehl, Williamstown, Mass. Alan Pechacek, Sioux City, Iowa	Pechacek, 1 up					
Lynn Yturri, Ontario, Ore. Kermit Zarley, Jr., Seattle, Wash.	Zarley, 1 up, 20 hls.	Zarley, 4 and 2				
William A. Sechrest, Kansas City, Mo. Kenneth L. Folkes, Concord, N.C.	Sechrest, 3 and 2					
Ronald L. Wright, Denver, Colo. Gary E. Allen, Tucson, Ariz.	Wright, 9 and 8	Sechrest, 1 up	Zarley, 5 and 4			
Robert L. Clark, Lakewood, Calif. Berigan Cooper, Madison, Ind.	Clark, 1 up, 19 hls.					
E. Phillip Scherer, Louisville, Ky. Jerry Bridges, Whitehall, Ohio	Bridges, 4 and 2	Clark, 1 up, 20 hls.				
John W. Levinson, Highland Park, Ill. Dennis Ahern, Detroit, Mich.	Levinson, 4 and 3					
Alan R. York, Auburndale, Mass. Frank Ahern, San Francisco, Calif.	Ahern, 4 and 3	Levinson, 4 and 3	Levinson, 2 and 1	Zarley, 2 and 1	Zarley, 5 and 4	
Steve Lyles, Scottsville, Ky. David E. Bast, New Orleans, La.	Bast, 6 and 5					
Bill LaShell, Manhattan, Kans. Fred R. Kucker, Rochester, N.Y.	LaShell, 1 up	LaShell, 2 up				
Gary M. Pageau, Detroit, Mich. Dennis Shaffer, Lancaster, Calif.	Shaffer, 7 and 6					
James E. Gurry, Andover, Mass. Robert L. Shephard, Phoenix, Ariz.	Shephard, 5 and 3	Shephard, 1 up	LaShell, 5 and 4			
Tom J. Thomas, Bloomington, Ind. Michael V. McMahon, Carrolton, Ga.	McMahon, 4 and 3					
Peter Geertsen, Eugene, Ore. Mike Malarkey, Signal Mountain, Tenn.	Malarkey, 3 and 2	McMahon, 4 and 3				
W. Daniel Boone, Chevy Chase, Md. Ernie Segale, Jr., Stockton, Calif.	Boone, 5 and 4					
Bruce Richards, Bellevue, Wash. Robert B. Kostelecky, La Jolla, Calif.	Richards, 3 and 1	Richards, 5 and 4	McMahon, 2 and 1	McMahon, 2 up		
Bill Todd Lusk, Kenner, La. John A. Abernethy, Johnson City, Tenn.	Abernethy, 4 and 3					
James S. Easterwood, Seattle, Wash. Clifford Davis, Menlo Park, Calif.	Easterwood, 2 and 1	Easterwood, 1 up				
Marc Yahn, Snyder, N.Y. Richard Anderson, Fargo, N.D.	Anderson, 4 and 3					
R. Jay Sigel, Narberth, Pa. James S. Wilson, Omaha, Neb.	Sigel, 6 and 4	Sigel, 7 and 6	Easterwood, 3 and 2			
Jimmy Gabrielsen, Athens, Ga. Reid Holbrook, Kansas City, Kans.	Gabrielsen, 6 and 5					
John Peterson, Coralville, Iowa Richard A. McCauley, Pine Bluff, Ark.	McCauley, 3 and 2	Gabrielsen, 5 and 4				
Robert Peterson, Minneapolis, Minn. Mike Davis, Long Beach, Calif.	Peterson, 2 and 1					
John J. O'Donnell, Baltimore, Md. Robert Understein, Bethesda, Md.	Understein, 1 up	Peterson, 2 up	Gabrielsen, 5 and 4	Gabrielsen, 5 and 4	McMahon, 2 up	McMahon, 3 and 2

LOWER HALF

Semi-Final (18 Holes)	5th Round (18 Holes)		4th Round (18 Holes)	3rd Round (18 Holes)	2nd Round (18 Holes)	1st Round (18 Holes)
				Lee, 2 and 1	Shemano, 3 and 2	Gary Shemano, San Francisco, Calif. Craig Goldate, Memphis, Tenn.
			Lee, 5 and 4		Lee, 7 and 5	Larry J. Lee, Spokane, Wash. Robert Lucas, Minneapolis, Minn.
				Waxman, 2 up	Kopra, 4 and 3	James B. Crummett, Kansas City, Kans. Bronislaus Kopra, Jr., Buffalo, N.Y.
		Lee, 2 and 1			Waxman, 4 and 3	Gerald Tanaka, Honolulu, Hawaii William Waxman, Cincinnati, Ohio
				Dean, 8 and 7	Dean, 5 and 4	Gilbert O. Dean, Jr., Little Rock, Ark. Glenn P. Phillips, Harahan, La.
			Small, 5 and 4		Lewis, 6 and 4	Gary Lewis, Shenandoah, Iowa Harry Corbin, Wichita, Kans.
				Small, 2 and 1	Flory, 2 and 1	Thomas D. Flory, Annapolis, Md. John Yoder, Annandale, Va.
	Lee, 2 up				Small, 1 up	Robert Small, Long Beach, Calif. Kenny Roach, Irwin, Pa.
				Kirovac, 5 and 3	L. Righter, 3 and 2	Lance Righter, Bethesda, Md. Robert A. Wagner, Owosso, Mich.
			Riley, 2 and 1		Kirovac, 3 and 1	Robert R. Kirovac, Sharon, Mass. John Manahan, Rochester, Minn.
				Riley, 5 and 4	Williams, 3 and 2	Mike Williams, Columbia, Mo. Edward C. Basso, Mamaroneck, N.Y.
		Riley, 1 up, 20 hls.			Riley, 7 and 6	William Wade, Freeport, Texas Michael Riley, San Diego, Calif.
				Silveyra, 4 and 3	Silveyra, 4 and 3	Bill Whitney, Wellington, Kans. Augie Silveyra, Jr., Chula Vista, Calif.
			O'Brien, 2 and 1		Shipley, 5 and 3	Dan Shipley, Erie, Pa. Arthur Berliner, San Francisco, Calif.
				O'Brien, 3 and 2	Peters, 2 and 1	Dallas Peters, Jr., Urbana, Ill. Ralph C. Whitmire, Easley, S.C.
Lee, 3 and 2					O'Brien, 3 and 2	Pat O'Brien, Kilgore, Texas William M. Welch, III, Kennewick, Wash.
				Lake, 2 and 1	R. Righter, 3 and 2	Larry Joseph, Ann Arbor, Mich. Ronald A. Righter, Cheverly, Md.
			Lake, 2 up		Lake, 2 up	Gerald Lake, Walpole, Mass. Robert H. Droz, Salt Lake City, Utah
				Murray, 2 up	Murray, 1 up	Fred Murray, San Clemente, Calif. Jeffrey Pass, Ladue, Mo.
		Leffingwell, 6 and 5			Taylor, 1 up	Charles Kohr, Decatur, Ill. Norman Taylor, Dallas, Texas
				Harris, 2 up	Harmon, 2 and 1	James Manthis, Minneapolis, Minn. Claude Harmon, Jr., New Rochelle, N.Y.
			Leffingwell, 1 up, 21 hls.		Harris, 3 and 2	Labron Harris, Jr., Stillwater, Okla. Gary A. Lazane, Ventura, Calif.
				Leffingwell, 4 and 2	Moore, 5 and 3	John Alich, Burlingame, Calif. Ernest L. Moore, Jr., Columbia, S.C.
	Leffingwell, 2 up				Leffingwell, 6 and 5	Frederick C. Leffingwell, Jr., Miami Shores, Fla. Jimmy Ferriell, Jr., Louisville, Ky.
				Boutell, 6 and 5	Boutell, 8 and 7	Richard Brooks, Ferndale, Mich. George W. Boutell, Phoenix, Ariz.
			Stockton, 5 and 3		Linscott, 1 up	Daniel Linscott, Oconomowoc, Wis. Tommy Settle, Owensboro, Ky.
				Stockton, 2 up	Abrams, 4 and 2	Stanton V. Abrams, Pawtucket, R.I. Jack West, Thornwood, N.Y.
		Stockton, 5 and 3			Stockton, 5 and 4	Steve H. Hixon, Oklahoma City, Okla. David K. Stockton, San Bernardino, Calif.
				Cornett, 3 and 2	Cornett, 2 and 1	Randy Glover, Cheraw, S.C. Herman Cornett, Hattiesburg, Miss.
			Cornett, 1 up, 19 hls.		Henoch, 2 and 1	Richard R. Jennings, Lubbock, Texas Frederick E. Henoch, La Porte, Ind.
				Kruse, 3 and 2	Enslow, 5 and 3	Robert Enslow, Burlingame, Calif. Carl P. Beckdolt, Lake Tahoe, Calif.
					Kruse, 1 up	Mark R. Gordon, San Diego, Calif. Allan Kruse, Mount Prospect, Ill.

GIRLS' JUNIOR CHAMPIONSHIP

VARE TROPHY

Presented in August, 1949, by

GLENNA COLLETT VARE
(Mrs. Edwin H. Vare, Jr.)
Women's Amateur Champion 1922-25-28-29-30-35

HISTORY

1949–Miss Marlene Bauer, of Los Angeles, only 15 years of age and 5 feet 3 inches tall, became the first USGA Girls' Junior Champion by defeating Miss Barbara Bruning, of Chappaqua, N.Y., 2 up, in the final match. Thirty-three girls not yet 18 years old entered the competition at the Philadelphia Country Club. It was the first national title won by Miss Bauer, who began playing golf when she was 3 years old. Miss Bauer scored 73 while defeating Miss Barbara Romack, Sacramento, Calif., by 3 and 1 in her semi-final match.

1950–Miss Patricia Lesser, of Seattle, Wash., won the second Girls' Junior Championship by defeating Miss Mary Kathryn (Mickey) Wright, of La Jolla, Calif., 4 and 2 in the final match. Eighteen girls competed at the Wanakah Country Club, Hamburg, N.Y. Miss Barbara Romack, of Sacramento, was the medalist with a 79. Miss Wright won a special driving competition with a total of 680 yards for three balls.

1951–Miss Arlene Brooks, of Pasadena, Calif., won three matches on the 18th green, the last of these a 1-up victory in the final over Miss Barbara McIntire, of Toledo, Ohio. Miss Brooks holed a 30-foot putt on the final green against Miss McIntire to decide their match. Miss McIntire's score of 76 earned her the qualifying medal. The semi-finalists were Miss Charlene Cross, of Winchester, Ky., and Miss Mickey Wright. The Onwentsia Club, Lake Forest, Ill., was the site of the Championship.

1952–The first playing of the Girls' Junior Championship on the West Coast at the Monterey Peninsula Country Club, Pebble Beach, Calif., attracted an entry of 49. Miss Wright, the runnerup in 1950, defeated Miss Barbara McIntire, of Heather Downs, Ohio, 1 up in the final match. The defending Champion, Miss Arlene Brooks was eliminated by Miss Anne Quast, a 14-year-old from Everett, Wash., in the second round. Miss McIntire defeated Miss Quast, 2 and 1, in one semi-final; Miss Wright defeated Miss Judy Bell, of Wichita, 2 and 1, in the other. Miss Wright and Miss Quast tied for the Qualifying medal with scores of 76.

1953–Miss Millie Meyerson, of Los Angeles, Calif., whose brother Eddie had been a finalist in the 1952 Junior Amateur Championship, went east to win the fifth Girls' Junior Championship at The Country Club, Brookline, Mass. Miss Meyerson defeated Miss Holly Jean Roth, of Milwaukee, by 4 and 2 in the final match. Three players were co-medalists with qualifying scores of 77–Miss Anne Richardson, of Columbus, Ohio; Miss Berridge Long, of Huntington, W. Va.; and Miss Jacqueline P. Yates, of Honolulu.

1954–Miss Margaret (Wiffi) Smith, of Guadalajara, Mexico, the Mexican Champion and a semi-finalist in the 1953 Women's Amateur Championship, defeated Miss Sue Driscoll, of Normandy, Mo., 5 and 4, at the Gulph Mills Golf Club, near Philadelphia, in August-September. Both were 17. There was a large entry of 64 girls, 59 of whom started. Miss Ruth Jessen, of Seattle, Wash., the Pacific Northwest Champion, set a qualifying record of 75, and there was a tie at 85 for the last of the 16 places in match play, also a new low. Miss Mildred Meyerson, the Champion, failed to qualify by four strokes, and Miss Holly Jean Roth, runnerup to her, failed by five.

1955–Two young ladies from the Pacific Northwest came together in the final at the Florence (S.C.) Country Club, in August, 1955. Miss Carole Jo Kabler, 17, of Sutherlin, Ore., made four birdies in 15 holes and defeated Miss JoAnne Gunderson, 16, of Kirkland, Wash., 4 and 3. Miss Kabler was the Oregon Women's Champion. Another Pacific Northwest player, Miss Anne Quast, 17, of Everett, Wash., was defeated in the semi-finals, along with Miss Betsy Cullen, 16, of Tulsa, Okla. The entry reached 72 and set a new record. However, an all-match-play form was being tried for the first time, and this caused an unusually large number of withdrawals. Thus only 57 started, as against 59 the previous year. These players represented 24 states, the District of Columbia and Mexico. The youngest was Sharon Klump, of Toledo, Ohio, who had turned 11 the previous March. The smallest was Sandra Haynie, 12, of Midland, Texas, who stood 4 feet 6 inches and weighed 66 pounds. Miss Wiffi Smith was too old to defend.

1956–Miss JoAnne Gunderson, 17, of the Sand Point Country Club, Seattle, Wash., the runnerup in the previous year, defeated Miss Clifford Ann Creed, 17, of Opelousas, La., 4 and 3, with the finest golf yet displayed in a Girls' Junior final, at the Heather Downs Country Club, Toledo, Ohio. Miss Gunderson played the first nine in 33, three under women's par, and was still three under when she won the match.

She went to the final of the Women's Amateur Championship the following week. For a brief period thereafter both the Girls' Junior and the Women's Amateur trophies were held by the same Club, since Miss Pat Lesser, the 1955 Women's Amateur Champion, was a club-mate of Miss Gunderson. After a one-year trial with an all-match-play form, an 18-hole qualifying round was restored; there were, however, 32 places at stake instead of 16 as in the years preceding 1955. The entry of 70 was a near record, as was the starting field of 58. Miss Mary Mills, 16, of Gulfport, Miss., set a new qualifying record with a 74, one over par. Seven girls tied for the last six places at 90 and a two-hole playoff was required. Miss Sharon Fladoos, of Dubuque, Iowa, was the surprise of the Championship, gaining the semi-finals at the age of 13. Miss Carole Jo Kabler was over the age limit and could not defend.

1957–In the longest final to date, Miss Judy Eller, 16, of Old Hickory, Tenn., ran down a 25-foot putt on the 20th green for a birdie 3 to defeat Miss Beth Stone, 17, of Muskogee, Okla., 1 up, at the Lakewood Country Club, Denver, Colo. Miss Eller was the Tennessee Champion. Miss Patsy Hahn, 17, of Wilmington, Del., won the qualifying medal with a three-over-par 78, and the highest score to qualify was 92. Miss Judy Torluemke, 12 years old and 67 pounds, of Washington, Iowa, had missed qualifying by two strokes the previous year, but she made the grade with an 87 and was again the youngest player. The entry was 52 and there were 51 starters. Miss JoAnne Gunderson had passed the age limit and was ineligible to defend.

1958–Miss Eller, now 17, became the first Champion to repeat in a USGA junior event by defeating Miss Sherry Wheeler, 17, of Glasgow, Ky., 1 up, at the Greenwich Country Club, Greenwich, Conn. In the semi-final, Miss Wheeler had needed only four pars for a 68 after defeating Miss Joyce Denson, 17, of Atlanta, Ga., and she played out the bye holes to make a 70. Miss Connie Robinson, 17, of Pasadena, Calif., was medalist with 78, six over par. The youngest qualifier was Miss Mimi Grandle, 13, of Cincinnati, Ohio, who scored 91 and earned a place in a one-hole playoff. There was a record entry of 84 and a starting field of 77, representing 24 states. Mrs. Glenna Collett Vare, of Philadelphia, six times Women's Amateur Champion and donor of the trophy, refereed the final and presented the prize. The Round Hill Club entertained 25 first round losers in a consolation which was won by Miss Judy Hoetmer, of Seattle, Wash., with a 75.

1959–Miss Judy Rand, 16, of Aurora, Ohio, won the Championship when she defeated Miss Marcia Hamilton, of Evansville, Ind., by 5 and 3 in the final. Miss Rand's semi-final victory over Miss Diana Hoke, of Pittsburgh, on the 19th hole was the most stirring match at the Manor Country Club course in suburban Washington. Miss Rand had competed in the last five Championships. The Championship included the relatives of several well-known professionals. Miss Hoke is a granddaughter of Bobby Cruickshank and Miss Hamilton's uncle is Bob Hamilton. The quarter-finalists were equally divided among 16-year-olds and 17-year-olds. A record 96 girls entered and 85 started. Entries set a record for the fourth straight year.

GIRLS' JUNIOR CHAMPIONSHIP

DATE	WINNER, RUNNER-UP	SCORE	SITE	ENTRY
1949 (Aug.)	Miss Marlene Bauer d. Miss Barbara Bruning	2 up	Philadelphia C.C., (Bala Course), Philadelphia, Pa. All Match Play	33
1950 (Aug.-Sept.)	Miss Patricia Ann Lesser d. Miss Mary K. (Mickey) Wright	4 & 2	Wanakah C.C., Hamburg, N.Y. Medalist—79: Miss Barbara Romack	18
1951 (Aug.)	Miss Arlene Brooks d. Miss Barbara McIntire	1 up	Onwentsia Club, Lake Forest, Ill. Medalist—76: Miss Barbara McIntire	32
1952 (Aug.)	Miss Mary K. (Mickey) Wright d. Miss Barbara McIntire	1 up	Monterey Peninsula C.C., Pebble Beach, Calif. Co-Medalists—76: Miss Mary K. (Mickey) Wright Miss Anne Quast	49
1953 (Aug.)	Miss Mildred Meyerson d. Miss Holly Jean Roth	4 & 2	The Country Club, Brookline, Mass. Co-Medalists—77: Miss Berridge Long Miss Anne Richardson Miss Jacqueline P. Yates	46
1954 (Aug.-Sept.)	Miss Margaret Smith d. Miss Sue Driscoll	5 & 3	Gulph Mills G.C., Bridgeport, Pa. Medalist—75: Miss Ruth Jessen	64
1955 (Aug.)	Miss Carole Jo Kabler d. Miss JoAnne Gunderson	4 & 3	Florence C.C., Florence, S.C. All Match Play	64
1956 (Aug.)	Miss JoAnne Gunderson d. Miss Clifford Ann Creed	4 & 3	Heather Downs C.C., Toledo, Ohio Medalist—†74: Miss Mary Mills	70
1957 (Aug.)	Miss Judy Eller d. Miss Beth Stone	1 up, 20 hls.	Lakewood C.C. Denver, Colo. Medalist—78: Miss Patricia Ann Hahn	52
1958 (Aug.)	Miss Judy Eller d. Miss Sherry Wheeler	1 up	Greenwich C.C., Greenwich, Conn. Medalist—78: Miss Connie Robinson	84
1959 (Aug.)	Miss Judy Rand d. Miss Marcia Hamilton	5 & 3	Manor C.C., Rockville, Md. Co-Medalists—76: Miss Diana Hoke Miss Andrea L. Schaffer	96

1949
FIRST GIRLS' JUNIOR CHAMPIONSHIP

Held at the Philadelphia Country Club (Bala Course), Philadelphia, Pa., August 15-19. 33 Entries, 28 Starters.

1st Round (18 Holes)	2nd Round (18 Holes)	3rd Round (18 Holes)	Semi-Finals (18 Holes)	Final (18 Holes)	
Miss Mary Ann Villegas, New Orleans, La.	Miss Villegas,				
Miss Leona Sayre, Plymouth, Pa.	8 and 6	Miss Villegas,			
Miss Jo Ann Nelson, Maryland, Md.	Miss Nelson,	3 and 2			
Miss Esther Reid, Tully-Secane, Pa.	4 and 2		Miss Bauer,		
Miss Marlene Bauer, California C.C., Calif.	Miss Bauer,		8 and 7		
Miss Mary Ann Brunner, Plymouth, Pa.	by default	Miss Bauer,		Miss Bauer, 3 and 1	
Miss Janet McIntosh, Hyde Park, Ohio	Miss Frank,	8 and 7			
Miss Judy Frank, Aldecress, N.J.	by default				
Miss Patricia Leith, Elgin, Ill.	Miss Leith,				
Miss Anne Lawson, Sandy Run, Pa.	8 and 7	Miss Romack,			
Miss Barbara Romack, Sacramento Women's, Calif.	Miss Romack,	5 and 4			
Miss Georgine Reid, Tully-Secane, Pa.	5 and 3		Miss Romack,		Miss Marlene Bauer, 2 up
Miss Leila Fisher, Blue Hill, Mass.	Miss Fisher,		5 and 4		
Miss Joan M. Hessdorfer, Melrose, Pa.	8 and 7	Miss Fisher,			
Miss Dorothy Anne Twilley, Druid Hills, Ga.	Miss Twilley,	1 up, 19 hls.			
Miss Ann Zeddies, Exmoor, Ill.	4 and 3				
Miss Ida H. McDowell, Linville, N.C.	Miss Hoenstine,				
Miss Suzanne Hoenstine, Overbrook, Pa.	by default	Miss Reed,			
Miss Nancy Reed, Richland, Tenn.	Miss Reed,	7 and 6			
Miss Anne F. McAvoy, Phoenixville, Pa.	4 and 3		Miss Bruning,		
Miss Virginia Dennehy, Onwentsia, Ill.	Miss Bruning,		1 up		
Miss Barbara Bruning, Whippoorwill, N.Y.	4 and 3	Miss Bruning,		Miss Bruning, 6 and 5	
Miss Alice Marie Emhardt, Speedway, Ind.	Miss Lowenstein,	6 and 5			
Miss Dorothy L. Lowenstein, Fenway, N.Y.	1 up				
Miss Barbara Blakely, Anniston, Ala.	Miss Blakely,				
Miss Glenna C. Vare, Jr., Philadelphia Country C., Pa.	6 and 4	Miss Blakely,			
Miss Nancy Keplinger, Hempstead, N.Y.	Miss Keplinger,	1 up			
Miss Deborah Jane Carver, Plymouth, Pa.	10 and 8		Miss Blakely,		
Miss Anne Eskridge, Woodholme, Md.	Miss Eskridge,		1 up, 19 hls.		
Miss Virginia C. Poad, Bala, Pa.	6 and 4	Miss McIntire,			
Miss Barbara McIntire, Heather Downs, Ohio	Miss McIntire,	9 and 7			
Miss Alberta Moeltner, Knoll, N.J.	by default				

No Qualifying Round.
The first word after the player's name is the name of the player's club.

1950
SECOND GIRLS' JUNIOR CHAMPIONSHIP

Held at the Wanakah Country Club, Hamburg, N.Y., August 28-September 1. 18 Entries, 18 Starters.
Yardage—6,313. Par 75.

Qualifying Score	1st Round (18 Holes)	2nd Round (18 Holes)	Semi-Finals (18 Holes)	Final Round (18 Holes)	
79	*Miss Barbara Romack, Del Paso, Calif.	Miss Romack			
94	Miss Marlene Gesell, Westfield, Minn.	6 and 5	Miss Lesser,		
85	Miss Patricia Ann Lesser, Sand Point, Wash.	Miss Lesser,	2 and 1		
97	Miss Anne L. Harvey, Niagara Falls, N.Y.	8 and 7		Miss Lesser,	Miss Patricia Ann Lesser, 4 and 2
82	Miss Barbara McIntire, Heather Downs, Ohio	Miss Emhardt,		9 and 8	
95	Miss Alice Marie Emhardt, Speedway, Ind.	3 and 1	Miss Emhardt,		
86	Miss Barbara Blakely, Anniston, Ala.	Miss Blakely,	3 and 1		
101	Miss Patricia Buell, Niagara Falls, N.Y.	8 and 6			
82	Miss Virginia Dennehy, Onwentsia, Ill.	Miss Dennehy,			
95	Miss Leila Fisher, Blue Hill, Mass.	3 and 2	Miss Wright,		
86	Miss Mary K. Wright, La Jolla, Calif.	Miss Wright,	3 and 2		
99	Miss Janet Mack, Niagara Falls, N.Y.	4 and 3		Miss Wright,	
83	Miss Katharine McKinnon, West Palm Beach, Fla.	Miss McKinnon,		2 and 1	
95	Miss Anne F. McAvoy, Phoenixville, Pa.	4 and 3	Miss McKinnon,		
91	Miss Esther Reid, Tully-Secane, Pa.	Miss Reid,	2 up		
104	Miss Suzanne Nagell, Transit Valley, N.Y.	6 and 4			

*Medalist.
The first word after the player's name is the name of the player's club.

1951
THIRD GIRLS' JUNIOR CHAMPIONSHIP

Held at the Onwentsia Club, Lake Forest, Ill., August 13-17. 32 Entries, 30 Starters.
Yardage—6,368. Par 75.

Qualifying Score	1st Round (18 Holes)	2nd Round (18 Holes)	Semi-Finals (18 Holes)	Final Round (18 Holes)	
76	*Miss Barbara McIntire, Heather Downs, Ohio	Miss McIntire,			
90	Miss Leila Fisher, La Jolla, Calif.	6 and 5	Miss McIntire,		
85	Miss Donna Knox, Meridian Hills, Ind.	Miss Knox,	5 and 4		
94	Miss Barbara Blakely, Anniston, Ala.	2 and 1		Miss McIntire,	Miss Arlene Brooks, 1 up
84	Miss Charlene Cross, Winchester, Ky.	Miss Cross,		4 and 3	
91	Miss Martha Mumby, Mission Valley, Calif.	4 and 3	Miss Cross,		
86	Miss Virginia Dennehy, Onwentsia, Ill.	Miss Dennehy,	1 up		
96	Miss Gay Miller, Quincy, Ill.	4 and 3			
83	Miss Mary K. Wright, La Jolla, Calif.	Miss Wright,			
91	Miss Faye Matzie, Fox Hill Men's, Calif.	5 and 3	Miss Wright,		
85	Miss Constance Oldershaw, Spokane, Wash.	Miss Oldershaw,	4 and 3		
94	Miss Nadyne MacGranick, Brynwood, Wis.	7 and 6		Miss Brooks,	
84	Miss Janet McIntosh, Maketewah, Ohio	Miss McIntosh,		1 up	
93	Miss Julie Quarles, Kenosha, Wis.	8 and 6	Miss Brooks,		
[illegible]	Miss Arlene Brooks, Annandale, Calif.	Miss Brooks,	1 up		
96	Miss Suzanne Hoenstine, Overbrook, Pa.	6 and 5			

*Medalist.
The first word after the player's name is the name of the player's club.

1952
FOURTH GIRLS' JUNIOR CHAMPIONSHIP

Held at the Monterey Peninsula Country Club, Pebble Beach, Calif., August 18-21. 49 Entries, 43 Starters.
Yardage—6,053. Par 74.

Qualifying Score	1st Round (18 Holes)	2nd Round (18 Holes)	Semi-Finals (18 Holes)	Final Round (18 Holes)
76	*Miss Anne Quast, Everett, Wash.	Miss Quast, 3 and 2		
82	Miss Berridge Long, Guyan, W. Va.		Miss Quast, 7 and 6	
80	Miss Arlene Brooks, Annandale, Calif.	Miss Brooks, 1 up, 19 hls.		
87	Miss Mildred Meyerson, Brentwood, Calif.			Miss McIntire, 2 and 1
79	Miss Barbara McIntire, Heather Downs, Ohio	Miss McIntire, 6 and 5		
86	Miss Mary Stallard, Fort Washington, Calif.		Miss McIntire, 5 and 4	
81	Miss Ruth Jessen, Inglewood, Wash.	Miss Jessen, 7 and 6		
90	Miss Sharon V. Johnson, Reno, Nevada			
76	*Miss Mary K. Wright, La Jolla, Calif.	Miss Wright, 7 and 6		
86	Miss Thyra Hilburn, San Gabriel, Calif.		Miss Wright, 5 and 4	
80	Miss Judy Frank, Aldecress, N.J.	Miss Frank, 4 and 3		
89	Miss Jane E. Lange, Lakewood, Calif.			Miss Wright, 2 and 1
79	Miss Janet McIntosh, Maketewah, Ohio	Miss McIntosh, 3 and 2		
86	Miss Margaret Smith, Guadalajara, Mexico		Miss Bell, 4 and 3	
81	Miss Judy Bell, Crestview, Kans.	Miss Bell, 9 and 7		
90	Miss Linda Tarsky, Brentwood, Calif.			

Miss Mary K. (Mickey) Wright, 1 up

*Medalists.
The first word after the player's name is the name of the player's club, except in the case of a foreign entrant.

1953
FIFTH GIRLS' JUNIOR CHAMPIONSHIP

Held at The Country Club, Brookline, Mass., August 17-21. 46 Entries, 41 Starters.
Yardage—5,850. Par 72.

Qualifying Score	1st Round (18 Holes)	2nd Round (18 Holes)	Semi-Finals (18 Holes)	Final Round (18 Holes)
77	*Miss Anne Richardson, Columbus, Ohio	Miss Richardson, 2 and 1		
82	Miss Judy Bell, Wichita, Kans.		Miss Roth, 2 up	
81	Miss Ann Rutherford, Carlisle, Pa.	Miss Roth, 2 up		
87	Miss Holly Jean Roth, Milwaukee, Wis.			Miss Roth, 2 and 1
77	*Miss Jacqueline P. Yates, Honolulu, T.H.	Miss Yates, 3 and 2		
83	Miss Susan J. Inman, Brattleboro, Vt.		Miss Yates, 2 and 1	
82	Miss Margaret Smith, Guadalajara, Mexico	Miss Smith, 2 and 1		
87	Miss Eileen A. Deschamps, Wenham, Mass.			
77	*Miss Berridge Long, Huntington, W. Va.	Miss Long, 3 and 2		
83	Miss Joanne F. Goodwin, Plymouth, Mass.		Miss Mintz, 1 up, 22 hls.	
81	Miss Judith Mintz, Great Neck, N.Y.	Miss Mintz, 5 and 4		
87	Miss Susan A. Casey, Tulsa, Okla.			Miss Meyerson, 1 up, 20 hls.
81	Miss Carole Ann Genesio, Oreland, Pa.	Miss Toski, 2 and 1		
84	Miss Joan Toski, Adams, Mass.		Miss Meyerson, 5 and 4	
82	Miss Mildred Meyerson, Los Angeles, Calif.	Miss Meyerson, 6 and 5		
87	Miss Leona Sayre, Norristown, Pa.			

Miss Mildred Meyerson, 4 and 2

*Medalists.

1954
SIXTH GIRLS' JUNIOR CHAMPIONSHIP

Held at the Gulph Mills Golf Club, Bridgeport, Pa., August 30-September 3. 64 Entries, 59 Starters. Yardage—6,068. Par 74.

Qualifying Score	1st Round (18 Holes)	2nd Round (18 Holes)	Semi-Finals (18 Holes)	Final Round (18 Holes)	
75	*Miss Ruth Jessen, Seattle, Wash.	Miss Jessen, 8 and 7			
81	Miss Eleanor C. Howard, Bridgeport, Conn.		Miss Jessen, 6 and 5		
80	Miss Elizabeth Bobel, Harmony, R.I.	Miss Bobel, 1 up, 19 hls.			
82	Miss Judith Mintz, Great Neck, N.Y.			Miss Driscoll, 3 and 1	
78	Miss Sue Driscoll, University City, Mo.	Miss Driscoll, 1 up			
82	Miss Diane Reed, Denver, Colo.		Miss Driscoll, 6 and 5		
81	Miss Elizabeth Dargie, Oxford, Mass.	Miss Cullen, 4 and 3			
84	Miss Betsy Cullen, Tulsa, Okla.				Miss Margaret Smith, 5 and 3
76	Miss Margaret Smith, La Canada, Calif.	Miss Smith, 5 and 4			
81	Miss Carole Jo Kabler, Sutherlin, Ore.		Miss Smith, 7 and 5		
81	Miss R. Sandra Stone, Endicott, N.Y.	Miss Stone, 1 up, 19 hls.			
83	Miss Kaya Caldwell, Kansas City, Kans.			Miss Smith, 5 and 4	
80	Miss Joan Toski, East Orange, N.J.	Miss Bell, 1 up			
82	Miss Judy Bell, Wichita, Kans.		Miss Sayre, 2 and 1		
81	Miss Leona Sayre, Norristown, Pa.	Miss Sayre, 1 up			
85	Miss Glenda Felkner, Coral Gables, Fla.				

*Medalist.

1955
SEVENTH GIRLS' JUNIOR CHAMPIONSHIP

Held at the Florence Country Club, Florence, S.C., August 15-19. 72 Entries, 64 Starters.
Yardage—6,053. Par 74.
Championship entirely at match play.

1st Round (18 Holes)	2nd Round (18 Holes)	3rd Round (18 Holes)	4th Round (18 Holes)	Semi-Finals (18 Holes)	Final Round (18 Holes)
Miss Florie McLeod, Florence, S.C.	Miss Edsall, default				
Miss Katharine V. Edsall, Hendersonville, N.C.		Miss Edsall, 1 up			
Miss Bernice Schipman, Florence, S.C.	Miss Musser, default				
Miss Mary Ann Musser, Ellicott City, Md.			Miss Cullen, 1 up		
BYE—Miss Sandra Lewars Clifford, Mexico City, Mexico	Miss Clifford				
Miss Betsy Cullen, Tulsa, Okla.	Miss Cullen, 7 and 6	Miss Cullen, 4 and 3		Miss Cullen, 1 up, 19 hls.	
Miss Helen Marie Weiland, Phoenixville, Pa.					
Miss Karen Anderson, Lansdowne, Pa.	Miss West, 3 and 2				
Miss Paula Ann West, Sacramento, Calif.		Miss Phillips, 1 up, 19 hls.			
Miss Bonnie Ann Locher, Buffalo, N.Y.	Miss Phillips, 6 and 5				
Miss Nancy Phillips, Newton, N.C.			Miss Phillips, 1 up		
Miss Judith Ann Moulton, Devon, Pa.	Miss Kreager, 7 and 6				
Miss Jill Kreager, Tulsa, Okla.		Miss Kreager, 3 and 1			Miss Kabler, 2 and 1
BYE—Miss Carol Ann Pflug, W. Hempstead, N.Y.	Miss Pflug				
Miss Margot Morton, Indiana, Pa.	Miss Wheeler, 1 up				
Miss Sherry Wheeler, Glasgow, Ky.		Miss Kabler, 4 and 2			
Miss Carole Jo Kabler, Sutherlin, Ore.	Miss Kabler, 7 and 6				
Miss Gayle Terwilliger, Snyder, N.Y.			Miss Kabler, 5 and 4		
Miss Judy C. Eller, Old Hickory, Tenn.	Miss Eller, 1 up, 19 hls.				
Miss Darlene Hough, South Gate, Calif.		Miss Eller, 4 and 3		Miss Kabler, 2 and 1	
BYE—Miss Mary J. Hewitt, Greenville, S.C.	Miss Hewitt				
Miss Glenda Felkner, Coral Gables, Fla.	Miss Felkner, 10 and 8				
Miss Celia Ann McDuffie, Florence, S.C.		Miss Felkner, 1 up			
Miss Barbara Lou Borneman, Buffalo, N.Y.	Miss Howard, 3 and 2				
Miss Eleanor Cynthia Howard, Bridgeport, Conn.			Miss Sayre, 3 and 2		
Miss Sharon Gabrielsen, Athens, Ga.	Miss Gabrielsen, 3 and 1				
Miss Marie Evans Riccoboni, Sumter, S.C.		Miss Sayre, 5 and 4			
Miss Judy Rand, Framingham, Mass.	Miss Sayre, 6 and 5				
Miss Leona Sayre, Norristown, Pa.					Miss Carole Jo Kabler, 4 and 3
Miss Sandra Jane Haynie, Midland, Texas	Miss Mills, 4 and 2				
Miss Mary Bentley Mills, Gulfport, Miss.		Miss Rand, 1 up			
Miss Eileen Patricia Myers, Arlington, Va.	Miss Rand, 1 up				
Miss Marcia Rand, Framingham, Mass.			Miss Mintz, 3 and 2		
BYE—Miss Judith Mintz, Great Neck, N.Y.	Miss Mintz				
		Miss Mintz, 6 and 5			
Miss Deborah Hodge Wilder, Kensington, Md.	Miss Wilder, 3 and 2				
Miss Sandra Lou Christensen, York, Pa.				Miss Quast, 1 up	
Miss Anne Quast, Marysville, Wash.	Miss Quast, 7 and 6				
Miss Ann Middlemas, Panama City, Fla.		Miss Quast, 4 and 3			
Miss Constance Gorsuch, Greensboro, N.C.	Miss Denson, 5 and 4				
Miss Gladys Joyce Denson, Decatur, Ga.			Miss Quast, 1 up, 19 hls.		
Miss Meriam H. Bailey, Evanston, Ill.	Miss Bailey, 10 and 8				
Miss Sharon Klump, Toledo, Ohio		Miss Bailey, 7 and 6			Miss Gunderson, 2 and 1
BYE—Miss Carole Joy Coulson, Wynnewood, Pa.	Miss Coulson				
Miss Janice Lee Butler, West Lawn, Pa.	Miss Schiller, 5 and 4				
Miss C. Jane Schiller, Salisbury, Md.		Miss Lombard, 2 and 1			
Miss V. Dana Lombard, Weston, Mass.	Miss Lombard, 3 and 2				
Miss Roseann Walley, Youngstown, Ohio			Miss Creed, 5 and 4		
BYE—Miss Barbara Ann Diggs, Rockville, Md.	Miss Diggs				
		Miss Creed, 9 and 8			
Miss Clifford Ann Creed, Opelousas, La.	Miss Creed, default				
Miss Celeste Allen, Florence, S.C.				Miss Gunderson, 1 up	
Miss Margaret E. Simpson, Athens, Ga.	Miss Hahn, 8 and 7				
Miss Patricia Ann Hahn, Wilmington, Del.		Miss Finkbeiner, 8 and 7			
BYE—Miss Susan A. Finkbeiner, Toledo, Ohio	Miss Finkbeiner				
			Miss Gunderson, 8 and 7		
Miss Carole Burdeshaw, Griffin, Ga.	Miss Gunderson, 6 and 5				
Miss JoAnne Gunderson, Kirkland, Wash.		Miss Gunderson, 8 and 7			
Miss Nancy J. McDuffie, Florence, S.C.	Miss Addison, 9 and 8				
Miss Elaine Addison, Clinton, S.C.					

1956
EIGHTH GIRLS' JUNIOR CHAMPIONSHIP

Held at the Heather Downs Country Club, Toledo, Ohio, August 27-31.
Yardage—6,348. Par 73. 70 Entries, 58 Starters

Qualifying Score	1st Round (18 Holes)	2nd Round (18 Holes)	3rd Round (18 Holes)	Semi-Finals (18 Holes)	Final Round (18 Holes)	Champion
74	*Miss Mary Mills, Gulfport, Miss.	Miss Mills, 5 and 4	Miss Creed, 1 up	Miss Creed, 6 and 4	Miss Creed, 4 and 3	Miss JoAnne Gunderson, 4 and 3
86	Miss Gail DePietro, Castro Valley, Calif.					
82	Miss Clifford Ann Creed, Opelousas, La.	Miss Creed, 6 and 5				
89	Miss Janice L. Butler, Wyomissing, Pa.					
82	Miss Mary Ann Sherry, Pittsburgh, Pa.	Miss Sherry, 1 up, 19 hls.	Miss Sherry, 1 up			
88	Miss Elizabeth C. Harshaw, Grove City, Pa.					
83	Miss Andrea Cohn, Waterloo, Iowa	Miss Dack, 5 and 4				
90	Miss Jacquelyn Dack, Wichita, Kans.					
80	Miss Sherry Wheeler, Glasgow, Ky.	Miss Pettit, 1 up	Miss Pettit, 2 up	Miss Musser, 2 and 1		
87	Miss Vicki Pettit, Wichita, Kans.					
83	Miss Constance A. Gorsuch, Greensboro, N.C.	Miss Rand, 7 and 5				
90	Miss Judy Rand, Aurora, Ohio					
82	Miss Darlene Hough, Norwalk, Calif.	Miss Musser, 3 and 2	Miss Musser, 1 up			
88	Miss Mary Ann Musser, Ellicott City, Md.					
84	Miss Glenda Felkner, Coral Gables, Fla.	Miss Felkner, 1 up				
90	Miss Marcia Rand, Aurora, Ohio					
78	Miss JoAnne Gunderson, Kirkland, Wash.	Miss Gunderson, 4 and 3	Miss Gunderson, 4 and 3	Miss Gunderson, 1 up, 19 hls.	Miss Gunderson, 4 and 3	
86	Miss Kathy Fawcett, Creve Coeur, Mo.					
82	Miss Margot Morton, Indiana, Pa.	Miss Hahn, 1 up, 19 hls.				
89	Miss Patricia A. Hahn, Wilmington, Del.					
82	Miss Judy C. Eller, Old Hickory, Tenn.	Miss Phillips, 1 up, 19 hls.	Miss Bruni, 5 and 4			
88	Miss Nancy Phillips, Newton, N.C.					
84	Miss Joanne Bruni, Laredo, Texas	Miss Bruni, 7 and 6				
90	Miss Roseann Walley, Youngstown, Ohio					
80	Miss Sharon Fladoos, Dubuque, Iowa	Miss Fladoos, 6 and 5	Miss Fladoos, 6 and 5	Miss Fladoos, 5 and 4		
87	Miss Susan A. Finkbeiner, Toledo, Ohio					
83	Miss Margaret Barton, Columbus, Ohio	Miss Hoke, 1 up, 20 hls.				
90	Miss Diana Hoke, Pittsburgh, Pa.					
82	Miss Carol A. Mann, Flossmoor, Ill.	Miss Hull, 2 and 1	Miss Hull, 5 and 3			
88	Miss Julie Hull, Anderson, Ind.					
85	Miss Kaya Caldwell, Kansas City, Mo.	Miss Caldwell, 4 and 3				
90	Miss Rosemarie Mesina, Pittsburgh, Pa.					

*Medalist.

1957
NINTH GIRLS' JUNIOR CHAMPIONSHIP

Held at the Lakewood Country Club, Denver, Colo., August 12-16.
Yardage—6,208. Par 75.
Yardage—6,208. Par 75. 52 Entries, 51 Starters.

Qualifying Score	1st Round (18 Holes)	2nd Round (18 Holes)	3rd Round (18 Holes)	Semi-Finals (18 Holes)	Final Round (18 Holes)	
78	*Miss Patricia Ann Hahn, Wilmington, Del.	Miss Hahn, 1 up				
84	Miss Patricia Gail Dailey, San Antonio, Texas		Miss Hahn, 7 and 6			
82	Miss Jeannie Carol Richey, Villisca, Iowa	Miss Painter, 2 and 1				
87	Miss Martha Painter, Corpus Christi, Texas			Miss Cohn, 1 up, 19 hls.		
80	Miss Andrea Cohn, Waterloo, Iowa	Miss Cohn, 4 and 2				
85	Miss Judy M. Hoetmer, Seattle, Wash.		Miss Cohn, 7 and 6			
83	Miss Judy Rand, Aurora, Ohio	Miss Rand, 1 up			Miss Eller, 3 and 2	
89	Miss Donna Litke, State College, Pa.					
79	Miss Sharon Fladoos, Dubuque, Iowa	Miss Eller, 6 and 5				
84	Miss Judy Eller, Old Hickory, Tenn.		Miss Eller, 8 and 6			
82	Miss Janet Kirby, Whittier, Calif.	Miss Kirby, 1 up				
87	Miss Karen Schull, Kansas City, Mo.			Miss Eller, 5 and 4		
81	Miss Elaine Woodman, Wichita, Kans.	Miss Woodman, 4 and 3				
85	Miss Margot Morton, Indiana, Pa.		Miss Harshaw, 1 up			
84	Miss Betsy Harshaw, Grove City, Pa.	Miss Harshaw, 3 and 2				
91	Miss Lillian R. Lea, Fairfax, Va.					Miss Judy Eller, 1 up, 20 Holes
79	Miss Constance Gorsuch, Greensboro, N.C.	Miss Gorsuch, 3 and 2				
84	Miss Kaya Caldwell, Kansas City, Mo.		Miss Gorsuch, 5 and 4			
82	Miss Sandra Haynie, Austin, Texas	Miss Haynie, 6 and 4				
87	Miss Judith Torluemke, Washington, Iowa			Miss Bruni, 4 and 3		
81	Miss Joanne Bruni, Laredo, Texas	Miss Bruni, 5 and 4				
85	Miss Lida Fee Matthews, Portsmouth, Ohio		Miss Bruni, 1 up, 20 hls.			
83	Miss Vicki Pettit, Wichita, Kans.	Miss Pettit, 5 and 3				
89	Miss Karen Widmer, Paullina, Iowa				Miss Stone, 4 and 3	
80	Miss Jacquelyn Dack, Wichita, Kans.	Miss Dack, 6 and 5				
84	Miss Gail De Pietro, Pleasanton, Calif.		Miss Hull, 2 up			
83	Miss Julie Hull, Anderson, Ind.	Miss Hull, 3 and 2				
88	Miss Karen Swanson, Sacramento, Calif.			Miss Stone, 5 and 4		
81	Miss Sherry Wheeler, Glasgow, Ky.	Miss Stone, 2 and 1				
85	Miss Beth Stone, Muskogee, Okla.		Miss Stone, 1 up, 19 hls.			
84	Miss Barbara Beuckman, Belleville, Ill.	Miss Beuckman, 2 and 1				
92	Miss Susan Cherniack, Stamford, Conn.					

*Medalist.

1958

TENTH GIRLS' JUNIOR CHAMPIONSHIP

Held at the Greenwich Country Club, Greenwich, Conn., August 11-15.
Yardage—6,303. Par 72. 84 Entries, 77 Starters.

Qualifying Score	1st Round (18 Holes)	2nd Round (18 Holes)	3rd Round (18 Holes)	Semi-Finals (18 Holes)	Final Round (18 Holes)	
78	*Miss Connie Robinson, Pasadena, Calif.	Miss C. Robinson,				
86	Miss Donna O'Brien, Richmond, Va.	5 and 4	Miss Fladoos,			
82	Miss Sharon Fladoos, Dubuque, Iowa	Miss Fladoos,	9 and 7			
88	Miss Kaya Caldwell, Kansas City, Mo.	1 up		Miss Hoke,		
80	Miss Judy Rand, Aurora, Ohio	Miss Rand,		2 and 1		
87	Miss Donna L. Litke, State College, Pa.	5 and 3	Miss Hoke,			
84	Miss Diana Hoke, Pittsburgh, Pa.	Miss Hoke,	1 up, 19 hls.			
91	Miss Miriam Grandle, Cincinnati, Ohio	7 and 5			Miss Eller, 4 and 3	
79	Miss Judy Eller, Old Hickory, Tenn.	Miss Eller,				
86	Miss Carlene Hotz, Tulsa, Okla.	4 and 2	Miss Eller,			
83	Miss Judy Hoetmer, Seattle, Wash.	Miss Morton,	1 up, 19 hls.			
89	Miss Margot Morton, Indiana, Pa.	2 up		Miss Eller,		
81	Miss Jacquelyn Leary, Paoli, Pa.	Miss Leary,		5 and 4		
88	Miss Carol Smith, Phoenix, Ariz.	5 and 4	Miss Dailey,			
85	Miss Judith Torluemke, Ellisville, Mo.	Miss Dailey,	3 and 2			
91	Miss Patricia Dailey, San Antonio, Texas	5 and 3				Miss Judy Eller, 1 up
79	Miss Heidi Prentice, Winnetka, Ill.	Miss J. Robinson,				
86	Miss June Robinson, Portland, Ore.	3 and 2	Miss Wheeler,			
82	Miss Sherry Wheeler, Glasgow, Ky.	Miss Wheeler,	6 and 4			
89	Miss Marjorie W. Sessions, Bristol, Conn.	6 and 5		Miss Wheeler,		
81	Miss Patty David, Tulsa, Okla.	Miss David,		7 and 6		
87	Miss Mary Lowell, Hayward, Calif.	4 and 3	Miss David,			
84	Miss Helen Weiland, Phoenixville, Pa.	Miss Black,	5 and 4			
91	Miss Virginia F. Black, Franklin Lakes, N.J.	4 and 3			Miss Wheeler, 6 and 4	
80	Miss Joyce Denson, Atlanta, Ga.	Miss Denson,				
86	Miss Susan Kunakoff, Montebello, Calif.	2 up	Miss Denson,			
83	Miss Linda Leader, Schenectady, N.Y.	Miss Leader,	4 and 3			
90	Miss Gayle Terwilliger, Snyder, N.Y.	1 up		Miss Denson,		
81	Miss Sandra Haynie, Austin, Texas	Miss Haynie,		1 up		
88	Miss Lillian R. Lea, Fairfax, Va.	7 and 5	Miss Haynie,			
85	Miss Joyce Smith, Shreveport, La.	Miss Smith,	3 and 2			
91	Miss Joanne Batchelor, Silver Spring, Md.	4 and 3				

*Medalist.

1959
ELEVENTH GIRLS' JUNIOR CHAMPIONSHIP

Held at the Manor Country Club, Rockville, Md. August 17-21.
Yardage—6,162. Par 73. 96 Entries, 85 Starters.

Qualifying Score	1st Round (18 Holes)	2nd Round (18 Holes)	3rd Round (18 Holes)	Semi-Finals (18 Holes)	Final Round (18 Holes)	
76	*Miss Andrea L. Schaffer, San Francisco, Calif.	Miss Schaffer, 3 and 2				
84	Miss Donna M. O'Brien, Richmond, Va.		Miss Hamilton, 2 and 1			
80	Miss Marcia G. Hamilton, Evansville, Ind.	Miss Hamilton, 2 and 1				
85	Miss Martha Painter, Corpus Christi, Texas			Miss Hamilton, 1 up		
79	Miss Sandra Haynie, Austin, Texas	Miss Haynie, 2 and 1				
85	Miss Patricia Ann Keating, Great Neck, N.Y.		Miss Haynie, 6 and 5			
82	Miss Jane Hawkins, Mount Pleasant, Iowa	Miss Hawkins, 4 and 3				
88	Miss Louise J. Dumler, Cincinnati, Ohio				Miss Hamilton, 1 up	
77	Miss Darlene Y. Anderson, St. Louis Park, Minn.	Miss Anderson, 6 and 4				
84	Miss Donna Litke, State College, Pa.		Miss Sorenson, 4 and 2			
81	Miss Carol Sorenson, Janesville, Wis.	Miss Sorenson, 5 and 4				
87	Miss Marianne Gable, Arcadia, Calif.			Miss Sorenson, 1 up, 19 hls.		
80	Miss Judith Torluemke, St. Louis, Mo.	Miss Loftfield, 3 and 1				
85	Miss Judy Loftfield, Phoenix, Ariz.		Miss Shook, 5 and 3			
83	Miss Patricia Shook, Saugatuck, Mich.	Miss Shook, 6 and 5				
89	Miss Robin Beard, Fleetwood, Pa.					Miss Judy Rand, 5 and 3
76	*Miss Diana Hoke, Pittsburgh, Pa.	Miss Hoke, 6 and 5				
84	Miss Mary Lowell, Hayward, Calif.		Miss Hoke, 5 and 4			
80	Miss Margot Morton, Indiana, Pa.	Miss Morton, 7 and 5				
87	Miss Nancy Way, Grand Rapids, Mich.			Miss Hoke, 5 and 4		
80	Miss Ann Baker, Maryville, Tenn.	Miss David, 6 and 5				
85	Miss Patricia David, Tulsa, Okla.		Miss David, 4 and 2			
83	Miss Patricia A. Park, Metropolis, Ill.	Miss Park, 2 and 1				
89	Miss Robbye Lee King, Norfolk, Va.				Miss Rand, 1 up, 19 hls.	
79	Miss Judy Rand, Aurora, Ohio	Miss Rand, 4 and 3				
84	Miss Pennie Page, Bridgton, Maine		Miss Rand, 2 up			
81	Miss Martha Page, Bridgton, Maine	Miss M. Page, 4 and 3				
88	Miss Jeannie Kay Thompson, Tulsa, Okla.			Miss Rand, 4 and 3		
80	Miss Sharon Fladoos, Dubuque, Iowa	Miss Prentice, 2 and 1				
85	Miss Heidi Prentice, Winnetka, Ill.		Miss Woodman, 1 up			
83	Miss Jane Bostrom, Hyattsville, Md.	Miss Woodman, 2 and 1				
89	Miss June J. Woodman, Wichita, Kans.					

*Tied for Medalist.

SENIOR AMATEUR CHAMPIONSHIP

CHAMPIONSHIP TROPHY

Presented in September, 1955

by Frederick L. Dold
Member of the United States Golf Association Executive Committee 1950-54

HISTORY

1955–The Senior Amateur Championship was established in 1955 as a result of a remarkable growth in senior golf. Many senior associations had come into being on district, state and sectional levels. The oldest was the United States Seniors' Golf Association, which limited itself to 850 members and had a substantial waiting list: Most of the others also were similar to private clubs, conducting fine, enjoyable tournaments for their members. However, as there was no one event open to members of all USGA Regular Member Clubs, the USGA was requested to inaugurate such a competition. Thus was born the USGA Senior Amateur Championship, for members of USGA Regular Member Clubs who were 55 years old and had handicaps not exceeding 10. One hundred twenty-eight players qualified through 18-hole sectional rounds, and they competed in another 18-hole qualifying round at the Championship site for 32 places in match play. The match play comprised one 18-hole round each day. The first Championship was held at the Belle Meade Country Club, Nashville, Tenn., in September-October, and J. Wood Platt, 56, of the Saucon Valley Country Club, Bethlehem, Pa., defeated George Studinger, of San Francisco, Calif., 5 and 4. Platt was two under par in the final. The medalist was Martin M. Issler, of West Orange, N.J., who equalled par with a 72. Sixteen tied for the last ten places at 79. The Championship attracted 370 entrants. Thirty states and the District of Columbia were represented among the qualifiers.

1956–Frederick J. Wright, Jr., 58, of the Oakley Country Club, Watertown, Mass., a member of the 1923 Walker Cup Team, became the second Senior Amateur Champion by defeating J. Clark Espie, 57, of Indianapolis, Ind., 4 and 3, at the Somerset Country Club, St. Paul, Minn., in August, 1956. The medalist was Weller Noble, 65, of Berkley, Calif., who scored a two-over-par 72, the same score which won the medal the first year. The defending champion, J. Wood Platt, lost in the third round to Wright. The entry dropped to 282. The qualifying limit fell on 10 players tied at 79, also the same score as in the first year, for the last four places. In the first round Thomas C. Robbins, of Mamaroneck, N.Y., went 21 holes to defeat Perry T. Taylor, Huntington, W. Va., the longest match thus far.

1957–In a reversal of the 1956 final, J. Clark Espie, 58, of the Hillcrest Country Club, Indianapolis, Ind., defeated Frederick J. Wright, Jr., 59, of Watertown, Mass., 2 and 1, at the Ridgewood Country Club, Ridgewood, N.J. in September-October.
Wright had beaten Espie, 4 and 3, the previous year and seemed on the way to another victory when he was 3 up with seven to play. J. Wood Platt, of Philadelphia, Pa., the first Senior Amateur Champion, lost in the first round to Christopher A. Carr, of Hamburg, N.Y. In the same round, Judd L. Brumley, of Greenville, Tenn., went 22 holes to defeat William L. Goodloe, Sr., of Valdosta, Ga., the longest match of the Championship thus far. The medalist was Thomas M. Green, Jr., 55, of Seattle, Wash., who scored a two-over-par 73. Eleven tied for the last nine places at 81. Runcie B. Martin, of Duluth, Minn., the oldest qualifier at 72, was playing 52 years after his first appearance in a USGA Championship, the Amateur of 1905.

1958–Thomas C. Robbins, 65, of West End, N.C., became the oldest winner by defeating John W. Dawson, 55, of Palm Desert, Calif., 2 and 1, at the Monterey Peninsula Country Club, Pebble Beach, Calif., in September-October. J. Clark Espie, 59, of Indianapolis, Ind., the defending Champion, established a new qualifying record with a one-under-par 71 but lost to Robbins in the semi-final, 2 up. Eight players tied at 79 for the last of the 32 qualifying places. Chick Evans, 68, of Chicago, who had played in all four Championships, was among the qualifiers for match play for the first time and won two matches.

1959–J. Clark Espie, 60, of Indianapolis, Ind., the 1957 Senior Amateur Champion, won again at the Memphis Country Club, Memphis, Tenn. His margin in the final was 3 and 1 over J. Wolcott Brown, of Manasquan, N.J. In the five Senior Amateur Championships played thus far, Espie had won twice, been runnerup once, and a semi-finalist and qualifying medalist on a fourth occasion. In 1959 he participated in the longest match to date in the history of the competition–a 24-hole match which he won in the second round against Larry E. Stage, of Lafayette, Ind. Other semi-finalists were George Dawson, of Chicago, and William E. Norvell, Jr., of Chattanooga. Defending Champion Thomas C. Robbins, of Pinehurst, N.C., missed qualifying for the Championship flight of 32. There was a record entry of 391. There was no handicap limit for the first time.

SENIOR AMATEUR CHAMPIONSHIP

DATE	WINNER, RUNNER-UP	SCORE	SITE	ENTRY
1955 (Sept.-Oct.)	J. Wood Platt d. George Studinger	5 & 4	Belle Meade C.C., Nashville, Tenn. Medalist–72: Martin M. Issler	370
1956 (Aug.)	Frederick J. Wright d. J. Clark Espie	4 & 3	Somerset C.C., St. Paul, Minn. Medalist–72: Weller Nobel	282
1957 (Sept.-Oct.)	J. Clark Espie d. Frederick J. Wright	2 & 1	Ridgewood C.C., Ridgewood, N.J. Medalist–73: Thomas M. Green, Jr.	349
1958 (Sept.-Oct.)	Thomas C. Robbins d. John W. Dawson	2 & 1	Monterey Peninsula C.C., Pebble Beach, Calif. Medalist–†71: J. Clark Espie	370
1959 (Oct.)	J. Clark Espie d. J. Wolcott Brown	3 & 1	Memphis C.C., Memphis, Tenn. Co-Medalists: 73: J. Wolcott Brown, George Dawson	391

†Record qualifying score, 18 holes.

1955
FIRST SENIOR AMATEUR CHAMPIONSHIP

Held at the Belle Meade Country Club, Nashville, Tenn., September 26-October 1.
Yardage—6,470. Par 72. 370 Entries, 120 Sectional Qualifiers, 119 Starters.

Qualifying Score	1st Round (18 Holes)	2nd Round (18 Holes)	3rd Round (18 Holes)	Semi-Finals (18 Holes)	Final (18 Holes)	
78	John R. Chappell, Jr., C.C. of Virginia, Va.	Noble,				
77	Weller Noble, Claremont, Calif.	5 and 4	Snekser,			
77	Peter M. Snekser, Brookfield, N.Y.	Snekser,	1 up, 19 hls.			
79	Paul Dickinson, Dornick Hills, Okla.	3 and 2		Rankin,		
74	Allen R. Rankin, Scioto, Ohio	Rankin,		4 and 3		
79	Dr. Joe B. Hibbitts, Jr., Belle Meade, Tenn.	2 and 1	Rankin,			
78	Frank J. English, Algonquin, Mo.	Ackerman,	4 and 3			
78	James H. Ackerman, Springdale, N.J.	4 and 2			Platt, 3 and 2	
79	Philip W. Ransom, Wanakah, N.Y.	Ransom,				
79	Stanlee Hampton, Belle Meade, Tenn.	1 up	Issler,			
72	*Martin M. Issler, Essex County, N.J.	Issler,	1 up, 19 hls.			
79	Don L. Lambert, St. Louis, Mo.	2 and 1		Platt,		
75	Perry T. Taylor, Guyan, W. Va.	Platt,		4 and 3		
76	J. Wood Platt, Saucon Valley, Pa.	4 and 3	Platt,			
76	Douglas W. Hill, Hyde Park, Ohio	Hill,	4 and 2			J. Wood Platt, 5 and 4
76	Eugene Bellville, Hillcrest, Mo.	5 and 4				
78	J. Murray Hunt, Pasatiempo, Calif.	Studinger,				
79	George Studinger, Lake Merced, Calif.	3 and 2	Studinger,			
76	Col. C.D. McAllister, C.C. of Orlando, Fla.	Quittner,	3 and 2			
79	Egon F. Quittner, Old York Road, Pa.	3 and 1		Studinger,		
79	J.J. Osplack, Plum Hollow, Mich.	McWane,		3 and 1		
76	William McWane, Birmingham, Ala.	2 up	McWane,			
75	Vincent Fitzgerald, Garden City G.C., N.Y.	Marston,	1 up, 20 hls.			
79	John Marston, Dallas, Texas	2 and 1				
76	Leslie B. Hoss, Tulsa, Okla.	Hoss,			Studinger, 6 and 5	
79	George H. Treadwell, Memphis, Tenn.	2 and 1	Hoss,			
77	George E. Edmondson, Palma Ceia, Fla.	Schulz,	2 up			
77	Fred Schulz, Glen Flora, Ill.	4 and 2		Watkins,		
77	Ewing Watkins, Chattanooga, Tenn.	Watkins,		6 and 4		
78	Elfred Beck, Southern Hills, Okla.	5 and 4	Watkins,			
75	Thomas C. Robbins, Winged Foot, N.Y.	Brumley,	1 up			
75	Judd L. Brumley, Biltmore Forest, N.C.	5 and 3				

*Medalist.
The first word after the player's name is the name of the player's club.

1956
SECOND SENIOR AMATEUR CHAMPIONSHIP

Held at the Somerset Country Club, St. Paul, Minn., August 20-25.
Yardage–6,387. Par 70. 282 Entries, 120 Sectional Qualifiers, 119 Starters.

Qualifying Score	1st Round (18 Holes)	2nd Round (18 Holes)	3rd Round (18 Holes)	Semi-Finals (18 Holes)	Final (18 Holes)	
77	Judd L. Brumley, Biltmore Forest, N.C.	Brumley, 6 and 4	Brumley, 5 and 4	Manion, 2 up	Wright, 7 and 6	Frederick J. Wright, 4 and 3
76	Robert W. Gammon, Keller, Minn.					
79	William H. Pressing, Anderson, Ind.	Pressing, 2 up				
77	Leslie B. Hoss, Tulsa, Okla.					
77	Maurice R. Smith, Indian Hills, Mo.	Smith, 2 and 1	Manion, 2 and 1			
78	Egon F. Quittner, Old York Road, Pa.					
78	James S. Manion, Normandie, Mo.	Manion, 1 up, 19 hls.				
74	Charles L. Hodgman, Woodhill, Minn.					
78	Paul Dickinson, Dornick Hills, Okla.	Platt, 3 and 2	Platt, 1 up	Wright, 1 up		
77	J. Wood Platt, Saucon Valley, Pa.					
76	Thomas C. Robbins, Winged Foot, N.Y.	Robbins, 1 up, 21 hls.				
76	Perry T. Taylor, Guyan, W. Va.					
77	Martin M. Issler, Essex County, N.J.	Issler, 1 up	Wright, 5 and 3			
72	*Weller Noble, Claremont, Calif.					
76	Frank Justin, Sr., Big Foot, Wis.	Wright, 5 and 3				
75	Frederick J. Wright, Oakley, Mass.					
75	George Studinger, Lake Merced, Calif.	Studinger, 3 and 2	Studinger, 5 and 3	Andrews, 4 and 3	Espie, 5 and 4	
77	Harry G. Silverberg, Green Gables, Colo.					
77	Ray W. Roberson, Highland, Ind.	Roberson, 3 and 2				
78	Edward F. Brady, Sr., Brook Hollow, Texas					
79	Forrest Andrews, Glen Oak, Ill.	Andrews, 4 and 3	Andrews, 3 and 2			
78	Col. Nicholas T. Grosch, Twin Brooks, N.J.					
79	Donald Hammond, Green Spring Valley, Md.	Hammond, 2 and 1				
78	George L. Hardy, Evanston, Ill.					
79	Paul W. Horn, Lehigh, Pa.	Horn, 5 and 4	Horn, 1 up	Espie, 4 and 2		
78	W.M. Willingham, Norwood Hills, Mo.					
78	Dr. J.B. Harris, Iowa State College, Iowa	Harris, 4 and 3				
76	Harry Packham, Rancho, Calif.					
76	Eugene Bellville, Hillcrest, Mo.	Espie, 4 and 3	Espie, 1 up, 19 hls.			
73	J. Clark Espie, Hillcrest, Ind.					
77	C. Ed Spurlin, Virginia, Calif.	McAllister, 2 and 1				
78	Col. C.D. McAllister, Orlando, Fla.					

*Medalist.
The first word after the player's name is the name of the player's club.

1957
THIRD SENIOR AMATEUR CHAMPIONSHIP

Held at the Ridgewood Country Club, Ridgewood, N.J., September 30-October 5.
Yardage—6,597. Par 71. 349 Entries, 120 Sectional Qualifiers, 120 Starters.

Qualifying Score	1st Round (18 Holes)	2nd Round (18 Holes)	3rd Round (18 Holes)	Semi-Finals (18 Holes)	Final (18 Holes)	
80	Arthur E. Wittig, Plum Hollow, Mich.	Ryder, 1 up				
78	Harold B. Ryder, Sankaty Head, Mass.		Ryder, 3 and 2			
77	Christopher A. Carr, Wanakah, N.Y.	Carr, 8 and 7				
79	J. Wood Platt, Saucon Valley, Pa.			Espie, 5 and 3		
79	J. Clark Espie, Hillcrest, Ind.	Espie, 2 and 1				
79	Martin M. Issler, Essex County, N.J.		Espie, 2 and 1			
81	Carl E. Haymond, Los Angeles, Calif.	Fitzgerald, 1 up, 20 hls.				
79	Vincent Fitzgerald, Garden City, N.Y.				Espie, 4 and 2	
77	John W. Roberts, Scioto, Ohio	Roberts, 6 and 5				
80	Robert U. Davidson, Blue Hills, Mo.		Winters, 1 up			
79	Dr. Sutro A. Frost, Silverado, Calif.	Winters, 4 and 3				
81	John M. Winters, Jr., Southern Hills, Okla.			Winters, 1 up, 19 hls.		
81	John Dowling, Mahopac, N.Y.	Dowling, 2 and 1				
81	Sydney Goldstone, Metropolis, N.Y.		Taylor, 5 and 4			
79	Perry T. Taylor, Guyan, W. Va.	Taylor, 3 and 2				
81	Ralph L. Sawyer, Hillcrest, Mass.					J. Clark Espie, 2 and 1
78	James A. Swink, Belle Haven, Va.	Green, 6 and 5				
73	*Thomas M. Green, Jr., Seattle, Wash.		Green, 2 and 1			
74	William L. Goodloe, Sr., Valdosta, Ga.	Brumley, 1 up, 22 hls.				
76	Judd L. Brumley, Biltmore Forest, N.C.			McAlvin, 2 up		
81	James H. McAlvin, Onwentsia, Ill.	McAlvin, 4 and 3				
78	A.L. (Jim) Miller, Bob O'Link, Ill.		McAlvin, 3 and 2			
78	Russell P. Scholl, Crown Point, Vt.	Scholl, 1 up, 19 hls.				
78	Gail Cave, Wilshire, Calif.				Wright, 2 and 1	
81	Harry C. Wils, Tam O'Shanter, Ill.	McWane, 4 and 3				
81	William McWane, C.C. of Birmingham, Ala.		Robbins, 5 and 4			
78	Thomas C. Robbins, Winged Foot, N.Y.	Robbins, 5 and 4				
81	Fred E. Crawford, Metacomet, R.I.			Wright, 4 and 3		
80	John N. Ledbetter, Jr., Scarsdale, N.Y.	Dunkel, 1 up, 19 hls.				
75	Paul A. Dunkel, Ridgewood, N.J.		Wright, 3 and 2			
80	Roy L. Corey, Drumlins, N.Y.	Wright, 6 and 5				
77	Frederick J. Wright, Oakley, Mass.					

*Medalist.
The first word after the player's name is the name of the player's club.

1958
FOURTH SENIOR AMATEUR CHAMPIONSHIP

Held at the Monterey Peninsula Country Club, Pebble Beach, Calif., September 29-October 4.
Yardage—6,236, 6,251. Par 72. 370 Entries, 120 Sectional Qualifiers, 120 Starters.

Qualifying Score	1st Round (18 Holes)	2nd Round (18 Holes)	3rd Round (18 Holes)	Semi-Finals (18 Holes)	Final (18 Holes)	
77	John W. Dawson, Eldorado, Calif.	Dawson, 2 and 1				
78	John M. Winters, Jr., Southern Hills, Okla.		Dawson, 5 and 4			
78	Paul Dickinson, Dornick Hills, Okla.	C. McCarthy, 5 and 4				
77	Calvin T. McCarthy, Salem, Mass.			Dawson, 6 and 5		
75	Adrian C. McManus, University-Sequoia, Calif.	McAlvin, 2 and 1				
75	James H. McAlvin, Onwentsia, Ill.		Ryder, 3 and 2			
76	John B. Ferguson, Jr., Great Southern, Miss.	Ryder, 2 and 1			Dawson, 2 and 1	
77	Harold B. Ryder, Sankaty Head, Mass.					
78	Maurice R. Smith, Indian Hills, Mo.	M. Smith, 1 up, 20 hls.				
78	Ray W. Roberson, Highland, Ind.		McGuire, 7 and 5			
77	William McWane, C.C. of Birmingham, Ala.	McGuire, 3 and 2				
76	John W. McGuire, Highland, Ind.			McDade, 3 and 2		
74	Ross McDade, Jr., Barbara Worth, Calif.	McDade, 3 and 2				Thomas C. Robbins, 2 and 1
79	Vincent Fitzgerald, Garden City, N.Y.		McDade, 5 and 4			
77	Bradford F. Oxnard, Metacomet, R.I.	Oxnard, 4 and 3				
75	Lyle Decker, San Jose, Calif.					
76	John W. Roberts, Scioto, Ohio	Roberts, 3 and 2				
77	Llewellyn Power, Overlake, Wash.		Quittner, 1 up, 22 hls.			
76	Egon F. Quittner, Old York Road, Pa.	Quittner, 2 and 1				
77	Howard A. Frame, Menlo, Calif.			Robbins, 3 and 1		
77	Martin F. McCarthy, Columbia, Md.	M. McCarthy, default				
78	Frank H. Patterson, Lakewood, Texas		Robbins, 2 and 1			
76	Thomas C. Robbins, Pinehurst, N.C.	Robbins, 4 and 3			Robbins, 2 up	
77	R.H. Guelich, Jr., Park C.C. of Buffalo, N.Y.					
78	Edward M. Smith, Upper Montclair, N.J.	Espie, 2 and 1				
71	*J. Clark Espie, Hillcrest, Ind.		Espie, 6 and 4			
76	Thomas M. Green, Jr., Seattle, Wash.	Williams, 6 and 4				
77	Charles W. Williams, San Jose, Calif.			Espie, 4 and 3		
77	Charles Evans, Jr., Edgewater, Ill.	C. Evans, 2 and 1				
77	F. Howard Evans, Santa Ana, Calif.		C. Evans, 5 and 4			
77	George S. Sperry, Oakmont, Calif.	Barnes, 1 up				
78	Walter E. Barnes, Forest Hills, Ill.					

*Medalist.
The first word after the player's name is the name of the player's club.

1959
FIFTH SENIOR AMATEUR CHAMPIONSHIP

Held at the Memphis Country Club, Memphis, Tenn., October 5-10.
Yardage—6,362. Par 70. 391 Entries, 120 Sectional Qualifiers, 120 Starters.

Qualifying Score	1st Round (18 Holes)	2nd Round (18 Holes)	3rd Round (18 Holes)	Semi-Finals (18 Holes)	Final (18 Holes)	
78	Minos L. Fletcher, Jr., Belle Meade, Tenn.	Stage,				
79	Larry E. Stage, Lafayette, Ind.	3 and 2				
77	Marvin W. Clark, Grants Pass, Ore.	Espie,	Espie,			
79	J. Clark Espie, Jr., Hillcrest, Ind.	5 and 3	1 up, 24 hls.			
77	David E. Rose, Beechmont, Ohio	Rose,		Espie,		
79	Albert A. Villegas, New Orleans, La.	4 and 3		5 and 3		
80	Matt C. Gallaway, Lockhaven, Ill.	McCarthy,	McCarthy,			
80	Martin F. McCarthy, Columbia, Md.	1 up, 19 hls.	2 and 1			
73	*George Dawson, Glen Oak, Ill.	Dawson,				
80	Dewey P. Bowen, Atlanta Athletic, Ga.	8 and 7			Espie, 5 and 4	
79	John W. McGuire, Highland, Ind.	McGuire,	Dawson,			
78	Lemuel B. Stevens, Belle Meade, Tenn.	3 and 1	3 and 2			
77	L.W. Ramsey, Westwood, Ind.	Taylor,		Dawson,		
76	Perry T. Taylor, Guyan, W. Va.	4 and 3		2 and 1		
79	Arnold Minkley, LaGorce, Fla.	Minkley,	Taylor,			
78	George Treadwell, Memphis, Tenn.	2 and 1	4 and 3			J. Clark Espie, Jr., 3 and 1
79	Ross McDade, Jr., Barbara Worth, Calif.	McDade,				
77	John W. Roberts, Scioto, Ohio	3 and 2				
78	Nicholas T. Grosch, Twin Brooks, N.J.	Brown,	Brown,			
73	*J. Wolcott Brown, Manasquan River, N.J.	6 and 5	5 and 4			
79	Richard H. Guelich, Jr., Park C.C. of Buffalo, N.Y.	Guelich,		Brown,		
79	Fred E. Crawford, Metacomet, R.I.	1 up, 21 hls.		3 and 1		
77	Richard T. Toney, Westwood Hills, Mo.	Greer,	Greer,			
80	J. Ripley Greer, Memphis, Tenn.	6 and 4	3 and 2			
78	Col. C.D. McAllister, C.C. of Orlando, Fla.	McAllister,			Brown, 2 up	
78	Ray W. Roberson, Highland, Ind.	4 and 3				
76	Bradford F. Oxnard, Metacomet, R.I.	Oxnard,	McAllister,			
79	Frank B. Edwards, C.C. of Spartanburg, S.C.	4 and 3	2 and 1			
76	William E. Norvell, Jr., Chattanooga, Tenn.	Norvell,		Norvell,		
77	Charles Evans, Jr., Edgewater, Ill.	2 up		3 and 2		
78	George E. Edmondson, Palma Ceia, Fla.	Edmondson,	Norvell,			
80	Neil Smith, Dornick Hills, Okla.	3 and 1	1 up			

*Co-Medalists.
The first word after the player's name is the name of the player's club.

WALKER CUP MATCH

UNITED STATES GOLF ASSOCIATION

INTERNATIONAL CHALLENGE TROPHY

Presented in May, 1921, by

GEORGE H. WALKER

President of the United States Golf Association, 1920

HISTORY

The Walker Cup competition was begun in the wake of World War I with a view to stimulating golf interest on both sides of the Atlantic. It was born in an era of dawning internationalism and grew, at least in part, out of two international matches between Canada and the United States. In 1919, the Royal Canadian Golf Association invited the USGA to send an amateur team to Canada. The invitation was accepted, and William C. Fownes, Jr., was appointed Captain. His 10-man team consisted of John G. Anderson, Eben M. Byers, Charles Evans, Jr., Robert A. Gardner, Robert T. Jones, Jr., Oswald Kirkby, Max R. Marston, Francis D. Ouimet, George Ormiston and Jerome D. Travers. Playing foursomes in the morning and singles in the afternoon, the Americans defeated the Canadians, 12 to 3, at the Hamilton (Ont.) Golf Club on July 25, 1919. The USGA Team won a return match the following year, in September, at the Engineers Country Club, in Roslyn, N.Y., 10 to 4.

Simultaneously, British and Americans were seriously seeking each other's Championships. In the spring of 1920, Bob Gardner had gone to the final of the British Amateur at Muirfield, losing to Cyril Tolley on the 37th hole. The United States Amateur that fall also had an international aspect. In addition to members of the Canadian team, Tolley, Roger Wethered, Lord Charles Hope and Tommy Armour came from Great Britain. Most of these failed to qualify, and Armour, the last foreign contender, was beaten by Ouimet in the third round.

The Executive Committee of the USGA, meanwhile, was invited abroad to confer with the Royal and Ancient Golf Club's Rules Committee regarding the advisability of amending or modifying various rules. The invitation was accepted and the USGA representatives sailed in the spring of 1920. The conferees met frequently in England and Scotland and played many of the well-known links.

Among the participants was George Herbert Walker of the National Golf Links of America, Southampton, N.Y., President of the USGA in 1920. Mr. Walker had been a low-handicap player in St. Louis and was a keen advocate of the game.

Upon the Executive Committee's return to the United States, the possibility of international team matches was discussed. The idea so appealed to Mr. Walker that, at a meeting of the Committee at the Links Club, in Manhattan, on the afternoon of December 21, 1920, he presented a plan for an international golf Championship and offered to donate an International Challenge Trophy. When the newspapers printed the news, they called it, to Mr. Walker's chagrin, the "Walker Cup," and the name has stuck.

Early in 1921 the USGA invited all countries interested in golf to send teams to compete for the Trophy, but no country was able to accept that year. The American urge for international competition was rampant, however, and Fownes, who had twice assembled the amateur teams which played against Canada, rounded up a third team in the spring of 1921 and took it to Hoylake, England, where in an informal match it defeated a British team, 9 to 3, on the day before the British Amateur.

If there had been any sentiment that the Americans could not provide adequate competition, this must have dispelled it. The members of that informal United States team were: Charles Evans, Jr., William C. Fownes, Jr., Jesse P. Guilford, Paul Hunter, Robert T. Jones, Jr., Francis D. Ouimet, J. Wood Platt and Frederick J. Wright, Jr. They won all four of the morning foursomes and five of the eight afternoon singles.

Although the Americans were not successful in the British Amateur, Wright did go to the quarter-finals and Jock Hutchison later that year won the British Open, after a playoff with Roger Wethered.

The following spring, the Royal and Ancient Golf Club of St. Andrews, Scotland, announced that it would send a team to compete for the Walker Cup in the United States.

1922–Howard F. Whitney, who had succeeded Mr. Walker as President of the USGA in 1921, made the arrangements for the match, selecting as the site Mr. Walker's home club, the National Golf Links of America. The dates were Monday and Tuesday, August 28 and 29.

The plan was for each side to select eight players and to play foursomes the first day and singles the second day.

The team selected to represent the United States was again captained by Fownes. The other members were Charles Evans, Jr., Robert A. Gardner, Jesse P. Guilford, Robert T. Jones, Jr., Max R. Marston, Francis D. Ouimet, Jess W. Sweetser and Rudolf E. Knepper, who did not play. Guilford held the Amateur Championship.

Robert Harris was nominated to Captain the

British team. His side consisted of Cyril J. H. Tolley, Roger H. Wethered, Colin C. Aylmer, C. V. L. Hooman, W. B. Torrance, John Caven and W. Willis Mackenzie. A notable absentee was Ernest W. E. Holderness, the British Champion, who was unable to make the trip.

Bernard Darwin, the golf writer of the *Times* of London, came with the team as a correspondent. When Harris fell ill before the match, Darwin was invited to compete in his place and serve as playing Captain. He defeated Fownes, 3 and 1, in an interesting singles match after losing the first three holes.

In the final singles match, Hooman defeated Sweetser on the first extra hole. It was the only extra-hole match ever played in Walker Cup competitions. Since that time, matches which finish even have not been played out.

Although many of the matches in that first meeting were close, the United States won three of the four foursomes and the first five of the eight singles to score an 8 to 4 victory in the first official match for the Walker Cup.

The members of the British team went from the National to Brookline, Mass., for the United States Amateur at The Country Club and only Tolley went as far as the quarter-finals in quest of the title which Sweetser won so impressively.

1923—An invitation to send a team to St. Andrews, Scotland, to defend the cup was quickly accepted the following winter, and the Americans nearly received their come-uppance in May, 1923. There had been many changes in personnel. Robert A. Gardner succeeded William C. Fownes, Jr., as Captain, and 10 players were selected so that alternates would be available on the scene. In addition to Gardner, Francis Ouimet, Jess Sweetser and Max Marston continued as members. S. Davidson Herron, Harrison R. Johnston, J. F. Neville, George V. Rotan, Dr. O. F. Willing and Frederick J. Wright, Jr., replaced Evans, Fownes, Guilford and Jones, who was studying at Harvard.

In the British Amateur at Deal, which preceded the Match, Ouimet went to the semi-finals, along with Douglas Grant, a fellow-American who was living abroad. Roger Wethered defeated Robert Harris, 7 and 6, in the final, and he remained the only Briton who has won a British Amateur in a year when a United States Walker Cup Team was playing abroad until 1963 when Michael S. R. Lunt defeated John D. Blackwell at St. Andrews.

On the first day of the Match at St. Andrews, with Cyril Tolley and Roger Wethered leading off, the British won three of the four foursomes, so that the Americans went into the eight singles needing five victories to tie and six to win. The prospect became even more gloomy when most of the Americans were trailing in their singles matches at noon. At one point the Team, collectively, had been 24 holes down.

Then their competitive fire was kindled. Ouimet, 2 down with three to play, made 3s on the 34th and 36th holes to halve Wethered and equal the course record of 70. He holed an 18-foot putt around a partial stymie on the 36th. Rotan, who had been six down after 14 holes, rallied to win 11 of the next 12 holes and defeat Mackenzie, 6 and 4. Marston, who had been 1 down at noon, came back to beat W. L. Hope, 5 and 4. Wright, 2 down with three to play, won the last three holes, the final one with a seven-foot putt for a birdie 3, to defeat Holderness.

These comebacks, coupled with Gardner's 1-up victory over Harris, the British Captain, tied the match, and the decision rode on Dr. Willing and William A. Murray. They were the last on the course, and they were even with three holes to play. Dr. Willing won the 34th and 35th to give the United States a 6-to-5 victory and retain the Cup.

In his report to the Executive Committee, Howard F. Whitney, Chairman of the International Matches and Relations Committee, wrote:

"Your committee is of the opinion that international competition in golf has done as much for the development of the game as any other factor."

1924—Another Match was scheduled for September, 1924, at the Garden City Golf Club. Captain Gardner's American team was particularly strong that year; every member had been a Cup player. The United States won, 9 to 3, over Captain Cyril Tolley's side, although not one of the Americans clinched a victory earlier than the 33rd green.

This Match was the last to be played on an annual basis. It was felt that the financial strain of annual Matches was too severe and that interest might drop if the Matches were played too frequently. A decision was made to meet in alternate years thereafter.

1926—In 1926, the Americans, again Captained by Gardner, went first to Muirfield, Scotland, for the British Amateur. Jess Sweetser, suffering severely from near-pneumonia, became the first American-born winner of that Championship. Then the team, comprising a nucleus of veterans with George Von Elm and the two youngsters, Roland MacKenzie, who was only 17, and Watts Gunn, returned to St. Andrews for the Match and defended the Cup by the narrowest of margins.

Bob Jones, who later that year was to win his first British Open, started his series of one-sided victories in singles play by defeating Cyril Tolley, 12 and 11. Jones never was defeated in five singles matches in Walker Cup competition from the first Match through his retirement after the 1930 season. The Americans, however, won only six contests against Captain Harris's side, and their 6 to 5 victory traced to Von Elm's tie with Major Charles O. Hezlet in a grim singles contest on the final day.

1928—Jones set the pace in 1928 when he defeated T. Philip Perkins, 13 and 12, in the first singles match. It was the widest margin in the history of the series. Only T. A. Torrance was able to win a point for Great Britain as the United States won, 11-1. Torrance defeated Charles Evans, Jr., 1 up. Watts Gunn won his singles match over Ronald R. Hardman, 11 and 10.

1930—George J. Voigt and Donald K. Moe joined the team in 1930, and Moe won one of the great matches of the series from James A. (Bill) Stout. Stout played the course in 68 in the morning and stood 4 up. He started the afternoon round 3-3-3 and went 7 up, and he was still 7 up with 13 to play. Moe then took back every one of the seven holes and won the match with a birdie 3 on the last hole. His score for the round was 67. After the match, Stout remarked reverently: "That was not golf; that was a visitation from the Lord!" The United States won, 10-7.

1932–Upon Jones' retirement, Francis Ouimet, who had participated in every International Match, took over the Captaincy in 1932 and retained it for six matches, through 1949. His personal record reveals four victories and two defeats in eight singles matches and five wins and three losses in eight foursomes. He last played in 1934 at St. Andrews but continued as a non-playing Captain.

The personnel of the teams changed rapidly, too, after the Jones era, as Charles H. Seaver, Gus T. Moreland, George T. Dunlap, Jr., William Howell, Jack Westland, a player in 1932 and 1934 and again in 1953; Maurice J. McCarthy, Jr., W. Lawson Little, Jr., John Goodman, the veteran H. Chandler Egan, who played in 1934 at the age of 50; John W. Fischer, Albert E. Campbell, Reynolds Smith, Charles R. Yates, Walter Emery, Harry L. Givan, Ed White, Charles R. Kocsis, Marvin H. Ward, Raymond E. Billows and Fred Haas, Jr., successively entered the scene in the prewar years.

They were capable replacements for the veterans of the early matches. At The Country Club in 1932, when the Match was played during a total eclipse of the sun, the biggest dent the British made in the Cup was by Leonard G. Crawley. He not only won the only point for Captain T. A. Torrance's side, defeating George J. Voigt by a hole, but his errant iron shot to the 18th green at noon hit the Cup on the fly. The Americans won the dented Cup, 8 to 1. The British side that year included two brothers, Rex. W. and W. Lister Hartley, and they were paired together in the first foursome.

1934–Playing at St. Andrews in 1934, the Americans won their eighth successive victory, by 9 to 2. The British side was Captained by the Hon. Michael Scott, who had won the 1933 British Amateur at the age of 55 and the following year became the oldest competitor in the Walker Cup series. Again the American invasion included a victory in the British Amateur as Lawson Little won at Prestwick.

1936–The British went down fighting in 1936, even though they lost the only shutout of the series, 9-0. In the foursomes at Pine Valley, Alec Hill and Cecil Ewing were 7 down to George Voigt and Harry Givan with 11 to play. They squared the match on the 35th hole and halved the last to gain a tie. Jock McLean, of the British Team, nearly carried away our Amateur Championship; Johnny Fischer had to play the last three holes in birdies to beat him on the 37th green in the final.

1938–The succession of nine victories, the last four decisive, set the stage for the come-uppance which had been so narrowly averted in 1923. There was every reason for the Americans to be confident again when they went to Scotland in 1938, and Charles R. Yates won the British Amateur at Troon, prior to the Walker Cup, to increase this confidence.

The British, however, were most serious. Captain John B. Beck, whose wife was later to captain the 1954 British Curtis Cup Team, conducted trials for a squad of players in an effort to end the American string of victories. When the teams met at St. Andrews, the British won two and halved another of the four foursomes to take a lead they never relinquished. An indication of their excellence was the fact that James Bruen, Jr., and Harry G. Bentley, 3 down at noon, came back with an approximate 68 to halve John Fischer and Charles R. Kocsis.

The Americans needed five victories in singles to insure defense of the Cup. Ward played the Old Course in 67 in the first round and beat Frank Pennink, 12 and 11. Fischer, 4 down at noon, was six under 4s for 16 holes in the afternoon to beat Leonard Crawley. Yates also won. But their victories were not enough. Great Britain finally took possession of the Cup, 7 to 4.

1947–It took a decade for the United States to regain the Cup. World War II intervened and no Match was played until the USGA sent a team to St. Andrews in 1947. Under normal circumstances, the Match would have been played in this country, but postwar conditions would have made the trip difficult for the British.

The Match was another close one, closer than the score indicated. Captain Ouimet's side won two foursomes, and Captain Beck's side won two. After 18 holes of singles play, four British players were ahead and four Americans were leading. It was anyone's Match, but the Americans were equal to the occasion. Bud Ward, three down at noon, played 15 holes in three under 4s to beat Leonard Crawley, 5 and 3, in the No. 1 contest. Frank Stranahan, 2 down at noon, went to the turn in 34 and defeated Charles Stowe, 2 and 1. The four Americans who had been ahead at noon held their advantages, and the United States regained the Cup, 8 to 4. The Team stayed abroad for the British Amateur, at Carnoustie, and Willie Turnesa won.

Only one member of this 1947 Team had played in 1938–Bud Ward. In the War decade, Ted Bishop, Dick Chapman, Fred Kammer, Smiley Quick, Skee Riegel, Stranahan and Turnesa achieved Cup status and took over from the veterans. William C. Turnesa replaced Ouimet as Captain in 1951. These players were joined in the following two Cup Matches by William C. Campbell, Charles R. Coe, John Dawson, Robert W. Knowles, Bruce McCormick, Harold D. Paddock and Sam Urzetta.

1949–When the Match was next held in the United States at the Winged Foot Golf Club, Mamaroneck, N.Y., it was not so close. Laddie Lucas, a left-handed golfer, provided outstanding leadership as a non-playing Captain, but United States skill with the sand wedge and putter could not be overcome. Ronnie White, the British lead-off player, won his singles and his foursome, the latter with Joe Carr, but these were the only points the British took. The United States won, 10 to 2.

1951–This superiority was maintained at Birkdale, although on English soil the margin was a less emphatic 6 to 3. After 18 holes of first-day foursomes, the British led in three matches and the fourth was even, but Captain Turnesa's men rallied to win two of the foursomes and halve the other two. The next day they won four and halved one of the eight singles. Paddock saved the half after being 3 down with four to play and 2 down with two to play, finishing 3-4-3-4. White again was the mainstay of the British side, playing 35 holes in three under 4s to edge Coe in singles after pairing with Carr to halve his foursome. White had never been defeated in Cup play.

Following the Match, Richard D. Chapman won the British Amateur, defeating Coe in an all-American final.

During this visit, representatives of the Royal and Ancient Golf Club and of the USGA met in London and St. Andrews, with representatives of Australia and Canada, and drafted a uniform code of Rules. Thus the series which had developed in part from the 1920 conference on Rules itself spawned another and very successful conference on Rules.

1953—The United States proved clearly superior in depth when the Teams met in 1953 at the Kittansett Club, Marion, Mass. This Match was played in calm weather and sultry heat which belied the seaside setting, and Captain Charles R. Yates' team won for the 13th time, 9 to 3.

The United States won the first three of the four foursomes on the first day, and although the British played bravely and stubbornly, it seemed throughout the day that they were fated to trail. The most spectacular play came in the third foursome, where James G. Jackson and Gene A. Littler played alternate strokes in par over 32 holes to defeat the two Scotsmen, Roy C. MacGregor and James C. Wilson 3 and 2. This was a Whirlaway sort of a victory, for Jackson and Littler were three down playing from the fourth tee.

Wilson chipped in for a birdie 3 to win the first hole and then Jackson discovered and reported while walking up the second fairway that he had 16 clubs in his bag, two more than the Rules allowed. He had neglected to remove his brassie and an extra wedge.

The penalty is, of course, disqualification; and the first reaction of the Executive Committee was to invoke it. However, the British asserted their desire to win their points on their play of the game. The Committee then yielded and modified the penalty to two holes, the number which Jackson had played in inadvertent violation, as it was empowered to do by the Rules. Since the British already had won the first hole, the United States pair was penalized the second and third holes and was sent to the fourth tee three down. They were still 3 down at the turn, but a homecoming 33 gained them five holes and a lead they never relinquished.

It was in the singles play on the second day, however, that the heroic match occurred. The United States won six of the eight singles, and certainly incurred no embarrassment over the second engagement, in which Ronald J. White, of Great Britain, defeated Richard D. Chapman, a member of the Kittansett Club, 1 up.

After 30 holes, Chapman was 3 up. It looked very much as if White, who had gone unbeaten in both foursomes and singles in three previous matches but had lost his foursome the day before, had come altogether to the end of his string. But not so.

White played the last six holes in three birdies and three pars, three 3s and three 4s, to win four of them and his fourth successive Walker Cup singles. Chapman survived the first two birdies and was still 1 up with two to play, but White hit a superb half shot from the rough with a No. 4 iron on the 35th and ran in a 10-foot putt for a birdie 3 to square the match. The last hole is a 455-yarder into a strong breeze which had sprung up at the end of the day, and White was handsomely on with his second while Chapman was bunkered near the green. The match turned when Chapman did not explode quite close enough to match White's par 4. White's score was 77-70–147 and Chapman, even with 7s on the 15th hole in each round, did two 74s.

1955—St. Andrews' Old Course, the site of the British Team's best showings in earlier Matches, was again the host course. Britain's only victory, in 1938, had come there. Twice the score at St. Andrews had been 6 to 5, with one match halved. Only one member of the 1955 American side had gone as far as the final of the United States Amateur—Dale Morey, runnerup in 1953. The United States' margin of victory in the 1955 Match, 10 to 2, therefore came as something of a surprise. Harvie Ward, who was to win the Amateur Championship in both 1955 and 1956, played brilliantly to defeat Britain's Ronnie White, 6 and 5, in singles. It was the first defeat in Walker Cup competition for White, who had won four earlier singles matches. William C. Campbell, Captain of the United States Team, declined to put himself in the lineup for either day of the Match even though he was one of the strongest and certainly the most experienced American player. Following the match, Lt. Joseph W. Conrad won the British Amateur Championship. It marked the eighth consecutive occasion on which a member of the visiting United States Walker Cup Team had won.

1957—The Walker Cup Match, played at the Minikahda Club, Minneapolis, Minn., in September, 1957, resulted in the 15th United States victory, but not without a real struggle. The 8-3 score (one match was halved) conveys nothing of the drama which led Captain Charles R. Coe to remark at the presentation: "At about 3 o'clock this afternoon I thought the Walker Cup was halfway across the Atlantic." Coe was referring to the stage where the balance lay with three singles matches which were even with six, five and two holes to go. The United States won all three. The highlight of the singles on the second day was Billy Joe Patton's magnificent, yet typical comeback when he rallied from a five-hole lunch-time deficit to beat the British Amateur Champion, R. Reid Jack, by one hole. Patton completed the 6,550-yard par 71 course in 68, eight strokes less than his morning round. Both teams included seven new faces. The British side was under the captaincy of Gerald Micklem, a member of several former Teams.

1959—The 17th Match resulted in a 9-3 victory for the American Team. Play was over the Muirfield Links, home of The Honourable Company of Edinburgh Golfers, 20 miles east of Edinburgh, Scotland. The margin of victory could almost be traced to American superiority in the late holes. Six of the 12 matches went to the 35th or 36th greens and America won five of those six. The American Team of five veterans and four youngsters won all four foursomes the first day and five of the eight singles. Charles R. Coe, of Oklahoma City, the 1958 Amateur Champion, was playing Captain of the unusually strong American team which included Jack W. Nicklaus, Deane R. Beman, and Thomas D. Aaron, all of whom became outstanding professionals in later years. Beman later won the British Amateur defeating William Hyndman, III, a team-mate, in another All-American final.

THE WALKER CUP MATCH

Year	Winner		Loser		Site
1922	United States,	8	Great Britain,	4	National Golf Links of America, Southampton, New York
1923	United States,	6	Great Britain,	5	St. Andrews, Scotland
	one match halved				
1924	United States,	9	Great Britain,	3	Garden City Golf Club, Garden City, New York
1926	United States,	6	Great Britain,	5	St. Andrews, Scotland
	one match halved				
1928	United States,	11	Great Britain,	1	Chicago Golf Club, Wheaton, Illinois
1930	United States,	10	Great Britain,	2	Royal St. George's Golf Club, Sandwich, England
1932	United States,	8	Great Britain,	1	The Country Club, Brookline, Massachusetts
	three matches halved				
1934	United States,	9	Great Britain,	2	St. Andrews, Scotland
	one match halved				
1936	United States,	9	Great Britain,	0	Pine Valley Golf Club, Clementon, New Jersey
	three matches halved				
1938	Great Britain,	7	United States,	4	St. Andrews, Scotland
	one match halved				
1947	United States,	8	Great Britain,	4	St. Andrews, Scotland
1949	United States,	10	Great Britain,	2	Winged Foot Golf Club, Mamaroneck, New York
1951	United States,	6	Great Britain,	3	Birkdale Golf Club, Southport, England
	three matches halved				
1953	United States,	9	Great Britain,	3	Kittansett, Marion, Massachusetts
1955	United States,	10	Great Britain,	2	St. Andrews, Scotland
1957	United States,	8	Great Britain,	3	Minikahda Club, Minneapolis, Minnesota
	one match halved				
1959	United States,	9	Great Britain,	3	Honourable Company of Edinburgh Golfers, Muirfield, Scotland

1922
INTERNATIONAL MATCH FOR THE WALKER CUP

Held at the National Golf Links of America, Southampton, N.Y.
August 28 and 29

FOURSOMES

Great Britain and Ireland	Points	United States	Points
Cyril J.H. Tolley and Bernard Darwin	0	Jesse P. Guilford and Francis D. Ouimet (8 and 7)	1
Roger H. Wethered and Colin C. Aylmer (5 and 4)	1	Charles Evans, Jr., and Robert A. Gardner	0
W.B. Torrance and C.V.L. Hooman	0	Robert T. Jones, Jr., and Jess W. Sweetser (3 and 2)	1
John Caven and W. Willis Mackenzie	0	Max R. Marston and William C. Fownes, Jr. (2 and 1)	1
Total	1	Total	3

SINGLES

Great Britain and Ireland	Points	United States	Points
Cyril J.H. Tolley	0	Jesse P. Guilford (2 and 1)	1
Roger H. Wethered	0	Robert T. Jones, Jr. (3 and 2)	1
John Caven	0	Charles Evans, Jr. (5 and 4)	1
Colin C. Aylmer	0	Francis D. Ouimet (8 and 7)	1
W.B. Torrance	0	Robert A. Gardner (7 and 5)	1
W. Willis Mackenzie (6 and 5)	1	Max R. Marston	0
Bernard Darwin (3 and 1)	1	William C. Fownes, Jr.	0
C.V.L. Hooman (1 up, 37 holes)	1	Jess W. Sweetser	0
Total	3	Total	5
Grand Total—Great Britain and Ireland	4	Grand Total—United States	8

Captain—Robert Harris

Captain—William C. Fownes, Jr. Reserve—Rudolf E. Knepper

1923
INTERNATIONAL MATCH FOR THE WALKER CUP

Held at St. Andrews, Scotland
May 18 and 19

FOURSOMES

Great Britain and Ireland	Points	United States	Points
Cyril J.H. Tolley and Roger H. Wethered (6 and 5)	1	Francis D. Ouimet and Jess W. Sweetser	0
Robert Harris and C.V.L. Hooman	0	Robert A. Gardner and Max R. Marston (7 and 6)	1
Ernest W.E. Holderness and William L. Hope (1 up)	1	George V. Rotan and S. Davidson Herron	0
John Wilson and William A. Murray (4 and 3)	1	Harrison R. Johnston and J. F. Neville	0
Total	3	Total	1

SINGLES

Great Britain and Ireland	Points	United States	Points
Roger H. Wethered (halved)	0	Francis D. Ouimet (halved)	0
Cyril J. H. Tolley (4 and 3)	1	Jess W. Sweetser	0
Robert Harris	0	Robert A. Gardner (1 up)	1
W. Willis Mackenzie	0	George V. Rotan (5 and 4)	1
William L. Hope	0	Max R. Marston (6 and 5)	1
Ernest W.E. Holderness	0	Frederick J. Wright, Jr. (1 up)	1
John Wilson (1 up)	1	S. Davidson Herron	0
William A. Murray	0	Dr. O.F. Willing (2 and 1)	1
Total	2	Total	5
Grand Total—Great Britain and Ireland	5	Grand Total—United States	6

Captain—Robert Harris

Captain—Robert A. Gardner

1924
INTERNATIONAL MATCH FOR THE WALKER CUP

Held at the Garden City Golf Club, Garden City, N.Y.
September 12 and 13

FOURSOMES

Great Britain and Ireland	Points	United States	Points
Edward F. Storey and William A. Murray	0	Max R. Marston and Robert A. Gardner (3 and 1)	1
Cyril J.H. Tolley and Major Charles O. Hezlet	0	Jesse P. Guilford and Francis D. Ouimet (2 and 1)	1
Hon. Michael Scott and Robert Scott, Jr. (1 up)	1	Robert T. Jones, Jr., and William C. Fownes, Jr.	0
T. A. Torrance and O. C. Bristowe	0	Jess W. Sweetser and Harrison R. Johnston (4 and 3)	1
Total	1	Total	3

SINGLES

Great Britain and Ireland	Points	United States	Points
Cyril J.H. Tolley (1 up)	1	Max R. Marston	0
Major Charles O. Hezlet	0	Robert T. Jones, Jr. (4 and 3)	1
William A. Murray	0	Charles Evans, Jr. (2 and 1)	1
Edward F. Storey	0	Francis D. Ouimet (1 up)	1
Hon. Michael Scott (7 and 6)	1	Jess W. Sweetser	0
William L. Hope	0	Robert A. Gardner (3 and 2)	1
T.A. Torrance	0	Jesse P. Guilford (2 and 1)	1
Dennis Kyle	0	Dr. O.F. Willing (3 and 2)	1
Total	2	Total	6
Grand Total—Great Britain and Ireland	3	Grand Total—United States	9

Captain—Cyril J.H. Tolley

Captain—Robert A. Gardner

1926
INTERNATIONAL MATCH FOR THE WALKER CUP

Held at St. Andrews, Scotland
June 2 and 3

FOURSOMES

Great Britain and Ireland	Points	United States	Points
Roger H. Wethered and Sir Ernest W.E. Holderness (5 and 4)	1	Francis D. Ouimet and Jesse P. Guilford	0
Cyril J.H. Tolley and Andrew Jamieson, Jr.	0	Robert T. Jones, Jr., and Watts Gunn (4 and 3)	1
Robert Harris and Major Charles O. Hezlet	0	George Von Elm and Jess W. Sweetser (8 and 7)	1
Edward F. Storey and Hon. W.G. E. Brownlow	0	Robert A. Gardner and Roland R. MacKenzie (1 up)	1
Total	1	Total	3

SINGLES

Great Britain and Ireland	Points	United States	Points
Cyril J.H. Tolley	0	Robert T. Jones, Jr. (12 and 11)	1
Sir Ernest W.E. Holderness	0	Jess W. Sweetser (4 and 3)	1
Roger H. Wethered (5 and 4)	1	Francis D. Ouimet	0
Major Charles O. Hezlet (halved)	0	George Von Elm (halved)	0
Robert Harris (2 and 1)	1	Jesse P. Guilford	0
Hon. W.G.E. Brownlow	0	Watts Gunn (9 and 8)	1
Edward F. Storey (2 and 1)	1	Roland R. MacKenzie	0
Andrew Jamieson, Jr. (5 and 4)	1	Robert A. Gardner	0
Total	4	Total	3
Grand Total—Great Britain and Ireland	5	Grand Total—United States	6

Captain—Robert Harris

Captain—Robert A. Gardner

1928
INTERNATIONAL MATCH FOR THE WALKER CUP

Held at the Chicago Golf Club, Wheaton, Ill.
August 30 and 31

FOURSOMES

Great Britain and Ireland	Points	United States	Points
T. Philip Perkins and Dr. William Tweddell	0	Jess W. Sweetser and George Von Elm (7 and 6)	1
Major Charles O. Hezlet and William L. Hope	0	Robert T. Jones, Jr., and Charles Evans, Jr. (5 and 3)	1
T. A. Torrance and Edward F. Storey	0	Francis D. Ouimet and Harrison R. Johnston (4 and 2)	1
John B. Beck and Dr. A.R. MacCallum	0	Watts Gunn and Roland R. MacKenzie (7 and 5)	1
Total	0	Total	4

SINGLES

Great Britain and Ireland	Points	United States	Points
T. Philip Perkins	0	Robert T. Jones, Jr. (13 and 12)	1
Dr. William Tweddell	0	George Von Elm (3 and 2)	1
Major Charles O. Hezlet	0	Francis D. Ouimet (8 and 7)	1
William L. Hope	0	Jess W. Sweetser (5 and 4)	1
Edward F. Storey	0	Harrison R. Johnston (4 and 2)	1
T.A. Torrance (1 up)	1	Charles Evans, Jr.	0
Ronald H. Hardman	0	Watts Gunn (11 and 10)	1
Capt. G.N.C. Martin	0	Roland R. MacKenzie (2 and 1)	1
Total	1	Total	7
Grand Total—Great Britain and Ireland	1	Grand Total—United States	11

Captain—Dr. William Tweddell

Captain—Robert T. Jones, Jr.   Reserve—M.J. McCarthy, Jr.

1930
INTERNATIONAL MATCH FOR THE WALKER CUP

Held at the Royal St. George's Golf Club, Sandwich, England
May 15 and 16

FOURSOMES

Great Britain and Ireland	Points	United States	Points
Cyril J.H. Tolley and Roger H. Wethered (2 up)	1	George Von Elm and George J. Voigt	0
Rex W. Hartley and T.A. Torrance	0	Robert T. Jones, Jr., and Dr. O. F. Willing (8 and 7)	1
Sir Ernest W.E. Holderness and James A. Stout	0	Roland R. MacKenzie and Donald K. Moe (2 and 1)	1
William Campbell and John N. Smith	0	Harrison R. Johnston and Francis D. Ouimet (2 and 1)	1
Total	1	Total	3

SINGLES

Great Britain and Ireland	Points	United States	Points
Cyril J.H. Tolley	0	Harrison R. Johnston (5 and 4)	1
Roger H. Wethered	0	Robert T. Jones, Jr. (9 and 8)	1
Rex W. Hartley	0	George Von Elm (3 and 2)	1
Sir Ernest W.E. Holderness	0	George J. Voigt (10 and 8)	1
John N. Smith	0	Dr. O.F. Willing (2 and 1)	1
T.A. Torrance (7 and 6)	1	Francis D. Ouimet	0
James A. Stout	0	Donald K. Moe (1 up)	1
William Campbell	0	Roland R. MacKenzie (6 and 5)	1
Total	1	Total	7
Grand Total—Great Britain and Ireland	2	Grand Total—United States	10

Captain—Roger H. Wethered

Captain—Robert T. Jones, Jr.

1932
INTERNATIONAL MATCH FOR THE WALKER CUP

Held at The Country Club, Brookline, Mass.
September 1 and 2

FOURSOMES

Great Britain and Ireland	Points	United States	Points
Rex W. Hartley and W. Lister Hartley	0	Jess W. Sweetser and George J. Voigt (7 and 6)	1
T.A. Torrance and John G. DeForest	0	Charles H. Seaver and Gus T. Moreland (6 and 5)	1
James A. Stout and John Burke	0	Francis D. Ouimet and George T. Dunlap, Jr. (7 and 6)	1
Eric W. Fiddian and Eric A. McRuvie	0	Donald K. Moe and William Howell (5 and 4)	1
Total	0	Total	4

SINGLES

Great Britain and Ireland	Points	United States	Points
T.A. Torrance (halved)	0	Francis D. Ouimet (halved)	0
James A. Stout (halved)	0	Jess W. Sweetser (halved)	0
Rex W. Hartley	0	Gus T. Moreland (2 and 1)	1
John Burke (halved)	0	Jack Westland (halved)	0
Leonard G. Crawley (1 up)	1	George J. Voigt	0
W. Lister Hartley	0	Maurice J. McCarthy, Jr. (3 and 2)	1
Eric W. Fiddian	0	Charles H. Seaver (7 and 6)	1
Eric A. McRuvie	0	George T. Dunlap, Jr. (10 and 9)	1
Total	1	Total	4
Grand Total—Great Britain and Ireland	1	Grand Total—United States	8

Captain—T.A. Torrance

Captain—Francis D. Ouimet

1934
INTERNATIONAL MATCH FOR THE WALKER CUP

Held at St. Andrews, Scotland
May 11 and 12

FOURSOMES

Great Britain and Ireland	Points	United States	Points
Roger H. Wethered and Cyril J. H. Tolley	0	John G. Goodman and W. Lawson Little, Jr. (8 and 6)	1
Harry G. Bentley and Eric W. Fiddian	0	Gus T. Moreland and Jack Westland (6 and 5)	1
Hon. Michael Scott and Samuel L. McKinlay	0	H. Chandler Egan and Max R. Marston (3 and 2)	1
Eric A. McRuvie and Jack McLean (4 and 2)	1	Francis D. Ouimet and George T. Dunlap, Jr.	0
Total	1	Total	3

SINGLES

Great Britain and Ireland	Points	United States	Points
Hon. Michael Scott	0	John G. Goodman (7 and 6)	1
Cyril J.H. Tolley	0	W. Lawson Little, Jr. (6 and 5)	1
Leonard G. Crawley	0	Francis D. Ouimet (5 and 4)	1
Jack McLean	0	George T. Dunlap, Jr. (4 and 3)	1
Eric W. Fiddian	0	John W. Fischer (5 and 4)	1
Samuel L. McKinlay	0	Gus T. Moreland (3 and 1)	1
Eric A. McRuvie (halved)	0	Jack Westland (halved)	0
T.A. Torrance (4 and 3)	1	Max R. Marston	0
Total	1	Total	6
Grand Total—Great Britain and Ireland	2	Grand Total—United States	9

Captain—Hon. Michael Scott

Captain—Francis D. Ouimet

1936
INTERNATIONAL MATCH FOR THE WALKER CUP

Held at the Pine Valley Golf Club, Clementon, N.J.
September 2 and 3

FOURSOMES

Great Britain and Ireland	Points	United States	Points
Hector Thomson and Harry G. Bentley	0	John G. Goodman and Albert E. Campbell (7 and 5)	1
Jack McLean and John D.A. Langley	0	Reynolds Smith and Ed White (8 and 7)	1
Gordon B. Peters and J. Morton Dykes (halved)	0	Charles R. Yates and Walter Emery (halved)	0
G. Alec Hill and R. Cecil Ewing (halved)	0	Harry L. Givan and George J. Voigt (halved)	0
Total	0	Total	2

SINGLES

Great Britain and Ireland	Points	United States	Points
Hector Thomson	0	John G. Goodman (3 and 2)	1
Jack McLean	0	Albert E. Campbell (5 and 4)	1
R. Cecil Ewing	0	John W. Fischer (8 and 7)	1
G. Alec Hill	0	Reynolds Smith (11 and 9)	1
Gordon B. Peters	0	Walter Emery (1 up)	1
J. Morton Dykes	0	Charles R. Yates (8 and 7)	1
Harry G. Bentley (halved)	0	George T. Dunlap, Jr. (halved)	0
John D.A. Langley	0	Ed White (6 and 5)	1
Total	0	Total	7
Grand Total—Great Britain and Ireland	0	Grand Total—United States	9

Captain—Dr. William Tweddell   Reserve—P.B. Lucas

Captain—Francis D. Ouimet

1938
INTERNATIONAL MATCH FOR THE WALKER CUP

Held at St. Andrews, Scotland
June 3 and 4

FOURSOMES

Great Britain and Ireland	Points	United States	Points
Harry G. Bentley and James Bruen, Jr. (halved)	0	John W. Fischer and Charles R. Kocsis (halved)	0
Gordon B. Peters and Hector Thomson (4 and 2)	1	John G. Goodman and Marvin H. Ward	0
Alexander T. Kyle and Charles Stowe	0	Charles R. Yates and Raymond E. Billows (3 and 2)	1
J.J. Frank Pennink and Leonard G. Crawley (3 and 1)	1	Reynolds Smith and Fred Haas, Jr.	0
Total	2	Total	1

SINGLES

Great Britain and Ireland	Points	United States	Points
James Bruen, Jr.	0	Charles R. Yates (2 and 1)	1
Hector Thomson (6 and 4)	1	John G. Goodman	0
Leonard G. Crawley	0	John W. Fischer (3 and 2)	1
Charles Stowe (2 and 1)	1	Charles R. Kocsis	0
J.J. Frank Pennink	0	Marvin H. Ward (12 and 11)	1
R. Cecil Ewing (1 up)	1	Raymond E. Billows	0
Gordon B. Peters (9 and 8)	1	Reynolds Smith	0
Alexander T. Kyle (5 and 4)	1	Fred Haas, Jr.	0
Total	5	Total	3
Grand Total—Great Britain and Ireland	7	Grand Total—United States	4

Captain—John B. Beck

Captain—Francis D. Ouimet

1947
INTERNATIONAL MATCH FOR THE WALKER CUP

Held at St. Andrews, Scotland
May 16 and 17

FOURSOMES

Great Britain and Ireland	Points	United States	Points
Joseph B. Carr and R. Cecil Ewing	0	Stanley E. Bishop and Robert H. (Skee) Riegel (3 and 2)	1
Leonard G. Crawley and Percy B. Lucas (5 and 4)	1	Marvin H. Ward and Smiley L. Quick	0
Alexander T. Kyle and James C. Wilson	0	William P. Turnesa and A. Frederick Kammer, Jr. (5 and 4)	1
Ronald J. White and Charles Stowe (4 and 3)	1	Frank R. Stranahan and Richard D. Chapman	0
Total	2	Total	2

SINGLES

Great Britain and Ireland	Points	United States	Points
Leonard G. Crawley	0	Marvin H. Ward (5 and 3)	1
Joseph B. Carr (5 and 3)	1	Stanley E. Bishop	0
Gerald H. Micklem	0	Robert H. (Skee) Riegel (6 and 5)	1
R. Cecil Ewing	0	William P. Turnesa (6 and 5)	1
Charles Stowe	0	Frank R. Stranahan (2 and 1)	1
Ronald J. White (4 and 3)	1	A. Frederick Kammer, Jr.	0
James C. Wilson	0	Smiley L. Quick (8 and 6)	1
Percy B. Lucas	0	Richard D. Chapman (4 and 3)	1
Total	2	Total	6
Grand Total—Great Britain and Ireland	4	Grand Total—United States	8

Captain—John B. Beck

Captain—Francis D. Ouimet   Reserve—George S. Hamer, Jr.

1949
INTERNATIONAL MATCH FOR THE WALKER CUP

Held at the Winged Foot Golf Club, Mamaroneck, N.Y.
August 19 and 20

FOURSOMES

Great Britain and Ireland	Points	United States	Points
Joseph B. Carr and Ronald J. White (3 and 2)	1	Raymond E. Billows and William P. Turnesa	0
James Bruen, Jr., and S. Max McCready	0	Charles R. Kocsis and Frank R. Stranahan (2 and 1)	1
R. Cecil Ewing and Gerald H. Micklem	0	Stanley E. Bishop and Robert H. (Skee) Riegel (9 and 7)	1
Kenneth G. Thom and Arthur H. Perowne	0	John W. Dawson and Bruce N. McCormick (8 and 7)	1
Total	1	Total	3

SINGLES

Great Britain and Ireland	Points	United States	Points
Ronald J. White (4 and 3)	1	William P. Turnesa	0
S. Max McCready	0	Frank R. Stranahan (6 and 5)	1
James Bruen, Jr.	0	Robert H. (Skee) Riegel (5 and 4)	1
Joseph B. Carr	0	John W. Dawson (5 and 3)	1
R. Cecil Ewing	0	Charles R. Coe (1 up)	1
Kenneth G. Thom	0	Raymond E. Billows (2 and 1)	1
Arthur H. Perowne	0	Charles R. Kocsis (4 and 2)	1
Gerald H. Micklem	0	James B. McHale, Jr. (5 and 4)	1
Total	1	Total	7
Grand Total—Great Britain and Ireland	2	Grand Total—United States	10

Captain—Percy B. Lucas   Reserve—Ernest B. Millward

Captain—Francis D. Ouimet

1951
INTERNATIONAL MATCH FOR THE WALKER CUP

Held at the Birkdale Golf Club, Southport, England
May 11 and 12

FOURSOMES

Great Britain and Ireland	Points	United States	Points
Ronald J. White and Joseph B. Carr (halved)	0	Frank R. Stranahan and William C. Campbell (halved)	0
R. Cecil Ewing and John D.A. Langley (halved)	0	Charles R. Coe and James B. McHale, Jr. (halved)	0
Alex T. Kyle and Ian Caldwell	0	Richard D. Chapman and Robert W. Knowles, Jr. (1 up)	1
James Bruen, Jr., and John L. Morgan	0	William P. Turnesa and Sam Urzetta (5 and 4)	1
Total	0	Total	2

SINGLES

Great Britain and Ireland	Points	United States	Points
S. Max McCready	0	Sam Urzetta (4 and 3)	1
Joseph B. Carr (2 and 1)	1	Frank R. Stranahan	0
Ronald J. White (2 and 1)	1	Charles R. Coe	0
John D.A. Langley	0	James B. McHale, Jr. (2 up)	1
R. Cecil Ewing	0	William C. Campbell (5 and 4)	1
Alex T. Kyle (2 up)	1	William P. Turnesa	0
Ian Caldwell (halved)	0	Harold D. Paddock, Jr. (halved)	0
John L. Morgan	0	Richard D. Chapman (7 and 6)	1
Total	3	Total	4
Grand Total—Great Britain and Ireland	3	Grand Total—United States	6

Captain—Raymond Oppenheimer

Captain—William P. Turnesa

Reserve—Dr. F.W.G. Deighton

1953
INTERNATIONAL MATCH FOR THE WALKER CUP

Held at the Kittansett Club, Marion, Mass.
September 4 and 5

FOURSOMES

Great Britain and Ireland	Points	United States	Points
Joseph B. Carr and Ronald J. White	0	Sam Urzetta and Kenneth Venturi (6 and 4)	1
John D.A. Langley and Arthur H. Perowne	0	E. Harvie Ward, Jr., and Jack Westland (9 and 8)	1
James C. Wilson and Roy C. MacGregor	0	James G. Jackson and Gene A. Littler (3 and 2)	1
Gerald H. Micklem and John L. Morgan (4 and 3)	1	William C. Campbell and Charles R. Coe	0
Total	1	Total	3

SINGLES

Great Britain and Ireland	Points	United States	Points
Joseph B. Carr	0	E. Harvie Ward, Jr. (4 and 3)	1
Ronald J. White (1 up)	1	Richard D. Chapman	0
Gerald H. Micklem	0	Gene A. Littler (5 and 3)	1
Roy C. MacGregor	0	Jack Westland (7 and 5)	1
Normand V. Drew	0	Donald R. Cherry (9 and 7)	1
James C. Wilson	0	Kenneth Venturi (9 and 8)	1
John L. Morgan (3 and 2)	1	Charles R. Coe	0
John D.A. Langley	0	Sam Urzetta (3 and 2)	1
Total	2	Total	6
Grand Total—Great Britain	3	Grand Total—United States	9

Captain—Lt. Col. A.A. Duncan

Captain—Charles R. Yates

1955
INTERNATIONAL MATCH FOR THE WALKER CUP

Held at St. Andrews, Scotland
May 20 and 21

FOURSOMES

Great Britain and Ireland	Points	United States	Points
Joseph B. Carr and Ronald J. White	0	E. Harvie Ward, Jr. and Donald R. Cherry (1 up)	1
Gerald H. Micklem and John L. Morgan	0	William J. Patton and Richard L. Yost (2 and 1)	1
Ian Caldwell and Ernest B. Millward	0	Joseph W. Conrad and Dale Morey (3 and 2)	1
David A. Blair and J. Robert Cater	0	Bruce H. Cudd and James G. Jackson (5 and 4)	1
Total	0	Total	4

SINGLES

Great Britain and Ireland	Points	United States	Points
Ronald J. White	0	E. Harvie Ward, Jr. (6 and 5)	1
Philip F. Scrutton	0	William J. Patton (2 and 1)	1
Ian Caldwell (1 up)	1	Dale Morey	0
Joseph B. Carr	0	Donald R. Cherry (5 and 4)	1
David A. Blair (1 up)	1	Joseph W. Conrad	0
Ernest B. Millward	0	Bruce H. Cudd (2 up)	1
R. Cecil Ewing	0	James G. Jackson (6 and 4)	1
John L. Morgan	0	Richard L. Yost (8 and 7)	1
Total	2	Total	6
Grand Total—Great Britain and Ireland	2	Grand Total—United States	10

Non-playing Captain—G. Alec Hill

Captain—William C. Campbell

1957
INTERNATIONAL MATCH FOR THE WALKER CUP

Held at the Minikahda Club, Minneapolis, Minn.
August 30 and 31

FOURSOMES

Great Britain and Ireland	Points	United States	Points
Joseph B. Carr and Dr. F W.G. Deighton	0	Rex Baxter, Jr. and William J. Patton (2 and 1)	1
Alan F. Bussell and Philip F. Scrutton	0	William C. Campbell and Dr. Frank M. Taylor, Jr. (4 and 3)	1
R. Reid Jack and Douglas Sewell (1 up)	1	Arnold S. Blum and Charles R. Kocsis	0
Dr. Alec E. Shepperson and Guy B. Wolstenholme (halved)	0	Hillman Robbins, Jr. and E. Mason Rudolph (halved)	0
Total	1	Total	2

SINGLES

Great Britain and Ireland	Points	United States	Points
R. Reid Jack	0	William J. Patton (1 up)	1
Joseph B. Carr	0	William C. Campbell (3 and 2)	1
Alan Thirlwell	0	Rex Baxter, Jr. (4 and 3)	1
Dr. F.W.G. Deighton	0	William Hyndman, III (7 and 6)	1
Alan F.Bussell (2 and 1)	1	Joe E. Campbell	0
Douglas Sewell	0	Dr. Frank M. Taylor, Jr. (1 up)	1
Philip F. Scrutton	0	E. Mason Rudolph (3 and 2)	1
Guy B. Wolstenholme (2 and 1)	1	Hillman Robbins, Jr.	0
Total	2	Total	6
Grand Total—Great Britain and Ireland	3	Grand Total—United States	8

Non-playing Captain—Gerald H. Micklem

Non-playing Captain—Charles R. Coe

1959
INTERNATIONAL MATCH FOR THE WALKER CUP

Held at the Honourable Company of Edinburgh Golfers, Muirfield, Scotland
May 15 and 16

FOURSOMES

Great Britain and Ireland	Points	United States	Points
R. Reid Jack and Douglas N. Sewell	0	E. Harvie Ward, Jr. and Dr. Frank M. Taylor, Jr. (1 up)	1
Joseph B. Carr and Guy B. Wolstenholme	0	William Hyndman, III and Thomas D. Aaron (1 up)	1
Michael F. Bonallack and Arthur H. Perowne	0	William J. Patton and Charles R. Coe (9 and 8)	1
Michael S.R. Lunt and Alec E. Shepperson	0	H. Ward Wettlaufer and Jack W. Nicklaus (2 and 1)	1
Total	0	Total	4

SINGLES

Great Britain and Ireland	Points	United States	Points
Joseph B. Carr (2 and 1)	1	Charles R. Coe	0
Guy B. Wolstenholme	0	E. Harvie Ward, Jr. (9 and 8)	1
R. Reid Jack (5 and 3)	1	William J. Patton	0
Douglas N. Sewell	0	William Hyndman, III (4 and 3)	1
Alec E. Shepperson (2 and 1)	1	Thomas D. Aaron	0
Michael F. Bonallack	0	Deane R. Beman (2 up)	1
Michael S.R. Lunt	0	H. Ward Wettlaufer (6 and 5)	1
W. Dickson Smith	0	Jack W. Nicklaus (5 and 4)	1
Total	3	Total	5
Grand Total—Great Britain and Ireland	3	Grand Total—United States	9

Non-playing Captain—Gerald H. Micklem

Captain—Charles R. Coe

Reserve—David M. Marsh

CURTIS CUP MATCH

WOMEN'S INTERNATIONAL CUP

Presented in May, 1932, by

MISS HARRIOT S. CURTIS and MISS MARGARET CURTIS
Women's Amateur Champion 1906 — Women's Amateur Champion 1907-1911-1912

HISTORY

The idea of an international women's match was discussed at a meeting of the Women's Eastern Golf Association in 1924. Meetings involving representatives of the WEGA, the British Ladies' Golf Union and the French Golf Union took place in 1924, 1927 and 1929. The major obstacle was financing the teams.

In 1930 Miss Glenna Collett arranged for a group of American women amateur golfers to play a British team abroad. The arrangements were unofficial insofar as the USGA was concerned. However, this was an almost immediate prelude to the institution of the first Curtis Cup Match in 1932.

The Ladies' Golf Union agreed to the matches in February, 1931. During the spring of 1931 the USGA decided to assume financial responsibility for the United States Team and to undertake administration of the matches.

The Curtis Cup, first offered by Miss Harriot Curtis and Miss Margaret Curtis in 1927, was accepted by the USGA and finally, in November, 1932, by the British Ladies' Golf Union with the proviso that France might join the matches whenever it felt able to do so.

The Misses Curtis were both former USGA Women's Amateur Champions. Miss Harriot Curtis won in 1906; Miss Margaret Curtis in 1907, 1911 and 1912. Their vision led to the following inscription on the trophy: "To stimulate friendly rivalry between the women golfers of many lands."

1932–The Curtis Cup series was inaugurated with three foursomes and six singles, all in one day. The United States Team outscored the British Isles by 5½ to 3½ on May 21 at the Wentworth Golf Club, Wentworth, England. The Americans swept the foursomes. Miss Helen Hicks and Miss Virginia Van Wie of the United States team scored 68 for the 17 holes they played in a 2-and-1 victory over Miss Enid Wilson and Mrs. J. B. Watson. In the singles, Miss Joyce Wethered, Miss Wilson, and Miss Diana Fishwick scored victories for the British Isles while Miss Van Wie and Mrs. L. D. Cheney scored the only two victories for the Americans. In the No. 1 match between two great players, Miss Wethered defeated Mrs. Glenna Collett Vare, Jr., 6 and 4. The match between Miss Molly Gourlay and Mrs. O. S. Hill was halved.

1934–The United States rallied to sweep five of the six singles matches and won by 6½ to 2½ over the British Isles in the first Curtis Cup Match held in the United States. The Match was played September 27 and 28 at the Chevy Chase Club, Chevy Chase, Md. Both teams scored 1½ points in the foursomes, played in a severe rainstorm. The lone singles victory for the British Isles came when Mrs. J. B. Walker defeated Mrs. Frank Goldthwaite, 3 and 2.

1936–The first tie occurred in the 1936 Match, 4½ to 4½. Miss Jessie Anderson, of the British Isles, sank a 21-foot putt at the home green to defeat Mrs. L. D. Cheney, 1-up, in the last match. The teams had tied in the foursomes with 1½ points each. In the singles, Mrs. Vare, Miss Charlotte Glutting, and Miss Maureen Orcutt won for the United States, and Mrs. Andrew M. Holm and Mrs. Marjorie Ross Garon scored for the British Isles. The Americans then led, 4½ to 3½, before Miss Anderson's dramatic putt. All matches were played in one day, at the King's Course, Gleneagles, Scotland. The Cup remained in the United States for the next two years. The British, captained by Miss Doris Chambers, graciously declined to share the trophy after the tie, declaring they had not won any claim to it.

1938–The American Team rallied to win five of the six singles and take the Match by 5½ to 3½. The outcome was determined by the last match of the day when Miss Charlotte Glutting won the final three holes to defeat Miss Nan Baird, 1 up, to assure the United States' victory. The British led, 2½ to ½, after the foursomes. The singles matches were hard fought, going at least as far as the 17th green. The match was played at the Essex County Club, Manchester, Mass.

1948–After a lapse of 10 years because of World War II, the Curtis Cup series was resumed in May with the United States winning, 6½ to 2½, for its fourth victory in the five matches to date. The Americans held a 2-1 edge after the foursomes and then won four singles matches and halved another. One of the high points came when Miss Louise Suggs, the American Champion, climaxed an uphill battle by winning the final two holes to halve her match with Miss Philomena Garvey. America's highly-regarded partners in foursomes, Miss Suggs and Miss Grace

Lenczyk, were upset by Miss Jacqueline Gordon and Miss Jean Donald, 3 and 2. The Match was played over two days at the Birkdale Golf Club, Birkdale, England.

1950–The United States won the Curtis Cup for the fifth time and did so by the largest margin, 7½ to 1½, at the Country Club of Buffalo, Williamsville, N.Y. Matches were at 36 holes for the first time. After winning two of the three foursomes, the Americans took five singles matches and halved another for a total of 5½ points out of a possible six. The only American loss during the two days came when Miss Helen Sigel and Miss Peggy Kirk were defeated in foursomes by Miss Frances Stephens and Miss Elizabeth Price, 1 down. The halved singles match was played by Miss Stephens and Mrs. Mark A. Porter, Champions of their countries in 1949. Going to the 34th tee, Miss Stephens was 3 down. She finished par-birdie-par to win all three holes and halve the match.

1952–The British Isles Team scored its first victory in cold, blustery weather at the Muirfield Course of the Honourable Company of Edinburgh Golfers in Scotland in early June. After winning two of the three foursomes to take a 2-1 lead, the British were tied, 4-4, with one match still on the course. The deciding game saw Miss Elizabeth Price, of the British side, take command over Miss Grace DeMoss. One of the most thrilling matches was between Miss Jean Donald, of Britain, and Miss Dorothy Kirby. Miss Donald was 5-up with 11 holes to play, but Miss Kirby tied the match at the 35th hole. Miss Donald's second shot on the final hole was bunkered. She scored a 5, while Miss Kirby made a par 4 to climax a great comeback victory.

1954–The United States regained the Curtis Cup at the East Course of the Merion Golf Club, Ardmore, Pa., in early September. The Americans won the three foursomes and went on to score a 6-3 triumph. Miss Frances Stephens, then the British Women's Amateur Champion, won a point for her side with a 1-up victory over Miss Mary Lena Faulk, the 1953 United States Women's Amateur Champion. Miss Faulk, 1 down, scored a birdie 2 on the 35th hole to tie the match, but Miss Stephens came back to hole a 24-foot putt on the 36th green to decide it.

1956–The British Isles gained possession of the Curtis Cup for the second time by superior play in the singles matches. Down 2-1 after the foursomes, the British took four of six singles to regain the Cup, 5 to 4. The last match to finish was vital. It pitted two players undefeated in singles play in earlier Matches, Miss Polly Riley and Mrs. Frances Stephens Smith. Miss Riley climaxed a comeback by evening the match on the 32nd hole and again on the 34th. After halving the 35th hole, Miss Riley took a one-over-par 6 on the final hole while Mrs. Smith got down in 5 for the victory and the Match. Winds of 45 miles per hour lashed sleet across the course during the foursomes play. The Match was played at the Prince's Golf Club, Sandwich Bay, England.

1958–The British Isles Curtis Cup Team made the best showing of any British amateur golf team to visit this country to that time, and the tenth match for the Cup resulted in a tie, 4½ to 4½, at the Brae Burn Country Club, West Newton, Mass. Under the terms of the Match, the holder retains the Cup in case of a tie, so it remained in Britain. The British took a 2-1 lead in the foursomes, but the Americans came back strongly in the singles, following the example of their Champion, Miss JoAnne Gunderson, who defeated the British Champion, Mrs. George Valentine, 2 up. With two matches coming to the home hole, the United States actually was in the lead, 4-3. However, Miss Barbara McIntire, who seemingly had had her match with Mrs. Angela Ward Bonallack in hand, had to come from nowhere on the last hole to gain a half for the United States; and, as it had two years earlier, the decision then rode on the contest between Miss Polly Riley and Mrs. Frances Stephens Smith. Mrs. Smith managed to bring a 1 up lead to the final hole and won it also for Britain to create the tie. Both Captains used the same six players in foursomes and singles.

THE CURTIS CUP MATCH

1932	United States,	5½	Great Britain & Ireland,	3½	Wentworth Golf Club, Wentworth, Eng.
1934	United States,	6½	Great Britain & Ireland,	2½	Chevy Chase Club, Chevy Chase, Md.
1936	United States,	4½	Great Britain & Ireland,	4½	King's Course, Gleneagles, Scotland
1938	United States,	5½	Great Britain & Ireland,	3½	Essex County Club, Manchester, Mass.
1948	United States,	6½	Great Britain & Ireland,	2½	Birkdale Golf Club, Southport, England
1950	United States,	7½	Great Britain & Ireland,	1½	C. C. of Buffalo, Williamsville, N. Y.
1952	Great Britain & Ireland,	5	United States,	4	Honourable Company of Edinburgh Golfers, Muirfield, Scotland
1954	United States,	6	Great Britain & Ireland,	3	Merion G.C., (East Course), Ardmore, Pa.
1956	Great Britain & Ireland,	5	United States,	4	Prince's G. C., Sandwich Bay, England
1958	Great Britain & Ireland,	4½	United States,	4½	Brae Burn C. C., West Newton, Mass.

1932
INTERNATIONAL MATCH FOR THE CURTIS CUP

Held at the Wentworth Golf Club, Wentworth, England

May 21

FOURSOMES

Great Britain and Ireland	Points	United States	Points
Miss Joyce Wethered and Miss Wanda Morgan	0	Mrs. Glenna Collett Vare and Mrs. O.S. Hill (1 up)	1
Miss Enid Wilson and Mrs. J.B. Watson	0	Miss Virginia Van Wie and Miss Helen Hicks (2 and 1)	1
Miss Molly Gourlay and Miss Doris Park	0	Miss Maureen Orcutt and Mrs. L.D. Cheney (1 up)	1
Total	0	Total	3

SINGLES

Great Britain and Ireland	Points	United States	Points
Miss Joyce Wethered (6 and 4)	1	Mrs. Glenna Collett Vare	0
Miss Enid Wilson (2 and 1)	1	Miss Helen Hicks	0
Miss Wanda Morgan	0	Miss Virginia Van Wie (2 and 1)	1
Miss Diana Fishwick (4 and 3)	1	Miss Maureen Orcutt	0
Miss Molly Gourlay (halved)	½	Mrs. O.S. Hill (halved)	½
Miss Elsie Corlett	0	Mrs. L.D. Cheney (4 and 3)	1
Total	3½	Total	2½
Grand Total—Great Britain and Ireland	3½	Grand Total—United States	5½

Captain—Miss Joyce Wethered

Captain—Miss Marion Hollins   Reserve—Mrs. Harley G. Higbie

1934
INTERNATIONAL MATCH FOR THE CURTIS CUP

Held at the Chevy Chase Club, Chevy Chase, Md.

September 27 and 28

FOURSOMES

Great Britain and Ireland	Points	United States	Points
Miss Molly Gourlay and Miss Pamela Barton (halved)	½	Miss Virginia Van Wie and Miss Charlotte Glutting (halved)	½
Miss Diana Fishwick and Miss Wanda Morgan	0	Miss Maureen Orcutt and Mrs. L.D. Cheney (2 up)	1
Miss Diana Plumpton and Mrs. J. B. Walker (2 and 1)	1	Mrs. O.S. Hill and Miss Lucile Robinson	0
Total	1½	Total	1½

SINGLES

Great Britain and Ireland	Points	United States	Points
Miss Diana Fishwick	0	Miss Virginia Van Wie (2 and 1)	1
Miss Molly Gourlay	0	Miss Maureen Orcutt (4 and 2)	1
Miss Pamela Barton	0	Mrs. L.D. Cheney (7 and 5)	1
Miss Wanda Morgan	0	Miss Charlotte Glutting (3 and 2)	1
Miss Diana Plumpton	0	Mrs. O.S. Hill (3 and 2)	1
Mrs. J.B. Walker (3 and 2)	1	Mrs. Frank Goldthwaite	0
Total	1	Total	5
Grand Total—Great Britain and Ireland	2½	Grand Total—United States	6½

Captain—Miss Doris Chambers   Reserve—Mrs. George Coats

Captain—Mrs. Glenna Collett Vare   Reserve—Miss Marion Miley

1936
INTERNATIONAL MATCH FOR THE CURTIS CUP

Held at King's Course, Gleneagles, Scotland

May 6

Great Britain and Ireland	Points	United States	Points
Miss Wanda Morgan and Mrs. Marjorie Ross Garon (halved)	½	Mrs. Glenna Collett Vare and Miss Patty Berg (halved)	½
Miss Pamela Barton and Mrs. J.B. Walker	0	Miss Maureen Orcutt and Mrs. L.D. Cheney (2 and 1)	1
Miss Jessie Anderson and Mrs. Andrew M. Holm (3 and 2)	1	Mrs. O.S. Hill and Miss Charlotte Glutting	0
Total	1½	Total	1½

SINGLES

Great Britain and Ireland	Points	United States	Points
Miss Wanda Morgan	0	Mrs. Glenna Collett Vare (3 and 2)	1
Mrs. Andrew M. Holm (4 and 3)	1	Miss Patty Berg	0
Miss Pamela Barton	0	Miss Charlotte Glutting (1 up)	1
Mrs. J.B. Walker	0	Miss Maureen Orcutt (1 up)	1
Miss Jessie Anderson (1 up)	1	Mrs. L.D. Cheney	0
Mrs. Marjorie Ross Garon (7 and 5)	1	Mrs. O.S. Hill	0
Total	3	Total	3

Grand Total—Great Britain and Ireland	4½	Grand Total—United States	4½

Captain—Miss Doris Chambers
Reserves—Miss Phyllis Wade, Miss Bridget Newell

Captain—Mrs. Glenna Collett Vare
Reserves—Miss Marion Miley, Mrs. Frank Goldthwaite

1938
INTERNATIONAL MATCH FOR THE CURTIS CUP

Held at the Essex County Club, Manchester, Mass.

September 7 and 8

FOURSOMES

Great Britain and Ireland	Points	United States	Points
Mrs. Andrew M. Holm and Miss Clarrie Tiernan (2 up)	1	Mrs. Julius A. Page, Jr., and Miss Maureen Orcutt	0
Miss Jessie Anderson and Miss Elsie Corlett (1 up)	1	Mrs. Glenna Collett Vare and Miss Patty Berg	0
Mrs. J.B. Walker and Miss Phyllis Wade (halved)	½	Miss Marion Miley and Miss Kathryn Hemphill (halved)	½
Total	2½	Total	½

SINGLES

Great Britain and Ireland	Points	United States	Points
Mrs. Andrew M. Holm	0	Mrs. Julius A. Page, Jr. (6 and 5)	1
Miss Jessie Anderson	0	Miss Patty Berg (1 up)	1
Miss Elsie Corlett	0	Miss Marion Miley (2 and 1)	1
Mrs. J.B. Walker	0	Mrs. Glenna Collett Vare (2 and 1)	1
Miss Clarrie Tiernan (2 and 1)	1	Miss Maureen Orcutt	0
Miss Nan Baird	0	Miss Charlotte Glutting (1 up)	1
Total	1	Total	5

Grand Total—Great Britain and Ireland	3½	Grand Total—United States	5½

Captain—Mrs. R.H. Wallace-Williamson

Non-playing Captain—Miss Frances E. Stebbins

1948
INTERNATIONAL MATCH FOR THE CURTIS CUP

Held at the Birkdale Golf Club, Birkdale, England

May 21 and 22

FOURSOMES

Great Britain and Ireland	Points	United States	Points
Miss Jacqueline Gordon and Miss Jean Donald (3 and 2)	1	Miss Louise Suggs and Miss Grace Lenczyk	0
Miss Philomena Garvey and Mrs. Zara Bolton	0	Mrs. Glenna Collett Vare and Miss Dorothy Kirby (4 and 3)	1
Miss Maureen Ruttle and Mrs. Val Reddan	0	Miss Dorothy Kielty and Mrs. Julius A. Page, Jr. (5 and 4)	1
Total	1	Total	2

SINGLES

Great Britain and Ireland	Points	United States	Points
Miss Philomena Garvey (halved)	½	Miss Louise Suggs (halved)	½
Miss Jean Donald (2 up)	1	Miss Dorothy Kirby	0
Miss Jacqueline Gordon	0	Miss Grace Lenczyk (5 and 3)	1
Mrs. Andrew M. Holm	0	Mrs. Julius A. Page, Jr. (3 and 2)	1
Miss Maureen Ruttle	0	Miss Polly Riley (3 and 2)	1
Mrs. Zara Bolton	0	Miss Dorothy Kielty (2 and 1)	1
Total	1½	Total	4½
Grand Total—Great Britain and Ireland	2½	Grand Total—United States	6½

Captain—Miss Doris E. Chambers
Reserve—Mrs. A.C. Critchley

Captain—Mrs. Glenna Collett Vare

1950
INTERNATIONAL MATCH FOR THE CURTIS CUP

Held at the Country Club of Buffalo, Williamsville, N.Y.

September 4 and 5

FOURSOMES

Great Britain and Ireland	Points	United States	Points
Miss Jean Donald and Mrs. George Valentine	0	Mrs. Dorothy Germain Porter and Miss Beverly Hanson (3 and 2)	1
Miss Frances Stephens and Miss Elizabeth Price (1 up)	1	Miss Helen Sigel and Miss Peggy Kirk	0
Miss Philomena Garvey and Miss Jeanne Bisgood	0	Miss Dorothy Kielty and Miss Dorothy Kirby (6 and 5)	1
Total	1	Total	2

SINGLES

Great Britain and Ireland	Points	United States	Points
Miss Frances Stephens (halved)	½	Mrs. Dorothy Germain Porter (halved)	½
Mrs. George Valentine	0	Miss Polly Riley (7 and 6)	1
Miss Jean Donald	0	Miss Beverly Hanson (6 and 5)	1
Miss Philomena Garvey	0	Miss Dorothy Kielty (3 and 1)	1
Miss Jeanne Bisgood	0	Miss Peggy Kirk (1 up)	1
Miss Elizabeth Price	0	Miss Grace Lenczyk (5 and 4)	1
Total	½	Total	5½
Grand Total—Great Britain and Ireland	1½	Grand Total—United States	7½

Captain—Mrs. A.C. Critchley

Captain—Mrs. Glenna Collett Vare

1952
INTERNATIONAL MATCH FOR THE CURTIS CUP

Held at the Links of The Honourable Company of Edinburgh Golfers, Muirfield, Scotland

June 6 and 7

FOURSOMES

Great Britain and Ireland	Points	United States	Points
Miss Jean Donald and Miss Elizabeth Price (3 and 2)	1	Miss Dorothy Kirby and Miss Grace DeMoss	0
Miss Frances Stephens and Mrs. George Valentine	0	Miss Claire Doran and Miss Marjorie Lindsay (6 and 4)	1
Miss Moira Paterson and Miss Philomena Garvey (2 and 1)	1	Miss Polly Riley and Miss Patricia O'Sullivan	0
Total	2	Total	1

SINGLES

Great Britain and Ireland	Points	United States	Points
Miss Jean Donald	0	Miss Dorothy Kirby	1
Miss Frances Stephens (2 and 1)	1	Miss Marjorie Lindsay	0
Miss Moira Paterson	0	Miss Polly Riley (6 and 4)	1
Miss Jeanne Bisgood (6 and 5)	1	Miss Mae Murray	0
Miss Philomena Garvey	0	Miss Claire Doran (3 and 2)	1
Miss Elizabeth Price (3 and 2)	1	Miss Grace DeMoss	0
Total	3	Total	3
Grand Total—Great Britain and Ireland	5	Grand Total—United States	4

Captain—Lady Katherine Cairns Reserve—Mrs. P.J. McCann

Captain—Mrs. Frank Goldthwaite

1954
INTERNATIONAL MATCH FOR THE CURTIS CUP

Held at the Merion Golf Club (East Course), Ardmore, Pa.

September 2 and 3

FOURSOMES

Great Britain and Ireland	Points	United States	Points
Miss Frances Stephens and Miss Elizabeth Price	0	Miss Mary Lena Faulk and Miss Polly Riley (6 and 4)	1
Mrs. George Valentine and Miss Philomena Garvey	0	Miss Claire Doran and Miss Patricia Lesser (6 and 5)	1
Mrs. R.T. Peel and Miss Janette Robertson	0	Miss Dorothy Kirby and Miss Barbara Romack (6 and 5)	1
Total	0	Total	3

SINGLES

Great Britain and Ireland	Points	United States	Points
Miss Frances Stephens (1 up)	1	Miss Mary Lena Faulk	0
Miss Jeanne Bisgood	0	Miss Claire Doran (4 and 3)	1
Miss Elizabeth Price	0	Miss Polly Riley (9 and 8)	1
Miss Philomena Garvey (3 and 1)	1	Miss Dorothy Kirby	0
Mrs. George Valentine	0	Mrs. Grace DeMoss Smith (4 and 3)	1
Miss Janette Robertson (3 and 1)	1	Miss Joyce Ziske	0
Total	3	Total	3
Grand Total—Great Britain and Ireland	3	Grand Total—United States	6

Captain—Mrs. John B. Beck

Captain—Mrs. Harrison F. Flippin

1956
INTERNATIONAL MATCH FOR THE CURTIS CUP

Held at Prince's Golf Club, Sandwich Bay, Kent, England

June 8 and 9

FOURSOMES

Great Britain and Ireland	Points	United States	Points
Mrs. George Valentine and Miss Philomena Garvey	0	Miss Patricia Lesser and Miss Margaret Smith (2 and 1)	1
Mrs. Roy Smith and Miss Elizabeth Price (5 and 3)	1	Miss Polly Riley and Miss Barbara Romack	0
Miss Janette Robertson and Miss Veronica Anstey	0	Miss Mary Ann Downey and Mrs. Philip J. Cudone (6 and 4)	1
Total	1	Total	2

SINGLES

Great Britain and Ireland	Points	United States	Points
Mrs. George Valentine (6 and 4)	1	Miss Patricia Lesser	0
Miss Philomena Garvey	0	Miss Margaret Smith (9 and 8)	1
Mrs. Roy Smith (1 up)	1	Miss Polly Riley	0
Miss Janette Robertson	0	Miss Barbara Romack (6 and 4)	1
Miss Angela Ward (4 and 3)	1	Miss Mary Ann Downey	0
Miss Elizabeth Price (7 and 6)	1	Miss Jane Nelson	0
Total	4	Total	2
Grand Total—Great Britain and Ireland	5	Grand Total—United States	4

Captain—Mrs. Sloan Bolton Reserve—Mrs. Nigel Howard

Captain—Mrs. Harrison F. Flippin

1958
INTERNATIONAL MATCH FOR THE CURTIS CUP

Held at Brae Burn Country Club, West Newton, Mass.

August 8 and 9

FOURSOMES

Great Britain and Ireland	Points	United States	Points
Mrs. Angela Ward Bonallack and Miss Elizabeth Price (2 and 1)	1	Miss Barbara Romack and Miss Polly Riley	0
Miss Janette Robertson and Mrs. Frances Smith (3 and 2)	1	Miss JoAnne Gunderson and Miss Anne Quast	0
Miss Bridget Jackson and Mrs. George Valentine	0	Miss Barbara McIntire and Mrs. Ann Casey Johnstone (6 and 5)	1
Total	2	Total	1

SINGLES

Great Britain and Ireland	Points	United States	Points
Mrs. George Valentine	0	Miss JoAnne Gunderson (2 up)	1
Mrs. Angela Ward Bonallack (halved)	½	Miss Barbara McIntire (halved)	½
Miss Elizabeth Price	0	Miss Anne Quast (4 and 2)	1
Miss Janette Robertson (3 and 2)	1	Mrs. Ann Casey Johnstone	0
Miss Bridget Jackson	0	Miss Barbara Romack (4 and 2)	1
Mrs. Frances Smith (2 up)	1	Miss Polly Riley	0
Total	2½	Total	3½
Grand Total—Great Britain and Ireland	4½	Grand Total—United States	4½

Non-playing Captain—Miss Daisy Ferguson
Reserve—Miss Dorothea T. Sommerville

Non-playing Captain—Mrs. Charles Dennehy
Reserves—Miss Meriam Bailey, Miss Anne Richardson

WORLD AMATEUR TEAM CHAMPIONSHIP

THE EISENHOWER TROPHY

Presented in October, 1958
by American Friends of Golf
through The Royal and Ancient Golf Club
and The Royal and Ancient Golf Club
of St. Andrews, Scotland

HISTORY

1958—A plan for a World Amateur Team Championship was conceived by the United States Golf Association and presented to the Royal and Ancient Golf Club of St. Andrews, Scotland, in March, 1958. The two governing bodies agreed to join hands in implementing the idea. As a result, a planning conference was held in Washington, D.C., in May. Representatives of national amateur golf associations in 35 countries attended, airplane transportation being provided by American friends of golf and with the cooperation of the Department of State. The conference created the World Amateur Golf Council, with 32 member organizations, to conduct the Championship. Friends of American golf presented a handsome silver trophy which, with President Eisenhower's approval, was named "The Eisenhower Trophy." The inscription reads: "To foster friendship and sportsmanship among the Peoples of the World." The first Championship was held over the old course at St. Andrews, Scotland, in October, 1958, and 115 players representing 29 countries assembled to compete over four rounds of stroke play. Each country was allowed four players. Each team's score each day was the total of its three best individual scores, and the sum of the daily totals was the team total for the Championship. At the conclusion of the four rounds, Australia set up a score of 918 and appeared to be the winner until the United States came from nowhere to tie. William Hyndman, III, of Philadelphia, in the last group, made a great 3 at the 17th, where par would be 4, and a solid 4 at the 18th for an individual 72 to create the tie. Great Britain-Ireland was one stroke away, New Zealand was fourth at 921, and Argentina was fifth at 940. In the 18-hole playoff, the Australians finished brilliantly to score 222 and win by two strokes. Their ultimate margin resulted from birdie 3s on the last hole by Bruce Devlin and Robert Stevens, team Captain. The lowest individual scores for the 72 holes were 301s by Hyndman, Devlin, and Reid Jack, of Great Britain.

WORLD AMATEUR TEAM CHAMPIONSHIP FOR THE EISENHOWER TROPHY

1958—At St. Andrews, Scotland (Old Course)

*Australia	918	Italy	963	Japan	1006
United States	918	Belgium	964	Brazil	1009
Great Britain & Ireland	919	Philippines	970	Venezuela	1015
New Zealand	921	Spain	974	Finland	1017
Argentina	940	India	981	Malaya	1029
Canada	945	Switzerland	981	Norway	1040
South Africa	945	Bermuda	985	Republic of China	1049
France	949	Germany	998	Portugal	1049
Sweden	957	Kenya	998	Austria	1071
		Netherlands	1005	Iceland	1084

*Won in play-off with United States: Australia, 222; United States, 224.

1958
FIRST WORLD AMATEUR TEAM CHAMPIONSHIP
FOR THE EISENHOWER TROPHY

Held at the Old Course, St. Andrews, Scotland, October 8-11 and 13.
Yardage—6,996. Par 72. 29 Team Entries.

Team score consisted of three best individual scores in each round.
*Indicates Captain.

		1st Rd.	2nd Rd.	3rd Rd.	4th Rd.	72-Hole Score	Play-Off
AUSTRALIA	Grand total	244	226	221	227	918	222
Douglas W. Bachli		81	77	78	79	(315)	77
Peter A. Toogood		84	76	71	79	(310)	75
Bruce W. Devlin		81	73	74	73	(301)	72
*Robert F. Stevens		82	77	76	75	(310)	75
UNITED STATES	Grand total	233	232	225	228	918	224
Charles R. Coe		74	77	76	[illegible]	(305)	73
William Hyndman, III		79	77	73	72	(301)	78
William J. Patton		80	78	76	79	(313)	75
Dr. Frank M. Taylor, Jr.		81	79	76	78	(314)	76
*Robert T. Jones, Jr.							
GREAT BRITAIN AND IRELAND	Grand total	227	234	230	228	919	
Joseph B. Carr		79	84	78	76	(317)	
R. Reid Jack		72	77	74	78	(301)	
Arthur H. Perowne		81	78	79	75	(313)	
Guy B. Wolstenholme		76	79	78	77	(310)	
*Gerald H. Micklem							
NEW ZEALAND	Grand total	236	226	225	234	921	
Robert J. Charles		74	74	76	81	(305)	
John D. Durry		81	78	77	83	(319)	
Stuart G. Jones		81	75	80	78	(314)	
Edward J. MacDougall		88	77	72	75	(312)	
*James A. Scouler							
ARGENTINA	Grand total	236	242	232	230	940	
Carlos Bracht		85	82	75	81	(323)	
Oscar E. Cella		78	79	79	79	(315)	
Jorge C. Ledesma, Jr.		82	81	78	73	(314)	
Hugo Nicora		76	82	83	78	(319)	
*Dr. Eduardo H. Maglione							
CANADA	Grand total	240	241	228	236	945	
Douglas Bajus		79	80	77	81	(317)	
Bruce Castator		79	84	76	81	(320)	
Eric Hanson		82	79	83	81	(325)	
Robert Kidd		83	82	75	74	(314)	
*John M. Blair							
SOUTH AFRICA	Grand total	246	231	229	239	945	
James R. Boyd		81	82	77	81	(321)	
Denis Hutchinson		82	75	78	83	(318)	
Arthur A. Stewart		86	89	78	79	(332)	
Arthur Walker		83	74	74	79	(310)	
*Maurice Tom Jackson							
FRANCE	Grand total	242	240	231	236	949	
Henri de Lamaze		77	77	75	78	(307)	
Marius Bardana		83	85	77	84	(329)	
Roger Lagarde		83	81	79	74	(317)	
Jean-Pierre Hirigoyen		82	82	82	84	(330)	
*Jacques Leglise							
SWEDEN	Grand total	251	242	227	237	957	
Gunnar Carlander		82	79	72	80	(313)	
Rune Karlfeldt		89	84	76	80	(329)	
Gustaf A. Bielke		84	81	79	79	(323)	
Bengt Moller		85	82	79	78	(324)	
*Sune Malmstrom							
ITALY	Grand total	246	239	237	241	963	
Franco Bevione		81	83	81	80	(325)	
Nadi Berruti		85	77	79	83	(324)	
Angelo Croce		80	79	77	78	(314)	
Alberto Schiaffino		89	85	81	84	(339)	
*Conte Giuseppe Sabini							

First World Amateur Team Championship – Continued

		1st Rd.	2nd Rd.	3rd Rd.	4th Rd.	72-Hole Score
BELGIUM	Grand total	245	250	229	240	964
Jacques Moerman		78	84	77	84	(323)
Eric Tavernier		80	85	73	79	(317)
Freddy Rodesch		87	83	79	78	(327)
Paul Rolin		94	83	81	83	(341)
*J. A. du Vivier						
PHILIPPINES	Grand total	248	245	239	238	970
Luis Silverio		75	81	77	75	(308)
Alex Prieto		86	85	85	89	(345)
Francisco Reyes, Jr.		87	79	89	82	(337)
Mel Gana		87	86	77	81	(331)
*Manuel J. Gonzalez						
SPAIN	Grand total	249	254	234	237	974
Juan A. Andreu		90	82	83	80	(335)
Duke of Fernan-Nunez		85	84	75	82	(326)
*Ivan Maura		81	88	76	75	(320)
Luis Rezola		83	90	88	84	(345)
INDIA	Grand total	244	251	237	249	981
*I. S. Malik		82	92	83	89	(346)
R. K. Pitamber		77	90	77	79	(323)
Capt. P. G. Sethi		85	77	80	82	(324)
A. S. Malik		86	84	80	88	(338)
SWITZERLAND	Grand total	249	244	248	245	981
Olivier Barras		82	78	80	82	(322)
Andre Barras		85	89	85	86	(345)
Peter Gutermann		82	80	87	77	(326)
John Panchaud		89	86	78	87	(340)
*Hans Schweizer						
BERMUDA	Grand total	249	251	240	245	985
*George E. Wardman		80	80	79	82	(321)
Ronald A. Dwyer		87	87	82	88	(344)
C. H. Ford Hutchings		82	84	79	77	(322)
Richard S. L. Pearman		88	88	87	86	(349)
GERMANY	Grand total	260	260	241	237	998
Hans Lampert		84	83	81	80	(328)
Erik Sellschopp		86	85	77	85	(333)
Werner Goetz		99	93	91	82	(365)
Jean Phillipps		90	92	83	75	(340)
*Heinz O. Krings						
KENYA	Grand total	253	259	239	247	998
*William N. B. Loudon		94	87	87	84	(352)
Alistair J. Robertson		85	86	81	88	(340)
Peter G. Tait		84	86	79	82	(331)
Christopher D. Sykes		84	92	79	81	(336)
NETHERLANDS	Grand total	250	256	253	246	1005
Dr. J. F. Dudok van Heel		82	82	81	81	(326)
A. F. Knappert		83	83	83	77	(326)
W. F. Smit		85	96	93	88	(362)
W. van Moorsel		88	91	89	91	(359)
*A. M. Groskamp						
JAPAN	Grand total	250	255	244	257	1006
Kiyoshi Ishimoto		80	85	79	85	(329)
Ichizo Oguri		85	85	83	88	(341)
Junzo Shibamoto		88	85	82	85	(340)
Naoyasu Nabeshima		85	85	87	87	(344)
*Shun Nomura						
BRAZIL	Grand total	253	262	249	245	1009
Sylvio Pinto Freire, Jr.		85	88	83	82	(338)
Humberto C. de Almeida		80	87	85	86	(338)
Joao Barbosa Correa		88	87	81	82	(338)
Raul Borges		99	90	90	81	(360)
*Seymour G. Marvin						
VENEZUELA	Grand total	264	261	242	248	1015
*Jack Corrie		98	83	81	78	(340)
Guillermo Behrens		90	86	85	87	(348)
Jack Alexandre, Jr.		87	100	81	85	(353)
Fernan Frias		87	92	80	85	(344)

First World Amateur Team Championship – Continued

		1st Rd.	2nd Rd.	3rd Rd.	4th Rd.	72-Hole Score
FINLAND	Grand total	265	255	242	255	1017
Jalo Gronlund		84	87	81	82	(334)
Mauri Vikstrom		87	79	80	86	(332)
Eero Hanninen		94	89	81	87	(351)
*Taavi Pohjanpalo		98	100	86	92	(376)
MALAYA	Grand total	262	257	252	258	1029
*W. J. Gibb		84	83	87	85	(339)
J. C. Hutcheson		83	96	80	87	(346)
J. W. R. Muraille		95	87	90	86	(358)
K. C. MacNair		97	87	85	87	(356)
NORWAY	Grand total	261	262	263	254	1040
John Johansen		87	86	91	85	(349)
Kare Kittilsen		87	87	86	91	(351)
Eric Osland		87	91	87	84	(349)
Einar Wahlstrom		100	89	90	85	(364)
*Arild Wahlstrom						
CHINA, REPUBLIC OF	Grand total	269	268	260	252	1049
Chang Tung-Chang		80	84	78	78	(320)
Jeffrey Koo		94	85	91	87	(357)
Richard Koo		95	99	91	87	(372)
*Eddie Tseng						
PORTUGAL	Grand total	259	269	265	256	1049
*Visconde de Pereira Machado		85	90	86	91	(352)
Duarte Espirito Santo Silva		85	88	87	90	(350)
Jose de Sousa e Melo		92	104	92	83	(371)
Manuel de Brito e Cunha		89	91	93	83	(356)
AUSTRIA	Grand total	268	272	269	262	1071
Heinrich Harrer		86	91	99	88	(364)
Hugo Hild		95	92	92	88	(367)
Alexander Maculan		87	89	83	86	(345)
Attilio Conte de Smecchia		100	92	94	94	(380)
*Hugo M. Eckelt						
ICELAND	Grand total	278	277	273	271	1084
*Magnus Gudmundsson		83	87	85	81	(336)
Olafur Agust Olafsson		95	94	93	102	(384)
Hermann Ingimarssen		95	96	85	96	(372)
Sveinn Avsaeksson		105	99	95	94	(393)

AMERICAS GOLF CUP MATCH

THE AMERICAS GOLF CUP

Presented to the

Royal Canadian Golf Association
Asociacion Mexicana de Golf
United States Golf Association

in August, 1952, by

JEROME P. BOWES, JR.
President of the Western Golf Association, 1950-1951

HISTORY

1952–The United States played an unofficial match against Canada prior to the 1951 Amateur Championship and was considering the institution of a regular series when the Western Golf Association proposed to sponsor a team for a match with Mexico. The USGA suggested combining the two proposals into a tripartite match, and the Western Golf Association graciously acceded. The Americas Cup subsequently was presented to the Royal Canadian Golf Association, the Asociacion Mexicana de Golf, and the USGA by Jerome P. Bowes, Jr., of Chicago, Ill., President of the Western Golf Association during 1950 and 1951. The United States Team narrowly won the first match played at the Seattle Golf Club, Seattle, Wash. The final score was United States, 12; Canada, 10; Mexico, 5.

The first three players in the Canadian line-up defeated simultaneously both their Mexican and United States opponents. It appeared to be United States depth, rather than first line strength, which turned the tide. The competition took the form of three 36-hole three-ball "sixsomes" on the first day and six 36-hole three-ball matches on the second day. In each encounter, representatives of one country played simultaneously against the other two, one point being awarded for each victory and all matches being played to a conclusion.

1954–The second match was held at the London Hunt and Country Club, London, Ontario, and the United States Team again narrowly finished ahead of the Canadians. The final score was United States, 14; Canada, 13; Mexico, 0. The United States won two of the three foursomes against Canada. The one-point difference in these was decisive. In the six singles matches between American and Canadian players, none was decided before the 35th hole was completed. Three were finished at the home hole, one went 37 holes and the other 38. Don Cherry won the No. 1 match for the United States from Canada's Nick Weslock after two extra holes. Billy Joe Patton played the last three holes in birdie-par-birdie to defeat Walter McElroy by 2 and 1. Charles R. Coe, 3 down after 29 holes, won four in a row and defeated Phil Farley, 1 up. Canada's points in singles matches against the Americans were earned by Donald Doe, Moe Norman and Douglas Silverberg.

1956–The United States won a clear-cut victory in the third match while the host Mexican Team defeated Canada to finish second. The score was United States, 29½; Mexico, 13; Canada, 11. The competition was staged at the Club Campestre at Mexico City. Harvie Ward, winner of the 1955 and 1956 United States Amateur Championships, won all four of his singles matches and teamed with Billy Joe Patton to earn four more points in the foursomes. Patton, too, was unbeaten in the singles. The format was changed to two separate 18-hole encounters each day, thus doubling the number of points available. Tied matches were not played to a conclusion, the point being split between the two sides. Three-ball "sixsomes" were again played on the first day and three-ball matches on the second.

1958–On the Lake Course of the Olympic Country Club, prior to the Amateur Championship, the United States led and Canada was second in each of the four phases of the competition and the totals were: United States, 30; Canada, 17; Mexico, 7. The teams played three 18-hole three-ball "sixsome" matches in the morning and six 18-hole three-ball matches in the afternoon on each of two days. Billy Joe Patton, the United States Captain, and Dr. Frank M. Taylor, Jr., who played the No. 1 singles the first day, won all their matches in two three-balls and one "sixsome" to earn all six points available to them. Charles R. Coe played in all four rounds without defeat but was halved twice in "sixsomes" to earn seven of a possible eight points. Gary Cowan, 19, of Canada, swept both his three-ball matches, in which he played No. 2 and then No. 1, and shared in two wins and two ties in "sixsomes" for seven points.

THE AMERICAS GOLF CUP MATCH

Year				Site
1952	U. S. 12	Canada 10	Mexico 5	Seattle Golf Club, Seattle, Washington
1954	U. S. 14	Canada 13	Mexico 0	London Hunt and Country Club, London, Ontario, Canada
1956	U. S. 29½	Mexico 13	Canada ...11½	Club Campestre de la Ciudad de Mexico, D. F.
1958	U. S. 30	Canada 17	Mexico 7	Olympic C. C. (Lake Course), San Francisco, California

1952
FIRST INTERNATIONAL MATCH FOR THE AMERICAS CUP
Held at the Seattle Golf Club, Seattle, Wash.

CANADA	MEXICO	UNITED STATES
Percy Clogg	Reynaldo Avila	William C. Campbell
Phil Farley	Carlos Belmont	Charles R. Coe
Peter C. Kelly	Percy Clifford	Joseph F. Gagliardi
Jerry Kesselring	Alejandro Cumming	Frank R. Stranahan
Walter McElroy	Fernando Gonzales	Sam Urzetta
Nick K. Weslock	Roberto Morris	Kenneth Venturi
		E. Harvie Ward, Jr.

FOURSOMES

CANADA	vs. Mex.	vs. U.S.	MEXICO	vs. Can.	vs. U.S.	UNITED STATES	vs. Can.	vs. Mex.
McElroy Kesselring	1 up (39 holes)	0	Avila Gonzales	0	0	Ward Venturi	11 and 10	10 and 8
Weslock Farley	0	1 up	Clifford Morris	1 up	1 up	Stranahan Coe	0	0
Clogg Kelly	1 up	0	Belmont Cumming	0	0	Urzetta Gagliardi	6 and 4	5 and 4
Total	2	1		1	1		2	2

SINGLES

CANADA	vs. Mes.	vs. U.S.	MEXICO	vs. Can.	vs. U.S.	UNITED STATES	vs. Can.	vs. Mex.
McElroy	10 and 9	4 and 3	Morris	0	0	Stranahan	0	9 and 8
Kesselring	11 and 9	1 up (38 holes)	Gonzales	0	0	Ward	0	13 and 11
Weslock	12 and 10	3 and 2	Avila	0	0	Coe	0	9 and 8
Farley	9 and 8	0	Cumming	0	0	Campbell	6 and 5	10 and 8
Clogg	0	0	Belmont	3 and 2	0	Venturi	10 and 9	12 and 11
Kelly	0	0	Clifford	10 and 8	2 and 1	Urzetta	11 and 10	0
Total	4	3		2	1		3	5
Grand Total	6	4		3	2		5	7

SUMMARY OF TEAM POINTS

	Canada	Mexico	United States
Foursomes	2	1	
Singles	4	2	
Totals	6	3	
Foursomes	1		2
Singles	3		3
Totals	4		5
Foursomes		1	2
Singles		1	5
Totals		2	7
Foursome Totals	3	2	4
Singles Totals	7	3	8
Grand Totals	10	5	12

1954
SECOND INTERNATIONAL MATCH FOR THE AMERICAS CUP
Held at the London Hunt and Country Club, London, Ont., Canada, August 12 and 13

CANADA	MEXICO	UNITED STATES
Donald Doe	Carlos Belmont	William C. Campbell
Philip Farley	Alejandro Cumming	Don Cherry
Robert Fleming	Juan A. Estrada	Charles R. Coe
Walter McElroy	Fernando Mendez	Joseph W. Conrad
Moe Norman	Roberto Morris, Jr.	Dale Morey
Douglas Silverberg	Carlos Porras	William J. Patton
Nick K. Weslock	Antonio Rivas	E. Harvie Ward, Jr.

FOURSOMES

CANADA	vs. Mex.	vs. U.S.	MEXICO	vs. Can.	vs. U.S.	UNITED STATES	vs. Can.	vs. Mex.
Weslock McElory	12 and 11	4 and 3	Cumming Mendez	0	0	Campbell Patton	0	6 and 5
Farley Silverberg	6 and 5	0	Estrada Morris	0	0	Cherry Morey	1 up	8 and 7
Doe Fleming	9 and 8	0	Porras Rivas	0	0	Ward Conrad	5 and 4	11 and 10
Total	3	1		0	0		2	3

SINGLES

CANADA	vs. Mex.	vs. U.S.	MEXICO	vs. Can.	vs. U.S.	UNITED STATES	vs. Can.	vs. Mex.
Weslock	9 and 8	0	Rivas	0	0	Cherry	1 up (38 holes)	8 and 7
McElory	7 and 5	0	Morris	0	0	Patton	2 and 1	7 and 6
Doe	7 and 5	1 up	Mendez	0	0	Morey	0	7 and 6
Norman	7 and 6	1 up (37 holes)	Belmont	0	0	Campbell	0	7 and 6
Farley	7 and 5	0	Cumming	0	0	Coe	1 up	8 and 6
Silverberg	7 and 5	1 up	Estrada	0	0	Ward	0	8 and 7
Total	6	3		0	0		3	6
Grand Total	9	4		0	0		5	9

SUMMARY OF TEAM POINTS

	Canada	Mexico	United States
Foursomes	3	0	
Singles	6	0	
Totals	9	0	
Foursomes	1	0	2
Singles	3	0	3
Totals	4	0	5
Foursomes		0	3
Singles		0	6
Totals		0	9
Foursome Totals	4	0	5
Singles Totals	9	0	9
Grand Totals	13	0	14

1956
THIRD INTERNATIONAL MATCH FOR THE AMERICAS CUP

Held at the Club Campestre de la Ciudad de Mexico, D.F., October 27 and 28.
All Matches at 18 Holes

CANADA	MEXICO	UNITED STATES
Douglas Bajus	Alejandro Cumming	Joe Campbell
Robert Kidd	Juan A. Estrada	William C. Campbell, Captain
George Knudson	Tomas Lehman	Joseph W. Conrad
Joseph LeBlanc	Ignacio Lopez, Jr.	William J. Patton
Jerry Magee	Fernando Mendez	Hillman Robbins, Jr.
Gordon MacKenzie	Antonio Rivas	Kenneth Venturi
Douglas Silverberg	Armando Rivero	E. Harvie Ward, Jr.
Non-playing Captain: James P. Anglin	Non-playing Captain: Pedro Suinaga	

FOURSOMES

	CANADA	vs. Mex.	vs. U.S.	MEXICO	vs. Can.	vs. U.S.	UNITED STATES	vs. Can.	vs. Mex.
a.m.:	Magee, Knudson	5 & 4	0	Estrada, Rivero	0	0	Ward, Patton	3 & 2	5 & 4
	Kidd, Silverberg	2 & 1	0	Rivas, Lopez	0	0	Venturi, J. Campbell	6 & 4	5 & 4
	LeBlanc, MacKenzie	0	0	Cumming, Mendez	3 & 2	0	Conrad, Robbins	3 & 1	1 up
	Points, a.m.	2	0		1	0		3	3
p.m.:	Magee, Knudson	0	0	Cumming, Mendez	2 & 1	0	Venturi, J. Campbell	2 & 1	1 up
	Silverberg, Bajus	0	0	Estrada, Lehman	4 & 3	halved	Conrad, Robbins	3 & 2	halved
	LeBlanc, MacKenzie	0	0	Rivas, Lopez	2 & 1	0	Ward, Patton	3 & 2	4 & 3
	Points, p.m.	0	0		3	½		3	2½
	Total	2	0		4	½		6	5½

SINGLES

	CANADA	vs. Mex.	vs. U.S.	MEXICO	vs. Can.	vs. U.S.	UNITED STATES	vs. Can.	vs. Mex.
a.m.:	Magee	2 up	0	Lopez	0	0	Ward	1 up	2 & 1
	Kidd	halved	0	Rivas	halved	0	Conrad	3 & 2	2 & 1
	LeBlanc	3 & 2	0	Mendez	0	0	Patton	1 up	2 & 1
	Knudson	halved	1 up	Lehman	halved	1 up	Robbins	0	0
	Silverberg	0	halved	Estrada	2 & 1	2 & 1	J. Campbell	halved	0
	MacKenzie	halved	0	Cumming	halved	0	W. Campbell	3 & 2	6 & 5
	Points, a.m.	3½	1½		2½	2		4½	4
p.m.:	LeBlanc	0	0	Rivas	1 up	0	Ward	2 & 1	3 & 2
	Magee	6 & 4	3 & 1	Mendez	0	0	Conrad	0	5 & 4
	Kidd	4 & 3	0	Lopez	0	0	Patton	4 & 3	7 & 5
	Bajus	0	0	Estrada	4 & 2	1 up	Robbins	4 & 2	0
	Knudson	2 & 1	halved	Cumming	0	0	J. Campbell	halved	2 & 1
	Silverberg	0	0	Lehman	3 & 2	0	W. Campbell	3 & 2	2 & 1
	Points, p.m.	3	1½		3	1		4½	5
	Total	6½	3		5½	3		9	9
	GRAND TOTAL	8½	3		9½	3½		15	14½

SUMMARY OF TEAM POINTS

	Canada	Mexico	United States
Foursomes	2	4	
Singles	6½	5½	
Totals	8½	9½	
Foursomes	0		6
Singles	3		9
Totals	3		15
Foursomes		½	5½
Singles		3	9
Totals		3½	14½
Foursome Totals	2	4½	11½
Singles Totals	9½	8½	18
Grand totals	11½	13	29½

1958
FOURTH INTERNATIONAL MATCH FOR THE AMERICAS CUP

Held at the Olympic Country Club, San Francisco, Calif.
September 5 and 6
All Matches at 18 Holes

CANADA	MEXICO	UNITED STATES
Douglas Bajus	Juan A. Estrada	Rex Baxter, Jr.
Gordon R. Ball	Enrique Farias, Jr.	Charles R. Coe
Bruce Castator	Ignacio Lopez, Jr.	William Hyndman, III
Gary Cowan	Fernando Mendez	William J. Patton, Captain
Eric Hanson	Jose L. Ortega	Hillman Robbins, Jr.
John Johnston	Rafael Quiroz	Dr. Frank M. Taylor, Jr.
Robert Kidd	Mauricio Urdaneta	E. Harvie Ward, Jr.
Non-playing Captain: V.C. Holdroyd	Non-playing Captain: Rodolfo Patron	

September 5—FOURSOMES

CANADA	vs. Mex.	vs. U.S.	MEXICO	vs. Can.	vs. U.S.	UNITED STATES	vs. Can.	vs. Mex.
Castator Hanson	0	0	Lopez Farias	2 up	2 & 1	Robbins Ward	2 up	0
Kidd Johnston	5 & 3	0	Urdaneta Mendez	0	0	Hyndman Taylor	1 up	3 & 2
Bajus Cowan	5 & 4	halved	Estrada Ortega	0	0	Coe Baxter	halved	2 & 1
Points, Foursomes	2	½		1	1		2½	2

September 5—SINGLES

CANADA	vs. Mex.	vs. U.S.	MEXICO	vs. Can.	vs. U.S.	UNITED STATES	vs. Can.	vs. Mex.
Castator	0	0	Estrada	1 up	0	Taylor	6 & 5	6 & 4
Cowan	7 & 6	3 & 2	Quiroz	0	0	Ward	0	4 & 3
Ball	0	0	Lopez	3 & 1	0	Coe	6 & 4	4 & 3
Bajus	2 & 1	0	Urdaneta	0	0	Baxter	2 up	2 & 1
Johnson	2 & 1	halved	Mendez	0	0	Hyndman	halved	5 & 4
Kidd	1 up	0	Ortega	0	0	Patton	3 & 1	2 up
Points, Singles	4	1½		2	0		4½	6
Totals, Sept. 5	6	2		3	1		7	8

September 6—FOURSOMES

CANADA	vs. Mex.	vs. U.S.	MEXICO	vs. Can.	vs. U.S.	UNITED STATES	vs. Can.	vs. Mex.
Castator Ball	0	0	Mendez Farias	1 up	0	Robbins Patton	6 & 5	2 up
Bajus Cowan	4 & 3	halved	Lopez Ortega	0	0	Ward Coe	halved	3 & 2
Johnston Kidd	halved	0	Estrada Urdaneta	halved	0	Baxter Hyndman	6 & 5	6 & 4
Points, Foursomes	1½	½		1½	0		2½	3

September 6—SINGLES

CANADA	vs. Mex.	vs. U.S.	MEXICO	vs. Can.	vs. U.S.	UNITED STATES	vs. Can.	vs. Mex.
Cowan	6 & 5	5 & 3	Lopez	0	0	Robbins	0	4 & 3
Hanson	halved	0	Farias	halved	0	Coe	6 & 4	8 & 6
Castator	halved	0	Estrada	halved	0	Patton	2 & 1	1 up
Johnston	3 & 2	0	Ortega	0	0	Ward	3 & 2	4 & 2
Bajus	2 & 1	4 & 3	Urdaneta	0	halved	Baxter	0	halved
Kidd	4 & 3	0	Mendez	0	0	Taylor	2 & 1	5 & 4
Points, Singles	5	2		1	½		4	5½
Totals, Sept. 6	6½	2½		2½	½		6½	8½
Grand Total	12½	4½		5½	1½		13½	16½

SUMMARY OF TEAM POINTS

	Canada	Mexico	United States
Foursomes	3½	2½	
Singles	9	3	
Totals	12½	5½	
Foursomes	1		5
Singles	3½		8½
Totals	4½		13½
Foursomes		1	5
Singles		½	11½
Totals		1½	16½
Foursome Totals	4½	3½	10
Single Totals	12½	3½	20
Grand Totals	17	7	30

Part Two

1960 - 1980

OPEN CHAMPIONS

GARY PLAYER
1965

LEE TREVINO
1968-71

ARNOLD PALMER
1960

OPEN CHAMPIONS

BILL CASPER, JR.
1959-66

GENE LITTLER
1961

HALE IRWIN
1974-79

OPEN CHAMPIONSHIP

CHAMPIONSHIP CUP

Presented in 1895 by the

UNITED STATES GOLF ASSOCIATION

Original trophy destroyed by fire September, 1946.

Replaced by the Association in 1947.

HISTORY

1960—Arnold Palmer, 31, of Ligonier, Pa., made a record comeback in the final round to win the Championship. He trailed Mike Souchak, the 54-hole leader at 208, by seven strokes entering the last round. Palmer birdied six of the first seven holes, was out in 30, and finished with a 65. Palmer had a score of 72-71-72-65—280 at the par-71 Cherry Hills Country Club near Denver, Colo. Jack Nicklaus, of Columbus, Ohio, recorded the lowest score ever made by an amateur in the Open with his 71-71-69-71—282 to take second place. This was the highest finish by an amateur since John Goodman won the Championship in 1933. Besides his record comeback, Palmer set one other record and tied a third. His 65 was the lowest score ever in the fourth round by a winner. His 30 on the first nine tied the mark for the lowest nine-hole score in an Open set by James B. McHale, Jr., an amateur, in 1947. Souchak, the 36-hole leader with a record 68-67—135, tied for third at 283 with E.J. (Dutch) Harrison, Ted Kroll, Dow Finsterwald, Julius Boros and Jack Fleck. Ben Hogan made a gallant try for an unprecedented fifth Open victory. Needing only pars (5 and 4) on the final two holes for a score of 280, Hogan went 4 over par with a 6 and a 7. He finished in a tie for ninth at 284 with Jerry Barber and amateur Don Cherry. The three-day gallery, estimated at 43,878, was a USGA Championship record, as was the opening-day crowd of 14,067. The total prize money, announced originally as $50,000, was increased by a bonus to $60,720 in the Championship proper. In addition, $1,300 was awarded in 13 Sectional Qualifying Championships to make the gross a record $62,020. Two other records were established. Art Wall, Jr. recorded the lowest 36-hole score in Sectional Qualifying history with a 63-65—128 at the Twin Hills Country Club, Oklahoma City, Okla. The entry reached a new high of 2,453. Fifty-six Districts held local qualifying rounds and there were 13 Sectional Qualifying Championships, all at 36 holes.

1961—Gene A. Littler, 30, of San Diego, Calif., the only player to break par twice, won the Championship by a single stroke with rounds of 73-68-72-68—281 at the par-70 Oakland Hills Country Club near Detroit. With this victory Littler became the eighth player in history to win both the Open and Amateur Championships. Doug Sanders, the 54-hole leader, and Bob Goalby were tied for second place at 282. Amateur Jack Nicklaus, runner-up in 1960, and Mike Souchak finished in a tie for fourth with 284s. The first-round was led by Bobby Brue with a 69. Sanders and Bob Rosburg shared the lead at 36 holes with 139. Thirteen contenders had scores ranging from 210 through 214 entering the final round. Sanders' 210 led, with Littler three shots behind. When all other contenders finished at 282 or higher, it settled down to a Littler-Sanders duel. After Littler took a one-over-par 5 on the final hole for 68, Sanders came to the 72nd hole needing a birdie for a 71 to tie. His third shot from off the front edge of the green barely missed the cup. Oakland Hills was a somewhat less stringent test than in 1951 when Ben Hogan won with 287. Only two rounds were played under par in 1951 while 18 were recorded in 1961. Defending Champion Arnold Palmer just made the cut at 149 but scored two 70s the final day for a 289 total. Ben Hogan, also at 289, failed to finish in the first ten for the first time since 1940 (except when sickness prevented him from starting in 1949 and 1957). Four former Open Champions, Cary Middlecoff, Julius Boros, Lew Worsham, and Ed Furgol, failed to make the 36-hole cut. A record gallery estimated at 47,975 saw the Championship, 4,097 more than the previous record of 43,878 set in 1960 in Denver. The last two days' attendance set records. There were 20,439 on the final day (3,912 more than the record of 16,527 in 1957) and 15,225 the second day (474 more than the record of 14,751 in 1960). The entry was 2,449. A record prize fund of $68,300 was awarded. In addition to the Championship prize money of $60,500 for professionals, a total of $7,800 was awarded in the Sectional Qualifying Championships. Fifty-eight districts held Local Qualifying rounds and there were 13 Sectional Qualifying Championships.

1962—In his first year as a professional, Jack Nicklaus, 22, won the 62nd Open Championship at the Oakmont Country Club, Oakmont, Pa. Not since the days of Bob Jones had the same person been the latest winner of both the Open and the Amateur Championships. The Open was decided by an 18-hole playoff after Nicklaus and Arnold Palmer, the 1960 Champion, tied at 283, one under par. During the playoff Nicklaus went ahead by one stroke on the first hole; led by four strokes after six holes; and eventually won by 71 to 74. It was the first victory as a professional for Nicklaus, who won the Amateur Championship in 1959 and 1961. On the third day, before 24,492 spectators, the greatest gallery in the history of the Open, Nicklaus and Palmer staged a classic duel during the final holes. They were tied after 67 holes and both parred in. On the 72nd green

Nicklaus missed a 15 foot putt for a birdie and then watched Palmer, playing in the next group, fail to make a 20-foot putt for a birdie. Nicklaus' scores were 72-70-72-69–283. Palmer's rounds were 71-68-73-71–283. Nicklaus, renowned for his long driving, was also a remarkable putter: he three-putted only once in 90 holes on the testing Oakmont greens. Palmer, on the other hand, three-putted 10 times. The first-round leader was Gene Littler, the defending Champion, who scored 69. After 36 holes Palmer and Bob Rosburg were tied at 139. Palmer and Bobby Nichols shared the 54-hole lead at 212. During the last day six players–Nicklaus, Palmer, Rosburg, Nichols, Phil Rodgers and Gary Player–held the lead at various times. Nichols and Rodgers, who made an 8 on the par-4 17th hole during the first round, tied for third at 285. Deane R. Beman, whose 67 in the fourth round was the lowest 18-hole score of the Championship, was low amateur with 293; Beman finished tied for 14th. Records were established in both entries and attendance. The entry of 2,474 surpassed the 2,453 mark set in 1960. The three-day attendance was 62,300, far ahead of the previous record of 47,975 set in 1961. Prize money of $73,800 in the Championship proper included bonuses of $2,500 each to Nicklaus and Palmer in the playoff; Nicklaus received $17,500 all told. Additionally, $7,800 was awarded to professionals in 13 Sectional Qualifying Championships, for a grand total of $81,600 for the entire Championship. Ben Hogan, who was not exempt from qualifying for the first time since 1941, was prevented by bursitis in a shoulder from trying to qualify sectionally.

1963–Julius Boros won the Championship for the second time by defeating Arnold Palmer and Jacky Cupit in an 18-hole playoff at The Country Club, Brookline, Mass. Strong and gusty winds caused playing conditions as severe as any in the Open's history, and the lowest 72-hole scores of 293 were nine over par, the highest since 1935, when Sam Parks won with 299 at Oakmont. Boros' rounds were 71-74-76-72. In the playoff, with the wind diminished, Boros won handily with a 70. Cupit shot 73 and Palmer 76. Boros was the first of the three to finish the fourth round. He birdied the 16th and the 17th holes in the only strong finish by a contender. Palmer missed a putt of two feet on the 71st. Cupit lost a two-stroke lead with 6 on the par-4 71st. The last contender on the course, Cupit then narrowly missed holing a 15-foot putt for a birdie on the home green. Paul Harney, who finished before Boros, went one over par on the last hole and finished one stroke behind the leaders. Tony Lema failed to par either of the last two holes and tied with Bruce Crampton and Billy Maxwell at 295. The wind, which came up at mid-day during the first round and was always a factor thereafter, blew in gusts up to 35 miles per hour during Saturday's two rounds and changed direction frequently. Of 409 rounds played in the Championship only 14 were par 71 or better, Bob Gajda was the first-round leader with 69; after 36 holes Palmer, Cupit, and Dow Finsterwald were tied at 142; and Cupit led after 54 holes with 218. Boros, 43 years old, became the oldest American to win the Championship. Ted Ray of England was 26 days older on the day he won in 1920. Only Ben Hogan compiled a better record in the Open than Boros since World War II. In nine of 13 starts Boros was among the first 10. He also won in 1952. Jack Nicklaus, the defending Champion, failed to qualify for the final 36 holes. He scored 76-77–153, one stroke over the cutoff score. For the first time, no amateur qualified for the final 36 holes. Prize money was a record $96,350, including $88,550 in the Championship proper and $7,800 in 13 Sectional Qualifying Championships. Boros' share was $17,500, including a $1,500 bonus which went to each of the three in the playoff. Professionals who did not qualify to play the last 36 holes were rewarded for the first time, each receiving $150. The Championship honored the 50th anniversary of Francis Ouimet's historic Open victory at The Country Club.

1964–Ken Venturi made the 1964 Open a most memorable Championship. After compiling an outstanding amateur record and enjoying much early success as a professional, Venturi lapsed into a 3-year slump beginning in 1961. He won less than $4,000 in 1963. Then, in the 1964 Open, Venturi made a remarkable comeback at the Congressional Country Club, Washington, D.C. His 72-hole total was 278, two above the record 276, with rounds of 72-70-66-70; Tommy Jacobs was second with 282. Adding to the drama was Venturi's physical condition on a brutally hot and humid Saturday. Six strokes behind after 36 holes, Venturi turned in 30, five under par, on Saturday morning, and was six under par when he went over par on the 17th and 18th holes. He appeared exhausted after this third round of 66 and there was doubt that he could play the fourth round. A doctor examined him and permitted him to play on. Venturi continued to hit brilliant strokes, overhauled the 54-hole leader, Jacobs, and, walking almost painfully, parred the last four holes to finish four strokes ahead of Jacobs. First prize was $17,000. Arnold Palmer's 68 was the only sub-par round on the first day. Palmer followed with a 69 but did not retain his lead because Jacobs, after a first round of 72, made an astounding 64 on the second day, concluding with a 60-foot putt for a birdie on the home green. His 64 tied the record for the lowest round in an Open, set by Lee Mackey, Jr. in 1950. Jacobs' third-round score of 70 put him at 206, two strokes ahead of Venturi and six ahead of Palmer, who slipped to a 75 in the third round. Bob Charles, the 1963 British Open Champion, made a strong rally with a final round of 68 to finish third at 283. Low amateur was John Farquhar, of Amarillo, Texas, with 297. Defending Champion Julius Boros had back trouble and his 36-hole score of 154 did not make the cut. Total attendance for the Championship was 55,498, second only to the record of 62,300 for three days at Oakmont in 1962.

1965–Gary Player, 29, of South Africa, became the first foreigner to win the Open Championship since Ted Ray in 1920. Player defeated Kel Nagle, a 44-year-old Australian, in a playoff at the Bellerive Country Club, St. Louis. They had tied after 72 holes with totals of 282, two over par. Player built a five-stroke lead after eight holes of the playoff and won, 71 to 74. At the prize-giving ceremony after the playoff, Player announced that he would return $25,000 of his $26,000 prize to the USGA, asking that $5,000 be earmarked for cancer relief work and $20,000 to promote junior golf. His rounds in the Championship proper were 70-70-71-71–282. Player, appeared to have a safe lead of three strokes with only three holes to play in the fourth round. Then he went two over par on the par-3 16th hole, just as Nagle birdied the par-5 17th. They parred in to tie; both narrowly missed long putts for birdies on the home green. Nagle was the first-round leader with 68; Player led after 36 and 54 holes with totals of 140 and 211. Frank Beard, a 26-year-old professional from Louisville, finished third with 284. Deane Beman, twice National Amateur Champion from Bethesda, Md., was low amateur; he tied for 11th at 290. Defending Champion Ken Venturi, his hands ailing because of a circulatory problem, failed to qualify for the final 36 holes. The prize money was $123,890 in the Championship proper and $7,800 in Sectional Qualifying, for a grand total of $131,690—an Open record. Attendance, including the playoff, was 72,052—another record. The format was changed to spread the 72 holes over four days; thus, for the first time in Open history two rounds were not scheduled for one day.

1966—Bill Casper, Jr., 34, from Peacock Gap, Calif., became the 11th player to win the Open a second time when he defeated Arnold Palmer, of Ligonier, Pa., in a playoff over the Lake Course of the Olympic Country Club, San Francisco. He won previously in 1959. Casper and Palmer had tied after 72 holes at 278, two under par and matching the second lowest score in Open history. Twice Casper had to come from behind—once in the final round and again in the playoff. With nine holes to play in the Championship proper, Casper trailed Palmer by seven strokes. On the back nine Casper caught Palmer by scoring 32 against Arnold's 39. No one in Championship history had ever before come from seven strokes behind with nine to play and tied for the lead. Palmer had gone out in 32 in the fourth round and needed par on the last six holes to score 274 and break by two strokes the Open scoring record of 276 set in 1948 by Ben Hogan. Palmer lost a stroke at the 10th, another at the 13th, two at the 15th and then two more at the par-5 16th. Casper squared with a par 4 against Palmer's 5 at the 17th. He had then recovered seven strokes in eight holes, five strokes in three holes! In the playoff, Palmer raced ahead again with 33 on the out-going nine to Casper's 35. Then Palmer saw his lead erased when Bill holed a putt of fully 50 feet for a birdie on the par-3 13th. From there Casper steadily built up his lead and finished the round with 69—one under par. Palmer shot 73. In the five rounds Casper was under Olympic's forthright par 70 in four rounds. In the Championship proper he scored 69-68-73-68—278, and then 69 in the playoff. Palmer scored 71-66-70-71—278 and 73. He and Casper shared the lead at the end of 36 holes at 137 and then Arnold went three strokes ahead after 54 holes with 207. Jack Nicklaus was third with 285, seven strokes behind Casper and Palmer. Rives McBee, an obscure young professional from Midland, Texas, equalled the Open's single round scoring record with 64 in the second round. It was set originally by Lee Mackey, Jr., in 1950 and equalled first by Tommy Jacobs in 1964. John Miller, a 19-year-old member of Olympic and the 1964 United States Junior Amateur Champion, was low amateur and tied for eighth place with 290. Gary Player, the defending Champion, finished in a tie for 15th place with a score of 293. The prize money was $147,490 in the Championship proper and $7,800 in sectional Qualifying for a grand total of $155,290, an Open record.

1967—Jack W. Nicklaus, 27, of Columbus, Ohio, set a new Open scoring record of 275 over the Baltusrol Golf Club's Lower Course, Springfield, N.J., in winning his second Championship. The previous record was 276, established by Ben Hogan at the Riviera Country Club, Los Angeles, in 1948. Nicklaus thus became the 12th player to win the Open more than once, he won previously in 1962. At Baltusrol, Nicklaus had rounds of 71, 67, 72, and a closing 65, which equalled the final round record. He won by four strokes over Arnold Palmer, of Latrobe, Pa., who had 279. For the first time since 1954 an amateur held the outright lead in the Open. Martin A. Fleckman, 23, of Port Arthur, Texas, scored 67 in the first round and took a two-stroke lead over seven others, who had 69. Fleckman scored 73 in the second round and fell three strokes behind Palmer, who had 69-68—137. Nicklaus was then second, one stroke behind Palmer. A third-round 69 put Fleckman in the lead again, the first time an amateur had led so late in the Championship since 1933 when John Goodman won. Fleckman had 209; one stroke behind were Nicklaus, Palmer, and Bill Casper, Jr., the defending Champion. The Open soon developed into a duel between Nicklaus and Palmer, who played together. Fleckman scored 80 and finished in a tie for 18th place; Casper scored 72 and finished fourth. Palmer went ahead of Nicklaus briefly at the second hole, but Nicklaus caught him with a birdie at the third and never was behind again. Beginning with the third hole, Nicklaus birdied five of the next six, scored 31 on the front nine and was then four strokes ahead of Palmer. A bogey 5 on 10 and birdies on 13 and 14 left Nicklaus needing one more birdie to break the record. He came to the par-5 18th still needing that one birdie, drove off the fairway on the right, hit a bad recovery, then a magnificent 1-iron to the green, and holed a 21-foot putt for his 65 and 275. Palmer became the first player to score less than 280 in the Open twice. The estimated attendance of 88,414 was the largest on record. The prize money was $169,400 in the Championship proper, and $8,400 in Sectional Qualifying for a grand total of $177,800, an Open record. Entries reached a new high of 2,649.

1968—Lee B. Trevino, 28, from Horizon City, Texas, played four rounds under par, equalled the 72-hole record of 275, and won by four strokes over the East Course of the Oak Hill Country Club, Rochester, N.Y. Trevino scored 69-68-69-69 and became the first player in Open history to play all four regulation rounds under par and in the 60s. Trevino's 275 tied the record set by Jack Nicklaus the previous year. Nicklaus was second to Trevino at 279. Bert Yancey, of Tallahassee, Fla., led the first round with 67—three under par. Yancey was then two strokes ahead of Trevino and Charles Coody, of Abilene, Texas. Yancey followed with 68, giving him a 36-hole score of 135. This tied the record set by Mike Souchak at the 1960 Open at Cherry Hills, Denver. Yancey was then two strokes ahead of Trevino. Yancey held the lead after three rounds with 70 for 205, one better than the previous record 206 established by Tommy Jacobs at Congressional Country Club, in 1964. Despite his record score, Yancey was only one stroke ahead of Trevino as the final round began, for Trevino had matched the previous record of 206. Nicklaus was third with 212, and Bobby Nichols fourth with 213. Nicklaus began the final round by scoring birdies on two of the first four holes. Yancey and Trevino, meanwhile, each scored 5 on the par-4 first hole. Trevino caught Yancey when Yancey made a 4 on the par-3 third, then went ahead to stay when Yancey went over par on the ninth. He added a stroke to his lead on each of the next four holes. John S. Spray, of Cedar Rapids, Iowa, equalled the record for the final round with 65 and tied Don Bies, of Seattle, Wash., for fifth place. Richard L. Siderowf, of Westport, Conn., was low amateur with 300. Entries reached a record total of 3,007, and the prize money of $188,800 also was a record.

1969–Orville Moody, 35, of Yukon, Okla. had spent 14 years in the Army before joining the Professional Golfers' Association tournament circuit in 1967. He won the United States Open Championship in his second full year on the tour with rounds of 71-70-68-72 for a 72-hole score of 281 at the Cypress Creek Course of the Champions Golf Club, Houston, Texas. Moody won by one stroke over Deane R. Beman, Bethesda, Md.; Al Geiberger, Santa Barbara, Calif.; and Bob Rosburg, St. Louis. All three had scores of 282. Moody had played in the Open only once before and had failed to survive the 36-hole cutoff in 1962. He rose to the rank of sergeant in the Army, then left the service in 1967 and qualified for the tour at the Approved Tournament Players School that fall. Bob Murphy, the 1965 United States Amateur Champion, was the first-round leader with a score of 66–four under par. Miller Barber was next with 67, followed by Beman and Geiberger. Beman took the lead the next day with a 36-hole score of 137. Barber and Murphy were tied for second at 138 and Rosburg, the 1959 PGA Champion, was fourth with 139. Barber scored 68 in the third round and seemed to be turning the Championship into a runaway. He had a 54-hole score of 206, one stroke above the 54-hole record, and was three strokes ahead of second-place Moody, whose 68 gave him a 54-hole total of 209. Beman and Bunky Henry were tied for third at 210, followed by Rosburg at 211. Geiberger was among five players at 212. Barber collapsed in the final round, shooting 78 and dropping to a tie for sixth place. Moody went ahead to stay at the 12th where he salvaged a par 3 and Barber took 5. At one time eight players were within two strokes of one another and all of them were playing the last nine holes. Moody was the steadiest in the closing moments. He went over par on the 14th hole, then made pars on all the rest. Geiberger scored 70 in the final round, the best of the leaders, and might have tied had he not three-putted the 16th hole. Rosburg missed a three-foot putt on the 18th after a brilliant recovery from a bunker, and Beman holed a 15-foot birdie putt on the final green. For the second time in Open history no amateur survived the 36-hole cutoff. This happened previously in 1963. Entries reached an all-time high of 3,397 and the prize money of $205,300 was also a record.

1970–Tony Jacklin, 25, of Scunthorpe, England, the British Open Champion became the first Briton to win the United States Open Championship in 50 years when he played four rounds in seven under par at the Hazeltine National Golf Club, Chaska, Minn. He was the first Englishman to win since Ted Ray in 1920. Jacklin was the only player in the field to score under par. He played rounds of 71-70-70-70–281, and won by seven strokes over Dave Hill, who had 288. This was the largest winning margin since James M. Barnes won by nine strokes at the Columbia Country Club, Washington, in 1921. Jacklin increased his lead after every round. Winds of over 40 miles per hour blew all through the first round, and Jacklin's 71 was best by two strokes. He increased his lead to three strokes after 36 holes, and to four after 54. He appeared to be slipping when he went a stroke above par on both the seventh and eighth holes of the final round, but he then sank a 30-foot birdie putt on the ninth and was never threatened. The Championship was marked by the unusual circumstance of Hill, the leading challenger to Jacklin after the first round, severely criticizing the golf course. Orville Moody, the 1969 Champion, failed to survive the 36-hole cutoff, the fifth Champion in eight years to fail. Prize money was $195,700 in the Championship proper and $7,800 in Sectional Qualifying, a grand total of $203,500. The entry reached 3,605, a record, and attendance was 75,878, second only to 1967 when 88,414 attended at Baltusrol Golf Club, Springfield, N.J. At 7,151 yards Hazeltine was the second longest course ever to be the site of a USGA Championship.

1971–Lee Trevino, 31, defeated Jack Nicklaus, 31, in a playoff at the Merion Golf Club, Ardmore, Pa. Both players had scored 280 for the 72 holes and Trevino scored 68 in the playoff against a 71 by Nicklaus. Nicklaus twice left shots in bunkers–once on the second hole, again on the third, to allow Trevino to take a two-stroke lead. Nicklaus never was able to catch Trevino, although several times he narrowed the margin to one stroke. Trevino had rounds of 70-72-69-69–280, and Nicklaus scored 69-72-68-71–280. Both had chances to win outright on the 72d hole, but they both missed putts. Trevino was ready to stroke a six-foot putt for a par 4 and 279 when a spectator fell from a bulletin board causing a distracting noise. Trevino backed away, and then missed the putt. Nicklaus had a 14-foot putt for a birdie on the final hole and barely missed. James B. Simons, a 21-year-old amateur from Butler, Pa., needed a birdie on the last hole to tie Nicklaus and Trevino, but he drove into the rough, gambled on reaching the green with a wood, and failed. He made 6 and finished in a tie for fifth with 283. Robert R. Rosburg, of French Lick, Ind., three-putted the 72d and tied for third with James J. Colbert, Jr., of Prairie Creek, Ark., at 282. Labron Harris, Jr., Stillwater, Okla., shot 67 and led the first round. Bob Erickson, of Sanford, Fla., and Colbert shared the second round lead at 138. Simons shot 65 in the third round, one stroke above the Open's single-round record set initially at Merion in 1950, and took the 54-hole lead with 207, two strokes ahead of Nicklaus, who was in second place. Simons still led after nine holes of the final round, but made a 5 on the par 4 10th to fall into a tie with Nicklaus, and then Trevino played a great 8-iron 15 inches from the hole on the 12th and made a birdie and forced a three-way tie. Trevino went ahead with a birdie on the 14th and held the lead until he made 5 on the par 4 18th, setting up the playoff. For the sixth time in nine years the defending Champion failed to survive the 36-hole cutoff. Tony Jacklin shot 152 and was eliminated. The entry was 4,279, the largest for any USGA Championship ever. Prize money totalled $200,000, with $192,200 awarded to professionals in the Championship proper and another $7,800 in

Sectional Qualifying Championships. This was the 13th USGA event held at Merion; no other Club had been host to so many.

1972—Jack Nicklaus, 32, won his third Open Championship with a score of 290 at the Pebble Beach Golf Links, Pebble Beach, California. Only Willie Anderson, Bob Jones, and Ben Hogan won as many: each won four. Nicklaus either led or was tied for the lead throughout and finished three strokes ahead of Bruce Crampton, of Australia. Arnold Palmer was third with 294, while Lee Trevino, the defending Champion, tied for fourth with Homero Blancas at 295. The winning score was the highest since 1963 when Julius Boros, Jacky Cupit, and Arnold Palmer scored 293 to tie for first place. Boros won the eventual playoff. Pebble Beach was not only the most scenic course ever host to the Open, but also was as stern a test of golfing skill as the Open has presented. As testimony to its difficulty, only 48 of the 150 starters scored lower than 80 on both the first two days, and only 40 rounds of par-72 or lower were played by the 70 contestants who finished 72 holes. Low score the first day was 71, with six players tied for the lead, the most ever to tie for the lead after the first round and the most ever to tie for the lead after any round since 1896, the second year of the Open. They were Nicklaus; Orville Moody, 1969 Champion; Juan Rodriguez; Mason Rudolph; Tom Shaw; and Kermit Zarley, Jr. Scoring improved the second day with 15 players shooting par or better. Lanny Wadkins and Arnold Palmer both scored 68, low for the Championship. Wadkins moved into a tie for first place at 144, while Palmer was seventh with 145. Six players were again tied for the lead: Nicklaus, Homero Blancas, Bruce Crampton, Cesar Sanudo, Wadkins, and Zarley. On the third day Pebble Beach continued to plague the field when only 13 players were able to match or better par. Nicklaus, with a 72, ended the day in sole possession of first place with a 216 total—even par. Bruce Crampton and Kermit Zarley shared second place with Lee Trevino at 217. Trevino had been hospitalized with a slight case of bronchial pneumonia the week preceding the Open, but he was still the only player in the field to improve on his scores in the first three rounds. The third day was highlighted by Jerry McGee's hole-in-one on the par-3, 180-yard 5th hole—the first scored in an Open since 1956. To thoroughly upset the rules of probability, Bobby Mitchell holed his tee shot on the same hole the next day. The last day was sunny but windy—not a day for low-scoring. In fact, there were only two final-day scores of par or better; a 70 by Mason Rudolph and a 72 by Jim Simons, one of three amateurs to play the entire 72 holes. The final round could hardly have been more dramatic: Trevino was grouped with Nicklaus, whom he beat in a playoff for the 1971 title. The anticipated duel did not develop, however. Trevino finally succumbed to physical ills and could not keep up. Nicklaus was apparently in full command of the Championship after nine holes and had increased his lead to four strokes, with Trevino, Crampton, and Arnold Palmer his closest pursuers. The 10th and 12th holes nearly changed the complexion of the Championship. On the 10th Nicklaus was blown off balance by a sudden gust of wind as he drove. His drive soared over a cliff and onto the beach below. Nicklaus elected to take a one-stroke penalty and dropped outside the hazard. He then hit a 2-iron, but the ball landed short and to the right of the green on the steep bank of the cliff and again in the lateral water hazard. He was able to play the ball as it lay, however, and got on with a wedge and two-putted for a 6. His lead was cut from four strokes to two. Nicklaus parred the 11th, then came to the 12th. Palmer, two holes ahead of him, had made a par-3 at the 12th and was only one stroke behind on the scoreboard. On the 555-yard, par-5 14th Palmer had an eight-foot putt for a birdie. Meantime, on the 12th, Nicklaus hit a 3-iron shot over the green into a terrible lie. He needed two more shots to reach the green, eight feet away from a bogey-4. The Open Championship finally hinged on the play of two shots by Palmer and Nicklaus. If Palmer made his and Nicklaus missed, Palmer would be ahead. If they both sank, they would be tied. Palmer's putt eased by the edge and Nicklaus holed his to retain the lead. Palmer then bogied the 15th and 16th holes to end his challenge. Nicklaus parred 13 and 14; birdied 15; parred 16, and then hit the flagstick on the par-3, 218-yard 17th hole with a 1-iron shot that left him only a six-inch putt for a birdie. Four strokes ahead of Bruce Crampton, Nicklaus played the 18th hole cautiously, three-putting for a bogey 6.

There were 4,196 acceptable entries filed for the 1972 Open, of which 1,661 were from amateurs, more than in any previous year. Fourteen of them made it into the Championship proper, after local and sectional qualifying rounds, and three finished 72 holes. Prize money totalled $202,400, with $194,600 going to professionals in the Championship proper and $7,800 in Sectional Qualifying Championships.

1973—John Miller, 26, shot a record score of 63 in the final round and won the 73d Open Championship with a 72-hole score of 279 at the Oakmont Country Club, Oakmont, Pa. Miller won by one stroke over John Schlee, 34, at 280. Tom Weiskopf, 32, was third with 281. Miller's 279 was only the 10th score under 280 in the history of the Open. He shot rounds of 71, 69, 76 and 63. The 63 was one stroke under the previous record of 64 shared by three men. It was set first by Lee Mackey, Jr., at the Merion Golf Club, Ardmore, Pa., in 1950. Tommy Jacobs shot 64 at the Congressional Country Club, Bethesda, Md., in 1964, and Rives McBee equalled it at the Olympic Country Club, San Francisco, in 1966. Miller's 279 was also the lowest 72-hole score in five Opens at Oakmont; the previous low was 283, set by Ben Hogan in 1953 and matched by both Arnold Palmer and Jack Nicklaus in 1962 when Nicklaus defeated

Palmer in a playoff. Four men shared the 54-hole lead, the most ever, and Miller was six strokes behind. Tied at 210 were Julius Boros, 53, Arnold Palmer, 43, John Schlee, 34, and Jerry Heard, 26. Tom Weiskopf was next at 211. Miller, with 216, began the last round an hour ahead of the leaders, and with three holes to play, only Weiskopf and Schlee could catch him. Weiskopf needed three birdies and made one, Schlee needed two and made one, although they both had opportunities. Weiskopf missed a short putt on the 17th, Schlee missed a longer putt at 17, but almost holed a chip shot at 18. Miller had nine birdies and one bogey in his round of 63, and his putt on the 18th hit the hole and spun out. Rain fell on 27 days during May, and Oakmont was hit by a heavy rainstorm on the Tuesday before the Open began. Consequently, Oakmont was not so severe a test as it had been for four previous Open Championships. Gary Player, the 1965 Champion, shot 67 in the first round, equalling the lowest single round for an Open at Oakmont until then. He led by three strokes over Raymond Floyd, Lee Trevino, and Jim Colbert. A record 19 players broke par the next day. Gene Borek, a club professional from East Norwich, N. Y., who was admitted into the field as an alternate when Dave Hill withdrew, led scoring with 65. Player shot 70 and still led by one stroke over Jim Colbert. Player had 137 for 36 holes, Colbert had 138. At that stage Miller had 140 and was tied with Jack Nicklaus and Bob Charles. A heavy rain fell Saturday morning, making Oakmont easier to play. Jerry Heard shot 66, John Schlee 67, Palmer and Boros 68s to cause the four-man tie after three rounds. In the fourth round Miller birdied the first four holes, bogied the eighth and birdied the ninth to make the turn in 32. He was then one under par for 63 holes. Coming in, he birdied the 11th through the 13th, parred the 14th, and birdied the 15th to finish five under par for the 72 holes. Palmer had a chance to go five under if he could birdie the 11th, but he missed a four-foot putt and followed with bogies on the 12th, 13th, and 14th. Schlee had made a remarkable comeback. His tee shot on the first hole had been unplayable and he made 6 on the par-4 hole. Still he was within one stroke of Miller with one hole to play when his second shot on the 18th hit the green and rolled off the back. He had to chip, and almost made the shot. The Open has been played at Oakmont five times, and since the golf course has remained basically the same, more Opens have been played over Oakmont than over any other course. Baltusrol Golf Club, Springfield, N. J. has been the site of five Opens, too, but they have been played over at least three different courses. One other record was broken and another tied. Sam Snead, who played in his fourth National Championship at Oakmont (three Opens, and the 1951 PGA Championship), played through his 27th Open, breaking a record he shared with Gene Sarazen. Nine men broke par for 72 holes, matching the record set at the Canterbury Golf Club, Cleveland, Ohio in 1946. Marvin M. Giles III, Richmond, Va. the current Amateur Champion, was low amateur with 290, good for 17th place. In the second round Giles finished 2-3-3-3 against a par of 4-3-4-4 and shot 69. Entries reached 3,580, and the starting field of 150 was composed of 137 professionals and 13 amateurs. Of the amateurs, Giles and Gary Koch survived the 36-hole cut. Prize money totalled $227,200, a record, of which $219,400 was distributed to professionals in the Championship proper and $7,800 in Sectional Qualifying Championships.

1974—Hale Irwin, 29, won by two strokes over Forrest Fezler with a seven-over-par score of 287 over the West Course of the Winged Foot Golf Club, Mamaroneck, N. Y. Fezler shot 289 while Lou Graham and Bert Yancey tied for third at 290. Irwin's best previous Open finish was in 1971 when he tied for 19th place. At Winged Foot he had 18-hole scores of 73, 70, 71, and 73, with 13 birdies, 18 bogies, and one hole where he went two over par. His score was the highest in relation to par since 1963 when a score of nine above par tied after 72 holes and caused a playoff. The 1974 Open was decided on the last two holes where Irwin holed a 10-foot putt for a par on the 17th as Fezler was making a bogey 5 on the 18th. Irwin saved his Championship by playing a 2-iron approach to the 18th 20 feet from the hole and making par 4. Winged Foot was a very difficult course for the Open. Gary Player was the only man in the field to equal par in the first round; he led by one stroke over Graham, Mike Reasor, and Jim Colbert. Irwin was three strokes behind at that time. Of the 150 men who began play that day, only 23 were under 75 for the first round. Scoring was somewhat better the second day. Hubert Green shot 67, which was to be the lowest round of the Championship, and three others were under par 70. In all, 38 men were under 75 and four matched par 70. Player maintained a share of the lead after 36 holes with 73 and 143. Also at 143 were Arnold Palmer, Raymond Floyd, and Irwin. Among those who failed to survive the 36-hole cut, which fell at 153, were Lee Trevino, Bill Casper, Ken Venturi, Gene Littler and Tony Jacklin, all former Open Champions; Craig Stadler, the 1973 U. S. Amateur Champion; and John Schlee, runnerup to John Miller in the 1973 Open. Player was out in 36 in the third round, and then shot 41 on the second nine for 77. With that he fell from contention. Palmer shot 73 and fell to third at 216. Tom Watson, 23, led after shooting 69 for a 54-hole score of 213. Watson saved a bogey 5 and his lead with a superb bunker shot on the 18th to within six inches of the hole. Irwin at this point was in second place at 214 after a 71 in the third round. Fezler was in sixth place at 219, behind Frank Beard and Bert Yancey, at 218. Palmer dropped from contention early in the final round. He three-putted the second hole from 12 feet and his approach to the short sixth dropped into a bunker. Watson holed two sizable putts for pars on the first two holes, and then three-putted the fourth and fifth. Irwin three-putted the fourth along with Watson, but he made a par 5 on the fifth to catch up. Then Irwin holed a 35-foot birdie putt on the ninth to go ahead to stay. At this point Irwin was five over par for the 63 holes while Watson was six over and Fezler was nine over. Watson's game collapsed entirely on the second nine; he shot 41 and 79 for a 72-hole score of 292. Irwin faltered slightly, too. He bogied four of the next seven holes, offset by two birdies, and he was seven over par playing the 17th. Fezler, meanwhile, had saved pars on both 16 and 17 by holing difficult putts, but he missed the 18th green and made 5, giving him 70 for the round and 289 for 72 holes. At this point Irwin holed a 10-foot putt to save his par on the 17th. He followed with another par on the 18th and won by two strokes. The entry of 3,914 was the third largest in Open history. Prize money totalled $227,700.

1975—Lou Graham, 37, defeated John Mahaffey, 27, in an 18-hole playoff over the No. 3 Course of the Medinah Country Club, Medinah, Ill. after both men scored three-over par 287s in regulation play. Graham shot 71 in the playoff and Mahaffey shot 73. Bob Murphy, Frank Beard, Ben Crenshaw and Hale Irwin, the 1974 Champion, tied for third with 288. Graham could have won outright with a par 4 on the 72nd hole, but after a perfectly placed tee shot in center fairway he hit his 6-iron approach into a greenside bunker and made 5, dropping him into a tie with Mahaffey, who had already finished. In the playoff Graham went ahead by scoring a birdie on the fourth hole, and he was never caught. He extended his lead to three strokes after the 10th hole and still led by two with one hole to play. On the 18th, however, Graham hooked his tee shot into the left rough creating the possibility of a tie if he lost a stroke to par and Mahaffey birdied the hole. Graham, however, played a low 4-iron to the edge of the green and saved par, winning by two strokes. Pat Fitzsimons, with a hole-in-one on the 187-yard second, and Tom Watson shared the first day lead with 67s. Jim Wiechers was a stroke behind in third place, while Arnold Palmer, Lanny Wadkins, Grier Jones and Peter Oosterhuis, were tied for fourth at 69. Eight players were under par and seven others matched it. Graham shot 74 to stand seven strokes back of the leaders, while Mahaffey had 73. Play of the second round was interrupted by an electrical storm. When it resumed Tom Watson shot 68, which—coupled with his opening 67—put him in the lead by three strokes over Ben Crenshaw, who also scored 68. Watson's total of 135 equalled the 36-hole record first set by Mike Souchak in 1960 and equalled by Bert Yancey in 1968. Fitzsimons was third at 140 with 67-73. Jim Wiechers shot 73 and was tied for fourth at 141 with Terry Dill (72-69) and Lee Trevino (72-69). Graham, meanwhile, shot 72 and was 11 strokes behind. Mahaffey stood at 144. Eleven players had sub-par rounds and ten others were at even par for the day. In the third round, Frank Beard shot 67 and climbed from a tie for tenth place after 36 holes into a three-stroke lead after 54 with 210. Fitzsimons and Watson were tied for second at 213. Lou Graham shot one of the day's four sub-par rounds and moved into a tie for fourth at 214 with Peter Oosterhuis and Crenshaw. Mahaffey was at 216, tied for tenth place. In the final round, Beard shot 78 and fell into a tie for third place with Bob Murphy, Crenshaw and Irwin. Beard lost his chance when he bogeyed 17 and 18 and Crenshaw fell back by scoring 5 on the 17th, a par 3 hole. Jack Nicklaus lost a stroke on each of the last three holes and finished two strokes behind at 289. Prize money totalled $235,700; Graham received $40,000 and Mahaffey $20,000. The entry of 4,214 was the second largest in Open history. Attendance for the Championship proper reached 97,345, setting a new record, while the playoff, on a Monday, was viewed by 6,246.

1976—Jerry Pate played one of the more memorable shots in Open history and won the 1976 Championship with a score of 277 at the Atlanta Athletic Club, Duluth, Ga. Pate, 22, was leading three players by one stroke on the 72nd hole, a 460-yard, par-4 with a lake in front of the green. From the right rough he hit a 5-iron shot within two feet of the cup and scored a birdie 3. He won by two strokes over Al Geiberger and Tom Weiskopf. John Mahaffey, grouped with Pate, hit his second shot into the lake, made 5, and finished with 280, tied for fourth place with Butch Baird. Pate was remarkably consistent. He shot rounds of 71, 69, 69, and 68 over the four days. Mike Reid, a 21-year-old amateur from Seattle, Wash., scored three-under par 67, the only sub-par score of the first round, and led by three strokes over five others tied at 70. Reid shot 81 in the second round, followed by 80-72 for a 300 total, which tied him with John Fought, of Portland, Ore., as low amateur. Mahaffey shot 68 in the second round and led with 138 for 36 holes, followed by Geiberger at 139. Ben Crenshaw, Rod Funseth and Pate tied for third at 140. Mahaffey continued to lead after the third round with 207, while Pate finished two strokes behind. Geiberger was at 210, while Weiskopf stood at 211. Crenshaw went two over par and was at 212. The day was marred by rain and lightning which delayed play for one hour and 26 minutes. Mahaffey led by six strokes at one stage during the third round, but bogied 16 and 17 to finish the day just two strokes ahead of Pate. Pate was four over par after the first four holes, but then made three birdies and an eagle and finished the round with 69, one under par. Mahaffey clung to his lead as late as the 15th hole of the final round, but bogied the final three holes, scored 73 and dropped into a tie for fourth place. Geiberger and Weiskopf, playing just ahead of Pate and Mahaffey, seemed to be in position to win the Championship, but both drove poorly on the 72nd hole and played their second shots short of the water hazard and saved their par-4s. Pate then played his dramatic 5-iron out of the rough, over the pond, and onto the 72nd green for the Championship. Prize money came to $253,000, including $500 to each professional who started but did not make the 36-hole cut. Attendance reached a new high of 113,084 for four days, 15,739 over the record established in 1975 at the Medinah Country Club, Medinah, Ill. Another Open record was set when 4,436 players filed entries; this was 157 more than filed in 1971, when the Open was held at the Merion Golf Club, Ardmore, Pa.

1977—Hubert Green, 30, held or shared the lead in all four rounds of the Championship at the Southern Hills Country Club, Tulsa, Okla., and scored 278, two under par; Lou Graham, the 1975 Champion, was second with 279. Graham's scores of 68-68-136 for the last two rounds equalled an Open record. Green had rounds of 69, 67, 72, 70. Another Open record fell when seven players tied for the first-round lead with 69, one under par. Green shared the 18-hole lead with Tom Purtzer, Terry Diehl, Rod Funseth, Grier Jones, Florentino Molina, and Larry Nelson. After 36 holes Green held the lead alone with 136. Terry Diehl was second at 137 and Tom Purtzer was third at 138. Green shot a 72 in the third round and led Andy Bean by one stroke with 208. Bean shot 68 for 209. Six players tied at 210, even par, and four more were at 211. As the final round began, 12 players were within two strokes of one another. When Green began the final round with birdies at the third and fourth holes, he was four under par and led by four strokes. Green lost strokes on both the ninth and 10th holes and was then two under par. Graham then scored four birdies on the second nine and missed still another from eight feet on the 17th, or 71st hole of the Championship. Green birdied the 16th after playing a wedge shot only two feet from the hole, followed with a par 4 on the 17th, and lost another stroke at the 18th where he drove into the rough and hit his approach into a bunker. He holed a three-foot putt to avoid a playoff with Graham, who had already finished. Tom Weiskopf finished third with 281. Prize money reached $284,990 with $227,990 awarded in the Championship proper and $15,000 in Sectional Qualifying Championships. Entries reached 4,726, a record.

1978—Andy North, 28, of Madison, Wis., won the Open Championship at the Cherry Hills Country Club, Englewood, Colo., with a score of 285, one over par. Dave Stockton and J.C. Snead tied for second place with 286. North had rounds of 70, 70, 71, 74. Hale Irwin was the first-round leader with 69, two under par. Only three other players bettered par 71 in the first round. North shot 70 and shared second place with Snead and Bob Clampett, an 18-year-old amateur. Six players finished the first round with 71, even par, including Bill Casper and Gary Player. After 36 holes, North held a two-stroke lead at 140, two under par, after a second consecutive 70 that included a 30-foot birdie putt on the long par 4 18th hole. In second place at 142, even par, were Snead, Player, and Jack Nicklaus. Nicklaus added a 69 to his opening-round 73. A stroke back, at 143, were Irwin, Clampett, Mark Hayes, and Lee Treviño. North shot a 71 in the third round for 211 and a one-stroke lead over Player, who shot 70 for 212. Three strokes behind North were Snead and Stockton, who had 72 and 70 respectively, for 214. North once again birdied the difficult 18th hole, dropping a 45-foot putt. In the final round, North made birdies on the fourth and fifth holes to go four under par. He gave back three strokes with bogies at the eighth, ninth, and 10th holes, recovered quickly with birdies at the 11th and 13th holes, but then went bogey -double bogey on the next two holes. Stockton birdied the 15th hole to cut North's lead to one stroke, but could manage only a par-par-bogey finish on the last three holes. Snead needed a birdie at the final hole, but he made par 4 instead. On the final hole, North needed a 5 to win the Championship. He played a 3-iron tee shot into the right rough. He played out with an 8-iron, but the ball landed in the opposite rough, left and short of the green. He misplayed his wedge pitch, and the ball fell short, into a greenside bunker. He played an excellent bunker shot, leaving himself a four-foot putt to win the Championship. North stepped away from the putt twice because the wind was affecting his concentration. When he finally reset himself, he stroked the ball firmly into the hole. The lowest 18-hole score of the Championship was 68, which was shot by John Miller in the third round and matched by Tom Weiskopf and Mike McCullough in the fourth round. Sixty-one professionals and two amateurs made the 36-hole cut at 151, nine over par. Bob Clampett was the low amateur with a 297 total, 13 over par. Prize money reached a record $310,200 with $295,200 awarded in the Championship proper and $15,000 in the Sectional Qualifying Championships. A record 4,897 entries were received for the Championship.

1979—Hale Irwin, 34, of Frontenac, Mo., became the 14th player to win the Open Championship more than once. Irwin won with a score of 284 for 72 holes, even par, at Inverness Club, Toledo, Ohio. Two strokes behind, at 286, were Gary Player and Jerry Pate, two former Open Champions. Irwin had rounds of 74-68-67-75. Five players shared the first round lead with 70, one under par. They were Lou Graham, 1975 Open Champion, Andy Bean, Tom Purtzer, Keith Fergus, and Lon Hinkle. At 71 were Pate, Jim Colbert, Larry Nelson, Dana Quigley, Bill Rogers, Tom Weiskopf, and Amateur Champion John Cook. After 36 holes, Nelson and Purtzer, with second-round scores of 68 and 69 respectively, shared the lead at 139. Irwin began the second round by holing birdie putts of 15 and 12 feet on the first two holes. He added birdies on the 10th, 11th, and 12th holes to go five under par for the day, but he lost strokes at both the 16th and 17th holes and finished with 68, three strokes behind the leader at 142. In the third round, Irwin took the lead when he shot 67, giving him a 54-hole score of 209, three strokes ahead of the field. Weiskopf, who had 74 in the second round, came back with a 67 and moved into second place with a 212 score. Tied for third place at 214 were Purtzer, who dropped back with 75, and Pate who moved into contention with 69. Irwin had built his lead to four strokes over Weiskopf through 12 holes of the third round, On the 13th hole, a par 5, Weiskopf played a 4-iron second shot just eight feet from the hole and scored an eagle 3. Irwin, playing directly behind him, then played a 2-iron shot that came to rest just three feet from the hole. He matched Weiskopf's eagle. In the last round, Pate and Purtzer, playing together in the next to last group, made early runs at the lead, but eventually fell out of contention. Irwin, paired with Weiskopf in the final group, played the first nine in 35. On the second nine he drove into the rough four times but, after 16 holes, he was five strokes ahead of both Weiskopf and Player. On the 17th hole, he hit his second shot into a greenside bunker, played his bunker shot over the back of the green, chipped back to 12 feet and two-putted for a double-bogey 6. Weiskopf bogeyed the 17th hole to pick up only one stroke. With one hole to play, Irwin led Player, who had finished with a 68, and Pate by three strokes and Weiskopf by four. Both Player and Pate had birdied the 18th hole. Irwin pushed his tee shot into the right rough and then pulled his approach into the left greenside bunker. He played a fine bunker shot to within six feet of the hole and two-putted for a bogey 5 to win the Championship. Sixty professionals and three amateurs made the 36-hole cut at 151, nine over par. Fred Couples was the low amateur with a 302 total. Prize money reached a record $330,400 with $315,400 awarded in the Championship proper and $15,000 in the Sectional Qualifying Championships. The 4,853 entries was short of the record of 4,897 for the 1978 Open Championship.

1980—Jack Nicklaus, 40, of Dublin, Ohio, won his fourth Open Championship, shooting a record score of 272, eight under par, over the Lower Course of the Baltusrol Golf Club, in Springfield, New Jersey. Nicklaus joined Willie Anderson, Bob Jones, and Ben Hogan as the only men to win the Open four times. In setting his record score, Nicklaus was three strokes under the previous record of 275 that he set in 1967 over the same course. Nicklaus also joined Julius Boros, Hogan, and Ted Ray as the only golfers to win the Open after they passed 40. In posting rounds of 63-71-70-68-272, Nicklaus either led or was tied for the lead throughout. He finished two strokes ahead of Isao Aoki, of Japan, with whom he played all four days. Aoki's 274 total thus became the second lowest 72-hole score in Open history, Keith Fergus, Lon Hinkle, and Tom Watson tied for third place at 276, the only other players to break par for the 72 holes. Nicklaus and Tom Weiskopf shared the first round lead with scores of eight-under-par 63. These were the lowest scores in the Open since John Miller's final round 63 in the 1973 Open at Oakmont. Nicklaus had a chance to break the record and score 62, but he missed a three-foot birdie putt at the 18th hole. Three players—Fergus, Hinkle, and Mark Hayes—shot 66, three others had 67, and altogether, 19 players broke par 70, a record for the first round. The low scoring was due, in part, to early week rainstorms which softened Baltusrol's true and very fast greens. When the Championship was over, 51 rounds were played under par, the most ever. In the second round, Nicklaus held on for 71, despite losing four strokes to par in mid-round. His 36-hole total of 134, another Open record, gave him a two-stroke lead over Aoki, Fergus, Hinkle, and Mike Reid. Aoki shot a second straight 68 for 136 and had only 23 putts for the round, including just 10 on the second nine. In his first round he had 27 putts, so for two rounds he had just 50 putts. After 54 holes, Nicklaus and Aoki were tied for the lead at 204, another Open record. Hinkle was third at 205, followed by Watson, Hayes and Fergus at 206. Hubert Green had 65, which included eight consecutive 3s from the ninth hole through the 16th. He had two 3s earlier in the round, 10 for the day. In the final round, Nicklaus went ahead by one stroke when Aoki made a bogey 5 at the second hole. Nicklaus birdied the par-4 third hole from five feet to go two strokes ahead. Aoki birdied the eighth hole to cut his deficit to one stroke, but he bogeyed the ninth as Nicklaus made par, and never again was he closer than two strokes. As they stood on the 17th tee, they remained two strokes apart. Both men birdied the 17th, Nicklaus from 20 feet, Aoki from five feet. Aoki's pitch shot to the 18th, another par 5, almost went into the hole, but once again both men birdied. Nicklaus had a final round 68 to Aoki's 70. Sixty-one professionals and two amateurs made the 36-hole cut at 146, four over par, the lowest cut in Open history. Gary Hallberg was the low amateur with a 285 total. Arnold Palmer competed in his 28th consecutive Open dating back to 1953. Prize money reached a record $356,700 with $341,700 awarded in the Championship proper and $15,000 in the Sectional Qualifying Championships. The 4,812 entries was short of the record of 4,897 for the 1978 Open Championship. More than 102,000 spectators attended, the second largest number in Open history.

OPEN CHAMPIONSHIP

DATE	WINNER, RUNNER-UP	SCORE	SITE	ENTRY
1960 (June)	Arnold Palmer	280	Cherry Hills, C.C.,	2,453
	*Jack Nicklaus	282	Englewood, Colo.	
1961 (June)	Gene Littler	281	Oakland Hills, C.C.,	2,449
	Doug Sanders	282	Birmingham, Mich.	
	Bob Goalby	282		
1962 (June)	Jack Nicklaus	283-71	Oakmont, C.C.,	2,475
	Arnold Palmer	283-74	Oakmont, Pa.	
1963 (June)	Julius Boros	293-70	The Country Club,	2,392
	Jacky Cupit	293-73	Brookline, Mass.	
	Arnold Palmer	293-76		
1964 (June)	Ken Venturi	278	Congressional C.C.,	2,341
	Tommy Jacobs	282	Washington, D.C.	
1965 (June)	Gary Player	282-71	Bellerive C.C.,	2,271
	Kel Nagle	282-74	St. Louis, Mo.	
1966 (June)	Bill Casper, Jr.	278-69	Olympic C.C.,	2,475
	Arnold Palmer	278-73	San Francisco, Calif.	
1967 (June)	Jack Nicklaus	275	Baltusrol G.C., (Lower Course),	2,651
	Arnold Palmer	279	Srpingfield, N.J.	
1968 (June)	Lee B. Trevino	275	Oak Hill C.C., (East Course),	3,007
	Jack Nicklaus	279	Rochester, N.Y.	
1969 (June)	Orville Moody	281	Champions G.C. (Cypress Creek Course),	3,397
	Deane R. Beman	282	Houston, Texas	
	Al Geiberger	282		
	Robert R. Rosburg	282		
1970 (June)	Tony Jacklin	281	Hazeltine National G.C.,	3,605
	Dave Hill	288	Chaska, Minn.	
1971 (June)	Lee Trevino	280-68	Merion G.C.,	4,279
	Jack Nicklaus	280-71	(East Course),	
			Ardmore, Pa.	
1972 (June)	Jack Nicklaus	290	Pebble Beach G.L.,	4,196
	Bruce Crampton	293	Pebble Beach, Calif.	
1973 (June)	John Miller	279	Oakmont C. C.,	3,580
	John Schlee	280	Oakmont, Pa.	
1974 (June)	Hale Irwin	287	Winged Foot G.C.,	3,914
	Forrest Fezler	289	(West Course),	
			Mamaroneck, N.Y.	
1975 (June)	Lou Graham	287-71	Medinah C.C.,	4,214
	John Mahaffey	287-73	(No. 3 Course),	
			Medinah, Ill.	
1976 (June)	Jerry Pate	277	Atlanta Athletic C.	4,436
	Tom Weiskopf	279	Duluth, Ga.	
	Al Geiberger	279		
1977 (June)	Hubert Green	278	Southern Hills C.C.	4,608
	Lou Graham	279	Tulsa, Okla.	
1978 (June)	Andy North	285	Cherry Hills C.C.	§4,897
	J. C. Snead	286	Englewood, Colo.	
	Dave Stockton	286		
1979 (June)	Hale Irwin	284	Inverness Club	4,853
	Gary Player	286	Toledo, Ohio	
	Jerry Pate	286		
1980 (June)	Jack Nicklaus	†272	Baltusrol G.C. (Lower Course)	4,812
	Isao Aoki	274	Springfield, N.J.	

*Denotes Amateur
†Record Score
§Record Entry

*Record score for stroke play.

1960
SIXTIETH OPEN CHAMPIONSHIP

Held at the Cherry Hills Country Club, Englewood, Colo., June 16-18.
Yardage—7,004. Par 71.
2,453 Entries, 150 Qualifiers, 150 Starters.
Fifty-five contestants who completed 72 holes.

						Score	Money Prize
1	Arnold Palmer, Laurel Valley G.C., Ligonier, Pa.	72	71	72	65	280	$14,400.00
2	*Jack Nicklaus, Scioto C.C., Columbus, Ohio	71	71	69	71	282	------
3	E. J. (Dutch) Harrison, Old Warson C.C., St. Louis, Mo.	74	70	70	69	283	$ 3,950.00
	Julius Boros, Mid Pines C., Southern Pines, N.C.	73	69	68	73	283	3,950.00
	Mike Souchak, Grossinger C.C., Grossinger, N.Y.	68	67	73	75	283	3,950.00
	Ted Kroll, DeSoto Lakes G. & C.C., Bradenton, Fla.	72	69	75	67	283	3,950.00
	Jack Fleck, El Caballero C.C., Los Angeles, Calif.	70	70	72	71	283	3,950.00
	Dow Finsterwald, Tequesta C.C., Tequesta, Fla.	71	69	70	73	283	3,950.00
9	Ben Hogan, Fort Worth, Texas	75	67	69	73	284	1,950.00
	Jerry Barber, Wilshire C.C., Los Angeles, Calif.	69	71	70	74	284	1,950.00
	*Don Cherry, Wichita Falls C.C., Wichita Falls, Texas	70	71	71	72	284	-----
12	George Bayer, Gleneagles G.C., Lemont, Ill.	72	72	73	69	286	1,240.00
	Paul Harney, Auburn, Mass.	73	70	72	71	286	1,240.00
	Bill Casper, Jr., Apple Valley, Calif.	71	70	73	72	286	1,240.00
15	Bob Harris, Sunset Ridge C.C., Winnetka, Ill.	73	71	71	72	287	840.00
	Johnny Pott, Shreveport C.C., Shreveport, La.	75	68	69	75	287	840.00
17	Dave Marr, Houston, Texas	72	73	70	73	288	630.00
	Donald E. Whitt, DeAnza Desert C.C., Borrego Springs, Calif.	75	69	72	72	288	630.00
19	Gary Player, Killarney G.C., Johannesburg, S. Africa	70	72	71	76	289	472.50
	Bob Goalby, St. Clair C.C., Belleville, Ill.	73	70	72	74	289	472.50
	Sam Snead, Greenbrier G. & T.C., White Sulphur Springs, W. Va.	72	69	73	75	289	472.50
	Jackson D. Bradley, River Oaks C.C., Houston, Texas	73	73	69	74	289	472.50
23	Lloyd Mangrum, Apple Valley C.C., Apple Valley, Calif.	72	73	71	74	290	390.00
	Ken Venturi, Palo Alto Hills C.C., Palo Alto, Calif.	71	73	74	72	290	390.00
	Al Feminelli, Dellwood C.C., New City, N.Y.	75	71	71	73	290	390.00
	Robert R. Rosburg, Brookridge G. & C.C., Overland Park, Kans.	72	75	71	72	290	390.00
27	Lionel P. Hebert, Lafayette, La.	73	72	71	75	291	367.50
	Robert J. Shave, Jr., Manakiki G.C., Willoughby, Ohio	72	71	71	77	291	367.50
	Richard A. Stranahan, Alameda G.C., Alameda, Calif.	70	73	73	75	291	367.50
	Claude Harmon, Winged Foot G.C., Mamaroneck, N.Y.	73	73	75	70	291	367.50
31	M.R. (Chick) Harbert, Livonia, Mich.	72	74	69	77	292	360.00
	Harold L. Kneece, Greenville C.C., Greenville, S.C.	76	71	71	74	292	360.00
33	Rex Baxter, Jr., Amarillo C.C., Amarillo, Texas	79	67	76	71	293	330.00
	Doug Ford, Paradise C.C., Crystal River, Fla.	73	72	70	78	293	330.00
	Huston L. LaClair, Jr., C.C. of Birmingham, Birmingham, Ala.	70	74	76	73	293	330.00
36	Frank E. Boynton, Norfolk, Va.	73	72	75	73	293	330.00
	Dave Douglas, St. Louis C.C., Clayton, Mo.	75	71	76	71	293	330.00
38	Stan Dudas, North Hills C.C., North Hills, Pa.	71	74	73	76	294	300.00
	David Ragan, Dubsdread C.C., Orlando, Fla.	71	72	78	73	294	300.00
	Bruce Crampton, Beverley Park G.C., Sydney, Australia	70	71	75	78	294	300.00
	Al Mengert, Echo Lake C.C., Westfield, N.J.	75	71	74	74	294	300.00
42	Bill Johnston, Timpanogos G.C., Provo, Utah	73	74	73	75	295	300.00
43	Art Wall Jr., Pocono Manor C.C., Pocono Manor, Pa.	72	73	78	73	296	270.00
	Henry Ransom, St. Andrews G.C., St. Andrews, Ill.	69	76	73	78	296	270.00
	Cary Middlecoff, Memphis, Tenn.	77	70	72	77	296	270.00
46	Charles L. Sifford, Los Angeles, Calif.	74	70	77	76	297	260.00
	Doug Sanders, LaGorce, C.C., Miami Beach, Fla.	70	68	77	82	297	260.00
	Jim Turnesa, Ryewood C.C., Rye, N.Y.	76	71	72	78	297	260.00
49	Frank R. Stranahan, Paradise C.C., Crystal River, Fla.	72	73	74	79	298	240.00
	Sam Penecale, Whitemarsh Valley C.C., Philadelphia, Pa.	73	73	77	75	298	240.00
	Walter Burkemo, Franklin Hills C.C., Franklin, Mich.	74	72	72	80	298	240.00
	Howie Johnson, Houston, Texas	72	75	74	77	298	240.00
53	Bob Verwey, Benoni Lake G.C., Benoni, Transvaal, S.A.	75	72	79	75	301	240.00
54	Robert L. Watson, Fairview C.C., Elmsford, N.Y.	72	73	73	84	302	240.00
55	Robert Goetz, Tulsa C.C., Tulsa, Okla.	73	74	74	85	306	240.00

*Gold medals awarded to all amateurs.
Prize money totaling $60,720 awarded to professionals.

1961
SIXTY-FIRST OPEN CHAMPIONSHIP

Held at the Oakland Hills Country Club, Birmingham, Mich., June 15-17.
Yardage—6,907. Par 70.
2,449 Entries, 150 Qualifiers, 150 Starters.

Fifty-seven contestants who completed 72 holes.

						Score	Money Prize
1	Gene Littler, Singing Hills G.C., El Cajon, Calif.	73	68	72	68	281	$14,000.00
2	Bob Goalby, Paradise C.C., Crystal River, Fla.	70	72	69	71	282	6,000.00
	Doug Sanders, Ojai C.C., Ojai, Calif.	72	67	71	72	282	6,000.00
4	Mike Souchak, Grossinger C.C., Grossinger, N.Y.	73	70	68	73	284	4,000.00
	*Jack Nicklaus, Scioto C.C., Columbus, Ohio	75	69	70	70	284	-----
6	Dow Finsterwald, Tequesta C.C., Jupiter, Fla.	72	71	71	72	286	2,616.66
	Eric Monti, Hillcrest C.C., Los Angeles, Calif.	74	67	72	73	286	2,616.67
	Doug Ford, Tuckahoe, N.Y.	72	69	71	74	286	2,616.67
9	Jacky D. Cupit, Pine Crest C.C., Longview, Texas	72	72	67	76	287	1,750.00
	Gardner E. Dickinson, Jr., Tequesta C.C., Jupiter, Fla.	72	69	71	75	287	1,750.00
	Gary Player, Langhorne C.C., Langhorne, Pa.	75	72	69	71	287	1,750.00
12	Al Geiberger, Valley C. of Montecito, Santa Barbara, Calif.	71	70	73	74	288	1,250.00
	*Deane R. Beman, Bethesda C.C., Bethesda, Md.	74	72	72	70	288	-----
14	Dave Douglas, St. Louis C.C., Clayton, Mo.	72	72	75	70	289	900.00
	Ben Hogan, Fort Worth, Texas	71	72	73	73	289	900.00
	Arnold Palmer, C.C. of Miami, Miami, Fla.	74	75	70	70	289	900.00
17	Bill Casper, Jr., Apple Valley C.C., Apple Valley, Calif.	74	71	73	72	290	625.00
	E.J. (Dutch) Harrison, Olympic C., San Francisco, Calif.	74	71	76	69	290	625.00
	Sam Snead, Greenbrier G. & T.C., White Sulphur Springs, W.Va.	73	70	74	73	290	625.00
	Kel Nagle, Pymble G.C., Sydney, N.S.W., Australia	71	71	74	74	290	625.00
21	Robert R. Rosburg, Meriwether C.C., Portland, Ore.	72	67	74	78	291	500.00
22	Jim Ferrier, Burbank, Calif.	74	72	71	75	292	410.00
	Tommy Bolt, Paradise C.C., Crystal River, Fla.	70	73	73	76	292	410.00
	Bruce Crampton, Beverley Park G.C., Sydney, Australia	71	71	74	76	292	410.00
	Bobby Brue, North Hills C.C., Menomonee Falls, Wis.	69	72	73	78	292	410.00
	Billy Maxwell, Dallas, Texas	73	74	72	73	292	410.00
27	Jack Fleck, Deauville C.C., Los Angeles, Calif.	73	71	79	70	293	375.00
	Ted Kroll, Tamarac G. & C.C., Fort Lauderdale, Fla.	78	69	73	73	293	375.00
29	M. R. (Chick) Harbert, Port St. Lucie C.C., Port St. Lucie, Fla.	75	71	69	79	294	350.00
	Jerry Steelsmith, Glendale, Calif.	74	74	72	74	294	350.00
	Robert W. Harrison, Riviera C.C., Pacific Palisades, Calif.	79	70	71	74	294	350.00
	Milon Marusic, Algonquin G.C., Glendale, Mo.	75	74	71	74	294	350.00
	*Edward L. Brantly, Signal Mountain G&CC, Sig. Mountain, Tenn.	75	70	72	77	294	----
34	Herman Scharlau, Oakwood C.C., Kansas City, Mo.	75	69	73	78	295	325.00
	Bob Harris, Sunset Ridge C.C., Winnetka, Ill.	75	67	78	75	295	325.00
	Jerry Barber, Wilshire C.C., Los Angeles, Calif.	75	72	76	72	295	325.00
	Gene Coghill, Penfield C.C., Penfield, N.Y.	76	73	74	72	295	325.00
38	Jimmy Ferree, Old Town C., Winston-Salem, N.C.	73	72	78	73	296	312.50
	Marty Furgol, Cog Hill G.C., Lemont, Ill.	71	73	76	76	296	312.50
40	Wes Ellis, Jr., Mountain Ridge C.C., West Caldwell, N.J.	74	72	74	77	297	300.00
	Joe Taylor, Berry Hills C.C., Charleston, W. Va.	76	71	74	76	297	300.00
42	Bill Farrell, Baltusrol G.C., Springfield, N.J.	76	71	77	74	298	300.00
	Dick Mayer, La Jolla, Calif.	75	73	75	75	298	300.00
	*Wm. Hyndman III, Huntingdon Valley C.C., Huntingdon Valley, Pa.	73	75	73	77	298	----
45	Mason Rudolph, Clarksville G. & C.C., Clarksville, Tenn.	78	70	72	79	299	275.00
	Robert J. Shave, Jr., Manakiki C.C., Willoughby, Ohio	73	75	74	77	299	275.00
	Doug Higgins, Diamond Oaks C.C., Fort Worth, Texas	76	73	75	75	299	275.00
	Frank Stranahan, Inverness C., Toledo, Ohio	73	76	76	74	299	275.00
49	Jay Hebert, Lafayette, La.	77	71	77	75	300	275.00
	*Edward Meister, Jr., Kirtland C.C., Willoughby, Ohio	78	71	75	76	300	----
51	Dave Hill, Denver, Colorado	76	71	75	79	301	250.00
	Bob Bruno, Countryside G.C., Countryside, Ill.	78	71	77	75	301	250.00
	Rex Baxter, Jr., Amarillo C.C., Amarillo, Texas	71	78	75	77	301	250.00
54	Jackson Bradley, River Oaks C.C., Houston, Texas	75	73	78	76	302	250.00
55	Paul Harney, Auburn, Mass.	71	77	75	81	304	250.00
	Charles Malchaski, Brookwood C.C., Addison, Ill.	76	73	77	78	304	250.00
57	Jack Lumpkin, Echo Lake C.C., Westfield, N.J.	73	76	81	79	309	250.00

*Gold medals awarded to all amateurs.
Prize money totaling $68,300 awarded to professionals as follows: Championship—$60,500; Sectional Qualifying Championships—$7,800.

1962
SIXTY-SECOND OPEN CHAMPIONSHIP

Held at the Oakmont Country Club, Oakmont, Pa., June 14-17.
Yardage—6,894. Par 71. 2,475 Entries, 150 Starters.

Fifty-one contestants who completed 72 holes.

						Score	Money Prize
1	Jack Nicklaus, Tucson National G.C., Tucson, Ariz.	72	70	72	69	283	$17,500.00†
2	Arnold D. Palmer, C.C. of Miami, Miami, Fla.	71	68	73	71	283	10,500.00†
3	Phil Rodgers, La Jolla C.C., La Jolla, Calif.	74	70	69	72	285	5,500.00
	Bobby Nichols, Midland C.C., Midland, Texas	70	72	70	73	285	5,500.00
5	Gay Brewer, Jr., Paradise C.C., Crystal River, Fla.	73	72	73	69	387	4,000.00
6	Tommy Jacobs, Bermuda Dunes C.C., Bermuda Dunes, Calif.	74	71	73	70	288	2,750.00
	Gary Player, Ponte Vedra G.C., Ponte Vedra, Fla.	71	71	72	74	288	2,750.00
8	Gene A. Littler, Rancho Bernardo C.C., San Diego, Calif.	69	74	72	75	290	1,766.66
	Billy Maxwell, Tropicana C.C., Las Vegas, Nev.	71	70	75	74	290	1,766.67
	Doug Ford, Tam O'Shanter C.C., Brookville, N.Y.	74	75	71	70	290	1,766.67
11	Doug Sanders, Ojai Valley Inn & C.C., Ojai, Calif.	74	74	74	69	291	1,325.00
	Art Wall, Jr., Pocono Manor C.C., Pocono Manor, Pa.	73	72	72	74	291	1,325.00
13	Robert R. Rosburg, Meriwether C.C., Portland, Ore.	70	69	74	79	292	1,100.00
14	Bob Goalby, St. Clair C.C., Belleville, Ill.	73	74	73	73	293	975.00
	Mike Souchak, Grossinger C.C., Grossinger, N.Y.	75	73	72	73	293	975.00
	*Deane R. Beman, Chatmoss C.C., Martinsville, Va.	74	72	80	67	293	----
17	Bo Wininger, Odessa, Texas	73	74	69	78	294	800.00
	Jay Hebert, Doral C.C., Miami, Fla.	75	72	73	74	294	800.00
	Jacky D. Cupit, Pinecrest C.C., Longview, Texas	73	72	72	77	294	800.00
	Don Whitt, San Diego, Calif.	73	71	75	75	294	800.00
	Earl Stewart, Jr., Oak Cliff C.C., Dallas, Texas	75	73	75	71	294	800.00
22	Miller Barber, Apawamis C., Rye, N.Y.	73	70	77	75	295	650.00
23	Lionel Hebert, Lafayette, La.	75	72	75	74	296	575.00
	Gardner Dickinson, Jr., Tequesta C.C., Jupiter, Fla.	76	74	75	71	296	575.00
25	Stan Leonard, Vancouver, Canada	72	73	78	74	297	500.00
	*Edward L. Meister, Jr., Kirtland C.C., Willoughby, Ohio	78	72	76	71	297	----
27	Frank Boynton, Corpus Christi, Texas	71	75	74	78	298	450.00
28	Mason Rudolph, Clarksville G. & C.C., Clarksville, Tenn.	74	74	73	78	299	400.00
	Paul Harney, Pacton, Mass.	73	73	71	82	299	400.00
	Dave Douglas, St. Louis C.C., Clayton, Mo.	74	70	72	83	299	400.00
	Dean Refram, Medinah C.C., Medinah, Ill.	75	73	77	74	299	400.00
	Joe Campbell, Idlewold C.C., Pendleton, Ind.	78	71	72	78	299	400.00
33	Jerry Pittman, Southern Hills C.C., Tulsa, Okla.	75	72	75	78	300	375.00
	Gene Coghill, Penfield C.C., Penfield, N.Y.	74	76	73	77	300	375.00
	J. C. Goosie, East Bay C.C., Largo, Fla.	71	79	75	75	300	375.00
36	Daniel D. Sikes, Jr., Selva Marina C.C., Atlantic Beach, Fla.	74	72	78	77	301	375.00
	Wesley Ellis, Jr., Mountain Ridge C.C., West Caldwell, N.J.	73	73	77	78	301	375.00
38	Fred Hawkins, Coronado C.C., El Paso, Texas	73	77	77	75	302	350.00
	Bob McCallister, Claremont, Calif.	76	74	74	78	302	350.00
	Joe Moore, Jr., San Antonio, Texas	77	73	74	78	302	350.00
	Pete Cooper, Palm Beach National G.C., Palm Beach, Fla.	74	76	74	78	302	350.00
	Sam Snead, Greenbrier Hotel & C., White Sulphur Springs, W. Va.	76	74	78	74	302	350.00
43	Charles Sifford, Los Angeles, Calif.	75	74	76	78	303	325.00
	Al Balding, Markland Wood G.C., Etobicoke, Ont., Canada	73	77	78	75	303	325.00
45	Bruce Crampton, Sydney, Australia	75	73	75	81	304	325.00
	*William Hyndman, III, Huntingdon Valley C.C., Huntingdon Valley, Pa.	73	76	78	77	304	----
	*John H. Guenther, Jr., Berkshire C.C., Reading, Pa.	72	78	75	79	304	----
48	Johnny Pott, Gulf Hills C.C., Ocean Springs, Miss.	75	75	75	80	305	325.00
	*Robert Gardner, Montclair C.C., Montclair, N.J.	76	74	77	78	305	----
50	Charles W. Garlena, Gallitzin, Pa.	74	72	82	81	309	312.50
	Edward A. Rubis, Oxford C.C., Chicopee Falls, Mass.	76	74	81	78	309	312.50

*Amateur.
Playoff—June 17: Nicklaus, 71; Palmer, 74.
†Includes $2,500 bonus to each player in playoff.
Prize money totaling $81,600 awarded to professionals as follows: Championship— $73,800; Sectional Qualifying Championships— $7,800.

1963
SIXTY-THIRD OPEN CHAMPIONSHIP

Held at The Country Club, Brookline, Mass., June 20–23.
Yardage–6,870. Par–71.
2,392 Entries, 150 Qualifiers, 150 Starters.

Fifty-one Contestants who completed 72 holes.

						Score	Money Prize
1	†Julius Boros, Mid Pines Club, Southern Pines, N.C.	71	74	76	72	293	$17,500.00*
2	†Jacky D. Cupit, Mountain View C.C., Corona, Calif.	70	72	76	75	293	8,500.00*
3	†Arnold Palmer, Laurel Valley C.C., Ligonier, Pa.	73	69	77	74	293	8,500.00*
4	Paul Harney, Sunset Oaks C.C., Sunset, Calif.	78	70	73	73	294	5,000.00
5	Billy Maxwell, Tropicana C.C., Las Vegas, Nev.	73	73	75	74	295	3,166.66
	Bruce Crampton, Sydney, Australia	74	72	75	74	295	3,166.67
	Tony Lema, San Leandro, Calif.	71	74	74	76	295	3,166.67
8	Gary Player, Arawak C., Paradise Is., Nassau, Bahamas	74	75	75	72	296	1,875.00
	Walter Burkemo, Franklin Hills C.C., Franklin, Mich.	72	71	76	77	296	1,875.00
10	Daniel D. Sikes, Jr., Selva Marina C.C., Atlantic Beach, Fla.	77	73	73	74	297	1,550.00
11	Don January, Walnut Valley G.C., Walnut, Calif.	72	74	78	75	299	1,400.00
12	Dow H. Finsterwald, Tequesta C.C., Tequesta, Fla.	73	69	79	79	300	1,175.00
	Dave Ragan, Dubsdread G.C., Orlando, Fla.	78	74	74	74	300	1,175.00
14	Michael Fetchick, Glen Head C.C., Glen Head, N.Y.	74	76	77	75	302	900.00
	Lionel P. Hebert, Lafayette, La.	71	79	76	76	302	900.00
	Bobby Nichols, Midland C.C., Midland, Texas	74	75	75	78	302	900.00
	Davis M. Love, Jr., Charlotte C.C., Charlotte, N.C.	71	74	78	79	302	900.00
	Dean Refram, Medinah C.C., Medinah, Ill.	72	71	80	79	302	900.00
19	Robert J. Charles, DeSoto Lakes G.C., Sarasota, Fla.	74	76	76	77	303	725.00
	Ken Still, Fircrest G.C., Tacoma, Wash.	76	75	78	74	303	725.00
21	Dave Marr, Hot Springs, Ark.	75	74	77	78	304	525.00
	Gardner E. Dickinson, Jr., Tequesta C.C., Tequesta, Fla.	76	71	78	79	304	525.00
	Jack Burke, Champions G.C., Houston, Texas	75	76	78	75	304	525.00
	Doug Sanders, Ojai Valley Inn & C.C., Ojai, Calif.	77	74	75	78	304	525.00
	Gene A. Littler, Rancho Bernardo, La Jolla, Calif.	75	77	80	72	304	525.00
	Bob McCallister, Mountain View C.C., Corona, Calif.	75	77	76	76	304	525.00
27	Otto Greiner, Knickerbocker C.C., Tenafly, N.J.	74	75	76	80	305	400.00
	Mason Rudolph, Lehigh Acres C.C., Lehigh Acres, Fla.	76	75	78	76	305	400.00
	Ted Makalena, Ala Wai C.C., Honolulu, Hawaii	75	77	76	77	305	400.00
30	Bill Ogden, North Shore C.C., Glenview, Ill.	73	76	78	79	306	387.50
	Robert G. Goetz, Tulsa, Okla.	79	72	80	75	306	387.50
32	Sam Reynolds, Hickory Hills C.C., Springfield, Mo.	79	72	79	77	307	366.66
	Phil Rodgers, Perdido Bay G.C., Perdido Bay, Fla.	77	74	77	79	307	366.66
	Al Balding, Maryland Wood G.C., Etobicoke, Ont., Canada	73	78	77	79	307	366.67
	Tommy Jacobs, Bermuda Dunes C.C., Bermuda Dunes, Calif.	73	78	81	75	307	366.67
	Bill Johnston, Arizona C.C., Phoenix, Ariz.	77	75	76	79	307	366.67
	Mike Souchak, Grossinger C.C., Grossinger, N.Y.	77	75	82	73	307	366.67
38	Jay Hebert, Lafayette, La.	73	76	83	77	309	350.00
	Ed Furgol, Westmoreland C.C., Export, Pa.	74	78	79	78	309	350.00
40	Art Wall, Jr., Pocono Manor, C.C., Pocono Manor, Pa.	73	77	76	84	310	337.50
	Frank E. Boynton, Corpus Christi C.C., Corpus Christi, Texas	74	78	77	81	310	337.50
42	George Bayer, South Pasadena, Calif.	76	74	81	80	311	325.00
	Sam Snead, Greenbrier G. & T.C., White Sulphur Springs, W. Va.	74	75	79	83	311	325.00
44	Stan Thirsk, Kansas City C.C., Shawnee Mission, Kans.	73	77	79	83	312	325.00
	Jimmy Clark, Huntington Beach C.C., Huntington Beach, Calif.	74	74	84	80	312	325.00
46	Bob Gajda, Forest Lake C.C., Bloomfield Hills, Mich.	69	80	84	80	313	300.00
47	Ross Coon, Jr., Canterbury G.C., Cleveland, Ohio	78	71	85	80	314	300.00
	William Gabal, Baden, Pa.	76	76	81	81	314	300.00
49	Paul E. Kelly, Sleepy Hollow C.C., Scarsborough, N.Y.	72	79	80	85	316	300.00
50	Thomas D. Aaron, Gainesville, Ga.	77	74	91	78	320	300.00
	Bob Harris, Sunset Ridge C.C., Winnetka, Ill.	73	79	86	82	320	300.00

†Playoff; 18 holes, June 23–Boros, 70; Cupit, 73; Palmer, 76.
*Includes $1,500 bonus to each player in playoff.

Prize money totaling $96,350 awarded to professionals as follows:
Championship–$88,550; Sectional Qualifying Championships–$7,800.

1964
SIXTY-FOURTH OPEN CHAMPIONSHIP

Held at Congressional Country Club, Washington, D.C., June 18–20.
Yardage–7,053. Par 70.
2,341 Entries, 150 Qualifiers, 150 Starters.

Fifty-four contestants who completed 72 holes.

						Score	Money Prize
1	Ken Venturi, Paradise C.C., Crystal River, Fla.	72	70	66	70	278	$17,000.00
2	Tommy Jacobs, Bermuda Dunes C.C., Bermuda Dunes, Calif.	72	64	70	76	282	8,500.00
3	Bob Charles, De Soto Lakes G.C., Sarasota, Fla.	72	72	71	68	283	6,000.00
4	Billy Casper, Mountain View C.C., Corona, Calif.	71	74	69	71	285	5,000.00
5	Gay Brewer, Jr., Dallas, Texas	76	69	73	68	286	3,750.00
	Arnold Palmer, Laurel Valley C.C., Ligonier, Pa.	68	69	75	74	286	3,750.00
7	Bill Collins, Grossinger C.C., Grossinger, N.Y.	70	71	74	72	287	3,000.00
8	Dow Finsterwald, Broadmoor G.C., Colorado Springs, Colo.	73	72	71	72	288	2,500.00
9	Robert Rosburg, Meriwether C.C., Hillsboro, Ore.	73	73	70	73	289	1,950.00
	Johnny Pott, Gulf Hills Ranch & C.C., Ocean Springs, Miss.	71	73	73	72	289	1,950.00
11	George Bayer, Incline Village C.C., Incline Village, Nev.	75	73	72	71	291	1,333.33
	Don January, Dallas Texas	75	73	74	69	291	1,333.33
	Gene A. Littler, La Jolla C.C., La Jolla, Calif.	73	71	74	73	291	1,333.34
14	Terry Dill, Muleshoe C.C., Muleshoe, Texas	73	73	75	71	292	900.00
	Ed Furgol, Westmoreland C.C., Export, Pa.	72	74	72	74	292	900.00
	Bobby Nichols, Mountain View C.C., Corona, Calif.	72	72	76	72	292	900.00
	Al Geiberger, Carlton Oaks C.C., Carlton Oaks, Calif.	74	70	75	73	292	900.00
	Bruce Crampton, Sydney, Australia	72	71	75	74	292	900.00
	Raymond L. Floyd, St. Andrews C.C., St. Andrews, Ill.	73	70	72	77	292	900.00
20	Tony Lema, San Leandro, Calif.	71	72	75	75	293	700.00
21	Lionel P. Hebert, Lafayette, La.	73	74	72	75	294	625.00
	Bill Ogden, North Shore C.C., Glenview, Ill.	73	73	73	75	294	625.00
23	Ted Makalena, Ala Wai G.C., Honolulu, Hawaii	73	74	75	73	295	475.00
	Dudley Wysong, Jr., McKinney C.C., McKinney, Texas	74	73	75	73	295	475.00
	Jack Nicklaus, Scioto C.C., Columbus, Ohio	72	73	77	73	295	475.00
	Gary Player, Arawak C., Nassau, Bahamas	75	74	72	74	295	475.00
27	Charles Sifford, Los Angeles, Calif.	72	70	77	77	296	400.00
28	Jacky Cupit, Mountain View C.C., Corona, Calif.	75	71	75	76	297	400.00
	Labron Harris, Jr., Turner's Lodge, Burneyville, Okla.	72	76	74	75	297	400.00
	Don Fairfield, Perdido Bay C.C., Perdido Bay, Fla.	75	72	74	76	297	400.00
	*John Farquhar, Amarillo C.C., Amarillo, Texas	74	73	77	73	297	----
32	Tom Nieporte, Piping Rock C., Locust Valley, N.Y.	73	73	76	76	298	375.00
	Doug Sanders, Ojai Valley Inn & C.C., Ojai, Calif.	74	74	76	74	298	375.00
34	Sam Snead, Greenbrier G.C., White Sulphur Springs, W. Va.	77	72	75	75	299	368.75
	Mason Rudolph, Lehigh Acres C.C., Lehigh Acres, Fla.	76	73	74	76	299	368.75
	Monte Bradley, Meadowbrook C.C., Ballwin, Mo.	75	74	73	77	299	368.75
	Paul Scodeller, Navy-Marine G.C., Honolulu, Hawaii	72	76	72	79	299	368.75
	*William C. Campbell, Guyan G. & C.C., Huntington, W. Va.	71	73	79	76	299	----
39	Paul Harney, Sunset Oaks C.C., Rocklin, Calif.	75	73	79	73	300	350.00
	Larry E. Beck, Whispering Pines C.C., Whispering Pines, N.C.	77	73	75	75	300	350.00
	George W. Archer, Gilroy G. & C.C., Gilroy, Calif.	75	74	76	75	300	350.00
42	Robert Panasiuk, Hydeaway G.C., Elmstead, Ont., Canada	72	78	78	73	301	350.00
43	Davis M. Love, Jr., Charlotte C.C., Charlotte, N.C.	77	72	71	82	302	325.00
44	Daniel D. Sikes, Jr., Ponte Vedra C., Ponte Vedra Beach, Fla.	77	73	76	77	303	325.00
	Bill Martindale, Jacksonville, Fla.	72	76	80	75	303	325.00
	David Boies, Brownwood, Texas	73	72	83	75	303	325.00
47	Rex Baxter, Jr., Amarillo, Texas	76	73	76	80	305	325.00
48	Robert (Skee) Riegel, York Road G.C., Jamison, Pa.	80	70	82	74	306	300.00
49	Ron Howell, Woodmont C.C., Rockville, Md.	78	72	78	79	307	300.00
50	M. R. (Chick) Harbert, Port St. Lucie C.C., Fort Pierce, Fla.	76	74	80	78	308	300.00
	*Jerry M. Greenbaum, Standard C., Atlanta, Ga.	75	74	80	79	308	----
52	Jimmy Clark, Argyle C.C., Silver Spring, Md.	73	77	78	81	309	300.00
53	Bryant Hiskey, Galena Park, Texas	78	72	78	83	311	300.00
54	William Gabal, Baden Pa.	76	73	83	80	312	300.00

*Gold medals awarded to all amateurs.
Prize money totaling $95,400 awarded to professionals as follows:
Championship–$87,600; Sectional Qualifying Championships–$7,800.

1965
SIXTY-FIFTH OPEN CHAMPIONSHIP

Held at Bellerive Country Club, St. Louis, Mo., June 17–21.
Yardage–7,191. Par–70.
2,271 Entries, 150 Qualifiers, 150 Starters.

Fifty contestants who completed 72 holes.

						Score	Money Prize
1	†Gary Player, Johannesburg, South Africa	70	70	71	71	282	$26,000.00+
2	†Kel Nagle, Pymble C.C., Sydney, Australia	68	73	72	69	282	13,500.00+
3	Frank Beard, Seneca G.C., Louisville, Ky.	74	69	70	71	284	9,000.00
4	Julius Boros, Mid Pines Club, Southern Pines, N.C.	72	75	70	70	287	6,500.00
	Al Geiberger, Carlton Oaks C.C., Santee, Calif.	70	76	70	71	287	6,500.00
6	Raymond L. Floyd, St. Andrews C.C., St. Andrews, Ill.	72	72	76	68	288	4,500.00
	Bruce Devlin, Sydney, Australia	72	73	72	71	288	4,500.00
8	Tony Lema, San Leandro, Calif.	72	74	73	70	289	2,500.00
	Gene A. Littler, Dunes C.C., Las Vegas, Nev.	73	71	73	72	289	2,500.00
	Dudley Wysong, Jr., Casper C.C., Casper, Wyo.	72	75	70	72	289	2,500.00
11	Doug Sanders, Ojai Valley Inn & C.C., Ojai, Calif.	77	73	69	71	290	1,650.00
	Mason Rudolph, Lehigh Acres C.C., Lehigh Acres, Fla.	69	72	73	76	290	1,650.00
	*Deane R. Beman, Congressional C.C., Bethesda, Md.	69	73	76	72	290	-----
14	Billy Maxwell, Greentree C.C., Indianapolis, Ind.	76	73	71	71	291	1,500.00
15	Steve R. Oppermann, McLaren Park G.C., San Francisco, Calif.	72	77	73	70	292	1,400.00
16	Gay Brewer, Jr,, Dallas, Texas	72	74	71	76	293	1,300.00
17	Billy Casper, Peacock Gap C.C., Peacock Gap, Calif.	73	73	76	72	294	1,087.50
	Bob Verwey, Houghton G.C., Johannesburg, South Africa	73	74	75	72	294	1,087.50
	Charles Huckaby, Woodmere Club, Woodmere, N.Y.	73	74	73	74	294	1,087.50
	George Knudson, Oakdale G. & C.C., Toronto, Ont., Canada	80	69	73	72	294	1,087.50
21	Eric Monti, Hillcrest C.C., Los Angeles, Calif.	76	71	75	73	295	925.00
	Gardner Dickinson, Jr., Lost Tree Village, Fla.	77	73	71	74	295	925.00
23	Lou Graham, Nashville, Tenn.	70	77	76	73	296	850.00
24	Ted Kroll, Franklin Hills C.C., Franklin, Mich.	76	74	72	75	297	732.50
	Sam Snead, Greenbrier G.C., White Sulphur Springs, W. Va.	75	71	77	74	297	732.50
	Labron Harris, Jr., Turner's Lodge G.C., Burnyville, Okla.	74	76	74	73	297	732.50
	Wesley Ellis, Jr., Mountain Ridge C.C., W. Caldwell, N.J.	73	76	77	71	297	732.50
28	Dean Refram, Medinah C.C., Medinah, Ill.	71	79	72	76	298	630.00
	Ernest J. (Dutch) Harrison, Forest Hills G.& C.C., Ellisville, Mo.	78	72	72	76	298	630.00
	Tommy Jacobs, Bermuda Dunes C.C., Bermuda Dunes, Calif.	76	71	74	77	298	630.00
	Terry Wilcox, Siwanoy C.C., Bronxville, N.Y.	74	73	73	78	298	630.00
32	Jack Nicklaus, Columbus, Ohio	78	72	73	76	299	550.00
	Miller Barber, Pecan Valley C.C., San Antonio, Texas	72	76	74	77	299	550.00
	Gordon Jones, Rio Pinar C.C., Orlando, Fla.	71	74	75	79	299	550.00
	Bruce Crampton, Sydney, Australia	74	76	72	77	299	550.00
36	Duff Lawrence, Scioto C.C., Columbus, Ohio	73	73	75	79	300	495.00
	Daniel D. Sikes, Jr., Selva Marina C.C., Atlantic Beach, Fla.	72	78	75	75	300	495.00
38	Robert R. Rosburg, Meriwether C.C., Hillsboro, Ore.	73	75	75	78	301	480.00
	*Edgar M. Tutwiler, Jr., Highlands G & C.C., Indianapolis, Ind.	77	73	76	75	301	----
40	Rex Baxter, Jr., Houston, Texas	70	75	79	78	302	455.00
	Juan Rodriguez, Dorado Beach, C.C., Dorado Beach, P.R.	78	72	77	75	302	455.00
	Tom Weiskopf, Bedford, Ohio	76	72	77	77	302	455.00
	Dick Hendrickson, Laurel Oak C.C., Gibbsboro, N.J.	74	76	72	80	302	455.00
44	Dick Hart, Hinsdale G.C., Hinsdale, Ill.	74	75	80	74	303	420.00
	Bill Ogden, North Shore C.C., Glenview, Ill.	75	73	79	76	303	420.00
	Jack Lumpkin, Oak Hill C.C., Rochester, N.Y.	74	74	74	81	303	420.00
47	Sam Carmichael, Martinsville C.C., Martinsville, Ind.	76	74	76	78	304	400.00
48	Robert G. Reith, Minikahda Club, Minneapolis, Minn.	73	76	73	83	305	385.00
	Paul E. Kelly, Sleepy Hollow C.C., Scarborough, N.Y.	75	74	78	78	305	385.00
50	Franklin R. Keller, Normandie G.C., St. Louis, Mo.	77	73	79	78	307	370.00

†Playoff: 18 holes, June 21–Player, 71; Nagle, 74.
+Includes $1,000.00 bonus to each player in playoff.
*Gold medals awarded to all amateurs.
Prize money totaling $131,690 awarded to professionals as follows:
Championship–$123,890; Sectional Qualifying Championships–$7,800.

1966
SIXTY-SIXTH OPEN CHAMPIONSHIP

Held at Olympic Country Club, San Francisco, Calif., June 16-20.
Yardage—6,719. Par 70.
Sixty-four contestants who completed 72 holes:

						Score	Money Prize
1	†Bill Casper, Jr., Peacock Gap C.C., Peacock Gap, Calif.	69	68	73	68	278	$26,500.00+
2	†Arnold Palmer, Laurel Valley, Pa.	71	66	70	71	278	14,000.00+
3	Jack Nicklaus, Scioto C.C., Columbus, Ohio	71	71	69	74	285	9,000.00
4	Tony Lema, Marco Island C.C., Marco Island, Fla.	71	74	70	71	286	6,500.00
	Dave Marr, Goodyear G. & C.C., Litchfield Park, Ariz.	71	74	68	73	286	6,500.00
6	Phil Rodgers, La Jolla C.C., La Jolla, Calif.	70	70	73	74	287	5,000.00
7	Bobby Nichols, Louisville, Ky.	74	72	71	72	289	4,000.00
8	Wesley Ellis, Jr., Mountain Ridge C.C., W. Caldwell, N.J.	71	75	74	70	290	2,800.00
	Doug Sanders, Ojai Valley C.C., Ojai, Calif.	70	75	74	71	290	2,800.00
	Mason Rudolph, Clarksville, Tenn.	74	72	71	73	290	2,800.00
	*John Miller, Olympic C.C., San Francisco, Calif.	70	72	74	74	290	-----
12	Ben Hogan, Fort Worth, Texas	72	73	76	70	291	2,200.00
13	Rod Funseth, Esmeralda G.C., Spokane, Wash.	75	75	69	73	292	1,900.00
	Rives McBee, Midland C.C., Midland, Texas	76	64	74	78	292	1,900.00
15	Gary Player, Castle Harbour G.C., Bermuda	78	72	74	69	293	1,700.00
	*Robert Murphy, Lone Palm C.C., Lakeland, Fla.	73	72	75	73	293	-----
17	George W. Archer, Gilroy C.C., Gilroy, Calif.	74	72	76	72	294	1,430.00
	Don January, Dallas, Texas	73	73	75	73	294	1,430.00
	Ken Venturi, California G.C., So. San Francisco, Calif.	73	77	71	73	294	1,430.00
	Julius Boros, Mid Pines C., Southern Pines, N.C.	74	69	77	74	294	1,430.00
	Frank Beard, Seneca G.C., Louisville, Ky.	76	74	69	75	294	1,430.00
22	Dave Hill, Hiwan G.C., Evergreen, Colo.	72	71	79	73	295	1,175.00
	Bob Verwey, Houghton G.C., Johannesburg, S. Africa	72	73	75	75	295	1,175.00
	Walter Burkemo, Detroit G.C., Detroit, Mich.	76	72	70	77	295	1,175.00
	Bob Goalby, St. Clair C.C., Belleville, Ill.	71	73	71	80	295	1,175.00
26	Miller Barber, Pecan Valley C.C., San Antonio, Texas	74	76	77	69	296	997.50
	Robert J. Shave, Jr., Philadelphia C.C., Gladwyne, Pa.	76	71	74	75	296	997.50
	Bruce Devlin, Sea Pines Plantation, Hilton Head Island, S.C.	74	75	71	76	296	997.50
	Al Mengert, Tacoma C. & G.C., Tacoma, Wash.	67	77	71	81	296	997.50
30	Al Geiberger, Carlton Oaks C.C., Santee, Calif.	75	75	74	73	297	920.00
	Vince Sullivan, Metuchen C.C., Metuchen, N.J.	77	73	73	74	297	920.00
	Tommy Aaron, Gainesville, Ga.	73	75	71	78	297	920.00
	*Deane R. Beman, Bethesda C.C., Bethesda, Md.	75	76	70	76	297	----
34	Kel Nagle, Pymble G.C., St. Ives, Australia	70	73	81	74	298	870.00
	Thomas R. Veech, North Hills C.C., Menomonee Falls, Wis.	72	73	77	76	298	870.00
36	Don Massengale, Jacksboro C.C., Jacksboro, Texas	68	79	78	74	299	790.00
	Bob Wolfe, Middle Bay C.C., Oceanside, N.Y.	77	72	76	74	299	790.00
	Ken Still, Fircrest G.C., Tacoma, Wash.	73	74	77	75	299	790.00
	Gay Brewer, Jr., Dallas, Texas	73	76	74	76	299	790.00
	Gene Bone, Bay Pointe G.C., Walled Lake, Mich.	74	76	72	77	299	790.00
	Billy Maxwell, Greentree C.C., Indianapolis, Ind.	73	74	74	78	299	790.00
	*Charles W. Harrison, Atlanta Athletic Club C.C., Atlanta, Ga.	72	77	80	70	299	----
	*Edgar M. Tutwiler, Jr., Highland G.& C.C., Indianapolis, Ind.	73	78	76	72	299	----
44	Robert R. Rosburg, Springbrook C.C., Leeds, Me.	77	73	75	75	300	697.50
	Juan (Chi-Chi) Rodriguez, Dorado Beach G.C., Dorado, P.R.	74	76	73	77	300	697.50
	George Knudson, Oakdale G. & C.C., Downsview, Ont., Canada	75	76	72	77	300	697.50
	Tom Nieporte, Piping Rock Club, Locust Valley, N.Y.	71	77	74	78	300	697.50
48	Gene Littler, La Jolla C.C., La Jolla Calif.	68	83	72	78	301	655.00
	George Bayer, Incline Village C.C., Incline Village, Nev.	75	74	78	74	301	655.00
	Steve Oppermann, McLaren Park G.C., San Francisco, Calif.	73	76	74	78	301	655.00
	Gardner Dickinson, Jr., Lost Tree C., Lost Tree Village, Fla.	75	74	78	74	301	655.00
52	Charles Coody, Fort Worth, Texas	76	75	76	75	302	625.00
	Tom Shaw, Meriwether C.C., Hillsboro, Ore.	75	74	73	80	302	625.00
54	Lee B. Trevino, Horizon G.C., El Paso, Texas	74	73	78	78	303	600.00
	Johnny Bulla, Century C.C., Scottsdale, Ariz.	73	76	77	77	303	600.00
	Gene Borek, Pine Hollow C.C., East Norwich, N.Y.	75	76	77	75	303	600.00
57	Lee Elder, Oxon Blades G.C., Washington, D.C.	74	77	74	79	304	565.00
	Bruce Crampton, Sydney, Australia	74	72	80	78	304	565.00
	Claude K. King, Cavalier G. & Yacht C., Virginia Beach, Va.	74	77	77	76	304	565.00
	David Jimenez, Chevy Chase Club, Chevy Chase, Md.	75	73	81	75	304	565.00
61	Stan Thirsk, Kansas City C.C., Shawnee Mission, Kans.	72	79	72	82	305	540.00
	*Hale S. Irwin, Jr., Boulder C.C., Boulder, Colo.	75	75	78	77	305	----
63	Herb Hooper, Willow Oaks C.C., Richmond, Va.	73	76	85	72	306	530.00
64	Joe Zakarian, Del Rio G. & C.C., Modesto, Calif.	77	74	79	80	310	520.00

†Playoff: 18 holes, June 20—Casper, 69; Palmer, 73.
+Includes $1,500 bonus to each player in playoff. *Gold medals awarded to all amateurs.
Prize money totaling $155,290 awarded to professionals as follows:
Championship—$147,490; Sectional Qualifying Championships—$7,800.

1967
SIXTY-SEVENTH OPEN CHAMPIONSHIP

Held at Baltusrol Golf Club (Lower Course), Springfield, N.J., June 15–18.
Yardage–7,015. Par 70.
2,651 Entries, 150 Qualifiers, 150 Starters.

Sixty-four contestants who completed 72 holes.

						Score	Money Prize
1	Jack Nicklaus, Scioto C.C., Columbus, Ohio	71	67	72	65	275	$30,000.00
2	Arnold Palmer, Laurel Valley C.C., Ligonier, Pa.	69	68	73	69	279	15,000.00
3	Don January, Dallas, Texas	69	72	70	70	281	10,000.00
4	Bill Casper, Jr., Bonita, Calif.	69	70	71	72	282	7,500.00
5	Lee B. Trevino, Horizon Hills C.C., El Paso, Texas	72	70	71	70	283	6,000.00
6	Bob Goalby, Tamarisk C.C., Palm Springs, Calif.	72	71	70	71	284	4,166.67
	Deane R. Beman, Bethesda C.C., Bethesda, Md.	69	71	71	73	284	4,166.67
	Gardner Dickinson, Jr., Lost Tree Club, Lost Tree Village, Fla.	70	73	68	73	284	4,166.66
9	Kel Nagle, Pymble Golf Club, Sydney, Australia	70	72	72	71	285	2,566.67
	Art Wall, Jr., Honesdale G.C., Honesdale, Pa.	69	73	72	71	285	2,566.67
	Dave Marr, Goodyear Golf and C.C., Litchfield Park, Ariz.	70	74	70	71	285	2,566.66
12	Al Balding, Markland Wood C.C., Etobicoke, Ont., Canada	75	72	71	68	286	2,000.00
	Gary Player, Castle Harbour G. & C.C., Bermuda	69	73	73	71	286	2,000.00
	Wesley Ellis, Jr., Westchester C.C., Rye, N.Y.	74	69	70	73	286	2,000.00
15	Tom Weiskopf, Marco Island, Fla.	72	71	74	70	287	1,800.00
16	Jerry Pittman, The Creek Club, Locust Valley, N.Y.	72	72	75	69	288	1,650.00
	E.J. (Dutch) Harrison, Forest Hills G. & C.C., Ellisville, Mo.	70	76	72	70	288	1,650.00
18	Paul Harney, Pleasant Valley C.C., Sutton, Mass.	71	75	72	71	289	1,475.00
	Bob Verwey, Houghton G.C., Johannesburg, So. Africa	75	71	69	74	289	1,475.00
	Dave Hill, Evergreen, Colo.	76	69	69	75	289	1,475.00
	Miller Barber, Pecan Valley C.C., San Antonio, Texas	71	71	69	78	289	1,475.00
	*Martin A. Fleckman, Port Arthur C.C., Port Arthur, Texas	67	73	69	80	289	-----
23	Billy Farrell, The Stanwich Club, Greenwich, Conn.	76	71	73	70	290	1,275.00
	Bobby Nichols, Louisville, Ky.	74	71	73	72	290	1,275.00
	Howie Johnson, Canyon C.C., Palm Springs, Calif.	74	73	71	72	290	1,275.00
	Bruce Devlin, Cleveland, Ohio	72	68	77	73	290	1,275.00
	*Robert J. Murphy, Jr., Lone Palm G.C., Lakeland, Fla.	73	73	75	69	290	-----
28	Lou Graham, Nashville, Tenn.	71	75	76	69	291	1,063.34
	Charles Coody, Fort Worth, Texas	77	71	75	68	291	1,063.34
	Michael Fetchick, Glen Head C.C., Glen Head, N.Y.	73	71	76	71	291	1,063.33
	Ken Venturi, California G.C., San Francisco, Calif.	74	74	72	71	291	1,063.33
	Labron Harris, Jr., Lakeside G.C., Stillwater, Okla.	75	71	72	73	291	1,063.33
	Al Geiberger, Carlton Oaks C.C., Santee, Calif.	71	73	73	74	291	1,063.33
34	Doug Sanders, Shamrock C.C., Tulsa, Okla.	76	72	74	70	292	940.00
	Ben Hogan, Ft. Worth, Texas	72	72	76	72	292	940.00
	Tom Nieporte, Piping Rock Club, Locust Valley, N.Y.	72	71	74	75	292	940.00
37	Rod Funseth, Esmeralda G.C., Spokane, Wash.	78	69	75	71	293	900.00
38	Mason Rudolph, LeHigh Acres C.C., LeHigh Acres, Fla.	78	70	75	71	294	850.00
	Raymond Floyd, St. Andrews C.C., St. Andrews, Ill.	74	74	73	73	294	850.00
	Gay Brewer, Jr., Dallas, Texas	74	70	76	74	294	850.00
	Donald W. Bies, Seattle G.C., Seattle, Wash.	71	73	72	78	294	850.00
42	Butch Baird, Carlton Oaks C.C., Santee, Calif.	72	73	77	73	295	785.00
	Bob McCallister, Mountain View C.C., Corona, Calif.	75	73	74	73	295	785.00
	Juan Rodriguez, Dorado Beach G.C., Dorado Beach, P.R.	69	75	76	75	295	785.00
	Bert Yancey, Killen Estates and C.C., Tallahassee, Fla.	72	73	71	79	295	785.00
46	R.H. (Dick) Sikes, Springdale C.C., Springdale, Ark.	74	74	76	72	296	755.00
	Bruce Cudd, Columbia-Edgewater C.C., Portland, Ore.	73	73	75	75	296	755.00
48	Steve Oppermann, McLeran Park G.C., San Francisco, Calif.	73	73	76	75	297	715.00
	Don Essig, III, Hillcrest C.C., Indianapolis, Ind.	75	72	75	75	297	715.00
	Tom Strange, Bow Creek G. & C.C., Virginia Beach, Va.	72	73	76	76	297	715.00
	Frank Boynton, Mayfield C.C., South Euclid, Ohio	74	72	74	77	297	715.00
	Bob Zimmerman, Moraine C.C., Dayton, Ohio	73	75	72	77	297	715.00
	Ted Kroll, Franklin Hills C.C., Franklin, Mich.	73	72	74	78	297	715.00
54	Frank Beard, Wildwood C.C., Louisville, Ky.	73	73	77	75	298	655.00
	Rocky Thompson, Wichita Falls C.C., Wichita Falls, Texas	75	71	77	75	298	655.00
	Bobby Clark, Lakewood, Calif.	76	71	75	76	298	655.00
	Carl Unis, Ozaukee C.C., Mequon, Wis.	74	72	75	77	298	655.00
	Bob Hold, Sportland G.C., Wheatridge, Colo.	71	71	78	78	298	655.00
	Cesar Sanudo, Singing Hills C.C., El Cajon, Calif.	73	73	79	73	298	655.00
60	Dick Lotz, Hayward, Calif.	76	67	80	76	299	615.00
	Rives McBee, Midland C.C., Midland, Texas	76	72	73	78	299	615.00
62	Mac Hunter, Riviera C.C., Pacific Palisades, Calif.	75	72	78	75	300	600.00
63	Jimmy Ferriell, Jr., Summit Hills C.C., Fort Mitchell, Ky.	73	73	81	75	302	600.00
64	Chuck Scally, Scally's G.C., Coraopolis, Pa.	73	74	79	80	306	600.00

*Gold medals awarded to all amateurs.
Prize money totaling $177,800 awarded to professionals as follows:
Championship–$169,400; Sectional Qualifying Championships–$8,400.

1968
SIXTY-EIGHTH OPEN CHAMPIONSHIP

Held at Oak Hill Country Club, (East Course), Rochester, N.Y., June 13-16.
Yardage—6,962. Par 70.
3,007 Entries, 150 Qualifiers, 150 Starters.

Sixty-three contestants who completed 72 holes.

						Score	Prize Money
1	Lee B. Trevino, Horizon Hills C.C., Horizon City, Texas	69	68	69	69	275	$30,000.00
2	Jack Nicklaus, Scioto C.C., Columbus, Ohio	72	70	70	67	279	15,000.00
3	Bert Yancey, Killearn G. & C.C., Tallahassee, Fla.	67	68	70	76	281	10,000.00
4	Bobby Nichols, Louisville, Ky.	74	71	68	69	282	7,500.00
5	Donald Bies, Seattle G.C., Seattle, Wash.	70	70	75	69	284	5,500.00
	John S. Spray, Cedar Rapids, Iowa	73	75	71	65	284	5,500.00
7	Bob Charles, Christchurch, New Zealand	73	69	72	71	285	3,750.00
	Jerry Pittman, The Creek Club, Locust Valley, N.Y.	73	67	74	71	285	3,750.00
9	Gay Brewer, Jr., Dallas, Texas	71	71	75	69	286	2,516.67
	Bill Casper, Jr., Bonita, Calif.	75	68	71	72	286	2,516.67
	Bruce Devlin, Palm Aire C.C., Pompano Beach, Fla.	71	69	75	71	286	2,516.67
	Al Geiberger, Carlton Oaks C.C., Santee, Calif.	72	74	68	72	286	2,516.67
	Sam Snead, Greenbrier G. & T.C., White Sulphur Springs, W. Va.	73	71	74	68	286	2,516.66
	David K. Stockton, Arrowhead C.C., San Bernardino, Calif.	72	73	69	72	286	2,516.66
15	Daniel D. Sikes, Jr., Hidden Hills C.C., Jacksonville, Fla.	71	71	73	72	287	1,900.00
16	George Archer, Gilroy C.C., Gilroy, Calif.	74	72	73	69	288	1,633.34
	Julius Boros, Mid Pines C., Southern Pines, N.C.	71	71	71	75	288	1,633.34
	Charles Coody, Abilene C.C., Abilene, Texas	69	71	72	76	288	1,633.33
	Rod Funseth, Almaden C.C., San Jose, Calif.	74	72	69	73	288	1,633.33
	Dave Hill, Jackson C.C., Jackson, Mich.	74	68	74	72	288	1,633.33
	Gary Player, Castle Harbour G. & C.C., Tuckers Town, Bermuda	76	69	70	73	288	1,633.33
22	Benson R. McLendon, Jr., Birmingham, Ala.	72	76	70	71	289	1,425.00
	Hugh Royer, Jr., Columbus C.C., Columbus, Ga.	75	72	73	69	289	1,425.00
24	Miller Barber, Woodlawn C.C., Sherman, Texas	74	68	78	70	290	1,203.75
	Roberto DeVicenzo, Ranelagh G.C., Ranelagh, Argentina	72	76	72	70	290	1,203.75
	Robert Erickson, Steger, Ill.	75	68	72	75	290	1,203.75
	Don January, Dallas, Texas	71	75	71	73	290	1,203.75
	Bob Lunn, Haggin Oaks G.C., Sacramento, Calif.	74	73	73	70	290	1,203.75
	Pat Schwab, Crestmont C.C., West Orange, N.J.	76	70	75	69	290	1,203.75
	Tom Weiskopf, Bedford, Ohio	75	72	70	73	290	1,203.75
	Larry Ziegler, Terre DuLac C.C., Bonne Terre, Mo.	71	71	74	74	290	1,203.75
32	Bill Collins, Brae Burn C.C., Purchase, N.Y.	71	72	76	72	291	1,020.00
	Terry Dill, Austin C.C., Austin, Texas	74	71	73	73	291	1,020.00
	Dave Marr, Goodyear G. & C.C., Litchfield Park, Ariz.	70	72	74	75	291	1,020.00
	Robert J. Murphy, Jr., Lone Palm G. C., Lakeland, Fla.	76	71	70	74	291	1,020.00
	Charles L. Sifford, Los Angeles, Calif.	75	69	75	72	291	1,020.00
37	Harold R. Henning, Johannesburg, South Africa	75	68	76	73	292	950.00
	Doug Sanders, Shamrock C.C., Tulsa, Okla.	73	72	73	74	292	950.00
39	Billy Farrell, The Stanwich Club, Greenwich, Conn.	70	72	74	77	293	897.50
	Bob Goalby, St. Clair C.C., Belleville, Ill.	76	71	73	73	293	897.50
	Mac Hunter, Riviera C.C., Pacific Palisades, Calif.	75	73	74	71	293	897.50
	Gibby Gilbert, Hillcrest C.C., Hollywood, Fla.	73	72	76	72	293	897.50
43	Al Balding, Plantation C.C., Crystal River, Fla.	70	76	71	77	294	860.00
	Dave Eichelberger, Ridgewood C.C., Waco, Texas	74	73	76	71	294	860.00
	Labron E. Harris, Jr., Lakeside G.C., Stillwater, Okla.	70	72	77	75	294	860.00
46	Bruce Crampton, Bahama Reef C.C., Grand Bahama Island	75	72	75	73	295	835.00
	Bob Dickson, Shamrock C.C., Tulsa, Okla.	76	70	75	74	295	835.00
48	Ronnie Reif, Costa Mesa G.C., Costa Mesa, Calif.	72	74	74	76	296	815.00
	Robert Stone, Rockwood C.C., Independence, Mo.	75	72	75	74	296	815.00
50	Monty Kaser, Wichita, Kansas	73	72	75	77	297	795.00
	Art Wall, Jr., Honesdale C.C., Honesdale, Pa.	74	74	75	74	297	795.00
52	Frank Beard, Big Spring C.C., Lousiville, Ky.	76	72	73	77	298	765.00
	Homero Blancas, Jr., Houston, Texas	72	75	74	77	298	765.00
	Billy Maxwell, Greentree C.C., Indianapolis, Ind.	72	74	78	74	298	765.00
	Kel Nagle, Pymble G.C., St. Ives, Australia	72	75	76	75	298	765.00
56	Gene Borek, Pine Hollow C.C., East Norwich, N.Y.	73	74	76	76	299	740.00
57	Paul Harney, Pleasant Valley C.C., Sutton, Mass.	74	73	78	75	300	730.00
	*Richard L. Siderowf, Birchwood C.C., Westport, Conn.	71	76	76	77	300	----
59	Arnold Palmer, Laurel Valley G.C., Ligonier, Pa.	73	74	79	75	301	720.00
60	*Jack W. Lewis, Jr., Florence C.C., Florence, S.C.	73	75	80	74	302	----
	Al Chandler, Columbia C.C., Columbiá, Mo.	74	72	78	78	302	710.00
62	Johnny Pott, Broadwater Beach C.C., Broadwater Beach, Miss.	76	72	76	79	303	700.00
63	*James Simons, Butler C.C., Butler, Pa.	75	73	81	81	310	----

*Gold medals awarded to all amateurs.
Prize money totaling $188,800 awarded to professionals as follows:
Championship—$181,000; Sectional Qualifying Championships—$7,800.

1969
SIXTY-NINTH OPEN CHAMPIONSHIP

Held at Champions Golf Club, (Cypress Creek Course), Houston, Texas, June 12-15.
Yardage—6,967. Par 70.
3,397 Entries, 150 Qualifiers, 150 Starters.

Sixty-eight contestants who completed 72 holes.

						Score	Prize Money
1	Orville J. Moody, Yukon, Okla.	71	70	68	72	281	$30,000.00
2	Deane R. Beman, Bethesda C.C., Bethesda, Md.	68	69	73	72	282	11,000.00
	Al Geiberger, Santa Barbara, Calif.	68	72	72	70	282	11,000.00
	Robert R. Rosburg, Westwood C.C., St. Louis, Mo.	70	69	72	71	282	11,000.00
5	Bob Murphy, Jr., Bartow, Fla.	66	72	74	71	283	7,000.00
6	Miller Barber, Woodlawn C.C., Sherman, Texas	67	71	68	78	284	5,000.00
	Bruce Crampton, Bahama Reef C.C., Grand Bahama Island	73	72	68	71	284	5,000.00
	Arnold Palmer, Laurel Valley G.C., Ligonier, Pa.	70	73	69	72	284	5,000.00
9	Bunky Henry, Flat Creek C., Peachtree City, Ga.	70	72	68	75	285	3,500.00
10	George Archer, Gilroy C.C., Gilroy, Calif.	69	74	73	70	286	2,800.00
	Bruce Devlin, Palm Aire C.C., Pompano Beach, Fla.	73	74	70	69	286	2,800.00
	Dave Marr, Goodyear G. & C.C., Litchfield Park, Ariz.	75	69	71	71	286	2,800.00
13	Julius Boros, Mid Pines C., Southern Pines, N.C.	71	73	70	73	287	1,888.89
	Charles Coody, Abilene C.C., Abilene, Texas	72	68	72	75	287	1,888.89
	Dale Douglass, Ft. Morgan, Colo.	76	69	70	72	287	1,888.89
	Raymond Floyd, Lake Havasu C.C., Lake Havasu City, Ariz.	79	68	68	72	287	1,888.89
	Dave Hill, Hiwan C.C., Evergreen, Colo.	73	74	70	70	287	1,888.89
	Howie Johnson, Canyon C.C., Palm Springs, Calif.	72	73	72	70	287	1,888.89
	Dean Refram, Boca Raton, Fla.	69	74	70	74	287	1,888.89
	Phil Rodgers, La Jolla, Calif.	76	70	69	72	287	1,888.89
	Kermit M. Zarley, Jr., Houston, Texas	74	72	70	71	287	1,888.88
22	Robert J. Stanton, New Orleans, La.	74	70	71	73	288	1,500.00
	Tom Weiskopf, Columbus, Ohio	69	75	71	73	288	1,500.00
	Bert Yancey, Killearn G. & C.C., Tallahassee, Fla.	71	71	74	72	288	1,500.00
25	Joe E. Campbell, Whittle Springs G.C., Knoxville, Tenn.	73	74	73	69	289	1,300.00
	Richard Crawford, Bella Vista C.C., Bella Vista, Ark.	70	75	73	71	289	1,300.00
	Tony Jacklin, Sea Island C.C., Sea Island, Ga.	71	70	73	75	289	1,300.00
	Bobby W. Mitchell, Danville G.C., Danville, Va.	72	74	66	77	289	1,300.00
	Jack Nicklaus, Scioto C.C., Columbus, Ohio	74	67	75	73	289	1,300.00
	David K. Stockton, Westlake G.C., Westlake Village, Calif.	75	69	72	73	289	1,300.00
31	Rich Bassett, C.C. of Miami, Miami, Fla.	73	74	69	74	290	1,140.00
	Bobby Cole, Cleveland, Ohio	73	72	72	73	290	1,140.00
	Bob E. Smith, Del Paso C.C., Sacramento, Calif.	76	67	72	75	290	1,140.00
	Jerry Steelsmith, Santa Barbara, Calif.	72	72	75	71	290	1,140.00
	Bobby Nichols, Firestone C.C., Akron, Ohio	74	74	72	70	290	1,140.00
36	Homero Blancas, Jr., Houston, Texas	72	73	69	77	291	1,070.00
	George A. Knudson, Oakdale G. & C.C., Downsview, Ont., Canada	70	70	76	75	291	1,070.00
38	Daniel D. Sikes, Jr., Hidden Hills C.C., Jacksonville, Fla.	74	74	72	72	292	1,030.00
	Sam Snead, Greenbrier G.C., White Sulphur Springs, W. Va.	71	77	70	74	292	1,030.00
40	Tommy Aaron, Callaway Gardens G.C., Pine Mountain, Ga.	71	72	73	77	293	995.00
	Bill Casper, Jr., Los Angeles, Calif.	74	73	72	74	293	995.00
42	Al Balding, Etobicoke, Ont., Canada	74	73	73	74	294	955.00
	Bert Greene, Fort Lauderdale, Fla.	78	70	74	72	294	955.00
	Bob Lunn, Haggin Oaks G.C., Sacramento, Calif.	71	72	76	75	294	955.00
	John Miller, San Francisco G.C., San Francisco, Calif.	71	70	80	73	294	955.00
	Jack C. Montgomery, Broadmoore G.C., Norman, Okla.	74	73	72	75	294	955.00
	Mike Souchak, Oakland Hills C.C., Birmingham, Mich.	72	73	74	75	294	955.00
48	Don Bies, Seattle G.C., Seattle, Wash.	78	70	70	77	295	915.00
	Gary Player, Castle Harbour G. & C.C., Tuckers Town, Bermuda	71	75	72	77	295	915.00
50	Frank Beard, Louisville, Ky.	72	73	73	78	296	895.00
	Robert Stone, Rockwood C.C., Independence, Mo.	74	72	75	75	296	895.00
52	Bill Collins, Brae Burn C.C., Purchase. N. Y.	75	72	73	77	297	865.00
	Lionel P. Hebert, Lafayette, La.	74	73	77	73	297	865.00
	Robert Joe Payne, Elks C.C., Mt. Vernon, Ill.	71	74	73	79	297	865.00
	John Schlee, Dallas, Texas	74	74	78	71	297	865.00
56	Bill Ogden, North Shore C.C., Glenview, Ill.	76	72	75	75	298	835.00
	Ken Still, Fircrest G.C., Tacoma, Wash.	74	74	72	78	298	835.00
58	Pete Brown, Los Angeles, Calif.	74	74	74	77	299	805.00
	Jack Ewing, Jr., Bakersfield C.C., Bakersfield, Calif.	70	76	80	73	299	805.00
	Labron E. Harris, Jr., Lakeside G.C., Stillwater, Okla.	71	75	75	78	299	805.00
	Larry W. Hinson, Douglas G. & C.C., Douglas, Ga.	73	75	76	75	299	805.00
	Rives McBee, Midland C.C., Midland, Texas	71	77	76	75	299	805.00
	David K. Philo, Timuquana C.C., Jacksonville, Fla.	71	74	78	76	299	805.00
64	Martin Bohen, Elmwood C.C., White Plains, N.Y.	72	75	74	81	302	800.00
65	Dave Eichelberger, Ridgewood C.C., Waco, Texas	76	71	76	80	303	800.00
	Dow Finsterwald, Broadmoor G.C., Colorado Springs, Colo.	77	71	77	78	303	800.00
67	Lee Elder, Washington, D.C.	74	73	79	82	308	800.00
68	Chuck Courtney, La Jolla C.C., La Jolla, Calif.	72	76	80	82	310	800.00

Qualifying score for last 36 holes—148. Prize money totaling $205,300 awarded to professionals as follows: Championship—$196,900; Sectional Qualifying Championships—$8,400.

1970
SEVENTIETH OPEN CHAMPIONSHIP

Held at Hazeltine National Golf Club, Chaska, Minnesota, June 18-21.
Yardage—7,151. Par 72. 3,605 Entries, 150 Starters.

Seventy-two contestants who completed 72 holes.

						Score	Money Prize
1	Tony Jacklin, The Cloisters, Sea Island, Ga.	71	70	70	70	281	$30,000.00
2	Dave Hill, Evergreen, Colo.	75	69	71	73	288	15,000.00
3	Robert J. Lunn, Haggin Oaks G.C., Sacramento, Calif.	77	72	70	70	289	9,000.00
	Bob Charles, Christchurch, New Zealand	76	71	75	67	289	9,000.00
5	Ken Still, Fircrest G.C., Tacoma, Wash.	78	71	71	71	291	7,000.00
6	Miller Barber, Woodlawn C.C., Sherman, Texas	75	75	72	70	292	6,000.00
7	Gay Brewer, Jr., Dallas, Texas	75	71	71	76	293	5,000.00
8	Billy Casper, Bonita, Calif.	75	75	71	73	294	3,325.00
	Larry Ziegler, Terre Dulac C.C., Terre Dulac, Mo.	75	73	73	73	294	3,325.00
	Bruce Devlin, Cleveland, Ohio	75	75	71	73	294	3,325.00
	Lee B. Trevino, El Paso, Texas	77	73	74	70	294	3,325.00
12	Julius Boros, Mid Pines C., Southern Pines, N.C.	73	75	70	77	295	2,150.00
	Gene Littler, La Jolla C.C., La Jolla, Calif.	77	72	71	75	295	2,150.00
	Bobby W. Mitchell, Danville G.C., Danville, Va.	74	78	74	69	295	2,150.00
	Howie Johnson, Canyon C.C., Palm Springs, Calif.	75	72	75	73	295	2,150.00
	Joel Goldstrand, Worthington C.C., Worthington, Minn.	76	76	71	72	295	2,150.00
	Bobby Cole, Cleveland, Ohio	78	75	71	71	295	2,150.00
18	Al Balding, Chippewa C.C., South Hampton, Ont., Canada	75	74	75	72	296	1,675.00
	John L. Miller, San Francisco G.C., San Francisco, Calif.	79	73	73	71	296	1,675.00
	Randy Wolff, Beaumont C.C., Beaumont, Texas	78	67	76	75	296	1,675.00
	Paul Harney, Pleasant Valley C.C., Worcester, Mass.	78	73	75	70	296	1,675.00
22	Raymond Floyd, Lake Havasu G.C., Lake Havasu, Ariz.	78	73	70	76	297	1,452.00
	Bert Yancey, Palm Aire C.C., Pompano Beach, Fla.	81	72	73	71	297	1,452.00
	Ted Hayes, Atlanta, Ga.	79	73	73	72	297	1,452.00
	Frank Beard, Louisville, Ky.	75	73	79	70	297	1,452.00
	Richard Crawford, Bella Vista C.C., Bella Vista Village, Ark.	74	71	76	76	297	1,452.00
27	Juan A. Rodriguez, Dorado Beach G.C., Dorado Beach Hotel, P.R.	73	77	75	73	298	1,280.00
	Mason Rudolph, Lehigh Acres G. & C.C., Lehigh Acres, Fla.	73	75	73	77	298	1,280.00
	Daniel D. Sikes, Jr., Hidden Hills C.C., Jacksonville, Fla.	81	69	72	76	298	1,280.00
30	Kel Nagle, Pymble G.C., Sydney, Australia	78	75	73	73	299	1,150.00
	George Archer, Gilroy G.C., Gilroy, Calif.	76	73	77	73	299	1,150.00
	Tom Weiskopf, Columbus, Ohio	76	73	78	72	299	1,150.00
	Bruce Crampton, Bahama Reef C.C., Grand Bahama Island, Bahamas	79	71	74	75	299	1,150.00
	Dave Marr, The Mount Washington, Bretton Woods, N.H.	82	69	74	74	299	1,150.00
	Bunky Henry, Farrington G. & Tennis C., Atlanta, Ga.	80	68	77	74	299	1,150.00
36	Tony Evans, Highland C.C., Fayetteville, N.C.	74	75	75	77	301	1,031.67
	Kermit Zarley, Jr., Houston, Texas	76	76	74	75	301	1,031.67
	Dean Refram, Boca Raton, Fla.	79	74	74	74	301	1,031.67
	Don Bies, Seattle G.C., Seattle, Wash.	75	76	76	74	301	1,031.67
	Bob Goalby, Belleville, Ill.	78	74	75	74	301	1,031.6[illegible]
	Robert F. Erickson, Flossmoor, Ill.	80	72	79	70	301	1,031.6[illegible]
	*John D. Mahaffey, Jr., Pecan Valley G.C., San Antonio, Texas	77	73	74	77	301	MEDAL
	*Ben Crenshaw, Austin C.C., Austin, Texas	75	73	77	76	301	MEDAL
44	Gary Player, Castle Harbour G. & B.C., Tucker's Town, Bermuda	80	73	75	74	302	975.00
	Dick Smith, Hi-Point Golf Farm, Ivyland, Pa.	76	77	76	73	302	975.00
46	Hugh Royer, Jr., Columbus C.C., Columbus, Ga.	77	76	73	77	303	940.00
	Tommy Aaron, Callaway Gardens, Pine Mountain, Ga.	77	76	74	76	303	940.00
	Monty Kaser, Wichita, Kans.	76	77	74	76	303	940.00
	Lou Graham, Richland C.C., Nashville, Tenn.	76	75	76	76	303	940.00
	Bobby Nichols, Firestone C.C., Akron, Ohio	75	73	80	75	303	940.00
51	Rives R. McBee, Las Colinas C.C., Irving, Texas	78	73	74	79	304	900.00
	J. Steve Spray, Indianola, Iowa	78	74	74	78	304	900.00
	Jack Nicklaus, Scioto C.C., Columbus, Ohio	81	72	75	76	304	900.00
54	Bert Greene, Sun River G.C., Sun River, Ore.	77	75	80	73	305	850.00
	Fred Marti, Goose Creek C.C., Baytown, Texas	75	78	77	75	305	850.00
	Rolf Deming, Riverside C.C., Menominee, Mich.	77	76	76	76	305	850.00
	Al Mengert, Gearhart G.C., Gearhart By The Sea, Ore.	76	77	76	76	305	850.00
	John Cook, Rolling Green C.C., Hamel, Minn.	77	75	77	76	305	850.00
	Dewitt T. Weaver, Jr., Atlanta C.C., Atlanta, Ga.	82	71	74	78	305	850.00
	Arnold D. Palmer, Laurel Valley G.C., Ligonier, Pa.	79	74	75	77	305	850.00
61	George Knudson, Oakdale G. & C.C., Downsview, Ont., Canada	82	71	76	77	306	805.00
	Chris Blocker, Hillcrest C.C., Lubbock, Texas	78	75	78	75	306	805.00
63	Wayne C. Yates, Indian Hills C.C., Marietta, Ga.	78	75	79	75	307	800.00
64	Robert R. Rosburg, French Lick Sheraton Hotel G.C., French Lick, Ind.	79	73	76	80	308	800.00
	Charles Coody, Abilene, Texas	78	74	80	76	308	800.00
66	Claude Harmon, Jr., Thunderbird C.C., Palm Springs, Calif.	80	72	76	82	310	800.00
	Leon Crump, Eastwood G.C., Charlotte, N.C.	78	75	78	79	310	800.00
	*Marvin Giles, III, Boonsboro C.C., Lynchburg, Va.	76	76	78	80	310	----
69	Gene Borek, Pine Hollow C.C., East Norwich, N.Y.	80	73	78	80	311	800.00
	Jim Wiechers, Atherton, Calif.	76	75	81	79	311	800.00
	Jerry L. McGee, Lake Worth, Fla.	80	73	78	80	311	800.00
72	Davis M. Love, Jr., Atlanta C.C., Marietta, Ga.	77	76	88	74	315	800.00

Prize money totaling $203,500 awarded to professionals as follows:
Championship—$195,700; Sectional Qualifying Championship—$7,800.
*Amateur.

1971
SEVENTY-FIRST OPEN CHAMPIONSHIP

Held at Merion Golf Club (East Course), Ardmore, Pennsylvania, June 17–20.
Yardage–6,544/6,528. Par 70. 4,279 Entries 150 Qualifiers, 150 Starters.

Sixty-four contestants who qualified for 72-hole holes.

						Score	Prize Money
1	†Lee Trevino, El Paso, Texas	70	72	69	69	280	$30,000.00
2	†Jack Nicklaus, Scioto C.C., Columbus, Ohio	69	72	68	71	280	15,000.00
3	Robert R. Rosburg, French Lick Sheraton C.C., French Lick, Ind.	71	72	70	69	282	9,000.00
	James J. Colbert, Jr., Prairie Creek C.C., Prairie Creek, Ark.	69	69	73	71	282	9,000.00
5	*James Simons, Butler C.C., Butler, Pa.	71	71	65	76	283	MEDAL
	John L. Miller, San Francisco G.C., San Francisco, Calif.	70	73	70	70	283	6,500.00
	George Archer, Gilroy C.C., Gilroy, Calif.	71	70	70	72	283	6,500.00
8	Raymond Floyd, Lake Havasu G.C., Lake Havasu City, Ariz.	71	75	67	71	284	5,000.00
9	Gay Brewer, Jr., Dallas, Texas	70	70	73	72	285	3,325.00
	Bert Yancey, Palm Aire C.C., Pompano Beach, Fla.	75	69	69	72	285	3,325.00
	Larry W. Hinson, Glassy Gap G.C., Beech Mountain, N.C.	71	71	70	73	285	3,325.00
	Bobby Nichols, Firestone C.C., Akron, Ohio	69	72	69	75	285	3,325.00
13	*Lanny Wadkins, Meadowbrook C.C., Richmond, Va.	68	75	75	68	286	MEDAL
	Jerry M. Heard, Visalia C.C., Visalia, Calif.	73	71	73	69	286	2,220.00
	Jerry L. McGee, Lake Worth, Fla.	72	67	77	70	286	2,220.00
	Bob Charles, Christchurch G.C., New Zealand	72	75	69	70	286	2,220.00
	Bobby Cole, Cleveland, Ohio	72	71	72	71	286	2,220.00
	Juan A. (Chi Chi) Rodriguez, Dorado Beach G.C., Dorado Beach, P.R.	70	71	73	72	286	2,220.00
19	Bob Goalby, St. Clair C.C., Belleville, Ill.	68	76	74	69	287	1,700.00
	Homero Blancas, Jr., Houston, Texas	71	71	75	70	287	1,700.00
	Hale Irwin, Prairie Creek C.C., Rogers, Ark.	72	73	72	70	287	1,700.00
	Dave Eichelberger, Ridgewood C.C., Waco, Texas	72	72	70	73	287	1,700.00
	Ken Still, Fircrest G.C., Tacoma, Wash.	71	72	69	75	287	1,700.00
24	Dick Lotz, Graeagle Meadows G.C., Graeagle, Calif.	72	72	73	71	288	1,500.00
	Bob E. Smith, Del Paso C.C., Sacramento, Calif.	71	74	71	72	288	1,500.00
	Arnold Palmer, Laurel Valley G.C., Ligonier, Pa.	73	68	73	74	288	1,500.00
27	Bruce Devlin, Hialeah, Fla.	72	69	71	77	289	1,253.34
	Don January, Royal Oaks C.C., Dallas, Texas	75	73	71	70	289	1,253.34
	Ralph W. Johnston, New Smyrna Beach C.C., New Smyrna Beach, Fla.	70	75	73	71	289	1,253.34
	Robert Lunn, Haggin Oaks G.C., Sacramento, Calif.	71	73	71	74	289	1,253.33
	Bobby W. Mitchell, Pine Tree G.C., Kernersville, N.C.	72	74	72	71	289	1,253.33
	Orville Moody, Lago Vista C.C., Lago Vista, Texas	71	71	76	71	289	1,253.33
	Gary Player, International G.C., Atlanta, Ga.	76	71	72	70	289	1,253.33
	John L. Schroeder, La Jolla C.C., La Jolla, Calif.	73	72	69	75	289	1,253.33
	Kermit Zarley, Jr., Houston, Texas	74	70	72	73	289	1,253.33
	*Ben Crenshaw, Austin C.C., Austin, Texas	74	74	68	73	289	MEDAL
37	Bob Erickson, Mayfair C.C., Sanford, Fla.	71	67	73	79	290	1,080.00
	Lou Graham, Richland C.C., Nashville, Tenn.	75	72	70	73	290	1,080.00
	John Lister, Timaru G.C., Timaru, New Zealand	73	75	72	70	290	1,080.00
	Gene Littler, La Jolla C.C., La Jolla, Calif.	74	74	71	71	290	1,080.00
	Doug Sanders, Sharpstown C.C., Houston, Texas	68	75	71	76	290	1,080.00
42	Julius Boros, C.C. Aventura, Miami, Fla.	74	71	73	74	292	997.50
	Dale Douglass, Applewood G.C., Golden, Colo.	70	74	74	74	292	997.50
	Mason Rudolph, Lehigh Acres C.C., Lehigh Acres, Fla.	72	75	71	74	292	997.50
	John Schlee, Preston Trail G.C., Dallas, Texas	70	73	77	72	292	997.50
46	Paul Harney, Pleasant Valley C.C., Worcester, Mass.	73	74	72	74	293	960.00
	Labron Harris, Jr., Prairie Creek C.C., Prairie Creek, Ark.	67	77	76	73	293	960.00
	Chuck Courtney, La Jolla C.C., La Jolla, Calif.	74	73	77	69	293	960.00
49	Bruce Crampton, Bahama Reef C.C., Freeport, Grand Bahama Island	73	73	71	77	294	915.00
	Bobby Greenwood, Fairfield Glade G.C., Crossville, Tenn.	73	74	73	74	294	915.00
	Robert Risch, Alondra Park C.C., Torrance, Calif.	74	74	73	73	294	915.00
	Charles L. Sifford, Los Angeles, Calif.	75	72	69	78	294	915.00
	Art Silverstrone, Pine Brook C.C., Bell Mead, N.J.	74	70	76	74	294	915.00
	Don Bies, Seattle G.C., Seattle, Wash.	71	74	72	77	294	915.00
55	Deane Beman, Bethesda C.C., Bethesda, Md.	72	73	70	80	295	870.00
	Bob Dickson, Muskogee C.C., Muskogee, Okla.	73	74	76	72	295	870.00
	Al Geiberger, Santa Barbara, Calif.	71	71	75	78	295	870.00
	*Danny Yates, Atlanta C.C., Atlanta, Ga.	72	75	76	72	295	MEDAL
59	Miller Barber, Woodlawn C.C., Sherman, Texas	73	73	72	78	296	850.00
60	Gene Borek, Pine Hollow C.C., East Norwich, N.Y.	75	71	75	76	297	835.00
	Roy Pace, Alpine G.C., Longview, Texas	72	76	73	76	297	835.00
62	Ronnie Reif, Carlton Oaks C.C., Santee, Calif.	73	72	75	78	298	820.00
63	Charles Coody, Prairie Creek C.C., Prairie Creek, Ark.	70	76	75	79	300	810.00
	*James B. Masserio, Duquesne G.C., Pittsburgh, Pa.	71	75	77	79	302	MEDAL

†Playoff, June 21, 1971, Lee Trevino 68, Jack Nicklaus 71.
Prize money totaling $200,000 awarded to professionals as follows:
Championship–$192,200; Sectional Qualifying Championship–$7,800.
*Amateur.

1972
SEVENTY-SECOND OPEN CHAMPIONSHIP

Held at Pebble Beach Golf Links, Pebble Beach, California, June 15-18.
Yardage–6,812. Par 72. 4,196 Entries, 150 Qualifiers, 150 Starters.

Seventy contestants who completed 72 holes.

						Score	Money Prize
1	Jack Nicklaus, Scioto C.C., Columbus, Ohio	71	73	72	74	290	$30,000.00
2	Bruce Crampton, Bahama Reef C.C., Freeport, Grand Bahamas	74	70	73	76	293	15,000.00
3	Arnold Palmer, Laurel Valley G.C., Ligonier, Pa.	77	68	73	76	294	10,000.00
4	Lee Trevino, El Paso, Texas	74	72	71	78	295	7,500.00
	Homero Blancas, Houston, Texas	74	70	76	75	295	7,500.00
6	Kermit Zarley, Jr., Houston, Texas	71	73	73	79	296	6,000.00
7	John L. Miller, Palmetto Dunes G.C., Hilton Head Island, S.C.	74	73	71	79	297	5,000.00
8	Tom Weiskopf, Columbus, Ohio	73	74	73	78	298	4,000.00
9	Cesar Sanudo, Singing Hills C.C., El Cajon, Calif.	72	72	78	77	299	3,250.00
	Juan Rodriguez, Dorado Beach G.C., Dorado Beach, P.R.	71	75	78	75	299	3,250.00
11	Don January, Royal Oaks C.C., Dallas, Texas	76	71	74	79	300	2,500.00
	Bert Yancey, Palm Aire C.C., Pompano Beach, Fla.	75	79	70	76	300	2,500.00
	Bobby Nichols, Firestone C.C., Akron, Ohio	77	74	72	77	300	2,500.00
	Billy Casper, Chula Vista, Calif.	74	73	79	74	300	2,500.00
15	Gary Player, International G.C., Atlanta, Ga.	72	74	75	78	301	1,900.00
	Don Massengale, Elmwood C.C., White Plains, N.Y.	72	81	70	78	301	1,900.00
	Orville Moody, Lago Vista C.C., Lago Vista, Texas	71	77	79	74	301	1,900.00
	*James Simons, Butler C.C., Butler, Pa.	75	75	79	72	301	– – – –
19	Lou Graham, Richland C.C., Nashville, Tenn.	75	73	75	79	302	1,750.00
	*Tom Kite, Jr., C.C. of Austin, Austin, Texas	75	73	79	75	302	– – – –
21	Paul Harney, Pleasant Valley C.C., Worcester, Mass.	79	72	75	77	303	1,625.00
	Al Geiberger, Santa Barbara, Calif.	80	74	76	73	303	1,625.00
	Bobby Mitchell, Pine Tree G.C., Kernersville, N.C.	74	80	73	76	303	1,625.00
	Charles Sifford, Los Angeles, Calif.	79	74	72	78	303	1,625.00
25	Gay Brewer, Jr., Dallas, Texas	77	77	72	78	304	1,427.00
	Lanny Wadkins, Bermuda Run G. & C.C., Clemmons, N.C.	76	68	79	81	304	1,427.00
	Jim Wiechers, Silverado C.C., Napa, Calif.	74	79	69	82	304	1,427.00
	Rod Funseth, Almaden C.C., San Jose, Calif.	73	73	84	74	304	1,427.00
29	Lee Elder, Washington, D.C.	75	71	79	80	305	1,217.00
	Miller Barber, Woodlawn C.C., Sherman, Texas	76	76	73	80	305	1,217.00
	Julius Boros, C.C. Aventura, Miami, Fla.	77	77	74	77	305	1,217.00
	Jerry Heard, Visalia C.C., Visalia, Calif.	73	74	77	81	305	1,217.00
	Dave Hill, Park Hill C.C., Denver, Colo.	74	78	74	79	305	1,217.00
	Dave Eichelberger, Ridgewood C.C., Waco, Texas	76	71	80	78	305	1,217.00
	Tom Watson, Kansas City C.C., Shawnee Mission, Kansas	74	79	76	76	305	1,217.00
36	Larry Hinson, Glassy Gap G.C., Beech Mountain, N.C.	78	73	72	83	306	1,090.00
	Hale Irwin, Prairie Creek C.C., Rogers, Ark.	78	72	73	83	306	1,090.00
	Barry Jaeckel, Riviera C.C., Pacific Palisades, Calif.	78	69	82	77	306	1,090.00
	Brian Allin, Santa Barbara, Calif.	75	76	77	78	306	1,090.00
40	Tony Jacklin, Elsham, England	75	78	71	83	307	994.00
	George Rives, Briarwood C.C., Tyler, Texas	80	73	79	75	307	994.00
	Jerry McGee, Lake Worth, Fla.	79	72	71	85	307	994.00
	Tom Shaw, Inverrary C.C., Inverrary, Fla.	71	79	80	77	307	994.00
	Billy Ziobro, Tammy Brook C.C., Cresskill, N.J.	76	77	77	77	307	994.00
	Ron Cerrudo, Silverado C.C., Napa, Calif.	77	77	76	77	307	994.00
	Mason Rudolph, Lehigh Acres C.C., Lehigh Acres, Fla.	71	80	86	70	307	994.00
47	Bobby Cole, Cleveland, Ohio	72	76	79	81	308	930.00
	Ron Letellier, North Hills C.C., Manhasset, N.Y.	75	77	74	82	308	930.00
	David Graham, Emerald Hills C.C., Hollywood, Fla.	77	77	79	75	308	930.00
	Gibby Gilbert, Pembroke Pines, Fla.	77	77	77	77	308	930.00
	John Schroeder, La Jolla C.C., La Jolla, Calif.	78	75	75	80	308	930.00
52	Tom Jenkins, Houston, Texas	73	80	75	81	309	890.00
	Mike Butler, The Olympic Club, San Francisco, Calif.	78	73	77	81	309	890.00
	Ralph Johnston, New Smyrna Beach G.C., New Smyrna Beach, Fla.	74	72	79	84	309	890.00
55	Michael Hill, Jackson C.C., Jackson, Mich.	75	77	75	83	310	835.00
	Bobby Greenwood, Fairfield G.C., Crossville, Tenn.	77	75	72	86	310	835.00
	Jim Hardy, Killeen, Texas	78	76	79	77	310	835.00
	Tim Collins, Greenville C.C., Greenville, S.C.	79	71	81	79	310	835.00
	Bob Brue, Ozaukee C.C., Mequon, Wis.	77	75	79	79	310	835.00
	Martin Bohen, Leewood G.C., Eastchester, N.Y.	77	76	77	80	310	835.00
	Hubert Green, Birmingham, Ala.	75	76	78	81	310	835.00
	Tommy Aaron, Calloway Gardens G.C., Pine Mountain, Ga.	76	76	77	81	310	835.00
63	Bob Murphy, Delray Dunes G.C., Delray Beach, Fla.	79	74	83	75	311	800.00
	Jim Colbert, Jr., Overland Park, Kansas	74	79	76	82	311	800.00
65	George Archer, Gilroy C.C., Gilroy, Calif.	74	74	77	87	312	800.00
	Bruce Devlin, Sheoah G.C., Orlando, Fla.	75	78	74	85	312	800.00
67	Austin Straub, Huntington C.C., Huntington, N.Y.	76	77	75	87	315	800.00
	Dick Hendrickson, Vincentown, N.J.	80	74	79	82	315	800.00
69	Dwight Nevil, Pecan Valley G.C., San Antonio, Texas	76	77	81	82	316	800.00
70	*Daniel O'Neill, Moon Brook C.C., Jamestown, N.Y.	78	76	77	86	317	– – – –

*Amateur.

1973
SEVENTY-THIRD OPEN CHAMPIONSHIP

Held at Oakmont Country Club, Oakmont, Pennsylvania, June 14-17.
Yardage—6,921. Par 71. 3,580 Entries, 150 Qualifiers, 150 Starters.
Sixty-five contestants who completed 72 holes.

						Score	Money Prize
1	John Miller, Palmetto Dunes C.C., Hilton Head Island, S. C.	71	69	76	63	279	$35,000.00
2	John H. Schlee, Preston Trails G.C., Dallas, Texas	73	70	67	70	280	18,000.00
3	Tom Weiskopf, Columbus, Ohio	73	69	69	70	281	13,000.00
4	Arnold Palmer, Laurel Valley G.C., Ligonier, Pa.	71	71	68	72	282	9,000.00
	Lee Trevino, El Paso, Texas	70	72	70	70	282	9,000.00
	Jack Nicklaus, Scioto C.C., Columbus, Ohio	71	69	74	68	282	9,000.00
7	Lanny Wadkins, Bermuda Run G. & C.C., Clemmons, N. C.	74	69	75	65	283	6,000.00
	Julius Boros, C.C. of Aventura, Miami, Fla.	73	69	68	73	283	6,000.00
	Jerry Heard, Visalia C.C., Visalia, Caif.	74	70	66	73	283	6,000.00
10	Jim Colbert, Overland Park, Kansas	70	68	74	72	284	4,000.00
11	Bob Charles, Christchurch G.C., Christchurch, New Zealand	71	69	72	74	286	3,500.00
12	Gary Player, River Oaks C.C., Grand Island, N. Y.	67	70	77	73	287	3,000.00
13	Ralph Johnston, Garden City C.C., Garden City, N. Y.	71	73	76	68	288	2,333.34
	Al Geiberger, San Vicente C.C., Ramona, Calif.	73	72	71	72	288	2,333.33
	Larry Ziegler, Terre DeLac C.C., St. Louis, Mo.	73	74	69	72	288	2,333.33
16	Raymond Floyd, Lake Havasu G.C., Lake Havasu, Ariz.	70	73	75	71	289	1,900.00
17	*Marvin Giles III, C.C. of Virginia, Richmond, Va.	74	69	74	73	290	Medal
18	Rocky Thompson, Wichita Falls C.C., Wichita Falls, Texas	73	71	71	76	291	1,775.00
	Gene Littler, LaJolla, Calif.	71	74	70	76	291	1,775.00
20	Bobby Nichols, Firestone C.C., Akron, Ohio	75	71	74	73	293	1,600.00
	Denny Lyons, Niagara Falls C.C., Lewiston, N. Y.	72	74	75	72	293	1,600.00
	Rod Funseth, Silverado C.C., Napa, Calif.	75	74	70	74	293	1,600.00
	Hale Irwin, Boulder C.C., Boulder, Colo.	73	74	75	71	293	1,600.00
	Bob Murphy, Delray Dunes G.C., Delray Beach, Fla.	77	70	75	71	293	1,600.00
25	Miller Barber, Woodlawn C.C., Sherman, Texas	74	71	71	78	294	1,382.50
	Frank Beard, Hurstbourne C.C., Louisville, Ky.	74	75	68	77	294	1,382.50
	Tom Shaw, Inverrary C.C., Inverrary, Fla.	73	71	74	76	294	1,382.50
	Bert Yancey, Palm Aire C.C., Pompano Beach, Fla.	73	70	75	76	294	1,382.50
29	John D. Mahaffey, Jr., Champions G.C., Houston, Texas	74	72	74	75	295	1,212.00
	Charles Coody, Apopka, Fla.	74	74	73	74	295	1,212.00
	Juan A. Rodriguez, Dorado Beach G.C., Dorado Beach, P. R.	75	71	75	74	295	1,212.00
	Sam Snead, Greenbrier G.C., White Sulphur Springs, W. Va.	75	74	73	73	295	1,212.00
	Don Bies, Seattle G.C., Seattle, Wash.	77	73	73	72	295	1,212.00
34	Brian Allin, Santa Barbara, Calif.	78	67	74	77	296	1,110.00
	George Archer, Amana, Iowa	76	73	74	73	296	1,110.00
	Robert F. Erickson, San Antonio, Texas	73	74	76	73	296	1,110.00
	Larry Wise, Silver Spring, Md.	74	73	76	73	296	1,110.00
38	Gene Borek, Pine Hollow C.C., East Norwich, N. Y.	77	65	80	75	297	1,060.00
39	Mac Hunter, Riviera C.C., Pacific Palisades, Calif.	77	73	72	76	298	1,000.00
	Deane Beman, Bethesda C.C., Bethesda, Md.	73	75	75	75	298	1,000.00
	Bill Ziobro, Tammy Brook C.C., Cresskill, N. J.	77	69	77	75	298	1,000.00
	Cesar Sanudo, Singing Hills C.C., El Cajon, Calif.	75	73	76	74	298	1,000.00
	Paul Moran, Jr., Haverhill G. & C.C., Haverhill, Mass.	75	74	76	73	298	1,000.00
	Dave Stockton, Westlake G.C., Westlake, Calif.	77	73	77	71	298	1,000.00
45	Tommy Aaron, Callaway Gardens G.C., Pine Mountain, Ga.	78	71	72	78	299	930.00
	Art Wall, Jr., Honesdale G.C., Honesdale, Pa.	73	77	71	78	299	930.00
	Roger Ginsberg, Willow Ridge C.C., Harrison, N. Y.	74	75	73	77	299	930.00
	Joe E. Campbell, Whittle Springs G.C., Knoxville, Tenn.	74	76	74	75	299	930.00
	Grier S. Jones, Wichita C.C., Wichita, Kans.	73	76	76	74	299	930.00
	Forrest Fezler, Indian Wells C.C., Indian Wells, Calif.	78	69	80	72	299	930.00
	Robert Lee Elder, Washington, D. C.	72	77	78	72	299	930.00
52	Butch Baird, Miami Beach, Fla.	75	74	75	76	300	880.00
	Tony Jacklin, Sea Island G.C., Sea Island, Ga.	75	75	73	77	300	880.00
	Larry E. Wood, Durham, N. C.	79	71	76	74	300	880.00
55	David W. Glenz, Coos C.C., Coos Bay, Ore.	76	74	71	80	301	855.00
	Chris Blocker, Hyde Park G.C., Jacksonville, Fla.	73	76	78	74	301	855.00
57	*Gary Koch, Temple Terrace G. & C.C., Temple Terrace, Fla.	74	74	79	75	302	Medal
58	John A. Gentile, Round Hill C., Greenwich, Conn.	72	74	78	79	303	820.00
	David Graham, Emerald Hills C.C., Hollywood, Fla.	73	77	77	76	303	820.00
	Bob Goalby, St. Clair C.C., Belleville, Ill.	72	77	79	75	303	820.00
	Jim Jamieson, Tarpon Springs, Fla.	74	76	79	74	303	820.00
	John Lister, Timaru G.C., Timaru, New Zealand	76	74	80	73	303	820.00
63	Greg Powers, Richland C.C., Nashville, Tenn.	79	70	77	79	305	800.00
	Tom Joyce, The Stanwich C., Greenwich, Conn.	78	70	81	76	305	800.00
65	George Bayer, Detroit G.C., Detroit, Mich.	72	77	82	79	310	800.00

Prize money totaling $227,200 awarded to professionals as follows: Championship—$182,400; prizes for 74 professionals who did not return scores for 72 holes—$37,000; Sectional Qualifying Championships—$7,800.

*Amateur

1974
SEVENTY-FOURTH OPEN CHAMPIONSHIP

Held at Winged Foot Golf Club, Mamaroneck, New York, June 13-16
Yardage—6,961. Par 70. 3,914 Entries, 150 Qualifiers, 150 Starters.

						Score	Money Prize
1	Hale Irwin, Boulder, Colo.	73	70	71	73	287	$35,000.00
2	Forrest Fezler, Indian Wells C.C., Indian Wells, Calif.	75	70	74	70	289	18,000.00
3	Bert Yancey, Killearn G. & C.C., Tallahassee, Fla.	76	69	73	72	290	11,500.00
	Lou Graham, Richland C.C., Nashville, Tenn.	71	75	74	70	290	11,500.00
5	Tom Watson, Kansas City C.C., Shawnee Mission, Kans.	73	71	69	79	292	8,000.00
	Arnold Palmer, Laurel Valley G.C., Ligonier, Pa.	73	70	73	76	292	8,000.00
	Jim Colbert, Saddlebrook C.C., Wesley Chapel, Fla.	72	77	69	74	292	8,000.00
8	Gary Player, River Oaks G.&C.C., Grand Island, N. Y.	70	73	77	73	293	5,500.00
	Tom Kite, Jr., C.C. of Austin, Austin, Texas	74	70	77	72	293	5,500.00
10	Brian Allin, Santa Barbara, Calif.	76	71	74	73	294	3,750.00
	Jack Nicklaus, Scioto C.C., Columbus, Ohio	75	74	76	69	294	3,750.00
12	Frank Beard, Louisville, Ky.	77	69	72	77	295	2,633.34
	John D. Mahaffey, Jr., Champions G.C., Houston, Texas	74	73	75	73	295	2,633.33
	Larry Zeigler, Terre Dulac C.C., Terre Dulac, Mo.	78	68	78	71	295	2,633.33
15	Tom Weiskopf, Columbus, Ohio	76	73	72	75	296	1,933.34
	Raymond Floyd, Lake Havasu City G.C., Lake Havasu City, Ariz.	72	71	78	75	296	1,933.33
	Mike Reasor, Seattle, Wash.	71	76	76	73	296	1,933.33
18	Dale Douglass, Colorado Springs, Colo.	77	72	72	76	297	1,700.00
	David Graham, Emerald Hills G.C., Hollywood, Fla.	73	75	76	73	297	1,700.00
	Allen Geiberger, San Vicente C.C., Ramona, Calif.	75	76	78	68	297	1,700.00
21	J. C. Snead, Hot Springs, Ark.	76	71	76	75	298	1,575.00
	Leonard Thompson, Robbers Roost G.C., North Myrtle Beach., S. C.	75	75	76	72	298	1,575.00
23	Bobby W. Mitchell, Pine Tree G.C., Kernersville, N. C.	77	73	73	76	299	1,450.00
	Bruce Crampton, Sidney, Australia	72	77	76	74	299	1,450.00
	Larry Hinson, Douglas, Ga.	75	76	75	73	299	1,450.00
26	Lanny Wadkins, Bermuda Run G.&C.C., Clemmons, N. C.	75	73	76	76	300	1,300.00
	Hubert M. Green, Colony Club, Panama City Beach, Fla.	81	67	76	76	300	1,300.00
	Jim Jamieson, Innisbroook G.C., Tarpon Springs, Fla.	77	73	75	75	300	1,300.00
	Juan A. Rodriguez, Dorado Beach G.C., Dorado Beach, P. R.	75	75	77	73	300	1,300.00
30	Rik Massengale, Jacksboro C.C., Jacksboro, Texas	79	72	74	76	301	1,160.00
	David W. Glenz, Miami, Fla.	76	74	75	76	301	1,160.00
	Rod Funseth, Silverado C.C., Napa, Calif.	73	75	78	75	301	1,160.00
	Jerry McGee, East Palestine, Ohio	77	72	78	74	301	1,160.00
	Ron Cerrudo, Silverado C.C., Napa, Calif.	78	75	75	73	301	1,160.00
35	Bob E. Smith, Del Paso C.C., Sacramento, Calif.	77	74	73	78	302	1,060.00
	John Miller, Palmetto Dunes C.C., Hilton Head Island, S. C.	76	75	74	77	302	1,060.00
	Steve Melnyk, Bay Meadows C.C., Jacksonville, Fla.	74	79	73	76	302	1,060.00
	Don Iverson, La Crosse, Wis.	74	77	76	75	302	1,060.00
	John H. Buczek, Plainfield C.C., Plainfield, N. J.	73	73	83	73	302	1,060.00
40	Kermit Zarley, Jr., Clear Lake C.C., Clear Lake, Texas	74	73	78	78	303	980.00
	Mark S. Hayes Kicking Bird G.C., Edmond, Okla.	73	77	76	77	303	980.00
	Homero Blancas, Stone Creek Cove, Anderson, S. C.	77	71	79	76	303	980.00
	Dave Eichelberger, Ridgewood C.C., Waco, Texas	76	77	76	74	303	980.00
	Dave Stockton, Westlake C.C., Westlake, Calif.	79	74	78	72	303	980.00
45	Robert P. Stone, Shenandoah C.C., Lee's Summit, Mo.	75	74	77	78	304	935.00
	Tom Ulozas, Madison G.C., Madison, N. J.	77	75	74	78	304	935.00
	Jerry Heard, Visalia C.C., Visalia, Calif.	73	77	75	79	304	935.00
	Jim Dent, Los Angeles, Calif.	76	73	79	76	304	935.00
49	Lynn Janson, C.C. of Lansing, Lansing, Mich.	77	74	77	77	305	905.00
	Bobby Nichols, Firestone C.C., Akron, Ohio	72	77	80	76	305	905.00
51	James B. Masserio, Pittsburgh, Pa.	75	75	76	80	306	880.00
	George Knudson, Oakdale G.&C.C., Toronto, Ont., Canada	78	75	75	78	306	880.00
	Mike McCullough, Coshocton, Ohio	76	76	74	80	306	880.00
54	Alan Tapie, Newport Beach, Calif.	77	74	77	79	307	845.00
	Jack Rule, Jr., Englewood, Colo.	78	75	73	81	307	845.00
	Bob Zender, Evanston, G.C., Skokie, Ill.	77	73	79	78	307	845.00
	Barney Thompson, Riviera C.C., Lesage, W. Va.	72	77	80	78	307	845.00
	*Jay Haas, St. Clair C.C., Belleville, Ill.	78	73	79	77	307	Medal
58	Edward L. Pearce, Carrollwood Village G. & T.C., Tampa, Fla.	75	71	84	78	308	820.00
59	Charles Sifford, Los Angeles, Calif.	77	76	76	80	309	810.00
60	Tom Shaw, Inverrary C.C., Inverrary, Fla.	77	76	78	81	312	800.00
61	Jim Simons, Butler C.C., Butler, Pa.	77	72	81	83	313	800.00
	Roy W. Pace, Alpine G.C., Longview, Texas	74	76	78	85	313	800.00
	*Andy Bean, Univ. of Fla. G.C., Gainesville, Fla.	74	76	83	81	314	Medal
	*William Hyndman, III, Huntingdon Valley G.C., Huntingdon Valley, Pa.	79	72	82	81	314	Medal
63	Bruce Summerhays, Cameron Park G.&C.C., Shingle Springs, Calif.	77	76	79	83	315	800.00

Prize money totaling $227,700 awarded to professionals as follows:
Championship—$182,400; prizes for 75 professionals who did not return scores for 72 holes—$37,500; Sectional Qualifying Championships—$7,800.

*Amateur

1975
SEVENTY-FIFTH OPEN CHAMPIONSHIP

Held at Medinah Country Club (No. 3 Course), Medinah, Illinois, June 19-22
Yardage—7,032. Par 71. 4,214 Entries, 150 Qualifiers, 150 Starters

						Score	Money Prize
1	†Lou Graham, Richland C.C., Nashville, Tenn.	74	72	68	73	287	$40,000.00
2	†John D. Mahaffey, Jr., Champions G.C., Houston, Texas	73	71	72	71	287	20,000.00
3	Bob Murphy, Delray Dunes C.C., Delray Beach, Fla.	74	73	72	69	288	10,875.00
	Hale S. Irwin, St. Louis, Mo.	74	71	73	70	288	10,875.00
	Ben Crenshaw, C.C. of Austin, Austin, Texas	70	68	76	74	288	10,875.00
	Frank Beard, Hurstbourne C.C., Louisville, Ky.	74	69	67	78	288	10,875.00
7	Jack Nicklaus, Muirfield Village C.C., Dublin, Oh.	72	70	75	72	289	7,500.00
	Peter Oosterhuis, Pacific Harbour, Deuba, Fiji Islands	69	73	72	75	289	7,500.00
9	Tom Watson, Kansas City, Mo.	67	68	78	77	290	5,000.00
	Arnold Palmer, Laurel Valley G.C., Ligonier, Pa.	69	75	73	73	290	5,000.00
	Pat Fitzsimons, Salem C.C., Salem, Ore.	67	73	73	77	290	5,000.00
12	Andy North Gainesville G.&C.C., Gainesville, Fla.	75	72	72	72	291	2,800.00
	Ray Floyd, Lake Havasu G.C., Lake Havasu, Ariz.	76	71	72	72	291	2,800.00
14	Jim Wiechers, Island C., Hilton Head Island, S.C.	68	73	76	75	292	2,025.00
	Rik Massengale, Charlotte, N.C.	71	74	71	76	292	2,025.00
	Eddie Pearce, Orange Tree G.C., Orlando, Fla.	75	71	70	76	292	2,025.00
	Joe Inman, Jr., River Hills Plantation G.C., Clover, S.C.	72	72	71	77	292	2,025.00
18	Grier Jones, Wichita C.C., Wichita, Kans.	69	73	79	72	293	1,675.00
	Gary Groh, Bridgman, Mich.	73	74	73	73	293	1,675.00
	Terry Dill, Austin, Texas	72	69	77	75	293	1,675.00
	Hubert Green, Bay Point Yacht & C.C., Panama City, Fla.	74	73	68	78	293	1,675.00
	*Jerome K. Pate, Pensacola C.C., Pensacola, Fla.	79	70	72	72	293	Medal
	*Jay Haas, St. Clair C.C., Belleville, Ill.	74	69	72	78	293	Medal
24	Dale Douglass, Boulder C.C., Boulder, Colo.	71	77	72	74	294	1,452.00
	Kermit Zarley, Clear Lake C.C., Clear Lake, Texas	73	71	75	75	294	1,452.00
	Brian Allin, Santa Barbara, Calif.	76	70	73	75	294	1,452.00
	Forrest Fezler, Indian Wells C.C., Indian Wells, Calif.	73	75	71	75	294	1,452.00
	Miller Barber, Woodlawn C.C., Sherman, Texas	74	71	71	78	294	1,452.00
29	Tommy Aaron, Callaway Gardens C.C., Callaway Gardens, Ga.	73	71	82	69	295	1,193.34
	Nate Starks, St. Petersburg, Fla.	75	72	76	72	295	1,193.34
	Jerry Heard, Visalia, Calif.	77	67	78	73	295	1,193.34
	Steve Melynk, Amelia Links G.C., Amelia Island, Fla.	75	73	74	73	295	1,193.33
	Ed Sneed, Palm Aire C.C., Pompano Beach, Fla.	75	74	73	73	295	1,193.33
	David Graham, Hollywood, Fla.	71	76	74	74	295	1,193.33
	Tom Weiskopf, Columbus, Ohio	75	71	74	75	295	1,193.33
	Don January, Plano Municipal G.C., Plano, Texas	72	75	73	75	295	1,193.33
	Lee Trevino, El Paso, Texas	72	69	75	79	295	1,193.33
38	Lanny Wadkins, Bermuda Run G.&C.C., Clemmons, N.C.	69	77	77	73	296	1,040.00
	Johnny Miller, Silverado C.C., Napa, Calif.	75	72	76	73	296	1,040.00
	Julius Boros, C.C. of Aventura, Miami Beach, Fla.	72	77	72	75	296	1,040.00
	John H. Schlee, Preston Trail C.C., Dallas, Texas	75	73	72	76	296	1,040.00
	Allen Geiberger, Silver Lakes C.C., Silver Lakes, Calif.	72	72	74	78	296	1,040.00
43	Dave Stockton, Westlake G.C., Westlake, Calif.	73	73	77	74	297	985.00
	Gary Player, Johannesburg, South Africa	75	73	72	77	297	985.00
45	Doug Sanders, Woodlands C.C., Woodlands, Texas	75	73	76	74	298	955.00
	Richard M. Rhyan, Jr., Bridgeview G.C., Columbus, Ohio	74	70	77	77	298	955.00
	Gibby Gilbert, Pembroke Pines, Fla.	71	76	74	77	298	955.00
	Bob E. Smith, Wailea C.C., Maui, Hawaii	78	71	72	77	298	955.00
49	Bob Stanton, Diamond Head C.C., Bay St. Louis, Miss.	77	72	78	72	299	905.00
	Bob Gilder, Corvallis C.C., Corvallis, Ore.	76	71	77	75	299	905.00
	J. C. Snead, Hot Springs, Va.	76	73	75	75	299	905.00
	Beau Baugh, Admicatty G.C., Rockledge, Fla.	77	72	73	77	299	905.00
	Gary Robinson, Oasis D.R, Plymouth, Mich.	72	72	76	79	299	905.00
	Gene Littler, La Jolla C.C., La Jolla, Calif.	74	73	73	79	299	905.00
	*Lance Ten Broeck, Beverly C.C., Chicago, Ill.	71	74	79	75	299	Medal
56	Wally Armstrong, Indianapolis C.C., Indianapolis, Ind.	73	74	77	76	300	865.00
	Lynn C. Janson, C.C. of Lansing, Lansing, Mich.	71	73	78	78	300	865.00
58	Robert Pansiuk, Hydeaway G.C., Tecumseh, Canada	76	71	76	78	301	845.00
	Frank Conner, San Antonio, Texas	72	72	76	81	301	845.00
60	Marty Fleckman, New Caney, Texas	71	77	79	76	303	830.00
61	Bill Rogers, Northridge C.C., Texarkana, Texas	75	73	81	75	304	820.00
62	Jack Ewing, Capistrano Beach, Calif.	76	73	77	79	305	810.00
63	Jack Connelly, Huntingdon Valley C.C., Huntingdon Valley, Pa.	75	74	78	79	306	800.00
	Bob Goalby, The Springs C., Rancho Mirage, Calif.	72	74	80	80	306	800.00
65	Mike Reasor, Seattle, Wash.	72	74	82	80	308	800.00
66	Carlton P. White, II, Washington Valley G.C., Washington Valley, N.J.	74	75	76	86	311	800.00
67	Stanton Altgelt, Royal Oaks C.C., Dallas, Texas	76	72	87	77	312	800.00

†Playoff, June 23, 1975, Lou Graham 71, John Mahaffey, Jr. 73.
Prize money totaling $244,000 awarded to professionals as follows:
Championship—$236,200; Sectional Qualifying Championship $7,800.

*Amateur.

1976
SEVENTY-SIXTH OPEN CHAMPIONSHIP

Held at Atlanta Athletic Club (Highlands Course), Duluth, Georgia, June 17-20
Yardage—7,015. Par 70. 4,436 Entries, 150 Qualifiers, 150 Starters

						Score	Money Prize
1	Jerome K. Pate, Pensacola C.C., Pensacola, Fla.	71	69	69	68	277	$42,000.00
2	Allen Geiberger, Silver Lakes Resort, Silver Lakes, Calif.	70	69	71	69	279	18,000.00
	Tom Weiskopf, Columbus, Ohio	73	70	68	68	279	18,000.00
4	Butch Baird, Miami Beach, Fla.	71	71	71	67	280	11,250.00
	John D. Mahaffey, Jr., Riverhill C.C., Kerrville, Texas	70	68	69	73	280	11,250.00
6	Hubert M. Green, Bay Point Yacht & C.C., Panama City Fla.	72	70	71	69	282	9,500.00
7	Tom Watson, Steamboat Village C.C., Steamboat Springs, Colo.	74	72	68	70	284	8,500.00
8	Ben Crenshaw, C.C. of Austin, Austin, Texas	72	68	72	73	285	7,000.00
	Lyn Lott, Douglas, Ga.	71	71	70	73	285	7,000.00
10	Johnny Miller, Silverado C.C., Napa, Calif.	74	72	69	71	286	5,500.00
11	Rod Funseth, Silverado C.C., Napa, Calif.	70	70	72	75	287	4,000.00
	Jack Nicklaus, Muirfield Village G.C., Muirfield, Ohio	74	70	75	68	287	4,000.00
13	Raymond Floyd, Lake Havasu C.C., Lake Havasu, Ariz.	70	75	71	72	288	3,000.00
14	Mark S. Hayes, Kickingbird G.C., Edmond, Okla.	74	74	70	71	289	2,310.00
	Don January, Dallas, Texas	71	74	69	75	289	2,310.00
	Michael E. Morley, Minot C.C., Minot, N.D.	71	71	70	77	289	2,310.00
	Andy North, Gainesville G. & C.C., Gainesville, Fla.	74	72	69	74	289	2,310.00
	J. C. Snead, Hot Springs, Va.	73	69	71	76	289	2,310.00
19	Danny Edwards, The Greens G. & Racquet C., Oklahoma City, Okla.	73	75	70	72	290	1,875.00
	Randy Glover, Wellman C.C., Johnsonville, S.C.	72	74	76	68	290	1,875.00
21	Dave Eichelberger, Ridgewood C.C., Waco, Texas	73	70	74	74	291	1,775.00
	Larry G. Nelson, Pinetree C.C., Kennesaw, Ga.	75	74	70	72	291	1,775.00
23	Joe Inman, Jr., River Hills Plantation C.C., Clover, S.C.	75	73	74	70	292	1,650.00
	Gary Player, Johannesburg, South Africa	72	77	73	70	292	1,650.00
	Calvin Peete, South Bay, Fla.	76	69	74	73	292	1,650.00
26	Hale Irwin, Frontenac, Mo.	75	72	75	71	293	1,540.00
	Tom Jenkins, Houston, Texas	72	74	75	72	293	1,540.00
28	Lou Graham, Richland C.C., Nashville, Tenn.	75	74	72	73	294	1,412.00
	Barry Jaeckel, The Golf C., Kahului, Maui, Hawaii	74	77	69	74	294	1,412.00
	Grier S. Jones, Wichita C.C., Wichita, Kans	76	69	71	78	294	1,412.00
	Wayne Levi, Mohawk Valley C.C., Little Falls, N.Y.	74	73	74	73	294	1,412.00
	Bob E. Smith, Wailea G.C., Wailea, Maui, Hawaii	72	75	74	73	294	1,412.00
33	Terry Diehl, Oak Hill C.C., Pittsford, N.Y.	71	72	76	76	295	1,330.00
	Rik Massengale, Jacksboro C.C., Jacksboro, Texas	70	78	70	77	295	1,330.00
35	Robert Lee Elder, Washington, D.C.	72	75	78	71	296	1,280.00
	Vic Regalado, Tijuana C.C., Tijuana, Mexico	75	76	71	74	296	1,280.00
	Bobby Wadkins, Richmond, Va.	76	72	72	76	296	1,280.00
38	Miller Barber, Woodlawn C.C., Sherman, Texas	76	72	79	70	297	1,200.00
	Charles Coody, Maitland, Fla.	75	76	70	76	297	1,200.00
	John A. Gentile, East Point C.C., Palm Beach Gardens, Fla.	77	74	73	73	297	1,200.00
	Lon Hinkle, Carlton Oaks G.C., Santee, Calif.	75	74	70	78	297	1,200.00
	Mike Shea, New Orleans, La.	72	73	72	80	297	1,200.00
	Fuzzy Zoeller, New Albany C.C., New Albany, Ind.	72	75	73	77	297	1,200.00
44	Kermit Zarley, Jr., Clear Lake C.C., Clear Lake, Texas	75	73	75	75	298	1,150.00
	Thomas Purtzer, Moon Valley C.C., Phoenix, Ariz.	73	75	73	77	298	1,150.00
	Tim Collins, Greenville C.C., Greenville, S.C.	73	76	72	77	298	1,150.00
47	Tommy Aaron, Pine Isle, Lake Lanier Island, Ga.	75	73	76	75	299	1,120.00
	Bruce Lietzke, Beaumont C.C., Beaumont, Texas	76	73	77	73	299	1,120.00
	Eddie Pearce, Orange Tree C.C., Orlando, Fla.	80	71	76	72	299	1,120.00
50	Carlton P. White, II, Washington Valley G.C., Washington, N.J.	75	75	75	75	300	1,090.00
	Gene Littler, La Jolla C.C., La Jolla, Calif.	76	75	71	78	300	1,090.00
	Arnold Palmer, Laurel Valley G..C, Ligonier, Pa.	75	75	75	75	300	1,090.00
	*Michael D. Reid, Broadmoor G.C., Seattle, Wash.	67	81	80	72	300	Medal
	*John Fought, Tualatin C.C., Tualatin, Ore.	79	72	72	77	300	Medal
55	Peter A. Oosterhuis, Mission Hills G.C., Palm Springs, Calif.	73	75	74	79	301	1,060.00
	Joey D. Dills, Southern Hills C.C., Tulsa, Okla.	77	73	74	77	301	1,060.00
	Jim Colbert, Saddlebrook C.C., Wesley Chapel, Fla.	74	76	73	78	301	1,060.00
58	John A. Jacobs, Round Hill G. & C.C., Alamo, Calif.	75	75	74	78	302	1,035.00
	Bob Gilder, Corvallis C.C., Corvallis, Ore.	75	74	75	78	302	1,035.00
60	Bruce Devlin, Walden G.C., Conroe, Texas	75	73	81	74	303	1,015.00
	George A. Cadle, Indian Wells C.C., Indian Wells, Calif.	79	71	77	76	303	1,015.00
62	Bobby Stroble, Metro G.C., Albany, Ga.	77	70	82	76	305	1,000.00
	*Martin R. West, III, Columbia C.C., Chevy Chase, Md.	73	73	80	79	305	Medal
	*Bruce Douglass, Thorny Lea G.C., Brockton, Mass.	73	76	75	81	305	Medal
65	Gene Borek, Sunningdale C.C., Scarsdale, N.Y.	74	74	76	83	307	1,000.00
66	Jim Ferree, Westmoreland C.C., Export, Pa.	76	73	80	82	311	1,000.00

Prize money totaling $268,000 awarded to professionals as follows:
Championship—$253,000; Sectional Qualifying Championships $15,000.

*Amateur

1977
SEVENTY-SEVENTH OPEN CHAMPIONSHIP

Held at Southern Hills Country Club, Tulsa, Oklahoma, June 16-19.
Yardage—6,873. Par 70. 4,608 Entries, 150 Qualifiers, 153 Starters.

						Score	Money Prize
1	Hubert M. Green, Birmingham, Ala.	69	67	72	70	278	$45,000.00
2	Lou Graham, Richland C.C., Nashville, Tenn.	72	71	68	68	279	23,500.00
3	Tom Weiskopf, Columbus, Ohio	71	71	68	71	281	16,000.00
4	Thomas W. Purtzer, Moon Valley C.C., Phoenix, Ariz.	69	69	72	72	282	13,000.00
5	Jay Haas, St. Clair C.C., Belleville, Ill.	72	68	71	72	283	10,875.00
	Gary S. Jacobson, Minnetonka, Minn.	73	70	67	73	283	10,875.00
7	Tom Watson, Steamboat Village C.C., Steamboat Springs, Colo.	74	72	71	67	284	8,000.00
	Lynn Lott, Douglas G.C., Douglas. Ga.	73	73	68	70	284	8,000.00
	Terry Diehl, Oak Hill C.C., Pittsford, N.Y.	69	68	73	74	284	8,000.00
10	Allen Geiberger, Santa Barbara, Calif.	70	71	75	69	285	4,100.00
	Peter A. Oosterhuis, Mission Hills C.C., Rancho Mirage, Calif.	71	70	74	70	285	4,100.00
	Michael McCullough, Los Angeles, Calif.	73	73	69	70	285	4,100.00
	Jack Nicklaus, Muirfield Village G.C., Dublin, Ohio	74	68	71	72	285	4,100.00
	Rod Funseth, Silverado C.C., Napa, Calif.	69	70	72	74	285	4,100.00
	Gary Player, Johannesburg, South Africa	72	67	71	75	285	4,100.00
16	Steve Melnyk, Amelia Links, Amelia Island, Fla.	70	73	70	73	286	2,400.00
	Joseph C. Inman, River Hills Plantation, Clover, S.C.	70	70	72	74	286	2,400.00
	Wally Armstrong, Orlando, Fla.	71	70	70	75	286	2,400.00
19	Jerry McGee, E. Palestine, Ohio	76	69	76	66	287	1,887.50
	Bill Kratzert, III, Ft. Wayne C.C., Ft. Wayne, Ind.	73	69	75	70	287	1,887.50
	Arnold D. Palmer, Laurel Valley G.C., Ligonier, Pa.	70	72	73	72	287	1,887.50
	Bruce A. Lietzke, Tyrrell Park G.C., Beaumont, Texas	74	68	71	74	287	1,887.50
23	Ron R. Streck, Cedar Ridge C.C., Tulsa, Okla.	73	73	71	71	288	1,700.00
	Sam M. Adams, Boone, N.C.	70	69	76	73	288	1,700.00
	Andy Bean, Sugar Hills Woods G.C., Homosassa, Fla.	71	70	68	79	288	1,700.00
26	Gay Brewer, Jr., Palm Springs, Calif.	73	72	70	74	289	1,600.00
27	George Archer, Reno, Nev.	73	72	74	71	290	1,412.50
	Michael E. Morley, Ahwatukee C.C., Phoenix, Ariz.	70	73	74	73	290	1,412.50
	Lee Trevino, Santa Teresa C.C., Santa Teresa, N.M.	74	70	73	73	290	1,412.50
	J. C. Snead, Hot Springs, Va.	72	75	68	75	290	1,412.50
	John Miller, Silverado C.C., Napa, Calif.	71	73	70	76	290	1,412.50
	Tom Kite, Jr., Horseshoe Bay C.C., Marble Falls, Texas	71	73	70	76	290	1,412.50
	John Lister, Timaru G.C., Timaru, New Zealand	72	73	68	77	290	1,412.50
	Donald E. Padgett, II, Woodland C.C., Carmel, Ind.	70	74	66	80	290	1,412.50
35	Rod Curl, Riverview G. & C.C., Redding, Calif.	75	71	73	72	291	1,270.00
	Graham V. Marsh, Golf St. Cyprien, St. Cyprien, Elne, France	74	72	72	73	291	1,270.00
	Grier S. Jones, Wichita C.C., Wichita, Kans.	69	75	72	75	291	1,270.00
	Jim Simons, Turtle Creek G.C., Tequesta, Fla.	75	67	71	78	291	1,270.00
39	Rik Massengale, Charlotte, Texas	71	72	77	72	292	1,210.00
	Florentino Molina, Ituzaingo G.C., Buenos Aires, Argentina	69	76	75	72	292	1,210.00
41	Hale Irwin, Frontenac, Mo.	73	71	77	72	293	1,180.00
	Mark S. Hayes, Oak Tree G.C., Oklahoma City, Okla.	76	68	73	76	293	1,180.00
	Gilmer B. Morgan, II, Wewoka, Okla.	76	70	69	78	293	1,180.00
44	Fuzzy Zoeller, New Albany C.C., New Albany, Ind.	73	69	79	73	294	1,150.00
	Bruce Fleisher, Grossinger's G. C., Liberty, N.Y.	73	69	74	78	294	1,150.00
	Phillip Hancock, Greenville, Ala.	74	73	72	75	294	1,150.00
47	Raymond Floyd, Lake Havasu G.C., Lake Havasu, Ariz.	73	73	78	71	295	1,125.00
	David E. Canipe, Highland C.C., Fayetteville, N.C.	74	73	70	78	295	1,125.00
49	George Burns, III, Delray Beach, Fla.	70	75	76	75	296	1,095.00
	Jim Dent, St. Petersburg, Fla.	76	71	74	75	296	1,095.00
	Ben Crenshaw, C.C. of Austin, Austin, Texas	74	71	72	79	296	1,095.00
	Morris Hatalsky, Daytona Beach, Fla.	70	74	72	80	296	1,095.00
53	Bill Mallon, John's Island C., Vero Beach, Fla.	73	71	77	77	298	1,070.00
54	John Melnick, Sea Island G.C., St. Simons Island, Ga.	71	75	78	75	299	1,055.00
	Larry G. Nelson, Pinetree C.C., Kennesaw, Ga.	69	75	78	77	299	1,055.00
	*Lindy Miller, Shady Oaks C.C., Ft. Worth, Texas	73	73	76	77	299	Medal
57	Bob E. Smith, Wialea C.C., Wialea, Maui, Hawaii	70	77	77	76	300	1,040.00
58	Vince Bizik, Overland Park, Kans.	71	76	76	79	302	1,030.00
	*John Fought, Tualatin C.C., Portland, Ore.	73	74	78	77	302	Medal
60	Juan A. (Chi Chi) Rodriguez, Rio Mar G.C., Palmer, Puerto Rico	74	71	75	84	304	1,020.00

Prize money totaling $284,990 awarded to professionals as follows:
Championship—$227,990; prizes for 84 professionals who did not return scores for 54 holes—$42,000; Sectional Qualifying Championship $15,000.

*Amateur

1978

SEVENTY-EIGHTH OPEN CHAMPIONSHIP

Held at Cherry Hills Country Club, Englewood, Colorado, June 15-18.
Yardage—7,083. Par 71. 4,897 Entries, 150 Qualifiers, 153 Starters.

						Score	Money Prize
1	Andy North, Makoma G.C., Madison, Wis.	70	70	71	74	285	$45,000.00
2	J. C. Snead, Hot Springs, Va.	70	72	72	72	286	19,750.00
	Dave Stockton, Westlake North Ranch, Westlake Village, Calif.	71	73	70	72	286	19,750.00
4	Tom Weiskopf, Columbus, Ohio	77	73	70	68	288	13,000.00
	Hale Irwin, Kapalua G.C., Kapalua, Maui, Hawaii	69	74	75	70	288	13,000.00
6	Tom Watson, Steamboat Village C.C., Steamboat Springs, Colo.	74	75	70	70	289	7,548.34
	Andy Bean, Grenelefe Golf & Racquet Club., Cypress Gardens, Fla.	72	72	71	74	289	7,548.34
	Bill Kratzert, Ft. Wayne C.C., Ft. Wayne, Ind.	72	74	70	73	289	7,548.33
	Jack Nicklaus, Muirfield Village G.C., Dublin, Ohio	73	69	74	73	289	7,548.33
	John Miller, San Francisco G.C., San Francisco, Calif.	78	69	68	74	289	7,548.33
	Gary Player, Johannesburg, South Africa	71	71	70	77	289	7,548.33
12	Raymond Floyd, Miami, Fla.	75	70	76	70	291	3,400.00
	Lee Trevino, Santa Teresa C.C., Santa Teresa, N.M.	72	71	75	73	291	3,400.00
	Joe Inman, Jr., River Hills C.C., Clover, S.C.	72	72	74	73	291	3,400.00
	Mike McCullough, Los Angeles, Calif.	75	75	73	68	291	3,400.00
16	Robert Shearer, Bay Tree G.C., N. Myrtle Beach, S.C.	78	72	71	71	292	2,650.00
	Jerry Pate, Shoal Creek C.C., Birmingham, Ala.	73	72	74	73	292	2,650.00
	Artie McNickle, Sacramento, Calif.	74	75	70	73	292	2,650.00
	Severiano Ballesteros, Pedrena G.C., Santander, Spain	75	69	71	77	292	2,650.00
20	Wally Armstrong, Maitland, Fla.	73	73	74	73	293	2,287.50
	Phillip Hancock, Greenville C.C., Greenville, Ala.	71	73	75	74	293	2,287.50
	Tom Kite, Jr., C.C. of Austin, Austin, Texas	73	73	70	77	293	2,287.50
	Bruce A. Lietzke, Tyrrell Park G.C., Beaumont, Texas	72	73	72	76	293	2,287.50
24	Dale Douglass, Boulder C.C., Boulder, Colo.	74	75	74	72	295	2,100.00
	Victor Regalado, Tijuana C.C., Tijuana, Mexico	74	72	73	76	295	2,100.00
	Tom Purtzer, Moon Valley C.C., Phoenix, Ariz.	75	72	72	76	295	2,100.00
27	Peter Oosterhuis, Mission Hills C.C., Rancho Mirage, Calif.	72	72	78	74	296	1,950.00
	Jerry McGee, E. Palestine, Ohio	74	76	71	75	296	1,950.00
	Pat McGowan, Colusa G.&C.C., Colusa, Calif.	74	73	72	77	296	1,950.00
30	Charles Coody, Fairway Oaks G.&R.C., Abilene, Texas	74	76	76	71	297	1,800.00
	Rod Curl, Riverview G.&C.C., Redding, Calif.	78	72	74	73	297	1,800.00
	Lee Elder, Washington, D.C.	76	73	73	75	297	1,800.00
	Bill Casper, Mapleton, Utah	71	76	73	77	297	1,800.00
	*Bob Clampett, Carmel Valley G.&C.C., Carmel, Calif.	70	73	80	74	297	Medal
35	Raymond Cragun, Rio Rancho C.C., Rio Rancho, N.M.	79	71	76	72	298	1,566.67
	Lou Graham, Richland C.C., Nashville, Tenn.	78	72	74	74	298	1,566.67
	Gene Littler, La Jolla C.C., La Jolla, Calif.	73	75	77	73	298	1,566.67
	Miller Barber, Woodlawn C.C., Sherman, Texas	74	73	76	75	298	1,566.67
	Leonard Thompson, Bay Hill C., Orlando, Fla.	74	76	73	75	298	1,566.67
	Ed Fiori, Sugar Creek C.C., Sugarland, Texas	74	73	74	77	298	1,566.67
	Mark Hayes, Oak Tree G.C., Edmond, Okla.	73	70	76	79	298	1,566.66
	Steve Melnyk, Amelia Links G.C., Amelia Island, Fla.	79	71	69	79	298	1,566.66
	Mac McLendon, Pine Harbor Resort, Pell City, Ala.	75	73	69	81	298	1,566.66
44	Bob Gilder, Corvallis, Ore.	76	74	74	75	299	1,430.00
	Bill Rogers, Northridge C.C., Texarkana, Texas	79	69	73	78	299	1,430.00
46	Bobby Wadkins, Meadowbrook C.C., Richmond, Va.	71	78	77	74	300	1,350.00
	George Burns, III, Quail Ridge G.&T.C., Delray Beach, Fla.	74	76	78	72	300	1,350.00
	Juan A. (Chi Chi) Rodriquez, Rio Mar G.C., Palmer, Puerto Rico	74	73	77	76	300	1,350.00
	Ed Sneed, Palm Aire C.C., Pompano Beach, Fla.	78	70	75	77	300	1,350.00
	Wayne Levi, Mohawk Valley C.C., Herkimer, N.Y.	76	73	74	77	300	1,350.00
	Tom Ulozas, Bamm Hollow C.C., Lincroft, N.J.	73	73	75	79	300	1,350.00
52	Bobby Nichols, Firestone C.C., Akron, Ohio	74	72	80	75	301	1,290.00
53	Nate Starks, St. Petersburg, Fla.	74	75	78	75	302	1,275.00
	Allen Geiberger, Santa Barbara, Calif.	71	74	78	79	302	1,275.00
55	Harry Toscano, New Wilmington, Pa.	74	75	75	79	303	1,255.00
	Dick McClean, Carmel, Calif.	78	71	72	82	303	1,255.00
57	Bill Brask, Eden Prairie, Minn.	71	76	78	79	304	1,240.00
	*Jim Holtgrieve, Westborough C.C., Glendale, Mo.	79	71	78	76	304	Medal
59	Dave Eichelberger, Ridgewood C.C., Waco, Texas	77	71	80	77	305	1,230.00
60	Mike Morley, Ahwatukee C.C., Phoenix, Ariz.	77	73	78	80	308	1,220.00
61	Walter Zembriski, Orlando, Fla.	76	73	84	76	309	1,210.00
62	Bob E. Smith, Honolulu, Hawaii	74	73	82	81	310	1,200.00
63	Al Chandler, Columbia C.C., Columbia, Mo.	75	75	76	86	312	1,200.00

Prize money totaling $310,200.00 awarded to professionals as follows:
Championship—$247,200.00; prizes for 80 professionals who did not return scores for 72 holes—$48,000.00; Sectional Qualifying Championship $15,000.00.

***Amateur**

1979
SEVENTY-NINTH OPEN CHAMPIONSHIP

Held at Inverness Club, Toledo, Ohio, June 14-17.
Yardage—6,982. Par 71. 4,853 Entries, 153 Qualifiers, 153 Starters.

						Score	Money Prize
1	Hale Irwin, Kapalua G.C., Kapalua Maui, Hawaii	74	68	67	75	284	$50,000.00
2	Gary Player, Johannesburg, South Africa	73	73	72	68	286	22,250.00
	Jerry Pate, Shoal Creek, Mountain Brook, Ala.	71	74	69	72	286	22,500.00
4	Bill Rogers, Northridge C.C., Texarkana, Texas	71	72	73	72	288	13,733.34
	Larry Nelson, Pine Tree C.C., Kennesaw, Ga.	71	68	76	73	288	13,733.33
	Tom Weiskopf, Paradise Valley, Ariz.	71	74	67	76	288	13,733.33
7	David Graham, The Hamlet, Delray Beach, Fla.	73	73	70	73	289	10,000.00
8	Tom Purtzer, Phoenix, Ariz.	70	69	75	76	290	9,000.00
9	Jack Nicklaus, Muirfield Village G.C., Dublin, Ohio	74	77	72	68	291	7,500.00
	Keith Fergus, Sugar Creek C.C., Sugarland, Texas	70	77	72	72	291	7,500.00
11	Ed Sneed, Columbus, Ohio	72	73	75	73	293	4,340.00
	Andy North, Nakoma G.C., Madison, Wis.	77	74	68	74	293	4,340.00
	Ben Crenshaw, C.C. of Austin, Austin, Texas	75	71	72	75	293	4,340.00
	Calvin Peete, Clewiston, Fla.	72	75	71	75	293	4,340.00
	Lee Elder, Langston G.C., Washington, D.C.	74	72	69	78	293	4,340.00
16	Jim Simons, Turtle Creek C., Tequesta, Fla.	74	74	78	68	294	2,833.34
	Graham Marsh, Club St. Cyprion, France	77	71	72	74	294	2,833.33
	Bob Gilder, Corvallis, Ore.	77	70	69	78	294	2,833.33
19	Lee Trevino, Royal Oaks C.C., Dallas, Texas	77	73	73	72	295	2,410.00
	D. A. Weibring, Red Run G.C., Royal Oak, Mich.	74	76	71	74	295	2,410.00
	Lanny Wadkins, Bermuda Run G&CC, Clemmons, N.C.	73	74	71	77	295	2,410.00
	Bobby Walzel, Missouri City, Texas	74	72	71	78	295	2,410.00
	Allen Geiberger, Santa Barbara, Calif.	74	74	69	78	295	2,410.00
24	Hubert Green, Shoal Creek, Mountain Brook, Ala.	74	77	73	72	296	2,200.00
25	Wayne Levi, Mohawk Valley C.C., Herkimer, N.Y.	77	73	75	72	297	2,000.00
	Michael Reid, Riverside C.C., Provo, Utah	74	75	74	74	297	2,000.00
	Lou Graham, Richland C.C., Nashville, Tenn.	70	75	77	75	297	2,000.00
	Bobby Nichols, Firestone C.C., Akron, Ohio	76	75	71	75	297	2,000.00
	Bob Murphy, Delray Dunes G.C., Boynton Beach, Fla.	72	79	69	77	297	2,000.00
	Andy Bean, Grenelefe G & Racquet C., Haines City, Fla.	70	76	71	80	297	2,000.00
	Bob E. Smith, Del Paso C.C., Sacramento, Calif.	77	71	69	80	297	2,000.00
32	Lynn Janson, Green Ridge C.C., Grand Rapids, Mich.	77	71	77	73	298	1,725.00
	Dale Douglass, Colorado Springs, Colo.	72	76	76	74	298	1,725.00
	Howard Twitty, Arizona Biltmore G.C., Phoenix, Ariz.	73	78	71	76	298	1,725.00
	Juan Rodriguez, Dorado Beach Hotel, Dorado Beach, P.R.	73	76	71	78	298	1,725.00
36	Isao Aoki, Tokyo, Japan	73	77	76	73	299	1,560.00
	Jim Dent, St. Petersburg, Fla.	75	76	75	73	299	1,560.00
	John Mahaffey, Champions G.C., Houston, Texas	77	73	74	75	299	1,560.00
	David Stockton, Westlake Vlg. North Ranch, Westlake, Calif.	75	70	78	76	299	1,560.00
	Bill Kratzert, Ft. Wayne C.C., Ft. Wayne, Ind.	77	73	73	76	299	1,560.00
41	Larry Ziegler, The Concord Hotel & C.C., Kiamesha Lake, N.Y.	77	72	78	73	300	1,430.00
	Jack Renner, Palm Springs, Calif.	76	75	75	74	300	1,430.00
	Bruce Lietzke, Shangri-La Resort, Afton, Okla.	74	77	73	76	300	1,430.00
	Jim Nelford, Orem, Utah	75	76	73	76	300	1,430.00
	James Colbert, Jr., Wesley Chapel, Fla.	71	74	78	77	300	1,430.00
	Dana Quigley, Barrington, R.I.	71	78	74	77	300	1,430.00
47	Forrest Fezler, Hollister, Calif.	73	77	73	78	301	1,360.00
48	George Burns, III, Quail Ridge G. & T.C., Delray Beach, Fla.	74	73	78	77	302	1,312.50
	Greg Norman, United Kingdom	76	74	74	78	302	1,312.50
	Frank Conner, San Antonio, Texas	73	78	73	78	302	1,312.50
	Rod Funseth, Silverado C.C., Napa, Calif.	73	74	74	81	302	1,312.50
	*Fred Couples, Beacon Hill C.C., Seattle, Wash.	76	74	80	72	302	Medal
53	David Edwards, Oak Tree G.C., Edmond, Okla.	74	76	84	70	304	1,265.00
	Edward Pearce, Bay Hill C., Orlando, Fla.	75	75	76	78	304	1,265.00
	Joseph Inman, Jr., River Hills C.C., Clover, S.C.	72	77	75	80	304	1,265.00
	Lon Hinkle, Royal Oaks C.C., Dallas, Texas	70	77	76	81	304	1,265.00
	*John Cook, Muirfield Village G.C., Dublin, Ohio	71	80	77	76	304	Medal
	*Joe Rassett, Turlock G.&C.C., Turlock, Calif.	75	75	77	77	304	Medal
59	Eric Batten, Pasatiempo G.C., Santa Cruz, Calif.	74	76	77	78	305	1,235.00
	Arnold Palmer, Laurel Valley G.C., Ligonier, Pa.	76	73	75	81	305	1,235.00
61	John Gentile, Birchwood C.C., Westport, Conn.	73	75	77	81	306	1,220.00
62	Mac McLendon, Pine Harbor C.C., Pell City, Ala.	77	74	80	78	309	1,210.00
63	Tony Peterson, Mission Hills C.C., Shawnee Mission, Kans.	74	75	84	79	312	1,200.00

Prize money totaling $330,400.00 awarded to professionals as follows:
Championship—$269,200.00; prizes for 77 professionals who did not return scores for 72 holes—$46,200.00; Sectional Qualifying Championship $15,000.00

*Amateur

1980
EIGHTIETH OPEN CHAMPIONSHIP

Held at Baltusrol Golf Club (Lower Course), Springfield, New Jersey, June 12-15
Yardage—7,076. Par 70. 4,812 Entries, 154 Qualifiers, 154 Starters

						Score	Money Prize
1	Jack Nicklaus, Muirfield Village G.C., Dublin, Ohio	63	71	70	68	272	$55,000.00
2	Isao Aoki, Golf Kikaku, Tokyo, Japan	68	68	68	70	274	29,500.00
3	Keith Fergus, Sugar Creek C.C., Sugarland, Texas	66	70	70	70	276	17,400.00
	Tom Watson, Kansas City, Mo.	71	68	67	70	276	17,400.00
	Lon Hinkle, Carrollton, Texas	66	70	69	71	276	17,400.00
6	Mike Reid, Riverside C.C., Provo, Utah	69	67	75	69	280	11,950.00
	Mark Hayes, Oak Tree G.C., Edmond, Okla.	66	71	69	74	280	11,950.00
8	Andy North, Nakoma G.C., Madison, Wis.	68	75	72	67	282	8,050.00
	Hale Irwin, Kapalua G.C., Kapalua Maui, Hawaii	70	70	73	69	282	8,050.00
	Ed Sneed, The Golf Club, Columbus, Ohio	72	70	70	70	282	8,050.00
	Mike Morley, Bloomington, Minn.	73	68	69	72	282	8,050.00
12	Joe Hager, Northwood Club, Dallas, Texas	72	70	71	70	283	4,387.50
	Bobby Wadkins, Meadowbrook C.C., Richmond, Va.	72	71	68	72	283	4,387.50
	Bruce Devlin, Raveneaux C.C., Houston, Texas	71	70	70	72	283	4,387.50
	Lee Trevino, Dallas, Texas	68	72	69	74	283	4,387.50
16	Curtis Strange, Kingsmill, Va.	69	74	71	70	284	2,891.67
	Gil Morgan, Oak Tree G.C., Edmond, Okla.	73	70	70	71	284	2,891.67
	Joe Inman, Jr., River Hills C.C., Clover, S.C.	74	69	69	72	284	2,891.67
	Pat McGowan, Colusa G.&C.C., Colusa, Calif.	69	69	73	73	284	2,891.67
	Bill Rogers, Northridge C.C., Texarkana, Texas	69	72	70	73	284	2,891.66
	Craig Stadler, Edgewood G.C., Stateline, Nev.	73	67	69	75	284	2,891.66
22	J.C. Snead, Ponte Vedra, Florida	69	71	73	72	285	2,400.00
	Jim Simons, Turtle Creek Club, Tequesta, Florida	70	72	71	72	285	2,400.00
	*Gary Hallberg, Rolling Green C.C., Arlington Heights, Ill.	74	68	70	73	285	Medal
	Peter Jacobsen, Portland, Oregon	70	69	72	74	285	2,400.00
26	Mark Lye, Silverado C.C., Napa, Calif.	68	72	77	69	286	2,275.00
	Jay Haas, Charlotte, N.C.	67	74	70	75	286	2,275.00
28	Calvin Peete, Belle Glade C.C., Belle Glade, Fla.	67	76	74	70	287	2,125.00
	George Burns, III, Quail Ridge G.C., Delray Beach, Fla.	75	69	73	70	287	2,125.00
	John Mahaffey, Champions G.C., Houston, Texas	72	73	69	73	287	2,125.00
	David Edwards, Oak Tree G.C., Edmond, Okla.	73	68	72	74	287	2,125.00
32	Jack Newton, Myrtle Beach, S.C.	72	71	74	71	288	1,900.00
	Ben Crenshaw, C.C. of Austin, Austin, Texas	72	73	71	72	288	1,900.00
	Bob Gilder, Corvallis, Oregon	72	68	74	74	288	1,900.00
	Jerry McGee, East Palestine, Ohio	72	72	70	74	288	1,900.00
	Hubert Green, Shoal Creek C.C., Shoal Creek, Ala.	73	73	65	77	288	1,900.00
37	Tom Weiskopf, Paradise Valley, Ariz.	63	75	76	75	289	1,760.00
38	Artie McNickle, Sacramento, Calif.	76	70	72	72	290	1,630.00
	*Bob Clampett, Carmel Valley G.& C.C., Carmel, Calif.	72	74	71	73	290	Medal
	Tim Simpson, Ansley G.C., Atlanta, Ga.	70	73	73	74	290	1,630.00
	Rod Curl, Riverview G. & C.C., Redding, Calif.	73	71	72	74	290	1,630.00
	Gene Littler, Rancho Santa Fe, Calif.	72	68	75	75	290	1,630.00
	James Dent, St. Petersburg, Fla.	72	72	70	76	290	1,630.00
	Bruce Lietzke, Shangri-La Resort, Afton, Okla.	71	72	70	77	290	1,630.00
45	Scott Simpson, Stardust C.C., San Diego, Calif.	73	72	73	73	291	1,530.00
	Wayne Levi, Mohawk Valley C.C., Little Falls, N.Y.	72	71	73	75	291	1,530.00
47	Charles Coody, Fairway Oaks G.&Racquet C., Abilene, Texas	72	71	74	75	292	1,470.00
	David Graham, The Hamlet G.C., Delray Beach, Fla.	72	73	72	75	292	1,470.00
	Raymond Floyd, Scarlet Oaks, Scarlet Oaks, W.Va.	67	79	71	75	292	1,470.00
	James Colbert, Jr., Wesley Chapel, Fla.	72	69	74	77	292	1,470.00
51	Dave Stockton, Keystone Ranch C.C., Keystone, Colo.	73	73	77	70	293	1,410.00
	Lou Graham, Richland C.C., Nashville, Tenn.	73	71	72	77	293	1,410.00
53	John Cook, Muirfield Village G.C., Dublin, Ohio	71	71	77	75	294	1,385.00
	Fuzzy Zoeller, New Albany C.C., New Albany, Ind.	75	70	72	77	294	1,385.00
55	Tommy McGinnis, Fox Meadows G.C., Memphis, Tenn.	69	71	81	74	295	1,370.00
56	Ron Streck, Cedar Ridge C.C., Tulsa, Okla.	72	71	76	77	296	1,355.00
	Lance Ten Broeck, Beverly C.C., Chicago, Ill.	73	71	71	81	296	1,355.00
58	Charles Beck, Gates Four G.&C.C., Fayetteville, N.C.	76	70	77	74	297	1,340.00
59	Jeff Mitchell, Hillcrest C.C., Lubbock, Texas	69	75	73	81	298	1,330.00
60	Bob Walzel, Missouri City, Texas	73	70	81	75	299	1,310.00
	Phil Hancock, Pensacola C.C., Pensacola, Fla.	76	70	75	78	299	1,310.00
62	Larry Nelson, Acworth, Ga.	70	74	76	79	299	1,310.00
63	Arnold Palmer, Laurel Valley C.C., Ligonier, Pa.	73	73	77	78	301	1,300.00

Prize money totaling $356,700.00 awarded to professionals as follows:
Championship—$295,500.00; prizes for 77 professionals who did not return scores for 72 holes—$46,200.00; Sectional Qualifying Championship $15,000.00

*Amateur

AMATEUR CHAMPIONSHIP

HAVEMEYER TROPHY

Presented in 1894 by

THEODORE A. HAVEMEYER

First President of the United States Golf Association

Original trophy destroyed by fire November, 1925. Replaced in January, 1926, by

EDWARD S. MOORE

Treasurer of the United States Golf Association, 1922-25

HISTORY

1960—Deane R. Beman, 22, of Silver Spring, Md., won at the St. Louis Country Club, Clayton, Mo., when he defeated Robert W. Gardner, of New York City, by 6 and 4 in the last match. Beman thus became the ninth player in history to win both the United States and the British Amateur Championships; he won the British title in 1959. The Amateur Championship had an international flavor as champions from seven foreign countries competed. The best showing by a visitor was by Capt. P.G. Sethi, the Champion of India, who advanced to the third round before bowing to Gardner, 4 and 3. Defending Champion Jack W. Nicklaus, of Columbus, Ohio, lost in the fourth round to Charles F. Lewis, of Little Rock, Ark., 5 and 3; Lewis was playing in his first Amateur. This was in contrast to Nicklaus' play in the third round when he was seven under par for 13 holes in eliminating Phil Rodgers, 6 and 5. Lewis and John Farquhar, of Amarillo, Texas, were the semi-finalists. This was the first time any of the last four had advanced so far in the Amateur. Beman defeated Farquhar, 5 and 4, and Gardner ousted Lewis, 2 and 1. In the scheduled 36-hole final match, Beman got out in front early and stayed there. He was 1-up at the end of the first nine, 3-up at the end of the first 18, and finally closed out the match on the 32nd hole. Beman was approximately seven under par for the week. There was a record entry of 1,737.

1961—Jack W. Nicklaus, 21, of Columbus, Ohio, won his second Championship in three years to become the 14th player to win at least twice. Nicklaus was 20 strokes under par for 112 holes and lost but 19 holes at the Pebble Beach Golf Links, Pebble Beach, Calif. Nicklaus was never over par at the end of any of his seven matches. He scored the largest margin in the final match since 1955 by defeating H. Dudley Wysong, Jr., of McKinney, Texas, 8 and 6. Nicklaus finished the morning round in 69, three under par, for a 4-up lead over Wysong. Nicklaus won the first four holes in the afternoon round to go 8 up and finally ended the match on the 30th hole. The record entry of 1,995 included most members of both United States and British Walker Cup Teams. Joseph B. Carr was the last British survivor. He advanced to the semi-finals before bowing to Wysong, 2 down. Besides Nicklaus, Charles B. Smith advanced the furthest of any other United States Walker Cup Team member. Smith went to the quarter-finals before losing to Marion C. Methvin, Jr., 5 and 4. Methvin subsequently lost to Nicklaus by 9 and 8 in the semi-finals. Nicklaus' total margin of victory of 21 holes in the last three rounds is tied for eighth in the all-time records. Bob Jones' advantage of 37 holes for the last three rounds in 1928 heads the list. William C. Campbell set a new qualifying record when he scored 67-64—131 at the Guyan Golf and Country Club in Huntington, W. Va.

1962—Labron Harris, Jr., of Enid, Okla., was five holes down to A. Downing Gray of Pensacola, Fla., after the morning round, then rallied to defeat Gray by 1 up in the final match on the No. 2 Course of the Pinehurst Country Club, Pinehurst, N.C. Gray's splendid morning round of 70, 2 under par, was offset by Harris' 72 in the afternoon. Harris needed to play only eight holes in the afternoon to draw even, then went ahead permanently on the 28th hole. Twenty years old and a graduate of Oklahoma State University, Harris had qualified previously for the Amateur Championship in 1961, when he lost in the first round. Gray, 24, an insurance salesman, had never entered the Championship before. The Championship was remarkable for the early-round defeats of many former Champions and other prominent players by younger qualifiers. Among those who failed to survive either the first or second rounds were Charles R. Coe, Amateur Champion in 1949 and 1958; William Hyndman, III, runner-up in 1955 and a member of the USGA International Teams since 1959; Robert Gardner, runner-up in 1960; and H. Dudley Wysong, Jr., runner-up in 1961 to Jack Nicklaus. Patton, 40, was the only man over 30 years of age to reach the quarter-final round. He lost to Harris by 3 and 1 in one semi-final match. Charles Coody, of Forth Worth, an Air Force Lieutenant, was the other semi-finalist. Gray beat him by 3 and 2. The course's yardage of 7,051 was the longest ever for a USGA event. Charles Evans, Jr., made his 50th appearance in the Amateur Championship, something no one else has ever done. He lost in the first round. Former President Eisenhower was a spectator during the afternoon round of the final match.

1963—Deane R. Beman, 25, Bethesda, Md., won the Championship for the second time, defeating R.H. Sikes, of Springdale, Ark., by 2 and 1 in the final round at the Wakonda Club, Des Moines, Iowa. It was the third major Amateur Championship won by Beman, the British Amateur Champion in 1959 and the United States Champion in 1960. Beman won five holes in succession from Sikes after being 3 down after the 14th. Sikes, the 1961 and 1962 Amateur Public Links Champion, drew even after 26, but

Beman played flawless golf from there in. Sikes defeated Charles R. Coe, of Oklahoma City, by 2 and 1 in the semi-final round. Coe, the 1949 and 1958 Champion, had won 55 matches in the Championship, two less than the record 57 won by Charles Evans, Jr. Evans, after competing in 50 consecutive Amateur Championships, did not start in 1963 because of illness. The other semi-finalist, and the only one of the four not a member of recent USGA International Teams, was George Archer, 25, a 6' 5" ranch employee from Gilroy, Calif. Archer lost to Beman by 5 and 4. Labron Harris, Jr., the 1962 Champion from Stillwater, Okla., lost in the third round to Walter Stahl of Cleveland, Ohio, by 2 and 1. Quarter-finalists included Stahl; Richard Guardiola, of Cleveland; John C. Owens, of Lexington, Ky.; and John S. (Steve) Spray, of Indianola, Iowa.

1964–William C. Campbell, 41, of Huntington, W.Va., who had qualified 21 times, finally won the Amateur Championship at the Canterbury Golf Club, Cleveland, Ohio. Campbell had been a semi-finalist in 1949 and had advanced to the fifth round five other times. Campbell defeated Edgar M. Tutwiler, Jr., of Indianapolis, Ind., by 1 up in the final. They had been opponents many times in the West Virginia State Championship; Tutwiler had defeated Campbell six of the seven times they met in the final. Their match at Cleveland, played on a day interspersed with a chilling mist and showers, went down to the final green where Campbell stood aside to watch Tutwiler's 15-foot putt for a win curl off at the cup. The match was even after 18 holes. Fifteen of the afternoon round holes were halved. Campbell, 1 down after 28 holes, got back to even with a birdie at the par-3 29th. They then halved until the 215-yard 35th, which Campbell won with a par. The Championship was played under a revised format which had 150 players come to the site to play 36 holes of stroke play over two days to determine 64 qualifiers for match play. The co-medalists were Robert Greenwood, Jr., Cookeville, Tenn., and Marvin M. Giles, III, Lynchburg, Va., who scored 143. The semi-finalists were John Mark Hopkins, Texas City, Texas, who lost to Campbell by 3 and 1, and Dave Eichelberger, Waco, Texas, who was defeated, 3 and 2, by Tutwiler. Deane Beman, the defending Champion, qualified readily at 149 but lost in the first round to Vernon S. Novak, Jr., College Park, Md., by 4 and 2.

1965–Robert J. Murphy, Jr., of Nichols, Fla., won the first Amateur Championship he entered with a 72-hole score of 291 at the Southern Hills Country Club, Tulsa, Okla. It was the first Amateur Championship to be decided entirely at stroke play. The format provided for four 18-hole rounds in as many days. Murphy, a 22-year-old senior at the University of Florida, had taken up golf in a required physical education class at 18. Murphy's rounds were 73-69-76-73–291. Bob Dickson, of Muskogee, Okla., a student at Oklahoma State University, was the runner-up at 292. Dickson had the misfortune to carry a 15th club in his bag for the first two holes of the second round and so incurred a penalty of four strokes; the club was not his and he did not use it. Dickson recovered from the penalty to lead after 70 holes. Murphy, already in with 291, waited as Dickson went one over par on each of the final two holes. Don Allen, of Rochester, a member of the 1965 Walker Cup Team, tied for third at 293 with Cesar Sanudo, of El Cajon, Calif. William C. Campbell, of Huntington, W.Va., the 1964 Champion, tied for eighth with 296. Charles R. Coe, of Oklahoma City, was the 54-hole leader at 217 and finished with an 80.

1966–Gary Cowan, 27, of Kitchener, Ontairo, Canada, became the first foreign player to win the U.S. Amateur Championship since C. Ross (Sandy) Somerville in 1932. Somerville is from London, Ontario, about 70 miles from Kitchener. Cowan defeated Deane R. Beman, Bethesda, Md., in a playoff, 75-76, after they both scored 285 for 72 holes of the Championship proper over the East Course of the Merion Golf Club, Ardmore, Pa. Beman, the 1960 and 1963 Champion, appeared to have the Championship won as late as the 72nd hole. However, his approach went into a bunker, his recovery went over the green and then he stubbed a chip shot. He scored 6 on the hole, a par-4. Cowan made up three strokes in two holes to catch Beman. After 16 holes of the playoff Cowan and Beman were tied. Cowan missed the green on his tee shot to the 17th and Beman carried to within 12 feet of the hole. However, Cowan got down in two for a par 3 while Beman three-putted, falling a stroke behind. Ron Cerrudo, of San Rafael, Calif., might have tied Cowan and Beman, but missed an 18-inch putt on the home green. He tied for third with Jack W. Lewis, Jr., of Florence, S.C., and A. Downing Gray, of Pensacola, Fla., with 286. The defending Champion, Robert J. Murphy, Jr., of Nichols, Fla., tied for 20th place. The Championship was televised nationally for the first time.

1967–Robert B. Dickson, 23, of McAlester, Okla., became the first player since 1935 to win both the British and the United States Amateur Championships in the same year–the "Little Slam." Dickson won by one stroke over Marvin Giles, III, over the West Course of the Broadmoor Golf Club, Colorado Springs, Colo., scoring 285 for 72 holes. The last player to win both in the same year was W. Lawson Little, Jr., in 1934 and 1935. Dickson led every round with scores of 71-71-74-69. He seemed to have the Championship won when Giles scored a bogey 5 on the 15th hole, giving Dickson a two-stroke lead. However, Giles then scored a birdie 3 on the 17th, and Dickson drove into the woods on the par-4 18th. He was given a free lift from interference by overhead television cables, played to the fairway, and then onto the green seven feet from the hole. He made the putt for his par and the Championship. Gary Cowan, the defending Champion from Kitchener, Ontario, Canada, scored 298 and tied for 18th place. The Championship was delayed one day when the course became unplayable because of rain. The final two rounds were played in one day.

1968–Bruce Fleisher, 19, of Miami, Fla., became the fourth youngest winner since the Amateur Championship began in 1895. He scored a record 284 for 72 holes at the Scioto Country Club, Columbus, Ohio, and won by one stroke over Marvin Giles, III. It was the second consecutive year that Giles lost the Championship by one stroke. Fleisher was one month short of his 20th birthday. Robert A. Gardner won the 1909 Championship at the age of 19 years 5 months; Jack Nicklaus won in 1959 at 19 years 8 months; and Louis N. James won in 1902 at 19 years, 10 months. Fleisher was the second player to win in his first attempt since the Championship was converted to stroke play in 1965. Fleisher had rounds of 73-70-71-70, and was never more than two strokes off the lead. Michael Bonallack, the British Amateur Champion from Thorpe Bay, England; Jack Veghte, of Clearwater, Fla.; and Allen Miller, III, of Pensacola, Fla., shared the first-round lead at 71, one over par. Fleisher and Hubert M. Green, of Birmingham, Ala., were tied at 143 after two rounds, and Fleisher held a two-stroke lead over Green after the third round, 214-216. Giles was then six strokes behind with 220. Fleisher played the first nine holes of the final round in 34 and seemed an easy winner, for he was then four strokes in front of Giles and Green. Giles played the first nine in 32, and by the 17th hole he was within one stroke of Fleisher. The issue wasn't settled until Fleisher made a par 4 at the 18th. Giles scored 65 in the final round, setting a tournament and course record. The best previous 18-hole score in an all-stroke-play Amateur was 67 by Gary Cowan and Deane Beman in 1966, and by Jack Ewing in 1967. The best previous 72-hole score was 285 by Cowan and Beman in 1966, and by Robert B. Dickson in 1967. The entry of 2,057 set a record.

1969–Steve Melnyk, 22, of Brunswick, Ga., played four rounds at Oakmont Country Club near Pittsburgh in 286 strokes, only three strokes higher than Jack Nicklaus and Arnold Palmer when they tied for the Open Championship in 1962, and Ben Hogan when he won the 1953 Open Championship over the same course. Melnyk won by five strokes over Marvin (Vinny) Giles, III, of Lynchburg, Va., who had 291. Allen Miller, of Pensacola, Fla., was third with 293. This was the third consecutive year in which Giles finished second. Melnyk led every round and was the only player in the field to return scores under Oakmont's par of 71. He had rounds of 70-73-73-70. He led Rick Jones, a reinstated amateur, and Giles by two strokes after the first round, and Miller by three after 36 holes. He led by six strokes after the first nine of the third round, but lost control of his game and needed a birdie 3 on the final hole to preserve a three-stroke lead over Miller and Giles after 54. He lost another stroke of his lead with a bogey 5 on the first hole of the final round and then led Giles by two strokes. However, he birdied the second as Giles made a bogey 5, and then scored an eagle 3 on the par-5 fourth with an explosion shot from a bunker into the hole. His lead then was six strokes, and he increased it to eight by the end of the first nine. The Oakmont course was so difficult that only four rounds were played under par and only six rounds equalled par. By contrast, 11 sub-par scores were returned at Merion Golf Club, Ardmore, Pa., in the 1966 Amateur Championship. The entry again increased to 2,142.

1970—Five records were set and two more tied when Jerry L. (Lanny) Wadkins won by one stroke over Thomas O. Kite, Jr., at the Waverley Country Club, Portland, Ore. Wadkins scored 67-73-69-70–279 to set the 72-hole record and lowest first-round score. Kite set records for 36 holes (136) and 54 holes (207), and the 36-hole cutoff score was 148, the fifth record. Kurt Cox shot 65 in the second round to equal the single round record set by Marvin M. (Vinnie) Giles III, in 1968. Kite appeared to have the Championship won as he played the 15th hole. Here he overshot the green, failed to reach it with a short chip, got on in four, then took two putts for a 6 and fell a stroke behind Wadkins, who was playing with him. Then began a strange series of holes. Both Wadkins and Kite made birdies on the 206-yard par 3 16th, they followed with two over par 6s on the 448-yard 17th, Kite almost hitting his second shot into the Willamette River along the right side of the fairway, and then they both made birdie 4s on the 577-yard 18th. Wadkins putted first and holed out from 20 feet. Kite followed with a birdie putt of 10 feet, and finished with a 72-hole score of 280. The previous record had been 284 set in 1968 by Bruce Fleisher at the Scioto Country Club, Columbus, Ohio. Three players tied the old record. They were Gary Cowan, of Canada, the 1966 Champion, James R. Gabrielsen, and James B. Simons. Two players scored holes in one. Gene Howard, of Chicago, scored one on the 11th hole during the second round, and Scott Bess, of Columbia, Mo., scored another on the sixth hole during the third round. At 6,469 yards, the course was the shortest during the post World War II era, and 16 sub-par rounds were played. The entry was 1,853.

1971–Gary Cowan, 32, of Kitchener, Ontario, Canada, made an eagle 2 on the last hole to score 280 and win by three strokes over Eddie Pearce, of Temple Terrace, Fla., over the South Course of the Wilmington Country Club, Wilmington, Del. It was the second Amateur Championship for Cowan, who had won in 1966. Marvin Giles, III, of Richmond, was third with 284; his record then for a five-year period was three second-place finishes, one third and one sixth. Giles scored 68-69–137 for the last 36 holes, breaking his own record of 138 set in 1968. Cowan was tied with James McLean, of Seattle, after 13 holes of the final round, then played the last five holes in three under par to win. He was one stroke ahead of Pearce with one hole to play, hit his drive into deep rough on the 18th and was in danger of making a 5 on the par 4 hole. Then he hit a 9-iron shot into the hole for the eagle. Martin West, of Chevy Chase, Md., led the first round with 67, equalling the record for the lowest first round score. Pearce and McLean each shot 67 in the second round and shared the 36-hole lead at 139. Cowan went ahead with 69 in the third round giving him 210 for 54 holes. Cowan is the first player to have won the Amateur twice at stroke play. Lanny Wadkins, the 1970 Champion, and Steve Melnyk, the 1969 Champion, became professionals during 1971 and were not eligible to play. The entry was 2,327, a record.

1972–Marvin M. (Vinny) Giles, III, of Richmond, Va., after nine years of disappointment, won the Championship at the Charlotte Country Club, Charlotte, N. C., with a one-over par total of 285, three strokes ahead of runners-up Ben Crenshaw, of Austin, Texas, and Mark S. Hayes, of Fort Jackson, S. C. Marty West, of Washington, D. C., was fourth. Since 1964, when he was co-medalist, Giles had been runner-up three times (1967-68-69), was third in 1971, and sixth in 1970. Giles was four strokes off the lead after the first round with a 73 to 69s by Greg Stuhler, of Atlanta, Ga., and Mark Pfeil, of Palos Verdes, Calif. In the second round, however, Giles shot 68, equalling the best round of the Championship. Only Charlie Harrison, of Atlanta, Ga., matched it. Giles was then a stroke ahead with

141. Bruce Robertson, of San Mateo, Calif., was second at 142, and Bob Bryant, of Charlotte, was third at 143. In the third round Giles began as if he would run away from the field; he birdied the second by holing a 12-foot putt, the fifth on a 40-footer, the seventh with another 12-footer, and the tenth. He was then five strokes up on his closest pursuers, Robertson and Hayes. Giles then bogied the next three holes and completed the round in one-over par 72 and 213 for 54 holes. He was a stroke ahead of Hayes, two ahead of Robertson, and four ahead of Crenshaw and West. In the final round Hayes took the lead with a birdie on the third hole after Giles went a stroke above par on the second. Hayes increased his lead to two strokes with a birdie on the 7th, but lost one of them when he bogied the 8th. After nine holes, Hayes was the leader, Giles was second, West was in third place, and Crenshaw was fourth. Giles drew even again when Hayes bogied the 10th hole. Then he hit a 4-iron shot to within four feet of the 13th hole and made a birdie, and stroked a wedge shot five feet from the hole on the 14th for another birdie. After 68 holes he stood three strokes ahead of Hayes, four ahead of Crenshaw, and five in front of West. Robertson, who had taken a 40 on the first nine, was out of contention. On the 15th Giles took a double-bogie 6, but Hayes made a 5, so Giles still had a two-stroke lead with three holes to play. It was all over when Giles hit a 6-iron second shot out of the rough onto the 16th green and holed an 18-foot putt for a birdie. He bogied the 17th, but it was inconsequential, for he had a three-stroke lead with one hole to play. The Amateur field changes very rapidly. Although Bill Campbell, of Huntington, W. Va., was playing in his 29th Amateur Championship, 62 per cent of those who answered a questionnaire posed by the USGA were playing their first Amateur and 14 per cent were competing for only the second time. Of the 150 who played in 1971, only 29 were in the field at Charlotte. The age range is interesting, also. Twenty per cent were under 19 years of age; 19 per cent were in the 20-21 bracket; 15 per cent were 22-24; 16 per cent were 25-29, while the remainder were 30 and over. In summary, 70 per cent were under 30. The entry reached 2,295. Gary Cowan, of Kitchener, Ontario, Canada, the 1971 Champion, decided to devote more time to his family and business and did not compete.

1973—After eight years at stroke play, the Championship reverted to match play. It was won by Craig Stadler, 20, of La Jolla, Calif., who was in his third year at the University of Southern California. Stadler defeated David Strawn, 23, of Charlotte, N. C., 6 and 5, in the final at Inverness Club, Toledo, Ohio. On the day before the final Stadler also defeated both Richard Siderowf, 1973 British Amateur Champion, 2 and 1, in the quarter-final round, and Marvin (Vinny) Giles III, who was the defending United States Champion, 3 and 1, in the semi-final round. Giles had led the United States Walker Cup Team to a 14 to 10 victory over Great Britain and Ireland the week before, and nineteen rounds in 14 days left him "drawing energy from (his) imagination." Stadler won the first three holes, and although Giles twice cut Stadler's lead to one hole, he could never draw even. At the end he bogied the 16th and 17th holes, losing 3 and 1. Aside from the morning 18 holes of the final, Stadler was taken to the 18th hole only once. In the fourth round he defeated Allen Sussell, Villanova, Pa., 1 up. In 147 holes he was three strokes over par. Strawn had one extra-hole match. He defeated Hugh Stuart, British Walker Cup team member, in 19 holes, in the fourth round. In the semi-final round, Strawn defeated William C. Campbell, 6 and 5. Campbell, 50, was in his 30th Amateur Championship and had won in 1964, the last time it was played at match play. The final match, at 36 holes, was never in doubt; Stadler was 4 up after nine and 7 up after 18. In the afternoon, Strawn cut Stadler's lead to 5 up by winning the first two holes. The next two holes determined the outcome of the match. Strawn hit his tee shot on the par-3 third to within 40 feet of the hole, while Stadler hit into a greenside bunker. Stadler, however, came out four feet from the hole and saved a half. On the fourth hole, Stadler drove into the right rough while Strawn was nicely on the fairway. Stadler then hit a 3-iron from the rough that carried to the green and stopped six inches from the hole for a conceded birdie. Strawn twice again cut the lead to five holes, but a tee shot that caught the trees on the ninth and an out-of-bounds third shot settled the outcome. The final four holes were halved in regulation pars, giving Stadler a 6 and 5 margin.

The entry was 2,110 and 200 started, with 72 matches played the first day. The weather was extremely hot with the temperature above 90 degrees every day.

1974—In the second year after it was changed back to match play, the Amateur Championship was won by Jerome K. (Jerry) Pate, of Pensacola, 20, a student at the University of Alabama. Pate defeated John R. Grace, of Fort Worth, Texas, 2 and 1, in the 36-hole final round at the Ridgewood Country Club, Ridgewood, N. J. Among others, Pate defeated Ed Tutwiler, of Indianapolis, Ind., 1964 runnerup who was playing in his 16th Amateur; Bill Campbell, 51, of Huntington, West Virginia, 1964 Champion playing in his 31st; George Burns, III, of Port Washington, N. Y., a 25-year old soft-drink salesman who had won two important tournaments in 1974; and Curtis Strange, 19, Virginia Beach, Va., the National Collegiate Athletic Association Champion from Wake Forest. Pate defeated Campbell, 4 and 2, in the quarter-final round. He was 2 down after seven holes and won six of the next nine. He defeated Strange, 2 and 1, in the semi-final round. Grace, a real estate salesman, had an easier time than Pate in reaching the final round. He won his first three matches by 4 and 3, 6 and 5, and 6 and 4. He was never down until the fifth hole of the fourth round when Bill Harvey, of Greensboro, N. C., scored a birdie and went 1 up. Grace won the match, 5 and 3, and then shot 31 on the first nine against Brian Willard, of Silver Spring, Md., and won, 6 and 5. Grace won his semi-final match, 3 and 1, from Gary Koch of Temple Terrace, Fla. In the final round Pate hit his first tee shot out of bounds and Grace quickly went one up. By the end of eight holes, however, Pate was two up after a couple of birdies and a loosely played hole by Grace. Beginning with the 12th hole, Grace won three of the next four with a pair of birdies and two pars, to go ahead by one, and then Pate drew even with a birdie on the 16th. The 17th was halved, then Grace went 1 up with a par four on the 18th where Pate again hit a wild drive. Grace began the final 18 by scoring birdies on the first two holes and taking a lead of 3 up. Pate cut the lead to 1 up after eight, and the final nine began with Grace 1 up. Grace birdied the 10th to assume a 2 up lead once more. Pate, however, met the challenge, winning the 11th and once again was 1 down. Pate settled the Championship by winning three consecutive holes—the 14th with a par, the 15th and 16th with birdies. He was then 2 up with two to play. The match ended when they halved the 17th in par 5s. The Championship was memorable for several reasons. Pate won the first time he qualified; Campbell went to the quarter-final round after reaching the semi-final round in 1973, and won two extra-hole matches, one of 25 holes; the entry reached 2,420, a new record. Craig Stadler, the 1973 Champion, was eliminated in the first round.

1975—For the second consecutive year the Championship had a Florida-Texas finale and once again the Florida player won. Fred Ridley, of Cypress Gardens, Fla., defeated Keith Fergus, of Houston, Texas, 2 up, in the 36-hole final round over the Country Club of Virginia's James River Course in Richmond. In winning the Championship Ridley defeated some of the best known players in the field, including Curtis Strange, of Virginia Beach, Va., who had won the North and South and the Eastern Amateur Championships earlier in 1975, and Andy Bean, of Lakeland, Fla., the current Western Amateur Champion, both by 2 and 1. He defeated Strange in the sixth round and Bean in the semi-final round. Ridley was taken to the final hole only twice, first when he defeated Jack Veghte, of Clearwater, Fla., on the 19th hole in the quarter-final round, and against Fergus in the final. Fergus went to the last hole only against Ridley, and he was behind in only three matches before the final against Ridley. He went ahead quickly, taking a 2-up lead after three holes, but Ridley pulled even after six. Ridley had made only four birdies on the previous 116 holes he had played, but then he made six on the last 12 holes of the morning round, and went to luncheon with a 5-up lead. He increased his lead to 6 up after the first hole of the afternoon portion, but by the end of the first nine, Fergus had cut Ridley's lead to two holes. Ridley once again began to pull away and with five holes to play led by 4 up. Fergus then won 14, 15, and 16, and with two holes to play he was just one hole behind. Both men went one over par on the 17th, and Ridley won the match on the 18th, a par-4 hole, when Fergus hit his second shot well over the green and was short with his third. Jerome K. Pate, the 1974 Champion, had become a professional earlier in the year and was not eligible to defend his title. Marvin M. Giles, III, the 1975 British Amateur Champion and 1972 United States Champion, lost in the first round, while John Grace, runnerup in 1974, was eliminated in the third round. The entry reached 2,258, surpassing the previous high of 2,420 of 1974.

1976—Bill Sander, of Kenmore, Wash., defeated C. Parker Moore, Jr., from Laurens, S. C., 8 and 6, in their scheduled 36-hole final match at the Bel-Air Country Club, Los Angeles, Calif. It was the greatest margin of victory in the Championship since 1961, when Jack Nicklaus beat Dudley Wysong by the same score. Fred Ridley, of Winter Haven, Fla., the 1975 Champion, was eliminated in the fourth round by Jim Mason, from Kirkwood, Mo., in 20 holes. William C. Campbell, of Huntington, W. Va., played in his 33rd Amateur Championship. He lost in the fourth round. In advancing to the final round, Sander defeated Mason in the semifinals, 8 and 7, and Skeeter Heath, of Hampton, Va., 1 up, in the quarterfinals. In the fifth round Sander defeated Jim Blair, of Logan, Utah, in 19 holes. Moore defeated Richard L. Siderowf, 1976 British Amateur Champion, from Westport, Conn., 2 and 1, in the fourth round and Mike Reid, Pacific Coast Amateur Champion, of Seattle, Wash., 1 up, in the quarterfinals. In the semifinals he defeated Stan Souza of Honolulu, in 19 holes, winning the 19th with a birdie. Sander played the first nine holes of the final match in 34, two under par, and stood 5-up. Moore won holes 12 through 15 to stand just one down, but lost the last three holes of the morning round and went to lunch 4 down. Sander started the afternoon round by winning the first hole with a birdie and was 7 up after the seventh hole. He lost the eighth hole—the only one he lost in the afternoon—but then birdied 11 and 12 to close out the match, 8 and 6. Entries reached 2,681, exceeding the record of 2,528 set in 1975 by 153.

1977—John Fought, 22, of Portland, Ore., a quarter-finalist in 1976, played his last 37 holes in one under par to win the Amateur Championship at the Aronimink Golf Club, in Newton Square, Pa. Fought defeated Doug Fischesser, of Connersville, Ind., 9 and 8, in the scheduled 36-hole final round. This was the largest margin of victory since 1955, when Harvie Ward defeated Bill Hyndman by the same score. Fischesser defeated several well-known players on his way to the final, among them Marty West, a former Walker Cup player; Buddy Alexander, the 1977 Eastern Amateur Winner; Peter McEvoy, the 1977 British Amateur Champion and British Walker Cupper; and Michael Brannan, an American Walker Cupper. In the semi-finals he defeated Ralph Landrum, of Elsmere, Ky. Fought defeated Vinny Giles, the 1972 Champion; Michael Kelley, a member of the British Walker Cup Team; Doug Clarke, the 1977 Trans-Mississippi Champion; and Jay Sigel, a Walker Cup player and member of Aronimink. Against Sigel in the semi-finals, Fought played the last nine holes in even par to win, 2 up. Bill Sander, the 1976 Champion, lost in the third round. Other former Champions —Bill Campbell (1964) and Gary Cowan (1966 and 1971)—lost in the second and third rounds, respectively. This was Campbell's 34th Championship. His victory in the first round was his 52nd in the Amateur. He was then tied with Harvie Ward in the number of matches won, five behind Chick Evans. (He also played in all eight Amateurs conducted at stroke play.) Fred Ridley, the 1975 Champion, lost in the third round. The final match was fairly even through the first 14 holes, but then Fischesser played the last four holes of the morning round and the first hole of the afternoon in six over par and lost them all. From only 2 down he dropped to 7 down. After nine holes of the afternoon round Fought was 8 up. The match ended when Fought birdied the 10th hole. The entry of 3,017 exceeded the record set in 1976 by 536.

1978—John Cook, 20, of Upper Arlington, Ohio, was nine under par in eight matches as he won the Amateur Championship at the Plainfield Country Club, Plainfield, N.J. Cook defeated Scott Hoch, of Raleigh, N.C., 5 and 4, in the scheduled 36-hole final. Among those he defeated were Doug Clarke, winner of the 1977 Southern Amateur and 1976 Trans-Miss Championships; Henri De Lozier, a semi-finalist and quarter-finalist in the 1975 and 1973 Amateurs, respectively; Kalua Makalena, the Hawaiian Open Champion; and, in a semi-final match, Michael Peck, the 1977 and 1978 Pacific 8 Champion. Meanwhile, Hoch breezed through his half of the draw until his semi-final match with Bob Clampett, whose 1978 accomplishments included victories in the Porter Cup and Western Amateur, and low amateur in the Open. For the first time in Amateur history, both semi-final matches were decided in extra holes. Cook and Peck played two under par golf for the first 18 holes. Cook settled the match with a birdie 3 on the second extra hole, a long par 4. Hoch and Clampett were playing even-par golf through the first 18 holes. Hoch won with a par 4, also at the 20th hole. In the final, Cook jumped to a quick 2-up lead after two holes. Hoch stayed close, however, and was one down after the first nine holes, despite scoring 40 to Cook's 37. Cook responded with 32 on the second nine, including five birdies, and led 5 up at the lunch break. Cook won the first three holes of the afternoon round with a par-birdie-birdie start to take an 8-up lead, the widest margin of the match. Hoch closed the gap slightly, but could come no closer than 5 down. Cook holed a four-foot par putt at the 32nd hole to win the Championship. In those 32 holes, there were 14 birdies—Cook had eight and Hoch six. Two former Amateur Champions—Marvin Giles, III, (1972) and Fred Ridley (1975)—were entered. Giles lost in the second round, Ridley in the first round. Doug Fischesser, the runner-up in the 1977 Amateur, lost in the fifth round. Jay Sigel, a semi-finalist in the 1977 Amateur, lost in the fourth round. The field included four members of the 1977 U.S. Walker Cup Team—Ridley, Sigel, Vance Heafner, who lost in the third round, and Gary Hallberg, who lost his first match. Dale Morey, twice the Senior Amateur Champion and runner-up in the 1953 Amateur, lost in the third round. He was competing in his 26th Amateur. A record for entries was established for the fifth consecutive year. The 3,035 entries exceeded the previous high of 2,950 set in 1977.

1979—Mark O'Meara, 22, of St. Charles, Ill., was four under par for 29 holes as he defeated John Cook, the 1978 Champion, 8 and 7, in the final match. The Championship was played at the Canterbury Golf Club, Cleveland, Ohio, under a revised format. Two hundred eighty-two players competed at the Championship site. They played 36-holes stroke play to decide the 64 qualifiers for match play. Two golf courses—Canterbury and Shaker Heights Country Club—were used for the qualifying stage. Bob Clampett, of Carmel, Calif., was the medalist with a course-record five under par 66 at Canterbury and a two under par 68 at Shaker Heights. His 36-hole total of 134 established a record qualifying score. Sixty-five players had scores of 146 or better, the lowest 36-hole cut-off score in the history of the Championship. Thirteen players tied for the final 12 spots for match play and played off. Clampett was eliminated in the third round by Gary Hallberg in a 21-hole match. O'Meara qualified with 142, one over par. He defeated Kel Devlin, 4 and 3; Hal Sutton, 1 up; was one under par in a 3 and 2 victory over Tom Carlton; rallied from a two-hole deficit with four to play to defeat David Ogrin with a par on the 20th hole; and won, 3 and 1, over Joe Rassett in the semi-finals. Cook qualified with 140, one under par. He was one under par in defeating Robert Wrenn, 3 and 1; one over in defeating Wayne Player 1 up; two under in a 26-hole match against Lennie Clements, the longest extra-hole match of the week; three under in a 4 and 3 decision over Gary Hallberg, the 1979 NCAA Champion; and even par in the semi-finals against Cecil Ingram, whom he defeated, 5 and 3. Cook had a chance to become the 16th two-time Amateur Champion and the first to successfully defend the title since E. Harvie Ward, Jr., in 1956. Cook won two of the first four holes in the final match and then lost the next, five holes—only one to a birdie—and O'Meara took a 3-up lead. With two holes to play in the morning round, O'Meara had a two-hole lead. He birdied the 17th and parred the 18th to take a 4-up lead at lunch. O'Meara had a morning round of 70, one under par, and Cook had 74. In the afternoon, they halved the first four holes with pars. O'Meara won the fifth through the seventh holes with birdies and the eighth hole with a par to take an 8-up lead with 3 holes to play. Cook won the 10th with a birdie, but O'Meara ended the match with a birdie on the 11th hole. He played the 11 holes of the afternoon in three under par. O'Meara hit 24 of 29 greens in the match and missed just three fairways. Entries jumped to a record 3,916, surpassing by 881 the previous high of 3,035 in 1978.

1980—Hal Sutton, 22, of Shreveport, Louisiana, was four under par for 28 holes as he defeated Bob Lewis, Jr., of Warren, Ohio, 9 and 8, in the final match at the Country Club of North Carolina, in Pinehurst. Using the format introduced a year earlier, 282 players competed at the site, playing 36 holes of stroke play over two days to determine the 64 competitors for match play. Two golf courses were used during stroke play—the Country Club of North Carolina and the No. 2 course of the Pinehurst Country Club. Fred Couples, of Seattle, Washington, was the medalist, at 139, with a round of 69 at the Pinehurst Country Club and 70 at the Country Club of North Carolina. Sutton shot 145 and Lewis shot 146. Lewis was a former professional golfer who was reinstated two years previously. At 35, he was the oldest player to reach the semi-final round and the oldest to reach the final since the Amateur was restored to match play in 1973. For 109 holes of match play, Sutton was 13 under par. For 145 holes, including the stroke play rounds, he was 12 under par. Lewis was two over par for 108 holes of match play and two more over par for the 36 holes of stroke play. In the final match, Sutton played the first nine in 35 strokes, one under par, and held a two hole lead. He won three more holes on the second nine, and at the end of 14 holes was 5 up. Lewis won his first hole of the match at the 15th with a par 4 as Sutton three-putted from 70 feet. They went to lunch with Sutton 5 up. After lunch, Lewis did not win another hole. Sutton went 6 up with a par 3 at the third, where Lewis hit his tee shot into the water, won the sixth with another par, and then birdied both the eighth and ninth holes. The match ended when both players parred the 10th hole. William C. Campbell, the 1964 Champion, made his 34th appearance in the Amateur championship, a record surpassed only by Charles Evans, Jr., who played in 50. The USGA accepted a record 4,008 entries, surpassing the previous record of 3,916 in 1979.

AMATEUR CHAMPIONSHIP

DATE	WINNER, RUNNER-UP	SCORE	SITE	ENTRY
1960 (Sept.)	Deane R. Beman d. Robert W. Gardner	6 & 4	St. Louis C.C., Clayton, Mo.	1,737
1961 (Sept.)	Jack W. Nicklaus d. H. Dudley Wysong, Jr.	8 & 6	Del Monte G. & C.C., Pebble Beach Golf Links, Calif.	1,995
1962 (Sept.)	Labron E. Harris, Jr. d. Downing Gray	1 up	Pinehurst C.C., (No. 2 Course), Pinehurst, N.C.	2,044
1963 (Sept.)	Deane R. Beman d. Richard H. Sikes	2 & 1	Wakonda Club, Des Moines, Iowa	1,768
1964 (Sept.)	William C. Campbell d. Edgar M. Tutwiler	1 up	Canterbury G.C., Cleveland, Ohio Co-Medalists—143: Marvin M. Giles, III Robert Greenwood, Jr.	1,562
		All Stroke Play		
1965 (Sept.)	Robert J. Murphy, Jr. Robert B. Dickson	291 292	Southern Hills C.C., Tulsa, Okla.	1,476
1966 (Aug.-Sept.)	Gary Cowan Deane R. Beman	285-75 285-76	Merion G.C. (East Course), Ardmore, Pa.	1,902
1967 (Aug.-Sept.)	Robert B. Dickson Marvin M. Giles, III	285 286	Broadmoor G.C., (West Course), Colorado Springs, Colo.	1,784
1968 (Aug.)	Bruce Fleisher Marvin M. Giles, III	284 285	Scioto C.C. Columbus, Ohio	2,057
1969 (Aug.)	Steven N. Melnyk Marvin M. Giles III	286 291	Oakmont C.C. Oakmont, Pa.	2,142
1970 (Sept.)	Lanny Wadkins Tom Kite, Jr.	*279 280	Waverley C.C., Portland, Ore.	1,853
1971 (Sept.)	Gary Cowan Eddie Pearce	280 283	Wilmington C.C., (South Course), Wilmington, Del.	2,327
1972 (Aug.-Sept.)	Marvin Giles, III Mark S. Hayes Ben Crenshaw	285 288 288	Charlotte C. C., Charlotte, N.C.	2,295
		All Match Play		
1973 (Aug.-Sept.)	Craig Stadler d. David Strawn	6 & 5	Inverness C. C., Toledo, Ohio	2,110
1974 (Aug.)	Jerome K. Pate d. John P. Grace	2 & 1	Ridgewood C. C., Ridgewood, N.J.	2,420
1975 (Aug.)	Fred Ridley d. Keith Fergus	2 up	C. C. of Virginia (James River Course) Richmond, Va.	2,528
1976 (Aug.-Sept.)	Bill Sander d. C. Parker Moore, Jr.	8 & 6	Bel-Air C.C., Los Angeles, Calif.	2,681
1977 (Aug.-Sept.)	John Fought d. Doug Fischesser	9 & 8	Aronimink G. C., Newtown Square, Pa.	2,950
1978 (Aug.-Sept.)	John Cook d. Scott Hoch	5 & 4	Plainfield C. C., Plainfield, N.J.	3,035
1979 (Aug.-Sept.)	Mark O'Meara d. John Cook	8 & 7	Canterbury G.C. Cleveland, Ohio Medalist—†134: Bob Clampett	3,916
1980 (Aug.)	Hal Sutton d. Bob Lewis	9 & 8	C.C. of North Carolina Pinehurst, N.C. Medalist—139 Fred Couples	§4,008

*Record score, stroke play. †Record qualifying score in Championship proper. §Record Entry.

AMATEUR CHAMPIONS

ROBERT DICKSON
1967

GARY COWAN
1966-71

WILLIAM C. CAMPBELL
1964

1960
SIXTIETH AMATEUR CHAMPIONSHIP

Held at the St. Louis Country Club, Clayton, Mo., September 12-17.
Yardage—6,616, 6,589. Par 71. 1,737 Entries, 200 Qualifiers, 200 Starters.
Championship entirely at match play.

FINAL ROUND (36 Holes)—Deane R. Beman defeated Robert W. Gardner, 6 up and 4 to play.

UPPER

FIRST QUARTER

1st Round (18 Holes)	2nd Round (18 Holes)	3rd Round (18 Holes)	4th Round (18 Holes)	5th Round (18 Holes)	6th Round (18 Holes)	
William Welch, III, Tri-City, Wash.	Johnston,					
M. O. Johnston, Jr., La Jolla, Calif.	2 up	Tindall, 3 and 2				
Peter T. Cook, Riviera, Fla.	Tindall,					
William L. Tindall, Olympic Hills, Wash.	3 and 2		Root, 3 and 1			
BYE—Harry Root, III, Palma Ceia, Fla.	Root					
George P. Swift, Jr., Columbus, Ga.	Wettlaufer,	Root, 3 and 2				
H. Ward Wettlaufer, C.C. of Buffalo, N.Y.	3 and 2			Root, 5 and 4		
Harold G. Williams, Jr., Westchester, N.Y.	Welsh,					
Alex Welsh, Rockford, Ill.	6 and 5	Welsh, 1 up				
BYE—Robert C. Smith, Rose City, Ore.	Smith					
Joseph F. Switzer, Sunset, Mo.	Birmingham,		Birmingham, 1 up			
John Birmingham, Oakmont, Pa.	6 and 5	Birmingham, 5 and 4				
BYE—Pursie E. Pipes, Green Hill, Ill.	Pipes				Gardner, 7 and 5	
Bruce W. Devlin, Goulburn, Australia	Stewart,					
William L. Stewart, Hickory Hills, Mo.	2 and 1	Stewart, 2 up				
BYE—George Dawson, Glen Oak, Ill.	Dawson		Ware, 6 and 5			
BYE—Murray Vernon, Jr., Greenwich, Conn.	Vernon					
Lewis W. Oehmig, Chattanooga, Tenn.	Ware,	Ware, 2 and 1				
Cobby Ware, Augusta, Ga.	4 and 3			Gardner, 5 and 4		
Dr. Arthur F. Butler, Glendora, Calif.	Butler,					
James R. English, Columbine, Colo.	6 and 5	Gardner, 4 and 3				
BYE—Robert W. Gardner, Knollwood, N.Y.	Gardner		Gardner, 4 and 3			
Capt. P.G. Sethi, New Delhi, India	Sethi,					
Edwin B. Hopkins, Jr., Abilene, Texas	4 and 2	Sethi, 7 and 6				
Gordon Aamoth, Jr. Fargo, N.D.	Simon,					Gardner, 1 up
Gaylon Simon, St. Andrews, Ill.	5 and 4					
BYE—Bert Burdick, Baton Rouge, La.	Burdick					
Bruce J. Campbell, Fredericksburg, Va.	Gabrielsen,	Burdick, 2 up				
James R. Gabrielsen, Athens, Ga.	5 and 3		Burdick, 4 and 3			
BYE—John N.C. Cameron, Dallas, Texas	Cameron					
Delane Thompson, Wichita Falls, Texas	Thompson,	Thompson, 3 and 2		Burdick, 1 up, 21 hls.		
H. Dudley Wysong, Jr., Northwood, Texas	5 and 4					
Robert O. Wolsborn, Riverside, Ore.	Fay,					
Robert Fay, Jr., Evansville, Ind.	4 and 3	Webb, 5 and 4				
BYE—Jack Webb, G. & C.C., Atlantic, Iowa	Webb		Blair, 2 and 1			
John B. McGarry, Eagle Haven, Va.	Johnston,					
Ralph W. Johnston, Garden City, N.Y.	4 and 3	Blair, 4 and 3				
BYE—Jim Tom Blair, Meadowbrook, Mo.	Blair				Spray, 5 and 3	
BYE—Hugh A. Burchfiel, Old Warson, Mo.	Burchfiel					
Thomas D. Aaron, Chattahoochee, Ga.	Aaron,	Aaron, 7 and 5				
William R. Hogan, Milburn, Kans.	3 and 1		Spray, 5 and 3			
BYE—Robert O. McCall, Gary, Ind.	McCall					
John S. Spray, Wakonda, Iowa	Spray,	Spray, 3 and 2				
Thomas Shaw, Rose City, Ore.	3 and 2			Spray, 3 and 2		
BYE—H. H. Edwards, Twin Hills, Okla.	Edwards					
Thomas F. Brown, Purdue Univ., Ind.	Rossi,	Edwards, 2 and 1				
Lloyd C. Rossi, Diablo, Calif.	5 and 4		Draper, 4 and 3			
BYE—Tom Draper, Red Run, Mich.	Draper					
Charles Rosen II, Lakewood, La.	Courtney,	Draper, 1 up				
Charles Courtney, La Jolla, Calif.	2 and 1					

SEMI-FINAL ROUND (36 Holes)—Robert W. Gardner defeated Charles F. Lewis, 2 up and 1 to play.

The first word after the player's name is the name of his club, except in the case of a foreign entrant.

HALF

SECOND QUARTER

6th Round (18 Holes)	5th Round (18 Holes)		4th Round (18 Holes)	3rd Round (18 Holes)	2nd Round (18 Holes)	1st Round (18 Holes)
					Caplin, 1 up	Tyler Caplin, Michigan Publinx, Mich.
				Liechty, 1 up, 20 hls.		John A. Abernethy, Johnson City, Tenn.
					Liechty, 1 up	John H. Liechty, Finkbine, Iowa
						Alfred Sams, Idle Hour, Ga.
			Sucher, 2 and 1			
					Harris	BYE—James L. Harris, Oakwood, Okla.
				Sucher, 2 and 1		
					Sucher, 2 and 1	James C. McCoy, Lake Worth, Fla.
						Richard Sucher, Ozaukee, Wis.
		Ward, 3 and 2				
					Ward, 1 up	E. Harvie Ward, Jr., San Francisco, Calif.
				Ward, 4 and 3		John W. Owens, St. Joseph, Mo.
					Williams	BYE—Jack S. Williams, Plainview, Texas
			Ward, 4 and 2			
					Blocker, 3 and 1	Clarence Norsworthy, Jr., Norwood Hills, Mo.
				Arasin, 1 up		Chris Blocker, Jal, N.M.
					Arasin	BYE—Frank W. Arasin, Shamokin, Pa.
	Wild, 1 up, 20 hls.					
					Harvey, 3 and 1	Stephen Oppermann, Green Hills, Calif.
				Harvey, 8 and 7		Bill Harvey, Sedgefield, N.C.
					O'Neill	BYE—John J. O'Neill, III, Sherwood Forest, La.
			Harvey, 3 and 2			
					Sykes	BYE—James D. Sykes, Old York Road, Pa.
				Chapman, 4 and 3		
					Chapman, 4 and 3	Edwin D. Preisler, Cleveland, Ohio
						Richard D. Chapman, Oyster Harbors, Mass.
		Wild, 3 and 1				
					Coker, 6 and 4	Peter C. Klass, Interlachen, Minn.
				Wild, 2 and 1		Hulen Coker, Mission Valley, Calif.
					Wild	BYE—Claude C. Wild, Jr., Burning Tree, Md.
			Wild, 1 up, 19 hls.			
					Wittenberg, 2 up	Jimmy Wittenberg, Memphis, Tenn.
				Semple, 1 up		Edgar M. Baber, Hermitage, Va.
					Semple	BYE—Harton S. Semple, Allegheny, Pa.
Lewis, 4 and 3						
					Wood	BYE—Walter W. Wood, C.C. of Birmingham, Ala.
				Penrose, 2 and 1		
					Penrose, 3 and 2	John J. Penrose, Jr., La Gorce, Fla.
			Lohren, 6 and 5			Howard Everitt, Atlantic City, N.J.
					Lohren	BYE—Carl A. Lohren, Brooke Manor Farms, Md.
				Lohren, 4 and 3		
					Thornton, 1 up, 19 hls.	Juan A. Estrada, Durando, Mexico
						John B. Thornton, Oak Hill, N.Y.
		Lohren, 2 up				
					Carmichael	BYE—Sam Carmichael, Martinsville, Ind.
				Carmichael, 7 and 5		
					Fehlig, 3 and 2	Bob Galloway, Old Town, N.C.
			Carmichael, 2 and 1			Eugene A. Fehlig, Westborough, Mo.
					Woodward	BYE—Harvey E. Woodward, Lakepointe, Mich.
				Woodward, 2 up		
					Evans, 1 up	Ralph T. Strafaci, Hempstead, N.Y.
	Lewis, 4 and 3					Earle W. Evans, Wichita, Kans.
					Nicklaus, 1 up	John J. Donohue, Jr., Wakonda, Iowa
				Nicklaus, 4 and 3		Jack W. Nicklaus, Scioto, Ohio
					Finke	BYE—Kenneth Finke, Tucson, Ariz.
			Nicklaus, 6 and 5			
					Hixon, 3 and 2	George Hixon, Twin Hills, Okla.
				Rodgers, 3 and 1		Mark J. Stuart, Jr., Winged Foot, N.Y.
					Rodgers	BYE—Pfc. Phil Rodgers, Torrey Pines, Calif.
		Lewis, 5 and 3				
					Siderowf, 4 and 3	Warren Tibbetts, Manchester, N.Y.
				Siderowf, 8 and 7		Richard L. Siderowf, Indian Hill, Conn.
					Coscolluela	BYE—Agustin Coscolluela, Jr., Rizal, Philippines
			Lewis, 6 and 4			
					Lewis, 4 and 2	Seymour N. Black, California, Calif.
				Lewis, 3 and 2		Charles F. Lewis, C.C. of Little Rock, Ark.
					Meister, 3 and 2	George W. Sinderson, Indian Hills, Mo.
						Edward L. Meister, Jr., Kirkland, Ohio

THIRD QUARTER

1st Round (18 Holes)	2nd Round (18 Holes)	3rd Round (18 Holes)	4th Round (18 Holes)	5th Round (18 Holes)	6th Round (18 Holes)	
Richard D. Davies, Annandale, Calif.	Davies, 1 up, 23 hls.					
John Wood, II, Cincinnati, Ohio		Howell, 6 and 5				
Richard L. Howell, Woodhill, Minn.	Howell, 2 and 1					
Eugene McBride, Wichita Falls, Texas			Howell, 2 and 1			
BYE–Richard Smith, Davenport, Iowa	R. Smith					
		R. Smith, 2 and 1				
Mike Conroy, Oakland Hills, Mich.	Grindrod, 1 up, 19 hls.			Garrett, 1 up		
Walter M. Grindrod, Durban, South Africa						
Herbert S. Abraham, Ridgeway, Tenn.	Garrett, 3 and 2					
John J. Garrett, River Oaks, Texas		Garrett, 5 and 4				
BYE–Richard Guardiola, Shaker Heights, Ohio	Guardiola					
			Garrett, 3 and 1			
James E. Iverson, Siwanoy, N.Y.	Iverson, 2 and 1					
Dan Carmichael, Columbus, Ohio		Jemison, 1 up, 20 hls.			Farquhar, 3 and 2	
BYE–Elbert S. Jemison, Jr., C.C. of Birmingham, Ala.	Jemison					
James G. Jackson, Greenbriar Hills, Mo.	Jackson, 2 up					
Terry D. Wilcox, Oak Hills, Okla.		Jackson, 1 up, 19 hls.				
BYE–Carlos Raffo, Lima, Peru	Raffo		Winton, 4 and 3			
BYE–Roger T. McManus, Kenwood, Ohio	McManus	Winton, 1 up				
Lloyd S. Monroe, Upper Montclair, N.J.	Winton, 1 up			Farquhar, 1 up		
Kent Winton, Stanford University, Calif.						
D.A. Traynham, Paris Mountain, S.C.	Traynham, 1 up	Coe, 1 up				
Peter Green, Orchard Lake, Mich.						
BYE–Charles R. Coe, Oklahoma City, Okla.	Coe		Farquhar, 2 up			
John Farquhar, Amarillo, Texas	Farquhar, 1 up, 19 hls.	Farquhar, 1 up, 19 hls.				Farquhar, 3 and 1
Robert E. Bither, Ruth Lake, Ill.						
Fred Kammer, Jr., C.C. of Detroit, Mich.	Kammer, 2 and 1					
Dr. Edgar R. Updegraff, Tucson, Ariz.						
BYE–Richard Foutche, Berry Hills, W. Va.	Foutche	Guenther, 4 and 3				
John H. Guenther, Jr., Hershey, Pa.	Guenther, 1 up, 19 hls.		Guenther, 6 and 5			
Warren A. Colton, Jr., Arizona, Ariz.						
BYE–Alan M. Jensen, Corvallis, Ore.	Jensen	Ledesma, 3 and 1		Guenther, 6 and 5		
Jack Bumgarner, Silver Lake, Fla.	Ledesma, 8 and 6					
Jorge C. Ledesma, Buenos Aires, Argentina						
William C. Campbell, Guyan, W. Va.	Campbell, 2 and 1	Campbell, 6 and 5				
Harlan Lane, Pine Forest, Texas						
BYE–James M. Hoak, Wakonda, Iowa	Hoak		Liljeholm, 2 up			
Larry E. Beck, Kinston, N.C.	Beck, 4 and 3	Liljeholm, 5 and 4			Brownlee, 6 and 5	
Herman E. Kleinecke, III, Galveston, Texas						
BYE–Thomas Liljeholm, Rose City, Ore.	Liljeholm					
BYE–Harry Duccilli, Jr., Wyoming, Ohio	Duccilli	Eisinger, 1 up, 19 hls.				
James Grant, III, Wethersfield, Conn.	Eisinger, 1 up, 19 hls.		Brownlee, 4 and 3			
John O. Eisinger, Jr., Congressional, Md.						
BYE–Phillip Brownlee, Scarboro, Ont., Canada	Brownlee	Brownlee, 3 and 2		Brownlee, 5 and 4		
Richard A. Jennings, Lubbock, Texas	Astleford, 1 up					
Robert L. Astleford, Field Club of Omaha, Neb.						
BYE–Richard Crawford, El Dorado, Ark.	Crawford	Crawford, 1 up				
Dickie Crosby, Lake Hills, Ind.	D. Smith, 8 and 7		Lowry, 4 and 3			
David W. Smith, Jr., Gaston, N.C.						
BYE–Jackson D. Rule, Jr., Finkbine, Iowa	Rule	Lowry, 2 and 1				
Robert Lowry, Jr., Huntsville, Ala.	Lowry, 2 and 1					
Erv Parent, Seattle, Wash.						

SEMI-FINAL ROUND (36 Holes)—Deane R. Beman defeated John Farquhar, 5 up and 4 to play.

CHAMPIONSHIP HALF

FOURTH QUARTER

1st Round (18 Holes)

- Harry H. Haverstick, Jr., Lancaster, Pa.
- Charles Evans, Jr., Edgewater, Ill.
- William J. Patton, Mimosa Hills, N.C.
- Truman F. Connell, Tequesta, Fla.
- BYE–Robert W. Teyro, Guyan, West Va.
- Frederick Paine, Jr., Oakmont, Pa.
- Glenn L. Gray, Edmonton, Alberta, Canada
- Thomas A. Stephenson, Blue Hills, Mo.
- Richard L. Yost, Columbia-Edgewater, Ore.
- BYE–Mike M. Andonian, Sylvan Glen, Mich.
- P.V. Wise, Ardsley, N.Y.
- William E. McBride, Argyle, Md.
- BYE–Verne E. Callison, Sacramento, Calif.
- Edgar Bradley, Kenwood, Ohio
- Leslie R. Fowler, Boulder, Colo.
- BYE–Robert Sweeny, Seminole, Fla.
- BYE–George E. Victor, Glen View, Ill.
- John R. Suisman, Bloomfield, Conn.
- Gerald L. Schreiber, Evansville, Ind.
- John O. Levinson, Waukegan, Ill.
- James H. Dolan, III, Hillcrest, Mass.
- BYE–Dale Morey, Mimosa Hills, N.C.
- Deane R. Beman, Bethesda, Md.
- Claude L. Wright, Cherry Hills, Colo.
- BYE–William M. Deemer, Virginia Tech, Va.
- BYE–William Hyndman, IV, Huntingdon Valley, Pa.
- Thomas W. Milligan, Hinsdale, Ill.
- David Goldman, Sr., Brookhaven, Texas
- BYE–Neil C. Croonquist, Interlachen, Minn.
- Richard Poe, Oak Memorial, Mo.
- Dean Refram, Medinah, Ill.
- James M. Peelor, Dutchess, N.Y.
- Robert Dredge, Soangetaha, Ill.
- BYE–Robert J. Scherer, Sullivan, Ill.
- BYE–Frank Bellino, Tippecanoe, Ohio
- Donald E. Albert, Brookside, Ohio
- William Hyndman, III, Huntingdon Valley, Pa.
- Anthony J. Blom, Jr., Maketewah, Ohio
- William W. Farish, Cypress Point, Calif.
- BYE–J. Clark Espie, Jr., Hillcrest, Ind.
- Cal Carlson, Cloquet, Minn.
- Gerald F. Cundari, Portland, Ore.
- BYE–Frank A. Dalvito, Cedar Hill, N.J.
- Alfred King, Wichita Falls, Texas
- Arnold S. Blum, Idle Hour, Ga.
- BYE–Charles H. Weston, Jr., Portland, Ore.
- Bruce Cudd, Columbia-Edgewater, Ore.
- Gene Andrews, California, Calif.
- Eugene Dahlbender, Jr., Adams Park, Ga.
- Donald D. Stickney, Ohio State University, Ohio

2nd Round (18 Holes)

- Haverstick, 7 and 6
- Patton, 1 up
- Teyro
- Paine, 2 and 1
- Yost, 3 and 2
- Andonian
- Wise, 1 up
- Callison
- Fowler, 1 up
- Sweeny
- Victor
- Suisman, 6 and 5
- Dolan, 2 and 1
- Morey
- Beman, 1 up
- Deemer
- Hyndman IV
- Milligan, 1 up
- Croonquist
- Refram, 3 and 2
- Dredge, 6 and 5
- Scherer
- Bellino
- Hyndman III, 2 and 1
- Farish, 2 and 1
- Espie
- Cundari, 4 and 3
- Dalvito
- Blum, 4 and 3
- Weston
- Andrews, 2 and 1
- Dahlbender, 1 up, 21 hls.

3rd Round (18 Holes)

- Patton, 2 and 1
- Paine, 6 and 5
- Yost, 2 and 1
- Wise, 2 up
- Fowler, 3 and 2
- Suisman, 1 up, 19 hls.
- Dolan, 1 up, 21 hls.
- Beman, 2 up
- Milligan, 7 and 6
- Croonquist, 1 up
- Scherer, 3 and 2
- Hyndman III, 5 and 3
- Farish, 3 and 2
- Cundari, 4 and 3
- Blum, 4 and 3
- Andrews, 2 up

4th Round (18 Holes)

- Paine, 2 and 1
- Wise, 1 up
- Suisman, 1 up
- Beman, 6 and 5
- Milligan, 2 and 1
- Hyndman III, 3 and 2
- Farish, 1 up
- Andrews, 1 up

5th Round (18 Holes)

- Paine, 1 up, 19 hls.
- Beman, 7 and 5
- Hyndman III, 5 and 4
- Andrews, 2 and 1

6th Round (18 Holes)

- Beman, 4 and 3
- Hyndman III, 1 up, 19 hls.

Beman, 1 up, 19 hls.

1961
SIXTY-FIRST AMATEUR CHAMPIONSHIP

Held at the Del Monte Golf and Country Club, Pebble Beach Golf Links, Calif., September 11-16.
Yardage—6,747. Par 72. 1,995 Entries, 200 Qualifiers, 200 Starters.
Championship entirely at match play.

FINAL ROUND (36 Holes)—Jack W. Nicklaus defeated H. Dudley Wysong, Jr., 8 up and 6 to play.

UPPER

FIRST QUARTER

1st Round (18 Holes)	2nd Round (18 Holes)	3rd Round (18 Holes)	4th Round (18 Holes)	5th Round (18 Holes)	6th Round (18 Holes)	
Ralph M. Bogart, Chevy Chase, Md.	Bogart, 4 and 2					
James F. Tingley, Nassau, N.Y.		Bogart, 1 up				
Wilson H. Madden, Elyria, Ohio	Madden, 4 and 3					
Michael T. Bowers, Indian Canyon, Wash.			Thomas, 3 and 2			
BYE—Thomas J. Thomas, Bloomington, Ind.	Thomas	Thomas, 1 up, 20 hls.				
Fred Scrutchfield, Twin Hills, Okla.	Cochran, 5 and 3			Hopkins, 3 and 2		
Robert E. Cochran, Norwood Hills, Mo.						
Gaylon Simon, St. Andrews, Ill.	Hoffman, 2 and 1					
Jon Hoffman, Worthington, Minn.		Stanovich, 4 and 3				
BYE—Martin Stanovich, Tam O'Shanter, Ill.	Stanovich		Hopkins, 1 up			
Donald P. Scanlon, Westchester, N.Y.	Scanlon, 4 and 3					
Clifford DeWitt, Rose City, Ore.		Hopkins, 2 up				
BYE—Edwin B. Hopkins, Jr., Abilene, Texas	Hopkins				Wysong, 4 and 3	
George G. Creagh, Belle Meade, Tenn.	Ward, 5 and 4					
E. Harvie Ward, Jr., San Francisco, Calif.		Ward, 7 and 5				
BYE—Harlan Lane, Pine Forest, Texas	Lane		Wysong, 4 and 3			
BYE—H. Dudley Wysong, Jr., McKinney, Texas	Wysong	Wysong, 2 up				
William C. Campbell, Guyan, W. Va.	Gard, 1 up			Wysong, 3 and 2		
Andrew J. Gard, Wayland, Mass.						
Ronnie D.B.M. Shade, Edinburgh, Scotland	Shade, 3 and 2					
Dr. Edgar R. Updegraff, Tucson, Ariz.		Shade, 2 up				
BYE—Joseph F. Carr, Wachusett, Mass.	Carr		Shade, 2 up			
Howie Katchen, Green Gables, Colo.	Goldburg, 6 and 4					
Ronald W. Goldburg, Braidburn, N.J.		Goldburg, 1 up				
Richard T. Barrett, Riverside, Ore.	J.M. Hoak, 2 and 1					Wysong, 6 and 5
James M. Hoak, Wakonda, Iowa						
BYE—Irving Fermon, Kernwood, Mass.	Fermon	Zemljak, 6 and 4				
Edward Zemljak, Butte, Mont.	Zemljak, 1 up, 19 hls.					
Dr. Donald J. Keith, Mission Valley, Calif.			Sikes, 1 up, 19 hls.			
BYE—Richard H. Sikes, Springdale, Ark.	Sikes	Sikes, 3 and 1				
Charles Henton, Spokane, Wash.	Cudd, 7 and 5			Sikes, 4 and 2		
Bruce Cudd, Columbia-Edgewater, Ore.						
Harry D. Allers, Lake Wales, Fla.	Beman, 1 up					
Deane R. Beman, Bethesda, Md.		Patton, 2 up				
BYE—William J. Patton, Mimosa Hills, N.C.	Patton		Patton, 3 and 1			
Daniel B. James, Green Hills, Calif.	James, 3 and 2					
Don Harman, Mission Valley, Calif.		James, 1 up				
BYE—Andre E. Huycke, Oswego, Ore.	Huycke				Norville, 1 up	
BYE—John H. Andersen, Oak Park, Ill.	Andersen	Andersen, 5 and 4				
Jack House, Milburn, Kans.	House, 5 and 4					
John G. Hendrickson, Philadelphia Cricket, Pa.			Norville, 2 and 1			
BYE—Martin J. Christmas, Sussex, England	Christmas	Norville, 1 up, 21 hls.				
William T. Loesch, Brae Burn, Texas	Norville, 4 and 2			Norville, 2 up		
Richard S. Norville, Oklahoma City, Okla.						
BYE—C.A. Smith, III, Arbor Hills, Mich.	C.A. Smith	C.A. Smith, 3 and 2				
Dick Lotz, Kiote Hills, Calif.	Lotz, 3 and 1					
John Farquhar, Amarillo, Texas			Fowler, 2 and 1			
BYE—Lloyd J. Pitzer, Edgewater, Ill.	Pitzer	Fowler, 6 and 5				
Labron E. Harris, Jr., Oakwood, Okla.	Fowler, 3 and 2					
Glen Fowler, Twin Hills, Okla.						

SEMI-FINAL ROUND (36 Holes)—H. Dudley Wysong, Jr., defeated Joseph B. Carr, 2 up.

The first word after the player's name is the name of his club, except in the case of a foreign entrant.

SECOND QUARTER

HALF

6th Round (18 Holes)	5th Round (18 Holes)		4th Round (18 Holes)	3rd Round (18 Holes)	2nd Round (18 Holes)	1st Round (18 Holes)
					McCarthy, 5 and 4	James P. McCarthy, Joliet, Ill.
				Connell, 4 and 3		Charles Evans, Jr., Edgewater, Ill.
					Connell, 3 and 2	Truman Connell, Tequesta, Fla.
			Taylor, 1 up			Frank P. Hixon, San Gabriel, Calif.
					Siderowf	BYE—Richard L. Siderowf, Indian Hill, Conn.
				Taylor, 2 and 1	Taylor, 2 and 1	Dr. Frank M. Taylor, Jr., Red Hill, Calif.
		Courtney, 2 up				Marshall Trammell, Belle Meade, Tenn.
					Bohannon, 1 up	James G. Jackson, Greenbriar Hills, Mo.
				Draper, 2 and 1		David E. Bohannon, Peninsula, Calif.
					Draper	BYE—Tom Draper, Red Run, Mich.
			Courtney, 3 and 2		Courtney, 5 and 4	Charles Courtney, La Jolla, Calif.
				Courtney, 5 and 4		James Walker, Ayrshire, Scotland
					Babick	BYE—John Babick, Lakeside, Calif.
	Carr, 2 and 1				Spengler, 4 and 3	Richard Price, Longview, Wash.
				Greenwood, 1 up		Paul J. Spengler, Jr., Meadow, Calif.
					Greenwood	BYE—M. Harris Greenwood, River Oaks, Texas
			Marsh, 1 up, 20 hls.		Stephenson	BYE—Thomas A. Stephenson, Blue Hills, Mo.
				Marsh, 2 and 1	Marsh, 1 up, 19 hls.	James W. Mallory, Spokane, Wash.
						Samuel E. Marsh, Paris Mt., S.C.
		Carr, 2 and 1			Wright, 1 up	James R. Neumann, Walnut Hills, Mich.
				Carr, 6 and 5		Claude L. Wright, Cherry Hills, Colo.
					Carr	BYE—Joseph B. Carr, Dublin, Ireland
			Carr, 3 and 2		Wood, 4 and 3	John Wood, II, Cincinnati, Ohio
				Thompson, 2 and 1		Ray Barnhart, Medinah, Ill.
					Thompson	BYE—Urban T. Thompson, Jr., Deauville, Calif.
Carr, 1 up					Slattery	BYE—Lester A. Slattery, Jr., Normandie, Mo.
				T.C. Hoak, 2 and 1	T.C. Hoak, 3 and 2	Richard Killian, Westside, Okla.
			T.C. Hoak, 1 up			Thomas C. Hoak, Interlachen, Minn.
					Gabrielsen	BYE—James R. Gabrielsen, Athens, Ga.
				Mitchell, 2 and 1	Mitchell, 1 up	Joseph F. Mitchell, Coral Ridge, Fla.
		Francis, 6 and 5				Daniel B. Hogan, Oyster Harbors, Mass.
					Coe	BYE—Charles R. Coe, Oklahoma City, Okla.
				Coe, 5 and 4	Nichols, 2 and 1	John Nichols, Rio Hondo Men's, Calif.
			Francis, 1 up			Thomas J. Rose, Town, Minn.
					Green	BYE—Peter Green, Orchard Lake, Mich.
				Francis, 2 and 1	Francis, 1 up	Ross E. Mitchell, Hillcrest, Texas
	Francis, 3 and 2					Gene Francis, Wheatley Hills, N.Y.
					Tindall, 3 and 2	George Archer, Harding Park, Calif.
				Hoover, 1 up		William L. Tindall, Olympic Hills, Wash.
					Hoover	BYE—Frank W. Hoover, Bakersfield, Calif.
			Hoover, 2 and 1		Garrett, 6 and 5	Richard G. Leckey, Lakewood, Fla.
				Garrett, 2 and 1		Wright L. Garrett, Danville, Va.
		Hoover, 6 and 4			Marlatt	BYE—Gordon R. Marlatt, Eugene, Ore.
					Huddy, 2 up	Gordon Huddy, Sheffield, England
				Huddy, 2 up		Donald Welch, Butte, Mont.
					Lynch	BYE—Terrence R. Lynch, Town, Minn.
			English, 1 up, 20 hls.		English, 3 and 2	Harry L. Newby, Jr., Cloquet, Minn.
				English, 3 and 2		James R. English, Columbine, Colo.
					R.C. Smith, 2 and 1	Robert C. Smith, Top-O-Scott Men's, Ore.
						Pete Bostwick, Jr., Meadow Brook, N.Y.

THIRD QUARTER

1st Round (18 Holes)	2nd Round (18 Holes)	3rd Round (18 Holes)	4th Round (18 Holes)	5th Round (18 Holes)	6th Round (18 Holes)	
R. Keith Alexander, Calgary, Canada	Westland, 5 and 4					
Jack Westland, Everett, Wash.		James, 6 and 4				
Alfred N. Bell, Jr., C.C. of Columbus, Ga.	James, 3 and 2					
Frank M. James, C.C. of Grinnell, Iowa			Clecak, 2 and 1			
BYE—Charles Kocsis, Red Run, Mich.	Kocsis					
		Clecak, 3 and 1				
Anthony J. Clecak, Yolo Fliers, Calif.	Clecak, 2 and 1					
Louis F. Rosanova, Tam O'Shanter, Ill.				Humm, 2 and 1		
John J. Humm, Rockville Links, N.Y.	Humm, 5 and 4					
Lido Landi, Green Hills, Calif.						
BYE—D.W. Frame, Surrey, England	Frame	Humm, 2 and 1				
			Humm, 1 up			
John N.C. Cameron, Dallas, Texas	Cameron, 2 and 1					
Raymon C. Stoker, Odessa, Texas		Allen, 6 and 4				
Donald C. Allen, C.C. of Rochester, N.Y.	Allen				Nicklaus, 3 and 1	
Richard J. Giddings, Del Rio, Calif.	Giddings, 2 and 1					
Jerry Greenbaum, Standard Town, Ga.		Edwards, 2 and 1				
BYE—William L. Edwards, Cherry Valley, N.Y.	Edwards					
			Nicklaus, 5 and 4			
BYE—Jack W. Nicklaus, Scioto, Ohio	Nicklaus					
		Nicklaus, 4 and 3				
Bill Stewart, Hickory Hills, Mo.	Krieger, 2 and 1			Nicklaus, 2 and 1		
Donald R. Krieger, Columbia—Edgewater, Ore.						
Don C. Voth, Portage, Ohio	Voth, 4 and 3					
John R. Kreger, Kenwood, Md.		King, 2 and 1				
BYE—David A. King, St. Davids, Pa.	King					
			D.W. Smith, 4 and 3			
John Lotz, Kiote Hills, Calif.	Lotz, 6 and 5					
Thomas O. Edwards, Beacon Hill, Wash.		D.W. Smith, 3 and 2				
Ira J. Hopkins, Jr., Los Altos, Calif.	D.W. Smith, 4 and 2					
David W. Smith, Jr., Gaston, N.C.						Nicklaus, 4 and 3
BYE—Kenneth G. Storey, Olympic Hills, Wash.	Storey					
		Gardner, 3 and 2				
Billy Nicks, Lakeside, Calif.	Gardner, 4 and 2					
Robert Gardner, Knollwood, N.Y.			Blancas, 2 and 1			
BYE—Homero Blancas, Jr., Champions, Texas	Blancas					
		Blancas, 2 and 1				
James B. West, Astoria, Ore.	Care, 5 and 4			Carmichael, 3 and 1		
William H. Care, Jr., Atlantic City, N.J.						
Vincent C. Greene, Meadowbrook, Mo.	Carmichael, 5 and 4					
Samuel H. Carmichael, Martinsville, Ind.		Carmichael, 3 and 2				
BYE—Michael Lunt, Birmingham, England	Lunt					
			Carmichael, 4 and 3			
James G. Littlejohn, Midland, Texas	Littlejohn, 4 and 2					
Roger Maxwell, Peach Tree, Calif.		Weston, 3 and 2				
BYE—Charles H. Weston, Jr., Portland, Ore.	Weston				Carmichael, 3 and 2	
BYE—Kenneth Finke, Tucson, Ariz.	Finke					
		Finke, 1 up, 19 hls.				
Stephen Stimac, Contra Costa, Calif.	Wilcox, 1 up					
Terry D. Wilcox, Oak Hills, Okla.			Finke, 4 and 3			
BYE—Kermit Zarley, Jr., Glen Acres, Wash.	Zarley					
		Colbert, 2 and 1				
James J. Colbert, Jr., Santa Fe Hills, Mo.	Colbert, 1 up			Finke, 2 and 1		
Jim Mooney, Jr., Encanto Men's, Ariz.						
BYE—Jerry E. Jackson, Kokomo, Ind.	Jackson					
		Jackson, 1 up				
Robert A. Roos, Jr., Olympic, Calif.	Ware, 3 and 2					
Cobby Ware, Augusta, Ga.			Jackson, 5 and 4			
BYE—William M. Deemer, Virginia Tech, Va.	Deemer					
		Andrews, 3 and 2				
Gene Andrews, California C.C. Men's Assoc., Calif.	Andrews, 2 and 1					
Gary C. Wright, Cherry Hills, Colo.						

SEMI-FINAL ROUND (36 Holes)—Jack W. Nicklaus defeated Marion C. Mithvin, Jr., 9 up and 8 to play.

CHAMPIONSHIP HALF

FOURTH QUARTER

6th Round (18 Holes)	5th Round (18 Holes)		4th Round (18 Holes)	3rd Round (18 Holes)	2nd Round (18 Holes)	1st Round (18 Holes)
Methvin, 5 and 4	Methvin, 2 up	Methvin, 3 and 2	Davies, 2 and 1	Davies, 5 and 4	Semple, 5 and 4	Pandell Savic, Ohio State University, Ohio Harton S. Semple, Allegheny, Pa.
					Davies 1 up	William Hyndman, III, Huntingdon Valley, Pa. Richard D. Davies, Annandale, Calif.
				Yates, 1 up	Kuntz	BYE–William R. Kuntz, Bonnie Briar, N.Y.
					Yates, 5 and 4	Charles S. McDowell, Princess Anne, Va. Richard L. Yates, Corpus Christi, Texas
			Methvin, 4 and 3	Methvin, 3 and 2	Birmingham, 5 and 4	John R. Birmingham, Oakmont, Pa. Charles L. VanLinge, Stanford University, Calif.
					Methvin	BYE–Marion C. Methvin, Jr., Riverdale, Ark.
				Wettlaufer, 1 up	Wettlaufer, 1 up, 19 hls.	H. Ward Wettlaufer, Atlanta Athletic, Ga. Edward Richitelli, Newark, Del.
					Yenny	BYE–John R. Yenny, Greater Alton Golfer's Assn. Ill.
		Hanen, 1 up, 19 hls.	Dahlbender, 4 and 2	Barton, 6 and 4	Chapman, 3 and 2	Alex Welsh, Rockford, Ill. Brian H.G. Chapman, Hertfordshire, England
					Barton	BYE–Robert K. Barton, Scioto, Ohio
				Dahlbender, 3 and 2	Dahlbender	BYE–Eugene V. Dahlbender, Jr., North Fulton, Ga.
					Johnston, 2 and 1	William A. Bergman, Cedar Rapids, Iowa M.O. Johnston, Jr., La Jolla, Calif.
			Hanen, 2 and 1	Stuart, 2 up	Stuart, 5 and 4	Mark J. Stuart, Jr., Winged Foot, N.Y. William I. Buppert, III, Bethesda, Md.
					Cordingley	BYE–William A. Cordingley, Edina, Minn.
				Hanen, 2 and 1	Hanen, 4 and 3	Richard D. Hanen, Coos, Ore. Charles F. Lewis, III, C.C. of Little Rock, Ark.
					Greenwood	BYE–Jimmy M. Greenwood, River Oaks, Texas
	C.B. Smith, 3 and 1	C.B. Smith, 1 up, 19 hls.	Spray, 2 and 1	Durham, 3 and 2	Hulverson	BYE–Tom Hulverson, Sunset, Mo.
					Durham, 2 and 1	John Hedlund, Oswego Lake, Ore. Herbert A. Durham, Brook Hollow, Texas
				Spray, 2 and 1	Boos	BYE–Robert W. Boos, Los Angeles, Calif.
					Spray, 1 up, 19 hls.	John S. Spray, Wakonda, Iowa Hugh D. Thompson, Wichita Falls, Texas
			C.B. Smith, 1 up, 20 hls.	C.B. Smith, 5 and 4	C.B. Smith, 1 up	Quin Flowers, Jr., Dothan, Ala. Charles B. Smith, Gaston, N.C.
					Hornbuckle	BYE–Tom Hornbuckle, Jr., Albuquerque, N.M.
				Pieper, 3 and 2	Minnich	BYE–Paul A. Minnich, Elyria, Ohio
					Pieper, 2 up	James D. Ward, Riviera, W. Va. Ernest Pieper, Jr., San Jose, Calif.
		Olshan, 1 up, 19 hls.	McManus, 1 up	McManus, 3 and 2	Towns, 2 up	Kenneth J. Towns, Green Hills, Calif. Daniel M. Keefe, Oakley, Mass.
					McManus	BYE–Roger T. McManus, Kenwood, Ohio
				Bonallack, 2 and 1	Morey, 4 and 2	Dale Morey, Mimosa Hills, N.C. Robert Littler, Jr., Athens, Ohio
					Bonallack	BYE–Michael F. Bonallack, Essex, England
			Olshan, 1 up	Olshan, 1 up, 19 hls.	Stickney, 2 and 1	Denny Lyons, Moon Brook, N.Y. Donald D. Stickney, Ohio State University, Ohio
					Olshan	BYE–Marvin Olshan, Harrison, N.Y.
				Newcomb, 2 up	Drimak, 5 and 4	Ronald P. McCall, Beaumont, Texas Ronald Drimak, Yorba Linda, Calif.
					Newcomb, 6 and 5	Frank Arasin, Shamokin Valley, Pa. William K. Newcomb, Jr., Logansport, Ind.

1962
SIXTY-SECOND AMATEUR CHAMPIONSHIP

Held at the Pinehurst Country Club, No. 2 Course, Pinehurst, N.C., September 17-22.
Yardage—7,051. Par 72. 2,044 Entries, 200 Starters.
Championship proper entirely at match play.

FINAL ROUND—Labron E. Harris, Jr., defeated Downing Gray, 1 up.

FIRST QUARTER

UPPER

1st Round (18 Holes)	2nd Round (18 Holes)	3rd Round (18 Holes)	4th Round (18 Holes)	5th Round (18 Holes)	6th Round (18 Holes)	
Neil Croonquist, Interlachen, Minn.	Croonquist, 1 up, 19 hls.					
Pete Bostwick, Jr., Meadow Brook, N.Y.		Blancas, 3 and 1				
James N. Pulliam, Forest Lake, S.C.	Blancas, 2 and 1					
Homero Blancas, Jr., Champions, Texas			Blancas, 6 and 4			
BYE—Tillman O. Berg, Jr., Laurelwood, Ore.	Berg					
		Allen, 6 and 4				
Albert W. Allen, Jr., Palmetto, Fla.	Allen, 5 and 4					
James C. Deemer, Paradise Point, N.C.				Blancas, 1 up, 24 hls.		
Norando Nannini, Sunset Valley Tee, Ill.	Farish, 4 and 3					
William W. Farish, Cypress Point, Calif.		Farish, 1 up				
BYE—Ted Bishop, Pine Brook, Mass.	Bishop					
			Beman, 7 and 6			
Tom Hornbuckle, Albuquerque, N.M.	Cleveland, 2 and 1					
James R. Cleveland, Jr., Druid Hills, Ga.		Beman, 6 and 5				
BYE—Deane R. Beman, Bethesda, Md.	Beman				Blancas, 1 up	
Burr Melvin, James River, Va.	Ade, 1 up					
Carl F. Ade, Jr., Indian Hills, Kansas		Marad, 5 and 4				
BYE—David Marad, Wollaston, Mass.	Marad					
			Marad, 2 and 1			
BYE—Harold B. Bolas, Columbine, Colo.	Bolas					
		Bolas, 3 and 2				
William H. Care, Jr., Atlantic City, N.J.	Little, 1 up, 19 hls.					
Roger G. Little, Carmel, N.C.				Marad, 3 and 2		
H. Ward Wettlaufer, CC of Buffalo, N.Y.	Carmichael, 5 and 4					
Dan Carmichael, Columbus, Ohio		Carmichael, 4 and 3				
BYE—Kenny Pinns, Indian Wells, Calif.	Pinns					
			Burdick, 1 up			
James A. Grant, III, Wethersfield, Conn.	Grant, 2 and 1					
Bruce Richards, Overlake, Wash.		Burdick, 4 and 3				
Charles W. Harrison, Atlanta, Ga.	Burdick, 1 up					Harris, 2 and 1
Bert C. Burdick, Baton Rouge, La.						
BYE—Donald Stickney, Ohio State Univ., Ohio	Stickney					
		Stickney, 2 and 1				
Ray G. Terry, Timuquana, Fla.	Terry, 1 up					
William Hyndman, III, Huntingdon Valley, Pa.			Harris, 2 and 1			
BYE—Don Placke, Sunset, Mo.	Placke					
		Harris, 2 and 1				
Labron E. Harris, Jr., Oakwood, Okla.	Harris, 2 and 1					
Roger Ginsberg, Harrison, N.Y.				Harris, 5 and 4		
John G. Hendrickson, Philadelphia Cricket, Pa.	Hendrickson, 2 and 1					
Larry N. Cassady, Marietta, Ohio		Hendrickson, 5 and 3				
BYE—John R. Suisman, Tumblebrook, Conn.	Suisman					
			Hopkins, 3 and 1			
Richard Martinez, California Men's, Calif.	Martinez, 2 and 1					
Richard L. Latimer, Columbia, Md.		Hopkins, 3 and 1				
BYE—Edwin B. Hopkins, Jr., Abilene, Kans.	Hopkins				Harris, 1 up, 21 hls.	
BYE—William Crooks, Johnstown, Pa.	Crooks					
		Edwards, 6 and 5				
William L. Edwards, Cherry Valley, N.Y.	Edwards, 1 up					
Pat Foy Brady, Penrose Park, N.C.			Edwards, 5 and 4			
BYE—John Peterson, Dunedin Isles, Fla.	Peterson					
		Peterson, 1 up, 20 hls.				
John M. Owen, Jr., Manor, Md.	Larkin, 2 and 1					
Robert Larkin, Kenwood, Ohio				Sikes, 3 and 2		
BYE—Edward J. Korylak, Rancho, Calif.	Korylak					
		Korylak, 3 and 2				
Kenneth T. Finke, Tucson, Ariz.	Finke, 1 up, 20 hls.					
Robert W. Corley, Jackson, Mich.			Sikes, 1 up			
BYE—Richard H. Sikes, Springdale, Ark.	Sikes					
		Sikes, 1 up				
Lloyd S. Monroe, Upper Montclair, N.J.	Monroe, 4 and 3					
Clarence McC. Ellerbe, Jr., Columbia, S.C.						

SEMI-FINAL ROUND (36 Holes)—Labron E. Harris, Jr., defeated William J. Patton, 3 and 1

HALF

SECOND QUARTER

6th Round (18 Holes)		5th Round (18 Holes)	4th Round (18 Holes)	3rd Round (18 Holes)	2nd Round (18 Holes)	1st Round (18 Holes)
					Cortazzo,	Frank P. Cortazzo, Orchard Hills, N.J.
				Albert,	2 and 1	Ralph T. Strafaci, Jr., Hempstead, N.Y.
				2 and 1	Albert,	Winnie C. Cole, Bayou DeSiard, La.
			McKey,		3 and 2	Donald E. Albert, Brookside, Ohio
			1 up		Merchant	BYE–Frank J. Merchant, Myers Park, N.C.
				McKey,		
				by default	McKey,	John D. McKey, Jr., CC of Orlando, Fla.
		McKey, 1 up			6 and 5	Charles E. Mac Callum, Tamarac, Fla.
					Allen,	James B. Allen, Jr., Athens, Ga.
				Chapman,	1 up	John O. Levinson, Glen Flora, Ill.
				1 up	Chapman	BYE–Richard D. Chapman, Pinehurst, N.C.
			Chapman,			
			2 and 1		Key,	Victor Cuiss, CC of Jackson, Mich.
				McCormick,	5 and 4	James W. Key, CC of Columbus, Ga.
				1 up	McCormick	BYE–Bruce McCormick, San Gabriel, Calif.
	Patton, 2 and 1				Green,	Glenn Gray, Alberta, Canada
				Knighton,	4 and 3	Peter Green, Orchard Lake, Mich.
				3 and 1	Knighton	BYE–Knute Knighton, Manor, Md.
			Knighton,			
			3 and 2		Butler	BYE–Dr. Arthur F. Butler, Glendora, Calif.
				Norville,		
				3 and 2	Norville,	Ben Lane, Jr., Amarillo, Texas
					1 up, 19 hls.	Richard S. Norville, Oklahoma City, Okla.
		Patton, 4 and 3			Smith,	William E. Kufta, Wethersfield, Conn.
				Zimmerman,	1 up	Thomas M. Smith, Greensburg, Pa.
				2 and 1	Zimmerman	BYE–Jack E. Zimmerman, Men's Assn. Dayton, Ohio
			Patton,			
			4 and 2		Patton,	Earl J. Stamer, Sr., Normandie, Mo.
				Patton,	3 and 2	William J. Patton, Mimosa Hills, N.C.
				4 and 2	Ferguson	BYE–William M. Ferguson, Wakonda, Iowa
Patton, 7 and 6					Davidson	BYE–William G. Davidson, Carlisle, Pa.
				Griffith,		
				5 and 3	Griffith,	James A. Head, Jr., Birmingham, Ala.
			Stuart,		1 up	David Griffith, Charlotte, N.C.
			2 and 1		Durkee	BYE–A. Bruce Durkee, Tedesco, Mass.
				Stuart,		
				5 and 3	Stuart,	Mark J. Stuart, Jr., Winged Foot, N.Y.
		Littler, 3 and 2			2 up	Alex Welsh, Rockford, Ill.
					Sher	BYE–James Sher, Westwood, Mo.
				Updegraff,		
				5 and 4	Updegraff,	Dr. Edgar R. Updegraff, Tucson, Ariz.
			Littler,		3 and 1	Arthur D. Hudnutt, Elyria, Ohio
			4 and 3		Chase	BYE–Ronald A. Chase, City Park, Colo.
				Littler,		
				6 and 5	Littler,	Robert Littler, Jr., Athens, Ohio
	Gabrielsen, 5 and 4				4 and 2	John Farquhar, Amarillo, Texas
					Gabrielsen,	Gene L. Lookabill, Carolina, N.C.
				Gabrielsen,	3 and 1	James R. Gabrielsen, Athens, Ga.
				5 and 3	Vickers	BYE–James W. Vickers, Wichita, Kans.
			Gabrielsen,			
			1 up		Stahl,	James L. Wiechers, Los Altos, Calif.
				Stahl,	1 up	Walter Stahl, Jr., Acacia, Ohio
				5 and 4	Keyser	BYE–Dick Keyser, Claremont, Calif.
		Gabrielsen, 2 and 1			Wysong,	Harold Foreman, Lake Shore, Ill.
				Justa,	4 and 3	H. Dudley Wysong, Jr., McKinney, Texas
				1 up	Justa	BYE–Edwin A. Justa, Benvenue, N.C.
			Justa,			
			3 and 2		Leer,	John B. Thornton, Oak Hill, N.Y.
				Mitchell,	4 and 3	Dr. Jack R. Leer, Highland, Ind.
				3 and 2	Mitchell,	James B. McHale, Jr., Aronimink, Pa.
					1 up	Ross E. Mitchell, Hillcrest, Texas

1962 AMATEUR CHAM

LOWER

THIRD QUARTER

1st Round (18 Holes)	2nd Round (18 Holes)	3rd Round (18 Holes)	4th Round (18 Holes)	5th Round (18 Holes)	6th Round (18 Holes)	
William R. Gerringer, Hampton, Va.	Gerringer, 3 and 2					
Charles R. Coe, Oklahoma City, Okla.		Gerringer, 6 and 4				
David A. Hasslen, Ortonville Men's, Minn.	Hasslen, 19 hls.					
William C. Ogilvy, Columbia-Edgewater, Ore.			Allen, 3 and 2			
BYE—Robert W. Allen, Wampanoag, Conn.	Allen					
Dan B. Winters, Abilene, Texas		Allen, 1 up		Allen, 2 up		
Arnold S. Blum, Idle Hour, Ga.	Blum, 6 and 4					
Keely A. Grice, Jr., Myers Park, N.C.	Roos, 2 up					
Robert A. Roos, Jr., Olympic, Calif.						
BYE—Dean N. Lind, Forest Hills, Ill.	Lind	Roos, 3 and 2				
Dexter H. Daniels, Lake Region Yacht, Fla.			Roos, 2 and 1			
Tom W. Matey, Highland, Ind.	Matey, 7 and 6					
BYE—John P. Ward, Onondaga, N.Y.	Ward	Matey, 3 and 1			Coody, 3 and 2	
Karl H. Schmidt, Fairlawn, Ohio	Sigel, 3 and 2					
Jay Sigel, Bala, Pa.						
BYE—Kermit M. Zarley, Jr., Yakima, Wash.	Zarley	Sigel, 1 up				
BYE—Dr. Sam W. Valuck, City Park, Colo.	Valuck		Coody, 3 and 2			
R. L. McDonald, Jr., Finley of UNC, N.C.	Coody, 4 and 2	Coody, 6 and 5		Coody, 4 and 3		
Charles Coody, Ridglea, Texas						
Dr. Charles L. Updegraff, Boone, Iowa	Jackson, 2 and 1					
James G. Jackson, Algonquin, Mo.						
BYE—James O. Watts, Boonsboro, Va.	Watts	Jackson, 6 and 5				
E. M. Mauro, Jr., Metacomet, R.I.	Finger, 3 and 2		Roccisano, 1 up			
Sherman Finger, III, Westmoreland, Ill.						
Tim Holland, La Gorce, Fla.	Roccisano, 3 and 2	Roccisano, 1 up				
Joseph D. Roccisano, Split Rock, N.Y.						Coody, 2 up
BYE—Roger T. McManus, Kenwood, Ohio	McManus					
Andrew J. Gard, Wayland, Mass.	Blair, 2 up	Blair, 2 and 1				
Jim Tom Blair, St. Louis, Mo.			Cullinane, 2 up			
BYE—Richard Sucher, Ozaukee, Wis.	Sucher					
Richard Canon, San Angelo, Texas	Cullinane, 3 and 2	Cullinane, 4 and 3		Cullinane, 2 up		
Anthony J. Cullinane, Bethesda, Md.						
Ted Richards, Jr., Bel-Air, Calif.	Bryan, 1 up					
John F. Bryan, CC of Fairfield, Conn.		Bryan, 1 up				
BYE—Michael V. McMahon, Lakewood, Fla.	McMahon		Ward, 3 and 2			
E. Harvie Ward, Jr., San Francisco, Calif.	Ward, 3 and 2					
Calvin W. Cooke, Mesa, Ariz.		Ward, 1 up				
BYE—Holly P. Toler, Sweetwater, Texas	Toler				Newcomb, 2 up	
BYE—Walter E. Beckjord, Cincinnati, Ohio	Beckjord	Beckjord, 2 and 1				
Samuel E. Marsh, Paris Mountain, S.C.	Grace, 3 and 2					
Thomas J. Grace, Detroit, Mich.			Beckjord, 5 and 4			
BYE—Randolph Snider, Westwood, Texas	Snider	Snider, 1 up, 20 hls.				
Harry H. Haverstick, Jr., Lancaster, Pa.	Cowan, 5 and 4			Newcomb, 1 up, 21 hls.		
Gary Cowan, Ontario, Canada						
BYE—Michael M. Dore, Fairmount, N.J.	Dore	Dore, 4 and 3				
John H. McCormick, Jr., Timuquana, Fla.	Harvey, 6 and 4					
Ernest W. Harvey, Sedgefield, N.C.			Newcomb, 5 and 3			
BYE—John M. Babick, Lakeside, Calif.	Babick	Newcomb, 3 and 2				
William K. Newcomb, Jr., Kokomo, Ind.	Newcomb, 4 and 3					
Albert L. Kelley, Jr., Palmetto, Fla.						

SEMI-FINAL ROUND (36 Holes)—Downing Gray defeated Charles Coody, 3 up and 2 to play.

The first word after the player's name is the name of his club, except in the case of a foreign entrant.

PIONSHIP – Continued

HALF

FOURTH QUARTER

6th Round (18 Holes)		5th Round (18 Holes)	4th Round (18 Holes)	3rd Round (18 Holes)	2nd Round (18 Holes)	1st Round (18 Holes)
					Desjardins, 4 and 3	Raymond Solinger, Branch Brook, N.J. Paul Desjardins, Miami Shores, Fla.
				Desjardins, 4 and 2		
					Klass, 2 and 1	Fred L. Mueller, Manor, Md. Peter C. Klass, Wayzata, Minn.
			Desjardins, 2 and 1			
					Swift	BYE–George P. Swift, Jr., Columbus, Ga.
				Folkes, 3 and 2		
		Desjardins, 3 and 2			Folkes, 1 up	Russell Glover, Florence, S.C. Kenneth L. Folkes, Old Town, N.C.
					Rheim, 5 and 4	Ralph Johnston, Garden City, N.Y. James E. Rheim, San Diego, Calif.
				Rheim, 1 up		
					Donaho	BYE–William R. Donaho, Lakeside, Texas
			Davies, 3 and 2			
					Davies, 1 up, 21 hls.	Richard D. Davies, Annandale, Calif. Joe Cormack, Jr., Skokie, Ill.
				Davies, 2 and 1		
					Browning	BYE–David R. Browning, Ames, Iowa
	Desjardins, 3 and 1					
					Tutwiler, 4 and 3	Edgar M. Tutwiler, Jr., Berry Hills, W. Va. George W. Boutell, Phoenix, Ariz.
				Tutwiler, 5 and 4		
					McBride	BYE–Joseph A. McBride, Arcola, N.J.
			Smith, 2 and 1			
					Semple	BYE–Harton S. Semple, Sewickley, Pa.
				Smith, 8 and 6		
					Smith, 7 and 5	Charles B. Smith, Gaston, N.C. H. H. Edwards, Quail Creek, Okla.
		Smith, 4 and 3				
					Brennan, 2 and 1	Thomas E. Brennan, Jr., Savannah, Ga. Ralph Ellstrom, Dearborn, Mich.
				Brennan, 4 and 3		
					Nield	BYE–Samuel J. Nield, Winged Foot, N.Y.
			Harmon, 2 up			
					Astleford, 4 and 3	**Robert L. Astleford, Field Club, Omaha, Neb.** Ralph M. Bogart, Chevy Chase, Md.
				Harmon, 1 up		
					Harmon	BYE–Don Harmon, Stardust, Calif.
Gray, 1 up						
					Methvin	BYE–Marion C. Methvin, Jr., Riverdale, Ark.
				Methvin, 1 up		
			Methvin, 5 and 3			
					Campbell, 3 and 2	William C. Campbell, Guyan, W. Va. John R. Hughes, Jr., Starmount Forest, N.C.
					Wise	BYE–Paul T. Wise, Ardsley, N.Y.
				Wise, 4 and 3		
		Gray, 3 and 2				
					Briggs, 3 and 2	James O'Bey, Wachusett, Mass. William M. Briggs, Jr., Columbia, Md.
					Thompson, 4 and 3	Ben M. Schulein, Jr., Westwood, Mo. Hugh D. Thompson, Wichita Falls, Texas
				Sussel, 1 up, 20 hls.		
			Gray, 1 up, 20 hls.			
					Sussel	BYE–Allan Sussel, White Manor, Pa.
					Heck	BYE–Marion E. Heck, Salem, Ohio
				Gray, 1 up		
					Gray, 3 and 2	Richard Crawford, El Dorado, Ark. Downing Gray, Pensacola, Fla.
	Gray, 3 and 2					
					Louis, 3 and 2	Mark E. Darnell, Purdue Univ., Ind. Michael W. Louis, Glen View, Ill.
				Galloway, 1 up		
			Reed, 2 and 1			
					Galloway	BYE–Bob Galloway, Old Town, N.C.
					Siderowf, 8 and 7	Charles Evans, Jr., Edgewater, Ill. Richard L. Siderowf, Indian Hill, Conn.
				Reed, 1 up, 20 hls.		
					Reed	BYE–Thomas K. Reed, Broomfield, Colo.
		Colbert, 5 and 4				
					Tullio, 1 up, 19 hls.	John C. Tullio, Aurora, Ohio Lewis W. Oehmig, Chattanooga, Tenn.
				Tullio, 1 up		
			Colbert, 4 and 2			
					Easterly	BYE–Harry W. Easterly, Jr., Virginia, Va.
					Penrose, 4 and 2	Robert Gardner, Montclair, N.J. John J. Penrose, Jr., Torresdale, Pa.
				Colbert, 2 and 1		
					Colbert, 3 and 2	James J. Colbert, Jr., Santa Fe Hills, Mo. Erv Parent, Seattle, Wash.

1963
SIXTY-THIRD AMATEUR CHAMPIONSHIP

Held at the Wakonda Club, Des Moines, Iowa, September 9-14.
Yardage—6,896. Par 72. 1,768 Entries, 200 Qualifiers, 200 Starters.
Championship entirely at match play.
FINAL ROUND—Deane R. Beman defeated Richard H. Sikes, 2 up and 1 to play.

UPPER

FIRST QUARTER

1st Round (18 Holes)	2nd Round (18 Holes)	3rd Round (18 Holes)	4th Round (18 Holes)	5th Round (18 Holes)	6th Round (18 Holes)	
Davis Eichelberger, Ridgewood, Texas	Eichelberger, 2 and 1	Eichelberger, 2 and 1				
John R. Hughes, Jr., Starmount Forest, N.C.						
Robert W. Millen, Piping Rock, N.Y.	Spangler, 5 and 4					
Richard L. Spangler, Jr., C.C. of Lincoln, Neb.			Lotz, 4 and 3			
BYE—Robert W. Gardner, Montclair, N.J.	Gardner	Lotz, 1 up				
James W. Paul, Piping Rock, N.Y.	Lotz, 1 up			Lotz, 3 and 2		
John Lotz, Olympic, Calif.						
Andrew J. Gard, Wayland, Mass.	Riley, 1 up					
Mike Riley, Stardust, Calif.		Porter, 1 up, 19 hls.				
BYE—Joe Porter, III, Arizona, Ariz.	Porter					
John C. Doser, Vero Beach, Fla.	Johns, 1 up		Hendrich, 1 up, 19 hls.			
Alfred M. Johns, Port Charlotte Men's, Fla.		Hendrich, 2 and 1				
BYE—William E. Hendrich, Riviera, Fla.	Hendrich				Archer, 3 and 2	
Harvey E. Woodard, Lochmoor, Mich.	Woodard, 1 up					
Paul B. Short, Oakbourne, La.		Horn, 2 and 1				
BYE—Rodney Horn, Hillcrest, Mo.	Horn					
BYE—A. Downing Gray, Pensacola, Fla.	Gray		Archer, 1 up			
Robert Lunn, Harding Park, Calif.	Archer, 3 and 2	Archer, 4 and 3				
George W. Archer, Harding Park, Calif.						
Richard Yates, Corpus Christi, Texas	Yates, 1 up, 20 hls.			Archer, 3 and 1		
William L. Edwards, Garden City, N.Y.		Estrada, 4 and 3				
BYE—Juan Antonio Estrada, Sonora, Mexico	Estrada		Estrada, 4 and 3			
John Jacobs, Candlewood, Calif.	Jacobs, 2 and 1					
Jack Malloy, Oklahoma City, Okla.		Morey, 6 and 5				
Dale Morey, Mimosa Hills, N.C.	Morey, 1 up					Archer, 1 up
Thomas Weiskopf, Ohio State Univ., Ohio						
BYE—John Liechty, Elmwood, Iowa	Liechty	Liechty, 5 and 3				
Dr. Edgar R. Updegraff, Tucson, Ariz.	James, 3 and 2					
Frank M. James, C.C. of Grinnell, Iowa			Olson, 1 up			
BYE—Dr. Philip A. Olson, Hazeltine National, Minn.	Olson	Olson, 5 and 4				
Charles L. Tinkham, Brae Burn, Mass.	Culligan, 6 and 5			Olson, 1 up, 19 hls.		
Thomas Culligan, III, California, Calif.						
Stephen R. Oppermann, McLean Park, Calif.	Bell, 6 and 4					
Lawrence G. Bell, Saucon Valley, Pa.		Cowan, 5 and 4				
BYE—Gary Cowan, Kitchener, Ont., Canada	Cowan		McKey, 5 and 4			
Dr. John D. McKey, C.C. of Orlando, Fla.	McKey, 3 and 1					
Verne Burnett, Wethersfield, Conn.		McKey, 4 and 2				
BYE—Eugene Carello, Franklin County, Ill.	Carello				Spray, 1 up	
BYE—Dillard A. Traynham, Paris Mountain, S.C.	Traynham	Traynham, 1 up, 20 hls.				
Ted Hale, Pine Forest, Texas	Hale, 2 and 1					
John A. Kuhlman, La Grange, Ill.			Traynham, 1 up			
BYE—Dr. Herbert Klontz, Quail Creek, Okla.	Klontz	Klontz, 2 and 1				
Rafael Quiroz, Monterrey, Nuevo Leon, Mexico	Cole, 2 up			Spray, 5 and 4		
W. Clayton Cole, Bayou DeSiard, La.						
BYE—Paul Tarnow, Jr., Palma Ceia, Fla.	Tarnow	Spray, 4 and 3				
John S. Spray, Wakonda, Iowa	Spray, 6 and 4					
Martin J. Bohen, Las Vegas, Nev.			Spray, 4 and 3			
BYE—William J. Curley, Jr., Springhaven, Pa.	Curley	Curley, 1 up, 21 hls.				
William B. Hamilton, Anniston, Ala.	Hogan, 5 and 4					
Daniel B. Hogan, Oyster Harbors, Mass.						

SEMI-FINAL ROUND (36 Holes)—Deane R. Beman defeated George W. Archer, 5 up and 4 to play.

The first word after the player's name is the name of his club, except in the case of a foreign entrant.

HALF

SECOND QUARTER

6th Round (18 Holes)	5th Round (18 Holes)		4th Round (18 Holes)	3rd Round (18 Holes)	2nd Round (18 Holes)	1st Round (18 Holes)
					Wright, 2 and 1	Gary C. Wright, Cherry Hills, Colo.
				Switzer, 2 and 1		Charles Courtney, La Jolla, Calif.
					Switzer, 4 and 3	Joseph F. Switzer, Old Warson, Mo.
						William H. Brafford, LaGrange, Ill.
			Gabrielsen, 4 and 3		Hoffer	BYE–Harry E. Hoffer, Sleepy Hollow, W. Va.
				Gabrielsen, 1 up	Gabrielsen, 4 and 3	James R. Gabrielsen, Athens, Ga.
		Beman, 1 up				Marshall Trammell, Belle Meade, Tenn.
					Beman, 7 and 5	Richard L. Latimer, Columbia, Md.
				Beman, 4 and 3		Deane R. Beman, Bethesda, Md.
					Polk	BYE–Charles M. Polk, II, St. Louis, Mo.
			Beman, 2 up		Greene, 4 and 3	Samuel B. Hartung, Baltusrol, N.J.
				Kocsis, 4 and 2		Charles Greene, Deane Hill, Tenn.
	Beman, 1 up, 19 hls.				Kocsis	BYE–Charles Kocsis, Red Run, Mich.
					Meerdink, 3 and 2	James F. O'Hara, C.C. of Maryland, Md.
				Meerdink, 1 up, 19 hls.		C. Barry Meerdink, Park Lane, La.
					Gumlia	BYE–David E. Gumlia, Univ. of Minn., Minn.
			Meerdink, 1 up		Sylveyra	BYE–Augustin Sylveyra, Tijuana, Baja, Mexico
				Liff, 2 and 1	Liff, 5 and 3	Earl R. Liff, Green Acres, Ill.
		Meerdink, 1 up				Norman S. Miller, Beauclerc, Fla.
					Blair, 1 up	Lambert L. Nagler, Spokane, Wash.
				Blair, 7 and 6		Jim Tom Blair, Meadowbrook, Mo.
					Spangler	BYE–Jeffrey S. Spangler, Northwood, N.J.
			Astleford, 1 up		Crooks, 1 up	Douglas H. Silverberg, Calgary, Alberta, Canada
				Astleford, 6 and 4		William Crooks, Sunnehanna, Pa.
Beman, 6 and 5					Astleford	BYE–Robert L. Astleford, Field Club, Neb.
					McKey	BYE–John D. McKey, Jr., C.C. of Orlando, Fla.
				Harris, 6 and 5	Harris, 8 and 6	Labron E. Harris, Jr., Oakwood, Okla.
			Stahl, 2 and 1			William C. Cowardin, Jr., James River, Va.
					Valuck	BYE–Dr. Sam W. Valuck, Meadow Hills, Colo.
				Stahl, 2 and 1	Stahl, 1 up	Rodney Bliss, Jr., Wakonda, Iowa
		Stahl, 6 and 5				Walter Stahl, Acacia, Ohio
					Mackenzie	BYE–Reed K. Mackenzie, Eau Claire, Wis.
				Jackson, 3 and 2	Jackson, 4 and 3	John W. Hedlund, Oswego Lake, Ore.
			Cochran, 2 and 1			James G. Jackson, Greenbriar Hills, Mo.
					Cochran	BYE–Robert E. Cochran, Norwood Hills, Mo.
				Cochran, 3 and 2	Hardin, 4 and 2	Howard J. Klein, Kokomo, Ind.
	Stahl, 1 up, 21 hls.					Hord W. Hardin, Bellerive, Mo.
					Francis, 2 and 1	Richard S. Norville, Oklahoma City, Okla.
				Coe, 4 and 3		Gene Francis, Wheatley Hills, N.Y.
					Coe	BYE–Bob Coe, Jr., Knox County, Ill.
			Coe, 3 and 2		O'Brien, 6 and 5	Patrick J. O'Brien, Sherwood Forest, La.
				O'Brien, 7 and 5		E.A. McCardell, Jr., Newton, Iowa
		Stockton, 3 and 2			Proctor	BYE–John A. Proctor, III, Olympia Fields, Ill.
					Attwell, 3 and 1	Kirby Attwell, River Oaks, Texas
				Attwell, 2 up		Mauricio Urdaneta, Mexico City, Mexico
					Culp	BYE–John D. Culp, Jr., St. Andrews, Ill.
			Stockton, 2 and 1		Stockton, 4 and 3	William Hyndman, III, Huntingdon Valley, Pa.
				Stockton, 6 and 5		David K. Stockton, Arrowhead, Calif.
					Carroll, 1 up	Robert L. Carroll, Blue Hills, Mo.
						Alex Antonio Jr., Squaw Creek, Ohio

THIRD QUARTER

1st Round (18 Holes)	2nd Round (18 Holes)	3rd Round (18 Holes)	4th Round (18 Holes)	5th Round (18 Holes)	6th Round (18 Holes)	
Merrill L. Carlsmith, Hilo, Hawaii	Green, 3 and 2					
Peter J. Green, Orchard Lake, Mich.		Green, 3 and 2				
J.D. Turner, Perry, Iowa	Compiano, 3 and 2					
Ralph J. Compiano, Hyperion Field, Iowa			Jewell, 1 up			
BYE—Fred L. Mueller, Manor, Md.	Mueller					
		Jewell, 3 and 2				
James W. Jewell, Indiana University, Ind.	Jewell, 3 and 1			Owens, 3 and 1		
Charles B. Smith, Gaston, N.C.						
Walter G. Atwood, Blackhawk, Wis.	Harvey, 1 up					
Ernest W. Harvey, Sedgefield, N.C.		Harvey, 3 and 2				
BYE—Fletcher Jones, Bel Air, Calif.	Jones					
			Owens, 1 up			
Frank A. Dalvito, Cedar Hill, N.J.	Dalvito, 4 and 2					
Arthur W. Schwartz, Piping Rock, N.Y.		Owens, 5 and 3				
BYE—John C. Owens, Lexington, Ky.	Owens					
					Owens, 2 up	
Vernon S. Novak, Jr., Univ. of Maryland, Md.	Palmer, 2 and 1					
Ray Palmer, Grosse Ile, Mich.		Palmer, 1 up				
BYE—Neil Croonquist, Interlachen, Minn.	Croonquist					
			Campbell, 6 and 5			
BYE—Marvin M. Giles, III, Boonsboro, Va.	Giles					
		Campbell, 4 and 2				
Dick M. Murphy, Texarkana, Ark.	Campbell, 3 and 2			Campbell, 4 and 3		
William C. Campbell, Guyan, W. Va.						
Arthur D. Hudnutt, Elyria, Ohio	Patton, 3 and 2					
William J. Patton, Mimosa Hills, N.C.		Patton, 3 and 2				
BYE—Frederick E. Franz, Crystal Lake, Ill.	Franz					
			Greenwood, 4 and 2			
Bruce E. Rotte, Kenwood, Ohio	Greenwood, 4 and 3					
Robert S. Greenwood, Jr., Arnold Center, Tenn.		Greenwood, 3 and 2				
Richard L. Siderowf, Birchwood, Conn.	Siderowf, 1 up					
Tom Draper, Red Run, Mich.						Sikes, 6 and 4
BYE—Rodney Bliss, III, Wakonda, Iowa	Bliss					
		Bliss, 4 and 2				
Gregg McHatton, Candlewood, Calif.	McHatton, 1 up					
David M. Good, Spring Valley, W. Va.			Bliss, 4 and 3			
BYE—Buddy Hamilton, Tascoa, Texas	Hamilton					
		Butler, 1 up				
Dr. Arthur F. Butler, Glendora, Calif.	Butler, 1 up			Tutwiler, 6 and 5		
Roger H. Holstein, Fort Belvoir, Va.						
Tomas Lehman, Mexico City, Mexico	Tutwiler, 4 and 3					
Edgar M. Tutwiler, Jr., Berry Hills, W.Va.		Tutwiler, 5 and 3				
BYE—Peter W. Parish, Albuquerque, N.M.	Parish					
			Tutwiler, 2 and 1			
David Griffith, Charlotte, N.C.	Griffith, 3 and 1					
Thomas B. Evans, Jr., Wilmington, Del.		Griffith, 6 and 5				
BYE—E. Sheldon Blades, Jr., Talbot, Md.	Blades					
					Sikes, 1 up	
BYE—Sam D. Kocsis, Atlas Valley, Mich.	Kocsis					
		Sikes, 5 and 3				
Jerry M. Greenbaum, Standard, Ga.	Sikes, 3 and 2					
Richard H. Sikes, Fayetteville, Ark.			Sikes, 1 up			
BYE—Tom W. Matey, Knollwood, Ill.	Matey					
		Lotz, 1 up, 19 hls.				
Dodd Fischer, Eugene, Ore.	Lotz, 2 and 1			Sikes, 2 and 1		
Dick Lotz, Olympic, Calif.						
BYE—Frank J. Moroney, Galloping Hill, N.J.	Moroney					
		Ferriell, 1 up				
Thomas K. Reed, Broomfield, Colo.	Ferriell, 3 and 2					
James A. Ferriell, Jr., Seneca, Ky.			Ferriell, 4 and 3			
BYE—William Wakeham, Victoria, B.C., Canada	Wakeham					
		Zemljak, 4 and 2				
Edgar F. Bradley, Kenwood, Ohio	Zemljak, 1 up					
Edward F. Zemljak, Butte, Mont.						

SEMI-FINAL ROUND (36 Holes)—Richard H. Sikes defeated Charles R. Coe, 2 up and 1 to play.

PIONSHIP
HALF

FOURTH QUARTER

6th Round (18 Holes)	5th Round (18 Holes)	4th Round (18 Holes)	3rd Round (18 Holes)	2nd Round (18 Holes)	1st Round (18 Holes)
				Chew, 1 up	Ted Adams, Encanto, Ariz. James H. Chew, Prairie Dunes, Kans.
			McBee, 1 up	McBee, 1 up	James Hoak, Jr., Wakonda, Iowa Rives R. McBee, N. Texas State College, Texas
		Coe, 7 and 5		James	BYE—Daniel B. James, Green Hills, Calif.
			Coe, 6 and 5	Coe, 3 and 1	William P. Castleman, Jr., Greenbrier, W. Va. Charles R. Coe, Oklahoma City, Okla.
		Coe, 2 and 1		Dorman, 1 up	Roy E. Marquette, DuPont, Del. William P. Dorman, Freeport, Ill.
			Allen, 5 and 4	Allen	BYE—Donald C. Allen, C.C. of Rochester, N.Y.
		Allen, 2 and 1		**J. Cleveland, 4 and 2**	Kenneth L. Folkes, Old Town, N.C. James R. Cleveland, Jr., Capital City, Ga.
			Birmingham, 6 and 5	Birmingham	BYE—John Birmingham, Oakmont, Pa.
	Coe, 8 and 7			Peterson, 4 and 3	James A. Jamieson, Short Hills, Ill. Les Peterson, Univ. of Minnesota, Minn.
			Peterson, 7 and 6	Brauer	BYE—Luis Brauer, Tlalpan, Mexico City, Mexico
		Thompson, 1 up		**R. Cleveland**	BYE—Roger Cleveland, Virginia, Calif.
			Thompson, 1 up	Thompson, 1 up, 19 hls.	Bill Garrett, Wichita Falls, Texas James C. Thompson, Jr., C.C. of Austin, Texas
		Thompson, 2 and 1		Murphy, 3 and 2	Pat Foy Brady, Penrose Park, N.C. Dan P. Murphy, Texarkana, Ark.
			Pidlaski, 4 and 2	Pidlaski	BYE—William Pidlaski, Winnipeg, Man., Canada
		Harvey, 4 and 3		Harvey, 2 up	Robert C. Harvey, Jr., Milburn, Kans. Murray Kleimon, Brandywine, Del.
			Harvey, 6 and 4	Dreyfus	BYE—John Dreyfus, Century, N.Y.
Coe, 6 and 4				Hanson	BYE—Eric Hanson, Etobicoke, Ont., Canada
			English, 2 and 1	English, 2 and 1	James A. Grant, III, Wethersfield, Conn. James R. English, Columbine, Colo.
		Gordon, 1 up, 19 hls.		Gordon	BYE—Fred L. Gordon, Clarmond, Iowa
			Gordon, 2 and 1	Boutell, 7 and 5	Loyal H. Chapman, Minneapolis, Minn. George W. Boutell, Phoenix, Ariz.
		Mitchell, 4 and 3		Davies, 6 and 4	Richard D. Davies, St. Andrews, Fife, Scotland Richard G. Babbitt, Mauh-Nah-Tee-See, Ill.
			Mitchell, 2 and 1	Mitchell	BYE—Ross E. Mitchell, Lubbock, Texas
		Mitchell, 4 and 3		Gilbert	BYE—Jim Gilbert, Singing Hills, Calif.
			Kunsaw, 1 up	Kunsaw, 4 and 3	Albert J. Gray, Jr., Moundsville, W. Va. Andrew Kunsaw, Preakness Valley, N.J.
	Guardiola, 2 and 1			Timbrook, 6 and 4	Brian McGuinn, Marshfield, Mass. Henry Timbrook, Jr., Lake Merced, Calif.
			Timbrook, 5 and 3	Blancas	BYE—Homero Blancas, Jr., Champions, Texas
		McManus, 5 and 4		McManus, 4 and 2	Roger T. McManus, Congress Lake, Ohio Mark Hopkins, Pine Forest, Texas
		Guardiola, 3 and 1	McManus, 1 up, 19 hls.	Andrade	BYE—Mike Andrade, Brook Hollow, Texas
			Guardiola, 3 and 2	Farquhar, 5 and 4	Jose Luis Ortega, Mexico City, Mexico John Farquhar, Amarillo, Texas
				Guardiola	BYE—Richard Guardiola, Shaker Heights, Ohio
		Guardiola, 3 and 1	Norbury, 2 and 1	Norbury, 4 and 3	Donald M. Norbury, Wildwood, N.J. Jerry P. Potter, Bayshore, Fla.
				Brooks, 1 up	Wilson Brooks, Cherokee Town, Ga. Frederick H. Ewald, Oakland Hills, Mich.

1964
SIXTY-FOURTH AMATEUR CHAMPIONSHIP

Held at the Canterbury Golf Club, Cleveland, Ohio, September 14-19.
Yardage—6,863. Par 71. 1,562 Entries, 150 Qualifiers, 150 Starters.

Qualifying Score	1st Round (18 Holes)	2nd Round (18 Holes)	3rd Round (18 Holes)	4th Round (18 Holes)	Semi-Finals (36 Holes)	Final (36 Holes)	
143	*Marvin M. Giles, III, Boonsboro, Va.	Giles, 5 and 4					
150	Tom W. Matey, Knollwood, Ill.		Patton, 4 and 2				
148	William J. Patton, Mimosa Hills, N.C.	Patton, 4 and 3					
152	Peter Green, Orchard Lake, Mich.			Campbell, 5 and 4			
146	William C. Campbell, Guyan, W. Va.	Campbell, 1 up, 20 hls.					
151	George Blocker, Jr., Jal, N.M.		Campbell, 1 up				
149	Harry Toscano, Jr., New Castle, Pa.	Toscano, 6 and 5					
153	Neil C. Croonquist, Interlachen, Minn.				Campbell, 1 up, 19 hls.		
145	Dale Morey, Sedgefield, N.C.	Morey, 2 and 1					
151	John D. McKey, Jr., C.C. of Orlando, Fla.		Morey, 3 and 2				
149	James L. Wiechers, Sharon Heights, Calif.	Wiechers, 5 and 4					
153	Robert W. Allen, Wampanoag, Conn.			Morey, 1 up			
146	Bill Harvey, Sedgefield, N. C.	Siderowf, 1 up					
151	Richard Siderowf, Birchwood, Conn.		Kocsis, 4 and 3				
149	Charles Kocsis, Red Run, Mich.	Kocsis, 4 and 3					
153	Gardner R. Thompson, Pleasant Valley, Mass.					Campbell, 3 and 1	
145	James G. Jackson, Greenbriar Hills, Mo.	Hopkins, 2 and 1					
151	John M. Hopkins, Texas City, Texas		Hopkins, 1 up				
148	Dr. Edgar R. Updegraff, Tucson, Ariz.	Updegraff, 3 and 2					
152	Melvin Stevens, Western, Mich.			Hopkins, 3 and 2			
146	Ralph F. Schlicht, Blackhawk, Wis.	Boldt, 1 up, 19 hls.					
151	Robert Boldt, Shadow Hills, Ore.		Boldt, 2 and 1				
149	Grier S. Jones, Wichita, Kans.	Birmingham, 5 and 4					
153	John R. Birmingham, Oakmont, Pa.				Hopkins, 3 and 2		
146	Gerald L. Schreiber, Evansville, Ind.	Schreiber, 4 and 3					
151	Robert C. Harvey, Jr., Milburn, Kans.		Schreiber, 5 and 4				
149	Richard Guardiola, Shaker Heights, Ohio	Milligan, 2 and 1					
153	Thomas W. Milligan, Hinsdale, Ill.			Smith, 4 and 3			
147	Charles B. Smith, Gaston, N.C.	Smith, 2 and 1					
151	Thomas W. Barnes, Jr., Atlanta Athletic, Ga.		Smith, 4 and 3				
150	James A. Nordine, Chagrin Valley, Ohio	McManus, 1 up					
153	Roger T. McManus, Congress Lake, Ohio						William C. Campbell, 1 up
143	*Robert Greenwood, Jr., Arnold AF, Tenn.	Greenwood, 1 up					
150	Wright Garrett, Danville, Va.		Eichelberger, 2 and 1				
148	Dr. Robert R. Reilly, Highland, Pa.	Eichelberger, 2 and 1					
152	Davis Eichelberger, Ridgewood, Texas			Eichelberger, 3 and 1			
146	James A. Grant, III, Wethersfield, Conn.	Grant, 1 up					
151	Donald E. Albert, Brookside, Ohio		Cerrudo, 1 up				
149	Ronald J. Cerrudo, Castlewood, Calif.	Cerrudo, 3 and 1					
153	Alfred M. Johns, Port Charlotte, Fla.				Eichelberger, 3 and 1		
145	Jimmy Allen, Athens, Ga.	Kammer, 6 and 5					
151	Fred Kammer, Jr., C.C. of Detroit, Mich.		Kammer, 1 up				
149	Robert B. Dickson, Muskogee, Okla.	Dickson, 6 and 5					
153	Ron Jamison, University of Maryland, Md.			Allen, 1 up			
147	Robert W. Gardner, Baltusrol, N.J.	St. Germain, 1 up					
151	James R. St. Germain, Meadowbrook, Mich.		Allen, 4 and 3				
150	David M. Good, Spring Valley, W. Va.	Allen, 3 and 2					
153	Donald C. Allen, C.C. of Rochester, N.Y.					Tutwiler, 3 and 2	
145	Charles H. Greene, Deane Hill, Tenn.	Colbert, 2 and 1					
151	James J. Colbert, Jr., Sante Fe Hills, Mo.		Colbert, 7 and 6				
148	John O. Eisinger, Jr., Congressional, Md.	Eisinger, 6 and 5					
152	Edwin D. Preisler, Beechmont, Ohio			Ferrell, 2 and 1			
146	Robert O. McCall, Gary, Ind.	Ferrell, 3 and 2					
151	William E. Ferrell, Jr., C.C. of Mobile, Ala.		Ferrell, 1 up				
149	Deane R. Beman, Congressional, Md.	Novak, 4 and 2					
153	Vernon S. Novak, Jr., University of Md., Md.				Tutwiler, 1 up, 20 hls.		
146	Edgar M. Tutwiler, Jr., Highlands, Ind.	Tutwiler, 2 and 1					
151	Jim L. Awtrey, Elks, Okla.		Tutwiler, 1 up				
149	Jack Thornton, Oak Hill, N.Y.	Spengler, 3 and 1					
153	Paul Spengler, Jr., Waialae, Hawaii			Tutwiler, 1 up			
147	A. Downing Gray, Pensacola, Fla.	Gray, 3 and 2					
152	James R. Cleveland, Jr., Capital City, Ga.		Spooner, 1 up 20 hls.				
150	Rives R. McBee, Eastern Hills, Texas	Spooner, 2 and 1					
153	Leo J. Spooner, Northland, Minn.						

*Co-Medalists.
The first word after the player's name is the name of the player's club.

1965
SIXTY-FIFTH AMATEUR CHAMPIONSHIP

Held at Southern Hills Country Club, Tulsa, Okla., September 15-18.
Yardage—6,917. Par 71.
1,476 Entries, 150 Qualifiers, 150 Starters.

Sixty-six contestants who completed 72 holes.

						Score
1	Robert J. Murphy, Jr., Lone Palm C.C., Lakeland, Fla.	73	69	76	73	291
2	Robert B. Dickson, Muskogee, Okla.	71	75	72	74	292
3	Donald C. Allen, C.C. of Rochester, Rochester, N.Y.	70	74	76	73	293
	Cesar Sanudo, Carlton Oaks C.C., Santee, Calif.	71	76	72	74	293
5	James W. Vickers, Wichita C.C., Wichita, Kansas	69	77	73	75	294
6	Charles H. Greene, Deane Hill C.C., Knoxville, Tenn.	76	75	72	72	295
	Rodney Horn, Milburn C.C., Overland Park, Kans.	74	77	70	74	295
8	Thomas W. Barnes, Jr., Atlanta Athletic Club, Atlanta, Ga.	70	79	76	71	296
	Ronald J. Cerrudo, Castlewood C.C., Pleasanton, Calif.	76	78	70	72	296
	William C. Campbell, Guyan G. & C.C., Huntington, W. Va.	73	71	75	77	296
	James A. Grant, III, Wethersfield, C.C., Wethersfield, Conn.	69	75	74	78	296
12	A. Downing Gray, Pensacola C.C., Pensacola, Fla.	81	70	73	73	297
	Jack W. Lewis, Jr., Florence C.C., Florence, S.C.	76	79	69	73	297
	Charles W. Harrison, Atlanta Athletic Club, Atlanta, Ga.	77	73	71	76	297
	Charles R. Coe, Southern Hills C.C., Tulsa, Okla.	72	73	72	80	297
16	John Farquhar, Amarillo C.C., Amarillo, Texas	73	79	71	75	298
17	George W. Boutell, Phoenix C.C., Phoenix, Ariz.	75	76	75	73	299
	Edgar M. Tutwiler, Jr., Highland C.C., Indianapolis, Ind.	76	75	75	73	299
19	Robert Greenwood, Jr., Cookeville C.C., Cookeville, Tenn.	78	77	74	71	300
	William J. Patton, Mimosa Hills G.C., Morganton, N.C.	73	76	78	73	300
	Howard Everitt, Pine Tree G.C., Boynton Beach, Fla.	74	76	76	74	300
	Ralph M. Bogart, Chevy Chase Club, Chevy Chase, Md.	75	79	70	76	300
23	Tom Culligan, California G.C., So. San Francisco, Calif.	76	74	77	74	301
	Charles Lewis, Santee, Calif.	71	79	77	74	301
	Robert Littler, Jr., Athens C.C., Athens, Ohio	74	77	74	76	301
	Sandy C. Saddler, Forfar, Angus, Scotland	75	79	71	76	301
27	Rodney Foster, Bradford, Yorkshire, England	79	75	76	72	302
	Leon Anderson, Hobbs C.C., Hobbs, N.M.	76	79	75	72	302
	Bill Holstead, Weeks Park G.A., Wichita Falls, Texas	78	73	75	76	302
	Lee S. Davis, Jr., Los Angeles C.C., Los Angeles, Calif.	75	77	74	76	302
31	Gordon B. Gosh, Glasgow, Scotland	76	75	79	73	303
	Benny Castloo, Mineola C.C., Mineola, Texas	72	79	78	74	303
	Edwin B. Hopkins, Jr., Brook Hollow G.C., Dallas, Texas	76	77	75	75	303
	Jim A. Jamieson, Short Hills C.C., East Moline, Ill.	75	79	74	75	303
	Neil Croonquist, Interlachen C.C., Minneapolis, Minn.	76	74	77	76	303
	Robert Lowry, Jr., Huntsville C.C., Huntsville, Ala.	75	72	79	77	303
	Sherman Finger, Westmoreland C.C., Wilmette, Ill.	78	76	72	77	303
38	Joseph B. Carr, Sutton, Dublin, Ireland	77	77	77	73	304
	E. Harvie Ward, Jr., San Francisco G.C., San Francisco, Calif.	77	78	75	74	304
	Robert E. Stroope, El Dorado Men's G.A., Houston, Texas	76	76	77	75	304
	William Hyndman, III, Huntingdon Valley C.C., Abington, Pa.	75	78	76	75	304
	Charles B. Smith, Gaston C.C., Gastonia, N.C.	73	79	75	77	304
	Jim Tom Blair, Meadowbrook C.C., Ballwin, Mo.	71	81	74	78	304
	Dennis Rouse, Bayshore Golfers Club, Miami Beach, Fla.	74	76	73	81	304
45	Dr. Edgar R. Updegraff, Tucson C.C., Tucson, Ariz.	76	77	75	77	305
	John R. Birmingham, Oakmont C.C., Oakmont, Pa.	82	73	76	74	305
	Eugene Dahlbender, Jr., No. Fulton G.A., Atlanta, Ga.	78	73	79	75	305
	J. Mark Hopkins, Texas City C.C., Texas City, Texas	76	77	73	79	305
	William Hyndman, IV, Huntingdon Valley C.C., Abington, Pa.	75	76	74	80	305
	Ray Terry, Timuquana C.C., Jacksonville, Fla.	70	80	74	81	305
51	Dan Carmichael, Columbus C.C., Columbus, Ohio	77	77	77	75	306
	Roger Brown, Lakeside G.C., Stillwater, Okla.	76	75	77	78	306
53	Michael F. Bonallack, Thorpe Bay, Essex, England	72	79	78	78	307
	Richard J. Sucher, Ozaukee C.C., Mequoh, Wis.	75	73	80	79	307
55	James McHugh, Wayland C.C., Wayland, Mass.	76	79	79	74	308
	Marion Heck, Fort Meyers Men's G.A., Fort Meyers, Fla.	76	76	79	77	308
	John T. Thornton, Oak Hills C.C., San Antonio, Texas	76	77	77	78	308
	William F. Hall, Fayetteville C.C., Fayetteville, Ark.	73	75	78	82	308
	Dale Morey, Willow Creek G.C., High Point, N.C.	72	74	76	86	308
60	Peter Green, Orchard Lake C.C., Orchard Lake, Mich.	76	76	81	77	310
	Richard D. Davies, Annandale G.C., Pasadena, Calif.	75	76	75	84	310
62	Davis Eichelberger, Ridgewood C.C., Waco, Texas	77	76	79	80	312
63	Ron Schmedemann, Manhattan C.C., Manhattan, Kansas	75	78	78	82	313
64	Richard Guardiola, Shaker Heights C.C., Shaker Heights, Ohio	81	74	82	77	314
65	Robert C. Smith, Little River Inn C.C., Little River, Calif.	79	76	80	81	316
66	John D. Phillips, Lincoln Greens G.C., Springfield, Ill.	72	82	80	84	318

1966
SIXTY-SIXTH AMATEUR CHAMPIONSHIP

Held at Merion Golf Club (East Course), Ardmore, Pa., August 31-September 4.
Yardage—6,509. Par 70.
1,902 Entries, 146 Qualifiers, 150 Starters.

Sixty-seven contestants who completed 72 holes.

						Score
1	Gary Cowan, Westmount G.C., Kitchener, Ontario, Canada	74	72	72	67	285+
2	Deane R. Beman, Bethesda C.C., Bethesda, Md.	71	67	76	71	285+
3	Jack W. Lewis, Jr., Florence C.C., Florence, S.C.	73	69	75	69	286
	Ronald Cerrudo, G.C. of California, San Francisco, Calif.	70	75	70	71	286
	A. Downing Gray, Pensacola C.C., Pensacola, Fla.	74	72	68	72	286
6	Donald C. Allen, C.C. of Rochester, Rochester, N.Y.	71	72	73	71	287
	Richard L. Siderowf, Birchwood C.C., Westport, Conn.	71	73	72	71	287
8	James A. Grant, III, Wethersfield C.C., Wethersfield, Conn.	74	75	70	70	289
	Michael E. Morley, Papago G.C., Phoenix, Ariz.	71	74	70	74	289
10	Lewis W. Oehmig, Chattanooga G. & C.C., Chattanooga, Tenn.	74	71	75	70	290
11	Edgar M. Tutwiler, Jr., Highland G. & C.C., Indianapolis, Ind.	72	77	72	70	291
	Charles W. Harrison, Atlanta A.C., Atlanta, Ga.	73	75	70	73	291
13	Nick Weslock, Mississaugua G. & C.C., Port Credit, Ont., Canada	76	74	70	72	292
	William C. Campbell, Guyan G. & C.C., Huntington, W. Va.	74	69	76	73	292
	Robert B. Dickson, Muskogee C.C., Muskogee, Okla.	77	72	69	74	292
16	James Rheim, San Diego C.C., Chula Vista, Calif.	75	70	75	73	293
	Robert Littler, Jr., Athens C.C., Athens, Ohio	71	76	73	73	293
18	Jerry (Lanny) Wadkins, Jr., Meadowbrook C.C., Richmond, Va.	75	75	73	71	294
	Leonard S. Thompson, Scotch Meadows C.C., Laurinburg, N.C.	71	74	74	75	294
20	Robert J. Murphy, Jr., Lone Palm C.C., Lakeland, Fla.	73	76	73	73	295
	Ron Schmedemann, Manhattan C.C., Manhattan, Kansas	74	69	77	75	295
	William J. Patton, Mimosa Hills, G.C., Morganton, N.C.	73	73	74	75	295
	Roger T. McManus, Congress Lake C., Hartville, Ohio	69	73	74	79	295
24	James P. King, Sunny Jim G.C., Medford, N.J.	72	78	77	69	296
	H. Ward Wettlaufer, Pinetree C.C., Kennesaw, Ga.	73	74	71	78	296
26	Bill Harvey, Sedgefield C.C., Greensboro, N.C.	76	74	74	73	297
	Bunky Henry, Valdosta C.C., Valdosta, Ga.	73	78	73	73	297
	Thomas W. Beck, Southern Hills C.C., Tulsa, Okla.	74	77	72	74	297
29	R. Hunter McDonald, Oakland Hills C.C., Birmingham, Mich.	75	77	75	71	298
	Sherman W. Finger III, Kishwaukee C.C., DeKalb, Ill.	75	77	69	77	298
31	Marty Fleckman, Port Arthur C.C., Port Arthur, Texas	74	75	77	73	299
	Robert E. Cole, Geduld G.C., Springs, Transvaal, South Africa	80	72	71	76	299
33	Robert R. Kirouac, Sharon C.C., Sharon, Mass.	72	79	78	71	300
	Jack Ewing, Jr., Bakersfield C.C., Bakersfield, Calif.	76	75	74	75	300
	John P. Cain, Champions G.C., Houston, Texas	80	72	72	76	300
	Stanley E. Bishop, Pine Brook C.C., Weston, Mass.	79	73	71	77	300
	Gerard M. Courville, Shorehaven G.C., East Norwalk, Conn.	73	72	77	78	300
38	Bob Boldt, Oswego Lake C.C., Lake Oswego, Ore.	73	77	78	73	301
	Frederick Jones, Brookside G. & C.C., Worthington, Ohio	79	73	75	74	301
	Marvin M. Giles III, Boonsboro C.C., Lynchburg, Va.	76	73	78	74	301
	Howard Everitt, Delray Beach, Fla.	75	76	74	76	301
	Thomas M. Smith, Greensburg C.C., Greensburg, Pa.	73	79	73	76	301
	Arthur Brunn, Wilkes-Barre Municipal G.A., Wilkes-Barre, Pa.	73	73	78	77	301
	Terrance L. Dear, University Golfers' Assn., Albuquerque, N.M.	77	73	74	77	301
45	Cameron P. Quinn, West Warwick C.C., West Warwick, R.I.	76	72	78	76	302
46	Charles Kocsis, Red Run G.C., Royal Oak, Mich.	73	76	78	76	303
	Michael E. Riley, Singing Hills C.C., El Cajon, Calif.	77	75	73	78	303
	Guy L. Bill, Sequoyah C.C., Oakland, Calif.	76	74	74	79	303
49	William Hyndman III, Huntingdon Valley C.C., Abington, Pa.	72	76	80	76	304
	Dick Runkle, Los Angeles C.C., Los Angeles, Calif.	71	79	77	77	304
	Kai G. Thomsen, Marin G.C., Novato, Calif.	72	79	76	77	304
	Lamont Kaser, MacDonald Park G.C., Wichita, Kansas	74	76	73	81	304
53	Gerald McFerren, Forsgate C.C., Jamesburg, N.J.	71	77	78	79	305
	Jerry Greenbaum, Standard Town & C.C., Atlanta, Ga.	70	78	75	82	305
55	Arnold Blum, Idle Hour G. & C.C., Macon, Ga.	75	75	80	77	307
	Robert W. Kuntz, Winged Foot G.C., Mamaroneck, N.Y.	75	76	79	77	307
	Dr. Edgar R. Updegraff, Tucson C.C., Tucson, Ariz.	72	79	78	78	307
58	Edward L. Meister Jr., Kirtland C.C., Willoughby, Ohio	76	76	78	78	308
	James G. Jackson, Greenbrier Hills C.C., Kirkwood, Mo.	76	75	77	80	308
	Truman F. Connell, Pine Tree G.C., Delray Beach, Fla.	77	74	76	81	308
	Dan Carmichael, Columbus C.C., Columbus, Ohio	78	74	75	81	308
	Gary C. Wright, Cherry Hills C.C., Englewood, Colo.	75	76	75	82	308
63	Harold R. Eller, Old Hickory G.C., Old Hickory, Tenn.	75	77	83	75	310
	Ralph F. Schlicht, Blackhawk C.C., Madison, Wis.	75	73	85	77	310
65	Robert M. Beirne, Riverton C.C., Riverton, N.J.	74	76	80	81	311
	M.O. Johnston, Jr., La Jolla C.C., La Jolla, Calif.	76	75	77	83	311
67	Eugene A. Howard, Bob O'Link G.C., Highland Park, Ill.	76	76	83	80	315

+Play-off: 18 holes, Sept. 4—Cowan, 75; Beman, 76.

1967
SIXTY-SEVENTH AMATEUR CHAMPIONSHIP

Held at Broadmoor Golf Club (West Course), Colorado Springs, Colo., August 30-September 2.
Yardage—6,946. Par 70.
1,784 Entries, 150 Qualifiers, 150 Starters.

Fifty-two contestants who completed 72 holes.

						Score
1	Robert B. Dickson, McAlester C.C., McAlester, Okla.	71	71	74	69	285
2	Marvin M. Giles III, Boonsboro C.C., Lynchburg, Va.	76	69	72	69	286
3	Ronald J. Cerrudo, California G.C., San Francisco, Calif.	75	73	73	68	289
4	A. Downing Gray, Pensacola C.C., Pensacola, Fla.	75	72	70	73	290
5	Robert J. Murphy, Jr., Lone Palm G.C., Lakeland, Fla.	77	75	69	70	291
6	Marty Fleckman, Port Arthur C.C., Port Arthur, Texas	74	73	70	75	292
7	Jack Ewing, Jr., Bakersfield C.C., Bakersfield, Calif.	78	75	75	67	295
	William C. Campbell, Guyan G. & C.C., Huntington, W. Va.	78	70	74	73	295
	Robert E. Smith, Del Paso C.C., Sacramento, Calif.	78	70	76	71	295
	Doug Olson, Rogue Valley C.C., Medford, Ore.	73	73	71	78	295
11	Donald C. Allen, C.C. of Rochester, Rochester, N.Y.	74	76	72	74	296
	Jay Sigel, Aronimink G.C., Newtown Square, Pa.	73	75	73	75	296
13	Grier S. Jones, Wichita C.C., Wichita, Kans.	77	77	73	70	297
	James Simons, Butler C.C., Butler, Pa.	79	74	69	75	297
	John H. Liechty, Elmwood C.C., Marshalltown, Iowa	76	76	74	71	297
16	Thomas S. Watson, Kansas City C.C., Shawnee Mission, Kans.	78	75	74	71	298
	Gary Cowan, Westmount G.C., Kitchener, Ontario, Canada	73	74	74	77	298
	John Miller, The Olympic Club, San Francisco, Calif.	81	74	69	74	298
19	Larry W. Hinson, Johnson City C.C., Johnson City, Tenn.	78	73	74	75	300
20	Edgar M. Tutwiler, Jr., Highland C.C., Indianapolis, Ind.	78	76	72	75	301
	Mickey McDonald, Champions G.C., Houston, Texas	77	77	75	72	301
	Benson R. McLendon, Jr., Bonnie Crest C.C., Montgomery, Ala.	77	76	75	73	301
	Steven N. Melnyk, Brunswick C.C., Brunswick, Ga.	79	76	70	76	301
24	John Farquhar, Amarillo C.C., Amarillo, Texas	80	74	76	72	302
	John R. Birmingham, Oakmont C.C., Oakmont, Pa.	80	73	73	76	302
	Warren L. Simmons, Shawnee C.C., Milford, Del.	78	74	77	73	302
	Jack Veghte, East Bay C.C., Largo, Fla.	76	75	73	78	302
	John Baldwin, Plandome C.C., Plandome, N.Y.	77	73	77	75	302
	Richard Spears, Port Jervis C.C., Port Jervis, N.Y.	80	69	74	79	302
30	Michael J. Nesbit, Bethesda C.C., Bethesda, Md.	74	77	74	78	303
	Peter J. Green, Orchard Lake C.C., Orchard Lake, Mich.	81	74	74	74	303
32	Mahlon Moe, Spokane C.C., Spokane, Wash.	76	77	76	75	304
33	Cameron P. Quinn, West Warwick C.C., West Warwick, R.I.	74	75	78	78	305
34	Michael A. Mitchell, El Dorado Men's G.A., Houston, Texas	81	73	76	76	306
	Edward L. Everett, Idle Hour G. & C.C., Macon, Ga.	77	76	76	77	306
	Robert O. McCall, Gary C.C., Gary, Ind.	77	75	79	75	306
	Ray Leach, The Olympic Club, San Francisco, Calif.	79	76	72	79	306
38	James M. English, Columbine C.C., Littleton, Colo.	78	75	76	78	307
	Stanley J. Thompson, Jr., Midland C.C., Midland, Mich.	82	73	77	75	307
	Ralph M. Bogart, Chevy Chase Club, Chevy Chase, Md.	78	77	73	79	307
41	Bill Harvey, Sedgefield Club, Greensboro, N.C.	78	72	81	78	309
	Brian Willard, Burning Tree Club, Bethesda, Md.	81	74	78	76	309
43	Jeff Parry, Zanesville C.C., Zanesville, Ohio	78	75	78	79	310
	Harvey Smith, Atlantic City C.C., Northfield, N.J.	79	75	80	76	310
45	Dr. Harry Duccilli, Jr., Wyoming G.C., Wyoming, Ohio	77	75	79	80	311
46	James G. Jackson, Greenbriar Hills C.C., Kirkwood, Mo.	80	75	78	79	312
47	Michael T. Norman, Muskogee G.C., Muskogee, Okla.	77	76	75	85	313
	Miles Childers, Amarillo C.C., Amarillo, Texas	79	76	81	77	313
49	Don Hawken, Jr., Marin C.C., Novato, Calif.	81	72	76	85	314
50	Morris B. Beecroft, Jr., James River C.C., Newport News, Va.	80	74	81	83	318
	Roger Z. Brown, Lakeside Golf Ass'n., Stillwater, Okla.	80	75	80	83	318
52	Terrence Curran, Kansas City C.C., Shawnee Mission, Kansas	81	74	85	79	319

1968
SIXTY-EIGHTH AMATEUR CHAMPIONSHIP

Held at Scioto Country Club, Columbus, Ohio, August 28-31.
Yardage—6,762. Par 70.
2,057 Entries, 150 Qualifiers, 150 Starters.

Fifty-nine contestants who completed 72 holes.

						Score
1	Bruce Fleisher, C.C. of Miami, Miami, Fla.	73	70	71	70	284
2	Marvin M. Giles, III, Boonsboro C.C., Lynchburg, Va.	75	72	73	65	285
3	John Bohmann, Chaparral C.C., Seguin, Texas	74	73	74	67	288
4	Hubert M. Green, C.C. of Birmingham, Birmingham, Ala.	72	71	73	73	289
5	Robert Barbarossa, Coral Ridge C.C., Ft. Lauderdale, Fla.	75	72	70	74	291
	Rik Massengale, Jacksboro G. & C.C., Jacksboro, Texas	73	75	74	69	291
7	Jack W. Lewis, Jr., Florence C.C., Florence, S.C.	74	74	70	75	293
8	William J. Patton, Mimosa Hills G.C., Morganton, N.C.	78	74	71	71	294
	Allen L. Miller, III, Pensacola C.C., Pensacola, Fla.	71	76	74	73	294
	Gary Cowan, Westmount G.C., Kitchener, Ont., Canada	78	75	73	68	294
11	John R. Birmingham, Oakmont C.C., Oakmont, Pa.	76	74	69	77	296
	Jerry Courville, Shorehaven G.C., East Norwalk, Conn.	73	73	75	75	296
	Rodney D. Curl, Riverview G. & C.C., Redding, Calif.	75	74	73	74	296
	Michael F. Bonallack, Thorpe Hall G.C., Essex, England	71	73	75	77	296
15	Robert Bramson, Brentwood C.C., Los Angeles, Calif.	76	71	77	73	297
16	Dale Morey, Willow Creek G.C., High Point, N.C.	72	73	76	77	298
17	Donald C. Allen, C.C. of Rochester, Rochester, N.Y.	73	76	77	73	299
	Roger T. McManus, Congress Lake Club, Hartville, Ohio	81	72	76	70	299
19	James B. Belton, Gaston C.C., Gastonia, N.C.	78	75	75	72	300
	Jack Veghte, East Bay C.C., Largo, Fla.	71	79	75	75	300
	E. Wayne Jackson, Jr., James River C.C., Newport News, Va.	73	79	76	72	300
	James Simons, Butler C.C., Butler, Pa.	73	78	77	72	300
	Frank F. Schmidt, Scarlet and Gray G.C., Columbus, Ohio	73	78	78	71	300
	Robert A. Roos, Jr., Peninsula G. & C.C., San Mateo, Calif.	80	73	76	71	300
25	Jerry M. Greenbaum, Standard Club, Atlanta, Ga.	73	76	77	75	301
	Bruce Ashworth, Paradise Valley C.C., Las Vegas, Nev.	75	78	74	74	301
	Edgar M. Tutwiler, Jr., Highland G. & C.C., Indianapolis, Ind.	75	75	77	74	301
	Thomas S. Watson, Kansas City C.C., Shawnee Mission, Kans.	75	75	72	79	301
	Michael Dow Taylor, Northwood C.C., Meridian, Miss.	73	77	78	73	301
	Jack Hesler, Scioto C.C., Columbus, Ohio	79	74	75	73	301
	Joseph C. Inman, Jr., Starmount Forest C.C., Greensboro, N.C.	77	72	72	80	301
	John P. Cain, Champions G.C., Houston, Texas	77	77	76	71	301
33	Robert Greenwood, Jr., Cookeville G. & C.C., Cookeville, Tenn.	76	74	71	81	302
	Lewis W. Oehmig, Chattanooga G. & C.C., Sugarland, Texas	72	77	75	78	302
	Thomas W. Jenkins, Riverbend C.C., Sugarland, Texas	73	76	75	78	302
	James Conace, Brookside G. & C.C., Worthington, Ohio	72	76	79	75	302
	Gerald L. Schreiber, Evansville C.C., Evansville, Ind.	77	75	77	73	302
	William C. Campbell, Guyan G. & C.C., Huntington, W. Va.	76	76	79	71	302
39	Robert (Yank) Heisler, Jr., Twin Lakes C.C., Kent, Ohio	76	77	72	78	303
	Thomas Culligan, San Mateo, Calif.	76	74	81	72	303
	Robert B. Huber, Jr., Hershey C.C., Hershey, Pa.	79	74	75	75	303
	Chip Stewart, Oak Cliff C.C., Dallas, Texas	77	70	81	75	303
43	Richard L. Siderowf, Birchwood C.C., Westport, Conn.	72	76	77	79	304
	John F. Disosway, Langley AFB G.C., Langley AFB, Va.	75	73	79	77	304
45	Donald M. Norbury, Buena Vista C.C., Buena, N.J.	74	74	77	80	305
	Jim Ward, Riviera C.C., Lesage, W. Va.	75	72	80	78	305
	William Hyndman, IV, Huntingdon Valley C.C., Abington, Pa.	75	77	77	76	305
48	Paul Erhardt, III, Sakima C.C., Carney Point, N.J.	74	75	81	76	306
	F.C. Bradley, Riviera C.C., Pacific Palisades, Calif.	79	74	77	76	306
	Stanley E. Bishop, Woodland G.C., Auburndale, Mass.	80	73	77	76	306
51	Neil Croonquist, Interlachen C.C., Edina, Minn.	78	72	79	78	307
52	Barry Jaeckel, Riviera C.C., Los Angeles, Calif.	78	75	75	80	308
53	James Shade, Norfolk C.C., Norfolk Neb.	76	78	76	79	309
54	John G. Capers, III, Merion G.C., Ardmore, Pa.	82	72	80	77	311
	Brad F. Lozares, Hillview G.C., Santa Clara, Calif.	78	74	81	78	311
	Robert J. Afton, Scarlet and Gray G.C., Columbus, Ohio	79	73	80	79	311
57	Eric Hanson, Scarboro G. & C.C., Scarborough, Ont., Canada	76	75	83	78	312
58	Robert W. Willson, Fort Myers Men's Golf Ass'n., Fort Myers, Fla.	77	72	82	82	313
59	Michael Thompson, Champaign C.C., Champaign, Ill.	76	76	84	79	315

1969
SIXTY-NINTH AMATEUR CHAMPIONSHIP

Held at Oakmont Country Club, Oakmont, Pennsylvania, August 27-30.
Yardage—6,670. Par 71.
2,142 Entries, 150 Qualifiers, 150 Starters.

Sixty-one contestants who completed 72 holes.

						Score
1	Steven N. Melnyk, Brunswick C.C., Brunswick, Ga.	70	73	73	70	286
2	Marvin M. Giles III, Boonsboro C.C., Lynchburg, Va.	72	75	72	72	291
3	Allen L. Miller, III, Pensacola C.C., Pensacola, Fla.	77	69	73	74	293
4	Robert I. Zender, Evanston G.C., Skokie, Ill.	75	78	72	70	295
5	John Farquhar, Amarillo C.C., Amarillo, Texas	73	74	76	73	296
	Thomas S. Watson, Kansas City C.C., Shawnee Mission, Kans.	74	75	72	75	296
7	Dr. Edgar R. Updegraff, Tuscon C.C., Tucson, Ariz.	74	77	73	73	297
8	Rodney Foster, Bradford G.C., Yorkshire, England	75	77	74	72	298
	Charles R. Coe, Oklahoma City G.C., Oklahoma City, Okla.	76	77	72	73	298
10	Bruce Ashworth, Paradise Valley C.C., Las Vegas, Nev.	74	73	76	76	299
11	Eddie Pearce, Temple Terrace G. & C.C., Temple Terrace, Fla.	77	74	76	73	300
	Lloyd Liebler, Elizabeth Manor G. & C.C., Portsmouth, Va.	75	77	75	73	300
	Lanny Wadkins, Meadowbrook C.C., Richmond, Va.	81	73	71	75	300
14	Andrew North, Cherokee C.C., Madison, Wis.	73	80	75	73	301
	Bruce Critchley, Sunningdale G.C., Sunningdale, Berkshire, England	78	77	73	73	301
	Michael F. Bonallack, Thorpe Hall G.C., Thorpe Bay, Essex, England	77	74	76	74	301
	James Masserio, Duquesne G. Ass'n., Pittsburgh, Pa.	74	74	77	76	301
	Bob Allard, Corvallis C.C., Corvallis, Ore.	77	76	71	77	301
	Joseph C. Inman Jr., Starmount Forest C.C., Greensboro, N.C.	75	74	73	79	301
20	William Hyndman III, Huntingdon Valley C.C., Abington, Pa.	76	75	75	76	302
	James Rheim, Lakewood C.C., New Orleans, La.	73	75	76	78	302
22	Chip Stewart, Brookhaven C.C., Dallas, Texas	77	77	75	74	303
	David K. Oakley, Westwood C.C., Vienna, Va.	76	78	74	75	303
	Edgar M. Tutwiler, Jr., Highland G. & C.C., Indianapolis, Ind.	79	71	75	78	303
25	John Bohmann, Chaparral C.C., Seguin, Texas	80	74	76	74	304
	Geoff Marks, Trentham G.C., Staffordshire, England	83	71	76	74	304
	Roger T. McManus, Congress Lake C., Hartville, Ohio	77	72	77	78	304
	John M. Jackson, Jr., Papago G.C., Phoenix, Ariz.	79	72	75	78	304
	Richard L. Siderowf, Birchwood C.C., Westport, Conn.	75	77	71	81	304
30	Rian McNally, Castlewood C.C., Pleasanton, Calif.	75	73	84	73	305
	Chester Sanok, Upper Montclair C.C., Upper Montclair, N.J.	75	78	76	76	305
	Vaughn Moise, Lakewood C.C., New Orleans, La.	74	81	74	76	305
	L. Peter Tupling, Tankersley Park G.C., Yorkshire, England	78	77	74	76	305
	Gary Cowan, Westmount G.C., Kitchener, Ontario, Canada	79	76	74	76	305
	Donald C. Allen, C.C. of Rochester, Rochester, N.Y.	73	78	77	77	305
	C.W. Green, Dumbarton C.C., Dumbarton, Scotland	75	74	77	79	305
37	Thomas O. Kite, Jr., C.C. of Austin, Austin, Texas	77	75	77	77	306
	Rick Jones, Brookside G. & C.C., Worthington, Ohio	72	80	75	79	306
39	Michael King, Reading G.C., Reading, Berks, England	80	75	77	75	307
	William C. Campbell, Guyan G. & C.C., Huntington, W. Va.	75	78	77	77	307
	James C. Bostwick, Meadow Brook C., Jericho, N.Y.	78	71	79	79	307
42	Dr. R.H. Watson, Carmel C.C., Charlotte, N.C.	77	77	80	74	308
	James D. Sykes, Huntingdon Valley C.C., Abington, Pa.	81	75	77	75	308
	Dean S. Overturf, Houston C.C., Houston, Texas	80	73	76	79	308
45	Edward T. Barry, Charles River C.C., Newton Centre, Mass.	79	76	77	77	309
	John Govern, Vestal Hills C.C., Binghamton, N.Y.	73	77	81	78	309
	Kenneth L. Scott, Atlanta C.C., Atlanta, Ga.	78	74	79	78	309
48	Paul W. Purtzer, Moon Valley C.C., Phoenix, Ariz.	80	76	77	77	310
	Jay Sigel, Aronimink G.C., Newtown Square, Pa.	77	79	73	81	310
50	Michael E. Gery, Lafayette C.C., Lafayette, Ind.	80	73	81	77	311
	Tommy Mullinax, Greer G. & C.C., Greer, S.C.	81	73	80	77	311
52	William M. Lehman, Lake Geneva C.C., Lake Geneva, Wis.	78	76	84	74	312
	Bruce C. Hollowell, Hickory Hills C.C., Springfield, Mo.	74	78	85	75	312
	Frank F. Schmidt, Scarlet and Gray G.C., Columbus, Ohio	78	77	79	78	312
55	Peter J. Benka, Addington G.C., Addington, Surrey, England	79	75	81	78	313
56	Gary L. Holloman, Fort Gordon G.C., Augusta, Ga.	80	76	80	80	316
	Arnold Blum, Idle Hour G. & C.C., Macon, Ga.	76	80	80	80	316
	Kent L. Englemeier, Brooke Manor C.C., Rockville, Md.	77	77	80	82	316
59	William F. Crooks, Sunnehanna C.C., Johnstown, Pa.	79	77	82	80	318
60	Russell Helwig, Branch Brook G.C., Belleville, N.J.	80	73	82	84	319
61	Michael J. Nilon, The Springhaven C., Wallingford, Pa.	77	78	86	79	320

1970
SEVENTIETH AMATEUR CHAMPIONSHIP

Held at Waverley Country Club, Portland, Ore., September 2-5.
Yardage—6,496. Par 70. 1,853 Entries, 150 Starters.

61 contestants who completed 72 holes.

						Score
1	Lanny Wadkins, Meadowbrook C.C., Richmond, Va.	67	73	69	70	279
2	Tom Kite, Jr., C.C. of Austin, Austin, Texas	69	67	71	73	280
3	Gary Cowan, West Mount G.C., Kitchener, Ont., Canada	69	70	73	72	284
	James R. Gabrielsen, Peachtree G.C., Atlanta, Ga.	75	67	69	73	284
	James B. Simons, Butler C.C., Butler, Pa.	69	72	69	74	284
6	Marvin Giles, III, Boonsboro C.C., Lynchburg, Va.	73	70	71	71	285
7	Richard A. Spears, Port Jervis, N.Y.	71	69	75	71	286
8	William C. Campbell, Guyan G. & C.C., Huntington, W. Va.	73	72	72	70	287
	Allen L. Miller, III, Pensacola C.C., Pensacola, Fla.	70	71	73	73	287
	Steve Melnyk, Hidden Hills C.C., Jacksonville, Fla.	71	68	74	74	287
11	Gary C. Sanders, Los Coyotes C.C., Buena Park, Calif.	68	78	68	74	288
	John Farquhar, Amarillo C.C., Amarillo, Texas	71	71	71	75	288
13	Drue R. Johnson, Crawford County C.C., Robinson, Ill.	71	76	72	70	289
	David Glenz, Coos C.C., Coos Bay, Ore.	72	70	73	74	289
	Steve C. Walker, Pinehurst C.C., Pinehurst, N.C.	73	72	70	74	289
16	Scott Bess, Columbia, C.C., Columbia, Mo.	70	75	73	72	290
	Robert I. Zender, Evanston G.C., Skokie, Ill.	73	71	73	73	290
18	George E. Haines, Jr., Somerset Hills, C.C., Bernardsville, N.J.	71	74	72	73	290
	Michael Killian, Seminole Lake C.C., Seminole, Fla.	69	73	74	74	290
	Bill Harvey, Sedgefield C., Greensboro, N.C.	69	76	71	74	290
21	Terry Diehl, Oak Hill C.C., Rochester, N.Y.	74	73	74	70	291
	Joseph C. Inman, Jr., Starmount Forest C.C., Greensboro, N.C.	72	73	75	71	291
	Jay Sigel, Aronimink G.C., Newtown Square, Pa.	75	70	72	74	291
24	Andrew S. North, Panorama C.C., Conroe, Texas	71	75	73	73	292
	Ben Duncan, Jr., Gadsden C.C., Quincy, Fla.	71	73	72	76	292
26	Tom Watson, Kansas City C.C., Shawnee Mission, Kans.	74	68	76	75	293
	Eddie Pearce, Bardmoor G. & C.C., Largo, Fla.	72	72	74	75	293
28	Fred Haney, Rock Creek Men's G.C., Portland, Ore.	70	77	72	75	294
	Barry Jaeckel, Riviera C.C., Pacific Palisades, Calif.	72	76	74	72	294
	Thomas W. Jenkins, Riverbend C.C., Sugarland, Texas	72	75	73	74	294
	Larry McAtee, Lakewood C.C., Lakewood, Colo.	75	72	73	74	294
	Donald D. Dodgen, Ridglea C.C., Ft. Worth, Texas	71	72	76	75	294
	Bruce Hollowell, Hickory Hills C.C., Springfield, Mo.	74	74	71	75	294
	Eugene A. Howard, Bob O'Link G.C., Highland Park, Ill.	74	72	72	76	294
35	Melvin Stevens, Western G. & C.C., Detroit, Mich.	71	72	78	74	295
	Bill Hoffer, Elgin C.C., Elgin, Ill.	70	74	77	74	295
	John Grace, C.C. of Detroit, Grosse Pointe Farms, Mich.	71	76	73	75	295
	Jim Shade, Norfolk C.C., Norfolk, Neb.	71	73	75	76	295
	Jim Brady, Inglewood C.C., Kenmore, Wash.	75	71	72	77	295
	Kurt Cox, Chapparal C.C., Seguin, Texas	76	65	74	80	295
41	Paul Erhardt, Sakima C.C., Carney's Point, N.J.	75	73	71	77	296
42	Donald C. Allen, C.C. of Rochester, Rochester, N.Y.	73	72	78	74	297
	Patrick C. Fitzsimons, Illahe Hills C.C., Salem, Ore.	75	70	78	74	297
	David A. King, Bethesda C.C., Bethesda, Md.	74	73	75	75	297
	Jeff Radder, Blackhawk C.C., Madison, Wis.	75	70	74	78	297
46	Mickey Van Gerbig, Seminole G.C., N. Palm Beach, Fla.	72	73	79	74	298
	Charles L. Sullivan, Jr., Green Valley C.C., Suisun, Calif.	73	74	77	74	298
48	Worth W. Calfee, Cavalier G. & Yacht C., Virginia Beach, Va.	71	75	76	76	298
	Wayne McDonald, Wyldewood G.C., Oakville, Ont., Canada	76	70	74	76	298
50	Warner Berry, Silverado C.C., Napa, Calif.	74	72	73	80	299
	Elvis Larkin, Huntsville C.C., Huntsville, Ala.	76	72	77	74	299
	Edward L. Meister, Jr., Kirtland C.C., Willoughby, Ohio	75	73	75	76	299
	Phillip J. McGleno, Jr., Green River G.C., Corona, Calif.	71	77	75	76	299
54	James Hilderbrand, C.C. of Ashland, Ashland, Ohio	75	72	76	77	300
	Charles Major, C.C. of Birmingham, Birmingham, Ala.	72	76	74	78	300
	Gary M. Burton, Ridgeview C.C., Duluth, Minn.	73	74	74	79	300
57	Michael G. Kallan, Pine Brook C.C., Winston-Salem, N.C.	74	73	77	77	301
	Ray Beallo, The Sharon Club, Sharon Center, Ohio	75	72	75	79	301
59	**Gary P. Floan, Manito G. & C.C., Spokane, Wash.**	70	75	78	79	302
	Jim Petralia, Quail Lake Men's C., Moreno, Calif.	73	74	76	79	302
	Craig Griswold, Oswego Lake C.C., Lake Oswego, Ore.	71	77	73	81	302

1971
SEVENTY-FIRST AMATEUR CHAMPIONSHIP

Held at Wilmington Country Club, Wilmington, Del., September 1–4.
Yardage—6,872. Par—71.
2,327 Entries, 149 Qualifiers. 150 Starters.

64 contestants who completed 72-hole holes.

						Score
1	Gary Cowan, Westmount G.C., Kitchener, Ontario, Canada	70	71	69	70	280
2	Eddie Pearce, Temple Terrace G. & C.C., Temple Terrace, Fla.	70	69	73	71	283
3	Marvin Giles, III, C.C. of Virginia, Richmond, Va.	74	73	68	69	284
4	James C. McLean, Rainier G.C., Seattle, Wash.	72	67	73	73	285
5	Ben Crenshaw, C.C. of Austin, Austin, Texas	73	70	72	71	286
6	Tom Culligan, Peninsula G. & C.C., San Mateo, Calif.	74	71	69	74	288
	Martin West, Columbia C.C., Chevy Chase, Md.	67	76	68	77	288
8	Richard A. Bendall, Jr., Danville G.C., Danville, Va.	73	76	69	72	290
9	Bradley M. Schuchat, Des Moines G. & C.C., W. Des Moines, Iowa	77	69	70	75	291
	Gilmer Morgan, Oakwood C.C., Enid, Okla.	72	72	72	75	291
11	Frederick Kask, Wethersfield C.C., Wethersfield, Conn.	75	73	74	70	292
	Stephen Benson, Lincolnshire C.C., Crete, Ill.	77	71	73	71	292
	Dennis Walters, Battleground G.A., Freehold, N.J.	71	80	71	70	292
14	William C. Campbell, Guyan G. & C.C., Huntington, W.Va.	74	72	70	77	293
	Cameron P. Quinn, West Warwick C.C., West Warwick, R.I.	71	73	74	75	293
	Jerry Courville, Shorehaven G.C., East Norwalk, Conn.	73	71	73	76	293
	Tom Kite, Jr., C.C. of Austin, Austin, Texas	71	76	70	76	293
18	George E. Haines, Jr., Somerset Hills C.C., Bernardsville, N.J.	69	73	80	72	294
	William A. Kratzert, III, Fort Wayne C.C., Fort Wayne, Ind.	71	73	76	74	294
	William Hyndman, III, Huntingdon Valley C.C., Huntingdon Valley, Pa.	70	74	73	77	294
21	Andrew S. North, Panorama G.C., Conroe, Texas	79	73	71	72	295
	Logan Jackson, Pinehurst C.C., Pinehurst, N.C.	74	75	75	71	295
	John E. Mills, Jr., Riverside G. Ass'n., Portland, Me.	73	76	73	73	295
	Jimmy Smith, East Bay C.C., Clearwater, Fla.	75	71	75	74	295
	Douglas Ballenger, Worthington Valley C.C., Owings Mills, Md.	75	76	70	74	295
	Arthur S. Russell, Riverside C.C., Lake Jackson, Texas	76	72	73	74	295
	David L. Newquist, Milburn G. & C.C., Overland Park, Kans.	75	71	74	75	295
28	Joseph C. Inman, Jr., Pinehurst C.C., Pinehurst, N.C.	73	74	77	72	296
	David M. Gurley, Glen View C., Golf, Ill.	73	72	80	71	296
	Gary R. Artz, Firestone C.C., Akron, Ohio	74	76	74	72	296
	Nick Weslock, Mississaugua G. & C.C., Port Credit, Ontario, Canada	70	78	73	75	296
32	Tommy Valentine, Chattahoochee G.C., Gainesville, Ga.	74	70	77	76	297
	Stanton Altgelt, Royal Oaks C.C., Dallas, Texas	74	70	76	77	297
	Stephen E. Graves, Scarlet & Gray C., Columbus, Ohio	72	73	75	77	297
	Jim Ahern, Hillcrest G. & C.C., Yankton, S.D.	71	74	75	77	297
36	Bill Schumaker, Elks C.C., Fort Wayne, Ind.	76	76	76	70	298
	Corker Deloach, Forest Cove C.C., Houston, Texas	77	73	74	74	298
	Bruce Lietzke, Bear Creek G.C., Houston, Texas	73	76	73	76	298
	Danny Edwards, Lakeside G.A., Stillwater, Okla.	74	73	72	79	298
40	Richard L. Siderowf, Birchwood C.C., Westport, Conn.	73	75	73	78	299
41	Terrence J. Diehl, Brook-Lea C.C., Rochester, N.Y.	73	74	79	74	300
	Bruce C. Hollowell, Hickory Hills C.C., Springfield, Mo.	72	74	76	78	300
	Joe D. Dills, Muskogee C.C., Muskogee, Okla.	75	71	75	79	300
44	Bill Rogers, Forest Cove C.C., Houston, Texas	74	71	78	78	301
45	Kenneth Peyre-Ferry, Indian Spring G.C., Marlton, N.J.	75	75	75	77	302
46	John Farquhar, Amarillo C.C., Amarillo, Texas	77	75	76	75	303
	Alan Tapie, Rio Hondo Men's G.C., Downey, Calif.	75	76	73	79	303
	John Granger, Colonial C.C., Fort Worth, Texas	78	71	74	80	303
	Robert H. Boyle, George Miler C.C., Summerville, S.C.	70	72	75	86	303
50	Howard Twitty, Phoenix C.C., Phoenix, Ariz.	75	76	81	72	304
	John R. Birmingham, Oakmont C.C., Oakmont, Pa.	73	79	75	77	304
	David A. Huske, Glen Oak C.C., Glen Ellyn, Ill.	78	70	77	79	304
	Robert R. Morris, Crawford County C.C., Robinson, Ill.	75	75	73	81	304
	Lawrence B. Stubblefield, Mid-Pacific C.C., Lanikai, Hawaii	73	73	76	82	304
55	Paul W. Purtzer, Moon Valley C.C., Phoenix, Ariz.	76	74	78	77	305
	Mike Phillips, Blue Hills C.C., Kansas City, Mo.	74	73	78	80	305
	Ben Duncan, Jr., Gadsen C.C., Quincy, Fla.	80	70	75	80	305
58	Donald C. Allen, C.C. of Rochester, Rochester, N.Y.	76	74	76	80	306
	Edgar Tutwiler, Highland G. & C.C., Indianapolis, Ind.	75	72	74	85	306
60	Jim Schreiber, Ouilmette G.C., Wilmette, Ill.	79	73	78	77	307
	Peter V. Bisconti, Jr., Westchester C.C., Rye, N.Y.	78	74	77	78	307
	George F. Burns, III, Plandome C.C., Plandome, N.Y.	74	74	78	81	307
63	Harry E. Fischer, Brookside Men's G.C., Brookside, Calif.	77	75	79	79	310
64	Arthur D. Hudnutt, Elyria C.C., Elyria, Ohio	74	77	86	83	320

AMATEUR CHAMPIONSHIP

1972
SEVENTY-SECOND AMATEUR CHAMPIONSHIP

Held at Charlotte Country Club, Charlotte, N.C., August 30–September 2.
Yardage–6,811. Par 71. 2,295 Entries, 143 Qualifiers, 150 Starters.

Sixty-five contestants who completed 72 holes.

						Score
1	Marvin M. Giles III, C.C. of Virginia, Richmond, Va.	73	68	72	72	285
2	Mark S. Hayes, Twin Hills G. & C.C., Oklahoma City, Okla.	73	72	69	74	288
	Ben Crenshaw, C.C. of Austin, Austin, Texas	71	75	71	71	288
4	Martin R. West III, Columbia C.C., Chevy Chase, Md.	73	71	73	72	289
5	Charles W. Harrison, Atlanta C.C., Marietta, Ga.	74	77	68	71	290
6	Bruce Robertson, Olympic Club, San Francisco, Calif.	70	72	73	77	292
7	Douglas S. Ballenger, Worthington Valley C.C., Owings Mills, Md.	72	72	73	77	294
	Michael P. Killian, Seminole Lake C.C., Seminole, Fla.	77	75	72	70	294
9	Dale Morey, Willow Creek G.C., High Point, N.C.	73	77	72	73	295
10	John R. Birmingham, Oakmont C.C., Oakmont, Pa.	76	73	73	74	296
	Robert Lee Bryant, Lenoir C.C., Lenoir, N.C.	72	71	74	79	296
12	Gary Jacobson, Wayzata C.C., Wayzata, Minn.	75	74	69	79	297
	Arthur Russell, Riverside C.C., Lake Jackson, Texas	75	70	77	75	297
	Richard Ehrmanntraut, Highland Park G.C., St. Paul, Minn.	74	74	75	74	297
15	David A. King, Bethesda C.C., Bethesda, Md.	70	74	77	77	298
	William J. Mallon, Framingham C.C., Framingham, Mass.	75	72	81	70	298
17	James R. Gabrielsen, Peachtree G.C., Atlanta, Ga.	76	75	72	76	299
	Danny Edwards, Kicking Bird Men's Golf Assn., Edmond, Okla.	79	73	75	72	299
	R. P. (Dick) Horne, The Club at Snee Farm, Mt. Pleasant, S.C.	76	73	77	73	299
20	Gregory E. Stuhler, East Lake G.C., Atlanta, Ga.	69	77	78	76	300
	Bruce Hollowell, Hickory Hills C.C., Springfield, Mo.	70	74	81	75	300
	Bill Rogers, Bear Creek G.C., Houston, Texas	76	71	79	74	300
23	Wally Payne, Colonial C.C., Fort Worth, Texas	72	74	74	81	301
	James A. Wittenberg, Jr., Colonial C.C., Memphis, Tenn.	71	73	77	80	301
	William C. Campbell, Guyan G. & C.C., Huntington, W. Va.	80	72	72	77	301
	Clayton V. Heafner, Jr., MacGregor Downs C.C., Cary, N.C.	76	76	76	73	301
	William J. Patton, Mimosa Hills G.C., Morganton, N.C.	74	78	74	75	301
	Richard L. Siderowf, G.C. at Aspetuck, Easton, Conn.	74	79	75	73	301
29	L. Kipp Minter, C.C. of Orlando, Orlando, Fla.	77	76	75	74	302
	John P. Grace, C.C. of Detroit, Grosse Pointe Farms, Mich.	72	75	82	73	302
	Robert S. Brow, Coronado Men's G.C., Coronado, Calif.	76	73	76	77	302
	Larry Zee, Tan-Tara C.C., Pendleton, N.Y.	76	73	79	74	302
33	Mark Pfeil, Palos Verdes G.C., Palos Verdes Estates, Calif.	69	76	83	75	303
	William Hyndman III, Huntingdon Valley C.C., Huntingdon Valley, Pa.	79	75	74	75	303
	Steve Groves, Scarlet & Gray C., Columbus, Ohio	72	76	71	84	303
	Jay Haas, St. Clair C.C., Bellville, Ill.	81	70	79	73	303
	Bill Musselman, Harmony Landing G.C., Goshen, Ky.	74	79	74	76	303
	Robert T. Byman, Flatirons C.C., Boulder, Colo.	76	77	77	73	303
39	Larry J. Tiziani, Chippewa Falls Elks C., Chippewa Falls, Wis.	77	74	74	79	304
	Charles Borner, Jr., North Platte C.C., North Platte, Neb.	76	75	78	75	304
	Robert F. Widener, Wedgewood C.C., Medina, Ohio	78	72	78	76	304
42	Robert E. Wadkins, Meadowbrook C.C., Richmond, Va.	78	74	75	78	305
	Robert W. Dumas, Saugahatchee C.C., Auburn, Ala.	74	77	78	76	305
	Jamie Gough III, Army Navy C.C., Arlington, Va.	76	77	71	81	305
	Donald E. Bliss, Norwood Hills C.C., St. Louis, Mo.	77	77	78	73	305
	Robert T. Carlson, Glenacres G. & C.C., Seattle, Wash.	77	75	79	74	305
47	Skeeter Heath, Williamsburg C.C., Williamsburg, Va.	77	77	71	81	306
	Thomas W. Barnes, Jr., Dunwoody C.C., Dunwoody, Ga.	77	74	78	77	306
	James C. McLean, Rainier G. & C.C., Seattle, Wash.	75	74	83	74	306
50	George Haines, Jr., Somerset Hills C.C., Bernardsville, N.J.	77	76	73	81	307
	Larry Griffin, Lakewood C.C., New Orleans, La.	75	77	75	80	307
	Duane F. Haley, Hop Meadow C.C., Simsbury, Conn.	74	79	79	75	307
53	John P. Cain, Brae Burn C.C., Houston, Texas	76	78	76	78	308
54	David H. Hanten, Huron C.C., Huron, S.D.	77	73	81	77	308
	Stewart M. Alexander III, Lakewood C.C., St. Petersburg, Fla.	73	81	76	78	308
56	Charles J. Canepa, Hiwan G.C., Evergreen, Colo.	76	75	81	78	310
	Philip Kenny, Bob O'Link G.C., Highland Park, Ill.	78	75	78	79	310
58	Robert C. MacWhinnie Nottingham C.C., Eighty Four, Pa.	76	78	81	77	312
	William B. Boles, Jr., Wilson C.C., Wilson, N.C.	76	77	80	79	312
60	William W. Gerber III, Lafayette C.C., Jamesville, N.Y.	77	76	81	79	313
61	Kirk Padgett, Colorado Springs C.C., Colorado Springs, Colo.	74	79	82	79	314
62	Frank Boyd, C.C. of Birmingham, Birmingham, Ala.	75	76	88	76	315
	Charles E. Smith, York Temple C.C., Worthington, Ohio	78	75	78	84	315
64	Gene Rucker, Miami, Fla.	80	74	82	80	316
65	Robert F. Vickers, Wichita C.C., Wichita, Kans.	77	77	82	82	318

WOMEN'S OPEN CHAMPIONS

SUSIE BERNING
1968-72-73

DONNA CAPONI
1969-70

JO ANNE CARNER
1971-76

1973
SEVENTY-THIRD AMATEUR CHAMPIONSHIP

Held at Inverness Club, Toledo, Ohio, August 28 - September 2.
Yardage—6,765. Par 71. 2,110 Entries, 200 Qualifiers, 200 Starters.
Championship entirely at match play.

FINAL ROUND—Craig Stadler defeated David Strawn, 6 and 5.

FIRST QUARTER

UPPER

1st Round (18 Holes)	2nd Round (18 Holes)	3rd Round (18 Holes)	4th Round (18 Holes)	5th Round (18 Holes)	6th Round (18 Holes)	
Donald E. Kelly, Auburn, Ind	Kelly,					
Gregory R. Wolff, Doylestown, Pa.	6 and 4	Sigel,				
Donnie DeAngelis, Norristown, Pa.	Sigel,	5 and 3				
Jay Sigel, Aronimink, Pa.	21 holes		Sigel,			
BYE - Ron Milanovich, Chicora, Pa.	Milanovich	Milanovich,	2 and 1			
Dennis M. Spencer, Sylvania, Ohio	Spencer,	1 up		Koch, 6 and 4		
John C. Davies, Royal, Mid-Surrey, England	2 up					
Gary Koch, Temple Terrace, Fla.	Koch,					
Dennis L. Smith, Memphis, Tenn.	19 holes	Koch,			Campbell, 3 and 1	
BYE - Charlie Eddie, Los Gatos, Calif.	Eddie	2 up	Koch,			
Joe Harper, Columbus, Ohio	Pfaff,		19 holes			
Tony Pfaff, Austin, Texas	19 holes	Cooke,				
BYE - L. Graham Cooke, Dorion, Quebec, Canada	Cooke	4 and 3				
Mack Murray, Jr., Jackson Beach, Fla.	Campbell					
William C. Campbell, Huntington, W. Va.	7 and 6	Campbell,				
BYE - Mark Tinder, Pebble Beach, Calif.	Tinder	6 and 4	Campbell,	Campbell, 2 and 1		
BYE - Richard W. Sharp, Memphis, Tenn.	Sharp	Sharp,	6 and 5			
Richard Karbowski, Sutton, Mass.	Aqualino,	5 and 3				
Nicholas J. Aqualino, Crofton, Md.	19 holes					
W. Laird Robertson, Havertown, Pa.	Robertson,					
Robert R. Shelton, Monroe, La.	19 holes	Morey,				
BYE - Dale Morey, High Point, N. C.	Morey	5 and 3				Campbell, 2 and 1
Timothy Wickenhauser, Alton, Ill.	Wickenhauser,		Morey,			
John A. Krumrine, Hollidaysburg, Pa.	3 and 1	Marucci,	1 up			
BYE - George E. Marucci, Jr., Havertown, Pa.	Marucci	4 and 3				
BYE - Donn A. Daus, Shaker Heights, Ohio	Daus	Daus,				
Kent C. Byers, Lake Oswego, Ore.	Byers,	5 and 3				
Bob Edgerton, Raleigh, N. C.	1 up		Metcalfe,			
BYE - Taylor B. Metcalfe, Wyoming, Ohio	Metcalfe		5 and 4	Metcalfe, 5 and 4		
Trevor Homer, Walsall, Broadway, England	Grose,	Metcalfe,				
Terry L. Grose, Lima, Ohio	4 and 2	2 and 1				
Bruce Dobbs, Ypsilanti, Michigan	Hyndman,					
William Hyndman III, Huntingdon Valley, Pa.	6 and 5	Hyndman,				
BYE - Robert W. Dumas, Auburn, Ala.	Dumas	4 and 3	Hyndman,			
BYE - Paul Hanczaryk, Crofton, Md.	Hanczaryk		4 and 3			
Larry Pagel, Tucson, Ariz.	Vickers,	Vickers,			Kratzert, 20 holes	
Robert F. Vickers, Wichita, Kans.	2 and 1	3 and 2				
Danny Simmons, Brandon, Fla.	Boeka,					
Jerry Boeka, Borger, Texas	2 up	Kratzert,				
BYE - Wm. A. Kratzert III, Ft. Wayne, Ind.	Kratzert	5 and 4				
Donald E. Albert, Columbus, Ohio	Fought,		Kratzert,			
John Fought, Tualatin, Ore.	2 and 1	Fought,	4 and 2	Kratzert, 5 and 4		
BYE - Jeffrey Pomerantz, Fairfield, Conn.	Pomerantz	21 holes				
William J. Mallon, Framingham, Mass.	Mallon,					
Bill Warner, Des Moines, Iowa	4 and 3	Ault,				
BYE - Robert Ault, Albuquerque, N. M.	Ault	1 up				
Michael M. Fox, Jacksonville, Fla.	Fox,					
Charles Gibson, Arcata, Calif.	1 up	Fox,	Ault,			
Mike Dale, Summerlea, Dorion, Quebec, Canada	Lenz,	1 up	2 and 1			
Thomas Lenz, Sewickley, Pa.	3 and 2					

SEMI-FINAL ROUND (18 Holes)—David Strawn defeated William C. Campbell, 6 up and 5 to play.

SECOND QUARTER

HALF	6th Round (18 Holes)	5th Round (18 Holes)	4th Round (18 Holes)	3rd Round (18 Holes)	2nd Round (18 Holes)	1st Round (18 Holes)
Strawn, 3 and 2	Strawn, 6 and 5	Strawn, 19 holes	Stuart, 4 and 2	Stuart, 1 up	Stuart, 3 and 2	Hugh B. Stuart, Forres, Scotland
						Kevin P. Morris, North Salem, N. Y.
					Bodin, 1 up	John P. Bodin, Decatur, Ga.
						John Hood, South Bend, Ind.
				Keim, 4 and 2	Keim	BYE - James W. Keim, Jr., Erie, Pa.
					McFerren, 1 up	Patrick J. Lindsey, Toledo, Ohio
						Gerald F. McFerren, Crofton, Md.
			Strawn, 3 and 2	Baskins, 2 and 1	Pfeil, 4 and 3	Mark Pfeil, Palos Verdes Estates, Calif.
						Stanley Moore, Jr., Miami Shores, Fla.
					Baskins	BYE - David Baskins, Reno, Nev.
				Strawn, 4 and 3	Strawn, 4 and 3	David Strawn, Concord, N. C.
						Robert C. Impaglia, Auburn, N. Y.
					Ohanian	BYE - Michael Ohanian, Watertown, Mass.
		Harvey, 1 up	Harvey, 4 and 3	Remsen, 8 and 7	Payne, 5 and 4	A. Jerome Freeland, St. Louis, Mo.
						Wally Payne, Fort Worth, Texas
					Remsen	BYE - Richard Remsen, Jr., Buck Hill Falls, Pa.
				Harvey, 1 up	Granger	BYE - John R. Granger, Fort Worth, Texas
					Harvey, 5 and 4	Bill Harvey, Greensboro, N. C.
						Richard Vershure, Lake Orion, Mich.
			Andrews, 1 up	Andrews, 2 and 1	Andrews, 20 holes	Harold P. Andrews, Jackson, Mich.
						Robert C. Macwhinnie, McMurray, Pa.
					Goethals	BYE - Glenn Goethals, Princeton, N. J.
				Edwards, 6 and 5	Moore, 5 and 4	Marion E. Moore, Orangeburg, S. C.
						Scott Ittersagen, Homewood, Ill.
					Edwards	BYE - Dan Edwards, Edmond, Okla.
	deLozier, 1 up	deLozier, 4 and 2	Bonallack, 19 holes	Mason, 2 and 1	Blair	BYE - James Blair, Logan, Utah
					Mason, 1 up	Edward L. Meister, Jr., Willoughby, Ohio
						James D. Mason, Duluth, Ga.
				Bonallack, 4 and 3	Steiner	BYE - Ned Steiner, West Caldwell, N. J.
					Bonallack, 5 and 4	Henry H. Russell, Miami Beach, Fla.
						Michael F. Bonallack, Thorpe Bay, Essex, England
			deLozier, 6 and 5	deLozier, 3 and 2	deLozier, 1 up	Henri deLozier, Crofton, Md.
						Stephen Scrafford, Erie, Pa.
					Bryant	BYE - Robert L. Bryant, Lenoir, N. C.
				Creagh, 1 up	Green	BYE - Charles Green, Dumbarton, Scotland
					Creagh, 2 up	George G. Creagh, Nashville, Tenn.
						Harry L. Newby, Jr., Cloquet, Minn.
		Ballenger, 1 up	Ballenger, 1 up	Hancock, 4 and 3	Levine, 3 and 2	Ronald Levine, Miami Beach, Fla.
						Brian Shanks, Phoenix, Ariz.
					Hancock	BYE - Phillip Hancock, Greenville, Ala.
				Ballenger, 6 and 5	Ballenger, 3 and 2	Doug Ballenger, Owings Mills, Md.
						Brian M. Kneasfsey, Huntington, W. Va.
					Mazza	BYE - John Mazza, Mackeyville, Pa.
			Alexander, 1 up	Alexander, 2 up	Alexander, 1 up	Stewart Alexander III, St. Petersburg, Fla.
						Andy Bean, Lakeland, Fla.
					Brookreson	BYE - David Brookreson, Huntingdon Valley, Pa.
				Kocsis, 6 and 4	Cass, 1 up	Richard Cass, Northport, N. Y.
						Robert E. Hoyt, Houston, Texas
					Kocsis, 4 and 2	J. P. Thompson III, Greenville, S. C.
						Charles Kocsis, Royal Oak, Mich.

THIRD QUARTER LOWER

1st Round (18 Holes)	2nd Round (18 Holes)	3rd Round (18 Holes)	4th Round (18 Holes)	5th Round (18 Holes)	6th Round (18 Holes)	
Steve Dropkin, River Vale, N. J.	Dropkin, 6 and 5					
Dallan Ragland, Fresno, Calif.		Stadler, 2 and 1				
Craig Stadler, LaJolla, Calif.	Stadler, 4 and 2					
William L. Oliver, Jr., Wichita, Kans.			Stadler, 6 and 4			
BYE - Kenneth W. McMaster, San Jose, Calif.	McMaster	Edman, 4 and 2		Stadler, 1 up		
James H. Edman, Jr., Suisun, Calif.	Edman, 3 and 2					
Thomas M. Sultzer, Kennett Square, Pa.						
James S. Porter, Upland, Calif.	Lutz, 2 and 1					
Norman Lutz, Pawtucket, R. I.		Sussel, 1 up				
BYE - Allen Sussel, Ambler, Pa.	Sussel		Sussel, 1 up			
William Hoppman III, Lexington, Ky.	Borner, 4 and 3				Stadler, 3 and 1	
Charles L. Borner, Jr., North Platte, Neb.		Borner, 23 holes				
BYE - Edgar R. Updegraff, Tucson, Ariz.	Updegraff					
David E. Canipe, Fayetteville, N. C.	Canipe, 2 and 1					
Douglas S. Rouse, Evergreen, Colo.		Canipe, 3 and 1				
BYE - George Kelley, Turlock, Calif.	Kelley		Canipe, 2 and 1			
BYE - Martin R. West III, Chevy Chase, Md.	West	Hickle, 5 and 4				
Peter Oppenheim, Salem, Mass.	Hickle, 2 and 1			Spooner, 1 up		
Frederick C. Hickle, Tucson, Ariz.						
John Tuft, Seattle, Wash.	Foster, 8 and 7					
Rodney Foster, Bradford, Yorkshire, England		Rowland, 2 and 1				
BYE - Fred A. Rowland, Olathe, Kans.	Rowland		Spooner, 3 and 2			Stadler, 2 and 1
Leo J. Spooner, Duluth, Minn.	Spooner, 4 and 2					
Jimmy Goss, Dallas, Texas		Spooner, 2 and 1				
BYE - Dennis Sullivan, Miami, Fla.	Sullivan					
BYE - John M. Darr, Fort Lauderdale, Fla.	Darr	Ten Broeck, 4 and 2				
Tom Case, Jr., Fort Myers, Fla.	TenBroeck, 5 and 4					
Lance TenBroeck, Chicago, Ill.			TenBroeck, 20 holes			
BYE - Wm. T. G. Milne, Crieff, Perthshire, Eng.	Milne	Jacobsen, 4 and 3		Hedges, 5 and 4		
Peter Jacobsen, Portland, Ore.	Jacobsen, 5 and 4					
Charles J. Prezioso, Jr., Columbia, S. C.						
Jim Stevenson, Bellevue, Wash.	Pittinger, 2 and 1					
Lyndon Pittinger, Oklahoma City, Okla.		Hedges, 1 up				
BYE - Peter J. Hedges, Beckham, Kent, England	Hedges		Hedges, 2 up		Siderowf, 2 up	
BYE - David M. Thore, Reidsville, N. C.	Thore	Peterson, 4 and 3				
Richard C. Peterson, Cincinnati, Ohio	Peterson, 2 up					
James L. Clements, Jr., Louisville, Ky.						
Jerry Courville, Norwalk, Conn.	Courville, 5 and 3					
Marc A. Rosenbaum, Miami Beach, Fla.		Courville, 4 and 3				
BYE - J. Franklin Rose, Topeka, Kans.	Rose		Courville, 21 holes			
Curtis Strange, Portsmouth, Va.	Strange, 2 and 1			Siderowf, 19 holes		
Bill Argabrite, Kingsport, Tenn.		Strange, 6 and 4				
BYE - Michael P. Killian, Largo, Fla.	Killian					
Jeffrey E. Lindsey, Salem, Ore.	Lindsey, 3 and 1					
Daniel A. Ybema, Rockport, Mich.		Lindsey, 4 and 3				
BYE - David H. Hanten, Huron, S. D.	Hanten		Siderowf, 2 and 1			
Kenneth Krieger, Denver, Colo.	Burns, 4 and 2					
Tommy Burns, Selma, Ala.		Siderowf, 4 and 3				
John E. Sutter, Westfield, Mass.	Siderowf, 3 and 1					
Richard L. Siderowf, Westport, Conn.						

SEMI-FINAL ROUND (18 Holes)—Craig Stadler defeated Marvin Giles III, 3 up and 1 to play.

HALF

FOURTH QUARTER

Half	6th Round (18 Holes)	5th Round (18 Holes)	4th Round (18 Holes)	3rd Round (18 Holes)	2nd Round (18 Holes)	1st Round (18 Holes)
Giles, 5 and 3	Gray, 1 up	Gray, 2 and 1	Streck, 3 and 2	Streck, 2 and 1	Shockley, 2 up	Stewart Shockley, Overland Park, Kansas Sale Omohundro, Sherman, Texas
					Streck, 5 and 4	Ronald R. Streck, Broken Arrow, Okla. Roy L. Hanks, Jr., Dallas, Texas
				Massimi, 4 and 2	Mann	BYE - Robert J. Mann, Mequon, Wis.
					Massimi, 3 and 2	Fred J. Massimi, Jr., Haworth, N. J. Howard K. Clark, Moortown, Leeds, England
			Gray, 3 and 2	Gray, 3 and 1	Smyers, 3 and 2	George E. Haines, Jr., Bernardsville, N. J. Steve Smyers, Houston, Texas
					Gray	BYE - A. Downing Gray, Pensacola, Fla.
				Haney, 2 and 1	Haney, 6 and 5	Mike Haney, Glendale, Calif. Bob Bailey, Hinsdale, Ill.
					Schmidt	BYE - Frank F. Schmidt, Columbus, Ohio
		Rogers, 9 and 8	Rogers, 3 and 2	Rogers, 6 and 5	Rogers, 4 and 2	Bill Rogers, Houston, Texas John Phillips, Springfield, Ill.
					Reid	BYE - Michael D. Reid, Seattle, Wash.
				Brauch, 2 and 1	Brauch	BYE - Timothy Brauch, Denver, Colo.
					Ehrmanntraut, 4 and 2	Richard Ehrmanntraut, St. Paul, Minn. Richard Norville, Oklahoma City, Okla.
			Cain, 2 and 1	Cain, 4 and 3	Cain, 4 and 3	James Beaman, Jr., Brownsville, Texas Rick Cain, Brooks, Ky.
					D'Aunoy	BYE - Rick D'Aunoy, New Orleans, La.
				Lee, 4 and 2	Burns, 5 and 3	Van Gillen, Conroe, Texas George Burns III, East Williston, N. Y.
					Lee	BYE - Stan Lee, Eden Isle, Ark.
	Giles, 2 up	Giles, 4 and 3	Forrest, 3 and 2	Forrest, 1 up	Forrest	BYE - Steve Forrest, Mt. Airy, N. C.
					King, 3 and 2	Jeffrey Radder, Sheboygan, Wis. Michael King, Reading, Berkshire, England
				Green, 1 up	Dills	BYE - Joey D. Dills, Muskogee, Okla.
					Green, 6 and 5	Peter J. Green, Orchard Lake, Mich. Gary Longfellow, Lakewood, Colo.
			Giles, 3 and 2	Giles, 3 and 1	vanGerbig, 2 and 1	Mickey vanGerbig, North Palm Beach, Fla. Wm. W. Harris, Jr., Fort Worth, Texas
					Giles	BYE - Marvin Giles III, Richmond, Va.
				Yates, 4 and 3	Yates	BYE - Danny Yates, Atlanta, Ga.
					Gerber, 5 and 4	Charles R. Hastie, Atlanta, Ga. Wm. W. Gerber III, Jamesville, N. Y.
		Harrison, 4 and 3	Haas, 2 up	Stuhler, 7 and 5	Stuhler, 5 and 4	Montford T. Johnson III, Amarillo, Texas Gregory E. Stuhler, Decatur, Ga.
					Congdon	BYE - Bruce G. Congdon, Foxboro, Mass.
				Haas, 4 and 3	Haas, 5 and 4	Ronald Perry, Los Angeles, Calif. Jay Haas, Belleville, Ill.
					Runkle	BYE - Dick Runkle, Los Angeles, Calif.
			Harrison, 3 and 2	Birmingham, 3 and 2	Ellis, 9 and 7	Lessely Noel, Hunt Valley, Md. James Ellis, Virginia Beach, Va.
					Birmingham	BYE - John R. Birmingham, Oakmont, Pa.
				Harrison, 8 and 7	Green, 20 holes	Michael Barge, Fargo, N. D. Dennis C. Green, St. Louis, Mo.
					Harrison, 2 and 1	Paul Davis, Whitevale, Ontario, Canada Charles N. Harrison, Atlanta, Ga.

1974
SEVENTY-FOURTH AMATEUR CHAMPIONSHIP

Held at Ridgewood Country Club, Ridgewood, New Jersey, August 26-31
Yardage—6,754 Par 71. 2,420 Entries, 200 Qualifiers, 200 Starters.
Championship entirely at match play.

FINAL ROUND (36 Holes)—Jerome K. Pate defeated John P. Grace, 2 and 1.

FIRST QUARTER

1st Round (18 Holes)	2nd Round (18 Holes)	3rd Round (18 Holes)	4th Round (18 Holes)	5th Round (18 Holes)	UPPER 6th Round (18 Holes)	
Thomas P. Miller, New Philadelphia, Ohio	Brauch,					
Timothy Brauch, Lafayette, Colo.	2 and 1	Brauch,				
Daniel J. Bogdan, Schenectady, N. Y.	Haas,	3 and 1				
Jay Haas, Belleville, Ill.	8 and 7		Lejko,			
Morris B. Beecroft, Jr., Newport News, Va.	Beecroft		2 and 1			
BYE		Lejko,				
Stephen T. Lejko, Jr., Bethesda, Md.	Lejko,	23 holes		Lejko, 2 and 1		
Brian Gaddy, Arcadia, Calif.	19 holes					
Patrick R. McGowan, Colusa, Calif.	DePiro,					
James DePiro, Belleville, N. J.	2 and 1	Kutz,				
Dale Kutz, Kansas City, Mo.	Kutz	2 up				
BYE			Kutz,			
Robert C. Ault, Columbus, Ohio	Ault,		1 up			
Van Gillen, Jr., Conroe, Texas	2 and 1	Ault,				
Joe Hager, Dallas, Texas	Hager	6 and 4			Campbell, 19 holes	
BYE						
Roger Simpkins, College Park, Md.	Simpkins,					
Raymond E. Cragun, Albuquerque, N. M.	2 and 1	Jennings,				
Jed Jennings, Bellvue, Wash.	Jennings	1 up				
BYE			Campbell,			
William C. Campbell, Huntington, W. Va.	Campbell		4 and 3			
BYE		Campbell,				
Michael O. Reid, Kirkland, Wash.	Choate,	25 holes		Campbell, 5 and 4		
Warren J. Choate, Montoursville, Pa.	1 up					
Gary M. Ostrega, Bensenville, Ill.	Ostrega,					
William F. Mitchell, Stratton Mt., Vt.	3 and 2	Ostrega,				
Lewis W. Oehmig, Lookout Mt., Tenn.	Oehmig	3 and 1				
BYE			Ostrega,			
Stewart M. Alexander, III, St. Petersburg, Fla.	Alexander,		4 and 3			
Richard Hurvitz, New Rochelle, N. Y.	4 and 3	Murray,				
Mack R. Murray, Jr., Green Cove Sprgs., Fla.	Murray	1 up				
BYE						Pate, 4 and 2
Beau Baugh, Whittier, Calif.	Baugh					
BYE		Pate,				
Robert E. Young, Jr., Dunwoody, Ga.	Pate,	4 and 3				
Jerome K. Pate, Pensacola, Fla.	4 and 2		Pate,			
Gaylord E. Davis, Lake Oswego, Ore.	Davis		1 up			
BYE		Tutwiler,				
Edgar M. Tutwiler, Jr., Indianapolis, Ind.	Tutwiler,	4 and 3				
Michael L. Barr, Sanger, Calif.	3 and 1			Pate, 2 and 1		
Donald Crowell, Palos Verdes Pensl., Calif.	Crowell,					
Bill Voyles, Marietta, Ga.	1 up	Tinder,				
Mark Tinder, Pebble Beach, Calif.	Tinder	3 and 2				
BYE			Burns,			
George F. Burns, III, Port Wash., N. Y.	Burns		19 holes			
BYE		Burns,				
Leo J. Spooner, Duluth, Minn.	Spooner,	5 and 4				
Robert M. Murphy, Garden City, N. Y.	3 and 1				Pate, 1 up	
Curtis E. Wagner, Atlanta, Ga.	Wagner,					
Thomas H. O'Melia, Grove Hill, Ala.	1 up	Wagner,				
Michael M. Fox, Jacksonville, Fla.	Fox	6 and 5				
BYE			Hyndman,			
Robert E. Hoyt, Houston, Texas	Hyndman,		3 and 2			
William Hyndman, III, Huntingdon Valley, Pa.	1 up	Hyndman,				
Bruce Furman, Waterloo, Ia.	Furman	3 and 1				
BYE				Fergus, 6 and 5		
John D. Tuft, Seattle, Wash.	Fabel,					
Brad Fabel, Madisonville, Ky.	2 up	Lenz,				
Thomas Lenz, Aliquippa, Pa.	Lenz	2 and 1				
BYE			Fergus,			
Keith Fergus, Houston, Texas	Fergus,		2 up			
Bob Mase, E. Lansing, Mich.	4 and 2	Fergus,				
David Baskins, Reno, Nev.	Ihnot,	3 and 1				
Jim Ihnot, Minneapolis, Minn.	4 and 2					

SEMI-FINAL ROUND (18 Holes)—Jerome K. Pate defeated Curtis Strange, 2 and 1.

HALF			SECOND QUARTER			
	6th Round (18 Holes)	5th Round (18 Holes)	4th Round (18 Holes)	3rd Round (18 Holes)	2nd Round (18 Holes)	1st Round (18 Holes)
					Sibbick, 2 and 1	D. Michael Good, Columbus, Ohio
				Sibbick, 1 up		William Sibbick, Martinsville, Va.
					Lis, 1 up	Lawrence B. Lis, Avella, Pa.
			Sibbick, 4 and 3			Craig Stadler, La Jolla, Calif.
					Branca	Donald L. Branca, Salt Lake City, Utah
				Branca, 1 up		BYE
					Cook, 3 and 2	O. Gordon Brewer, Jr., Huntingdon Valley, Pa.
		Courville, 4 and 3				John Cook, Rolling Hills Estates, Calif.
					Caprera, 3 and 2	Robert G. Caprera, Southbridge, Mass.
				Caprera, 4 and 2		Don Beattie, Pompano Beach, Fla.
					Preston	Michael Preston, Cream Ridge, N. J.
			Courville, 1 up			BYE
					Courville, 1 up	Dennis C. Green, St. Louis, Mo.
				Courville, 4 and 3		Jerry Courville, Norwalk, Conn.
					Archer	James S. Archer, Shawnee Mission, Kans.
	Courville, 1 up					BYE
					Heath, 5 and 4	Skeeter Heath, Hampton, Va.
				Heath, 3 and 2		H. Clare Shepard, Birmingham, Mich.
					Mikles	Lee Mikles, Camarillo, Calif.
			Heath, 2 and 1			BYE
					Harrison	Charles W. Harrison, Atlanta, Ga.
				Harrison, 3 and 2		BYE
					Tryon, 6 and 5	William Tryon, Jr., Elmira, N. Y.
		Heath, 1 up				James N. Manuel, Las Vegas, Nev.
					Horne, 4 and 3	David S. Ishii, Lihue, Hawaii
				West, 2 and 1		Dick Horne, Mt. Pleasant, S. C.
					West	Martin R. West, III, Bethesda, Md.
			West, 4 and 3			BYE
					Jones, 3 and 2	Dr. Amos Jones, Atlanta, Ga.
				Jones, 1 up		J. B. Johnston, Jr., New Canaan, Conn.
					Harris	John R. Harris, Edina, Minn.
Strange, 2 and 1						BYE
					Nash	Arthur Nash, Kent, Ohio
				Strange, 2 and 1		BYE
					Strange, 4 and 3	Mark Boyajian, Belleville, Ill.
			Strange, 3 and 1			Curtis Strange, Virginia Beach, Va.
					Steiner	Ned Steiner, W. Caldwell, N. J.
				Joseph, 1 up		BYE
					Joseph, 4 and 3	Kenn L. Teel, Jr., San Clemente, Calif.
		Strange, 4 and 3				Jim Joseph, Chicago, Ill.
					Scott, 3 and 2	Mark Winstrom, Omaha, Neb.
				Lee, 5 and 4		Curt Scott, Louisville, Ky.
					Lee	Stan Lee, Baton Rouge, La.
			Allen, 2 and 1			BYE
					Allen	Donald C. Allen, Rochester, N. Y.
				Allen, 4 and 3		BYE
					Kuntz, 2 up	Vincent A. Scarpetta, Jr., Jermyn, Pa.
	Strange, 1 up					Robert W. Kuntz, Larchmont, N. Y.
					Mallon, 4 and 3	Jack S. Stevens, Wichita, Kans.
				Mallon, 7 and 5		Bill Mallon, Framingham, Mass.
					Stein	Doug Stein, Great Neck, N. Y.
			Mallon, 21 holes			BYE
					Ridley, 4 and 3	Edward Meister, Jr., Willoughby, Ohio
				Ridley, 19 holes		Fred S. Ridley, Winter Haven, Fla.
					Terban	Howard Terban, Newton, Mass.
		Mallon, 3 and 2				BYE
					Hollowell, 2 up	Bruce C. Hollowell, Springfield, Mo.
				Hollowell, 19 holes		David Martin, Williamsville, N. Y.
					Fairchild	Robert M. Fairchild, Bay Village, Ohio
			Gray, 6 and 5			BYE
					Gray, 5 and 4	A. Downing Gray, Pensacola, Fla.
				Gray, 4 and 3		Stuart Francis, Madison, Ohio
					Corzilius, 3 and 2	Bruce Douglass, Stoughton, Mass.
						David N. Corzilius, Wilmington, Del.

THIRD QUARTER — LOWER

1st Round (18 Holes)	2nd Round (18 Holes)	3rd Round (18 Holes)	4th Round (18 Holes)	5th Round (18 Holes)	6th Round (18 Holes)	
Richard B. Tucker, Virginia Beach, Va.	Arnold,					
Julian R. Arnold, Miami, Fla.	4 and 2	Arnold,				
William H. Wellman, Huntington, W. Va.	Magee	4 and 2				
Frank D. Magee, Meadowbrook, Pa.	5 and 4		Arnold,			
David Ferrell, Mobile, Ala.	Ferrell		2 up			
BYE		Siderowf,		Arnold, 2 and 1		
James R. Johnson, Levelland, Texas	Siderowf,	3 and 2				
Richard L. Siderowf, Westport, Conn.	8 and 7					
Frank F. Schmidt, Delaware, Ohio	Schmidt,					
Todd Crandall, Ashtabula, Ohio	1 up	Byman,				
Robert T. Byman, Raleigh, N. C.	Byman	6 and 5				
BYE			Byman,			
Brian Shanks, Phoenix, Arizona	Shanks,		4 and 3			
Don Sowers, Whitfield, Pa.	5 and 4	Shanks,				
Luther P. Godwin, Poplar Bluff, Mo.	Godwin	21 holes			Sucher, 1 up	
BYE						
James Nosewicz, Aurora, Colo.	Veghte,					
Jack Veghte, Clearwater, Fla.	2 and 1	Sucher,				
Richard Sucher, Mequon, Wis.	Sucher	2 and 1				
BYE			Sucher,			
Henri de Lozier, Hyattsville, Md.	de Lozier		2 and 1			
BYE		Jacobsen,				
Del de Windt, Bloomfield Hills, Mich.	Jacobsen,	4 and 3		Sucher, 1 up		
Peter Jacobsen, Portland, Ore.	3 and 2					
Fred Behymer, Jr., Potterville, Mich.	Behymer,					
William W. Gerber, III, Jamesville, N. Y.	1 up	Rouse,				
Douglas S. Rouse, Boulder, Colo.	Rouse	1 up				
BYE			Rouse,			
Michael J. Sullivan, Ocala, Fla.	Sullivan,		3 and 2			
Marvin M. Rockholt, Memphis, Tenn.	4 and 2	Sullivan,				
Mark Witt, Norman, Okla.	Witt	6 and 5				Grace, 2 up
BYE						
David T. Pelz, Beltsville, Md.	Pelz					
BYE		Willard,				
Brian C. Willard, Silver Spring, Md.	Willard,	19 holes				
James F. Morris, Springfield, Mo.	3 and 1		Willard,			
Michael Brannan, Salinas, Calif.	Brannan		4 and 3			
BYE		Haines,				
George E. Haines, Jr., Far Hills, N. J.	Haines,	5 and 4		Willard, 1 up		
Bob Bailey, Oak Park, Ill.	2 and 1					
Dennis M. Spencer, Sylvania, Ohio	Popa,					
Thomas T. Popa, Columbus, Ohio	1 up	Brown,				
Walter J. Brown, Jr., Melrose, Mass.	Brown	3 and 2				
BYE			Lewis,			
William A. Lewis, Florence, S. C.	Lewis		3 and 2			
BYE		Lewis,				
Gary W. Yohe, West Chester, Pa.	Bedillion,	7 and 5			Grace, 6 and 5	
Mark Bedillion, Austin, Texas	3 and 1					
Vincent L. Head, Tampa, Fla.	Head,					
Don Shevorski, Upland, Calif.	2 and 1	Harvey,				
Bill Harvey, Jamestown, N. C.	Harvey	4 and 3				
BYE			Harvey,			
Tom R. Jones, Tulsa, Okla.	Jones,		1 up			
John R. Sterchi, Jr., Knoxville, Tenn.	3 and 2	Jones,				
Bob Edgerton, Raleigh, N. C.	Edgerton	6 and 5		Grace, 5 and 3		
BYE						
Larry Mattox, Columbia, S. C.	Mattox,					
Dennis M. Sullivan, Grant Park, Ill.	1 up	Mattox,				
Charles G. Hancock, Greenville, Ala.	Hancock	1 up				
BYE			Grace,			
Glen Sullivan, Lexington, Mass.	Sullivan,		6 and 4			
Taylor B. Metcalfe, Cincinnati, Ohio	3 and 1	Grace,				
Donnell J. Smith, The Dalles, Ore.	Grace,	6 and 5				
John P. Grace, Fort Worth, Texas	4 and 3					

SEMI-FINAL ROUND (18 Holes)—John P. Grace defeated Gary Koch, 3 and 1

HALF

FOURTH QUARTER

	6th Round (18 Holes)	5th Round (18 Holes)	4th Round (18 Holes)	3rd Round (18 Holes)	2nd Round (18 Holes)	1st Round (18 Holes)
					Allen,	Robert M. Allen, II, Yardley, Pa.
				Giles,	5 and 4	Stanley Moore, Jr., Miami, Fla.
				4 and 3	Giles,	Marvin Giles, III, Richmond, Va.
			Cooke,		5 and 3	Keith Mohan, Flint, Mich.
			1 up		Cooke	L. Graham Cooke, Quebec, Canada
				Cooke,		BYE
				3 and 2	Irey,	Chester Sanok, Montclair, N. J.
		Pomerantz, 4 and 3			2 and 1	Roc D. Irey, Mansfield, Ohio
					Heyl,	Richard E. Heyl, Sterling, Va.
				Heyl,	5 and 4	E. R. Updegraff, Tucson, Ariz.
				5 and 4	Colaguori	Richard Colaguori, Long Branch, N. J.
			Pomerantz,			BYE
			2 and 1		Pomerantz,	Michael Milligan, Bloomington, Ill.
				Pomerantz,	1 up	Jeffrey Pomerantz, Weston, Conn.
				5 and 3	Wishart	Lawrence Wishart, Reno, Nev.
	Pomerantz, 4 and 3					BYE
					Gabrielsen,	J. P. Thompson, III, Greenville, S. C.
				Blooston,	6 and 5	James R. Gabrielsen, Atlanta, Ga.
				3 and 2	Blooston	Richard J. Blooston, Edina, Minn.
			Fischesser,			BYE
			3 and 2		Fischesser	Doug Fischesser, Niles, Mich.
				Fischesser,		BYE
				19 holes	Short,	Leslie R. Fowler, Boulder, Colo.
		Green, 1 up			2 and 1	Kerry P. Short, S. Vineland, Ontario, Canada
					Green,	Peter J. Green, Franklin, Mich.
				Green,	5 and 4	Roger Null, Davenport, Iowa
				1 up	DeBernardi	Richard C. DeBernardi, Roseburg, Ore.
			Green,			BYE
			1 up		Streck,	Ronald R. Streck, Tulsa, Okla.
				Fox,	19 holes	Lindy Miller, Ft. Worth, Texas
				20 holes	Fox	Thomas K. Fox, Jr., Glen Head, N. Y.
Koch, 6 and 4						BYE
					Enger	Robert B. Enger, Lake Quivira, Kans.
				Edwards,		BYE
				4 and 3	Edwards,	David Edwards, Edmond, Okla.
			Koch,		4 and 3	James G. Tuttle, Jr., Albermarle, N. C.
			2 and 1		Koch	Gary Koch, Temple Terrace, Fla.
				Koch,		BYE
				2 and 1	Cooper,	W. Rhode Hill, Atlanta, Ga.
		Koch, 1 up			3 and 2	Lance Cooper, Miami, Fla.
					Reaume,	Jeffrey Reaume, Ypsilanti, Mich.
				Reaume,	22 holes	John E. Kenny, Jr., Northfield, Ill.
				3 and 2	Sigel	Jay Sigel, Berwyn, Pa.
			Heafner,			BYE
			5 and 3		Nash	David S. Nash, Weymouth, Mass.
				Heafner,		BYE
				4 and 3	Heafner,	Clayton V. Heafner, Cary, N. C.
	Koch, 1 up				3 and 2	Peter A. Wallenborn, III, Roanoke, Va.
					Simmons,	Randal M. Simmons, Shreveport, La.
				Simmons,	4 and 3	Ronald Pelton, Downey, Calif.
				4 and 3	Smith	Charles E. Smith, Delaware, Ohio
			Simmons,			BYE
			1 up		Gibbs,	John T. Gibbs, III, Augusta, Ga.
				Bean,	1 up	Fred van Bargen, Rockville, Md.
				1 up	Bean	Andy Bean, Lakeland, Fla.
		Houston, 21 holes				BYE
					Kovar,	Warren Kovar, Houston, Texas
				Saylor,	3 and 2	John P. Kyle, Beltsville, Md.
				5 and 3	Saylor	Tim Saylor, East Bend, N. C.
			Houston,			BYE
			3 and 2		Sylvan,	John R. Birmingham, Pittsburgh, Pa.
				Houston,	3 and 2	Gus Sylvan, III, Columbia, S. C.
				2 and 1	Houston,	Bill Celli, Piedmont, Calif.
					7 and 5	Shelby Houston, Shreveport, La.

1975
SEVENTY-FIFTH AMATEUR CHAMPIONSHIP

Held at Country Club of Virginia (James River Course), Richmond, Virginia, August 26-31
Yardage—6,672. Par 70. 2,528 Entries, 200 Qualifiers, 200 Starters
Championship entirely at match play.

FINAL ROUND (36 Holes)—Fred S. Ridley defeated Keith Fergus, 2 Up.

FIRST QUARTER

1st Round (18 Holes)	2nd Round (18 Holes)	3rd Round (18 Holes)	4th Round (18 Holes)	5th Round (18 Holes)	UPPER 6th Round (18 Holes)	
Gunnar Bennett, Lake Forest, Ill.	Bennett,					
Charles H. Whitehill, Pittsburgh, Pa.	4 and 3	Robb,				
Lenoir C. Keesler, Charlotte, N.C.	Robb,	4 and 2				
Robert Robb, College Park, Ga.	2 and 1		Andrachak,			
Johnny Andrachak, Hollywood, Fla.	Andrachak		2 and 1			
BYE		Andrachak,				
Gregory H. Morey, Los Angeles, Calif.	Alexander,	2 and 1				
Stewart M. Alexander, III, St. Petersburg, Fla.	3 and 2					
Paul Haire, Memphis, Tenn.	Haire,			Haire, 19 holes		
Haynes Richardson, Newport News, Va.	2 and 1	Haire,				
Shane Fox, Abilene, Texas	Fox	3 and 1				
BYE			Haire,			
Gene A. Ploucha, Mt. Morris, Mich.	Jacobsen,		3 and 2			
Peter Jacobsen, Portland, Ore.	2 and 1	Dunaway,				
Shuford Dunaway, Charlotte, N.C.	Dunaway	1 up				
BYE						
Vincent A. Scarpetta, Jr., Jermyn, Pa.	Scarpetta,				Kenny, 1 up	
Reid Brannon, Cincinnati, Ohio	4 and 2	Kenny,				
Philip B. Kenny, Northbrook, Ill.	Kenny	6 and 4				
BYE			Kenny,			
John P. Grace, Fort Worth, Texas	Grace		2 and 1			
BYE		Grace,				
Richard Smith, Virginia Beach, Va.	Mason,	4 and 3				
James T. Mason, Kirkwood, Mo.	4 and 3					
Rogert T. McManus, Hartville, Ohio	McManus,			Kenny, 5 and 3		
Doug H. Fichesser, Connersville, Ind.	2 and 1	English,				
Jeffrey S. English, Shawnee Mission, Kans.	English	5 and 4				
BYE			Vershure,			
Skeeter Heath, Hampton, Va.	Heath,		3 and 1			
Christopher K. Campbell, Inverness, Fla.	3 and 1	Vershure,				
Rick Vershure, Pontiac, Mich.	Vershure	1 up				
BYE						
Walter J. Brown, Jr., Melrose, Mass.	Brown					Bean, 1 up
BYE		Bean,				
Andy Bean, Lakeland, Fla.	Bean,	4 and 3				
Gary A. Tinney, Pensacola, Fla.	8 and 6		Bean,			
Paul Tankersley, Clovis, N.M.	Tankersley		3 and 2			
BYE		Jacobson,				
Judd Silverman, Toledo, Ohio	Jacobson,	2 and 1				
Gary D. Jacobson, Minnetonka, Minn.	6 and 4					
Jeffrey H. Hadley, Rye, N.Y.	Radder,			Bean, 4 and 2		
Rick Radder, Edina, Minn.	2 and 1	Hyndman,				
William Hyndman, III, Huntingdon Valley, Pa.	Hyndman	5 and 4				
BYE			Puett,			
E. Michael Petit, Knoxville, Tenn.	Petit		19 holes			
BYE		Puett,				
Aly Trompas, San Diego, Calif.	Puett,	3 and 2				
Roane Puett, Austin, Texas	19 Holes					
Brian L. Shanks, Phoenix, Ariz.	Shanks,				Bean, 2 and 1	
John Cudd, Augusta, Ga.	20 holes	Shanks,				
Jay H. Rothenberger, Ft. Lauderdale, Fla.	Rothenberger	5 and 4				
BYE			Byman,			
Jerry Cundari, Portland, Ore.	Byman,		8 and 6			
Robert T. Byman, Raleigh, N.C.	3 and 2	Byman,				
Robert G. Caprera, Southbridge, Mass.	Caprera	8 and 6				
BYE						
Thomas Bartolacci, Fallsington, Pa.	De Francesco,			Byman, 3 and 1		
Wayne De Francesco, McLean, Va.	19 holes	De Francesco,				
Jerry Courville, Norwalk, Conn.	Courville	3 and 2				
BYE			De Francesco,			
Gary C. Wright, Englewood, Colo.	Rose,		2 and 1			
J. Franklin Rose, Topeka, Kans.	6 and 5	Rose,				
Andy Hyjek, Cedar Grove, N.J.	Gause,	5 and 3				
Bobby W. Gause, Columbia, S.C.	6 and 5					

SEMI-FINAL ROUND (18 Holes)—Fred S. Ridley defeated Andy Bean, 2 and 1.

HALF

SECOND QUARTER

6th Round (18 Holes)	5th Round (18 Holes)	4th Round (18 Holes)	3rd Round (18 Holes)	2nd Round (18 Holes)	1st Round (18 Holes)
				Witt,	Mark Witt, Norman, Okla.
			Bliss,	19 holes	Bernard A. Dunne, Jr., Pitman, N.J.
			1 up	Bliss,	Donald Bliss, Earth City, Mo.
		Bliss,		6 and 5	Jon W. Dunn, Oakmont, Pa.
		2 up		Alberts	Dennis H. Alberts, Albuquerque, N.M.
			Willard,		BYE
			2 and 1	Willard,	James H. Frick, Jr., Stamford, Conn.
				7 and 6	Brian Willard, Silver Spring, Md.
	Strange, 5 and 4			Jacobs,	Mark Rohde, Marshalltown, Ia.
			Jacobs,	3 and 2	John J. Jacobs, IV, Riverside, Calif.
			2 and 1	Malehorn	Edward L. Malehorn, York Haven, Pa.
		Strange,			BYE
		4 and 2		Strange,	Curtis Strange, Virginia Beach, Va.
			Strange,	5 and 4	Richard C. Peterson, Cincinnati, Ohio
			4 and 3	Thames	Woody Thames, Beaumont, Texas
					BYE
Ridley, 2 and 1				Brannan,	Michael Brannan, Salinas, Calif.
			Brannan,	4 and 3	James W. Hamilton, Raleigh, N.C.
			8 and 7	Carson	Craig L. Carson, Columbus, Ohio
		Kelley,			BYE
		5 and 4		Kelley	Ronald K. Kelley, Richmond, Va.
			Kelley,		BYE
			20 holes	Haynes,	Patrick R. McGowan, Colusa, Calif.
				19 holes	Lamar Haynes, Shreveport, La.
	Ridley, 4 and 3			Kircher,	John G. Kircher, Pittsford, N.Y.
			Waitt,	1 up	Charles W. Harrison, Atlanta, Ga.
			2 and 1	Waitt	Rocky Waitt, Wichita, Kans.
		Ridley,			BYE
		2 and 1		Ridley,	Steve Summers, Dallas, Texas
			Ridley,	5 and 3	Fred S. Ridley, Winter Haven, Fla.
			3 and 1	Mangan	Robert T. Mangan, Olympia Fields, Ill.
					BYE
Ridley, 19 holes				Goethals	Glenn Goethals, Cincinnati, Ohio
			Britton,		BYE
			5 and 4	Britton,	William Britton, Staten Island, N.Y.
		Jones,		4 and 3	Donald Taylor, Taylors, S.C.
		3 and 1		Fowler	Leslie R. Fowler, Boulder, Colo.
			Jones,		BYE
			2 and 1	Jones,	Tom Jones, Jr., Tulsa, Okla.
	Jones, 6 and 4			4 and 3	Greg Zorilla, Yonkers, N.Y.
				Ashley,	William A. Landis, Jefferson City, Mo.
			Gray,	3 and 2	Guy Ashley, Boston, Mass.
			6 and 5	Gray	A. Downing Gray, Pensacola, Fla.
		Jacobsen,			BYE
		2 up		Woodley	William K. Woodley, Barksdale AFB, La.
			Jacobsen,		BYE
			3 and 2	Jacobsen,	David Jacobsen, Portland, Ore.
Veghte, 1 up				19 holes	Jay Blumenfeld, Millburn, N.J.
				Morey,	Dale Morey, High Point, N.C.
			Goodwin,	5 and 3	Kirk Goss, Chickasha, Okla.
			1 up	Goodwin	Barton Goodwin, Houston, Texas
		Goodwin,			BYE
		5 and 3		Young,	Robert E. Young, Jr., Dunwoody, Ga.
			McBride,	1 up	Martin R. West, III, Bethesda, Md.
			5 and 3	McBride	Michael McBride, Ridgewood, N.J.
	Veghte, 19 holes				BYE
				Veghte,	Jack Veghte, Clearwater, Fla.
			Veghte,	4 and 3	Roger Simpkins, Chevy Chase, Md.
			2 up	Ward	Jim Ward, Huntingon, W. Va.
		Veghte,			BYE
		2 and 1		Lum,	Bob Abbey, Huntington Beach, Calif.
			Mallon,	1 up	Wren Lum, Mobile, Ala.
			2 and 1	Mallon,	Bill Mallon, Framingham, Mass.
				2 and 1	Gary Treater, Warren, Ohio

THIRD QUARTER — LOWER

1st Round (18 Holes)	2nd Round (18 Holes)	3rd Round (18 Holes)	4th Round (18 Holes)	5th Round (18 Holes)	6th Round (18 Holes)	
William L. Cheairs, Memphis, Tenn.	Hartoin,					
Ronald J. Hartoin, Cincinnati, Ohio	3 and 2	Norman,				
Charles H. Beck, Jr., Fayetteville, N.C.	Norman,	4 and 3				
Mark Norman, Bloomington, Minn.	6 and 5		Mayo,			
Jeffrey Pomerantz, Fairfield, Conn.	Pomerantz		2 up			
BYE		Mayo,		Boyajian, 3 and 1		
William Payne Stewart, Springfield, Mo.	Mayo,	3 and 1				
Steve Mayo, Knoxville, Tenn.	5 and 3					
Stuart Francis, Madison, Ohio	Simpson,					
Tim Simpson, Atlanta, Ga.	2 and 1	Boyajian,				
Mark Boyajian, Belleville, Ill.	Boyajian	1 up				
BYE			Boyajian,			
James M. Phillips, Westport, Conn.	Ziemski,		6 and 5			
Bruce Ziemski, Dudley, Mass.	5 and 3	Ziemski,			Boyajian, 3 and 2	
Richard L. Siderowf, Westport, Conn.	Siderowf	1 up				
BYE						
Paul Schock, Sioux Falls, S.D.	Allen,					
Donald C. Allen, Rochester, N.Y.	5 and 4	Saunders,				
Dennis Saunders, ,Yorba Linda, Calif.	Saunders	3 and 2				
BYE			Saunders,			
John D. McKey, Jr., Delray Beach, Fla.	McKey		2 up			
BYE		Fitzgibbon,		Mitchell, 2 up		
James A. Fitzgibbon, Coral Gables, Fla.	Fitzgibbon,	3 and 2				
George E. Graefe, III, Jamesville, Md.	4 and 2					
Marshall Marraccini, Elizabeth, Pa.	Marraccini,					
Michael D. Reid, Kirkland, Wash.	20 holes	Trombley,				
William J. Trombley, Dallas, Texas	Trombley	4 and 3				
BYE			Mitchell,			
Paul M. Darwin, Fort Worth, Texas	Mitchell,		5 and 4			
William F. Mitchell, Stratton Mt., Vt.	2 and 1	Mitchell,				deLozier, 3 and 2
Thomas S. Delcher, Erdenheim, Pa.	Delcher	6 and 4				
BYE						
Douglas Nelson, Little Falls, N.J.	Nelson					
BYE		Nelson,				
Mark B. Andrew, Albemarle, N.C.	Andrew,	3 and 2				
Bruce Hollowell, Springfield, Mo.	3 and 2		deLozier,			
Dave DeRosa, East Wayne, N.J.	DeRosa		3 and 2			
BYE		deLozier,		deLozier, 3 and 2		
Keith Mohr, Mt. Pleasant, Mich.	deLozier,	5 and 4				
Henri deLozier, Silver Spring, Md.	19 holes					
Ken Moran, Suffolk, Va.	Flax,					
Jeffrey Flax, Richmond, Va.	4 and 3	Reaume,				
Jeffrey F. Reaume, Ypsilanti, Mich.	Reaume	3 and 2				
BYE			Reaume,			
James R. Gabrielsen, Atlanta, Ga.	Gabrielsen		1 up			
BYE		Holtgrieve,			deLozier, 3 and 2	
W. Nicholas Neumann, III, Des Moines, Ia.	Holtgrieve,	2 and 1				
Jim Holtgrieve, Kirkwood, Mo.	6 and 4					
Bryan Beymer, Huntington, W. Va.	Beymer,					
Patrick Chapman, San Leandro, Calif.	2 and 1	DuPre,				
David DuPre, Columbia, S.C.	DuPre	2 up				
BYE			DuPre,			
Thomas R. Evans, Northbrook, Ill.	Evans,		3 and 2			
Ludwig Schenk, Mansfield, Ohio	1 up	Evans,		DuPre, 3 and 2		
Jay Haas, Belleville, Ill.	Haas	19 holes				
BYE						
Michael W. Donald, Hollywood, Fla.	Brown,					
Mills Brown, Phoenix, Ariz.	20 holes	Streck,				
Ronald R. Streck, Tulsa, Okla.	Streck	6 and 4				
BYE			Padgett,			
Kirk Padgett, Colorado Springs, Colo.	Padgett,		1 up			
Ray Montgomery, III, Louisville, Ky.	4 and 3	Padgett,				
Clayton V. Heafner, Cary, N.C.	Heafner,	19 holes				
Stephen A. Smith, New York, N.Y.	3 and 1					

SEMI-FINAL ROUND (18 Holes)—Keith Fergus defeated Henri deLozier, 3 and 2.

HALF

FOURTH QUARTER

	6th Round (18 Holes)	5th Round (18 Holes)	4th Round (18 Holes)	3rd Round (18 Holes)	2nd Round (18 Holes)	1st Round (18 Holes)
					Brown, 1 up	Ted Huff, Winter Haven, Fla.
				Brown, 2 up		Russell C. Brown, Phoenix, Ariz.
					Sigel, 6 and 5	Gustaf J. Sylvan, III, Columbia, S.C.
			Loeffler, 5 and 3			Jay Sigel, Berwyn, Pa.
					Van Dyne	Charles Van Dyne, Prairie Village, Kans.
				Loeffler, 1 up		BYE
					Loeffler, 3 and 2	Charles C. Moyer, Wood River, Neb.
		Loeffler, 1 up				William R. Loeffler, Englewood, Colo.
					Ten Broeck, 5 and 4	Michael Preston, Cream Ridge, N.J.
				Ten Broeck, 2 and 1		Lance Ten Broeck, Chicago, Ill.
					Pate	Alan T. Pate, Mobile, Ala.
			Douglass, 20 holes			BYE
					Marucci, 4 and 3	Tom Culligan, San Mateo, Calif.
				Douglass, 20 holes		George Marucci, Jr., Wayne, Pa.
					Douglass	Bruce R. Douglass, Stoughton, Mass.
	Loeffler, 4 and 3					BYE
					Price, 3 and 2	Stanlye J. Price, III, Pittsburgh, Pa.
				Price, 19 holes		Douglas D. Lumpkin, Knoxville, Tenn.
					Giles	Marvin Giles, III, Richmond, Va.
			Price, 1 up			BYE
					Liner	George L. Liner, III, Chattanooga, Tenn.
				Voyles, 4 and 3		BYE
					Voyles, 5 and 4	William F. Voyles, Marietta, Ga.
		Price, 2 and 1				Robert T. Ladd, Pittsford, N.Y.
					Hoyt, 5 and 4	Raymond J. Vanyo, San Bernardino, Calif.
				Beutler, 1 up		Robert E. Hoyt, Houston, Texas
					Beutler	John Allen Beutler, Hayden Lake, Ida.
			Spencer, 2 and 1			BYE
					Marrello, 4 and 3	Philip G. Lumsden, Arlington, Texas
				Spencer, 3 and 2		Fran Marrello, Waterbury, Conn.
Fergus, 3 and 2					Spencer	Dennis M. Spencer, Sylvania, Ohio
						BYE
					Holmes	James W. Holmes, Aiken, S.C.
				Holmes, 2 and 1		BYE
					Kelley, 1 up	Thomas Kelley, Ft. Wayne, Ind.
			Holmes, 2 and 1			William C. Campbell, Huntington, W. Va.
					Summa	Gerry L. Summa, Larchwood, Iowa
				Baldwin, 6 and 4		BYE
					Baldwin, 1 up	John C. Baldwin, Chicago, Ill.
		Hoyt, 3 and 2				Bobby Brow, Coronado, Calif.
					Smyers, 3 and 2	Steven R. Smyers, Houston, Texas
				Hoyt, 3 and 1		James T. Meyer, Cherry Hill, N.J.
					Hoyt	D. Scott Hoyt, Menlo Park, Calif.
			Hoyt, 2 and 1			BYE
					de Windt	Del de Windt, Bloomfield Hills, Mich.
				de Windt, 3 and 2		BYE
					Zabell, 4 and 3	Harold Harder, Madison, Wis.
	Fergus, 3 and 2					David Zabell, Columbus, Ohio
					Wallenborn, 1 up	Richard Sucher, Mequon, Wis.
				Wallenborn, 3 and 2		Peter A. Wallenborn, III, Roanoke, Va.
					Strafaci	Frank D. Strafaci, Jr., Miami, Fla.
			Fergus, 4 and 3			BYE
					Fergus, 4 and 3	Keith Fergus, Houston, Texas
				Fergus, 3 and 2		Joe Videtta, Canton, Mass.
					Simpson	Scott Simpson, San Diego, Calif.
		Fergus, 4 and 2				BYE
					Timyan, 3 and 1	Mark Timyan, Grand Blanc, Mich.
				Bilbo, 1 up		David Thore, Reidsville, N.C.
					Bilbo	Robert F. Bilbo, Beltsville, Md.
			Bilbo, 19 holes			BYE
					Anderson, 1 up	Robert J. Anderson, Minneapolis,, Minn.
				Fabel, 7 and 6		Albert Highducheck, Syracuse, N.Y.
					Fabel, 4 and 3	Brad Fabel, Madisonville, Ky.
						Stephen W. Prugh, Spokane, Wash.

1976
SEVENTY-SIXTH AMATEUR CHAMPIONSHIP

Held at Bel-Air Country Club, Los Angeles, California, August 31-September 5
Yardage—6,507. Par 70. 2,681 Entries, 200 Qualifiers, 200 Starters
Championship entirely at match play.

FINAL ROUND (36 Holes)—Bill Sander defeated C. Parker Moore, Jr., 8 and 6

UPPER

FIRST QUARTER

1st Round (18 Holes)	2nd Round (18 Holes)	3rd Round (18 Holes)	4th Round (18 Holes)	5th Round (18 Holes)	6th Round (18 Holes)	
William A. Sibbick, Jr., Martinsville, Va.	Marucci,					
George E. Marucci, Jr., Havertown, Pa.	2 and 1	Levin,				
William G. Moody, III, Athens, Ga.	Levin,	4 and 2				
Don Levin, Sacramento, Calif.	6 and 5		Tinder,			
Mark E. Tinder, Monterey, Calif.	Tinder,		4 and 3			
BYE	Bye	Tinder,				
Harvey Ortof, Bayside, N.Y.	Harrison,	1 up		Tinder, 4 and 3		
Britt Harrison, Beaumont, Texas	5 and 4					
Randall M. Mahar, Portland, Ore.	Clarke,					
Douglas Clarke, La Jolla, Calif.	3 and 2	Gibbs,				
John T. Gibbs, III, Augusta, Ga.	Gibbs,	2 up				
BYE	Bye		Gibbs,			
Richard C. Peterson, Cincinnati, Ohio	Cusick,		1 up			
Reggie Cusick, Benton, Ark.	3 and 2	Jones,				
Tommy R. Jones, Bartlesville, Okla.	Jones,	4 and 3			Tinder, 5 and 3	
BYE	Bye					
James G. Harrison, Ontario, Canada	Harrison,					
Michael Preston, Matawan, N.J.	1 up	Evans,				
Thomas R. Evans, Lake Forest, Ill.	Evans,	2 up				
BYE	Bye		Hancock,			
Larry Collins, Walnut, Calif.	Collins,		5 and 4	Ten Broeck, 4 and 3		
BYE	Bye	Hancock,				
Phillip Hancock, Greenville, Ala.	Hancock,	3 and 2				
William D. Brafford, Orchard Lake, Mich.	2 and 1					
Charles E. Smith, Worthington, Ohio	Creagh,					
George G. Creagh, Nashville, Tenn.	4 and 2	Creagh,				
Bill Loeffler, Englewood, Colo.	Loeffler,	19 holes				
BYE	Bye		Ten Broeck,			
Bruce A. Scamehorn, Winter Haven, Fla.	McGinnis,		2 and 1			
Thomas W. McGinnis, Jr., Latrobe, Pa.	4 and 3	Ten Broeck,				
Lance Ten Broeck, Chicago, Ill.	Ten Broeck,	2 and 1				Souza, 19 holes
BYE	Bye					
Nathan G. Pomeroy, Sun City, Ariz.	Pomeroy,					
BYE	Bye	Miller,				
Lindy Miller, Ft. Worth, Texas	Miller,	5 and 4				
Monte Schauer, Victoria, Texas	3 and 2		Powers,			
Foster C. Bradley, Jr., Hollywood, Calif.	Bradley,		3 and 2			
BYE	Bye	Powers,				
Michael F. Powers, Oakland, Calif.	Powers,	3 and 1		Souza, 2 up		
J. Scott Porter, Richmond, Ind.	4 and 3					
Mark J. Balen, East Aurora, N.Y.	Simmons,					
Randy Simmons, Shreveport, La.	4 and 3	Souza,				
Stan K. M. Souza, Honolulu, Hawaii	Souza,	2 and 1				
BYE	Bye		Souza,			
Doug Roxburgh, Vancouver, B.C.	Roxburgh,		3 and 2			
BYE	Bye	Roxburgh,				
Harold Garrison, Albuquerque, N.M.	Garrison,	8 and 7			Souza, 19 holes	
Steven Gebert, Wichita, Kans.	8 and 6					
Mark Boyajian, Belleville, Ill.	Boyajian,					
Wade Adams, Dallas, Texas	2 and 1	Boyajian,				
Jack Van Ess, Comstock Park, Mich.	Van Ess,	2 and 1				
BYE	Bye		Strange,			
Craig Meyer, Hastings, Neb.	Strange,		3 and 2			
Allan Strange, Portsmouth, Va.	3 and 2	Strange,		Strange, 4 and 3		
Dr. R. T. Tschetter, Sioux Falls, S.D.	Tschetter,	5 and 3				
BYE	Bye					
Chick Hunter, Charlotte, N.C.	Pini,					
Bryan Pini, Santa Cruz, Calif.	1 up	Pini,				
Henri C. de Lozier, Jr., Chevy Chase, Md.	de Lozier,	3 and 2				
BYE	Bye		Pini,			
Phil Whitler, Springfield, Ill.	Rassett,		1 up			
Joe Rassett, Turlock, Calif.	6 and 5	Rassett,				
Charles D. Schnebly, Daytona Beach, Fla.	Schnebly,	6 and 5				
David P. Watson, Harahan, La.	2 up					

SEMI-FINAL ROUND (18 Holes)—C. Parker Moore, Jr., defeated Stan K. M. Souza, 19 holes.

HALF

SECOND QUARTER

Half	6th Round (18 Holes)	5th Round (18 Holes)	4th Round (18 Holes)	3rd Round (18 Holes)	2nd Round (18 Holes)	1st Round (18 Holes)
Moore, 1 up	Moore, 2 and 1	Hays, 6 and 4	Donald, 2 and 1	Simpson, 2 and 1	Simpson, 4 and 3	Douglas Kaczenski, Westhampton, N.Y. Tim Simpson, Atlanta, Ga.
					Armstrong, 4 and 2	Douglas P. Nelson, Wayne, N.J. Roger Armstrong, Oakland, Calif.
				Donald, 1 up	Veghte, Bye	Jack Veghte, St. Petersburg, Fla. BYE
					Donald, 20 holes	Michael W. Donald, Statesboro, Ga. Brian E. Gaddy, Pasadena, Calif.
			Hays, 19 holes	Marello, 2 and 1	Hoffman, 2 and 1	Tom Hoffman, Mankato, Minn. William A. Hoffer, Elgin, Ill.
					Marello, Bye	Fran Marello, Watertown, Conn. BYE
				Hays, 1 up	Gray, 3 and 2	A. Downing Gray, Pensacola, Fla. Louis Buttermark, Staten Island, N.Y.
					Hays, Bye	Greg Hays, Fayetteville, Ark. BYE
		Moore, 2 and 1	Siderowf, 5 and 4	Barnes, 5 and 4	Billings, 2 and 1	Guy R. Billings, Haslett, Mich. Bruce C. Hollowell, Springfield, Mo.
					Barnes Bye	Edward T. Barnes, Jr., Kennesaw, Ga. BYE
				Siderowf, 2 and 1	Boros, Bye	Julius Boros, Jr., Miami Beach, Fla. BYE
					Siderowf, 1 up	Richard L. Siderowf, Purchase, N.Y. Michael Barge, Fargo, N.D.
			Moore, 4 and 3	Farrow, 3 and 1	Cain, 3 and 1	Richard W. Cain, Louisville, Ky. Greg W. Ramsey, Colorado Springs, Colo.
					Farrow, Bye	Gregory P. Farrow, Marlton, N.J. BYE
				Moore, 1 up	Horne, 2 up	John J. Jacobs, IV, Riverside, Calif. Dick Horne, Mt. Pleasant, S.C.
					Moore, Bye	C. Parker Moore, Jr., Laurens, S.C. BYE
	Reid, 1 up	Reid, 3 and 2	Heisler, 2 and 1	Edwards, 3 and 2	Edwards, Bye	David Edwards, Edmond, Okla. BYE
					Tutwiler, 4 and 3	Matt Ellison, Ventura, Calif. Ed Tutwiler, Indianapolis, Ind.
				Heisler, 2 and 1	Heisler, Bye	Kim F. Heisler, Aurora, Ohio BYE
					Norton, 3 and 2	Peter Teravainen, Duxbury, Mass. Steve Norton, Reading, Pa.
			Reid, 3 and 1	Reid, 4 and 3	Davis, 3 and 2	Phil C. Gibbs, Olathe, Kans. Lee Davis, Los Angeles, Calif.
					Reid, Bye	Michael D. Reid, Seattle, Wash. BYE
				Cavanaugh, 2 and 1	Hubbert, Bye	John J. Hubbert, III, Oreland, Pa. BYE
					Cavanaugh, 5 and 3	Gilbert C. Cavanaugh, Jericho, N.Y. Thomas R. Fairgrieve, Grosse Ile, Mich.
		Mohr, 6 and 5	Landsberg, 1 up	Keith, 3 and 2	Keith, 3 and 2	Dr. Don Keith, San Diego, Calif. James C. Kilduff, Lebanon, Ohio
					Updegraff, Bye	Dr. Edgar R. Updegraff, Tucson, Ariz. BYE
				Landsberg, 19 holes	Landsberg, 1 up	Douglas R. Ehle, Dallas, Texas Richard D. Landsberg, Urbandale, Iowa
					Sucher, Bye	Richard J. Sucher, Mequon, Wis. BYE
			Mohr, 1 up	Mohr, 2 and 1	Mohr, 1 up	Terry S. Roberts, San Diego, Calif. Wesley G. Mohr, Jr., Houston, Texas
					Runkle, Bye	Dick Runkle, Los Angeles, Ca. BYE
				Milanovich, 3 and 2	Milanovich, 19 holes	Ronald Milanovich, Brookville, Pa. Jerry J. Orebaugh, Houston, Texas
					Jacobsen, 7 and 5	Todd Barker, Salt Lake City, Utah Peter Jacobsen, Portland, Ore.

THIRD QUARTER

1st Round (18 Holes)	2nd Round (18 Holes)	3rd Round (18 Holes)	4th Round (18 Holes)	5th Round (18 Holes)	6th Round (18 Holes)	
Lennie Clements, Poway, Calif.	Clements, 1 up					
David Zabell, Columbus, Ohio		Clements, 2 and 1				
Brian Willard, Silver Spring, Md.	Spiller, 3 and 2					
Lindsey W. Spiller, Baton Rouge, La.			Adcock, 2 and 1			
Wesley M. Adcock, Columbus, Miss.	Adcock, Bye					
BYE		Adcock, 5 and 4		Adcock, 2 and 1		
Michael W. Soli, DeKalb, Ill.	Soli, 4 and 3					
Dan Forsman, Los Altos, Calif.						
H. Stroud Cole, Monroe, La.	Cole, 1 up					
Taylor Metcalfe, Wyoming, Ohio		Cole, 3 and 2				
Carey E. Shulten, Grand Prairie, Texas	Shulten, Bye					
BYE			Brewer, 2 and 1			
Gary Cowan, Kitchener, Ontario, Canada	Cowan, 7 and 6					
David Richards, Chambersburg, Pa.		Brewer, 3 and 2			Mason, 1 up	
O. Gordon Brewer, Jr., Huntingdon Valley, Pa.	Brewer, Bye					
BYE						
Chris Voges, Tarzana, Calif.	Alexander, 6 and 5					
Stewart M. Alexander, Lakewood, Fla.		Mason, 2 up				
James T. Mason, Kirkwood, Mo.	Mason, Bye					
BYE			Mason, 3 and 2			
James E. Jackson, Glendale, Mo.	Jackson, Bye					
BYE		Goettel, 1 up				
Richard D. Gordon, Jr., Daly City, Calif.	Goettel, 20 holes					
Dennis R. Goettel, Carthage, Mo.				Mason, 20 holes		
Mike Stoll, Beaverton, Ore.	Stoll, 2 and 1					
Mark W. Curlett, Coatesville, Pa.		Ridley, 4 and 3				
Fred S. Ridley, Cypress Gardens, Fla.	Ridley, Bye					
BYE			Ridley, 2 and 1			
Kevin Canada, Richmond, Va.	Jurkowitz, 3 and 2					
Warren Jurkowitz, Miami, Fla.		Kask, 3 and 2				
Frederick Kask, Wethersfield, Conn.	Kask, Bye					
BYE						Mason, 1 up
John Farquhar, Lubbock, Texas	Farquhar, Bye					
BYE		Mobley, 5 and 4				
Anthony J. Cullinane, Chevy Chase, Md.	Mobley, 5 and 4					
Ronald L. Mobley, Dothan, Ala.			Fought, 2 and 1			
John Susko, San Francisco, Calif.	Susko, Bye					
BYE		Fought, 4 and 3				
Bruce Dobbs, Ypsilanti, Mich.	Fought, 4 and 3					
John Fought, Tulatin, Ore.				Fought, 3 and 1		
Charles Van Dyne, Prairie Village, Kans.	Van Dyne, 3 and 1					
Edward K. Knox, Tallahassee, Fla.		Sonnier, 5 and 3				
Randolph J. Sonnier, Lafayette, La.	Sonnier, Bye					
BYE			Duren, 3 and 2			
Richard Clark, Ashville, N.C.	Clark, Bye					
BYE		Duren, 19 holes				
Bruce R. Douglass, Brockton, Mass.	Duren, 2 and 1					
Gary Duren, Austin, Minn.					Fought, 19 holes	
David George, Westlake Village, Calif.	Eaton, 6 and 5					
Robert L. Eaton , Greeley, Colo.		Heafner, 2 up				
Clayton V. Heafner, Cary, N.C.	Heafner, Bye					
BYE			Heafner, 5 and 4			
David C. Vihlen, Homestead, Fla.	Vihlen, 1 up					
Philip B. Kenny, Highland Park, Ill.		Walter, 6 and 5				
Joseph L. Walter, Baltimore, Md.	Walter, Bye					
BYE				Campregher, 3 and 1		
Aldo R. Butera, Danbury, Conn.	Brodie, 23 holes					
John R. Brodie, Sharon Heights, Calif.		Brodie, 1 up				
David A. Ogrin, Waukegan, Ill.	Ogrin, Bye					
BYE			Campregher, 3 and 1			
Marvin M. Giles, III, Richmond, Va.	Reese, 20 holes					
Donald Reese, West River, Mich.		Campregher, 2 and 1				
Kirk Goss, Stillwater, Okla.	Campregher, 20 holes					
Tony Campregher, Salton City, Calif.						

SEMI-FINAL ROUND (18 Holes)—Bill Sander defeated James T. Mason, 8 and 7.

HALF

FOURTH QUARTER

Half	6th Round (18 Holes)	5th Round (18 Holes)	4th Round (18 Holes)	3rd Round (18 Holes)	2nd Round (18 Holes)	1st Round (18 Holes)
Sander, 1 up	Sander, 19 holes	Sander, 2 and 1	Roberts, 1 up	Roberts, 7 and 6	Roberts, 4 and 3	John Hendricks, White Bear Lake, Minn. Kelly Roberts, London, Ont., Canada
					Godwin, 1 up	Lawrence B. Lis, Wellsburg, W. Va. Luther Godwin, St. Louis, Mo.
				Gonzáles, 4 and 2	Gonzales, Bye	Jaime Gonzales, Rio de Janeiro, Brazil BYE
					Lamb, 1 up	Peter Nisselson, Mamaroneck, N.Y. Charles R. Lamb, Yuma, Ariz.
			Sander, 3 and 2	George, 19 holes	George, 4 and 3	Jeffrey C. George, Douglas, Wyo. Stephen M. Foehl, Rumson, N.J.
					Rose, Bye	J. Franklin Rose, Topeka, Kansas BYE
				Sander, 4 and 2	Sander, 1 up	D. Scott Hoyt, Menlo Park, Calif. Bill Sander, Kenmore, Wash.
					Money, Bye	Monte Carlo Money, Las Vegas, Nev. BYE
		Blair, 5 and 3	Campbell, 2 and 1	Campbell, 5 and 4	Spencer, 20 holes	Dennis M. Spencer, Sylvania, Ohio Peter Young, Harrison, N.Y.
					Campbell, Bye	William C. Campbell, Huntington, W. Va. BYE
				Hallberg, 1 up	Duhon, Bye	Alton Duhon, Los Angeles, Calif. BYE
					Hallberg, 3 and 2	Tim Graham, Baton Rouge, La. Gary Hallberg, Barrington, Ill.
			Blair, 3 and 1	Mikles, 3 and 2	Kimbrough, 5 and 4	Kriss Kimbrough, Napa, Calif. Warren MacGregor, Santa Maria, Calif.
					Mikles, Bye	Lee Mikles, Camarillo, Calif. BYE
				Blair, 2 up	Diniz, 1 up	Priscillo G. Diniz, Sao Paulo, Brazil Gordon C. Johnson, Worcester, Mass.
					Blair, Bye	James C. Blair, III, Logan, Utah BYE
	Heath, 1 up	Heath, 7 and 5	Sigel, 6 and 4	Wright, 1 up	Wright, Bye	John R. Wright, Coral Gables, Fla. BYE
					Hopper, 2 up	Gerry Simoni, Riverside, Calif. James D. Hopper, Goleta, Calif.
				Sigel, 4 and 3	Sigel, Bye	Jay Sigel, Newtown Square, Pa. BYE
					Roskopf, 2 and 1	David J. Hilgenberg, Iowa City, Ia. Richard J. Roskopf, Portland, Ore.
			Heath, 8 and 7	Heath, 2 and 1	Harrison, 5 and 4	Charles W. Harrison, Marietta, Ga. Stephen Saal, Akron, Ohio
					Heath, Bye	Skeeter Heath, Hampton, Va. BYE
				Steiner, 3 and 2	Steiner, Bye	Ned Steiner, West Caldwell, N.J. BYE
					Mathews, 4 and 3	Patrick J. Coffey, Boulder, Colo. Mark S. Mathews, Phoenix, Ariz.
		Fuhrer, 2 and 1	Fairchild, 3 and 2	Cain, 3 and 2	Gusmus, 5 and 4	Robert T. Byman, Raleigh, N.C. Frank Gusmus, Jr., Germantown, Tenn.
					Cain, Bye	John Cain, Houston, Texas BYE
				Fairchild, 5 and 4	Fairchild, 20 holes	Robert M. Fairchild, Cleveland, Ohio Eric Evans, Thousand Oaks, Calif.
					Scrafford, Bye	Steve Scrafford, Gainesville, Fla. BYE
			Fuhrer, 19 holes	Levenson, 2 and 1	Gabrielsen, 4 and 3	James R. Gabrielsen, Atlanta, Ga. Warren Aune, Dallas, Texas
					Levenson, Bye	Gavin N. Levenson, Johannesburg, S. A. BYE
				Fuhrer, 2 and 1	Peck, 1 up	Michael Peck, Overland Park, Kans. Guy Ashley, Brockton, Mass.
					Fuhrer, 4 and 3	Harry L. Newby, III, Cloquet, Minn. Frank B. Fuhrer, III, Pittsburgh, Pa.

1977
SEVENTY-SEVENTH AMATEUR CHAMPIONSHIP

Held at Aronimink Golf Club, Newtown Square, Pennsylvania, August 31-September 5.
Yardage—6,958. Par 70. 2,950 Entrants, 200 Qualifiers, 200 Starters.
Championship entirely at match play.

FINAL ROUND (36 Holes)—John Fought defeated Doug H. Fischesser, 9 and 8.

FIRST QUARTER — UPPER

1st Round (18 Holes)	2nd Round (18 Holes)	3rd Round (18 Holes)	4th Round (18 Holes)	5th Round (18 Holes)	6th Round (18 Holes)	
Eric P. Sellers, Quincy, Ill.	Carlton,					
Thomas Carlton, Augusta, Ga.	3 and 2	Carlton,				
Mel Baum, Jr., Camillus, N.Y.	Baum,	1 up, 19 holes				
Taylor Metcalf, Wyoming, Ohio	2 and 1					
John Cook, Arlington, Ohio	Cook,		Cook,			
BYE	Bye		7 and 6			
Paul B. Godwin, Poplar Bluff, Mo.	Godwin,	Cook,				
W. Ray Laird, III, Sioux Falls, S.D.	3 and 1	4 and 2				
Peter Teravainen, Duxbury, Mass.	Hostetter,			Cook,		
Sherman E. Hostetter, Beaver Falls, Pa.	3 and 2			2 and 1		
Jeff Walser, Edmond, Okla.	Walser,	Hostetter,				
BYE	Bye	5 and 4				
Paul McKellar, Glasgow, Scotland	Padgett,		Padgett,			
Kirk Padgett, Colorado Springs, Colo.	3 and 2		4 and 2			
Stephen Long, Lubbock, Texas	Long,	Padgett,				
BYE	Bye	2 and 1				
Jim Holtgrieve, Kirkwood, Mo.	Gray,				Bond,	
Thomas Gray, Prescott, Ariz.	3 and 2				4 and 3	
James Dee, Ridgewood, N.J.	Dee,	Gray,				
BYE	Bye	5 and 3				
Frank Fuhrer, III, Pittsburgh, Pa.	Fuhrer,		Stark,			
BYE	Bye		7 and 6			
John Stark, San Antonio, Texas	Stark,	Stark,				
Mark L. Crabtree, Fort Collins, Colo.	4 and 3	4 and 2		Bond,		
Bill Sander, Seattle, Wash.	Sander,			5 and 4		
Radford A. Yaun, Liberty, N.Y.	1 up, 19 holes	Sander,				
Rik Jones, Youngstown, Ohio	Jones,	2 and 1				
BYE	Bye		Bond,			
Timothy Bond, Aberdeen, Wash.	Bond,		1 up, 21 holes			
Mike Davino, Red Bank, N.J.	3 and 2	Bond,				
Kevin Harrison, Beaumont, Texas	Harrison,	3 and 2				
BYE	Bye					Landrum, 6 and 5
Mike Milligan, Bloomington, Ill.	Milligan,					
BYE	Bye	Deeble,				
Peter Deeble, North Humberland, England	Deeble,	3 and 2				
Arthur Whaley, Wilmington, Del.	1 up		Powers,			
James S. Joseph, Homewood, Ill.	Joseph,		3 and 2			
BYE	Bye	Powers,				
Allen M. Powers, Jr., North August, S.C.	Powers,	1 up, 19 holes				
Mark E. Tinder, Monterey, Calif.	4 and 2			Powers,		
Mel Collins, Jr., Long Beach, Calif.	Simpson,			1 up		
Scott Simpson, San Diego, Calif.	4 and 3	Simpson,				
Kim F. Heisler, Aurora, Ohio	Heisler,	3 and 2				
BYE	Bye		Young,			
George G. Creagh, Nashville, Tenn.	Creagh,		3 and 2			
BYE	Bye	Young,				
Greg Young, Killeen, Texas	Young,	1 up				
Carl B. Everett, Wilmington, Del.	1 up				Landrum,	
Mathew P. Seitz, Ellsworth, Kans.	Seitz,				4 and 3	
John Parsons, Newtown, Conn.	2 and 1	Murray,				
Gordon Murray, Barrhead, Scotland	Murray,	6 and 5				
BYE	Bye		Murray,			
James W. Holmes, Aiken, S.C.	Holmes,		2 and 1			
James E. Johnson, Dallas, Texas	4 and 2	Morey,				
Dale Morey, High Point, N.C.	Morey,	1 up, 20 holes				
BYE	Bye			Landrum,		
Michael Z. Wilson, Tupelo, Miss.	Landrum,			1 up		
Ralph L. Landrum, Elsmere, Ky.	1 up, 21 holes	Landrum,				
Stan K. Souza, Honolulu, Hawaii	Souza,	5 and 3				
BYE	Bye		Landrum,			
Jon R. Chaffee, Austin, Minn.	Holland,		4 and 3			
Mike Holland, Bishopville, S.C.	2 and 1	Holland,				
Robert W. Cole, Columbus, Ohio	Pacuk,	6 and 5				
John P. Pacuk, Jacksonville, Fla.	1 up, 19 holes					

SEMI-FINAL ROUND (18 Holes)—Doug H. Fischesser, defeated Ralph L. Landrum, 1 up

HALF

SECOND QUARTER

Fischesser, 3 and 2

6th Round (18 Holes)	5th Round (18 Holes)	4th Round (18 Holes)	3rd Round (18 Holes)	2nd Round (18 Holes)	1st Round (18 Holes)
				Bakst,	Clark M. Miyazaki, Wahiana, Hawaii
			Grace,	2 up	Kenneth S. Bakst, Great Neck, N.Y.
			4 and 3	Grace,	Michael W. Ancel, Newport News, Va.
		Grace,		5 and 4	John P. Grace, Ft. Worth, Texas
		2 up		Holbrook,	William A. Holbrook, III, Rome, Ga.
			Holbrook,	Bye	BYE
			1 up	Choate,	Warren J. Choate, Montoursville, Pa.
	McEvoy,			2 and 1	Allan L. Beck, Minot, N.D.
	2 and 1			Israelson,	Bill Israelson, Bemidji, Minn.
			McEvoy,	4 and 3	Gary Noto, New Orleans, La.
			5 and 4	McEvoy,	Peter McEvoy, Birmingham, England
		McEvoy,		Bye	BYE
		1 up		Humrickhouse,	Scott R. Humrickhouse, Raleigh, N.C.
			Humrickhouse,	1 up	Steven C. Broadwell, Midland, Mich.
			1 up, 19 holes	Yates,	Danny Yates, Atlanta, Ga.
Fischesser,				Bye	BYE
1 up				Fischesser,	Scott W. Cooke, Warwick, R.I.
			Fischesser,	1 up	Doug H. Fischesser, Connersville, Ind.
			1 up	West,	Martin R. West, III, Bethesda, Md.
		Fischesser,		Bye	BYE
		4 and 3		Alexander,	Stewart Alexander, St. Petersburg, Fla.
			Alexander,	Bye	BYE
			2 and 1	Bromley,	Dennis M. Saunders, Yorba Linda, Calif.
	Fischesser,			3 and 2	Jim Bromley, Paoli, Pa.
	3 and 1			Hallberg,	Gary Hallberg, Barrington, Ill.
			Hallberg,	6 and 5	Harvey Ortof, Woodside, N.Y.
			6 and 4	Bernstein,	Robert Bernstein, Grand Blanc, Mich.
		Hanefeld,		Bye	BYE
		2 up		Hanefeld,	Brett Harrison, Beaumont, Texas
			Hanefeld,	1 up	Kirk C. Hanefeld, Somersworth, N.H.
			6 and 5	Kemp,	Harcourt Kemp, Louisville, Ky.
				Bye	BYE
				Sluman,	Jeffrey Sluman, Brockport, N.Y.
			Brannan,	Bye	BYE
			2 and 1	Brannan,	Warren Gittlen, Harrisburg, Pa.
		Brannan,		5 and 3	Michael Brannan, Salinas, Calif.
		4 and 3		Sibbick,	William A. Sibbick, Jr., Martinsville, Va.
			Hopson,	Bye	BYE
			3 and 2	Hopson,	Jerry Anderson, Scarborough, Ont., Canada
	Brannan,			1 up	Michael H. Hopson, Athens, Texas
	4 and 3			Nelson,	Allan Brodie, Glasgow, Scotland
			Nelson,	3 and 2	Warren E. Nelson, Medford, Mass.
			1 up, 19 holes	Baker,	Carl Baker, Houston, Texas
		Nelson,		Bye	BYE
		2 and 1		Butler,	Arthur F. Butler, Jr., Glendora, Calif.
			Gregg,	Bye	BYE
			6 and 5	Gregg,	Ricky L. Gregg, Knoxville, Tenn.
Brannan,				6 and 5	Kenny Limes, Tulsa, Okla.
2 and 1				Moody,	Griff Moody, III, Athens, Ga.
			Moody,	5 and 4	John C. Baldwin, Chicago, Ill.
			4 and 3	Edwards,	David Edwards, Edmond, Okla.
		Moody,		Bye	BYE
		1 up		Ortega,	Charles Ortega, Montecito, Calif.
			Pini,	3 and 2	Mark S. Allen, Brunswick, Ga.
			5 and 4	Pini,	Bryan Pini, Santa Cruz, Calif.
	King,			Bye	BYE
	1 up			Harris,	H. Dane Harris, Jr., Hot Springs, Ark.
			King,	4 and 3	Jim Patrone, Boca Raton, Fla.
			2 up	King,	Steven W. King, Lawrence, Kans.
		King,		Bye	BYE
		2 and 1		Anton,	Thomas P. Anton, Columbus, Ga.
			Miller,	4 and 3	Denny Gallagher, Cincinnati, Ohio
			1 up	Miller,	Robert M. Allen, II, Allentown, Pa.
				4 and 3	Lindy Miller, Fort Worth, Texas

THIRD QUARTER — LOWER

1st Round (18 Holes)	2nd Round (18 Holes)	3rd Round (18 Holes)	4th Round (18 Holes)	5th Round (18 Holes)	6th Round (18 Holes)	
Richard A. Long, Bartlesville, Okla.	Daly,					
Stephen X. Daly, St. Charles, Ill.	1 up, 19 holes	Clarke,				
J. D. Olsen, Des Moines, Iowa	Clarke,	3 and 2				
Douglas Clarke, La Jolla, Calif.	5 and 4		Clarke,			
O. Gordon Brewer, Jr., Huntingdon Valley, Pa.	Brewer,		6 and 4			
BYE	Bye	Brewer,				
Jim Unruh, Tulsa, Okla.	Unruh,	1 up		Fought,		
Kent C. Myers, Lake Oswego, Ore.	2 and 1			1 up		
Bill Manor, Garland, Texas	Manor,					
Michael Giacini, Garden City, N.Y.	2 and 1	Fought,				
John Fought, Portland, Ore.	Fought,	6 and 5				
BYE	Bye		Fought,			
Michael Peck, Prairie Village, Kans.	Peck,		1 up			
Alan D. Fadel, Sylvania, Ohio	3 and 2	Peck,				
James H. Gibbons, Beaverton, Ore.	Gibbons,	1 up, 19 holes			Fought,	
BYE	Bye				4 and 3	
William D. Bevan, Jacksonville, Fla.	Snyder,					
Kenneth D. Snyder, Jr., Winter Haven, Fla.	2 and 1	Gaddy,				
Brian E. Gaddy, Arcadia, Calif.	Gaddy,	5 and 4				
BYE	Bye		Kelley,			
Allen R. Waddell, Arlington, Texas	Waddell,		2 up			
BYE	Bye	Kelley,				
Michael Kelley, Scarborough, England	Kelley,	4 and 3		Kelley,		
Wallace Adams, Jr., Glenwood, Ga.	2 and 1			4 and 3		
Michael P. Toomey, Crofton, Md.	Toomey,					
Vance Heafner, Cary, N.C.	1 up	Van Dyne,				
Charles Van Dyne, Prairie Village, Kans.	Van Dyne,	3 and 1				
BYE	Bye		Simoni,			
Terry May, Longwood, Fla.	Forgash,		1 up			
Michael Forgash, Wayne, Pa.	1 up	Simoni,				
Gerry Simoni, Upland, Calif.	Simoni,	5 and 4				
BYE	Bye					
Matt King, Nashville, Tenn.	King,					Fought, 3 and 1
BYE	Bye	Sutton,				
Hal E. Sutton, Shreveport, La.	Sutton,	7 and 5				
Thomas F. Randolph, Jr., Menlo Park, Calif.	5 and 3		Sutton,			
Fred S. Ridley, Winter Haven, Fla.	Ridley,		3 and 2			
BYE	Bye	Ridley,				
Michael Bourne, Newark, Del.	Spadafora,	2 up		Hackstadt,		
Paul J. Spadafora, Middletown, Ohio	3 and 1			1 up		
James T. Crowley, Fanwood, N.J.	Campbell,					
William C. Campbell, Huntington, W. Va.	5 and 3	Druga,				
Jack Druga, Pittsburgh, Pa.	Druga,	1 up				
BYE	Bye		Hackstadt,			
R. David Hackstadt, Birmingham, Ala.	Hackstadt,		3 and 2			
BYE	Bye	Hackstadt,				
Thomas J. Loyd, Columbia, Mo.	Loyd,	1 up, 20 holes			Giles,	
Marshall Marraccini, Elizabeth, Pa.	4 and 3				1 up	
Ian Hutcheon, Monifieth, Scotland	Hutcheon,					
James A. Fitzgerald, Gaithersburg, Md.	4 and 2	Hutcheon,				
Raymond Warobick, Brookfield, Wis.	Warobick,	6 and 5				
BYE	Bye		Hutcheon,			
Steven Waugl, Vidalia, Ga.	Waugl		1 up, 19 holes			
Glenn Ray Apple, Olmsted Falls, Ohio	5 and 3	Waugl,				
Jack Veghte, Clearwater, Fla.	Veghte,	3 and 2				
BYE	Bye			Giles,		
Randy Sonnier, Lafayette, La.	Croonquist,			1 up		
Dan Croonquist, St. Paul, Minn.	1 up, 19 holes	Giles,				
Marvin Giles, III, Richmond, Va.	Giles,	3 and 2				
BYE	Bye		Giles,			
Gary Schroeder, Winter Park, Fla.	Schroeder,		2 up			
John E. Duggan, Plantation, Fla.	5 and 3	Rassett,				
Joe Rassett, Turlock, Calif.	Rassett,	1 up				
Gregg Wolff, Philadelphia, Pa.	3 and 2					

SEMI-FINAL ROUND (18 Holes)—John Fought defeated Jay Sigel, 2 up

HALF

FOURTH QUARTER

	6th Round (18 Holes)	5th Round (18 Holes)	4th Round (18 Holes)	3rd Round (18 Holes)	2nd Round (18 Holes)	1st Round (18 Holes)
					Cowan,	Jay W. Vincent, S. Norwalk, Conn.
				Cowan,	6 and 4	Gary Cowan, Kitchener, Ont., Canada
				4 and 2	King,	Darrell Welker, Plantation, Fla.
			McGowan,		4 and 3	David A. King, Beltsville, Md.
			2 and 1		Mitchell,	Chris Mitchell, Spokane, Wash.
				McGowan,	Bye	BYE
				1 up	McGowan,	Chris Pollard, Richmond, Va.
		McGowan,			2 and 1	Patrick R. McGowan, Colusa, Calif.
		2 and 1			Gazecki,	John Gazecki, Tacoma, Wash.
				Gazecki,	4 and 3	William Bergin, Marietta, Ga.
				1 up	Davies,	John Davies, London, England
			Mankulish,		Bye	BYE
			5 and 3		Mankulish,	Gary Mankulish, Greenbelt, Md.
				Mankulish,	2 and 1	H. B. Wanen, II, Tulsa, Okla.
				5 and 4	Rowse,	James K. Rowse, San Jose, Calif.
	Sigel,				Bye	BYE
	3 and 1				Jones,	Backman J. Jones, Tampa, Fla.
				Sigel,	3 and 2	Richard J. McClear, Birmingham, Mich.
				1 up	Sigel,	Jay Sigel, Berwyn, Pa.
			Sigel,		Bye	BYE
			1 up		Johnson,	Gordon C. Johnson, Worcester, Mass.
				Reese,	Bye	BYE
				2 and 1	Reese,	Donald Reese, Troy, Ala.
		Sigel,			2 up	Brent Murray, Portland, Ore.
		3 and 1			Sanok,	David Sanok, Montclair, N.J.
				de Windt,	1 up, 21 holes	Barry L. Black, Spartanburg, S.C.
				1 up	de Windt,	Del de Windt, Bloomfield Hills, Mich.
			Apelgren,		Bye	BYE
			2 and 1		Apelgren,	Scott Hoch, Raleigh, N.C.
				Apelgren,	1 up, 20 holes	Dallas Apelgren, N. Palm Beach, Fla.
				1 up	Schroeder,	Sephen W. Schroeder, Atherton, Calif.
Sigel, 6 and 4					Bye	BYE
					Walsh,	Dennis B. Walsh, Groves, Texas
				Ojala,	Bye	BYE
				7 and 6	Ojala,	David Ojala, Houston, Texas
			Ojala,		1 up, 19 holes	Richard Siderowf, Westport, Conn.
			1 up		King,	Andy King, DeKalb, Ill.
				Krieger,	Bye	BYE
				3 and 2	Krieger,	Lawrence C. Hicks, Greensboro, N.C.
		Lyle,			6 and 5	Ken Krieger, Aurora, Colo.
		1 up			Snyder,	Michael P. Toliuszis, Chicago, Ill.
				Lyle,	4 and 2	Jack Snyder, Charlottesville, Va.
				3 and 2	Lyle,	Sandy Lyle, Shropshire, England
			Lyle,		Bye	BYE
			2 and 1		Mooney,	Mitch Mooney, Albuquerque, N.M.
				Mooney,	Bye	BYE
				1 up	Armstrong,	Eddie Lyons, Shreveport, La.
	Balen,				1 up	Roger Armstrong, Oakland, Calif.
	1 up				Martin,	Bill May, Homestead, Fla.
				Balen,	1 up	Steve Martin, Dundee, Scotland
				1 up, 20 holes	Balen,	Mark J. Balen, Lackawanna, N.Y.
			Balen,		Bye	BYE
			2 and 1		Meyers,	William C. Meyers, Phoenix, Ariz.
				Meyers,	5 and 4	Ronald O. Gaiser, Jr., Birmingham, Ala.
				1 up, 19 holes	Anton,	Terrence Anton, Columbus, Ga.
		Balen,			Bye	BYE
		2 and 1			Kern,	Terrence J. Sawyer, Morrisville, Pa.
				Reynolds,	2 and 1	Jeff Kern, Tucson, Ariz.
				1 up	Reynolds,	Tom Reynolds, Raleigh, N.C.
			Reynolds,		Bye	BYE
			1 up		Watson,	Bill Britton, Staten Island, N.Y.
				Lipe,	2 and 1	David P. Watson, Metrairie, La.
				7 and 6	Lipe,	James W. Lipe, Jr., Ypsilanti, Mich.
					2 and 1	David K. Brookreson, Overland Park, Kans.

1978
SEVENTY-EIGHTH AMATEUR CHAMPIONSHIP

Held at Plainfield Country Club, Plainfield, New Jersey, August 29-September 3.
Yardage—6,865. Par 72. 3,035 Entries, 201 Qualifiers, 201 Starters.
Championship entirely at match play.

FINAL ROUND (36 Holes)—John Cook defeated Scott Hoch, 5 and 4.

FIRST QUARTER — UPPER

1st Round (18 Holes)	2nd Round (18 Holes)	3rd Round (18 Holes)	4th Round (18 Holes)	5th Round (18 Holes)	6th Round (18 Holes)	
Andrew G. Soley, Cedar Lake, Ind.	Soley,					
Patrick J. Venker, Bloomington, Ill.	4 and 3	Soley,				
Doug Hanzel, Orange Village, Ohio	Hanzel,	3 and 2				
George J. Zahringer, III, New York, N.Y.	3 and 1		Soley,			
Fred M. Hansen, Houston, Texas	Hansen,		3 and 1			
BYE	Bye	Hansen,				
Todd Smith, Raleigh, N.C.	Smith,	2 and 1				
William R. Loeffler, Englewood, Colo.	3 and 2			Soley,		
Jodie Mudd, Louisville, Ky.	Lee,			1 up		
David Lee, Englewood, Colo.	4 and 3	Van Ingen,				
Peter Van Ingen, Glen Head, L.I., N.Y.	Van Ingen,	5 and 4				
BYE	Bye		Holtgrieve,			
Mickey Yokoi, Los Angeles, Calif.	Yokoi,		1 up			
David Hackstadt, Birmingham, Ala.	1 up	Holtgrieve,				
Jim Holtgrieve, Kirkwood, Mo.	Holtgrieve,	2 and 1				
BYE	Bye				Moody,	
Stephen A. Smith, New York, N.Y.	Smith,				2 and 1	
James Taylor, Norfolk, Va.	4 and 3	Davis,				
Lee Davis, Newport Beach, Calif.	Davis,	3 and 2				
BYE	Bye		Davis,			
Lynn Stone, Chino, Calif.	Stone,		2 up			
BYE	Bye	Fellinger,				
Phillip R. Estep, Conroe, Texas	Fellinger,	5 and 4				
Steve Fellinger, Ontario, Canada	3 and 2			Moody,		
Walter S. Cisco, Palatine, Ill.	Harvey,			1 up		
Bill Harvey, Jamestown, N.C.	1 up	Moody,				
Griff Moody, III, Athens, Ga.	Moody,	6 and 5				
BYE	Bye		Moody,			
Mike Klein, Scottsbluff, Neb.	Klein,		3 and 2			Peck, 3 and 2
Carter H. Parry, Jr., Sarasota, Fla.	1 up	Klein,				
Donald K. Hurter, Honolulu, Hawaii	Hurter,	3 and 2				
BYE	Bye					
Hal Sutton, Shreveport, La.	Sutton,					
BYE	Bye	Sutton,				
Tony Ciconte, Kensington, Md.	Ciconte,	4 and 2				
Kent Stauffer, Marshburg, Pa.	2 and 1		Peck,			
John Ervasti, London, Ont., Canada	Ervasti,		1 up			
BYE	Bye	Peck,				
Michael Peck, Prairie Village, Kans.	Peck,	5 and 3				
Frederick C. Hickle, Tucson, Ariz.	3 and 2			Peck,		
Jon Heselwood, Selah, Wash.	Choate,			2 and 1		
Warren J. Choate, Williamsport, Pa.	5 and 3	Choate,				
Bill Israelson, Bemidji, Minn.	Israelson,	2 and 1				
BYE	Bye		West,			
Christopher M. Gutilla, Fresno, Calif.	Gutilla,		4 and 2			
BYE	Bye	West,				
Martin R. West, III, Bethesda, Md.	West,	4 and 3				
Mike Hughett, Lincoln, Neb.	2 and 1				Peck,	
Gerald Gutknecht, Hillsborough, Calif.	Buttner,				2 and 1	
William Buttner, Plymouth, Mass.	5 and 4	Buttner,				
Anthony J. Cullinane, Chevy Chase, Md.	Cullinane,	1 up				
BYE	Bye		Buttner,			
Dale Morey, High Point, N.C.	Morey,		1 up, 20 holes			
Hinton Leigh, Columbia, S.C.	4 and 3	Morey,				
Robert R. Tway, III, Marietta, Ga.	Tway,	1 up				
BYE	Bye			Levin,		
Ricky L. Gregg, Knoxville, Tenn.	Griggs,			1 up		
Stephen P. Griggs, Winter Park, Fla.	1 up, 22 holes	Griggs,				
Steve Hayles, Willowdale, Ont., Canada	Hayles,	1 up				
BYE	Bye		Levin,			
John J. Hubbert, III, Washington, Pa.	Levin,		1 up			
Don Levin, Elk Grove, Calif.	2 and 1	Levin,				
Michael Burke, Jr., Allenhurst, N.J.	Burke,	3 and 2				
Bill Heldmar, Tulsa, Okla.	5 and 4					

SEMI-FINAL ROUND (18 holes)—John Cook defeated Michael Peck, 1 up, 20 holes.

SECOND QUARTER

HALF	6th Round (18 Holes)	5th Round (18 Holes)	4th Round (18 Holes)	3rd Round (18 Holes)	2nd Round (18 Holes)	1st Round (18 Holes)
					Clarke,	Jeffrey W. Goettman, Springfield, Ohio
				Clarke,	1 up	Douglas Clarke, San Diego, Calif.
				3 and 1	Cleaver,	Thomas F. Cleaver, Tampa, Fla.
			Clarke,		6 and 5	Joe Jackson, Richardson, Texas
			4 and 2		Barry,	E. T. Barry, Needham, Mass.
				Behl,	Bye	BYE
				1 up	Behl,	David Benham, West Bloomfield, Mich.
		Cook,			1 up	John S. Behl, Lakeland, Fla.
		1 up			Cook,	Joe Malench, Edwardsville, Ill.
				Cook,	6 and 4	John Cook, Upper Arlington, Ohio
				2 and 1	Hart,	James P. Hart, Jr., Endwell, N.Y.
			Cook,		Bye	BYE
			4 and 3		Whaley,	Arthur Whaley, Wilmington, Del.
				Whaley,	1 up	Bryant P. Barnes, Shawnee Mission, Kans.
				6 and 4	Ghioto,	Ralph C. Ghioto, Jr., Tampa, Fla.
	Cook,				Bye	BYE
	5 and 3				Giles,	Randy Reifers, Dublin, Ohio
				Coldwater,	5 and 4	Marvin Giles, III, Richmond, Va.
				2 and 1	Coldwater,	Cleve A. Coldwater, Huntsville, Ala.
			Carlton,		Bye	BYE
			6 and 5		Long,	Richard A. Long, Bartlesville, Okla.
				Carlton,	Bye	BYE
				1 up	Carlton,	Thomas M. Carlton, Augusta, Ga.
		De Lozier,			1 up	Geno Celano, Walton Beach, Fla.
		1 up, 21 holes			Chaffee,	Jon Chaffee, Austin, Minn.
				De Lozier,	6 and 5	Jim Rowse, San Jose, Calif.
				5 and 4	De Lozier,	Henri De Lozier, Silver Spring, Md.
			De Lozier,		Bye	BYE
			4 and 3		Haskell,	Richard D. Haskell, Jr., Brookline, Mass.
				Burns,	4 and 3	Kevin King, Spring, Texas
				5 and 3	Burns,	Timothy Burns, Clarks Summit, Pa.
					Bye	BYE
Cook, 5 and 3					Camp,	Mitchell A. Camp, Columbus, Ohio
				Dee,	Bye	BYE
				6 and 5	Dee,	Louis J. Moore, Wyoming, Ohio
			Dee,		6 and 5	James Dee, Ridgewood, N.J.
			3 and 2		Robbins,	Hillman Robbins, III, Memphis, Tenn.
				Robbins,	Bye	BYE
				4 and 3	Dobbs,	Bob Dickerson, Dallas, Texas
		Makalena,			2 and 1	Bruce Dobbs, Ypsilanti, Mich.
		2 and 1			Chapin,	Toby W. Chapin, Statesboro, Ga.
				Chapin,	4 and 2	Ricky L. Price, Prescott, Ariz.
				5 and 4	Hallberg,	Gary Hallberg, Barrington, Ill.
			Makalena,		Bye	BYE
			1 up		Long,	Stephen Long, Lubbock, Texas
				Makalena,	Bye	BYE
				1 up, 20 holes	Makalena,	Kalua Makalena, Wahiawa, Hawaii
	Makalena,				1 up	Patrick Delaney, Findlay, Ohio
	1 up, 19 holes				Haines,	Paul Rooney, Sioux Falls, S.D.
				Morgan,	4 and 3	George E. Haines, Jr., Ambler, Pa.
				1 up, 20 holes	Morgan,	Jefferson D. Morgan, Milledgeville, Ga.
			Fischesser,		Bye	BYE
			4 and 2		Rasset,	Tommy Settle, Shelbyville, Ky.
				Fischesser,	2 and 1	Joe Rasset, Turlock, Calif.
				2 and 1	Fischesser,	Doug H. Fischesser, Connersville, Ind.
		Fischesser,			Bye	BYE
		3 and 2			Doss,	Richard Price, Albuquerque, N.M.
				Muller,	1 up	Greg Doss, Rolla, Mo.
				4 and 3	Muller,	Enrique Muller, Mexico
			Muller,		Bye	BYE
			3 and 2		Duhon,	Alton Duhon, Los Angeles, Calif.
				Kuromoto,	3 and 2	John P. Dewey, Clyde, Ohio
				7 and 6	Kuromoto,	Tom Mase, East Lansing, Mich.
					5 and 4	Masahiro Kuromoto, Mountain City, Tenn.

THIRD QUARTER

LOWER

1st Round (18 Holes)	2nd Round (18 Holes)	3rd Round (18 Holes)	4th Round (18 Holes)	5th Round (18 Holes)	6th Round (18 Holes)
Brent Murray, Portland, Ore.	Murray, 2 up				
Eric Evans, Conoga Park, Calif.		Boles, 4 and 3			
Dr. William B. Boles, Wilson, N.C.	Boles, 1 up, 19 holes				
Michael D. Taylor, Meridian, Miss.			Pernice, 1 up		
Charles L. Bolling, Jr., Rosemont, Pa.	Bolling, Bye				
BYE		Pernice, 4 and 2			
Thomas C. Pernice, Jr., Kansas City, Mo.	Pernice, 3 and 1				
William Britton, Staten Island, N.Y.				Hoch, 7 and 5	
Leon J. Chill, Jr., Middleburg Heights, Ohio	Chill, 1 up				
Robb Pomerantz, Des Moines, Iowa		Hoch, 4 and 3			
Scott Hoch, Raleigh, N.C.	Hoch, Bye				
BYE			Hoch, 7 and 5		
Jim Evans, Atherton, Calif.	Gizzarelli, 2 and 1				
Gene Gizzarelli, Hialeah, Fla.		Gizzarelli, 3 and 1			
William Blalock, Atlanta, Ga.	Blalock, Bye				
BYE					Hoch, 4 and 3
Robert B. Wrenn, Jr., Midlothian, Va.	Wrenn, 2 and 1				
Stewart Alexander, Statesboro, Ga.		Wrenn, 3 and 2			
David Abell, Ft. Pierce, Fla.	Abell, Bye				
BYE			Wrenn, 3 and 1		
Terry S. Roberts, San Diego, Calif.	Roberts, Bye				
BYE		Roberts, 2 and 1			
Thomas Gray, Prescott, Ariz.	Cooley, 2 and 1				
Bob Cooley, Athens, Ohio				Wrenn, 5 and 4	
Jere F. Davis, Knoxville, Tenn.	Sigel, 1 up, 20 holes				
Jay Sigel, Berwyn, Pa.		Sigel, 8 and 6			
John F. Deitz, Albany, N.Y.	Dietz, Bye				
BYE			Sigel, 1 up		
Lyle L. Panepinto, Marrero, La.	Gleeton, 3 and 1				
Thomas R. Gleeton, Cheshire, Conn.		Fuhrer, 1 up			
Frank Fuhrer, III, Pittsburgh, Pa.	Fuhrer, Bye				
BYE					Hoch, 4 and 2
Ronald B. Hill, Fernandina Beach, Fla.	Hill, Bye				
BYE		Knox, 6 and 5			
James M. Woodward, Oklahoma City, Okla.	Knox, 4 and 3				
Thomas E. Knox, Greensboro, N.C.			Kotz, 1 up		
Robert B. Kotz, Morrisville, Pa.	Kotz, Bye				
BYE		Kotz, 4 and 3			
Paul Krochnke, Denver, Colo.	Krochnke, 2 and 1				
Lee Booker, Naples, Fla.				Kotz, 2 and 1	
David Lane, Chelmsford, Mass.	Lane, 2 and 1				
James R. Fankhauser, Vienna, W. Va.		Lane, 6 and 5			
Madden Hatcher, III, Columbus, Ga.	Hatcher, Bye				
BYE			Lane, 3 and 2		
Kenneth J. Green, Danbury, Conn.	Green, Bye				
BYE		Player, 2 and 1			
Flynt Lincoln, Springfield, Mass.	Player, 3 and 2				
Wayne Player, Johannesburg, S. Africa					Burk, 1 up
Britt Lindsey, Abilene, Texas	Simmons, 2 and 1				
Calvin Simmons, Edina, Minn.		Heafner, 4 and 3			
Vance Heafner, Cary, N.C.	Heafner, Bye				
BYE			Burk, 1 up, 25 holes		
Steven Liebler, Portsmouth, Va.	Liebler, 2 and 1				
Ronald G. Brewer, Maryland Heights, Mo.		Burk, 6 and 4			
Robert W. Burk, Palm Harbor, Fla.	Burk, Bye				
BYE				Burk, 1 up, 19 holes	
Daniel B. Forsman, Mountain View, Calif.	Francis, 4 and 3				
Stuart Francis, New York, N.Y.		Francis, 2 up			
James C. Robertson, Ardmore, Pa.	Robertson, Bye				
BYE			Sanders, 2 and 1		
Jay Rustman, Deerfield, Ill.	Rustman, 1 up				
Danny Yates, Atlanta, Ga.		Sanders, 3 and 2			
Jeff Sanders, Portland, Ore.	Sanders, 3 and 1				
Gerald McFerren, Phoenix, Ariz.					

SEMI-FINAL ROUND (18 holes)—Scott Hoch defeated Bob Clampett, 1 up, 20 holes.

HALF

FOURTH QUARTER

Half	6th Round (18 Holes)	5th Round (18 Holes)	4th Round (18 Holes)	3rd Round (18 Holes)	2nd Round (18 Holes)	1st Round (18 Holes)
					McCallister,	Charles Meade, Winter Park, Fla.
				Clampett,	2 up	Blaine McCallister, Monehans, Texas
				5 and 4	Clampett,	Mike Keliher, Brentwood, Tenn.
			Clampett,		3 and 2	Bob Clampett, Carmel, Calif.
			3 and 2		Johnson,	James E. Johnson, Dallas, Texas
				Johnson,	Bye	BYE
				3 and 1	Pallot,	John Pallot, Coral Gables, Fla.
		Clampett,			6 and 5	Jeff Mawhorr, Shelby, Ohio
		3 and 2			Jones,	B. John Jones, Tampa, Fla.
				Jones,	3 and 2	Jim Kane, San Mateo, Calif.
				3 and 1	Bond	Tim Bond, Aberdeen, Wash.
			Jones,		Bye	BYE
			1 up		Johnson,	Jeffrey B. Johnson, Mansfield, Ohio
				Johnson,	2 up	Robert J. Heath, Stillwater, Okla.
				1 up, 19 holes	Jones,	Howard W. Jones, Columbia, Md.
	Clampett,				Bye	BYE
	6 and 4				Marraccini,	Fred S. Ridley, Lyndhurst, Ohio
				DeSantis,	5 and 4	Marshall Marraccini, Elizabeth, Pa.
				2 and 1	DeSantis,	Marc Melendez, Santa Barbara, Calif.
			Croonquist,		1 up	Dave DeSantis, Tucson, Ariz.
			1 up		DeLong,	Dave DeLong, Portland, Ore.
				Croonquist,	Bye	BYE
				1 up	Croonquist,	Thomas M. Lee, Englewood, Colo.
		Spittle,			2 and 1	Dan Croonquist, St. Paul, Minn.
		3 and 2			Jones,	Ward G. Jones, Siloam Springs, Ark.
				Spittle,	1 up, 19 holes	Bill Holstead, Wichita Falls, Texas
				4 and 3	Spittle,	Rod Spittle, Niagara Falls, Ont., Canada
			Spittle,		Bye	BYE
			1 up		Marney,	Mark Marney, Wichita, Kans.
				Mazza,	1 up	Dr. John F. Harbottle, Tacoma, Wash.
				7 and 5	Mazza,	John Mazza, Edinboro, Pa.
Clampett, 4 and 2					Bye	BYE
					Higgins,	Brad Higgins, Ft. Worth, Texas
				Balen,	Bye	BYE
				3 and 1	Balen,	Mark J. Balen, Lackawanna, N.Y.
			Ward,		4 and 3	Fran Marrello, Waterbury, Conn.
			3 and 2		Schneider,	Lance Schneider, Cincinnati, Ohio
				Ward,	Bye	BYE
				3 and 2	Ward,	Jim Ward, Huntington, W.Va.
		Owen,			1 up	Michael J. Gove, Seattle, Wash.
		2 and 1			Fairchild,	Chester Sanok, Montclair, N.J.
				O'Meara,	4 and 2	Robert M. Fairchild, Lakewood, Ohio
				5 and 3	O'Meara	Mark O'Meara, Mission Viejo, Calif.
			Owen,		Bye	BYE
			1 up, 19 holes		Warobick,	Raymond L. Warobick, Brookfield, Wis.
				Owen,	Bye	BYE
				4 and 3	Owen,	Joseph Flood, La Jolla, Calif.
	Owen,				1 up, 19 holes	Steve C. Owen, Haines City, Fla.
	1 up				Martinson,	Lee Martinson, Wyckoff, N.J.
				Martinson,	2 and 1	Michael T. Moraghan, Litchfield, Conn.
				2 and 1	Grace,	John P. Grace, Ft. Worth, Texas
			DeFrancesco,		Bye	BYE
			6 and 5		DeFrancesco,	Steve Waugh, Vidalia, Ga.
				DeFrancesco,	3 and 1	Wayne DeFrancesco, McLean, Va.
				3 and 1	Detweiler,	Marlin Detweiler, Akron, Pa.
		Monneyham,			Bye	BYE
		1 up			DeSanders,	Lee DeSanders, Dallas, Texas
				Monneyham,	3 and 1	Peter Teravainen, Duxbury, Mass.
				3 and 2	Monneyham,	William J. Monneyham, Houston, Texas
			Monneyham,		Bye	BYE
			2 up		Pelaez,	Kevin J. Walsh, Seminole, Fla.
				Nash,	1 up, 19 holes	Carlos Pelaez, Vera Cruz, Mexico
				1 up	Nash,	Ted Nash, Dallas, Texas
					3 and 1	Tom Reynolds, Raleigh, N.C.

1979
SEVENTY-NINTH AMATEUR CHAMPIONSHIP

Held at the Canterbury Golf Club, Cleveland, Ohio, August 28-September 2.
Yardage—6,837. Par 71. 3,916 Entries, 282 Starters at this Site, 64 Qualifiers.

Qualifying Score	1st Round (18 Holes)	2nd Round (18 Holes)	3rd Round (18 Holes)	4th Round (18 Holes)	Semi Finals (18 Holes)	Final (36 Holes)
*134	Bob Clampett, Carmel, Calif.	Clampett,				
144	Bryan Pini, Santa Cruz, Calif.	1 up	Clampett,			
143	Timmy Baker, Hampton, Va.	Baker,	5 and 4			
145	John Salamone, Pittsford, N.Y.	1 up		Hallberg,		
141	Gary Hallberg, Barrington, Ill.	Hallberg,		1 up, 21 holes		
145	Dan Croonquist, St. Paul, Minn.	4 and 3	Hallberg,			
144	Kevin Arnold, Hilton Head Island, S.C.	West,	1 up			
146	Martin West, III, Rockville, Md.	5 and 4			Cook,	
140	John Cook, Dublin, Ohio	Cook,			4 and 3	
144	Robert Wrenn, Midlothian, Va.	3 and 1	Cook,			
143	Wayne Player, Johannesburg, So. Africa	Player,	1 up			
146	Tom Henderson, Columbus, Ohio	3 and 1		Cook,		
142	Lennie Clements, Poway, Calif.	Clements,		1 up, 26 holes		
145	John Grace, Fort Worth, Texas	5 and 3	Clements,			
144	Rick Fehr, Seattle, Wash.	Fehr,	6 and 5			
146	Marshall Stewart, Raleigh, N.C.	2 and 1				Cook,
139	Michael Gove, Seattle, Wash.	Gove,				5 and 3
144	John Morse, Marshall, Mich.	1 up, 19 holes	Gove,			
143	Clyde Rego, Kunia, Hawaii	Rego,	4 and 3			
145	David Lane, Chelmsford, Mass.	1 up, 19 holes		Gove,		
142	Mike Peck, Prairie Village, Kans.	Peck,		4 and 3		
145	Mike Hendrickson, Grand Blanc, Mich.	2 and 1	Peck,			
144	Mitch Mooney, Albuquerque, N.M.	Borg,	1 up, 20 holes			
146	Rick Borg, Worthington, Ohio	1 up			Ingram,	
141	Robert Tway, Marietta, Ga.	Zahringer,			1 up	
145	George Zahringer, Sands Point, N.Y.	4 and 3	Zahringer,			
143	Ron Morgan, Clemmons, N.C.	Morgan,	5 and 4			
146	John McKey, Boynton Beach, Fla.	2 up		Ingram,		
142	Brian Gaddy, Pasadena, Calif.	Ingram,		3 and 2		
145	Cecil Ingram, Birmingham, Ala.	1 up	Ingram,			
144	William McLaughlan, El Paso, Texas	McLaughlin,	5 and 4			
146	Scott Stoner, Camp Hill, Pa.	1 up, 19 holes				
138	Tim Graham, Baton Rouge, La.	Graham,				
144	Tom Reynolds, Raleigh, N.C.	3 and 2	Goldstein,			
143	Stephen Goldstein, Huntsville, Ala.	Goldstein,	1 up			
145	Larry Lis, Avella, Pa.	3 and 1		Ogrin,		
142	Jodie Mudd, Louisville, Ky.	Wood,		4 and 2		
145	William Wood, Birmingham, Ala.	1 up, 19 holes	Ogrin,			
144	David Ogrin, Waukegan, Ill.	Ogrin,	1 up			
146	A. Downing Gray, Pensacola, Fla.	4 and 3			O'Meara,	
141	Frank Fuhrer, Pittsburgh, Pa.	Fuhrer,			1 up, 20 holes	
144	David Ojala, Houston, Texas	6 and 4	Carlton,			
143	Mitchell Camp, Columbus, Ohio	Carlton,	5 and 4			
146	Thomas Carlton, Augusta, Ga.	2 and 1		O'Meara,		
142	Mark O'Meara, St. Charles, Ill.	O'Meara,		3 and 2		
145	Kel Devlin, Spring, Texas	4 and 3	O'Meara,			
144	Hal Sutton, Shreveport, La.	Sutton,	1 up			
146	Jay Sigel, Berwyn, Pa.	2 and 1				O'Meara,
140	Scott Hoch, Raleigh, N.C.	Hoch,				3 and 1
144	Rafael Alarcon, Guadalajara, Mexico	1up, 19 holes	Siderowf,			
143	Richard Siderowf, Westport, Conn.	Siderowf,	6 and 5			
145	Joel Peattie, Port Huron, Mich.	4 and 3		Siderowf,		
142	Tom Inskeep, Fort Wayne, Ind.	Fischesser,		2 and 1		
145	Doug Fischesser, Connersville, Ind.	5 and 4	Stewart,			
144	Wm. Payne Stewart, Springfield, Mo.	Stewart,	3 and 2			
146	Brent Murray, Portland, Ore.	1 up, 19 holes			Rassett,	
141	Nicholas Beauvy, Los Angeles, Calif.	Bliss,			6 and 5	
145	Donald Bliss, Laguna Hills, Calif.	2 up	Kelley,			
144	Tom Kelley, Fort Wayne, Ind.	Kelley,	2 up			
146	Griff Moody, Athens, Ga.	4 and 3		Rassett,		
142	Fred Couples, Seattle, Wash.	Couples,		6 and 4		
145	Scott Nicholas, Rockford, Ill.	4 and 3	Rassett,			
144	Joe Rassett, Turlock, Calif.	Rassett,	2 and 1			
146	Jerry Courville, So. Norwalk, Conn.	3 and 2				

Mark O'Meara, 8 and 7

*Medalist

1980
EIGHTIETH AMATEUR CHAMPIONSHIP

Held at Country Club of North Carolina, Pinehurst, North Carolina, August 26-31.
Yardage—7,161. Par 72. 4008 Entries, 282 Starters at this site, 64 Qualifiers.

Qualifying Score	1st Round (18 Holes)	2nd Round (18 Holes)	3rd Round (18 Holes)	4th Round (18 Holes)	Semi-Finals (18 Holes)	Final (36 Holes)
*139	Fred Couples, Seattle, Wash.	Couples,				
148	Donald Bliss, El Toro, Calif.	3 and 1	Couples,			
146	Thomas Knox, Greensboro, N.C.	Slaughter,	4 and 3			
150	John Slaughter, Abilene, Texas	4 and 3		Couples,		
145	Jay Don Blake, Logan, Utah	Blake,		3 and 2		
149	Stu Ingraham, Cleona, Pa.	3 and 1	Blake,			
148	Tom Kelley, Fort Wayne, Ind.	Kuramoto,	3 and 2			
150	Masahiro Kuramoto, Tokyo, Japan	3 and 1			Holtgrieve,	
143	Bob Wolcott, Dickson, Tenn.	Wolcott,			5 and 3	
149	Mark Drury, Brunswick, Ga.	1 up, 20 holes	Holtgrieve,			
147	Jim Holtgrieve, Kirkwood, Mo.	Holtgrieve,	2 up			Sutton,3 and 2
150	Bill Harvey, Greensboro, N.C.	1 up		Holtgrieve,		
145	Mark Brooks, Fort Worth, Texas	Brooks,		5 and 4		
149	Steve Haskins, El Paso, Texas	2 and 1	Brooks,			
148	Gary Cowan, Kitchner, Canada	Cowan,	5 and 4			
151	Woody Thames, Beaumont, Texas	4 and 2				
143	Joe Rassett, Turlock, Calif.	Rassett,				
148	Richard Pearson, Bradenton, Fla.	3 and 1	Gallagher,			
147	Jim Gallagher, Marion, Ind.	Gallagher,	1 up			
150	Thad Daber, Durham, N.C.	3 and 1		Sutton,		
145	Hal Sutton, Shreveport, La.	Sutton,		5 and 4		
149	Charles Bolling, Rosemont, Pa.	4 and 3	Sutton,			
148	Willie Wood, Tucson, Ariz.	Wood,	1 up			
151	Mark O'Meara, Laguna Niguel, Calif.	2 up			Sutton,	
145	Dick Siderowf, Westport, Conn.	Siderowf,			2 up	
149	Brad Faxon, Barrington, R.I.	5 and 4	Siderowf,			Hal Sutton,9 and 8
147	David O'Kelly, Marshfield, Mass.	Allen,	3 and 2			
150	Don Allen, Rochester, N.Y.	1 up		Mudd,		
146	Jodie Mudd, Louisville, Ky.	Mudd		3 and 2		
149	Fred Funk, College Park, Md.	2 up	Mudd,			
148	David Sann, Dallas, Texas	Sann,	2 up			
151	Brooks Burkhardt, Gainesville, Fla.	3 and 2				
141	Thomas Lehman, Alexandria, Minn.	McMillian,				
148	Jeff McMillian, Stillwater, Okla.	3 and 2	Rose,			
147	Clarence Rose, Goldsboro, N.C.	Rose,	5 and 4			
150	Brian Mogg, Tacoma, Wash.	2 up		Rose		
145	Allen Doyle, LaGrange, Ga.	Doyle,		2 up		
149	Flynt Lincoln, Somers, Conn.	5 and 3	Doyle,			
148	Keith Clearwater, Rancho Murieta, Calif.	Clearwater,	1 up			
151	Glen Luikart, Springfield, Ore.	2 up			Von Tacky,	
144	Roy McMillin, Phoenix, Ariz.	Mills,			3 and 1	
149	Nolan Mills, Charlotte, N.C.	3 and 2	Mills,			
147	David Ogrin, Waukegan, Ill.	Jones,	2 and 1			Lewis,4 and 2
150	Steven Jones, Yuma, Colo.	1 up, 20 holes		Von Tacky,		
145	Dick Von Tacky, Titusville, Pa.	Von Tacky,		5 and 4		
149	Gary Marlowe, Rockville, Md.	6 and 5	Von Tacky,			
148	Peter Green, Franklin, Mich.	Green,	4 and 3			
151	Don Burwell, Miami Lakes, Fla.	2 and 1				
143	Jay Sigel, Berwyn, Pa.	Sigel,				
148	Rafael Alarcon, Guadalajara, Mexico	1 up	Sigel,			
147	William Ploeger, Columbus, Ga.	Ploeger,	5 and 3			
150	William Argabrite, Nashville, Tenn.	1 up		Sigel,		
145	Bob Tway, Marietta, Ga.	Tway,		1 up		
149	Mark Davis, Mesa, Ariz.	2 and 1	Tway,			
148	Jeff Mawhorr, Shelby, Ohio	Mawhorr,	4 and 3			
151	Tim Jarman, Excelsior Springs, Mo.	2 up			Lewis,	
145	John Paul Cain, Houston, Texas	Hoffer,			4 and 3	
149	Bill Hoffer, Elgin, Ill.	2 and 1	Smith,			
147	Michael Neece, Irving, Texas	Smith,	1 up			
150	Stuart Smith, Rocklin, Calif.	2 and 1		Lewis,		
146	Bob Lewis, Warren, Ohio	Lewis,		6 and 4		
150	Tom Pernice, Kansas City, Mo.	2 and 1	Lewis,			
148	Bill Tuten, Palatka, Fla.	Tuten,	1 up			
151	Michael Healy, Sarasota, Fla.	1 up				

* Medalist

WOMEN'S AMATEUR CHAMPIONSHIP

CHAMPIONSHIP CUP

Presented in 1896 by
ROBERT COX

Gorgie Edinburg Golf Association
Golfer and Graduate of St. Andrews'

HISTORY

1960–Miss JoAnne Gunderson, 21, of Kirkland, Wash., won the Championship for the second time when she defeated Miss Jean Ashley, 21, of Chanute, Kans., 6 and 5 in the final. Miss Gunderson won her first Women's Amateur title in 1957. Miss Gunderson played 122 holes in 17 strokes over women's par at the Tulsa Country Club, Tulsa, Okla. Miss Ashley, playing in her first Amateur Championship, eliminated the defending Champion, Miss Barbara McIntire, 1-up, in the quarter-finals and Mrs. Ann Casey Johnstone, by 1-up, in the semi-finals. Miss Gunderson defeated Miss Judy Eller, of Old Hickory, Tenn., 2-up, in the other semi-final match. There were 109 entrants and 102 starters.

1961–Mrs. Jay D. (Anne Quast) Decker, 23, of Mercer Island, Wash., established the USGA record for the largest margin of victory in a final match. She defeated Miss Phyllis Preuss, of Pompano Beach, Fla., 14 and 13, at the Tacoma Country and Golf Club, Tacoma, Wash. This topped the previous record of 13 and 12 set by Mrs. Glenna Collett Vare in the final of the 1928 Women's Amateur. Mrs. Decker also held a record 12-up lead after the morning round, surpassing the mark of 10-up established by Mrs. Vare in 1928. Mrs. Decker became the 11th two-time winner of the Championship; she won her first title in 1958. Mrs. Decker played superlative golf all week and finished nine under par for 112 holes. She never finished any of her seven rounds worse than even par and lost only six holes during the Championship. Miss Roberta Albers, of Temple Terrace, Fla., became the youngest player ever to reach the semi-finals. She was but 14 years 8 months. Miss Marlene Bauer was the youngest previously; she was 15 when she reached the semi-finals in 1949. Miss JoAnne Gunderson, the defending Champion, was eliminated in the second round by Miss Mary Lowell, who had won the USGA Girls' Junior Championship the previous week. In the semi-finals, Mrs. Decker defeated Mrs. Gaines Wilson, Jr., 5 and 4, and Miss Preuss defeated Miss Albers, 2 and 1. The entry was 107.

1962–Miss JoAnne Gunderson, of Kirkland, Wash., won the Women's Amateur Championship for the third time. She concluded with a performance she described as the best of her career–a 9-and-8 triumph over 17-year old Ann Baker of Maryville, Tenn., in the final match. The Champion was credited with an unofficial 70, two under par, for the first 18 holes of the final. She made eight 3s in the round, and had four birdies and one eagle. The Championship was played at the Country Club of Rochester, N.Y. Miss Gunderson had won previously in 1957 and in 1960, and was runnerup in 1956. She barely avoided defeat in the quarter-final round when she holed a six-foot putt on the 18th to halve Miss Barbara Williams. Miss Gunderson won the match on the 20th hole. Mrs. Anne Quast Decker, the defending Champion, lost to Miss Patricia Hahn by 5 and 4 in the quarter-final round. All eight playing members of the United States Curtis Cup team competed, as did Miss Polly Riley, the non-playing Captain. Five British Curtis Cup Team members entered. Mrs. Frances Smith, the non-playing British Captain, and Miss Sheila Vaughan, of the British Team, both advanced to the fourth round. The draw brought about a second-round match between mother and daughter–Mrs. George M. Trainor and Anne Trainor, members of the host club. Mrs. Trainor won by 4 and 3. Miss Althea Gibson, former United States and Wimbledon tennis champion, was among the entrants. She lost in the second round.

1963–Mrs. Anne Quast Welts, of Mount Vernon, Wash., joined her contemporary, Miss JoAnne Gunderson of Providence, R.I., as a three-time Women's Amateur Champion at the Taconic Golf Club, Williamstown, Mass. Between them they had won six of the previous seven Championships. Mrs. Welts eliminated Miss Gunderson in the semi-final round by 3 and 2 and then defeated Miss Peggy Conley, of Spokane, Wash., by 2 and 1 in the 36-hole final. The Championship match ended with Mrs. Welts, a superb putter, holing a putt of 17 feet for a half. She had advanced to at least the quarter-final round of every Women's Amateur Championship since 1955, when she was 17 years old. Mrs. Welts defeated Miss Gunderson in their only other meeting in the Women's Amateur Championship in the semi-final round in 1958. Miss Conley, 16, was the youngest player ever to reach the final round. She also was runnerup in the 1963 Girls' Junior Championship in the week immediately preceding the Women's Amateur. The other semi-finalist was Miss Carol Sorenson, of Janesville, Wis., the 1960 Girls' Junior

Champion. She lost to Miss Conley, 1 down. Miss Janis Ferraris, of San Francisco, attempting to become the first winner of both the Girls' Junior and Women's Championships in the same year, was eliminated by Mrs. Welts in the quarter-final round. There were 12 extra-hole matches in the first round, five more than there had ever been in any one round of the Championship.

1964–Miss Barbara McIntire, of Colorado Springs, Colo., won for the second time by defeating Miss JoAnne Gunderson, by 3 and 2 in the final at the Prairie Dunes Country Club, Hutchinson, Kans. Miss McIntire first won in 1959. At links-like Prairie Dunes, Miss McIntire staged a strong rally in the afternoon round of the final. She was three down after 21 holes. It marked the third major Championship victory for Miss McIntire, who also won the British Women's Amateur in 1960. Mrs. Welts, the defending Champion, entered although she was expecting the birth of a child in November. Her 36-hole qualifying score of 162 failed to qualify her for match play. Qualifying at the site was resumed after a 13-year interruption. Miss McIntire, Miss Gunderson and Miss Polly Riley, shared the medal with totals of 151. The losing semi-finalists were Mrs. Paul Dye, Jr., Indianapolis, Ind., who lost to Miss Gunderson by 5 and 4, and Miss Robbye King, Norfolk, Va., who was defeated, 3 and 1, by Miss McIntire.

1965–Miss Jean Ashley, of Chanute, Kansas, three down after 19 holes in the final, rallied to defeat Mrs. Welts, by 5 and 4, at the Lakewood Country Club, Denver, Colo. Miss Ashley, 26, a third-grade teacher, was the runnerup in 1960. Her victory thwarted Mrs. Welts' bid to win the Championship for a fourth time. From 1957 through 1964 the Championship had been won only by Mrs. Welts, Miss Barbara McIntire, and Miss JoAnne Gunderson. Miss McIntire, the defending Champion, lost to Miss Ashley in the quarter-final round. Miss Gunderson did not enter. The defeated semi-finalists were Miss Connie June Day, of Chattanooga, Tenn., who lost to Miss Ashley by 2 and 1, and Miss Polly Riley, who lost to Mrs. Welts on the 19th hole. Miss Riley, who had been an entrant 20 times, advanced to the quarter-final round or better on nine occasions. The medalist was Miss Lida Fee Matthews, of Portsmouth, Ohio, with 74-74–148.

1966–In the longest final match in the history of the USGA, Mrs. JoAnne Gunderson Carner, of Seekonk, Mass., defeated Mrs. Marlene Stewart Streit, of Toronto, Canada, in 41 holes at the Sewickley Heights Golf Club, Sewickley, Pa., and won her fourth Championship. Mrs. Streit might have defeated Mrs. Carner but her 13-foot putt on the 36th hole hit the back of the cup and bounced out. In the extra holes, Mrs. Streit executed a series of remarkable recoveries to stay in contention until the 41st, where Mrs. Carner won with a par. Losing semi-finalists were Mrs. Teddy Boddie, of Shreveport, La., who lost to Mrs. Carner, 1 down, and Miss Roberta Albers, of Temple Terrace, Fla., who lost to Mrs. Streit, 1 down. Mrs. Boddie defeated Mrs. Welts, 1 up, in the quarter-finals. Mrs. Welts had reached the quarter-finals 11 times in 12 years. The Championship also brought to light Miss Shelley Hamlin, a 17-year-old schoolgirl from Fresno, Calif. Miss Hamlin scored 143 in the qualifying round, five strokes lower than the previous 36-hole qualifying record of 148, established by Miss Lida Fee Matthews in 1965. Miss Hamlin had 73 in the first round and 70 in the second, another record.

1967–Miss Mary Lou Dill, 19, of Houston, Texas, defeated Miss Ashley, 5 and 4, in the final at the Annandale Golf Club, Pasadena, Calif. It was the third time Miss Ashley had been to the final, and the first time for Miss Dill. Miss Ashley was the 1965 Champion. Miss Dill took a lead of 6 up in the first 18 holes and never permitted the result to come into doubt. Twice Miss Dill was taken 19 holes before winning–by Mrs. Nancy Roth Syms, of Hollywood, Fla., in the first round, and by Miss Peggy Conley, of Spokane, Wash., in the semi-finals. Miss Dill was 3 down with 6 to play against Miss Conley, won four of the next five, lost the 18th and won with a par on the 19th. Mrs. Carner, the defending Champion, was eliminated in the first round by 16-year-old Miss Marianne Cox, of Santa Ana, Calif., 2 and 1. Miss Phyllis Preuss, of Pompano Beach, Fla., had the low qualifying score of 76-72–148.

1968–Mrs. Carner won her fifth Women's Amateur Championship by defeating Mrs. Welts, 5 and 4, at the Birmingham Country Club, Birmingham, Mich. Mrs. Carner thus had earned only one less Championship than Mrs. Glenna Collett Vare, who won six between 1922 and 1935; no one has won as many. Mrs. Welts was a three-time Champion, and in 11 of the previous 13 years either she or Mrs. Carner reached the final round. Mrs. Welts had gone to at least the quarter-finals in 12 of the previous 14 Championships. Mrs. Carner was 1 up after the morning 18-hole round, and 2 up after 11 holes in the afternoon. Mrs. Carner then scored consecutive birdies on the 12th and 13th and pitched to within 18 inches of the hole for a par and a win on the 14th, thus closing out the match. Against Miss Catherine Lacoste, of Paris, France, Mrs. Carner put on a devastating finish to win her semi-final match. Miss Lacoste was even with Mrs. Carner after 11 holes. Mrs. Carner then scored with a par on the 12th and three consecutive birdies, winning, 4 and 3. Mrs. Welts defeated Miss Joyce Kazmierski, of Detroit, 2 and 1, in the other semi-final match. Miss Lacoste was qualifying medalist with 143, one under par. This score equalled the record for 36-hole qualifying set by Miss Shelley Hamlin in 1966.

1969–Miss Catherine Lacoste climaxed a profound year by winning the United States Women's Amateur Championship at the Las Colinas Country Club, Irving, Texas. Miss Lacoste defeated Miss Shelley Hamlin, of Fresno, Calif., 3 and 2. Miss Lacoste already had won the 1969 British Ladies Championship, the French and the Spanish ladies' titles and in 1967 had become the only amateur ever to win the United States Women's Open Championship. Miss Lacoste took a three-hole lead over Miss Hamlin after nine holes of the first round. Miss Hamlin then played the next 25 holes in even par, but made up no ground. Miss Lacoste surrendered nothing to this fine scoring and closed out the match on the 34th hole. Miss Lacoste was three down to Mrs. Welts after 10 holes of their semi-final match, but rallied to win, 2 and 1. Mrs. Welts then had reached at least the quarter-final round in 13 of 15 championships. Mrs. Carner, the 1968 Champion, lost in the first round to Mrs. Sam Furrow, of Concord, Tenn., and became a professional before the 1970 Championship was played. Miss Nancy Hager, 16, of Dallas, reached the semi-final round and lost, 1 up, to Miss Hamlin. Mrs. Teddy Boddie, of Shreveport, La., scored 147 and led the qualifying round. Her 69 in the first round of qualifying was a record single-round score for the qualifying round.

1970—Miss Martha Wilkinson, of Whittier, Calif., defeated Miss Cynthia Hill, of St. Petersburg, Fla., 3 and 2, in the final match at the Wee Burn Country Club, Darien, Conn. Miss Wilkinson and Miss Hill were close friends and had been travelling together and playing in tournaments since the Women's Open Championship in June. Twice during the final round Miss Hill hit approaches to the 16th hole into a creek. She recovered the lost hole in the morning and went to lunch leading, 1 up. However, she was 2 down playing the 16th in the afternoon, and when she made 6 she had lost the match. All four semi-finalists were members of the 1970 Curtis Cup Team. Miss Wilkinson defeated Miss Shelley Hamlin, of Fresno, Calif., 5 and 4, and Miss Hill defeated Miss Jane Bastanchury, 2 up. Miss Wilkinson was medalist with 150, while both Miss Hill and Miss Hamlin had to survive a playoff to reach match play. All but one member of the British Isles Curtis Cup Team played, but none survived the second round.

1971–Miss Laura Baugh, of Long Beach, Calif., became the second 16-year-old Women's Amateur Champion and probably the youngest when she defeated Miss Beth Barry, of Dauphin Island, Ala., 1 up, at the Atlanta Country Club, Atlanta, Ga. Miss Baugh was age 16 years, 2 months, 21 days when she won. Mis Beatrix Hoyt was 16 years, 3 months, 4 days of age when she won in 1896. Miss Baugh, a high school student in Long Beach, defeated two former Champions. She eliminated Mrs. Mark A. Porter, of Riverton, N.J., 3 and 1, in the second round, and Miss Barbara McIntire, Colorado Springs, Colo. 1 up, in the quarter-final round. Mrs. Porter was the 1949 Champion and Miss McIntire won in 1959 and 1964. Miss Barry was 3-up on Miss Baugh after eight holes of the final match, but Miss Baugh pulled even after 16 holes. Miss Barry then won the 18th and went to lunch leading, 1 up. After nine holes of the afternoon round Miss Baugh held a 1-up lead. Miss Barry birdied the 12th with a 30-foot putt, but Miss Baugh won the 15th with a par. They halved the remainder of the holes. Among Miss Barry's victims were Miss Martha Wilkinson, the defending Champion, and Miss Polly Riley a member of six Curtis Cup Teams. Miss Connie June Day, of Chattanooga, and Miss Jane Bastanchury, of Whitter, Calif., each scored 150, low score in the 36-hole qualifying round. The entry was 102.

1972–Miss Mary Budke, of Dundee, Ore., won at the St. Louis Country Club, Clayton, Mo., in her second attempt. In 1971, at the age of 17, she was eliminated in the second round of match play. Miss Budke defeated Miss Cynthia Hill, of St. Petersburg, Fla., 5 and 4, in the 36-hole final. Miss Hill was runnerup to Mrs. Martha Wilkinson Kirouac in the 1970 Championship. Miss Budke barely qualified for match play, scoring 79-81-160. In her first round match against Miss Lancy Smith, a member of the 1972 Curtis Cup Team, Miss Budke scored a 77 and won, 1-up. Miss Budke was only one over par for 16 holes in her second match, defeating Miss Phyliss Preuss, a veteran of five Curtis Cup Teams, 3 and 2. In her quarter-final match against Miss Mary Bea Porter, Miss Budke lost five of the first six holes, won the 7th and 8th, and lost the 9th to go four down. She then won five holes before Miss Porter evened the match at the 18th with a birdie. But on the 19th Miss Porter hit two bunker shots out of bounds and lost. The semi-final match against Mrs. Barbara White Boddie also went extra holes. Mrs. Boddie had been playing perhaps the best golf of the Championship, scoring just two over par in her three matches and beating all her opponents by the same 6 and 5 margin. She eliminated the defending Champion, Miss Laura Baugh, Miss Marilynn Palmer, of Vancouver, British Columbia, Canada, and Mrs. Nancy Roth Syms. Mrs. Boddie was 1 up at the 18th, and then called a one-stroke penalty on herself when her ball moved at address deep in the rough. She conceded the hole to Miss Budke and they went to the 19th. Miss Budke parred the hole and Mrs. Boddie bogied. Against Cynthia Hill in the final round, Miss Budke shot a morning round of 75, to go 1-up, despite a hole-in-one by Miss Hill on the 145-yard seventh. In the afternoon, Miss Budke birdied the first hole to go 2-up and went 3-up at the eighth. Miss Hill birdied the ninth, but lost the 10th to fall three back. Miss Budke clinched the match at the 12th with a par when Miss Hill had to crawl under a fir tree to play her second shot. In the 32 holes of the final match, Miss Budke was only three over par.

1973—Miss Carol Semple, of Sewickley, Pa., won the Championship at Montclair Golf Club, Montclair, N. J., defeating Mrs. Anne Quast Sander, of Seattle, Wash., 1 up. In six previous attempts, Miss Semple had never advanced beyond the second round. Miss Semple was able to win only one of her matches before the 17th hole, while Mrs. Sander did not go beyond the 15th hole before the final. Miss Semple defeated Miss Mary Budke, the defending Champion from Dundee, Ore., 2 and 1, and Miss Bonnie Lauer, the National Women's Intercollegiate Champion from Union Lake, Mich., 1 up. Against Miss Lauer she was 2 down with three holes to play, but finished birdie-par-birdie to win all three holes and the match. In the final round, Miss Semple won the first three holes and was 1 up after nine. Mrs. Sander then won four holes against two for Miss Semple on the second nine and held a 1 up lead after 18 holes. In the afternoon round, Miss Semple won the first hole with a par and the match was even. Miss Semple then played some loose golf and was 3 down after five holes. The sixth was halved and then Miss Semple birdied three of the next four holes to pull even once again. Mrs. Sander won the 11th, but lost the 15th when she drove into a fairway bunker. They halved the 16th in par 3s and Miss Semple went ahead with a par 4 on the 17th where Mrs. Sander drove into the rough and made 5. The 18th was halved in par 5s. The presentation was unusual in that Lynford Lardner, Jr., President of the USGA, stepped aside so that Miss Semple could receive the Championship trophy from her father, Harton S. Semple, a USGA Vice-President. This was the 14th time in the last 19 Championships that Mrs. Sander reached at least the quarter-final round. The entry was 154.

1974—Miss Cynthia Hill, of Colorado Springs, Colo., twice runnerup, defeated Miss Carol Semple, the defending Champion from Sewickley, Pa., 5 and 4 in the 36-hole final round at the Broadmoor Golf Club, Seattle, Wash. Miss Hill had lost in the final round in both 1970 and 1972. Miss Semple was attempting to become the first to win consecutive Championships since Betty Jameson in 1939 and 1940. Earlier in 1974 she had won the British Ladies' Championship. Medalist was Miss Debbie Massey, of Bethlehem, Pa., with a two-under par 70. She was eliminated in the semi-final round by Miss Hill, 4 and 2. The other semi-finalist was Miss Peggy Conley, from Spokane, Wash. Miss Conley, runnerup in the 1963 Championship, was eliminated by Miss Semple, 3 and 1. In the morning round of the final match Miss Hill was seven over par and Miss Semple 12 over, with Miss Hill 3 up. The afternoon produced much better golf. Miss Hill was two under par with 12 pars and two birdies on the 14 holes played, while Miss Semple was even par, with two birdies offsetting two bogies. Miss Hill did not let up after establishing her 3-up lead in the morning, and went 4 up on the first hole of the final 18, where Miss Semple three-putted. Miss Hill won the short par-3 fifth hole with a birdie to go 5 up, then birdied the par-4, 315-yard eighth hole to stand 6 up. Miss Semple came back on the 369-yard ninth hole with a birdie 3 to cut Miss Hill's lead to 5 up, but lost the par-3 11th with a bogie to Miss Hill's par 3, to go 6 down again. Miss Semple birdied the 13th to stand 5 down with five to play, and Miss Hill ended the match by matching Miss Semple's par 3 on the 14th hole. The entry was 121.

1975—Miss Beth Daniel, of Charleston, S. C., defeated Miss Donna Horton, from Jacksonville, Fla., 3 and 2, in the 36-hole final at Brae Burn Country Club, West Newton, Mass. Miss Daniel was appearing in her first Championship, while Miss Horton reached the semi-final round in 1973 and the second round in both 1972 and 1974. Medalist was Mrs. Nancy Roth Syms, of Colorado Springs, Colo., who scored a two-under par 71; she lost to Miss Carol Semple, of Sewickley, Pa., in the second round. Miss Semple was then defeated by Miss Daniel in the third round. The defending Champion, Miss Cynthia Hill, of Colorado Springs, Colo., lost in the second round to Miss Marilyn Palmer, from Kamloops, B. C. With Miss Daniel and Miss Horton in the semi-final round were Miss Noreen Friel, of Woburn, and Jeanne-Marie Boylan, of Milton; it was the first time since 1911, when Miss Margaret Curtis and Eleanor Allen made the round of four, that two Massachusetts players had reached the semi-finals. In the final round Miss Daniel won the fourth hole with a birdie 4, then lost three in a row—five through seven—to stand 2-down. The next three holes were halved in par. Miss Daniel then won five of the next seven holes while Miss Horton could win only the 15th, where she had a birdie. The 18th was halved and the players went to lunch with Miss Daniel standing 2-up. The had played the first 18 holes in 2 hours, 45 minutes. In the afternoon Miss Horton squared the match after eight holes, but Miss Daniel went 1-up with a birdie on the ninth. Miss Horton drew even again with a birdie 4 on the 10th. The 11th and 12th were halved in pars and then Miss Daniel made par-5s on the 13th and 14th while Miss Horton hooked out-of-bounds on the 13th and was short of the green in three on the 14th. Miss Daniel was then 2-up with four to play. The 15th was halved in pars and Miss Daniel closed out the match scoring a birdie on the 16th, where she holed a 15-foot sidehill putt. The match took only 5 hours, 5 minutes, about the time it takes U. S. Open contestants to play 18 holes. There were 154 entries.

1976—Miss Donna Horton, of Jacksonville, Fla., defeated Miss Marianne Bretton, from San Diego, Calif., 2 and 1, in the 36-hole final at the Del Paso Country Club, Sacramento, Calif. Miss Horton reached the semifinals in 1973 and was runner-up in 1975, while Miss Bretton was appearing in her first Women's Amateur Championship. Miss Beth Daniel, of Charleston, S. C., the 1975 Champion, was medalist with two-under-par 70, which tied the 18-hole qualifying record set by Miss Debbie Massey in 1974. Miss Daniel was eliminated in the first round by Miss Dale Shaw, of Sidney, British Columbia, Canada. The losing semifinalists were Miss Rise Alexander, of Gresham, Ore., and Miss Pat Cornett, from Salinas, Calif. On her way to the final, Miss Bretton defeated former Wo men's Amateur Champions Miss Carol Semple and Miss Mary Budke. In the final round Miss Bretton won the first two holes and was 3-up at the end of nine. The match turned around on the second nine where Miss Bretton had six bogies, four in succession on holes 15 through 18. The morning round ended with the match even. In the afternoon, Miss Bretton began with another birdie on the first hole, to take the lead, 1-up, and she was still 1-up after 10 holes. Miss Horton then won the 11th with a par to pull even and holed a 10-foot putt for a birdie on the 13th to go ahead for the first time in the match. She added another hole to her lead with a par on the 15th and led 2-up with three holes to play. Both women scored pars on the 16th, and the match ended when they both scored 6 on the 17th hole, a par 4. There were 157 entries, the highest number since 1958. The Championship was previously played at the Del Paso Country Club in 1957.

1977—Miss Beth Daniel, 22, of Charleston, S. C., won her second Women's Amateur in three years by defeating Mrs. Cathy Sherk, of Fonthill, Canada, 3 and 1, at the Cincinnati Country Club, Cincinnati, Ohio. Mrs. Donna Horton White, the 1976 Champion, had become a professional earlier in the year. Miss Mary Lawrence, of Canton, N. Y., was medalist with a score of 72, one stroke under par. She was defeated in the first round by Miss Mary Elizabeth Murphy, of Naples, Fla. In the semi-final round Miss Daniel defeated Mrs. Nancy Hager Hammer, of Dallas, Texas, 3 and 1, and Mrs. Sherk won, 9 and 8, from Miss Brenda Goldsmith, of San Antonio, Texas, who played even though she had a cracked rib. Mrs. Sherk was one under par. This equalled the largest winning margin in an 18-hole match in the history of the Championship. Miss Daniel and Mrs. Hammer played their semi-final match evenly until Miss Daniel went ahead to stay with birdies on the 12th and 14th holes. In the 36-hole final round, Miss Daniel could gain no more than a two hole advantage through the morning round. Mrs. Sherk won the sixth and seventh holes of the afternoon round to even the match, and then hit the eighth green in regulation while Miss Daniel was bunkered. Miss Daniel recovered to save her par, however, and Mrs. Sherk three-putted to lose the hole. Miss Daniel again was 1 up. She birdied the 12th and 14th to go 3 up, and then holed from 12 feet to halve the 15th. Mrs. Sherk holed her 6-iron second shot for an eagle 2 at the 16th, but she lost the 17th and the match when Miss Daniel holed a putt from 14 feet.

1978—Mrs. Cathy Sherk, 28, of Fonthill, Ontario, Canada, became the first foreign player to win the Women's Amateur Championship since Miss Catherine Lacoste, of France, in 1969. She defeated Mrs. Judith J. Oliver, of Sewickley, Pa., 4 and 3, in the scheduled 36-hole final at the Sunnybrook Golf Club, Plymouth Meeting, Pa. Mrs. Sherk reached the final in 1977, but lost, 3 and 1, to Miss Beth Daniel, who had also won the 1975 Championship, Mrs. Ian Robertson, of Glasgow, Scotland, was the medalist with an even-par 72, but lost her first-round match. The qualifying round reduced the starting field of 154 players to 64 for match play. Twelve players had to compete for the final six qualifying places in a playoff that was delayed until the following morning because of darkness. From the quarter-final round on, Mrs. Sherk defeated three members of the 1978 U.S. Curtis Cup Team to win the Championship—Pat Cornett, Cynthia Hill, and finally Mrs. Oliver. Miss Hill, the 1974 Women's Amateur Champion, gave Mrs. Sherk her closest match, taking her to the final hole. Mrs. Sherk, 1 up going to the 18th hole, overshot the green with her approach. She played a delicate pitch from the rough at the back of the green, then holed a short par putt to preserve the victory. Miss Hill had eliminated Miss Daniel the previous day, 1 up, in a quarter-final match. Mrs. Oliver also had a scare in her semi-final match with Miss Mary Hafeman. She needed a five-foot birdie putt on the first extra hole to win. When she holed the putt, it was the first time she had been ahead all day. In the final match, Mrs. Sherk birdied the eighth hole of the morning round, which put her ahead to stay. She was 3 up at the lunch break. In the afternoon, she increased her lead to 4 up after 24 holes. Mrs. Oliver cut the lead in half by winning the next two holes. Mrs. Sherk countered by winning three of the next four holes for a five-hole lead, the largest of the match. She closed out the match with a par 3 on the 15th hole, the 33rd hole of the match. Three other former Champions—Mrs. Mark A. Porter (1949), Miss Mary Budke (1972), and Miss Carol Semple (1973)—also qualified for match play. Mrs. Porter and Miss Semple lost in the second round. Miss Budke lost her first round match. A first-round match between Miss Denise Hermida and Mrs. Carole Caldwell, of the British Curtis

Cup Team, went nine extra holes before Miss Hermida won with a birdie. The match tied the Women's Amateur record for most extra holes, set in the 1950 Championship when Miss Mae Murray defeated Miss Fay Crocker in the fourth round. The Championship received a record 207 entries, exceeding the previous high of 201 in 1939.

1979—Carolyn Hill, 20, of Placentia, Calif., was nine under par in six matches at the Memphis Country Club, Memphis, Tenn. Miss Hill defeated Patty Sheehan, of Reno, Nev., 7 and 6, in the 36-hole final. Kathy Baker, of Clover, S. C., was the medalist with an 18-hole qualifying score of 71, one under par. Miss Baker, playing in her first Women's Amateur, reached the quarter finals where she lost, 4 and 3, to Miss Sheehan. In the 18-hole qualifying round, 71 players had scores of 79 or better, the lowest cut-off score in the history of the Championship. A playoff involving 17 players decided the final 10 places in match play. Miss Hill and Miss Sheehan both qualified with scores of 73. Miss Hill was three under par in defeating Beth Barry, a former Women's Amateur runner-up; two under in her 5 and 4 victory over Lynn Connelly; even par in eliminating Mitzi Edge, 2 and 1; one under in her 6 and 5 quarter-final victory over Lori Castillo, the Women's APL Champion; and one over in defeating Peggy Kirsch, 5 and 4, in the semi-finals. Miss Sheehan was even par in defeating Bie-Shyun Huang with a birdie on the 20th hole; two under in her next two victories, over Laurie Reichenbach, 5 and 4, and Sue Ertl, 7 and 6; one under in defeating Kathy Baker in the quarter-finals; and even par in eliminating Vicki Singleton, 4 and 3, in the semi-finals. In the final, Miss Hill won the first hole with a par as Miss Sheehan three-putted. Miss Hill was 2 up after the first nine holes. She stretched the lead to 5 up after 14 holes. Miss Sheehan won the 16th and 17th, but lost the 18th and was four down at lunch. For the first 18 holes, Miss Hill had 71 and Miss Sheehan 74. Miss Hill played the first nine holes of the afternoon in 33, three under par, and was 6 up. She won the 10th with a par 3, and the match ended when they halved the 11th and 12th holes in pars. Miss Hill was four under par and hit 21 of 23 fairways on the driving holes in the final. The Championship drew a record 273 entries, exceeding the previous high of 207 in 1978.

1980—Mrs. Juli Simpson Inkster, 20, of Santa Cruz, California, a bride of three weeks, defeated Patti Rizzo, 20, of Hialeah, Florida, 2 up, in the 18-hole final match at the Prairie Dunes Country Club, in Hutchinson, Kansas. Dorothy Lasker, of Hinsdale, Illinois, was medalist with a 36-hole score of 147, three over par. Miss Lasker reached the second round where she lost, 2 up, to Phyllis Preuss. Mrs. Inkster and Miss Rizzo had scores of 150 and 151 respectively. Eight players were involved in a playoff to decide the final two places in match play. On her way to the final, Mrs. Inkster defeated among others, Maureen Madill of Northern Ireland, the 1979 British Champion, 7 and 6; and Carol Semple, of Sewickley, Pa., the 1973 Women's Amateur Champion and 1974 British Champion, 2 and 1, in the semi-finals. The 10th, a par 3, was a pivotal hole in the final match. Miss Rizzo was 2 down, but she had a short birdie putt. Mrs. Inkster, however, holed a downhill 20-foot putt for a birdie. Miss Rizzo made her putt for a half, and then won the 11th with another birdie. Had she won the 10th, the match would have been even. Mrs. Inkster took a 2-up lead with a birdie on the 13th green, lost the 16th, and won the 18th with a par when Miss Rizzo's approach was short of the green. The starting field of 150 included 15 past United States Curtis Cup team members, including Polly Riley, Barbara McIntire, and Mrs. Anne Quast Sander, each of whom played on six teams. Miss McIntire, who won the 1964 Women's Amateur at Prairie Dunes, qualified for match play but lost her first round match. The USGA received a record 281 entries, surpassing the previous record of 273 in 1979.

WOMEN'S AMATEUR CHAMPIONSHIP

DATE	WINNER, RUNNER-UP	SCORE	SITE	ENTRY
1960 (Aug.)	Miss JoAnne Gunderson d. Miss Jean Ashley	6 & 5	Tulsa C.C., Tulsa, Okla.	109
1961 (Aug.)	Mrs. Jay D. Decker (Anne Quast) d. Miss Phyllis Preuss	14 & 13	Tacoma C. & G.C., Tacoma, Wash.	107
1962 (Aug.)	Miss JoAnne Gunderson d. Miss Anne Baker	9 & 8	C.C. of Rochester, Rochester, N.Y.	**128
1963 (Aug.)	Mrs. David Welts (Anne Quast) d. Miss Peggy Conley	2 & 1	Taconic Golf Club, Williamstown, Mass.	**128
1964 (Aug.)	Miss Barbara McIntire d. Miss JoAnne Gunderson	3 & 2	Prairie Dunes C.C., Hutchinson, Kans. Co-Medalists—151: Miss JoAnne Gunderson Miss Barbara McIntire Miss Polly Riley	93
1965 (Aug.)	Miss Jean Ashley d. Mrs. David Welts (Anne Quast)	5 & 4	Lakewood C.C., Denver, Colo. Medalist—148: Miss Lida Fee Matthews	88
1966 (Aug.)	Mrs. Don R. Carner (JoAnne Gunderson) d. Mrs. J. Douglas Streit (Marlene Stewart)	1 up, 41 hls.	Sewickley Heights G.C., Sewickley, Pa. Medalist—143*: Miss Shelley Hamlin	115
1967 (Aug.)	Miss Mary Lou Dill d. Miss Jean Ashley	5 & 4	Annandale G.C., Pasadena, Calif. Medalist—148: Miss Phyllis Preuss	119
1968 (Aug.)	Mrs. Don R. Carner (JoAnne Gunderson) d. Mrs. David Welts (Anne Quast)	5 & 4	Birmingham C.C., Birmingham, Mich. Medalist—143*: Miss Catherine Lacoste	110
1969 (Aug.)	Miss Catherine Lacoste d. Miss Shelley Hamlin	3 & 2	Las Colinas C.C., Irving, Texas Medalist—147: Mrs. Teddy B. Boddie	103
1970 (Aug.)	Miss Martha Wilkinson d. Miss Cynthia Hill	3 & 2	Wee Burn C.C., Darien, Conn. Medalist—150: Miss Martha Wilkinson	139
1971 (Aug.)	Miss Laura Baugh d. Miss Beth Barry	1 up	Atlanta C.C., Atlanta, Ga. Co-Medalist—150: Miss Jane Bastanchury	102
1972 (Aug.)	Miss Mary Budke d. Miss Cynthia Hill	5 & 4	St. Louis C. C., St. Louis, Mo. Medalist—148: Mrs. William Flenniken, Jr.	134
1973 (Aug.)	Miss Carol Semple d. Mrs. Stephen Sander (Anne Quast)	1 up	Montclair G. C., Montclair, N.J. Medalist—74: Mrs. Kaye Potter	142
1974 (Aug.)	Miss Cynthia Hill d. Miss Carol Semple	5 & 4	Broadmoor G. C., Seattle, Wash. Medalist—70†: Miss Deborah Massey	121
1975 (Aug.)	Miss Beth Daniel d. Miss Donna Horton	3 & 2	Brae Burn C. C., West Newton, Mass. Medalist—71: Mrs. Nancy Syms	154
1976 (Aug.)	Miss Donna Horton d. Miss Marianne Bretton	2 & 1	Del Paso C. C., Sacramento, Calif. Medalist—70†: Miss Beth Daniel	157
1977 (Aug.)	Miss Beth Daniel d. Mrs. Cathy Sherk	3 & 1	Cincinnati C. C., Cincinnati, Ohio Medalist—72: Miss Mary Lawrence	162
1978 (Aug.)	Mrs. Cathy Sherk d. Mrs. Judith Oliver	4 & 3	Sunnybrook G. C. Plymouth Meeting, Pa. Medalist—72: Mrs. Ian Robertson	207
1979 (Aug.)	Miss Carolyn Hill d. Miss Patty Sheehan	7 & 6	Memphis C. C. Memphis, Tenn. Medalist—71: Miss Kathy Baker	*273
1980 (Aug.)	Mrs. Juli Simpson Inkster d. Miss Patti Rizzo	2 up	Prairie Dunes C.C. Hutchinson, Kans. Medalist—147: Miss Dorothy Lasker	§281

**Limited entry.
*Record Qualifying score, 36 holes.
†Record Qualifying score, 18 holes.
§Record entry.

WOMEN'S AMATEUR CHAMPIONS

LAURA BAUGH
1971

BETH DANIEL
1975-77

ANNE QUAST
1958-61-63

CATHERINE LACOSTE
1969

1960
SIXTIETH WOMEN'S AMATEUR CHAMPIONSHIP

Held at the Tulsa Country Club, Tulsa, Okla., August 22-27.
Yardage—6,150. Par 71. 109 Entries, 102 Starters.
Championship entirely at match play.

FINAL ROUND (36 Holes)—Miss JoAnne Gunderson defeated Miss Jean Ashley, 6 and 5.

UPPER HALF

1st Round (18 Holes)	2nd Round (18 Holes)	3rd Round (18 Holes)	4th Round (18 Holes)	5th Round (18 Holes)	Semi-Final (18 Holes)	
Miss Judy Torluemke, Triple A, Mo.	Miss Torluemke, 3 and 1					
Miss Kaya Caldwell, Santa Fe Hills, Mo.		Mrs. Johnstone, 4 and 2				
Mrs. Raleigh C. Hall, Tulsa, Okla.	Mrs. Johnstone, 7 and 6					
Mrs. Anne Casey Johnstone, Mason City, Iowa			Mrs. Johnstone, 5 and 3			
BYE—Mrs. James R. Biddick, Tulsa, Okla.	Mrs. Biddick	Mrs. Biddick, 1 up				
Miss Marcia G. Hamilton, El Rio, Ariz.	Miss Bostrom, 1 up			Mrs. Johnstone, 2 and 1		
Miss Jane Bostrom, Prince Georges, Md.						
Mrs. Fred Apostoli, Lake Merced, Calif.	Miss Holmes, 2 and 1					
Miss Nancy E. Holmes, Town, Tenn.		Miss Holmes, 2 and 1				
BYE—Miss Melinda Magly, Silverado, Calif.	Miss Magly		Miss White, 6 and 5			
Miss Kathie Martin, Rhinelander, Wis.	Miss Cranston, 7 and 6					
Miss Elanne M. Cranston, Annandale, Calif.		Miss White, 6 and 5			Mrs. Johnstone, 2 and 1	
BYE—Miss Barbara Fay White, Broadmoor, La.	Miss White					
Mrs. Dale Fleming McNamara, Kahkwa, Pa.	Mrs. Gregory, 1 up					
Mrs. Ann Gregory, Chicago Women's, Ill.		Miss Newton, 4 and 3				
BYE—Miss Kathleen Newton, Acacia, Ohio	Miss Newton		Miss Newton, 1 up, 20 hls.			
Miss Karen Schull, Blue Hills, Mo.	Miss Schull, 2 up	Miss Schull, 4 and 3				
Mrs. J.J. Freeman, Jr., C.C. of Little Rock, Ark.						
BYE—Miss Joan Gavigan, Merrill Hills, Wis.	Miss Gavigan			Miss Quast, 4 and 3		
Miss Ann Baker, Green Meadow, Tenn.	Miss Quast, 1 up, 19 hls.	Miss Quast, 2 up				
Miss Anne Quast, Everett, Wash.						
BYE—Miss Carol Sorenson, Janesville, Wis.	Miss Sorenson		Miss Quast, 7 and 5			
Mrs. Dena Dobson, Oakwood, Okla.	Miss Rich, 4 and 2	Miss Rich, 4 and 3				
Miss Frances Rich, Northwood, Texas						
BYE—Mrs. Maurice Glick, Woodholme, Md.	Mrs. Glick					Miss Ashley, 1 up
Miss Maureen Crum, Cleveland Heights, Fla.	Miss Wheeler, 5 and 4	Miss Wheeler, 7 and 6				
Miss Sherry Wheeler, Glasgow, Ky.						
BYE—Miss Mary Carey, Ridge, Ill.	Miss Carey		Miss McIntire, 1 up			
Miss Barbara McIntire, Tequesta, Fla.	Miss McIntire, 7 and 6	Miss McIntire, 3 and 1				
Miss Gwen Brownlee, Tulsa, Okla.						
BYE—Miss Sharon Fladoos, Dubuque, Iowa	Miss Fladoos			Miss McIntire, 2 and 1		
Miss Margaret Jones, Fort Mitchell, Ky.	Miss Jones, 1 up	Miss Jones, 2 up				
Miss Jean R. Bell, Acacia, Ohio						
BYE—Miss Linda Collins, Turlock, Calif.	Miss Collins		Miss Williams, 3 and 1			
Miss Heidi Prentice, Westmoreland, Ill.	Miss Prentice, 7 and 6	Miss Williams, 3 and 2				
Miss Pam Kingsbury, Wichita, Kans.					Miss Ashley, 1 up	
Miss Barbara Williams, Richmond, Calif.	Miss Williams, 2 and 1					
Mrs. Helen Sigel Wilson, Philadelphia, Pa.						
Miss Patty David, Tulsa, Okla.	Miss Hull, 4 and 3	Miss Riley, 1 up				
Miss Julie Hull, Edgewood, Ind.						
BYE—Miss Polly Riley, River Crest, Texas	Miss Riley		Miss Ashley, 1 up, 21 hls.			
Miss Jean Ashley, Chanute, Kans.	Miss Ashley, 5 and 4	Miss Ashley, 3 and 2				
Mrs. Sam Schwartzkopf, Hillcrest, Neb.						
Mrs. Elsie C. Hoke, Chartiers, Pa.	Mrs. Semple, 3 and 1			Miss Ashley, 5 and 3		
Mrs. Harton S. Semple, Allegheny, Pa.						
Mrs. Frank Stranahan, Inverness, Ohio	Mrs. Stranahan, 3 and 1	Mrs. Stranahan, 2 up				
Miss Susie Maxwell, Lincoln Park, Okla.						
BYE—Miss Linda Anderson, Olympia, Wash.	Miss Anderson		Miss Hoke, 4 and 2			
Mrs. Martha Griffith, Shady Oaks, Texas	Mrs. Patch, 1 up	Miss Hoke, 1 up, 21 hls.				
Mrs. Peter Patch, Orinda, Calif.						
BYE—Miss Diana Hoke, Chartiers, Pa.	Miss Hoke					

The first word after the player's name is the name of her club, except in the case of a foreign entrant.

LOWER HALF

	Semi-Final (18 Holes)	5th Round (18 Holes)	4th Round (18 Holes)	3rd Round (18 Holes)	2nd Round (18 Holes)	1st Round (18 Holes)
					Miss Hutchison, 3 and 1	Mrs. Joseph J. Miller, Hot Springs, Ark.
				Mrs. Dommers, 2 up		Miss Anna May Hutchison, Rancho, Calif.
					Mrs. Dommers	BYE—Mrs. Paul Dommers, Mauh-Nah-Tee-See, Ill.
			Miss Mills, 6 and 4		Miss Mills, 4 and 3	Miss Mary Mills, Great Southern, Miss.
				Miss Mills, 3 and 2		Miss Judy Rand, Aurora, Ohio
		Miss Matson, 5 and 4			Miss Sowell	BYE—Miss Wanda Sowell, Austin, Texas
					Miss Phillips, 4 and 2	Miss Doris Phillips, St. Clair, Ill.
				Miss Matson, 1 up		Miss Carrie Hoiles, Alliance, Ohio
					Miss Matson	BYE—Miss Natasha Matson, Rolling Hills, Kans.
			Miss Matson, 4 and 2		Mrs. Robbins, 8 and 6	Mrs. Carle Robbins, Hardscrabble, Ark.
				Miss Clifford, 4 and 3		Miss Margo Ann Michaelis, Orange Brook, Fla.
	Miss Gunderson, 7 and 6				Miss Clifford	BYE—Miss Sandra Clifford, Club de Golf Mexico, Mexico
					Miss Gunderson, 6 and 5	Miss Betsy Cullen, Tulsa, Okla.
				Miss Gunderson, 3 and 1		Miss JoAnne Gunderson, Sand Point, Wash.
			Miss Gunderson, 6 and 5		Miss Burns	BYE—Miss Marjorie Burns, Starmount Forest, N.C.
		Miss Gunderson, 1 up			Miss Abbott, 1 up, 19 hls.	Miss Lorraine Abbott, Sylvania, Ohio
				Miss Abbott, 4 and 3		Mrs. Charles Menninger, Twin Hills, Okla.
					Miss Gable, 3 and 2	Miss Jane Thomas, San Francisco, Calif.
						Miss Marianne Gable, Santa Anita Women's, Calif.
					Miss Janssen	BYE—Miss Mary Patton Janssen, Farmington, Va.
				Miss Janssen, 4 and 3	Mrs. Messinger, 7 and 5	Mrs. Grant Messinger, Northwood, Texas
			Miss Spuzich, 5 and 4			Miss Jeanie Butler, Harlingen, Texas
					Mrs. Perrin, 3 and 2	Mrs. Richard C. Beveridge, Tulsa, Okla.
Miss Gunderson, 2 up				Miss Spuzich, 4 and 2		Mrs. Gordon Perrin, Tulsa, Okla.
					Miss Spuzich	BYE—Miss Sandra Spuzich, Speedway, Ind.
					Miss Palmer, 1 up	Miss Sandra Palmer, Glen Garden, Texas
				Miss Bell, 5 and 4		Miss Phyllis Preuss, Pompano Beach, Fla.
			Miss Bell, 4 and 3		Miss Bell	BYE—Miss Judy Bell, Wichita, Kans.
					Miss Haynie, 6 and 5	Mrs. Ed Oberholtzer, Tulsa, Okla.
				Miss Haynie, 3 and 2		Miss Sandra Haynie, Capitol City, Texas
		Miss Cohn, 5 and 4			Dr. Whitaker	BYE—Dr. Jo Ann Whitaker, Glen Lakes, Texas
					Miss Roth, 6 and 5	Miss Nancy L. Roth, Elks, Ind.
				Miss Roth, 1 up, 19 hls.		Mrs. L.G. Sutter, Southern Hills, Okla.
					Miss Glanville, 3 and 1	Mrs. C.D. Elwell, Ranchland Hill, Texas
			Miss Cohn, 1 up			Miss Harriet Glanville, Recreation Park, Calif.
					Miss Cohn	BYE—Miss Andrea Cohn, Sunnyside, Iowa
	Miss Eller, 3 and 2			Miss Cohn, 5 and 4	Mrs. Wilcox, 1 up, 19 hls.	Mrs. George E. Wilcox, Jr., Miami Shores, Fla.
						Miss Charlotte Schulz, Wichita Falls, Texas
					Miss Eller, 7 and 5	Miss Judy Eller, Old Hickory, Tenn.
				Miss Eller, 2 and 1		Mrs. Sam Israel, Jr., Lakewood, La.
					Miss Stone	BYE—Miss Beth Stone, Muskogee, Okla.
			Miss Eller, 2 and 1		Miss Mann, 1 up, 19 hls.	Miss Carol Mann, Olympia Fields, Ill.
				Miss Mann, 8 and 6		Mrs. Gaines Wilson, Jr., Big Spring, Ky.
		Miss Eller, 2 and 1			Mrs. Savage, 5 and 4	Mrs. Howard Savage, Mohawk, Okla.
						Mrs. Gertrude Marshall, Southern Hills, Okla.
				Miss Lowell, 1 up	Miss Lowell	BYE—Miss Mary Lowell, Alameda Municipal, Calif.
					Miss Loftfield, 4 and 3	Miss Carlene Hotz, Oaks, Okla.
			Mrs. Dye, 7 and 5			Miss Judy Kay Loftfield, Arizona, Ariz.
					Miss Thompson	BYE—Miss Jeannie Thompson, Tulsa, Okla.
				Mrs. Dye, 6 and 4	Mrs. Dye, 4 and 2	Mrs. Paul Dye, Jr., C.C. of Indianapolis, Ind.
						Miss Judy Kimball, Hyperion Field, Iowa

1961
SIXTY-FIRST WOMEN'S AMATEUR CHAMPIONSHIP

Held at the Tacoma Country and Golf Club, Tacoma, Washington, August 21-26.

Yardage—6,297. Par 73. 107 Entries, 102 Starters.

Championship entirely at match play.

FINAL ROUND (36 Holes)—Mrs. Anne Quast Decker defeated Miss Phyllis Preuss 14 and 13.

UPPER HALF

1st Round (18 Holes)	2nd Round (18 Holes)	3rd Round (18 Holes)	4th Round (18 Holes)	5th Round (18 Holes)	Semi-Final (18 Holes)	
Miss Gloria Fay, Bellingham, Wash.	Miss Fay, 7 and 5					
Mrs. Barbara L. Potter, St. Joseph, Mo.		Miss Hoetmer, 6 and 5				
Miss Tina Powell, Elks.Allenmore, Wash.	Miss Hoetmer, 6 and 4					
Miss Judy Hoetmer, Sand Point, Wash.			Miss Hoetmer, 5 and 4			
BYE—Miss Mary Lowell, Alameda, Calif.	Miss Lowell	Miss Lowell, 1 up, 19 hls.				
Miss Kathryn L. Farrer, Decatur, Ala.	Miss Gunderson, 5 and 4			Miss Hoetmer, 1 up		
Miss JoAnne Gunderson, Sand Point, Wash.						
BYE—Miss Mary Ann Doctor, White Beeches, N.J.	Miss Doctor	Miss Spuzich, 3 and 2				
Mrs. Barbara D. Hartson, Claremont, Calif.	Miss Spuzich, 2 and 1					
Miss Sandra Spuzich, Speedway, Ind.			Miss Spuzich, 1 up			
Miss Gail De Pietro, Castlewood, Calif.	Miss De Pietro, 7 and 6					
Miss Melinda Magly, Indian Valley, Calif.		Miss De Pietro, 3 and 2				
BYE—Mrs. Fred Zwahlen, Jr., Corvallis, Ore.	Mrs. Zwahlen				Mrs. Wilson, 2 up	
Mrs. Lee Ghilarducci, Sacramento Women's, Calif.	Mrs. Ghilarducci, 5 and 3					
Miss Jean R. Bell, Acacia, Ohio		Mrs. Ghilarducci, 7 and 6				
BYE—Miss Sherry Ann Taylor, Twin Hills, Okla.	Miss Taylor		Mrs. Ghilarducci, 2 and 1			
Miss Karen Swanson, Del Paso, Calif.	Miss Anderson, 7 and 6					
Miss Linda Anderson, Olympia, Wash.		Miss Anderson, 1 up				
Mrs. Harton S. Semple, Allegheny, Pa.	Mrs. Johnstone, 5 and 4			Mrs. Wilson, 8 and 6		
Mrs. Anne Casey Johnstone, Mason City, Iowa						
BYE—Mrs. Gaines Wilson, Jr., Big Spring, Ky.	Mrs. Wilson	Mrs. Wilson, 3 and 2				
Miss Carol M. Hartson, San Diego, Calif.	Mrs. Skala, 3 and 2					
Mrs. Carole Jo Skala, Roseburg, Ore.			Mrs. Wilson, 1 up, 19 hls.			
Miss Lea C. Mouncier, Olympia, Wash.	Miss Hull, 1 up					
Miss Julie Hull, Anderson, Ind.		Miss Hull, 6 and 4				
BYE—Mrs. Pat Brewitt, Kitsap, Wash.	Mrs. Brewitt					**Mrs. Decker, 5 and 4**
Miss Janet MacWha, Vancouver, Canada	Miss MacWha, 5 and 4					
Miss Ruth P. Wilson, Vancouver, Canada		Miss MacWha, 3 and 1				
BYE—Mrs. Martin Fopp, Elk's Allenmore, Wash.	Mrs. Fopp		Miss MacWha, 2 up			
Miss Carol Sorenson, Janesville, Wis.	Miss Sorenson, 7 and 6					
Mrs. E.C. Kip Finch, C.C. of New Canaan, Conn.		Mrs. Fife, 1 up		Mrs. Miller, 1 up, 19 hls.		
Mrs. N. Matson Fife, Rolling Hills, Kans.	Mrs. Fife, 3 and 2					
Dr. JoAnne Whitaker, Glen Lakes, Texas						
BYE—Miss Jacqueline King, Alameda, Calif.	Miss King	Miss Robinson, 2 up				
Mrs. Patricia Ann Lesser Harbottle, Tacoma, Wash.	Miss Robinson, 4 and 2					
Miss June Robinson, Rose City, Ore.			Mrs. Miller, 4 and 3			
Miss Frances Rich, Northwood, Texas	Miss Rich, 5 and 4					
Mrs. George E. Wilcox, Jr., Miami Shores, Fla.		Mrs. Miller, 1 up			Mrs. Decker, 5 and 3	
BYE—Mrs. Ruth White Miller, California, Calif.	Mrs. Miller					
Miss Sue DeVoe, Rogue Valley, Ore.	Miss Daniel, 5 and 3					
Miss Mary Lou Daniel, Iroquois, Ky.		Mrs. Cole, 3 and 1				
BYE—Mrs. Betty Stanhope Cole, Edmonton, Canada	Mrs. Cole		Miss Riley, 1 up			
Miss Polly Riley, River Crest, Texas	Miss Riley, 7 and 5					
Miss Carrie Lou Hoiles, Alliance, Ohio		Miss Riley, 4 and 3		Mrs. Decker, 3 and 2		
BYE—Miss Carla Jean Glasgow, Candlewood, Calif.	Miss Glasgow					
Miss Judy Rand, Aurora, Ohio	Miss Rand, 7 and 5					
Miss Margaret Martin, Belmont Hills, Ohio		Miss Rand, 3 and 2				
BYE—Miss Diana Hoke, Chartiers, Pa.	Miss Hoke		Mrs. Decker, 6 and 5			
Mrs. Anne Quast Decker, Broadmoor, Wash.	Mrs. Decker, 5 and 3					
Miss Judy Torluemke, St. Louis Amateur Athletic Ass'n., Mo.		Mrs. Decker, 4 and 2				
BYE—Miss Sharon Fladoos, Dubuque, Iowa	Miss Fladoos					

The first word after the player's name is the name of her club, except in the case of a foreign entrant.

LOWER HALF

Semi-Final (18 Holes)	5th Round (18 Holes)		4th Round (18 Holes)	3rd Round (18 Holes)	2nd Round (18 Holes)	1st Round (18 Holes)
					Miss Williams, 1 up	Miss Wanda Sowell, Glen Garden, Texas
				Miss Williams, 1 up, 21 hls.		Miss Barbara Williams, Richmond, Calif.
					Miss Glanville	BYE—Miss Harriet Glanville, Meadowlark, Calif.
			Miss Williams, 4 and 3		Miss Baker, 1 up, 21 hls.	Miss Ann Baker, Green Meadow, Tenn.
				Miss Newton, 1 up		Miss Joan Gavigan, Troy, Ohio
					Miss Newton, 3 and 2	Miss Kathleen Newton, Acacia, Ohio
		Miss McIntire, 5 and 4				Mrs. Frank Donaldson, Yorba Linda, Calif.
					Miss Maxwell	BYE—Miss Susie Maxwell, Lincoln Park, Okla.
				Miss McIntire, 4 and 2	Miss McIntire, 4 and 2	Miss Barbara McIntire, Tequesta, Fla.
			Miss McIntire, 5 and 4			Miss Jean Ashley, Chanute, Kans.
					Miss Gable, 7 and 5	Miss Mary Carey, Beverly, Ill.
				Miss Gable, 3 and 2		Miss Marianne Gable, California, Calif.
					Miss Bell	BYE—Miss Barbara Bell, Peninsula, Wash.
	Miss Preuss, 3 and 2				Miss Edwards, 3 and 1	Mrs. Floyd L. Ratliff, Stockdale, Calif.
				Miss Preuss, 5 and 4		Miss Joan Edwards, Columbia-Edgewater, Ore.
					Miss Preuss	BYE—Miss Phyllis Preuss, Pompano Beach, Fla.
			Miss Preuss, 1 up		Miss Phillips, 3 and 1	Mrs. Frank Stranahan, Inverness, Ohio
				Miss Price, 1 up, 21 hls.		Miss Doris Phillips, St. Clair, Ill.
					Miss Price, 3 and 2	Mrs. Robert Ihlanfeldt, Inglewood, Wash.
						Miss Elizabeth Price, Tilford, England
		Miss Preuss, 7 and 6			Mrs. Baty	BYE—Mrs. Jack Baty, Fircrest, Wash.
				Miss Byrne, 2 up	Miss Byrne, 6 and 5	Mrs. Del Walker, Virginia, Calif.
			Miss Michaelis, 1 up			Miss Bonnie Byrne, California, Calif.
					Miss Michaelis, 6 and 5	Miss Jeanie Butler, Harlingen, Texas
				Miss Michaelis, 1 up, 19 hls.		Miss Margo Ann Michaelis, Orange Brook, Fla.
					Miss Wheeler	BYE—Miss Sherry Wheeler, Glasgow, Ky.
Miss Preuss, 2 and 1					Miss Janssen, 3 and 2	Miss Elanne M. Cranston, Annandale, Calif.
				Miss Janssen, 2 and 1		Miss Mary Patton Janssen, Farmington, Va.
					Miss Burns	BYE—Miss Marjorie Burns, Starmount Forest, N.C.
			Miss Janssen, 2 and 1		Miss Thomas, 4 and 3	Miss Claudia Lindor, Everett, Wash.
				Miss Thomas, 1 up		Miss Jane Thomas, San Francisco, Calif.
					Mrs. Pennington, 1 up, 19 hls.	Mrs. John Pennington, C.C. of Buffalo, N.Y.
						Miss Karen Ellen Ford, Overlake, Wash.
		Miss Albers, 5 and 4			Miss Cohn	BYE—Miss Andrea Cohn, Sunnyside, Iowa
				Miss Eller, 5 and 4	Miss Eller, 3 and 1	Mrs. S.M. Hopkins, Los Altos, Calif.
			Miss Albers, 5 and 3			Miss Judy Eller, Old Hickory, Tenn.
					Miss Albers, 5 and 4	Miss Patricia Dwyer, Waverley, Ore.
				Miss Albers, 4 and 3		Miss Roberta A. Albers, Temple Terrace, Fla.
					Mrs. Hulscher	BYE—Mrs. Henry Hulscher, Fircrest, Wash.
	Miss Albers, 7 and 5				Miss McCoy, 1 up, 19 hls.	Miss Susan McCoy, Inglewood, Wash.
				Miss Roth, 5 and 4		Miss Peggy Rutledge, Los Angeles, Calif.
					Miss Roth	BYE—Miss Nancy Roth, Elks, Ind.
			Miss Schull, 1 up		Miss Sheldon, 5 and 3	Miss Bridget Jackson, Birmingham, England
				Miss Schull, 4 and 2		Miss Harriet Sheldon, Bakersfield, Calif.
		Miss Schull, 1 up			Miss Schull	BYE—Miss Karen Schull, Blue Hills, Mo.
					Miss Jennett, 2 and 1	Miss Sue Jennett, Oswego Lake, Ore.
				Miss Jennett, 2 and 1		Miss Barbara Fay White, East Ridge, La.
					Miss Thompson	BYE—Miss Jeannie Thompson, Tulsa, Okla.
			Miss Jennett, 2 and 1		Maj. Amizich, 1 up	Miss Judy Bell, Wichita, Kans.
				Maj. Amizich, 1 up, 19 hls.		Major Amelia D. Amizich, Presidio, Calif.
					Mrs. Straub	BYE—Mrs. Betse Straub, Mesa Verde Women's, Calif.

1962

SIXTY-SECOND WOMEN'S AMATEUR CHAMPIONSHIP

Held at the Country Club of Rochester, Rochester, New York, August 27-September 1.
Yardage—6,161. Par 72. 128 Entries, 128 Starters.
Championship entirely at match play.

FINAL ROUND (36 Holes)—Miss JoAnne Gunderson defeated Miss Ann Baker, 9 and 8.

UPPER HALF

1st Round (18 Holes)	2nd Round (18 Holes)	3rd Round (18 Holes)	4th Round (18 Holes)	5th Round (18 Holes)	Semi Final (18 Holes)	
Mrs. E. C. Kip Finch, New Canaan, Conn. Miss Ellen H. Gery, Palmetto, Fla.	Miss Gery, 2 up					
Mrs. Natasha Fife, Rolling Hills, Kans. Miss Lou Evans, Ontario, Canada	Mrs. Fife, 8 and 7	Mrs. Fife, 5 and 4				
Mrs. Joseph A. Nesbitt, Westchester, N.Y. Mrs. Ann Gregory, Chicago's Women's, Ill.	Mrs. Nesbitt, 6 and 4					
Miss JoAnne Gunderson, Sand Point, Wash. Miss Nancy Gunther, CC of Troy, N.Y.	Miss Gunderson, 7 and 5	Miss Gunderson, 4 and 3	Miss Gunderson, 5 and 4			
Miss Jean R. Bell, Acacia, Ohio Miss Rae Milligan, Alberta, Canada	Miss Milligan, 6 and 5					
Miss Maggie Martin, Belmont Hills, Ohio Miss Lida Fee Matthews, Elks, Ohio	Miss Martin, 1 up	Miss Milligan, 1 up				
Miss Nancy E. Holmes, Town & Country, Tenn. Miss Shirley M. Woodley, Ontario, Canada	Miss Holmes, 5 and 4					
Miss Carrie Hoiles, Alliance, Ohio Miss Diana Hoke, Chartiers, Pa.	Miss Hoke, 3 and 1	Miss Holmes, 1 up	Miss Holmes, 4 and 2	Miss Gunderson, 5 and 4		
Mrs. Helen Sigel Wilson, Philadelphia, Pa. Miss Margaret Jones, Fort Mitchell, Ky.	Mrs. Wilson, 1 up					
Miss Sandra Spuzich, Speedway, Ind. Miss Barbara J. Williams, Richmond, Calif.	Miss Williams, 1 up	Miss Williams, 1 up				
Miss Judy M. Bell, Broadmoor, Colo. Miss Mary Ann Doctor, Cedar Brook, N.Y.	Miss Bell, 2 up					
Mrs. Anthony F. Rose, Antlers, N.Y. Miss Mary Lou Daniel, Iroquois, Ky.	Mrs. Rose, 1 up	Miss Bell, 3 and 2	Miss Williams, 3 and 2			
Miss Polly Riley, River Crest, Texas Mrs. Maurice Glick, Woodholme, Md.	Miss Riley, 5 and 3					
Mrs. George E. Wilcox, Jr., Miami Shores, Fla. Miss Karen Schull, Blue Hills, Mo.	Miss Schull, 7 and 6	Miss Schull, 1 up				
Miss Mary Ann Downey, Baltimore, Md. **Miss Nancy Roth, Elks', Ind.**	Miss Downey, 1 up					
Mrs. Charles Keating, Corning, N.Y. Miss Ann Lesley Irvin, St. Anne's-on-Sea, England	Miss Irvin, 6 and 5	Miss Downey, 1 up	Miss Schull, 1 up	Miss Williams, 4 and 3	Miss Gunderson, 1 up, 20 hls.	
Miss Roberta A. Albers, Temple Terrace, Fla. Mrs. Francis Smith, Liverpool, England	Mrs. Smith, 2 and 1					
Miss Patsy E. Johnson, Spartanburg, S.C. Mrs. John M. Dyson, Huntingdon Valley, Pa.	Miss Johnson, 1 up, 19 hls.	Mrs. Smith, 1 up, 19 hls.				
Mrs. Phillip H. Allen, Bellevue, N.Y. Miss Anne Richardson, Columbus, Ohio	Miss Richardson, 5 and 4					
Miss Judy Jones, Canterbury, Ohio Mrs. Emma B. Kutzer, Lafayette, N.Y.	Miss Jones, 6 and 5	Miss Richardson, 6 and 5	Mrs. Smith, 1 up			
Miss Jean Ashley, Chanute, Kansas Miss Bonnie Byrne, Women's Aux. of Calif., Calif.	Miss Byrne, 1 up					
Miss Maureen Orcutt, White Beeches, N.J. Miss Renee M. Powell, Clearview, Ohio	Miss Orcutt, 2 up	Miss Orcutt, 3 and 2				
Miss Cynthia Buzan, Speedway, Ind. Mrs. Gaines P. Wilson, Jr., Big Springs, Ky.	Mrs. Wilson, 4 and 3					
Miss Kathleen Newton, Acacia, Ohio Mrs. Harry J. Nevil, Jr., Cooperstown, N.Y.	Mrs. Nevil, 1 up	Mrs. Nevil, 1 up, 19 hls.	Mrs. Nevil, 4 and 3	Mrs. Nevil, 1 up, 20 hls.		Miss Gunderson, 3 and 2
Miss Althea Gibson, Englewood, N.J. Miss Jeanie Butler, Harlingen, Texas	Miss Gibson, 2 and 1					
Mrs. John B. Whitacre, Jr., Brookside, Ohio Mrs. Paul Dye, Jr., Meridian Hills, Ind.	Mrs. Dye, 6 and 5	Mrs. Dye, 2 up				
Miss Mary Ellen Driscoll, New Brunswick, Canada **Mrs. Scott Probasco, Jr., Chattanooga, Tenn.**	Mrs. Probasco, 3 and 1					
Miss Sheila Vaughan, Liverpool, England Miss Martha Kosar, Silver Lake, Ohio	Miss Vaughn, 3 and 2	Miss Vaughan, 5 and 3	Miss Vaughan, 2 and 1			
Miss Connie Day, Brainerd, Tenn. Mrs. John Pennington, Buffalo, N.Y.	Miss Day, 3 and 1					
Mrs. Joanne Creason, Colonial, Pa. Mrs. Roslyn Swift Berger, Westwood, N.Y.	Mrs. Berger, 7 and 5	Mrs. Berger, 1 up				
Miss Phyllis Preuss, Pompano Beach, Fla. Miss Sherry Taylor, Town Hills, Okla.	Miss Preuss, 6 and 5					
Mrs. James P. Lee, Huntington, N.Y. Miss Sue Lance, Woodland Hills, Calif.	Mrs. Lee, 2 and 1	Miss Preuss, 1 up, 19 hls.	Miss Preuss, 1 up, 20 hls.	Miss Preuss, 1 up, 19 hls.	Miss Preuss, 4 and 2	

The first word after the player's name is the name of her club, except in the case of a foreign entrant.

LOWER HALF

Semi-Final (18 Holes)	5th Round (18 Holes)		4th Round (18 Holes)	3rd Round (18 Holes)	2nd Round (18 Holes)	1st Round (18 Holes)
Miss Baker, 1 up	Miss Hahn, 5 and 4	Mrs. Decker, 3 and 2	Mrs. Decker, 3 and 2	Mrs. Trainor, 4 and 3	Mrs. Trainor 4 and 2	Mrs. Jean Trainor, Rochester, N.Y. Miss Donna Kosar, Silver Lake, Ohio
					Miss Trainor, 1 up	Miss Anne Trainor, Rochester, N.Y. Miss Joan Edwards, Columbia-Edgewater, Ore.
				Mrs. Decker, 5 and 4	Miss Burns, 6 and 5	Miss Marjorie Burns, Starmount Forest, N.C. Miss Carla Jean Glasgow, Candlewood, Calif.
					Mrs. Decker, 8 and 7	Mrs. Anne Quast Decker, Broadmoor, Wash. Miss Helen I. Reynolds, Manchester, Conn.
			Miss Rand, 3 and 2	Miss Porter, 5 and 4	Miss King, 1 up	Mrs. J. Peter Bush, Rochester, N.Y. Mrs. Jacqueline King, Alameda, Calif.
					Miss Porter, 5 and 4	Miss Ruth Porter, Bath, England Miss Mary Lowell, Alameda, Calif.
				Miss Rand, 4 and 2	Miss Rand, 4 and 3	Mrs. Marjorie Burris, Mohawk, N.Y. Miss Judith Rand, Aurora, Ohio
					Mrs. Cooperstein 4 and 3	Mrs. Walter M. Cooperstein, Harbor Hills, N.Y. Miss Heidi Prentice, Westmoreland, Ill.
		Miss Hahn, 2 up	Miss Gavigan, 1 up	Miss Fladoos, 2 and 1	Miss O'Sullivan, 2 and 1	Miss Patricia O'Sullivan, Race Brook, Conn. Miss Clifford Ann Creed, Rapidas, La.
					Miss Fladoos, 7 and 6	Miss Sharon Lee Fladoos, Dubuque, Iowa Mrs. John F. Youker, Glens Falls, N.Y.
				Miss Gavigan, 2 and 1	Miss Gavigan, 2 and 1	Miss Joan Gavigan, Troy, Ohio Miss Margaret M. Cramer, Antlers, N.Y.
					Mrs. Maurer, 4 and 3	Miss Katherine Helleur, Toronto, Canada Mrs. Linda Collins Maurer, Turlock, Wis.
			Miss Hahn, 2 up	Miss Ferraris, 3 and 1	Miss Ferraris, 6 and 4	Miss Janis Ferraris, Presidio, Calif. Miss Lois Ward, Park, N.Y.
					Mrs. Cronin, 5 and 4	Miss Judith Ann Taylor, Speedway, Ind. Mrs. Grace Lenczyk Cronin, Indian Hill, Conn.
				Miss Hahn, 5 and 3	Mrs. Coupe, 1 up	Mrs. Douglas Coupe, Schuyler Meadows, N.Y. Miss Marianne Gable, California, Calif.
					Miss Hahn, 1 up	Miss Kay Herbert, Lawrence Park, Pa. Miss Patricia Hahn, Du Pont, Del.
	Miss Baker, 2 and 1	Miss McLachlan, 3 and 2	Miss McIntire, 3 and 2	Miss King, 1 up	Miss King, 4 and 3	Miss Mary Patton Janssen, Farmington, Va. Miss Robbye Lee King, Army-Navy, Va.
					Miss Purdy, 3 and 2	Miss Gail S. Purdy, Glens Falls, N.Y. Mrs. Joseph Malia, Spring Valley, Mass.
				Miss McIntire, 2 and 1	Miss Hilton, 3 and 1	Miss Sue Hilton, London, Canada Miss Evelyn A. Sawyer, Race Brook, Conn.
					Miss McIntire, 4 and 3	Miss Barbara McIntire, Broadmoor, Colo. Miss Gail Harvey, Willowdale, Canada
			Miss McLachlan, 1 up, 19 hls.	Mrs. Semple, 2 and 1	Mrs. Semple, 2 and 1	Mrs. Harton S. Semple, Allegheny, Pa. Mrs. Jeffrey R. Smythe, Nottingham Knoll, N.Y.
					Miss Sorenson, 5 and 4	Miss Carol Sorenson, Janesville, N.Y. Miss Janet C. MacLeod, Buffalo, N.Y.
				Miss McLachlan, 4 and 3	Miss Michaelis, 6 and 5	Miss Mary B. Darling, Montreal, Canada Miss Margo Ann Michaelis, Orange Brook, Fla.
					Miss McLachlan, 7 and 5	Miss Marcia McLachlan, Ridgewood, Conn. Miss Janet MacWha, Vancouver, Canada
		Miss Baker, 5 and 4	Miss High, 1 up	Miss Weiland, 2 and 1	Miss Logan, 4 and 3	Miss Mary Anne Lopez, Palmetto, Fla. Miss Terry Logan, Forest Hills Field, N.J.
					Miss Weiland, 8 and 6	Miss Helen M. Weiland, Aronimink, Pa. Miss Katherine Cartwright, Ontario, Canada
				Miss High, 2 and 1	Miss Jennett, 1 up, 19 hls.	Mrs. William C. Warren, III, Rochester, N.Y. Miss Sue Jennett, Oswego Lake, Ore.
					Miss High, 2 and 1	Miss Jean Roberts, Birmingham, England Miss Brenda High, Glasgow, Ky.
			Miss Baker, 7 and 6	Miss Baker, 3 and 2	Miss Crum, 1 up, 19 hls.	Mrs. Barbara Fitton, Elks, Ohio Miss Maureen Crum, Plant City, Fla.
					Miss Baker, 7 and 5	Mrs. Ann Casey Johnstone, Mason City, Iowa Miss Ann Baker, Green Meadow, Tenn.
				Miss Carroll, 4 and 3	Miss Carroll, 5 and 4	Miss Sally Carroll, Wheeling, W. Va. Mrs. Robert Lyle, Montreal, Canada
					Mrs. Creed, 1 up	Miss Jeannie Thompson, Tulsa, Okla. Mrs. Eddie Creed, Toronto, Canada

1963

SIXTY-THIRD WOMEN'S AMATEUR CHAMPIONSHIP

Held at the Taconic Golf Club, Williamstown, Mass., August 19-24.

Yardage—6,195. Par 72. 128 Entries, 128 Starters. Championship entirely at match play.

FINAL ROUND (36 Holes)—Mrs. Anne Quast Welts defeated Miss Peggy Conley, 2 up and 1 to play.

UPPER HALF

1st Round (18 Holes)	2nd Round (18 Holes)	3rd Round (18 Holes)	4th Round (18 Holes)	5th Round (18 Holes)	Semi-Final (18 Holes)	
Miss Mary Carey, Beverly, Ill.	Miss Marinaro, 1 up	Miss Marinaro, 6 and 4	Miss Marinaro, 7 and 6	Mrs. Semple, 1 up	Miss Sorenson, 4 and 3	Miss Conley, 1 up
Miss Terry Marinaro, Belmont, Calif.						
Miss Maggie Martin, Belmont Hills, Ohio	Miss Martin, 1 up					
Mrs. Paul Dye, Jr., Meridian Hills, Ind.						
Miss Barbara Fay White, East Ridge, La.	Miss White, 7 and 5	Miss White, 1 up				
Mrs. Richard H. Semple, Jr., Allegheny, Pa.						
Miss Carrie Hoiles, Alliance, Ohio	Mrs. Posey, 5 and 3					
Mrs. Barbara L. Posey, Lake Chabot, Calif.						
Miss Judy Rand, Aurora, Ohio	Miss Shook, 21 holes	Miss Shook, 3 and 2	Mrs. Semple, 3 and 2			
Miss Patti Shook, South Haven, Mich.						
Miss Melinda Magly, Meadow, Calif.	Miss Magly, 21 holes					
Miss Martha Kosar, Silver Lake, Ohio						
Mrs. Grace Lenczyk Cronin, Indian Hill, Conn.	Mrs. Jones, 20 holes	Mrs. Semple, 2 and 1				
Mrs. Mae Murray Jones, Burlington, Vt.						
Mrs. Margaret Paul, Pequabuck, Conn.	Mrs. Semple, 5 and 4					
Mrs. Harton S. Semple, Allegheny, Pa.						
Miss Carol Sorenson, Janesville, Wis.	Miss Sorenson, 4 and 3	Miss Sorenson, 5 and 4	Miss Sorenson, 4 and 3	Miss Sorenson, 1 up		
Mrs. Ann Gregory, Chicago Women's C.C., Ill.						
Mrs. E.C.K. Finch, C.C. of New Canaan, Conn.	Mrs. Burke, 4 and 3					
Mrs. J.T. Burke, Florham Park Women's G.A., N.J.						
Mrs. Donald K. McClusky, Worcester, Mass.	Mrs. McClusky, 1 up	Miss Carroll, 4 and 3				
Mrs. Barbara Fitton, Elks, Hamilton, Ohio						
Miss Sylvia Maurycy, Edison, N.Y.	Miss Carroll, 2 and 1					
Miss Sally Carroll, Wheeling, W. Va.						
Miss Linda Lewis, Florence, Ala.	Miss Lewis, 1 up	Miss Lewis, 5 and 4	Miss King, 3 and 1			
Mrs. Maurice Glick, Woodholme, Md.						
Miss Susan L. Rich, Skaneateles, N.Y.	Mrs. Kane, 6 and 5					
Mrs. John B. Kane, Whitemarsh Valley, Pa.						
Miss Robbye King, Army Navy, Va.	Miss King, 4 and 2	Miss King, 2 and 1				
Mrs. Linda C. Maurer, Plattsburgh AFB, N.Y.						
Miss Barbara McIntire, Broadmoor, Colo.	Miss Fleitas, 1 up					
Miss Elizabeth H. Fleitas, Wilmington, Del.						
Mrs. Linda Smythe, Catskill, N.Y.	Miss Glasscock, 2 and 1	Miss Holmes, 9 and 8	Miss Holmes, 3 and 2	Miss Bell, 2 and 1	Miss Conley, 3 and 2	
Miss Becky Glasscock, Pine Bluff, Ark.						
Miss Barbara Jo Gabrielsen, Athens, Ga.	Miss Holmes, 3 and 2					
Miss Nancy E. Holmes, Town & Country, Tenn.						
Mrs. Charles F. Spalding, Round Hill, Conn.	Mrs. Spalding, 3 and 2	Mrs. Spalding, 21 holes				
Mrs. Joseph A. Nesbitt, Westchester, N.Y.						
Miss Susan Gregory, Pine Bluff, Ark.	Miss Purdy, 7 and 5					
Miss Gail Purdy, Glens Falls, N.Y.						
Miss Brenda High, Glasgow, Ky.	Miss Austin, 20 holes	Mrs. Nydle, 6 and 5	Miss Bell, 5 and 3			
Miss Debbie Austin, Teugega, N.Y.						
Miss Emily Gail, Grosse Ile, Mich.	Mrs. Nydle, 2 up					
Mrs. Fred W. Nydle, Ottumwa, Iowa						
Miss Judy Bell, Broadmoor, Colo.	Miss Bell, 1 up	Miss Bell, 1 up				
Miss Donna Leary, Southington, Conn.						
Miss Diana Hoke, Chartiers, Pa.	Miss Riley, 19 holes					
Miss Polly Riley, River Crest, Texas						
Mrs. T.R. Garlington, Jr., Capital City, Ga.	Mrs. Coupe, 4 and 2	Miss Lance, 4 and 3	Miss Lance, 3 and 1	Miss Conley, 6 and 4		
Mrs. A. Van Vechten Coupe, Schuyler Meadows, N.Y.						
Miss Barbara Williams, Richmond, Calif.	Miss Lance, 3 and 2					
Miss Susan Lance, Woodland Hills, Calif.						
Mrs. George M. Trainor, C.C. of Rochester, N.Y.	Mrs. Trainor, 19 holes	Mrs. Erickson, 2 and 1				
Mrs. Margaret M. Cramer, Antlers, N.Y.						
Mrs. John E. Erickson, Nakoma, Wis.	Mrs. Erickson, 5 and 4					
Miss Marcia Knapp, Shephard Hills, N.Y.						
Miss Jane Schiller, Green Hill Yacht, Md.	Miss Schiller, 3 and 1	Miss Schiller, 3 and 2	Miss Conley, 2 and 1			
Miss Gloria Ehret, Ridgewood, Conn.						
Mrs. Helen L. Manheimer, Metropolis, N.Y.	Mrs. Manheimer, 19 holes					
Mrs. Anthony F. Rose, Antlers, N.Y.						
Miss Phyllis Preuss, Pompano Beach, Fla.	Miss Conley, 3 and 2	Miss Conley, 2 and 1				
Miss Peggy Conley, Spokane, Wash.						
Miss Rhonda Glenn, West Palm Beach, Fla.	**Miss Glenn, 4 and 3**					
Miss Lida Fee Matthews, Elks, Portsmouth, Ohio						

The first word after the player's name is the name of her club, except in the case of a foreign entrant.

LOWER HALF

Semi-Final (18 Holes)	5th Round (18 Holes)		4th Round (18 Holes)	3rd Round (18 Holes)	2nd Round (18 Holes)	1st Round (18 Holes)
Mrs. Welts, 3 and 2	Miss Gunderson, 5 and 4	Mrs. Wilson, 4 and 3	Miss Ashley, 1 up	Miss Lowell, 6 and 5	Miss Lowell, 3 and 1	Miss Mary Lowell, Alameda Women's Club, Calif. Mrs. Alexander F. Munro, Innis Arden, Conn.
					Mrs. Stranahan, 2 and 1	Miss Jeanie Butler, Harlingen, Texas Mrs. Frank Stranahan, Inverness, Ohio
				Miss Ashley, 4 and 3	Miss Ashley, 6 and 5	Mrs. Anna Sampson, Haverhill, Mass. Miss Jean Ashley, Broadmoor, Colo.
					Miss Willoughby, 2 and 1	Miss Roberta Albers, Temple Terrace, Fla. Miss Marguerite K. Willoughby, Tedesco, Mass.
			Mrs. Wilson, 5 and 4	Mrs. Wilson, 2 and 1	Mrs. Wilson, 3 and 2	Miss Linda Leader, Mohawk, N.Y. **Mrs. Helen Sigel Wilson, Philadelphia, Pa.**
					Mrs. Fife, 21 holes	Miss Jane Woodworth, Mt. Pleasant, Mass. Mrs. Natasha Fife, Rolling Hills, Kans.
				Mrs. McConnell, 20 holes	Mrs. McConnell, 4 and 3	Mrs. Max Kutzer, Lafayette, N.Y. Mrs. Jeanne McConnell, Amherst, Mass.
					Mrs. Daniels, 2 and 1	**Mrs. Dixon H. Daniels, C.C. of Pittsfield, Mass.** Mrs. James E. Thomas, Winchester, Mass.
		Miss Gunderson, 3 and 2	Mrs. Berger, 2 up	Mrs. Berger, 8 and 7	Miss Tobin, 22 holes	Miss Betty Tobin, Framingham, Mass. Miss Connie June Day, Chattanooga, Tenn.
					Mrs. Berger, 8 and 7	**Mrs. Roslyn Swift Berger, Westwood, N.Y.** Mrs. George E. Wilcox, Jr., Miami Shores, Fla.
				Miss McLachlan, 2 up	Miss McLachlan, 1 up	Miss Margaret Jones, Fort Mitchell, Ky. Miss Marcia McLachlan, Ridgewood, Conn.
					Miss Mines, 2 and 1	Mrs. J. Albert Hayes, Philadelphia, Pa. Miss Betty Mines, Metacomet, R.I.
			Miss Gunderson, 5 and 4	Mrs. O'Connor, 19 holes	Mrs. Dempsey, 1 up	Mrs. Thorne Dempsey, Southward Ho, N.Y. Mrs. Raymond S. Patton, Hartford, Conn.
					Mrs. O'Connor, 6 and 4	Mrs. Irving G. Kaufmann, Century, N.Y. Mrs. Robert J. O'Connor, Charles River, Mass.
				Miss Gunderson, 7 and 6	Miss Gunderson 6 and 5	Miss JoAnne Gunderson, Rhode Island, R.I. **Mrs. William C. Warren, C.C. of Rochester, N.Y.**
					Miss Johnson, 5 and 4	**Miss Patricia E. Johnson, C.C. of Spartanburg, S.C.** **Miss Nancy Gunther, C.C. of Troy, N.Y.**
	Mrs. Welts, 4 and 3	**Miss Ferraris, 4 and 3**	Miss Palmer, 1 up	Miss Palmer, 1 up	Miss Burns, 1 up	Miss Claudette A. LaBonte, Plymouth, Mass. Miss Marjorie Burns, Starmount Forest, N.C.
					Miss Palmer, 3 and 2	Miss Patricia B. O'Sullivan, Race Brook, Conn. Miss Sandra Palmer, Glen Garden, Texas
				Miss Daniel, 4 and 2	Miss Daniel, 8 and 6	Miss Mary Lou Daniel, Iroquois, Ky. Mrs. Arthur Flash, Quaker Ridge, N.Y.
					Miss Sawyer, 8 and 7	Miss Mary Alice Sawyer, Forest Park, Md. Mrs. Jean Zaiko, Indian Hill, Conn.
			Miss Ferraris, 1 up	Miss Phillips, 2 and 1	Miss Phillips, 4 and 3	Miss Doris Phillips, Norwood Hills, Mo. Miss Susan J. Pompeo, Wachusett, Mass.
					Miss Powell, 21 holes	Miss Renee Powell, Clearview Par & Birdie, Ohio Mrs. Edward S. McAuliffe, Wellesley, Mass.
				Miss Ferraris, 2 and 1	Miss Baker, 2 and 1	Miss Ann Baker, Green Meadow, Tenn. Miss Kay Hebert, Lawrence Park, Pa.
					Miss Ferraris, 1 up	Miss Jean Bryant, Paris Mountain, S.C. Miss Janis Ferraris, Presidio, Calif.
		Mrs. Welts, 6 and 5	Mrs. Probasco, 19 holes	Mrs. Probasco, 4 and 3	Mrs. MacGee, 2 and 1	Miss Irene Tworig, Taconic, Mass. Mrs. Edwin E. MacGee, Blue Hills, Mo.
					Mrs. Probasco, 4 and 3	Mrs. Robert Ihlanfeldt, Inglewood, Wash. Mrs. Scott L. Probasco, Jr., Chattanooga, Tenn.
				Miss Hilton, 4 and 3	Miss Hilton, 19 holes	Mrs. Joseph Malia, Spring Valley, Mass. Miss Sue Hilton, London, Ont., Canada
					Miss Ward, 19 holes	Mrs. Alfred Slaner, Quaker Ridge, N.Y. **Miss Lois Ward, Park C.C. of Buffalo, N.Y.**
			Mrs. Welts, 2 and 1	Miss Roth, 1 up	Miss Rose, 5 and 3	**Miss Carol A. Beinbrink, St. George's, N.Y.** Miss Marcella Rose, Meadow Lake Acres, Mo.
					Miss Roth, 1 up	Miss Nancy Roth, Elks, Elkhart, Ind. Mrs. William Tracy, Essex Fells, N.J.
				Mrs. Welts, 5 and 4	Miss Hull, 3 and 1	**Mrs. J. Peter Bush, C.C. of Rochester, N.Y.** Miss Julie Hull, Anderson, Ind.
					Mrs. Welts, 6 and 5	**Mrs. John Pennington, C.C. of Buffalo, N.Y.** **Mrs. Anne Quast Welts, Seattle, Wash.**

1964
SIXTY-FOURTH WOMEN'S AMATEUR CHAMPIONSHIP

Held at the Prairie Dunes Country Club, Hutchinson, Kans., August 17-22.
Yardage—6,001. Par 73. 93 Entries, 81 Starters.

Qualifying Score	1st Round (18 Holes)	2nd Round (18 Holes)	3rd Round (18 Holes)	Semi-Finals (18 Holes)	Final (36 Holes)	
151	*Miss JoAnne Gunderson, Sand Point, Wash.	Miss Gunderson, 6 and 5				
157	Miss Jean Ashley, Broadmoor, Colo.		Miss Gunderson, 1 up			
155	Miss Barbara Fay White, East Ridge, La.	Miss White, 1 up				
158	Miss Nancy Roth, Elks, Ind.			Miss Gunderson, 3 and 2		
152	Mrs. Philip J. Cudone, Montclair, N.J.	Miss Ehret, 3 and 2				
157	Miss Gloria J. Ehret, Ridgewood, Conn.		Mrs. Ihlanfeldt, 4 and 2			
156	Mrs. Donna Gilliam, California, Calif.	Mrs. Ihlanfeldt, 1 up				
159	Mrs. Robert Ihlanfeldt, Inglewood, Wash.				Miss Gunderson, 5 and 4	
151	*Miss Polly Riley, River Crest, Texas	Mrs. Dye, 3 and 2				
157	Mrs. Paul Dye, Jr., C.C. of Indianapolis, Ind.		Mrs. Dye, 3 and 2			
155	Miss Phyllis Preuss, Coral Ridge, Fla.	Miss Preuss, 4 and 3				
159	Miss Sally Carroll, Wheeling, W. Va.			Mrs. Dye, 3 and 2		
154	Miss Susan Gregory, Pine Bluff, Ark.	Miss Gregory, 4 and 3				
157	Miss Janis Ferraris, Presidio, Calif.		Miss Gregory, 5 and 3			
156	Miss Nicki Nordstrom, Minnesota Valley, Minn.	Mrs. Bailey, 3 and 2				
160	†Mrs. James W. Bailey, Wellshire, Colo.					Miss Barbara McIntire, 3 and 2
151	*Miss Barbara McIntire, Broadmoor, Colo.	Miss McIntire, 3 and 2				
157	Miss Sharon K. Miller, Battle Creek, Mich.		Miss McIntire, 3 and 1			
155	Miss Peggy S. Conley, Spokane, Wash.	Mrs. Probasco, default				
158	Mrs. Scott L. Probasco, Jr., Chattanooga, Tenn.			Miss McIntire, 2 and 1		
154	Miss Patti Shook, Saginaw, Mich.	Miss Varangot, 2 up				
157	Miss Brigitte Varangot, St. Germain, France		Mrs. Weiss, 1 up			
156	Miss Susan Lance, Woodland Hills, Calif.	Mrs. Weiss, 1 up				
159	Mrs. Jason Weiss, Broadmoor, Ind.				Miss McIntire, 3 and 1	
152	Miss Carol Sorenson, Janesville, Wis.	Miss Sorenson, 5 and 3				
157	Miss Judy Bell, Broadmoor, Colo.		Miss Rose, 3 and 2			
155	Miss Marcella Rose, Meadow Lake Acres, Mo.	Miss Rose, 2 and 1				
159	Miss Carla Jean Glasgow, California, Calif.			Miss King, 2 and 1		
154	Miss Marsha Houghton, Del Rio, Calif.	Miss Masters, 6 and 5				
158	Miss Margie Masters, Ottawa, Ont., Canada		Miss King, 4 and 3			
157	Miss Robbye King, Commissioned Officers', Va.	Miss King, 4 and 3				
160	†Miss Ann Baker, Green Meadow, Tenn.					

*Medalists.
†Qualified in playoff. Losers in playoff: Mrs. Karen Shull MacGee, Indian Hills, Kans.; Miss Patsy E. Johnson, Spartanburg, S.C.

1965
SIXTY-FIFTH WOMEN'S AMATEUR CHAMPIONSHIP

Held at the Lakewood Country Club, Denver, Colo., August 23-28.
Yardage–6,175. Par 73. 88 Entries, 84 Starters.

Qualifying Score	1st Round (18 Holes)	2nd Round (18 Holes)	3rd Round (18 Holes)	Semi-Finals (18 Holes)	Final (36 Holes)	
148	*Miss Lida Fee Matthews, Elks, Ohio	Miss Matthews, 1 up				
156	Mrs. Frank Stranahan, Inverness, Ohio		Miss Matthews, 4 and 3			
153	Mrs. Karen S. MacGee, Indian Hills, Kansas	Miss Preuss, 5 and 4				
158	Miss Phyllis Preuss, Coral Ridge, Florida			Miss Riley, 1 up		
152	Miss Polly Riley, River Crest, Texas	Miss Riley, 3 and 1				
157	Miss Patti Shook, Saginaw, Mich.		Miss Riley, 2 and 1		Mrs. Welts, 1 up, 19 hls.	
154	Miss Sue Lance, Woodland Hills, Calif.	Miss Lance, 2 and 1				
159	Mrs. Helen Sigel Wilson, Philadelphia, Pa.					
149	Mrs. Anne Quast Welts, Broadmoor, Wash.	Mrs. Welts, 3 and 2				
156	Miss Brigitte Varangot, Saint-Germain, France		Mrs. Welts, 8 and 7			
153	Mrs. Gordon Street, Jr., Chattanooga, Tenn.	Miss Milliken, 4 and 3				
159	Miss Lesley Milliken, Bartow, Florida			Mrs. Welts, 3 and 1		
152	Miss Harriet Glanville, Meadowlark, Calif.	Miss Glanville, 7 and 6				
158	Miss Doris Phillips, Norwood Hills, Mo.		Miss Bell, 1 up			
155	Miss Judy Bell, Broadmoor, Colo.	Miss Bell, 4 and 2				Miss Jean Ashley, 5 and 4
159	Miss Susan Moore, Arizona, Ariz.					
149	Miss Barbara Fay White, Broadmoor, La.	Miss White, 5 and 4				
156	Mrs. Harton S. Semple, Allegheny, Pa.		Miss White, 2 and 1			
153	Miss Carol Sorenson, Janesville, Wis.	Miss Sorenson, 4 and 3				
159	Mrs. Paul Dye, Jr., Crooked Stick, Ind.			Miss Day, 2 and 1		
152	Miss Shelley Hamlin, University-Sequoia, Calif.	Miss Day, 3 and 2				
157	Miss Connie June Day, Chattanooga, Tenn.		Miss Day, 3 and 2			
155	Mrs. Scott L. Probasco, Jr., Chattanooga, Tenn.	Mrs. Probasco, 1 up, 21 hls.				
159	Miss Rhonda Glenn, Lake Worth, Fla.					
152	Miss Roberta A. Albers, Temple Terrace, Fla.	Miss Albers, 5 and 4				
157	Miss Marsha Houghton, Del Rio, Calif.		Miss Ashley, 2 and 1		Miss Ashley, 2 up	
154	Miss Jean Ashley, Broadmoor, Colo.	Miss Ashley, 5 and 4				
159	Miss Patricia Johnson, Spartanburg, S.C.			Miss Ashley, 2 and 1		
153	Miss Marcella Rose, Meadow Lake Acres, Mo.	Miss Rose, 3 and 1				
158	Miss Pamela Sue Fox, Corvallis, Oregon		Miss McIntire, 3 and 2			
155	Miss Barbara McIntire, Broadmoor, Colo.	Miss McIntire, 3 and 1				
160	†Miss Becky Glasscock, Riverdale, Ark.					

*Medalist.
†Qualified in playoff. Losers in playoff: Miss Jane Bastanchury, Miss Gail Sykes, Miss Carol J. Sorensen.

1966
SIXTY-SIXTH WOMEN'S AMATEUR CHAMPIONSHIP

Held at the Sewickley Heights Golf Club, Sewickley, Pa., August 8-13.
Yardage—6,120. Par 73. 115 Entries, 111 Starters.

Qualifying Score	1st Round (18 Holes)	2nd Round (18 Holes)	3rd Round (18 Holes)	Semi-Finals (18 Holes)	Final (36 Holes)	
143	*Miss Shelley Hamlin, University-Sequoia, Calif.	Miss Hamlin, 5 and 4				
160	Mrs. I.C. Robertson, Dunaverty, Scotland		Mrs. Welts, 19 holes			
158	**Mrs. Anne Quast Welts, Seattle, Washington**	Mrs. Welts, 1 up				
162	Mrs. Michael J. Skala, Speedway "500", Ind.			Mrs. Boddie, 1 up		
153	**Mrs. Barbara White Boddie, Broadmoor, La.**	Mrs. Boddie, 4 and 3				
161	Miss Peggy Conley, Spokane, Wash.		Mrs. Boddie, 4 and 2			
158	Miss Barbara McIntire, Broadmoor, Colo.	Miss McIntire, 3 and 2			Mrs. Carner, 1 up	
162	Mrs. Paul Dye, Jr., Crooked Stick, Ind.					
152	**Mrs. JoAnne Gunderson Carner, Sand Point, Wash.**	Mrs. Carner, 7 and 6				
161	Miss Ita Burke, Elm Park, Ireland		Mrs. Carner, 3 and 2			
158	**Miss Mary Lou Dill, Humble, Texas**	Miss Kazmierski, 5 and 4				
162	Miss Joyce Kazmierski, Grosse Ile, Mich.			Mrs. Carner, 4 and 3		
157	Miss Pamela Sue Fox, Corvallis, Ore.	Mrs. Weiss, 2 up				Mrs. JoAnne Gunderson Carner, 41 Holes
161	Mrs. Jason Weiss, Hillcrest, Ind.		Miss Martin, 4 and 3			
159	Miss Maggie Martin, Belmont Hills, Ohio	Miss Martin, 3 and 1				
163	†Miss Jean Bryant, Paris Mountain, S.C.					
149	Miss Judy Bell, Broadmoor, Colo.	Miss Bell, 19 holes				
160	**Mrs. Dorothy Germain Porter, Riverton, N.J.**		Miss Albers, 3 and 2			
158	Miss Roberta A. Albers, Temple Terrace, Fla.	Miss Albers, 2 and 1				
162	Miss Lesley A. Milliken, Cleveland Hgts., Fla.			Miss Albers, 3 and 2		
155	Mrs. William Flenniken, Janesville, Wis.	Miss Rose, 1 up				
161	Miss Marcella Rose, Meadow Lakes Acres, Mo.		Miss Rose, 20 holes			
159	**Mrs. Paul F. Klinefelter, Philadelphia Cricket, Pa.**	Mrs. Klinefelter, 4 and 3			Mrs. Streit, 1 up	
163	Miss Robbye King, Army Navy, Va.					
153	**Mrs. Marlene Stewart Streit, Lookout Pt., Ont., Canada**	Mrs. Streit, 2 and 1				
161	Miss Kathleen Ahern, Dallas Athletic, Texas		Mrs. Streit, 6 and 5			
158	Miss Brigitte Varangot, St.-Germain, France	Miss Downey, 5 and 4				
162	Miss Mary Ann Downey, Baltimore, Md.			Mrs. Streit, 3 and 1		
157	Mrs. Gordon P. Street, Jr., Chattanooga, Tenn.	Mrs. Street, 4 and 3				
162	**Mrs. Scott L. Probasco, Jr., Chattanooga, Tenn.**		Miss Matthews, 19 holes			
160	Miss Elizabeth Chadwick, Bramall, England	Miss Matthews, 4 and 3				
163	†Miss Lida Fee Matthews, Elks, Ohio					

*Medalist.
†Qualified in playoff. Losers in playoff: Miss Phyllis Preuss, Miss Maureen Crum.

1967
SIXTY-SEVENTH WOMEN'S AMATEUR CHAMPIONSHIP

Held at the Annandale Golf Club, Pasadena, Calif., August 14-19.
Yardage—6,062. Par 72. 119 Entries, 119 Starters.

Qualifying Score	1st Round (18 Holes)	2nd Round (18 Holes)	3rd Round (18 Holes)	Semi-Finals (18 Holes)	Final (36 Holes)	
148	*Miss Phyllis Preuss, Coral Ridge, Fla.	Miss Preuss, 5 and 4				
157	Miss Candace Michaeloff, Columbia, Minn.		Miss Preuss, 6 and 4			
154	**Mrs. Anne Quast Welts, Seattle, Wash.**	Miss Rose, 1 up				
160	Miss Marcella Rose, Meadow Lake Acres, Mo.			Miss Preuss, 1 up		
152	Miss Jane Bastanchury, California, Calif.	Miss Bastanchury, 2 and 1				
159	**Mrs. Barbara White Boddie, Broadmoor, La.**		Miss Bastanchury, 3 and 1		Miss Ashley, 5 and 4	
156	Miss Judy Bell, Broadmoor, Colo.	Miss Bell, 6 and 5				
160	Mrs. Jay Hopkins, Los Altos, Calif.					
150	Miss Martha Wilkinson, Yorba Linda, Calif.	Miss Wilkinson, 2 and 1				
159	Mrs. Michael Skala, Roseburg, Ore.		Miss Wilkinson, 3 and 2			
156	**Mrs. Claudine Cros Rubin, Lamorlaye, France**	Mrs. Rubin, 2 up				
160	Mrs. Mildred Stanley, Griffith Park, Calif.			Miss Ashley, 3 and 2		
154	Miss Connie Day, Chattanooga, Tenn.	Miss Ashley, 2 and 1				Miss Mary Lou Dill, 5 and 4
160	Miss Jean Ashley, Chanute, Kans.		Miss Ashley, 2 and 1			
157	Miss Shelley Hamlin, University Sequoia, Calif.	Miss Harmon, 1 up				
161	†Miss Margaret Harmon, River Bend, Tenn.					
150	Miss Roberta Albers, Temple Terrace, Fla.	Miss Albers, 3 and 1				
158	Miss Dorothy Germain, Blytheville, Ark.		Miss Cox, 3 and 2			
155	**Mrs. JoAnne Gunderson Carner, Kirkbrae, R.I.**	Miss Cox, 2 and 1				
160	Miss Marianne Cox, Santa Ana, Calif.			Miss Dill, 2 up		
153	Mrs. Nancy Syms, Elks, Ind.	Miss Dill, 19 holes				
160	Miss Mary Lou Dill, Humble, Texas		Miss Dill, 4 and 2			
156	Miss Joyce Kazmierski, Grosse Ile, Mich.	Miss Lauer, default			Miss Dill, 19 holes	
160	Miss Bonnie Lauer, Edgewood, Mich.					
151	Miss Barbara McIntire, Broadmoor, Colo.	Miss McIntire, 5 and 4				
159	Miss Marie Strand, Green Hills, Calif.		Mrs. Probasco, 1 up			
156	Miss Jan Webber, Fig Garden, Calif.	Mrs. Probasco, 5 and 4				
160	**Mrs. Scott L. Probasco, Jr., Chattanooga, Tenn.**			Miss Conley, 1 up		
154	Miss Peggy Conley, Spokane, Wash.	Miss Conley, 1 up				
160	Miss Maureen Crum, Lone Palm, Fla.		Miss Conley, 1 up			
157	Mrs. Paul Dye, Jr., Crooked Stick, Ind.	Miss Huntsberger, 19 holes				
160	†Miss Jane Huntsberger, Las Posas, Calif.					

*Medalist.
†Qualified in playoff. Losers in playoff: Miss Susan Lance, Miss Polly Riley.

1968
SIXTY-EIGHTH WOMEN'S AMATEUR CHAMPIONSHIP

Held at the Birmingham Country Club, Birmingham, Mich., August 12-17.
Yardage—6,170. Par 72. 110 Entries, 107 Starters.

Qualifying Score	1st Round (18 Holes)	2nd Round (18 Holes)	3rd Round (18 Holes)	Semi-Finals (18 Holes)	Final (36 Holes)	
143	*Miss Catherine Lacoste, Chantaco, France	Miss Lacoste, 21 Holes				
155	Miss Margaret Jones, Fort Mitchell, Ky.		Miss Lacoste, 3 and 2			
154	Mrs. Patti Boice, Saginaw, Mich.	Miss Webber, 4 and 3				
155	Miss Jan Webber, Fig Garden, Calif.					
151	Miss Jane Bastanchury, California, Calif.	Miss Bastanchury, 2 and 1		Miss Lacoste, **1 up**		
155	Miss Joyce Ann Jackson, Altadena Valley, Ala.					
154	Miss Kaye Beard, Campbellsville, Ky.	Miss Beard, 3 and 2	Miss Bastanchury, 3 and 2			
156	Miss Jane Blalock, Portsmouth, N.H.				Mrs. Carner, 4 and 3	
148	Miss Betty Burfeindt, Wahconah, Mass.	Miss Hill, 3 and 1				
155	Miss Cynthia Hill, South Haven, Mich.					
154	Miss Penelope Ann Burrows, Formley Ladies, England	Mrs. Dye, 8 and 7	Mrs. Dye, 3 and 1			
156	Mrs. Paul Dye, Jr., Crooked Stick, Ind.					
153	**Mrs. JoAnne Gunderson Carner, Kirkbrae, R.I.**	Mrs. Carner, **1 up**		Mrs. Carner, 4 and 3		
155	Miss Barbara-Jo Gabrielsen, Athens, Ga.					
154	Miss Shelley Hamlin, University-Sequoia-Sunnyside, Calif.	Miss Semple, **1 up**	Mrs. Carner, 3 and 1			
157	†Miss Carol Semple, Allegheny, Pa.					**Mrs. JoAnne Gunderson Carner, 5 and 4**
147	**Miss Joyce Kazmierski, Grosse Ile, Mich.**	Miss Kasmierski, 3 and 1				
155	Miss Mary Margaret Dwyer, Seneca Lake, N.Y.					
154	Miss Barbara McIntire, Broadmoor, Colo.	Mrs. Oldham, 19 Holes	Miss Kazmierski, 19 Holes			
156	Mrs. Karen Oldham, Congress Lake, Ohio					
153	Miss Vivien I. Saunders, Banstead Downs, England	Miss Saunders, 2 and 1		Miss Kazmierski, 4 and 3		
155	Miss Carol Jean Sorensen, Meadowbrook Town, Wis.					
154	**Miss Mary Lou Dill, Baywood, Texas**	Miss Dill, 4 and 3	Miss Saunders, 19 Holes			
156	Miss Peggy Conley, Spokane, Wash.				Mrs. Welts, 2 and 1	
149	**Mrs. Anne Quast Welts, Bellingham, Wash.**	Mrs. Welts, 3 and 1				
155	Miss Connie Day, Chattanooga, Tenn.					
154	Mrs. John Rathmell, Houston, Texas	Mrs. Rathmell, 5 and 3	Mrs. Welts, 5 and 4			
156	Miss Mariann Eichelberger, Huntingdon Valley, Pa.					
153	Miss Phyllis Preuss, Coral Ridge, Fla.	Miss Preuss, 6 and 4		Mrs. Welts, 5 and 4		
155	Miss Pam Higgins, Groveport, Ohio					
154	**Miss Margaret Harmon, River Bend, Tenn.**	Mrs. Skala, 3 and 2	Miss Preuss, **1 up**			
157	†Mrs. Michael J. Skala, El Dorado Royal, Calif.					

*Medalist.
†Qualified in playoff. Losers in playoff: Miss Patricia O'Brien, Miss Marcella Rose, Miss Martha Wilkinson.

1969
SIXTY-NINTH WOMEN'S AMATEUR CHAMPIONSHIP

Held at the Las Colinas Country Club, Irving, Texas, August 11-16.
Yardage—6,022. Par 72. 103 Entries, 101 Starters.

Qualifying Score	1st Round (18 Holes)	2nd Round (18 Holes)	3rd Round (18 Holes)	Semi-Finals (18 Holes)	Final (36 Holes)	
147	***Mrs. Barbara White Boddie, Broadmoor, La.**	Mrs. Boddie, 5 and 4				
157	Miss Nancy E. Holmes, Town & Country, Tenn.		Mrs. Boddie, 3 and 1			
152	Miss Cynthia Hill, Pasadena, Fla.	Miss Matthews, 4 and 3				
159	Miss Lida Fee Matthews, Elks, Ohio			Miss Hamlin, 1 up		
149	Miss Shelley Hamlin, University-Sequoia-Sunnyside, Calif.	Miss Hamlin, 3 and 2				
158	Miss Roberta A. Albers, Temple Terrace, Fla.		Miss Hamlin, 2 and 1			
155	Miss Jane Bastanchury, California, Calif.	Mrs. Berkmeyer, 1 up				
160	†Mrs. Richard Berkmeyer, Norwood Hills, Mo.				Miss Hamlin, 1 up	
148	Miss Martha Wilkinson, California, Calif.	Miss Dailey, 5 and 4				
158	Miss Dianne Dailey, Frankfort, Ky.		Miss Dailey, 3 and 2			
154	Mrs. William Flenniken, Rolling Hills, Colo.	Mrs. Flenniken, 1 up				
159	Miss Phyllis Preuss, Coral Ridge, Fla.			Miss Hager, 2 and 1		
150	Miss Nancy Hager, Northwood, Texas	Miss Hager, 2 and 1				
159	Miss D.M. Everard, Hallamshire, England		Miss Hager, 6 and 5			
157	Miss Bonnie Lauer, Edgewood, Mich.	Miss Lauer, 2 and 1				
160	†Miss Jan Schulte, Lebanon, Pa.					Miss Catherine Lacoste, 3 and 2
148	**Mrs. Anne Quast Welts, Everett, Wash.**	Mrs. Welts, 2 and 1				
157	Mrs. John Rathmell, Houston, Texas		Mrs. Welts, 1 up			
153	Mrs. Paul Dye, Jr., Crooked Stick, Ind.	Mrs. Dye, 2 and 1				
159	**Miss Mary Lou Dill, Baywood, Texas**			Mrs. Welts, 1 up		
150	**Mrs. JoAnne Gunderson Carner, Kirkbrae, Mass.**	Mrs. Furrow, 2 and 1				
158	Mrs. Sam Furrow, Fox Den, Tenn.		Miss Germain, 19 Holes			
156	Miss Dorothy Germain, Blytheville, Ark.	Miss Germain, 1 up				
160	†Mrs. W.B. Mahan, Corpus Christi, Texas				Miss Lacoste, 2 and 1	
148	**Miss Catherine Lacoste, Chantaco, France**	Miss Lacoste, 2 and 1				
158	Miss Polly Riley, River Crest, Texas		Miss Lacoste, 1 up			
155	Miss Constance E. Hirschman, York, Pa.	Miss Hirschman, 20 Holes				
159	Mrs. Michael J. Skala, El Dorado Royal, Calif.			Miss Lacoste, 4 and 2		
151	Miss Barbara McIntire, Broadmoor, Colo.	Miss Fassinger, 3 and 2				
159	Miss Mary Jane Fassinger, New Castle, Pa.		Miss Fassinger, 3 and 1			
157	Miss Jan Webber, Fig Garden, Calif.	Mrs. Porter, 3 and 2				
160	**†Mrs. Dorothy Germain Porter, Riverton, N.J.**					

*Medalist.
†Qualified in playoff. Losers in playoff: Miss Noni Schneider, Miss Mary E. Shea.

1970
SEVENTIETH WOMEN'S AMATEUR CHAMPIONSHIP

Held at the Wee Burn Country Club, Darien, Conn., August 17-22.
Yardage—6,240. Par 74. 139 Entries, 134 Starters.

Qualifying Score	1st Round (18 Holes)	2nd Round (18 Holes)	3rd Round (18 Holes)	Semi-Finals (18 Holes)	Final (18 Holes)
150*	Miss Martha Wilkinson, Whittier, Calif.	Miss Wilkinson, 1 up			
159	Miss Nancy Hager, Dallas, Texas		Miss Wilkinson, 2 and 1		
156	Mrs. Marlene Stewart Streit, Fonthill, Ont., Canada	Mrs. Boice, 5 and 4			
161	Mrs. Patti Boice, Saginaw, Mich.			Miss Wilkinson, 2 and 1	
154	Miss Connie Day, Chattanooga, Tenn.	Mrs. Porter, 4 and 3			
160	Mrs. Dorothy Germain Porter, Riverton, N.J.		Mrs. Porter, 7 and 6		
157	Miss Julia Greenhalgh, Blackburn, Lancashire, Eng.	Miss Wilkins, 20 hls.			
161	Miss Mardell J. Wilkins, Long Beach, Calif.				Miss Wilkinson, 5 and 4
153	Miss Sally Little, Cape Town, South Africa	Miss Dailey, 3 and 2			
160	Miss Dianne Dailey, Frankfort, Ky.		Miss Baugh, 3 and 2		
156	Miss Laura Baugh, Cocoa, Fla.	Miss Baugh, 20 hls.			
161	Mrs. I.C. Robertson, Glasgow, Scotland			Miss Hamlin, 4 and 3	
155	Miss Barbara McIntire, Colorado Springs, Colo.	Miss Schneider, 19 hls.			
160	Miss Noni Schneider, Fair Oaks, Calif.		Miss Hamlin, 1 up		
157	Miss Dinah Oxley, W. Byfleet, Surrey, England	Miss Hamlin, 4 and 3			
162+	Miss Shelley Hamlin, Fresno, Calif.				Miss Martha Wilkinson, 3 and 2
153	Mrs. Richard J. Canney, Centreville, Va.	Mrs. Canney, 2 and 1			
159	Miss Carol Semple, Sewickley, Pa.		Mrs. Canney, 6 and 5		
156	Mrs. Albert B. Bower, Pelham, N.Y.	Mrs. Bower, 20 hls.			
161	Miss Joan B. Lawrence, Dunfermline, Scotland			Miss Hill, 19 hls.	
154	Miss Mary A. McKenna, Dublin, Ireland	Miss McKenna, 20 hls.			
160	Miss Polly Riley, Fort Worth, Texas		Miss Hill, 6 and 5		
157	Mrs. Marcia Dolan, Danbury, Conn.	Miss Hill, 19 hls.			
162+	Miss Cynthia Hill, St. Petersburg, Fla.				Miss Hill, 2 up
154	Mrs. Paul Dye, Jr., Carmel, Ind.	Mrs. Dye, 3 and 2			
160	Miss Mary Everard, Sheffield, Yorkshire, England		Miss Bastanchury, 5 and 3		
156	Miss Jane Bastanchury, Whittier, Calif.	Miss Bastanchury, 5 and 3			
161	Miss Kathryn Phillips, Shipley, Yorkshire, England			Miss Bastanchury, 5 and 3	
155	Miss Phyllis Preuss, Fort Lauderdale, Fla.	Miss Lauer, 2 and 1			
160	Miss Bonnie Lauer, Union Lake, Mich.		Miss Lauer, 2 and 1		
158	Miss Peggy Harmon, Shelbyville, Tenn.	Miss Harmon, 1 up			
162+	Miss Doris Kostrinsky, Armonk, N.Y.				

*Medalist.

1971
SEVENTY-FIRST WOMEN'S AMATEUR CHAMPIONSHIP

Held at the Atlanta Country Club, Atlanta, Georgia, August 16–21.
Yardage—6,117. Par—72.
102 Entries, 102 Starters.

Qualifying Score	1st Round (18 Holes)	2nd Round (18 Holes)	3rd Round (18 Holes)	Semi-Finals (18 Holes)	Finals (18 Holes)	
150	*Miss Connie Day, Chattanooga, Tenn.	Fassinger,				
160	Miss Mary Jane Fassinger, New Castle, Pa.	5 and 4	Fassinger,			
156	Miss Hollis Stacy, Savannah, Ga.	Webber,	2 and 1			
161	Miss Janet Webber, Fresno, Calif.	5 and 4		Wilkinson,		
154	Miss Phyllis Preuss, Ft. Lauderdale, Fla.	Johnson,		3 and 1		
161	Miss Judith Jane Johnson, Pittsburgh, Pa.	1 up	Wilkinson,			
158	Miss Martha Wilkinson, Whittier, Calif.	Wilkinson,	2 and 1			
163	Mrs. Margaret Simpson Brass, Orlando, Fla.	7 and 6			Barry, 2 and 1	
151	Mrs. Barbara White Boddie, Shreveport, La.	Boddie,				
160	Miss Lida Fee Matthews, Portsmouth, Ohio	4 and 3	Harmon,			
157	Miss Nancy Hager, Dallas, Texas	Harmon,	22 holes			
162	Miss Margaret E. Harmon, Palm Bay, Fla.	2 and 1		Barry,		
155	Miss Beth Barry, Dauphin Island, Ala.	Barry,		3 and 1		
161	Miss Polly Riley, Fort Worth, Texas	3 and 1	Barry,			
159	Miss Dorothy Germain, Blytheville, Ark.	Germain,	3 and 1			
164	Miss Judi Jehle, Montgomery, Ala.	20 holes				Miss Laura Baugh, 1 up
150	*Miss Jane Bastanchury, Whittier, Calif.	McIntire,				
160	Miss Barbara McIntire, Colorado Springs, Colo.	2 up	McIntire,			
156	Mrs. Nancy Roth Syms, Colorado Springs, Colo.	Syms,	2 and 1			
162	Miss Bonnie Lauer, Union Lake, Mich.	7 and 5		Baugh,		
155	Miss Cynthia Hill, St. Petersburg, Fla.	Porter,		1 up		
161	Mrs. Dorothy Germain Porter, Riverton, N.J.	3 and 1	Baugh,			
159	Miss Laura Baugh, Long Beach, Calif.	Baugh,	3 and 1			
164	Miss Carol Semple, Sewickley, Pa.	2 up			Baugh, 21 holes	
154	Miss Katherine Hite, St. Simons Island, Ga.	Budke,				
160	Miss Mary Budke, Dundee, Ore.	1 up	Shea,			
157	Miss Mary Elizabeth Shea, Los Angeles, Calif.	Shea,	2 and 1			
163	Mrs. B.L. Stanley, Long Beach, Calif.	19 holes		Smith,		
156	Miss Lancy Smith, Williamsville, N.Y.	Smith,		5 and 3		
161	Miss Helen J. Kirkland, Cadiz, Ohio	19 holes	Smith,			
160	Miss Martha Jones, Decatur, Ala.	Finucan,	2 and 1			
164	Miss Jessie E. Finucan, Summerville, S.C.	5 and 4				

*Co-medalists.

1972
SEVENTY-SECOND WOMEN'S AMATEUR CHAMPIONSHIP

Held at the St. Louis Country Club, St. Louis, Missouri, August 14-19.
Yardage—6,138. Par—72. 134 Entries, 115 Starters.

Qualifying Score	1st Round (18 Holes)	2nd Round (18 Holes)	3rd Round (18 Holes)	Semi-Finals (18 Holes)	Final (36 Holes)
148	*Mrs. William Flenniken, Jr., Golden, Colo.	Mrs. Flenniken, 4 and 2			
159	Miss Maria E. Astrologes, Valparaiso, Ind.		Miss Daniel, 1 up, 20 holes		
156	Miss Elizabeth Daniel, Toronto, Ontario, Canada	Miss Daniel, 1 up, 19 holes			
160	Miss Hollis Stacy, Savannah, Ga.			Miss Hill, 2 and 1	
154	Miss Donna Horton, Kinston, N.C.	Miss Horton, 7 and 6			
160	Mrs. Karen Schull MacGee, Overland Park, Kans.		Miss Hill, 4 and 3		
158	Miss Debra Jan Rhodes, North Wilkesboro, N.C.	Miss Hill, 3 and 2			Miss Hill, 3 and 1
162	Miss Cynthia Hill, St. Petersburg, Fla.				
153	Mrs. Martha Wilkinson Kirouac, Whittier, Calif.	Mrs. Kirouac, 1 up, 20 holes			
159	Mrs. Patti S. Boice, Saginaw, Mich.		Mrs. Kirouac, 3 and 1		
157	Miss Kaye Beard, Campbellsville, Ky.	Mrs. Dye, 1 up			
161	Mrs. Paul Dye, Jr., Carmel, Ind.			Mrs. Kirouac, 8 and 7	
154	Miss Carol Semple, Sewickley, Pa.	Miss Massey, 4 and 3			
160	Miss Deborah Massey, Bethlehem, Pa.		Miss Massey, 7 and 5		
158	Miss Janey Fassinger, New Castle, Pa.	Miss Fassinger, 2 and 1			
162	Miss Paula M. Eger, Kirkwood, Mo.				Miss Mary Anne Budke, 5 and 4
151	Miss Laura Baugh, Long Beach, Calif.	Miss Baugh, 4 and 3			
159	Mrs. Jane Bastanchury Booth, Whittier, Calif.		Miss Baugh, 4 and 2		
156	Miss Janet Anne Coles, Aptos, Calif.	Miss Holmes, 1 up			
161	Miss Nancy E. Holmes, Nashville, Tenn.			Mrs. Boddie, 6 and 5	
154	Mrs. Barbara White Boddie, Shreveport, La.	Mrs. Boddie, 6 and 5			
160	Mrs. Nancy Roth Syms, Colorado Springs, Colo.		Mrs. Boddie, 6 and 5		
158	Miss Marilyn Palmer, British Columbia, Canada	Miss Palmer, 2 up			
162	Mrs. Richard Deal, Auburn, Wash.				Miss Budke, 1 up, 19 holes
154	Miss Janet Webber, Fresno, Calif.	Miss Porter, 1 up			
159	Miss Mary Bea Porter, San Luis Rey Downs, Calif.		Miss Porter, 1 up		
157	Miss Nancy Hager, Dallas, Texas	Miss Albers, 6 and 4			
161	Miss Roberta A. Albers, Medina, Ohio			Miss Budke, 1 up, 19 holes	
155	Miss Lancy Smith, Snyder, N.Y.	Miss Budke, 1 up			
160	Miss Mary Anne Budke, Dayton, Ore.		Miss Budke, 3 and 2		
158	Miss Lida Fee Matthews, Portsmouth, Ohio	Miss Preuss, 1 up			
162	Miss Phyllis Preuss, Ft. Lauderdale, Fla.				

*Medalist

1973
SEVENTY-THIRD WOMEN'S AMATEUR CHAMPIONSHIP

Held at the Montclair Golf Club, Montclair, New Jersey, August 13-18.
Yardage 6,032. Par-72. 154 Entries, 142 Starters, 64 Qualifiers.

Qualifying Score	1st Round (18 Holes)	2nd Round (18 Holes)	3rd Round (18 Holes)	4th Round (18 Holes)	Semi-Finals (18 Holes)	Final (36 Holes)	
74	*Mrs. Kaye Potter, Louisville, Ky.	Mrs. Oliver,					
80	Mrs. John C. Oliver III, Pittsburgh, Pa.	6 and 4	Mrs. Sander,				
78	Mrs. Anne Quast Sander, Seattle, Wash.	Mrs. Sander,	7 and 6				
81	Mrs. Mary M. Cushing, Ann Arbor, Mich.	5 and 4		Mrs. Sander,			
77	Miss Margaret E. Harmon, Palm Bay, Fla.	Miss Harmon,		5 and 4			
81	Miss Cynthia K. Booker, Wickliffe, Ohio	19 holes	Miss Harmon,				
79	Mrs. Albert B. Bower, Pelham, N. Y.	Mrs. Fitzgerald,	4 and 2				
82	Mrs. Edward Fitzgerald, Hershey, Pa.	2 and 1			Mrs. Sander,		
75	Miss Marianne Stangeland, Long Beach, Calif.	Miss Eger,			5 and 3		
80	Miss Paula M. Eger, Kirkwood, Mo.	1 up	Miss Conley,				
78	Miss Peggy Conley, Spokane, Wash.	Miss Conley,	2 and 1				
82	Miss Judy Whalon, Rumford, R. I.	6 and 5		Miss Conley,			
77	Mrs. David Johnstone, West Orange, N. J.	Mrs. Johnstone,		6 and 4			
81	Mrs. Scott L. Probasco, Jr., Chattanooga, Tenn.	4 and 3	Miss Webber,				
79	Miss Janet Webber, Fresno, Calif.	Miss Webber,	2 and 1				
82	Miss Katherine Linney, Plainfield, N. J.	2 up					
75	Miss Nancy Hager, Dallas, Texas	Miss Hager,				Mrs. Sander, 4 and 3	
80	Mrs. Gwen Straub, Wilton, Conn.	20 holes	Miss Preuss,				
78	Miss Phyllis Preuss, Ft. Lauderdale, Fla.	Miss Preuss,	5 and 4				
81	Miss Nancy Porter, Ardmore, Pa.	5 and 4		Miss Barry,			
77	Miss Beth Barry, Dauphin Island, Ala.	Miss Barry,		2 and 1			
81	Mrs. Mildred M. Stanley, Long Beach, Calif.	6 and 4	Miss Barry,				
79	Miss Suzanne Jackson, La Grange, Ga.	Miss Smith,	20 holes				
82	Miss Lancy Smith, Williamsville, N. Y.	2 up			Miss Horton,		
76	Miss Cynthia Hill, Colorado Springs, Colo.	Mrs. Booth,			4 and 3		
80	Mrs. Jane Bastanchury Booth, Whittier, Calif.	5 and 3	Mrs. Booth,				
79	Mrs. Philip J. Cudone, Myrtle Beach, S. C.	Mrs. Kinnicutt	7 and 6				
82	Mrs. Lida Matthews Kinnicutt, West Hartford, Conn.	2 and 1		Miss Horton,			
78	Miss Donna Horton, Jacksonville, Fla.	Miss Horton,		2 and 1			
81	Miss Susan M. O'Connor, Rancho La Costa, Calif.	1 up	Miss Horton,				
80	Mrs. Frances English, Indianapolis, Ind.	Miss Shea,	3 and 2				
82	Miss Mary E. Shea, Los Angeles, Calif.	1 up					Miss Carol Semple, 1 up
75	Miss Julie Greene, Barrington, R. I.	Miss Greene,					
80	Miss Barbara McIntire, Colorado Springs, Colo.	1 up	Miss Greene,				
78	Miss Deborah Ann Massey, Bethlehem, Pa.	Miss Massey,	2 and 1				
81	Miss Janice Johnson, Owensboro, Ky.	7 and 6		Miss Semple,			
77	Miss Carol Semple, Sewickley, Pa.	Miss Semple,		4 and 3			
81	Miss Denise L. Bebernes, Santa Maria, Calif.	2 up	Miss Semple,				
79	Miss Marilyn Palmer, Vancouver, B. C., Canada	Miss O'Brien,	1 up				
82	Miss Pat O'Brien, Pittsfield, Mass.	2 and 1			Miss Semple,		
76	Miss Liana Zambresky, Pebble Beach, Calif.	Miss Zambresky,			2 and 1		
80	Mrs. Jean Ashley Crawford, Rye, N. Y.	3 and 2	Miss Alcott,				
79	Miss Amy Alcott, Pacific Palisades, Calif.	Miss Alcott,	7 and 5				
82	Miss Martha Jones, Decatur, Ala.	19 holes		Miss Budke,			
78	Mrs. Robert A. Young, Weston, Conn.	Miss Budke,		20 holes			
81	Miss Mary Budke, Dundee, Ore.	6 and 5	Miss Budke,				
80	Miss Patricia Bradley, Andover, Mass.	Miss Laughlin,	2 and 1				
82	Miss Ann R. Laughlin, Riverton, N. J.	3 and 2					
75	Miss Nancy Lopez, Roswell, N. M.	Miss Lauer,				Miss Semple, 1 up	
80	Miss Bonnie Lauer, Union Lake, Mich.	3 and 2	Miss Lauer,				
78	Miss Deborah A. Simourian, Auburndale, Mass.	Miss Simourian,	5 and 3				
82	Miss Dale Lundquist, Savannah, Ga.	2 up		Miss Lauer,			
77	Miss Noreen Friel, Andover, Mass.	Miss Friel,		2 and 1			
81	Miss Carolyn Hill, Placentia, Calif.	1 up	Miss Miller,				
79	Miss Linda Parker, Gadsden, Ala.	Miss Miller,	4 and 3				
82	Miss Alice Miller, Marysville, Calif.	2 up			Miss Lauer,		
77	Mrs. A. Sherburne Hart, Springfield, N. J.	Mrs. Hart,			2 up		
80	Miss Sue Vail, Moundsville, W. Va.	1 up	Mrs. Hart,				
79	Mrs. Mark A. Porter, Riverton, N. J.	Mrs. Porter,	19 holes				
82	Mrs. Marcia Dolan, Danbury, Conn.	2 and 1		Mrs. Hart,			
78	Miss Dale Shaw, Victoria, B. C., Canada	Miss Shaw,		3 and 2			
81	Miss Karen Dremonas, Hammond, Ind.	9 and 7	Miss Morse,				
80	Miss Catherine C. Morse, Pittsford, N. Y.	Miss Morse,	1 up				
82	Mrs. Robert Wilkinson Kirouac, Barrington, R. I.	5 and 3					

*Medalist

1974

SEVENTY-FOURTH WOMEN'S AMATEUR CHAMPIONSHIP

Held at the Broadmoor Golf Club, Seattle, Washington, August 12-17
Yardage—5,942. Par 72. 121 Entries, 114 Starters, 64 Qualifiers.

Qualifying Score		1st Round (18 Holes)	2nd Round (18 Holes)	3rd Round (18 Holes)	4th Round (18 Holes)	Semi-Finals (18 Holes)	Final (36 Holes)
70	*Miss Deborah Massey, Bethlehem, Pa.	Miss Massey, 5 and 3					
80	Miss Martha Jane Southern, National City, Ca.		Miss Massey, 3 and 2				
77	Miss Shelley Gates, Mill Valley, Calif.	Miss Alcott, 6 and 5					
81	Miss Amy Alcott, Los Angeles, Calif.			Miss Massey, 3 and 2			
75	Miss Deborah Meisterlin, Buena Park, Calif.	Mrs. Guthrie, 19 holes					
80	Mrs. Wayne E. Guthrie, Spokane, Wash.		Mrs. Guthrie, 4 and 3				
78	Miss Mary McKenna, Dublin, Ireland	Miss Horton, 19 holes					
82	Miss Donna Horton, Jacksonville, Fla.				Miss Massey, 1 up		
75	Miss Lancy Smith, Snyder, N. Y.	Mrs. Shorb, 3 and 2					
80	Mrs. Basil A. Shorb, III, York, Pa.		Miss Floyd, 5 and 3				
78	Miss Marlene E. Floyd, Palm Springs, Calif.	Miss Floyd, 19 holes					
82	Miss Pamela J. Palmieri, Santa Rosa, Calif.			Miss O'Brien, 2 and 1			
76	Mrs. Nancy Roth Syms, Colorado Springs, Colo.	Mrs. Syms, 2 and 1					
81	Mrs. John I. Maurer, Turlock, Calif.		Miss O'Brien, 3 and 2				
79	Miss Sandra Burns, Pittsburgh, Pa.	Miss O'Brien, 2 up					
82	Miss Pat O'Brien, Pittsfield, Mass.					Miss Hill, 4 and 2	
73	Miss Cynthia Hill, Colorado Springs, Colo.	Miss Hill, 4 and 3					
80	Miss Carol Gillen, Van Nuys, Calif.		Miss Hill, 2 and 1				
78	Miss Debby Stewart, Long Beach, Calif.	Miss Stewart, 3 and 2					
81	Miss Mary Elizabeth Shea, Los Angeles, Calif.			Miss Hill, 4 and 3			
76	Mrs. Nancy Fitzgerald, Hershey, Pa.	Miss Hager, 2 and 1					
80	Miss Nancy Hager, Dallas, Texas		Miss Hager, 5 and 3				
79	Miss Harriet Glanville, Long Beach, Calif.	Miss Glanville, 19 holes					
82	Miss Dian L. Murphy, Medford, Ore.				Miss Hill, 5 and 3		
75	Miss Phyllis Preuss, Colorado Springs, Colo.	Miss Preuss, 1 up					
80	Miss Barbara McIntire, Colorado Springs, Colo.		Mrs. Emory, 3 and 2				
78	Mrs. Pam F. Emory, Philadelphia, Pa.	Mrs. Emory, 2 and 1					
82	Miss Rise Jeananne Alexander, Gresham, Ore.			Mrs. Stanley, 1 up			
77	Mrs. B. L. Stanley, Los Angeles, Calif.	Mrs. Stanley, 3 and 2					
81	Miss Kay Kennedy, Dayton, Ohio		Mrs. Stanley, 2 up				
80	Mrs. Paul Dye, Jr., Delray Beach, Fla.	Miss Hand, 1 up					
82	Miss Elaine Hand, Douglas, Ga.						Miss Cynthia Hill, 5 and 4
73	Mrs. Anne Quast Sander, Seattle, Wash.	Mrs. Sander, 5 and 4					
80	Miss Carolyn Hill, Placentia, Calif.		Mrs. Sander, 4 and 3				
77	Miss Carol LeFeuvre, Channel Islands, England	Miss Morse, 2 and 1					
81	Miss Catherine Morse, Pittsford, N. Y.			Miss Conley, 20 holes			
75	Miss Peggy Conley, Spokane, Wash.	Miss Conley, 4 and 2					
80	Miss Cathy Reynolds, Springfield, Mo.		Miss Conley, 2 up				
78	Miss Mary Budke, Dayton, Ore.	Miss Martin, 6 and 4					
82	Miss Margaret Martin, St. Clairsville, Ohio				Miss Conley, 2 and 1		
75	Miss Nancy Lopez, Roswell, N. M.	Miss Barrow, 1 up					
80	Miss Barbara Ann Barrow, Chula Vista, Calif.		Miss Barry, 1 up				
78	Miss Beth Barry, Mobile, Ala.	Miss Barry, 6 and 4					
82	Miss Heather D. Clifford, Hampshire, England			Miss Barry, 2 and 1			
76	Miss Bonnie Lauer, Orchard Lake, Mich.	Miss Lauer, 2 and 1					
81	Mrs. J. Douglas Streit, Stouffville, Ont.		Miss Lauer, 4 and 3				
79	Miss Brenda Moyers, Tulsa, Okla.	Miss Vetrano, 3 and 2					
82	Miss Barbara Vetrano, San Francisco, Calif.					Miss Semple, 3 and 1	
74	Miss Nancy Aaronson, El Paso, Texas	Miss Booker, 2 up					
80	Miss Cynthia Kathryn Booker, Clarkston, Mich.		Miss Booker, 3 and 2				
78	Mrs. Jay Hopkins, Pebble Beach, Calif.	Mrs. Hopkins, 4 and 3					
82	Miss Liz Culver, Seattle, Wash.			Miss Goldsmith, 2 and 1			
76	Miss Brenda Anne Goldsmith, San Antonio, Texas	Miss Goldsmith, 1 up					
81	Miss Marianne Stangeland, Long Beach, Calif.		Miss Goldsmith, 1 up				
79	Miss Beverley Davis, Jacksonville, Fla.	Miss Cornett, 2 up					
82	Miss Patricia Cornett, Salinas, Calif.				Miss Semple, 2 up		
75	Mrs. Jane B. Booth, Whittier, Calif.	Mrs. Booth, 1 up					
80	Miss Marga B. Stubblefield, Kailua, Hawaii		Mrs. Booth, 2 and 1				
78	Mrs. I. C. Robertson, Glasgow, Scotland	Mrs. Robertson, 3 and 2					
82	Miss Teresa Weinshilbaum, Ponca City, Okla.			Miss Semple, 1 up			
77	Miss Carol Semple, Sewickley, Pa.	Miss Semple, 6 and 4					
81	Miss Laura Goodwin, Tulsa, Okla.		Miss Semple, 1 up				
80	Miss Robin Walton, Clarkston, Wash.	Mrs. Oliver, 2 and 1					
82	Mrs. Judith J. Oliver, Pittsburgh, Pa.						

*Medalist

1975

SEVENTY-FIFTH WOMEN'S AMATEUR CHAMPIONSHIP

Held at Brae Burn Country Club, West Newton, Massachusetts, August 11-16
Yardage—6,134. Par 73. 154 Entries, 150 Starters, 64 Qualifiers

Qualifying Score	1st Round (18 Holes)	2nd Round (18 Holes)	3rd Round (18 Holes)	4th Round (18 Holes)	Semi-Finals (18 Holes)	Final (36 Holes)
*71	Mrs. Nancy Roth Syms, Colorado Springs, Colo.	Mrs. Syms,				
78	Mrs. Marcia Dolan, Danbury, Conn.	3 and 1	Miss Semple,			
76	Miss Connie Chillemi, Naples, Fla.	Miss Semple,	2 and 1			
80	Miss Carol Semple, Sewickley, Pa.	19 holes		Miss Daniel,		
75	Miss Nancy M. Lopez, Roswell, N.M.	Miss Lopez,		5 and 4		
79	Miss Alice Miller, Marysville, Calif.	4 and 2	Miss Daniel,			
78	Miss Beth Daniel, Charleston, S.C.	Miss Daniel,	2 up			
81	Miss Susie Conklin, Montreal, Que., Canada	6 and 4			Miss Daniel,	
74	Miss Sara Jane Stuhler, Fort Johnson, N.Y.	Miss Barrow,			19 holes	
79	Miss Barbara Ann Barrow, Chula Vista, Calif.	4 and 3	Miss Smith,			
77	Miss Lancy Smith, Snyder, N.Y.	Miss Smith,	1 up			
81	Miss Janice F. Palmer, Rydal, Pa.	4 and 2		Miss Greene,		
76	Miss Holly Hartley, Oceanside, Calif.	Miss Greene,		19 holes		
80	Miss Julie Greene, Barrington, R.I.	6 and 5	Miss Greene,			
78	Miss Julie Stanger, Phoenix, Ariz.	Miss Goldsmith,	2 up			Miss Daniel, 19 holes
81	Miss Brenda Anne Goldsmith, San Antonio, Tex.	20 holes				
74	Miss Mary Budke, Dayton, Ore.	Miss Budke,				
79	Miss Sally Tomlinson, Oakland, Calif.	2 up	Miss Conley,			
76	Miss Peggy Conley, Spokane, Wash.	Miss Conley,	1 up			
80	Mrs. Connie Shorb, York, Pa.	3 and 2		Miss Friel,		
75	Miss Patricia Cornett, Salinas, Calif.	Miss Cornett,		3 and 2		
80	Miss Carolyn Hill, Placentia, Calif.	5 and 4	Miss Friel,			
78	Miss Paula Wagasky, Odenton, Md.	Miss Friel,	2 and 1			
81	Miss Noreen Friel, Woburn, Mass.	4 and 3			Miss Friel,	
75	Mrs. Mark A. Porter, Cinnaminson, N.J.	Miss Laughlin,			3 and 1	
79	Miss Ann R. Laughlin, Riverton, N.J.	5 and 4	Miss Laughlin,			
78	Miss Dale Lundquist, Savannah, Ga.	Miss Lundquist,	20 holes,			
81	Miss Kathy Westlund, Greensburg, Pa.	7 and 5		Miss Laughlin,		
76	Miss Pam Palmieri, Santa Rosa, Calif.	Miss Davis,		2 and 1		
80	Miss Beverley Davis, Jacksonville, Fla.	2 up	Miss Howe,			
78	Miss Pat O'Brien, Pittsfield, Mass.	Miss Howe,	3 and 1			Miss Beth Daniel, 3 and 2
82	Miss Lauren Howe, Colorado Springs, Colo.	4 and 3				
72	Miss Donna Horton, Jacksonville, Fla.	Miss Horton,				
79	Miss Kyle O'Brien, Indianapolis, Ind.	5 and 4	Miss Horton,			
76	Miss Dale Shaw, Sidney, B.C., Canada	Mrs. Shapiro,	5 and 4			
80	Mrs. Carmen E. Shapiro, Santurce, P.R.	2 and 1		Miss Horton,		
75	Mrs. Martha Wilkinson Kirouac, Barrington, R.I.	Miss Shea,		3 and 2		
80	Miss Mary E. Shea, Los Angeles, Calif.	5 and 4	Miss Shea,			
78	Miss Mary-Beth King, Limekiln, Pa.	Miss King,	2 up			
81	Miss Debby Wynn Stewart, Long Beach, Calif.	6 and 5			Miss Horton,	
75	Miss Deborah Massey, Bethlehem, Pa.	Mrs. Streit,			3 and 2	
79	Mrs. J. Douglas Streit, Stouffville, Ont., Can.	2 and 1	Mrs. Streit,			
77	Miss Marlene E. Floyd, Palm Desert, Calif.	Miss Floyd,	1 up			
81	Miss Barbara McIntire, Colorado Springs, Colo.	1 up		Mrs. Oliver,		
76	Miss Martha P. Jones, Decatur, Ala.	Miss Jones,		1 up		
80	Miss Lyda Hill, Colorado Springs, Colo.	5 and 3	Mrs. Oliver,			
78	Mrs. Judith J. Oliver, Pittsburgh, Pa.	Mrs. Oliver,	3 and 1			Miss Horton, 2 and 1
82	Miss Phyllis Preuss, Colorado Springs, Colo.	3 and 2				
74	Miss Cynthia Hill, Colorado Springs, Colo.	Miss Hill, ·				
79	Mrs. Stephen P. Sander, Lundin Links, Fife, Scotland	4 and 2	Miss Palmer,			
77	Miss Marilyn Palmer, Kamloops, B.C., Canada	Miss Palmer,	5 and 3			
80	Mrs. Robert Meyers, Ormond Beach, Fla.	1 up		Miss Morse,		
76	Miss Shelley A. Gates, Mill Valley, Calif.	Mrs. Crawford,		2 up		
80	Mrs. Charles T. Crawford, Rye, N.Y.	3 and 2	Miss Morse,			
78	Miss Janet Webber, Atlanta, Ga.	Miss Morse,	6 and 5			
81	Miss Catherine Morse, Pittsford, N.Y.	4 and 3			Miss Boylan,	
75	Miss Beth Barry, Mobile, Ala.	Miss Barry,			2 and 1	
79	Miss Marianne A. Stangeland, Long Beach, Calif.	3 and 2	Miss Boylan,			
78	Mrs. Carol A. Bostock, Scottsdale, Ariz.	Miss Boylan,	2 and 1			
81	Miss Jeanne-Marie Boylan, Milton, Mass.	20 holes		Miss Boylan,		
76	Miss Myra Van Hoose, Lexington, Ky.	Miss Van Hoose,		4 and 3		
80	Mrs. Frances English, Indianapolis, Ind.	3 and 2	Miss Van Hoose,			
78	Miss Deborah A. Simourian, Lincoln, Mass.	Miss Lawrence,	2 and 1			
82	Miss Mary A. Lawrence, Canton, N.Y.	1 up				

*Medalist

1976

SEVENTY-SIXTH WOMEN'S AMATEUR CHAMPIONSHIP

Held at Del Paso Country Club, Sacramento, California, August 16-21
Yardage—6,175. Par 72. 157 Entries, 150 Starters, 64 Qualifiers

Qualifying Score	1st Round (18 Holes)	2nd Round (18 Holes)	3rd Round (18 Holes)	4th Round (18 Holes)	Semi-Finals (18 Holes)	Final (36 Holes)
*70	Miss Beth Daniel, Charleston, S.C.	Miss Shaw, 1 up	Miss Shaw, 3 and 1	Miss Shaw, 2 and 1	Miss Alexander, 22 holes	Miss Bretton, 7 and 6
78	Miss Dale Shaw, Sidney, B.C., Canada					
77	Miss April Bain, Williamsville, N.Y.	Mrs. Fitzgerald, 1 up				
80	Mrs. Nancy Fitzgerald, Indianapolis, Ind.					
76	Miss Mary Murphy, Naples, Fla.	Miss Murphy, 2 up	Mrs. English, 19 holes			
79	Miss Judy Bell, Colorado Springs, Colo.					
78	Miss Shelley Gates, San Rafael, Calif.	Mrs. English, 5 and 4				
80	Mrs. Frances English, Indianapolis, Ind.					
74	Miss Beverley Davis, Jacksonville, Fla.	Miss Stewart, 1 up	Miss Morse, 3 and 2	Miss Alexander, 2 up		
79	Miss Martha Stewart, Long Beach, Calif.					
77	Miss Catherine Morse, Rochester, N.Y.	Miss Morse, 4 and 2				
80	Miss Kathryn Young, Portland, Ore.					
76	Miss Rise Alexander, Gresham, Ore.	Miss Alexander, 19 holes	Miss Alexander, 1 up			
79	Mrs. Margaret Harmon Brady, Gautier, Miss.					
78	Miss Sue Peterson, Rockford, Ill.	Miss Morgan, 3 and 2				
81	Miss Mary Morgan, Houston, Texas					
73	Miss Nancy Lopez, Albuquerque, N.M.	Miss Lopez, 7 and 5	Miss Lopez, 2 up	Miss Lopez, 5 and 3	Miss Bretton, 1 up	
78	Mrs. J. Engesser, Long Beach, Calif.					
77	Mrs. Nancy Syms, Colorado Springs, Colo.	Miss Preuss, 19 holes				
80	Miss Phyliss Preuss, Colorado Springs, Colo.					
76	Mrs. John Maurer, Turlock, Calif.	Miss Waynick, 8 and 7	Miss Waynick, 19 holes,			
79	Miss Elizabeth Waynick, Roanoke, Va.					
78	Mrs. J. Callaghan, Los Angeles, Calif.	Miss Hill, 5 and 4				
81	Miss Cynthia Hill, Colorado Springs, Colo.					
75	Miss Carol Semple, Sewickley, Pa.	Miss Semple, 4 and 3	Miss Bretton, 19 holes	Miss Bretton, 5 and 4		
79	Miss Mary Racicot, Riverside, Calif.					
77	Miss Marianne Bretton, San Diego, Calif.	Miss Bretton, 1 up				
80	Miss Robin Walton, Lewiston, Idaho					
77	Miss Brenda Goldsmith, San Antonio, Texas	Mrs. Uihlein, 1 up	Miss Budke, 2 up			
79	Mrs. Noreen Friel Uihlein, Reading, Pa.					
78	Miss Mary Budke, Dayton, Ore.	Miss Budke, 5 and 4				
81	Miss Beth Barry, Dauphin Island, Ala.					
72	Miss Donna Horton, Jacksonville, Fla.	Miss Horton, 3 and 2	Miss Horton, 8 and 7	Miss Horton, 3 and 2	Miss Horton, 19 holes	Miss Horton, 1 up
78	Miss Chris Johnson, Arcata, Calif.					
77	Mrs. Janet Webber McCoy, Marietta, Ga.	Mrs. Harsh, 6 and 5				
80	Mrs. Diane Harsh, Long Beach, Calif.					
76	Miss Helen Kirkland, Colorado Springs, Colo.	Miss Kirkland, 5 and 4	Miss Kirkland, 2 and 1			
79	Miss Marylin Palmer, Vancouver, B.C.					
78	Miss Deborah Simourian, Auburndale, Ma.	Miss Skelly, 2 up				
80	Miss Deborah Skelly, San Antonio, Texas					
74	Miss Deborah Massey, Bethlehem, Pa.	Miss Massey, 6 and 4	Miss Massey, 2 and 1	Miss Massey, 1 up		
79	Mrs. Candace Meyers, Whittier, Calif.					
77	Miss Mary-Beth King, Bernville, Pa.	Miss King, 2 up				
80	Miss Harriet Glanville, Long Beach, Calif.					
77	Miss Debbie Raso, Cape Coral, Fla.	Miss Barrow, 6 and 5	Miss Barrow, 7 and 6			
79	Miss Barbara Barrow, El Cajon, Calif.					
78	Miss Dayna Benson, Whittier, Calif.	Miss Greene, 3 and 1				
81	Miss Julie Greene, Barrington, R.I.					
74	Miss Lauren Howe, Colorado Springs, Colo.	Miss Howe, 7 and 5	Miss Howe, 2 and 1	Miss Cornett, 23 holes	Miss Cornett, 2 up	
78	Miss Cathy Reynolds, Springfield, Mo.					
77	Mrs. Judith J. Oliver, Pittsburgh, Pa.	Mrs. Oliver, 3 and 2				
80	Miss Lyda Hill, Colorado Springs, Colo.					
76	Miss Patricia Cornett, Salinas, Calif.	Miss Cornett, 6 and 4	Miss Cornett, 1 up			
79	Mrs. Jerry Keil, Sylvania, Ohio					
78	Miss Sherri Turner, Greenville, S.C.	Miss Coles, 5 and 3				
81	Miss Janet Coles, Salinas, Calif.					
76	Miss Patty Sheehan, Reno, Nev.	Miss Sheehan, 3 and 2	Miss Sheehan, 7 and 6	Miss Sheehan, 4 and 2		
79	Miss Jeanne Boylan, Newton Centre, Mass.					
77	Miss Joan Bennett, Long Beach, Calif.	Mrs. Woodruff, 5 and 4				
80	Mrs. Sandy Woodruff, San Jose, Calif.					
77	Mrs. J. Douglas Streit, Ontario, Canada	Mrs. Streit, 3 and 2	Miss Dorado, 19 holes			
80	Mrs. Jane Bastanchury Booth, Whittier, Calif.					
78	Miss Mary Mulflur, Portland, Ore.	Miss Dorado, 4 and 2				
81	Miss Pilar Dorado, Hayward, Calif.					

Miss Donna Horton, 2 and 1

*Medalist

1977

SEVENTY-SEVENTH WOMEN'S AMATEUR CHAMPIONSHIP

Held at Cincinnati Country Club, Cincinnati, Ohio, August 8-13.
Yardage—5,978. Par 73. 162 Entries, 150 Starters, 64 Qualifiers.

Qualifying Score	1st Round (18 Holes)	2nd Round (18 Holes)	3rd Round (18 Holes)	4th Round (18 Holes)	Semi-Finals (18 Holes)	Final (36 Holes)	
*72	Miss Mary Lawrence, Canton, N.Y.	Miss Murphy,					
79	Miss Mary Elizabeth Murphy, Naples, Fla.	2 and 1	Miss Walton,				
77	Miss Robin Walton, Clarkston, Wash.	Miss Walton,	2 and 1				
81	Miss Deborah Ann Skelly, San Antonio, Texas	4 and 2		Miss Preuss,			
75	Miss Denise Hermida, Brandon, Fla.	Miss Preuss,		5 and 3			
80	Miss Phylis Preuss, Colorado Springs, Colo.	1 up, 20 holes	Miss Preuss,				
79	Miss Connie Day, Cleveland, Tenn.	Miss Reynolds,	3 and 2				
81	Miss Catherine Reynolds, Springfield, Mo.	4 and 3			Mrs. Sherk,		
74	Mrs. Cathy Sherk, Port Colborne, Ont. Canada	Mrs. Sherk,			4 and 2		
80	Mrs. Margaret Harmon Brady, Theodore, Ala.	7 and 5	Mrs. Sherk,				
78	Miss Debbie Raso, Cape Coral, Fla.	Miss Powell,	4 and 3				
81	Miss Cynthia F. Powell, Winchester, Ky.	4 and 3		Mrs. Sherk,			
76	Mrs. Judy Clark, Bridgeton, N.J.	Mrs. Clark,		2 and 1			
81	Mrs. Myra V. Norsworthy, Lexington, Ky.	2 and 1	Mrs. Clark,				
79	Mrs. Marcia Dolan, Danbury, Conn.	Mrs. Dolan,	1 up				
81	Miss Betty Glynn Baird, Louisville, Ky.	4 and 3				Mrs. Sherk,	
73	Miss Patty Sheehan, Reno, Nev.	Miss Sheehan,				9 and 8	
80	Miss Nancy Aaronson, El Paso, Texas	2 and 1	Miss Sheehan,				
78	Miss Laurie Ann Rinker, Stuart, Fla.	Miss Hafeman,	7 and 5				
81	Miss Mary Hafeman, West Bend, Wis.	1 up, 20 holes		Miss Ogrin,			
75	Miss Nancy Porter, Cinnaminson, N.J.	Miss Porter,		1 up, 19 holes			
80	Miss Cathy Hanlon, Palos Verdes, Calif.	6 and 5	Miss Ogrin,				
79	Miss Rise J. Alexander, Portland, Ore.	Miss Orgin,	1 up, 19 holes				
81	Miss Alicia A. Ogrin, Waukegan, Ill.	4 and 3					
74	Mrs. Noreen Friel Uihlein, Hershey, Pa.	Miss Dailey,			Miss Goldsmith,		
80	Miss Dianne Dailey, Winston-Salem, N.C.	2 up	Miss Dailey,		1 up		
79	Miss Terri Moody, Athens, Ga.	Miss Moody,	4 and 2				
81	Miss Charlene McLear, Barrington, Ill.	3 and 1		Miss Goldsmith,			
77	Mrs. Jerry N. Keil, Toledo, Ohio	Miss Garbacz,		1 up			
81	Miss Lori L. Garbacz, South Bend, Ind.	1 up	Miss Goldsmith,				
79	Miss Brenda Goldsmith, San Antonio, Texas	Miss Goldsmith,	3 and 2				
81	Miss Betsy L. Waynick, Greensboro, N.C.	5 and 4					Miss Beth Daniel, 3 and 1
73	Miss Beth Daniel, Charleston, S.C.	Miss Daniel,					
80	Miss Barbara Riedl, Sidney, Ohio	1 up	Miss Daniel,				
77	Miss Helen J. Kirkland, Colorado Springs, Colo.	Miss Kirkland,	7 and 6				
81	Miss Lyda Hill, Colorado Springs, Colo.	4 and 3		Miss Daniel,			
75	Miss Lancy Smith, Snyder, N.Y.	Miss Smith,		3 and 2			
80	Miss Nancy Hoins, Leavenworth, Kans.	2 up					
79	Miss Martha Jones, Houston, Texas	Miss Stanley,	Mrs. Stanley,				
81	Miss Mildred M. Stanley, Los Angeles, Calif.	1 up, 19 holes	1 up				
74	Miss Barbara Hoffmeister, Rifle, Colo.	Mrs. Potter,			Miss Daniels,		
80	Mrs. Kaye Potter, Louisville, Ky.	3 and 1			2 and 1		
78	Miss Elaine Hand, Douglas, Ga.	Miss Hand,	Miss Hand,				
81	Mrs. Nancy Roth Syms, Colorado Springs, Colo.	3 and 2	4 and 3				
77	Miss Lauren Howe, Colorado Springs, Colo.	Miss Greene,		Miss Greene,			
81	Miss Julie Greene, Barrington, R.I.	2 and 1		1 up			
79	Mrs. Judith J. Oliver, Sewickley, Pa.	Mrs. Kensler,	Miss Greene,				
81	Mrs. Tamara Bowman Kensler, Orlando, Fla.	6 and 4	5 and 4				
74	Miss Janet Anderson, Slippery Rock, Pa.	Miss Anderson,				Miss Daniel,	
80	Miss Sally Gunter Austin, Raeford, N.C.	3 and 2	Miss Anderson,			3 and 2	
78	Miss Kellii Doherty, Buena Park, Calif.	Miss Doherty,	2 and 1				
81	Miss Nancy Ann Bunton, Huntington, W.Va.	4 and 3		Miss Anderson,			
76	Mrs. William Flenniken, Hillrose, Colo.	Mrs. Flenniken,		3 and 2			
81	Miss Melissa McGeorge, Richardson, Texas	2 and 1	Mrs. Sander,				
79	Mrs. Stephen P. Sander, Berkshire, England	Mrs. Sander,	2 and 1				
81	Miss Lucille H. Ray, Ft. Mill, S.C.	3 and 2			Mrs. Hammer,		
75	Mrs. Nancy Hager Hammer, Dallas, Texas	Mrs. Hammer,			2 and 1		
80	Miss Jeanne-Marie Boylan, Milton, Mass.	4 and 3	Mrs. Hammer,				
79	Miss Beth Barry, Mobile, Ala.	Mrs. English,	2 and 1				
81	Mrs. Frances English, Indianapolis, Ind.	1 up, 20 holes		Mrs. Hammer,			
77	Miss Patricia Cornett, Salinas, Calif.	Mrs. Booth,		2 and 1			
81	Mrs. Jane B. Booth, Whittier, Calif.	3 and 2	Mrs. Hardy,				
79	Mrs. Susan Shinn Hardy, Tucson, Ariz.	Mrs. Hardy,	3 and 2				
81	Mrs. Kevin Kirby, Sioux Falls, S.D.	1 up, 19 holes					

*Medalist

1978

SEVENTY-EIGHTH WOMEN'S AMATEUR CHAMPIONSHIP

Held at Sunnybrook Golf Club, Plymouth Meeting, Pennsylvania, August 14-19.
Yardage—6,105. Par 72. 207 Entries, 150 Starters, 64 Qualifiers.

Qualifying Score	1st Round (18 Holes)	2nd Round (18 Holes)	3rd Round (18 Holes)	4th Round (18 Holes)	Semi-Finals (18 Holes)	Final (36 Holes)	
*72	Mrs. Ian Robertson, Glasgow, Scotland	Miss Hession,					
78	Miss Therese Hession, Indianapolis, Ind.	3 and 1	Mrs. Dolan,				
77	Mrs. Marcia Dolan, Danbury, Conn.	Mrs. Dolan,	1 up				
80	Miss Deborah Skelly, San Antonio, Texas	3 and 1		Miss Swanson,			
75	Miss Tamara Bowman, Orlando, Fla.	Miss Swanson,		4 and 3			
79	Miss Ann Swanson, Seattle, Wash.	4 and 2	Miss Swanson,				
77	Mrs. Leslie Shannon, Hialeah, Fla.	Miss O'Brien,	6 and 5				
80	Miss Kyle O'Brien, Indianapolis, Ind.	1 up, 19 holes			Miss Hafeman,		
74	Mrs. Carole Caldwell, London, England	Miss Hermida,			3 and 2		
79	Miss Denise Hermida, Brandon, Fla.	1 up, 27 holes	Miss Hartley,				
77	Miss Debbie Raso, Cape Coral, Fla.	Miss Hartley,	4 and 3				
80	Miss Holly Hartley, Oceanside, Calif.	1 up		Miss Hafeman,			
76	Miss Dianne Dailey, Winston-Salem, N.C.	Miss Hafeman,		4 and 3			
79	Miss Mary Hafeman, West Bend, Wis.	1 up	Miss Hafeman,				
78	Miss Patty Sheehan, Reno, Nev.	Miss Sheehan,	1 up				
81	Miss Vanessa Marvin, St. Andrews, Scotland	3 and 2				Mrs. Oliver,	
74	Miss Laurie Rinker, Stuart, Fla.	Miss Singleton,				1 up, 19 holes	
79	Miss Vicki Singleton, Oberlin, Ohio	1 up	Miss Singleton,				
77	Miss Phyllis Preuss, Colorado Springs, Colo.	Miss Preuss,	3 and 2				
80	Miss Sarah LeVeque, Springfield, Ill.	2 up		Miss Singleton,			
76	Miss Lancy Smith, Snyder, N.Y.	Miss Baxter,		3 and 2			
79	Miss Lisa Baxter, Los Gatos, Calif.	1 up	Miss Simpson,				
78	Miss Caroline McLean Gowan, Greenville, S.C.	Miss Simpson,	5 and 3				
81	Miss Juli Simpson, Santa Cruz, Calif.	5 and 4					
74	Miss Carol Semple, Sewickley, Pa.	Miss Semple,			Mrs. Oliver,		
79	Miss Nina Foust, Ramseur, N.C.	6 and 4			4 and 3		
77	Miss Elaine Hand, Douglas, Ga.	Miss Pearson,	Miss Pearson,				
80	Miss Leslie Pearson, Ft. Lauderdale, Fla.	2 up	3 and 2				
77	Miss Debbie Hall, Corpus Christi, Texas	Miss Hall,		Mrs. Oliver,			
79	Miss Cynthia Kessler, Orchard Park, N.Y.	5 and 3		4 and 3			
78	Mrs. Judith Oliver, Sewickley, Pa.	Mrs. Oliver,	Mrs. Oliver,				
81	Miss Nathalie Jeanson, Compiegne, France	2 and 1	2 and 1				Mrs. Cathy Sherk, 4 and 3
74	Miss Lyda Hill, Colorado Springs, Colo.	Miss Hill,					
78	Miss Lynn Stiffler, Waycross, Ga.	4 and 2	Mrs. Sherk,				
77	Mrs. Cathy Sherk, Colborne, Ont., Canada	Mrs. Sherk,	5 and 3				
80	Miss Pam Miller, Libertyville, Ill.	5 and 4					
76	Miss Sally Voss, Bethesda, Md.	Miss Voss,		Mrs. Sherk,			
79	Miss Sally Austin, Wesley Chapel, Fla.	3 and 1		3 and 2			
78	Miss Nancy Porter, Cinnaminson, N.J.	Miss Porter,	Miss Voss,				
80	Miss Cynthia Powell, Winchester, Ky.	1 up	1 up				
74	Miss Beth Barry, Mobile, Ala.	Mrs. Porter,			Mrs. Sherk,		
79	Mrs. Mark Porter, Cinnaminson, N.J.	4 and 3			7 and 6		
77	Miss Tegwen Perkins, Wales, G.B.	Miss Perkins,	Miss Perkins,				
80	Mrs. Paul Dye, Delray Beach, Fla.	4 and 3	2 up				
77	Miss Lori Garbacz, South Bend, Ind.	Miss Ogrin,		Miss Cornett,			
79	Miss Alicia Ogrin, Waukegan, Ill.	1 up		1 up			
78	Miss Helen Kirkland, Colorado Springs, Colo.	Miss Cornett,	Miss Cornett,				
81	Miss Pat Cornett, Salinas, Calif.	2 and 1	2 and 1			Mrs. Sherk,	
74	Miss Carolyn Hill, Placentia, Calif.	Miss Hill,				1 up	
79	Miss Christine Desch, Hampton Bays, N.Y.	1 up	Miss Hill,				
77	Miss Jan Rapp, Dallas, Texas	Miss Rapp,	3 and 2				
80	Miss Beverley Davis, Jacksonville, Fla.	3 and 1		Miss Cynthia Hill,			
76	Miss Cynthia Hill, Colorado Springs, Colo.	Miss Hill,		2 and 1			
79	Miss Julie Cole, Orlando, Fla.	7 and 5	Miss Hill,				
78	Miss Lisa Goedecke, Los Altos, Calif.	Miss Goedecke,	3 and 2				
81	Miss Ann Laughlin, Riverton, N.J.	2 up			Miss Hill,		
75	Miss Terri Moody, Athens, Ga.	Miss O'Brien,			1 up		
79	Miss Patricia O'Brien, Pittsfield, Mass.	1 up, 20 holes	Miss O'Brien,				
77	Miss Nancy Maunder, Crofton, Md.	Mrs. Fitzgerald,	1 up				
80	Mrs. Edward Fitzgerald, Indianapolis, Ind.	1 up, 19 holes		Miss Daniel,			
77	Miss Beth Daniel, Charleston, S.C.	Miss Daniel,		4 and 2			
80	Miss Liza Abood, Bethesda, Md.	6 and 5	Miss Daniel,				
78	Miss Christa Johnson, Arcata, Calif.	Miss Johnson,	6 and 4				
81	Miss Mary Budke, Dayton, Ore.	2 and 1					

*Medalist

1979

SEVENTY-NINTH WOMEN'S AMATEUR CHAMPIONSHIP

Held at Memphis Country Club, Memphis, Tennessee, August 13-18.
Yardage—6,077. Par 72. 273 Entries, 150 Starters, 64 Qualifiers.

Qualifying Score	1st Round (18 Holes)	2nd Round (18 Holes)	3rd Round (18 Holes)	4th Round (18 Holes)	Semi-Finals (18 Holes)	Final (36 Holes)
*71	Kathy Baker, Clover, S.C.	Baker, 3 and 1				
77	Cindy Pleger, Athens, Ga.		Baker, 2 up			
75	Cathy Cook, Columbus, Ohio	Kluver, 5 and 4				
78	Lisa Kluver, Alexandria, Minn.			Baker, 3 and 1		
75	Mary Beth Sullivan, Houston, Texas	Sullivan, 5 and 3				
77	Jane Sirmons, St. Petersburg, Fla.		Sullivan, 3 and 2			
76	Melissa Whitmire, Hendersonville, N.C.	Whitmire, 2 and 1				
79	Mary Lou Mulflur, Gresham, Ore.				Sheehan, 4 and 3	
73	Patty Sheehan, Reno, Nev.	Sheehan, 1 up, 20 holes				
77	Bie-Shyun Huang, Taipei, Taiwan		Sheehan, 5 and 4			
76	Brenda Goldsmith, San Antonio, Texas	Reichenbach, 4 and 3				
78	Laurie Reichenbach, Mayfield Heights, Ohio			Sheehan, 7 and 6		
75	Patti Rizzo, Hialeah, Fla.	Jones, 2 and 1				
78	Rose E. Jones, Albuquerque, N.M.		Ertl, 2 up			
76	Betsy Seitz, Edina, Minn.	Ertl, 2 up				
79	Sue Ertl, Ionia, Mich.					Sheehan, 4 and 3
73	Colleen Walker, Bradenton, Fla.	Walker, 1 up, 20 holes				
77	Jennifer Davis, Northridge, Calif.		Skinner, 1 up, 19 holes			
75	Nancy Rubin, New Kensington, Pa.	Skinner, 2 and 1				
78	Valerie Skinner, North Platte, Neb.			Singleton, 4 and 3		
75	Kristen Allen, East Derry, N.H.	Uihlein, 3 and 2				
78	Noreen Uihlein, New Bedford, Mass.		Singelton, 1 up			
76	Vicki Singleton, Oberlin, Ohio	Singleton, 3 and 1				
79	Marcia Dolan, Danbury, Conn.					
74	Terri Moody, Athens, Ga.	Moody, 3 and 2			Singleton, 2 and 1	
77	Pat Cornett, Salinas, Calif.					
76	Donna Kimes, West Chester, Pa.	Kimes, 3 and 2	Moody, 5 and 3			
79	Ann Swanson, Seattle, Wash.					
75	Mary Moore, Boca Raton, Fla.	Barberio, 3 and 1		Moody, 4 and 3		
78	Debbie Barberio, Oceanside, Calif.					
76	Therese Hession, Indianapolis, Ind.	Hession, 4 and 3	Barberio, 2 and 1			
79	Mary Hafeman, West Bend, Wis.					
72	Carol Semple, Sewickley, Pa.	Anderson, 1 up				
77	Marla Anderson, Jacksonville, Fla.		Kirsch, 5 and 4			
75	Juli Simpson, Santa Cruz, Calif.	Kirsch, 1 up, 19 holes				
78	Peggy Kirsch, Duluth, Minn.					
75	Nancy Fitzgerald, Indianapolis, Ind.	McDougall, 6 and 5		Kirsch, 3 and 2		
78	Mari McDougall, Midlothian, Ill.					
76	Beverley Davis, Raeford, N.C.	Davis, 6 and 5	Davis, 2 and 1			
79	Jane Geddes, Summerville, S.C.					
74	Lancy Smith, Snyder, N.Y.	Smith, 5 and 3			Kirsch, 3 and 1	
77	Dorothy Lasker, Hinsdale, Ill.					
76	Becky Pearson, Delray Beach, Fla.	Pearson, 4 and 3	Smith, 5 and 3			
78	Jill Nesbitt, Berwyn, Pa.					
75	Kelley Spooner, Delray Beach, Fla.	Spooner, 2 and 1		Smith, 2 and 1		
78	Susan Fromuth, Chesterfield, Mo.					
76	Jeannette Kerr, Honolulu, Hawaii	Kerr, 2 up	Kerr, 3 and 2			
79	Lida Kinnicutt, Bloomfield, Conn.					Hill, 5 and 3
73	Carolyn Hill, Placentia, Calif.	Hill, 5 and 4				
77	Beth Barry, Mobile, Ala.		Hill, 5 and 4			
76	Lynn Connelly, North Palm Beach, Fla.	Connelly, 1 up				
78	Martha Jones, Houston, Texas			Hill, 2 and 1		
75	Pamela Miller, Libertyville, Ill.	Miller, 3 and 1				
78	Toni Wiesner, Ft. Worth, Texas		Edge, 1 up			
76	Mitzi Edge, Augusta, Ga.	Edge, 4 and 2				
79	Carol Donald, Athens, Ga.				Hill, 6 and 5	
74	Leslie Shannon, Hialeah, Fla.	Lee, 1 up, 20 holes				
77	Tanna Lee, Ft. Smith, Ark.		Castillo, 4 and 3			
76	Laurie Rinker, Stuart, Fla.	Castillo, 4 and 3				
79	Lori Castillo, Honolulu, Hawaii			Castillo, 5 and 3		
75	Sheree Muirhead, South Africa	Muirhead, 7 and 6				
78	Lisa Baxter, Los Gatos, Calif.		Ranta, 6 and 4			
76	Ann Ranta, Lake Worth, Fla.	Ranta, 7 and 5				
79	Karen Plamondon, Ypsilanti, Mich.					

Carolyn Hill, 7 and 6

*Medalist

1980
EIGHTIETH WOMEN'S AMATEUR CHAMPIONSHIP

Held at Prairie Dunes Country Club, Hutchinson, Kansas, August 11-16
Yardage—6,026. Par 72. 281 Entries, 150 Starters, 64 Qualifiers.

Qualifying Score	1st Round (18 Holes)	2nd Round (18 Holes)	3rd Round (18 Holes)	4th Round (18 Holes)	Semi-Finals (18 Holes)	Final (18 Holes)
*147	Dorothy Lasker, Hinsdale, Ill.	Lasker, 2 and 1				
157	Lynn Thompson, Loveland, Ohio		Preuss, 2 up			
154	Phyllis Preuss, Colorado Springs, Colo.	Preuss, 5 and 4				
158	Susan Hundley, Columbus, Ind.			Semple, 4 and 3		
152	Deborah Petrizzi, Austin, Texas	Semple, 3 and 2				
158	Carol Semple, Sewickley, Pa.		Semple, 3 and 1			
156	Helen Kirkland, Colorado Springs, Colo.	Kirkland, 4 and 2				
159	Brenda Pictor, Columbus, Miss.				Semple, 1 up, 20 holes	
150	Mrs. Judith Oliver, Sewickley, Pa.	Hanlon, 1 up				
157	Cathy Hanlon, Palos Vrd, Est., Calif.		Hanlon, 7 and 6			
156	Debbie Hall, San Jose, Calif.	Slivinsky, 2 and 1				
159	Paula Slivinsky, Brewster, N.Y.			Hanlon, 4 and 3		
153	Mrs. William Flenniken, Eugene, Ore.	Anderson, 4 and 3				
158	Marla Anderson, Jacksonville, Fla.		Gowan, 2 up			
156	Allison Finney, Winnetka, Ill.	Gowan, 1 up, 19 holes				
160	Caroline Gowan, Greenville, S.C.					Inkster 2 and 1
150	Mari McDougall, Midlothian, Ill.	Barberio, 1 up				
157	Debbie Barberio, Oceanside, Calif.		Davis, 1 up, 19 holes			
155	Brenda Goldsmith, San Antonio, Texas	Davis, 3 and 2				
158	Jennifer Davis, Northridge, Calif.			Davis, 2 and 1		
153	Lori Castillo, Honolulu, Hawaii	Castillo, 5 and 3				
158	Julie Kintz, Atlantis, Fla.		Clark, 1 up			
156	Lori Clark, Des Moines, Iowa	Clark, 7 and 6				
160	Barbara McIntire, Colorado Springs, Colo.				Inkster, 3 and 2	
150	Mrs. Juli Simpson Inkster, Santa Cruz, Calif.	Inkster, 7 and 6				
158	Maureen Madill, C. Derry, N. Ireland		Inkster, 4 and 2			
156	Lauri Merten, Phoenix, Ariz.	Barrett, 2 up				
159	Betsy Barrett, Syracuse, N.Y.			Inkster, 6 and 5		
154	Ann Zahn, Crystal Bay, Minn.	Zahn, 5 and 4				
158	Laurie Blair, Wichita, Kans.		Pleger 1 up			
156	Cindy Pleger, Athens, Ga.	Pleger, 3 and 2				
161	Jennifer Gaddy, Venice, Fla.					Juli Simpson Inkster 2 up
149	Mitzi Edge, Augusta, Ga.	Edge, 6 and 5				
157	Betsy Seitz, Edina, Minn.		Bowman, 3 and 2			
155	Tamara Bowman, Orlando, Fla.	Bowman, 2 and 1				
158	Mary Murphy, Naples, Fla.			McKenna, 6 and 4		
152	Mary McKenna, Co. Dublin, Ireland	McKenna, 3 and 2				
158	Denise Hermida, Brandon, Fla.		McKenna, 3 and 2			
156	Theresa Schreck, Spokane, Wash.	Cook, 2 and 1				
159	Cathy Cook, Upper Arlington, Ohio				McKenna, 5 and 4	
150	Valerie Skinner, No. Platte, Neb.	Skinner, 1 up				
157	Cynthia Schreyer, Peachtree City, Ga.		Bauer, 3 and 2			
156	Cynthia Kelliher, Riverton, Wyo.	Bauer, 2 and 1				
159	Kim Bauer, Conroe, Texas			Bauer, 1 up		
153	Rose Jones, Albuquerque, N.M.	Jones, 4 and 2				
158	Linda Bowman, San Rafael, Calif.		Jones, 4 and 2			
156	Terri Moody, Athens, Ga.	Moody, 1 up				
160	Melissa Whitmire, Hendersonville, N.C.					Rizzo, 3 and 2
150	Lancy Smith, Snyder, N.Y.	Smith, 5 and 4				
157	Denise Strebig, San Bernardino, Calif.		Miller 4 and 3			
155	Pamela Miller, Libertyville, Ill.	Miller, 4 and 2				
158	Mary Hafeman, West Bend, Wis.			Miller, 1 up		
153	Rae Rothfelder, No. Ft. Worth, Texas	Rothfelder, 2 and 1				
158	Penny Hammel, Decatur, Ill.		Scanlon, 2 and 1			
156	Sally Austin, Raeford, N.C.	Scanlon, 1 up, 19 holes				
160	Kerry Scanlon, Rye, N.Y.				Rizzo 5 and 4	
151	Patti Rizzo, Hialeah, Fla.	Rizzo, 5 and 4				
158	Debbie McClung, Farmers Branch, Texas		Rizzo, 1 up, 19 holes			
156	Mrs. Leslie Shannon, Miami, Fla.	Daniel, 3 and 2				
159	Carla Daniel, Wilmington, N.C.			Rizzo 4 and 3		
154	Karin Mundinger, Toronto, Ont., Canada	Mundinger, 5 and 3				
158	Laurie Rinker, Stuart, Fla.		Mundinger, 1 up			
157	Lida Kinnicutt, Bloomfield, Conn.	Kinnicutt, 5 and 3				
161	Kristen Allen, East Derry, N.H.					

*Medalist

WOMEN'S OPEN CHAMPIONSHIP

CHAMPIONSHIP TROPHY

Presented in July, 1953, by the
UNITED STATES GOLF ASSOCIATION

HISTORY

1960–Miss Betsy Rawls won her fourth Women's Open Championship with a score of 292 at the Worcester Country Club, Worcester, Mass. Worcester was the site of the men's Open Championship in 1925, and was the first club to entertain the two Open Championships. Miss Rawls' rounds of 76-73-68-75 gave her a one-stroke advantage over Miss Joyce Ziske, of Waterford, Wis., who posted 75-74-71-73–293. Miss Ziske moved into a two-stroke lead over Miss Rawls at the 63-hole mark, but Miss Rawls' 35 on the final nine gave her the edge. Miss Ziske needed a par 4 on the final hole to tie, but took a 5. Her second shot went over the green and she subsequently missed a four-foot putt. Miss Mickey Wright, the Champion in 1958 and 1959, set a fast pace as she led throughout the first three rounds with 71-71-75; she slipped to 82 in the final round for a 299 total. This put her in fifth place behind Mrs. Marlene Bauer Hagge and Miss Mary Lena Faulk, who were tied for third at 298. Miss Judy Torluemke, 15 years old, of St. Louis, Mo., was the youngest player in history to win low amateur honors, with 326. The prize money was $7,200. Miss Rawls won $1,800.

1961–Miss Mickey Wright, 26, won her third Championship in four years with rounds of 72-80-69-72–293. Miss Wright termed this her "most satisfying victory as it transpired on such a marvelous test of the game", the Lower Course of the Baltusrol Golf Club, Springfield, N.J. Miss Wright played the final 36 holes in 141, three below par, to pull away from the field. She was six strokes ahead of runnerup Miss Betsy Rawls. Miss Wright used her extreme distance to great advantage over the 6,372-yard par-72 course. She needed only 73 strokes on the four par-5 holes during the Championship–seven under par. Miss Wright played nearly flawless golf during the final round for her six-stroke margin. Miss Ruth Jessen finished third with 300 and Miss Louis Suggs continued her achievement of being the only player to finish in the top ten in every USGA Women's Open with her fourth-place 301 score. The Championship was marked by record galleries estimated at 2,754 the first day, 3,081 the second day, and 3,757 the final day. The total of 9,592 was 2,394 more than the previous record of 7,198 set in 1959. The prize money was $8,000, with Miss Wright's check totaling $1,800.

1962–Mrs. Murle MacKenzie Lindstrom, of Cape Girardeau, Mo., overcame a five-stroke deficit in the final round to win with a score of 301 at the Dunes Golf and Beach Club, Myrtle Beach, S.C. Mrs. Lindstrom scored 78-74-76-73–301. She was not regarded as a serious contender until well along in the fourth round, since she was six, four, and five strokes behind the leaders after each of the first three rounds. Mrs. Lindstrom, who had never before won a professional tournament, recorded no score higher than 5 on any hole with the exception of the 550-yard 13th–a feat unmatched by any other player in a field of 67. Her final round of 73 was played in a persistent rain. Miss Ruth Jessen, the first-round leader with 72, was tied for the lead after 36 holes, and was again the sole leader after 54 with 223. She relinquished the lead to Mrs. Lindstrom during the final nine holes and eventually tied for second place at 303 with Miss Jo Ann Prentice. Miss Jessen and Miss Shirley Englehorn were the only players who matched the par of 72. High winds which confronted the field for three rounds gave way to Saturday afternoon's rain. Miss Mickey Wright hoped to become the first four-time winner of the Women's Open since the USGA adopted sponsorship of the Championship in 1953. She seemed ideally placed to accomplish this when she was tied with Miss Jessen at 148 after 36 holes. In Saturday morning's third round, however, Miss Wright soared to 81 and then concluded with 77 for a 306 and a tie for fourth place with Miss Louise Suggs. Miss Suggs continued her record of being the only player to finish in the low 10 every year since 1953. The purse for the winner was $1,800. Miss JoAnne Gunderson, who later in the year won the Women's Amateur Championship for the third time, was the low amateur at 313.

1963–Miss Mary Mills' first victory as a professional occurred in the Open Championship, just as had Mrs. Murle Lindstrom's one year earlier. Miss Mills, 23, scored 289 with rounds of 71-70-75-73 at the Kenwood Country Club in Cincinnati. The winning total was three under par. Her 36-hole score of 141 set a record. Miss Mills had been the Mississippi Amateur Champion eight consecutive years, 1954-61. She was a graduate of Millsaps College, where she majored in philosophy. There was a tie for second at 292 between Miss Louise Suggs and Miss Sandra Haynie. Miss Suggs has been runnerup four times, and she was returning to competition after a year's absence. After a poor start, Mrs. Lindstrom finished with rounds of 74 and 71 for a 303 total and a tie for seventh place. The prize money reached a USGA high of $9,000. Part of the final round was televised locally for the first time. Miss Mickey Wright, three times the Champion, did not start.

1964–Miss Wright became the first four-time Women's Open Champion under USGA sponsorship by defeating Miss Ruth Jessen in an 18-hole playoff at the San Diego Country Club, Chula Vista, Calif. They had tied at 290, three under par. Miss Wright played flawless golf in the playoff, posting a 70 to Miss Jessen's 72. To make the playoff, Miss Wright had to get down in two from a bunker at the 72nd hole. Minutes earlier Miss Jessen had played a full wood shot that came to rest three feet from the hole on the final green to set up a birdie. First prize was $2,200; Miss Jessen earned $1,320. The low amateur was Miss Barbara McIntire, Colorado Springs, Colo., with 304. Miss McIntire later won the Women's Amateur title. Miss Judy Bell, an amateur from Colorado Springs, had a phenomenal third round of 31-36–67, matching the record score for 18 holes in the Women's Open set by Miss Marilynn Smith in 1952. Physical discomfort caused by a skin reaction to sunshine required Miss Bell to wear gloves on both hands during the round. Miss Wright led or tied for the lead after every round. She, Miss Shirley Englehorn, and Mrs. Marlene Bauer Hagge had 71 in the first round; Miss Wright was alone in the lead after 36 holes at 142; Miss Wright, Miss Englehorn and Miss Smith all had 217 after 54 holes. Miss Louise Suggs, who had finished in the top 10 in the 11 previous Women's Opens, did not enter.

1965–Miss Carol Mann, of Towson, Md., after an indifferent opening round of 78, scored 70, 70 and 72 to win with a total of 290. The runnerup was Mrs. Kathy Cornelius, the 1956 Champion, whose brilliant 69, three under par, in the final round gave her a total of 292. Miss Mann, 6 feet 3 inches tall, played the final three holes in two pars and a birdie. Her prize was $4,000, a record for this Championship, and part of $17,780 distributed among 28 professionals who completed 72 holes. Mrs. Cornelius was six under par for 20 par-3 holes played and had four straight 2s at the 163-yard eighth hole. Miss Marilynn Smith, who has competed in all 13 USGA Women's Open Championships, was third at 294. Mrs. Helen Sigel Wilson, of Gladwyne, Pa., shared fifth place with 296 and thus set a record low score for an amateur in the Open. Miss Catherine Lacoste, of France, was second low amateur at 304. Miss Mickey Wright, the defender and four times the Champion, was unable to start because of a hand injury. Miss Margie Masters, a professional from Australia, finished with a 67 to tie the record score for one round. The final round was telecast nationally for the first time and the last two rounds were played in two days instead of one as before.

1966–Miss Sandra Spuzich, 29, won the first Championship of her professional career by one stroke over Miss Carol Mann, of Towson, Md., the defending Champion. Miss Spuzich scored 75-74-76-72–297 at the Hazeltine National Golf Club, Chaska, Minn. In the final round Miss Spuzich birdied both the par-3 16th to go one stroke ahead of Miss Mann and the par-4 17th to go two strokes ahead. Miss Mann almost tied when her putt for a birdie on the 18th hit the hole. It stayed out, however, and her par 4 gained only one stroke on Miss Spuzich, who needed five strokes on the home hole. The opening-round 71 of Miss Mickey Wright was the lowest single round of the Championship and the only score under par 72. Seventeen-year-old Miss Shelley Hamlin, of Fresno, Calif., was low amateur with 311 and tied for ninth place.

1967–For the first time since the Championship began in 1946, an amateur won the Women's Open. Miss Catherine Lacoste, of Paris, France, scored 294 at the Cascades Course of the Virginia Hot Springs Golf and Tennis Club, Hot Springs, Va., and won by two strokes over Miss Susie Maxwell, Oklahoma City, Okla., and Miss Beth Stone of Muskogee, Okla. Miss Lacoste scored 71 in the first round and was one stroke behind Miss Sandra Haynie, of Fort Worth, Texas. A superb 70 in the second round gave her a five-stroke lead over Miss Maxwell and Miss Margie Masters, of Largo, Fla. She maintained her lead at five strokes even though scoring 74 in the third round. She then had a 54-hole score of 215, and Miss Masters had 220. Miss Lacoste increased her lead to seven strokes early in the final round, began to play poorly, and her lead subsequently dwindled to one stroke. She recovered near the end of the round, scored a birdie on the 17th hole and a par 3 on the 18th, and finished with her 294 total. Miss Louise Suggs, of Delray Beach, Fla., seriously challenged Miss Lacoste through the final round. She was nine strokes behind when the round began, but made up eight of those strokes through the 15th hole. However, her third stroke to the 16th hole embedded in the bank of a water hazard, and she scored two-over-par 7. Miss Stone was one stroke behind with three holes to play, and parred in. Miss Lacoste's mother once won the British Women's Amateur Championship; her father, Rene Lacoste, was a great tennis Champion.

1968–Mrs. Susie Maxwell Berning, of Crystal Bay, Nev., a bride of seven weeks, led every round in winning the Women's Open Championship at Moselem Springs Golf Club, Fleetwood, Pa. Mrs. Berning, co-runnerup in 1967, became one of six players who won after leading every round. Her score was five-over-par 289, and included a 69 in the first round. Her 71 in the final round equalled the lowest closing-round score by a Champion. Miss Mickey Wright, of Dallas, was runnerup, three strokes behind Mrs. Berning with 292. Miss Wright scored 68 in the final round, a record finish. Miss Carol Mann and Miss Marilynn Smith tied for third at 295. Miss Catherine Lacoste tied for 13th place with 302. Miss Phyllis Preuss, of Fort Lauderdale, Fla., was low amateur; she scored 300 and was tied for ninth place. Mrs. Berning had rounds of 69-73-76-71. She led Miss Wright by one stroke after 18 holes, and increased her lead to four strokes over Mrs. Murle Lindstrom after 36. She still led by two strokes over Miss Mann after 54 holes. Miss Wright, playing ahead of Mrs. Berning in the final round, came in with her 68, and only excellent play under pressure preserved Mrs. Berning's victory. Mrs. Berning received $5,000 prize money. A total of $24,950 was distributed among the professionals. Miss Wright's $2,200 increased her record prize winnings for the Open to $12,435. A record number of 104 players entered, of whom 65 were professionals, another record.

WOMEN'S OPEN CHAMPIONSHIP

1969–Miss Donna Caponi, of Burbank, Calif., scored 294 at the Scenic Hills Country Club, Pensacola, Fla., and won by one stroke over Miss Peggy Wilson, of Boca Raton, Fla. Miss Kathy Whitworth, of Richardson, Texas, was third with 296. It was the first tournament victory for Miss Caponi since she became a professional in 1965. Her scores were 74-76-75-69, and the last round was the lowest ever shot by a winner. Miss Caponi did not take the lead until the final round when she scored an eagle 3 on the par-5 15th hole. She made a par on the 16th, went one over on the 17th, and then was delayed in playing the 18th by an electrical storm. After hitting her drive, Miss Caponi had to wait in the clubhouse for 15 minutes while play was suspended. Far from being unnerved by the delay, Miss Caponi then made a birdie 4 on the hole to win the championship. A different player led each round. Miss Wilson went ahead at the beginning with a first-round 71. Miss JoAnn Prentice took the 36-hole lead with 144, then gave way to Miss Ruth Jessen, who led at 54 holes with 220. For the second consecutive year Miss Phyllis Preuss, of Pompano Beach, Fla., was low amateur. Miss Preuss' score was 304. Miss Caponi received a money prize of $5,000 and prize money totalling $31,040 was awarded, a record. Of the field of 99 who entered, 70 were professionals, a record.

1970–Miss Donna Caponi became the second player to defend the Championship successfully, matching not only the performance of Miss Mickey Wright in 1958-59, but also equalling Miss Wright's record score of 287 set in 1959. Miss Caponi played rounds of 69-70-71-77, at the Muskogee Country Club, Muskogee, Okla., and was well ahead after 54 holes with a record score of 210. However, she almost was tied on the final hole, a par 4. Miss Caponi and Miss Spuzich were playing together, and after 71 holes Miss Caponi was just one stroke ahead. There she hit her third shot over the green, played a very poor fourth and had to sink a four-foot putt for a 6. Miss Spuzich had just missed a six foot putt that would have given her a par 4 and a tie. Miss Caponi equalled two other records. Her 69 equalled the lowest first round score, and her 139 matched the previous low 36-hole total. Miss Cynthia Hill, of St. Petersburg, Fla., was low amateur with 294. The entry reached 131, a record.

1971–Mrs. JoAnne Gunderson Carner led every round and won by seven strokes over Miss Kathy Whitworth at the Kahkwa Club, Erie, Pa. Mrs. Carner had rounds of 70-73-72-73–288. She became the fourth player to have won both the Women's Amateur and the Women's Open. She became a professional in the fall of 1969 after winning her fifth Women's Amateur. Mrs. Carner was tied with Miss Donna Caponi after the first round when each scored 70. Miss Caponi had won the Championship the two previous years. Mrs. Carner went two strokes ahead of Miss Caponi after 36 holes with 143, and Miss Caponi was only one stroke behind after 12 holes of the third round. Then, however, Miss Caponi began making bogies and shot 77. Miss Mary Mills then took over second place at 220, five strokes behind Mrs. Carner, with 215. Miss Mills shot 82 in the final round and Miss Caponi had another 77. Miss Whitworth shot 72 to move into second place at 295. Miss Caponi tied for third place at 299, with Miss Jane Blalock, Miss Mickey Wright, and Miss Jane Bastanchury, an amateur. Three of the first 10 scorers were amateurs. In addition to Miss Bastanchury they were Miss Shelley Hamlin, and Miss Martha Wilkinson, the current Women's Amateur Champion. Prize money for the professionals totalled $34,450, and first prize was $5,000. Eighty-six professionals entered, a record. The most previously was 79 in 1970.

1972–Mrs. Susie Maxwell Berning, the 1968 Women's Open Champion, won at Winged Foot Golf Club, Mamaroneck, N. Y., with a score of 299. Mrs. Berning shot rounds of 79-73-76-71 to finish one stroke ahead of Miss Pam Barnett, Miss Kathy Ahern, and Mrs. Judy Rankin. She joined a select group of six who have won the Women's Open at least twice. Mrs. Berning's golf at Winged Foot was erratic. Her opening 79 was the poorest start by a Champion since 1953, when the USGA first conducted the Women's Open, while her closing 71 was one of just eight rounds that matched or bettered par in the 212 rounds played by the 53 contestants who finished 72 holes. The Championship was decided on the 200-yard, par-3 17th hole in the last round. Mrs. Berning came to the 17th trailing Miss Barnett by one stroke. She then made one of the most rewarding shots of her career: her tee shot carried the green and came down some 20 feet from the hole. Mrs. Berning sank her putt for a birdie 2, parred the 18th and was home with a 71 and a 299 total. Moments later, Miss Barnett came to the 17th. She was short of the green with a 4-wood, chipped up weakly, and missed an eight-foot putt, scoring one-over-par 4 to fall a stroke behind Mrs. Berning. She finished with a 72 for the round, tying for second place with Judy Rankin and Kathy Ahern. Miss Ahern's final-day 70 was the lowest score of the Championship. Heavy rains the week before had threatened to cause a postponement of the Championship, and caused Winged Foot to play especially long. Mrs. JoAnne Gunderson Carner, the defending Champion, started with a 79 and was never in contention. Miss Marilynn Smith finished 72 holes in her 20th consecutive Open, a record which no one else has matched. Miss Shirley Englehorn, recipient of the Ben Hogan Award in 1967, had not played tournament golf in over a year following an operation to fuse ankle bones, and, furthermore, she had not walked 18 holes until the week before the Championship. Yet she led after the first round with a 72 and held her lead with a 75 in the second round for 147. The next day she could not keep up the pace and scored an 82. Of the 57 amateur golfers who started the Championship, nine finished 72 holes. Mrs. Jane Bastanchury Booth, leading amateur in the 1971 Open, again led, scoring 304 to tie for sixth place. Miss Nancy Porter, another amateur, scored a hole in one on the par-3, 164-yard sixth hole with a 3-iron. There was a record entry of 176, of which 92 were professionals, also a new record. Only 150 played, however, because the USGA imposed a limit for the first time. Prize money amounted to $38,350, a new record. Of this amount, $6,000 was awarded to the winner, another new high.

1973 Mrs. Susie Maxwell Berning became

the third player to win the Championship three times when she shot 72-77-69-72—290, and won by five strokes at the Country Club of Rochester, Rochester, N.Y. Miss Gloria Ehret and Miss Shelley Hamlin were second with 295. Mrs. Berning won the Championship previously in 1968 and 1972. Miss Mickey Wright won the Championship in 1958-59-61-64 and Miss Betsy Rawls in 1951-53-57-60. Miss Marilynn Smith extended her own record by completing 72 holes; since 1953 she had played through 21 Women's Opens. Miss Cynthia Hill, an amateur, also set a new record with 68 in the opening round; this was the lowest first round score ever shot in the Women's Open. Mrs. Anne Quast Sander, three-time winner of the U.S. Women's Amateur Championship, was the low amateur. She finished fourth with a score of 296. Miss Pam Higgins was tied with Mrs. Berning going into the final round. She bogied the first hole to Mrs. Berning's par, then played even with Mrs. Berning for the next four holes. On the sixth, both players were in a greenside bunker in two. Miss Higgins made a marvelous recovery to within three feet of the hole, while Mrs. Berning played a poor shot out. Mrs. Berning bogied and it appeared that Miss Higgins would pick up at least one stroke and pull even. She 3-putted, however, to let Mrs. Berning go two strokes up. That was the end for Miss Higgins. A bogie on the 8th and a double bogie on the 10th ended her challenge. She shot 79 and finished fifth. The only other contender was Miss Hamlin, who started the final round three strokes behind the leaders. After a 38 on the first nine she was four behind Mrs. Berning. She then birdied the 10th and chipped in at the 12th for another birdie and was only one stroke behind Mrs. Berning. She then three-putted the 13th and never recovered.

The entry reached 150 and 142 started. Prize money totaled $39,490, a record. Mrs. Berning's share was $6,000.

1974—Miss Sandra Haynie birdied the last two holes at the LaGrange Country Club, LaGrange, Ill., to win the Championship by one stroke over Miss Carol Mann and Miss Beth Stone. Miss Haynie played consistent rounds of 73-73-74-75—295. Mrs. JoAnne Carner, the 1971 Champion, and Miss Kathy Whitworth tied for fourth place at 297, a stroke behind Miss Mann and Miss Stone. With nine holes to play in the last round, Mrs. Carner led the field by two strokes. She lost two strokes to par with a 5 on the 13th hole, and by then five players had the Championship within reach. They were Mrs. Carner, Miss Haynie, Miss Whitworth, Miss Stone, and Miss Mann. All but Miss Stone made two-over-par 6s on the 16th, Miss Stone was first to complete the 72 holes; she finished with 296. Miss Mann birdied the 18th to match her and Miss Haynie was then one stroke behind with two holes to play. She holed a 70-foot putt for a birdie on the 17th, and came to the 18th needing another birdie to win. She holed a putt of about 15 feet for her 295, and this left only Mrs. Carner with a chance to catch her. Mrs. Carner, however, needed an eagle 3 on the 18th, and her pitch from off the green did not fall. She made a par 5 and dropped to fourth place. It is interesting to note that while Miss Haynie birdied the last two holes, she had only three other birdies through the first 70 holes of the Championship. Miss Debbie Massey was low amateur with 299, good for a tie for seventh place with Mrs. Donna Caponi Young, Champion in 1969 and 1970. Miss Massey was among 14 amateurs, including the entire 1974 Curtis Cup Team, to survive the 36-hole cut. Miss Kathy Ahern equalled the first round record with 68 and held a three-stroke lead over Miss Massey and Mrs. Young, with 71s. Miss Ahern, however, played the next three rounds in 76, 81, and 82 and finished in 28th place at 307. Her second round 76 was still good enough to earn a tie for first place with Miss Mann and Miss Massey at 144. Miss Haynie was then two strokes behind at 146, tied with Bonnie Lauer, another amateur. Ruth Jessen had 77 in the opening round, added 71 in the second, and when she shot a second 71 in the third round she took the 54-hole lead at 219. Miss Haynie was then second at 220, tied with Sandra Spuzich and Mrs. Carner. Miss Jessen, troubled by physical problems throughout her career, was playing in only her second tournament of the year. She slipped from contention in the final round by shooting 81. The single round record for the Women's Open was matched in the last round by Miss Bonnie Bryant, a left-hander. Miss Bryant shot 67, matching the record set by Miss Judy Bell, an amateur, in 1964. A total of 155 players entered the Championship and 150 started. Prize money totalled $40,000.

1975—Miss Sandra Palmer scored 71 in the third round—one of only two sub-par rounds all week—and added a par 72 the final day to win the 23rd Women's Open Championship by four strokes with seven-over par 295 at the Atlantic City Country Club, Northfield, N.J. Tied for second were

Miss Nancy Lopez, of Roswell, New Mexico, an amateur; Mrs. JoAnne Carner, the 1971 Champion; and Miss Sandra Post. Miss Lopez was U. S. Girls' Junior Champion in 1972 and 1974. Miss Susie McAllister was fifth. Mrs. Judy Rankin, who tied for second in 1972, led after 18 holes with par 72, a stroke ahead of Mrs. Carner, Miss Lopez, and Miss Judy Kimball. Miss Palmer, meanwhile, shot 78 and trailed the leader by six strokes. Miss Post added a 73 to her first-round 74 to take the early 36-hole lead at 147; she was later tied by Miss Lopez, who shot 74. Tied for third were Mrs. Rankin, and Miss Diane Patterson, at 149. Mrs. Carner, Miss Laura Baugh, and Miss Sally Little, whose 70 was the best round of the entire Championship, were at 150, while Miss Palmer was five strokes behind at 152. On the third day, however, Miss Palmer shot a one-under par 71 and went into a tie for the lead at 223 with Miss Little, who had 73, and Miss Post, who shot 76. One stroke back were Mrs. Carner, Miss Lopez, and Miss Debbie Austin, while Miss Sandra Haynie, the defending Champion, and Miss Amy Alcott, 1973 U. S. Girls' Junior Champion, were two strokes behind. The winds that had hampered play all week grew stronger the final day and only Miss Palmer, Miss McAllister and Miss Maria Astrolges were able to play par rounds. Miss Palmer held her lead by playing the front nine in even par 37, while Miss Post fell two behind with 39. Mrs. Carner, on 38, was also two strokes back, and Miss Lopez was three behind with 39. Miss Little had 42 going out and Miss Austin had 40; both were out of contention. Miss Palmer played holes 10 through 14 in one under par, and Mrs. Carner lost another stroke and was three behind after 14 holes. She then bogied the 15th and was able only to match Miss Palmer's three finishing holes. Miss Lopez shot one-over par 36 on the home nine, losing sole possession of second place by putting too boldly at the 18th green and losing a stroke to par. Her finish, however, was the best by an amateur since Miss Catherine Lacoste won the Championship in 1967. Seven other amateurs played through 72 holes. There were 175 entries and prize money totaled $55,000.

1976—Mrs. JoAnne Carner, who won the Championship in 1971, defeated Miss Sandra Palmer, the defending Champion, 76 to 78, in an 18-hole playoff after both had scored eight-over-par 292 at the Rolling Green Golf Club, Springfield, Delaware County, Pa. It was the first playoff since 1964 and only the fourth since 1953, when the USGA first conducted the Championship. Miss Jane Blalock was third at 296 and Miss Susie McAllister was fourth with 297. Miss Beth King, of Bernville, Pa., was low amateur at 303. A record was set when another amateur, Miss Nancy Porter of Cinnaminson, N. J., made a hole-in-one on the 135-yard 16th hole the second day; this was only the fourth hole-in-one in the Championship's history—and Miss Porter made two of them. Miss Connie Chillemi led after the first round with a two-under-par 69, one of only four sub-par scores in the four rounds. Tied for second were Miss Palmer and Mrs. Mary Lou Crocker at 70, while Mrs. Carner had 71. In the second round Mrs. Carner shot another 71 to take the lead at 142, two strokes ahead of Miss Palmer, who had 74. Miss Pat Bradley was third at 145. Miss Chillemi, just 18 years old, shot 84 and Mrs. Crocker scored 80. Mrs. Carner shot 77 in the third round, her worst round of the year, and lost the lead to Miss Palmer, who had a score of 217 for 54 holes. Mrs. Carner was two strokes behind at 219. Miss Blalock moved into contention at 220. The Championship was decided between Mrs. Carner and Miss Palmer in the fourth round. Miss Blalock fell behind with 76. Mrs. Carner took the lead with pars on the first 10 holes, while Miss Palmer bogied four of the first five. Miss Palmer caught her on the 15th, but Mrs. Carner, playing ahead of Miss Palmer, went ahead again with a birdie on the 17th. Moments later Miss Palmer also birdied. Both women scored par-5s on the 18th, forcing the playoff. Mrs. Carner shot a 73 in the fourth round, while Miss Palmer had 75. In the playoff, Mrs. Carner birdied the first hole and led by two strokes after nine holes, and by four strokes after 13. Mrs. Carner then lost five strokes on the next three holes and fell one stroke behind Miss Palmer. Mrs. Carner then birdied the 17th and scored a par on the 18th as Miss Palmer dropped a stroke on each. Mrs. Carner won the playoff by two strokes. The entry reached 205 and for the first time sectional qualifying was required to reduce the field to the 150 starters. Sectional qualifying was conducted at three locations. Prize money totalled $60,000, a record.

1977—Hollis Stacy, 23, led all four rounds at the Hazeltine National Golf Club, Chaska, Minn., and won her fourth USGA Championship. Miss Stacy had a 72-hole score of 292 and won by two strokes over Nancy Lopez, with 294. Jo Anne Carner was third with 295. All three were former Girls'

Junior Champions. (Miss Stacy had won three consecutive Girls' Juniors from 1969 through 1971). After the first round, Miss Stacy led by two strokes with 70, the only sub-par round of the day. Tied for second at even par 72 were Jan Stephenson, Jane Blalock, Joyce Kazmierski, and Amy Alcott, also a former Girls' Junior Champion. Miss Stacy added 73 in the second round to lead by two strokes with 143 after 36 holes. Miss Lopez, playing her first tournament as a professional, moved into second place with a second-round 72 and a total of 145. Mrs. Carner also had 72 for a 146 total and third place. At the end of the third round Miss Stacy's lead was cut to one stroke when she shot 75 for 218. Jan Stephenson moved back into contention with an even par 72 for 219. Miss Lopez remained two behind at 220, and Mrs. Carner was four strokes behind at 222. In the final round both Miss Stacy and Miss Lopez shot 74 and Mrs. Carner shot 73. Miss Stephenson dropped behind with 79 and finished in a tie for fourth place at 298. Miss Beth Daniel, of Charleston, S. C., was the low amateur with a total of 308. Later in the year she won the Women's Amateur. The entry reached 197, and again regional qualifying determined the 150 players for the Championship proper. A total of $75,000 was awarded in prize money, a record.

1978—Miss Hollis Stacy, 24, of Savannah, Ga., became only the fourth player to win two consecutive Women's Open Championships. She won her second at the Country Club of Indianapolis, in Indianapolis, Indiana. She also became the youngest player to win the Women's Open twice. She had rounds of 70, 75, 72, 72 for a 289 total, five over par. Mrs. JoAnne Carner and Miss Sally Little tied for second place, one stroke behind, with scores of 290. Miss Little's final round of 65, six under par, established a Women's Open single-round scoring record. It was the fifth USGA Championship for Miss Stacy (she had won three consecutive Girls' Junior Championships from 1969 through 1971). Only Bob Jones (9), Mrs. Carner (8), and Mrs. Glenna Collett Vare (6), have won more USGA events. Mrs. Donna Caponi Young led the first round with 68, three under par, equalling the lowest first round ever shot in the Women's Open. Second place was shared by Miss Stacy and two other players with rounds of 70. Mrs. Carner and Miss Little had first-round scores of 73 and 75, respectively. Three players—Mrs.Donna Horton White, Miss Nancy Lopez, and Miss Carol Semple, an amateur—shared the 36-hole lead at 144, two over par. At 145 were Miss Stacy with 75 and Mrs. Carner with 72, along with Miss Cynthia Hill, an amateur. Mrs. Young fell two strokes off the pace at 146 after scoring 78. Miss Little shot another 75 and was six strokes behind at 150. Miss Stacy shot 72 in the third round, giving her a 54-hole total of 217, four over par. Mrs. Carner moved into second place with 73 for 218, one stroke behind. Mrs. Young also had 73 to stay close at 219, tied with Miss Jane Blalock, who moved into contention with an even-par 71. Miss Little added still another 75 for a 225 total, eight strokes behind Miss Stacy. The 36-hole leaders didn't do well in the third round. Miss Semple dropped four strokes behind with 77, for 221; Mrs. White and Miss Lopez turned in identical 79s for 223 totals, six strokes behind the leader. Lightning and heavy rain caused play of the last round to be suspended twice. The lead changed hands six times between Miss Stacy and Mrs. Carner, who were playing together. When Miss Little completed her round of 65, Miss Stacy and Mrs. Carner still had six holes to play. At the 16th hole, Miss Stacy, five over par, went ahead to stay. Mrs. Carner bogied the hole to fall into a tie with Miss Little at six over par. It remained that way going to the final hole. There, Miss Stacy hit her 1-iron tee shot very fat. Mrs. Carner also used a 1-iron and pushed her shot into some trees. Both second shots landed in the rough, short of the green. Mrs. Carner pitched her ball to within 10 feet of the hole. Miss Stacy's shot came to rest four feet above the hole. Mrs. Carner ran in her par putt, but Miss Stacy wasted no time in holing her four-foot par putt for the Championship. Miss Carol Semple, of Sewickley, Pa., the 1973 Women's Amateur Champion, was the low amateur with 297. The Championship established new records for number of entries and for prize money. There were 297 entries, exceeding the previous high of 205 in 1976. A total of $100,000 in prize money was awarded.

1979—Miss Jerilyn Britz, 36, of Luverne, Minn., won the Women's Open Championship at the Brooklawn Country Club, Fairfield, Conn., with a score of 284, even par, the lowest 72-hole total since the USGA assumed sponsorship of the Championship in 1953. Miss Britz had rounds of 70-70-75-69. Debbie Massey and Sandra Palmer, the 1975 Champion, tied for second place at 286. Miss Britz and Miss Massey were the first-round co-leaders with rounds of 70, one under par. Six players were a stroke behind at 71. Among them were Hollis Stacy, Sally Little, former Champion Sandra Spuzich, Jane Blalock, Pam Higgins and Cathy Morse. Miss Palmer was three strokes behind at 73. In the second round, Miss Britz shot another 70 for a total of 140, two under par. Two strokes back at even par 142 were Miss Massey who shot 72, Miss Palmer, who moved into contention with 69, and Miss Little, who added a second 71. Susie Berning had a second-round 66, five-under-par, the lowest round in the 1979 Championship, one stroke above the Women's Open record of 65, set by Miss Little in 1978. In the third round, Miss Britz had a 75 that dropped her into second place at 215, three strokes behind Miss Massey, who had 70 for a 54-hole total of 212, one under par. Tied for third place, at 216, four strokes back, were Miss Palmer and Miss Little, both with 74s, and Mrs. Berning with a 71. In the final round, Miss Massey lost two strokes to par on both the sixth and seventh holes and eventually finished the first nine in 41. Meanwhile, Miss Little and Miss Britz had scores of 34 and 35, respectively, and were tied for the lead at one over par. Miss Little bogeyed the 13th and 14th holes to fall back to three over par. Miss Britz bogeyed the 12th hole, but she birdied the 11th and 14th and parred the rest to finish at even par. Miss Massey birdied the 12th hole to go three over par. After playing the 13th and 14th holes in par, she ran in consecutive birdie putts from 15 feet on the 15th, 30 feet on the 16th, and six feet on the 17th. She was then tied with Miss Britz with one hole to play. Miss Massey's final drive rolled into a very narrow divot hole on the left edge of the fairway. She punched a 4-iron shot short of the green, her pitch shot ran 10 feet above the hole, and she three-putted for a 6. Miss Britz, meanwhile, played the hole routinely and two-putted from 15 feet for a par 4 to win the Championship. A Women's Open attendance four-day record of 41,200 was set. Fifty-three professionals and three amateurs made the 36-hole cut at 152, 10 over par. Terri Moody was the low amateur with a 297 total. The Championship established new records for number of entries and for prize money. There were 335 entries, exceeding the previous high of 297 on 1978. A total of $125,000 in prize money was awarded.

1980—Amy Alcott, 24, of Santa Monica, California, won the 1980 Championship at the Richland Country Club, Nashville, Tennessee, setting the 72-hole scoring record with 280. The previous record, of 284, was set in 1979 by Jerilyn Britz. Hollis Stacy was second, with 289, nine strokes behind Miss Alcott. Miss Alcott had rounds of 70-70-68-72. She was four under par, the fifth sub-par 72-hole score since the USGA assumed sponsorship in 1953. Temperatures reached beyond 100 degrees every day. By winning, Miss Alcott became the 22nd player to win more than one USGA Championship. She won the Girls' Junior in 1973. The first-round co-leaders were Miss Alcott and Barbara Moxness, with rounds of 70, one under par. Seven others were two strokes back. Miss Britz, the defending champion, shot 78 and eventually missed the 36-hole cut, with a 156 total. With a second consecutive 70, for 140, Miss Alcott opened her lead to four strokes after 36 holes. Tied for second place, at 144, were Mrs. Donna Caponi Young and Penny Pulz, who both shot 72, and Mrs. Moxness, with 74. Miss Stacy had 71 and was six strokes back, at 146, tied with Mrs. JoAnne Carner, Mrs. Nancy Lopez-Melton, and Mrs. Janet Alex. Miss Alcott increased her lead to eight strokes after the third round with a 68, three under par. Her 208 total established a new 54-hole Women's Open record, surpassing Mrs. Young's 210, set in 1970. Miss Stacy, with a 70, was alone in second place, at 216. Sharing third place, at 217, nine strokes back, were Mrs. Lopez-Melton, who had 71, Sandra Post, with 70, and Beth Daniel, with 69. Throughout the final round, no one could mount a serious challenge. With one hole to play, Miss Alcott was 10 strokes ahead of Miss Stacy; she hit a bad tee shot on the 18th and lost a stroke to par. Fifty-eight professionals and only two amateurs, the fewest ever, made the 36-hole cut at 153, 11 over par. Mrs. Judith Oliver was the low amateur with a 306 total. The Championship received 337 entries. A record $140,000 in prize money was awarded.

WOMEN'S OPEN CHAMPIONSHIP

DATE	WINNER, RUNNER-UP	SCORE	SITE	ENTRY
1960 (July)	Miss Betsy Rawls	292	Worcester C.C.,	57
	Miss Joyce Ziske	293	Worcester, Mass.	
1961 (June-July)	Miss Mickey Wright	293	Baltusrol G.C., (Lower Course),	85
	Miss Betsy Rawls	299	Springfield, N.J.	
1962 (June)	Mrs. Murle Lindstrom	301	Dunes G. & Beach Club,	70
	Miss Ruth Jessen	303	Myrtle Beach, S.C.	
	Miss JoAnn Prentice	303		
1963 (July)	Miss Mary Mills	289	Kenwood C.C., (Kenview Course),	84
	Miss Sandra Haynie	292	Cincinnati, Ohio	
	Miss Louise Suggs	292		
1964 (July)	Miss Mickey Wright	290-70	San Diego C.C.,	57
	Miss Ruth Jessen	290-72	Chula Vista, Calif.	
1965 (July)	Miss Carol Mann	290	Atlantic City C.C.,	84
	Mrs. Kathy Cornelius	292	Northfield, N.J.	
1966 (July)	Miss Sandra Spuzich	297	Hazeltine National G.C.,	101
	Miss Carol Mann	298	Minneapolis, Minn.	
1967 (June-July)	*Miss Catherine Lacoste	294	Virginia Hot Springs G. & T.C.,	98
	Miss Susie Maxwell	296	(Cascades Course),	
	Miss Beth Stone	296	Hot Springs, Va.	
1968 (July)	Mrs. Susie Maxwell Berning	289	Moselem Springs G.C.,	104
	Miss Mickey Wright	292	Fleetwood, Pa.	
1969 (July)	Miss Donna Caponi	294	Scenic Hills C.C.,	99
	Miss Peggy Wilson	295	Pensacola, Fla.	
1970 (July)	Miss Donna Caponi	287	Muskogee C.C.,	139
	Miss Sandra Haynie	288	Muskogee, Okla.	
	Miss Sandra Spuzich	288		
1971 (June)	Mrs. JoAnne Gunderson Carner	288	Kahkwa C.,	149
	Miss Kathy Whitworth	295	Erie, Pa.	
1972 (June-July)	Mrs. Susie Maxwell Berning	299	Winged Foot G.C.,	176
	Miss Kathy Ahern	300	Mamaroneck, N.Y.	
	Miss Pam Barnett	300		
	Mrs. Judy Rankin	300		
1973 (July)	Mrs. Susie Maxwell Berning	290	C.C. of Rochester	150
	Miss Shelley Hamlin	295	Rochester, N.Y.	
	Miss Gloria Ehret	295		
1974 (July)	Miss Sandra Haynie	295	La Grange C. C.,	155
	Miss Beth Stone	296	La Grange, Ill.	
	Miss Carol Mann	296		
1975 (July)	Miss Sandra Palmer	295	Atlantic City, C. C.,	175
	*Miss Nancy Lopez	299	Northfield, N.J.	
	Mrs. JoAnne Carner	299		
	Miss Sandra Post	299		
1976 (July)	Mrs. JoAnne Carner	292-76	Rolling Green G.C.	205
	Miss Sandra Palmer	292-78	Springfield,	
			Delaware Co., Pa.	
1977 (July)	Miss Hollis Stacy	292	Hazeltine National G. C.,	197
	Miss Nancy Lopez	294	Chaska, Minn.	
1978 (July)	Miss Hollis Stacy	289	C.C. of Indianapolis,	297
	Mrs. JoAnne Carner	290	Indianapolis, Ind.	
	Miss Sally Little	290		
1979 (July)	Miss Jerilyn Britz	284	Brooklawn C. C.	335
	Miss Debbie Massey	286	Fairfield, Conn.	
	Miss Sandra Palmer	286		
1980 (July)	Miss Amy Alcott	†280	Richland C.C.	§337
	Miss Hollis Stacy	289	Nashville, Tenn.	

*Denotes Amateur
†Record Score
§Record Entry

1960
EIGHTH WOMEN'S OPEN CHAMPIONSHIP

Held at Worcester Country Club, Worcester, Mass., July 21-23.
Yardage–6,137. Par 72. 57 Entries, 53 Starters.
Forty-one contestants who completed 72 holes.

						Score	Money Prize
1	Miss Betsy Rawls, Spartanburg C.C., Spartanburg, S.C.	76	73	68	75	292	$1,800.00
2	Miss Joyce Ziske, Rivermoor C.C., Waterford, Wis.	75	74	71	73	293	1,200.00
3	Mrs. Marlene Bauer Hagge, Paradise C.C., Crystal River, Fla.	74	74	75	75	298	725.00
	Miss Mary Lena Faulk, Sea Island G.C., Sea Island, Ga.	75	72	76	75	298	725.00
5	Miss Mickey Wright, San Diego C.C., Chula Vista, Calif.	71	71	75	82	299	500.00
6	Miss Wiffi Smith, St. Clair River C.C., St. Clair, Mich.	75	76	73	76	300	400.00
7	Miss Beverly Hanson, Eldorado C.C., Palm Desert, Calif.	75	77	77	72	301	350.00
8	Miss Fay Crocker, Club de Golf del Uruguay, Montevideo, Uruguay	74	76	76	76	302	300.00
9	Miss Louise Suggs, Castle View, C.C., Atlanta, Ga.	78	77	72	77	304	225.00
	Miss Marilynn Smith, French Lick Sheraton C.C., French Lick, Ind.	72	72	83	77	304	225.00
	Miss Kathy Whitworth, Jal C.C., Jal, N.M.	75	73	80	76	304	225.00
12	Miss Betty Jameson, San Antonio C.C., San Antonio, Texas	78	74	77	77	306	141.66
	Miss Barbara Romack, Del Paso C.C., Sacramento, Calif.	80	78	73	75	306	141.67
	Miss Ruth Jessen, Cincinnati, Ohio	76	77	78	75	306	141.67
15	Miss Murle MacKenzie, Happy Acres G. & C.C., Webster, N.Y.	75	80	76	78	309	100.00
16	Miss Gloria Armstrong, Lake Chabot G.C., Oakland, Calif.	78	78	80	77	313	
17	Miss Patty Berg, St. Andrews G.C., St. Andrews, Ill.	80	76	78	80	314	
18	Miss Wanda Sanches, Baton Rouge, La.	77	77	81	81	316	
19	Mrs. Mary Ann Reynolds, Tippecanoe Lake C.C., Leesburg, Ind.	81	78	79	79	317	
20	Mrs. Betty Bush, Tequesta C.C., Tequesta, Fla.	83	79	77	79	318	
	Mrs. Peggy Kirk Bell, Pine Needles C.C., Southern Pines, N.C.	79	77	81	81	318	
22	Mrs. Jacqueline N. Pung, Daly City, Calif.	81	80	80	79	320	
23	Miss Bonnie Randolph, Naples Beach & G.C., Naples, Fla.	77	77	87	80	321	
24	*Miss Judy Torluemke, Triple A Club, St. Louis, Mo.	85	81	80	80	326	
25	Miss Gloria Fecht, Pine Needles C.C., Southern Pines, N.C.	86	79	82	81	328	
26	*Miss Sally Carroll, Wheeling C.C., Wheeling, W. Va.	86	81	77	85	329	
27	*Miss Claudette A. LaBonte, Segregansett C.C., Taunton, Mass.	82	83	79	86	330	
28	*Mrs. Edward Stumpp, Wheeling C.C., Wheeling, W. Va.	83	83	81	85	332	
29	*Mrs. Donald K. McClusky, Worcester C.C., Worcester, Mass.	83	81	87	82	333	
	Miss JoAnn Prentice, Birmingham, Ala.	80	85	81	87	333	
31	*Mrs. Edward J. McAuliffe, Charles River C.C., Newton Centre, Mass.	82	82	85	85	334	
	Miss Cynthia Sullivan, Florence C.C., Florence, S.C.	81	85	83	85	334	
33	Mrs. Bettye Mims Danoff, Lakewood C.C., Dallas, Texas	87	81	80	87	335	
34	*Miss Diana Hoke, Chartiers C.C., Pittsburgh, Pa.	84	84	83	85	336	
35	*Miss Joanne Goodwin, Haverhill C.C., Haverhill, Mass.	85	81	82	89	337	
36	Miss Dana Lombard, Weston G.C., Weston, Mass.	85	85	85	85	340	
37	*Miss Betty June Bobel, Valley C.C. on Ledgemont, W. Warwick, R.I.	86	84	84	87	341	
38	*Miss Gail Purdy, Glens Falls C.C., Glens Falls, N.Y.	81	86	84	92	343	
39	*Mrs. Harton S. Semple, Allegheny C.C., Sewickley, Pa.	84	89	89	82	344	
40	Miss Barbara Rotvig, Univ. of Michigan G.C., Ann Arbor, Mich.	86	87	84	89	346	
41	*Mrs. John G. Gager, Worcester C.C., Worcester, Mass.	86	87	92	89	354	

*Amateur.
Prize money totaling $7,200 awarded to professionals.

1961
NINTH WOMEN'S OPEN CHAMPIONSHIP

Held at Baltusrol Golf Club (Lower Course), Springfield, N.J., June 29-July 1.
Yardage—6,372. Par 72. 85 Entries, 82 Starters.
Forty-one contestants who completed 72 holes.

						Score	Money Prize
1	Miss Mickey Wright, Oak Cliff C.C., Dallas, Texas	72	80	69	72	293	$1,800.00
2	Miss Betsy Rawls, Spartanburg C.C., Spartanburg, S.C.	74	76	73	76	299	1,200.00
3	Miss Ruth Jessen, Inglewood C.C., Seattle, Wash.	75	73	77	75	300	800.00
4	Miss Louise Suggs, Atlanta, Ga.	78	74	76	73	301	650.00
5	Miss Marilynn Smith, French Lick Sheraton C.C., French Lick, Ind.	77	74	77	75	303	500.00
6	Miss JoAnn Prentice, Birmingham, Ala.	72	76	80	76	304	400.00
7	Miss Barbara Romack, Del Paso C.C., Sacramento, Calif.	77	77	78	74	306	350.00
	*Mrs. Marlene Stewart Streit, Lookout Point G.C., Fonthill, Ont., Canada	74	77	77	78	306	----
9	Miss Mary Lena Faulk, Sea Island G.C., Sea Island, Ga.	78	77	80	73	308	312.50
	Miss Shirley Englehorn, Esmeralda G.C., Spokane, Wash.	80	73	78	77	308	312.50
	*Mrs. Philip J. Cudone, Forest Hill Field C., Bloomfield, N.J.	77	76	75	80	308	----
12	Miss Fay Crocker, Club de Golf del Uruguay, Montevideo, Uruguay	76	83	77	73	309	262.50
	Miss Murle MacKenzie, Pinellas Park, Fla.	78	79	78	74	309	262.50
14	Mrs. Kathy Cornelius, Phoenix, Ariz.	76	80	73	82	311	212.50
	Miss Carol Mann, Olympia Fields C.C., Olympia Fields, Ill.	80	75	77	79	311	212.50
16	Miss Kathy Whitworth, Jal C.C., Jal, N.M.	81	81	77	74	313	180.00
17	Miss Sybil Griffin, Par Haven G.R., Baton Rouge, La.	82	77	77	79	315	160.00
18	Miss Patty Berg, St. Andrews G.C., St. Andrews, Ill.	82	83	77	74	316	140.00
19	Mrs. Gerda Whalen, Par 3 G.C., LaGrange, Ill.	80	82	77	78	317	122.50
	Mrs. Marlene Hagge, Pine Tree G.C., Delray Beach, Fla.	80	84	75	78	317	122.50
21	Miss Betty Jameson, San Antonio C.C., San Antonio, Texas	81	81	79	77	318	
	Miss Barbara E. Greene, Dodge County G.C., Eastman, Ga.	80	80	81	77	318	
	*Miss Anne Richardson, Columbus C.C., Columbus, Ohio	75	76	83	84	318	
24	*Mrs. Helen Sigel Wilson, Philadelphia Country C., Gladwyne, Pa.	74	81	81	83	319	
25	Miss Beverly Hanson, Indian Wells C.C., Palm Springs, Calif.	83	80	78	79	320	
	*Miss Judy Torluemke, Triple A G.C., St. Louis, Mo.	82	78	78	82	320	
	Miss Judy Kimball, Sioux City, Iowa	78	79	85	78	320	
28	Miss Beth Stone, Muskogee C.C., Muskogee, Okla.	82	81	77	81	321	
29	*Miss Marianne Gable, California C.C., Whittier, Calif.	81	79	80	82	322	
	Mrs. Peggy Kirk Bell, Pine Needles C.C., Southern Pines, N.C.	86	78	78	80	322	
	Miss Wanda J. Sanches, River Oaks C.C., Houston, Texas	82	82	79	79	322	
32	Miss Gloria Armstrong, Oakland, Calif.	81	84	82	76	323	
33	*Miss Phyllis Preuss, Pompano Beach C.C., Pompano Beach, Fla.	81	83	78	83	325	
	*Mrs. Harton S. Semple, Allegheny C.C., Sewickley, Pa.	86	81	80	78	325	
35	*Miss Marjorie Burns, Starmount Forest C.C., Greensboro, N.C.	81	85	78	82	326	
36	*Miss Judy Rand, Aurora C.C., Aurora, Ohio	79	81	85	83	328	
37	*Mrs. Bruce McGhie, Apawamis C., Rye, N.Y.	80	81	87	81	329	
38	*Mrs. Barbara Fitton, Elks C.C., Hamilton, Ohio	82	85	81	82	330	
39	*Miss Gail Purdy, Glens Falls C.C., Glens Falls, N.Y.	84	84	81	85	334	
40	*Miss Doris Phillips, St. Clair C.C., Belleville, Ill.	83	85	84	83	335	
41	*Miss Nancy Roth, Sunset G.C., Hollywood, Fla.	81	87	82	86	336	

*Amateur.
Prize money totaling $8,000 awarded to professionals.

1962
TENTH WOMEN'S OPEN CHAMPIONSHIP

Held at Dunes Golf and Beach Club, Myrtle Beach, S.C., June 28-30.
Yardage—6,400. Par 72. 70 Entries, 67 Starters.

Forty-one contestants who completed 72 holes.

						Score	Money Prize
1	Mrs. Murle Lindstrom, Cape Girardeau C.C., Mo.	78	74	76	73	301	$1,800.00
2	Miss Ruth Jessen, Delray Beach C.C., Delray Beach, Fla.	72	76	75	80	303	1,000.00
	Miss JoAnn Prentice, Columbia C.C., Columbia, S.C.	75	77	73	78	303	1,000.00
4	Miss Louise Suggs, Cincinnati, Ohio	80	77	74	75	306	575.00
	Miss Mickey Wright, Oak Cliff C.C., Dallas, Texas	75	73	81	77	306	575.00
6	Miss Shirley Englehorn, Esmeralda G.C., Spokane, Wash.	81	72	79	75	307	375.00
	Miss Mary Lena Faulk, Sea Island G.C., Sea Island, Ga.	78	74	78	77	307	375.00
8	Mrs. Marlene Bauer Hagge, Pine Tree G.C., Delray Beach, Fla.	76	75	81	76	308	312.50
	Miss Shirley G. Spork, Palm Desert, Calif.	77	77	79	75	308	312.50
10	Miss Mary Mills, Gulf Hills G.C., Ocean Springs, Miss.	78	79	77	75	309	262.50
	Miss Kathy Whitworth, Jal C.C., Jal, N.M.	80	78	73	78	309	262.50
12	Miss Barbara Romack, Del Paso C.C., Sacramento, Calif.	76	76	81	78	311	225.00
13	Miss Patty Berg, St. Andrews G.C., St. Andrews, Ill.	85	75	75	77	312	190.00
	Mrs. Kathy Cornelius, Scottsdale, Ariz.	79	79	78	76	312	190.00
15	Miss Marilynn Smith, Tequesta C.C., Jupiter, Fla.	79	77	80	77	313	160.00
	*Miss JoAnne Gunderson, Sand Point C.C., Seattle, Wash.	82	74	77	80	313	PIN
17	*Miss Clifford Ann Creed, Rapides G. & C.C., Alexandria, La.	79	78	75	84	316	PIN
18	Miss Carol Mann, Olympia Fields C.C., Olympia Fields, Ill.	82	79	80	76	317	140.00
19	Mrs. Peggy Kirk Bell, Pine Needles C.C., Southern Pines, N.C.	80	82	79	77	318	122.50
	Mrs. Jacqueline N. Pung, Daly City, Calif.	76	83	75	84	318	122.50
21	Miss Betsy Rawls, Spartanburg C.C., Spartanburg, S.C.	86	74	80	79	319	
	Miss Sandra Haynie, Eastern Hills C.C., Garland, Texas	77	83	83	76	319	
23	*Miss Mary Anne Lopez, Palmetto C.C., Miami, Fla.	77	81	82	80	320	
	*Miss Nancy Roth, Sunset G.C., Hollywood, Fla.	78	83	79	80	320	
	Miss Judy Kimball, Sioux City, Iowa	78	77	75	90	320	
26	*Miss Polly Riley, River Crest C.C., Forth Worth, Texas	81	75	87	79	322	
	Miss Judy Torluemke, Chattanooga G. & C.C., Chattanooga, Tenn.	79	81	82	80	322	
	*Mrs. Paul Dye, Jr., Indianapolis,C.C., Indianapolis, Ind.	78	78	84	82	322	
29	Miss Beth Stone, Muskogee C.C., Muskogee, Okla.	82	81	82	78	323	
30	Miss Lesbia Lobo, San Antonio, Texas	82	82	78	83	325	
31	Miss Sherry Wheeler, Glasgow G. & C.C., Glasgow, Ky.	85	81	83	77	326	
32	Miss Betty Jameson, San Antonio C.C., San Antonio, Texas	79	83	82	83	327	
	*Mrs. Philip J. Cudone, Forest Hill Field C., Bloomfield, N.J.	84	80	76	87	327	
34	Miss Gloria Armstrong, Lake Chabot G.C., Oakland, Calif.	84	79	82	83	328	
	Miss Sybil Griffin, Par Haven G.R., Baton Rouge, La.	83	82	86	77	328	
	*Miss Anne Richardson, Columbus C.C., Columbus, Ohio	83	82	81	82	328	
37	*Miss Doris Phillips, Norwood Hills C.C., St. Louis, Mo.	81	83	83	87	334	
38	Mrs. Margaret Ann Allen, Radium C.C., Albany, Ga.	90	76	86	84	336	
39	*Miss Maureen Crum, Plant City G. & C.C., Plant City, Fla.	82	84	83	88	337	
40	*Miss Pamela Barnett, Myers Park C.C., Charlotte, N.C.	87	78	87	86	338	
41	Miss Sandra McClinton, Seguin, Texas	85	78	86	102	351	

*Amateur.
Prize money totaling $8,000 awarded to professionals.

1963
ELEVENTH WOMEN'S OPEN CHAMPIONSHIP

Held at Kenwood Country Club (Kenview Course), Cincinnati, Ohio, July 18-20.
Yardage—6,444. Par 73. 84 Entries, 82 Starters.
Forty contestants who completed 72 holes.

						Score	Money Prize
1	Miss Mary Mills, Gulf Hills Dude Ranch & CC., Gulf Hills, Miss.	71	70	75	73	289	$2,000.00
	Miss Sandra Haynie, Houston, Texas	75	72	73	72	292	1,000.00
	Miss Louise Suggs, Delray Beach, Florida	72	72	75	73	292	1,000.00
4	Miss Clifford Ann Creed, Rapides G. & C.C., Alexandria, La.	71	75	79	74	299	650.00
5	Miss Ruth Jessen, San Luis Rey C.C., Bonsall, Calif.	72	78	77	75	302	450.00
	Miss Kathy Whitworth, Jal C.C., Jal, N.M.	75	74	80	73	302	450.00
7	Miss Mary Lena Faulk, Sea Island G.C., Sea Island, Ga.	75	73	76	79	303	312.50
	Mrs. Kathy Cornelius, Scottsdale C.C., Scottsdale, Ariz.	76	75	77	75	303	312.50
	Miss Patsy Hahn, DuPont C.C., Wilmington, Del.	74	73	78	78	303	312.50
	Mrs. Murle Lindstrom, Pleasant Valley C.C., Sutton, Mass.	83	75	74	71	303	312.50
11	Miss Betsy Rawls, Spartanburg C.C., Spartanburg, S.C.	75	77	72	80	304	237.50
	Miss Judy Kimball, Sioux City, Iowa	72	78	79	75	304	237.50
13	Miss Carol Mann, Druid Hills G.C., Atlanta, Ga.	75	76	78	76	305	190.00
	Mrs. Marlene B. Hagge, Pine Tree C.C., Boynton Beach, Fla.	80	72	77	76	305	190.00
	*Miss Phyllis Preuss, Pompano Beach C.C., Pompano Beach, Fla.	76	73	79	77	305	----
16	Miss Sandra A. Spuzich, Speedway G.C., Indianapolis, Ind.	79	77	75	75	306	160.00
17	Mrs. Jacqueline N. Pung, Daly City, Calif.	76	73	79	79	307	150.00
18	Miss Shirley G. Spork, Indian Wells C.C., Palm Desert, Calif.	79	73	77	79	308	135.00
	Miss Marilynn Smith, Tequesta C.C., Tequesta, Fla.	75	76	76	81	308	135.00
20	Miss Betty Jameson, San Antonio C.C., San Antonio, Texas	75	79	80	75	309	125.00
21	*Miss Sally Carroll, Wheeling C.C., Wheeling, W. Va.	77	78	80	75	310	----
22	Miss Shirley Englehorn, Rancho G.C., Los Angeles, Calif.	77	79	78	77	311	113.34
	Miss Sybil J. Griffin, Delray Beach, Fla.	79	76	78	78	311	113.33
	Miss Gail Davis, Victoria C.C., Riverside, Calif.	78	72	84	77	311	113.33
25	*Mrs. Helen Sigel Wilson, Philadelphia C.C., Gladwyne, Pa.	81	72	79	80	312	----
	*Miss Margaret Jones, Ft. Mitchell C.C., Ft. Mitchell, Ky.	81	76	75	80	312	----
	Miss Sandra McClinton, Seguin, Texas	82	75	76	79	312	100.00
28	Miss JoAnn Prentice, Columbia C.C., Columbia, S.C.	77	75	83	79	314	100.00
29	Miss Patty Berg, St. Andrews G.C., St. Andrews, Ill.	77	79	78	81	315	33.34
	Miss Beth Stone, Muskogee C.C., Muskogee, Okla.	75	81	80	79	315	33.33
	Miss Andrea Cohn, Sunnyside C.C., Waterloo, Iowa	75	78	86	76	315	33.33
32	*Miss Judy Rand, Aurora C.C., Aurora, Ohio	79	77	80	80	316	
	Miss Gloria Armstrong, Oakland, Calif.	81	78	76	81	316	
34	Miss Judy Torluemke, Green Valley C.C., Lafayette Hills, Pa.	77	80	79	81	317	
35	*Miss Brenda Ann High, Glasgow C.C., Glasgow, Ky.	84	74	78	82	218	
36	Mrs. John H. Germain, Owensboro C.C., Owensboro, Ky.	80	78	81	81	320	
37	Miss Gloria J. Fecht, Bermuda Dunes C.C., Bermuda Dunes, Calif.	77	80	83	81	321	
38	*Miss Doris Phillips, Norwood Hills C.C., St. Louis, Mo.	78	80	81	83	322	
39	*Miss Marcella Rose, Meadow Lake Acres C.C., Jefferson City, Mo.	79	76	83	85	323	
40	Major Amelia Amizich, Fort Campbell G.C., Fort Campbell, Ky.	82	77	90	77	326	

*Amateur. Gold, silver and bronze pins were awarded to the amateurs returning the lowest three scores.
Prize money totaling $9,000 awarded to professionals.

1964
TWELFTH WOMEN'S OPEN CHAMPIONSHIP

Held at the San Diego Country Club, Chula Vista, Calif., July 9-11.
Yardage–6,470. Par 73. 57 Entries, 53 Starters.
Forty-three contestants who completed 72 holes.

						Score	Money Prize
1	†Miss Mickey Wright, Oak Cliff C.C., Dallas, Texas	71	71	75	73	290	$2,200.00
2	†Miss Ruth Jessen, San Luis Rey G.C., Bonsall, Calif.	72	73	74	71	290	1,320.00
3	Miss Shirley Englehorn, Rancho G.C., Los Angeles, Calif.	71	78	68	74	291	797.50
	Miss Marilynn Smith, The Trelawny C., Runaway Bay, Jamaica, W.I.	75	70	72	74	291	797.50
5	Miss Sandra Haynie, Phoenix, Ariz.	78	73	70	74	295	550.00
6	Miss Peggy Wilson, El Camino C.C., Oceanside, Calif.	73	77	72	74	296	440.00
7	Miss JoAnn Prentice, Perdido Bay C.C., Pensacola, Fla.	78	73	76	71	298	371.25
	Mrs. Marlene B. Hagge, Perdido Bay C.C., Pensacola, Fla.	71	76	74	77	298	371.25
9	Miss Kathy Whitworth, Pecan Valley C.C., San Antonio, Texas	76	76	75	73	300	330.00
10	Miss Patty Berg, St. Andrews G.C., St. Andrews, Ill.	76	74	77	75	302	302.50
11	Miss Mary Mills, Gulf Hills Ranch & C.C., Gulf Hills, Miss.	79	75	75	75	304	275.00
	*Miss Barbara McIntire, Broadmoor G.C., Colorado Springs, Colo.	76	76	77	75	304	----
13	Mrs. Jacqueline N. Pung, Mauna Kea Beach Hotel G.C., Hawaii	73	79	76	78	306	247.50
14	*Miss Judy Bell, Broadmoor G.C., Colorado Springs, Colo.	79	78	67	83	307	----
15	Miss Beverly Hanson, Westward Ho G.C., Indio, Calif.	78	80	76	74	308	209.00
	Miss Sandra McClinton, Seguin, Texas	72	78	75	83	308	209.00
	*Miss Nancy Roth, Elks G. & C.C., Elkhart, Ind.	74	78	75	81	308	----
18	Mrs. Kathy Cornelius, Scottsdale, Ariz.	80	75	76	78	309	176.00
	*Miss Barbara Fay White, Broadmoor G.C., Shreveport, La.	80	75	72	82	309	----
	*Miss Susan Lance, Woodland Hills C.C., Woodland Hills, Calif.	74	79	79	77	309	----
21	*Miss Susan O'Connor, Coronado G.C., Coronado, Calif.	75	77	80	78	310	----
22	Miss Betsy Rawls, Spartanburg C.C., Spartanburg, S.C.	81	77	76	77	311	159.50
	Miss Gloria Armstrong, Lake Chabot G.C., Oakland, Calif.	74	77	80	80	311	159.50
24	Miss Barbara Romack, Grossinger C.C., Grossinger, N.Y.	79	76	81	80	316	137.50
	Miss Betty Hicks, Bella Vista G.C., Mexico City, Mexico	82	79	79	76	316	137.50
	Miss Wanda J. Sanches, Sunset C.C., St. Louis, Mo.	78	83	77	78	316	137.50
27	Mrs. Alice Bauer Hovey, Long Boat Key G.C., Sarasota, Fla.	76	79	80	82	317	121.00
28	*Mrs. Linda C. Maurer, Plattsburgh AFB G.C., Plattsburgh, N.Y.	80	79	80	82	321	----
	*Miss Jean Ashley, Broadmoor G.C., Colorado Springs, Colo.	78	81	80	82	321	----
	*Miss Janis Ferraris, Presidio G.C., San Francisco, Calif.	77	77	82	85	321	----
31	*Miss Mary Lowell, Alameda Women's G.C., Alameda, Calif.	79	81	80	83	323	----
	*Miss Carla Jean Glasgow, California C.C., Whittier, Calif.	82	79	76	86	323	----
	Miss Susie Maxwell, Southern Hills C.C., Tulsa, Okla.	76	88	76	84	324	121.00
34	*Mrs. Donna Gilliam, California C.C., Whittier, Calif.	83	78	82	83	326	----
	*Mrs. Dora Donaldson, Rancho Santa Fe G.C., Calif.	79	83	80	84	326	----
	*Miss Jan Tarble, Bel-Air C.C., Los Angeles, Calif.	79	86	82	79	326	----
37	Miss Connie Robinson, South Hills C.C., West Covina, Calif.	82	77	84	85	328	110.00
38	Miss Jeanette Rector, Singing Hills C.C., El Cajon, Calif.	85	79	83	82	329	110.00
39	*Mrs. Harton S. Semple, Allegheny C.C., Sewickley, Pa.	80	85	80	85	330	----
40	Miss Joanne Winter, Indian Bend C.C., Scottsdale, Ariz.	84	81	82	84	331	110.00
	*Mrs. Theodore C. Enger, Coronado G.C., Coronado, Calif.	80	82	82	87	331	----
	*Miss Janet Moseley, Balboa Park G.C., San Diego, Calif.	79	86	78	88	331	----
43	*Mrs. Maxine P. Van Evera, Coronado Women's G.C., Calif.	86	79	83	93	341	----

†Playoff: 18 holes, July 12–Miss Wright, 70; Miss Jessen, 72.
*Amateur. Gold, silver, and bronze pins were awarded to the amateurs returning the lowest three scores.
Prize money for each professional increased 10 per cent above amount originally announced. Prize money totaling $9,900 was awarded.

1965
THIRTEENTH WOMEN'S OPEN CHAMPIONSHIP

Held at Atlantic City Country Club, Northfield, N.J., July 1-4.
Yardage—6,220. Par 72. 84 Entries, 81 Starters.
Forty-one contestants who completed 72 holes.

						Score	Money Prize
1	Miss Carol Mann, Towson, Md.	78	70	70	72	290	$4,000.00
2	Mrs. Kathy Cornelius, Rancho Santa Fe, Calif.	71	75	77	69	292	2,000.00
3	Miss Marilynn Smith, Runaway Bay G.C., Jamaica, W.I.	75	74	74	71	294	1,200.00
4	Miss Mary Mills, Gulf Hills G.C., Ocean Springs, Miss.	76	76	70	73	295	900.00
5	Miss Susie Maxwell, Southern Hills C.C., Tulsa, Okla.	75	75	75	71	296	800.00
	*Mrs. Helen Sigel Wilson, Philadelphia C.C., Gladwyne, Pa.	78	72	75	71	296	----
7	Miss Ruth Jessen, San Luis Rey G.C., Bonsall, Calif.	77	76	71	75	299	700.00
8	Miss Louise Suggs, Delray Beach, Fla.	76	77	71	76	300	600.00
9	Miss Margie Masters, Woodlands, Victoria, Australia	81	74	79	67	301	550.00
10	Miss Clifford Ann Creed, Rapides G.C., Alexandria, La.	77	76	76	73	302	485.00
	Miss Judy Torluemke, Ocean Reef C.C., N. Key Largo, Fla.	76	74	72	80	302	485.00
12	Miss Sandra Haynie, Euless, Texas	80	76	77	70	303	430.00
	Mrs. Marlene Bauer Hagge, Perdido Bay C.C., Pensacola, Fla.	72	82	72	77	303	430.00
14	*Miss Catherine Lacoste, Chantaco G.C., Paris, France	79	73	77	75	304	----
15	Miss Andrea Cohn, Willowood C.C., Flint, Mich.	78	80	75	72	305	395.00
	Miss Sandra Palmer, Glen Garden C.C., Ft. Worth, Texas	76	81	77	71	305	395.00
	*Miss Nancy Roth, Elks G.C., Elkhart, Ind.	79	77	80	69	305	----
18	Miss Barbara Romack, Del Paso C.C., Sacramento, Calif.	79	74	74	79	306	375.00
	Miss Kathy Whitworth, Pecan Valley C.C., San Antonio, Texas	79	74	81	72	306	375.00
20	Miss Donna Caponi, Elkins Ranch G.C., Fillmore, Calif.	78	79	75	75	307	360.00
21	*Mrs. Anne Quast Welts, Seattle G.C., Seattle, Wash.	74	79	76	79	308	----
22	Miss Patty Berg, St. Andrews G.C., W. Chicago, Ill.	79	77	80	73	309	350.00
	*Mrs. Marlene Stewart Streit, Lookout Point G.C., Fonthill, Canada	79	73	80	77	309	----
	*Mrs. Scott L. Probasco, Jr., Chattanooga G.C., Chattanooga, Tenn.	80	74	76	79	309	----
25	Mrs. Peggy Kirk Bell, Pine Needles C.C., Southern Pines, N.C.	81	77	77	75	310	340.00
26	Miss Judy Kimball, Lakewood C.C., Dallas, Texas	82	75	78	76	311	315.00
	Miss Gail Davis, Victoria C.C., Riverside, Calif.	79	76	79	77	311	315.00
	Miss JoAnn Prentice, Perdido Bay C.C., Pensacola, Fla.	80	77	74	80	311	315.00
	Miss Betsy Rawls, Spartanburg C.C., Spartanburg, S.C.	75	79	74	83	311	315.00
30	Mrs. Ann Casey Johnstone, Stephens College C.C., Columbia, Mo.	82	76	77	78	313	290.00
31	Miss Sandra Spuzich, Speedway G.C., Indianapolis, Ind.	81	78	79	76	314	280.00
32	Miss Betsy Cullen, Tulsa C.C., Tulsa, Okla.	78	80	77	80	315	270.00
	*Miss Sharon K. Miller, Battle Creek C.C., Battle Creek, Mich.	79	80	76	80	315	----
34	*Miss Renee M. Powell, East Canton, Ohio	82	77	79	78	316	----
	*Miss Phyllis Preuss, Coral Ridge C.C., Ft. Lauderdale, Fla.	79	77	83	77	316	----
36	*Miss Jan Ferraris, Presidio G.C., San Francisco, Calif.	80	78	82	78	318	----
37	Miss Gloria Armstrong, Delray Beach G.C., Delray Beach, Fla.	77	81	82	79	319	260.00
	*Mrs. Dorothy Germain Porter, Riverton C.C., Riverton, N.J.	82	77	82	78	319	----
39	*Miss Loretta Perlstein, Linwood C.C., Linwood, N.J.	78	80	76	87	321	----
40	Miss Sybil Griffin, Cypress Creek C.C., Boynton Beach, Fla.	78	79	86	79	322	250.00
41	*Miss Carla Jean Glasgow, California C.C., Whittier, Calif.	79	79	86	83	327	----

*Amateur. Gold, silver and bronze pins were awarded to the amateurs returning the lowest three scores.
Prize money totaling $17,780 was awarded.

1966
FOURTEENTH WOMEN'S OPEN CHAMPIONSHIP

Held at Hazeltine National Golf Club, Minneapolis, Minn., June 30-July 3.
Yardage—6,325. Par 72. 101 Entries, 99 Starters.
Forty-three contestants who completed 72 holes.

						Score	Money Prize
1	Miss Sandra Spuzich, Speedway G.C., Speedway, Ind.	75	74	76	72	297	$4,000.00
2	Miss Carol Mann, Towson, Md.	73	78	75	72	298	2,000.00
3	Miss Mickey Wright, Oak Cliff C.C., Dallas, Texas	71	78	77	73	299	1,200.00
4	Miss Clifford Ann Creed, Rapides G. & C.C., Alexandria, La.	76	75	76	76	303	900.00
5	Miss Sandra Haynie, Colonial C.C., Fort Worth, Texas	79	75	78	74	306	750.00
	Miss Kathy Whitworth, Pecan Valley C.C., San Antonio, Texas	80	74	76	76	306	750.00
7	Miss Judy Torluemke, Ocean Reef G.C., N. Key Largo, Fla.	77	78	79	73	307	600.00
8	Miss Mary Mills, Gulf Hills Ranch & G.C., Gulf Hills, Miss.	79	73	76	80	308	550.00
9	Miss Shirley Englehorn, Brookhaven C.C., Dallas, Texas	83	77	75	76	311	446.00
	Miss Barbara Romack, Del Paso C.C., Sacramento, Calif.	80	77	77	77	311	446.00
	Miss Susie Maxwell, Southern Hills C.C., Tulsa, Okla.	80	79	75	77	311	446.00
	Miss Peggy Wilson, San Luis Rey C.C., Bonsall, Calif.	76	76	81	78	311	446.00
	Miss Gloria Ehret, Ridgewood C.C., Danbury, Conn.	82	75	75	79	311	446.00
	*Miss Shelley Hamlin, University-Sequoia C.C., Fresno, Calif.	81	74	80	76	311	----
15	Miss Sharon K. Miller, Battle Creek C.C., Battle Creek, Mich.	75	77	77	84	313	390.00
	*Mrs. Anne Quast Welts, Broadmoor G.C., Seattle, Wash.	79	78	77	79	313	----
17	Miss JoAnn Prentice, Perdido Bay C.C., Perdido Bay, Fla.	78	78	80	78	314	380.00
18	Miss Patty Berg, Interlachen C.C., Minneapolis, Minn.	80	81	80	74	315	355.00
	Miss Sandra Palmer, River Lake C.C., Dallas, Texas	83	78	79	75	315	355.00
	Miss Donna M. Caponi, Los Angeles, Calif.	74	82	81	78	315	355.00
	Miss Jan Ferraris, Olympic Club, San Francisco, Calif.	78	81	76	80	315	355.00
	*Miss Joyce Kazmierski, Grosse Ile G. & C.C., Grosse Ile, Mich.	75	77	82	81	315	----
	*Miss Roberta Albers, Temple Terrace G. & C.C., Temple Terrace, Fla.	75	82	81	77	315	----
24	*Miss Peggy S. Conley, Spokane G. & C.C., Spokane, Wash.	77	83	80	76	316	----
25	Mrs. Marlene B. Hagge, Perdido Bay C.C., Pensacola, Fla.	78	83	77	79	317	320.00
	Miss Cynthia Sullivan, C.C. of South Carolina, Florence, S.C.	79	83	75	80	317	320.00
	Miss Judy Kimball, Lakewood C.C., Dallas, Texas	82	75	79	81	317	320.00
28	Miss Margie Masters, Victoria, Australia	81	79	82	76	318	290.00
	Miss Mary Lena Faulk, Pine Needles G.C., Southern Pines, N.C.	85	77	79	77	318	290.00
	Miss Candy Phillips, Temple Terrace G. & C.C., Temple Terrace, Fla.	81	77	79	81	318	290.00
31	Miss Betsy Cullen, Tulsa C.C., Tulsa, Okla.	80	77	81	82	320	265.00
	Mrs. Althea Gibson Darben, Englewood G.C., Englewood, N.J.	79	75	81	85	320	265.00
33	Miss Louise Suggs, Pine Tree G.C., Delray Beach, Fla.	83	78	80	80	321	250.00
	*Mrs. Paul Dye, Crooked Stick G.C., Carmel, Ind.	79	79	83	80	321	----
	*Miss Renee Powell, Clearview Par & Birdie C., East Canton, Ohio	79	83	76	83	321	----
36	Miss Marilynn Smith, Runaway Bay C.C., Jamaica, W.I.	85	73	83	81	322	240.00
37	Miss Penny Zavichas, Pueblo, Colo.	79	82	80	83	324	230.00
38	Miss Gloria Armstrong, Delray Beach C.C., Delray Beach, Fla.	81	79	87	79	326	215.00
	Mrs. David C. Fischer, Meadowbrook C.C., Ballwin, Mo.	83	78	81	84	326	215.00
	*Miss Polly Riley, River Crest C.C., Fort Worth, Texas	83	76	85	82	326	----
41	*Mrs. Donna Gilliam, California C.C., City of Industry, Calif.	78	78	89	82	327	----
42	*Miss Robbye King, Army Navy C.C., Arlington, Va.	84	78	84	82	328	----
43	*Miss Carol Ellis, Midland Hills C.C., St. Paul, Minn.	80	82	84	85	331	----

*Amateur. Gold, silver and bronze pins were awarded to the amateurs returning the lowest three scores.
Prize money totaling $20,680 was awarded.

1967
FIFTEENTH WOMEN'S OPEN CHAMPIONSHIP

Held at Virginia Hot Springs Golf and Tennis Club, (Cascades Course), Hot Springs, Va., June 29-July 2.
Yardage—6,191. Par 71. 98 Entries, 94 Starters.
Forty-one contestants who completed 72 holes.

						Score	Money Prize
1	*Miss Catherine Lacoste, Chantaco G.C., Saint Jean De Luz, France	71	70	74	79	294	------
2	Miss Susie Maxwell, Bogie Hills C.C., Oklahoma City, Okla.	71	75	76	74	296	$3,600.00
	Miss Beth Stone, Muskogee C.C., Muskogee, Okla.	75	76	71	74	296	3,600.00
4	Miss Sandra Haynie, Colonial C.C., Fort Worth, Texas	70	79	77	71	297	1,033.33
	Mrs. Murle Lindstrom, Pine Valley C.C., Fort Wayne, Ind.	75	74	73	75	297	1,033.33
	Miss Louise Suggs, Pine Tree G.C., Delray Beach, Fla.	76	74	74	73	297	1,033.33
7	Miss Margie Masters, East Bay C.C., Largo, Fla.	73	73	74	80	300	750.00
8	Miss Sharon K. Miller, Battle Creek C.C., Battle Creek, Mich.	76	80	74	71	301	630.00
	Miss Clifford Ann Creed, East Bay C.C., Largo, Fla.	75	75	76	75	301	630.00
	Miss Marilynn Smith, Runaway Bay C.C., Jamaica, W.I.	75	77	72	77	301	630.00
11	Miss Judy Torluemke, Ocean Reef C.C., N. Key Largo, Fla.	78	81	70	73	302	550.00
	Miss Shirley Englehorn, Purple Sage G.C., Caldwell, Idaho	73	74	76	79	302	550.00
	*Miss Dorothy Germain, Blytheville C.C., Blytheville, Ark.	75	78	79	70	302	----
14	Miss Sybil Griffin, Cypress Creek C.C., Boynton Beach, Fla.	71	79	75	78	303	520.00
15	Miss Betsy Rawls, Spartanburg C.C., Spartanburg, S.C.	73	82	75	75	305	470.00
	Miss Kathy Whitworth, Coronado Springs C.C., Coronado Springs, N.M.	81	76	73	75	305	470.00
	Miss Judy Kimball, Pleasant Valley C.C., Worcester, Mass.	78	76	73	78	305	470.00
	Miss Lesley Holbert, Ocean Reef C.C., N. Key Largo, Fla.	79	73	74	79	305	470.00
	*Mrs. Nancy Roth Syms, Elks G. & C.C., Elkhart, Ind.	76	75	78	76	305	----
20	Mrs. Marlene Bauer Hagge, Longboat Key C.C., Sarasota, Fla.	79	80	73	74	306	420.00
	Miss Carol Mann, Olympia Fields C.C., Olympia Fields, Ill.	77	72	82	75	306	420.00
	Miss Peggy Wilson, San Luis Rey C.C., Bonsall, Calif.	80	72	79	75	306	420.00
23	Mrs. Gerda Whalen, Northmoor C.C., Highland Park, Ill.	80	76	79	72	307	390.00
	Miss Sandra Palmer, St. Lucie C.C., Port St. Lucie, Fla.	80	76	76	75	307	390.00
	Miss Donna M. Caponi, De Bell G.C., Burbank, Calif.	74	76	76	81	307	390.00
26	*Mrs. Anne Quast Welts, Seattle G.C., Seattle, Wash.	78	78	75	77	308	----
27	Miss Sandra Spuzich, Speedway G.C., Indianapolis, Ind.	77	79	77	76	309	355.00
	Miss Mary Mills, Sunkist C.C., Biloxi, Miss.	84	75	73	77	309	355.00
	Miss Betsy Cullen, Tulsa C.C., Tulsa, Okla.	72	79	77	81	309	355.00
	Miss Kathy Ahern, Pharoahs C.C., Corpus Christi, Texas	78	74	74	83	309	355.00
31	Miss Sharron Moran, La Costa C.C., Carlsbad, Calif.	76	83	78	73	310	330.00
32	Miss Gloria Ehret, Ridgewood C.C., Danbury, Conn.	76	79	76	80	311	320.00
33	Miss JoAnn Prentice, Columbia C.C., Columbia, S.C.	81	76	78	77	312	305.00
	Miss Jan Ferraris, Olympic Club, San Francisco, Calif.	76	83	75	78	312	305.00
35	Miss Renee Powell, Clearview Par & Birdie G.C., E. Canton, Ohio	82	76	79	76	313	285.00
	Miss Barbara Romack, Atlantis C.C., Atlantis, Fla.	77	77	80	79	313	285.00
37	Mrs. Kathy Cornelius, Rancho Santa Fe G.C., Rancho Santa Fe, Calif.	76	78	80	81	315	270.00
	*Miss Barbara Jo Gabrielsen, Athens C.C., Athens, Ga.	73	78	81	83	315	----
39	Miss Patty Berg, St. Andrews G.C., West Chicago, Ill.	77	82	77	80	316	260.00
40	Miss Jean Bryant, Greenville, S.C.	75	80	82	83	320	250.00
41	*Mrs. Scott L. Probasco, Jr., Chattanooga G. & C.C., Chattanooga, Tenn.	78	79	84	80	321	----

*Amateur. Gold, silver and bronze pins were awarded to the amateurs returning the lowest three scores.
Prize money totaling $25,000 was awarded.

1968
SIXTEENTH WOMEN'S OPEN CHAMPIONSHIP

Held at Moselem Springs Golf Club, Fleetwood, Pa., July 4-7.
Yardage—6,232. Par 71. 104 Entries, 98 Starters.
Forty-four contestants who completed 72 holes.

						Score	Money Prize
1	Mrs. Susie Maxwell Berning, Incline Village G.C., Crystal Bay, Nev.	69	73	76	71	289	$5,000.00
2	Miss Mickey Wright, Oak Cliff C.C., Dallas, Texas	70	78	76	68	292	2,200.00
3	Miss Marilynn Smith, Runaway Bay C.C., Runaway Bay, Jamaica, W.I.	72	76	74	73	295	1,125.00
	Miss Carol Mann, Royal Oak Racquet & C.C., Cincinnati, Ohio	71	76	73	75	295	1,125.00
5	Miss Kathy Whitworth, Richardson, Texas	75	74	73	74	296	800.00
	Mrs. Murle Lindstrom, Pine Valley C.C., Fort Wayne, Ind.	73	73	75	75	296	800.00
7	Miss Clifford Ann Creed, East Bay G. & C.C., Largo, Fla.	77	73	76	71	297	680.00
8	Mrs. Gerda Whalen, Northmoor C.C., Highland Park, Ill.	75	72	79	73	299	630.00
9	Miss Sandra Spuzich, Speedway G.C., Indianapolis, Ind.	75	75	78	72	300	570.00
	Mrs. Judy Torluemke Rankin, Hogan Park G.C., Midland, Texas	75	76	74	75	300	570.00
	*Miss Phyllis Preuss, Coral Ridge C.C., Ft. Lauderdale, Fla.	73	76	73	78	300	----
12	Miss Sandra Post, Oakville G. & C.C., Oakville, Ont., Canada	73	76	77	75	301	540.00
13	Miss Pam Barnett, Menomonee Falls, Wis.	77	75	74	76	302	510.00
	Miss Judy Kimball, Pleasant Valley C.C., Worcester, Mass.	77	76	70	79	302	510.00
	*Miss Shelley Hamlin, University-Sequoia Sunnyside C.C., Fresno, Calif.	79	77	74	72	302	----
	*Miss Catherine Lacoste, Chantaco G.C., Saint Jean De Luz, France	74	78	77	73	302	----
17	Miss Sharron Moran, Park Ridge C.C., Park Ridge, Ill.	78	73	78	74	303	460.00
	Miss Mary Mills, Edgewater G.C., Biloxi, Miss.	80	74	73	76	303	460.00
	Miss Ruth Jessen, Seattle, Wash.	72	77	77	77	303	460.00
	*Mrs. Nancy Roth Syms, Elks G. & C.C., Elkhart, Ind.	77	79	75	72	303	----
21	Miss Sandra Palmer, St. Lucie C.C., Port St. Lucie, Fla.	76	77	76	75	304	430.00
	*Mrs. Dorothy Germain Porter, Riverton C.C., Riverton, N.J.	79	77	76	72	304	----
23	Miss Jane Woodworth, Sunset G.C., Hollywood, Fla.	75	80	78	72	305	395.00
	Miss Betsy Cullen, Tulsa C.C., Tulsa, Okla.	77	76	78	74	305	395.00
	Miss Donna Caponi, De Bell G.C., Burbank, Calif.	76	79	76	74	305	395.00
	Miss JoAnn Prentice, Columbia C.C., Columbia, S.C.	74	75	81	75	305	395.00
	Miss Mary Lou Daniel, Audubon C.C., Louisville, Ky.	82	73	73	77	305	395.00
	Miss Sandra Haynie, Colonial C.C., Fort Worth, Texas	78	78	72	77	305	395.00
29	Miss Gail Davis, Victoria C.C., Riverside, Calif.	75	76	82	73	306	340.00
	Miss Patty Berg, St. Andrews G.C., West Chicago, Ill.	75	77	78	76	306	340.00
	Miss Sybil Griffin, Cypress Creek C.C., Boynton Beach, Fla.	75	75	79	77	306	340.00
	Miss Louise Suggs, Pine Tree G.C., Delray Beach, Fla.	75	76	77	78	306	340.00
	Miss Margie Masters, East Bay G. & C.C., Largo, Fla.	77	73	74	82	306	340.00
	*Mrs. Anne Quast Welts, Bellingham G. & C.C., Bellingham, Wash.	78	74	76	78	306	----
35	Miss Linda L. Craft, Eastern Hills C.C., Garland, Texas	75	77	78	77	307	310.00
36	Miss Sharon K. Miller, Battle Creek C.C., Battle Creek, Mich.	79	76	77	76	308	295.00
	Miss Betsy Rawls, Spartanburg C.C., Spartanburg, S.C.	74	76	79	79	308	295.00
38	Miss Kathleen Ahern, Pharoahs C.C., Corpus Christi, Texas	76	78	76	79	309	280.00
39	Mrs. Althea Gibson Darben, Montclair, N.J.	78	77	78	78	311	270.00
40	*Miss Roberta Albers, Temple Terrace G. & C.C., Temple Terrace, Fla.	75	80	81	79	315	----
	*Mrs. Helen Sigel Wilson, Philadelphia C.C., Gladwyne, Pa.	79	77	79	80	315	----
42	*Miss Lancy Smith, Park C.C., Williamsville, N.Y.	79	76	82	80	317	----
43	Miss Lesley Holbert, Ocean Reef Club, N. Key Largo, Fla.	81	73	85	82	321	260.00
	*Mrs. Paul Dye, Jr., Crooked Stick G.C., Carmel, Ind.	79	76	87	79	321	----

*Amateur. Gold, silver and bronze pins were awarded to the amateurs returning the lowest three scores.
Prize money totaling $24,950 was awarded.

1969
SEVENTEENTH WOMEN'S OPEN CHAMPIONSHIP

Held at Scenic Hills Country Club, Pensacola, Fla., June 26-29.
Yardage—6,308. Par 73. 99 Entries, 98 Starters.
Forty-three contestants who completed 72 holes.

						Score	Money Prize
1	Miss Donna Caponi, De Bell G.C., Burbank, Calif.	74	76	75	69	294	$5,000.00
2	Miss Peggy Wilson, Boca Raton, Fla.	71	76	75	73	295	2,500.00
3	Miss Kathy Whitworth, Richardson, Texas	76	78	69	73	296	1,500.00
4	Miss JoAnn Prentice, Columbia C.C., Columbia, S.C.	73	71	79	75	298	1,033.34
	Miss Sybil Griffin, Cypress Creek C.C., Boynton Beach, Fla.	73	76	77	72	298	1,033.33
	Miss Ruth Jessen, Tamarisk C.C., Palm Springs, Calif.	73	72	75	78	298	1,033.33
7	Miss Shirley Englehorn, Indian Wells C.C., Indian Wells, Calif.	72	76	77	76	301	850.00
8	Miss Mary Mills, Sunkist C.C., Biloxi, Miss.	75	80	71	76	302	718.00
	Mrs. Murle Lindstrom, Mission Valley C.C., Venice, Fla.	74	79	74	75	302	718.00
	Miss Mickey Wright, Dallas, Texas	76	79	76	71	302	718.00
	Mrs. Clifford Ann Creed Gordon, East Ridge G. & C.C., Shreveport, La.	76	76	75	75	302	718.00
	Miss Louise Suggs, Pine Tree G.C., Delray Beach, Fla.	76	78	75	73	302	718.00
13	Miss Sandra Spuzich, Speedway G.C., Indianapolis, Ind.	76	72	79	76	303	620.00
	Mrs. Kathy Cornelius, Green Tree G. & Tennis Club, Victorville, Calif.	80	74	76	73	303	620.00
	Miss Sandra Haynie, Runaway Bay G.C., Bridgeport, Texas	76	73	74	80	303	620.00
16	Miss Beth Stone, Ocean Reef C., North Key Largo, Fla.	77	74	74	79	304	560.00
	Mrs. Susie Maxwell Berning, Incline Village G.C., Incline Village, Nev.	78	78	75	73	304	560.00
	Miss Marilynn Smith, Jupiter, Fla.	80	74	77	73	304	560.00
	*Miss Phyllis Preuss, Coral Ridge C.C., Ft. Lauderdale, Fla.	79	77	79	69	304	----
20	Mrs. Gerda Whalen, River Plantation C.C., Conroe, Texas	78	78	76	73	305	503.34
	Miss Betsy Rawls, Spartanburg C.C., Spartanburg, S.C.	77	80	76	72	305	503.33
	Mrs. Susan Little, Brae Burn C.C., Houston, Texas	74	78	77	76	305	503.33
23	Miss Sharon K. Miller, Battle Creek C.C., Battle Creek, Mich.	75	79	75	77	306	475.00
	Miss Sherry Wilder, Royal Oak C.C., Titusville, Fla.	78	75	76	77	306	475.00
	*Miss Shelley Hamlin, University Sequoia Sunnyside C.C., Fresno, Calif.	86	72	76	72	306	----
26	Miss Carol Mann, Royal Oak Racquet & C.C., Cincinnati, Ohio	77	78	77	75	307	455.00
	Mrs. Marlene B. Hagge, Longboat Key C.C., Sarasota, Fla.	80	75	76	76	307	455.00
28	Miss Jane Blalock, Portsmouth C.C., Portsmouth, N.H.	77	76	81	75	309	440.00
29	Miss Betsy Cullen, Tulsa C.C., Tulsa, Okla.	78	77	76	79	310	420.00
	Miss Sharron Moran, Shamrock C.C., Tulsa, Okla.	82	76	76	76	310	420.00
	Miss Signa Jean Quandt, Pasadena C.C., St. Petersburg, Fla.	78	80	75	77	310	420.00
32	Miss Sandra Palmer, Fort Worth, Texas	78	80	76	78	312	400.00
	*Miss Connie Day, Chattanooga G. & C.C., Chattanooga, Tenn.	76	81	80	75	312	----
	*Mrs. Scott L. Probasco, Jr., Chattanooga G. & C.C., Chattanooga, Tenn.	76	76	76	84	312	----
35	Miss Judy Kimball, Pleasant Valley C.C., Sutton, Mass.	76	80	79	79	314	390.00
36	Miss Kathy Ahern, Phoenix, Ariz.	76	82	78	79	315	380.00
	*Mrs. Paul Dye, Jr., Crooked Stick G.C., Carmel, Ind.	79	78	80	78	315	----
38	*Miss Beth Barry, Isle Dauphine C.C., Dauphin Island, Ala.	79	79	79	79	316	----
	*Miss Lancy Smith, The Park C.C., Williamsville, N.Y.	80	78	82	76	316	----
40	Miss Pam Barnett, Reno, Nev.	80	77	79	81	317	360.00
	Miss Debbie Austin, Oneida, N.Y.	76	81	79	81	317	360.00
	Miss Joyce Kazmierski, Colorado Springs, Colo.	77	75	82	83	317	360.00
43	Miss Lesley Holbert, C.C. of Miami, Miami, Fla.	79	76	82	81	318	340.00

*Amateur. Gold, silver and bronze pins were awarded to the amateurs returning the lowest three scores.
Prize money totaling $31,040 was awarded.

1970
EIGHTEENTH WOMEN'S OPEN CHAMPIONSHIP

Held at Muskogee Country Club, Muskogee, Okla., July 2-5.
Yardage—6,210. Par 71. 131 Entries, 126 Starters.

Forty contestants who completed 72 holes.

						Score	Money Prize
1	Miss Donna Caponi, North Hollywood, Calif.	69	70	71	77	287	$5,000.00
2	Miss Sandra Haynie, Runaway Bay G.C., Runaway Bay, Texas	71	72	71	74	288	2,000.00
	Miss Sandra Spuzich, Speedway G.C., Indianapolis, Ind.	72	72	70	74	288	2,000.00
4	Miss Sandra Palmer, Lake Arrowhead C.C., Lake Arrowhead, Calif.	73	71	71	74	289	1,100.00
	Miss Kathy Whitworth, Ocean Shores C.C., Ocean Shores, Wash.	71	71	76	71	289	1,100.00
6	Miss Sharon K. Miller, Battle Creek C.C., Battle Creek, Mich.	70	77	74	69	290	900.00
7	Miss JoAnn Prentice, Columbia C.C., Columbia, S.C.	72	75	70	74	291	850.00
8	Miss Carol Mann, Royal Oak Racquet & C.C., Cincinnati, Ohio	69	70	77	76	292	800.00
9	Miss Shirley Englehorn, Indian Wells C.C., Indian Wells, Calif.	70	74	74	75	293	725.00
	Miss Clifford Ann Creed, East Bay G. & C.C., Largo, Fla.	73	73	74	73	293	725.00
11	Miss Peggy J. Wilson, University Park C.C., Boca Raton, Fla.	71	75	75	73	294	670.00
	Miss Marilynn Smith, The Yacht & C.C., Stuart, Fla.	72	73	77	72	294	670.00
	*Miss Cynthia Hill, Pasadena G.C., St. Petersburg, Fla.	72	70	75	77	294	PIN
14	Mrs. Gerda Whalen, River Plantation G.C., Conroe, Texas	71	74	75	75	295	620.00
	Miss Kathy Ahern, Phoenix, Ariz.	71	74	76	74	295	620.00
	Miss Betsy Rawls, Spartanburg C.C., Spartanburg, S.C.	72	75	77	71	295	620.00
17	Mrs. Michael J. Skala, El Dorado Royal C.C., Shingle Springs, Calif.	72	74	79	71	296	580.00
	*Miss Jane Fassinger, New Castle C.C., New Castle, Pa.	71	73	78	74	296	PIN
19	Miss Janie Blalock, Portsmouth C.C., Portsmouth, N.H.	73	74	77	73	297	550.00
	Miss Pam Barnett, Charlotte, N.C.	77	68	80	72	297	550.00
21	Miss Judy Kimball, Pleasant Valley C.C., Worcester, Mass.	75	74	73	76	298	497.50
	Mrs. Murle Lindstrom, Mission Valley G. & C.C., Venice, Fla.	73	76	73	76	298	497.50
	Mrs. Susan M. Little, Houston C.C., Houston, Texas	74	74	79	71	298	497.50
	Mrs. Joanne Gunderson Carner, Palm Beach Nat'l. G.C., Lake Worth, Fla.	73	74	78	73	298	497.50
	*Miss Jane Bastanchury, California C.C., Whittier, Calif.	74	74	75	75	298	PIN
26	Miss Betsy Cullen, Tulsa C.C., Tulsa, Okla.	71	77	76	75	299	455.00
	Miss Gloria Ehret, Riverlakes C.C., Dallas, Texas	74	75	74	76	299	455.00
	Mrs. Althea Gibson Darben, East Orange, N.J.	73	75	74	77	299	455.00
	Mrs. Marlene B. Hagge, DeSoto Lakes C.C., Sarasota, Fla.	72	76	74	77	299	455.00
	*Miss Shelley Hamlin, University Sequoia-Sunnyside C.C., Fresno, Calif.	73	75	76	75	299	----
31	Miss Patty Berg, St. Andrews G.C., Chicago, Ill.	74	75	76	75	300	430.00
32	*Miss Nancy Hager, Northwood C., Dallas, Texas	75	72	79	75	301	----
	*Miss Martha Jett, Western Hills C.C., Little Rock, Ark.	76	74	78	73	301	----
34	Miss Lesley Holbert, C.C. of Miami, Miami, Fla.	75	75	75	77	302	415.00
	Miss Sharron Moran, Morton Grove, Ill.	72	76	74	80	302	415.00
36	Miss Kathy Farrer, Birmingham C.C., Birmingham, Ala.	76	74	78	77	305	400.00
37	Miss Mickey Wright, Shady Oaks C.C., Fort Worth, Texas	71	78	79	78	306	390.00
38	Miss Gail Denenberg, Orange County G.C., Middletown, N.Y.	76	72	81	79	308	370.00
	Miss Betty Burfeindt, Canaan, N.Y.	76	73	78	81	308	370.00
	Miss Norma Diane Owens, Wellman C.C., Johnsonville, S.C.	76	74	76	82	308	370.00

*Amateur.
Prize money totaling $31,150 was awarded.

1971
NINETEENTH WOMEN'S OPEN CHAMPIONSHIP

Held at Kahkwa Club, Erie, Pennsylvania, June 24–27.
Yardage—6,306 Par 72
141 Entries, 134 Starters.

Fifty-four contestants who qualified for 72-hole holes.

						Score	Money Prize
1	Mrs. JoAnne Gunderson Carner, Palm Beach National C.C., Lake Worth, Fla.	70	73	72	73	288	$5,000.00
2	Miss Kathy Whitworth, Richardson, Texas	73	77	73	72	295	2,500.00
3	Miss Jane Blalock, C.C. of New Seabury, Mashpee, Mass.	75	73	74	77	299	1,233.34
	Miss Donna Caponi, No. Hollywood, Calif.	70	75	77	77	299	1,233.33
	Miss Mickey Wright, Shady Oaks C.C., Fort Worth, Texas	73	75	75	76	299	1,233.33
	*Miss Jane Bastanchury, California C.C., Whittier, Calif.	72	77	76	74	299	PIN
7	Mrs. Kathy Cornelius, Sierra Estrella G.C., Phoenix, Ariz.	73	78	73	76	300	875.00
	Miss Lesley Holbert, Hialeah, Fla.	71	75	81	73	300	875.00
9	*Miss Shelley Hamlin, University-Sequoia Sunnyside C.C., Fresno, Calif.	77	76	73	75	301	PIN
	*Miss Martha Wilkinson, California C.C., Whittier, Calif.	74	78	77	72	301	PIN
11	Mrs. Murle Lindstrom Breer, Nashville, Tenn.	75	72	77	78	302	775.00
	Miss Mary Mills, Broadwater Beach G. & C.C., Biloxi, Miss.	75	72	73	82	302	775.00
13	Mrs. Gerda Whalen Boykin, Plantation C.C., Conroe, Texas	77	75	78	73	303	690.00
	Miss Betsy Cullen, Tulsa C.C., Tulsa, Okla.	76	76	76	75	303	690.00
15	Mrs. Sandra Post Elliott, Lido G.C., Oakville, Ontario, Canada	79	77	76	72	304	610.00
	Mrs. Marlene B. Hagge, De Soto Lakes C.C., Sarasota, Fla.	74	78	75	77	304	610.00
	Miss Carol Mann, Hunt Valley Inn & G.C., Hunt Valley, Md.	75	77	76	76	304	610.00
	Miss Pam Higgins, Palm Springs G.C., Palm Springs, Calif.	77	77	76	74	304	610.00
	Miss Beth Stone, Muskogee, Okla.	74	77	73	80	304	610.00
	Miss Sandra Haynie, Runaway Bay G.C., Runaway Bay, Texas	75	78	78	73	304	610.00
21	Miss Mary Lou Daniel, Louisville, Ky.	74	79	76	77	306	530.00
	Miss Marilynn Smith, Yacht & C.C., Stuart, Fla.	74	77	79	76	306	530.00
23	Miss JoAnn Prentice, Columbia C.C., Columbia, S.C.	77	74	77	79	307	500.00
24	Miss Pam Barnett, Myers Park C.C., Charlotte, N.C.	77	80	75	76	308	485.00
	Miss Sharon K. Miller, Battle Creek C.C., Battle Creek, Mich.	74	82	73	79	308	485.00
	*Mrs. Marlene Stewart Streit, Lookout Point C.C., Fonthill, Ontario, Canada	76	78	77	77	308	----
27	Mrs. Susie Maxwell Berning, Incline Village G.C., Incline Village, Nev.	80	76	77	76	309	465.00
	Miss Judy Kimball, Pleasant Valley C.C., Sutton, Mass.	77	77	76	79	309	465.00
29	Miss Kathy Ahern, Phoenix, Ariz.	78	79	74	79	310	430.00
	Miss Debbie Austin, Oneida Silversmiths G.C., Oneida, N.Y.	78	80	78	74	310	430.00
	Miss Hisako Higuchi, Osaka, Japan	79	79	77	75	310	430.00
	Miss Barbara Myers, Cherry Hill C.C., Andrews, S.C.	78	81	73	78	310	430.00
	Miss Sandra Spuzich, Speedway G.C., Indianapolis, Ind.	78	81	75	76	310	430.00
34	Miss Sue Roberts, Columbus, Ohio	78	81	77	75	311	395.00
	Miss Louise Suggs, Pine Tree G.C., Delray Beach, Fla.	81	74	77	79	311	395.00
36	Miss Betsy Rawls, Spartanburg C.C., Spartanburg, S.C.	77	78	81	77	313	380.00
37	Miss Sandra Palmer, Lake Arrowhead C.C., Lake Arrowhead, Calif.	79	78	78	79	314	355.00
	Miss Clifford Ann Creed, East Bay G. & C.C., Largo, Fla.	82	76	79	77	314	355.00
	Mrs. Michael J. Skala, El Dorado Royal C.C., Shingle Springs, Calif.	79	74	80	81	314	355.00
	Miss Cynthia Sullivan, Doral C.C., Miami, Fla.	77	80	78	79	314	355.00
41	*Miss Connie Day, Chattanooga G. & C.C., Chattanooga, Tenn.	80	76	78	80	314	----
	*Mrs. Dorothy Germain Porter, Riverton C.C., Riverton, N.J.	75	84	79	76	314	----
43	*Miss Lida Fee Matthews, Elks C.C., Portsmouth, Ohio	73	82	76	84	315	----
	*Miss Lancy Smith, Park C.C., Williamsville, N.Y.	76	83	79	77	315	----
45	Miss Jan Ferraris, C.C. of New Seabury, Mashpee, Mass.	77	80	82	77	316	330.00
46	Miss Sherry Wilder, Grand Rapids, Mich.	80	79	81	77	317	320.00
47	*Miss Sally Little, Metropolitan G.C., Cape Town, South Africa	78	79	76	85	318	----
48	Miss Sharon Moran, Morton Grove, Ill.	79	80	78	82	319	310.00
49	Miss Janet Tina Caponi, Lakeside G.C. of Hollywood, North Hollywood, Calif.	76	79	86	79	320	295.00
	Miss Kathy McMullen, Bradenton, Fla.	80	77	81	82	320	295.00
51	Miss Gail Denenberg, Orange County G.C., Middletown, N.Y.	75	81	77	88	321	280.00
52	Miss DeDe Owens, Wellman C.C., Johnsonville, S.C.	77	78	83	84	322	270.00
53	Miss V. Joyce Kazmierski, Detroit, Mich.	79	80	81	83	323	255.00
	Mrs. Sue Little, Houston C.C., Houston, Texas	82	75	86	80	323	255.00

*Amateur. Golf, silver and bronze pins were awarded to the amateurs returning the lowest three scores.
Prize money totaling $34,450 was awarded.

1972
TWENTIETH WOMEN'S OPEN CHAMPIONSHIP

Held at Winged Foot Golf Club (East Course), Mamaroneck, New York
June 29–July 2
Yardage–6,226. Par 72. 176 Entries, 150 Starters.
Fifty-three contestants who completed 72 holes.

						Score	Money Prize
1	Mrs. Susie Maxwell Berning, Incline Village C.C., Incline Village, Nev.	79	73	76	71	299	$6,000.00
2	Miss Kathy Ahern, Denton, Texas	74	80	76	70	300	2,200.00
	Miss Pam Barnett, Hickory Hills C.C., Pascagoula, Miss.	73	76	75	76	300	2,200.00
	Mrs. Judy Torluemke Rankin, Midland, Texas	76	75	76	73	300	2,200.00
5	Miss Betty Burfeindt, Canaan, N.Y.	75	78	74	75	302	1,500.00
6	Miss Mickey Wright, Pine Tree G.C., Delray Beach, Fla.	77	80	76	71	304	1,350.00
	*Mrs. Jane Bastanchury Booth, California C.C., Whittier, Calif.	79	75	78	72	304	PIN
	Miss Gloria Ehret, Riverlakes C.C., Dallas, Texas	74	74	80	76	304	1,350.00
9	Miss Carol Mann, Hunt Valley Inn & G.C., Hunt Valley, Md.	79	77	78	71	305	1,150.00
	*Miss Carol Semple, Allegheny C.C., Sewickley, Pa.	79	79	74	73	305	PIN
	Miss Jocelyne Bourassa, Shawinigan G.C., Shawinigan, Quebec, Canada	76	75	78	76	305	1,150.00
12	Miss Sharon K. Miller, Battle Creek C.C., Battle Creek, Mich.	79	74	79	74	306	1,025.00
	Miss Betsy Cullen, Lakeway C.C., Austin, Texas	73	78	78	77	306	1,025.00
14	Miss Hisako Higuchi, Los Angeles, Calif.	78	77	79	73	307	852.00
	Miss Janie Blalock, C.C. of New Seabury, Waquoit, Mass.	78	78	77	74	307	852.00
	Miss JoAnn Prentice, Tuckaway G.C., Oneonta, Ala.	79	78	75	75	307	852.00
	Miss Sandra Haynie, Runaway Bay Resort, Runaway Bay, Texas	83	76	73	75	307	852.00
	Miss Shirley Englehorn, Indian Wells C.C., Palm Desert, Calif.	72	75	82	78	307	852.00
19	Miss Shelley Hamlin, University Sequoia-Sunnyside C.C., Fresno, Calif.	78	74	79	77	308	630.00
	Miss Sandra Palmer, Glen Garden G. & C.C., Fort Worth, Texas	78	76	77	77	308	630.00
	Miss Sue Roberts, Columbus, Ohio	77	78	76	77	308	630.00
	Miss Kathy Whitworth, Richardson, Texas	79	79	72	78	308	630.00
	Mrs. Kathy Cornelius, Sierra Estrella G.C., Phoenix, Ariz.	74	80	75	79	308	630.00
	Miss Betsy Rawls, Lakeway C.C., Austin, Texas	77	76	74	81	308	630.00
25	Mrs. Gerda Wnalen Boykin, River Plantation C.C., Conroe, Texas	81	76	81	71	309	530.00
	Mrs. Donna Caponi Young, Woodland Hills, Calif.	80	75	75	79	309	530.00
27	Mrs. Marlene B. Hagge, Palm-Aire at Sarasota, Sarasota, Fla.	78	79	80	73	310	500.00
28	Miss Peggy Wilson, University Park C.C., Boca Raton, Fla.	78	75	82	76	311	490.00
29	Miss Mary Mills, Hickory Hills C.C., Pascagoula, Miss.	80	78	78	76	312	465.00
	Miss Debbie Austin, Oneida, N.Y.	80	76	79	77	312	465.00
	Mrs. JoAnne Gunderson Carner, Palm Beach Nat'l. G. & C.C., Lake Worth, Fla.	79	79	75	79	312	465.00
	Miss Clifford Ann Creed, Rapides G. & C.C., Alexandria, La.	79	74	78	81	312	465.00
33	*Miss Laura Baugh, California C.C., Whittier, Calif.	79	80	77	78	314	PIN
34	Mrs. Murle Lindstrom Breer, Par Golf Center, Fort Wayne, Ind.	83	76	82	74	315	425.00
	*Mrs. Nancy Roth Syms, Broadmoor G.C., Colorado Springs, Colo.	81	79	78	77	315	----
	Miss DeDe Owens, Losantiville C.C., Cincinnati, Ohio	77	75	85	78	315	425.00
	Miss Pam Higgins, Palm Springs G.C., Palm Springs, Calif.	77	78	81	79	315	425.00
	Miss Marilynn Smith, The Yacht & C.C., Stuart, Fla.	76	80	80	79	315	425.00
39	Miss Louise Suggs, Pine Tree G.C., Delray Beach, Fla.	78	80	82	76	316	400.00
40	Miss Sally Little, Cleveland, Ohio	82	79	81	75	317	390.00
41	Miss Judy Kimball, Pleasant Valley C.C., Sutton, Mass.	76	83	83	77	319	375.00
	*Mrs. Paul Dye, Jr., Crooked Stick G.C., Carmel, Ind.	78	80	82	79	319	----
	Miss Barbara Myer, Cherry Hill C.C., Andrews, S.C.	78	82	80	79	319	375.00
44	Mrs. Mary Lou Daniel Crocker, Iroquois G.C., Louisville, Ky.	79	82	82	77	320	360.00
45	Miss Renee Powell, Clearview G.C., East Canton, Ohio	84	76	85	76	321	340.00
	*Mrs. Martha Wilkinson Kirouac, California C.C., Whittier, Calif.	79	82	82	78	321	----
	*Mrs. Marlene Stewart Streit, Lookout Point G.C., Fonthill, Ontario, Canada	78	81	81	81	321	----
	Miss Masako (Marbo) Sasaki, Los Angeles, Calif.	74	80	84	83	321	340.00
	Miss Jan Ferraris, C.C. of New Seabury, Waquoit, Mass.	80	78	79	84	321	340.00
50	Mrs. Janet Caponi LePera, Toftrees C.C. & Lodge, State College, Pa.	82	79	84	77	322	315.00
	Miss LeNore Beserra, Calabasas Park C.C., Calabasas, Calif.	78	82	81	81	322	315.00
52	*Miss Connie Day, Chattanooga G. & C.C., Chattanooga, Tenn.	77	82	90	80	329	----
53	*Miss Judith Jane Johnson, Fox Chapel G.C., Pittsburgh, Pa.	82	79	89	80	330	----

*Amateur.

1973

TWENTY-FIRST WOMEN'S OPEN CHAMPIONSHIP

Held at Country Club of Rochester, Rochester, New York

July 19-22

Yardage—6,120. Par 72. 150 Entries, 142 Starters.

Fifty-nine contestants who completed 72 holes.

						Score	Money Prize
1	Mrs. Susie Maxwell Berning, Incline Village C.C., Incline Village, Nev.	72	77	69	72	290	$6,000.00
2	Miss Gloria Ehret, Spring Valley C.C., Dallas, Texas	75	75	74	71	295	2,500.00
	Miss Shelley Hamlin, Sunnyside C.C., Fresno, Calif.	76	70	75	74	295	2,500.00
4	*Mrs. Anne Quast Sander, Broadmoor G.C., Seattle, Wash.	74	72	76	74	296	PIN
5	Miss Pam Higgins, Palm Springs G.C., Palm Springs, Calif.	72	76	70	79	297	1,600.00
6	Mrs. Judy Torluemke Rankin, Midland C.C., Midland, Texas	77	72	75	74	298	1,400.00
	Miss Mary Mills, University Park C.C., Boca Raton, Fla.	74	73	75	76	298	1,400.00
	Miss Sandra Palmer, del Safari C.C., Palm Desert, Calif.	76	72	74	76	298	1,400.00
9	Miss Janie Blalock, C.C. of New Seabury, Cape Cod, Mass.	78	76	72	73	299	1,116.67
	Miss Sue Roberts, Columbus, Ohio	71	81	73	74	299	1,116.67
	Mrs. Mary Lou Crocker, Iroquois G.C., Louisville, Ky.	75	78	69	77	299	1,116.67
12	Miss Sandra Spuzich, Speedway G.C., Indianapolis, Ind.	75	79	74	72	300	975.00
	Miss Carole Jo Skala, El Dorado Royal C.C., Shingle Springs, Calif.	78	74	74	74	300	975.00
14	*Miss Beth Barry, Isle Dauphine C.C., Dauphin Island, Ala.	74	74	78	75	301	PIN
	Miss Margie Masters, Belleair, Fla.	74	75	78	74	301	875.00
	Miss Sharon K. Miller, Battle Creek C.C., Battle Creek, Mich.	73	69	78	81	301	875.00
17	*Miss Mary Budke, Riverwood G.C., Dundee, Ore.	77	76	76	73	302	PIN
	Mrs. Murle Lindstrom Breer, Richland C.C., Nashville, Tenn.	76	75	75	76	302	720.00
	Miss Susie McAllister, Beaumont, Texas	77	75	76	74	302	720.00
	Mrs. Kathy Cornelius, Goodyear G. & C.C., Litchfield Park, Ariz.	74	77	76	75	302	720.00
	Mrs. Mary Dwyer Horner, Seneca Lake C.C., Geneva, N. Y.	75	76	76	75	302	720.00
	Miss Marilynn Smith, Mariner Sands C.C., Stuart, Fla.	75	76	75	76	302	720.00
23	*Miss Liana Zambresky, Monterey Peninsula C.C., Pebble Beach, Calif.	75	78	75	75	303	—
	*Mrs. Jane Bastanchury Booth, California C.C., Whittier, Calif.	73	74	77	79	303	—
25	*Miss Hollis Stacy, Savannah G.C., Savannah, Ga.	77	77	73	77	304	—
	*Mrs. Marlene Stewart Streit, Lookout Point G.C., Fonthill, Ontario, Canada	72	76	78	78	304	—
	Miss Amie Amizich, Bardmoor G. & C.C., Largo, Fla.	75	78	76	75	304	580.00
	Mrs. Donna Caponi Young, Woodland Hills, Calif.	78	73	76	77	304	580.00
	Miss Laura Baugh, California C.C., Long Beach, Calif.	73	79	77	75	304	580.00
30	Miss Jan Ferraris, C.C. of New Seabury, Cape Cod, Mass.	78	71	78	78	305	520.00
	Mrs. Barbara White Boddie, Broadmoor G.C., Shreveport, La.	70	81	79	75	305	520.00
	Miss Kathy Whitworth, Errol Estate Inn & C.C., Apopka, Fla.	78	74	76	77	305	520.00
33	*Miss Cynthia Hill, Broadmoor G.C., Colorado Springs, Colo.	68	79	79	80	306	—
	Miss Betty Burfeindt, Palm Springs, Calif.	80	73	74	79	306	490.00
35	*Miss Carol Semple, Allegheny C.C., Sewickley, Pa.	73	77	81	76	307	—
	*Miss Brenda Goldsmith, Pecan Valley G.C., San Antonio, Texas	76	76	77	78	307	—
	Miss V. Joyce Kazmierski, Barwick G.C., Delray Beach, Fla.	79	75	78	75	307	470.00
	Miss Gail Denenberg, Orange County G.C., Middletown, N. Y.	75	80	75	77	307	470.00
	Miss Beth Stone, LaGorce C.C., Miami Beach, Fla.	78	75	76	78	307	470.00
40	Mrs. Janet Caponi LePera, Toftrees C.C. & Lodge, State College, Pa.	77	74	79	78	308	435.00
	Miss Clifford Ann Creed, Rapides Golf & C..C., Alexandria, La.	76	79	75	78	308	435.00
	Miss Kathy Martin, Los Robles Greens C.C., Thousand Oaks, Calif.	73	73	82	80	308	435.00
	Miss Catherine M. Duggan, Ft. Lauderdale C.C., Ft. Lauderdale, Fla.	78	77	72	81	308	435.00
44	Miss Brenda High, Park Mammouth G. Resort, Park City, Ky.	77	78	77	77	309	395.00
	Miss Judy Kimball, Pleasant Valley C.C., Sutton, Mass.	75	77	78	79	309	395.00
	Mrs. Andy C. Fischer, Sugar Valley C.C., Dayton, Ohio	78	76	77	78	309	395.00
	Miss JoAnn Washam, Woodhaven C.C., Ft. Worth, Texas	78	76	75	80	309	395.00
48	Miss Katherine M. Hite, Florence C.C., Florence, S. C.	81	72	78	80	311	370.00
49	Mrs. JoAnne Carner, Palm Beach National G. & C.C., Lake Worth, Fla.	75	75	82	80	312	345.00
	Miss Mardell J. Wilkins, Vista, Calif.	78	77	77	80	312	345.00
	Miss Sandra Post, Oakville G. & C.C., Oakville, Ontario, Canada	78	77	77	80	312	345.00
	Miss Kathy Farrer, Woodhaven C.C., Ft. Worth, Texas	78	75	79	80	312	345.00
53	Miss Kathleen Ahern, Ft. Worth, Texas	75	78	79	81	313	315.00
	Miss Betsy Rawls, Lakeway C.C., Austin, Texas	71	82	84	76	313	315.00
55	Mrs. Mary Alice Canney, Chantilly National G. & C.C., Centreville, Va.	76	79	79	80	314	300.00
56	Miss Karolyn K. Kertzman, Carlton Oaks C.C., Santee, Calif.	80	74	85	80	319	290.00
57	*Mrs. Richard Meister, Lawrence Park G.C., Lawrence Park, Pa.	77	78	84	81	320	—
	Miss Joyce Deese, Northridge, Calif.	78	77	79	86	320	280.00
59	Miss Mary Bryan, Errol Estate Inn & C.C., Apopka, Fla.	80	75	83	84	322	270.00

*Amateur. Gold, silver, and bronze pins were awarded to the amateurs returning the lowest three scores.

Prize money totaling $39,490 was awarded.

1974

TWENTY-SECOND UNITED STATES WOMEN'S OPEN CHAMPIONSHIP

Held at La Grange Country Club, La Grange, Illinois, July 18-21

Yardage—6,266. Par 72. 155 Entries, 150 Starters.

						Score	Money Prize
1	Miss Sandra Haynie, Dallas, Texas	73	73	74	75	295	$6,073.75
2	Miss Beth Stone, La Gorce C.C., Miami Beach, Fla.	75	74	76	71	296	2,573.75
	Miss Carol Mann, Towson, Md.	72	72	77	75	296	2,573.75
4	Miss Kathy Whitworth, Errol Estate Inn & C. C., Apopka, Fla.	75	77	74	71	297	1,623.75
	Mrs. JoAnne Carner, Palm Beach National G. & C.C., Lake Worth, Fla.	77	72	71	77	297	1,623.75
6	Miss Sandra Post, Cypress Creek C.C., Boynton Beach, Fla.	81	72	71	74	298	1,473.75
7	Mrs. Donna Caponi Young, Los Angeles, Calif.	71	76	79	73	299	1,373.75
	*Miss Deborah Massey, Saucon Valley C.C., Bethlehem, Pa.	71	73	80	75	299	PIN
9	Miss Ruth Jessen, Pinetop C.C., Pinetop, Ariz.	77	71	71	81	300	1,273.75
	*Mrs. Jane Bastanchury Booth, California C.C., Whittier, Calif.	76	74	76	74	300	PIN
11	Mrs. Susie Maxwell Berning, Keauhou-Kona C.C., Kona, Hawaii	73	77	75	76	301	1,173.75
12	Miss Sandra Spuzich, Indianapolis, Ind.	74	74	72	82	302	1,123.75
	*Miss Bonnie Lauer, Edgewood C.C., Union Lake, Mich.	74	72	80	76	302	PIN
14	Miss Bonnie Bryant, Oakland, Calif.	77	78	81	67	303	998.75
	Mrs. Murle Lindstrom Breer, Bardmoor C.C., St. Petersburg, Fla.	77	77	76	73	303	998.75
	Miss Sue Roberts, Fountains G.C., West Palm Beach, Fla.	82	72	72	77	303	998.75
	Miss Hollis Stacy, Savannah G.C., Savannah, Ga.	77	75	72	79	303	998.75
18	Mrs. Carole Jo Skala, Cameron Park C.C., Shingle Springs, Calif.	77	74	79	74	304	833.75
	Miss Gail Denenberg, Orange County G.C., Middletown, N. Y.	77	74	78	75	304	833.75
	Miss Mary Mills, University Park C.C., Boca Raton, Fla.	78	76	75	75	304	833.75
	*Mrs. Anne Quast Sander, Broadmoor G.C., Seattle, Wash.	74	78	76	76	304	——
	*Miss Nancy Lopez, Albuquerque C.C., Albuquerque, N. M.	77	73	77	77	304	——
23	*Miss Lancy Smith, Park C.C., Williamsville, N. Y.	73	82	75	75	305	——
24	Miss Clifford Ann Creed, Bayou Oaks G. & C.C., Sulphur, La.	77	75	81	73	306	713.75
	Miss Gloria Ehret, Spring Valley C.C., Dallas, Texas	78	75	79	74	306	713.75
	Miss Maria E. Astrologes, Mission Valley C.C., Laurel, Fla.	75	76	74	81	306	713.75
	*Miss Carol Semple, Allegheny C.C., Sewickley, Pa.	81	74	74	77	306	——
28	Mrs. Mary Lou Crocker, Iroquois G.C., Louisville, Ky.	75	76	82	74	307	623.75
	Mrs. Kathy Cornelius, Pueblo Club Las Hadas, Manzanillo, Mexico	76	75	79	77	307	623.75
	Miss Debbie Austin, Fountains G.C., West Palm Beach, Fla.	76	73	80	78	307	623.75
	Miss Kathy Ahern, Woodhaven C.C., Ft. Worth, Texas	68	76	81	82	307	623.75
	*Mrs. Judith J. Oliver, Fox Chapel G.C., Pittsburgh, Pa.	78	72	79	78	307	——
33	Miss Laura Baugh, The Hamlet, Delray Beach, Fla.	76	79	77	76	308	568.75
	Miss Sally Little, Mission Hills C.C., Rancho Mirage, Calif.	76	76	76	80	308	568.75
35	Miss JoAnn Prentice, Tockaway Golf Club, Onconta, Ala.	78	77	81	73	309	548.75
	Miss Louise Suggs, Pine Tree G.C., Delray Beach, Fla.	80	74	79	76	309	548.75
	*Miss Cynthia Hill, Broadmoor G.C., Colorado Springs, Colo.	72	79	79	79	309	——
	*Miss Peggy S. Conley, Spokane C.C., Spokane, Wash.	73	74	79	83	309	——
39	Miss Jane Blalock, Portsmouth, N. H.	76	76	79	79	310	523.75
	Miss Diane Patterson, Longview, Texas	79	74	77	80	310	523.75
	Miss Shelley Hamlin, Sunnyside C.C., Fresno, Calif.	77	77	76	80	310	523.75
42	*Miss Martha Jones, Decatur C.C., Decatur, Ala.	74	79	79	79	311	——
	*Miss Mary Budke, Riverwood G.C., Dundee, Ore.	77	75	79	80	311	——
44	Miss Marlene B. Hagge, DeSoto Lakes C.C., Sarasota, Fla.	77	76	84	75	312	488.75
	Miss Pam Higgins, Palm Springs G.C., Palm Springs, Calif.	74	80	83	75	312	488.75
	Miss Carla Jean Glasgow, El Caballero C.C., Tarzana, Calif.	76	74	85	77	312	488.75
	Miss Jan Stephenson, Canyon C.C., Palm Springs, Calif.	81	74	80	77	312	488.75
48	Miss Betsy Cullen, Tulsa, Okla.	81	74	82	77	314	463.75
	*Miss Nancy Hager, Northwood Club, Dallas, Texas	76	78	81	79	314	——
	*Miss Beth Barry, Isle Dauphine C.C., Dauphin Island, Ala.	76	76	81	81	314	——
51	Miss Christl Pastore, Pine Needles C.C., Southern Pines, N. C.	81	74	80	80	315	448.75
	Miss Sharon K. Miller, Battle Creek C.C., Battle Creek, Mich.	77	78	80	80	315	448.75
53	Miss JoAnn Washam, Dallas, Texas	75	72	87	82	316	433.75
54	Miss Liana Zambresky, Monterey Penninsula C.C., Pebble Beach, Calif.	78	77	86	82	323	423.75

*Amateur

1975
TWENTY-THIRD UNITED STATES WOMEN'S OPEN CHAMPIONSHIP

Held at Atlantic City Country Club, Northfield, New Jersey, July 17-20
Yardage—6,165 Par 72. 175 Entries, 150 Starters

						Score	Money Prize
i	Miss Sandra Palmer, Glen Garden G.&C.C., Fort Worth, Texas	78	74	71	72	295	$8,044.77
2	Miss Sandra Post, Cypress Creek C.C., Boynton Beach, Florida	74	73	76	76	299	4,044.77
	Mrs. JoAnne Carner, Palm Beach National G.&C.C., Lake Worth, Florida	73	77	74	75	299	4,044.77
	*Miss Nancy Lopez, New Mexico Military Inst. G.C., Roswell, N.M.	73	74	77	75	299	PIN
5	Miss Susie McAllister, Beaumont, Texas	79	75	74	72	300	2,444.77
6	Miss Sandra Haynie, Lake Country Estates, Fort Worth, Texas	74	77	74	76	301	2,244.77
7	Miss Kathy Whitworth, Errol Estate Inn & C.C., Apopka, Florida	76	76	75	75	302	2,044.77
8	Miss Debbie Austin, Fountains G.C., Lake Worth, Florida	76	76	72	79	303	1,944.77
9	Miss Sally Little, Johannesburg, S. Africa	80	70	73	81	304	1,744.77
	Mrs. Judy Rankin, Kings Mill on the James, Williamsburg, Va.	72	77	79	76	304	1,744.76
	Miss Jocelyne Bourassa, Bromont G.C., Bromont, Quebec, Canada	77	76	75	76	304	1,744.76
12	Mrs. Gerda Boykin, River Plantation C.C., Conroe, Texas	78	78	75	74	305	1,494.76
	Miss Maria Astrologes, Mission Valley C.C., Venice, Florida	81	73	79	72	305	1,494.76
14	Miss Laura Baugh, The Hamlet, Delray Beach, Florida	76	74	76	80	306	1,319.76
	Miss Jane Blalock, Highland Beach, Florida	75	76	80	75	306	1,319.76
16	Miss Diane Patterson, Longview, Texas	75	74	79	79	307	1,194.76
	Miss Pat Bradley, Nashua C.C., Nashua, N.H.	78	77	78	74	307	1,194.76
	Mrs. Donna Caponi Young, Los Angeles, Calif.	81	74	77	75	307	1,194.76
19	Miss Amy Alcott, Riviera C.C., Pacific Palisades, Calif.	75	76	74	83	308	1,019.76
	Mrs. Mary Lou Crocker, Iroquois G.C., Louisville, Kentucky	79	76	73	80	308	1,019.76
	Miss Beth Stone, Muskogee, Okla.	76	75	77	80	308	1,019.76
	Miss Kathy McMullen, Bradenton, Florida	80	76	75	77	308	1,019.76
23	Miss Kathy Postlewait, Coosa Valley C.C., Sylacauga, Alabama	75	76	82	76	309	894.76
	*Miss Barbara Ann Barrow, Singing Hills C.C., El Cajon, Calif.	79	76	76	78	309	PIN
25	Miss Sue Roberts, Fountains G.C., Lake Worth, Florida	78	79	76	77	310	774.76
	Miss Marilyn J. S. Smith, Shandow G.C., Wellington, N.Z.	79	78	75	78	310	774.76
	Miss Silvia Bertolaccini, Ranelagh G.C., Buenos Aires, Argentina	77	78	79	76	310	774.76
	Miss Gloria Ehret, Country Place, Carrollton, Texas	81	76	79	74	310	774.76
	*Miss Deborah A. Massey, Saucon Valley C.C., Bethlehem, Pa.	81	72	75	82	310	PIN
30	Miss Judy Kimball, North Platte C.C., North Platte, Nebraska	73	83	79	76	311	684.76
	*Miss Peggy S. Conley, Spokane C.C., Spokane, Wash.	78	80	74	79	311	
32	Miss Mardell Wilkins, Mission Viejo, Calif.	80	78	75	79	312	654.76
33	Miss Betsy Cullen, Tulsa C.C., Tulsa, Okla.	76	77	80	80	313	594.76
	Mrs. Mary A. Canney, Chantilly Nat'l G.&C.C., Centreville, Virginia	77	80	77	79	313	594.76
	Miss Kathy Ahern, Arlington, Texas	76	82	77	78	313	594.76
36	Miss Jan Stephenson, Canyon C.C., Palm Springs, Calif.	79	78	79	78	314	534.76
	*Miss Donna Horton, Willow Lakes G.&C.C., Jacksonville, Florida	81	77	78	78	314	
	*Miss Carol Semple, Allegheny C.C., Sewickley, Pa.	80	78	77	79	314	
39	Mrs. Michael J. Skala, Cameron Park C.C., Shingle Springs, Calif.	79	79	77	80	315	504.76
	*Miss Beth Barry, Isle Dauphin C.C., Dauphin Island, Alabama	80	78	76	81	315	
41	Miss Mary Mills, University Park C.C., Boca Raton, Florida	81	75	80	80	316	474.76
42	Miss Shelley Hamlin, Sunnyside C.C., Fresno, Calif.	77	81	79	80	317	434.76
	Miss Mary K. Wolfe, Dallas Texas	81	76	81	79	317	434.76
44	Miss Kathy Martin, Los Robles Greens C.C., Thousand Oaks, Calif.	77	80	80	81	318	404.76
45	Miss Pam Barnett, University Park C.C., Boca Raton, Florida	79	78	79	84	320	374.76
	Miss Joyce Kazmierski, Williston Highlands C.C., Williston, Florida	81	75	84	80	320	374.76
47	Miss LeNore Beserra, Lakeside G.C., Toluca Lake, Calif.	82	76	88	75	321	344.76
	*Miss Martha Jones, Decatur C.C., Decatur, Alabama	81	77	84	79	321	
49	Miss Janet C. Aulisi, Maplewood C.C., Maplewood, N.J.	78	77	90	77	322	334.76
50	Miss Pam Higgins, Palm Springs G.C., Palm Springs, Calif.	75	82	87	79	323	324.76

*Amateur. Gold, silver, and bronze pins were awarded to the amateurs returning the lowest three scores.
Prize money totaling $55,000. was awarded.

1976
TWENTY-FOURTH UNITED STATES WOMEN'S OPEN CHAMPIONSHIP

Held at Rolling Green Golf Club, Springfield, Delaware County, Pennsylvania, July 8-11
Yardage—6,066. Par 71. 205 Entries, 150 Starters

						Score	Prize Money
1	†Mrs. JoAnne Carner, Palm Beach National G.C., Lake Worth, Fla.	71	71	77	73	292	$9,054.28
2	†Miss Sandra Palmer, Cathedral Canyon C.C., Palm Springs, Calif.	70	74	73	75	292	5,554.28
3	Miss Jane Blalock, Portsmouth, N.H.	75	72	73	76	296	3,454.29
4	Miss Susie McAllister, Beaumont, Texas	76	78	70	73	297	2,654.29
5	Miss Amy Alcott, Riviera C.C., Pacific Palisades, Calif.	72	75	78	74	299	2,329.29
	Miss Sharon K. Miller, Battle Creek C.C., Battle Creek, Mich.	75	75	77	72	299	2,329.29
7	Miss Silvia Bertolaccini, Champions G.C., Houston, Texas	78	73	74	75	300	2,054.29
8	Mrs. Susie Berning, Keauhou-Kona C.C., Kona, Hawaii	73	76	79	75	303	1,954.29
	*Miss Mary-Beth C. King, Heidelberg C.C., Bernville, Pa.	76	74	76	77	303	PIN
10	Mrs. Carole Jo Skala, Cameron Park C.C., Shingle Springs, Calif.	78	77	72	78	305	1,854.29
	*Miss Deborah Massey, Saucon Valley C.C., Bethlehem, Pa.	75	74	74	82	305	PIN
	*Miss Carol Semple, Allegheny C.C., Sewickley, Pa.	71	77	82	75	305	PIN
13	Miss V. Joyce Kazmierski, Barwick G.C., Delray Beach, Fla.	74	75	81	76	306	1,604.29
	Miss Gloria Ehret, Country Place, Carrollton, Texas	77	75	76	78	306	1,604.29
	Mrs. Hisako Higuchi Matsui, Tokyo, Japan	72	77	78	79	306	1,604.29
	Miss JoAnn Washam, Dallas, Texas	75	77	74	80	306	1,604.29
17	Miss Peggy Conley, Spokane C.C., Spokane, Wash.	74	80	77	76	307	1,229.29
	Mrs. Judy T. Rankin, Mission Hills C.C., Palm Springs, Calif.	79	75	79	74	307	1,229.29
	Miss Jan Stephenson, Canyon C.C., Palm Springs, Calif.	79	76	75	77	307	1,229.29
	Miss Sandra Spuzich, Speedway G.C., Indianapolis, Ind.	76	78	74	79	307	1,229.29
	Miss Pat Bradley, Nashua C.C., Nashau, N.H.	74	71	81	81	307	1,229.29
	Miss Betty Burfeindt, Palmetto Dunes Resort, Hilton Head, S.C.	77	74	76	80	307	1,229.29
23	Miss Hollis Stacy, Moss Creek Plantation G.C., Hilton Head, S.C.	75	80	75	78	308	1,004.29
	Miss Bonnie Lauer, Edgewood C.C., Union Lake, Mich.	73	80	77	78	308	1,004.29
	Miss Ai-Yu Tu, Tam-Sui C.C., Taipei, Taiwan	79	77	76	76	308	1,004.29
26	Miss Judy Kimball, Camelback C.C., Scottsdale, Ariz.	76	76	76	81	309	834.29
	Mrs. Mary Lou Crocker, Iroquois G.C., Louisville, Ky.	70	80	81	78	309	834.29
	Mrs. Marlene B. Hagge, La Quinta Cove C.C., La Quinta, Calif.	76	78	77	78	309	834.29
	Miss Sandra Post, Indian Spring C.C., Boynton Beach, Fla.	74	80	77	78	309	834.29
30	Miss Mary Mills, University Park C.C., Boca Raton, Fla.	75	77	77	81	310	729.28
	Miss Connie Chillemi, Cypress Creek C.C., Orlando, Fla.	69	84	78	79	310	729.28
32	*Miss Nancy Porter, Merion G.C., Ardmore, Pa.	76	77	76	82	311	—
	Miss Laura Baugh, Hamlet C.C., Delray Beach, Fla.	75	75	81	80	311	684.28
34	*Miss Barbara Barrow, Singing Hills C.C., El Cajon, Calif.	79	77	82	74	312	609.28
	Miss Marlene Floyd, Cleveland, Ohio	77	77	81	77	312	609.28
	Miss Jo Ann Prentice, Tuckaway G.C., Oneonta, Ala.	77	79	80	76	312	609.28
	Miss Masako Sasaki, Tokyo, Japan	83	73	79	77	312	609.28
	Miss Clifford Ann Creed, Bayou Oaks G. & C.C., Sulpher, La.	77	77	79	79	312	609.28
39	*Miss Lauren Howe, The C.C. of Colorado, Colorado Springs, Colo.	74	79	81	79	313	—
	Miss Beth Stone, Muskogee, Okla.	75	79	80	79	313	507.62
	Mrs. Mary D. Horner, Chace Lake C.C., Birmingham, Ala.	80	74	80	79	313	507.61
	Miss Jocelyne Bourassa, Bromont G.C., Bromont, Quebec, Canada	78	77	77	81	313	507.61
43	*Mrs. Nancy Roth Syms, The Broadmoor G.C., Colorado Springs, Colo.	77	78	79	80	314	—
44	Miss Kathy Postlewait, Coosa Valley C.C., Sylacauga, Ala.	80	75	82	78	315	464.28
45	Miss Marilyn J. S. Smith, Shandon G.C., Wellington, N.Z.	78	78	82	78	316	444.28
46	Miss Penny Pulz, San Francisco, Calif.	79	75	85	78	317	424.28
47	Miss Maria Astrologes, Mission Valley C.C., Venice, Fla.	77	76	80	86	319	399.28
	Miss Janet C. Aulisi, West Caldwell, N.J.	83	73	84	79	319	399.28
49	Mrs. Mary A. Canney, Chantilly National G. & C.C., Centreville, Va.	76	76	86	82	320	384.28
50	*Mrs. Lida M. Kinnicutt, The Hartford G.C., West Hartford, Conn.	75	79	86	85	325	—

*Amateur. Gold, silver, and bronze pins were awarded to the amateurs returning the lowest three scores.
Prize money totaling $60,000 was awarded.
†Playoff: 18 Holes, July 12 - Mrs. Carner, 76; Miss Palmer, 78.

1977
TWENTY-FIFTH WOMEN'S OPEN CHAMPIONSHIP

Held at Hazeltine National Golf Club, Chaska, Minnesota, July 21-24.
Yardage—6,313. Par 72. 197 Entries, 151 Starters.

						Score	Money Prize
1	Ms. Hollis Stacy, Savannah, Ga.	70	73	75	74	292	$11,040.44
2	Miss Nancy Marie Lopez, Albuquerque C.C., Albuquerque, N.M.	73	72	75	74	294	7,040.44
3	Mrs. JoAnne Carner, Palm Beach National G. & C.C., Lake Worth, Fla.	74	72	76	73	295	4,540.44
4	Miss Amy Alcott, Riviera C.C., Pacific Palisades, Calif.	72	77	75	74	298	2,923.78
	Miss Pat Bradley, Marco Island C.C., Marco Island, Fla.	77	72	79	70	298	2,923.77
	Miss Jan Stephenson, La Quinta, Calif.	72	75	72	79	298	2,923.77
7	Miss Susie McAllister, Round Hill C.C., Alamo, Calif.	76	80	73	70	299	2,340.44
8	Mrs. Donna Caponi Young, Los Angeles, Calif.	76	77	77	70	300	2,140.44
9	Miss Jane Blalock, Boca West C.C., Boca Raton, Fla.	72	78	77	74	301	2,040.44
10	Miss Sally Little, Bent Tree C.C., Dallas, Texas	81	75	72	74	302	1,790.44
	Miss JoAnn Prentice, Tuckaway G.C., Oneonta, Ala.	77	76	77	72	302	1,790.44
	Mrs. Judy T. Rankin, Mission Hills C.C., Palm Springs, Calif.	75	77	78	72	302	1,790.44
	Miss Kathy Whitworth, Richardson, Texas	74	76	79	73	302	1,790.44
14	Miss Sandra Post, Cypress Creek C.C., Boynton Beach, Fla.	73	80	72	78	303	1,540.44
15	Miss Sandra Spuzich, Ironwood IX, Golden, Colo.	76	78	75	75	304	1,465,44
	Mrs. Mary Lou Crocker, Iroquois G.C., Louisville, Ky.	77	74	81	72	304	1,465.44
17	Miss Betsy Cullen, Tulsa, Okla.	80	74	73	78	305	1,315.44
	Miss Carol Mann, Towson, Md.	76	76	77	76	305	1,315.44
	Miss Peggy Conley, Spokane C.C., Spokane, Wash.	74	76	78	77	305	1,315.44
	Ms. Debbie Austin, Columbus, Ohio	74	75	78	78	305	1,315.44
21	Miss Laura Baugh, The Canyon C.C., Palm Springs, Calif.	77	80	75	74	306	1,190.44
22	Miss Debbie Massey, Saucon Valley C.C., Bethlehem, Pa.	76	79	76	76	307	1,115.44
	Miss Pam Higgins, Palm Springs, Calif.	75	74	83	75	307	1,115.43
24	Miss Bonnie Lauer, Edgewood C.C., Union Lake, Mich.	76	80	80	72	308	1,040.43
	*Miss Beth Daniel, C.C. of Charleston, Charleston, S.C.	76	77	81	74	308	PIN
26	Miss Marlene Floyd, Hilton Head G.C., Hilton Head, S.C.	79	76	80	74	309	975.43
	Miss Janet A. Coles, Corral de Tierra, Salinas, Calif.	79	78	73	79	309	975.43
28	Miss Sandra Palmer, Boca Lago C.C., Boca Raton, Fla.	74	81	78	77	310	855.43
	Miss Joyce Kazmierski, Barwick G.C., Delray Beach, Fla.	72	83	80	75	310	855.43
	Miss Beth Stone, Muskogee, Okla.	80	73	80	77	310	855.43
	Miss Silvia Bertolaccini, Dallas, Texas	78	75	80	77	310	855.43
	Miss Susan O'Connor, Costa Mesa, Calif.	75	81	75	79	310	855.43
	Miss Michelle Walker, Faversham G.C., Faversham, Kent, England	75	76	79	80	310	855.43
34	Mrs. Donna Horton White, Beaucleric C.C., Jacksonville, Fla.	80	77	77	77	311	720.43
	Miss Mary Mills, Boca Raton Hotel G.C., Boca Raton, Fla.	78	77	79	77	311	720.43
	Miss Dorothy Germain, Pine Needles C.C., Southern Pines, N.C.	81	76	74	80	311	720.43
37	Miss Penny Pulz, San Francisco, Calif.	79	78	78	77	312	640.43
	Miss Alexandra Reinhardt, Albuquerque, N.M.	82	75	78	77	312	640.43
	Miss Diane Patterson, Dallas, Texas	78	79	78	77	312	640.43
	Mrs. Murle Lindstrom Breer, Savannah Inn & C.C., Savannah, Ga.	75	80	77	80	312	640.43
	*Miss Brenda Goldsmith, Pecan Valley G.C., San Antonio, Texas	79	75	80	78	312	PIN
42	Miss Louise Bruce, Carlton Oaks C.C., Santee, Calif.	79	77	77	80	313	590.43
	*Miss Catherine Reynolds, Hickory Hills C.C., Springfield, Mo.	77	76	79	81	313	PIN
44	Miss Eva Chang, Taiwan Tamsui G. & C.C., Taiwan	77	80	81	77	315	575.43
	Mrs. Cathy Mant, Snee Farm C.C., Mt. Pleasant, S.C.	79	70	88	78	315	575.43
46	Ms. Bonnie Bryant, Minneapolis, Minn.	76	81	83	76	316	560.43
47	Miss Kathy Ahern, Denton, Texas	78	79	81	79	317	545.43
	Miss Clifford Ann Creed, Bayou Oaks C.C., Sulpher, La.	81	76	81	79	317	545.43
49	Miss Shirley Englehorn, Desert Island C.C., Rancho Mirage, Calif.	78	79	77	85	319	530.43
50	*Mrs. Myra V. Norsworthy, Big Elm C.C., Lexington, Ky.	80	76	82	84	322	—
51	*Miss Christine Desch, Southampton G.C., Southampton, N.Y.	79	77	82	89	327	—

*Amateur. Gold, silver, and bronze pins were awarded to the amateurs returning the lowest three scores. Prize money totaling $75,000.00 was awarded.

1978

TWENTY-SIXTH WOMEN'S OPEN CHAMPIONSHIP

Held at Country Club of Indianapolis, Indianapolis, Indiana, July 20-23.
Yardage—6,115. Par 71. 297 Entries, 150 Starters.

						Score	Money Prize
1	Miss Hollis Stacy, Savannah, Ga.	70	75	72	72	289	$15,000.00
2	Mrs. JoAnne Carner, Palm Beach Nat'l. G. & C.C. Lake Worth ,Fla.	73	72	73	72	290	7,000.00
	Miss Sally Little, Dallas, Texas	75	75	75	65	290	7,000.00
4	Miss Pam Higgins, Palm Springs, Calif.	74	73	75	71	293	4,650.00
	Miss Jane Blalock, Portsmouth, N.H.	74	74	71	74	293	4,650.00
6	Mrs. Donna Horton White, The Wellington C., W. Palm Bch., Fla.	72	72	79	71	294	3,260.00
	Miss Kathy Martin, Los Robles Greens G.C., Thousand Oaks, Calif.	76	74	71	73	294	3,260.00
	Mrs. Donna Caponi Young, North Ranch C.C., Westlake, Calif.	68	78	73	75	294	3,260.00
9	Miss Sandra Post, Cypress Creek C.C., Boynton Bch., Fla.	78	73	74	70	295	2,533.33
	Miss Nancy Lopez, Albuquerque C.C., Albuquerque, N.M.	71	73	79	72	295	2,533.33
	Miss Peggy Conley, Spokane C.C., Spokane, Wash.	75	76	70	74	295	2,533.33
12	Miss Amy Alcott, Riviera C.C., Pacific Palisades, Calif.	75	75	75	71	296	2,150.00
	Mrs. Robert C. Meyers, Riviera C.C., Ormond Beach, Fla.	75	73	76	72	296	2,150.00
	Miss Janet A. Coles, Carmel Valley C.C., Carmel, Calif.	71	80	72	73	296	2,150.00
	Miss Joann Washam, Auburn G.C., Auburn, Wash.	72	77	73	74	296	2,150.00
16	Miss Pat Bradley, Nashua C.C., Nashua, N.H.	76	75	76	70	297	1,800.00
	Miss Marlene B. Hagge, La Quinta Hotel C.C. La Quinta, Calif.	76	75	75	71	297	1,800.00
	Mrs. Murle Breer, Savannah Inn & C.C., Savannah, Ga.	75	77	73	72	297	1,800.00
	*Miss Carol Semple, Allegheny C.C., Sewickley, Pa.	73	71	77	76	297	Pin
20	Miss Betsy King, Heidelberg C.C., Bernville, Pa.	74	74	79	71	298	1,500.00
	Miss Jan Stephenson, La Quinta, Calif.	75	72	77	74	298	1,500.00
	Miss Mary Dwyer, Geneva, N.Y.	75	77	71	75	298	1,500.00
23	Miss Mickey Wright, Sandpiper C.C., Port St. Lucie, Fla.	74	77	77	71	299	1,275.00
	Miss Laura Baugh, Canyon C.C., Palm Springs, Calif.	73	74	76	76	299	1,275.00
	Miss Kathy McMullen, Carrollton, Texas	78	76	74	71	299	1,275.00
	Miss Bonnie Lauer, Palm Desert, Calif.	73	76	76	74	299	1,275.00
	*Miss Juli Simpson, Pasatiempo G.C., Santa Cruz, Calif.	80	72	72	75	299	Pin
28	Miss Jerilyn Britz, Coronado G.C., Scottsdale, Ariz.	74	73	78	75	300	1,120.00
	Miss Sharon K. Miller, Battle Creek C.C., Battle Creek, Mich.	72	76	77	75	300	1,120.00
	Miss Mary B. Mills, Boca Raton, Fla.	76	76	73	75	300	1,120.00
31	Miss Shelley L. Hamlin, Sunnyside C.C., Fresno, Calif.	72	76	81	72	301	1,000.00
	Miss Janet C. Aulisi, Bent Tree G. & C.C., Sarasota, Fla.	76	78	73	74	301	1,000.00
	Miss Beth Stone, Muskogee, Okla.	75	76	75	75	301	1,000.00
34	Miss Kathy Whitworth, Trophy C., Dallas Texas	76	75	78	73	302	864.00
	Miss Beth E. Solomon, Tri-County G.C., Middletown, Ind.	76	77	76	73	302	864.00
	Miss Sandra Palmer, Boca Lago C.C., Boca Raton, Fla.	77	77	75	73	302	864.00
	Miss Janet L. Anderson, Greenville, C.C., Greenville, Pa.	72	75	81	74	302	864.00
	Miss Alexandra Reinhardt, Columbine C.C., Littleton, Colo.	70	77	77	78	302	864.00
39	Miss Clifford A. Creed, Bayou Oaks G. & C.C., Sulphur, La.	76	75	77	75	303	766.00
	Miss Vicki Fergon, Palm Springs, Calif.	70	81	76	76	303	766.00
	Miss Sandra Spuzich, Ironwood IX, Golden, Colo.	74	77	74	78	303	766.00
	Miss Betty Burfeindt, Palm Springs, Calif.	74	75	83	71	303	766.00
	Miss Sue Roberts, Columbus, Ohio	79	73	78	73	303	766.00
	*Miss Cynthia Hill, Broadmoor G.C., Colorado Springs, Colo.	71	74	83	75	303	Pin
45	Mrs. Mary Alice Canney, Chantilly Nat'l. G & C.C., Centreville, Va.	77	74	80	73	304	715.00
	Mrs. Roberta A. Speer, Forest Hills C.C., Richmond, Ind.	80	74	77	73	304	715.00
	Miss Deborah A. Massey, Saucon Valley C.C., Bethlehem, Pa.	76	76	77	75	304	715.00
	Miss Penny Pulz, San Francisco, Calif.	75	76	77	76	304	715.00
49	Miss Lily Wu, Tamsui G & C.C., Taiwan	76	74	82	73	305	675.00
	Miss Louise Bruce, Singing Hills C.C., El Cajon, Calif.	77	76	74	78	305	675.00
	Miss Joann Prentice, Tuckaway G.C., Oneonta, Ala.	79	74	74	78	305	675.00
	Miss Dorothy Germain, Pine Needles Ldg. & C.C., Sthrn. Pines, N.C.	74	75	77	79	305	675.00
53	Miss Marilyn J.S. Smith, Shandon G.C., Wellington, N. Zealand	79	74	79	75	307	650.00
	Mrs. Judy Rankin, Mission Hills G.C., Rancho Mirage, Calif.	73	75	83	76	307	650.00
	Miss Betsy Cullen, Tulsa, Okla.	78	74	76	79	307	650.00
	*Miss Beth Daniel, C.C. of Charleston, Charleston, S.C.	75	78	77	77	307	——
57	Miss Margie Masters, Tarpon Woods C.C., Palm Harbor, Fla.	78	76	74	80	308	650.00
	*Miss Holly Hartley, Marine Mem. G.C., Camp Pendleton, Calif.	73	76	78	81	308	——
59	*Mrs. Judith J. Oliver, Allegheny C.C., Sewickley, Pa.	75	79	79	77	310	——
60	Ms. Sue Kenney, Pompano Park Par 60, Pompano Bch., Fla.	78	74	77	82	311	650.00
61	*Mrs. Peggy Kirby, Minnehaha C.C., Sioux Falls, S.D.	78	75	78	81	312	——
62	Miss Judy Kimball, Camelback C.C., Scottsdale, Ariz.	74	75	83	82	314	650.00
	Miss Carla J. Glasgow, Piping Rock C., Locust Valley, N.Y.	75	79	81	79	314	650.00
64	Miss Constance Chillemi, Silver Spgs. Shores G. & C.C., Ocala, Fla.	78	76	80	82	316	650.00
	*Miss Debbie Hall, Corpus Christi C.C., Corpus Christi, Texas	73	81	78	84	316	——
66	Miss Alice Miller, Plumas Lake G.C., Marysville, Calif.	80	74	83	80	317	650.00

*Amateur. Gold, silver, and bronze pins were awarded to the amateurs returning the lowest three scores.
Prize money totaling $105,199.99 was awarded.

1979
TWENTY-SEVENTH WOMEN'S OPEN

Held at Brooklawn Country Club, Fairfield, Connecticut, July 12-15.
Yardage—6,010. Par 71. 335 Entries, 153 Starters.

						Score	Money Prize
1	Jerilyn Britz, Luverne C.C., Luverne, Minn.	70	70	75	69	284	$19,000.00
2	Sandra Palmer, Boca Lago C.C., Boca Raton, Fla.	73	69	74	70	286	9,200.00
	Deborah Massey, Saucon Valley C.C., Bethlehem, Pa.	70	72	70	74	286	9,200.00
4	Sally Little, Dallas, Texas	71	71	74	71	287	6,500.00
5	Susie Berning, Keauhou Kona C.C., Kona, Hawaii	79	66	71	73	289	4,566.67
	Mary Dwyer, Geneva, New York	73	71	74	71	289	4,566.67
	Jo Ann Washam, Dallas Texas	76	74	72	67	289	4,566.66
8	Joyce Kazmierski, Williston Highlands C.C., Williston, Fla.	76	72	72	70	290	3,400.00
	Laura Baugh, The Canyon C.C., Palm Springs, Calif.	73	72	77	68	290	3,400.00
	Donna C. Young, N. Ranch C.C., Los Angeles, Calif.	72	74	74	70	290	3,400.00
11	Amelia Rorer, Jenkintown, Pa.	73	73	77	69	292	2,775.00
12	Sandra Post, Cypress Creek C.C., Boynton Beach, Fla.	72	75	74	71	292	2,775.00
	Nancy Lopez, Palm Coast G.C., Palm Coast, Fla.	73	73	73	73	292	2,775.00
	Jane Blalock, Portsmouth, N.H.	71	73	74	74	292	2,775.00
15	Murle Breer, Sheraton Savannah Inn & C.C., Savannah, Ga.	76	74	70	73	293	2,350.00
	Hollis Stacy, The Landings on Skidaway Island, Savannah, Ga.	71	75	74	73	293	2,350.00
	Penny Pulz, Visalia, Calif.	73	72	75	73	293	2,350.00
	Sandra Spuzich, Indianapolis, Ind.	71	73	74	75	293	2,350.00
19	Silvia Bertolaccini, Dallas, Texas	75	74	71	74	294	2,100.00
20	Shelly Hamlin, Sunnyside C.C., Fresno, Calif.	78	70	80	67	295	1,750.00
	Lori Garbacz, South Bend, Ind.	76	74	74	71	295	1,750.00
	Beth Daniel, Seabrook C., Seabrook Island, S.C.	78	70	72	75	295	1,750.00
	Janet Coles, Carmel Valley C.C., Carmel, Calif.	75	71	74	75	295	1,750.00
	Pam Higgins, Rancho Mirage, Calif.	71	72	77	75	295	1,750.00
	Donna H. White, The Wellington C., Wellington, Fla.	74	74	71	76	295	1,750.00
26	Jan Stephenson, Oklahoma City, Okla.	75	74	74	73	296	1,292.00
	Judy Rankin, Mission Hills C.C., Palm Springs, Calif.	76	68	78	74	296	1,292.00
	Pat Bradley, Nashua C.C., Nashua, N.H.	77	70	74	75	296	1,292.00
	Alexandra Reinhardt, Albuquerque, N.M.	74	76	68	78	296	1,292.00
	Cathy Morse, Oak Hill C.C., Rochester, N.Y.	71	75	72	78	296	1,292.00
31	Susie McAllister, Beaumont, Texas	76	75	75	71	297	1,105.00
	Sue Roberts, Columbus, Ohio	75	74	76	72	297	1,105.00
	*Terri Moody, Athens C.C., Athens, Ga.	76	73	74	74	297	Pin
34	Kathleen McMullen, Carrollton, Texas	76	75	73	74	298	1,030.00
35	Kathryn A. Young, New York City, N.Y.	75	72	75	77	299	975.00
	Judy Clark, Frenchmans Creek G.C., N. Palm Beach, Fla.	75	72	79	73	299	975.00
37	Vicki Fergon, Palm Springs, Calif.	79	73	75	73	300	920.00
	Kathy Postlewait, Still Waters G.C., Dadeville, Ala.	78	72	77	73	300	920.00
	Amy Alcott, Kutschers C.C., Monticello, N.Y.	77	70	76	77	300	920.00
40	Bonnie Lauer, Palm Desert, Calif.	73	78	76	74	301	870.00
	Kathy Whitworth, Trophy C., Dallas, Texas	73	79	74	75	301	870.00
	*Carol Semple, Allegheny, C.C., Sewickley, Pa.	77	75	74	75	301	Pin
43	Marlene Hagge, La Quinta Hotel C.C., La Quinta, Calif.	78	74	76	74	302	825.00
	Alice Ritzman, Buffalo Hills C.C., Kalispell, Mont.	74	76	77	75	302	825.00
	Jan Ferraris, San Francisco, Calif.	74	76	77	75	302	825.00
	Kathy Hite, Florence C.C., Florence, S.C.	73	72	79	78	302	825.00
47	Maria A. Combs, Wakonda C.C., Des Moines, Iowa	74	76	79	74	303	790.00
	Cathy R. Thompson, Hickory Hills C.C., Springfield, Mo.	76	75	75	77	303	790.00
	Elaine Hand, Douglas G.&C.C., Douglas, Ga.	76	71	78	78	303	790.00
50	Alice Miller, Plumas Lake G.C., Marysville, Calif.	77	75	78	74	304	770.00
51	Kathy Ahern, Phoenix, Ariz.	75	75	77	78	305	755.00
	Jo Ann Prentice, Tuckaway G.C., Oneonta, Ala.	75	77	74	79	305	755.00
53	Janet Alex, West Sunbury, Pa.	79	73	79	75	306	750.00
54	Hellen B. Duntz, Pleasant Valley C.C., Sutton, Mass.	73	77	82	75	307	750.00
55	Muffin Spencer-Devlin, Quail Ridge C.C., Delray Beach, Fla.	74	76	82	80	312	750.00
56	*Alicia Ogrin, Bonnie Brook G.C., Waukegan, Ill.	75	75	83	85	318	Pin

*Amateur. Gold, silver, and bronze pins were awarded to the amateurs returning the lowest three scores.
Prize money totaling $127,270.00 was awarded.

1980
TWENTY-EIGHTH WOMEN'S OPEN CHAMPIONSHIP

Held at Richland Country Club, Nashville, Tennessee, July 10-13.
Yardage—6,229. Par 71. 337 Entries, 150 Starters

						Score	Money Prize
1	Amy Alcott, Riviera C.C., Pacific Palisades, Calif.	70	70	68	72	280	$20,047.50
2	Hollis Stacy, Savannah G.C., Savannah, Ga.	75	71	70	73	289	11,347.50
3	Kathy McMullen, Emmaus, Pa.	74	73	71	73	291	8,547.50
4	Judy Clark, Frenchmen's Creek, N. Palm Beach, Fla.	75	73	73	71	292	6,347,50
	Donna Caponi Young, Los Angeles, Calif.	72	72	75	73	292	6,347.50
6	Louise Bruce, Singing Hills C.C., El Cajon, Calif.	73	74	73	73	293	4,847.50
	Lori Garbacz, South Bend, Ind.	72	76	75	71	294	3,964.17
	Jane Blalock, Boca Raton, Fla.	76	71	71	76	294	3,964.17
	Nancy Lopez-Melton, Jack Nicklaus G. Center, Mason, Ohio	74	72	71	77	294	3,964.16
10	Patty Hayes, Suntree C.C., Melbourne, Fla.	75	72	74	74	295	3,085.00
	JoAnne Carner, Palm Beach Nat'l. G.&C.C., Lake Worth, Fla.	74	72	74	75	295	3,085.00
	Eva Chang, Carlsbad, Calif.	74	74	72	75	295	3,085.00
	Beth Daniel, Seabrook Island G.C. Seabrook Island, S.C.	76	72	69	78	295	3,085.00
14	Penny Pulz, Cleveland, Ohio	72	72	77	75	296	2,747.50
15	Shelly Hamlin, Sunnyside C.C., Fresno, Calif.	78	73	71	75	297	2,647.50
16	Marlene Floyd, Mission Hills C.C., Rancho Mirage, Calif.	72	76	76	74	298	2,397.50
	Dorothy Germain, Pine Needles Lodges & C.C., So. Pines S.C.	75	76	72	75	298	2,397.50
	Pat Bradley, Marco Island C.C., Marco Island, Fla.	74	74	74	76	298	2,397.50
	Cathy Morse, Oak Hill C.C., Rochester, N.Y.	74	74	72	78	298	2,397.50
20	Sally Little, Delray Beach, Fla.	74	76	76	73	299	2,047.50
	Bonnie Lauer, Palm Desert, Calif.	76	73	75	75	299	2,047.50
	Barbara Moxness, Singing Hills C.C., San Diego, Calif.	70	74	75	80	299	2,047.50
23	Pat Meyers, Oceanside C.C., Ormond Beach, Fla.	75	73	77	75	300	1,702.50
	Alison Sheard, Royal Durban G.C., South Africa	77	73	75	75	300	1,702.50
	Ai-Yu Tu, Osaka, Japan	75	73	72	80	300	1,702.50
	Sandra Post, Indian Spring C.C., Boynton Beach, Fla.	79	68	70	83	300	1,702.50
27	Mary Dwyer, Geneva, N.Y.	76	75	77	73	301	1,434.17
	Laura Baugh, Argyle, Texas	81	71	73	76	301	1,434.17
	Janet Alex, Grove City C.C., Grove City, Pa.	72	74	77	78	301	1,434.16
30	Debbie Austin, Alexandria, Va.	76	75	78	73	302	1,229.50
	Gail Hirata, Montebello, Calif.	75	76	78	73	302	1,229.50
	Sandra Spuzich, Cypress Creek C.C., Boynton Beach, Fla.	78	72	75	77	302	1,229.50
	Barbara Barrow, Lamas Santa Fe C.C., Solana Beach, Calif.	78	73	72	79	302	1,229.50
	Becky Pearson, Boca Del Mar C.C., Boca Raton, Fla.	77	76	76	73	302	1,229.50
35	Bonnie Bryant, Minneapolis, Minn.	76	76	77	74	303	1,087.50
	Kathy Ahern, Arlington, Texas	73	76	77	77	303	1,087.50
	Martha Hansen, St. Paul, Minn.	72	76	77	78	303	1,087.50
38	Kathy Hite, Florence, S.C.	77	71	80	76	304	1,047.50
39	Carole Charbonnier, Geneva G.C., Geneva, Switzerland	78	75	77	75	305	1,027.50
40	*Judith Oliver, Allegheny G.C. Sewickley, Pa.	75	76	80	75	306	Medal
	Susie McAllister, Beaumont, Texas	75	75	78	78	306	977.50
	Beth Solomon, Tri-County G.C., Middletown, Ind.	76	76	76	78	306	977.50
	Barbara Mizrahie, Indonesia	81	71	76	78	306	977.50
	Myra Van Hoose, Lexington G.C., Lexington, Ky.	75	77	72	82	306	977.50
45	Beth Stone, Muskogee, Okla.	78	73	79	77	307	907.50
	Debby Rhodes, Calusa C.C., Miami, Fla.	75	75	79	78	307	907.50
	Donna White, Wellington, Forest Hill, Fla.	74	76	78	79	307	907.50
48	Alice Ritzman, Ahwatukee C.C., Phoenix, Ariz.	76	74	83	76	309	837.50
	Mary Mills, Hunters Run, Boynton Beach, Fla.	76	75	79	79	309	837.50
	*Lida M. Kinnicutt, The Hartford G.C., W. Hartford, Conn.	77	76	77	79	309	Medal
	Kathryn Young, Portland, Ore.	72	77	80	80	309	837.50
	Marty Dickerson, Forest Hills, G.C. Middletown, Ohio	74	77	77	81	309	837.50
53	Marlene Hagge, La Quinta Hotel G.C., La Quinta, Calif.	76	76	81	77	310	777.50
	Cathy Mant, Columbia-Edgewater C.C., Portland, Ore.	78	75	79	78	310	777.50
	Silvia Bertolaccini, Palm-Aire, Pompano Beach, Fla.	78	72	77	83	310	777.50
56	Betty Burfeindt, Palm Springs, Calif.	74	78	80	79	311	757.50
57	Angie Tsai, Osaka, Japan	78	74	83	77	312	742.50
	Cynthia Kessler, Tri-County C.C., Forestville, N.Y.	80	73	77	82	312	742.50

*Amateur. Gold and silver pins were awarded to the amateurs returning the lowest two scores.
Prize money totaling $140,000.00 was awarded

AMATEUR PUBLIC LINKS CHAMPIONSHIP

STANDISH CUP

Presented in June, 1922, by

JAMES D. STANDISH, JR.

Chairman, United States Golf Association Public and Municipal Golf Courses Committee

WARREN G. HARDING TROPHY

Presented in June, 1923, by

HON. WARREN G. HARDING

President of the United States of America

HISTORY

1960–California swept the honors in the first USGA Championship ever played outside the continental United States–at the Ala Wai Golf Course in Honolulu, Hawaii. Verne Callison, 41, a tavern owner from Sacramento, Calif., won the title when he defeated Tyler Caplin, a member of the Michigan State golf team from East Lansing, Mich., by 7 and 6 in the final. Callison became the oldest Public Links Champion. Another honor went to California when the Pasadena team won the sectional team Championship and the Warren G. Harding Trophy with a three-man score of 453 for 36 holes, four better than second-place Honolulu. Members of the Pasadena team were Harlan Stevenson, Richard Clover, and Ray Swedo, Jr. In the semi-final matches, Callison defeated Mike Andonian, of Pontiac, Mich., 1 up, and Caplin ousted Bob McMasters, of Royal Oak, Mich., 5 and 4. The entry was 2,718.

1961–Richard H. Sikes, a 21-year-old student at the University of Arkansas, became the third player in history and the first in 14 years to win both the qualifying medal and the Championship. Sikes, who carried his own bag throughout the Championship, rallied from a three-hole deficit after 14 holes to defeat John Molenda, of Detroit, 4 and 3, in the final. Sikes won the medal with a five-under-par 70-65–135, a two-stroke edge over David Bettencourt, of Honolulu, Hawaii. Sikes was four under par through 130 holes of match play. An outstanding putter the entire week, Sikes had 59 one-putt greens for 166 holes of play, including qualifying. His closest match came in the semi-finals when he defeated John Schlee, of Memphis, Tenn., 2 and 1. Molenda defeated Lt. Cmdr. Lou Gifford, of Jacksonville, Fla., 1 up in the other semi-final match. The team Championship was won by Honolulu with a score of 428. Members of the Honolulu team were Bettencourt, Owen T. Douglass, Jr., and Hung Soo Ahn. This was the second Championship at the 6,358-yard Rackham Golf Course in Detroit, Mich., and the entry reached 2,409.

1962–Sikes became the second man in the history of the Amateur Public Links Championship to defend the title successfully. He did so by defeating Hung Soo Ahn, a 32-year-old draftsman from Honolulu, by 2 and 1 in the 36-hole final match at the Sheridan Park Golf Course, Tonawanda, N.Y. Carl F. Kauffmann won consecutively in 1927, 1928, and 1929. Charles Ferrera, Amateur Public Links Champion in 1931 and 1933, was the only other two-time winner. Sikes, three down to Ahn after the morning round, rallied to win at the 35th hole. He was four under par for the day. Sikes' semi-final round victim was Warren E. Stout, Speedway, Ind., who lost by 4 and 3. The other semi-finalist was Wayne Breck, of Scottsdale, Ariz., who lost to Ahn by one hole. Sikes, 22 and a student at the University of Arkansas, later advanced to the fifth round of the Amateur Championship for the second straight year and was then selected to represent the United States in the World Amateur Team Championship. Seattle won the team Championship with a score of 451. The defending Champion Honolulu team was second with 453. George Archer, of San Francisco, was medalist with 73-72–145.

1963–Robert Lunn, 18, of San Francisco, defeated Stephen Oppermann, 21, of South San Francisco, by 1 up in the final at the Haggin Oaks Municipal Golf Course, Sacramento, Calif. Richard H. Sikes' bid to become the second three-time Champion ended in the quarter-final round when he lost to Dante Vicini, 49, a glass-worker from Ottawa, Ill. Vicini won on the 19th hole after being 2 down with two to play. Sikes had won 15 consecutive matches in the Championships of 1961-62-63. Lunn, the 12th Californian to win the title, was four under par in 134 holes of match play. He defeated Jerry Yuke, of Sacramento, by 3 and 1 in the semi-final round. Oppermann beat Vicini, 4 and 3, in the other semi-final. John Joseph, of Hayward, Calif., was medalist with 141, three under par. Seventeen players engaged in a sudden death playoff for the last four positions in match play. The playoff required two hours for four extra holes. The longest match in the Championship's history took place in the first round when Clyde Sniffen, of Everett, Wash., defeated Hung Soo Ahn, of Honolulu, the 1962 runnerup, at the 25th hole. Toledo won the team Championship with a score of 443. The winning team consisted of Hubert Farmer, Andrew Holmes and Leonard Pietras.

1964–William McDonald, a 20-year-old college student from Topeka, Kans., reached the final round although suffering from severe blisters on his feet. One up after the morning round of the final, McDonald was rushed to a hospital for treatment; he returned to play 15 holes in one under par to defeat Dean Wilson, Jr., of Omaha, Neb., by 5 and 3. The Championship was played at the Francis A. Gross Golf Course, Minneapolis, Minn. Los Angeles won the team Championship for the eighth time, with an aggregate of 435. The medalist was Steve Oppermann, a San Franciscan who had been runner-up in 1963. Oppermann's 36-hole total was 135. Defending Champion Robert Lunn lost in the quarter-final round. For the first time, Alaska was awarded a qualifying site and 12 players from that State entered to seek the one qualifier's place allotted.

1965–Arne Dokka, a semi-finalist in 1964, won the 1965 title by defeating Leo Zampedro, a fireman from Warren, Ohio, by the record margin of 10 and 9 in the final match at the North Park Golf Course, Pittsburgh. Dokka, 21, was a senior at California State College in Los Angeles. A native of Norway, he came to the United States with his parents at the age of 14. Defending Champion Bill McDonald, of Topeka, Kansas, lost in the third round. The team competition was won by Phoenix, Ariz., with an aggregate of 445. Tom Takaguchi, of Honolulu, failed to qualify although he scored a hole-in-one during the second qualifying round. The youngest player, Jim Masserio, 16, of Pittsburgh, lost in the second round. Three weeks later he won the Junior Amateur Championship.

1966–Monty Kaser, 24, of Wichita, Kans., defeated Dave Ojala, 21, of Two Harbors, Minn., by 6 and 5, in the final match at the Brown Deer Park Golf Course, Milwaukee. This was the fourth attempt for Kaser, an employee in the payroll department of an aircraft factory. Arne Dokka, of Studio City, Calif., was medalist with 72-65–137, but lost in the fourth round to George Demling, of Louisville. Demling had quit his job in order to play. Dokka's 65 broke the course record, which was set by Gary Player in an exhibition match. The team competition was won by Pittsburgh with an aggregate score of 449.

1967–The Amateur Public Links Championship was played at 72 holes stroke play for the first time, and the changed format resulted in the oldest male Champion in USGA history, other than the Senior Amateur Champion. Verne Callison, 48, of Sacramento, Calif., staged a spectacular finish to score 287 at the Jefferson Park Golf Course, Seattle, Wash., and win by one stroke over Ronald Stokley, of Park Ridge, Ill. The oldest previous USGA Champion was Jack Westland, who won the 1952 United States Amateur at 47. Callison became the fourth player to win the Championship more than once. He won previously in 1960 at 41, and even then was the oldest Public Links Champion. At Seattle he finished birdie-par-eagle-par–three under on the last four holes. The team competition was won by Dayton, Ohio, in a playoff with Atlanta after they tied with aggregate scores of 436.

1968–Gene Towry, of Richardson, Texas, won the second Amateur Public Links Championship conducted entirely at stroke play with a 72-hole score of 292 over the Tenison Memorial Municipal Golf Course in Dallas. Towry, an electrical engineer, once had been a professional and was reinstated to amateur status before 1957, when he was runnerup to Don Essig. Robert Unger, of Milwaukee, Wis., was second at 294. Verne Callison, of Sacramento, Calif., and Michael Keck, New Orleans, La., tied for third at 298. Towry was 12 over par for the four rounds with 18-hole scores of 74-71-75-72.

1969–John Jackson, Jr., of Tempe, Ariz., shot 79 in the first round, then followed with scores of 70-73-70 to win by two strokes with 292. Tied for second at 294 were Art Fujita, of Honolulu; Fred Lufkin, of Spokane, Wash.; Steve Cook, of Long Beach, Calif.; and Joe Andron, Jr., of Erie, Pa. The Championship was played over the Downing Golf Course in Erie, Pa. Jackson's victory returned the title to the college boys, who had not won since the Championship was changed to stroke play in 1967. Jackson was a student at Arizona State University in Tempe. With 18 holes to play, Jackson was five strokes behind Larry Zee, of Tonawanda, N.Y. Zee shot 81 and dropped out of contention. Fujita was leading with nine holes to play, but he made bogies on five of the next seven holes. Lufkin made a two-over-par 6 on the final hole when a par 4 would have tied Jackson. Pasadena, Calif., won the team Championship. The entry of 3,754 was the largest ever for any USGA competition.

1970–Robert Risch, 22, of Gardena, Calif., won the Championship by three strokes over Mike Zimmerman, of Kettering, Ohio, over the demanding Cog Hill No. 4 Golf Course, Lemont, Ill. Risch had scores of 72-72-72-76–293. Ted Meier, 18, of Joliet, Ill., led after two rounds with 69-73–142, then shot 85 in the third. Risch led by five strokes after 54 holes and never really was threatened in the final 18. Later in the year he became a professional. The entry reached record proportions–4,015, the largest for any USGA competition to that time.

1971–Fred Haney, 21, won by five strokes with a score of 290 at the difficult Papago Golf Course in Phoenix in mid-July. Bob Blomberg, 26, of Alameda, Calif., was second with 295, and four players tied for third at 297. They were Tom Olson, of Phoenix; Kenny Rucker, of Houston; Gary Balliet, of Pontiac, Mich.;, and Archie Dadian, of South Milwaukee, Wis. Dadian was a former professional and the other three were college students. Haney and Blomberg were tied at 220 after 54 holes, and then Haney shot 70 in the last round against 75 by Blomberg. Haney had round of 74-71-75-70–290, while Blomberg shot 77-72-71-75–295. The entry reached 4,174, a record total, but for the first time since 1963 the entry for the Amateur Public Links was less than the entry for the Open Championship. The 1971 Open entry totalled 4,279.

1972–Bob Allard, of Portland, Ore., won the Championship in an 18-hole playoff with Rick Schultz, of Omaha, Neb., scoring a 71 to Schultz' 74. Both had scored 285 over the regulation 72 holes, a record low score for the Championship since it was converted to stroke play in 1967. Match play was in effect from 1922 until 1967. Allard, 23, had rounds of 70-73-73 and Schultz, 22, had scored 70-71-75 to be two strokes off the lead at 216 after 54 holes. They both scored 69 in the final round to tie and force a playoff, the first in the Championship's stroke-play history. In the playoff, Allard's straight driving and dependable short-irons led to three birdies, whereas Schultz could not manage one. The Championship was held at the Coffin Golf Course, Indianapolis, Ind., a relatively short course at 6,360 yards with a par of 70. However, only 12 rounds of sub-par golf were played. This was the third Amateur Public Links Championship played at Coffin Golf Course, more than any other course. Third place was won by Dan Elliot, with rounds of 68-70-76-74–288; his 36-hole total of 138 tied the record set in 1967 and led the City of Portland to its second consecutive team title. He, Allard, and Lynn McSherry scored a total of 430 for the first two rounds to beat the second-place team from Phoenix, Ariz. by seven strokes and retain the Warren G. Harding Trophy. Fourth place was shared by Richard Ehrmanntraut, of St. Paul, Minn.; Gene Rucker, of Miami, Fla., and Dennis Smith, from Memphis, Tenn. Ehrmanntraut's final round of 66 was low for the Championship. There were 3,743 acceptable entries for the Championship, with the 150 eventual starters being decided by 36-hole qualifying rounds held at 50 locations.

1973—Stan Stopa, of New Orleans, La., won the Championship by one stroke over Gary Hitch, of Santa Barbara, Calif., and Philip T. Reichel, Minneapolis, Minn., with a 72-hole total of 294, 10 over par. The Championship was held at the Flanders Valley Golf Course, Flanders, N. J. It was the first Public Links Championship held in New Jersey. Stopa started poorly, shooting 76-76 in the first two rounds and was nine strokes behind Reichel, who led after 36 holes with 143. Play was stopped twice during the third round because of severe electrical storms, with high winds and driving rain. There were delays of 35 and 90 minutes, but the field finally completed the day's round. Reichel still led with 217 for 54 holes after a round of 74, but Stopa gained four strokes on Reichel with 70, and with 18 holes to play he was five strokes behind. After 17 holes of the final round, Reichel, Hitch, and Stopa were tied. Reichel three-putted the 17th, Hitch bogied the 18th, and when Stopa made two steady pars, the Championship was his. In the Team Championship, Seattle, Wash., won the Warren G. Harding Trophy, defeating Detroit in a playoff. The entry was 3,653, the largest for any USGA Championship in 1973.

1974—Charles Barenaba, 20-year old student from the island of Oahu, became the third Hawaiian to hold a national Championship when he took the Amateur Public Links title at the No. 1 Course at Brookside Golf Club, Pasadena, Calif. It was quite appropriate that a Hawaiian should win because 187 Hawaiians entered the 1974 Championship, out of an entry of 3,948, and nine qualified for the Championship proper. Barenaba scored a two-over par 290, defeating Frank Mazion, a 33-year-old airlines maintenance man from San Francisco, by two strokes. Jim Everham, a 47-year-old mail carrier from Seattle, Wash., was third at 293. Spencer Sappington, of Manchester, Mo., led after the first and second rounds on scores of 68 and 73, but he shot 78 in the third round and finished tied for fifth. His 68 was the lowest round of the Championship. Randy Barenaba, 17-year-old brother of Charles, tied Sappington. San Francisco won the Warren G. Harding Trophy as the Team Champion. Mazion, Tom Smith, and Lamar Bass made up the San Francisco Team which shot 442. Honolulu was second at 444. Barenaba entered the final 18 holes one stroke ahead of Mazion and increased his lead to two when Mazion bogied the second hole. By the end of nine holes, however, Mazion had made up three strokes and was in the lead. Mazion then lost two strokes to par on the 10th and Barenaba went ahead by one. Barenaba saved a bogie on the 12th by ricocheting a shot off a brick wall to where he had a clear shot at the green and eventually holed a six-foot putt. Barenaba then increased his lead to two strokes on the 13th and the remaining holes were halved.

1975—Randyn Barenaba, 18, whose brother Charles won the Public Links Amateur Championship in 1974, kept the title in the family by defeating Allan Yamamoto on the 37th hole of their final match at the Wailua Golf Course on the island of Kauai. Both finalists were from Hawaii, and the Team representing Honolulu won the Warren G. Harding

Trophy Cup in three-man-team competition. Yamamoto, from Honolulu and David Ishii, of Lihue, were co-medalists with 144, even par. In the final match, Barenaba was 1-up after the morning round. He was 1-down, however, after nine holes of the afternoon round when Yamamoto, 40, scored four birdies for a medal 32 to Barenaba's 34. The next seven holes were halved, but Yamamoto was bunkered on the par-3 17th hole and bogied while Barenaba birdied. The match was square after the scheduled 36 holes. On the extra hole, a 520-yard par 5, Barenaba pitched to within three feet of the cup and Yamamoto was 35 feet away. He putted six feet past the hole and when he missed coming back, he conceded the birdie and the match to Barenaba. A field of 4,601 players filed entries, a record for any Championship conducted by the USGA.

1976—Eddie Mudd, of Louisville, Ky., defeated Archie Dadian, South Milwaukee, Wis., on the first extra hole of their scheduled 36-hole final match at the Bunker Hills Golf Course, Coon Rapids, Minn. Medalist was Jeff Thomas, of Boise, Idaho, with four-under par 140. Defending Champion, Randyn Barenaba, of Hawaii, was beaten in the second round by Arthur Fujita, also from Hawaii. Detroit, Mich. won the team competition for the Warren G. Harding Trophy. Mudd, a 22-year-old college senior, was 2-up on Dadian, 42, after 18 holes. Dadian won the 20th and 21st holes to pull even, and was 1-up with two holes to play. Mudd then birdied the 35th hole to square the match and they halved the 36th, forcing extra holes. Mudd won on the 37th when Dadian went two over par. Mudd was one over. A field of 4,015 filed entries.

1977—Jerry Vidovic, 20, of Blue Island, Ill., defeated Jeff Kern, Tucson, Ariz., 4 and 2, in the final at the Brown Deer Park Golf Course in Madison, Wis. This was the third time that the Amateur Public Links Championship was played at Brown Deer Park. Vidovic was co-medalist with Peter Jacobi, of Dayton, Ohio. Both scored 142 for 36 holes—even par. No one had been both Champion and medalist since R. H. Sikes, in 1961. Jacobi lost in the third round to Kim Hubbart, of Spokane, Wash., 3 and 2. Hubbard lost to Kern in the semi-final round. Vidovic defeated Spencer Sappington, of Manchester, Mo., 4 and 3, in the other semi-final. Vidovic played the morning round of the final in 70, one under par, and took a 3-up lead to lunch. In the afternoon he scored ten consecutive pars before making a bogey at the 11th and a double-bogey at the 13th. He still led by three holes. The match ended when Vidovic won the 16th. The Tacoma, Wash., Team of C. Peter Niles, Jeff Baker and Bill Gunderson won the Warren G. Harding Trophy for the Team Championship. The entry of 3,703 was well under the record 4,601 set in 1975.

1978—Dean Prince, 40, of Santa Rosa, Calif., survived a 14-man playoff for the last 11 places in match play, and went on to win the Amateur Public Links Championship, defeating Tony Figueredo, of Miami, Fla., 5 and 3, in the final. The Championship was played at the Bangor Municipal Golf Course in Bangor, Maine. It was the first USGA event ever played in Maine. The medalist was Mike Campbell, of Louisville, Ky., who had 138, two under par, in the 36-hole qualifying round. He lost to Kim Hubbard in a first-round 20-hole match. Fourteen players, including Prince, had 153 totals to force a playoff for the final 11 places in the 64-player match-play draw. Prince birded the first extra hole to qualify. Jerry Vidovic, the defending Champion, qualified with 149, but lost in the second round to Samuel Hunt, 1 up. In the semi-final matches, Prince eliminated Dale Loeslein on the 19th hole, and Figueredo defeated Doug Ward, 5 and 3. Prince led, 3 up, after the first five holes of the final match. He birdied the second and fourth holes during the stretch. Figuerdo cut his deficit to one hole after the first nine. Prince then won three holes on the second nine and took a 4-up lead at lunch. Figueredo could come no closer than within three holes the rest of the match. The match ended when the 14th hole was halved in par. The Louisville, Ky., Team of Mike Campbell, Jodie Mudd, and Vaughan Jones won the Team Championship. There were 3,929 entries, short of the record of 4,601 set in 1975.

1979—Dennis Walsh, 35, of Groves, Tex., defeated Eric Mork, of Wichita, Kans., 4 and 4, in the final at the West Delta Gold course, Portland, Ore. Walsh, a technical shift foreman for an oil company, was also co-medalist with Vic Wilk, of Sepulveda, Calif., with 36-hole qualifying scores of 140, two under par. Wilk lost in the quarter-finals to Roy Biancalana, 3 and 2. Walsh was never more than one over par in any match. He defeated Ted Brodzik, 2 and 1; Arthur Fujita, the 1969 runner-up, 6 and 4; Art Diaz, 3 and 2; Jeff Short, 1 up; and Jodie Mudd, 2 and 1, in the semi-finals.

Mork, who got into the Championship as second alternate, defeated Baker Maddera, 4 and 3; Steven Johnson, 3 and 2; Michael Taylor, 2 and 1; Thomas Hines, 2 and 1; and was three under par in eliminating Roy Biancalana, 5 and 4, in the semi-finals. In the scheduled 36-hole final, Mork birdied the first two holes for a two-hole lead. Walsh took advantage of Mork's inconsistency over the next seven holes and had a 1 up lead after the first nine holes. After 18 holes, Walsh was 2 up. In the afternoon round, Walsh rain a 20-foot birdie putt on the first hole to extend his lead to 3 up. Walsh increased his lead to 6 up with six holes to play. Mork won the 13th and 14th holes with pars and was four down with four holes to play. But at the 15th hole, Walsh holed a 25-foot putt for a birdie 3 to win the Championship. Walsh was one under par for 33 holes in the final, including a 69, two under par, in the morning round. Winners of the Team Trophy were Art Diaz, Anthony Grimes, and Jim Blanford, of Phoenix, Ariz., with a 36-hole team total of 431, two strokes better than the team from Chicago, Ill. The 4,170 entries was short of the record of 4,601 entries set in 1975.

1980—Jodie Mudd, 20, of Louisville, Kentucky, won the Championship with a 9 and 8 victory over Richard Gordon, 24, of Santa Clara, California, at the Edgewood Tahoe Golf Course in Stateline, Nevada, the first time a USGA competition had been played in Nevada. Mudd, a junior at Georgia Southern College, is the brother of Eddie Mudd, the 1976 Champion. Their father, Edward Mudd, Jr., serves on the USGA Public Links Committee. Billy Tuten, of Palatka, Florida, and David Ogrin, of Waukegan, Illinois, tied for medalist with scores of 144, even par. Mudd was only pressed in his first round match against George Beebe, winning, 2 and 1. He won his other matches by scores of 8 and 7, 6 and 5, 6 and 4, and 3 and 2. Gordon had closer matches, winning 1 up, 3 and 2, 2 and 1, 1 up, and 3 and 1. In the final match, Mudd shot a 69 in the morning, including four birdies on the second nine, for a 9 up lead before lunch. Mudd maintained his lead in the afternoon and finished even par over 28 holes. Mudd's margin of victory was the second largest in the 55-year history of the Championship. In 1965, Arne Dokka defeated Leo Zampedro 10 and 9 in the final. Winners of the Team Trophy were the Los Angeles team of Vic Wilk, Mickey Yokoi, and Lynn Stone with a 36-hole score of 464, three strokes ahead of a team from San Francisco. The USGA received 4,416 entries, second only to the record 4,601 set in 1975.

AMATEUR PUBLIC LINKS CHAMPIONSHIP

DATE	WINNER, RUNNER-UP	SCORE	SITE	ENTRY
1960 (July)	Verne Callison d. Tyler Caplin	7 & 6	Al Wai G.C., Honolulu, Hawaii Co-Medalists—146: Owne T. Douglass, Jr. Richard H. Hopwood Harlan Stevenson	2,718
1961 (July)	Richard H. Sikes d. John A. Molenda	4 & 3	Rackham G.C. Detroit, Mich. Medalist—135: Richard H. Sikes	2,409
1962 (July)	Richard H. Sikes d. Hung Soo Ahn	2 & 1	Sheridan Park G.C., Tonawanda, N.Y. Medalist—145: George Archer	2,241
1963 (July)	Robert Lunn d. Stephen Oppermann	1 up	Haggin Oaks Municipal G.C., Sacramento, Calif. Medalist—141: John Jospeh	2,358
1964 (July)	William McDonald d. Dean Wilson, Jr.	5 & 3	Francis A. Gross G.C., Minneapolis, Minn. Medalist—135: Steve Oppermann	2,692
1965 (July)	Arne Dokka d. Leo Zampedro	10 & 9	North Park G.C., Pittsburgh, Pa. Medalist—144: Stanley Poploski	2,683
1966 (July)	Lamont Kaser d. Dave Ojala	6 & 5	Brown Deer Park G.C., Milwaukee, Wis. Medalist—137: Arne Dokka	2,912
		All Stroke Play		
1967 (July) Ronald Stokley 288	Verne Callison	287 Seattle, Wash.	Jefferson Park G.C.,	2,849
1968 (July)	Gene Towry Robert R. Unger	292 294	Tenison Memorial Municipal G.C., Dallas, Texas	3,316
1969 (July)	John M. Jackson, Jr. Arthur S. Fujita Fred Lufkin	292 294 294	Downing G.C., Erie, Pa.	3,754
Steven F. Cook 294	Joseph Andron, Jr.	294		
1970 (July)	Robert Risch Mike Zimmerman	293 296	Cog Hill No. 4 G.C. Lemont, Ill.	4,015
1971 (July)	Fred Haney Bob Bloomberg	290 295	Papago G.C. Phoenix, Ariz.	4,174
1972 (July)	Bob Allard Rick Schultz	285-71 285-74	Coffin Municipal G. C., Indianapolis, Ind.	3,743
1973 (July)	Stan Stopa Gary Hitch Philip Reichel	294 295 295	Flanders Valley G. C., Flanders, N.J.	3,653
1974 (July)	Charles Barenaba, Jr. Frank Mazion	290 292	Brookside G.C., Pasadena, Calif.	3,948
		Match Play		
1975 (July)	Randyn Barenaba d. Alan Yamamoto	1 up, 37 holes	Wailua G.C., Kauai, Hawaii Co-Medalists—144: Alan Yamamoto David Ishii	§4,601
1976 (July)	Eddie Mudd d. Archie Dadian	1 up, 37 holes	Bunker Hills G. C., Coon Rapids, Minn. Medalist—140: Jeffrey Thomas	4,105
1977 (July)	Jerry Vidovic d. Jeff Kern	4 & 2	Brown Deer Park G. C., Milwaukee, Wis. Co-Medalists—142: Jerry Vidovic Peter Jacobi	3,703
1978 (July)	Dean Prince d. Tony Figueredo	5 & 3	Bangor Municipal G. C., Bangor, Maine Medalist—138: Mike Campbell	3,929
1979 (July)	Dennis Walsh d. Eric Mork	4 & 3	West Delta S. C., Portland, Ore. Co-Medalists—140: Dennis Walsh Vic Wilk	4,170
1980 (July)	Jodie Mudd d. Rick Gordon	9 & 8	Edgewood Tahoe G.C. Stateline, Nev. Co-Medalists—144: David Ogrin Billy Tuten	4,416

Record qualifying score, 134, by James C. Clark Jr., in 1946.
§ Record entry

AMATEUR PUBLIC LINKS TEAM CHAMPIONSHIP

DATE	WINNER	TEAM SCORE	SITE	ENTRY
1960 (July)	Pasedena, Calif.	453	Ala Wai G.C., Honolulu, Hawaii	26
1961 (July)	Honolulu, Hawaii	428	Rackham G.C. Detroit, Mich.	28
1962 (July)	Seattle, Wash.	451	Sheridan Park, G.C., Tonawanda, N.Y.	28
1963 (July)	Toledo, Ohio	443	Haggin Oaks Municipal G.C., Sacramento, Calif.	30
1964 (July)	Los Angeles, Calif.	435	Francis A. Gross G.C. Minneapolis, Minn.	26
1965 (July)	Phoenix, Ariz.	445	North Park G.C. Pittsburgh, Pa.	27
1966 (July)	Pittsburgh, Pa.	449	Brown Deer Park G.C., Milwaukee, Wis.	32
1967 (July)	Dayton, Ohio	436	Jefferson Park G.C., Seattle, Wash.	29
1968 (July)	Dallas, Texas	447	Tenison Memorial Municipal G.C., Dallas, Texas	28
1969 (July)	Pasadena, Calif.	447	Downing Golf Course, Erie, Pa.	27
1970 (July)	Chicago, Ill.	445	Cog Hill No. 4 Golf Course, Lemont, Ill.	30
1971 (July)	Portland, Ore.	441	Papago Golf Course, Phoenix, Ariz.	30
1972 (July)	Portland, Ore.	430	Coffin Municipal G. C., Indianapolis, Ind.	28
1973 (July)	Seattle, Wash.	457	Flanders Valley G. C., Flanders, N.J.	30
	Runner-up: Detroit, Mich.	457		
1974 (July)	San Francisco, Calif.	442	Brookside G. C., Pasadena, Calif.	31
1975 (July)	Honolulu, Hawaii	439	Wailua G. C., Kauai, Hawaii	32
1976 (July)	Detroit, Mich.	446	Bunker Hills G. C., Coon Rapids, Minn.	35
1977 (July)	Tacoma, Wash.	440	Brown Deer Park G. C., Milwaukee, Wisc.	35
1978 (July)	Louisville, Ky.	440	Bangor Municipal G. C., Bangor, Maine	37
1979 (July)	Phoenix, Ariz.	431	West Delta G. C. Portland, Ore.	36
1980 (July)	Los Angeles, Calif.	464	Edgewood Tahoe G.C. Stateline, Nev.	36

1960

THIRTY-FIFTH AMATEUR PUBLIC LINKS CHAMPIONSHIP

Held at the Ala Wai Golf Course, Honolulu, Hawaii, July 11-16.

Yardage–6,677. Par 71. 2,718 Entries, 150 Qualifiers, 150 Starters.

Qualifying Score	1st Round (18 Holes)	2nd Round (18 Holes)	3rd Round (18 Holes)	4th Round (18 Holes)	Semi-Finals (18 Holes)	Final (36 Holes)	
148	Tom Dixon, Daly City, Calif.	Ahn, 2 and 1					
148	Hung Soo Ahn, Honolulu, Hawaii		Ahn, 1 up, 19 hls.				
156	**William A. Wright, Seattle, Wash.**	Douglass, 3 and 2					
146	***Owen T. Douglass, Jr., Honolulu, Hawaii**			Callison, 3 and 2			
154	Verne Callison, Sacramento, Calif.	Callison, 1 up					
152	Gene Hansen, Minneapolis, Minn.		Callison, 1 up				
152	Masa Kaya, Honolulu, Hawaii	Kaya, 4 and 3					
153	Brown Cullen, Jr., Louisville, Ky.				Callison, 2 and 1		
155	Mike Stolarik, Waukegan, Ill.	Brown, 2 and 1					
153	Clifford Brown, Cleveland, Ohio		Brown, 2 and 1				
155	Hank Magnaris, San Francisco, Calif.	Magnaris, 4 and 3					
155	H.C. Miracle, Jr., Washington, D.C.			Takiguchi, 1 up			
154	**Tom Takiguchi, Honolulu, Hawaii**	Takiguchi, 2 and 1					
156	**Wallace Smith, Pontiac, Mich.**		Takiguchi, 4 and 3				
149	James T. McMurtrey, San Leandro, Calif.	Barrett, 3 and 2					
152	Richard T. Barrett, Portland, Ore.					Callison, 1 up	
152	David Bettencourt, Honolulu, Hawaii	Borseth, 1 up, 20 hls.					
155	Ray Borseth, Minneapolis, Minn.		Essig, 4 and 3				
151	Tommy Jenkins, Jacksonville, Fla.	Essig, 2 and 1					
148	Don Essig, III, Indianapolis, Ind.			Claveran, 1 up			
156	**Bernie Salter, Tacoma, Wash.**	Leonard, 5 and 4					
153	Kenneth M. Leonard, Portland, Ore.		Claveran, 3 and 2				
150	Richard Clover, Norwalk, Calif.	Claveran, 5 and 3					
147	Felix G. Claveran, Stockton, Calif.				Andonian, 3 and 2		
146	*Richard H. Hopwood, Phoenix, Ariz.	Hopwood, 4 and 2					
154	Walter F. Russell, Aurora, Colo.		Andonian, 1 up				
156	**Charles J. McKay, Kailua, Hawaii**	Andonian, 2 and 1					
150	Mike Andonian, Pontiac, Mich.			Andonian, 1 up, 19 hls.			
153	Edward Gladysz, Brookfield, Ohio	Gladysz, 3 and 2					
153	William R. Graham, Miami, Fla.		Stevenson, 5 and 3				
146	*Harlan Stevenson, Long Beach, Calif.	Stevenson, 3 and 2					
151	Elmer Clites, Antioch, Calif.						Verne Callison, 7 and 6
152	Hal McCommas, Dallas, Texas	Valuck, 1 up					
152	Dr. Sam W. Valuck, Denver, Colo.		Valuck, 2 and 1				
148	Jack H. Omuro, Honolulu, Hawaii	Nelson, 1 up, 19 hls.					
152	William O. Nelson, Denver, Colo.			McMasters, 1 up			
151	Stephen M. Swain, Sr., Los Angeles, Calif.	Latawiec, 2 and 1					
156	**Chester W. Latawiec, Minneapolis, Minn.**		McMasters, 1 up				
152	Eugene Lake, Toledo, Ohio	McMasters, 5 and 4					
151	Robert L. McMasters, Royal Oak, Mich.				McMasters, 3 and 1		
149	James E. Everham, Seattle, Wash.	Everham, 2 and 1					
153	**Lamont A. Kaser, Wichita**, Kans.		Huff, 3 and 2				
152	Frank H. Huff, Phoenix, Ariz.	Huff, 2 and 1					
156	**Charles Beyer, Fargo, North Dakota**			Santoki, 5 and 4			
150	Marshall Dallas, Seattle, Wash.	Roach, 3 and 2					
155	Joe Roach, Pacoima, Calif.		Santoki, 3 and 2				
151	Toshio Santoki, Honolulu, Hawaii	Santoki, 3 and 2					
152	Brian Goldsworthy, Salt Lake City, Utah					Caplin, 5 and 4	
153	Tyler Caplin, East Lansing, Mich.	Caplin, 2 and 1					
156	**Robert Mueller, Greendale, Wis.**		Caplin, 4 and 3				
154	Bob Ludlow, Indianapolis, Ind.	Campagni, 1 up					
154	Julio Campagni, Highwood, Ill.			Caplin, 4 and 2			
155	Robert A. Howe, Los Angeles, Calif.	Carson, 1 up					
156	**John Carson, Atlanta, Ga.**		Carson, 3 and 2				
151	Emil Esposito, Franklin Park, Ill.	Campbell, by default					
154	Frank Campbell, Jacksonville, Fla.				Caplin, 2 up		
151	Michael C. Rashkow, Miami, Fla.	Karlin, 7 and 6					
155	Robert E. Karlin, Denver, Colo.		Karlin, 1 up				
154	Takeo Kaneshina, Honolulu, Hawaii	O'Neill, 2 up					
149	Dr. Joseph J. O'Neill, Pasadena, Calif.			Dixon, 4 and 3			
153	Floyd E. Dixon, Memphis, Tenn.	Dixon, 4 and 3					
154	Remo Crovetti, Highwood, Ill.		Dixon, 1 up				
150	Charles Farrington, Kokomo, Ind.	Stewart, 3 and 2					
154	James F. Stewart, Dallas, Texas						

*Medalists.

Thirty-fourth Amateur Public Links Team Championship, Harding Trophy, 26 Entries, July 11-12: Won by Pasadena, California team, 453 for 36 holes (Harlan Stevenson, 146; Richard Clover, 150; Ray Swedo, Jr., 157); second Honolulu, Hawaii team 457 (Hung Soo Ahn, 148; Daniel K.W. Kop, 157; Masa Kaya, 152); third, Denver, Colo. team 458 (Dr. Sam W. Valuck, 152; William O. Nelson, 152; Walter F. Russell, 154).

1961
THIRTY-SIXTH AMATEUR PUBLIC LINKS CHAMPIONSHIP

Held at the Rackham Golf Course, Detroit, Michigan, July 10-15.

Yardage—6,538. Par 70. 2,409 Entries, 150 Qualifiers, 150 Starters.

Qualifying Score	1st Round (18 Holes)	2nd Round (18 Holes)	3rd Round (18 Holes)	4th Round (18 Holes)	Semi-Finals (36 Holes)	Final (36 Holes)	
135	*Richard H. Sikes, Wichita, Kans.	Sikes, 5 and 4					
147	Forrest T. Jones, Bloomington, Ind.		Sikes, 4 and 3				
144	Roy Cullenbine, Detroit, Mich.	Douglass, 3 and 2					
149	Owen T. Douglass, Jr., Honolulu, Hawaii			Sikes, 3 and 2			
142	Brown Cullen, Jr., Louisville, Ky.	Kolenda, 1 up					
148	Thomas P. Kolenda, Grand Rapids, Mich.		Pietras, 1 up, 19 hls.				
145	Leonard Pietras, Toledo, Ohio	Pietras, 4 and 2					
150	Tom Randall, New Orleans, La.				Sikes, 3 and 1		
141	William B. Kelley, Jr., Coraopolis, Pa.	Kelley, 2 up					
147	C.A. Ducker, Sr., Charleston, S.C.		Kelley, 4 and 3				
145	Douglas Wilson, Ypsilanti, Mich.	Turner, 3 and 2					
150	Hans R. Turner, Seattle, Wash.			Kelley, 4 and 3			
143	Alex Solanics, Cleveland, Ohio	Solanics, 6 and 5					
149	Mike Stolarik, Waukegan, Ill.		Clites, 3 and 1				
146	Elmer Clites, Antioch, Calif.	Clites, 6 and 5					
150	Carl L. Yung, Dayton, Ohio					Sikes, 2 and 1	
138	John Schlee, Memphis, Tenn.	Schlee, 2 up					
147	Dick Hopwood, Phoenix, Ariz.		Schlee, 4 and 3				
144	David Graska, Oshkosh, Wis.	Graska, 2 and 1					
149	Murphy Street, Baltimore, Md.			Schlee, 2 up			
142	Masa Kaya, Honolulu, Hawaii	Law, 2 and 1					
148	James Law, Harper Woods, Mich.		Law, 1 up				
145	Robert Murray, Xenia, Ohio	Murray, 3 and 2					
150	John Tershin, Seattle, Wash.				Schlee, 2 and 1		
142	Frank W. Campbell, Leeds, Ala.	Campbell, 4 and 3					
148	Robert Reynolds, Normandy, Mo.		Campbell, 6 and 5				
145	Don Pilarski, Kewanee, Ill.	May, 7 and 5					
150	LeRoy May, Racine, Wis.			Campbell, 2 and 1			
144	William Curtis, Farmington, Mich.	Curtis, 5 and 3					
149	Larry Madison, Chicago, Ill.		Atkins, 1 up				
146	Roy W. Atkins, Portland, Ore.	Atkins, 3 and 2					
150	Wayne H. Osborne, Oak Park, Ill.						Richard H. Sikes, 4 and 3
137	David Bettencourt, Honolulu, Hawaii	Bettencourt, 7 and 6					
147	William Crowe, Phoenix, Ariz.		Hughey, 2 and 1				
144	James E. Hughey, Memphis, Tenn.	Hughey, 2 and 1					
149	Herb Howe, Minneapolis, Minn.			Lunn, 2 up			
142	Hung Soo Ahn, Honolulu, Hawaii	Ahn, 4 and 3					
148	Donnie Robinson, Louisville, Ky.		Lunn, 1 up				
145	Bob Lunn, San Francisco, Calif.	Lunn, 1 up					
150	H.C. Miracle, Jr., Washington, D.C.				Molenda, 2 and 1		
141	John A. Molenda, Detroit, Mich.	Molenda, 4 and 3					
148	Woodrow Gray, Oklahoma City, Okla.		Molenda, 4 and 3				
145	Tom Dixon, Daly City, Calif.	Smith, 2 and 1					
150	Wallace Smith, Pontiac, Mich.			Molenda, 2 up			
144	Clifford Brown, Cleveland, Ohio	Graham, 3 and 2					
149	William R. Graham, Miami, Fla.		Wright, 2 and 1				
146	David B. Brown, Detroit, Mich.	Wright, 5 and 4					
150	William A. Wright, Seattle, Wash.					Molenda, 1 up	
140	Gerald J. Thomas, Beloit, Wis.	Tanaka, 5 and 4					
147	Thomas T. Tanaka, Honolulu, Hawaii		Tanaka, 2 and 1				
145	Glen L. Baxstrom, Denver, Colo.	Baxstrom, 3 and 2					
149	**Richard J. Habes, Jr., Sodus, N.Y.**			Andonian, 3 and 1			
143	Kaye Don Walker, Spokane, Wash.	Cook, 5 and 3					
148	Dennis Cook, Pasadena, Calif.		Andonian, 1 up, 20 hls.				
146	Mike M. Andonian, Pontiac, Mich.	Andonian, 5 and 4					
150	John C. Kurach, Detroit, Mich.				Gifford, 1 up		
142	Jim Ferriell, Jr., Louisville, Ky.	Ferriell, 1 up					
148	Ron Ghidina, Peoria, Ill.		Peterson, 1 up, 19 hls.				
145	Lamont A. Kaser, Wichita, Kans.	Peterson, 1 up					
150	Gary Peterson, Minneapolis, Minn.			Gifford, 2 and 1			
144	Thomas C. Jenkins, Jacksonville, Fla.	Jenkins, 1 up, 19 hls.					
149	Gene Lake, Toledo, Ohio		Gifford, 1 up				
146	Lou Gifford, Jacksonville, Fla.	Gifford, 6 and 4					
150	Joe Pennington, Jr., Phoenix, Ariz.						

*Medalist.

Thirty-fifth Amateur Public Links Team Championship, Harding Trophy, 20 Entries, July 10-11: Won by Honolulu, Hawaii, Team, 428 for 36 holes (David Bettencourt, 137; Hung Soo Ahn, 142; Owen T. Douglass, Jr., 149); second, Wichita, Kansas, Team, 431 (Lamont A. Kaser, 145; Richard H. Sikes, 135; David M. Dunn, 151); third, **Memphis, Tennessee Team, 438 (John** Schlee, 138; James E. Hughey, 144; Joseph J. Columbus, 156).

1962
THIRTY-SEVENTH AMATEUR PUBLIC LINKS CHAMPIONSHIP

Held at the Sheridan Park Golf Course, Tonawanda, N.Y., July 9-14.
Yardage—6,697. Par 70. 2,241 Entries, 150 Starters.

Qualifying Score	1st Round (18 Holes)	2nd Round (18 Holes)	3rd Round (18 Holes)	4th Round (18 Holes)	Semi-Finals (18 Holes)	Finals (36 Holes)
145†	George Archer, San Francisco, Calif.	Archer, 3 and 2				
153	Fred Lufkin, Spokane, Wash.		**Oppermann,** 4 and 3			
151	Roy G. Widstrom, Minneapolis, Minn.	Oppermann, 4 and 2				
155	Stephen Oppermann, Millbrae, Calif.			Farmer, 2 and 1		
149	Richard Potzner, Los Angeles, Calif.	Potzner, 3 and 2				
155	**James Masuyama, Kailua, Hawaii**		Farmer, 3 and 2			
152	Hubert Farmer, Toledo, Ohio	Farmer, 4 and 3			Sikes, 7 and 6	
156	Paul Franke, Louisville, Ky.					
148	John Joseph, Hayward, Calif.	Joseph, 6 and 5				
154	John R. Floch, Troy, Mich.		Joseph, **by default**			
151	James Walker, Jr., New York, N.Y.	Dixon, 3 and 1				
156	David Dixon, Memphis, Tenn.			Sikes, 1 up		
150	Richard H. Sikes, Springdale, Ark.	Sikes, 3 and 2				
155	Thomas F. Hovey, Utica, N.Y.		Sikes, 3 and 2			
152	William Rist, Chesterland, Ohio	Rist, 1 up				Sikes, 4 and 3
157*	J. L. Blakenship, Memphis, Tenn.					
147	Gene Hansen, Minneapolis, Minn.	Peterson, 3 and 2				
154	Gary C. Peterson, Minneapolis, Mo.		Kaser, 4 and 3			
151	Andrew Holmes, Toledo, Ohio	Kaser, 3 and 2				
156	Lamont A. Kaser, Wichita, Kans.			Strout, 1 up		
150	**Chester W. Latawiec, Minneapolis, Minn.**	Latawiec, 2 and 1				
155	Val Bleech, Flint, Mich.		Strout, 2 and 1			
152	Warren E. Strout, Speedway, Ind.	Strout, 1 up, 19 hls.			Strout, 2 up	
157*	Thomas D. Balliet, Pontiac, Mich.					
148	John B. Wade, Jr., Memphis, Tenn.	Seamster, 1 up, 19 hls.				
154	Jay Seamster, San Diego, Calif.		Tindall, 1 up, 22 hls.			
151	William L. Tindall, Seattle, Wash.	Tindall, 1 up, 19 hls.				
156	Francis J. Hoch, Oklahoma City, Okla.			Howe, 1 up		
151	Herb Howe, Minneapolis, Minn.	Howe, 4 and 3				
155	Joseph Lazor, Cleveland, Ohio		Howe, 1 up			
153	Earvin Scott, Seattle, Wash.	Scott, 1 up				Richard H. Sikes, 2 and 1
157*	Gregory Dikilato, Kailua, Hawaii					
146	Lalu Sabotin, Warren, Ohio	Sabotin, 1 up, 19 hls.				
153	E. Arthur St. John, Oklahoma City, Okla.		Sabotin, 2 and 1			
151	Clarence Davenport, New Rochelle, N.Y.	Davenport, 5 and 4				
155	Nello Campagni, Highwood, Ill.			Ahn, 3 and 1		
149	Hung Soo Ahn, Honolulu, Hawaii	Ahn, 7 and 6				
155	Allan Yamamoto, Honolulu, Hawaii		Ahn, 4 and 3			
157*	Tim Sweborg, Dunlap, Ill.	Sweborg, 5 and 4			Ahn, 1 up, 19 hls.	
152	Richard Hopwood, Phoenix, Ariz.					
148	Bert Greene, Eastman, Ga.	Wilson, 2 and 1				
154	Douglas Wilson, Ypsilanti, Mich.		Wilson, 2 and 1			
151	Archie Dadian, Milwaukee, Wis.	Dadian, 6 and 5				
156	Leon R. Radde, Minneapolis, Minn.			Heedt, 4 and 3		
151	Alan Heedt, Peoria, Ill.	Heedt, 7 and 6				
155	Jack Pfeiffer, Indianapolis, Ind.		Heedt, 2 and 1			
153	William Scarbrough, Jr., Jacksonville, Fla.	Scarbrough, 3 and 2				Ahn, 1 up
157*	Orlis G. Caskey, Dayton, Ohio					
147	Kenneth Storey, Seattle, Wash.	Storey, 4 and 3				
154	David A. Wernicke, Jr., Milwaukee, Wis.		Schlee, 5 and 4			
151	Bill Arakawa, Honolulu, Hawaii	Schlee, 1 up, 19 hls.				
156	John Schlee, Memphis, Tenn.			Schlee, 5 and 4		
150	Tom Sisolak, Waukegan, Ill.	Harrington, 2 and 1				
155	Denis J. Harrington, Indianapolis, Ind.		Massey, 2 and 1			
152	O. T. Douglass, Jr., Honolulu, Hawaii	Massey, 1 up, 21 hls.			Breck, 2 and 1	
157*	Raymond Massey, Miami, Fla.					
149	John C. Kurach, Detroit, Mich.	Kurach, 5 and 4				
155	Edwin L. Jones, Peoria, Ill.		Kaya, 2 and 1			
152	Masa Kaya, Honolulu, Hawaii	Kaya, 1 up				
156	Arnold Salinas, Dallas, Texas			Breck, 4 and 3		
151	Wayne T. Breck, Scottsdale, Ariz.	Breck, 5 and 4				
155	Reese R. Berry, Indianapolis, Ind.		Breck, 2 and 1			
153	William Curtis, Farmington, Mich.	Poploski, 1 up, 19 hls.				
157*	Stanley P. Poploski, Pittsburgh, Pa.					

†Medalist.
*Qualified in playoff.
Thirty-sixth Amateur Public Links Team Championship, Harding Trophy, 28 Entries, July 9-10: Won by Seattle, Wash. Team, 451 for 36 holes (William Lloyd Tindall, 151; Earvin Scott, 153; Kenneth Storey, 147); second Honolulu, Hawaii Team, 452 (Bill Arakawa, 151; Masa Kaya, 152; Hung Soo Ahn, 149); third San Francisco, Calif. Team, 453 (George Archer, 145; James T. McMurtrey, 160; John Joseph, 148).

1963
THIRTY-EIGHTH AMATEUR PUBLIC LINKS CHAMPIONSHIP

Held at the Haggin Oaks Municipal Golf Course, Sacramento, Calif., July 8-13.
Yardage—6,702. Par 72. 2,358 Entries, 150 Qualifiers, 149 Starters.

Qualifying Score	1st Round (18 Holes)	2nd Round (18 Holes)	3rd Round (18 Holes)	4th Round (18 Holes)	Semi-Final (36 Holes)	Final (36 Holes)	
141	*John Joseph, Hayward, Calif.	Smith, 4 and 3	Castagnetto, 3 and 2	Castagnetto, 3 and 2	Oppermann, 4 and 3	Oppermann, 4 and 3	Robert Lunn, 1 up
152	Wallace J. Smith, Pontiac, Mich.						
149	Andrew Holmes, Toledo, Ohio	Castagnetto, 3 and 2					
154	Ed Castagnetto, Jr., San Francisco, Calif.						
146	Wendell Kop, Honolulu, Hawaii	Kitsuwa, 3 and 2	Kitsuwa, 1 up				
153	Naomitsu Kitsuwa, Honolulu, Hawaii						
151	Richard Potzner, Los Angeles, Calif.	Potzner, 1 up, 19 hls.					
154	Dick Hopwood, Phoenix, Ariz.						
144	Hubert Farmer, Toledo, Ohio	Farmer, 3 and 2	Omuro, 1 up	Oppermann, 3 and 1			
152	Les W. Klabunde, Garden Grove, Calif.						
150	Bill Dorece, Racine, Wis.	Omuro, 4 and 3					
154	Jack H. Omuro, Honolulu, Hawaii						
147	Steve Oppermann, San Francisco, Calif.	Oppermann, 3 and 2	Oppermann, 2 and 1				
153	Rolf Deming, Minneapolis, Minn.						
151	Thomas Huber, Minneapolis, Minn.	Huber, 2 up					
155	**Lee M. Evans, Indianapolis, Ind.**						
143	Foster C. Bradley, Los Angeles, Calif.	Vicini, 3 and 2	Vicini, 5 and 4	Vicini, 2 and 1	Vicini, 1 up, 19 hls.		
152	Dante C. Vicini, Ottawa, Ill.						
150	Edward Briegel, Ann Arbor, Mich.	Latawiec, 4 and 3					
154	**Chester W. Latawiec, Minneapolis, Minn.**						
146	Tom Randall, New Orleans, La.	Cullen, 4 and 3	Cullen, 4 and 2				
153	Brown Cullen, Jr., Louisville, Ky.						
151	George E. Bass, Sacramento, Calif.	Bass, 3 and 2					
154	Samuel E. Lima, Hazel Park, Mich.						
145	R.H. Sikes, Wichita, Kansas	Sikes, 6 and 5	Sikes, 5 and 4	Sikes, 3 and 2			
152	David Hellman, Waukegan, Ill.						
150	Arnold Salinas, Dallas, Texas	Kurach, 1 up					
154	John Kurach, Detroit, Mich.						
149	John Schlee, Memphis, Tenn.	Schlee, 3 and 2	Schlee, 5 and 4				
153	James McMurtrey, San Leandro, Calif.						
152	Paul Joseph Franke, Louisville, Ky.	Franke, 6 and 5					
155	**Ernie Arnone, Renton, Wash.**						
142	Leroy Beasley, Dallas, Texas	Beasley, 1 up, 19 hls.	Sniffen, 3 and 2	Osborne, 1 up	Yuke, 1 up	Lunn, 3 and 1	
152	James E. Everham, Seattle, Wash.						
150	Clyde E. Sniffen, Everett, Wash.	Sniffen, 1 up,25 hls.					
154	Hung Soo Ahn, Honolulu, Hawaii						
146	Robert Lucas, Minneapolis, Minn.	Creasey, 2 and 1	Osborne, 1 up, 19 hls.				
153	Paul Creasey, Sacramento, Calif.						
151	Dennis Reger, Spokane, Wash.	Osborne, 3 and 2					
154	Wayne Osborne, Oak Park, Ill.						
145	Leonard Fiocca, Macomb, Ill.	Fiocca, 1 up	Fiocca, 2 and 1	Yuke, 3 and 1			
152	Mike Panniccia, Fresno, Calif.						
150	Leonard A. Pietras, Toledo, Ohio	Pietras, 1 up, 19 hls.					
154	Mike Bellows, Fresno, Calif.						
148	Edward T. Barnes, Jr., Atlanta, Ga.	Bisesi, 4 and 2	Yuke, 4 and 2				
153	Donel Vince Bisesi, Miami, Fla.						
151	Douglas B. King, Sacramento, Calif.	Yuke, 1 up					
155	**Jerry Yuke, Sacramento, Calif.**						
144	Daniel J. Scott, Seattle, Wash.	Scott, 2 and 1	Scott, 4 and 3	Scott, 4 and 3	Lunn, 1 up, 19 hls.		
152	Robert E. Smith, Sacramento, Calif.						
150	Marty Boehne, St. Paul, Minn.	Boehne, 1 up					
154	Robert Wright, Seattle, Wash.						
147	George B. Cram, Jr., Bismarck, N.D.	Cram, 2 and 1	Cram, 5 and 4				
153	Verne Perry, Jr., Portland, Ore.						
151	Robert Unger, Milwaukee, Wis.	Wheeler, 4 and 3					
154	Jim Wheeler, Peoria, Ill.						
146	Henry Suico, Oakland, Calif.	Suico, 3 and 2	Abbott, 5 and 4	Lunn, 5 and 4			
152	Philip N. Anderson, Spokane, Wash.						
151	Jerry Abbott, Tulsa, Okla.	Abbott, 1 up, 20 hls.					
154	William A. Giese, Woodale, Ill.						
149	Leon Anderson, Hobbs, New Mexico	Lunn, 5 and 4	Lunn, 3 and 2				
153	Robert Lunn, San Francisco, Calif.						
152	David C. Bettencourt, Honolulu, Hawaii	Kaser, 2 and 1					
155	**Lamont A. Kaser, Wichita, Kansas**						

*Medalist.

Amateur Public Links Team Championship, Harding Trophy, 30 Entries, July 8-9: Won by Toledo, Ohio, Team, 443 for 36 holes (Hubert Farmer, 144; Andrew Holmes, 149; Leonard Pietras, 150); Second, Long Beach, Calif., Team, 446 (Foster C. Bradley, 143; Richard Potzner, 151; Les W. Klabunde, 152); third place tie, Minneapolis, Minn., Team, 451 (Thomas Huber, 151; Chester W. Latawiec, 153; Robert Lucas, 146) and Peoria, Ill., Team, (Jim Wheeler, 154; Dante Vicini, 152; Leonard Fiocca, 145).

1964
THIRTY-NINTH AMATEUR PUBLIC LINKS CHAMPIONSHIP

Held at Francis A. Gross Golf Course, Minneapolis, Minn., July 13-18.
Yardage—6,593. Par 70. 2,692 Entries, 150 Qualifiers, 150 Starters.

Qualifying Score	1st Round (18 Holes)	2nd Round (18 Holes)	3rd Round (18 Holes)	4th Round (18 Holes)	Semi-Finals (36 Holes)	Final (36 Holes)	
135	*Steve Oppermann, San Francisco, Calif.	Carlson, 1 up, 19 hls.	Carlson, 1 up	Dokka, 1 up, 23 hls.	Dokka, 2 and 1	Wilson, 1 up, 38 hls.	William McDonald, 5 and 3
147	James Carlson, Hopkins, Minn.						
145	Gregory Dikilato, Kailua, Oahu, Hawaii	Dikilato, 3 and 2					
149	Brian M. Field, Minneapolis, Minn.						
143	Arne Dokka, Sherman Oaks, Calif.	Dokka, 4 and 3	Dokka, 1 up, 20 hls.				
148	Robert Rychert, Pittsburgh, Pa.						
146	Robert E. Smith, Sacramento, Calif.	Smith, 5 and 4					
150	**David Carter, Lesage, W. Va.**						
142	Dave Graska, Oshkosh, Wis.	Stolarik, 1 up	Adamczyk, 3 and 2	Adamczyk, 1 up, 19 hls.			
147	Mike Stolarik, Waukegan, Ill.						
146	Vincent Adamczyk, Pasadena, Calif.	Adamczyk, 3 and 2					
149	Maurice Driggins, Chattanooga, Tenn.						
145	Foster C. Bradley, Santa Monica, Calif.	Bradley, 7 and 6	Yee, 2 up				
148	Harry Boback, Jr., Erie, Pa.						
147	Alfred E. Krol, Mt. Clemens, Mich.	Yee, 1 up, 19 hls.					
150	**Clarence Yee, Honolulu, Hawaii**						
142	Dennis P. Murphy, Anchorage, Alaska	Murphy, 4 and 3	Murphy, 7 and 6	Murphy, 2 up	Wilson, 1 up		
147	Robert Turner, Cleveland, Ohio						
146	Thomas D. Balliet, Pontiac, Mich.	Balliet, 1 up					
149	Ken Friend, Chicago, Ill.						
144	Steve Whitman, San Francisco, Calif.	Whitman, 2 and 1	Whitman, 5 and 4				
148	Philip N. Anderson, Spokane, Wash.						
147	Eugene Lake, Toledo, Ohio	Lake, 1 up					
150	**Kenneth G. Storey, Seattle, Wash.**						
143	J.L. Blankenship, Memphis, Tenn.	Blankenship, 4 and 2	Blankenship, 3 and 1	Wilson, 3 and 1			
148	Gary L. Bray, Memphis, Tenn.						
146	George E. Bass, Citrus Heights, Calif.	Holmes, 1 up					
149	Andrew Holmes, Toledo, Ohio						
145	John C. MacMurray, Havertown, Pa.	MacMurray, 2 and 1	Wilson, 7 and 6				
149	Barry N. Klein, Baltimore, Md.						
147	Curtis H. Sifford, Los Angeles, Calif.	Wilson, 3 and 2					
150	**Dean Wilson, Jr., Omaha, Nebr.**						
141	George H. Welsh, Dayton, Ohio	Welsh, 1 up	Hawkins, 4 and 2	Smith, 4 and 3	McDonald, 1 up, 19 hls.	McDonald, 8 and 6	
147	Ron Pelias, New Orleans, La.						
145	Hubert Farmer, Toledo, Ohio	Hawkins, 1 up, 24 hls.					
149	Robert F. Hawkins, Takoma Park, Md.						
144	Robb R. Smith, Big Spring, Texas	Smith, 1 up	Smith, 1 up, 19 hls.				
148	Jinri Shinsato, Honolulu, Hawaii						
147	Robert Korsch, Pittsburgh, Pa.	Korsch, 3 and 1					
150	James Law, Harper Woods, Mich.						
142	William McDonald, Topeka, Kans.	McDonald, 2 up	McDonald, 1 up	McDonald, 1 up, 19 hls.			
147	Eddie Leonard, Detroit, Mich.						
146	Buddy McEwen, Nashville, Tenn.	Michaeloff, 3 and 2					
149	Wally Michaeloff, Minneapolis, Minn.						
145	Warren L. Simmons, Albuquerque, N.M.	Simmons, 2 and 1	Simmons, 1 up, 21 hls.				
148	Richard Taylor, Phoenix, Ariz.						
147	Robert Unger, Milwaukee, Wis.	Unger, 1 up					
150	**David Hicks, Duluth, Minn.**						
142	William J. Farkas, Phoenix, Ariz.	Farkas, 3 and 2	Adams, 3 and 2	Adams, 1 up	Adams, 1 up		
147	James T. McMurtrey, San Leandro, Calif.						
146	Donald G. Mosher, Hopkins, Minn.	Adams, 1 up					
149	Yates Adams, Jr., High Point, N.C.						
145	Billy Shelton, Jacksonville, Fla.	Shelton, 2 and 1	Shelton, 2 and 1				
148	Jerry Diamond, Peoria, Ill.						
147	Ras Allen, Dallas, Tex	Allen, 3 and 2					
150	**David Liebau, Erie, Pa.**						
143	Wallace C. Mizell, Jacksonville, Fla.	Arakawa, 2 and 1	Lunn, 1 up, 19 hls.	Lunn, 5 and 4			
148	Bill Arakawa, Honolulu, Hawaii						
146	Robert Lunn, San Francisco, Calif.	Lunn, 1 up					
149	Paul Franke, Louisville, Ky.						
145	**Chester W. Latawiec, Col. Heights, Minn.**	Latawiec, 3 and 1	Lee, 1 up				
149	Salvatore Pomante, Center Line, Mich.						
147	Kyu Num Lee, Keneohe, Hawaii	Lee, 2 and 1					
150	**Tom Randall, Metairie, La.**						

*Medalist.

Amateur Public Links Team Championship, Harding Trophy, 26 Entries, July 13-14: Won by Los Angeles, Calif., Team, 435 for 36 holes (Foster C. Bradley, 145; Arne Dokka, 143; Curtis H. Sifford, 147); Second, San Francisco, Calif., Team, 437 (John Steddin, 158; Steve Oppermann, 135; Steve Whitman, 144); Third, Toledo Team, 441 (Andrew Holmes, 149; Hubert Farmer, 145; Eugene Lake, 147).

1965
FORTIETH AMATEUR PUBLIC LINKS CHAMPIONSHIP

Held at the North Park Golf Course, Pittsburgh, Pa., July 12-17.

Yardage—6,781. Par 71. 2,683 Entries, 150 Qualifiers, 150 Starters.

Qualifying Score	1st Round (18 Holes)	2nd Round (18 Holes)	3rd Round (18 Holes)	4th Round (18 Holes)	Semi-Finals (18 Holes)	Final (18 Holes)	
144	*Stanley Poploski, Pittsburgh, Pa.	Poploski,					
151	Paul Creasey, Sacramento, Calif.	1 up	Poploski,				
149	James B. Masserio, Pittsburgh, Pa.	Masserio,	1 up				
153	Richard E. Johnson, Minneapolis, Minn.	4 and 3		Zampedro,			
147	Lee Evans, Indianapolis, Ind.	Evans,		5 and 4			
151	Francis E. Clifford, Boston, Mass.	5 and 4	Zampedro,				
150	Leo Zampedro, Warren, Ohio	Zampedro,	3 and 2				
154	George Cogbill, Dyersburg, Tenn.	3 and 1			Zampedro, 3 and 1		
146	Wendell Kop, Honolulu, Hawaii	Kop,					
151	Bill O'Connor, Los Angeles, Calif.	5 and 3	Kop,				
150	Dave Wernicke, River Hills, Wis.	Wernicke,	1 up				
153	Regis Votilla, Pittsburgh, Pa.	3 and 2		Kop,			
147	Dennis Ewing, Dallas, Texas	Ewing,		3 and 1			
152	David M. Cooper, Metairie, La.	1 up	Ewing,				
151	Charles W. Butler, Doraville, Ga.	Butler,	1 up, 21 hls.				
154	Galen Sorenson, Harlan, Iowa	2 up				Zampedro, 2 and 1	
146	Richard E. Heyl, Falls Church, Va.	Heyl,					
151	Danny Koroly, Twinsburg, Ohio	1 up, 19 hls.	Heyl,				
150	Jim P. Caires, San Leandro, Calif.	Harbist,	7 and 6				
153	Francis Harbist, Pittsburgh, Pa.	2 up		Bailey,			
147	Alan Jon Bailey, Cedar Rapids, Iowa	Bailey,		6 and 5			
152	Henry A. Birk, Indianapolis, Ind.	1 up	Bailey,				
151	Joe Pugh, Baltimore, Md.	Pugh,	1 up				
154	Mike M. Andonian, Pontiac, Mich.	5 and 4			Bailey, 3 and 2		
146	Les Wimp, Tempe, Ariz.	Wimp,					
151	Ray Uccelletti, Philadelphia, Pa.	2 and 1	Wimp,				
150	Lalu Sabotin, Warren, Ohio	Majka,	5 and 4				
154	Ed Majka, Brooklyn, N.Y.	3 and 2		Roney,			
148	Arthur C. Ellis, Wilmette, Ill.	Ellis,		1 up			
152	Geoffrey Ames, Glenview, Ill.	1 up, 19 hls.	Roney,				
151	George Roney, Pittsburgh, Pa.	Roney,	7 and 5				
155	Jim Wheeler, East Peoria, Ill.	3 and 2					Arne Dokka, 10 and 9
146	Sonny Ewing, Dallas, Texas	Ewing,					
151	Moreno C. Caso, Seattle, Wash.	3 and 2	Eichstaedt,				
149	Robert S. Eichstaedt, Miami, Fla.	Eichstaedt,	6 and 4				
153	Walt Smola, Omaha, Neb.	2 up		Eichstaedt,			
147	Tom Schenke, Phoenix, Ariz.	Schenke,		1 up, 19 hls.			
152	John Makitka, Carnegie, Pa.	1 up	Schenke,				
151	Bill Farkas, Jr., Phoenix, Ariz.	Farkas,	3 and 2				
154	Lavon E. Griffin, Sacramento, Calif.	7 and 6			Dokka, 5 and 4		
146	Hubert S. Farmer, Toledo, Ohio	Farmer,					
151	George Madsen, Racine, Wis.	1 up	Farmer,				
150	Wayne Etherton, St. Charles, Ill.	Etherton,	3 and 2				
153	Dale F. Lingenbrink, Seattle, Wash.	2 and 1		Dokka,			
148	Arne Dokka, Studio City, Calif.	Dokka,		2 and 1			
152	Carl L. Yung, Kettering, Ohio	3 and 2	Dokka,				
151	Frank Burka, Pittsburgh, Pa.	Latawiec,	1 up				
155	Chester W. Latawiec, Col. Hgts., Minn.	2 and 1				Dokka, 5 and 3	
146	**William McDonald, Topeka, Kansas**	McDonald,					
151	Richard Hardcastle, Warson Woods, Mo.	4 and 3	McDonald,				
150	H. E. Harris, No. Little Rock, Ark.	Petersen,	5 and 4				
153	Robert C. Petersen, Minneapolis, Minn.	2 and 1		Schroder,			
147	Richard Taylor, Phoenix, Ariz.	Boone,		2 and 1			
152	**Thomas Boone, Jr., Chattanooga, Tenn.**	1 up	Schroder,				
151	James Schroder, San Francisco, Calif.	Schroder,	3 and 2				
154	Steve Whitman, San Francisco, Calif.	2 and 1			Schroder, 5 and 4		
146	Ronald Greenbach, San Francisco, Calif.	Jacob,					
151	Andrew A. Jacob, McKees Rocks, Pa.	1 up	Jacob,				
150	Daniel Hogan, Denver, Colo.	Hogan,	1 up				
154	Richard A. Johnson, Englewood, Colo.	5 and 4		Grier,			
148	Clinton B. Whitney, Denver, Colo.	Whitney,		4 and 3			
153	Paul G. Snow, Denver, Colo.	1 up	Grier,				
151	Arnold J. Schuessler, Sandusky, Ohio	Grier,	3 and 2				
155	Rafus Grier, Dayton, Ohio	3 and 2					

*Medalist.

Amateur Public Links Team Championship, Harding Trophy, 27 Entries, July 12, 13—Won by Phoenix, Ariz., Team, 445 for 36 holes (Tom Schenke, 147; Richard Taylor, 147; Bill Farkas, Jr., 151); Second, Pasadena, Calif., Team, 454 (Arne Dokka, 148; Bill O'Connor, 151; Gerald Gallardo, 155); Third, Sacramento, Calif., Team, 465 (Paul Creasey, 151; Ed Griffin, 154; Sam Stassi, 160).

1966
FORTY-FIRST AMATEUR PUBLIC LINKS CHAMPIONSHIP

Held at the Brown Deer Park Golf Course, Milwaukee, Wis., July 11-16.

Yardage—6,765. Par 71. 2,912 Entries, 150 Qualifiers, 150 Starters.

Qualifying Score	1st Round (18 Holes)	2nd Round (18 Holes)	3rd Round (18 Holes)	4th Round (18 Holes)	Semi-Finals (36 Holes)	Final (36 Holes)	
137	*Arne Dokka, Studio City, Calif.	Dokka, 19 holes					
152	Michael J. Moriarty, San Francisco, Calif.		Dokka, 6 and 5				
151	Herb Bolden, Denver, Colo.	Bolden, 3 and 2					
154	Robert L. Clarke, Niagara Falls, N.Y.			Dokka, 3 and 2			
148	Mike T. O'Connell, Carthage, Ill.	O'Connell, 20 holes					
153	Rick Richards, Fresno, Calif.		Blankenship, 1 up				
152	J.L. Blankenship, Memphis, Tenn.	Blankenship, 2 and 1					
155	Cliff Schmitt, Aun Prairie, Wis.				Demling, 5 and 4		
146	George Demling, Louisville, Ky.	Demling, 6 and 5					
153	William Curtis, Detroit, Mich.		Demling, 6 and 5				
151	Richard E. Johnson, Minneapolis, Minn.	Johnson, 19 holes					
154	Masa Kaya, Honolulu, Hawaii			Demling, 2 and 1			
149	George Cogbill, Dyersburg, Tenn.	Bevilacqua, 6 and 5					
153	Louis Bevilacqua, Philadelphia, Pa.		Reynolds, 19 holes				
152	George C. Siconolfi, Miami, Fla.	Reynolds, 2 and 1					
155	Robert T. Reynolds, Normandy, Mo.					Kaser, 3 and 2	
144	Lamont A. Kaser, Wichita, Kans.	Kaser, 3 and 2					
153	Robert T. Wallace, Sherman Oaks, Calif.		Kaser, 3 and 2				
151	Allen G. Birmingham, Scottsdale, Ariz.	Birmingham, 5 and 4					
154	John E. Peters, Dyersburg, Tenn.			Kaser, 2 and 1			
149	Dennis Ewing, Dallas, Texas	Graska, 4 and 3					
153	David C. Graska, Oshkosh, Wis.		Yamamoto, 1 up				
152	George M. Yamamoto, Anahola, Kauai, Hawaii	Yamamoto, 5 and 4					
155	Robert Barto, Warren, Ohio				Kaser, 4 and 2		
147	Stanley P. Poploski, Pittsburgh, Pa.	Poploski, 19 holes					
153	Barry Baumgardner, Dayton, Ohio		Anderson, 4 and 3				
152	Norb Anderson, St. Paul, Minn.	Anderson, 3 and 2					
154	Ernest Godina, Stockton, Calif.			Anderson, 3 and 2			
150	Les Wimp, Tempe, Ariz.	Wimp, 3 and 2					
154	Russell Helwig, Bloomfield, N.J.		Wimp, 4 and 3				
152	Thomas D. Balliet, Pontiac, Mich.	Miller, 4 and 3					
156	Lawrence J. Miller, New Orleans, La.						Lamont A. Kaser, 6 and 5
141	Ralph Colla, Jr., Youngstown, Ohio	Wernicke, 3 and 1					
152	David Wernicke, Jr., River Hills, Wis.		Carter, 3 and 2				
151	John Whittle, Batavia, Ill.	Carter, 6 and 5					
154	David Carter, Huntington, W. Va.			Powers, 20 holes			
149	Don Powers, Litchfield Park, Ariz.	Powers, 1 up					
153	Mills Rendell, Palatine, Ill.		Powers, 3 and 2				
152	Mike Andonian, Camarillo, Calif.	Abihai, 2 up					
155	Benjamin Abihai, Wailuku, Maui, Hawaii				Powers, 2 and 1		
147	Curtis Sifford, Los Angeles, Calif.	Taylor, 2 and 1					
153	Richard Taylor, Phoenix, Ariz.		Rudis, 4 and 3				
151	Roy Widstrom, Minneapolis, Minn.	Rudis, 5 and 4					
154	Paul Rudis, Tumwater, Wash.			Rudis, 19 holes			
150	Leo Zampedro, Warren, Ohio	Zampedro, 3 and 1					
154	Dennis Ross, Albuquerque, N.M.		Yung, 19 holes				
152	Lou Kane, Pittsburgh, Pa.	Yung, 4 and 3					
156	Carl Yung, Kettering, Ohio					Ojala, 7 and 6	
145	Dave Ojala, Two Harbors, Minn.	Ojala, 5 and 4					
153	John Jackson, Tempe, Ariz.		Ojala, 1 up				
151	Hubert Farmer, Toledo, Ohio	Farmer, 2 and 1					
154	Allan Thompson, Pleasant Ridge, Mich.			Ojala, 2 up			
149	Wayne Etherton, St. Charles, Ill.	Etherton, 4 and 3					
153	Mike Keck, New Orleans, La.		Etherton, 4 and 2				
152	Jack Omuro, Honolulu, Hawaii	Omuro, 2 and 1					
155	Leonard Dahl, Oakwood, N.Y.				Ojala, 2 and 1		
148	James Walker, Detroit, Mich.	Walker, 3 and 2					
153	Daniel Hogan, Denver, Colo.		Heyl, 5 and 3				
152	Frank Perpich, N. Miami Beach, Fla.	Heyl, 2 and 1					
155	Richard Heyl, Sterling, Va.			Heyl, 2 up			
151	Roger Watson, High Point, N.C.	Watson, 5 and 3					
154	Joseph Lenahan, Louisville, Ky.		Bisesi, 19 holes				
152	Gene Hay, Decatur, Ga.	Bisesi, 4 and 2					
156	Don Bisesi, Martinsville, Ind.						

*Medalist.

Amateur Public Links Team Championship, Harding Trophy, 32 Entries, July 11, 12: Won by Pittsburgh, Pa. Team 449 for 36 holes (Ralph Colla Jr., 141; Stanley Poploski, 147; David Graham, 161); Second, Pasadena, Calif. Team 452 (Curtis Sifford, 147; Robert Wallace, 153; Mike Andonian, 152); Third, Memphis, Tenn. Team 455 (George Cogbill, 149; J.L. Blankenship, 152; John Peters, 154).

1967
FORTY-SECOND AMATEUR PUBLIC LINKS CHAMPIONSHIP

Held at the Jefferson Park Golf Course, Seattle, Wash., July 12-15.
Yardage—6,329. Par 70. 2,849 Entries, 150 Qualifiers, 150 Starters.

Sixty-five contestants who completed 72 holes.

						Score
1	Verne Callison, Sacramento, Calif.	72	72	71	72	287
2	Ronald Stokley, Park Ridge, Ill.	75	68	75	70	288
3	James E. Everham, Seattle, Wash.	74	69	71	75	289
4	Richard Robertson, Pontiac, Mich.	78	72	71	69	290
	Jim McMurtrey, San Leandro, Calif.	73	73	70	74	290
	Philip Torres, Alameda, Calif.	75	69	69	77	290
7	Ray Swedo, Pico Rivera, Calif.	73	69	73	76	291
	M.J. Zimmerman, Kettering, Ohio	69	69	74	79	291
9	Whitney T.F. Kam, Honolulu, Hawaii	75	72	70	75	292
	Michael San Filippo, Miami, Fla.	72	76	69	75	292
11	Lloyd Watts, Jr., Allandale, Fla.	74	74	75	71	294
	Donald J. Scott, Seattle, Wash.	72	73	73	76	294
13	Kene Bensel, Spokane, Wash.	72	78	73	72	295
	Gary A. Panks, Scottsdale, Ariz.	70	73	77	75	295
15	James Law, Harper Woods, Mich.	73	72	80	71	296
	John Calabria, Rochester, N.Y.	75	72	75	74	296
	Gene Hay, Decatur, Georgia	75	69	77	75	296
	Arthur Ellis, Wilmette, Ill.	74	72	73	77	296
19	Gilbert Frey, Portland, Ore.	74	73	78	72	297
	Richard Whitfield, Vero Beach, Fla.	73	77	75	72	297
	Allan W. Thompson, Pleasant Ridge, Mich.	74	72	77	74	297
	John Jackson, Jr., Tempe, Ariz.	70	76	74	77	297
	David M. Graham, Pittsburgh, Pa.	78	69	73	77	297
	Rick Richards, Fresno, Calif.	75	69	72	81	297
	Daniel Hogan, Denver, Colo.	73	72	71	81	297
26	Dan Anderson, Jr., Dallas, Texas	76	73	81	68	298
	Ray Chamberlin, Libertyville, Ill.	74	74	75	75	298
	Alan E. Heedt, Peoria, Ill.	76	72	74	76	298
	Roy G. Widstrom, Minneapolis, Minn.	73	74	73	78	298
30	Bill Arakawa, Honolulu, Hawaii	74	72	79	74	299
	Emile J. Lochbaum, Atlanta, Ga.	74	74	76	75	299
	Billy Eaton, Chino, Calif.	79	67	77	76	299
	Gene Gilliatte, French Lick, Ind.	71	77	75	76	299
34	Graham Walker, Rochester, Mich.	71	76	81	72	300
	Dennis Wash, Groves, Texas	73	71	82	74	300
	Jim Frye, Jr., Oak Harbor, Wash.	76	72	73	79	300
	Robert J. McLeod, Jr., Atlanta, Ga.	73	71	74	82	300
38	Mike M. Andonian, Camarillo, Calif.	76	74	77	74	301
	Arthur S. Fujita, Honolulu, Hawaii	68	79	78	76	301
	Mike Nixon, Memphis, Tenn.	70	76	77	78	301
	Eric Wilson, Memphis, Tenn.	73	71	78	79	301
	David A. Wernicke, Jr., River Hills, Wis.	72	76	74	79	301
43	Thomas R. Tindall, Seattle, Wash.	75	75	78	74	302
	Chris Scena, Denver, Colo.	76	72	80	74	302
	Mason West, Memphis, Tenn.	74	75	75	78	302
	J.W. White, Dallas, Texas	71	74	77	80	302
	Mark A. Yingling, Ottumwa, Iowa	75	74	71	82	302
48	Donny Powers, Litchfield Park, Ariz.	74	74	80	75	303
	Richard C. Larson, Bellevue, Wash.	73	76	78	76	303
	Jim Albus, Staten Island, N.Y.	74	75	71	83	303
51	Hans R. Turner, Seattle, Wash.	76	73	79	76	304
	William Mathews, St. Louis, Mo.	74	76	78	76	304
	Robert A. Marks, Elkhorn, Wis.	76	73	76	79	304
	Harold A. Bishop, Starke, Fla.	81	69	74	80	304
	Richard E. Johnson, Minneapolis, Minn.	75	72	76	81	304
56	Ronnie Benandi, Chalmette, La.	73	76	80	76	305
	Harvey Bryant, Oklahoma City, Okla.	76	70	82	77	305
	William Homeyer, Minneapolis, Minn.	72	74	80	79	305
	Clayton Koschel, New Orleans, La.	73	75	82	75	305
60	Bill Cunningham, Hilo, Hawaii	74	75	76	81	306
61	Don Splonick, Phoenix, Ariz.	75	74	76	82	307
62	Bob Balnis, Chicago, Ill.	76	72	79	82	309
63	Michael R. Mathisen, Peoria, Ill.	74	74	82	82	312
64	Ted Rochwalski, Chicago, Ill.	74	76	81	83	314
65	Timo Kilpelainen, Framington, Mich.	73	77	82	83	315

Forty-second Amateur Public Links Team Championship, Harding Trophy (29 Team Entries)—
July 12, 13: Won by Dayton, Ohio team (M.J. Zimmerman, 138, Daniel L. Robison, 153, Rafus Grier, 145) **in sudden-death playoff with Atlanta, Ga. team** (Emile J. Lochbaum, 148, Gene Hay, 144, Robert McLeod, 144) after tie at 436 for 36 holes.

1968
FORTY-THIRD AMATEUR PUBLIC LINKS CHAMPIONSHIP

Held at the Tenison Memorial Municipal Golf Course, Dallas, Texas, July 10-13.
Yardage—6,578. Par 70. 3,316 Entries, **149 Qualifiers**, 150 Starters.

Fifty-five contestants who completed 72 holes.

						Score
1	Gene Towry, Richardson, Texas	74	71	75	72	292
2	Robert R. Unger, Milwaukee, Wis.	73	75	74	72	294
3	Verne E. Callison, Sacramento, Calif.	77	71	76	74	298
	Michael Keck, New Orleans, La.	74	74	77	73	298
5	Paul M. Langager, Orem, Utah	72	74	78	75	299
6	Tom Olson, Phoenix, Ariz.	74	77	75	74	300
7	Phillip R. Freer, Jr., Rocklin, Calif.	74	77	75	75	301
	Wendell Kop, Honolulu, Hawaii	**75**	73	79	74	301
	Joseph E. Lenahan, Louisville, Ky.	77	73	78	73	301
10	David M. Graham, Pittsburgh, Pa.	75	78	75	74	302
	James P. Miller, Hialeah, Fla.	80	69	79	74	302
12	Don A. Maddox, Wichita, Kans.	71	78	79	75	303
	Vernon S. Petersen, Cortland, Neb.	74	78	74	77	303
14	William Mathews, St. Louis, Mo.	77	75	75	77	304
	George M. Yamamoto, Anahola, Kauai, Hawaii	73	76	77	78	304
	Wayne Shircliff, Indianapolis, Ind.	**79**	**74**	**75**	76	304
	Bill Bakken, Minneapolis, Minn.	77	77	74	76	304
	Ernest H. McCray, Denton, Texas	77	76	79	72	304
19	Harold A. Bishop, II, Starke, Fla.	78	77	73	77	305
	Ray Uccelletti, Bluebell, Pa.	76	74	77	78	305
	Robert J. McLeod, Jr., Atlanta, Ga.	79	77	76	73	305
22	James E. Everham, Seattle, Wash.	81	74	74	77	306
	Arnold Salinas, Dallas, Texas	74	79	77	76	306
	Bob Austin, Euclid, Ohio	80	74	75	77	306
	Thomas Pendlebury, Ann Arbor, Mich.	78	78	72	78	306
	Ray Arinno, Sacramento, Calif.	78	76	74	78	306
	Gary Schaefer, Sandusky, Ohio	77	78	76	75	306
	John W. Lugo, Jr., Los Angeles, Calif.	75	75	78	78	306
	Tom Fussaro, Oakmont, Pa.	75	79	75	77	306
	John Steddin, Daly City, Calif.	78	78	80	70	306
	Pleas Jones, Jr., Memphis, Tenn.	74	75	77	80	306
32	Lt. Chester Gorgas, Arlington, Va.	75	76	71	85	307
	Tom Evans, Dallas, Texas	71	78	76	82	307
	Harold G. Lane, Chattanooga, Tenn.	75	75	80	77	307
	Will M. Sowles, Memphis, Tenn.	77	74	81	75	307
36	Robert H. Blomberg, Alameda, Calif.	77	79	75	77	308
37	Frank J. Perpich, North Miami Beach, Fla.	79	77	77	76	309
	John U. Law, Birmingham, Mich.	78	78	77	76	309
39	Wayne Kancko, Seattle, Wash.	80	76	75	79	310
	Robert A. Marks, Elkhorn, Wis.	74	82	77	77	310
	Les Mattocks, Greeley, Colo.	71	81	76	82	310
	Michael E. McCullough, Bowling Green, Ohio	77	78	77	78	310
	Gary Hitch, Ventura, Calif.	75	76	83	76	310
44	Tommy Jackson, Dallas, Texas	75	74	78	84	311
	Joseph R. Harbin, Indianapolis, Ind.	78	77	74	82	311
	Walter A. Law, Dayton, Ohio	74	78	77	82	311
	David A. Wernicke, Jr., River Hills, Wis.	77	78	77	79	311
	Walter Livingston, Lower Burrell, Pa.	80	75	78	78	311
49	Morris Masten, Indianapolis, Ind.	81	75	80	76	312
50	Raymond Swedo, Pico Rivera, Calif.	78	79	77	79	313
51	Michael R. Fermoyle, Minneapolis, Minn.	76	81	81	76	314
52	Paul A. O'Kane, San Francisco, Calif.	76	81	81	78	316
	Chris Scena, Denver, Colo.	76	77	82	81	316
54	Donald Goldstein, Oak Park, Mich.	76	80	83	84	323
55	Michael R. Mathisen, Peoria, Ill.	79	76	85	88	328

Forty-Third Amateur Public Links Team Championship, Harding Trophy (28 Team Entries)—July 10, 11: Won by Dallas, Texas Team 447 for 36 holes (Tom Evans, 149, Gene Towry, 145, Arnold Salinas, 153); Second, Memphis, Tennessee Team 458 (Pleas Jones, Jr., 149, Will M. Sowles, 151, Thurmon Glass, Jr., 158); Third, Indianapolis, Indiana 464 (Joseph R. Harbin, 155, Morris Masten, 156, Wayne Shircliff, 153).

1969
FORTY-FOURTH AMATEUR PUBLIC LINKS CHAMPIONSHIP

Held at the Downing Golf Course, Erie, Pa., July 9-12.
Yardage—6,954. Par 71. 3,754 Entries, **149 Qualifiers, 150 Starters.**

Sixty-one contestants who completed 72 holes.

						Score
1	**John M. Jackson, Jr., Tempe, Ariz.**	79	70	73	70	292
2	Arthur S. Fujita, Honolulu, Hawaii	73	72	74	75	294
	Fred Lufkin, Spokane, Wash.	74	71	73	76	294
	Steven F. Cook, Long Beach, Calif.	69	73	76	76	294
	Joseph Andron, Jr., Erie, Pa.	75	73	70	76	294
6	Gene Towry, Richardson, Texas	75	71	75	74	295
	Charles Barenaba, Jr., Laie, Oahu, Hawaii	75	75	69	76	295
8	Douglas Pool, Phoenix, Ariz.	75	76	71	74	296
	Ronald E. Benson, North St. Paul, Minn.	73	75	72	76	296
10	John L. Calabria, Rochester, N.Y.	75	74	73	75	297
11	George R. Cascino, Hillside, Ill.	75	78	73	72	298
	Gary D. Navarro, Wichita, Kans.	78	70	75	75	298
	Lalu Sabotin, Warren, Ohio	74	73	75	76	298
	Larry Zee, Tonawanda, N.Y.	75	71	71	81	298
15	Robert H. Blomberg, Alameda, Calif.	70	77	77	75	299
	Fred Haney, Forest Grove, Ore.	79	73	72	75	299
17	Brian E. Gaddy, Arcadia, Calif.	73	78	76	73	300
	David M. Cooper, Metairie, La.	77	72	76	75	300
	Jim Pfleider, Anoka, Minn.	77	73	74	76	300
20	Dale Seaton, Hialeah, Fla.	74	80	75	72	301
	Bill McDonough, W. Hempstead, N.Y.	79	75	74	73	301
	Elwin Fanning, Seattle, Wash.	71	80	73	77	301
23	Peter E. Friedes, Lake Bluff, Ill.	74	77	76	75	302
	Sherman W. Keeney II, York, Pa.	74	75	76	77	302
	Danny Joe May, Bloomington, Ind.	75	75	75	77	302
	Jim Goshdigian, Pasadena, Texas	74	76	74	78	302
	Steve Cole, Vallejo, Calif.	80	68	73	81	302
28	Dennis Satyshur, Erie, Pa.	75	77	80	71	303
	George Madsen, Racine, Wis.	79	74	78	72	303
	Wayne E. Jacobs, York, Pa.	74	78	77	74	303
	Ken Lindsay, Jacksonville, Ark.	75	77	74	77	303
	Jim Everham, Seattle, Wash.	79	75	72	77	303
	Warren H. Butler, Minneapolis, Minn.	74	77	74	78	303
	Joe Ungvary, Cleveland, Ohio	74	78	73	78	303
	Steven Mitchell, Homestead, Fla.	75	76	73	79	303
36	John Nelson, Columbus, Ohio	79	75	77	73	304
	Wendell Kop, Honolulu, Hawaii	75	77	77	75	304
	Phillip J. Arinno, Sacramento, Calif.	76	77	76	75	304
	Timothy J. Gibson, Portland, Ore.	76	76	73	79	304
40	Gary Schaefer, Sandusky, Ohio	77	74	78	76	305
41	Tom Olson, Phoenix, Ariz.	76	75	78	78	307
	Marshall Fine, Brookline, Mass.	76	77	76	78	307
43	Timothy Brauch, Denver, Colo.	75	75	79	79	308
	William Cunningham, Hilo, Hawaii	77	74	78	79	308
	Wade Jordan, Huntsville, Texas	77	76	76	79	308
46	Geoffrey Searcy, Jacksonville, Fla.	78	74	78	79	309
	Dennis Cashman, Chicago, Ill.	76	76	78	79	309
48	Jerry Potter, Miami, Fla.	80	74	78	78	310
	Steve Foulston, Wichita, Kans.	76	75	78	81	310
50	Walter Lee Livingston, Lower Burrell, Pa.	81	72	77	81	311
	Bill Homeyer, Minneapolis, Minn.	76	77	77	81	311
52	Wallace Smith, Pontiac, Mich.	76	77	79	80	312
	Robert G. Davis, Southfield, Mich.	79	75	73	85	312
54	Peter J. Konek, Wichita, Kans.	78	73	83	80	314
	Bill Callahan, Erie, Pa.	77	76	79	82	314
	Matthew Slavin, Pasadena, Calif.	77	77	78	82	314
	John Abramchuk, Jr., Springfield, Pa.	78	76	77	83	314
58	George Rask, Pittsburgh, Pa.	80	73	82	81	316
	Rodney Allen, Dallas, Texas	74	78	80	84	316
	Francis Harbist, Pittsburgh, Pa.	76	78	78	84	316
61	Chet Latawiec, Colonial Heights, Minn.	78	76	84	83	321

Forty-fourth Amateur Public Links Team Championship, Harding Trophy (27 Team Entries)— July 9, 10: Won by Pasadena, Calif. Team 447 for 36 holes (Matt Slavin, 154, Brian Gaddy, 151, Steve Cook, 142); Second, Wichita, Kans. Team 450 (Gary Navarro, 148, Steve Foulston, 151, Peter J. Konek, 151); Third, Phoenix, Ariz. Team 451 (John M. Jackson, 149, Douglas Pool, 151, Tom Olson, 151).

1970
FORTY-FIFTH AMATEUR PUBLIC LINKS CHAMPIONSHIP

Held at the Cog Hill No. 4 Golf Course, Lemont, Ill., July 8-11.
Yardage—6,656. Par 72. 4,015 Entries, 150 Starters.

Fifty-nine contestants who completed 72 holes.

1	Robert Risch, Gardena, Calif.	72	72	73	76	293
2	Mike Zimmerman, Kettering, Ohio	76	73	73	74	296
3	Archie Dadian, South Milwaukee, Wis.	72	79	73	76	300
	Jerry W. Denver, Wichita, Kans.	77	74	72	77	300
5	Eddie Post, Fort Smith, Ark.	77	72	76	76	301
6	Harold A. Bishop III, Starke, Fla.	75	75	76	76	302
	Gary Balliet, Rochester, Mich.	75	76	75	76	302
8	Larry Zee, Tonawanda, N.Y.	74	78	79	72	303
	Ted Meier, Joliet, Ill.	69	73	85	76	303
10	Richard Mortenson, Long Beach, Calif.	77	79	74	74	304
	Bill Manor, Dallas, Texas	73	82	74	75	304
	Harold G. Lane, Chattanooga, Tenn.	79	74	74	77	304
	Bob Augustine, Chicago, Ill.	76	76	74	78	304
	Michael J. Moriarty, San Francisco, Calif.	77	73	75	79	304
15	Frank Phillips, Bethel Park, Pa.	78	76	76	75	305
	Miro Vidovic, Blue Island, Ill.	77	74	78	76	305
	Bob Henry, Torrance, Calif.	74	72	82	77	305
	Cyril Shettleroe, Tucson, Ariz.	75	76	76	78	305
19	Don Simon, Scottsdale, Ariz.	76	76	76	78	306
	Don Splonick, Austin, Texas	79	75	81	71	306
	Raymond D. Arinno, Sacramento, Calif.	70	81	77	78	306
	Alton Duhon, Los Angeles, Calif.	74	74	79	79	306
	Nelson M. Broach, Richmond, Va.	73	78	76	79	306
24	Rod Sumpter, Grand Blanc, Mich.	75	78	77	77	307
	Steve G. Johnson, North Branch, Minn.	75	77	77	78	307
26	Tom Pendlebury, Trenton, Mich.	76	76	80	76	308
	Marlen Vogt, Woodside, N.Y.	74	76	79	79	308
28	John W. Gostele III, Long Grove, Ill.	81	76	79	73	309
	Keith Mohan, Grand Blanc, Mich.	80	71	80	78	309
	Allan Yamamoto, Honolulu, Hawaii	78	76	76	79	309
31	Morris Masten, Indianapolis, Ind.	83	75	80	72	310
	Bill Bakken, Minneapolis, Minn.	78	78	77	77	310
	Steve Cole, Seattle, Wash.	77	77	75	81	310
34	Bill Malley, Hayward, Calif.	81	76	76	78	311
	Wendell Kop, Honolulu, Hawaii	76	73	78	84	311
36	Paul Kump, Jr., Renton, Wash.	81	77	77	77	312
	Bob Astleford, Omaha, Neb.	75	82	77	78	312
	Robert M. McAfee, San Rafael, Calif.	79	77	75	81	312
39	Joel O. Cork, Speedway, Ind.	78	78	84	73	313
	Michael S. Poulsen, Peoria, Ill.	80	75	82	76	313
	Lance Suzuki, Kahuku, Hawaii	78	79	79	77	313
42	Dennis G. Kowalski, Minneapolis, Minn.	78	77	80	79	314
	John M. Jackson, Jr., Tempe, Ariz.	80	78	76	80	314
	John O. Weaver, Richmond, Va.	76	79	77	82	314
45	Bufford Jones, Jr., Lithia Springs, Ga.	80	76	79	80	315
	Donald Gary Strametz, Lynwood, Calif.	79	77	79	80	315
	John E. Taylor, Minneapolis, Minn.	76	82	77	80	315
	Christopher Smith, Portland, Ore.	78	77	78	82	315
49	Tom Olson, Phoenix, Ariz.	74	82	78	82	316
	Louis Kane, Pittsburgh, Pa.	78	79	81	78	316
	John Moore, Pittsburgh, Pa.	83	75	78	80	316
	Mike Clayton, Oklahoma City, Okla.	78	80	75	83	316
53	Gary Schaefer, Sandusky, Ohio	77	78	84	79	318
54	William Mathews, St. Louis, Mo.	84	74	81	80	319
	Gary Lindeblad, Spokane, Wash.	75	80	82	82	319
56	Ronnie Kaser, Wichita, Kans.	80	78	82	80	320
	Steven Leonard, Downers Grove, Ill.	75	83	81	81	320
	Ken Honeysuckle, Little Rock, Ark.	77	79	78	86	320
59	Stan B. Stopa, New Orleans, La.	74	83	80	84	321

Forty-fifth Amateur Public Links Inter-city Team Championship, Harding Trophy (30 Team Entries) – July 8, 9: Won by Chicago, Ill. Team 445 for 36 holes (Miro Vidovic, 151, Bob Augustine, 152, Ted Meier, 142); Second, Pasadena, Calif. Team 450 (Richard Mortenson, 156, Bob Henry, 146, Alton Duhon, 148); Third, Phoenix, Ariz. Team 459 (Tom Olson, 156, Don Simon, 152, Cyril Shettleroe, 151).

1971
FORTY-SIXTH AMATEUR PUBLIC LINKS CHAMPIONSHIP

Held at the Papago Golf Course, Phoenix, Arizona, July 14-17.
Yardage—6,956 Par—72 4,174 Entries, 150 Qualifiers, 150 Starters.

Sixty-four contestants who completed 72-hole holes.

						SCORE
1	Fred Haney, Forest Grove, Calif.	74	71	75	70	290
2	Robert H. Blomberg, Alameda, Calif.	77	72	71	75	295
3	Tom Olson, Phoenix, Ariz.	73	73	76	75	297
	Kenny Rucker, Houston, Texas	75	74	74	74	297
	Gary A. Balliet, Pontiac, Mich.	73	71	77	76	297
	Archie Dadian, South Milwaukee, Wis.	74	71	76	76	297
7	Michael Sheely, Sacramento, Calif.	73	77	76	72	298
	Christopher J. Pinckney, Charleston, S.C.	75	74	75	74	298
9	Kent J. Brown, Ventura, Calif.	73	76	77	73	299
10	Bill Meyers, Phoenix, Ariz.	80	74	73	73	300
	Eddie Post, Fort Smith, Ark.	77	78	72	73	300
	Bob Allard, Portland, Ore.	73	74	78	75	300
	Lance Suzuki, Kahuku, Oahu, Hawaii	75	74	74	77	300
14	David F. York, Tacoma, Wash.	81	72	79	69	301
	John Miranov, Warren, Mich.	74	77	75	75	301
	Frederick L. Good, Jr., San Diego, Calif.	80	73	71	77	301
	Rodney Velasquez, Hayward, Calif.	73	74	75	79	301
	Gary Navarro, Wichita, Kans.	76	72	74	79	301
19	Mark Braman, Portland, Ore.	76	73	81	72	302
	Ike Meitzen, Victoria, Texas	77	70	81	74	302
	Ted Meier, Joliet, Ill.	75	76	76	75	302
	Ron Jumper, Peoria, Ill.	78	73	76	75	302
	Bill Malley, Hayward, Calif.	77	72	75	78	302
	Gary Schaefer, Sandusky, Ohio	76	73	74	79	302
	Lee Carter, Dallas, Texas	73	73	75	81	302
26	Adam Carvalho, Hilo, Hawaii	76	76	78	73	303
	Robert Masterana, Las Vegas, Nev.	76	79	73	75	303
28	Phillip Freer, Jr., Rocklin, Calif.	75	75	78	76	304
	William R. McDonald, Pontiac, Mich.	76	75	77	76	304
	Mark Wolfla, Indianapolis, Ind.	81	70	77	76	304
	John Moore, Pittsburgh, Pa.	78	76	74	76	304
	Arthur S. Fujita, Kapaa, Kauai, Hawaii	76	76	75	77	304
33	Robert G. Harris, Jacksonville, Fla.	78	77	76	74	305
	Morris Masten, Indianapolis, Ind.	74	74	81	76	305
	William Robert Dudich, McKees Rocks, Pa.	79	75	75	76	305
	Buford Jones, Lithia Springs, Ga.	77	75	76	77	305
	Gene Rucker, Miami, Fla.	74	78	73	80	305
38	Arlen R. Peacock, Salt Lake City, Utah	77	75	81	73	306
	Jack Shollenberger, Reading, Pa.	76	77	79	74	306
	Jim Stalarow, Glen Head, N.Y.	74	78	79	75	306
	Paul Franke, Louisville, Ky.	74	77	79	76	306
	Ron Schmid, Columbus, Ohio	76	75	77	78	306
43	Thomas Huber, Minneapolis, Minn.	76	77	76	78	307
	Homer Dunn, Englewood, Colo.	80	74	74	79	307
	Allan Thompson, Pleasant Ridge, Mich.	77	75	75	80	307
46	Don Splonick, Austin, Texas	76	73	83	76	308
	Merritt Cook, Jr., Lombard, Ill.	76	75	77	80	308
	Rodney D. Lidenberg, Fargo, N.D.	78	70	78	82	308
49	John R. Dodd, Scottsdale, Ariz.	75	74	83	77	309
	Spencer Sappington, Phoenix, Ariz.	77	74	81	77	309
	Steven Mitchell, Homestead, Fla.	78	76	78	77	309
52	Gary M. Hitch, Ventura, Calif.	76	77	80	77	310
53	Paul Loth, Racine, Wis.	78	77	77	79	311
	John Tuft, Seattle, Wash.	77	73	81	80	311
55	Dennis Barr, Bloomington, Minn.	77	78	79	78	312
	Steve Work, Englewood, Colo.	78	76	79	79	312
	Clark Stevens, Wichita, Kans.	79	75	78	80	312
	Peter Owens, Livonia, Mich.	72	80	79	81	312
59	Nello Campagni, Highwood, Ill.	76	77	82	80	315
60	Joe Dargay, Minneapolis, Minn.	81	74	79	82	316
61	Tom Delaney, New York, N.Y.	79	76	83	79	317
62	Michael S. Murani, Town of Tonawanda, N.Y.	75	79	81	84	319
63	Mike Fermoyle, Minneapolis, Minn.	78	76	85	81	320
64	Emile J. Lochbaum, Atlanta, Ga.	78	76	81	87	322

Forty-sixth Amateur Public Links Inter-city Team Championship, Harding Trophy (30 Team Entries) — July 14, 15: Won by Portland, Ore. Team 441 for 36 holes (Bob Allard, 147, Mark Braman, 149, Fred Haney, 145); Second, Phoenix, Ariz. Team 451 (Tom Olson, 146, Spencer Sappington, 151, Bill Meyers, 154); Third, San Francisco, Calif. Team 456 (Robert H. Blomberg, 149, Patrick J. Chapman, 158, Bill Malley, 149).

1972
FORTY-SEVENTH AMATEUR PUBLIC LINKS CHAMPIONSHIP

Held at the Coffin Municipal Golf Course, Indianapolis, Indiana, July 12-15
Yardage -6,360. Par 70. 3,743 Entries, 150 Qualifiers, 150 Starters.

Sixty-one contestants who completed 72 holes.

						Score
1	†Bob Allard, Portland, Ore.	70	73	73	69	285
2	†Rick Schultz, Omaha, Neb.	70	71	75	69	285
3	Dan Elliot, Portland, Ore.	68	70	76	74	288
4	Dennis L. Smith, Memphis, Tenn.	70	72	75	72	289
	Gene Rucker, Miami, Fla.	75	71	71	72	289
	Richard Ehrmanntraut, St. Paul, Minn.	75	68	80	66	289
7	Morris Masten, Indianapolis, Ind.	73	70	73	74	290
8	Thurman Glass, Jr., Memphis, Tenn.	69	77	72	73	291
	Robert H. Blomberg, Alameda, Calif.	70	72	76	73	291
10	Steven Ryan, Phoenix, Ariz.	68	72	77	75	292
	Stan Stopa, New Orleans, La.	73	73	74	72	292
12	Bill Yarc, Waukegan, Ill.	72	76	76	69	293
	Tommy Jackson, Dallas, Texas	71	71	79	72	293
14	Geoffrey Searcy, Jacksonville, Fla.	72	74	74	74	294
	Lloyd D. McWilliams, Cherry Valley, Ill.	74	69	81	70	294
16	John E. Zett, Jr., Amarillo, Texas	70	72	72	81	295
	Lamar Bass, San Francisco, Calif.	76	72	71	76	295
	Lynn McSherry, Portland, Ore.	72	77	74	72	295
19	Harold A. Bishop III, Starke, Fla.	74	73	73	76	296
	Bill Von Wald, N. St. Paul, Minn.	73	75	75	73	296
21	Richard R. Barbarics, Secane, Pa.	72	75	76	74	297
	Al B. Souza, Jr., Honolulu, Hawaii	73	76	68	80	297
	Tom Clark, Ypsilanti, Mich.	67	78	77	75	297
	John Moore, McKees Rock, Pa.	76	71	77	73	297
	Jim Burgess, Sacramento, Calif.	72	72	80	73	297
26	John R. Dodd, Glendale, Ariz.	74	71	77	76	298
	Glen C. Mankowski, Des Moines, Iowa	77	73	73	75	298
	Bill Deeble, Jr., Long Beach, Calif.	70	76	74	78	298
	Steven L. Barnett, Anderson, Ind.	74	74	75	75	298
	Arthur Fujita, Kapaa, Hawaii	74	74	76	74	298
	Joe Ungvary, Akron, Ohio	76	72	77	73	298
32	Jerry Frey, Chambersburg, Pa.	75	70	75	79	299
	Richard A. Garcia, Jr., Bensenville, Ill.	74	76	73	76	299
	Gordon J. Gutierrez, Sacramento, Calif.	71	78	74	76	299
	Tom Herzan, St. Paul, Minn.	72	74	77	76	299
	John E. Grant, Fairborn, Ohio	74	75	75	75	299
	James R. Kuntz, Webster, N.Y.	74	77	73	75	299
	Robert Ludlow, Indianapolis, Ind.	76	72	76	75	299
	Steven Cole, Seattle, Wash.	75	74	78	72	299
	Dennis Barr, Bloomington, Minn.	72	78	77	72	299
41	Steve Ralston, No. Little Rock, Ark.	74	72	76	78	300
	Edward F. Selser, Jr., New Orleans, La.	77	73	76	74	300
43	Mark Wolfla, Indianapolis, Ind.	75	76	73	77	301
	Gary A. Balliet, Rochester, Mich.	76	69	78	78	301
	Philip N. Anderson, Spokane, Wash.	75	76	75	75	301
	Michael Lanigan, Minneapolis, Minn.	76	75	76	74	301
47	Val Beatriz, Hayward, Calif.	72	76	76	78	302
48	Gerald A. Garber, New Rochelle, N.Y.	77	72	76	78	303
	Stephen C. Boller, Overland Park, Kansas	73	78	76	76	303
	Merritt Cook, Jr., Lombard, Ill.	75	76	76	76	303
51	Robert F. Hawkins, Takoma Park, Md.	78	72	79	75	304
	Thomas L. Jacobsen, Schaumburg, Ill.	72	79	81	72	304
53	Henry H. Seymour, Falls Church, Va.	78	73	75	79	305
54	William R. McDonald, Pontiac, Mich.	75	75	79	77	306
	Don Richmond, Auburn, Wash.	74	74	82	76	306
56	Carl Patron, Detroit, Mich.	76	74	77	80	307
	David N. Corzilius, Wilmington, Del.	76	75	77	79	307
	Bill Cunningham, Hilo, Hawaii	72	78	78	79	307
59	William O. Nelson, Arvada, Colo.	74	73	82	79	308
60	Wally A. Lowe, Boise, Idaho	74	76	81	80	311
61	Daniel J. Desmond, Jr., W. Roxbury, Mass.	74	76	85	78	313

†Playoff, July 16, Bob Allard 71, Rick Schultz 74.

Forty-seventh Amateur Public Links Inter-city Team Championship, Harding Trophy (28 Team Entries)—July 14-15: Won by Portland, Ore. Team 430 for 36 holes (Dan Elliot, 138; Lynn McSherry, 149; Bob Allard, 143); Second, Phoenix, Ariz. Team 437 (John R. Dodd, 145; Wayne D. Ackman, 152; Steven Ryan, 140); Third, Edina, Minn. Team 443 (Richard Ehrmanntraut, 143; Bill Von Wald, 148; Steve Howe, 152).

1973
FORTY-EIGHTH AMATEUR PUBLIC LINKS CHAMPIONSHIP

Held at the Flanders Valley Golf Course, Flanders, New Jersey, July 11-14
Yardage—6,522. Par 71. 3,653 Entries, 159 Qualifiers, 159 Starters.
Fifty-nine contestants who completed 72 holes.

						Score
1	Stan Stopa, New Orleans, La.	76	76	70	72	294
2	Gary Hitch, Santa Barbara, Calif.	70	74	77	74	295
	Philip T. Reichel, Minneapolis, Minn.	71	72	74	78	295
4	Dennis L. Smith, Memphis, Tenn.	72	79	74	71	296
5	Spencer Sappington, Ballwin, Mo.	72	75	75	75	297
6	William McDonald, Pontiac, Mich.	74	77	75	73	299
	John Tuft, Seattle, Wash.	76	74	75	74	299
	Archie Dadian, South Milwaukee, Wis.	76	73	75	75	299
	Gary Robinson, Ypsilanti, Mich.	76	75	72	76	299
10	James Meitzen, Victoria, Texas	73	77	79	71	300
	Jerry Frey, Chambersburg, Pa.	77	77	73	73	300
	Gil Torres, San Jose, Calif.	74	78	75	73	300
	Thomas E. Proben, Detroit, Mich.	73	74	78	75	300
14	Leo Hayden, Jacksonville, Fla.	74	79	76	73	302
	Daniel Nishimoto, Honolulu, Hawaii	76	73	75	78	302
16	John Moore, Pittsburgh, Pa.	75	74	81	73	303
	Mike Lindsey, Scottsdale, Ariz.	76	76	76	75	303
	William McDonald, Seattle, Wash.	75	77	75	76	303
	William W. Helenius, Worcester, Mass.	74	74	77	78	303
20	John R. Dodd, Phoenix, Ariz.	78	75	77	74	304
	Val Beatriz, Oakland, Calif.	74	79	75	76	304
	William Mathews, St. Louis, Mo.	75	76	75	78	304
	Donald Gosztyla, Detroit, Mich.	74	75	76	79	304
	Rock Hutcheson, Riverdale, Ga.	75	74	74	81	304
25	Mike Sheely, Sacramento, Calif.	70	82	78	75	305
	Bob Martin, San Bruno, Calif.	79	76	75	75	305
	Jim Camella, Pittsburgh, Pa.	75	72	80	78	305
	Richard R. Barbarics, Secane, Pa.	72	78	75	80	305
29	Jerry Denver, Wichita, Kans.	76	80	77	73	306
	Rick J. Simmons, Phoenix, Ariz.	72	79	80	75	306
	Donald Samatulski, Bridgeport, Conn.	76	77	77	76	306
	Dave Wernicke, River Hills, Wis.	76	75	78	77	306
33	Bill Von Wald, North St. Paul, Minn.	77	75	84	71	307
	Will M. Sowles, Memphis, Tenn.	77	78	80	72	307
	Tony Marimon, Houston, Texas	69	81	79	78	307
	Charles Uram, Carnegie, Pa.	75	77	77	78	307
	Tom Studer, Joliet, Ill.	76	80	73	78	307
	Robert V. Holmes, Omaha, Neb.	72	80	74	81	307
39	Ted Meier, Joliet, Ill.	80	75	79	74	308
	Morris Masten, Indianapolis, Ind.	76	73	82	77	308
	Fred L. Shultz, York, Pa.	76	73	81	78	308
42	Greg Dikilato, Honolulu, Hawaii	74	79	81	75	309
	Bob McLeod, Hapeville, Ga.	76	80	78	75	309
	James Kuntz, Webster, N. Y.	75	80	78	76	309
	D. William Dickens, East Lansing, Mich.	73	77	81	78	309
46	Rick Roskopf, Beaverton, Ore.	75	81	80	74	310
47	Paul Loth, Racine, Wis.	80	75	83	73	311
48	D. Alvin Stanfield, Chattanooga, Tenn.	79	77	79	77	312
49	Peter Owens, Livonia, Mich.	78	78	81	77	314
	Richard T. Dallagiacomo, Anderson, Calif.	74	78	82	80	314
	Raymond Sanfrey, Erie, Pa.	76	79	76	83	314
52	Nick Mastroni, Bridgeport, Conn.	80	76	79	80	315
	Lynn Yturri, Scottsdale, Ariz.	75	81	76	83	315
54	John Trahon, Brookline, Mass.	77	78	83	78	316
	Steve Dallas, Seattle, Wash.	79	76	81	80	316
56	George Werner, Little Falls, N. J.	76	78	81	82	317
	Thomas M. Woodard, Denver, Colo.	77	76	78	86	317
58	Harley R. Hooper, Jr., Sacramento, Calif.	74	81	77	86	318
59	Duane Paiva, Hilo, Hawaii	78	77	87	79	321

Forty-eighth Amateur Public Links Inter-city Team Championship, Harding Trophy (30 Team Entries), July 11-12: Won by Seattle, Wash. Team, 457 for 36 holes (John Tuft, 150; William McDonald, 152; Steve Dallas, 155); Playoff with Detroit, Mich. Team, 457 (Thomas E. Proben, 147; Gary Robinson, 151; Keith Mohan, 159); Third, Sacramento, Calif. Team, 459 (Mike Sheely, 152; Richard T. Dallagiacomo, 152; Harley R. Hooper, Jr., 155).

1974

FORTY-NINTH AMATEUR PUBLIC LINKS CHAMPIONSHIP

Held at the Brookside Golf Club (No. 1 Course) Pasadena, California July 10-13
Yardage—6,791. Par 72. 3,948 Entries, 150 Qualifiers, 150 Starters.

						Score
1	Charles Barenaba, Jr., Laie, Hawaii	70	71	74	75	290
2	Frank Mazion, San Francisco, Calif.	72	71	73	76	292
3	Jim Everham, Seattle, Wash.	75	74	70	74	293
4	Thomas Proben, Detroit, Mich.	74	76	72	72	294
5	Randy Barenaba, Laie, Hawaii	73	77	72	74	296
	Spencer Sappington, Manchester, Mo.	68	73	78	77	296
7	Fred Lufkin, Spokane, Wash.	75	72	72	78	297
8	W. Keith Mohan, Flint, Mich.	71	77	72	78	298
	Jack Koski, Modesto, Calif.	72	75	73	78	298
	Lamar Bass, San Francisco, Calif.	74	76	74	74	298
	Gary Hitch, Ventura, Calif.	76	72	77	73	298
	Thomas S. Smith, San Francisco, Calif.	73	76	72	77	298
13	Gene R. Parr, Richfield, Minn.	73	71	81	74	299
	Archie Dadian, South Milwaukee, Wis.	76	72	77	74	299
	Steve Barnett, Anderson, Ind.	75	77	76	71	299
	Robert J. Lee, Seattle, Wash.	75	73	73	78	299
17	Bruce L. Wallace, Jacksonville, Fla.	72	77	78	73	300
	Art Diaz, Phoenix, Ariz.	74	72	74	80	300
19	Mark Nielsen, Portland, Ore.	75	77	74	75	301
	Allan W. Thompson, Pleasant Ridge, Mich.	75	75	76	75	301
	Alfred Morton, Washington, D. C.	77	75	73	76	301
	Mack Christensen, Salt Lake City, Utah	74	71	77	79	301
	Gary Navarro, Wichita, Kans.	75	78	74	74	301
24	Daniel I. Villarreal, Houston, Texas	75	76	74	77	302
	Lloyd McWilliams, Cherry Valley, Ill.	76	74	79	73	302
26	Snell Lancaster, Jacksonville, Fla.	79	75	75	74	303
	Richard C. Larson, Bellevue, Wash.	75	78	75	75	303
	Thomas C. Jensen, San Mateo, Calif.	77	75	77	74	303
29	Mike Stoll, Portland, Ore.	72	81	77	74	304
	John Miranov, Warren, Mich.	75	76	72	81	304
	Jan D. Jakovac, Napa, Calif.	75	75	77	77	304
32	Allan Yamamoto, Honolulu, Hawaii	73	78	74	80	305
	Mark De Grazier, San Orego, Calif.	78	73	74	80	305
	Keith B. Williams, Seattle, Wash.	78	75	74	78	305
35	Stan Souza, Honolulu, Hawaii	71	82	75	78	306
	Cliff Frisby, Memphis, Tenn.	74	74	75	83	306
	Richard R. Barbarics, Secane, Pa.	79	70	78	79	306
	Harvey Ortof, Woodside, N. Y.	78	72	75	81	306
	James Meitzen, Victoria, Texas	77	76	76	77	306
	Hung Soo Ahn, Honolulu, Hawaii	73	80	77	76	306
41	James Covelli, Racine, Wis.	76	78	78	75	307
42	Leo Glutting, Mullica Hill, N. J.	80	72	77	79	308
	Randy Manuella, Sandusky, Ohio	77	76	76	79	308
	Jim Sanders, Philadelphia, Pa.	78	75	75	80	308
	Glen Babula, Oxnard, Calif.	75	75	76	82	308
	Scott Bridges, Irving, Texas	76	73	79	80	308
	Todd W. Read, Hollywood, Fla.	77	77	76	78	308
48	Vaughan E. Jones, Louisville, Ky.	71	76	80	82	309
	Thomas Huber, Minneapolis, Minn.	76	78	77	78	309
	Ken Hyland, Jr., Hartville, Ohio	74	78	78	79	309
	Ronald Janicki, Annandale, Va.	74	76	73	86	309
	Ronald L. Skiles, Monessen, Pa.	71	82	78	78	309
53	Keith D. Larsen, Piscataway, N. J.	74	76	81	79	310
	Eddie Mudd, Louisville, Ky.	72	81	76	81	310
	Rodney J. Sumpter, Grand Blanc, Mich.	76	77	80	77	310
56	Robin McCool, Phoenix, Ariz.	77	74	81	79	311
	Robert D. Bohn, Golden Valley, Minn.	79	74	79	79	311
58	Mason West, Memphis, Tenn.	75	79	79	80	313
	Peter Allen Owens, Livonia, Mich.	75	75	84	79	313
60	James T. Kioski, Belleville, Ill.	76	76	82	81	315

Forty-ninth Amateur Public Links Inter-city Team Championship, Harding Trophy (31 Team Entries), July 10, 11: Won by San Francisco, Calif. Team, 442 for 36 holes (Frank Mazion, 143; Lamar Bass, 150; Thomas S. Smith, 149); Second, Honolulu, Hawaii Team, 444 (Charles Barenaba, 141; Randy Barenaba, 150; Stan K. M. Souza, 153); Third, Highland, Mich. Team, 448 (John Miranov, 150; W. Keith Mohan, 148; Allan W. Thompson, 150).

1975
FIFTIETH AMATEUR PUBLIC LINKS CHAMPIONSHIP

Held at Wailua Golf Course, Kauai, Hawaii, July 7-12
Yardage—6,874. Par 72. 4,601 Entries, 159 Starters, 64 Qualifiers

Qualifying Score	1st Round (18 Holes)	2nd Round (18 Holes)	3rd Round (18 Holes)	4th Round (18 Holes)	Semi-Finals (18 Holes)	Final (36 Holes)	
*144	Alan Yamamoto, Honolulu, Hawaii	Yamamoto, 2 up					
152	Gary Noto, New Orleans, La.		Yamamoto, 3 and 2				
150	Scott Wood, Dallas, Texas	Wood, 20 holes					
153	Dr. Gerard Wilson, Carmichael, Calif.			Yamamoto, 1 up			
148	Rickie D'Aunoy, Metairie, La.	Blomberg, 1 up					
153	Robert Blomberg, Alameda, Calif.		Johnson, 6 and 4				
151	Steven Johnson, Rush City, Minn.	Johnson, 2 up					
154	James P. Kuntz, Webster, N.Y.				Yamamoto, 5 and 3		
147	Chris Marszalek, Arlington Hgts., Ill.	Marszalek, 4 and 3					
152	Chris Mitchell, Spokane, Wash.		Marszalek, 1 up				
151	Eddie Mudd, Louisville, Ky.	Rickett, 4 and 3					
154	Joe Pat Rickett, Houston, Texas			Salmans, 1 up			
149	Charles Uram, Carnegie, Pa.	Proben, 6 and 5					
153	Robert Proben, Detroit, Mich.		Salmans, 4 and 3				
151	Larry Roy, Detroit, Mich.	Salmans, 2 and 1					
155	Van Salmans, Chicago, Ill.					Yamamoto, 1 up	
145	Mark Sollenberger, Tempe, Ariz.	Sollenberger, 20 holes					
152	James Barnes, Bellevue, Wash.		Knuth, 3 and 2				
150	Stephen Knuth, Toledo, Ohio	Knuth, 1 up					
154	Ray Doege, Houston, Texas			Zebroski, 2 and 1			
148	John Zebroski, Brookfield, Ohio	Zebroski, 19 holes					
153	Michael Kanoff, Jr., Harrisburg, Pa.		Zebroski 19 holes				
151	Todd Christensen, Robbins Dale, Minn.	Proben, 3 and 2					
155	Thomas E. Proben, Detroit, Mich.				Richard, 3 and 1		
147	Peter Owens, Livonia, Mich.	Owens, 4 and 3					
153	William Maynard, Louisville, Ky.		Mohan, 6 and 5				
151	Keith Mohan, Flint, Mich.	Mohan, 4 and 3					
154	Jim Bartak, Omaha, Neb.			Richard, 4 and 3			
149	Spencer Sappington, St. Louis, Mo.	Sappington, 4 and 2					
153	David Wernicke, Jr., River Hills, Wis.		Richard, 3 and 1				
152	Gene George, Erie, Pa.	Richard, 2 up					
155	Ronald Richard, Fort Smith, Ark.						Randyn Barenaba, 37 holes
*144	David Ishii, Lihue, Hawaii	Gutz, 5 and 4					
152	Reynold Gutz, Warren, Mich.		Iverson, 2 up				
150	Joe Runte, Seattle, Wash.	Iverson, 2 up					
154	Richard Iverson, Portland, Ore.			Konek, 4 and 3			
148	Gary Pinns, Lombard, Ill.	Meyers, 2 up					
153	Bill Meyers, Phoenix, Ariz.		Konek, 1 up				
151	Wendell Kop, Honolulu, Hawaii	Konek, 3 and 2					
155	Peter Konek, Wichita, Kans.				Dadian, 1 up		
147	Joe Springer, Durand, Wis.	Bellmar, 7 and 6					
153	Mike Bellmar, Los Alamitos, Calif.		Bellmar, 3 and 2				
151	John Susko, San Francisco, Calif.	Deckert, 5 and 4					
154	Kenneth Deckert, Omaha, Neb.			Dadian, 3 and 1			
149	George Yamamoto, Anahola, Hawaii	Dadian, 2 and 1					
153	Archie Dadian, S. Milwaukee, Wis.		Dadian, 19 holes				
151	Jim Bixler, Richland, Wash.	Bixler, 5 and 4					
155	Doug Black, College Park, Ga.					Barenaba, 1 up	
146	James McMurtrey, Danville, Calif.	Hitch, 7 and 6					
152	Gary Hitch, Ventura, Calif.		Bahensky, 3 and 2				
150	Dan Bahensky, Lincoln, Neb.	Bahensky, 4 and 3					
154	Robert Chrestman, Metairie, La.			Barenaba, 1 up			
149	Edward Campos, Daly City, Calif.	Campos, 3 and 2					
153	Ron Skiles, Monesen, Pa.		Barenaba, 2 and 1				
151	Randyn Barenaba, Laie, Hawaii	Barenaba, 1 up					
155	John R. Hand, Jr., Alton, Ill.				Barenaba, 4 and 3		
148	Tony Campregher, Huntington Beach, Calif.	Campregher, 3 and 2					
153	John Tuft, Seattle, Wash.		Campregher, 5 and 3				
151	Tim Mehl, Mission, Kans.	Mehl, 3 and 1					
154	Kenneth Ezell, Jacksonville, Fla.			Anton, 1 up			
150	Daniel Nishimoto, Kapaa, Hawaii	Jackson, 1 up					
153	Matthew Jackson, Jr., Jacksonville, Fla.		Anton, 4 and 3				
152	Frank Mazion, San Francisco, Calif.	Anton, 5 and 4					
153	Terrence P. Anton, Doraville, Ga.						

*Co-Medalists

Fiftieth Amateur Public Links Inter-city Team Championship, Harding Trophy (32 Team Entries), July 7, 8: Won by Honolulu, Hawaii Team, 439 for 36 holes (Allan Yamamoto, 144; Wendell Kop, 151; David S. Ishii, 144); Second, Pittsburgh, Pa. Team, 450 (John T. Zebroski, Jr., 148; Ron Skiles, 153; Charles Uram, 149); Third, San Francisco, Calif. Team, 452 (Frank Mazion, 152; John Susko, 151; Edward Campos, 149).

1976
FIFTY-FIRST AMATEUR PUBLIC LINKS CHAMPIONSHIP

Held at Bunker Hills Golf Course, Coon Rapids, Minnesota, July 12-17
Yardage—6,745. Par 72. 4,015 Entries, 159 Starters, 64 Qualifiers

Qualifying Score	1st Round (18 Holes)	2nd Round (18 Holes)	3rd Round (18 Holes)	4th Round (18 Holes)	Semi-Finals (18 Holes)	Final (36 Holes)
*140	Jeffrey Thomas, Boise, Idaho	Sexton,				
152	Frank Sexton, Barboursville, W.Va.	2 and 1	Roskopf,			
148	Ken Allard, Ann Arbor, Mich.	Roskopf,	3 and 2			
154	Rick Roskopf, Beaverton, Ore.	3 and 2		Roskopf,		
146	Carlton Dienstbach, Wichita, Kans.	Mohan,		4 and 3		
153	W. Keith Mohan, Grand Blanc, Mich.	2 and 1	West,			
151	Mason West, Memphis, Tenn.	West,	2 up			
155	Robert Dangerfield, S. Monroe, La.	1 up			Roskopf,	
145	Chris Marszalek, Arlington Heights, Ill.	Marszalek,			5 and 4	
152	Art Diaz, Phoenix, Ariz.	2 up	Marszalek,			
150	Vincent Glowacki, Houston, Texas	Glowacki,	4 and 3			
154	Clyde Rego, Kunia, Oahu, Hawaii	2 and 1		Pallis,		
147	Ned Weaver, Orville, Ohio	Pallis,		2 and 1		
154	Randy Pallis, Torrance, Calif.	4 and 3	Pallis,			
152	Tommy Williams, Kansas City, Mo.	Dirtadian,	2 and 1			
155	Armen Dirtadian, Tucson, Ariz.	6 and 5				Dadian,
144	Reid Schronce, Charlotte, N.C.	Schronce,				7 and 6
152	Dale Loeslein, Fairview, Pa.	6 and 5	Dadian,			
148	Archie Dadian, S. Milwaukee, Wis.	Dadian,	1 up			
154	John Osborne, New Market, Va.	4 and 3		Dadian,		
147	Ben Lantz, Omaha, Neb.	Lantz,		5 and 3		
154	Jim Covelli, Racine, Wis.	4 and 2	DiMuccio,			
152	Bill Von Wald, Maplewood, Minn.	DiMuccio,	2 and 1			
155	John DiMuccio, New Castle, Pa.	2 and 1			Dadian,	
146	Rick Radder, Edina, Minn.	Radder,			1 up	
153	Frank Mazion, San Francisco, Calif.	4 and 3	Radder,			
150	Eric Mork, Wichita, Kans.	Mork,	1 up			
155	Jerry Kidney, Littleton, Colo.	3 and 2		Peterson,		
148	Robert Allen, Lockport, Ill.	Sappington,		1 up		
154	Spencer Sappington, Manchester, Mo.	3 and 2	Peterson,			
152	Jim Peterson, Scottsdale, Ariz.	Peterson,	3 and 2			
155	Mike Harmon, Clarkston, Ga.	4 and 3				
143	Peter Jacobs, Dayton, Ohio	Witte,				
152	Terry Witte, Phoenix, Ariz.	2 and 1	Adams,			
148	Bill Adams, Starke, Fla.	Adams,	2 and 1			
154	Adrian Schjetnan, Houston, Texas	19 holes		Mudd,		
146	Eddie Mudd, Louisville, Ky.	Mudd,		1 up		
153	Robert Madsen, Coral Gables, Fla.	2 and 1	Mudd,			
151	Steve Varnett, Anderson, Ind.	Hyland,	3 and 2			
155	Ken Hyland, Hartville, Ohio	3 and 1			Mudd,	
145	Robert Proben, Detroit, Mich.	R. Proben,			5 and 3	
153	Paul F. Smith, Belleville, Ill.	3 and 1	Hubbart,			
150	Kim Hubbart, Spokane, Wash.	Hubbart,	5 and 4			
154	James Hughes, New Orleans, La.	5 and 3		Hubbart,		
148	Damon Bahensky, Lincoln, Neb.	Bahensky,		19 holes		
154	Buddy Rountree, Ft. Lauderdale, Fla.	1 up	Coston,			
152	Jeff Coston, Seattle, Wash.	Coston,	3 and 2			
155	Gary Noto, New Orleans, La.	2 and 1				Mudd,
144	Victor Wolfe, Livermore, Calif.	Wolfe,				2 up
152	Thomas Jacobsen, Schaumburg, Ill.	1 up	Wolfe,			
149	Thomas Proben, Detroit, Mich.	T. Proben,	1 up			
154	Bill Gundersen, Woodinville, Wash.	6 and 5		Wolfe,		
147	James Fellner, Pewaukee, Wis.	Fellner,		1 up		
154	Robert Hawkins, Takoma Park, Md.	5 and 4	Fellner,			
152	Mark Winstrom, Omaha, Neb.	Winstrom,	3 and 2			
155	Rick Spaeth, Boise, Idaho	3 and 2			Hitch,	
146	Gene Parr, Richfield, Minn.	Parr,			3 and 2	
153	Michael Spellman, Peoria, Ill.	2 and 1	Hitch,			
151	John Van Vleck, Farmington, Mich.	Hitch,	3 and 1			
155	Gary Hitch, Ventura, Calif.	7 and 6		Hitch,		
148	Robert Holdstein, Woodbury, N.J.	Barenaba,		1 up		
154	Randy Barenaba, Oahu, Hawaii	20 holes	Fujita,			
152	Steve Sands, Reno, Nev.	Fujita,	3 and 2			
155	Arthur Fujita, Kopoa, Hawaii	3 and 2				

Eddie Mudd, 1 up, 37 holes

*Medalist

Fifty-First Amateur Public Links Inter-city Team Championship, Harding Trophy, 35 Team Entries, July 12, 13: Won by Detroit, Mich. Team, 446 for 36 holes (W. Keith Mohan, 153; Ken Allard, 148; Robert Proben, 145), Second, Omaha, Neb. Team, 447 (Ben Lantz, 147; Damon Bahensky, 148; Mark Winstrom, 152); Third, Boise, Idaho Team, 452 (Craig Collins, 157; Jeffrey Thomas, 140; Rick Spaeth, 155).

1977
FIFTY-SECOND AMATEUR PUBLIC LINKS CHAMPIONSHIP

Held at Brown Deer Park Golf Course, Milwaukee, Wisconsin, July 11-16.
Yardage—6,608. Par 71. 3,732 Entries, 159 Starters, 64 Qualifiers.

Qualifying Score	1st Round (18 Holes)	2nd Round (18 Holes)	3rd Round (18 Holes)	4th Round (18 Holes)	Semi-Finals (18 Holes)	Final (36 Holes)
*142	Jerry Vidovic, Blue Island, Ill.	Vidovic,				
150	Mike Morrow, Stow, Ohio	1 up	Vidovic,			
148	Joe Leslie, Highland, Ind.	Leslie,	4 and 3			
152	Gary Neuschel, Tonawanda, N.Y.	8 and 6		Vidovic,		
146	Matt Ellison, Ventura, Calif.	Hetzler,		1 up		
151	Gregory Hetzer, Seal Beach, Calif.	5 and 4	Hetzler,			
150	Bill Kokott, S. Milwaukee, Wis.	Jackson,	19 holes			
153	Matthew Jackson, Jacksonville, Fla.	2 and 1			Vidovic,	
146	Dave Kluver, Phoenix, Ariz.	Smith,			5 and 4	
151	Ashley Smith, Oakland, Calif.	3 and 2	Smith,			
149	Jeff Teal, Rochester, Minn.	Uram,	2 up			
153	Charles Uram, Carnegie, Pa.	6 and 4		Brodzik,		
148	Michael Shepard, Wichita, Kans.	Shepard,		5 and 3		
152	Gary Lutz, Westland, Mich.	8 and 7	Brodzik,			
150	Walter Brodzik, Lancaster, N.Y.	Brodzik,	1 up			
154	William Grant, Kokomo, Ind.	3 and 2				Vidovic,
143	Bill Gundersen, Redmond, Wash.	Roskopf,				4 and 3
151	Richard Roskopf, Beaverton, Ore.	2 and 1	Newton,			
149	John Newton, Lexington, Ky.	Newton,	1 up, 19 holes			
152	Richard Gordon, Redwood City, Calif.	2 and 1		Sappington,		
147	Archie Dadian, S. Milwaukee, Wis.	Dahm,		2 and 1		
152	Robert Dahm, Fargo, N.D.	2 and 1	Sappington,			
150	Spencer Sappington, Manchester, Mo.	Sappington,	2 up			
154	Tom Yellin, Audobon, Tenn.	3 and 2			Sappington,	
146	Stephen Shawler, Fairborn, Ohio	Nelson,			4 and 2	
151	David Nelson, Reno, Nev.	3 and 2	Moore,			
149	Thomas Proben, Redford, Mich.	Moore,	2 and 1			
153	Ed Moore, Tucker, Ga.	5 and 4		Moore,		
148	Bill Moretti, St. Louis, Mo.	Walsh,		3 and 1		
152	Larry Walsh, Atlanta, Ga.	1 up, 22 holes	Walsh,			
150	Dale Loeslein, Fairview, Pa.	Loeslein,	2 and 1			
154	Pat Shinners, Greensburg, Pa.	4 and 3				
*142	Peter Jacobi, Dayton, Ohio	Jacobi,				
151	Kevin Packard, Twin Falls, Idaho	5 and 4	Jacobi,			
149	Jim Petterson, Scottsdale, Ariz.	Anderson,	1 up			
152	Dan Anderson, Minneapolis, Minn.	3 and 2		Hubbart,		
146	Kim Hubbart, Spokane, Wash.	Hubbart,		3 and 2		
151	Dan Aylwin, New Smyrna Beach, Fla.	4 and 3	Hubbart,			
150	Tom Dixon, Carmichael, Calif.	Dixon,	3 and 2			
153	Tom Brugger, Miami Shores, Fla.	2 and 1			Hubbart,	
146	Bobby Proben, Redford, Mich.	Proben,			4 and 3	
151	Frank Swopes, Chattanooga, Tenn.	4 and 3	Proben,			
149	Warren Sasse, Lincoln, Neb.	Sasse,	3 and 1			
153	Larry Edwards, Denton, Texas	3 and 2		McGaughey,		
148	John Van Vleck, Farmington, Mich.	Peters,		1 up, 19 holes		
152	Al Peters, Milwaukee, Wis.	5 and 4	McGaughey,			
150	David Ogrin, Waukegan, Ill.	McGaughey,	1 up			
154	Patrick McGaughey, Troy, Mich.	3 and 2				Kern,
146	C. Peter Niles, Seattle, Wash.	Niles,				2 and 1
151	Jeff Baker, Seattle, Wash.	6 and 5	Diaz,			
149	Arthur Diaz, Phoenix, Ariz.	Diaz,	4 and 3			
152	Richard Graen, Rochester, Minn.	1 up, 19 holes		Figueredo,		
147	Robert Girvan, Kenduskeg, Maine	Figueredo,		6 and 4		
152	Tony Figueredo, Miami, Fla.	5 and 3	Figueredo,			
150	Jody Mudd, Louisville, Ky.	Mudd,	2 up			
154	Harlon Hendrick, Port Arthur, Texas	6 and 5			Kern,	
146	Les Kamm, Escondido, Calif.	Kamm,			1 up, 19 holes	
151	Dee Conton, Reno, Nev.	1 up	Martins,			
150	Brandon Kop, Honolulu, Hawaii	Martins,	6 and 5			
153	Bruce Martins, Ware, Mass.	1 up		Kern,		
148	Jeff Kern, Tucson, Ariz.	Kern,		4 and 3		
152	Tony Moya, Greeley, Colo.	2 and 1	Kern,			
150	Richard Sieradzki, Waianae, Hawaii	Hueber,	1 up			
154	David Hueber, Memphis, Tenn.	20 holes				

Jerry Vidovic, 4 and 2

*Co-Medalists

Fifty-second Amateur Public Links Inter-city Team Championship, Harding Trophy (35 Team Entries), July 11, 12: Won by Tacoma, Washington, Team, 440 for 36 holes (C. Peter Niles, 146; Jeff Baker, 151; Bill Gundersen, 143); Second, Dayton, Ohio, Team, 450 (Peter H. Jacobi, 142; Stephen E. Shawler, 146; John C. Elbin, 162) Third, Buffalo, New York, Team, 452 (Walter Brodzik, 150; Gary Neuschel, 152; Dale Loeslein, 150).

1978

FIFTY-THIRD AMATEUR PUBLIC LINKS CHAMPIONSHIP

Held at Bangor Municipal Golf Course, Bangor, Maine, July 10-15.
Yardage—6,674. Par 70. 3,929 Entries, 159 Starters, 64 Qualifiers.

Qualifying Score	1st Round (18 Holes)	2nd Round (18 Holes)	3rd Round (18 Holes)	4th Round (18 Holes)	Semi-Finals (18 Holes)	Final (36 Holes)
*138	Mike Campbell, Louisville, Ky.	Hubbard, 1 up, 20 holes				
150	Kim Hubbard, Spokane, Wash.		Clatworthy, 2 up			
148	Gregg Clatworthy, Janesville, Wis.	Clatworthy, 6 and 5				
152	Paul Trittler, St. Louis, Mo.			Monday, 2 and 1		
146	Dan Monday, San Gabriel, Calif.	Monday, 1 up				
151	John Zebroski, Brookfield, Ohio		Monday, 2 up			
149	Scott Watkins, Scottsdale, Ariz.	McDonald, 1 up, 20 holes				
153	William McDonald, Royal Oak, Mich.				Figueredo, 2 and 1	
145	Kenny Rucker, Houston, Texas	Figueredo, 3 and 2				
151	Tony Figueredo, Miami, Fla.		Figueredo, 5 and 3			
148	Jeff Thomas, Racine, Wis.	Everham, 1 up				
152	Jim Everham, Seattle, Wash.			Figueredo, 1 up, 20 holes		
147	David Nelson, Reno, Nev.	Mork, 5 and 4				
152	Eric Mork, Wichita, Kans.		Mork, 1 up			
149	Tom Studer, Plainfield, Ill.	Susko, 1 up				
153	John Susko, San Francisco, Calif.					Figueredo, 5 and 3
144	Philip Pleat, Manchester, N.H.	Pleat, 2 up				
150	Charles Pifer, Miami, Fla.		Pleat, 3 and 2			
148	James Sullivan, Canton, Mass.	Martin, 4 and 3				
152	Peter Martin, Smyrna, Ga.			Ward, 4 and 2		
147	Doug Ward, Little Rock, Ark.	Ward, 3 and 2				
151	Robert DePopolo, Canton, Mass.		Ward, 2 up			
149	David Ogrin, Waukegan, Ill.	Ogrin, 3 and 2				
153	Bill Curtis, Farmington, Mich.				Ward, 4 and 3	
145	Samuel Hunt, McRae, Ga.	Hunt, 6 and 5				
151	Homer Dunn, Englewood, Colo.		Hunt, 1 up			
149	Jerry Vidovic, Blue Island, Ill.	Vidovic, 4 and 3				
153	John Kerins, W. Middlesex, Pa.			Hunt, 2 and 1		
147	Richard Graen, Rochester, Minn.	Graen, 2 and 1				
152	Allan Ericson, Jacksonville, Fla.		Mehl, 1 up			
149	Lenny Clements, Poway, Calif.	Mehl, 4 and 2				
153	Timothy Mehl, Overland Park, Kans.					
144	Art Diaz, Phoenix, Ariz.	Parr, 3 and 2				
150	Gene Parr, Minneapolis, Minn.		Parr, 2 up			
148	Gary Neuschel, Tonawanda, N.Y.	Neuschel, 1 up				
152	Lee Shortridge, St. Paul, Minn.			Mudd, 1 up		
147	Jodie Mudd, Louisville, Ky.	Mudd, 3 and 2				
151	Dr. Gustav Kozina, Lake Bluff, Ill.		Mudd, 2 up			
149	Robert Darling, Jr., Cumberland Center, Maine	Darling, 1 up				
153	Rod Pafford, Essexville, Mich.				Prince, 3 and 2	
145	Dee Conton, Reno, Nev.	Conton, 3 and 2				
151	Richard Merino, Broomfield, Colo.		Prince, 3 and 2			
149	Jerry Minor, Clackamas, Ore.	Prince, 1 up				
153	Dean Prince, Santa Rosa, Calif.			Prince, 5 and 4		
147	Marv Blemly, Dearborn, Mich.	Blemly, 3 and 2				
152	Jay Robinson, Tigard, Ore.		Blemly, 5 and 4			
149	John DeLuise, Raleigh, N.C.	DeLuise, 3 and 2				
153	Michael Blais, State Line, Nev.					Prince, 1 up, 19 holes
145	Robert Blomberg, Alameda, Calif.	Blomberg, 4 and 3				
151	Jim Smith, Bowling Green, Ohio		Blomberg, 5 and 4			
148	Mike Bellmar, Seal Beach, Calif.	Papovlias, 6 and 4				
152	Tom Papovlias, Brockton, Mass.			Blomberg, 6 and 5		
147	Bobby Proben, Redford, Mich.	DeWulf, 4 and 3				
151	David DeWulf, Rochester, Mich.		DeWulf, 5 and 3			
149	Tom Sandie, Des Moines, Iowa	Rudis, 1 up, 19 holes				
153	Paul Rudis, Olympia, Wash.				Loeslein, 2 up	
146	Bruce Anderson, Minneapolis, Minn.	Anderson, 1 up, 20 holes				
151	Mark Mathews, Phoenix, Ariz.		Anderson, 1 up			
149	Gary Griggs, El Cajon, Calif.	Griggs, 2 and 1				
153	Lance Taketa, Hilo, Hawaii			Loeslein, 2 up		
148	John Johnson, Madison Heights, Mich.	Loeslein, 4 and 3				
152	Dale Loeslein, Fairview, Pa.		Loeslein, 6 and 5			
150	Michael Taylor, Milwaukee, Wis.	Taylor, 4 and 3				
153	Roy Widstrom, Minneapolis, Minn.					

Dean Prince, 5 and 3

*Medalist

Fifty-third Amateur Public Links Inter-city Team Championship, Harding Trophy (37 Team Entries), July 10, 11: Won by Louisville, Kentucky Team, 440 for 36 holes (Jodie Mudd, 147; Mike Campbell, 138; Vaughan E. Jones, 155); Second, Reno, Nevada Team, 447 (David C. Nelson, 147; Dee Conton, 145; Bruce F. Handy, 155); Third, Portland, Maine Team, 449 (Philip Pleat, 144; Robert E. Darling, Jr., 149; Ronald O. Brown, Jr., 156).

1979
FIFTY-FOURTH AMATEUR PUBLIC LINKS CHAMPIONSHIP

Held at West Delta Golf Course, Portland, Oregon, July 16-21.
Yardage—6,394. Par 71. 4,170 Entries, 159 Starters, 64 Qualifiers.

Qualifying Score	1st Round (18 Holes)	2nd Round (18 Holes)	3rd Round (18 Holes)	4th Round (18 Holes)	Semi-Finals (18 Holes)	Final (36 Holes)
*140	Dennis Walsh, Groves, Texas	Walsh,				
147	Ted Brodzik, Lancaster, N.Y.	2 and 1	Walsh,			
145	James Dunn, Webster Groves, Mo.	Fujita,	6 and 4			
149	Arthur Fujita, Kapaa, Hawaii	1 up		Walsh,		
143	Thomas Smith, San Francisco, Calif.	Davis,		3 and 2		
148	Mark Davis, Mesa, Ariz.	3 and 2	Diaz,			
146	Art Diaz, Phoenix, Ariz.	Diaz,	2 and 1			
149	John Powers, Miami, Fla.	1 up			Walsh,	
142	Jeff Short, Van Nuys, Calif.	Short,			1 up	
147	Patrick McGaughey, St. Clair Shores, Mich.	1 up	Short,			
145	Marc Arnette, Orange Park, Fla.	May,	2 and 1			
149	Dan May, Burlington, Ind.	1 up, 21 holes		Short,		
145	William McDonald, Royal Oak, Mich.	Parr,		2 up		
148	Gene Parr, Minneapolis, Minn.	1 up, 19 holes	Parr,			
146	Gary Schultz, New Orleans, La.	White,	1 up			
150	Tim White, Richmond, Va.	1 up				Walsh,
141	Jim Blandford, Scottsdale, Ariz.	Blandford,				2 and 1
147	Denny Thompson, Louisville, Ky.	4 and 3	Blandford,			
145	Merritt Cook, Jr., Lombard, Ill.	Cook,	2 up			
149	James Cichra, Pittsburgh, Pa.	1 up		Mudd,		
144	Jodie Mudd, Louisville, Ky.	Mudd,		3 and 2		
148	Jesse Allen, Tacoma, Wash.	2 and 1	Mudd,			
146	Robert Hawkins, Dallas, Texas	Hawkins,	4 and 2			
150	Larry Opatz, Bloomington, Minn.	2 and 1			Mudd,	
143	John Jannone, San Diego, Calif.	Jannone,			2 and 1	
147	Roger Ferrec, Upper Saddle River, N.J.	5 and 4	Hawkins,			
145	Rod Nuckolls, Wichita, Kans.	Hawkins,	2 and 1			
149	Robert F. Hawkins, Takoma Park, Md.	1 up		Perkins,		
145	Gary Borst, Carson City, Nev.	Perkins,		4 and 3		
149	Lawrence Perkins, Allentown, Pa.	2 and 1	Perkins,			
147	William Himm, Livonia, Mich.	Jorg,	3 and 2			
150	Stephen Jorg, Kailua-Koua, Hawaii	1 up				Dennis Walsh, 4 and 3
*140	Vic Wilk, Sepulveda, Calif.	Wilk,				
147	Dee Conton, Reno, Nev.	4 and 3	Wilk,			
145	Joseph Bowman, Omaha, Neb.	Bowman,	3 and 1			
149	Robert Imlay, San Diego, Calif.	2 and 1		Wilk,		
144	Tony Grimes, Safford, Ariz.	Grimes,		2 up		
148	Kirk Jones, Hollywood, Fla.	5 and 3	Grimes,			
146	George Lucas, Atlanta, Ga.	Pasquali,	2 and 1			
149	Mike Pasquali, Kokomo, Ind.	4 and 3			Biancalana,	
142	John Susko, San Francisco, Calif.	Robidoux,			3 and 2	
147	Art Robidoux, Brunswick, Ohio	5 and 3	Robidoux,			
145	David DeWulf, Rochester, Mich.	Caster,	2 and 1			
149	Mike Caster, Wichita, Kans.	1 up		Biancalana,		
145	Sam Hunt, McRae, Ga.	Maloney,		2 and 1		
149	Brian Maloney, Pearl River, N.Y.	1 up	Biancalana,			
147	Roy Biancalana, Franklin Park, Ill.	Biancalana,	1 up, 22 holes			
150	Tim Macken, Portland, Ore.	1 up				Mork,
141	David Ogrin, Waukegan, Ill.	Taylor,				5 and 4
147	Michael Taylor, Milwaukee, Wis.	2 and 1	Taylor,			
145	Paul Trittler, St. Louis, Mo.	Trittler,	1 up, 19 holes			
149	Bruce Anderson, Minneapolis, Minn.	2 and 1		Mork,		
144	Steven Johnson, Elk River, Minn.	Johnson,		2 and 1		
148	Jerry Wilson, Fair Oaks, Calif.	1 up, 20 holes	Mork,			
146	Eric Mork, Wichita, Kans.	Mork,	3 and 2			
150	Baker Maddera, Pine Mountain, Ga.	4 and 3			Mork,	
143	Thomas Hines, Lehue, Hawaii	Hines,			2 and 1	
148	Leo Glutting, Mullica Hill, N.J.	2 and 1	Hines,			
146	Paul Rudis, Olympia, Wash.	Poulsen,	3 and 1			
149	Michael Poulsen, Peoria, Ill.	5 and 4		Hines,		
145	Archie Dadien, S. Milwaukee, Wis.	Dadian,		1 up		
149	Dru Lammle, Omaha, Neb.	4 and 3	Kelley,			
147	Ken Kelley, Waller, Texas	Kelley,	2 up			
150	Daniel Patch, Pittsburgh, Pa.	1 up				

*Co-Medalists

Fifty-fourth Amateur Public Links Inter-city Team Championship, Harding Trophy (36 Team Entries), July 16, 17: Won by Phoenix, Arizona Team, 431 for 36 holes (Artie Diaz, 146; Anthony Grimes, 144; Jim Blandford, 141); Second, Chicago, Illinois Team, 433 (Merritt Cook, 145; Roy Biancalana, 147; Dave Ogrin, 141); Third, Los Angeles, California Team, 434 (Jeff Short, 142; Roger Fagan, 152; Vic Wilk, 140).

1980

FIFTY-FIFTH AMATEUR PUBLIC LINKS CHAMPIONSHIP

Held at Edgewood Tahoe Golf Course, Stateline, Nevada, July 14-19
Yardage—7,127. Par 72. 4,416 Entries, 159 Starters, 64 Qualifiers.

Qualifying Score	1st Round (18 Holes)	2nd Round (18 Holes)	3rd Round (18 Holes)	4th Round (18 Holes)	Semi-Finals (18 Holes)	Final (36 Holes)	
•144	David Ogrin, Waukegan, Ill.	Ogrin, 6 and 5					
159	Tom Porsch, Harrisburg, Pa.		Ogrin, 5 and 4				
155	John Hamarik, Jr., Youngstown, Ohio	Hamarik, 5 and 4					
161	Edward Briegel, Ann Arbor, Mich.			Ogrin, 5 and 4			
153	Edward Terasa, Green Bay, Wis.	Terasa, 2 up					
160	Mike Kerr, Livonia, Mich.		Malley, 4 and 3				
157	Bill Malley, Hayward, Calif.	Malley, 2 and 1					
162	Michael Tennant, Champaign, Ill.				Ogrin, 4 and 2		
149	Jim Carter, Mesa, Ariz.	Biancalana, 6 and 5				Mudd, 3 and 2	
159	Roy Biancalana, Franklin Park, Ill.		Biancalana, 2 and 1				
157	Mark Paithorp, La Mesa, Calif.	Gabrielson, 1 up, 19 holes					
161	Gary Gabrielson, Minneapolis, Minn.			Walsh, 2 and 1			
154	Russell Orth, Dallas, Texas	Walsh, 1 up					
160	Dennis Walsh, Groves, Texas		Walsh, 6 and 5				
158	Donald Green, Ft. Lauderdale, Fla.	Dalpos, 2 and 1					
162	Richard Dalpos, Lemont, Ill.						
148	Gwin Richards, Las Vegas, Nev.	Bentley, 3 and 1					
159	Scott Bentley, El Cajon, Calif.		Hurter, 4 and 3				
156	Donald Hurter, Honolulu, Hawaii	Hurter, 1 up					
161	Ken Schreiber, Evansville, Ind.			Hurter, 2 and 1			
154	Bill McDonald, Royal Oaks, Mich.	McDonald, 2 and 1					
160	Peter Jacobi, Scottsdale, Ariz.		McDonald, 1 up				
158	Coe Power, Eugene, Ore.	Power, 1 up					Jodie Mudd, 9 and 8
162	David Nelson, Reno, Nev.				Mudd, 6 and 5		
151	Jodie Mudd, Louisville, Ky.	Mudd, 2 up					
159	George Beebe, Waverly, Iowa		Mudd, 8 and 7				
157	Jerome Yochum, McMurray, Pa.	Yochum, 2 and 1					
161	Joe Malay, Weiser, Idaho			Mudd, 6 and 5			
155	Marc Redman, Bloomington, Minn.	Hill, 3 and 2					
160	Steve Hill, Houston, Texas		Hill, 3 and 1				
159	Roger Tennyson, Pinehurst, N.C.	Tennyson, 2 up					
162	Danny May, Kokomo, Ind.						
•144	Billy Tuten, Palatka, Fla.	Tuten, 3 and 2					
159	Rob Boldt, Walnut Creek, Calif.		Tuten, 1 up, 19 holes				
156	Michael Diffley, Woodhaven, N.Y.	Schjetnan, 4 and 3					
161	Adrian Schjetnan, Houston, Texas			Tuten, 4 and 3			
153	Bruce Jenkins, Little Rock, Ark.	Cromie, 8 and 7					
160	James Cromie, N. Hollywood, Calif.		Nilles, 5 and 4				
157	Vic Wilk, Sepulveda, Calif.	Nilles, 2 and 1					
162	Peter Nilles, Seattle, Wash.				Tuten, 2 and 1	Gordon, 3 and 1	
150	Rick Burgess, Stockton, Calif.	Burgess, 2 and 1					
159	Harlon Hendrick, Vidor, Texas		Burgess, 3 and 2				
157	Daniel Nishimoto, Kapaa, Hawaii	Nishimoto, 2 and 1					
161	Gary Schaefer, Sandusky, Ohio			Kilthau, 2 and 1			
154	Eddie Kilthau, Phoenix, Ariz.	Kilthau, 2 and 1					
160	Douglas Surine, Philadelphia, Pa.		Kilthau, 2 and 1				
158	Gary Schultz, New Orleans, La.	McDonald, 1 up					
162	Steve McDonald, Portland, Ore.						
148	Mickey Yokoi, Los Angeles, Calif.	Hunt, 4 and 3					
159	Samuel Hunt, McRae, Ga.		Hunt, 4 and 3				
156	Mark Crabtree, Norman, Okla.	Blandford, 4 and 3					
161	Jim Blandford, Scottsdale, Ariz.			Hunt, 4 and 3			
154	Tony Grimes, Phoenix, Ariz.	Grimes, 1 up					
160	Jeff Baechler, Louisville, Ky.		Martin, 3 and 2				
158	Peter Martin, Clarkston, Ga.	Martin, 4 and 3					
162	Gene Parr, Minneapolis, Minn.				Gordon, 1 up		
151	Richard Gordon, Santa Clara, Calif.	Gordon, 1 up					
160	Leo Glutting, Mullica Hill, N.J.		Gordon, 3 and 2				
157	Alan Wojcik, Parma, Ohio	Crawford, 5 and 4					
162	Daryl Crawford, Phoenix, Ariz.			Gordon, 2 and 1			
155	Jim Stefanich, Joliet, Ill.	Stefanich, 2 and 1					
160	Mark Gardner, Mead, Wash.		Stefanich, 1 up, 19 holes				
159	Lynn Stone, Chino, Calif.	Stone, 4 and 2					
162	Rennie Sasse, Lincoln, Neb.						

•Co-medalist

Fifty-fifth Amateur Public Links Inter-city Team Championship, Harding Trophy (36 Team Entries), July 14, 15: Won by Los Angeles, California Team, 464 for 36 holes (Mickey Yokoi, 148; Lynn Stone, 159; Vic Wilk, 157); Second, San Francisco, California Team, 467 (William Malley, 157; Richard Gordon, Jr., 151; Robert B. Boldt, 159); Third, Chicago, Illinois Team, 468 (Jim Stefanich, 155; Dave Ogrin, 144; Jim Waring, 169).

WOMEN'S AMATEUR PUBLIC LINKS CHAMPIONSHIP

CHAMPIONSHIP TROPHY

Presented in January 1977 by

ROBERT F. DWYER

Member of the United States Golf Association Executive Committee

1962-1974

HISTORY

1977—Miss Kelly Fuiks, 19, of Phoenix, Ariz., defeated Miss Kathy Williams, of La Cresent, Minn., 1 up, to become the first Women's Amateur Public Links Champion. The Championship was played at the Yahara Hills Golf Course (East Course) in Madison, Wis. Miss Fuiks also helped Arizona win the Team Championship played in conjunction with the qualifying rounds. Mrs. Diana Schwab, of Kettering, Ohio, was medalist with a score of 149, on rounds of 73 and 76. She was defeated in the third round by Miss Barbara Hoffmeister, of Rifle, Colo., 1 up. Miss Fuiks defeated Miss Hoffmeister, her teammate at Arizona State University, 2 and 1, in the semi-final round. In the other semi-final match, Miss Williams defeated Miss Lenore Muraoka, of Honolulu, 1 up. The Championship drew an entry of 686 players.

1978—Miss Kelly Fuiks, 20, of Phoenix, Ariz., defeated Mrs. Diana Schwab, of Kettering, Ohio, 5 and 4, to win her second consecutive Women's Amateur Public Links Championship. The Championship, originated in 1977, was played at the Myrtlewood Golf Course (Palmetto Course) in Myrtle Beach, S.C. The co-medalists with 36-hole scores of 151 were Miss Kathy Williams, of Minneapolis, Minn., the 1977 runner-up; and Miss Jeanne Hartman, of Miami, Fla. Miss Williams lost in the first round to Laura Bencriscutto, 5 and 4. Miss Hartman lost a quarter-final match to Mrs. Schwab, the 1977 medalist, 1 up. In the semi-final round, Miss Fuiks defeated Miss Sarah LeVeque, a 1977 quarter-finalist, 1 up, and Mrs. Schwab, also a 1977 quarter-finalist, ousted Miss Debbie Johnston, 3 and 2. In the final, Miss Fuiks was 3 up after the first nine holes. The lead was increased to five holes with birdies at the 10th and 11th holes. She closed out the match by holing a five-foot putt at the 14th hole. The Miami, Fla., Team of Miss Hartman, Miss Patrice Rizzo, and Miss Pam Elders, won the Team Championship. The 658 entries was short of the 686 received for the first WAPL in 1977.

1979—Miss Lori Castillo, 18, of Honolulu, defeated Becky Pearson, of Miami, Fla., 2 up, in the final played at the Braemar Golf Course, Edina, Minn. Miss Castillo joined a very select group. Only three other players—Charles (Chick) Evans, Jr., Bob Jones, and Jack Nicklaus—have held two USGA Championships simultaneously. She was also the Girl's Junior Champion. She was not only the first woman player to hold concurrent titles, but also the youngest player, at 18 years, nine months, and 16 days old. Kelly Fuiks, the defending champion, and Lauri Merten, both of Phoenix, Ariz., were the co-medalists with 6-over-par scores of 152. Both, however, lost their first-round matches. Miss Castillo's first two matches were very close. She had to win the 18th hole in her first match against Miss Lea Larson to square the match, and she eventually won on the 20th hole. She defeated Nicki Reuterfeldt, 1 up, in the second round. In her quarter-final match, she played even-par golf to defeat Lenore Muraoka, 4 and 2, and then defeated Holly Morris, 5 and 4, in the semi-finals. Miss Pearson had an easier route to the finals, reaching the 16th hole only once. She defeated Linda Finders, 4 and 2; was five under par in defeating Lois Drafke, 4 and 3; was one under par in defeating Cheryl Wilson, 7 and 6, in the quarter-finals; and defeated Marianne Huning, 4 and 3, in the semi-finals. In the final, Miss Castillo went 1 up three times in the first 10 holes, but three times Miss Pearson came back to even the match. Miss Castillo won the 11th and 12th holes to go 2 up, but Miss Pearson won the 13th and 14th to even the match again. Miss Castillo won the 17th hole with a 15 foot putt for a birdie 2 and then won the 18th hole with a par. Winners of the Team Trophy were Sarah LeVeque, Becky Beach, and Lois Drafke, of Chicago, Ill., with a 36-hole team total of 461, 11 strokes better than the team from Phoenix, Ariz. A record 695 entries were received, exceeding the previous high of 686 for the inaugural WAPL Championship in 1977.

1980—Lori Castillo, 19, of Honolulu, Hawaii, won her second consecutive Women's Amateur Public Links Championship, defeating Pamela Miller, 21, of Libertyville, Illinois, 2 and 1, in the final. The Championship was played at the Center Square Golf Club, in Center Square, Pennsylvania. For Miss Castillo, the 1978 Girls' Junior Champion, it was her third USGA title. In winning, Miss Castillo not only won the qualifying medal, but also equalled or broke all the existing records. All 120 starters played 36 holes to determine the 32 competitors in match play. Miss Castillo followed her first round 77 with a one under par 71, establishing a new single round scoring record. Her two-day total of 148 also established the 36-hole record. After 36 holes of stroke play, 32 players were at 163 or better, the lowest cutoff score since the championship was started in 1977. Miss Castillo never trailed in any match, losing only six holes in 72 holes of match play. She won her first matches by a margin of 26 holes. In her first two matches she didn't lose a hole, winning by 7 and 6 and by 9 and 7, a WAPL record for the largest winning margin in one match. In the final match, both Miss Castillo and Miss Miller were excellent from tee to green, and even though they each had many birdie chances, the only birdie on the front nine was by Miss Castillo on the fourth hole from six feet. Miss Castillo made the nine-hole turn in par 36 and Miss Miller in 38. Miss Castillo opened a two-hole lead at the 11th, but Miss Miller won the 12th. At the 13th, Miss Castillo went two up again, and when they halved the next three holes, Miss Castillo stood dormie two playing the 17th. They halved in par to end the match. Miss Castillo was one over par, Miss Miller five over. For the second consecutive year, a team from the Chicago area won the Team Championship with a record tying score of 459, 15 strokes ahead of Dayton, Ohio at 474. The members of the winning team were Pamela Miller, Alicia Ogrin, and Penny Hammel. The USGA received a record 728 entries, surpassing the previous high of 695 in 1979.

WOMEN'S AMATEUR PUBLIC LINKS CHAMPIONSHIP

DATE	WINNER, RUNNER-UP	SCORE	SITE	ENTRY
1977 (June-July)	Miss Kelly Fuiks d. Miss Kathy Williams	1 up	Yahara Hills G.C., Madison, Wis. Medalist—149: Mrs. Diana Schwab	686
1978 (June-July)	Miss Kelly Fuiks d. Mrs. Diana Schwab	5 & 4	Myrtlewood G. C., (Palmetto Course) Myrtle Beach, S.C. Medalist—151: Miss Kathy Williams	658
1979 (June-July)	Miss Lori Castillo d. Miss Becky Pearson	2 up	Braemar G. C., Edina, Minn. Co-Medalists—152: Miss Kelly Fuiks Miss Lauri Merten	695
1980 (June)	Miss Lori Castillo d. Miss Pam Miller	2 and 1	Center Square G.C., Center Square, Pa. Medalist—†148: Lori Castillo	§728

§ Record entry
† Record qualifying score

WOMEN'S AMATEUR PUBLIC LINKS TEAM CHAMPIONSHIP

DATE	WINNER	SCORE	SITE	ENTRY
1977 (June-July)	Phoenix, Ariz.	472	Yahara Hills G. C. Madison, Wis.	§21
1978 (June-July)	Miami, Fla.	459	Myrtlewood G. C., (Palmetto Course) Myrtle Beach, S.C.	20
1979 (June-July)	Chicago, Ill.	461	Braemar G.C. Edina, Minn.	18
1980 (June)	Chicago, Ill.	459	Center Square G.C., Center Square, Pa.	§21

§Record Entry

1977

FIRST WOMEN'S AMATEUR PUBLIC LINKS CHAMPIONSHIP

Held at Yahara Hills Golf Course (East Course), Madison, Wisconsin, June 29-July 3.
Yardage—6,107. Par 72. 688 Entries, 120 Starters, 32 Qualifiers.

Qualifying Score	1st Round (18 Holes)	2nd Round (18 Holes)	3rd Round (18 Holes)	Semi-Finals (18 Holes)	Final (18 Holes)	
*149	Mrs. Diana L. Schwab, Kettering, Ohio	Mrs. Schwab,				
163	Miss Linda Pierson, Austin, Texas	6 and 5	Mrs. Schwab,			
161	Miss Jeanne Hartman, Bellevue, Ohio	Miss Hartman,	3 and 2			
166	Mrs. Karen Plamondon, Ypsilanti, Mich.	3 and 1		Miss Hoffmeister,		
157	Miss Laura Bencriscutto, Racine, Wis.	Miss Keblish,		1 up		
164	Miss Sherrie Ann Keblish, Miami, Fla.	19 holes	Miss Hoffmeister,			
162	Miss Barbara Hoffmeister, Rifle, Colo.	Miss Hoffmeister,	5 and 4			
167	Miss Janina Parrott, Detroit, Mich.	4 and 3			Miss Fuiks,	
155	Miss Kelly Fuiks, Phoenix, Ariz.	Miss Fuiks,			2 and 1	
163	Mrs. Terri Maier, Racine, Wis.	5 and 4	Miss Fuiks,			
161	Miss Lori Castillo, Honolulu, Hawaii	Miss Castillo,	3 and 2			
167	Miss Holley Morris, Golden, Colo.	5 and 4		Miss Fuiks,		
157	Miss Carole Holland, Edmonds, Wash.	Miss Creveling,		3 and 1		Miss Kelly Fuiks, 1 up
165	Miss Marianne Creveling, Alhambra, Calif.	19 holes	Ms. Wheaton,			
162	Mrs. Mary Hutchison, Warren, Ohio	Ms. Wheaton,	1 up			
167	Ms. Debra Wheaton, San Pedro, Calif.	2 and 1				
154	Miss Sarah LeVeque, Springfield, Ill.	Miss LeVeque				
163	Miss Laurie Stokien, Washington, D.C.	7 and 5	Miss LeVeque,			
161	Mrs. Chris Epperly, Springfield, Va.	Mrs. Welch,	5 and 4			
166	Mrs. Jeanne Welch, Simsbury, Conn.	19 holes		Miss Williams,		
157	Miss Kathy Williams, LaCrescent, Minn.	Miss Williams,		3 and 2		
164	Miss Ann Gardner, Country Club Hills, Ill.	1 up	Miss Williams,			
162	Miss Lauri Merten, Phoenix, Ariz.	Miss Merten,	4 and 2			
167	Miss Dana Jennings, Denver, Colo.	2 and 1			Miss Williams,	
155	Miss Julie Stanger, Phoenix, Ariz.	Miss Stanger,			1 up	
164	Miss Maureen Nedwick, Miami, Fla.	5 and 3	Miss Muraoka,			
161	Miss Lenore Muraoka, Honolulu, Hawaii	Miss Muraoka,	1 up, 20 holes			
167	Mrs. Katherine Perry, Laguna Hills, Calif.	7 and 5		Miss Muraoka,		
159	Dr. Lea Larson, Clarksville, Tenn.	Dr. Larson,		3 and 1		
166	Miss Carol Hochsprung, Denver, Colo.	4 and 2	Miss Rego,			
162	Miss Brenda Rego, Kunia, Hawaii	Miss Rego,	2 and 1			
167	Miss Brenda Lunsford, Winnipeg, Manitoba, Can.	7 and 6				

*Medalist

First Women's Amateur Public Links Inter-city Team Championship, Team Trophy (21 Team Entries). June 29, 30: Won by Phoenix, Arizona, Team, 472 for 36 holes (Julie Stanger, 155; Kelly Fuiks, 155; Lauri Merten, 162); Second, Honolulu, Hawaii, Team, 484 (Lori C. Castillo, 161; Brenda Rego, 162; Lenore K. Muraoka, 161); Third, Denver, Colorado, Team, 495 (Barbara Hoffmeister, 162; Carol J. Hochsprung, 166; Holley Morris, 167).

1978

SECOND WOMEN'S AMATEUR PUBLIC LINKS CHAMPIONSHIP

Held at Myrtlewood Golf Course (Palmetto Course), Myrtle Beach, South Carolina, June 28-July 2.
Yardage—6,211. Par 72. 658 Entries, 120 Starters, 32 Qualifiers.

Qualifying Score	1st Round (18 Holes)	2nd Round (18 Holes)	3rd Round (18 Holes)	Semi-Finals (18 Holes)	Final (18 Holes)
*151	Miss Kathy Williams, Minneapolis, Minn.	Miss Bencriscutto,			
158	Miss Laura Bencriscutto, Racine, Wis.	5 and 4	Miss Fuiks,		
155	Miss Kelly Fuiks, Phoenix, Ariz.	Miss Fuiks,	1 up, 20 holes		
162	Miss Holley Morris, Golden, Colo.	4 and 3		Miss Fuiks,	
153	Miss Pamela Elders, Leisure City, Fla.	Miss Elders,		1 up	
161	Miss Penny Hammel, Decatur, Ill.	1 up	Miss Elders,		
155	Miss Mary Elizabeth Boozer, Lawrence, Kans	Miss Boozer,	4 and 3		
165	Mrs. Ann Pearson, Dodge Center, Minn.	3 and 2			Miss Fuiks,
152	Miss Barbara Hoffmeister, Rifle, Colo.	Miss Hoffmeister,			1 up
161	Miss Brenda Lunsford, Winnipeg, Manitoba	1 up	Miss Hoffmeister,		
155	Miss Patrice Marie Rizzo, Hialeah, Fla.	Miss Rizzo,	2 and 1		
162	Miss Linda Hawk, Indianapolis, Ind.	6 and 5		Miss LeVeque,	
154	Miss Jo Anne Cesar, Phoenix, Ariz.	Miss Spencer,		7 and 6	
162	Miss Deborah Spencer, Honolulu, Hawaii	1 up	Miss LeVeque,		
156	Miss Sarah LeVeque, Springfield, Ill.	Miss LeVeque,	4 and 3		
165	Miss Janice Schulte, Wichita, Kans.	5 and 4			
*151	Miss Jeanne Hartman, Miami, Fla.	Miss Hartman,			
158	Mrs. Christine Epperly, Springfield, Va.	6 and 5	Miss Hartman,		
155	Miss Althea Tome, Honolulu, Hawaii	Miss Drafke,	1 up		
162	Miss Lois Drafke, Downers Grove, Ill.	2 up		Mrs. Schwab,	
154	Miss Joan Garety, Caro, Mich.	Miss Garety,		1 up	
162	Mrs. Mary Hutchinson, Warren, Ohio	1 up	Mrs. Schwab,		
156	Miss Lauri Merten, Phoenix, Ariz.	Mrs. Schwab,	5 and 4		
165	Mrs. Diana Schwab, Kettering, Ohio	3 and 1			Mrs. Schwab,
153	Miss Lenore Muraoka, Honolulu, Hawaii	Miss Muraoka,			2 and 1
161	Miss Marianne Creveling, Alhambra, Calif.	2 and 1	Miss Johnston,		
155	Miss Debbie Johnston, Kankakee, Ill.	Miss Johnston,	1 up, 19 holes		
164	Miss Kathy Patton, Plano, Texas	7 and 5		Miss Johnston,	
154	Miss Irene Zuniga, Santa Ana, Calif.	Miss Zuniga,		3 and 2	
162	Miss Lou Anne Gibson, Santa Ana, Calif.	5 and 4	Miss Lauther,		
157	Miss Janice Japar, Seattle, Wash.	Miss Lauther,	2 and 1		
165	Miss Dawn Lauther, Myrtle Beach, S.C.	1 up, 20 holes			

Miss Kelly Fuiks, 5 and 4

*Co-Medalists

Second Women's Amateur Public Links Inter-city Team Championship, Team Trophy (20 Team Entries), June 28, 29: Won by Miami, Florida Team, 459 for 36 holes (Patrice Marie Rizzo, 155; Pamela R. Elders, 153; Jeanne Hartman, 151); Second, Honolulu, Hawaii Team, 470 (Lenore K. Muraoka, 153; Althea Tome, 155; Deborah Spencer, 162); Third, Plainfield, Illinois Team, 472 (Sarah LeVeque, 156; Penny Hammel, 161; Debbie Johnston, 155).

1979
THIRD WOMEN'S AMATEUR PUBLIC LINKS CHAMPIONSHIP

Held at Braemar Golf Course, Edina, Minnesota, June 27-July 1.
Yardage—6,099. Par 73. 695 Entries, 120 Starters, 32 Qualifiers.

Qualifying Score	1st Round (18 Holes)	2nd Round (18 Holes)	3rd Round (18 Holes)	Semi-Finals (18 Holes)	Final (18 Holes)
*152	Kelly Fuiks, Phoenix, Ariz.	Varty,			
161	Kelly Varty, Elk River, Minn.	2 up	Huning,		
157	Marianne Huning, San Gabriel, Calif.	Huning,	1 up		
166	Amanda Presto, Greenwich, Conn.	2 and 1		Huning,	
155	Becky Beach, Champaign, Ill.	Tome,		6 and 4	
163	Althea Tome, Honolulu, Hawaii	5 and 4	Tome,		
158	Jane Sirmons, St. Petersburg, Fla.	Sirmons,	1 up		
167	Dana Jennings, Denver, Colo.	4 and 3			Pearson,
153	Lois Drafke, Downers Grove, Ill.	Drafke,			4 and 3
162	Julie Loebs, Myrtle Beach, S.C.	2 and 1	Pearson,		
157	Becky Pearson, Miami, Fla.	Pearson,	4 and 3		
166	Linda Finders, St. Charles, Mo.	4 and 2		Pearson,	
156	Mary Jane McClure, Ft. Wayne, Ind.	Schwab,		7 and 6	
164	Diana Schwab, Kettering, Ohio	2 up	Wilson,		
160	Deborah Johnston, Kankakee, Ill.	Wilson,	1 up, 19 holes		
168	Cheryl Wilson, Houston, Texas	2 and 1			
*152	Lauri Merten, Phoenix, Ariz.	Elders,			
161	Pamela Elders, Leisure City, Fla.	3 and 1	Morris,		
157	Holley Morris, Golden, Colo.	Morris,	3 and 2		
166	Carole Holland, Edmonds, Wash.	5 and 3		Morris,	
155	Ann Soderman, Newgulf, Texas	Soderman,		5 and 4	
164	Peggy Gustafson, Brenham, Texas	4 and 3	Flom,		
159	Cynthia Flom, Honolulu, Hawaii	Flom,	2 and 1		
168	Kelly Merten, Phoenix, Ariz.	1 up			Castillo,
153	Sarah LeVeque, Springfield, Ill.	Muraoka,			4 and 3
162	Lenore Muraoka, Honolulu, Hawaii	1 up	Muraoka,		
158	Kay Cornelius, Scottsdale, Ariz.	Cornelius,	1 up		
167	Kristie Tovson, Waite Park, Minn.	3 and 1		Castillo,	
156	Lori Castillo, Honolulu, Hawaii	Castillo,		4 and 2	
165	Lea Larson, Clarksville, Tenn.	1 up, 20 holes	Castillo,		
160	Nicki Reuterfeldt, Coon Rapids, Minn.	Reuterfeldt,	1 up		
168	Lisa Porambo, Seattle, Wash.	4 and 3			

Winner: Lori Castillo, 2 up

*Co-Medalists

Third Women's Amateur Public Links Inter-city Team Championship, Team Trophy (18 Team Entries), June 27, 28: Won by Chicago, Illinois Team, 461 for 36 holes (Sarah LeVeque, 153; Becky Beach, 155; Lois Drafke, 153); Second, Phoenix, Arizona Team, 472 (Kelly Fuiks, 152; Lauri Merten, 152; Kelly Merten, 168); Third, Miami, Florida Team, 476 (Becky Pearson, 157; Jane Sirmons, 158; Pamela Elders, 161).

1980
FOURTH WOMEN'S AMATEUR PUBLIC LINKS CHAMPIONSHIP

Held at Center Square Golf Club, Center Square, Pennsylvania, June 25-29
Yardage—6,139. Par 72. 728 Entries, 120 Starters, 32 Qualifiers.

Qualifying Score	1st Round (18 Holes)	2nd Round (18 Holes)	3rd Round (18 Holes)	Semi-Finals (18 Holes)	Final (18 Holes)	
*148	Lori Castillo, Honolulu, Hawaii	Castillo, 7 and 6				
160	Ann Soderman, Newgulf, Texas		Castillo, 9 and 7			
156	Ginger Fulton, South Vienna, Ohio	Fulton, 2 up				
162	Cathy Lynne Hockin, Hanover Park, Ill.			Castillo, 3 and 1		
151	Cynthia Flom, Honolulu, Hawaii	Flom, 1 up				
160	Jamie Wise, Dayton, Ohio		Flom, 4 and 3			
157	Julie Loebs, Myrtle Beach, S.C.	Loebs, 2 and 1				
163	Kay Cornelius, Scottsdale, Ariz.				Castillo, 5 and 3	
151	Maria Sera, Bloomington, Ind.	Farr, 1 up				
160	Heather Farr, Phoenix, Ariz.		Farr, 2 and 1			
156	Alicia Ann Ogrin, Waukegan, Ill.	Forse, 1 up, 20 holes				
162	Nancy Forse, Anderson, Ind.			Farr, 2 and 1		
153	Lisa Kimbro, Houston, Texas	Kimbro, 6 and 5				
161	Theresa Schreck, Spokane, Wash.		Kimbro, 2 and 1			
158	Diana Schwab, Kettering, Ohio	Schwab, 6 and 5				
163	Joan Ash, Youngstown, Ohio					Lori Castillo, 2 and 1
149	Lauri Merten, Phoenix, Ariz.	Merten, 5 and 4				
160	Michelle Hiskey, College Park, Md.		Munno, 2 and 1			
156	Sherrie Ann Keblish, Miami, Fla.	Munno, 2 and 1				
162	Angela Munno, College Park, Md.			Hammel, 2 and 1		
152	Penny Hammel, Decatur, Ill.	Hammel, 1 up				
160	Izzy Johnson, Hanover, N.H.		Hammel, 2 and 1			
158	Andrea Hodel, Birmingham, Mich.	Hodel, 2 up				
163	Jacquie Galbraith, Mission Viejo, Calif.				Miller, 4 and 3	
151	Pam Miller, Libertyville, Ill.	Miller, 4 and 3				
160	Kelly Merten, Phoenix, Ariz.		Miller, 3 and 1			
157	Jody Christensen, St. Louis Park, Minn.	Maier, 1 up, 20 holes				
162	Terri Maier, Racine, Wis.			Miller, 2 and 1		
154	Pamela Elders, Leisure City, Fla.	Elders, 4 and 2				
162	Carol Ludvigson, Flossmoor, Ill.		Morris, 2 up			
159	Holley Morris, Golden, Colo.	Morris, 2 and 1				
163	Denise Bratzler, Carson City, Nev.					

*Medalist

Fourth Women's Amateur Public Links Inter-city Team Championship, Team Trophy (21 Team Entries), June 25, 26: Won by Chicago, Illinois Team, 459 for 36 holes (Penny Hammel, 152; Pamela Miller, 151; Alicia Ogrin, 156); Second, Dayton, Ohio Team, 474 (Diana Schwab, 158; Ginger Fulton, 156; Jamie Wise, 160); Third, Phoenix, Arizona Team, 477 (Lauri Merten, 149; Heather Farr, 160; Denise Martinez, 168).

JUNIOR AMATEUR CHAMPIONSHIP

CHAMPIONSHIP TROPHY

Presented in August, 1948, by the

UNITED STATES GOLF ASSOCIATION

HISTORY

1960–The State of Washington produced its second consecutive Junior Amateur Champion in William L. Tindall, 17, of Seattle. He defeated Robert L. Hammer, 17, of Sarasota, Fla., 2 and 1, in the final. This followed the victory of Larry J. Lee, of Spokane, the previous year and marked the first time consecutive Champions had come from the same state. The Championship was played at the Milburn Golf and Country Club, Overland Park, Kans. The entry reached a record 1,445; this was the 11th successive year in which the entry had increased. Both semi-final matches went extra holes for the first time. Tindall defeated Bruce Fischer, 15, of Manning, Iowa, 1 up in 19 holes; Hammer ousted Sherman Finger, III, 16, of Evanston, Ill., 1 up in 20 holes. A 28-hole match won by Michael Eiserman, of Independence, Mo., over Patrick Honeycutt, of Memphis, Tenn., equaled the all-time USGA record for most extra holes in a match; George Von Elm and Maurice McCarthy, Jr., were the first to play 10 extra holes, in the 1930 Amateur Championship. Robert R. Kirouac, of Sharon, Mass., became the third player in history to play in five Junior Amateur Championships. He joined Jack Nicklaus and John Konsek in this select group.

1961–Charles S. McDowell, of Virginia Beach, Va., became the youngest winner of the Championship at 16 years one month, with his 2 up victory over Jay Sigel, 17, of Whitemarsh, Pa., at the Cornell University Golf Course, Ithaca, N.Y. McDowell replaced as youngest Champion Mason Rudolph, who was 16 years two months when he won in 1950. During the final match McDowell held a 2 up lead after nine holes but Sigel won the next two holes to even the match. McDowell won the 13th hole with a par while Sigel missed a putt from two feet. After halving four straight holes, McDowell won the 18th. In the semi-final matches, McDowell defeated George Boutell, 17, of Phoenix, Ariz., 2 up, and Sigel defeated Bob Haldeen, of Sterling, Colo., 3 and 2. The Championship drew a record entry of 1,885. Rain caused postponement of the first day's play so that the final was played on Sunday, August 6, rather than Saturday, August 5, as originally scheduled.

1962–The opponents in the final match were teammates on the golf team of Bellarmine High School, San Jose, Calif. Jim Wiechers, 17, of Los Altos, overcame Jim Sullivan, also 17, of Sacramento, by 4 and 3 to win the Championship at the Lochmoor Club, Grosse Pointe, Mich. The match included an eagle by Wiechers on the third hole, a par-5, where he holed out a pitch shot across a bunker. Wiechers played 113 holes in only three over par. His opponents included the defending Champion, Charles McDowell, of Virginia Beach, Va., whose bid to become the first two-time Champion, ended in the semi-final round, 2 and 1. Bob Carson, 15, of Long Beach, was the third Californian to advance to the semi-final round. Terry Hurst, of Honolulu, made the third hole-in-one in the history of the Championship with a four iron on the 187-yard fourth hole in a third-round match against Wiechers. The Championship continued to grow at a remarkable rate. There were 2,090 entrants contesting for 127 qualifiers places at 53 sites. The number of entrants comfortably surpassed the record of 1,885 set the previous year and marked the 13th consecutive year in which the entry has increased.

1963–Greg McHatton, 16, of Whittier, Calif., defeated Richard Bland, of Tulsa, by 4 and 3 in the final at the Florence Country Club, Florence, S.C. McHatton's semi-final victim was 15-year-old Billy Herbert, of Roanoke, Va., 3 and 1. Bland eliminated Mike Thorp, of Louisville, Ky., on the 19th hole in the other semi-final after being 4 down as late as the 11th hole. McHatton, outdriving Bland by 30 to 40 yards, was 6 up at the turn in the final, which required only one hour 47 minutes for its 15 holes. Herbert beat the only foreign player in the field, Enrique Sterling, Jr., of Mexico City, by 1 up in the fifth round. the entry of 2,230 was a record for the 14th consecutive year.

1964–John Miller, 17, of San Francisco, won both the qualifying medal and the Championship at the Eugene Country Club, Eugene, Ore. It was the first time that the Championship included stroke play qualifying at the site. The 64 low scorers from a field of 150 survived for match play. Miller's qualifying scores were 71-68–139, three under par. Miller's opponent in the 18-hole final match was Enrique Sterling, Jr., of Mexico City. Miller won by 2 and 1. Sterling was the first foreign player to reach the final. Gregg McHatton, the defending Champion, lost in the quarter-final round. A handicap requirement of 10 strokes or better was introduced for the first time and the total entry fell to 1,583 after the record entry of 2,230 in 1963.

1965–James B. Masserio, 16, of Pittsburgh, became the first resident of the Northeast to win the Junior Amateur Championship. He was even par while defeating Lloyd Liebler, Portsmouth, Va., by 3 and 2 in the final match on the South Course of the Wilmington Country Club, Wilmington, Del. Liebler, only 14 years of age, 5 feet 5 and 130 pounds, is the youngest player to reach the final round. The losing semi-finalists were Mike Spang, 15, Tualatin, Ore., and Gary Bennett, 16, Dillsburg, Pa. All the semi-finalists were young enough to be eligible to play again in 1966. The co-medalists, with 148, six over par, were Bob Barbarossa, St. Cloud, Minn., and Arthur Russell, Lake Jackson, Texas.

1966–In the third all-California final in the history of the Junior Amateur Championship, 16-year-old Gary Sanders, of Buena Park, defeated Ray Leach, of Novato, 2 up, at the California Country Club, Whittier, Calif. Sanders' margin might have been bigger, but he committed a breach of the Rules by lifting his ball to clean it twice on the 12th hole. The Rules at that time permitted a ball to be lifted for the purpose of cleaning it only once on each green. Instead of winning the hole, he lost it, but still won the Championship. Losing semi-finalists were Lanny Wadkins, of Richmond, Va., and Tom Kite, Austin, Texas.

1967–John Crooks, 17, of Winston-Salem, N.C., became the second Easterner in three years to win the Junior Amateur Championship. He defeated Andy North, 17, of Madison, Wis., 2 and 1, at the Twin Hills Golf and Country Club, Tulsa, Okla. North was 6 down to Crooks after nine holes of their 18-hole final. He then scored birdies on four of the next seven holes and was 2 down playing the 17th. They halved the 17th and Crooks won the match. Gary Sanders, the defending Champion, lost his first round match to Tyler Chase, of Hamden, Conn., in 19 holes.

1968–Eastern domination of the United States Junior Amateur Championship continued as Eddie Pearce, 16, of Temple Terrace, Fla., defeated William B. Harman, Jr., of Wilmington, Del., 6 and 5, at The Country Club, Brookline, Mass. It was the third victory for an Easterner in the last four Championships. Pearce went ahead at the first hole of the final and steadily built on his lead, closing out the match with a birdie 4 on the 12th hole. Pearce had uncanny command of the par 5s. He played 17 of them in the course of the Championship, and was 15 under par. He won 15 of them, lost one and halved one. Gary Koch of Sarasota, Fla., lead the qualifying with 145 for 36 holes.

1969–The Junior Amateur Championship returned to California for the first time since 1966 as Aly Trompas, of San Diego, defeated Eddie Pearce, of Temple Terrace, Fla., 3 and 1, at the Spokane Country Club, Spokane, Wash. Pearce was attempting to become the first player in the history of the Championship to win twice. He is the second player ever to reach the final twice. Mason Rudolph lost to Gay Brewer in the 1949 final, then won over Charles Beville the next year. Three times Trompas played spectacular recovery shots, winning one hole with a birdie and saving halves on the other two. Richard Monkman, of Wilmington, Del., was medalist with 146. Gregory Shreaves, of Salisbury, Md., and David Eger, of Charlotte, N.C., were the losing semi-finalists.

1970–Gary Koch, 16, became the second Junior Amateur Champion from Tampa, Fla., within three years. Eddie Pearce, the 1968 Champion, was the other. Koch defeated Mike Nelms, 16, of Hixson, Tenn., by 8 and 6 in the final at the Athens Country Club, Athens, Ga. The margin was the largest ever in a final match. Aly Trompas, the 1969 Champion, was trying for a second consecutive title, but he was defeated by Koch, 3 and 1, in the quarter-final round. Mike Fambrough, of Valdosta, Ga., and Randall L. Transou, of Bethania, N.C., were the losing semi-finalists. Koch had a formidable reputation when he arrived for the Championship. He already had won the Florida Open and led local qualifying for the 1970 U.S. Open by 11 strokes with a 36-hole score of 136.

1971–The Championship continued to be exchanged between players from Florida and California when Michael Brannan, of Salinas, Calif., defeated Robert M. Steele, of Dunkirk, N.Y., 4 and 3, at the Manor Country Club in Rockville, Md. Brannan succeeded Gary Koch, of Temple Terrace, Fla., as Champion. The 1969 Champion was from California and the 1968 Champion from Florida. Brannan was 15 years, 8 months of age when he won, the youngest Champion ever. He won six matches, and in the 92 holes he played he was only 12 over par. In the final Brannan won the first five holes and was 6-up after nine holes. Curtis Strange, of Virginia Beach, Va., was medalist with 142. Michael D. Reid, of Aurora, Colo., and John J. O'Neal, of Carmel, Ind., were the losing semi-finalists.

1972–The California/Florida domination of the Championship was ended when Bob Byman, 17, of Boulder, Colo., defeated Scott Simpson, of San Diego, Calif., 2 and 1, in the final round at the Brookhaven Country Club. Dallas, Texas. Since 1968 the Champion had come from one of those two states. Mike Brannan, of Salinas, Calif., the 1971 Champion, was upset in the first round by Ron Kilby, of Houston, Texas, 3 and 2. Byman, the qualifying medalist with a 144, was forced to go 18 holes in only one of his six match-play rounds; Jim Stewart, of the Republic of Singapore, took him 19 holes before losing in the semi-final match. In the final round against Scott Simpson, Byman was 4-up after eight holes. Simpson rallied with a winning birdie on the 1[illegible]th hole, halved the next three, and won 15 and 16 to pull to within one hole. The 17th was his downfall, however; he hit his drive into water and three-putted from 20 feet to lose the hole and the match. A high school student, Byman won the Colorado State Amateur Championship in 1971. He qualified for the Open in 1972–the youngest player in the field.

1973—In the fourth all-California final, Jack Renner, 17, of San Diego, defeated Michael Brannan, of Salinas, the 1971 Champion, in 20 holes, over the Willow Glen course of the Singing Hills Country Club, El Cajon, Calif. It was the first final match to go extra holes in 26 years of the Championship. Renner was three down after 14 holes against Brannan and he caught him at the 18th. He holed birdie putts of 10 feet on both the 15th and 16th, halved the 17th, and won the 18th when Brannan missed a $3\frac{1}{2}$ footer. Both boys birdied the

19th hole, Brannan from 30 feet and Renner from nine. Renner won the 20th with a par 4; Brannan was just off the green in three, 22 feet from the hole. He putted and missed. No Champion has ever repeated. Brannan was, however, only the third player to reach the final twice. Eddie Pearce was Champion in 1968 and runnerup in 1969, while Mason Rudolph was runnerup in 1949 and Champion in 1950. The Willow Glen course was the longest—6,935 yards—ever used for the Junior Championship. Two other records were tied in the qualifying rounds. Robert Donald, of Athens, Ga., scored 71-68—139, equalling the marks set by John Miller in 1964 at the Eugene (Ore.) Country Club. The 68 and the 139 total are both record scores. The entry totaled 1,325.

1974—For the fifth time and second consecutive year, the Championship had an all-California final. Dave Nevatt, of Merced, defeated Mark Tinder, from Pebble Beach, 4 and 3, in the final at the Brooklawn Country Club, Fairfield, Conn. To illustrate the strength of the California delegation, 1,453 boys entered the Championship; these 1,453 played 18-hole qualifying rounds at various sites throughout the country for 150 places. The 150 qualifiers then played 36 holes at the Brooklawn Country Club to determine the 64 starters for match play. Nineteen California juniors made the trip to Connecticut, 13 qualified for match play, and two were in the final. The losing semi-finalists were Bob Griffin of Denver, and Bill Loeffler, from Englewood, Colo. Charles H. Beck, Jr., of Fayetteville, N. C., was medalist with 143. In the final round, Nevatt went into the lead on the first hole. Tinder won the second, and Nevatt went into the lead again on the third, increased his lead to two up on the sixth, and won the ninth hole with another birdie, to go 3 up. The match was actually decided on the 10th hole, 140-yard par-3. Here Tinder was on the green with his tee shot, while Nevatt was in high rough back of the green. Nevatt hit a wedge to the edge of the sloping green and the ball rolled to within two feet of the hole. Nevatt holed the putt and crushed Tinder's hopes for a comeback. Tinder won the 12th with a birdie, but Nevatt took the 14th and 15th with pars, to end the match.

1975—Brett Mullin, a big 6-foot-4, 195-pound 17-year old from Riverside, became the fourth Californian in the past five years to win the Junior Amateur and the 12th in the Championship's 28 years. He defeated Scott Templeton of Willington, Kans., 2 and 1, at the Richland Country Club, Nashville, Tenn. Gary Pinns, of Lombard, Ill., was medalist with 72-68—140. He lost to Mullin on the 19th hole in the semi-final round. The other losing semi-finalist was Rob Brewster, of Orchard Lake, Mich., whom Templeton defeated, 4 and 3. Templeton, only 15, was playing in his first United States Junior Amateur Championship, and he held a 2-up lead over Mullin after nine holes of their scheduled 18-hole final match. Mullin pulled even by winning the 12th with a bogey and the 14th when Templeton three-putted. Mullin won the 15th and 16th to go 2-up, and the match ended when they halved the 17th hole. There were 1,898 entries filed, the highest number since 1963, when there were no limitations on handicaps. Now an entrant cannot have a USGA handicap of more than eight strokes.

1976—Madden Hatcher, III, of Columbus, Ga., ended the California domination of the Junior Championship by defeating Doug Clarke from La Jolla, 3 and 2, at the Hiwan Golf Club, Evergreen, Colo. California juniors had won four of the previous five Championships. However, two Californians, Robert Clampett, of Carmel, and Andy Blossom, from Stockton, were co-medalists with 144. Losing semifinalists were Steve Jones, of Yuma, Colo., who lost to Hatcher, 5 and 4, and Mike McGee, of Middletown, Ohio, who was eliminated by Clarke, 4 and 3. Hatcher went 3-up on Clarke after the first four holes of the final match and never was caught. The entry reached 1,957, besting last year's figure by 59. This represents the highest number of entries filed since 1963.

1977—Willard Wood, 16, of Lake Charles, La., played superbly to win both the qualifying medal and the Championship over the Scarlet Course of the Ohio State University Golf Course, in Columbus, Ohio. Wood led the qualifying round by six strokes with a 36-hole score of 141, and scored six birdies as he defeated David Games, of Bellflower, Calif., 4 and 3, in the final. Wood was only the second player to become both medalist and Junior Amateur Champion. John Miller, later the Open Champion, was the first. Wood's 68 in the second round of qualifying equalled Miller's record for a single round, set in 1964, when Miller won. Wood, who was only 5-foot-5 and weighed 120 pounds, defeated Corey Pavin, of Oxnard, Calif., 1 up, in one semi-final, and Games defeated Eric

Evans, of Canoga Park, Calif., 1 up, in the other. California once again dominated the Championship winning 13 of the 64 qualifying places and three of the four places in the final round. Madden Hatcher, III, the 1976 Champion, lost in the second round. The entry of 2,046 was the highest since 1963 when there was no handicap limit. In 1977 an entrant must have had a USGA handicap of not more than eight strokes.

1978—Donald Hurter, 17, of Honolulu, Hawaii, rallied from an early four-hole deficit to defeat Keith Banes, of La Mirada, Calif., 1 up, in 21 holes, in the final of the Junior Amateur Championship, played on the South Course of the Wilmington Country Club, in Wilmington, Del. At the same time, the Girls' Junior Championship was being conducted over the North Course. This was the first time that the USGA had conducted two national championships simultaneously at the same golf club. Willard Wood, of Tucson, Ariz., the defending Champion, was medalist for an unprecedented second time with a 36-hole score of 141, matching his total of a year ago. He lost to Banes, however, in a semi-final match, 1 up. In the other semi-final, Hurter eliminated Chris Perry, 6 and 5. In the final, Hurter overcame Banes's four-hole lead to level the match after 15 holes. Banes regained the lead at the 16th hole, where Hurter bogied. Hurter ran in an 18-foot putt for a halve on the 17th hole to stay within one hole. Banes then three-putted the 18th hole to send the match into extra holes. At the third extra hole, a par 5, Banes's ball lay five, just three feet from the hole. Hurter then played his fourth stroke from a bunker. His ball deflected off Banes's ball and came to rest three feet from the hole. Hurter holed the putt to end the match. The 2,013 entries represented the fourth largest field in the history of the event.

1979—Jack Larkin, 17, of Atlanta, Ga., played even-par golf to defeat Billy Tuten, of Palatka, Fla., 1 up, in the final at the Moss Creek Golf Club, Hilton Head Island, S. C. Nathaniel Crosby, of Hillsborough, Calif., and Rick Fehr, of Seattle, Wash., were the co-medalists with 36-hole qualifying scores of 148. Crosby lost in the second round, 3 and 2, to Webb Heintzelman, and Fehr lost, 2 and 1, to Wright Waddell in the quarter-finals. Larkin qualified with scores of 82 and 77 for 159, but he was never over par in his matches. He defeated Stuart Smith, 2 and up; Donnie Cude, 7 and 6; Greg Tebutt, 6 and 5; Webb Heintzelman, 1 up; and Tommy Moore, 2 and 1. Tuten defeated Peter Parsons, 3 and 2; Mark Visintainer, 6 and 4; Ty Roush, 2 and 1; Mark Tschetter, 1 up; and Wright Waddell, 1 up, in the semi-finals. In the final, Tuten won the first hole with a par. Larkin birdied the second and fourth holes to take a one-hole lead. When Tuten three-putted the fifth hole, Larkin went 2 up, the widest margin of the match. Tuten won the 10th and 17th holes with pars to even the match. On the final hole, Tuten drove into the left rough one foot behind a small pine tree. With his stroke impeded by the tree, he shanked his second shot into the trees and the ball was lost. Meanwhile, Larkin had hit his best drive of the day and played his second shot onto the back of the green. After an unsuccessful search for his ball, Tuten conceded the match. The 1,848 entries was short of the record of 2,230 set in 1963.

1980—Eric Johnson, 17, of Eugene, Oregon, overcame a steady rain and won the final match, 4 and 3, over Bruce Soulsby, 17, a New Zealander living in Columbus, Ohio. Three golfers shot 68 the first day of the match, equalling the 18-hole scoring record. Kurt Beck, of Pittsburgh, Pennsylvania, broke the record with 66 in the second round. Ralden Chang, 16, of Ewa Beach, Hawaii, equalled the 36-hole record of 139. Johnson twice went extra holes, defeating Kent Caldwell on the 19th hole and Jerry Haas on the 20th. Johnson won the first two holes of the final match, but Soulsby was even after five. Johnson went ahead for good when he won the sixth hole with a par. He was 3 up after nine holes and finally closed out the match with six foot putt for par at the 15th hole. Johnson was even par for the match. Play on the final day was competed despite three delays caused by lightning. Arnold Palmer was the guest speaker at the contestants' dinner the Sunday night before the Championship. The USGA received 1,694 entries for the Championship, well short of the record 2,230 in 1963.

THE JUNIOR AMATEUR CHAMPIONSHIP

DATE	WINNER, RUNNER-UP	SCORE	SITE	ENTRY
1960 (Aug.)	William L. Tindall d. Robert L. Hammer	2 & 1	Milburn G. & C.C., Overland Park, Kans.	1,445
1961 (Aug.)	Charles S. McDowell d. Jay Sigel	2 up	Cornell Univ. G.C., Ithaca, N.Y.	1,885
1962 (Aug.)	James L. Wiechers d. James Sullivan	4 & 3	Lochmoor Club, Grosse Pointe Woods, Mich.	2,090
1963 (July-Aug.)	Gregg McHatton d. Richard Bland	4 & 3	Florence C.C., Florence, S.C.	§2,230
1964 (July-Aug.)	John Miller d. Enrique Sterling, Jr.	2 & 1	Eugene C.C., Eugene, Ore. Medalist—†139: John Miller	1,583
1965 (Aug.)	James Masserio d. Lloyd Liebler	3 & 2	Wilmington C.C., (South Course) Wilmington, Del. Co-Medalists—148: Robert Barbarossa Arthur Russell	1,600
1966 (Aug.)	Gary Sanders d. Ray Leach	2 up	California C.C., Whittier, Calif. Medalist—143: Terry Jastrow	1,464
1967 (Aug.)	John T. Crooks d. Andy North	2 & 1	Twin Hills G. & C.C., Oklahoma City, Okla. Medalist—141: Allen Brooks	1,484
1968 (Aug.)	Eddie Pearce d. W. B. Harman, Jr.	6 & 5	The Country Club, Brookline, Mass. Medalist—145: Gary Koch	1,599
1969 (July-Aug.)	Aly Trompas d. Eddie Pearce	3 & 1	Spokane C.C., Spokane, Wash. Medalist—146: Richard Monkman	1,337
1970 (July-Aug.)	Gary Koch d. Mike Nelms	8 & 6	Athens C.C. Athens, Ga. Medalist—141: Mike Fambrough	1,444
1971 (Aug.)	Michael Brannan d. Robert M. Steele	4 & 3	Manor C.C., Rockville, Md. Medalist—142: Curtis Strange	1,545
1972 (Aug.)	Robert T. Byman d. Scott Simpson	2 & 1	Brookhaven C. C., Dallas, Texas Medalist—144: Robert T. Byman	1,492
1973 (July-Aug.)	Jack Renner d. Mike Brannan	1 up, 20 holes	Singing Hills C. C., El Cajon, Calif. Medalist—†139: Robert Donald	1,325
1974 (July)	David Nevatt d. Mark Tinder	4 & 3	Brooklawn C. C., Bridgeport, Conn. Medalist—143: Charles H. Beck, Jr.	1,453
1975 (July-Aug.)	Bert Mullin d. Scott Templeton	2 & 1	Richland C. C., Nashville, Tenn. Medalist—140: Gary Pinns	1,898
1976 (Aug.)	Madden Hatcher, III d. Doug Clarke	3 & 2	Hiwan G. C., Evergreen, Colo. Co-medalists—144: Andy Blossom Robert Clampett	1,957
1977 (July)	Willard Wood d. David Games	4 & 3	Ohio State University G. C., (Scarlet Course), Columbus, Ohio Medalist—141: Willard Wood	2,039
1978 (Aug.)	Donald Hurter d. Keith Banes	1 up, 21 holes	Wilmington C. C., (South Course) Wilmington, Del. Medalist—141: Willard Wood	2,019
1979 (July-Aug.)	Jack Larkin d. Billy Tuten	1 up	Moss Creek G. C. Hilton Head Island, S. C. Co-Medalists—148: Nathaniel Crosby Rick Fehr	1,848
1980 (July-Aug.)	Eric Johnson d. Bruce Soulsby	4 & 3	Pine Lake C.C. Orchard Lake, Mich. Medalist—†139: Ralden Chang	1,694

† Record qualifying score
§ Record entry

1960
THIRTEENTH JUNIOR AMATEUR CHAMPIONSHIP

Held at the Milburn Golf and Country Club, Overland Park, Kans., August 3-6.
Yardage—6,565. Par 71. 1,445 Entries, 128 Qualifiers, 128 Starters.
FINAL ROUND (18 Holes) – William L. Tindall defeated Robert L. Hammer, 2 up and 1 to play.

UPPER HALF

1st Round (18 Holes)	2nd Round (18 Holes)	3rd Round (18 Holes)	4th Round (18 Holes)	5th Round (18 Holes)	Semi-Final (18 Holes)	
Brian Hirsch, Lake Charles, La.	Hirsch, 2 up	Hirsch 3 and 2	Regnier 4 and 3	Regnier, 5 and 4	Fischer, 2 and 1	Tindall, 1 up, 19 hls.
Jamie Gough, III, Arlington, Va.						
Phil Scherer, Louisville, Ky.	Scherer, 4 and 2					
Frank Warner, Edina, Minn.						
Stephen Sundstrom, E. Aurora, N.Y.	Sundstrom, 2 and 1	Regnier, 5 and 4				
Grant Lawton, Portland, Ore.						
William Regnier, LaPorte, Ind.	Regnier, 3 and 2					
Glen R. Noland, Jr., Kansas City, Mo.						
Dennis Bond, Cincinnati, Ohio	Bond, 2 and 1	Metzker, 7 and 6	Placido, 1 up			
James M. Grant, San Antonio, Texas						
Roger Garrett, Tucson, Arizona	Metzker, 3 and 1					
Gary Metzker, Seattle, Wash.						
Philip A. Roth, Los Angeles, Calif.	Roth, 1 up, 22 hls.	Placido, 8 and 6				
William F. Malone, Atlanta, Ga.						
Robert Placido, Portsmouth, R.I.	Placido, 2 and 1					
William Hershey, Landover, Md.						
Alan Cooke, Sioux Falls, S.D.	Tomlinson, 6 and 5	Straub, 3 and 2	Thomas, 2 up	Fischer, 1 up		
Robert Tomlinson, Richmond, Va.						
William A. Burke, Brockton, Mass.	Straub 1 up, 20 hls.					
Austin Straub, Woodhaven, N.Y.						
Don Lackey, Borger, Texas	Mathiason, 1 up	Thomas, 1 up				
Mark O. Mathiason, Fargo, N.D.						
Robert Zender, Skokie, Ill.	Thomas 2 and 1					
Robert W. Thomas, Greenville, N.C.						
Terry Small, Long Beach, Calif.	Small, 3 and 2	Small, 1 up	Fischer, 3 and 2			
Michael G. Jackson, Birmingham, Mich.						
James Offer, Clayton, Mo.	Berliner, 6 and 5					
Art Berliner, Daly City, Calif.						
Joe Dreps, Lewiston, Idaho	Dreps, 5 and 4	Fischer, 2 and 1				
David A. Outland, Birmingham, Ala.						
Benjamin A. Skinker, III, Chevy Chase, Md.	Fischer, 1 up					
Bruce Fischer, Manning, Iowa						
Johnny Stevens, Wichita, Kans.	Stevens, 6 and 5	Jelks, 2 and 1	Tindall, 3 and 2	Tindall, 1 up	Tindall, 7 and 6	
Dave Graska, Oshkosh, Wis.						
Joe W. Jelks, Jr., Greenville, S.C.	Jelks, 4 and 3					
Joel Kaye, Phoenix, Ariz.						
William L. Tindall, Seattle, Wash.	Tindall, 1 up	Tindall, 3 and 2				
John Einhorn, San Diego, Calif.						
Gary Shemano, San Francisco, Calif.	Shemano, 6 and 5					
Fred J. Cook, Danville, Ill.						
Thomas Hahn, Arlington, Va.	Schultz, 5 and 4	Harmon, 2 and 1	Harmon, 6 and 5			
Rick Schultz, Aurora, Ill.						
Claude Harmon, Jr., New Rochelle, N.Y.	Harmon, 6 and 5					
Robert A. Wagner, Owosso, Mich.						
Ken Wilson, Hastings, Neb.	Antonio, 4 and 3	Hanten, 2 and 1				
Alex Antonio, Jr., Vienna, Ohio						
Dave Hanten, Huron, S.D.	Hanten, 2 up					
Anthony Romano, Beverly, Mass.						
Roger Cleveland, Lakewood, Calif.	Cleveland, 4 and 2	Finkelstein, 1 up	Finkelstein, 2 and 1	Hedrick, 4 and 3		
Alex Sanderson, Texarkana, Ark.						
Michael V. McMahon, Orlando, Fla.	Finkelstein, 2 and 1					
Maury A. Finkelstein, Savannah, Ga.						
Craig D. Goldate, Memphis, Tenn.	Goldate, 1 up	DiPadua, 2 and 1				
Henry L. Warner, Alexandria, Va.						
Luther M. Vaughan, Jr., Houston, Texas	DiPadua, 5 and 4					
Pasco DiPadua, W. Warwick, R.I.						
John E. Dement, Meridian, Miss.	Hedrick, 5 and 4	Hedrick, 1 up, 20 hls.	Hedrick, 3 and 2			
Don Hedrick, Lexington, N.C.						
Del McAllister, Plymouth, Mich.	Knox, 5 and 4					
King Knox, Lancaster, Pa.						
James Polsinelli, Kansas City, Mo.	Hadlock, 3 and 2	Hadlock, 3 and 2				
James M. Hadlock, Marshall, Texas						
William J. Bailes, Vienna, W. Va.	Snyder, 6 and 4					
Bill Snyder, Columbus, Ohio						

LOWER HALF

Semi-Final (18 Holes)	5th Round (18 Holes)		4th Round (18 Holes)	3rd Round (18 Holes)	2nd Round (18 Holes)	1st Round (18 Holes)
Hammer, 1 up, 20 holes	Hammer, 6 and 4	Hammer, 4 and 3	Price, 2 up	Price, 1 up	McCormick, 2 and 1	Rodney Bliss, III, Des Moines, Iowa Bill McCormick, Long Beach, Calif.
					Price, 2 and 1	Mike Price, New Albany, Ind. Barry Friedman, Daly City, Calif.
				Gorman, 2 and 1	Gruidl, 5 and 4	Gerald Gruidl, Minneapolis, Minn. Gerald C.P. Eckert, Albany, N.Y.
					Gorman, 6 and 4	Robert D. Andrews, Lincoln, Neb. Jay Gorman, Portland, Ore.
			Hammer, 2 and 1	Munn, 6 and 4	Schiefelbein, 3 and 1	Jeff Andrick, San Antonio, Texas Brad Schiefelbein, Tucson, Ariz.
					Munn, 5 and 3	Richard Munn, Victoria, B.C., Canada John R. Banion, Detroit, Mich.
				Hammer, 4 and 3	Williams, 1 up	Pete Williams, Englewood, Colo. Martin Garber, Bethesda, Md.
					Hammer, 2 and 1	Leonard Fiocca, Harvey, Ill. Robert L. Hammer, Sarasota, Fla.
		Brigham, 4 and 3	Hutchins, 1 up, 19 hls.	McDowell, 2 and 1	McDowell, 1 up	Michael Hoke, LaPorte, Ind. Bryan L. McDowell, Humble, Texas
					Cook, 5 and 4	Frank H. Kirk, Kansas City, Mo. Thomas H. Cook, Fargo, N.D.
				Hutchins, 2 and 1	Baker, 2 and 1	Robert J. Baker, Jr., Charleston, S.C. Jim Farrell, Ogden, Utah
					Hutchins, 4 and 3	Stephen Brown, Arlington, Va. Thomas A. Hutchins, Jr., Boise, Idaho
			Brigham, 3 and 2	Gurry, 1 up	Pageau, 4 and 3	Raymond E. Waller, Des Moines, Iowa Gary M. Pageau, Detroit, Mich.
					Gurry, 3 and 2	Lawrence P. Malpica, Conway, Ark. James E. Gurry, Andover, Mass.
				Brigham, 3 and 1	Brigham, 3 and 2	Dennis Troy, Scotch Plains, N.J. Thomas Brigham, San Mateo, Calif.
					Aden, 1 up, 19 hls.	Gordon Aden, Spokane, Wash. Desmond P. Curran, Kansas City, Mo.
	Finger, 4 and 3	Eiserman, 3 and 2	Adler, 6 and 4	Maloney, 3 and 2	Kling, 7 and 6	John C. Keohane, Jr., Minneapolis, Minn Jarett B. Kling, Rochester, N.Y.
					Maloney, 2 and 1	Gary S. Markland, Little Rock, Ark. Michael J. Maloney, Wayne, Pa.
				Adler, 1 up	Adler, 4 and 3	Gary Adler, Columbus, Ohio Scott Smith, Tulsa, Okla.
					Difloure, 4 and 3	John King, Litchfield Park, Ariz. John B. Difloure, Las Vegas, Nev.
			Eiserman, 1 up	Barnes, 2 up	Barnes, 4 and 3	Dennis Smith, Upland, Calif. Thomas W. Barnes, Jr., Atlanta, Ga.
					Meissner, 2 and 1	Richard E. Meissner, Silver Spring, Md. James G. Bush, New Orleans, La.
				Eiserman, 2 and 1	O'Donnell, 2 and 1	John O'Donnell, Baltimore, Md. Charles H. Mendell, Foxboro, Mass.
					Eiserman, 1 up, 28 hls.	Michael W. Eiserman, Independence, Mo. Patrick Honeycutt, Memphis, Tenn.
		Finger, 1 up	Finger, 2 and 1	Lyles, 1 up, 19 hls.	Lyles, 3 and 2	Steve Lyles, Scottsville, Ky. Carl Hoss, Twin Falls, Idaho
					Kirovac, 8 and 7	Phil Skover, Northville, Mich. Robert Kirovac, Sharon, Mass.
				Finger, 6 and 5	Finger, 3 and 2	Kent B. Kittle, Bethesda, Md. Sherman Finger, III, Wilmette, Ill.
					O'Brien, 3 and 2	Mike Malarkey, Signal Mt., Tenn. Patrick O'Brien, Artesia, N.M.
			Diaz, 7 and 6	Livingston, 2 and 1	Livingston, 4 and 3	David Livingston, Tulsa, Okla. Tom Clark, Ann Arbor, Mich.
					Boutell, 6 and 4	Thomas B. Thomsen, Hastings, Neb. George W. Boutell, Phoenix, Ariz.
				Diaz, 3 and 2	Nelson, 1 up, 19 hls.	Bruce Richards, Medina, Wash. Kent P. Nelson, Longmont, Colo.
					Diaz, 8 and 7	Joe R. Diaz, Whittier, Calif. Stephen Cox, Bloomington, Ill.

1961
FOURTEENTH JUNIOR AMATEUR CHAMPIONSHIP

Held at the Cornell University Golf Course, Ithaca, N.Y., August 2-5.
Yardage—6,593 Par 71. 1,885 Entries, 128 Qualifiers, 128 Starters.
FINAL ROUND (18 Holes) – Charles S. McDowell defeated Jay Sigel, 2 up.

UPPER HALF

1st Round (18 Holes)	2nd Round (18 Holes)	3rd Round (18 Holes)	4th Round (18 Holes)	5th Round (18 Holes)	Semi-Final (18 Holes)	
William C. Sutton, St. Louis, Mo. Byron, Wood, Eugene, Ore.	Wood, 6 and 5	Wood, 1 up, 22 hls.	Wood, 2 and 1	Boutell, 2 and 1	Boutell, 3 and 2	McDowell, 2 up
Steve Whitman, San Francisco, Calif. Claude Harmon, Jr., New Rochelle, N.Y.	Whitman, 2 and 1					
Denny Gallagher, Mt. Gilead, Ohio Michael Goodart, Roswell, N.M.	Gallagher, 7 and 6	Gallagher, 2 up				
Dale Vaught, Albuquerque, N.M. Michael Kress, Pittsburgh, Pa.	Kress, 6 and 5					
Robert Barclay, W. Peabody, Mass. George W. Boutell, Phoenix, Ariz.	Boutell, 3 and 2	Boutell, 4 and 3	Boutell, 5 and 4			
Wally Blessey, New Orleans, La. Robert Pettingill, Port Huron, Mich.	Blessey, 5 and 4					
Jamie Gough, III, Arlington, Va. Mark Whitaker, Prairie Village, Kans.	Gough, 3 and 2	Gough, 5 and 4				
Patton Kincaid, Jr., Lebanon, Ky. Chris Miel, Stanton, Mich.	Miel, 4 and 3					
James E. Greber, W. Orange, N.J. Bob Post, Patuxent River, Md.	Greber, 4 and 3	Gerring, 1 up	Richardson, 3 and 2	McLendon, 3 and 2		
Bill Hesler, Prairie Village, Kans. Jim Gerring, Union, S.C.	Gerring, 2 and 1					
Thomas R. Elkins, Lake Charles, La. Robert W. Thomas, Greenville, N.C.	Elkins, 1 up, 21 hls.	Richardson, 4 and 2				
John G. Richardson, Jr., Ft. Smith, Ark. Joseph Lanahan, Louisville, Ky.	Richardson, 1 up					
Paul R. Sinelli, Detroit, Mich. Richard Cunningham, Fresno, Calif.	Cunningham, 4 and 2	Cunningham, 1 up	McLendon, 1 up			
Robert L. Abbott, Dallas, Texas Duncan S. Wall, Westfield, Mass.	Abbott, 6 and 5					
Peter Strupp, Phoenix, Ariz. Stephen H. Probst, Oreland, Pa.	Probst, 6 and 5	McLendon, 2 up				
Benson R. McLendon, Montgomery, Ala. George Pulver, Saratoga Springs, N.Y.	McLendon, 2 and 1					
C. L. Allen, Jr., Tulsa, Okla. Brian E. Bovard, Jackson, Mich.	Allen, 1 up	Allen, 1 up	McDowell, 3 and 2	McDowell, 3 and 2	McDowell, 3 and 2	
Carl DiCesare, Rochester, N.Y. Paul Wilderson, III, Sioux City, Iowa	DiCesare, 6 and 5					
John McKey, Jr., Orlando, Fla. Derek Kent, Galion, Ohio	McKey, 3 and 1	McDowell, 2 and 1				
William W. Cowgill, New Vienna, Ohio Charles S. McDowell, Virginia Beach, Va.	McDowell, 5 and 3					
Roger Cleveland, Lakewood, Calif. Greg Pitzer, Waukegan, Ill.	Cleveland, 3 and 1	Cleveland, 6 and 5	Cleveland, 2 and 1			
Jim Gittleman, Alma, Mich. Ora A. Kincaid, III, Lebanon, Ind.	Kincaid, 2 and 1					
Blaine Hibbard, Jr., Shawnee Mission, Kans. James Klutz, Arlington, Va.	Hibbard, 5 and 4	Lehman, 3 and 2				
James Lehman, Lake Geneva, Wis. Thomas H. Garrett, St. Paul, Minn.	Lehman, 2 and 1					
Tom Tindall, Seattle, Wash. William C. Stork, Columbia, S.C.	Stork, 4 and 3	Smith, 4 and 3	Troncatty, 2 and 1	Troncatty, 5 and 4		
Thomas J. Bracken, Waterbury, Conn. Lyford Smith, North Conway, N.H.	Smith, 2 up					
Steve Potter, Louisville, Ky. James Troncatty, Sacramento, Calif.	Troncatty, 4 and 3	Troncatty, 5 and 4				
William R. Cigich, Bethesda, Md. William J. Rahling, Waukegan, Ill.	Cigich, 1 up					
Don Chapman, San Diego, Calif. Jeff Wood, Sunbury, Ohio	Chapman, 2 up	Wilcox, 7 and 6	Wilcox, 2 and 1			
James R. Chester, Jr., Macon Ga. Brian Wilcox, Thornhill, Ont., Canada	Wilcox, 4 and 2					
Craig Goldate, Memphis, Tenn. Robert Francis, Tulsa, Okla.	Goldate, 2 and 1	Goldate, 2 and 1				
Laurence S. Webster, Lincoln, Neb. Fred Ewald, Birmingham, Mich.	Ewald, 3 and 1					

LOWER HALF

Semi-Final (18 Holes)	5th Round (18 Holes)		4th Round (18 Holes)	3rd Round (18 Holes)	2nd Round (18 Holes)	1st Round (18 Holes)
				Chotlos, 3 and 2	Hutchins, 4 and 2	Tom Hutchins, Jr., Boise, Idaho Peter R. George, Port Huron, Mich.
			Haldeen, 4 and 3		Chotlos, 3 and 2	Joe Wood, Takoma Park, Md. Bay Chotlos, Topeka, Kans.
				Haldeen, 1 up	McCutcheon, 1 up, 19 hls.	Jack Ewing, Bakersfield, Calif. Mike McCutcheon, Little Rock, Ark.
		Haldeen, 3 and 1			Haldeen, 6 and 5	James P. Rusher, Ellington, Conn. Robert Haldeen, Sterling, Colo.
				Fanning, 4 and 3	Iversen, 3 and 2	Tom Iversen, Clinton, Iowa Edward Waldron, Glens Falls, N.Y.
			Antonio, 4 and 2		Fanning, 5 and 4	Gary Ackerman, Jackson, Ohio Elwin Fanning, Seattle, Wash.
				Antonio, 5 and 4	Antonio, 4 and 3	James Johnson, Pleasonton, Calif. Alex Antonio, Jr., Vienna, Ohio
	Haldeen, 3 and 2				Mulliken, 1 up	John W. Mulliken, Champaign, Ill. Tom Wrenn, Jr., Chattanooga, Tenn.
				Carton, 3 and 1	Carton, 1 up, 19 hls.	Richard Groebel, Phoenix, Ariz. Kevin K. Carton, Milburn, N.J.
			Aden, 6 and 4		Wood, 7 and 6	Thomas O'Hare, St. Louis, Mo. Donald M. Wood, Carmel, Ind.
				Aden, 1 up	Aden, 2 up	Patrick J. Day, Detroit Lakes, Minn. Gordon E. Aden, Spokane, Wash.
		Aden, 2 and 1			Glover, 6 and 5	Lynn P. Westcott, Ontario, Ore. Russell Glover, Florence, S.C.
				Haap, 2 up	Haap, 2 and 1	Larry Furlong, Joliet, Ill. Tim Haap, Cucamonga, Calif.
			Chew, 2 and 1		Gottschalk, 5 and 4	Stanley J. Thompson, Jr., Midland, Mich. Gary Gottschalk, Dubuque, Iowa
				Chew, 6 and 5	Barnes, 1 up, 20 hls.	Richard Schmidt, Bethesda, Md. Larry L. Barnes, Hastings, Neb.
Sigel, 3 and 2					Chew, 4 and 3	James H. Chew, Hutchinson, Kans. Charles B. Lyon, Prairie Village, Kans.
				Wiechers, 4 and 3	Schmitz, 4 and 3	Robert Schmitz, Groveport, Ohio William P. Hewitt, Idaho Falls, Idaho
			Wiechers, 4 and 3		Wiechers, 6 and 5	James Wiechers, Los Altos, Calif. George Shull, Chevy Chase, Md.
				Spragens, 3 and 2	Spragens, 3 and 2	Melvin S. Rifman, Ellicott City, Md. Robert Spragens, Lebanon, Ky.
		Wiechers, 8 and 6			Parco, 4 and 3	George Thorn, Marietta, Ohio Michael F. Parco, Jr., Ft. Eire, Canada
				Leftwich, 5 and 4	Leftwich, 1 up	Robert Leftwich, Houston, Texas Jeff Alpert, Woodbridge, Conn.
			Bayley, 1 up, 20 hls.		Holman, 2 and 1	James K. Holman, Skokie, Ill. Bruce Fisher, Manning, Iowa
				Bayley, 6 and 4	Fox, 6 and 5	Randall E. Fox, Needham, Mass. Richard Pearce, St. Louis, Mo.
	Sigel, 3 and 1				Bayley, 4 and 3	Volney P. Bayley, Jr., Walled Lake, Mich. Daniel Mazzilli, Jr., Yonkers, N.Y.
				Martin, 1 up	Martin, 7 and 6	Michael Gocke, Bridgeport, W. Va. William Martin, Benton, Ark.
			Sigel, 4 and 2		Eiserman, 5 and 4	Gary Pollock, Erie, Pa. Michael Eiserman, Independence, Mo.
				Sigel, 4 and 3	Fonagy, 6 and 4	Jimmy Day, Laurel, Miss. John L. Fonagay, Jr., Hamburg, N.Y.
		Sigel, 4 and 2			Sigel, 1 up	Jay Sigel, Whitemarsh, Pa. Ernest Denham, Louisville, Ky.
				Moe, default	Duffy 3 and 1	James E. Duffy, Jr., Fairfax, Va. Michael E. Hastings, Waxahachie, Texas
			Nusbaum, 2 and 1		Moe, 5 and 3	Joseph Langston, Jr., Rock Hill, S.C. Mahlon Moe, Spokane, Wash.
				Nusbaum, 2 and 1	Flood, 1 up, 19 hls.	Anthony D. Romano, Beverly, Mass. Tim Flood, Phoenix, Ariz.
					Nusbaum, 2 and 1	Peter Williams, Denver, Colo. Andrew Nusbaum, Salina, Kans.

1962
FIFTEENTH JUNIOR AMATEUR CHAMPIONSHIP

Held at the Lochmoor Club, Grosse Pointe Woods, Mich., August 1-4.
Yardage—6,724. Par 72. 2,090 Entries, 128 Starters.

FINAL ROUND (18 Holes)—James L. Wiechers defeated James Sullivan, 4 and 3.

UPPER HALF

1st Round (18 Holes)	2nd Round (18 Holes)	3rd Round (18 Holes)	4th Round (18 Holes)	5th Round (18 Holes)	Semi-Final (18 Holes)	
John F. King, Scottsdale, Ariz.	Hankey, 5 and 3					
Douglas Hankey, St. Johns, Mich.		Mayhew, 3 and 2				
Edwin L. Murphy, Wheeling, W. Va.	Mayhew, 6 and 5					
Stephen L. Mayhew, Carmel, Ind.			Hyndman, 2 and 1			
John Campbell, Independence, Mo.	Hyndman, 6 and 5					
Tom Hyndman, Abington, Pa.		Hyndman, 6 and 5				
Phil Aldridge, Bloomington, Ill.	Spragens, 5 and 4					
Roger Spragens, Jr., Lebanon, Ky.				Jewett, 4 and 3		
William Cowgill, Cincinnati, Ohio	Cowgill, 4 and 2					
Joe Connolly, Pasadena, Calif.		Cowgill, 1 up				
Tom Davis, Columbus. Ohio	Corbett, 1 up, 20 hls.					
Lawrence Corbett, Rockville Centre, N.Y.			Jewett, 2 and 1			
Harold R. Eller, Old Hickory, Tenn.	Eller, 3 and 2					
Fred Kell, Jr., Normandy, Mo.		Jewett, 2 up				
Bob Jewett, Fort Myers, Fla.	Jewett, 6 and 5					
James S. Usich, Avon, Conn.					Wiechers, 1 up, 19 hls.	
Stephens J. Robbins, Portsmouth, N.H.	Robbins, 6 and 5					
Marc Eason, Oak Park, Mich.		Robbins, 3 and 2				
Billy Herbert, Roanoke, Va.	Herbert, 3 and 1					
Kent Carter, Wichita, Kans.			Robbins, 3 and 2			
Joe Jelks, Jr., Greenville, S.C.	Jelks, 4 and 2					
D. Leith Anderson, Hinsdale, Ill.		Jelks, 3 and 1				
David L. Oliphant, North Platte, Neb.	Bowers, 4 and 3					
Robert Bowers, Springfield, Va.				Wiechers, 3 and 2		
Fred Huebner, Bay City, Mich.	Schroeder, 5 and 4					
John Schroeder, La Jolla, Calif.		Hurst, 2 and 1				
Bryan L. McDowell, Humble, Texas	Hurst, 1 up, 19 hls.					
Terry Hurst, Oahu, Hawaii			Wiechers, 5 and 4			
Michael Pixley, Rochester, N.Y.	Wiechers, 4 and 2					
James L. Wiechers, Los Altos, Calif.		Wiechers, 3 and 2				
Loy Martin, Jr., Tulsa, Okla.	Martin, 2 up					
Robert E. Allen, Shawnee Mission, Kans.						Wiechers, 2 and 1
Norman Waara, Portland, Mich.	Barnes, 3 and 2					
Thomas W. Barnes, Jr., Atlanta, Ga.		Barnes, 4 and 2				
William L. Vernor, Edwardsville, Ill.	Dau, 4 and 2					
Charles F. Dau, Des Moines, Iowa			Hastings, 3 and 2			
John G. Owen, Arlington, Va.	Owen, 7 and 6					
Anthony Ande, Louisville, Ky.		Hastings, 1 up, 19 hls.				
Michael E. Hastings, Waxahachie, Texas	Hastings, 5 and 4					
Robert Centeno, Saticoy, Calif.				McDowell, 2 and 1		
Charles S. McDowell, Virginia Beach, Va.	McDowell, 2 and 1					
Tom Hennings, Avon, Ohio		McDowell, 1 up				
David G. Bennett, Florence, S.C.	Bennett, 3 and 2					
David M. Strapp, Columbus, Ohio			McDowell, 1 up, 19 hls.			
Joe Potter, Phoenix, Ariz.	Potter, 4 and 3					
Elliott C. Pachter, Dodson, Mo.		Potter, 5 and 3				
Joseph V. Smith, Jr., Newburgh, N.Y.	Smith, 4 and 3					
Donald M. Wood, Carmel, Ind.					McDowell, 4 and 3	
Elwin Fanning, Seattle, Wash.	Fanning, 4 and 2					
John R. Krogh, Portland, Ore.		Fanning, 2 and 1				
Roger Manwell, Marysville, Calif.	Manwell, 5 and 4					
William M. Bewley, Glasgow, Ky.			Klahn, 5 and 4			
Gary Klahn, Arlington, Va.	Klahn, 5 and 3					
Mike Spann, Jr., Burlington, N.C.		Klahn, 1 up				
Mike Riley, San Diego, Calif.	Riley, 5 and 3					
Mike Kurzynowski, Jackson, Mich.				Bethea, 5 and 4		
Robert Barclay, Peabody, Mass.	Barclay, 4 and 3					
Mike Harper, Twin Falls, Idaho		Barclay, 4 and 2				
James Penna, Spokane, Wash.	Penna, 5 and 3					
Robert A. Simons, Overland Park, Kans.			Bethea, 5 and 3			
Morrison C. Bethea, Reidsville, N.C.	Bethea, 6 and 5					
John Lorenzen, Jr., Port Huron, Mich.		Bethea, 2 and 1				
Ronald J. Cerrudo, Pleasanton, Calif.	Cerrudo, 4 and 3					
William Rahling, Waukegan, Ill.						

LOWER HALF

Semi-Final (18 Holes)	5th Round (18 Holes)		4th Round (18 Holes)	3rd Round (18 Holes)	2nd Round (18 Holes)	1st Round (18 Holes)
				Schmedemann, 6 and 5	Keen, 3 and 2	Brian Keen, Walled Lake, Mich. Denis G. Manley, London, Ohio
			Frederickson, 1 up		Schmedemann, 6 and 5	Rick Talt, Whittier, Calif. Ron Schmedemann, Manhattan, Kans.
				Frederickson, 5 and 3	Baske, 3 and 2	Ronald Philo, Ballston Spa, N.Y. James R. Baske, Benton Harbor, Mich.
		Fruge, 5 and 4			Frederickson, 1 up, 19 hls.	Tony Frederickson, Ft. Belvoir, Va. Joseph Lenahan III, Louisville, Ky.
				Fruge, 1 up, 21 hls.	Anthony, 3 and 2	John Baer, Woodbridge, Conn. Richard Anthony, Andalusia, Ala.
			Fruge, 2 and 1		Fruge, 2 and 1	Don Fruge, Meridian, Miss. James R. Carlson, Bemidji, Minn.
				Hackett, 3 and 1	Sowles, 1 up, 19 hls.	Will Sowles, Memphis, Tenn. John Mulliken, Champaign, Ill.
	Sullivan, 2 and 1				Hackett, 7 and 6	J.B. Meredith, Jr., Charleston, W. Va. Thomas S. Hackett, Lancaster, Pa.
				Glover, 5 and 4	Turner, 4 and 3	Thomas Carson, Columbus, Ohio Randall Turner, Springfield, Mo.
			Sullivan, 2 and 1		Glover, 1 up	Russell Glover, Florence, S.C. Allen Jones, Honolulu, Hawaii
				Sullivan, 1 up	Sullivan, 6 and 5	James Sullivan, Sacramento, Calif. Kenny L. Brown, Denton, Texas
		Sullivan, 2 and 1			Watson, 4 and 3	George Dunham, Corunna, Mich. William W. Watson, III, Catonsville, Md.
				Meissner, 9 and 8	Diesing, 1 up, 20 hls.	Robert J. Rosenberg, Chicago, Ill. John Diesing, Jr., Omaha, Neb.
			Roby, 2 up		Meissner, 2 up	Andrew Nusbaum, Jr., Salina, Kans. Richard E. Meissner, Silver Spring, Md.
				Roby, 6 and 5	McCutcheon, 1 up	Mike McCutcheon, Little Rock, Ark. Don Brooks, Royal Oak, Mich.
Sullivan, 2 up					Roby, 1 up, 19 hls.	Peter Roby, Rochester, N.Y. Alex Antonio, Jr., Vienna, Ohio
				Polumbus, 4 and 2	Schweitzer, 1 up	David Schweitzer, Louisville, Ky. Rick Adell, Seattle, Wash.
			Polumbus, 1 up		Polumbus, 1 up, 19 hls.	Richard T. Polumbus, Denver, Colo. Don Baranco, Jr., Caldwell, Idaho
				Malarkey, 3 and 2	Malarkey, 6 and 5	Mike Malarkey, Signal Mountain, Tenn. T. J. Schmekpeper, Glenwood, Minn.
		Polumbus, 1 up			Leslie, 6 and 5	Tim Leslie, Highland, Ind. Tony Gage, Detroit, Mich.
				Jacobs, 2 and 1	Cheek, 3 and 2	Edwin W. Cheek, Pittsburgh, Pa. Richard Schmidt, Bethesda, Md.
			Jacobs, 1 up		Jacobs, 6 and 4	Michael Goodart, Roswell, N.M. John Jacobs, Whittier, Calif.
				Garrett, 1 up	Brill, 3 and 1	William Heston, Zanesville, Ohio David Brill, Moses Lake, Wash.
	Carson, 2 and 1				Garrett, 1 up, 19 hls.	Thomas H. Garrett, III, St. Paul, Minn. Theodore J. Kondratko, Dearborn, Mich.
				Kittle, 3 and 1	Langston, 5 and 4	Robert Sawyer, Shawnee Mission, Kans. Joseph W. Langston, Jr., Rock Hill, S.C.
			Kittle, 2 up		Kittle, 6 and 5	John T. Holmes, New Orleans, La. Kent Kittle, Bethesda, Md.
				Abbott, 2 and 1	Massar, 1 up	Terry A. Massar, Atlanta, Ga. Derek Kent, Galion, Ohio
		Carson, 3 and 2			Abbott, 2 up	William M. Martin, Benton, Ark. Robert Lee Abbott, Dallas, Texas
				Carson, 4 and 2	Carson, 5 and 3	Richard G. Meeker, Kent, Ohio Bob Carson, Long Beach, Calif.
			Carson, 2 and 1		Hanten, 4 and 3	Dennis K. Moore, St. Louis, Mo. Dave Hanten, Huron, S.D.
				Baldwin, 4 and 3	Baldwin, 3 and 2	John C. Baldwin, Plandome, N.Y. Michael Thorp, Louisville, Ky.
					Proffitt, 1 up, 20 hls.	Craig Proffitt, Muscatine, Iowa Kent Cadey, Belmont, Mich.

1963
SIXTEENTH JUNIOR AMATEUR CHAMPIONSHIP

Held at the Florence Country Club, Florence, S.C., July 31-August 3.
Yardage—6,513. Par 71. 2,230 Entries, 128 Qualifiers, 128 Starters.
FINAL ROUND (18 Holes)—Gregg McHatton defeated Richard Bland, 4 up and 3 to play.

UPPER HALF

1st Round (18 Holes)	2nd Round (18 Holes)	3rd Round (18 Holes)	4th Round (18 Holes)	5th Round (18 Holes)	Semi-Final (18 Holes)	
Richard Bland, Tulsa, Okla. Marvin M. Nixon, Nashville, Tenn.	Bland, 7 and 6					
William Waldman, Ellington, Conn. Allen Powers, Orangeburg, S.C.	Powers, 2 and 1	Bland, 3 and 2				
Russell Wing, Bellevue, Wash. Stephen M. Falender, Indianapolis, Ind.	Wing, 1 up					
Marc R. Carlson, Lawrence, Kans. Charles Wood, Winston-Salem, N.C.	Carlson, 2 up	Wing, 2 and 1	Bland, 1 up			
David Volpitto, Augusta, Ga. Dennis Troy, Olympia Fields, Ill.	Troy, 2 up					
Charles Sleichter, Severna Park, Md. Stephen Poweska, Rochester, N.Y.	Sleichter, 5 and 4	Sleichter, 3 and 2				
Don Fruge, Meridian, Miss. Denny Alexander, Fort Worth, Texas	Fruge, 6 and 4					
Thomas S. Ruch, Louisville, Ky. Ned Story, St. Charles, Mo.	Story, 2 and 1	Fruge, 1 up, 19 hls.	Sleichter, 3 and 2	Bland, 6 and 5		
John G. Richardson, Fort Smith, Ark. Theodore O. Turner, Norristown, Pa.	Richardson, 6 and 5					
Douglas Marriott, Chevy Chase, Md. Tim Flood, Phoenix, Ariz.	Marriott, 2 up	Richardson, 2 and 1				
George S. Bock, Lincoln, Neb. Robert Hammond, Kalamazoo, Mich.	Hammond, 3 and 2					
Thomas C. Apple, Telford, Pa. John A. Broadbent, Union, N.J.	Broadbent, 2 up	Broadbent, 1 up	Broadbent, 1 up			
Ronald Pence, Clarkston, Wash. Dennis G. Tull, Kansas City, Mo.	Tull, 4 and 3					
Dave Gibson, Spokane, Wash. James Q. Ball, Towson, Md.	Ball, 2 and 1	Ball, 4 and 3				
Robert Bernstein, Flint, Mich. Grier Jones, Wichita, Kans.	Jones, 7 and 6					
Jimmy P. Clayton, Kermit, Texas Melvin Weinberger, Weston, Mass.	Weinberger, 4 and 3	Jones, 2 up	Jones, 3 and 2	Jones, 3 and 2	Bland, 6 and 4	
Michael A. Thorp, Louisville, Ky. Donald C. Baker, Fort Belvoir, Va.	Thorp, 4 and 2					
Ken Sawyer, Guilford College, N.C. Robert Hodgson, Hollywood, Fla.	Sawyer, 6 and 5	Thorp, 2 and 1				
Mike Kurzynowski, Jackson, Mich. Kenneth Engle, Tucson, Ariz.	Engle, 4 and 3					
Mike Long, Joliet, Ill. Terence Block, Vienna, Ohio	Block, 1 up, 19 hls.	Block, 5 and 3	Thorp, 2 and 1			
Steve Beltzer, Grand Island, Neb. Jim Sher, St. Louis, Mo.	Sher, 5 and 3					
Michael Regan, Bethesda, Md. Robert H. Earle, Sharon, Mass.	Earle, 5 and 4	Earle, 4 and 3				
John Kontak, Schofield Barracks, Hawaii Dale Vaught, Albuquerque, N.M.	Vaught, 2 and 1					
Gary Gottschalk, Dubuque, Iowa John Lauri, Mt. Clemens, Mich.	Gottschalk, 3 and 1	Vaught, 1 up	Vaught, 1 up, 20 hls.	Thorp, 1 up		
Johnnie Tinnat, Fort Knox, Ky. Dennis Troy, Jamesburg, N.J.	Troy, 5 and 4					
Charles Lynch, Minneapolis, Minn. James P. Rusher, Ellington, Conn.	Rusher, 1 up, 21 hls.	Rusher, 1 up				
David H. Nore, Twin Falls, Idaho John Cowan, Urbana, Ohio	Cowan, 2 and 1					
Paul D. Elcano, Jr., Reno, Nev. Gary Ostrin, Minneapolis, Minn.	Ostrin, 1 up	Ostrin, 3 and 2	Rusher, 3 and 2			
Robert S. Jewett, Fort Myers, Fla. Stephen Butterfield, Columbus, Ohio	Jewett, 8 and 6					
Pete Bell, Fort Riley, Kansas Jack Lewis, Jr., Florence, S.C.	J. Lewis, 6 and 5	J. Lewis, 1 up				
Cole Mendenhall, Mt. Clemens, Mich. Leonard Studinger, Burlingame, Calif.	Studinger, 8 and 7					
Dennis Moore, St. Louis, Mo. Ronnie Acree, Ferncreek, Ky.	Acree, 5 and 4	Studinger, 3 and 2	Studinger, 1 up	Rusher, 2 and 1	Thorp, 1 up, 19 hls.	Bland, 1 up, 19 hls.

LOWER HALF

Semi-Final (18 Holes)	5th Round (18 Holes)		4th Round (18 Holes)	3rd Round (18 Holes)	2nd Round (18 Holes)	1st Round (18 Holes)
				Sterling, 2 and 1	Spann, 6 and 4	John Long, Placentia, Calif. Mike Spann, Jr., Burlington, N.C.
			Sterling, 4 and 2		Sterling, 6 and 4	Enrique Sterling, Jr., Mexico, D.F. John Krogh, Portland, Ore.
		Sterling, 2 and 1		Cook, 1 up, 22 hls.	Fair, 3 and 2	James Ed Fair, San Francisco, Calif. Richard Hoak, Sioux City, Iowa
					Cook, 5 and 4	Harvey Cook, Memphis, Tenn. John Musterman, Louisville, Ky.
				Govus, 2 and 1	Johnson, 2 and 1	J.B. Meredith, Jr., S. Charleston, W. Va. Don Johnson, Spokane, Wash.
			Stewart, 1 up, 19 hls.		Govus, 2 and 1	David Govus, Atlanta, Ga. Bob Kulp, Jr., Winston-Salem, N.C.
				Stewart, 6 and 5	Stewart, 2 and 1	Michael Goodart, Roswell, N.M. Earl Stewart, III, Dallas, Texas
	Herbert, 1 up				Nickey, 2 and 1	John Nickey, Memphis, Tenn. Hank Bonde, Detroit Lakes, Minn.
				Herbert, 5 and 4	Main, 2 and 1	Doug Main, Flint, Mich. Jay Morelli, Farmingdale, N.Y.
			Herbert, 3 and 2		Herbert, 8 and 7	Tom Ogden, Troy, N.Y. Billy Herbert, Roanoke, Va.
		Herbert, 6 and 5		Malarkey, 5 and 4	Malarkey, 6 and 5	Mike Malarkey, Signal Mountain, Tenn. Jack Arnst, Jackson, Mich.
					Potter, 3 and 1	Stephen Potter, Louisville, Ky. John V. Mattson, Jr., Oak Park, Ill.
				Hoard, 1 up	Hoard, 1 up	Edgar Hoard, Atlanta, Ga. John French, Birmingham, Mich.
			Hoard, 2 up		White, 1 up	Larry E. White, Chattanooga, Tenn. James Gerring, Union, S.C.
				Audeoud, 8 and 6	Monkman, 1 up	Eddie Polk, Oklahoma City, Okla. James P. Monkman, Wilmington, Del.
McHatton, 3 and 1					Audeoud, 1 up, 20 hls.	John D. Richart, Ann Arbor, Mich. Lynn Audeoud, San Bernardino, Calif.
				Cheek, 2 and 1	McClutcheon, 4 and 3	Ronald J. Pelias, New Orleans, La. Mike McClutcheon, Little Rock, Ark.
			Robinson, 4 and 3		Cheek, 3 and 2	William W. Watson, Cantonsville, Md. Edwin Cheek, Pittsburgh, Pa.
				Robinson, 3 and 2	Robinson, 5 and 4	Denny Robinson, Coronado, Calif. William R. Cook, Twin Falls, Idaho
		Van Doren, 1 up			deHebreard, 5 and 4	David deHebreard, Indianapolis, Ind. Thomas Killeen, Columbus, Ohio
				Van Doren, 4 and 3	Aldridge, 2 and 1	Phillip Aldridge, Bloomington, Ill. Greg Pitzer, Waukegan, Ill.
			Van Doren, 3 and 1		Van Doren, 4 and 3	John Van Doren, Kenmore, Wash. Rick Burton, Whittier, Calif.
				Penney, 2 and 1	Penney, 3 and 2	Richard D. Penney, Freeport, Texas Pete Butler, Columbus, Ohio
	McHatton, 5 and 3				W. Lewis, 2 and 1	Jack Holmes, Jr., Villa Grove, Ill. Wayne Lewis, Rochester, N.Y.
				McHatton, 6 and 4	McHatton, 3 and 2	Michael Ihlenfeld, Slippery Rock, Pa. Gregg McHatton, Whittier, Calif.
			McHatton, 2 up		Hamilton, 6 and 4	Robert D. Rice, Clarksburg, W. Va. Richard Hamilton, Atlantic Beach, Fla.
				Taylor, 6 and 4	Taylor, 6 and 5	Charles Taylor, Jr., Signal Mountain, Tenn. Bowen White, Shawnee Mission, Kans.
		McHatton, 2 and 1			Simons, 6 and 4	Robert A. Simons, Overland Park, Kans. Eric Fraunfelter, Middletown, Ohio
				Galvin, 1 up, 21 hls.	Carson, 8 and 6	Derek Kent, Gallion, Ohio Bob Carson, Long Beach, Calif.
			Good, 3 and 2		Galvin, 2 up	James Galvin, Glenn Dale, Md. Jeff Blankenburg, Richland, Mich.
				Good, 2 and 1	Good, 1 up	Thomas O'Hare, St. Louis, Mo. David M. Good, Huntington, W. Va.
					Foster, 1 up	Robert Foster, Columbia, S.C. Richard Anthony, Andalusia, Ala.

1964
SEVENTEENTH JUNIOR AMATEUR CHAMPIONSHIP

Held at the Eugene Country Club, Eugene, Oregon, July 28-August 1.
Yardage—6,627. Par 71. 1,583 Entries, 150 Qualifiers, 150 Starters..

Qualifying Score	1st Round (18 Holes)	2nd Round (18 Holes)	3rd Round (18 Holes)	4th Round (18 Holes)	Semi-Finals (18 Holes)	Final (18 Holes)	
139	*John Miller, San Francisco, Calif.	Miller,					
151	Louis Anderson, Alexandria, Va.	3 and 2	Miller,				
149	Leonard S. Thompson, Laurinburg, N.C.	Estes,	5 and 4				
153	David Estes, Bloomington, Ind.	2 up		Miller,			
147	Lloyd T. Wright, Fort Worth, Texas	Pitzer,		4 and 3			
152	Gregory Pitzer, Culver City, Calif.	1 up, 19 hls.	Pitzer,				
150	Richard Eller, Old Hickory, Tenn.	Eller,	2 and 1				
154	Steve Cole, Seattle, Wash.	3 and 2			Miller, 1 up		
144	Jack W. Lewis, Jr., Florence, S.C.	Thompson,					
151	Jeff Thompson, Greenville, S.C.	2 and 1	Hayes,				
149	Mark S. Hayes, Oklahoma City, Okla.	Hayes,	2 and 1				
154	Steve Dunning, Warrenton, Ore.	1 up		Barbarossa,			
147	Robert Barbarossa, Fort Lauderdale, Fla.	Barbarossa,		1 up			
153	Mike Bergstrom, Lebanon, Ore.	5 and 4	Barbarossa,				
150	Richard Harmon, New Rochelle, N.Y.	Harmon,	3 and 2				
154	James W. Andrews, Stillwater, Okla.	1 up, 21 hls.				Miller, 6 and 5	
143	Bob Archer, Culver City, Calif.	Cisco,					
151	Stephen Cisco, Ottawa, Ill.	2 up	Cisco,				
149	Daniel Scott, Seattle, Wash.	Holloway,	1 up, 19 hls.				
154	Clay M. Holloway, Murfreesboro, Tenn.	2 and 1		St. Germain,			
147	Joseph Lenahan, Louisville, Ky.	Murphy,		3 and 2			
152	Charles F. Murphy, Jr., Albany, N.Y.	2 up	St. Germain,				
150	James R. St. Germain, Northville, Mich.	St. Germain,	5 and 4				
154	John Lampman, Indio, Calif.	4 and 3			St. Germain, 5 and 4		
145	Gregg McHatton, Whittier, Calif.	McHatton,					
152	Ross D. Bartschy, Jr., Columbus, Ohio	1 up, 19 hls.	McHatton,				
149	William Pabarcus, Honolulu, Hawaii	Pabarcus,	3 and 1				
154	Bruce G. Walters, Pikesville, Ky.	1 up, 20 hls.		McHatton,			
148	Sonny Fowler, Baton Rouge, La.	Fowler,		4 and 3			
153	Tommy Medlin, Monroe, N.C.	3 and 2	Sleichter,				John Miller, 2 and 1
150	Charles H. Sleichter, Severna Park, Md.	Sleichter,	5 and 3				
155	Mark Gustafson, Corvallis, Ore.	2 and 1					
141	Vincent F. Glowacki, La Marque, Texas	Glowacki,					
151	Thomas E. Samuels, Jr., Memphis, Tenn.	8 and 7	Noble,				
149	Randy Noble, Montebello, Calif.	Noble,	4 and 3				
153	Jim Deloach, Dallas, Texas	5 and 4		Noble,			
147	Jack Chapman, San Francisco, Calif.	Chapman,		5 and 3			
152	Allen Lee Hovious, Oxford, Miss.	1 up, 19 hls.	Spears,				
150	Cyril Shettleroe, Tucson, Ariz.	Spears,	4 and 3				
154	Richard Spears, Port Jervis, N.Y.	6 and 5			Sterling, 1 up		
145	John D. Richart, Ann Arbor, Mich.	Richart,					
152	Scott Springer, Wichita, Kans.	6 and 5	Richart,				
149	James P. Monkman, Wilmington, Del.	Monkman,	6 and 5				
154	Phillip Armbruster, Fern Creek, Ky.	4 and 3		Sterling,			
148	Enrique Sterling, Jr., Mexico, D.F.	Sterling,		2 and 1			
153	Donald Rambo, Little Rock, Ark.	6 and 4	Sterling,				
150	Michael Goodart, Roswell, N.M.	Goodart,	2 and 1			Sterling, 2 and 1	
154	Hank Bonde, III, Detroit Lakes, Minn.	7 and 6					
143	Jerry M. Heard, Visalia, Calif.	Heard,					
151	Bill Harris, Fort Lauderdale, Fla.	5 and 4	Green,				
149	Wayne Palessiro, Fort Ontario, Calif.	Green,	1 up, 20 hls.				
154	Hubert M. Green, Birmingham, Ala.	1 up		Green,			
147	John Grace, Detroit, Mich.	Grace,		4 and 3			
153	Ronald Moore, Whittier, Calif.	2 and 1	Grace,				
150	R. Charles Nearhoff, Whittier, Calif.	Baca,	7 and 5				
154	Michael J. Baca, Albuquerque, N.M.	2 and 1			Green, 3 and 2		
147	James Catalano, Needham, Mass.	Thompson,					
152	Barney Thompson, Huntington, W. Va.	2 and 1	Engle,				
150	Ken Engle, Tucson, Ariz.	Engle,	1 up, 20 hls.				
154	Mike Davis, Portland, Ore.	1 up		Grant,			
149	Tommy O'Kane, San Francisco, Calif.	English,		3 and 2			
153	James M. English, Evergreen, Colo.	5 and 4	Grant,				
151	Bruce M. Grant, Atlanta, Ga.	Grant,	3 and 1				
155	Steve Morrison, Portland, Ore.	1 up					

*Medalist.

1965
EIGHTEENTH JUNIOR AMATEUR CHAMPIONSHIP

Held at the Wilmington Country Club (South Course), Wilmington, Delaware, August 3-7.
Yardage—6,724. Par 71. 1,600 Entries, 150 Qualifiers, 150 Starters.

Qualifying Score	1st Round (18 Holes)	2nd Round (18 Holes)	3rd Round (18 Holes)	4th Round (18 Holes)	Semi-Finals (18 Holes)	Final (18 Holes)	
148	*Robert Barbarossa, St. Cloud, Minn.	Barbarossa, 3 and 2	Morris, 3 and 1	Trompas, 1 up, 19 hls.	Masserio, 1 up, 19 hls.	Masserio, 2 and 1	James Masserio, 3 and 2
158	Allen L. Miller III, Pensacola, Fla.						
154	Robert Dyer, Melrose, Mass.	Morris, 3 and 2					
159	Ed Morris, San Jose, Calif.						
151	Gregory Trompas, San Diego, Calif.	Trompas, 1 up, 19 hls.	Trompas, 1 up				
158	Wally Howard, Greenville, N.C.						
156	Jerry L. Wadkins, Jr., Richmond, Va.	Ash, 3 and 2					
160	Brian Ash, Buena Park, Calif.						
150	Bruce Ashworth, Las Vegas, Nev.	Lind, 4 and 3	Cheek, 6 and 5	Masserio, 4 and 3			
158	James R. Lind, Skokie, Ill.						
155	John Grace, Detroit, Mich.	Cheek, 3 and 2					
160	Mike Cheek, Pinehurst, N.C.						
153	Don Padgett, II, Selma, Ind.	Masserio, 3 and 1	Masserio, 4 and 3				
159	James Masserio, Pittsburgh, Pa.						
157	Steven Cisco, Ottawa, Ill.	Cisco, 1 up					
161	Dennis R. Metzler, Dillsburg, Pa.						
149	Bruce P. Lopucki, Ypsilanti, Mich.	Lopucki, 1 up, 19 hls.	Lopucki, 4 and 3	Lopucki, 3 and 1	Spang, 3 and 2		
158	Michael A. Jonson, Seattle, Wash.						
155	Lee E. Edmundson, Ludington, Mich.	Edmundson, 2 up					
159	Paul Schultz, Louisville, Ky.						
152	Forrest Fezler, San Jose, Calif.	Fezler, 6 and 5	Fezler, 1 up				
159	Michael T. Dougherty, Newtown Square, Pa.						
156	Stuart J. Friedman, Broken Arrow, Okla.	Friedman, 2 and 1					
160	George Tepley, Chattanooga, Tenn.						
151	Mark S. Hayes, Oklahoma City, Okla.	Hayes, 3 and 1	Klenk, 1 up, 19 hls.	Spang, 6 and 5			
158	Jerry D. Gray, Salina, Kansas						
155	Dan Klenk, Medinah, Ill.	Klenk, 1 up, 19 hls.					
160	Mike Ray, Millbrae, Calif.						
153	Richard Ward, Santee, Calif.	Spang, 1 up	Spang, 5 and 3				
159	Michael Spang, Tualatin, Ore.						
158	Don Rambo, North Little Rock, Ark.	Rambo, 5 and 3					
161	Michael Crider, St. Louis, Mo.						
148	*Arthur Russell, Lake Jackson, Texas	Simpson, 1 up, 19 hls.	Simpson, 4 and 3	Bennett, 2 and 1	Bennett, 5 and 4	Liebler, 1 up, 20 hls.	
158	Bob Simpson, Louisville, Ky.						
155	Kevin Reid, Avon, Conn.	Smith, 4 and 3					
159	Stephen S. Smith, Roseburg, Ore.						
152	Gary Bennett, Dillsburg, Pa.	Bennett, 2 and 1	Bennett, 4 and 2				
159	Peter Hummel, Columbus, Ohio						
156	Stephen J. Smith, Columbia, Mo.	Tyler, 1 up, 19 hls.					
160	Richard Tyler, Englewood, Colo.						
151	Lyle Wehrman, Jr., Diablo, Calif.	Clement, 6 and 4	Clement, 7 and 5	Clement, 4 and 3			
158	Zack Clement, Shaker Heights, Ohio						
155	William H. Young, Sparrows Pt., Md.	Bogan, 3 and 2					
160	Stephen W. Bogan, Montebello, Calif.						
153	Kent L. Engelmeier, Rockville, Md.	Engelmeier, 5 and 4	Alkire, 3 and 2				
159	Phillip Armbruster, Fern Creek, Ky.						
157	Phillip B. Alkire, Wash. Court House, Ohio	Alkire, 5 and 4					
161	Michael Micka, Jr., Bethesda, Md.						
150	Robert Stuart, Mamaroneck, N.Y.	Stuart, 4 and 3	Stuart, 2 and 1	Stuart, 4 and 3	Liebler, 4 and 3		
158	Howard Swartz, Baltimore, Md.						
155	Joseph C. Inman, Jr., Greensboro, N.C.	Inman, 3 and 2					
160	James R. Weeks, Culver City, Calif.						
152	Theodore N. Coia, Wethersfield, Conn.	Coia, 4 and 2	Coia, 3 and 2				
159	Mike Clipko, Niagara Falls, N.Y.						
157	William Lemon, Charleston, S.C.	Battaglia, 1 up					
161	Robert J. Battaglia, Clarence, N.Y.						
151	Lloyd Liebler, Portsmouth, Va.	Liebler, 5 and 3	Liebler, 7 and 5	Liebler, 3 and 1			
158	John T. Baynard, St. Petersburg, Fla.						
156	William Scott, Detroit, Mich.	Scott, 1 up					
160	Paul Samanchik, Wayne, N.J.						
154	Barry Jaekel, Pacific Palisades, Calif.	Kerr, 3 and 2	Gingrich, 4 and 2				
159	Michael H. Kerr, Hewlett Harbor, N.Y.						
158	Robert Viets, Kettering, Ohio	Gingrich, 1 up, 23 hls.					
161	Ike Gingrich, Atlanta, Ga.						

*Co-Medalist.

1966

NINETEENTH JUNIOR AMATEUR CHAMPIONSHIP

Held at the California Country Club, Whittier, California, August 2-6.
Yardage—6,743. Par 72. 1,464 Entries, 150 Qualifiers, 150 Starters.

Qualifying Score	1st Round (18 Holes)	2nd Round (18 Holes)	3rd Round (18 Holes)	4th Round (18 Holes)	Semi-Finals (18 Holes)	Final (18 Holes)
143	*Terry Jastrow, Midland, Texas	Jastrow, 3 and 2				
156	Steve C. Hakes, Coronado, Calif.		Wadkins, 2 and 1			
152	Lanny Wadkins, Richmond, Va.	Wadkins, 5 and 4				
157	Henry C. Walters, Florence, S.C.			Wadkins, 6 and 5		
150	Edmund Thompson III, Bryn Mawr, Pa.	Thompson, 3 and 2				
156	Wayne Blanchard, New Bedford, Mass.		Thompson, 3 and 2			
154	Kent L. Engelmeier, Rockville, Md.	Engelmeier, 3 and 2				
159	Richard A. Stevens, Waterbury, Conn.				Wadkins, 2 and 1	
149	Lloyd Liebler, Portsmouth, Va.	Kalbfleisch, 3 and 1				
156	Tom Kalbfleisch, Louisville, Ky.		Teasdall, 3 and 1			
153	Bill Teasdall, Bonsall, Calif.	Teasdall, 7 and 6				
158	Mark A. Hirsch, East Norwich, N.Y.			Bohn, 1 up		
151	Steven M. Falender, Indianapolis, Ind.	Garriss, 4 and 3				
157	Marshall H. Garriss, Jr., Kailua, Hawaii		Bohn, 4 and 3			
154	Stephen E. Bohn, Roseville, Calif.	Bohn, 5 and 4				
159	Robert J. Murphy, Wilmington, Del.					Sanders, 2 and 1
148	Billy Ziobro, Warrenville, N.J.	Ziobro, 6 and 5				
156	Ralph Colla, Jr., Youngstown, Ohio		Ziobro, 2 and 1			
153	Danny Yates, Atlanta, Ga.	Yates, 1 up				
157	Forrest O. Fezler, San Jose, Calif.			Guernsey, 5 and 4		
150	Arthur Russell, Lake Jackson, Texas	Russell, 7 and 6				
157	Edward L. Burke, Woodbridge, Conn.		Guernsey, 1 up			
154	Rusty Guernsey, Bellingham, Wash.	Guernsey, 2 up				
159	Steve L. Ross, Herndon, Calif.				Sanders, 6 and 5	
149	Andy North, Madison, Wis.	North, 1 up				
156	Tim Cheney, Portland, Ore.		North, 5 and 3			
154	Jimmy Wittenberg, Jr., Memphis, Tenn.	Masserio, 2 and 1				
158	James B. Masserio, Pittsburgh, Pa.			Sanders, 4 and 3		
151	Gary Sanders, Buena Park, Calif.	Sanders, 4 and 3				
157	Edwin W. Cheek, Pittsburgh, Pa.		Sanders, 4 and 3			
155	Kent Clark, Medford, Ore.	Clark, 3 and 2				
159	Howard Barrow, Jr., Mattapoisett, Mass.					Gary Sanders, 2 up
148	Michael Micka, Bethesda, Md.	Micka, 2 and 1				
156	Lynn Summerhays, Salt Lake City, Utah		Simons, 2 and 1			
152	James Simons, Butler, Pa.	Simons, 1 up				
157	James Carney, Centerville, Iowa			Simons, 4 and 2		
150	Ralph A. Smallman III, Birmingham, Ala.	Cheney, 1 up				
156	Jack Cheney, Jr., Little Rock, Ark.		Cheney, 3 and 1			
154	Eddie Pearce, Temple Terrace, Fla.	Pearce, 3 and 2				
159	Dave Penso, Palos Verdes Estates, Calif.				Leach, 3 and 1	
149	Ray Leach, Novato, Calif.	Leach, 5 and 3				
156	Bill Scott, Detroit, Mich.		Leach, 3 and 2			
154	Bernard J. Smith, Jr., Owensboro, Ky.	Smith, 4 and 3				
158	Michael J. Knorre, Spokane, Wash.			Leach, 1 up		
151	James Schiavenza, Milpitas, Calif.	Schiavenza, 19 holes				
157	George Waterhouse, Charlotte, N.C.		Trompas, 1 up			
155	Tim Wickenhauser, Alton, Ill.	Trompas, 2 and 1				
159	Greg Trompas, San Diego, Calif.					Leach, 3 and 2
149	Robert G. Hamilton, Culver City, Calif.	Hamilton, 2 up				
156	John A. Cameron, Dallas, Texas		Boles, 2 and 1			
153	William B. Boles, Jr., Wilson, N.C.	Boles, 1 up				
158	Jerry Lammers, Detroit, Mich.			Boles, 1 up		
150	Brad Lucy, San Francisco, Calif.	Matthews, 1 up				
157	David Matthews, Fayetteville, Ark.		Miller, 4 and 3			
154	Allen L. Miller III, Pensacola, Fla.	Miller, 4 and 3				
159	Michael Achterberg, Fresno, Calif.				Kite, 1 up	
150	Bruce Ashworth, Henderson, Nev.	Ashworth, 8 and 6				
156	Bart Schuerman, Pocatello, Idaho		Kite, 3 and 2			
154	Thomas O. Kite, Jr., Austin, Texas	Kite, 2 and 1				
158	Paul Schultz, Louisville, Ky.			Kite, 2 and 1		
151	James Brady, Bothell, Wash.	Brady, 1 up				
157	Gary Bennett, Florence, S.C.		Reardon, 3 and 1			
156	James M. English, Littleton, Colo.	Reardon, 2 and 1				
159	Timothy Reardon, Worthington, Ohio					

*Medalist

1967
TWENTIETH JUNIOR AMATEUR CHAMPIONSHIP

Held at Twin Hills Golf and Country Club, Oklahoma City, Okla., August 1-5.
Yardage—6,556. Par 71. 1,484 Entries, 149 Qualifiers, 150 Starters.

Qualifying Score	1st Round (18 Holes)	2nd Round (18 Holes)	3rd Round (18 Holes)	4th Round (18 Holes)	Semi-Finals (18 Holes)	Final (18 Holes)	
141	*Allen Brooks, Medford, Ore.	Brooks, 3 and 2					
153	Bill Killea, Elmsford, N.Y.		Brooks, 6 and 5				
151	Wade Mayo, Atlanta, Ga.	Mayo, 3 and 2					
156	Stephen H. Spragins, Rockville, Md.			Brooks, 19 holes			
148	Geoffrey Becker, Daly City, Calif.	Becker, 2 and 1					
155	Gary W. Holland, Wichita, Kans.		Becker, 2 and 1				
152	Bruce W. McKenzie, Alamogordo, N.M.	McKenzie, 3 and 2					
157	Andrew J. Stone, Dallas, Texas				Brooks, 2 and 1		
147	Bruce Ashworth, Las Vegas, Nev.	Ashworth, 4 and 3					
154	William Harman, Jr., Wilmington, Del.		Ashworth, 3 and 2				
152	Joe Burden, Clinton, Iowa	McLean, 4 and 3					
157	James C. McLean, Seattle, Wash.			Ashworth, 1 up			
149	Ted Goin, Seminole, Okla.	Burns, 1 up					
155	Tommy Burns, Selma, Ala.		Kallam, 4 and 3				
153	Michael G. Kallam, Winston-Salem, N.C.	Kallam, 19 holes					
158	Charles Smith, Bellingham, Mass.					North, 5 and 3	
143	Michael P. Killian, Seminole, Fla.	North, 4 and 3					
154	Andy North, Madison, Wis.		North, 7 and 6				
151	Stephen Bohn, Roseville, Calif.	Armstrong, 19 holes					
156	Craig Armstrong, Sacramento, Calif.			North, 2 up			
149	Brian Inkster, Los Altos, Calif.	Inkster, 20 holes					
155	Ted Lindsay, Jr., Ft. Lauderdale, Fla.		Inkster, 2 up				
153	Jack Cheney, Jr., N. Little Rock, Ariz.	Cheney, 5 and 3					
158	Brad Masingill, Payette, Idaho				North, 2 and 1		
147	Joey D. Dills, Muskogee, Okla.	Dills, 2 and 1					
154	William Dutch, Wheaton, Ill.		Dills, 2 and 1				
152	Tyler E. Chase, Hamden, Conn.	Chase, 19 holes					
157	Gary Sanders, Buena Park, Calif.			Bradford, 2 up			
150	Jim Bradford, Buena Park, Calif.	Bradford, 2 and 1					
156	John R. Rice, Gibsonia, Pa.		Bradford, 2 and 1				
153	Don Splonick, Phoenix, Ariz.	Splonick, 20 holes					
158	David Pettersson, Cleveland, Ohio						John T. Crooks, 2 and 1
142	James Simons, Butler, Pa.	Simson, 4 and 3					
154	Paul Simson, Chatham, N.J.		Simson, 20 holes				
151	Robert Goldman, Dallas, Texas	Fezler, 25 holes					
156	Forrest Fezler, San Jose, Calif.			Taylor, 20 holes			
149	Robert Lapic, Millbrae, Calif.	Sharp, 3 and 2					
155	Steven Sharp, Salt Lake City, Utah		Taylor, 4 and 3				
153	Tim Taylor, Memphis, Tenn.	Taylor, 1 up					
158	Tommy Suber, Whitmire, S.C.				Taylor, 4 and 3		
147	Thomas O. Kite, Jr., Austin, Texas	Hensley, 3 and 1					
154	G. Geoffrey Hensley, Cincinnati, Ohio		Hensley, 3 and 2				
152	Chris Pigott, Washington, D.C.	Pigott, 20 holes					
157	John S. Davis, Overland Park, Kans.			Benson, 4 and 3			
150	Vic Benson, Tulsa, Okla.	Benson, 2 up					
155	Lee Moss, Lubbock, Texas		Benson, 5 and 3				
153	John R. Hoehl, Jr., Coral Gables, Fla.	Hoehl, 2 and 1					
158	Robert Stenson II, Greenwich, Conn.					Crooks, 20 holes	
147	William M. Mosser, Garland, Texas	Mosser, 2 up					
154	Eddie Vossler, Oklahoma City, Okla.		Mosser, 6 and 5				
151	Terry Diehl, Rochester, N.Y.	Harpster, 1 up					
157	Pete Harpster, Tulsa, Okla.			Crooks, 1 up			
149	John T. Crooks, Winston-Salem, N.C.	Crooks, 7 and 5					
155	Rick Matteoli, Healdsburg, Calif.		Crooks, 2 and 1				
153	Mark Engelman, Grand Blanc, Mich.	Penso, 4 and 3					
158	David R. Penso, Palos Verdes Estates, Calif.				Crooks, 4 and 3		
148	Lloyd B. Liebler, Portsmouth, Va.	Hatalsky, 1 up					
155	Morris Hatalsky, San Diego, Calif.		Eaton, 19 holes				
152	Jack W. Steinmeyer, Tulsa, Okla.	Eaton, 4 and 3					
157	William G. Eaton, Jr., Riverside, Calif.			Eaton, 1 up			
150	William Kratzert III, Fort Wayne, Ind.	DeLozier, 3 and 2					
156	Michael C. DeLozier, Sedalia, Mo.		DeLozier, 4 and 2				
153	Tim Arnold, Falls Church, Va.	Alexander, 1 up					
158	Charles A. Alexander, W. Frankfort, Ill.						

*Medalist.

1968
TWENTY-FIRST JUNIOR AMATEUR CHAMPIONSHIP

Held at The Country Club, Brookline, Mass., July 30-August 3.
Yardage—6,743. Par 72. 1,599 Entries, 150 Qualifiers, 150 Starters.

Qualifying Score	1st Round (18 Holes)	2nd Round (18 Holes)	3rd Round (18 Holes)	4th Round (18 Holes)	Semi-Finals (18 Holes)	Final (18 Holes)	
145	*Gary Koch, Sarasota, Fla.						
158	Stephen Brown, San Diego, Calif.	S. Brown, 4 and 3					
156	William W. Brown, Jacksonville, Ark.						
160	Joe Burden, Clinton, Iowa	W. Brown, 1 up	W. Brown, 2 and 1				
153	William Kratzert, III, Fort Wayne, Ind.						
159	Richard W. Monkman, Wilmington, Del.	Monkman, 1 up					
157	Joel Eastman, Peoria, Ill.						
161	William Harmon, Mamaroneck, N.Y.	Harmon, 1 up	Harmon, 5 and 4	Brown, 2 and 1			
152	Bruce A. Lietzke, Beaumont, Texas						
159	Phil Sasich, Billings, Mont.	Lietzke, 3 and 2					
157	Alan Helfer, Westport, Conn.						
160	Jamie Frith, Bloomfield Hills, Mich.	Helfer, 2 and 1	Lietzke, 7 and 5				
155	Jeffrey Jerrel, Marietta, Ga.						
160	William F. Macholl, Wickliffe, Ohio	Macholl, 6 and 5					
158	Thomas Loyd, Carthage, Mo.						
161	Randy S. Tickner, Baytown, Texas	Loyd, 4 and 3	Macholl, 19 holes	Lietzke, 1 up	Lietzke, 5 and 4		
150	Eddie Pearce, Temple Terrace, Fla.						
158	Jeff Reaume, Ypsilanti, Mich.	Pearce, 4 and 2					
156	Jim Fisher, Beatrice, Neb.						
160	Brad Masingill, Payette, Idaho	Masingill, 1 up	Pearce, 2 and 1				
154	Charles J. Canepa, Evergreen, Colo.						
160	Jim Sparkman, Ocean Shores, Wash.	Sparkman, 23 holes					
157	Michael L. Dobzinski, Hartford, Conn.						
161	Mike Lynch, Bryn Mawr, Pa.	Lynch, 4 and 3	Sparkman, 1 up	Pearce, 1 up			
153	Richard A. Bendall, Jr., Danville, Va.						
159	Bruce Digiacinto, Dallas, Texas	Bendall, 6 and 5					
157	Wes Gilliland, Hixson, Tenn.						
160	Brian E. Butler, Albuquerque, N.M.	Gilliland, 9 and 8	Bendall, 5 and 3				
155	Richard Adams, Johnson City, N.Y.						
160	Arthur E. Burke, III, Greenfield, Mass.	Burke, 25 holes					
158	Tom Haase, Wickliffe, Ohio						
161	Douglas Ballenger, Owings Mills, Md.	Haase, 4 and 3	Burke, 4 and 2	Bendall, 2 and 1	Pearce, 4 and 3	Pearce, 2 and 1	
148	W.B. Harman, Jr., Wilmington, Del.						
158	James S. Porter, Cucamonga, Calif.	Harman, 2 and 1					
156	Neil Spitalny, Voorheesville, N.Y.						
160	Don Leonard, San Jose, Calif.	Leonard, 2 and 1	Harman, 2 and 1				
153	Gary Vanier, Oakland, Calif.						
159	Stacy Russell, Scottsville, Ky.	Russell, 2 and 1					
157	Mike Smith, Selma, Ala.						
161	Timothy P. Brauch, Denver, Colo.	Smith, 4 and 3	Smith, 1 up	Harman, 4 and 3			
152	Paul Darwin, Fort Worth, Texas						
159	Frederick D. Schick, Cranston, R.I.	Darwin, 2 up					
157	Mike Barnett, Missoula, Mont.						
160	John Shirai, Lihue, Kauai, Hawaii	Shirai, 3 and 1	Darwin, 2 and 1				
155	Bobby Wadkins, Richmond, Va.						
160	Lyman J. Doane, II, Stoneham, Mass.	Wadkins, 6 and 4					
158	Edward W. Morrison, Jr., Huntington, W. Va.						
161	Os Hillman, Jr., Columbia, S.C.	Morrison, 19 holes	Wadkins, 5 and 4	Wadkins, 4 and 3	Harman, 7 and 5		
151	Ben Crenshaw, Austin, Texas						
159	David Eger, Charlotte, N.C.	Crenshaw, 6 and 4					
156	Roger Osterling, Cromwell, Conn.						
160	Bruce Titus, Los Angeles, Calif.	Osterling, 20 holes	Crenshaw, 2 and 1				
154	John Brizendine, Long Beach, Calif.						
160	Denny Colvin, Yakima, Wash.	Brizendine, 6 and 4					
158	Stephen Groves, Lancaster, Ohio						
161	David L. Newquist, Overland Park, Kans.	Newquist, 2 up	Newquist, 3 and 2	Crenshaw, 4 and 3			
153	Larry Zee, Tonawanda, N.Y.						
159	Larry Griffin, New Orleans, La.	Griffin, 2 up					
157	John Vander Meiden, Spring Lake, Mich.						
160	William R. Hoft, Chapel Hill, N.C.	Hoft, 3 and 2	Griffin, 5 and 4				
155	Henry Walters, Florence, S.C.						
160	Marcus Long, Jr., Blacksburg, Va.	Long, 1 up					
158	Chris Hansen, Olympia Fields, Ill.						
162	Steven Nicot, San Diego, Calif.	Nicot, 4 and 3	Long, 7 and 6	Griffin, 3 and 1	Griffin, 1 up	Harman, 1 up	Eddie Pearce, 6 and 5

*Medalist.

1969
TWENTY-SECOND JUNIOR AMATEUR CHAMPIONSHIP

Held at Spokane Country Club, Spokane, Washington, July 29-August 2.
Yardage—6,493. Par 70. 1,337 Entries, 150 Qualifiers, 150 Starters.

Qualifying Score	1st Round (18 Holes)	2nd Round (18 Holes)	3rd Round (18 Holes)	4th Round (18 Holes)	Semi-Finals (18 Holes)	Final (18 Holes)	
146	*Richard Monkman, Wilmington, Del.	Monkman, 3 and 2					
154	Charlie Lockett, Grenada, Miss.		Monkman, 2 up				
152	Kim Heisler, Aurora, Ohio	Heisler, 1 up					
156	Mark Schechter, Aliquippa, Pa.			Pearce, 2 up			
148	Eddie Pearce, Temple Terrace, Fla.	Pearce, 6 and 5					
155	Gary Rodin, Minneapolis, Minn.		Pearce, 5 and 4				
152	Robert Elliott, Austin, Texas	Bradford, 2 and 1					
157	Jim Bradford, Whittier, Calif.				Pearce, 4 and 3		
148	Marvin Rockholt, Memphis, Tenn.	Jarvis, 2 up					
154	Don E. Jarvis, East Norwich, N.Y.		Solomon, 3 and 1				
152	Gary Solomon, Coral Gables, Fla.	Solomon, 20 holes					
157	Michael Lander, Grand Forks, N.D.			Jerrel, 2 up			
151	Jeffrey L. Jerrel, Marietta, Ga.	Jerrel, 2 up					
156	Bill McCloskey, Tantallon, Md.		Jerrel, 3 and 2				
153	Gary Koch, Temple Terrace, Fla.	Koch, 6 and 5					
157	William C. Currie, Bend, Ore.					Pearce, 2 up	
147	Arthur Burke, III, Greenfield, Mass.	Burke, 5 and 4					
154	Scott Rovenger, Coral Gables, Fla.		Leonard, 1 up				
152	Don Leonard, San Jose, Calif.	Leonard, 2 and 1					
156	Billy Bowie, Memphis, Tenn.			Leonard, 1 up			
150	Jay Dean Haas, Belleville, Ill.	Shipley, 5 and 4					
155	David Shipley, Salinas, Calif.		Shipley, 3 and 2				
153	Gregory M. Milan, Bloomington, Ind.	Milan, 3 and 2					
157	Tom Warren, Decatur, Ill.				Shreaves, 2 up		
148	David Miller, Fresno, Calif.	Shreaves, 4 and 3					
155	Gregory Shreaves, Quantico, Md.		Shreaves, 1 up				
152	Larry Zee, Tonawanda, N.Y.	Zee, 4 and 3					
157	Timothy Brauch, Denver, Colo.			Shreaves, 6 and 5			
151	Kevin Morris, New Milford, Conn.	Morris, 1 up					
156	Dean May, Longview, Wash.		Bench, 3 and 2				
153	Kevin Bench, Dallas, Texas	Bench, 2 and 1					
157	Fred Ridley, Winter Haven, Fla.						Aly Trompas, 3 and 1
147	Joseph Heinz, Waterloo, Iowa	Heinz, 4 and 3					
154	Jerry Rollins, Tulsa, Okla.		Myers, 5 and 3				
152	Mack Christensen, Salt Lake City, Utah	Myers, 1 up					
156	Tim Myers, Portland, Ore.			Hurley, 3 and 2			
149	Joe Dills, Muskogee, Okla.	Swanson, 6 and 5					
155	Steve Swanson, Galesburg, Ill.		Hurley, 3 and 2				
153	Dennis Hurley, Ft. Mitchell, Ky.	Hurley, 3 and 2					
157	West Campbell, Yakima, Wash.				Eger, 4 and 3		
148	David Eger, Charlotte, N.C.	Eger, 4 and 3					
154	Stan A. Lee, Heier Springs, Ark.		Eger, 3 and 2				
152	Steve Marshall, Huntingdon Valley, Pa.	Brown, 1 up					
157	Thomas E. Brown, Oklahoma City, Okla.			Eger, 2 up			
151	John McDonald, Fallbrook, Calif.	Abbey, 3 and 2					
156	Robert G. Abbey, Huntington, Calif.		Matteoli, 2 and 1				
153	Rick Matteoli, Healdsburg, Calif.	Matteoli, 4 and 3					
157	Harold Perry, Jr., Honolulu, Hawaii					Trompas, 7 and 5	
147	Gary Gant, Indianapolis, Ind.	Mallon, 3 and 1					
154	William J. Mallon, Framingham, Mass.		Mallon, 5 and 3				
152	Jeff Urban, Arlington, Va.	Urban, 6 and 4					
157	Gary Mankulish, Greenbelt, Md.			Strong, 2 and 1			
150	James A. Strong, Ukiah, Calif.	Strong, 5 and 4					
155	Mike Barnett, Missoula, Mont.		Strong, 1 up				
153	Jim Beabout, Englewood, Colo.	Beabout, 7 and 5					
157	David Grandstaff, Palo Alto, Calif.				Trompas, 3 and 2		
148	Aly Trompas, San Diego, Calif.	Trompas, 2 and 1					
155	C. Pen Barenaba, Jr., Honolulu, Hawaii		Trompas, 1 up				
152	Dennis Conrad, Hamburg, N.Y.	Conrad, 4 and 2					
157	Robert Swahn, Omaha, Neb.			Trompas, 3 and 2			
151	William Bassler, Jr., Catonsville, Md.	Bassler, 5 and 4					
156	Mancil Davis, Dallas, Texas		Bassler, 3 and 2				
154	Scott B. Gillespy, Dallas, Texas	Nilmeier, 1 up					
158	Conrad Nilmeier, Fresno, Calif.						

*Medalist

1970
TWENTY-THIRD JUNIOR AMATEUR CHAMPIONSHIP

Held at Athens Country Club, Athens, Ga., July 28-August 1.
Yardage—6,674. Par 71. 1,444 Entries, 150 Starters.

Qualifying Score	1st Round (18 Holes)	2nd Round (18 Holes)	3rd Round (18 Holes)	4th Round (18 Holes)	Semi-Finals (18 Holes)	Final (18 Holes)	
141*	Mike Fambrough, Valdosta, Ga.	Fambrough,					
154	Conrad Nilmeier, Fresno, Calif.	3 and 2	Fambrough.				
152	Daniel A. Ybema, Rockford, Mich.	Omohundra,	1 up				
157	Sale Omohundra, Sherman, Texas	4 and 2		Fambrough,			
150	Jim Stevenson, Belleville, Wash.	Hamilton,		3 and 2			
156	James Hamilton, Evansville, Ind.	2 up	Long,				
153	David Long, Cascade, Mich.	Long,	4 and 3				
157	Ronald Josepher, Miami, Fla.	19 hls.			Fambrough, 2 and 1		
148	Bob McClearen, Atlanta, Ga.	Hager,					
155	Joe Hager, Dallas, Texas	1 up	Hager,				
152	David Martin, Spencerport, N.Y.	Martin,	4 and 3				
157	Robert Hoyt, Fort Worth, Texas	2 up		Hager,			
151	Benjamin F. Brundred, Bethesda, Md.	Ray,		3 and 1			
156	Davis Ray, Meridian, Miss.	2 and 1	Lodge,				
154	Paul W. Lodge, Caldwell, Idaho	Lodge,	2 and 1				
158†	Doug Miller, Pittsford, N.Y.	7 and 6				Koch, 2 up	
146	Aly Trompas, San Diego, Calif.	Trompas,					
155	Bobby Brow, Coronado, Calif.	3 and 1	Trompas,				
152	Wesley S. Kono, Honolulu, Hawaii	Kono,	7 and 5				
157	Bobby Crowley, Irving, Texas	4 and 3		Trompas,			
150	Wally Payne, Fort Worth, Texas	Payne,		2 up			
156	Peter A. Wallenborn, Roanoke, Va.	2 and 1	Payne,				
154	Frank H. Reynolds, Signal Mt., Tenn.	Reynolds,	6 and 4				
158	Jack Burton, Miami, Fla.	19 hls.			Koch, 3 and 1		
149	Gary Mankulish, Glenn Dale, Md.	Mankulish,					
155	Bradley H. Hyland, Grosse Isle, Mich.	1 up	Long,				
153	Stephen R. Golub, San Francisco, Calif.	Long,	3 and 2				
157	James M. Long, Jr., San Diego, Calif.	2 and 1		Koch,			
152	John Fought, Tualatin, Ore.	Frith,		7 and 6			
156	Jamie Frith, Birmingham, Mich.	2 up	Koch,				
154	Gary Koch, Temple Terrace, Fla.	Koch,	5 and 3				
158	Richard A. Serian, Troy, N.Y.	3 and 2					Gary Koch, 8 and 6
145	Bruce Robertson, San Mateo, Calif.	Robertson,					
155	Robert Fields, Tulsa, Okla.	4 and 2	Stansel,				
152	Howard Randolph, Tulsa, Okla.	Stansel,	2 and 1				
157	Robert E. Stansel, Park Hills, Ky.	3 and 2		Transou,			
150	Russell Hulser, Pompano Beach, Fla.	Hulser,		3 and 2			
156	Keith Kollmeyer, Honolulu, Hawaii	3 and 1	Transou,				
153	Randall L. Transou, Bethania, N.C.	Transou,	4 and 2				
158	John K. Abendroth, San Francisco, Calif.	3 and 2			Transou, 2 up		
148	David E. Canipe, Fayetteville, N.C.	Canipe,					
155	David Baskins, Reno, Nevada	7 and 6	Joseph,				
153	Jim Joseph, Homewood, Ill.	Joseph,	4 and 2				
157	John Manning, Billings, Mont.	19 hls.		Joseph,			
151	Larry Pagel, New Tucson, Ariz.	Pagel,		1 up			
156	Jud Vance, Hattiesburg, Miss.	6 and 5	Booth,				
154	Kim Heisler, Aurora, Ohio	Booth,	3 and 2				
158	Douglas A. Booth, San Diego, Calif.	3 and 2				Nelms, 1 up	
146	Steve Scrafford, Erie, Pa.	Scrafford,					
155	Patrick L. McCormick, Atlantic Beach, Fla.	2 and 1	Scrafford,				
152	Eddie Lowry, Louisville, Ky.	Lowry,	4 and 2				
157	Steven Kulich, Benton Harbor, Mich.	3 and 2		Lye,			
151	Mark Lye, Napa, Calif.	Lye,		6 and 4			
156	Robert Strahan, Fairfield, Calif.	6 and 4	Lye,				
154	Steve Robertson, Costa Mesa, Calif.	Robertson,	2 and 1				
158	Steve Smyers, Houston, Texas	3 and 2			Nelms, 2 and 1		
149	Tony Maltese, Jr., Whittier, Calif.	Hoyt,					
156	Nathan B. Hoyt, Rome, Ga.	1 up	Phillips,				
153	Curtis Strange, Virginia Beach, Va.	Phillips,	20 hls.				
157	Mike Phillips, Aliquippa, Pa.	2 up		Nelms,			
152	Jeff Hadley, Rye, N.Y.	Blowers,		1 up			
156	Steve Blowers, McDermott, Ohio	5 and 4	Nelms,				
154	Mike Nelms, Hixson, Tenn.	Nelms,	1 up				
158	Michael C. Aronstein, Monroe, N.Y.	2 and 1					

*Medalist

1971
TWENTY-FOURTH JUNIOR AMATEUR CHAMPIONSHIP

Held at Manor Country Club, Rockville, Md., August 3–17.
Yardage–6,410. Par 70. 1,559 Entries, 150 Starters.

Qualifying Score	1st Round (18 Holes)	2nd Round (18 Holes)	3rd Round (18 Holes)	4th Round (18 Holes)	5th Round (18 Holes)	Semi-Finals (18 Holes)	Final (18 Holes)
142	Curtis Strange, Virginia Beach, Va.	Hyland, 20 holes					
153	Bradley Hyland, Grosse Ile, Mich.		Steele, 19 holes				
150	Robert M. Steele, Dunkirk, N.Y.	Steele, 1 up					
154	David Ishii, Honolulu, Hawaii			Steele, 3 and 2			
148	David E. Canipe, Fayetteville, N.C.	Canipe, 2 up					
153	James M. McNamara, Jr., Balboa, Canal Zone		Adams, 2 and 1				
151	Jim Adams, Fayetteville, N.C.	Adams, 4 and 3					
155	Jim Ruziecki, Lawndale, Calif.				Steele, 3 and 2		
146	Blake Watt, Moundsville, W. Va.	Watt, 19 Holes					
153	Dan V. Mitchell, Philadelphia, Miss.		Kolbus, 3 and 2				
151	Paul Kilbus, Alamo, Calif.	Kolbus, 7 and 5					
155	Harold R. Payne, Hurricane, W. Va.			Goss, 6 and 5			
149	Michael Nelms, Chattanooga, Tenn.	Nelms, 2 and 1					
154	Robert Chapman, Northville, Mich.		Goss, 19 holes				
152	Rick Cavalar, Polson, Mont.	Goss, 1 up					
156	Jimmy Goss, Dallas, Texas					Steele, 4 and 3	
145	Steve Dietz, Columbus, Ohio	Dietz, 1 up					
153	Terry Knight, Costa Mesa, Calif.		Dietz, 5 and 4				
150	David Gookin, Verona, Pa.	Perpich, 2 up					
155	Mike Perpich, Louisville, Ky.			Sezna, 4 and 3			
149	James W. Stewart, Singapore, Malaysia	Sezna, 4 and 3					
154	David Sezna, Westchester, Pa.		Sezna, 3 and 1				
152	Rod Iverson, Arkansas City, Kans.	Iverson, 20 holes					
155	Mark T. Pfeil, Pewaukee, Wis.				Reid, 19 holes		
148	Michael D. Reid, Aurora, Colo.	Reid, 3 and 1					
153	Don L. Dormer, Pebble Beach, Calif.		Reid, 3 and 1				
151	Mike Landram, Indianapolis, Ind.	Landram, 2 up					
155	Ralph D. Nevern, Spokane, Wash.			Reid, 3 and 2			
150	Douglas E. Lauer, Everett, Wash.	Lauer, 3 and 2					
154	Jeff Thomsen, Twin Falls, Idaho		Lauer, 1 up				
152	Lee Carter, Jr., Dallas, Texas	Carter, 5 and 4					
156	H.B. Warren, Tulsa, Okla.						Michael Brannan, 4 and 3
145	Clark Stevens, Wichita, Kans.	Stevens, 2 and 1					
153	Patrick R. McGowan, Colusa, Calif.		O'Neal, 2 up				
150	John J. O'Neal, Carmel, Ind.	O'Neal, 1 up					
154	Ron Hartoin, Cincinnati, Ohio			O'Neal, 3 and 1			
149	Eddie Lowry, Louisville, Ky.	Lowry, 4 and 2					
153	Skip Talbert, Warner Robins, Ga.		Lowry, 6 and 5				
152	Hal B. Freeman, Russellville, Ky.	Hiestand, 19 holes					
155	Ed Hiestand, Nashville, Tenn.				O'Neal, 1 up		
147	Jay Dean Haas, Belleville, Ill.	Haas, 5 and 4					
153	Robert Fields, Tulsa, Okla.		Ruland, 2 and 1				
151	Doug Ruland, Pacific Palisades, Calif.	Ruland, 4 and 3					
155	James T. Hayes, Columbia, Md.			Ruland, 19 holes			
149	Robert G. Caprera, Southbridge, Mass.	Barenaba, 2 and 1					
154	C. Pen Barenaba, Jr., Honolulu, Hawaii		Viner, 20 holes				
152	Robert V. Viner, Jr., Norbeck, Md.	Viner, 5 and 4					
156	Terry McPartland, Dallas, Texas					Brannan, 3 and 2	
146	Mike Phillips, Aliquippa, Pa.	Phillips, 3 and 1					
153	John Alexander, Portland, Ore.		Brannan, 2 up				
150	Michael Brannan, Salinas, Calif.	Brannan, 8 and 7					
155	Scott Frye, Jacksonville, Fla.			Brannan, 5 and 4			
149	Meredith Lyemance, Birmingham, Ala.	Brewton, 2 up					
154	Stephen Brewton, McMurray, Pa.		Brewton, 2 up				
152	William A. Lewis, Florence, S.C.	Lewis, 5 and 3					
155	Scott Simpson, San Diego, Calif.				Brannan, 2 up		
148	Joseph Flood, La Jolla, Calif.	Flood, 3 and 2					
153	Bill Chapman, Charlotte, N.C.		Flood, 4 and 3				
151	Fred Farris, Tulsa, Okla.	Farris, 6 and 5					
155	Bill Dunsmore, Palo Alto, Calif.			Flood, 1 up			
150	Eric Batten, Santa Cruz, Calif.	Ahern, 19 holes					
154	Jim Ahern, Burlingame, Calif.		Ahern, 5 and 4				
153	Allen J. Clay, Cincinnati, Ohio	Clay, 3 and 2					
157	Sammy Trahan, New Orleans, La.						

1972
TWENTY-FIFTH JUNIOR AMATEUR CHAMPIONSHIP

Held at Brookhaven Country Club, Dallas, Texas, August 1-5
Yardage—6,921. Par—72. 1,492 Entries, 150 Starters.

Qualifying Score	1st Round (18 Holes)	2nd Round (18 Holes)	3rd Round (18 Holes)	4th Round (18 Holes)	Semi-Finals (18 Holes)	Final (18 Holes)
144	*Robert T. Byman, Boulder, Colo.	Byman, 3 and 2				
152	Bruce Disbrow, Riverton, N.J.		Byman, 3 and 1			
149	Dave Simpson, San Diego, Calif.	Gordon, 4 and 2				
155	Rick Gordon, Menlo Park, Calif.			Byman, 5 and 4		
147	John Pacuk, Jacksonville, Fla.	Pacuk, 3 and 2				
153	Mark J. Balen, Hamburg, N.Y.		Pacuk, 4 and 3			
151	Ken McMaster, San Jose, Calif.	Mitchell, 1 up, 19 holes				
156	Teddy D. Mitchell, Oklahoma City, Okla.				Byman, 3 and 2	
145	Joe Dawn, Jr., Gastonia, N.C.	Souza, 1 up, 19 holes				
153	Stanley M. Souza, Honolulu, Hawaii		Souza, 4 and 2			
150	Harry Taylor, Jr., Old Hickory, Tenn.	Taylor, 4 and 3				
155	Gordon L. Booker, Jr., Clarkston, Mich.			Souza, 3 and 2		
147	Jack Renner, San Diego, Calif.	Renner, 9 and 8				
154	Jim Russell, Indianapolis, Ind.		Ward, 1 up, 23 holes			
152	David C. Rasco, Shreveport, La.	Ward, 3 and 2				
156	Daniel Ward, Portsmouth, Va.					Byman, 1 up, 19 hol
145	Skeeter Heath, Williamsburg, Va.	Stewart, 7 and 5				
153	James W. Stewart, Singapore, Republic of Singapore		Stewart, 4 and 3			
150	Jay Guthrie, Wheeling, W.Va.	Guthrie, 2 and 1				
155	Jerrel A. Horne, Elberton, Ga.			Stewart, 7 and 6		
147	Mark Heisler, Aurora, Ohio	Lange, 3 and 2				
154	Chris Lange, Bryn Mawr, Pa.		O'Rear, 2 up			
152	Martin O'Rear, Jr., Arlington, Va.	O'Rear, 3 and 1				
156	Lance M. TenBroeck, Chicago, Ill.				Stewart, 4 and 2	
146	Tommy R. Jones, Tulsa, Okla.	Jones, 7 and 6				
153	Lyle Beaver, Columbus, Ohio		Jones, 4 and 3			
150	Doug B. Thomas, New Brunswick, N.J.	Whiteside, 2 and 1				
155	Steven R. Whiteside, Midland, Texas			Day, 1 up		
149	Jimmy Riddle, Madisonville, Ky.	Riddle, 4 and 3				
154	South Smith, Akron, Ohio		Day, 2 and 1			
152	James R. Day, North Palm Beach, Fla.	Day, 4 and 3				
156	Lyndon F. Pittinger, Oklahoma City, Okla.					Robert T. Byman, 2 and 1
145	Bryan Stiegman, Dallas, Texas	Miller, 1 up				
153	Lindy Miller, Fort Worth, Texas		Miller, 2 and 1			
149	Carl Ho, Honolulu, Hawaii	Holmes, 2 and 1				
155	James Holmes, Aiken, S.C.			Miller, 2 and 1		
147	Curtis Strange, Virginia Beach, Va.	Strange, 3 and 2				
153	Ted Mills, Sunol, Calif.		Strange, 2 and 1			
152	Robert E. Hoyt, Houston, Texas	McGinnis, 4 and 3				
156	Daniel McGinnis, Memphis, Tenn.				Gilliland, 3 and 2	
146	Hunt Gilliland, Hixon, Tenn.	Gilliland, 1 up				
153	Joe Hager, Dallas, Texas		Gilliland, 2 and 1			
150	Bill Eldridge, Augusta, Ark.	Fabel, 2 up				
155	Brad Fabel, Madisonville, Ky.			Gilliland, 3 and 1		
148	Michael Brannan, Salinas, Calif.	Kilby, 3 and 2				
154	Ronald Kilby, Houston, Texas		Kilby, 3 and 2			
152	Reinhold Schmieding, Bloomfield Hills, Mich.	Schmieding, 1 up				
156	William Cunningham, Loudonville, N.Y.					Simpson, 5 and 3
145	Ray Cragun, Rio Rancho Estates, N.M.	Cragun, 5 and 3				
153	Bob Pando, San Jose, Calif.		O'Linger, 2 and 1			
150	Arthur R. O'Linger, Berlin, Md.	O'Linger, 2 and 1				
155	James D. Dixon, Houston, Texas			Simpson, 1 up		
147	Scott Simpson, San Diego, Calif.	Simpson, 1 up, 19 holes				
154	Tony Campregher, Salton City, Calif.		Simpson, 2 and 1			
152	Gary Domagalski, East Lansing, Mich.	Domagalski, 1 up				
156	Scott Alexander, Portland, Ore.				Simpson, 1 up	
146	Charles E. Wallace, Long Beach, Calif.	Wallace, 1 up				
153	James T. Mason, Kirkwood, Mo.		Wansker, 1 up			
151	Matt Doyle, Menlo Park, Calif.	Wansker, 4 and 3				
155	Robert J. Wansker, Charlotte, N.C.			Galloway, 1 up, 19 holes		
149	James R. Henderson, Virginia Beach, Va.	Galloway, 1 up				
154	Larry Galloway, Columbus, Ohio		Galloway, 1 up, 19 holes			
152	Peter Sexton, Reno, Nev.	Shanks, 3 and 2				
157	Brian L. Shanks, Phoenix, Ariz.					

*Medalist

1973
TWENTY-SIXTH JUNIOR AMATEUR CHAMPIONSHIP

Held at Singing Hills Country Club, El Cajon, California, July 31 - August 4
Yardage—6,935. Par- 72. 1,325 Entries, 150 Starters. 64 Qualifiers.

Qualifying Score	1st Round (18 Holes)	2nd Round (18 Holes)	3rd Round (18 Holes)	4th Round (18 Holes)	Semi-Finals (18 Holes)	Final (18 Holes)	
139	*Robert M. Donald, Athens, Ga.	Yaun,					
152	Radford Yaun, Liberty, N. Y.	6 and 4	Pearson,				
148	Scott Pearson, Columbia, Mo.	Pearson,	1 up				
154	Lee Mikles, Camarillo, Calif.	6 and 5		Brannan,			
147	Paul Stitt, Bethaney, Okla.	Brannan,		7 and 6			
153	Michael Brannan, Salinas, Calif.	3 and 2	Brannan,				
150	Brian L. Sund, Edina, Minn.	Sund,	6 and 5				
155	David Kenyon, Missoula, Mont.	2 up			Brannan,		
146	William Sibbick, Martinsville, Va.	Sibbick,			3 and 2		
153	Curt McMaster, San Jose, Calif.	7 and 5	Sibbick,				
150	Jimmy Riddle, Madisonville, Ky.	Talbott,	2 up				
154	Steve Talbott, Snyder, Texas	1 up		Sibbick,			
148	Raymond Cragun, Albuquerque, N. M.	Cragun,		5 and 4			
153	Scott Spradley, Jr., Shelby, N. C.	1 up	Cragun,				
151	Tony Tabor, Edmond, Okla.	DeCastro,	7 and 6				
156	Gary DeCastro, Joplin, Mo.	5 and 4				Brannan,	
145	Lindy Miller, Ft. Worth, Texas	Saunders,				5 and 4	
152	Dennis Saunders, Yorba Linda, Calif.	1 up	Saunders,				
149	Ralph Guarasci, Columbus, Ohio	McAvoy,	6 and 5				
154	Mark McAvoy, Jr., Somerville, N. J.	5 and 4		Loeslein,			
147	Paul Marchand, Franklin, Ind.	Binegar,		2 and 1			
153	Mark Binegar, Medford, Ore.	3 and 2	Loeslein,				
151	Dale Loeslein, Fairview, Pa.	Loeslein,	19 holes				
156	Steven Liebler, Portsmouth, Va.	3 and 2			Simpson,		
147	Scott Simpson, San Diego, Calif.	Simpson,			5 and 4		
153	Chris Mitchell, Spokane, Wash.	2 up	Simpson,				
150	John Miller, Dubuque, Iowa	Miller,	2 and 1				
155	Ross Strehlow, Wilmar, Minn.	3 and 1		Simpson,			
148	Tom Costello III, Santa Rosa, Calif.	Costello,		2 and 1			
154	Randy Stevenson, Auburn, Mass.	3 and 2	Fort,				
152	Harry Bauer, Wheeling, W. Va.	Fort,	3 and 1				
156	Doug Fort, Pekin, Ill.	3 and 2					Jack Renner, 20 holes
143	Jack Renner, San Diego, Calif.	Renner,					
152	Jim Appel, Los Alamitos, Calif.	2 up	Renner,				
149	James Becker, Marietta, Ga.	Becker,	4 and 3				
154	Clyde Rego, Kunia, Hawaii	5 and 4		Renner,			
147	Lex Murray, Santa Rosa, Calif.	Murray,		2 and 1			
153	Ryan Hamilton, Mobank, Texas	2 and 1	Campregher,				
151	Tony Campregher, Huntington Beach, Calif.	Campregher,	3 and 2				
155	Charles Adams, Dallas, Texas	19 holes			Renner,		
146	Chip Beck, Fayetteville, N. C.	Beck,			5 and 3		
153	Kirk Hanefeld, Somersworth, N. H.	1 up	Brewster,				
150	Robert Brewster, Orchard Lake, Mich.	Brewster,	2 and 1				
155	Arthur Whaley, Wilmington, Del.	8 and 6		Brewster,			
148	Lyndon Pittinger, Oklahoma City, Okla.	Rountree,		2 and 1			
154	Buddy Rountree, Ft. Lauderdale, Fla.	4 and 3	Rountree,				
152	Timothy M. Wahl, Gainesville, Fla.	Hill,	5 and 3				
156	Dave Hill, Riverside, Calif.	2 and 1				Renner,	
145	Frank Gardner, Montgomery, Ala.	Chaffee,				3 and 2	
153	Jon R. Chaffee, Austin, Minn.	3 and 1	Fabel,				
150	Brad Fabel, Madisonville, Ky.	Fabel,	1 up				
154	Wendell Tom, Honolulu, Hawaii	5 and 4		Fabel,			
148	Eric Batten, Santa Cruz, Calif.	Reid,		3 and 2			
153	Bob Reid, Statesville, N. C.	2 up	Britton,				
151	William Britton, New York, N. Y.	Britton,	5 and 4				
156	Vytas Kisielius, Sidney, Ohio	5 and 4			Fabel,		
147	Mark Balen, Lackawanna, N. Y.	Olsen,			4 and 3		
153	Steve Olsen, Marietta, Ga.	2 and 1	Cater,				
150	Walt Ranzau, San Jose, Calif.	Cater,	2 and 1				
155	Kim Cater, Pebble Beach, Calif.	19 holes		Barenaba,			
148	Bill Sander, Seattle, Wash.	Sander,		21 holes			
154	Bill Helmbacher, St. Louis, Mo.	19 holes	Barenaba,				
152	Poneu R. Barenaba, Laie, Oahu, Hawaii	Barenaba,	4 and 2				
156	S. Trent Ash, Newton, Kansas	2 and 1					

*Medalist; tied record qualifying score set by John Miller in 1964.

1974
TWENTY-SEVENTH JUNIOR AMATEUR CHAMPIONSHIP

Held at Brooklawn Country Club, Bridgeport, Connecticut, July 23-27
Yardage—6,595. Par 71. 1,453 Entered, 150 Starters, 64 Qualifiers.

Qualifying Score	1st Round (18 Holes)	2nd Round (18 Holes)	3rd Round (18 Holes)	4th Round (18 Holes)	Semi-Finals (18 Holes)	Final (18 Holes)
143	*Charles H. Beck, Jr., Fayetteville, N. C.	Walter, 3 and 2				
153	Joseph L. Walter, Baltimore, Md.		Herbert, 1 up			
151	Joel Herbert, Anderson, S. C.	Herbert, 3 and 2				
156	Todd Awe, Jefferson City, Mo.			Abell, 19 holes		
148	Robert DeFalco, Sutton, Mass.	DeFalco, 4 and 3				
155	Randall Banks, Fairfax, Va.		Abell, 3 and 2			
152	David Abell, Port St. Lucie, Fla.	Abell, 2 and 1				
157	Allan Menne, Jr., West Palm Beach, Fla.				Tinder, 6 and 5	
147	Thomas Rogan, Racine, Wis.	Gove, 1 up				
154	Mike Gove, Seattle, Wash.		Gove, 1 up			
151	Rob Brewster, Detroit, Mich.	Brewster, 2 and 1				
157	William P. Stewart, Springfield, Mo.			Tinder, 6 and 5		
150	Mark Tinder, Pebble Beach, Calif.	Tinder, 3 and 2				
156	James Day, N. Palm Beach, Fla.		Tinder, 3 and 2			
153	Chris Witcher, Atlanta, Ga.	Miller, 2 and 1				
158	John S. Miller, Peosta, Iowa					Tinder, 4 and 2
145	Robert Blum, Buena Park, Calif.	Hicks, 3 and 2				
154	Tommy Hicks, Germantown, Tenn.		Hicks, 2 and 1			
151	Scott Vidimos, Gary, Ind.	Gutilla, 1 up				
156	Chris Gutilla, Fresno, Calif.			Hicks, 2 and 1		
150	Mitchell Bleznak, Bloomfield Hills, Mich.	Magargal, 6 and 5				
156	Steven Magargal, Worthington, Mass.		Sindelar, 4 and 3			
153	David P. Lane, Andover, Mass.	Sindelar, 4 and 2				
157	Joseph Sindelar, Horseheads, N. Y.				Griffin, 1 up	
147	Brett Mullin, Riverside, Calif.	Mullin, 2 up				
155	Mark Balen, Hamburg, N. Y.		Griffin, 4 and 2			
151	Robert Hakes, Coronado, Calif.	Griffin, 19 holes				
157	Robert Griffin, Denver, Colo.			Griffin, 2 and 1		
150	Michael Peck, Overland Park, Kans.	Peck, 6 and 5				
156	Donald Hammond, Frederick, Md.		Heselwood, 19 holes			
153	Michael Burke, Deal, N. J.	Heselwood, 3 and 1				
158	John Heselwood, Selah, Wash.					David Nevatt, 4 and 3
145	Mitch Mooney, Warrenton, Ore.	Mooney, 3 and 1				
154	Mike Hall, Smyrna, Del.		Mooney, 3 and 1			
151	Glen Luikart, Grants Pass, Ore.	Brow, 19 holes				
156	Smokey Brow, Coronado, Calif.			Mooney, 4 and 3		
149	Tom Costello, Santa Rosa, Calif.	Renner, 3 and 2				
155	Jim Renner, El Cajon, Calif.		Loeslein, 5 and 4			
152	Dale Loeslein, Fairview, Pa.	Loeslein, 20 holes				
157	Mickey Ray, Somerset, Ky.				Nevatt, 6 and 4	
147	Chris Mitchell, Spokane, Wash.	Mitchell, 3 and 2				
155	Stephen R. Smith, Martinsville, Va.		Nevatt, 20 holes			
151	David Nevatt, Merced, Calif.	Nevatt, 3 and 2				
157	Butch Creek, Lafayette, Tenn.			Nevatt, 7 and 5		
150	Brian Sund, Minneapolis, Minn.	Rose, 2 and 1				
156	Jerry Rose, Fresno, Calif.		Starnes, 19 holes			
153	Lanee Lailer, San Marcos, Texas	Starnes, 3 and 2				
158	Jim Starnes, Gaithersburg, Md.					Nevatt, 2 and 1
146	Eric S. Smith, Martinsville, Va.	E. Smith, 4 and 3				
154	Michael Aitken, New Rochelle, N. Y.		E. Smith, 2 and 1			
151	Joe Rassett, Turlock, Calif.	Rassett, 6 and 5				
156	Joe Knox, Wilmington, Del.			Loeffler, 5 and 3		
150	David Ogrin, Waukegan, Ill.	Regner, 2 up				
156	Scot Regner, Milwaukee, Wis.		Loeffler, 1 up			
153	Bill Loeffler, Englewood, Colo.	Loeffler, 1 up				
157	Jerome Kroc, Austin, Minn.				Loeffler, 3 and 2	
147	Len Stone, Ontario, Calif.	Jacobs, 19 holes				
155	Randy Jacobs, Ft. Worth, Texas		Jacobs, 1 up			
152	Scott Teller, N. Kingstown, R. I.	Teller, 2 up				
157	Gary Pinns, Glen Ellyn, Ill.			Backlund, 19 holes		
150	Daniel Delekta, McConnellsville, N. Y.	Jones, 6 and 5				
156	Gregg Jones, Colorado Springs, Colo.		Backlund, 4 and 3			
153	Gary Backlund, Calabasas Park, Calif.	Backlund, 3 and 2				
158	Jon Levin, Tarzana, Calif.					

*Medalist

1975
TWENTY-EIGHTH JUNIOR AMATEUR CHAMPIONSHIP

Held at Richland Country Club, Nashville, Tennessee, July 29-August 2
Yardage—6,668. Par 71. 1,898 Entries, 150 Starters, 64 Qualifiers

Qualifying Score	1st Round (18 Holes)	2nd Round (18 Holes)	3rd Round (18 Holes)	4th Round (18 Holes)	Semi-Finals (18 Holes)	Final (18 Holes)
*140	Gary Pinns, Lombard, Ill.	Pinns,				
153	Mike Cook, Cartersville, Ga.	3 and 2	Pinns,			
150	David Sann, Dallas, Texas	Sann,	2 and 1			
156	Gary Hallberg, Barrington, Ill.	2 up		Pinns,		
149	Scott W. Cooke, Warwick, R.I.	Jones,		3 and 2		
154	John Jones, Tampa, Fla.	2 and 1	Jones,			
152	Eric S. Smith, Martinsville, Va.	Smith,	3 and 1			
157	Frank Mebane, III, Sanford, Fla.	7 and 6			Pinns,	
148	Matt King, Nashville, Tenn.	King,			3 and 2	
154	Rick Borg, Worthington, Ohio	3 and 1	King,			
151	Michael Hall, Smyrna, Del.	Zaruba,	2 and 1			
157	Harry A. Zaruba, Jr., Claveland, Ohio	2 and 1		King,		
150	Douglas Clarke, La Jolla, Calif.	Cupit,		20 holes		
155	Maxie Cupit, III, Yazoo City, Miss.	20 holes	Cupit,			
152	Mike Keliher, Brentwood, Tenn.	Hartoin,	5 and 4			
158	Mike Hartoin, Cincinnati, Ohio	19 holes				Mullin, 19 holes
145	Brett Mullin, Riverside, Calif.	Mullin,				
154	Frank Fuhrer, III, Pittsburgh, Pa.	4 and 3	Mullin,			
151	Kenny Kraatz, Del Mar, Calif.	Kraatz,	8 and 6			
156	Tom Aiello, Severna Park, Md.	2 and 1		Mullin,		
149	Craig A. Anderson, Los Angeles, Calif.	Anderson,		4 and 3		
155	Timothy Marchese, Omaha, Neb.	3 and 2	Roth,			
152	Jeffrey Roth, Plymouth, Mich.	Roth,	19 holes			
157	Ralph Mathews, Andalusia, Ala.	3 and 2			Mullin,	
149	David Abell, Pierce, Fla.	Abell,			4 and 2	
154	Jeff Sluman, Rochester, N.Y.	3 and 2	Smith,			
151	Jeff Smith, Oskaloosa, Iowa	Smith,	3 and 2			
157	Michael Aitken, Bronxville, N. Y.	3 and 2		Smith,		
150	Clyde Rego, Kunia, Hawaii	Rego,		2 and 1		
156	Lou Yannotti, Westport, Conn.	2 up	Rego,			
153	Philip Vescove, Austin, Texas	Vescove,	4 and 2			
158	Sam Pavlis, Knoxville, Tenn.	3 and 1				Brett Mullin, 2 and 1
144	Kalua Makalena, Wahiawa, Hawaii	Makalena,				
154	Jim Kane, San Mateo, Calif.	1 up	Makalena,			
150	Steve Bond, Elbertson, Ga.	Bond,	19 holes			
156	John Broach, Solomons, Md.	20 holes		Makalena,		
149	Mike McGee, Middleton, Ohio	Hanrahan,		19 holes		
155	Mark Hanrahan, Kansas City, Mo.	4 and 3	Whaley,			
152	Arthur Whaley, Wilmington, Del.	Whaley,	4 and 2			
157	John T. Gentry, Springfield, Mo.	4 and 3			Brewster,	
149	David A. Ogrin, Waukegan, Ill.	Ogrin,			6 and 5	
154	Stuart Rumph, Montezuma, Ga.	3 and 2	Newman,			
151	Arthur Greenfeder, Miami, Fla.	Newman,	4 and 3			
157	William Newman, Scotch Plains, N. J.	1 up		Brewster,		
150	Rob Brewster, Orchard Lake, Mich.	Brewster,		5 and 4		
155	Mark Powell, Baton Rouge, La.	1 up	Brewster,			
153	Monte Watson, Midland, Texas	Watson,	19 holes			
158	John White, St. Catharines, Ont., Can.	19 holes				Templeton, 4 and 3
147	Wayne DeFrancesco, McLean, Va.	DeFrancesco,				
154	David Games, Paramount, Calif.	7 and 6	Hines,			
151	Tommy M. Hines, Lihue, Kauai, Hawaii	Hines,	1 up			
156	Chris Hall, Marietta, Ga.	19 holes		Hines,		
149	Erick Gott, San Marino, Calif.	Gott,		3 and 2		
155	Patrick J. Venker, Bloomington, Ill.	3 and 2	Sadowski,			
152	Bryan Norton, Salina, Kans.	Sadowski,	1 up			
158	Joseph G. Sadowski, Hickory, N. C.	6 and 4			Templeton,	
149	Vince Vines, Odessa, Texas	Vines,			1 up	
154	Steven B. Magargal, Worthington, Mass.	2 and 1	Cater,			
151	Kimble T. Cater, Pebble Beach, Calif.	Cater,	2 and 1			
157	Stanley Sargent, Sunrise, Fla.	6 and 4		Templeton,		
150	Tod Hensarling, Lafayette, La.	Christiansen,		5 and 4		
156	Vance Christiansen, Ogden, Utah	4 and 3	Templeton,			
153	Robert Tway, Marietta, Ga.	Templeton,	6 and 5			
158	Scott Templeton, Wellington, Kans.	21 holes				

*Medalist

1976
TWENTY-NINTH JUNIOR AMATEUR CHAMPIONSHIP

Held at Hiwan Golf Club, Evergreen, Colorado, August 3-7
Yardage—6,942. Par 71. 1,957 Entries, 150 Starters, 64 Qualifiers

Qualifying Score	1st Round (18 Holes)	2nd Round (18 Holes)	3rd Round (18 Holes)	4th Round (18 Holes)	Semi-Finals (18 Holes)	Final (18 Holes)
*144	Robert Clampett, Jr., Carmel, Calif.	Clampett,				
153	Douglas C. Maddox, Baytown, Mo.	2 and 1	Clampett,			
150	Bryan Pini, Santa Cruz, Calif.	Pini,	19 holes			
154	David Abell, Ft. Pierce, Fla.	3 and 1		Fuhrer,		
148	Larry K. Jones, Milford, Del.	Fuhrer,		5 and 4		
153	Frank Fuhrer, III, Pittsburgh, Pa.	20 holes	Fuhrer,			
152	Robert Peters, Tucson, Ariz.	Horne,	1 up			
155	John R. Horne, Plainview, Texas	5 and 4			Hatcher,	
147	Mike Cook, Cartersville, Ga.	Cook,			1 up	
153	Doug Klumpp, Vincennes, Ind.	7 and 6	Wrenn,			
151	Kirk Herrick, Saginaw, Mich.	Wrenn,	4 and 2			
154	Robert Wrenn, Jr., Midlothian, Va.	5 and 4		Hatcher,		
148	Jeff McMillian, Stillwater, Okla.	Hatcher,		20 holes		
154	Madden Hatcher, III, Columbus, Ga.	3 and 2	Hatcher,			
152	Eric Costa, Fresno, Calif.	Asmundson,	5 and 4			
156	Philip Asmundson, Wilton, Conn.	6 and 5				Hatcher,
145	Donald DuBois, Glendora, Calif.	DuBois,				5 and 4
153	M. Scott Bullek, Yakima, Wash.	2 and 1	DuBois,			
150	Bill Rullman, Portland, Ore.	Nakazaki,	19 holes			
154	Tracy Nakazaki, Los Angeles, Calif.	1 up		DuBois,		
148	Colin Bork, Brookings, S.D.	White,		4 and 3		
154	Henry White, Salt Lake City, Utah	19 holes	Sauer,			
152	Scott A. Harris, Roseau, Minn.	Sauer,	1 up			
155	Bob Sauer, Bloomfieid Hills, Mich.	3 and 1			Jones,	
147	Steven M. Liebler, Portsmouth, Va.	Smith,			1 up	
153	Jeffrey S. Smith, Oskaloosa, Iowa	19 holes	Smith,			
151	Raymond Perez, III, Hamburg, N.Y.	Perez,	6 and 4			
155	Cutts Benedict, Williamstown, Mass.	2 up		Jones,		
149	C. Alex Moore, Chesterfield, Mo.	Chill,		5 and 4		
154	Leon Chill, Middleburg Heights, Ohio	1 up	Jones,			
153	Robert M. Shaw, Salisbury, N.C.	Jones,	5 and 4			
156	Steven G. Jones, Yuma, Colo.	1 up				
*144	Andrew C. Blossom, Jr., Stockton, Calif.	Blossom,				
153	Jack Druga, Pittsburgh, Pa.	20 holes	McGee,			
150	Tommy Hines, Li Hue, Hawaii	McGee,	5 and 4			
154	Mike McGee, Middletown, Ohio	2 up		McGee,		
148	Bryan Norton, Salina, Kans.	Bisdorf,		1 up		
154	Lawrence J. Bisdorf, Denver, Colo.	5 and 3	Bisdorf,			
152	Willard Wood, Jr., Lake Charles, La.	Bracken,	1 up			
155	John Bracken, Seattle, Wash.	19 holes			McGee,	
147	David Farina, Hingham, Mass.	Duncan,			1 up	
153	Bruce Duncan, El Paso, Texas	1 up	Smith,			
151	E. Todd McGrew, Oklahoma City, Okla.	Smith,	3 and 2			
154	Handler Smith, Jr., San Marcos, Texas	7 and 5		Smith,		
149	Doug Nelle, Austin, Texas	Raber,		1 up		
154	Steve Raber, Santa Barbara, Calif.	1 up	Moreno,			
153	Jess Moreno, China Lake, Calif.	Moreno,	4 and 3			
156	Stuart Rumph, Tifton, Ga.	2 and 1				Clarke,
146	Mark A. Lawrence, Richmond, Va.	Rowse,				4 and 3
153	Jim Rowse, San Jose, Calif.	6 and 4	Rowse,			
151	John Turnbull, Scotch Plains, N.J.....	Stanger,	1 up			
154	Robert Stanger, Cleveland, Ohio	7 and 6		Clarke,		
148	Douglas Clarke, La Jolla, Calif.	Clarke,		3 and 2		
154	John Ashworth, Escondido, Calif.	4 and 2	Clarke,			
152	Rick Christie, Northfield, Minn.	Christie,	4 and 3			
156	Jerry Rose, Fresno, Calif.	3 and 2			Clarke,	
147	Bruce Rice, Pueblo, Colo.	Nash,			3 and 2	
153	Scott Nash, Portland, Ore.	2 and 1	Stewart,			
152	Craig Stewart, Milpitas, Calif.	Stewart,	4 and 3			
155	Jay Smith, Lafayette, Ind.	4 and 3		King,		
149	Matt King, Nashville, Tenn.	King,		4 and 3		
154	Mike Petrovich, Ft. Worth, Texas	5 and 4	King,			
153	Dave DeLong, Portland, Ore.	DeLong,	1 up			
156	Roy McMillin, Tempe, Ariz.	4 and 3				

Madden Hatcher, III, 3 and 2

*Co-Medalists

1977
THIRTIETH JUNIOR AMATEUR CHAMPIONSHIP

Held at Ohio State University (Scarlet Course) Columbus, Ohio, July 26-30.
Yardage—6,879. Par 72. 2,039 Entries, 150 Starters, 64 Qualifiers.

Qualifying Score	1st Round (18 Holes)	2nd Round (18 Holes)	3rd Round (18 Holes)	4th Round (18 Holes)	Semi-Finals (18 Holes)	Final (18 Holes)
*141	Willard Wood, Lake Charles, La.	Wood,				
158	Rick Cramer, Ft. Collins, Colo.	1 up	Wood,			
155	James Stuart, Duluth, Minn.	Pidgeon,	5 and 3			
161	Brian Pidgeon, Des Moines, Iowa	3 and 2		Wood,		
152	Bill Porter, Jr., McNary, Ore.	Nick,		3 and 2		
159	Joe Nick, Okmulgee, Okla.	3 and 1	Nick,			
156	Jack N. Brown, Sumter, S.C.	Brown,	1 up, 19 holes			
162	Peter Prokop, Youngstown, Ohio	1 up, 19 holes			Wood,	
149	Billy Corbett, San Rafael, Calif.	Corbett,			7 and 5	
159	Mark D. Anderson, Pensacola, Fla.	1 up, 21 holes	Corbett,			
156	Michael Stanton, San Luis Obispo, Calif.	Stanton,	4 and 2			
161	Mark Redman, Bloomington, Minn.	2 up		Allenspach,		
154	Bob McNiff, Muskegon, Mich.	Frey,		2 up		
159	Michael A. Frey, Lombard, Ill.	3 and 2	Allenspach,			
157	Mitch Allenspach, Oxford, Ohio	Allenspach,	9 and 8			
163	David Abell, Ft. Pierce, Fla.	1 up, 19 holes				Wood,
148	Bob Wolcott, Dickson, Tenn.	Nash,				1 up
158	Scott Nash, Portland, Ore.	2 up	Hendrix,			
155	Robert Wrenn, Jr., Midlothian, Va.	Hendrix,	2 and 1			
161	Mark Hendrix, Austin, Texas	2 and 1		Dickinson,		
153	Charles Dickinson, Jr., Modesto, Calif.	Dickinson,		2 and 1		
159	Rick Wampler, Champaign, Ill.	4 and 3	Dickinson,			
156	James T. Gallagher, Jr., Marion, Ind.	Hatcher,	3 and 2			
162	Madden Hatcher, III, Columbus, Ga.	2 up			Pavin,	
151	Corey Pavin, Oxnard, Calif.	Pavin,			2 and 1	
159	Jess Moreno, China Lake, Calif.	2 and 1	Pavin,			
156	John Perles, Bloomfield Hills, Mich.	Perles,	1 up, 20 holes			
162	Brandon Kop, Honolulu, Hawaii	3 and 2		Pavin,		
155	Joey Sadowski, Hickory, N.C.	Sadowski,		6 and 5		
160	Brian Noto, New Orleans, La.	4 and 2	Sadowski,			
157	Barry W. Pearce, Jackson, Tenn.	Pearce,	2 and 1			
163	Ryan Gordon, Columbus, Ohio	disqualified				
147	David Games, Bellflower, Calif.	Games,				
158	Ryan Ramey, Honolulu, Hawaii	1 up	Games,			
155	Steven L. Hart, Tequesta, Fla.	Hart,	2 and 1			
161	Patrick J. Rielly, Jr., La Canada, Calif.	5 and 3		Games,		
152	Robert J. Giuffra, Jr., Bronxville, N.Y.	Mittlehauser,		1 up, 19 holes		
159	Timothy Mittlehauser, Cincinnati, Ohio	5 and 4	Ladehoff,			
156	Rick Bautista, Irving, Texas	Ladehoff,	1 up			
162	Greg Ladehoff, Clinton, Iowa	1 up, 19 holes			Games,	
151	Bob Clampett, Jr., Carmel, Calif.	Taylor,			2 and 1	
159	Mark Taylor, Rockford, Ill.	1 up, 19 holes	Taylor,			
156	Tom Walters, Dayton, Ohio	Walters,	1 up			
161	Tim Donohue, Sioux Falls, S.D.	3 and 2		Yerger,		
154	William Barrett, Spring Valley, Calif.	Barrett,		5 and 4		
160	Bill Wrobbel, Sylvania, Ohio	4 and 3	Yerger,			
157	John Yerger, Johnstown, Pa.	Yerger,	5 and 3			
163	John Gilbert, Jr., Succasunna, N.J.	1 up, 20 holes				Games,
149	Eric Evans, Canoga Park, Calif.	Evans,				1 up
158	Doug Hoffmann, Lindale, Texas	3 and 2	Evans,			
155	Storm Gleim, Sumner, Wash.	McGuinness,	2 up			
161	Bill McGuinness, Woodbury, N.J.	2 and 1		Evans,		
154	David Farina, Hingham, Mass.	Allenspach,		2 and 1		
159	Mark Allenspach, Oxford, Ohio	4 and 3	Allenspach,			
156	Tom Pernice, Jr., Kansas City, Mo.	Pernice,	4 and 3			
163	Mark P. Sivara, Ft. Lewis, Wash.	4 and 3			Evans,	
152	Larry Gosewehr, Frankfort, Ind.	Gosewehr,			4 and 2	
159	George Wolfe, Johnstown, Pa.	2 and 1	Gosewehr,			
156	Gary Battistoni, East Aurora, N.Y.	Pallot,	9 and 7			
162	John Pallot, Coral Gables, Fla.	6 and 4		Gosewehr,		
155	David E. Craig, Danville, Va.	Craig,		1 up		
160	Steven Russell, Amarillo, Texas	1 up	Leuthke,			
157	Edward Luethke, Los Altos, Calif.	Luethke,	2 up			
163	David L. Hobby, Newport Beach, Calif.	4 and 3				

Willard Wood, 4 and 3

*Medalist

1978
THIRTY-FIRST JUNIOR AMATEUR CHAMPIONSHIP

Held at Wilmington Country Club (South Course), Wilmington, Delaware, August 8-12.
Yardage—6,708. Par 71. 2,019 Entries, 150 Starters, 64 Qualifiers.

Qualifying Score	1st Round (18 Holes)	2nd Round (18 Holes)	3rd Round (18 Holes)	4th Round (18 Holes)	Semi-Finals (18 Holes)	Final (18 Holes)
*141	Willard Wood, Tucson, Ariz.	Wood,				
156	Mark Brooks, Ft. Worth, Texas	2 and 1	Wood,			
153	Mark Sivara, Tacoma, Wash.	Sivara,	4 and 3			
157	Lee Bosch, Winnemucca, Nev.	1 up		Wood,		
151	Monty Leong, San Diego, Calif.	Burns,		2 and 1		
156	Timothy Burns, Clarks Summit, Pa.	4 and 3	Haley,			
155	Mike Heinen, Enid, Okla.	Haley,	3 and 1			
158	Robert Haley, III, Nashville, Tenn.	3 and 2			Wood,	
148	Patrick Reilly, Jr., La Canada, Calif.	Loveless,			2 and 1	
156	Thomas Loveless, Silver Springs, Md.	2 and 1	Loveless,			
154	Greg Sullivan, Pittsburgh, Pa.	Thorn,	3 and 1			
158	Roger Thorn, East Wenatchee, Wash.	1 up		Gilreath,		
152	Bruce Jenkins, Little Rock, Ark.	Bybee,		1 up		
157	Doug Bybee, Brigham City, Utah	1 up	Gilreath,			
155	Carter Mize, Columbus, Ga.	Gilreath,	1 up			
159	Scott Gilreath, Montgomery, Ala.	1 up				Banes,
143	Keith Banes, La Mirada, Calif.	Banes,				1 up
156	Matt Woods, Columbia, Mo.	6 and 5	Banes,			
153	Steven Audas, Birmingham, Mich.	Audas,	2 and 1			
157	Brent Bonney, Shelby, Ohio	6 and 5		Banes,		
151	Greg Tebbutt, Bettendorf, Iowa	Tebbutt,		1 up, 19 holes		
156	Michael Chadwick, Lafayette, Ind.	5 and 3	Tebbutt,			
155	Jay Smith, Lafayette, Ind.	Smith,	7 and 5			
158	Daniel Berta, Canon City, Colo.	8 and 6			Banes,	
149	John Corzilius, Wilmington, Del.	Clark,			2 and 1	
156	Bobby Clark, Jr., Copper Hill, Va.	5 and 4	Mogg,			
154	Brian Mogg, Tacoma, Wash.	Mogg,	3 and 2			
158	Mark Levander, Thousand Oaks, Calif.	4 and 3		Mogg,		
152	Kevin Orona, Morro Bay, Calif.	Orona,		3 and 2		
157	Dean Johnson, Phoenix, Ariz.	4 and 3	Emmons,			
156	Romilly Emmons, Swampscott, Mass.	Emmons,	3 and 2			
159	Kirk Schooley, Columbus, Ind.	4 and 3				
143	Craig Davis, Valencia, Calif.	Delsing,				
156	Jay Delsing, St. Louis, Mo.	4 and 3	Delsing,			
153	Gary Krueger, Valparaiso, Ind.	Krueger,	4 and 3			
157	Don Plohg Griffith, Ind.	6 and 5		Delsing,		
151	Michael Larson, Lake Oswego, Ore.	Mac,		1 up, 19 holes		
156	Ron Mac, Westfield, Mass.	2 and 1	LeDonne,			
155	Dennis LeDonne, Fullerton, Calif.	LeDonne,	7 and 6			
158	Bert Buehler, Napa, Calif.	2 and 1			Hurter,	
149	Donald Hurter, Honolulu, Hawaii	Hurter,			1 up, 21 holes	
156	Scott Beard, Louisville, Ky.	5 and 4	Hurter,			
154	Robert Meyer, Sacramento, Calif.	Meyer,	1 up			
158	Robert Addington, Dallas, Texas	6 and 4		Hurter,		
152	Nolan Mills, Charlotte, N.C.	Mills,		4 and 3		
157	Norman Chapman, Spartanburg, S.C.	2 and 1	Mills,			
155	Ernest Echols, Jr., Charlottesville, Va.	Ohrman,	5 and 4			
159	Mark Ohrman, Bethel Park, Pa.	1 up				Hurter,
146	Chris Hughes, Madison, Conn.	Hughes,				6 and 5
156	Clayton Uselton, Tullahoma, Tenn.	5 and 3	Vybihal,			
153	Martin Vybihal, Clinton, N.J.	Vybihal,	2 up			
158	Stuart Smith, Rocklin, Calif.	5 and 4		Martin,		
151	Jack Kraemer, Cincinnati, Ohio	Kraemer,		1 up, 19 holes		
157	Kurt Oldson, Richland, Wash.	2 up	Martin,			
155	Buddy Martin, Pittsburgh, Pa.	Martin,	1 up			
158	Bill Tanner, San Antonio, Texas	1 up, 20 holes			Perry,	
150	Chris Perry, Edina, Minn.	Perry,			2 and 1	
156	Mark Diamond, Roslyn Estates, N.Y.	4 and 3	Perry,			
154	Roger Lyon, Madera, Calif.	Lyon,	6 and 5			
158	Scott Fjelstul, Decorah, Iowa	3 and 2		Perry,		
152	Brandan Kop, Honolulu, Hawaii	Finn,		6 and 5		
157	Tom Finn, Chadds Ford, Pa.	1 up	Steffan,			
156	Robert Steffan, West Allis, Wis.	Steffan,	4 and 3			
159	Jeffrey Davis, Gloucester, Mass.	1 up				

Donald Hurter, 1 up, 21 holes

*Medalist

1979
THIRTY-SECOND JUNIOR AMATEUR CHAMPIONSHIP

Held at Moss Creek Golf Club, Hilton Head Island, South Carolina, July 31-August 4.
Yardage—6,850. Par 72. 1,848 Entries, 150 Starters, 64 Qualifiers.

Qualifying Score	1st Round (18 Holes)	2nd Round (18 Holes)	3rd Round (18 Holes)	4th Round (18 Holes)	Semi-Finals (18 Holes)	Final (18 Holes)
*148	Nathaniel Crosby, Hillsborough, Calif.	Crosby,				
157	Tom Moshier, Kingsburg, Calif.	3 and 1	Heintzelman,			
154	Webb Heintzelman, Bethesda, Md.	Heintzelman,	3 and 2			
160	Michael Grace, Clarence, N.Y.	2 and 1		Heintzelman,		
152	David Hughes, El Paso, Texas	Hughes,		1 up		
158	Jay Townsend, Chagrin Falls, Ohio	6 and 4	Hughes,			
156	Jeff Combe, Fresno, Calif.	Combe,	2 and 1			
161	James McGowan, Colusa, Calif.	2 up			Larkin,	
150	Greg Tebbutt, Bettendorf, Iowa	Tebbutt,			1 up	
158	Chris Byrd, Chattanooga, Tenn.	1 up	Tebbutt,			
155	Brad Worthington, Trumbull, Conn.	Kaufman,	1 up, 19 holes			
160	Jeff Kaufman, Birmingham, Ala.	3 and 2		Larkin,		
154	Stuart Smith, Rocklin, Calif.	Larkin,		6 and 5		
159	Jack Larkin, Atlanta, Ga.	2 up	Larkin,			
157	James Phillips, II, Pittsford, N.Y.	Cude,	7 and 6			
161	Donnie Cude, Burns, Tenn.	4 and 3				Larkin,
149	Ignacio De Leon, Jr., Sugar Land, Texas	Ivan,				2 and 1
158	Steve Ivan, Pueblo, Colo.	2 and 1	Ivan,			
154	Peter Huber, Tucson, Ariz.	Hartsema,	3 and 2			
160	Doug Hartsema, Muskegon, Mich.	2 up		Ivan,		
153	Thomas Homa, Fairfield, Conn.	Homa,		7 and 5		
158	Edward Cuff, La Mesa, Calif.	1 up, 21 holes	Johnson,			
157	Patrick Fitzgerald, Lexington, Ky.	Johnson,	1 up, 19 holes			
161	Eric Johnson, Eugene, Ore.	2 and 1			Moore,	
151	Tommy Moore, New Orleans, La.	Moore,			3 and 2	
158	Tom Williams, Mason, Ohio	3 and 1	Moore,			
156	Mark Kittrell, Gilbert, S.C.	Foltz,	6 and 5			
161	Jerry Foltz, Las Vegas, Nev.	1 up, 22 holes		Moore,		
154	William Beverley, Jr., Irving, Texas	Beverley,		1 up		
159	Chris Caplinger, Edmond, Okla.	4 and 3	Beverley,			Jack Larkin, 1 up
157	Eugene Elliott, Bettendorf, Iowa	Elliott,	2 up			
161	Michael Hoss, Manassas, Va.	1 up				
*148	Rick Fehr, Seattle, Wash.	Fehr,				
158	Steven Bosdosh, Mt. Pleasant, Pa.	3 and 1	Fehr,			
154	Scott Inman, Springfield, Va.	Inman,	4 and 3			
160	Patrick Shaw, Fall River, Mass.	4 and 3		Fehr,		
152	Eric Booker, Naples, Fla.	Baker,		3 and 2		
158	David Baker, Wahiawa, Hawaii	1 up, 20 holes	Weaver,			
156	Brad Weaver, Cordova, Tenn.	Weaver,	6 and 5			
161	Cary Vossler, La Quinta, Calif.	4 and 3			Waddell,	
151	Greg Ladehoff, Clinton, Iowa	Ivy,			2 and 1	
158	Michael Ivy, Huntington Beach, Calif.	1 up, 19 holes	Von Thaden,			
155	Gregg Von Thaden, Atherton, Calif.	Von Thaden,	4 and 3			
160	Ed Vietmeier, Pittsburgh, Pa.	5 and 4		Waddell,		
154	Tom Martine, Neenah, Wis.	Martine,		6 and 5		
159	Mike Walker, Santee, Calif.	8 and 6	Waddell,			
157	Wright Waddell, Columbus, Ga.	Waddell,	1 up			
161	Mike Kingsrud, Fargo, N.D.	1 up				Tuten,
149	Billy Tuten, Falatka, Fla.	Tuten,				1 up
158	Peter Persons, Macon, Ga.	3 and 2	Tuten,			
155	Mike Heinen, Enid, Okla.	Visintainer,	6 and 4			
160	Mark Visintainer, Spokane, Wash.	1 up, 21 holes		Tuten,		
153	Doug Thompson, Laguna Niguel, Calif.	Roush,		2 and 1		
159	Ty Roush, Mason, W.Va.	1 up	Roush,			
157	Jerry Haas, Belleville, Ill.	Howell,	3 and 2			
161	James Howell, Newton, N.J.	2 up			Tuten,	
151	Chris Perry, Edina, Minn.	Perry,			1 up	
158	Chris Anderson, Wilmington, Del.	6 and 5	Tschetter,			
156	Ralph De Stefano, Jr., Poughkeepsie, N.Y.	Tschetter,	2 and 1			
161	Michael Tschetter, Sioux Falls, S.D.	2 and 1		Tschetter,		
154	Paul Ellington, Jr., Louisville, Ky.	Roberts,		5 and 4		
159	Daniel Roberts, Ypsilanti, Mich.	4 and 3	Roberts,			
157	Sandy Pierce, Houston, Texas	Pierce,	2 up			
161	Jay Cooper, Miami, Fla.	1 up, 19 holes				

*Co-Medalists

1980
THIRTY-THIRD JUNIOR AMATEUR CHAMPIONSHIP

Held at Pine Lake Country Club, Orchard Lake, Michigan, July 29-August 2
Yardage—6,484. Par 70. 1,694 Entries, 150 Starters, 64 Qualifiers.

Qualifying Score	1st Round (18 Holes)	2nd Round (18 Holes)	3rd Round (18 Holes)	4th Round (18 Holes)	Semi-Finals (18 Holes)	Final (18 Holes)	
*139	Ralden Chang, Ewa Beach, Hawaii	Chang,					
151	Jeff Combe, Clovis, Calif.	4 and 3	Chang,				
147	Jimmy Matuszewski, Euless, Texas	Matuszewski,	1 up				
154	Ronald Poe, Pebble Beach, Calif.	1 up		Chang,			
145	Richard Fehr, Seattle, Wash.	Fehr,		2 and 1			
152	Dennis Paulson, Costa Mesa, Calif.	1 up, 19 holes	Fehr,				
149	Steve Hull, Severna Park, Md.	Hull,	4 and 2				
155	John Pazdan, Greenville, S.C.	6 and 4			Soulsby,		
144	Greg Tebbut, Bettendorf, Iowa	Robinson,			2 and 1		
152	Tim Robinson, Coronado, Calif.	4 and 3	Taylor,				
148	James Watterson, Pittsburgh, Pa.	Taylor,	3 and 1				
154	Bruce Taylor, Atherton, Calif.	2 and 1		Soulsby,			
146	Bruce Soulsby, Columbus, Ohio	Soulsby,		4 and 3		Soulsby, 5 and 4	
153	Rick Fansler, Fresno, Calif.	1 up	Soulsby,				
150	Scott Erickson, Villa Park, Calif.	Erickson,	2 and 1				
155	James Keck, Powell, Ohio	3 and 2					
143	Rob Boldt, Walnut Creek, Calif.	Storch,					
151	Marty Storch, Louisville, Ky.	1 up	Storch,				
148	Daniel Roberts, Ypsilanti, Mich.	Roberts,	2 and 1				
154	Mark Bueter, Dublin, Ohio	1 up, 23 holes		Restifo,			
146	Ken Saal, Wadsworth, Ohio	Restifo,		2 and 1			
152	Blase Restifo, Aurora, Ohio	2 and 1	Restifo,				
149	Michael Hoss, Manassas, Va.	Vincent,	2 up				
155	Jay Vincent, High Point, N.C.	3 and 1			Restifo,		
144	Todd Smith, Rochester, Ind.	Reding,			3 and 1		Johnson, 1 up, 20 holes
152	Steve Reding, Stillwater, Okla.	3 and 2	Coombs,				
149	Randy Stevenson, Miami Lakes, Fla.	Coombs,	3 and 2				
154	Kevin Coombs, Woodland Hills, Calif.	2 and 1		Hinkelman			
146	Thomas Borah, Seekonk, Mass.	Hinkelman,		1 up, 20 holes			
153	Erick Hinkelman, Fair Oaks, Calif.	2 and 1	Hinkelman,				
150	Danny Coughlin, Redding, Calif.	Coughlin,	3 and 2				
155	Charles Altenbern, Fort Morgan, Colo.	5 and 4					
140	Robert Meyer, Sacramento, Calif.	Meyer,					
151	W. Page Greenwood, Dover, De.	1 up, 19 holes	Meyer,				
148	Chris Webb, Shreveport, La.	Kaercher,	3 and 1				
154	Dan Kaercher, St. Louis, Mo.	1 up		Meyer,			
146	Sandy Pierce, Houston, Texas	Wing,		3 and 2			
152	James Wing, Rochester, N.Y.	2 and 1	Wing,				
149	David Baker, Wahiawa, Hawaii	Baker,	1 up, 23 holes				
155	Robert Burns, Lake City, Fla.	2 and 1			Johnson,		
144	Kurt Beck, Pittsburgh, Pa.	Caldwell,			4 and 2		
152	Kent Caldwell, Lilburn, Ga.	2 and 1	Caldwell,				
148	Mark Thaxton, Burlington, N.C.	Gustafson,	1 up			Eric Johnson, 4 and 3	
154	Kevin Gustafson, Leawood, Kans.	4 and 2		Johnson,			
146	Eric Johnson, Eugene, Ore.	Johnson,		1 up, 19 holes			
153	Mark Gilmartin, Reno, Nev.	8 and 7	Johnson,				
150	Bret Burroughs, University City, Mo.	Burroughs,	6 and 4				
155	Leonard Hartlage, Louisville, Ky.	2 and 1					
144	Jamie McGonagill, Mesa, Ariz.	Kase,					
151	Adam Kase, Socorro, N.M.	1 up, 20 holes	Haas,				
148	Jerry Haas, Belleville, Ill.	Haas,	4 and 3				
154	Cliff Stone, Sandston, Va.	4 and 3		Haas,			
146	James Howell, Newton, N.J.	Stewart,		1 up, 19 holes			
153	Jeff Stewart, Wooster, Ohio	7 and 5	Hamilton,				
149	Tommy Moore, New Orleans, La.	Hamilton,	2 and 1				
155	W. Todd Hamilton, Biggsville, Ill.	2 and 1					
145	Mark Drury, Brunswick, Ga.	Lane,			Haas,		
152	Greg Lane, Orange, Calif.	4 and 3	Lane,		1 up, 19 holes		
149	Greg Sweatt, Rock Hill, S.C.	Jackson,	4 and 2				
154	David Jackson, Monticello, Fla.	2 and 1		Kelson,			
147	Scott Klute, Richmond, Ind.	Kelson,		2 and 1			
153	James Kelson, Grand Prairie, Texas	1 up	Kelson,				
150	Raymond Hajjar, Birmingham, Mich.	Hajjar,	4 and 3				
155	George Stone, Centereach, N.Y.	8 and 6					

* Medalist

GIRLS' JUNIOR CHAMPIONSHIP

VARE TROPHY

Presented in August, 1949, by

GLENNA COLLETT VARE
(Mrs. Edwin H. Vare, Jr.)
Women's Amateur Champion 1922-25-28-29-30-35

HISTORY

1960–Miss Carol Sorenson, 17, of Janesville, Wis., followed the longest route to the Championship since it began, by defeating Miss Sharon Fladoos, of Dubuque, Iowa, by 2 and 1. It was only in this final match that Miss Sorenson's opponents failed to carry her at least as far as the 18th green. The maximum number of holes through six rounds, excepting extra holes, is 108. But Miss Sorenson had to play 109. The total included a victorious 20th hole in the third round. Miss Sorenson's finest comeback was in her semi-final match with Miss Judy Torluemke, of St. Louis, Mo., when she won 1-up after being 3 down with 5 to play. Miss Sorenson and defending Champion Judy Rand, of Aurora, Ohio, who bowed out in the second round, were co-medalists with one-under-par 76s. A total of 91 girls competed in the Championship at The Oaks Country Club, in Tulsa, Okla. Miss Margot Morton, 17, of Indiana, Pa., played in her seventh Championship, a record for the event.

1961–Miss Mary Lowell, 17, of Hayward, Calif., became the sixth Californian and the ninth West Coast player to win in the 13-year history of the Championship. Miss Lowell defeated Miss Margaret Martin, of St. Clairsville, Ohio, 1 up, at the Broadmoor Golf Club, Seattle, Wash. Miss Lowell held leads of 3 up on two occasions but each time Miss Martin cut the lead to 1. The last time was on the 16th hole. They halved the final two holes and Miss Lowell preserved her margin. In the semi-finals, both decided 1 up, Miss Lowell defeated Miss Judy Torluemke, of St. Louis, Mo., and Miss Martin defeated Miss Jeannie Thompson, of Tulsa, Okla. A field of 69 from 18 states and Canada competed over the 6,270-yard Broadmoor course. Co-medalists at 78 were Miss Ann Baker, of Marysville, Tenn., and Miss Mary Lou Daniel, of Louisville, Ky.

1962–Miss Mary Lou Daniel, 17, of Louisville, Ky., defeated Miss Mary Alice Sawyer, 17, of Baltimore, Md., by 2 up in the final match at the Country Club of Buffalo, Williamsville, N.Y. Miss Daniel played a 30-yard approach shot to within three feet of the 18th hole to insure her triumph. An unusual number of girls under 17 qualified for the Championship Flight of 32; in all, there were 21 in the flight who would be eligible for the competition again. Fifteen-year-old Roberta Albers, of Temple Terrace, Fla., was the medalist with 74, which broke the women's course record at the Country Club of Buffalo by one stroke. Miss Albers, a semi-finalist in the 1962 Women's Amateur Championship, lost in the third round. Miss Albers was not the only gifted player who failed to survive an early-round match. Miss Ann Baker, who two weeks later was runnerup in the Women's Amateur Championship, lost in the first round to Miss Renee M. Powell, the first Negro to compete in the Championship.

1963–Miss Janis Ferraris, of San Francisco, and Miss Peggy Conley, of Spokane, Wash., tied for the medal in the qualifying round with scores of 74 at the Wolfert's Roost Country Club, Albany, N.Y. The two girls, both 16, then made their way through the draw to the final round. Miss Ferraris won by 2 up and was credited with a score of approximately 73. The other semi-finalists were Miss Roberta Albers, of Temple Terrace, Fla., and Miss Jacqueline Fladoos, of Dubuque, Iowa, whose sister Sharon was the 1960 runnerup. For the first time a rule limiting accepted entries to 120 was applied when 138 girls filed entry.

1964–Miss Peggy Conley, 17, of Spokane, Wash., who had been runnerup in both the 1963 Girls' Junior and Women's Amateur Championships, had little trouble winning the Girls' title in 1964. She was the medalist at 154 and no opponent carried her past the 16th hole in five matches. Miss Conley was later selected as a member of the Curtis Cup Team, the youngest so honored. Miss Laura MacIvor, Fort Walton Beach, Fla., lost by 6 and 5 in the final match; Miss Conley was even par for the 13 holes. Miss Janis Ferraris, of San Francisco, the 1963 Champion, lost in the quarter-final round to Miss Lou Dill, Houston, Texas, by 1 up.

1965–Miss Gail Sykes, 17, of Schenectady, N.Y., qualified with 167, 19 strokes more than that of the medalist, Miss Shelley Hamlin, Fresno, Calif. But when the two met in the second round of match play Miss Sykes defeated Miss Hamlin, 3 and 2. Miss Sykes went on to win the Championship by defeating Miss Mary Louise Pritchett, Raleigh, N.C., 5 and 4, in the final match at the Hiwan Golf Club, Evergreen, Colo., 7,500 feet high in the Rocky Mountains. Miss Sykes defeated Miss Kathy Hutson, Lubbock Texas, in a semi-final match; in the other Miss Pritchett beat the 1964 runnerup, Miss Laura MacIvor, Fort Walton Beach, Florida.

1966–For the second consecutive year a golfer who qualified with a score 19 strokes higher than the medalist's won the Girls' Junior Championship. Miss Claudia Ann Mayhew, of Woodland, Ind., qualified with 167 and defeated Miss Kathleen Ahern, of Dallas, 3 and 2, in the final at the Longue Vue Club, Verona, Pa. Miss Ahern was the medalist with 148.

Miss Mayhew also defeated Miss Shelley Hamlin, low amateur in the Women's Open and record-breaking medalist in the Women's Amateur. Defeated semi-finalists were Miss Pamela Sue Fox, Corvallis, Ore., who lost to Miss Ahern, and Miss Mariann Eichelberger, Abington, Pa., loser to Miss Mayhew.

1967–Miss Elizabeth (Doll) Story, 16, of Oriskany, N.Y., defeated Miss Liana Zambresky, 16, of Pebble Beach, Calif., 5 and 4, at the Hacienda Golf Club, La Habra, Calif. In a spectacular display of putting skill Miss Story went four under par after eight holes and was 5 up on Miss Zambresky. Miss Janet Webber, 17, of Fresno, Calif., was the medalist with 152. Her first-round 72 was a record for a stroke play round.

1968–Miss Margaret Harmon, 17, of Shelbyville, Tenn., played relentless par golf and defeated Miss Kaye Beard, also 17, 3 and 2, at the Flint Golf Club, Flint, Mich. Miss Beard took an early lead with two birdies and went 2 up. Miss Harmon gradually went ahead by scoring 14 consecutive pars, a birdie at the 15th, and another par at the 16th. The medalist was 15-year-old Miss Nancy Hager, of Dallas, who scored 147 for 36 holes and set a new qualifying record. The total entry reached 130, setting a record.

1969–Hollis Stacy, of Savannah, Ga., became the youngest player ever to win the Girls' Junior Championship when she defeated Mary Jane Fassinger, of New Castle, Pa., 1 up, at the Brookhaven Country Club, Dallas, Texas. Miss Stacy was 15 years, 4 months, 24 days of age when she won. Marlene Bauer won the first Girls' Junior Championship in 1949 at the age of 15 years, 6 months, 3 days. Both Miss Stacy and Miss Fassinger played superb golf in the final. Miss Stacy was 3 up after eight holes, but then Miss Fassinger played holes 9 through 13 in four under par to even the match. Miss Stacy went ahead with a par 5 at the 14th, and they halved the remaining holes. Miss Martha Jones, of Decatur, Ala., was the medalist and lost to Miss Stacy in the semi-finals. Miss Suzanne Jackson, of Highland, Ga., was the other semi-finalist.

1970–Miss Hollis Stacy, of Savannah, Ga., became only the second to win consecutive Girls' Junior Championships when she defeated Miss Janet Aulisi, of West Caldwell, N.J., 1 up, at the Apawamis Club, Rye, N.Y. Miss Stacy had won in 1969 and was eligible to play again in 1970. She had one close match, defeating Miss Mollie Anderson, of Morro Bay, Calif., in 19 holes in the first round. Miss Elizabeth Pooley, of Gainesville, Fla., and Miss Mary Budke, of Dayton, Ore., were the losing semi-finalists. Miss Budke eliminated Miss Nancy Hager, of Dallas, 4 and 3, in the first round. Miss Hager was a member of the U.S. Curtis Cup Team. Miss Louise Bruce, of La Mesa, Calif., was the medalist with 163.

1971–Hollis Stacy, of Savannah, Ga., became the first player to win three successive Girls' Junior Championships when she defeated Amy Alcott, of Los Angeles, in 19 holes at the Augusta Country Club, Augusta, Ga. Other than Miss Stacy, only Willie Anderson, Mrs. Glenna Collett Vare, Miss Virginia Van Wie, and Mrs. Philip Cudone have won three USGA Championships in successive years. Anderson won the Open in 1903-04-05, Mrs. Vare the Women's Amateur in 1928-29-30, Miss Van Wie the Women's Amateur in 1932-33-34, and Mrs. Cudone won four successive Senior Women's Amateur Championships in 1968-69-70-71. Miss Stacy was four under par for the 19 holes she needed to defeat Miss Alcott, 15. From the third hole through the 17th neither girl made a bogey; between them they made nine birdies, and going to the 18th Miss Stacy led by one hole. Miss Alcott won the 18th with a par, and Miss Stacy won with a 15-foot birdie putt on the 19th. Miss Stacy hit 15 greens, Miss Alcott 14, Janet Aulisi, of West Caldwell, N.J., was the medalist with 152. Losing semi-finalists were Mary Budke, of Dayton, Ore., and Donna Horton, of Kinston, N.C. On her way to the Championship Miss Stacy defeated Laura Baugh, of Long Beach, Calif., in the quarter-final round. The following week Miss Baugh won the Women's Amateur Championship.

1972–Miss Nancy Lopez, Roswell, New Mexico, won the Championship in her first attempt at the age of 15. She defeated Miss Catherine Morse, Rochester, N. Y., 1-up, in the final round at the Jefferson City Country Club, Jefferson City, Mo. Miss Lopez had been her state's Women's Amateur Champion since she was 12. Miss Laura Baugh of Long Beach, Calif., the 1971 Women's Amateur Champion, was eliminated in the second round by Miss Janet Aulisi, West Caldwell, N. J., and Miss Amy Alcott, the qualifying medalist with a 151, and 1971 runnerup, was defeated by Miss Barbara Barrow, Chula Vista, Calif., in the quarter-final round. Miss Aulisi, runner-up to Miss Hollis Stacy in 1970, was defeated in turn by Miss Janis Jones, Phoenix, Ariz. On her way to the final, Miss Lopez won handily, requiring only 55 holes to win four matches. Miss Morse, on the other hand, was forced to the 18th hole in two of her four matches and took 63 holes to reach the final. Miss Morse began the final round by winning the first three holes, but Miss Lopez drew even at nine. They continued all even until the 16th where Miss Morse, a strong player, amazed the gallery by driving over a tree at the bend of the sharply dog-legged par-4, 315-yard hole to within 30 feet of the green. She birdied the hole and went 1 up with two to play. Miss Lopez won 17 with a birdie and the 18th with a par.

1973—Miss Amy Alcott, Los Angeles, won in her fourth attempt, defeating Miss Mary Lawrence, Canton, N. Y., 6 and 5, in the final round at the Somerset Hills Country Club, Bernardsville, N. J. Miss Alcott first played in the Girls' Junior Championship in 1969, when she was defeated in the opening round by Miss Hollis Stacy, the eventual winner. Miss Stacy went on to win the Championship in 1970 and 1971. Miss Alcott had been a player of promise since 1971, when she was runnerup to Miss Stacy. She was medalist in 1972, but she lost in the quarter-finals. Miss Nancy Lopez, Roswell, N. M., the defending Champion, was eliminated in the second round by Miss Becky Pearson, North

Branch, Minn. Miss Pearson won, 1 up. Miss Lopez scored 71-73—144 in the qualifying rounds; both the 71 and the 144 total established new records. Miss Alcott was extended only by Miss Alice Miller, Marysville, Calif. Miss Miller, one of seven California girls who qualified in the field of 32, took Miss Alcott 19 holes in the third round. Miss Alcott won her other matches by the scores of 5 and 4; 5 and 3; and 6 and 5. Miss Lawrence, on the other hand, was hard pressed to make the final round. She comes from a town close to the Canadian border where, because of the climate, the golf season is only about four months long. Her performance, therefore, was remarkable. Miss Alcott birdied the first and sixth holes and had a 6 up lead after nine holes. They halved the 10th and 11, then Miss Lawrence won her first hole of the match—the par-3 12th—when Miss Alcott overshot the green into an unplayable lie and took a bogey. It was all over at the 13th, however, when Miss Alcott made a birdie 3, striking a 5-iron from the rough to within six feet of the cup and holing the putt. Miss Lawrence could only make a par. The 6 and 5 victory tied the record for the widest winning margin in a final match, set in 1964 by Miss Peggy Conley over Miss Laura MacIvor. The entry was 98 girls.

1974—Nancy Lopez, of Roswell, N. M., won her second Championship in three years, defeating Lauren Howe, of Colorado Springs, 7 and 6, in the final round at the Columbia-Edgewater Country Club, Portland, Ore. This was the most decisive margin of victory in the final round in the Championship's 26 years. Miss Lopez and Miss Howe, the 15-year-old daughter of a Colorado Springs club professional, were easily the most consistent players in the field of 91 who started play with 36 holes of stroke play qualifying for 32 places in match play. Miss Howe won matches with scores of 7 and 6, 4 and 3, and 6 and 4, and before meeting Miss Lopez had only one close match. She won by 2 and 1 over Carolyn Hill, of Placentia, Calif. Miss Hill, who made it into the semi-final round in 1973, was the 1974 medalist with a 151 total. In her five matches Miss Lopez was par, par, four under, one under, two under. Elaine Hand, of Douglas, Ga., played the first nine holes of her match with Miss Lopez in eight pars and a birdie, and was 1 down. Miss Lopez won the match, 3 and 2. In the final round Miss Howe quickly lost two holes by pulling her tee shots into the woods, and Miss Lopez made a birdie on the par-5 fifth hole to go 4 up. Miss Lopez closed out the match on the 13th hole; she had scored 11 pars and two birdies.

1975—Miss Dayna Benson, 17, of Anaheim, Calif., won the Championship from Miss Kyle O'Brien, of Indianapolis, with a remarkable shot. With the match even, Miss O'Brien was on the final green at the Dedham (Mass.) Country and Polo Club in three. Miss Benson, meanwhile, had played her third shot over the green into a flower bed. Under a Local Rule adopted expressly for the Championship, however, the flower bed was designated ground under repair and Miss Benson was allowed to drop her ball without penalty outside the flower bed. Even with relief Miss Benson was left with a difficult shot over a slope to the hole cut at the back of the green. When Miss Benson played the shot she seemed to hit it too hard and the ball appeared certain to roll well past the hole. Instead the ball hit the flagstick and dropped into the hole for a birdie 4 that won the hole and the match. The Championship was plagued by bad weather. One day was lost completely to the rain, with the result that the quarter-final and semi-final rounds were played on the same day in the rain. There were 113 entrants and of the 32 who qualified for match play, six were from California, four reached the quarter-finals and three were in the semi-final round. Miss Benson was co-medalist with Beverley Davis, of Jacksonville, Fla., and Lauren Howe, from Colorado Springs, Colo., runner-up to Nancy Lopez in the 1974 Championship.

1976—In an all-California final, Miss Pilar Dorado, of Hayward, defeated Miss Kellii Doherty, from Buena Park, 3 and 2, at the Del Rio Golf and Country Club, Modesto, Calif. It was only the third time the Girls' Junior Championship had been held in California. Of the 129 entrants, 13 California youngsters qualified for match play, and of those, three reached the semifinal round. Medalist was Miss Lauren Howe, of Colorado Springs, Colo., who was co-medalist in 1975 and runnerup to Miss Nancy Lopez in 1974. Miss Howe tied Miss Lopez' record for low 18-hole qualifying score (71), but missed by two strokes matching her 36-hole qualifying record of 144, set in 1973. Miss Howe was defeated by Miss Lisa Johnson, of Buena Park, 1-up, in the first round. Miss Cathy Curry, Columbus, Neb., defeated Miss Denise Hermida, of Brandon, Fla., on the 23rd hole. This was the longest match ever in the Girls' Junior. Miss Curry advanced to the semifinal round, where she lost to Miss Doherty. The other losing semifinalist was Miss LuLong Hartley, of Oceanside, Calif. In the final round, Miss Dorado quickly went 2-up with a birdie and a par on the first two holes and then birdied the seventh to go 3-up. After nine holes, she was two under par. Miss Dorado won the 10th and 11th and was 5-up, but Miss Doherty then won the 13th and 14th with birdies. She was then three down with four to play. The match ended when the girls halved the 15th and 16th holes.

1977—Two 17-year-olds met at the Guyan Golf and Country Club, in Huntington, W. Va., and Miss Althea Tome, of Honolulu, defeated Miss Melissa McGeorge, of Richardson, Texas, 3 and 2, in the final round. Miss Tome was the first Hawaiian to win the Girls' Junior. Neither girl was able to take more than a one hole advantage until the 13th, where Miss Tome won to go 2 up. She then won the 14th hole with the only birdie of the match. The match ended after both the 15th and 16th holes were halved. Miss Mary Murphy, of Naples, Fla., led the qualifying round with 144, even par. This equalled the record set by Miss Nancy Lopez in 1973. Miss Murphy took Miss Tome to the 19th hole in the second round. Miss Tome also went 19 holes in her semi-final round in defeating Miss LuLong Hartley, of Oceanside, Calif. Miss McGeorge defeated Miss Kim Bauer, of Conroe, Texas, 3 and 2, in her semi-final match. At 5,777 yards, Guyan became the shortest course to entertain the Championship.

1978—Miss Lori Castillo, 17, of Honolulu, kept the Girls' Junior Championship Trophy in Hawaii for the second consecutive year by defeating Miss Jenny Lidback, of Baton Rouge, La., 4 and 2, in the final over the North Course of the Wilmington Country Club, in Wilmington, Del. Miss Althea Tome, the 1977 Champion, was also from Honolulu. Miss Mary Barrett, of El Cajon, Calif., was medalist with a score of 146 for 36 holes. She was defeated in the first round by Miss Shannon McAleer, 3 and 2. In one semi-final, Miss Castillo, who had lost to Miss Tome in a 1977 quarter-final match, defeated Miss Cathy Hanlon, 2 and 1. Miss Lidback, just 15 years old, eliminated Miss Cindy Pleger, 6 and 5, in the other semi-final. She barely made the match-play field after scoring 164 in qualifying play. She birdied the first extra hole in a five-way playoff for the last place in the 32-player match-play draw. In the final, Miss Castillo won three of the first four holes and maintained that lead after the first nine. Miss Lidback bogied the 10th hole to drop four holes behind. Finally, at the 16th hole, a par 3, Miss Lidback bunkered her tee shot and bogied the hole. Miss Castillo parred the hole to end the match.

1979—Miss Penny Hammel, 17, of Decatur, Ill., birdied four of the last eight holes to defeat Amy Benz, of Clearwater, Fla., in the final at the Pleasant Valley Country Club, Little Rock, Ark. Miss Benz was the medalist with a record 36-hole qualifying score of 142. Laurie Burns shot 70 on the first day of qualifying for a new 18-hole record. The conditions of play were changed to allow 64 girls to qualify for match play rather than 32. The 64th player to qualify for match play had the same score—164—as the 32nd player to qualify for match play in 1978. Miss Hammel reached the final by defeating Jane Abood, 5 and 4; Caroline Gowan, 4 and 3; Joanne Pacillo, 5 and 4; Sharon Barrett, 1 up; and Kathe Kingston, 2 and 1, in the semi-finals. Miss Benz defeated Christine Smith, 2 up; Gail Flanagan, 1 up in 20 holes after Miss Flanagan three-putted the 18th; Robin Wohltman, 6 and 5; Jenny Lidback, the 1978 runner-up, 1 up, when Miss Lidback three-putted the final hole; and Laurie Burns, 2 up, in the semi-finals. In the final, Miss Benz won the first two holes with pars. Miss Hammel came back to win the third hole with a par as Miss Benz three-putted, and the fifth hole with a birdie to even the match. Miss Benz won the sixth with a birdie, but Miss Hammel parred the seventh to even the match again. Miss Benz went 1 up with a par on the ninth hole, but Miss Hammel birdied four of the next eight holes to close out the match. A record 176 entries were received, exceeding the previous high of 172 in 1978.

1980—Laurie Rinker, 17, of Stuart, Florida, won the Championship in her sixth try by defeating Libby Akers, 15, of French Lick, Indiana, 5 and 4, in the final match at the Crestview Country Club, in Wichita, Kansas. Miss Rinker played in her first Girls' Junior in 1975 at the age of 12. Miss Rinker played only 86 holes in wining her six matches. In the first three rounds she played only 37 holes by winning, 8 and 7, 5 and 3, and 8 and 7. She won her quarter-final match by 3 and 1, and in her semi-final match, against 15-year-old Heather Farr, Miss Rinker had to hole a seven foot birdie putt on the 17th and halve the 18th to win, 1 up. She shot 73, one over par. Miss Rinker was off to a slow start in the final with a double bogey 6 at the first hole and a bogey five at the second, but she was only 1 down. From there on her golf was superb; she missed only one green the rest of the way. She played the first nine in 39 strokes; Miss Akers shot 41. Miss Rinker then won the 10th, 11th, and 13th holes to go 5 up. She closed out the match by halving the 14th hole. The medalist was Cynthia Schreyer, of Peachtree, Georgia, with a 36 hole score of 151. There was a playoff at 168 for the 64th place in the match play. The USGA received 162 entries, short of the record 176 received in 1979.

GIRLS' JUNIOR CHAMPIONSHIP

DATE	WINNER, RUNNER-UP	SCORE	SITE	ENTRY
1960 (Aug.)	Miss Carol Sorenson d. Miss Sharon Fladoos	2 & 1	The Oaks C.C., Tulsa, Okla. Co-Medalists—76: Miss Judy Rand Miss Carol Sorenson	91
1961 (Aug.)	Miss Mary Lowell d. Miss Margaret Martin	1 up	Broadmoor G.C., Seattle, Wash. Co-Medalists—78: Miss Ann Baker Miss Mary Lou Daniel	69
1962 (Aug.)	Miss Mary Lou Daniel d. Miss Mary Sawyer	2 up	C.C. of Buffalo, Williamsville, N.Y. Medalist—†74: Miss Roberta Albers	119
1963 (Aug.)	Miss Janis Ferraris d. Miss Peggy Conley	2 up	Wolfert's Roost C.C., Albany, N.Y. Co-Medalists—†74: Miss Janis Ferraris Miss Peggy Conley	121
1964 (Aug.)	Miss Peggy Conley d. Miss Laura MacIvor	6 & 5	Leavenworth C.C., Leavenworth, Kans. Medalist—154: Miss Peggy Conley	126
1965 (Aug.)	Miss Gail Sykes d. Miss Mary Louise Pritchett	5 & 4	Hiwan G.C., Evergreen, Colo. Medalist—148: Miss Shelley Hamlin	88
1966 (Aug.)	Miss Claudia Ann Mahew d. Miss Kathleen Ahern	3 & 2	Longue Vue C., Verona, Pa. Medalist—148: Miss Kathleen Ahern	115
1967 (Aug.)	Miss Elizabeth Story d. Miss Liana Zambresky	5 & 4	Hacienda G.C., La Habra, Calif. Medalist—152: Miss Janet Webber	107
1968 (Aug.)	Miss Margaret Harmon d. Miss Kaye Beard	3 & 2	Flint G.C., Flint, Mich. Medalist—147: Miss Nancy Hager	130
1969 (Aug.)	Miss Hollis Stacy d. Miss Jane Fassinger	1 up	Brookhaven C.C., (Championship Course) Dallas, Texas Medalist—151: Miss Martha Jones	115
1970 (Aug.)	Miss Hollis Stacy d. Miss Janet Aulisi	1 up	Apawamis Club, Rye, N.Y. Medalist—163: Miss Louise Bruce	85
1971 (Aug.)	Miss Hollis Stacy d. Miss Amy Alcott	1 up, 19 hls.	Augusta C.C. Augusta, Ga. Medalist—152: Miss Janet Aulisi	105
1972 (Aug.)	Miss Nancy Lopez d. Miss Catherine Morse	1 up	Jefferson City C. C., Jefferson City, Mo. Medalist—151: Miss Amy Alcott	93
1973 (Aug.)	Miss Amy Alcott d. Miss Mary Lawrence	6 & 5	Somerset Hills, C. C., Bernardsville, N.J. Medalist—144: Miss Nancy Lopez	98
1974 (Aug.)	Miss Nancy Lopez d. Miss Lauren Howe	7 & 5	Columbia-Edgewater C. C., Portland, Ore. Medalist—151: Miss Carolyn Hill	102
1975 (Aug.)	Miss Dayna Benson d. Miss Kyle O'Brien	1 up	Dedham C. & Polo C., Dedham, Mass. Co-Medalists—148: Miss Dayna Benson Miss Beverley Davis Miss Lauren Howe	113
1976 (Aug.)	Miss Pilar Dorado d. Miss Kellii Doherty	3 & 2	Del Rio G. & C. C., Modesto, Calif. Medalist—146: Miss Lauren Howe	129
1977 (Aug.)	Miss Althea Tome d. Miss Melissa McGeorge	3 & 2	Guyan G. & C. C., Huntington, W. Va. Medalist—144: Miss Mary Murphy	127
1978 (Aug.)	Miss Lori Castillo d. Miss Jenny Lidback	4 & 2	Wilmington C. C., (North Course) Wilmington, Del. Medalist—146: Miss Mary Barrett	172

Girls' Junior Championship (Continued)

DATE	WINNER, RUNNER-UP	SCORE	SITE	ENTRY
1979 (Aug.)	Miss Penny Hammel d. Miss Amy Benz	2 & 1	Pleasant Valley C. C., Little Rock, Ark. Medalist—††142: Miss Amy Benz	§176
1980 (Aug.)	Miss Laurie Rinker d. Miss Libby Akers	5 & 4	Crestview C.C., Wichita, Kans. Medalist—151: Cynthia Schreyer	162

†† Record qualifying score, 18 holes.
§ Record Entry.

1960
TWELFTH GIRLS' JUNIOR CHAMPIONSHIP

Held at the Oaks Country Club, Tulsa, Okla., August 15-19.
Yardage—6,272. Par 77. 91 Entries, 84 Starters.

Qualifying Score	1st Round (18 Holes)	2nd Round (18 Holes)	3rd Round (18 Holes)	Semi-Finals (18 Holes)	Final Round (18 Holes)	
76	*Miss Judy Rand, Aurora, Ohio	Miss Rand, 4 and 2				
85	Miss Joan Gavigan, Waukesha, Wis.		Miss Haynie, 2 up			
81	Miss Sandra Haynie, Austin, Texas	Miss Haynie, 8 and 6				
86	Miss Eledra Woodman, Wichita, Kans.			Miss Fladoos, 2 up		
80	Miss Sharon Fladoos, Dubuque, Iowa	Miss Fladoos, 7 and 6				
85	Miss Margaret Jones, Fort Mitchell, Ky.		Miss Fladoos, 4 and 3			
84	Miss Sue Jennett, Portland, Ore.	Miss Jennett, 2 up				
87	Miss Carrie Hoiles, Alliance, Ohio				Miss Fladoos, 3 and 2	
79	Miss Ann Baker, Maryville, Tenn.	Miss Baker, 1 up				
85	Miss Mary Ann Doctor, Haworth, N.J.		Miss Baker, 8 and 7			
82	Miss Jane Bostrom, Landover, Md.	Miss Carey, 2 and 1				
87	Miss Mary Carey, Chicago, Ill.			Miss Baker, 1 up		
81	Miss Marianne Gable, Arcadia, Calif.	Miss Gable, 2 and 1				
86	Miss Suzanne Marks, Tulsa, Okla.		Miss Prentice, 4 and 3			
84	Miss Heidi Prentice, Wilmette, Ill.	Miss Prentice, 3 and 2				
88	Miss Mary Lou Daniel, Louisville, Ky.					Miss Carol Sorenson, 2 and 1
76	*Miss Carol Sorenson, Janesville, Wis.	Miss Sorenson, 2 up				
85	Miss Nancy Jean Way, Grand Rapids, Mich.		Miss Sorenson, 1 up			
82	Miss Nan Gauthier, Corning, Iowa	Miss Thompson, 8 and 7				
87	Miss Jeannie Thompson, Tulsa, Okla.			Miss Sorenson, 1 up, 20 hls.		
80	Miss Patricia Shook, South Haven, Mich.	Miss Albers, 4 and 2				
85	Miss Roberta Albers, Tampa, Fla.		Miss Albers, 4 and 2			
84	Miss Suzy Williams, Monongahela, Pa.	Miss Loftfield, 1 up				
87	Miss Judy Kay Loftfield, Phoenix, Ariz.				Miss Sorenson, 1 up	
80	Miss Brenda High, Glasgow, Ky.	Miss Campbell, 1 up				
85	Miss Mary Jo Campbell, Independence, Mo.		Miss Torluemke, 5 and 4			
82	Miss Judy Torluemke, St. Louis, Mo.	Miss Torluemke, 7 and 5				
87	Miss Nancy Fawcett, Normandy, Mo.			Miss Torluemke, 4 and 3		
81	Miss Mary Lowell, Alameda, Calif.	Miss Lowell, 1 up, 21 hls.				
86	Miss Joan Edwards, Portland, Ore.		Miss King, by default			
84	Miss Jeanie Butler, Harlingen, Texas	Miss King, 2 and 1				
88	Miss Robbye Lee King, Arlington, Va.					

*Tied for Medalist.

1961
THIRTEENTH GIRLS' JUNIOR CHAMPIONSHIP

Held at the Broadmoor Golf Club, Seattle, Wash., August 14-18.
Yardage—6,270. Par 74. 69 Entries, 69 Starters.

Qualifying Score	1st Round (18 Holes)	2nd Round (18 Holes)	3rd Round (18 Holes)	Semi-Finals (18 Holes)	Final Round (18 Holes)	
78	*Miss Mary Lou Daniel, Louisville, Ky.	Miss Daniel, 2 up				
83	Miss Joan Edwards, Portland, Ore.		Miss Albers, 4 and 3			
81	Miss Roberta Albers, Temple Terrace, Fla.	Miss Albers, 4 and 3				
86	Miss Robyn Bohen, Las Vegas, Nev.			Miss Martin, 2 and 1		
79	Miss Gayle Hitchens, N. Van'vr., B.C., Canada	Miss Hitchens, 1 up				
84	Miss Gayle Blockhus, Seattle, Wash.		Miss Martin, 4 and 2			
81	Miss Margaret Martin, St. Clairsville, Ohio	Miss Martin, 5 and 4			Miss Martin, 1 up	
87	Miss Jane Woodworth, Hollywood, Fla.					
79	Miss Jeannie Thompson, Tulsa, Okla.	Miss Thompson, 3 and 2				
83	Miss Michele Yapp, Santa Cruz, Calif.		Miss Thompson, 1 up			
81	Miss Joan Gavigan, Troy, Ohio	Miss Gavigan, 5 and 4				
86	Miss Terry Marinaro, Fresno, Calif.			Miss Thompson, 6 and 4		
81	Miss Sue Lance, Woodland Hills, Calif.	Miss Sawyer, 3 and 1				
85	Miss Mary Alice Sawyer, Baltimore, Md.		Miss Sawyer, 3 and 2			
82	Miss Carol Marie Hartson, San Diego, Calif.	Miss Hartson, 3 and 1				Miss Mary Lowell, 1 up
88	Miss Suzy Williams, Monongahela, Pa.					
78	*Miss Ann Baker, Maryville, Tenn.	Miss Baker, 2 up				
83	Miss Mary Ann Doctor, Haworth, N.J.		Miss Baker, 3 and 1			
81	Miss Margo Ann Michaelis, Hollywood, Fla.	Miss Knutsen, 2 and 1				
86	Miss Mary Knutsen, Warrenton, Ore.			Miss Torluemke, 2 and 1		
80	Miss Lesley Holbert, Medina, Wash.	Miss Holbert, 3 and 2				
85	Miss Janis Ferraris, San Francisco, Calif.		Miss Torluemke, 3 and 2			
82	Miss Judy Torluemke, St. Louis, Mo.	Miss Torluemke, 5 and 3			Miss Lowell, 1 up	
88	Miss Mary Doyle, Portland, Ore.					
79	Miss Mary Carey, Chicago, Ill.	Miss Lowell, 3 and 2				
83	Miss Mary Lowell, Hayward, Calif.		Miss Lowell, 5 and 4			
81	Miss Peggy Conley, Spokane, Wash.	Miss Butler, 2 and 1				
86	Miss Jeanie Butler, Harlingen, Texas			Miss Lowell, 3 and 2		
81	Miss Kathryn Farrer, Decatur, Ala.	Miss Farrer, 1 up				
85	Miss Jacqueline King, Newark, Calif.		Miss Farrer, 1 up, 20 hls.			
83	Miss Carrie Lou Hoiles, Alliance, Ohio	Miss Moorehead, 2 and 1				
89	Miss Elizabeth Moorehead, Diablo, Calif.					

*Tied for Medalist.

1962
FOURTEENTH GIRLS' JUNIOR CHAMPIONSHIP

Held at the Country Club of Buffalo, Williamsville, N.Y., August 20-24.
Yardage—6,102. Par 72. 119 Entries, 115 Starters.

Qualifying Score	1st Round (18 Holes)	2nd Round (18 Holes)	3rd Round (18 Holes)	Semi-Finals (18 Holes)	Finals (18 Holes)	
74*	Miss Roberta Albers, Temple Terrace, Fla.	Miss Albers, 5 and 4				
84	Miss Susan Blazer, Dallas, Texas		Miss Albers, 4 and 3			
87	Miss Joyce Kazmierski, Detroit, Mich.	Miss Kazmierski, 5 and 4				
82	Miss V. Ann Beadle, Belton, Mo.			Miss Ferraris, 4 and 3		
80	Miss Janis Ferraris, San Francisco, Calif.	Miss Ferraris, 1 up				
86	Miss Elizabeth Tobin, Framingham, Mass.		Miss Ferraris, 3 and 2		Miss Daniel, 1 up, 20 hls.	
83	Miss Brenda High, Glasgow, Ky.	Miss High, 6 and 4				
88	Miss Susan Gregory, Pine Bluff, Ark.					
80	Miss Mary Lou Daniel, Louisville, Ky.	Miss Daniel, 4 and 3				
86	Miss Sandra Post, Milton, Ontario		Miss Daniel, 2 up			
87	Miss Barbara Severino, Aurora, Ohio	Miss Severino, 4 and 2				
83	Miss Martha G. Kosar, Cuyahoga Falls, Ohio			Miss Daniel, 4 and 3		
81	Miss Bonnie Werner, Menomonee Falls, Wis.	Miss Werner, 1 up				Miss Mary Lou Daniel, 2 up
87	Miss Terry Marinaro, Fresno, Calif.		Miss Werner, 1 up			
84	Miss Marsha Houghton, Modesto, Calif.	Miss Houghton, 1 up				
88	Miss Jacqueline King, Alameda, Calif.					
85	Miss Renee Powell, E. Canton, Ohio	Miss Powell, 2 and 1				
79	Miss Ann Baker, Maryville, Tenn.		Miss Powell, 1 up			
83	Miss Jeanie Butler, Harlingen, Texas	Miss Butler, 4 and 3				
87	Miss Elaine D. Beguin, Penfield, N.Y.			Miss Sawyer, 1 up, 21 hls.		
80	Miss Mary A. Sawyer, Baltimore, Md.	Miss Sawyer, 2 and 1				
87	Miss Sandra Paine, West Orange, N.J.		Miss Sawyer, 3 and 2			
84	Miss Mary Carey, Chicago, Ill.	Miss Carey, 7 and 5			Miss Sawyer, 4 and 3	
88	Miss Barbara Nelson, Dearborn, Mich.					
80	Miss Sherry Taylor, Oklahoma City, Okla.	Miss Taylor, 3 and 2				
86	Miss Zonnie Tracy, Essex Fells, N.J.		Miss Yapp, 2 and 1			
88	Miss Michele Yapp, Santa Cruz, Calif.	Miss Yapp, 5 and 3				
83	Miss Susan Pompeo, Leicester, Mass.			Miss Lance, 6 and 5		
82	Miss Margo Ann Michaelis, Hollywood, Fla.	Miss Michaelis, 6 and 5				
87	Miss Betty Fassinger, New Castle, Pa.		Miss Lance, 2 and 1			
84	Miss Sue Lance, Woodland Hills, Calif.	Miss Lance, 3 and 2				
89	Miss Patricia Reeves, Seattle, Wash.					

*Medalist.

1963

FIFTEENTH GIRLS' JUNIOR CHAMPIONSHIP

Held at the Wolfert's Roost Country Club, Albany, N.Y., August 12-16.

Yardage—6,002. Par 72. 121 Entries, 121 Starters.

Qualifying Score	1st Round (18 Holes)	2nd Round (18 Holes)	3rd Round (18 Holes)	Semi-Finals (18 Holes)	Final (18 Holes)	
74	*Miss Janis Ferraris, San Francisco, Calif.	Miss Ferraris, 1 up	Miss Ferraris, 1 up, 21 hls.	Miss Ferraris, 2 and 1	Miss Ferraris, 3 and 1	Miss Janis Ferraris, 2 up
83	Miss Sandra Paine, West Orange, N.J.					
81	Miss Betsy Fassinger, New Castle, Pa.	Miss Fassinger, 2 and 1				
85	Miss Michele Yapp, Santa Cruz, Calif.					
80	Miss Carol J. Sorensen, Racine, Wis.	Miss MacIvor, 6 and 4	Miss MacIvor, 4 and 2			
84	Miss Laura A. MacIvor, Eglin AFB, Fla.					
82	Miss Elaine D. Beguin, Penfield, N.Y.	Miss Beguin, 4 and 3				
85	Miss Gaile Burnell, Lafayette, Ind.					
75	Miss Roberta Albers, Temple Terrace, Fla.	Miss Albers, 7 and 6	Miss Albers, 4 and 2	Miss Albers, 2 and 1		
84	Miss Becky Glasscock, Pine Bluff, Ark.					
82	Miss Lesley Holbert, Bellevue, Wash.	Miss Dwyer, 1 up, 19 hls.				
85	Miss Mary M. Dwyer, Canandaigua, N.Y.					
81	Miss Terry Marinaro, Fresno, Calif.	Miss Marinaro, 4 and 3	Miss Marinaro, 6 and 5			
84	Miss Gail Anne Sykes, Ballston Spa, N.Y.					
83	Miss Sandra Post, Milton, Ont., Canada	Miss Post, 7 and 6				
85	Miss Sondrea M. Lees, Copetown, Ont., Canada					
74	*Miss Peggy Conley, Spokane, Wash.	Miss Conley, 4 and 2	Miss Conley, 4 and 2	Miss Conley, 2 and 1	Miss Conley, 2 and 1	
84	Miss Renee Powell, East Canton, Ohio					
82	Miss Jane Blalock, Greenland, N.H.	Miss Blalock, 1 up, 19 hls.				
85	Miss Susan Jayne Pompeo, West Boylston, Mass.					
81	Miss Jeanie Butler, Harlingen, Texas	Miss Butler, 6 and 4	Miss Butler, 4 and 3			
84	Miss Constance E. Hirschman, York, Pa.					
83	Miss Sherry Taylor, Oklahoma City, Okla.	Miss Taylor, 3 and 2				
85	Miss Carolyn Ploysa, Lancaster, N.Y.					
79	Miss Ann Fulkerson, Whittier, Calif.	Miss Fladoos, 1 up, 19 hls.	Miss Fladoos, 2 and 1	Miss Fladoos, 1 up		
84	Miss Jacqueline Mary Fladoos, Dubuque, Iowa					
82	Miss Shirley Walley, Hubbard, Ohio	Miss Houghton, 1 up, 19 hls.				
85	Miss Marsha Houghton, Modesto, Calif.					
81	Miss Sue Lance, Woodland Hills, Calif.	Miss Lance, 1 up, 19 hls.	Miss Lance, 6 and 4			
84	Miss Carol Boyes, Whitevale, Ont., Canada					
83	Miss Susan Basolo, Muskogee, Okla.	Miss Basolo, 1 up				
86	Miss Susan Gregory, Pine Bluff, Ark.					

*Medalists.

1964
SIXTEENTH GIRLS' JUNIOR CHAMPIONSHIP

Held at the Leavenworth Country Club, Leavenworth, Kans., August 10-15.
Yardage—5,801. Par 72. 126 Entries, 108 Starters.

Qualifying Score	1st Round (18 Holes)	2nd Round (18 Holes)	3rd Round (18 Holes)	Semi-Finals (18 Holes)	Final (18 Holes)	
154	*Miss Peggy Conley, Spokane, Wash.	Miss Conley, 3 and 2				
163	Miss Karin Hayes, Kansas City, Mo.		Miss Conley, 7 and 6			
161	Miss Judy Jehle, Montgomery, Ala.	Miss Jehle, 4 and 2				
166	Miss Lynn Mercer, Bethesda, Md.			Miss Conley, 3 and 2		
159	Miss Jacqueline Mary Fladoos, Dubuque, Iowa	Miss Fladoos, 3 and 1				
165	Miss Debbie Austin, Rome, N.Y.		Miss Fladoos, 1 up			
163	Miss Janice Elias, Cascade, Mich.	Miss Elias, 2 and 1			Miss Conley, 5 and 4	
167	Miss Constance E. Hirschman, York, Pa.					
157	Miss Janis Ferraris, San Francisco, Calif.	Miss Ferraris, 3 and 2				
164	Miss Susan Gregory, Pine Bluff, Ark.		Miss Ferraris, 2 and 1			
162	Miss Susan Lance, Woodland Hills, Calif.	Miss Lance, 3 and 1				
166	Miss Becky Glasscock, Pine Bluff, Ark.			Miss Dill, 1 up		
159	Miss Jane Bastanchury, Whittier, Calif.	Miss Bastanchury, 1 up				
166	Miss Diane Keppen, Arcadia, Calif.		Miss Dill, 3 and 1			
163	Miss Lou Dill, Houston, Texas	Miss Dill, 1 up				Miss Peggy Conley, 6 and 5
167	Miss Karen Hagberg, Glendora, Calif.					
156	Miss Laura MacIvor, Fort Walton Beach, Fla.	Miss MacIvor, 4 and 2				
164	Miss Paulette Erickson, Atlanta, Ga.		Miss MacIvor, 1 up			
161	Miss Rita J. Weihe, Bellingham, Wash.	Miss Marsalis, 4 and 3				
166	Miss Valerie J. Marsalis, Shreveport, La.			Miss MacIvor, 5 and 3		
159	Miss Roberta Albers, Temple Terrace, Fla.	Miss Albers, 1 up				
165	Miss Cynthia Hill, South Haven, Mich.		Miss Albers, 4 and 3			
163	Miss Tamara Sue Bowman, Atlantic Beach, Fla.	Miss Bowman, 1 up, 19 hls.			Miss MacIvor, 3 and 2	
167	Miss Kristen Gilbertson, Stillwater, Minn.					
157	Miss Mary Louise Pritchett, Raleigh, N.C.	Miss Hutson, 3 and 1				
165	Miss Kathy Hutson, Lubbock, Texas		Miss Evans, 2 and 1			
162	Miss Jackie Evans, Topeka, Kans.	Miss Evans, 1 up				
166	Miss Shirley Walley, Hubbard, Ohio			Miss Morris, 3 and 2		
160	Miss Susan Basolo, Muskogee, Okla.	Miss Basolo, 4 and 3				
166	Miss Jane Huntsberger, Carmarillo, Calif.		Miss Morris, 1 up, 19 hls.			
163	Miss Carmen M. Piasecki, South Bend, Ind.	Miss Morris, 6 and 5				
167	Miss Linda Morris, Orlando, Fla.					

*Medalist.

1965
SEVENTEENTH GIRLS' JUNIOR CHAMPIONSHIP

Held at the Hiwan Golf Club, Evergreen, Colo., August 16-21.
Yardage—6,041. Par 73. 88 Entries, 88 Starters.

Qualifying Score	1st Round (18 Holes)	2nd Round (18 Holes)	3rd Round (18 Holes)	Semi-Finals (18 Holes)	Final (18 Holes)	
148	*Miss Shelley Hamlin, Fresno, Calif.	Miss Hamlin, 7 and 5	Miss Sykes, 3 and 2	Miss Sykes, 2 and 1	Miss Sykes, 2 and 1	Miss Gail A. Sykes, 5 and 4
163	Miss Carolyn Finley, Huntington Beach, Calif.					
161	Miss Lou Dill, Houston, Texas	Miss Sykes, 2 and 1				
167	Miss Gail A. Sykes, Ballston Spa, N.Y.					
158	Miss Lesley A. Milliken, Bartow, Fla.	Miss Milliken, 4 and 3	Miss Milliken, 2 and 1			
164	Miss Betsy Fassinger, New Castle, Pa.					
163	**Miss Carol Semple, Sewickley, Pa.**	Miss Sorensen, 5 and 4				
168	**Miss Carol J. Sorensen, Racine, Wis.**					
157	Miss Kathy Hutson, Lubbock, Texas	Miss Hutson, 1 up, 20 hls.	Miss Hutson, 3 and 2	Miss Hutson, 1 up		
164	Miss Claudia Ann Mayhew, Carmel, Ind.					
162	Miss Marsha Houghton, Modesto, Calif.	Miss Houghton, 2 and 1				
167	Miss Jacqueline Mary Fladoos, Dubuque, Iowa					
160	Miss Debbie Austin, Rome, N.Y.	Miss Austin, 1 up	Miss Austin, 2 and 1			
167	Miss Kristen Gilbertson, Stillwater, Minn.					
163	Miss Jackie Evans, Topeka, Kansas	Miss Evans, 6 and 5				
169	Miss Lynn Mercer, Bethesda, Md.					
154	Miss Jane Bastanchury, Whittier, Calif.	Miss Bastanchury, 4 and 3	Miss Bastanchury, 3 and 2	Miss MacIvor, 4 and 3	Miss Pritchett, 1 up	
164	Miss Carmen Maria Piasecki, South Bend, Ind.					
161	Miss Diane Keppen, Los Angeles, Calif.	Miss Keppen, 6 and 4				
167	Miss Mary M. Dwyer, Geneva, N.Y.					
159	Miss Laura A. MacIvor, Ft. Walton Beach, Fla.	Miss MacIvor, 1 up	Miss MacIvor, 4 and 2			
166	Miss Jill Endicott, Anaheim, Calif.					
163	Miss Janet Crow, Santa Barbara, Calif.	Miss Crow, 3 and 2				
168	Miss Janet Webber, Fresno, Calif.					
158	Miss Kathleen Ahern, Dallas, Texas	Miss Ahern, 3 and 2	Miss Ahern, 1 up	Miss Pritchett, 5 and 4		
164	Miss Dian Murphy, Ashland, Ore.					
162	Miss Karen Hagberg, Glendora, Calif.	Miss Hagberg, 2 and 1				
168	Miss Susan Basolo, Muskogee, Okla.					
161	Miss Mary Louise Pritchett, Raleigh, N.C.	Miss Pritchett, 1 up	Miss Pritchett, 4 and 2			
167	Miss Linda Fuller, Union Lake, Mich.					
163	Miss Martha Wilkinson, Yorba Linda, Calif.	Miss Phillips, 1 up				
170	Miss Candice R. Phillips, Mobile, Ala.					

*Medalist.

1966
EIGHTEENTH GIRLS' JUNIOR CHAMPIONSHIP

Held at the Longue Vue Club, Verona, Pa., August 15-20.
Yardage—5,907. Par 73. 115 Entries, 105 Starters.

Qualifying Score	1st Round (18 Holes)	2nd Round (18 Holes)	3rd Round (18 Holes)	Semi-Finals (18 Holes)	Final (18 Holes)	
148	*Miss Kathleen Ahern, Dallas, Texas	Miss Ahern, 4 and 3	Miss Ahern, 5 and 3	Miss Ahern, 5 and 4	Miss Ahern, 4 and 3	Miss Claudia Ann Mayhew, 3 and 2
170	Miss Carol Semple, Allegheny, Pa.					
164	Miss Kaye Beard, Campbellsville, Ky.	Miss Beard, 2 up				
174	Miss Janet A. Schulte, Lebanon, Pa.					
162	Miss Elizabeth Story, Cedar Lake, N.Y.	Miss Story, 5 and 3	Miss Story, 5 and 4			
172	Miss Kathy Hutson, Lubbock, Texas					
166	Miss Gwen E. Bennett, Monterey, Calif.	Miss Bennett, 2 and 1				
176	Miss Marilyn R. Karch, Regal, Canada					
159	Miss Katherine M. Hite, Florence, S.C.	Miss Hite, 1 up	Miss Fox, 5 and 4	Miss Fox, 3 and 2		
172	Miss Janet Webber, Fig Garden, Calif.					
165	Miss Pamela Sue Fox, Corvallis, Oregon	Miss Fox, 7 and 5				
176	Miss Nancy Porter, Riverton, N.J.					
164	Miss Mary Jane Fassinger, Castle Hills, Pa.	Miss Fassinger, 4 and 3	Miss Hagberg, 7 and 6			
173	Miss Jackie Evans, Lackland, Texas					
167	Miss Karen Hagberg, Glendora, Calif.	Miss Hagberg, 4 and 3				
177	Miss Sandra M. Baker, Sycamore Hills, Ohio					
155	Miss Shelley Hamlin, University-Sequoia, Calif.	Miss Hamlin, 4 and 3	Miss Hamlin, 3 and 1	Miss Mayhew, 2 and 1	Miss Mayhew, 2 and 1	
171	Miss Julie Savoy, Oak Bourne, La.					
164	Miss Mary Louise Pritchett, Carolina, N.C.	Miss Pritchett, 3 and 2				
175	Miss Beth Reese, Huntingdon Valley, Pa.					
162	Miss Martha Wilkinson, Yorba Linda, Calif.	Miss Wilkinson, 3 and 1	Miss Mayhew, 4 and 3			
172	Miss Patricia M. O'Brien, Pittsfield, Mass.					
167	Miss Claudia Ann Mayhew, Woodland, Ind.	Miss Mayhew, 5 and 4				
177	Miss Nancy Elizabeth May, Bemidji, Minn.					
160	Miss Carmen M. Piasecki, Erskine Park, Ind.	Miss Eichelberger, 3 and 2	Miss Eichelberger, 3 and 2	Miss Eichelberger, 1 up		
172	Miss Mariann Eichelberger, Huntingdon, Pa.					
166	Miss Nancy Hager, Northwood, Texas	Miss Hager, 6 and 4				
176	Miss Cynthia Patricia Meyers, Riviera, Fla.					
164	Miss Marsha Houghton, Del Rio, Calif.	Miss Houghton, 19 holes	Miss Harmon, 2 and 1			
173	Miss Judi Jehle, Bonnie Crest, Ala.					
169	Miss Margaret E. Harmon, Suburban, Ga.	Miss Harmon, 7 and 5				
177	Miss Janice F. Palmer, Huntingdon Valley, Pa.					

*Medalist.

1967

NINETEENTH GIRLS' JUNIOR CHAMPIONSHIP

Held at the Hacienda Golf Club, La Habra, Calif., August 7-12.
Yardage—5,888. Par 73. 107 Entries, 107 Starters.

Qualifying Score	1st Round (18 Holes)	2nd Round (18 Holes)	3rd Round (18 Holes)	Semi-Finals (18 Holes)	Final (18 Holes)	
152	*Miss Janet Webber, Fig Garden, Calif.	Miss Duggan, 19 holes	Miss Fassinger, 5 and 4	Miss Story, 3 and 1	Miss Story, 3 and 2	Miss Elizabeth Story, 5 and 4
164	Miss Catherine Duggan, Fort Lauderdale, Fla.					
159	Miss Mary Jane Fassinger, New Castle, Pa.	Miss Fassinger, 5 and 4				
168	Miss Jane Renner, San Diego, Calif.					
156	Miss Elizabeth Story, Cedar Lake, N.Y.	Miss Story, 4 and 3	Miss Story, 3 and 2			
166	Miss Cindy L. Kobleski, Fircrest, Wash.					
162	Miss Susie Long, Glen Lakes, Texas	Miss Long, 6 and 5				
169	Miss Barbara Bazik, Stardust, Calif.					
156	Miss Margaret Harmon, River Bend, Tenn.	Miss Harmon, 6 and 4	Miss Harmon, 5 and 3	Miss Harmon, 21 holes		
166	Miss Susan Meze, Aptos Beach, Calif.					
161	Miss Catherine Rea, Montecito, Calif.	Miss Rea, 1 up				
168	Miss Judy McClure, Mountain View, Calif.					
158	Miss Marianne Cox, Santa Ana, Calif.	Miss Cox, 3 and 2	Miss Hager, 6 and 4			
167	Miss Coreen Brunham, Regal, Alberta, Canada					
163	Miss Nancy Hager, Northwood, Texas	Miss Hager, 20 holes				
170	Miss Hollis Stacy, Savannah, Ga.					
153	Miss Marsha Houghton, Del Rio, Calif.	Miss Houghton, 4 and 2	Miss Zambresky, 20 holes	Miss Zambresky, 2 and 1	Miss Zambresky, 5 and 4	
166	Miss Sandra Burns, Wildwood, Pa.					
160	Miss Liana Zambresky, Monterey, Calif.	Miss Zambresky, 6 and 5				
168	Miss Karolyn Kertzman, Carloton, Calif.					
157	Miss Cathy Gaughan, Eugene, Ore.	Miss Gaughan, 3 and 2	Miss Michaeloff, 2 and 1			
167	Miss Darcy Lepir, South Shore, N.Y.					
163	Miss Candace L. Michaeloff, Columbia, Minn.	Miss Michaeloff, 4 and 3				
169	Miss Susan Rapp, Bonita, Calif.					
156	Miss Kaye Beard, Campbellsville, Ky.	Miss Beard, 7 and 5	Miss Grove, 19 holes	Miss Grove, 3 and 2		
166	Miss Janice Palmer, Huntingdon, Pa.					
161	Miss Debbie Anne Grove, Chula Vista, Calif.	Miss Grove, 5 and 4				
169	Miss Robin Watson, Meadowbrook, Ark.					
159	Miss Mary Bea Porter, Los Coyotes, Calif.	Miss Porter, default	Miss Porter, 2 up			
167	Miss Julie Savoy, Oakbourne, La.					
163	Miss Jo Ann Washam, Green River, Wash.	Miss Washam, 1 up				
170	Miss Patricia Cooke, Potowomut, R.I.					

*Medalist.

1968
TWENTIETH GIRLS' JUNIOR CHAMPIONSHIP

Held at the Flint Golf Club, Flint, Mich., August 5-10.
Yardage—6,056. Par 74. 130 Entries, 120 Starters.

Qualifying Score	1st Round (18 Holes)	2nd Round (18 Holes)	3rd Round (18 Holes)	Semi-Finals (18 Holes)	Final (18 Holes)	
147	*Miss Nancy Hager, Dallas, Texas	Miss Hager, 5 and 4	Miss Harmon, 3 and 2	Miss Harmon, 2 and 1	Miss Harmon, 3 and 2	Miss Margaret Harmon, 3 and 2
159	Miss Debbie Anne Grove, Bonita, Calif.					
156	Miss Margaret E. Harmon, Shelbyville, Tenn.	Miss Harmon, 5 and 3				
163	Miss Marla Lynn Dietzen, Anderson, Ind.					
151	Miss Elizabeth Story, New Hartford, N.Y.	Miss McClure, 5 and 4	Miss McClure, 2 and 1			
161	Miss Judy McClure, Pomona, Calif.					
158	Miss Cynthia L. Kobleski, Tacoma, Wash.	Miss Savoy, 2 up				
163	Miss Julie Savoy, Lafayette, La.					
150	Miss Susan Rapp, Bonita, Calif.	Miss Rapp, 3 and 2	Miss Rapp, 4 and 2	Miss Rapp, 19 holes		
160	Miss Susan Harman, Cedar Rapids, Iowa					
157	Miss Bobbe Lichty, Waterloo, Iowa	Miss Laughlin, 2 and 1				
163	Miss Ann R. Laughlin, Riverton, N.J.					
155	Miss Tamara Sue Bowman, Atlantic Beach, Fla.	Miss Bowman, default	Miss Jett, 19 holes			
162	Miss Candace Ann Sibbick, Martinsville, Va.					
159	Miss Ellen Joann Dost, Sterling, Va.	Miss Jett, 4 and 3				
164	Miss Martha Jett, Little Rock, Ark.					
148	Miss Mary Jane Fassinger, New Castle, Pa.	Miss Fassinger, 2 and 1	Miss Fassinger, 5 and 4	Miss Fassinger, 4 and 3	Miss Beard, 1 up	
160	Miss Susan Dougherty, Redmond, Wash.					
157	Miss Gail Williams, Medford, Ore.	Miss Williams, 5 and 4				
163	Miss Wendy Hodgson, McConnellsville, N.Y.					
152	Miss Vicki Zimmerman, Mequon, Wis.	Miss Eichelberger, 2 and 1	Miss Cox, 1 up			
162	Miss Mariann Eichelberger, Abington, Pa.					
158	Miss Marianne Cox, Santa Ana, Calif.	Miss Cox, 4 and 3				
163	Miss Sandra Burns, Allison Park, Pa.					
151	Miss Mary Budke, Dundee, Oregon	Miss Zambresky, 4 and 2	Miss Eger, 3 and 2	Miss Beard, 3 and 2		
161	Miss Liana F. Zambresky, Pebble Beach, Calif.					
158	Miss Paula Eger, Kirkwood, Mo.	Miss Eger, 19 holes				
163	Miss Karolyn Kertzman, Santee, Calif.					
155	Miss Kaye Beard, Campbellsville, Ky.	Miss Beard, 5 and 4	Miss Beard, 1 up			
162	Miss Barbara Russell, Oklahoma City, Okla.					
159	Miss Susan Meze, Rio Del Mar, Calif.	Miss Lauer, 1 up				
164	Miss Bonnie Lauer, Union Lake, Mich.					

*Medalist.

1969
TWENTY-FIRST GIRLS' JUNIOR CHAMPIONSHIP

Held at the Brookhaven Country Club (Championship Course), Dallas, Texas, August 4-9.
Yardage—6,113. Par 73. 115 Entries, 106 Starters.

Qualifying Score	1st Round (18 Holes)	2nd Round (18 Holes)	3rd Round (18 Holes)	Semi-Finals (18 Holes)	Final (18 Holes)	
151	*Miss Martha Jones, Decatur, Ala.	Miss Jones,				
163	Miss Karen Cox, Pharoahs, Texas	5 and 3	Miss Jones,			
160	Miss Vilma Haderer, Miami Shores, Fla.	Miss Bruce,	6 and 5			
165	Miss Louise Bruce, Bonita, Calif.	1 up		Miss Jones,		
155	Miss Janet Ann Coles, Aptos Beach, Calif.	Miss Coles,		20 holes		
164	Miss Pamela Spikes, Prairie, Ark.	4 and 3	Miss Weinshilboum,			
161	Miss Jane Renner, San Diego, Calif.	Miss Weinshilboum,	5 and 4		Miss Stacy, 1 up	
165	Miss Teresa Weinshilboum, Ponca City, Okla.	2 and 1				
153	Miss Hollis Stacy, Savannah, Ga.	Miss Stacy,				
163	Miss Amy Alcott, Los Angeles, Calif.	3 and 2	Miss Stacy,			
160	Miss Beverley Huntsman, Valle Verde, Calif.	Miss Collins,	4 and 3			
165	Miss Frances Collins, Amarillo, Texas	5 and 3		Miss Stacy,		
159	Miss Martha Jett, Western Hills, Ark.	Miss Jett,		3 and 2		
164	Miss Diane Lukken, Oaks, Okla.	3 and 2	Miss Jett,			Miss Hollis Stacy, 1 up
161	Miss Jonya Stapp, Miami, Fla.	Miss Long,	3 and 2			
166	Miss Susie Long, Glen Lakes, Texas	3 and 2				
152	Miss Nancy Hager, Northwood, Texas	Miss Hager,				
163	Miss Laura Baugh, Recreation Park, Calif.	1 up	Miss Hager,			
160	Miss Deborah Skinner, Bonita, Calif.	Miss Skinner,	2 and 1			
165	Miss Vicki Mallea, Broadmore, Idaho	1 up		Miss Fassinger,		
157	Miss Mollie Anderson, Morro Bay, Calif.	Miss Wines,		1 up		
164	Miss Debbie Wines, Arizona, Arizona	1 up	Miss Fassinger,			
161	Miss Mary Jane Fassinger, New Castle, Pa.	Miss Fassinger,	3 and 2		Miss Fassinger, 7 and 6	
165	Miss Karen Dremonas, Woodmar, Ind.	8 and 6				
155	Miss Mary Budke, Riverwood, Ore.	Miss Eger,				
163	Miss Paula Eger, Greenbriar Hills, Mo.	21 holes	Miss Jackson,			
160	Miss Sara Stuhler, Antlers, N.Y.	Miss Jackson,	1 up			
165	Miss Suzanne Jackson, Highland, Ga.	3 and 1		Miss Jackson,		
159	Miss Marguerite Mahon, Brook-lea, N.Y.	Miss Tynar,		2 and 1		
165	Miss Pam Tynar, Kayouche Coulee, La.	2 and 1	Miss Grove,			
162	Miss Debbie Grove, Bonita, Calif.	Miss Grove,	1 up			
166	Miss Donna Adwell, Ravenwood, Tenn.	4 and 2				

* Medalist.
The first word after the player's name is the name of the player's club.

1970
TWENTY-SECOND GIRLS' JUNIOR CHAMPIONSHIP

Held at the Apawamis Club, Rye, N.Y., August 10-15.
Yardage—6,091. Par 73. 85 Entries, 75 Starters.

Qualifying Score	1st Round (18 Holes)	2nd Round (18 Holes)	3rd Round (18 Holes)	Semi-Finals (18 Holes)	Final (18 Holes)	
163*	Miss Louise Bruce, La Mesa, Calif.	Miss Laughlin, 2 and 1				
175	Miss Ann Laughlin, Riverton, N.J.		Miss Pooley, 2 up			
170	Miss Elizabeth Pooley, Gainseville, Fla.	Miss Pooley, 2 and 1				
177	Miss Paula Eger, Kirkwood, Mo.			Miss Pooley, 19 hls.		
166	Miss Laura Baugh, Long Beach, Calif.	Miss Baugh, 5 and 3				
176	Miss Susan Lynn, River Vale, N.J.		Miss Baugh, 7 and 5			
172	Miss Paula Wagasky, Odenton, Md.	Miss Wagasky, 6 and 5			Stacy, 2 up	
178	Miss Dana Griswold, Lake Oswego, Ore.					
165	Miss Mollie Anderson, Morro Bay, Calif.	Miss Stacy, 19 hls.				
176	Miss Hollis Stacy, Savannah, Ga.		Miss Stacy, 5 and 4			
171	Miss Sara Stuhler, Fort Johnson, N.Y.	Miss Stuhler, 20 hls.				
177	Miss Melanie Schiller, Waterloo, Iowa			Miss Stacy, 4 and 2		Miss Hollis Stacy, 1 up
170	Miss Martha Jones, Decatur, Ala.	Miss Goldsmith, 2 and 1				
177	Miss Brenda Goldsmith, San Antonio, Texas		Miss Hyatt, 5 and 3			
172	Miss Jane Renner, San Diego, Calif.	Miss Hyatt, 3 and 2				
180	Miss Wendy Hyatt, Placentia, Calif.					
165	Miss Laura Beeken, Pittsburgh, Pa.	Miss Beeken, 2 and 1				
175	Miss Janet Coles, Aptos, Calif.		Miss Beeken, 19 hls.			
171	Miss Barbara Haverty, New Carrollton, Md.	Miss Skinner, 2 and 1				
177	Miss Deborah Skinner, Bonita, Calif.			Miss Budke, 8 and 6		
168	Miss Nancy Hager, Dallas, Texas	Miss Budke, 4 and 3				
176	Miss Mary Budke, Dayton, Ore.		Miss Budke, 4 and 3			
172	Miss Debra Grove, Bonita, Calif.	Miss Kircher, 3 and 1			Aulisi, 19 holes	
180	Miss Mary Kircher, Pittsford, N.Y.					
165	Miss Karen Dremonas, Hammond, Ind.	Miss Aulisi, 6 and 5				
176	Miss Janet Aulisi, W. Caldwell, N.J.		Miss Aulisi, 6 and 4			
171	Miss Suzanne Jackson, La Grange, Ga.	Miss Mahon, 2 up				
178	Miss Marguerite Mahon, Rochester, N.Y.			Miss Aulisi, 1 up		
170	Miss Hali Edison, Sherman Oaks, Calif.	Miss Ferro, 2 and 1				
177	Miss Cynthia Ferro, Belleville, N.J.		Miss Long, 2 up			
175	Miss Susie Long, Dallas, Texas	Miss Long, 2 up				
181	Miss Margaret McCartney, Clinton, Md.					

*Medalist.
+Qualified in playoff.

1971
TWENTY-THIRD GIRLS' JUNIOR CHAMPIONSHIP

Held at Augusta Country Club, Augusta, Georgia, August 9–14.
Yardage–6,052. Par 73. 105 Entries, 100 Starters.

Qualifying Score	1st Round (18 Holes)	2nd Round (18 Holes)	3rd Round (18 Holes)	Semi-Finals (18 Holes)	Final (18 Holes)
152	*Miss Janet Aulisi, W. Caldwell, N.J.	Miss Aulisi,			
166	Miss Marguerite Mahon, Rochester, N.Y.	3 and 2	Miss Coles,		
159	Miss Janet Anne Coles, Aptos, Calif.	Miss Coles,	3 and 1		
169	Miss Debra Miller, Titusville, Fla.	21 Holes		Miss Horton,	
156	Miss Donna Horton, Kinston, N.C.	Miss Horton,		5 and 3	
168	Miss Deborah Simourian, Lincoln, Mass.	7 and 6	Miss Horton,		
164	Miss Noreen Friel, Woburn, Mass.	Miss Friel,	2 up		
171	Miss Becky Pearson, N. Branch, Minn.	8 and 6			Miss Stacy, 2 and 1
156	Miss Laura Baugh, Long Beach, Calif.	Miss Baugh,			
167	Miss Patricia Cornett, Salinas, Calif.	2 and 1	Miss Baugh,		
161	Miss Margie Leno, Milwaukee, Wis.	Miss Leno,	4 and 2		
170	Miss Hellene Spencer, Merrick, N.Y.	1 up		Miss Stacy,	
157	Miss Hollis Stacy, Savannah, Ga.	Miss Stacy,		19 Holes	
169	Miss April Bain, Williamsville, N.Y.	8 and 7	Miss Stacy,		
166	Miss Dawn Young, Warner Robbins, Ga.	Miss Young,	5 and 3		
172	Miss Nancy White, Atlantic Beach, Fla.	4 and 3			Miss Hollis Stacy, 19 Holes
153	Miss Amy Alcott, Los Angeles, Calif.	Miss Alcott,			
167	Miss Linda Hart, McAllen, Texas	3 and 1	Miss Alcott,		
160	Miss Cynthia Booker, Clarkston, Mich.	Miss Booker,	7 and 6		
170	Miss Elaine Hand, Douglas, Ga.	3 and 2		Miss Alcott,	
157	Miss Louise Bruce, La Mesa, Calif.	Miss Bruce,		2 and 1	
168	Miss Debby Marsalis, Shreveport, La.	3 and 2	Miss Bruce,		
165	Miss LuAnn Thames, San Antonio, Texas	Miss Thames,	4 and 3		
171	Miss Patricia Morrison, Abilene, Kans.	1 up			Miss Alcott, 21 Holes
156	Miss Mary Budke, Dayton, Ore.	Miss Budke,			
168	Miss Shelley Grose, New Albany, Ind.	2 and 1	Miss Budke,		
163	Miss Barbara Barrow, Chula Vista, Calif.	Miss Barrow,	5 and 4		
170	Miss Mary Beth Morgan, Houston, Texas	2 and 1		Miss Budke,	
159	Miss Myra Van Hoose, Lexington, Ky.	Miss Skinner,		2 and 1	
169	Miss Deborah Skinner, Chula Vista, Calif.	3 and 1	Miss Skinner,		
166	Miss Cynthia Ferro, Belleville, N.J.	Miss Ferro,	19 Holes		
172	Miss Denise Snellman, Mobile, Ala.	3 and 2			

*Medalist.

1972
TWENTY-FOURTH GIRLS' JUNIOR CHAMPIONSHIP

Held at Jefferson City Country Club, Jefferson City, Missouri, August 7-12.
Yardage—6,125. Par—72. 93 Entries, 85 Starters.

Qualifying Score	1st Round (18 Holes)	2nd Round (18 Holes)	3rd Round (18 Holes)	Semi-Finals (18 Holes)	Final (18 Holes)	
151	*Miss Amy Alcott, Los Angeles, Calif.	Miss Alcott, 5 and 4				
169	Miss Elanine Hand, Douglas, Ga.		Miss Alcott, 2 up			
165	Miss Joan Nesset, Edina, Minn.	Miss Nesset, 3 and 2				
171	Miss Connie Chillemi, Deland, Fla.			Miss Barrow, 2 and 1		
162	Miss Julie Gumlia, Bemidji, Minn.	Miss Gumlia, 3 and 2				
170	Miss Becky Pearson, North Branch, Minn.		Miss Barrow, 4 and 3			
167	Miss Barbara Barrow, Chula Vista, Calif.	Miss Barrow, 4 and 2			Miss Morse, 1 up	
173	Miss Terry Williams, Homestead, Fla.					
159	Miss Myra Van Hoose, Lexington, Ky.	Miss Van Hoose, 1 up, 19 holes				
170	Miss Anne Theis, Buffalo, Minn.		Miss Van Hoose, 1 up			
165	Miss Cynthia Booker, Clarkston, Mich.	Miss Booker, 3 and 2				
172	Miss Shelley Grose, N. Albany, Ind.			Miss Morse, 7 and 5		
164	Miss Alice Miller, Marysville, Calif.	Miss Miller, 5 and 4				
171	Miss Kimberly Fisher, Buckingham, Pa.		Miss Morse, 1 up			
168	Miss Catherine Morse, Rochester, N.Y.	Miss Morse, 5 and 4				
173	Miss Margaret McCartney, Indian Harbor, Fla.					Miss Nancy Lopez, 1 up
155	Miss Laura Baugh, Long Beach, Calif.	Miss Baugh, 3 and 2				
169	Miss Linda Hart, McAllen, Texas		Miss Aulisi, 4 and 3			
165	Miss Janet Aulisi, W. Caldwell, N.J.	Miss Aulisi, 4 and 3				
171	Miss Dawn Young, Warner Robbins, Ga.			Miss Jones, 1 up		
164	Miss Brenda Goldsmith, San Antonio, Texas	Miss Goldsmith, 8 and 6				
171	Miss Jane Jensen, Watertown, Minn.		Miss Jones, 3 and 2			
168	Miss Lee Burke, Shreveport, La.	Miss Jones, 1 up, 19 holes			Miss Lopez, 9 and 8	
173	Miss Janis Jones, Phoenix, Ariz.					
159	Miss Nancy Lopez, Roswell, N.M.	Miss Lopez, 4 and 3				
170	Miss Mary Kircher, Pittsford, N.Y.		Miss Lopez, 6 and 4			
166	Miss Lori Nelson, West Chester, Pa.	Miss Nelson, 1 up, 21 holes				
173	Miss Sherry Donovan, Memphis, Tenn.			Miss Lopez, 3 and 2		
168	Miss Marianne Stangeland, Long Beach, Calif.	Miss Stangeland, 3 and 2				
171	Miss Mary Beth Morgan, Houston, Texas		Miss Stangeland, 3 and 2			
169	Miss Robin Walton, Clarkston, Wash.	Miss Walton, 2 and 1				
174	Miss Judy Snellman, Mobile, Ala.					

*Medalist

1973
TWENTY-FIFTH GIRLS' JUNIOR CHAMPIONSHIP

Held at Somerset Hills Country Club, Bernardsville, New Jersey, August 6 - 11.
Yardage—5,838, 5,813. Par 73, 72. 98 Entries, 97 Starters.

Qualifying Score	1st Round (18 Holes)	2nd Round (18 Holes)	3rd Round (18 Holes)	Semi-Finals (18 Holes)	Final (18 Holes)
144	*Miss Nancy Lopez, Roswell, N. M.	Miss Lopez, 20 holes	Miss Pearson, 1 up	Miss Hill, 4 and 2	Miss Lawrence, 1 up
162	Miss Sharon Lang, North Palm Beach, Fla.				
158	Miss Becky Pearson, North Branch, Minn.	Miss Pearson, 4 and 2			
165	Miss Constance Chillemi, Naples, Fla.				
155	Miss Carolyn Hill, Placentia, Calif.	Miss Hill, 5 and 3	Miss Hill, 4 and 3		
163	Miss Brenda Rego, Kunia, Hawaii				
161	Miss Patti Morrison, Abilene, Kansas	Miss Morrison, 1 up			
167	Miss Deborah Skelly, San Antonio, Texas				
154	Miss Pamela Lang, North Palm Beach, Fla.	Miss Daniel, 4 and 2	Miss Daniel, 5 and 4	Miss Lawrence, 2 and 1	
163	Miss Elizabeth Daniel, Charleston, S. C.				
159	Miss Lori Nelson, West Chester, Pa.	Miss Nelson, 4 and 2			
166	Miss Diane Bohl, Urbana, Ohio				
158	Miss Mary Lawrence, Canton, N. Y.	Miss Lawrence, 6 and 4	Miss Lawrence, 1 up		
164	Miss Sherri Donovan, Memphis, Tenn.				
162	Miss Marianne Stangeland, Long Beach, Calif.	Miss Nesset, 1 up			
167	Miss Joan Nesset, Edina, Minn.				
150	Miss Amy Alcott, Los Angeles, Calif.	Miss Alcott, 5 and 4	Miss Alcott, 5 and 3	Miss Alcott, 19 holes	Miss Alcott, 6 and 5
163	Miss Marilyn Martyniak, St. Helena, Calif.				
158	Miss Vicki Tabor, Waco, Texas	Miss Turner, 4 and 3			
166	Miss Sherri Turner, Greenville, S. C.				
156	Miss Alice Miller, Marysville, Calif.	Miss Miller, 3 and 1	Miss Miller, 4 and 2		
164	Miss Julie Gumlia, Bemidji, Minn.				
162	Miss Linda Hart, McAllen, Texas	Miss Hart, 4 and 2			
167	Miss Denise Snellman, Mobile, Ala.				
155	Miss Debby Stewart, Long Beach, Calif.	Miss Stewart, 4 and 2	Miss Stewart, 2 and 1	Miss King, 1 up	
163	Miss Janet Eastman, Arcadia, Calif.				
160	Miss Elaine Hand, Douglas, Ga.	Miss Hand, 3 and 1			
166	Miss Rise Alexander, Portland, Ore.				
158	Miss Terri Thoreson, Snoqualmie, Wash.	Miss Thoreson, 6 and 4	Miss King, 1 up		
164	Miss Desiree Alley, Waukegan, Ill.				
162	Miss Mary-Beth King, Limekiln, Pa.	Miss King, 3 and 2			
168	Miss Sue Goodwin, Pulaski, N. Y.				

Winner: Miss Amy Alcott, 6 and 5

*Medalist

1974
TWENTY-SIXTH GIRLS' JUNIOR CHAMPIONSHIP

Held at Columbia Edgewater Country Club, Portland, Oregon, August 5-10
Yardage 6,086. Par 73. 102 Entries, 91 Starters.

Qualifying Score	1st Round (18 Holes)	2nd Round (18 Holes)	3rd Round (18 Holes)	Semi-Finals (18 Holes)	Final (18 Holes)
151	*Miss Carolyn Hill, Placentia, Calif.	Miss Hill, 2 up			
162	Miss Kyle O'Brien, Indianapolis, Ind.		Miss Howe, 2 and 1		
157	Miss Lauren Howe, Colorado Springs, Colo.	Miss Howe, 7 and 6			
166	Miss Denise Gualco, El Macero, Calif.			Miss Howe, 4 and 3	
156	Miss Therese Hession, Indianapolis, Ind.	Miss Hession, 3 and 1			
164	Miss Vikki Staton, Alexandria, Va.		Miss Gumlia, 19 holes		Miss Howe, 6 and 4
160	Miss Connie Chillemi, Naples, Fla.	Miss Gumlia, 2 and 1			
167	Miss Julie Gumlia, Bemidji, Minn.				
154	Miss Debby Stewart, Long Beach, Calif.	Miss Stewart, 2 up			
163	Miss Sherry Lynn Wood, Austin, Texas		Miss Stanger, 2 and 1		
159	Miss Julie Stanger, Phoenix, Ariz.	Miss Stanger, 5 and 4			
166	Miss Mary Beth Murphy, Naples, Fla.			Miss Stanger, 4 and 3	
157	Miss Deborah Ann Skelly, San Antonio, Texas	Miss Johnson, 20 holes			Miss Nancy Lopez, 7 and 5
164	Miss Christa A. Johnson, Arcata, Calif.		Miss Keblish, 2 and 1		
161	Miss Lisa Ann Baxter, Los Gatos, Calif.	Miss Keblish, 1 up			
168	Miss Sherrie Ann Keblish, Miami, Fla.				
153	Miss Nancy Lopez, Roswell, N. M.	Miss Lopez, 9 and 7			
162	Miss Jo Anne Cesar, Phoenix, Ariz.		Miss Lopez, 3 and 2		
158	Miss Dayna Benson, Anaheim, Calif.	Miss Gregory, 20 holes			
166	Miss Paula Elaine Gregory, Alamo, Calif.			Miss Lopez, 5 and 3	
156	Miss Beverley Davis, Jacksonville, Fla.	Miss Garbacz, 20 holes			
164	Miss Lori Garbacz, South Bend, Ind.		Miss Garbacz, 1 up		
161	Miss Beth Boozer, Lawrence, Kans.	Miss Boozer, 5 and 4			Miss Lopez, 3 and 2
168	Miss Betsy Barrett, Syracuse, N. Y.				
155	Miss Elaine Hand, Douglas, Ga.	Miss Hand, 1 up			
163	Miss Kellii L. P. Doherty, Fullerton, Calif.		Miss Hand, 3 and 2		
160	Miss Beth Daniel, Charleston, S. C.	Miss Nelson, 1 up			
167	Miss Lori Nelson, West Chester, Pa.			Miss Hand, 5 and 3	
157	Miss Holly Hartley, Oceanside, Calif.	Miss Reynolds, 4 and 3			
165	Miss Cathy Reynolds, Springfield, Mo.		Miss Reynolds, 5 and 3		
161	Miss Terri Jo Heacock, Cypress, Calif.	Miss Hoins, 3 and 1			
169	Miss Nancy Hoins, Leavenworth, Kans.				

*Medalist

1975
TWENTY-SEVENTH GIRLS' JUNIOR CHAMPIONSHIP

Held at Dedham Country & Polo Club, Dedham, Massachusetts, August 4-9
Yardage—5,643. Par 72. 113 Entries, 109 Starters

Qualifying Score	1st Round (18 Holes)	2nd Round (18 Holes)	3rd Round (18 Holes)	Semi-Finals (18 Holes)	Final (18 Holes)	
*148	Miss Beverley Davis, Jacksonville, Fla.	Miss Davis, 2 and 1				
163	Miss Terri Moody, Athens, Ga.		Miss Davis, 2 and 1			
158	Miss LuLong Hartley, Oceanside, Calif.	Miss Hartley, 7 and 5				
166	Miss Robin Sue Hall, Lavernia, Texas			Miss Hartley, 3 and 2		
153	Miss Holly Hartley, Oceanside, Calif.	Miss Hartley, 2 and 1				
165	Miss Kathy Butera, Northampton, Mass.		Miss Hartley, 4 and 3		Miss O'Brien, 1 up	
162	Miss Nancy Narkon, Manchester, Conn.	Miss Lawrence, 5 and 3				
167	Miss Kathleen Lawrence, Canton, N.Y.					
148	Miss Lauren Howe, Colorado Springs, Colo.	Miss Baxter, Default				
164	Miss Lisa Baxter, Los Gatos, Calif.		Miss Baxter, 4 and 3			
160	Miss Betty Baird, Louisville, Ky.	Miss Baird, 4 and 2				
166	Miss Peggy Sue Gustafson, Brenham, Texas			Miss O'Brien, 2 and 1		
155	Miss Lori Garbacz, South Bend, Ind.	Miss Garbacz, 19 holes				
165	Miss Lynn Marriott, Herkimer, N.Y.		Miss O'Brien, 2 and 1			Miss Dayna Benson, 1 up
163	Miss Kyle O'Brien, Indianapolis, Ind.	Miss O'Brien, 7 and 6				
169	Miss Lene Jordan, Fairfax, Va.					
*148	Miss Dayna Benson, Anaheim, Calif.	Miss Benson, 2 and 1				
164	Miss Alicia Ogrin, Waukegan, Ill.		Miss Benson, 6 and 5			
160	Miss JoAnne Cesar, Phoenix, Ariz.	Miss Cesar, 5 and 4				
166	Miss Laura Jean Vautrain, Wallingford, Conn.			Miss Benson, 2 and 1		
154	Miss Carolyn Hill, Placentia, Calif.	Miss Elders, 2 and 1				
165	Miss Pamela Elders, Leisure City, Fla.		Miss Chillemi, 19 holes		Miss Benson, 5 and 3	
162	Miss Connie Chillemi, Naples, Fla.	Miss Chillemi, 7 and 5				
168	Miss Sally Voss, Bethesda, Md.					
150	Miss Debby Stewart, Long Beach, Calif.	Miss Stewart, 6 and 5				
164	Miss Kathy Williams, LaCrescent, Minn.		Miss Stewart, 1 up			
161	Miss Judy Shock, Bexley, Ohio	Miss Murphy, 5 and 3				
167	Miss Mary Elizabeth Murphy, Naples, Fla.			Miss Stewart, 3 and 1		
158	Miss Theresa Hession, Indianapolis, Ind.	Miss Hession, 19 holes				
165	Miss Charlotte Allen, Louisville, Ky.		Miss Hession, 6 and 5			
163	Miss Monica O'Hare, Parkville, Mo.	Miss O'Hare, 4 and 2				
169	Miss Mary Wilkinson, Beverly, Mass.					

*Co-Medalists

1976
TWENTY-EIGHTH GIRLS' JUNIOR CHAMPIONSHIP

Held at Del Rio Golf and Country Club, Modesto, California, August 9-14
Yardage—6,194. Par 75. 129 Entries, 123 Starters

Qualifying Score	1st Round (18 Holes)	2nd Round (18 Holes)	3rd Round (18 Holes)	Semi-Finals (18 Holes)	Final (18 Holes
*146	Miss Lauren Howe, Colorado Springs, Colo.	Miss Johnson,			
162	Miss Lisa Johnson, Buena Park, Calif.	1 up	Miss Johnson,		
160	Miss Betsy Barrett, Syracuse, N.Y.	Miss Fulton,	3 and 2		
164	Miss Julie Fulton, San Diego, Calif.	1 up		Miss Curry,	
157	Miss Althea Tome, Honolulu, Hawaii	Miss Tome,		6 and 5	
163	Miss Pamela K. Miller, Libertyville, Ill.	3 and 1	Miss Curry,		
161	Miss Catherine Curry, Columbus, Neb.	Miss Curry,	5 and 3		
165	Miss Denise Hermida, Brandon, Fla.	23 holes			Miss Doherty,
156	Miss Cathy Hanlon, Palos Verdes Estates, Calif.	Miss Stiffler,			1 up
163	Miss Lynn Stiffler, Waycross, Ga.	1 up	Miss Jordan,		
160	Miss Michelle Jordan, Fairfax, Va.	Miss Jordan,	1 up		
164	Miss Joanne Marie Pacillo, Torrance, Calif.	7 and 6		Miss Doherty,	
158	Miss Kellii Doherty, Buena Park, Calif.	Miss Doherty,		2 up	
164	Miss Suzy Shultz, Coronado, Calif.	5 and 4	Miss Doherty,		
162	Miss Terri Moody, Athens, Ga.	Miss Moody,	3 and 2		
165	Miss Bari Brandwynne, Las Vegas, Nev.	7 and 5			
153	Miss LuLong Hartley, Oceanside, Calif.	Miss Hartley,			
163	Miss Denise Marie Strebig, San Bernardino, Calif.	2 and 1	Miss Hartley,		
160	Miss Laurie Ann Rinker, Stuart, Fla.	Miss Rinker,	2 and 1		
164	Miss Diana Doyle, Monterey, Calif.	5 and 4		Miss Hartley,	
157	Miss Carolyn Hill, Placentia, Calif.	Miss Hill,		2 up	
163	Miss Genevieve A. Huvendick, Lansing, Kans.	5 and 4	Miss Varty,		
161	Miss Kelly Varty, Elk River, Minn.	Miss Varty,	1 up		
165	Miss Debra Spencer, Kaneohe, Oahu, Hawaii ..	2 and 1			Miss Dorado,
157	Miss Laura Hurlbut, Woodland Hills, Calif.	Miss Hurlbut,			3 and 1
163	Miss Martha Fay Stewart, Long Beach, Calif.	4 and 3	Miss Wood,		
160	Miss Deanie Wood, Lake Charles, La.	Miss Wood,	2 up		
165	Miss Nancy Peck, Eugene, Ore.	3 and 2		Miss Dorado,	
158	Miss Pilar Ruth Dorado, Hayward, Calif.	Miss Dorado,		3 and 2	
164	Miss Mary Elizabeth Murphy, Naples, Fla.	6 and 5	Miss Dorado,		
162	Miss Lynda Wimberly, Brentwood, Tenn.	Miss Wimberly,	2 and 1		
165	Miss Ann Feist, Phoenix, Ariz.	3 and 2			

Miss Pilar Ruth Dorado, 3 and 2

*Medalist

1977
TWENTY-NINTH GIRLS' JUNIOR CHAMPIONSHIP

Held at Guyan Golf and Country Club, Huntington, West Virginia, August 1-6.
Yardage—5,777. Par 72. 127 Entries, 120 Starters.

Qualifying Score	1st Round (18 Holes)	2nd Round (18 Holes)	3rd Round (18 Holes)	Semi-Finals (18 Holes)	Final (18 Holes)
*144	Miss Mary E. Murphy, Naples, Fla.	Miss Murphy,			
155	Miss Patrice Rizzo, Hialeah, Fla.	4 and 2	Miss Tome,		
153	Miss Althea Tome, Honolulu, Hawaii	Miss Tome,	1 up, 19 holes		
156	Miss Lauri Merten, Phoenix, Ariz.	5 and 3		Miss Tome,	
150	Miss Lori Castillo, Honolulu, Hawaii	Miss Castillo,		3 and 1	
156	Miss Lene Jordan, Fairfax, Va.	4 and 3	Miss Castillo,		
153	Miss Linda Brown, Bartlesville, Okla.	Miss Brown,	3 and 2		
157	Miss Kristi Elton, Alexandria, Minn.	1 up, 20 holes			Miss Tome,
149	Miss Betty Baird, Louisville, Ky.	Miss Stiffler,			1 up, 19 holes
155	Miss Lynn Stiffler, Waycross, Ga.	1 up	Miss Hanolon,		
153	Miss Cathy Hanolon, Palos Verdes Estates, Calif.	Miss Hanolon,	6 and 5		
157	Miss Sheree Muirhead, Johannesburg, S. Africa	4 and 3		Miss Hartley,	
151	Miss Kathy Williams, LaCrescent, Minn.	Miss Williams,		3 and 2	
156	Miss Charlotte Grant, Lookout Mountain, Tenn.	4 and 3	Miss Hartley,		
154	Miss LuLong Hartley, Oceanside, Calif.	Miss Hartley,	2 and 1		
158	Miss Marie de Lorenzi, Oceanside, Calif.	1 up, 21 holes			
148	Miss Laurie Rinker, Stuart, Fla.	Miss Rinker,			
155	Miss Elizabeth Waynick, Roanoke, Va.	7 and 6	Miss McGeorge,		
153	Miss Melissa McGeorge, Richardson, Texas	Miss McGeorge,	2 and 1		
157	Miss Mary Beth Lange, Rosemont, Pa.	1 up, 19 holes		Miss McGeorge,	
150	Miss Anne Rush, Thompkinsville, Ky.	Miss Rush,		1 up	
156	Miss Kris Hanson, Granite Falls, Minn.	1 up	Miss Hammell,		
153	Miss Penny Hammell, Decatur, Ill.	Miss Hammell,	4 and 3		
158	Miss Cathy Cook, Columbus, Ohio	2 and 1			Miss McGeorge,
149	Miss Catherine Curry, Columbus, Neb.	Miss Varty,			3 and 2
155	Miss Kelly Varty, Elk River, Minn.	1 up, 19 holes	Miss Varty,		
153	Miss Denise Strebig, San Bernardino, Calif.	Miss Strebig,	1 up, 22 holes		
157	Miss Mari McDougall, Midlothian, Ill.	1 up		Miss Bauer,	
152	Miss Mary Kathryn Baker, Clover, S. C.	Miss Headings,		2 up	
156	Miss Diane Headings, Palm Beach, Fla.	4 and 2	Miss Bauer,		
154	Miss Kim Bauer, Conroe, Texas	Miss Bauer,	6 and 4		
158	Miss Jennifer Graff, Philadelphia, Pa.	8 and 6			

Miss Althea Tome, 3 and 2

*Medalist

1978
THIRTIETH GIRLS' JUNIOR CHAMPIONSHIP

Held at Wilmington Country Club (North Course), Wilmington, Delaware, August 7-12.
Yardage—5,872. Par 72. 172 Entries, 120 Starters, 32 Qualifiers.

Qualifying Score	1st Round (18 Holes)	2nd Round (18 Holes)	3rd Round (18 Holes)	Semi-Finals (18 Holes)	Final (18 Holes)
*146	Miss Mary Barrett, Spring Valley, Calif.	McAleer, 3 and 2			
158	Miss Shannon McAleer, Mobile, Ala.		Castillo, 7 and 5		
156	Miss Lori Castillo, Honolulu, Hawaii	Castillo, 4 and 2			
161	Miss Marla Anderson, Jacksonville, Fla.			Castillo, 1 up	
154	Miss Dana Howe, Colorado Springs, Colo.	Howe, 6 and 4			
160	Miss Jennifer Graff, Philadelphia, Pa.		Howe, 5 and 4		
157	Miss Mary Enright, San Leandro, Calif.	Enright, 1 up			
162	Miss Michelle Jordan, Fairfax, Va.				Castillo, 2 and 1
147	Miss Cathy Hanlon, Palos Verdes, Calif.	Hanlon, 2 and 1			
160	Miss Beverly Boozer, Lawrence, Kans.		Hanlon, 6 and 5		
157	Miss Rae Rothfelder, Ft. Worth, Texas	Rothfelder, 3 and 2			
161	Miss Kris Hanson, Granite Falls, Minn.			Hanlon, 1 up	
154	Miss Diane Headings, Wesley Chapel, Fla.	Baker, 1 up, 21 holes			
160	Miss Mary Baker, Clover, S.C.		Baker, 1 up		
158	Miss Kelly Varty, Elk River, Minn.	Varty, 4 and 3			
163	Miss Viveca Vanderpriff, Arlington, Texas				
147	Miss Kris Monaghan, Los Alamos, N.M.	Burba, 4 and 3			
158	Miss Janice Burba, Tulsa, Okla.		Pleger, 2 up		
156	Miss Valerie Skinner, N. Platte, Neb.	Pleger, 1 up			
161	Miss Cindy Pleger, Athens, Ga.			Pleger, 3 and 2	
154	Miss Martha Stacy, Savannah, Ga.	Stacy, 4 and 3			
160	Miss Joanne Pacillo, Torrance, Calif.		Stacy, 2 and 1		
157	Miss Carol Hogan, Oceanside, Calif.	Hogan, 1 up			
163	Miss Jacqueline Bertram, Austin, Texas				Lidback, 6 and 5
153	Miss Lynn Stiffler, Waycross, Ga.	Stiffler, 5 and 3			
160	Miss Kathe Kingston, East Point, Ga.		Kelly, 2 up		
157	Miss Mary Beth Corrigan, Amsterdam, N.Y.	Kelly, 1 up, 20 holes			
161	Miss Anne Kelly, Tucson, Ariz.			Lidback, 3 and 2	
155	Miss Laurie Rinker, Stuart, Fla.	Quinlan, 1 up, 21 holes			
160	Miss Sally Quinlan, E. Dennis, Mass.		Lidback, 4 and 3		
158	Miss Julie Fulton, San Diego, Calif.	Lidback, 2 up			
164	Miss Jenny Lidback, Baton Rouge, La.				

Miss Lori Castillo, 4 and 2

*Medalist

1979
THIRTY-FIRST GIRLS' JUNIOR CHAMPIONSHIP

Held at Pleasant Valley Country Club, Little Rock, Arkansas, August 6-11.
Yardage—5,802. Par 72. 176 Entries, 120 Starters, 64 Qualifiers.

Qualifying Score	1st Round (18 Holes)	2nd Round (18 Holes)	3rd Round (18 Holes)	4th Round (18 Holes)	Semi-Finals (18 Holes)	Final (18 Holes)
*142	Amy Benz, Clearwater, Fla.	Benz,				
159	Christine Smith, Littleton, Colo.	2 up	Benz,			
156	Gail Flanagan, Scarsdale, N.Y.	Flanagan,	1 up, 20 holes			
162	Cathy Nelson, Omaha, Neb.	3 and 2		Benz,		
151	Heather Farr, Phoenix, Ariz.	Farr,		6 and 5		
161	Hilary Rack, Santa Barbara, Calif.	7 and 5	Wohltman,			
158	Robin Wohltman, Independence, Kans.	Wohltman,	3 and 2			
163	Rhonda Weldon, Enid, Okla.	3 and 1			Benz,	
150	Jenny Lidback, Baton Rouge, La.	Lidback,			1 up	
160	Kandi Kessler, Charlottesville, Va.	5 and 3	Lidback,			
158	Pamela Meany, Holbrook, Mass.	Abare,	5 and 4			
163	Robin Abare, Forsyth, Ga.	1 up, 19 holes		Lidback,		
154	Linda Mescan, York, Pa.	Mescan,		4 and 3		
161	Sandra Stubbe, Miami, Fla.	1 up, 20 holes	Mescan,			
159	Lise Russell, New City, N.Y.	Russell,	2 and 1			
164	Flori Prono, Northridge, Calif.	4 and 2				Benz,
146	Laurie Burns, Plantation, Fla.	Burns,				2 up
160	Tammy Towles, Titusville, Fla.	2 and 1	Burns,			
156	Janet Groene, Cushing, Okla.	Davis,	2 and 1			
162	Cindy Davis, Bowie, Md.	3 and 2		Burns,		
154	Cheryl Stacy, Findlay, Ohio	C. Stacy		5 and 4		
161	Lavon Seabolt, Melrose Park, Ill.	5 and 4	C. Stacy,			
159	Martha Stacy, Savannah, Ga.	M. Stacy,	4 and 2			
163	Nancy Harris, Roseau, Minn.	3 and 2			Burns,	
151	Denise King, Miami, Fla.	King,			1 up	
161	Andre Marchand, Luling, La.	5 and 4	King,			
158	Karen Jones, Rockville, Md.	Alderete,	4 and 2			
163	Loretta Alderete, Rancho Mirage, Calif.	2 and 1		Lofland,		
156	Sharon Hadley, Eugene, Ore.	Ellis,		1 up		
162	Joan Ellis, Tampa, Fla.	4 and 3	Lofland,			
159	Lucy Lofland, Newton, N.C.	Lofland,	2 and 1			
164	Julie Oppie, Arlington, Texas	6 and 4				
145	Rae Rothfelder, Ft. Worth, Texas	Rothfelder,				
160	Denise Bratzler, Carson City, Nev.	4 and 3				
156	Viveca Vandergriff, Arlington, Texas	Pacillo,	Pacillo,			
162	Joanne Pacillo, Torrance, Calif.	5 and 3	4 and 3			
152	Penny Hammel, Decatur, Ill.	Hammel,		Hammel,		
161	Jane Abood, Bethesda, Md.	5 and 4		5 and 4		
158	Caroline Gowan, Greenville, S.C.	Gowan,	Hammel,			
163	Susan Davis, Arden Hills, Minn.	4 and 2	4 and 3		Hammel,	
150	Sharon Barrett, Spring Valley, Calif.	Barrett,			1 up	
161	Debra Greiner, Hibbing, Minn.	3 and 2	Barrett,			
158	Kris Hanson, Granite Falls, Minn.	Vendetti,	5 and 4			
163	Kathy Vendetti, Hopedale, Mass.	3 and 1		Barrett,		
155	Charlotte McGinnis, Huntington, W.Va.	Quintana		3 and 2		
161	Graciela Quintana, Caracas, Venezuela	4 and 2	Schreyer,			
159	Cynthia Schreyer, Peach Tree City, Ga.	Schreyer,	4 and 2			
164	Kathy Budai, Glendale, Ariz.	4 and 2				Hammel,
147	Kelly Merten, Phoenix, Ariz.	Brock,				2 and 1
160	Lori Brock, Dallas, Texas	4 and 2	Brock,			
157	Laurie Rinker, Stuart, Fla.	Rinker,	1 up			
162	Susan Yantis, San Antonio, Texas	1 up		Jordan,		
154	Holley Morris, Golden, Colo.	Morris,		3 and 2		
161	Laurie Brower, Orange, Calif.	7 and 6	Jordan,			
159	Diane Dickman, Modesto, Calif.	Jordan,	1 up, 19 holes			
163	Michelle Jordan, Fairfax, Va.	5 and 4			Kingston,	
151	Brenda Corrie, Santo Domingo, Dominican Rep.	Richard,			1 up, 19 holes	
161	Deb Richard, Manhattan, Kans.	1 up	Stiffler,			
158	Lynn Stiffler, Waycross, Ga.	Stiffler,	4 and 3			
163	Jill Prince, Amarillo, Texas	5 and 4		Kingston,		
156	Kathe Kingston, East Point, Ga.	Kingston,		1up		
162	Meredith McQuaig, Battle Creek, Mich.	4 and 3	Kingston,			
159	Mary Hession, Indianapolis, Ind.	Hession,	2 up			
164	Susan Fromuth, Chesterfield, Mo.	1 up				

Penny Hammel, 2 and 1

*Medalist

1980
THIRTY-SECOND GIRLS' JUNIOR CHAMPIONSHIP

Held at Crestview Country Club (North Course), Wichita, Kansas, August 4-9
Yardage—6,129. Par 72. 162 Entries, 150 Starters, 64 Qualifiers.

Qualifying Score	1st Round (18 Holes)	2nd Round (18 Holes)	3rd Round (18 Holes)	4th Round (18 Holes)	Semi-Finals (18 Holes)	Final (18 Holes)
*151	Cynthia Schreyer, Peach Tree City, Ga.	Marsh,				
163	Allison Marsh, Jameston, N.C.	1 up	Hadley,			
159	Sharon Hadley, Eugene, Ore.	Hadley,				
165	Michelle Bell, Melrose, Mass.	5 and 4		Dunlap,		
156	Lise Russell, New City, N.Y.	Dunlap,		4 and 2		
164	Page Dunlap, Sarasota, Fla.	3 and 1	Dunlap,			
161	Hilary Rack, Santa Barbara, Calif.	Marchand,	2 and 1			
167	Andre Marchand, Luling, La.	1 up, 25 holes			Farr,	
154	Debra Richard, Manhattan, Kans.	Shipman,			3 and 2	
163	Kim Shipman, Dallas, Texas	3 and 2	Shipman,			
160	Christine Dristy, Annadale, Va.	Dristy,	5 and 4			
166	Amy Dover, Jasper, Texas	1 up, 21 holes		Farr,		
157	Sherri Steinhauer, Madison, Wis.	Farr,		8 and 6		
164	Heather Farr, Phoenix, Ariz.	1 up, 19 holes	Farr,			Rinker, 1 up
161	Lisa Christie, Northfield, Minn.	Christie,	7 and 5			
167	Beth Ehlert, Austin, Texas	2 and 1				
153	Laurie Rinker, Stuart, Fla.	Rinker,				
163	Flori Prono, Northridge, Calif.	8 and 7	Rinker,			
160	Michelle Berteotti, Pittsburgh, Pa.	Bradley,	5 and 3			
166	Lisa Bradley, Emporia, Kans.	5 and 3		Rinker,		
157	Lori Brock, Dallas, Texas	Billek,		8 and 7		
164	Susan Billek, Oldsmar, Fla.	4 and 2	Atkins,			
161	Angela Atkins, Missouri City, Texas	Atkins,	2 and 1			
167	Deirdre Anderson, Baltimore, Md.	3 and 2			Rinker	
155	Theresa Schreck, Spokane, Wash.	Schreck,			3 and 1	Lauri Rinker, 5 and 4
163	Joanne Pacillo, Torrance, Calif.	3 and 2	Mockett			
160	Martha Foyer, Carmel, Ind.	Mockett,	2 and 1			
166	Nancy Mockett, Newport, Calif.	1 up		Mockett,		
158	Jamie DeWeese, Rochester, N.Y.	Okazaki,		7 and 6		
165	Terri Okazaki, Gardena, Calif.	1 up	Okazaki,			
162	Jill Prince, Amarillo, Texas	Fuertges,	4 and 2			
167	Kathryn Fuertges, Hays, Kans.	1 up, 19 holes				
152	Jody Rosenthal, Edina, Minn.	Rosenthal				
163	Elizabeth Smart, Shawnee Mission, Kans.	2 up	Cornelius,		Hathaway, 1 up, 22 holes	
159	Kay Cornelius, Scottsdale, Ariz	Cornelius,	1 up, 19 holes			
165	Laurie Brower, Villa Park, Calif.	1 up, 19 holes		Skalicky,		
156	Kelly Skalicky, Avon, Minn.	Skalicky,		2 and 1		
164	Cathy Mockett, Newport Beach, Calif.	1 up	Skalicky,			
161	Susan Fromuth, Chesterfield, Mo.	Fromuth,	5 and 3			
167	Diane Nixon, Rochester, N.Y.	6 and 4				
154	Viveca Vandergriff, Arlington, Texas	Vandergriff,				
163	Sara Timms, Spartanburg, S.C.	7 and 6	Hathaway,			
160	Jacqueline Nicoletti, San Diego, Calif.	Hathaway,	2 and 1			Akers, 3 and 1
166	Edithe Hathaway, Oceanside, Calif.	1 up, 21 holes		Hathaway,		
158	Susan Thompson, Garden Grove, Calif.	Thompson,		4 and 3		
164	Brenda Corrie, Santo Domingo, Dominican Rep.	3 and 1				
162	Pamela Meany, Holbrook, Mass.	Meany,	3 and 2			
167	Cathy Hicks, Safford, Ariz.	5 and 3				
153	Jenny Lidback, Baton Rouge, La.	Andreoli,				
163	Cara Andreoli, Wethersfield, Conn.	1 up, 19 holes	Morris			
160	Holley Morris, Golden, Colo.	Morris,	3 and 2			
166	Denise King, Miami, Fla.	3 and 2		Morris,		
157	Lisa Stanley, Melbourne, Fla.	Bridge,		1 up, 19 holes		
164	Lynda Bridge, Hollister, Calif.	4 and 3	Bridge,			
161	Kandi Kessler, Charlottesville, Va.	Kessler,	2 and 1			
167	Carey Ruffer, Conroe, Texas	5 and 4				
156	Kathy Kostas, Palmdale, Calif.	Drinnon,				
163	Juanita Drinnon, Chattanooga, Tenn.	1 up	Towles,		Akers,	
161	Meredith McCuaig, Battle Creek, Mich.	Towles,	3 and 2		1 up	
167	Tammy Towles, Titusville, Fla.	2 and 1		Akers,		
159	Diane Gioia, St. Louis, Mo.	Akers,		2 and 1		
165	Libby Akers, French Lick, Ind.	4 and 3	Akers,			
162	Rita Moore, Dallas, Texas	Moore,	2 and 1			
168	Valerie Faulker, Jackson, N.J.	2 and 1				

*Medalist

SENIOR AMATEUR CHAMPIONSHIP

CHAMPIONSHIP TROPHY

Presented in September, 1955

by Frederick L. Dold

Member of the United States Golf Association Executive Committee 1950-54

HISTORY

1960–Michael Cestone, age 55, of Montclair, N.J., competed in his first Senior Amateur Championship at Oyster Harbors Club, Osterville, Mass., and finished as winner. He defeated David Rose, 56, Cleveland, Ohio, on the 20th hole of the final match. Other semi-finalists were W.B. McConnell, Kennett Square, Pa., and Edward E. Lowery, San Francisco, Calif. Weather played a large part in the Championship. Steady rain fell on the day scheduled for the qualifying and continued into the following day, causing cancellation of play both days. The USGA Senior Championship Committee was forced to extend the Championship one day, to Sunday, and to schedule two match rounds on Saturday. The Committee also decided to permit the use of automotive transportation on the double-round day. Defending Champion J. Clark Espie, Jr., Indianapolis, Ind., withdrew because carts were to be permitted in the emergency, contrary to the published conditions of the tournament. The medalist was S.S. Rockey, of Los Angeles, who shot 74. A record 517 entered the Championship–126 more than the previous high.

1961–Dexter H. Daniels, 56, of Winter Haven, Fla., won the Senior Amateur Championship on his first attempt. He defeated Col. William K. Lanman, Jr., also 56, of Golf, Ill., in the final match by 2 and 1. The finalists, after five days of play under serene weather conditions at the Southern Hills Country Club, Tulsa, Okla., were confronted with a wind that blew in gusts up to 35 miles per hour. Daniels, 2 up after nine holes, maintained that lead through the 16th and ended the match by halving the 17th. Joseph Morrill, Jr., of Great Barrington, Mass., was the medalist at the site of the Championship with a 74, three over par. Seven men who advanced to the quarter-final round of the 1960 Senior Amateur Championship competed at Southern Hills but only Richard H. Guelich, of Hamburg, N.Y., was able to equal his 1960 performance. Guelich lost to Lanman in a semi-final match.

1962–Merrill L. Carlsmith, a 56-year-old Hawaii attorney, won the eighth Senior Amateur Championship by defeating Willis H. Blakely, Portland, Ore., by 4 and 2 in the final match at the Evanston Golf Club, Skokie, Ill. Carlsmith saved his strongest efforts for the last two matches. He was even par against Michael Cestone, the 1960 Champion, through 17 holes of their semi-final, and only one over par in the final against Blakely, the Oregon State and Pacific Northwest Senior Champion. The field, considered by many to be the strongest ever for this event, produced 31 scores of 77 or better in the qualifying round. Previously, the lowest score required to qualify had been 78. Dexter H. Daniels, the defending Champion, was automatically awarded the 32nd qualifying berth. He lost in the first round to David E. Rose, the 1960 runnerup. Three men playing in the event for the first time shared the qualifying medal with scores of 72–James M. Johnson, LaDue, Mo.; William S. Terrell, Charlotte, N.C., and Henry L. Robison, Albuquerque, N.M. There was a record entry of 525.

1963–Merrill L. Carlsmith, became the first to defend the title successfully. He defeated William D. Higgins, of San Francisco, by 3 and 2 at the Sea Island Golf Club, Sea Island, Ga. This was the third appearance in the Championship for the 57-year-old Hilo attorney and the first for Higgins, also 57. Egon F. Quittner, Jenkintown, Pa., defeated Maurice R. Smith, Charlotte, N.C., in the first round after nine extra holes, an overtime record for the Championship by three holes. A new all-match play format was introduced. The original entry of 494 was reduced by Sectional Qualifying to 128 for the Championship proper. On Friday, the only day of two rounds, players were permitted to use automotive transportation for the first time under original conditions of a USGA Championship.

1964–William D. Higgins, 58, of San Francisco, won the Senior Amateur Championship at the Waverley Country Club, Portland, Ore., after losing in the final round in 1963. Higgins birdied the last two holes to win his semi-final match 1 up from David Goldman, Sr., of Dallas. He then beat Edward Murphy, a member of the host club, by 2 and 1 in the final. Merrill L. Carlsmith, of Hilo, Hawaii, was seeking an unprecedented third straight Championship but he was defeated in the second round by Ralph Swan, of Vancouver, Wash., by 3 and 2. The format was altered to 36 holes of qualifying at the site to determine 32 players for match play. A.L. (Jim) Miller, 71, turned in a remarkable qualifying performance to earn the medal with scores of 74-76–150.

1965–Robert B. Kiersky, 57, of Oakmont, Pa., won the 1965 Championship at the Fox Chapel Golf Club, Pittsburgh, by defeating George C. Beechler, Prineville, Ore., on the 19th hole. On the extra hole, 405 yards long, Kiersky two-putted for his par, but Beechler was short with his second and took three to get down. Two former Champions lost in the semi-final round. Merrill L. Carlsmith, winner in 1962 and 1963, lost to Beechler; William D. Higgins, San Francisco, the 1964 Champion, was ousted by Kiersky. Curtis Person, Sr., of Memphis, Tenn., won the medal with 149.

1966–For the second consecutive year George C. Beechler reached the final of the Senior Amateur Championship and met defeat. Dexter H. Daniels, of Winter Haven, Fla., defeated Beechler, 1 up, at the Tucson National Golf Club, Tucson, Ariz. Robert B. Kiersky, of Delray Beach, Fla., the defending Champion, lost in the third round to Merrill L. Carlsmith, the Champion in 1962 and 1963. Two former Amateur Champions played: Jack Westland, the 1952 Amateur Champion from Pebble Beach, Calif., lost in the first round to Curtis Person, Sr., of Memphis, and Richard D. Chapman, of Oyster Harbors, Mass., was defeated in the third round by David Goldman, Sr., of Dallas. Person was medalist with 143.

1967–Raymond Palmer, 55, of Lincoln Park, Mich., won the Championship the first year he was eligible. In the final he defeated Walter D. Bronson, of Chicago, 3 and 2, at the Shinnecock Hills Golf Club, Southampton, N.Y. Dexter H. Daniels, of Winter Haven Fla., the defending Champion, failed to qualify for match play. Palmer, J. Wolcott Brown, of Sea Girt, N.J., and David Goldman, Sr., of Dallas, tied for medalist with 153.

1968–Curtis Person, Sr., 58, of Memphis, Tenn., barely qualified for match play, then won the Championship. He defeated Ben Goodes, 55, of Reidsville, Tenn., 2 and 1, in the final. Person escaped a sudden-death playoff for a qualifying position by one stroke. He won his first match in 20 holes, and his next three by 1 up. Person was 1 down after 13 holes against Goodes, won the 14th with a birdie, and the 15th and 17th with pars. John Tullio, Aurora, Ohio, was qualifying medalist with 146. The entry of 674 set a record.

1969–Curtis Person Sr., of Memphis, Tenn., became the second to defend the title successfully when he defeated David Goldman, Sr., of Dallas 1 up, at the Wichita Country Club, Wichita, Kans. Merrill Carlsmith, of Hilo, Hawaii, won successive Championships in 1962-63. For the second consecutive year Person barely qualified for the match play phase. His 36-hole score of 154 was one stroke under the cutoff. The par-3 holes made the difference in the final match; Person won three of the four with pars. The match was even after 10 holes, then Person won the par-3 11th when Goldman missed the green. The halved the remainder of the holes with Person holing a 10-foot putt for par on the 18th. Goldman was medalist with 146.

1970—Gene Andrews, 57, of Hacienda Heights, Calif., won the Senior Amateur Championship by defeating James Ferrie, of Indian Wells, Calif., 1 up at the California Golf Club of San Francisco, South San Francisco, Calif. Andrews was a former Amateur Public Links Champion and a former member of the Walker Cup Team. He was the first Senior Amateur Champion ever to have won another USGA Championship and was the second former Walker Cup player to have done so. Frederick J. Wright, Jr., the 1956 Champion, was a member of the 1923 Walker Cup Team; Andrews was on the 1961 Team. Andrews won two extra hole matches, defeating Robert E. Cochran, of Normandy, Mo., in 21 holes, and Ernest Pieper, Jr., of San Jose, Calif., in 19. He won the final by sinking a 27-foot putt on the final hole. Curtis Person, Sr., Champion in 1968 and 1969, lost in the first round to Truman Connell, of Delray Beach, Fla. Bruce N. McCormick, of San Gabriel, Calif., was medalist with 147. The entry of 683 was a record.

1971–The 1971 Championship drew what was probably the best field in the history of the Senior Amateur, and it was won by Tom Draper, 57, of Troy, Mich. Draper defeated Ernest Pieper, Jr., of San Juan Bautista, Calif., 3 and 1, in the final at the Sunnybrook Golf Club, Plymouth Meeting, Pa. Among players competing for the first time were William Hyndman, III., who had been runnerup in the British Amateur in 1969 and 1970. Hyndman was eliminated by Pieper in the semi-final round. Draper was 1 up on Pieper after playing fine bunker shots on holes 9, 13, and 14, birdied the 152-yard 15th with a tee shot 30 inches from the hole to go 2 up, and hit a 2-iron 15 feet from the hole on the 183-yard 17th to win another hole and end the match. Draper also defeated Bob Cochran, of St. Louis, a former Walker Cup player and medalist at 148, and Truman Connell, of Boynton Beach, Fla., the current American Seniors Champion. Draper also defeated William F. Colm, of Pebble Beach, Calif., in the semi-final round. Gene Andrews, the 1970 Champion, did not defend.

1972–Lewis W. Oehmig, 56, of Lookout Mountain, Tenn., won the Senior Amateur Championship at the Sharon Golf Club, Sharon Center, Ohio, in his initial attempt, beating Ernest Pieper, San Juan Bautista, Calif., on the 20th hole. This was the second successive year that Pieper was runnerup. Tom Draper, the defending Champion, failed to qualify for match play. Three of Oehmig's victories were extra hole matches, and in each he had to make a sizable putt or hit his approach shot close to the hole. He defeated Edward L. Meister, Jr., Willoughby, Ohio, on the 19th hole with a birdie; Bill Hyndman, Huntingdon Valley, Pa., on the 20th hole by making an 18-foot putt, and Pieper on the 20th hole of the final round after squaring the match on the 18th with a 30-foot birdie putt. He also beat Timothy Holland, Wenham, Mass., 3 and 2, in the first round, and Curtis Person, Memphis, Tenn., 2 and 1, in the quarter-finals. Person, Senior Champion in 1968 and 1969, played an impeccable round against Oehmig, but caught him on a day when Oehmig shot 15 pars and two birdies. Hyndman was the medalist with 71-74-145. In his match with Oehmig, Hyndman was two up after nine holes and was still one up after 17. On the 18th Oehmig hit his approach shot four feet from the flagstick and made his birdie, sending the match into extra holes. On the 20th he holed an 18-footer to beat Hyndman. Senior amateur golf continues to burgeon, with the result that there were 617 entries and another strong field.

1973—Bill Hyndman, of Huntingdon Valley, Pa., won the Senior Amateur Championship at the Onwentsia Club, Lake Forest, Ill., defeating Harry Welch, of Salisbury, N. C., 3 and 2. This victory marked the end of a long quest for Hyndman; for more than 20 years he had been one of the country's leading amateurs, but he had never won a national Championship. He had been runnerup in the 1955 U. S. Amateur and had been the finalist in the British Amateur Championships of 1959-69-70. He had also reached the semi-finals in the Senior Championship, 1971 and 1972. The defending Champion, Lew Oehmig, of Lookout Mountain, Tenn., was eliminated in the first round. Hyndman defeated Bill Trepsas, Stoughton, Mass., 2 and 1 in his first match, then Ernest Pieper, San Juan Bautista, Calif., by the same margin in his second round. Two down to Pieper after nine holes, Hyndman scored four birdies in eight holes for a four-under par 31 to win the match. Pieper was even with par on the second nine. In the final round against Welch, Hyndman won the first hole and was never behind. Hyndman either won or saved holes on three occasions by brilliant recoveries from greenside bunkers. It should be noted that Hyndman and Welch played their match—16 holes—in only two hours and 20 minutes. Co-medalists were the new Champion and Sam Friedman, of Fort Walton Beach, Fla., with scores of 73-74—147. A total of 633 entered the Championship.

1974—In his first year of eligibility, Dale Morey, of High Point, N. C., defeated Lew Oehmig, the 1972 Champion from Lookout Mountain, Tenn., 4 and 2 in the final round at the Harbour Town Golf Links, Hilton Head Island, S. C. The defending Champion, Bill Hyndman, of Huntingdon Valley, Pa., was eliminated by Oehmig in the third round, 1 up. Morey was runnerup to Gene Littler in the 1953 Amateur Championship, but he had never won a national Championship. On his way to the final he defeated Ed Meister, of Willoughby, Ohio, 6 and 5; Wally Sezna, West Chester, Pa., 4 and 3; John Humm, Rockville Centre, N. Y., 2 up, and Ed Tutwiler, of Indianapolis, Ind., 3 and 2 in the semi-final round. Tutwiler was medalist in the 36-hole qualifying with 144, two over par. Morey won four of the first five holes in the final round but Oehmig rallied and was only 1 down playing the 14th when he became involved in one of a series of Rules decisions that were made during the Championship; in all, Oehmig was party to three such incidents. His tee shot on the 152-yard, par-3 hole came to rest within the confines of a water hazard. Electing to play the ball, because he was not entitled to relief without penalty, Oehmig took his stance and then soled his club. The Referee had no choice but to invoke Rule 33-1b and advise Oehmig that he had lost the hole. Morey won the 15th hole to go 3 up with three to play. Oehmig conceded the 16th hole and the match to Morey. The entry of 743 set a new record.

1975—William F. Colm became the third Californian to win a USGA Championship during 1975. He defeated fellow-Californian Stephen Stimac, 4 and 3, in the final of the Senior Amateur Championship at the Carmel Valley Golf and Country Club, Carmel, Calif. Players from 37 states competed for the Championship, but when it was over the winner was the man who traveled the shortest distance—nine miles. Colm lives in Pebble Beach. He had been a semi-finalist in 1971, and in 1970, 1972, and 1973 he lost in the first round. Stimac, of Walnut Creek, had never advanced beyond the second round before, but he kept winning his matches, including his quarter-final round against former Walker Cupper Bob Cochran, which went 19 holes. It was a week of upsets; two former Champions—Dale Morey, of High Point, N. C., and Lew Oehmig, from Lookout Mountain, Tenn., were eliminated in the first round. William Hyndman, III, of Huntingdon Valley, Pa., who won the Championship in 1973, was defeated in the second round, after defeating Oehmig in the first. Hyndman did set a record, however; he was medalist for the third time, shooting 73-70—143. His 143 tied the 36-hole qualifying record score, set by Curtis Person, Sr., in 1966. In the final round, Colm was 4-up after nine holes, as Stimac had six bogies and couldn't win a hole, even when Colm bogied three times. The first four holes of the home nine were halved in par, then Stimac won his first hole with a par on the short 14th to stand three down with four to play. Colm, however, closed the match out on the next hole, striking a six-iron to within five feet of the cup and holing the putt for a birdie-3 on the 363-yard hole. There were 737 entries.

1976—Lewis W. Oehmig, 60, of Lookout Mountain, Tenn., who had won the Tennessee Amateur in 1937 at 21, won the Senior Amateur Championship for the second time. He defeated John Richardson, 55, of Laguna Niguel, Calif., 4 and 3 in the final round at the Cherry Hills Country Club, Englewood, Colo. Oehmig won previously in 1972. The Championship was played in erratic weather—showers and temperatures in the 50s. Oehmig and Dale Morey, High Point, N. C., were the only former Champions among the 32 who qualified for match play. Richardson eliminated Morey in the second round. Richardson also defeated Ed Tutwiler, of Indianapolis, the medalist. In the final round, Richardson, 1961 California Amateur Champion, consistently outdrove Oehmig, but he could not match Oehmig's short game. In the 15 holes played, Oehmig had five conceded birdies and lost only two holes. He three-putted both. On the first hole Richardson drove into a lateral water hazard and conceded a birdie to Oehmig. Holes two and three were halved, then Richardson drew even when Oehmig three-putted the fourth green. Oehmig then won four holes in succession to go 4-up. Oehmig three-putted again, on the 10th, to stand 3-up. Both players birdied the 11th and halved the 12th, 13th and 14th with pars. The match ended on the 15th, where Oehmig put his tee shot within 12 feet of the hole and Richardson hit into a bunker. The entry reached 833, breaking the record 743 set in 1974.

1977—Dale Morey, of High Point, N. C., became the fifth man to win a second Senior Amateur Championship when he defeated Lewis W. Oehmig, the defending Champion, 4 and 3, in the final round at the Salem Country Club, Peabody, Mass. Oehmig was from Lookout Mountain, Tenn. It was the second time that Morey defeated Oehmig in the final. In 1974 Morey won 4 and 2. Morey was also medalist with 72-71—143, equalling the record low score for the qualifying round. Oehmig was in the final for the fourth time, a record. He also won twice, in 1972 and 1976. Three of the four semi-finalists were former Champions. Oehmig defeated Bill Hyndman, the 1973 Champion, in 19 holes in a semi-final match after being 3-down. In the other semi-final, Morey defeated Harry Welch, of Salisbury, N. C., 5 and 4. Morey won three of the first five holes of the final match, and was 2 up after eight. On the ninth hole, Oehmig reached the green in regulation, but Morey was 30 yards short. Morey's approach shot hit the flagstick, however, and dropped alongside the hole. He made his par. Oehmig three-putted to go 3 down with nine holes to play. He could not recover. The entry of 797 was short of the record 833 established the previous year.

1978—In an all-Texas final, Keith K. Compton, of Marble Falls, defeated John Kline, of Houston, 1 up, to win the Senior Amateur Championship at the Pine Tree Golf Club, in Delray Beach, Fla. Both men were retired Air Force generals and close friends. The medalist was William Stewart, of Springfield, Mo., who had a 143 total, one under par, to equal the 36-hole record for lowest qualifying score in this event. Stewart lost in the second round to Dick Hopwood, 1 up. In the semi-final round, Kline defeated Ed Tutwiler on the 23rd hole in the longest match of the week. Compton was two under par and eliminated defending Champion Dale Morey, 4 and 3, in the other semi-final match. In the final, Compton and Kline were even coming to the final hole, a par 4. Both players reached the green in two. Kline three-putted from 30 feet. Compton was 40 feet away, but two-putted for a winning par. Two other former Champions, William Hyndman, III, and Lewis W. Oehmig, qualified for the 32-player match play draw. Hyndman lost to Compton in the third round, 3 and 2. Oehmig lost to Richard Remsen in the second round, 1 up. William C. Campbell, the 1964 Amateur Champion, made his debut in senior golf. However, he was eliminated by Oehmig in the first round, 1 up. A record 930 entries were received, exceeding the 833 who entered in 1976.

1979—William C. Campbell, 56, of Huntington, W. Va., the 1964 Amateur Champion, won the Senior Amateur Championship by defeating Lewis Oehmig, of Lookout Mountain, Tenn., 2 and 1, in the final at the Chicago Golf Club, Wheaton, Ill. Campbell became the only golfer to have won both the Amateur and Senior Amateur titles. Oehmig, twice Senior Amateur Champion, was playing in the final match for the fifth time. Campbell and Dale Morey, of High Point, N. C., were co-medalists with scores of 143, equalling the 36-hole record held previously by four other golfers. Morey lost in the second round, 3 and 2, to Allan Sussel. Campbell eliminated Oren Shiro, 2 and 1; Dr. Edgar Updegraff, 6 and 5; shot 69 in a 1-up quarter-final victory over Les Fowler; and defeated Robert Willits in the semi-finals, 8 and 6. Oehmig defeated Dick Lytle, 5 and 4; Kenneth Weavil, 4 and 3; Wally Sezna, 4 and 3; and Sussel, 1 up, in the semi-finals. In the final, Oehmig won the first hole with a par and Campbell the second hole with a birdie. The match remained even until the ninth hole. Campbell went 1 up with a par to Oehmig's double-bogey. On the 17th, Oehmig was still 1 down with two to play. He was in good position off the tee, but Campbell drove his ball into a fairway bunker. Campbell could pitch out only 80 yards, but Oehmig's shot carried over the green. He chipped well past the hole and three-putted for a double-bogey 6. Campbell played his third shot onto the green and two-putted for a 5 to win the Championship. The Chicago Golf Club, one of the five USGA Charter Member Clubs, was the host to its 10th USGA national or international competition. The Championship received a record of 1,023 entries, exceeding the previous high of 930 in 1978.

1980—William C. Campbell, 57, of Huntington, West Virginia, won his second consecutive Senior Amateur Championship by scoring a 3 and 2 victory over Keith K. Compton, 64, of San Antonio, Texas, the 1978 champion. The event was held on the Cascades Course of the Virginia Hot Springs Golf & Tennis Club, in Hot Springs, Virginia. Campbell joined Merrill Carlsmith (1962-63) and Curtis Person (1968-69) as the only players to successfully defend the Senior Amateur title. For the second consecutive year, Campbell also was medalist, with a 36 hole score of 147, three over par. Campbell was three under par in his first round match, three over par in the second round and one over par in the quarter-finals. In the semi-finals, his match with Dr. Ed Updegraff was even through nine holes. Both players birdied the 12th hole, a par 5, to remain even. Campbell then birdied the 13th from 10 feet, the 15th from 12 feet, and closed out the match with a six-foot putt for a birdie at the 16th. Campbell was two over par. Campbell won three of the first four holes of the final match and was never caught. The USGA received 1,000 entries, short of the record 1,023 set in 1979.

SENIOR AMATEUR CHAMPIONSHIP

DATE	WINNER, RUNNER-UP	SCORE	SITE	ENTRY
1960 (Sept.)	Michael Cestone d. David Rose	1 up, 20 hls.	Oyster Harbors C., Osterville, Mass. Medalist–74: S. S. Rockey	517
1961 (Sept.)	Dexter H. Daniels d. Col. William K. Lanman, Jr.	2 & 1	Southern Hills C.C., Tulsa, Okla. Medalist–74: Joseph Morrill, Jr.	481
1962 (Sept.)	Merrill L. Carlsmith d. Willis H. Blakely	4 & 2	Evanston G.C., Skokie, Ill. Co-Medalists–72: James M. Johnson Henry L. Robison William S. Terrell	525
1963 (Oct.)	Merrill L. Carlsmith d. William D. Higgins	3 & 2	Sea Island G.C., Sea Island, Ga. All Match Play	494
1964 (Oct.)	William D. Higgins d. Edward Murphy	2 & 1	Waverley C.C., Portland, Ore. Medalist–150: A. L. (Jim) Miller	357
1965 (Oct.)	Robert B. Kiersky d. George Beechler	1 up, 19 hls.	Fox Chapel G.C., Pittsburgh, Pa. Medalist–149: Curtis Person, Sr.	448
1966 (Sept.- Oct.)	Dexter H. Daniels d. George Beechler	1 up	Tucson National G.C., Tucson, Ariz. Medalist—†† 143: Curtis Person, Sr.	449
1967 (Sept.)	Ray Palmer d. Walter D. Bronson	3 & 2	Shinnecock Hills G.C., Southampton, N.Y. Co-Medalists–153: J. Wolcott Brown David Goldman Ray Palmer	563
1968 (Sept.)	Curtis Person, Sr. d. Ben Goodes	2 & 1	Atlanta C.C., Atlanta, Ga. Medalist–146: John C. Tullio	674
1969 (Sept.)	Curtis Person, Sr. d. David Goldman	1 up	Wichita C.C., Wichita, Kans. Medalist–146: David Goldman	576
1970 (Sept.)	Gene Andrews d. James Ferrie	1 up	California G.C. of San Francisco, South San Francisco, Calif. Medalist–147: Bruce McCormick	683
1971 (Sept.)	Tom Draper d. Ernest Pieper, Jr.	3 & 1	Sunnybrook G.C., Plymouth Meeting, Pa. Medalist–148: Robert E. Cochran	661
1972 (Sept.)	Lewis W. Oehmig d. Ernest Pieper, Jr.	1 up, 20 holes	Sharon G. C., Sharon Center, Ohio Medalist—145: William Hyndman, III	617
1973 (Sept.)	William Hyndman, III d. Harry Welch	3 & 2	Onwentsia Club, Lake Forest, Ill. Co-Medalists—147: Sam Friedman William Hyndman, III	633
1974 (Sept.)	Dale Morey d. Lewis W. Oehmig	4 & 2	Harbour Town G. L., Hilton Head Island, S. C. Medalist—144: Ed Tutwiler	743
1975 (Sept.)	William F. Colm d. Stephen Stimac	4 & 3	Carmel Valley G. & C. C., Carmel, Calif. Medalist—††143: William Hyndman, III	737
1976 (Sept.)	Lewis W. Oehmig d. John Richardson	4 & 3	Cherry Hills C. C., Englewood, Colo. Medalist—145: Ed Tutwiler	833
1977 (Sept.)	Dale Morey d. Lewis W. Oehmig	4 & 3	Salem C. C., Peabody Mass. Medalist—§143: Dale Morey	789
1978 (Oct.)	Keith K. Compton d. John Kline	1 up	Pine Tree G. C., Delray Beach, Fla. Medalist—§143: William Stewart	930
1979 (Sept.)	William C. Campbell d. Lewis W. Oehmig	2 & 1	Chicago G. C., Wheaton, Ill. Co-Medalists—§143 Dale Morey William C. Campbell	§1,023

Senior Amateur Championship (Continued)

DATE	WINNER, RUNNER-UP	SCORE	SITE	ENTRY
1980 (Sept.)	William C. Campbell d. Keith K. Compton	3 & 2	Virginia Hot Springs G.&T.C. (Cascades Course), Hot Springs, Va. Medalist—147: William C. Campbell	1,000

Record qualifying score, 18 holes, 71, by J. Clark Espie, in 1958.
†† Record qualifying score, 36 holes.
§ Record Entry.

SENIOR and SENIOR WOMEN'S CHAMPIONS

LEWIS W. OEHMIG
1972-76

CAROLYN CUDONE
1968-69-70-71-72

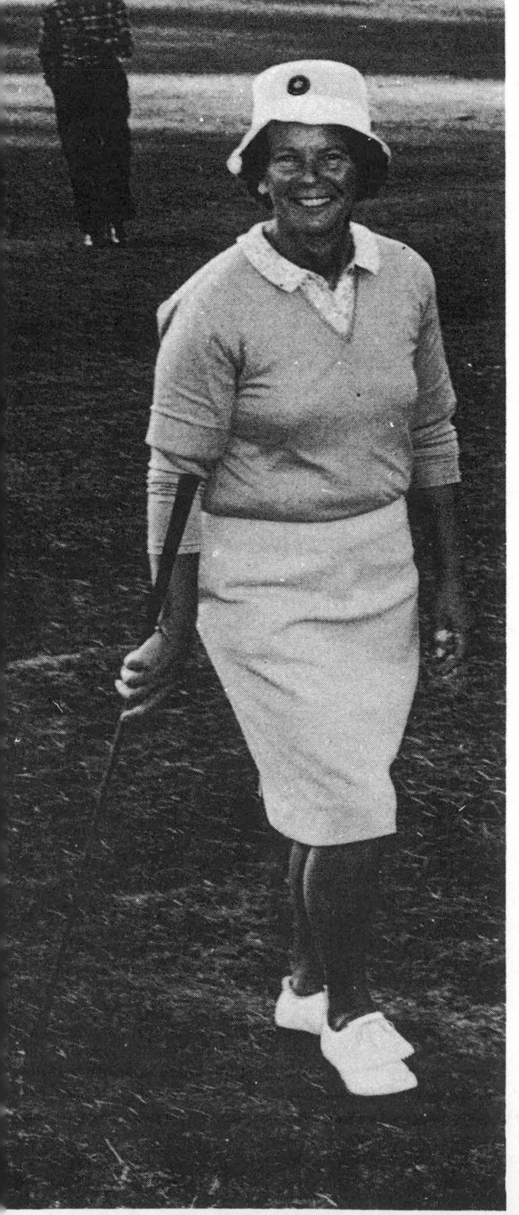

DALE MOREY
1974-77

1960
SIXTH SENIOR AMATEUR CHAMPIONSHIP

Held at the Oyster Harbors Club, Osterville, Mass., September 19-25.
Yardage 6,597. Par 72. **517 Entries,** 120 Sectional Qualifiers, 120 Starters.

Qualifying Score	1st Round (18 Holes)	2nd Round (18 Holes)	3rd Round (18 Holes)	Semi-Finals (18 Holes)	Final (18 Holes)	
78	Willard B. McConnell, Kennett Square, Pa.	McConnell, 7 and 5	McConnell, 2 and 1	McConnell, 5 and 3	Cestone, 2 and 1	Michael Cestone, 1 up, 20 holes
81	Loyal R. Safford, Cohassett, Mass.					
82	George Haggarty, C.C. of Detroit, Mich.	Molinari, 3 and 2				
77	James J. Molinari, Harding Park, Calif.					
82	Karl Krupitza, En-Joie, N.Y.	Krupitza, 3 and 2	Pope, 3 and 2			
78	A.L. (Jim) Miller, Bob O'Link, Ill.					
82	Charles T. Robinson, Millbrook, Conn.	Pope, 5 and 3				
77	John D. Pope, Sr., Wayland, Mass.					
78	Dr. John C. Mercer, Oak Hill, Mass.	Mercer, 1 up, 19 hls.	Brown, 3 and 2	Cestone, 1 up, 21 hls.		
77	Jesse A. Mason, New Haven, Conn.					
79	J. Wolcott Brown, Manasquan River, N.J.	Brown, 2 and 1				
82	John W. McGuire, Highland, Ind.					
81	Edward M. Smith, Upper Montclair, N.J.	Cestone, 7 and 6	Cestone, 6 and 5			
77	Michael Cestone, Forsgate, N.J.					
79	Ralph L. Sawyer, Marlboro, Mass.	McAllister, 1 up, 19 hls.				
80	Col. C.D. McAllister, C.C. of Orlando, Fla.					
80	Herman C. Wilke, Wethersfield, Conn.	Wilke, 4 and 3	Guelich, 2 and 1	Rose, 1 up, 20 hls.	Rose, 2 up	
77	George E. Hale, University, N.M.					
82	Richard H. Guelich, Jr., Wanakah, N.Y.	Guelich, 3 and 1				
81	James H. Ackerman, Springdale, N.J.					
74	*S.S. Rockey, Los Angeles, Calif.	Rockey, 5 and 4	Rose, 4 and 3			
80	Calvin T. McCarthy, Salem, Mass.					
80	Thomas C. Robbins, Pinehurst, N.C.	Rose, 6 and 4				
78	David E. Rose, Beechmont, Ohio					
78	Frank D. Ross, Wampanoag, Conn.	Ross, 2 up	McAlvin, 2 and 1	Lowery, 2 and 1		
78	William K. Lanman, Jr., Glen View, Ill.					
82	Roy L. Corey, Drumlins, N.Y.	McAlvin, 3 and 1				
82	James H. McAlvin, Onwentsia, Ill.					
82	John W. Roberts, Bob O'Link, Ill.	Lowery, 3 and 1	Lowery, 3 and 2			
75	Edward E. Lowery, California, Calif.					
78	Egon F. Quittner, Old York Road, Pa.	Ledbetter, 4 and 3				
80	John N. Ledbetter, Jr., Scarsdale, N.Y.					

*Medalist
The first word after the player's name is the name of the player's club.

1961
SEVENTH SENIOR AMATEUR CHAMPIONSHIP

Held at the Southern Hills Country Club, Tulsa, Okla., October 2-7. Yardage—6,476. Par 71. 481 Entries, 119 Sectional Qualifiers, 120 Starters.

Qualifying Score	1st Round (18 Holes)	2nd Round (18 Holes)	3rd Round (18 Holes)	Semi-Finals (18 Holes)	Final Round (18 Holes)	
80	Bob Tobin, Shore View, N.Y.	Guelich, 1 up, 21 hls.				
80	Richard H. Guelich, Jr., Wanakah, N.Y.		Guelich, 2 and 1			
75	John J. Driver, Atlas Valley, Mich.	Driver, 2 and 1				
79	Willis H. Blakely, Waverley, Ore.			Guelich, 1 up		
81	Robert E. Bilbrough, Milburn, Kans.	Payseur, 5 and 4				
79	Ted B. Payseur, North Shore, Ill.		Payseur, 1 up			
77	Francis Francis, Nassau, Bahamas	Francis, 5 and 4			Lanman, 2 and 1	
82	Egon F. Quittner, Old York Road, Pa.					
80	E.H. Carrington, Mohawk Men's, Okla.	Roberts, 1 up				
79	John W. Roberts, Bob O'Link, Ill.		Roberts, 1 up, 19 hls.			
75	Lewis Lacey, Twin Hills, Okla.	Lacey, 2 up				
80	James H. Ackerman, Springdale, N.J.			Lanman, 1 up, 19 hls.		
DC	Michael Cestone, Forsgate, N.J.	Freydberg, 1 up				Dexter H. Daniels, 2 and 1
79	Herman M. Freydberg, Metropolis, N.Y.		Lanman, 3 and 2			
78	Col. William K. Lanman, Jr., Glen View, Ill.	Lanman, 4 and 3				
82	Floyd M. James, Wampanoag, Conn.					
75	George Dawson, Glen Oak, Ill.	Dawson, 3 and 2				
78	Edward F. Schwartz, Indian Hills, Mo.		Dawson, 6 and 5			
81	James H. McAlvin, Onwentsia, Ill.	McAlvin, 1 up				
81	Archie J. Gonzales, Covington, La.			Dawson, 4 and 3		
77	Dr. John C. Mercer, Oak Hill, Mass.	Mercer, 6 and 5				
81	A.J. Ruffini, Canterbury, Ohio		Carlsmith, 3 and 2			
82	J. Wolcott Brown, Manasquan River, N.J.	Carlsmith, 7 and 6			Daniels, 2 and 1	
78	Merrill L. Carlsmith, Hilo, Hawaii					
79	Dexter H. Daniels, Lake Region, Fla.	Daniels, 1 up, 20 hls.				
80	J. Ripley Greer, Memphis, Tenn.		Daniels, 5 and 3			
80	John M. Winters, Jr., Southern Hills, Okla.	Morrill, 3 and 2				
74	*Joseph Morrill, Jr., Wyantenuck, Mass.			Daniels, 2 and 1		
81	Judd L. Brumley, Biltmore Forest, N.C.	Taylor, 3 and 1				
80	C.C. Taylor, Durban, Natal, South Africa		Taylor, 5 and 4			
81	Clarence P. Kay, Twin Hills, Okla.	Kay, 4 and 3				
79	William J. McGlone, Hiawatha, Minn.					

*Medalist.

DC—Defending Champion, not required to qualify.

The first word after the player's name is the name of player's club, except in the case of a foreign entrant.

1962
EIGHTH SENIOR AMATEUR CHAMPIONSHIP

Held at the Evanston Golf Club, Skokie, Ill., October 1-6.
Yardage—6,414. Par 70. 525 Entries, 120 Starters.

Qualifying Score	1st Round (18 Holes)	2nd Round (18 Holes)	3rd Round (18 Holes)	Semi-Finals (18 Holes)	Final Round (18 Holes)
77	Joseph Morrill, Jr., Wyantenuck, Mass.	Morrill,			
72*	James M. Johnson, Algonquin, Mo.	2 up	Ross,		
76	Frank D. Ross, Wampanoag, Conn.	Ross,	1 up, 19 hls.		
73	P. T. Taylor, Guyan, W. Va.	2 and 1		Carlsmith,	
75	Merrill L. Carlsmith, Hilo, Hawaii	Carlsmith,		1 up	
76	Eugene Brown, Berkshire, Pa.	3 and 2	Carlsmith,		
75	William L. Goodloe, Sr., Valdosta, Ga.	Dawson,	2 and 1		Carlsmith, 3 and 1
73	George Dawson, Glen Oak, Ill.	3 and 2			
76	John J. Driver, Atlas Valley, Mich.	Driver,			
72*	William S. Terrell, Charlotte, N.C.	1 up	McAlvin,		
75	Lewie Lacy, Twin Hills, Okla.	McAlvin,	2 and 1		
75	James H. McAlvin, Onwentsia, Ill.	1 up		Cestone,	
77	Francis Francis, Nassau, Bahamas	Cestone,		3 and 1	
75	Michael Cestone, Forsgate, N.J.	2 and 1	Cestone,		
74	Edward E. Lowery, California, Calif.	Russell,	4 and 3		Merrill L. Carlsmith, 4 and 2
77	Jack Russell, Clearwater, Fla.	3 and 2			
76	H. Gordon Adkins, James River, Va.	Adkins,			
74	Willard B. McConnell, Kennett Square, Pa.	5 and 4	Lanman,		
75	John E. Lehman, Bob O'Link, Ill.	Lanman,	1 up, 21 hls.		
74	Col. William K. Lanman, Jr., Glen View, Ill.	4 and 3		Lanman,	
73	Franklin G. Clement, Onwentsia, Ill.	Clement,		1 up, 22 hls.	
75	Thomas C. Robbins, Pinehurst, N.C.	1 up, 21 hls.	Clement,		
74	David E. Rose, Beechmont, Ohio	Rose,	3 and 2		Blakely, 4 and 3
DC	Dexter Daniels, Lake Region, Fla.	2 and 1			
72*	Henry L. Robison, Albuquerque, N.M.	Robison,			
76	L. W. Ramsey, Westwood, Ind.	3 and 1	Robison,		
73	Dr. Alfred J. Keck, Garden City, N.Y.	James,	2 up		
76	Floyd M. James, Wampanoag, Conn.	3 and 1		Blakely,	
76	George Groote, Medinah, Ill.	Blakely,		1 up, 19 hls.	
77	Willis H. Blakely, Waverley, Ore.	3 and 2	Blakely,		
75	James H. Ackerman, Springdale, N.J.	Guelich,	2 up		
76	Richard H. Guelich, Wanakah, N.Y.	1 up, 19 hls.			

DC—Defending Champion not required to qualify.
*Co-medalists.
The first word after the player's name is the name of player's club, except in the case of a foreign entrant.

1963
NINTH SENIOR AMATEUR CHAMPIONSHIP

Held at the Sea Island Golf Club, Sea Island, Ga., October 7-12.
Yardage–6,532. Par 71. 494 Entries, 128 Qualifiers, 128 Starters.

FINAL ROUND (18 Holes)–Merrill L. Carlsmith defeated William D. Higgins, 3 up and 2 to play.

UPPER HALF

1st Round (18 Holes)	2nd Round (18 Holes)	3rd Round (18 Holes)	4th Round (18 Holes)	5th Round (18 Holes)	Semi-Final (18 Holes)	
Harry P. Franzoni, Rutland, Vt.	Franzoni, 6 and 5					
Marshall J. Wylie, Four Hills, N.M.		Franzoni, 1 up				
Arthur G. Peterson, Oak Hill, Mass.	Peterson, 1 up, 19 hls.					
James M. Johnson, Algonquin, Mo.			McAlvin, 3 and 2			
George E. Edmondson, Palma Ceia, Fla.	McAlvin, 5 and 3					
James H. McAlvin, Onwentsia, Ill.		McAlvin, 1 up				
William N. Smith, Jr., Paradise Valley, Ariz.	Smith, 3 and 1					
A.L. (Jim) Miller, Bob O'Link, Ill.				McAlvin, 2 and 1		
Thomas C. Robbins, Pinehurst, N.C.	Simon, 2 up					
Jack L. Simon, Oakwood, Ohio		Simon, 5 and 3				
Harold F. Ludwig, Sr., California, Calif.	Ludwig, 1 up					
Gilbert Hattier, Metairie, La.			McCarthy, 2 up			
Martin F. McCarthy, Columbia, Md.	McCarthy, 2 and 1					
Roy L. Corey, Nottingham, N.Y.		McCarthy, 4 and 2				
John W. Baymiller, Lancaster, Pa.	Baymiller, 4 and 3					
Willard B. McConnell, Kennett Square, Pa.					Higgins, 1 up	
David E. Rose, Beechmont, Ohio	Rose, 5 and 3					
Douglas E. Mattison, Prince Georges, Md.		Daniels, 4 and 2				
Charles Evans, Jr., Edgewater, Ill.	Daniels, 5 and 4					
Dexter H. Daniels, Lake Region Yacht, Fla.			Daniels, 4 and 2			
William J. McGlone, Hiawatha, Minn.	McGlone, 1 up					
Joseph S. Garske, Midland Hills, Minn.		McGlone, 1 up				
Lionel MacDuff, Salem, Mass.	Mac Duff, 2 and 1					
Rock F. Zammiello, Gaston, N.C.				Higgins, 2 and 1		
Rudy Taggesell, Columbia Edgewater, Ore.	Higgins, 1 up					
William D. Higgins, Olympic Club, Calif.		Higgins, 2 and 1				
J. Ripley Greer, Memphis, Tenn.	Croxton, 3 and 2					
Jacob D. Croxton, North Fulton, Ga.			Higgins, 5 and 3			
Charles P. Redick, Columbia, Md.	Andrews, 1 up					
Forrest Andrews, Broadmoor, Colo.		Davis, 3 and 1				
Sidney P. Davis, Berry Hills, W. Va.	Davis, 4 and 3					
Floyd E. Lasher, Woodhill, Minn.						Higgins, 3 and 2
A. Wayne Braden, Manor, Md.	Braden, 3 and 2					
Roy G. Taylor, East Bay, Fla.		Taylor, 4 and 3				
John W. Roberts, Scioto, Ohio	Taylor, 3 and 2					
Rollin P. Taylor, Detroit, Mich.			Haggarty, 1 up			
George Haggarty, C.C. Detroit, Mich.	Haggarty, 2 up					
James L. Garard, Old Elm, Ill.		Haggarty, 8 and 6				
Leslie B. Hoss, Southern Hills, Okla.	Moore, 3 and 2					
Henry L. Moore, Oakwoods, N.C.				Haggarty, 3 and 2		
Robert R. Bell, Brookside, Ohio	V. Cestone, 5 and 4					
Victor T. Cestone, Knoll, N.J.		Cestone, 5 and 4				
Paul W. Horn, C.C. Scranton, Pa.	Horn, 1 up					
Casimer A. Mohn, Alcoma, Pa.			Coffin, 4 and 2			
Bruce A. Coffin, Tedesco, Mass.	Coffin, 5 and 3					
H.D. Ackerman, Mirror Lake, Mo.		Coffin, 3 and 2				
Michael Cestone, Forsgate, N.J.	M. Cestone, 2 and 1					
Hugh A. Johnson, C.C. Buffalo, N.Y.					Haggarty, 1 up	
L.B. Peterson, James River, Va.	Randall, 1 up					
Edward H. Randall, Palmetto, Fla.		McManus, 1 up				
George D. Wiggins, Albuquerque, N.M.	McManus, 4 and 3					
Adrian C. McManus, Bay Hill, Fla.			Brown, 3 and 2			
Thomas P. Newcomb, Dornick Hills, Okla.	Mallozzi, 5 and 3					
Robert E. Mallozzi, Shorehaven, Conn.		Brown, 3 and 2				
J. Wolcott Brown, Manasquan River, N.J.	Brown, 3 and 2					
Paul C. Swiech, Chartiers, Pa.				Brown, 2 and 1		
John P. Ryan, Leewood, N.Y.	Daro, 3 and 1					
August F. Daro, Bob O'Link, Ill.		Daro, 2 and 1				
Travis A. Stephenson, North Fulton, Ga.	Lutz, 3 and 1					
Robert T. Lutz, California, Calif.			Blakely, 5 and 3			
Willis H. Blakely, Waverley, Ore.	Blakely, 4 and 3					
Herman C. Wilke, Wethersfield, Conn.		Blakely, 3 and 1				
Paul Dickinson, Dornick Hills, Okla.	Bullock, 2 and 1					
Gordon S. Bullock, Gainesville, Fla.						

LOWER HALF

Semi-Final (18 Holes)	5th Round (18 Holes)		4th Round (18 Holes)	3rd Round (18 Holes)	2nd Round (18 Holes)	1st Round (18 Holes)
Carlsmith, 3 and 2	Morrill, 4 and 3	Morrill, 1 up	Morrill, 2 up	Bergelin, 1 up, 19 hls.	Breslin, 1 up	Chess Lagomarsino, Jr., Peachtree, Ga. Roger W. Breslin, Arcola, N.J.
					Bergelin, 4 and 3	Dr. Millard S. Rosenblatt, Tualatin, Ore. John O. Bergelin, Meceola, Mich.
				Morrill, 2 and 1	Stilwell, 3 and 2	E. Logan Chitwood, Northwood, Miss. Theodore D. Stilwell, Plum Hollow, Mich.
					Morrill, 2 and 1	Bob Tobin, Shore View, N.Y. Joseph Morrill, Jr., Wyantenuck, Mass.
			Brown, 2 and 1	Brown, 5 and 4	Brown, 1 up	Eugene Brown, Berkshire, Pa. Orrin H. Davison, Peninsula, Calif.
					Allan, 5 and 4	Joseph Allan, Suburban, N.J. Richard E. MacDonald, Warwick, R.I.
				Kellerman, 5 and 4	Kellerman, 3 and 2	Karl F. Kellerman, Columbia, Md. John J. Byrne, Kenwood, Ohio
					James, 5 and 3	Charles W. Braughton, Highland, Ind. Floyd M. James, Wampanoag, Conn.
		Lanman, 7 and 6	Spurlin, 4 and 2	Pope, 2 and 1	Murphy, 1 up	Edward Murphy, Waverley, Ore. N.D. Harter, Quail Creek, Okla.
					Pope, 2 and 1	Robert Lowry, Huntsville, Ala. John D. Pope, Sr., South Shore, Mass.
				Spurlin, 3 and 2	Treadwell, 1 up	Robert L. Poer, Arizona, Ariz. George Treadwell, Sr., Memphis, Tenn.
					Spurlin, 5 and 4	Major William K. Sebasky, Rutland, Vt. C.E. Spurlin, Virginia, Calif.
			Lanman, 3 and 2	Lanman, 6 and 5	E. Ames, 6 and 4	Eugene L. Ames, San Antonio, Texas Matt C. Galloway, Lockhaven, Ill.
					Lanman, 2 and 1	William K. Lanman, Glen View, Ill. Frank A. Prat[illegible]r, Cypress Lake, Fla.
				Binkley, 4 and 3	Binkley, 2 and 1	James G. Fearing, Statesville, N.C. William J. Binkley, Miami Valley, Ohio
					Quittner, 1 up, 27 hls.	Maurice R. Smith, Charlotte, N.C. Egon F. Quittner, Old York Road, Pa.
	Carlsmith, 2 and 1	Carlsmith, 4 and 3	Carlsmith, 1 up	Goodloe, 5 and 4	Goodloe, 2 and 1	William L. Goodloe, Sr., Valdosta, Ga. William O. Vantine, Brackenridge Heights, Pa.
					J. Ames, 4 and 2	Dr. John C. Mercer, Oak Hill, Mass. John D. Ames, Onwentsia, Ill.
				Carlsmith, 5 and 4	Carlsmith, 6 and 4	Merrill L. Carlsmith, Hilo, Hawaii Joseph S. Gillin, Rolling Hills, Okla.
					Norvell, 7 and 6	W.E. Norvell, Jr., Chattanooga, Tenn. Garibaldi F. Serafini, Shore View, N.Y.
			Charlton, 5 and 4	Charlton, 4 and 3	Guelich, 6 and 4	Richard H. Guelich, Jr., Wanakah, N.Y. William J. Yates, Charlotte, N.C.
					Charlton, 4 and 2	Edward D. Charlton, Lincoln Greens, Ill. Frank D. Ross, Wampanoag, Conn.
				Sikes, 1 up, 19 hls.	Sikes, 4 and 3	Leon R. Sikes, Sr., Cleveland Heights, Fla. Robert F. Nichols, Tipton, Ind.
					Lowery, 3 and 2	Hubert H. Holland, Hermitage, Va. Edward E. Lowery, California, Calif.
		Severino, 6 and 5	Severino, 3 and 2	Severino, 7 and 6	Langhorn, 2 and 1	Ernest L. Langhorn, Berry Hills, W. Va. Theodore R. Miller, Royal Oaks, Wash.
					Severino, 1 up	Severino P. Severino, Aurora, Ohio Prescott K. Bearce, Plymouth, Mass.
				Quinn, 3 and 2	Quinn, 3 and 1	James P. Quinn, Blue Hills, Mo. Charles H. Black, Jr., Peachtree, Ga.
					Sakolosky, 5 and 3	John L. Lauritsen, Columbia, Md. Peter Sakolosky, Bull's Eye, Wis.
			Gonzales, 1 up, 21 hls.	Moore, 1 up	Adkins, 2 up	Herman M. Freydberg, Metropolis, N.Y. H. Gordon Adkins, James River, Va.
					Moore, 5 and 3	Clayton J. Carpenter, Anderson, Ind. Dr. Clarence E. Moore, Hershey, Pa.
				Gonzales, 6 and 5	Bellville, 8 and 7	Eugene Bellville, Hillcrest, Mo. O.M. Masters, Bellevue, N.Y.
					Gonzales, 3 and 2	Howell W. Anderson, Wilson, N.C. Archie J. Gonzales, St. John, La.

1964
TENTH SENIOR AMATEUR CHAMPIONSHIP

Held at the Waverley Country Club, Portland, Ore., October 5-10.
Yardage—6,399. Par 72. 357 Entries, 119 Sectional Qualifiers, 120 Starters.

Qualifying Score	1st Round (18 Holes)	2nd Round (18 Holes)	3rd Round (18 Holes)	Semi-Finals (18 Holes)	Final (18 Holes)	
150	*A.L. (Jim) Miller, Bob O'Link, Ill.	Lacy, 5 and 4	Rapp, 2 and 1	Murphy, default	Murphy, 2 up	William D. Higgins, 2 and 1
158	Lewie Lacy, Twin Hills, Okla.					
155	James M. Johnson, Algonquin, Mo.	Rapp, 2 and 1				
160	Eddie Rapp, Royal Oaks, Wash.					
153	J. Wolcott Brown, Manasquan River, N.J.	Andrews, 1 up, 19 hls.	Murphy, 4 and 3			
159	Francis H. Andrews, Waverley, Ore.					
156	Edward Murphy, Waverley, Ore.	Murphy, 7 and 6				
161	Harry Craviotto, Del Monte, Calif.					
152	Dr. Melvin Aspray, Spokane, Wash.	Aspray, 4 and 3	Aspray, 4 and 3	Aspray, 3 and 2		
159	Dewey P. Bowen, Atlanta Athletic, Ga.					
155	James J. Molinari, Harding Park, Calif.	Molinari, 3 and 2				
161	Aaron Morris, Woodmont, Tenn.					
154	Merrill L. Carlsmith, Hilo, Hawaii	Carlsmith, 3 and 2	Swan, 3 and 2			
159	William K. Lanman, Jr., Glen View, Ill.					
157	Willis H. Blakely, Waverley, Ore.	Swan, 3 and 1				
162	Ralph E. Swan, Royal Oaks, Wash.					
152	David Goldman, Sr., Dallas Athletic, Texas	Goldman, 1 up	Goldman, 4 and 3	Goldman, 5 and 3	Higgins, 1 up	
158	Robert L. Mitenbuler, Tripoli, Wis.					
155	William F. Zieske, Minnesota Valley, Minn.	Zieske, 1 up				
160	David E. Rose, Beechmont, Ohio					
154	Richard E. MacDonald, Agawam Hunt, R.I.	Hunter, 2 and 1	James, 1 up			
159	Dr. Max R. Hunter, Olympia, Wash.					
157	John H. Wolfe, Bellefonte, Ky.	James, 5 and 4				
161	Floyd M. James, Wampanoag, Conn.					
152	Joseph Morrill, Jr., Wyantenuck, Mass.	Morrill, 2 and 1	Morrill, 4 and 2	Higgins, 2 and 1		
159	H.D. (Dutch) Ackerman, Mirror Lake, Mo.					
155	Henry L. Robison, Albuquerque, N.M.	Baymiller, 1 up				
161	John W. Baymiller, Lancaster, Pa.					
154	George W. Sinderson, Indian Hills, Kans.	Sinderson, 4 and 3	Higgins, 3 and 1			
160	W.W. Giddings, Jr., Del Rio, Calif.					
158	William D. Higgins, Olympic, Calif.	Higgins, 6 and 5				
162	Henry L Schuldener, Metropolis, N.Y.					

*Medalist.

1965
ELEVENTH SENIOR AMATEUR CHAMPIONSHIP

Held at the Fox Chapel Golf Club, Pittsburgh, Pa., October 4-9.
Yardage—6,299. Par 70. 448 Entries, 119 Sectional Qualifiers, 120 Starters.

Qualifying Score	1st Round (18 Holes)	2nd Round (18 Holes)	3rd Round (18 Holes)	Semi-Finals (18 Holes)	Final (18 Holes)	
149	*Curtis Person, Sr., Colonial, Tenn.	Quinn, 1 up				
159	James P. Quinn, Blue Hills, Mo.		Quinn, 5 and 4			
157	A.L. (Jim) Miller, Bob O'Link, Ill.	McCue, 4 and 3				
161	Capt. John K. McCue, New Orleans, La.			Beechler, 3 and 1		
155	George C. Beechler, Prineville, Oregon	Beechler, 4 and 2				
161	Lewie Lacy, Twin Hills, Okla.		Beechler, 3 and 2			
158	Victor G. Rose, Anderson, Ind.	Rose, 2 and 1				
162	Leon R. Sikes, Lost Tree, Fla.				Beechler, 1 up	
152	David Goldman, Dallas Athletic, Texas	Goldman, 2 up				
160	Jack Westland, Cypress Point, Calif.		Goldman, 1 up			
158	Richard C. Freed, The Country Club, Utah	Watson, 5 and 4				
161	John C. Watson, Williams, W. Va.			Carlsmith, 3 and 2		
156	Merrill L. Carlsmith, Hilo, Hawaii	Carlsmith, 3 and 2				
161	Joseph Morrill, Jr., Wyantenuck, Mass.		Carlsmith, 3 and 2			
159	Nolan S. Hatcher, Turtle Point, Ala.	Moller, 2 and 1				
163	Lawrence F. Moller, Quincy, Ill.					Robert B. Kiersky, 1 up, 19 hls.
151	Robert B. Kiersky, Oakmont, Pa.	Kiersky, 4 and 3				
160	E. Douglas Gunter, Virginia, Va.		Kiersky, 5 and 3			
157	Henry L. Robison, Albuquerque, N.M.	Moore, 3 and 2				
161	Dr. Clarence E. Moore, Harrisburg, Pa.			Kiersky, 1 up		
156	William K. Lanman, Glen View, Ill.	Croxton, 1 up				
161	Jacob D. Croxton, North Fulton, Ga.		Steptoe, 1 up			
159	Edward J. Steptoe, Runaway Brook, Mass.	Steptoe, 6 and 4				
162	Willard B. McConnell, Kennett Square, Pa.				Kiersky, 3 and 2	
154	William D. Higgins, Olympic Club, Calif.	Higgins, 2 and 1				
160	John R. Jacob, Congress Lake, Ohio		Higgins, 1 up			
158	A.J. Jordan, Chartiers, Pa.	Saettele, 1 up, 19 hls.				
162	Leo G. Saettele, Brookside, Pa.			Higgins, 1 up, 22 hls.		
156	Charlie O. Murphy, Atlanta, Ga.	Keating, 3 and 2				
161	Edward Keating, Ekwanok, Vt.		Brown, 1 up			
159	Charles A. Totten, Pittsburgh Field, Pa.	Brown, 1 up				
163	J. Wolcott Brown, Manasquan River, N.J.					

*Medalist.
The first word after the player's name is the name of the player's club.

1966
TWELFTH SENIOR AMATEUR CHAMPIONSHIP

Held at the Tucson National Golf Club, Tucson, Ariz., September 26-October 1.
Yardage—6,585. Par 72. 449 Entries, 119 Sectional Qualifiers, 120 Starters.

Qualifying Score	1st Round (18 Holes)	2nd Round (18 Holes)	3rd Round (18 Holes)	Semi-Finals (18 Holes)	Final (18 Holes)	
143	*Curtis Person, Sr., Colonial, Tenn.	Person, 3 and 2				
152	Jack Westland, Cypress Point, Calif.		Ferrie, 4 and 3			
148	James Ferrie, Virginia, Calif.	Ferrie, 4 and 3				
154	G.W. Addison, Jal, N.J.			Daniels, 3 and 2		
146	Marcel J. Bellande, Sunkist, Miss.	Bellande, 2 and 1				
153	J.D. Shriver, California, Calif.		Daniels, 3 and 2			
150	John K. McCue, New Orleans, La.	Daniels, 4 and 3				
154	Dexter H. Daniels, Lake Region, Fla.				Daniels, 2 and 1	
145	Richard D. Chapman, Oyster Harbors, Mass.	Chapman, 3 and 2				
152	James P. Quinn, Blue Hills, Mo.		Chapman, 4 and 3			
149	Alan Howard, Rock Island Arsenal, Ill.	Dowell, 3 and 2				
154	Walter A. Dowell, Newport, Ark.			Goldman, 1 up		
147	David Goldman, Dallas Athletic, Texas	Goldman, 2 and 1				
154	Anderson Borthwick, Chula Vista, Calif.		Goldman, 20 holes			
151	John E. Lehman, Bob O'Link, Ill.	Lehman, 23 holes				
155	Webster Wilder, Ft. Sam Houston, Texas					Dexter H. Daniels, 1 up
145	George C. Beechler, Prineville, Ore.	Beechler, 3 and 2				
152	Edwin D. Preisler, Beechmont, Ohio		Beechler, 6 and 4			
148	Arthur Hays, Interlachen, Minn.	H. Lanman, 2 and 1				
154	Henry Lanman, Sante Fe, N.M.			Beechler, 2 and 1		
147	George F. Kerrigan, Meadow, Calif.	W. Lanman, 1 up				
153	William K. Lanman, Glen View, Ill.		Keating, 4 and 2			
151	J. Ripley Greer, Memphis, Tenn.	Keating, 5 and 3				
155	Edward L. Keating, Ekwanok, Vt.				Beechler, 3 and 2	
146	Merrill L. Carlsmith, Hilo, Hawaii	Carlsmith, 2 up				
153	Randall R. Ahern, Red Run, Mich.		Carlsmith, 3 and 2			
149	Cecil C. Dees, Oakmont, Calif.	Lowery, 2 and 1				
154	Edward E. Lowery, Cypress Point, Calif.			Carlsmith, 20 holes		
148	J. E. Bernolfo, Jr., The Country Club, Utah	Brothers, 2 and 1				
154	Mack Brothers, Jr., Belle Meade, Tenn.		Kiersky, 3 and 2			
151	Robert B. Kiersky, Pine Tree, Fla.	Kiersky, 19 holes				
155	Lawrence F. Moller, Quincy, Ill.					

*Medalist.
The first word after the player's name is the name of the player's club.

1967

THIRTEENTH SENIOR AMATEUR CHAMPIONSHIP

Held at the Shinnecock Hills Golf Club, Southampton, N.Y., September 25-30.
Yardage—6,429. Par 70. 563 Entries, 119 Sectional Qualifiers, 120 Starters.

Qualifying Score	1st Round (18 Holes)	2nd Round (18 Holes)	3rd Round (18 Holes)	Semi-Finals (18 Holes)	Final (18 Holes)	
153	*J. Wolcott Brown, Manasquan River, N.J.	Brown, 1 up				
160	Stanley J. Matczak, Jr., Avon, Conn.		Brown, 2 and 1			
157	Curtis Person, Sr., Colonial, Tenn.	Person, 3 and 1				
162	Anthony P. Brown, Springhaven, Pa.			Petrone, 1 up		
154	George L. Marchant, Charles River, Mass.	Harris, 1 up				
161	Norton C. Harris, Key West, Fla.		Petrone, 2 up			
159	Sam Petrone, Hubbard Heights, Conn.	Petrone, 5 and 4				
163	William K. Lanman, Glen View, Ill.				Palmer, 2 up	
153	*Raymond Palmer, Grosse Ile, Mich.	Palmer, 4 and 2				
161	Andrew Gard, Runaway Brook, Mass.		Palmer, 1 up			
158	Burton B. Resnik, Woodbridge, Conn.	Beechler, 6 and 5				
162	George C. Beechler, Prineville, Ore.			Palmer, 7 and 5		
156	Alan Howard, Rock Island Arsenal, Ill.	Howard, 6 and 5				
162	Martin F. McCarthy, Columbia, Md.		Howard, 2 up			
160	John R. Butler, River Oaks, Texas	Butler, 4 and 3				Raymond Palmer, 3 and 2
163	Milton Frank, Four Seasons, Mo.					
153	*David Goldman, Dallas, Texas	Chapman, 2 up				
160	Richard D. Chapman, Kittansett, Mass.		Chapman, 1 up			
157	Knox M. Young, Jr., Shannopin, Pa.	Young, 2 and 1				
162	Steve Dunford, The Country Club, Utah			Chapman, 3 and 2		
155	Bruce N. McCormick, San Gabriel, Calif.	McCormick, 20 holes				
162	Edwin D. Preisler, Beechmont, Ohio		Ferrie, 1 up			
159	J. William Pierce, Raritan Valley, N.J.	Ferrie, 3 and 2				
163	James Ferrie, Virginia, Calif.				Bronson, 5 and 4	
154	Joseph Greene, Seminole, Fla.	Kowal, 2 and 1				
161	Henry J. Kowal, Dutchess, N.Y.		Bronson, 6 and 4			
158	Walter D. Bronson, Chicago, Ill.	Bronson, 1 up				
163	Charles Lynch, New Orleans, La.			Bronson, 4 and 3		
156	George F. Kerrigan, Meadow, Calif.	Kerrigan, 4 and 3				
162	Dewey P. Brown, Atlanta, Ga.		Kerrigan, 1 up			
160	Merrill L. Carlsmith, Hilo, Hawaii	Carlsmith, 2 and 1				
163	Harry Craviotto, Carmel Valley, Calif.					

*Medalist.
The first word after the player's name is the name of the player's club.

1968
FOURTEENTH SENIOR AMATEUR CHAMPIONSHIP

Held at the Atlanta Country Club, Atlanta, Ga., September 23-28.
Yardage—6,516. Par 72. 674 Entries, 120 Sectional Qualifiers, 120 Starters.

Qualifying Score	1st Round (18 Holes)	2nd Round (18 Holes)	3rd Round (18 Holes)	Semi-Finals (18 Holes)	Final (18 Holes)	
146	*John C. Tullio, Aurora, Ohio	Brothers, 4 and 2				
154	Mack Brothers, Jr., Belle Meade, Tenn.		Brothers, 2 up			
152	Merrill L. Carlsmith, Hilo, Hawaii	Carlsmith, 5 and 4				
156	Nolan S. Hatcher, Turtle Point, Ala.			Howard, 5 and 4		
151	Alan Howard, Rock Island, Ill.	Howard, 21 holes				
155	Rodney Bliss, Jr., Wakonda, Iowa		Howard, 2 up			
154	George C. Beechler, Prineville, Ore.	Beechler, 3 and 2				
157	Norton Harris, Key West, Fla.				Person, 1 up	
149	John Purdum, Sharon, Ohio	Purdum, 1 up				
155	Dexter H. Daniels, Lake Region, Fla.		Person, 1 up			
153	Donald O'Brien, Virginia, Va.	Person, 20 holes				
156	Curtis Person, Sr., Colonial, Tenn.			Person, 1 up		
152	T. Desmond Sullivan, Essex County, N.J.	Sullivan, 5 and 3				
156	Raleigh M. Selby, Henderson, Texas		Sullivan, 2 up			
154	Webster Wilder, Oak Hills, Texas	Wilder, 2 and 1				Curtis Person, Sr., 2 and 1
157	Homer Starks, Fairview, Pa.					
148	Collins Gaines, Jr., Glen Lakes, Texas	Kiersky, 19 holes				
155	Robert B. Kiersky, Pine Tree, Fla.		Kiersky, 2 and 1			
153	John M. Ross, Canyon Crest, Calif.	Ross, 2 and 1				
156	J. Wolcott Brown, Manasquan River, N.J.			Kiersky, 4 and 3		
151	Walter A. Dowell, Newport, Ark.	Dowell, 25 holes				
155	Knox M. Young, Jr., Shannopin, Pa.		Dowell, 2 and 1			
154	Ernest Pieper, Jr., San Jose, Calif.	Pieper, 3 and 1				
157	A. J. Jordan, Chartiers, Pa.				Goodes, 2 and 1	
150	Robert C. Loufek, Rock Island, Ill.	Loufek, 5 and 4				
155	David M. McLelland, Jr., Taconic, Mass.		Goodes, 2 up			
153	Ben Goodes, Pennrose Park, N.C.	Goodes, 20 holes				
157	J. William Pierce, Raritan Valley, N.J.			Goodes, 6 and 5		
152	Francis J. McCarthy, Transit Valley, N.Y.	McCarthy, 4 and 3				
156	Edwin C. Dayton, Fox Hills, Mich.		Robison, 2 and 1			
154	Arthur B. Patchin, Augusta, Ga.	Robison, 2 and 1				
157	Henry L. Robison, Albuquerque, N.M.					

*Medalist.
The first word after the player's name is the name of the player's club.

1969
FIFTEENTH SENIOR AMATEUR CHAMPIONSHIP

Held at the Wichita Country Club, Wichita, Kans., September 15-20.
Yardage—6,485. Par 71. 576 Entries, 119 Sectional Qualifiers, 120 Starters.

Qualifying Score	1st Round (18 Holes)	2nd Round (18 Holes)	3rd Round (18 Holes)	Semi-Finals (18 Holes)	Final (18 Holes)	
146	*David Goldman, Sr., Brookhaven, Texas	Goldman, 3 and 2	Goldman, 5 and 4	Goldman, 2 up	Goldman, 3 and 2	Curtis Person, Sr., 1 up
153	Ernest Pieper, Jr., San Jose, Calif.					
152	Rodney Bliss, Jr., Wakonda, Iowa	Bliss, 6 and 5				
155	James R. Kerr, Glen Oak, Ill.					
151	Robert E. Cochran, Norwood Hills, Mo.	Cochran, 3 and 2	Cochran, 4 and 2			
154	Walter D. Bronson, Chicago, Ill.					
153	Richard Stevenson, Claremont, Calif.	Stevenson, 2 up				
155	Marcus W. Smith, Horizon Hills, Texas					
148	George C. Beechler, Prineville, Ore.	Beechler, 4 and 3	Palmer, 5 and 4	Loufek, 2 and 1		
154	Edward L. Keating, Tucson, Ariz.					
152	Raymond Palmer, Grosse Ile, Mich.	Palmer, 4 and 3				
155	John H. Soellner, Sr., Terrace Park, Ohio					
152	Robert C. Loufek, Rock Island, Ill.	Loufek, 19 holes	Loufek, 4 and 3			
154	Bud McKinney, Dallas, Texas					
153	O.H. Washam, Twin Hills, Okla.	Robison, 1 up				
155	Henry L. Robison, Albuquerque, N.M.					
148	Alan Howard, Rock Island, Ill.	Howard, 1 up	Howard, 4 and 3	Carlsmith, 1 up	Person, 4 and 3	
154	Fred L. Gordon, Clarmond, Iowa					
152	Burt G. Kling, Oak Hill, N.Y.	Marshall, 20 holes				
155	Raymond R. Marshall, Lubbock, Texas					
151	Raleigh M. Selby, Henderson, Texas	Carlsmith, 2 and 1	Carlsmith, 1 up			
154	Merrill L. Carlsmith, Oahu, Hawaii					
153	Ralph V. Ellstrom, Dearborn, Mich.	Ellstrom, 4 and 3				
155	O.W. Nelson, Rolling Hills, Colo.					
150	Edwin D. Preisler, Beechmont, Ohio	Bjorklund, 2 and 1	Bjorklund, 6 and 5	Person, 3 and 2		
154	Leonard T. Bjorklund, Interlachen, Minn.					
152	Jack Westland, Cypress Point, Calif.	Gold, 4 and 3				
155	Lynn Gold, Mohawk, Okla.					
152	W.E. Gowdy, Meadowlark, Calif.	Person, 2 and 1	Person, 2 and 1			
154	Curtis Person, Sr., Colonial, Tenn.					
153	Tom Draper, Red Run, Mich.	Giddings, 5 and 4				
155	Richard J. Giddings, San Joaquin, Calif.					

*Medalist.
The first word after the player's name is the name of the player's club.

1970
SIXTEENTH SENIOR AMATEUR CHAMPIONSHIP

Held at the California Golf Club of San Francisco, South San Francisco, Calif., September 21-26.
Yardage—6,440. Par 72. 683 Entries, 130 Starters.

Qualifying Score	1st Round (18 Holes)	2nd Round (18 Holes)	3rd Round (18 Holes)	Semi-Finals (18 Holes)	Final (18 Holes)
147*	Bruce N. McCormick, San Gabriel, Calif.	McCormick, 2 and 1			
154	Arthur Gee, Woodmar, Ind.		McCormick, 1 up		
153	Frank Toronto, Northridge, Calif.	Stimac, 4 and 3			
156	Stephen Stimac, Contra Costa, Calif.			Pieper, 5 and 4	
150	Ernest Pieper, Jr., San Jose, Calif.	Pieper, 2 and 1			
156	Theodore Sall, Green Valley, Pa.		Pieper, 1 up		
154	Raymond E. Palmer, Grosse Ile, Mich.	Palmer, 4 and 3			Andrews, 19 holes
158	George L. Marchant, Charles River, Mass.				
149	Robert E. Cochran, Norwood Hills, Mo.	Cochran, 6 and 5			
155	Eugene P. Zuspann, Cherry Hills, Colo.		Andrews, 21 hls.		
153	David (Spec) Goldman, Brookhaven, Texas	Andrews, 3 and 2			
157	Gene Andrews, California, Calif.			Andrews, 5 and 4	
152	Dick Giddings, San Joaquin, Calif.	Maniaci, 3 and 1			
156	Sam Maniaci, Cedarbrook, Pa.		Maniaci, 4 and 3		
154	Robert K. Bronson, Riverside, Ore.	Bronson, 2 and 1			
158+	Raleigh M. Selby, Henderson, Texas				
148	Curtis Person, Sr., Colonial, Tenn.	Connell, 2 and 1			
155	Truman F. Connell, Pine Tree, Fla.		Connell, 4 and 3		
153	W. F. Colm, Monterey Peninsula, Calif.	Bolas, 5 and 4			
157	Harold B. Bolas, Columbine, Colo.			Fahy, 2 and 1	
152	Robert E. Fahy, Quail Lake, Calif.	Fahy, 4 and 3			
156	Sheldon G. Braun, Clovernook, Ohio		Fahy, 2 and 1		
154	Ed Castagnetto, Cypress Hills, Calif.	Preisler, 1 up			
158	Edwin Preisler, Beechmont, Ohio				Ferrie, 3 and 1
149	Art B. Patchin, Augusta, Ga.	Kershaw, 2 up			
156	Henry G. Kershaw, Papago, Ariz.		Bliss, 1 up		
153	Andrew Augaitis, Dayton, Ohio	Bliss, 4 and 3			
157	Rodney Bliss, Jr., Wakonda, Iowa			Ferrie, 1 up	
153	Leo S. Case, Oakbourne, La.	Stevenson, 1 up			
156	Richard G. Stevenson, Claremont, Calif.		Ferrie, 4 and 3		
154	James Ferrie, Indian Wells, Calif.	Ferrie, 3 and 1			
158	B. J. Leonard, Paradise Valley, Ariz.				

Gene Andrews, 1 up

*Medalist.
The first word after the player's name is the name of the player's club.

1971
SEVENTEENTH SENIOR AMATEUR CHAMPIONSHIP

Held at the Sunnybrook Golf Club, Plymouth Meeting, Pennsylvania, September 20–25.
Yardage–6,492 Par–72.
655 Entries. 150 Sectional Qualifiers, 150 Starters.

Qualifying Score	1st Round (18 Holes)	2nd Round (18 Holes)	3rd Round (18 Holes)	Semi-Finals (18 Holes)	Final (18 Holes)	
148	*Robert E. Cochran, St. Louis, Mo.	Cochran,				
155	Aubrey L. Wolf, Jr., Houston, Texas	5 and 4	Draper,			
154	George W. Sinderson, Shawnee Mission, Kans.	Draper,	1 up			
157	Tom Draper, Troy, Mich.	3 and 2		Draper,		
152	Truman Connell, Boynton Beach, Fla.	Connell,		21 holes		
156	Burr Melvin, Newport News, Va.	5 and 4	Connell,			
155	Eugene P. Zuspann, Denver, Colo.	Sullivan,	4 and 3		Draper, 5 and 4	
158	Desmond Sullivan, Myrtle Beach, S.C.	1 up				
150	Edward P. Martin, Lexington, Mass.	Colm,				
156	William F. Colm, Pebble Beach, Calif.	19 holes	Colm,			
154	Curtis Person, Sr., Memphis, Tenn.	Person,	4 and 2			
157	William H. Zimmerman, Columbus, Ga.	2 and 1		Colm,		
153	Ed Somerville, River Forest, Ill.	Beyer,		3 and 2		
157	H. Lloyd Beyer, Jr., Bryn Mawr, Pa.	4 and 3	Davis,			
155	Howard Everitt, Tequesta, Fla.	Davis,	6 and 5			Tom Draper, 3 and 1
159	J. Bishop Davis, Melvin Village, N.H.	1 up				
149	David (Spec) Goldman, Dallas, Texas	Sezna,				
156	W.W. Sezna, Greenville, Del.	3 and 2	Pieper,			
154	Ernest Pieper, Jr., San Juan Bautista, Calif.	Pieper,	2 and 1			
157	Jack House, Mission, Kans.	2 and 1		Pieper,		
153	James R. Kerr, Chicago, Ill.	Kerr,		8 and 6		
157	William V. Kuhl, Albuquerque, N.M.	6 and 5	Kerr,			
155	Samual W. Maniaci, Glenside, Pa.	Price,	2 and 1			
158	Richard H. Price, Wichita, Kans.	2 up			Pieper, 4 and 2	
152	William Hyndman, III, Huntingdon Valley, Pa.	Hyndman,				
156	Merrill L. Carlsmith, Hilo, Hawaii	5 and 4	Hyndman,			
154	Rodney Bliss, Jr., Des Moines, Iowa	Bliss,	5 and 4			
157	William J. Deupree, Jr., Covington, Ky.	4 and 2		Hyndman,		
153	Edward L. Meister, Jr., Willoughby, Ohio	Meister,		4 and 3		
157	O.H. Washam, Oklahoma City, Okla.	2 up	Meister,			
155	Aulick Burke, Bristol, Va.	Burke,	5 and 4			
159	Cecil Wheat, Huntington Beach, Calif.	3 and 2				

*Medalist.

1972
EIGHTEENTH SENIOR AMATEUR CHAMPIONSHIP

Held at Sharon Golf Club, Sharon Center, Ohio, September 18-23, 1972.
Yardage—6,750. Par—72. 617 Entries. 150 Sectional Qualifiers, 150 Starters.

Qualifying Score	1st Round (18 Holes)	2nd Round (18 Holes)	3rd Round (18 Holes)	Semi-Finals (18 Holes)	Final (18 Holes)	
145	*William Hyndman, III, Huntingdon Valley, Pa.	Hyndman,				
152	Harvey Breaux, Homestead, Fla.	2 and 1	Hyndman,			
150	Harold Foreman, Glencoe, Ill.	Foreman,	4 and 3			
153	Eugene Zuspann, Englewood, Colo.	3 and 2		Hyndman,		
147	John Tullio, Willoughby, Ohio	Sinderson,		1 up		
153	George Sinderson, Prairie Village, Kansas	2 up	Simonson,			
151	Harry Simonson, Madison, Wis.	Simonson,	1 up			
154	W. F. Colm, Pebble Beach, Calif.	1 up, 19 holes			Oehmig,	
147	Lewis W. Oehmig, Lookout Mountain, Tenn.	Oehmig,			1 up, 20 holes	
152	Timothy Holland, Wenham, Mass.	3 and 2	Oehmig,			
151	Truman Connell, Delray Beach, Fla.	Meister,	1 up, 19 holes			
154	Edward L. Meister, Jr., Willoughby, Ohio	2 and 1		Oehmig,		
149	Howard Everitt, Jupiter, Fla.	Everitt,		2 and 1		
153	Francis McCarthy, Grand Island, N.Y.	5 and 4	Person,			
151	James Ferrie, Indian Wells, Calif.	Person,	2 and 1			
154	Curtis Person, Sr., Memphis, Tenn.	1 up, 21 holes				Lewis W. Oehmig,
146	Eugene Taano, Menlo Park, Calif.	Goldman,				1 up, 20 holes
152	David Goldman, Sr., Dallas, Texas	1 up, 20 holes	Pieper,			
150	William R. Coffey, Fort Worth, Texas	Pieper,	1 up			
153	Ernest Pieper, San Jose, Calif.	6 and 5		Pieper,		
148	Bruce McCormick, San Gabriel, Calif.	McCormick,		6 and 5		
153	Wilbur Bartels, Kansas City, Mo.	4 and 3	Giddings,			
151	R. J. Giddings, Fresno, Calif.	Giddings,	1 up, 19 holes			
154	Andrew Augaitis, Dayton, Ohio	6 and 5			Pieper,	
147	Richard Price, Wichita, Kansas	Price,			5 and 4	
153	John Wood, II, Cincinnati, Ohio	2 and 1	Price,			
151	Raymond Palmer, Grosse Ile, Mich.	Braun,	4 and 3			
154	Sheldon Braun, Sr., Cincinnati, Ohio	5 and 4		Price,		
149	W. W. Sezna, West Chester, Pa.	Sezna,		3 and 2		
153	Ralph Ellstrom, Dearborn, Mich.	3 and 2	Sezna,			
152	Henry C. Felts, Charlotte, N.C.	Felts,	3 and 2			
154	Webster Wilder, San Antonio, Texas	1 up				

*Medalist

1973
NINETEENTH SENIOR AMATEUR CHAMPIONSHIP

Held at Onwentsia Club, Lake Forest, Illinois, September 17 - 22.
Yardage—6,450. Par—71. 633 Entries. 150 Sectional Qualifiers, 150 Starters.

Qualifying Score	1st Round (18 Holes)	2nd Round (18 Holes)	3rd Round (18 Holes)	Semi-Finals (18 Holes)	Final (18 Holes)
147	*William Hyndman III, Huntingdon Valley, Pa.	Hyndman,			
156	William Trepsas, Stoughton, Mass.	2 and 1	Hyndman,		
153	Ernest Pieper, San Juan Bautista, Calif.	Pieper,	2 and 1		
156	Richard Payne, Norfolk, Va.	2 and 1		Hyndman,	
150	Dr. Gene Taano, Menlo Park, Calif.	Taano,		19 holes	
156	Jay Gaines, Libertyville, Ill.	8 and 7	Taano,		Hyndman, 2 and 1
155	Harold Foreman, Northbrook, Ill.	Foreman,	1 up		
158	Merle Getten, Sioux Falls, S. D.	22 holes			
148	Howard Everitt, Oakbrook, Ill.	Everitt,			
156	Jim Young, Kokomo, Ind.	2 and 1	Everitt,		
153	Edward L. Meister, Jr., Willoughby, Ohio	Sullivan,	1 up		
157	Desmond Sullivan, Myrtle Beach, S. C.	4 and 3		Everitt,	
152	Sam Maniaci, Glenside, Pa.	Maniaci,		2 and 1	
156	J. B. Bernolfo, Jr., Salt Lake City, Utah	4 and 3	Maniaci,		
155	Eugene Zuspann, Denver, Colo.	Reed,	1 up		
158	George Reed, Milwaukee, Wis.	5 and 4			William Hyndman III, 3 and 2
147	*Sam Friedman, Walton Beach, Fla.	Forkey,			
156	Raymond Forkey, Holden, Mass.	2 up	Welch,		
153	Harry Welch, Salisbury, N. C.	Welch,	4 and 3		
157	Neil Cronquist, Minneapolis, Minn.	3 and 2		Welch,	
151	Lewis M. Martin, St. Clairsville, Ohio	Hightower,		4 and 3	
156	Buck Hightower, Atlanta, Ga.	5 and 3	Hightower,		
155	George Victor, Golf, Ill.	Draper,	2 up		Welch, 1 up
158	Tom Draper, Troy, Mich.	2 and 1			
148	Richard Giddings, Fresno, Calif.	Giddings,			
156	O. W. (Red) Nelson, Wheatridge, Colo.	7 and 5	Giddings,		
155	Fred Gordon, Belmond, Iowa	Atkinson,	1 up		
157	William Atkinson, Houston, Texas	3 and 2		Giddings,	
153	Lewis Oehmig, Lookout Mountain, Tenn.	Zimmerman,		21 holes	
156	William Zimmerman, Columbus, Ga.	3 and 2	Sezna,		
156	W. F. Colm, Bakersfield, Calif.	Sezna,	1 up		
158	W. W. Sezna, Greenville, Del.	2 up			

*Co-medalists

1974
TWENTIETH SENIOR AMATEUR CHAMPIONSHIP

Held at Harbour Town Golf Links, Hilton Head Island, South Carolina, September 23-28
Yardage—6,310. Par 71. 743 Entries. 150 Sectional Qualifiers. 150 Starters.

Qualifying Score	1st Round (18 Holes)	2nd Round (18 Holes)	3rd Round (18 Holes)	Semi-Finals (18 Holes)	Final (18 Holes)	
144	*Ed Tutwiler, Indianapolis, Ind.	Tutwiler,				
159	Erv Parent, Seattle, Wash.	2 and 1	Tutwiler,			
157	Truman Connell, Pompano Beach, Fla.	Connell,	19 holes			
161	John McCue, Orlando, Fla.	3 and 1		Tutwiler,		
155	John Pottle, Linville, N. C.	Pottle,		4 and 3		
160	Paul Tulga, Columbus, Ohio	2 up	Pottle,			
157	James Manzone, Riverhead, N. Y.	Manzone,	1 up			
162	Eugene Zuspann, Englewood, Colo.	20 holes				
149	Dale Morey, High Point, N. C.	Morey,			Morey, 3 and 2	
160	Edward L. Meister, Jr., Willoughby, Ohio	6 and 5	Morey,			
157	Walter Sezna, West Chester, Pa.	Sezna,	4 and 3			
161	George Victor, Golf, Ill.	2 and 1		Morey,		
156	Robert A. Roos, San Mateo, Calif.	Roos,		2 up		
161	O. H. Washam, Oklahoma City, Okla.	1 up	Humm,			
158	John Humm, Rockville Centre, N. Y.	Humm,	19 holes			
163	H. B. Bolas, Littleton, Colo.	1 up				Dale Morey, 4 and 2
146	William Hyndman, III, Huntingdon Valley, Pa.	Hyndman,				
160	Robert Cochran, Normandy, Mo.	19 holes	Hyndman,			
157	George Reed, Oconomowoc, Wis.	Reed,	4 and 3			
161	R. M. Arnold, Greenwood, S. C.	2 up		Oehmig,		
156	K. K. Compton, Fort Worth, Texas	Compton,		1 up		
160	Herbert Elliott, Rock Island, Ill.	6 and 4	Oehmig,			
158	Lewis Oehmig, Lookout Mt., Tenn.	Oehmig,	2 and 1			
162	Saul Gealer, Los Angeles, Calif.	4 and 2			Oehmig, 2 up	
155	Neil Croonquist, Edina, Minn.	Croonquist,				
160	Sheldon Braun, Jr., Cincinnati, Ohio	2 and 1	Nannini,			
157	Karl Schmidt, Sharon Center, Ohio	Nannini,	3 and 2			
162	Norando Nannini, Lake Bluff, Ill.	4 and 3		Nannini,		
156	John Wood, II, Cincinnati, Ohio	Wood,		20 holes		
161	Floyd Burdette, Royal Oak, Mich.	19 holes	Pottle,			
158	Maj. Gen. John Kline, Ormond Beach, Fla.	Pottle,	5 and 4			
163	George Pottle, Pinehurst, N. C.	1 up				

*Medalist

1975
TWENTY-FIRST SENIOR AMATEUR CHAMPIONSHIP

Held at Carmel Valley Golf and Country Club, Carmel, California, September 22-27
Yardage—6,310. Par 71. 737 Entries, 132 Sectional Qualifiers, 132 Starters

Qualifying Score	1st Round (18 Holes)	2nd Round (18 Holes)	3rd Round (18 Holes)	Semi-Finals (18 Holes)	Final (18 Holes)	
*143	William Hyndman, III, Huntingdon Valley, Pa.	Hyndman,				
152	Lewis Oehmig, Lookout Mt., Tenn.	5 and 4	Cochran,			
150	Lyle Gray, Atherton, Calif.	Cochran,	2 and 1			
153	Bob Cochran, Chesterfield, Mo.	5 and 4		Stimac,		
148	Dr. Paul Travis, Downey, Calif.	Palacio,		19 holes		
152	Matias Palacio, San Rafael, Calif.	1 up	Stimac,			
151	Stephen Stimac, Walnut Creek, Calif.	Stimac,	3 and 1		Stimac, 2 up	
154	David MacHarg, Pinehurst, N.C.	2 and 1				
147	George Reed, Brookfield, Wis.	Reed,				
152	George Pottle, Spring Lake, N.J.	19 holes	Getten,			
151	David Goldman, Sr., Dallas, Texas	Getten,	19 holes			
154	Merle Getten, Sioux Falls, N.D.	8 and 6		Miller,		
149	John McNiff, Salem, Mass.	Connell,		5 and 4		William F. Colm, 4 and 3
153	Truman Connell, Pompano Beach, Fla.	1 up	Miller,			
151	John Miller, Edina, Minn.	Miller,	4 and 3			
155	Amel Pascuzzi, Portland, Ore.	5 and 3				
145	Ed Tutwiler, Indianapolis, Ind.	Swift,				
152	George Swift, Columbus, Ga.	20 holes	Colm,			
151	William F. Colm, Pebble Beach, Calif.	Colm,	1 up			
154	Richard Remsen, Locust Valley, N.Y.	2 up		Colm,		
148	James Tingley, Glen Cove, N.Y.	Tingley,		2 up		
153	James Manzone, Melville, N.Y.	5 and 4	Tingley,			
151	John Kline, Houston, Texas	Kline,	2 up			
154	Paul Tulga, Columbus, Ohio	20 holes				
148	Henry Edwards, Oklahoma City, Okla.	Edwards,			Colm, 2 up	
152	Dale Morey, High Point, N.C.	1 up	Compton,			
151	K. K. Compton, Fort Worth, Texas	Compton,	22 holes			
154	Erv Parent, Seattle, Wash.	1 up		Compton,		
149	Dr. Gene Taano, Menlo Park, Calif.	Tatum,		2 and 1		
153	Frank Tatum, Jr., San Francisco, Calif.	2 and 1	Tatum,			
152	W. D. Bronson, Oak Brook, Ill.	Bronson,	2 and 1			
155	Richard Jennings, Lubbock, Texas	1 up				

*Medalist

1976
TWENTY-SECOND SENIOR AMATEUR CHAMPIONSHIP

Held at Cherry Hills Country Club, Englewood, Colorado, September 20-25
Yardage—6,653. Par 72. 833 Entries, 132 Sectional Qualifiers, 132 Starters

Qualifying Score	1st Round (18 Holes)	2nd Round (18 Holes)	3rd Round (18 Holes)	Semi-Finals (18 Holes)	Final (18 Holes)	
*145	Ed Tutwiler, Indianapolis, Ind.	Richardson,				
153	John Richardson, Laguna Niguel, Calif.	3 and 2	Richardson,			
150	Dale Morey, High Point, N.C.	Morey,	3 and 2			
155	Ernest Pieper, Pebble Beach, Calif.	3 and 1		Richardson,		
148	Frank Guernsey, Houston, Texas	Baty,		1 up		
153	Jack Baty, Tacoma, Wash.	1 up	Baty,			
152	Arnold Horelick, Pittsburgh, Pa.	Horelick,	2 and 1			
155	John W. Kline, Houston, Texas	1 up			Richardson,	
147	Harry Welch, Salisbury, N.C.	Welch,			1 up	
153	Byron Swedberg, Rock Island, Ill.	6 and 4	Welch,			
151	William R. Hogan, Prairie Village, Kans.	G. Pottle,	4 and 2			
155	George W. Pottle, Spring Lake, N.J.	3 and 2		Hightower,		
149	John P. Morrell, Charlotte, N.C.	Morrell,		1 up		
154	Ralph M. Bogart, Kensington, Md.	2 and 1	Hightower,			Lewis W. Oehmig, 4 and 3
152	Charles Hightower, Duluth, Ga.	Hightower,	2 and 1			
155	Frank D. Tatum, Jr., San Francisco, Calif.	2 up				
146	William H. Zimmerman, Columbus, Ga.	J. Pottle,				
153	John Pottle, Linville, N.C.	4 and 3	J. Pottle,			
151	Frank Hardison, Laguna Beach, Calif.	White,	1 up			
155	J. B. White, Lubbock, Texas	1 up		Schmidt,		
149	Peter J. Zaccagnino, Jr., Hartford, Conn.	Schmidt,		3 and 1		
153	Karl Schmidt, Akron, Ohio	5 and 4	Schmidt,			
152	Clark E. Creed, New Britain, Conn.	Turner,	2 and 1			
155	Paul J. Turner, St. Paul, Minn.	4 and 3			Oehmig,	
148	Wally Sezna, Greenville, Del.	McCormick,			2 and 1	
153	Bruce McCormick, Temple City, Calif.	1 up	Oehmig,			
151	Lewis W. Oehmig, Lookout Mt., Tenn.	Oehmig,	5 and 4			
155	Chris Kappas, Racine, Wis.	7 and 6		Oehmig,		
149	Ralph Bevan, Wichita, Kans.	Giddings,		5 and 3		
154	Dick Giddings, Fresno, Calif.	1 up	Giddings,			
152	John J. Humm, Baldwin, N.Y.	Humm,	20 holes			
156	Robert Cochran, Chesterfield, Mo.	5 and 4				

*Medalist

1977
TWENTY-THIRD SENIOR AMATEUR CHAMPIONSHIP

Held at Salem Country Club, Peabody, Massachusetts, September 19-24.
Yardage—6,638. Par 72. 789 Entries, 144 Sectional Qualifiers, 144 Starters.

Qualifying Score	1st Round (18 Holes)	2nd Round (18 Holes)	3rd Round (18 Holes)	Semi-Finals (18 Holes)	Final (18 Holes)	
*143	Dale Morey, High Point, N.C.	Morey,				
155	Robert Morris, Rockville, Md.	1 up, 20 holes	Morey,			
154	Walter McDonald, Warner Robins, Ga.	McDonald,	1 up			
157	Darrell Nelson, Detroit Lake, Minn.	2 and 1		Morey,		
152	Harry Welch, Salisbury, N.C.	Welch,		5 and 4		
156	Ed Richitelli, Newark, Del.	3 and 2	Welch,			
155	Keith Compton, Ft. Worth, Texas	Lytle,	4 and 2			
158	Richard Lytle, Pacific Palisades, Calif.	5 and 3			Morey,	
151	John Jacobs, Cedar Ridge, Iowa	Patton,			5 and 4	
156	William J. Patton, Morganton, N.C.	3 and 2	Weavil,			
154	Kenneth Weavil, Winston Salem, N.C.	Weavil,	3 and 2			
158	James Tingley, Glen Cove, N.Y.	4 and 3		Weavil,		
154	Ed Tutwiler, Indianapolis, Ind.	Croonquist,		2 and 1		Dale Morey, 4 and 3
156	Neil Croonquist, Minneapolis, Minn.	1 up	Updegraff,			
155	Ed Updegraff, Tucson, Ariz.	Updegraff,	1 up, 20 holes			
158	John Pottle, Linville, N.C.	3 and 2				
147	John Morrell, Charlotte, N.C.	Morrell,				
155	Truman Connell, Pompano Beach, Fla.	3 and 2	Hyndman,			
152	William Hyndman, Huntingdon Valley, Pa.	Hyndman,	6 and 5			
158	John Richardson, Laguna Niguel, Calif.	6 and 4		Hyndman,		
153	Ralph Bogart, Kensington, Md.	Bogart,		3 and 2		
156	John Frithsen, Gloucester, Mass.	1 up, 20 holes	Humm,			
155	John Humm, Baldwin, N.Y.	Humm,	3 and 2			
158	Tom Forkner, Duluth, Ga.	3 and 2			Oehmig,	
151	Earl Burt, Paradise Valley, Ariz.	Burt,			1 up, 19 holes	
156	Paul Severin, Richmond, Va.	1 up, 19 holes	Oehmig,			
155	Lewis W. Oehmig, Lookout Mt., Tenn.	Oehmig,	3 and 2			
158	John Field, Brattleboro, Vt.	3 and 2		Oehmig,		
154	Karl Schmidt, Akron, Ohio	Schmidt,		4 and 3		
157	Anthony Maragno, Gloversville, N.Y.	1 up, 19 holes	Schmidt,			
155	Richard Remsen, Locust Valley, N.Y.	Remsen,	2 and 1			
159	John Miller, Minneapolis, Minn.	1 up				

*Medalist

1978
TWENTY-FOURTH SENIOR AMATEUR CHAMPIONSHIP

Held at Pine Tree Golf Club, Delray Beach, Florida, October 2-7.
Yardage—6,431. Par 72. 930 Entries, 145 Sectional Qualifiers, 145 Starters, 32 Qualifiers.

Qualifying Score	1st Round (18 Holes)	2nd Round (18 Holes)	3rd Round (18 Holes)	Semi-Finals (18 Holes)	Final (18 Holes)
*143	William Stewart, Springfield, Mo.	Stewart,			
152	Neil Croonquist, Minneapolis, Minn.	5 and 4	Hopwood,		
148	Dick Hopwood, Scottsdale, Ariz.	Hopwood,	1 up		
154	John Jacobs, Cedar Rapids, Iowa	1 up, 19 holes		Tutwiler,	
146	Ed Tutwiler, Indianapolis, Ind.	Tutwiler,		3 and 2	
153	Warren Tibbetts, Manchester, N.H.	4 and 3	Tutwiler,		
152	Vernon Ray, Jacksonville, Fla.	Ray,	4 and 3		
155	Henry Russell, Miami Beach, Fla.	3 and 1			Kline,
145	William Trombley, Dallas, Texas	Trombley,			1 up, 23 holes
153	Joe King, Birmingham, Ala.	5 and 4	Kline,		
151	William Patton, Morganton, N.C.	Kline,	4 and 3		
154	John Kline, Houston, Texas	1 up		Kline,	
147	William Campbell, Huntington, W.Va.	Oehmig,		5 and 4	
153	Lewis Oehmig, Lookout Mountain, Tenn.	1 up	Remsen,		
152	Richard Remsen, Locust Valley, N.Y.	Remsen,	1 up		
155	Edgar Updegraff, Tucson, Ariz.	2 and 1			
145	Dale Morey, High Point, N.C.	Morey,			
152	Grover Poole, Jonesboro, Ark.	5 and 4	Morey,		
149	Billy Napier, Orlando, Fla.	Kuntz,	1 up		
154	Robert Kuntz, Larchmont, N.Y.	6 and 4		Morey,	
147	Kenneth Weavil, Winston-Salem, N.C.	Weavil,		1 up	
153	Ralph Levy, Memphis, Tenn.	4 and 3	Weavil,		
152	A. M. Walker, Tuscaloosa, Ala.	Severin,	3 and 2		
155	Paul Severin, Ashland, Va.	8 and 6			Compton,
146	J. R. Ferguson, Dallas, Texas	Ferguson,			4 and 3
153	Don Bridge, Norfolk, Neb.	2 and 1	Hyndman,		
151	William Hyndman, Huntingdon Valley, Pa.	Hyndman,	1 up		
155	Robert Vaughn, Martinsburg, W.Va.	7 and 6		Compton,	
148	John Morrell, Charlotte, N.C.	Morrell,		3 and 2	
154	J. B. White, Lubbock, Texas	6 and 5	Compton,		
152	K. K. Compton, Marble Falls, Texas	Compton,	5 and 3		
155	Loyal Chapman, Minneapolis, Minn.	5 and 4			

K. K. Compton, 1 up

*Medalist

1979
TWENTY-FIFTH SENIOR AMATEUR CHAMPIONSHIP

Held at Chicago Golf Club, Wheaton, Illinois, September 17-22.
Yardage—6,572. Par 71. 1,023 Entries, 144 Sectional Qualifiers, 144 Starters.

Qualifying Score	1st Round (18 Holes)	2nd Round (18 Holes)	3rd Round (18 Holes)	Semi-Finals (18 Holes)	Final (18 Holes)
*143	Dale Morey, High Point, N.C.	Morey,			
152	Lyle Gray, Atherton, Calif.	3 and 2	Sussel,		
150	Allan Sussel, Bala Cynwyd, Pa.	Sussel,	4 and 2		
153	Robert Lochridge, Lake Bluff, Ill.	1 up, 19 holes		Sussel,	
149	Roger Hurd, Northfield, Ill.	Hurd,		2 and 1	
153	Vernon Ray, Jacksonville, Fla.	2 up	Hoff,		
151	John Kline, Houston, Texas	Hoff,	1 up, 21 holes		
154	Robert Hoff, Rochester, N.Y.	1 up, 19 holes			Oehmig,
145	Kenneth Weavil, Winston Salem, N.C.	Weavil,			1 up
152	Robert Cochran, Chesterfield, Mo.	3 and 2	Oehmig,		
151	Lewis W. Oehmig, Lookout Mountain, Tenn.	Oehmig,	5 and 4		
153	Dick Lytle, Chula Vista, Calif.	4 and 2		Oehmig,	
150	Karl H. Schmidt, Akron, Ohio	Trombley,		4 and 3	
153	William J. Trombley, Dallas, Texas	1 up, 19 holes	Sezna,		
151	W. W. Sezna, Greenville, Del.	Sezna,	3 and 2		
154	Tom Draper, Boca Raton, Fla.	1 up, 19 holes			
*143	William C. Campbell, Huntington, W.Va.	Campbell,			
152	Oren R. Shiro, Waterville, Maine	2 and 1	Campbell,		
151	Edgar R. Updegraff, Tuscon, Ariz.	Updegraff,	6 and 5		
153	Byron Swedberg, Moline, Ill.	1 up		Campbell,	
150	Leslie R. Fowler, Boulder, Colo.	Fowler,		1 up	
153	Harold Gould, Alexandria, Va.	5 and 4	Fowler,		
151	Truman Connell, Pompano Beach, Fla.	Connell,	2 and 1		
154	Charlie Van Ooteghem, Rock Island, Ill.	6 and 4			Campbell,
146	W. Brown McDonald, Warner Robins, Ga.	Morrell,			8 and 6
152	John P. Morrell, Charlotte, N.C.	1 up, 20 holes	Giddings,		
151	Harry W. Easterly, Jr., Richmond, Va.	Giddings,	4 and 3		
154	Dick Giddings, Fresno, Calif.	1 up, 19 holes		Willits,	
150	Jack Fraser, Atlanta, Ga.	Remsen,		1 up, 19 holes	
153	Richard Remsen, Jr., Locust Valley, N.Y.	4 and 3	Willits,		
151	Glenn H. Johnson, Detroit, Mich.	Willits,	3 and 2		
155	Robert Willits, Kansas City, Mo.	3 and 2			

William C. Campbell, 2 and 1

*Co-Medalists

1980
TWENTY-SIXTH SENIOR AMATEUR CHAMPIONSHIP

Held at Virginia Hot Springs Golf and Tennis Club (Cascades Course), Hot Springs, Virginia, September 15-20
Yardage—6,486. Par 71. 1,000 Entries, 144 Sectional Qualifiers, 144 Starters.

Qualifying Score	1st Round (18 Holes)	2nd Round (18 Holes)	3rd Round (18 Holes)	Semi-Finals (18 Holes)	Final (18 Holes)	
*147	William C. Campbell, Huntington, W. Va.	Campbell, 5 and 4				
155	Gene Christensen, Minneapolis, Minn.					
153	Robert Rowland, Portsmouth, Va.	Simons, 2 and 1	Campbell, 2 and 1			
156	Joseph Simons, N. Myrtle Beach, S.C.					
151	Neil Croonquist, Minneapolis, Minn.	Croonquist, 4 and 3		Campbell, 3 and 2		
156	T.A. Avarello, Fort Worth, Texas		Baker, 6 and 5			
154	Robert T. Baker, Ft. Collins, Colo.	Baker, 2 up				
158	William Trombley, Dallas, Texas				Campbell, 3 and 2	
150	E.R. Updegraff, Tucson, Ariz.	Updegraff, 3 and 2				
156	Robert Wallace, Pensacola, Fla.		Updegraff, 2 and 1			
154	Wally Senza, Greenville, Del.	Sussel, 2 and 1				
156	Allan Sussel, Bala-Cynwyd, Pa.			Updegraff, 3 and 1		
152	Lee Mackey, Birmingham, Ala.	Mackey, 6 and 5				William C. Campbell, 3 and 2
156	Harry Forbes, St. Joseph, Mich.		Mackey, 2 up			
155	John Morrell, Charlotte, N.C.	Jackson, 5 and 4				
159	James Jackson, Kirkwood, Mo.					
148	William Hyndman, III, Huntingdon Valley, Pa.	Hyndman, 2 and 1				
155	Robert F. Hoff, Rochester, N.Y.		Hyndman, 7 and 5			
154	Robert Myers, Indianapolis, Ind.	Myers, 1 up, 19 holes				
156	Landon G. Buchanan, Roanoke, Va.			Hopkins, 3 and 2		
151	Edwin Hopkins, Whitney, Texas	Hopkins, 4 and 2				
156	Paul Weis, Westerville, Ohio		Hopkins, 2 and 1			
155	Edward Clark, Franconia, N.H.	Clark, 1 up, 19 holes			Compton, 4 and 3	
159	Dale Morey, High Point, N.C.					
150	Lewis W. Oehmig, Lookout Mtn., Tenn.	Oehmig, 4 and 2				
156	Rowland Ferguson, Dallas, Texas		Compton, 5 and 3			
154	K.K. Compton, San Antonio, Texas	Compton, 4 and 3				
158	W.F. Colm, Pebble Beach, Calif.			Compton, 2 and 1		
152	John W. Kline, Houston, Texas	Kline, 2 and 1				
156	Earl Burt, Paradise Valley, Ariz.		Kline, 4 and 3			
155	Charlie Van Ooteghem, Rock Island, Ill.	Van Ooteghem, 4 and 3				
159	J.D. Johnson, Hagerstown, Md.					

*Medalist

SENIOR WOMEN'S AMATEUR CHAMPIONSHIP

Championship Trophy

Presented in October 1962 by the

United States Golf Association and Friends of Senior Golf

HISTORY

1962–The inauguration of a Senior Women's Amateur Championship followed the same pattern that preceded the start of the Senior Amateur Championship in 1955. A number of senior women's associations had come into being on various levels, but no one event was open to members of all USGA Regular Member Clubs. The request to begin such a competition was approved by the Executive Committee in January, 1962. The addition of the Championship to the USGA schedule meant that every man, woman and child golfer has an opportunity to compete in a USGA Championship. The format decided upon was a 54-hole stroke play competition over three days. Competitors must be at least 50 years old. In addition to the Championship proper, it was decided to award prizes in three age groups: A–50 through 54 years; B–55 through 59 years; and C–60 years and over. The first Championship was played at the Manufacturers' Golf and Country Club, Oreland, Pa. Miss Maureen Orcutt, Englewood, N.J., a reporter for the New York *Times*, won the Championship with a total of 240 through three consecutive rounds of 80. Miss Orcutt had twice been runnerup in the Women's Amateur Championship and was a member of the first four Curtis Cup Teams. Her first USGA Championship victory was particularly gratifying. The runnerup, seven strokes behind, was Mrs. Glenna Collett Vare, Bryn Mawr, Pa., six times the Women's Amateur Champion. In the age group competitions Mrs. Allison Choate, Rye, N.Y., was the A winner; Miss Orcutt won in the B section; and Mrs. Theodore W. Hawes earned the C award. The entry for the first Championship was 96.

1963–Mrs. Allison Choate, of Rye, N.Y., went four extra holes on top of an 18-hole playoff round to win the second Championship at The Country Club of Florida, Delray Beach. Mrs. Choate trailed Miss Maureen Orcutt of Englewood, N.J., the defending Champion, by four strokes with five holes to play in the regulation 54-hole stroke play Championship and capped her rally with a 25-foot putt for a birdie 4 on the 54th hole. Each scored 239. Next day in a playoff, Miss Orcutt again seemed on the way to a successful defense when she led by three strokes with three holes remaining. A bunker at the 16th proved her undoing and they finished in a tie at 81. On the fourth extra hole of sudden death, Mrs. Choate won with a birdie 2. Mrs. William R. Kirkland, Jr., of New York, was third with 241 for 54 holes. Next, at 247, was the six time former Women's Amateur Champion, Mrs. Glenna Collett Vare, of Philadelphia. In age class competition, Mrs. Choate repeated in Class A (50-54); Miss Orcutt in Class B (55-59) and Mrs. Vare won Class C (60 and over).

1964–Mrs. Hulet P. Smith, of Pebble Beach, Calif., a former national badminton champion who took up golf in 1944, won the third Senior Women's Amateur Championship with 81-79-87–247 at the Del Paso Country Club, Sacramento, Calif. Her winning margin was one stroke over Mrs. William R. Kirkland, Jr., of New York. The defending Champion, Mrs. Allison Choate, of Rye, N.Y., shared third place with Mrs. Maurice Glick, of Pikesville, Md., at 249. Mrs. Smith led by four strokes after 36 holes, lost the lead to Mrs. Kirkland midway of the final round, then regained the advantage with three holes to play. Mrs. Kirkland's 15-foot putt for a tie barely slipped past the hole at the final green. In age class competition, Mrs. Smith won Class A (50-54); Mrs. Aubrey E. Babson, of Novato, Calif., won Class B (55-59) with 254; and Mrs. C.D. Lee, of El Paso, Texas, won Class C (60 and over) with 251.

1965–Mrs. Smith became the only 1964 USGA Champion to defend a title successfully when she won her second straight Senior Women's Amateur Championship. Her score was 242 at the Exmoor Country Club, Highland Park, Ill., an improvement of five strokes over her winning total in 1964. In second place was Mrs. John S. Haskell, Titusville, Pa., with 245. The Champion and the runnerup, paired together on the final round, were all even with three holes to play. The critical hole was the 16th, a par-4, where Mrs. Smith made a birdie as Mrs. Haskell went one over par. In age class competition, Mrs. Smith won Class A (50-54); Mrs. Frank D. Mayer, Glencoe, Ill., won Class B (55-59) with 249; and Mrs. E.L. Cooley, Winnetka, Ill., won Class C (60 and over) with 257.

1966–Miss Maureen Orcutt, of Englewood, N.J., became the second repeat winner at the Lakewood County Club, New Orleans, when she scored 242. Miss Orcutt won the first Senior Women's Amateur in 1962. Mrs. Frank Goldthwaite of River Crest, Texas, was second with 248 and Mrs. Glenna Collett Vare, of Philadelphia, was third with 250. Mrs. Hulet P. Smith, of Pebble Beach, Calif., did not defend her title. She had won the two previous years. The three leaders represented different age classes. Miss Orcutt represented the 55-59-year-old division, Mrs. Goldthwaite the 50-54-year-old division, and Mrs. Vare the 60-and-over division.

1967–Mrs. Marge Mason, of Englewood, N.J., set a new scoring record of 236 for 54-hole Senior set a new scoring record of 236 at the Atlantic City Country Club, Northfield, N.J., and won by four strokes over Mrs. Hulet P. Smith, of Pebble Beach, Calif. The old record was 239, set by Mrs. Allison Choate and Miss Maureen Orcutt, of Englewood, N.J., in 1963. Mrs. Mason opened with 77 and was two strokes ahead of Mrs. Smith. She added 80 in the second round to take a three-stroke lead, and had a closing 79. Miss Orcutt, the defending Champion, scored 258 and never was a factor.

1968–Mrs. Philip Cudone, of Myrtle Beach, S.C., led every round at the Monterey Peninsula Country Club, Pebble Beach, Calif., and won by a record 10 strokes over Mrs. Hulet P. Smith, of Pebble Beach. Mrs. Cudone scored 236 for the 54 holes and equalled the Championship record set in 1967 by Mrs. Marge Mason, of Ridgewood, N.J. Mrs. Smith, the Champion in 1964 and 1965, scored 246, one stroke better than Mrs. Mason, who had 247. Mrs. Cudone was pursued closely by Mrs. Smith throughout the first two rounds. Mrs. Cudone started with 80 and was two strokes ahead of Mrs. Smith. Both ladies scored 79 in the second round. Mrs. Cudone had 77 in the last round; Mrs. Smith's final round was 85. In age class competition, Mrs. Cudone won Class A (50-54); Mrs. Smith won Class B (55-59); and Miss Maureen Orcutt, Englewood, N.J., won Class C (60 and over) with 255. For the first time the entry limit of 120 was surpassed and some entries had to be rejected.

1969–Mrs. Cúdone won her second consecutive Championship by defeating Mrs. Lowell D. Brown, of Tyler, Texas, in a playoff at the Ridglea Country Club, Fort Worth, Texas. Both ladies equalled the scoring record of 236 for the regulation 54 holes, and then Mrs. Cudone scored 76 in the playoff against 84 by Mrs. Brown. With nine holes to play in the Championship proper, Mrs. Cudone held a five-stroke lead over Mrs. Brown. Mrs. Cudone then lost four strokes to Mrs. Brown in the first three holes of the home nine, and three-putted the 18th to allow Mrs. Brown to pull even. In the playoff Mrs. Cudone birdied three of the first four holes and was never caught.

1970—Mrs. Philip Cudone, of Myrtle Beach, S.C., became the first player since the 1930s to hold a USGA Championship three consecutive years by winning the Senior Women's Amateur Championship at the Coral Ridge Country Club, Fort Lauderdale, Fla., with a record score of 231 for 54 holes. Mrs. Cudone won previously in 1968 and 1969. Miss Virginia Van Wie was the last to win three straight–the 1932-33-34 Women's Amateur Championships. Mrs. Cudone played rounds of 78-75-78 and bettered by five strokes the record 236 she shared with Mrs. Marge Mason. Mrs. Paulette Lee, of Coral Gables, Fla., was second with 239. Mrs. Cudone was four strokes ahead after the first round, and increased the margin to 12 after the second. The entry was 68.

1971–Mrs. Philip Cudone, of Myrtle Beach, S.C. became the first player ever to win a USGA Championship four consecutive years. Mrs. Cudone scored 77-81-78–236 at the Sea Island Golf Club, Sea Island, Ga., to win by one stroke over Mrs. Ann Gregory, of Chicago. Mrs. Gregory's scores were 77-82-78–237. Four other players had won three. They were Willie Anderson (Open, 1903-04-05), Mrs. Glenna Collett Vare (Women's Amateur, 1928-29-30), Miss Virginia Van Wie (Women's Amateur, 1932-33-34), and Miss Hollis Stacy (Girls' Junior, 1969-70-71). Mrs. Cudone led Mrs. Gregory by one stroke going into the final round and birdied the par 3 third. Mrs. Gregory went one over on the hole and Mrs. Cudone's lead was then three strokes. It remained the same until the 17th where Mrs. Cudone bogied and Mrs. Gregory birdied, cutting the lead to one stroke again. Mrs. Cudone got down in two from 35 feet on the home hole to win.

1972–Mrs. Philip Cudone, of Myrtle Beach, S. C., won her fifth consecutive Championship at the Manufacturers' Golf and Country Club, Oreland, Pa., and thus established a record. Only seven other players won as many as three consecutive USGA Championships. They are Willie Anderson (Open); Miss Beatrix Hoyt (Women's Amateur); Mrs. Alexa Stirling Fraser (Women's Amateur); Mrs. Glenna Collett Vare (Women's Amateur); Miss Virginia Van Wie (Women's Amateur); Miss Hollis Stacy (Girls' Junior), and Carl Kauffmann (Amateur Public Links). After a shaky first round of 82 which left her in a tie for seventh place with Mrs. I. Wayne Rutter, of Buffalo, N. Y., Mrs. Cudone scored 76-73 in the last two rounds for a total of 231, six strokes ahead of Mrs. Rutter, the runnerup. Mrs. Rutter kept pace with Mrs. Cudone for the first two days, shooting 82-76, but scored 79 in the last round against Mrs. Cudone's 73. In third place was Mrs. Helen Sigel Wilson, of Philadelphia, runnerup in the Women's Amateur Championship in 1941 and 1948. Mrs. Cudone's 231 total equalled the Championship record she set in 1970 at Coral Ridge Country Club, Fort Lauderdale, Fla. Her 73 was a competitive course record for the difficult Manufacturers' course, which measured 5,832 yards. The field was composed of 85 players from 24 states. This was the second Senior Women's Championship for the Manufacturers' Golf and Country Club, which was host to the inaugural in 1962.

1973—For the first time in five years the senior women had a new Champion. Mrs. David L. Hibbs, of Long Beach, Calif., concluded Mrs. Philip J. Cudone's custody of the Senior Women's Amateur Championship by scoring 229 for 54 holes at the San Marcos Country Club, Chandler, Ariz., in her second attempt. Mrs. Cudone, of Myrtle Beach, S. C., had won every year since 1968. Mrs. Hibbs' 229 set a record; the previous record of 231 was first set by Mrs. Cudone in 1970. Mrs. I. Wayne Rutter, of Williamsville, N. Y., was runnerup for the second year in succession, with a score of 235, six strokes back of Mrs. Hibbs. Mrs. James Roessler, of San Jose, Calif., was third at 236, while Mrs. Cudone finished fourth, one stroke back with 237. In the first round Mrs. Hibbs scored a four-over-par 8 on the first hole, but recovered and shot 77, tying Mrs. Cudone for second place. At the end of the day, Mrs.

Rutter led with 76. Mrs. Hibbs shot even par 74 the second day and took a six-stroke lead with a 36-hole score of 151. Mrs. Rutter was second with 157, Mrs. Cudone third at 158, and Mrs. Roessler fourth with 159. Both Mrs. Rutter and Mrs. Cudone shot 81, while Mrs. Roessler had an 80. Mrs. Hibbs shot 78 in the final round to Mrs. Rutter's 78 and Mrs. Cudone's 79. Mrs. Roessler had a 77 to pull ahead of Mrs. Cudone into third place. There were 98 entries—the second largest in the 12-year history of the Championship—and 95 starters.

1974—Mrs. Justine B. Cushing, of New York City, won the Championship with a 54-hole score of 231 over the 5,992-yard Lakewood Golf Club course in Point Clear, Ala. Mrs. Philip Cudone, was second at 233. Mrs. Cudone had won the Championship five consecutive years and was bidding to join Mrs. Glenna Collett Vare as the only woman to have won six United States Championships. Mrs. Vare won the United States Women's Amateur Championship six times between the years 1922 and 1935. Mrs. Gwen Hibbs, of Long Beach, Calif., the defending Champion and Mrs. Mark Porter, of Cinnaminson, N. J., tied for third place, seven strokes back. Mrs. Nancy Rutter, runnerup in 1972 and 1973, had a lost ball and scored a 10 on the first hole. She finished with a total score of 245 and placed sixth in the field of 118. Mrs. Cushing and Mrs. Hibbs started with 77 in the first round. Mrs. Cudone shot a 79, while Mrs. Porter, the 1949 United States Women's Amateur Champion, scored a 78. Mrs. Porter took the lead, by one stroke, after the second round with a 76 for 154 while both Mrs. Cushing and Mrs. Cudone shot 78s, giving them 155 for 36 holes. Mrs. Hibbs shot 83 in the second round and never challenged again. Mrs. Porter increased her lead to two strokes after three holes of the final round, but she lost two strokes to par on the fourth as Mrs. Cushing birdied. Mrs. Cushing was then a stroke ahead, and when she finished the first nine in 36, she led Mrs. Cudone by three strokes and Mrs. Porter by five. Mrs. Cushing finished the round with a 76, matched by Mrs. Cudone, while Mrs. Porter shot 84. The 76s by Mrs. Cushing and Mrs. Cudone in the last round and by Mrs. Porter in the second were the low rounds of the Championship. Mrs. Porter's 76 included an eagle three on the 408-yard, par-5 ninth hole. There were 122 entries and 119 starters from 28 states and Washington, D. C.

1975—Mrs. Albert Bower, of Pelham, N.Y. improved her score in every round and won the 14th United States Senior Women's Championship a day before her 53rd birthday. Mrs. Bower opened with 82, shot 79 in the second round, and finished with 73, for a 54-hole score of 234. Mrs. Bower won by six strokes over Mrs. Philip Cudone, of Myrtle Beach, S. C. with 240. Mrs. Mark Porter, of Cinnaminson, N. J., was third with 243. The Championship was played at the Rhode Island C. C., West Barrington, R. I. The defending champion, Mrs. Justine B. Cushing, from Glen Head, N.Y. finished in a tie for eighth place. Mrs. Cudone, who had won this event five times shared the first day lead with Mrs. Porter at 79, and took sole possession of first place with another 79 the second day. Mrs. Bower was in third place, three strokes behind Mrs. Cudone. Mrs. Porter shot an 81—despite six three-putt greens—and was in second place. In the final round Mrs. Bower picked up nine strokes on Mrs. Cudone, who could manage only an 82. Mrs. Porter added an 83. Mrs. Bower's closing 73, the only sub-par round of the Championship, included four birdies. There were 109 entrants, representing 22 states and the District of Columbia.

1976—Mrs. Cecile Maclaurin, of Savannah, Ga., the only player in the field to break 80 in every round, won the Championship over the Dunes Course of the Monterey Peninsula Country Club, Pebble Beach, Calif. Playing in her first Senior Women's Championship, Mrs. Maclaurin scored 78-75-77—230 for the 54 holes and won by seven strokes over Mrs. Lyle Bowman, from San Rafael, Calif. Mrs. Wayne Rutter, of Williamsville, N. Y., runnerup in 1972 and 1973, finished third at 240. The 1975 Champion, Mrs. Albert Bower, of Pelham, N. Y., was fifth with 246. Mrs. Philip J. Cudone, who won the Championship five times (1968 through 1972) and was runner-up twice, finished in fourth place. Mrs. Bowman led by three strokes after the first round with a par 75, Mrs. Maclaurin was second at 78, and Mrs. Justine Cushing, 1974 Champion, was third at 79. Mrs. Maclaurin took the lead after the second round with 153, while Mrs. Bowman added an 80 to her opening 75 for 155. Mrs. Rutter moved into third place at 157. There was no change in the top three the final day. Mrs. Maclaurin shot a 77, while Mrs. Bowman had 82 and Mrs. Rutter scored 83. One hundred-sixty-one players filed entries—a record; the field, however, is limited to 120, based on handicaps.

SENIOR WOMEN'S AMATEUR CHAMPIONSHIP

1977—Mrs. Mark A. Porter, of Cinnaminson, N. J., became the first Women's Amateur Champion (1949) to win the Senior Women's Championship. Mrs. Porter shot 75-77-78—230 for 54 holes at the Dunes Golf and Beach Club, in Myrtle Beach, S. C. She birdied the 18th hole, a par 5, to win by one stroke over Mrs. Paul Dye, Jr., of Delray Beach, Fla. Mrs. Dye had rounds of 79-77-75—231. They were the only players to break 80 for all three rounds. Mrs. Phillip J. Cudone, of Myrtle Beach, was third with rounds of 81-76-78—235. Mrs. Cudone won the Group 2 competition. Mrs. Robert MacLaurin, the defending Champion, from Savannah, Ga., finished fourth with a score of 236. The entry was 120.

1978—Mrs. Paul Dye, Jr., of Delray Beach, Fla., defeated Mrs. Robert H. Maclaurin, of Savannah, Ga., in an 18-hole playoff, 76-79, to win the Senior Women's Amateur Championship at the Rancho Bernardo Golf Club, in San Diego, Calif. It was the third playoff since the Championship was originated in 1962, and the first since 1969. Both players had completed the regulation 54 holes with 232 totals. Mrs. Dye had rounds of 74-75-83, and Mrs. Maclaurin, 76-81-75. Entering the final round, Mrs. Dye led Mrs. Paul G. Black by seven strokes and Mrs. Maclaurin and three others by eight strokes. In the playoff, Mrs. Dye parred the first nine holes for 35 and a four-stroke lead. Mrs. Maclaurin cut the lead to two strokes after 16 holes. Mrs. Dye scored pars on the last two holes. Mrs. Ellen Bowering just missed the playoff with a 233 total to finish third. The defending Champion, Mrs. Mark A. Porter, tied for seventh place with a 239 total. In the age-group competition, Group 1 was won by Mrs. Dye with her 232; Group 2, by Mrs. Black, 237; Group 3, by Mrs. James A. Roessler, 242; and Group 4, by Mrs. Frank Fisk, 257.

1979—Mrs. Paul Dye, Jr., 52, of Delray Beach, Fla., won her second consecutive Senior Women's Amateur Championship with a record score of 223, 10 over par. Mrs. Dye had rounds of 70-77-76 at the Hardscrabble Country Club, Fort Smith, Ark. She became only the fourth golfer to repeat as Champion. Her winning score was six strokes better than the previous record of 229, set by Mrs. David L. Hibbs in 1973. Her opening round of 70, one under par, establishing a single-round scoring record, was three strokes better than the previous record of 73 set by two former Champions, Mrs. Philip J. Cudone, in 1972, and Mrs. Albert Bower, in 1975. Mrs. Cecile H. Maclaurin, a former Champion, was runner-up for the second straight year. She had a 230 total. Mrs. Mildred M. Stanley was third, with 231. Mrs. Bower was fourth, with 236, and Mrs. Mark A. Porter, another former Champion, was fifth, with 237. Mrs. Dye's first-round 70 gave her an eight-stroke lead; Mrs. Maclaurin and Mrs. Stanley were tied for second place with rounds of 78. Mrs. Maclaurin cut the deficit to four strokes in the second round with a 73, the best score of the day, for a 151 total as Mrs. Dye slipped to a 77 for a total of 147. On the second hole of the final round, after Mrs. Maclaurin missed a 15-foot birdie putt, Mrs. Dye made a 10-foot putt to save par, and her four-stroke lead was never seriously challenged after that. Mrs. Dye had a final round 76 to Mrs. Maclaurin's 79. The final round was actually a race for second place. Mrs. Stanley had 74, the best score of the day, but Mrs. Maclaurin holed a 12-foot birdie putt on the final green to edge her for second place. In the age-group competition, Group 1 was won by Mrs. Dye; Group 2 by Mrs. Bower; Group 3 by Mrs. Janet Blair; and Group 4 by Mrs. Ann Gregory. There were 123 entries, short of the record of 161 set in 1976.

1980—Mrs. Mark A. Porter, 56, of Cinnaminson, New Jersey, won her second Senior Women's Amateur with a 54-hole score of 236, five over par, at the Sea Island Golf Club, in Sea Island, Georgia. Mrs. Porter had rounds of 81-80-75. Mrs. Cecile Maclaurin, the 1976 Champion, was the runner-up for the third consecutive year, with a 237 total. Mrs. Albert Bower, the 1975 Champion, finished third at 239. Defending Champion Mrs. Paul Dye, Jr. was 12th, at 246. Mrs. Maclaurin led the first round with 78, one over par. At 79 were Mrs. Lois Hodge, Mrs. Nancy Black, and Mrs. Kathryn Salley. Mrs. Bower was alone at 80. Mrs. Porter was in a group of eight players at 81. Mrs. Dye was at 82. On the second day, Mrs. Betty Probasco, playing in her first Senior Women's Amateur, took the lead with an even par 77 for a total of 158. Mrs. John Germain, also with 77, was one stroke back at 159. Mrs. Maclaurin slipped to an 82 and a share of third place with Mrs. Mildred Stanley at 160, two strokes behind Mrs. Probasco. Mrs. Porter had an 80 for a 161 total. After nine holes of the final round, Mrs. Porter had a score of 37 and stood one stroke ahead of Mrs. Probasco and two strokes ahead of Mrs. Maclaurin, Mrs. Bower, Mrs. Germain, Mrs. Hodge, and Mrs. Louise Wilson. Mrs. Porter made three birdies on the final nine, and after 16 holes she was three strokes ahead of Mrs. Maclaurin. Mrs. Maclaurin picked up two strokes in the last two holes with a par and a birdie. In the age group competition, Group 1 was won by Mrs. Maclaurin (237); Group 2 by Mrs. Porter (236); Group 3 by Mrs. Ruth Miller (253); and Group 4 by Mrs. Ann Gregory (245). Mrs. Gregory, the 1971 runner-up at Sea Island, not only won her age group by 19 strokes but she finished in a tie for ninth place in the overall Championship. A record 186 entries were accepted, surpassing the previous mark of 161 in 1976.

SENIOR WOMEN'S AMATEUR CHAMPIONSHIP

DATE	WINNER, RUNNER-UP	SCORE	SITE	ENTRY
1962 (Oct.)	Miss Maureen Orcutt Mrs. Edwin H. Vare, Jr. (Glenna Collett)	240 247	Manufacturers' G. & C.C., Oreland, Pa.	96
1963 (Oct.-Nov.)	Mrs. Allison Choate Miss Maureen Orcutt	239-81-17 239-81-19	C.C. of Florida, Delray Beach, Fla.	91
1964 (Oct.)	Mrs. Hulet P. Smith Mrs. William Kirkland	247 248	Del Paso C.C., Sacramento, Calif.	53
1965 (Oct.)	Mrs. Hulet P. Smith Mrs. John S. Haskell	242 245	Exmoor C.C., Highland Park, Ill.	70
1966 (Oct.)	Miss Maureen Orcutt Mrs. Frank Goldthwaite	242 248	Lakewood C.C. New Orleans, La.	68
1967 (Oct.)	Mrs. Marge Mason Mrs. Hulet P. Smith	236 240	Atlantic City C.C., Northfield, N.J.	80
1968 (Oct.)	Mrs. Philip J. Cudone Mrs. Hulet P. Smith	236 246	Monterey Peninsula C.C., Pebble Beach, Calif.	120
1969 (Oct.)	Mrs. Philip J. Cudone Mrs. Lowell D. Brown	236-76 236-84	Ridglea C.C., Forth Worth, Texas	79
1970 (Oct.)	Mrs. Philip J. Cudone Mrs. Paulette Lee	231 239	Coral Ridge C.C., Fort Lauderdale, Fla.	68
1971 (Oct.)	Mrs. Philip J. Cudone Mrs. Ann Gregory	236 237	Sea Island G.C., Sea Island, Ga.	111
1972 (Sept.)	Mrs. Philip J. Cudone Mrs. I. Wayne Rutter	231 237	Manufacturers' G. & C.C., Oreland, Pa.	94
1973 (Nov.)	Mrs. David L. Hibbs Mrs. I. Wayne Rutter	229 235	San Marcos C. C., Chandler, Ariz.	98
1974 (Oct.)	Mrs. Justine B. Cushing Mrs. Philip J. Cudone	231 233	Lakewood G. C., Point Clear, Ala.	122
1975 (Oct.)	Mrs. Albert Bower Mrs. Philip J. Cudone	234 240	Rhode Island C. C., West Barrington, R.I.	109
1976 (Sept.-Oct.)	Mrs. Cecile H. Maclaurin Mrs. Lyle O. Bowman	230 237	Monterey Peninsula C. C., Pebble Beach, Calif.	161
1977 (Oct.)	Mrs. Mark A. Porter Mrs. Paul Dye, Jr.	230 231	Dunes G. and B. C., Myrtle Beach, S. C.	120
1978 (Sept.)	Mrs. Paul Dye, Jr. Mrs. Cecile H. Maclaurin	232-76 232-79	Rancho Bernardo G. C., San Diego, Calif.	143
1979 (Sept.)	Mrs. Paul Dye, Jr., Mrs. Cecile H. Maclaurin	†223 230	Hardscrabble C. C., Fort Smith, Ark.	123
1980 (Sept.)	Mrs. Mark A. Porter d. Mrs. Cecile H. Maclaurin	236 237	Sea Island G.C., Sea Island, Ga.	§186

† Record score
§ Record entry
1 Sudden death playoff, 4 holes

1962
FIRST SENIOR WOMEN'S AMATEUR CHAMPIONSHIP

Held at Manufacturers' Golf and Country Club, Oreland, Pa., October 17-19.
Yardage—5,923. Par 73. 96 Entries, 91 Starters.

Letters preceding names denote age groups for
supplementary prize competition, as follows:
A—50 through 54 years; B—55 through 59 years; C—60 years and over.

All starters eligible for all three rounds. The 59 low scores plus ties:

						Score
1	B	Miss Maureen Orcutt, White Beeches, N.J.	80	80	80	240
2	B	Mrs. Glenna Collett Vare, Philadelphia, Pa.	86	80	81	247
3	A	Mrs. Allison Choate, Apawamis, N.Y.	80	85	85	250
4	B	Mrs. William Hockenjos, Jr., Baltusrol, N.J.	82	86	83	251
5	A	Mrs. Maurice Glick, Woodholme, Md.	85	86	82	253
6	B	Mrs. Charles F. Bartholomew, Dedham Country and Polo, Mass.	82	86	86	254
7	B	Mrs. John Pennington, C.C. of Buffalo, N.Y.	87	79	89	255
8	A	Mrs. Henry B. Jackson, The Country Club, Mass.	90	87	79	256
	C	Mrs. Theodore W. Hawes, Baltusrol, N.J.	86	85	85	256
10	A	Mrs. Marie M. Shehadi, Maplewood, N.J.	82	87	90	259
	B	Mrs. Harrison F. Flippin, Merion, Pa.	83	89	87	259
12	A	Mrs. Gerald R. Hellenbeck, Catskill, N.J.	86	87	87	260
	A	Mrs. Frances W. Lack, Wilmington, Del.	84	87	89	260
14	A	Mrs. Lloyd W. Dennis, Jr., Washington, Va.	85	91	87	263
	A	Mrs. Philip Somervell, Riverton, N.J.	88	84	91	263
16	B	Mrs. Ralph I. Raynor, Manufacturers', Pa.	89	87	88	264
17	A	Mrs. Reinert M. Torgerson, Cherry Valley, N.Y.	92	87	87	266
	A	Mrs. Robert Stimming, Las Posas, Calif.	83	90	93	266
19	B	Miss Jane Chalfant, West Chester, Pa.	90	88	89	267
20	A	Mrs. James S. Sherman, Sadaquada, N.Y.	90	89	89	268
21	A	Mrs. Anthony J. DeLisio, Woodstock, N.Y.	93	91	85	269
	B	Mrs. Willard Howard, The Country Club, Mass.	91	92	86	269
	A	Mrs. Emerson Y. Glendhill, Wilmington, Del.	89	88	92	269
24	A	Mrs. James Dorment, Montclair, N.J.	99	86	85	270
	A	Mrs. Albert R. Braun, East Orange, N.J.	86	95	89	270
26	A	Mrs. L. W. Smead, Oakland Hills, Mich.	92	86	93	271
	C	Mrs. J. Stuart Brown, Allegheny, Pa.	85	92	94	271
28	A	Mrs. Stanley A. Foster, Innis Arden, Conn.	90	90	92	272
	A	Mrs. James A. Swink, Belle Haven, Va.	86	89	97	272
30	B	Mrs. William Renner, Hempstead, N.Y.	94	96	83	273
	B	Mrs. Sally Francis, Apawamis, N.Y.	94	96	83	273
	B	Mrs. Thaddeus C. Owings, C.C. of York, Pa.	85	98	90	273
	C	Mrs. W. G. Boggs, Allegheny, Pa.	93	90	90	273
	A	Mrs. Charles S. Hale, III, Philadelphia Country, Pa.	84	97	92	273
35	B	Mrs. Hugh T. Nicolson, Wilmington, Del.	93	91	90	274
36	B	Mrs. Robert M. Ackerman, Century, N.Y.	90	96	90	276
	B	Mrs. Harald H. Gade, Gulph Mills, Pa.	90	98	88	276
	A	Mrs. Clement B. Newbold, Sunnybrook, Pa.	90	93	93	276
39	B	Mrs. William R. Bryant, Detroit, Mich.	91	92	96	279
40	B	Mrs. Christopher M. Turman, Sunnybrook, Pa.	92	95	93	280
	B	Mrs. George Salinett, Cazenovia, N.Y.	93	93	94	280
	A	Mrs. Marie D. Rowland, G.C. of Avon, Conn.	90	94	96	280
	A	Mrs. Philip H. Foote, Maplewood, N.J.	91	90	99	280
44	B	Mrs. Landra B. Platt, Chevy Chase, Md.	95	92	94	281
	A	Mrs. Walter Perry, Jr., Rhode Island, R.I.	94	93	94	281
46	B	Mrs. Samuel B. Crocker, Columbia, Md.	91	91	100	282
	C	Mrs. George R. Johnson, Philadelphia Cricket, Pa.	93	89	100	282
48	C	Mrs. Stuart H. Patterson, Pinehurst, N.C.	96	97	92	285
	B	Mrs. Winthrop Dow, Dedham Country & Polo, Mass.	100	89	96	285
	A	Mrs. John O. Saeger, Lehigh, Pa.	88	101	96	285
	C	Mrs. David H. Henderson, Congressional, Washington, D.C.	88	100	97	285
52	C	Mrs. Isabel M. Seiffert, Park C.C. of Buffalo, N.Y.	100	94	92	285
	B	Miss Winifred M. Faunce, Brooke Manor Farms, Md.	98	94	94	286
	A	Mrs. Ruth McCullough, Huntingdon Valley, Pa.	98	97	92	286
55	B	Mrs. Hugh F. Carroll, Lehigh, Pa.	98	98	92	288
	A	Mrs. John S. Connolly, Washington Va.	98	96	94	288
	A	Mrs. George L. Buck, Reading, Pa.	96	94	98	288
58	B	Mrs. James Medart, Glen Echo, Mo.	98	94	97	289
59	C	Mrs. Walter S. Heazlitt, New Albany, Ind.	93	102	95	290
	A	Mrs. Donald Strachan, Springdale, N.J.	92	101	97	290
	C	Mrs. William L. McGiverin, C.C. of Detroit, Mich.	94	95	101	290

The first word after the player's name is the name of the player's club.

1963
SECOND SENIOR WOMEN'S AMATEUR CHAMPIONSHIP

Held at The Country Club of Florida, Delray Beach, Fla., October 30-November 1.
Yardage—6,225. Par 75. 91 Entries, 85 Starters.
Letters preceding names denote age groups as follows:
A—50 through 54 years; B—55 through 59 years; C—60 years and over.

All starters eligible for all three rounds. **The 61 low scores:**

						Score
1	†A	Mrs. Allison Choate, Apawamis, N.Y.	80	81	78	239
2	†B	Miss Maureen Orcutt, White Beeches, N.J.	76	85	78	239
3	A	Mrs. William R. Kirkland, Jr., Meadow Brook, N.Y.	81	81	79	241
4	C	Mrs. Edwin H. Vare, Jr., C.C. of Florida, Fla.	85	85	77	247
5	A	Mrs. Maurice Glick, Woodholme, Md.	82	82	84	248
6	B	Mrs. Harrison Flippin, Merion, Pa.	84	84	81	249
	B	Mrs. John Pennington, C.C. of Buffalo, N.Y.	85	83	81	249
8	B	Mrs. Charles E. Eastman, Greenwich, Conn.	87	84	81	252
	B	Mrs. Willard Howard, The Country Club, Mass.	83	81	88	252
	A	Mrs. F.K. Thayer, Jr., Piping Rock, N.Y.	84	82	86	252
11	B	Mrs. Reinert M. Torgerson, Cherry Valley, N.Y.	84	84	86	254
12	A	Miss Betty S. Abernethy, Fox Chapel, Pa.	84	88	83	255
	A	Mrs. Anthony J. DeLisio, Woodstock, N.Y.	93	84	78	255
14	C	Mrs. Charles F. Bartholomew, Dedham, Mass.	89	84	85	258
15	B	Mrs. George M. Boughton, C.C. of Florida, Fla.	85	90	84	259
16	C	Mrs. Walborg Menzel, Delray Beach, Fla.	88	87	85	260
17	B	Mrs. Mark McGarry, Sunset, Fla.	85	87	89	261
	A	Mrs. Lloyd W. Dennis, Jr., Washington, Va.	86	84	91	261
	A	Mrs. William G. Hamilton, Jr., Huntingdon Valley, Pa.	87	86	88	261
20	B	Mrs. Sally Francis, Apawamis, N.Y.	89	85	88	262
	A	Mrs. George Brantley, Okefenokee, Ga.	88	87	87	262
	B	Mrs. Thomas Findley, Augusta, Ga.	88	90	84	262
	B	Mrs. Ralph I. Raynor, Manufacturers, Pa.	91	87	84	262
24	A	Mrs. Stanley A. Foster, Innis Arden, Conn.	89	87	87	263
25	A	Mrs. L.W. Smead, Oakland Hills, Mich.	87	88	90	265
26	B	Miss Winifred M. Faunce, Brooke Manor, Md.	87	91	88	266
27	B	Mrs. John J. Corson, Washington, Va.	89	93	86	268
28	C	Mrs. Belle G. Allen, James River, Va.	92	89	88	269
29	C	Mrs. Theodore W. Hawes, Baltusrol, N.J.	91	92	88	271
30	B	Miss Helen Ruff, Rolling Road, Md.	90	88	94	272
	B	Mrs. Boyd Everett, Indian Hill, Ill.	91	90	91	272
32	A	Mrs. John J. Farrell, Baltusrol, N.J.	90	89	94	273
	A	Mrs. Sidney M. Smith, Standard Town, Ga.	97	88	88	273
	B	Mrs. Samuel B. Crocker, Chevy Chase, Md.	95	87	91	273
	A	Mrs. Charles S. Hale, Philadelphia, Pa.	92	92	89	273
	C	Mrs. Winfield L. Waters, Big Spring, Ky.	86	95	92	273
	A	Mrs. W.D. Matthews, Ottawa, Ont., Canada	91	88	94	273
38	B	Miss Ruth E. Jepson, Wallingford, Conn.	87	93	94	274
	C	Mrs. Robert Seiffert, Park C.C. of Buffalo, N.Y.	87	96	91	274
40	B	Mrs. Robert M. Ackerman, Century, N.Y.	92	94	89	275
	B	Mrs. Harold H. Gade, Gulph Mills, Pa.	93	91	91	275
42	B	Mrs. Hugh F. Carroll, Lehigh, Pa.	90	92	94	276
43	C	Mrs. P.H. Waggoner, Hendersonville, N.C.	91	89	97	277
	A	Mrs. Elizabeth A. Hanna, C.C. of Fairfax, Va.	92	95	90	277
	C	Mrs. David H. Henderson, Congressional, Md.	87	94	96	277
46	A	Mrs. Thomas A. Burdeshaw, Griffin Ladies, Ga.	95	89	94	278
	A	Mrs. E.N. Rhodes, Sr., Ottawa, Ont., Canada	96	93	89	278
48	A	Mrs. Clement B. Newbold, Sunnybrook, Pa.	95	92	92	279
	A	Mrs. Frank S. Sims, Onwentsia, Ill.	97	93	89	279
	B	Mrs. James R. Medart, Glen Echo, Mo.	98	93	88	279
51	C	Mrs. George Johnson, Philadelphia Cricket, Pa.	96	92	92	280
	A	Mrs. Louise Hayes, Palma Ceia, Fla.	92	97	91	280
53	C	Mrs. Allen B. Laing, Plainfield, N.J.	88	98	95	281
	C	Mrs. Stuart H. Patterson, Pinehurst, N.C.	96	94	91	281
	A	Mrs. Joseph E. Waugh, Brooke Manor, Md.	91	91	99	281
	A	Mrs. James C. Gentle, Sunnybrook, Pa.	91	99	91	281
57	B	Mrs. Joseph C. Dey, Jr., The Creek, N.Y.	101	94	87	282
58	C	Mrs. J. Stuart Brown, Allegheny, Pa.	88	96	99	283
	A	Mrs. R.E. Cameron, Greenbriar Hills, Mo.	93	95	95	283
	B	Mrs. Eugene V. Homans, Maidstone, N.Y.	95	92	96	283
	C	**Mrs. Clyde A. Fisher, Sylvania, Ohio**	98	90	95	283

†Playoff. 18 holes, November 2—Mrs. Choate, 81-5-5-5-2; Miss Orcutt, 81-5-5-5-4.
The first word after the player's name is the name of player's club except in the case of a foreign entrant.

1964
THIRD SENIOR WOMEN'S AMATEUR CHAMPIONSHIP

Held at Del Paso Country Club, Sacramento, Calif., October 14-16.
Yardage—6,019. Par 72. 53 Entries, 50 Starters.
Letters preceding names denote age groups as follows:
A—50 through 54 years; B—55 through 59 years; C—60 years and over.

All starters eligible for all three rounds. The 44 low scores:

						Score
1	A	Mrs. Hulet P. Smith, Monterey Peninsula, Calif.	81	79	87	247
2	A	Mrs. William R. Kirkland, Jr., Meadow Brook, N.Y.	81	83	84	248
3	A	Mrs. Allison Choate, Apawamis, N.Y.	86	83	80	249
	A	Mrs. Maurice Glick, Woodholme, Md.	85	83	81	249
5	A	Mrs. Mike Baimas, Sacramento Women's, Calif.	84	84	83	251
	C	Mrs. C.D. Lee, El Paso, Texas	78	88	85	251
7	B	Mrs. Aubrey E. Babson, Marine, Calif.	83	86	85	254
	A	Mrs. Robert Stimming, Las Posas, Calif.	82	83	89	254
9	C	Mrs. James Montgomery, Oakmont, Calif.	89	81	86	256
10	A	Miss Elizabeth Brand, Del Paso, Calif.	87	85	89	261
11	B	Mrs. Sydney Grossman, Hillcrest, Calif.	87	88	88	263
12	A	Mrs. Fred S. Shehadi, Maplewood, N.J.	85	90	89	264
	A	Mrs. Nathan D. Wise, Peach Tree, Calif.	85	89	90	264
	A	Mrs. E.A. Boyd, Del Paso, Calif.	90	84	90	264
15	A	Mrs. Anthony J. DeLisio, Twaalskill, N.Y.	91	86	88	265
	A	Mrs. Jack Chew, Sacramento Women's, Calif.	86	89	90	265
17	A	Mrs. Rose M. Valerio, Sacramento Women's, Calif.	91	86	89	266
18	A	Mrs. Stanley Freeman, Sierra View, Calif.	87	91	89	267
19	B	Mrs. Donald E. Clark, San Diego, Calif.	87	92	91	270
	C	Mrs. K. Kenneth Smith, Irvine Coast, Calif.	91	88	91	270
21	B	Mrs. Landra B. Platt, Chevy Chase, Md.	95	88	89	272
22	A	Mrs. C.L. Warren, North Ridge, Calif.	92	90	91	273
	B	Mrs. Robert M. Ackerman, Century, N.Y.	96	90	87	273
24	A	Mrs. Aubrey Rawlins, San Francisco, Calif.	91	91	92	274
25	B	Mrs. Calvin Tilden, San Francisco, Calif.	90	94	91	275
	A	Mrs. John H. Gaw, Green Hills, Calif.	94	90	91	275
	B	Mrs. E.J. Rake, Meadow, Calif.	92	92	91	275
	A	Mrs. Thomas E. Ough, Sacramento Women's, Calif.	92	90	93	275
29	C	Mrs. A. Watt Bruner, Sequoyah, Calif.	94	89	93	276
	C	Mrs. W.W. Campbell, Los Angeles, Calif.	96	91	89	276
31	C	Mrs. Roxanna Setrakian, Olympic, Calif.	93	91	94	278
	A	Mrs. John H. Lowe, Santa Ana, Calif.	92	88	98	278
33	B	Mrs. H.W. Jerry, Ridgemoor, Ill.	95	94	91	280
34	A	Mrs. Arthur Wallace, Del Paso, Calif.	98	95	90	283
35	C	Mrs. Tanya McLaughlin, Phoenix, Ariz.	92	99	93	284
	B	Mrs. George L. Haneberg, Santa Ana, Calif.	93	93	98	284
37	B	Mrs. Le Roy Krusi, Claremont, Calif.	96	96	96	288
	B	Mrs. Ellard Pless, Irvine Coast, Calif.	95	97	96	288
39	B	Mrs. Harry N. Hensler, Meadow, Calif.	98	96	99	293
40	C	Mrs. M.A. Greenfield, Richmond, Calif.	105	99	94	298
41	A	Mrs. Herbert J. Johnson, Del Paso, Calif.	104	97	98	299
42	B	Mrs. Thomas K. McManus, Claremont, Calif.	100	102	98	300
43	A	Mrs. Dorothy W. Wolfe, Bellefonte, Ky.	106	103	101	310
44	B	Mrs. Don Thomas, Richmond, Calif.	106	104	105	315

The first word after the player's name is the name of the player's club.

1965
FOURTH SENIOR WOMEN'S AMATEUR CHAMPIONSHIP

Held at Exmoor Country Club, Highland Park, Ill., October 13-15.
Yardage–6,025. Par 72. 70 Entries, 66 Starters.
Letters preceding names denote age groups as follows:
A–50 through 54 years; B–55 through 59 years; C–60 years and over.

All starters eligible for all three rounds. The 61 low scores:

						Score
1	A	Mrs. Hulet P. Smith, Monterey Peninsula, Calif.	81	81	80	242
2	A	Mrs. John S. Haskell, Wanango, Pa.	88	79	78	245
3	B	Mrs. Frank D. Mayer, Lake Shore, Ill.	84	81	84	249
4	B	Mrs. Allison Choate, Apawamis, N.Y.	84	88	83	255
5	A	Mrs. Victor Ryden, Flint, Mich.	86	89	81	256
	A	Mrs. Mike Baimas, Bing Maloney Women's, Calif.	84	88	84	256
	A	Mrs. Maurice Glick, Woodholme, Md.	82	89	85	256
8	C	Mrs. E.L. Cooley, Indian Hill, Ill.	87	86	84	257
9	A	Mrs. Frank Goldthwaite, River Crest, Texas	90	87	83	260
	A	Mrs. Robert M. Monsted, New Orleans, La.	89	87	84	260
11	A	Mrs. Lawrence H. Selz, Northmoor, Ill.	84	91	86	261
12	B	Mrs. Howard C. Seehausen, Inverness, Ill.	91	90	81	262
	B	Mrs. John Pennington, Buffalo, N.Y.	92	83	87	262
14	A	Mrs. Henry Doubilet, Hollywood, N.J.	85	86	92	263
15	C	Mrs. Charles F. Bartholomew, Brae Burn, Mass.	83	88	93	264
16	A	Mrs. Fred Shehadi, Maplewood, N.J.	94	88	83	265
	A	Miss Elizabeth Brand, Del Paso, Calif.	89	87	89	265
18	A	Mrs. Edgar Reynolds, Lansing, Mich.	88	86	92	266
19	C	Mrs. W.K. Powell, San Angelo, Texas	87	87	93	267
	B	Mrs. Thomas E. Nolan, New Castle, Pa.	92	88	87	267
	B	Mrs. Almon Smith, B.P.O. Elks Lodge #48, Mich.	94	83	90	267
22	C	Mrs. J. Stuart Brown, Allegheny, Pa.	92	87	89	268
	C	Mrs. Ralph I. Raynor, Manufacturers, Pa.	85	93	90	268
24	C	Mrs. H.F.C. Brown, Racine, Wis.	97	89	83	269
	A	Mrs. Allyn G. Bonnie, Valley, Colo.	91	88	90	269
26	C	Mrs. H.W. Jerry, Ridgemoor, Ill.	88	90	92	270
27	A	Mrs. L.W. Smead, Oakland Hills, Mich.	88	91	92	271
28	B	Mrs. G.B. Gordon, Mount Bruno, Quebec, Canada	94	88	90	272
29	C	Mrs. Sally Francis, Apawamis, N.Y.	95	88	90	273
	A	Mrs. Clarence M. Loane, Woodmar, Ind.	92	91	90	273
	B	Mrs. Robert M. Ackerman, Century, N.Y.	86	96	91	273
	A	Mrs. C. Horton Smith, New Orleans, La.	88	88	97	273
33	B	Mrs. Boyd N. Everett, Indian Hill, Ill.	95	88	91	274
	A	Mrs. Edward C. Grelle, Barrington Hills, Ill.	93	89	92	274
35	A	Mrs. Stanley A. Foster, Innis Arden, Conn.	94	90	91	275
	B	Mrs. George Haneberg, Santa Ana, Calif.	93	88	94	275
37	A	Mrs. Arthur M. Rogers, Quail Hollow, N.C.	93	93	90	276
38	A	Mrs. Walter Perry, Jr., Rhode Island, R.I.	92	95	91	278
	A	Mrs. Lloyd W. Dennis, Jr., Washington, Va.	95	95	88	278
	B	Mrs. W.D. Matthews, Royal Ottawa, Canada	95	90	93	278
41	C	Mrs. Stuart H. Patterson, Pinehurst, N.C.	94	91	95	280
42	B	Mrs. V.J. Hultman, Glen Flora, Ill.	94	99	91	284
43	B	Mrs. John E. Lehman, Lake Geneva, Wis.	93	96	96	285
	B	Mrs. Landra B. Platt, Chevy Chase, Md.	93	94	98	285
	B	Mrs. Samuel B. Crocker, Chevy Chase, Md.	92	96	97	285
46	B	Mrs. William M. Walker, Jr., Exmoor, Ill.	90	95	101	286
47	A	Mrs. E.J. Somerville, Jr., Butterfield, Ill.	98	97	92	287
48	C	Mrs. Perry Pennington, Exmoor, Ill.	100	93	97	290
49	A	Mrs. Sidney W. Blackman, Conewango Valley, Pa.	103	99	89	291
	B	Miss Ada K. Rew, Glen View, Ill.	97	100	94	291
	A	Mrs. David A. Root, Gary, Ind.	98	99	94	291
	A	Mrs. D.J. Moos, Woodhill, Minn.	103	98	90	291
53	B	Mrs. Lester M. Cohn, Northmoor, Ill.	97	97	98	292
54	A	Mrs. Robert F. Edgar, Winnetka, Ill.	100	101	98	299
55	B	Mrs. James R. Medart, Glen Echo, Mo.	104	94	102	300
56	C	Mrs. W.L. Waters, Big Spring, Ky.	104	102	95	301
57	C	Mrs. Walter S. Heazlitt, New Albany, Ind.	101	105	96	302
58	C	Mrs. L. Norman Dilley, Greenville, Pa.	101	107	96	304
59	B	Mrs. DeWitt S. Schwartz, East Aurora, N.Y.	102	103	100	305
60	B	Mrs. Arthur N. Johnson, Hot Springs, Ark.	102	102	104	308
61	C	Mrs. Reid Johnson, Philadelphia Cricket, Pa.	119	103	96	318

The first word after the player's name is the name of the player's club.

1966
FIFTH SENIOR WOMEN'S AMATEUR CHAMPIONSHIP

Held at Lakewood Country Club, New Orleans, La., October 5-7.
Yardage—6,090. Par 72. 68 Entries, 63 Starters.
Letters preceding names denote age groups as follows:
A—50 through 54 years; B—55 through 59 years; C—60 years and over.

All starters eligible for all three rounds. The 56 low scores:

						Score
1	B	Miss Maureen Orcutt, White Beeches, N.J.	84	79	79	242
2	A	Mrs. Frank Goldthwaite, River Crest, Texas	83	85	80	248
3	C	Mrs. Edwin H. Vare, Jr., Philadelphia, Pa.	87	82	81	250
4	C	Mrs. C.D. Lee, El Paso, Texas	80	84	87	251
5	B	Mrs. Maurice Glick, Woodholme, Md.	81	88	86	255
6	B	Mrs. Thomas E. Nolan, New Castle, Pa.	88	86	82	256
7	A	Mrs. John S. Haskell, Wanango, Pa.	89	87	81	257
	A	Miss Lucille M. Busch, Oakmont, Calif.	89	85	83	257
9	B	Mrs. Allison Choate, Apawamis, N.Y.	89	86	83	258
10	C	Mrs. Charles F. Bartholomew, Brae Burn, Mass.	84	86	89	259
11	A	Mrs. Frederic C. Paffard, Jr., Allegheny, Pa.	86	87	89	262
	A	Mrs. Robert M. Monsted, New Orleans, La.	85	84	93	262
13	A	Mrs. Lowell D. Brown, Marshall Lakeside, Texas	91	83	90	264
14	A	Mrs. Sam Israel, Jr., Lakewood, La.	89	89	88	266
15	A	Mrs. A.J. Bryant, Rockland, N.Y.	88	91	89	268
	C	Mrs. Ralph I. Raynor, Manufacturers, Pa.	89	89	90	268
17	B	Mrs. Thomas Findley, Augusta, Ga.	89	94	86	269
	A	Mrs. Clyde T. Webb, Jackson, Ill.	91	91	87	269
19	A	Mrs. Rose M. Valerio, Sacramento Women's, Calif.	97	92	84	273
	A	Mrs. Larry Martin, Atlanta Athletic, Ga.	93	96	84	273
21	C	Mrs. Theodore W. Hawes, Baltusrol, N.J.	91	92	91	274
	A	Mrs. John Jay McDonald, Pass Christian Isles, Miss.	87	93	94	274
	B	Mrs. Fred Shehadi, Maplewood, N.J.	88	93	93	274
	B	Mrs. James Durham, Pass Christian Isles, Miss.	93	89	92	274
25	A	Mrs. Althea Casteix, St. John, La.	90	96	89	275
26	A	Mrs. Allyn G. Bonnie, Valley, Colo.	95	86	96	277
27	A	Miss Elizabeth S. Brand, Del Paso, Calif.	96	96	88	280
28	A	Mrs. Henry Doubilet, Hollywood, N.J.	93	99	90	282
	A	Mrs. Clarence M. Loane, Woodmar, Ind.	97	92	93	282
30	C	Mrs. George Reid Johnson, Philadelphia Cricket, Pa.	90	101	92	283
	C	Mrs. J. Stuart Brown, Allegheny, Pa.	96	94	93	283
	C	Mrs. Winfield L. Waters, Big Spring, Ky.	91	96	96	283
	A	Mrs. D.J. Moos, Woodhill, Minn.	96	91	96	283
34	B	Mrs. Robert M. Ackerman, Century, N.Y.	94	99	91	284
	B	Mrs. Sidney M. Smith, Standard Town, Ga.	97	95	92	284
	A	Mrs. John T. Rausch, Danville, Ill.	95	92	97	284
	B	Mrs. John J. Farrell, Baltusrol, N.J.	91	94	99	284
38	B	Mrs. Willard Howard, The Country Club, Mass.	93	99	93	285
39	B	Mrs. C. Horton Smith, New Orleans, La.	100	94	95	289
	A	Mrs. Walter Perry, Jr., Rhode Island, R.I.	96	96	97	289
	A	Mrs. David A. Root, Gary, Ind.	92	99	98	289
	C	Mrs. Edward W. Wentworth, Edgewood, Pa.	92	96	101	289
43	B	Mrs. Landra B. Platt, Chevy Chase, Md.	93	100	97	290
	A	Mrs. David B. Weir, Zanesville, Ohio	94	95	101	290
45	A	Mrs. William J. Harrison, New Orleans, La.	98	100	96	294
46	A	Mrs. Paul C. McWilliams, New Orleans, La.	99	97	100	296
47	B	Mrs. John Brazeal, Bellevue, Kansas	100	103	95	298
48	A	Mrs. Arthur G. Levy, Lakewood, La.	106	100	96	302
	A	Mrs. Sidney W. Blackman, Conewango Valley, Pa.	109	97	96	302
	B	Mrs. W.H. Henderson, Metairie, La.	105	100	97	302
51	B	Mrs. Charles F. Lynch, New Orleans, La.	100	98	108	306
52	C	Mrs. Walter S. Heazlitt, New Albany, Ind.	102	106	99	307
	C	Mrs. L. Norman Dilley, Greenville, Pa.	100	100	107	307
54	A	Mrs. Hyder F. Brewster, New Orleans, La.	103	103	104	310
55	C	Mrs. W.K. Cousins, St. John, La.	104	95	112	311
56	C	Mrs. True Davis, St. Joseph, Mo.	112	113	121	346

The first word after the player's name is the name of player's club.

1967
SIXTH SENIOR WOMEN'S AMATEUR CHAMPIONSHIP

Held at Atlantic City Country Club, Northfield, N.J., October 4-6.
Yardage—5,929. Par 73. 80 Entries, 80 Starters.
Letters preceding names denote age groups as follows:
A—50 through 54 years; B—55 through 59 years; C—60 years and over.

All starters eligible for all three rounds. The 63 low scores:

						Score
1	A	Mrs. Marge Mason, Ridgewood, N.J.	77	80	79	236
2	A	Mrs. Hulet P. Smith, Monterey Peninsula, Calif.	79	81	80	240
3	C	Mrs. John Pennington, Buffalo, N.Y.	82	80	83	245
4	A	Mrs. John S. Haskell, Wanango, Pa.	83	86	80	249
5	C	Mrs. Edwin H. Vare, Jr., Philadelphia, Pa.	84	80	86	250
	A	Mrs. Henry Doubilet, Hollywood, N.J.	81	87	82	250
7	B	Mrs. Allison Choate, Apawamis, N.Y.	86	84	81	251
8	B	Mrs. F.K. Thayer, Jr., Piping Rock, N.Y.	82	85	86	253
	B	Mrs. William G. Hamilton, Jr., Huntingdon Valley, Pa.	82	86	85	253
10	A	Mrs. W. Lincoln Boyden, Myopia Hunt, Mass.	85	80	[illegible]	254
	A	Mrs. W.R. Monro, Hercules, Del.	82	86	86	254
	A	Mrs. E.C. Kip Finch, New Canaan, Conn.	82	84	88	254
13	A	Mrs. Douglas C. Coupe, Schuyler Meadows, N.Y.	87	91	77	255
	B	Mrs. Emerson Y. Gledhill, Wilmington, Pa.	84	80	91	255
	A	Mrs. Vincent de Paul Larkin, Nassau, N.Y.	88	81	86	255
16	A	Mrs. Frederic C. Paffard, Jr., Allegheny, Pa.	86	90	81	257
17	C	Miss Maureen Orcutt, White Beeches, N.J.	83	86	89	258
	B	Mrs. James S. Sherman, Yahnundasis, N.Y.	82	95	81	258
19	B	Mrs. Philip Somervell, Riverton, N.J.	87	88	84	259
	B	Mrs. Joseph A. Nesbitt, Westchester, N.Y.	86	89	84	259
	A	Mrs. Thomas McDarby, Dean, N.J.	85	92	82	259
22	C	Mrs. Charles F. Bartholomew, Brae Burn, Mass.	86	89	85	260
	B	Mrs. Thomas E. Rhodes, Allegheny, Pa.	89	87	84	260
24	A	Mrs. Andre L. Sayles, Edison, N.Y.	86	90	85	261
25	C	Mrs. Harrison F. Flippin, Merion, Pa.	88	90	84	262
26	C	Mrs. Harald H. Gade, Gulph Mills, Pa.	86	93	84	263
27	B	Mrs. James Dorment, Montclair, N.J.	89	89	86	264
	B	Miss Marion Fairfield, Nashua, N.H.	88	88	88	264
29	B	Mrs. Llewellyn W. Smead, Oakland Hills, Mich.	90	91	85	266
30	B	Mrs. George H. Edwards, Bala, Pa.	85	92	90	267
31	B	Mrs. Edward J. Somerville, Jr., Butterfield, Ill.	91	87	90	268
32	A	Mrs. George J. Brady, Scarsdale, Conn.	88	89	92	269
	A	Mrs. Cyril Crabb, Spring Brook, N.J.	88	92	89	269
	C	Mrs. Willard Howard, The Country Club, Mass.	90	93	86	269
35	B	Miss Betty S. Abernethy, Fox Chapel, Pa.	88	92	90	270
	B	Mrs. Philip H. Foote, Maplewood, N.J.	90	90	90	270
37	B	Mrs. W. Lynn Hendrickson, Riverton, N.J.	88	95	88	271
38	B	Mrs. Fred Shehadi, Maplewood, N.J.	88	95	89	272
	A	Miss Elizabeth S. Brand, Del Paso, Calif.	92	88	92	272
	C	Mrs. H.F.C. Brown, Racine, Wis.	91	93	88	272
	B	Mrs. John J. Bryne, Atlantic City, N.J.	92	92	88	272
42	C	Miss Ruth E. Jepson, Wallingford, Conn.	89	90	94	273
	B	Mrs. C. Joseph Burnett, Plymouth, Pa.	93	89	91	273
	A	Mrs. Henry C. Trainer, St. Davids, Pa.	88	88	97	273
	A	Mrs. Maurice Burke, North Ridge, Calif.	93	91	89	273
	C	Mrs. Ralph I. Raynor, Manufacturers, Pa.	88	97	88	273
	B	Mrs. Norman M. Lack, Wilmington, Del.	90	90	93	273
48	A	Mrs. Robert C. Tyo, Baltimore, Md.	94	93	88	275
49	B	Mrs. Morton Bright, Riviera, Fla.	89	93	95	277
50	C	Mrs. C.M. Turman, Sunnybrook, Pa.	92	93	94	279
	B	Mrs. Reginald T. Blauvelt, Jr., Baltusrol, N.J.	88	99	92	279
	A	Mrs. DeLong H. Monahan, Merion, Pa.	92	98	89	279
53	B	Mrs. Gertrud de Markovic, Prince of Wales, N.J.	89	94	98	281
	C	Mrs. Herbert N. Allen, James River, Va.	97	96	88	281
55	B	Mrs. John J. Farrell, Baltusrol, N.J.	90	98	95	283
56	B	Mrs. Dean Stapp, St. Davids, Pa.	93	102	89	284
57	A	Mrs. Sidney W. Blackman, Conewango Valley, Pa.	95	94	96	285
	C	Mrs. W.L. Waters, Big Spring, Ky.	87	94	104	285
	C	Mrs. Lewis F. Gadbois, Brookfield, N.Y.	95	95	95	285
60	C	Mrs. Rufus Nelson, Concord, N.H.	93	96	97	286
	A	Mrs. Ralph Trimble Kent, Whitford, Pa.	96	100	90	286
	B	Mrs. Charles Novotny, New Haven, Conn.	99	95	92	286
	A	Mrs. Howard Hobson, Augusta, Ga.	97	97	92	286

The first word after the player's name is the name of the player's club.

1968
SEVENTH SENIOR WOMEN'S AMATEUR CHAMPIONSHIP

Held at Monterey Peninsula Country Club, Pebble Beach, Calif., October 2-4.
Yardage—5,935. Par 75. 120 Entries, 120 Starters.
Letters preceding names denote age groups as follows:
A—50 through 54 years; B—55 through 59 years; C—60 years and over.

All starters eligible for all three rounds. The 62 low scores:

						Score
1	A	Mrs. Philip J. Cudone, The Dunes, S.C.	80	79	77	236
2	B	Mrs. Hulet P. Smith, Monterey Peninsula, Calif.	82	79	85	246
3	A	Mrs. Marge Mason, Ridgewood, N.J.	87	80	80	247
4	A	Mrs. Philip G. Johnson, Fircrest, Wash.	85	85	79	249
5	B	Mrs. Ruth McCullah, Riviera, Calif.	82	84	84	250
6	A	Mrs. Jack Damerel, Annandale, Calif.	83	85	84	252
7	A	Mrs. Charles T. Brooke, Los Altos, Calif.	87	82	84	253
8	A	Mrs. Jack Fenton, Sierra View, Calif.	83	86	85	254
	A	Mrs. Douglass C. Coupe, Schuyler Meadows, N.Y.	82	86	86	254
10	A	Mrs. David P. Stephenson, San Antonio, Texas	84	89	82	255
	A	Mrs. Charles A. Cary, Sequoyah, Calif.	87	84	84	255
	B	Mrs. Harry Hamilton, Monterey Peninsula, Calif.	86	85	84	255
	C	Miss Maureen Orcutt, White Beeches, N.J.	84	84	87	255
14	A	Mrs. Allan A. Ryan, Red Hook, N.Y.	88	85	85	258
15	B	Mrs. Allison Choate, Apawamis, N.Y.	87	87	85	259
16	A	Mrs. Harold Stone, Hacienda, Calif.	94	82	84	260
17	B	Mrs. Fred Wetmore, Aptos Beach, Calif.	85	88	88	261
18	A	Miss Mildred Jude, Alameda Womens, Calif.	89	89	84	262
	B	Mrs. Thomas E. Rhodes, Allegheny, Pa.	87	89	86	262
	A	Mrs. James D. Berry, Jr., Wanango, Pa.	85	90	87	262
21	A	Mrs. Henry Doubilet, Hollywood, N.J.	88	87	88	263
22	B	Miss Betty S. Abernethy, Fox Chapel, Pa.	88	90	86	264
	A	Mrs. Joseph R. Ray, The Country Club, Utah	88	86	90	264
24	B	Miss Lucille M. Busch, Oakmont, Calif.	91	83	91	265
25	A	Mrs. Robert M. Monsted, New Orleans, La.	87	88	91	266
26	A	Mrs. John S. Haskell, Wanango, Pa.	90	90	87	267
27	A	Mrs. Robert M. Young, Tacoma, Wash.	90	91	87	268
	C	Mrs. Charles F. Bartholemew, Brae Burn, Mass.	96	84	88	268
29	A	Mrs. Clinton Adams, Sacramento Women's, Calif.	89	90	90	269
	B	Mrs. John H. Gaw, Green Hills, Calif.	88	90	91	269
	C	Mrs. Gene Shields, Riverside, Ore.	90	88	91	269
	A	Mrs. Stanley Polland, Annandale, Calif.	92	86	91	269
33	A	Mrs. David L. Hibbs, Eldorado Women's, Calif.	92	92	86	270
	B	Mrs. James S. Sherman, Yahnundasis, N.Y.	91	93	86	270
	A	Mrs. Les Darby, Riverside, Ore.	91	92	87	270
	B	Mrs. Almon Smith, Grand Rapids, Mich.	90	90	90	270
37	A	Mrs. Thomas Johnson, Rhode Island, R.I.	91	90	90	271
	A	Mrs. Raymond Ford Moreland, Fox Chapel, Pa.	93	88	90	271
39	C	Mrs. Donald Wilson, Del Paso, Calif.	91	91	90	272
	A	Mrs. Frederic C. Paffard, Jr., Allegheny, Pa.	92	90	90	272
	C	Mrs. H.W. Jerry, Paradise Valley, Ariz.	95	83	94	272
	A	Mrs. Reeves Kennedy, Riviera, Calif.	89	88	95	272
43	B	Mrs. Robert Stimming, Las Pasas, Calif.	92	91	90	273
44	A	Mrs. Morris Friedman, Brentwood, Calif.	94	91	89	274
	A	Miss Elizabeth S. Brand, Del Paso, Calif.	91	89	94	274
46	B	Mrs. C.W. Bruner, San Diego, Calif.	94	92	89	275
	A	Mrs. Roland Wise, Sacramento Women's, Calif.	99	86	90	275
	C	Mrs. Theodore W. Hawes, Baltusrol, N.J.	91	94	90	275
	B	Mrs. John Lowe, Santa Ana, Calif.	87	94	94	275
	C	Mrs. Edmund Hill Shea, Los Angeles, Calif.	92	90	93	275
51	B	Mrs. Paul Johnson, El Dorado Women's, Calif.	94	93	89	276
	A	Mrs. Charles W. Bonner, San Joaquin, Calif.	94	93	89	276
	B	Mrs. Charles G. DeKay, Presidio Army, Calif.	89	96	91	276
	C	Mrs. Sydney Grossman, Hillcrest, Calif.	91	92	93	276
55	A	Mrs. Michael E. Reed, Arrowhead, Calif.	95	93	89	277
	C	Mrs. Harry Hensler, Meadow, Calif.	94	93	90	277
	A	Mrs. Allen T. Mitchell, Jr., Deauville, Calif.	91	96	90	277
	B	Mrs. Lawrence H. Selz, Northmoor, Ill.	97	88	92	277
59	A	Mrs. Ted L. Fix, Fircrest, Wash.	98	89	91	278
	A	Mrs. Lamont Odett, Antelope Valley, Calif.	93	89	96	278
	A	Mrs. Charles F. Hamlin, University-Sequoia, Calif.	96	94	88	278
	B	Mrs. Allan Jones, Lake Elizabeth, Calif.	95	88	95	278

The first word after the player's name is the name of the player's club.

1969

EIGHTH SENIOR WOMEN'S AMATEUR CHAMPIONSHIP

Held at Ridglea Country Club, Fort Worth, Texas, October 1-3.

Yardage—5,650. Par 73. 79 Entries, 74 Starters.

Letters preceding names denote age groups as follows:

A—50 through 54 years; B—55 through 59 years; C—60 years and over.

All starters eligible for all three rounds. The 66 low scores:

						Score
1	†A	Mrs. Philip J. Cudone, The Dunes, S.C.	80	77	79	236
2	†B	Mrs. Lowell D. Brown, Willow Brook, Texas	79	80	77	236
3	A	Mrs. Marge Mason, Ridgewood, N.J.	75	82	83	240
	C	Miss Maureen Orcutt, White Beeches, N.J.	78	79	83	240
5	A	Mrs. Raymond F. Moreland, Fox Chapel, Pa.	87	81	77	245
6	B	Mrs. Allison Choate, Apawamis, N.Y.	80	86	80	246
7	A	Mrs. William L. Mosher, Jr., Orchard Lake, Mich.	80	81	86	247
8	A	Mrs. Paul W. Graham, El Dorado, Kans.	79	83	86	248
9	A	Mrs. Douglass C. Coupe, Schuyler Meadows, N.Y.	81	83	85	249
	A	Mrs. Frank H. Murray, Village, Calif.	84	77	88	249
	A	Miss Mary Louise Baker, Wildwood, Ky.	82	82	85	249
	B	Mrs. Frank Goldthwaite, River Crest, Texas	85	81	83	249
13	B	Mrs. John S. Haskell, Wanango, Pa.	82	84	84	250
	C	Mrs. G. William Bibby, Cumberland, Md.	83	86	81	250
	B	Mrs. James D. Berry, Jr., Wanango, Pa.	81	85	84	250
16	B	Mrs. Dorothy Franey Langkop, Brookhaven, Texas	81	83	87	251
	A	Mrs. Peck Westmoreland, Austin, Texas	86	80	85	251
18	A	Mrs. Drury S. Blair, Brookhaven, Texas	83	85	84	252
	A	Mrs. T. William Selman, Glen Oak, Ill.	84	85	83	252
	A	Mrs. Jack Munger, Dallas, Texas	86	83	83	252
21	A	Mrs. Robert M. Monsted, New Orleans, La.	82	82	89	253
22	C	Mrs. Theodore W. Hawes, Baltusrol, N.J.	86	87	81	254
	A	Mrs. William K. Stripling, Jr., River Crest, Texas	80	88	86	254
	C	Mrs. W.K. Powell, San Angelo, Texas	84	88	82	254
25	A	Mrs. Henry Doubilet, Hollywood, N.J.	85	81	89	255
26	A	Mrs. David P. Stephenson, San Antonio, Texas	90	81	85	256
27	B	Mrs. Thomas E. Rhodes, Allegheny, Pa.	83	83	91	257
	A	Mrs. Frederic Paffard, Jr., Allegheny, Pa.	86	82	89	257
29	C	Mrs. Paul H. Streit, Chevy Chase, Md.	91	83	84	258
	B	Mrs. A.G. Bonnie, Valley, Colo.	90	86	82	258
31	B	Mrs. James D. Flower, Allegheny, Pa.	87	83	90	260
32	B	Miss Helen Crews, Pharoahs, Texas	92	86	86	264
	A	Mrs. W.C. Castleberry, Dallas, Texas	90	89	85	264
	B	Mrs. John Lowe, Santa Ana, Calif.	89	87	88	264
35	C	Mrs. Agatha Lee, El Paso, Texas	90	91	84	265
	A	Mrs. John L. Surber, Oak Hills, Texas	84	90	91	265
	C	Mrs. H. W. Jerry, Ridgemoor, Ill.	89	87	89	265
38	B	Mrs. John J. Farrell, Baltusrol, N.J.	91	89	87	267
	A	Mrs. Norman Moize, Lakewood, Texas	91	86	90	267
40	A	Mrs. R.C. Hausinger, Ridglea, Texas	87	92	89	268
	C	Mrs. E.G. Brown, Diamond Oaks, Texas	89	90	89	268
42	B	Mrs. Howard W. Moore, Ridglea, Texas	93	88	90	271
	A	Mrs. E.A. Polumbus, Jr., Cherry Hills, Colo.	94	85	92	271
	B	Mrs. Frank Kottek, Coral Ridge, Fla.	93	88	90	271
	B	Mrs. H.A. Watson, Glen Lakes, Texas	86	93	92	271
	C	Mrs. James R. Medart, Glen Echo, Mo.	90	93	88	271
47	B	Mrs. E.E. Finch, Ridglea, Texas	91	93	88	272
	A	Mrs. Nelson Aregood, Rolling Hills, Colo.	93	93	86	272
49	A	Mrs. J. Hugh E. Davis, Baltusrol, N.J.	92	84	97	273
50	C	Mrs. John S. Brazeal, Bellevue, Kans.	94	91	89	274
51	B	Mrs. J.W. Newman, Diamond Oaks, Texas	89	99	87	275
	A	Mrs. Bill Kile, Jr., San Angelo, Texas	91	90	94	275
53	B	Mrs. Leon N. Roulier, Colby, Kans.	93	91	92	276
54	C	Mrs. J.R. Brown, Amarillo, Texas	90	94	94	278
	A	Mrs. C.L. Kramlich, Coral Ridge, Fla.	97	89	92	278
56	A	Mrs. Leo W. O'Dell, Ridglea, Texas	99	95	85	279
	C	Mrs. W. L. Waters, Big Spring, Ky.	96	94	89	279
58	A	Mrs. R. M. Park, Pinecrest, Texas	89	98	93	280
59	A	Mrs. Elmer C. Knott, Ridglea, Texas	97	93	93	283
60	C	Mrs. James K. Ellis, San Antonio, Texas	98	94	93	285
61	C	Mrs. C. C. Miller, Glen Garden, Texas	95	98	93	286
62	C	Mrs. W. Archer Maley, Corpus Christi, Texas	96	102	94	292
63	B	Mrs. Otha Lee Blythe, Waxahachie, Texas	96	101	96	293
64	A	Mrs. Pauline Delaney, Diamond Oaks, Texas	98	99	99	296
	C	Mrs. Justus Laube, Knickerbocker, N.J.	101	97	98	296
66	C	Mrs. Gay Younger, Roy H. Laird, Texas	99	103	99	301

†Playoff: 18 holes, October 4—Mrs. Cudone, 76; Mrs. Brown, 84.

The first word after the player's name is the name of the player's club.

1970

NINTH SENIOR WOMEN'S AMATEUR CHAMPIONSHIP

Held at Coral Ridge Country Club, Fort Lauderdale, Fla., October 7-9.
Yardage—5,856. Par 74. 68 Entries, 67 Starters.

Letters preceding names denote age groups for supplementary prize competition, as follows:

A—50 through 54 years; B—55 through 59 years; C—60 years and over.
All starters eligible for all three rounds. The 60 low scores:

						Score
1	A	Mrs. Philip J. Cudone, The Dunes, S.C.	78	75	78	231
2	A	Mrs. Paulette Lee, Coral Gables, Fla.	88	77	74	239
3	A	Mrs. Robert M. Young, Tacoma, Wash.	82	83	85	250
4	C	Miss Maureen Orcutt, White Beeches, N.J.	82	86	83	251
5	B	Mrs. Henry Doubilet, Hollywood, N.J.	84	81	87	252
6	A	Mrs. Mary Gillette Brown, Coral Gables, Fla.	88	80	85	253
	B	Mrs. Dorothy Franey Langkop, Brookhaven, Texas	86	85	82	253
8	A	Mrs. Drury S. Blair, Brookhaven, Texas	88	83	83	254
	A	Mrs. E. C. Kip Finch, New Canaan, Conn.	82	86	86	254
10	B	Mrs. William L. Mosher, Jr., Orchard Lake, Mich.	87	84	84	255
11	A	Mrs. Raymond F. Moreland, Fox Chapel, Pa.	86	85	85	256
	A	Mrs. Marge Mason, Ridgewood, N.J.	87	84	85	256
13	B	Mrs. Douglass C. Coupe, Schuyler Meadows, N.Y.	91	82	86	259
	B	Mrs. James D. Berry, Jr., Wanango, Pa.	90	84	85	259
15	A	Mrs. Robert Lyle, Kanawaki, Quebec, Canada	86	85	89	260
16	C	Mrs. John Pennington, Buffalo, N.Y.	87	87	87	261
17	A	Miss Mary Lou Baker, Wildwood, Ky.	89	82	93	264
18	B	Mrs. Audre L. Sayles, Edison, N.Y.	89	88	90	267
19	A	Mrs. Peter A. Mazza, Atlantis, Fla.	87	93	88	268
	C	Mrs. Charles F. Bartholomew, Brae Burn, Mass.	92	88	88	268
21	A	Mrs. T. William Selman, Glen Oak, Ill.	94	87	89	270
	C	Mrs. Harrison F. Flippin, Merion, Pa.	92	86	92	270
23	A	Mrs. Elizabeth M. Blatner, Colonie, N.Y.	88	93	90	271
24	B	Mrs. John S. Haskell, Wanango, Pa.	91	91	90	272
	A	Miss Lois S. Straus, Standard, Ky.	94	90	88	272
26	A	Mrs. Frederic C. Paffard, Jr., Allegheny, Pa.	89	90	94	273
	A	Mrs. Edward A. Ballman, Lockhaven, Ill.	96	87	90	273
28	B	Mrs. Thomas E. Rhodes, Allegheny, Pa.	93	92	90	275
29	B	Mrs. Edward G. Kelley, The Oaks, Okla.	91	95	90	276
30	A	Mrs. Bernard M. Halpern, Westmoreland, Pa.	93	94	90	277
	B	Mrs. Robert P. McDermott, Atlantis, Fla.	95	89	93	277
32	C	Mrs. Almon Smith, Elks, Mich.	87	90	101	278
33	A	Mrs. E. A. Polumbus, Jr., Cherry Hills, Colo.	95	93	91	279
	B	Miss Betty S. Abernethy, Fox Chapel, Pa.	97	94	88	279
	C	Mrs. James S. Sherman, Yahnundasis, N.Y.	91	92	96	279
36	B	Mrs. Ray Schwartz, Normandie, Mo.	91	93	97	281
	C	Mrs. Thomas E. Nolan, New Castle, Pa.	86	95	100	281
38	B	Mrs. Henry J. Noerling, Columbia, N.Y.	103	92	87	282
	B	Mrs. W. W. Munsey, Tamarac, Fla.	95	93	94	282
	C	Mrs. Philip H. Foote, Maplewood, N.J.	98	86	98	282
41	A	Mrs. Paul W. Adams, New Haven,Conn.	95	94	94	283
	B	Mrs. J. Hugh E. Davis, Baltusrol, N.J.	95	93	95	283
	C	Mrs. Ralph I. Raynor, Manufacturers, Pa.	94	97	92	283
44	C	Mrs. Lewis F. Gadbois, Brookfield, N.Y.	95	98	93	286
	C	Mrs. J. Stuart Brown, Allegheny, Pa.	96	95	95	286
46	C	Mrs. Edward W. Wentworth, Tamarac, Fla.	97	101	89	287
47	B	Mrs. John J. Farrell, Baltusrol, N.J.	100	98	91	289
	B	Mrs. Gertrud de Markovic, Prince of Wales, Santiago, Chile	91	97	101	289
	B	Miss Helen Crews, Pharaohs, Texas	96	96	97	289
	C	Mrs. Loren Fletcher, Willow Brook, Texas	97	96	96	289
51	B	Mrs. Frank Kottek, Coral Ridge, Fla.	95	94	102	291
	C	Mrs. Justus Laube, Knickerbocker, N.J.	93	102	96	291
53	C	Mrs. Winfield L. Waters, Big Springs, Ky.	90	100	103	293
54	B	Mrs. James D. Black, Atlantis, Fla.	96	93	105	294
55	C	Mrs. William L. May, Shady Hollow, Ohio	95	101	99	295
56	B	Mrs. Sidney W. Blackman, Conewango Valley, Pa.	106	95	95	296
57	B	Mrs. Grace Duvivier, Winnemucca, Nevada	103	98	99	300
58	C	Mrs. William J. Greenfield, Ponce de Leon, Fla.	99	107	97	303
59	B	Mrs. Wade W. Hildinger, Atlantis, Fla.	102	103	99	304
	C	Mrs. L. Norman Dilley, Greenville, Pa.	103	100	101	304

The first word after the player's name is the name of player's club.

1971
TENTH SENIOR WOMEN'S AMATEUR CHAMPIONSHIP

Held at Sea Island Golf Club, Sea Island, Ga., September 29–October 1.
Yardage–5,711 Par 75. 103 Entries, 103 Starters.

Letters preceding names denote age groups for supplementary prize competition, as follows:

A–50 through 54 years; B–55 through 59 years; C–60 years and over:
All Starters eligible for all three rounds. The 60 low scores:

						Score
1	A	Mrs. Philip J. Cudone, The Dunes, S.C.	77	81	78	236
2	A	Mrs. Ann Gregory, Chicago Women's, Ill.	77	82	78	237
3	A	Mrs. Harton S. Semple, Allegheny, Pa.	82	85	78	245
4	A	Mrs. Thorne Dempsey, Piping Rock, N.Y.	84	84	81	249
5	B	Mrs. Henry Doubilet, Hollywood, N. J.	86	82	83	251
6	A	Mrs. Drury Shelton Blair, Brookhaven, Texas	83	82	88	253
7	B	Miss Lucille M. Busch, Montgomery Village, Md.	85	81	89	255
8	A	Miss Josephine S. Smith, Merion, Pa.	85	83	88	256
9	A	Mrs. Raymond F. Moreland, Fox Chapel, Pa.	88	88	82	258
10	B	Mrs. Edward G. Kelley, Oaks, Okla.	84	86	89	259
	B	Mrs. Frederic C. Paffard, Jr., Allegheny, Pa.	85	86	88	259
	A	Mrs. Donald O'Brien, C.C. of Virginia, Va.	82	87	90	259
13	B	Mrs. Robert P. McDermott, Atlantis, Fla.	91	87	82	260
	A	Mrs. Frank Cush, Argyle, Md.	89	87	84	260
	A	Mrs. William E. Gilmore, Parkersburg, W. Va.	86	87	87	260
16	B	Mrs. Audre L. Sayles, Edison, N.Y.	86	90	85	261
	B	Mrs. Larry Martin, Atlanta Athletic, Ga.	86	89	86	261
	C	Mrs. Thomas Findley, Pinehurst, N.C.	88	86	87	261
19	B	Mrs. Robert M. Monsted, New Orleans, La.	88	84	91	263
20	A	Mrs. James F. Reinhardt, High Meadows, N.C.	87	91	86	264
	C	Mrs. Allison Choate, Apawamis, N.Y.	91	85	88	264
	B	Mrs. Douglass C. Coupe, Schuyler Meadow, N.Y.	88	87	89	264
23	A	Mrs. Sam DuBose, Okefenokee, Ga.	90	87	88	265
	C	Miss Betty S. Abernethy, Fox Chapel, Pa.	89	88	88	265
	A	Miss Nellie G. Randall, Chicago Women's, Ill.	88	87	90	265
	A	Mrs. Alice E. Lissner, Brunswick, Ga.	90	85	90	265
26	B	Mrs. Thomas R. Oleson, Brae Burn, Mass.	89	94	85	268
	A	Mrs. Eben C. Clark, Dedham, Mass.	92	85	91	268
	B	Mrs. Ruth ven Vaux, Sea Pines, S.C.	85	91	92	268
29	A	Mrs. Edward H. Gerry, Piping Rock, N.Y.	87	97	85	269
	C	Mrs. L.W. Smead, Oakland Hills, Mich.	91	90	88	269
	B	Mrs. Donald J. Mercer, Baltusrol, N.J.	90	89	90	269
32	C	Mrs. Lloyd W. Dennis, Jr., Washington, Va.	88	93	89	270
	B	Mrs. Henry J. Noerling, Columbia, N.Y.	91	89	90	270
	A	Mrs. Reeves Kennedy, Riviera, Calif.	88	91	91	270
35	A	Miss Lois Straus, The Standard, Ky.	93	93	85	271
	B	Mrs. James D. Berry, Jr., Wanango, Pa.	93	89	89	271
	C	Mrs. Freeman Darby, Sea Island, Ga.	87	89	95	271
38	B	Mrs. Harold Howard, C.C. of Lansing, Mich.	90	96	86	272
	B	Mrs. Allyn G. Bonnie, Valley, Colo.	87	97	88	272
	A	Mrs. Paul W. Admas, Round Hill, Conn.	86	92	94	272
	A	Mrs. Henry M. Weston, Crown Point, Vt.	91	86	95	272
42	A	Miss Evelyn S. Smith, Merion, Pa.	91	93	89	273
	C	Mrs. Charles F. Bartholomew, Brae Burn, Mass.	93	85	95	273
44	A	Mrs. George R. Thurman, Firestone, Ohio	93	92	89	274
	B	Mrs. C. Frank Pollen, Skokie, Ill.	92	92	90	274
	B	Mrs. James B. Baldwin, Piping Rock, N.Y.	89	95	90	274
47	A	Miss Mary Lou Baker, Wildwood, Ky.	96	88	91	275
	A	Mrs. Seymour Holub, Shackamaxon, N. J.	95	94	86	275
	A	Mrs. William Marshall, Sea Island, Ga.	88	96	91	275
50	A	Mrs. E.M. Blatner, Colonie, N.Y.	91	94	91	276
51	A	Mrs. T. William Selman, Glen Oak, Ill.	93	91	93	277
52	A	Mrs. Bernard Halpern, Westmoreland, Pa.	95	96	88	279
	C	Mrs. Winthrop Dow, Sea Pines, S.C.	95	89	95	279
54	C	Mrs. F.K. Thayer, Jr., Piping Rock, N.Y.	91	97	92	280
55	B	Mrs. Sidney W. Blackman, Sea Pines, S.C.	93	96	92	281
	C	Miss Marion Fairfield, Nashua, N.H.	94	94	93	281
	C	Mrs. Frederick Bellinger, Atlanta Athletic, Ga.	93	95	93	281
	B	Mrs. Peter A. Mazza, Atlantis, Fla.	96	91	94	281
59	B	Mrs. George D. Brantley, Okefenokee, Ga.	94	98	90	282
	B	Mrs. Clarence M. Loane, Woodmar, Ind.	100	91	91	282
	A	Mrs. Edward A. Ballman, Lackhaven, Ill.	98	92	92	282
	B	Mrs. Howard R. Finn, Crown Point, Vt.	97	92	93	282
	B	Mrs. John Barnes, Sea Island, Ga.	97	90	95	282

The first word after the player's name is the name of the player's club.

1972
ELEVENTH SENIOR WOMEN'S AMATEUR CHAMPIONSHIP

Held at Manufacturers' Golf and Country Club, Oreland, Pa., September 27-29.
Yardage—5,832. Par 74. 94 Entries, 85 Starters.

Letters preceding names denote age groups for supplementary prize competition, as follows:

A–50 through 54 years; B–55 through 59 years; C–60 years and over:

All starters eligible for all three rounds. The 67 low scores:

						Score
1	A	Mrs. Philip J. Cudone, Myrtle Beach, S.C.	82	76	73	231
2	A	Mrs. I. Wayne Rutter, Williamsville, N.Y.	82	76	79	237
3	A	Mrs. Charles Wilson, Gladwyne, Pa.	80	81	79	240
4	A	Mrs. Theron U. Lyman, Basking Ridge, N.J.	79	85	82	246
5	A	Mrs. Ann Gregory, Gary, Ind.	80	86	83	249
	B	Mrs. George M. Trainor, Rochester, N.Y.	84	79	86	249
7	C	Mrs. Edwin H. Vare, Jr., Narragansett, R.I.	86	84	83	253
	B	Mrs. Douglass C. Coupe, Rochester, N.Y.	85	84	84	253
9	A	Mrs. Edwin M. Burke, Far Hills, N.J.	84	83	87	254
10	A	Mrs. Drury S. Blair, Dallas, Texas	88	84	83	255
11	A	Mrs. Raymond F. Moreland, Pittsburgh, Pa.	86	90	80	256
	B	Mrs. Gene Genesio, Elkins Park, Pa.	81	89	86	256
	A	Mrs. Maurice D. Mosher, Chaddsford, Pa.	83	83	90	256
14	A	Mrs. John B. Kane, Jr., North Wales, Pa.	78	92	87	257
	C	Miss Maureen Orcutt, Englewood, N.J.	81	87	89	257
16	B	Mrs. Frederic C. Paffard, Jr., Sewickley, Pa.	86	85	87	258
17	B	Mrs. Marge Mason, West Englewood, N.J.	84	93	82	259
	A	Mrs. William E. Gilmore, Vienna, W. Va.	89	85	85	259
	B	Mrs. James G. B. Perkins, Jr., Abington, Pa.	87	86	86	259
	B	Mrs. James D. Berry, Jr., Titusville, Pa.	85	83	91	259
21	A	Mrs. Harton S. Semple, Sewickley, Pa.	87	87	86	260
22	B	Mrs. Audre L. Sayles, Schenectady, N.Y.	87	87	88	262
23	C	Mrs. Allison Choate, Rye, N.Y.	89	88	86	263
	B	Mrs. John S. Haskell, Titusville, Pa.	91	86	86	263
	C	Mrs. William G. Hamilton, Jr., Rydal, Pa.	86	88	89	263
	B	Mrs. William L. Mosher, Jr., Bloomfield Hills, Mich.	91	82	90	263
27	A	Mrs. DeWitt L. Alexandre, Far Hills, N.J.	90	88	86	264
	B	Mrs. Henry Doubilet, Elberon, N.J.	85	90	89	264
29	A	Mrs. Eugene L. Frazier, Ardmore, Pa.	84	95	87	266
	C	Mrs. Harrison F. Flippin, Douglasville, Pa.	86	88	92	266
	B	Mrs. Maitland Alexander, Sewickley, Pa.	85	88	93	266
32	A	Mrs. Donald O'Brien, Richmond, Va.	92	86	89	267
33	C	Mrs. George H. Edwards, Lansdowne, Pa.	93	91	84	268
	A	Miss Nellie G. Randall, College Park, Ga.	93	88	87	268
	B	Miss Lois S. Straus, Louisville, Ky.	92	96	90	268
36	A	Mrs. Eben Clark, Dover, Mass.	96	89	84	269
	B	Mrs. Paul W. Adams, Greenwich, Conn.	91	90	88	269
38	A	Mrs. Frank Cush, Washington, D.C.	88	89	93	270
	A	Mrs. I. M. Scott, Meadowbrook, Pa.	91	86	93	270
40	C	Mrs. Philip Somervell, Riverton, N.J.	88	92	91	271
	A	Mrs. Seymour Holub, East Orange, N.J.	87	87	97	271
42	A	Mrs. Morris Katz, Philadelphia, Pa.	91	92	90	273
	A	Mrs. Percy R. Pyne III, Far Hills, N.J.	89	87	97	273
44	A	Mrs. Henry M. Weston, Claremont, N.H.	89	102	83	274
	A	Mrs. John D. Matsinger, Media, Pa.	94	91	89	274
46	C	Mrs. Ralph I. Raynor, Wyncote, Pa.	91	94	91	276
47	B	Mrs. Frank O'Neill, Bryn Athyn, Pa.	92	94	93	279
	A	Mrs. Nathan Lewis Smith, Jr., Baltimore, Md.	94	91	94	279
	A	Mrs. Anthony Genesio, Glenside, Pa.	89	93	97	279
50	A	Mrs. Kate H. Guest, Hanover, N.H.	91	95	94	280
51	C	Mrs. Emily M. Fentress, Haverford, Pa.	89	97	97	283
	C	Mrs. Joseph Frelinghuysen, Morristown, N.J.	90	95	98	283
53	A	Mrs. Bernard Halpern, Pittsburgh, Pa.	93	95	96	284
	C	Mrs. John J. Farrell, Springfield, N.J.	93	94	97	284
55	C	Mrs. Christopher M. Turman, Jenkintown, Pa.	91	96	98	285
	B	Mrs. Butler Cox, Rochester, N.Y.	95	95	95	285
57	B	Mrs. E. Smith Jackson, Providence, R.I.	95	93	100	288
58	B	Mrs. E. A. Polumbus, Jr., Englewood, Colo.	95	95	100	290
	B	Miss Mary Lou Baker, Louisville, Ky.	99	92	99	290
60	B	Mrs. George E. Fissel, Williamsport, Pa.	94	100	99	293
61	A	Mrs. Theodore Hartung, Louisville, Ky.	96	100	100	296
62	C	Mrs. Bernice E. Wood, Los Angeles, Calif.	103	94	101	298
	C	Mrs. Clement B. Newbold, Jenkintown, Pa.	100	99	99	298
64	B	Mrs. Howard R. Finn, Springfield, Vt.	100	97	104	301
65	C	Mrs. Winfield L. Waters, Louisville, Ky.	103	103	96	302
66	C	Mrs. C. Joseph Burnett, Plymouth Meeting, Pa.	103	103	103	309
67	C	Mrs. DeWitt S. Schwartz, East Aurora, N.Y.	101	106	103	310

1973
TWELFTH SENIOR WOMEN'S AMATEUR CHAMPIONSHIP

Held at San Marcos Country Club, Chandler, Arizona, November 7 - 9.
Yardage—5,891 Par 74. 98 Entries, 95 Starters.

Letters preceding names denote age groups for supplementary prize competition, as follows:
A—50 through 54 years; B—55 through 59 years; C—60 years and over:
All Starters eligible for all three rounds. The low scores:

						Score
1	B	Mrs. David L. Hibbs, Long Beach, Calif.	77	74	78	229
2	A	Mrs. I. Wayne Rutter, Williamsville, N. Y.	76	81	78	235
3	B	Mrs. James Roessler, San Jose, Calif.	79	80	77	236
4	B	Mrs. Philip J. Cudone, Myrtle Beach, S. C.	77	81	79	237
5	B	Mrs. Douglass C. Coupe, Rochester, N. Y.	82	78	78	238
6	C	Miss Maureen Orcutt, Durham, N. C.	80	81	79	240
	B	Mrs. Justine B. Cushing, New York, N. Y.	81	80	79	240
8	B	Mrs. James A. Hume, Incline Village, Nev.	82	82	78	242
	A	Mrs. Charles R. Stimpson, Rancho Santa Fe, Calif.	79	83	80	242
10	B	Mrs. Robert M. Young, Tacoma, Wash.	84	82	77	243
	A	Mrs. William Windatt, Phoenix, Ariz.	85	80	78	243
12	A	Mrs. Allen Georgenson, La Habra, Calif.	86	79	79	244
13	A	Mrs. Martin Leach, Monterey, Calif.	84	78	83	245
	A	Mrs. Edwin M. Burke, Far Hills, N. J.	82	77	86	245
15	C	Mrs. Hulet Smith, Pebble Beach, Calif.	78	82	86	246
16	B	Mrs. Frederic C. Paffard, Jr., Sewickley, Pa.	83	82	82	247
	B	Mrs. George M. Trainor, Rochester, N. Y.	82	82	83	247
18	B	Mrs. Raymond F. Moreland, Pittsburgh, Pa.	83	86	79	248
	B	Mrs. Henry Doubilet, Elberon, N. J.	89	79	80	248
	B	Mrs. Charles F. Hamlin, Fresno, Calif.	86	81	81	248
21	B	Mrs. W. A. Willmarth, Tucson, Ariz.	90	81	78	249
	B	Mrs. Marge Mason, West Englewood, N. J.	85	82	82	249
23	B	Mrs. Les Darby, Portland, Ore.	89	78	84	251
	C	Mrs. Frank T. Fisk, Vashon, Wash.	79	85	87	251
25	A	Mrs. H. J. Baker, Green Valley, Ariz.	90	82	81	253
	B	Mrs. John S. Haskell, Titusville, Pa.	83	88	82	253
	A	Mrs. Jimmy A. Thompson, Montebello, Calif.	82	87	84	253
	A	Mrs. Charles W. Peckinpaugh, Toledo, Ohio	84	84	85	253
	A	Mrs. Paul W. Graham, El Dorado, Kans.	86	81	86	253
	A	Mrs. Murray Gordon, New York, N. Y.	81	84	88	253
31	A	Mrs. Henry M. Weston, Claremont, N. H.	82	91	81	254
32	A	Mrs. Thomas S. Harrison, Jr., Milwaukie, Ore.	86	80	89	255
	B	Mrs. W. K. Stripling, Jr., Ft. Worth, Texas	83	81	91	255
34	B	Mrs. Lamont Odett, Palmdale, Calif.	83	94	79	256
35	A	Mrs. Graham J. Barbey, Astoria, Ore.	83	87	87	257
	B	Mrs. Edward A. Ballman, East Alton, Ill.	85	84	88	257
37	B	Mrs. Robert M. Monsted, New Orleans, La.	90	83	85	258
	A	Mrs. Philip Long, Colorado Springs, Colo.	90	83	85	258
	B	Mrs. Grace Duvivier, Winnemucca, Nev.	89	80	89	258
40	C	Mrs. Allison Choate, Rye, N. Y.	87	85	88	260
41	A	Mrs. H. J. Guernsey, Jr., Tempe, Ariz.	90	88	83	261
	C	Mrs. James D. Berry, Jr., Titusville, Pa.	87	86	88	261
43	B	Mrs. Joan C. Barthold, Sedona, Ariz.	84	93	85	262
	C	Mrs. Frank Goldthwaite, Ft. Worth, Texas	89	86	87	262
	A	Mrs. S. A. Hendrickson, Cortland, N. Y.	85	88	89	262
46	C	Mrs. Ben E. Glasgow, Capleville, Tenn.	91	88	84	263
	A	Miss Frances Rich, Dallas, Texas	93	83	87	263
	A	Miss Nellie G. Randall, College Park, Ga.	92	84	87	263
	B	Mrs. Donald J. Mercer, Summit, N. J.	85	89	89	263
50	B	Mrs. J. Hugh E. Davis, Short Hills, N. J.	87	87	90	264
51	B	Mrs. Reeves Kennedy, Pacific Palisades, Calif.	93	84	88	265
	B	Mrs. Victor C. Folsom, Green Valley, Ariz.	83	94	88	265
53	A	Mrs. Dan Siegel, Frontenac, Mo.	89	90	87	266
	A	Mrs. George H. Van Tassel, Blairstown, N. J.	93	85	88	266
55	B	Mrs. Audre L. Sayles, Schenectady, N. Y.	89	89	89	267
56	B	Mrs. Edward G. Kelley, La Canada, Calif.	88	91	89	268
57	B	Mrs. E. A. Dorsey, Denver, Colo.	89	89	91	269
	C	Mrs. Ida Mae Powell, San Angelo, Texas	87	88	94	269
59	A	Mrs. Peck Westmoreland, Lockhart, Texas	98	85	87	270
	B	Mrs. Roland Wise, Sacramento, Calif.	94	88	88	270
	A	Mrs. Seymour Holub, East Orange, N. J.	88	89	93	270
62	C	Mrs. W. W. Campbell, Los Angeles, Calif.	98	87	86	271
	B	Mrs. Fred Shantz, Tucson, Ariz.	96	87	88	271
	B	Mrs. Elizabeth M. Blatner, Altamont, N. Y.	91	91	89	271
	C	Mrs. Harrison F. Flippin, Douglassville, Pa.	89	88	94	271
66	B	Mrs. Robert Skok, Mesa, Ariz.	92	91	89	272
	A	Mrs. Scott Bower, Jr., Dallas, Texas	90	90	92	272
68	B	Mrs. John L. Surber, San Antonio, Texas	88	91	93	272

1974
THIRTEENTH SENIOR WOMEN'S AMATEUR CHAMPIONSHIP

Held at Lakewood Golf Club, Point Clear, Alabama, October 9-11
Yardage—5,992. Par 74. 122 Entries. 119 Starters.

Letters preceding names denote age groups for supplementary prize competition, as follows:
A—50 through 54 years; B—55 through 59 years; C—60 years and over:
All Starters eligible for all three rounds. The low scores:

						Score
1	B	Mrs. Justine B. Cushing, New York, N. Y.	77	78	76	231
2	B	Mrs. Philip J. Cudone, Myrtle Beach, S. C.	79	78	76	233
3	B	Mrs. David L. Hibbs, Long Beach, Calif.	77	83	78	238
	A	Mrs. Mark A. Porter, Cinnaminson, N. J.	78	76	84	238
5	A	Mrs. John Hume, Birmingham, Mich.	81	80	81	242
6	A	Mrs. I. Wayne Rutter, Buffalo, N. Y.	82	83	80	245
7	A	Mrs. Harton S. Semple, Sewickley, Pa.	80	81	86	247
8	A	Mrs. Jimmy A. Thompson, Montebello, Calif.	87	78	83	248
9	C	Miss Maureen Orcutt, Durham, N. C.	79	88	83	250
10	B	Mrs. George M. Trainor, Rochester, N. Y.	85	84	82	251
11	A	Mrs. Frank Cush, Washington, D. C.	86	84	83	253
12	B	Mrs. Raymond F. Moreland, Pittsburgh, Pa.	86	87	81	254
	C	Mrs. John S. Haskell, Titusville, Pa.	85	87	82	254
	A	Mrs. Charles Stimpson, Rancho Santa Fe, Calif.	83	86	85	254
15	A	Mrs. Ann Gregory, Gary, Ind.	87	85	83	255
	A	Mrs. Gordon R. McGrath, Glen Head, N. Y.	89	83	83	255
	B	Mrs. Frederic C. Paffard, Jr., Sewickley, Pa.	88	80	87	255
18	B	Mrs. William E. Gilmore, Vienna, W. Va.	88	88	83	259
19	B	Mrs. Wilson Evans, Peoria, Ill.	83	92	85	260
	A	Mrs. Nick Melnyk, Brunswick, Ga.	86	88	86	260
21	A	Mrs. Nellie G. Randall, College Park, Ga.	84	92	85	261
22	A	Mrs. Harry W. Roberts, Dadeville, Ala.	85	94	83	262
	C	Miss Lucille M. Busch, Poway, Calif.	92	86	84	262
	C	Mrs. James D. Berry, Jr., Titusville, Pa.	84	90	88	262
25	A	Mrs. Robert McKee, Grosse Pointe Shores, Mich.	89	89	85	263
	B	Mrs. Henry Doubilet, Elberon, N. J.	89	88	86	263
27	B	Mrs. Charles W. Peckinpaugh, Toledo, Ohio	92	81	91	264
28	A	Mrs. Bruce Gilliland, Kimball, Neb.	87	91	87	265
	A	Mrs. Ben H. Freeman, Lafayette, La.	87	87	91	265
	A	Mrs. Leonard L. Shertzer, Jr., Montgomery, Ala.	87	86	92	265
31	A	Mrs. Richard H. Semple, Jr., Sewickley, Pa.	84	91	92	267
	B	Mrs. Robert M. Monsted, New Orleans, La.	88	87	92	267
33	B	Mrs. Douglass C. Coupe, Rochester, N. Y.	88	90	90	268
	A	Mrs. Charles F. Troxel, Ft. Lauderdale, Fla.	87	89	92	268
35	A	Mrs. Amos Huguley, Jr., West Point, Ga.	94	88	87	269
36	A	Mrs. Henry M. Weston, Springfield, Vt.	89	97	84	270
	B	Mrs. E. A. Polumbus, Jr., Englewood, Colo.	91	89	90	270
38	B	Mrs. Russell B. Sell, Birmingham, Ala.	92	91	89	272
39	A	Mrs. George H. Van Tassel, Blairstown, N. J.	92	92	89	273
	B	Mrs. Scott Bower, Jr., Dallas, Texas	91	91	91	273
41	B	Mrs. William P. Snyder, III, Sewickley, Pa.	91	93	90	274
	B	Mrs. Edward A. Ballman, East Alton, Ill.	91	96	87	274
43	A	Mrs. Dan Siegel, Frontenac, Mo.	92	93	91	276
	C	Miss Betty S. Abernethy, Pittsburgh, Pa.	92	92	92	276
45	A	Mrs. Edward Poitevent, New Orleans, La.	92	93	92	277
	B	Mrs. Frances M. Pitman, Point Clear, Ala.	94	91	92	277
	B	Mrs. Audre L. Sayles, Schenectady, N. Y.	87	95	95	277
48	B	Mrs. Margot F. Reck, St. Joseph, Mo.	95	93	90	278
49	B	Mrs. Edison Casey, St. Marys, Ga.	97	92	90	279
	C	Mrs. Thomas A. Burdeshaw, Hampton, Ga.	96	90	93	279
	B	Mrs. J. Hugh E. Davis, Short Hills, N. J.	89	95	95	279
	C	Mrs. Lowell D. Brown, Flint, Texas	91	90	98	279
53	C	Mrs. Joseph McPhillips, Point Clear, Ala.	90	97	93	280
	C	Mrs. Theodore W. Hawes, Delray Beach, Fla.	91	96	93	280
	C	Mrs. J. Stuart Brown, Sewickley, Pa.	95	92	93	280
	A	Mrs. E. J. Mittelbronn, Jr., Chalmette, La.	90	94	96	280
57	A	Mrs. Celeste V. Phipps, Englewood, N. J.	95	95	91	281
	A	Mrs. Morris W. Newman, Metairie, La.	94	94	93	281
	A	Mrs. Roger Sherman, Pensacola, Fla.	92	96	93	281
	A	Mrs. Arthur Randol, Jr., Lafayette, La.	91	96	94	281
	C	Mrs. C. Horton Smith, Metairie, La.	92	95	94	281
62	B	Mrs. Robert M. Whiting, Mobile, Ala.	95	94	93	282
	C	Mrs. Howard R. Finn, Springfield, Vt.	97	92	93	282
	A	Mrs. John Hineman, Dighton, Kans.	94	90	98	282
65	B	Mrs. John J. McDonald, Bay St. Louis, Miss.	98	93	92	283
	C	Miss Faith Clark, Chevy Chase, Md.	90	100	93	283
	A	Mrs. Emil A. Kremer, Tuscaloosa, Ala.	101	89	93	283
	A	Miss Cynthia Brants, Alna, Maine	97	90	96	283
69	B	Mrs. Hal McCall, Tuscaloosa, Ala.	96	93	95	284
		Mrs. George H. Thomas, Lafayette, La.	92	97	95	284

1975
FOURTEENTH SENIOR WOMEN'S AMATEUR CHAMPIONSHIP

Held at Rhode Island Country Club, West Barrington, Rhode Island, October 1-3
Yardage—5,985. Par 74. 109 Entries, 107 Starters

Letters preceding names denote age groups for supplementary prize competition, as follows
A—50 through 54 years; B—55 through 59 years; C—60 years and over
All Starters eligible for all three rounds. The 65 low scores:

						Score
1	A	Mrs. Albert B. Bower, Pelham, N.Y.	82	79	73	234
2	B	Mrs. Philip J. Cudone, Myrtle Beach, S.C.	79	79	82	240
3	A	Mrs. Mark A. Porter, Cinnaminson, N.J.	79	81	83	243
4	A	Mrs. I. Wayne Rutter, Williamsville, N.Y.	81	82	83	246
5	A	Mrs. Thorne Dempsey, Stony Brook, N.Y.	87	84	81	252
6	B	Mrs. E. C. K. Finch, New Caanan, Conn.	83	89	86	258
	A	Mrs. Paul G. Black, Greenbush, Mass.	89	82	87	258
8	B	Mrs. Justine B. Cushing, Glen Head, N.Y.	83	90	86	259
	B	Mrs. Richard B. Redfield, West Hartford, Conn.	85	86	88	259
10	A	Mrs. Winslow V. Grant, Bangor, Maine	89	91	82	262
11	B	Mrs. Karl G. Clement, Glen Head, N.Y.	87	90	86	263
	B	Mrs. George M. Trainor, Rochester, N.Y.	88	88	87	263
	A	Mrs. Harton S. Semple, Sewickley, Pa.	84	91	88	263
14	B	Mrs. Frederic C. Paffard, Jr., Sewickley, Pa.	90	91	83	264
	B	Mrs. Edwin M. Burke, Far Hills, N.J.	84	93	87	264
	B	Mrs. Drury Shelton Blair, Dallas, Texas	88	89	87	264
17	A	Mrs. William E. Gilmore, Vienna, W.Va.	83	94	88	265
18	C	Mrs. Thomas E. Rhodes, Sewickley, Pa.	90	91	86	267
	B	Mrs. Raymond S. Patton, West Hartford, Conn.	86	90	91	267
	C	Miss Maureen Orcutt, Durham, N.C.	84	90	93	267
21	B	Mrs. Frank Cush, Washington, D.C.	88	93	87	268
	A	Mrs. Gordon R. McGrath, Glen Head, N.Y.	88	91	89	268
	A	Mrs. Richard DeRuvo, Hudson, Mass.	84	90	94	268
24	A	Mrs. James Pickrel, Pompano Beach, Fla.	86	89	94	269
25	A	Miss Claire R. Nolan, Waltham, Mass.	89	93	88	270
	A	Mrs. Percy R. Pyne, III, Far Hills, N.J.	91	89	90	270
27	C	Mrs. Douglass C. Coupe, Rochester, N.Y.	91	94	86	271
	C	Mrs. Joseph Frelinghuysen, Far Hills, N.J.	92	89	90	271
29	A	Mrs. Ralph W. Petrone, Blacksburg, Va.	93	92	87	272
	C	Mrs. John S. Haskell, Titusville, Pa.	92	90	90	272
	B	Mrs. Donald K. McClusky, Worcester, Mass.	7	94	91	272
	C	Mrs. W. L. Boyden, Wenham, Mass.	90	89	93	272
33	B	Mrs. Charles W. Peckinpaugh, Toledo, Ohio	86	96	91	273
	C	Miss Lucille M. Busch, Poway, Calif.	89	91	93	273
35	B	Mrs. Ann Gregory, Gary, Ind.	88	94	92	274
36	B	Mrs. C. George Taylor, Providence, R.I.	95	92	88	275
	B	Mrs. Raymond F. Moreland, Pittsburgh, Pa.	92	93	90	275
	C	Mrs. E. Brainard Graves, Providence, R.I.	91	93	91	275
	A	Mrs. John B. Mitsock, Warwick, R.I.	90	93	92	275
40	A	Mrs. Harold Wolfson, Providence, R.I.	96	91	89	276
	B	Mrs. Leslie W. Sampson, Bradford, Mass.	91	95	90	276
	A	Mrs. Eileen T. Kenefick, Needham, Mass.	88	96	92	276
	B	Mrs. Thomas Johnson, Barrington, R.I.	90	91	95	276
44	A	Mrs. Paul F. Hartz, West Barrington, R.I.	91	98	89	278
	A	Mrs. Charles Stimpson, Rancho Santa Fe, Calif.	94	91	93	278
	A	Mrs. Joseph B. Rudnick, Keyport, N.J.	89	92	97	278
47	B	Mrs. Amos Huguley, Jr., West Point, Ga.	94	90	95	279
	C	Mrs. Allison Choate, Rye, N.Y.	92	95	92	279
49	B	Mrs. Reeves L. Kennedy, Pacific Palisades, Calif.	93	92	95	280
50	B	Mrs. Henry M. Weston, Claremont, N.H.	92	97	93	282
	B	Miss Barbara Groves, South Dartmouth, Mass.	97	92	93	282
	B	Mrs. Bernard Halpern, Pittsburgh, Pa.	93	92	97	282
53	A	Mrs. Dot Roe, Westport, Conn.	93	97	93	283
	C	Mrs. Walter Perry, Jr., Barrington, R.I.	94	96	93	283
	B	Mrs. Genevieve Lanyon, Westhampton Beach, N.Y.	97	88	98	283
56	C	Mrs. Audre L. Sayles, Schenectady, N.Y.	94	92	98	284
57	B	Mrs. Richard P. Owsley, Hubbard, Ohio	88	102	95	285
	B	Mrs. Edward H. Gerry, Mill Neck, N.Y.	94	94	97	285
59	A	Mrs. Dan Siegel, Chesterfield, Mo.	99	92	97	288
60	B	Mrs. DeWitt L. Alexandre, Far Hills, N.J.	91	101	97	289
	C	Mrs. Harold L. Howard, Lansing, Mich.	94	98	97	289
62	C	Mrs. James E. Hollis, Providence, R.I.	93	97	100	290
63	C	Mrs. Francis K. Thayer, Jr., Locust Valley, N.Y.	97	97	97	291
	B	Mrs. Seymour Holub, East Orange, N.J.	92	102	97	291
65	B	Mrs. Frank Stackhouse, Short Hills, N.J.	97	100	95	292

1976
FIFTEENTH SENIOR WOMEN'S AMATEUR CHAMPIONSHIP

Held at Monterey Peninsula Country Club, (Dunes Course), Pebble Beach, California, September 29-October 1
Yardage—5,968. Par 75. 161 Entries, 150 Starters

Letters preceding names denote age groups for supplementary prize competition, as follows:
A—50 through 54 years; B—55 through 59 years; C—60 years and over.
All Starters eligible for all three rounds. The 65 low scores:

						Score
1	A	Mrs. Cecile H. Maclaurin, Savannah, Ga.	78	75	77	230
2	A	Mrs. Lyle O. Bowman, San Rafael, Calif.	75	80	82	237
3	A	Mrs. I. Wayne Rutter, Williamsville, N.Y.	80	77	83	240
4	B	Mrs. Philip J. Cudone, Myrtle Beach, S.C.	81	81	82	244
5	A	Mrs. Albert B. Bower, Pelham, N.Y.	85	80	81	246
6	B	Mrs. Helen Sigel Wilson, Gladwyne, Pa.	84	80	84	248
	A	Mrs. Peter Patch, Lafayette, Calif.	82	84	82	248
8	B	Mrs. Ann Gregory, Gary, Ind.	83	84	85	252
	A	Mrs. Kenneth Rowe, Suisun, Calif.	80	89	83	252
10	B	Mrs. Justine B. Cushing, Glen Head, N.Y.	79	84	90	253
	B	Mrs. Ruth White Miller, Long Beach, Calif.	81	84	88	253
	B	Mrs. Jimmy A. Thompson, Montebello, Calif.	83	87	83	253
13	B	Mrs. William E. Gilmore, Vienna, W.Va.	84	84	86	254
14	C	Mrs. Hulet Smith, Pebble Beach, Calif.	83	91	81	255
15	A	Mrs. John E. Cann, Mill Valley, Calif.	84	85	88	257
16	A	Mrs. Phyllis LaSorella, Pebble Beach, Calif.	87	83	89	259
	B	Mrs. Kathleen McDonald, Pebble Beach, Calif.	87	84	88	259
	C	Mrs. Frank Fisk, Vashon, Wash.	90	90	79	259
19	A	Mrs. Alma Robertson, Napa, Calif.	85	85	90	260
	A	Mrs. Edward W. Mueller, Davenport, Iowa	87	84	89	260
	B	Mrs. Thomas S. Harrison, Jr., Milwaukie, Ore.	88	85	87	260
22	C	Miss Lucille M. Busch, Poway, Calif.	84	86	92	262
	C	Mrs. Ann J. Griffel, Eldora, Iowa	90	83	89	262
	A	Mrs. Robert L. Golden, Redondo Beach, Calif.	86	87	89	262
25	B	Mrs. James A. Roessler, San Jose, Calif.	90	85	88	263
	A	Mrs. George MacGibbon, Minnetonka, Minn.	89	88	86	263
27	B	Mrs. Raymond F. Moreland, Pittsburgh, Pa.	88	87	89	264
	B	Mrs. David L. Hibbs, Long Beach, Calif.	91	86	87	264
	C	Mrs. Harry A. Hamilton, Pebble Beach, Calif.	88	91	85	264
	A	Mrs. Charles Stimpson, Rancho Santa Fe, Calif.	89	90	85	264
31	A	Mrs. William S. Windatt, Phoenix, Ariz.	91	85	89	265
32	A	Mrs. Penelope LaGrange, Pebble Beach, Calif.	88	88	90	266
	C	Miss Peggy Rutledge, Beverly Hills, Calif.	91	86	89	266
	A	Mrs. Maurice D. Mosher, Chadds Ford, Pa.	91	87	88	266
	A	Miss Janet Seagle, Morristown, N.J.	89	90	87	266
36	A	Mrs. John H. Belser, Monterey, Calif.	87	90	90	267
	A	Mrs. Murray Gordon, New York, N.Y.	91	89	87	267
	B	Mrs. Paul G. Black, Greenbush, Mass.	90	92	85	267
	A	Mrs. Allen Georgenson, La Habra, Calif.	90	92	85	267
40	B	Mrs. Amos Huguley, Jr., West Point, Ga.	87	90	92	269
	C	Mrs. Douglass C. Coupe, Rochester, N.Y.	88	90	91	269
	C	Mrs. Charles G. DeKay, Pebble Beach, Calif.	86	91	92	269
	C	Mrs. James A. Hume, Incline Village, Nev.	93	95	81	269
44	C	Mrs. Allison Choate, Rye, N.Y.	90	88	92	270
	C	Mrs. Charles A. Cary, Oakland, Calif.	88	91	91	270
46	B	Miss Nellie G. Randall, College Park, Ga.	87	91	93	271
	A	Mrs. John B. Kirkley, Jonesboro, Ark.	89	90	92	271
	A	Mrs. Al M. Loeb, Sacramento, Calif.	93	86	92	271
	B	Mrs. Charles F. Hamlin, Fresno, Calif.	92	88	91	271
50	C	Mrs. Thomas Rhodes, Sewickley, Pa.	92	87	93	272
	B	Mrs. Robert M. Young, Tacoma, Wash.	87	93	92	272
	C	Mrs. Roland Wise, Sacramento, Calif.	90	92	90	272
53	A	Mrs. Everett Boothe, Modesto, Calif.	91	93	89	273
	B	Mrs. G. W. Baatz, Los Altos, Calif.	92	92	89	273
55	A	Mrs. Kenneth W. Sliger, Sandy, Ore.	91	88	95	274
	C	Mrs. Kermit Pearson, San Jose, Calif.	88	96	90	274
	C	Mrs. Lois M. Webb, Sunnyvale, Calif.	91	93	90	274
	B	Mrs. Lewis Keller, Sacto, Calif.	97	87	90	274
	C	Mrs. E. C. Kip Finch, New Canaan, Conn.	98	87	89	274
	C	Mrs. Henry Doubilet, Elberon, N.J.	97	90	87	274
61	B	Mrs. James A. Searle, Delray Beach, Fla.	91	90	94	275
	B	Mrs. Legh F. Knowles, Napa, Calif.	94	88	93	275
	C	Mrs. Frederic C. Pafford, Jr., Sewickley, Pa.	95	87	93	275
	A	Mrs. William S. Tally, San Jose, Calif.	93	94	88	275
65	B	Mrs. W. W. Forsman, St. Louis, Mo.	95	90	91	276

1977
SIXTEENTH SENIOR WOMEN'S AMATEUR CHAMPIONSHIP

Held at Dunes Golf and Beach Club, Myrtle Beach, South Carolina, October 5-7.
Yardage 5,793. Par 73. 120 Entries, 120 Starters.

Letters preceding names denote age groups for supplementary prize competition, as follows:
A—50 through 54 years; B—55 through 59 years; C—60 through 64 years; D—65 and over.
All Starters eligible for all three rounds. The 65 low scores:

						Score
1	A	Mrs. Mark A. Porter, Riverton, N.J.	75	77	78	230
2	A	Mrs. Paul Dye, Jr., Carmel, Ind.	79	77	75	231
3	B	Mrs. Philip J. Cudone, Myrtle Beach, S.C.	81	76	78	235
4	A	Mrs. Robert H. Maclaurin, Savannah, Ga.	80	78	78	236
5	B	Mrs. Nick Melnyk, Brunswick, Ga.	83	79	76	238
6	A	Mrs. Winslow V. Grant, Bangor, Maine	77	76	86	239
7	A	Mrs. Albert B. Bower, Pelham, N.Y.	79	81	80	240
8	B	Mrs. I. Wayne Rutter, Williamsville, N.Y.	82	82	79	243
	A	Miss Harriet Glanville, Long Beach, Calif.	83	80	80	243
10	B	Mrs. Jimmy A. Thompson, Long Beach, Calif.	83	83	79	245
	B	Mrs. William E. Gilmore, Vienna, W.Va.	83	77	85	245
12	A	Mrs. John H. Germain, Houston, Texas	81	80	85	246
13	B	Mrs. Paul G. Black, Marshfield, Mass.	75	81	92	248
14	A	Mrs. Jean W. Hester, Cookeville, Tenn.	86	83	80	249
	A	Mrs. Laura M. Cann, Fairfax, Calif.	83	84	82	249
16	C	Mrs. Ann Gregory, Gary, Ind.	81	85	84	250
17	A	Miss Sally Carroll, Wheeling, W.Va.	83	83	85	251
18	B	Mrs. Justine B. Cushing, Jericho, N.Y.	87	80	85	252
	A	Mrs. D. R. Pifer, Riviera Beach, Fla.	89	78	85	252
20	C	Mrs. George M. Trainor, Rochester, N.Y.	86	85	82	253
	A	Mrs. Dorothy Linsin, St. Louis, Mo.	85	84	84	253
	B	Mrs. Ruth White Miller, Whittier, Calif.	84	84	85	253
23	B	Mrs. Jack R. McCarty, Prairie Village, Kans.	85	82	87	254
24	C	Mrs. Douglass C. Coupe, Rochester, N.Y.	84	88	83	255
	C	Mrs. Hulet Smith, Pebble Beach, Calif.	85	85	85	255
	A	Mrs. Oren Palmer, Clemmons, N.C.	82	87	86	255
	B	Mrs. Wallace Palmer, Hilton Head Island, S.C.	83	83	89	255
28	A	Mrs. Harold M. Selm, Benton Harbor, Mich.	85	85	86	256
	B	Mrs. Raymond F. Moreland, Pittsburgh, Pa.	85	86	85	256
	B	Mrs. Jane C. Covington, Orangeburg, S.C.	89	79	88	256
31	A	Dr. Jo Anne Whitaker, Oldsmar, Fla.	89	85	84	258
	B	Miss Frances Rich, Bainbridge, Ga.	86	87	85	258
33	B	Mrs. Charles F. Troxel, Ft. Lauderdale, Fla.	84	87	88	259
34	A	Mrs. John B. Whitacre, Jr., Canton, Ohio	89	86	85	260
	A	Mrs. Ralph W. Petrone, Blacksburg, Va.	87	87	86	260
36	B	Miss Nellie G. Randall, Atlanta, Ga.	90	84	87	261
	B	Mrs. Drury S. Blair, Dallas, Texas	84	89	88	261
	A	Mrs. J. Lewis Rawls, Jr., Suffolk, Va.	86	87	88	261
39	B	Mrs. Harry J. Nevil, Jr., Cooperstown, N.Y.	87	88	87	262
40	B	Mrs. Reeves L. Kennedy, Pacific Palisades, Calif.	92	89	83	264
	A	Mrs. Joan Grunewald, Ft. Lauderdale, Fla.	90	89	85	264
	A	Mrs. John B. Kirkley, Jonesboro, Ark.	92	85	87	264
	A	Mrs. Charles Stimpson, Rancho Santa Fe, Calif.	89	87	88	264
44	A	Mrs. Edward W. Mueller, Bettendorf, Iowa	91	91	83	265
	B	Dr. Mary F. Callaghan, Whittier, Calif.	89	88	88	265
	C	Mrs. Henry Doubilet, Deal, N.J.	89	86	90	265
	D	Mrs. George H. Edwards, Springfield, Pa.	90	91	85	266
48	B	Mrs. W. W. Forsman, St. Louis, Mo.	94	90	83	267
	A	Mrs. Rita Houston, Green Bay, Wis.	88	89	90	267
	C	Mrs. Kathryn L. Anhalt, Branch, Wis.	89	85	93	267
	D	Mrs. Allison Choate, Rye, N.Y.	84	89	94	267
52	C	Mrs. Fontella Howard, Lansing, Mich.	91	89	88	268
	A	Mrs. Richard Wright, Humble, Texas	95	85	88	268
	B	Miss Josephine S. Smith, Ardmore, Pa.	93	86	89	268
	A	Mrs. Anne F. Gookin, Oklahoma City, Okla.	88	90	90	268
	A	Mrs. Nancy K. Stumpp, Wheeling, W.Va.	91	86	91	268
57	A	Mrs. B. E. Kirkendall, Wilmington, N.C.	89	93	87	269
	C	Miss Lucille M. Busch, San Diego, Calif.	89	89	91	269
59	A	Mrs. Joseph L. Crowder, Columbia, S.C.	91	88	91	270
	C	Mrs. Frederic C. Paffard, Jr., Sewickley, Pa.	89	89	92	270
	A	Mrs. Chris J. Miller, Farmington, Mich.	86	88	96	270
62	A	Mrs. William C. Warren, Rochester, N.Y.	89	94	88	271
	B	Mrs. Joseph C. Zirkle, Woodbridge, Va.	93	86	92	271
	B	Mrs. James A. Searle, Delray Beach, Fla.	94	84	93	271
65	B	Mrs. Amos Huguley, Jr., West Point, Ga.	95	91	86	272

1978

SEVENTEENTH SENIOR WOMEN'S AMATEUR CHAMPIONSHIP

Held at Rancho Bernardo Golf Club, San Diego, California, September 27-29.
Yardage—5,853. Par 73. 143 Entries, 120 Starters.

Letters preceding names denote age groups for supplementary prize competition, as follows:
A—50 through 54 years; B—55 through 59 years; C—60 through 64 years; D—65 and over.
All Starters eligible for all three rounds. The 65 low scores:

						Scor
1	*A	Mrs. Paul Dye, Jr., Delray Beach, Fla.	74	75	83	23[illegible]
2	*A	Mrs. Robert H. Maclaurin, Savannah, Ga.	76	81	75	23[illegible]
3	A	Mrs. Ellen Bowering, Bonita, Calif.	78	79	76	233
4	A	Miss Harriet Glanville, Long Beach, Calif.	79	78	79	236
5	B	Mrs. Paul G. Black, Greenbush, Mass.	81	75	81	237
6	A	Mrs. John H. Germain, Houston, Texas	80	78	80	238
7	B	Mrs. Peggy Patch, Lafayette, Calif.	82	78	79	239
	A	Mrs. Mark A. Porter, Cinnaminson, N.J.	79	80	80	239
	A	Mrs. Rosemary Mueller, Davenport, Iowa	81	76	82	239
10	B	Mrs. James P. Lee, Coral Gables, Fla.	79	80	82	241
11	C	Mrs. James A. Roessler, San Jose, Calif.	82	78	82	242
	B	Mrs. William E. Gilmore, Vienna, W. Va.	78	81	83	242
13	C	Mrs. James A. Hume, Rancho Santa Fe, Calif.	84	82	77	243
14	B	Mrs. William Windatt, Sedona, Ariz.	81	84	79	244
	A	Miss Polly Riley, Fort Worth, Texas	84	79	81	244
16	A	Mrs. Muriel J. Lewis, San Diego, Calif.	84	84	78	246
	C	Mrs. Marsh E. Shumaker, Glendora, Calif.	77	81	88	246
18	A	Mrs. Phyllis LaSorella, Pebble Beach, Calif.	85	83	79	247
19	B	Mrs. Elizabeth Lett, Palm Springs, Calif.	82	87	79	248
	A	Mrs. George MacGibbon, Minnetonka, Minn.	81	86	81	248
	C	Mrs. David L. Hibbs, Long Beach, Calif.	85	80	83	248
22	B	Mrs. Allen Georgenson, La Habra, Calif.	89	81	80	250
	C	Mrs. Roland Wise, Sacramento, Calif.	84	84	82	250
	A	Mrs. Leila A. Turner, Mesa, Ariz.	79	86	85	250
25	A	Mrs. Lyle Bowman, San Rafael, Calif.	84	87	80	251
	A	Mrs. F. R. Schroeder, Jr., La Jolla, Calif.	80	90	81	251
	A	Mrs. Mary Merwin, Sunrise, Fla.	84	81	86	251
	B	Mrs. Winslow V. Grant, Bangor, Maine	81	83	87	251
29	A	Mrs. Anne F. Gookin, Monument, Colo.	83	85	84	252
	A	Mrs. Julie A. Bescos, Long Beach, Calif.	84	81	87	252
31	A	Mrs. Roger R. Linsin, St. Louis, Mo.	86	82	86	254
32	A	Mrs. Aileen Terry, Berkeley, Calif.	88	86	81	255
	A	Mrs. Arthur J. Johns, Chula Vista, Calif.	87	86	82	255
	C	Mrs. Raymond F. Moreland, Pittsburgh, Pa.	91	82	82	255
	B	Mrs. Ruth White Miller, Long Beach, Calif.	86	85	84	255
	B	Mrs. Jan R. Nichols, Solana Beach, Calif.	88	81	86	255
37	B	Mrs. Charles L. Keenoy, Dayton, Ohio	88	83	85	256
	C	Mrs. John S. Haskell, Titusville, Pa.	87	83	86	256
	A	Mrs. Laura Gruner, San Diego, Calif.	87	83	86	256
	A	Mrs. D. R. Pifer, Jupiter, Fla.	85	84	87	256
	B	Mrs. Lois M. Webb, Sunnyvale, Calif.	85	82	89	256
	C	Mrs. Howard A. Powers, Marysville, Wash.	81	84	91	256
43	B	Mrs. James Pickrel, Pompano Beach, Fla.	84	86	87	257
	C	Mrs. Grant H. Messinger, Del Mar, Calif.	85	84	88	257
	D	Mrs. Frank Fisk, Vashon, Wash.	80	88	89	257
	C	Mrs. Ann Griffel, Eldora, Iowa	83	85	89	257
	A	Mrs. Roy E. Kiner, San Diego, Calif.	85	80	92	257
48	B	Mrs. Jimmy A. Thompson, Montebello, Calif.	88	84	86	258
	B	Mrs. Jack R. McCarty, Kansas City, Mo.	85	85	88	258
	A	Mrs. Richard Wright, San Antonio, Texas	91	78	89	258
51	A	Mrs. Edward A. Hanske, Edina, Minn.	91	87	81	259
	C	Mrs. Frederic C. Paffard, Sewickley, Pa.	89	88	82	259
	D	Mrs. Ann Gregory, Gary, Ind.	85	89	85	259
	A	Mrs. John B. Kirkley, Jonesboro, Ark.	85	87	87	259
55	A	Mrs. Rita Houston, Green Bay, Wis.	88	87	85	260
	C	Mrs. Charles Eckstrom, Tacoma, Wash.	86	87	87	260
	B	Mrs. Harold Hirsh, Los Angeles, Calif.	89	84	87	260
	A	Mrs. Aldora Lucchesi, Modesto, Calif.	85	87	88	260
59	C	Miss Lois Straus, Louisville, Ky.	84	91	86	261
	B	Mrs. Maurice D. Mosher, Chadds Ford, Pa.	82	88	91	261
	D	Mrs. Allison Choate, Rye, N.Y.	86	84	91	261
62	C	Mrs. James D. Berry, Jr., Titusville, Pa.	89	89	84	262
	A	Dr. Joanne Whitaker, Crystal Beach, Fla.	91	87	84	262
	A	Mrs. Ricardo M. Senteno, Roswell, N.M.	88	88	86	262
65	C	Mrs. E. A. Dorsey, Jr., Denver, Colo.	88	84	90	262

*Playoff. 18 holes, September 30—Mrs. Dye, 76, Mrs. Maclaurin, 79.

1979
EIGHTEENTH SENIOR WOMEN'S AMATEUR CHAMPIONSHIP

Held at Hardscrabble Country Club, Fort Smith, Arkansas, September 26-28.
Yardage—5,712. Par 71. 123 Entries, 109 Starters.

Letters preceding names denote age groups for supplementary prize competition, as follows:
A—50 through 54 years; B—55 through 59 years; C—60 through 64 years; D—65 and over.
All Starters eligible for all three rounds. The 65 low scores:

						Score
1	A	Mrs. Paul Dye, Jr., Delray Beach, Fla.	70	77	76	223
2	A	Mrs. Robert H. Maclaurin, Savannah, Ga.	78	73	79	230
3	A	Mrs. Mildred M. Stanley, Los Angeles, Calif.	78	79	74	231
4	B	Mrs. Albert B. Bower, Pelham, N.Y.	79	78	79	236
5	B	Mrs. Mark A. Porter, Cinnaminson, N.J.	79	79	79	237
6	A	Mrs. Ellen Bowering, Bonita, Calif.	79	77	82	238
7	B	Mrs. Naoma Galles, Port Angeles, Wash.	81	82	77	240
8	B	Mrs. John H. Germain, Houston, Texas	82	79	80	241
	A	Mrs. John B. Whitacre, Waynesburg, Ohio	80	79	82	241
10	A	Mrs. Natalie Gamble, Grosse Point Isle, Mich.	81	81	80	242
11	B	Mrs. Ruth W. Miller, Long Beach, Calif.	78	84	81	243
12	A	Mrs. A. F. Munro, Greenwich, Conn.	83	84	78	245
	B	Mrs. James Pickrel, Pompano Beach, Fla.	83	83	79	245
	A	Mrs. Thomas Hodge, San Jose, Calif.	80	83	82	245
15	A	Miss Polly Riley, Fort Worth, Texas	84	80	82	246
16	A	Mrs. George Nowotny, Tulsa, Okla.	79	84	84	247
	A	Mrs. Roger Linsin, St. Louis, Mo.	84	78	85	247
18	D	Mrs. Ann Gregory, Gary, Ind.	81	88	79	248
	A	Mrs. Clyde Collins, Enid, Okla.	80	86	82	248
20	B	Mrs. Jimmy A. Thompson, Montebello, Calif.	81	87	81	249
	A	Dr. Joanne Whitaker, Crystal Beach, Fla.	79	84	86	249
22	A	Mrs. Walton Horton, Beaufort, S.C.	84	84	82	250
	A	Mrs. Anne F. Gookin, Monument, Colo.	84	84	82	250
	A	Mrs. D. R. Pifer, Jupiter, Fla.	88	79	83	250
	A	Mrs. Mary Merwin, Sunrise, Fla.	86	78	86	250
26	A	Mrs. Julian A. Salley, Columbia, S.C.	85	83	83	251
	B	Mrs. Frank Richart, Ann Arbor, Mich.	84	83	84	251
	A	Mrs. Nancy MacGibbon, Minnetonka, Minn.	86	81	84	251
29	A	Mrs. Tom Sewell, Pasadena, Texas	86	87	79	252
	C	Mrs. Drury Shelton Blair, Dallas, Texas	87	83	82	252
	B	Mrs. F. R. Schroeder, Jr., La Jolla, Calif.	83	85	84	252
32	B	Mrs. Harton S. Semple, Sewickley, Pa.	85	85	83	253
	B	Mrs. William E. Gilmore, Vienna, W. Va.	85	82	86	253
	B	Mrs. Paul G. Black, Greenbush, Mass.	86	79	88	253
35	A	Mrs. Rosemary Mueller, Davenport, Iowa	79	85	90	254
36	D	Mrs. Lucille M. Busch, San Diego, Calif.	88	87	81	256
	C	Mrs. Frederic C. Pafford, Jr., Sewickley, Pa.	82	88	86	256
38	B	Mrs. Richard Wright, San Antonio, Texas	87	85	85	257
39	C	Mrs. Raymond Moreland, Pittsburgh, Pa.	87	87	84	258
40	C	Mrs. W. W. Forsman, St. Louis, Mo.	90	86	84	260
	A	Mrs. Bruce L. Hilkene, Birmingham, Mich.	89	85	86	260
42	A	Mrs. Marion T. Wise, East Point, Ga.	87	92	82	261
	C	Mrs. Grant H. Messinger, Del Mar, Calif.	88	90	83	261
	D	Mrs. Sue Faurot, Columbia, Mo.	83	91	87	261
	A	Mrs. John B. Kirkley, Jonesboro, Ark.	88	85	88	261
46	C	Mrs. Kathryn L. Anhalt, Manitowoc, Wis.	87	91	84	262
	B	Mrs. Ann K. Troxel, Suches, Ga.	89	89	84	262
	B	Mrs. Charles Stimpson, Rancho Santa Fe, Calif.	88	89	85	262
	C	Mrs. Dorothy G. Benham, Friendship, Texas	86	87	89	262
50	D	Mrs. Ann Griffel, Eldora, Iowa	88	90	97	265
	B	Mrs. John P. Call, San Diego, Calif.	86	89	90	265
52	A	Mrs. Barbara D. Hartson, Phoenix, Ariz.	91	90	85	266
	D	Mrs. Allison Choate, Rye, N.Y.	92	85	89	266
	A	Mrs. Harold Selm, Stevensville, Mich.	88	87	91	266
55	B	Mrs. Harry Hatlan, Ballwin, Mo.	87	91	89	267
	B	Mrs. Robert S. McKee, Grosse Point Shores, Mich.	87	90	90	267
	C	Mrs. Amos Huguley, Jr., West Point, Ga.	83	93	91	267
58	C	Mrs. Walter H. Hoffman, Springfield, Mo.	89	92	87	268
	C	Mrs. Henry Doubilet, Elberon, N.J.	90	91	87	268
	B	Mrs. Bruce Gilliland, Kimball, Neb.	88	88	92	268
61	A	Mrs. Sidney O. Lee, Minnetonka, Minn.	91	87	91	269
62	D	Mrs. James Berry, Jr., Titusville, Pa.	86	96	89	271
63	D	Mrs. Allyn G. Bonnie, Denver, Colo.	86	93	93	272
64	C	Miss Mary Lou Baker, Louisville, Ky.	92	92	89	273
	C	Mrs. Jack R. McCarty, Kansas City, Mo.	92	92	89	273

1980
NINETEENTH SENIOR WOMEN'S AMATEUR CHAMPIONSHIP

Held at Sea Island Golf Club, Sea Island, Georgia, September 24-26
Yardage—6,053. Par 77. 186 Entries, 120 Starters

Letters preceding names denote age groups for supplementary prize competition, as follows:
A—50 through 54 years; B—55 through 59 years; C—60 through 64 years; D—65 and over.
All starters eligible for all three rounds. The 65 low scores.

1	B	Mrs. Mark A. Porter, Cinnaminson, N.J.	81	80	75	236
2	A	Mrs. Robert H. MacLaurin, Savannah, Ga.	78	82	77	237
3	B	Mrs. Albert B. Bower, Pelham, N.Y.	80	83	76	239
4	A	Mrs. Thomas Hodge, San Jose, Calif.	79	84	77	240
5	B	Mrs. John H. Germain, Houston, Texas	82	77	83	242
6	A	Mrs. Gaines P. Wilson, Jr., Louisville, Ky.	81	80	82	243
	A	Mrs. Mildred M. Stanley, Los Angeles, Calif.	81	79	83	243
	A	Mrs. Scott L. Probasco, Jr., Lookout Mountain, Tenn.	81	77	85	243
	D	Mrs. Ann Gregory, Gary, Ind.	84	81	80	245
	B	Mrs. Roy E. Thomas, Winter Haven, Fla.	81	82	82	245
	B	Mrs. I. Wayne Rutter, Williamsville, N.Y.	82	81	82	245
12	A	Mrs. Paul Dye, Jr., Delray Beach, Fla.	82	84	80	246
13	A	Mrs. Andrew Sage, Locust Valley, N.Y.	81	84	82	247
14	B	Mrs. Gordon McGrath, Glen Head, N.Y.	81	85	83	249
15	A	Mrs. George Nowotny, Tulsa, Okla.	85	84	81	250
	A	Miss Nancy G. Hollenbeck, Annandale, Va.	85	83	82	250
17	B	Mrs. Nick Melnyk, Brunswick, Ga.	84	82	85	251
18	B	Mrs. Nancy MacGibbon, Minnetonka, Minn.	83	83	86	252
	A	Mrs. Walton B. Horton, Beaufort, S.C.	84	80	88	252
20	C	Mrs. Ruth W. Miller, Long Beach, Calif.	86	83	84	253
	B	Mrs. Paul G. Black, Greenbush, Mass.	79	87	87	253
22	B	Mrs. Peggy Patch, Lafayette, Calif.	82	88	84	254
	A	Mrs. Frank H. Featherston, Charlottesville, Va.	85	85	84	254
	A	Mrs. D.R. Pifer, Jupiter, Fla.	83	86	85	254
	B	Mrs. William E. Gilmore, Vienna, W.Va.	83	85	86	254
	A	Mrs. Anne F. Gookin, Monument, Colo.	83	82	89	254
27	A	Mrs. Natalie Gamble, Grosse Point Isle, Mich.	90	83	82	255
	A	Mrs. Tom Jones, Amarillo, Texas	81	88	86	255
	A	Mrs. John B. Whitacre, Jr., Canton, Ohio	82	87	86	255
	A	Mrs. John B. Eshelman, Lancaster, Pa.	87	82	86	255
31	A	Mrs. Edie Creed, Ontario, Canada	86	85	85	256
	A	Mrs. Margarita F. Lillard, Terrace Park, Ohio	84	86	86	256
	A	Mrs. Blancke Noyes, Darien, Conn.	85	81	90	256
	A	Mrs. Ellen R. Bowering, Bonita, Calif.	85	81	90	256
35	B	Mrs. H. Foster Hamilton, Charleston, S.C.	88	86	83	257
	A	Miss Polly Riley, Fort Worth, Texas	82	88	87	257
37	C	Mrs. Charles T. Eckstrom, Tacoma, Wash.	85	90	83	258
	A	Mrs. Lucille Penner, Virginia Beach, Va.	87	86	85	258
	B	Mrs. James Pickrel, Pompano Beach, Fla.	85	82	91	258
40	A	Mrs. Clyde Collins, Enid, Okla.	85	84	90	259
41	A	Mrs. Julian A. Salley, Columbia, S.C.	79	93	88	260
	C	Mrs. Justine B. Cushing, Glen Head, N.Y.	89	82	89	260
43	A	Mrs. John H. Flagg, Tampa, Fla.	83	90	88	261
	C	Mrs. Harold Fink, Scarsdale, N.Y.	86	86	89	261
	B	Mrs. J. Lewis Rawls, Jr., Suffolk, Va.	85	83	93	261
46	B	Mrs. Frank E. Richart, Ann Arbor, Mich.	87	92	83	262
	B	Mrs. Betty A. O'Neill, Shaker Heights, Ohio	87	92	83	262
	A	Mrs. Elizabeth Wren, Williamsburg, Va.	92	85	85	262
	A	Mrs. Robert W. Hacker, Moline, Ill.	85	88	89	262
50	B	Mrs. Betse Straub, Long Beach, Calif.	97	83	84	264
	D	Mrs. Ann J. Griffel, Eldora, Iowa	90	86	88	264
	A	Mrs. Mary Lou Moreau, Jefferson City, Mo.	85	87	92	264
	A	Mrs. A.F. Munro, Greenwich, Conn.	87	84	93	264
54	B	Mrs. Penelope E. Thompson, Pebble Beach, Calif.	94	86	85	265
	B	Mrs. Harton S. Semple, Sewickley, Pa.	87	89	89	265
56	B	Mrs. Evelyn M. Grant, Bangor, Maine	85	96	85	266
	B	Mrs. William Tracy, Sea Pines, S.C.	92	87	87	266
	A	Mrs. Colleen Carmichael, Toronto, Ontario, Canada	85	93	88	266
	D	Mrs. Douglass C. Coupe, Rochester, N.Y.	92	86	88	266
	B	Mrs. Rosemary Mueller, Davenport, Iowa	92	86	88	266
	A	Mrs. Lawrence Hester, Cookeville, Tenn.	89	87	90	266
	C	Mrs. Joy R. Fish, New Orleans, La.	88	86	92	266
63	C	Mrs. Frederick C. Pafford, Jr., Sewickley, Pa.	92	90	85	267
	A	Mrs. Mary Merwin, Sunrise, Fla.	89	94	84	267
	C	Mrs. Raymond Moreland, Pittsburgh, Pa.	87	93	87	267

SENIOR OPEN CHAMPIONSHIP

FRANCIS OUIMET TROPHY

Presented in 1980 by

GOLFERS OF MASSACHUSETTS

HISTORY

1980—The Senior Open Championship, for players age 55 and over, was established in 1980 as a result of the remarkable growth in senior golf, both at the professional and amateur levels. The Championship was played over the East Course of the Winged Foot Golf Club, in Mamaroneck, New York. The USGA accepted 631 entrants, among them former U.S. Open Champions Lew Worsham, Julius Boros, Ed Furgol, Jack Fleck, and Tommy Bolt. The only former U.S. Amateur Champion entered was William C. Campbell. Roberto De Vicenzo, 57, of Buenos Aires, Argentina, won the Championship. His winning score of 285, one over par, comprised rounds of 74-73-68-70. He was four strokes ahead of Campbell, 57, of Huntington, West Virginia. De Vicenzo and Campbell were the only players to break 290. Art Wall, Jr., was third, at 290; Charles Sifford was fourth, at 295, and tied for fifth were amateur Ed Tutwiler and professionals Mike Fetchick and Hampton Auld, at 296. Four players shared the first round lead at 72—Mike Fetchick, Ted Kroll, Charles Sifford, and Bill Tromley, an amateur. De Vicenzo had 74 and Campbell shot 76. Campbell took the lead in the second round with 68, three under par, and Wall had 71, to move into second place at 145. Boros was third, at 146, and De Vicenzo was fourth at 147. De Vicenzo went ahead for the first time with 68 in the third round, giving him 215 for 54 holes, two strokes better than Wall, with 217. Campbell shot another 76 and was grouped with Boros and Kroll at 220. Wall and De Vicenzo were paired together in the final round, and De Vicenzo maintained his two-stroke advantage through seven holes. De Vicenzo increased his lead to three strokes at the eighth, where Wall three-putted. De Vicenzo shot 70 in the last round, and Wall shot 73. Campbell played the final nine in 32, scoring birdies in three of the last four holes, to finish at 69 for the day and 289 for the 72 holes, one stroke ahead of Wall. The final two days of the Senior Open were nationally televised. Thirty-five professionals and 16 amateurs made the 36-hole cut at 156, 14 over par. A total of $100,000 in prize money was awarded.

SENIOR OPEN CHAMPIONSHIP

DATE	WINNER, RUNNER-UP	SCORE	SITE	ENTRY
1980 (June)	Roberto De Vicenzo William C. Campbell	285 289	Winged Foot G.C. (East Course) Mamaroneck, N.Y.	631

1980
FIRST UNITED STATES SENIOR OPEN CHAMPIONSHIP

Held at Winged Foot Golf Club (East Course), Mamaroneck, New York, June 26-29
Yardage—6,619. Par 71. 631 Entries, 150 Qualifiers, Starters

						Score	Money Prize
1	Roberto De Vicenzo, Buenos Aires, Argentina	74	73	68	70	285	$20,000.00
2	*William C. Campbell, Guyan G. & C.C., Huntington, W.Va.	76	68	76	69	289	Medal
3	Art Wall, Jr., Sonoita, Ariz.	74	71	72	73	290	10,000.00
4	Charles Sifford, Sleepy Hollow G.C., Brecksville, Ohio	72	77	71	75	295	6,000.00
5	*Ed Tutwiler, Crooked Stick G.C., Carmel, Ind.	81	72	68	75	296	Medal
	Michael Fetchick, Dix Hills, N.Y.	72	77	78	69	296	4,750.00
	Hampton Auld, Edgewood C.C., Charleston, W.Va.	75	73	74	74	296	4,750.00
8	Julius Boros, Turnberry Isle C.C., Miami, Fla.	73	73	74	77	297	3,800.00
	Ted Kroll, Cold Spring G.C., Cold Spring Harbor, N.Y.	72	77	71	77	297	3,800.00
10	Gaylon Simon, Blossom Trails, Benton Harbor, Mich.	76	74	76	72	298	3,200.00
11	Jay Hebert, Champions G.C., Houston, Texas	80	73	75	71	299	2,800.00
	Fred Hawkins, Antioch, Ill.	74	75	73	77	299	2,800.00
	Tommy Bolt, Tarpon Woods C.C., Palm Harbour, Fla.	77	72	72	78	299	2,800.00
14	Jerry Barber, Griffith Park G. Crse, Los Angeles, Calif.	79	73	75	73	300	2,400.00
15	Freddie Haas, Metairie, La.	76	75	78	72	301	2,100.00
	Jack Fleck, Buena Park, Calif.	76	74	78	73	301	2,100.00
17	George Thomas, Elcona C.C., Elkhart, Ind.	75	75	78	74	302	1,700.00
	*Lew Oehmig, Lookout Mountain G.C., Lookout Mountain, Tenn.	75	75	77	75	302	Medal
	Bob Duden, Glendoveer G.C., Portland, Or.	76	72	77	77	302	1,700.00
20	Jim Shaw, Eberhart Park G.C., Mishawaka, Ind.	80	75	72	76	303	1,500.00
21	Bill Johnston, Paradise Valley C.C., Paradise Valley, Ariz.	73	78	76	77	304	1,350.00
	Al Besselink, Beaumont, Texas	75	72	79	78	304	1,350.00
23	Travis L. Hudson, Sr., Musgrove C.C., Jasper, Ala.	77	79	75	74	305	1,200.00
24	Doug Ford, Sabal Palms G.C., Longwood, Fla.	79	77	77	73	306	1,125.00
	Jackson Bradley, Atascocita G.C., Humble, Texas	73	79	77	77	306	1,125.00
26	William Kozak, Westbrock G.C., Welland, Ontario, Canada	77	72	80	78	307	1,025.00
	*John Kline, Champions G.C., Houston, Texas	74	82	73	78	307	Medal
	Chuck Scally, Scally G.C., Coraopolis, Pa.	76	75	76	80	307	1,025.00
29	*Don Adderton, Willow Creek G.C., High Point, N.C.	79	75	78	76	308	Medal
	Herman Scharlau, Oakwood C.C., Kansas City, Mo.	76	75	79	78	308	927.50
	Eli Marovich, Duquesne G.C., West Mifflin, Pa.	73	78	75	82	308	927.50
32	Murry Jacobs, Wildcreek G. Crse, Sparks, Nev.	78	78	80	73	309	825.00
	Joe Sodd, Olympic Hills G.C., Eden Prairie, Minn.	75	76	79	79	309	825.00
	Vernon Thwaites, Southwest Point G.C., Kingston, Tenn.	76	78	72	83	309	825.00
35	*Nick Weslock, Glen Abbey, Ontario, Canada	80	73	76	81	310	Medal
36	*Glenn H. Johnson, Grosse Ile C.C., Grosse Ile, Mich.	79	76	80	76	311	Medal
	*William J. Trombley, Dallas Athletic C., Dallas, Texas	72	77	83	79	311	Medal
38	Bob Gajda, Forest Lane G.C., Bloomfield Hills, Mich.	74	80	76	82	312	760.00
	*W. Brown McDonald, Houston Lake C.C., Perry, Ga.	77	76	77	82	312	Medal
40	Hans Merrell, Mount Vernon G.C., Mount Vernon, Ohio	80	74	81	79	314	730.00
	*Kenneth G. Weavil, Pine Brook C.C., Winston Salem, N.C.	76	79	76	83	314	Medal
42	Milon Marusic, Algonquin G.C., Glendale, Mo.	79	77	80	79	315	700.00
	Robert E. Cochran, Meadowbrook C.C., Ballwin, Mo.	79	73	82	81	315	Medal
44	Arthur Doering, JDM Country Club, Palm Beach Gardens, Fla.	79	77	75	85	316	670.00
45	Michael Homa, H. Smith Richardson G.C., Fairfield, Conn.	76	79	80	82	317	640.00
46	*Dale Morey, C.C. of North Carolina, Pinehurst, N.C.	81	75	79	83	318	Medal
	*Fletcher Wall, Sapona C.C., Lexington, N.C.	78	76	80	84	318	Medal
48	*Richard Remsen, Jr., Piping Rock G.C., Locust Valley, N.Y.	81	75	84	79	319	Medal
49	*Robert L. Morris, Argyle G.C., Silver Spring, Md.	78	78	84	80	320	Medal
50	*Harry Welch, Kannapolis G.C., Kannapolis, N.C.	83	73	81	85	322	Medal
51	Bill Chaddock, Center City G. Crse, Oceanside, Calif.	79	76	88	91	334	610.00

15 Money prizes were divided among the 44 professionals who did not make the cut. The amount involved is $7,160. Accordingly, $7,160 was divided equally among the 44 professionals, $162.73 was given to 32 professionals and $162.72 given to 12 professionals for a total of $7,160.00

*Amateur

WALKER CUP MATCH

UNITED STATES GOLF ASSOCIATION

INTERNATIONAL CHALLENGE TROPHY

Presented in May, 1921, by

GEORGE H. WALKER

President of the United States Golf Association, 1920

HISTORY

1961–The Walker Cup series made its first visit to the West Coast of the United States when the 1961 Match was played at the Seattle Golf Club, Seattle, Wash. The United States side won over Great Britain for the 17th time in 18 Matches. The score was 11 to 1, equaling the record margin of 1928. Martin J. Christmas, the youngest member of the British Team at 21, defeated Charles B. Smith, of Gastonia, N.C., 3 and 2, for Great Britain's one victory. The Hon. Jack Westland, a member of the House of Representatives for his native Washington, served as Captain of the American Team at the course where he had won the Amateur Championship in 1952 at age 47. The British Team was under the captaincy of Charles D. Lawrie.

1963–The United States, behind by 6 to 3 after the first day, rallied to win by a score of 12 to 8, with four matches halved, at Turnberry, Scotland. American superiority in foursomes was decisive. The United States won six, lost one, and halved one of the alternate stroke matches. The British prevailed in singles with seven wins, six losses, and three halves. For the first time, matches were played over 18 holes. The United States won all four foursomes on the morning of the second day for a 7-to-6 lead and then took five singles in the afternoon when Britain could win only two matches and halve a third. Charles R. Coe was on the winning side three times and halved his other match for the United States. In the singles, Britain's David Sheahan defeated the Amateur Champions of both the United States and Great Britain–Labron Harris, Jr., and Richard Davies, the Californian who had won the British title in 1962. Joseph B. Carr set a record for playing appearances in the Match. He had been a member of the British side nine consecutive times. Francis Ouimet played eight times for the United States. The Match was played on Turnberry's Ailsa Course, restored since World War II, when it was part of an R.A.F. Airfield. The winning team was captained by Richard S. Tufts, USGA President in 1956-57.

1965–The first tie in the history of the Walker Cup Match came about at the Baltimore Country Club's Five Farms East Course when the United States Team rallied during the second day's singles matches to pull even at 11-11. Great Britain, captained by the veteran Walker Cup player, Joseph B. Carr, of Ireland, led by 8 to 3 at the end of the first day and 10 to 5 after the foursomes of the second day. The Americans then won six of eight singles and tied the other. The Captain for the United States Team was John W. Fischer, the Amateur Champion in 1936. Edgar M. Tutwiler, the oldest member of the American team at 46 years, began the American rally by coming from behind to defeat Ronnie Shade by 5 and 3. Tutwiler's feat seemed to inspire his teammates. Eventually, it appeared likely that the British would be denied even a tie. The climactic match was between Clive Clark, a 20-year-old Englishman, and Mark Hopkins. Hopkins was 1 up coming to the 18th hole and needed only to halve that hole to earn the point that would win the Match for the United States. Clark, on in two, 35 feet from the cup, watched as Hopkins put his third close to the hole. Clark then holed his putt.

1967–The United States won eight of 10 matches and halved one on the first day to take an 8-1 lead, took five points the next day and won, 13-7. The match was played at the Royal St. George's Golf Club, Sandwich, England. It was the 19th victory for the United States in 21 matches. The superiority of the United States in the singles matches was decisive. Americans won 12 and lost four singles, and won four and lost three foursomes. William C. Campbell, of Huntington, W. Va., had a hand in winning four points for the United States. He teamed with Jack W. Lewis, Jr., to win two foursome matches, and won both his singles. Lewis and Robert B. Dickson, of McAlester, Okla., won three points each for the United States. Sandy Saddler, Michael F. Bonallack, and Tom Craddock each had a hand in winning two points for the British Team. Jess W. Sweetser, of Washington, D.C., the 1922 United States Amateur Champion and 1926 British Amateur Champion, was non-playing Captain of the American Team. Dickson later won the British Amateur.

1969–Despite taking a 7-3 lead after the first day's play, the United States was hard-pressed to score a 10-8 victory over Great Britain and Ireland at the Milwaukee Country Club, Milwaukee, Wis. The United States won only two singles matches and one foursome for three points on the second day, while Great Britain-Ireland won three singles matches and two foursomes. The match was decided on the last two holes. Allen Miller, of the United States, was 1 up on Michael G. King with two holes to play and saved losing two holes with superb pitches after missing the green on both the 17th and 18th. Richard L. Siderowf, of the United States, was one down to Bruce Critchley, but saved a half with a par 4 on the

18th. Bruce Fleisher, the 1968 United States Amateur Champion, was five down with six holes to play against Michael Bonallack, the British Amateur Champion and Walker Cup Team Captain, then won five consecutive holes to halve their first singles match. Bonallack won, 5 and 4, the second day. Siderowf won three of a possible four points. No one else won so many. The victory was the 20th for the United States. Great Britain-Ireland had won once (1938), and the 1965 match was halved. William J. Patton was non-playing Captain of the American Team.

1971—On the 50th anniversary of the first informal match between British and American amateurs, Great Britain and Ireland won the Walker Cup for the second time, defeating the United States, 13-11, at St. Andrews, Scotland. Formal competition between the United States and Great Britain and Ireland began in 1922, and the 1971 Match was the 23d in the series. The British won last in 1938 at St. Andrews, and tied in 1965 at Baltimore. Great Britain and Ireland opened the 1971 Match by sweeping all four of the foursomes competitions the first morning. The United States then won six of the eight afternoon singles matches and halved one other. After the first day the United States led, 6½-5½. The United States then won two foursomes the morning of the second day, halved another, and with eight singles matches remaining led, 9-7. The tide swung to the British in the singles. Hugh B. Stuart, of Britain, defeated Vinny Giles, 2 and 1. Warren Humphreys, of Britain, holed two monstrous birdie putts on the 15th and 16th, and then won the 17th when Steve Melnyk, his opponent made 6, to win his match, 2 and 1. Charles W. Green, of Britain, won the 16th to go 1 up over Allen Miller, but Miller won the 17th to pull even, and then Green won the 18th with a par 4, beating Miller, 1 up. Roddy Carr, of Britain, was 2 up on Jim Simons with two to play. Simons won the 17th, but Carr holed a 30-foot birdie on the 18th to win, 2 up; Bill Hyndman, of the United States, was bunkered on the 16th and lost the hole and Dave Marsh won, 1 up. Jim Gabrielsen, of the United States, lost the 17th and the match to George Macgregor, 1 up. Only Lanny Wadkins and Tom Kite won their singles matches for the United States. Michael F. Bonallack was the playing Captain for Great Britain and Ireland, and John M. Winters, Jr., was non-playing Captain for the United States.

1973—After losing the Match in 1971 for only the second time in the 50-year history of the competition, the United States won again, 14 to 10, at The Country Club, Brookline, Mass. It was the 24th meeting of Teams representing Great Britain and Ireland and the United States, and the 21st victory for the United States. Great Britain and Ireland's only previous victory had been in 1938 at St. Andrew's, Scotland. The Americans got off to a 3½ to ½ lead in the first morning's foursomes. The United States teams of Richard Siderowf, the British Amateur Champion, and Mark Pfeil; Danny Edwards and Jimmy Ellis; and Doug Ballenger and Marty West all won their matches. In the first match, Marvin M. Giles III, the United States Amateur Champion, and Gary Koch rallied after being two down with three to play and won a half with Michael King and Peter Hedges. In the afternoon's singles the British won five matches to three for the United States. Giles, Siderowf, and Edwards were the only winners for the American Team. The first day's play ended with the United States leading by only one point, 6½ to 5½. In the second day's foursomes, the American Side once more scored 3½ points to the British Team's ½. At morning's close, the United States led, 10-6, and still needed 2½ points in the afternoon's singles to regain the Cup. These 2½ points were extremely hard won. With every match at least as far along as the eighth hole, the British led every one. Giles finally holed a 12-foot birdie putt on the 18th to halve his match with Charles Green and win a half point; Edwards was 2 down to Trevor Homer after nine holes and won 12, 14, 16, and 17; and West, one down to Michael King after 15, won 16, 17, and 18 to win the Walker Cup Match. Edwards was the only player on either Side to win four points. The Country Club became the first American club to have entertained the Match twice. Non-playing Captains were Dr. David Marsh, for Great Britain and Ireland, and Jess Sweetser, for the United States. Sweetser won the 1922 United States Amateur Championship at The Country Club.

1975—In the 25th meeting of Teams representing Great Britain and Ireland and the United States, the Americans won for the 22nd time, 15½ to 8½, at the Old Course, St. Andrews, Scotland. Great Britain and Ireland's only victories, in 1938 and 1971, were won at St. Andrews. One Match—at Baltimore Country Club, Five Farms, Baltimore, Md. in 1965—ended all square. The magic of St. Andrews did not hold for the Great Britain-Ireland Team this time, however, although it began the Match on a winning note when Mark James and Richard Eyles defeated Jerry Pate and Dick Siderowf, 1-up, in the first foursomes match. The Americans then won the three remaining foursomes of the morning, with George Burns-Craig Stadler, Jay Haas-Curtis Strange and Vinny Giles-Gary Koch teaming extremely well. Burns and Stadler won their match 5 and 4, and stood four under par for the 14 holes required. Haas and Strange were out in 34, two under par, while Giles and Koch shot 35 on the first nine. Haas and Strange won their match 2 and 1, while Giles and Koch won by 5 and 4. In the afternoon's singles, Pate, the 1974 Amateur Champion, lost to Mark James, the English Amateur Champion, 2 and 1. Great Britain-

Ireland won another half point when John Davies tied with Strange, and another full point in the next match as Pat Mucare, a 27-year-old Irishman, defeated Dick Siderowf, 1-up. The United States then won four of the remaining five matches and halved the other. The first day ended with the United States leading, 8 points to 4. In the second day's foursomes, each Team won two points, and with only the eight single matches remaining the Americans led by four points, 10 to 6 and needed just 2½ to win the Walker Cup. Ian Hutcheon defeated Jerry Pate, 3 and 2, in the first singles match in the afternoon cutting the American's lead to three points. The British got no closer after that. Strange and Koch won 4 and 3 and 5 and 4, respectively, but then John Davies won for Great Britain-Ireland, defeating George Burns, 2 and 1. When Grace won, however, the Match was decided. Stadler and Campbell won their Matches and Marvin M. (Vinny) Giles, III, halved Peter Hedges in the final matches of the day. Curtis Strange led the United States with 3½ points of a possible four, while Koch, Stadler and Haas all had three points. James won three points for the British-Irish side. Campbell kept intact his record of never having lost a Walker Cup singles match. Non-playing Captains were Dr. David Marsh for Great Britain and Ireland and Dr. Edgar R. Updegraff for the United States.

1977—Even though only one member of its Team had previous Walker Cup experience, the United States defeated Great Britain and Ireland, 16-8, to win its 23rd match in the 26-match series. Richard L. Siderowf had played for the United States three times previously. The Match was played at the Shinnecock Hills Golf Club, in Southampton, N. Y., one of the five Charter Member Clubs of the United States Golf Association. The Walker Cup Match is played over two days with four 18-hole foursome matches each morning and eight 18-hole singles matches each afternoon. The United States led from the first match and was never really threatened. The Americans won three of the four foursomes the first day and six of the eight singles matches and led 9-3. After winning two foursomes the second day, the United States led by 11-5 and needed just two points in the afternoon singles to win. Lindy Miller and John Fought, the first two Americans off the tee, won and decided the outcome. Fought and Miller each won four points, the maximum, for the United States. Scott Simpson, Vance Heafner and Jay Sigel played in three matches and won three points each. The match began with the United States winning the first two foursome matches of the first day, with Fought and Heafner defeating Peter McEvoy, the British Amateur Champion, and Sandy Lyle in the first match and Miller and Simpson defeating John Davies and Michael Kelley in the second. Ian Hutcheon and Peter Deeble, of British Team then defeated Siderowf and Gary Hallberg in the third match. With two holes to play in the last foursome, Alan Brodie and Steve Martin were leading Jay Sigel and Michael Brannan with a chance to even the standing. The Americans won the 17th, however, to pull even, and then Brannan played a marvelous 2-iron just three feet from the hole on the 18th. Sigel holed the putt for a birdie 3, and the United States was ahead to stay. The British-Irish Team rallied the next day. After nine holes of the foursomes, they were leading in all four matches. Then the Fought-Heafner and Miller-Simpson teams wore down their opponents and won their matches, the British and Irish won the other two and a split. The Americans won five of the eight singles matches in the afternoon. Lewis W. Oehmig was non-playing Captain of the United States Team, and Sandy Saddler was non-playing Captain of the Team from Great Britain and Ireland.

1979—The United States won the 27th International Match for the Walker Cup for its 24th victory in the series which began in 1922. Great Britain and Ireland has won twice, and one Match has ended in a tie. The United States won, 15½ - 8½, at the Honourable Company of Edinburgh Golfers, Muirfield, Gullane, Scotland. The Match was much closer than the final score indicated. Fourteen of the 24 matches were decided on the 17th or 18th holes. Of those 14, the United States won seven, lost four, and halved the other three. The first morning's foursomes matches were split, 2-2. The Scott Hoch-Jay Sigel and Doug Fischesser-Jim Holtgrieve teams both won by 1 up margins for the United States side. The combinations of Geoffrey Goodwin-Ian Hutcheon and Allan Brodie—Iain Carslaw won for the British-Irish side by 2 up and 2 and 1, respectively. In the afternoon singles matches, Doug Clarke, 8 and 7; Holtgrieve, 6 and 4; Michael Gove, 3 and 2; Hoch, 9 and 7; and Sigel, match halved, gave the American side 4½ points. Hoch was two under par in his victory over James Buckley. It was the widest margin ever recorded in an 18-hole Walker Cup singles match. After the first day's play, the United States led 6½-5½. On the second day the teams once again split the foursomes matches, 2-2. The Hoch-Sigel combination won again, 4 and 3, for the American side, and McEvoy-Marchbank won, 2 and 1, for the British side. The other two foursomes matches were halved. The United States still had only an 8½-7½ lead. At one point during the afternoon singles matches of the second day, Great Britain and Ireland was ahead in five matches, even in two, and behind in only one. The United States rallied on the final nine holes to win seven of the eight matches. Hoch was three under par in his 3 and 1 victory over McEvoy. Sigel and Hal Sutton also won by 3 and 1 margins. Clarke and Michael Peck both won, 2 and 1, and Gove and Griff Moody both won by 3 and 2. Only Brodie won a point for the British-Irish side. Peck won the decisive point when he holed a birdie putt at the 17th to defeat Hutcheon. All 10 Americans contributed to their winning 15½ point total. Richard Siderowf, a member of four U.S. Walker Cup Teams and the 1973 and 1976 British Amateur Champion, was the non-playing Captain of the United States Team. Rodney Foster, a member of five British Walker Cup Teams, was the non-playing Captain of the Great Britain and Ireland Team.

WALKER CUP MATCH

DATE	WINNER		RUNNER-UP		SITE
1961	United States,	11	Great Britain & Ireland,	1	Seattle G.C., Seattle, Wash.
1963	United States,	12	Great Britain & Ireland,	8	Ailsa Course, Turnberry, Scotland
	four matches halved				
1965	Great Britain & Ireland,	11	United States,	11	Baltimore C.C., Five Farms, Baltimore, Md.
	two matches halved				
1967	United States,	13	Great Britain & Ireland,	7	Royal St. George's G.C., Sandwich, England
	four matches halved				
1969	United States,	10	Great Britain & Ireland,	8	Milwaukee C.C., Milwaukee, Wisc.
	six matches halved				
1971	Great Britain & Ireland,	13	United States,	11	St. Andrews, Scotland
	two matches halved				
1973	United States,	14	Great Britain & Ireland,	10	The Country Club, Brookline, Mass.
1975	United States,	15½	Great Britain & Ireland,	8½	St. Andrews, Scotland
1977	United States,	16	Great Britain & Ireland,	8	Shinnecock Hills G.C., Southampton, N.Y.
1979	United States,	15½	Great Britain & Ireland,	8½	Honourable Company of Edinburgh Golfers, Muirfield, Scotland

1961
INTERNATIONAL MATCH FOR THE WALKER CUP

Held at the Seattle Golf Club, Seattle, Washington
September 1 and 2

FOURSOMES

Great Britain and Ireland

	Points
James Walker and Brian H.G. Chapman	0
David A. Blair and Martin J. Christmas	0
Joseph B. Carr and Gordon Huddy	0
Michael F. Bonallack and Ronald D.B.M. Shade	0
Total	0

United States

	Points
Deane R. Beman and Jack W. Nicklaus (6 and 5)	1
Charles R. Coe and Donald R. Cherry (1 up)	1
William Hyndman, III, and Robert W. Gardner (4 and 3)	1
Robert E. Cochran and Eugene S. Andrews (4 and 3)	1
Total	4

SINGLES

Great Britain and Ireland

	Points
Michael F. Bonallack	0
Michael S.R. Lunt	0
James Walker	0
David W. Frame	0
Joseph B. Carr	0
Martin J. Christmas (3 and 2)	1
Ronald D.B.M. Shade	0
David A. Blair	0
Total	1
Grand Total—Great Britain and Ireland	1

Non-playing Captain—C.D. Lawrie

United States

	Points
Deane R. Beman (3 and 2)	1
Charles R. Coe (5 and 4)	1
Dr. Frank M. Taylor, Jr. (3 and 2)	1
William Hyndman, III (7 and 6)	1
Jack W. Nicklaus (6 and 4)	1
Charles B. Smith	0
Robert W. Gardner (1 up)	1
Donald R. Cherry (5 and 4)	1
Total	7
Grand Total—United States	11

Non-playing Captain—Jack Westland

1963
INTERNATIONAL MATCH FOR THE WALKER CUP

Held at the Ailsa Course, Turnberry, Scotland
May 24 and 25

May 24

FOURSOMES

Great Britain and Ireland	Points	United States	Points
Michael F. Bonallack and Stuart W.T. Murray (4 and 3)	1	William J. Patton and R.H. Sikes	0
Joseph B. Carr and Charles W. Green	0	A. Downing Gray, Jr. and Labron E. Harris, Jr. (2 up)	1
Michael S.R. Lunt and David B. Sheahan	0	Deane R. Beman and Charles R. Coe (5 and 3)	1
J.F. David Madeley and Ronald D.B.M. Shade (halved)	0	Robert W. Gardner and Dr. Edgar R. Updegraff (halved)	0
Total	1	Total	2

SINGLES

Great Britain and Ireland	Points	United States	Points
Stuart W.T. Murray (3 and 1)	1	Deane R. Beman	0
Martin J. Christmas	0	William J. Patton (3 and 2)	1
Joseph B. Carr (7 and 5)	1	R.H. Sikes	0
David B. Sheahan (1 up)	1	Labron E. Harris, Jr.	0
Michael F. Bonallack (1 up)	1	Richard E. Davies	0
Sandy Saddler (halved)	0	Charles R. Coe (halved)	0
Ronald D.B.M. Shade (4 and 3)	1	A. Downing Gray, Jr.	0
Michael S.R. Lunt (halved)	0	Charles B. Smith (halved)	0
Total	5	Total	1
Friday's Total	6	Friday's Total	3

May 25

FOURSOMES

Great Britain and Ireland	Points	United States	Points
Michael F. Bonallack and Stuart W.T. Murray	0	William J. Patton and R.H. Sikes (1 up)	1
Michael S.R. Lunt and David B. Sheahan	0	A. Downing Gray, Jr., and Labron E. Harris, Jr. (3 and 2)	1
Charles W. Green and Sandy Saddler	0	Robert W. Gardner and Dr. Edgar R. Updegraff (3 and 1)	1
J.F. David Madeley and Ronald D.B.M. Shade	0	Deane R. Beman and Charles R. Coe (3 and 2)	1
Total	0	Total	4

SINGLES

Great Britain and Ireland	Points	United States	Points
Stuart W.T. Murray	0	William J. Patton (3 and 2)	1
David B. Sheahan (1 up)	1	Richard D. Davies	0
Joseph B. Carr	0	Dr. Edgar R. Updegraff (4 and 3)	1
Michael F. Bonallack	0	Labron E. Harris, Jr. (3 and 2)	1
Michael S.R. Lunt	0	Robert W. Gardner (3 and 2)	1
Sandy Saddler (halved)	0	Deane R. Beman (halved)	0
Ronald D.B.M. Shade (2 and 1)	1	A. Downing Gray, Jr.	0
Charles W. Green	0	Charles R. Coe (4 and 3)	1
Total	2	Total	5
Saturday's Total	2	Saturday's Total	9
Grand Total—Great Britain and Ireland	8	Grand Total—United States	12

Non-playing Captain—C.D. Lawrie

Non-playing Captain—Richard S. Tufts

1965
INTERNATIONAL MATCH FOR THE WALKER CUP

Held at the Baltimore Country Club
Five Farms Old Course, Baltimore, Maryland
September 3 and 4

September 3

FOURSOMES

Great Britain and Ireland	Points	United States	Points
Michael Lunt and Gordon Cosh (1 up)	1	William C. Campbell and A. Downing Gray, Jr.	0
Michael Bonallack and Clive Clark (halved)	0	Deane R. Beman and Donald C. Allen (halved)	0
Rodney Foster and Gordon Clark	0	William J. Patton and Edgar M. Tutwiler (5 and 4)	1
Peter Townsend and Ronald D.B.M. Shade (2 and 1)	1	John Mark Hopkins and Davis Eichelberger	0
Total	2	Total	1

SINGLES

Great Britain and Ireland	Points	United States	Points
Michael Bonallack	0	William C. Campbell (6 and 5)	1
Rodney Foster	0	Deane R. Beman (2 up)	1
Ronald D.B.M. Shade	1	A. Downing Gray, Jr.	0
Clive Clark (5 and 3)	1	John Mark Hopkins	0
Peter Townsend (3 and 2)	1	William J. Patton	0
Sandy Saddler (2 and 1)	1	Dale Morey	0
Gordon Cosh (2 up)	1	Donald C. Allen	0
Michael Lunt (2 and 1)	1	Dr. Edgar R. Updegraff	0
Total	6	Total	2
Friday's Total	8	Friday's Total	3

September 4

FOURSOMES

Great Britain and Ireland	Points	United States	Points
Sandy Saddler and Rodney Foster	0	William C. Campbell and A. Downing Gray, Jr. (4 and 3)	1
Ronald D.B.M. Shade and Peter Townsend (2 and 1)	1	Deane R. Beman and Davis Eichelberger	0
Gordon Cosh and Michael Lunt	0	Edgar M. Tutwiler and William J. Patton (2 and 1)	1
Clive Clark and Michael Bonallack (2 and 1)	1	Donald C. Allen and Dale Morey	0
Total	2	Total	2

SINGLES

Great Britain and Ireland	Points	United States	Points
Rodney Foster	0	William C. Campbell (3 and 2)	1
Sandy Saddler	0	Deane R. Beman (1 up)	1
Ronald D.B.M. Shade	0	Edgar M. Tutwiler (5 and 3)	1
Gordon Cosh (4 and 3)	1	Donald C. Allen	0
Peter Townsend	0	A. Downing Gray, Jr. (1 up)	1
Clive Clark (halved)	0	John Mark Hopkins (halved)	0
Michael Bonallack	0	Davis Eichelberger (5 and 3)	1
Michael Lunt	0	William J. Patton (4 and 2)	1
Total	1	Total	6
Saturday's Total	3	Saturday's Total	8
Grand Total—Great Britain and Ireland	11	Grand Total—United States	11

Captain—Joseph B. Carr

Non-playing Captain—John W. Fischer

1967
INTERNATIONAL MATCH FOR THE WALKER CUP

Held at Royal St. George's Golf Club, Sandwich, England
May 19 and 20

May 19

FOURSOMES

Great Britain and Ireland	Points	United States	Points
Ronald D.B.M. Shade and Peter A. Oosterhuis (halved)	0	Robert J. Murphy, Jr., and Ronald J. Cerrudo (halved)	0
Rodney Foster and Sandy Saddler	0	William C. Campbell and Jack W. Lewis, Jr. (1 up)	1
Michael Bonallack and Michael F. Attenborough	0	A. Downing Gray, Jr., and Edgar M. Tutwiler (4 and 2)	1
Joseph B. Carr and Tom Craddock	0	Robert B. Dickson and James A. Grant (3 and 1)	1
Total	0	Total	3

SINGLES

Great Britain and Ireland	Points	United States	Points
Ronald D.B.M. Shade	0	William C. Campbell (2 and 1)	1
Rodney Foster	0	Robert J. Murphy, Jr. (2 and 1)	1
Michael Bonallack (halved)	0	A. Downing Gray, Jr. (halved)	0
Michael F. Attenborough	0	Ronald J. Cerrudo (4 and 3)	1
Peter A. Oosterhuis	0	Robert B. Dickson (6 and 4)	1
Tom Craddock	0	Jack W. Lewis, Jr. (2 and 1)	1
A.K. Pirie (halved)	0	Donald C. Allen (halved)	0
Sandy Saddler (3 and 2)	1	Martin A. Fleckman	0
Total	1	Total	5
Friday's Total	1	Friday's Total	8

May 20

FOURSOMES

Great Britain and Ireland	Points	United States	Points
Michael Bonallack and Tom Craddock (2 up)	1	Robert J. Murphy, Jr. and Ronald J. Cerrudo	0
Sandy Saddler and A.K. Pirie	0	William C. Campbell and Jack W. Lewis, Jr. (1 up)	1
Ronald D.B.M. Shade and Peter A. Oosterhuis (3 and 1)	1	A. Downing Gray, Jr. and Edgar M. Tutwiler	0
Rodney Foster and Dudley J. Millensted (2 and 1)	1	Donald C. Allen and Martin A. Fleckman	0
Total	3	Total	1

SINGLES

Great Britain and Ireland	Points	United States	Points
Ronald D.B.M. Shade	0	William C. Campbell (3 and 2)	1
Michael Bonallack (4 and 2)	1	Robert J. Murphy, Jr.	0
Sandy Saddler (3 and 2)	1	A. Downing Gray	0
Rodney Foster (halved)	0	Ronald J. Cerrudo (halved)	0
A.K. Pirie	0	Robert B. Dickson (4 and 3)	1
Tom Craddock (5 and 4)	1	Jack W. Lewis, Jr.	0
Peter A. Oosterhuis	0	James A. Grant (1 up)	1
Dudley J. Millensted	0	Edgar M. Tutwiler (3 and 1)	1
Total	3	Total	4
Saturday's Total	6	Saturday's Total	5
Grand Total–Great Britain and Ireland	7	Grand Total–United States	13

Captain–Joseph B. Carr

Non-playing Captain–Jess W. Sweetser

1969
INTERNATIONAL MATCH FOR THE WALKER CUP

Held at Milwaukee Country Club, Milwaukee, Wisconsin
August 22 and 23

August 22

FOURSOMES

Great Britain and Ireland	Points	United States	Points
Michael Bonallack and Tom Craddock	0	Marvin Giles III and Steve Melnyk (3 and 2)	1
Peter Benka and Bruce Critchley (halved)	0	Bruce Fleisher and Allen Miller	0
Charles Green and Andrew Brooks (3 and 2)	1	Lanny Wadkins and Richard L. Siderowf	0
Rodney Foster and Geoffrey Marks	0	William Hyndman III and Joseph Inman, Jr. (2 and 1)	1
Total	1	Total	2

SINGLES

Great Britain and Ireland	Points	United States	Points
Michael Bonallack (halved)	0	Bruce Fleisher (halved)	0
Charles Green	0	Marvin Giles III (1 up)	1
Bruce Critchley	0	Allen Miller III (1 up)	1
Leonard Tupling	0	Richard L. Siderowf (6 and 5)	1
Peter Benka (3 and 1)	1	Steve Melnyk	0
Geoffrey Marks (1 up)	1	Lanny Wadkins	0
Michael King	0	John Bohmann (2 and 1)	1
Rodney Foster	0	Dr. Edgar R. Updegraff (6 and 5)	1
Total	2	Total	5
Friday's Total	3	Friday's Total	7

August 23

FOURSOMES

Great Britain and Ireland	Points	United States	Points
Charles Green and Andrew Brooks (halved)	0	Marvin Giles III and Steve Melnyk (halved)	0
Peter Benka and Bruce Critchley (2 and 1)	1	Bruce Fleisher and Allen Miller III	0
Rodney Foster and Michael King	0	Richard L. Siderowf and Lanny Wadkins (6 and 5)	1
Michael Bonallack and Peter Tupling (4 and 3)	1	Dr. Edgar R. Updegraff and John Bohmann	0
Total	2	Total	1

SINGLES

Great Britain and Ireland	Points	United States	Points
Michael Bonallack (5 and 4)	1	Bruce Fleisher	0
Bruce Critchley (halved)	0	Richard L. Siderowf	0
Michael G. King	0	Allen Miller III (1 up)	1
Tom Craddock (halved)	0	Marvin Giles III (halved)	0
Peter Benka	0	Joseph Inman, Jr. (2 and 1)	1
Andrew Brooks (4 and 3)	1	John Bohmann	0
Charles W. Green (halved)	0	William Hyndman III (halved)	0
Geoffrey Marks (3 and 2)	1	Dr. Edgar R. Updegraff	0
Total	3	Total	2
Saturday's Total	5	Saturday's Total	3
Grand Total—Great Britain and Ireland	8	Grand Total—United States	10

Captain—Michael Bonallack

Non-playing Captain—William J. Patton

1971
INTERNATIONAL MATCH FOR THE WALKER CUP

Held at St. Andrews, Scotland
May 26 and 27

May 26

FOURSOMES

Great Britain and Ireland	Points	United States	Points
Michael Bonallack and Warren Humphreys (1 up)	1	Lanny Wadkins and James B. Simons	0
Charles W. Green and Roderick J. Carr (1 up)	1	Steven Melnyk and Marvin Giles, III	0
David M. Marsh and George Macgregor (2 and 1)	1	Allen L. Miller, III and John Farquhar	0
John S. Macdonald and Rodney Foster (2 and 1)	1	William C. Campbell and Thomas O. Kite, Jr.	0
Total	4	Total	0

SINGLES

Great Britain and Ireland	Points	United States	Points
Charles W. Green	0	Lanny Wadkins (1 up)	1
Michael Bonallack	0	Marvin Giles, III (1 up)	1
Geoffrey C. Marks	0	Allen L. Miller, III (1 up)	1
John S. Macdonald	0	Steven Melnyk (3 and 2)	1
Roderick J. Carr (even)	½	William Hyndman, III	½
Warren Humphreys	0	James R. Gabrielsen (1 up)	1
Hugh B. Stuart (3 and 2)	1	John Farquhar	0
Rodney Foster	0	Thomas O. Kite, Jr. (3 and 2)	1
Total	1½	Total	6½
Wednesday Total – Great Britain and Ireland	5½	Wednesday Total – United States	6½

May 27

FOURSOMES

Great Britain and Ireland	Points	United States	Points
Geoffrey C. Marks and Charles W. Green	0	Steven Melnyk and Marvin Giles, III (1 up)	0
Hugh B. Stuart and Roderick J. Carr (1 up)	1	Lanny Wadkins and James R. Gabrielsen	0
David M. Marsh and Michael Bonallack	0	Allen L. Miller, III and John Farquhar (5 and 4)	1
John S. Macdonald and Rodney Foster (even)	½	William C. Campbell and Thomas O. Kite, Jr. (even)	½
Total	1½	Total	2½

SINGLES

Great Britain and Ireland	Points	United States	Points
Michael Bonallack	0	Lanny Wadkins (3 and 1)	1
Hugh B. Stuart (2 and 1)	1	Marvin Giles, III	0
Warren Humphreys (2 and 1)	1	Steven Melnyk	0
Charles W. Green (1 up)	1	Allen L. Miller, III	0
Roderick J. Carr (2 up)	1	James B. Simons	0
George Macgregor (1 up)	1	James R. Gabrielsen	0
David M. Marsh (1 up)	1	William Hyndman, III	0
Geoffrey C. Marks	0	Thomas O. Kite, Jr. (3 and 2)	1
Total	6	Total	2
Thursday's Total	7½	Thursday's Total	4½
Grand Total – Great Britain and Ireland	13	Grand Total – United States	11

Captain – Michael F. Bonallack

Non-playing Captain – John M. Winters, Jr.

1973
TWENTY-FOURTH INTERNATIONAL MATCH FOR THE WALKER CUP

Held at The Country Club, Brookline, Massachusetts
August 24 and 25

August 24
FOURSOMES

Great Britain and Ireland	Points	United States	Points
Michael King and Peter Hedges (halved)	½	Marvin Giles III and Gary Koch (halved)	½
Hugh Stuart and John Davies	0	Richard Siderowf and Mark Pfeil (5 and 4)	1
Charles Green and William Milne	0	Dan Edwards and James Ellis (2 and 1)	1
Rodney Foster and Trevor Homer	0	Douglas Ballenger and Martin West III (2 and 1)	1
Total	½	Total	3½

SINGLES

Great Britain and Ireland	Points	United States	Points
Hugh Stuart	0	Marvin Giles III (5 and 4)	1
Michael Bonallack	0	Richard Siderowf (4 and 2)	1
John Davies (1 up)	1	Gary Koch	0
Howard Clark (2 and 1)	1	Martin West III	0
Rodney Foster	0	Dan Edwards (2 up)	1
Michael King (1 up)	1	Michael Killian	0
Charles Green (1 up)	1	William Rogers	0
William Milne (4 and 3)	1	Mark Pfeil	0
Total	5	Total	3
Friday's Total—Great Britain and Ireland	5½	Friday's Total —United States	6½

August 25
FOURSOMES

Great Britain and Ireland	Points	United States	Points
Rodney Foster and Trevor Homer	0	Marvin Giles III and Gary Koch (7 and 5)	1
Howard Clark and John Davies (halved)	½	Richard Siderowf and Mark Pfeil (halved)	½
Peter Hedges and Michael King	0	Dan Edwards and James Ellis (2 and 1)	1
Hugh Stuart and William Milne	0	William Rogers and Michael Killian (1 up)	1
Total	½	Total	3½

SINGLES

Great Britain and Ireland	Points	United States	Points
Charles Green (halved)	½	Marvin Giles III (halved)	½
John Davies (3 and 2)	1	Richard Siderowf	0
Trevor Homer	0	Dan Edwards (2 and 1)	1
Hugh Stuart (5 and 4)	1	James Ellis	0
Michael King	0	Martin West III (2 up)	1
Howard Clark	0	Mark Pfeil (1 up)	1
William Milne (2 and 1)	1	Michael Killian	0
Peter Hedges (halved)	½	Gary Koch (halved)	½
Total	4	Total	4
Saturday's Total	4½	Saturday's Total	7½
Grand Total—Great Britain and Ireland	10	Grand Total—United States	14

Non-Playing Captain—Dr. David Marsh

Non-Playing Captain—Jess W. Sweetser

1975
TWENTY-FIFTH INTERNATIONAL MATCH FOR THE WALKER CUP

Held at St. Andrews, Scotland
May 28 and 29

May 28
FOURSOMES

Great Britain and Ireland	Points	United States	Points
Mark James and Richard Eyles	1	Jerome K. Pate and Richard Siderowf	0
John Davies and Martin Poxon	0	George Burns III and Craig Stadler (5 and 4)	1
Charles Green and Hugh Stuart	0	Jay Haas and Curtis Strange (2 and 1)	1
George Macgregor and Ian Hutcheon	0	Marvin Giles III and Gary Koch (5 and 4)	1
Total	1	Total	3

SINGLES

Great Britain and Ireland	Points	United States	Points
Mark James (2 and 1)	1	Jerome K. Pate	0
John Davies (halved)	½	Curtis Strange (halved)	½
Paddy Mulcare (1 up)	1	Richard Siderowf	0
Hugh Stuart	0	Gary Koch (3 and 2)	1
Martin Poxon	0	John Grace (3 and 1)	1
Ian Hutcheon (halved)	½	William C. Campbell (halved)	½
Richard Eyles	0	Jay Haas (2 and 1)	1
George Macgregor	0	Marvin Giles III (3 and 2)	1
Total	3	Total	5
Wednesday's Total—Great Britain and Ireland	4	Wednesday's Total—United States	8

May 29
FOURSOMES

Great Britain and Ireland	Points	United States	Points
Paddy Mulcare and Ian Hutcheon (1 up)	1	Jerome K. Pate and Richard Siderowf	0
Charles Green and Hugh Stuart	0	George Burns III and Craig Stadler (1 up)	1
Mark James and Richard Eyles (4 and 3)	1	William C. Campbell and John Grace	0
Peter Hedges and John Davies	0	Jay Haas and Curtis Strange (3 and 2)	1
Total	2	Total	2

SINGLES

Great Britain and Ireland	Points	United States	Points
Ian Hutcheon (3 and 2)	1	Jerome K. Pate	0
Paddy Mulcare	0	Curtis Strange (4 and 3)	1
Mark James	0	Gary Koch (5 and 4)	1
John Davies (2 and 1)	1	George Burns III	0
Charles Green	0	John Grace (2 and 1)	1
George Macgregor	0	Craig Stadler (3 and 2)	1
Richard Eyles	0	William C. Campbell (2 and 1)	1
Peter Hedges (halved)	½	Marvin Giles III (halved)	½
Total	2½	Total	5½
Thursday's Total	4½	Thursday's Total	7½
Grand Total—Great Britain and Ireland	8½	Grand Total—United States	15½

Non-playing Captain—Dr. David Marsh

Non-playing Captain—Dr. Edgar R. Updegraff

1977
TWENTY-SIXTH MATCH FOR THE WALKER CUP

Held at Shinnecock Hills Golf Club, Southampton, Long Island, New York, August 26 and 27.
Yardage—6,740. Par 70.

August 26
FOURSOMES

Great Britain and Ireland	Points	United States	Points
Peter McEvoy and Sandy Lyle	0	John Fought and Vance Heafner (4 and 3)	1
John Davies and Michael Kelley	0	Scott Simpson and Lindy Miller (5 and 4)	1
Ian Hutcheon and Peter Deeble (1 up)	1	Dick Siderowf and Gary Hallberg	0
Alan Brodie and Steve Martin	0	Jay Sigel and Mike Brannan (1 up)	1
Total	1	Total	3

SINGLES

Great Britain and Ireland	Points	United States	Points
Peter McEvoy	0	Lindy Miller (2 up)	1
Ian Hutcheon	0	John Fought (4 and 3)	1
Gordon Murray	0	Scott Simpson (7 and 6)	1
John Davies	0	Vance Heafner (4 and 3)	1
Alan Brodie (4 and 3)	1	Bill Sander	0
Steve Martin (3 and 2)	1	Gary Hallberg	0
Sandy Lyle	0	Fred Ridley (2 up)	1
Paul McKellar	0	Jay Sigel (5 and 4)	1
Total	2	Total	6
Friday's Total—Great Britain and Ireland	3	Friday's Total—United States	9

August 27
FOURSOMES

Great Britain and Ireland	Points	United States	Points
Ian Hutcheon and Peter Deeble	0	John Fought and Vance Heafner (4 and 3)	1
Peter McEvoy and John Davies	0	Lindy Miller and Scott Simpson (2 up)	1
Alan Brodie and Steve Martin (6 and 4)	1	Dick Siderowf and Bill Sander	0
Gordon Murray and Michael Kelley (4 and 3)	1	Fred Ridley and Mike Brannan	0
Total	2	Total	2

SINGLES

Great Britain and Ireland	Points	United States	Points
Steve Martin	0	Lindy Miller (1 up)	1
John Davies	0	John Fought (2 and 1)	1
Alan Brodie (2 and 1)	1	Bill Sander	0
Peter McEvoy	0	Gary Hallberg (4 and 3)	1
Michael Kelley (2 and 1)	1	Dick Siderowf	0
Ian Hutcheon (2 up)	1	Mike Brannan	0
Sandy Lyle	0	Fred Ridley (5 and 3)	1
Peter Deeble	0	Jay Sigel (1 up)	1
Total	3	Total	5
Saturday's Total—Great Britain and Ireland	5	Saturday's Total United States	7
Grand Total—Great Britain and Ireland	8	Grand Total United States	16

Non-playing Captain—Sandy Saddler

Non-playing Captain Lewis W. Oehmig

1979
TWENTY-SEVENTH INTERNATIONAL MATCH FOR THE WALKER CUP

Held at the Honourable Company of Edinburgh Golfers, Muirfield, Gullane, Scotland
May 30 and 31

May 30

FOURSOMES

Great Britain and Ireland	Points	United States	Points
Peter McEvoy and Brian Marchbank	0	Scott Hoch and Jay Sigel (1 up)	1
Geoff Godwin and Ian Hutcheon (2 up)	1	Martin West, III, and Hal Sutton	0
Gordon Brand and Michael Kelley	0	Doug Fischesser and Jim Holtgrieve (1 up)	1
Allan Brodie and Iain Carslaw (2 and 1)	1	Griff Moody, III, and Michael Gove	0
Total	2	Total	2

SINGLES

Great Britain and Ireland	Points	United States	Points
Peter McEvoy (even)	½	Jay Sigel (even)	½
John Davies	0	Doug Clarke (8 and 7)	1
Ian Hutcheon	0	Jim Holtgrieve (6 and 4)	1
Brian Marchbank (1 up)	1	Michael Peck	0
Geoff Godwin (3 and 2)	1	Griff Moody, III	0
Michael Kelley (3 and 2)	1	Doug Fischesser	0
Allan Brodie	0	Michael Gove (3 and 2)	1
James Buckley	0	Scott Hoch (9 and 7)	1
Total	3½	Total	4½
Wednesday's Total	5½	Wednesday's Total	6½

May 31

FOURSOMES

Great Britain and Ireland	Points	United States	Points
Geoff Godwin and Gordon Brand	0	Scott Hoch and Jay Sigel (4 and 3)	1
Michael Kelley and Ian Hutcheon (even)	½	Martin West, III, and Hal Sutton (even)	½
Peter McEvoy and Brian Marchbank (2 and 1)	1	Doug Fischesser and Jim Holtgrieve	0
Iain Carslaw and Allan Brodie (even)	½	Doug Clarke and Michael Peck (even)	½
Total	2	Total	2

SINGLES

Great Britain and Ireland	Points	United States	Points
Peter McEvoy	0	Scott Hoch (3 and 1)	1
Gordon Brand	0	Doug Clarke (2 and 1)	1
Geoff Godwin	0	Michael Gove (3 and 2)	1
Ian Hutcheon	0	Michael Peck (2 and 1)	1
Allan Brodie (3 and 2)	1	Martin West, III	0
Michael Kelley	0	Griff Moody, III (3 and 2)	1
Brian Marchbank	0	Hal Sutton (3 and 1)	1
Iain Carslaw	0	Jay Sigel (3 and 1)	1
Total	1	Total	7
Thursday's Total	3	Thursday's Total	9
Grand Total—Great Britain and Ireland	8½	Grand Total—United States	15½

Non-playing Captain—Rodney Foster

Non-playing Captain—Richard L. Siderowf

CURTIS CUP and WALKER CUP TEAMS

1964 U.S. CURTIS CUP TEAM

1965 MATCH WALKER CUP

CURTIS CUP MATCH

WOMEN'S INTERNATIONAL CUP

Presented in May, 1932, by

MISS HARRIOT S. CURTIS and MISS MARGARET CURTIS
Women's Amateur Champion 1906 — Women's Amateur Champion 1907-1911-1912

HISTORY

1960–The United States team won the Curtis Cup for the first time since 1954 in scoring a victory by 6½ to 2½. The Match was played at the Lindrick Golf Club, Worksop, Nottinghamshire, England. The Americans took a 2-1 lead in foursomes and went on to win four singles and halve another. In the singles, Miss JoAnne Gunderson defeated Mrs. Angela Ward Bonallack, 2 and 1; Miss Anne Quast defeated Miss Janette Robertson, 2 up; Miss Judy Eller defeated Miss Philomena Garvey, 4 and 3; Miss Judy Bell defeated Miss Belle McCorkindale, 8 and 7; and Miss Barbara McIntire and Miss Elizabeth Price were all even after 36 holes. A gallery estimated at 12,000 viewed the last day's singles competition.

1962–The United States Team scored a decisive 8-1 victory over the British Isles at the Broadmoor Golf Club, Colorado Springs, Colo. Mrs. Alastair Frearson earned the only point for the visitors by defeating Miss Judy Bell, 8 and 7, after the Americans had won all three foursomes matches. The Americans, five of whom were members of the victorious 1960 Team, scored remarkably low on a course considered to be a very severe test for women. Mrs. Anne Quast Decker, the United States Champion, was credited with a 74 in the morning round of her singles and then played the first nine holes in the afternoon in 36; Mrs. Decker and Miss Barbara McIntire produced a 74 in the foursomes; Miss Phyllis Preuss scored 75 in singles; Miss Clifford Ann Creed a 76. The British side was largely the product of a training program sponsored by the Ladies' Golf Union for juniors. Five of the eight British players were new to Curtis Cup competition; three were still in their teens. The non-playing Captains were Mrs. Frances Stephens Smith for the British Isles and Miss Polly Riley for the United States.

1964–With first-time players accounting for 6½ points, the United States Team scored a 10½-7½ victory at the Royal Porthcawl Golf Club, Porthcawl, South Wales. The competition was extremely close throughout. After the morning foursomes on the first day, the British led 2-1. The United States drew even at 4½ each by winning three and halving one of the afternoon singles matches. On the final day, the foursomes were divided, and after the first three singles matches each team had 7½ points. The United States rookies, Misses Peggy Conley, Barbara Fay White, and Carol Sorenson, provided the winning points in the last three singles matches. Miss Conley, at 17 the youngest player ever to compete for the United States in the Curtis Cup Match, won both her singles; she did not compete in the foursomes. Miss JoAnne Gunderson, of the United States, and Mrs. Marley Spearman, of the British Isles, played a memorable match on the final afternoon; it was halved with each player scoring 71, two under par. The day before, Miss Gunderson was four under par in her singles victory over Mrs. Angela Ward Bonallack. The non-playing Captains were Mrs. Theodore W. Hawes for the United States and Miss Elsie Corlett for the British Isles.

1966–A vastly more experienced United States team scored a decisive 13-5 victory over the British Isles team at the Virginia Hot Springs Golf and Tennis Club, Hot Springs, Va. Strong finishes by the teams of Miss Phyllis Preuss and Miss Jean Ashley, and that of Mrs. Anne Quast Welts and Miss Barbara McIntire helped the United States to a 2½-½ lead at the end of the morning foursomes on opening day. Only Miss Ita Burke was able to win a singles match for the British in the afternoon, although Miss Susan Armitage won a half. At the end of the first day the United States was ahead, 7-2. On the second day the British Isles Team was able to win only two matches. Miss Burke teamed with Miss Elizabeth Chadwick to win a foursomes match from Mrs. Welts and Miss McIntire, and Mrs. Angela Ward Bonallack defeated Miss Ashley in singles. All the Americans had been in Curtis Cup play before: only three of the British had been. The non-playing captains were Mrs. S. M. Bolton for the British Isles and Mrs. Mark A. Porter for the United States.

1968–In a very close match, the United States defeated the British Isles, 10½-7½, at the Royal County Down Golf Club, Newcastle, Northern Ireland. With three singles matches undetermined late on the second day, the score was tied at 7½-7½. Then Miss Peggy Conley, of the United States, defeated Mrs. Margaret Pickard, 1 up, to put the Americans ahead. Miss Mary Lou Dill followed with a 4-and-2 victory over Mrs. Ann Howard, and finally Miss Phyllis Preuss defeated Miss Bridget Jackson, 2 and 1. Miss Ann Irwin was outstanding for the British Isles, and Miss Preuss had the best record for the United States. Both won 3½ of a possible 4 points. This was the United States' 11th victory in 14 matches. Non-playing Captains were Mrs. S. M. Bolton for the

British Isles, and Mrs. Robert M. Monsted, for the United States.

1970—The United States won the 16th International Match for the Curtis Cup, 11½-6½, at the Brae Burn Country Club, West Newton, Mass., for its 12th victory in the series. The British Isles had won two, and two matches had been tied. The British Isles took the lead after the foursomes matches of the first day, 2-1, and with one match remaining had a chance to end the first day's play tied at 4½-4½. However, Mrs. Paul Dye, Jr., of the United States, rallied from being two down with four to play, won the next three holes from Miss Julia Greenhalgh, and put the United States ahead to stay, 5½-3½. The United States won 2½ of a possible 3 points in the morning foursomes of the second day, led, 8-4, with only the singles remaining, then won 3½ of a possible 6 in the afternoon. Miss Jane Bastanchury, of the United States, was the only player on either side to win both her singles matches, and teamed with Miss Shelley Hamlin to win a foursomes. Non-playing Captains were Miss Jeanne Bisgood for the British Isles, Mrs. Philip Cudone for the United States.

1972—The United States won the 17th International Match for the Curtis Cup, 10 to 8, at the Western Gailes Golf Club in Ayrshire, Scotland, for its 13th victory in the series that began in 1932. The two-point margin of victory was the narrowest since 1958, when the Teams played to a tie. Great Britain and Ireland last won in 1956. The British Isles led, 2 to 1, after the first morning's foursomes, but in the afternoon's singles the United States won four matches, lost only one and halved one, a classic match between the Women's Champions of the United States and Great Britain. Miss Laura Baugh, the U.S. Champion, was constantly outdriven by Miss Michelle Walker, the British Champion, and she was two down after 10 holes. She squared the match on the 15th, where Miss Walker was bunkered, and the match ended even. Both shot 75. The United States Team took a 7 to 5 lead after the foursomes on the final day. The pivotal match was between the American team of Miss Beth Barry and Miss Hollis Stacy and the British pair of Mrs. I. C. Robertson and Mrs. Diane Frearson. Miss Barry and Miss Stacy were four down with only six to play, but they salvaged a half and preserved the two-point lead. The British Team then rallied in the afternoon singles as Miss Walker, Miss Mary McKenna, and Miss Mary Everard all won their matches. To that point, only Laura Baugh had been able to score a point for the United States. With two matches left to be played, the Teams were even, 8 to 8. Miss Lancy Smith, a doubtful starter because of illness, then defeated Mrs. Diane Frearson, 3 and 2, to ensure a tie, and then Miss Barry defeated Miss Kathryn Phillips, also by 3 and 2, to win the victory for the United States. Miss Walker won 3½ of four points and was the only undefeated player on either Side. Miss Baugh and Miss Barry led the Americans in points scored with 2½ each. Miss Barbara McIntire, who first was a member of the United States Team in 1958, played in her sixth International Match for the Curtis Cup and scored two points. Mrs. Jean Ashley Crawford, a member of the United States Team in 1962-66-68, was non-playing Captain. Mrs. Frances Stephens Smith, who played on the Great Britain and Ireland Team from 1950 through 1960, was the non-playing Captain for the British Isles.

1974—The United States won the 18th International Match for the Curtis Cup, 13 to 5, at the San Francisco Golf Club in a fog-bound, chilly setting. The 8-point margin equalled that of the 1966 Match, and it brought the United States its 14th victory in 18 matches. Great Britain and Ireland won twice, and two matches ended in ties. At the end of the first day's foursomes, the Teams were tied; both had won a match, while one match was halved. In the afternoon's singles, four of the six matches went to the 18th hole; the United States won four, halved one, and lost one. Mrs. Jane Bastanchury Booth, Miss Debbie Massey, Miss Bonnie Lauer, and Miss Beth Barry all won, while Miss Maureen Walker won for the British and Irish side. Miss Cynthia Hill and Miss Tegwen Perkins halved. At the end of the day's play, the United States was ahead, 6 points to 3. The next day the United States Team won two of the three foursomes to take an 8 to 4 lead, and in the afternoon's singles, the United States won five of six matches. Only Miss Mary McKenna was able to win a point for Great Britain and Ireland. Mrs. Booth was the leading point-winner on either side, with two singles and two foursomes victories. In three Curtis Cup Matches Mrs. Booth won seven of a possible nine points. Mrs. Allison Choate was the non-playing Captain for the United States, while Mrs. I. C. Robertson, who played in five previous Matches was non-playing Captain for Great Britain and Ireland.

1976—The United States won the 19th International Match for the Curtis Cup, 11½ to 6½, at Royal Lytham and St. Annes Golf Club, St. Annes-On-Sea, Lancashire, England, playing in bitter, rainy, windy weather the first day and in sunny, yet windy weather the next. This was the 15th victory for the United States in 19 Matches; Great Britain and Ireland won twice and two Matches ended in ties. The American side won two of the first day's foursomes while Great Britain and Ireland took one. In the afternoon singles, the United States gained 4½ points, winning four matches and halving another. Miss Beth Daniel, Mrs. Nancy Roth Syms, Miss Nancy Lopez and Miss Deborah Massey all won. Only Mrs. Dinah Henson was able to win a point for Great Britain and Ireland, while Miss Barbara Barrow, for the United

States, and Miss Julia Greenhalgh halved. At the end of the first day, the United States led, 6½ to 2½, needing only three points to assure the victory. In the next day's foursomes the United States gained two more points and needed just one more to win. Miss Beth Daniel supplied that point, defeating Mrs. Dinah Henson, 3 and 2, in the first singles match of the afternoon. After Miss Daniel closed out her match, the Great Britain-Ireland Team won three of the remaining five matches. Miss Daniel, the 1975 United States Women's Amateur Champion, was the only player on either side to win four points. Miss Tegwin Perkins led the Great Britain-Ireland side with three points. Miss Deborah Massey also had three points, while Misses Hill, Lopez and Horton each added two. Miss Barbara McIntire, U. S. Amateur Champion in 1959 and 1964, was the non-playing Captain. Mrs. I. C. Robertson, a former Scottish Women's Amateur Champion, was the non-playing Captain for the Great Britain and Ireland side. The gallery, despite the wind and rain, reached 5,000.

1978—The United States won the 20th International Match for the Curtis Cup for its 16th victory in the series, which began in 1932. Great Britain and Ireland have won twice, and two Matches have ended in ties. The United States won, 12-6, at the Apawamis Club, in Rye, N.Y. The Match was much closer than the final score indicated, because the individual matches were very competitive. Seven of the 18 matches were decided on the 18th green. Of those seven, Americans won four and halved the other three, which proved to be the deciding factor. Great Britain and Ireland won two of the first three foursomes matches on the first day and halved the third for an early 2½-½ lead. In the afternoon, the United States won four of the six singles matches and halved one other. Miss Beth Daniel, Miss Cynthia Hill, Mrs. Judith Oliver, and Miss Lancy Smith all won. Only Miss Mary Everard won a point for Great Britain and Ireland, while Miss Carolyn Hill, for the United States, and Mrs. Carole Caldwell, halved their match. The first day ended with the United States holding a 5-4 lead. On the second day, the United States won all three foursomes matches to increase its lead to 8-4. The Americans needed just two points from the six afternoon singles matches for a victory. When Miss Daniel defeated Miss Mary McKenna, 2 and 1, in the first singles match, the United States needed just one more point to win. Miss Pat Cornett, although off late in the fourth match, supplied that point by defeating Mrs. Caldwell, 3 and 2. After Miss Cornett closed out her match, the United States won one and halved two of the four remaining matches. Miss Muriel Thomson, of Great Britain-Ireland, defeated Miss Carolyn Hill in the other. All eight American players contributed at least one point to the victory. Mrs. Helen Sigel Wilson, runner-up in both the 1941 and 1948 Women's Amateur Championships and a member of the 1950 and 1966 Curtis Cup Teams, was the non-playing Captain of the United States Team. Mrs. Carol Comboy, Chairman of the British Selection Committee, was the non-playing Captain of the Great Britain and Ireland side.

1980—The United States won the 21st Match 13-5, for its 17th victory in the series. The 13-5 score equalled the largest winning team margin set in 1966 and 1974. The Match was played at the St. Pierre Golf Club, in Chepstow, Wales. Patty Sheehan and Lori Castillo won their first day's foursomes match, 5 and 3, and their teammates halved the other two matches to give the United States an early 2-1 lead. In one halved match, Terri Moody of the United States holed a par putt of 18 feet at the 18th, as she and partner Lancy Smith halved Mary McKenna and Claire Nesbitt. Carol Semple and Judy Oliver, of the United States, were one down to Maureen Madill and Carole Caldwell coming to the 18th. Miss Semple's tee shot stopped 10 feet from the cup and Mrs. Oliver holed it to cause another halved match. In the afternoon singles, the United States won four of the six matches and halved the other two. Miss Sheehan played the last nine holes one under par to defeat Mary McKenna 3 and 2. Mary Hafeman, of the United States, was four down at the 15th tee, but won the final four holes to halve Lynda Moore. Lancy Smith halved her match with Claire Nesbitt. The United States led 7-2 at the end of the first day. On the second day, the United States won all three foursomes matches to stretch its lead to 10-2. Miss Smith and Miss Moody won five consecutive holes on the first nine and won, 6 and 5. Miss Sheehan and Miss Castillo won the first three holes and maintained that lead for a 3 and 2 decision. Mrs. Oliver and Miss Semple provided the 10th and deciding point for the American side as Mrs. Oliver holed a par putt of 30 feet at the final hole for a 1 up victory over Tegwen Thomas and Miss Moore. At this stage, Great Britain and Ireland had not won a match. In the final afternoon's singles, both sides won three matches apiece. Miss Hafeman, who had won the final four holes of her first singles match, won the first six holes from Jane Connachan—10 in a row. She won the match 6 and 5. Eight of the matches over the two days were decided at the 18th hole. Great Britain and Ireland won only one of these. The United States won three and the other four were halved. Miss Sheehan was the leading point winner with four of a possible four. In none of her matches was she extended beyond the 16th hole. All eight American players contributed at least one point to the victory. Mrs. Nancy Roth Syms, a member of the 1964, 1966, and 1976 Curtis Cup Teams, was the non-playing Captain of the United States Team. Mrs. Carol Comboy again was non-playing Captain of Great Britain and Ireland.

CURTIS CUP MATCH

1960	United States,	6½	Great Britain & Ireland, 2½	Lindrick G.C., Worksop, England
1962	United States,	8	Great Britain & Ireland, 1	Broadmoor, G.C., (East Course), Colorado Springs, Colo.
1964	United States,	10½	Great Britain & Ireland, 7½	Royal Porthcawl G.C., Porthcawl, Wales
1966	United States,	13	Great Britain & Ireland, 5	Virginia Hot Springs G.&T.C., (Cascades Course), Hot Springs, Va.
1968	United States,	10½	Great Britain & Ireland, 7½	Royal County Down G.C., Newcastle, Northern Ireland
1970	United States,	11½	Great Britain & Ireland, 6½	Brae Burn, C.C., West Newton, Mass.
1972	United States,	10	Great Britain & Ireland, 8	Western Gailes, Ayrshire, Scotland
1974	United States,	13	Great Britain & Ireland, 5	San Francisco G.C., San Francisco, Calif.
1976	United States,	11½	Great Britain & Ireland, 6½	Royal Lytham & St. Annes G.C., St. Annes-On-Sea, Lancashire, England
1978	United States,	12	Great Britain & Ireland, 6	Apawamis Club, Rye, N.Y.
1980	United States,	13	Great Britain & Ireland, 5	St. Pierre G.&C.C., Chepstow, Wales

1960
INTERNATIONAL MATCH FOR THE CURTIS CUP

Held at Lindrick Golf Club, Worksop, Nottinghamshire, England

May 20 and 21

FOURSOMES

Great Britain and Ireland	Points	United States	Points
Mrs. Angela Ward Bonallack and Miss Elizabeth Price (1 up)	1	Miss JoAnne Gunderson and Miss Barbara McIntire	0
Miss Belle McCorkindale and Miss Janette Robertson	0	Miss Judy Eller and Miss Anne Quast (4 and 2)	1
Miss Ruth Porter and Mrs. Frances Smith	0	Miss Joanne Goodwin and Mrs. Ann Casey Johnstone (3 and 2)	1
Total	1	Total	2

SINGLES

Great Britain and Ireland	Points	United States	Points
Miss Elizabeth Price (halved)	½	Miss Barbara McIntire (halved)	½
Mrs. Angela Ward Bonallack	0	Miss JoAnne Gunderson (2 and 1)	1
Miss Janette Robertson	0	Miss Anne Quast (2 up)	1
Miss Philomena Garvey	0	Miss Judy Eller (4 and 3)	1
Miss Belle McCorkindale	0	Miss Judy Bell (8 and 7)	1
Miss Ruth Porter (1 up)	1	Miss Joanne Goodwin	0
Total	1½	Total	4½
Grand Total—Great Britain and Ireland	2½	Grand Total—United States	6½

Non-playing Captain—Mrs. Maureen Garrett

Non-playing Captain—Mrs. Henri Prunaret

1962
INTERNATIONAL MATCH FOR THE CURTIS CUP

Held at Broadmoor Golf Club, Colorado Springs, Colorado

August 17 and 18

FOURSOMES

Great Britain and Ireland	Points	United States	Points
Mrs. Angela Ward Bonallack and Mrs. Marley Spearman	0	Mrs. Anne Quast Decker and Miss Barbara McIntire (7 and 5)	1
Miss Ann Irvin and Miss Sheila Vaughan	0	Miss Clifford Ann Creed and Miss JoAnne Gunderson (4 and 3)	1
Mrs. Alastair Frearson and Miss Ruth Porter	0	Miss Jean Ashley and Mrs. Anna Casey Johnstone (8 and 7)	1
Total	0	Total	3

SINGLES

Great Britain and Ireland	Points	United States	Points
Mrs. Marlev Spearman	0	Mrs. Anne Quast Decker (5 and 4)	1
Mrs. Angela Ward Bonallack	0	Miss JoAnne Gunderson (2 and 1)	1
Mrs. Alastair Frearson (8 and 7)	1	Miss Judy Bell	0
Miss Jean Roberts	0	Miss Phyllis Preuss (1 up)	1
Miss Sally Bonallack	0	Miss Clifford Ann Creed (6 and 5)	1
Miss Sheila Vaughan	0	Miss Barbara McIntire (5 and 4)	1
Total	1	Total	5
Grand Total—Great Britain and Ireland	1	Grand Total—United States	8

Non-playing Captain—Mrs. Frances Smith

Non-playing Captain—Miss Polly Riley

1964
INTERNATIONAL MATCH FOR THE CURTIS CUP

Held at the Royal Porthcawl Golf Club, Porthcawl, South Wales
September 11 and 12

September 11

FOURSOMES

Great Britain - Ireland	Points	United States	Points
Mrs. Marley Spearman and Mrs. Angela Ward Bonallack (2 and 1)	1	Miss Barbara McIntire and Miss Phyllis Preuss	0
Miss Bridget Jackson and Miss Susan Armitage	0	Miss Carol Sorenson and Miss Barbara Fay White (8 and 6)	1
Miss Sheila Vaughan and Miss Ruth Porter (3 and 2)	1	Miss JoAnne Gunderson and Miss Nancy Roth	0
Total	2	Total	1

SINGLES

Great Britain - Ireland	Points	United States	Points
Miss Marley Spearman (halved)	½	Miss Barbara McIntire (halved)	½
Mrs. Angela Ward Bonallack	0	Miss JoAnne Gunderson (6 and 5)	1
Miss Joan Lawrence	0	Miss Peggy Conley (1 up)	1
Miss Julia Greenhalgh	0	Miss Barbara Fay White (3 and 2)	1
Miss Bridget Jackson (4 and 3)	1	Miss Carol Sorenson	0
Miss Ruth Porter (1 up)	1	Miss Nancy Roth	0
Total	2½	Total	3½
Friday's Total	4½	Friday's Total	4½

September 12

FOURSOMES

Great Britain - Ireland	Points	United States	Points
Mrs. Marley Spearman and Mrs. Angela Ward Bonallack (6 and 5)	1	Miss Barbara McIntire and Miss Phyllis Preuss	0
Miss Susan Armitage and Miss Bridget Jackson	0	Miss JoAnne Gunderson and Miss Nancy Roth (2 up)	1
Miss Ruth Porter and Miss Sheila Vaughan (halved)	½	Miss Carol Sorenson and Miss Barbara Fay White (halved)	½
Total	1½	Total	1½

SINGLES

Great Britain - Ireland	Points	United States	Points
Mrs. Marley Spearman (halved)	½	Miss JoAnne Gunderson (halved)	½
Miss Joan Lawrence	0	Miss Barbara McIntire (4 and 2)	1
Miss Julia Greenhalgh (5 and 3)	1	Miss Phyllis Preuss	0
Miss Bridget Jackson	0	Miss Peggy Conley (1 up)	1
Mrs. Angela Ward Bonallack	0	Miss Barbara Fay White (3 and 2)	1
Miss Ruth Porter	0	Miss Carol Sorenson (3 and 2)	1
Total	1½	Total	4½
Saturday's Total	3	Saturday's Total	6
Grand Total—Great Britain and Ireland	7½	Grand Total—United States	10½

Non-playing Captain—Miss Elsie Corlett

Non-playing Captain—Mrs. T.W. Hawes

1966
INTERNATIONAL MATCH FOR THE CURTIS CUP

Held at Cascades Course, Virginia Hot Springs Golf and Tennis Club, Hot Springs, Virginia
July 29 and 30

July 29

FOURSOMES

Great Britain - Ireland	Points	United States	Points
Mrs. Angela Ward Bonallack and Miss Susan Armitage	0	Miss Jean Ashley and Miss Phyllis Preuss (1 up)	1
Mrs. I.C. Robertson and Miss Joan Hastings (halved)	½	Mrs. Anne Quast Welts and Miss Barbara McIntire (halved)	½
Miss Elizabeth Chadwick and Miss Pamela Tredinnick	0	Mrs. Barbara White Boddie and Mrs. Carol Sorenson Flenniken (1 up)	1
Total	½	Total	2½

SINGLES

Great Britain - Ireland	Points	United States	Points
Mrs. I.C. Robertson	0	Miss Jean Ashley (1 up)	1
Miss Susan Armitage (halved)	½	Mrs. Anne Quast Welts (halved)	½
Mrs. Angela Ward Bonallack	0	Mrs. Barbara White Boddie (3 and 2)	1
Miss Elizabeth Chadwick	0	Mrs. Nancy Roth Syms (2 up)	1
Miss Ita Burke (3 and 1)	1	Mrs. Helen Sigel Wilson	0
Miss Marjory Fowler	0	Mrs. Carol Sorenson Flenniken (3 and 1)	1
Total	1½	Total	4½
Total July 29	2	Total July 29	7

July 30

FOURSOMES

Great Britain - Ireland	Points	United States	Points
Mrs. Angela Ward Bonallack and Miss Susan Armitage	0	Miss Jean Ashley and Miss Phyllis Preuss (3 and 1)	1
Miss Elizabeth Chadwick and Miss Ita Burke (1 up)	1	Mrs. Anne Quast Welts and Miss Barbara McIntire	0
Mrs. I.C. Robertson and Miss Joan Hastings	0	Mrs. Barbara White Boddie and Mrs. Carol Sorenson Flenniken (2&1)	1
Total	1	Total	2

SINGLES

Great Britain - Ireland	Points	United States	Points
Mrs. Angela Ward Bonallack (2 and 1)	1	Miss Jean Ashley	0
Mrs. I.C. Robertson (halved)	½	Mrs. Anne Quast Welts (halved)	½
Miss Susan Armitage	0	Mrs. Barbara White Boddie (3 and 2)	1
Miss Pamela Tredinnick (halved)	½	Mrs. Nancy Roth Syms (halved)	½
Miss Elizabeth Chadwick	0	Miss Phyllis Preuss (3 and 2)	1
Miss Ita Burke	0	Mrs. Carol Sorenson Flenniken (2 and 1)	1
Total	2	Total	4
Total July 30	3	Total July 30	6
Grand Total—Great Britain and Ireland	5	Grand Total—United States	13

Non-playing Captain—Mrs. S.M. Bolton

Non-playing Captain—Mrs. Dorothy Germain Porter

1968
INTERNATIONAL MATCH FOR THE CURTIS CUP

Held at Royal County Down Golf Club, Newcastle, County Down, Northern Ireland
June 14 and 15

June 14

FOURSOMES

Great Britain - Ireland	Points	United States	Points
Mrs. I.C. Robertson and Miss Ann Irvin (6 and 5)	1	Miss Shelley Hamlin and Mrs. Anne Quast Welts	0
Mrs. Margaret Pickard and Miss Vivien Saunders (3 and 2)	1	Miss Mary Lou Dill and Miss Peggy Conley	0
Mrs. Ann Howard and Miss Pamela Tredinnick	0	Miss Phyllis Preuss and Miss Jean Ashley (1 up)	1
Total	2	Total	1

SINGLES

Great Britain - Ireland	Points	United States	Points
Miss Ann Irvin (3 and 2)	1	Mrs. Anne Quast Welts	0
Miss Vivien Saunders	0	Miss Shelley Hamlin (1 up)	1
Mrs. I.C. Robertson	0	Miss Roberta Albers (1 up)	1
Miss Bridget Jackson (halved)	½	Miss Peggy Conley (halved)	½
Miss Dinah Oxley (halved)	½	Miss Phyllis Preuss (halved)	½
Mrs. Margaret Pickard (2 up)	1	Miss Jean Ashley	0
Total	3	Total	3
Total June 14	5	Total June 14	4

June 15

FOURSOMES

Great Britain - Ireland	Points	United States	Points
Mrs. I.C. Robertson and Miss Ann Irvin (halved)	½	Miss Mary Lou Dill and Miss Peggy Conley (halved)	½
Mrs. Margaret Pickard and Miss Vivien Saunders	0	Miss Shelley Hamlin and Mrs. Anne Quast Welts (2 and 1)	1
Miss Dinah Oxley and Miss Pamela Tredinnick	0	Miss Phyllis Preuss and Miss Jean Ashley (5 and 4)	1
Total	½	Total	2½

SINGLES

Great Britain - Ireland	Points	United States	Points
Miss Ann Irvin (3 and 2)	1	Miss Shelley Hamlin	0
Mrs. I.C. Robertson (halved)	½	Mrs. Anne Quast Welts (halved)	½
Miss Vivien Saunders (halved)	½	Miss Roberta Albers (halved)	½
Mrs. Margaret Pickard	0	Miss Peggy Conley (1 up)	1
Mrs. Ann Howard	0	Miss Mary Lou Dill (4 and 2)	1
Miss Bridget Jackson	0	Miss Phyllis Preuss (2 and 1)	1
Total	2	Total	4
Total June 15	2½	Total June 15	6½
Grand Total—Great Britain and Ireland	7½	Grand Total—United States	10½

Non-playing Captain—Mrs. S.M. Bolton

Non-playing Captain—Mrs. Robert M. Monsted

1970

INTERNATIONAL MATCH FOR THE CURTIS CUP

Held at Brae Burn Country Club, West Newton, Massachusetts
August 7 and 8

August 7

FOURSOMES

Great Britain – Ireland	Points	United States	Points
Miss Dinah Oxley and Miss Mary McKenna (4 and 3)	1	Miss Shelley Hamlin and Miss Jane Bastanchury	0
Mrs. I. C. Robertson and Miss Ann Irvin	0	Miss Phyllis Preuss and Miss Martha Wilkinson (4 and 3)	1
Miss Mary Everard and Miss Julia Greenhalgh (5 and 3)	1	Miss Cynthia Hill and Miss Jane Fassinger	0
Total	2	Total	1

SINGLES

Great Britain – Ireland	Points	United States	Points
Miss Dinah Oxley	0	Miss Jane Bastanchury (5 and 3)	1
Miss Ann Irvin	0	Miss Martha Wilkinson (1 up)	1
Mrs. I. C. Robertson (even)	½	Miss Shelley Hamlin (even)	½
Miss Mary McKenna (4 and 2)	1	Miss Phyllis Preuss	0
Mrs. Margaret Pickard	0	Miss Nancy Hager (5 and 4)	1
Miss Julia Greenhalgh	0	Mrs. Paul Dye, Jr. (1 up)	1
Total	1½	Total	4½
Total August 7	3½	Total August 7	5½

August 8

FOURSOMES

Great Britain – Ireland	Points	United States	Points
Miss Dinah Oxley and Miss Mary McKenna	0	Miss Phyllis Preuss and Miss Martha Wilkinson (6 and 4)	1
Mrs. I. C. Robertson and Miss Ann Irvin	0	Miss Shelley Hamlin and Miss Jane Bastanchury (1 up)	1
Miss Mary Everard and Miss Julia Greenhalgh (even)	½	Miss Cynthia Hill and Mrs. Paul Dye, Jr. (even)	½
Total	½	Total	2½

SINGLES

Great Britain – Ireland	Points	United States	Points
Miss Dinah Oxley (even)	½	Miss Shelley Hamlin (even)	½
Miss Ann Irvin	0	Miss Jane Bastanchury (4 and 3)	1
Mrs. I. C. Robertson	0	Miss Phyllis Preuss (1 up)	1
Miss Julia Greenhalgh (6 and 4)	1	Miss Martha Wilkinson	0
Miss Mary Everard (4 and 3)	1	Miss Nancy Hager	0
Miss Mary McKenna	0	Miss Cynthia Hill (2 and 1)	1
Total	2½	Total	3½
Total August 8	3	Total August 8	6
Grand Total–Great Britain and Ireland	6½	Grand Total–United States	11½

Non-playing Captain–Miss Jeanne Bisgood

Non-playing Captain–Mrs. Philip Cudone

1972

INTERNATIONAL MATCH FOR THE CURTIS CUP

Held at Western Gailes, Ayrshire, Scotland
June 9 and 10

June 9

FOURSOMES

Great Britain – Ireland	Points	United States	Points
Miss Beverley Huke and Miss Mary Everard	0	Miss Laura Baugh and Mrs. Martha Wilkinson Kirouac	1
Mrs. I.C. Robertson and Mrs. Diane Frearson	1	Mrs. Jane Bastanchury Booth and Miss Barbara McIntire	0
Miss Michelle Walker and Miss Mary McKenna	1	Miss Beth Barry and Miss Hollis Stacy	0
Total	2	Total	1

SINGLES

Great Britain – Ireland	Points	United States	Points
Miss Michelle Walker	½	Miss Laura Baugh	½
Mrs. I.C. Robertson	0	Mrs. Jane Bastanchury Booth	1
Miss Mary Everard	0	Mrs. Martha Wilkinson Kirouac	1
Miss Dinah Oxley	0	Miss Barbara McIntire	1
Miss Kathryn Phillips	1	Miss Lancy Smith	0
Miss Mary McKenna	0	Miss Beth Berry	1
Total	1½	Total	4½
Total June 9	3½	Total June 9	5½

June 10•

FOURSOMES

Great Britain – Ireland	Points	United States	Points
Miss Michelle Walker and Miss Mary McKenna	1	Miss Laura Baugh and Mrs. Martha Wilkinson Kirouac	0
Mrs. I.C. Robertson and Mrs. Diane Frearson	½	Miss Beth Barry and Miss Hollis Stacy	½
Miss Mary Everard and Miss Beverley Huke	0	Mrs. Jane Bastanchury Booth and Miss Barbara McIntire	1
Total	1½	Total	1½

SINGLES

Great Britain – Ireland	Points	United States	Points
Miss Michelle Walker	1	Mrs. Jane Bastanchury Booth	0
Miss Mary McKenna	1	Mrs. Martha Wilkinson Kirouac	0
Mrs. I.C. Robertson	0	Miss Laura Baugh	1
Miss Mary Everard	1	Miss Barbara McIntire	0
Mrs. Diane Frearson	0	Miss Lancy Smith	1
Miss Kathryn Phillips	0	Miss Beth Barry	1
Total	3	Total	3
Total June 10	4½	Total June 10	4½
Grand Total-Great Britain–Ireland	8	Grand Total-United States	10

Non-playing Captain–Mrs. Frances Smith

Non-playing Captain–Mrs. Jean Ashley Crawford

1974
INTERNATIONAL MATCH FOR THE CURTIS CUP

Held at San Francisco Golf Club, San Francisco, California
August 2 and 3

August 2
FOURSOMES

Great Britain—Ireland	Points	United States	Points
Miss Jennifer Lee-Smith and Miss Carol LeFeuvre	0	Mrs. Anne Quast Sander and Mrs. Jane Bastanchury Booth (6 and 5)	1
Miss Mary McKenna and Miss Julia Greenhalgh	½	Miss Carol Semple and Miss Cynthia Hill	½
Miss Mary Everard and Miss Maureen Walker (5 and 4)	1	Miss Mary Budke and Miss Bonnie Lauer	0
Total	1½	Total	1½

SINGLES

Great Britain—Ireland	Points	United States	Points
Miss Maureen Walker (2 and 1)	1	Miss Carol Semple	0
Miss Mary McKenna	0	Mrs. Jane Bastanchury Booth (5 and 3)	1
Miss Mary Everard	0	Miss Deborah Massey (1 up)	1
Miss Tegwen Perkins	½	Miss Cynthia Hill	½
Miss Jennifer Lee-Smith	0	Miss Bonnie Lauer (6 and 4)	1
Miss Julia Greenhalgh	0	Miss Beth Barry (1 up)	1
Total	1½	Total	4½
Total August 2	3	Total August 2	6

August 3
FOURSOMES

Great Britain—Ireland	Points	United States	Points
Miss Mary McKenna and Miss Maureen Walker	0	Mrs. Anne Quast Sander and Mrs. Jane Bastanchury Booth (5 and 4)	1
Miss Julia Greenhalgh and Miss Tegwen Perkins (3 and 2)	1	Miss Carol Semple and Miss Cynthia Hill	0
Miss Mary Everard and Miss Carol LeFeuvre	0	Miss Mary Budke and Miss Bonnie Lauer (5 and 3)	1
Total	1	Total	2

SINGLES

Great Britain—Ireland	Points	United States	Points
Miss Mary Everard	0	Mrs. Anne Quast Sander (4 and 3)	1
Miss Julia Greenhalgh	0	Mrs. Jane Bastanchury Booth (7 and 5)	1
Miss Maureen Walker	0	Miss Carol Semple (2 and 1)	1
Miss Carol LeFeuvre	0	Miss Deborah Massey (6 and 5)	1
Miss Mary McKenna (2 and 1)	1	Miss Bonnie Lauer	0
Miss Tegwen Perkins	0	Miss Mary Budke (5 and 4)	1
Total	1	Total	5
Total August 3	2	Total August 3	7
Grand Total—Great Britain—Ireland	5	Grand Total—United States	13

Non-playing Captain—Mrs. I. C. Robertson

Non-playing Captain—Mrs. Allison Choate

1976
INTERNATIONAL MATCH FOR THE CURTIS CUP

Held at Royal Lytham and St. Annes Golf Club, St. Annes-On-Sea, Lancashire, England
June 11-12

June 11
FOURSOMES

Great Britain—Ireland	Points	United States	Points
Mrs. Dinah Oxley Henson and Miss Suzanne Cadden	0	Miss Deborah Massey and Miss Donna Horton (3 and 2)	1
Miss Mary McKenna and Miss Julia Greenhalgh	0	Miss Beth Daniel and Miss Cynthia Hill (3 and 2)	1
Miss Ann Irvin and Miss Tegwen Perkins (3 and 2)	1	Mrs. Nancy Roth Syms and Miss Carol Semple	0
Total	1	Total	2

SINGLES

Great Britain—Ireland	Points	United States	Points
Miss Ann Irvin	0	Miss Beth Daniel (4 and 3)	1
Mrs. Dinah Oxley Henson (1 up)	1	Miss Cynthia Hill	0
Miss Mary McKenna	0	Mrs. Nancy Roth Syms (1 up)	1
Miss Suzanne Cadden	0	Miss Nancy Lopez (3 and 1)	1
Miss Tegwen Perkins	0	Miss Deborah Massey (1 up)	1
Miss Julia Greenhalgh (halved)	½	Miss Barbara Barrow (halved)	½
Total	1½	Total	4½
Total June 11	2½	Total June 11	6½

June 12
FOURSOMES

Great Britain—Ireland	Points	United States	Points
Miss Ann Irvin and Miss Suzanne Cadden	0	Miss Beth Daniel and Miss Cynthia Hill (4 and 3)	1
Miss Mary McKenna and Mrs. Ann Stant	0	Miss Nancy Lopez and Miss Barbara Barrow (4 and 2)	1
Mrs. Dinah Oxley Henson and Miss Tegwen Perkins (2 and 1)	1	Miss Carol Semple and Mrs. Nancy Roth Syms	0
Total	1	Total	2

SINGLES

Great Britain—Ireland	Points	United States	Points
Mrs. Dinah Oxley Henson	0	Miss Beth Daniel (3 and 2)	1
Miss Jennifer Lee Smith	0	Miss Deborah Massey (3 and 2)	1
Miss Tegwen Perkins (1 up)	1	Miss Cynthia Hill	0
Miss Mary McKenna (1 up)	1	Miss Carol Semple	0
Miss Julia Greenhalgh (2 and 1)	1	Mrs. Nancy Roth Syms	0
Miss Suzanne Cadden	0	Miss Donna Horton (6 and 5)	1
Total	3	Total	3
Total June 12	4	Total June 12	5
Grand Total—Great Britain and Ireland	6½	Grand Total—United States	11½

Non-playing Captain—Mrs. I. C. Robertson

Non-playing Captain—Miss Barbara McIntire

1978
INTERNATIONAL MATCH FOR THE CURTIS CUP

Held at the Apawamis Club, Rye, New York
August 4-5

August 4

FOURSOMES

Great Britain and Ireland	Points	United States	Points
Miss Julia Greenhalgh and Miss Vanessa Marvin (3 and 2)	1	Miss Beth Daniel and Miss Brenda Goldsmith	0
Miss Mary Everard and Miss Muriel Thomson (2 and 1)	1	Miss Cynthia Hill and Miss Lancy Smith	0
Miss Tegwen Perkins and Miss Mary McKenna (halved)	½	Miss Patricia Cornett and Miss Carolyn Hill (halved)	½
Total	2½	Total	½

SINGLES

Great Britain and Ireland	Points	United States	Points
Miss Vanessa Marvin	0	Miss Beth Daniel (5 and 4)	1
Miss Mary Everard (7 and 6)	1	Mrs. Noreen Uihlein	0
Miss Julia Greenhalgh	0	Miss Cynthia Hill (2 and 1)	1
Miss Tegwen Perkins	0	Mrs. Judith Oliver (2 and 1)	1
Mrs. Angela Uzielli	0	Miss Lancy Smith (4 and 3)	1
Mrs. Carole Caldwell (halved)	½	Miss Carolyn Hill (halved)	½
Total	1½	Total	4½
Total August 4	4	Total August 4	5

August 5

FOURSOMES

Great Britain and Ireland	Points	United States	Points
Miss Mary Everard and Miss Muriel Thomson	0	Miss Cynthia Hill and Miss Lancy Smith (1 up)	1
Miss Tegwen Perkins and Miss Mary McKenna	0	Miss Brenda Goldsmith and Miss Beth Daniel (1 up)	1
Miss Julia Greenhalgh and Miss Vanessa Marvin	0	Mrs. Noreen Uihlein and Mrs. Judith Oliver (4 and 3)	1
Total	0	Total	3

SINGLES

Great Britain and Ireland	Points	United States	Points
Miss Mary McKenna	0	Miss Beth Daniel (2 and 1)	1
Miss Julia Greenhalgh (halved)	½	Mrs. Judith Oliver (halved)	½
Miss Mary Everard (halved)	½	Mrs. Noreen Uihlein (halved)	½
Mrs. Carole Caldwell	0	Miss Patricia Cornett (3 and 2)	1
Miss Muriel Thomson (2 and 1)	1	Miss Carolyn Hill	0
Miss Tegwen Perkins	0	Miss Lancy Smith (2 up)	1
Total	2	Total	4
Total August 5	2	Total August 5	7
Grand Total—Great Britain and Ireland	6	Grand Total—United States	12
Non-playing Captain—Mrs. Carol Comboy		Non-playing Captain—Mrs. Helen Sigel Wilson	

1980

TWENTY-FIRST INTERNATIONAL MATCH FOR THE CURTIS CUP

Held at the St. Pierre Golf and Country Club, Chepstow, Gwent, Wales

June 6-7

June 6

FOURSOMES

Great Britain and Ireland	Points	United States	Points
Miss Mary McKenna and Miss Claire Nesbitt (Halved)	½	Miss Lancy Smith and Miss Terri Moody (Halved)	½
Mrs. Tegwen Thomas and Miss Gillian Stewart	0	Miss Patty Sheehan and Miss Lori Castillo (5 & 3)	1
Miss Maureen Madill and Mrs. Carole Caldwell (Halved)	½	Mrs. Judy Oliver and Miss Carol Semple (Halved)	½
Total	1	Total	2
SINGLES			
Miss Mary McKenna	0	Miss Patty Sheehan (3 and 2)	1
Miss Claire Nesbitt (Halved)	½	Miss Lancy Smith (Halved)	½
Miss Jane Connachan	0	Miss Brenda Goldsmith (2 up)	1
Miss Lynda Moore (Halved)	½	Miss Mary Hafeman (Halved)	½
Miss Maureen Madill	0	Miss Carol Semple (4 and 3)	1
Mrs. Carole Caldwell	0	Mrs. Judy Oliver (1 up)	1
Total	1	Total	5
Total June 6	2	Total June 6	7

June 7

FOURSOMES

Great Britain and Ireland	Points	United States	Points
Mrs. Carole Caldwell and Miss Maureen Madill	0	Miss Patty Sheehan and Miss Lori Castillo (3 & 2)	1
Miss Mary McKenna and Miss Claire Nesbitt	0	Miss Lancy Smith and Miss Terri Moody (6 & 5)	1
Mrs. Tegwen Thomas and Miss Lynda Moore	0	Mrs. Judy Oliver and Miss Carol Semple (1 up)	1
Total	0	Total	3
SINGLES			
Miss Maureen Madill	0	Miss Patty Sheehan (5 and 4)	1
Miss Mary McKenna (5 and 4)	1	Miss Lori Castillo	0
Miss Gillian Stewart (5 and 4)	1	Miss Lancy Smith	0
Miss Jane Connachan	0	Miss Mary Hafeman (5 and 4)	1
Miss Lynda Moore (1 up)	1	Miss Brenda Goldsmith	0
Mrs. Tegwen Thomas	0	Miss Carol Semple (4 and 3)	1
Total	3	Total	3
Total June 7	3	Total June 7	6
Grand Total-Great Britain and Ireland	5	Grand Total-United States	13

Non-playing Captain—Mrs. Carol Comboy

Non-playing Captain—Mrs. Nancy Roth Syms

WORLD AMATEUR TEAM CHAMPIONSHIP

THE EISENHOWER TROPHY

Presented in October, 1958
by American Friends of Golf
through The Royal and Ancient Golf Club
and The Royal and Ancient Golf Club
of St. Andrews, Scotland

HISTORY

1960—The United States scored an impressive victory in the second Championship at Merion Golf Club, Ardmore, Pa. Led by Jack Nicklaus' brilliant 11-under-par 269 total for the four days, the United States team won by 42 strokes. The team had daily three-best scores of 208-205-203-218 for a total of 834. Australia was second with 219-220-215-222—876. Great Britain and Ireland, tied with Australia for second going into the last day, finished third with 218-215-221-227—881. A total of 126 players from 32 teams competed (11 more players and three more teams than in the first Championship) over the par 70 Merion East course. Although prizes are not awarded for individual scoring, the calibre of play by the leaders is worthy of note. Nicklaus' great scoring came on rounds of 66-67-68-68 for his 269 total—a fabulous score for a great course. Deane R. Beman, the United States Amateur Champion, had second best individual score of 71-67-69-75—282. Bruce Devlin, of Australia, was third among the leaders with 288. The other two members of the United States team, Robert W. Gardner and William Hyndman, III, both scored 289.

1962—The United States dueled with Canada from the outset and eventually won its second straight victory by the narrow margin of 854 to Canada's 862. The Championship was played in Asia for the first time, at the Fuji Golf Course, Kawana, Japan, some 75 miles southwest of Tokyo. Twenty-three countries were represented. After the first round, the United States led with 212, to Canada's 215. The lead shifted during a rainy second round which ended with Canada leading the United States, 432 to 438. The Americans rebounded strongly in the third round to regain the lead, 649 to 651. William J. Patton, the first American to play in the fourth round, scored 81, but the other three Americans played superbly. Deane R. Beman scored 66; Richard H. Sikes, the Amateur Public Links Champion in both 1961 and 1962, recorded his third 69; and Labron Harris, Jr., the 1962 Amateur Champion, scored 70. The team representing Great Britain and Ireland was third, as it was in both 1958 and 1960, with a total of 872. Gary Cowan, of Canada, was the low individual scorer with 280, three strokes lower than Sikes and six lower than Beman. Juan Antonio Estrada, of Mexico, had the fourth best individual score of 287. Estrada, Beman, and Ronald D. B. M. Shade of Great Britain and Ireland, each had one round of 66, four under par. The Republic of China Team, which had finished 26th and 21st in the earlier Championships, exhibited remarkable progress by finishing sixth with a total of 892, one stroke ahead of Australia, the 1958 Champion. The event was enriched by the girls and young ladies who served as caddies, clad in blue-trousered uniforms, white caps and veils, gloves, and sneakers. John D. Ames, a former USGA President, was the winning team's nonplaying Captain; he was an original Joint Chairman of the World Amateur Golf Council.

1964 The Team of Great Britain and Ireland led after every round in winning the Eisenhower Trophy for the first time. The margin at the end was two strokes over Canada, 895 to 897; New Zealand was third with 900 and the defending United States Team was fourth with 908 at the Olgiata Golf Club, Rome, Italy. A record number of 33 countries and 132 golfers competed. The weather made scoring extremely difficult. After a sunny and fairly mild opening round, high winds sent scores upward the second day. The weather continued rainy and blustery for the last two days, and the final round had heavy downpours which produced much casual water. Par of 72 for the testing course was beaten only six times and was tied 12 times. The lowest individual score was 294, six over par, by Min-Nan Hsieh of the Republic of China. After the first round, Great Britain-Ireland led by four strokes over Italy with 214 to 218 after rounds of 70 by Ronald Shade and 72 by Rodney Foster and Michael Lunt. The United States rallied strongly on the second day and moved to within one stroke of the leaders, helped considerably by a 72 by Dale Morey and steady rounds by William C. Campbell and Edgar M. Tutwiler, Jr. Great Britain-Ireland opened the margin, however, to five strokes over the United States and Canada after the third round, and held on for the Championship on the rainy final day despite a remarkable surge on the closing holes by Keith Alexander of the Canadian Team. Needing birdies on the last five holes to bring his Team into a tie for the Championship, Alexander made four in succession from the 14th through the 17th holes. But he was bunkered on his approach to the home green, went one over par on the hole, and the courageous rally fell two strokes short. The non-playing Captain for the winning British Team was Joseph B. Carr, who had been in the three previous Eisenhower Trophy events as a competitor.

1966—Australia won by two strokes over the United States, 877-879, at the Club de Golf Mexico,

Mexico City. This was the second victory for Australia, which won the inaugural competition in 1958. Australia's lone sub-par round in 16 tries was a 68 by Kevin Hartley on opening day. This helped give the team a six-stroke lead over South Africa, with the United States 10th. Australia went seven strokes ahead in the second round, but dropped a stroke behind South Africa after the third round. Bobby Cole, the British Amateur Champion, scored one 70 for South Africa and Dave Symonds another. Deane R. Beman, United States Amateur Champion of 1960 and 1963, almost saved the American cause. In the final round he went out in 36 and then scored four birdies on the home nine for 69. But this wasn't enough. Harry Berwick, paired with Beman, scored 72 for Australia; Hartley had 73, and both Phil Billings and Kevin Donohoe had 74. Great Britain and Ireland, the defending Champion, finished third with 883 and South Africa was fourth with 884. Host Mexico finished fifth with 889. Ronnie Shade, of Great Britain and Ireland, had the lowest individual score of 283. Shade had rounds of 74, 69, 72 and 68. D. H. Dwyer was non-playing Captain of the winning team.

1968 The United States came from seven strokes behind in the final round to win its third Championship. The margin was by one stroke over Great Britain and Ireland, 868 to 869. Twenty-six countries were represented at the Royal Melbourne Golf Club in Australia. Australia, the defending Champion, took a two-stroke lead over Great Britain and Ireland in the first round, 216-218, with the United States third at 220. The United States went ahead in the second round with 431 against 433 for Great Britain and Ireland. Marvin Giles, III, scored 68 for the United States in the second round, and Richard L. Siderowf had 69. However, Michael F. Bonallack, British Champion, had a 66 in the third round, equalling the championship record, and led his team to the seven-stroke lead over the United States, 640-647. At one point in the final round Great Britain and Ireland led by 11 strokes, but the United States made up the deficit. The decision went to the final hole where Siderowf made a three-foot putt for 5. Ronald D. B. M. Shade could have tied for Great Britain and Ireland by sinking a six-footer; his putt, nicked the edge of the hole and stayed out. The United States scored 221 in the final round; the British, 229. Bonallack and Giles each scored 286 for 72 holes over the 6,946-yard, par-73 course and were the low individual scorers, although this category is not officially recognized. The United States Team comprised Bruce Fleisher, the national Champion; Jack Lewis, Jr., Giles and Siderowf, with non-playing Captain William C. Campbell, who had played in the 1964 Championship.

1970—The United States led every round and won the World Amateur Team Championship by 15 strokes over New Zealand with a score of 854. New Zealand scored 869 and South Africa 870. It was the fourth victory for the United States in seven matches. The four United States Team Members had only one score as high as 74, and in the first two rounds Marvin (Vinnie) Giles III, had the experience of shooting two 73s and having neither of them count in the team total. The United States led by one stroke over South Africa after 18 holes, then increased its lead to seven strokes at 36 holes, and to nine after 54 holes. Thirty-six teams competed in the Championship at the Real Club de la Puerta de Heirro in Madrid, Spain, the most ever. Since this is a team competition, individual scoring is not officially recognized. However, the score of Victor Regalado, of Mexico, is worth noting. Regalado shot 72-67-71-70—280. Dale Hayes, of South Africa, had the next lowest score of 283. Lanny Wadkins was low for the United States, with 286, Allen Miller had 287, and Giles 289. Tom Kite had three rounds totalling 215, but was ill during the final round and did not play. Non-playing Captain for the United States Team was Clarence W. Benedict.

1972—The United States retained the Eisenhower Trophy, coming from three strokes behind Australia after three rounds and finishing five strokes ahead. It was the third successive victory for the United States and its fifth in the eight matches played. In contrast to its victory in 1970 when it led every round, the United States Team was nine strokes behind after the first round, seven strokes back after the second, and still three strokes behind going into the final round. A magnificent rally on the final day, however, put the American Team five strokes ahead of runnerup Australia, 865 to 870. South Africa finished third at 878, a stroke ahead of Spain. Fittingly enough, Argentina, the host country, led after the first day; its three best scores over the par-71 Olivos Golf Club course, situated in Buenos Aires, totalled 212. Australia and Spain were tied for second at 215 while the United States was well back at 221. The Australians took over first place with a 434 total after 36 holes on a 69 by Anthony Gresham. Argentina and Spain were tied for second at 437, while the United States had 441. In the third round, however, Ben Crenshaw shot a 69, Vinny Giles added 70, and Mark Hayes scored 71 for an aggregate of 210. On the final day Crenshaw shot 68, Giles had 71 and Hayes 75. Australia shot a team total of 222. Awards are not given for individual performances, but it should be noted that Gresham led the field with a total of 285 on scores of 70-69-73-73; Crenshaw and Giles tied at 287, Crenshaw shooting 74-76-69-68, and Giles 73-73-70-71. Teams from non-English-speaking nations did particularly well. Argentina finished fifth, Spain fourth, and Japan ninth. The progress made by these countries and some others in the 32-team field portends a happy trend in International Golf. Wm. Ward Foshay was the non-playing Captain of the United States Team.

1974—A well-balanced United States Team composed of George Burns, III, Gary Koch, Jerry Pate, and Curtis Strange won the World Amateur Team Championship at the Cajuiles Golf Club, La Romana, Dominican Republic. This was the fourth consecutive victory for the United States, and its sixth in nine Championships. The winning score of 888 was the third highest ever and the highest since 1964, when 895 won. Scoring is done on the basis of a Team's three best scores out of four, each day, for the four days of the Championship. Japan, which finished ninth in 1972 and tied for 23rd place only 10 years ago, was second, with a total of 898. Brazil, at 901, was third, led by Jayme Gonzalez, who is a student at Oklahoma State University. Gonzalez tied Jerry Pate for individual low score with 294 for 72 holes. The United States led after each day's play, and all four men contributed to the victory. Pate shot 73 the first day, while Burns added a 74 and Strange contributed 77. Koch took 79. Brazil was second at 225, Japan was third, and South Africa and Great Britain and Ireland were tied for fourth. The next day Gary Koch posted a new course record of 70. Pate had his only bad day, scoring a 77, but Burns had a 76 and Curtis Strange, although ill all during the Championship, added a 75 to increase the United States lead to five strokes. South Africa was now second, Japan third, Brazil fourth, and Great Britain and Ireland fifth. Burns matched Koch's 70 on the third day, Pate had a 73, and Koch shot a 76. The Americans were seven strokes ahead of Japan, while Brazil and South Africa were tied for third. During the final round the United States' lead was cut to just one stroke. Strange and Koch had finished with scores of 77 and 76, respectively, while Japan's Satoski Yamazaki had a 71 and Ginjiro Nakabe a 76. It was then up to Burns and Pate. Pate played the first nine in two under par and finished with 71. Burns had 77, but the two remaining Japanese players could score only 80 and 81 and slipped further behind. The low score of the Championship was 70, scored by Koch, Burns, Jose Diniz, of Brazil, and Japan's Ginjiro Nakabe. Thirty-five nations and 138 players competed. Hord Hardin was non-playing Captain.

1976—Great Britain and Ireland had at least a tie for the lead in every round and won the 10th World Amateur Team Championship by two strokes over Japan at the Penina Golf Club, Portimao, Algarve, Portugal. This was the second time that Great Britain and Ireland won; it was also the second consecutive time that Japan finished second. Great Britain and Ireland had a total score of 892 while Japan had 894. The United States, which had won six previous Championships, finished fifth. Great Britain and Ireland shared the first round lead with South Africa at 219, and Sweden and Rhodesia tied for third place at 223. David Suddards led South Africa with 71 while M. J. Kelly shot 72 for Great Britain and Ireland. Both South Africa and Great Britain-Ireland had team totals of 224 in the second round and once again shared the lead at 443. Japan moved into contention with 220, behind a 71 by Masahiro Kuramoto. Japan was then four strokes behind the co-leaders at 447, and there was a further three-stroke gap back to Australia and the Republic of China. T. M. Chen shot 69 for China, the best single round of the Championship, as his team scored 221 for the round. Great Britain and Ireland took a clear two-stroke lead after the third round even though its team total went up to 225. South Africa, with three of its players scoring in the 80s, dropped well off the pace at 682, which was 14 strokes behind Great Britain and Ireland, which had 668. Japan, Australia and the United States shared second place at 670. The United States had the best single round team total of the competition with a score of 217. Fred Ridley shot 70, Richard L. Siderowf 72, and Bill Sander, shot 75. The next day Ian Hutcheon shot 71 and Great Britain and Ireland kept its two-stroke lead and won the Championship. Japan also had 224, but Australia slipped to 227 and the United States fell well behind with 231. Individual scores have no standing in the World Amateur Team Championship, but it is worth noting that Hutcheon and T. M. Chen each shot 293, the lowest 72-hole total of any players. Hutcheon had rounds of 73, 73, 76, and 71, while Chen had scores of 75, 69, 73, and 76. Thirty-eight teams competed, the most ever.

1978—The United States regained possession of the Eisenhower Trophy with an impressive 13-stroke victory in the 11th World Amateur Team Championship at the Pacific Harbour Golf and Country Club, in Fiji. The United States has now won seven times since the inaugural event in 1958. The 13-stroke victory was the second largest winning margin in the event's history. The United States had won by 42 strokes at the Merion Golf Club, Ardmore, Pa., in 1960. The 1978 team had scores of 213-220-219-221 for its winning total of 873. Canada finished in second place with 886, followed by Australia, 891; New Zealand, 895; and Sweden, 914. Great Britain and Ireland, the defending Champion, finished in sixth place, with 919. The United States led by eight strokes after the first round on scores of 69 by Bob Clampett, 70 by Scott Hoch, and 74 by Jay Sigel. The 213 total was the lowest single-round team score of the event. Great Britain and Ireland and Sweden were tied for second place at 221. Australia and Canada were next at 222. Mikael Sorling had 70 for Sweden, and Brian Marchbank shot 72 for Great Britain and Ireland to lead their respective teams. In the second round, the United States had 220 for a 433 total and increased its lead to 11 strokes on scores of 71 by Clampett, 73 by John Cook, and 76 by Hoch. Canada moved into second place at 444, led by Gary Cowan, who had 71. After 54 holes, the United States had a 652 total, 17 strokes ahead of its nearest competition, Canada and Australia, tied at 669. The United States' third-round total of 219 included scores of 71 by Clampett, 73 by Cook, and 75 by Sigel. Cowan had 71 to pace Canada, and Peter Sweeney shot 71 for Australia. On the final day, Canada sealed second place with a round of 217, the lowest team score of the day, including 69 by Doug Roxburgh, 71 by Cowan, and 77 by David Mick. The United States' final-round 221 included 72 by Cook, 73 by Hoch, and 76 by both Sigel and Clampett. While individual scores are not officially recognized, Clampett had 69-71-71-76—287 for the lowest 72-hole score. Roxburgh was next with 72-74-74-69—289. The 69's by Clampett and Roxburgh were the low single round scores of the event. The non-playing Captain of the United States Team was Harton S. Semple, a former USGA President. The 24 team entries was the second lowest total ever. The 1972 Championship in Japan had 23 entries.

1980—The United States led every round and won the 12th World Amateur Team Championship by 27 strokes for its eighth victory. The Championship was played on the No. 2 Course at the Pinehurst Country Club, in Pinehurst, North Carolina. The margin of victory was the second largest ever. The United States had won by 42 strokes in 1960 at the Merion Golf Club, in Ardmore, Pennsylvania. The 1980 team had daily scores of 211-211-217-209 for its winning total of 848, 16 under par. South Africa was second, with 875, followed by the Republic of China, (Taiwan), 884; Japan, 887; Australia, Canada, and Great Britain and Ireland tied at 890; and Sweden, 894. The United States led by eight strokes after the first day on scores of 68 by Hal Sutton, 71 by Jay Sigel, and 72 by Jim Holtgrieve. South Africa and the Republic of China were tied for second place at 219. In the second round, the United States matched its first-day total on rounds of 69 by Sutton, and 71s by Sigel and Holtgrieve and had a 422 total. With 217 in the third round, the United States increased its lead to 14 strokes over South Africa. The Americans shot 209 in the last round, the lowest daily team score of the week. While individual scores are not officially recognized, Sutton had 68-69-71-68—276, 12 under par, for the lowest 72-hole score. His two 68s were the lowest single round scores of the event. The non-playing Captain of the United States team was Harry W. Easterly, Jr., of Richmond, Virginia. The 39 team entries were the most ever, breaking the previous record of 38, set in 1976 when the Championship was played in Algarve, Portugal.

WORLD AMATEUR TEAM CHAMPIONSHIP

1960—At Merion Golf Club, Ardmore, Pa. (East Course)

Team	Score	Team	Score	Team	Score
United States	834	Italy	935	Norway	979
Australia	876	France	937	Peru	999
Great Britain & Ireland	881	Germany	940	Bermuda	1001
South Africa	893	Philippines	942	Austria	1005
New Zealand	895	Denmark	952	Netherlands	1008
Canada	906	Japan	954	Finland	1023
Mexico	909	Belgium	960	Portugal	1035
Rhodesia & Nyasaland	914	Venezuela	962	United Arab Republic	1045
Argentina	917	Brazil	972	Malaya	1099
Sweden	923	India	975	Ceylon	1104
		Republic of China	977		
		Switzerland	977		

1962—At Fuji Golf Course, Kawana, Japan

Team	Score	Team	Score	Team	Score
United States	854	South Africa	896	Sweden	943
Canada	862	Japan	902	Switzerland	947
Great Britain & 1 Ireland	874	Argentina	905	Spain	961
New Zealand	882	Italy	912	Brazil	964
Mexico	887	Germany	926	Bermuda	980
Republic of China	892	Philippines	929	Peru	985
Australia	893	India	931	Malaya	1036
		Hong Kong	942	Pakistan	1056

1964—At Olgiata Golf Club, Rome, Italy

Team	Score	Team	Score	Team	Score
Great Britain & Ireland	895	Spain	942	Chile	965
Canada	897	Southern Rhodesia	943	Japan	965
New Zealand	900	Sweden	946	Philippines	967
United States	908	India	949	Germany	971
Australia	910	Northern Rhodesia	949	Brazil	977
Republic of China	911	Denmark	952	Netherlands	978
Italy	911	Venezuela	954	Peru	1006
Argentina	913	Belgium	955	Malaysia	1019
Mexico	917	Switzerland	959	Portugal	1025
France	922	Austria	960	Iceland	1043
South Africa	929	Bermuda	964	Uruguay	1059

1966—At Club de Golf Mexico, Mexico City

Team	Score	Team	Score	Team	Score
Australia	877	France	908	Bermuda	947
United States	879	Sweden	908	Venezuela	950
Great Britain & Ireland	883	Chile	909	Switzerland	952
South Africa	884	Belgium	912	Jamaica	956
Mexico	889	Rhodesia	915	Denmark	957
Canada	890	India	916	Uruguay	958
Republic of China	892	Zambia	929	Peru	983
Japan	894	Brazil	932	Iceland	1024
Germany	900	Philippines	938	Dominican Republic	1033
New Zealand	905	Guatemala	939	Puerto Rico	1070
Italy	905	Spain	940		

1968—At Royal Melbourne Golf Club, Victoria, Australia

Team	Score	Team	Score	Team	Score
United States	868	Japan	908	Switzerland	954
Great Britain & Ireland	869	Germany	910	Korea	956
Canada	885	France	912	Papua/New Guinea	958
Australia	886	Argentina	916	Bermuda	971
South Africa	889	India	925	Brazil	976
Mexico	893	Malaysia	930	Hong Kong	981
New Zealand	895	Spain	939	Chile	983
Republic of China	900	Italy	947	Libya	1021
		Philippines	950	Venezuela	1067

1970—At Real Club de la Puerta de Hierro, Madrid, Spain

Team	Score	Team	Score	Team	Score
United States	854	Sweden	901	Denmark	930
New Zealand	869	Germany	903	Bermuda	934
South Africa	870	Italy	904	Netherlands	938
Australia	871	Belgium	909	Portugal	939
Mexico	873	Brazil	909	Papua/New Guinea	940
Canada	880	Argentina	917	Chile	943
Great Britain & Ireland	882	Venezuela	918	Hong Kong	955
Japan	883	Korea	919	Finland	957
France	886	Colombia	923	Peru	982
Philippines	889	Switzerland	925	Pakistan	1013
China	890	Austria	929	Guatemala	1017
Spain	892	Norway	929	Iceland	1018

WORLD AMATEUR TEAM CHAMPIONSHIP FOR THE EISENHOWER TROPHY

1972—At Olivos Golf Club, Buenos Aires, Argentina

United States	865	Republic of China	907	Malaysia	938
Australia	870	Italy	912	Ecuador	951
South Africa	878	Sweden	913	Panama	952
Spain	879	Brazil	915	Peru	957
Argentina	884	Chile	916	Bermuda	963
New Zealand	884	Netherlands	925	Uruguay	964
Great Britain & Ireland	888	Belgium	927	Korea	978
Canada	889	Mexico	927	Dominican Republic	985
Japan	891	Portugal	927	Bahamas	1007
France	903	Switzerland	929	El Salvador	1021
Germany	905	Colombia	930		

1974—At the Campo de Golf, Cajuiles, La Romana, Dominican Republic

United States	888	Spain	941	Korea	985
Japan	898	Rhodesia	942	Panama	988
Brazil	901	New Zealand	947	Ecuador	989
South Africa	908	Venezuela	956	Jamaica	990
Australia	916	Switzerland	959	Norway	990
Great Britain & Ireland	922	Italy	960	Dominican Republic	998
Republic of China	928	Papua/New Guinea	961	Puerto Rico	1003
Argentina	931	Mexico	962	Bermuda	1004
Canada	932	Netherlands	964	Bahamas	1046
France	936	Chile	969	Iceland	1109
Sweden	936	Belgium	970	El Salvador	1126
Germany	939	Colombia	980		

1976—At the Penina Golf Club, Portimao, Algarve, Portugal

Great Britain & Ireland	892	Mexico	935	Finland	964
Japan	894	Spain	937	Netherlands	966
Australia	897	Brazil	939	Bermuda	974
Republic of China	898	Chile	941	Venezuela	974
United States	901	Italy	944	Portugal	977
Canada	906	Papua/New Guinea	944	Israel	1002
Sweden	911	Denmark	946	Dominican Republic	1011
South Africa	912	Korea	947	Sri Lanka	1020
Rhodesia	914	Norway	947	Bahamas	1042
Switzerland	914	Germany	949	El Salvador	1047
Argentina	922	Malaysia	950	Costa Rica	1078
New Zealand	923	Belgium	955	Puerto Rico	1079
France	930	Austria	964		

1978—At the Pacific Harbour Golf and Country Club, Fiji

United States	873	Japan	935	Austria	969
Canada	886	Italy	944	Bermuda	969
Australia	891	Spain	944	Brazil	972
New Zealand	895	Switzerland	945	Belgium	980
Sweden	914	Argentina	949	Thailand	982
Great Britain & Ireland	919	India	958	Fiji	985
France	923	Papua/New Guinea	960	Hong Kong	986
Germany	933	Netherlands	963	Korea	1001

1980—At Pinehurst Country Club, No. 2 Course, Pinehurst, N.C.

United States	848	Philippines	923	Austria	947
South Africa	875	Brazil	924	Denmark	947
Republic of China	884	Germany	924	Venezuela	952
Japan	887	France	926	Norway	953
Australia	890	Colombia	927	Fiji	971
Canada	890	Korea	929	Bermuda	979
Great Britain & Ireland	890	Chile	935	Portugal	984
Sweden	894	India	935	Papua/New Guinea	991
Mexico	899	Netherlands	935	Israel	1002
New Zealand	902	Switzerland	935	Dominican Republic	1003
Spain	904	Zimbabwe	935	Guatemala	1009
Argentian	917	Hong Kong	944	El Salvador	1043
Italy	917	Belgium	945	Puerto Rico	1077

1960
SECOND WORLD AMATEUR TEAM CHAMPIONSHIP
FOR THE EISENHOWER TROPHY

Held at the Merion Golf Club, Ardmore, Pennsylvania, September 28-October 1.
Yardage—6,694. Par 70. 32 Team Entries.

Team score consisted of best three individual scores in each round.
*Indicates Captain.

		1st Rd.	2nd Rd.	3rd Rd.	4th Rd.	72-Hole Score
UNITED STATES	Grand total	208	413	616		834
Deane R. Beman		71	67	69	75	(282)
Robert W. Gardner		71	71	68	79	(289)
William Hyndman, III		71	76	67	75	(289)
Jack W. Nicklaus		66	67	68	68	(269)
Total best 3, daily		208	205	203	218	
*Totton P. Heffelfinger						
AUSTRALIA	Grand total	219	439	654		876
Edward Ball		77	75	73	76	(301)
Jack Coogan		73	80	74	78	(305)
Bruce W. Devlin		74	70	70	74	(288)
*Eric G. Routley		72	75	72	72	(291)
Total best 3, daily		219	220	215	222	
GREAT BRITAIN AND IRELAND	Grand total	218	433	654		881
Michael F. Bonallack		73	72	73	78	(296)
Joseph B. Carr		78	70	72	81	(301)
Douglas N. Sewell		74	73	76	74	(297)
Guy B. Wolstenholme		71	75	76	75	(297)
Total best 3, daily		218	215	221	227	
*Charles O. Lawrie						
SOUTH AFRICA	Grand total	220	445	660		893
Walter M. Grindrod		79	80	78	83	(320)
Johannes G. LeRoux		74	75	72	74	(295)
Reginald R. Taylor		72	73	70	84	(299)
Arthur Walker		74	77	73	76	(300)
Total best 3, daily		220	225	215	233	
*Elgar B. Pagden						
NEW ZEALAND	Grand total	217	442	662		895
Robert J. Charles		70	75	70	76	(291)
Walter J. Godfrey		74	76	74	77	(301)
Stuart G. Jones		80	74	76	80	(310)
Ross R. Newdick		73	76	82	82	(313)
Total best 3, daily		217	225	220	233	
*Douglas O. Whyte						
CANADA	Grand total	230	450	672		906
R. Keith Alexander		76	72	77	83	(308)
Gary Cowan		78	80	72	80	(310)
John Johnston		76	77	81	79	(313)
Robert L. Wylie		79	71	73	75	(298)
Total best 3, daily		230	220	222	234	
*R. Bruce Forbes						
MEXICO	Grand total	217	442	669		909
Juan Antonio Estrada		71	72	76	75	(294)
Roberto Halpern		73	79	77	83	(312)
Rafael Quiroz		73	79	74	82	(308)
Mauricio Urdaneta		75	74	79	91	(319)
Total best 3, daily		217	225	227	240	
*Rodrigo Medelin						
RHODESIA AND NYASALAND	Grand total	224	450	673		914
Benny Brews		72	76	70	85	(303)
John Drysdale		75	76	75	80	(306)
Dave Proctor		79	82	78	79	(318)
Ken Treloar		77	74	82	82	(315)
Total best 3, daily		224	226	223	241	
*Bob Shackleton						
ARGENTINA	Grand total	225	453	677		917
Roberto Benito, Jr.		75	80	76	80	(311)
Guillermo Carman		81	80	89	81	(331)
Jorge C. Ledesma, Jr.		72	74	76	81	(303)
Angel R. Monguzzi		78	74	72	79	(303)
Total best 3, daily		225	228	224	240	
*Horacio H. Vignoles						

		1st Rd.	2nd Rd.	3rd Rd.	4th Rd.	72-Hole Score
SWEDEN	Grand total	227	455	684		923
Gustaf Adolf Bielke		73	74	73	83	(303)
Rune Karlfeldt		79	81	81	81	(322)
Lennart Leinborn		79	77	75	79	(310)
Goran Lindeblad		75	77	85	79	(316)
Total best 3, daily		227	228	229	239	
*Erik Runfelt						
ITALY	Grand total	227	456	689		935
Eduardo Bergamo		77	77	79	83	(316)
Nadi Berruti		71	77	82	83	(313)
Franco Bevione		82	82	78	88	(330)
Alberto Schiaffino		79	75	76	80	(310)
Total best 3, daily		227	229	233	246	
*Don Francesco Ruspoli						
FRANCE	Grand total	226	458	690		937
Marius Bardana		75	79	77	82	(313)
Jean Pierre Cros		75	78	86	86	(325)
Patrick Cros		81	83	78	—	—
Henri de Lamaze		76	75	77	79	(307)
Total best 3, daily		226	232	232	247	
*Jacques Leglise						
GERMANY	Grand total	236	466	692		940
Walter Bruehne		78	73	78	79	(308)
Hans Lampert		85	77	76	85	(323)
Peter Moeller		77	—	74	87	—
Erik Sellschopp		81	80	76	84	(321)
Total best 3, daily		236	230	226	248	
*Heinz O. Krings						
PHILIPPINES	Grand total	230	459	691		942
Augustin Coscolluela, Jr.		76	75	82	82	(315)
Melanio Gana		76	79	81	86	(322)
Alejandro Prieto		81	85	77	83	(326)
Luis F. Silverio		78	75	74	87	(314)
Total best 3, daily		230	229	232	251	
*Manuel J. Gonzalez						
DENMARK	Grand total	230	461	704		952
Herluf Hansen		78	78	78	86	(320)
John Jacobsen		77	77	82	78	(314)
Henrik Lund		75	76	83	84	(318)
Erik Staerk		85	82	87	90	(344)
Total best 3, daily		230	231	243	248	
*Mogens Bredfeldt						
JAPAN	Grand total	237	468	713		954
Kiyoshi Ishimoto		78	79	81	81	(319)
Takeaki Kaneda		83	76	82	81	(322)
Ginjiro Nakabe		84	83	82	86	(335)
Makoto Tanaka		76	76	84	79	(315)
Total best 3, daily		237	231	245	241	
*Shun Nomura						
BELGIUM	Grand total	231	473	717		960
Jacques Moerman		76	82	85	78	(321)
Freddy Rodesch		75	79	81	83	(318)
Eric Tavernier		80	83	86	82	(331)
Phillippe Washer		82	81	78	83	(324)
Total best 3, daily		231	242	244	243	
*Henry Van Den Bosch						
VENEZUELA	Grand total	245	476	714		962
Alfredo A. Behrens		74	76	80	83	(313)
E. A. (Jack) Corrie		91	81	78	84	(334)
Julio L. Torres		89	77	80	90	(336)
*Rafael E. Vaamonde		82	78	81	81	(322)
Total best 3, daily		245	231	238	248	
BRAZIL	Grand total	235	479	718		972
Humberto de Almeida		78	78	73	80	(309)
Joao Barbossa		78	84	85	84	(331)
Fernando Chaves Barcellos		80	83	85	90	(338)
Carlos Sozio		79	83	81	—	—
Total best 3, daily		235	244	239	254	
*Seymour G. Marvin						

		1st Rd.	2nd Rd.	3rd Rd.	4th Rd.	72-Hole Score
INDIA	Grand total	233	477	722		975
A. S. Malik		78	81	85	91	(335)
I. S. Malik		77	91	85	89	(342)
R. K. Pitamber		78	81	83	77	(319)
Capt. P. G. Sethi		78	82	77	87	(324)
Total best 3, daily		233	244	245	253	
*J. L. Esplen						
CHINA, REPUBLIC OF	Grand total	237	477	717		977
C. C. Chen		76	77	79	84	(316)
Jeffrey Koo		82	89	82	92	(345)
Stanley Shen		93	101	—	108	—
Chang Tung-Chang		79	74	79	84	(316)
Total best 3, daily		237	240	240	260	
*T. Y. Lee						
SWITZERLAND	Grand total	238	486	729		977
Olivier Barras		78	85	86	82	(331)
Otto Dillier		83	83	74	86	(326)
Peter Gutermann		77	83	83	80	(323)
*Hans Schweizer		94	82	88	89	(353)
Total best 3, daily		238	248	243	248	
NORWAY	Grand total	239	482	722		979
Jan Aaseth		82	80	85	86	(333)
John Johansen		78	84	79	88	(329)
Kaare Kittilsen		79	82	85	83	(329)
Arve Pedersen		86	81	76	92	(335)
Total best 3, daily		239	243	240	257	
*Arild Wahlstrom						
PERU	Grand total	242	500	745		999
Luis Fraser		87	93	89	85	(354)
Luis Larrabure		86	91	83	90	(350)
Alfonso Noriega		82	88	—	101	—
Carlos A. Raffo		74	79	73	79	(305)
Total best 3, daily		242	258	245	254	
*Gabriel Tudela						
BERMUDA	Grand total	243	495	743		1001
Joseph T. DeCosta		82	81	81	90	(334)
James A. Pearman		85	87	84	88	(344)
Richard S. L. Pearman		76	88	89	80	(333)
George E. Wardman		85	84	83	90	(342)
Total best 3, daily		243	252	248	258	
*Lt. Gen. Sir Julian A. Gascoigne						
AUSTRIA	Grand total	244	491	739		1005
Hugo Hild		82	80	85	94	(341)
Fritz Jonak		82	83	91	93	(349)
Alexander Maculan		80	86	81	88	(335)
Klaus Nierlich		88	84	82	85	(339)
Total best 3, daily		244	247	248	266	
*Hugo Von Eckelt						
NETHERLANDS	Grand total	250	495	747		1008
Robbie E. van Erven Dorens		82	88	84	92	(346)
Jani A. R. Roland Holst		85	94	82	86	(347)
Ajef F. Knappert		83	81	86	83	(333)
Joan F. Dudok van Heel		87	76	88	92	(343)
Total best 3, daily		250	245	252	261	
*Tonny M. Groskamp						
FINLAND	Grand total	246	505	769		1023
Jalo Gronlund		77	87	89	84	(337)
Pentti E. Nurminen		91	83	89	90	(353)
*T. Nystrom		87	89	90	86	(352)
Mauri O. Vikstrom		82	90	86	84	(342)
Total best 3, daily		246	259	264	254	
PORTUGAL	Grand total	250	509	756		1035
Nuno Alberto de Brito e Cunha		83	85	80	92	(340)
*Visconde de Pereira Machado		85	86	82	93	(346)
Jose de Sousa e Melo		90	90	92	95	(367)
Duarte Espirito Santo Silva		82	88	85	94	(349)
Total best 3, daily		250	259	247	279	

Second World Amateur Team Championship – Continued

		1st Rd.	2nd Rd.	3rd Rd.	4th Rd.	72-Hole Score
UNITED ARAB REPUBLIC	Grand total	263	518	774		1045
Vladimir Blazek		84	84	87	86	(341)
Marwan Djeddaoui		84	80	81	95	(340)
*Dr. Zakaria Taher		95	91	88	90	(364)
Total best 3, daily		263	255	256	271	
MALAYA	Grand total	263	534	816		1099
E. S. Choong		94	94	96	98	(382)
T. S. Leong		85	94	94	106	(379)
Patrick Lim		84	90	92	88	(354)
H. Y. Loh		98	87	99	97	(381)
Total best 3, daily		263	271	282	283	
*William H. Day						
CEYLON	Grand total	271	536	818		1104
*W. Pinsiri Fernando		83	75	89	81	(328)
C. Upali Senanayake		86	89	91	88	(354)
Dr. J. Francis Silva		102	101	102	117	(422)
Total best 3, daily		271	265	282	286	

1962

THIRD WORLD AMATEUR TEAM CHAMPIONSHIP FOR THE EISENHOWER TROPHY

Held at the Fuji Golf Course, Kawana, Japan, October 10-13.
Yardage—6,587. Par 70. 23 Team Entries.

Team score consisted of best three individual scores in each round.
*Indicates Captain.

		1st Rd.	2nd Rd.	3rd Rd.	4th Rd.	72-hole Score
UNITED STATES	Grand total	212	438	649		854
Deane R. Beman		70	80	70	66	(286)
Labron Harris, Jr.		74	77	72	70	(292)
William J. Patton		74	73	72	81	(300)
Richard H. Sikes		69	76	69	69	(283)
Total best 3, daily		212	226	211	205	
*John D. Ames						
CANADA	Grand total	215	432	651		862
Gary Cowan		68	71	72	69	(280)
William Wakeham		76	73	72	78	(299)
Nick Weslock		71	73	75	73	(292)
Robert Wylie		77	78	80	69	(304)
Total best 3, daily		215	217	219	211	
*Dr. Jack E. Leddy						
GREAT BRITAIN AND IRELAND	Grand total	222	444	658		874
Michael F. Bonallack		74	80	69	70	(293)
Martin J. Christmas		73	80	73	78	(304)
A. C. Saddler		79	76	72	70	(297)
Ronald D. B. M. Shade		75	66	74	76	(291)
Total best 3, daily		222	222	214	216	
*Charles D. Lawrie						
NEW ZEALAND	Grand total	218	442	660		882
Walter J. Godfrey		69	80	73	73	(295)
Stuart G. Jones		77	76	73	81	(307)
Ross C. Murray		75	72	76	76	(299)
Ross R. Newdick		74	76	72	73	(295)
Total best 3, daily		218	224	218	222	
*V. C. Hollis						
MEXICO	Grand total	225	457	672		887
Hector Alvarez		73	78	72	71	(294)
Juan Antonio Estrada		73	79	69	66	(287)
Roberto Halpern		79	76	78	78	(311)
Tomas Lehman		87	78	74	79	(318)
Total best 3, daily		225	232	215	215	
*Rodrigo Medellin						
CHINA, REPUBLIC OF	Grand total	225	453	675		892
Tung Chan Chang		75	85	75	76	(311)
Chien Chin Chen		73	75	74	73	(295)
Min Nan Hsieh		77	78	77	73	(305)
Chi Hsiung Kuo		78	75	73	71	(297)
Total best 3, daily		225	228	222	217	
*I Wen Lin						
AUSTRALIA	Grand total	230	455	675		893
Douglas Bachli		79	76	78	79	(312)
*Phillip K. Billings		81	72	75	67	(295)
Tom Crow		77	77	72	73	(299)
Kevin L. Donohoe		74	77	73	78	(302)
Total best 3, daily		230	225	220	218	
SOUTH AFRICA	Grand total	223	456	678		896
B. Franklin		77	82	81	78	(318)
J. Hayes		79	73	75	74	(301)
Johannes G. LeRoux		73	79	77	74	(303)
Reginald C. Taylor		73	81	70	70	(294)
Total best 3, daily		223	233	222	218	
*H. E. P. Watermeyer						
JAPAN	Grand total	227	457	678		902
Yoshikane Hirose		76	74	77	74	(301)
*Kiyoshi Ishimoto		71	77	75	76	(299)
Naomoto Nabeshima		81	83	73	74	(311)
Ginjiro Nakabe		81	83	73	74	(311)
Total best 3, daily		227	230	221	224	

		1st Rd.	2nd Rd.	3rd Rd.	4th Rd.	72-hole Score
ARGENTINA	Grand total	225	458	680		905
Oscar E. Cella		86	78	73	74	(311)
*Jorge C. Ledesma, Jr.		70	80	72	79	(301)
Hugo Nicora		83	80	79	78	(320)
Raul Travieso		72	75	77	73	(297)
Total best 3, daily		225	233	222	225	
ITALY	Grand total	228	461	688		912
Franco Bevione		77	83	77	79	(316)
Carlo Cobianchi		80	76	78	73	(307)
Angelo Croce		75	74	72	79	(300)
Lorenzo Silva		76	84	78	72	(310)
Total best 3, daily		228	233	227	224	
*Conte Giuseppe Sabini						
GERMANY	Grand total	231	476	699		926
Walter Bruehne		73	78	74	73	(298)
Peter Moeller		80	81	78	78	(317)
Helge Rademacher		81	86	81	76	(324)
Erik Sellschopp		78	87	71	81	(317)
Total best 3, daily		231	245	223	227	
*Heinz O. Krings						
PHILIPPINES	Grand total	232	470	696		929
Alex Montelibano		81	86	80	84	(331)
Alex Prieto		77	76	88	80	(321)
Luis F. Silverio		74	80	71	70	(295)
Dick Villalon		81	82	75	83	(321)
Total best 3, daily		232	238	226	233	
*Manuel J. Gonzalez						
INDIA	Grand total	233	473	700		931
J. H. Forman		82	88	79	78	(327)
Ashok S. Malik		76	79	75	77	(307)
P. K. Pitamber		80	83	80	76	(319)
Capt. P. G. Sethi		77	78	73	79	(307)
Total best 3, daily		233	240	227	231	
*H. S. Malik						
HONG KONG	Grand total	236	473	715		942
George G. D. Carter		76	77	83	79	(315)
A. W. J. Kim Hall		78	80	79	73	(310)
John D. Mackie		82	84	80	75	(321)
Alan F. Sutcliffe		84	80	83	84	(331)
Total best 3, daily		236	237	242	227	
*Graeme D. Nicholl						
SWEDEN	Grand total	242	481	713		943
Gustaf Adolf Bielke		79	78	75	81	(313)
Per Olof Johansson		81	85	80	76	(322)
Claes Johncke		82	79	77	74	(312)
Rune Karlfeldt		85	82	82	80	(329)
Total best 3, daily		242	239	232	230	
*Olle Isaksson						
SWITZERLAND	Grand total	235	478	715		947
Olivier Barras		77	81	75	76	(309)
Otto Dillier		79	82	79	78	(318)
Peter Gutermann		79	80	83	82	(324)
Rudolf Muller		83	85	88	78	(334)
Total best 3, daily		235	243	237	232	
*Antoine Barras						
SPAIN	Grand total	240	482	721		961
Duke of Fernan-Nunez		80	84	78	79	(321)
Ivan Maura		79	79	82	84	(324)
Francisco Sanchiz		81	82	82	77	(322)
Juan de Sentmenat		82	81	79	89	(331)
Total best 3, daily		240	242	239	240	
*Juan Antonio Andreu						
BRAZIL	Grand total	240	486	735		964
Humberto de Almeida		81	84	84	75	(324)
Joao J. Barbosa		81	83	87	76	(327)
Carlos A. Sozio		78	79	80	78	(315)
Nestor L. Sozio, Jr.		84	89	85	78	(336)
Total best 3, daily		240	246	249	229	
*Nestor Sozio, Sr.						

		1st Rd.	2nd Rd.	3rd Rd.	4th Rd.	72-hole Score
BERMUDA	Grand total	245	500	739		980
George McLachlan		85	87	84	86	(342)
James A. Pearman		86	83	83	81	(333)
Richard S. L. Pearman		83	89	81	80	(335)
George E. Wardman		75	85	75	80	(315)
Total best 3, daily		245	255	239	241	
*Capt. A. R. Francis						
PERU	Grand total	245	497	740		985
Maxwell Cooper		81	83	82	81	(327)
Miguel Grau		82	87	78	79	(326)
Ricardo Hernandez		90	94	85	85	(354)
Arnie Lidback		82	82	83	85	(332)
Total best 3, daily		245	252	243	245	
*Gabriel Tudela						
MALAYA	Grand total	268	528	785		1036
Patrick Lim		93	93	88	87	(361)
Henry W. Liu		93	87	83	87	(350)
Too Joon Loke		91	87	86	85	(349)
Choong Ewe Seong		84	86	90	79	(339)
Total best 3, daily		268	260	257	251	
*Tun Sir Henry H. S. Lee						
PAKISTAN	Grand total	265	529	797		1056
*R. D. Habib		95	92	92	94	(373)
M. M. Hashim Khan		90	92	96	87	(365)
M. Ibrahim Musa		86	80	90	80	(336)
Tajuddin Salimi		89	94	86	92	(361)
Total best 3, daily		265	264	268	259	

1964
FOURTH WORLD AMATEUR TEAM CHAMPIONSHIP
FOR THE EISENHOWER TROPHY

Held at the Olgiata Golf Club, Rome, Italy, October 7-10.
Yardage—6,879. Par 72. 33 Team Entries.

Team score consisted of best three individual scores in each round.
*Indicates Captain.

		1st Rd.	2nd Rd.	3rd Rd.	4th Rd.	72-Hole Score
GREAT BRITAIN AND IRELAND	Grand total	214	445	671		895
Michael F. Bonallack		80	76	77	78	(311)
Rodney Foster		72	79	75	75	(301)
Michael S. R. Lunt		72	76	79	74	(301)
Ronald D. B. M. Shade		70	81	74	75	(300)
Total best 3, daily		214	231	226	224	
*Joseph B. Carr						
CANADA	Grand total	224	451	676		897
R. Keith Alexander		76	75	72	74	(297)
Gary Cowan		77	85	79	74	(315)
Douglas H. Silverberg		74	80	78	73	(305)
Nick Weslock		74	72	75	77	(298)
Total best 3, daily		224	227	225	221	
*W. Arthur Johnston						
NEW ZEALAND	Grand total	225	448	677		900
John D. Durry		76	81	76	75	(308)
Stuart G. Jones		80	77	78	79	(314)
Edward J. McDougall		72	76	77	74	(299)
Ross C. Murray		77	70	76	74	(297)
Total best 3, daily		225	223	229	223	
*Philip L. Phillipps						
UNITED STATES	Grand total	221	446	676		908
Deane R. Beman		74	79	75	75	(303)
William C. Campbell		73	77	77	79	(306)
Dale Morey		75	72	78	80	(305)
Edgar M. Tutwiler, Jr.		74	76	80	78	(308)
Total best 3, daily		221	225	230	232	
*Isaac B. Grainger						
AUSTRALIA	Grand total	223	453	682		910
B. J. Baker		75	83	79	79	(316)
Phillip K. Billings		76	76	75	77	(304)
Tom L. Crow		72	78	76	77	(303)
K. W. Hartley		77	76	78	74	(305)
Total best 3, daily		223	230	229	228	
*J. W. Wilson						
CHINA, REPUBLIC OF	Grand total	219	452	679		911
Chien Chin Chen		73	81	86	80	(320)
Min Nan Hsieh		72	77	72	73	(294)
Sheng San Hsu		83	79	76	82	(320)
Chi Hsiung Kuo		74	77	79	79	(309)
Total best 3, daily		219	233	227	232	
*K. U. Dzung						
ITALY	Grand total	218	449	682		911
Carlo Bordogna		76	79	78	76	(309)
Angelo Croce		70	75	75	79	(299)
Alberto Schiaffino		72	77	80	77	(306)
Lorenzo Silva		76	81	80	76	(313)
Total best 3, daily		218	231	233	229	
*A. Lang						
ARGENTINA	Grand total	220	456	685		913
Hernan Fernandez		74	86	77	77	(314)
Jorge C. Ledesma, Jr.		73	83	81	76	(313)
Angel R. Monguzzi		74	79	79	77	(309)
Raul Travieso		73	74	73	75	(295)
Total best 3, daily		220	236	229	228	
*Dr. Edwardo H. Maglione						

Fourth World Amateur Team Championship – Continued

		1st Rd.	2nd Rd.	3rd Rd.	4th Rd.	72-Hole Score
MEXICO	Grand total	219	453	684		917
Juan Antonio Estrada		72	74	75	77	(298)
Tomas Lehman		73	81	78	75	(307)
Raphael Quiroz		76	79	78	81	(314)
Enrique Sterling		74	83	79	84	(320)
Total best 3, daily		219	234	231	233	
*Julio Orvananos						
FRANCE	Grand total	228	461	690		922
Patrick Cros		77	77	74	75	(303)
Herve Frayssineau		74	80	77	77	(308)
Alexis Godillot		78	78	82	81	(319)
Gaetan Mourgue d'Algue		77	78	78	80	(313)
Total best 3, daily		228	233	229	232	
*Pierre Maeght						
SOUTH AFRICA	Grand total	223	457	691		929
Murray Grindrod		79	80	78	79	(316)
David Symons		73	78	78	75	(304)
Reginald C. Taylor		83	79	78	85	(325)
Dorian Wharton-Hood		71	77	79	84	(311)
Total best 3, daily		223	234	234	338	
*Dennis P. Adams						
SPAIN	Grand total	228	465	706		942
Luis Alvarez de Bohorques		74	77	90	87	(328)
Duke of Fernan Nunez		79	81	79	78	(317)
Ivan Maura		75	90	80	80	(325)
Francisco Sanchiz		82	79	82	78	(321)
Total best 3, daily		228	237	241	236	
*Juan Antonio Andreu						
SOUTHERN RHODESIA	Grand total	230	467	704		943
Dr. R. A. Cahi		81	88	88	84	(341)
Gordon Owen		85	84	82	76	(327)
M. J. Reinders		73	74	77	81	(305)
R. W. White		76	79	78	82	(315)
Total best 3, daily		230	237	237	239	
*Charles C. W. Ingham						
SWEDEN	Grand total	237	474	711		946
Gunnar Carlander		80	83	81	78	(322)
Lennart Leinborn		76	81	81	78	(316)
Claes Johncke		82	79	78	79	(318)
Bengt Moller		81	77	78	84	(320)
Total best 3, daily		237	237	237	235	
*Major Erik Runfelt						
INDIA	Grand total	231	464	706		949
A. S. Malik		79	83	82	78	(322)
S. S. Malik		79	81	84	85	(329)
*R. K. Pitamber		75	81	86	81	(323)
P. G. Sethi		77	71	76	84	(308)
Total best 3, daily		231	233	242	243	
NORTHERN RHODESIA	Grand total	223	464	710		949
John Drysdale		75	90	82	81	(328)
Phil Dunne		72	80	81	80	(313)
Jackie Muir		80	80	83	78	(321)
Ken Treloar		76	81	83	82	(322)
Total best 3, daily		223	241	246	239	
*Alister D. McLean						
DENMARK	Grand total	230	479	717		952
John Jacobsen		80	84	82	80	(326)
Nils Elsoe Jensen		75	85	78	74	(312)
Niels Thygesen		81	84	84	85	(334)
Ole Wilberg Jorgensen		75	81	78	81	(315)
Total best 3, daily		230	249	238	235	
*Steen Damgaard						
VENEZUELA	Grand total	231	476	711		954
*Manuel Bernardez		79	84	77	77	(317)
R. Keith Guise		72	79	78	82	(311)
Fernan Frias		80	86	81	84	(331)
Jose M. Stuyck		82	82	80	87	(331)
Total best 3, daily		231	245	235	243	

Fourth World Amateur Team Championship – Continued

		1st Rd.	2nd Rd.	3rd Rd.	4th Rd.	72-Hole Score
BELGIUM	Grand total	232	480	718		955
Jacques Moerman		76	84	80	78	(318)
Freddy Rodesch		79	89	82	75	(325)
Baron Paul Rolin		77	85	77	87	(326)
Philippe Washer		79	79	81	84	(323)
Total best 3, daily		232	248	238	237	
*Jacques Du Vivier						
SWITZERLAND	Grand total	232	466	715		959
Andre Barras		86	84	92	86	(348)
Otto Dillier		75	74	76	83	(308)
Peter Gutermann		77	76	86	83	(322)
Rudolf Muller		80	84	87	78	(329)
Total best 3, daily		232	234	249	244	
*Antoine Barras						
AUSTRIA	Grand total	239	486	717		960
*Fritz Jonak		86	83	89	90	(348)
Alexander Maculan		76	84	81	79	(320)
Klaus Nierlich		79	80	74	79	(312)
Wolfgang Pollak		84	84	76	85	(329)
Total best 3, daily		239	247	231	243	
BERMUDA	Grand total	233	480	721		964
Ford Hutchings		79	82	80	81	(322)
Brendan Ingham		76	80	78	84	(318)
Louis Moniz		80	85	88	82	(335)
George Wardman		78	85	83	80	(326)
Total best 3, daily		233	247	241	243	
*Capt. A. R. Francis						
CHILE	Grand total	238	478	720		965
Arturo Mori		86	88	89	86	(349)
Christian Prieto		77	87	80	83	(327)
Eric van der Valk		81	79	81	77	(318)
Jaime R. Vergara		80	74	81	85	(320)
Total best 3, daily		238	240	242	245	
*Manuel J. Diaz						
JAPAN	Grand total	227	475	720		965
Ginjiro Nakabe		80	83	84	80	(327)
Yoshikane Hirose		77	84	85	81	(327)
*Kiyoshi Ishimoto		70	81	78	84	(313)
Hiroshi Morimoto		—	84	83	85	(—)
Total best 3, daily		227	248	245	245	
PHILIPPINES	Grand total	236	484	728		967
Alex Prieto		76	85	85	83	(329)
Alberto Silverio		81	87	84	84	(336)
*Luis F. Silverio		79	82	80	78	(319)
Willie Villalon		85	81	80	78	(324)
Total best 3, daily		236	248	244	239	
GERMANY	Grand total	236	483	721		971
Klaus R. Bez		80	88	81	86	(335)
Walter Bruehne		77	80	81	79	(317)
Peter Moeller		79	85	76	85	(325)
Nils Wirichs		83	82	83	86	(334)
Total best 3, daily		236	247	238	250	
*Heinz O. Krings						
BRAZIL	Grand total	229	483	728		977
Fernando Chaves Barcellos		78	91	87	83	(339)
Robert Falkenburg		76	83	79	84	(322)
Carlos Sozio		75	84	79	82	(320)
Nestor L. Sozio, Jr.		84	87	91	85	(347)
Total best 3, daily		229	254	245	249	
*Seymour G. Marvin						
NETHERLANDS	Grand total	237	485	730		978
Ajef F. Knappert		77	88	79	82	(326)
Jani A. R. Roland Holst		85	85	86	88	(344)
Joan F. Dudok van Heel		82	85	86	85	(338)
Robbie E. van Erven Dorens		78	78	80	81	(317)
Total best 3, daily		237	248	245	248	
*A. M. Groskamp						

Fourth World Amateur Team Championship – Continued

		1st Rd.	2nd Rd.	3rd Rd.	4th Rd.	72-Hole Score
PERU	Grand total	242	502	754		1006
Miguel Grau		75	87	83	82	(327)
Ricardo Hernandez		81	89	87	83	(340)
Maxwell Cooper		86	84	85	87	(342)
Guillermo Salazar		86	89	84	88	(347)
Total best 3, daily		242	260	252	252	
*Giorgio Nassano						
MALAYSIA	Grand total	255	507	770		1019
Sulaiman Bin Bluah		88	80	90	78	(336)
Darwis Deren		80	84	84	83	(331)
Rashid Mallal		91	98	90	89	(368)
Brian R. Marks		87	88	89	88	(352)
Total best 3, daily		255	252	263	249	
*Alfred S. Machado						
PORTUGAL	Grand total	251	508	764		1025
Fernando P. Coelho		82	89	84	90	(345)
Jorge J. de Figueiredo		83	85	92	90	(350)
Daniel B. Lane		86	84	86	81	(337)
Dr. Manuel Leao		94	88	86	91	(359)
Total best 3, daily		251	257	256	261	
*Manuel Brito e Cunha						
ICELAND	Grand total	253	518	784		1043
Petur Bjornsson		93	—	90	90	(—)
Magnus Gudmundsson		80	83	83	82	(328)
Gunnar Solnes		85	86	93	87	(351)
Ottar Yngvason		88	96	96	94	(374)
Total best 3, daily		253	265	266	259	
*S. Einarsson						
URUGUAY	Grand total	257	528	797		1059
Francisco Etcheverry		87	88	85	83	(343)
*Dr. Carlos Giambruno		88	100	98	99	(385)
Pablo Paullier		82	83	86	80	(331)
Fernando Valdez		—	—	—	—	—
Total best 3, daily		257	271	269	262	

1966
FIFTH WORLD AMATEUR TEAM CHAMPIONSHIP
FOR THE EISENHOWER TROPHY

Held at the Mexico Golf Club, Mexico City, Mexico, October 27-30.
Yardage—7,125. Par 72. 32 Team Entries.

Team score consisted of best three individual scores in each round.
*Indicates Captain.

		1st Rd.	2nd Rd.	3rd Rd.	4th Rd.	72-Hole Score
AUSTRALIA	Grand total	214	435	658		877
Harry W. Berwick		74	75	74	72	(295)
Phillip K. Billings		72	74	74	74	(294)
Kevin L. Donohoe		75	72	75	74	(296)
Kevin W. Hartley		68	78	77	73	(296)
Total best 3, daily		214	221	223	219	
*Daniel H. Dwyer						
UNITED STATES	Grand total	226	443	663		879
Deane R. Beman		76	73	73	69	(291)
Ronald J. Cerrudo		76	73	74	74	(297)
A. Downing Gray		76	80	73	75	(304)
Robert J. Murphy, Jr.		74	71	74	73	(292)
Total best 3, daily		226	217	220	216	
*Jess W. Sweetser						
GREAT BRITAIN AND IRELAND	Grand total	228	443	666		883
Michael F. Bonallack		77	70	76	77	(300)
Gordon B. Cosh		77	76	75	73	(301)
Ronald D. B. M. Shade		74	69	72	68	(283)
Peter M. Townsend		77	79	84	76	(316)
Total best 3, daily		228	215	223	217	
*Joseph B. Carr						
SOUTH AFRICA	Grand total	220	442	657		884
Robert E. Cole		72	75	70	77	(294)
Comrie J. DuToit		74	77	78	75	(304)
Jonathan A. Fourie		74	72	75	77	(298)
David H. Symons		75	75	70	75	(295)
Total best 3, daily		220	222	215	227	
*L. Henri Marquard						
MEXICO	Grand total	230	446	667		889
Juan Antonio Estrada		78	72	74	73	(297)
Roberto Halpern		76	71	73	75	(295)
Tomas Lehman		77	73	74	75	(299)
Agustin Silveyra		77	82	76	74	(309)
Total best 3, daily		230	216	221	222	
*Javier Padilla						
CANADA	Grand total	223	445	670		890
Keith Alexander		73	73	76	75	(297)
Gary Cowan		75	73	75	72	(295)
Douglas Silverberg		80	78	77	75	(310)
Nick Weslock		75	76	74	73	(238)
Total best 3, daily		223	222	225	220	
*E. Duncan Millican						
CHINA, REPUBLIC OF	Grand total	225	449	670		892
Chien Chin Chen		74	73	78	72	(297)
Ming Chong Ho		75	78	71	75	(299)
Sheng San Hsu		76	75	75	75	(301)
Yee Shone Shay		78	76	75	76	(305)
Total best 3, daily		225	224	221	222	
*K. U. Dzung						
JAPAN	Grand total	228	452	678		894
Yoshikane Hirose		77	78	79	75	(309)
Ginjiro Nakabe		76	73	73	69	(291)
Shohei Nishida		78	74	75	72	(299)
Akihiro Teramoto		75	77	78	76	(306)
Total best 3, daily		228	224	226	216	
*Taiichi Okahashi						
GERMANY	Grand total	224	452	675		900
Walter Bruehne		74	73	73	75	(295)
Friedrich Carl Janssen		76	77	71	75	(299)
Peter Jochums		75	78	79	77	(309)
Christian Strenger		75	78	79	75	(307)
Total best 3, daily		224	228	223	225	
*Jan Bruegelmann						

		1st Rd.	2nd Rd.	3rd Rd.	4th Rd.	72-Hole Score
NEW ZEALAND	Grand total	222	446	675		905
John D. Durry		78	75	81	78	(312)
Stuart G. Jones		74	76	78	76	(304)
Ross C. Murray		75	73	75	78	(301)
Bruce A. Stevens		73	76	76	76	(301)
Total best 3, daily		222	224	229	230	
*Richard F. Mackie						
ITALY	Grand total	230	451	679		905
Franco Bevione		77	85	84	76	(322)
Angelo Croce		76	70	74	74	(294)
Alberto Schiaffino		77	77	77	79	(310)
Lorenzo Silva		78	74	77	76	(305)
Total best 3, daily		230	221	228	226	
*Count Giuseppe Sabini						
FRANCE	Grand total	229	453	678		908
Patrick Cros		71	71	72	76	(290)
Herve Frayssineau		82	75	76	78	(311)
Alex Godillot		79	80	81	77	(317)
Gaetan Mourgue D'Algue		79	78	77	77	(311)
Total best 3, daily		229	224	225	230	
*Roland Raffard						
SWEDEN	Grand total	226	452	681		908
Hans Hedjersson		73	75	76	77	(301)
Thure Holmstrom		78	81	80	77	(316)
Claes Johncke		75	79	76	79	(309)
Magnus Lindberg		78	72	77	73	(300)
Total best 3, daily		226	226	229	227	
*Erik Torudd						
CHILE	Grand total	225	455	682		909
Guy Barroilhet		76	78	75	80	(309)
Mauricio Galeno		76	78	79	75	(308)
Eric van der Valk		78	74	73	75	(300)
Jaime R. Vergara		73	82	84	77	(316)
Total best 3, daily		225	230	227	227	
*Manuel J. Diaz						
BELGIUM	Grand total	232	453	685		912
Jacques Moerman		78	75	78	75	(306)
Frederic Rodesch		80	76	77	75	(308)
Baron Paul Rolin		77	71	84	81	(313)
Philippe Toussaint		77	75	77	77	(306)
Total best 3, daily		232	221	232	227	
*Jacques du Vivier						
RHODESIA	Grand total	223	457	683		915
Douglas Black		79	84	78	79	(320)
Peter J. Matkovich		76	75	81	81	(313)
Michael J. Reinders		74	—	73	81	(—)
Robert W. White		73	75	75	72	(295)
Total best 3, daily		223	234	226	232	
*Guy C. Molyneux						
INDIA	Grand total	221	448	677		916
A. S. Malik		73	83	80	83	(319)
S. S. Malik		83	82	84	81	(330)
Ashok Mehra		73	75	76	85	(309)
*Major P. G. Sethi		75	70	73	75	(293)
Total best 3, daily		221	227	229	239	
ZAMBIA	Grand total	228	470	697		929
Malcolm Cordukes		78	80	84	79	(321)
John F. Drysdale		76	84	72	78	(310)
Simon Hobday		74	81	77	76	(308)
Ken Treloar		82	81	78	78	(319)
Total best 3, daily		228	242	227	232	
*Alister D. McLean						
BRAZIL	Grand total	235	465	698		932
Humberto C. de Almeida		79	79	82	79	(319)
Robert Falkenburg		78	75	79	78	(310)
Mario Gonzalez, Jr.		80	82	79	80	(321)
Carlos A. Sozio		78	76	75	77	(306)
Total best 3, daily		235	230	233	234	
*Jesse S. Rinehart, Jr.						

Fifth World Amateur Team Championship – Continued

		1st Rd.	2nd Rd.	3rd Rd.	4th Rd.	72-Hole Score
PHILIPPINES	Grand total	229	468	702		938
Emil G. Gaston		78	86	84	81	(329)
*Manuel J. Gonzales		86	82	87	82	(337)
Alejandro Montelibano		79	75	74	78	(306)
Luis F. Silverio		72	82	76	77	(307)
Total best 3, daily		229	239	234	236	
GUATEMALA	Grand total	231	471	700		939
Angel Arturo Casellas		79	80	82	83	(324)
Juan Jose Hermosilla		77	83	78	80	(318)
Mario Perez		85	83	75	82	(325)
Adolfo Rios		75	77	76	77	(305)
Total best 3, daily		231	240	229	239	
*Oscar Escobar						
SPAIN	Grand total	234	464	704		940
Duke of Fernan Nunez		81	83	86	76	(326)
Alvaro Rezola		81	77	81	92	(331)
Jose Gancedo		76	73	74	74	(297)
Alvaro Muro		77	80	85	86	(328)
Total best 3, daily		234	230	240	236	
*Juan A. Andreu						
BERMUDA	Grand total	236	475	709		947
Ford Hutchings		80	88	77	74	(319)
Brendan Ingham		80	77	78	82	(317)
Louis Moniz		76	74	79	82	(311)
Richard S. L. Pearman		85	89	80	86	(340)
Total best 3, daily		236	239	234	238	
*George Wardman						
VENEZUELA	Grand total	232	471	712		950
Jacques Alexander, Jr.		74	76	78	79	(307)
*Fernan Frias		79	84	83	76	(322)
Jack Strange		92	86	88	91	(357)
Alirio Yanes		79	79	80	83	(321)
Total best 3, daily		232	239	241	238	
SWITZERLAND	Grand total	239	479	718		952
Otto F. Dillier		79	79	77	79	(314)
Dr. Peter Gutermann		81	78	82	75	(316)
Rudi Muller		79	83	81	80	(323)
Michael Rey		82	85	81	84	(332)
Total best 3, daily		239	240	239	234	
*Gregory Trippi						
JAMAICA	Grand total	242	478	724		956
L. L. Delapenha		87	82	84	76	(329)
M. S. Elder		79	80	83	75	(317)
H. E. T. McDonald, Jr.		82	79	89	88	(338)
I. Sturdy		81	77	79	81	(318)
Total best 3, daily		242	236	246	232	
*Michael Elder						
DENMARK	Grand total	237	480	714		957
Klaus Hove		78	85	83	—	(—)
John Jacobsen		79	76	77	79	(311)
Nils Elsoe Jensen		83	86	79	78	(326)
Ole Pfeiffer		80	82	78	86	(326)
Total best 3, daily		237	243	234	243	
*Steen Damgaard						
URUGUAY	Grand total	242	481	724		958
Orlin Jacobson		81	80	78	78	(317)
Pable Paullier		79	76	82	75	(312)
Victor Paullier		86	93	83	85	(347)
*Peter Stanham		82	83	87	81	(333)
Total best 3, daily		242	239	243	234	
PERU	Grand total	246	485	739		983
Maxwell Cooper		86	85	88	84	(343)
Miguel Grau		80	79	81	77	(317)
Ricardo Hernandez		81	80	87	84	(332)
Fernando de Osma		85	80	86	83	(334)
Total best 3, daily		246	239	254	244	
*Luis Larrabure						

Fifth World Amateur Team Championship – Continued

		1st Rd.	2nd Rd.	3rd Rd.	4th Rd.	72-Hole Score
ICELAND	Grand total	262	513	771		1024
Magnus Gudmundsson		86	80	85	79	(330)
Th. Kjerbo		98	94	88	89	(369)
O. B. Ragnarsson		88	88	96	91	(363)
Ottar Yngvason		88	83	85	85	(341)
Total best 3, daily		262	251	258	253	
*O. A. Olafsson						
DOMINICAN REPUBLIC	Grand total	268	528	782		1033
Ramon Baez		92	87	86	83	(348)
Dionisio Bernal		89	88	92	100	(369)
Jack Corrie		87	85	78	76	(326)
Bernardo Pichardo		95	92	90	92	(369)
Total best 3, daily		268	260	254	251	
*Jaime Luis Bou						
PUERTO RICO	Grand total	272	544	817		1070
Richard Bernhard		94	92	89	87	(362)
John Keith Clark		95	95	96	83	(369)
Fred W. Thon		90	87	93	92	(362)
*Juan N. Torruella		88	93	91	83	(355)
Total best 3, daily		272	272	273	253	

1968

SIXTH WORLD AMATEUR TEAM CHAMPIONSHIP FOR THE EISENHOWER TROPHY

Held at the Royal Melbourne Golf Club, Black Rock, Victoria, Australia, October 9-12.
Yardage—6,946. Par 73. 26 Team Entries.

Team score consisted of best three individual scores in each round.
*Indicates Captain.

		1st Rd.	2nd Rd.	3rd Rd.	4th Rd.	72-Hole Score
UNITED STATES	Grand total	220	431	647		868
Bruce Fleisher		77	76	73	75	(301)
Marvin Giles, III		74	68	71	73	(286)
Jack W. Lewis, Jr.		72	74	72	78	(296)
Richard L. Siderowf		74	69	73	73	(289)
Total best 3, daily		220	211	216	221	
*William C. Campbell						
GREAT BRITAIN AND IRELAND	Grand total	218	433	640		869
*Michael F. Bonallack		72	72	66	76	(286)
Gordon B. Cosh		79	74	71	79	(303)
Peter A. Oosterhuis		70	71	72	76	(289)
Ronald D. B. M. Shade		76	72	70	77	(295)
Total best 3, daily		218	215	207	229	
CANADA	Grand total	225	440	662		885
Gary Cowan		73	69	72	79	(293)
Jim Doyle		79	73	79	71	(302)
John Johnston		74	75	80	76	(305)
Robert L. Wylie		78	73	71	76	(298)
Total best 3, daily		225	215	222	223	
*John A. Swanson						
AUSTRALIA	Grand total	216	438	660		886
Harry W. Berwick		80	74	79	74	(307)
Kevin L. Donohoe		68	75	72	76	(291)
Anthony Y. Gresham		76	75	74	76	(301)
Kevin W. Hartley		72	73	76	76	(297)
Total best 3, daily		216	222	222	226	
*G. H. Mocatta						
SOUTH AFRICA	Grand total	225	443	663		889
Hugh J. Baiocchi		79	70	74	74	(297)
Comrie J. DuToit		75	76	74	75	(300)
John A. Fourie		72	75	74	77	(298)
David H. Symons		78	73	72	77	(300)
Total best 3, daily		225	218	220	226	
*L. Henri Marquard						
MEXICO	Grand total	222	433	665		893
Ernesto Perez		72	69	72	78	(291)
Juan Antonio Estrada		87	72	80	71	(310)
Victor Regalado		74	70	83	79	(306)
Tomas Lehman		76	76	80	79	(311)
Total best 3, daily		222	211	232	228	
*Mauricio Urdaneta						
NEW ZEALAND	Grand total	224	447	670		895
John D. Durry		76	75	75	79	(305)
Edward J. McDougall		75	75	77	75	(302)
Ross C. Murray		75	74	72	73	(294)
Bruce A. Stevens		74	74	76	77	(301)
Total best 3, daily		224	223	223	225	
*Philip L. Phillipps						
CHINA, REPUBLIC OF	Grand total	226	450	673		900
Chien-Chin Chen		76	75	75	72	(298)
Ming-Chung Ho		75	74	72	75	(296)
Yee-Shone Shay		79	75	76	80	(310)
Sheng-San Hsu		75	79	78	83	(315)
Total best 3, daily		226	224	223	227	
*K. U. Dzung						
JAPAN	Grand total	228	447	674		908
Shoichiro Maeda		85	84	81	80	(330)
Shinji Morikawa		79	73	77	83	(312)
Ginjiro Nakabe		76	73	71	76	(296)
Kenichi Yamada		73	73	79	78	(303)
Total best 3, daily		228	219	227	234	
*Taiichi Okahashi						

		1st Rd.	2nd Rd.	3rd Rd.	4th Rd.	72-Hole Score
GERMANY	Grand total	229	458	682		910
Walter Bruehne		77	77	75	75	(304)
Gerhard Koenig		77	74	75	78	(304)
Christian Strenger		75	80	79	75	(309)
Jurgen Th. Weghmann		77	78	74	84	(313)
Total best 3, daily		229	229	224	228	
*Jan Bruegelmann						
FRANCE	Grand total	227	456	679		912
Didier Charmat		85	77	82	78	(322)
Herve Frayssineau		76	74	74	78	(302)
Alexis Godillot		75	78	74	77	(304)
*Gaetan Mourgue d'Algue		76	78	75	84	(313)
Total best 3, daily		227	229	223	233	
ARGENTINA	Grand total	226	447	680		916
Jorge de Azcuenaga		74	73	77	84	(308)
*Jorge C. Ledesma		77	77	78	79	(311)
Roberto Monguzzi		75	71	78	79	(303)
Alberto E. Texier		80	82	79	78	(319)
Total best 3, daily		226	221	233	236	
INDIA	Grand total	231	453	686		925
Vikram Chopra		94	85	84	84	(347)
A. S. Malik		79	79	78	82	(318)
*R. K. Pitamber		76	71	78	78	(303)
P. G. Sethi		76	72	77	79	(304)
Total best 3, daily		231	222	233	239	
MALAYSIA	Grand total	239	463	696		930
Zainal Abidin		84	76	75	71	(306)
Kwan C. Choo		84	78	79	89	(330)
Darwis Deran		79	83	79	83	(324)
Jalal Deran		76	70	84	80	(310)
Total best 3, daily		239	224	233	234	
*Edmund Yong						
SPAIN	Grand total	232	464	700		939
Santiago Fernandez		78	78	79	83	(318)
Jose Gancedo		75	77	77	73	(302)
Alvaro Muro		81	77	80	84	(322)
Roman Taya		79	82	81	83	(325)
Total best 3, daily		232	232	236	239	
*Juan A. Andreu						
ITALY	Grand total	230	472	701		947
Stefano Cimatti		80	86	78	82	(326)
Alberto Croze		79	84	76	84	(323)
*Alberto Schiaffino		75	76	75	81	(307)
Lorenzo Silva		76	82	84	83	(325)
Total best 3, daily		230	242	229	246	
PHILIPPINES	Grand total	236	469	702		950
Alan Gaston		78	78	79	87	(322)
Nilo Lizares		86	84	91	96	(357)
Jose Ma. Santos		86	79	78	82	(325)
Luis Silverio		72	76	76	79	(303)
Total best 3, daily		236	233	233	248	
*Edmundo Unson						
SWITZERLAND	Grand total	234	467	709		954
Gilles Bagnoud		79	78	79	79	(315)
Dr. Peter Gutermann		74	76	81	81	(312)
Anton Matti		81	79	82	85	(327)
Peter Muller		83	81	84	88	(336)
Total best 3, daily		234	233	242	245	
*Gregory Trippi						
KOREA, REPUBLIC OF	Grand total	238	468	713		956
Yuong Chang Kim		74	76	77	74	(301)
Kyu Won Lee		84	74	83	88	(329)
Moon Koo Lee		80	84	85	81	(330)
*Yung Jun Park		94	80	93	88	(355)
Total best 3, daily		238	230	245	243	
PAPUA/NEW GUINEA	Grand total	243	478	719		958
Wayne Brittain		81	84	83	84	(332)
*John Keating		81	79	81	80	(321)
Ian Trevena		84	82	84	79	(329)
John Wilkinson		81	74	77	80	(312)
Total best 3, daily		243	235	241	239	

		1st Rd.	2nd Rd.	3rd Rd.	4th Rd.	72-Hole Score
BERMUDA	Grand total	241	485	722		971
Brendan J. Ingham		82	76	78	86	(322)
Louis Moniz		79	81	74	79	(313)
Llewellyn Tucker		80	87	90	89	(346)
*George E. Wardman		85	93	85	84	(347)
Total best 3, daily		241	244	237	249	
BRAZIL	Grand total	257	496	735		976
Robert Falkenburg		87	82	77	84	(330)
Robert Falkenburg, II		89	93	88	81	(351)
Lee Smith		92	80	81	87	(340)
Carlos A. Sozio		81	77	81	76	(315)
Total best 3, daily		257	239	239	241	
*Seymour G. Marvin						
HONG KONG	Grand total	250	494	740		981
K. G. Finlayson		80	84	85	76	(325)
C. R. Cribben		88	81	80	82	(331)
A. W. J. Kim Hall		93	83	82	83	(341)
*J. D. Mackie		82	80	84	87	(333)
Total best 3, daily		250	244	246	241	
CHILE	Grand total	247	490	738		983
Guy Barroilhet		79	81	82	77	(319)
Francisco Condon		86	83	86	91	(346)
Mauricio Galeno		86	83	83	88	(340)
Eric van der Valk		82	79	83	80	(324)
Total best 3, daily		247	243	248	245	
*Francisco Reutter						
LIBYA	Grand total	264	513	764		1021
Miland Gamudi		88	82	93	89	(352)
Abdul Afid Sadek		89	85	80	86	(340)
Hadi Sasi		88	83	85	90	(346)
Abdalla Zguzi		88	84	86	82	(340)
Total best 3, daily		264	249	251	257	
*Muftah Salem						
VENEZUELA	Grand total	261	537	800		1067
Rafael Vaamonde		97	97	83	93	(370)
Gustavo Kalen		81	91	88	89	(349)
Carlos Plaza A.		83	88	92	85	(348)
Total best 3, daily		261	276	263	267	
*William S. Waldrip						

1970
SEVENTH WORLD AMATEUR TEAM CHAMPIONSHIP
FOR THE EISENHOWER TROPHY

Held at the Real Club de la Puerta de Hierro, Madrid, Spain, September 23-26.
Yardage—7,043. Par 72. 36 Team Entries.

Team score consists of best three individual scores in each round.
*Indicates Captain

		1st Rd.	2nd Rd.	3rd Rd.	4th Rd.	72-hole Score
UNITED STATES	Grand total	213	426	640		854
Marvin Giles, III		73	73	71	72	(289)
Tom Kite, Jr.		71	70	74	—	——
Allen L. Miller, III		72	71	71	73	(287)
Lanny Wadkins		70	72	72	72	(286)
Total best 3, daily		213	213	214	214	
*Clarence W. Benedict						
NEW ZEALAND	Grand total	220	434	652		869
Geoffrey Edward Clarke		75	71	71	74	(291)
Stuart Gwyn Jones		75	70	75	73	(293)
Edward John McDougall		72	73	73	70	(288)
Ross Cheyne Murray		73	73	74	75	(295)
Total best 3, daily		220	214	218	217	
*Peter K. H. Smyth						
SOUTH AFRICA	Grand total	214	433	649		870
Hugh J. Baiocchi		72	80	73	73	(298)
John A. Fourie		73	75	75	74	(297)
Dale Hayes		70	71	68	74	(283)
Dave H. Symons		72	73	76	79	(300)
Total best 3, daily		214	219	216	221	
*C. Oldridge						
AUSTRALIA	Grand total	224	439	651		871
Kevin L. Donohoe		81	70	70	75	(296)
Terry R. Gale		76	71	71	78	(296)
Tony Y. Gresham		71	74	71	71	(287)
Kevin W. Hartley		77	74	75	74	(300)
Total best 3, daily		224	215	212	220	
*Jack D. Tomlinson						
MEXICO	Grand total	221	433	653		873
Héctor Alvarez		78	71	73	75	(297)
Enrique Farias		74	79	76	75	(304)
Tomas Lehman		75	74	78	75	(302)
Victor Regalado		72	67	71	70	(280)
Total best 3, daily		221	212	220	220	
*Muricio Urdaneta						
CANADA	Grand total	218	434	662		880
Keith Alexander		72	71	77	77	(297)
Gary Cowan		73	73	76	73	(295)
Stu Hamilton		75	75	75	73	(288)
Wayne McDonald		73	72	77	72	(294)
Total best 3, daily		218	216	228	218	
*J. Campbell McLean						
GREAT BRITAIN AND IRELAND	Grand total	222	438	663		882
*Michael Bonallack		75	74	75	75	(299)
Rodney Foster		75	69	79	76	(299)
Charlie Green		74	75	74	73	(296)
Geoffrey Marks		73	73	76	71	(293)
Total best 3, daily		222	216	225	219	
JAPAN	Grand total	223	445	665		883
Kenichi Yamada		73	75	74	68	(290)
Tsutomu Irie		78	73	76	77	(304)
Tetsuo Sakata		80	83	77	81	(321)
Nobuo Takahashi		72	74	70	73	(289)
Total best 3, daily		223	222	220	218	
*Taiichi Okahashi						
FRANCE	Grand total	226	447	669		886
Didier Charmat		84	72	77	82	(313)
Herve Frayssineau		78	72	73	74	(297)
Alexis Godillot		74	77	72	69	(292)
*Roger Lagarde		74	78	77	74	(303)
Total best 3, daily		226	221	222	217	

Seventh World Amateur Team Championship – Continued

		1st Rd.	2nd Rd.	3rd Rd.	4th Rd.	72-hole Score
PHILIPPINES	Grand total	221	441	664		889
Luis Silverio		74	77	81	75	(307)
Tomas Manotoc		78	71	71	75	(294)
Miguel Preysler		78	75	74	75	(302)
Edmundo Unson, Jr.		69	74	78	82	(303)
Total best 3, daily		221	220	223	225	
*Leonardo M. Guinto						
CHINA	Grand total	223	447	669		890
Ming-Chung Ho		72	75	73	71	(291)
Tung-Chan Chang		81	80	73	78	(312)
Chien-Chin Chen		74	72	76	74	(269)
Cheng-Hsiung Li		77	77	76	76	(306)
Total best 3, daily		223	224	222	221	
*K.U. Dzung						
SPAIN	Grand total	224	448	666		892
Jose Gancedo		72	75	74	75	(296)
Javier Viladomiu		77	75	70	75	(297)
Eduardo de la Riva		76	74	76	76	(302)
Ivan Maura		76	76	74	77	(303)
Total best 3, daily		224	224	218	226	
*Juan A. Ruiz de Alda						
SWEDEN	Grand total	228	455	679		901
Hans Hedjerson		73	75	75	75	(298)
Claes Johncke		75	76	74	78	(303)
Magnus Lindberg		81	76	75	71	(303)
Sven Tumba		80	78	76	76	(310)
Total best 3, daily		228	229	224	222	
*Ola Bergovist						
GERMANY	Grand total	226	450	676		703
Heinrich Adam		76	75	75	77	(303)
Walter Bruehne		75	75	77	81	(308)
Peter Jochmus		80	74	76	77	(304)
Jan G. Muller		75	75	75	73	(298)
Total best 3, daily		226	224	226	227	
*Jan Bruegelmann						
ITALY	Grand total	219	448	681		904
Stefano Cimatti		79	79	80	78	(316)
Baldovino Dassu		73	72	79	71	(295)
Alberto Schiaffino		71	83	75	76	(305)
Lorenzo Silva		75	78	79	76	(308)
Total best 3, daily		219	229	233	223	
*Umberto Nordio						
BELGIUM	Grand total	230	458	632		(909)
Jacky Moerman		77	79	73	—	—
Freddy Rodesch		76	74	81	74	(305)
Philip Toussaint		77	75	71	75	(298)
George Boomer		78	81	80	78	(317)
Total best 3, daily		230	228	224	227	
*Jacques Du Vivier						
BRAZIL	Grand total	228	445	676		909
Jose Joaquim Barbosa		83	77	84	78	(322)
Carlos Alfredo Sozio		75	72	80	79	(306)
Jaime Gonzalez		76	70	77	77	(300)
Lee Smith		77	75	74	78	(304)
Total best 3, daily		228	217	231	233	
*Jesse S. Rinehart, Jr.						
ARGENTINA	Grand total	226	462	692		(917)
Alberto Barreira		75	79	75	76	(305)
Carlos Bracht		79	84	80	85	(348)
*Jorge C. Ledesma, Jr.		77	80	76	76	(303)
Roberto H. Monguzzi		74	77	79	73	(303)
Total best 3, daily		226	236	230	225	
VENEZUELA	Grand total	231	460	682		918
Jonathan Coles		75	75	76	75	(301)
Gustabo Kalen		82	77	79	83	(321)
Carlos Plaza		76	77	72	81	(306)
Fernan Frias		80	82	74	80	(316)
Total best 3, daily		231	229	222	236	
*Juan Brunet						

Seventh World Amateur Team Championship – Continued

		1st Rd.	2nd Rd.	3rd Rd.	4th Rd.	72-hole Score
KOREA	Grand total	228	454	684		919
SungLong Kim		78	74	77	80	(306)
HongSoo Kim		75	79	82	80	(316)
YoungChang Kim		75	74	75	75	(299)
GiuWon Lee		78	78	78	86	(320)
Total best 3, daily		228	226	230	235	
*YungJun Park						
COLOMBIA	Grand total	233	460	693		923
*Diego Correa Gomez		79	79	73	74	(305)
Emillo Sardi Aparicio		78	73	81	75	(307)
Juan Pablo Gutierrez L		83	76	79	81	(319)
Fernando Arriola Sierra		76	78	90	81	(325)
Total best 3, daily		233	227	233	230	
SWITZERLAND	Grand total	227	452	690		925
Thomas Fortmann		75	76	79	80	(310)
Dr. Peter Gutermann		76	74	82	78	(310)
Jurg Pesko		76	79	77	77	(309)
Michel Rey		76	75	83	80	(314)
Total best 3, daily		227	225	238	235	
*Alfred Schwarzenbach						
AUSTRIA	Grand total	228	467	697		929
Max Lamberg		71	79	76	75	(299)
Alexander Maculan		79	86	82	80	(327)
Klaus Nierlich		78	78	73	77	(306)
Helmuth Reichel		79	82	81	84	(326)
Total best 3, daily		228	239	230	232	
*Gunther Jack						
NORWAY	Grand total	233	461	701		929
Johan J. Horn		78	76	81	75	(310)
Yngve Eriksen		80	76	80	78	(314)
Lars Musaeus, Jr.		84	76	81	82	(323)
Erik Donnestad		75	76	79	75	(305)
Total best 3, daily		233	228	240	228	
*Erik Olav						
DENMARK	Grand total	236	465	692		930
Niels Elsoe		84	83	81	80	(328)
Klaus Hove		78	75	76	79	(308)
John Jacobsen		79	77	74	80	(310)
Henry Knudsen		79	77	77	79	(312)
Total best 3, daily		236	229	227	238	
*Erik Nohrlind						
BERMUDA	Grand total	235	469	704		934
Ford Hutchings		83	76	77	81	(317)
Brendan J. Ingham		79	80	78	79	(316)
Louis Moniz		78	78	80	73	(309)
Keith Pearman		78	80	80	78	(316)
Total best 3, daily		235	234	235	230	
*George Wardman						
NETHERLANDS	Grand total	234	467	704		938
Piet-Hein Streutgers		77	75	80	85	(317)
Lout Mangelaar Meertens		79	79	76	79	(313)
Victor Swane		78	79	81	78	(314)
Jaap Van Neck		79	80	82	77	(318)
Total best 3, daily		234	233	237	234	
*Richard Rahusen						
PORTUGAL	Grand total	227	465	707		939
Nuno A. De Brito e Cunha		73	78	79	72	(302)
Jose Lara de Sousa e Melo		77	79	86	79	(321)
Daniel Lane		77	81	84	84	(326)
Antonio Carmona Santos		82	82	79	81	(324)
Total best 3, daily		227	238	242	232	
*Visconde Periera Machado						
PAPUA/NEW GUINEA	Grand total	237	464	701		940
John T. Keating		76	74	75	79	(304)
Ian N. Trevena		85	82	86	83	(336)
John Wilkinson		76	76	79	82	(313)
James Wu		87	77	83	78	(325)
Total best 3, daily		237	227	237	239	

Seventh World Amateur Team Championship – Continued

		1st Rd.	2nd Rd.	3rd Rd.	4th Rd.	72-hole Score
CHILE	Grand total	233	465	705		943
Mauricio Galeno		80	82	80	81	(323)
Eric van der Valk		77	74	80	74	(305)
Francisco Condon		76	82	84	86	(328)
Guy Barroilhet		81	76	80	83	(320)
Total best 3, daily		233	232	240	238	
*Armando Chellew						
HONG KONG	Grand total	242	479	714		955
J. D. Mackie		85	80	84	87	(336)
C. R. Cribben		80	79	78	78	(315)
Bertie To, Jr.		82	83	78	83	(326)
H. M. P. Miles		80	78	79	80	(317)
Total best 3, daily		242	237	235	241	
*J. D. Clague						
FINLAND	Grand total	244	487	721		957
Jalo Gronlund		88	79	77	78	(322)
Juhani Hamalainen		85	80	79	78	(322)
Harri Safonoff		82	90	81	80	(333)
Karl Salonen		77	84	78	82	(321)
Total best 3, daily		244	243	234	236	
*Kaj Salenius						
PERU	Grand total	240	484	731		982
Felipe Osma		87	90	88	91	(356)
Carlos A. Raffo		76	81	77	83	(317)
Enrique Grau		80	82	86	87	(335)
Guillermo Salazar E.		84	81	84	81	(330)
Total best 3, daily		240	244	247	251	
*Luis Larrabure L.						
PAKISTAN	Grand total	254	505	758		1013
*M. M. Hashim Khan		83	79	83	85	(331)
Mohammed Hassan Musa		87	93	82	85	(347)
Masud Ahmed		84	81	88	87	(340)
Asad I. A. Khan		92	91	90	85	(358)
Total best 3, daily		254	251	253	255	
GUATEMALA	Grand total	264	513	767		1017
Adolfo Rios S.		90	79	82	84	(335)
*Oscar Escobar		96	99	104	94	(393)
Juan Jose Hermosilla		89	83	85	83	(340)
Roberto Cottone		85	87	87	83	(342)
Total best 3, daily		264	249	254	250	
ICELAND	Grand total	262	517	772		1018
Thorbjoern Kjaerbo		84	80	85	92	(341)
Thorarinn B. Jonsson		95	86	94	95	(370)
Johann Benediktsson		93	90	90	95	(368)
Gunniaugur Ragnarsson		85	89	80	89	(343)
Total best 3, daily		262	255	255	276	
*Johann Eyjolfsson						

1972
EIGHTH WORLD AMATEUR TEAM CHAMPIONSHIP
FOR THE EISENHOWER TROPHY

Held at the Olivos Golf Club, Buenos Aires, Argentina, October 18-21.
Yardage—6,684. Par 71. 32 Team Entries.

Team score consists of best three individual scores in each round.
*Indicates Captain

		1st Rd.	2nd Rd.	3rd Rd.	4th Rd.	72-hole Score
UNITED STATES	Grand Total	221	441	651		865
Ben Crenshaw		74	76	69	68	(287)
Marvin M. Giles III		73	73	70	71	(287)
Mark S. Hayes		74	71	71	75	(291)
Martin R. West III		76	76	76	79	(307)
Total best 3, daily		221	220	210	214	
*Wm. Ward Foshay						
AUSTRALIA	Grand Total	215	434	648		870
Michael F. Cahill		74	75	75	76	(300)
Terrence Ross Gale		71	80	68	77	(296)
Anthony Gresham		70	69	73	73	(285)
Noel Anthony Ratcliffe		75	75	73	73	(296)
Total best 3, daily		215	219	214	222	
*Graham Ronald Keane						
SOUTH AFRICA	Grand Total	224	442	656		878
Coen Dreyer		77	72	70	75	(294)
Johann Murray		72	74	72	78	(296)
Kevin Suddards		79	79	74	79	(311)
Neville Sundelson		75	72	72	69	(288)
Total best 3, daily		224	218	214	222	
*Cliff Anderson						
SPAIN	Grand Total	217	437	659		879
Eduardo de la Riva		72	71	72	73	(288)
Jose Gancedo		76	75	75	75	(301)
Nicasio Sagardia		73	74	75	75	(297)
Roman Taya		72	76	78	72	(298)
Total best 3, daily		217	220	222	220	
*Alvaro Alvarez-Alouso						
ARGENTINA	Grand Total	212	437	661		884
Horacio Carbonetti		72	75	76	75	(298)
Luis Angel Daneri		80	76	75	75	(306)
Juan Carlos Devoto		70	74	80	75	(299)
Roberto H. Monguzzi		70	76	73	73	(292)
Total best 3, daily		212	225	224	223	
*Guillermo Ehrman						
NEW ZEALAND	Grand Total	223	441	662		884
Geoffrey E. Clarke		77	76	74	77	(304)
Stuart Gwyn Jones		74	71	76	74	(295)
Edward John McDougall		76	78	72	72	(298)
Ross Cheyne Murray		73	71	75	76	(295)
Total best 3, daily		223	218	221	222	
*John George Slade						
GREAT BRITAIN AND IRELAND	Grand Total	218	439	662		888
*Michael F. Bonallack		71	73	75	76	(295)
Charles W. Green		74	73	73	75	(295)
Trevor W. B. Homer		79	75	78	79	(311)
Hugh B. Stuart		73	75	75	75	(298)
Total best 3, daily		218	221	223	226	

CANADA	Grand Total	221	439	667		889
Keith Alexander		73	79	78	73	(303)
Dave Barr		74	72	75	78	(299)
Doug Roxburgh		75	75	80	73	(303)
Nick Weslock		74	71	75	76	(296)
Total best 3, daily		221	218	228	222	
JAPAN	Grand Total	221	449	673		891
Tsutomu Irie		74	77	74	72	(297)
Tetsuo Sakata		71	76	74	79	(300)
Kasunari Takahashi		77	75	80	76	(308)
Zenjiro Takano		76	78	76	70	(300)
Total best 3, daily		221	228	224	218	
*Naomoto Nabeshima						
FRANCE	Grand Total	222	449	674		903
Alexis Godillot		75	72	78	77	(302)
Roger Lagarde		75	78	73	78	(304)
Philippe Ploujoux		73	77	80	75	(305)
Michel Tapia		74	79	74	77	(304)
Total best 3, daily		222	227	225	229	
*Claude-Roger Cartier						
GERMANY	Grand Total	217	444	673		905
Friedrich C. Jannsen		70	78	76	75	(299)
Jan G. Muller		77	72	77	78	(304)
Veit Pagel		70	77	76	80	(303)
Christian Strenger		79	83	84	79	(325)
Total best 3, daily		217	227	229	232	
*Jan Bruegelmann						
CHINA	Grand Total	228	454	681		907
Chien-Chi Chen		81	79	80	79	(319)
Fa Hung		77	70	75	75	(297)
Tze-Chi Lu		80	82	75	74	(311)
Lung-Tsu Tsai		71	77	77	77	(302)
Total best 3, daily		228	226	227	226	
*George C. Chen						
ITALY	Grand Total	226	453	684		912
Luca Fabrini		78	84	82	77	(321)
Delio Lovato		74	74	73	76	(297)
Alberto Schiaffino		75	76	81	75	(307)
Lorenzo Silva		77	77	77	79	(310)
Total best 3, daily		226	227	231	228	
*Emilio Pallaviccino						
SWEDEN	Grand Total	229	445	683		913
Olle Dahlgren		75	75	73	76	(299)
Claes Johncke		77	79	77	76	(309)
Jan Rube		77	77	80	83	(317)
Mikael Sorling		79	74	78	78	(309)
Total best 3, daily		229	226	228	230	
*Stig-Lennart Alehammar						
BRAZIL	Grand Total	226	464	690		915
Joao Barbosa Correa		82	84	78	80	(324)
Jayme Gonzalez		77	80	75	72	(304)
Ricardo Rossi		76	74	73	76	(299)
Carlos Sozio		73	84	78	77	(312)
Total best 3, daily		226	238	226	225	
*Jesse Rinehart						

CHILE	Grand Total	241	464	692		916
Benjamin Astaburuaga		82	79	84	81	(326)
Mauricio Galeno		81	79	73	75	(308)
Ricardo Orellana		83	71	77	76	(307)
Felipe Taverne		78	73	78	73	(302)
Total best 3, daily		241	223	228	224	
*Francisco Condon						
NETHERLANDS	Grand Total	236	471	700		925
Jaa Van Neck		76	84	78	76	(314)
Teun Roosenburg		85	82	83	87	(337)
Piet Hein Streutgers		83	76	75	73	(307)
Victor Swane		77	77	76	76	(306)
Total best 3, daily		236	235	229	225	
*Richard Rahusen						
BELGIUM	Grand Total	230	460	686		927
Ives Mahaim		80	76	80	86	(322)
Ives Brose		76	83	76	84	(319)
Benoit Dumont		77	78	75	77	(307)
*Freddy Rodesch		77	76	75	80	(308)
Total best 3, daily		230	230	226	241	
MEXICO	Grand Total	229	463	691		927
*Mauricio Urdaneta		76	83	84	80	(323)
Enrique Farias		79	81	77	79	(316)
Carlos A. Perez		77	75	73	78	(303)
Ricardo Vega		76	78	78	79	(311)
Total best 3, daily		229	234	228	236	
PORTUGAL	Grand Total	235	465	700		927
Nuno A. De Brito E Cunha		77	74	79	76	(306)
Jose Lar De Sousa E Melo		76	76	78	72	(302)
Pedro D'Homee Caupers		82	80	78	81	(321)
Ricardo M. Holroyd Soares		88	82	90	79	(339)
Total best 3, daily		235	230	235	227	
*Tito Lagos						
SWITZERLAND	Grand Total	235	466	692		929
Thomas Fortmann		79	77	77	80	(313)
*Peter Gutermann		79	80	82	78	(319)
Yves Hofstetter		83	80	75	82	(320)
Martin Kessler		77	74	74	79	(304)
Total best 3, daily		235	231	226	237	
COLOMBIA	Grand Total	233	457	697		930
Diego Correa		77	75	80	77	(309)
Fernando Arriola		77	77	80	82	(316)
Ricardo Sala		84	80	82	87	(333)
Emilio Sardi		79	72	80	74	(305)
Total best 3, daily		233	224	240	233	
*Jaime C. Leyva						
MALAYSIA	Grand Total	229	462	702		938
K. C. Choo		79	78	86	78	(321)
Jalal Deran		76	80	77	79	(312)
Rashid Mallal		80	81	86	80	(327)
Saad Yusof		74	75	77	79	(305)
Total best 3, daily		229	233	240	236	
*D. J. A. Hamid						
ECUADOR	Grand Total	235	476	718		951
Carlos M. Cobo		89	84	85	80	(338)
Fernando Fiore		74	75	76	75	(300)
Isidro Icaza		77	88	82	78	(325)
Anthony Gittes		84	82	84	80	(330)
Total best 3, daily		235	241	242	233	

PANAMA Grand Total	242	479	717		952
Francisco Arias	77	84	88	83	(332)
Jaime de la Guardia	83	81	79	77	(320)
Leo Dehlinger	82	76	74	77	(309)
Anibal Galindo	83	80	85	81	(329)
Total best 3, daily	242	237	238	235	
*Jose Domingo de la Rosa					
PERU Grand Total	235	479	718		957
Gullermo Gamon	79	81	79	80	(319)
Luis Grana	79	81	78	79	(317)
Hector Loli	80	83	83	80	(326)
Alejandro Morales	77	82	82	80	(321)
Total best 3, daily	235	244	239	239	
*Carlos Ortega					
BERMUDA Grand Total	234	476	716		963
*Brendan J. Ingham	77	79	81	84	(321)
Louis T. Moniz	80	83	82	81	(326)
Keith Pearman	78	80	77	82	(317)
Noel Van Putten	79	83	82	85	(329)
Total best 3, daily	234	242	240	247	
URUGUAY Grand Total	238	482	731		964
Franci Etcheverry Ferber	76	79	82	76	(313)
Pablo Paullier	83	82	84	79	(328)
Victor Paullier	79	88	87	78	(332)
Francisco Vidiella	83	83	83	82	(331)
Total best 3, daily	238	244	249	233	
*Fernando Valdez					
KOREA Grand Total	258	502	740		978
Michael Han	90	82	81	83	(336)
Inbae Kim	90	87	84	80	(341)
Huh Kwansoo	83	77	76	75	(311)
Lee Soon Young	85	85	81	88	(339)
Total best 3, daily	258	244	238	238	
*Kwang Soo Huh					
DOMINICAN REPUBLIC Grand Total	245	498	741		985
Jack Corrie	82	84	79	76	(321)
Luis F. Henriquez	91	88	87	81	(347)
Arturo Pellerano	84	84	78	87	(333)
Salomon Melgen	79	85	86	89	(339)
Total best 3, daily	245	253	243	244	
*Maximo Bonetti					
BAHAMAS Grand Total	253	507	758		1007
Valdo Prosa	85	86	84	87	(342)
*Robert Slatter	84	80	85	82	(331)
Basil Smith	84	88	82	83	(337)
Michael Taylor	85	91	87	84	(347)
Total best 3, daily	253	254	251	249	
EL SALVADOR Grand Total	250	505	759		1021
Guillermo Aceto	87	91	93	87	(358)
Mauricio Alvarez	80	81	78	85	(324)
Henry Daubin	89	90	92	90	(361)
Jaime Munguia	83	84	84	90	(341)
Total best 3, daily	250	255	254	262	
*Francisco Lima					

1974
NINTH WORLD AMATEUR TEAM CHAMPIONSHIP
FOR THE EISENHOWER TROPHY

Held at the Camp de Golf, Cajuiles, La Romana, Dominican Republic, October 30-November 2

Yardage—6,744. Par 72. 35 Team Entries.

*Team Captain

	First Round	Second Round	Third Round	Fourth Round	72-Hole Score
United States Grand Total	224	445	664		888
George F. Burns, III	74	76	70	77	(297)
Gary Koch	79	70	76	76	(301)
Jerome K. Pate	73	77	73	71	(294)
Curtis Strange	77	75	77	77	(306)
Total best 3, daily	224	221	219	224	
*Hord W. Hardin					
Japan	226	452	671		898
Ginjiro Nakabe	83	80	70	76	(309)
Tsutomu Irie	75	77	73	80	(305)
Tetsuo Sakata	78	74	77	81	(310)
Satoshi Yamazaki	73	75	76	71	(295)
Total best 3, daily	226	226	219	227	
*Naomoto Nabeshima					
Brazil	225	454	675		901
Jayme Gonzalez	73	74	74	73	(294)
Jose Diniz	73	80	70	77	(300)
Ricardo Rossi	79	75	77	79	(310)
Rafael Navarro	79	80	86	76	(321)
Total best 3, daily	225	229	221	226	
*Jesse S. Rinehart, Jr.					
South Africa	227	450	675		908
Coen Dreyer	76	75	73	80	(304)
Jeff Hawkes	79	72	79	75	(305)
Robbie Meier	72	76	73	81	(302)
Neville Sundelson	80	79	80	78	(317)
Total best 3, daily	227	223	225	233	
*C. R. Anderson					
Australia	235	466	695		916
Terry Gale	78	75	75	72	(300)
Tony Gresham	78	78	77	75	(308)
Colin Kaye	83	78	77	79	(317)
Phil Wood	79	81	77	74	(311)
Total best 3, daily	235	231	229	221	
*F. J. Foley					
Great Britain and Ireland	227	460	688		922
John Davies	75	80	74	78	(307)
Richard Eyeles	78	78	77	77	(310)
Peter J. Hedges	74	84	77	83	(318)
Ian C. Hutcheon	78	75	78	79	(310)
Total best 3, daily	227	233	228	234	
*J. J. F. Pennink					
China	243	470	698		928
Ter-Kuei Chang	84	77	76	77	(314)
Tje-Ming Cheng	76	80	84	73	(313)
Wen-Nung Hung	83	73	73	80	(309)
Kuo-Chih, Charles Liao	84	77	79	84	(324)
Total best 3, daily	243	227	228	230	
*Wei-Hsiang Lu					
Argentina	239	466	697		931
Horacio Carbonetti	79	74	76	82	(311)
Juan Devoto	78	79	76	78	(311)
Jorge Ledesma	82	83	79	80	(324)
Roberto Monguzzi	84	74	80	76	(314)
Total best 3, daily	239	227	231	234	
*Adolfo B. Cambiaso					

	First Round	Second Round	Third Round	Fourth Round	72-Hole Score
Canada Grand Total	238	477	701		932
Douglas Roxburgh	84	78	72	73	(307)
Kenneth Doig	82	82	85	83	(332)
Bruce Brewer	79	82	77	78	(316)
Pierre Archambault	77	79	75	80	(311)
Total best 3, daily	238	239	224	231	
*Bruce Forbes					
France	245	475	710		936
Patrick Cotton	82	78	79	77	(316)
Alexis Godillot	79	79	81	75	(314)
George Leven	84	74	78	80	(316)
Philippe Ploujoux	86	78	78	74	(316)
Total best 3, daily	245	230	235	226	
*Roger Lagarde					
Sweden	237	471	706		936
Olle Dahalgren	78	80	79	78	(315)
Hans Hedjerson	80	76	78	74	(308)
Goran Lundqvist	83	80	81	84	(328)
Jan Rube	79	78	78	78	(313)
Total best 3, daily	237	234	235	230	
*Magnus Lindberg					
Germany	242	474	705		939
Veit Pagel	80	76	76	74	(306)
Uwe Nievert	87	82	78	80	(327)
Christoph Stadler	81	77	77	80	(315)
Peter Jochums	81	79	81	85	(326)
Total best 3, daily	242	232	231	234	
*Jan Brugelmann					
Spain	237	479	708		941
Jose Gancedo	76	77	76	78	(307)
Nicasio Sagardia	88	88	80	77	(333)
Eduardo de la Riva	80	77	74	78	(309)
Roman Taya	81	88	79	82	(330)
Total best 3, daily	237	242	229	233	
*Alvaro Alvarez-Alonso					
Rhodesia	247	480	708		942
George Howard Harvey	84	80	76	81	(321)
Mark William McNulty	83	76	86	77	(322)
Denis Leslie Watson	80	80	75	76	(311)
Edward Arthur Webber	85	77	77	81	(320)
Total best 3, daily	247	233	228	234	
*Gerald F. Taylor					
New Zealand	241	478	714		947
Richard Coombes	80	81	78	78	(317)
Edward McDougall	81	78	78	79	(316)
Ross Murray	82	79	80	78	(319)
Michael Nicholson	80	80	86	77	(323)
Total best 3, daily	241	237	236	233	
*Kenneth Stephen					
Venezuela	241	484	720		956
Gustavo Larrazabal	81	84	75	77	(317)
Carlos Plaza	79	78	83	80	(320)
Jonathan Coles	81	81	78	79	(319)
Carlos Whaite	83	93	84	85	(345)
Total best 3, daily	241	243	236	236	
*Freddy Alcantara					
Switzerland	245	487	720		959
Ives Hofstetter	82	84	80	77	(323)
Martin Kessler	83	79	76	82	(320)
Michel Rey	87	83	85	80	(335)
Johnny Storjohann	80	80	77	83	(320)
Total best 3, daily	245	242	233	239	
*Gregory Trippi					

	First Round	Second Round	Third Round	Fourth Round	72-Hole Score
Italy Grand Total	240	481	713		960
G. Sita	83	80	78	92	(333)
Antonio Lionello	80	87	79	86	(332)
Lorenzo Silva	80	81	76	80	(317)
Massimo Mannelli	80	80	78	81	(319)
Total best 3, daily	240	241	232	247	
Papua New Guinea	245	479	710		961
John Keating	81	80	82	81	(324)
Wayne Brittain	86	86	75	92	(339)
Greg Fennell	83	77	79	87	(326)
Tony Gover	81	77	77	83	(318)
Total best 3, daily	245	234	231	251	
*D. A. Hutchinson					
Mexico	248	479	719		962
Jose Ortega	81	92	80	82	(335)
Tomas Lehman	83	79	80	80	(322)
Oscar Fernandez	88	75	82	81	(326)
Rafael Fajer	84	77	80	82	(323)
Total best 3, daily	248	231	240	243	
*Mauricio Urdaneta					
Netherlands	248	487	731		964
Victor Swane	88	83	84	72	(327)
J. J. Van Neck	83	84	83	82	(332)
T. Trienen	84	78	78	80	(320)
Carel Braun	81	78	83	81	(323)
Total best 3, daily	248	239	244	233	
*W. E. L. Mangelaar Meertens					
Chile	250	494	732		969
Mauricio Galeno	84	86	85	86	(341)
Felipe Taverne	84	80	76	73	(313)
Edmund Grasty	83	83	77	82	(325)
Roberto Desmaras	83	81	85	82	(331)
Total best 3, daily	250	244	238	237	
*Francisco Condon					
Belgium	242	481	727		970
*Freddy Rodesch	82	84	81	86	(333)
Benoit Dumont	85	80	85	79	(329)
John Bigwood	80	81	88	85	(334)
E. Boyer	80	78	80	79	(317)
Total best 3, daily	242	239	246	243	
Colombia	250	494	729		980
Fernando Sanchez	82	82	77	85	(326)
Alberto Evers	85	79	89	84	(337)
*Gustavo Giraldo	83	83	73	82	(321)
Alfonso Linares	90	85	85	86	(346)
Total best 3, daily	250	244	235	251	
Korea	250	497	749		985
*Won Taek Park	89	90	86	85	(350)
Young Chang Kim	79	82	81	77	(319)
Il Keun Kim	82	83	87	78	(330)
Mee Rang Kim	93	82	85	81	(341)
Total best 3, daily	250	247	252	236	
Panama	251	500	746		988
Leo Dehlinger	84	77	78	78	(317)
Francisco Arias	86	86	83	76	(331)
Anibal Galindo	81	86	85	88	(340)
*Antonio de Janon	95	91	96	D	(282)
Total best 3, daily	251	249	246	242	

	First Round	Second Round	Third Round	Fourth Round	72-Hole Score
Ecuador Grand Total	260	505	739		989
Fernando Fiore	81	73	76	86	(316)
Isidro Ycaza	94	85	89	82	(350)
Danilo Murtinho	87	90	77	87	(341)
Joe Monge	92	85	83	82	(342)
Total best 3, daily	260	243	236	250	
*Rafael Miranda					
Jamaica	244	498	742		990
Stafford Demercado	86	87	84	89	(346)
Herman McDonald	87	86	85	90	(348)
Ian Sturdy	77	83	85	85	(330)
Bill Ward	81	85	75	74	(315)
Total best 3, daily	244	254	244	248	
Norway	255	501	745		990
*Westye Hoegh	85	93	84	80	(342)
Petter Donnestad	84	80	81	83	(328)
Asbjorn Ramnefjell	88	84	85	82	(339)
Alexander Vik	86	82	79	83	(330)
Total best 3, daily	255	246	244	245	
Dominican Republic	257	507	753		998
Luis Henriquez	85	88	82	88	(343)
Jack Corrie	79	82	80	84	(321)
Luis Hernandez	96	85	87	84	(352)
Ramon Baez, Jr.	93	83	84	77	(337)
Total best 3, daily	257	250	246	245	
*Maximo Pellerano					
Puerto Rico	244	495	748		1,003
Butch James	82	83	84	88	(337)
Victor Morales	79	85	84	79	(327)
Welby Van Horn	97	92	85	88	(362)
*James Teale	83	83	90	91	(347)
Total best 3, daily	244	251	253	255	
Bermuda	250	496	751		1,004
*Brendan Ingham	85	88	85	83	(341)
Bill Pitt	81	79	86	86	(332)
Louis Moniz	87	80	84	84	(335)
Noel Van Putten	84	87	86	87	(344)
Total best 3, daily	250	246	255	253	
Bahamas	261	509	779		1,046
Mike Taylor	82	82	87	88	(339)
J. Moree	95	88	95	90	(368)
Brendan Lynch	96	85	94	91	(366)
Valdo Prosa	84	81	89	89	(343)
Total best 3, daily	261	248	270	267	
*Fred Higgs					
Iceland	288	578	846		1,109
T. Kjaerbo	96	91	88	94	(369)
J. Holton	103	99	97	89	(388)
J. Benediktsson	95	103	93	88	(379)
E. Gudnason	97	100	87	86	(370)
Total best 3, daily	288	290	268	263	
*K. Bjarnason					
El Salvador	282	570	844		1,126
Mauricio Alvarez	91	97	98	85	(371)
Jose Duran	98	101	88	101	(388)
Guillermo Aceto	93	90	88	96	(367)
Total best 3, daily	282	288	274	282	
*Gustavo Longoria					

1976
TENTH WORLD AMATEUR TEAM CHAMPIONSHIP
FOR THE EISENHOWER TROPHY

Held at the Penina Golf Club, Portimao, Algarve, Portugal, October 13-16

Yardage—6,940. Par 73. 38 Team Entries

*Team Captain

	First Round	Second Round	Third Round	Fourth Round	72-Hole Score
Great Britain and Ireland Grand Total	219	443	668		892
John C. Davies	74	75	76	77	(302)
Ian C. Hutcheon	73	73	76	71	(293)
M. J. Kelly	72	76	75	78	(301)
Steve Martin	75	78	74	76	(303)
Total best 3, daily	219	224	225	224	
*Sandy Sadler					
Japan	227	447	670		894
Ginjiro Nakabe	80	74	80	73	(307)
Micho Mori	76	76	77	78	(307)
Tetsuo Sakata	76	75	71	83	(305)
Masahiro Kuramoto	75	71	75	73	(294)
Total best 3, daily	227	220	223	224	
*Noamoto Nabeshima					
Australia	230	450	670		897
Chris Bonython	75	79	83	78	(315)
*Tony Gresham	79	78	70	77	(304)
Colin Kaye	84	72	74	80	(310)
Phil Wood	76	70	76	72	(294)
Total best 3, daily	230	220	220	227	
Republic of China	229	450	673		898
C. C. Chen	79	76	79	83	(317)
H. C. Lu	79	76	77	75	(307)
C. S. Shen	75	80	73	74	(302)
T. M. Chen	75	69	73	76	(293)
Total best 3, daily	229	221	223	225	
*Wei-Hsiang Lu					
United States	224	453	670		901
John Fought	72	73	76	78	(299)
Fred S. Ridley	74	77	70	77	(298)
Bill Sander	78	79	75	80	(312)
Richard L. Siderowf	78	80	72	76	(306)
Total best 3, daily	224	229	217	231	
*Philip H. Strubing					
Canada	227	453	678		906
Keith Alexander	75	72	75	75	(297)
Rob Jackson	80	81	77	77	(315)
Jim Nelford	77	77	73	76	(303)
Doug Roxburg	75	77	79	78	(309)
Total best 3, daily	227	226	225	228	
*R. Bruce Forbes					
Sweden	223	452	684		911
Hans Hedjerson	73	80	78	72	(303)
Jan Rube	75	71	81	77	(304)
Goran Lundquist	75	84	76	80	(315)
Michael Sorling	79	78	78	78	(313)
Total best 3, daily	223	229	232	227	
*Magnus Lindberg					
South Africa	219	443	682		912
G. N. Levenson	73	73	80	77	(303)
David Suddards	71	74	83	77	(305)
R. Stewart	75	77	77	82	(311)
P. M. Todt	77	80	82	76	(315)
Total best 3, daily	219	224	239	230	
*W. M. Kerr					
Rhodesia	223	451	677		914
George Harvey	79	78	81	80	(318)
Anthony Johnstone	80	83	77	83	(323)
Nicky Price	73	74	73	82	(302)
Teddy Webber	71	76	76	75	(298)
Total best 3, daily	223	228	226	237	
*Dick Cahi					

	First Round	Second Round	Third Round	Fourth Round	72-Hole Score
Switzerland Grand Total	226	453	680		914
Michael Rey	73	73	75	78	(299)
Yves Hofstetter	79	78	82	75	(314)
Tommy Fortmann	74	76	76	81	(307)
Johnny Storjohan	84	81	76	84	(325)
Total best 3, daily	226	227	227	234	
*Ruedi Muller					
Argentina	230	460	690		922
Horacio Carbonetti	72	79	78	77	(306)
Luis Carbonetti	79	77	77	78	(311)
Roberto H. Monguzzi	79	74	75	77	(305)
Jorge M. Ocampo	87	86	80	81	(334)
Total best 3, daily	230	230	230	232	
*Jorge Ledesma					
New Zealand	224	457	685		923
Alex N. Bonnington	76	79	77	83	(315)
Peter M. Burney	76	80	77	84	(317)
Geoffrey E. Clarke	74	74	78	76	(302)
Edward J. McDougall	74	80	74	79	(307)
Total best 3, daily	224	233	228	238	
*John G. Slade					
France	230	464	697		930
Thierry Planchin	74	85	83	81	(323)
Alexis Godillot	79	75	81	80	(315)
Philippe Ploujoux	77	79	74	77	(307)
Patrick Lemaire	89	80	78	76	(323)
Total best 3, daily	230	234	233	233	
*Hubert Chesneau					
Mexico	235	471	706		935
Rafael Alarcon	77	74	81	81	(313)
Juan A. Estrado	84	79	80	78	(321)
Roberto Lebrija	79	84	82	75	(320)
Jose Martinez	79	83	74	76	(312)
Total best 3, daily	235	236	235	229	
*Ricardo Alarcon					
Spain	233	469	707		937
Jose Gancedo	80	78	84	81	(323)
Santiago Fernandez	80	78	84	79	(321)
Eduardo de la Riva	75	80	76	72	(303)
Roman Taya	78	95	78	79	(330)
Total best 3, daily	233	236	238	230	
*Alvaro Alvarez Alonso					
Brazil	235	469	700		939
Jamie Gonzales	77	78	70	76	(301)
Jose Priscillo G. Diniz	77	77	81	81	(316)
Ricardo R. Rossi	81	81	80	85	(327)
Rafael Navarro	83	79	84	82	(328)
Total best 3, daily	235	234	231	239	
*J. S. Rinehart, Jr.					
Chile	237	475	707		941
Felipe Taverne	83	79	78	76	(316)
Michael Grasty	79	77	76	82	(314)
Ricardo Orellana	78	82	81	76	(317)
Thomas Boetigger	80	82	78	86	(326)
Total best 3, daily	237	238	232	234	
*Humberto Magliochetti					
Italy	242	477	709		944
Stefano Betti	77	79	76	81	(313)
Massimo Mannelli	84	79	79	78	(320)
Guiseppe Sita	86	81	89	79	(335)
Lorenzo Silva	81	77	77	78	(313)
Total best 3, daily	242	235	232	235	
*Pierro Cora					
Papau-New Guinea	239	476	713		944
*John Keating	83	81	82	88	(334)
Greg Fennell	77	77	79	72	(305)
Tony Gover	81	79	76	79	(315)
Phillip Frame	81	84	84	80	(329)
Total best 3, daily	239	237	237	231	

	First Round	Second Round	Third Round	Fourth Round	72-Hole Score
Denmark Grand Total	238	475	708		946
Lars Jacobsen	80	77	80	81	(318)
Henry Knudsen	81	79	77	77	(314)
Ryan Olsen	77	81	78	83	(319)
Ole Wiberg	83	82	78	80	(323)
Total best 3, daily	238	237	233	238	
*Erik Staerk					
Korea	236	474	713		947
*Yung Chang Kim	76	79	76	80	(311)
Mi Rank Kim	78	78	80	77	(313)
Chang Whan Cho	89	81	92	79	(341)
Chong Min Lee	82	84	83	78	(327)
Total best 3, daily	236	238	239	234	
Norway	231	467	702		947
Per Berge	83	82	81	81	(327)
Petter Donnestad	83	75	86	85	(329)
Asbjorn Ramnefjell	75	83	78	83	(319)
Alexander M. Vik	73	79	76	81	(309)
Total best 3, daily	231	236	235	245	
*Aksel Gresvig					
Germany	235	465	711		949
Jan G. Muller	83	75	83	78	(319)
Veit Pagel	80	79	81	79	(319)
Christoph Stadler	78	77	82	81	(318)
Christian Strenger	77	78	83	85	(323)
Total best 3, daily	235	230	246	238	
*Jan Brugelmann					
Malaysia	241	474	710		950
Eshak Bluah	81	77	77	84	(319)
Nazamuddin Yusof	83	83	81	84	(331)
Sahabuddin Yusof	86	79	82	77	(234)
Tan Yee Khan	77	77	78	79	(311)
Total best 3, daily	241	233	236	240	
*D. J. A. Hamid					
Belgium	231	473	713		955
F. Rodesch	78	78	79	80	(315)
J. Rolin	84	83	82	84	(333)
Benoit Dumont	78	84	85	83	(330)
Y. Mahaim	75	81	79	79	(314)
Total best 3, daily	231	242	240	242	
*P. Rolin					
Finland	243	478	720		964
*Patrik Hallamaa	85	80	81	83	(329)
Harry Safonoff	86	82	87	92	(347)
Kary Salonen	74	75	80	81	(310)
Timo Sipponen	84	80	81	80	(325)
Total best 3, daily	243	235	242	244	
Austria	238	480	724		964
Max Lamberg	76	78	83	77	(314)
Franz Laimer	89	86	86	83	(344)
Klaus Nierlich	76	80	75	80	(311)
Florian Stolz	86	84	92	87	(349)
Total best 3, daily	238	242	244	240	
*Gunther Jungk					
Netherlands	241	486	730		966
C. A. Braun	79	82	79	84	(324)
V. van Dam	81	82	87	91	(341)
J. J. van Neck	83	85	84	77	(329)
V. C. Swane	81	81	81	75	(318)
Total best 3, daily	241	245	244	236	
*R. E. Van Erven Dorens					
Bermuda	242	482	723		974
*Brendan J. Ingham	78	80	87	82	(327)
Louiz Monoz	90	83	82	88	(343)
Hav Trott	79	79	78	84	(320)
R. Blake Marshall	85	81	81	85	(332)
Total best 3, daily	242	240	241	251	

		First Round	Second Round	Third Round	Fourth Round	72-Hole Score
Venezuela	Grand Total	241	488	731		974
*Jonathan Coles		82	82	86	81	(331)
Gustavo Larrazabal		79	85	80	82	(326)
Carlos Whaite		80	81	82	94	(337)
Luiz E. Plaza		83	84	81	80	(328)
Total best 3, daily		241	247	243	243	
Portugal		248	489	734		977
Nuno A. Brito e Cunha		84	78	82	77	(321)
Jose Sousa e Melo		82	82	78	86	(328)
Jorge Soares		87	94	90	87	(358)
Pedro Caupers		82	81	85	80	(328)
Total best 3, daily		248	241	245	243	
*Fernando Costa Cabral						
Israel		248	500	750		1002
Laurie Been		80	78	84	74	(316)
Barry Mandel		80	86	86	92	(344)
Neil Shochet		92	91	95	86	(364)
Jonathan Eting		88	88	80	93	(349)
Total best 3, daily		248	252	250	252	
*Michael Ossip						
Dominican Republic		248	508	760		1011
Edwin A. Corrie		82	88	83	84	(337)
Luiz F. Henriquez		80	84	85	81	(330)
Salomon Melgen		87	88	84	86	(345)
Jose B. Lahoz		86	95	88	94	(363)
Total best 3, daily		248	260	252	251	
*Bernardo E. Pichardo						
Sri Lanka		265	515	763		1020
F. E. Captain		90	83	84	89	(346)
W. J. Barsenbach		88	85	82	88	(343)
Dr. C. Thural Rahaj		92	92	82	86	(352)
*W. P. Fernando		87	82	87	83	(339)
Total best 3, daily		265	250	248	257	
Bahamas		254	519	789		1042
Bob Slatter		85	93	86	85	(349)
Brendan Lynch		99	87	90	86	(362)
*Michael Taylor		89	87	94	82	(352)
Basil Smith		80	91	99	102	(372)
Total best 3, daily		254	265	270	253	
El Salvador		256	522	785		1047
Guillermo Aceto M.		96	93	104	100	(393)
*Jose Maria Duran		93	98	89	86	(366)
Mauricio Alvarez		81	88	83	88	(340)
Carlos M. Gurdian		82	85	91	88	(346)
Total best 3, daily		256	266	263	262	
Costa Rica		256	528	797		1078
Ramon Jimenez		80	94	82	97	(353)
Xavier Gonzalez		83	84	91	93	(351)
Arturo Montealegre		93	94	96	91	(374)
Enrique Herrero		96	106	99	99	(400)
Total best 3, daily		256	272	269	281	
*Alfonso Filloy						
Puerto Rico		274	555	815		1079
Fred Thon		94	95	85	87	(361)
*James Teale		92	95	86	90	(363)
Joe Passarel		91	94	89	87	(361)
Carlos Bolivar		91	92	97	96	(376)
Total best 3, daily		274	281	260	264	

1978
ELEVENTH WORLD AMATEUR TEAM CHAMPIONSHIP
FOR THE EISENHOWER TROPHY

Held at the Pacific Harbour Golf and Country Club, Fiji, October 18-21.

Yardage—6,317. Par 72. 24 Team Entries.

*Team Captain	First Round	Second Round	Third Round	Fourth Round	72-Hole Score
United States Grand Total	213	433	652		873
Bob Clampett	69	71	71	76	(287)
John Cook	75	73	73	72	(293)
Scott Hoch	70	76	75	73	(294)
Jay Sigel	74	81	75	76	(306)
Total best 3, daily	213	220	219	221	
*Harton S. Semple					
Canada	222	444	669		886
Gary Cowan	73	71	77	71	(292)
David Mick	77	77	76	77	(307)
Doug Roxburgh	72	74	74	69	(289)
Yves Tremblay	78	82	75	78	(313)
Total best 3, daily	222	222	225	217	
*Geordie R. Hilton					
Australia	222	445	669		891
Christopher Bonython	75	82	81	77	(315)
Anthony Gresham	75	75	77	71	(298)
Peter Sweeney	76	73	71	74	(294)
Philip Wood	72	75	76	77	(300)
Total best 3, daily	222	223	224	222	
*Neil Titheridge					
New Zealand	227	446	675		895
Geoffrey Clarke	71	76	72	71	(290)
Paul Hartstone	80	73	81	77	(311)
Phillip Mosley	76	70	81	72	(299)
Frank Nobilo	80	84	76	77	(317)
Total best 3, daily	227	219	229	220	
*Brian Mahar					
Sweden	221	451	679		914
Goran Lundqvist	76	75	77	82	(310)
Jan Rube	77	79	79	75	(310)
Mikael Sorling	70	76	75	78	(299)
Bjorn Svedin	75	81	76	82	(314)
Total best 3, daily	221	230	228	235	
*Magnus Lindberg					
Great Britain and Ireland	221	450	688		919
Gordon Brand	77	74	83	80	(314)
Allan Brodie	76	79	78	78	(311)
Brian Marchbank	72	77	80	79	(308)
Peter McEvoy	73	78	80	74	(305)
Total best 3, daily	221	229	238	231	
*Sandy Saddler					
France	230	466	702		923
Francois Illouz	75	79	80	74	(308)
Jean Mouhica	81	85	83	84	(333)
Thierry Planchin	81	80	79	73	(313)
Philippe Ploujoux	74	77	77	74	(302)
Total best 3, daily	230	236	236	221	
*Hubert Chesneau					
Germany	231	471	700		933
Kai Flint	93	81	79	81	(334)
Thomas Hubner	80	83	78	77	(318)
Veit Pagel	79	78	83	89	(329)
Christian Strenger	72	81	72	75	(300)
Total best 3, daily	231	240	229	233	
*Harry Cotterell					

	First Round	Second Round	Third Round	Fourth Round	72-Hole Score
Japan Grand Total	235	461	703		935
*Ginjiro Nakabe	78	76	85	77	(316)
Tetsuo Sakata	78	75	85	78	(316)
Funimori Sano	79	82	80	84	(325)
Masao Shioda	80	75	77	77	(309)
Total best 3, daily	235	226	242	232	
Italy	235	474	705		944
Franco Gigliarelli	83	74	76	83	(316)
Antonio Lionello	80	78	77	81	(316)
Alberto Schiaffino	73	87	85	78	(323)
Lorenzo Silva	82	88	78	80	(328)
Total best 3, daily	235	239	231	239	
*Giuseppe Sabini					
Spain	238	475	713		944
Gonzaga Escauriaza	80	85	80	84	(329)
Nicasio Sagardia	82	80	80	75	(317)
*Roman Taya	76	77	80	75	(308)
Alfonso Vidaor	82	80	78	81	(321)
Total best 3, daily	238	237	238	231	
Switzerland	235	475	711		945
Francis Boillat	78	82	77	78	(315)
Markus Frank	75	87	81	78	(321)
Yves Hofstetter	82	79	85	80	(326)
Johnny Storjohann	82	79	78	78	(317)
Total best 3, daily	235	240	236	234	
*Ruedi Muller					
Argentina	245	486	719		949
Luis Carbonetti	80	82	78	78	(318)
Luis Daneri	83	77	87	75	(322)
Jorge Eiras	82	82	75	77	(316)
Oscar Vetere	83	85	80	79	(327)
Total best 3, daily	245	241	233	230	
*Jorge C. Ledesma					
India	239	484	729		958
*P. G. Sethi	80	79	81	77	(317)
Alan Singh	81	85	84	75	(325)
Lakshman Singh	78	81	80	77	(316)
Vikramjit Singh	85	86	86	86	(343)
Total best 3, daily	239	245	245	229	
Papua New Guinea	246	488	723		960
Greg Fennell	81	80	72	73	(306)
P. Giles	82	85	87	88	(342)
*John Keating	83	77	83	80	(323)
J. Wu	86	88	80	84	(338)
Total best 3, daily	246	242	235	237	
Netherlands	239	489	723		963
Bart Nolte	82	83	81	85	(331)
Victor Swane	81	85	74	84	(324)
Jaap Van Neck	78	82	79	80	(319)
Barend Van Dam	80	87	82	76	(325)
Total best 3, daily	239	250	234	240	
*Robert Van Erven Dorens					
Austria	239	491	731		969
*Klaus Nierlich	72	83	78	83	(326)
Rudi Bondenseer	85	87	83	87	(342)
Johann Lamberg	82	85	86	76	(329)
Max Lamberg	87	84	79	79	(329)
Total best 3, daily	239	252	240	238	

	First Round	Second Round	Third Round	Fourth Round	72-Hole Score
Bermuda Grand Total	238	481	724		969
*Llewellyn Tucker	87	89	76	87	(339)
Luis Moniz	82	85	85	79	(331)
Kim Swan	77	77	88	79	(321)
Hav Trott	79	81	82	91	(333)
Total best 3, daily	238	243	243	245	
Brazil	247	491	727		972
Roberto Gomez	84	94	80	84	(342)
Rafael Gonzalez	87	80	80	81	(328)
Marco Ruberti	85	82	76	85	(328)
Marcello Stallone	78	82	80	80	(320)
Total best 3, daily	247	244	236	245	
*Jesse S. Rinehart, Jr.					
Belgium	243	494	739		980
Benoit Dumont	84	83	86	77	(330)
Bruno Dupont	77	84	83	82	(326)
Thierry Goossens	82	84	79	82	(327)
*Philippe Relecom	88	86	83	82	(339)
Total best 3, daily	243	251	245	241	
Thailand	249	494	742		982
Tamsak Ansusinha	87	81	84	78	(330)
*Pratuang Nop-Ubol	86	82	80	82	(330)
Santa Pestonji	85	82	91	80	(338)
Thongplew Rungsang	78	82	84	85	(329)
Total best 3, daily	249	245	248	240	
Fiji	252	502	745		985
Rahim Buksh	91	87	85	87	(350)
Raymond Fisher	81	83	87	84	(335)
Rafiq Mohammed	86	85	82	80	(333)
Eremasi Lutunatabua	85	82	76	76	(319)
Total best 3, daily	252	250	243	240	
*Reginald John Woodman					
Hong Kong	254	497	737		986
David Chan	98	84	85	86	(353)
Mark Chow	80	81	81	86	(328)
Yau Tak	87	78	83	80	(328)
Alex Tang	87	84	76	83	(330)
Total best 3, daily	254	243	240	249	
*Gordon Macwhinnie					
Korea	254	508	753		1001
*Chang Hwan Cho	83	91	86	86	(346)
Byong Hoon Kim	84	77	76	77	(314)
Dae Soon Kim	87	86	83	85	(341)
Total best 3, daily	254	254	245	248	

1980
TWELFTH WORLD AMATEUR TEAM CHAMPIONSHIP
FOR THE EISENHOWER TROPHY

Held at Pinehurst Country Club (No. 2 Course), Pinehurst, North Carolina, October 8-11
Yardage—6,960, Par 72. 39 Team Entries

*Team Captain		1st Rd.	2nd Rd.	3rd Rd.	4th Rd.	72-Hole Score
UNITED STATES	Grand total		422	639		848
Jim Holtgrieve		72	71	72	70	(285)
Jay Sigel		71	71	75	77	(294)
Hal Sutton		68	69	71	68	(276)
Robert R. Tway, IV		72	71	74	71	(288)
Total best 3, Daily		211	211	217	209	
*Harry W. Easterly, Jr.						
SOUTH AFRICA	Grand total		435	653		875
E. Groenewald		74	75	73	76	(298)
D. Lindsay-Smith		73	71	74	80	(298)
Wayne Player		72	73	77	76	(298)
D. Suddards		79	72	71	70	(292)
Total best 3, Daily		219	216	218	222	
*C. Sampson						
REPUBLIC OF CHINA	Grand total		440	661		884
Dong-Liang Chang		81	74	78	78	(311)
Tze-Chung Chen		69	70	71	72	(282)
Chun-Lung Wu		76	86	79	81	(322)
Ching-Chi Yuan		74	77	72	73	(296)
Total best 3, Daily		219	221	221	223	
*Gen. Wei-Hsiang Lu						
JAPAN	Grand total		442	667		887
*Tetsuo Sakata		73	70	76	72	(291)
Tatsuhiko Asakawa		77	77	79	74	(307)
Masayuki Naito		73	72	73	74	(292)
Fuminori Sano		79	77	76	78	(310)
Total best 3, Daily		223	219	225	220	
AUSTRALIA	Grand total		456	669		890
A.Y. Gresham		77	77	71	72	(297)
J.A. Kelly		80	80	73	76	(309)
J.L. Senior		79	74	80	77	(310)
P.J. Sweeney		75	74	69	73	(291)
Total best 3, Daily		231	225	213	221	
*J.R. Higson						
CANADA	Grand total		442	667		890
Graham Cooke		74	77	77	78	(306)
Stu Hamilton		76	79	74	72	(301)
Greg Olson		78	70	74	75	(297)
Richard Zokol		71	74	80	76	(301)
Total best 3, Daily		221	221	225	223	
*Geordie Hilton						
GREAT BRITAIN AND IRELAND	Grand total		446	667		890
Gordon Brand		80	74	79	76	(309)
Ian Hutcheon		77	74	71	77	(299)
Peter McEvoy		82	73	79	74	(308)
Roman Rafferty		72	70	71	73	(286)
Total best 3, Daily		229	217	221	223	
*Rodney Foster						
SWEDEN	Grand total		451	674		894
Per Anderson		76	74	75	76	(301)
Anders Johnsson		72	75	75	71	(293)
Goeran Lundqvist		82	74	82	75	(313)
Jan Rube		84	73	73	74	(304)
Total best 3, Daily		230	221	223	220	
*Jan Blomqvist						
MEXICO	Grand total		445	673		899
Rafael Alarcon		73	77	78	78	(306)
Ignacio de Leon		72	75	84	74	(305)
Jose Martinez		79	72	73	81	(305)
Carlos Pelaez		76	80	77	74	(307)
Total best 3, Daily		221	224	228	226	
*Jose Gomez Canibe						
NEW ZEALAND	Grand total		455	670		902
Michael E. Barltrop		80	75	71	75	(301)
Geoffrey E. Clarke		77	78	72	80	(307)
Paul E.Hartstone		77	74	75	77	(303)
Colin E. Taylor		75	77	72	86	(310)
Total best 3, Daily		229	226	215	232	
*J. Barry Forrest						

TWELFTH WORLD AMATEUR TEAM CHAMPIONSHIP (Continued)

SPAIN Grand total		454	678		904
Eduardo de Lariva	77	70	72	75	(294)
Jesus L. Moreno	77	82	74	78	(311)
Roman Taya	84	79	78	83	(324)
Alfonso Vidaor	76	75	80	73	(304)
Total best 3, Daily	230	224	224	226	
*Luis Sartorius					
ARGENTINA Grand total		459	686		917
Jorge de Ascuenago	83	80	78	76	(317)
Augusto M. Bruchman	78	80	79	83	(320)
Luis G. Carbonetti	77	76	74	76	(303)
Miguel Prado	72	76	75	79	(302)
Total best 3, Daily	227	232	227	231	
*Ivar Brostrom					
ITALY Grand total		455	686		917
Andrea Canessa	78	73	75	76	(302)
Marco Durante	77	76	77	79	(309)
Antonio Lionello	77	74	79	76	(306)
Lorenzo Silva	79	78	79	79	(315)
Total best 3, Daily	232	223	231	231	
*Stefano Cimatti					
PHILIPPINES Grand total		461	692		923
Guillermo Ababa, Jr.	74	78	79	80	(311)
Eduardo Bagtas	78	76	76	80	(310)
Tomas Manotoc	77	79	79	77	(312)
Francisco Minoza	78	78	76	74	(306)
Total best 3, Daily	229	232	231	231	
*Teodoro Lovina					
BRAZIL Grand total		461	689		924
Carlos H. Dluhosch	72	80	77	80	(309)
Roberto T. Gomez	80	76	82	78	(316)
J. Rafael Gonzalez	78	79	72	77	(306)
Ricardo R. Rossi	83	76	79	87	(325)
Total best 3, Daily	230	231	228	235	
*Jesse S. Rinehart, Jr.					
GERMANY Grand total		466	686		924
Hans G. Reiter	81	76	77	78	(312)
Ulrich Schulte	75	77	71	79	(302)
Christoph Stadler	81	77	72	81	(311)
Ralf Thielemann	80	77	80	83	(320)
Total best 3, Daily	236	230	220	238	
*Jan Brugelmann					
FRANCE		462	691		926
Herve Frayssineau Grand total	74	77	76	81	(308)
Alexis Goddillot	79	79	77	74	(309)
Francoise Illouz	84	86	87	82	(328)
Thierry Planchin	76	77	78	80	(311)
Total best 3, Daily	229	233	229	235	
*Jean-Louis Dupont					
COLUMBIA Grand total		469	694		927
Albert Evers	83	78	74	82	(317)
Jorge Luis Herrera	81	80	76	77	(314)
Ivan Renjifo	78	76	81	80	(315)
Richardo Ronderos	81	75	75	76	(307)
Total best 3, Daily	240	229	225	233	
*Enrique Samper					
KOREA Grand total		468	695		929
*Byong Hoon Kim	70	80	81	79	(310)
Joo Heun Kim	75	79	68	75	(297)
Myon Kim	78	88	78	81	(325)
Kyong Chul Park	87	86	85	80	(338)
Total best 3, Daily	223	245	227	234	
CHILE Grand total		469	703		935
Sebastian Aninat	86	81	77	85	(329)
Benjamin Astaburuaga	83	84	81	82	(330)
A. Morales	78	79	80	75	(312)
Felipe Taverne	75	73	77	75	(300)
Total best 3, Daily	236	233	234	232	
*Francisco Reutter					
INDIA Grand total		461	694		935
*P. G. Sethi	80	77	79	82	(318)
A.S. Malik	79	79	77	77	(312)
Laksham Singh	77	75	77	83	(312)
Vikramjit Singh	79	74	81	82	(316)
Total best 3, Daily	235	226	233	241	

TWELFTH WORLD AMATEUR TEAM CHAMPIONSHIP (Continued)

NETHERLANDS Grand total		465	699		935
Carel Braum	83	83	82	81	(329)
Erik Hertzberger	76	81	81	85	(323)
Bart Nolte	79	73	74	76	(302)
Jaap Van Neck	78	78	79	79	(314)
Total best 3, Daily	233	232	234	236	
*Anton Frederick Knappert					
SWITZERLAND Grand total		473	702		935
C.A. Bagnoud	83	83	76	80	(322)
Ivan Couturier	88	76	79	83	(326)
Carlo Rampone	79	79	78	74	(310)
Johnny Storjohann	79	77	75	79	(310)
Total best 3, Daily	241	232	229	233	
*Ruedi Muller					
ZIMBABWE Grand total		473	703		935
Tony Hatchwell	83	78	83	79	(323)
Hennie Heyns	80	80	78	82	(320)
John Pritchard	76	77	75	77	(305)
Garry Taylor	82	82	77	76	(317)
Total best 3, Daily	238	235	230	232	
*Dick Cahi					
HONG KONG Grand total		473	705		944
Cam Gribben	86	87	78	78	(329)
Don Innes	86	76	82	82	(326)
Alex Tang	77	73	72	79	(301)
Tang Siu Wing	81	80	82	86	(329)
Total best 3, Daily	244	229	232	239	
*J.D. Mackie					
BELGIUM Grand total		472	706		945
*Eric Boyer de la Giroday	80	78	75	80	(313)
Olivier Buysse	80	87	78	84	(329)
Thierry Goossens	80	75	81	78	(314)
Patrick Bonnelance	84	79	82	81	(326)
Total best 3, Daily	240	232	234	239	
AUSTRIA Grand total		473	710		947
V. Berlinger	85	78	84	83	(330)
J. Lamberg	79	78	81	79	(317)
M. Lamberg	83	82	78	75	(318)
K. Nierlich	78	77	78	88	(321)
Total best 3, Daily	240	233	237	237	
*L. Stolz					
DENMARK Grand total		470	706		947
Klaus Eldrup-Jorgensen	84	79	79	81	(323)
Christian Pein	81	79	77	79	(316)
Jacob Rasmussen	79	75	80	86	(320)
Anders Sorensen	80	76	83	81	(320)
Total best 3, Daily	240	230	236	241	
*Ole Pheiffer					
VENEZUELA Grand total		477	709		952
Armando Cabrera	83	79	82	90	(334)
Carlos Plaza	85	80	79	86	(330)
Luis E. Plaza	79	79	78	75	(311)
Carlos Whaite	77	86	75	82	(320)
Total best 3, Daily	239	238	232	243	
*Freddy Alcantara					
NORWAY Grand total		477	712		953
Eric Bjerkholt	80	79	78	80	(317)
Olaf Eie	79	82	83	83	(327)
Asbjorn Ramnefjell	82	80	79	78	(319)
Tore Sviland	78	81	78	83	(320)
Total best 3, Daily	237	240	235	241	
*Theo Holm					
FIJI Grand total		486	728		971
Veera Gounden	82	80	80	79	(321)
Vilikesa Kalou	81	79	82	83	(325)
Vijay Singh	84	80	80	81	(325)
Ulaisai Tabutoci	87	84	87	85	(343)
Total best 3, Daily	247	239	242	243	
*Tony Cooper					

TWELFTH WORLD AMATEUR TEAM CHAMPIONSHIP (Continued)

BERMUDA Grand total		505	742		979
Brendan J. Ingham	88	84	82	87	(341)
Noel (Red) Smith	88	86	83	87	(344)
Kim Swan	78	81	78	73	(310)
Eric Hav Trott	89	88	77	77	(331)
Total best 3, Daily	254	251	237	237	
*J. Thomas Smith					
PORTUGAL Grand total		481	728		984
Jose Luis Correia	80	80	85	84	(329)
Nuno Brito E. Cunha	84	79	79	83	(325)
Jose Sousa E. Melo	81	80	84	89	(334)
Antonio Dantes Oliveira	81	83	84	89	(337)
Total best 3, Daily	242	239	247	256	
*Rodrigo Maria de Vivar					
PAPUA NEW GUINEA Grand total		495	746		991
Greg Fennel	81	77	77	82	(317)
P. Giles	91	83	89	89	(352)
Kundi Umba	89	79	89	77	(334)
Jimmy Wu	86	83	85	86	(340)
Total best 3, Daily	256	239	251	245	
*Darcy Williams					
ISRAEL Grand total		509	752		1002
Laurie Been	85	83	86	79	(333)
Leon Eting	89	84	83	86	(342)
Neil Schochet	85	87	80	85	(337)
Barry Shaked	87	85	80	87	(339)
Total best 3, Daily	257	252	243	250	
*Robert Mandel					
DOMINICAN REPUBLIC Grand total		496	749		1003
Ramon Baez	81	82	88	81	(332)
Edwin A. Corrie	85	82	81	84	(332)
Edgar Pichardo	85	81	86	89	(341)
Guillermo Pumarol	86	90	86	91	(353)
Total best 3, Daily	251	245	253	254	
*Juan Santoni					
GUATEMALA Grand total		509	757		1009
*Manuel Ortiz	88	89	85	87	(349)
Roberto Cottone	87	84	82	88	(341)
Gustavo Staebler	85	84	82	78	(329)
Alfonso Toledo	89	81	84	87	(341)
Total best 3, Daily	260	249	248	252	
EL SALVADOR Grand total		512	778		1043
*Guillermo Aceto	97	97	92	101	(387)
Maurico Alvarez	82	82	87	90	(341)
Jose Maria Duran	84	91	93	85	(353)
Jaime Munguia	89	84	87	90	(350)
Total best 3, Daily	255	257	266	265	
PUERTO RICO Grand total		532	805		1077
*Jim Teale	93	86	89	93	(361)
Elvyn Cordova	92	85	92	89	(358)
Juan Ramos	91	87	92	93	(363)
Carlos Vicente	91	88	93	90	(362)
Total best 3, Daily	274	258	273	272	

WOMEN'S WORLD AMATEUR TEAM CHAMPIONSHIP

THE ESPIRITO SANTO TROPHY

Presented in October 1964
by Mrs. Espirito Santo Silva of Portugal

HISTORY

1964–The Women's World Amateur Team Championship was instituted by the French Golf Federation on a suggestion by the United States Golf Association. The first playing was held at the St. Germain Golf Club, near Paris, France, in October and proved an immediate success, under the able chairmanship of the Vicomtesse de Saint-Sauveur. With an entry of 25 teams and 75 players, the Championship became an established member of golf's family of events. The World Amateur Golf Council assumed sponsorship of future events. The host French team won by one stroke over the United States, 588 to 589. Each team was allowed three players; each day the two best individual scores made up the team's score. The sum of the four daily totals gave the team total for the Espirito Santo Trophy. Led by Miss Catherine Lacoste, who began with rounds of 72 and 71, the French girls opened a two-stroke lead over the United States after 36 holes with England another two strokes behind. Miss Carol Sorenson, with 72, and Miss Barbara Fay White, with 73, sent the United States into the lead after three rounds, 440 to 441. On the final day, the two teams dueled throughout, and France finally prevailed when Miss Lacoste finished with a strong 73 and the United States' Champion, Miss Barbara McIntire, encountered bunker trouble and played the last two holes in three over par. Miss Lacoste shared the low individual score for 72 holes with Miss Sorenson at 294. She is the daughter of former tennis champion Rene Lacoste and former French and British golf champion Mme. Simone Thion de la Chaume Lacoste.

1966–The United States Team led every round and won the second Women's World Amateur Team Championship at the Mexico City Country Club, Mexico City. The United States ladies, playing without the services of Mrs. JoAnne Gunderson Carner, the National Champion, scored 580. Canada was second with 589, followed by France with 597. France was the defending Champion. Seventeen-year-old Shelley Hamlin, who replaced Mrs. Carner shortly before the team left for Mexico, scored 72s in the last two rounds, the best scores for the American Team over the final 36 holes. Mrs. Anne Quast Welts and Mrs Barbara White Boddie each had 71s earlier. Mrs. Boddie's score counted in each of the four rounds. Mrs. Marlene Stewart Streit, of Canada, former United States Women's Amateur Champion and runnerup to Mrs. Carner earlier in the year, had the low individual score of 289–one over par. Mrs. Boddie was second with 292 and Miss Catherine Lacoste, of France, was third with 295. Mrs. Theodore W. Hawes was non-playing Captain of the American Team. It was the first Women's Team Championship under the auspices of the World Amateur Golf Council.

1968–The United States Team retained the Women's World Amateur Team Championship at the Victoria Golf Club near Melbourne, Australia. Both Australia and France challenged seriously, and not until the final round did the United States establish a clear lead. The American score was 616. Australia was second with 621, and France third at 622. France and the United States tied at 156 in the first round, and France went ahead with a 36-hole score of 308, against 310 for Australia and 312 for the United States. The three Teams were within one stroke of one another after 54 holes: the United States and Australia tied at 463, and France had 464. The United States then pulled ahead. Miss Shelley Hamlin scored 75, and Miss Jane Bastanchury scored 78, giving the United States 153 for the final round. Both Australia and France scored 158. Mrs. Anne Quast Welts, the third American player, contributed significantly in previous rounds. Although individual honors are not awarded, Miss Catherine Lacoste, of France, had the low score of 307, and Miss Marea Hickey, of Australia, had 308. Mrs. John Pennington was non-playing Captain of the United States Team.

1970–Trailing by two strokes going into the final round, the United States made up the deficit and won the Women's World Amateur Team Championship by one stroke over France at the R.S.H.E. Club de Campo, in Madrid, Spain. Miss Martha Wilkinson, the United States Champion, and Miss Jane Bastanchury, combined for a score of 151 in the last round while Mrs. Catherine Lacoste De Prado, and Mrs. Claudine Cros Rubin combined for 154 for France. The United States had a total of 598 and France 599. It was a struggle between these two teams throughout the competition. France took the lead in the first round with 141 on superb rounds of 70 by Mrs. Rubin and 71 by Miss Brigitte Varangot. The United States then was four strokes behind with 145. France increased its lead to seven strokes after the second round, but with Miss Bastanchury shooting 74 and Miss Wilkinson 75 in the third round, the United States cut its deficit to two strokes. In the dramatic final round, Miss Wilkinson was grouped with Mrs. De Prado, and after nine holes they were stroke-for-stroke. Miss Wilkinson then continued to play steadily and picked up four strokes on Mrs. De Prado over the next eight holes. The French lead then was dissapated and they trailed by one stroke at the 18th. There Mrs. De Prado had to hole a 30-foot putt to force a tie. She missed, and when Miss Wilkinson made her putt from two feet, the United States had won. Twenty-two teams entered the competition, second only to the 25 which entered the first Championship in 1964. Miss Sally Knight Little, of South Africa, was the only player in the field to score under 300. Miss Little shot 76-74-74-75–299. Miss Bastanchury was low for the United States, scoring 73-78-74-77–302. Mrs. De Prado and Mrs. Marlene Stewart Streit, of Canada, also had 302. Miss Wilkinson scored 303, and Miss Cynthia Hill, the other United States player, had 305. Mrs. Henri Prunaret was non-playing Captain of the United States Team.

1972–The United States won its fourth consecutive Championship at the Hindu Country Club, Buenos Aires, Argentina, defeating Teams from 19 other nations. The United States combined Team total–in which the two lowest scores made by the three players each day were counted–was 583, four strokes lower than runnerup France. The Americans led the first round with 140 on a 68 by Mrs. Jane Bastanchury Booth, which equalled the course record, and a 72 by Miss Laura Baugh. The United States was then five-strokes ahead of Canada and seven ahead of Japan. The play of the Canadian Team was highlighted by a 68 by Mrs. Marlene Streit, who was playing in her third Championship. France was far back with 156, 16 strokes off the lead. The American Team increased its lead the second day to 13 strokes on a 72 by Miss Mary Budke while Mrs. Booth and Miss Baugh both shot 73s. Argentina and Sweden were tied for second, while France was 18 strokes behind. The third round, however, saw a complete turn-around by the French and American Teams. Mrs. Claudine Clos Rubin, who had played for France in all the Championships from 1964, shot a 68, matching the earlier rounds of Mrs. Booth and Mrs. Streit, and Miss Brigitte Varangot added a one-under par 71 for a 139, the lowest daily team score of the Championship. Meantime, the United States could do no better than a 76 and two 77s. In one day France had made up 14 strokes on the American team and was in second place, four strokes behind. Sweden was third, seven strokes away. The United States rallied, however, on the final day to retain the Championship. Miss Budke, U.S. Amateur Champion, first off for the United States, shot a 74 against Miss Varangot's 76. Miss Baugh followed with a 72 against Miss Anne Mari Palli's 74. In the last group, Mrs. Booth and Mrs. Rubin played brilliant golf, realizing that the outcome might determine the Championship. Both were one under par after the 13th hole when word reached them that the United States players had finished 74-72 and the pressure was off. The United States led by four strokes; France was second; Sweden was third, and Australia was fourth. Mrs. Booth, who played on the 1968-70 United States Teams, was low individual scorer with a 291 total for the four rounds, one stroke ahead of Mrs. Rubin and Mrs. Streit, Mrs. Robert M. Monsted was non-playing Captain for the United States.

1974—The United States won its fifth consecutive Championship at Campo de Golf, Cajuiles, Dominican Republic, defeating the second-place Teams of South Africa and Great Britain and Ireland by a record margin of 16 strokes. The United States had a total score of 620; the runnersup had 636. Australia was fourth at 637, Spain fifth with 639, and Italy sixth at 640. Twenty-two countries and 65 players participated. The American Team was composed of Miss Cynthia Hill, Miss Debbie Massey, and Miss Carol Semple. Scoring was on the basis of the two lowest scores for each day, for four days. The American girls came back very strong after what could have been disaster on the very first day. Miss Massey was so woozy from medication that she almost withdrew after the first nine holes. She three-putted eight greens for a 45. She continued, however, and finished with 84. Normally such a score would be discarded, but it counted because Miss Semple, playing behind Miss Massey, committed a Rules infraction and she was disqualified for the round. Without Miss Massey's 84, therefore, the American girls would have had no score for the first round and would have been eliminated; with it, they were only one stroke behind Italy, the first-round leader at 159 and tied with France and Great Britain and Ireland. Miss Hill had scored two-over par 76, the low score of the day, to give the United States a team score of 160. The American girls took the lead after the second day's play, going four strokes ahead of Italy. Miss Massey led the United States with a two-under par 72, while both Miss Hill and Miss Semple had 79s. After that, the American girls were never challenged. On the third day Miss Hill and Miss Massey added 79 and 77, respectively and increased the lead to 10 strokes. In the final round Miss Hill shot 73 after going two over for nine holes and finished with a 72-hole score of 307, the low individual score of the Championship. Miss Massey was next with 314, followed by Miss Jane Lock, of Australia, at 315. Low score for the entire Championship—a 71 on the last day—was shot by Mrs. Catherine Lacoste de Prado, a former United States Women's Amateur and Women's Open Champion. In the field were Liv Wollin, of Sweden, and Brigitte Varangot, of France, who are the only players who have participated in all six Championships. Playing, also, were two 14-year-old girls—Maria de la Guardia and Silvia Corrie, who were representing the host nation, the Dominican Republic. Mrs. Allison Choate was the non-playing Captain for the United States Team.

1976—The United States built its lead steadily through the four rounds of the seventh Women's World Amateur Team Championship and finally won by 17 strokes over France at the Vilamoura Golf Club, Algarve, Portugal. This was the sixth victory for the United States and the third time France finished second. France is the only other country to have won. The Championship was between those two teams throughout the four rounds. Nancy Lopez shot 72 in the opening round, the lowest 18-hole score of the competition, and combined with Debbie Massey to give the United States the lead, 152-154, over France. Italy and the Republic of China shared third place at 157, five strokes off the lead. The next day the United States extended its lead to seven strokes with another team total of 152 on a 75 by Miss Lopez and 77 by Miss Massey. This gave the United States a 36-hole score of 304 against 311 by France. By then Italy and South Africa were tied for third at 316 with Canada another stroke back at 317. The United States picked up another two strokes in the third round and extended its lead to nine, 451-460, even though France had its best one-round score of the competition. Mrs. Catherine Lacoste de Prado shot 75 and Miss Anne Marie Palli shot 74, giving France 149 for the day. However, Miss Lopez shot 73 and Miss Massey 74 and the United States had 147. In the last round the United States simply pulled away, scoring 154 on 77s by both Miss Lopez and Miss Donna Horton against 162 for France. Brazil matched the U. S. total of 154 and moved into third place ahead of Italy. Miss Lopez had scores of 72, 75, 73, and 77 and finished the four rounds with a 72-hole score of 297. Mrs. Lacoste had the next best total of 307 on rounds of 76, 77, 75, and 79, and Miss Massey had 309. Individual scores, however, are not recognized. The entry reached 25 countries, the most since the first Championship in 1964 when 25 countries also competed.

1978—Australia overcame a two-stroke deficit on the last four holes to win the eighth Women's World Amateur Team Championship, played at the Pacific Harbour Golf and Country Club in Fiji. It was the first victory for Australia; six of the first seven Championships had been won by the United States and the other by France. Australia finished one stroke ahead of Canada, 596-597. Miss Jane Lock, of the Australian Team, played the last four holes in two under par with an eagle and three pars. At the 15th hole, a par 5, she reached the green with a drive and a 4-iron and holed a four-foot putt for an eagle that tied Australia with Canada. When Mrs. Cathy Sherk, of the Canadian Team, bogied the 17th hole, a par 3, Australia held a one-stroke lead. The Australian Team needed a par 4 from Miss Lock on the final hole to win the Championship. At the 18th hole, she pulled her 5-iron approach to the left of the green, behind a small tree. Her pitch shot came to rest three feet from the hole and she made the putt to save her par. Australia began the final round with a six-stroke lead over Canada, the United States, and Great Britain and Ireland. France finished the event in third place with a 602 total. The United States and Great Britain and Ireland tied for fourth place with scores of 605. The Australian Team comprised Miss Lock, Miss Edwina Kennedy (the British Ladies Champion), and Mrs. Lindy Goggin. The non-playing Captain was Mrs. R.D. Bridges. While no official recognition is given to individual performances, the U.S. Women's Amateur Champion, Mrs. Sherk, had rounds of 72-74-76-72—294 for the lowest 72-hole total. Next were Miss Lock, Miss Beth Daniel of the United States, and Miss Miki Oda, of Japan, all at 298. Miss Lock had 73-72-75-78; Miss Daniel had 75-71-74-78; and Miss Oda had 74-73-77-74. A pair of second-round 71s by Miss Daniel and Miss Kennedy, were the lowest single-round scores of the event. Fourteen teams competed, the fewest number of entries since the event was inaugurated in 1964.

1980—The United States regained possession of the Espirito Santo Trophy by winning the ninth Women's World Amateur Team Championship at the No. 2 Course of the Pinehurst Country Club, in Pinehurst, North Carolina. It was the U.S. Team's seventh victory. With daily team scores of 151-145-148-144, the United States posted a total of 588, four under par. Australia, the 1978 Champion finished seven strokes behind, at 595. France and Spain tied for third place at 610. Australia took the first round lead with a 150 total on scores of 73 by Edwina Kennedy and 77 by Lindy Goggin. The United States was a stroke behind. After two rounds, the United States and Australia were tied, at 296. The U.S. team had a second-round 145 on scores of 70 by Miss Rizzo and 75 by Mrs. Inkster. A third round 148 on 74s by Mrs. Inkster and Carol Semple gave the United States a 54-hole total of 444, three strokes ahead of Australia, and then the Americans shot 144 on the final day, the lowest daily team score of the week. Miss Semple and Mrs. Inkster shot 71 and 73, respectively. While no official recognition is given to individual performances, Patti Rizzo had rounds of 73-70-75-76—294, two under par, for the lowest 72-hole total. Edwina Kennedy, the only other player to equal or better par, was at 296. The non-playing Captain of the United States team was Miss Elizabeth S. Brand, of Sacramento, California. The Championship drew a record 28 entries.

WOMEN'S WORLD AMATEUR TEAM CHAMPIONSHIP FOR THE ESPIRITO SANTO TROPHY

1964—At St. Germain Golf Club, St. Germain (Paris), France

France	588	Scotland	624	Chile	645
United States	589	Belgium	626	Japan	649
England	597	South Africa	627	Argentina	658
Canada	606	Wales	634	Spain	663
Australia	613	Ireland	637	Portugal	668
New Zealand	616	Italy	641	Denmark	682
Sweden	616	Philippines	641	Bermuda	689
Germany	621	Netherlands	641	Austria	713
Mexico	624				

1966—At Mexico City Country Club, Mexico City

United States	580	Mexico	613	Spain	647
Canada	589	New Zealand	613	Japan	648
France	597	South Africa	613	Brazil	659
Belgium	611	Sweden	617	Venezuela	690
Great Britain & Ireland	612	Australia	621	Chile	703
Italy	613	Netherlands	625	Bermuda	711
Germany	631				

1968—At Victoria Golf Club, Victoria, Australia

United States	616	Argentina	651	Netherlands	665
Australia	621	New Zealand	653	Japan	666
France	622	Philippines	654	Mexico	670
Sweden	638	Italy	655	Republic of China	671
Canada	643	South Africa	659	Bermuda	773
Great Britain & Ireland	649	Belgium	661		

1970—R.S.H.E. Club de Campo, Madrid, Spain

United States	598	Germany	630	New Zealand	653
France	599	Belgium	631	Brazil	663
South Africa	606	Italy	632	Japan	670
Canada	610	Sweden	632	Uruguay	672
Argentina	624	China	633	Switzerland	673
Great Britain & Ireland	626	Spain	634	Norway	676
Australia	629	Netherlands	640	Venezuela	697
		Philippines	642		

1972—At The Hindu Country Club, Buenos Aires, Argentina

United States	583	Argentina	605	South Africa	638
France	587	Spain	610	Chile	643
Sweden	594	Italy	612	Brazil	653
Australia	601	New Zealand	621	Peru	665
Canada	602	Germany	622	Colombia	666
Great Britain & Ireland	602	Netherlands	624	Uruguay	680
Japan	602	Belgium	628		

1974—At the Campo de Golf, Cajuiles, La Romana, Dominican Republic

United States	620	Switzerland	654	Chile	692
Great Britain & Ireland	636	Canada	655	Jamaica	712
South Africa	636	Japan	657	Dominican Republic	718
Australia	637	Brazil	665	Puerto Rico	722
Spain	639	Netherlands	668	Venezuela	732
Italy	640	New Zealand	676	Bermuda	814
France	647	Argentina	682		
Sweden	650	Belgium	687		

1976—At the Vilamoura Golf Club, Algarve, Portugal

United States	605	Germany	641	Denmark	685
France	622	Sweden	641	Mexico	685
Brazil	626	Japan	643	Norway	701
Italy	635	Great Britain & Ireland	645	Sri Lanka	701
Australia	636	Argentina	649	Rhodesia	702
Canada	636	Switzerland	663	Portugal	762
Republic of China	638	Netherlands	669	Dominican Republic	777
South Africa	639	Belgium	674		
Spain	639	Chile	677		

1978—At the Pacific Harbour Golf and Country Club, Fiji

Australia	596	Japan	610	Switzerland	635
Canada	597	New Zealand	614	Argentina	640
France	602	Sweden	616	Italy	644
United States	605	Spain	625	Fiji	737
Great Britain & Ireland	605	Germany	632		

WOMEN'S WORLD AMATEUR TEAM CHAMPIONSHIP FOR THE ESPIRITO SANTO TROPHY

1980—At Pinehurst Country Club, Pinehurst, North Carolina

United States	588	Japan	628	Colombia	663
Australia	595	New Zealand	630	Zimbabwe	666
France	610	Republic of China	633	Peru	668
Spain	610	Germany	635	Chile	671
Great Britain & Ireland	615	South Africa	638	Mexico	681
Italy	621	Argentina	643	Venezuela	685
Sweden	621	Netherlands	643	Bermuda	711
Canada	622	Belgium	649	Guatemala	713
Switzerland	622	Brazil	649	Fiji	739
		Norway	651		

1964
FIRST WOMEN'S WORLD AMATEUR TEAM CHAMPIOSNHIP FOR THE ESPIRITO SANTO TROPHY

Sponsored by The French Golf Federation

Held at the St. Germain Golf Club, St. Germain (Paris), France, Oct. 1-4.
Yardage—5,933. Par 72. 25 Team Entries.

Team score consisted of best two individual scores in each round.
*Indicates Captain.

		1st Rd.	2nd Rd.	3rd Rd.	4th Rd.	72-hole Score
FRANCE	Grand total	147	293	441		588
Miss Claudine Cros		76	75	75	74	(300)
Miss Catherine Lacoste		72	71	78	73	(294)
Miss Brigitte Varangot		75	76	73	77	(301)
Total best 2, daily		147	146	148	147	
*Vicomtesse de Saint-Sauveur						
UNITED STATES	Grand total	148	295	440		589
Miss Barbara McIntire		80	73	78	76	(307)
Miss Carol Sorenson		75	74	72	73	(294)
Miss Barbara F. White		73	78	73	76	(300)
Total best 2, daily		148	147	145	149	
*Mrs. Theodore W. Hawes						
ENGLAND	Grand total	148	297	446		597
*Miss Bridget Jackson		73	78	79	82	(312)
Miss Ruth Porter		80	74	77	76	(307)
Mrs. Marley Spearman		75	75	72	75	(297)
Total best 2, daily		148	149	149	151	
CANADA	Grand total	149	305	460		606
*Mrs. G. A. Cole		80	86	81	81	(328)
Miss Gail Harvey		73	77	75	72	(297)
Miss Joanne Goulet		76	79	80	74	(309)
Total best 2, daily		149	156	155	146	
AUSTRALIA	Grand total	154	311	463		613
Miss Gail Corry		79	81	77	77	(314)
Miss Betty J. Dalgleish		79	82	83	73	(317)
Mrs. Ray Thomas		75	76	75	77	(303)
Total best 2, daily		154	157	152	150	
*Miss Jean Derrin						
NEW ZEALAND	Grand total	154	312	467		616
Miss Jane Butler		77	78	80	81	(316)
Miss Pat Harrison		77	81	78	73	(309)
*Mrs. J. Mangan		80	80	77	76	(313)
Total best 2, daily		154	158	155	149	
SWEDEN	Grand total	156	309	462		616
Miss Liv Forsell		77	75	78	73	(303)
Mrs. Britt Mattsson		79	80	83	82	(324)
Miss Cecilia Perslow		82	78	75	81	(316)
Total best 2, daily		156	153	153	154	
*Mrs. Margaretha Murray						
GERMANY	Grand total	157	313	465		621
Mrs. Alex P. Gutermann		82	78	78	78	(316)
Miss Monika Moller		80	78	74	78	(310)
Miss Monica Steegmann		77	83	79	83	(322)
Total best 2, daily		157	156	152	156	
*Mrs. Waldemar Strenger						
MEXICO	Grand total	158	318	473		624
Miss Fela Chavez		78	81	80	73	(312)
Mrs. Ana Luisa Hernandez de Ortega		80	79	75	78	(312)
Miss Maria Luisa Martinez		91	85	86	85	(347)
Total best 2, daily		158	160	155	151	
*Mrs. Raul Valdes						
SCOTLAND	Grand total	158	318	469		624
Miss Joan B. Lawrence		83	82	74	77	(316)
*Mrs. Mary Roberts		80	83	85	78	(326)
Mrs. Ian C. Robertson		78	78	77	79	(312)
Total best 2, daily		158	160	151	155	

First Women's World Amateur Team Championship — Continued

		1st Rd.	2nd Rd.	3rd Rd.	4th Rd.	72-hole Score
BELGIUM	Grand total	154	314	472		626
Mrs. Jacques Francois		76	84	86	82	(328)
Mrs. Fr. Engel-Jacquet		78	82	74	77	(311)
Mrs. Pierre Leysen		85	78	84	77	(324)
Total best 2, daily		154	160	158	154	
*Mrs. Helene Chaudoir						
SOUTH AFRICA	Grand total	156	314	467		627
Mrs. Jeanette Burd		82	80	79	81	(322)
Mrs. Jacqueline Mercer		78	80	75	85	(318)
Mrs. Mary Clemence		78	78	78	79	(313)
Total best 2, daily		156	158	153	160	
*Mrs. Helen Wilson						
WALES	Grand total	164	320	476		634
Mrs. R. Oliver		84	80	79	82	(325)
*Miss P. Roberts		83	79	78	76	(316)
Mrs. Marcus Wright		81	77	78	83	(319)
Total best 2, daily		164	156	156	158	
IRELAND	Grand total	163	323	482		637
Miss Elisabeth Barnett		78	81	79	82	(320)
Miss Ita Burke		86	82	80	73	(321)
*Mrs. Zelie Fallon		85	79	81	82	(327)
Total best 2, daily		163	160	159	155	
NETHERLANDS	Grand total	159	316	482		641
Miss Annie van Lanschot		80	84	82	78	(324)
Miss Anneke van Riemsdijk		80	78	84	81	(323)
*Mrs. Roely Sauter		79	79	88	81	(327)
Total best 2, daily		159	157	166	159	
ITALY	Grand total	162	320	482		641
*Mrs. Tommaso Goldschmid		81	75	78	77	(311)
Miss Marina Ragher		90	83	84	86	(343)
Mrs. Mario Tadini		81	84	85	82	(332)
Total best 2, daily		162	158	162	159	
PHILIPPINES	Grand total	159	323	481		641
Miss Dominga Capati		79	81	87	82	(329)
Miss Mercedes Feliciano		95	84	75	84	(338)
Miss Nora M. Mateo		80	83	83	78	(324)
Total best 2, daily		159	164	158	160	
*Mrs. Enrique Valles						
CHILE	Grand total	166	325	484		645
Mrs. Sara Garcia de Raby		80	75	82	79	(316)
Miss Gabriela Gazitua		86	84	77	82	(329)
Miss Maria-Angelica Segovia		91	91	89	88	(359)
Total best 2, daily		166	159	159	161	
*Mr. M. Jorge Perez						
JAPAN	Grand total	168	325	484		649
Miss Tamako Izutani		84	76	79	83	(322)
*Mrs. Tokusaburo Kosaka		84	81	80	85	(330)
Miss Hiroko Matsunami		84	81	85	82	(332)
Total best 2, daily		168	157	159	165	
ARGENTINA	Grand total	159	327	491		658
*Mrs. Margarita Mackinlay de Maglione		81	80	82	84	(327)
Miss Cecilia Palacio		78	88	82	83	(331)
Mrs. Adelina J. de Rodriguez		86	93	90	87	(356)
Total best 2, daily		159	168	164	167	
SPAIN	Grand total	169	330	499		663
*Mrs. Mercedes Etchart de Artiach		84	79	82	78	(323)
Mrs. Emma Villacieros de Garcia-Ogara		85	82	88	86	(341)
Mrs. Rosa Cuito de Serra		89	90	87	93	(359)
Total best 2, daily		169	161	169	164	
PORTUGAL	Grand total	164	333	496		668
Miss Barbara de Brito e Cunha		84	82	79	83	(328)
*Mrs. Vera Costa Lennox		90	88	97	90	(365)
Mrs. Salette de Sousa e Melo		80	87	84	89	(340)
Total best 2, daily		164	169	163	172	

First Women's World Amateur Team Championship – Continued

		1st Rd.	2nd Rd.	3rd Rd.	4th Rd.	72-hole Score
DENMARK	Grand total	173	354	513		682
Mrs. Bjorg Dam		86	93	84	86	(349)
Miss Vibeke Knudsen		87	—	75	96	(—)
Mrs. K. Siegumfeldt		88	88	92	83	(351)
Total best 2, daily		173	181	159	169	
*Mrs. Kaja Gammeltoft						
BERMUDA	Grand total	168	338	518		689
Mrs. Brock Park		83	79	88	83	(333)
Mrs. Tom Smith		91	94	92	96	(373)
Mrs. George Wardman		85	91	92	88	(356)
Total best 2, daily		168	170	180	171	
*Lady Dill						
AUSTRIA	Grand total	183	362	542		713
Miss C. Csernohorszky		98	95	92	88	(373)
Miss Christa Leixner		97	92	92	92	(373)
*Mrs. Marie Sernetz		86	87	88	83	(344)
Total best 2, daily		183	179	180	171	

1966
SECOND WOMEN'S WORLD AMATEUR TEAM CHAMPIONSHIP
FOR THE ESPIRITO SANTO TROPHY

Held at the Mexico City Country Club, Mexico City, Mexico, October 20-23.
Yardage–6,260. Par 72. 19 Team Entries.

Team score consisted of best two individual scores in each round.
*Indicates Captain.

		1st Rd.	2nd Rd.	3rd Rd.	4th Rd.	72-hole Score
UNITED STATES	Grand total	145	289	435		580
Mrs. Teddy B. Boddie		74	71	74	73	(292)
Miss Shelley Hamlin		80	75	72	72	(299)
Mrs. Anne Quast Welts		71	73	76	78	(298)
Total best 2, daily		145	144	146	145	
*Mrs. Theodore W. Hawes						
CANADA	Grand total	150	298	443		589
Miss Gayle Hitchens		76	78	75	76	(305)
Mrs. Gail Harvey Moore		77	77	78	72	(304)
Mrs. Marlene Stewart Streit		74	71	70	74	(289)
Total best 2, daily		150	148	145	146	
*Miss Kay Helleur						
FRANCE	Grand total	147	297	447		597
Miss Claudine Cros		75	77	77	77	(306)
Miss Catherine Lacoste		74	73	75	73	(295)
Miss Brigitte Varangot		73	79	75	78	(305)
Total best 2, daily		147	150	150	150	
*Vicomtesse de Saint-Sauveur						
BELGIUM	Grand total	150	301	459		611
Mrs. Fr. Engel-Jacquet		79	84	78	76	(317)
Miss Corinne Reybroeck		72	75	81	76	(304)
Miss Loulou van den Berghe		78	76	80	78	(312)
Total best 2, daily		150	151	158	152	
*Mrs. Helen Chaudoir						
GREAT BRITAIN AND IRELAND	Grand total	155	310	459		612
Miss Ita Burke		80	83	82	81	(326)
*Miss Ruth Porter		78	78	80	75	(311)
Mrs. Ian C. Robertson		77	77	69	78	(301)
Total best 2, daily		155	155	149	153	
ITALY	Grand total	146	304	457		613
*Mrs. Tommaso Goldschmid		72	80	79	80	(311)
Miss Marina Ragher		74	78	74	76	(302)
Mrs. Marion Tadini		78	83	87	83	(331)
Total best 2, daily		146	158	153	156	
MEXICO	Grand total	157	311	459		613
Miss Fela Chavez		85	77	77	76	(315)
Miss Florencia Hernandez		72	77	73	78	(300)
Mrs. Elena Larralde		87	80	75	80	(322)
Total best 2, daily		157	154	148	154	
*Mrs. Luz de Lourdes Fernandez						
NEW ZEALAND	Grand total	154	307	459		613
Mrs. Patricia Bull		78	77	76	75	(306)
Mrs. Jane Little		76	76	76	80	(308)
Miss Natalie White		81	77	84	79	(321)
Total best 2, daily		154	153	152	154	
*Mrs. E. Burrowes						
SOUTH AFRICA	Grand total	152	302	454		613
Miss Judy Angel		78	87	77	82	(324)
Miss Jill Kennedy		77	78	75	78	(308)
Mrs. Jacqueline Mercer		75	72	80	81	(308)
Total best 2, daily		152	150	152	159	
*Mrs. Esther Gallie						

Second Women's World Amateur Team Championship – Continued

		1st Rd.	2nd Rd.	3rd Rd.	4th Rd.	72-hole Score
SWEDEN	Grand total	154	309	458		617
Miss Liv Forsell		76	73	70	79	(298)
Mrs. Birgit Forssman		79	86	80	81	(326)
Miss Nina Rehnqvist		78	82	79	80	(319)
Total best 2, daily		154	155	149	159	
*Mrs. Sven Bernstrom						
AUSTRALIA	Grand total	158	317	469		621
Miss Gail Corry		84	86	84	77	(331)
Miss Marea Hickey		79	80	78	75	(312)
Mrs. Ray Thomas		79	79	74	86	(318)
Total best 2, daily		158	159	152	152	
*Mrs. J. D. Fisher						
NETHERLANDS	Grand total	159	309	471		625
Mrs. J. Eschauzier		83	81	82	80	(326)
Miss Annie van Lanschot		81	75	82	78	(316)
Miss Anneke van Riemsdyk		78	75	80	76	(309)
Total best 2, daily		159	150	162	154	
*Mrs. A. Swane						
GERMANY	Grand total	159	316	475		631
Miss Monika Moeller		83	78	81	77	(319)
Miss Marion Petersen		76	79	78	79	(312)
Miss Monica Steegmann		86	85	82	84	(337)
Total best 2, daily		159	157	159	156	
*Mrs. Waldemar Strenger						
SPAIN	Grand total	163	324	487		647
Mrs. Mercedes de Artiach		84	77	85	78	(324)
Miss Teresa Bagaria		84	84	87	82	(337)
*Mrs. Emma de Garcia Ogara		79	85	78	86	(328)
Total best 2, daily		163	161	163	160	
JAPAN	Grand total	165	321	489		648
Miss Tamako Izutani		83	83	84	83	(333)
Miss Takako Kiyomoto		82	73	84	78	(317)
Miss Seiko Sato		87	84	85	81	(337)
Total best 2, daily		165	156	168	159	
*Mrs. Asako Kosaka						
BRAZIL	Grand total	167	331	491		659
Miss Margot M. Brand		79	83	84	85	(331)
Miss Gitta Grant		88	81	79	83	(331)
Mrs. Irene Ribeiro		89	86	81	85	(341)
Total best 2, daily		167	164	160	168	
*Mrs. Evelyn M. Brand						
VENEZUELA	Grand total	169	349	521		690
*Mrs. Hope P. de Nestares		83	91	83	82	(339)
Mrs. Luisa M. de Sabater		88	89	90	87	(334)
Mrs. Margaret Murray-Wilson		86	95	89	90	(360)
Total best 2, daily		169	180	172	169	
CHILE	Grand total	177	351	533		703
Mrs. Raquel R. T. de Edwards		90	91	94	88	(363)
Miss Gabriela Gazitua		89	83	88	82	(342)
Mrs. Violet J. de Vermehren		88	93	94	91	(366)
Total best 2, daily		177	174	182	170	
*Marcelo Taverne						
BERMUDA	Grand total	168	351	534		711
Mrs. M. J. Brewer		83	89	95	90	(357)
Mrs. Brock Park		86	94	93	88	(361)
Mrs. Graham Rosser		85	95	90	89	(359)
Total best 2, daily		168	183	183	177	
*Mrs. George Wardman						

1968
THIRD WOMEN'S WORLD AMATEUR TEAM CHAMPIONSHIP FOR THE ESPIRITO SANTO TROPHY

Held at Victoria Golf Club, Cheltenham, Victoria, Australia, October 2-5.
Yardage—6,040. Par 73. 17 Team Entries.

Team score consisted of best two individual scores in each round.
*Indicates Captain.

		1st Rd.	2nd Rd.	3rd Rd.	4th Rd.	72-hole Score
UNITED STATES	Grand total	156	312	463		616
Miss Jane Bastanchury		78	80	76	78	(312)
Miss Shelley Hamlin		82	76	76	75	(309)
Mrs. Anne Quast Welts		78	80	75	80	(313)
Total best 2, daily		156	156	151	153	
*Mrs. John Pennington						
AUSTRALIA	Grand total	158	310	463		621
Miss Elizabeth Blackmore		79	80	80	81	(320)
Miss Marea Hickey		81	75	75	77	(308)
Mrs. Ray Thomas		79	77	78	86	(320)
Total best 2, daily		158	152	153	158	
*Mrs. M. Dawson						
FRANCE	Grand total	156	308	464		622
Mrs. Claudine Cros Rubin		81	75	81	82	(319)
Miss Catherine Lacoste		75	81	75	76	(307)
Miss Brigitte Varangot		83	77	82	83	(325)
Total best 2, daily		156	152	156	158	
*Vicomtesse de Saint-Sauveur						
SWEDEN	Grand total	161	323	479		638
Miss Liv Forsell		82	77	78	77	(314)
Miss Louise Johansson		80	85	86	87	(338)
Miss Nina Rehnqvist		81	88	78	82	(329)
Total best 2, daily		161	162	156	159	
*Mrs. Sven Bernstrom						
CANADA	Grand total	158	322	481		643
Mrs. Robert Borthwick		80	85	80	—	(—)
Mrs. J. B. Moore		85	83	79	81	(328)
Miss Marilyn Palmer		78	81	81	81	(321)
Total best 2, daily		158	164	159	162	
*Mrs. Robert Lyle						
GREAT BRITAIN AND IRELAND	Grand total	163	321	482		649
Miss Mary Everard		82	90	84	84	(340)
Mrs. Diane Frearson		81	83	86	86	(336)
*Mrs. Ian C. Robertson		86	75	77	83	(321)
Total best 2, daily		163	158	161	167	
ARGENTINA	Grand total	168	329	492		651
Mrs. Maria Julia Caserta de Aftalion		87	82	81	77	(327)
*Mrs. Carmen Baca Castex de Conen		88	79	82	82	(331)
Miss Marta Saenz Valiente		81	86	84	85	(336)
Total best 2, daily		168	161	163	159	
NEW ZEALAND	Grand total	165	332	489		653
Miss Glennis Taylor		88	89	81	82	(340)
Miss Natalie B. White		83	84	79	84	(330)
*Mrs. D. A. Whitehead		82	83	78	82	(325)
Total best 2, daily		165	167	157	164	
PHILIPPINES	Grand total	168	328	493		654
Miss Mercedes Filiciano		89	79	83	79	(330)
Miss Nora Mateo		86	88	88	82	(344)
Miss Vicky Pertierra		82	81	82	90	(335)
Total best 2, daily		168	160	165	161	
*Mrs. Carmel Romero						
ITALY	Grand total	161	325	486		655
*Mrs. Tommaso Goldschmid		80	90	83	85	(338)
Miss Marina Ragher		87	83	81	84	(335)
Mrs. Marion Tadini		81	81	80	87	(329)
Total best 2, daily		161	164	161	169	

Third Women's World Amateur Team Championship – Continued

		1st Rd.	2nd Rd.	3rd Rd.	4th Rd.	72-hole Score
SOUTH AFRICA	Grand total	168	330	491		659
Mrs. Jeanette Burd		86	79	81	81	(327)
Mrs. Rita Easton		82	87	85	87	(341)
Mrs. Felicity Wassenaar		92	83	80	87	(342)
Total best 2, daily		168	162	161	168	
*Mrs. Mary Holdsworth						
BELGIUM	Grand total	167	330	492		661
Miss Francoise Berard		89	85	84	91	(349)
*Miss Louise van den Berghe		86	35	89	85	(345)
Miss Corinne Reybroeck		81	78	78	84	(321)
Total best 2, daily		167	163	162	169	
NETHERLANDS	Grand total	172	334	498		665
Miss Alice Janmaat		87	81	81	83	(332)
Miss Priscilla Sauter		87	86	83	84	(340)
Miss Joyce de Witt Puyt		85	81	83	84	(333)
Total best 2, daily		172	162	164	167	
*Mrs. Dody Swane						
JAPAN	Grand total	169	332	499		666
Miss Haruko Ifuku		89	79	80	87	(335)
Miss Fasako Masui		80	84	87	81	(332)
Miss Masako Satomi		89	86	88	86	(349)
Total best 2, daily		169	163	167	167	
*Mrs. Atsuko Nishimura						
MEXICO	Grand total	168	339	509		670
Miss Fela Chavez		87	88	84	80	(339)
Miss Florencia Hernandez		85	91	89	81	(346)
*Mrs. Elena de Larralde		83	83	86	83	(335)
Total best 2, daily		168	171	170	161	
CHINA, REPUBLIC OF	Grand total	165	331	501		671
Miss Eva Chang		82	82	87	85	(336)
Miss Yu Hwa Pan		88	84	83	85	(340)
Miss Ming Yeh Wu		83	92	88	89	(352)
Total best 2, daily		165	166	170	170	
*Mrs. Pearl Niu						
BERMUDA	Grand total	196	390	579		773
Mrs. A. W. Card		95	98	91	98	(382)
Mrs. E. Graham Gibbons		101	96	99	96	(392)
Mrs. Eric N. Parker		105	108	98	106	(417)
Total best 2, daily		196	194	189	194	
*Mrs. Rendell Arton						

1970
FOURTH WOMEN'S WORLD AMATEUR TEAM CHAMPIONSHIP FOR THE ESPIRITO SANTO TROPHY

Held at the R.S.H.E. Club de Campo, Madrid, Spain, Sept. 30–October 3.
Yardage–6,221 Par 73. 22 Team Entries.

Team score consisted of best two individual scores in each round.
*Indicates Captain.

		1st Rd.	2nd Rd.	3rd Rd.	4th Rd.	72-hole Score
UNITED STATES	Grand total	145	298	447		598
Miss Jane Bastanchury		73	78	74	77	(302)
Miss Cynthia Hill		72	78	77	78	(305)
Miss Martha Wilkinson		79	75	75	74	(303)
Total best 2, daily		145	153	149	151	
*Mrs. Henri Prunaret						
FRANCE	Grand total	141	291	445		599
Mrs. Catherine Lacoste De Prado		74	74	76	78	(302)
Mrs. Claudine Cros-Rubin		70	76	81	76	(303)
Miss Brigitte Varangot		71	76	78	79	(304)
Total best 2, daily		141	150	154	154	
*Vicomtesse de Saint-Sauveur						
SOUTH AFRICA	Grand total	154	306	456		606
Miss Judy Angel		81	78	77	75	(311)
Mrs. Jeanette Joan Burd		78	83	76	76	(313)
Miss Sally Knight Little		76	74	74	75	(299)
Total best 2,daily		154	152	150	150	
*Mrs. Esther M. Gallie						
CANADA	Grand total	150	300	453		610
Mrs. Marlene Streit		75	73	75	79	(302)
Miss Jocelyne Bourassa		75	77	78	78	(308)
Mrs. Gail Moore		80	87	78	80	(325)
Total best 2, daily		150	150	153	157	
*Mrs. Barbara Turnbull						
ARGENTINA	Grand total	154	308	469		624
Mrs. Maria Julia Caserta de Aftalion		78	77	83	77	(315)
Miss Silvia Bertolaccini		80	82	86	85	(333)
*Miss Beatriz Rossello		76	77	78	78	(309)
Total best 2, daily		154	154	161	155	
GREAT BRITAIN AND IRELAND	Grand total	155	311	468		626
Miss Mary McKenna		79	80	82	85	(326)
Miss Dinah Oxley		76	77	75	77	(305)
*Miss Julia Greenhalgh		79	79	83	81	(312)
Total best 2, daily		155	156	157	158	
AUSTRALIA	Grand total	151	313	469		629
Mrs. Robyn Nancy Dummett		82	83	79	83	(327)
Miss Lindy Gay Jennings		76	82	84	78	(329)
Miss Rhys Wright		75	80	77	82	(314)
Total best 2, daily		151	162	156	160	
*Mrs. R. D. Bridges						
GERMANY	Grand total	155	316	469		630
Miss Marietta Gutermann		78	81	77	81	(316)
Miss Marion Peterson		77	81	76	81	(315)
Miss Katharina Trebitsch		86	80	90	80	(336)
Total best 2, daily		155	161	153	161	
*Mrs. Lieselotte Strenger						
BELGIUM	Grand total	157	316	467		632
Miss Louise Van Den Berghe		82	87	86	85	(340)
Miss Corinne Reybroeck		75	77	73	80	(305)
Miss Marie Anne Toussaint		90	82	78	88	(338)
Total best 2, daily		157	159	151	165	
*Francoise Francois						
ITALY	Grand total	156	317	471		632
*Mrs. Tommaso Goldschmid		77	85	81	78	(321)
Miss Marina Ragher		79	82	73	83	(317)
Miss Bianca Martini Crotti		84	79	84	87	(334)
Total best 2, daily		156	161	154	161	

Fourth Women's World Amateur Team Championship – Continued

		1st Rd.	2nd Rd.	3rd Rd.	4th Rd.	72-hole Score
SWEDEN	Grand total	154	317	474		632
Miss Christina Westerberg		78	85	85	81	(329)
Mrs. Birgit Forssman		81	84	82	85	(332)
Miss Liv Forsell		76	79	75	77	(307)
Total best 2, daily		154	163	157	158	
*Mrs. Anne-Marie Brynolf						
CHINA, REPUBLIC OF	Grand total	155	314	468		633
*Miss Eva Chih-Hsia Chang		76	81	74	81	(312)
Miss Ming-Yueh Wu		80	78	80	84	(322)
Miss Yu-Hwa Pan		79	82	86	86	(333)
Total best 2, daily		155	159	154	165	
SPAIN	Grand total	160	321	473		634
Mrs. Emma Villacieros de Garcia-Ogara		80	82	82	86	(330)
Marquesa de Artasona		81	79	76	79	(315)
Condesa de Albox		80	84	76	82	(322)
Total best 2, daily		160	161	152	161	
*Mrs. Mercedes E. de Artiach						
NETHERLANDS	Grand total	157	323	481		640
Miss Alice Janmaat		82	80	76	79	(317)
Miss Marischka Swane		79	86	82	82	(329)
Miss Joyce de Witt Puyt		78	87	84	80	(329)
Total best 2, daily		157	166	158	159	
*Mrs. J. P. Eschanzier-Schiff						
PHILIPPINES	Grand total	159	323	483		642
Miss Mercedes Feliciano		79	82	84	83	(328)
Miss Nora Mateo		80	82	80	85	(327)
Miss Vicky Pertierra		80	82	80	76	(318)
Total best 2, daily		159	164	160	159	
*Mrs. Teresa Lao						
NEW ZEALAND	Grand total	160	322	486		653
Miss Glennis Taylor		79	86	85	81	(331)
Miss Heather Booth		81	82	—	87	–
Miss Cushla Sullivan		81	80	79	86	(326)
Total best 2, daily		160	162	164	167	
*Mrs. Brenda Grenall						
BRAZIL	Grand total	162	329	494		663
Mrs. Elizabeth N. Noronha		78	82	80	84	(324)
*Mrs. Yolanda Figueiredo		84	85	85	85	(339)
Mrs. Irene Ribeiro		87	92	89	88	(356)
Total best 2, daily		162	167	165	169	
JAPAN	Grand total	173	340	508		670
Miss Masuyo Toyama		91	87	83	76	(337)
Miss Fusako Masui		89	81	85	87	(342)
Miss Kazuko Kobayashi		84	86	86	86	(342)
Total best 2, daily		173	167	168	162	
*Mrs. Atsuko Nishimura						
URUGUAY	Grand total	173	332	502		672
Mrs. Madelon Paez Vilaro		90	89	—	92	–
Mrs. Rosina F. de Pons		90	82	85	88	(345)
*Mrs. Gladys C. de Bragard		83	77	85	92	(327)
Total best 2, daily		173	159	170	170	
SWITZERLAND	Grand total	162	330	503		673
Miss Jacqueline Stucki		82	90	88	86	(344)
Miss Margrit Burki		87	84	—	94	–
Miss Astrid Bek		80	84	85	84	(333)
Total best 2, daily		162	168	173	170	
*Mrs. Germaine Ust						
NORWAY	Grand total	169	333	500		676
Miss Bebban Bjorge		84	82	82	89	(337)
Miss Vivi Horn		88	90	88	90	(356)
Miss Mette Rinde		85	82	85	87	(339)
Total best 2, daily		169	164	167	176	
*Mrs. Ruth Waaler						
VENEZUELA	Grand total	176	350	517		697
Mrs. Susana Ortega		87	82	81	89	(337)
Miss Elizabeth Tovar		89	92	89	97	(367)
Miss Doris Wright		95	93	86	91	(365)
Total best 2, daily		176	174	167	180	
*Mrs. Hope Nestares						

1972
FIFTH WOMEN'S WORLD AMATEUR TEAM CHAMPIONSHIP FOR THE ESPIRITO SANTO TROPHY

Held at the Hindu Country Club, Buenos Aires, Argentina, Oct. 11-14.
Yardage–6,117. Par 72. 20 Team Entries.

Team score consisted of best two individual scores in each round.
*Indicates Captain.

		1st Rd.	2nd Rd.	3rd Rd.	4th Rd.	72-hole Score
UNITED STATES	Grand Total	140	285	438		583
Miss Laura Baugh		72	73	77	72	(294)
Mrs. Jane Bastanchury Booth		68	73	77	73	(291)
Miss Mary Anne Budke		78	72	76	74	(300)
Total best 2, daily		140	145	153	145	
*Mrs. Robert M. Monsted						
FRANCE	Grand Total	156	303	442		587
Miss Anne Marie Palli		85	77	77	74	(313)
Mrs. Claudine Cros Rubin		80	73	68	71	(292)
Miss Brigitte Varangot		76	74	71	76	(297)
Total best 2, daily		156	147	139	145	
*Mrs. Lally Segard						
SWEDEN	Grand Total	148	298	445		594
Mrs. Birgit Forssman		78	81	77	80	(316)
Miss Christina Westerberg		75	79	73	73	(300)
Mrs. Liv Wollin		73	71	74	76	(294)
Total best 2, daily		148	150	147	149	
*Ms. Margaretha Murray						
AUSTRALIA	Grand Total	151	300	451		601
Mrs. Heather R. Bleeck		77	78	79	74	(308)
Mrs. Gayle G. Gannon		74	73	74	79	(300)
Mrs. Sandra M. McCaw		79	76	77	76	(308)
Total best 2, daily		151	149	151	150	
*Mrs. E. H. Griffith						
CANADA	Grand Total	145	302	452		602
Mrs. Gayle Borthwick		77	83	81	78	(319)
Miss Marilyn Palmer		80	80	77	76	(313)
Mrs. Marlene Streit		68	77	73	74	(292)
Total best 2, daily		145	157	150	150	
*Mrs. J. H. Todd						
GREAT BRITAIN AND IRELAND	Grand Total	151	299	453		602
*Miss Mary Everard		77	74	75	77	(303)
Mrs. Ian C. Robertson		75	74	79	74	(302)
Miss Michelle Walker		76	77	85	75	(313)
Total best 2, daily		151	148	154	149	
JAPAN	Grand Total	147	299	449		602
Miss Takako Kiyomoto		71	74	73	76	(294)
Miss Kazuko Kobayashi		76	82	79	77	(314)
Mrs. Michiko Tachibana		82	78	77	85	(322)
Total best 2, daily		147	152	150	153	
*Mrs. Akiko Azakami						
ARGENTINA	Grand Total	151	298	452		605
Mrs. Maria Julia Caserta de Aftalion		78	82	79	75	(314)
Miss Silvia Bertolaccini		78	74	78	79	(309)
Miss Betriz Rosello		73	73	76	78	(300)
Total best 2, daily		151	147	154	153	
*Ms. Margarita Mackinlay de Maglione						
SPAIN	Grand Total	151	305	457		610
Marquesa de Artasona		73	77	77	76	(303)
Miss Elena Corominas		78	77	77	78	(310)
*Mrs. Emma V. de Garcia-Ogara		81	79	75	77	(312)
Total best 2, daily		151	154	152	153	

ITALY	Grand Total	157	312	461		612
Miss Marina Ragher		82	78	78	77	(315)
*Mrs. Isa Goldschmid		80	77	71	74	(302)
Miss Bianca Martini		77	87	82	79	(325)
Total best 2, daily		157	155	149	151	
NEW ZEALAND	Grand Total	158	315	467		621
Mrs. S. R. S. Bannan		78	78	76	83	(315)
Miss Susan Hamilton		81	79	76	78	(314)
Miss Marilyn Smith		80	80	79	76	(315)
Total best 2, daily		158	157	152	154	
*Mrs. H. W. Mullaney						
GERMANY	Grand Total	152	308	464		622
Ms. Barbara Bohm		73	79	79	81	(312)
Miss Marion Petersen		79	77	81	77	(314)
Ms. Jeannette Weghmann		79	81	77	83	(320)
Total best 2, daily		152	156	156	158	
*Mrs. Lieselotte Strenger						
NETHERLANDS	Grand Total	154	311	467		624
Miss Alice Janmaat		77	77	77	78	(309)
Mrs. Annie M. Sandbach		77	82	79	—	—
Miss Marischka Swane		77	80	84	79	(320)
Total best 2, daily		154	157	156	157	
*Mrs. B. J. Verspyck						
BELGIUM	Grand Total	159	309	463		628
Miss Corinne Reybroeck		77	75	74	82	(308)
Miss Marie Anne Reybroeck		96	84	90	93	(363)
*Miss Louise Van der Berghe		82	75	80	83	(320)
Total best 2, daily		159	150	154	165	
SOUTH AFRICA	Grand Total	165	317	477		638
Miss Judy Angel		84	81	79	88	(332)
Miss Cheran Gerber		85	73	81	78	(317)
Mrs. Jenny Nellmapius		81	79	85	83	(328)
Total best 2, daily		165	152	160	161	
*Mrs. Esther M. Gallie						
CHILE	Grand Total	161	324	487		643
Ms. Ximena Bernales		83	81	82	88	(334)
Ms. Patricia de Fernandes		84	83	85	73	(325)
Ms. Marina Raab		78	82	81	83	(324)
Total best 2, daily		161	163	163	156	
BRAZIL	Grand Total	161	326	484		653
Mrs. Yolanda Figueiredo		80	82	80	85	(327)
Miss Gitta Grant		82	83	78	89	(332)
Mrs. Emy Nomura		81	88	85	84	(338)
Total best 2, daily		161	165	158	169	
*Ms. Marina de Nioac						
PERU	Grand Total	166	331	496		665
Ms. Cecilia Barreda		84	80	84	87	(335)
Ms. Jennifer Bayly		94	96	94	99	(383)
*Ms. Juana de Nari		82	85	81	82	(330)
Total best 2, daily		166	165	165	169	
COLOMBIA	Grand Total	166	330	498		666
Ms. Beatriz de Gaviria		84	83	84	87	(338)
Ms. Elisa Pardo		82	81	84	87	(334)
*Ms. Gloria de Pardo		86	86	88	81	(341)
Total best 2, daily		166	164	168	168	
URUGUAY	Grand Total	176	345	513		680
*Mrs. Gladys C. de Bragard		89	83	81	80	(333)
Ms. Carmen T. de Oelsner		90	86	87	87	(350)
Ms. Sheila Rumassa		87	89	94	88	(358)
Total best 2, daily		176	169	168	167	

1974
SIXTH WOMEN'S WORLD AMATEUR TEAM CHAMPIONSHIP
FOR THE ESPIRITO SANTO TROPHY

Held at the Campo de Golf, Cajuiles, La Romana, Dominican Republic, October 22-25

Yardage—6,212. Par 74. 22 Team Entries.

*Team Captain	First Round	Second Round	Third Round	Fourth Round	72-Hole Score
United States Grand Total	160	311	467		620
Miss Cynthia Hill	76	79	79	73	(307)
Miss Deborah Massey	84	72	77	81	(314)
Miss Carol Semple	D	79	88	80	
Total best 2, daily	160	151	156	153	
*Mrs. Allison Choate					
Great Britain and Ireland	160	317	477		636
Miss Mary McKenna	80	82	81	80	(323)
*Miss Julia Greenhalgh	80	84	79	81	(324)
Miss Tegwen Perkins	90	75	86	79	(330)
Total best 2, daily	160	157	160	159	
South Africa	162	321	482		636
Lisle Nel	79	83	80	86	(328)
Alison Sheard	83	81	81	74	(319)
Jenny Bruce	86	78	84	80	(328)
Total best 2, daily	162	159	161	154	
*Mrs. J. S. Dowie Dunn					
Australia	168	323	481		637
Miss J. Lock	83	76	79	77	(315)
Mrs. M. Parsons	85	79	79	87	(330)
Mrs. H. W. Cavill	86	82	86	79	(333)
Total best 2, daily	168	155	158	156	
*Miss H. Hawkeswood					
Spain	165	319	481		639
Marquesa de Artasona	81	75	80	82	(318)
Emma Garcia-Ogara	84	88	84	87	(343)
Carmen Maestre	84	79	82	76	(321)
*Condesa de Albox	165	154	162	158	
Italy	159	315	477		640
Federica Dassu	78	79	79	80	(317)
Marina Ciaffi Ragher	81	77	89	83	(330)
Eva Ragher	90	83	83	87	(343)
Total best 2, daily	159	156	162	163	
France	160	325	495		647
Mrs. Catherine Lacoste de Prado	78	84	88	71	(321)
Miss Brigitte Varangot	82	85	82	85	(334)
Mrs. Martine Giraud	84	81	88	81	(334)
Total best 2, daily	160	165	170	152	
*Mrs. Lally Segard					
Sweden	168	329	487		650
Miss Anna Skense	83	81	77	82	(323)
Mrs. Liv Wollin	85	80	81	81	(327)
Miss Monica Anderson	90	85	85	84	(344)
Total best 2, daily	168	161	158	163	
*Mrs. Margartha Murray					
Switzerland	164	332	498		654
Ms. Carole Charbonnier	82	84	88	78	(332)
Miss Marie Christine Werra	82	84	80	78	(324)
*Mrs. Verena Salvisberg	91	89	86	88	(354)
Total best 2, daily	164	168	166	156	
Canada	164	328	496		655
Miss Marilyn Palmer	81	87	85	84	(337)
Mrs. Betty Cole	83	80	83	75	(321)
Mrs. Susan Wickware	90	84	85	85	(344)
Total best 2, daily	164	164	168	159	
*Mrs. Julia Diditch					
Japan	167	332	495		657
Miss Masu Arakawa	82	84	86	84	(336)
Mrs. Haruko Ishii	85	91	83	82	(341)
Miss Machiko Yamada	86	81	80	80	(327)
Total best 2, daily	167	165	163	162	
*Noamoto Nabeshima					

		First Round	Second Round	Third Round	Fourth Round	72-Hole Score
Brazil	Grand Total	168	337	501		665
Elizabeth Noronha		83	83	81	86	(333)
Ingrid Buchi		85	88	89	82	(344)
Maria Alice Gonzalez		86	86	83	82	(337)
Total best 2, daily		168	169	164	164	
*Mrs. Yolanda Figueiredo						
Netherlands		165	332	504		668
Miss Alice Janmaat		80	87	80	82	(329)
Miss Priscilla Sauter		85	87	92	87	(351)
Miss Narischka Swane		92	80	92	82	(346)
Total best 2, daily		165	167	172	164	
*Mrs. Yvonne Spitzen						
New Zealand		175	342	517		676
Miss Frances Pere		87	84	87	79	(337)
Mrs. V. A. Bishop		88	83	88	86	(345)
Miss S. Boag		94	87	89	80	(350)
Total best 2, daily		175	167	175	159	
*Mrs. H. Mullaney						
Argentina		168	340	512		682
Miss Beatriz Rosello		83	89	86	85	(343)
Miss Maria Teran		85	85	86	86	(342)
Maria Aftalion		87	87	90	85	(349)
Total best 2, daily		168	172	172	170	
*Mrs. Margarita M. de Maglione						
Belgium		172	341	513		687
Miss Corinne Reybroeck		80	80	83	85	(328)
*Miss Louise van den Berghe		92	93	93	89	(367)
Ms. Francoise Wagheneire		95	89	89	98	(371)
Total best 2, daily		172	169	172	174	
Chile		177	355	529		692
Ms. Ximena Bernales		87	86	85	80	(338)
Ms. Maria Pia Aguirre		90	92	89	83	(354)
Total best 2, daily		177	178	174	163	
*Oscar Galeno						
Jamaica		181	358	538		712
Dorothy Mahfood		89	88	89	89	(355)
Pauline Laman		92	89	91	85	(357)
Susanne Rebhan		104	94	101	97	(396)
Total best 2, daily		181	177	180	174	
Dominican Republic		185	359	540		718
Maria de la Guardia		87	90	92	91	(360)
*Mrs. Jacqueline de Jesus		98	84	90	87	(359)
Miss Silvia Corrie		103	96	91	98	(388)
Total best 2, daily		185	174	181	178	
*Mrs. Norma de Lahoz						
Puerto Rico		183	366	552		722
*Mrs. Tati Shapiro		91	87	90	84	(352)
Linda Lupica		92	96	96	86	(370)
Sally Gonzalez		105	106	99	104	(414)
Total best 2, daily		183	183	186	170	
Venezuela		189	370	551		732
Angeles Alcantara		91	91	89	94	(365)
Elena Larrazabal		98	99	92	89	(378)
Doris Wright		99	90	97	92	(378)
Total best 2, daily		189	181	181	181	
*Freddy Alcantara						
Bermuda		208	413	620		814
Phillys Ahern		102	103	103	102	(410)
Glenda Todd		106	106	105	95	(412)
*Mrs. Joan Foulger		117	102	104	99	(422)
Total best 2, daily		208	205	207	194	

1976
SEVENTH WOMEN'S WORLD AMATEUR TEAM CHAMPIONSHIP FOR THE ESPIRITO SANTO TROPHY

Held at the Vilamoura Golf Club, Algarve, Portugal, October 6-9

Yardage—6,181. Par 73. 25 Team Entries.

*Team Captain		First Round	Second Round	Third Round	Fourth Round	72-Hole Score
United States	Grand Total	152	304	451		605
Donna Horton		81	77	77	77	(312)
Nancy Lopez		72	75	73	77	(297)
Deborah Massey		80	77	74	78	(309)
Total best 2, daily		152	152	147	154	
*Mrs. Harton S. Semple						
France		154	311	460		622
Catherine Lacoste de Prado		76	77	75	79	(307)
Anne Marie Palli		78	80	74	83	(315)
M. Christine Ubald-Bocquet		81	88	83	87	(339)
Total best 2, daily		154	157	149	162	
*Martine Giraud						
Brazil		160	320	472		626
Laura M. dos Santos		84	87	84	83	(338)
Maria Alice Gonzalez		81	76	80	75	(312)
Elisabeth Noronha		79	84	72	79	(314)
Total best 2, daily		160	160	152	154	
*Yolanda Figueiredo						
Italy		157	316	473		635
Isa Goldschmidt		85	82	79	81	(327)
Marina Ragher		77	83	80	83	(323)
Frederica Dassu		80	77	78	81	(316)
Total best 2, daily		157	159	157	162	
Australia		160	320	477		636
Jane Lock		81	78	75	83	(317)
Sandra McCaw		79	82	82	81	(324)
Karen Permezel		83	87	82	78	(330)
Total best 2, daily		160	160	157	159	
*Mrs. J. S. Bailey						
Canada		161	317	474		636
G. (Betty) Cole		87	78	84	80	(329)
Marylin Palmer		83	78	80	82	(329)
Dale Shaw		78	82	77	84	(321)
Total best 2, daily		161	156	157	162	
*Miss Sally Basler						
Republic of China		157	318	475		638
Ming-Ching Huang		80	81	82	82	(325)
Yu-Hsia Tai		78	83	75	81	(317)
Mei-Chen Chen		79	80	82	85	(326)
Total best 2, daily		157	161	157	163	
*Miss Pearl Niu						
South Africa		159	316	476		639
Jenny Bruce		83	77	79	82	(321)
Cheran Gerber		84	81	81	81	(327)
Alison Sheard		76	80	81	82	(319)
Total best 2, daily		159	157	160	163	
*E. V. Britt						
Spain		162	322	479		639
Cristina Marsans		84	82	83	82	(331)
Elena Corominas		84	87	80	79	(330)
Carmen Maestre		78	78	77	81	(314)
Total best 2, daily		162	160	157	160	
*Emma Garcia-Ogara						

	First Round	Second Round	Third Round	Fourth Round	72-Hole Score
Germany Grand Total	164	324	479		641
Barbara Bohm	80	80	74	84	(318)
Marietta Guttermann	89	84	84	78	(335)
Susan Schultz	84	80	81	84	(329)
Total best 2, daily	164	160	155	162	
*Lieselotte Strenger					
Sweden	165	323	482		641
Hillewi Hagstrom	89	79	82	85	(335)
Pia Nilsson	86	83	86	85	(340)
*Liv Wollin	79	79	77	74	(309)
Total best 2, daily	165	158	159	159	
Japan	158	321	487		643
Haruko Ishii	78	87	84	79	(328)
Machiko Yamada	86	83	82	79	(330)
Yumiko Kanoh	80	80	85	77	(322)
Total best 2, daily	158	163	166	156	
*Miss Yoshiko Kosaka					
Great Britain and Ireland	164	326	488		645
Jennifer Lee Smith	82	80	86	80	(328)
Mary McKenna	85	83	79	77	(324)
Catherine Panton	82	82	83	80	(327)
Total best 2, daily	164	162	162	157	
*Mrs. F. G. M. Baker					
Argentina	160	330	489		649
Maria J. C. de Aftalion	85	88	80	84	(337)
*Amanda S. de Felizia	81	87	84	82	(334)
Beatriz Rossello	79	83	79	78	(319)
Total best 2, daily	160	170	159	160	
Switzerland	166	337	503		663
Carole Charbonnier	81	86	84	78	(329)
Verena Salvisberg	85	91	86	83	(345)
Marie-Christine de Werra	86	85	82	82	(335)
Total best 2, daily	166	171	166	160	
*Peter Salvisberg					
Netherlands	166	337	502		669
Alice Janmaat	84	84	88	82	(338)
Nicole B. Spits	88	87	83	85	(343)
Marischka Zegger-Swane	82	89	82	88	(341)
Total best 2, daily	166	171	165	167	
*Mrs. Yvonne Spitzen					
Belgium	172	343	509		674
Maguy Brose	88	91	94	89	(362)
Marie Anne Toussaint	91	85	84	93	(353)
Francoise de Wagheneire	84	86	82	76	(328)
Total best 2, daily	172	171	166	165	
*Mrs. Josephine Leysen					
Chile	168	338	509		677
*Patricia Fernandez	88	90	91	84	(353)
Maria Pia Valdez	80	85	95	87	(347)
Beatriz Steeger	93	85	80	84	(342)
Total best 2, daily	168	170	171	168	
Denmark	175	344	513		685
*Marete Meiland	87	87	85	86	(345)
Annette Hagdrup	88	84	84	86	(342)
Tina Pors	90	85	90	86	(351)
Total best 2, daily	175	169	169	172	

		First Round	Second Round	Third Round	Fourth Round	72-Hole Score
Mexico	Grand Total	167	338	513		685
Maria Luisa Martinez		93	92	99	83	(367)
Luz de Lourdes Fernandez		86	90	89	95	(360)
Fela Chaves de Subirats		81	81	86	89	(337)
Total best 2, daily		167	171	175	172	
*Mrs. S. W. de Gutierrez						
Norway		172	349	524		701
Lilly Gulliksen		86	86	88	94	(354)
Vivi Marstrand		89	91	89	86	(355)
Mette Reuss		86	91	87	91	(355)
Total best 2, daily		172	177	175	177	
*Anniken Langaard						
Sri Lanka		176	360	534		701
Tiru Fernando		82	83	82	81	(328)
*W. P. Fernando		94	101	92	86	(373)
Total best 2, daily		176	184	174	167	
Rhodesia		177	352	527		702
Anne Esson		90	97	91	90	(368)
Jean Freeman		93	87	84	90	(354)
Joan Walker		87	88	100	85	(360)
Total best 2, daily		177	175	175	175	
*Mrs. Dorothy Martin						
Portugal		193	392	577		762
Graca Medina		96	102	94	98	(390)
Veronica Oliveira e Silva		110	103	107	104	(424)
Teresa Mata		97	97	91	87	(372)
Total best 2, daily		193	199	185	185	
Dominican Republic		208	397	580		777
*Jacquelin de Jesus		103	96	93	100	(392)
Silvia Corrie		112	102	90	101	(405)
Susan Fellow		105	93	97	97	(392)
Total best 2, daliy		208	189	183	197	

1978
EIGHTH WOMEN'S WORLD AMATEUR TEAM CHAMPIONSHIP
FOR THE ESPIRITO SANTO TROPHY

Held at the Pacific Harbour Golf and Country Club, Fiji, October 10-13.

Yardage—5,823. Par 72. 14 Team Entries.

*Team Captain	First Round	Second Round	Third Round	Fourth Round	72-Hole Score
Australia Grand Total	149	292	443		596
Lindy Goggin	79	77	76	75	(307)
Edwina Kennedy	76	71	78	79	(304)
Jane Lock	73	72	75	78	(298)
Total best 2, daily	149	143	151	153	
*Mrs. R. D. Bridges					
Canada	147	296	449		597
Marilyn Palmer	75	75	80	76	(306)
Cathy Sherk	72	74	76	72	(294)
Stacey West	80	80	77	81	(318)
Total best 2, daily	147	149	153	148	
*Marlene Streit					
France	146	299	455		602
Nathalie Jeanson	73	76	85	89	(323)
Marie Laure Lorenzi	74	77	77	73	(301)
Catherine Lacoste de Prado	73	78	79	74	(304)
Total best 2, daily	146	153	156	147	
*Martine Giraud					
United States	152	301	449		605
Beth Daniel	75	71	74	78	(298)
Cynthia Hill	77	78	75	78	(308)
Judith Oliver	77	84	74	86	(321)
Total best 2, daily	152	149	148	156	
*Mrs. Frank Lovell					
Great Britain and Ireland	145	296	449		605
Mary Everard	73	77	75	80	(305)
Julia Greenhalgh	72	76	78	77	(303)
Muriel Thomson	83	75	78	79	(315)
Total best 2, daily	145	151	153	156	
*Mrs. Carol Comboy					
Japan	148	301	452		610
Hauko Ishii	85	80	74	84	(323)
Miki Oda	74	73	77	74	(298)
Machiko Yamada	74	84	81	88	(327)
Total best 2, daily	148	153	151	158	
*Miss Yoshiko Kosaka					
New Zealand	153	303	455		614
Liz Douglas	82	76	78	77	(313)
Cherry Kingham	75	74	74	82	(305)
Heather Ryan	78	82	78	—	
Total best 2, daily	153	150	152	159	
*Mrs. T. D. Munro					
Sweden	149	302	450		616
Karsten Ehrnlund	74	—	—	—	
Charlotte Montgomery	78	73	72	87	(310)
*Liv Wollin	75	80	76	79	(310)
Total best 2, daily	149	153	148	166	
Spain	156	315	471		625
Marta Figueras	78	84	85	75	(322)
Carmen Maestre	79	79	77	79	(314)
*Cristina Marsans	78	80	79	80	(317)
Total best 2, daily	156	159	156	154	

		First Round	Second Round	Third Round	Fourth Round	72-Hole Score
Germany	Grand Total	167	323	475		632
Barbara Bohm		85	78	83	87	(333)
Susanne Schultz		82	78	76	80	(316)
Marion Thannhauser		86	80	76	77	(319)
Total best 2, daily		167	156	152	157	
*Harry Cotterell						
Switzerland		153	309	472		635
Carole Charbonnier		76	78	82	79	(315)
Marie de Werra		80	78	81	85	(324)
Regine Lautens		77	84	84	84	(329)
Total best 2, daily		153	156	163	163	
*Ruedi Muller						
Argentina		160	311	471		640
Susanna Garmendia		78	74	83	85	(320)
*Beatriz Rossello		82	83	79	85	(329)
Amanda de Felizia		85	77	81	84	(327)
Total best 2, daily		160	151	160	169	
Italy		157	317	480		644
Minette Marazza		90	83	78	87	(338)
Guenda Moavero		78	80	91	92	(341)
Marina Buscani Ragher		79	80	85	77	(321)
Total best 2, daily		157	160	163	164	
*Isa Goldschmid						
Fiji		183	364	539		737
Anna Dunn		90	89	86	96	(361)
Lydia Manueli		98	99	89	102	(388)
Adi Sai Tuivanuavou		93	92	104	104	(393)
Total best 2, daily		183	181	175	198	
*Mrs. Doris Leys						

1980
NINTH WOMEN'S WORLD AMATEUR TEAM CHAMPIONSHIP FOR THE ESPIRITO SANTO TROPHY

Held at Pinehurst Country Club (No. 2 Course), Pinehurst, North Carolina, October 1-4
Yardage—5,940. Par 74. 28 Team Entries

*Team Captain	1st Rd.	2nd Rd.	3rd Rd.	4th Rd.	72-Hole Score
UNITED STATES Grand total	151	296	444		588
Juli Simpson Inkster	78	75	74	73	(300)
Patrice M. Rizzo	73	70	75	76	(294)
Carol Semple	78	79	74	71	(302)
Total best 2	151	145	148	144	
*Miss Elizabeth S. Brand					
AUSTRALIA Grand total	150	296	447		595
Lindy Goggin	77	75	75	72	(299)
Edwina Kennedy	73	71	76	76	(296)
Jane Lock	87	77	79	82	(325)
Total best 2	150	146	151	148	
*Mrs. R. D. Bridges					
FRANCE Grand total	158	308	464		610
Eliane Berthet	79	77	80	77	(313)
Marie-Laure de Lorenzi	79	80	77	71	(307)
Cecilia Mourgue D'Algue	79	73	79	75	(306)
Total best 2	158	150	156	146	
*Mrs. Martine Giraud					
SPAIN Grand total	159	304	454		610
Ana Monfort de Albox	79	77	82	81	(319)
Marta Figueras-Dotti	80	70	71	77	(298)
Carmen Maestre de Pellon	80	75	79	79	(313)
Total best 2	159	145	150	156	
*Emma V. de Garcia-Ogara					
GREAT BRITAIN & IRELAND Grand total	156	310	459		615
Jane Connachan	78	73	76	81	(308)
Maureen Madill	81	82	73	81	(317)
Belle Robertson	78	81	76	75	(310)
Total best 2	156	154	149	156	
*Marie O'Donnell					
ITALY Grand total	158	313	469		621
Emanuela Braito	80	81	83	78	(322)
Marina Buscaini	83	80	79	82	(324)
Federica Dassu	78	75	77	74	(304)
Total best 2	158	155	156	152	
*Lunella Rivetti					
SWEDEN Grand total	156	310	464		621
Viveca Hoff	77	77	79	80	(313)
Pia Nilsson	79	77	75	77	(308)
Liv Wollin	79	82	80	85	(326)
Total best 2	156	154	154	157	
*Barbro Montgomery					
CANADA Grand total	160	311	466		622
Barbara Bunkowsky	81	73	78	85	(317)
Lynn Cooke	80	84	80	78	(322)
Judy Ellis	80	78	77	78	(313)
Total best 2	160	151	155	156	
*Mrs. Marlene Streit					
SWITZERLAND Grand total	157	315	467		622
Annette Hadorn	84	79	78	81	(322)
Regine Lautens	80	79	81	80	(320)
Marie Christine de Werra	77	85	74	75	(311)
Total best 2	157	158	152	155	
*Mrs. Monica Wieland					
JAPAN Grand total	159	316	473		628
*Mrs. Haruko Ishii	86	83	81	83	(333)
Miss Toshi Matsubara	82	79	82	75	(318)
Miss Haruyo Miyazawa	77	78	76	80	(311)
Total best 2	159	157	157	155	

NINTH WOMEN'S WORLD AMATEUR TEAM CHAMPIONSHIP (Continued)

NEW ZEALAND	Grand total	157	314	467		630
Mrs. W. R. Douglas		79	79	79	82	(319)
Mrs. B. Rhodes		78	78	74	84	(314)
Miss J. Scandrett		90	82	81	81	(334)
Total best 2		157	157	153	163	
*Mrs. H.A. Williams						
REPUBLIC OF CHINA	Grand total	160	315	472		633
Li-Ying Chen		79	87	84	83	(333)
Bie-Shyun Huang		81	81	78	85	(325)
Hsiu-Tien Su		83	74	79	78	(314)
Total best 2		160	155	157	161	
*Mrs. Lan Hsun-hsun Huang						
GERMANY	Grand total	160	313	471		635
Ursula Beer		89	75	81	83	(328)
Sabine Blecher		79	81	78	82	(320)
Dr. Barbara Boehm		81	78	80	82	(321)
Total best 2		160	153	158	164	
*H. Biemer						
SOUTH AFRICA	Grand total	160	321	477		638
Vicky Farrell		80	79	75	81	(315)
Rae Hast		80	84	83	85	(332)
Sheree Muirhead		80	82	81	80	(323)
Total best 2		160	161	156	161	
*L. van Diggelen						
ARGENTINA	Grand total	160	326	487		643
Susana B. Garmendia		75	79	78	77	(309)
Maria E. Noguerol		85	87	86	79	(337)
Beatriz G. Rossello		90	87	83	81	(341)
Total best 2		160	166	161	156	
*Ivar F. W. Brostrom						
NETHERLANDS	Grand total	162	321	483		643
Joyce Heyster		81	80	81	83	(325)
Alice Janmaat		83	79	87	78	(327)
Ineke Keunen		81	84	81	82	(328)
Total best 2		162	159	162	160	
*Mrs. Anneke Tuyt						
BELGIUM	Grand total	169	332	486		649
Isabelle Declercq		84	82	74	80	(320)
Marie-Noelle Herkens		85	85	87	83	(340)
Francoise de Wagheneire		90	81	80	84	(335)
Total best 2		169	163	154	163	
*Louise Vandenberghe						
BRAZIL	Grand total	162	320	483		649
Isabel D. Lopes		84	78	86	92	(340)
Elizabeth Nickhorn		80	80	81	83	(324)
Tiemi Nomura		82	87	82	83	(334)
Total best 2		162	158	163	166	
*Dora Nardy						
NORWAY	Grand total	167	329	489		651
Reidun S. Dirdal		83	83	82	81	(329)
Lilly Gulliksen		84	81	78	81	(324)
Mette Reuss		87	81	83	84	(335)
Total best 2		167	162	160	162	
*Anne-Marie Giortz						
COLOMBIA	Grand total	171	335	501		663
Patricia Gonzalez		89	79	83	79	(330)
*Gloria de Pardo		88	86	85	83	(342)
Monica Tamayo		83	85	83	84	(335)
Total best 2		171	164	166	162	
ZIMBABWE	Grand total	168	336	498		666
Vivienne Browning		84	84	81	90	(339)
Linda Turnbull		88	86	96	85	(355)
Rowena Wepener		84	84	81	83	(332)
Total best 2		168	168	162	168	
*Mrs. Ann Swift						
PERU	Grand total	169	332	494		668
Mariza Alzamora		87	83	84	88	(342)
Alicia Dibos		82	80	78	86	(326)
Juana M. de Nari		87	83	85	89	(344)
Total best 2		169	163	162	174	
*Enrique Dibos						
CHILE	Grand total	169	329	502		671
Maria Pia Aguirre		86	87	84	85	(342)
Ana Maria Cambiaso		87	79	90	89	(345)
Beatriz Steeger		83	81	89	84	(337)
Total best 2		169	160	173	169	
*Ana Maria Cambiaso						

NINTH WOMEN'S WORLD AMATEUR TEAM CHAMPIONSHIP (Continued)

MEXICO Grand total	171	338	513		681
Carolina Fernandez	86	84	97	94	(361)
Pilar Guzman	96	92	89	90	(367)
Adriana Ramirez	85	83	86	78	(332)
Total best 2	171	167	175	168	
*Patricia de Fuentes					
VENEZUELA Grand total	171	339	508		685
Angeles Alcantara	86	84	86	89	(345)
Graciela Quintana	85	84	83	90	(342)
Gracielo Plaza	93	85	95	88	(361)
Total best 2	171	168	169	177	
*Freddy Alcantara					
BERMUDA Grand total	181	360	539		711
Judithanne L. Astwood	91	89	87	85	(352)
Barbara Mulder	102	101	103	102	(408)
Ginette Spinucci	90	90	92	87	(359)
Total best 2	181	179	179	179	
*Mrs. Rendell Arton					
GUATEMALA Grand total	170	362	535		713
Nancy D. de Noguera	88	101	93	95	(377)
Florencia H. de Rolz	82	91	80	83	(336)
Total best 2	170	192	173	178	
FIJI Grand total	183	366	551		739
Anna Dunn	87	86	90	89	(352)
Tuli Naisara	96	98	99	103	(396)
Myrtle Pickering	105	97	95	99	(396)
Total best 2	183	183	185	188	
*Mrs. Heather Hughan					

WOMEN'S TEAM MATCH

United States vs. Europe

HISTORY

1968—Following the Curtis Cup Match, the United States played a match against a team representing the Continent of Europe at St. Cloud Golf Club, Paris, France. The Continent of Europe won, 10½-7½. The Europeans took a 5½-3½ lead the first day, and increased it to 7-5 in the foursomes the second day. The United States could not make up the difference in the concluding series of singles, when in the first three matches Miss Catherine Lacoste, of France, defeated Miss Shelley Hamlin; Mrs. Claudine Cros Rubin, of France, defeated Mrs. Anne Quast Welts; and Miss Marina Ragher, of Italy, defeated Miss Roberta Albers. Miss Ragher scored 3½ of a possible 4 points for Europe, the best score of any contestant on either side. Non-playing Captains were Vicomtesse de Saint-Sauveur, of France, for Europe, and Mrs. Robert M. Monsted, for the United States.

1968
WOMEN'S TEAM MATCH

Held at St. Cloud Golf Club, Paris, France
June 19 and 20

June 19

Continental Europe	Points	United States	Points
FOURSOMES			
Miss Catherine Lacoste and Mrs. Claudine Rubin	0	Miss Shelley Hamlin and Mrs. Anne Quast Welts (6 and 4)	1
Miss Brigitte Varangot and Mrs. Isa Goldschmid (1 up)	1	Miss Mary Lou Dill and Miss Peggy Conley	0
Mrs. Odile Garaialde and Miss Marina Ragher (2 and 1)	1	Miss Jean Ashley and Miss Phyllis Preuss	0
Total	2	Total	1
SINGLES			
Miss Catherine Lacoste (4 and 3)	1	Mrs. Anne Quast Welts	0
Mrs. Claudine Rubin	0	Miss Shelley Hamlin (5 and 4)	1
Miss Marina Ragher (2 and 1)	1	Miss Roberta Albers	0
Mrs. Odile Garaialde	0	Miss Peggy Conley (2 and 1)	1
Miss Brigitte Varangot (4 and 3)	1	Miss Phyllis Preuss	0
Mrs. Isa Goldschmid (halved)	½	Miss Jean Ashley (halved)	½
Total	3½	Total	2½
Total June 19	5½	Total June 19	3½

June 20

Continental Europe	Points	United States	Points
FOURSOMES			
Miss Catherine Lacoste and Mrs. Claudine Rubin (5 and 3)	1	Miss Shelley Hamlin and Mrs. Anne Quast Welts	0
Mrs. Isa Goldschmid and Miss Brigitte Varangot	0	Miss Phyllis Preuss and Miss Jean Ashley (3 and 2)	1
Mrs. Odile Garaialde and Miss Marina Ragher (halved)	½	Miss Peggy Conley and Miss Mary Lou Dill (halved)	½
Total	1½	Total	1½
SINGLES			
Miss Catherine Lacoste (4 and 3)	1	Miss Shelley Hamlin	0
Mrs. Claudine Rubin (1 up)	1	Mrs. Anne Quast Welts	0
Miss Marina Ragher (3 and 1)	1	Miss Roberta Albers	0
Miss Corinne Reybroeck	0	Miss Phyllis Preuss (1 up)	1
Mrs. Isa Goldschmid	0	Miss Peggy Conley (2 and 1)	1
Mrs. Odile Garaialde (halved)	½	Miss Jean Ashley (halved)	½
Total	3½	Total	2½
Total June 20	5	Total June 20	4
Grand Total—Continental Europe	10½	Grand Total—United States	7½

Non-playing Captain—Vicomtesse de Saint-Sauveur

Non-playing Captain—Mrs. Robert M. Monsted

SENIOR WORLD AMATEUR TEAM CHAMPIONSHIP

THE SHUN NOMURA TROPHY

Presented in October, 1967
by the Japanese Friends of Golf through the
Japan Golf Association

HISTORY

1967–On a suggestion by the USGA, the World Amateur Golf Council inaugurated a Senior World Amateur Team Championship for golfers 55 years of age and older. It was played for the first time in November, 1967, over the No. 2 Course of the Pinehurst Country Club, Pinehurst, N.C., and it was won by the United States with a team score of 903. Canada was second with 920, and Australia third with 940. Eleven countries participated in the competition for the Shun Nomura Trophy presented by Friends of Golf in Japan through the Japan Golf Association. Each team was allowed four players; each day the three best individual scores made up the team's score. The sum of the four daily totals determined the winner. Robert B. Kiersky and Raymond Palmer led the United States to the victory. Kiersky, the 1965 Senior Amateur Champion of the USGA, scored 297 for the four rounds, and Palmer, the current Champion, scored 301. Those were the low individual scores. Lionel Bowditch, of Australia, was next with 302. The United States took an eight-stroke lead over Canada and Great Britain and Ireland after the first round, and increased the advantage daily. J. Ellis Knowles, six times Champion of the United States Seniors Golf Association, was non-playing Captain.

1969–The United States led every one of the four rounds and won the World Senior Amateur Team Championship for the second time. The final score was 908. Canada was second with 929, Great Britain and Ireland was third with 931. The United States led Great Britain and Ireland by five strokes after the first round, then increased its lead to 11 strokes after two rounds and 21 after three. David (Spec) Goldman, United States, was low individual for the competition with a 72-hole score of 298. Dr. George B. Bigelow, of Canada, had the second lowest individual score of 305. Curtis Person, Sr., was Captain of the American team. The competition was conducted over the Old Course at St. Andrews, Scotland.

WORLD SENIOR AMATEUR TEAM CHAMPIONSHIP FOR THE SHUN NOMURA TROPHY

1967–At Pinehurst Country Club (No. 2 Course), Pinehurst, N.C.

United States	903	Japan	959	Bermuda	1007
Canada	920	France	971	Switzerland	1047
Australia	940	Germany	975	Italy	1053
Great Britain & Ireland	941	Zambia	982		

1969–At Royal and Ancient Golf Club (Old Course), St. Andrews, Scotland

United States	908	Germany	963	Portugal	1029
Canada	929	Japan	978	Italy	1029
Great Britain & Ireland	931	France	979	Mexico	1040
		Sweden	980	Switzerland	1058
South Africa	953	Bermuda	1009		

1967
FIRST WORLD SENIOR AMATEUR TEAM CHAMPIONSHIP
FOR THE SHUN NOMURA TROPHY

Held at the Pinehurst Country Club, No. 2 Course, Pinehurst, N.C., November 15-18.
Yardage—6,415. Par 72. 11 Team Entries.

Team score consisted of best three individual scores in each round.
*Indicates Captain.

		1st Rd.	2nd Rd.	3rd Rd.	4th Rd.	72-hole Score
UNITED STATES	Grand total	226	449	679		903
George C. Beechler		78	74	80	82	(314)
David Goldman		76	77	78	77	(308)
Robert B. Kiersky		73	75	73	76	(297)
Raymond Palmer		77	74	79	71	(301)
Total best 3, daily		226	223	230	224	
*J. Ellis Knowles						
CANADA	Grand total	234	461	693		920
Dr. George B. Bigelow		82	76	74	82	(314)
*Phil Farley		76	76	81	76	(309)
George C. Hevenor, Sr.		83	75	81	75	(314)
Jack B. Nash		76	77	77	76	(306)
Total best 3, daily		234	227	232	227	
AUSTRALIA	Grand total	240	472	707		940
*Jack C. Barkel		80	79	81	79	(319)
Lionel Bowditch		78	74	75	75	(302)
Lou D. Carson		82	86	84	80	(332)
William J. Welch		85	79	79	79	(322)
Total best 3, daily		240	232	235	233	
GREAT BRITAIN AND IRELAND	Grand total	234	469	706		941
*Harry G. Bentley		77	73	82	74	(306)
Stanley L. Elliott		81	84	86	84	(335)
Francis Francis		78	78	74	78	(308)
+Charles Stowe		79	dq	81	83	
Total best 3, daily		234	235	237	235	
+Signed incorrect scorecard						
JAPAN	Grand total	244	475	719		959
Zenjiro Hirano		83	79	83	83	(328)
Dr. Makoto Katayama		84	79	82	82	(327)
*Naoyas Nabeshima		83	79	79	84	(325)
Isamu Sekiguchi		78	73	84	75	(310)
Total best 3, daily		244	231	244	240	
FRANCE	Grand total	242	493	738		971
Marius Bardana		83	78	79	73	(313)
Michel Carlhian		87	92	90	83	(352)
Max Corre		86	85	87	81	(339)
Georges Huet		73	88	79	79	(319)
Total best 3, daily		242	251	245	233	
*Jacques Leglise						
GERMANY	Grand total	245	482	734		975
Walter Asendorf		81	84	89	85	(339)
Anjo Lacinik		82	79	81	77	(319)
*Dr. Kurt Muller		82	78	87	81	(328)
August K. Weyhausen		83	80	84	83	(330)
Total best 3, daily		245	237	252	241	
ZAMBIA	Grand total	249	496	740		982
John Lavelle		83	80	84	84	(331)
Ronald E. Norris		85	85	90	76	(336)
Pieter J. Terblanche		84	84	80	90	(338)
George J. van Niekerk		82	83	80	82	(327)
Total best 3, daily		249	247	244	242	
*William Cobbett-Tribe						
BERMUDA	Grand total	255	502	752		1007
Dr. Morris Fulton		90	81	94	85	(350)
A. Brock Park		84	85	85	88	(342)
Robert Scott		90	91	88	87	(356)
*George E. Wardman		81	81	77	83	(322)
Total best 3, daily		255	247	250	255	

First World Senior Amateur Team Championship – Continued

		1st Rd.	2nd Rd.	3rd Rd.	4th Rd.	72-hole Score
SWITZERLAND	**Grand total**	264	524	791		1047
*Antoine Barras		88	87	91	88	(354)
Max Reymond		86	87	86	85	(344)
Robert Weber		93	99	91	89	(372)
Herman Wirth		90	86	90	83	(349)
Total best 3, daily		264	260	267	256	
ITALY	Grand total	261	530	790		1053
Ercole Remigi		91	88	83	89	(351)
Guiseppe Sabini		82	96	87	87	(352)
*Leone Valmaggia		88	92	90	87	(357)
Mario Veneziani		93	89	91	94	(367)
Total best 3, daily		261	269	260	263	

1969
SECOND WORLD SENIOR AMATEUR TEAM CHAMPIONSHIP FOR THE SHUN NOMURA TROPHY

Held at the Royal and Ancient Golf Club (Old Course), St. Andrews, Scotland, October 1-4.
Yardage—6,581. Par 72. 13 Team Entries.

Team score consists of three best individual scores in each round.
*Indicates Captain.

		1st Rd.	2nd Rd.	3rd Rd.	4th Rd.	72-hole Score
UNITED STATES	Grand total	230	456	679		908
*Curtis Person, Sr.		78	79	75	74	(306)
Merrill L. Carlsmith		77	77	74	79	(307)
David Goldman		75	73	74	76	(298)
Robert C. Loufek		78	76	80	79	(313)
Total best 3, daily		230	226	223	229	
CANADA	Grand total	236	467	700		929
Dr. George B. Bigelow		80	73	76	76	(305)
James C. Boeckh		85	80	81	83	(329)
Phil Farley		82	78	79	74	(313)
Jack Nash		74	80	78	79	(311)
Total best 3, daily		236	231	233	229	
*Ray Getliffe						
GREAT BRITAIN AND IRELAND	Grand total	235	470	703		931
*A. D. Cave		82	80	77	81	(320)
A. L. Bentley		81	78	80	73	(312)
A. Kyle		77	77	84	79	(317)
R. Pattinson		77	80	76	76	(309)
Total best 3, daily		235	235	233	228	
SOUTH AFRICA	Grand total	240	473	711		953
Eric L. Dalton		77	76	80	79	(312)
John Fisher		82	83	78	87	(330)
Julian Jourdan		85	74	88	78	(325)
Charles C. Taylor		81	83	80	86	(330)
Total best 3, daily		240	233	238	242	
*Hugh Kelly						
GERMANY	Grand total	243	473	718		963
*A. K. Weyhausen		84	89	88	81	(342)
Dr. Peter Fehring		86	77	83	83	(329)
Anjo Lacinik		79	78	84	86	(327)
Jean Phillipps		80	75	78	81	(314)
Total best 3, daily		243	230	245	245	
JAPAN	Grand total	247	484	736		978
*Naoyas Nabeshima		79	77	86	79	(321)
Tatsuo Fujimoto		87	81	83	81	(332)
Hiroshi Ikenaga		83	80	87	84	(334)
Kaneshige Yoshikawa		85	80	83	82	(330)
Total best 3, daily		247	237	252	242	
FRANCE	Grand total	244	486	726		979
Marius Bardana		78	81	81	81	(321)
Michel Carlhian		87	85	87	91	(350)
Georges Huet		83	78	80	85	(326)
Jacques de Saint-Sauveur		83	83	79	87	(332)
Total best 3, daily		244	242	240	253	
*Jacques Leglise						
SWEDEN	Grand total	254	496	749		980
*L. Bunke		86	85	87	79	(337)
L. Floberg		83	—	84	80	(—)
G. Nygren		85	80	89	76	(330)
G. Nystrom		86	77	82	76	(321)
Total best 3, daily		254	242	253	231	
BERMUDA	Grand total	260	516	764		1009
*George Ervin Wardman		82	82	79	77	(320)
Dr. Morris Crawford Fulton		92	86	86	87	(351)
A. Brock Park		94	88	94	91	(367)
Robert Harrison Scott		86	91	83	81	(341)
Total best 3, daily		260	256	248	245	

Second World Senior Amateur Team Championship – Continued

		1st Rd.	2nd Rd.	3rd Rd.	4th Rd.	72-hole Score
PORTUGAL	Grand total	263	516	775		1029
*Viscount Pereira Machado		90	90	89	86	(355)
Manuel de Brito E. Cunha		97	82	88	86	(353)
Brodie Lennox		80	*81	82	82	(325)
Frederico Burnay Mendonca		93	99	95	88	(375)
Total best 3, daily		263	253	259	254	
ITALY	Grand total	261	522	783		1029
*Leone Valmaggia		86	88	92	90	(356)
Peitro Camera		93	90	85	84	(352)
Dino Mondolfi		89	85	84	82	(340)
Mario Sposito		86	88	—	80	(—)
Total best 3, daily		261	261	261	246	
MEXICO	Grand total	255	517	780		1040
Pedro del Villar		81	85	95	86	(347)
Rodrigo Medellin		88	90	84	86	(348)
Ignacio Diaz		86	87	84	88	(345)
*Pedro R. Suinaga-Lujan		97	91	100	93	(381)
Total best 3, daily		255	262	263	260	
SWITZERLAND	Grand total	265	526	794		1058
*Antoine Barras		89	89	92	94	(364)
Ernst Plattner		88	84	90	90	(352)
Max Reymond		91	88	89	88	(356)
Herman Wirth		88	89	89	86	(352)
Total best 3, daily		265	261	268	264	

AMERICAS GOLF CUP MATCH

THE AMERICAS GOLF CUP

Presented to the

Royal Canadian Golf Association
Asociacion Mexicana de Golf
United States Golf Association

in August, 1952, by

JEROME P. BOWES, JR.
President of the Western Golf Association, 1950-1951

HISTORY

1960–The United States won only after staging a rally to finish with 21½ points, to 20 for Canada and 12½ for Mexico. This was the fifth Americas Golf Cup Match and the United States team had won each time. The teams played at the Ottawa Hunt and Golf Club, Ottawa, Canada. The United States had only one point after the first morning's play and was second behind Canada at the end of the day. The United States team did not move into the lead until the next-to-last three-ball match on the final day when Donald R. Cherry, of Wichita Falls, Texas, defeated both Bob Wylie, Canada, by 2 and 1, and Hector Alvarez, Mexico, by 3 and 1. Gary Cowan, of Canada, participated in winning 6½ out of eight possible points.

1961–The sixth Match was played at the Monterrey Country Club, which nestles among beautiful jagged-peak mountains of Monterrey, Mexico. The final tally was: United States, 29; Canada, 14; Mexico, 11. The Mexican team led after the first morning's three-ball "sixsomes" with 4½ points to 4 for the United States and ½ for Canada. But that afternoon the Americans pulled away in individual play and kept going throughout the second day. For the United States, Deane Beman, Robert Gardner and William Hyndman, III, each won all four possible points in individual play. Charles R. Coe served as playing Captain, just as he did for the inaugural match in 1952. The Americas Cup, normally played for every other year, was advanced from 1962 to 1961 to avoid conflict with the 1962 World Amateur Team Championship.

1963–The United States maintained its perfect record by winning for the seventh time at the Wakonda Club, Des Moines, Iowa, with 26½ points to 19½ for Canada and 8 for Mexico. The United States took the lead during the opening day's "sixsomes" with 4½ points to Canada's 3½. The Canadians trailed by only 1½ points after the first day, but the United States solidified its lead by gaining 2½ of 3 possible points against Canada in the second day's "sixsomes." Charles R. Coe and R. H. Sikes both participated in winning seven of eight possible points for the United States. William J. Patton, the United States Captain for the second time, helped his side win 5½ points of a possible 6. Patton had won 12 singles points in the series without a loss or tie. Gary Cowan, of Canada, who had never lost in 12 previous singles matches, was defeated by both Coe and Mexico's Juan Estrada on the first day.

1965–The United States had won all seven Matches prior to 1965, but Canada ended the domination at the St. Charles Country Club, Winnipeg, Canada, with a point score of 22, compared to 19½ for the United States and 12½ for Mexico. After the first of the Match's two days Canada had 9½ points, Mexico 9 and the United States 8½. Every member of the Canadian team had played before in the series. The winning Captain was Bruce Forbes, President of the Royal Canadian Golf Association. Doug Silverberg, of Canada, won all four of his points in the "sixsomes" play, paired with Bill Pidlaski, and took three of four points in the three-ball play. William C. Campbell, the reigning United States Amateur Champion, won all eight of his possible points.

1967–The United States built up a 9-6 lead over Canada during the first day's play, but then was hard pressed to win its eighth victory in nine Matches. The final totals were 14½ for the United States, 11½ for Canada, and 10 for Mexico. The site was the Guadalajara Country Club, Guadalajara, Mexico. On the morning of the second day, Mexico swept all four of its "sixsomes" points, and with four singles matches remaining the United States led with 9½ points, followed by Canada with 7½, and Mexico with 7. Robert B. Dickson and William C. Campbell then won 3½ of a possible 4 singles points, assuring the victory for the United States. Dickson was the leading point-maker, participating in 6½. Next was Keith Alexander, of Canada, with 5, and then Hector Alvarez, of Mexico, with 4½. Dr. Edgar Undegraff, a former competitor, was nonplaying Captain of the United States Team. The series was discontinued after the 1967 match.

1960	U. S. 21½	Canada 20	Mexico ...12½	Ottawa Hunt and Golf Club, Ottawa, Canada
1961	U. S. 29	Canada 14	Mexico 11	Monterrey C. C., Monterrey, Mexico
1963	U. S. 26½	Canada ...19½	Mexico 8	Wakonda Club, Des Moines, Iowa
1965	Canada 22	U. S. 19½	Mexico ...12½	St. Charles C. C., Winnipeg, Manitoba, Canada
1967	U. S. 14½	Canada ...11½	Mexico 10	Guadalajara C. C., Guadalajara, Jal., Mexico

1960
FIFTH INTERNATIONAL MATCH FOR THE AMERICAS CUP
Held at the Ottawa Hunt Golf Club, Ottawa, Canada
August 11 and 12
All Matches at 18 Holes

CANADA	MEXICO	UNITED STATES
R. Keith Alexander	Hector Alvarez	Deane R. Beman
Phil Brownlee	Juan Antonio Estrada	Don Cherry
Gary Cowan	Fernando Garza	Charles R. Coe
John Johnston	Roberto Halpern	William Hyndman, III, Captain
Nick Weslock	Tomas Lehman	John Konsek
Ron Willey	Rafael Quiroz	Jack W. Nicklaus
Bob Wylie	Mauricio Urdaneta	Dr. Frank Taylor
Non-playing Captain:	Non-playing Captain	
E. Duncan Millican	Rodrigo Medelin	

August 11–FOURSOMES

CANADA	vs. Mex.	vs. U.S.	MEXICO	vs. Can.	vs. U.S.	UNITED STATES	vs. Can.	vs. Mex.
Johnston Willey	halved	1 up	Quiroz Urdaneta	halved	1 up	Nicklaus Beman	0	0
Wylie Alexander	2 & 1	3 & 2	Alvarez Estrada	0	2 & 1	Coe Cherry	0	0
Cowan Brownlee	7 & 6	2 & 1	Halpern Lehman	0	0	Taylor Konsek	0	4 & 3
Points, Foursomes	2½	3		½	2		0	1

August 11–SINGLES

CANADA	vs. Mex.	vs. U.S.	MEXICO	vs. Can.	vs. U.S.	UNITED STATES	vs. Can.	vs. Mex.
Johnston	3 & 2	0	Alvarez	0	0	Nicklaus	3 & 2	6 & 5
Cowan	6 & 5	4 & 3	Quiroz	0	0	Coe	0	4 & 2
Wylie	halved	0	Lehman	halved	halved	Hyndman	1 up	halved
Alexander	0	0	Estrada	2 up	halved	Beman	2 up	halved
Willey	3 & 2	0	Halpern	0	0	Taylor	2 & 1	4 & 3
Brownlee	2 up	0	Urdaneta	0	halved	Konsek	1 up	halved
Points, Singles ...	4½	1		1½	1½		5	4½
Totals, Aug. 11 ...	7	4		2	3½		5	5½

August 12–FOURSOMES

CANADA	vs. Mex.	vs. U.S.	MEXICO	vs. Can.	vs. U.S.	UNITED STATES	vs. Can.	vs. Mex.
Johnston Willey	0	1 up	Urdaneta Quiroz	1 up	4 & 3	Nicklaus Beman	0	0
Cowan Brownlee	1 up	0	Estrada Alvarez	0	halved	Hyndman .... Taylor	2 & 1	halved
Wylie Alexander	0	1 up	Halpern Lehman	3 & 2	0	Coe Cherry	0	1 up
Points, Foursomes	1	2		2	1½		1	1½

August 12–SINGLES

CANADA	vs. Mex.	vs. U.S.	MEXICO	vs. Can.	vs. U.S.	UNITED STATES	vs. Can.	vs. Mex.
Brownlee	4 & 2	0	Halpern	0	0	Nicklaus	2 & 1	4 & 3
Johnston	2 & 1	halved	Lehman	0	0	Coe	halved	2 & 1
Cowan	halved	4 & 3	Urdaneta	halved	3 & 2	Hyndman	0	0
Alexander	halved	0	Estrada	halved	halved	Beman	1 up	halved
Wylie	0	0	Alvarez	2 & 1	0	Cherry	2 & 1	3 & 1
Willey	1 up	halved	Garza	0	0	Konsek	halved	1 up
Points, Singles ...	4	2		2	1½		4	4½
Totals, Aug. 12 ...	5	4		4	3		5	6
Grand Total	12	8		6	6½		10	11½

SUMMARY OF TEAM POINTS

	Canada	Mexico	United States
Foursomes	3½	2½	
Singles	8½	3½	
Totals	12	6	
Foursomes	5		1
Singles	3		9
Totals	8		10
Foursomes		3½	2½
Singles		3	9
Totals		6½	11½
Foursome Totals	8½	6	3½
Singles Totals	11½	6½	18
Grand Totals	20	12½	21½

1961
SIXTH INTERNATIONAL MATCH FOR THE AMERICAS CUP

Held at the Club Campestre Monterrey, A.C., Monterrey City, N.L., Mexico
October 21 and 22
All Matches at 18 Holes

CANADA	MEXICO	UNITED STATES
R. Keith Alexander	Hector Alvarez	Deane R. Beman
Gary Cowan	Juan Antonio Estrada	Charles R. Coe, Captain
Ted Homenuik	Enrique Farias	Robert W. Gardner
John Johnston	Roberto Halpern	William Hyndman, III
Bert Ticehurst	Tomas Lehman	Jack W. Nicklaus
Nick Weslock	Rafael Quiroz	Charles B. Smith
Robert Wylie	Mauricio Urdaneta	H. Dudley Wysong, Jr.
Non-playing Captain:	Non-playing Captain:	
Albert Rolland	Rodrigo Medellin	

October 21—FOURSOMES

CANADA	vs. Mex.	vs. U.S.	MEXICO	vs. Can.	vs. U.S.	UNITED STATES	vs. Can.	vs. Mex.
Wylie Weslock	halved	0	Urdaneta Quiroz	halved	0	Nicklaus Wysong	3 & 1	2 & 1
Ticehurst Cowan	0	0	Estrada Farias	4 & 3	3 & 2	Hyndman Gardner	2 & 1	0
Johnston Alexander	0	0	Alvarez Halpern	2 & 1	3 & 2	Coe Smith	1 up	0
Points, Foursome	½	0		2½	2		3	1

October 21—SINGLES

CANADA	vs. Mex.	vs. U.S.	MEXICO	vs. Can.	vs. U.S.	UNITED STATES	vs. Can.	vs. Mex.
Cowan	1 up	halved	Lehman	0	halved	Nicklaus	halved	halved
Alexander	4 & 3	halved	Farias	0	0	Wysong	halved	6 & 4
Johnston	0	0	Estrada	5 & 4	0	Beman	6 & 4	2 & 1
Wylie	0	0	Alvarez	5 & 4	0	Hyndman	5 & 4	2 & 1
Weslock	4 & 3	0	Quiroz	0	0	Gardner	2 & 1	4 & 3
Homenuik	0	0	Halpern	5 & 3	0	Smith	5 & 4	3 & 2
Points, Singles	3	1		3	½		5	5½
Totals, Oct. 21	3½	1		5½	2½		8	6½

October 22—FOURSOMES

CANADA	vs. Mex.	vs. U.S.	MEXICO	vs. Can.	vs. U.S.	UNITED STATES	vs. Can.	vs. Mex.
Weslock Cowan	2 & 1	0	Urdaneta Quiroz	0	0	Nicklaus Wysong	2 & 1	3 & 2
Johnston Ticehurst	0	0	Estrada Farias	2 & 1	0	Smith Beman	2 & 1	1 up
Alexander Wylie	4 & 3	2 & 1	Alvarez Halpern	0	halved	Gardner Coe	0	halved
Points, Foursomes	2	1		1	½		2	2½

October 22—SINGLES

CANADA	vs. Mex.	vs. U.S.	MEXICO	vs. Can.	vs. U.S.	UNITED STATES	vs. Can.	vs. Mex.
Weslock	5 & 3	halved	Farias	0	0	Nicklaus	halved	5 & 3
Cowan	2 & 1	1 up	Urdaneta	0	0	Wysong	0	2 up
Alexander	1 up	0	Lehman	0	0	Hyndman	1 up	5 & 4
Wylie	0	0	Estrada	1 up	0	Gardner	2 & 1	1 up
Johnston	2 & 1	halved	Halpern	0	0	Smith	halved	1 up
Ticehurst	halved	0	Alvarez	halved	0	Beman	2 & 1	3 & 2
Points, Singles	4½	2		1½	0		4	6
Totals, Oct. 22	6½	3		2½	½		6	8½
Grand Total	10	4		8	3		14	15

SUMMARY OF TEAM POINTS

	Canada	Mexico	United States
Foursomes	2½	3½	
Singles	7½	4½	
Totals	10	8	
Foursomes	1		5
Singles	3		9
Totals	4		14
Foursomes		2½	3½
Singles		½	11½
Totals		3	15
Foursome Totals	3½	6	8½
Single Totals	10½	5	20½
Grand Totals	14	11	29

1963
SEVENTH INTERNATIONAL MATCH FOR THE AMERICAS CUP

Held at the Wakonda Club, Des Moines, Iowa
September 5 and 6
All Matches at 18 holes

CANADA	MEXICO	UNITED STATES
R. Keith Alexander	Luis Brauer	Deane R. Beman
Gary Cowan	Juan Antonio Estrada	Charles R. Coe
Bill Pidlaski	Tomas Lehman	Richard D. Davies
Douglas Silverberg	Jose Luis Ortega	Labron Harris, Jr.
Bert Ticehurst	Rafael Quiroz	William J. Patton, Captain
Bill Wakeham	Agustin Silveyra	Richard H. Sikes
Nick Weslock	Mauricio Urdaneta	Dr. Edgar R. Updegraff
Non-playing Captain:	Non-playing Captain:	
E. Duncan Millican	Guillermo Vidales	

CANADA	vs. Mex.	vs. U.S.	MEXICO	vs. Can.	vs. U.S.	UNITED STATES	vs. Can.	vs. Mex.
Weslock			Ortega			Beman		
Ticehurst	0	0	Lehman	3 & 2	0	Coe	4 & 3	3 & 2
Cowan			Urdaneta			Harris		
Wakeham	4 & 2	halved	Quiroz	0	0	Patton	halved	4 & 2
Silverberg			Estrada			Sikes		
Alexander	2 & 1	2 & 1	Silveyra	0	0	Updegraff	0	2 & 1
Points, Foursomes	2	1½		1	0		1½	3

September 5—SINGLES

CANADA	vs. Mex.	vs. U.S.	MEXICO	vs. Can.	vs. U.S.	UNITED STATES	vs. Can.	vs. Mex.
Weslock	3 & 2	halved	Brauer	0	0	Harris	halved	3 & 2
Cowan	0	0	Estrada	1 up	0	Coe	4 & 2	2 & 1
Ticehurst	6 & 5	3 & 2	Lehman	0	0	Beman	0	2 & 1
Silverberg	4 & 2	4 & 2	Ortega	0	0	Davies	0	1 up
Alexander	0	0	Urdaneta	3 & 2	0	Sikes	5 & 4	5 & 3
Pidlaski	1 up	5 & 3	Silveyra	0	halved	Updegraff	0	halved
Points, Singles	4	3½		2	½		2½	5½
Totals, Sept. 5	6	5		3	½		4	8½

September 6—FOURSOMES

CANADA	vs. Mex.	vs. U.S.	MEXICO	vs. Can.	vs. U.S.	UNITED STATES	vs. Can.	vs. Mex.
Weslock			Estrada			Coe		
Ticehurst	8 & 7	0	Urdaneta	0	0	Harris	1 up	9 & 7
Cowan			Ortega			Sikes		
Wakeham	0	0	Lehman	3 & 2	0	Patton	2 up	1 up
Silverberg			Silveyra			Beman		
Alexander	0	halved	Quiroz	3 & 2	2 up	Davies	halved	0
Points, Foursomes	1	½		2	1		2½	2

September 6—SINGLES

CANADA	vs. Mex.	vs. U.S.	MEXICO	vs. Can.	vs. U.S.	UNITED STATES	vs. Can.	vs. Mex.
Weslock	4 & 2	3 & 2	Estrada	0	0	Harris	0	1 up
Cowan	2 & 1	2 & 1	Brauer	0	0	Coe	0	2 up
Ticehurst	4 & 3	0	Ortega	0	0	Patton	3 & 2	6 & 5
Wakeham	3 & 1	0	Lehman	0	0	Updegraff	3 & 2	4 & 2
Silverberg	0	0	Quiroz	4 & 3	halved	Beman	2 & 1	halved
Alexander	1 up	0	Silveyra	0	0	Sikes	6 & 5	7 & 6
Points, Singles	5	2		1	½		4	5½
Totals, Sept. 6	6	2½		3	1½		6½	7½
Grand Total	12	7½		6	2		10½	16

SUMMARY OF TEAM POINTS

	Canada	Mexico	United States
Foursomes	3	3	
Singles	9	3	
Totals	12	6	
Foursomes	2		4
Singles	5½		6½
Totals	7½	2	10½
Foursomes		1	5
Singles		1	11
Totals		2	16
Foursome Totals	5	4	9
Singles Totals	14½	4	17½
Grand Totals	19½	8	26½

1965
EIGHTH INTERNATIONAL MATCH FOR THE AMERICAS CUP

Held at the St. Charles Country Club, Winnipeg, Manitoba, Canada
August 6 and 7
All Matches 18 Holes

CANADA	MEXICO	UNITED STATES
Keith Alexander	Juan A. Estrada	Donald C. Allen
Gary Cowan	Robert Halpern	William C. Campbell
John Johnston	Tomas Lehman	Davis Eichelberger
Bill Pidlaski	Jorge Molinar	A. Downing Gray
Doug Silverberg	Agustin Silveyra	John Mark Hopkins
Bert Ticehurst	Mauricio Urdaneta	Dale Morey
Nick Weslock	Ricardo Vega	Edgar M. Tutwiler, Jr.
Non-playing Captain:	Non-playing Captain:	Non-Playing Captain:
R. Bruce Forbes	Armando Damy	John M. Winters, Jr.

August 6—FOURSOMES

CANADA	vs. Mex.	vs. U.S.	MEXICO	vs. Can.	vs. U.S.	UNITED STATES	vs. Can.	vs. Mex.
Weslock Alexander	0	0	Molinar Lehman	2 & 1	0	Campbell Gray	1 up	1 up
Cowan Johnston	6 & 4	5 & 4	Estrada Silveyra	0	0	Morey Tutwiler	0	2 & 1
Silverberg Pidlaski	3 & 2	3 & 2	Halpern Urdaneta	0	0	Hopkins Eichelberger	0	1 up
Points, Foursomes	2	2		1	0		1	3

August 6—SINGLES

CANADA	vs. Mex.	vs. U.S.	MEXICO	vs. Can.	vs. U.S.	UNITED STATES	vs. Can.	vs. Mex.
Weslock	0	0	Vega	3 & 2	0	Campbell	5 & 4	3 & 2
Cowan	0	4 & 3	Urdaneta	3 & 2	5 & 4	Gray	0	0
Alexander	halved	halved	Estrada	halved	4 & 2	Morey	halved	0
Silverberg	0	2 & 1	Lehman	4 & 3	5 & 3	Tutwiler	0	0
Johnston	halved	0	Halpern	halved	0	Hopkins	2 up	3 & 2
Ticehurst	2 & 1	3 & 2	Silveyra	0	2 & 1	Allen	0	0
Points, Singles	2	3½		4	4		2½	2
Totals, August 6	4	5½		5	4		3½	5

August 7—FOURSOMES

CANADA	vs. Mex.	vs. U.S.	MEXICO	vs. Can.	vs. U.S.	UNITED STATES	vs. Can.	vs. Mex.
Cowan Johnston	2 & 1	0	Lehman Molinar	0	0	Campbell Gray	3 & 2	5 & 4
Weslock Alexander	3 & 2	4 & 3	Estrada Silveyra	0	2 & 1	Hopkins Eichelberger	0	0
Silverberg Pidlaski	5 & 4	2 & 1	Halpern Urdaneta	0	0	Morey Allen	0	3 & 2
Points, Foursomes	3	2		0	1		1	2

August 7—SINGLES

CANADA	vs. Mex.	vs. U.S.	MEXICO	vs. Can.	vs. U.S.	UNITED STATES	vs. Can.	vs. Mex.
Johnson	halved	0	Urdaneta	halved	0	Campbell	2 up	2 & 1
Silverberg	4 & 3	4 & 3	Estradas	0	1 up	Tutwiler	0	0
Weslock	1 up	0	Lehman	0	0	Hopkins	5 & 4	5 & 4
Ticehurst	0	0	Halpern	1 up	0	Gray	4 & 3	5 & 4
Alexander	4 & 3	2 & 1	Vega	0	0	Morey	0	3 & 2
Cowan	5 & 4	4 & 2	Molinar	0	0	Eichelberger	0	1 up
Points, Singles	4½	3		1½	1		3	5
Totals, August 7	7½	5		1½	2		4	7
Grand Total	11½	10½		6½	6		7½	12

SUMMARY OF TEAM POINTS

	CANADA	MEXICO	UNITED STATES
Foursomes	5	1	
Singles	6½	5½	
Totals	11½	6½	
Foursomes	4		2
Singles	6½		5½
Totals	10½		7½
Foursomes		1	5
Singles		5	7
Totals		6	12
Foursomes Totals	9	2	7
Singles Totals	13	10½	12½
Grand Totals	22	12½	19½

1967
NINTH INTERNATIONAL MATCH FOR THE AMERICAS CUP

Held at the Guadalajara Country Club, Guadalajara, Jalisco, Mexico
October 7 and 8
All Matches at 18 Holes

CANADA	MEXICO	UNITED STATES
Keith Alexander	Hector Alvarez	Donald C. Allen
Gary Cowan	Juan Antonio Estrada	William C. Campbell
John Johnston	Roberto Halpern	Robert B. Dickson
Ben Kern	Tomas Lehman	Marvin Giles, III
John Russell	Rafael Quiroz	A. Downing Gray
Non-playing Captain:	Non-playing Captain:	Non-playing Captain:
Phil Farley	Mauricio Urdaneta	Dr. Edgar R. Updegraff

October 7—FOURSOMES

CANADA	vs. Mex.	vs. U.S.	MEXICO	vs. Can.	vs. U.S.	UNITED STATES	vs. Can.	vs. Mex.
Cowan / Alexander	1 up	0	Lehman / Halpern	0	0	Dickson / Giles	4 & 3	3 & 2
Johnston / Russell	2 & 1	1 up	Estrada / Quiroz	0	0	Campbell / Gray	0	1 up
Points, Foursome	2	1		0	0		1	2

SINGLES

CANADA	vs. Mex.	vs. U.S.	MEXICO	vs. Can.	vs. U.S.	UNITED STATES	vs. Can.	vs. Mex.
Cowan	0	0	Alvarez	2 and 1	0	Dickson	1 up	4 & 3
Johnston	0	0	Estrada	4 & 3	2 up	Giles	4 & 3	0
Alexander	3 & 2	2 & 1	Lehman	0	0	Campbell	0	2 & 1
Kern	3 & 2	0	Quiroz	0	0	Allen	2 & 1	3 & 2
Points, Singles	2	1		2	1		3	3
Totals, Oct. 7	4	2		2	1		4	5

October 8—FOURSOMES

CANADA	vs. Mex.	vs. U.S.	MEXICO	vs. Can.	vs. U.S.	UNITED STATES	vs. Can.	vs. Mex.
Johnston / Russell	0	½	Estrada / Lehman	1 up	1 up	Dickson / Giles	½	0
Cowan / Alexander	0	4 & 3	Halpern / Alvarez	1 up	2 & 1	Allen / Gray	0	0
Points, Foursomes	0	1½		2	2		½	0

SINGLES

CANADA	vs. Mex.	vs. U.S.	MEXICO	vs. Can.	vs. U.S.	UNITED STATES	vs. Can.	vs. Mex.
Kern	0	0	Halpern	0	0	Dickson	5 & 4	6 & 5
Johnston	½	½	Alvarez	1 up	½	Campbell	2 & 1	½
Cowan	7 & 5	5 & 4	Lehman	½	1 up	Gray	½	0
Alexander	3 & 1	0	Estrada	0	0	Allen	0	1 up
Points, Singles	2½	1½		1½	1½		2½	2½
Totals, October 8	2½	3		3½	3½		3	2½
Grand Total	6½	5		5½	4½		7	7½

SUMMARY OF TEAM POINTS

	Canada	Mexico	United States
Foursomes	2	2	
Singles	4½	3½	
Totals	6½	5½	
Foursomes	2½		1½
Singles	2½		5½
Totals	5		7
Foursomes		2	2
Singles		2½	5½
Totals		4½	7½
Foursome Totals	4½	4	3½
Singles Totals	7	6	11
Grand Totals	11½	10	14½

Part Three

1981 - 1990

OPEN CHAMPIONSHIP

CHAMPIONSHIP CUP

Presented in 1895 by the

UNITED STATES GOLF ASSOCIATION

Original trophy destroyed by fire September, 1946.

Replaced by the Association in 1947.

HISTORY

1981—David Graham, 35, became the first Australian to win the Open Championship, shooting 273, seven under par, over the East Course of the Merion Golf Club in Ardmore, Pennsylvania. Graham, who resides in Dallas, Texas, is the 20th foreign-born player to win the Open. However, 16 of the 20 had already emigrated to the United States. The four overseas champions were Harry Vardon of England in 1900, Ted Ray of England in 1920, Gary Player of South Africa in 1965 and Tony Jacklin of England in 1970. Graham is the first foreign-born champion since Jacklin. Graham's final round 67, three under par, was one of the finest ever played in the Open. It brought him from three strokes behind 54-hole leader George Burns when the fourth round began to three strokes ahead when the Championship ended. His 273 total brought him to within one stroke of the Open record for 72 holes, set at 272 a year earlier by four-time Open Champion Jack Nicklaus at the Baltusrol Golf Club. Graham finished with rounds of 68-68-70-67—273. Burns finished in a tie for second place with Bill Rogers at 276. John Cook and John Schroeder tied for fourth place at 279, the only other players to break par for the 72 holes. Five players, including Nicklaus, finished at even-par 280. The 36-hole cut fell at 147, only one stroke lower than it was 10 years earlier at Merion. Lee Trevino, who won that Open, missed the cut this time. An overnight rain before the third round made the greens softer and very receptive to approach shots. Burns added a 68, his third consecutive round under par, and increased his lead from one stroke to three over Graham, who shot 70. Burns had 203 for three rounds, setting an Open record for 54 holes. The third day produced the low round of the Championship—a 64, six under par, by Ben Crenshaw. It put him only six strokes behind at 209. The final round was really a duel between Graham and Burns, although Rogers remained a threat all day. Graham put the heat on Burns right away with birdies on the first two holes to close within one stroke. Graham caught up at the fourth hole when Burns made a bogey 6. Graham gave back the stroke with a three-putt bogey on the fifth and that's how the contest remained until the 10th, a short par 4. Burns' pitch shot found the front bunker. He came out 15 feet from the hole and took two putts for a bogey. Burns and Graham were tied once again and remained that way through 13 holes. Graham forged into the lead with birdie putts of six feet on the 14th and 10 feet on the 15th. Burns made a bogey at the 16th to fall three behind, but chipped in on the par-3 17th to get one stroke back. Rogers, who was playing steady golf all day, was actually just one stroke behind Graham and Burns until Graham made his birdies at the 14th and 15th holes. A bogey 5 at the 16th all but ended Rogers' bid for the Championship, but a marvelous birdie at the 18th earned him a tie for second place with Burns, who made bogey at the final hole. Graham parred in from the 16th hole for a three-stroke victory. His putt from 18 feet on the final hole to tie the Open scoring record hit the cup and stayed out. Rassett, the low amateur with a 294 total, received a gold medal. Arnold Palmer competed in his 29th consecutive Open, dating back to 1953. Prize money reached a record $361,730 with $346,730 awarded in the Championship proper and $15,000 in the Sectional Qualifying Championships. The USGA received a record 4,946 entries, breaking the record of 4,897 set in 1978. More than 78,000 spectators attended the Open Championship at Merion.

1982—In one of the most memorable moments in Open history, Tom Watson birdied the 17th hole at Pebble Beach by pitching into the cup from off the green and won his first Open Championship. Jack Nicklaus finished second. Watson, 32, from Kansas City, Missouri, won with the scores of 72-72-68-70—282, six under par. Nicklaus shot 74-70-71-69—284. This was the fourth time Nicklaus finished as runner-up in the Open, tying a record shared by Sam Snead, Bob Jones, and Arnold Palmer. Bobby Clampett, Dan Pohl, and Bill Rogers tied for third, at 286. Gary Koch, Jay Haas, Lanny Wadkins and defending champion David Graham tied for sixth at 287. They were the only other players under par for the 72 holes. The first round co-leaders, at 70, were Rogers, the 1981 British Open Champion, and Bruce Devlin, who, at 44, was a part-time Tour player. One stroke back at 71 were four players, including Danny Edwards, who was five under for the first six holes; Clampett, from nearby Carmel, Calif.; Calvin Peete; Terry Diehl; and Jim King. Watson birdied three of the last four holes and finished with 72, tied with eight others. In the second round, Devlin shot 69 and took the lead at 139 for 36 holes. Larry Rinker moved into second place at 141 with a 67. Scott Simpson was next at 142, following a 69. Rogers slipped to 73 and was tied at 143 with Andy North, the 1978 Open Champion, Peete, and Lyn Lott. Nicklaus came back from an opening 74 and shot 70 for a 144 total to tie Watson, who had a second consecutive 72;

Clampett; Tom Kite; and George Burns. Burns had an unusual round of 72. After an opening par 4 on the first hole, he birdied the next six holes. His 30 on the first nine equalled the Open's nine-hole record. He played the second nine in 42. Watson made his move in the third round with a 68 to tie Rogers for the lead, at 212, four under par. Rogers had 69. They were two strokes ahead of Devlin, who shot 75, for 214; Burns; Simpson; and Graham. Nicklaus was three strokes behind at 215. Nicklaus began his final round with a bogey at the first hole and a par at the second, and then put together a string of five consecutive birdies, from the third through the seventh. At that moment he was tied for the lead with Rogers, who was five under through the fifth, one stroke ahead of Watson and Devlin. Devlin birdied the sixth for a momentary share of the lead at five under, but he lost three strokes on the seventh and the ninth and fell from contention. Nicklaus dropped to three under with bogies at the eighth and 11th holes. With nine holes to play, Rogers and Watson were tied for the lead at four under par, and Nicklaus, playing two holes ahead, was three under. Rogers, starting the second nine with bogies at the 10th and 12th, dropped to two under, and there he remained. Watson, on the other hand, saved par from the edge of a cliff at the 10th and birdied the 11th to go five under. Watson dropped a shot to par at the 12th. When Nicklaus birdied the 15th, they were tied for the lead once again at four under par. Nicklaus parred the last three holes for 69 and a 72-hole score of 284. At the long, par-5 14th, Watson holed a 35-foot putt from the collar, and with that birdie moved one stroke ahead of Nicklaus. After a par at the 15th, Watson missed his first fairway of the round, pushing his tee shot into a bunker at the 16th, and made a bogey 5. Watson was four under par once again and back in a tie with Nicklaus. At the long par-3 17th, Watson hit a 2-iron shot that drew more than he had planned. The ball hit on the left edge of the green, then hopped into the rough between two bunkers, 18 feet from the hole. Using his sand wedge, Watson popped the ball out of the grass. It dropped onto the collar of the green and ran right into the hole. Needing a par-5 to win, Watson played the 18th hole carefully—3-wood from the tee, 7-iron for his second shot, 9-iron onto the green. His 20-foot putt fell in for a birdie. Sixty-four professionals and two amateurs made the 36-hole cut at 151, seven over par. Nathaniel Crosby, the 1981 Amateur Champion, received a gold medal as low amateur, with a 303 total. Arnold Palmer competed in his 30th consecutive Open, dating back to 1953. Prize money reached a record $385,000, with $370,000 awarded in the Championship proper and $15,000 in the Sectional Qualifying Championships. The USGA received a record 5,255 entries, breaking the previous high of 4,946 set in 1981.

1983—Larry Nelson, 35, played the last 36 holes in 132 strokes—10 under par—and won by one stroke over Tom Watson, the 1982 Champion. Nelson, from Marietta, Georgia, shot 75-73-65-67—280, four under par, at the Oakmont Country Club, in Oakmont, Pennsylvania, near Pittsburgh. Nelson's 65 and 67 were the two lowest single rounds of the Championship. His 132 broke the former 36-hole record of 136, set by Gene Sarazen, in 1932. It had been matched six times. Watson had 72-70-70-69—281. Gil Morgan, the only other golfer to break par for the Championship, shot 73-72-70-68—283. Calvin Peete and Severiano Ballesteros tied for fourth place, at 286. The first round co-leaders at 69, two under par, were Ballesteros, John Mahaffey, and Bob Murphy. Mahaffey won the 1978 PGA Championship at Oakmont. Nelson's opening 75 left him six strokes off the lead. Second-round play was interrupted for two and a half hours by a severe electrical storm in the early afternoon. Two spectators, struck by lightning near the second green, were taken to a hospital for treatment and later released. Through it all, Mahaffey managed a 72 and shared the 36-hole lead, at 141, one under par, with Joe Rassett, a first-year professional, who had posted rounds of 72 and 69. Watson and Raymond Floyd shared third place, at 142. Peete moved into contention with 68 and a total of 143, the same as Ballesteros, who shot 74, and Hal Sutton, with 73-70. Murphy dropped out of contention with 81. Because of the rain delay, 38 contestants, including Peete, had to complete their second rounds on Saturday morning. Sixty-nine professionals and two amateurs made the 36-hole cut, at 151, nine over par. Nelson, with 148, made the cut by only three strokes. Six over par as the third round began, Nelson dropped to seven over with a bogey at the third hole. After a par 5 on the fourth, Nelson played the next 14 holes of the third round in seven under par, to finish at 65, and then played the last 18 holes in four under. By shooting 65 in the third round, Nelson passed all but three men who were ahead of him—Watson, Ballesteros, and Peete. At 54 holes, Ballesteros and Watson were the co-leaders, at 212, on rounds of 69 and 70 respectively. Nelson was at 213, tied with Peete, who had 70. Floyd was next, at 214, followed by Morgan, at 215. Ballesteros and Watson were paired for the last round, behind Nelson and Peete. After a few holes, Watson began pulling away from the field. Six birdies on the first nine and he was out in 31, five strokes better than Ballesteros. Nelson was out in 33, and although he passed Ballesteros and Peete, he was losing strokes to Watson. Watson, however, lost strokes on the 10th and 12th, and Nelson, only one stroke behind by then, caught him with a birdie on the 14th. It was his fifth birdie of the round. As Nelson was playing the 15th and Watson was playing the 14th, play was suspended because of another thunderstorm. Completion of the final round was carried over to Monday. Play resumed at 10 o'clock with Watson facing a 35-foot putt on the 14th and with Nelson playing his tee shot to the 16th. Watson two-putted for his par 4 and Nelson played his tee shot onto the left side of the 16th green, about 62 feet from the hole. Nelson holed the putt for a birdie 2, and led for the first time. When Nelson three-putted the 18th, Watson missed a five-foot putt for a par on the 17th that would have pulled him even. Nelson played the final 32 holes in 114 strokes, 11 under par, and the last 27 of these in 99 strokes, seven under. On 16 of the last 32 holes, Nelson's approaches were within 15 feet of the hole, and on nine holes he was within 10 feet of the cup with his shots to the greens. Brad Faxon, a member of the 1983 U.S. Walker Cup Team, received a gold medal as low amateur, with a 302 total. Arnold Palmer competed in his 31st consecutive Open, dating back to 1953. He tied the record previously set by Gene Sarazen. Palmer had played in the last four Opens held at Oakmont. Prize money reached a record $506,184, with $72,000 going to Nelson. The USGA accepted 5,039 entries.

1984—Fuzzy Zoeller, 32, shot 67 and defeated Greg Norman in an 18-hole playoff. Norman shot 75. By shooting 276 for the 72 holes, Zoeller and Norman became the first men to be under par in four Opens played at Winged Foot Golf Club, in Mamaroneck, New York. Par is 280. The lowest previous score was 282, by Billy Casper, in 1959. Norman and Zoeller finished five strokes in front of Curtis Strange, of Kingsmill, Virginia, whose 69-70-74-68—281 would have won any previous Open at Winged Foot. John Miller, the 1973 Open champion, and Jim Thorpe shared fourth, at 282, while Hale Irwin, who led for most of the first three rounds, shot 79 on the final day and finished sixth, at 284. In the first round 18 players bettered or equaled par. Irwin and Thorpe, at 68, shared the lead with Hubert Green, the 1977 champion, and Mike Donald. Seve Ballesteros, Strange, and Jay Sigel, 1982 and 1983 U.S. Amateur champion, were at 69, with Norman at par 70. Irwin 39, added 68 and led after 36-holes with 136, but Zoeller shot 66, the lowest round ever during an Open at Winged Foot, to stand at 137. Norman had 68 for 138, along with David Canipe. Both Irwin and Zoeller shot 69 in the third round, Irwin led by a stroke, at 205, and Norman and Thorpe had 207. While Irwin and Thorpe faded in the fourth round, Zoeller and Norman pulled away. Zoeller holed consecutive birdie putts of 20, 22, 20, and 15 feet on the third through sixth holes, gaining five strokes on Irwin, and by then only Norman and Zoeller were in contention. Zoeller led by three strokes with nine holes to play, but Norman pulled even at the 17th and saved par on the 18th by holing a 45-foot putt after hitting his approach into a grandstand and being given relief without penalty. After both men birdied the first hole of the playoff, Zoeller birdied the second from 68 feet and gained three strokes when Norman made 6. Zoeller made the turn in 34 and led by five strokes, went ahead by seven on the 14th, by eight after 15 holes, and by nine after 16. Norman's birdie, at 17, trimmed the margin to eight. Sigel, a contender for 36 holes, and Richard Fehr were low amateurs. Arnold Palmer missed qualifying after playing in 31 consecutive Opens. He is tied with Gene Sarazen for the most consecutive Opens played. Prize money reached a record $596,925, with $95,000 going to Zoeller.

1985—Andy North, 35, shot a final-round 74 to win his second U.S. Open title at Oakland Hills Country Club in Birmingham, Michigan. The win makes North, who was the 1978 Open champion, the 15th player to win the Championship more than once. His total of 279, one under par, was one stroke better than that of Tze-Chung Chen, Denis Watson and Dave Barr. Lanny Wadkins, Payne Stewart and Severiano Ballesteros tied for fifth at 281. Chen recorded the first double-eagle in U.S. Open history on the second hole of the first round on his way to a course-record 65, one stroke better than Fred Couples. Five players were tied for third at one-under-par 69. Chen, 26, shot 69 in the second round to retain his one-stroke advantage; it was one of a record 24 sub-par rounds on the second day. His two-round total of 134 tied the Open record set by Jack Nicklaus in 1980. North, who shot 65, moved into a second-place tie at 135 with Jay Haas, who shot 66. Rick Fehr was fourth at 136, two shots behind Chen. Watson, who also shot a round of 65, was three strokes off the lead. Chen tied another Open record the following day with another 69. His 54-hole total of 203 matched that of George Burns in 1981. Chen was two strokes ahead of North, who shot 70. The rest of the field had fallen back. Barr was in third place, five strokes behind Chen. Chen built his lead to four strokes after just two holes of the final round and maintained his lead until the fifth hole. There, Chen took a "double-par" eight, including a double-hit, and slipped to four under par, even with North. North opened a two-stroke lead over Barr and Stewart after eight holes, but bogeyed the ninth, 10th and 11th to fall one stroke behind Barr, who had birdied the 12th. North, Chen and Barr shared the lead after Chen birdied the 12th, North birdied the 13th and Barr bogeyed the 13th. Chen and Barr each bogeyed two of the remaining holes to finish at even par. North, who saved par on the 17th from the right green-side bunker, held a two-stroke lead as he played the 18th. North bogeyed the hole and won the Championship. Scott Verplank, the 1984 Amateur Champion, shot two rounds of 69 and was the low amateur at 289. Nicklaus missed the cut, breaking his string of 21 consecutive Opens in which he had played 72 holes. The USGA accepted a record 5,274 entries for the Championship.

1986—Raymond Floyd, 43, shot a final-round 66 to win the U.S. Open at Shinnecock Hills Golf Club in Southampton, New York, and became the oldest player ever to win the championship. Floyd's 279, one under par, was two strokes better than Lanny Wadkins and Chip Beck, who each shot 65 in the final round to finish at 281. Lee Trevino and Hal Sutton were at 282, three shots behind Floyd. Bob Tway was the only player to equal par for the first round, which was played in cold rain and high winds. Tway led Greg Norman by one stroke and six golfers—Tom Watson, David Frost, Rick Fehr, Kenny Knox, Tsuneyuki Nakajima and Denis Watson—by two strokes. Under much better conditions, Norman shot 68 in the second round giving him a 36-hole total of 139 and a three-stroke lead over Trevino and Denis Watson. Tway slipped to a 73 and a fourth place tie with Tom Watson and Floyd, four behind Norman. Danny Edwards missed the cut despite tying a U.S. Open record by playing the second nine in 30 strokes. Norman retained his lead after 54 holes, shooting 71 for 210, one stroke ahead of Trevino, who shot 69, and Sutton, who shot 66. Tway was alone in fourth place at 212. Floyd, Denis Watson, Payne Stewart and Mike Reid were at 213. Lennie Clements duplicated Edwards' feat of a day earlier when he shot 30 for the first nine. After three rounds, 14 players were within four strokes of the lead. The chase remained close throughout the final day. After one hole, Trevino and Sutton had caught Norman, but the three of them faltered on the ensuing holes and Ben Crenshaw took a one-stroke lead with birdies on the third, fourth, fifth and sixth holes. When Crenshaw bogeyed the seventh, Mark McCumber gained the lead. At one time nine men shared the lead. Wadkins and Beck, playing well ahead of the leaders, posted one-over 72-hole totals of 281. Beck shot 30 on the second nine (missing a three-foot putt on the 18th that would have given him a record 29). Payne Stewart, with birdies on the 11th and 12th, took a two-stroke lead over Beck, Wadkins and Floyd, who also birdied 11. Floyd birdied while Stewart bogeyed the 13th and the two were tied for the lead. Floyd birdied the 16th to go under par for the first time in the championship and parred in for the victory. The USGA accepted a record 5,410 entries for the championship.

1987—Scott Simpson, 31 birdied the 14th, 15th and 16th holes of the final round to overtake Tom Watson and win the U.S. Open at The Olympic Club in San Francisco. Simpson's 71-68-70-68—277, three under par, was one stroke better than Watson, who shot 72-65-71-70—278. They were the only players to better par for the championship. Seve Ballesteros finished third at 282, two over par and five strokes behind Simpson. Ben Crenshaw shot a 67 and held a one-stroke lead after the first day. Trailing him were six top foreign golfers and the defending U.S. Open champion. In second place at two-under par 68 were Ballesteros of Spain, Japan's Tommy Nakajima and 1986 Open champion Raymond Floyd. Two strokes behind Crenshaw were South African Nick Price, Denis Watson of Zimbabwe and West Germany's Bernhard Langer. Ten golfers posted scores of even-par 70. Tom Watson, who shot a second-round 65, and Mark Wiebe, who shot 67, share the 36-hole lead at three-under-par 137. They were two of 24 golfers who broke par for the round, tying a record set in the second round of the 1985 Open at Oakland Hills. One stroke behind the leaders were Nakajima, Langer, Jack Nicklaus, Jim Thorpe and John Cook. A record 77 golfers completed 36 holes within 10 strokes of the lead and made the cut at seven-over-par 147. For only the third time, however, no amateurs survived the cut. After a third-round 71, Watson held the lead by himself. One stroke behind were Simpson and Keith Clearwater, who fired a third-round 64, tying the record for a third round in the Open set by Crenshaw in 1981 and tying the course record set by Rives McBee in the 1966 U.S. Open. Two strokes off the lead at even par was Lennie Clements, who shot a third consecutive 70. Wiebe shot 77 and fell out of contention. Early in the final round, the leaders played erratically, allowing nine golfers to be within one stroke of the lead at one point. Through 13 holes, however, all but Simpson and Watson fell back and Watson led by one. Simpson caught Watson by sinking a five-foot birdie putt at the 14th. Watson, one group and one hole behind, birdied 14 at nearly the same instant that Simpson birdied 15. Simpson took the lead when he holed a 15-footer at 16 for his third consecutive birdie. He finished his round by saving par from a greenside bunker at 17 and a two-putt at 18. Watson holed a six foot par putt at 17 and needed a birdie at the 18th to force a playoff. His approach came to rest about 45 feet short of the hole. His birdie putt broke just before reaching the hole and came to rest six inches away. The USGA accepted a record 5,696 entries for the championship.

1988—Curtis Strange, 33, of Kingsmill, Virginia, shot even-par 71 in an 18-hole playoff to defeat England's Nick Faldo by four strokes at The Country Club in Brookline, Massachusetts. It was the third Open played at The Country Club and the third that was decided by a playoff. Francis Ouimet defeated Harry Vardon and Ted Ray in 1913; Julius Boros defeated Jacky Cupit and Arnold Palmer in 1963. Strange and Faldo completed 72 holes in six-under-par 278. Faldo shot 72-67-68-71—278 and Strange shot 70-67-69-72. Two strokes behind were D.A. Weibring, Mark O'Meara and Steve Pate. Paul Azinger and 1987 Champion Scott Simpson finished three strokes behind the leaders at three-under-par 281. Bob Gilder, Mike Nicolette and 1988 Masters winner Sandy Lyle shared the first-round lead at three-under-par 68. Five golfers—Simpson, Azinger, Seve Ballesteros, Larry Mize and Dick Mast—were one stroke behind at 69. Strange, Lanny Wadkins and Craig Stadler finished in 70. The good scoring continued in the second round, led by Simpson's 66. His 36-hole total of 135, seven under par, placed him one stroke ahead of Mize, who had a second-round 67. Simpson became the first defending champion to lead after 36 holes since 1941, when 1940 Champion Lawson Little held the second-round lead. Strange and Gilder trailed Simpson by two strokes; Faldo and Lyle were four strokes off the pace.

Strange emerged as the leader after the third round by shooting 69 for a 54-hole total of 206, one stroke better than Simpson, who posted a 72; Gilder, who shot 70; and Faldo, who moved into the tie for second with a 68. Weibring, who shot 68, and Mize with a third-round 72 were two strokes behind. In the final round, it became a two-man battle as Strange and Faldo's closest competitors faltered. Faldo, the 1987 British Open Champion, moved a stroke in front when Strange bogeyed the second and third holes, but Strange birdied the par-3 seventh to pull even. They remained tied until the 16th, where Strange holed a 25-footer to save par and Faldo bogeyed. Faldo drew even again when Strange bogeyed the 17th. Strange saved par from the front bunker on 18 and the two finished tied at 278. In the playoff, Strange birdied the fourth and seventh, went out in 34 and held a one-stroke lead. Curtis stretched his lead to two when Faldo bogeyed the 11th, but he gave the stroke back with a bogey at the 12th. Strange sank an 18-foot birdie putt at the 13th and Faldo bogeyed, pushing the American's lead to three strokes. Faldo birdied the 14th, but bogeyed three of the final four holes for 75 to Strange's 71. Bill Mayfair, the 1987 U.S. Amateur Champion, was the only amateur to make the cut, which came at 146. He finished with 287. The USGA accepted a record 5,775 entries for the championship.

1989—Curtis Strange, 34 became the sixth man to win consecutive Open championships, and the first in 38 years, scoring 278 at the Oak Hill Country Club, in Rochester, New York, and winning by one stroke over Mark McCumber, Chip Beck, and Ian Woosnam, a Welshman playing in his first U.S. Open. By winning two successive championships, Strange followed Willie Anderson (1903-04-05), John McDermott (1911-12), Bob Jones (1929-30), Ralph Guldahl (1937-38), and Ben Hogan (1950-51). Rochester had been hit by heavy rains throughout the spring, and a heavy downpour Friday night threatened to postpone the third round, but through superb work by the Oak Hill grounds crew, and with help from the fire department of the town of Pittsford, which sent a high-capacity pumper to help drain a flooded fairway, the round was completed on schedule. Strange shot 71 in the first round and stood five strokes behind the leaders. Bernhard Langer, Payne Stewart, and Jay Don Blake shot 66. On a day of low scoring, 21 broke par 70. Although Oak Hill played harder in the second round, with only 15 men breaking par, the round began with four men scoring holes in one within an hour and a half. Doug Weaver, Mark Wiebe, Jerry Pate, and Nick Price each holed 7-iron tee shots on the sixth, a par 3 of 167 yards. Strange shot 64 and with 135 for 36 holes led Tom Kite by one stroke. Kite shot 69. The rain fell so heavily the night after the second round that Oak Hill was flooded and unplayable the following morning. In order to complete the third round, the field was split in two, with the lower scorers playing in threes from the first tee, and the higher scorers from the 10th. With three bogeys and no birdies. Strange shot 73 and fell into third place, three strokes behind Kite, with another 69, and two behind Scott Simpson. When Kite birdied the third hole of the fourth round, he suddenly shot three strokes ahead of the field, but then he drove into a creek on the fifth hole, made 7 on a par 4, and fell from the lead. He finished with a 78, and dropped into ninth place. Playing steady par golf, Strange moved into the lead after the 10th. He parred the first 15 holes, and made his first birdie in 35 holes on the 16th, opening his lead to two strokes over McCumber, Beck, and Woosnam. With a three-putt for bogey on the 18th, Strange scored 70 in the fourth round and still won by a stroke.

1990—Hale Irwin became the fifth player to win three or more U.S. Opens, defeating Mike Donald on the 19th hole of a playoff, at Medinah Country Club, in Medinah, Illinois. Irwin and Donald each shot eight under par 280 for four rounds. Each then shot 74, two over par, in an 18-hole playoff and then Irwin holed an eight-foot putt for a birdie on the first extra playoff hole. Leading by one stroke, Donald had bogeyed the 18th by hooking his drive into the trees. By winning, Irwin, 45, became the oldest U.S. Open champion. Raymond Floyd had won at 43, in 1986. Irwin had won previously in 1974 and 1979. Irwin had received a special exemption from the USGA. He completed 72 holes by shooting 31 on the second nine and 67 for the last round, holing a twisting 45-foot putt on the 72nd green. Donald, 34, was among the leaders from the beginning, shooting 67 in his opening round. He was one of 39 players who broke par for the first round, nearly doubling the former record number of 21, set in 1989, at Oak Hill, in Rochester, New York. The four-day total of 124 with rounds under par shattered the previous record of 64, set in 1988, at The Country Club, in Brookline, Mass. For the championship, 28 players finished under par for 72 holes; the previous high was 11, also at The Country Club. Nick Faldo and Billy Ray Brown tied for third place, at 281. Each missed makeable putts on the final hole. Scott Simpson was nine under par early in the third round before falling back and finishing in a tie for 14th place, at 3 under par 285. Curtis Strange was in position to win a third consecutive Open after shooting 68 in the third round, which left him just two strokes behind Donald and Brown. But Strange slipped to 75 in the fourth round and tied for 21st place.

OPEN CHAMPIONSHIP

DATE	WINNER, RUNNER-UP	SCORE	SITE	ENTRY
1981 (June)	David Graham	273	Merion G.C.,	4,946
	Bill Rogers	276	(East Course)	
	George Burns	276	Ardmore, Pa.	
1982 (June)	Tom Watson	282	Pebble Beach G.L.,	5,255
	Jack Nicklaus	284	Pebble Beach, Calif.	
1983 (June)	Larry Nelson	280	Oakmont C.C.,	5,039
	Tom Watson	281	Oakmont, Pa.	
1984 (June)	Fuzzy Zoeller	276-67	Winged Foot G.C.,	5,195
	Greg Norman	276-75	Mamaroneck, N.Y.	
1985 (June)	Andy North	279	Oakland Hills C.C.,	5,274
	Denis Watson	280	Birmingham, Mich.	
	Dave Barr	280		
	Tze-Chung Chen	280		
1986 (June)	Raymond Floyd	279	Shinnecock Hills G.C.,	5,410
	Lanny Wadkins	281	Southampton, N.Y.	
	Chip Beck	281		
1987 (June)	Scott Simpson	277	The Olympic Club,	5,696
	Tom Watson	278	(Lake Course)	
			San Francisco, Calif.	
1988 (June)	Curtis Strange	278-71	The Country Club,	5,775
	Nick Faldo	278-75	Brookline, Mass.	
1989 (June)	Curtis Strange	278	Oak Hill C.C.,	5,786
	Ian Woosnam	279	Rochester, N.Y.	
	Chip Beck	279		
	Mark McCumber	279		
1990 (June)	Hale Irwin	280-74-3	Medinah C.C.,	*6,198
	Mike Donald	280-74-4	(No. 3 Course)	
			Medinah, Ill.	

*Record Entry.

1981
EIGHTY-FIRST OPEN CHAMPIONSHIP

Merion Golf Club (East Course), Ardmore, Pennsylvania, June 18-21
Yardage—6,544 (6,528). Par 70. †4,946 Entries, 156 Qualifiers, 156 Starters.

						Score	Money Prize
1	David Graham, Preston Trail, Dallas, Texas	68	68	70	67	273	$55,000.00
2	Bill Rogers, Northridge C.C., Texarkana, Texas	70	68	69	69	276	24,650.00
	George Burns, III, Quail Ridge G. & T.C., Boynton Bch. Fla.	69	66	68	73	276	24,650.00
4	John Cook, Muirfield Village G.C., Dublin, Ohio	68	70	71	70	279	16,200.00
	John Schroeder, Del Mar, Calif.	71	68	69	71	279	16,200.00
6	Frank Conner, San Antonio, Texas	71	72	69	68	280	9,920.00
	Lon Hinkle, Royal Oaks, Dallas, Texas	69	71	70	70	280	9,920.00
	Samuel T. Rachels, Sandestin, Destin, Fla.	70	71	69	70	280	9,920.00
	Jack Nicklaus, Muirfield Village G.C., Dublin, Ohio	69	68	71	72	280	9,920.00
	Juan A. Rodriguez, Dorado Bch. C.C., Puerto Rico	68	73	67	72	280	9,920.00
11	Isao Aoki, Tokyo, Japan	72	71	71	67	281	5,500.00
	Jim Thorpe, Buffalo, N.Y.	66	73	70	72	281	5,500.00
	Ben Crenshaw, C.C. of Austin, Austin, Texas	70	75	64	72	281	5,500.00
14	Mark Hayes, Oak Tree G.C., Edmond, Okla.	71	70	72	69	282	3,616.67
	Calvin Peete, Eastwood C.C., Fort Meyers, Fla.	73	72	67	70	282	3,616.67
	Lanny Wadkins, Royal Oaks C.C., Dallas, Texas	71	68	72	71	282	3,616.66
17	Curtis Strange, Williamsburg, Va.	71	69	72	71	283	2,950.00
	Bruce Lietzke, Shangri-La Resort, Afton, Okla.	70	71	71	71	283	2,950.00
	Jack Renner, Lomas Santa Fe C.C., San Diego, Calif.	68	71	72	72	283	2,950.00
20	Tom Kite, C.C. of Austin, Austin, Texas	73	74	67	70	284	2,550.00
	Michael Reid, Riverside C.C., Provo, Utah	71	72	69	72	284	2,550.00
	Larry Nelson, La Quinta Hotel & G.C., La Quinta, Calif.	70	73	69	72	284	2,550.00
23	Johnny Miller, Napa, Calif.	69	71	73	72	285	2,350.00
	Tom Watson, Kansas City, Mo.	70	69	73	73	285	2,350.00
	Scott Simpson, Stardust C.C., San Diego, Calif.	72	67	71	75	285	2,350.00
26	Jim Colbert, Las Vegas, Nev.	71	69	77	69	286	2,100.00
	Gary Player, Johannesburg, South Africa	72	72	71	71	286	2,100.00
	Rik Massengale, Charlotte, Texas	70	75	70	71	286	2,100.00
	Craig Stadler, Reno, Nev.	71	76	68	71	286	2,100.00
	Bruce Devlin, Waldon on Lake Conroe, Conroe, Texas	73	71	70	72	286	2,100.00
	Jerry Pate, Shoal Creek, Shoal Creek, Ala.	70	69	72	75	286	2,100.00
	Tommy Valentine, Gainesville, Ga.	69	68	72	77	286	2,100.00
33	J.C. Snead, Glade Springs, Daniels, W. Va.	67	77	73	70	287	1,827.50
	Lee Elder, Langston G.C., Washington, D.C.	72	74	71	70	287	1,827.50
	Greg Norman, Springfield, Va.	71	67	73	76	287	1,827.50
	Billy Kratzert, Ft. Wayne C.C., Ft. Wayne, Ind.	69	69	73	76	287	1,827.50
37	Hubert Green, Shoal Creek C.C., Shoal Creek, Ala.	69	76	71	72	288	1,660.00
	Peter Jacobsen, Saddlebrook G.R. Wesley Chapel, Fla.	71	74	71	72	288	1,660.00
	Raymond Floyd, Scarlet Oaks C.C., Nitro, W. Va.	75	72	68	73	288	1,660.00
	Forrest Fezler, Killearn C.C., Tallahassee, Fla.	70	72	71	75	288	1,660.00
41	Roger Maltbie, San Jose C.C., San Jose, Calif.	71	74	74	70	289	1,570.00
	Severiano Ballesteros, Doral Hotel & C.C., Miami, Fla.	73	69	72	75	289	1,570.00
43	Leonard Thompson, Bay Hill C., Orlando, Fla.	75	71	74	70	290	1,453.00
	Thomas Gray, Antelope Hills G.C., Prescott, Ariz.	75	72	73	70	290	1,453.00
	Tim Simpson, Ansley G.C., Atlanta, Ga.	70	75	74	71	290	1,453.00
	Andy North, Nakoma G.C., Madison, Wis.	73	74	72	71	290	1,453.00
	Keith Fergus, Sugarland, Texas	74	71	73	72	290	1,453.00
	Mick Soli, Shady Oaks G.C., Amboy, Ill.	77	69	72	72	290	1,453.00
	Bob Ackerman, Detroit G.C., Detroit, Mich.	68	78	71	73	290	1,453.00
	D.A. Weibring, Plano, Texas	71	72	72	75	290	1,453.00
	Mike Peck, Milburn G. & C.C., Overland Park, Kans.	76	68	71	75	290	1,453.00
	Bobby Wadkins, Meadowbrook C.C., Richmond, Va.	70	72	71	77	290	1,453.00
53	Bobby Nichols, Naples, Fla.	71	71	78	71	291	1,350.00
	Steve Melnyk, Amelia Isl. Plantation, Amelia Isl., Fla.	70	75	73	73	291	1,350.00
	Mark McNulty, Randpark G.C., South Africa	72	69	75	75	291	1,350.00
	Gary Hallberg, Cleveland, Ohio	70	77	69	75	291	1,350.00
	Jim Nelford, Pleasant Grove, Utah	74	73	69	75	291	1,350.00
58	Joe Hager, Northwood C., Dallas, Texas	74	73	77	68	292	1,310.00
	Hale Irwin, Kapalua G.C., Kapalua Maui, Hawaii	72	75	73	72	292	1,310.00
	Ray Carrasco, Rancho San Joaquin, Irvine, Calif.	74	71	73	74	292	1,310.00
	Greg Powers, Killearn C.C., Tallahassee, Fla.	73	73	72	74	292	1,310.00
	George Archer, Gilroy, Calif.	76	69	70	77	292	1,310.00
	Jim Simons, Turtle Creek C., Tequesta, Fla.	78	69	67	78	292	1,310.00
64	Charlie Gibson, Phoenix, Ariz.	75	72	71	75	293	1,300.00
65	Bill Pelham, Champions G.C., Houston, Texas	73	73	73	75	294	1,300.00
	Morris Hatalsky, Daytona Beach, Fla.	71	76	72	75	294	1,300.00
	*Joseph Rassett, Turlock G. & C.C., Turlock, Calif.	70	70	78	76	294	Medal
68	Dave Barr, Kelowna G. & C.C., Canada	74	72	73	76	295	1,300.00
69	Mark Lye, Silverado C.C., Napa, Calif.	70	72	76	78	296	1,300.00
70	Kip Byrne, Jr., C.C. of Miami, Hialeah, Fla.	74	72	79	75	300	1,300.00

Prize money totaling $361,730.00 awarded to professionals as follows: Championship—$305,930.00; prizes for 68 professionals who did not return scores for 72 holes—$40,800.00; Sectional Qualifying Championship—$15,000.00

*Amateur †Record Entry

1982
EIGHTY-SECOND OPEN CHAMPIONSHIP

Pebble Beach Golf Links, Pebble Beach, California, June 17-20.
Yardage — 6,825 (6,791). Par 72. †5,255 Entries, 153 Qualifiers, 153 Starters.

						Score	Money Prize
1	Tom Watson, Kansas City, Mo.	72	72	68	70	282	$60,000.00
2	Jack Nicklaus, Muirfield Village G.C., Dublin, Ohio	74	70	71	69	284	34,506.00
3	Bobby Clampett, Carmel Valley Ranch, Carmel, Calif.	71	73	72	70	286	14,967.00
	Dan Pohl, Canadian Lakes C.C., Mecosta, Mich.	72	74	70	70	286	14,967.00
	Bill Rogers, Texarkana, Texas	70	73	69	74	286	14,967.00
6	Gary Koch, Carrollwood Vlg. G. & C.C., Tampa, Fla.	78	73	69	67	287	8,011.00
	Jay Haas, Charlotte, N.C.	75	74	70	68	287	8,011.00
	Lanny Wadkins, Preston Trail G.C., Dallas, Texas	73	76	67	71	287	8,011.00
	David Graham, Preston Trail G.C., Dallas, Texas	73	72	69	73	287	8,011.00
10	Calvin Peete, Cape Coral G. & R.C., Cape Coral, Fla.	71	72	72	73	288	6,332.00
	Bruce Devlin, Walden on Lk. Conroe, Montgomery, Texas	70	69	75	74	288	6,332.00
12	Charles Beck, Gates Four G. & C.C., Fayetteville, N.C.	76	75	69	69	289	5,510.67
	Danny Edwards, Oak Tree G.C., Edmond, Okla.	71	75	73	70	289	5,510.67
	Lyn Lott, Douglas G. & C.C., Douglas, Ga.	72	71	75	71	289	5,510.66
15	Fuzzy Zoeller, New Albany C.C., New Albany, Ind.	72	76	71	71	290	4,661.00
	J. C. Snead, Ponte Vedra Beach, Fla.	73	75	71	71	290	4,661.00
	Larry Rinker, Orlando, Fla.	74	67	75	74	290	4,661.00
	Scott Simpson, Stardust C.C., San Diego, Calif.	73	69	72	76	290	4,661.00
19	Hal Sutton, Shreveport C.C., Shreveport, La.	73	76	72	70	291	4,008.34
	Larry Nelson, LaQuinta Hotel & G.R., La Quinta, Calif.	74	72	74	71	291	4,008.33
	Ben Crenshaw, Austin, Texas	76	74	68	73	291	4,008.33
22	Joe Hager, Los Rios C.C., Plano, Texas	78	72	72	70	292	3,403.72
	Gene Littler, Rancho Santa Fe G.C., Rancho Santa Fe, Calif.	74	75	72	71	292	3,403.72
	Andy North, Nakoma G.C., Madison, Wis.	72	71	77	72	292	3,403.72
	Mike Brannan, Glendale, Ariz.	75	74	71	72	292	3,403.71
	John Mahaffey, The Woodlands, Woodlands, Texas	77	72	70	73	292	3,403.71
	Gil Morgan, Oak Tree G.C., Edmond, Okla.	75	75	68	74	292	3,403.71
	Craig Stadler, Mission Hills C.C., Rancho Mirage, Calif.	76	70	70	76	292	3,403.71
29	Tom Kite, Green Tree C.C., Midland, Texas	73	71	75	74	293	3,006.00
30	George Burns, Grossinger's Hotel, Grossinger, N.Y.	72	72	70	80	294	2,718.00
	Isao Aoki, Tokyo, Japan	77	74	72	71	294	2,718.00
	Jack Renner, Lomas Santa Fe C.C., Solana Beach, Calif.	74	71	77	72	294	2,718.00
	Greg Powers, Killearn C.C., Tallahassee, Fla.	77	71	74	72	294	2,718.00
	Peter Oosterhuis, Mission Hills C.C., Rancho Mirage, Calif.	73	78	67	76	294	2,718.00
	Jim Thorpe, Buffalo, N.Y.	72	73	72	77	294	2,718.00
	Don Bies, Seattle G.C., Seattle, Wash.	73	74	74	73	294	2,718.00
37	Terry Diehl, Oak Hill C.C., Rochester, N.Y.	71	77	75	72	295	2,430.50
	Bob Gilder, Carmel Valley Ranch, Carmel, Calif.	73	76	74	72	295	2,430.50
39	Tom Weiskopf, Paradise Valley, Ariz.	74	77	73	72	296	2,175.00
	Lou Graham, Richland C.C., Nashville, Tenn.	75	73	74	74	296	2,175.00
	Curtis Strange, Williamsburg, Va.	74	73	74	75	296	2,175.00
	Rod Nuckolls, Rolling Hills C.C., Wichita, Kans.	78	73	69	76	296	2,175.00
	Hale Irwin, Kapalua G.C., Maui, Hawaii	76	75	68	77	296	2,175.00
	Kermit Zarley, Friendswood, Texas	75	74	69	78	296	2,175.00
45	Johnny Miller, Los Angeles, Calif.	78	69	78	72	297	1,855.00
	Dave Stockton, Keystone Ranch, Keystone, Colo.	79	71	73	74	297	1,855.00
	Woody Blackburn, Orange Park, Fla.	75	73	73	76	297	1,855.00
	Lon Hinkle, Carrollton, Texas	73	75	69	80	297	1,855.00
49	Ray Floyd, Monte Carlo C.C., Ft. Pierce, Fla.	78	73	75	72	298	1,599.00
	Clarence Rose, Goldsboro G.C., Goldsboro, N.C.	73	78	73	74	298	1,599.00
	Bob Shearer, Bay Tree G. Pltn., N. Myrtle Beach, S.C.	75	75	72	76	298	1,599.00
	Skeeter Heath, Kingsmill on James, Williamsburg, Va.	73	74	74	77	298	1,599.00
53	Butch Baird, Miami Beach, Fla.	72	75	78	74	299	1,409.34
	Larry Ziegler, Emerald Hills C.C., Hollywood, Fla.	77	74	73	75	299	1,409.33
	Vance Heafner, MacGregor Downs C.C., Cary, N.C.	75	74	74	76	299	1,409.33
56	Tom Sieckmann, Omaha, Neb.	77	73	75	76	301	1,358.00
	Ron Streck, Tulsa, Okla.	72	77	75	77	301	1,358.00
58	Mark O'Meara, Irving, Texas	77	74	77	74	302	1,336.00
59	*Nathaniel Crosby, Miami, Fla.	77	73	76	77	303	Medal
60	Bobby Wadkins, Brandermill C.C., Midlothian, Va.	73	74	82	75	304	1,319.00
61	*Corey Pavin, Las Posas C.C., Camarillo, Calif.	77	74	78	75	304	Medal
62	Jim King, Fontainebleau C.C., Miami, Fla.	71	77	80	77	305	1,300.00
	Kenny Knox, Capital City C.C., Tallahassee, Fla.	76	75	77	77	305	1,300.00
	Lloyd Monroe, Wykagyl C.C., New Rochelle, N.Y.	79	70	78	78	305	1,300.00
65	William Israelson, Bemidji Town & C.C., Bemidji, Minn.	76	69	80	83	308	1,300.00
66	Doug Tewell, Oak Tree G.C., Edmond, Okla.	75	75	79	90	319	1,300.00

Prize money totaling $385,000.00 awarded to professionals as follows: Championship — $325,000.00; prizes for 75 professionals who did not return scores for 72 holes — $45,000.00; Sectional Qualifying Championship — $15,000.00.

***Amateur †Record Entry**

1983
EIGHTY-THIRD OPEN CHAMPIONSHIP

Oakmont Country Club, Oakmont, Pennsylvania, June 16-20.
Yardage — 6,972. Par 71. 5,039 Entries, 153 Qualifiers, 153 Starters.

						Score	Money Prize
1	Larry Nelson, La Quinta Hotel & G.C., La Quinta, Calif.	75	73	65	67	280	$72,000.00
2	Tom Watson, Kansas City C.C., Kansas City, Mo.	72	70	70	69	281	44,000.00
3	Gil Morgan, Oak Tree G.C., Edmond, Okla.	73	72	70	68	283	29,000.00
4	Calvin Peete, Cape Coral C.C., Cape Coral, Fla.	75	68	70	73	286	17,968.50
	Severiano Ballesteros, Doral Hotel & C.C., Miami, Fla.	69	74	69	74	286	17,968.50
6	Hal Sutton, Shreveport, La.	73	70	73	71	287	13,254.00
7	Lanny Wadkins, Preston Trail G.C., Dallas, Texas	72	73	74	69	288	12,088.00
8	David Graham, Preston Trail G.C., Dallas, Texas	74	75	73	69	291	10,711.00
	Ralph Landrum, World of Golf, Florence, Ky.	75	73	69	74	291	10,711.00
10	Chip Beck, Highland C.C., Fayetteville, N.C.	73	74	74	71	292	8,976.34
	Craig Stadler, Tahoe-Donner C.C., Lake Tahoe, Nev.	76	74	73	69	292	8,976.33
	Andy North, Nakoma G.C., Madison, Wis.	73	71	72	76	292	8,976.33
13	Scott Simpson, Makaha Valley C.C., Honolulu, Hawaii	73	71	73	76	293	6,993.72
	Ray Floyd, Monte Carlo C.C., Ft. Pierce, Fla.	72	70	72	79	293	6,993.72
	Jim Thorpe, Buffalo, N.Y.	75	70	75	73	293	6,993.72
	Pat McGowan, Pine Needles Lodges, Southern Pines, N.C.	75	71	75	72	293	6,993.71
	David Ogrin, Cog Hill G. & C.C., Lemont, Ill.	75	69	75	74	293	6,993.71
	Lennie Clements, La Jolla C.C., La Jolla, Calif.	74	71	75	73	293	6,993.71
	Mike Nicolette, Santa Barbara, Calif.	76	69	73	75	293	6,993.71
20	Tom Kite, Green Tree C.C., Midland, Texas	75	76	70	73	294	5,554.50
	Griff Moody, Athens C.C., Athens, Ga.	76	72	73	73	294	5,554.50
	Gary Player, Johannesburg, South Africa	73	74	76	71	294	5,554.50
	D.A. Weibring, Jr., Shipyard Plantation, Hilton Hd., S.C.	71	74	80	69	294	5,554.50
24	Gary Koch, Avila G.& C.C., Tampa, Fla.	78	71	72	74	295	5,017.00
	Tom Weiskopf, Paradise Valley, Ariz.	75	73	74	73	295	5,017.00
26	Bob Ford, Oakmont C.C., Oakmont, Pa.	76	73	75	72	296	4,464.67
	Ken Green, Richter Park G.C., Danbury, Conn.	77	73	71	75	296	4,464.67
	Mark Hayes, Oak Tree G.C., Edmond, Okla.	75	72	74	75	296	4,464.67
	Joey Rassett, Turlock G. & C.C., Turlock, Calif.	72	69	78	77	296	4,464.67
	Tommy Nakajima, Richardson, Texas	75	74	74	73	296	4,464.66
	Curtis Strange, Kingsmill on James, Williamsburg, Va.	74	72	78	72	296	4,464.66
32	Tim Simpson, Ansley G.C., Atlanta, Ga.	76	74	73	74	297	4,013.50
	Roger Maltbie, San Jose C.C., San Jose, Calif.	76	72	69	80	297	4,013.50
34	Ron Terry, Ruggles G.C., Aberdeen, Md.	75	75	73	75	298	3,686.60
	Andy Bean, Grenelefe G. & T. Resort, Grenelefe, Fla.	76	75	73	74	298	3,686.60
	John Mahaffey, The Woodlands, Woodlands, Texas	69	72	79	78	298	3,686.60
	Mike Sullivan, Ocala, Fla.	74	76	74	74	298	3,686.60
	Peter Jacobsen, Saddlebrook Resort, Wesley Chapel, Fla.	75	75	77	71	298	3,686.60
39	Hale Irwin, Kapalua G.C., Maui, Hawaii	72	76	75	76	299	3,267.50
	Bob Gilder, Carmel Valley Ranch, Carmel, Calif.	75	74	75	75	299	3,267.50
	Keith Fergus, Sugarland, Texas	76	72	79	72	299	3,267.50
	Skeeter Heath, Kingsmill on James, Williamsburg, Va.	73	76	74	76	299	3,267.50
43	Jay Haas, Charlotte, N.C.	74	74	74	78	300	2,847.20
	Mike Reid, Provo, Utah	75	75	78	72	300	2,847.20
	Wayne Levi, Whitesboro, N.Y.	74	76	74	76	300	2,847.20
	J.C. Snead, Ponte Vedra Beach, Fla.	76	73	76	75	300	2,847.20
	Jack Nicklaus, Muirfield Village G.C., Dublin, Ohio	73	74	77	76	300	2,847.20
48	Nick Price, Haines City, Fla.	72	77	72	80	301	2,520.50
	Scott Hoch, Bay Hill C. & L., Orlando, Fla.	74	77	74	76	301	2,520.50
50	Bob Murphy, Delray Dunes C.C., Boynton Beach, Fla.	69	81	74	78	302	2,104.89
	Lou Graham, Richland C.C., Nashville, Tenn.	71	77	78	76	302	2,104.89
	Bob Shearer, Bay Tree G. Plantn., N. Myrtle Beach, S.C.	76	74	75	77	302	2,104.89
	Robert Boyd, Jr., Charleston, S.C.	76	75	74	77	302	2,104.89
	Greg Norman, Orlando, Fla.	74	75	81	72	302	2,104.89
	*Brad Faxon, Rhode Island C.C., Barrington, R.I.	77	74	75	76	302	Medal
	Frank Conner, Tapatio Spgs. Hotel, Tapatio Spgs., Texas	72	74	81	75	302	2,104.89
	Mark McNulty, Johannesburg, South Africa	75	76	75	76	302	2,104.89
	Forrest Fezler, Tallahassee, Fla.	75	76	74	77	302	2,104.89
	Peter Oosterhuis, Mission Hills C.C., Rancho Mirage, Calif.	75	76	77	74	302	2,104.89
60	Hubert Green, Bay Point Y. & C.C., Panama City, Fla.	74	74	76	79	303	1,907.00
	Arnold Palmer, Laurel Valley G.C., Ligonier, Pa.	74	75	78	76	303	1,907.00
	Donnie Hammond, Longwood, Fla.	74	73	81	75	303	1,907.00
63	*John Sherman, Kansas City C.C., Shawnee Mission, Kans.	80	71	79	74	304	Medal
64	Bob Eastwood, Dry Creek Ranch G.C., Galt, Calif.	75	76	80	74	305	1,898.00
65	Bruce Devlin, Northgate Forest C.C., Houston, Texas	70	79	77	80	306	1,898.00
	Bobby Wadkins, Brandermill C.C., Midlothian, Va.	71	77	81	77	306	1,898.00
67	Jim Nelford, Gallagher's Canyon, Kelownabr, Col.	72	79	79	77	307	1,898.00
68	Jim Booros, Allentown Muni. G. Course, Allentown Pa.	72	79	82	77	310	1,898.00
	Rocky Thompson, Paris G. & C.C., Paris, Texas	76	75	79	80	310	1,898.00
70	Hsu Sheng-San, Taiwan G. & C.C., Taiwan	74	77	80	81	312	1,898.00

Prize money totaling $506,184.00 awarded to professionals as follows: Championship—$459,384.00; prizes for 75 professionals who did not return scores for 72 holes—$46,800.00.

*Amateur

1984
EIGHTY-FOURTH OPEN CHAMPIONSHIP

Winged Foot Golf Club (West Course), Mamaroneck, New York, June 14-17
Yardage—6,930. Par 70. 5,195 Entries, 154 Qualifiers, 154 Starters

						Score	Money Prize
1	† Fuzzy Zoeller, New Albany C.C., New Albany, Ind.	71	66	69	70	276	$94,000.00
2	† Greg Norman, Orlando, Fla.	70	68	69	69	276	47,000.00
3	Curtis Strange, Kingsmill G.C., Williamsburg, Va.	69	70	74	68	281	36,000.00
4	Johnny Miller, Los Angeles, Calif.	74	68	70	70	282	22,335.00
	Jim Thorpe, Buffalo, N.Y.	68	71	70	73	282	22,335.00
6	Hale Irwin, Kapalua G.C., Kapalua, Maui, Hawaii	68	68	69	79	284	16,238.00
7	Peter Jacobsen, Saddlebrook R., Wesley Chapel, Fla.	72	73	73	67	285	14,237.00
	Mark O'Meara, Palm Desert, Calif.	71	74	71	69	285	14,237.00
9	Fred Couples, LaQuinta Hotel & C.C., LaQuinta, Calif.	69	71	74	72	286	12,122.00
	Lee Trevino, Dallas, Texas	71	72	69	74	286	12,122.00
11	Tom Watson, Kansas City C.C., Kansas City, Mo.	72	72	74	69	287	9,891.40
	Andy Bean, Grenelefe Resort, Grenelefe, Fla.	70	71	75	71	287	9,891.40
	Jay Haas, Greenville, S.C.	73	73	70	71	287	9,891.40
	Lanny Wadkins, Preston Trail G.C., Dallas, Texas	72	71	72	72	287	9,891.40
	Tim Simpson, Springbrook C.C., Lawrenceville, Ga.	72	71	68	76	287	9,891.40
16	Hal Sutton, Shreveport, La.	72	72	74	70	288	7,799.40
	Tom Purtzer, Desert Highlands G.C., Scottsdale, Ariz.	73	72	72	71	288	7,799.40
	Lennie Clements, LaJolla C.C., LaJolla, Calif.	69	76	72	71	288	7,799.40
	Isao Aoki, Cleveland, Ohio	72	70	72	74	288	7,799.40
	Mark McCumber, Ravines Resort, Middleburg, Fla.	71	73	71	73	288	7,799.40
21	Chip Beck, Fayetteville, N.C.	72	74	71	72	289	6,575.50
	Gil Morgan, Oak Tree G.C., Edmond, Okla.	70	74	72	73	289	6,575.50
	David Graham, Preston Trail, Dallas, Texas	71	72	70	76	289	6,575.50
	Jack Nicklaus, Muirfield Vlg. G.C., Dublin, Ohio	71	71	70	77	289	6,575.50
25	Scott Simpson, Makaha Valley C.C., Makaha Valley, Hawaii	72	75	74	69	290	5,717.80
	Bill Glasson, Singing Hills, San Diego, Calif.	72	75	71	72	290	5,717.80
	Joe Hager, Plano Municipal G.C., Plano, Texas	74	73	71	72	290	5,717.80
	Peter Oosterhuis, Mission Hills G&C.C., Rancho Mirage, Calif.	73	71	71	75	290	5,717.80
	Mike Sullivan, Ravines, Middleburg, Fla.	70	73	70	77	290	5,717.80
30	John Mahaffey, Woodlands Inn & C.C., Woodlands, Texas	72	74	77	68	291	5,031.25
	Jim Albus, Poping Rock Club, Locust Valley, N.Y.	77	69	74	71	291	5,031.25
	Seve Ballesteros, Doral Hotel & C.C., Miami, Fla.	69	73	74	75	291	5,031.25
	Hubert Green, Bay Point Y.&C.C., Panama City, Fla.	68	75	72	76	291	5,031.25
34	Tony Sills, Sherman Oaks, Calif.	73	72	76	71	292	4,573.50
	Gary Koch, Avila G.&C.C., Tampa, Fla.	74	71	75	72	292	4,573.50
	George Burns, Foxhill C.C., Baiting Hollow, N.Y.	72	74	74	72	292	4,573.50
	Mike Donald, Coral Springs, Fla.	68	78	74	72	292	4,573.50
38	Patrick McGowan, Pine Needles Ldg.&C.C., Southern Pines, N.C.	74	72	77	70	293	4,060.20
	James Colbert, Las Vegas, Nev.	71	73	77	72	293	4,060.20
	David Ogrin, Cog Hill G.&C.C., Lemont, Ill.	74	72	74	73	293	4,060.20
	D.A. Weibring, Shipyard Plantation, Hilton Head, S.C.	76	71	73	73	293	4,060.20
	Steven Hart, Turtle Creek C.C., Tequesta, Fla.	73	73	72	75	293	4,060.20
43	Mark Hayes, Oak Tree G.C., Edmond, Okla.	72	74	75	73	294	3,373.86
	Mark Balen, Crag Burn C.C., E. Aurora, N.Y.	71	75	75	73	294	3,373.86
	Barry Jaeckel, Palm Desert, Calif.	75	72	73	74	294	3,373.86
	*Jay Sigel, Aronimink G.C., Newtown Square, Pa.	69	72	78	75	294	MEDAL
	Steven Liebler, Cavalier G.&Y.C., Virginia Bch., Va.	71	75	73	75	294	3,373.86
	*Richard Fehr, Sand Point C.C., Seattle, Wash.	73	74	72	75	294	MEDAL
	Gary Player, Johannesburg, South Africa	74	72	72	76	294	3,373.86
	Jack Renner, Lomas Santa Fe C.C., Solana Beach, Calif.	73	71	73	77	294	3,373.85
	Philip Blackmar, Padre Island C.C., Corpus Christi, Texas	74	71	71	78	294	3,373.85
52	Raymond Floyd, Monte Carlo C.C., Ft. Pierce, Fla.	72	72	77	74	295	2,801.67
	Mike Reid, Provo, Utah	70	72	77	76	295	2,801.67
	Morris Hatalsky, Pelican Bay C.C., Daytona Beach, Fla.	70	73	69	83	295	2,801.66
55	Nick Faldo, Cleveland, Ohio	71	76	77	72	296	2,544.00
	Griff Moody, Athens C.C., Athens, Ga.	76	71	76	73	296	2,544.00
57	Bill Rogers, Texarkana, Texas	71	73	76	77	297	2,471.00
58	Mitch Adcock, Errol Estate, Apopka, Fla.	73	72	79	74	298	2,443.00
59	Mike Nicolette, Ponte Vedra, Fla.	73	72	74	80	299	2,413.00
60	Dan Forsman, Scottsdale, Ariz.	72	73	80	76	301	2,373.50
	Bill Britton, Staten Island, N.Y.	73	74	77	77	301	2,373.50
62	Rafael Alarcon, Guadalajara C.C., Guadalajara, Mexico	72	71	79	80	302	2,325.00
	David Canipe, Alhambra G. & T.C., Orlando, Fla.	69	69	81	83	302	2,325.00

†Playoff, June 18, Zoeller 67, Norman 75.

Prize money totaling $596,925.00 awarded to professionals as follows: Championship—546,525.00; prizes for 84 professionals who did not return scores for 72 holes—50,400.00

*Amateur

1985
EIGHTY-FIFTH OPEN CHAMPIONSHIP

Oakland Hills Country Club, Birmingham, Michigan, June 13-16
Yardage—6,996. Par 70. +5,274 Entries, 156 Qualifiers, 156 Starters

						Score	Money Prize
1	Andy North, Nakoma G.C., Madison, Wis.	70	65	70	74	279	$103,000.00
2	Denis Watson, Plantation G&C.C., Venice, Fla.	72	65	73	70	280	39,185.00
	Dave Barr, Kelowna G.&C.C., Kelowna, Canada	70	68	70	72	280	39,185.00
	Tze-Chung Chen, Monterey Park, Calif.	65	69	69	77	280	39,185.00
5	Lanny Wadkins, Preston Trail G.C., Dallas, Texas	70	72	69	70	281	18,458.67
	Payne Stewart, C.C. of Heathrow, Lake Mary, Fla.	70	70	71	70	281	18,458.67
	Seve Ballesteros, Doral C.C., Miami, Fla.	71	70	69	71	281	18,458.66
8	Johnny Miller, Salt Lake City, Utah	74	71	68	69	282	14,921.00
9	Fuzzy Zoeller, New Albany C.C., New Albany, Ind.	71	69	72	71	283	12,439.75
	Corey Pavin, Las Posas C.C., Camarillo, Calif.	72	68	73	70	283	12,439.75
	Jack Renner, Lomas Santa Fe C.C., Solana Beach, Calif.	72	69	72	70	283	12,439.75
	Rick Fehr, Sand Point C.C., Seattle, Wash.	69	67	73	74	283	12,439.75
13	Tom Kite, Jr., Austin, Texas	69	70	71	74	284	10,738.00
14	Hale Irwin, Kapalua G.C., Kapalua, Maui, Hawaii	73	72	70	70	285	10,237.00
15	Greg Norman, Orlando, Fla.	72	71	71	72	286	8,397.50
	Don Pooley, La Paloma C.C., Tucson, Ariz.	73	69	73	71	286	8,397.50
	Scott Simpson, Makaha Valley C.C., Makaha Valley, Hawaii	73	73	68	72	286	8,397.50
	Mark O'Meara, Escondido, Calif.	72	67	75	72	286	8,397.50
	Joey Sindelar, Horseheads, N.Y.	72	72	69	73	286	8,397.50
	Tony Sills, Wood Ranch C.C., Thousand Oaks, Calif.	75	70	71	70	286	8,397.50
	Andy Bean, Lakeland, Fla.	69	72	73	72	286	8,397.50
	Jay Haas, Greenville, N.C.	69	66	77	74	286	8,397.50
23	Tom Sieckmann, Highland C.C., Omaha, Neb.	73	73	70	71	287	6,344.63
	Hal Sutton, Shreveport C.C., Shreveport, La.	74	71	74	68	287	6,344.63
	Raymond Floyd, Monte Carlo C.C., Ft. Pierce, Fla.	72	67	73	75	287	6,344.63
	David Graham, Preston Trail G.C., Dallas, Texas	73	72	74	68	287	6,344.63
	Mike Reid, Provo, Utah	69	75	70	73	287	6,344.62
	Gil Morgan, Oak Tree G.C., Edmond, Okla.	71	72	72	72	287	6,344.62
	David Frost, Johannesburg, S. Africa	74	68	74	71	287	6,344.62
	Frederick Funk, Univ. of Maryland G.C., College Park, Md.	75	70	72	70	287	6,344.62
31	Bruce Lietzke, Shangri-La Resort, Afton, Okla.	72	71	74	71	288	5,431.00
	Curtis Strange, Kingsmill G.C., Williamsburg, Va.	71	68	76	73	288	5,431.00
	Peter Jacobsen, Portland, Ore.	71	73	72	72	288	5,431.00
34	Loren Roberts, San Luis Obispo C.C., San Luis Obispo, Calif.	74	71	74	70	289	4,994.00
	Jim Thorpe, Crag Burn, East Aurora, N.Y.	73	69	74	73	289	4,994.00
	Skeeter Heath, Kingsmill G.C., Williamsburg, Va.	70	70	77	72	289	4,994.00
	Scott Hoch, Bay Hill C.& L., Orlando, Fla.	73	72	71	73	289	4,994.00
	*Scott Verplank, Brookhaven C.C., Dallas, Texas	77	69	74	69	289	MEDAL
39	Larry Nelson, Marietta, Ga.	71	71	77	71	290	4,433.40
	John Mahaffey, The Woodlands, Woodlands, Texas	72	70	75	73	290	4,433.40
	Larry Mize, Columbus, Ga.	72	73	70	75	290	4,433.40
	Fred Couples, LaQuinta Hotel C.C., LaQuinta, Calif.	66	78	73	73	290	4,433.40
	Bill Glasson, Singing Hills G.& C.C., El Cajon, Calif.	70	71	75	74	290	4,433.40
44	Ronnie Black, Northshore C.C., Portland, Texas	71	69	76	75	291	3,996.50
	Danny Edwards, Oak Tree G.C., Edmond, Okla.	72	69	73	77	291	3,996.50
46	Tim Simpson, Springbrook C.C., Lawrenceville, Ga.	74	72	72	74	292	3,496.17
	Wayne Levi, New Hartford, N.Y.	75	71	70	76	292	3,496.17
	Bobby Wadkins, Brandermill C.C., Midlothian, Va.	72	69	75	76	292	3,496.17
	Frank Conner, Pecan Valley G.C., San Antonio, Texas	74	68	77	73	292	3,496.17
	Jeff Sanders, Beaverton, Ore.	71	75	73	73	292	3,496.16
	Ed Fiori, Statford, Texas	72	71	76	73	292	3,496.16
52	Dick Mast, Cypress Creek C.C., Orlando, Fla.	71	71	77	74	293	2,887.00
	Rafael Alarcon, Guadalajara C.C., Guadalajara, Mexico	73	72	72	76	293	2,887.00
	Morris Hatalsky, Daytona Beach, Fla.	71	72	77	73	293	2,887.00
	Bill Israelson, Bemidji T.& C.C., Bemidji, Minn.	71	72	75	75	293	2,887.00
56	Peter Oosterhuis, Mission Hills C.C., Rancho Mirage, Calif.	73	71	76	74	294	2,698.00
57	Brad Faxon, Rhode Island C.C., Barrington, R.I.	71	72	77	75	295	2,667.00
58	Lee Rinker, Martin Downs, Stuart, Fla.	74	69	75	78	296	2,606.34
	Ken Mattiace, Sawgrass C.C., Ponte Vedra, Fla.	74	72	73	77	296	2,606.33
	Gene Sauers, Statesboro, Ga.	70	73	80	73	296	2,606.33
61	Bob Eastwood, Stockton, Calif.	72	73	80	74	299	2,539.00
	Ken Green, Richter Park, Danbury, Conn.	73	73	79	74	299	2,539.00
63	Jeff Grygiel, Towne Isle G.C., Kirkville, N.Y.	73	70	76	81	300	2,539.00
64	Curt Byrum, Hillsview Municipal G.Crse., Pierre, S. D.	71	75	80	76	302	2,539.00
	*Jay Sigel, Aronimink G.C., Newtown Square, Pa.	76	69	78	79	302	MEDAL
66	Gregory Chapman, Champions G.C., Houston, Texas	75	71	80	78	304	2,539.00

Prize money totaling $664,756.00 awarded to professionals as follows: Championship—604,356.00; prizes for 84 professionals who did not return scores for 72 holes—50,400.00

+Record Entry

*Amateur

1986
EIGHTY-SIXTH OPEN CHAMPIONSHIP

Shinnecock Hills Golf Club, Southampton, New York, June 12-15
Yardage—6,912. Par 70. +5,410 Entries, 156 Starters.

						Score	Money Prize
1	Raymond Floyd, Monte Carlo C.C., Ft. Pierce, Fla.	75	68	70	66	279	$115,000.00
2	Lanny Wadkins, Preston Trail G.C., Dallas, Texas	74	70	72	65	281	47,646.00
	Chip Beck, Sea Palms G.&R.C., St. Simons Island, Ga.	75	73	68	65	281	47,646.00
4	Lee Trevino, Dallas, Texas	74	68	69	71	282	26,269.00
	Hal Sutton, Shreveport, La.	75	70	66	71	282	26,269.00
6	Ben Crenshaw, Austin C.C., Austin, Texas	76	69	69	69	283	19,009.00
	Payne Stewart, C.C. at Heathrow, Lake Mary, Fla.	76	68	69	70	283	19,009.00
8	Jack Nicklaus, Muirfield Village G.C., Dublin, Ohio	77	72	67	68	284	14,500.75
	Bernhard Langer, Monte Carlo C.C., Ft. Pierce, Fla.	74	70	70	70	284	14,500.75
	Mark McCumber, Ravines R.&C.C., Middleburg, Fla.	74	71	68	71	284	14,500.75
	Bob Tway, Oak Tree G.C., Edmond, Okla.	70	73	69	72	284	14,500.75
12	Denis Watson, The Plantation G. & C.C., Venice, Fla.	72	70	71	72	285	11,870.00
	Greg Norman, Windstar Naples Bay, Naples, Fla.	71	68	71	75	285	11,870,00
14	Mark Calcavecchia, Bear Lakes C.C., W. Palm Beach, Fla.	75	75	72	65	287	11,028.00
15	David Frost, Grenelefe, Fla.	72	72	77	67	288	8,884.66
	Fuzzy Zoeller, New Albany C.C., New Albany, Ind.	75	74	71	68	288	8,884.66
	Craig Stadler, Rancho Santa Fe, Calif.	74	71	74	69	288	8,884.66
	Gary Koch, Innisbrook Resort, Tarpon Springs, Fla.	73	73	71	71	288	8,884.66
	Joey Sindelar, The Polo Club, Boca Raton, Fla.	81	66	70	71	288	8,884.66
	Jodie Mudd, Shawnee G.C., Louisville, Ky.	73	75	69	71	288	8,884.66
	Bobby Wadkins, Brandermill C.C., Midlothian, Va.	75	69	72	72	288	8,884.66
	David Graham, Preston Trail G.C., Dallas, Texas	76	71	69	72	288	8,884.66
	Scott Verplank, Brookhaven C.C., Dallas, Texas	75	72	67	74	288	8,884.66
24	Dave Eichelberger, TPC, Ponte Vedra Beach, Fla.	80	70	72	67	289	6,461.80
	Andy Bean, Lakeland, Fla.	76	72	73	68	289	6,461.80
	Don Pooley, La Paloma C.C., Tucson, Ariz.	75	71	74	69	289	6,461.80
	Calvin Peete, Fiddlesticks C.C., Ft. Myers, Fla.	77	73	70	69	289	6,461.80
	Larry Mize, Columbus, Ga.	75	71	73	70	289	6,461.80
	Larry Rinker, Winter Park, Fla	77	71	70	71	289	6,461.80
	Severiano Ballesteros, Doral C.C., Miami, Fla.	75	73	68	73	289	6,461.80
	Tom Watson, Kansas City, Mo.	72	71	71	75	289	6,461.80
	Lenny Clements, San Diego, Calif.	75	72	67	75	289	6,461.80
	Mike Reid, Provo, Utah	74	73	66	76	289	6,461.80
34	Paul Azinger, River Wilderness, Parrish, Fla.	78	72	70	70	290	5,575.00
35	Tom Kite, Riverplace C.C., Austin, Texas	74	74	73	70	291	5,170.20
	Philip Blackmar, Rockport C.C, Rockport, Texas	75	75	70	71	291	5,170.20
	Larry Nelson, Metropolitan Club, Atlanta, Ga.	75	73	70	73	291	5,170.20
	John Cook, Mission Hills C.C., Rancho Mirage, Calif.	75	73	70	73	291	5,170.20
	*Sam Randolph, La Cumbre C.C., Santa Barbara, Calif.	79	71	68	73	291	Medal
	Mark McNulty, Johannesburg, South Africa	75	72	68	76	291	5,170.20
41	Mark O'Meara, Escondido, Calif.	76	73	71	72	292	4,566.00
	Bruce Fleisher, Westview C.C., Miami, Fla.	76	73	71	72	292	4,566.00
	Roger Maltbie, San Jose C.C., San Jose, Calif.	76	70	73	73	292	4,566.00
	Doug Tewell, Oak Tree G.C., Edmond, Okla.	74	73	71	74	292	4,566.00
45	Kenny Knox, Golden Eagle G.C., Tallahassee, Fla.	72	76	74	71	293	3,963.00
	Dave Barr, Kananaskis C.C., Canmore, Alberta, Canada	75	73	73	72	293	3,963.00
	Sandy Lyle, Surrey, England	78	71	72	72	293	3,963.00
	Mark Lye, Silverado C.C., Napa, Calif.	80	70	70	73	293	3,963.00
	Johnny Miller, Boca West C.C., Boca Raton, Fla.	76	72	71	74	293	3,963.00
50	David Hobby, Santa Ana C.C., Santa Ana, Calif.	76	74	71	73	294	3,427.00
	Barry Jaeckel, Palm Desert, Calif.	75	74	71	74	294	3,427.00
	Mac O'Grady, Palm Springs, Calif.	75	69	73	77	294	3,427.00
53	Tsuneyuki Nakajima, Narita City, Japan	72	72	78	73	295	3,092.00
	Bill Glasson, Singing Hills C.C., San Diego, Calif.	76	74	69	76	295	3,092.00
55	Hubert Green, Shoal Creek, Birmingham, Ala.	75	75	75	71	296	2,914.50
	Bill Israelson, Hazeltine National C.C., Chaska, Minn.	79	71	72	74	296	2,914.50
	Greg Powers, Tallahassee, Fla.	80	70	72	74	296	2,914.50
	Wayne Levi, New Hartford, N.Y.	77	70	74	75	296	2,914.50
59	Frank Conner, San Antonio, Texas	75	73	77	72	297	2,791.00
	Tze-Chung Chen, Lincou C.C., Taiwan	76	72	75	74	297	2,791.00
	Peter Jacobsen, Lake Oswego, Ore.	76	72	73	76	297	2,791.00
62	Rick Fehr, Bellevue, Wash.	72	77	75	74	298	2,761.00
	Jeff Sluman, Oak Hill C.C., Rochester, N.Y.	75	74	75	74	298	2,761.00
	David Ogrin, Cog Hill G.& C.C, Lemont, Ill.	76	73	74	75	298	2,761.00
65	Richard Mast, Cypress Creek G.C., Orlando, Fla.	76	74	76	74	300	2,761.00
66	Howard Twitty, Arizona Biltmore, Phoenix, Ariz.	79	71	75	76	301	2,761.00
67	Andy North, Nakoma G.C., Madison, Wis.	79	71	77	75	302	2,761.00
68	Michael Malaska, Fairbanks Ranch C.C., Rancho Santa Fe., Calif.	74	74	80	75	303	2,761.00
69	Peter Oosterhuis, Mission Hills C.C., Rancho Mirage, Calif.	78	70	78	78	304	2,761.00
70	Bradford Greer, Mission Hills C.C., Rancho Mirage, Calif.	73	72	79	76	305	2,761.00

Prize money totaling $718,248.94 awarded to professionals as follows: Championship—669,048.94; prizes for 84 professionals who did not return scores for 72 holes—49,200.00

+Record Entry

*Amateur

1987
EIGHTY-SEVENTH OPEN CHAMPIONSHIP

The Olympic Club (Lake Course), San Francisco, California, June 18-21
Yardage—6,709. Par 70. +5,696 Entries, 156 Starters.

						Score	Money Prize
1	Scott Simpson, Makaha Valley C.C., Honolulu, Hawaii	71	68	70	68	277	$150,000.00
2	Tom Watson, Kansas City, Mo.	72	65	71	70	278	75,000.00
3	Seve Ballesteros, La Manga, Spain	68	75	68	71	282	46,240.00
4	Bobby Wadkins, Brandermill C.C., Midlothian, Va.	71	71	70	71	283	24,542.80
	Curtis Strange, Kingsmill on James, Williamsburg, Va.	71	72	69	71	283	24,542.80
	Bernhard Langer, Anhausen, West Germany	69	69	73	72	283	24,542.80
	Ben Crenshaw, Austin Texas	67	72	72	72	283	24,542.80
	Larry Mize, Columbus, Ga.	71	68	72	72	283	24,542.80
9	Dan Pohl, The Boulders, Carefree, Ariz.	75	71	69	69	284	15,004.20
	Tsuneyuki Nakajima, Narita City, Japan	68	70	74	72	284	15,004.20
	Mac O'Grady, Palm Springs, Calif.	71	69	72	72	284	15,004.20
	Jim Thorpe, Buffalo, N.Y.	70	68	73	73	284	15,004.20
	Lennie Clements, Pala Mesa Resort, San Diego, Calif.	70	70	70	74	284	15,004.20
14	Bob Eastwood, Stockton, Calif.	73	66	75	71	285	12,065.34
	Isao Aoki, Tokyo, Japan	71	73	70	71	285	12,065.33
	Tim Simpson, Springbrook C.C., Lawrenceville, Ga.	76	66	70	73	285	12,065.33
17	Jodie Mudd, Shawnee G.C., Louisville, Ky.	72	75	71	68	286	9,747.29
	Jim Woodward, Quail Creek C.C., Oklahoma City, Okla.	71	74	72	69	286	9,747.29
	Mark Calcavecchia, Bear Lakes C.C., W. Palm Beach, Fla.	73	68	73	72	286	9,747.29
	David Frost, Cape Town, South Africa	70	72	71	73	286	9,747.29
	Masashi Ozaki, Funabashi, Japan	71	69	72	74	286	9,747.28
	Nick Price, Orlando, Fla.	69	74	69	74	286	9,747.28
	Kenny Knox, Golden Eagle G.C., Tallahassee, Fla.	72	71	69	74	286	9,747.28
24	Don Pooley, La Paloma C.C., Tucson, Ariz.	74	72	72	69	287	7,719.72
	Jay Don Blake, St. George, Utah	70	75	71	71	287	7,719.72
	Steve Pate, Simi Valley, Calif.	71	72	72	72	287	7,719.72
	Craig Stadler, Rancho Santa Fe, Calif.	72	68	74	73	287	7,719.71
	Danny Edwards, PGA West, La Quinta, Calif.	72	70	72	73	287	7,719.71
	Peter Jacobsen, Portland, Ore.	72	71	71	73	287	7,719.71
	John Mahaffey, The Woodlands, The Woodlands, Texas	72	72	67	76	287	7,719.71
31	Ken Green, West Palm Beach, Fla.	71	74	75	68	288	6,554.60
	Tony Sills, Santa Monica, Calif.	71	70	75	72	288	6,554.60
	Hal Sutton, Shreveport, La.	74	70	70	74	288	6,554.60
	Dale Douglass, Phoenix, Ariz.	70	73	69	76	288	6,554.60
	Keith Clearwater, Orem, Utah	74	71	64	79	288	6,554.60
36	Scott Hoch, Orlando, Fla.	72	70	77	70	289	5,626.00
	Sandy Lyle, London, England	70	74	72	73	289	5,626.00
	Lanny Wadkins, Preston Trail G.C., Dallas, Texas	73	71	72	73	289	5,626.00
	Denis Watson, Links of Tryon, Gowansville, S.C.	69	74	72	74	289	5,626.00
	Rodger Davis, Terranora, Australia	75	68	72	74	289	5,626.00
	Barry Jaeckel, Palm Desert, Calif.	73	70	72	74	289	5,626.00
	John Cook, Mission Hills C.C., Rancho Mirage, Calif.	70	68	76	75	289	5,626.00
43	Sam Randolph, La Cumbre G.C., Santa Barbara, Calif.	71	71	76	72	290	4,856.67
	Raymond Floyd, Miami Beach, Fla.	68	73	76	73	290	4,856.67
	Wayne Grady, Orlando, Fla.	73	70	74	73	290	4,856.66
46	Roger Maltbie, San Jose C.C., San Jose, Calif.	73	73	75	70	291	4,240.00
	Ralph Landrum, Devou Park G.& T.C., Covington, Ky.	72	71	74	74	291	4,240.00
	Fred Couples, La Quinta Hotel & C.C., La Quinta, Calif.	72	71	73	75	291	4,240.00
	Tom Kite, Austin, Texas	76	69	70	76	291	4,240.00
	Jack Nicklaus, Muirfield Village G.C., Dublin, Ohio	70	68	76	77	291	4,240.00
51	Joey Sindelar, Polo Club, Boca Raton, Fla.	75	71	75	71	292	3,462.15
	David Hobby, Santa Ana C.C., Santa Ana, Calif.	77	70	73	72	292	3,462.15
	Gil Morgan, Oak Tree G.C., Edmond, Okla.	72	71	76	73	292	3,462.14
	David Graham, Preston Trails, Dallas, Texas	71	76	72	73	292	3,462.14
	Ed Dougherty, Edgemont C.C., Edgemont, Pa.	73	67	78	74	292	3,462.14
	Greg Norman, Queensland, Australia	72	69	74	77	292	3,462.14
	Mark McCumber, Summer Beach Resort, Amelia Island, Fla.	72	72	69	79	292	3,462.14
58	Bob Lohr, Orlando, Fla.	76	67	79	71	293	3,178.00
	Duffy Waldorf, Calabasas Park, Calabasas, Calif.	74	69	75	75	293	3,178.00
	Mike Smith, Selma C.C., Selma, Ala.	73	71	74	75	293	3,178.00
	Eddie Kirby, Kirkbrae C.C., Lincoln, R.I.	73	69	75	76	293	3,178.00
	Jack Renner, Lomas Santa Fe C.C., Solana Beach, Calif.	73	73	71	76	293	3,178.00
	Mark Wiebe, Bear Creek G.C., Lakewood, Colo.	70	67	77	79	293	3,178.00
	Gene Sauers, Statesboro, Ga.	72	69	73	79	293	3,178.00
	Bob Gilder, Carmel Valley Ranch, Carmel, Calif.	72	72	70	79	293	3,178.00
66	Russ Cochran, Paducah, Ky.	71	69	81	73	294	3,165.00
	Mark McNulty, Johannesburg, South Africa	73	72	73	76	294	3,165.00
68	Tom Purtzer, La Quinta Hotel & G.C., La Quinta, Calif.	74	73	77	71	295	3,165.00
	Jose-Maria Olazabal, San Sebastian, Spain	76	69	76	74	295	3,165.00
	Bob Tway, Oak Tree G.C., Edmond, Okla.	70	71	79	75	295	3,165.00
71	Donnie Hammond, Longwood, Fla.	75	71	76	74	296	3,165.00
	Jim Carter, Mesa, Ariz.	75	72	75	74	296	3,165.00
73	Gary Hallberg, Taos G.C., Taos, N.M.	71	72	69	85	297	3,165.00
74	David Ogrin, Cog Hill G.& C.C., Lemont, Ill.	74	72	74	78	298	3,165.00
75	Dave Eichelberger, TPC, Ponte Vedra, Fla.	72	75	77	76	300	3,165.00
	Fred Wadsworth, Columbus, Ga.	75	71	77	77	300	3,165.00
77	David Rummells, Orlando, Fla.	74	73	76	78	301	3,165.00

Prize money totaling $869,204.00 awarded to professionals as follows: Championship—$823,004.00; prizes for 77 professionals who did not return scores for 72 holes—$46,200.00.

+ Record Entry

1988
EIGHTY-EIGHTH OPEN CHAMPIONSHIP

Held at The Country Club, Brookline, Massachusetts, June 16-20
Yardage—7,010. Par 71. +5,775 Entries, 156 Starters.

						Score	Money Prize
1	†Curtis Strange, Kingsmill on the James, Williamsburg, Va.	70	67	69	72	278	$180,000.00
2	†Nick Faldo, Ascot, England	72	67	68	71	278	90,000.00
3	Steve Pate, Simi Valley, Calif.	72	69	72	67	280	41,370.00
	Mark O'Meara, PGA West, LaQuinta, Calif.	71	72	66	71	280	41,370.00
	D.A. Weibring, Plano, Texas	71	69	68	72	280	41,370.00
6	Paul Azinger, Sarasota, Fla.	69	70	76	66	281	25,414.50
	Scott Simpson, Makaha Valley C.C., Makaha Valley, Hawaii	69	66	72	74	281	25,414.50
8	Fuzzy Zoeller, New Albany C.C., New Albany, Ind.	73	72	71	66	282	20,903.50
	Bob Gilder, Corvallis C.C., Corvallis, Ore.	68	69	70	75	282	20,903.50
10	Payne Stewart, C.C. at Heathrow, Lake Mary, Fla.	73	73	70	67	283	17,870.50
	Fred Couples, Rancho Mirage, Calif.	72	67	71	73	283	17,870.50
12	Ben Crenshaw, Austin, Texas	71	72	74	67	284	14,781.20
	Dan Pohl, The Boulders, Carefree, Ariz.	74	72	69	69	284	14,781.20
	Andy Bean, Windstar C.C., Naples, Fla.	71	71	72	70	284	14,781.20
	Lanny Wadkins, Preston Trail C.C., Dallas, Texas	70	71	70	73	284	14,781.20
	Larry Mize, Columbus, Ga.	69	67	72	76	284	14,781.20
17	Raymond Floyd, Miami Beach, Fla.	73	72	73	67	285	11,981.25
	Mark McNulty, Harare, Zimbabwe	73	72	72	68	285	11,981.25
	Hale Irwin, Kapalua G.C., Kapalua Maui, Hawaii	71	71	72	71	285	11,981.25
	Joey Sindelar, Polo Club of Boca Raton, Boca Raton, Fla.	76	68	70	71	285	11,981.25
21	Peter Jacobsen, Doral C.C., Doral, Fla.	76	70	76	64	286	10,344.75
	Chip Beck, Sea Palms Golf Resort, St. Simons Island, Ga.	73	72	71	70	286	10,344.75
	Bob Eastwood, Stockton, Calif.	74	72	69	71	286	10,344.75
	Scott Hoch, Bay Hill, Orlando, Fla.	71	72	71	72	286	10,344.75
25	Bob Tway, Oak Tree G.C., Edmond, Okla.	77	68	73	69	287	8,855.84
	Mark Wiebe, Littleton, Colo.	75	70	73	69	287	8,855.84
	Dave Barr, Richmond, British Columbia, Canada	73	72	72	70	287	8,855.83
	Sandy Lyle, Surrey, England	68	71	75	73	287	8,855.83
	Jay Haas, Thorn Blade G.C., Greenville, S.C.	73	67	74	73	287	8,855.83
	Craig Stadler, Rancho Santa Fe, Calif.	70	73	71	73	287	8,855.83
	*Bill Mayfair, Camelback G.C., Scottsdale, Ariz.	71	72	71	73	287	Medal
32	Seve Ballesteros, Santander, Spain	69	74	72	73	288	7,726.00
	Mark McCumber, Summer Beach Resort, Amelia Island, Fla.	72	72	71	73	288	7,726.00
	Tommy Nakajima, Japan	74	72	69	73	288	7,726.00
	Ken Green, W. Palm Beach, Fla.	72	70	70	76	288	7,726.00
36	David Ishii, Pearl C.C., Aiea, Hawaii	73	73	75	68	289	7,002.50
	Mark Lye, Silverado C.C., Napa, Calif.	75	71	71	72	289	7,002.50
	Tom Kite, Austin, Texas	72	69	73	75	289	7,002.50
	Tom Watson, Kansas City C.C., Mission Hills, Kan.	74	71	69	75	289	7,002.50
40	Chip Johnson, C.C. of Halifax, Halifax, Mass.	72	72	76	70	290	6,014.86
	Danny Edwards, PGA West G.C., LaQuinta, Calif.	72	73	74	71	290	6,014.86
	Lee Trevino, Dallas, Texas	73	73	73	71	290	6,014.86
	Mike Nicolette, Buffalo Grove, Ill.	68	73	77	72	290	6,014.86
	Dan Halldorson, Cambridge, Ill.	72	71	74	73	290	6,014.85
	Nick Price, Orlando, Fla.	72	74	71	73	290	6,014.85
	Clarence Rose, Goldsboro, N.C.	75	71	68	76	290	6.014.85
47	Kent Stauffer, Longue Vue Club, Verona, Pa.	72	72	78	69	291	5,119.00
	David Graham, Preston Trail, Dallas, Texas	77	69	74	71	291	5,119.00
	Rodger Davis, Terranora, Australia	73	73	71	74	291	5,119.00
50	Buddy Gardner, Birmingham C.C., Birmingham, Ala.	72	73	75	72	292	4,492.25
	John Cook, Mission Hills C.C., Rancho Mirage, Calif.	73	68	78	73	292	4,492.25
	Dick Mast, Cypress Creek C.C., Boynton Beach, Fla.	69	75	75	73	292	4,492.25
	Isao Aoki, Tokyo, Japan	71	74	71	76	292	4,492.25
54	David Edwards, Oak Tree G.C., Edmond, Okla.	76	69	75	73	293	4,044.00
55	Kenny Perry, Franklin C.C., Franklin, Ky.	74	71	77	72	294	3,896.50
	Dennis Trixler, California G.C., San Francisco, Calif.	72	73	76	73	294	3,896.50
	Roger Maltbie, San Jose C.C., San Jose, Calif.	75	71	74	74	294	3,896.50
	Jim Carter, Mesa, Ariz.	74	72	70	78	294	3,896.50
59	Robert Wilkin, Wolf Creek G.C., Olathe, Kan.	74	71	77	73	295	3,751.50
	Steven Bowman, Tyler, Texas	71	72	75	77	295	3,751.50
61	Jim Hallet, Bass River G.C., South Yarmouth, Mass.	72	74	77	73	296	3,691.00
62	Larry Nelson, Marietta, Ga.	78	67	80	72	297	3,691.00
	Mike Calcavecchia, Bear Lakes C.C., West Palm Beach, Fla.	74	69	78	76	297	3,691.00
64	Hal Sutton, Shreveport, La.	74	72	75	77	298	3,691.00
65	Jerry Haas, St. Clair C.C., Belleville, Ill.	73	73	73	80	299	3,691.00

† Playoff, June 20, 1988, Curtis Strange 71, Nick Faldo 75.
Prize money totaling $1,006,764.00 awarded to professionals as follows: Championship—$918,764.00, prizes for 88 professionals who did not return scores for 72 holes—$88,000.00.

+ Record Entry
* Amateur

1989
EIGHTY-NINTH OPEN CHAMPIONSHIP

Held at Oak Hill Country Club (East Course), Rochester, New York, June 15-18
Yardage—6,902. Par 70. Record 5,786 Entries, 156 Starters.

						Score	Money Prize
1	Curtis Strange, Kingsmill on the James, Williamsburg, Va.	71	64	73	70	278	$200,000.00
2	Ian Woosnam, Oswestry, Wales	70	68	73	68	279	67,823.00
	Chip Beck, Sea Palms Golf Resort, St. Simon Isl., Ga.	71	69	71	68	279	67,823.00
	Mark McCumber, Ravines G.C., Ponte Vedra Beach, Fla.	70	68	72	69	279	67,823.00
5	Brian Claar, Eastlake Woodlands, Oldsmar, Fla.	71	72	68	69	280	34,345.00
6	Masashi Ozaki, Funabashi Chiba, Japan	70	71	68	72	281	28,220.50
	Scott Simpson, Makaha Valley C.C., Makaha Valley, Hawaii	67	70	69	75	281	28,220.50
8	Peter Jacobsen, Lake Oswego, Ore.	71	70	71	70	282	24,307.00
9	Hubert Green, Shoal Creek, Shoal Creek, Ala.	69	72	74	68	283	19,968.50
	Paul Azinger, Sarasota, Fla.	71	72	70	70	283	19,968.50
	Jose Maria Olazabal, San Sebastian, Spain	69	72	70	72	283	19,968.50
	Tom Kite, Austin, Texas	67	69	69	78	283	19,968.50
13	Payne Stewart, Orlando, Fla.	66	75	72	71	284	15,634.00
	Mark Lye, Silverado C.C., Fort Myers, Fla.	71	69	72	72	284	15,634.00
	Scott Hoch, Orlando, Fla.	70	72	70	72	284	15,634.00
	Tom Pernice, Jr., Lees Summit, Mo.	67	75	68	74	284	15,634.00
	Larry Nelson, Marietta, Ga.	68	73	68	75	284	15,634.00
18	David Frost, Dallas, Texas	73	72	70	70	285	13,013.00
	Nick Faldo, Ascot, England	68	72	73	72	285	13,013.00
	Jay Don Blake, St. George, Utah	66	71	72	76	285	13,013.00
21	Steve Elkington, Humble, Texas	70	70	78	68	286	11,306.00
	D.A. Weibring, Riverside G.C., Plano, Texas	70	74	73	69	286	11,306.00
	Nolan Henke, Vines C.C., Fort Myers, Fla.	75	69	72	70	286	11,306.00
	Bill Glasson, Oceanside, Calif.	73	70	70	73	286	11,306.00
	Fred Couples, Palm Beach Polo Club, West Palm Beach, Fla.	74	71	67	74	286	11,306.00
26	Robert Wrenn, Wintergreen, Richmond, Va.	74	71	73	69	287	9,983.67
	Raymond Floyd, Turnberry Isle Yacht, Miami Beach, Fla.	68	74	74	71	287	9,983.67
	Don Pooley, La Paloma C.C., Tucson, Ariz.	74	69	71	73	287	9,983.67
29	Scott Taylor, Sleepy Hollow C.C., Scarborough, N.Y.	69	71	76	72	288	9,006.50
	Hal Sutton, Shreveport, La.	69	75	72	72	288	9,006.50
	Emlyn Aubrey, Eastwood Fairways, Bossier City, La.	69	73	73	73	288	9,006.50
	Dan Pohl, The Boulders, Phoenix, Ariz.	71	71	73	73	288	9,006.50
33	Brad Faxon, Orlando, Fla.	73	70	75	71	289	9,006.50
	Joey Sindelar, Polo Club, Horseheads, N.Y.	67	77	74	71	289	7,576.60
	Davis Love, III, Sea Island G.C., Sea Island, Ga.	71	74	73	71	289	7,576.60
	Billy Mayfair, Camelback G.C., Phoenix, Ariz.	72	69	76	72	289	7,576.60
	Daniel Forsman, Provo, Utah	70	70	76	73	289	7,576.60
	Isao Aoki, Tokyo, Japan	70	70	75	74	289	7,576.60
	Larry Mize, Columbus, Ga.	72	72	71	74	289	7,576.60
	Greg Norman, Grand Cypress Resort, Orlando, Fla.	72	68	73	76	289	7,576.60
	Edward Kirby, Kirkbrae C.C., Cumberland, R.I.	70	70	73	76	289	7,576.60
	Mark Wiebe, Highlands Ranch, Colo.	69	71	72	77	289	7,576.60
43	Severiano Ballesteros, Santander, Spain	75	70	76	69	290	6,281.00
	Clark Dennis, Mira Vista C.C., Fort Worth, Texas	72	72	72	74	290	6,281.00
	Jack Nicklaus, Muirfield Village G.C., Dublin, Ohio	67	74	74	75	290	6,281.00
46	Steven Jones, Phoenix, Ariz.	69	75	77	70	291	5,485.80
	John Mahaffey, The Woodlands, Houston, Texas	77	68	74	72	291	5,485.80
	Tom Watson, Kansas City C.C., Kansas City, Mo.	76	69	73	73	291	5,485.80
	Richard Zokol, Whistler G.C., Richmond B.C., Canada	71	69	76	75	291	5,485.80
	Ken Green, West Palm Beach, Fla.	73	72	71	75	291	5,485.80
51	Tom Sieckmann, Highland C.C., Dallas, Texas	73	71	74	74	292	4,690.00
	Jodie Mudd, Atlanta, Ga.	73	71	74	74	292	4,690.00
	Steve Pate, Richmond, Va.	74	69	73	76	292	4,690.00
54	Hale Irwin, Kapalua G.C., Kapalua, Hawaii	74	70	79	70	293	4,299.80
	Ronnie Black, Scottsdale, Ariz.	71	74	76	72	293	4,299.80
	David Ogrin, The Club at Sonterra, San Antonio, Texas	73	72	73	75	293	4,299.80
	Webb Heintzelman, Glenn Dale C.C., Bethesda, Maryland	72	70	75	76	293	4,299.80
	Chris Perry, Dublin, Ohio	76	67	72	78	293	4,299.80
59	Bernhard Langer, Anhausen, W. Germany	66	78	77	73	294	4,120.00
	Clarence Rose, Goldsboro, N.C.	70	75	73	76	294	4,120.00
61	David Graham, Preston Trail G.C., Dallas, Texas	73	72	77	73	295	4,099.00
	Mark Calcavecchia, North Palm Beach, Fla.	74	70	74	77	295	4,099.00
63	Don Halldorson, Cambridge, Ill.	72	70	76	78	296	4,099.00
	Tony Sills, TPC of Southwind, Memphis, Tenn.	72	72	71	81	296	4,099.00
	*Gregory Lesher, Lebanon C.C., Lebanon, PA	70	72	76	78	296	Medal
66	Bobby Wadkins, Rivers Bend C.C., Richmond, Va.	73	72	75	77	297	4,099.00
67	Dillard Pruitt, Greenville C.C., Greenville, S.C.	68	74	81	75	298	4,099.00
	Ed Humenik, Allen Park, Miss.	73	72	76	77	298	4,099.00
69	Doug Weaver, Orlando, Fla.	72	73	80	75	300	4,099.00
	John Daly, Bay Ridge C.C., Dardanelle, Ariz.	74	67	80	79	300	4,099.00
71	Kurt Beck, Valley Brook C.C., Pittsburgh, Pa.	68	73	83	77	301	4,099.00

Prize money totaling $1.1 million awarded to professionals.
*Amateur

1990
NINETIETH OPEN CHAMPIONSHIP

Medinah Country Club (No. 3 Course), Medinah, Illinois, June 14-18
Yardage—7,195. Par 72. Record 6,198 Entries, 156 Starters.

						Score	Money Prize
1	Hale Irwin, Kapalua, Maui, Hawaii	69	70	74	67	280-74-3	$220,000.00
	Mike Donald, Hollywood, Fla.	67	70	72	71	280-74-4	110,000.00
3	Nick Faldo, Surrey, England	72	72	68	69	281	56,878.50
	Billy Ray Brown, Missouri City, Tex.	69	71	69	72	281	56,878.50
5	Greg Norman, Queensland, Australia	72	73	69	69	283	33,271.33
	Tim Simpson, Reynolds Plantation, Ga.	66	69	75	73	283	33,271.33
	Mark Brooks, Fort Worth, Tex.	68	70	72	73	283	33,271.33
8	Steve Jones, Phoenix, Ariz.	67	76	74	67	284	22,236.67
	Craig Stadler, San Diego, Calif.	71	70	72	71	284	22,236.67
	Scott Hoch, Orlando, Fla.	70	73	69	72	284	22,236.67
	Tom Sieckmann, Omaha, Neb.	70	74	68	72	284	22,236.67
	Jose Maria Olazabal, Spain	73	69	69	73	284	22,236.67
	Fuzzy Zoeller, Williamsburg, Va.	73	70	68	73	284	22,236.67
14	Jim Benepe, Sheridan, N.Y.	72	70	73	70	285	15,712.43
	John Huston, Innsbrook, Fla.	68	72	73	72	285	15,712.43
	John Inman, Rosewell, Ga.	72	71	70	72	285	15,712.43
	Scott Simpson, Kailua, Hawaii	66	73	73	73	285	15,712.43
	Larry Mize, Columbus, Ga.	72	70	69	74	285	15,712.43
	Jeff Sluman, Naples, Fla.	66	70	74	75	285	15,712.43
	Larry Nelson, Marietta, Ga.	74	67	69	75	285	15,712.43
21	Steve Elkington, Sydney, Australia	73	71	73	69	286	12,843.33
	Ian Woosnam, Wales	70	70	74	72	286	12,843.33
	Curtis Strange, Kingsmill, Va.	73	70	68	75	286	12,843.33
24	Masashi Ozaki, Japan	73	72	74	68	287	11,308.80
	Webb Heintzelman, Bethesda, Md.	70	75	74	68	287	11,308.80
	Corey Pavin, Kauai, Hawaii	74	70	73	70	287	11,308.80
	Billy Tuten, Palatka, Fla.	74	70	72	71	287	11,308.80
	Paul Azinger, Sarasota, Fla.	72	72	69	74	287	11,308.80
29	*Phil Mickelson, San Diego, Calif.	74	71	71	72	288	Medal
	Chip Beck, Chicago, Ill.	71	71	73	73	288	10,022.00
	Mike Hulbert, Orlando, Fla.	76	66	71	75	288	10,022.00
	Brian Claar, Palm Harbor, Fla.	70	71	71	76	288	10,022.00
33	Tom Byrum, Onida, S.D.	70	75	74	70	289	8,221.15
	Kirk Triplett, Pullman, Wash.	72	70	75	72	289	8,221.15
	Bob Lohr, Orlando, Fla.	71	74	72	72	289	8,221.15
	Isao Aoki, Tokyo, Japan	73	69	74	73	289	8,221.15
	David Frost, Dallas, Tex.	72	72	72	73	289	8,221.15
	Bob Tway, Edmond, Okla.	69	72	74	74	289	8,221.15
	Steve Pate, Orlando, Fla.	75	68	72	74	289	8,221.15
	Bobby Wadkins, Richmond, Va.	71	73	71	74	289	8,221.15
	Seve Ballesteros, Sandander, Spain	73	69	71	76	289	8,221.15
	Jack Nicklaus, Dublin, Ohio	71	74	68	74	289	8,221.15
	Jim Gallagher, Jr., W. Palm Beach, Fla.	71	69	72	77	289	8,221.15
	Ted Schulz, Louisville, Ky.	73	70	69	77	289	8,221.15
	Mike Reid, Provo, Utah	70	73	68	78	289	8,221.15
46	Craig Parry, Sydney, Australia	72	71	68	79	290	6,687.00
47	Dave Barr, Alberta, Canada	74	71	75	71	291	6,140.50
	Mark McCumber, Jacksonville, Fla.	76	68	74	73	291	6,140.50
	Robert Thompson, Huntsville, Tex.	71	73	72	75	291	6,140.50
	Dave Rummells, West Branch, Iowa	73	71	70	77	291	6,140.50
51	Ray Stewart, British Columbia, Can.	70	74	73	75	292	5,184.40
	Bill Glasson, North Las Vegas, Nev.	71	73	72	76	292	5,184.40
	Andy North, Vail, Colo.	74	71	71	76	292	5,184.40
	Greg Twiggs, Rancho Mirage, Calif.	72	70	73	77	292	5,184.40
	Lanny Wadkins, Dallas, Tex.	72	72	70	78	292	5,184.40
56	Tom Kite, Austin, Tex.	75	70	74	74	293	4,694.25
	Blaine McCallister, Ft. Stockton, Tex.	71	72	75	75	293	4,694.25
	*David Duval, Ponte Verde Beach, Fla.	72	72	72	77	293	
	Bob Gilder, Corvallis, Ore.	71	70	74	78	293	4,694.25
	Gil Morgan, Edmond, Okla.	70	72	73	78	293	4,694.25
61	Scott Verplank, Edmond, Okla.	72	69	77	76	294	4,529.50
	Robert Gamez, Las Vegas, Nev.	72	73	73	76	294	4,529.50
63	Ronan Rafferty, Northern Ireland	75	70	73	78	296	4,507.00
64	David Graham, Dallas, Tex.	72	73	74	79	298	4,507.00
65	Howard Twitty, Phoenix, Ariz.	73	72	77	77	299	4,507.00
66	Brad Faxon, Orlando, Fla.	70	74	76	81	301	4,507.00
67	Michael E. Smith, McDowell Lk., Ala.	72	72	82	80	306	4,507.00
68	Randy Wylie, Knoxville, Tenn.	70	75	81	82	308	4,507.00

Prize money of $1.2 million awarded to professionals.

*Amateur

AMATEUR CHAMPIONSHIP

HAVEMEYER TROPHY

Presented in 1894 by

THEODORE A. HAVEMEYER

First President of the United States Golf Association

Original trophy destroyed by fire November, 1925. Replaced in January, 1926, by

EDWARD S. MOORE

Treasurer of the United States Golf Association, 1922-25

HISTORY

1981—Nathaniel Crosby, 19, of Hillsborough, California, won the Amateur Championship in a dramatic fashion usually reserved for other members of his famous family. The Championship was played over the Lake Course of the Olympic Club in San Francisco, not more than 15 miles from the Crosby home. He was down in four of his six matches and each time he played the shots he needed to win. Crosby defeated fellow Californian Brian Lindley, 24, of Fountain Valley, 1 up, 37 holes, settling the matter with a birdie putt of 20 feet on the first extra hole. It was the first time that a final had gone more than 36 holes since 1950. In the 36 holes of stroke play that preceded match play, Joe Rassett, of Turlock, California, led the starting field of 282 with a qualifying score of 145, to capture medalist honors. The field included members of both the American and British Walker Cup Teams. Crosby and Lindley both made match play with 152 totals. Defending Champion and Walker Cupper Hal Sutton also made it with 151. Rassett lost his second round match to Bill Bergin, 2 and 1, and Sutton bowed to Walker Cup teammate and two-time Amateur Public Links Champion Jodie Mudd, 2 up. Before reaching the final, Crosby's sternest test came from Willie Wood in the semi-final round. Wood had Crosby 3 down after eight holes, but going to the 16th hole, the match was even. Crosby then played three marvelous bunker shots, the first to save a half in par at the 16th; the second, a spectacular shot from the lower of two bunkers to the right of the 17th green to within two feet for another par to win the hole; and the third for another par at the 18th to win the match, 2 up. In the other semi-final match, Lindley defeated Walker Cupper Bob Lewis, Jr., 3 and 2. Lewis had lost in the final to Sutton in 1980. In the morning round of the final match, neither player was able to establish a comfortable lead. Lindley was ahead, 1 up, at the lunch break on a 74 to Crosby's 76, four and six over par, respectively. As the afternoon round began, Lindley pulled further ahead, winning the second hole with a bogey, the third with a par 3 and the seventh with a birdie 3 to go four up. Crosby won the ninth with a par 4, but Lindley had a three hole lead with seven to play. But when he lost the 12th and 13th, his lead was down to one hole. Lindley chipped in for a birdie 3 at the 14th to go 2 up. Both played excellent tee shots on the par-3 15th and halved the hole with birdie putts of eight feet or less. Both had their problems at the 16th, a par 5. Lindley was in the front bunker in three. Crosby was off the back of the green, also in three. But, Crosby chipped 10 feet past and holed the putt for a winning par as Lindley faltered. Crosby needed only a bogey 5 to win the 17th and the match was even. Both made par 4s on the 18th. On the first extra hole, a par 5, both players were on the edge of the green in three shots. Lindley chipped close and had a short putt for a par. Crosby then holed his curling left-to-right putt of 20 feet to cap a remarkable comeback. For a moment, Crosby thought that he had missed the putt as the ball waited on the lip of the cup for an instant before falling in. Crosby became only the fifth golfer to win the Amateur Championship before his 20th birthday. The difficult weather conditions sent the scores soaring, even Crosby's. Though he won, Crosby was 33 over par for 120 holes of match play. Add his score of 152 for the 36 holes of stroke play and he was 45 over par for 156 holes. Still, he made the critical shots, the type that win championships. William C. Campbell, the 1964 Amateur Champion, made his 37th appearance in the Championship, a record surpassed only by Charles Evans, Jr., who played in 50. The USGA accepted 3,525 entries, short of the record 4,008 for the 1980 Championship.

1982—Jay Sigel, 38, of Berwyn, Pennsylvania, became the oldest Amateur Champion since 1964, winning at The Country Club, in Brookline, Massachusetts. William C. Campbell won the Amateur Championship in 1964 at the age of 41. Ironically, Campbell was the referee in the morning round of the final match. Sigel competed in his first Amateur Championship in 1962. He won in his 16th attempt, defeating David Tolley, 22, of Roanoke, Virginia, 8 and 7, in the 36-hole final match. Despite some uncharacteristically sloppy play on the first nine of the morning round, Sigel took a five-hole advantage into the afternoon round. He built the lead to seven holes before Tolley mounted a small comeback, winning the fifth and sixth holes to narrow the margin to five. But Sigel rolled in a birdie putt of 40 feet on the seventh to open a six-hole advantage. He won the match on the 11th hole when Tolley conceded a short par putt. Nathaniel Crosby, of Hillsborough, California, the 1981 Champion, qualified easily for match play with a 149 total, but lost to Tom Pernice, Jr., of Kansas City, Missouri, on the 19th hole of the first round.

Pernice birdied both the 18th and 19th holes. Robert Stanger, Jr., of Durham, North Carolina, and Bob Lewis, Jr., of Warren, Ohio, shared medalist at 141, one under par. Stanger was eliminated in the third round by Jim Hallet, of South Yarmouth, Massachusetts, 2 and 1, while Sigel defeated Lewis, 3 and 2, in the first round. All 282 starters played one round each at The Country Club and the Charles River Country Club. Sixty-three players qualified with a score of 151 or better, while the 64th qualifier, Mark Brooks, of Ft. Worth, Texas, survived a 12-man playoff for the final spot after posting a 152. Jess Sweetser, who won the 1922 Amateur Championship at The Country Club, was the featured speaker at the players' dinner. Roger Brown, of Ponca City, Oklahoma, recorded the lone hole-in-one of the Championship, on the 237-yard 11th hole at Charles River. He failed to qualify for match play, however, The USGA accepted 3,685 entries, short of the record 4,008 for the 1980 Championship.

1983—Jay Sigel, 39, of Berwyn, Pennsylvania, became the eighth man to win consecutive Amateur Championships, when he defeated Chris Perry, of Edina, Minnesota, 8 and 7, at the North Shore Country Club, in Glenview, Illinois. Sigel was the first since E. Harvie Ward, Jr., in 1955-56, to win consecutive Amateur titles. After qualifying with a 148 total, Sigel was taken to extra holes twice. He was three down with four holes to play against George MacDonald, of Virginia Beach, Virginia, but made consecutive birdies on the 15th, 16th and 17th to square the match, then birdied the first extra hole to win. In the third round, Sigel was six under par in defeating Eric Peterson, of Fresno, California, 5 and 3. He built an early 2-up lead in his quarterfinal match, against Roy Biancalana, of Franklin Park, Illinois, but Biancalana squared the match and forced extra holes. Sigel won with a birdie from 12 feet on the 19th. In the semifinals, Sigel won, 3 and 2, against, Clark Burroughs, of Overland Park, Kansas. Burroughs was the qualifying medalist, with 139. Perry, the son of Jim Perry, a former major league pitcher, was among 14 players who shot 150 in the qualifying rounds, and after winning one of the six available places in match play in a playoff, had to survive three extra-hole matches. He defeated Tim Straub, the U.S. Junior Amateur Champion, from Orchard Park, New York, John Erickson, of Palos Verdes Estates, California, and Clifton Pierce of Lawton, Oklahoma, all on the 19th. Pierce had been 1 up going to the 17th against Perry in the semifinal, but he hit his tee shot out of bounds. In the final, Sigel was 2 up after nine holes and 3 up after 18 holes. He was devastating in the afternoon. Out in 33, Sigel won five of the first nine holes and stood 8 up. In sequence, he won the second and fifth with birdies, the sixth with a par, the seventh with another birdie and the ninth with a par. They halved the 10th and 11th holes to end the match. Sigel had only two bogeys during the 29 holes of the final match. The USGA accepted entries from 3,553 players.

1984—Scott Verplank, 20, of Dallas, Texas, defeated Sam Randolph, of Santa Barbara, California, 4 and 3, in the final at the Oak Tree Golf Club, in Edmond, Oklahoma. Verplank, a student at Oklahoma State University, was the medalist, with a score of 137 over the two courses at Oak Tree. Twice he had close calls in match play. In the semifinals, he holed an eight-foot par putt on the 18th green to defeat Randy Sonnier, of Woodlands, Texas, 1-up. Against Peter Persons, of Macon, Georgia, in the quarterfinals, Verplank was 2 down after 10 holes, but he won the 11th 12th, 15th, and 16th holes. Meanwhile, Randolph was extended to the 18th hole just once. In the first round he defeated Tom McKnight, of Galex, Virginia, 2-up. Randolph moved into the final with a surprisingly easy 7 and 5 semifinal victory over Jerry Haas, of Belleville, Illinois. Its start delayed two hours because of rain, the final became a contrast of putting fortunes, with Verplank salvaging either halves or wins with putts ranging from four to 10 feet while Randolph missed a half-dozen putts inside five feet. In the morning round, Randolph led, 2 up, through 16 holes, but he lost both the 17th and 18th when he missed short putts, leaving the match even at lunch. The pattern repeated itself in the afternoon. Randolph took control with a par on the first hole as Verplank bogeyed, but as the rain began to ease, Verplank squared the match at the third, made three successive birdies beginning at the eighth hole and went ahead for the first time. His 25-foot birdie on the 15th ended the match. Jay Sigel, of Berwyn, Pennsylvania, only the eighth man ever to win two successive U.S. Amateurs, in 1982 and 1983, lost in the first round, 3 and 1, to Rocco Mediate, of Greensburg, Pennsylvania.

1985—Sam Randolph, 21, of Santa Barbara, California, defeated Peter Persons of Macon, Georgia, 1 up, at Montclair Golf Club, West Orange, New Jersey. Randolph, a student at the University of Southern California, earned medalist honors with 134, tying a record set by Bob Clampett in 1979. Randolph defeated Mike Schuchart of Lincoln, Nebraska, 1 up, in a first round match and proceeded to the final without again having to play the 18th hole. In the semi-finals he defeated Jack Kay, Jr., of Don Mills, Ontario, Canada, who had earlier eliminated 1984 champion Scott Verplank, 4 and 3. Persons, a graduate of the University of Georgia, was twice extended to the 18th green on his way to the final. His semifinal opponent was Chip Drury, a college teammate from Brunswick, Georgia, whom he eliminated 3 and 1. After losing the second hole in the final, Persons won the fifth with a birdie, the seventh with a par and the ninth with a birdie to take a 2-up lead. Randolph stormed back, winning the next five holes to go 3 up. After Persons won the 15th, Randolph birdied the 16th to regain his three-hole edge. Persons then won the 17th and 18th and was only one down as the afternoon began. Neither golfer could manage more than a 1-up lead during the afternoon. Persons evened the match on the 19th hole, only to fall behind again on the 20th. Persons pulled even again on the 21st hole. This pattern continued, with Randolph gaining a lead and Persons pulling even, until the 31st hole when Persons gained his first lead in the match since the 10th hole. Randolph evened the match with a birdic on the 32nd hole. After the 33rd and 34th were halved with pars, Randolph's approach from the right rough on the 35th stopped two feet from the hole and the birdie gave him a one-hole lead. On the final hole, Randolph made a par after blasting from the right greenside bunker to within eight feet to gain the victory. The USGA accepted 3,816 entries for the Championship.

1986—Buddy Alexander, 33, the golf coach at Louisiana State University in Baton Rouge, defeated Chris Kite of Hiddenite, North Carolina, 5 and 3, at Shoal Creek in Shoal Creek, Alabama. Len Mattiace, 18, earned medalist honors with a five-under-par total of 137. He was defeated by Kite in the second round, 1 up. Kite was taken to the 17th hole in his next three matches. He defeated Brian Montgomery of Bristow, Oklahoma, the 1986 U.S. Junior Amateur champion, 3 and 1, in their semifinal match. Alexander defeated 1984 U.S. Mid-Amateur champion Mike Podolak on the 19th hole in the first round. He was not severely tested again until the quarter-finals, when he downed Todd Hamilton, 2 and 1. He defeated Bob Lewis, Jr., 5 and 4, to gain his spot in the final. Kite was 2-up after six holes of the 36-hole final, but his lead was cut to one hole when Alexander birdied the par-3 eighth. The margin went back to two when Alexander three-putted the ninth. Alexander squared the match with a par on the 10th and a birdie on the 11th and earned his first lead of the match with a par on the 16th. A scrambling birdie on the par-5 17th to a three-putt par by Kite gave Alexander a 2-up lead after the morning round. Alexander's lead grew to three holes when Kite bogeyed the 20th hole; but Kite birdied the 22nd, 23rd and 24th holes to pull within one again. That was as close as he got, however, as Alexander birdied the 25th and won the 27th with a par to go 3 up again. The 30th and 31st holes were halved with birdies and Alexander closed out the match with birdies on the next two holes. The USGA accepted a record 4,071 entries for the championship.

1987—Bill Mayfair, 21 of Scottsdale, Arizona, defeated Eric Rebmann of Plantation, Florida, 4 and 3, in the final at the Jupiter Hills Club in Jupiter, Florida. Mayfair became the first player ever to win the U.S. Amateur and Amateur Public Links Championships. He won the APL in 1986. Scott Gump of Rockledge, Florida, earned the qualifying medal at three-under-par 141, two strokes better than fellow Floridians Miles McConnell and Nolan Henke. Gump was eliminated in the semifinal round by Rebmann, who defeated two-time champion Jay Sigel in a quarterfinal match. Mayfair twice was extended to extra holes on his way to the final. He defeated Scott Mayne of Warwick, Bermuda, on the 19th hole in the first round and eliminated McConnell in the quarterfinals. He defeated Stephen Ford of Melbourne, Florida, 3 and 2, to reach the final against Rebmann. Mayfair won the fourth hole with a birdie, then lost the advantage when Rebmann birdied the fifth. Mayfair regained the lead at the seventh and increased to 2 up with a par at the eighth. Rebmann pulled even by winning the ninth and 11th with pars. Mayfair held a 1-up lead after the morning round, but Rebmann squared the match with a birdie at the 20th. Mayfair took the lead for good when Rebmann three-putted at the 22nd hole. Mayfair built his lead to 2 up at the 26th and 3 up at the 29th. He held that edge at the 33rd hole, where he closed Rebmann out with a par. Buddy Alexander, the 1986 champion, failed to qualify for match play. He was eliminated in a playoff in which 25 players battled for nine spots in match play. The USGA accepted a record 4,085 entries for the championship.

1988—Eric Meeks, 23, of Walnut, California, defeated Danny Yates of Atlanta, 7 and 6, in the final, played over the Cascades Course of the Virginia Hot Springs Golf and Tennis Club. Tom McKnight of Galax, Virginia, earned the qualifying medal at five-under-par 137, one stroke better than Meeks. McKnight was eliminated in the first round by David Lind of Chicago, runner-up in the 1987 U.S. Mid-Amateur, 2 and 1. Meeks did not have an easy path to the final. He was extended to the 18th hole or beyond in four matches. He defeated Randy Haag of Danville, California, 1 up, in the first round. After a 4-and-3 victory over Fred Benton of Jacksonville Beach, Florida, in his second match, Meeks eliminated two-time U.S. Amateur champion Jay Sigel on the 21st hole. Meeks then edged University of Arizona teammate Robert Gamez of Las Vegas, Nevada, and David Toms of Bossier City, Louisiana, 1 up, to gain his place in the final. Yates had a much easier time in his half of the draw. None of his matches reached the 18th hole until the semifinal round, where Doug Martin of Van Buren, Ohio, the 1984 U.S. Junior Amateur champion, stretched Yates to the 18th before Yates eliminated him, 1 up. Meeks gained an early advantage in the 36-hole final, winning the first four holes with two birdies and two pars, but Yates won the sixth, seventh and eighth and was just one down through nine. Meeks then won the 12th through the 15th holes and was 5 up through 17. He lost the 18th when he three-putted, but still held a four-hole lead after the morning round. The afternoon round began in the same fashion as the morning round. Meeks won the first six holes and was 10 up with 12 to play. Yates again fought back, winning the eighth with a birdie and the 10th and 11th with pars. The 12th was halved with pars to end the match. The USGA accepted a record 4,320 entries for the championship.

1989—Chris Patton, a 21-year old senior at Clemson University, defeated Danny Green, 3 and 1, at the Merion Golf Club, in Ardmore,

Pennsylvania. Playing in his first Amateur, Patton went ahead by three holes at the end of the first 18, and held his lead through the afternoon round. At the time the match ended, Patton stood at even par. Patton had played well all week. He reached match play with a two-round score of 142, five strokes off Eoghan O'Connell's medalist total of 137. He won his first two matches by scores of 2 and 1, and 5 and 4. He cleared his biggest hurdle in the quarterfinal round, against Michael Podolak, of Oxbow, North Dakota. Paton and Podolak were all square after 18 holes and then halved the first extra hole with double bogeys. Patton, however, won the 20th with a par. He went on to defeat Mike Brannan, in the semifinals, 2 and 1. Walker Cup players were, for the most part, eliminated early in match play. O'Connell, who had played for Great Britain and Ireland a week earlier, was eliminated in the second round by Brannan. Phil Mickelson, from the United States Walker Cup team, who qualified at 138, was defeated in the first round of match play by Ted Himka, of Reston, Washington. Jay Sigel, playing in his home area, was the last survivor among the Walker Cup players. Twice the Amateur champion, Sigel, 45, lost an extra hole match to Green in the quarterfinals.

1990—Phil Mickelson, 20, of San Diego, California, won both the qualifying medal and the championship, defeating Manny Zerman by 5 and 4, at Cherry Hills Country Club, in Denver. A left-hander, Mickelson, a junior at Arizona State University, led the morning round by three holes. Zerman, also 20, and a former high school teammate of Mickelson's, closed to within one hole in the afternoon, but Mickelson regained a comfortable advantage by winning holes 10 and 11. Mickelson birdied five of the last 12 holes, and played the 32 holes of the match in five under par. He had defeated David Eger, 38, in his semifinal match, 4 and 3, but he had been extended to the 18th hole or beyond in three of his earlier matches. In his second and tightest match, he defeated Jeff Thomas, New Jersey state amateur champion, on the 20th hole. After opening the qualifying with 71, Mickelson shot a record score of 64 on the second day, and a 36-hole total of 135.

AMATEUR CHAMPIONSHIP

DATE	WINNER, RUNNER-UP	SCORE	SITE	ENTRY
1981 (Sept.)	Nathaniel Crosby d. Brian Lindley	1 up, 37 holes	The Olympic Club, (Lake Course) San Francisco, Calif. Medalist—145: Joe Rassett	3,525
1982 (Sept.)	Jay Sigel d. David Tolley	8 & 7	The Country Club, Brookline, Mass. Co-Medalists—141: Bob Lewis, Jr. Robert Stanger, Jr.	3,685
1983 (Aug.-Sept.)	Jay Sigel d. Chris Perry	8 & 7	North Shore C.C., Glenview, Ill. Medalist—139: Clark Burroughs	3,553
1984 (Aug.-Sept.)	Scott Verplank d. Sam Randolph	4 & 3	Oak Tree G.C., Edmond, Okla. Medalist—137: Scott Verplank	3,679
1985 (Aug.-Sept.)	Sam Randolph d. Peter Persons	1 up	Montclair G.C., West Orange, N.J. Medalist—†134: Sam Randolph	3,816
1986 (Aug.)	Stewart Alexander d. Chris Kite	5 & 3	Shoal Creek, Shoal Creek, Ala. Medalist—137: Len Mattiace	4,069
1987 (Aug.)	Bill Mayfair d. Eric Rebmann	4 & 3	Jupiter Hills Club, Jupiter, Fla. Medalist—141: Scott Gump	4,084
1988 (Aug.)	Eric Meeks d. Danny Yates	7 & 6	Va. Hot Springs G. & T.C, Hot Springs, Va. Medalist—137: Tom McKnight	4,320
1989 (Aug.)	Chris Patton d. Danny Green	3 & 1	Merion G.C., Ardmore, Pa. Medalist—137: Eoghan O'Connell	4,603
1990 (Aug.)	Phil Mickelson d. Manny Zerman	5 & 4	Cherry Hills C.C., Denver, Colo. Medalist—135: Phil Mickelson	§4,765

†Record Qualifying Score
§Record Entry

1981
EIGHTY-FIRST AMATEUR CHAMPIONSHIP

The Olympic Club (Lake Course), San Francisco, California, September 1-6
Yardage—6,679. Par 70. 3,525 Entries, 282 Starters at this site, 64 Qualifiers.

Qualifying Score	1st Round (18 Holes)	2nd Round (18 Holes)	3rd Round (18 Holes)	4th Round (18 Holes)	Semi-Finals (18 Holes)	Final (36 Holes)	
*145	Joe Rassett, Turlock, Calif.	Rassett,					
153	Danny Mijovic, Willowdale, Ontario, Canada	3 and 2	Bergin,				
151	William Hadden, III, Hamden, Conn.	Bergin,	2 and 1				
155	William Bergin, Marietta, Ga.	5 and 4					
150	Bob Lewis, Jr., Warren, Ohio	Lewis,		Lewis,			
154	Kevin DeNike, Bettendorf, Iowa	2 and 1	Lewis,	1 up			
152	William Hyndman, III, Huntington Valley, Pa.	Aune,	5 and 4				
155	Gregory Aune, Dallas, Texas	4 and 3					
148	Robert Wrenn, Midlothian, Va.	Morse,			Lewis,		
154	John Morse, Ypsilanti, Mich.	1 up	Morse,		1 up		
152	Peter Deeble, Northumberland, England	Deeble,	5 and 4				
155	Keith Westover, Burnaby, B.C., Canada	3 and 1		Morse,			
151	Jacky Lee, Jr., Houston, Texas	Banke,		5 and 4			
155	Dana Banke, Castro Valley, Calif.	2 up	Faxon,				
153	Bradford Faxon, Jr., Barrington, R.I.	Faxon,	6 and 5				
156	Stephen Schroeder, Menlo Park, Calif.	5 and 4				Lindley,	
148	Greg Twiggs, LaJolla, Calif.	Tentis,				3 and 2	
154	David Tentis, White Bear Lake, Minn.	6 and 5	Tentis,				
152	Tom Pernice, Jr., Raytown, Mo.	Pernice,	2 and 1				
155	Ray Leach, San Ramon, Calif.	2 and 1					
150	John Hamarik, Youngstown, Ohio	Rafferty,		Tentis,			
155	Ronan Rafferty, Warrenpoint, N. Ireland	3 and 2		1 up, 20 holes			
152	Bill Holstead, Wichita Falls, Texas	Hutcheon,	Rafferty,				
156	Ian Hutcheon, Dundee, Scotland	1 up	2 and 1		Lindley,		
149	Michael Barnblatt, San Mateo, Calif.	McGee,			2 and 1		
154	Mike McGee, Middletown, Ohio	1 up	Lindley,				Nathaniel Crosby, 1 up, 37 holes
152	Brian Lindley, Fountain Valley, Calif.	Lindley,	2 and 1				
155	Ron Commans, Westlake Village, Calif.	1 up					
151	Jim Holtgrieve, Des Peres, Mo.	Gaddy,		Lindley,			
155	Brian Gaddy, Pasadena, Calif.	1 up, 19 holes		3 and 2			
153	Mark Maness, Lincoln, Neb.	Miyazaki,	Gaddy,				
156	Clark Miyazaki, Wahiawa, Hawaii	1 up	4 and 3				
147	Corey Pavin, Oxnard, Calif.	DeLuca					
154	Tony DeLuca, Vienna, Va.	3 and 1	Michael,				
151	Robert Michael, Sarasota, Fla.	Michael,	1 up, 20 holes				
155	John Childs, Kennesaw, Ga.	3 and 1		Michael,			
150	William Boles, Wilson, N.C.	Krueger,		4 and 2			
155	Gary Krueger, Valparaiso, Ind.	4 and 3	Krueger,				
152	Joey Sadowski, Hickory, N.C.	Sadowski,	3 and 2				
155	Robert Lohr, Loveland, Ohio	4 and 3			Crosby,		
148	Chris Tucker, Midland, N.C.	Wolcott,			5 and 4		
154	Bob Wolcott, Jr., Dickson, Tenn.	2 and 1	Crosby,				
152	Nathaniel Crosby, Hillsborough, Calif.	Crosby,	2 and 1				
155	Frank Fuhrer, III, Pittsburgh, Pa.	2 and 1		Crosby,			
151	Hal Sutton, Shreveport, La.	Mudd,		2 and 1		Crosby,	
155	Jodie Mudd, Louisville, Ky.	2 up				2 up	
153	Steve Hart, Tequesta, Fla.	Hart,	Hart,				
156	John Gagai, Ironton, Ohio	4 and 2	4 and 3				
148	Colin Dalgleish, Helensburgh, Scotland	Dalgleish,					
154	Gregory Brown, Columbus, Ohio	1 up, 19 holes	Carter,				
152	John Sherman, Shawnee Mission, Kans.	Carter,	3 and 1				
155	Jim Carter, Mesa, Ariz.	7 and 6		Carter,			
151	Jay Siegel, Berwyn, Pa.	Sigel,		1 up			
155	James Chew, Tulsa, Okla.	6 and 5	Grace,				
153	Marshall Marraccini, McKeesport, Pa.	Grace,	4 and 2				
156	John Grace, Ft. Worth, Texas	3 and 2			Wood,		
149	Jay Delsing, St. Louis, Mo.	Delsing,			3 and 2		
154	Terry Kahl, Aurora, Colo.	2 and 1	Lee,				
152	David Lee, Littleton, Colo.	Lee,	1 up, 20 holes				
155	Jack Veghte, Clearwater, Fla.	3 and 2		Wood,			
151	Geoffrey Godwin, Essex, England	Sucher,		1 up			
155	Richard Sucher, Mequon, Wis.	2 up	Wood,				
153	Wright Waddell, Columbus, Ga.	Wood,	4 and 2				
156	Willie Wood, Oklahoma City, Okla.	1 up					

*Medalist

1982
EIGHTY-SECOND AMATEUR CHAMPIONSHIP

The Country Club, Brookline, Massachusetts, August 31 - September 5.
Yardage — 6,896. Par 72. 3,685 Entries, 282 Starters at this site, 64 Qualifiers.

Qualifying Score	1st Round (18 Holes)	2nd Round (18 Holes)	3rd Round (18 Holes)	4th Round (18 Holes)	Semifinals (18 Holes)	Final (36 Holes)
*141	Bob Lewis, Jr., Warren, Ohio	Sigel,				
149	Jay Sigel, Berwyn, Pa.	3 and 2	Sigel,			
146	Taylor Metcalfe, Wyoming, Ohio	Metcalfe,	1 up, 21 holes			
150	Larry Seligmann, Houston, Texas	1 up, 19 holes				
144	Billy Andrade, Bristol, R.I.	Reifers,		Sigel,		
150	Randy Reifers, Dublin, Ohio	4 and 3	Taylor,	3 and 1		
147	Julian Taylor, Youngstown, Ohio	Taylor,	5 and 3			
151	John Slaughter, Abilene, Texas	2 up				
144	Chris Perry, Edina, Minn.	Perry,			Sigel,	
149	John Baldwin, New York, N.Y.	3 and 1	Tentis,		4 and 3	
147	David Tentis, White Bear Lake, Minn.	Tentis,	1 up			
151	Thomas Ross, Royal Oak, Mich.	5 and 4				
145	Craig Steinberg, Studio City, Calif.	Steinberg,		Tentis,		
150	Randy Watkins, Jackson, Miss.	1 up	Heninger,	4 and 3		
147	Brad Heninger, San Jose, Calif.	Heninger,	6 and 4			
151	Daniel Wilkins, Laconia, N.H.	4 and 3				
143	Richard Fehr, Seattle, Wash.	Fehr,				Sigel,
149	Andrew Magee, Dallas, Texas	1 up	Fehr,			1 up
146	Kevin Klier, Rockland, Mass.	Klier,	7 and 6			
151	Ross Johnson, Rome, Ga.	3 and 1		Fehr,		
145	Bob Wolcott, Jr., Dickson, Tenn.	Briggs,		4 and 3		
150	Danny Briggs, Paris, Texas	5 and 4	Slater,			
147	Greg Starkman, Beverly Hills, Calif.	Slater,	3 and 2			
151	Kevin Slater, San Diego, Calif.	2 up			Fehr,	
144	Brad Faxon, Somerset, Mass.	Biancalana,			5 and 4	
150	Roy Biancalana, Franklin Park, Ill.	1 up	Biancalana,			
147	Jeff Johnson, Ventura, Calif.	Johnson,	1 up, 20 holes			
151	Mark Plummer, Augusta, Maine	4 and 3		Humenik,		
146	Edward Humenik, Allen Park, Mich.	Humenik,		2 up		
150	David Jackson, Monticello, Fla.	5 and 4	Humenik,			
148	Ron Delaney, Portland, Ore.	Ruschioni,	5 and 3			
151	James Ruschioni, Leominster, Mass.	6 and 4				
*141	Robert Stanger, Jr., Durham, N.C.	Stanger,				
149	Stan Bickel, Bellevue, Ky.	2 up	Stanger,			
146	Willie Wood, Stillwater, Okla.	Lipski,	1 up			
150	Gary Lipski, Cockeysville, Md.	1 up		Hallet,		
145	Donald Bliss, Chesterfield, Mo.	Reiser,		2 and 1		
150	Troy Reiser, Ft. Worth, Texas	2 and 1	Hallet,			
147	James Hallet, S. Yarmouth, Mass.	Hallet,	1 up, 20 holes		Hallet,	
151	Jimmy Squires, Conroe, Texas	2 and 1			1 up, 20 holes	
144	Eric Johnson, Eugene, Ore.	Johnson,				
150	Bill Halstead, Wichita Falls, Texas	2 and 1	Krapfel,			
147	Timothy Krapfel, Columbia, S.C.	Krapfel,	2 up			
151	David Lee, Littleton, Colo.	2 and 1		Krapfel,		
146	Martin West, Rockville, Md.	Frandsen,		1 up		
150	Kent Frandsen, Lebanon, Ind.	3 and 2	Frandsen,			Tolley,
148	James Gallagher, Marion, Ind.	Gallagher,	1 up, 20 holes			1 up
151	James Delsing, St. Louis, Mo.	3 and 1				
143	Tom Pernice, Jr., Kansas City, Mo.	Pernice,				
149	Nathaniel Crosby, Hillsborough, Calif.	1 up, 19 holes	Holtgrieve,			
146	Jim Holtgrieve, St. Louis, Mo.	Holtgrieve,	5 and 4			
151	James Kilduff, Summit, N.J.	2 up		Holtgrieve,		
145	Brian Mogg, Tacoma, Wash.	Delong,		2 up		
150	Dave Delong, Portland, Ore.	1 up	Delong,			
147	Frank Fuhrer, Pittsburgh, Pa.	Fuhrer,	3 and 2			
151	Chip Hall, Jacksonville Beach, Fla.	7 and 5			Tolley,	
144	Kevin Dillen, Paris, Texas	Dillen,			1 up, 21 holes	
150	Charles Harrison, Marietta, Ga.	4 and 3	Pavin,			
147	Corey Pavin, Oxnard, Calif.	Pavin,	5 and 4			
151	Joe Tamburino, San Jose, Calif.	5 and 4		Tolley,		
146	John Ervasti, London, Ont., Canada	Ervasti,		3 and 2		
150	David Boeff, Rochester, N.Y.	1 up	Tolley,			
148	David Tolley, Roanoke, Va.	Tolley,	4 and 2			
152	Mark Brooks, Ft. Worth, Texas	6 and 5				

Jay Sigel, 8 and 7

*Co-Medalists

1983
EIGHTY-THIRD AMATEUR CHAMPIONSHIP

North Shore Country Club, Glenview, Illinois, August 30-September 4
Yardage—6,988. Par 72. 3,553 Entries, 282 Starters at this site, 64 Qualifiers

Qualifying Score	1st Round (18 Holes)	2nd Round (18 Holes)	3rd Round (18 Holes)	4th Round (18 Holes)	Semifinals (18 Holes)	Final (36 Holes)	
*139	Clark Burroughs, Overland Park, Kans.	Burroughs, 3 and 2					
148	Brian Mogg, Tacoma, Wash.		Burroughs, 2 and 1				
146	William Smunk, Charleston, S.C.	Smunk, 1 up, 20 holes					
149	Chris Young, Arlington, Texas			Burroughs, 1 up			
144	Jerry Haas, Belleville, Ill.	Haas, 1 up, 19 holes					
148	Fred Wadsworth, Columbus, Ga.		Haas, 1 up, 22 holes				
147	Joe Tamburino, San Jose, Calif.	Tamburino, 1 up					
149	Jim Holtgrieve, St. Louis, Mo.						
143	Bob Lewis, Jr., Warren, Ohio	Lewis, 1 up			Burroughs, 1 up		
148	John Given, Carmi, Ill.		Horne, 1 up				
147	Dick Horne, Mt. Pleasant, S.C.	Horne, 1 up					
149	Pat Stephens, Richmond, Ky.						
145	Andrew Magee, Norman, Okla.	Utley, 2 and 1		Utley, 4 and 3			
149	Stan Utley, West Plaines, Mo.		Utley, 5 and 4				
148	John Schoonover, Boise, Id.	Mondry, 1 up, 19 holes					
150	Josh Mondry, Franklin, Mich.					Sigel, 3 and 2	
143	Billy Tuten, Palatka, Fla.	Tuten, 5 and 4					
148	William Ludwig, Independence, Mo		Tuten, 7 and 5				
147	Andy Dillard, Tyler, Texas	Murdock, 1 up, 19 holes					
149	Mike Murdock, Memphis, Tenn.						
145	John Baldwin, New York, N.Y.	Timyan, 2 and 1		Biancalana, 6 and 4			
149	Mark Timyan, Grand Blanc, Mich.		Biancalana, 4 and 2				
147	Roy Biancalana, Franklin Park, Ill.	Biancalana, 4 and 3					
150	Rock Gentile, Matawan, N.J.						
143	Marty West, Rockville, Md.	West, 3 and 2			Sigel, 1 up, 19 holes		
148	John Perles, Palos Verdes, Calif.		Peterson, 2 up				
147	Eric Peterson, Fresno, Calif.	Peterson, 2 and 1					
149	Bob Wolcott, Dickson, Tenn.			Sigel, 5 and 3			
145	George MacDonald, Virginia Beach, Va.	MacDonald, 2 up					
149	Mark Plummer, Augusta, Me.		Sigel, 1 up, 19 holes				
148	Jay Sigel, Berwyn, Pa.	Sigel 3 and 2					
150	Bruce Soulsby, Columbus, Ohio						Jay Sigel, 8 and 7
142	Fred Dupre, Natchez, Miss.	Dupre, 4 and 3					
148	Dan Ybema, Comstock Park, Mich.		Dupre, 1 up, 20 holes				
146	Brian Tennyson, Evansville, Ind.	Moyers, 5 and 4					
149	Robert Moyers, New Market, Va.			Pierce, 1 up			
144	Clifton Pierce, Lawton, Okla.	Pierce, 4 and 3					
148	Steve Russell, Amarillo, Texas		Pierce, 6 and 5				
147	Gregg Von Thaden, Menlo Park, Calif.	Parker, 4 and 3					
149	Richard Parker, Lebanon, N.H.						
143	Jim Hallet, South Yarmouth, Mass.	Hallet, 3 and 2					
148	Jeff Maggert, Woodlands, Texas		Hallet, 3 and 2		Pierce, 5 and 4		
147	Randy Sonnier, Woodlands, Texas	Sonnier, 3 and 2					
149	Robert Friend, Pittsburgh, Pa.			Inman, 4 and 3			
145	John Inman, Greensboro, N.C.	Inman, 6 and 4					
149	Danny Yates, Atlanta, Ga.		Inman, 6 and 5				
148	Charles Raulerson, Jacksonville, Fla.	Raulerson, 2 and 1					
150	Randy Nichols, Connersville, Ind.						
143	Wayne Case, Thousand Oaks, Calif.	Slaughter, 2 and 1				Perry, 1 up, 19 holes	
148	John Slaughter, Abilene, Texas		Slaughter, 3 and 1				
147	Mark Fuller, Yukon, Okla.	Fuller, 4 and 3					
149	Chris Anderson, Wilmington, Del.			Perry, 3 and 1			
145	Eric Johnson, Eugene, Ore.	Straub, 1 up					
149	Tim Straub, Orchard Park, N.Y.		Perry, 1 up, 19 holes				
148	Ted Schulz, Louisville, Ky.	Perry, 2 up					
150	Chris Perry, Edina, Minn.						
144	Doug Doxsie, Seattle, Wash.	Erickson, 5 and 4			Perry, 1 up, 19 holes		
148	John Erickson, Palos Verdes Estates, Calif.		Erickson, 2 and 1				
147	Stacy Richburg, Starkville, Miss.	Crosby, 2 and 1					
149	Nathaniel Crosby, Miami, Fla.			Erickson, 3 and 2			
145	Billy Andrade, Bristol, R.I.	Andrade, 3 and 1					
149	Roger Thorn, Wenatchee, Wash.		Andrade, 5 and 3				
148	Robert Anderson, Downey, Calif.	Welch, 1 up, 19 holes					
150	George Welch, Kilgore, Texas						

*Medalist

1984
EIGHTY-FOURTH AMATEUR CHAMPIONSHIP

Oak Tree Golf Club, Edmond, Oklahoma, August 28-September 2
Yardage—6,951. Par 71. 3,679 Entries, 282 Starters at this site, 64 Qualifiers

Qualifying Score	1st Round (18 Holes)	2nd Round (18 Holes)	3rd Round (18 Holes)	4th Round (18 Holes)	Semifinals (18 Holes)	Final (36 Holes)	
*137	Scott Verplank, Dallas, Texas	Verplank, 3 and 2					
148	Dillard Pruitt, Greenville, S.C.		Verplank, 3 and 1				
145	Scott Inman, Springfield, Va.	Estes, 2 up					
149	Bob Estes, Abilene, Texas			Verplank, 5 and 4			
144	Greg Turner, Norman, Okla.	Turner, 3 and 1					
149	Mike Swartz, Phoenix, Ariz.		Turner, 2 and 1				
147	Douglas Farr, Monroe, La.	Pierce, 3 and 2					
150	Cliff Pierce, Lawton, Okla.				Verplank, 1 up		
142	Jay Sigel, Berwyn, Pa.	Mediate, 3 and 1					
148	Rocco Mediate, Greensburg, Pa.		Persons, 1 up				
146	Peter Persons, Macon, Ga.	Persons, 4 and 2					
150	Charles Kline, Warren, Ohio			Persons, 3 and 2			
145	Nolan Henke, Fort Myers, Fla.	Walker, 4 and 2					
149	Daryl Walker, Conroe, Texas		Burroughs, 2 up				
147	Clark Burroughs, Overland Park, Kans.	Burroughs, 4 and 3					
150	Jeff Butler, Coral Springs, Fla.					Verplank, 1 up	
141	Jerry Foltz, Tucson, Ariz.	Sonnier 2 and 1					
148	Randy Sonnier, Woodlands, Texas		Sonnier, 1 up				
146	John Schoonover, Boise, Idaho	Schoonover, 2 and 1					
150	Gordon Brewer, Huntingdon Valley, Pa.			Sonnier, 3 and 2			
144	Mark Thaxton, Winston-Salem, N.C.	Webb, 3 and 1					
149	Gary Webb, Dallas, Texas		Webb, 4 and 2				
147	Jeff Brehaut, Los Altos Hills, Calif.	Linck, 2 and 1					
150	Cary Linck, McKinney, Texas				Sonnier, 3 and 2		
144	Darryl Donovan, Oklahoma City, Okla.	Hoffer, 7 and 6					
148	Bill Hoffer, Elgin, Ill.		Maggert, 1 up, 20 holes				
146	James Benepa, Sheridan, Wyo.	Maggert, 3 and 2					
150	Jeff Maggert, Woodlands, Texas			Love, 3 and 3			
145	Davis Love, St. Simons Island, Ga.	Love, 4 and 3					
149	John Delong, Portland, Ore.		Love, 2 and 1				Scott Verplank, 4 and 3
148	Jim Holtgrieve, St. Louis, Mo.	Holtgrieve, 4 and 3					
150	Mark Phillips, Studio City, Calif.						
140	Scott Dunlap, Sarasota, Fla.	Dunlap 6 and 4					
148	Randy Nichols, Connersville, Ind.		Dunlap 4 and 3				
145	Steven Serotte, Amherst, N.Y.	Serotte, 1 up					
149	Charles Smith, Delaware, Ohio			Haas, 4 and 3			
144	Jerry Haas, Belleville, Ill.	Haas 4 and 2					
149	Rick Schuller, Fairfax, Va.		Haas, 2 up				
147	Johnny Stevens, Wichita, Kans.	Stevens, 5 and 4					
150	Howie Johnson, Palm Springs, Calif.				Haas, 2 up		
143	Ed Kirby, Cumberland, R.I.	Kirby, 1 up					
148	Ted Hensarling, Lafayette, La.		Lewis, 2 up				
146	Jim Guerra, Glen Ridge, N.J.	Lewis, 3 and 2					
150	Bob Lewis, Warren, Ohio			Lewis, 2 up			
145	Griffin Rudolph, Clarksville, Tenn.	Carter, 3 and 2					
149	Jim Carter, Mesa, Ariz.		Hamilton, 3 and 2				
147	Todd Hamilton, Oquawka, Ill.	Hamilton, 4 and 3					
150	Brian Watts, Carrollton, Texas					Randolph, 7 and 5	
142	Sam Randolph, Santa Barbara, Calif.	Randolph, 2 up					
148	Tom McKnight, Galax, Va.		Randolph, 4 and 2				
146	Mark Timyan, Grand Blanc, Mich.	Timyan, 5 and 4					
150	Andie Parks, Forest City, N.C.			Randolph, 4 and 3			
145	Danny Mijovic, Willowdale, Ontario, Canada	Mijovic, 2 and 1					
149	Bob Young, Atlanta, Ga.		Kase, 1 up				
147	John Inman, Greensboro, N.C.	Kase, 2 and 1			Randolph, 4 and 3		
150	Adam Kase, Socorro, N.M.						
144	Ron Gekalka, Lynwood, Ill.	Utley, 2 up					
149	Stan Utley, West Plains, Mo.		Utley 2 and 1				
147	Bard Larsen, Houston, Texas	Larsen, 1 up					
150	Greg Sweatt, Rock Hill, S.C.			Cuff, 1 up, 19 holes			
145	Richard Miller, Columbus, Ohio	Miller, 2 and 1					
149	Jarrett Sharp, LaFollette, Tenn.		Cuff, 3 and 1				
148	Roger Gunn, Napa, Calif.	Cuff, 3 and 2					
150	Edward Cuff, La Mesa, Calif.						

*Medalist

1985
EIGHTY-FIFTH AMATEUR CHAMPIONSHIP

Montclair Golf Club, West Orange, New Jersey, August 27-September 1
Yardage—6,362. Par 70. 3,816 Entries, 282 Starters, 64 Qualifiers

Qualifying Score	1st Round (18 Holes)	2nd Round (18 Holes)	3rd Round (18 Holes)	4th Round (18 Holes)	Semifinals (18 Holes)	Final (36 Holes)
*134	Sam Randolph, Santa Barbara, Calif.	Randolph,				
147	Mike Schuchart, Lincoln, Neb.	1 up	Randolph,			
145	Thomas Lape, Lebanon, Pa.	Trauner,	2 and 1			
145	Mark Trauner, Armonk, N.Y.	1 up, 19 holes		Randolph,		
143	Steven Serotte, Amherst, N.Y.	Serotte,		5 and 4		
146	David Brookreson, Huntingdon Valley, Pa.	6 and 4	Serotte,			
143	Woody Austin, Tampa, Fla.	Perry,	1 up			
146	Mitchell Perry, Spring Lake, N.C.	2 and 1			Randolph,	
142	Brandt Jobe, Littleton, Colo.	Bendall,			2 and 1	
147	Richard Bendall, Lynchburg, Va.	4 and 3	Blewett,			
144	Michael Blewett, Burlingame, Calif.	Blewett,	1 up			
145	Robert Hughes, Watertown, N.Y.	2 and 1		Sigel,		
142	Jay Sigel, Berwyn, Pa.	Sigel,		4 and 2		
146	Kirk Triplett, Reno, Nev.	2 and 1	Sigel,			
144	Karl Zoller, Chesterland, Ohio	Zoller,	1 up			
146	Jerry Haas, Belleville, Ill.	1 up, 19 holes				Randolph,
141	Patrick Fogarty, Oyster Bay, N.Y.	Fogarty,				4 and 3
147	Carter Fasick, Milford, Mass.	2 and 1	Kay,			
144	Howard Logan, Jr., Shelbyville, Ken.	Kay,	4 and 3			
145	Jack Kay, Jr., Ontario, Canada	1 up, 19 holes		Kay,		
142	Len Mattiace, Ponte Vedra, Fla.	Hartlage,		1 up		
146	Leonard Hartlage, Floyds Knobs, Ind.	3 and 2	Bradley,			
143	James Guerra, Glen Ridge, N.J.	Bradley,	6 and 5			
146	Michael Bradley, Valrico, Fla.	4 and 2			Kay,	
141	Allen Doyle, LaGrange, Ga.	Doyle,			1 up	
147	Wesley Mohr, Jr., Houston, Texas	1 up	Lewis,			
144	Robert Lewis, Jr., Warren, Ohio	Lewis,	5 and 4			
145	Pat Herzog, Alexandria, Minn.	2 and 1		Verplank,		
142	Scott Verplank, Dallas, Texas	Verplank,		1 up, 19 holes		
146	Randy Sonnier, Woodlands, Texas	1 up, 20 holes	Verplank,			
143	James Benepe, III, Evanston, Ill.	Benepe,	3 and 1			
146	Dean Paulson, Costa Mesa, Calif.	6 and 4				Sam Randolph, 1 up
137	Duffy Waldorf, Tarzana, Calif.	Waldorf,				
147	Roger Brown, Arkansas City, Kans.	5 and 4	Waldorf,			
145	Lamar Haynes, Dallas, Texas	Haynes,	1 up, 19 holes			
145	Jim Carter, Mesa, Ariz.	1 up		Hamilton,		
143	Todd Hamilton, Oquakwa, Ill.	Hamilton,		8 and 7		
146	Mike Ketcham, Ottumwa, Iowa	2 and 1	Hamilton,			
143	Billy Andrade, Bristol, R.I.	Andrade,	1 up, 20 holes			
146	James Brown, Paducah, Ky.	3 and 2			Drury,	
141	James Estes, Rockville, Md.	Marucci,			1 up	
147	George Marucci, Villanova, Pa.	1 up	Johnson,			
144	Clark Burroughs, Overland Park, Kan.	Johnson,	2 up			
145	Kevin Johnson, Pembroke, Mass.	1 up		Drury,		
142	Peter Baker, Staffordshire, England	Drury,		5 and 3		
146	Chip Drury, Brunswick, Ga.	3 and 2	Drury,			
143	James Sorenson, Bloomington, Minn.	Sorenson,	3 and 2			
146	Louis Brown, Newman, Ga.	5 and 4				Persons,
140	Kevin Whipple, Duncan, Okla.	Farlow,				3 and 1
147	Sam Farlow, Birmingham, Ala.	1 up, 19 holes	Farlow,			
144	John Schoonover, Boise, Idaho	Maggert,	1 up, 19 holes			
145	Jeff Maggert, Woodlands, Texas	1 up		Farlow,		
142	Jim Holtgrieve, St. Louis, Mo.	Podolak,		5 and 3		
146	Mike Podolak, Fargo, N.D.	5 and 3	Podolak,			
143	Tim Robinson, Rancho Murieta, Calif.	Wilson,	4 and 3			
146	Jeffrey Wilson, Vallejo, Calif.	2 and 1			Persons,	
141	Paul Simson, Raleigh, N.C.	Simson,			1 up	
147	Donald Bliss, Chesterfield, Mo.	1 up	Simson,			
144	Sandy Stephen, Edinburgh, Scotland	Stephen,	4 and 3			
145	John Grace, Fort Worth, Texas	1 up, 21 holes		Persons,		
142	David Jackson, Monticello, Fla.	Jackson,		4 and 3		
146	Bret Burroughs, St. Louis, Mo.	2 up	Persons,			
143	Frank Ford, Charleston, S.C.	Persons,	2 up			
146	Peter Persons, Macon, Ga.	2 and 1				

*Medalist

1986
EIGHTY-SIXTH AMATEUR CHAMPIONSHIP

Shoal Creek, Shoal Creek, Alabama, August 26-31
Yardage—6,981. Par 72. +4,071 Entries, 282 Starters, 64 Qualifiers

Qualifying Score	1st Round (18 Holes)	2nd Round (18 Holes)	3rd Round (18 Holes)	4th Round (18 Holes)	Semifinals (18 Holes)	Final (36 Holes)
*137	Len Mattiace, Ponte Vedra Beach, Fla.	Mattiace,				
149	Yasunobu Kuramoto, Stillwater, Okla.	2 up	Kite,			
147	Chris Kite, Hiddenite, N.C.	Kite,	1 up			
147	Eric Woods, Corona del Mar, Calif.	2 and 1		Kite,		
145	Jim Hagstrom, Grove City, Pa.	Hagstrom,		3 and 1		
148	Richard Holland, Bethesda, Md.	1 up, 21 holes	Hagstrom,			
145	Jay Sigel, Berwyn, Pa.	Voges,	4 and 3			
148	Mitch Voges, Simi Valley, Calif.	1 up, 20 holes			Kite,	
142	Bill Andrade, Bristol, R.I.	Andrade,			2 and 1	
149	Rob Huff, Boise, Idaho	3 and 1	Davis,			
146	Kevin King, Hilton Head Island, S.C.	Davis,	1 up, 20 holes			
147	Greg Davis, Portland, Ore.	3 and 2		Gustin,		
142	Chris Gustin, Birmingham, Ala.	Gustin,		3 and 2		
149	Robert Huxtable, Cathedral City, Calif.	5 and 3	Gustin,			
146	Bill Pelham, Houston, Texas	Franks,	3 and 2			
148	Todd Franks, Fort Worth, Texas	2 and 1				Kite
140	Bryan Sullivan, Kitty Hawk, N.C.	Sullivan,				3 and 1
149	Schley Purvis, Pearl, Miss.	1 up	Sullivan,			
146	Michael Lopuszynski, Rye, N.Y.	Harrington,	1 up, 19 holes			
147	Dennis Harrington, Columbus, Ohio	4 and 3		Montgomery,		
145	Brian Montgomery, Bristow, Okla.	Montgomery,		2 up		
149	Dave Esler, Wauconda, Ill.	5 and 4	Montgomery,			
146	Sam Farlow, Birmingham, Ala.	Kase	1 up			
148	Adam Kase, Socorro, N.M.	3 and 2			Montgomery,	
140	Ron McCann, Orlando, Fla.	McCann,			1 up	
149	Shawn Baker, Brattleboro, Vt.	3 and 2	McCann			
146	Jim Begwin, Ponca City, Okla.	Begwin,	1 up, 20 holes			
147	Jim Holtgrieve, St. Louis, Mo.	1 up		Smith,		
144	Robert McDonnell, Ormond Beach, Fla.	Smith,		4 and 2		
149	Mike Smith, Conway, Ark.	2 and 1	Smith,			
146	Bill Loeffler, Littleton, Colo.	Loeffler,	1 up			
148	John Parson, Avon, Conn.	3 and 2				
138	Tim Straub, Orchard Park, N.Y.	Straub,				
149	Jeff Teal, Minneapolis, Minn.	2 and 1	Sorenson,			
147	Brian Connor, Enola, Pa.	Sorenson,	1 up,			
147	Jim Sorenson, Bloomington, Minn.	5 and 4		Henke,		
145	Gregory Jones, Mobile, Ala.	Jones,		3 and 1		
148	Downing Gray, Pensacola, Fla.	3 and 2	Henke,			
146	Nolan Henke, Fort Myers, Fla.	Henke,	3 and 2			
148	Kevin Hester, Worcester, Mass.	4 and 3			Ro. Lewis,	
141	David Jackson, Monticello, Fla.	Jackson,			4 and 3	
149	Paul Spadafora, Durham, N.C.	2 and 1	Pfister,			
146	Edward Pfister, Marilla, N.Y.	Pfister,	1 up, 19 holes			
147	Steve Flesch, Edgewood, Ky.	5 and 4		Ro. Lewis,		
143	Steve Maddalena, Jackson, Miss.	Baker,		2 and 1		
149	Jonathan Baker, Orem, Utah	2 and 1	Ro. Lewis,			
146	Robert Lewis, Warren, Ohio	Ro. Lewis,	2 and 1			
148	Jack Kay, Toronto, Ontario, Canada	2 and 1				Alexander,
139	Brian Watts, Carollton, Texas	Watts,				6 and 4
149	Michael Bradley, Valrico, Fla.	3 and 2	Hayes,			
147	Bob Estes, Abilene, Texas	Hayes,	4 and 3			
147	John Hayes, Appleton, Wis.	2 up		Alexander,		
145	Stewart Alexander, Baton Rouge, La.	Alexander,		4 and 2		
149	Michael Podolak, Fargo, N.D.	1 up, 19 holes	Alexander,			
146	Jeff Cranford, Odessa, Texas	Cranford,	8 and 6			
148	Steve Lamontagne, Satellite Beach, Fla.	2 up			Alexander,	
141	Bill Mayfair, Phoenix, Ariz.	Mayfair,			2 and 1	
149	Randal Lewis, Englewood, Colo.	4 and 3	Mayfair,			
146	George Zahringer, New York, N.Y.	McKnight,	5 and 4			
147	Tom McKnight, Galax, Va.	1 up, 19 holes		Hamilton,		
144	Randy Sonnier, Woodlands, Texas	Sonnier,		1 up, 20 holes		
149	Eddie Carmichael, Knoxville, Tenn.	3 and 1	Hamilton,			
146	Allen Doyle, LaGrange, Ga.	Hamilton,	1 up, 19 holes			
148	Todd Hamilton, Oquawka, Ill.	3 and 1				

Stewart Alexander, 5 and 3

+Record Entry
*Medalist

1987
EIGHTY-SEVENTH U.S. AMATEUR CHAMPIONSHIP

Jupiter Hills Club, Jupiter, Fla., August 25-30
Yardage—6,879. Par 72. +4,084 Entries, 288 Starters, 64 Qualifiers

Qualifying Score	1st Round (18 Holes)	2nd Round (18 Holes)	3rd Round (18 Holes)	4th Round (18 Holes)	Semifinals (18 Holes)	Final (36 Holes)
*141	Scott Gump, Rockledge, Fla.	Gump,				
151	Orrin Vincent, III, Incline Village, Nev.	6 and 5	Gump,			
149	Len Mattiace, Ponta Vedra, Fla.	Mattiace,	1 up			
149	David Wettlaufer, Waterloo, Ontario, Canada	6 and 5		Gump,		
147	Mark Leetzow, Sarasota, Fla.	Leetzow,		7 and 6		
150	Michael Podolak, Hickson, N.D.	1 up, 20 holes	O'Neill,			
145	John O'Neill, Glendora, Calif.	O'Neill,	2 and 1			
150	Daniel Belden, Jr., Canton, Ohio	4 and 2			Gump,	
145	Larry Penley, Anderson, S.C	Rudolph,			4 and 3	
151	Harry Rudolph, La Jolla, Calif.	2 up	Rudolph,			
148	Russell Beiresdorf, Dallas, Texas,	Knapp,	4 and 2			
149	Tom Knapp, West Palm Beach, Fla.	5 and 3		Webb,		
146	Eric Epperson, Garland, Texas	Gregor,		1 up, 19 holes		
151	Mike Gregor, Huntingdon Valley, Pa.	4 and 2	Webb,			
148	Chris Webb, Shreveport, La.	Webb,	3 and 2			
149	David Miley, Menomonee Falls, Wis.	7 and 6				Rebmann,
144	Bob Lewis, Jr., Warren, Ohio	Lewis,				5 and 4
151	Art Roberson, Zebulon, N.C.	1 up	Dyer,			
148	Scott Warzecha, Fort Rucker, Ala.	Dyer,	5 and 3			
149	Thomas Dyer, Melrose, Mass.	2 up		Rebmann,		
147	Steve Stricker, Edgerton, Wis.	Rebmann,		2 and 1		
150	Eric Rebmann, Davie, Fla.	1 up	Rebmann,			
147	Jim Sorenson, Bloomington, Minn.	Ellis,	4 and 3			
150	Leslie Ellis, Belden, Miss.	1 up, 19 holes			Rebmann,	
144	Kevin Johnson, Pembroke, Mass.	Johnson,			2 up	
150	Matt Stokes, Columbus, Ohio	6 and 5	Sigel,			
148	Jay Sigel, Berwyn, Pa.	Sigel,	3 and 2			
149	Bradley Benbrook, Grover, Mo.	3 and 2		Sigel,		
147	George Zahringer, III, New York, N.Y.	Zahringer,		2 up		
150	Michael Smith, Beaumont, Texas	2 up	White,			
147	David White, Conroe, Texas	White,	1 up, 19 holes			
150	Andrew Brock, Wallingford, Conn.	3 and 2				
143	Miles McConnell, Valrico, Fla.	McConnell,				
151	John Wright, Gulf Shores, Ala.	6 and 4	McConnell,			
149	Randy Reifers, Dublin, Ohio	Tryba,	1 up,			
149	Ted Tryba, Wilkes-Barre, Pa.	5 and 4		McConnell,		
147	Keith Harris, Baytown, Texas	Harris,		2 and 1		
150	Henry Cagigal, Willow Park, Texas	1 up, 20 holes	Harris,			
147	Jonathan Nichols, Decatur, Ga.	Cole,	6 and 5			
150	Tom Cole, Oakland, Calif.	2 and 1			Mayfair,	
145	Bill Mayfair, Scottsdale, Ariz	Mayfair,			1 up, 20 holes	
151	Scott Mayne, Warwick, Bermuda	4 and 3	Mayfair,			
148	Martin West, III, Chevy Chase, Md.	Young,	1 up, 19 holes			
149	Robert Young, Jr., Atlanta, Ga.	1 up, 19 holes		Mayfair,		
146	Kevin Troyer, Grand Blanc, Mich.	Troyer,		6 and 5		
150	Douglas Dunakey, Waterloo, Iowa	3 and 2	Potter,			
148	Ben Furth, Santa Rosa, Calif.	Potter,	1 up, 19 holes			
149	Matthew Potter, Lakewood, Colo.	3 and 2				Mayfair,
143	Nolan Henke, Fort Myers, Fla.	Henke,				3 and 2
151	Bob Mason, St. Louis, Mo.	6 and 5	DeKock,			
148	David Brookreson, Huntingdon Valley, Pa.	DeKock,	1 up			
149	Nicholas DeKock, Cedar Rapids, Iowa	2 and 1		McNamara,		
147	Glen Day, Norman, Okla.	McNamara,		3 and 1		
150	Robert McNamara, Frankfort, Ky.	4 and 3	McNamara,			
147	David Toms, Benton, La.	Hart,	4 and 3			
150	Dudley Hart, Miami Beach, Fla.	3 and 2			Ford,	
144	Allen Doyle, La Grange, Ga.	Doyle,			2 and 1	
151	Joe Vennari, Ellicott City, Md.	4 and 3	Ford,			
148	Stephen Ford, Melbourne, Fla.	Ford,	1 up			
149	John Parsons, Palm Beach Gardens, Fla.	2 and 1		Ford,		
146	Vance Whicker, Greensboro, N.C.	Whicker,		1 up, 19 holes		
150	Troy Williams, Fresno, Calif.	1 up	Whicker,			
147	Patrick Duncan, Rancho Santa Fe, Calif.	Heffelman,	4 and 3			
149	Bob Heffelman, Akron, Ohio	1 up, 22 holes				

Bill Mayfair, 4 and 3

+ Record Entry
* Medalist

1988

EIGHTY-EIGHTH U.S. AMATEUR CHAMPIONSHIP

Virginia Hot Springs Golf and Tennis Club (Cascades Course), Hot Springs, Virginia, August 23-28
Yardage—6,663. Par 72. 4,320 Entries, 291 Starters, 64 Qualifiers

Qualifying Score	1st Round (18 Holes)	2nd Round (18 Holes)	3rd Round (18 Holes)	4th Round (18 Holes)	Semifinals (18 Holes)	Final (36 Holes)	
*137	Tom McKnight, Galax, Va.	Lind, 2 and 1					
148	David Lind, Chicago, Ill.		Lind, 3 and 2				
146	Ted Tryba, Wilkes Barre, Pa.	Tryba, 3 and 2					
146	William Spangler, Lincoln, Neb.			Lind, 1 up			
144	Chris DiMarco, Heathrow, Fla.	DeMarco, 3 and 1					
147	Dennis Postlewait, Winter Springs, Fla.		Alexander, 4 and 3				
144	Buddy Alexander, Gainesville, Fla.	Alexander, 1 up					
147	Kevin Wentworth, Manteca, Calif.				Martin, 4 and 3		
142	Jon Christian, Albert Lea, Minn.	Christian, 3 and 2					
148	Tom Knapp, North Palm Beach, Fla.		Martin, 3 and 2				
145	John Hayes, Appleton, Wis.	Martin, 6 and 5					
147	Doug Martin, Van Buren, Ohio			Martin, 2 and 1			
142	David Bishop, Plantation, Fla.	Wood, 6 and 5					
147	Chris Wood, Corona Del Mar, Calif.		Wood, 1 up				
145	Patrick Duncan, Rancho Santa Fe, Calif.	Sullivan, 4 and 3					
142	Robert Sullivan, Palatine, Ill.					Yates, 1 up	
141	Josh Mondry, Franklin, Mich.	Gai, 6 and 5					
148	Kevin Gai, Newington, Conn.		Larkin, 5 and 4				
146	Patrick Brady, Reidsville, N.C.	Larkin, 1 up					
146	Jack Larkin, Atlanta, Ga.			Larkin, 2 up			
143	David McCampbell, Marshall, Ind.	Goetze, 3 and 2					
147	Nicky Goetze, Hull, Ga.		Harris, 2 and 1				
145	Craig Steinberg, Van Nuys, Calif.	Harris, 1 up					
147	John Harris, Edina, Minn.				Yates, 5 and 4		
141	David Sutherland, Sacramento, Calif.	Sutherland, 3 and 2					
148	Craig Hainline, Wichita, Kan.		Baker, 1 up				
146	Tony Dupre, Newport Beach, Calif.	Baker, 5 and 3					
146	Jon Baker, Salt Lake City, Utah			Yates, 5 and 4			
143	Thomas Tolles, Cape Coral, Fla.	Tolles, 6 and 5					
147	Anthony Mollica, Columbus, Ohio		Yates, 3 and 2				
145	Danny Yates, Atlanta, Ga.	Yates, 3 and 2					
147	John Connelly, Oregon, Ohio						Eric Meeks, 7 and 6
138	Eric Meeks, Walnut, Calif.	Meeks, 1 up					
148	Randy Haag, Danville, Calif.		Meeks, 4 and 3				
148	Fred Benton, Jacksonville Beach, Fla.	Benton, 1 up, 20 holes					
146	Aaron Bengoechea, Billings, Mont.			Meeks, 1 up, 21 holes			
143	Jay Sigel, Berwyn, Pa.	Sigel, 1 up					
147	Brian Montgomery, Bristow, Okla.		Sigel, 1 up, 19 holes				
144	Orrin Vincent, San Diego, Calif.	Vincent, 1 up, 19 holes					
147	Robin McCool, Bethlehem, Pa.				Meeks, 1 up		
141	Bill Mayfair, Phoenix, Ariz.	Tuck, 4 and 2					
148	Wes Tuck, Trusville, Ala.		Gamez, 4 and 3				
145	Robert Gamez, Las Vegas, Nev.	Gamez, 1 up					
147	Kevin King, Hilton Head, S.C.			Gamez, 2 up			
148	Todd Parks, Madison, S.D.	Maddalena, 1 up					
147	Steve Maddalena, Jackson, Mich.		Maddalena, 4 and 2				
146	Brett Quigley, Barrington, R.I.	Widener, 3 and 2					
147	Jason Widener, Greensboro, N.C.					Meeks, 1 up	
139	Bob May, Lahabra, Calif.	May, 4 and 3					
148	Steve Lass, Altadena, Calif.		May, 2 and 1				
146	Andrew Pitts, Boone, N.C.	Pitts, 3 and 2					
146	Mark Sollenberger, Phoenix, Ariz.			Yellin, 1 up			
143	Brandt Jobe, Littleton, Colo.	Yellin, 3 and 2					
147	Tom Yellin, Cos Cob, Conn.		Yellin, 6 and 5				
145	Bill Hadden, North Haven, Conn.	Eger, 1 up					
147	David Eger, Ponte Vedra Beach, Fla.				Toms, 2 up		
141	John Isenhour, Salisbury, N.C.	Himka, 4 and 3					
148	Theodore Himka, Renton, Wash.		Toms, 3 and 2				
146	David Toms, Bossier City, La.	Toms, 6 and 5					
147	Harry King, North Little Rock, Ark.			Toms, 1 up, 21 holes			
143	Sam Stein, Richmond, Va.	Stein, 1 up, 19 holes					
147	Scott Frisch, Scottsdale, Ariz.		Stein, 1 up, 20 holes				
145	Geoff Sisk, Marshfield, Mass.	Sisk, 1 up					
147	Packard DeWitt, Fort Smith, Ark.						

*Medalist

1989
EIGHTY-NINTH U.S. AMATEUR CHAMPIONSHIP

Merion Golf Club, Ardmore, Pennsylvania, August 22-27
Yardage—6,523. Par 70. Record 4,603 Entries, 298 Starters, 64 Qualifiers

Qualifying Score	1st Round (18 Holes)	2nd Round (18 Holes)	3rd Round (18 Holes)	4th Round (18 Holes)	Semifinals (18 Holes)	Final (36 Holes)
*137	Eoghan O'Connell, Ireland	O'Connell, 2 up	Brannan, 4 and 3	Brannan, 3 and 1	Brannan, 2 up	Patton, 3 and 2
149	Tim Jackson, Memphis, Tenn.					
146	Michael Brannan, Trumbull, Conn.	Brannan, 3 and 2				
146	Lee Gerdes, Macon, Ga.					
145	O. Gordon Brewer, Huntingdon Valley, Pa.	Eger, 1 up	Eger, 2 and 1			
148	David Eger, Ponte Vedra Beach, Fla.					
145	Dave Ryan, Taylorville, Ill.	Ryan, 2 up				
148	Jim Lemon, Mesa, Ariz.					
143	John Grace, Fort Worth, Texas	Grace, 3 and 2	Satterfield, 2 and 1	Satterfield, 3 and 2		
149	Neil Roderick, Blackpyl, Wales					
146	Wright Waddell, Cataula, Ga.	Satterfield, 2 and 1				
147	Todd Satterfield, Athens, Ga.					
144	Tom Kelley, Fort Wayne, Ind.	Kelley, 5 and 4	Housen, 3 and 2			
149	Michael Mealia, Ontario, Canada					
146	Robert Housen, Brielle, N.J.	Housen, 2 and 1				
147	Tim Straub, Orchard Park, N.Y.					
142	Chris Patton, Fountain Inn, S.C.	Patton, 2 and 1	Patton, 5 and 4	Patton, 20 holes	Patton, 2 and 1	
149	Randal Lewis, Alma, Mich.					
146	Takahiro Nakagawa, Japan	Nakagawa, 19th				
147	Rudy Virga, Warrington, Pa.					
144	Watt Whatley, Forest, Miss.	Whatley, 3 and 1	Podolak, 6 and 5			
148	Scott DeSarrano, Farmers Branch, Texas					
145	Chip Travis, Clarendon Hills, Ill.	Podolak, 3 and 2				
148	Michael Podolak, Oxbow, N.D.					
142	John Isenhour III, Salisbury, N.C.	Isenhour, 2 and 1	Hobby, 2 and 1	Wentworth, 1 up		
149	Paul Hindsley, Glenview, Ill.					
146	Harry Freund, Arcadia, Calif.	Hobby, 1 up				
147	Tim Hobby, Alvin, Texas					
144	Kevin Wentworth, Manteca, Calif.	Wentworth, 2 up	Wentworth, 1 up			
148	Trev Anderson, Tempe, Ariz.					
146	Andrew Pitts, Hildebran, N.C.	Pitts, 2 up				
148	Mike McClung, Dallas, Texas					
138	Phil Mickelson Jr., San Diego, Calif.	Himka, 3 and 2	Himka, 21 holes	Himka, 3 and 1	Courville, 2 and 1	Green, 2 up
149	Ted Himka, Reston, Wash.					
146	Bob May, La Habra, Calif.	May, 5 and 3				
147	James Furyk, Manheim, Pa.					
145	Danny Yates, Atlanta, Ga.	Yates, 4 and 2	Hare, 19 holes			
148	Buddy Alexander, Gainesville, Fla.					
145	Darren Veitch, Ontario, Canada	Hare, 5 and 3				
148	Andrew Haire, Scotland					
143	Duke Delcher, Linwood, N.J.	Delcher, 4 and 3	Whittington, 2 and 1	Courville, 5 and 3		
149	James Brown, Paducah, Ky.					
146	Charles Whittington, Columbus, Ga.	Whittington, 5 and 3				
147	Ben Furth, San Francisco, Calif.					
144	Jerry Courville, Norwalk, Conn.	Courville, 2 and 1	Courville, 5 and 3			
149	Jim Milligan, Troon, Scotland					
146	Chris Cain, Knoxville, Tenn.	Geiberger, 6 and 4				
148	Brent Geiberger, Santa Barbara, Calif.					
142	Bryan Pemberton, Dublin, Calif.	Manson, 1 up	Green, 3 and 2	Green, 3 and 2	Green, 19 holes	
149	Jeff Manson, Long Beach, Calif.					
146	Danny Green, Jackson, Tenn.	Green, 1 up				
147	Paul Simson, Raleigh, N.C.					
145	Robert Gamez, Las Vegas, Nev.	Gamez, 2 and 1	Devers, 21 holes			
148	Greg Kennedy, Watkinsville, Ga.					
145	Paul Claxton, Vidalia, Ga.	Devers, 1 up				
148	Clayton Devers, Lake Quivira, Kan.					
143	Doug Martin, Norman, Okla.	Brookreson, 3 and 2	Brookreson, 5 and 4	Sigel, 2 and 1		
149	Dave Brookreson, Huntingdon Valley, Pa.					
146	Bruce Kenerson, Weston, Mass.	Goodes, 1 up				
147	Mike Goodes, Reidsville, N.C.					
144	Joel Hirsch, Chicago, Ill.	Sollenberger, 4 and 3	Sigel, 2 and 1			
148	Mark Sollenberger, Phoenix, Ariz.					
146	Jay Sigel, Berwyn, Pa.	Sigel, 3 and 1				
148	Dave Cunningham, Michigan City, Ind.					

Chris Patton, 3 and 1

*Medalist

1990
NINETIETH U.S. AMATEUR CHAMPIONSHIP

Cherry Hills Country Club, Denver, Colorado, August 21-26
Yardage—7,110. Par 71. Record 4,765 Entries, 309 Starters, 64 Qualifiers

Qualifying Score	1st Round (18 Holes)	2nd Round (18 Holes)	3rd Round (18 Holes)	4th Round (18 Holes)	Semifinals (18 Holes)	Final (36 Holes)
* 135	Phil Mickelson, San Diego, Ca	Mickelson,				
149	John Grace, Forth Worth, Texas	1 up	Mickelson,			
146	Jeffrey Thomas, South Plainfield, N.J.	Thomas,	6 and 5			
146	Jeff Lee, Dallas, Texas	20 holes		Mickelson,		
143	Justin Leonard, Dallas, Texas	Leonard,		1 up		
148	Diego Ventureira, Columbus, Ga.	2 up	Swingle,			
143	Michael Swingle, Seattle, Wa.	Swingle,	3 and 2			
148	Mitch Voges, Simi Valley, Calif.	3 and 2			Mickelson,	
142	Bob May, La Habra, Calif.	May,			1 up	
148	Bob Young Jr., Atlanta, Ga.	2 up	May,			
144	Marc St. Martin, Smithfield, R.I.	St. Martin,	4 and 2			
147	Rob McKelvey, Lawrenceville, Ga.	1 up		May,		
142	Bill Edwards, Moultrie, Ga.	Edwards,		22 holes		
148	Jeff Fulwiler, Albuquerque, N.M.	5 and 4	Edwards,			
144	Mark Davis, Shelby, N.C.	Davis,	1 up			
147	Kevin Wentworth, Manteca, Calif.	3 and 1				Mickelson,
140	David Edger, Ponte Vedra Beach, Fla.	Eger,				5 and 3
149	Duane Bock, East Hampton, N.Y.	6 and 5	Eger,			
145	Heath Fell, Lapeer, Mi.	Darling,	2 and 1			
146	Craig Darling, Green Bay, Wi.	3 and 2		Eger,		
143	D. Peter Keller Jr., Chatham, N.J.	Furyk,		5 and 4		
148	Jim Furyk, Manheim, Pa.	1 up	Furyk,			
144	Mark Miller, Houston, Texas	Miller,	4 and 2			
147	Chad Magee, Tyler, Texas	19th			Eger,	
141	Jay Sigel, Collegeville, Pa.	Sigel,			2 and 1	
148	Bill Hoefle, Ames, Ia.	2 up	Brannan,			
145	Todd Johnson, Livonia, Mi.	Brannan,	2 and 1			
146	Michael Brannan, Trumbull, Ct.	5 and 4		Brannan,		
143	Dave Cunningham, Michigan City, Ind.	Cozby,		1 up		
148	Cary Cozby, Bartlesville, Ok.	22 holes	Cozby,			
144	Briny Baird, Miami Beach, Fla.	Baird,	6 and 5			
147	Paul Melson, Plantation, Fla.	2 and 1				
137	Richard Holland, Washington, DC.	Holland,				
149	Michael Combs, Kennewick, Wa.	3 and 2	Albertsson,			
146	Hans Albertsson, Manchester, Vt.	Albertsson,	19 holes			
146	Steve Gill, Coppell, Texas	4 and 2		Albertsson,		
143	Gary Schroeder, Windermere, Fla.	Schroeder,		4 and 3		
148	Jeff Street, Tuscaloosa, Al.	3 and 2	Schroeder,			
143	Chip Stewart, Dallas, Texas	Veneziano,	2 and 1			
147	Jon Veneziano, Kensington, Ct.	4 and 3			Scherrer,	
141	John Harris, Edina, Mn.	Harris,			3 and 2	
148	Mark Drury, Brunswick, Ga.	4 and 3	Scherrer,			
145	Jaxon Brigman, Abilene, Texas	Scherrer,	19 holes			
147	Thomas Scherrer, Skaneateles, N.Y.	1 up		Scherrer,		
143	Chris Patton, Fountain, Inn, S.C.	Zambri,		4 and 3		
148	Chris Zambri, Thousand Oaks, Calif.	8 and 6	Zambri,			
144	Bryan Pemberton, Dublin, Calif.	Pemberton,	1 up			
147	Kevin Fairfield, Atlanta, Ga.	4 and 3				Zerman,
138	Perry Moss, Shreveport, L.A.	Moss,				4 and 2
149	Jimmy Johnston, Knoxville, Tenn.	1 up	Sposa,			
146	Michael Sposa, Dillard, Ga.	Sposa,	19 holes			
146	Christopher Dibble, Greeneville, Tenn.	1 up		Sposa,		
143	Bradley Klapprott, Iowa City, Ia.	Klapprott,		19 holes		
148	William Sibbick, Martinsville, Va.	1 up	Klapprott,			
143	Taichi Teshima, Norcross, Ga.	Sbarbaro,	4 and 2			
147	Keith Sbarbaro, San Diego, Calif.	1 up			Zerman,	
141	Chris Smith, Rochester, In.	Liner,			3 and 2	
148	Chris Liner, Athens, Tenn.	3 and 1	Reed,			
145	Terrence Miskell, Salinas, Calif.	Reed,	3 and 2			
146	Craig Reed, Gillette, Wy.	2 up		Zerman,		
143	Manny Zerman, Tucson, Az.	Zerman,		2 and 1		
148	Michael Etherington, Fayetteville, Ar.	4 and 3	Zerman,			
144	John Sosa, El Paso, Texas	Sosa,	3 and 2			
147	David Apperson, Memphis, Tenn.	3 and 2				

Phil Mickelson, 5 and 4

*Medalist

WOMEN'S AMATEUR CHAMPIONSHIP

CHAMPIONSHIP CUP

Presented in 1896 by
ROBERT COX

Gorgie Edinburg Golf Association
Golfer and Graduate of St. Andrews

HISTORY

1981—Juli Simpson Inkster, 21, of Los Altos, California, became the first golfer to win consecutive Women's Amateur Championships since Betty Jameson in 1939 and 1940. Inkster captured a dramatic 1 up victory over Lindy Goggin, of Tasmania, Australia, at the Waverley Country Club in Portland, Oregon. Patti Rizzo, of Hialeah, Florida, and Heather Farr, of Phoenix, Arizona, shared medalist honors with 36-hole scores of 147 to lead the 64 qualifiers for match play. Rizzo, the 1980 runner-up, was eliminated in the quarterfinals by Rose Jones, 2 and 1. Farr, playing in her first Women's Amateur, lost in the first round to Karin Mundinger, of Canada, 3 and 2. Inkster and Goggin qualified with scores of 156 and 154, respectively. Eight players were involved in a playoff to decide the final seven places in match play. To reach the semifinals, Inkster defeated Tanna Lee, of Ft. Smith, Arkansas, and Helen Kirkland, of Colorado Springs, Colorado, by identical 3 and 2 margins; Penny Hammel, the 1979 Girls' Junior Champion, of Decatur, Illinois, 4 and 3; and in the quarterfinals, Curtis Cupper Lancy Smith, of Snyder, New York, 2 and 1. Inkster's semifinal opponent, as in 1980, was Carol Semple, of Sewickley, Pennsylvania, her U.S. World Amateur teammate. Inkster defeated Semple, the former American and British Amateur Champion, 3 and 2. Goggin, whose husband was her caddie, made a serious bid to become the first Australian to win the U.S. Women's Amateur. She defeated Mary Callaghan, of Los Angeles, California, 3 and 2; Julie Kintz, of Atlantis, Florida, 1 up; Mary Beth Zimmerman, of Hillsboro, Illinois, 5 and 4; and, in the quarterfinals, Carol Hogan, of Delmar, California, 2 and 1. In the semifinals, Goggin was four down to Rose Jones with eight holes to play. She won the next five holes en route to a 1 up victory. The final match, for the most part, was played on even terms. They halved 11 of the 18 holes. Neither managed more than a one-hole lead. Through 15 holes, the match was even. At the long par-3 16th, Inkster left her tee shot to the right of the green and lost the hole to Goggin's par. One down, Inkster proceeded to birdie the final two holes and save her title. At the 17th, she made a birdie putt of 10 feet, then watched as Goggin missed from six feet. Inkster followed with a birdie putt of 12 feet on the final hole to clinch the victory. The USGA received 240 entries, short of the record 281 for the 1980 Championship.

1982—Mrs. Juli Simpson Inkster, 22, of Los Altos, California, became the fifth player to win the Women's Amateur Championship in three consecutive years, joining Beatrix Hoyt (1896-97-98), Alexa Stirling (1916-1919-20—World War I cancelled this championship in 1917-18), Glenna Collett Vare (1928-29-30), and Virginia Van Wie (1932-33-34). Her 18 consecutive match-play victories in this championship are one short of the 19 consecutive matches won by Miss Stirling and Mrs. Vare. Mrs. Inkster won with a 4 and 3 victory over Cathy Hanlon, of Palos Verdes Estates, California, on the South Course of the Broadmoor Golf Club, in Colorado Springs, Colorado. Both Mrs. Inkster and Miss Hanlon were members of the 1982 Curtis Cup Team. Penny Hammel, of Decatur, Illinois, tied the 36-hole qualifying record with 143, one under par, matching the score shot in 1966 by Shelley Hamlin and equalled two years later by Catherine Lacoste. Amy Benz, of Clearwater, Florida, shot 69 on the second day, matching the 18-hole record set by Barbara Fay White Boddie in 1969. The Misses Hammel and Benz both lost in the quarterfinals. Mrs. Inkster and Miss Hanlon qualified with scores of 148 and 151, respectively. Mrs. Inkster's first opponent nearly ended her quest for a third title. Matched against Caroline Gowan, of Greenville, South Carolina, Mrs. Inkster was three down after four holes. She fought back to go 1 up after 16, but lost the 17th to square the match. On the 18th, a par 4, Miss Gowan drove into a fairway bunker, then played a remarkable shot over the trees to within eight feet of the hole. Mrs. Inkster left her approach just short of the green, chipped poorly, but holed a 15-foot putt to save par. Miss Gowan missed her short birdie putt by an inch, and they went to extra holes. Mrs. Inkster birdied the 19th to win the match. In the second round, Mrs. Inkster eliminated Carol Semple, of Sewickley, Pennsylvania, 3 and 1. It marked the third consecutive year that Mrs. Inkster had defeated Miss Semple, a fellow Curtis-Cupper and former Women's Amateur Champion. Mrs. Inkster then ousted Robin Wohltman, of Independence, Kansas, 6 and 5; medalist Penny Hammel, 2 and 1, in the quarterfinals; and Lisa Kluver, of Alexandria, Minnesota, 3 and 2, in the semifinals. Miss Hanlon did not lose a single hole in three of her first five matches before the final. In those five matches she won 32 holes, halved 32, and lost only four. Mrs. Inkster's play throughout the week on the par 5s was awesome. Of the 28 she played, she earned conceded eagles twice, birdied 13, had par on 10, and bogeyed only three. In the final, she was 2 up after the first 18 holes. Miss Hanlon rallied after lunch, winning the first two holes of the afternoon round, and the match was even again. She won only one more hole all day, the ninth, with a par 5. Mrs. Inkster, meanwhile, birdied the fourth, sixth, eighth (a chip-in), 10th (halving the hole), and 11th holes to go three up with seven holes left. Her dominance of the par 5s was clearly demonstrated on the 12th hole. After a long tee shot, she played a 4-iron shot from 239 yards away that landed just short of the green, bounced towards the flagstick, and stopped just eight inches from the hole. Miss Hanlon conceded the eagle. They halved the 13th, 14th, and 15th holes and the match was over. Mrs. Inkster was five under par. During the 33 holes of the match, Mrs. Inkster made 10 birdies and one eagle. Miss Hanlon was one under; she made six birdies. The USGA received 262 entries, short of the record 281 set in 1980.

1983—Joanne Pacillo, 21, of Torrance, California, became the third consecutive Californian to win the Women's Amateur. She succeeded Carolyn Hill, Placentia (1979), and Juli Inkster, of Los Altos (1980-81-82). Miss Pacillo, a graduate of Stanford University, defeated Sally Quinlan, of Dennis, Massachusetts, 2 and 1, in the final. The Championship was played on the North Course of the Canoe Brook Country Club, in Summit, New Jersey. Mary Anne Widman, of Elmira, N.Y., was medalist, with 147, but she lost to Susan Marchese, of Omaha, Nebraska, 3 and 2, in the second round. Miss Pacillo and Miss Quinlan each qualified with 152. On her way to the final Miss Pacillo defeated, among others, Mrs. Anne Quast Sander, of Seattle, Washington, three times the Women's Amateur Champion, 2 up, and Mrs. Belle Robertson, of Glasgow, Scotland, 1981 British Champion, 1 up. Meanwhile, Miss Quinlan eliminated her college teammate Penny Hammel, of Decatur, Illinois, the Women's NCAA Champion, 4 and 3; and Nancy Taylor, of Tampa, Florida, the 1982 Women's Amateur Public Links Champion, 3 and 2. Miss Pacillo played the steadier golf in the final. Miss Quinlan had trouble controlling her drives and chose to play her 1-iron off most tees, conceding a distance advantage to Miss Pacillo. Miss Quinlan led only once, winning the third hole with a par-5, but Miss Pacillo squared it two holes later. Miss Pacillo was 2 up as the afternoon round began, and when Miss Quinlan three-putted the first green, Miss Pacillo was 3 up with 17 holes to play. Miss Quinlan began to close in, however, by winning the next two holes, but Miss Pacillo held a 2-up lead with nine holes to play. The next five holes were halved with pars, and then Miss Quinlan won the 15th, and Miss Pacillo countered with a birdie at the 16th. The match ended when the 17th was halved in par. The Championship attracted 259 entries.

1984—Deb Richard, 21, of Manhattan, Kansas, defeated Kimberly Williams, 21, of Bethesda, Maryland, on the 37th hole at the Broadmoor Golf Club, in Seattle, Washington. Miss Richard, a student at the University of Florida, qualified at 155, 11 strokes over par and 10 behind Claire Waite, of England, the medalist. Miss Waite lost in the first round to Kandi Kessler, of Charlottesville, Virginia, even though she was even par for the 20 holes. In the third round, against Heather Farr, of Scottsdale, Arizona, Miss Richard was 4 down after 15 holes, but she won the next five. The 36-hole final match was even 12 times. Miss Richard led most of the forenoon, holding a 2-up advantage after nine holes, but Miss Williams won three of the last four holes and was ahead by one hole at the luncheon break. Miss Richard carried a 2-up lead into the final nine holes in the afternoon, but Miss Williams caught her at the 17th. The 18th was halved, but Miss Richard birdied the 37th hole while Miss Williams three-putted. It was her third bogey on that hole in the match. Each player shot 157, Miss Williams scoring 73-78, plus her bogey 6, and Miss Richard shooting 75-78, plus her birdie 4. This was only the second final match of the Women's Amateur Championship to go to extra holes. The Championship attracted a record 290 entries.

1985—Michiko Hattori, 16, of Aichi, Japan, defeated Cheryl Stacy of Findlay, Ohio, 5 and 4, at Fox Chapel Golf Club in Pittsburgh, Pennsylvania. With the win, Hattori became the youngest Women's Amateur champion in 14 years and the first foreign-born winner of the championship in seven years. She also became the eighth golfer to win on her first attempt. Hattori and Stacy shared medalist honors in the Championship, at seven-over-par 151. Miss Hattori never played the 18th hole on her way to the final match. Her most severe test came in a 2 and 1 win over Pat Cornett of San Francisco, California, in the third round. Miss Hattori won by a 2 and 1 margin. She defeated Kim Gardner, 3 and 2, in the semifinal. Miss Stacy twice was extended to the 18th hole on her way to the final round. She defeated Lisa Marino of West Allen Park, Michigan, 1 up, in the first round and edged 1985 Women's Amateur Public Links champion Danielle Ammaccapane of Phoenix, Arizona, 1 up, in the semi-finals. In the final match, after losing the first hole with a double bogey, Stacy birdied the second and fourth holes to take a one-hole advantage. Hattori pulled even on the fifth, but Stacy regained the lead with a par on the seventh hole. She held that lead until the 12th when Hattori birdied to square the match. Stacy regained the lead on the 13th, but bogeyed the 15th, 17th and 18th and trailed by two holes heading into the afternoon round. Hattori held off a game comeback effort by Stacy, who birdied the third, sixth, seventh and eighth holes in the afternoon, but still could not square the match. Hattori held a 1-up lead after nine holes and increased it with a birdie at the 10th. Hattori parred the next four holes and closed out Stacy. The USGA accepted a record 329 entries for the Championship.

WOMEN'S AMATEUR CHAMPIONSHIP

1986—Kay Cockerill, 21, of Los Gatos, California, defeated Kathleen McCarthy of Fresno, California, 9 and 7, at Pasatiempo Golf Club in Santa Cruz, California. The margin of victory was the largest in the Women's Amateur since 1962 when JoAnne Gunderson defeated Ann Baker, 9 and 8. Pearl Sinn of Bellflower, California, and 1985 champion Michiko Hattori of Nagoya, Japan, shared medalist honors, each shooting 151, seven over par. Sinn advanced to the third round before losing to Carol Semple Thompson, 1 up. Hattori lost in the second round to British Curtis Cupper Trish Johnson, 2 up. Cockerill trailed in only one match. In the second round, France's Marie de Lorenzi-Taya was 1-up at the 10th, but Cockerill recovered for a 3-and-2 victory. In her semifinal, Cockerill eliminated Flori Prono of Northridge, California, 2 and 1. McCarthy was seriously challenged in the quarterfinals, where she downed Thompson, 1 up. She eliminated Danielle Ammaccapane of Phoenix, Arizona, 1 up, in the semifinals with a 20-foot birdie putt on the 18th hole. McCarthy won the first hole of the scheduled 36-hole final but did not win another until the 22d. In the meantime, Cockerill had won four holes on the first nine and three more on the second to lead 6 up after the morning round. Still 6 up after 26 holes, Cockerill won the 27th, 28th and 29th to close out the match. The USGA accepted a record 387 entries for the Championship.

1987—Kay Cockerill of Los Gatos, California, successfully defended her U.S. Women's Amateur title, defeating Tracy Kerdyk of Coral Gables, Florida, the 1987 Women's APL champion, 3 and 2, at the Rhode Island Country Club in Barrington. She became the first to win consecutive Women's Amateurs since Juli Inkster won the championship in 1980-81-82. Kerdyk and Michiko Hattori of Nagoya, Japan, shared medalist honors at three-over-par 147, one stroke ahead of Susan Ginter of Appleton, Wisconsin. It was Hattori's third consecutive qualifying medal in this championship. She was eliminated by Carol Semple Thompson in the third round, 4 and 3. Cockerill defeated Thompson in the quarterfinals, then ousted Nanci Bowen of Tifton, Georgia, 3 and 1, to reach the final. Kerdyk was extended to 22 holes by Kim Saiki of Redwood City, California, in the third round, then downed Leslie Shannon and Pat Milton to earn her trip to the final. Cockerill won the first three holes of the final, but Kerdyk played the sixth through the ninth in two under par and made the turn 1 up. Cockerill birdied the 12th to even the match and took the lead with a par at the 13th. She won the 15th, 16th and 17th, played in a driving rain, and was 4 up after the morning round. Play was suspended after Cockerill and Kerdyk had played their approaches to the 19th green. Play was resumed the following day. Cockerill sank a 35-foot putt at the 19th to go 5 up. Kerdyk reduced the lead to four holes on three occasions and got it to three at the 31st. Cockerill parred the last three holes to win the match. The USGA accepted 359 entries for the championship.

1988—Pearl Sinn, 21, of Bellflower, California, defeated Karen Noble of Convent Station, New Jersey, 6 and 5, in the final at the Minikahda Club in Minneapolis, Minn. Sinn is the first golfer to win the U.S. Women's Amateur Public Links and Women's Amateur Championships, and the first woman to win two USGA championships in the same year. Sinn won the qualifying medal with rounds of 71-69—140, and record for the championship. Michiko Hattori of Nagoya, Japan, who had shared the qualifying medal the past three years, placed second, three strokes behind Sinn. Sinn was extended past the 16th hole only once on her way to the final. In the quarterfinal round, Kelly Robbins of Mount Pleasant, Michigan, and Sinn were all square through 18 holes. After the 19th was halved with birdies, Sinn won the 20th with a par. Sinn advanced to the final by eliminating Pat Milton of Akron, Ohio, who reached the semifinals for the second consecutive year, 6 and 5. Noble defeated three past U.S. Women's Amateur Champions in succession on her way to the final match. She ousted Carol Semple Thompson, the 1973 champion, in the third round, 1 up. In the quarterfinals, she eliminated Anne Sander, who won the championship in 1958, 1961 and 1963, 6 and 5. She then defeated Hattori, the 1985 champion, with a birdie on the 19th hole. In the final, Noble lost two of the first five holes, then won the sixth, seventh and eighth to take a 1-up lead. Sinn rebounded, winning four holes in succession to give her a 3-up lead, which she held after the morning round. Sinn won three holes with pars early in the afternoon round to go 6 up. She won the match, 6 and 5, when the 13th was halved with birdies. The USGA accepted 357 entries for the championship.

1989—In a match between two teenagers, Vicki Goetze, of Hull, Georgia, became the third youngest U.S. Women's Amateur champion by defeating Brandie Burton, 17, of Rialto, California, 4 and 3, on the No. 2 course of the Pinehurst Country Club, in Pinehurst, North Carolina. A high-school junior, Miss Goetze was 16 years, 9 months and 19 days old on the day of the final. She was playing in her first U.S. Amateur Championship. A week earlier, Miss Burton had defeated Miss Goetze in a semifinal match in the Girls' Junior Championship. Miss Burton won the championship the next day. Miss Goetze ended the scheduled 36-hole match by scoring birdies on the 34th and 36th holes. Miss Burton won three of the first four holes of the Women's Amateur final, but Goetze went ahead to stay at the 13th. Although a short hitter, Miss Goetze won five of the nine par 5s played, even though Miss Burton had chances to reach several of those holes in two shots. Miss Goetze's play around the greens made the difference. She holed six birdie putts during the match, and was 1-under-par when it ended. Miss Goetze was one of the low qualifiers, and most of her matches were one-sided, except against Terri Thompson, of Savannah, Georgia. Miss Thompson had Miss Goetze two holes down with three to play, but Miss

Goetze won the match with three consecutive birdies. Her birdie on the 18th hole was a 30-foot putt from off the green. Pat Hurst, the 1986 Girls' Junior champion, led qualifying by shooting 69-74-143, but lost in the first round of match play. Three past champions reached match play. The others were Carol Semple Thompson (1973), Anne Sander (1963), and Michiko Hattori (1985), who also won at 16. Mrs. Thompson lost to Miss Goetze in the semifinals.

1990—Pat Hurst, 21, of San Leandro, California, scored a par 4 on the first extra hole and defeated Stephanie Davis of Bainbridge Island, Washington, at the Canoe Brook Country Club, in Summit, New Jersey. Three holes down after the morning round, Miss Hurst rallied and won four of the first eight holes in the afternoon round to go 1 up. Miss Davis then birdied the next to last hole to draw all square, and each player parred the final hole, sending the match to extra holes. The Women's Amateur is Miss Hurst's second USGA title; she had won the 1986 Girls' Junior. Miss Hurst defeated three members of the 1990 Curtis Cup team to reach the semifinals. From the second round through the quarterfinals, she defeated, in order, Katie Peterson, 3 and 1; Robin Weiss, 7 and 6; and Vicki Goetze, 1 up. Miss Hurst defeated Delphine Bourson 2 up in her semifinal match, using a strong second nine to gain the lead, just as she had done many times in the championship. A senior at San Jose State University, Miss Hurst capped her summer by playing for the United States in the U.S. Women's World Amateur Team Championship, in Christchurch, New Zealand. The United States won.

WOMEN'S AMATEUR CHAMPIONSHIP

DATE	WINNER, RUNNER-UP	SCORE	SITE	ENTRY
1981 (Aug.)	Mrs. Juli Simpson Inkster d. Mrs. Lindy Goggin	1 up	Waverley C.C., Portland, Ore. Co-Medalists—147: Miss Patti Rizzo Miss Heather Farr	240
1982 (Aug.)	Mrs. Juli Simpson Inkster d. Miss Cathy Hanlon	4 & 3	Broadmoor G.C., (South Course) Colorado Springs, Colo. Medalist—143: Miss Penny Hammel	262
1983 (Aug.)	Miss Joanne Pacillo d. Miss Sally Quinlan	2 & 1	Canoe Brook C.C., Summit, N.J. Medalist—147: Miss Mary Anne Widman	259
1984 (Aug.)	Miss Deb Richard d. Miss Kim Williams	1 up, 37 hls.	Broadmoor G.C., Seattle, Wash. Medalist—145: Miss Claire Waite	290
1985 (Aug.)	Miss Michiko Hattori d. Miss Cheryl Stacy	5 & 4	Fox Chapel C.C., Pittsburgh, Pa. Co-Medalists—151: Miss Michiko Hattori Miss Cheryl Stacy	329
1986 (Aug.)	Miss Kay Cockerill d. Miss Kathleen McCarthy	9 & 7	Pasatiempo G.C., Santa Cruz, Calif. Co-Medalists—148: Miss Pearl Sinn Miss Michiko Hattori	*387
1987 (Aug.)	Miss Kay Cockerill d. Miss Tracy Kerdyk	3 & 2	Rhode Island C.C., Barrington, R.I. Co-Medalists—147: Miss Michiko Hattori Miss Tracy Kerdyk	359
1988 (Aug.)	Miss Pearl Sinn d. Miss Karen Noble	6 & 5	Minikahda Club, Minneapolis, Minn. Medalist—140: Miss Pearl Sinn	357
1989 (July-Aug.)	Miss Vicki Goetze d. Miss Brandie Burton	4 & 3	Pinehurst C.C. (No. 2), Pinehurst, N.C. Medalist—143: Miss Pat Hurst	376
1990 (Aug.)	Miss Pat Hurst d. Miss Stephanie Davis	37 holes	Canoe Brook C.C., Summit, N.J. Medalist—144: Miss Vicki Goetze	384

*Record entry

1981
EIGHTY-FIRST WOMEN'S AMATEUR CHAMPIONSHIP

Waverley Country Club, Portland, Oregon, August 10-15
Yardage — 6,229. Par 72. 240 Entries, 159 Starters, 64 Qualifiers.

Qualifying Score	1st Round (18 Holes)	2nd Round (18 Holes)	3rd Round (18 Holes)	4th Round (18 Holes)	Semi-Finals (18 Holes)	Final (18 Holes)
*147	Patti Rizzo, Hialeah, Fla.	Rizzo, 3 and 2	Rizzo, 2 and 1	Rizzo, 2 and 1	Jones, 2 and 1	Goggin, 1 up
156	Leslie Shannon, Miami, Fla.					
154	Debbie McClung, Farmers Branch, Texas	Lasker, 4 and 3				
158	Dorothy Lasker, Hinsdale, Ill.					
151	Jane Geddes, Summerville, S.C.	Geddes, 4 and 3	Geddes, 1 up			
158	Kim Eaton, Greeley, Colo.					
156	Vicki Woodcock, Vancouver, B.C.	Schreck, 6 and 4				
159	Theresa Schreck, Spokane, Wash.					
150	Deborah Petrizzi, Austin, Texas	Petrizzi, 4 and 2	Petrizzi, 1 up	Jones, 2 and 1		
157	Cristina Artasona, Madrid, Spain					
155	Cathy Hanlon, Palos Verdes, Calif.	Hanlon, 2 and 1				
159	Jill Briles, Peoria, Ill.					
152	Rose Jones, Albuquerque, N.M.	Jones, 4 and 2	Jones, 6 and 4			
158	Jan Rikard, Gilbert, S.C.					
156	Susan Yantis, San Antonio, Texas	Yantis, 4 and 3				
160	Veronica Karaman, Fayetteville, N.C.					
148	Viveca Vandergriff, Arlington, Texas	Anderson, 1 up, 19 holes	Hogan, 1 up	Hogan, 4 and 3	Goggin, 2 and 1	
157	Marla Anderson, Jacksonville, Fla.					
155	Carol Hogan, Del Mar, Calif.	Hogan, 2 and 1				
159	Cathy Cook, Columbus, Ohio					
152	Kim Bauer, Conroe, Texas	Bauer, 1 up	Bauer, 1 up			
158	Heather Drew, Solana Beach, Calif.					
156	Jennifer Davis, Northridge, Calif.	Davis, 5 and 4				
159	Linda Hunt, Lubbock, Texas					
150	Kris Monaghan, Albuquerque, N.M.	Zimmerman, 4 and 3	Zimmerman, 3 and 1	Goggin, 5 and 4		
158	Mary Zimmerman, Hillsboro, Ill.					
156	Mari McDougall, Midlothian, Ill.	Flenniken, 2 and 1				
159	Carol Flenniken, Brush, Colo.					
154	Lindy Goggin, Tasmania, Australia	Goggin, 3 and 2	Goggin, 1 up			
158	Mary Callaghan, Los Angeles, Calif.					
156	Cheryl Stacy, Findlay, Ohio	Kintz, 4 and 3				
150	Julie Kintz, Atlantis, Fla.					
*147	Heather Farr, Phoenix, Ariz.	Mundinger, 3 and 2	Smith, 5 and 3	Smith, 8 and 7	Inkster, 2 and 1	Inkster, 3 and 2
156	Karin Mundinger, Toronto, Canada					
154	Lancy Smith, Snyder, N.Y.	Smith, 3 and 2				
159	Diane Calkins, Cleves, Ohio					
152	Mitzi Edge, Augusta, Ga.	Dye, 1 up	Rinker, 7 and 5			
158	Alice Dye, Delray Beach, Fla.					
156	Judith Oliver, Sewickley, Pa.	Rinker, 1 up				
159	Kellii Rinker, Placentia, Calif.					
150	Phyllis Preuss, Colorado Springs, Colo.	Hammel, 7 and 5	Hammel, 1 up	Inkster, 4 and 3		
157	Penny Hammel, Decatur, Ill.					
155	Kim Simmons, Charleston, S.C.	Simmons, 2 up				
159	Debbie Hall, San Jose, Calif.					
153	Tammy Wilborn, San Marino, Calif.	Kirkland, 2 and 1	Inkster, 3 and 2			
158	Helen Kirkland, Colorado Springs, Colo.					
156	Juli Inkster, Los Altos, Calif.	Inkster, 3 and 2				
160	Tanna Lee, Fort Smith, Ark.					
148	Amy Benz, Clearwater, Fla.	Benz, 3 and 2	Benz, 1 up, 20 holes	Benz, 3 and 2	Semple, 1 up	
157	Catherine Curry, Columbus, Neb.					
155	Mary Enright, San Leandro, Calif.	Enright, 2 and 1				
159	Carol Ludvigson, Flossmoor, Ill.					
152	Mary Hafeman, Jacksonville, Fla.	Hafeman, 1 up, 21 holes	Rothfelder, 1 up			
158	Patricia Cornett, San Francisco, Calif.					
156	Lynne Cooke, Vancouver, British Columbia	Rothfelder, 2 and 1				
160	Rae Rothfelder, Ft. Worth, Texas					
150	Carol Semple, Sewickley, Pa.	Semple, 1 up	Semple, 1 up	Semple, 3 and 2		
158	Anne Kelly, Tucson, Ariz.					
156	Anne Sander, Seattle, Wash.	Thomas, 3 and 2				
159	Barbara Thomas, Sibley, Iowa					
154	Kathy Baker, Clover, S.C.	Jeanson, 6 and 5	Figg, 2 and 1			
158	Nathalie Jeanson, Paris, France					
156	Cynthia Figg, Austin, Texas	Figg, 5 and 4				
160	Susan Sanders, Salem, Ore.					

Juli Inkster, 1 up

*Co-Medalists

1982
EIGHTY-SECOND WOMEN'S AMATEUR CHAMPIONSHIP

Broadmoor Golf Club (South Course), Colorado Springs, Colorado, August 16-21.
Yardage — 6,337. Par 72. 262 Entries, 144 Starters, 64 Qualifiers.

Qualifying Score	1st Round (18 Holes)	2nd Round (18 Holes)	3rd Round (18 Holes)	4th Round (18 Holes)	Semifinals (18 Holes)	Final (36 Holes)
*143	Penny Hammel, Decatur, Ill.	Hammel,				
157	Kathe Kingston, Marietta, Ga.	3 and 2	Hammel,			
155	Loretta Alderete, Rancho Mirage, Calif.	Kennedy,	1 up			
160	Edwina Kennedy, Sydney, Australia	3 and 1		Hammel,		
151	Denise Hermida, Brandon, Fla.	Hermida,		7 and 6		
159	Joan Ellis, Tampa, Fla.	2 and 1	Hermida,			
156	Liz Rowland, Portsmouth, Va.	Rosenthal,	1 up			
161	Jody Rosenthal, Edina, Minn.	3 and 1			Inkster,	
148	Juli Inkster, Los Altos, Calif.	Inkster,			2 and 1	
158	Caroline Gowan, Greenville, S.C.	1 up, 19 holes	Inkster,			
155	Carol Semple, Sewickley, Pa.	Semple,	3 and 1			
160	Lisa Stanley, Melbourne, Fla.	4 and 3		Inkster,		
152	Cindy Davis, Bowie, Md.	Davis,		6 and 5		
159	Barbara Wright, Salt Lake City, Utah	3 and 1	Wohltman,			
157	Theresa Schreck, Spokane, Wash.	Wohltman,	1 up			
162	Robin Wohltman, Independence, Kans.	1 up				Inkster,
147	Amy Benz, Clearwater, Fla.	Benz,				3 and 2
158	Kris Hanson, Granite Falls, Minn.	4 and 3	Benz,			
155	Mary McKenna, Dublin, Ireland	Furlong,	1 up, 19 holes			
160	Shirley Furlong, San Antonio, Texas	2 up		Benz,		
152	Jennifer Steiner, Palos Verdes Est., Calif.	Steiner,		5 and 4		
159	Mitzi Edge, Augusta, Ga.	2 and 1	Steiner,			
156	Mary B. Zimmerman, Hillsboro, Ill.	Hart,	2 and 1			
161	Kathleen Hart, Miami Beach, Fla.	3 and 2				
151	Lisa Kluver, Alexandria, Minn.	Kluver,				
159	Deb Richard, Manhattan, Kans.	6 and 5	Kluver,		Kluver,	
156	Helen Kirkland, Colorado Springs, Colo.	Thomas,	1 up		2 up	
161	Barbara Thomas, Sibley, Iowa	4 and 2		Kluver,		
154	Susan Sanders, Albuquerque, N.M.	Fromuth,		1 up, 20 holes		
160	Susan Fromuth, Chesterfield, Mo.	2 and 1	Quinlan,			
157	Sally Quinlan, Dennis, Mass.	Quinlan,	5 and 4			
162	Carol Slane, Auburn, Calif.	3 and 2				
146	Lindy Goggin, Tasmania, Australia	Goggin,				
158	Debbie Weldon, Laguna Beach, Caif.	5 and 3	Goggin,			
155	Lynn Connelly, Gainesville, Fla.	Connelly,	3 and 1			
160	Deborah Skelly, San Antonio, Texas	4 and 3		Goggin,		
151	Kathy Baker, Clover, S.C.	Baker,		3 and 2		
146	Debby Distefano, Webster, N.Y.	7 and 5	Baker,			
156	Lancy Smith, Snyder, N.Y.	Smith,	6 and 4			
161	Wilma Aitken, Scotland	4 and 3			Goggin,	
150	Anne Sander, Seattle, Wash.	Sander,			2 and 1	
158	Renee Headings, Skytop, Pa.	4 and 3	Grant,			
155	Charlotte Grant, Lookout Mtn., Tenn.	Grant,	4 and 3			
161	Amy Read, Olney, Ill.	2 and 1		Tomich,		
153	Kelly Skalicky, Avon, Minn.	Ray,		6 and 5		
160	Lucille Ray, Rockhill, S.C.	3 and 2	Tomich,			
157	Nancy Tomich, Upper St. Clair, Pa.	Tomich,	1 up, 19 holes			
162	Carol Flenniken, Brush, Colo.	2 and 1				
147	Kris Monaghan, Albuquerque, N.M.	Monaghan,				Hanlon,
158	Kitrina Douglas, Avon, England	6 and 5	Cook,			6 and 4
155	Lida Kinnicutt, Bloomfield, Conn.	Cook,	2 and 1			
160	Cathy Cook, Columbus, Ohio	1 up		Bozarth,		
152	Cindy Pleger, Athens, Ga.	Bozarth,		1 up		
159	Marci Bozarth, Lampassas, Texas	2 up	Bozarth,			
156	Yoshiko Ito, Tokyo, Japan	Ito,	2 and 1			
161	Rebecca Larson, Watertown, S.D.	2 up			Hanlon,	
151	Cathy Hanlon, Palos Verdes Est., Calif.	Hanlon,			5 and 4	
159	Cynthia Figg, Mt. Pleasant, Mich.	8 and 7	Hanlon,			
156	Dana Howe, Colorado Springs, Colo.	Zahn,	6 and 5			
161	Anne Zahn, Excelsior, Minn.	1 up		Hanlon,		
154	Brenda Pictor, Jacksonville, Fla.	Connachan,		3 and 2		
160	Jane Connachan, E. Lothian, Scotland	2 and 1	McDougall,			
157	Mari McDougall, Midlothian, Ill.	McDougall,	2 and 1			
162	Mary Ann Morrison, Houston, Texas	5 and 3				

Juli Inkster, 4 and 3

*Medalist

1983
EIGHTY-THIRD WOMEN'S AMATEUR CHAMPIONSHIP

Canoe Brook Country Club, Summit, New Jersey, August 15-20
Yardage—6,170. Par 72. 259 Entries, 144 Starters, 64 Qualifiers

Qualifying Score	1st Round (18 Holes)	2nd Round (18 Holes)	3rd Round (18 Holes)	4th Round (18 Holes)	Semifinals (18 Holes)	Final (36 Holes)
*147	Mary Anne Widman, Elmira, N.Y.	Widman,				
155	Deb Richard, Manhattan, Kans.	3 and 2	Marchese,			
152	Sara Timms, Spartanburg, S.C.	Marchese,	3 and 2			
158	Susan Marchese, Omaha, Neb.	3 and 2		Dickman,		
152	Lancy Smith, Snyder, N.Y.	Tschetter,		5 and 4		
157	Kristen Tschetter, Sioux Falls, S.D.	1 up	Dickman,			
154	Diane Dickman, Modesto, Calif.	Dickman,	2 up			
159	Denise King, Smyrna, Ga.	2 and 1				
150	Joan Ellis, Tampa, Fla.	Ellis,			Dickman,	
156	Jodi Logan, Sandusky, Ohio	2 and 1	Bozarth,		2 and 1	
153	Vicky Lakoff, Richmond, Ind.	Bozarth,	3 and 2			
158	Marci Bozarth, Ft. Worth, Texas	7 and 6				
152	Yoshiko Ito, Stillwater, Okla.	Read,		Bozarth,		
158	Amy Read, Olney, Ill.	2 and 1	Read	3 and 2		
155	Carol S. Thompson, Pittsburgh, Pa.	Thompson,	3 and 2			Pacillo,
159	Ann Swanson, Seattle, Wash.	1 up, 19 holes				2 up
149	Belle Robertson, Glasgow, Scotland	Robertson,				
156	Angela Atkins, Missouri City, Texas	1 up	Robertson,			
153	Julie Fulton, San Diego, Calif.	Fulton,	5 and 4			
158	Tammy Welborn, Pasadena, Calif.	2 and 1		Pacillo,		
152	Joanne Pacillo, Torrance, Calif.	Pacillo		1 up		
157	Anne Sander, Seattle, Wash.	1 up	Pacillo,			
154	Ann Laughlin, Riverton, N.J.	Laughlin,	3 and 2			
159	Tina Tombs, Bedford, N.H.	5 and 4			Pacillo,	
150	Dana Howe, Colorado Springs, Colo.	Howe,			3 and 2	
156	Robin Weiss, Ft. Pierce, Fla.	5 and 4	Howe,			
153	Charlotte Grant, St. Simons Island, Ga.	Cook,	3 and 2			
158	Cathy Cook, Akron, Ohio	1 up		Howe,		
152	Kathleen McCarthy, Fresno, Calif.	McCarthy,		3 and 1		
158	Michele Berteotti, Pittsburgh, Pa.	1 up	McCarthy,			
155	Brenda Pictor, Dunwoody Ga.	Pictor,	6 and 5			
159	Mitzi Edge, Augusta, Ga.	1 up				
148	Penny Hammel, Decatur, Ill.	Hammel,				
156	Julie Kintz, Atlantis, Fla.	3 and 2	Quinlan,			
152	Sally Quinlan, Dennis, Mass.	Quinlan,	4 and 3			
158	Susan Fromuth, Chesterfield, Mo.	1 up		Quinlan,		
152	Cheryl Anne Stacy, Findlay, Ohio	Stacy,		3 and 2		
157	Jamie DeWeese, Rochester, N.Y.	2 up	Taylor			
154	Nancy Taylor, Tampa, Fla.	Taylor,	1 up, 19 holes			
159	Marie-Laure DeLorenzi-Taya, Barcelona, Spain	2 up			Quinlan,	
150	Catherine Conheady, Rochester, N.Y.	Conheady,			2 and 1	
156	Kelli Antolock, Port Angeles, Wash.	3 and 2	Schreck,			
153	Theresa Schreck, Spokane, Wash.	Schreck,	5 and 4			
158	Gina Hull, Jacksonville, Fla.	7 and 6				
152	Jessica Supernaw, Houston, Texas	Supernaw,		Schreck,		
158	Nancy Harris, Minneapolis, Minn.	2 and 1	Shorb,	6 and 5		
155	Connie Shorb, York, Pa.	Shorb,	1 up			
159	Gail Flanagan, Scarsdale, N.Y.	4 and 3				Quinlan,
150	Rita Moore, Dallas, Texas	Moore,			Kostas,	3 and 2
156	Cindy Schreyer, Peachtree City, Ga.	1 up, 19 holes	Rosenthal,		3 and 2	
153	Kim Gardner, Larchmont, N.Y.	Rosenthal,	6 and 4			
158	Jody Rosenthal, Edina, Minn.	6 and 4		Kostas,		
152	Kathy Kostas, Palmdale, Calif.	Kostas,		4 and 3		
157	Cathy Tatum, Atlanta, Ga.	3 and 2	Kostas,			
155	Terri Lyn Carter, Clifton, Ariz.	Carter,	3 and 2			
159	Mary Wilkinson, Melrose, Mass.	2 and 1				
151	Jenny Lidback, Baton Rouge, La.	Lidback,				
157	Barbara Mucha, Parma Heights, Ohio	1 up	Lidback,			
153	Caroline Gowan, Greenville, S.C.	Gowan	3 and 1			
159	Nancy Porter-Engman, Cinnaminson, N.J.	1 up, 19 holes		Lidback,		
152	Heather Farr, Phoenix, Ariz.	Farr,		4 and 3		
158	Beverly D. Moose, Mt. Holly, N.C.	3 and 2	Farr,			
155	Regine Lautens, Geneva, Switzerland	Foyer,	1 up, 19 holes			
159	Martha Foyer, Carmel, Ind.	2 up				

Joanne Pacillo, 2 and 1

*Medalist

1984
EIGHTY-FOURTH WOMEN'S AMATEUR CHAMPIONSHIP

Broadmoor Golf Club, Seattle, Washington, August 13-18
Yardage—6,046. Par 72. +290 Entries, 144 Starters, 64 Qualifiers

Qualifying Score	1st Round (18 Holes)	2nd Round (18 Holes)	3rd Round (18 Holes)	4th Round (18 Holes)	Semifinals (18 Holes)	Final (36 Holes)
*145	Claire Waite, Swindon, England	Kessler,				
155	Kandi Kessler, Charlottesville, Va.	1 up, 20 holes	Kessler,			
153	Connie Shorb, York, Pa.	Shorb,	6 and 5			
157	Lynda Bridge, Hallister, Calif.	2 up		Kessler,		
151	Laurel Kean, Willoughby, Ohio	Ellis,		3 and 1		
157	Joan Ellis, Tampa, Fla.	2 up	Ellis,			
154	Joanne Pacillo, Palos Verdes, Calif	Pacillo,	2 and 1			
158	Jennifer Graff, Philadelphia, Pa.	5 and 4				
150	Barbara Ann Mucha, Parma Heights, Ohio	Mucha,			Slane,	
156	Page Dunlap, Sarasota, Fla.	2 and 1	McCarthy,		3 and 2	
153	Kathleen McCarthy, Fresno, Calif.	McCarthy,	6 and 4			
158	Cathy Mockett, Newport Beach, Calif.	1 up, 20 holes		Slane,		
152	Brenda Pictor, Atlanta, Ga.	Pictor,		3 and 2		
157	Leslie Shannon, Plantation, Fla	3 and 2	Slane,			
155	Kim Saiki, Costa Mesa, Calif.	Slane,	5 and 4			Richard,
159	Carol Slane, Auburn, Calif.	3 and 2				4 and 3
147	Anne Sander, Seattle, Wash.	Sander,				
156	Pamela Pruitt, Quincy, Ill.	6 and 5	Berteotti,			
153	Diane Calkins, Cincinnati, Ohio	Berteotti,	4 and 3			
158	Michele Berteotti, McMurray, Pa.	5 and 4		Berteotti,		
151	Lindy Goggin, Hobart, Tasmania, Australia	Goggin,		1 up, 19 holes		
157	Lee Ann Hammack, Oklahoma City, Okla.	5 and 4	Goggin,			
154	Susan Pager, Daphne, Ala.	Pager,	7 and 6			
158	Kristal Parker, Cable, Ohio	3 and 2			Richard,	
150	Tina Tombs, Bedford, N.H.	Dirks,			5 and 4	
156	Kimberly Dirks, Ft. Worth, Texas	1 up, 19 holes	Farr,			
154	Heather Farr, Scottsdale, Ariz.	Farr,	2 and 1			
158	Kathy Vendetti, Millis, Mass.	1 up		Richard,		
152	Cindy Scholefield, Los Angeles, Calif.	Read,		1 up, 19 holes		
157	Amy Read, Olney, Ill.	1 up	Richard,			
155	Deb Richard, Manhattan, Kans.	Richard,	2 and 1			
159	Lynn Dennison, Marion, Ohio	7 and 6				
147	Lancy Smith, Williamsville, N.Y.	Smith,				
156	Kim Gardner, Garches, France	5 and 4	Schreck,			
153	Danielle Ammaccapane, Phoenix, Ariz.	Schreck,	1 up			
158	Theresa Schreck, Spokane, Wash.	3 and 1				
151	Dorothy Pepper, Saratoga Springs, N.Y.	Brown,		Brown,		
157	Leslie Brown, Charlotte, N.C.	1 up	Brown,	3 and 2		
154	Carol S. Thompson, Sewickley, Pa.	Thompson,	1 up			
158	Lorraine Elder, Arlington, Va.	7 and 5			Rosenthal	
150	Jody Rosenthal, Golden Valley, Minn.	Rosenthal,			5 and 4	
156	Caroline Keggi, Waterbury, Conn.	4 and 3	Rosenthal,			
153	Ann Walsh, San Jose, Calif.	Schreyer,	5 and 4			
158	Cindy Schreyer, Peachtree City, Ga.	5 and 3		Rosenthal,		
152	Kerry Liedes, Maple Valley, Wash.	Yantis,		5 and 4		
157	Susan Yantis, San Antonio, Texas	1 up	Yantis,			
155	Lee Steffens, Springfield, N.J.	Liscio,	4 and 3			Williams,
159	Patricia Liscio, El Cajon, Calif.	4 and 3				1 up
148	Jill Briles, Peoria, Ill.	Cornett,				
156	Pat Cornett, San Francisco, Calif.	1 up, 22 holes	Cornett,			
153	Jenny Lidback, Baton Rouge, La.	Lidback,	1 up			
158	Margaret Kelt, Dallas, Texas	6 and 5		Williams,		
152	Kimberly Williams, Bethesda, Md.	Williams,		1 up		
157	Susan Marchese, Omaha, Neb.	2 and 1	Williams,			
155	Toni Wiesner, Grand Prairie, Texas	Weisner,	4 and 2			
159	Stacy Colborne, San Diego, Calif.	6 and 5			Williams,	
151	Adele Lukken, Tulsa, Okla.	Lukken,			1 up, 19 holes	
157	Pamela Wright, Aboyne, Scotland	3 and 2	Lukken,			
154	Diane Dickman, Modesto, Calif.	Dickman,	2 and 1			
158	Deborach McHaffie, Las Vegas, Nev.	2 and 1		Steiner,		
152	Tracy Kerdyk, Coral Gables, Fla.	Stacy,		1 up		
157	Cheryl Anne Stacey, Findlay, Ohio	3 and 2	Steiner,			
155	Jennifer Steiner, Palos Verdes, Calif.	Steiner,	4 and 2			
159	Mildred Stanley, Los Angeles, Calif.	4 and 3				

Deb Richard, 1 up, 37 holes

*Medalist

+ Record Entry

1985
EIGHTY-FIFTH WOMEN'S AMATEUR CHAMPIONSHIP

Fox Chapel Golf Club, Pittsburgh, Pennsylvania, August 5-10
Yardage—6,128. Par 72. +329 Entries, 120 Starters

Qualifying Score	1st Round (18 Holes)	2nd Round (18 Holes)	3rd Round (18 Holes)	4th Round (18 Holes)	Semifinals (18 Holes)	Final (18 Holes)
*151	Michiko Hattori, Aichi, Japan	Hattori,				
163	Brenda Pictor, Palmetto, Ga.	5 and 4	Hattori,			
159	Valerie Pamard, Paris, France	Pamard,	5 and 4			
159	Kathy Rogerson, Indiana, Pa.	5 and 4		Hattori,		
155	Kathe Kingston, East Point, Ga.	Lawson,		2 and 1		
161	Wendy Lawson, Daphne, Ala.	3 and 1	Cornett,			
156	Pat Cornett, San Francisco, Calif.	Cornett,	6 and 5			
161	Kathy Hart, Miami Beach, Fla.	3 and 2			Hattori,	
153	Lancy Smith, Snyder, N.Y.	Sander,			3 and 2	
162	Anne Sander, Seattle, Wash.	2 and 1	Ralls,			
157	Page Dunlap, Sarasota, Fla.	Ralls,	3 and 2			
160	Julie Ralls, Redmond, Wash.	5 and 4		K. Kessler,		
154	Jamie DeWeese, Rochester, N.Y.	DeWeese,		3 and 2		
162	Michelle Mackall, Kensington, Md.	1 up	K. Kessler,			
157	Kandi Kessler, Charlottesville, Va.	K. Kessler,	3 and 1			
160	Jill Briles, Peoria Heights, Ill.	1 up, 19 holes				Hattori,
152	Marianne Morris, Middletown, Ohio	Morris,				3 and 2
162	Jane Mennie, Australia	3 and 2	Lapaire,			
159	Sophie Lapaire, Los Angeles, Calif.	Lapaire,	3 and 2			
159	Elizabeth Fry, Adelphi, Md.	5 and 3		Michanowicz,		
155	Michelle Michanowicz, Pittsburgh, Pa.	Michanowicz,		4 and 3		
161	Nanci Bowen, Tifton, Ga.	1 up	Michanowicz,			
156	Martha Foyer, Carmel, Ind.	Foyer,	4 and 3			
160	Laura Mays, Augusta, Ga.	2 and 1			Gardner,	
152	Theresa Schreck, Spokane, Wash.	Schreck,			2 and 1	
162	Cecilia D'Algue, Paris, France	3 and 2	Dolan,			
158	Clare Dolan, Gaithersburg, Md.	Dolan,	2 and 1			
159	Cindy Mah-Lyford, Stratton Mountain, Vt.	2 and 1		Gardner,		
155	Cindy Schreyer, Peachtree City, Ga.	Schreyer,		5 and 3		
161	Nancy Kessler, Portland, Ore.	3 and 2	Gardner,			
156	Adele Lukken, Tulsa, Okla.	Gardner,	1 up, 21 holes			
161	Kim Gardner, Paris, France	4 and 2				
*151	Cheryl Stacy, Findlay, Ohio	Stacy,				
163	Lisa Marino, West Allen Park, Mich.	1 up	Stacy,			
159	Jane Kank, Elyria, Ohio	Thompson,	5 and 3			
159	Carol Semple Thompson, Sewickley, Pa.	3 and 2		Stacy,		
155	Dottie Pepper, Gansevoort, N.Y.	Pepper,		2 and 1		
161	Peggy Kirby, Sioux Falls, S.C.	4 and 3	Pepper,			
156	Brenda Corrie, Dominican Republic	Corrie,	3 and 1			
160	Kristin Lofye, Venice, Fla.	5 and 4			Stacy,	
153	Kim Williams, Bethesda, Md.	Williams,			5 and 4	
162	Jodi Figley, Aliquippa, Pa.	1 up	Baxter,			
158	Julie Baxter, Normal, Ill.	Baxter,	1 up			
159	Connie McCain, Crockett, Texas	4 and 3		Brennan,		
154	Diane Dickman, Modesto, Calif.	Lidback,		1 up, 20 holes		
161	Jenny Lidback, Baton Rouge, La.	3 and 1	Brennan,			
157	Martha Leach, Savannah, Ga.	Brennan,	1 up			
160	Valerie Brennan, Quincy, Ill.	6 and 4				Stacy,
152	Kathleen McCarthy, Fresno, Calif.	Logan,				1 up
162	Jody Logan, Sandusky, Ohio	3 and 1	Logan,			
159	Graciela Quintana, Venezuela	Quintana,	3 and 1			
159	Robin Waterhouse, Sanibel Island, Fla.	7 and 6		Ammaccapane,		
155	Amy Read, Olney, Ill.	Read,		1 up		
161	Caroline Keggi, Middlebury, Conn.	3 and 2	Ammaccapane,			
156	Danielle Ammaccapane, Phoenix, Ariz.	Ammaccapane,	1 up			
160	Pat Milton, Akron, Ohio	2 up			Ammaccapane,	
153	Leslie Shannon, Plantation, Fla.	Shannon,			2 and 1	
162	Lisa Neboda, Plantation, Fla.	1 up	Scholefield,			
158	Cindy Scholefield, Los Angeles, Calif.	Scholefield,	2 and 1			
159	Sarah Dekraay, Racine, Wis.	1 up		Scholefield,		
154	Laurel Kean, Painesville, Ohio	Kean,		1 up, 20 holes		
161	Carey Ruffer, Conroe, Texas	2 and 1	Kerdyk,			
157	Tracy Kerdyk, Coral Gables, Fla.	Kerdyk,	1 up			
160	Vickie Moran, Fairmont, W.Va.	3 and 2				

Michiko Hattori, 5 and 4

*Co-medalists
+Record Entry

1986
EIGHTY-SIXTH WOMEN'S AMATEUR CHAMPIONSHIP

Pasatiempo Golf Club, Santa Cruz, California, August 11-16
Yardage—6,005. Par 72. +387 Entries, 150 Starters, 64 Qualifiers

Qualifying Score	1st Round (18 Holes)	2nd Round (18 Holes)	3rd Round (18 Holes)	4th Round (18 Holes)	Semifinals (18 Holes)	Final (36 Holes)
*148	Pearl Sinn, Bellflower, Calif.	Sinn, 3 and 2				
162	Lorie Wilkes, Bartow, Fla.		Sinn, 5 and 3			
157	Chris Newton, Whitefish, Mont.	Edelen, 4 and 3				
157	Cathy Edelen, Lexington, Ky.			Thompson, 1 up		
154	Carol Semple Thompson, Pittsburgh, Pa.	Thompson, 2 and 1				
160	Lynda Wimberly, Apopka, Fla.		Thompson, 3 and 2			
154	Kimberly Williams, Potomac, Md.	McKenna, 2 up				
160	Mary McKenna, County Dublin, Ireland				McCarthy, 1 up	
151	Kimberly Gardner, Larchmont, N.Y.	Gardner, 1 up				
161	Lynne Scalberg, Aptos, Calif.		Gardner, 1 up, 21 holes			
155	Cindy Scholefield, Malibu, Calif.	Kerdyk, 4 and 3				
159	Tracy Kerdyk, Coral Gables, Fla.			McCarthy, 7 and 6		
152	Dana Lofland, Oxnard, Calif.	Kostas, 4 and 3				
161	Kathleen Kostas, Palmdale, Calif.		McCarthy, 5 and 4			
155	Kathleen McCarthy, Fresno, Calif.	McCarthy, 4 and 3				
159	Melissa McNamara, Tulsa, Okla.					McCarthy, 1 up
150	Danielle Ammaccapane, Phoenix, Ariz.	Ammaccapane, 4 and 2				
162	Kathy Quelland, Berlin, Md.		Ammaccapane, 2 and 1			
157	Cathy Mockett, Newport Beach, Calif.	Mockett, 2 and 1				
159	Jodi Ann Logan, Norwalk, Ohio			Ammaccapane, 6 and 5		
153	Claire Hourihane, County Dublin, Ireland	Hourihane, 3 and 2				
160	Mildred Stanley, Escondido, Calif.		Arnold, 2 and 1			
154	Sarah Dekraay, Racine, Wis.	Arnold, 1 up, 20 holes				
160	Dana Arnold, Modesto, Calif.				Ammaccapane, 4 and 2	
151	Caroline Keggi, Middlebury, Conn.	Keggi, 3 and 2				
162	Lois Ledbetter, Rockville, Md.		Keggi, 2 and 1			
156	Cindy Schreyer, Peachtree City, Ga.	Schreyer, 1 up, 19 holes				
159	Brenda Corrie, Santo Domingo, Dominican Rep.			Keggi, 4 and 3		
152	Sarah Lebrun, Owings Mills, Md.	Lebrun, 2 and 1				
161	Valerie Pamard, Paris, France		Cathrein, 2 and 1			
154	Ginger Brown, Hope, Ark.	Cathrein, 2 up				
160	Kim Cathrein, Salinas, Calif.					
*148	Michiko Hattori, Nagoya, Japan	Hattori, 6 and 5				
162	Leslie Shannon, Fort Lauderdale, Fla.		Johnson, 2 up			
157	Karen Davies, Berkshire, England	Johnson, 3 and 2				
158	Trish Johnson, Glamorgan, Wales			Johnson, 3 and 1		
153	Kandi Kessler, Charlottesville, Va.	Kessler, 3 and 2				
160	Cara Andreoli, Wethersfield, Conn.		Smith, 1 up, 19 holes			
160	Lancy Smith, Snyder, N.Y.	Smith, 4 and 3				
160	Donna Andrews, Lynchburg, Va.				Prono, 1 up, 19 holes	
151	Kathleen Rogerson, Indiana, Pa.	Rogerson, 1 up, 19 holes				
161	Sherry Andonian, Camarillo, Calif.		Prono, 2 and 1			
158	Flori Prono, Northridge, Calif.	Prono, 2 and 1				
159	Patricia Ehrhart, Dunlap, Ill.			Prono, 2 and 1		
152	Dottie Mochrie, Gansevoort, N.Y.	Mochrie, 2 and 1				
161	Pat Milton, Monroe Falls, Ohio		Mochrie, 6 and 4			
154	Susan Marchese, Omaha, Neb.	Cornett, 2 and 1				
159	Patricia Cornett, Greenbrae, Calif.					Cockerill, 2 and 1
149	Michelle Dobek, Chicopee, Mass.	Dobek, 3 and 2				
162	Joan Pitcock, Fresno, Calif.		Cornelius, 1 up			
157	Robin Hood, Oscola, Ind.	Cornelius, 2 and 1				
158	Kay Cornelius, Tucson, Ariz.			Redman, 4 and 3		
153	Michele Redman, Zanesville, Ohio	Redman, 4 and 3				
160	Karen Noble, Brookside, N.J.		Redman, 6 and 4			
154	Julie Ralls, Woodinville, Wash.	Ralls, 5 and 3				
160	Marilyn Horn, Mesa, Ariz.				Cockerill, 1 up	
151	Kay Cockerill, Los Gatos, Calif.	Cockerill, 4 and 2				
161	Libby Akers, French Lick, Ind.		Cockerill, 3 and 2			
156	Marie de Lorenzi-Taya, Paris, France	de Lorenzi-Taya, 3 and 2				
159	Ellie Gibson, Houston, Texas			Cockerill, 3 and 1		
152	Cecilia Mourgue d'Algue, Paris, France	Mourgue d'Algue, 4 and 2				
161	Aiko Hashimoto, Tokushima, Japan		Mourgue d'Algue, 7 and 6			
154	Kellie Stenzel, Geneva, N.Y.	Michanowicz, 1 up, 21 holes				
159	Michele Michanowicz, Fox Chapel, Pa.					

Kay Cockerill, 9 and 7

*Co-medalist
+Record Entry

1987
EIGHTY-SEVENTH WOMEN'S AMATEUR CHAMPIONSHIP

Rhode Island Country Club, Barrington, Rhode Island, August 17-23
Yardage—6,171. Par 73. 359 Entries, 150 Starters, 64 Qualifiers

Qualifying Score	1st Round (18 Holes)	2nd Round (18 Holes)	3rd Round (18 Holes)	4th Round (18 Holes)	Semifinals (18 Holes)	Final (36 Holes)
*147	Michiko Hattori, Nagoya, Japan	Hattori, 2 up				
160	Toni Wiesner, Fort Worth, Texas		Hattori, 3 and 2			
155	Kathryn Peterson, Plantation, Fla.	Peterson, 3 and 2				
155	Jodi Figley, Aliquippa, Pa.			Thompson, 4 and 3		
152	Sarah Lebrun, Garrison, Md.	Lebrun, 6 and 5				
157	Graciela Quintana, Caracas, Venezuela		Thompson, 1 up			
152	Carol Semple Thompson, Sewickley, Pa.	Thompson, 3 and 2				
157	Jean Zedlitz, Pleasanton, Calif.				Cockerill, 6 and 5	
150	Kay Cockerill, Los Gatos, Calif.	Cockerill, 3 and 2				
159	Michele Michanowicz, Oakmont, Pa.		Cockerill, 1 up			
154	Brenda Corrie, Santo Domingo, D.R.	Corrie, 1 up				
156	Asako Kita, Tochiga, Japan			Cockerill, 1 up		
150	Michele Lyford, Redlands, Calif.	Lyford, 3 and 2				
159	Kristin Lofye, Venice, Fla.		Lyford, 1 up			
154	Phyllis Preuss, Colorado Springs, Colo.	Arnold, 4 and 3				
156	Dana Arnold, Ripon, Calif.					Cockerill, 3 and 1
149	Robin Weiss, Lake Worth, Fla.	Thomas, 1 up				
159	Sue Thomas, Texarkana, Texas		Thomas, 7 and 6			
155	Courtney Myhrum, Waccabuc, N.Y.	Ruffer, 2 and 1				
156	Carey Ruffer, Montgomery, Texas			Sander, 6 and 4		
152	Anne Sander, Seattle, Wash.	Sander, 5 and 3				
158	Jean Bartholomew, Garden City, N.Y.		Sander, 4 and 3			
153	Lisa Marino, Grosse Ile, Mich.	Marino, 4 and 3				
157	Kristin Ericson, Isle of Palms, S.C.				Bowen, 5 and 4	
149	Pearl Sinn, Bellflower, Calif.	Scholefield, 1 up				
159	Cindy Scholefield, Los Angeles, Calif.		Scholefield, 7 and 6			
154	Diane Headings, Palm Beach, Fla.	Headings, 4 and 2				
156	Sarah Dekraay, Martinsville, Ind.			Bowen, 1 up, 23 holes		
151	Regine Lautens, Geneva, Switzerland	Hammack, 1 up, 19 holes				
158	Lee Ann Hammack, Oklahoma City, Okla.		Bowen, 2 and 1			
153	Katherine Rogerson, Indiana, Pa.	Bowen, 5 and 4				
156	Nanci Bowen, Tifton, Ga.					
*147	Tracy Kerdyk, Miami, Fla.	Kerdyk, 2 up				
159	Lynda Wimberly, Longwood, Fla.		Kerdyk, 2 and 1			
155	Kimberly Lasken, Whittier, Calif.	Lasken, 5 and 4				
155	Tracy Chapman, Martinsville, Ind.			Kerdyk, 1 up, 22 holes		
152	Susan Wineinger, Green Bay, Wis.	Redman, 4 and 2				
157	Michele Redman, Martinsville, Ind.		Saiki, 2 and 1			
152	Patricia Cornett, San Francisco, Calif.	Saiki, 2 and 1				
157	Kim Saiki, Redwood City, Calif.				Kerdyk, 5 and 4	
150	Dana Lofland, Oxnard, Calif.	Lofland, 1 up, 20 holes				
159	Kathleen McCarthy, Fresno, Calif.		Shannon, 3 and 2			
154	Leslie Shannon, Plantation, Fla.	Shannon, 2 and 1				
156	Caroline Keggi, Waterbury, Conn.			Shannon, 2 up		
150	Blue Kinander, Medinah, Ill.	McKenzie, 1 up				
158	Carolyn McKenzie, Paoli, Pa.		Orley, 1 up			
154	Ellie Gibson, Houston, Texas	Orley, 1 up				
156	Evelyn Orley, Kashacht, Switzerland					Kerdyk, 3 and 2
148	Susan Ginter, Appleton, Wis.	Ginter, 1 up, 21 holes				
159	Cathy Mockett, Newport Beach, Calif.		Kirouac, 4 and 2			
155	Nancy Kessler, Portland, Ore.	Kirouac, 3 and 1				
155	Martha Kirouac, Duluth, Ga.			Milton, 4 and 3		
152	Christina Barrett, Baltimore, Md.	Milton, 3 and 3				
157	Pat Milton, Akron, Ohio		Milton, 5 and 4			
153	Karen Engberg, Laguna Niguel, Calif.	Slaughter, 6 and 4				
157	Susan Slaughter, Blacksburg, Va.				Milton, 1 up	
150	Dina Ammaccapane, Paradise Valley, Ariz.	Koyama, 2 up				
159	Debbi Koyama, Industry City, Calif.		Koyama, 6 and 4			
154	Michelle Estill, Phoenix, Ariz.	Estill, 1 up				
156	Tiffany Maurycy, Schenectady, N.Y.			Koyama, 4 and 2		
151	Anne Cain, Athens, Ga.	Silverburg, 4 and 2				
158	Debbie Silverberg, Absecon, N.J.		Silverberg, 2 and 1			
154	Jane Kang, Elyria, Ohio	Kang, 2 up				
156	Diane Rama, Oreland, Pa.					

Kay Cockerill, 3 and 2

* Co-medalists

1988
EIGHTY-EIGTH WOMEN'S AMATEUR CHAMPIONSHIP

Minikahda Club, Minneapolis, Minnesota, August 8-13
Yardage—6,172. Par 72. 357 Entries, 147 Starters, 64 Qualifiers

Qualifying Score	1st Round (18 Holes)	2nd Round (18 Holes)	3rd Round (18 Holes)	4th Round (18 Holes)	Semifinals (18 Holes)	Final (36 Holes)
*140	Pearl Sinn, Bellflower, Calif.	Sinn,				
157	Sophie Louapre, St. Nom La Breteche, France	4 and 3	Sinn,			
154	Nadia Ste-Marie, Lake City, Fla.	Ste-Marie,	4 and 3			
154	Cindy Scholefield, Los Angeles, Calif.	3 and 2		Sinn,		
150	Evelyn Orley, Kusnacht, Switzerland	Orley,		3 and 2		
156	Missy Farr, Scottsdale, Ariz.	1 up, 19 holes	Orley,			
150	Amanda Nealy, Grants Pass, Ore.	Nealy,	1 up			
156	Sarah Lebrun, Garrison, Md.	3 and 2			Sinn,	
147	Jean Bartholomew, Garden City, N.Y.	Bartholomew,			1 up, 20 holes	
157	Caroline Bourtayre, Soustons, France	4 and 3	Robbins,			
152	Kelly Robbins, Mount Pleasant, Mich.	Robbins,	2 up			
155	Elizabeth Bowman, Bonita, Calif.	2 and 1		Robbins,		
148	Katie Peterson, Plantation, Fla.	Peterson,		2 and 1		
157	Phyllis Preuss, Colorado Springs, Colo.	2 and 1	Saiki,			
152	Nancy Harris, Chaska, Minn.	Saiki,	2 and 1			
155	Kim Saiki, Redwood City, Calif.	4 and 3				Sinn,
145	Christina Barrett, Baltimore, Md.	Barrett,				6 and 5
157	Alice Plain, South Bend, Ind.	5 and 4	Barrett,			
154	Pam McCloskey, Boca Raton, Fla.	Cain,	3 and 2			
154	Anne Marie Cain, Charlotte, N.C.	2 up		Milton,		
149	Susan Ginter, Appleton, Wis.	Milton,		1 up, 19 holes		
155	Pat Milton, Akron, Ohio	1 up, 19 holes	Milton,			
152	Deborah Lee, Martinsville, Ind.	Nedoba,	6 and 4			
155	Lisa Nedoba, Plantation, Fla.	2 and 1			Milton,	
147	Sheila Luginbuel, Afton, Okla.	Luginbuel,			2 and 1	
157	Ann Zahn, Chaska, Minn.	8 and 7	Bourson,			
153	Susan Wineinger, Green Bay, Wis.	Bourson,	1 up			
154	Delphine Bourson, St. Nom La Breteche, France	1 up, 23 holes		Bourson,		
149	Kate Hughes, White Bear Lake, Minn.	Hughes,		1 up		
156	Donna Andrews, Lynchburg, Va.	1 up	Hughes,			
152	Jodi Figley, Aliquippa, Pa.	Pamard,	3 and 2			
155	Valerie Pamard, Saint Cloud, France	1 up, 19 holes				
143	Michiko Hattori, Nagoya, Japan	Hattori,				
157	Elizabeth Haines, Ardmore, Pa.	7 and 6	Hattori,			
154	Terri Thompson, Savannah, Ga.	T. Thompson,	6 and 5			
154	Loretta Coleman, Greenwich, Conn.	6and 4		Hattori,		
150	Brandie Burton, San Bernardino, Calif.	Burton,		1 up, 20 holes		
156	Loren Milhench, Marion, Mass.	4 and 3	Burton,			
151	Vivian Overturf, Seal Beach, Calif.	Platt,	1 up			
155	Margaret Platt, Rye, N.Y.	2 and 1			Hattori,	
147	Cissye Meeks, Greenwood, Miss.	Keggi,			1 up	
157	Caroline Keggi, Waterbury, Conn.	1 up	Keggi,			
153	Robin Weiss, Lake Worth, Fla.	Weiss,	1 up			
155	Cathy Mockett, Newport Beach Calif.	1 up, 19 holes		Keggi,		
148	Leslie Shannon, Plantation, Fla.	Shannon,		6 and 4		
156	Lynn Bradley, Huntsville, Ala.	3and 2	Shannon,			
152	Kiernan Prechtl, Ormond Beach, Fla.	Smith,	2 and 1			
155	Lancy Smith, Williamsville, N.Y.	5 and 3				Noble,
145	Carol Semple Thompson, Sewickley, Pa.	C. Thompson				1 up, 19 holes
157	Kim Cathrein, Salinas, Calif.	3 and 2	C. Thompson,			
154	Christy Erb, Bonita, Calif.	Rogers,	2 and 1			
154	Liz Rogers, Virginia Beach, Va.	8 and 6		Noble,		
149	Karen Noble, Convent Station, N.J.	Noble,		1 up		
156	Tanna Lee, Fort Smith, Ark.	4 and 3	Noble,			
152	Michelle Wooding, Fircrest, Wash.	Golden,	3 and 1			
155	Katherine Golden, Jasper, Texas	1 up			Noble,	
147	Patricia Cornett, San Francisco, Calif.	Cornett,			5 and4	
157	Andrea Dornin, Miami Beach, Fla.	5 and 4	Cornett,			
153	Lorie Wilkes, Gainesville, Fal.	Weisner,	4 and 3			
155	Toni Weisner, Forth Worth Texas	5 and 4		Sander,		
149	Pat Hurst, Pleasanton, Calif.	Hurst,		6 and 5		
156	Peggy Kelly, Madison, Wis.	6 and 4	Sander,			
152	Anne Sander, Seattle, Wash.	Sander,	4 and 3			
155	Debbie Silverberg, Absecon, N.J.	3 and 2				

Pearl Sinn, 6 and 5

*Medalist

1989
EIGHTY-NINTH WOMEN'S AMATEUR CHAMPIONSHIP

Pinehurst Country Club (No. 2 Course), Pinehurst, North Carolina, July 31-August 5
Yardage—6,184. Par 73. 376 Entries, 143 Starters, 64 Qualifiers

Qualifying Score	1st Round (18 Holes)	2nd Round (18 Holes)	3rd Round (18 Holes)	4th Round (18 Holes)	Semifinals (18 Holes)	Final (18 Holes)
*143	Pat Hurst, San Leandro, Calif.	Figley,				
157	Jodi Figley, Aliquippa, Pa.	4 and 3	LeBrun,			
153	Sheila Luginbuel, Vinita, Okla.	LeBrun	2 up			
153	Sarah LeBrun, Owings Mills, Md.	3 and 2		Mockett,		
150	Leslie Shannon, Fort Lauderdale, Fla.	Shannon,		4 and 3		
154	La Ree Sugg, Petersburg, Va.	3 and 2	Mockett,			
150	Cathy Mockett, Newport Beach, Calif.	Mockett,	2 and 1			
154	Karen Weiss, St. Paul, Minn.	2 and 1			Mockett,	
148	Nanci Bowen, Athens, Ga.	Bowen			4 and 3	
155	Cathy Cook, Las Vegas, Nev.	2 up	Sander,			
152	Tanna Lee, Fort Smith, Ariz.	Sander,	4 and 3			
154	Anne Sander, Seattle, Wash.	3 and 2		Prechtl,		
149	Debbi Koyama, Monrovia, Calif.	Biron,		3 and 1		
155	Eve-Lyne Biron, Canada	20 holes	Prechtl,			
152	Keirnan Prechtl, Ormond Beach, Fla.	Prechtl,	2 and 1			
154	Page Marsh, Jamestown, N.C.	1 up				Burton,
145	Michiko Hattori, Nagoya, Japan	Gill,				1 up
156	Tonya Gill, Stone Mountain, Ga.	2 and 1	Gill,			
152	Missy Tuck, Trussville, Ala.	Tuck,	19 holes			
153	Stacey Arnold, Glen Ellyn, Ill.	1 up		Burton		
149	Brandie Burton, Rialto, Calif.	Burton,		4 and 3		
155	Elizabeth Bowman, Bonita, Calif.	7 and 6	Burton,			
150	Shirley Trier, Akron, Ohio	Robbins,	4 and 3			
154	Kelly Robbins, Mt. Pleasant, Mich.	5 and 3			Burton,	
147	Margaret Kelt, Dallas, Texas	Miller,			6 and 5	
156	Chris Miller, Sacramento, Calif.	1 up	Miller,			
152	Anna Acker, Marshfield, Wis.	Acker,	2 and 1			
153	Karen Noble, Brookside, N.J.	2 up		Miller,		
149	Leslye McDermott, Naples, Fla.	Smith,		3 and 2		
155	Lancy Smith, Snyder, N.Y.	4 and 2	Smith,			
151	Margie Muzik, Naperville, Ill.	Rundle,	2 and 1			
154	Emma Rundle, Coral Springs, Fla.	4 and 2				
144	Donna Andrews, Lynchburg, Va.	Andrews,				
157	Nancy Harris, Minnetonka, Minn.	3 and 2	Andrews,			
153	Jamille Jose, Carmichael, Calif.	Jose,	19 holes			
153	Loren Milhench, Marion, Mass.	3 and 2		Peterson,		
149	Debbie Eckroth, Harrisburg, Pa.	A. Moore,		4 and 3		
155	Adele Moore, Dallas, Texas	19 holes	Peterson,			
150	Katie Peterson, Plantation, Fla.	Peterson,	5 and 4			
154	Tina Paternostro, Williamsport, Pa.	3 and 2			Goetze,	
147	Vicki Goetze, Hull, Ga.	Goetze,			5 and 4	
156	Pam Holcombe, Quincy, Ill.	6 and 5	Goetze,			
152	Patricia Milton, Akron, Ohio	Milton,	1 up			
153	Diane Rama, Philadelphia, Pa.	1 up		Goetze,		
149	Robin Weiss, Palm Beach, Fla.	R. Weiss,		1 up		
155	Pam McCloskey, Boca Raton, Fla.	5 and 4	Thompson,			
152	Terri Thompson, Savannah, Ga.	Thompson,	7 and 6			
154	Wendy Modic, Chula Vista, Calif.	1 up				Goetze,
144	Jean Zedlitz, Pleasanton, Calif.	Zedlitz,				5 and 3
157	Paula Brzostowski, Pinehurst, N.C.	2 and 1	Zedlitz,			
153	Jennifer Myers, Bloomington, Ind.	Smither,	2 and 1			
153	Debbie Smither, Sarasota, Fla.	1 up		Platt,		
149	Dina Ammaccapane, Phoenix, Ariz.	Hanyak,		5 and 4		
155	Mary Hanyak, Boynton Beach Fla.	19 holes	Platt,			
150	Margaret Platt, Hastings-on-Hudson, NY	Platt,	4 and 2			
154	Kathy Moore, Argyle, Texas	4 and 3			C. Thompson,	
147	Carol Thompson, Sewickley, Pa.	C. Thompson,			1 up	
156	Jennifer Buchanan, Kimberly, Wis.	3 and 2	C. Thompson,			
152	Phyllis Preuss, Colorado Springs, Co.	Preuss,	3 and 2			
153	Natalie Galligan, West Newton, Mass.	1 up		C. Thompson,		
149	Suzanne Green, Franklin, Miss.	Bradley,		6 and 5		
155	Lynn Bradley, Huntsville, Ala.	4 and 3	D. Lee,			
152	Kate Hughes, Woodbury, Minn.	D. Lee,	5 and 4			
154	Deborah Lee, Canada	1 up				

Vicki Goetze, 4 and 3

*Medalist

1990
NINETIETH WOMEN'S AMATEUR CHAMPIONSHIP

Canoe Brook Country Club, Summit, New Jersey, August 6-11
Yardage—6,086. Par 72. 384 Entries, 147 Starters, 64 Qualifiers

Qualifying Score	1st Round (18 Holes)	2nd Round (18 Holes)	3rd Round (18 Holes)	4th Round (18 Holes)	Semifinals (18 Holes)	Final (18 Holes)
*144	Vicki Goetze, Hull, Ga.	Goetze, 3 and 2				
159	Pat Milton, Munroe Falls, Ohio		Geotze, 2 and 1			
155	Page Marsh Lea, Jamestown, N.C.	Marsh Lea 5 and 4				
155	Toni Wiesner, Fort Worth, Tex.			Goetze, 3 and 2		
152	Dana Arnold, Modesto, Calif.	Hartley, 4 and 3				
157	Polly Hartley, Oceanside, Calif.		Koch, 2 and 1			
152	Martina Koch, Germany	Koch, 2 and 1				
157	Gail Flanagan, New York, N.Y.				Hurst, 1 up	
150	Robin Weiss, Palm Beach, Fla.	Weiss 3 and 2				
159	Leslye McDermott, Naples, Fla.		Weiss, 1 up			
153	Julie Hall, England	Hall, 2 and 1				
155	Jane Fitzgerald, Kensington, Md.			Hurst, 7 and 6		
151	Pat Hurst, San Leandro, Calif.	Hurst, 1 up				
159	Jodi Figley, Aliquippa, Pa.		Hurst, 3 and 1			
153	Cathy Schaeffer, Fort Myers, Fla.	Peterson, 3 and 2				
156	Katie Peterson, Plantation, Fla.					Hurst, 2 up
145	Carol Semple Thompson, Sewickley, Pa.	Cornett-Iker, 1 up				
159	Pat Cornett-Iker, Corte Madera, Calif.		Bourson, 2 and 1			
154	Delphine Bourson, France	Bourson, 6 and 5				
155	Kristi Coats, Hattiesburg, Miss.			Bourson 3 and 2		
151	Debbie Eckroth, Harrisburg, Pa.	Slaughter, 7 and 5				
158	Susan Slaughter, Floyd, Va.		Slaughter, 5 and 4			
153	Aline Van Derhaegen, Belgium	Van Derhaegen, 22 holes				
157	Jane Egan, Sioux Falls, S.D.				Bourson, 5 and 4	
148	Amy Fruhwirth, Phoenix, Ariz.	Fruhwirth, 22 holes				
159	Karen Weiss, Roselawn, Minn.		Dobson, 2 and 1			
154	Helen Dobson, England	Dobson, 21 holes				
155	Helen Wadsworth, England			Dobson, 3 and 2		
151	Brandie Burton, Rialto, Calif.	Rogers, 21 holes				
158	Liz Rogers, Bradenton, Fla.		Rogers, 2 and 1			
153	Leslie Shannon, Fort Lauderdale, Fla.	Cain, 3 and 1				
157	Anne Marie Cain, Matthews, N.C.					Hurst, 37 holes
145	Kelly Robbins, Mt. Pleasant, Mich.	Robbins, 1 up				
159	Jill McGill, Denver, Colo.		Robbins, 7 and 6			
155	Janice Golden, Fall River, Mass.	Dunn, 1 up				
155	Moira Dunn, Utica, N.Y.			Robbins, 1 up		
152	Deborah Lee, Canada	Lee, 2 and 1				
157	Virginia Derby, York, Ala.		Lee, 2 and 1			
152	Terrill Samuel, Canada	Thomas, 1 up				
157	Vicki Thomas, Wales				Davis, 19 holes	
149	Kate Hughes, Woodbury, Minn.	Hughes, 4 and 3				
159	Carolyn Creekmore, Dallas, Tex		Hughes, 1 up			
153	Linzi Fletcher, England	Fletcher, 4 and 3				
155	Shannon Hardesty, Bloomington, Ind.			Davis, 3 and 2		
151	Stephanie Davis, Bainbridge Is., Wash.	Davis, 3 and 1				
158	Catriona Lambert, Scotland		Davis, 19 holes			
153	Susan Daou, Fort Pierce, Fla.	Daou, 1 up				
156	Erin O'Neil, Zephyrhills, Fla.					Davis, 4 and 2
145	Karen Noble, Brookside, N.J.	Noble, 6 and 5				
159	Lancy Smith, Snyder, N.Y.		Noble, 4 and 3			
155	Margaret Platt, Hasting, N.Y.	Platt, 1 up				
155	Kimberly Tyrer, Frankfort, N.Y.			Noble, 3 and 2		
151	Sally Voss Krueger, San Francisco, Calif.	Tobin, 19 holes				
158	Anne Marie Tobin, Peabody, Mass.		Tobin, 2 up			
153	Terri Thompson, Savannah, Ga.	Thompson, 4 and 3				
157	Elaine Farquharson, Scotland				Noble, 5 and 4	
148	Cathy Mockett, Tulsa, Okla.	Lee, 2 and 1				
159	Tanna Lee, Fort Smith, Ark.		Lee, 2 and 1			
154	Sarah Ingram, Nashville, Tenn.	Ingram, 6 and 4				
155	Marion McInerney, Dedham, Mass.			Lee, 20 holes		
151	Debbi Koyama, Monrovia, Calif.	Moore, 1 up				
158	Patty Moore, Charlotte, N.C.		Imrie, 4 and 2			
153	Kathryn Imrie, Scotland	Imrie, 3 and 2				
156	Jennifer Myers, Lancaster, Pa.					

*Medalist

WOMEN'S OPEN CHAMPIONSHIP

CHAMPIONSHIP TROPHY

Presented in July, 1953 by the

UNITED STATES GOLF ASSOCIATION

HISTORY

1981—Pat Bradley, 30, of Nashua, New Hampshire, won the 1981 Championship with a record score of 279, nine under par, at the La Grange (Illinois) Country Club. She was the third consecutive Champion to lower the Women's Open 72-hole scoring record. In 1979, Jerilyn Britz had brought it down from 287 to 284. One year later, Amy Alcott dropped it to 280. Bradley played absolutely stunning golf, yet won by only one stroke over Beth Daniel, who had 280. Bradley had rounds of 71-74-68-66 to Daniel's 69-74-69-68. It was the first USGA title for Bradley, whose best previous Open performance was a tie for fourth in 1977. From 1953, when the USGA assumed sponsorship, through 1980, par for 72 holes in the Women's Open had been bettered only seven times. In this Championship alone, five players finished below par, including Bradley, Daniel, Kathy Whitworth at 284, and Cynthia Hill and Bonnie Lauer, both with 287. When the 1981 Women's Open was over, 33 rounds had been played under par, the most ever. The first round co-leaders were Whitworth, playing in her 23rd Women's Open, and Daniel with 69s. Britz and Shelley Hamlin were one stroke back at 70. Bradley, Donna Caponi, Marlene Floyd, Dorothy Germain and Debbie Massey were in a group at 71. After the second round Whitworth with a 70 still had a share of the lead at 139, but was tied with Lauer, who shot 67. They were four strokes ahead of Floyd, Daniel and Massey at 143. Bradley, with a 74, fell six shots off the pace at 145. The third round produced no dramatic changes. Whitworth managed a 71, her third straight sub-par score, and clung to a one stroke lead at 210. Lauer at 211 and Daniel at 212 were close behind. Bradley, who cut her deficit in half with a 68, was fourth at 213. After nine holes of the final round, it was clear that the Championship would be settled between Bradley and Daniel. Paired together, they played perhaps the most spirited final round the Women's Open has known. Bradley broke the deadlock at the 15th hole with a birdie putt of nearly 70 feet. Daniel had all she could do to save par from a greenside bunker. But at the 16th, Daniel hooked her 4-iron to the left of the green and dropped a stroke to par. Bradley's lead was now two strokes. Daniel rallied at the par 3 17th hole with a birdie putt of eight feet, and so she was only one behind with the 18th, a 455-yard par 5, coming up. Knowing that she possibly could reach the green in two, Daniel played a big tee shot and then went for the green with a 3-wood. However, the ball hooked to the left of the green. Bradley's first two shots left her neatly in front of the green. She then lofted a soft sand wedge shot just two feet from the hole. Knowing that she would have to hole her pitch shot for an eagle, Daniel nearly did just that, barely missing the hole. Both players made their short putts for birdies; but Bradley, having played a glorious round of 66, was the winner. Daniel, with a superb 68, settled for second place. Whitworth, who finished third, became the first woman golfer to have won more than $1 million in a career. Fifty-eight professionals and 10 amateurs returned scores for 72 holes. The 36 hole cut was at 153, nine over par. Kathy Baker of Clover, South Carolina, was the low amateur with a 299 total. The Championship received a record 434 entries. A record $148,670 in prize money was awarded. A total of 37,900 spectators attended the four days of the Championship, second only to the 41,200 attendance record established in 1979.

1982—Janet Alex, 26, of West Sunbury, Pennsylvania, the only player to finish under par, won the Women's Open Championship with a score of 283, five under par, at the Del Paso Country Club, in Sacramento, California. It was her first victory as a professional. For the first time in Women's Open history, four players tied for second. They included former Women's Open Champion Sandra Haynie, former Women's Amateur Champion Donna H. White, two-time Women's Open and five-time Women's Amateur Champion JoAnne Carner, and two-time Women's Amateur Champion Beth Daniel. All four players finished at 289, one over par. Mrs. Alex, whose best previous finish in the Women's Open was a tie for 26th in 1981, had rounds of 70-73-72-68—283. Mrs. Carner, who earned her first Women's Amateur title at Del Paso in 1957, was the first-round leader, with 69, three under par. Mrs. Alex, Mrs. White, Miss Haynie, and Vicki Tabor were one stroke behind at 70. Mrs. Carner built her lead to three strokes by the end of the second round. She shot 70 for a 36-hole score of 139, five under par, tying the Women's Open record set by Donna Caponi and Carol Mann, in 1970, and equalled by Kathy Whitworth and Bonnie Lauer, in 1981. Beth Daniel moved into second place at 142 with a second consecutive 71. Mrs. Alex held third place with a 73 for 143. Mrs. Carner lost the lead in the third round with 75, for a total of 214. Miss Daniel shot still another 71, giving her the lead and a total of 213 for 54 holes. Mrs. Alex shot a par 72 for a third-place total of 215. Mrs. White, who won the 1976 Women's Amateur at Del Paso, was at 217 with a 73 for the day, and Miss Haynie, the 1974 Women's Open Champion, was next with 74 for 218. Miss Daniel and Mrs. Carner played together in the last round, with Mrs. Alex in the group just ahead. Mrs. Alex began with birdies on the first and third holes to go three under par, but so did Miss Daniel, who was then 5 under, three strokes ahead of Mrs. Carner and two ahead of Mrs. Alex. Mrs. Carner fought back, and when she birdied the sixth hole, she drew into a tie with Miss Daniel and passed Mrs. Alex by one stroke. The eighth hole was the first turning point. Mrs. Alex went ahead to stay when she birdied. Moments later, Mrs. Carner three-putted for a bogey and Miss Daniel called a penalty stroke on herself when her ball moved on the putting green after she had addressed it. She also bogeyed. The 13th, another par 5, was also a key hole. Once again Mrs. Alex birdied and picked up two strokes on both Mrs. Carner and Miss Daniel, who bogeyed. Mrs. Carner three putted again and Miss Daniel's second shot rolled under a tree, and she could not reach the green with her third. When Mrs. Alex birdied the 15th, it was all the cushion she needed. She finished with three pars on the closing holes for a final round of 68, four under par. Miss Daniel shot 76 and Mrs. Carner had another 75. They fell into a tie for second, with Miss Haynie and Mrs. White, who finished with 71 and 72, respectively. Fifty-six professionals and 12 amateurs returned scores for 72 holes. The 36-hole cut was at 154, 10 over par. Kathy Baker, of Clover, South Carolina, was the low amateur for the second consecutive year, with a 296 total. The Championship drew 360 entries, short of the record 434 entries received in 1981. A record $174,250.99 in prize money was awarded. An estimated crowd of 44,600 attended the four days of the Championship, breaking the previous attendance record of 41,200 set in 1979

1983—Jan Stephenson, 31, from Australia, became the third foreigner to win the Women's Open. She finished one stroke ahead of JoAnne Carner and Patty Sheehan in sweltering heat at the Cedar Ridge Country Club in Tulsa, Oklahoma. Despite daily temperatures in excess of 100 degrees, Miss Stephenson shot rounds of 72-73-71-74-290, six over par. Previous foreign champions were Fay Crocker, of Uraguay, who won in 1955, and Catherine Lacoste, of France, the 1967 Champion. Miss Sheehan and Betsy King shared the first-round lead, at 71. Miss Stephenson's round of 72 included a 6-iron shot for an eagle 2 on the 11th. She was tied with six other players, including former Women's Open Champion Pat Bradley. Defending Champion Janet Anderson shot 82 and missed the cut the following day. Mrs. Carner opened with an 81, which left her in 101st place. Miss Sheehan matched par 71 in the second round, giving her 142 for 36 holes and a three-stroke lead over Miss Stephenson, Debbie, Meisterlin, Dot Germain, and Lauren Howe, all tied for second place at 145. Mrs. Carner shot 70, for a total of 151. The day's low round was a 69 by 18-year-old Heather Farr, of Phoenix, Arizona. Miss Stephenson shot a consistent 71 in the third round and assumed the lead, at 216, three over par. Two strokes back, at 218, were Miss Meisterlin, with a second consecutive 73, and Miss Sheehan, who shot 76. Miss Bradley made a hole-in-one on the sixth, a 151-yard par-3, and shot 31 on the first nine. This tied the Women's Open record, set by Judy Bell, in 1964. Miss Bradley shot 40 on her incoming nine and 71 for the day. She tied for fourth place, at 219, with Miss Howe. Mrs. Carner shot 72, for a 223 total. She continued to climb when she birdied three of the first four holes in the last round. When Miss Stephenson lost two strokes at the third hole she fell into a temporary tie with Miss Meisterlin. Miss Stephenson regained the lead one hole later and settled down over the next 12 holes. With two holes left, she led Mrs. Carner and Miss Sheehan by three strokes and Patti Rizzo by four. Mrs. Carner finished with a 68, topped off by an off-balance wood shot from a fairway bunker that helped her salvage par at the 18th. Mrs. Carner shared second place with Miss Sheehan, who closed with a 73. It was Mrs. Carner's fourth runner-up finish in the Women's Open, a record she shares with Louise Suggs. Miss Farr was the low amateur, with 296. A record $200,000 in prize money was awarded, including $32,780 to Miss Stephenson. The USGA accepted 414 entries.

1984—Hollis Stacy, 30, became the fourth player to win three U.S. Women's Open championships when she shot 290, 2-over par, at the Salem Country Club, in Peabody, Massachusetts. Miss Stacy won previously in 1977 and 1978. With a final round of 69, the lowest score of the championship, Miss Stacy beat Rosie Jones by one stroke and Amy Alcott by two. Miss Alcott, the 1980 Champion, and JoAnn Washam tied at 71 in the first round. After 36 holes, Miss Jones and Penny Pulz had 144 and Miss Alcott 145. Donna Horton White then moved into a tie for the 54-hole lead with Miss Alcott, at 218, with Miss Stacy three strokes behind. A 6 on the fourth hole during the last round left Miss Stacy five strokes behind Miss Alcott and Betsy King, but Miss Stacy birdied the fifth and eighth to move within two strokes of the lead then shared by Miss Alcott, Mrs. White, and Miss Jones. Miss Stacy holed a 7-iron second shot for an eagle 2 at the 13th and a 20-foot birdie putt on the 16th to catch Miss Jones and Miss Alcott. Miss Stacy safely parred the 17th and 18th holes, but Miss Jones bogeyed and Miss Alcott lost two strokes to par. Miss Stacy's winning score was one stroke under the 291 shot by Babe Zaharias in winning the 1954 Women's Open at Salem. Dorothy Pepper was low amateur, with a score of 302. The USGA accepted a record 558 entries.

1985—Kathy Baker, 24, a member of the U.S. Curtis Cup Team and Women's World Amateur Team in 1982, shot 8-under-par 280 to win at Baltusrol Golf Club in Springfield, New Jersey for her first professional victory. Miss Baker finished three strokes ahead af Judy Clark, who finished second. Baker shared the first-round lead with Nancy Lopez and Janet Anderson at 70. Seven players—Clark, Betsy King, Lori Garbacz, Jackie Bertsch, Jan

WOMEN'S OPEN CHAMPIONSHIP

Stephenson and amateurs Kathleen McCarthy and Dottie Pepper—were one stroke behind. At the close of the second day, Lopez held the lead by herself after another round of 70. Vicki Alvarez and Janet Coles each shot second-round 69s to pull within one stroke of the lead. Baker trailed by two. She led by one after a third-round 68 put her at six-under-par 210. Lopez and Clark were one stroke behind at 211. Clark matched a Women's Open record with her round of 65. Lopez bogeyed three of the first four holes in the final round and fell out of contention, leaving Baker and Clark to battle for the Championship. Baker birdied the seventh and eighth holes and held a two-stroke lead after nine holes. Clark parred the first six holes of the second nine while Miss Baker birdied the 11th and 15th, but bogeyed the 10th and 14th, to hold onto her two-stroke advantage. At the 16th, Baker sank a four-foot birdie putt, while Clark bogeyed, giving Baker a four-stroke advantage and ensuring the win. McCarthy and Women's Amateur Public Links champion Danielle Ammaccapane shared low amateur honors at 297. The USGA accepted a record 626 entries for the Championship.

1986—Jane Geddes, 26, shot a one-under-par 71 to defeat Sally Little by two strokes in an 18-hole playoff at NCR Country Club in Dayton, Ohio. Geddes and Little completed 72 holes at one-under-par 287. It was Geddes' first professional victory. Beth Daniel led by one stroke after a first-round 70. Amy Benz, Silvia Bertolaccini and amateur Michele Redman were at 71. Play was delayed for one hour and 23 minutes during the first round due to rain. Judy Dickinson and Betsy King had 36-hole totals of 72-71—143 and shared the lead after the second round, which twice was interrupted by rain. Amy Alcott shot a second-round 69 for even-par 144, one stroke behind the leaders. A record 79 players within 10 strokes of Dickinson and King made the 36-hole cut at 153. The third round was delayed for two hours and 17 minutes due to more rain. King's 70 placed her at three-under par 213, one ahead of Okamoto, who recorded her second consecutive 69. Geddes began her final round at two over par and, after 11 straight pars, began her move with birdies on the 12th and 14th. That put her at even par, tied for second with Little and two strokes behind King. Little birdied the 15th to pull to within one stroke of King, who lost the lead for good on the 14th when she put her approach shot into a greenside bunker, played a poor pitch from there, and three putted for double-bogey 6. Little led at one under par with Geddes and King at even par. Geddes birdied the 17th to gain a share of the lead for the first time. She finished her bogey-free fourth round with another par for 74-74-70-69—287. Little finished with rounds of 73-72-72-70—287. King and Okamoto tied for third, one stroke off the lead. In the playoff, Geddes birdied the second hole to take a brief lead that she relinquished by bogeying the fourth. Little then birdied the fifth, sixth and seventh holes to take a three-stroke lead. Geddes picked up two strokes on the eighth by sinking a 12-foot birdie putt while Little was settling for bogey. Little bunkered her approach shot on the ninth and, after taking two to get out of the sand, took a double-bogey 6. Geddes' par gave her a one-stroke lead. Little recovered on the 10th with a birdie that brought her even. Geddes took the lead for good with a birdie on 14 and stretched it to two strokes when Little bogeyed the 15th. Geddes held that margin the rest of the way to win the championship. Geddes earned $50,000 for the win. Joan Pitcock of Fresno, California, finished at 294, tying the record for low score by an amateur. The USGA accepted a record 704 entries for the championship.

1987—Laura Davies, 23, of Ottershaw, England, shot one-under-par 71 in an 18-hole playoff to defeat Ayako Okamato by two strokes and JoAnne Carner by three strokes and win the 42d U.S. Women's Open at Plainfield Country Club in Edison, New Jersey. She had shot rounds of 72-70-72-71—285. Davies became the fourth foreign golfer to win the championship. Fay Crocker of Uruguay won in 1955, Catherine Lacoste of France won in 1967 and Jan Stephenson of Australia won in 1983. Bonnie Lauer and Dot Germain shot opening-round 69s to take the early lead. Rain interrupted the second round for one hour and 47 minutes. Davies' second-round 70 for a 36 hole total of 142 gave her a one-stroke advantage over Okamato, Sandra Palmer and Jody Rosenthal, each of whom shot 71. Carner was tied with Davies through 16 holes and was in position to take the lead when play was suspended far the day. She returned the next morning and bogeyed the 17th and 18th to fall two strokes back, tied with Nancy Lopez at 144. Sixty-eight players made the 36-hole cut at eight-over-par 152. A third-round 70 gave Okamoto a 54-hole total of 213, one stroke better than Davies, who posted an even-par 72. Martha Nause, who followed her opening-round 76 with rounds of 69 and 70, was in third place at 215. Carner, who shot 72, and Deedee Roberts, who shot 69, were in fourth, three strokes off the lead at 216. Only 40 of the 68 players got onto the course before rain caused a postponement of the fourth round until Monday. Okamato built her lead to three strokes with birdies at the second, third and sixth holes, but a double-bogey at the ninth and a birdie by Davies left them tied. After playing the first nine in two-under-par 34, Carner caught Davies and Okamoto, both of whom played the second nine in even par, with a birdie at the 15th. She took the lead when she holed a four-foot birdie putt on 17. However, Carner missed a five-foot par putt on 18 to force the first threeway playoff in Women's Open history. After the three parred the first three holes of the playoff Davies shouldered the first lead with a birdie at the fourth. Her lead grew to three when Okamoto and Carner each bogeyed two of the next three holes. Her lead was cut to two when she bogeyed the seventh. Carner birdied the ninth to cut the lead to one, and grabbed a share of the lead when Davies bogeyed the 10th. Okamoto was one stroke behind. Carner dropped strokes at the 11th and 13th to fall behind Okamoto. Davies birdied the 14th and 15th to lead Okamoto by three and Carner by four. She parred in for the championship Japan's Michiko Hattori earned low amateur honors at 297, nine over par. The USGA accepted a record 711 entries for the championship.

1988—Liselotte Neumann, 22, of Finspang, Sweden, led or shared the lead after every round and won the championship by three strokes over Patty Sheehan at Baltimore (Maryland) Country Club. Neumann's total of 67-72-69-69—277 seven under par, is the lowest score recorded in the championship, breaking the record held by Pat Bradley, who shot 279 in 1981. Colleen Walker and Dottie Mochrie tied for third at one-under-par 273, six strokes behind Neumann. Neumann's first-round 67 gave her a two-stroke lead over JoAnne Carner and Sally Quinlan. Six players—Sheehan, Mochrie, Walker, Amy Benz, Vicki Fergon and Shirley Furlong—shot one-under-par 70. Juli Inkster's 68, three under par earned her a share of the lead after the second round. Her 36-hole total of three-under-par 139, equalled that of Neumann, who shot 72, and Mochrie, who shot 69. Fergon and Tammie Green trailed by two at 141. Carner, Sheehan, Benz and Donna White stood at even-par 142. Sixty-seven golfers made the 36-hole cut at eight-over-par 150. Only two amateurs survived, tying the record for the fewest amateurs to make the cut. With a third-round 69, Neumann regained sole possession of the lead after 54 holes. Her total of 208 was two strokes ahead of Sheehan whose 68 left her at three-under-par 210. Walker and Green were four strokes behind Neumann at 212 after rounds of 68 and 71, respectively. Benz stood at even-par 213. When Sheehan birdied the seventh hole of the final round and Neumann double-bogeyed, Sheehan held the lead by herself, one stroke ahead af Neumann and Walker. After parring the eighth and ninth, Neumann birdied the 10th, 11th, 12th, 15th and 17th and won the championship going away. Sheehan was not able to match Neumann's pace and finished three strokes behind. Carol Semple Thompson, the 1973 Women's Amateur Champion shot 79-71-70-72—292 to earn low amateur honors, breaking the scoring record set by Catherine Lacoste when she won the championship in 1967. The USGA accepted 736 entries for the championship.

1989—Betsy King led from start to finish, shot 278 at the Indianwood Golf and Country Club, in Lake Orion, Michigan, and won by four strokes over Nancy Lopez, with 282. In her best finish in 11 previous Women's Opens, Miss King placed third. She jumped into the lead with a four-under-par 67 on the first day of play, faltered near the close of the third round, and slipped into a tie for the lead with Patty Sheehan, but Miss King birdied four of the first nine holes of the fourth round, and regained a comfortable lead. The Women's Open was Miss King's fifth victory of 1989, and one that she called special. Miss King and Miss Lopez each shot final rounds of 68, but the best round of the Championship was played by Ayako Okamoto who tied for 11th. Miss Okamoto equalled the Woman's Open record by shooting 65 in the fourth round. Miss Lopez was the runner-up for the third time. Four players broke par for 72 holes over the 6,109-yard course. Vicki Goetze was the low amateur, with a score of 300. She won the U.S. Women's Amateur Championship a month later.

1990—Betsy King won her second consecutive Women's Open by shooting a steady four under par total of 284 and edging Patty Sheehan by one stroke at the Atlanta Athletic Club, in Duluth, Georgia. Danielle Ammaccapane and Dottie Mochie who shot 66 on the final day, finished two strokes back, at 286. Vicki Goetze was low amateur for the second successive year, at 300. Rains over the first three days of the championship forced 36 holes to be played on the final day. Miss Sheehan led by 12 strokes early in the third round, and by 11 early in the final round before she fell from the lead by playing the last 33 holes in nine over par. Nineteen players shot sub-par scores in the first round, led by Miss Sheehan's and Jane Geddes's 66s, but after four rounds only five players remained under par. Before Miss King, Hollis Stacy had been the last to win successive Women's Opens, in 1977 and 1978.

WOMEN'S OPEN CHAMPIONSHIP

DATE	WINNER, RUNNER-UP	SCORE	SITE	ENTRY
1981 (July)	Miss Pat Bradley	279	LaGrange C.C.,	434
	Miss Beth Daniel	280	LaGrange, Ill.	
1982 (July)	Mrs. Janet Alex	283	Del Paso C.C.,	360
	Mrs. JoAnne Carner	289	Sacramento, Calif.	
	Miss Beth Daniel	289		
	Mrs. Donna White	289		
	Miss Sandra Haynie	289		
1983 (July)	Miss Jan Stephenson	290	Cedar Ridge C.C.,	414
	Mrs. JoAnne Carner	291	Tulsa, Okla.	
	Miss Patty Sheehan	291		
1984 (July)	Miss Hollis Stacy	290	Salem C.C.,	558
	Miss Rose Jones	291	Peabody, Mass.	
1985 (July)	Miss Kathy Baker	280	Baltusrol G.C.,	626
	Mrs. Judy Clark	283	Springfield, N.J.	
1986 (July)	Miss Jane Geddes	287-71	NCR C.C.,	704
	Miss Sally Little	287-73	Dayton, Ohio	
1987 (July)	Miss Laura Davies	285-71	Plainfield C.C.,	712
	Miss Ayako Okamoto	285-73	Plainfield, N.J.	
	Mrs. JoAnne Carner	285-74		
1988 (July)	Miss Liselotte Neumann	†277	Baltimore C.C.,	735
	Miss Patty Sheehan	280	Baltimore, Md.	
1989 (July)	Miss Betsy King	278	Indianwood G. & C.C.,	736
	Miss Nancy Lopez	282	Lake Orion, Mich.	
1990 (July)	Miss Betsy King	284	Atlanta Athletic Club	‡785
	Miss Patty Sheehan	285	(Riverside Course), Duluth, Ga.	

‡Record Entry
†Record Qualifying Score

1981
TWENTY-NINTH WOMEN'S OPEN CHAMPIONSHIP
La Grange Country Club, La Grange, Illinois, July 23-26
Yardage—6,204. Par 72. †434 Entries, 151 Qualifiers, 151 Starters.

						Score	Money Prize
1	Pat Bradley, Nashua Country Club, Nashua, N.H.	71	74	68	66	279	$22,000.00
2	Beth Daniel, Seabrook Island G.C., Seabrook Island, S.C.	69	74	69	68	280	12,500.00
3	Kathy Whitworth, Avon, Conn.	69	70	71	74	284	9,500.00
4	Cynthia Hill, Fort Lauderdale, Fla.	76	70	69	72	287	7,300.00
	Bonnie Lauer, Palm Desert, Calif.	72	67	72	76	287	7,300.00
6	Donna Caponi, Sherman Oaks, Calif.	71	74	72	73	290	4,562.50
	Marlene Floyd, Horseshoe Bay C.C., Horseshoe Bay, Texas	71	72	73	74	290	4,562.50
	JoAnne Carner, Palm Beach National G.&C.C., Lake Worth, Fla.	73	71	72	70	290	4,562.50
	Patty Sheehan, Palo Alto Hills C.C., Palo Alto, Calif.	74	74	72	74	290	4,562.50
10	Amelia Rorer, Jenkintown, Pa.	73	77	69	73	292	2,966.67
	Sally Little, Imperial Lakes C.C., Lakeland, Fla.	74	72	76	70	292	2,966.67
	Hollis Stacy, Savannah G.C., Savannah, Ga.	73	75	71	73	292	2,966.67
	Debbie Massey, Dolphin Head G.C., Hilton Head, S.C.	71	72	72	77	292	2,966.67
	Sandra Haynie, Carrollton, Texas	75	73	73	71	292	2,966.66
	Shelley Hamlin, Sunnyside C.C., Fresno, Calif.	70	75	75	72	292	2,966.66
16	Cathy Sherk, Lookout Point C.C., Canada	76	69	76	72	293	2,500.00
	Louise Parks, Singing Hills, El Cajon, Calif.	72	75	72	74	293	2,500.00
18	Dorothy Germain, Pine Needles L. & C.C., Southern Pines, N.C.	71	76	71	76	294	2,350.00
19	Julie Stanger, The Arizona Biltmore, Phoenix, Ariz.	74	75	74	72	295	2,200.00
	Amy Alcott, Princeville Resort, Kauai, Hawaii	75	73	72	75	295	2,200.00
21	Betsy King, Heidelberg C.C., Bernville, Pa.	75	75	73	73	296	1,950.00
	Kyle O'Brien, Hillcrest C.C., Indianapolis, Ind.	75	69	73	79	296	1,950.00
	Marlene Hagge, La Quinta Hotel G.C., La Quinta, Calif.	74	75	72	75	296	1,950.00
24	Vickie Fergon, Boca Raton, Fla.	77	73	72	76	298	1,700.00
	Dale Lundquist, Lutz, Fla.	73	72	74	79	298	1,700.00
26	Judy Clark, Frenchmen's Creek G.C., Juno Beach, Fla.	74	76	71	78	299	1,535.00
	Janet Alex, West Sunbury, Pa.	77	74	73	75	299	1,535.00
	* Kathy Baker, River Hills Plantation G.C., Clover, S.C.	75	77	74	73	299	Pin
29	Penny Pulz, Rancho Mirage, Calif.	80	68	72	80	300	1,380.00
	Sandra Palmer, La Quinta Hotel G.C., La Quinta, Calif.	77	75	74	74	300	1,380.00
	Jan Stephenson, Woodhaven C.C., Forth Worth, Texas	76	70	77	77	300	1,380.00
32	Mary Mills, Hunters Run, Boynton Beach, Fla.	79	74	75	73	301	1,255.00
	Sandra Post, Indian Spring C.C., Boyton Beach, Fla.	73	79	72	77	301	1,255.00
34	Jerilyn Britz, Deer Run G.C., Orlando, Fla.	70	81	75	76	302	1,160.00
	Debbie Austin, Haines City, Fla.	75	74	76	77	302	1,160.00
	* Patti Rizzo, La Gource C.C., Miami, Fla.	79	74	74	75	302	Pin
37	Barbara Moxness, Singing Hills C.C., San Diego, Calif.	74	79	76	74	303	1,080.00
	Marilyn J.S. Smith, Shandon G.C., New Zealand	74	75	79	75	303	1,080.00
	Murle Breer, Sheraton Savannah I.&C.C., Savannah, Ga.	74	73	76	80	303	1,080.00
40	Alexandra Reinhardt, Columbine C.C., Littleton, Colo.	77	75	75	77	304	1,020.00
	Laura Baugh-Cole, Argyle, Texas	73	76	76	79	304	1,020.00
	Mary A. Lawrence, Oaks North, San Diego, Calif.	75	73	75	81	304	1,020.00
43	Jeanette Kerr, Oahu C.C., Oahu, Hawaii	77	75	79	74	305	970.00
	Catherine Morse, Oak Hill C.C., Pittsford, N.Y.	72	81	77	75	305	970.00
	* Rose Jones, Ohio State Univ. Scarlet & Gray, Columbus, Ohio	75	76	77	77	305	Pin
46	* Jennifer Davis, Porter Valley C.C., Northridge, Calif.	75	76	79	76	306	—
	Connie Chillemi, Silver Springs Shore, Fla.	74	76	71	85	306	940.00
48	Kathyrn Young, Portland, Ore.	76	74	81	76	307	870.00
	Kathy Postlewait, Coosa Valley C.C., Sylacauga, Ala.	78	73	79	77	307	870.00
	Vicki Singleton, Elyria C.C., Elyria, Ohio	77	76	77	77	307	870.00
	* Lancy Smith, Park C.C., Williamsville, N.Y.	76	77	76	78	307	—
	Patty Hayes, Sun Tree C.C., Melbourne, Fla.	80	70	78	79	307	870.00
	Gail Hirata, Montebello, Calif.	76	76	74	81	307	870.00
	Judy Rankin, Mission Hills C.C., Rancho Mirage, Calif.	81	72	73	81	307	870.00
	* Cathy Hanlon, Palos Verdes G.C., Palos Verdes Ests., Calif.	79	72	74	82	307	—
56	Alice Miller, Plumas Lake G.C., Marysville, Calif.	78	74	79	77	308	790.00
	Joyce Kazmierski, Williston Highlands C.C., Williston, Fla.	75	75	80	78	308	790.00
	* Kris Monaghan, Univ. of New Mexico G.A., Albuquerque, N.M.	77	75	75	81	308	—
	* Edwina Kennedy, The Australian G.C., Australia	78	74	74	82	308	—
60	Sandra Spuzich, Indianapolis, Ind.	80	71	79	79	309	760.00
	* Laurie Rinker, Sandpiper Bay Resort, Port St. Lucie, Fla.	76	74	75	84	309	—
62	Chris Johnson, Arthur Pack Desert G.C., Tucson, Ariz.	75	75	78	82	310	730.00
	Kathy Ahern, Arlington, Texas	75	78	74	83	310	730.00
64	Peggy Conley, Spokane C.C., Spokane, Wash.	77	76	81	77	311	700.00
	Debbie Meisterlin, Del Mar, Calif.	77	75	80	79	311	700.00
	* Penny Hammel, Faries Park G.C., Decatur, Ill.	77	75	79	80	311	—
	Susie Berning, Keahou Kona C.C., Kona, Hawaii	78	75	79	80	311	700.00
68	Mary B. Porter, Hillcrest G.C., Sun City West, Ariz.	74	77	78	86	315	680.00

*Amateur. Gold and silver pins were awarded to the amateurs returning the lowest two scores. Prize money totaling $148,670.00 was awarded.
†Record Entry.

1982
THIRTIETH WOMEN'S OPEN CHAMPIONSHIP

Del Paso Country Club, Sacramento, California, July 22-25.
Yardage — 6,342. Par 72. 360 Entries, 150 Starters.

						Score	Money Prize
1	Janet Alex, Venice, Fla.	70	73	72	68	283	$27,315.00
2	JoAnne Carner, Palm Beach Nat'l G. & C.C., Lake Worth, Fla.	69	70	75	75	289	10,659.25
	Beth Daniel, Seabrook Island G.C., Seabrook Island, Fla.	71	71	71	76	289	10,659.25
	Donna White, Wellington G.C., Wellington, Fla.	70	74	73	72	289	10,659.25
	Sandra Haynie, Carrollton, Texas	70	74	74	71	289	10,659.25
6	Susie McAllister, Beaumont, Texas	77	70	75	71	293	5,673.00
7	Carole Jo Callison, Riverbend G. & C.C., Broderick, Calif.	76	69	72	77	294	4,539.67
	Nancy Lopez, Stafford, Texas	78	73	74	69	294	4,539.67
	Vicki Tabor, Baymeadows C.C., Jacksonville, Fla.	70	76	75	73	294	4,539.67
10	Beverley Cooper, Apopka, Fla.	73	72	76	74	295	3,637.33
	Stephanie Farwig, Houston, Texas	75	76	72	72	295	3,637.33
	Muffin Spencer-Devlin, Hunters Run G. & R.C., Boynton Beach, Fla.	76	71	76	72	295	3,637.33
13	Amy Alcott, Princeville Resort, Kauai, Hawaii	75	74	71	76	296	3,085.50
	Dale Eggeling, Innisbrook R. & G.C., Tarpon Springs, Fla.	72	74	76	74	296	3,085.50
	Sally Little, San Jose, Calif.	71	77	75	73	296	3,085.50
	Alexandra Reinhardt, Columbine C.C., Littleton, Colo.	73	75	71	77	296	3,085.50
	*Kathy Baker, River Hills C.C., Clover, S.C.	75	70	72	79	296	PIN
18	Sandra Palmer, La Quinta Hotel G.C., La Quinta, Calif.	78	71	75	73	297	2,744.00
	Lynn Adams, Kingsville, Texas	71	76	77	73	297	2,744.00
	*Amy Benz, Eastlake Woodlands, Palm Harbor, Fla.	79	70	72	76	297	PIN
21	Jeannette Kerr, Oahu C.C., Honolulu, Hawaii	74	77	71	76	298	2,474.00
	Pat Bradley, Nashua C.C., Nashua, N.H.	77	74	72	75	298	2,474.00
	Donna Caponi, Cleveland, Ohio	73	76	78	71	298	2,474.00
	Janet Coles, Carmel Valley Ranch, Carmel, Calif.	77	77	74	70	298	2,474.00
25	Yuko Moriguchi, Gifuseki C.C., Japan	73	74	77	75	299	2,178.50
	Jane Blalock, Boca Raton, Fla.	77	77	72	73	299	2,178.50
	Kathy Postlewait, Coosa Valley C.C., Sylacauga, Ala.	76	73	75	75	299	2,178.50
	Betsy King, Heidelberg C.C., Bernville, Pa.	75	77	76	71	299	2,178.50
29	*Carol Semple, Allegheny C.C., Sewickley, Pa.	76	72	74	78	300	—
	Bonnie Lauer, Palm Desert, Calif.	73	71	78	78	300	1,869.40
	*Juli Inkster, Los Altos G. & C.C., Los Altos, Calif.	75	77	77	71	300	—
	Terri Moody, Athens C.C., Athens, Ga.	73	79	72	76	300	1,869.40
	Nancy Rubin, Hillcrest C.C., Lower Burrell, Pa.	74	78	76	72	300	1,869.40
	Kathy Whitworth, Avon, Conn.	74	75	75	76	300	1,869.40
	Patty Sheehan, Palo Alto Hills G.C., Palo Alto, Calif.	78	75	76	71	300	1,869.40
36	Penny Pulz, Studio City, Calif.	78	75	76	72	301	1,700.00
	*Mary Zimmerman, Hillsboro C.C., Hillsboro, Ill.	72	74	77	78	301	—
38	Jerilyn Britz, Deer Run G.C., Casselberry, Fla.	74	79	74	75	302	1,620.00
	Ayako Okamoto, Daiwa Spinning Co. Ltd., Tokyo, Japan	74	76	74	78	302	1,620.00
40	Alice Ritzman, Phoenix, Ariz.	74	77	74	78	303	1,481.00
	Cathy Morse, Oak Hill C.C., Rochester, N.Y.	76	75	78	74	303	1,481.00
	Barbara Moxness, San Diego, Calif.	76	78	77	72	303	1,481.00
	*Anne Sander, Broadmoor G.C., Seattle, Wash.	77	76	75	75	303	—
44	Chris Johnson, Tucson, Ariz.	74	76	79	75	304	1,364.00
45	Valerie Skinner, N. Platte C.C., N. Platte, Neb.	75	73	79	78	305	1,310.00
	*Cindy Pleger, Athens, Ga.	78	74	75	78	305	—
	*Dana Howe, The C.C. of Colorado, Colorado Springs, Colo.	71	77	82	75	305	—
	*Caroline Gowan, Greenville C.C., Greenville, S.C.	77	74	78	76	305	—
49	Hollis Stacy, Savannah G.C., Savannah, Ga.	78	73	79	76	306	1,229.50
	Myra Van Hoose, Dunedin C.C., Dunedin, Fla.	74	78	78	76	306	1,229.50
51	Lauri Peterson, Maryvale G.C., Phoenix, Ariz.	81	70	78	78	307	1,124.50
	Jo Ann Washam, Coronado, Calif.	74	76	78	79	307	1,124.50
	*Deb Richard, Manhattan C.C., Manhattan, Kans.	75	76	76	81	308	—
	Cindy Flom, Randolph G.C., Tucson, Ariz.	79	74	78	77	308	1,027.00
	Lenore Muraoka, Honolulu, Hawaii	76	74	76	82	308	1,027.00
56	Patti Rizzo, Monte Carlo C.C., Fort Pierce, Fla.	75	78	76	80	309	944.33
	Jackie Bertsch, Plum Brook C.C., Sandusky, Ohio	77	77	83	72	309	944.33
	Kelly Fuiks, Grenelefe G. & T.C., Haines City, Fla.	80	74	75	80	309	944.33
59	Barbara Mizrahie, Los Angeles, Calif.	76	76	80	79	311	903.00
60	Gail Hirata, Upland Hills C.C., Upland Hills, Calif.	78	76	79	79	312	876.00
	Kathryn Young, Portland, Ore.	78	76	79	79	312	876.00
62	Julie Lynd, Industry Hills G.C., City of Industry, Calif.	75	78	84	76	313	850.00
63	Cathy Reynolds, Hickory Hills C.C., Springfield, Mo.	78	76	80	80	314	805.00
	Cathy Mant, Columbia Edgewater C., Portland, Ore.	79	75	80	80	314	805.00
65	Margaret Kirsch, Ridgeview C.C., Duluth, Minn.	79	74	82	83	318	779.00
66	*Carol Slane, Auburn Valley G. & C.C., Auburn, Calif.	78	75	86	81	320	—
67	Betsy Barrett, Whispering Pines, Myrtle Beach, S.C.	80	74	91	78	323	762.00
	*Denise Hermida, Brandon, Fla.	76	77	83	87	323	—
	Jan Stephenson, Orange Tree G.C., Phoenix, Ariz.	75	73	74	WD		

*Amateur. Gold and silver pins were awarded to the amateurs returning the lowest two scores. Prize money totaling $174,250.99 was awarded.

1983
THIRTY-FIRST WOMEN'S OPEN CHAMPIONSHIP

Cedar Ridge Country Club, Tulsa, Oklahoma, July 28-31
Yardage—6,298. Par 71. 414 Entries, 150 Starters

						Score	Money Prize
1	Jan Stephenson, Cedar Ridge C.C., Tulsa, Okla.	72	73	71	74	290	$32,780.00
2	JoAnne Carner, Palm Beach National, Lake Worth, Fla.	81	70	72	68	291	15,400.00
	Patty Sheehan, Plumas Pines G.C., Eureka, Calif.	71	71	76	73	291	15,400.00
4	Patti Rizzo, Monte Carlo C.C., Ft. Pierce, Fla.	75	74	73	70	292	9,659.00
5	Cathy Morse, Oak Hill C.C., Rochester, N.Y.	76	71	77	69	293	7,708.00
6	Dorothy Germain, Pine Needles Lodges, Southern Pines, N.C.	73	72	76	73	294	5,998.00
	Myra Van Hoose, East Lake Woodlands, Oldsmar, Fla.	77	72	72	73	294	5,998.00
8	Ayako Okamoto, Monte Carlo C.C., Ft. Pierce, Fla.	77	73	75	70	295	4,714.67
	Jane Lock, Huntingdale G.C., Melbourne, Australia	75	73	72	75	295	4,714.67
	Pat Bradley, Nashua C.C., Nashua, N.H.	72	76	71	76	295	4,714.66
11	Judy Clark, Frenchmen's Creek G.C., Juno, Fla.	79	76	70	71	296	3,895.00
	Rosie Jones, Paradise Hills C.C., Albuquerque, N.M.	76	74	73	73	296	3,895.00
	*Heather Farr, Camelback G.C., Paradise Valley, Ariz.	78	69	73	76	296	pin
	Amy Alcott, Princeville Resort, Kauai, Hawaii	75	74	71	76	296	3,895.00
15	Muffin Spencer-Devlin, Hntrs. Rn. G. & R.C., Boynton Bch. Fla.	78	76	70	73	297	3,312.00
	Janet Coles, Carmel Valley Ranch, Carmel, Calif.	72	75	75	75	297	3,312.00
	Jane Blalock, Portsmouth C.C., Portsmouth, N.H.	77	75	70	75	297	3,312.00
	Lauren Howe, C.C. of Colorado, Colorado Springs, Colo.	72	73	74	78	297	3,312.00
19	Valerie Skinner, N. Platte C.C., N. Platte, Neb.	79	71	75	73	298	2,950.00
	Sherrin Galbraith, Imperial Lakes C.C., Lakeland, Fla.	75	75	73	75	298	2,950.00
21	Dale Eggeling, Innisbrook, Tarpon Springs, Fla.	79	73	74	73	299	2,542.86
	Juli Inkster, Los Altos G. & C.C., Los Altos, Calif.	72	79	74	74	299	2,542.86
	Lori Garbacz, Boca West C., Boca Raton, Fla.	73	79	73	74	299	2,542.86
	Donna White, Wellington G.C., Wellington, Fla.	77	74	73	75	299	2,542.86
	Cynthia Hill, Pasadena G. & C.C., St. Petersburg, Fla.	79	71	73	76	299	2,542.86
	Becky Pearson, Camino Del Mar C.C., Boca Raton, Fla.	72	75	75	77	299	2,542.85
	Sandra Haynie, Eastern Hills C.C., Garland, Texas	74	74	74	77	299	2,542.85
28	Stephanie Farwig, Sugar Land, Texas	73	75	75	77	300	2,220.00
29	Barbara Mizrahie, Woodmont C.C., Ft. Lauderdale, Fla.	79	74	73	75	301	2,066.67
	Martha Nause, Amelia Is. Plantation, Fernandina Bch., Fla.	79	71	74	77	301	2,066.67
	Debbie Meisterlin, La Quinta H. & G.C., La Quinta, Calif.	72	73	73	83	301	2,066.66
32	Betsy King, Heidelberg C.C., Bernville, Pa.	71	78	78	75	302	1,880.00
	Yuko Moriguchi, Gifuzeki C.C., Japan	76	77	73	76	302	1,880.00
	Hollis Stacy, Long Cove C., Hilton Head, S.C.	78	74	72	78	302	1,880.00
35	Mindy Moore, Boca Raton, Fla.	79	74	79	71	303	1,640.00
	Beth Boozer, Alvamar G.C., Lawrence, Kans.	78	75	77	73	303	1,640.00
	Vicki Fergon, Highland Beach, Fla.	75	76	78	74	303	1,640.00
	Alice Miller, Plumas Lake G. & C.C., Marysville, Calif.	79	75	74	75	303	1,640.00
	Kathy Baker, River Hills C.C., Clover, S.C.	74	76	75	78	303	1,640.00
40	Jane Crafter, Pine Needles L. & C.C., Southern Pines, N.C.	75	76	73	80	304	1,340.00
	Judy Ellis, Westmount G. & C.C., Canada	80	75	77	72	304	1,340.00
	*Sherri Steinhauer, Nakoma G.C., Madison, Wis.	76	77	76	75	304	pin
	Peggy Conley, Spokane C.C., Spokane, Wash.	73	81	74	76	304	1,340.00
	*Kathleen McCarthy, San Joaquin C.C., Fresno, Calif.	74	74	79	77	304	pin
	*Cindy Davis, Prince Georges C.C., Mitchellville, Md.	79	72	76	77	304	pin
	Therese Hession, Hillcrest, C.C., Indianapolis, Ind.	77	77	73	77	304	1,340.00
	Beverly Davis, Hidden Hills G.C., Jacksonville, Fla.	76	77	73	78	304	1,340.00
48	*Lancy Smith, The Park C.C., Williamsville, N.Y.	78	78	71	78	305	—
	*Mary Anne Widman, Elmira C.C., Elmira, N.Y.	73	73	79	80	305	—
50	*Jody Rosenthal, Golden Valley C.C., Golden Valley, Minn.	78	76	76	77	307	—
	Debbie Hall, Dallas, Texas	76	79	75	77	307	1,084.00
	Marta Dotti, Monte Carlo C.C., Ft. Pierce, Fla.	78	75	76	78	307	1,084.00
	Carole Charbonnier, Geneva, Switzerland	74	78	76	79	307	1,084.00
	Lenore Muraoka, Honolulu, Hawaii	73	79	75	80	307	1,084.00
	Julie Pyne, Dallas, Texas	82	74	70	81	307	1,084.00
56	Vicki Tabor, Bay Meadows C.C., Jacksonville, Fla.	78	78	76	76	308	990.00
	Beverly Klass, Boca Raton, Fla.	77	78	76	77	308	990.00
58	Sandra Palmer, La Quinta H. & G.C., La Quinta, Calif.	77	77	81	74	309	950.00
	Gerda Boykin, River Plantation C.C., Conroe, Texas	81	73	79	76	309	950.00
60	Brenda Goldsmith, Pecan Valley G.C., San Antonio, Texas	80	76	75	80	311	910.00
	Sue Ertl, Bent Tree G. & R.C., Sarasota, Fla.	75	78	75	83	311	910.00
62	Pia Nilsson, Torekovs G. Klubb, Sweden	78	78	78	79	313	880.00
63	Barbara Thomas, Sibley C.C., Sibley, Iowa	75	81	80	78	314	840.00
	Dianne Dailey, Cardinal G.C., Greensboro, N.C.	81	75	78	80	314	840.00
	Kim Eaton, Butterfield, C.C., Oak Brook, Ill.	77	79	77	81	314	840.00
66	Mina Rodriguez, Golfcrest C.C., Pearland, Texas	74	78	83	81	316	800.00

*Amateur. Gold and silver pins were awarded to the amateurs returning the lowest two scores. Prize money totaling 200,000.00 was awarded.

1984
THIRTY-SECOND WOMEN'S OPEN CHAMPIONSHIP

Salem Country Club, Peabody, Massachusetts, July 12-15
Yardage—6,285. Par 72. +558 Entries, 150 Starters

						Score	Money Prize
1	Hollis Stacy, Los Angeles, Calif	74	72	75	69	290	$36,000.00
2	Rosie Jones, Paradise Hills C.C., Albuquerque, N.M.	73	71	75	72	291	19,500.00
3	Amy Alcott, Princeville, Kauai, Hawaii	71	74	73	74	292	13,008.00
	Lori Garvacz, Boca West Club, Boca Raton, Fla.	74	76	72	70	292	13,008.00
5	Betsy King, Heidelberg C.C., Bernville, Pa.	74	72	75	73	294	7,389.34
	Penny Pulz, Burbank, Calif.	75	69	78	72	294	7,389.33
	Patty Sheehan, Tahoe Donner G.C., Truckee, Calif.	73	77	74	70	294	7,389.33
8	Donna White, Wellington G.C., Wellington, Fla.	75	71	72	77	295	5,510.50
	Ayako Okamoto, Monte Carlo C.C., Ft. Pierce, Fla.	72	74	74	75	295	5,510.50
10	Beth Daniel, Richmond, Va.	76	76	73	72	297	4,746.00
	Kathy Whitworth, Trophy Club, Roanoke, Texas	73	75	75	74	297	4,746.00
12	Susan Fogleman, Atlantis, Fla.	74	77	74	73	298	4,374.00
13	Patti Rizzo, Monte Carlo C.C., Ft. Pierce, Fla.	75	71	78	75	299	3,892.75
	Pat Bradley, Nashua C.C., Nashua, N.H.	76	77	70	76	299	3,892.75
	Jo Ann Washam, Carrollton, Texas	71	78	77	73	299	3,892.75
	Vicki Alvarez, Jacksonville, Fla.	80	74	76	69	299	3,892.75
17	Cathy Hanlon Marino, Oakwood C.C., Enid, Okla.	76	73	74	77	300	3,381.00
	Lauri Peterson, Maryvale Municipal G.C., Phoenix, Ariz.	74	79	72	75	300	3,381.00
	Silvia Bertolaccini, Moody, Maine	74	75	76	75	300	3,381.00
20	Alice Miller, Marysville, Calif.	73	77	76	75	301	3,093.50
	JoAnne Carner, Palm Bch. Nat'l G.&C.C., Lake Worth, Fla.	77	79	73	72	301	3,093.50
22	Amy Benz, East Lake Woodlands G.&C.C., Oldsmar, Fla.	73	79	80	70	302	2,812.50
	Heather Drew, Lomas Santa Fe C.C., Solana Beach, Calif.	73	75	76	78	302	2,812.50
	Debbie Massey, Oyster Reef G.C., Hilton Head Is., S.C.	77	78	75	72	302	2,812.50
	Jerilyn Britz, Deer Run G.C., Casselbury, Fla.	76	75	77	74	302	2,812.50
	*Dorothy Pepper, McGregor Links C.C., Saratoga Spgs, N.Y.	77	75	75	75	302	Pin
27	Juli Inkster, Los Altos G.&C.C., Los Altos, Calif.	80	76	73	74	303	2,497.34
	Jan Stephenson, Fort Worth, Texas	72	81	71	79	303	2,497.33
	*Jody Rosenthal, Golden Valley C.C., Golden Valley, Minn.	79	72	74	78	303	Pin
	Marta Figueras-Dotti, Cleveland, Ohio	77	74	80	72	303	2,497.33
31	Val Skinner, North Platte C.C., North Platte, Neb.	78	76	75	75	304	2,250.00
	*Tina Tombs, Manchester C.C., Bedford, N.H.	77	74	78	75	304	Pin
	Martha Nause, Amelia Is. Plantation, Fernandina Bch., Fla.	75	77	77	75	304	2,250.00
	Carole Charbonnier, Crans-Sar-Sierreg C., Switzerland	74	76	77	77	304	2,250.00
35	Lisa Young, Prince Rupert G.C., Canada	74	76	79	76	305	1,980.20
	Judy Clark, Frenchmans Creek G.C., N. Palm Beach, Fla.	79	76	77	73	305	1,980.20
	Nancy Lopez, Palm Harbor G.C., Palm Coast, Fla.	77	79	75	74	305	1,980.20
	Charlotte Montgomery, Falsterboro G.C., Sweden	76	75	77	77	305	1,980.20
	Karin Mundinger, Cedarhurst, Canada	75	78	77	75	305	1,980.20
40	Jane Blalock, Portsmouth, N.H.	76	76	74	80	306	1,642.60
	Dale Eggeling, Royal Kaanapali G.C., Maui, Hawaii	78	77	73	78	306	1,642.60
	*Heather Farr, Camelback G.C., Paradise Valley, Ariz.	74	80	79	73	306	
	Jeannette Kerr, Oahu C.C., Honolulu, Hawaii	76	77	79	74	306	1,642.60
	Therese Hession, Hillcrest C.C., Indianapolis, Ind.	79	74	78	75	306	1,642.60
	Janice Gibson, Stillwater C.C., Stillwater, Okla.	74	79	74	79	306	1,642.60
46	Sally Little, Richmond, Va.	79	74	72	82	307	1,440.00
47	Sandra Haynie, Eastern Hills, C.C., Dallas, Texas	77	77	69	85	308	1,312.34
	Mary Beth Zimmerman,, Hillsboro C.C., Hillsboro, Ill.	78	77	80	73	308	1,312.33
	Muffin Spencer-Devlin, Hunters Run, Boynton Beach, Fla.	79	77	77	75	308	1,312.33
50	Kathy Baker, River Hills C.C., Clover, S.C.	78	77	74	80	309	1,177.34
	Donna Caponi, Wesley Chapel, Fla.	74	75	82	78	309	1,177.33
	Elaine Crosby, C.C. of Jackson, Jackson, Mich.	80	76	75	78	309	1,177.33
53	Jane Crafter, Pine Needles L.&C.C., Southern Pines, N.C.	78	78	77	77	310	1,102.67
	Laurie Rinker, Martin Downs C.C., Stuart, Fla.	77	74	86	73	310	1,102.67
	Kathryn Young, Portland, Ore.	76	73	82	79	310	1,102.66
56	Pia Nilsson, Torekovs G.K., Torekov, Sweden	76	80	75	80	311	1,046.00
	Myra Van Hoose, East Lake Woodlands, Oldsmar, Fla.	77	78	82	74	311	1,046.00
	*Kathe Kingston, Lakeside C.C., Atlanta, Ga.	76	80	79	76	311	—
59	Janet Anderson, Plantation G.&C.C., Venice, Fla.	76	79	76	81	312	1,013.00
	*Joan Ellis, Palma Ceia G.&C.C., Tampa, Fla.	72	80	82	81	315	—
61	Vicki Singleton, Elyria C.C., Elyria, Ohio	80	76	82	77	315	990.00
62	Sherri Turner, Greenville, S.C.	77	77	83	79	316	967.00

+ Record Entry

*Amateur. Gold and silver pins were awarded to the amateurs returning the lowest two scores. Prize money totaling $221,357.00 was awarded.

1985
†FORTIETH WOMEN'S OPEN CHAMPIONSHIP

Baltusrol Golf Club, Springfield, New Jersey, July 11-14
Yardage—6,274. Par 72. +626 Entries, 153 Starters

						Score	Money Prize
1	Kathy Baker, River Hills C.C., Clover, S.C.	70	72	68	70	280	$41,975.00
2	Judy Clark, Frenchmen's Creek C., N. Palm Beach, Fla.	71	75	65	72	283	21,700.00
3	Vicki Alavarez, Baymeadows C.C., Jacksonville, Fla.	72	69	71	75	287	16,800.00
4	Janet Coles, Carmel Valley Ranch, Carmel, Calif.	72	69	71	76	288	10,854.50
	Nancy Lopez, Del Lago C.C., Montgomery, Texas	70	70	71	77	288	10,854.50
6	Penny Pulz, Laguna Beach, Calif.	75	74	70	70	289	7,497.50
	Sally Little, The Hamlet, Delray Beach, Fla.	73	70	74	72	289	7,497.50
8	Ayako Okamoto, Monte Carlo C.C., Ft. Pierce, Fla.	72	74	73	71	290	5,893.34
	Jane Geddes, Diamond Oaks C.C., Ft. Worth, Texas	74	75	69	72	290	5,893.34
	Betsy King, Heidelberg C.C., Bernville, Pa.	71	73	71	75	290	5,893.34
11	Amy Alcott, Princeville Resort, Kauai, Hawaii	72	72	74	74	292	5,111.00
12	Chris Johnson, Haines City, Fla.	77	73	73	70	293	4,342.50
	Alice Miller, Marysville, Calif.	75	75	71	72	293	4,342.50
	Patty Sheehan, Tahoe Donner G.C., Tahoe Donner, Calif.	73	73	74	73	293	4,342.50
	Pat Bradley, Nashua C.C., Nashua, N.H.	74	75	71	73	293	4,342.50
	Jan Stephenson, The Foothills, Phoenix, Ariz.	71	74	73	75	293	4,342.50
	Cathy Morse, Oak Hill C.C., Rochester, N.Y.	73	74	69	77	293	4,342.50
18	Muffin Spencer Devlin, Hunters Run, Boynton Beach, Fla.	73	72	75	74	294	3,750.00
19	Barb Bunkowsky, Boca Pointe G.C., Boca Raton, Fla.	76	73	73	73	295	3,625.00
20	Lori Garbacz, Boca West C., Boca Raton, Fla.	71	76	76	73	296	3,229.17
	Stephanie Farwig, Mequon, Wis.	78	71	74	73	296	3,229.17
	Marlene Floyd, Cypress Lakes G.C., Fayetteville, N.C.	76	70	76	74	296	3,229.17
	Silvia Bertolaccini, Boca Raton, Fla.	76	72	74	74	296	3,229.17
	Cathy Marino, Milburn C.C., Overland Park, Kan.	75	70	74	77	296	3,229.17
	Janet Anderson, West Sunbury, Pa.	70	73	75	78	296	3,229.17
26	*Kathleen McCarthy, San Joaquin C.C., Fresno, Calif.	71	79	73	74	297	Pin
	Vickie Fergon, Deerfield Beach, Fla.	75	75	73	74	297	2,825.00
	Valerie Skinner, PGA West LaQuinta, LaQuinta, Calif.	73	74	73	77	297	2,825.00
	*Danielle Ammaccapane, Anasazi G.C., Phoenix, Ariz.	74	71	73	79	297	Pin
30	Pat Meyers, Riviera C.C., Ormond Beach, Fla.	75	72	77	74	298	2,428.57
	Susie Berning, Keauhou Kona C.C., Kailua Kona, Hawaii	80	71	72	75	298	2,428.57
	Kathy Whitworth, Roanoke, Texas	76	73	73	76	298	2,428.57
	Dawn Coe, March Meadows G.C., Canada	72	77	73	76	298	2,428.57
	Jane Blalock, Portsmouth, N.H.	74	76	71	77	298	2,428.57
	Kathy Postlewait, Deer Run C.C., Casselberry, Fla.	73	77	71	77	298	2,428.57
	Leann Cassaday, Virginia C.C., Long Beach, Calif.	76	73	71	78	298	2,428.57
37	Becky Pearson, Camino Del Mar C.C., Boca Raton, Fla.	75	75	76	73	299	2,087.50
	Jerilyn Britz, Deer Run C.C., Casselberry, Fla.	78	73	69	79	299	2,087.50
39	Sherri Turner, Greenville, S.C.	72	72	82	74	300	1,677.78
	Myra Blackwelder, Oldsmar, Fla.	75	75	76	74	300	1,677.78
	Dee Dee Lasker, Medinah C.C., Medinah, Ill.	73	78	75	74	300	1,677.78
	Marci Bozarth, Hancock Park G.C., Lampasas, Texas	74	76	74	76	300	1,677.78
	Dale Eggeling, Royal Kaanapali R., Maui, Hawaii	77	73	74	76	300	1,677.78
	Sandra Palmer, LaQuinta, LaQuinta, Calif.	77	74	73	76	300	1,677.78
	Jackie Bertsch, Plum Brook C.C., Sandusky, Ohio	71	76	76	77	300	1,677.78
	Donna Caponi, Wesley Chapel, Fla.	75	73	72	80	300	1,677.78
	Cynthia Hill, Pasadena G.C., St. Petersburg, Fla.	74	75	71	80	300	1,677.78
48	JoAnne Carner, Palm Beach Nat'l. G.&C.C., Lake Worth, Fla.	77	73	75	76	301	1,325.00
	Heather Farr, Camelback G.C., Scottsdale, Ariz.	75	73	76	77	301	1,325.00
50	Jody Rosenthal, Golden Valley C.C., Golden Valley, Minn.	76	75	76	75	302	1,250.00
	Lenore Muraoka, Devon, Pa.	76	73	76	77	302	1,250.00
	Barb Thomas, Sibley C.C., Sibley, Iowa	72	77	76	77	302	1,250.00
53	Rosie Jones, Paradise Hills C.C., Albuquerque, N.M.	76	75	76	76	303	1,200.00
54	Sherrin Galbraith, Imperial Lakes C.C., Lakeland, Fla.	76	71	76	81	304	1,175.00
55	*Dottie Pepper, McGregor Links C.C., Saratoga Springs, N.Y.	71	76	80	78	305	Pin
	Debbie Meisterlin, LaQuinta, LaQuinta, Calif.	77	73	75	80	305	1,150.00
57	Charlotte Montgomery, The Forest C.C., Ft. Myers, Fla.	75	75	79	77	306	1,125.00
58	Julie Cole, Bay Hill G.C., Orlando, Fla.	76	75	80	76	307	1,087.50
	Cathy Reynolds, Hickory Hills C.C., Springfield, Mo.	75	76	77	79	307	1,087.50
60	*Pearl Sinn, Bellflower G.C., Bellflower, Calif.	80	71	80	78	309	Pin
61	Diane Lang, Camino Del Mar C.C., Boca Raton, Fla.	73	77	78	82	310	1,037.50
	M.J. Smith, Shandon G.C., New Zealand	73	73	78	86	310	1,037.50

+Record Entry

*Amateur

†The decision has been made this year to include the Championships played from 1946 through 1952 when numbering Women's Opens.

1986
FORTY FIRST WOMEN'S OPEN CHAMPIONSHIP

NCR Country Club, Kettering, Ohio, July 10-13
Yardage—6,243. Par 72. +704 Entries, 153 Starters

						Score	Money Prize
1	†Jane Geddes, Irving, Texas	74	74	70	69	287	$50,000.00
2	†Sally Little, Big Canyon G.C., Irvine, Calif.	73	72	72	70	287	25,000.00
3	Ayako Okamoto, Monte Carlo C.C., Ft. Pierce, Fla.	76	69	69	74	288	16,534.50
	Betsy King, Heidelberg C.C., Bernville, Pa.	72	71	70	75	288	16,534.50
5	Pat Bradley, Nashua C.C., Nashua, N.H.	76	71	74	69	290	9,196.25
	Jody Rosenthal, Rio Verde C.C., Rio Verde, Ariz.	72	76	71	71	290	9,196.25
	Amy Alcott, Princeville Resort, Kauai, Hawaii	75	69	74	72	290	9,196.25
	Judy Dickinson, Frenchmen's Creek G.C., N. Palm Beach, Fla.	72	71	74	73	290	9,196.25
9	Cathy Morse, Oak Hill C.C., Rochester, N.Y.	75	71	75	70	291	6,801.00
	Deb Richard, Manhattan C.C., Manhattan, Kan.	76	69	72	74	291	6,801.00
11	Laura Davies, West Byfleet, England	75	73	73	72	293	5,805.33
	Jan Stephenson, The Foothills, Phoenix, Ariz.	72	78	70	73	293	5,805.33
	Hollis Stacy, Indian Wells, Calif.	73	72	73	75	293	5,805.33
14	Tammie Green, Zanesville C.C., Zanesville, Ohio	72	79	71	72	294	4,873.75
	Silvia Bertolaccini, Moody, Maine	71	77	73	73	294	4,873.75
	Ok-Hee Ku, Los Coyotes, Buena Park, Calif.	74	74	72	74	294	4,873.75
	Lauren Howe, Dallas, Texas	74	75	70	75	294	4,873.75
	*Joan Pitcock, Ft. Washington C.C., Fresno, Calif.	77	69	72	76	294	Pin
19	Chris Johnson, Tucson, Ariz.	76	71	73	75	295	4,244.00
	Nancy Scranton, Greenview G.C., Centralia, Ill.	78	71	71	75	295	4,244.00
21	Charlotte Montgomery, The Forest, Fort Myers, Fla.	75	74	75	72	296	3,676.50
	Sherri Turner, Greenville, S.C.	72	73	78	73	296	3,676.50
	Kathy Baker, River Hills C.C., Clover, S.C.	74	72	77	73	296	3,676.50
	Beth Daniel, Loxahatchee Club, Jupiter, Fla.	70	76	75	75	296	3,676.50
	Laurie Rinker, Stuart, Fla.	77	71	73	75	296	3,676.50
	Val Skinner, PGA West, La Quinta, Calif.	74	75	71	76	296	3,676.50
27	Patti Rizzo, Monte Carlo C.C., Ft. Pierce, Fla.	76	75	74	72	297	3,191.00
	Muffin Spencer-Devlin, Hunters Run, Boynton Beach, Fla.	77	76	70	74	297	3,191.00
	Lenore Muraoka, Devon, Pa.	73	73	75	76	297	3,191.00
30	*Michele Redman, Martinsville C.C., Martinsville, Ind.	71	77	79	71	298	Pin
	Lori Garbacz, Boca West Club, Boca Raton, Fla.	73	79	74	72	298	2,878.75
	Martha Nause, Amelia Island Plantation, Amelia Island, Fla.	72	75	72	79	298	2,878.75
	Debbie Massey, Cape Arundel G.C., Kennebunkport, Maine	75	73	71	79	298	2,878.75
	Penny Hammel, Decatur, Ill.	76	74	69	79	298	2,878.75
35	JoAnne Carner, Palm Beach National, Lake Worth, Fla.	75	78	74	72	299	2,582.00
	Kathy Kratzert, Ft. Wayne, C.C., Ft. Wayne, Ind.	73	74	78	74	299	2,582.00
	Rosie Jones, Paradise Hills G.C., Albuquerque, N.M.	77	75	73	74	299	2,582.00
	Cindy Mackey, Athens C.C., Athens, Ga.	78	73	73	75	299	2,582.00
	Jane Blalock, Concord, N.H.	73	77	73	76	299	2,582.00
40	Alice Miller, Marysville, Calif.	77	76	76	71	300	2.293.25
	Jerilyn Britz, Deer Run G.C., Casselberry, Fla.	72	74	78	76	300	2.293.25
	Alice Ritzman, Tempe, Ariz.	76	74	74	76	300	2,293.25
	Jane Crafter, Pine Needles Lodge, Southern Pines, N.C.	74	73	73	80	300	2.293.25
44	Sandra Palmer, La Quinta Hotel G.C., La Quinta, Calif.	75	76	76	74	301	1.911.62
	Becky Pearson, Camino Del Mar C.C., Boca Raton, Fla.	78	71	77	75	301	1,911.62
	*Tracy Kerdyk, Melreese G.C., Miami, Fla.	75	74	76	76	301	Pin
	Amy Benz, Dallas, Texas	71	78	76	76	301	1,911.62
	Betsy Barrett, Baldwinsville, N.Y.	74	77	74	76	301	1,911.62
	Barb Bunkowsky, Boca Pointe G.C., Boca Raton, Fla.	74	74	76	77	301	1,911.62
	Denise Strebig, San Bernardino, Calif.	76	73	75	77	301	1,911.62
	Patty Sheehan, Hidden Valley C.C., Reno, Nev.	73	77	72	79	301	1,911.62
	Pia Nilsson, Torekovs G. Klubb, Torekov, Sweden	74	76	74	77	301	1,911.62
53	Missie McGeorge, Denton, Texas	76	74	73	79	302	1,506.60
	Leann Cassaday, Virginia C.C., Long Beach, Calif.	77	76	77	72	302	1,506.60
	Penny Pulz, Camden C.C., Camden, S.C.	73	77	78	74	302	1,506.60
	Nancy Rubin, Lower Burrell, Pa.	77	74	76	75	302	1,506.60
	Beth Solomon, Tri County G.C., Middletown, Ind.	76	74	75	77	302	1,506.60
58	Janet Coles, Carmel Valley Ranch, Carmel Valley, Calif.	73	77	78	75	303	1,389.00
	*Kimberly Gardner, Winged Foot G.C., Mamaroneck, N.Y.	75	76	75	77	303	——
	*Michele Ann Michanowicz, Oakmont C.C., Oakmont, Pa.	78	73	74	78	303	——
61	Bonnie Lauer, Indian Wells, Calif.	76	77	74	77	304	1,364.00
	*Robin Hood, Morris Park C.C., South Bend, Ind.	77	72	77	78	304	——
	*Michiko Hattori, Nagoya Green C.C., Japan	76	76	73	79	304	——
	Lisa Young, Prince Rupert G.C., British Columbia	81	72	72	79	304	1,364.00
65	*Page Dunlap, Misty Creek C.C., Sarasota, Fla.	76	76	78	75	305	——
	Martha Foyer, Woodland C.C., Carmel, Ind.	79	73	77	76	305	1,324.00
	Sally Quinlan, Blue Rock G.C., S. Yarmouth, Mass.	77	72	79	77	305	1,324.00
	Kathy Whitworth, Roanoke, Texas	76	75	77	77	305	1,324.00
69	Kathy Postlewait, Deer Run C.C., Casselberry, Fla.	76	74	79	77	306	1,310.00
	Juli Inkster, Rancho Murieta, Los Altos, Calif.	80	72	78	76	306	1,310.00
71	Mary Beth Zimmerman, Hillsboro C.C., Hillsboro, Ill.	78	75	81	73	307	1,310.00
	Kathryn Young, Coronado G.C., Coronado, Calif.	73	77	80	77	307	1,310.00
	Susie McAllister, Beaumont, Texas	77	73	79	78	307	1,310.00
	*Cathy Edelen, Juniper Hills G.C., Frankfurt, Ky.	78	72	79	78	307	——
75	Jo Ann Washam, Irving, Texas	77	73	83	75	308	1,310.00
	*Caroline Keggi, The C.C. of Waterbury, Waterbury, Conn.	77	75	76	85	313	1,310.00
77	Jill Briles, C.C., of Peoria, Peoria Heights, Ill.	78	74	82	80	314	1,310.00
	*Dottie Pepper, McGregor Links C.C., Saratoga Springs, N.Y.	76	75	84	80	315	——
79	Adele Lukken, G.C. of Oklahoma, Broken Arrow, Okla.	74	79	85	78	316	1,310.00

†Playoff, July 14: Geddes 71, Little 73. +Record Entry *Amateur

1987
FORTY-SECOND WOMEN'S OPEN CHAMPIONSHIP

Plainfield Country Club, Plainfield, New Jersey, July 23-28
Yardage—6,284. Par 72. +712 Entries, 153 Starters.

						Score	Money Prize
1	†Laura Davies, Surrey, England	72	70	72	71	285	$55,000.00
2	†Ayako Okamoto, Tokyo, Japan	71	72	70	72	285	23,823.50
	†JoAnne Carner, Palm Beach Nat'l G. & C.C., Lake Worth, Fla.	74	70	72	69	285	23,823.50
4	Betsy King, Rail G.C., Springfield, Ill.	75	73	70	71	289	13,461.00
	Jody Rosenthal, Rio Verde C.C., Rio Verde, Ariz.	71	72	74	72	289	13,461.00
6	Debbie Massey, C.C. of Hilton Head, Hilton Head, S.C.	76	69	74	71	290	9,741.00
	Deedee Roberts, Sunset Ridge C.C., Northbrook, Ill.	74	73	69	74	290	9,741.00
8	Martha Nause, Amelia Island Plantation, Amelia Island, Fla.	76	69	70	76	291	8,390.00
9	Kathy Postlewait, Deer Run C.C., Casselberry, Fla.	70	79	73	70	292	7,111.00
	Sally Quinlan, Blue Rock G.C., South Yarmouth, Mass.	75	71	71	75	292	7,111.00
	Rosie Jones, Paradise Hills C.C., Albuquerque, N.M.	75	71	71	75	292	7,111.00
12	Dottie Mochrie, McGregor Links C.C., Saratoga Springs, N.Y.	73	72	77	71	293	5,939.00
	Marta Figueras-Dotti, Valderrama G.C., Madrid, Spain	77	70	74	72	293	5,939.00
	Amy Alcott, Princeville Resort, Kauai, Hawaii	72	71	76	74	293	5,939.00
15	Alice Ritzman, Tempe, Ariz.	76	74	73	71	294	5,256.00
	Tammie Green, Zanesville C.C., Zanesbille, Ohio	72	74	72	76	294	5,256.00
17	Deb Richard, Sweetwater C.C., Houston, Texas	72	73	75	75	295	4,790.50
	Sandra Palmer, LaQuinta H. & G.C., LaQuinta, Calif.	71	72	75	77	295	4,790.50
19	Michele Berteotti, Valley Brook C.C., McMurray, Pa.	73	74	79	70	296	4,394.50
	Cindy Rarick, Tucson National G.C., Tucson, Ariz.	74	71	76	75	296	4,394.50
21	Patty Sheehan, Los Gatos, Calif.	74	74	77	72	297	3,844.17
	Denise Strebig, San Bernardino, Calif.	74	78	73	72	297	3,844.17
	Sherri Turner, Greenville, S.C.	77	73	74	73	297	3,844.17
	Donna White, Wellington Club, Wellington, Fla.	77	72	74	74	297	3,844.17
	*Michiko Hattori, Nagoya Green C.C., Nagoya, Japan	78	73	71	71	297	Pin
	Nancy Lopez, Windstar Development, Naples, Fla.	73	71	77	76	297	3,844.16
	Amy Benz, Clearwater, Fla.	74	73	74	76	297	3,844.16
28	Lori Garbacz, Boca Raton, Fla.	77	72	77	72	298	3,291.00
	Jerilyn Britz, Deer Run C.C., Casselberry, Fla.	79	71	76	72	298	3,291.00
	Bonnie Lauer, Palm Desert, Calif.	69	76	76	77	298	3,291.00
	*Kathleen McCarthy, San Joaquin C.C., Fresno, Calif.	74	78	69	77	298	Pin
	Anne-Marie Palli, Ciboure, France	74	73	77	74	298	3,291.00
33	Hollis Stacy, Palm Desert, Calif.	76	76	75	72	299	2,857.58
	Marci Bozarth, Hancock Park G.C., Lampasas, Texas	72	73	81	73	299	2,857.57
	Nancy Ledbetter, Bent Tree C.C., Dallas, Texas	79	73	74	73	299	2,857.57
	Beth Daniel, The Loxahatchee Club, Jupiter, Fla.	73	75	77	74	299	2,857.57
	Cathy Morse, Oak Hill C.C., Rochester, N.Y.	74	74	76	75	299	2,857.57
	Dorothy Germain, Pine Needles L. & C.C., Southern Pines, N.C.	69	75	79	76	299	2,857.57
	Ok-Hee Ku, Mesa Verde C.C., Costa Mesa, Calif.	73	73	77	76	299	2,857.57
40	Juli Inkster, Rancho Murieta C.C., Rancho Murieta, Calif.	78	72	79	71	300	2,577.75
	Missie McGeorge, Denton, Texas	78	74	75	73	300	2,477.75
	Cathy Marino, Milburn C.C., Overland Park, Kan.	78	73	75	74	300	2,477.75
	Carolyn Hill, Alta Vista C.C., Placentia, Calif.	75	73	78	74	300	2,477.75
	*Cindy Scholefield, The Los Angeles C.C., Los Angeles, Calif.	75	74	72	79	300	Pin
45	Dale Eggeling, Quail Hollow G.C., Wesley Chapel, Fla.	76	74	77	74	301	2,271.50
	Kandi Kessler, Farmington C.C., Charlottesville, Va.	74	78	75	74	301	2,271.50
47	Judy Dickinson, Frenchmen's Creek G.C., N. Palm Beach, Fla.	77	71	78	76	302	2,134.50
	Dawn Coe, March Meadows G.C., Lake Cowichan, B.C., Canada	78	69	77	78	302	2,134.50
	*Kay Cockerill, La Rinconada C.C., Los Gatos, Calif.	73	74	76	79	302	Pin
49	Mary Beth Zimmerman, Hillsboro C.C., Hillsboro, Ill.	78	74	77	74	303	1,962.67
	Janet Coles, Carmel Valley Ranch, Carmel, Calif.	76	73	79	75	303	1,962.67
	M.J. Smith, Robin Dale C.C., Brandywine, Md.	75	75	78	75	303	1,962.66
	Silvia Bertolaccini, Moody, Maine	75	77	78	74	304	1,789.00
	Muffin Spencer-Devlin, Hunters Run G.C., Boynton Beach, Fla.	77	75	75	77	304	1,789.00
54	Sally Little, Big Canyon G.C., Irvine, Calif.	73	74	82	76	305	1,617.34
	Lauri Peterson, Gainey Ranch G.C., Scottsdale, Ariz.	77	75	76	77	305	1,617.33
	Betsy Barrett, San Jose, Calif.	76	74	76	79	305	1,617.33
57	Tammy Fredrickson, Annandale G.C., Pasadena, Calif.	76	76	77	77	306	1,511.50
	Joan Pitcock, Ft. Washington C.C., Fresno, Calif.	73	75	80	78	306	1,511.50
	*Dana Lofland, River Ridge G.C., Oxnard, Calif.	74	76	77	79	306	Pin
60	Debbie Skinner, Chula Vista, Calif.	76	75	79	77	307	1,472.00
	Caroline Pierce, Sweetwater C.C., Sugar Land, Texas	77	75	78	77	307	1,472.00
62	Susan Tonkin, Kooyonga G.C., Adelaide, Australia	74	76	76	82	308	1,445.00
63	Debby Rhodes, MacDill AFB G.C., Tampa, Fla.	77	75	75	82	309	1,428.00
64	*Leslie Shannon, Lago Mar C.C., Plantation, Fla.	74	75	82	80	311	Pin
65	Lulong Radler, Ft. Worth, Texas	79	73	80	81	313	1,414.00
	Margaret Kirsch, Eastpointe C.C., Palm Beach Gardens, Fla.	76	74	81	82	313	1,414.00
	Jane Geddes, Dallas, Texas	75	74	74	WD	—	—

†Playoff, July 28: Davies 71, Okamoto 73, Carner 74. +Record Entry *Amateur

1988
FORTY-THIRD WOMEN'S OPEN CHAMPIONSHIP

Baltimore Country Club (East Course), Baltimore, Maryland, July 21-24
Yardage—6,232. Par 71. †736 Entries, 153 Starters.

						Score	Money Prize
1	Liselotte Neumann, Finspang G.C., Finspang, Sweden	67	72	69	69	277	$70,000.00
2	Patty Sheehan, Los Gatos, Calif.	70	72	68	70	280	35,000.00
3	Dottie Mochrie, McGregor Links C.C., Saratoga Springs, N.Y.	70	69	76	68	283	21,679.00
	Colleen Walker, Brandon, Fla.	70	74	68	71	283	21,679.00
5	Jan Stephenson, Fort Worth, Texas	72	72	71	69	284	14,393.00
6	Michele Berteotti, Valley Brock C.C., Pittsburgh, Pa.	75	71	68	71	285	11,826.00
	Amy Benz, Delray Beach, Fla.	70	72	71	72	285	11,826.00
8	Kristi Albers, Vista Hills C.C., El Paso, Texas	73	70	72	71	286	9,726.00
	Juli Inkster, Rancho Murieta C.C., Rancho Murieta, Calif.	71	68	75	72	286	9,726.00
10	Vicki Fergon, Royal Oaks, C.C. Dallas, Texas	70	71	75	71	287	8,315.00
	Beth Daniel, Loxahatchee C., Jupiter, Fla.	77	71	66	73	287	8,315.00
12	Betsy King, Rail G.C., Springfield, Ill.	76	74	71	67	288	7,038.75
	Ayako Okamoto, Torrance, Calif.	75	73	71	69	288	7,038.75
	Kris Hanson, The Hills of Lakeway, Austin, Texas	73	72	73	70	288	7,038.75
	Nancy Lopez, Albany, Ga.	72	74	71	71	288	7,038.75
16	JoAnne Carner, Palm Beach National G. & C.C., Lake Worth, Fla.	69	73	76	71	289	5,954.00
	Nancy Brown, Greenview G.C., Centralia, Ill.	71	73	72	73	289	5,954.00
	Kay Cockerill, La Rinconada C.C., Los Gatos, Calif.	73	70	72	74	289	5,954.00
19	Christa Johnson, Tucson, Ariz.	73	74	73	70	290	5,070.60
	Mei Chi Cheng, Arcadia, Calif.	74	76	70	70	290	5,070.60
	Rosie Jones, Hilton Head Island, S.C.	74	70	74	72	290	5,070.60
	Marta Figueras-Dotti, Valderrama C.C., Madrid, Spain	77	71	69	73	290	5,070.60
	Tammie Green, Zanesville C.C., Zanesville, Ohio	71	70	71	78	290	5,070.60
24	Robin Hood, Riverside G.C., Grand Prairie, Texas	77	72	71	71	291	4,310.40
	Sally Quinlan, Blue Rock G.C., South Yarmouth, Mass.	69	75	74	73	291	4,310.40
	Deedee Lasker, San Diego, Calif.	73	71	74	73	291	4,310.40
	Judy Dickinson, Frenchmens Creek G.C., Tequesta, Fla.	71	76	71	73	291	4,310.40
	Donna White, Wellington Club, Wellington, Fla.	72	70	73	76	291	4,310.40
29	*Carol Semple Thompson, Allegheny C.C., Sewickley, Pa.	79	71	70	72	292	Pin
	Kathy Baker-Guadagnino, Boca Raton, Fla.	72	72	75	73	292	3,820.00
	Sherri Turner, Greenville, S.C.	73	72	73	74	292	3,820.00
	Jody Rosenthal, Rio Verde C.C., Rio Verde, Ariz.	74	73	71	74	292	3,820.00
33	Shelley Hamlin, Sunnyside C.C., Fresno, Calif.	74	74	73	72	293	3,468.00
	Debbie Massey, Bear Creek G.C., Hilton Head, S.C.	74	73	73	73	293	3,468.20
	Patti Rizzo, Monte Carlo C.C., Fort Pierce, Fla.	78	71	71	73	293	3,468.20
	Shirley Furlong, San Antonio, Texas	70	75	72	76	293	3,468.20
	Alice Ritzman, Tempe, Ariz.	73	74	70	76	293	3,468.20
38	Cathy Morse, Oak Hill C.C., Rochester, N.Y.	73	74	73	74	294	3,132.34
	Sally Little, Big Canyon C.C., Irvine, Calif.	71	75	72	76	294	3,132.33
	Janet Coles, Carmel Valley Ranch, Carmel, Calif.	72	71	74	77	294	3,132.33
41	Amy Alcott, Princeville Resort, Kauai, Hawaii	76	74	74	71	295	2,882.34
	Jane Geddes, Mission Hills C.C., Rancho Mirage, Calif.	74	76	73	72	295	2,882.33
	Dale Eggeling, Tampa Palms G. & C.C., Tampa, Fla.	76	72	72	75	295	2,882.33
44	Meg Mallon, San Vicente C.C., Ramona, Calif.	78	71	75	72	296	2,632.00
	*Brandie Burton, Arrowhead C.C., San Bernardino, Calif.	74	75	73	74	296	Pin
	Dawn Coe, March Meadows G.C., Lake Cowichan, B.C., Canada	74	72	74	76	296	2,632.00
	Sue Ertl, Sweetwater C.C., Sugar Land, Texas	74	72	73	77	296	2,632.00
48	Valerie Skinner, PGA West, LaQuinta, Calif.	75	72	78	72	297	2,424.00
	Heather Farr, Camelback G.C., Scottsdale, Ariz.	72	75	72	78	297	2,424.00
50	Laura Davies, West Byfleet, England	72	73	75	78	298	2,257.00
	Robin Walton, Clarkston, Wash.	73	75	72	78	298	2,257.00
52	Hollis Stacy, Wilshore C.C., Los Angeles, Calif.	77	70	76	76	299	2,090.50
	Kathy Postlewait, Tuscawilla C.C., Winter Springs, Fla.	74	72	74	79	299	2.090.50
54	Mary Beth Zimmerman, Hillsboro C.C., Hillsboro, Ill.	76	74	74	76	300	1,965.00
55	Mina Hardin, Golfcrest C.C., Pearland, Texas	75	74	81	71	301	1,839.25
	Martha Foyer, Woodland C.C., Carmel, Ind.	73	76	77	75	301	1,839.25
	Dorothy Germain, Pine Needles C.C., Southern Pines, N.C.	75	72	78	76	301	1,839.25
	Tracy Kerdyk, Melreese G.C., Miami, Fla.	73	74	76	78	301	1,839.25
59	Terry-Jo Myers, Eagle Ridge G.C., Fort Myers, Fla.	75	75	77	75	302	1,777.00
60	Carol French, Auburn Valley G. & C.C., Auburn, Calif.	74	75	79	75	303	1,736.34
	Cindy Figg-Currier, Hills of Lakeway, Austin, Texas	78	72	77	76	303	1,736.33
	Kristin Lofye, Misty Creek C.C., Sarasota, Fla.	77	71	75	80	303	1,736.33
63	Dale Reid, Ladybank G.C., Ladybank, England	73	76	75	80	304	1,718.00
64	Alison Nicholas, Birmingham, England	76	73	77	79	305	1,718.00
65	Marlene Brodzik-Davis, Dande Farms G.C., Akron, N.Y.	71	77	79	79	306	1,718.00
66	Jill Briles, C.C. of Peoria, Peoria, Ill.	75	74	77	81	307	1,718.00
67	Jane Crafter, Pine Needles C.C., Southern Pines, N.C.	74	71	85	80	310	1,718.00

†Record Entry
*Amateur

1989
FORTY-FOURTH WOMEN'S OPEN CHAMPIONSHIP

Indianwood Golf and Country Club (Old Course), Lake Orion, Michigan, July 13-16
Yardage—6,109. Par 71. Record 736 Entries, 155 Starters.

						Score	Money Prize
1	Betsy King, Heidelberg C.C., Limekiln, Pa.	67	71	72	68	278	$80,000.00
2	Nancy Lopez, Albany, Ga.	73	70	71	68	282	40,000.00
3	Penny Hammel, Decatur, Ill.	74	73	69	67	283	24,250.00
	Pat Bradley, Nashua C.C., Nashua, N.H.	73	74	68	68	283	24,250.00
5	Dottie Mochrie, McGregor Links C.C., Saratoga Springs, NY	72	70	75	67	284	15,043.00
	Lori Garbacz, Boca Raton, Fla.	71	70	73	70	284	15,043.00
7	Laura Davies, Ottershaw, England	73	71	75	66	285	11,931.00
	Vicki Fergon, Royal Oaks C.C., Dallas, Texas	72	74	69	70	285	11,931.00
9	Jane Geddes, Mission Hills C.C., Rancho Mirage, Calif.	70	72	72	72	286	9,974.00
	Colleen Walker, Bloomingdale G.C., Brandon, Fla.	72	69	71	74	286	9,974.00
11	Ayako Okamoto, Torrance, Calif.	76	72	74	65	287	8,304.00
	Danielle Ammaccapane, Phoenix, Ariz.	73	70	74	70	287	8,304.00
	Myra Blackwelder, Champions C.C., Oldsmar, Fla.	76	68	71	72	287	8,304.00
	Marie-Laure Delorenzi-Taya, Spain	68	74	71	74	287	8,304.00
15	Kim Bauer, Sugar Land, Texas	72	72	73	71	288	7,137.00
	Marta Figueras-Dotti, Valderrama C.C., Sarasota, Fla.	75	70	70	73	288	7,137.00
17	Gina Hull, Marsh Landing C.C., Jacksonville, Fla.	74	72	72	71	289	6,374.00
	JoAnne Carner, Palm Beach National, Palm Beach, Fla.	76	69	71	73	289	6,374.00
	Patty Sheehan, Middlebury G.C., Scotts Valley, Calif.	74	67	69	79	289	6,374.00
20	Shirley Furlong, San Antonio, Texas	74	75	73	68	290	5,392.00
	Liselotte Neumann, Finspang, Sweden	71	71	75	73	290	5,392.00
	Caroline Keggi, The C.C. of Waterbury, Waterbury, Conn.	71	73	73	73	290	5,392.00
	Beth Daniel, The Loxahatchee Club, Jupiter, Fla.	73	73	71	73	290	5,392.00
	Kathy Postlewait, Timacuan G.C., Casselberry, Fla.	77	70	70	73	290	5,392.00
	Donna Cusano-Wilkins, Fort Lauderdale, Fla.	71	72	71	76	290	5,392.00
26	Sally Quinlan, Blue Rock G.C., Dennis, Mass.	78	71	73	69	291	4,680.00
	Kim Shipman, Dallas, Texas	74	69	74	74	291	4,680.00
	Amy Alcott, Princeville Resort, Kauai, Hawaii	73	71	73	74	291	4,680.00
29	Donna White, Wellington Club, Wellington, Fla.	75	73	74	70	292	4,172.00
	Chris Johnson, Oro Valley C.C., Tucson, Ariz.	73	73	75	71	292	4,172.00
	Nancy Taylor, Bloomingdale G.C., Tampa, Fla	74	73	73	72	292	4,172.00
	Patrice Rizzo, Miami, Fla.	77	69	73	73	292	4,172.00
	Debbie Massey, Bear Creek G.C., Hilton Head Island, S.C.	71	72	75	74	292	4,172.00
34	Jody Rosenthal, Rio Verde C.C., Rio Verde, Ariz.	80	69	76	69	294	3,786.00
	Deborah McHaffie, Las Vegas C.C., Las Vegas, Nev.	71	73	80	70	294	3,786.00
	Cindy Rarick, Tucson National G.C., Tucson, Ariz.	75	73	73	73	294	3,786.00
37	Amy Benz, Boca Raton, Fla.	71	76	76	72	295	3,458.00
	Hollis Stacy, Wilshire C.C. Palm Desert, Calif.	78	70	73	74	295	3,458.00
	Kristi Albers, El Paso C.C., El Paso, Texas	71	73	75	76	295	3,458.00
	Sandra Haynie, Fort Myers, Fla.	72	73	74	76	295	3,458.00
41	Linda Hunt, Sweetwater C.C., Sugar Land, Texas	71	72	74	79	296	3,178.00
	Lenore Rittenhouse, Pauma Valley C.C., Pauma Valley, Cal.	73	72	72	79	296	3,178.00
43	Missie McGeorge, Fort Worth, Texas	74	73	77	73	297	2,758.00
	Allison Finney, Rancho Mirage, Calif.	74	74	76	73	297	2,758.00
	Kathy Guadagnino, Boca Raton, Fla.	76	74	74	73	297	2,758.00
	Peggy Kirsch, Lake Placid, Sebring, Fla.	76	70	77	74	297	2,758.00
	Maggie Will, Pinehurst C.C., Whiteville, N.C.	74	75	74	74	297	2,758.00
	Tammie Green, Zanesville C.C., Somerset, Ohio	77	67	77	76	297	2,758.00
	Alice Ritzman, Tempe, Ariz.	71	75	74	77	297	2,758.00
50	Lori West, Cardinal C.C., Greensboro, N.C.	76	73	75	74	298	2,292.00
	Valerie Skinner, PGA West, Palm Desert, Calif.	78	72	74	74	298	2,292.00
	Alison Nicholas, Harborne Birmingham, England	74	73	75	76	298	2,292.00
53	Nancy Rubin, Lower Burrell, Pa.	75	73	77	74	299	2,105.00
54	Deb Richard, Sweetwater C.C., Manhattan, Kan.	73	77	76	74	300	2,072.00
	a-Vicki Goetze, Jennings Mill, Hull Ga.	73	75	77	75	300	
56	Kris Monaghan, Albuquerque, N.M.	74	76	81	70	301	2,039.00
57	Angie Ridgeway, Red Fox C.C., Inman, S.C.	71	79	79	74	303	1,977.00
	Robin Walton, Hilton Head Island, S.C.	71	78	79	75	303	1,977.00
	Rosie Jones, Desert Mountain, Clarkston, Wash.	72	78	77	76	303	1,977.00
	Michelle McGann, Old Marsh G.C., Singer Island, Fla.	72	75	79	77	303	1,977.00
61	Pamela Wright, Houston, Texas	78	70	80	76	304	1,921.00

a = amateur

1990
FORTY-FIFTH WOMEN'S OPEN CHAMPIONSHIP

Atlanta Athletic Club (Riverside Course), Duluth, Georgia, July 12-15
Yardage—6,298. Par 72. Record 785 Entries, 156 Starters.

						Score	Money Prize
1	Betsy King, Limekiln, Pa.	72	71	71	70	284	$85,000.00
2	Patty Sheehan, Reno, Nevada	66	68	75	76	285	42,500.00
3	Danielle Ammaccapane, Phoenix, Ariz.	72	73	70	71	286	23,956.00
	Dottie Mochrie, Sarasota, Fla.	74	74	72	66	286	23,956.00
5	Mary E. Murphy, Naples, Fla.	70	74	69	74	287	15,904.00
6	Elaine Crosby, Fort Myers, Fla.	71	74	73	70	288	12,463.67
	Tammie Green, Somerset, Ohio	70	74	73	71	288	12,463.67
	Beth Daniel, Richmond, Va.	71	71	74	72	288	12,463.67
9	Colleen Walker, Brandon, Fla.	69	75	73	72	289	8,533.14
	Amy Alcott, Pacific Palisades, Cal.	72	72	72	73	289	8,533.14
	Sherrie E. Turner, Oak Ridge, N.C.	74	72	71	72	289	8,533.14
	Hollis Stacy, Palm Desert, Calif.	71	72	77	69	289	8,533.14
	Caroline S. Keggi, Waterbury, Conn.	67	75	73	74	289	8,533.14
	Meg Mallon, Ramona, Calif.	71	71	77	70	289	8,533.14
	Cathy Gerring, Dublin, Ohio	70	78	70	71	289	8,533.14
16	Missie McGeorge, Fort Worth, Tex.	72	74	72	72	290	6,726.50
	Rose Jones, Hilton Head Isl., S.C.	72	70	74	74	290	6,726.50
18	JoAnne Carner, Palm Beach, Fla.	73	71	70	77	291	6,287.00
19	Jody Anschutz, Rio Verde, Ariz.	72	73	74	73	292	5,423.86
	Nancy Lopez, Albany, Ga.	68	76	75	73	292	5,423.86
	Pat Bradley, Camp Hill, Pa.	74	70	75	73	292	5,423.86
	Alice Ritzman, Tempe, Ariz.	77	70	73	72	292	5,423.86
	Donna Andrews, Pinehurst, N.C.	75	72	73	72	292	5,423.86
	Jane Geddes, Orlando, Fla.	66	74	79	73	292	5,423.86
	Cindy Rarick, Tucson, Ariz.	73	74	70	75	292	5,423.86
26	Barbara Mucha, Parma Heights, Ohio	74	72	75	72	293	4,622.67
	Laura Davies, England	73	73	74	73	293	4,622.67
	Cindy Figg Currier, Austin, Tex.	76	72	73	72	293	4,622.67
29	Allison Finney, Winnetka, Ill.	73	73	71	77	294	4,221.33
	Debbie Massey, Bethlehem, Pa.	70	73	75	76	294	4,221.33
	Kathy Postlewait, Casselberry, Fla.	75	74	75	70	294	4,221.33
32	Pamela Wright, Scotland	72	74	74	75	295	3,693.75
	Martha Nause, Sheboygan, Wis.	75	71	76	73	295	3,693.75
	Nancy Rubin, Lower Burrell, Pa.	71	72	76	73	295	3,693.75
	Deb Richard, Sugar Land, Tex.	74	72	74	75	295	3,693.75
	Shirley Furlong, San Antonio, Tex.	71	71	77	76	295	3,693.75
	Hiromi Kobayashi, Torrance, Calif.	75	72	73	75	295	3,693.75
	Cathy Morse, Palm Beach Gardens, Fla.	73	75	74	73	295	3,693.75
	Ayako Okamoto, Japan	74	74	73	74	295	3,693.75
40	Janet Anderson, Phoenix, Ariz.	70	72	80	74	296	3,185.00
	Nancy Brown, Riverview, Fla.	72	75	74	75	296	3,185.00
	Susan Sanders, Phoenix, Ariz.	70	77	72	77	296	3,185.00
43	Gina Hull, Jacksonville, Fla.	73	72	78	74	297	2,817.00
	Jackie Gallagher, Marion, Ind.	74	73	74	76	297	2,817.00
	Cathy Marino, Overland Park, Kan.	71	77	78	71	297	2,817.00
	Alison Nicholas, England	75	73	74	75	297	2,817.00
	Heather L. Drew, Solana Beach, Cal.	75	74	74	74	297	2,817.00
48	Jan Stephenson, Fort Worth, Tex.	75	72	73	78	298	2,540.00
49	Kris Tschetter, Sioux Falls, S.D.	70	75	79	75	299	2,264.00
	Myra Blackwelder, Versailles, Ken.	75	71	78	75	299	2,264.00
	Jerilyn Britz, Luverne, Minn.	69	74	78	78	299	2,264.00
	Joan Delk, Norcross, Ga.	74	73	73	79	299	2,264.00
	Amy Benz, Boca Raton, Fla.	74	75	76	74	299	2,264.00
54	*Vicki Goetze, Hull, Ga.	72	73	76	79	300	Medal
	Liselotte Neumann, Lutz, Fla.	73	74	78	75	300	2,030.50
	Kay Cockerill, Los Gatos, Calif.	76	72	76	76	300	2,030.50
57	*Jennifer Myers, Lancaster, Pa.	71	76	79	75	301	
	Caroline Pierce, Sussex, England	75	73	79	74	301	1,990.00
59	Vicki Fergon, Dallas, Tex.	74	72	76	80	302	1,964.00
60	*Katie Peterson, Plantation, Fla.	75	74	81	73	303	
61	Dale Eggeling, Tampa, Fla.	75	73	75	81	304	1,941.00
62	*Kate Hughes, Woodbury, Minn.	76	73	81	77	307	
63	Nancy Harvey, Mesa, Ariz.	75	74	79	83	311	1,918.00

* = amateur
Prize money of approximately $500,000 awarded to professionals.

AMATEUR PUBLIC LINKS CHAMPIONSHIP

STANDISH CUP

Presented in June, 1922, by

JAMES D. STANDISH, JR.

Chairman, United States Golf Association Public and Municipal Golf Courses Committee

WARREN G. HARDING TROPHY

Presented in June, 1923, by

HON. WARREN G. HARDING

President of the United States of America

HISTORY

1981—Jodie Mudd, 21, of Louisville, Kentucky, became the first golfer in 19 years to win consecutive Amateur Public Links Championships. R.H. Sikes was the last to win two in a row in 1961 and 1962. Mudd defeated 1981 Dixie Amateur Champion Billy Tuten in the final, 3 and 2, on the Masters Course of the Bear Creek Golf World in Houston, Texas. Mudd beat the heat to keep the Public Links Trophy in the family for the third time in the past six years. Brother Eddie won the Amateur Public Links title in 1976. Roy Biancalana of Chicago, Illinois won medalist honors with a superb 36-hole score of 138 under difficult weather conditions. Mudd shot 141 to qualify easily for the match play. Biancalana exited in the first round falling to Mike Miles of Cypress, California, 1 up, in 19 holes. Mudd had some close calls en route to the final. After eliminating Greg Morrison of Richardson, Texas, 4 and 3, Mudd needed a birdie on the 18th to square his second match with Mark Saatzer of St. Cloud, Minnesota and then birdied the first extra hole to close it out. Next, Mudd was 3 down after 10 holes to Doug Hixon of Crooked River, Oregon, but won four in a row on the way to a 2 and 1 triumph. He swept to a 3 and 1 quarter-final victory over David Anthony of Nashville, Tennessee, and to a 2 and 1 semifinal decision against Danny Elkins of St. Petersburg, Florida. Tuten, the 1979 Junior Amateur runner-up and 1980 Amateur Public Links semifinalist from Palatka, Florida, defeated Richard Dalpos of Lemont, Illinois, 3 and 2; Phil Arinno of Citrus Heights, California, 2 up; Vic Wilk of Sepulveda, California, 1 up, 20 holes; Mark Seki of Kahului, Hawaii, 6 and 4; and Andrew Soley of Cedar Lake, Indiana, 2 up. Both Mudd and Tuten showed the strain of the heat and the competition in the 36-hole final. Mudd, however, was 3 up at the lunch break and 5 up through 28 holes. Tuten managed to win two more holes, but he pulled a birdie putt of five feet at the 15th, which cost him dearly. The match was over on the 16th hole. In August, Mudd became the first Amateur Public Links Champion since R.H. Sikes to be named to the United States Walker Cup Team. On a sad note, Mudd's father, Edward L. Mudd, a member of the USGA Public Links Committee, passed away in Louisville, not long after witnessing his son's victory in Houston. The Chicago Team, led by Biancalana's stylish play, won the Warren G. Harding Team Trophy, emblematic of the Amateur Public Links Team Championship. Biancalana combined with Soley and Nicholas Zambole of Palatine, Illinois, for a 435 total, 19 strokes better than the 454 of the Houston Team. The USGA received 4,318 entries, short of the record, 4601 set in 1975.

1982—Billy Tuten, 20, of Palatka, Florida, won the Amateur Public Links Championship by defeating Brad Heninger, of San Jose, California, 6 and 5, in the final at Eagle Creek Golf Course, in Indianapolis, Indiana. Tuten had previously been runner-up to Jodie Mudd in the 1981 Championship and semifinalist in 1980. He was also runner-up in the 1979 Junior Amateur Championship. Tuten is believed to be the first alternate player to win this Championship. He was included when Christopher Young, one of the Jacksonville, Florida, qualifiers, withdrew because of a business commitment. After qualifying with a 142 total, Tuten reached the final by defeating Tom Cotter, of St. Paul, Minnesota, 1 up; Gary Hitch, of Ventura, California, on the 21st hole; Dennis Dolci, of Sharon, Pennsylvania, 5 and 4; Jesse Patino, of Dallas, Texas, 6 and 4; and, in the semifinals, David Nelson, of Sparks, Nevada, 4 and 3. Heninger, who qualified with a 151 total, had an easier route to the final. He defeated Bryan Symonds, of Newburgh, Indiana, 7 and 6; Mike Davidson, of Paramount, California, 4 and 3; Andy Soley (a 1981 semifinalist), of Cedar Lake, Indiana, 2 and 1; Ken Kelley, of Waller, Texas, 3 and 2; and, in the semifinals, Steve Barnett, of Anderson, Indiana, 3 and 1. Tony Grimes, of Scottsdale, Arizona, was medalist with a 36-hole score of 140, including a course record 68 in the second round. He was defeated in the first round by Soley, 1 up. Led by the fine play of Grimes, Phoenix, Arizona, won the Warren G. Harding Trophy, emblematic of the Amateur Public Links Team Championship. Grimes teamed with Jimmy Carter and Bill Myers for a 288 total, six strokes better than the 294 of the Los Angeles team. The USGA received 4,312 entries, short of the record 4,601 set in 1975.

AMATEUR PUBLIC LINKS CHAMPIONSHIP

1983—Billy Tuten, 21, of Palatka, Florida, won a second successive Amateur Public Links title, defeating David Hobby, of Santa Ana, California, 3 and 1, at the Hominy Hill Golf Course, in Colts Neck, New Jersey. Tuten, who two months earlier had been a member of the victorious U.S. Walker Cup Team, qualified for match play easily with a 148 total. Enroute to the final, Tuten defeated Dean Prince of San Bruno, California, the 1978 APL Champion, 5 and 3, in the semifinal round. Hobby qualified with 149, and defeated Greg Twiggs, his college teammate, from San Diego State University, 3 and 1; and, in the semifinals, Mike Swartz, the reigning National Junior College Champion, 4 and 3. Tuten birdied two of the first four holes of the final to take a 2-up lead, but Hobby won the sixth and 13th holes to even the match. After both players birdied the par-5 14th, Hobby opened a two-hole lead by winning the 15th and 17th holes. As the afternoon round began, Hobby won two of the first three holes to increase his lead to 4 up with 15 to play. Tuten, however, won four of the next five holes, three with birdies, to even the match. Hobby eagled the ninth, to go 1 up, but Tuten won the 10th to pull even once again. When Hobby hit his tee shot on the par-3 11th into a pond, Tuten went ahead for good. Tuten went 2 up with a par at the 14th and closed out the match when he hit the par-5 17th in 2 and two-putted for a birdie. The Los Angeles team of Mike Miles, Jeff Johnson, and John Ledgerwood won the Warren G. Harding Team Trophy, emblematic of the Amateur Public Links Team Championship. They combined for a 292 total, three strokes better than the team from Des Moines, Iowa. Fifty-four teams competed. The USGA accepted entries from 4,533 players.

1984—Bill Malley, 29, a truck driver from Hayward, California, defeated Dirk Jones, of San Diego, California, 2 and 1, at the Indian Canyon Golf Course, in Spokane Washington. Jim Carter, of Phoenix, Arizona, was medalist with a record 132, eight strokes under par, Carter led Phoenix to the team championships and the Warren G. Harding Trophy with a score of 269. While Malley qualified at 145, Jones was two strokes back, at 147. The final match was a test of Malley's patience. He was three holes down on two occasions and did not claim the lead until the 31st hole. He closed out Jones on the 35th. The USGA accepted a record 4,814 entries and 46 teams competed in the team competition.

1985—Jim Sorenson, 22, of Bloomington, Minnesota, defeated Jay Cooper of Coral Gables, Florida, 12 and 11, to win the Championship at Wailua Golf Course in Lihue, Hawaii. Sorenson's margin of victory was the largest ever in the Amateur Public Links final. Robin McCool of Bethlehem, Pennsylvania, was medalist with a two-under-par 142 total. Sorenson completely dominated the final match. He was 7 up after nine holes and 11 up at the close of the morning round. He needed only seven holes of the afternoon round to close out Cooper. The Phoenix Arizona, team of Mike Swartz, Bill Mayfair and Robert Vessel won the Team Championship in a playoff over the team from St. Louis, Missouri. It was Phoenix's fourth team title in the last seven years. The USGA accepted 5,529 entries for the Championship, more than for any Championship in USGA history.

1986—Bill Mayfair, 19, of Phoenix, Arizona, defeated Jim Sorenson, the defending champion from Bloomington, Minnesota, at Tanglewood Park in Clemmons, North Carolina. Mayfair was co-medalist with Art Roberson of Zebulon, North Carolina, at one-under-par 139. Roberson was eliminated in the second round by Kevin Hayashi of Honolulu. Mayfair was extended to the 18th hole twice on his way to the final. He defeated Steve Rintoul of Eugene, Oregon, 2 and 1, in his semifinal match. Sorenson, on the other hand, was not seriously challenged until the semifinal round, when he edged Bryan Hancock of Athens, Georgia, 1 up. In the final, Sorenson won the first hole with a par, but lost the next two to go 1 down. Sorenson leveled the match with a par at the eighth hole, but Mayfair regained the lead immediately with birdies on the ninth and 10th. Mayfair's 2-up lead lasted until he bogeyed the 21st and 22nd holes. Birdies on the 24th, 26th and 28th hole, gave Mayfair the lead for good. He closed out the match by sinking a 33-foot birdie putt on the 34th hole, his 10th birdie in the final match. The Team Championship was won by Roberson, Larry Boswell and Mike Taylor, who represented Clemmons, North Carolina. Their total of 279 was three better than that of the team from Tucson, Arizona. The USGA accepted 5,427 entries for the championship.

1987—Kevin Johnson, 20, of Pembroke, Massachusetts, defeated Jimmy England of Gastonia, North Carolina, 10 and 9, to win the championship at Glenview Golf Course in Cincinnati, Ohio. The margin of victory was the second-largest in the championship's history, exceeded only by Jim Sorenson's 12-and-11 win over Jay Cooper in 1985. Garth Johnston, Eric Woods and 1979 APL champion Dennis Walsh shared the qualifying medal at two-under-par 142. All three were eliminated by the quarterfinals. Johnson never trailed in the final. He won the first four holes, seven of the first nine and held a seven-hole advantage after the morning round. He recorded seven birdies in 27 holes on the way to the victory. The San Francisco team of Frank Mazion, Rodney Wilson and Mark Sanchez won the team title with a 289 total, four ahead of Minneapolis and five ahead of San Diego. The USGA accepted 5,501 entries for the championship.

1988—Ralph Howe, III, 23, of West Sayville, New York, defeated 1987 champion Kevin Johnson of Pembroke, Massachusetts, on the 37th hole of the final at the Jackson Hole Golf and Tennis Club in Jackson, Wyoming. Howe is the first left-hander to win a USGA championship. Mike Foster of

Vacaville, California, won the qualifying medal with a 36-hole total of 66-70—136, six under par. He was eliminated in the second round by Kelly Manos of Cypress, California, 2 and 1. Howe, who qualified at 146, earned his place in the final round with a 2-up victory over Kyle McGee of Houston. Johnson eliminated Kevin Wentworth of Manteca, California, another lefthander, 3 and 1, in the other semifinal match. Howe birdied the first hole of the final to go 1 up and held that lead through nine. He won the 10th with a birdie to go 2 up, and increased his lead to three when Johnson double-bogeyed the 14th. It was the only hole that Johnson played over par in the final. Johnson won the 17th with a birdie and trailed by two holes after the morning round. The defending champion erased the deficit early in the afternoon round and, when Howe bogeyed the 11th, Johnson took his first lead of the final. The 12th through the 17th were halved with pars, and Howe squared the match when he birdied the 18th. Howe chipped in from the back fringe for birdie on the first extra hole to win the match. The Sacramento, California, team of Foster, Wentworth and David Sutherland won the Team Championship with a 281 total. The Northport, New York, team finished second, six strokes behind. The USGA accepted 5,283 entries for the championship.

1989—Tim Hobby, of Alvin, Texas, caught Henry Cagigal of Fort Worth, Texas, on the second nine of the first 18 holes, then built a three-hole lead and won by 4 and 3 in the Amateur Public Links Championship. He won the 14th, 16th, and 18th holes of the scheduled 36-hole match, and went to lunch 3 up. He extended his lead to five holes on the first nine in the afternoon, and Cagigal could get no closer than three holes down. There was, however, a marvelous contrast between the two finalists. Hobby was one of the many collegians in the field. Cagigal is a waiter. A senior at Baylor University, Hobby had attended the University of Houston on a basketball scholarship. He had scored eight three-point goals in one game, a record for the Southwest Conference. His record was broken during the 1988-89 season. Cog Hill was equal to its demanding reputation. Hobby was a combined 21 over par for 149 holes of stroke and match play. In the end, Hobby's putting skill led him to the title. Still, he insisted, "I'm a better free throw shooter than a putter."

1990—Michael Combs, 23, of Kennewick, Washington, built a six-hole lead through the first 19 holes, and coasted to a 4 and 3 victory over Terrence Miskell, 23, of Salinas, California, at Eastmoreland Golf Course, in Portland, Oregon. Combs, who was the qualifying medalist, at 141, went ahead on the seventh hole. He went 5 up with birdies on the 16th and 17th holes of the morning round, playing the second nine 32, three under par. Miskell made a serious challenge early in the afternoon when he won three consecutive holes, aided by a rules infraction which cost Combs the loss of a hole. Still 3 up, Combs fought back by winning holes 9 and 10, regaining a comfortable lead. Combs was on the verge of defeat twice in his earlier matches, winning both at the 19th hole. Miskell was forced to play the 18th hole only in his first match. A senior at the University of Washington, Combs becomes the fifth medalist to win the APL championship. Four others have been defeated in the final.

AMATEUR PUBLIC LINKS CHAMPIONSHIP

DATE	WINNER, RUNNER-UP	SCORE	SITE	ENTRY
1981 (July)	Jodie Mudd d. Billy Tuten	3 & 2	Bear Creek Golf World, (Masters Course) Houston, Texas Medalist—138: Roy Biancalana	4,318
1982 (July)	Billy Tuten d. Brad Heninger	6 & 5	Eagle Creek G.C., Indianapolis, Ind. Medalist—140: Tony Grimes	4,312
1983 (July)	Billy Tuten d. David Hobby	3 & 1	Hominy Hill G.C., Colts Neck, N.J. Medalist—142: Michael Miles	4,533
1984 (July)	Bill Malley d. Dirk Jones	2 & 1	Indian Canyon G.C., Spokane, Wash. Medalist—†132: Jim Carter	4,814
1985 (July)	Jim Sorenson d. Jay Cooper	12 & 11	Wailua C.C., Lihue, Hawaii Medalist—142: Robin McCool	5,519
1986 (July)	Bill Mayfair d. Jim Sorenson	3 & 2	Tanglewood Park, Clemmons, N.C. Co-Medalists—139: Adrian Roberson, Bill Mayfair	5,427
1987 (July)	Kevin Johnson d. Jimmy England	10 & 9	Glenview G.C., Cincinnati, Ohio Co-Medalists—142: Eric Woods, Garth Johnston, Dennis Walsh	5,501
1988 (July)	Ralph Howe d. Kevin Johnson	1 up, 37 holes	Jackson Hole G. & T.C., Jackson, Wyo. Medalist—136: Mike Foster	5,283
1989 (July)	Tim Hobby d. Henry Cagigal	4 & 3	Cog Hill G. & C.C., Lemont, Ill. Medalist—137: Robert Gamez	5,919
1990 (July)	Michael Combs d. Terrence Miskell	4 & 3	Eastmoreland G.C., Portland, Ore. Medalist—141: Michael Combs	§5,921

†Record Qualifying Score
§Record Entry

AMATEUR PUBLIC LINKS TEAM CHAMPIONSHIP

DATE	WINNER	SCORE	SITE	ENTRY
1981 (July)	Chicago, Ill.	435	Bear Creek Golf World, (Masters Course) Houston, Texas	34
1982 (July)	Phoenix, Ariz.	288 (36 hls., 2 men)	Eagle Creek G.C., Indianapolis, Ind.	42
1983 (July)	Los Angeles, Calif.	292	Hominy Hill G.C., Colts Neck, N.J.	44
1984 (July)	Phoenix, Ariz.	269	Indian Canyon G.C., Spokane, Wash.	46
1985 (July)	Phoenix, Ariz.* Runner-up: St. Louis, Mo.	297 297	Wailua C.C., Lihue, Hawaii	44
1986 (July)	Clemmons, N.C.	279	Tanglewood Park, Clemmons, N.C.	48
1987 (July)	San Francisco, Calif.	289	Glenview G.C., Cincinnati, Ohio	48
1988 (July)	Sacramento, Calif.	281	Jackson Hole G. & T.C., Jackson, Wyo.	48
1989 (July)	Las Vegas, Nev.	294	Cog Hill G. & C.C., Lemont, Ill.	46
1990 (July)	Portland, Ore.	292	Eastmoreland G.C., Portland, Ore.	§50

*Playoff
§Record Entry

1981
FIFTY-SIXTH AMATEUR PUBLIC LINKS CHAMPIONSHIP

Bear Creek Golf World (Masters Course), Houston, Texas, July 13-18
Yardage—6,953. Par 72. 4,318 Entries, 159 Starters, 64 Qualifiers.

Qualifying Score	1st Round (18 Holes)	2nd Round (18 Holes)	3rd Round (18 Holes)	4th Round (18 Holes)	Semi-Finals (18 Holes)	Final (36 Holes)
*138	Roy Biancalana, Franklin Park, Ill.	Miles,				
153	Mike Miles, Cypress, Calif.	1 up, 19 holes	Miles,			
150	Mike Neece, Irving, Texas	Kressly,	6 and 4			
155	L. Dee Kressly, Boise, Idaho	1 up, 19 holes				
148	Nick Zambole, Palatine, Ill.	Vanyo,		Miles,		
154	Ray Vanyo, San Bernardino, Calif.	5 and 3	Meyer,	7 and 6		
152	Dana Banke, Reno, Nev.	Meyer,	7 and 6			
156	Greg Meyer, Honolulu, Hawaii	3 and 2			Soley,	
146	David Baker, Wahiawa, Hawaii	Baker,			1 up	
154	Cliff Stone, Sandston, Va.	5 and 4	Baker,			
151	Jim Carter, Mesa, Ariz.	Carter,	4 and 3			
155	Jeff Mehler, Coconut Creek, Fla.	2 up		Soley,		
149	Andy Soley, Cedar Lake, Ind.	Soley,		4 and 2		
155	Bill McDonald, Royal Oak, Mich.	3 and 2	Soley,			
152	Wayne Sifford, Jacksonville, Fla.	Sifford,	1 up, 19 holes			
158	Brian Holt, Bridgeport, Conn.	1 up, 19 holes				Tuten,
145	Richard Dalpos, Lemont, Ill.	Tuten,				2 up
153	Billy Tuten, Palatko, Fla.	3 and 2	Tuten,			
151	Phill Arinno, Citrus Heights, Calif.	Arinno,	2 up			
155	David Nelson, Sparks, Nev.	2 and 1		Tuten,		
148	Vic Wilk, Sepulveda, Calif.	Wilk,		1 up, 20 holes		
155	Vaughan Jones, Louisville, Ky.	3 and 1	Wilk,			
152	Jim Neff, Kettering, Ohio	Neff,	3 and 2			
156	David Leiss, Houston, Texas	1 up			Tuten,	
147	Duane Standley, Madisonville, Texas	Standley,			6 and 4	
154	Frank Torres, Mesquite, Texas	7 and 6	Seki,			
152	Ken Chance, New Orleans, La.	Seki,	2 up			
155	Mark Seki, Kahului, Hawaii	5 and 3		Seki,		
150	Terry Tessary, Granite, Ill.	Tessary,		2 and 1		
155	Tom Jereb, Wickliffe, Ohio	5 and 4	Weber,			
153	Art Weber, Clearwater, Fla.	Weber,	3 and 2			
156	Jim Kurtzeborn, St. Louis, Mo.	2 and 1				
141	Jodie Mudd, Louisvile, Ky.	Mudd,				
153	Greg Morrison, Richardson, Texas	4 and 3	Mudd,			
150	Mark Saatzer, St. Cloud, Minn.	Saatzer,	1 up, 19 holes			
155	Bill Von Wald, Stillwater, Minn.	5 and 4				
148	Doug Hixson, Crooked River, Ore.	Hixson,		Mudd,		
155	Todd Palmaer, Carmichael, Calif.	2 and 1	Hixson,	2 and 1		
152	David McCollough, Walker, Iowa	Davidson,	6 and 4			
156	Mike Davidson, Paramount, Calif.	1 up			Mudd,	
146	Tony Grimes, Scottsdale, Ariz.	Grimes,			3 and 1	
154	Bill Morgan, Clemmons, N.C.	1 up	Anthony,			
152	David Anthony, Nashville, Tenn.	Anthony,	1 up			
155	Jerry Kidney, Littleton, Colo.	4 and 3		Anthony,		
150	Dennis Walsh, Groves, Texas	Walsh,		3 and 1		
155	Dean Prince, San Bruno, Calif.	2 up	Walsh,			
153	Steve Barnett, Anderson, Ind.	Barnett,	2 and 1			
156	John Laing, Farmington Hills, Mich.	2 and 1				Mudd,
145	Carl Poché, Metairie, La.	Poché				5 and 3
154	Ray Pontinen, Minneapolis, Minn.	6 and 5	Poché			
151	Don Burwell, Miami Lakes, Fla.	Burwell,	4 and 2			
155	Bob Allshouse, Greensburg, Pa.	2 and 1		Poché		
149	Ruben Lopez, Stafford, Texas	Lopez,		7 and 5		
155	Carl Campanelli, Newark, N.J.	3 and 1	Ward,			
152	Doug Ward, Little Rock, Ark.	Ward,	3 and 1			
156	Tom Heinen, Sartell, Minn.	4 and 3			Elkins,	
147	Mark Olson, Phoenix, Ariz.	Powell,			2 and 1	
154	Robert Powell, San Diego, Calif.	7 and 5	Everin,			
152	Roger Everin, New Britain, Conn.	Everin,	4 and 3			
155	Glenn Vaughn, Columbus, Ga.	3 and 1		Elkins,		
150	Danny Elkins, St. Petersburg, Fla.	Elkins,		3 and 2		
155	Tom Rogers, Corpus Christi, Texas	2 up	Elkins,			
153	Spencer Sappington, St. Louis, Mo.	Sappington	2 and 1			
156	Wes Weston, Las Vegas, Nev.	1 up, 19 holes				

Jodie Mudd, 3 and 2

*Medalist

Fifty-sixth Amateur Public Links Inter-city Team Championship, Harding Trophy (34 Team Entries), July 13, 14: Won by Chicago, Illinois Team, 435 for 36 holes (Nicholas Zambole, 148; Roy Biancalano, 138; Andy Soley, 149); Second, Houston, Texas Team, 454 (Jimmy Adams, 157; Duane Standley, 147; Dennis Walsh, 150); Third, Phoenix, Arizona Team, 457 (Mark Olson, 147; Larry Pagel, 159; Jim Carter, 151).

1982
FIFTY-SEVENTH AMATEUR PUBLIC LINKS CHAMPIONSHIP

Eagle Creek Golf Course, Indianapolis, Indiana, July 12-17.
Yardage — 7,107. Par 72. 4,312 Entries, 159 Starters, 64 Qualifiers.

Qualifying Score	1st Round (18 Holes)	2nd Round (18 Holes)	3rd Round (18 Holes)	4th Round (18 Holes)	Semifinals (18 Holes)	Final (36 Holes)
*140	Tony Grimes, Scottsdale, Ariz.	Soley,				
152	Andy Soley, Cedar Lake, Ind.	1 up	Soley,			
150	Martin Auch, Pontiac, Mich.	Auch,	2 and 1			
154	Charles Renfrow, Pontiac, Mich.	1 up		Heninger,		
148	Ray Pontinen, St. Louis Park, Minn.	Davidson,		2 and 1		
153	Mike Davidson, Paramount, Calif.	3 and 1	Heninger,			
151	Brad Heninger, San Jose, Calif.	Heninger,	4 and 3			
155	Bryan Symonds, Newburgh, Ind.	7 and 6			Heninger,	
146	Ken Kelley, Waller, Texas	Kelley,			3 and 2	
153	Greg King, Memphis, Tenn.	2 and 1	Kelley,			
151	Andy Morse, S. Weymouth, Mass.	Hixson,	4 and 2			
154	Doug Hixson, Crooked River, Ore.	2 and 1		Kelley,		
149	William Morgan, Winston-Salem, N.C.	Morgan,		1 up, 19 holes		
154	Mike Neece, Irving, Texas	1 up	Morgan,			
152	Shane Marvelli, Newton, Iowa	Jarvey,	5 and 4			
155	Dan Jarvey, Seattle, Wash.	4 and 2				Heninger,
144	Richard Miller, Columbus, Ohio	Wrobbel,				3 and 1
152	Bill Wrobbel, Tampa, Fla.	4 and 3	Barnett,			
150	Steve Barnett, Anderson, Ind.	Barnett,	2 up			
154	Bill Von Wald, Stillwater, Minn.	5 and 3		Barnett,		
148	Jim Carter, Mesa, Ariz.	Menante,		1 up, 19 holes		
153	Dean Menante, Reno, Nev.	1 up	Menante,			
151	Carl Cooper, Houston, Texas	Hawkins,	1 up			
155	Arnold Hawkins, San Francisco, Calif.	1 up			Barnett,	
148	Stan Bickel, Bellevue, Ky.	Haberkorn,			2 and 1	
153	Mike Haberkorn, Des Plains, Ill.	1 up	Tom,			
151	Wendell Tom, Honolulu, Hawaii	Tom,	6 and 5			
154	Jeff Brown, Elgin, Ill.	5 and 4		Huston,		
150	John Huston, Tarpon Springs, Fla.	Huston,		3 and 1		
154	Joe Ferrari, Stockton, Calif.	3 and 2	Huston,			
152	Hugh O'Neil, Jacksonville Beach, Fla.	O'Neil,	5 and 4			
155	Win Bruning, Palatine, Ill.	2 and 1				Billy Tuten, 6 and 5
142	Billy Tuten, Palatka, Fla.	Tuten,				
152	Tom Cotter, St. Paul, Minn.	1 up	Tuten,			
150	Jerry Nosewicz, Aurora, Colo.	Hitch,	1 up, 21 holes			
154	Gary Hitch, Ventura, Calif.	3 and 2		Tuten,		
148	Tim Koressel, Bloomington, Ind.	Walsh,		5 and 4		
153	Dennis Walsh, Groves, Texas	2 and 1	Dolci,			
151	Dennis Dolci, Sharon, Pa.	Dolci,	3 and 2			
155	Robert Tietz, St. Joseph, Mo.	6 and 5			Tuten,	
147	Archie Dadian, S. Milwaukee, Wis.	Silnik,			6 and 4	
153	Ray Silnik, Emmaus, Pa.	3 and 2	Patino,			
151	Denny Thompson, Louisville, Ky.	Patino,	1 up			
154	Jesse Patino, Dallas, Texas	3 and 2		Patino,		
150	Kirk Schooley, Columbus, Ind.	Schooley,		1 up, 20 holes		
154	Bruce Cavarno, Vista, Calif.	8 and 6	Schooley,			
152	Randy Haag, Houston, Texas	Johnson,	3 and 2			
155	Steve Johnson, Elk River, Minn.	4 and 3				Tuten,
145	Doug Harper, Chatsworth, Calif.	Harper,				4 and 3
153	Mike Hamblin, Twin Falls, Idaho	2 and 1	Brodzik,			
150	Ted Brodzik, Lancaster, N.Y.	Brodzik,	1 up, 23 holes			
154	Dan Hixson, Crooked River, Ore.	4 and 3		Anderson,		
149	Jeff Johnson, Ventura, Calif.	Johnson,		3 and 2		
153	Joe Cornwall, Salt Lake City, Utah	1 up, 20 holes	Anderson,			
151	Robert Anderson, Downey, Calif.	Anderson,	3 and 1			
155	Mike Sokalski, Coopersburg, Pa.	1 up, 19 holes			Nelson,	
148	Carl Von Hake, Las Vegas, Nev.	Von Hake,			1 up	
153	Dan Pelczarski, Pittsburgh, Pa.	1 up, 21 holes	Nelson,			
151	David Nelson, Sparks, Nev.	Nelson,	3 and 2			
155	John Miranov, Warren, Mich.	1 up		Nelson,		
150	Bill Reilly, Bethel Park, Pa.	Hubbart,		1 up		
154	Kim Hubbart, San Diego, Calif.	6 and 5	Hubbart,			
152	Ted Schulz, Louisville, Ky.	Jawor,	5 and 4			
155	Frank Jawor, Dearborn Heights, Mich.	1 up, 21 holes				

*Medalist

Fifty-seventh Amateur Public Links Inter-city Team Championship, Harding Trophy (42 Team Entries), July 12, 13: Won by Phoenix, Arizona, Team, 288 (Jimmy Carter, 148; Bill Myers, 163; Tony Grimes, 140); Second, Los Angeles, California, 294 (Doug Harper, 145; Gary Hitch, 154; Jeff Johnson, 149); Third, Jacksonville, Florida, 294 (Billy Tuten, 142; Hugh O'Neil, 152; Gary Reed, 163).

1983
FIFTY-EIGHTH AMATEUR PUBLIC LINKS CHAMPIONSHIP

Hominy Hill Golf Course, Colts Neck, New Jersey, July 11-16
Yardage—6,992. Par 72. 4,533 Entries, 159 Starters, 64 Qualifiers

Qualifying Score	1st Round (18 Holes)	2nd Round (18 Holes)	3rd Round (18 Holes)	4th Round (18 Holes)	Semifinals (18 Holes)	Final (36 Holes)	
*142	Michael Miles, Cypress, Calif.	Miles,					
151	Dennis Walsh, Groves, Texas	1 up, 19 holes	Miles,				
149	Kurt Bosen, Centerville, Utah	Bosen,	2 up				
153	Donald Berry, Roseville, Minn.	4 and 3		Prince,			
148	James Wright, Travis AFB, Calif.	Wright,		2 up			
152	Greg Harvey, Minneapolis, Minn.	1 up, 20 holes	Prince,				
150	Raymond Boone, Miami, Fla.	Prince,	4 and 3				
154	Dean Prince, San Bruno, Calif.	2 and 1			Prince,		
147	Gary Rusnak, Painesville, Ohio	Nieman,			1 up		
152	Charles Nieman, Crescent Springs, Ky.	3 and 2	Nieman,				
150	Jeff Johnson, Ventura, Calif.	Thompson,	5 and 3				
154	Allan Thompson, Pleasant Ridge, Mich.	2 and 1		Piscopink,			
149	Brian Tennyson, Evansville, Ind.	Tennyson,		1 up, 20 holes			
152	Jim Horvath, Dennis, Mass.	6 and 5	Piscopink,				
151	Thom Piscopink, Wayne, Mich.	Piscopink,	4 and 3				
155	John Kerins, West Middlesex, Pa.	1 up				Tuten,	
146	Angelo Petraglia, Belmar, N.J.	Gaus,				5 and 3	
151	Robert Gaus, St. Louis, Mo.	2 and 1	Patino,				
149	Bruce Zulaica, Alameda, Calif.	Patino,	3 and 2				
153	Jesse Patino, Dallas, Texas	1 up, 19 holes		Tuten,			
148	Billy Tuten, Palatka, Fla.	Tuten,		2 and 1			
152	Bill Reilly, Jr. Tallassee, Ala.	2 and 1	Tuten,				
150	Gregg Gamester, Tampa, Fla	Brown,	6 and 4				
155	Michael Brown, Philadelphia, Pa.	1 up, 19 holes			Tuten,		
148	Thomas Howe, Pearl River, N.Y.	Malay,			3 and 2		
152	Joe Malay, Weiser, Id.	4 and 3	Malay,				
150	Thomas Cotter, St. Paul, Minn.	Halpine,	5 and 4				
154	Paul Halpine, Omaha, Neb.	3 and 2		Roush,			
149	Allen Christ, Kenosha, Wis.	Roush,		3 and 2			
152	Gary Roush, Mason, W.V.	1 up	Roush,				
151	Philip Thomas, Oklahoma City, Okla.	McGregor,	4 and 2				
155	John McGregor, Sacramento, Calif.	4 and 2					Billy Tuten, 3 and 1
145	Michael McCoy, Des Moines, Iowa	McCoy,					
151	Tim Koressel, Bloomington, Ind.	1 up	Swartz,				
149	Michael Swartz, Phoenix, Ariz.	Swartz,	1 up, 22 holes				
153	Karl Elbrecht, St. Louis, Mo.	6 and 5		Swartz,			
148	David Graulau, Alma, Mich.	Cooper,		6 and 5			
152	Jay Byron Cooper, Coral Gables, Fla.	5 and 4	Cooper,				
150	Larry Pagel, Tucson Ariz.	Pagel,	2 up				
155	Robert Solden, Remsenburg, N.Y.	2 and 1			Swartz,		
147	Dennis Dolci, Sharon, Pa.	Dolci,			4 and 3		
152	Kevin Hall, Carson City, Nev.	2 and 1	Dolci,				
150	Raymond Silnik, Emmaus, Pa.	Silnik,	1 up				
154	Lance Taketa, Hilo, Hawaii	3 and 2		Terasa,			
149	Marc Dingman, Milan, Mich.	Terasa,		3 and 2			
152	Ed Terasa, Green Bay, Wis.	1 up	Terasa,				
151	Richard Miller, Columbus, Ohio	Miller,	3 and 2				
155	Don Burwell, Miami Lakes, Fla.	2 and 1				Hobby,	
146	Paul Rudis, Olympia, Wash.	Esler,				3 and 2	
152	Dave Esler, Wauconda, Ill.	1 up	Esler,				
150	Carl Cooper, Houston, Texas	Foltz,	1 up				
153	Jerry Foltz, Tucson, Ariz.	2 and 1		Morse,			
149	Roy Biancalana, Franklin Park, Ill.	Biancalana,		1 up			
152	Arnold Hawkins, San Francisco, Calif.	3 and 2	Morse,				
151	Andrew Morse, South Weymouth, Mass.	Morse,	3 and 1				
155	Gary Skaggs, Louisville, Ky.	4 and 2			Hobby,		
148	Brad Rosiar, Pontiac, Mich.	Uyehara,			4 and 3		
152	Les Uyehara, Honolulu, Hawaii	1 up, 19 holes	Tom,				
150	Dana John Kain, Ames, Iowa	Tom,	1 up, 19 holes				
154	Wendell Tom, Honolulu, Hawaii	3 and 2		Hobby,			
149	David Hobby, Santa Ana, Calif.	Hobby,		1 up			
152	Greg Twiggs, San Diego, Calif.	3 and 1	Hobby,				
151	Dean Menante, Reno, Nev.	Menante,	4 and 3				
155	Doug Leider, Bensenville, Ill.	1 up					

*Medalist

Fifty-eighth Amateur Public Links Inter-city Team Championship, Harding Trophy (44 Team Entries), July 11, 12: Won by Los Angeles, California, Team, 292 (Michael Miles, 142; John Ledgerwood, 158; Jeff Johnson, 150); Second, Des Moines, Iowa, 295 (Phil Wistrom, 159; Mike McCoy, 145; Dana Kain, 150); Third, Tie, Milwaukee, Wisconsin, 301 (Allen Christ, 149; Edward Terasa, 152; Dave Esler, 152); San Francisco, California, 301 (Arnold Hawkins, 152; Bruce Zulaica, 149; Dean Prince, 154). The two low individual scores of the three team members are used to calculate the team score.

1984
FIFTY-NINTH AMATEUR PUBLIC LINKS CHAMPIONSHIP

Indian Canyon Golf Course, Spokane, Washington, July 16-21
Yardage—6,296. Par 70. +4,814 Entries, 159 Starters, 64 Qualifiers

Qualifying Score	1st Round (18 Holes)	2nd Round (18 Holes)	3rd Round (18 Holes)	4th Round (18 Holes)	Semifinals (18 Holes)	Final (36 Holes)	
*132	Jim Carter, Mesa, Ariz.	Carter, 3 and 2					
146	Jay Thorseth, Sioux Falls, S.D.		Carter, 4 and 3				
143	Jeff Cook, Indianapolis, Ind.	Nielsen, 4 and 2					
148	Mark Nielsen, Portland, Ore.			Johnson, 1 up			
141	Edward Smith, Tempe, Ariz.	Smith, 2 and 1					
147	Kent Russell, Columbus, Ohio		Johnson, 3 and 2				
145	Steven Johnson, Elk River, Minn.	Johnson 2 and 1					
149	Eric Sexton, Sedgwick, Kans.				Jones, 1 up		
141	Brian Brugger, Milwaukee, Wis.	Jones, 7 and 5					
147	Dirk Jones, San Diego, Calif.		Jones, 3 and 2				
145	Kent Brown, Colville, Wash.	Brown 2 and 1					
148	Allen Norris, El Sobrante, Calif.			Jones, 1 up			
143	Leonard Hartlage, Floyds Knobs, Ind.	Hartlage, 2 and 1					
148	Craig Steinberg, North Hollywood, Calif.		Endres, 7 and 6				
145	Chris Endres, Glendale, Ariz.	Endres, 4 and 2					
150	Jerry Foltz, Tucson, Ariz.					Jones, 1 up	
140	Andy Parks, Forest City, N.C.	Parks, 3 and 2					
146	Robert Hawkins, Takoma Park, Md.		Parks, 2 up				
144	Jerry Sneve, Oroville, Wash,	Tate, 1 up, 23 holes					
148	Curtis Tate, Omaha, Neb.			Pontinen, 3 and 2			
142	Chris Vandell, Des Moines, Iowa	Vandell, 1 up, 20 holes					
148	Eric Reed, Louisville, Ky.		Pontinin, 2 up				
145	Ray Pontinen, Bloomington, Minn.	Pontinen, 2 up					
149	Philip Miranda, Miami, Fla.				Austin, 2 and 1		
141	Woody Austin, Tampa, Fla.	Austin, 6 and 4					
147	Wendell Tom, Honolulu, Hawaii		Austin, 2 and 1				
145	Tom Porsch, Harrisburg, Pa.	Porsch, 7 and 5					
149	Pete Morgan, Harwich, Mass.			Austin, 5 and 3			Bill Malley, 2 and 1
143	Douglas Hixson, Crooked River Ranch, Ore.	Opatz, 1 up					
148	Larry Opatz, Bloomington, Minn.		Standfield, 1 up				
146	Lewis Standfield, Dallas, Texas	Standfield, 3 and 2					
150	Roy Omoto, Torrance, Calif.						
134	Shawn Bellis, Aurora, Colo.	Bellis, 2 and 1					
146	Chuck Kletcke, Chicago, Ill.		Bietz, 4 and 3				
143	Kirk Triplett, Reno, Nev.	Bietz, 2 and 1					
148	Rich Bietz, Tempe, Ariz.			Beitz, 8 and 6			
142	Anthony Cuchessi, San Clemente, Calif.	Cuchessi, 1 up,					
147	Patrick Herzog, Alexandria, Minn.		Cuchessi, 2 and 1				
145	Donald Berry, Minneapolis, Minn.	Berry, 2 and 1					
149	Michael Wileman, St. Petersburg, Fla.				Tennyson, 1 up, 21 holes		
141	Brad Penfold, Brighton, Colo.	Cheatham, 3 and 2					
147	David Cheatham, Washington, Ill.		Cheatham, 2 and 1				
145	Charles Renfrow, Pontiac, Mich.	Bloom, 4 and 3					
149	Jeffrey Bloom, Seattle, Wash.			Tennyson, 6 and 5			
143	William Mitchell, Daytona Beach, Fla.	Mitchell, 2 up					
148	Thomas Piscopink, Wayne, Mich.		Tennyson, 5 and 4				
145	Brian Tennyson, Evansville, Ind.	Tennyson, 1 up, 19 holes					
150	Bill Von Wald, Stillwater, Minn.					Malley, 1 up	
141	John Von Lossow, Seattle, Wash.	Green, 5 and 4					
147	Chuck Green, Spokane, Wash.		Green, 2 and 1				
144	Brian Lindley, Costa Mesa, Calif.	Lindley, 4 and 2					
148	Jerry Butler, Memphis, Tenn.			Green, 1 up, 19 holes			
143	Dave Esler, Wauconda, Ill.	Kerr, 3 and 2					
148	Mike Kerr, Livonia, Mich.		Barrett, 2 and 1				
145	Sheldon Joyner, Eugene, Ore.	Barrett, 2 and 1					
149	Glen Barrett, Alexandria, Va.				Malley, 1 up		
141	Scott Masingill, Payette, Idaho	Masingill, 2 and 1					
147	Tom Hearn, Fort Pierce, Fla.		Malley, 1 up				
145	Bill Malley, Hayward, Calif.	Malley, 1 up					
149	William McDonald, Royal Oak, Mich.			Malley, 5 and 3			
143	Mark Mielke, Flushing, N.Y.	Mielke, 1 up					
148	Tony Welch, Indianapolis, Ind.		Jenson, 1 up				
146	Kenneth Jenson, Edmonds, Wash.	Jenson, 5 and 4					
150	Craig Apple, Prairie Village, Kans.						

*Medalist
+ Record Entry

Fifty-ninth Amateur Public Links Inter-city Team Championship, Harding Trophy (46 Team Entries), July 16, 17: Won by Phoenix, Arizona, Team, 269(Jim Carter, 132; Edward Smith, 141; Chris Endres, 145); Second, Denver, Colorado, 275 (Eric Hoos, 156; Shawn Bellis, 134; Brad Penfold, 141); Third, San Diego, California, 286 (Dirk Jones, 147; Brian Lindley, 144; Anthony Cuchessi, 142). The two low individual scores of the three team members are used to calculate the team score.

1985
SIXTIETH AMATEUR PUBLIC LINKS CHAMPIONSHIP

Wailua Golf Course, Kauai, Hawaii, July 15-20
Yardage—6,992. Par 72. +5,519 Entries, 159 Starters, 64 Qualifiers

Qualifying Score	1st Round (18 Holes)	2nd Round (18 Holes)	3rd Round (18 Holes)	4th Round (18 Holes)	Semifinals (18 Holes)	Final (36 Holes)
*142	Robin McCool, Bethlehem, Pa.	McCool,				
155	Dale Pecjak, San Diego, Calif.	1 up	Kain,			
152	Dana Kain, Ames, Iowa	Kain,	1 up			
152	Scott Munroe, Indianapolis, Ind.	3 and 2		Burroughs,		
149	Kevin Sutherland, Sacramento, Calif.	Malay,		2 and 1		
153	Joe Malay, Weiser, Idaho	2 and 1	Burroughs,			
149	Bret Burroughs, University City, Mo.	Burroughs,	3 and 2			
153	Brad Rosiar, Pontiac, Mich.	1 up			Cooper,	
146	Bill Mayfair, Phoenix, Ariz.	Topnick,			2 and 1	
154	Charles Topnick, Pittsburgh, Pa.	1 up	Cooper,			
151	Michael Kerr, Livonia, Mich.	Cooper,	3 and 2			
153	Jay Cooper, Coral Gables, Fla.	4 and 3		Cooper,		
146	Robert Burns, Lake City, Fla.	Teal,		4 and 3		
154	Jeff Teal, Minnetonka, Minn.	1 up, 19 holes	Teal,			
151	Edward Smith, Tempe, Ariz.	Smith,	2 and 1			
153	Tony Hill, Evansville, Ind.	5 and 4				Cooper,
144	Rick Garber, Redmond, Wash.	Garber,				2 and 1
155	Scott Matheson, S. Holland, Ill.	3 and 2	McDonald,			
151	David Sutherland, Sacramento, Calif.	McDonald,	3 and 2			
152	William McDonald, Royal Oak, Mich.	1 up, 19 holes		Biskind,		
148	Deron Doi, Lihue, Hawaii	Harris,		1 up, 20 holes		
153	Keith Harris, Baytown, Texas	2 and 1	Biskind,			
150	Ted Biskind, Beachwood, Ohio	Biskind,	1 up			
153	Tony Welch, Orlando, Fla.	3 and 2			D. Nishimoto,	
145	Larry Blanchard, Hollywood, Fla.	Vonderheide,			3 and 1	
154	Robert Vonderheide, Lafayette, La.	1 up	D. Nishimoto,			
151	Jason Nishimoto, Hilo, Hawaii	D. Nishimoto,	6 and 5			
152	Daniel Nishimoto, Kapaa, Hawaii	2 and 1		D. Nishimoto,		
148	Jim Knoesel, St. Louis, Mo.	Knoesel,		3 and 1		
153	Patrick Burke, West Covina, Calif.	1 up	Knoesel,			
150	Rodney Wilson, Petaluma, Calif.	Yogi,	2 and 1			
153	Steven Yogi, Honolulu, Hawaii	3 and 2				
143	Albert Austin, Tampa, Fla.	Holloway,				
155	Ted Holloway, Ontario, Ore.	1 up, 19 holes	Sneve,			
152	Jerry Sneve, Oroville, Wash.	Sneve,	4 and 3			
152	Jorge Badel, Lakewood, Calif.	7 and 6		Sneve,		
148	Kurt Bosen, Bountiful, Utah	Bosen,		5 and 4		
153	Dean Menante, Reno, Nev.	5 and 3	Driscoll,			
149	Jerry Driscoll, Topsfield, Mass.	Driscoll,	3 and 1			
153	David Lennox, Westerville, Ohio	3 and 1			Ferrara,	
146	Richard Brune, Cincinnati, Ohio	Brune,			1 up	
154	David Farnam, Seattle, Wash.	2 and 1	White,			
151	Ron Skayhan, Eugene, Ore.	White,	3 and 1			
152	Jeff White, Fort Wayne, Ind.	2 up		Ferrara,		
147	Shawn Bellis, Aurora, Colo.	Jonson,		1 up		
154	Edward Jonson, Bainbridge Island, Wash.	2 and 1	Ferrara,			
151	John Ferrara, Jr., Staten Island, N.Y.	Ferrara,	4 and 2			
153	Christopher Pinckney, Charleston, S.C.	4 and 3				Sorenson,
143	James Sorenson, Bloomington, Minn.	Sorenson,				4 and 2
155	Samuel Hunt, Chattanooga, Tenn.	4 and 3	Sorenson,			
151	William Sullivan, Marietta, Ga.	Tucker,	2 up			
152	Jim Tucker, Portland, Ore.	2 and 1		Sorenson,		
148	Philip Reichel, W. Minnetonka, Minn.	Reichel,		5 and 3		
153	Scott Hancock, Prescott, Ariz.	3 and 2	Walker,			
149	George Walker, Portland, Ore.	Walker,	2 and 1			
153	Larry Sock, Lincoln, Neb.	1 up			Sorenson,	
145	Wendell Tom, Aiea, Hawaii	Tom,			6 and 5	
154	Raymond Fuller, Pitman, N.J.	3 and 2	McPherson,			
151	Duane Miller, Tulsa, Okla.	McPherson,	2 and 1			
152	John McPherson, Stone Mountain, Ga.	2 and 1		McPherson,		
148	Michael Kingsrud, N. Fargo, N.D.	Kingsrud,		1 up		
153	Wade Jordan, Houston, Texas	7 and 5	Tyner,			
150	Tray Tyner, Sour Lake, Texas	Tyner,	1 up, 21 holes			
153	Michael Swartz, Phoenix, Ariz.	1 up				

James Sorenson, 12 and 11

+Record Entry

*Medalist

Fifty-ninth Amateur Public Links Inter-city Team Championship, Harding Trophy (44 Team Entries), July 15-16: Won by Phoenix, Team, 297 for 36 holes (Michael Swartz, 153; Bill Mayfair, 146; Robert Vessel, 158); Playoff with St. Louis Team, 297 (Jim Knoesel, 148; Bret Burroughs, 149); Third, Miami, Team, 298 (Jay Cooper, 153; David Freedman, 164; Larry Blanchard, 145). The two low individual scores of the three team members are used to calculate the team score.

1986
SIXTY-FIRST AMATEUR PUBLIC LINKS CHAMPIONSHIP

Tanglewood Park, Clemmons, North Carolina, July 14-19
Yardage—6,671. Par 70. 5,427 Entries, 159 Starters, 64 Qualifiers

Qualifying Score	1st Round (18 Holes)	2nd Round (18 Holes)	3rd Round (18 Holes)	4th Round (18 Holes)	Semifinals (18 Holes)	Final (36 Holes)	
*139	Art Roberson, Zebulon, N.C.	Roberson, 2 and 1					
152	Randy Winn, Boulder, Colo.		Hayashi, 5 and 4				
147	Kevin Hayashi, Honolulu, Hawaii	Hayashi, 2 and 1					
147	Scott Hancock, Prescott, Ariz.			Hayashi, 1 up, 20 holes			
144	Patrick Burke, West Covina, Calif.	Burke, 3 and 1					
150	Roger Cherico, Jacksonville, Fla.		Wurtz, 3 and 2				
144	Steve Wakulsky, Lansing, Mich.	Wurtz, 6 and 4					
150	Mark Wurtz, Port Ludlow, Wash.				B. Hancock, 4 and 3		
142	Greg Kraft, Clearwater, Fla.	Kraft, 3 and 2					
151	Perry Busse, Waverly, Iowa		Goydos, 4 and 3				
146	Paul Goydos, Long Beach, Calif.	Goydos, 3 and 1					
148	Bruce Oldendick, Florence, Ky.			B. Hancock, 3 and 2			
143	Pat Herzog, Alexandria, Minn.	Herzog, 4 and 3					
151	David McAtee, Evansville, Ind.		B. Hancock, 2 and 1				
146	Carl Seltzer, Grand Blanc, Mich.	B. Hancock, 6 and 5					
149	Bryan Hancock, Athens, Ga.					Sorenson, 1 up	
144	Brad Dixon, Florissant, Mo.	Dixon, 1 up, 24 holes					
151	Dana Kain, Ames, Iowa		Dixon, 2 and 1				
147	Henry Cagigal, Fort Worth, Texas	Cagigal, 4 and 3					
148	Garth Johnston, Rochester, Minn.			Sorenson, 2 and 1			
143	Jim Sorenson, Bloomington, Minn.	Sorenson, 4 and 3					
150	Brian Lindley, Costa Mesa, Calif.		Sorenson, 3 and 2				
146	Rob Huff, Boise, Idaho	Huff, 2 up					
149	Steve Barnett, Anderson, Ind.				Sorenson, 5 and 4		
141	Steve Schadewitz, Vancouver, Wash.	Schadewitz, 5 and 4					
151	Ralph Howe, West Sayville, N.Y.		Schadewitz, 7 and 6				
147	Mark Mason, El Cajon, Calif.	Mason, 2 and 1					
148	Wendell Tom, Aiea, Hawaii			Schadewitz 2 and 1			
143	Jerry Sneve, Oroville, Wash.	Sneve, 1 up, 19 holes					Bill Mayfair, 3 and 2
150	Scott Frisch, Scottsdale, Ariz.		Sneve, 4 and 2				
146	Dan Nishimoto, Kapaa, Hawaii	Nishimoto, 2 and 1					
149	Donald Clement, Myrtle Beach, S.C.						
*139	Bill Mayfair, Phoenix, Ariz.	Mayfair, 3 and 2					
151	Richard Anderson, Houston, Texas		Mayfair, 1 up				
147	Larry Silveira, Oakley, Calif.	Silveira, 1 up, 19 holes					
148	Jay Cooper, Coral Gables, Fla.			Mayfair, 1 up			
143	Rich Bietz, Tempe, Ariz.	Mudd, 5 and 4					
150	Tom Mudd, Louisville, Ky.		Mudd, 6 and 4				
145	Benny Bowen, Milan, Ga.	Bowen, 2 up					
149	Jim Lundstrom, Chatsworth, Calif.				Mayfair, 4 and 3		
142	Mike Taylor, Gastonia, N.C.	Taylor, 1 up, 22 holes					
151	Vaughan Jones, Louisville, Ky.		Taylor, 3 and 2				
146	Tom Rooney, Weymouth, Mass.	Wong, 3 and 2					
148	Brent Wong, Milwaukee, Wis.			Taylor, 1 up			
143	Mike Kerr, Livonia, Mich.	Kerr, 2 and 1					
150	Lester Kimber, Winston-Salem, N.C.		Gorgone, 5 and 4				
146	Sean Gorgone, Topsham, Maine	Gorgone, 4 and 3					
149	Jay Kurisu, Wailuku, Hawaii					Mayfair, 2 and 1	
140	Kevin Sutherland, Sacramento, Calif.	Sutherland, 7 and 6					
151	John Ferrara, Staten Island, N.Y.		Sutherland, 3 and 2				
147	Deron Doi, Lihue, Hawaii	Doi, 1 up, 19 holes					
148	Jimmy Morris, Bartow, Fla.			Armstrong, 1 up			
143	Ed Harper, San Clemente, Calif.	Metz, 2 and 1					
150	David Metz, Kittanning, Pa.		Armstrong, 3 and 2				
145	Jim Armstrong, Solana Beach, Calif.	Armstrong, 4 and 2					
149	Richard Garber, Corvallis, Ore.				Rintoul, 6 and 5		
141	Larry Boswell, Greensboro, N.C.	Boswell, 6 and 5					
151	Mike Maronge, Plaquemine, La.		Rintoul, 5 and 4				
147	Mark Small, Flossmoor, Ill.	Rintoul, 1 up, 22 holes					
148	Steve Rintoul, Eugene, Ore.			Rintoul, 1 up			
143	Terrence Miskell, Salinas, Calif.	Miskell, 1 up					
150	Dennis Walsh, Grove, Texas		Miskell, 4 and 3				
146	Steve Groom, Kansas City, Mo.	Prince, 1 up, 19 holes					
149	Dean Prince, San Bruno, Calif.						

*Co-medalists

Sixtieth Amateur Public Links Inter-city Team Championship, Harding Trophy (48 Team Entries), July 14-15: Won by Clemmons, N.C., Team, 279 for 36 holes (Adrian Roberson, 139; Michael Taylor, 142; Larry Boswell, 141); Second, Tucson Team, 282 (Bill Mayfair, 139; Armen Dirtadian, 153; Rich Bietz, 143); third, Los Angeles Team, 288 (Paul Goydos, 146; Patrick Burke, 144; Jim Lundstrom, 149). The two low individual scores of the three team members are used to calculate the team score.

1987
SIXTY-SECOND AMATEUR PUBLIC LINKS CHAMPIONSHIP

Glenview Golf Course, Cincinnati, Ohio, July 13-18
Yardage—6,777. Par 72. 5,501 Entries, 159 Starters, 64 Qualifiers

Qualifying Score	1st Round (18 Holes)	2nd Round (18 Holes)	3rd Round (18 Holes)	4th Round (18 Holes)	Semifinals (18 Holes)	Final (36 Holes)
*142	Eric Woods, Newport Beach, Calif.	Woods, 3 and 2				
152	John Ferrara, Staten Island, N.Y.		Woods, 6 and 4			
150	William Beck, Joliet, Ill.	Beck, 4 and 3				
150	John Moldovan, North Canton, Ohio			Woods, 3 and 2		
147	Guy Mertz, Longmont, Colo.	Brafford, 2 and 1				
151	William Brafford, Broken Arrow, Okla.		Langham, 4 and 3			
147	Glenn Przybylski, Palos Heights, Ill.	Langham, 1 up, 22 holes				
151	Franklin Langham, Thomson, Ga.				Johnson, 3 and 2	
145	Jim Sorenson, Bloomington, Minn.	Lindley, 3 and 1				
152	Brian Lindley, Long Beach, Calif.		Lindley, 5 and 4			
149	Scott Almquist, Santa Ana, Calif.	Almquist, 3 and 2				
151	Deron Doi, Lihue, Hawaii			Johnson, 1 up, 19 holes		
145	Frank Schiro, Jr., Indian Wells, Calif.	Schiro, 3 and 1				
152	Steve Cartano, Baltimore, Md.		Johnson, 3 and 2			
149	Alan Peters, Milwaukee, Wis.	Johnson, 2 and 1				
151	Kevin Johnson, Pembroke, Mass.					Johnson, 3 and 2
144	James Gilleon, Ocala, Fla.	Gilleon, 4 and 2				
152	Dean Prince, San Bruno, Calif.		Gilleon, 2 and 1			
149	Brian Carson, Downey, Calif.	Peterson, 3 and 1				
150	Scott Peterson, St. Paul, Minn.			Mayfair, 4 and 3		
146	Bill Mayfair, Phoenix, Ariz.	Mayfair, 5 and 4				
152	Chris Carr, Dayton, Ohio		Mayfair, 6 and 4			
148	Lawton Harrison, Neskowin, Ore.	Ma. Smith, 2 and 1				
151	Martin Smith, El Paso, Texas				Bridges, 1 up	
144	Brian Bridges, Whitehall, Ohio	Bridges, 5 and 4				
152	Trent Walker, Las Vegas, Nev.		Bridges, 3 and 2			
149	Frank Mazion, San Mateo, Calif.	Mazion, 1 up				
150	Mark Hayes, Birchwood, Minn.			Bridges, 3 and 2		
146	Ed Smith, Tempe, Ariz.	Ed Smith, 1 up				
152	Robert Buzard, Ellwood City, Pa.		Ed Smith, 2 up			
148	Tom Barry, St. Louis, Mo.	Cagigal, 1 up, 21 holes				
151	Henry Cagigal, Ft. Worth, Texas					
*142	Garth Johnston, Rochester, Minn.	Vanyo, 1 up, 20 holes				
152	Ray Vanyo, San Bernardino, Calif.		Vanyo, 1 up			
149	Ronald Marks, Castro Valley, Calif.	Sanchez, 2 and 1				
150	Mark Sanchez, Berkeley, Calif.			Munroe, 4 and 3		
147	Mark Mielke, Cedarhurst, N.Y.	Chandler, 3 and 2				
151	Gary Chandler, Mesquite, Texas		Munroe, 3 and 1			
147	Lamar Haynes, Nashville, Tenn.	Munroe, 1 up				
151	Scott Munroe, Indianapolis, Ind.				Wilson, 2 and 1	
145	Rodney Wilson, Petaluma, Calif.	Wilson, 2 and 1				
152	Wayne Woolfall, Chattanooga, Tenn.		Wilson, 4 and 3			
149	Thomas Kies, Lodi, Ohio	Kies, 2 up				
150	John Hearn, Honolulu, Hawaii			Wilson, 2 and 1		
145	Tony Chieffo, Granada Hills, Calif.	Chieffo, 2 and 1				
152	Paul Lopez, Ft. Worth, Texas		Von Lossow, 1 up, 21 holes			
148	John Von Lossow, Seattle, Wash.	Von Lossow, 1 up				
151	Richard Brune, Cincinnati, Ohio					
*142	Dennis Walsh, Groves, Texas	Walsh, 1 up, 20 holes				England, 2 and 1
152	Phil Reichel, Minnetonka, Minn.		Garber, 4 and 2			
149	Lee Shortridge, St. Paul, Minn.	Garber, 5 and 4				
150	Richard Garber, Corvallis, Ore.			England, 4 and 3		
147	Jimmy England, Gastonia, N.C.	England, 2 up				
151	Perry Busse, Waverly, Iowa		England, 3 and 2			
148	Doug Hutchins, Cincinnati, Ohio	Sedorcek, 5 and 4				
151	Robert Sedorcek, Kansas City, Kan.				England, 1 up, 19 holes	
144	Jeff Teal, St. Louis Park, Minn.	Teal, 1 up				
152	Eerik Kauppinen, Atlantis, Fla.		Teal, 4 and 3			
149	Terry Tessary, Granite City, Ill.	McNeil, 1 up				
150	Michael McNeil, Havana, Ill.			Mi. Smith, 2 and 1		
146	Perry Parker, Tustin, Calif.	Gamez, 2 and 1				
152	Robert Gamez, Las Vegas, Nev.		Mi. Smith, 1 up			
148	Michael Smith, Beaumont, Texas	Mi. Smith, 4 and 3				
151	Jay Muller, Omaha, Neb.					

Kevin Johnson, 10 and 9

* Co-medalists

Sixty-first Amateur Public Links Inter-city Team Championship, Harding Trophy (48 Team Entries), July 13-14; Won by San Francisco, California Team, 289 for 36 holes (Rodney Wilson, 145; Frank Mazion, 149; Mark Sanchez, 150); Second, Minneapolis, Minnesota Team, 293 (Lee Shortridge, 149; Jeff Teal, 144; Scott Peterson, 150); third, San Diego, California Team, 294 (Brian Lindley, 152; Patrick Mohan, 153; Eric Woods, 142). The two low individual scores of the three team members are used to calculate the team score.

1988

SIXTY-THIRD AMATEUR PUBLIC LINKS CHAMPIONSHIP

Jackson Hole Golf & Tennis Club, Jackson, Wyoming, July 11-16
Yardage—7,027. Par 72. 5,283 Entries, 159 Starters, 64 Qualifiers

Qualifying Score	1st Round (18 Holes)	2nd Round (18 Holes)	3rd Round (18 Holes)	4th Round (18 Holes)	Semifinals (18 Holes)	Final (36 Holes)
*136	Mike Foster, Vacaville, Calif.	Foster,				
151	Dan Reilly, Bethel Park, Pa.	2 and 1	Manos,			
148	Kelly Manos, Cypress, Calif.	Manos,	2 and 1			
148	Terry Tyson, Wauseon, Ohio	1 up, 19 holes		Boswell,		
145	Sean Gorgone, Brunswick, Maine	Gorgone,		7 and 6		
150	Michael Taylor, Milwaukee, Wis.	2 up	Boswell,			
145	Larry Boswell, Greensboro, N.C.	Boswell,	3 and 2			
150	Frank Mazion, San Mateo, Calif.	1 up, 20 holes			Johnson,	
143	Chris Vandell, Des Moines, Iowa	Vandell,			2 and 1	
150	Sean Pacetti, Palatka, Fla.	2 up	Sedorcek,			
147	Robert Sedorcek, Kansas City, Kan.	Sedorcek,	2 up			
149	Robert Rodriguez, West St. Paul, Minn.	7 and 5		Johnson,		
143	Doug Corby, Oakvile, Ontario, Canada	Corby,		1 up		
150	Tim Veach, Winston-Salem, N.C.	2 and 1	Johnson,			
147	Tony Chieffo, Granada Hills, Calif.	Johnson,	5 and 4			
149	Kevin Johnson, Pembroke, Mass.	5 and 4				Johnson,
142	Bill Mayfair, Phoenix, Ariz.	Mayfair,				3 and 1
150	Dan Hendrickson, Waterford, Conn.	4 and 3	Lindley,			
147	Brian Lindley, Long Beach, Calif.	Lindley,	1 up, 21 holes			
148	Shaun Haberstroh, Rapid City, S.D.	1 up, 20 holes		Wentworth		
145	David Bishop, Plantation, Fla.	Bishop,		7 and 6		
150	Rob Huff, Boise, Idaho	5 and 3	Wentworth,			
146	Kevin Wentworth, Manteca, Calif.	Wentworth,	6 and 4			
149	Bobby Bird, Shaker Heights, Ohio	3 and 2			Wentworth,	
143	Mike Sipula, Ottawa, Ill.	Sipula,			3 and 2	
150	Robert Baker, Little Rock, Ark.	1 up	Sipula,			
147	Mark Phillips, Eagle, Idaho	Brewster,	1 up			
149	Steve Brewster, Euless, Texas	2 up		Holmes,		
144	Mark Sperling, River Falls, Wis.	Hubbart,		1 up, 20 holes		
150	Kim Hubbart, Redmond, Wash.	2 up	Holmes,			
146	John Holmes, Brooklyn Park, Minn.	Holmes,	3 and 2			
149	Richard Blackwell, Grapevine, Texas	2 and 1				Ralph Howe, 1 up, 37 holes
138	Robert Goettlicher, Orange Park, Fla.	Goettlicher,				
151	Michael Stephens, Carmel, Ind.	5 and 4	Peterson,			
148	Scott Peterson, St. Paul, Minn.	Peterson,	1 up			
151	Rudy Mihelic, Merrillville, Ind.	3 and 2		McGee,		
145	Kyle McGee, Houston, Texas	McGee,		2 and 1		
150	David Gilpin, Horton, Mich.	4 and 2	McGee,			
145	Mike Glaesel, Arvada, Colo.	Glaesel,	3 and 1			
149	Greg Valdez, Tampa, Fla.	4 and 3			McGee,	
143	Scott Winn, Westerville, Ohio	Winn,			1 up, 19 holes	
150	Tom Jungkind, Birmingham, Ala.	3 and 2	Wardrup,			
147	John Wardrup, Corona Del Mar, Calif.	Wardrup,	3 and 2			
149	Todd Cresap, Minot, N.D.	5 and 4		Steinicke,		
144	Jack Steinicke, Concord, Ohio	Steinicke,		3 and 2		
150	Matthew Wiley, Canton, Mich.	1 up	Steinicke,			
146	Gerald Richardson, Beaumont, Texas	Richardson,	3 and 2			
149	Leif Carlson, Bloomington, Minn.	2 and 1				Howe,
141	P.J. Cowan, Hicksville, N.Y.	Cowan,				2 up
151	Chris Birdseye, Marietta, Ga.	1 up, 20 holes	Dunphy,			
147	Mike Dunphy, Perry, Iowa	Dunphy,	4 and 2			
148	Tim Wilson, Greenville, S.C.	2 up		Howe,		
145	David Sutherland, Sacramento, Calif.	Sutherland,		4 and 3		
150	Reginald Connell, St. Petersburg, Fla.	5 and 3	Howe,			
146	Ralph Howe, West Sayville, N.Y.	Howe,	4 and 3			
149	Michael Seek, Everett, Wash.	4 and 3			Howe,	
143	Joe Worden, Las Cruces, N.M.	Hogard,			2 and 1	
150	Larry Hogard, Flint, Mich.	2 up	Lundstrom,			
147	Jim Lundstrom, Mission Hills, Calif.	Lundstrom,	def.			
149	Rudy Zupetz, Minot, N.D.	1 up		Gomes,		
144	Tim Hegna, Bird Island, Minn.	Kuhn,		7 and 5		
150	Albert Kuhn, Drayton Plains, Mich.	2 and 1	Gamez,			
146	Robert Gamez, Las Vegas, Nev.	Gamez,	2 up			
149	William Kost, Lansing, Mich.	3 and 2				

* Medalist

Sixty-second Amateur Public Links Inter-city Team Championship, Harding Trophy (48 Team Entries), July 11-12; Won by Sacramento, California, Team, 281 for 36 holes (Mike Foster, 136; David Sutherland, 145; Kevin Wentworth, 146); second, Metropolitan New York Team, 287 (Ralph Howe, 146; P.J. Cowan 141); third, Jacksonville, Florida, Team, 288 (Robert Goettlicher, 138; Sean Pacetti, 150). The two low individual scores of the three team members are used to calculate the team score.

1989
SIXTY-FOURTH AMATEUR PUBLIC LINKS CHAMPIONSHIP

Cog Hill Golf and Country Club, Lemont, Illinois, July 17-22
Yardage—6,990. Par 72. Record 5,919 Entries, 156 Starters, 64 Qualifiers

Qualifying Score	1st Round (18 Holes)	2nd Round (18 Holes)	3rd Round (18 Holes)	4th Round (18 Holes)	Semifinals (18 Holes)	Final (18 Holes)
*137	Robert Gamez, Las Vegas, Nev.	Pieri,				
157	Scott Pieri, Fort Wayne, Ind.	1 up	Work,			
154	Jade Work, Palm Springs, Calif.	Work,	3 and 1			
154	David Farnam, Seattle, Wash.	3 and 2		Enriquez,		
151	Todd Gjesvold, Corvallis, Ore.	Enriquez,		2 and 1		
156	Sal Enriquez, Upland, Calif.	1 up	Enriquez,			
151	Thomas McGraw, Westminster, Colo.	Walsh,	5 and 3			
155	Dennis Walsh, Groves, Texas	3 and 2			Enriquez,	
147	Doug Martin, Norman, Okla.	Martin,			5 and 4	
157	Kurt Bilben, Chula Vista, Calif.	4 and 3	Martin,			
153	P.J. Cowan, Hicksville, N.Y.	Bauer,	6 and 5			
154	David Bauer, Phoenix, Ariz.	3 and 2		Haynes		
148	Howard Mash, Miami, Fla.	Haynes,		2 and 1		
156	Lamar Haynes, Nashville, Tenn.	1 up	Haynes,			
153	Chris Vandell, Des Moines, Iowa	Bull,	3 and 2			
154	Larry Bull, Boise, Idaho	4 and 3				Hobby,
145	Joseph Alfieri, Tampa, Fla.	Alfieri,				1 up
157	Jerry Mullen, Mililani, Hawaii	19 holes	Alfieri,			
153	Andrew Pitts, Hildebran, N.C.	Pitts,	2 and 1			
154	Jay Kurisu, Maui, Hawaii	3 and 2		Cornell,		
150	Fred Cornell, Clearwater, Fla.	Cornell,		19 holes		
156	Phil McClellan, Humble, Texas	3 and 2	Cornell,			
152	Geoffrey Griffin, Sacramento, Calif.	Griffin,	2 and 1			
155	Rob Huff, Boise, Idaho	19 holes			Hobby,	
146	Ralph Howe, Sayville, N.Y.	Acker,			2 up	
157	Frank Acker, Las Vegas, Nev.	3 and 2	Brafford,			
153	Bill Brafford, Broken Arrow, Okla.	Brafford,	2 and 1			
154	Mark Gilmartin, Reno, Nev.	1 up		Hobby,		
149	Terry Tessary, Granite City, Ill.	Tessary,		2 up		
156	Shaun Haberstroh, Rapid City, S.D.	19 holes	Hobby,			
152	Tim Hobby, Alvin, Texas	Hobby,	6 and 5			
155	Tom Piscopink, Wayne, Mich.	4 and 3				
141	Henry Cagigal, Fort Worth, Texas	Cagigal,				
157	Jonathan Sielsky, Northbrook, Ill.	4 and 3	Cagigal,			
154	Jim Webb, Des Moines, Iowa	Moss,	4 and 3			
154	Rob Moss, Parma, Ohio	19 holes		Cagigal		
150	Rob Mangini, Tempe, Ariz.	Mangini,		2 and 1		
156	Patrick Fitzpatrick, Austin, Texas	3 and 2	Mangini,			
152	Alan Peters, Milwaukee, Wis.	Peters,	1 up			
155	Robert Rodriguez, W. St. Paul, Minn.	3 and 2			Cagigal,	
147	Robert Baker, Little Rock, Ark.	Baker,			3 and 2	
157	Bob Johnson, Sterling, Va.	4 and 2	Baker,			
153	Richard Keene, Chattanooga, Tenn.	Keene,	2 and 1			
154	Kevin Moylan, Ft. Richardson, Ark.	5 and 4		Baker,		
148	Michael Kavka, So. Plainfield, N.J.	Kavka,		2 and 1		
156	Mark Small, Flossmoor, Ill.	2 up	Kresnak,			
153	Rick Petri, Greeley, Colo.	Kresnak,	19 holes			
154	Randy Kresnak, Kentwood, Mich.	1 up				Cagagil,
144	Howard Logan, Shelbyville, Ky.	Correll,				2 and 1
157	David Correll, Baltimore, Md.	1 up	Langham,			
153	Franklin Langham, Thomson, Ga.	Langham,	19 holes			
154	Jim Kiely, Plantation, Fla.	1 up		Langham,		
150	Trev Anderson, Tempe, Ariz.	Leutsch,		21 holes		
156	Edward Leutsch, Houston, Texas	6 and 5	Leutsch,			
152	David Metz, Library, Pa.	Metz,	2 and 1			
155	Jason Nishimoto, Hilo, Hawaii	3 and 2			Langham,	
147	Terrence Miskell, Fresno, Calif.	Miskell,			4 and 2	
157	Michael Owsik, Bryn Mawr, Pa.	19 holes	Olson,			
153	Glenn Apple, Medina, Ohio	Olson,	5 and 4			
154	Sam Olson, Anniston, Ala.	4 and 3		Olson,		
148	Chris Brooks, W. Palm Beach, Fla.	Russell,		3 and 2		
156	Terry Russell, Aurora, Colo.	4 and 2	Wickenhauser,			
153	Darren Channell, Lawrence, Kan.	Wickenhauser,	3 and 2			
154	Tim Wickenhauser, Worden, Ill.	19 holes				

Tim Hobby, 4 and 3

*Medalist

Sixty-third Amateur Public Links Inter-City Team Championship, Harding Trophy (46 Team Entries); Won by Las Vegas, Nevada, Team, 294 for 36 holes (Robert Gamez, 137; Frank Acker, 157); second, Tampa, Florida Team, 295 (Greg Valdes, 160; Joseph Alfieri, 145; Fred Cornell, 150); third, Miami, Florida Team, 296 (Jim Kiely, 154; Chris Brooks, 148; Howard Mash, 148). The two low individual scores of the three team members are used to calculate the team score.

1990
SIXTY-FIFTH AMATEUR PUBLIC LINKS CHAMPIONSHIP

Eastmoreland Golf Club, Portland, Oregon, July 16-21
Yardage—6,629. Par 71. Record 5,921 Entries, 155 Starters, 64 Qualifiers

Qualifying Score	1st Round (18 Holes)	2nd Round (18 Holes)	3rd Round (18 Holes)	4th Round (18 Holes)	Semifinals (18 Holes)	Final (36 Holes)	
*141	Michael Combs, Kennewick, Wash.	Combs, 5 and 4					
158	Tom Jungkind, Birmingham, Ala.		Combs, 19 holes				
155	Steve Harwell, Mooresville, N.C.	Harwell, 20 holes,					
155	George Yamamoto, Kapaa, Hawaii			Combs, 5 and 3			
151	Richard Keene, Chattanooga, Tenn.	Keene, 4 and 3					
156	David Nelson, Sparks, Nev.		Vickers, 4 and 3				
151	Warren Vickers, Corvallis, Ore.	Vickers, 7 and 5					
156	Benny Justice, Macon, Ga.				Combs, 19 holes		
147	Ron Schroeder, Pasadena, Texas	Schroeder, 19 holes					
157	David Cunningham, Michigan City, Ind.		Sipula, 1 up				
153	Tom Sipula, Ottawa, Ill.	Sipula, 2 up					
156	Royden Heirakuji, Makawao, Hawaii			Sipula, 2 and 1			
148	David Christenson, Spokane, Wash.	Christenson, 2 up					
157	Michael Kanoff, Harrisburg, Pa.		Christenson, 3 and 2				
153	Robert Wakeling, Monroe Falls, Ohio	Albertson, 1 up					
156	Brent Albertson, Caledonia, Mich.					Combs, 2 up	
146	Christopher Gorgone, Brunswick, Me.	Gorgone, 20 holes					
157	Jerry Michals, Redlands, Calif.		Gorgone, 1 up				
154	Tom McGraw, Westminister, Colo.	McGraw, 1 up					
155	Mark Hayes, White Bear Lake, Minn.			Baker, 1 up			
151	David Berganio, Jr., Sylmar, Calif.	Berganio, 20 holes					
157	Beau Yokomoto, Kaneohe, Hawaii		Baker, 2 and 1				
152	Robert Baker, Little Rock, Ark.	Baker, 5 and 4					
156	Richard Laing, Bonner Springs, Kan.				Baker, 5 and 4		
146	Kenny Ramsey, Houston, Texas	Brafford, 3 and 2					
157	Bill Brafford, Broken Arrow, Okla.		Shook, 2 and 1				
154	Jason Shook, Frankfort, Ill.	Shook, 19 holes					
155	Randy Arvidson, Portland, Ore.			Shook, 20 holes			
150	Mike Dunphy, Birmingham, Ala.	Hale, 2 and 1					
157	Tom Hale, Tacoma, Wash.		Crabtree, 4 and 3				
153	Mark Crabtree, Fort Collins, Colo.	Crabtree, 2 and 1					
156	Lance Taketa, Hilo, Hawaii						Michael Combs, 4 and 3
142	Terrence Miskell, Salinas, Calif.	Miskell, 1 up					
158	Darrel Baker, Fort Worth, Texas		Miskell, 6 and 5				
154	Jason Nishimoto, Hilo, Hawaii	Nishimoto, 1 up					
155	Keith Sbarbaro, San Diego, Calif.			Miskell, 4 and 3			
151	Dennis Walsh, Groves, Texas	Johnson, 3 and 1					
156	Steve Johnson, Elk River, Minn.		Dorman, 2 and 1				
151	Richard Beem, Las Cruces, N.M.	Dorman, 5 and 4					
156	Brent Dorman, Ocala, Fla.				Miskell, 2 and 1		
147	Jack O'Keefe, Little Rock, Ark.	O'Keefe, 5 and 4					
157	Chad Rogers, Lincoln, Neb.		O'Keefe, 6 and 4				
153	John Kueper, Carlyle, Ill.	Marsh, 3 and 2					
155	Brad Marsh, Cincinnati, Ohio			O'Keefe, 4 and 3			
150	Alistair Catto, S. Hadley, Mass.	Catto, 3 and 2					
157	Scott Lindgren, Richfield, Minn.		Catto, 2 up				
153	Cliff Kresge, Orlando, Fla.	Kresge, 1 up					
156	Larry Bull, Boise, Idaho					Miskell, 2 and 1	
145	Trev Anderson, Tempe, Ariz.	Anderson, 6 and 5					
158	Alan Peters, Milwaukee, Wis.		Guest, 3 and 2				
154	Jeff Guest, LaGrange, Ky.	Guest, 3 and 1					
155	Matt Plagmann, Phoenix, Ariz.			Guest, 1 up			
151	Frank Acker, Las Vegas, Nev.	Acker, 2 up					
157	Derek Dicks, Quincy, Ill.		Acker, 3 and 2				
152	Mark Gilmartin, Reno, Nev.	Gilmartin, 6 and 5					
156	Steve Anders, Brooklyn, Hgts., Ohio				Guest, 6 and 5		
147	Javier Sanchez, Redwood City, Calif.	Schmidt, 22 holes					
157	Mike Schmidt, Palmyra, Pa.		Schmidt, 2 and 1				
154	Robert Rullman, Beaverton, Ore.	Hancock, 4 and 3					
151	Bryan Hancock, Dunwoody, Ga.			Waitulavich, 19 holes			
150	Robert Fisher, Oakland, N.J.	Waitulavich, 4 and 3					
157	Gerald Waitulavich, Chesterfield, Mo.		Waitulavich, 1 up				
153	Michael Troy, Clarendon Hills, Ill.	Carlson, 1 up					
156	Leif Carlson, Bloomington, Minn.						

*Medalist

Sixty-fourth Amateur Public Links Inter-City Team Championship, Harding Trophy (50 Team Entries); Won by Portland, Oregon Team, 292 for 36 holes (Michael Combs, 141; Warren Vickers, 151; Randy Avidson, 155); second, Houston, Texas Team, 293 (Ron Schroeder, 147; Ken Ramsey, 146; Chris Brauner, 162); third, Boston, Massachusetts Team, 296 (Chris Gorgone, 146; Alistair Catto, 150; Warren Nelson, 175). The two low individual scores of the three team members are used to calculate the team score.

WOMEN'S AMATEUR PUBLIC LINKS CHAMPIONSHIP

CHAMPIONSHIP TROPHY

Presented in January 1977 by

ROBERT F. DWYER

Member of the United States Golf Association Executive Committee

1962-1974

HISTORY

1981—Mary Enright, 20, of San Leandro, California, won the Women's Amateur Public Links Championship by defeating Lauri Merten, of Phoenix, Arizona, 3 and 1, in the final at the Emerald Valley Golf Course in Creswell, Oregon. Enright was only the third different champion in the event's five year history. The medalist was 14-year-old Kay Cornelius, of Scottsdale, Arizona, who posted a 36-hole score of 152, four strokes better than anyone else in the field. Enright, who had won the California Women's Amateur title earlier in the year, advanced to match play with a 159 total. Merten, who only made the field as an alternate, had 158. Two-time champion Lori Castillo, of Honolulu, Hawaii, reached match play with a 156 total. Her string of 11 consecutive match victories ended in the second round when she lost on the first extra hole to Pam Elders. Enright reached the championship match by defeating Heidi Brice, of Lake Oswego, Oregon, 3 and 2; Susan Berdoy, of Litchfield Park, Arizona, 1 up; Janis Kleiman, of Rushville, Indiana, 1 up; and Beth Sierra, of Lansing, Michigan, 4 and 3. In the other bracket, Merten advanced by eliminating Nancy Taylor, of Phoenix, Arizona, 2 up; Libby Akers, of French Lick, Indiana, 6 and 5; Kay Cornelius, 3 and 1; and Lisa Bradley, of Emporia, Kansas, 2 and 1. Through eight holes of the final, Enright and Merten were even, each having won two holes to that point. Enright won the 9th with a birdie putt of 10 feet and then won the 10th with a par to go 2 up. Merten got one hole back with a par at the 12th. Enright then won the 15th with a birdie putt of 15 feet for a 2 up lead. At the 17th, her 20-foot birdie putt ended the match. The Phoenix, Arizona Team of Berdoy, Cornelius and Kelly Merten (Lauri's sister) won the team trophy with 473, outdistancing the second place team from Miami, Florida, by 26 strokes. The Championship drew 686 entries, as in the first event in 1977, but short of the 728 entries attracted in 1980.

1982—Nancy Taylor, 22, of Phoenix, Arizona, won the Women's Amateur Public Links Championship by defeating Kerri Clark, of North Las Vegas, Nevada, 2 and 1, at the Alvamar Golf Club, in Lawrence, Kansas. Miss Taylor became only the fourth different champion in the event's six-year history, and, at 22, was the oldest winner. Defending Champion Mary Enright, of San Leandro, California, qualified easily with 154, but she was defeated in the second round by Linda McEwen, of Lake Oswego, Oregon, 3 and 2. Lori Castillo, of Honolulu, Champion in 1979 and 1980, qualified at 155, but lost in the first round to Ann Walsh, of Walnut Creek, California, 2 and 1. The Portland, Oregon, team of Linda McEwen, Kareen Gibson, and Renee MacDonald won the Team Trophy with 476, four strokes ahead of the team from Phoenix, Arizona. The Championship drew a record 760 entries, exceeding the previous record of 728 received for the 1980 Championship at the Center Square (Pa.) Golf Club.

1983—One year after being eliminated by Nancy Taylor, Kelli Antolock, 21, of Port Angeles, Washington, won the Women's Amateur Public Links Championship, by defeating Miss Taylor, of Phoenix, Arizona, the defending Champion, 1 up, at the Ala Wai Golf Course, in Honolulu. Miss Antolock stood 2 up after 11 holes of the final, but Miss Taylor fought back to square the match at the 14th. Miss Antolock won the 17th when Miss Taylor's wind-blown approach shot bounced over the green. Her pitch stopped eight feet short and she missed the putt. Both players bogeyed the home hole, preserving Miss Antolock's winning margin. Penny Hammel, of Decatur, Illinois, won the qualifying medal, with a 143 total, establishing a new record by five strokes. Marci Bozarth, of Fort Worth, Texas, set a new single-round record, with 70, on the second day of qualifying. The Chicago, Illinois, team of Miss Hammel, Jennifer Reego, and Jacqueline Ryan won the Team Trophy with 297, seven strokes ahead of Phoenix, Arizona. Twenty-eight teams competed. The Championship drew a record 1,008 entries, surpassing the previous high of 760, set in 1982.

1984—Heather Farr, 19, of Scottsdale, Arizona, won her second USGA Championship by defeating Kristie Kolacny, of Grand Junction, Colorado, 3 and 2, at the Meadowbrook Golf Course, in Rapid City, South Dakota. Miss Farr, the 1982 Girls' Junior champion, was medalist, with 144. Miss Kolacny's qualifying score was 13 strokes higher than Miss Farr's. The final amounted to an all-Arizona matchup; Miss Farr is the No. 1 player for Arizona State University and Miss Kolacny is the top player on the University of Arizona team. Miss Farr won the first hole with a par, but Miss Kolacny was ahead by one hole with six to play. Miss Farr won the next four holes. The Athens, Georgia, team of Cindy Schreyer, Lori Gaffney and Kathe Kingston won the Team Trophy, with 308, three strokes better than Phoenix. Thirty-two teams competed.

WOMEN'S AMATEUR PUBLIC LINKS CHAMPIONSHIP

1985—Danielle Ammaccapane, 19, of Phoenix, Arizona, defeated Kristie Kolacny of Grand Junction, Colorado, 6 and 5, at Flanders Valley Golf Course in Flanders, New·Jersey. Ammaccapane was the medalist at one-over-par 145. In the final, Ammaccapane won two of the first three holes but Kolacny evened the match by winning the fourth and sixth holes. Ammaccapane won the seventh and, after the eighth was halved with pars, took control of the match, winning the ninth through the 13th holes to close out Kolacny. It was the second year in a row that Kolacny had fallen to a five-hole run by her opponent in the final. Phoenix won the Team Championship for the third time in the nine-year history of the event. The team of Lisa Cornelius, Michelle Estill and Lana Perhacs combined for a 300 total, three strokes better than both Miami, Florida, and Grand Junction, Colorado. The USGA accepted 878 entries for the Championship.

1986—Cindy Schreyer, 22, of Peachtree City, Georgia, defeated Victoria Goetze of Hull, Georgia, 3 and 2, at SentryWorld Golf Course in Stevens Point, Wisconsin. Danielle Ammaccapane, the 1985 champion, shot a record 142 to earn the qualifying medal; she lost in the quarterfinal round to Catherine Burton, 1 up. In the final, Schreyer won the first four holes, as well as the seventh, threatening to make this final the most lop-sided in the championship's history. Goetze, 13 and bidding to become the youngest USGA champion ever, won the ninth and 10th to pull to within three. Schreyer won the 11th and 12th, but Goetze came back again, winning the 13th and 14th. The two golfers halved the 15th and 16th to give Schreyer the victory. The 10th WAPL Team Championship was won by Phoenix, its record fourth team title. The team of Lee Ann Hammack, Kay Cornelius and Carol Berger combined for a 309 total, one stroke ahead of the Cleveland team and six better than Los Angeles. The USGA accepted a record 1,085 entries for the championship.

1987—Tracy Kerdyk, 21, of Coral Gables, Florida, defeated Pearl Sinn of Bellflower, Florida, 4 and 3, at Cog Hill Golf and Country Club in Lemont, Illinois. Sinn shot 148, four over par, to earn the qualifying medal, two strokes better than Kerdyk. Kerdyk and Sinn each survived one extra hole match on the way to the final. Kerdyk defeated Melissa Farr of Phoenix on the 19th hole in the quarterfinals. Sinn eliminated Shelley Sanders of Miami Lakes, Florida, in 19 holes in the semifinal round. In the final, Kerdyk birdied the second to take a one-hole advantage, but her bogey at the fourth squared the match. An eagle at the fifth and a winning par at the eighth gave Kerdyk a two-hole edge. Sinn won the ninth with par and the 11th with bogey to pull even again. Kerdyk sank a four-foot birdie putt to win the 12th and won the 13th with a par to regain her two-hole advantage. At the 14th, she sank a 60-foot chip for par and, when Sinn missed her par putt, Kerdyk was 3 up. A birdie at the par-5 15th sealed the match. The 11th WAPL Team Championship was won by Miami. The team of Kerdyk and Sanders combined for a 303 total, two strokes ahead of the Los Angeles team and eight better than Indianapolis. The USGA accepted 952 entries for the championship.

1988—Pearl Sinn, 20, of Bellflower, California, defeated Tami Jo Henningsen of Colorado Springs, Colorado, 2 and 1, in the final at Page Belcher Golf Course in Tulsa, Oklahoma. Lee Ann Hammack of Oklahoma City earned the qualifying medal at two-under-par 142, tying a championship record. Her second-round 68 was the lowest 18-hole score ever posted at the Women's APL. Hammack was eliminated in the quarterfinal round by Stacey Arnold of Glen Ellyn, Illinois, on the 19th hole. Sinn defeated Arnold, 6 and 5, in the semifinals. Henningsen advanced to the final by ousting Michelle Estill of Scottsdale, Arizona, 4 and 3. Through eight holes of the final, Sinn held a two-hole advantage, extending her string of holes without a bogey to 35. That skein ended when both players bogeyed the par-5 ninth. Henningsen squared the match when she birdied the par-4 10th and par-5 11th holes. After the 12th was halved with pars, Sinn regained the lead with birdies on the 13th and 14th holes. Both players parred the par-4 15th before lightning forced play to be suspended briefly. After the 16th was halved, Sinn closed out the match by sinking a 20-foot birdie putt on the par-3 17th. The Tulsa, Oklahoma, team of Hammack, Shana Radford and Alycya Rambin won the Team Championship by four strokes over Sácramento, California. The USGA accepted a record 1,052 entries for the championship.

1989—Pearl Sinn, 21, won her second consecutive Women's Amateur Public Links championship, defeating 19-year-old Kelli Akers, 2 and 1, in the final. One hole down after the ninth, Miss Sinn won holes 10 through 12 with an eagle and two birdies. She reached the final for the third straight year by defeating Michelle Estill, her teammate at Arizona State, 1-up, in a semifinal match on a ruling on the final hole that went against Miss Estill. The ruling stemmed from Miss Estill's moving a tree branch in her attempt to recover from trouble off the 18th fairway. The Committee's ruling added a penalty stroke to her score, giving her a bogey on the final hole. In her first three matches, Miss Sinn was never extended to the 17th hole. She won those early matches by scores of 3 and 2, 6 and 5, and 5 and 4. She and Curtis Strange, who won the U.S. Open, were the only two to repeat as USGA champions in 1989.

1990—Cathy Mockett, 22, scored four birdies and an eagle in the final match, and defeated Barbara Blanchar, 22, by 5 and 4, to win the Women's Amateur Public Links Championship. Miss Mockett, a senior at the University of Tulsa, won the first three holes, and then built a six-hole lead with an eagle 3 on the 12th hole. She was five under par when the

WOMEN'S AMATEUR PUBLIC LINKS CHAMPIONSHIP

match ended, on the 14th hole. Competing in her first WAPL championship, Miss Mockett qualified for match play with 154, eight strokes behind medalist Debbit Eckroth, who shot 146. However, Miss Eckroth and the three other lowest scorers in stroke play were defeated in the first round of match play. Miss Mockett advanced by winning her first and second rounds easily, and then rallied to win by one hole over both Jennifer Holt and Lori Stinson. Miss Mockett was the U.S. Girls' Junior champion in 1984. She was also named second alternate to the 1990 U.S. Curtis Cup team.

WOMEN'S AMATEUR PUBLIC LINKS CHAMPIONSHIP

DATE	WINNER, RUNNER-UP	SCORE	SITE	ENTRY
1981 (June)	Miss Mary Enright d. Miss Lauri Merten	3 & 1	Emerald Valley G.C., Creswell, Ore. Medalist—152: Miss Kay Cornelius	686
1982 (June)	Miss Nancy Taylor d. Miss Kerri Clark	2 & 1	Alvamar G.C., Lawrence, Kan. Medalist—148: Miss Alicia Ogrin	760
1983 (June)	Miss Kelli Antolock d. Miss Nancy Taylor	1 up	Ala Wai G.C., Honolulu, Hawaii Medalist—143: Miss Penny Hammel	1,008
1984 (June)	Miss Heather Farr d. Miss Kristie Kolacny	3 & 2	Meadowbrook G.C., Rapid City, S.D. Medalist—144: Miss Heather Farr	834
1985 (June)	Miss Danielle Ammaccapane d. Miss Kristie Kolacny	6 & 5	Flanders Valley G.C., Flanders, N.J. Medalist—145: Miss Danielle Ammaccapane	878
1986 (June)	Miss Cindy Schreyer d. Miss Vicki Goetze	3 & 2	Sentry World G.C., Stevens Point, Wis. Medalist—†142: Miss Danielle Ammaccapane	§1,085
1987 (June)	Miss Tracy Kerdyk d. Miss Pearl Sinn	4 & 3	Cog Hill G. & C.C., (No. 4 Course) Lemont, Ill. Medalist—148: Miss Pearl Sinn	952
1988 (June)	Miss Pearl Sinn d. Miss Tami Jo Henningsen	2 & 1	Page Belcher G.C., Tulsa, Okla. Medalist—142: Miss Lee Ann Hammack	1,052
1989 (June)	Miss Pearl Sinn d. Miss Kelli Akers	2 & 1	Indian Canyon G.C., Spokane, Wash. Medalist—†141: Miss Michelle Estill	1,020
1990 (June)	Miss Cathy Mockett d. Miss Barbara Blanchar	5 & 4	Hyland Hills G.C., Westminster, Colo. Medalist—146: Miss Debbie Eckroth	920

†Record Qualifying Score
§Record Entry

WOMEN'S AMATEUR PUBLIC LINKS TEAM CHAMPIONSHIP

DATE	WINNER, RUNNER-UP	SCORE	SITE	ENTRY
1981 (June)	Phoenix, Ariz.	473	Emerald Valley G.C., Creswell, Ore.	**20**
1982 (June)	Portland, Ore.	476	Alvamar G.C., Lawrence, Kan.	**22**
1983 (June)	Chicago, Ill.	297 (36 hls., 2 women)	Ala Wai G.C., Honolulu, Hawaii	**28**
1984 (June)	Athens, Ga.	308	Meadowbrook G.C., Rapid City, S.D.	**32**
1985 (June)	Phoenix, Ariz.	300	Flanders Valley G.C., Flanders, N.J.	**31**
1986 (June)	Phoenix, Ariz.	309	Sentry World G.C., Stevens Point, Wis.	**31**
1987 (June)	Miami, Fla.	303	Cog Hill G. & C.C., (No. 4 Course) Lemont, Ill.	**30**
1988 (June)	Tulsa, Okla.	291	Page Belcher G.C., Tulsa, Okla.	**32**
1989 (June)	Phoenix, Ariz.	*288	Indian Canyon G.C., Spokane, Wash.	**33**
1990 (June)	Albuquerque, N.M.	305	Hyland Hills, G.C., Westminster, Colo.	**§36**

§Record Entry
*Record Score

1981
FIFTH WOMEN'S AMATEUR PUBLIC LINKS CHAMPIONSHIP

Emerald Valley Golf Course, Creswell, Oregon, June 24-28
Yardage—6,108. Par 72. 686 Entries, 120 Starters, 32 Qualifiers.

Qualifying Score	1st Round (18 Holes)	2nd Round (18 Holes)	3rd Round (18 Holes)	Semi-Finals (18 Holes)	Final (18 Holes)
*152	Kay Cornelius, Scottsdale, Ariz.	Cornelius,			
163	Leigh Klasse, Westbrook, Minn.	2 and 1	Cornelius,		
159	Sherrie Ann Keblish, Miami, Fla.	Clark,	1 up, 19 holes		
165	Lori Clark, Des Moines, Iowa	1 up, 20 holes			
158	Lauri Merten, Phoenix, Ariz.	Merten,		Merten,	
165	Nancy Taylor, Phoenix, Ariz.	2 up	Merten,	3 and 1	
160	Elizabeth Ann Akers, French Lick, Ind.	Akers,	6 and 5		
167	Mahealani Souza, Honolulu, Hawaii	4 and 3			Merten,
156	Lori Castillo, Honolulu, Hawaii	Castillo,			2 and 1
164	Diane Escobedo, Phoenix, Ariz.	6 and 4	Elders,		
160	Pam Elders, Leisure City, Fla.	Elders,	1 up, 19 holes		
166	Julie Carmichael, Martinsville, Ind.	2 and 1			
159	Jody Christensen, St. Louis Park, Minn.	Christensen,		Bradley,	
165	Kerry Liedes, Hoquiam, Wash.	4 and 3		2 up	
162	Denise Martinez, Tempe, Ariz.	Bradley,	Bradley,		Mary Enright, 3 and 1
167	Lisa Bradley, Emporia, Kans.	1 up	1 up		
156	Susan Berdoy, Litchfield Park, Ariz.	Berdoy,			
163	Deborah Skelly, Bellaire, Texas	4 and 2	Enright,		
159	Mary Enright, San Leandro, Calif.	Enright,	1 up		
166	Heidi Brice, Lake Oswego, Ore.	3 and 2		Enright,	
158	Linda Branstetter, Albuquerque, N.M.	Kleiman,		1 up	
165	Janis Kleiman, Rushville, Ind.	1 up	Kleiman,		
161	Julie Fulton, Los Angeles, Calif.	Fulton,	4 and 3		
167	Denise Qualtire, Phoenix, Ariz.	2 and 1			Enright,
158	Marianne Huning, San Gabriel, Calif.	Huning,			4 and 3
164	Barbara Arrell, Minneapolis, Minn.	2 and 1	Sierra,		
160	Linda McEwen, Lake Oswego, Ore.	Sierra,	1 up	Sierra,	
167	Beth Sierra, East Lansing, Mich.	1 up		4 and 2	
159	Theresa Schreck, Spokane, Wash.	Merten,			
165	Kelly Merten, Phoenix, Ariz.	1 up	Merten,		
162	Nina Spatafora, St. Clair Shores, Mich.	Spatafora,	2 and 1		
168	Sandra Nakagaki, Honolulu, Hawaii	2 and 1			

*Medalist

Fifth Amateur Public Links Inter-city Team Championship Team Trophy (20 Team Entries), June 24, 25: Won by Phoenix, Arizona Team, 473 for 36 holes (Susie Berdoy, 156; Kay Cornelius, 152; Kelly Merten, 165); Second, Miami, Florida Team, 497 (Susan Smith, 178; Pam Elders, 160; Sherrie Keblish, 159); Third, Industry Hills, California Team, 499 (Patty Lopez, 169; Julie Fulton, 161; Flori Prono, 169).

1982
SIXTH WOMEN'S AMATEUR PUBLIC LINKS CHAMPIONSHIP

Alvamar Golf Club, Lawrence, Kansas, June 23-27.
Yardage—5,897. Par 72. †760 Entries, 120 Starters, 32 Qualifiers.

Qualifying Score	1st Round (18 Holes)	2nd Round (18 Holes)	3rd Round (18 Holes)	Semifinals (18 Holes)	Final (18 Holes)
*148	Alicia Ogrin, Waukegan, Ill.	Ogrin,			
159	Susan Thompson, Garden Grove, Calif.	8 and 7	Antolock,		
157	Kelli Antolock, Port Angeles, Wash.	Antolock,	2 and 1		
162	Denise Bratzler, Carson City, Nev.	5 and 3		Antolock,	
154	Mary Enright, San Leandro, Calif.	Enright,		6 and 5	
160	Leigh Klasse, Minneapolis, Minn.	2 and 1	McEwen,		
157	Linda McEwen, Lake Oswego, Ore.	McEwen,	3 and 2		
163	Lisa Kartheiser, Port Washington, Wis.	4 and 2			Taylor,
154	Kathleen Budai, Glendale, Ariz.	Budai,			1 up, 19 holes
159	Danielle Ammaccapane, Phoenix, Ariz.	2 up	Taylor,		
157	Nancy Taylor, Phoenix, Ariz.	Taylor,	3 and 2		
163	Michelle Bell, Melrose, Mass.	7 and 6		Taylor,	
156	Jan Kleiman, Rushville, Ind.	Cornelius,		3 and 2	
161	Kay Cornelius, Phoenix, Ariz.	3 and 1	Cornelius,		
158	Renee MacDonald, Grants Pass, Ore.	Lovander,	4 and 3		
164	Marilyn Lovander, Willmar, Minn.	1 up			
153	Holley Morris, Golden, Colo.	Clark,			
159	Kerri Clark, North Las Vegas, Nev.	1 up	Clark,		
157	Denise Martinez, Rio Rico, Ariz.	Lopez,	1 up		
162	Patricia Lopez, Northridge, Calif.	1 up, 19 holes		Clark,	
155	Lori Castillo, Honolulu, Hawaii	Walsh,		4 and 3	
160	Ann Walsh, Walnut Creek, Calif.	2 and 1	Walsh,		
158	Bev Boozer, Lawrence, Kans.	Harris,	4 and 3		
163	Nancy Harris, Roseau, Minn.	1 up			Clark,
154	Lucy Castaneda, Albuquerque, N.M.	Castaneda,			2 and 1
159	Mary McClure, Shelburn, Ind.	2 and 1	Schreck,		
157	Theresa Schreck, Spokane, Wash.	Schreck,	1 up		
163	Jamie Bronson, Kinsman, Ohio	3 and 2		Schreck,	
156	Marcie Bozarth, Lampasas, Texas	Bozarth,		1 up	
161	Kareen Gibson, Fall River Mills, Calif.	6 and 5	Kerdyk,		
159	Tracy Kerdyk, Coral Gables, Fla.	Kerdyk,	2 up		
164	Chris Lehmann, Thousand Oaks, Calif.	5 and 3			

Nancy Taylor, 2 and 1

*Medalist †Record Entry

Sixth Women's Amateur Public Links Inter-city Team Championship Team Trophy (22 Team Entries), June 23, 24: Won by Portland, Oregon, Team, 476 for 36 holes (Linda McEwen, 157; Kareen Gibson, 161; Renee MacDonald, 158); Second, Phoenix, Arizona, Team, 479 (Nancy Taylor, 157; Denise Martinez, 157; Kelly Douglass, 165); Third, Denver, Colorado, Team, 485 (Holley Morris, 153; Kristie Kolacny, 165; Susan Knox, 167).

1983
SEVENTH WOMEN'S AMATEUR PUBLIC LINKS CHAMPIONSHIP

Ala Wai Golf Course, Honolulu, Hawaii, June 22-26
Yardage—6,045. Par 72. +1,008 Entries, 120 Starters, 32 Qualifiers.

Qualifying Score	1st Round (18 Holes)	2nd Round (18 Holes)	3rd Round (18 Holes)	Semifinals (18 Holes)	Final (18 Holes)	
*143	Penny Hammel, Decatur, Ill.	Hammel, 6 and 5				
155	Lana Perhacs, Glendale, Ariz.		Hammel, 1 up, 19 holes			
153	Ann Soderman, Bellaire, Texas	Brown, 5 and 4				
157	Karen Brown, Twin Falls, Id.			Taylor, 1 up		
149	Nancy Taylor, Tampa, Fla.	Taylor, 2 and 1				
156	Marilyn Lovander, Willmar, Minn.		Taylor, 3 and 2			
154	Theresa Schreck, Spokane, Wash.	Schreck, 1 up				
158	Linda McEwen, Lake Oswego, Ore.				Taylor, 1 up, 19 holes	
148	Heather Farr, Phoenix, Arix.	Farr, 2 and 1				
156	Kerry Liedes, Aberdeen, Wash.		Farr, 2 and 1			
153	Juli Ordonez, Salinas, Calif.	Ordonez, 1 up				
157	Lucy Castaneda, Tijeras, N.M.			Harris, 3 and 2		
151	Nancy Harris, Minneapolis, Minn.	Harris, 3 and 2				
156	Jan Shiroma, Kaneone, Hawaii		Harris, 7 and 6			
154	Jennifer Reego, North Brook, Ill.	Reego, 1 up				
158	Tracy Kerdyk, Coral Gables, Fla.					Kelli Antolock, 1 up
146	Marci Bozarth, Ft. Worth, Texas	Billek, 3 and 2				
155	Susan Billek, Oldsmar, Fla.		Branstetter, 1 up			
153	Linda Branstetter, Albuquerque, N.M.	Branstetter, 1 up, 19 holes				
157	Kareen Gibson, Fall River Mills, Calif.			Branstetter, 1 up, 19 holes		
151	Michelle Bell, Melrose, Mass.	Skalicky, 2 and 1				
156	Kelly Skalicky, St. Paul, Minn.		Skalicky, 2 and 1			
154	Leigh Klasse, Minneapolis, Minn.	Klasse, 3 and 2				
158	Cindy Mueller, Belleville, ill.				Antolock, 4 and 2	
149	Kelli Antolock, Port Angeles, Wash.	Antolock, 2 up				
156	Jane Carlson, Las Vegas, Nev.		Antolock, 5 and 4			
153	Kathy Budai, Glendale, Ariz.	Budai, 1 up, 21 holes				
157	Lynn Dennison, Marion, Ohio			Antolock, 3 and 1		
151	Kris Hanson, Granite Falls, Minn.	Abascal, 3 and 2				
157	Cam Abascal, Ft. Lauderdale, Fla.		Abascal, 1 up			
155	Sherry Andonian, Camarillo, Calif.	Martinez, 6 and 5				
159	Denise Martinez, Tempe, Ariz.					

*Medalist +Record Entry

Seventh Women's Amateur Public Links Inter-city Team Championships Team Trophy (28 Team Entries), June 22, 23: Won by Chicago, Illinois Team, 297 for 36 holes (Penny Hammel 143; Jacqueline Ryan, 167; Jennifer Reego, 154); Second, Phoenix, Arizona Team, 304 (Lisa Cornelius, 162; Michelle Bell, 151; Kathy Budai, 153); Third, Tacoma, Washington Team, 305 (Kelli Antolock, 149; Kerry Liedes, 156; Rusty Galles, 159). The two low individual scores of the three team members are used to calculate the team score.

1984
EIGHTH WOMEN'S AMATEUR PUBLIC LINKS CHAMPIONSHIP

Meadowbrook Golf Course, Rapid City, South Dakota, June 20-24
Yardage—5,881. Par 72. 834 Entries, 120 Starters, 32 Qualifiers

Qualifying Score	1st Round (18 Holes)	2nd Round (18 Holes)	3rd Round (18 Holes)	Semifinals (18 Holes)	Final (18 Holes)	
*144	Heather Farr, Phoenix, Ariz.	Farr, 3 and 1				
158	Lynn Dennison, Marion, Ohio		Farr, 3 and 1			
155	Julie Baxter, Rutland, Ill.	Baxter, 1 up				
163	Judy Giovainni, Akron, Ohio			Farr, 3 and 2		
151	Theresa Schreck, Spokane, Wash.	Schreck, 2 and 1				
160	Karen Schulthes, Normal, Ill.		Antolock, 2 and 1			
157	Kelli Antolock, Port Angeles, Wash.	Antolock, 1 up				
164	Lana Perhacs, Glendale, Ariz.				Farr, 4 and 2	
149	Kerri Clark, Las Vegas, Nev.	Nakagaki, 3 and 2				
160	Sandra Nakagaki, Honolulu, Hawaii		Nakagaki, 3 and 2			
155	Catherine Nelson, Lincoln, Neb.	Pruett, 2 up				
163	Missy Pruett, Newburgh, Ind.			Kerdyk, 6 and 5		
153	Denise Martinez, Tempe, Ariz.	Martinez, 4 and 3				
163	Kerry Liedes, Seattle, Wash.		Kerdyk, 4 and 2			
158	Dee Forsberg, Farmington, Minn.	Kerdyk, 2 and 1				
165	Tracy Kerdyk, Coral Gables, Fla.					Heather Farr, 3 and 2
149	Sandra Persinger, Laurel, Md.	Persinger, 1 up, 20 holes				
158	Kay Cornelius, Scottsdale, Ariz.		Persinger, 4 and 3			
155	Kathe Kingston, Marietta, Ga.	Kingston, 3 and 2				
163	Leigh Klasse, Edina, Minn.			Kolacny, 3 and 2		
153	Cindy Schreyer, Peachtree City, Ga.	Ryan, 2 up				
162	Jacqueline Ryan, Lockport, Ill.		Kolacny, 1 up			
157	Kristie Kolacny, Grand Junction, Colo.	Kolacny, 7 and 5				
165	Rusty Galles, Port Angeles, Wash.				Kolacny, 2 and 1	
149	Danielle Ammaccapane, Phoenix, Ariz.	Ammaccapane, 7 and 6				
160	Dori O'Rourke, Sacramento, Calif.		Ammaccapane, 1 up, 19 holes			
157	Libby Akers, French Lick, Ind.	McEwen, 3 and 2				
164	Linda McEwen, Lake Oswego, Ore.			Ammaccapane, 6 and 4		
155	Francine Epstein, Van Nuys, Calif.	Epstein, 1 up, 19 holes				
163	Sarah Zwemke, Arvada, Colo.		Harris, 1 up			
158	Nancy Harris, Falcon Heights, Minn.	Harris, 2 and 1				
165	Kimberly Mann, Council Bluffs, Iowa					

*Medalist

Eighth Women's Amateur Public Links Inter-city Championships Team Trophy (32 Team Entries), June 20,21; Won By Athens, Georgia Team, 308 for 36 holes (Cindy Schreyer, 153; Kathe Kingston, 155; Lori Gaffney, 180); Second, Phoenix, Arizona Team, 311 (Danielle Ammaccapane, 149; Lana Perhacs, 164; Michelle Estill, 166); Third, Tacoma, Washington Team, 314 (Kerry Liedes, 163; Theresa Schreck, 149; Debra Brown, 180). The two low individual scores of the three team members are used to calculate the team score.

1985
NINTH WOMEN'S AMATEUR PUBLIC LINKS CHAMPIONSHIP

Flanders Valley Golf Course, Flanders, New Jersey, June 19-23
Yardage—5,808. Par 72. 878 Entries, 120 Starters, 32 Qualifiers

Qualifying Score	1st Round (18 Holes)	2nd Round (18 Holes)	3rd Round (18 Holes)	Semifinals (18 Holes)	Final (18 Holes)	
*145	Danielle Ammaccapane, Phoenix, Ariz.	Da. Ammaccapane,				
158	Judy Giovainni, Akron, Ohio	4 and 3	Da. Ammaccapane,			
155	Tami Jo Henningsen, Colorado Springs, Colo.	Liscio,	2 and 1			
155	Patricia Liscio, San Diego, Calif.	2 and 1		Da. Ammaccapane,		
151	Heather Farr, Phoenix, Ariz.	Farr,		2 and 1		
157	Elizabeth Akers, French Lick, Ind.	5 and 4	Farr,			
152	Lynn Dennison, Marion, Ohio	McHugh,	3 and 2			
157	Nancy McHugh, Vernon, Conn.	3 and 2			Da. Ammaccapane,	
149	Kristll Caldeira, Kaneohe, Hawaii	Mah-Lyford,			1 up	
158	Cindy Mah-Lyford, Stratton Mountain, Vt.	6 and 5	Mah-Lyford,			
153	Dawn Ginnaty, Rochester, Minn.	Klasse,	7 and 6			
156	Leigh Klasse, Minneapolis, Minn.	3 and 1		Schreyer,		Danielle Ammaccapane, 6 and 5
150	Cynthia Schreyer, Athens, Ga.	Schreyer,		7 and 6		
158	Lorie Wilkes, Bartow, Fla.	4 and 3	Schreyer,			
153	Charlaine Tatz, Westfield, N.J.	Tatz,	2 and 1			
156	Geralyn Repasky, Livonia, Mich.	1 up				
146	Sue Billek, Provo, Utah	Billek,				
158	Lynne Scalberg, Saratoga, Calif.	6 and 5	Schreck,			
154	Theresa Schreck, Spokane, Wash.	Schreck,	6 and 5			
155	Dina Ammaccapane, Phoenix, Ariz.	4 and 2		Kolacny,		
150	Lana Perhacs, Glendale, Ariz.	Perhacs,		1 up, 21 holes		
157	Carla Cantu, Newport News, Va.	3 and 2	Kolacny,			
153	Lori Gaffney, Des Moines, Iowa	Kolacny,	2 and 1			
156	Kristie Kolacny, Grand Junction, Colo.	5 and 3			Kolacny,	
149	Tracy Kerdyk, Coral Gables, Fla.	Kerdyk,			1 up, 22 holes	
158	Roberta Kokx, Grand Rapids, Mich.	2 and 1	Baxter,			
154	Susan Thompson, Plantation, Fla.	Baxter,	2 and 1			
155	Julie Baxter, Normal, Ill.	4 and 3		Baxter,		
150	Michelle Estill, Scottsdale, Ariz.	Fry,		4 and 3		
158	Elizabeth Fry, Adelphi, Md.	3 and 1	Fry,			
153	Ann Soderman, Houston, Texas	Soderman,	5 and 4			
156	Jane Carlson, Las Vegas, Nev.	5 and 3				

*Medalist

Ninth Women's Amateur Public Links Inter-city Championships Team Trophy (31 Team Entries), June 19, 20; Won by Phoenix, Arizona, Team, 300 for 36 holes (Michelle Estill, 150; Lisa Cornelius, 160; Lana Perhacs, 150); Tied for Second, Athens, Georgia, Team, 303 (Tracy Kerdyk, 149; Lori Wilkes, 158; Susan Thompson, 154); and Grand Junction, Colorado, Team, 303 (Sue Billek, 146; Kimberly Kell, 159; Michelle Reed, 160). The two low individual scores of the three team members are used to calculate the team score.

1986
TENTH WOMEN'S AMATEUR PUBLIC LINKS CHAMPIONSHIP

SentryWorld Golf Course, Stevens Point, Wisconsin, June 18-22
Yardage—5,926. Par 72. 1,085 Entries, 120 Starters, 32 Qualifiers

Qualifying Score	1st Round (18 Holes)	2nd Round (18 Holes)	3rd Round (18 Holes)	Semifinals (18 Holes)	Final (18 Holes)	
*142	Danielle Ammaccapane, Phoenix, Ariz.	Ammaccapane,				
163	Tina Becker, Fenton, Mich.	9 and 7	Ammaccapane,			
158	Natalie Gresham, Crosby, Texas	Sanders,	2 and 1			
158	Shelley Sanders, Miami Lakes, Fla.	3 and 2		Burton,		
156	Jennifer Holt, Las Vegas, Nev.	Burton,		1 up		
161	Catherine Burton, Winnipeg, Manitoba, Canada	5 and 4	Burton,			
156	Leigh Klasse, Minneapolis, Minn.	Klasse,	3 and 2			
161	Anne Staub, Cedar Rapids, Iowa	2 and 1			Schreyer,	
151	Cindy Mah-Lyford, Stratton Mountain, Vt.	Mah-Lyford,			3 and 2	
162	Kari Mangan, Omaha, Neb.	1 up, 19 holes	Mah-Lyford,			
157	Marlene Brodzik, Lancaster, N.Y.	Brodzik,	3 and 2			
159	Lee Ann Hammack, Oklahoma City, Okla.	1 up		Schreyer,		
152	Pearl Sinn, Bellflower, Calif.	Horner,		3 and 2		
162	Nicole Horner, Mililani, Hawaii	1 up	Schreyer,			Cindy Schreyer, 3 and 2
157	Cindy Schreyer, Athens, Ga.	Schreyer,	1 up, 19 holes			
159	Jan Shiroma, Kaneohe, Hawaii	2 up				
146	Tracy Kerdyk, Coral Gables, Fla.	Kerdyk,				
163	Ann Meyer, Minneapolis, Minn.	4 and 3	Kerdyk,			
158	Judy Giovainni, Akron, Ohio	Andonian,	4 and 2			
159	Sherry Andonian, Camarillo, Calif.	4 and 2		Goetze,		
154	Victoria Goetze, Hull, Ga.	Goetze,		1 up		
161	Dawn Ginnaty, Rochester, Minn.	7 and 6	Goetze,			
156	Victoria Abens, Woodridge, Ill.	Kokx,	2 and 1			
160	Roberta Kokx, Grand Rapids, Mich.	3 and 2			Goetze,	
150	Kay Cornelius, Tucson, Ariz.	Cornelius,			2 and 1	
162	Sherry Keblish, Miami, Fla.	1 up	Cornelius,			
157	Judy Greco, Los Alamitos, Calif.	Greco,	5 and 4			
159	Laura Mehall, Cleveland, Ohio	1 up, 19 holes		Cornelius,		
152	Tami Jo Henningsen, Colorado Springs, Colo.	Henningsen,		3 and 2		
162	Sarah Johnson, Wayzata, Minn.	5 and 4	Lofland,			
156	Susan Roll, Chadron, Neb.	Lofland,	1 up			
159	Dana Lofland, Oxnard, Calif.	1 up				

*Medalist

Tenth Women's Amateur Public Links Inter-city Championships Team Trophy (30 Team Entries), June 18, 19; Won by Phoenix, Arizona, Team, 309 for 36 holes (Lee Ann Hammack, 159; Kay Cornelius, 150; Carol Berger, 167); Second, Cleveland, Ohio, Team, 310 (Tami Jo Henningsen, 152; Lisa Paris, 168; Judy Giovainni, 158); Third, Los Angeles, California, Team, 316 (Sherry Andonian, 159; Judy Greco, 157). The two low individual scores of the team members are used to calculate the team score.

1987
ELEVENTH WOMEN'S AMATEUR PUBLIC LINKS CHAMPIONSHIP

Cog Hill Golf & Country Club, Lemont, Illinois, June 24-28
Yardage—5,886. Par 72. 952 Entries, 120 Starters, 32 Qualifiers

Qualifying Score	1st Round (18 Holes)	2nd Round (18 Holes)	3rd Round (18 Holes)	Semifinals (18 Holes)	Finals (18 Holes)	
*148	Pearl Sinn, Bellflower, Calif.	Sinn,				
164	Sherrie Keblish, Miami, Fla.	3 and 2	Sinn,			
160	Libby Akers, French Lick, Ind.	Akers,	2 and 1			
160	Kelly Lu Meyers, Rapid City, S.D.	3 and 2		Sinn,		
155	Nicole Kochaphum, Vallejo, Calif.	Kochaphum,		2 up		
162	Nancy Harris, Bloomington, Minn.	3 and 2	Mah-Lyford,			
156	Cindy Mah-Lyford, Stratton Mountain, Vt.	Mah-Lyford,	2 and 1			
162	Carol Rhoades, Jamestown, Pa.	3 and 2			Sinn,	
153	Amy Fruhwirth, Cypress, Calif.	Fruhwirth,			1 up, 19 holes	
163	Susan McGuire, State College, Pa.	2 and 1	Fruhwirth,			
159	Martha Lang, Geneva, Ill.	Lang,	3 and 1			
161	Jan Shiroma, Kaneohe, Hawaii	4 and 3		Sanders,		
153	Shelley Sanders, Miami Lakes, Fla.	Sanders,		5 and 3		
163	Nodjya Cook, Tipton, Ind.	4 and 2	Sanders,			
159	Julia Carmichael, Martinsville, Ind.	Dobek,	3 and 2			
161	Michelle Dobek, Chicopee, Mass.	2 and 1				Tracy Kerdyk, 4 and 3
150	Tracy Kerdyk, Coral Gables, Fla.	Kerdyk,				
164	Sarah Zwemke, Albuquerque, N.M.	5 and 4	Kerdyk,			
160	Jean Smith, Boise, Idaho	Hine,	2 and 1			
160	Leanne Hine, Olympia, Wash.	1 up, 20 holes		Kerdyk,		
155	Dawn Ginnaty, Rochester, Minn.	Farr,		1 up, 19 holes		
162	Missy Farr, Phoenix, Ariz.	2 and 1	Farr,			
157	Nicole Horner, Mililani, Hawaii	Burton,	4 and 3			
162	Catherine Burton, Winnipeg, Manitoba, Canada	3 and 1			Kerdyk,	
152	Dana Lofland, Oxnard, Calif.	Lofland,			3 and 1	
164	Susan Artemenko, Des Plaines, Ill.	4 and 2	Perhacs,			
160	Loree Hayes, Renton, Wash.	Perhacs,	2 and 1			
160	Lana Perhacs, Glendale, Ariz.	3 and 2		Chapman,		
154	Tracy Chapman, Indianapolis, Ind.	Chapman,		4 and 3		
163	Stacey Arnold, Glen Ellyn, Ill.	4 and 3	Chapman,			
158	Vicki Goetze, Hull, Ga.	Goetze,	3 and 2			
162	Ann Soderman, Houston, Texas	1 up, 20 holes				

* Medalist

Eleventh Women's Amateur Public Links Inter-city Championships Team Trophy (30 Team Entries), June 24, 25; Won by Miami, Florida, Team, 303 for 36 holes (Shelley Sanders, 153; Tracy Kerdyk, 150); Second, Los Angeles, California, Team, 305 (Dana Lofland, 152; Amy Fruhwirth, 153); Third, Indianapolis, Indiana, Team 311 (Tracey Chapman, 154; Julie Carmichael, 159; Libby Akers, 160). The two low individual scores of the team members are used to calculate the team score.

1988
TWELFTH WOMEN'S AMATEUR PUBLIC LINKS CHAMPIONSHIP

Page Belcher Golf Course, Tulsa, Oklahoma, June 22-26
Yardage—5,970. 1,051 Entries, 120 Starters, 32 Qualifiers

Qualifying Score	1st Round (18 Holes)	2nd Round (18 Holes)	3rd Round (18 Holes)	Semifinals (18 Holes)	Final (18 Holes)	
*141	Lee Ann Hammack, Oklahoma City, Okla.	Hammack,				
156	Kelly Lu Meyers, Rapid City, S.D.	3 and 2	Hammack,			
150	Missy Farr, Phoenix, Ariz.	Horner,	3 and 2			
150	Nicole Horner, Mililani Town, Hawaii	2 and 1		Arnold,		
148	Judy Giovainni, Akron, Ohio	Giovainni,		1 up, 19 holes		
154	Anne Marie Goslak, Brighton, Mich.	1 up	Arnold,			
149	Stacey Arnold, Glen Ellyn, Ill.	Arnold,	2 and 1			
154	Cindy Haley, Arlington, Texas	3 and 1			Sinn,	
145	Pearl Sinn, Bellflower, Calif.	Sinn,			6 and 5	
155	Kris Montplaisir, Mesa, Ariz.	4 and 2	Sinn,			
149	Shana Radford, Memphis, Tenn.	Radford,	1 up			
152	Kelly Holland, Lansing, Mich.	1 up		Sinn,		
146	Kim Saiki, Redwood City, Calif.	Saiki,		7 and 6		
155	Laurie Roche, Hamden, Conn.	2 up	Saiki,			
149	Becky Iverson, Gladstone, Mich.	Brown,	3 and 2			
152	Laura Brown, New Smyrna Beach, Fla.	2 and 1				
143	Tami Jo Henningsen, Colorado Springs, Colo.	Henningsen,				
155	Kelli Jo Ross, Burnsville, Minn.	1 up	Henningsen,			Pearl Sinn, 2 and 1
150	Loree Hayes, Tacoma, Wash.	Hayes,	3 and 2			
151	Tamerlane Carter, Austin, Texas	1 up		Henningsen,		
147	Nadia Ste-Marie, Lake City, Fla.	Ste-Marie,		3 and 1		
154	Sara Evens, Grafton, N.D.	3 and 2	Krafka,			
149	Natalie Gresham, Crosby, Texas	Krafka,	2 and 1			
154	Jodi Krafka, Minneapolis, Minn.	4 and 3			Henningsen,	
143	Michelle Estill, Scottsdale, Ariz.	Estill,			4 and 3	
155	Lisa Ikegami, Salt Lake City, Utah	3 and 2	Estill,			
150	Barbara Blanchar, Columbia, Mo.	Blanchar,	2 and 1			
152	Leanne Hine, Olympia, Wash.	1 up, 19 holes		Estill,		
147	Nicole Kochaphum, Vallejo, Calif.	Kochaphum,		5 and 4		
155	Heidi Brice, West Linn, Ore.	3 and 1	Kochaphum,			
149	Kelly Crawford, Rancho Cordova, Calif.	Akers,	2 and 1			
153	Kelli Akers, French Lick, Ind.	2 and 1				

*Medalist

Twelfth Women's Amateur Public Links Inter-city Championships Team Trophy (32 Team Entries), June 22, 23; Won by Tulsa, Oklahoma, Team, 291 for 36 holes (Lee Ann Hammack, 142; Shana Radford, 149; Alycya Rambin, 162); Second, Sacramento, California, Team, 296 (Kelly Crawford, 149; Nicole Kochaphum, 147); Third, Phoenix, Arizona, Team, 298 (Michelle Estill, 143; Kris Montplaisir, 155; Janice McCarley, 162). The two low individual scores of the team members are used to calculate the team score.

1989
THIRTEENTH WOMEN'S AMATEUR PUBLIC LINKS CHAMPIONSHIP

Indian Canyon Golf Course, Spokane, Washington, June 21-25
Yardage—5,666. Par 73. 1,020 Entries, 132 Starters, 32 Qualifiers

Qualifying Score	1st Round (18 Holes)	2nd Round (18 Holes)	3rd Round (18 Holes)	Semifinals (18 Holes)	Final (18 Holes)	
*141	Michelle Estill, Scottsdale, Ariz.	Estill,				
159	Jennie Holloway, Mount Dora, Fla.	2 and 1	Estill,			
154	Jean Smith, Boise, Idaho	Smith,	3 and 2			
154	Kareen Markle, Meridian, Idaho	4 and 3				
151	Michelle Wooding, Tacoma, Wash.	Wooding,		Estill,		
157	Sandy Ashley, Edmonds, Wash.	4 and 3		1 up		
152	Stacey Arnold, Glenn Ellyn, Ill.	Arnold,	Arnold,			
156	Kristi Montplaisir, Mesa, Ariz.	1 up	7 and 6			
149	Pearl Sinn, Bellflower, Calif.	Sinn,			Sinn,	
159	Lynne Mikulas, La Mesa, Calif.	3 and 2			1 up	
153	Karen Weiss, St. Pual, Minn.	Weiss,	Sinn,			
155	Anne Staub, Cedar Rapids, Iowa	4 and 3	6 and 5			
158	Kelly Meyers, Rapid City, S.D.	Meyers,		Sinn,		
149	Missy Farr, Phoenix, Ariz.	2 up		5 and 4		
156	Carri Wood, South Dennis, Mass.	Wood,	Wood,			
153	Nicole Horner, Mililani Town, Hawaii	1 up	19 holes			
146	Amy Fruhwirth, Cypress, Calif.	Fruhwirth,				
159	Pat Rogers, Eden Prairie, Minn.	5 and 3	Luginbuel,			
153	Sheila Luginbuel, Vinita, Okla.	Luginbuel,	3 and 1			
155	Gina Glodowski, Ogden, Utah	8 and 7		Luginbuel,		Pearl Sinn, 2 and 1
150	Robin Crowther, Las Cruces, N.M.	Crowther,		2 and 1		
157	Sara Evens, Grafton, N.D.	5 and 4	Crowther,			
152	Cathy Cook, Las Vegas, Nev.	Cook,	2 and 1			
156	Lorianne Johns, Tacoma, Wash.	5 and 4			Akers,	
147	Kelli Akers, French Lick, Ind.	Akers,			5 and 3	
159	Jennifer Mieras, Kentwood, Mich.	4 and 3	Akers,			
153	Barbara Blanchar, Columbia, Mo.	Blanchar,	1 up			
155	Dina Ammaccapane, Phoenix, Ariz.	2 and 1		Akers,		
158	Keiko Hamazaki, Westchester, Ill.	Hamazaki,		4 and 3		
149	Jodi Krafka, Minneapolis, Minn.	2 and 1	Hamazaki,			
156	Judy Giovainni, Akron, Ohio	Giovainni,	4 and 2			
152	Kay Schvaneveldt, Portland, Ore.	1 up				

*Medalist

Thirteenth Women's Amateur Public Links Inter-City Championship Trophy (Record 33 Team Entries); Won by Phoenix, Arizona, Team, Record 288 for 36 holes (Dina Ammaccapane, 155; Michelle Estill, 141; Pearl Sinn, 149); second, St. Paul, Minnesota, Team, 302 (Jodi Krafka, 149; Karen Weiss, 153); third, Portland, Oregon, Team, 303 (Michelle Wooding, 151; Kay Schvaneveldt, 152). The two low individual scores of the team members are used to calculate the team scores.

1990
FOURTEENTH WOMEN'S AMATEUR PUBLIC LINKS CHAMPIONSHIP

Westminister, Colorado, June 20-24
Yardage—6,025. Par 73. 920 Entries, 135 Starters, 32 Qualifiers

Qualifying Score	1st Round (18 Holes)	2nd Round (18 Holes)	3rd Round (18 Holes)	Semifinals (18 Holes)	Final (18 Holes)	
*146	Debbie Eckroth, Harrisburg, Pa.	Melanson, 20 holes				
160	Terri Melanson, W. Hollywood, Calif.		Hanson, 6 and 4			
155	Tracy Hanson, Rathdrum, Idaho	Hanson, 1 up				
156	Kelly Crawford, Rancho Cordova, Calif.			Hanson, 6 and 5		
152	Joyce Wilcox, East Hampton, Conn.	Ross, 2 up				
157	Kelli Ross, Burnsville, Minn.		Rizer, 3 and 1			
153	Joan Rizer, Bardstown, Ky.	Rizer, 19 holes				
157	Pattie Holthaus, The Woodlands, Texas				Blanchar, 3 and 1	
149	Stacey Arnold, Glen Ellyn, Ill.	Mieras, 1 up				
159	Jennifer Mieras, Kentwood, Mich.		Blanchar, 2 up			
155	Barbara Blanchar, Columbia, Mo.	Blanchar, 1 up				
156	Ann Guiberson, Lincoln, Neb.			Blanchar, 5 and 4		
151	Paige Gilbert, Phoenix, Ariz.	Gilbert, 6 and 5				
158	Krista Revterfeldt, Coon Rapids, Minn.		Gilbert, 5 and 4			Cathy Mockett, 5 and 4
154	Wendy Bigler, New Brighton, Minn.	Zebick, 3 and 2				
156	Kerry Zebick, Albuquerque, N.M.					
148	Kelly Meyers, Rapid City, S.D.	Holt, 3 and 2				
160	Jennifer Holt, Las Vegas, Nev.		Holt, 19 holes			
155	Alycya Rambin, Tulsa, Okla.	Rambin, 4 and 3				
156	Jenny Park, Lafayette, Calif.			Mockett, 1 up		
152	Jennie Holloway, Mount Dora, Fla.	Jacobs, 6 and 5				
158	Janina Jacobs, St. Clair Shores, Mich.		Mockett, 5 and 4			
154	Cathy Mockett, Tulsa, Okla.	Mockett, 6 and 5				
157	Nicole Horner, Mililani Town, Hawaii				Mockett, 1 up	
149	JoJo Robertson, Roswell, N.M.	Giovainni, 2 and 1				
160	Judy Giovainni, Akron, Ohio		Akers, 3 and 2			
155	Heather Hughes, Palo Alto, Calif.	Akers, 2 and 1				
156	Kelli Akers, French Lick, Ind.			Stinson, 1 up		
151	Karen Weiss, Roseville, Minn.	Weiss, 5 and 3				
158	Joy Cross-Garcia, Las Cruces, N.M.		Stinson, 4 and 3			
154	Lesly Ann Komoda, Pearl City, Hawaii	Stinson, 5 and 3				
156	Lori Stinson, Fort Wayne, Ind.					

*Medalist

Fourteenth Women's Amateur Public Links Inter-City Championship Trophy (Rercord 36 Team Entries); Won by Albuquerque, New Mexico, 305 for 36 holes (Kerry Zebick, 156; Jo Jo Robertson, 149; Joy Cross-Garcia, 158); second, Martinsville, Indiana, 307 (Kelli Akers, 156; Tracy Pace, 160; Lori Stinson, 156); third, Anoka, Minnesota, 308 (Kris Furlong, 168; Karen Weiss, 151; Kelli Ross, 157), and Philadelphia, Pennsylvania, 308 (Charlaine Tatz, 168; Debbie Eckroth, 146; Annette Kealoha, 162). The two low individual scores of the team members are used to calculate the team scores.

JUNIOR AMATEUR CHAMPIONSHIP

CHAMPIONSHIP TROPHY

Presented in August, 1948, by the

UNITED STATES GOLF ASSOCIATION

HISTORY

1981—Scott Erickson, 17, of Villa Park, California, won the Junior Amateur Championship in his home state by defeating Matt McCarley, of Camden, South Carolina, 4 and 3, at the Sunnyside Country Club in Fresno. Erickson became the 10th Californian to win the Junior Amateur in the last 20 years, but the first since 1975. Two other Californians, Mike Blewett of Burlingame, and Jeff Combe of Clovis, shared medalist honors with 36-hole even-par 144s after 36 holes of stroke play. Despite their fine stroke-play performances, Jerry Haas, Combe and Blewett all failed to survive the first round of match play. Erickson had little trouble qualifying with a fine 148 total, but McCarley could do no better than 155, one stroke under the cutoff score of 156. Erickson's early victims on his way to the Championship final were Peter Jordan, of Wooddale, Illinois, 1 up; Robert Park of Shawnee Mission, Kansas, 5 and 4; Kevin Earl of Pleasanton, California, 5 and 4; Louis Brown of Newnan, Georgia, 4 and 3; and, in the semifinals, Ken Miller, of Modesto, California, 1 up. McCarley had rather an easy time of it through his first five matches. He defeated Peter Savarino of Ann Arbor, Michigan, 3 and 2; Chris Webb of Shreveport, Louisiana, 4 and 3; James Kelson of Grand Prairie, Texas, 4 and 2; Mike Foley of Solana Beach, California, 5 and 3; and, in the semi-finals, Jim Benepe of Sheridan, Wyoming, 6 and 4. In the final match, Erickson took a three-hole lead early in the final match which McCarley was not able to overcome. Johnny Miller was the guest speaker at the contestants' dinner the Sunday night before the Championship. The USGA received 1,516 entries for the Championship, well short of the record 2,230 in 1963.

1982—Rich Marik, 17, of Anaheim, California, won the Junior Amateur Championship by defeating Tim Straub, 15, of Orchard Park, New York, 4 and 3, at the Crooked Stick Golf Club, in Carmel, Indiana. Marik became the second player from Yorba Linda Country Club to win the Championship in as many years; Scott Erickson won the 1981 Championship at Sunnyside Country Club, in Fresno, California, Tim Fleming, of Ocean Springs, Mississippi, was medalist with a 36-hole total of 144, even par. He advanced to the third round, where he lost to Bill McDonald, of Dalton, Georgia, 5 and 4. The cutoff score of 163 tied for the highest ever; it first was established in 1977 on the Scarlet Course at Ohio State University. The USGA received 1,701 entries for the Championship, well short of the record 2,230 in 1963.

1983—Tim Straub, 16, of Orchard Park, New York, won the Junior Amateur Championship, 1 up, over John Mahon, of Glendora, California, on the Old Course of Saucon Valley Country Club, in Bethlehem, Pennsylvania. Runner-up in the 1982 Championship, Straub thus became only the fourth player to reach the final twice. The others were Mason Rudolph (1949-50), Eddie Pearce (1968-69), and Mike Brannan (1971 and 1973). Straub qualified for match play with a 149 total, three strokes behind medalist Anthony Adams, of Toronto, Canada, who shot rounds of 74-72-146. Adams was eliminated in the second round by Robert McNamara, of Frankfort, Kentucky, 2 and 1. In the quarterfinals Straub was under par in defeating David Hillman, of Rye, New York, 6 and 5. In the semifinal round Straub faced Bob Estes, of Abilene, Texas, whom he had defeated in the 1982 quarterfinals. Straub played the last 11 holes even par to win 4 and 2. Although Straub bogeyed four of the first seven holes of the final match, he held a 1-up lead. He went 2-up with a par on the 10th. The most exciting moment of the match came at the 604-yard par-5 15th, where Mahon holed a winding 50-foot birdie putt and Straub matched it with a 4-footer of his own. Mahon won the 17th when Straub played a weak recovery from a greenside bunker. Only 1 up, Straub closed out the match with a par on the 18th. The Junior Amateur attracted 1,816 entries.

1984—Doug Martin, 17, of Findlay, Ohio, was never behind in six matches and became the fourth player to win both the qualifying medal and the championship. He defeated Brad Agee, of Conroe, Texas, 4 and 2, at the Wayzata Country Club, in Wayzata, Minnesota. The 1983 Ohio Junior champion, Martin took control early against Agee, winning the first five holes and seven of the first eight. He was four under par over those holes. Agee, who played the 18th hole just twice in winning his first five matches, won the ninth hole with a par, the 12th with a birdie and the 13th with a par. Martin was dormie after 14, and after Agee won the 15th, Martin ended the match with a birdie on the 16th.

1985—Charles Rymer, 17, of Fort Mill, South Carolina, defeated Gregory Lesher of Lebanon, Pennsylvania, on the 19th hole at Brookfield Country Club in Clarence, New York. Michael Watson of Rockville, Maryland and John Tighe, Jr., of Lake Worth, Florida, were co-medalists at two-over-par 146. Both lost their first-round matches.

Rymer held a three-hole lead after eight holes of the final match, but lost the ninth through the 12th to Lesher and trailed by one. Lesher, 16, won the 14th to go 2 up, but Rymer won the 15th to pull back to within one hole. Lesher won the 16th with a par to go dormie, but Rymer won the 17th with a birdie and the 18th with a par to force the match to an extra hole. On the 19th, after Rymer missed a seven-foot putt for a par, Lesher conceded Rymer's short bogey putt, then Lesher missed his own putt for bogey. The USGA accepted 2,068 entries for the Championship.

1986—Brian Montgomery, 17, of Bristow, Oklahoma, defeated Nicky Goetze of Hull, Georgia, 3 and 2, at Muirfield Village Golf Club in Dublin, Ohio. Michael Schafer of Fresno, California, shot 152 to earn the qualifying medal, the highest medalist score in the championship's history. Schafer was eliminated in the third round, 3 and 2, by Montgomery. In the final, Montgomery ran off to a three-hole lead by parring the first six holes while Goetze bogeyed the second, third and sixth, finding water on each. Montgomery then birdied the seventh to go 4 up. Goetze won the ninth with a par, then, with a par at the 12th and a birdie at the 13th, closed Montgomery's lead to one hole. Montgomery played his approach to the par-4 14th to within five feet of the hole and his birdie gave him a two-hole lead. Montgomery and Goetze halved the next three holes to give Montgomery the championship. The USGA accepted a record 2,320 entries for the championship. The old record of 2,230 was set in 1963.

1987—Brett Quigley, 17, of Barrington, Rhode Island, defeated Bill Heim of New Franken, Wisconsin, 1 up, to win the championship at Singletree Golf Club in Edwards, Colorado. Quigley became the 40th golfer to win the Junior Amateur. No one has repeated as champion. Harry Rudolph, Jr., of La Jolla, California, earned the qualifying medal with a 36-hole total of one-under-par 141, two strokes better than Quigley, Scott Peterson of Englewood, Colorado, and Jack O'Keefe of Little Rock, Arkansas. Quigley won the first three holes of the final, but Heim cut the margin to two holes when Quigley bogeyed the 11th. Quigley lost the 14th when he three-putted and led by only one hole. Quigley played cautiously down the stretch and parred the final two holes to preserve the win. The USGA accepted a record 2,349 entries for the championship.

1988—Jason Widener, 17, of Greensboro, North Carolina, defeated Brandon Knight of Denton, Texas, 1 up, in the final at Yale University Golf Club in New Haven, Connecticut. Brad Lehmann of Louisville, Kentucky, earned the qualifying medal with rounds of 66-74—140. His first-round 66 tied a championship record set by Kurt Beck in 1966. Lehmann was eliminated in the second round by William Power of Richmond, Virginia, 1 up. Widener, who qualified third at 143, was not extended past the 16th hole in any match on his way to the final. He defeated the second-low qualifier, Jon Veneziano of Kensington, Connecticut, 4 and 3, to earn his place in the final. Knight, on the other hand, survived two 19-hole matches—against Hank Smith of Waycross, Georgia, in the second round and David White of Little Rock, Arkansas, in the third round. Knight ousted Ronald Whittaker, also of Little Rock, 2 and 1, to reach the final. Birdies at the eighth and ninth holes gave Widener a 2-up advantage in the final. He stretched his lead to three holes with a par at the 12th, but Knight cut the lead to one hole with birdies at the 13th and 16th. Widener and Knight parred the final two holes, giving Widener the 1-up victory. The USGA accepted 2,087 entries for the championship.

1989—Seventeen-year-old David Duval defeated Austin Maki by one hole at Singing Hills Golf and Country Club, in El Cajon, California. From Ponte Verde Beach, Florida, Duval consistently outdrove his opponents by 20 to 40 yards. His drive, on the par 5 eighth hole was measured at 331 yards, leaving him only a 5 iron to the green. He birdied the hole and defeated Chris Riley, 3 and 2, in the semifinals. A fast-paced player, Riley played one match in 1 hour 50 minutes, and another in 2 hours 15 minutes. Duval fell behind Maki in the final by bogeying the first hole, pulled even on the 11th hole, and took the lead for the first time with a birdie on the 14th. Maki dropped two holes behind on the 15th when Duval hit a remarkable recovery shot over trees to within eight feet of the hole and two-putted for par. Duval slipped just once on the closing holes before parring the final hole to preserve his victory.

1990—Mathew Todd, 17, of Visalia, California, won the last three holes, two with birdies, and defeated Dennis Hillman, 17, of Rye, New York, the medalist, 1 up at Lake Merced Golf and Country Club, in Daly City, California. Todd lost four of the first eight holes. A par at the 12th hole pulled him to within 2 holes, setting the stage for a par-birdie-birdie finish. The two were all square after 17 holes, and Todd played a 90-yard wedge shot within three feet for a birdie. Hillman overclubbed into the back bunker and conceded the hole. Todd had failed to reach match play in his first Junior Amateur, in 1989, and had qualified in 1990 at 156, five strokes behind Hillman. He won his first match 1 up, and his second went 21 holes. He defeated 17-year-old Adam Thomas, from Baxley, Georgia, 3 and 2 in the semifinals. Hillman, meanwhile, was never extended to the 17th hole, and trailed only briefly in five matches leading up to the final. He beat 14-year-old Tiger Woods, of Cypress, California, in the semifinals.

JUNIOR AMATEUR CHAMPIONSHIP

DATE	WINNER, RUNNER-UP	SCORE	SITE	ENTRY
1981 (July-Aug.)	Scott Erickson d. Matt McCarley	4 & 3	Sunnyside C.C., Fresno, Calif. Co-Medalists—144: Jeff Combe Michael Blewett	1,516
1982 (July)	Richard Marik d. Tim Straub	4 & 3	Crooked Stick G.C., Carmel, Ind. Medalist—144: Tim Fleming	1,701
1983 (Aug.)	Tim Straub d. John Mahon	1 up	Saucon Valley C.C., Bethlehem, Pa. Medalist—146: Anthony Adams	1,816
1984 (July-Aug.)	Doug Martin d. Brad Agee	4 & 2	Wayzata C.C., Wayzata, Minn. Medalist—145: Doug Martin	1,877
1985 (July)	Charles Rymer d. Gregory Lesher	1 up, 19 hls.	Brookfield C.C., Clarence, N.Y. Co-Medalists—145: Michael Watson John Tighe, Jr.	2,068
1986 (July)	Brian Montgomery d. Nicky Goetze	2 & 1	Muirfield Village G.C., Dublin, Ohio Medalist—152: Michael Schafer	2,320
1987 (Aug.)	Brett Quigley d. Bill Heim	1 up	Singletree G.C., Vail, Colo. Medalist—141: Harry Rudolph, Jr.	§2,349
1988 (July)	Jason Widener d. Brandon Knight	1 up	Yale University G.C., New Haven, Conn. Medalist—140: Brad Lehmann	2,087
1989 (July)	David Duval d. Austin Maki	1 up	Singing Hills G. & C.C., El Cajon, Calif. Medalist—145: Chris Edgmon, Jason Worth Chris Riley and Brian Gay	2,025
1990 (July)	Mathew Todd d. Dennis Hillman	1 up	Lake Merced G. & C.C., Daly City, Calif. Medalist—151: Dennis Hillman	2,051

§Record Entry

1981
THIRTY-FOURTH JUNIOR AMATEUR CHAMPIONSHIP

Sunnyside Country Club, Fresno, California, July 28-August 1
Yardage—6,673. Par 72. 1,516 Entries, 150 Starters, 64 Qualifiers.

Qualifying Score	1st Round (18 Holes)	2nd Round (18 Holes)	3rd Round (18 Holes)	4th Round (18 Holes)	Semi-Finals (18 Holes)	Final (18 Holes)
*144	Jeff Combe, Clovis, Calif.	Maggert, 3 and 2				
152	Jeff Maggert, Woodlands, Texas					
150	James Benepe, III, Sheridan, Wyo.	Benepe, 4 and 3	Benepe, 3 and 2			
154	James Estes, Rockville, Md.					
148	Jerry Haas, Belleville, Ill.	Goyen, 1 up		Benepe, 1 up		
153	Keith Goyen, Flagstaff, Ariz.		Goyen, 4 and 2			
151	Bryan Hughett, Lincoln, Neb.	Hughett, 1 up, 19 holes			Benepe, 2 and 1	
155	Eric Samuelson, New Canaan, Conn.					
148	Robert Friend, Pittsburgh, Pa.	Fricke, 2 up				
153	James Fricke, Cincinnati, Ohio		Fricke, 2 and 1			
151	Josh Mondry, Franklin, Mich.	Le Master, 1 up				
155	Jeff Le Master, Galloway, Ohio			Stankowski, 5 and 4		
149	Patrick Brady, Reidsville, N.C.	Tingus, 2 and 1				
154	Mike Tingus, El Macero, Calif.		Stankowski, 2 and 1			
152	John Brellinthin, Edina, Minn.	Stankowski, 3 and 2				
156	Thomas Stankowski, Oxnard, Calif.					McCarley, 6 and 4
146	James Kelson, Grand Prairie, Texas	Kelson, 8 and 7				
153	Ken Collins, Selma, Calif.		Kelson, 1 up			
150	Charles Raulerson, Jr., Jacksonville, Fla.	Ushijima, 1 up		McCarley, 4 and 2		
155	Naka Ushijima, Burlingame, Calif.					
149	Francis Quinn, Jr., Northboro, Mass.	Webb, 1 up, 20 holes				
153	Chris Webb, Shreveport, La.		McCarley, 4 and 3			
152	Peter Savarino, Ann Arbor, Mich.	McCarley, 3 and 2			McCarley, 5 and 3	
155	Matt McCarley, Camden, S.C.					
148	Lenny Hartlage, Floyds Knobs, Ind.	Foley, 6 and 5				
153	Mike Foley, Solana Beach, Calif.					
151	Charles Willis, Moultrie, Ga.	Willis, 2 and 1	Foley, 4 and 2			
155	Michael Ketcham, Ottumwa, Iowa			Foley, 2 and 1		
150	Scott Dunlap, Sarasota, Fla.	Dunlap, 3 and 2				
154	Vincent Mazzi, Walnut Creek, Calif.		Dunlap, 2 and 1			
152	David Jackson, Monticello, Fla.	Jackson, 2 and 1				
156	John Haddock, Annandale, Va.					
*144	Michael Blewett, Burlingame, Calif.	Dargan, 3 and 1				
152	Fred Dargan, Bishopville, S.C.		Susser, 4 and 2			
150	Sam Susser, Corpus Christi, Texas	Susser, 4 and 2				
155	James Childs, Annapolis, Md.			Rebmann, 5 and 3		
149	Cass Bagley, Spokane, Wash.	Lopuszynski, 2 up				
153	Michael Lopuszynski, Rye, N.Y.		Rebmann, 1 up			
151	Eric Rebmann, Plantation, Fla.	Rebmann, 7 and 6				
155	Tony Rick, Milwaukee, Wis.					
148	Billy McDonald, Dalton, Ga.	McDonald, 1 up, 21 holes			Miller, 2 and 1	
153	Randy Wylie, Knoxville, Tenn.		Miller, 1 up			
151	Kenneth Miller, Modesto, Calif.	Miller, 5 and 3				
155	John Sinovic, Prairie Village, Kans.			Miller, 1 up		
149	Jerry Smith, Oskaloosa, Iowa	Smith, 2 and 1				
154	Donald Edwards, White Plains, N.Y.		Randolph, 8 and 7			
152	Sam Randolph, Santa Barbara, Calif.	Randolph, 4 and 3				
156	George Daves, Medford, Ore.					
147	Louis Brown, Newnan, Ga.	Brown, 3 and 2				
153	Chris Patrizi, Crosby, Texas		Brown, 7 and 6			Erickson, 1 up
150	Tim Fleming, Ocean Springs, Miss.	Fleming, 5 and 3				
155	Jeff Blake, Indianapolis, Ind.			Brown, 6 and 5		
149	Brian Mahon, San Diego, Calif.	Mahon, 4 and 3				
154	Ronald Speaker, Greeley, Colo.		Mahon, 4 and 2			
152	Matt Stokes, Groveport, Ohio	Waller, 2 and 1				
155	Rich Waller, Coral Gables, Fla.					
148	Scott Erickson, Villa Park, Calif.	Erickson, 1 up			Erickson, 4 and 3	
153	Peter Jordan, Wooddale, Ill.		Erickson, 5 and 4			
151	Eric Arnold, Modesto, Calif.	Park, 4 and 2				
155	Robert Park, Shawnee Mission, Kans.			Erickson, 5 and 4		
150	Michael Stone, New Bedford, Mass.	Earl, 3 and 1				
154	Kevin Earl, Pleasanton, Calif.		Earl, 6 and 4			
152	David Sodersten, Visalia, Calif.	Mann, 3 and 2				
156	William Mann, III, Bluffton, Ind.					

Scott Erickson, 4 and 3

*Co-Medalists

1982
THIRTY-FIFTH JUNIOR AMATEUR CHAMPIONSHIP

Crooked Stick Golf Club, Carmel, Indiana, July 27-31.
Yardage — 6,918/6,955. Par 72. 1,701 Entries, 150 Starters, 64 Qualifiers.

Qualifying Score	1st Round (18 Holes)	2nd Round (18 Holes)	3rd Round (18 Holes)	4th Round (18 Holes)	Semifinals (18 Holes)	Final (18 Holes)	
*144	Tim Fleming, Ocean Springs, Miss.	Fleming,					
157	Charley Berry, Jr., Las Vegas, Nev.	6 and 5	Fleming,				
154	Russell Barger, Oak Ridge, Tenn.	Barger,	2 and 1				
161	Bob Kollsmith, Cedar Rapids, Iowa	4 and 3		McDonald,			
153	Bill McDonald, Dalton, Ga.	McDonald,		5 and 4			
158	Mike Kingsrud, Fargo, N.D.	1 up, 25 holes	McDonald,				
155	Allyn Flores, Hanford, Calif.	Flores,	5 and 3				
162	Arnie Calvert, Perryville, Md.	3 and 1			Blewett,		
149	Lee Janzen, Lakeland, Fla.	Janzen,			8 and 7		
158	Patrick Chisholm, Birmingham, Mich.	2 up	Blewett,				
155	Michael Blewett, Burlingame, Calif.	Blewett,	1 up, 19 holes				
161	Peter Hoff, Rolling Hills Estates, Calif.	5 and 4		Blewett,			
154	John O'Neill, Arcadia, Calif.	O'Neill,		6 and 4			
160	Jonathan Roe, St. Paul, Minn.	1 up	Arasin,				
157	Michael Arasin, Old Bethpage, N.Y.	Arasin,	3 and 2				
162	Steve Larick, Seaford, Del.	2 and 1				Marik,	
146	Len Hartlage, Floyds Knobs, Ind.	Hartlage,				3 and 2	
158	Edward Pfister, III, Marilla, N.Y.	1 up, 20 holes	Hartlage,				
154	Mike Lopuszynski, Rye, N.Y.	Lopuszynski,	3 and 1				
161	Larry Bellorado, Jr., Melrose, Mass.	8 and 6		Hartlage,			
153	Matt Stokes, Groveport, Ohio	Stokes,		1 up, 19 holes			
159	Jeff Hannigan, E. Amherst, N.Y.	2 and 1	Stokes,				
156	Brian Lehnhard, Manassas, Va.	Lehnhard,	5 and 3				
162	Michael Tebbetts, San Diego, Calif.	5 and 3			Marik,		
152	Richard Marik, Anaheim, Calif.	Marik,			2 and 1		
158	Gary Nicklaus, N. Palm Beach, Fla.	2 and 1	Marik,				
155	George Daves, Medford, Ore.	Daves,	1 up				Richard Marik, 4 and 3
161	Chris Gustin, Birmingham, Ala.	1 up, 19 holes		Marik,			
154	Kevin Kozlowski, Valparaiso, Ind.	Kozlowski,		3 and 2			
161	Jeffrey Hunt, Olympia, Wash.	5 and 4	Hamilton,				
157	Todd Hamilton, Oquawka, Ill.	Hamilton,	3 and 2				
163	Matt Swanson, Farmers Branch, Texas	3 and 2					
146	James Estes, Rockville, Md.	Estes,					
158	Jim Johnson, El Macero, Calif.	2 up	Estes,				
154	Doug Lucci, Verona, N.J.	Roy,	2 up				
161	Scott Roy, Kent, Wash.	3 and 2		Estes,			
153	Kevin Leach, Rolling Hills Estates, Calif.	Edwards,		2 and 1			
159	Donald Edwards, White Plains, N.Y.	2 up	Edwards,				
156	John Sundberg, Boulder, Colo.	Sayad,	2 and 1				
162	Matt Sayad, Midland, Mich.	1 up, 19 holes			Estes,		
151	Michael Foley, Solana Beach, Calif.	Foley,			4 and 3		
158	Bill Mayfair, Phoenix, Ariz.	3 and 2	Foley,				
155	John Mollica, Columbus, Ohio	Mollica,	2 and 1				
161	Scott Beaugureau, Elk Grove Village, Ill.	2 and 1		Foley,			
154	Jim Vernon, Frankfort, Ky.	Stankowski,		1 up, 20 holes			
160	Tom Stankowski, Oxnard, Calif.	1 up	Stankowski,				
157	Chuck Scally, Jr., Coraopolis, Pa.	Scally,	6 and 4				
163	Darin Patrizi, Crosby, Texas	4 and 3				Straub,	
149	Jerry Sneve, Oroville, Wash.	Sneve,				2 and 1	
158	Brad Wilhite, Lawrence, Kans.	6 and 5	Sneve,				
155	Charley Winn, Wilmot, Wis.	Winn,	1 up				
161	David Sheffield, Sherman, Texas	4 and 3		Straub,			
153	Tom Hearn, Ft. Pierce, Fla.	Williams,		6 and 4			
160	Don Williams, Gainesville, Ga.	1 up	Straub,				
156	Tim Straub, Orchard Park, N.Y.	Straub,	1 up				
162	George Welsh, Charlotte, N.C.	1 up, 19 holes			Straub,		
153	Eric Rebmann, Plantation, Fla.	Estes,			1 up		
158	Bob Estes, Abilene, Texas	1 up	Estes,				
155	Paul Keating, Jr., Westwood, Mass.	Keating,	8 and 7				
162	John Andrews, Kokomo, Ind.	1 up		Estes,			
154	Robert McNamara, Frankfort, Ky.	McNamara,		3 and 2			
161	Dennis Andrus, Jr., Bloomfield Hills, Mich.	2 and 1	Cranston,				
157	Robert Lasken, Whittier, Calif.	Cranston,	3 and 1				
163	Riley Cranston, Los Altos, Calif.	2 and 1					

*Medalist

1983
THIRTY-SIXTH JUNIOR AMATEUR CHAMPIONSHIP

Saucon Valley Country Club, Bethlehem, Pennsylvania, August 2-6.
Yardage—6,773. Par 71. 1,816 Entries, 150 Starters, 64 Qualifiers.

Qualifying Score	1st Round (18 Holes)	2nd Round (18 Holes)	3rd Round (18 Holes)	4th Round (18 Holes)	Semifinals (18 Holes)	Final (18 Holes)	
*146	Anthony Adams, Don Mills, Ont. Canada	Adams,					
155	Chris Holzgang, Beaverton, Ore.	6 and 4	McNamara,				
152	Flint Nelson, Houston, Texas	McNamara,	2 and 1				
158	Robert McNamara, Frankfort, Ky.	6 and 4		Mahon,			
150	John Mahon, Glendora, Calif.	Mahon,		3 and 2			
157	Warren Vickers, Lewiston, Idaho	2 and 1	Mahon,				
154	Mark Phillips, Fresno, Calif.	Phillips,	4 and 3				
159	Mitchell Perry, Spring Lake, N.C.	2 up			Mahon,		
150	Brian Watts, Carrollton, Texas	Watts,			4 and 3		
156	Jeff Hull, Newark, Ohio	1 up, 20 holes	Mayfair,				
153	Bill Mayfair, Phoenix, Ariz.	Mayfair,	3 and 1				
159	Douglas Wherry, Englewood, Colo.	5 and 3		Silveira,			
152	John Dickey, Toledo, Ohio	Dickey,		2 and 1			
158	Mark Cero, Lebanon, Ind.	2 and 1	Silveira,				
154	Larry Silveira, Oakley, Calif.	Silveira,	3 and 1				
159	Kyle Robar, Sioux Falls, S.D.	3 and 1				Mahon,	
149	Jack Rudisill, III, Gastonia, N.C.	Strickland,				3 and 2	
156	Jim Strickland, Bothell, Wash.	2 and 1	Miskell,				
153	Terrence Miskell, Salinas, Calif.	Miskell,	1 up, 19 holes				
159	Johnny Ciotola, Dublin, Ohio	2 and 1		Mattiace,			
152	Don Edwards, White Plains, N.Y.	Edwards,		6 and 4			
157	Todd Satterfield, Bluefield, W. Va.	3 and 2					
154	Len Mattiace, Ponte Vedra Beach, Fla.	Mattiace,					
159	Dave Witt, Noblesville, Ind.	6 and 5	Mattiace,		McDonald,		
150	Robert Lasken, Whittier, Calif.	Curren,	6 and 5		1 up, 19 holes		
157	James Curran, W. Palm Beach, Fla.	2 and 1					
154	John Andrews, Kokomo, Ind.	Andrews,					
159	Mark Calhoun, Napa, Calif.	1 up	Andrews,				
152	Warren Reitz, Myrtle Beach, S.C.	Reitz,	5 and 3				
158	Michael Springer, Dinuba, Calif.	1 up		McDonald,			Tim Straub, 1 up
154	Bill McDonald, Dalton, Ga.	McDonald,		7 and 5			
160	Chris Clements, Hialeah, Fla.	1 up	McDonald,				
147	Bob Estes, Abilene, Texas	Estes,	1 up				
155	Don Williams, Gainesville, Ga.	3 and 2	Estes,				
153	Chris Dibble, Greeneville, Tenn.	Dibble	1 up				
159	Todd Tumminia, St. Louis, Mo.	6 and 4		Estes,			
151	Rob Huff, Eagle, Idaho	Toulson,		4 and 3			
157	Christopher Toulson, Knoxville, Tenn.	1 up	Berklich,				
154	Joseph Berklich, Grand Blanc, Mich.	Berklich,	6 and 5				
159	Michael Clements, Cincinnati, Ohio	7 and 6			Estes,		
150	Chris Gustin, Birmingham, Ala.	Kaufman,			4 and 3		
157	Chris Kaufman, Arlington, Texas	4 and 3	Sinovic,				
154	Will Tipton, Hallister, Calif.	Sinovic,	3 and 2				
159	John Sinovic, Shawnee Mission, Kans.	2 up		Turlington,			
152	Judson Kotas, Grosse Pointe City, Mich.	Kotas,		1 up			
158	John Barnes, Wooster, Ohio	1 up, 19 holes	Turlington,				
154	Andrew Debusk, Houston, Texas	Turlington,	4 and 3				
160	Mark Turlington, Temple Ter., Fla.	2 and 1				Straub,	
149	Tim Straub, Orchard Park, N.Y.	Straub,				4 and 2	
156	Anthony Perino, Thousand Oaks, Calif.	2 and 1	Straub,				
153	Jim Vernon, Frankfort, Ky.	Vernon,	2 and 1				
159	Timothy Cone, Ringoes, N.J.	5 and 4		Straub,			
152	Todd Tibke, Snohomish, Wash.	Kranick,		5 and 4			
158	Jody Kranick, Pittsburgh, Pa.	6 and 5	Kranick,				
154	Jeff Hellman, Hacienda Heights, Calif.	Hellman,	1 up, 19 holes				
159	Mike Lehman, Alexandria, Minn.	5 and 4			Straub,		
150	David Hillman, Rye, N.Y.	Hillman,			6 and 5		
157	Mickie Gallagher, Palm Beach Gardens, Fla.	5 and 4	Hillman,				
154	John Reynolds, Palm Beach Gardens, Fla.	Reynolds,	3 and 1				
159	Fred Benton, Jacksonville Beach, Fla.	5 and 3		Hillman,			
152	Barry Fabyan, Worthington, Ohio	Tryba,		1 up			
158	Ted Tryba, Wilkes-Barre, Pa.	5 and 4	Gunn,				
155	Robert Mancill, Kennett Square, Pa.	Gunn,	3 and 2				
160	Craig Gunn, Danville, Va.	3 and 2					

*Medalist

1984
THIRTY-SEVENTH JUNIOR AMATEUR CHAMPIONSHIP

Wayzata Country Club, Wayzata, Minnesota, July 31-August 4
Yardage—6,910. Par 72. 1,877 Entries, 150 Starters, 64 Qualifiers

Qualifying Score	1st Round (18 Holes)	2nd Round (18 Holes)	3rd Round (18 Holes)	4th Round (18 Holes)	Semifinals (18 Holes)	Final (18 Holes)
*145	Doug Martin, Van Buren, Ohio	Martin,				
155	John Crump, Jasper, Ala.	4 and 3	Martin,			
152	Bradley Geer, Edina, Minn.	Geer,	6 and 5			
156	Chris Haugen, Ames, Iowa	1 up, 23 holes		Martin,		
149	Bob May, La Habra, Calif.	May,		1 up		
155	Kurt Sowle, Appleton, Wis.	5 and 4	May,			
153	Grant Switzer, Arlington, Texas	Sciorra,	1 up, 21 holes			
157	Cary Sciorra, Trumbull, Conn.	5 and 4			Martin,	
148	Jeff Hellman, Rosemead, Calif.	Hellman,			1 up, 19 holes	
155	Chris Toulson, Knoxville, Tenn.	2 and 1	Rhees,			
153	Brad Flinders, Worthington, Ohio	Rhees,	1 up, 21 holes			
157	Ryan Rhees, Orem, Utah	2 and 1		Knoesel,		
151	Jim Webb, Des Moines, Iowa	Smyre,		1 up, 20 holes		
156	Frederic Smyre, Gastonia, N.C.	1 up	Knoesel,			
154	Joseph Berklich, Grand Blanc, Mich.	Knoesel,	1 up, 21 holes			
158	James Knoesel, St. Louis, Mo.	3 and 1				Martin,
146	Ken Tanigawa, Los Angeles, Calif,	Boepple,				3 and 1
155	Matt Boepple, Columbia, S.C.	4 and 2	Cole,			
152	James Corey, Fairfield, Calif.	Cole,	2 and 1			
156	Clete Cole, Kennesaw, Ga.	4 and 3		Ogden,		
150	Uly Grisette, Advance, N.C.	Grisette,		1 up		
155	Alan Rosen, Springfield, Mich.	2 up	Ogden,			
154	John Ogden, Kansas City, Kans.	Ogden,	1 up, 20 holes			
157	Bruce Bulina, Mississauga, Ont., Canada	2 and 1			Ogden,	
149	Mark Cero, Lebanon, Ind.	Holzgang,			6 and 5	
155	Chris Holzgang, Beaverton, Ore.	3 and 2	Smith,			
153	Malcom Smith, Huntington, N.Y.	Smith,	4 and 3			
157	Doug Giorgio, III, Savannah, Ga.	1 up		Smith,		
151	Matt Peterson, Mortanton, N.C.	Peterson,		4 and 2		
156	Eric Schreiber, Pittsburgh, Pa.	6 and 4	Peterson,			
154	William Davis, III, Decatur, Ga.	Davis,	1 up, 19 holes			
158	Barry Fabyan, Worthington, Ohio	3 and 1				
146	Brad Agee, Conroe, Texas	Agee,				
155	Tim Hobby, Alvin, Texas	5 and 3	Agee,			
152	Michael Heisterkamp, Troy, Mich.	Gleaton,	2 up			
156	Todd Gleaton, Hope Mills, N.C.	4 and 3		Agee		
150	Jeff Guest, Lagrange, Ky.	Clark,		5 and 3		
155	Sean Clark, Danville, Calif.	1 up, 20 holes	Clark,			
154	Michael Watson, Rockville, Md.	Ziats	1 up			
157	Ray Ziats, Jr., Clifton Springs, N.Y.	5 and 4			Agee,	
148	Tim Straub, Orchard Park, N.Y.	Adams,			2 and 1	
155	Anthony Adams, Don Mills, Ont., Canada	4 and 3	Adams,			
153	David Cunningham, Michigan City, Ind.	Glaesel,	5 and 4			
157	Mike Glaesel, Arvada, Colo.	1 up		Christensen,		
151	Shannon Radke, Minot, N.D.	Radke,		1 up		
156	Rodney Austin, Lakewood, Calif.	1 up	Christensen,			
154	Don Christensen, Edmonds, Wash.	Christensen,	2 and 1			
158	Chris Keim, Erie, Pa.	1 up				Agee,
147	Bill Mayfair, Phoenix, Ariz	Mayfair,				3 and 1
155	O.D. Vincent, Zephyr Cove, Nev.	5 and 4	Mayfair,			
152	Jim Strickland, Mill Creek, Wash.	Strickland,	6 and 5			
157	George Vincent, Teague, Texas	3 and 1		Simms,		
151	Neil Simms, Honolulu, Hawaii	Simms,		1 up, 19 holes		
156	Stephen White, La Canada, Calif.	3 and 1	Simms,			
154	Chris Smith, Rochester, Ind.	Smith,	4 and 2			
158	Nick Deets, Lafayette, Ind.	1 up			Simms,	
149	Terrence Miskell, Salinas, Calif.	Wood,			5 and 4	
155	William Wood, Des Moines, Iowa	6 and 5	Wood,			
153	Monte Lee Scheinblum, Villa Park, Calif.	Marston,	5 and 3			
157	Todd Marston, Jackson, Mich.	1, up 21 holes		Wood,		
151	Brian Montgomery, Bristow, Okla.	Montgomery,		5 and 4		
156	Stephen Sear, Monte Sereno, Calif.	1 up	Wilcox,			
155	Bob Bremer, Wilmington, Del.	Wilcox,	4 and 2			
158	Tim Wilcox, Rancho Mirage, Calif.	1 up				

Doug Martin, 4 and 2

*Medalist

1985
THIRTY-EIGHTH JUNIOR AMATEUR CHAMPIONSHIP

Brookfield Country Club, Clarence, New York, July 23-27
Yardage—6,813. Par 72. 2,068 Entries, 153 Starters, 64 Qualifiers

Qualifying Score	1st Round (18 Holes)	2nd Round (18 Holes)	3rd Round (18 Holes)	4th Round (18 Holes)	Semifinals (18 Holes)	Final (18 Holes)	
*146	Michael Watson, Rockville, Md.	Ahmann,					
161	Mark Ahmann, Sioux City, Iowa	1 up	Lee,				
157	Alan Wood, Irving, Texas	Lee,	5 and 3				
157	Randy Lee, Houston, Texas	4 and 2		Karcher,			
153	Steven Chambless, St. Simons Island, Ga.	Eltz,		6 and 4			
159	Matthew Eltz, Dallas, Texas	4 and 3	Karcher,				
154	John Karcher, Darien, Conn.	Karcher,	4 and 3				
159	Kurt Sandness, Eden Prairie, Minn.	1 up			Lesher,		
152	Ken Tanigawa, Los Angeles, Calif.	Tanigawa,			3 and 2		
160	Brian Bridges, Whitehall, Ohio	7 and 5	Tamiya,				
156	Gregory Cox, Missouri City, Texas	Tamiya,	1 up, 20 holes				
158	Troy Tamiya, Hilo, Hawaii	1 up, 19 holes		Lesher,			
152	Jason Bittick, Yorba Linda, Calif.	Lesher,		1 up			
160	Gregory Lesher, Lebanon, Pa.	2 and 1	Lesher,				
156	Phil Mickelson, San Diego, Calif.	Tucker,	1 up, 20 holes				
158	Philip Tucker, Orem, Utah	2 and 1				Lesher,	
148	Dudley Hart, Miami Beach, Fla.	Passolt,				4 and 3	
161	Rick Passolt, Edina, Minn.	1 up	Dibble,				
157	Tim Dunlavey, Erie, Pa.	Dibble,	1 up, 20 holes				
158	Christopher Dibble, Greeneville, Tenn.	3 and 2		Wentworth,			
152	Kevin Wentworth, Manteca, Calif.	Wentworth,		4 and 3			
159	William Morlan, Largo, Fla.	2 up	Wentworth,				
155	Jim Geiser, Snohomish, Wash.	Geiser,	3 and 1				
158	Mike Foster, Vacaville, Calif.	1 up			Wentworth,		
150	John Bizik, Grove, Okla.	Bizik,			1 up, 20 holes		
161	Chris Smith, Rochester, Ind.	2 and 1	Bizik,				
157	Ben Furth, San Francisco, Calif.	Furth,	3 and 2				
158	Pat Carter, Lesage, W.Va.	2 and 1		B. Wood,			
152	Bill Wood, Des Moines, Iowa	B. Wood,		3 and 2			
159	William Hyndman, V, Huntingdon Valley, Pa.	1 up	B. Wood,				
155	Robert Moss, Parma, Ohio	Brownfield,	5 and 4				
158	Patrick Brownfield, Tacoma, Wash.	4 and 2					Charles Rymer, 1 up, 19 holes
*146	John Tighe, Lake Worth, Fla.	Vietmeier,					
161	Gordon Vietmeier, Pittsburgh, Pa.	1 up	White,				
157	Stephen White, La Canada, Calif.	White,	6 and 5				
158	Kevin Youngblood, Broken Arrow, Okla.	1 up		White,			
153	Steven Spencer, Amagansett, N.Y.	Serrao,		3 and 2			
159	Stephen Serrao, Virginia Beach, Va.	1 up, 19 holes	Serrao,				
154	William Tipton, Hollister, Calif.	Tipton,	3 and 1				
159	John Greenagel, Fergus Falls, Minn.	5 and 4			Cero,		
152	Mark Cero, Lebanon, Ind.	Cero,			2 and 1		
160	John Connelly, Perrysburg, Ohio	4 and 3	Cero,				
156	Bruce Kenerson, Weston, Mass.	Kenerson,	1 up, 19 holes				
158	Michael Finney, New Orleans, La.	3 and 2		Cero,			
152	O.D. Vincent, Zephyr Cove, Nev.	Vincent,		1 up, 19 holes			
160	Greg Wilhelm, Findlay, Ohio	6 and 4	Vincent,				
155	Craig Kanada, Lake Oswego, Ore.	Kanada,	1 up, 19 holes				
158	Dee Green, Roswell, N.M.	1 up				Rymer,	
148	Jon Worrell, Douglas, Ga.	Worrell,				2 and 1	
161	Mike Seek, Everett, Wash.	1 up	Worrell,				
157	Clayton Devers, Kansas City, Kan.	Stone,	3 and 2				
158	Steve Stone, Toledo, Ohio	3 and 2		Rymer,			
153	Sean Pacetti, Palatka, Fla.	Pacetti,		5 and 4			
159	Hub Goyen, III, Scottsdale, Ariz.	4 and 3	Rymer,				
155	Charles Rymer, Fort Mill, S.C.	Rymer,	3 and 2				
159	Mickey Moore, Lynchburg, Va.	4 and 2			Rymer,		
152	Ronald Ewing, Merced, Calif.	Ewing,			6 and 4		
160	Christopher Gorgone, Topsham, Maine	6 and 4	Ewing,				
156	Tom Wilson, Grosse Pointe Shores, Mich.	Schafer,	2 up				
158	Mike Schafer, Fresno, Calif.	1 up		Dean,			
152	Robert Gamez, Las Vegas, Nev.	Smyre,		1 up			
160	Deric Smyre, Gastonia, N.C.	3 and 2	Dean,				
155	Brett Dean, Evergreen, Colo.	Dean,	1 up				
158	Ted Kreider, Walnut, Calif.	2 and 1					

*Co-medalists

1986
THIRTY-NINTH JUNIOR AMATEUR CHAMPIONSHIP

Muirfield Village Golf Club, Dublin, Ohio, July 22-26
Yardage—7,042. Par 72. +2,320 Entries, 153 Starters, 64 Qualifiers

Qualifying Score	1st Round (18 Holes)	2nd Round (18 Holes)	3rd Round (18 Holes)	4th Round (18 Holes)	Semifinals (18 Holes)	Final (18 Holes)
*152	Michael Schafer, Fresno, Calif.	Schafer, 1 up				
165	Timothy Herron, Wayzata, Minn.		Schafer, 2 and 1			
161	Tim Logsdon, Louisville, Ky.	Smith, 5 and 4				
161	Chris Smith, Rochester, Ind.			Montgomery, 4 and 3		
156	Brian Montgomery, Bristow, Okla.	Montgomery, 1 up, 19 holes				
163	John Aber, Greensburg, Pa.		Montgomery, 4 and 3			
156	Gordon Leith, Stanford, Calif.	Leith, 8 and 6				
163	Keith Brennan, Edina, Minn.				Montgomery, 4 and 3	
154	Hub Goyen, III, Scottsdale, Ariz.	Goyen, 2 and 1				
164	Gregory Lesher, Lebanon, Pa.		Jukes, 1 up			
159	Jean-Paul Hebert, Houston, Texas	Jukes, 3 and 1				
162	David Jukes, Toronto, Ontario, Canada			Jukes, 1 up		
155	Chris Cupit, Dunwoody, Ga.	Cupit, 5 and 4				
164	Peter Lugowski, Des Moines, Iowa		Stone, 1 up, 20 holes			
159	Stephen Stone, Toledo, Ohio	Stone, 5 and 4				
162	Brent Milam, Corpus Christi, Texas					Montgomery, 2 up
153	Kent Wiese, Huntington Beach, Calif.	Spiher, 2 and 1				
165	Michael Spiher, Granger, Ind.		Pemberton, 1 up			
160	Bryan Pemberton, Pleasanton, Calif.	Pemberton, 3 and 2				
161	Robert Bodde, Vermilion, Ohio			Pemberton, 3 and 2		
155	Joel Hartwell, N. Myrtle Beach, S.C.	Kanada, 1 up, 19 holes				
163	Craig Kanada, Lake Oswego, Ore.		Wehnes, 3 and 2			
158	Warren Vickers, Lewiston, Idaho	Wehnes, 5 and 4				
163	Robert Wehnes, Santa Monica, Calif.				Pemberton, 1 up, 19 holes	
154	David Patterson, Lutherville, Md.	Johnston, 2 and 1				
165	James Johnston, Jr., Concord, Tenn.		Johnston, 4 and 2			
160	Kyle Kauffman, Woodlands, Texas	Woda, 1 up				
161	Steven Woda, Crofton, Md.			Lee, 1 up		
155	David Renzulli, Southport, Conn.	Lee, 2 up				
163	Jeff Lee, Dallas, Texas		Lee, 3 and 2			
158	Nick Cusick, Wichita, Kan.	Cusick, 3 and 1				
163	Jerome Andrews, River Forest, Ill.					
153	Jim Sanders, Dallas, Texas	Strickland, 5 and 4				
165	Mark Strickland, El Cajon, Calif.		Witham, 1 up			
160	Troy Witham, Rockland, Maine	Witham, 2 and 1				
161	Todd Fischer, Pleasanton, Calif.			Witham, 5 and 4		
155	Brad Sutterfield, Salt Lake City, Utah	Sutterfield, 4 and 3				
163	Scott Ford, Lake Worth, Fla.		Sutterfield, 3 and 2			
156	Francis Holroyd, Augusta, Ga.	Holroyd, 2 and 1				
163	Chris Chapman, Conroe, Texas				Goetze, 5 and 3	
154	Bob May, La Habra, Calif.	May, 3 and 2				
164	Fred Widicus, Annandale, Va.		May, 6 and 5			
159	Todd Barranger, Phoenix, Ariz.	Barranger, 1 up				
162	Chris Greenwood, Valdese, N.C.			Goetze, 2 and 1		
155	Nicky Goetze, Hull, Ga.	Goetze, 7 and 6				
164	Brian Colucci, Half Moon Bay, Calif.		Goetze, 1 up			
159	David Cunningham, Michigan City, Ind.	Wentworth, 2 and 1				
162	Kevin Wentworth, Manteca, Calif.					Goetze, 2 and 1
153	Carito Villaroman, Iligan, Philippines	Villaroman, 3 and 2				
165	Lawrence Ordonio, Aiea, Hawaii		Villaroman, 5 and 3			
160	John Bizik, Grove, Okla.	Kaminski, 5 and 4				
161	Kevin Kaminski, Wilkes-Barre, Pa.			Villaroman, 5 and 4		
155	Greg McDonald, Dalton, Ga.	McDonald, 4 and 3				
163	Andy Gingerich, York, Pa.		Sargent, 5 and 4			
158	David Woliner, Brick, N.J.	Sargent, 4 and 2				
163	Bowen Sargent, Brentwood, Tenn.				Villaroman, 1 up, 19 holes	
154	Brett Dean, Evergreen, Colo.	Couey, 1 up				
165	Voyed Couey, McComb, Miss.		Dargan, 2 and 1			
159	John Sosa, El Paso, Texas	Dargan, 3 and 2				
161	Robert Dargan, Jr., Columbia, S.C.			Mickelson, 5 and 3		
155	Phil Mickelson, San Diego, Calif.	Mickelson, 4 and 2				
163	Brennan Little, St. Thomas, Ontario, Canada		Mickelson, 2 and 1			
158	Grant Halverson, Rockford, Ill.	Bishop, 1 up, 19 holes				
162	David Bishop, Plantation, Fla.					

Brian Montgomery, 2 and 1

+Record Entry

*Medalist

1987
FORTIETH JUNIOR AMATEUR CHAMPIONSHIP

Singletree Golf Club, Edwards, Colorado, August 4-8
Yardage—7,038. Par 71.+2,349 Entries, 153 Starters, 64 Qualifiers

Qualifying Score	1st Round (18 Holes)	2nd Round (18 Holes)	3rd Round (18 Holes)	4th Round (18 Holes)	Semifinals (18 Holes)	Final (18 Holes)
*141	Harry Rudolph, Jr., La Jolla, Calif.	Rudolph,				
156	Jeff Manson, Long Beach, Calif.	1 up	Rudolph,			
151	Greg Cox, Missouri City, Texas	Cox,	2 and 1			
151	Thomas Hurley, Darien, Conn.	1 up		Rudolph,		
148	Daniel Seawell, Anderson, S.C.	Seawell,		2 up		
154	Michael Melendez, Merced, Calif.	2 up	Seawell,			
148	Paul Stankowski, Oxnard, Calif.	Stankowski,	1 up			
154	Brian Gay, Daleville, Ala.	1 up			Albertsson,	
146	William Moore, Sacramento, Calif.	South,			2 and 1	
155	Kevin South, Richmond, Va.	DQ	Whittaker,			
151	Ronald Whittaker, Little Rock, Ark.	Whittaker,	5 and 4			
153	Rob Conrad, Crystal Lake, Ill.	3 and 2		Albertsson,		
145	Hans Albertsson, Manchester, Vt.	Albertsson,		7 and 6		
155	Lance Reid, Denver, N.C.	2 up	Albertsson,			
150	Jim Furyk, Manheim, Pa.	Wittenburg,	1 up			
153	Darren Wittenburg, Arizona City, Ariz.	6 and 5				Heim,
143	Scott Petersen, Englewood, Colo.	Petersen,				5 and 4
156	Jeff Wolff, Ft. Worth, Texas	2 and 1	Petersen,			
151	Marshall Smith, Miami, Okla.	Smith,	2 and 1			
152	Chris Chuck, Jacksonville, Fla.	3 and 1		Petersen,		
147	Keven Pomarleau, E. Wenatchee, Wash.	Pomarleau,		3 and 2		
154	John Miller, Jr., Napa, Calif.	1 up, 19 holes	Pomarleau,			
150	Darin Osborn, Taft, Calif.	Spiher,	5 and 4			
154	Michael Spiher, Granger, Ind.	2 and 1			Heim,	
144	Matthew Dodge, Pittsburgh, Pa.	Dodge,			5 and 3	
155	Pete Lugowski, Des Moines, Iowa	4 and 3	Snortland,			
151	Jerry Hounchell, Troy, Ohio	Snortland,	1 up, 20 holes			
152	Brett Snortland, Conroe, Texas	5 and 3		Heim,		
147	Bill Heim, New Franken, Wis.	Heim,		5 and 4		
154	Charles Kaminsky, Cincinnati, Ohio	3 and 2	Heim,			
150	Hans Haas, Fort Worth, Texas	Haas,	5 and 3			
154	Todd Kolb, Sioux Falls, S.D.	3 and 1				
143	Brett Quigley, Barrington, R.I.	Quigley,				
156	Grant Russell, Amarillo, Texas	3 and 1	Quigley,			
151	Cameron Martin, Eugene, Ore.	Dargan,	2 and 1			
152	Robert Dargan, Jr., Columbia, S.C.	5 and 4		Quigley,		
148	Charlie Wi, Thousand Oaks, Calif.	Wi,		1 up		
154	Jason Hill, Rockwall, Texas	8 and 7	Hendee,			
149	Thomas Sipula, Ottawa, Ill.	Hendee,	1 up, 19 holes			
154	Neal Hendee, Duluth, Ga.	1 up			Quigley,	
145	Phil Mickelson, San Diego, Calif.	Mickelson,			1 up	
155	Jimmuy Chang, Westlake Village, Calif.	2 up	Krak,			
151	Taggart Wylie, Knoxville, Tenn.	Krak,	1 up			
153	Greg Krak, Palm Beach Gardens, Fla.	3 and 1		Krak,		
146	Scott De Serrano, Farmers Branch, Texas	De Serrano,		2 and 1		
155	David Hathaway, Lenoxdale, Mass.	1 up	M. Weir,			
150	Michael Weir, Brights Grove, Ontario, Canada	M. Weir,	5 and 3			
153	William Maynard, Clarksville, Tenn.	4 and 2				
143	Jack O'Keefe, Little Rock, Ark.	Emery,				Quigley,
156	Michael Emery, Massillion, Ohio	4 and 3	Emery,			3 and 2
151	Jim Beavers, Senatobia, Miss.	Knight,	2 up			
152	Brandon Knight, Denton, Texas	2 up		Whittemore,		
147	William Banks, Rome, Ga.	Banks,		3 and 2		
154	Jonathan Wiser, Pacific Palisades, Calif.	3 and 2	Whittemore,			
149	Jon Whittemore, Sarasota, Fla..	Whittemore,	2 up			
154	Collin Stoops, Freeport, Ill.	6 and 5			Whittemore,	
145	Jaimie Burns, Gainesville, Fla.	Burns,			3 and 2	
155	Michael Montgomery, Seattle, Wash.	4 and 3	Burns,			
151	Jeffrey Junk, Washington Court House, Ohio	Goetze,	3 and 2			
152	Nicky Goetze, Hull, Ga.	5 and 3		Sosa,		
146	John Sosa, El Paso, Texas	Sosa,		2 and 1		
154	Ben Weir, Moline, Ill.	6 and 5	Sosa,			
150	Douglas Gregor, Huntingdon Valley, Pa.	Goalby,	5 and 4			
153	Kevin Goalby, Belleville, Ill.	5 and 4				

Brett Quigley, 1 up

+ Record Entry

* Medalist

1988
FORTY-FIRST JUNIOR AMATEUR CHAMPIONSHIP

Yale University Golf Course, New Haven, Connecticut, July 26-30
Yardage—6,620. Par 70. 2,087 Entries, 156 Starters, 64 Qualifiers

Qualifying Score	1st Round (18 Holes)	2nd Round (18 Holes)	3rd Round (18 Holes)	4th Round (18 Holes)	Semifinals (18 Holes)	Final (18 Holes)
*140	Brad Lehmann, Louisville, Ky.	Lehman,				
155	Brian Kortan, Yankton, S.D.	3 and 2	Power, 1 up			
151	William Power, Richmond, Va.	Power,				
151	Austin Maki, Costa Mesa, Calif.	1 up, 19 holes		Whittaker, 1 up		
147	Andrew Price, Morristown, Tenn.	Price,				
153	Rick Tramontin, Portola Valley, Calif.	3 and 2	Whittaker, 4 and 3			
148	Ronald Whittaker, Little Rock, Ark.	Whittaker,				
152	Richard Breed, Wethersfield, Conn.	2 and 1			Whittaker, 1 up, 21 holes	
146	Joon Lee, Fullerton, Calif.	Lee,				
154	Kevin Lamair, Citrus Heights, Calif.	3 and 2	Lee, 6 and 4			
150	John Barrett, Milwaukee, Wis.	Barrett,				
151	Robert Wakeling, Stow, Ohio	3 and 2		Lee, 4 and 3		
146	Ben Walter, Menomonie, Wis.	Frazar,				
154	Harrison Frazar, Dallas, Texas	1 up	Frazar, 3 and 1			
150	Scott Hoffman, Omaha, Neb.	Hoffman,				
152	Carl Ste-Marie, Lake City, Fla.	3 and 2				Knight, 2 and 1
144	Jean-Paul Hebert, Houston, Texas	Hebert,				
154	Robby Loving, Wichita Falls, Texas	5 and 3	Weinstein, 3 and 2			
150	Adam Weinstein, Shaker Heights, Ohio	Weinstein,				
151	Brad Lanning, Sarasota, Fla.	5 and 4		Rudosky, 4 and 2		
147	Jeff Makohon, Saskatoon, Saskatchewan, Canada	Makohon,				
153	Ted Snavely, Portland, Ore.	3 and 2	Rudosky, 1 up, 19 holes			
148	Micah Rudosky, Peoria, Ariz.	Rudosky,				
152	Steven Van Alstyne, Bakersfield, Calif.	2 up			Knight, 5 and 4	
145	Hunter Albright, Great Falls, Va.	Albright,				
154	Steve Isley, Burlington, N.C.	3 and 2	White, 2 and 2			
150	Dominick Saratore, Buchanan, Mich.	White,				
151	David White, Little Rock, Ark.	3 and 2		Knight, 1 up, 19 holes		
147	Harold Jones, Augusta, Ga.	Knight,				
153	Brandon Knight, Denton, Texas	2 and 1	Knight, 1 up, 19 holes			
149	Hank Smith, Waycross, Ga.	Smith,				
152	Jonathan Kaye, Phoenix, Ariz.	6 and 5				
142	Jon Veneziano, Kensington, Conn.	Veneziano,				
155	Kevin Hammer, Boynton Beach, Fla.	2 and 1	Veneziano, 3 and 2			
151	Gregory Raleigh, Renton, Wash.	Raleigh,				
151	Brad Montgomery, Sugar Land, Texas	2 and 1		Veneziano, 1 up		
147	Louis O'Keefe, Lynnfield, Mass.	Watson,				
153	Dusti Watson, Galesburg, Ill.	2 and 1	Duval, 3 and 1			
148	Brent Mumford, Melbourne, Fla.	Duval,				
152	David Duval, Ponte Vedra Beach, Fla.	6 and 5			Veneziano, 3 and 1	
145	William Richards, Essex Fells, N.J.	Bennett,				
154	Ben Bennett, Blackshear, Ga.	2 up	Bennett, 4 and 2			
150	Brian Gay, Daleville, Ala.	Gay,				
151	Hans Albertsson, Manchester, Vt.	2 and 1		Ruotolo, 3 and 2		
146	Jaxon Brigman, Abilene, Texas	Brigman,				
153	Eric Peterson, Idaho Falls, Idaho	2 up	Ruotolo, 3 and 1			
149	Jeffrey Ruotolo, Rochester, N.Y.	Ruotolo,				
152	James Van Etten, Etters, Pa.	7 and 6				Widener, 4 and 3
143	Jason Widener, Greensboro, N.C.	Widener,				
155	Frederick Chew, Oakland, Calif.	3 and 2	Widener, 5 and 4			
151	Jon Whittemore, Sarasota, Fla.	Bock,				
151	Brian Bock, Lincoln, Neb.	1 up		Widener, 6 and 5		
147	Larry Barber, Sherman, Texas	Barber,				
153	Chip Richter, Mechanicsburg, Pa.	1 up	Aycock, 3 and 2			
148	Macon Bycem Spartanburg, S.C.	Aycock,				
152	Matthew Aycock, Rockport, Texas	2 and 1			Widener, 4 and 3	
145	Brent Bostick, Duncan, Okla.	Bostick,				
154	James Tegeler, Renton, Wash.	5 and 3	Bostick, 1 up, 19 holes			
150	David Jones, Augusta, Ga.	D. Jones,				
151	Joseph Ring, Madison, Wis.	1 up, 19 holes		Labritz, 1 up, 19 holes		
146	Ren Budde, Argyle, Texas	Labritz,				
153	Robert Labritz, Hobe Sound, Fla.	1 up	Labritz, 1 up, 19 holes			
149	Brandon Goethals, Redding, Calif.	Goethals,				
152	Matt Gogel, Tulsa, Okla.	2 up				

Jason Widener, 1 up

*Medalist

1989
FORTY-SECOND JUNIOR AMATEUR CHAMPIONSHIP

Singing Hills Golf and Country Club, El Cajon, California, July 25-29
Yardage—6,670. Par 70. 2,025 Entries, 157 Starters, 64 Qualifiers

Qualifying Score	1st Round (18 Holes)	2nd Round (18 Holes)	3rd Round (18 Holes)	4th Round (18 Holes)	Semifinals (18 Holes)	Final (18 Holes)	
*145	Chris Riley, San Diego, Calif.	Riley, 4 and 3					
154	Rob Booth, Gladwyne, Pa.		Riley, 2 up				
150	Chris Stutts, Leoma, Tenn.	Stutts, 3 and 1					
150	Steve White, Dalton, Ga.			Riley, 5 and 4			
149	Keith Cutler, Haverhill, Mass.	Huff, 2 and 1					
153	Phillip Huff, Portola Valley, Calif.		Huff, 21 holes				
149	Jim Ousley, Kokomo, Ind.	Ousley, 1 up					
153	Shannon Sykora, Garland, Texas				Riley, 2 and 1		
146	Justin Leonard, Dallas, Texas	Leonard, 4 and 3					
154	Lex Tarumianz, Lookout Mountain, Tenn.		Leonard, 3 and 2				
150	Todd Demsey, Rancho Santa Fe, Cal.	Hughes, 19 holes					
152	Rick Hughes, Columbia, N.J.			Leonard, 4 and 3			
146	Kevin Kemp, Greensboro, N.C.	Vanko, 1 up					
153	Ken Vanko, St. Charles, Ill.		Vanko, 19 holes				
150	Jon Horowitz, Nashua, N.H.	Horowitz, 2 and 1					
152	Casey Martin, Eugene, Ore.					Duval, 3 and 2	
*145	Chris Edgmon, Edmond, Okla.	Edgmon, 5 and 4					
154	Brent Winston, Sheridan, Ark.		Duval, 3 and 2				
150	Chad Dawson, Frankfort, Ky.	Duval, 3 and 2					
151	David Duval, Ponte Vedra, Fla.			Duval, 4 and 2			
148	Trip Kuehne, Dallas, Texas	Kuehne, 6 and 4					
153	Marshall Butler, Louisville, Ky.		Kuehne, 4 and 2				
149	Tony Cilla, Scottsdale, Ariz.	Graville, 5 and 3					
152	Lance Graville, Corcoran, Calif.				Duval, 3 and 2		
146	Casey Magner, Winnetka, Ill.	Magner, 2 and 1					
154	Brian Bartolec, Hudson, Ohio		Bangert, 6 and 5				
150	Ben Bangert, Odessa, Texas	Bangert, 4 and 3					
151	Mark Swygert, Blythewood, S.C.			Bangert, 4 and 3			
148	Reynold Lee, Pearl City, Hawaii	Lee, 19 holes					
153	Tom Traficano, Mesa, Ariz.		McEntee, 2 and 1				
149	Leland McEntee, Doylestown, Pa.	McEntee, 3 and 1					
152	Billy Faeth, Bakersfield, Calif.						David Duval, 3 and 2
*145	Brian Gay, Daleville, Ala.	Gay, 1 up					
154	Joe Summerhays, Heber, Utah		Gay, 3 and 1				
150	Jeff Morgenstern, Fresno, Calif.	Morgenstern, 2 and 1					
151	Brian Bock, Lincoln, Neb.			Gay, 3 and 1			
149	Ron Whittaker, Little Rock, Ark.	Bateman, 5 and 4					
153	Brian Bateman, Monroe, La.		Bateman, 4 and 3				
149	Chad Phillips, Fenton, Mo.	Phillips, 4 and 2					
153	Fred Chew III, Oakland, Calif.				Bratton, 1 up		
146	Macon Byce, Spartanburg, S.C.	Bergstrom, 2 and 1					
154	Matt Bergstrom, Burlington, Wash.		Bergstrom, 19 holes				
150	Andrew Price, Morristown, Tenn.	Price, 3 and 1					
152	Eric Shaffer, Fairmont, W.V.			Bratton, 5 and 3			
147	Alan Bratton, College Station, Texas	Bratton, 4 and 3					
153	Christian Chernock, Orange, Conn.		Bratton, 4 and 2				
150	Trey Sones, Windermere, Fla.	Sones, 3 and 2					
152	Rich Vaughan, Spokane, Wash.					Maki, 22 holes	
*145	Jason Worth, Des Moines, Iowa	Worth, 4 and 2					
154	Craig Uyehara, Honolulu, Hawaii		Begay, 4 and 3				
150	Notah Begay III, Albuquerque, N.M.	Begay, 2 and 1					
151	Eric Schroeder, Alameda, Calif.			Davis, 3 and 2			
148	Wyatt Rollins, Dalton, Ga.	Rollins, 2 and 1					
153	Phil Hurrle, Burnsville, Minn.		Davis, 6 and 5				
149	Mike Muehr, Bernardsville, NJ	Davis, 21 holes					
152	Edward Davis, Suisun, Calif.				Maki, 19 holes		
146	Matt Aycock, Rockport, Texas	Maki, 1 up					
154	Austin Maki, Costa Mesa, Calif.		Maki, 2 and 1				
150	Ted Snavely, Portland, Ore.	Snavely, 3 and 1					
151	Cory Okuna, Hilo, Hawaii			Maki, 3 and 2			
147	Kevin Hammer, Dillon, Colo.	Watso, 3 and 2					
153	Dusti Watson, Galesburg, Ill.		Tomaselli, 22 holes				
149	Henry Schlissberrg, E. Lansing, Mi.	Tomaselli, 3 and 2					
152	Joe Tomaselli, Jr., Plano, Texas						

*Co-medalists

1990
FORTY-THIRD JUNIOR AMATEUR CHAMPIONSHIP

Lake Merced Golf and Country Club, Daly City, California, July 24-28
Yardage—6,731. Par 72. 2,051 Entries, 153 Starters, 64 Qualifiers

Qualifying Score	1st Round (18 Holes)	2nd Round (18 Holes)	3rd Round (18 Holes)	4th Round (18 Holes)	Semifinals (18 Holes)	Final (18 Holes)
*151	Dennis Hillman, Rye, N.Y.	Hillman,				
165	Ryan Nakata, Aiea, Hawaii	7 and 6	Hillman,			
161	Ben Taylor, Jacksonville, Fla.	Taylor,	3 and 2			
161	Brad Sharpe, Waco, Texas	2 and 1		Hillman,		
158	Steve Burdick, Rocklin, Calif.	Burdick,		3 and 2		
163	Todd Pence, Cheney, Wash.	3 and 1	Chang,			
158	Joe Acosta, Visalia, Calif.	Chang,	19th hole			
163	Jerry Chang, Westlake Village, Calif.	1 up			Hillman,	
156	Troy Ferris, Norfolk, Va.	Graville,			4 and 3	
164	Lance Graville, Corcoran, Calif.	5 and 4	Graville,			
159	Brandt Ficken, Middleburg, Pa.	Spencer,	2 up			
162	Marc Spencer, Bradford, Mass.	4 and 3		Bradley,		
156	Eddie Davis, Suisun, Calif.	E. Davis,		4 and 3		
164	Craig Uyehara, Honolulu, Hawaii	1 up	Bradley,			
159	John Griffin, Terrell, Texas	Bradley	2 up			
162	Rob Bradley, Milford, N.J.	3 and 2				Hillman,
154	Tiger Woods, Cypress, Calif.	Woods,				3 and 2
164	Travis Williams, Greenwood, Miss.	2 up	Woods,			
160	Brian Johnson, Shreveport, La.	Johnson,	19th hole			
161	Grant Masson, Richardson, Texas	2 and 1		Woods,		
158	Brian Bateman, Monroe, La.	J. Davis,		7 and 6		
164	Jason Davis, Escondido, Calif.	1 up	Waggoner,			
158	Brian Waggoner, Old Hickory, Tenn.	Waggoner,	19th hole			
162	Brian Newton, Richardson, Texas	5 and 4			Woods,	
154	Nick Clinard, Gastonia, N.C.	Flippen,			3 and 2	
164	Jimmy Flippen, Jr., Danville, Va.	3 and 2	Campos,			
160	Dan Campos, Phoenix, Ariz.	Campos,	19th hole			
162	Jason Wight, Brigham City, Utah	21st hole		Begay,		
157	Notah Begay, Albuquerque, N.M.	Begay,		3 and 2		
164	Scott Carlson, Grafton, Wis.	4 and 3	Begay,			
159	Matt Filipowicz, Roswell, Ga.	Monahan,	19th hole			
162	Brenden Monahan, Belmont, Mass.	3 and 2				Mathew Todd, 1 up
153	Chris Dauk, Akron, Ohio	Dauk,				
165	Bill Lyle, Ann Arbor, Mich.	19 holes	Dauk,			
161	Aaron Berthiaume, Southbridge, Mass.	Berthiaume,	2 up			
161	Trevor Arts, Flower Mound, Texas	2 and 1		Biershenk,		
158	Tommy Biershenk, Inman, S.C.	Biershenk,		4 and 2		
163	Jason Bourgeois, Opelousas, La.	4 and 2	Biershenk,			
158	Travis Deibert, Doylestown, Pa.	Vaughan,	1 up			
163	Rick Vaughan, Spokane, Wash.	3 and 1			Todd,	
156	Mathew Todd, Visalia, Calif.	Todd,			3 and 1	
164	Jason Gore, Valencia, Calif.	1 up	Todd,			
159	Jason Freeman, Guthrie, Okla.	Freeman,	21st hole			
162	Troy Petracek, Crete, Neb.	4 and 3		Todd,		
156	Bobby Collins, Atlantis, Fla.	Lamberson,		4 and 3		
164	Colby Lamberson, Lake Forest, Ill.	2 and 1	Lamberson,			
159	Chad Dawson, Frankfort, Ky.	Riley,	2 and 1			
162	Chris Riley, San Diego, Calif.	6 and 4				Todd,
153	Lee McEntee, Doylestown, Pa.	McEntee,				3 and 2
164	Chris Crawford, Austin, Texas	4 and 3	McEntee,			
160	Bert Roney, Blue Springs, Mo.	Ogilvie,	3 and 2			
161	Joe Ogilvie, Lancaster, Ohio	2 up		McEntee,		
158	Mark Madson, Kailua Kona, Hawaii	Dragovich,		1 up		
163	Darren Dragovich, Yuba City, Calif.	3 and 2	Ormsby,			
158	Todd Ormsby, Peachtree, Ga.	Ormsby,	3 and 2			
163	Steve Reiter, Brandon, S.D.	20 holes			Thomas,	
154	Robert Murray, Harrisburg, Pa.	Segelke,			1 up	
164	John Segelke, Englewood, Colo.	6 and 5	Thomas,			
160	Adam Thomas, Baxley, Ga.	Thomas,	1 up			
162	Matt Beckett, Findlay, Ohio	2 up		Thomas,		
157	Scott Richardson, Laguna Niguel, Calif.	Richardson,		3 and 2		
164	Al Oh, Orange, Calif.	6 and 5	Faeth,			
159	Jason Enloe, Decatur, Ill.	Faeth,	1 up			
162	Billy Faeth, Bakersfield, Calif.	3 and 1				

*Medalist

GIRLS' JUNIOR CHAMPIONSHIP

VARE TROPHY

Presented in August, 1949, by

GLENNA COLLETT VARE
(Mrs. Edwin H. Vare, Jr.)
Women's Amateur Champion 1922-25-28-29-30-35

HISTORY

1981—Kay Cornelius, 14, of Scottsdale, Arizona, became the youngest champion in USGA history when she won the Girls' Junior Championship at the Illahe Hills Country Club, Salem, Oregon. Cornelius defeated Kim Simmons of Charleston, South Carolina, in the final, 2 and 1. Kay is the daughter of Kathy and Bill Cornelius, both golf professionals. Mrs. Cornelius was the 1956 U.S. Women's Open Champion. Cornelius, who won the Girls' Junior in her third attempt, still has three more years of eligibility before reaching her 18th birthday. Medalist honors were shared by Jamie De Weese, of Rochester, New York, and Kathy Kostas, of Palmdale, California. Both players were at 151. Cornelius reached match play with a 156 and Simmons also made it easily with 159. Cornelius had a very tough road enroute to the final. She defeated Juanita Drinnon of Chattanooga, Tennessee, 2 and 1; Sammie Souza of Honolulu, Hawaii, 4 and 3; Leslie Price of Ontario, Canada, 1 up; Debra Burris of Modesto, California, 1 up, 20 holes, after dropping a 40-foot putt for a birdie; and Heather Kuzmich of Ontario, Canada, who was hoping to become the first foreign player to win the Girls' Junior, 4 and 3. Simmons didn't have an easy time either. She defeated Diedra Bailey of Sapula, Oklahoma, 4 and 2; Deborah Moss of West Palm Beach, Florida, 1 up, 19 holes; Renee MacDonald of Grants Pass, Oregon, 1 up; Jamie De Weese, 3 and 2; and Page Dunlap of Sarasota, Florida, 4 and 3. In the final match, Cornelius opened her round par-birdie and was 2 up on the third tee. Simmons won the sixth with a birdie but Cornelius won the 9th and 10th holes with pars to go 3 up. Simmons got one hole back at the 16th with a par. When the 17th hole, a par-3, was halved in pars, the match was over. The Championship was played in hot, humid weather as temperatures rose to 100 degrees and above. The USGA accepted 131 entries, far short of the record 176 in 1979.

1982—Heather Farr, 17, of Phoenix, Arizona, won the Girls' Junior Championship in her fourth and final try, defeating Caroline Keggi, 17, of Middlebury, Connecticut, 2 and 1 in the final match. The Championship was played at the Greeley Country Club, in Greeley, Colorado. It was a week of record-breaking golf, beginning with two days of stroke-play qualifying for match play. Kathy McCarthy, of Fresno, California, scored two consecutive eagles in shooting a record 69, four under par, in the first round. On the second day, Melissa McNamara, of Tulsa, Oklahoma, equalled the 69, which, added to her opening 72, gave her the 36-hole qualifying record of 141, five under par, one stroke better than the record set by Amy Benz, in 1979. Miss McCarthy qualified second with a 76 for 145, one under par. Miss Farr, who qualified with 153, reached the final match by defeating Janet Soulsby, of Prudhoe, England, in a 19-hole semifinal match. Miss Soulsby, a member of the 1982 British Curtis Cup Team, was the first British Curtis Cupper to compete in the U.S. Girls' Junior. In the final match, Miss Keggi took an early 1-up lead with a par 3 at the second hole. Miss Farr pulled even with a birdie at the par-5 fourth hole. When Miss Keggi took three putts at both the fifth and sixth holes, Miss Farr was able to recover from errant drives to halve both holes. Miss Farr assumed a 2-up lead after the ninth, but she lost the 10th to Miss Keggi's par 3. She recovered her 2-up advantage when she parred the 12th. Miss Keggi won the 13th, but Miss Farr won the 14th with a bogey and the 15th with a birdie to go dormie three. The match ended at the 17th hole when they halved with birdies. Miss Keggi narrowly missed an eagle putt from 12 feet after Farr chipped her third shot to within one foot of the hole. The USGA accepted 167 entries, short of the record 176 received in 1976.

1983—Kim Saiki, 17, of Westminster, California, won the Girls' Junior Championship by defeating Buffy Klein, of Argyle, Texas, 2 and 1, at the Somerset Hills Country Club, in Bernardsville, New Jersey. Somerset Hills, which had been the host club in 1973, thus became the first club to hold two Girls' Junior Championships. Miss Saiki qualified for match play with 152, and in the semifinal defeated Kay Cornelius, of Phoenix, Arizona, the 1981 Champion, 1 up in 19 holes. Miss Saiki was 3 down against Miss Cornelius, but she squared the match by the 16th and holed a 20-foot birdie putt to win on the first extra hole. Miss Klein was not expected to reach the final, having qualified with 170, 20 strokes behind Melissa McNamara, of Tulsa, Oklahoma, the medalist. In the semifinals Miss Klein defeated Miss McNamara, who was medalist for the second consecutive year, 2 and 1. Miss Saiki won the first hole of the final match, but Miss Klein won three of the next four to take a 2-up lead. Miss Saiki fought back and closed out the match on the 17th. The Girls' Junior attracted 165 entries.

1984—Cathy Mockett, 16, of Newport Beach, California, defeated Michiko Hattori, of Aichigun,

Japan, 1 up, in the final played at the Mill Creek Country Club, in Bothell, Washington. Not only was Miss Mockett the third player to become medalist and champion, but she was also the second successive Californian to win. Kim Saiki, of Westminster, California, had won the 1983 Girls' Junior. Miss Hattori, who is 15, disposed of five opponents without playing the 18th hole. Miss Mockett, also had a relatively smooth path to the final, playing the 18th hole just once. In the final, the first nine belonged to Miss Mockett, who was one-under par and 2 up, but Miss Hattori strung together successive pars on holes 10 through 14 and Miss Mockett's lead disappeared. Miss Mockett won the 15th when Miss Hattori three-putted, but Miss Hattori won the 16th when Miss Mockett bunkered her approach. Miss Mockett missed a two-foot putt for a par that would have won the 17th hole, but on the 18th, she holed one of the same length for a bogey to win the match.

1985—Dana Lofland, 17, of Oxnard, California, defeated Amy Fruhwirth of Cypress, California, 4 and 3, to win the Girls' Junior Championship at St. Clair Country Club in Pittsburgh, Pennsylvania. Lofland thus became the fourth golfer to win the qualifying medal and the Championship, and the third successive Californian to win the Championship. Kim Saiki of Westminster and Cathy Mockett of Newport Beach won in 1983 and 1984, respectively. Only one of Fruhwirth's matches went to the final hole. That occurred in her semifinal match with Christy Erb of Bonita, California, which she won, 1 up. Lofland had a more difficult road to the final, twice winning on the final green and once on the 19th hole. She defeated Tracy Nakamura of Monterey Park, California, 3 and 2, in her semifinal match. The final match was all square through 10 holes. Lofland won the 11th with a birdie and the 12th and 13th with pars to go 3 up. The 14th was halved with pars and Lofland won the match on the par-3 15th when Fruhwirth three-putted from 45 feet. The USGA accepted 144 entries for the Championship.

1986—Pat Hurst, 17, of San Leandro, California, defeated Adele Moore of Dallas on the 20th hole to win the U.S. Girls' Junior Championship at Peach Tree Golf and Country Club in Marysville, California. Hurst became the fourth consecutive Californian to win the championship, joining Kim Saiki of Westminster (1983), Cathy Mockett of Newport Beach (1984) and Dana Lofland of Oxnard (1985). Michiko Hattori of Nagoya, Japan, the 1985 U.S. Women's Amateur Champion, was the medalist with a record 140, six under par. Moore eliminated Hattori in the quarterfinal round. In the final, Hurst birdied the second and third holes to go 2 up, but Moore won three of the next six holes and was 1 up through nine. Hurst then birdied the 12th to square the match and birdied the 16th to go 1 up. Moore won the 18th hole with an eagle 3, sending the match to extra holes. After matching par 4s on the 19th hole, Hurst nearly reached the par-5 second (20th) hole with her second shot. She chipped to five feet and made her birdie. Moore, who had missed the fairway with her drive, made six. The USGA accepted a record 193 entries for the championship.

1987—Michelle McGann, 17, of Riviera Beach, Florida, defeated Lynne Mikulas, La Mesa, California, 7 and 5, to win the championship at The Orchards Golf Course in South Hadley, Massachusetts. McGann became only the second Floridian to win the championship and the first player from outside of California to win since 1982. McGann shared medalist honors with Lisa Brandetsas of Snyder, New York, and Brandie Burton of Rialto, California, at seven-over-par 151, despite posting a 45 for the first nine holes of her second round. Brandetsas and Burton lost their first-round matches. McGann was extended to the 16th hole only twice on her way to the championship. In the semifinal round she eliminated Vicki Goetze of Hull, Georgia, 8 and 6. Mikulas, who only once was forced to the 17th in her matches, defeated Elizabeth Bowman of Bonita, California, 4 and 2, in the semifinals. After the first hole of the final was halved, McGann won the next six. She lost the eighth hole, but won the ninth and 10th to go 7 up. McGann birdied the 13th to close out the match. The USGA accepted a record 209 entries for the championship.

1988—Jamille Jose, 15, of Carmichael, California, defeated Debbie Parks of Phoenix, Arizona, 5 and 4, in the final at Golden Valley (Minnesota) Country Club. Brandie Burton of Rialto, California, who two weeks earlier was one of two amateurs to make the 36-hole cut at the U.S. Women's Open, earned the qualifying medal with a 36-hole total of 141, three under par. The second qualifying round was interrupted by severe thunderstorms and a tornado warning. Burton was eliminated in the quarterfinal round by Elizabeth Bowman of Bonita, California, 2 and 1. Parks, two down to Bowman with three to play in the semifinals, rallied to win on the 19th hole. Jose eliminated Vicki Goetze of Hull, Georgia, 3 and 2, in the other semifinal match to earn her place in the final. In the final, Parks won the first hole with a par, only to lose to a par by Jose at the second hole. Parks birdied the fourth to regain the lead. Still one down at the sixth, Jose took advantage of four consecutive bogeys by Parks, winning all four holes, to go 3 up. She extended her lead to 4 up with a birdie at the 10th. After Parks pulled to within three by birdieing the par-3 11th, Jose won the 12th with a par to regain her advantage. Jose closed out the match by sinking a four-foot birdie putt at the 14th. The USGA accepted 207 entries for the championship.

1989—Brandie Burton, 17, from Rialto, California, did what was expected of her by defeating Camie Hoshino, of Honolulu, by one hole, at Pine Needles Country Club, in Southern Pines, North Carolina. In her six matches, Miss Burton fell behind an opponent only in her semifinal match against Vicki Goetze, 16, from Hull, Georgia. She trailed by three holes early in the match, but she regrouped and took the lead for good on the 13th. She won by 1 up. Against Miss Hoshino, Miss Burton won three of the first four holes before she began missing greens on the second nine, but she hung on to win. At times, Miss Burton outdrove her opponents by as much as 50 yards, and could reach the greens of some par 5 holes with her second shots.

1990—Sandrine Mendiburu, 17, from St. Jean de Luz, France, birdied and won three consecutive holes on the second nine at Manasquan River Golf Club, in Brielle, New Jersey, to defeat Vicki Goetze, 17, of Hull, Georgia, 3 and 2, and become the Girls' Junior's first foreign champion. Miss Mendiburu, three times the French National Junior champion, made six birdies through 16 holes, and one-putted 11 greens. She has 22 putts overall. Miss Goetze, who was medalist by four strokes, at 147, added another in a series of near misses at the Girls' Junior. She was a quarterfinalist at age 13, and a semifinalist in each of the next three years. Both finalists had little trouble advancing through match play. Miss Mendiburu was challenged only once, in a 1 up victory over 13-year-old Erin O'Neill, of Zephyrhills, Florida, in the third round of match play. Miss Goetze was never extended beyond the 16th hole in her five matches before the final. Miss Mendiburu pulled all square with a birdie at the ninth hole in the final, then birdied holes 11 through 13 to take a 3 up lead, which she held through the remaining holes.

GIRLS' JUNIOR CHAMPIONSHIP

DATE	WINNER, RUNNER-UP	SCORE	SITE	ENTRY
1981 (Aug.)	Miss Kay Cornelius d. Miss Kim Simmons	2 & 1	Illahe Hills C.C., Salem, Ore. Co-Medalists—151: Miss Kathy Kostas Miss Jamie De Weese	131
1982 (Aug.)	Miss Heather Farr d. Miss Caroline Keggi	2 & 1	Greeley C.C., Greeley, Colo. Medalist—141: Miss Melissa McNamara	167
1983 (Aug.)	Miss Kim Saiki d. Miss Buffy Klein	2 & 1	Somerset Hills C.C., Bernardsville, N.J. Medalist—150: Miss Melissa McNamara	165
1984 (Aug.)	Miss Cathy Mockett d. Miss Michiko Hattori	1 up	Mill Creek C.C., Bothell, Wash. Medalist—146: Miss Cathy Mockett	145
1985 (Aug.)	Miss Dana Lofland d. Miss Amy Fruhwirth	4 & 3	St. Clair C.C., Pittsburgh, Pa. Medalist—148: Miss Dana Lofland	144
1986 (Aug.)	Miss Pat Hurst d. Miss Adele Moore	1 up, 20 hls.	Peach Tree G. & C.C., Marysville, Calif. Medalist—139: Miss Michiko Hattori	193
1987 (Aug.)	Miss Michelle McGann d. Miss Lynne Mikulas	7 & 5	The Orchards G.C., South Hadley, Mass. Co-Medalists—151: Miss Lisa Brandetsas Miss Michelle McGann Miss Brandie Burton	§209
1988 (Aug.)	Miss Jamille Jose d. Miss Debbie Parks	5 & 4	Golden Valley C.C., Golden Valley, Minn. Medalist—141: Miss Brandie Burton	207
1989 (July)	Miss Brandie Burton d. Miss Camie Hoshino	1 up	Pine Needles Lodges and C.C., Southern Pines, N.C. Medalist—138: Miss Brandie Burton	189
1990 (Aug.)	Miss Sandrine Mendiburu d. Miss Vicki Goetze	3 & 2	Manasquan River G.C., Brielle, N.J. Medalist—147: Miss Vicki Goetze	183

§ Record Entry.

1981
THIRTY-THIRD GIRLS' JUNIOR CHAMPIONSHIP

Illahe Hills Country Club, Salem, Oregon, August 3-8
Yardage—5,933. Par 72. 131 Entries, 105 Starters, 64 Qualifiers.

Qualifying Score	1st Round (18 Holes)	2nd Round (18 Holes)	3rd Round (18 Holes)	4th Round (18 Holes)	Semi-Finals (18 Holes)	Final (18 Holes)
*151	Kathy Kostas, Palmdale, Calif.	Kostas,				
162	Brenda Corrie, Santo Domingo, Dominican Rep.	3 and 1				
158	Heather Farr, Phoenix, Ariz.	Farr,	Kostas,			
166	Sarah Peters, Wichita, Kans.	4 and 2	3 and 1			
156	Susan Thompson, Garden Grove, Calif.	Thompson,		Kostas,		
164	Diane Dickman, Modesto, Calif.	1 up		1 up, 19 holes		
160	Sarah Lebrun, Owings Mills, Md.	Lebrun,	Thompson,		Kuzmich,	
167	Mary Ann Baney, Pittsburgh, Pa.	4 and 3	5 and 3		4 and 2	
155	Kim Saiki, Westminster, Calif.	Kuzmich,				
162	Heather Kuzmich, Ontario, Canada	3 and 2				
159	Cheryl Stacy, Findlay, Ohio	Stacy,	Kuzmich,			
167	Audrey Bendick, Ontario, Canada	5 and 3	1 up	Kuzmich,		
157	Kerry Liedes, Hoquiam, Wash.	Gardner,		3 and 2		
165	Kimberly Gardner, Garches, France	1 up, 19 holes				
161	Nancy Brown, Salinas, Calif.	Brown,	Brown,			
169	Cathy Hicks, Safford, Ariz.	4 and 2	2 and 1			Cornelius,
152	Flori Prono, Northridge, Calif.	Prono,				4 and 3
162	Susan Pager, Daphne, Ala.	3 and 2				
159	Laurie Brower, Villa Park, Calif.	Brower,	Prono,			
166	Caroline Keggi, Middlebury, Conn.	2 and 1	2 and 1	Burris,		
157	Robin Hood, Osceola, Ind.	Hood,		3 and 2		
164	Nancy Macagnone, Clearwater, Fla.	1 up	Burris,			
161	Debra Burris, Modesto, Calif.	Burris,	2 up			
168	Jennifer Warner, Lake Oswego, Ore.	5 and 3			Cornelius,	
156	Kay Cornelius, Scottsdale, Ariz.	Cornelius,			1 up, 20 holes	
163	Juanita Drinnon, Chattanooga, Tenn.	2 and 1	Cornelius,			
160	Sammie Souza, Honolulu, Hawaii	Souza,	4 and 3			
167	Stacy Colborne, Poway, Calif.	4 and 2				
158	Leslie Price, Ontario, Canada	Price,		Cornelius,		
166	Kris Tschetter, Sioux Falls, S.D.	3 and 2		1 up		
161	Donna Cusano, Ft. Lauderdale, Fla.	Cusano,	Price,			
169	Cathy Mockett, Newport Beach, Calif.	4 and 2	1 up, 21 holes			
*151	Jamie DeWeese, Rochester, N.Y.	DeWeese,				
162	Lynn Dennison, Marion, Ohio	5 and 4	DeWeese,			
158	Martha Foyer, Carmel, Ind.	Nixon,	6 and 4			
166	Diane Nixon, Rochester, N.Y.	2 and 1				
156	Donna Linder, Seguin, Texas	Linder,		DeWeese,		
164	Tamara Rehurek, San Gabriel, Calif.	3 and 2	Linder,	2 and 1		
160	Connie McCain, Crockett, Texas	McCain,	1 up			
167	Michele Michanowicz, Pittsburgh, Pa.	2 and 1			Simmons,	
155	Deborah Moss, W. Palm Beach, Fla.	Moss,			3 and 2	
162	Jane Harris, Bellvue, Wash.	2 and 1				
159	Kim Simmons, Charleston, S.C.	Simmons,	Simmons,			
167	Diedra Bailey, Sapula, Okla.	4 and 2	1 up, 19 holes			
157	Renee MacDonald, Grants Pass, Ore.	MacDonald,		Simmons,		
165	Renee Mack, Portland, Ore.	3 and 2		1 up		
161	Danielle Ammaccapane, Phoenix, Ariz.	Gilmartin,	MacDonald,			
169	Adrienne Gilmartin, Port Washington, N.Y.	3 and 2	7 and 5			Simmons,
153	Julie Cross, Salem, Ore.	Fisher,				4 and 3
162	Maureen Fisher, Central Islip, N.Y.	1 up, 19 holes				
159	Libby Akers, French Lick, Ind.	Akers,	Akers,			
166	Patricia McGonigle, Spokane, Wash.	4 and 3	4 and 2			
157	Kathleen McCarthy, Fresno, Calif.	Dunlap,		Dunlap,		
164	Page Dunlap, Sarasota, Fla.	3 and 2	Dunlap,	1 up, 19 holes		
161	Patti Berendt, San Diego, Calif.	Ruffer,	5 and 4			
168	Carey Ruffer, Conroe, Texas	2 and 1			Dunlap,	
156	Amy Dover, Jasper, Texas	Dover,			1 up	
163	Lisa Stanley, Melborne, Fla.	3 and 1				
160	Catherine Johnston, Enfield, N.C.	Johnston,	Dover,			
167	Julie Carmichael, Martinsville, Ind.	1 up, 20 holes	4 and 2	Dover,		
158	Lisa Bradley, Emporia, Kans.	Bradley,		5 and 4		
166	Paula Gamble, Kent, Wash.	3 and 1	Bradley,			
161	Kimberley Dirks, Ft. Worth, Texas	Dirks,	2 and 1			
169	Frances Dunn, Nassau, Bahamas	2 and 1				

Kay Cornelius, 2 and 1

*Co-Medalists

1982
THIRTY-FOURTH GIRLS' JUNIOR CHAMPIONSHIP

Greeley Country Club, Greeley, Colorado, August 9-14.
Yardage — 6,019. Par 73. 167 Entries, 150 Starters, 64 Qualifiers.

Qualifying Score	1st Round (18 Holes)	2nd Round (18 Holes)	3rd Round (18 Holes)	4th Round (18 Holes)	Semifinals (18 Holes)	Final (18 Holes)
*141	Melissa McNamara, Tulsa, Okla.	Mockett,				
160	Cathy Mockett, Newport Beach, Calif.	1 up	Kondik,			
157	Kimberly Lasken, Whittier, Calif.	Kondik,	2 and 1			
164	Stephanie Kondik, Houston, Texas	1 up		H. Farr,		
153	Heather Farr, Scottsdale, Ariz.	H. Farr,		3 and 2		
163	Adrienne Gilmartin, Pt. Washington, N.Y.	6 and 5	H. Farr,			
158	Sue Thomas, Texarkana, Texas	Thomas,	4 and 3			
166	Jane Kang, Elyria, Ohio	6 and 5			H. Farr,	
151	Brenda Corrie, Santo Domingo, Dom. Rep.	Corrie,			4 and 3	
161	Catherine Hadley, Irving, Texas	1 up	Corrie,			
158	Kathy Kostas, Palmdale, Calif.	Dirks,	4 and 2			
165	Kimberly Dirks, Ft. Worth, Texas	1 up		Corrie,		
155	Sarah Lebrun, Owings Mills, Md.	Lebrun,		5 and 3		
164	Diahnn Forsberg, Farmington, Minn.	2 up	Lebrun,			
160	Paula Gamble, Kent, Wash.	Gamble,	5 and 4			
167	Donna Linder, Sequin, Texas	2 and 1				H. Farr,
146	Carey Kresheck, DeKalb, Ill.	Kresheck,				1 up,
161	Christine Newton, Whitefish, Mont.	4 and 3	Soulsby,			19 holes
157	Janet Soulsby, England	Soulsby,	2 up			
165	Nicole Dutt, Las Vegas, Nev.	8 and 6		Soulsby,		
154	Kay Cornelius, Phoenix, Ariz.	Hood,		2 and 1		
163	Robin Hood, Osceola, Ind.	4 and 3	Pager,			
159	Cathleen Fritz, Punta Gorda, Fla.	Pager,	1 up, 19 holes			
166	Susan Pager, Daphe, Ala.	4 and 2			Soulsby,	
152	Kristal Parker, Cable, Ohio	Parker,			2 up	
162	Melissa Farr, Phoenix, Ariz.	4 and 3	Parker,			
158	Elizabeth Akers, French Lick, Ind.	Akers,	2 and 1			
166	Michelle Reed, Glenwood Springs, Colo.	5 and 4		Parker,		
156	Kimberly Gardner, Larchmont, N.Y.	Gardner,		1 up, 20 holes		
164	Patricia McGonigle, Spokane, Wash.	7 and 6	Gadbaw,			
160	Carey Ruffer, Conroe, Texas	Gadbaw,	3 and 1			
167	Tari Gadbaw, Appleton, Wis.	1 up				
145	Kathy McCarthy, Fresno, Calif.	McCarthy,				
160	Christa Wicks, Roseburg, Ore.	3 and 1	McCarthy,			
157	Michele Michanowicz, Pittsburgh, Pa.	Machado,	5 and 4			
165	Mary Machado, Lockeford, Calif.	1 up, 19 holes		McCarthy,		
153	Carolina Fernandez-Oro, Mexico City, Mex.	Fernandez-Oro,		1 up, 20 holes		
163	Vickie Moran, Fairmont, W. Va.	1 up, 19 holes	Fernandez-Oro,			
159	Kerre Duninsky, Lincoln, Neb.	Wilson,	6 and 4			
166	Melanie Wilson, Pensacola, Fla.	6 and 5			McCarthy,	
151	Kristen Tschetter, Sioux Falls, S.D.	Lofye,			8 and 7	
162	Kristin Lofye, Venice, Fla.	4 and 3	Lofye,			
158	Danielle Ammaccapane, Phoenix, Ariz.	Bartholomew,	4 and 3			
166	Jean Bartholomew, Garden City, N.Y.	4 and 3		Green,		
156	Page Dunlap, Sarasota, Fla.	Green,		3 and 2		
164	Paige Green, Kalamazoo, Mich.	1 up	Green,			
160	Michele Miller, Spring Valley, Ohio	Kase,	4 and 3			
167	Judy Kase, Socorro, N.M.	4 and 2				Keggi,
151	Michele Saiki, Westminster, Calif.	Keggi,				4 and 3
161	Caroline Keggi, Middlebury, Conn.	6 and 5	Keggi,			
158	Pearl Sin, Bellflower, Calif.	Taylor,	6 and 4			
165	Michelle Taylor, Allyn, Wash.	4 and 3		Keggi,		
154	Jamie DeWeese, Rochester, N.Y.	DeWeese,		2 and 1		
164	Nancy Macagnone, Clearwater, Fla.	6 and 5	Gamester,			
159	Cindy Mueller, Belleville, Ill.	Gamester,	6 and 4			
167	Robin Gamester, Tampa, Fla.	2 and 1			Keggi,	
153	Tracy Kerdyk, Coral Gables, Fla.	Kerdyk,			2 and 1	
162	Becky Whitworth, Colorado Springs, Colo.	5 and 4	Kerdyk,			
158	Nanci Bowen, Tifton, Ga.	Bowen,	1 up			
166	Tamala Sides, Lenoir, N.C.	6 and 5		Kerdyk,		
157	Karen Zielenski, Sacramento, Calif.	Zielenski,		6 and 5		
164	Debra Davis, East Dennis, Mass.	5 and 4	Ralls,			
160	Julie Ralls, Woodinville, Wash.	Ralls,	3 and 2			
167	Lisa Dooling, Warminster, Pa.	2 up				

Heather Farr, 2 and 1

*Medalist

1983
THIRTY-FIFTH GIRLS' JUNIOR CHAMPIONSHIP

Somerset Hills Country Club, Bernardsville, New Jersey, August 8-13.
Yardage—5,985. Par 72. 165 Entries, 150 Starters, 64 Qualifiers.

Qualifying Score	1st Round (18 Holes)	2nd Round (18 Holes)	3rd Round (18 Holes)	4th Round (18 Holes)	Semifinals (18 Holes)	Final (18 Holes)
*150	Melissa McNamara, Tulsa, Okla.	McNamara,				
165	Debbie Silverberg, Rydal, Pa.	4 and 2	McNamara,			
161	Nancy Macagnone, Clearwater, Fla.	Macagnone	4 and 2			
168	Marlene Brodzik, Lancaster, N.Y.	4 and 2		McNamara,		
158	Michele Lyford, Redlands, Calif.	Lyford,		1 up		
167	Jennifer Love, Richmond, Va.	4 and 3	Thomas,			
162	Sue Thomas, Texarkana, Texas	Thomas,	3 and 2			
170	Phyllis Conroy, St. James City, Fla.	1 up			McNamara,	
156	Page Dunlap, Sarasota, Fla.	Tucek,			6 and 4	
166	Krista Tucek, The Woodlands, Texas	3 and 1	Kelley,			
161	Tracy Nakamura, Monterey Park, Calif.	Kelley,	5 and 4			
169	Hope Kelley, W. Hartford, Conn.	2 and 1		Mockett,		
159	Heather Hodur, Glenview, Ill.	Hodur,		1 up		
168	Adele Moore, Dallas, Texas	1 up, 19 holes	Mockett,			
163	Cathy Mockett, Newport Beach, Calif.	Mockett,	2 and 1			
172	Heather Westphal, Midland, Mich.	5 and 3				Klein,
152	Dottie Pepper, Gansevoort, N.Y.	Pepper,				2 and 1
165	Catherine Stevens, Wichita, Kans.	8 and 6	Pepper,			
161	Sarah Peters, Wichita, Kans.	Peters,	2 up			
168	Cindy Mueller, Belleville, Ill.	1 up		Pepper,		
158	Melanie Wilson, Pensacola, Fla.	Pager,		6 and 4		
167	Susan Pager, Daphne, Ala.	1 up, 21 holes	Pager,			
162	Stephanie Kondik, Houston, Texas	Kondik,	4 and 3			
171	Joann Walker, Palm Springs, Calif.	4 and 3			Klein,	
157	Tracy Chapman, Indianapolis, Ind.	Gadbaw,			5 and 3	
166	Tari Sue Gadbaw, Appleton, Wis.	3 and 2	Klein,			
161	Ginger Brown, Hope, Ark.	Klein,	4 and 3			
170	Buffy Klein, Argyle, Texas	6 and 5		Klein,		
160	Clare Dolan, Gaithersburg, Md.	Dolan,		1 up, 20 holes		
168	Catherine Hadley, Irving, Texas	1 up	Rogerson,			
165	Katherine Rogerson, Indiana, Pa.	Rogerson,	2 up			
173	Adrienne Gilmartin, Port Wash., N.Y.	3 and 1				
152	Kim Saiki, Westminster, Calif.	Saiki,				
165	Carolina Fernandez, Atizapan, Mexico	7 and 6	Saiki,			
161	Elizabeth Macfie, Camden, S.C.	Macfie,	2 up			
168	Carey Ruffer, Conroe, Texas	2 and 1		Saiki,		
158	Lisa Nedoba, Plantation, Fla.	Nedoba,		3 and 2		
167	Jane Kang, Elyria, Ohio	4 and 3	Nedoba,			
162	Margaret Kelt, Dallas, Texas	Kelt,	1 up			
171	Barbara Ann Blanchar, Columbia, Mo.	2 up			Saiki,	
157	Julie Ralls, Woodinville, Wash.	Luginbuel,			2 and 1	
166	Sheila Luginbuel, Vinita, Okla.	3 and 2	Luginbuel,			
161	Lisa DePaulo, Solana Beach, Calif.	DePaulo,	3 and 2			
170	Elizabeth Fry, Adelphi, Md.	3 and 1		Sinn,		
159	Pearl Sinn, Bellflower, Calif.	Sinn,		5 and 4		
168	Beck Cross, Gadsden, Ala.	6 and 5	Sinn,			
164	Michelle Wooding, Tacoma, Wash.	Powers,	5 and 4			
172	April Rene Powers, Charlotte, N.C.	3 and 2				Saiki,
155	Tami Henningsen, Camarillo, Calif.	Henningsen,				1 up, 19 holes
166	Leigh Ann Mills, Coral Springs, Fla.	3 and 1	Henningsen,			
161	Lana Perhacs, Glendale, Ariz.	Perhacs,	6 and 5			
168	Catherine Bothe, Big Flats, N.Y.	1 up		Kerdyk,		
158	Tracy Kerdyk, Coral Gables, Fla.	Kerdyk,		4 and 2		
167	Christina Jae Barrett, Baltimore, Md.	7 and 6	Kerdyk,			
163	Danielle Ammaccapane, Phoenix, Ariz.	Hessenauer,	5 and 3			
172	Laura Hessenauer, Baltimore, Md.	3 and 1			Cornelius,	
157	Kay Cornelius, Phoenix, Ariz.	Cornelius,			2 and 1	
167	Nancy Kessler, Portland, Ore.	5 and 4	Cornelius,			
162	Lorie Anne Wilkes, Bartow, Fla.	Wilkes,	2 and 1			
170	Colleen Draeger, Scottsdale, Ariz.	2 up		Cornelius,		
160	Nanci Bowen, Tifton, Ga.	Bartholomew,		2 and 1		
168	Jean Bartholomew, Garden City, N.Y.	2 up	Bartholomew,			
165	Nadia St. Marie, Lake City, Fla.	Kern,	3 and 2			
173	Bilee Lynn Kern, Allentown, Pa.	1 up, 20 holes				

Kim Saiki, 2 and 1

*Medalist

1984
THIRTY-SIXTH GIRLS' JUNIOR CHAMPIONSHIP

Mill Creek Country Club, Bothell, Washington, August 6-11
Yardage—5,925, Par 72. 145 Entries, 150 Starters, 64 Qualifiers

Qualifying Score	1st Round (18 Holes)	2nd Round (18 Holes)	3rd Round (18 Holes)	4th Round (18 Holes)	Semifinals (18 Holes)	Final (18 Holes)
*146	Cathy Mockett, Newport Beach, Calif.	Mockett,				
160	Nanci Bowen, Tifton, Ga.	4 and 3	Mockett,			
156	Kimberly Belk, Kershaw, S.C.	Gallagher,	4 and 3			
163	Jacqueline Gallagher, Marion, Ind.	1 up		Mockett,		
154	Blakney Boggs, Dallas, Texas	Boggs,		4 and 2		
161	Paige Cribb, Georgetown, S.C.	3 and 2	Mc Guire,			
158	Suzy McGuire, Jamesville, N.Y.	McGuire,	1 up, 19 holes			
164	Debbie Silverberg, Ventor, N.J.	1 up, 19 holes			Mockett,	
151	Joan Pitcock, Fresno, Calif.	Pitcock,			1 up	
161	Christine Toogood, Reno, Nev.	3 and 2	Pitcock,			
157	Dana Lofland, Oxnard, Calif.	Lofland,	3 and 1			
163	Dana Arnold, Modesto, Calif.	3 and 1		Pitcock,		
155	Judith Schneider, Helena, Mont.	Werley,		2 and 1		
162	Wendy Werley, Littleton, Colo.	6 and 4	Brown,			
159	Christine Brown, Jacksonville Beach, Fla.	Brown,	3 and 2			
165	Michele Taylor, Bellevue, Wash.	4 and 3				Mockett,
149	Kay Cornelius, Scottsdale, Ariz.	Cornelius,				4 and 3
160	Nancy Kessler, Portland, Ore.	6 and 4	Cathrein,			
157	Kim Cathrein, Salinas, Calif.	Cathrein,	1 up			
163	Donna Andrews, Lynchburg, Va.	4 and 2		Cathrein,		
154	Clare Dolan, Gaithersburg, Md.	Miller,		4 and 3		
162	Chrissie Miller, Sacramento, Calif.	1 up	Platt,			
158	Margaret Platt, Elmsford, N.Y.	Platt,	1 up			
165	Melissa Farr, Phoenix, Ariz.	3 and 2			Cathrein,	
153	Kate Golden, Jasper, Texas	Golden,			4 and 3	
161	Margaret Kelt, Dallas, Texas	3 and 2	Golden,			
157	Aiko Hashimoto, Narutoshi, Japan	Hashimoto,	3 and 2			
164	Cathy Lorenze, Woodland Hills, Calif.	3 and 1		Golden,		
156	Karen Socha, Greeneville, Tenn.	Socha,		1 up, 19 holes		
162	Lara Mack, Portland, Ore.	5 and 3	Socha,			
159	Joye McAvoy, Windsor, Ont., Canada	McAvoy,	1 up			
165	Kathryn Hughes, Woodbury, Minn.	1 up				
147	Tami Jo Henningsen, Camarillo, Calif.	Henningsen,				
160	Adele Moore, Dallas, Texas	3 and 1	Lyford,			
156	Michele Lyford, Redlands, Calif.	Lyford,	1 up 19 holes			
154	Lana Perhacs, Glendale, Ariz.	1 up		Fry,		
154	Cissye Meeks, Greenwood, Miss.	Fry,		4 and 2		
161	Elizabeth Fry, Adelphi, Md.	5 and 3	Fry,			
158	Keri Arnold, Modesto, Calif.	Arnold,	3 and 1			
164	Krista Tucek, The Woodlands, Texas	1 up, 20 holes			Nedoba,	
153	Jean Zedlitz, Pleasanton, Calif.	Zedlitz,			2 and 1	
161	Inger Molina, Moscow, Idaho	3 and 1	Nedoba,			
157	Kathryn Peterson, Plantation, Fla.	Nedoba,	1 up			
163	Lisa Nedoba, Plantation, Fla.	3 and 2		Nedoba,		
156	Nadia Ste-Marie, Lake City, Fla.	Ste-Marie,		7 and 5		
162	Kathleen Klein, Kokomo, Ind.	3 and 2	Ste-Marie,			
159	Christi Parkes, Lawrenceburg, Tenn.	Parkes,	1 up, 19 holes			
165	Ellie Gibson, Houston, Texas	1 up				Hattori,
150	Julie Lynn Ralls, Woodinville, Wash.	Ralls,				2 and 1
161	Barbara Ann Blanchar, Columbia, Mo.	6 and 4	Bendick,			
157	Susan Wineinger, Green Bay, Wis.	Bendick,	4 and 2			
163	Audrey Bendick, Windsor, Ont., Canada	3 and 2		Thompson,		
154	Pearl Sinn, Belleflower, Calif.	Thompson,		5 and 4		
162	Terri Thompson, Savannah, Ga.	2 and 1	Thompson,			
158	Buffy Klein, Argyle, Texas	Haley,	6 and 5			
165	Cindy Haley, Bullard, Texas	1 up, 19 holes			Hattori,	
153	Amy Fruhwirth, Cypress, Calif.	Fruhwirth,			2 and 1	
161	Debbi Koyama, Monterey Park, Calif.	1 up, 20 holes	Hattori,			
157	Michiko Hattori, Aichigun, Japan	Hattori,	4 and 3			
164	Loren Milhench, Marion, Mass.	4 and 2		Hattori,		
156	Catherine Stevens, Wichita, Kans.	Stevens,		4 and 3		
162	Tracy Nakamura, Monterey Park, Calif.	2 up	Stevens,			
160	Christy Erb, Chula Vista, Calif.	Wooding,	1 up			
165	Michelle Wooding, Tacoma, Wash.	4 and 3				

Cathy Mockett, 1 up

*Medalist

1985
THIRTY-SEVENTH GIRLS' JUNIOR CHAMPIONSHIP

St. Clair Country Club, Pittsburgh, Pennsylvania, July 29-August 3
Yardage—5,975. Par 72. 144 Entries, 144 Starters, 64 Qualifiers

Qualifying Score	1st Round (18 Holes)	2nd Round (18 Holes)	3rd Round (18 Holes)	4th Round (18 Holes)	Semifinals (18 Holes)	Final (18 Holes)
*148	Dana Lofland, Oxnard, Calif.	Lofland,				
175	Maralynn Adams, San Jose, Calif.	7 and 6	Lofland,			
166	Christine Casingal, Lake Wales, Fla.	Ammaccapane,	2 up			
167	Dina Ammaccapane, Phoenix, Ariz.	1 up		Lofland,		
162	Debbie Koyama, Monterey Park, Calif.	Koyama,		1 up		
170	Barbara Koosa, Columbia, S.C.	2 and 1	Koyama,			
163	Carolyn McKenzie, Berwyn, Pa.	McKenzie,	8 and 6			
170	Tara Hipp, Gaithersburg, Md.	5 and 3			Lofland,	
158	Jodi Figley, Aliquippa, Pa.	Figley,			1 up, 19 holes	
173	Shirley Trier, Akron, Ohio	3 and 1	Figley,			
165	Joal Rieder, Charlotte, N.C.	Kroot,	7 and 6			
168	Ann Kroot, Carmel, Ind.	1 up, 20 holes		Lyford,		
158	Michele Lyford, Redlands, Calif.	Lyford,		5 and 3		
172	Kathy Highfill, Monroe, La.	5 and 3	Lyford,			
165	Tracy Lynne Taylor, Corvallis, Ore.	Taylor,	3 and 2			
168	Barbara Ann Blanchar, Columbia, Mo.	2 and 1				Lofland,
154	Jennifer Myers, Lancaster, Pa.	Myers,				3 and 2
174	Karen Noble, Brookside, N.J.	5 and 4	Trimble,			
166	Tina Trimble, Houston, Texas	Trimble,	6 and 4			
167	Michelle Paden, San Diego, Calif.	2 up		Trimble,		
161	Laura Dalessandro, Toms River, N.J.	Dalessandro,		2 and 1		
171	Krista Tucek, The Woodlands, Texas	3 and 2	Parker,			
163	Alexandria Kinander, Medinah, Ill.	Parker,	1 up, 19 holes			
169	Kristin Parker, The Woodlands, Texas	1 up			Nakamura,	
155	Jean Zedlitz, Pleasanton, Calif.	Zedlitz,			2 and 1	
173	Cheryl Riegel, Bossior City, La.	9 and 7	McAvoy,			
165	Sheryl Maize, Venice, Fla.	McAvoy,	1 up, 20 holes			
167	Joye McAvoy, Windsor, Ontario, Canada	3 and 2		Nakamura,		
161	Julie Rieger, Miami, Okla.	Rieger,		2 and 1		
171	Karen Socha, Greeneville, Tenn.	4 and 3	Nakamura,			
164	Tracy Nakamura, Monterey Park, Calif.	Nakamura,	5 and 3			
169	Ingrid Lundblad, Painesville, Ohio	5 and 3				Dana Lofland, 4 and 3
153	Pat Hurst, San Leandro, Calif.	Hurst,				
174	Erin Good, Sacramento, Calif.	4 and 3	Kelt,			
166	Margaret Kelt, Dallas, Texas	Kelt,	3 and 2			
167	Meg Cimino, Plant City, Fla.	3 and 2		Kelt,		
162	Melissa Farr, Phoenix, Ariz.	Farr,		2 and 1		
170	Mia Browning, Detroit, Mich.	4 and 2	Platt,			
163	Catherine Stevens, Wichita, Kan.	Platt,	4 and 3			
170	Margaret Platt, Elmsford, N.Y.	1 up			Erb,	
157	Michelle McGann, Riviera Beach, Fla.	Jones,			1 up	
173	Anne Jones, Louisville, Ky.	3 and 2	Erb,			
165	Donna Olexio, Portland, Ore.	Erb,	5 and 4			
168	Christy Erb, Bonita, Calif.	3 and 2		Erb,		
158	Laura Saiki, Westminster, Calif.	Saiki,		5 and 4		
172	Tracey Brawley, Sault Ste Marie, Ont., Canada	6 and 5	Gibson,			
164	Kristen Klein, Tampa, Fla.	Gibson,	4 and 3			
168	Ellie Gibson, Houston, Texas	4 and 3				Fruhwirth,
153	Michiko Hattori, Aichi, Japan	Hattori,				1 up
174	Kelli Ross, Burnsville, Minn.	7 and 5	Mockett,			
166	Cathy Mockett, Newport Beach, Calif.	Mockett,	1 up			
167	Sarah Jane Morton, Columbus, Ohio	3 and 1		Lee,		
162	Anne Cain, Springfield, Mo.	Cain,		1 up		
171	Deborah Doniger, Greenwich, Conn.	8 and 7	Lee,			
163	Chrissie Miller, Sacramento, Calif.	Lee,	1 up, 19 holes			
170	Deborah Lee, Dundas, Ontario, Canada	6 and 4			Fruhwirth,	
156	Amy Fruhwirth, Cypress, Calif.	Fruhwirth,			4 and 3	
173	Elizabeth Martin, Wickenburg, Ariz.	6 and 4	Fruhwirth,			
165	Stacie Konz, Chandler, Ariz.	Winkelman,	1 up			
167	Susan Winkelman, Belvidere, Ill.	4 and 3		Fruhwirth,		
159	Adele Moore, Dallas, Texas	Hundley,		4 and 3		
171	Sherry Hundley, Southern Pines, N.C.	1 up, 20 holes	Hundley,			
164	Lori Beth Poling, Baytown, Texas	Renaud,	2 and 1			
169	Sandra Renaud, Windsor, Ontario, Canada	4 and 2				

*Medalist

1986
THIRTY-EIGHTH GIRLS' JUNIOR CHAMPIONSHIP

Peach Tree Golf and Country Club, Marysville, California, August 4-9
Yardage—5,850. Par 73. 193 Entries, 150 Starters, 64 Qualifiers

Qualifying Score	1st Round (18 Holes)	2nd Round (18 Holes)	3rd Round (18 Holes)	4th Round (18 Holes)	Semifinals (18 Holes)	Final (18 Holes)
*140	Michiko Hattori, Nagoya, Japan	Hattori, 8 and 6				
161	Elizabeth Martin, Wickenburg, Ariz.		Hattori, 7 and 6			
156	Jennifer Holt, Las Vegas, Nev.	Holt, 6 and 5				
156	Meliza Goble, La Mirada, Calif.			Hattori, 2 and 1		
152	Anna Emmons, Conroe, Texas	Emmons, 4 and 3				
159	Tracy Lehman, Palm Desert, Calif.		Casingal, 2 and 1			
153	Kelli Ross, Burnsville, Minn.	Casingal, 5 and 4				
159	Christine Casingal, Lake Wales, Fla.				A. Moore, 1 up	
147	Adele Moore, Dallas, Texas	A. Moore, 6 and 5				
160	Piper Wagner, Missouri City, Texas		A. Moore, 2 up			
155	Mikki Records, Franklin, Ind.	Blackwell, 1 up				
157	Barbara Blackwell, Spring, Texas			A. Moore, 3 and 2		
148	Tina Trimble, Houston, Texas	Trimble, 2 and 1				
160	Patricia Corace, Gwynedd Valley, Pa.		Trimble, 1 up, 19 holes			
154	Kelly Ann Tilghman, N. Myrtle Beach, S.C.	Horner, 3 and 1				
157	Nicole Horner, Mililani, Hawaii					A. Moore, 4 and 3
144	Christy Erb, Bonita, Calif.	Erb, 1 up				
161	Gayle Jenkins, Palos Verdes, Calif.		Erb, 4 and 3			
156	Ann Kroot, Indianapolis, Ind.	Kroot, 4 and 3				
157	Leslie Green, Kingwood, Texas			Konz, 2 and 1		
150	Julie Rieger, Miami, Okla.	Brown, 2 up				
159	Laura Brown, New Smyrna Beach, Fla.		Konz, 2 and 1			
154	Tricia Konz, Chandler, Ariz.	Konz, 1 up				
158	Starla Yamada, Sandy, Utah				Konz, 1 up, 19 holes	
144	Dana Arnold, Modesto, Calif.	Arnold, 6 and 5				
161	Cathy Cordova, Mission Viejo, Calif.		Arnold, 1 up			
156	Shannon Hardesty, Crawfordsville, Ind.	Bowman, 7 and 6				
157	Elizabeth Bowman, Bonita, Calif.			Arnold, 2 and 1		
149	Stephanie Davis, Bainbridge Island, Wash.	Bell, 3 and 2				
159	Rachel Bell, Queensland, Australia		Bell, 3 and 2			
154	Stacy Smith, Grants Pass, Ore.	Kifer, 1 up				
158	Kellie Kifer, Seagoville, Texas					
142	Tracy Nakamura, Monterey Park, Calif.	Nakamura, 5 and 3				
161	Donna Lippstreu, Pleasanton, Calif.		Thompson, 4 and 2			
156	Anne Marie Goslak, Springtown, Pa.	Thompson, 6 and 4				
156	Terri Thompson, Savannah, Ga.			Thompson, 2 and 1		
152	Liza LaBelle, Minneapolis, Minn.	LaBelle, 4 and 2				
159	Lynne Mikulas, LaMesa, Calif.		LaBelle, 1 up			
154	Vivian Overturf, Huntington Beach, Calif.	Castellucci, 5 and 4				
158	Maria Castellucci, Orlando, Fla.				Lyford, 2 and 1	
147	Jodi Figley, Aliquippa, Pa.	Figley, 2 and 1				
161	Gia Kronske, Clearwater, Fla.		Lyford, 1 up, 20 holes			
155	Leigh Dickey, Missouri City, Texas	Lyford, 3 and 2				
157	Michele Lyford, Redlands, Calif.			Lyford, 1 up		
149	Martha Longoria, Corpus Christi, Texas	Wooding, 1 up				
160	Audrey Wooding, Tacoma, Wash.		Wooding, 1 up, 19 holes			
154	Christi Yong, Stockton, Calif.	Yong, 1 up				
158	Kathy Moore, Argyle, Texas					Hurst, 1 up, 19 holes
144	Vicki Goetze, Hull, Ga.	Goetze, 4 and 2				
161	Lisa Doble, Zionsville, Ind.		Goetze, 3 and 1			
156	Kristin Ryan, Noblesville, Ind.	Ryan, 5 and 3				
156	Amanda Nealy, Grants Pass, Ore.			Goetze, 2 and 1		
151	Brandie Burton, Rialto, Calif.	Burton, 5 and 3				
159	Ginger Lowe, Boise, Idaho		Burton, 3 and 1			
154	Angela Mills, French Lick, Ind.	Mills, 2 and 1				
158	Christine Lagow, Edina, Minn.				Hurst, 2 and 1	
146	Pat Hurst, San Leandro, Calif.	Hurst, 2 and 1				
161	Tammie Dougan, White Rock, B.C., Canada		Hurst, 2 and 1			
155	Carrie Leary, Newhall, Calif.	Kealoha, 3 and 2				
157	Annette Kealoha, Kaneohe, Hawaii			Hurst, 1 up		
149	Michelle McGann, Riviera Beach, Fla.	McGann, 4 and 3				
160	Leslye McDermott, Naples, Fla.		McGann, 4 and 3			
154	Tina Paternostro, Williamsport, Pa.	Paternostro, 1 up, 19 holes				
158	Kim Cayce, Potomac, Md.					

Pat Hurst, 1 up, 20 holes

*Medalist

1987
THIRTY-NINTH GIRLS' JUNIOR CHAMPIONSHIP

The Orchards Golf Course, South Hadley, Massachusetts, August 10-15
Yardage—5,843. Par 72.+209 Entries, 150 Starters, 64 Qualifiers

Qualifying Score	1st Round (18 Holes)	2nd Round (18 Holes)	3rd Round (18 Holes)	4th Round (18 Holes)	Semifinals (18 Holes)	Final (18 Holes)	
*151	Lisa Brandetsas, Perry, N.Y.	Castellucci, 2 and 1					
168	Maria Castellucci, Orlando, Fla.		Bowman, 2 and 1				
163	Kimberly Cayce, Potomac, Md.	Bowman, 3 and 2					
164	Elizabeth Bowman, Bonita, Calif.			Bowman, 5 and 4			
158	Barbara Blackwell, Spring, Texas	Blackwell, 5 and 3					
165	Jennifer Holt, Las Vegas, Nev.		Lippstreu, 4 and 2				
159	Donna Lippstreu, Pleasanton, Calif.	Lippstreu, 4 and 2					
165	Sandy Hamby, Houston, Texas				Bowman, 4 and 3		
155	Sue Veasey, Safety Harbor, Fla.	Veasey, 6 and 4					
167	Alisha Granson, Russiaville, Ind.		Gill, 1 up				
162	Starla Yamada, Sandy, Utah	Gill, 2 and 1					
164	Tonya Gill, Stone Mountain, Ga.			Gill, 4 and 3			
155	Christy Erb, Bonita, Calif.	Erb, 5 and 4					
167	Mary Dunne, Lauderdale-by-the-Sea, Fla.		Erb, 2 and 1				
162	Cathy Cordova, Mission Viejo, Calif.	Cordova, 2 up					
164	Vivian Overturf, Huntington Beach, Calif.					Mikulas, 4 and 2	
152	Tina Paternostro, Williamsport, Pa.	Paternostro, 6 and 4					
167	Beth Manczak, Eugene, Ore.		Paternostro, 1 up, 19 holes				
162	Lisa Weissmueller, Lexington, Ky.	Weissmueller, 1 up, 21 holes					
164	Nicole Kochaphum, Vallejo, Calif.			Arnold, 2 and 1			
157	Dana Arnold, Modesto, Calif.	Arnold, 2 up					
166	Stephanie Comstock, Jacksonville, Fla.		Arnold, 1 up				
160	Tricia Allen, Vallejo, Calif.	Allen, 1 up					
165	Meredith Loosse, Capertino, Calif.				Mikulas, 2 and 1		
153	Susan Slaughter, Floyd, Va.	Slaughter, 2 and 1					
167	Erin Haney, Santa Clara, Calif.		Sison, 4 and 3				
162	Bronwyn Burke, Houston, Texas	Sison, 3 and 2					
164	Marian Sison, Arlington, Va.			Mikulas, 3 and 2			
156	Lynne Mikulas, La Mesa, Calif.	Mikulas, 7 and 5					
166	Debbie Doniger, Greenwich, Conn.		Mikulas, 5 and 3				
161	Annette Kealoha, Sacramento, Calif.	Dickey, 2 and 1					
165	Leigh Dickey, Missouri City, Texas						Michelle McGann, 7 and 5
*151	Michelle McGann, Riviera Beach, Fla.	McGann, 4 and 3					
168	Kimberly Byham, Raleigh, N.C.		McGann, 3 and 2				
163	Stephanie Davis, Bainbridge Island, Wash.	Sugg, 1 up					
164	LaRee Sugg, Petersburg, Va.			McGann, 3 and 2			
158	Stephanie Martin, Camarillo, Calif.	Martin, 5 and 4					
165	Julie Shephard, Scottsdale, Ariz.		Martin, 2 up				
160	Tina Trimble, Houston, Texas	Trimble, 6 and 4					
165	Shannon Clark, Danville, Calif.				McGann, 3 and 2		
155	Adele Moore, Dallas, Texas	Moore, 5 and 4					
169	Liza LaBelle, Minneapolis, Minn.		Moore, 2 up				
162	Mandy Quattlebaum, Cabot, Ark.	Perry, 1 up, 19 holes					
164	Julie Perry, Burlingame, Calif.			Moore, 7 and 5			
155	Patricia Corace, Gwynedd Valley, Pa.	Corace, 3 and 2					
167	Jody Cosgrove, Kailua, Hawaii		Corace, 6 and 5				
161	Barbara Morace, East Longmeadow, Mass.	Augusta, 4 and 2					
164	Kim Augusta, Rumford, R.I.					McGann, 8 and 6	
*151	Brandie Burton, Rialto, Calif.	Stinson, 1 up					
167	Lori Stinson, Fort Wayne, Ind.		Malkin, 5 and 3				
163	Michelle Malkin, Grand Blanc, Mich.	Malkin, 3 and 2					
164	Nicole Horner, Mililani Town, Hawaii			Saiki, 4 and 3			
158	Tonya Blosser, Athens, Ohio	Blosser, 4 and 3					
166	Amy McDonald, Bloomington, Ind.		Saiki, 4 and 2				
160	Audrey Wooding, Tacoma, Wash.	Saiki, 5 and 4					
165	Laura Saiki, Redwood City, Calif.				Goetze, 3 and 2		
154	Terri Thompson, Savannah, Ga.	Thompson, 5 and 4					
167	Cynthia Isaac, Novato, Calif.		Thompson, 2 and 1				
162	Tricia Konz, Chandler, Ariz.	Konz, 3 and 2					
164	Angela Mills, French Lick, Ind.			Goetze, 1 up			
155	Vicki Goetze, Hull, Ga.	Goetze, 5 and 4					
167	Claudia Leyland, Orillia, Ontario, Canada		Goetze, 4 and 3				
161	Shirley Trier, Akron, Ohio	Trier, 1 up					
164	Coley Jordan, Richardson, Texas						

+ Record Entry

* Co-Medalists

1988
FORTIETH GIRLS' JUNIOR CHAMPIONSHIP

Golden Valley Country Club, Golden Valley, Minnesota, August 1-6
Yardage—5,721. Par 72. 207 Entries, 150 Starters, 64 Qualifiers

Qualifying Score	1st Round (18 Holes)	2nd Round (18 Holes)	3rd Round (18 Holes)	4th Round (18 Holes)	Semifinals (18 Holes)	Final (18 Holes)	
*141	Brandie Burton, Rialto, Calif.	Burton, 2 and 1					
163	Jessica Wood, Buies Creek, N.C.		Burton, 6 and 4				
158	Jill McGill, Englewood, Colo.	McGill, 2 and 1					
158	Nicole Horner, Mililani Town, Hawaii			Burton, 4 and 3			
153	Tina Trimble, Houston, Texas	Kochaphum, 1 up					
161	Nicole Kochaphum, Vallejo, Calif.		Kochaphum, 3 and 2				
153	Renee Heiken, Metamora, Ill.	Heiken, 1 up					
161	Shannon Clark, Danville, Calif.				Bowman, 2 and 1		
149	Mary Dunne, Lauderdale-by-the-Sea, Fla.	Landers, 5 and 4					
162	Stephanie Landers, Kingston, Ontario, Canada		Landers, 4 and 3				
156	Leann Lockin, Aurelia, Iowa	Kotoshirodo, 5 and 4					
159	Carrie Kotoshirodo, Pearl City, Hawaii			Bowman, 1 up			
149	Elizabeth Bowman, Bonita, Calif.	Bowman, 4 and 2					
162	Carol Pfaff, Hesston, Kan.		Bowman, 4 and 3				
156	Tana Re Figueras, San Diego, Calif.	Cosgrove, 5 and 4					
160	Jody-Marie Cosgrove, Kailua, Hawaii					Parks, 1 up, 19 holes	
147	Patricia Sinn, Bellflower, Calif.	Sinn, 4 and 3					
163	Gina Yoder, Nappanee, Ind.		Parks, 1 up, 19 holes				
157	Debbie Parks, Phoenix, Ariz.	Parks, 5 and 4					
158	Jeong Min Park, Alemeda, Calif.			Parks, 1 up			
151	Leta Lindley, Carlsbad, Calif.	Lindley, 6 and 4					
162	Stephanie Neill, Charlotte, N.C.		Lindley, 7 and 6				
154	Julie Perry, Burlingame, Calif.	Sunderman, 4 and 2					
161	Kristyl Sunderman, El Cajon, Calif.				Parks, 4 and 3		
147	Tricia Konz, Chandler, Ariz.	Konz, 6 and 5					
163	Justina Hopkins, Crystal River, Fla.		Konz, 3 and 2				
157	Kim Augusta, Rumford, R.I.	Augusta, 3 and 2					
159	Tracy Hanson, Rathdrum, Idaho			Konz, 4 and 2			
150	Maria Castellucci, Orlando, Fla.	Castellucci, 3 and 2					
162	Jennifer Vernon, Garland, Texas		Castellucci, 4 and 2				
155	Kimberley Tyrer, Frankfort, Ky.	Suhocki, 2 and 1					
160	Victoria Suhocki, Tucson, Ariz.						Jamille Jose, 5 and 4
147	Christy Erb, Bonita, Calif.	Erb, 6 and 4					
163	Kelly Cooper, Leawood, Kan.		Erb, 7 and 6				
158	Lisa Weissmueller, Lexington, Ky.	Pieroni, 2 and 1					
158	Angela Pieroni, Citrus Heights, Calif.			Myers, 1 up			
152	Mandy Quattlebaum, Cabot, Ark.	Quattlebaum, 3 and 2					
161	Allyson Greer, Millbrook, N.Y.		Myers, 4 and 2				
153	Laura Myers, Missouri City, Texas	Myers, 2 up					
161	Alisha Granson, Russiaville, Ind.				Goetze, 5 and 4		
148	Vicki Goetze, Hull, Ga.	Goetze, 5 and 4					
162	Marie Rouleau, St. Lambert, Quebec, Canada		Goetze, 2 and 1				
156	Stephanie Martin, Camarillo, Calif.	Cayce, 1 up					
159	Kimberly Cayce, Potomac, Md.			Goetze, 1 up			
150	Jennifer Holt, Las Vegas, Nev.	Holt, 1 up, 19 holes					
162	Tracy Cone, Vancouver, Wash.		Holt, 4 and 2				
155	Annette Kealoha, Sacramento, Calif.	Blosser, 2 and 1					
160	Tonya Blosser, Athens, Ohio					Jose, 1 up	
147	Lisa Brandetsas, Perry, N.Y.	Brandetsas, 2 and 1					
163	Sheri Vincent, San Diego, Calif.		Brandetsas, 3 and 1				
158	Sara Miley, Menomonee Falls, Wis.	Wong, 5 and 4					
158	Leanne Wong, Los Angeles, Calif.			Turner, 1 up, 21 holes			
152	Bronwyn Burke, Houston, Texas	Turner, 7 and 5					
161	Jennifer Turner, Austin, Texas		Turner, 2 up				
154	Sandrine Mendiburu, La Teste, France	Rambin, 1 up					
161	Alycya Rambin, Tulsa, Okla.				Jose, 3 and 2		
147	Jamille Jose, Carmichael, Calif.	Jose, 2 and 1					
162	Camie Hoshino, Hilo, Hawaii		Jose, 6 and 5				
157	Leslie Green, Kingwood, Texas	Roth, 1 up					
159	Shani Roth, Cleveland, Ohio			Jose, 4 and 3			
150	Donna Lippstreu, Pleasanton, Calif.	Lippstreu, 3 and 1					
162	Sandy Hamby, Houston, Texas		Lippstreu, 1 up, 19 holes				
155	Tonya Gill, Stone Mountain, Ga.	Gill, 4 and 3					
160	Sandra Haines, Scarborough, Ontario, Canada						

*Medalist

1989
FORTY-FIRST GIRLS' JUNIOR CHAMPIONSHIP

Pine Needles Lodges and Country Club, Southern Pines, North Carolina, July 24-29
Yardage—5,879. Par 72. 189 Entries, 149 Starters, 64 Qualifiers

Qualifying Score	1st Round (18 Holes)	2nd Round (18 Holes)	3rd Round (18 Holes)	4th Round (18 Holes)	Semifinals (18 Holes)	Final (18 Holes)
*138	Brandie Burton, Rialto, Calif.	Burton, 8 and 7				
162	Lisa Penske, Bethlehem, Pa.		Burton, 5 and 4			
157	Stacy Boville, Sault Ste Marie, Ontrio	Cone, 2 and 1				
157	Tracy Cone, Vancouver, Wash.			Burton, 2 and 1		
152	Jeong Min Park, Alameda, Calif.	Hawie, 2 and 1				
160	Gilda Hawie, Miami, Fla.		Hawie, 3 and 2			
153	Lauren Stivers, Palm Beach, Gardens, Fla.	Balch, 1 up				
160	Lisa Balch, San Angelo, Texas				Burton, 7 and 5	
148	Leta Lindley, Carlsbad, Calif.	Lindley, 3 and 2				
162	Tracy Dupre, Newport Beach, Calif.		Lindley, 2 up			
155	Kristin Krogsrud, Placerville, Calif.	Krogsrud, 19 hole				
159	Gwen Gravina, Miami Lakes, Fla.			Horner, 3 and 2		
149	Nicole Horner, Mililani Town, Hawaii	Horner, 3 and 2				
161	Laurie Robbins, Mount Pleasant, Mich.		Horner, 8 and 7			
155	Anzee Wilkins, Wade, N.C.	Wilkins, 5 and 4				
159	Linda Chen, Hacienda Heights, Calif.					Burton, 1 up
142	Vicki Goetze, Hull, Ga.	Goetze, 6 and 5				
162	Julie Chapman, Conroe, Texas		Goetze, 7 and 5			
156	Julie Jesswein, Grant Pass, Ore.	Welch, 1 up				
158	Tracy Welch, Winchester, Mass.			Goetze, 2 and 1		
151	Jill Hamasaki, Aiea, Hawaii	Hamasaki, 19 holes				
161	Kerri Slaughter, Chatham, Ontario, Canada		Hamasaki, 8 and 7			
154	Annie Deets, Lafayette, Ind.	Deets, 2 and 1				
160	Patricia Sinn, Bellflower, Calif.				Goetze, 7 and 5	
147	Emiles Klein, Studio City, Calif.	Sunderman, 3 and 2				
162	Kristyl Sunderman, El Cajon, Calif.		Sunderman, 19 holes			
155	Marie Josee Desbiens, Loretteville, Can.	Desbiens, 3 and 2				
158	Staci Aber, Greensburg, Pa.			Sison, 3 and 1		
150	Kim Augusta, Rumford, R.I.	Augusta, 2 and 1				
161	Leigh Casey, San Jose, Calif.		Sison, 3 and 1			
160	Stephanie Neill, Charlotte, N.C.	Sison, 7 and 5				
154	Marian Sison, Arlington, Va.					
139	Sandrine Mendiburu, Saint Jean De Lu, France	Mendiburu, 8 and 7				
162	Abby Pearsor, Florence, S.C.		Mendiburu, 7 and 6			
156	Kristi Joiner, Orlando, Fla.	Kuhn, 8 and 7				
157	Amanda Kuhn, Pinehurst, N.C.			Mendiburu, 2 and 1		
152	Barbara Paul, Clarksburg, N.J.	Paul, 5 and 4				
160	Meredith Loosse, Cupertino, Calif.		Turner, 3 and 2			
153	Jennifer Turner, Austin, Texas	Turner, 1 up				
160	Medley Sapp, Santa Maria, Calif.				Hoshino, 2 and 1	
147	Maria Castellucci, Orlando, Fla.	Castellucci, 5 and 4				
162	Melanie Gray, Cleveland, Tenn.		Castellucci, 5 and 4			
155	Stephanie Sparks, Wheeling, W. Va.	Sparks, 1 up				
159	Kellie Daniel, Tampa, Fla.			Hoshino, 3 and 1		
149	Tonya Blosser, Athens, Ohio	Blosser, 6 and 5				
161	Jill Cicora, Sarasota, Fla.		Hoshino, 1 up			
154	Camie Hoshino, Hilo, Hawaii	Hoshino, 4 and 3				
159	Alissa Lauder, Murillo, Ontario, Can.					Hoshino, 23 holes
141	Jill McGill, Englewood, Colo.	McGill, 9 and 7				
162	Ann Pohira, Winter Park, Fla.		Weber, 2 and 1			
156	Mary Jo Rollins, Colbert, Wash.	Weber, 3 and 2				
158	Kathy Weber, Derby, Kan.			Jose, 1 up (19)		
151	Tracy Hanson, Rathdrum, Idaho	Hanson, 2 and 1				
161	Leeanne Wong, Los Angeles, Calif.		Jose, 1 up			
153	Jamille Jose, Carmichael, Calif.	Jose, 7 and 5				
160	Susse Budde, Argyle, Texas				Jose, 2 and 1	
147	Stephanie Martin, Camarillo, Calif.	Martin, 6 and 5				
162	Nicole Granson, Russiaville, Ind.		Martin, 4 and 3			
155	Jennifer Choi, Beverly Hills, Calif.	Choi, 4 and 2				
158	Jeane Orr, Wichita, Kan.			Park, 2 and 1		
149	Jenny Park, Lafayette, Calif.	Park, 3 and 2				
161	Holly Reynolds, Morrisville, Vt.		Park, 8 and 7			
154	Erika Wicoff, Hartford City, Ind.	Herron, 3 and 2				
159	Alissa Herron, Wayzata, Minn.					

Brandie Burton, 1 up

*Medalist

1990
FORTY-SECOND GIRLS' JUNIOR CHAMPIONSHIP

Manasquan River Golf Club, Brielle, New Jersey, August 13-18
Yardage—6,036. Par 73. 183 Entries, 150 Starters, 64 Qualifiers

Qualifying Score	1st Round (18 Holes)	2nd Round (18 Holes)	3rd Round (18 Holes)	4th Round (18 Holes)	Semifinals (18 Holes)	Final (18 Holes)
*147	Vicki Goetze, Hull, Ga.	Goetze,				
170	Jennifer Lynch, Wateska, Ill.	7 and 5	Goetze,			
165	Angie Burkett, Modesto, Calif.	Kurmel,	4 and 2			
165	Lee Kurmel, Roseville, Calif.	5 and 4		Goetze,		
160	Kerry Zebick, Albuquerque, N.M.	Zebick,		8 and 6		
158	Tomoko Yamashita, Solana Beach, Calif.	3 and 2	Jesswein,			
161	Meredith Tucker, Rocky Mount, N.C.	Jesswein,	4 and 2			
168	Julie Jesswein, Grants Pass, Ore.	2 and 1			Goetze,	
156	Kelley Richardson, Macon, Ga.	Richardson,			5 and 3	
169	Andrea Baxter, Eagle, Idaho	2 and 1	Richardson,			
162	Skyli Yamada, Sandy, Utah	Yamada,	1 up			
167	Caren Felps, Kountze, Texas	5 and 3		Richardson,		
157	Alissa Herron, Wayata, Minn.	Herron,		6 and 4		
169	Stephanie Brockbank, Provo, Utah	6 and 5	Herron,			
162	Rachel Poston, Winter Park, Fla.	Poston,	4 and 2			
167	Caroline Peek, Cedartown, Ga.	5 and 4				Goetze,
153	Kristel Mourgue-D'Algue, France	Mourgue-D'Algue,				3 and 2
170	Ericka Wicoff, Hartford, City, Ind.	4 and 2	Garrett,			
164	Christine Garrett, Bloomington, Ill.	Garrett,	2 and 1			
166	Kristyl Sunderman, La Quinta, Calif.	2 and 1		Garrett,		
159	Lisa Balch, San Angelo, Texas	Santos,		1 up		
168	Shelly Santos, Houston, Texas	2 and 1	Santos,			
161	Staci Aber, Greensburg, Pa.	Biehl,	1 up			
168	Becky Biehl, Keokuk, Iowa	7 and 6			Garrett,	
155	Stephanie Neill, Charlotte, N.C.	Neill,			3 and 2	
170	Susan Wright, Canada	4 and 3	Materne,			
164	Nicole Materne, Spokane, Wash.	Materne,	19 holes			
166	Robin Buck, Edwardsville, Ill.	3 and 2		Bakhle,		
157	Barbara Jane Paul, Clarksburg, N.J.	Bakhle,		3 and 2		
168	Tara Bakhle, Canada	2 and 1	Bakhle,			
162	Jeong Ming Park, Alameda, Calif.	Gray,	4 and 3			
168	Melanie Gray, Cleveland, Tenn.	2 and 1				Sandrine Mendiburu, 3 and 2
151	Sandrine Mendiburu, Saint Jean De Lu, France	Mendiburu,				
170	Elizabeth Demane, Hillsdale, N.J.	8 and 7	Mendiburu,			
165	Mary Jo Rollins, Colbert, Wash.	Rollins,	4 and 3			
166	Mendy Cooper, Tumwater, Wash.	1 up		Mendiburu,		
160	Erin O'Neil, Zerpherhills, Fla.	O'Neil,		1 up		
168	Jill Hamasaki, Aiea, Hawaii	2 and 1	O'Neil,			
161	Jennifer Biehn, Scottsdale, Ariz.	Krizman,	5 and 4			
168	Jeanne Ann Krizman, South Bend, Ind.	1 up			Mendiburu,	
156	Julie Brand, Palm Beach Gardens, Fla.	Brand,			5 and 3	
169	Caroline Merrick, Cockeysville, Md.	6 and 5	Brand,			
162	Annie Deets, Lafayette, Ind.	Deets,	1 up			
167	Lisa Cornwell, Fayetteville, Ark.	6 and 4		Brand,		
157	Emilee Klein, Studio City, Calif.	Klein,		5 and 3		
169	Wendi Patterson, Atlanta, Ga.	5 and 3	Myers,			
162	Amy Lawrence, Portland, Ore.	Myers,	20 holes			
167	Kacie Myers, Venice, Fla.	3 and 2				Mendiburu,
152	Kathryn Weber, Derby, Kan.	Weber,				3 and 2
170	Jamie Koizumi, Kailua-Kona, Hawaii	5 and 4	Kuhn,			
164	Shannon Roth, Pepper Pike, Ohio	Kuhn,	4 and 3			
166	Amada Kuhn, Pinehurst, N.C.	2 up		Kuhn,		
160	Kirsten Krogsrud, Placerville, Calif.	Krogsrud,		2 and 1		
168	Jennifer Bartley, Houston, Texas	3 and 2	Krogsrud,			
161	Kim Marshall, Bermuda	Wong,	20 holes			
168	Leanne Wong, Los Angeles, Calif.	2 up			Booth,	
156	Kellee Booth, Coto De Caza, Calif.	Booth,			5 and 3	
169	Jennifer Choi, Beverly Hills, Calif.	1 up	Booth,			
162	Patricia Sinn, Bellflower, Calif.	Sinn,	2 up			
166	Dina Taylor, Debary, Fla.	4 and 3		Booth,		
157	Heather Bowie, Dover, Del.	Bowie,		5 and 4		
169	Kim Qually, Canada	2 and 1	Ward,			
162	Stephanie Sparks, Wheeling, W.V.	Ward,	1 up			
167	Wendy Ward, San Antonio, Texas	3 and 2				

*Medalist

SENIOR AMATEUR CHAMPIONSHIP

CHAMPIONSHIP TROPHY

Presented in September, 1955

by Frederick L. Dold

Member of the United States Golf Association Executive Committee, 1950-54

HISTORY

1981—Dr. Edgar R. Updegraff, 59, of Tucson, Arizona, won the Senior Amateur Championship at the Seattle (Wash.) Golf Club. It was the first USGA title of his long and distinguished amateur career. Updegraff had won many of the game's top amateur events including the Western and Pacific Coast Amateurs. He also was named to three U.S. Walker Cup teams and was non-playing captain of the 1975 team. In five previous Senior Amateur Championships, he had not gone past the semi-final round. At Seattle, he dominated his early round opponents and met Dale Morey, a two-time Senior Amateur Champion, in the final. Updegraff defeated Morey in a memorable match, 2 and 1. Updegraff, one of five brothers who all became doctors of medicine, dominated the Championship from the outset. He started by winning medalist honors with a 36-hole score of 148, four over par. He then won matches over Joseph Oppenheimer of Sun River, Oregon, 6 and 5; 1953 Amateur Public Links Champion Ted Richards of Los Angeles, 2 and 1; 1980 Senior Amateur semifinalist Ed Hopkins of Whitney, Texas, 6 and 4; and Roger McManus of Hartville, Ohio, 4 and 3. Morey, a two-time Walker Cupper, was bidding to become the first three-time winner of the Senior Amateur. He had won in 1974 and 1977. Morey defeated Gregory Dikilato of Kaneohe, Hawaii, 3 and 1; 1981 Senior Open low amateur Glenn H. Johnson of Detroit, Michigan, 3 and 1, John Zoller, the Executive Director of the Northern California Golf Association in Pebble Beach, 2 and 1; and Richard E. Riley of Phoenix, Arizona, 1 up. The Updegraff-Morey final produced quality golf. Updegraff made six birdies and Morey had three birdies of his own. The match was even through 15 holes. At the par 3 16th, Updegraff hit a long iron to within four feet of the hole, made the birdie putt and went 1 up for the first time in the match. The match ended on the 17th when Morey three-putted for a bogey. The 1981 Championship ended the two-year reign of William C. Campbell of Huntington, West Virginia who had won the Senior Amateur in 1979 and 1980. He lost in the second round to Zoller on the 19th hole. The USGA received 952 entries, short of the record 1,023 in 1979. By mere coincidence, Updegraff will have a rare opportunity for a national champion to defend on his home course when the Senior Amateur is played at the Tucson Country Club in 1982.

1982—Alton Duhon, 57, of Los Angeles, won the Senior Amateur Championship and became the second black ever to win a USGA Championship. Duhon defeated Dr. Edgar R. Updegraff, 2-up. Updegraff was attempting to defend his title on his home course, the Tucson Country Club, in Tucson, Arizona. After qualifying easily with a 36-hole score of 148, four over par, Duhon defeated John Zoller, the Executive Director of the Northern California Golf Association, from Pebble Beach, California, 2 and 1; William Scarbrough, from Jacksonville, Florida, 2 and 1; William Hyndman, III, the 1973 Senior Amateur Champion, from Huntingdon Valley, Pennsylvania, 3 and 1; and in the semifinals, Richard Giddings, from Pebble Beach, California, 7 and 6. Updegraff, who was bidding to become the third player to successfully defend his title and only the second player in USGA history to successfully defend his title on his home course, qualified easily at 146. He defeated Chris Kappas, of Ponte Vedra, Florida, 4 and 3; Billy Joe Patton, of Morganton, North Carolina, 4 and 3; William Kinsel, of San Luis Obispo, California, 6 and 4; and in the semifinals, Keith Barton, of Salt Lake City, Utah, 4 and 3. Duhon never trailed in the final match. After both players halved the first hole with birdies, Duhon went 2-up after six holes, but he lost the seventh and eighth, and the match was even with nine holes to play. The turning point came on the 14th, where Duhon dropped an eight-foot putt for a birdie. Duhon also rolled in a 35-footer on the 18th for a birdie to end the match. Roger McManus, of Hartville, Ohio, set two records in stroke-play qualifying. His second-round 70, two under par, broke the former record of 71, set in 1958 by J. Clark Espie. His 36 hole total of 142 broke the former record of 143, set by Curtis Person, Sr., in 1966, and matched by William Hyndman, III, in 1975; Dale Morey, in 1977; William Stewart, in 1978; and William C. Campbell and Morey, in 1979. The USGA accepted a record 1,104 entries, topping the previous mark of 1,023 set in 1979 at Pine Tree Golf Club, in Delray Beach, Florida.

1983—William Hyndman, III, 67, of Huntingdon Valley, Pennsylvania, became the oldest Champion in USGA history when he won the Senior Amateur Championship for the second time at the Crooked Stick Golf Club, in Carmel, Indiana. Hyndman, who had won this title in 1973, defeated Richard Runkle, 55, of Los Angeles, 1 up, in the final. Runkle only recently had become eligible for the Championship. Dr. Edgar R. Updegraff, of Tucson, Arizona, the 1981 Senior Amateur Champion and 1982 runner-up, was the qualifying medalist for the second time in three years, with rounds of 76-72-148. Updegraff lost in the second round to Willis Watkins, of Conway, Arkansas, 3 and 2. On his way to the final, Hyndman, a member of five U.S. Walker Cup teams, defeated Dale Morey, of High Point, North Carolina, twice the Senior Amateur Champion, 2 up. Runkle began quickly in the final, winning the first two holes, but Hyndman squared the match with a par at the third and a birdie at the fourth, rolling in a 45-foot putt. At the end of 16 holes, the match was even. Runkle missed a chance to win the 17th when he missed a putt from four feet. At the 18th, Hyndman's long tee shot left him with only a wedge shot to the green. Runkle's approach caught a bunker, and he eventually missed a 7-foot putt. Hyndman hit his approach 10 feet from the hole and two-putted to end the match. The Championship's format was altered. After 36 holes of stroke play qualifying, the low 64 players, rather than 32, continued into match play. The Championship attracted 1,102 entrants.

1984—Robert Rawlins, 55, of Dallas, Texas, became the youngest man to win the Senior Amateur Championship when he defeated Richard Runkle, 56, of Los Angeles, on the 19th hole at the Birmingham Country Club, in Birmingham, Michigan. William C. Campbell, of Huntington, West Virginia, was medalist, with 144. He lost to Runkle, 7 and 5, in the second round. Rawlins defeated Alton Duhon, the 1982 champion, on the 19th hole in one semifinal match while Runkle, who had finished second to William Hyndman, III, in 1983, defeated James Frost, 1-up, in the other. In the final, Runkle led, 1 up, after nine holes, but Rawlins birdied the 18th to even the match. Rawlins won the 19th when Runkle missed an 18-inch par putt. The USGA accepted a record 1,159 entries.

1985—Lewis Oehmig, 69, of Lookout Mountain, Tennessee, became the oldest person ever to win a USGA Championship and the first to win the Senior Amateur Championship three times when he defeated Edwin Hopkins, 61, of Whitney, Texas, on the 20th hole at Wild Dunes Beach and Racquet Club on Isle of Palms, South Carolina. Hopkins was medalist with 143, one stroke off the qualifying record. Hopkins had his sternest challenge on his way to the final in the third round when he defeated Ira Templeton of Hixson, Tennessee, on the 20th hole. In the semifinal, Hopkins eliminated Dempsey Ballard of San Antonio, Texas, 2 and 1. Oehmig was stretched to extra holes twice on his way to the final—in the first round he defeated Charles Sullivan of Peabody, Massachusetts, on the 20th hole and, in the second round he defeated Chris Kappas of Ponta Vedre, Florida, on the 20th hole. Oehmig defeated Clifford Taylor of Spring Lake, Michigan, 2 and 1, in the semifinal. Hopkins won the first hole of the final but Oehmig won the second, fourth and fifth holes to take a two-hole lead. Hopkins won the 12th, 13th and 14th to regain the lead and had a chance to win the match on the 17th but his putt for a winning par slid past the hole. Oehmig sank a 15-foot birdie putt on the 18th to send the match to extra holes. The 19th hole was halved with pars. Oehmig won the match on the 20th hole when Hopkins's pitch from behind the green did not hold the green and he settled for bogey. The USGA accepted a record 1,345 entries for the Championship.

1986—Bo Williams, 57, of Ocala, Florida, defeated John Harbottle of Tacoma, Washington, 3 and 2, in the final at Interlachen Country Club in Edina, Minnesota. William Hyndman, III, who won the championship in 1973 and 1983, shot 149 in qualifying to earn medalist honors, the fourth time he had won or shared the qualifying medal in this championship. Hyndman was eliminated in the quarterfinals by William Ludwig of Lees Summit, Missouri, 5 and 4. Williams had to play the 17th hole only once on his way to the final. In the fourth round he defeated Robert Marks of Elkhorn, Wisconsin, 2 and 1. Williams downed Ludwig, 3 and 2, in the semifinal round to earn his way into the final. Harbottle was extended to the 18th hole twice. He edged Joe Eason of Houston, 1 up, in his opening match and defeated Ed Tutwiler of Indianapolis by the same margin in the third round. A 4-and-3 victory over Marshall Trammell of Nashville, Tennessee, in the semifinals put Harbottle in the final. Harbottle holed a 10-foot putt to earn a half on the first hole and sank a birdie of the same length at the second to go 1 up; but he had four bogeys and a double bogey over the next six holes. Four up at that point, Williams held on for the victory. The USGA accepted a record 1,362 entries for the championship.

1987—John Richardson, 66, of Laguna Niguel, California, defeated James Kite, Jr., of Wolftown, Virginia, 5 and 4, at Saucon Valley Country Club, Bethlehem, Pennsylvania. Richardson also was the medalist, shooting three-over-par 145 and becoming the first golfer to win the medal and the championship in the same year since Ed Updegraff in 1981. Despite his impressive play, Richardson was tested often on his way to the championship. He trailed 1982 champion Alton Duhon by two holes through 13 before coming back to win on the 19th. He later defeated 1986 runner-up John Harbottle and three-time champion Lew Oehmig. Kite, a left-hander, was stretched to the 17th hole or further in each of his first four matches. His most decisive victory came in the semifinals where he ousted George Holland, 6 and 5. In the final, Richardson played superbly and held a 4-up advantage through nine holes. A birdie at the 12th increased the margin to five holes and Richardson held that lead for a 5-and-4 victory. The USGA accepted 1,465 entries for the championship.

1988—Clarence Moore, 59, of Winnsboro, South Carolina, defeated Bud Stevens of Plymouth, Michigan, 5 and 4, in the final at Milwaukee (Wisconsin) Country Club. John Harbottle of Tacoma, Washington, runner-up in the championship in 1986, and Richard Goerlich, Jr., of Tampa, Florida, shared medalist honors at 148. Harbottle advanced to the quarterfinals before losing to

James McMurtrey of Danville, California. Goerlich was a second-round loser to Bob Miller of Bay Village, Ohio. Moore's play was outstanding as he proceeded through the draw. In his closest match, he defeated Morris Beecroft of Newport News, Virginia, in the quarterfinals, 3 and 2. He eliminated Joe Simpson, of San Diego, California, father of 1987 U.S. Open champion Scott Simpson, 4 and 3, to reach the final. Stevens had a more difficult journey to the final. In the quarterfinals, he eliminated Bill Lee of Tulsa, Oklahoma, on the 20th hole. He then defeated McMurtrey, 1 up. Stevens won the first hole of the final and held that one-hole advantage through the fifth. Moore squared the match at the sixth, then took the lead for good at the eighth when he holed a shot from a greenside bunker for a birdie. Moore then won the ninth and 10th to go 3 up. After winning the 12th and 13th, Moore closed out the match when the 14th was halved with bogeys. The USGA accepted 1,440 entries for the championship.

1989—Bo Williams parred the first extra hole, at Lochinvar Golf Club, in Houston, Texas, and defeated Joe Simpson, the father of Scott Simpson, the 1987 U.S. Open champion, in the final. The win was his second. He also won the Senior Amateur in 1986. A 60-year-old car dealer from Ocala, Florida, Williams birdied two of the first eight holes, took a four-hole lead, but faltered a bit on the second nine and fell back to even after 16 holes. They halved the final two holes of the regulation 18 before Simpson three-putted the 19th. Simpson actually was the more accurate of the two, hitting 15 greens in regulation, but Williams one-putted eight greens and chipped in twice. At the end of the day Williams had but 26 putts for the 19 holes. Five strokes off the qualifying pace set by Frank Tenfel (147), Williams won five matches to reach the final. He won two of his early matches by scores of 3 and 2, and two more by 2 and 1 margins.

1990—Jackie Cummings, 55, holed a six-foot downhill birdie putt on the 16th hole and defeated Bobby Clark, 3 and 2, at Desert Forest Country Club, in Carefree, Arizona. Cummings, of Tuscaloosa, Alabama, went ahead with a par 4 on the 10th hole, and won the 15th hole with a par, then closed out the match by scoring the only birdie of his round on the 16th hole. On his route to the final, Cummings defeated Clarence Moore, of Winnsboro, South Carolina, the 1988 champion, 2 and 1 in the quarterfinals, and won his semifinal match over Rick Jones, from Youngstown, Ohio, by 3 and 2. Clark, 56, of Asheville, North Carolina, was extended to the 18th hole or beyond in two of his five matches. His toughest match was against Joe Simpson, of San Diego, California, the 1989 finalist, whom he defeated on the 21st hole. Bo Williams, of Ocala, Florida, the defending champion, was runner-up, at 151, after 36 holes of stroke play qualifying, but lost in the first round of match play.

SENIOR AMATEUR CHAMPIONSHIP

DATE	WINNER, RUNNER-UP	SCORE	SITE	ENTRY
1981 (Sept.)	Ed Updegraff d. Dale Morey	2 & 1	Seattle G.C., Seattle, Wash. Medalist—148: Ed Updegraff	952
1982 (Oct.)	Alton Duhon d. Ed Updegraff	2 up	Tucson C.C., Tucson, Ariz. Medalist—‡142: Roger T. McManus	1,104
1983 (Sept.)	William Hyndman, III d. Richard Runkle	1 up	Crooked Stick G.C., Carmel, Ind. Medalist—148: Ed Updegraff	1,102
1984 (Sept.)	Bob Rawlins d. Dick Runkle	1 up, 19 holes	Birmingham C.C., Birmingham, Mich. Medalist—144: William C. Campbell	1,159
1985 (Sept.-Oct.)	Lewis W. Oehmig d. Edwin Hopkins	1 up, 20 holes	Wild Dunes Beach & Racquet C., Isle of Palms, S.C. Medalist—145: Edwin Hopkins	1,345
1986 (Sept.)	R.S. Williams d. John Harbottle	3 & 2	Interlachen C.C., Edina, Minn. Medalist—149: William Hyndman, III	1,362
1987 (Sept.)	John Richardson d. James Kite, Jr.	5 & 4	Saucon Valley C.C., Bethlehem, Pa. Medalist—145: John Richardson	1,485
1989 (Sept.)	Bo Williams d. Joe Simpson	1 up, 19 holes	Lochinvar G.C., Houston, Tex. Medalist—147: Frank Tenfel	1,508
1990 (Oct.)	Jackie Cummings d. Bobby Clark	3 & 2	Desert Forest C.C., Carefree, Ariz. Medalist—150: William Godden	§1,658

‡Record Qualifying Score, 36 holes
§Record Entry

1981
TWENTY-SEVENTH SENIOR AMATEUR CHAMPIONSHIP

Seattle Golf Club, Seattle, Washington, September 21-26
Yardage—6,460. Par 72. 952 Entries, 144 Starters, 32 Qualifiers.

Qualifying Score	1st Round (18 Holes)	2nd Round (18 Holes)	3rd Round (18 Holes)	Semi-Finals (18 Holes)	Final (18 Holes)	
*148	E.R. Updegraff, Tucson, Ariz.	Updegraff, 6 and 5				
157	Joseph Oppenheimer, Sun River, Ore.		Updegraff, 2 and 1			
154	Ted Richards, Jr., Los Angeles, Calif.	Richards, 6 and 4				
158	D.D. Boney, El Paso, Texas					
152	John W. Kline, Houston, Texas	Kline, 6 and 5		Updegraff, 6 and 4		
157	Dick Hopwood, Scottsdale, Ariz.		Hopkins, 1 up, 19 holes			
155	Edwin B. Hopkins, Whitney, Texas	Hopkins, 1 up				
159	Donald Nehrenberg, Charlotte, N.C.				Updegraff, 4 and 3	
151	Roger McManus, Hartville, Ohio	McManus, 1 up, 19 holes				
157	George Swift, Jr., Columbus, Ga.		McManus, 4 and 3			
154	James E. Brooks, Cushing, Okla.	Levy, 3 and 2				
158	Ralph Levy, Jr., Memphis, Tenn.			McManus, 7 and 5		
153	John A. Miller, Naples, Fla.	Miller, 2 and 1				E.R. Updegraff, 2 and 1
157	Shaw McCutcheon, Spokane, Wash.		Bogart, 3 and 2			
155	Alton Duhon, Los Angeles, Calif.	Bogart, 1 up				
157	Ralph Bogart, Chevy Chase, Md.					
149	Lewis Oehmig, Lookout Mt., Tenn.	Tutwiler, 6 and 4				
157	Ed Tutwiler, Indianapolis, Ind.		Tutwiler, 3 and 1			
154	Allan Sussel, Bala-Cynwyd, Pa.	Zink, 1 up, 19 holes				
158	Robert S. Zink, Simsbury, Conn.			Riley, 1 up		
153	John W. Ridd, Jr., West Valley, Utah	Ridd, 5 and 4				
157	Frank D. Tatum, Jr., San Francisco, Calif.		Riley, 2 and 1			
155	Richard E. Riley, Phoenix, Ariz.	Riley, 4 and 3				
159	Osmond Boutwell, Mobile, Ala.				Morey, 1 up	
151	Jack Lovegren, San Jose, Calif.	Zoller, 1 up, 19 holes				
157	John Zoller, Pebble Beach, Calif.		Zoller, 1 up, 19 holes			
155	William J. Trombley, Dallas, Texas	Campbell 6 and 5				
159	William C. Campbell, Huntington, W. Va.			Morey, 2 and 1		
153	Glenn H. Johnson, Detroit, Mich.	Johnson, 1 up, 19 holes				
157	Earl F. Burt, Paradise Valley, Ariz.		Morey, 3 and 1			
156	Dale Morey, High Point, N.C.	Morey, 3 and 1				
159	Gregory Dikilato, Kaneohe, Hawaii					

*Medalist

1982
TWENTY-EIGHTH SENIOR AMATEUR CHAMPIONSHIP

Tucson Country Club, Tucson, Arizona, October 4-9.
Yardage — 6,601. Par 72. †1,104 Entries, 144 Starters, 32 Qualifiers.

Qualifying Score	1st Round (18 Holes)	2nd Round (18 Holes)	3rd Round (18 Holes)	Semifinals (18 Holes)	Final (18 Holes)	
*142	Roger McManus, Hartville, Ohio	McManus,				
151	Patrick Kaya, Wahiawa, Hawaii	2 and 1	Kinsel,			
148	William Kinsel, San Luis Obispo, Calif.	Kinsel,	4 and 3			
154	Rolland Seltz, St. Paul, Minn.	3 and 1		Updegraff,		
146	E. R. Updegraff, Tucson, Ariz.	Updegraff,		6 and 4		
153	Chris Kappas, Ponte Vedra Beach, Fla.	4 and 3	Updegraff,			
150	Leo Kubiak, Poway, Calif.	Patton,	4 and 3			
154	Billy Joe Patton, Morganton, N.C.	1 up, 19 holes			Updegraff,	
145	Keith Barton, Salt Lake City, Utah	Barton,			4 and 3	
152	Mike Lobosco, Whitestone, N.Y.	1 up	Barton,			
150	K. K. Compton, San Antonio, Texas	Compton,	1 up			
154	James Watts, Jr., Midlothian, Va.	6 and 5		Barton,		
148	Jack Van Ess, Grand Rapids, Mich.	Van Ess,		3 and 2		Alton Duhon, 2 up
153	Charles Morgan, St. Louis, Mo.	1 up, 21 holes	Van Ess,			
151	William Stewart, Springfield, Mo.	Gould,	2 up			
154	Harold Gould, Alexandria, Va.	1 up				
144	Marshall Trammel, Nashville, Tenn.	Giddings,				
151	Dick Giddings, Pebble Beach, Calif.	1 up, 20 holes	Giddings,			
149	John Ridd, West Valley, Utah	Trombley,	3 and 1			
154	William Trombley, Dallas, Texas	6 and 5		Giddings,		
146	John Owens, Lexington, Ky.	Owens,		2 and 1		
153	Ed Tutwiler, Indianapolis, Ind.	1 up, 22 holes	Owens,			
150	Robert Marks, Elkhorn, Wis.	Willits,	2 up			
154	Bob Willits, Kansas City, Mo.	1 up, 19 holes			Duhon,	
145	Dale Morey, High Point, N.C.	Riley,			7 and 6	
152	Dick Riley, Phoenix, Ariz.	2 and 1	Hyndman,			
150	William Hyndman, III, Huntingdon Valley, Pa.	Hyndman,	3 and 1			
154	Dick Lytle, Chula Vista, Calif.	2 and 1		Duhon,		
148	Alton Duhon, Los Angeles, Calif.	Duhon,		3 and 1		
153	John Zoller, Pebble Beach, Calif.	2 and 1	Duhon,			
151	Edwin Hopkins, Whitney, Texas	Scarbrough,	2 and 1			
154	William Scarbrough, Jacksonville, Fla.	7 and 5				

*Medalist

†Record Entry

1983
TWENTY-NINTH SENIOR AMATEUR CHAMPIONSHIP

Crooked Stick Golf Club, Carmel, Indiana, September 19-24.
Yardage—6,741 (6,716). Par 72. 1,102 Entries, 144 Starters, 64 Qualifiers.

Qualifying Score	1st Round (18 Holes)	2nd Round (18 Holes)	3rd Round (18 Holes)	4th Round (18 Holes)	Semifinals (18 Holes)	Final (18 Holes)
*148	Ed Updegraff, Tucson, Ariz.	Updegraff,				
162	Tom Moberg, Eau Claire, Wis.	5 and 4	Watkins,			
159	Willis Watkins, Conway, Ark.	Watkins,	3 and 2			
165	Raymond Pierson, Tucson, Ariz.	2 and 1		McCall,		
157	Keith Compton, San Antonio, Texas	Compton,		4 and 2		
164	Howard Derrick, Huntsville, Ala.	2 and 1	McCall,			
161	Robert McCall, Merrillville, Ind.	McCall,	5 and 4			
167	Richard Remsen, Locust Valley, N.Y.	2 and 1			Runkle,	
156	Keith Barton, Salt Lake City, Utah	Barton,			4 and 3	
164	John Campbell, Oskaloosa, Iowa	5 and 4	Frost,			
160	James Frost, Mercer Island, Wash.	Frost,	3 and 1			
166	George Swift, Columbus, Ga.	Default		Runkle,		
158	Richard Runkle, Los Angeles, Calif.	Runkle,		5 and 4		
165	James Cooley, Cincinnati, Ohio	3 and 2	Runkle,			
162	Robert Naudain, La Jolla, Calif.	Koressel,	3 and 2			
167	William Koressel, Pensacola, Fla.	5 and 4				Runkle,
154	Ted Richards, Los Angeles, Calif.	Sussel,				2 and 1
163	Allan Sussel, Bala-Cynwyd, Pa.	3 and 2	Sussel,			
160	James Brooks, Cushing, Okla.	Brooks,	7 and 6			
166	Bill Zimmerman, Columbus, Ga.	3 and 2		Garnero,		
157	Tony Garnero, St. Charles, Ill.	Garnero,		1 up		
164	Harry Duccilli, Wyoming, Ohio	2 up	Garnero,			
161	Karl Schmidt, Akron, Ohio	Bostock,	2 up			
167	Frank Bostock, Scottsdale, Ariz.	1 up			Spooner,	
157	Leo Spooner, Duluth, Minn.	Spooner,			3 and 2	
164	James Ostler, Frankfort, Ind.	7 and 6	Spooner,			
160	Harry Forbes, St. Joseph, Mich.	Forbes,	4 and 3			
166	George McCall, Austin, Texas	2 and 1		Spooner,		
159	John Zoller, Pebble Beach, Calif.	Zoller,		1 up, 19 holes		
165	Fred Zinn, Petoskev, Mich.	2 and 1	Zoller,			
162	Robert Myers, Indianapolis, Ind.	Myers,	4 and 3			
166	John Crump, Raytown, Mo.	5 and 4				
152	Dale Morey, High Point, N.C.	Morey,				
163	George Pottle, Southern Pines, N.C.	5 and 3	Morey,			
159	Weldon Mathis, Bethesda, Md.	Schutt,	6 and 5			
165	Roger Schutt, Indianapolis, Ind.	3 and 2		Morey,		
157	Ralph Bogart, Chevy Chase, Md.	Bogart,		5 and 4		
164	Robert Hoff, Rochester, N.Y.	3 and 2	Bogart,			
161	Lewis Leis, Los Angeles, Calif.	Cirigliano,	6 and 4			
167	Vincent Cirigliano, Birmingham, Mich.	5 and 3			Hyndman,	
156	Donald Crowell, W. Lake Village, Calif.	Crowell,			2 up	
164	Pete Dye, Delray Beach, Fla.	2 and 1	Hyndman,			
160	William Hyndman, III, Huntingdon Valley, Pa.	Hyndman,	3 and 2			
166	Joseph McDaniel, Carmel, Ind.	2 and 1		Hyndman,		
158	William Campbell, Huntington, W. Va.	Kubiak,		2 and 1		
165	Leo Kubiak, Escondido, Calif.	1 up, 21 holes	Kubiak,			
162	Robert Baker, Ft. Collins, Colo.	Welch,	6 and 4			
167	Harry Welch, Salisbury, N.C.	4 and 2				Hyndman,
155	Edwin Hopkins, Whitney, Texas	Hopkins,				2 up
163	A.J. Swann, Macon, Ga.	3 and 2	Ridd,			
160	John Ridd, W. Valley City, Utah	Ridd,	4 and 3			
166	Don Adderton, High Point, N.C.	5 and 4		Ridd,		
158	Lew Oehmig, Lookout Mountain, Tenn.	Poole,		4 and 3		
164	Grover Poole, Jonesboro, Ark.	3 and 2	Trombley,			
161	Bill Trombley, Dallas, Texas	Trombley,	5 and 4			
167	Deles Smith, Akron, Ohio	1 up			Ridd,	
161	Richard Riley, Phoenix, Ariz.	Kuhlman,			2 and 1	
164	John Kuhlman, Oak Brook, Ill.	3 and 2	Duhon,			
161	Alton Duhon, Los Angeles, Calif.	Duhon,	1 up, 19 holes			
167	James Wilson, Palm Desert, Calif.	2 up		Duhon,		
159	Bill Stewart, Springfield, Mo.	Silva,		5 and 4		
165	Don Silva, Pebble Beach, Calif.	5 and 3	McManus,			
162	Roger McManus, Hartville, Ohio	McManus,	6 and 5			
167	Robert Morris, Rockville, Md.	3 and 1				

William Hyndman, III, 1 up

*Medalist

1984
THIRTIETH SENIOR AMATEUR CHAMPIONSHIP

Birmingham Country Club, Birmingham, Michigan, September 17-22.
Yardage—6,467. Par 72. +1,159 Entries, 144 Starters, 64 Qualifiers.

Qualifying Score	1st Round (18 Holes)	2nd Round (18 Holes)	3rd Round (18 Holes)	4th Round (18 Holes)	Semifinals (18 Holes)	Final (18 Holes)
*144	William C. Campbell, Huntington, W. Va.	Campbell,				
157	James Brennan, Dothan, Ala.	4 and 3	Runkle,			
154	Richard Runkle, Los Angeles, Calif.	Runkle,	7 and 5			
159	Paul Wessel, East Moline, Ill.	4 and 3		Runkle,		
152	Dempsey Ballard, San Antonio, Texas	Ballard,		3 and 2		
158	Dick Flockenzier, Mansfield, Ohio	3 and 2	Ballard,			
155	Jim Kirk, Ardmore, Okla.	Kirk,	6 and 5			
160	Clyde Wilson, Hot Springs, Ark.	4 and 3			Runkle,	
149	Les Fowler, Boulder, Colo.	Fowler,			3 and 1	
158	Oren Shiro, Waterville, Maine	5 and 4	Oehmig,			
154	Lew Oehmig, Lookout Mountain, Tenn.	Oehmig,	1 up			
160	Ken Williams, Houston, Texas	2 and 1		Oehmig,		
153	Keith Barton, Bountiful, Utah	Barton,		8 and 6		
159	Lloyd Freden, Edina, Minn.	5 and 3	Clarke,			
156	Donald McLauchlan, Naperville, Ill.	Clarke,	4 and 2			
160	Robert Clarke, Walkertown, N.C.	1 up				Runkle,
148	Bill Hyndman, III, Huntingdon Valley, Pa.	Hyndman,				1 up
157	John Kline, Houston, Texas	1 up	Kappas,			
154	John Owens, Lexington, Ky.	Kappas,	2 and 1			
159	Chris Kappas, Ponte Vedra Beach, Fla.	1 up, 20 holes		Kappas,		
152	Roger McManus, Hartville, Ohio	Luke,		1 up, 19 holes		
159	Richard Luke, Green Valley, Ariz.	1 up, 19 holes	Fisher,			
155	Jerry Fisher, Matthews, N.C.	Fisher,	2 up			
160	Robert Willits, Kansas City, Mo.	2 and 1			Frost,	
150	James Frost, Mercer Island, Wash.	Frost,			1 up	
158	Frank Brunk, Jr., Orinda, Calif.	6 and 5	Frost,			
155	Delos Smith, Akron, Ohio	Levy,	5 and 3			
160	Ralph Levy, Memphis, Tenn.	1 up		Frost,		
153	Billy Napier, Orlando, Fla.	O'Hara,		5 and 3		
159	Pat O'Hara, Suisun, Calif.	1 up	Perlite,			
156	Jack Van Ess, Grand Rapids, Mich.	Perlite,	by default			
161	Thomas Perlite, San Francisco, Calif.	2 up				
147	Ed Updegraff, Tucson, Ariz.	Updegraff,				
157	James Wilson, Palm Desert, Calif.	1 up	Updegraff,			
154	Allan Sussel, Bala Cynwyd, Pa.	Sussel,	4 and 3			
159	George Holland, Seattle, Wash.	5 and 3		Duhon,		
152	Alton Duhon, Los Angeles, Calif.	Duhon,		3 and 2		
159	James Tingley, Glen Cove, N.Y.	6 and 4	Duhon,			
155	Dale Morey, High Point, N.C.	Morey,	4 and 3			
160	Duane Isham, Akron, Ohio	2 and 1			Duhon,	
150	Leo Kubiak, Escondido, Calif.	Spooner,			1 up, 21 holes	
158	Leo Spooner, Duluth, Minn.	3 and 2	Spooner,			
155	Ed Tutwiler, Indianapolis, Ind.	Tutwiler,	1 up			
160	Dave Dennis, Independence, Kan.	1 up, 21 holes		Spooner,		
153	Thomas Avarello, Ft. Worth, Texas	Franz,		4 and 2		
159	Frederic Franz, Crystal Lake, Ill.	2 up	Chapman,			
156	Loyal Chapman, Minneapolis, Minn.	Chapman,	1 up			
161	Rollie Seltz, St. Paul, Minn.	4 and 3				Rawlins,
149	Robert Hoff, Rochester, N.Y.	Taylor,				1 up, 19 holes
157	Clifford Taylor, Spring Lake, Mich.	1 up	Taylor,			
154	John McGarry, Weymouth, Mass.	McGarry,	2 and 1			
160	Takeo Kaneshina, Aiea, Hawaii	4 and 3		Taylor,		
152	Frank Campbell, Huntsville, Ala.	Garnero,		2 and 1		
159	Tony Garnero, St. Charles, Ill.	2 and 1	Garnero,			
156	Ken Weavil, Winston-Salem, N.C.	Riley,	2 and 1			
160	Richard Riley, Phoenix, Ariz.	2 up			Rawlins,	
151	Robert Rawlins, Dallas, Texas	Rawlins,			4 and 3	
158	Louis Button, San Antonio, Texas	2 up	Rawlins,			
155	William Scarbrough, Jr., Jacksonville, Fla.	Scarbrough,	7 and 6			
160	Leonard Napoli, Stratford, Conn.	1 up		Rawlins,		
153	Fred Zinn, Petoskey, Mich.	Zinn,		4 and 3		
159	Joseph Sylvester, Wilmington, Del.	3 and 2	Ornitz,			
156	Robert Ornitz, Delray Beach, Fla.	Ornitz,	2 and 1			
161	Robert Marks, Elkhorn, Wis.	1 up				

Robert Rawlins, 1 up, 19 holes

*Medalist +Record Entry

1985
THIRTY-FIRST SENIOR AMATEUR CHAMPIONSHIP

Wild Dunes Beach & Racquet Club, Isle of Palms, South Carolina, September 30-October 5
Yardage—6,377(6,342). Par 72. +1,345 Entries, 144 Starters, 64 Qualifiers

Qualifying Score	1st Round (18 Holes)	2nd Round (18 Holes)	3rd Round (18 Holes)	4th Round (18 Holes)	Semifinals (18 Holes)	Final (18 Holes)
*143	Edwin Hopkins, Dallas, Texas	Hopkins, 4 and 3				
157	Roy Ewing, Jr., Irving, Texas		Hopkins, 4 and 2			
154	Patrick Kaya, Schofield Barracks, Hawaii	Ehlebracht, 3 and 1				
154	Hank Ehlebracht, Indianapolis, Ind.			Hopkins, 1 up, 20 holes		
149	Hobart Manley, Jr., Savannah, Ga.	Fowler, 3 and 2				
155	Leslie Fowler, Boulder, Colo.		Templeton, 2 and 1			
149	Julian Arnold, Miami, Fla.	Templeton, 2 and 1				
155	Ira Templeton, Hixson, Tenn.				Hopkins, 3 and 1	
148	John Jacobs, Spencer, Iowa	Wallace, 3 and 1				
156	Robert Wallace, Pensacola, Fla.		Wallace, 5 and 4			
152	John Frithsen, Gloucester, Mass.	Frithsen, 1 up				
154	Jack Sweatt, York, S.C.			Wallace, 4 and 3		
148	Leo Kubiak, San Diego, Calif.	Kubiak, 2 and 1				
156	Alton Duhon, Los Angeles, Calif.		Anderson, 1 up			
152	Daniel Murray, LaVerne, Calif.	Anderson, 1 up				
155	William Anderson, Wyoming, Ohio					Hopkins, 2 and 1
145	Richard Runkle, Los Angeles, Calif.	Zinn, 1 up				
157	Fred Zinn, Petoskey, Mich.		Brooks, 2 up			
153	James Brooks, Tulsa, Okla.	Brooks, 3 and 2				
154	Robert Huff, Rochester, N.Y.			Holland, 1 up		
148	Richard Stackhouse, Boynton Beach, Fla.	Stackhouse, 2 up				
156	Jim Frost, Seattle, Wash.		Holland, 6 and 5			
151	George Holland, Seattle, Wash.	Holland, 1 up				
155	George McCall, Austin, Texas				Ballard, 1 up, 19 holes	
146	Oneil Hadnott, Pacific Palisades, Calif.	Hadnott, 4 and 2				
157	Charles Hightower, Duluth, Ga.		Hadnott, 1 up, 19 holes			
153	Valmour Poulin, Nashua, N.H.	Poulin, 1 up				
154	Fordie Pitts, Jr., Scituate, Mass.			Ballard, 5 and 4		
148	John Kline, Houston, Texas	Kline, 2 up				
156	Gerald Thompson, Ft. Lauderdale, Fla.		Ballard, 3 and 2			
151	Robert Cochran, Ballwin, Mo.	Ballard, 5 and 4				
155	Dempsey Ballard, San Antonio, Texas					
145	Robert Rawlins, Dallas, Texas	Kappas, 5 and 4				
157	Chris Kappas, Ponte Vedra, Fla.		Oehmig, 1 up, 20 holes			
153	Charles Sullivan, Peabody, Mass.	Oehmig, 1 up, 20 holes				
154	Lewis Oehmig, Lookout Mountain, Tenn.			Oehmig, 4 and 3		
149	Clarence Moore, Miami Beach, Fla.	Dye, 3 and 2				
155	Pete Dye, Carmel, Ind.		Ludwig, 3 and 1			
150	Hal Knuth, Franklin, Wis.	Ludwig, 1 up				
155	William Ludwig, Lee's Summit, Mo.				Oehmig, 1 up	
147	Glenn Johnson, Grosse Ile, Mich.	Johnson, 5 and 4				
156	Russell O'Hara, Suisun, Calif.		Vadnais, 3 and 2			
152	Robert Vadnais, Seattle, Wash.	Vadnais, 1 up, 19 holes				
154	Francis Hannaway, Peabody, Mich.			Vadnais, 6 and 4		
148	James Swanson, Rock Falls, Ill.	McLauchlan, 3 and 2				
156	D.A. McLauchlan, N. Riverside, Ill.		Napoli, 4 and 3			
152	John Morrell, Lake Wylie, S.C.	Napoli, 1 up, 19 holes				
155	Leonard Napoli, Stratford, Conn.					Oehmig, 2 and 1
145	Ed Updegraff, Tucson, Ariz.	Updegraff, 1 up, 19 holes				
157	W. Brown McDonald, Perry, Ga.		Updegraff, 6 and 5			
153	Romie Holder, Broken Arrow, Okla.	Scarbrough, 1 up				
154	William Scarbrough, Jacksonville, Fla.			Hyndman, 4 and 2		
149	Marshall Trammell, Nashville, Tenn.	Trammell, 5 and 4				
156	Eugene Hawks, Cuyahoga Falls, Ohio		Hyndman, 4 and 3			
151	William Hyndman, III, Huntingdon Valley, Pa.	Hyndman, 2 and 1				
155	Adam Freccia, Wilmington, Del.				Taylor, 1 up	
147	William Campbell, Huntington, W.Va.	Brafford, 3 and 1				
156	J.O. Brafford, Mesa, Ariz.		Brafford, 1 up			
153	Edward Nelson, Savannah, Ga.	Nelson, 3 and 2				
154	Pursie Pipes, Miami Beach, Fla.			Taylor, 3 and 2		
148	Frank Campbell, Sr., Huntsville, Ala.	F. Campbell, 2 and 1				
156	Robert Watson, Charlotte, N.C.		Taylor, 1 up			
151	Dale Morey, High Point, N.C.	Taylor, 1 up				
155	Clifford Taylor, Spring, Lake, Mich.					

Lewis Oehmig, 1 up, 20 holes

*Medalist
+Record entry

1986
THIRTY-SECOND SENIOR AMATEUR CHAMPIONSHIP

Interlachen Country Club, Edina, Minnesota, September 15-20
Yardage—6,537. Par 73. +1,362 Entries, 144 Starters, 64 Qualifiers

Qualifying Score	1st Round (18 Holes)	2nd Round (18 Holes)	3rd Round (18 Holes)	4th Round (18 Holes)	Semifinals (18 Holes)	Final (18 Holes)
*149	William Hyndman, III, Huntingdon Valley, Pa.	Hyndman, 6 and 4	Hyndman, 1 up	Hyndman, 1 up	Ludwig, 5 and 4	R. Williams, 3 and 2
163	John Pottle, Linville, N.C.					
159	Charles Harrison, Marietta, Ga.	Harrison, 2 and 1				
159	Miro Vidovic, Blue Island, Ill.					
157	Richard Spangler, Jr., Lincoln, Neb.	Spangler, 5 and 4	Duhon, 2 and 1			
162	Anthony Garnero, St. Charles, Ill.					
157	Alton Duhon, Los Angeles, Calif.	Duhon, 2 and 1				
161	Weldon Mathis, Bethesda, Md.					
156	Bill Bonney, Fairfield, Conn.	Moore, 1 up	Ludwig, 5 and 4	Ludwig, 3 and 2		
163	David Moore, Rancho Santa Fe, Calif.					
158	Hal Gould, Alexandria, Va.	Ludwig, 5 and 4				
160	William Ludwig, Lees Summit, Mo.					
156	Joe Simpson, San Diego, Calif.	Simpson, 4 and 3	Caldwell, 2 and 1			
163	Herbert Durham, Dallas, Texas					
158	W.B. Caldwell, Midland, Ga.	Caldwell, 1 up				
160	Fred Zinn, Petoskey, Mich.					
153	Robert Lewis, Fairfax, Va.	Burges, 2 and 1	Burges, 1 up	Marks, 5 and 3	R. Williams, 2 and 1	
163	Neil Burges, La Miranda, Calif.					
159	Jack Charron, Fort Worth, Texas	Wilson, 6 and 5				
159	Clyde Wilson, Hot Springs, Ark.					
157	Eugene Hawks, Cuyahoga Falls, Ohio	Marks, 1 up, 19 holes	Marks, 5 and 4			
162	Robert Marks, Elkhorn, Wis.					
158	Kenneth Murphy, Itasca, Ill.	Murphy, 1 up, 19 holes				
161	Laird Robertson, Ardmore, Pa.					
154	R.S. (Bo) Williams, Ocala, Fla.	R. Williams, 3 and 2	R. Williams, 8 and 7	R. Williams, 5 and 3		
163	Lawrence Carpenter, Short Hills, N.J.					
159	Charles Shuff, Laurel, Miss.	Mosman, 2 and 1				
160	Richard Mosman, Plano, Texas					
157	Lewis Oehmig, Lookout Mountain, Tenn.	Oehmig, 5 and 4	Owens, 1 up, 19 holes			
162	Robert Greene, San Rafael, Calif.					
158	John Owens, Lexington, Ky.	Owens, 2 and 1				
161	Robert Harris, Glenwood, Minn.					
152	Raymond Beeber, Portland, Ore.	Brooks, 1 up	Brooks, 1 up	Brooks, 1 up	Trammell, 5 and 3	Harbottle, 4 and 3
163	James Brooks, Cushing, Okla.					
159	Jim Williams, Ocala, Fla.	J. Williams, 5 and 3				
159	Hank Ehlebracht, Speedway, Ind.					
157	A.D. Dorsett, Salisbury N.C.	F. Campbell, 1 up, 20 holes	Beecroft, 4 and 3			
162	Frank Campbell, Huntsville, Ala.					
157	Morris Beecroft, Newport News, Va.	Beecroft, 3 and 1				
161	Harold Knuth, Racine, Wis.					
156	Ronald Allen, Mahwah, N.J.	Barnes, 2 and 1	Richards, 1 up	Trammell, 7 and 5		
163	Ed Barnes, Rome, Ga.					
159	Ted Richards, Los Angeles, Calif.	Richards, 2 and 1				
160	Lewis Leis, Pacific Palisades, Calif.					
157	Robert Hoff, Rochester, N.Y.	Trammell, 5 and 3	Trammell, 3 and 2			
162	Marshall Trammell, Nashville, Tenn.					
158	Paul Zimmermann, Solana Beach, Calif.	Zimmermann, 2 and 1				
160	Duane Haley, Bloomfield, Conn.					
153	Robert Wylie, Calgary, Alberta, Canada	Wylie, 4 and 3	Wylie, 2 and 1	Wylie, 1 up	Harbottle, 4 and 3	
163	Dempsey Ballard, San Antonio, Texas					
159	Allan Sussel, Bala Cynwyd, Pa.	Hightower, 2 up				
159	C.C. Hightower, Duluth, Ga.					
157	Ed Updegraff, Tucson, Ariz.	Updegraff, 4 and 3	Holland, 1 up, 19 holes			
162	Harold Campbell, Alpharetta, Ga.					
158	Daniel Murray, La Verne, Calif.	Holland, 1 up				
161	George Holland, Seattle, Wash.					
155	Ed Tutwiler, Indianapolis, Ind.	Tutwiler, 1 up	Tutwiler, 1 up	Harbottle, 1 up		
163	Morton Howard, Great Neck, N.Y.					
159	John Richardson, Laguna Niguel, Calif.	Richardson, 1 up, 19 holes				
160	Hobart Manley, Savannah, Ga.					
157	Bob Seawell, Penn Valley, Calif.	Seawell, 3 and 2	Harbottle, 3 and 2			
162	Anthony Blom, St. Bernard, Ohio					
158	Joe Eason, Houston, Texas	Harbottle, 1 up				
160	John Harbottle, Tacoma, Wash.					

R.S. (Bo) Williams, 3 and 2

+Record entry
*Medalist

1987
THIRTY-THIRD SENIOR AMATEUR CHAMPIONSHIP

Saucon Valley Country Club, Bethlehem, Pennsylvania, September 21-26
Yardage—6,428. Par 71. 1,485 Entries, 144 Starters, 64 Qualifiers

Qualifying Score	1st Round (18 Holes)	2nd Round (18 Holes)	3rd Round (18 Holes)	4th Round (18 Holes)	Semifinals (18 Holes)	Final (18 Holes)	Champion
*145	John Richardson, Laguna Niguel, Calif.	Richardson, 4 and 3					
157	Jack Tuthill, Lillian, Ala.		Richardson, 1 up, 19 holes				
154	Alton Duhon, Los Angeles, Calif.	Duhon, 2 and 1					
154	Eli Tullis, New Orleans, La.			Richardson, 3 and 2			
151	John Harbottle, Tacoma, Wash.	Harbottle, 3 and 2					
156	Marshall Trammell, Nashville, Tenn.		Harbottle, 4 and 2				
151	Frank Summers, Jr., Staunton, Va.	Gee, 1 up, 20 holes					
156	E.B. Gee, Jr., Blytheville, Ark.				Richardson, 1 up		
150	Jim Kirk, Ardmore, Okla.	Barnes, 3 and 2					
156	Ed Barnes, Jr., Rome, Ga.		Oehmig, 1 up, 19 holes				
153	Lewis Oehmig, Lookout Mountain, Tenn.	Oehmig, 1 up, 19 holes					
155	Charles McCormick, Winter Springs, Fla.			Oehmig, 2 and 1			
150	Duane Haley, Bloomfield, Conn.	Haley, 4 and 3					
156	Dean Cassell, Charlotte, N.C.		Haley, 2 up				
152	Wilburn Palmer, Camarillo, Calif.	Palmer, 1 up					
155	Vaughn Barker, Murray, Utah					Richardson, 2 and 1	
148	Richard Goerlick, Tampa, Fla.	Goerlich, 4 and 3					
157	Robert Clarke, Walkertown, N.C.		Sussel, 1 up				
154	Allan Sussel, Bala Cynwyd, Pa.	Sussel, 1 up					
155	Ed Tutwiler, Indianapolis, Ind.			Derrick, 1 up			
151	William Bogle, Poughkeepsie, N.Y.	Doyle, 3 and 2					
156	Allan Doyle, Longmeadow, Mass.		Derrick, 2 and 1				
152	Ken Weavil, Winston-Salem, N.C.	Derrick, 6 and 4					
155	Howard Derrick, Palm Beach Gardens, Fla.				Jacobs, 3 and 2		
148	R.S. Williams, Ocala, Fla.	Riley, 1 up, 19 holes					
156	Dick Riley, Phoenix, Ariz.		Moore, 1 up				
154	Ronald Moore, Englewood, Colo.	Moore, 1 up, 19 holes					
155	Ed Updegraff, Tucson, Ariz.			Jacobs, 7 and 6			
151	William Bonney, Fairfield, Conn.	Ikard, 2 and 1					
156	William Ikard, Santa Teresa, N.M.		Jacobs, 4 and 3				
152	John Jacobs, III, Cedar Rapids, Iowa	Jacobs, 3 and 2					
155	Frank Draper, Bellevue, Wash.						John Richardson, 5 and 4
146	William Dearman, Jackson, Miss.	Dearman, 2 up					
157	John Owens, Lexington, Ky.		Katula, 3 and 2				
154	Ted Katula, Greencastle, Ind.	Katula, 4 and 3					
154	Richard Stackhouse, Boynton Beach, Fla.			Holland, 1 up			
151	Ralph Levy, Jr., Memphis, Tenn.	Levy, 2 and 1					
156	Art Kramer, Horsham, Pa.		Holland, 5 and 4				
151	George Holland, Seattle, Wash.	Holland, 5 and 3					
156	Chris Kappas, Ponte Vedra Beach, Fla.				Holland, 5 and 4		
150	William Ludwig, Lees Summit, Mo.	Tenfel, 1 up, 25 holes					
156	Frank Tenfel, West Bend, Wis.		Tenfel, 1 up, 19 holes				
153	Anthony Garnero, St. Charles, Ill.	Garnero, 1 up					
155	Jack Dover, Etowah, N.C.			Darnell, 4 and 3			
150	Paul Minnich, Bay Village, Ohio	Darnell, 3 and 2					
156	Bobby Lee Darnell, Westminster, Calif.		Darnell, 2 up				
152	Richard Spangler, Lincoln, Neb.	Spangler, 3 and 2					
155	Amos Jones, Atlanta, Ga.						
148	Dick Estey, Portland, Ore.	Estey, 6 and 5				Kite, 6 and 5	
157	Franklin Simon, Los Angeles, Calif.		Estey, 3 and 2				
154	Fred Davis, Ocala, Fla.	Davis, 2 up					
154	Keith Barton, Pleasanton, Calif.			Wylie, 3 and 1			
151	Jack Van Ess, Grand Rapids, Mich.	Trofibio, 1 up, 20 holes					
156	Philip Trofibio, Endicott, N.Y.		Wylie, 3 and 2				
152	Edgar Bradley, Cincinnati, Ohio	Wylie, 2 and 1					
155	Robert Wylie, Calgary, Alberta, Canada				Kite, 1 up		
149	William Hyndman III, Huntingdon Valley, Pa.	Hyndman, 5 and 4					
156	Roger Dasch, Albany, Ore.		Hyndman, 3 and 2				
153	Patrick Keeley, Belleville, Ill.	Johnson, 2 up					
155	Glenn Johnson, Detroit, Mich.			Kite, 2 and 1			
151	Robert Zink, Lugoff, S.C.	Zink, 4 and 3					
156	Charles Ribelin, Dallas, Texas		Kite, 2 and 1				
152	James McMurtrey, Danville, Calif.	Kite, 1 up					
155	James Kite, Jr., Wolftown, Va.						

* Medalist

1988
THIRTY-FOURTH SENIOR AMATEUR CHAMPIONSHIP

Milwaukee Country Club, Milwaukee, Wisconsin, September 19-24
Yardage—6,603. Par 72. 1,440 Entries, 144 Starters, 64 Qualifiers

Qualifying Score	1st Round (18 Holes)	2nd Round (18 Holes)	3rd Round (18 Holes)	4th Round (18 Holes)	Semifinals (18 Holes)	Final (18 Holes)
*148	John Harbottle, Tacoma, Wash.	Harbottle, 7 and 5				
161	Chuck Ribelin, Dallas, Texas		Harbottle, 2 and 1			
156	Francis Pedersen, Deerfield, Ill.	Remsen, 1 up				
156	Richard Remsen, Jr., Locust Valley, N.Y.			Harbottle, 2 up		
153	Don Webster, Austin, Texas	Futch, 1 up				
159	Leo Futch, Pebble Beach, Calif.		Darnell, 1 up, 19 holes			
154	Bobby Darnell, Westminster, Calif.	Darnell, 5 and 3				
159	Hank Ehlebracht, Speedway, Ind.				McMurtrey, 3 and 2	
151	Fred Strebel, Hillsborough, Calif.	Strebel, 4 and 2				
160	Leonard Napoli, Stratford, Conn.		Strebel, 2 and 1			
155	John Kline, Houston, Texas	Kline, 3 and 2				
157	Charles Morgan, St. Louis, Mo.			McMurtrey, 5 and 4		
152	James Key, Columbus, Ga.	Key, 1 up				
160	Morton Howard, Great Neck, N.Y.		McMurtrey, 3 and 1			
155	Frank Tenfel, West Bend, Wis.	McMurtrey, 5 and 4				
157	James McMurtrey, Danville, Calif.					Stevens, 1 up
150	Robert Wylie, Calgary, Alberta, Canada	Wylie, 1 up				
160	Boyd Johnson, Franklin, Tenn.		Wylie, 6 and 5			
156	Robert Hardy, Boynton Beach, Fla.	Murray, 1 up				
157	Daniel Murray, LaVerne, Calif.			Stevens, 4 and 2		
153	Melvin Stevens, Plymouth, Mich.	Stevens, 5 and 3				
159	William Caldwell, III, Midland, Ga.		Stevens, 2 and 1			
154	Tommy Langley, High Point, N.C.	Langley, 1 up, 19 holes				
158	John Woodard, Jr., Surfside Beach, S.C.				Stevens, 1 up, 20 holes	
150	Bob Lowry, Huntsville, Ala.	Lowry, 7 and 5				
160	Bobby Flynn, Lexington, Ky.		Skeadas, 6 and 5			
156	Johnny Skeadas, Savannah, Ga.	Skeadas, 3 and 1				
157	Art Kramer, Horsham, Pa.			Lee, 5 and 4		
153	Anthony Blom, Jr., St. Bernard, Ohio	Blom, 3 and 2				
159	Karl Estes, Ponte Vedra Beach, Fla.		Lee, 2 and 1			
155	Bill Lee, Tulsa, Okla.	Lee, 2 up				
158	James Hutchinson, Accokeek, Md.					
*148	Richard Goerlich, Jr., Tampa, Fla.	Goerlich, 1 up, 19 holes				
161	Dave Dennis, Independence, Kan.		Miller, 6 and 5			
156	Ralph Bogart, Chevy Chase, Md.	Miller, 4 and 3				
156	Bob Miller, Bay Village, Ohio			Miller, 2 and 1		
153	John Owens, Lexington, Ky.	Owens, 1 up, 19 holes				
159	Ronald Moore, Englewood, Colo.		Owens, 3 and 2			
154	Oren Shiro, Waterville, Maine	Cowe, 1 up, 19 holes				
158	Mel Cowe, Halifax, Mass.				Simpson, 4 and 2	
151	Cleston Shaffran, Ypsilanti, Mich.	Williams, 5 and 4				
160	Bo Williams, Ocala, Fla.		Williams, 1 up, 22 holes			
156	Paul Minnich, Bay Village, Ohio	Dadian, 1 up, 20 holes				
157	Archie Dadian, South Milwaukee, Wis.			Simpson, 2 up		
152	James Kite, Jr., Wolftown, Va	McGuiness, 3 and 2				
159	John McGuiness, Des Moines, Iowa		Simpson, 4 and 3			
155	Clyde Wilson, Hot Springs, Ark.	Simpson, 5 and 4				
158	Joe Simpson, San Diego, Calif.					Moore, 4 and 3
150	Clarence Moore, Winnsboro, S.C.	Moore, 6 and 4				
160	Richard Mosman, Dallas, Texas		Moore, 5 and 4			
156	Lewis Oehmig, Lookout Mountain, Tenn.	Oehmig, 1 up, 21 holes				
157	Richard Spangler, Jr., Lincoln, Neb.			Moore, 7 and 5		
153	Dick Estey, Portland, Ore.	Campbell, 1 up				
159	Harold Campbell, Alpharetta, Ga.		Campbell, 6 and 5			
154	George Holland, Seattle, Wash.	Johnson, 1 up				
158	Glenn Johnson, Grosse Ile, Mich.				Moore, 3 and 2	
151	Dick Riley, Phoenix, Ariz.	Kelly, 5 and 4				
160	Donald Kelly, Naples, Fla.		Kelly, 2 and 1			
156	John Powers, Jr., St. Louis, Mo.	Powers, 6 and 4				
157	Pete Dye, Delray, Fla.			Beecroft, 5 and 4		
152	Fordie Pitts, Jr., Scituate, Mass.	Pitts, 1 up				
159	Charles Van Linge, Portola Valley, Calif.		Beecroft, 4 and 3			
155	James Frost, Mercer Island, Wash.	Beecroft, 1 up				
150	Morris Beecroft, Jr., Newport News, Va.					

Clarence Moore, 5 and 4

*Co-Medalists

1989
THIRTY-FIFTH SENIOR AMATEUR CHAMPIONSHIP

Lochinvar Golf Club, Houston, Texas, September 18-23
Yardage—6,510. Par 72. Record 1,508 Entries, 151 Starters, 64 Qualifiers

Qualifying Score	1st Round (18 Holes)	2nd Round (18 Holes)	3rd Round (18 Holes)	4th Round (18 Holes)	Semifinals (18 Holes)	Final (18 Holes)
*147	Frank Tenfel, West Bend, Wis.	Gunn, 3 and 1	Gunn, 2 up	Murray, 3 and 2	Williams, 3 and 2	Williams, 2 and 1
160	Harry Gunn, Olympia Falls, Ill.					
157	Richard Copeland, White Bear Lake, Mn.	Uelmen, 2 and 1				
157	David Uelmen, Mequon, Wis.					
154	Jim Kirk, Ardmore, Okla.	Kirk, 3 and 2	Murray, 3 and 2			
158	Walter Fugate, Macon, Ga.					
154	Daniel Murray, La Verne, Calif.	Murray, 4 and 2				
158	Richard Dalton, St. Louis, Mo.					
152	Sam Hall, Hattiesburg, Miss.	Hall, 3 and 2	Hall, 2 and 1	Williams, 2 and 1		
159	George Martin, Spring Lake Hts, N.J.					
156	Keith Barton, Pleasanton, Calif.	Bratina, 2 up				
158	Bill Bratina, Harrisburg, Pa.					
152	Bo Williams, Ocala, Fla.	Williams, 3 and 2	Williams, 2 and 1			
159	John Campbell, Oskaloosa, Iowa					
156	Milo Novotny, Sequim, Wash.	Kelly, 23 holes				
158	Don Kelly, Ft. Wayne, Ind.					
150	James Rivers, Monroe, La.	Samples, 1 up	Samples, 1 up	Demick, 20 holes	Lowry, 5 and 4	
160	Wayne Samples, Wichita, Kansas					
156	Marshall Trammell, Nashville, Tenn.	Cudd, 21 holes				
157	Bruce Cudd, Portland, Ore.					
153	Frederic Franz, Crystal Lake, Ill.	Demick, 1 up	Demick, 1 up			
159	Paul Demick, Boynton Beach, Fla.					
155	Eddie Pell, Charlotte, N.C.	Pell, 5 and 4				
158	William Brafford, Mesa, Ariz.					
150	Rick Jones, Youngstown, Ohio	Jones, 2 and 1	Jones, 4 and 3	Lowry, 4 and 3		
159	Bill Lee, Tulsa, Okla.					
156	Bud Lucas, Bedford, NY	Lucas, 2 and 1				
157	Edward Barry, Needham, Mass.					
153	Clarence Moore, Winnsboro, S.C.	Mizell, 3 and 2	Lowry, 3 and 2			
159	Wally Mizell, Jacksonville, Fla.					
155	Bob Lowry, Huntsville, Ala.	Lowry, 6 and 5				
158	Wayne Williams, Greenwood, Miss.					
148	Jack Van Ess, Grand Rapids, Mich.	Dearman, 2 up	Cassell, 4 and 2	Simpson, 4 and 2	Simpson, 3 and 2	Simpson, 3 and 2
160	William Dearman, Jackson, Mich.					
157	Melvin Stevens, Plymouth, Mich.	Casell, 19 holes				
157	Dean Cassell, Charlotte, NC					
154	Joe Simpson, San Diego, Calif.	Simpson, 1 up	Simpson, 2 and 1			
158	Bob Miller, Bay Village, Ohio					
155	Lewis Oehmig, Lookout Mountain, Tenn.	Matheson, 19 holes				
158	Don Matheson, Ft. Worth, Texas					
151	Jim McMurtrey, Danville, Calif.	Napoli, 19 holes	Riley, 5 and 4	Jones, 4 and 3		
159	Leonard Napoli, Stratford, Conn.					
156	Jim Morris, Rocky Face, Ga.	Riley, 3 and 1				
158	Dick Riley, Phoenix, Ariz.					
152	Warren Jones, San Mateo, Calif.	Jones, 4 and 2	Jones, 6 and 5			
159	Dean Daugherty, Sister, Ore.					
155	Elliott Phillips, New Albany, Ind.	Gee, 19 holes				
158	E.B. Gee, Blytheville, Ariz.					
150	Fred Strebel, Hillsborough, Calif.	Strebel, 6 and 5	Strebel, 2 and 1	Jones, 2 and 1	Jones 19 holes	
160	Richard Stearns, Ft. Washington, Md.					
157	Chuck Ribelin, Dallas, Texas	Chain, 20 holes				
157	Jerry Chain, Livingston, Texas					
153	Robert Jacobs, Edmonds, Wash.	Jones 3 and 1	Jones, 2 and 1			
158	Amos Jones, Atlanta, Ga.					
155	Philip Kistler, Roanoke, Va.	Kistler, 2 and 1				
158	Robert Bruce, Winnetka, Ill.					
151	Robert Wylie, Calgary, Alberta, Canada	Wylie, 1 up	Wylie, 5 and 4	Mangum, 4 and 3		
159	William Caldwell, Midland, Ga.					
156	Robert Harris, Glenwood, Minn.	Harris, 21 holes				
158	Don Webster, Austin, Texas					
152	Don White, Redmond, Wash.	Eaton, 2 and 1	Mangum, 5 and 3			
159	Robert Eaton, Greeley, Colo.					
155	Richard Mosman, Dallas, Texas	Mangum, 20 holes				
158	James Mangum, New Orleans, La.					

Bo Williams, 19 holes

*Medalist

1990
THIRTY-SIXTH SENIOR AMATEUR CHAMPIONSHIP

Desert Forest Country Club, Carefree, Arizona, October 15-20
Yardage—6,622. Par 72. Record 1,658 Entries, 160 Starters, 64 Qualifiers

Qualifying Score	1st Round (18 Holes)	2nd Round (18 Holes)	3rd Round (18 Holes)	4th Round (18 Holes)	Semifinals (18 Holes)	Final (18 Holes)	
*150	William Godden, Medford, Ore	Godden,					
163	Richard Peterson, Cincinnati, Ohio	4 and 3	Dadian,				
159	William Rodie, Phoenix, Ariz.	Dadian,	2 and 1				
159	Archie Dadian, S. Milwaukee, Wis.	2 and 1		Dadian,			
156	Richard Mosman, Dallas, Texas	Mangan,		1 up			
162	Robert Mangan, Olympia Fields, Ill.	3 and 2	Frost,				
156	Don Webster, Austin, Texas	Frost,	5 and 3				
162	James Frost, Mercer Island, Wash.	2 up			Woodard,		
155	Robert Rankin, Tarpon Springs, Fla.	Rankin,			4 and 3		
163	Robert Wylie, Alberta, Canada	5 and 4	Whitehead,				
159	Jerry Loeber, Locust Valley, N.Y.	Whitehead,	1 up				
160	Ken Whitehead, West Des Moines, Iowa	5 and 4		Woodard,			
155	Ellis Michael, Baton Rouge, La.	Woodard,		3 and 2			
163	John Woodard, Fayetteville, N.C.	1 up	Woodard,				
158	Robert Gunnell, Jamestown, N.Y.	Gunnell,	4 and 3				
161	Robert Hardy, Boynton Beach, Fla.	5 and 4				Clark,	
152	Joe Simpson, San Diego, Calif.	Simpson,				3 and 2	
163	Bob Mandeville, Scottsdale, Ariz.	3 and 2	Clark,				
159	Dennis Iden, Costa Mesa, Calif.	Clark,	21 holes				
160	Bobby Clark, Asheville, N.C.	4 and 3		Clark,			
155	Ed Hopkins, Whitney, Texas	Hopkins,		1 up			
162	Gene Hagen, Sioux City, Iowa	2 and 1	Hopkins,				
158	Paul Demick, Boynton Beach, Fla.	Estey,	3 and 2				
161	Dick Estey, Portland, Ore.	5 and 4			Clark,		
154	Jack Shubert, Altamonte Springs, Fla.	Shubert,			3 and 2		
163	Lewis Oehmig, Lookout Mountain, Tenn.	3 and 2	Veghte,				
159	Jack Veghte, Clearwater, Fla.	Veghte,	7 and 6				
160	Ronald Moore, Englewood, Colo.	1 up		Veghte,			
155	Dave Dennis, Independence, Kan.	Brennan,		2 and 1			
162	James Brennan, Dothan, Ala.	3 and 2	Brennan,				
158	Richard McClear, Birmingham, Mich.	Beecroft,	1 up				
161	Morris Beecroft, Newport News, Va	1 up					Cummings, 3 and 2
151	Bo Williams, Ocala, Fla.	Uebele,					
163	Herman Uebele, Laporte, Ind.	1 up	Kop,				
159	Wendell Kop, Honolulu, Hawaii	Kop,	2 and 1				
159	Leo Spooner, Duluth, Minn.	1 up		Cummings,			
156	Amos Jones, Atlanta, Ga.	Jones,		19 holes			
162	Larry Watts, LaQuinta, Calif.	2 and 1	Cummings,				
157	Jackie Cummings, Tuscaloosa, Ala.	Cummings,	3 and 1				
162	Harold Campbell, Alpharetta, Ga.	4 and 3			Cummings,		
155	Kent Myers, Bend, Ore.	Myers,			2 and 1		
163	Jack Flatt, Tempe, Ariz.	3 and 2	Moore,				
159	Clarence Moore, Winnsboro, S.C.	Moore,	4 and 3				
160	Robert Jacobs, Edmonds, Wash.	4 and 3		Moore,			
155	Frank Boydston, Phoenix, Ariz.	Boydston,		2 and 1			
163	John Loss, Burr Ridge, Ill.	20 holes	Boydston,				
158	Charles Green, Scotland	Ladin,	4 and 3				
161	Paul Ladin, Westlake Village, Calif.	3 and 2				Cummings,	
152	Rick Jones, Youngstown, Ohio	Jones,				3 and 2	
163	Jerry Fehr, Seattle, Wash.	2 and 1	Jones,				
159	John Procter, Carrollton, Texas	Procter,	2 up				
160	Joseph Estes, Atlanta, Ga.	5 and 4		Jones,			
156	Fred Strebel, Hillsborough, Calif.	Strebel		7 and 5			
162	Thomas Watrous, Birmingham, Mich.	3 and 1	Strebel,				
158	Paul Minnich, Bay Village, Ohio	Minnich,	4 and 3				
161	Joe Eason, Houston, Texas	4 and 3			Jones		
154	Dean Daugherty, Sisters, Ore.	Sullivan,			2 and 1		
163	Jeremiah Sullivan, Richfield, Wis.	3 and 2	Pell,				
159	Fordie Pitts, Scituate, Mass.	Pell,	6 and 5				
160	Eddie Pell, Charlotte, N.C.	2 and 1		McMurtrey,			
155	Jim McMurtrey, Danville, Calif.	McMurtrey,		4 and 3			
163	Maurice Oakes, Gretna, Va.	1 up	McMurtrey,				
158	Daniel Murray, LaVerne, Calif.	Murray,	by default				
161	Vaughn Barker, Murray, Utah	2 up					

*Medalist

SENIOR WOMEN'S AMATEUR CHAMPIONSHIP

Championship Trophy

Presented in October 1962 by the

United States Golf Association and Friends of Senior Golf

HISTORY

1981—Mrs. Mark A. Porter, 57, of Cinnaminson, New Jersey, won her second consecutive Senior Women's Amateur Championship and the third of the last five years with a 54-hole score of 238, 19 over par, at the Spring Lake (New Jersey) Golf Club. Mrs. Porter also had won in 1977 and 1980. Her rounds of 81-80-77 gave her a four stroke winning margin over Mrs. Paul Dye, Jr., the 1978 and 1979 Champion, who had a 242 total on rounds of 80-80-82. Both players are past members of the U.S. Curtis Cup team. Tied for third at 244 were Helen Sigel Wilson, another former Curtis Cup player and non-playing captain, and Mildred Stanley. Alberta Bower, the 1975 Champion, finished fifth at 247. Mrs. Porter, who was the 1949 Women's Amateur Champion, has now won two national titles 32 years apart, a USGA record. She also continues as the only golfer to win both the Women's Amateur and Senior Women's Amateur Championships and now belongs to a select group of 11 golfers who have won four or more USGA championships. The scores were unusually high because of the cold, windy conditions which persisted throughout the week. Mrs. Robert Ihlanfeldt was the first round leader with a 79, six over par. Five players were just one stroke back at 80: Mrs. Dye, Mrs. Bower, Mrs. Betty Probasco, Mrs. Louise Wilson and Mrs. Kathryn Salley. At 81, two strokes behind were Mrs. Porter and Mrs. Helen Sigel Wilson. After two rounds, Mrs. Dye took over the lead with a total of 160. A trio of players were one behind at 161 including Mrs. Helen Sigel Wilson, Mrs. Porter and Mrs. Ihlanfeldt. On the final day, Mrs. Dye was in control early. Helped by a birdie at the 8th hole, Mrs. Dye held a two stroke lead going into the final nine holes. However, Mrs. Porter matched par 37 on the final nine, including a birdie at the par-3 16th and a bogey at the par-5 17th where she three-putted. Mrs. Dye faltered with three bogeys and one double bogey on the final four holes and none of the other players could mount a serious challenge down the stretch. Mrs. Porter's closing round of 77 matched a second round 77 by Mrs. Lois Hodge as the best of the championship. Mrs. Dye was the champion of Group I (ages 50-54) and Mrs. Porter again was Group II champion (55-59). Mrs. Helen Wilson was Group III champion (60-64) and Mrs. Ann Gregory won her third successive Group IV Championship (65 and over). The USGA received 113 entries, far short of the record 186 received in 1980.

1982—Mrs. Robert Ihlanfeldt, 52, of Seattle, Washington, became the first Pacific Northwest resident to win the Senior Women's Amateur Championship, shooting a 54-hole score of 232, 13 over par, at Kissing Camels Golf Club, in Colorado Springs, Colorado. Mrs. Ihlanfeldt won by four strokes over Mrs. Mary Ann Morrison, of Houston, Texas, and by eight over Mrs. Betty Probasco, captain of the 1982 U.S. Curtis Cup Team, from Lookout Mountain, Tennessee. Mrs. Mark A. Porter, of Cinnaminson, New Jersey, the defending champion and winner of three of the last five, was unable to defend her title because of an injury. The first round produced a three-way tie for the lead between Mrs. Ihlanfeldt, Mrs. Morrison, and Mrs. Lois Hodge, of San Jose, California, all at 77, four over par. Mrs. Ihlanfeldt took a one-stroke lead over Mrs. Morrison and a two-stroke advantage over Mrs. Hodge with 80 the second day, as winds pushed the temperature to freezing. Mrs. Ihlanfeldt took command the third day, playing the first seven holes in one under par to open a five-stroke lead. She shot two-over-par 75, but she was never threatened. Mrs. Morrison had 78 for 236, while Mrs. Hodge, who was bothered by a bad back the entire week, shot 84 and tied for fourth, at 243, with 1978 and 1979 Champion Mrs. Paul Dye, Jr., of Delray Beach, Florida. Mrs. Probasco had 74, the lowest 18-hole score of the Championship, to finish third, at 240. Mrs. Ihlanfeldt was the Champion of Group I (ages 50-54), and Mrs. Dye was Group II Champion (55-59). Mrs. Nancy Black, of Greenbush, Massachusetts, was Group III Champion (60-64), and Mrs. Edith Paffard, of Sewickley, Pennsylvania, was Group IV Champion (65 and older). Mrs. Morrison and Mrs. Hodge completed an unusual triple by competing in the Senior Women's Amateur. They previously competed in the U.S. Women's Open and U.S. Women's Amateur earlier in the year. The USGA received 154 entries, short of the record 186 received for the 1980 Championship at Sea Island (Georgia) Golf Club.

1983—Mrs. Mark A. Porter, 59, of Cinnaminson, New Jersey, won her fourth Senior Women's Amateur Championship and her fifth USGA title with a 54-hole score of 234, at the Gulph Mills Golf Club, in King of Prussia, Pennsylvania. It was Mrs. Porter's third consecutive victory in the Senior Women's Amateur. She had missed the 1982 Championship because of an injury. Her previous victories were in 1977, 1980, and 1981. Winner of the 1949 U.S. Women's Amateur, Mrs. Porter had therefore won championships 34 years apart. This is a USGA record. She also moved within one Senior Women's Amateur Championship of Mrs. Carolyn Cudone's record of five, won consecutively between 1968 and 1972. The first-round leader was

Ms. Jean Thomas of Phoenix, Arizona, who shot 77, two strokes ahead of Mrs. Lois Hodge, of San Jose, California. Mrs. Edean Ihlanfeldt, the defending Champion, from Seattle, Washington, was tied for third, at 81, with Ms. Natalie Gamble, of Grosse Pointe Shores, Michigan, Ms. Eugenia Slaymaker (Gulph Mills women's Champion 14 times), of Villanova, Pennsylvania; and Mrs. Ceil Maclaurin, of Savannah, Georgia. Mrs. Porter opened with 83, marred by a triple-bogey 8 at the third hole. After shooting 77 in the second round, Mrs. Porter shared the lead with Mrs. Hodge, at 160, two strokes ahead of Mrs. Thomas and Mrs. Albert Bower, the 1975 Champion, from Charleston, South Carolina. Mrs. Slaymaker, Mrs. Gamble, and Ms. Barbara Young, of Westport, Connecticut, were tied at 165. Mrs. Porter shot 74 in the final round and opened an eight-stroke margin over Mrs. Hodge, who finished with 82. Mrs. Bower closed with 84 and finished third, 12 strokes back. Mrs. Porter had nine one-putt greens, for total of 27 putts. The key hole was the third, where Mrs. Porter reached the green in two with a 4-wood second and holed an 18-inch putt for an eagle 3. Mrs. Hodge was the Champion of Group I (ages 50-54), Mrs. Porter won Group II (ages 55-59), Mrs. Bower won Group III (ages 60-64), and Mrs. Ann Gregory, of Gary Indiana, won Group IV (ages 65 and above) for the fourth time. Mrs. Maureen Garrett, President of the Ladies' Golf Union of Great Britain and recipient of the 1983 USGA Bob Jones Award, attended the Championship. The USGA accepted 143 entries.

1984—Mrs. Constance Guthrie, 50, of Spokane, Washington, shot 227 for 54 holes and won by two strokes over Mrs. Janice Calin, of Edina, Minnesota, at the Tacoma Country and Golf Club, in Tacoma, Washington. The first-round lead was shared by Mrs. Lois Hodge, of Los Altos, California, and Mrs. Louise Wilson, of Louisville, Kentucky, both of whom shot 73, two strokes better than Mrs. Natalie Gamble, of Grosse Pointe Shores, Michigan, and Mrs. Alberta Bower, of Charleston, South Carolina. Mrs. Guthrie shot 76 with an eagle 3 on the 18th hole. Mrs. Guthrie moved strongly into the picture with 73 in the second round and shared the lead with Mrs. Calin. A 70 boosted Mrs. Calin into the tie and equalled the Championship's record low round, set in 1979 by Mrs. Paul Dye, Jr. At the end of nine holes of the final round, Mrs. Guthrie held a two stroke lead, and despite some shaky play on the fifth and sixth holes, both par-3s, still led by four after 10. On the 11th, a par 3, Mrs. Guthrie's tee shot plugged deep in a bunker, and when she made 5, Mrs. Calin pulled even. Mrs. Calin then four-putted the 12th hole and Mrs. Guthrie went ahead by two once again. Mrs. Dorothy Porter, four times the Senior Women's Amateur champion, finished third, at 231, tied with Mrs. Wilson. Mrs. Gamble was fifth, at 233. Mrs. Porter was the Group C (ages 60 through 64) champion; Mrs. Gamble won Group B (55 through 59); and Mrs. Helen M. Johnson, of Tacoma, Washington, won Group D (65 and over).

1985—Marlene Streit, 51, of Stouffville, Ontario, Canada, shot 224 for 54 holes to defeat Louise Wilson of Louisville, Kentucky, by three strokes at the Sheraton Savannah Resort and Country Club in Savannah, Georgia. Streit became the second golfer ever to win the Women's Amateur and Senior Women's Amateur. Dorothy Porter was the first to win both championships. Streit shot a two-under-par 70 in the opening round to take a three-stroke lead over Janice Calin of Edina, Minnesota, and Mrs. Dick Kaufman of San Antonio, Texas. Streit's round tied the Championship record set by Alice Dye in 1979 and tied by Calin last year. In the second round, Mildred Stanley of Escondido, California, shot a round of even-par 72 to gain a share of the lead with Streit. Four-time champion Dorothy Porter recorded her second consecutive round of two-over-par 74 to pull to within two strokes of the lead. Streit opened the final round with three pars to three bogeys for Stanley but could not build on that lead in the ensuing holes. At the 12th hole, Stanley had come back to within two strokes of the lead. Stanley bogeyed the 13th and double-bogeyed the 14th, however, and fell out of contention. Her round of 82 left her in a tie for third place. Streit finished with a round of 78. Wilson shot 76 to finish alone in second place. Stanley, Porter and 1984 Champion Constance Guthrie, who posted a final-round 72 (the best round of the day by four strokes) finished tied for third at 228. Streit was the winner for Group 1 (ages 50-54); Wilson was the Group 2 (ages 55-59) champion; Porter won Group 3 (ages 60-64) and Ruth White Miller of Placentia, California was the winner in Group 4 (ages 65 and over). The USGA received 184 entries for the Championship.

1986—Constance Guthrie, 52, of Spokane, Washington, shot 225 for 54 holes to win at Lakewood Golf Club in Point Clear, Alabama. Guthrie won her second Senior Women's Amateur win in three years. Marlene Streit of Stouffville, Ontario, Canada, the 1985 champion; Ceil Maclaurin of Savannah, Georgia, the 1976 winner; and Barbara Young of Westport, Connecticut, were tied for second, six strokes back. Guthrie took the first-round lead by shooting 73, one over par, three better than Maclaurin and Mary Jones of Champaign, Illinois. Guthrie faltered early in the second round, playing the first nine in 41. She came back in 35 and retained her three-stroke lead. Barbara McIntire's 72 gave her a 36-hole total of 152 and second place. June Mayson of nearby Mobile was alone in third, one stroke behind McIntire. No one challenged Guthrie on the final day. The 1984 champion shot another 76 to win the championship. McIntire's 83 left her 10 strokes back. Streit, who opened with an 83, rebounded with rounds of 75 and 73 to finish in the second-place tie. Guthrie was the winner for Group 1 (ages 50-54); Lois Hodge won Group 2 (ages 55-59); Maclaurin won Group 3 (ages 60-64); and Virginia Jarvis won Group 4 (ages 65 and above). The USGA received 137 entries for the championship.

SENIOR WOMEN'S AMATEUR CHAMPIONSHIP

1987—Anne Sander, 50, of Seattle, Washington, shot rounds of 72-80-76—228 to win the championship by three strokes over Harriet Hart of Ridgefield, Connecticut, and eight strokes over Charlotte Wood of Beaumont, Texas. The win was Sander's fourth in a USGA competition. She won the Women's Amateur in 1958, 1961 and 1963. Sander shot a two-under-par 72 in the first round, which was played on a day that featured heavy rain and gusty winds. She led Wood and Millie Zimring by five strokes. Sander was seven over par through six holes of the second round, but was one under par the rest of the way for a round of 80. Zimring's second 77 pulled her to within two strokes at 154. Hart stood another stroke back at 78-77—155. After parring the first hole of the final round, Zimring lost six strokes over the next five and fell from contention. Hart had cut Sander's lead to one stroke after six holes. The margin was still one after 11 holes. Sander then birdied the 12th and picked up another stroke when Hart bogeyed the 13th. Sander parred in for a three-stroke victory. Sander was the Group 1 winner (ages 50-54). Lois Hodge won Group 2 (ages 55-59), shooting 247; Dot Porter won Group 3 (ages 60-64) with a 245 total; and Helen Sigel Wilson won Group 4 (ages 65 and over) with 251. The USGA accepted 136 entries for the championship.

1988—Lois Hodge, 57, of Los Altos, California, shot rounds of 77-76-75—228 to win the championship by one stroke over 1985 Champion Marlene Streit of Stouffville, Ontario, Canada, and by two strokes over Harriet Hart of Ponte Vedra, Florida. Hodge had been runner-up in the 1983 championship. Belle Robertson, of Glasgow, Scotland, birdied four consecutive holes on the first nine in shooting two-over-par 75 to take the lead after the first round. She was two strokes ahead of Hodge, Hart and Joan Comisar of Cincinnati. Robertson bogeyed four consecutive holes early in the second round and fell from the lead. Four-time champion Dorothy Porter of Cinnaminson, New Jersey, shot the best round of the second day, a 75, to earn a share of the 36-hole lead. Her total of 153 tied her with Hart and Hodge, who each shot 77-76. Anne Sander of Seattle, Washington, the 1987 champion, was one stroke behind. After playing the first nine in 35, Hart held a three-stroke lead, but a double-bogey at the 10th and a bogey at the 11th left her tied with Hodge. The two remained tied, with Streit one stroke behind, until Hart drove into the water on the 17th and made another bogey. She also bogeyed the 18th to finish in third place. Hodge, playing a group ahead of Hart, parred the final five holes to secure the victory. Streit was the Group 1 winner (ages 50-54). Hodge won Group 2 (ages 55-59); Dot Porter won Group 3 (ages 60-64) with a 232 total; and Alberta Bower, the 1975 champion won Group 4 (ages 65 and over) with 238. The USGA accepted 182 entries for the championship.

1989—Anne Sander, a 52-year old career amateur, easily won the U.S. Senior Women's Amateur Championship, shooting 75-74-75-224, at the Tournament Players Course, in The Woodlands, Texas. She was so dominant that she held a 12-stroke lead with nine holes to play, and won by nine strokes over Alice Dye, of Delray Beach, Florida. Mrs. Dye, posted a score of 233, including a 75 in the final round. She birdied the final hole to prevent Mrs. Sander from winning by the largest margin in the event's 28-year history. Mrs. Sander, of Seattle, Washington, was one of eight former champions in the field. She had also won three Women's Amateur championships. Mrs. Sander went ahead in the second round, passing Betty Probasco, from Lookout Mountain, Tennessee, who had celebrated her 60th birthday by shooting a 73 in the first round. Mrs. Sander started slowly, with 41 for her first nine holes. She came back in 34, on the second, and played every nine holes in the 30s the rest of the way. Mrs. Dye, herself a two-time champion, easily won the 60-64 age group. The other two age bracket winners were former champions as well. Marlene Streit, the champion in 1985, won in the 55-59 age group, and Dorothy Porter, who had won four senior women's titles, won the 65-and-up age bracket.

1990—Anne Sander, of Seattle, Washington, made up five strokes in the last round, caught Marlene Streit, and then won the 18-hole playoff, at Del Rio Golf and Country Club, in Modesto. It was the second consecutive Senior Women's championship for Mrs. Sander, 53. She scrambled back into contention after an opening round of 80, then shot one-under-par 71 in the final round to tie Mrs. Streit at 225 for the 54 holes of regulation play. Mrs. Streit holed a 15-foot putt to par the final hole and force the playoff the next day. Mrs. Sander won by six strokes, 72-78, as she holed birdie putts from 10, 20, and 60 feet. She was seven strokes ahead with six holes to play. Mrs. Streit, of Ontario, Canada, led after the first and second rounds, shooting 72-77—149. Mary Ann Morrison, of Dubois, Wyoming, finished one stroke behind the leaders, at 226. While Mrs. Sander won the 50-54 age bracket, and Mrs. Streit the 55-59 division, Mildred Stanley captured the 60-64 age bracket, and Dorothy Porter was the winner among those 65 and over.

SENIOR WOMEN'S AMATEUR CHAMPIONSHIP

DATE	WINNER, RUNNER-UP	SCORE	SITE	ENTRY
1981 (Sept.-Oct.)	Mrs. Mark A. Porter	238	Spring Lake G.C.,	113
	Mrs. Paul Dye, Jr.	242	Spring Lake, N.J.	
1982 (Sept.-Oct.)	Mrs. Robert Ihlanfeldt	232	Kissing Camels G.C.,	154
	Mrs. Gary E. Morrison	236	Colorado Springs, Colo.	
1983 (Sept.)	Mrs. Mark A. Porter	234	Gulph Mills G.C.,	
	Mrs. Lois Hodge	242	King of Prussia, Pa.	
1984 (Sept.)	Mrs. Constance Guthrie	227	Tacoma C. & G.C.,	131
	Mrs. Janice Calin	229	Tacoma, Wash.	
1985 (Sept.)	Mrs. J. Douglas Streit	226	Sheraton Savannah Resort	184
	Mrs. Louise Wilson	228	& C.C.,	
			Savannah, Ga.	
1986 (Sept.)	Mrs. Constance Guthrie	225	Lakewood G.C.,	137
	Mrs. J. Douglas Streit	231	Point Clear, Ala.	
	Mrs. Barbara Young	231		
	Mrs. Cecile H. Maclaurin	231		
1987 (Sept.-Oct.)	Mrs. Anne Quast Sander	228	Manufacturers' G. & C.C.,	136
	Mrs. Harriet Hart	231	Oreland, Pa.	
1988 (Sept.)	Mrs. Lois Hodge	228	Sea Island G.C.,	184
	Mrs. J. Douglas Streit	229	Sea Island, Ga.	
1989 (Oct.)	Mrs. Anne Sander	224	Tournament Players Course,	119
	Mrs. Alic Dye	233	The Woodlands, Tex.	
1990 (Sept.)	Mrs. Anne Sander	225-72	Del Rio G. & C.C.,	133
	Mrs. Marlene Streit	225-78	Modesto, Calif.	

1981
TWENTIETH SENIOR WOMEN'S AMATEUR CHAMPIO

Spring Lake Golf Club, Spring Lake, New Jersey, September 30-October 2
Yardage—5,903. Par 73. 113 Entries, 101 Starters.

Letters preceding names denote age groups for supplementary prize competition, as follows:
A—50 through 54 years; B—55 through 59 years; C—60 through 64 years; D—65 and over.
All starters eligible for all three rounds. The 65 low scores:

						Score
1	B	Mrs. Mark A. (Dorothy) Porter, Cinnaminson, N.J.	81	80	77	238
2	A	Mrs. Paul (Alice O.) Dye, Jr., Delray Beach, Fla.	80	80	82	242
3	A	Mrs. Mildred M. Stanley, Los Angeles, Calif.	83	81	80	244
	C	Mrs. Helen Sigel Wilson, Gladwyn, Pa.	81	80	83	244
5	B	Mrs. Albert B. (Alberta L.) Bower, Pelham, N.Y.	80	82	85	247
6	A	Mrs. Thomas (Lois) Hodge, San Jose, Calif.	89	77	82	248
	A	Mrs. Gaines, P. (Louise) Wilson, Jr., Louisville, Ky.	80	83	85	248
8	A	Mrs. Robert (Edean) Ihlanfeldt, Seattle, Wash.	79	82	90	251
9	A	Mrs. Scott L. (Betty) Probasco, Jr., Lookout Mountain, Tenn.	80	92	82	254
	A	Dr. Joanne Whitaker, Crystal Beach, Fla.	85	84	85	254
	B	Mrs. Laura M. Cann, Mill Valley, Calif.	85	82	87	254
12	B	Mrs. I. Wayne (Nancy) Rutter, Williamsville, N.Y.	85	84	86	255
13	A	Miss Nancy G. Hollenbeck, Arlington, Va.	85	89	82	256
	B	Mrs. Robert H. (Cecile) MacLaurin, Savannah, Ga.	85	83	88	256
15	A	Miss Harriet Glanville, Long Beach, Calif.	87	87	83	257
	B	Mrs. John Germain, Houston, Texas	86	84	87	257
	A.	Mrs. Charlotte C. Neslie, Willow Grove, Pa.	82	85	90	257
18	A	Mrs. Janice Vining, Willowdale, Ontario, Canada	87	87	84	258
	D	Mrs. Ann Gregory, Gary, Ind.	86	86	86	258
	A	Mrs. Walton B. Horton, Beaufort, S.C.	90	82	86	258
21	A	Mrs. Joan Comisar, Cincinnati, Ohio	94	84	81	259
	C	Mrs. Paul G. (Nancy) Black, Greenbush, Mass.	94	81	84	259
	B	Mrs. Frank E. Richart, Ann Arbor, Mich.	93	81	85	259
	A	Mrs. Julian A. (Kathryn W.) Salley, Columbia, S.C.	80	89	90	259
25	A	Mrs. Andrew (Sara) Sage, Locust Valley, N.Y.	92	83	85	260
	B	Mrs. Nancy MacGibbon, Minnetonka, Minn.	85	90	85	260
	B	Mrs. Juanita Petrone, Blacksburg, Va.	83	91	86	260
	A	Mrs. Beverly A. Vanstrum, White Bear Lake, Minn.	87	83	90	260
	A	Mrs. Sheila Hopkins, Clover, S.C.	85	83	92	260
30	C	Mrs. William E. (Maxine) Gilmore, Vienna, W. Va.	84	89	89	262
31	A	Mrs. John B. Whitacre, Jr., Canton, Ohio	90	91	83	264
	B	Mrs. A.F. (Louise) Munro, Greenwich, Conn.	92	86	86	264
	B	Miss Carol Beinbrink, Stony Brook, N.Y.	87	88	89	264
34	A	Mrs. J.J. (S.) Kessler, Oshawa, Ontario, Canada	91	91	83	265
35	C	Mrs. Ruth W. Miller, Long Beach, Calif.	88	91	87	266
36	B	Mrs. Fay DeRuvo, Hudson, Mass.	89	89	89	267
	A	Mrs. Juanita Jones, Amarillo, Texas	87	92	88	267
	B	Mrs. J. Lewis (Mary Helen) Rawls, Jr., Suffolk, Va.	95	83	89	267
39	A	Mrs. Elizabeth Wren, Williamsburg, Va.	92	89	87	268
	B	Mrs. Edna A. Trombley, Dallas, Texas	95	86	87	268
	B	Mrs. Gordon (Grace M.) McGrath, Glen Head, N.Y.	90	86	92	268
42	A	Mrs. Rita Houston, Green Bay, Wis.	92	89	88	269
	D	Mrs. Frederick C. (Edith R.) Pafford, Jr., Sewickley, Pa.	90	90	89	269
	C	Mrs. W.W. Forsman, St. Louis, Mo.	87	90	92	269
45	A	Mrs. Edie Creed, Schomberg, Ontario, Canada	94	94	83	271
	C	Mrs. Raymond F. Moreland, Pittsburgh, Pa.	91	86	94	271
	A	Mrs. Betty Halloran, Paramus, N.J.	88	88	95	271
	A	Mrs. Anne Ravinski, Norfolk, Mass.	83	90	98	271
49	D	Mrs. Ann Griffel, Eldora, Iowa	98	88	86	272
	B	Miss Erma D. Keyes, Lancaster, Pa.	88	97	87	272
	A	Mrs. Grace E. Lenahan, Buffalo, N.Y.	91	87	94	272
52	A	Mrs. Frank H. (Jane G.) Featherston, Charlottesville, Va.	90	91	92	273
	C	Mrs. Kathryn L. Anhalt, Manitowoc, Wis.	89	90	94	273
	C	Mrs. Justine B. Cushing, Glen Head, N.Y.	85	92	96	273
55	D	Mrs. Patricia Stiming, Camarillo, Calif.	87	96	91	274
56	A	Mrs. Mary P. Merwin, Lauderdale, Fla.	94	91	90	275
	B	Mrs. Aldora Lucchesi, Modesto, Calif.	90	94	91	275
58	B	Mrs. Jean Hitchcock, Hingham, Mass.	89	94	93	276
	B	Mrs. Gretchen R. Gayton, Brookfield, Ohio	89	91	96	276
60	C	Miss Mary Lou Conner, Annandale, Va.	96	90	91	277
	C	Mrs. Jimmy A. Thompson, Montebello, Calif.	89	93	95	277
	A	Mrs. John B. Eshelman, Lancaster, Pa.	90	88	99	277
63	B	Mrs. Constance D. Lewis, Fairfield, Conn.	93	95	91	279
	A	Mrs. Colleen Carmichael, Toronto, Ontario, Canada	89	98	92	279
	A	Mrs. Lucille Penner, Virginia Beach Va.	94	90	95	279

1982
TWENTY-FIRST SENIOR WOMEN'S AMATEUR CHAMPIONSHIP

Kissing Camels Golf Club, Colorado Springs, Colorado, September 29 - October 1.
Yardage — 6,110. Par 73. 154 Entries, 120 Starters.

Letters preceding names denote age groups for supplementary prize competition, as follows:
A — 50 through 54 years; B — 55 through 59 years; C — 60 through 64 years; D — 65 and over.
All starters eligible for all three rounds. The 64 low scores:

						Score
1	A	Mrs. Robert Ihlanfeldt, Seattle, Wash.	77	80	75	232
2	A	Mrs. Gary E. Morrison, Houston, Texas	77	81	78	236
3	A	Mrs. Scott L. Probasco, Jr., Lookout Mountain, Tenn.	81	85	74	240
4	B	Mrs. Paul Dye, Delray Beach, Fla.	83	81	79	243
	A	Mrs. Thomas Hodge, San Jose, Calif.	77	82	84	243
6	A	Mrs. Mildred M. Stanley, Los Angeles, Calif.	81	85	78	244
7	A	Mrs. Louise Wilson, Louisville, Ky.	83	81	82	246
8	A	Mrs. Kathryn W. Salley, Columbia, S.C.	79	87	83	249
	A	Mrs. Sara W. Sage, Locust Valley, N.Y.	79	85	85	249
10	C	Mrs. Paul G. Black, Cohasset, Mass.	82	86	82	250
11	B	Mrs. Robert Maclaurin, Savannah, Ga.	89	81	81	251
12	A	Mrs. Gwen Oldaker, Calabasas Park, Calif.	85	89	79	253
	B	Mrs. Natalie Gamble, Grosse Pointe Shores, Mich.	78	89	86	253
14	A	Mrs. Joyce B. Mahoney, Springfield, Mo.	84	87	83	254
	A	Miss Nancy G. Hollenbeck, Arlington, Va.	84	86	84	254
	A	Mrs. Jan Calin, St. Paul, Minn.	82	85	87	254
17	B	Mrs. Phyllis LaSorella, Pebble Beach, Calif.	87	82	86	255
18	C	Mrs. Ruth White Miller, Whittier, Calif.	89	83	84	256
19	B	Mrs. Jean W. Hester, Cookeville, Tenn.	83	89	85	257
20	B	Dr. Joanne Whitaker, Tarpon Springs, Fla.	84	89	85	258
	A	Mrs. Walton B. Horton, Beaufort, S.C.	88	85	85	258
	C	Mrs. Peggy Patch, Lafayette, Calif.	85	87	86	258
	A	Mrs. Jody Gumlia, Edina, Minn.	84	85	89	258
24	D	Mrs. Frederick C. Paffard, Sewickley, Pa.	90	87	83	260
	B	Mrs. Shirley T. Baty, Tacoma, Wash.	83	91	86	260
26	B	Mrs. John H. Germain, Houston, Texas	81	95	85	261
	D	Mrs. William L. Mosher, Jr., West Bloomfield, Mich.	89	84	88	261
28	B	Mrs. Edna Trombley, Dallas, Texas	88	90	84	262
	A	Mrs. Herbert Fleming, Carmel, Calif.	89	86	87	262
	A	Miss Jean E. Kirkman, Burlington, N.C.	85	89	88	262
	D	Mrs. James A. Roessler, San Jose, Calif.	87	86	89	262
	C	Mrs. Claude Beeler, Oklahoma City, Okla.	84	88	90	262
33	C	Ms. Mary Hoffman, Springfield, Mo.	92	97	85	264
	C	Mrs. Jimmy A. Thompson, Whittier, Calif.	96	85	83	264
	B	Mrs. George Nowotny, Tulsa, Okla.	91	89	84	264
	C	Mrs. Jane Hibbard, Cascade, Mont.	85	94	85	264
	B	Mrs. Nancy L. MacGibbon, Minnetonka, Minn.	90	89	85	264
	A	Mrs. Kathleen Fiorella, Denver, Colo.	90	37	87	264
39	C	Mrs. George B. Campbell, Portland, Ore.	87	91	87	265
	B	Mrs. Ricardo M. Senteno, Roswell, N.M.	89	89	87	265
	A	Mrs. Marilyn M. Wolfe, Longmont, Colo.	84	89	92	265
42	C	Mrs. Beatrice C. McKee, Grosse Pointe Shores, Mich.	84	92	90	266
43	A	Mrs. Velma Thomas, La Quinta, Calif.	91	91	85	267
	A	Mrs. Ormand Birkland, Denver, Colo.	90	90	87	267
45	B	Mrs. Rita Houston, Green Bay, Wis.	89	92	87	268
	A	Mrs. Roland Bryant, Santee, S.C.	85	95	88	268
47	B	Mrs. Marg Georgenson, La Habra, Calif.	89	92	88	269
	C	Mrs. William E. Gilmore, Vienna, W.Va.	94	86	89	269
49	A	Mrs. Juanita Jones, Amarillo, Texas	88	96	86	270
	B	Mrs. Anne F. Gookin, Monument, Colo.	96	88	86	270
	B	Mrs. Richard Wright, Laredo, Texas	90	93	87	270
	B	Miss Carol Beinbrink, St. James, N.Y.	93	89	88	270
	B	Mrs. Betty Crittendon, Norman, Okla.	88	87	95	270
54	B	Mrs. Mary Lou Frazier, Albuquerque, N.M.	88	94	89	271
	C	Mrs. Charles T. Eckstrom, Tacoma, Wash.	93	88	90	271
56	B	Mrs. Jean Flockenzier, Mansfield, Ohio	90	92	90	272
	A	Miss Joanne E. Yonker, Denver, Colo.	87	92	93	272
58	B	Mrs. Laura M. Cann, Mill Valley, Calif.	90	96	87	273
	D	Mrs. Robert W. Stimming, Camarillo, Calif.	91	94	88	273
	D	Mrs. Ann Gregory, Gary, Ind.	90	92	91	273
61	A	Mrs. Roger R. Linson, Normandy, Mo.	93	94	87	274
	A	Mrs. Emily Borba, Upland, Calif.	92	91	91	274
63	B	Mrs. Fay De Ruvo, Hudson, Mass.	92	92	91	275
	B	Mrs. Charles Stimson, Rancho Santa Fe, Calif.	91	92	92	275

1983
TWENTY-SECOND SENIOR WOMEN'S AMATEUR CHAMPIONSHIP

Gulph Mills Golf Club, King of Prussia, Pennsylvania, September 28-30
Yardage—5,816. Par 74. 143 Entries, 120 Starters.

Letters preceding names denote age groups for supplementary prize competition, as follows:
A—50 through 54 years; B—55 through 59 years; C—60 through 64 years; D—65 and over.
All starters eligible for all three rounds. The 65 low scores:

						Score
1	B	Mrs. Dorothy G. Porter, Cinnaminson, N.J.	83	77	74	234
2	A	Mrs. Thomas Hodge, San Jose, Calif.	79	81	82	242
3	C	Mrs. Alberta L. Bower, Charleston, S.C.	81	81	84	246
	A	Mrs. Jean Thomas, Phoenix, Ariz.	77	85	84	246
5	B	Mrs. Cecile MacLaurin, Savannah, Ga.	81	87	79	247
	A	Mrs. Edean A. Ihlanfeldt, Seattle, Wash.	81	86	80	247
7	A	Ms. Barbara P. Young, Westport, Conn.	83	82	83	248
8	A	Mrs. Joan Comisar, Cincinnati, Ohio	84	84	84	252
	A	Ms. Sylvia Marlio, Marion, MA.	83	84	85	252
10	B	Mrs. Alice Dye, Delray Beach, Fla.	86	83	84	253
	B	Mrs. Natalie Gamble, Grosse Point Shores, Mich.	81	84	88	253
12	A	Mrs. Gary Morrison, Houston, Texas	84	88	82	254
	B	Mrs. Eugenia Slaymaker, Villanova, Pa.	81	84	89	254
14	A	Mrs. Shiela Hopkins, Lake Wylie, S.C.	87	79	89	255
15	C	Mrs. Helen S. Wilson, Gladwyne, Pa.	83	88	88	259
	B	Mrs. Pauline F. Whitacre, Canton, Ohio	90	81	88	259
17	C	Mrs. Dorothy S. Campbell, Portland, Ore.	84	90	86	260
	A	Mrs. Sue Kessler, Oshawa, Ont., Canada	89	89	72	260
19	B	Mrs. Lee B. Hilkene, Birmingham, Mich.	82	91	89	262
	A	Mrs. Joseph K. Gordon, Haverford, Pa.	83	88	91	262
	A	Mrs. Frances F. Stearns, Poughkeepsie, N.Y.	86	81	95	262
22	A	Mrs. Janice Calin, Edina, Minn.	85	86	92	263
23	B	Mrs. Sara W. Sage, Locust Valley, N.Y.	84	89	91	264
	A	Mrs. Mary Jane King, Newport News, Va.	87	84	93	264
25	A	Ms. Ann A. Richmond, Toronto, Ont., Canada	86	89	90	265
	C	Mrs. Paul G. Black, Hingham, Mass.	89	86	90	265
27	B	Ms. Monica L. LaCroix, Burlington, Vt.	89	87	90	266
28	C	Mrs. Grace M. McGrath, Glen Head, N.Y.	88	88	91	267
	A	Mrs. Walton B. Horton, Beaufort, S.C.	88	87	92	267
	C	Mrs. Annette C. Kane, Flourtown, Pa.	93	87	87	267
	A	Miss Nancy G. Hollenbeck, Annandale, Va.	92	86	89	267
32	C	Mrs. Ruth White Miller, Long Beach, Calif.	91	83	94	268
	B	Mrs. Dena M. Nowotny, Tulsa, Okla.	89	84	95	268
	B	Ms. Susan Rakestraw, Chester Springs, Pa.	89	91	88	268
	B	Mrs. Charlotte E. Neslie, Willow Grove, Pa.	86	91	91	268
36	C	Mrs. Nancy W. Rutter, Williamsville, N.Y.	92	84	93	269
	B	Mrs. Phyllis Germain, Houston, Texas	88	91	90	269
	B	Miss Erma D. Keyes, Lancaster, Pa.	91	89	89	269
39	B	Mrs. Nancy MacGibbon, Minnetonka, Minn.	95	85	90	270
	B	Mrs. Babbie Nalle, Philadelphia, Pa.	89	88	93	270
41	B	Ms. Florence E. Green, Haverford, Pa.	88	90	93	271
	B	Mrs. Lois M. Hanske, Edina Minn.	90	92	89	271
43	B	Mrs. Cameron Postle, Slidell, La.	86	92	94	272
	A	Mrs. Joan Stewart Ruvane, Durham, N.C.	86	93	93	272
	C	Mrs. Ruth Thompson, Whittier, Calif.	91	91	90	272
	A	Ms. Barbara D. Harrington, Luddington, Mich.	91	93	88	272
	B	Mrs. Gretchen R. Gayton, Brookfield, Ohio	96	88	88	272
48	C	Mrs. Frank E. Richart, Ann Arbor, Mich.	87	96	90	273
49	A	Mrs. Beverly A. Vanstrum, Dellwood WBL, Mich.	89	94	91	274
	D	Mrs. Ann Gregor, Gary, Ind.	94	95	85	274
51	A	Mrs. Kathryn W. Salley, Columbia, S.C.	93	90	92	275
	B	Mrs. Rita T. Houston, Green Bay, Wis.	86	95	94	275
	C	Ms. Josephine O. Marchant, Greenville, S.C.	93	94	88	275
	A	Mrs. Oraleze K. Rendleman, Tampa, Fla.	90	95	90	275
55	D	Mrs. Edith R. Paffard, Sewickley, Pa.	90	98	88	276
	B	Mrs. Lee Marr, Greenville, S.C.	90	95	91	276
57	A	Miss Elaine Forgie, Rochester, N.Y.	95	90	92	277
58	D	Mrs. Anne V. Coupe, Rochester, N.Y.	92	97	89	278
	A	Mrs. Nancy G. Harris, Villanova, Pa.	99	92	87	278
60	B	Mrs. Sue Herold, Wayne, Pa.	89	95	97	281
	A	Mrs. Kathryn D. Williams, Rockville, Md.	94	89	98	281
62	C	Mrs. Robert S. McKee, Grosse Point Shores, Mich.	98	92	92	282
	A	Ms. Elizabeth G. Haga, Prospect, Va.	94	94	94	282
	B	Mrs. Peggy Noyes, Darien, Conn.	92	96	94	282
65	D	Mrs. Justine B. Cushing, Glen Head, N.Y.	99	92	92	283

1984
TWENTY-THIRD SENIOR WOMEN'S AMATEUR CHAMPIONSHIP

Tacoma Country & Golf Club, Tacoma, Washington, September 26-28
Yardage—5,988. Par 74. 131 Entries, 120 Starters.

Letters preceding names denote age groups for supplementary prize competition, as follows:
A—50 through 54 years; B—55 through 59 years; C—60 through 64 years; D—65 and over.
All starters eligible for all three rounds. The 67 low scores:

						Score
1	A	Constance M. Guthrie, Spokane, Wash.	76	73	78	227
2	A	Janice Calin, Minneapolis, Minn.	79	70	80	229
3	C	Dorothy G. Porter, Cinnaminson, N.J.	77	75	79	231
	A	Louise Wilson, Louisville, Ky.	73	79	79	231
5	B	Natalie Gamble, Grosse Pointe Shores, Mich.	75	81	77	233
6	B	Lois Hodge, Los Altos, Calif.	73	80	81	234
7	A	Mrs. Robert Ihlanfeldt, Seattle, Wash.	78	77	79	234
8	A	Pat Harbottle, Tacoma, Wash.	78	78	80	236
	C	Alberta Bower, Charleston, S.C.	75	85	76	236
	B	Ceil MacLaurin, Savannah, Ga.	77	78	81	236
11	B	Mildred H. Stanley, Los Angeles, Calif.	76	81	80	237
12	A	Mrs. Betty Probasco, Lookout Mountain, Tenn.	80	79	80	239
13	B	Joan Damon, Kaneohe, Hawaii	80	82	81	243
14	A	Marie Lilliedoll, Davis, Calif.	81	81	84	246
15	A	Barbara P. Young, Westport, Conn.	83	78	86	247
16	B	Alice Dye, Delray Beach, Fla.	81	83	84	248
	B	Nancy G. Hollenbeck, Annandale, Va.	81	85	82	248
18	B	Electra Koeniger, Aberdeen, Wash.	84	84	81	249
	B	Barbara B. Wilson, Pleasanton, Calif.	80	88	81	249
20	B	Harriet Glanville, Long Beach, Calif.	87	81	82	250
	A	Liz Culver, Seattle, Wash.	82	82	86	250
	C	Shirley Fopp, Tacoma, Wash.	78	82	90	250
23	C	Phyllis Germain, Houston, Texas	84	86	81	251
	D	Helen M. Johnson, Tacoma, Wash,	83	83	85	251
25	C	Naoma Rusty Gales, Port Angeles, Wash.	87	86	79	252
26	C	Shirley T. Baty, Tacoma, Wash.	86	86	81	253
	B	Rita Houston, Green Bay, Wis.	84	84	85	253
	B	Dorothy June Rogers, Redmond, Wash.	83	87	83	253
29	C	Mrs. Paul G. Black, Hingham, Mass.	82	86	86	254
	C	Dorothy Stimpson, Rancho Santa Fe, Calif.	87	79	88	254
	C	Dorothy Campbell, Portland, Ore.	84	84	86	254
	C	Ruth Thompson, Whittier, Calif.	88	83	83	254
	C	June Sitts, Tacoma, Wash.	85	87	82	254
	A	Bev Mullins, Boise, Idaho	82	90	82	254
35	C	Mrs. John L. Hulteng, Haydenlake, Idaho	80	90	85	255
	D	Janet D. Blair, Dallas, Texas	83	88	84	255
	B	Mary F. Westhoven, San Antonio, Texas	85	85	85	255
38	A	Mary E. Conarro, Warren, Pa.	83	89	84	256
	B	Joyce O'Connor, Nanaimo, Canada	88	82	86	256
40	B	Doris McGuire, Aberdeen, Wash.	84	88	85	257
	A	Virginia Dennehy, Lake Forest, Ill.	82	87	88	257
	A	Gail Dils, Vancouver, Wash.	89	87	81	257
43	C	Ruth White Miller, Long Beach, Calif.	86	87	85	258
44	B	Laura M. Cann, Mill Valley, Calif.	80	86	93	259
45	A	Joanne D. Brown, Vancouver, Wash.	86	86	88	260
	A	Jean Marshall, Portland, Ore.	84	90	86	260
	B	Lois M. Hanske, Edina, Minn.	86	89	85	260
	B	Bea Catlow, Portland, Ore	90	86	84	260
49	D	Mrs. Charles Eckstrom, Tacoma, Wash.	84	86	91	261
50	A	Ellie Maloney, Seattle, Wash.	85	89	87	261
	A	Joanne Fleming, Carmel, Calif.	84	86	91	261
52	A	Robin Marcus, Portland, Ore.	86	88	88	262
	A	Janet Drake, Yakima, Wash.	85	88	89	262
	A	Karen H. Stuht, Bellevue, Wash.	91	83	88	262
	A	Margery Sue Crook, Eugene, Ore.	85	89	88	262
	B	Mrs. Kathryn W. Salley, Columbia, S.C.	86	89	87	262
	D	Ann Gregory, Gary, Ind.	94	89	79	262
58	B	Mrs. Nancy L. Gapinski, San Anselmo, Calif.	92	89	82	263
	A	Patty Bethune, Portland, Ore.	87	85	91	263
60	B	Jane T. Anderson, San Luis Obispo, Calif.	90	87	87	264
61	B	Ms. Mary E. Bell, Bellevue, Wash.	85	95	85	265
	B	Joanne Nichols, Bellevue, Wash.	85	87	93	265
63	B	Marjorie O. Urban, Tacoma, Wash.	90	88	88	266
	D	Edith R. Paffard, Sewickley, Pa.	87	87	92	266
	A	Frances Schaafsma, Westminster, Calif.	88	87	91	266
	B	Carol J. Commeford, Kaneohe, Hawaii	91	90	85	266
	D	Mrs. Walter E. Martin, Spokane, Wash.	93	89	84	266

1985
TWENTY-FOURTH SENIOR WOMEN'S AMATEUR CHAMPIONSHIP

Sheraton Savannah Resort & Country Club, Savannah, Georgia, September 25-27
Yardage—5,845. Par 73. 184 Entries, 124 Starters.

Letters preceding names denote age groups for supplementary prize competition, as follows:
A—50 through 54 years; B—55 through 59 years; C—60 through 64 years; D—65 and over.
All starters eligible for all three rounds. The 62 low scores:

						Score
1	A	Mrs. J. Douglas Streit, Stouffville, Ontario, Canada	70	76	78	224
2	B	Louise C. Wilson, Louisville, Ky.	74	77	76	227
3	B	Mildred M. Stanley, Escondido, Calif.	74	72	82	228
	C	Dorothy G. Porter, Cinnaminson, N.J.	74	74	80	228
	A	Constance M. Guthrie, Spokane, Wash.	80	76	72	228
6	A	Janice Calin, Edina, Minn.	73	81	77	231
7	B	Mrs. Betty R. Probasco, Lookout Mountain, Tenn.	76	76	80	232
	A	Mrs. Lamar Potts, Columbia, S.C.	78	78	76	232
9	A	Muffy Marlio, Marion, Mass.	74	75	85	234
10	B	Mrs. Frances F. Stearns, Poughkeepsie, N.Y.	77	80	78	235
	B	Lois F. Hodge, Los Altos, Calif.	76	78	81	235
12	B	Dena M. Nowotny, Tulsa, Okla.	82	77	77	236
	A	Mrs. Dick Kaufman, San Antonio, Texas	73	81	82	236
14	C	Nancy Rutter, Williamsville, N.Y.	78	80	79	237
	B	Ceil Maclaurin, Savannah, Ga.	76	82	79	237
16	C	Martha M. Smith, Virginia Beach, Va.	79	82	77	238
	B	Alice Dye, Delray Beach, Fla.	78	80	80	238
	A	Beverly M. Baetge, Richmond , Texas	78	80	80	238
	B	Mrs. Robert Ihlanfeldt, Seattle, Wash.	78	79	81	238
20	B	Natalie Gamble, Grosse Pointe Shores, Mich.	85	78	76	239
	B	Nancy Hollenbeck, Annandale, Va.	79	79	81	239
	A	Barbara Young, Westport, Conn.	80	76	83	239
23	B	Erma D. Keyes, Coatesville, Pa.	81	79	80	240
24	A	Pat Harbottle, Tacoma, Wash.	79	82	80	241
	C	Alberta L. Bower, Charleston, S.C.	75	79	87	241
26	B	Elizabeth Wren, Williamsburg, Va.	78	85	79	242
	A	Donna Cunning, Phoenix, Ariz.	83	81	78	242
28	A	Roberta S. Brown, Tampa, Fla.	79	84	80	243
29	C	Joanne B. Tracy, Hilton Head Island, S.C.	83	80	81	244
30	A	Harriet S. Hart, Ridgefield, Conn.	80	83	82	245
	A	Liz Culver, Seattle, Wash.	80	82	83	245
	D	Ruth White Miller, Placentia, Calif.	86	82	77	245
33	A	Joan H. Comisar, Cincinnati, Ohio	80	82	84	246
	B	Sara W. Sage, Locust Valley, N.Y.	84	83	79	246
	C	Anne S. Johnston, Highlands, N.C.	82	83	81	246
36	B	Pauline F. Whitacre, Canton, Ohio	80	85	82	247
37	B	Lucille Penner, Virginia Beach, Va.	82	83	83	248
38	C	Lee Marr, Greenville, S.C.	79	87	83	249
39	A	Joanne D. Brown, Vancouver, Wash.	83	86	81	250
	C	Evelyn M. Grant, Bangor, Maine	80	86	84	250
	A	Julie R. Madison, Jacksonville, Fla.	78	85	87	250
42	A	Emily L. Brown, Orange Park, Fla.	83	82	86	251
	C	Mrs. George B. Campbell, Portland, Ore.	79	85	87	251
	A	Charlene C. Baumgarten, Owensboro, Ky.	81	89	81	251
	A	Mary Reed Schneider, Sheldon, Iowa	82	84	85	251
	A	Phyllis D. Carlson, St. Paul, Minn.	79	86	86	251
	B	Dorie Scripsema, Grand Rapids, Mich.	85	87	79	251
	A	Gail B. Wiltshire, Lake Oswego, Ore.	87	83	81	251
49	B	Mary Jane King, Newport News, Va.	83	84	85	252
	C	Mary Helen Rawls, Suffolk, Va.	85	85	82	252
	A	Barbara Seale, Jasper, Texas	87	84	81	252
52	B	Rita Houston, Green Bay, Wis.	85	83	85	253
	B	Marjorie B. Chadsey, Greenwich, Conn.	82	85	86	253
54	B	Polly Riley, Fort Worth, Texas	86	84	84	254
	A	Mrs. Robert G. Bingham, Hilton Head Island, S.C.	83	87	84	254
	A	Retha D. Hankins, Knoxville, Tenn.	82	88	84	254
57	B	Juanita Jones, Amarillo, Texas	85	83	87	255
	B	Lois M. Hanske, Edina, Minn.	85	84	86	255
	A	Marie Lilliedoll, Davis, Calif.	84	84	87	255
	C	Mrs. Paul G. Black, Hingham, Mass.	84	84	87	255
	A	Elaine Forgie, Rochester, N.Y.	92	86	77	255
	B	Oraleze Rendleman, Tampa, Fla.	87	84	84	255

1986

TWENTY-FIFTH SENIOR WOMEN'S AMATEUR CHAMPIONSHIP

Lakewood Golf Club, Point Clear, Alabama, September 24-26
Yardage—5,835. Par 72. 137 Entries, 120 Starters.

Letter preceding names denote age groups for supplementary prize competition, as follows:
A—50 through 54 years; B—55 through 59 years; C—60 through 64 years; D—65 and over.
All starters eligible for all three rounds. The 64 low scores:

						Score
1	A	Constance Guthrie, Spokane, Wash.	73	76	76	225
2	A	Marlene Streit, Stouffville, Ontario, Canada	83	75	73	231
	A	Barbara Young, Westport, Conn.	77	80	74	231
	C	Ceil Maclaurin, Savannah, Ga.	76	78	77	231
5	A	June Mayson, Mobile, Ala.	77	76	79	232
6	A	Muffy Marlio, Marion, Mass.	82	81	70	233
7	A	Barbara McIntire, Colorado Springs, Colo.	80	72	83	235
8	A	Harriet Hart, Ridgefield, Conn.	79	82	76	237
	A	Carol Kaufman, San Antonio, Texas	79	79	79	237
	B	Lois Hodge, Los Altos, Calif.	83	75	79	237
11	B	Louise Wilson, Louisville, Ky.	81	80	77	238
	B	Mildred Stanley, Escondido, Calif.	77	83	78	238
13	B	Edean Ihlanfeldt, Seattle, Wash.	82	80	78	240
	A	Donna Cunning, Phoenix, Ariz.	82	80	78	240
15	A	Mary Ann Morrison, Houston, Texas	81	79	81	241
16	A	Marlene Miller, Lake Bluff, Ill.	81	83	78	242
17	B	Betty Probasco, Lookout Mountain, Tenn.	79	84	81	244
	B	Frances Stearns, Poughkeepsie, N.Y.	77	85	82	244
	C	Nancy Rutter, Williamsville, N.Y.	81	83	80	244
20	B	Alice Dye, Delray Beach, Fla.	80	84	81	245
	A	Liz Culver, Seattle, Wash.	80	83	82	245
	A	Diane Dill, Pasadena, Texas	80	82	83	245
	A	Pat Lesser Harbottle, Tacoma, Wash.	88	80	77	245
	C	Jean Hester, Cookeville, Tenn.	84	83	78	245
	C	Mary Jones, Champaign, Ill.	76	81	88	245
26	C	Dorothy Porter, Cinnaminson, N.J.	81	83	82	246
	C	Natalie Gamble, Grosse Point Shores, Mich.	84	86	76	246
	A	Beverly Baetge, Richmond, Texas	79	83	84	246
	A	Noreen McKay, Toronto, Ontario, Canada	79	82	85	246
30	C	Alberta Bower, Charleston, S.C.	83	86	78	247
	A	Mary Conarro, Warren, Pa.	81	81	85	247
32	A	Martha Hatlan, New Orleans, La.	82	81	85	248
	A	Julie Madison, Balsam, N.C.	81	85	82	248
	B	Edie Creed, Schomberg, Ontario, Canada	78	86	84	248
35	B	Mary Lou Scharf, Tulsa, Okla.	85	86	78	249
36	B	Sara Sage, Locust Valley, N.Y.	85	79	76	250
	A	Judy Bell, Colorado Springs, Colo.	86	80	84	250
38	B	Bobby Kuhn, Glendale, Calif.	87	85	79	251
	C	Grace McGrath, Glen Head, N.Y.	82	82	87	251
	A	Jane Moffat, Toronto, Ontario, Canada	82	88	81	251
	A	Ann Richmond, Toronto, Ontario, Canada	81	88	82	251
	C	Phyllis Germain, St. George, Utah	84	83	84	251
	B	Rita Houston, Green Bay, Wis.	82	84	85	251
44	B	Elizabeth Wren, Williamsburg, Va.	83	86	83	252
	B	Mary Anita Tripp, Indio, Calif.	83	84	85	252
	A	Janice Calin, Edina, Minn.	81	86	85	252
47	A	Barbara McGhie, East Haddam, Conn.	84	86	83	253
	D	Virginia Jarvis, Winfield, Kan.	83	86	84	253
	B	Dena Nowotny, Tulsa, Okla.	86	81	86	253
50	C	Helen Wright, Cibolo, Texas	88	88	79	255
	D	Nancy Black, Hingham, Mass.	87	85	83	255
	A	Mary Reed Schneider, Sheldon, Iowa	87	83	85	255
	D	Dorothy Campbell, Portland, Ore	83	85	87	255
54	A	Ann Potts, Columbia, S.C.	84	93	79	256
	B	Pauline Whitacre, Canton, Ohio	86	88	82	256
	B	Joanne Brown, Vancouver, Wash.	89	85	82	256
57	A	Emily Brown, Orange Park, Fla.	84	88	85	257
	B	Ellen Bowering, Bonita, Calif.	90	82	85	257
	B	Phyllis Carlson, St. Paul, Minn.	82	82	93	257
	A	Florence Strong, Ontonagon, Mich.	85	83	89	257
61	B	Lee Hilkene, Birmingham, Ala.	86	91	81	258
	B	Marjorie Chadsey, Greenwich, Conn.	84	91	83	258
	A	Diane Cornwall, Dallas, Texas	91	83	84	258
	A	Betty Von Rump, St. Louis, Mo.	82	88	88	258

1987

TWENTY-SIXTH SENIOR WOMEN'S AMATEUR CHAMPIONSHIP

September 30-October 2, 1987
Manufacturers' Golf and Country Club, Oreland, Pa.
Yardage—5,771. Par 74.

(1) ages 50-54
(2) ages 55-59
(3) ages 60-64
(4) ages 65 and above

					Score
1.	(1) Anne Sander, Seattle, Wash.	72	80	76	228
2.	(1) Harriet Hart, Ridgefield, Conn.	78	77	76	231
3.	(1) Charlotte Wood, Beaumont, Texas	77	82	77	236
4.	(1) Millie Zimring, Los Angeles, Calif.	77	77	83	237
5.	(1) Marlene Streit, Stouffville, Ontario, Canada	81	84	78	244
6.	(3) Dorothy Porter, Cinnaminson, N.J.	82	81	82	245
7.	(1) Betty Cole, Edmonton, Alberta, Canada	81	82	83	246
8.	(2) Lois Hodge, Los Altos, Calif.	84	81	82	247
9.	(1) Barbara Young, Westport, Conn.	85	85	78	248
10.	(1) Pat Harbottle, Tacoma, Wash.	83	87	78	248
	(2) Louise Wilson, Louisville, Ky.	80	85	83	248
12.	(1) Muffy Marlio, Marion, Mass.	80	83	86	249
13.	(1) Jane Moffat, Toronto, Ontario, Canada	84	86	80	250
14.	(2) Janice Vining, Don Mills, Ontario, Canada	83	84	84	251
	(4) Helen Sigel Wilson, Gladwyne, Pa.	84	81	86	251
	(2) Mildred Stanley, Escondido, Calif.	80	84	87	251
17.	(3) Alberta Bower, Charleston, S.C.	88	80	84	252
	(2) Frances Stearns, Poughkeepsie, N.Y.	79	85	88	252
19.	(2) Janice Calin, Edina, Minn.	82	85	87	254
20.	(1) Marlene Miller, Lake Bluff, Ill.	82	88	85	255
	(3) Alice Dye, Delray Beach, Fla.	86	83	86	255
22.	(2) Betty Probasco, Lookout Mountain, Tenn.	80	91	85	256
	(3) Ceil Maclaurin, Savannah, Ga.	88	82	86	256
	(1) Ginger Lamberson, New York, N.Y.	82	86	88	256
25.	(1) Meriam Bailey Leeke, Montague, Mich.	82	87	88	257
26.	(1) Barbara McGhie, East Haddam, Conn.	90	85	83	258
27.	(1) Judy Bell, Colorado Springs, Colo.	89	92	79	260
	(2) Juanita Jones, Amarillo, Texas	84	91	85	260
	(2) Edean Ihlanfeldt, Seattle, Wash.	83	86	91	260
30.	(2) Sheila Hopkins, Lake Wylie, S.C.	86	90	85	261
	(1) Jean Boynton, Willowdale, Ontario, Canada	87	88	86	261
32.	(3) Phyllis Germain, St. George, Utah	91	87	84	262
	(2) Charlotte Balick, Wilmington, Del.	85	86	91	262
34.	(1) Liz Culver, Seattle, Wash.	88	91	84	263
	(3) Erma Keyes, Coatesville, Pa.	91	87	85	263
	(1) Ann Beard, Essex Fells, N.J.	84	92	87	263
37.	(3) Elizabeth Wren, Williamsburg, Va.	90	90	-89	264
	(1) Sheila Selby, Lahaska, Pa.	88	91	85	264
	(1) Nancy Koustas, Dearborn, Mich.	84	89	91	264
40.	(2) Joanne Brown, Salem Ore.	85	91	89	265
	(3) Dena Nowotny, Tulsa, Okla.	89	86	90	265
42.	(1) Carol Barrett, Palm Desert, Calif.	91	87	88	266
	(1) Barbara McIntire, Colorado Springs, Colo.	86	95	85	266
	(1) Gertrude Dunn, Chadds Ford, Pa.	90	91	85	266
	(2) Daintry Snyder, Waterloo, Ontario, Canada	88	88	90	266
46.	(1) Elena Larralde, Monterrey, Mexico	87	90	90	267
	(4) Janet Beardsley, Centerville, Ohio	86	90	91	267
48.	(1) Heather Colhoun, Don Mills, Ontario, Canada	89	94	85	268
49.	(3) Marjorie Chadsey, Greenwich, Conn.	85	92	92	269
	(3) Charlotte Neslie, Willow Grove, Pa.	89	94	86	269
	(2) Ann Richmond, Toronto, Ontario, Canada	86	97	86	269
	(3) Ruth Scott, Rydal, Pa.	95	88	86	269
	(2) Patricia Lawson, Saskatoon, Saskatchewan, Canada	95	84	90	269
	(1) Maureen Paladino, New Castle, Pa.	91	89	89	269
	(3) Pauline Whitacre, Canton, Ohio	85	89	95	269
56.	(4) Virginina Jarvis, Winfield, Kan.	89	87	94	270
	(2) Betty Halloran, Paramus, N.J.	94	88	88	270
58.	(2) Walton Horton, Beaufort, S.C.	87	90	94	271
	(1) Eleanor Seibert, Island Heights, N.J.	93	90	88	271
	(3) Rita Houston, Green Bay, Wis.	89	94	88	271
	(4) Nancy Rutter, East Amherst, N.Y.	83	94	94	271
62.	(2) Patricia Kellam, Schenectady, N.Y.	88	92	92	272
	(2) Nancy Goodwin, Evanston, Ill.	89	92	92	272
	(1) Geraldine Street, Saskatoon, Saskatchewan, Canada	88	92	92	272

1987
TWENTY-SIXTH SENIOR WOMEN'S AMATEUR CHAMPIONSHIP
Continued

65.	(3) Olive Brown, Princeton, N.J.	91	94	88	273
	(2) Phyllis Carlson, St. Paul, Minn.	93	87	93	273
	(1) Noreen McKay, Toronto, Ontario, Canada	87	92	94	273
	(1) Anne Teel, Capistrano Beach, Calif.	93	89	91	273
	(4) Annette Kane, Flourtown, Pa.	85	94	94	273
70.	(1) Patsy Kavanagh, Pittsford, N.Y.	93	93	88	274
	(2) Kathryn Salley, Columbia, S.C.	91	96	87	274
72.	(3) Lee Hilkene, Birmingham, Mich.	88	91	96	275
	(2) Ruth Goldzier, Muttontown, N.Y.	90	89	96	275
	(3) Nancy MacGibbon, Minnetonka, Minn.	87	97	91	275
	(2) Patricia Brooke, Lakewood, N.J.	94	94	87	275
	(2) Mary Jane King, Newport News, Va.	97	88	90	275
77.	(2) Suzanne Herold, Paoli, Pa.	96	92	88	276
	(1) Carole Trombly, New Haven, Mich.	95	87	94	276
	(1) Dottie Blue, Northville, Mich.	91	96	89	276
	(2) Mary Anita Tripp, Indio, Calif.	92	91	93	276
81.	(2) Doris Kaufman, Blue Bell, Pa.	90	95	92	277
	(1) Barbara Hildebrand, Unionville, Ontario, Canada	95	90	92	277
	(1) Nancy Honebrink, Bloomington, Minn.	92	90	95	277
	(4) Bobbie Rose, Meadowbrook, Pa.	91	90	96	277
85.	(3) Anne Johnston, Highlands, N.C.	96	93	89	278
	(3) Constance Lewis, Fairfield, Conn.	95	93	90	278
	(3) Betty O'Neill, Chagrin Falls, Ohio	97	88	93	278
	(1) Virginia Dillon, Far Hills, N.J.	94	88	96	278
	(3) Shirley Durham, Rochester, N.Y.	92	89	97	278
90.	(1) Betty Forbes, Stuart, Fla.	91	96	92	279
91.	(2) Rosa Eshelman, Lancaster, Pa.	93	87	100	280
	(1) Susan Byrne, Toledo, Ohio	93	92	95	280
93.	(1) Linda Ellis, Hilton Head, S.C.	93	99	89	281
	(2) Margery Crook, Eugene, Ore.	96	93	92	281
	(4) Evelyn Moreland, Pittsburgh, Pa.	94	94	93	281
96.	(2) June Rogers, Redmond, Wash.	94	91	97	282
97.	(3) Jean Lee, York, Pa.	99	97	88	284
98.	(1) Judith Cooke, Collegeville, Pa.	94	89	92	285
	(1) Nora Jensen, Orinda, Calif.	94	86	105	285
100.	(2) Patricia MacCallum, Los Angeles, Calif.	97	95	95	287
	(1) Emily Brown, Orange Park, Fla.	100	93	94	287
	(3) Love Marshall, Merion Station, Pa.	96	94	97	287
103.	(2) Ray Gordon, Haverford, Pa.	96	100	92	288
104.	(2) Joanne Yonker, Denver, Colo.	100	95	95	290
105.	(3) Florence Green, Haverford, Pa.	103	93	95	291
	(2) Norma Cooper, Santa Rosa, Calif.	97	95	99	291
107.	(1) Donna Bodtker, Portland, Ore.	104	90	98	292
108.	(3) Jeanne Mercier, Rochester, N.Y.	97	100	96	293
	(2) Mildred Ball, Highland Mills, N.Y.	97	103	93	293
110.	(4) Frances Rich, St. Simons Island, Ga.	104	100	95	299
111.	(4) Helen Espey, Pompano Beach, Fla.	103	101	98	302
112.	(2) Becky Lee, Middletown, Ohio	96	103	108	307
113.	(4) Ruth White Miller, Placentia, Calif.	106	109	93	308
114.	(1) Mary Lou Wonderly, York, Pa.	108	102	99	309
115.	(4) Pauline Edwards, Lansdowne, Pa.	104	109	113	326
	(1) Anne Dooling, Warminster, Pa.	100	101		WD
	(2) Peggy Noyes, Darien, Conn.	93			WD
	(3) Natalie Gamble, Grosse Pointe Shores, Mich.	84	94		DQ

1988
TWENTY-SEVENTH SENIOR WOMEN'S AMATEUR CHAMPIONSHIP

September 28-30, 1988
Sea Island Golf Club, St. Simons Island, Ga.
Yardage—5,791. Par 73.

(1) ages 50-54
(2) ages 55-59
(3) ages 60-64
(4) ages 65 and above

					Score
1.	(2) Lois Hodge, Los Altos, Calif.	77	76	75	228
2.	(1) Marlene Streit, Stouffville, Ontario, Canada	79	76	74	229
3.	(1) Harriet Hart, Ponte Vedra, Fla.	77	76	77	230
4.	(1) Belle Robertson, Glasgow, Scotland	75	80	76	231
5.	(1) Anne Sander, Seattle, Wash.	78	76	78	232
	(3) Dorothy Porter, Cinnaminson, N.J.	78	75	79	232
7.	(2) Joan Comisar, Cincinnati, Ohio	77	81	79	237
8.	(4) Alberta Bower, Charleston, S.C.	82	82	74	238
	(1) Meriam Leeke, Montague, Mich.	83	78	77	238
	(2) Janice Calin, Lilydale, Minn.	82	78	78	238
11.	(2) Barbara Young, Westport, Conn.	80	76	83	239
12.	(2) Betty Probasco, Lookout Mountain, Tenn.	81	80	79	240
	(1) Odile Semelaigne, Tourny, France	79	80	81	240
14.	(1) Barbara McIntire, Colorado Springs, Colo.	80	82	79	241
	(3) Ceil Maclaurin, Savannah, Ga.	78	81	82	241
16.	(2) Frances Stearnes, Poughkeepsie, N.Y.	82	83	78	243
	(2) Louise Wilson, Louisville, Ky.	78	83	82	243
18.	(1) Jane Moffat, Toronto, Ontario, Canada	79	85	81	245
	(3) Alice Dye, Delray Beach, Fla.	79	83	83	245
	(1) Judy Bell, Colorado Springs, Colo.	81	80	84	245
21.	(4) Carolyn Cudone, Myrtle Beach, S.C.	81	84	82	247
22.	(4) Nancy Black, Hingham, Mass.	86	81	81	248
23.	(2) Edean Ihlanfeldt, Seattle, Wash.	82	84	83	249
	(2) Charlotte Balick, Wilmington, Del.	82	84	83	249
	(3) Sara Sage, Glen Cove, N.Y.	84	81	84	249
	(4) Nancy Rutter, East Amherst, N.Y.	80	84	85	249
	(1) Carol Barrett, Palm Desert, Calif.	87	84	78	249
	(1) Ginger Lamberson, New York, N.Y.	84	86	79	249
	(2) Mildred Stanley, Escondido, Calif.	83	85	81	249
	(2) Natalie Gamble, Grosse Pointe Shores, Mich.	85	83	81	249
31.	(2) June Mayson, Mobile, Ala.	78	88	84	250
	(2) Muffy Marlio, Marion, Mass.	85	83	82	250
33.	(3) Phyllis Germain, St. George, Utah	84	85	82	251
34.	(3) Dena Nowotny, Tulsa, Okla.	84	84	84	252
35.	(1) Sharon Pauly, West Palm Beach, Fla.	86	86	81	253
	(2) Jane Hawkins, Richmond, Va.	85	86	82	253
	(1) Mary Ellen Driscoll, Rothesay, New Brunswick, Canada	85	86	82	253
38.	(2) Annalies Eschauzier, Laag Keppel, Netherlands	83	84	87	254
	(2) Louise van den Berghe, Brabent, Belgium	89	82	83	254
	(4) Lally Segard, Paris, France	85	84	85	254
41.	(1) Carol Falk, Portland, Ore.	88	87	80	255
	(3) Alice Sampson, Kirkwood, Mo.	83	88	84	255
43.	(2) Anne Bouton, Boulogne, France	84	89	83	256
	(1) Heather Colhoun, Don Mills, Ontario, Canada	81	85	90	256
	(1) Betty Von Rump, St. Louis, Mo.	87	82	87	256
46.	(4) Jan Nichols, La Quinta, Calif.	80	91	86	257
47.	(2) Barbro Montgomery, Stockholm, Sweden	82	93	83	258
	(2) Marlene Miller, Lake Bluff, Ill.	95	81	82	258
	(2) Lucille Penner, Virginia Beach, Va.	85	89	84	258
	(1) Noreen McKay, Toronto, Ontario, Canada	87	85	86	258
	(1) Nancy Koustas, Dearborn, Mich.	89	83	86	258
	(1) Ann Potts, Columbia, S.C.	86	85	87	258
	(1) Ann Brandis, Asheville, N.C.	82	88	88	258
54.	(1) Martha Meyer, Atlanta, Ga.	89	85	85	259
	(4) Grace McGrath, Glen Head, N.Y.	88	84	87	259
	(1) Mary Schneider, Sheldon, Iowa	84	87	88	259
	(3) Jean Hester, Cookeville, Tenn.	83	86	90	259
58.	(2) Joyce Mahoney, Springfield, Mo.	85	95	80	260
	(3) Marg Lillard, Terrace Park, Ohio	84	89	87	260
	(3) Polly Riley, Fort Worth, Texas	85	88	87	260
	(1) Carol McCown, Portland, Ore.	85	88	87	260
62.	(2) Joanne Brown, Salem, Ore.	91	85	85	261
	(3) Rita Houston, Green Bay, Wis.	87	86	88	261
	(2) Mary Jane King, Newport News, Va.	85	86	90	261
65.	(3) Peggy Noyes, Darien, Conn.	86	91	85	262
	(2) Elaine Forgie, Rochester, N.Y.	84	92	86	262
	(2) Liz Culver, Seattle, Wash.	85	91	86	262
	(1) Ann Beard, Essex Fells, N.J.	93	82	87	262

1988
TWENTY-SEVENTH SENIOR WOMEN'S AMATEUR CHAMPIONSHIP
Continued

69.	(2) Brenda Helmer, Hilton Head Island, S.C.	86	91	86	263
	(4) Dorothy Campbell, Portland, Ore.	87	88	88	263
	(2) Patricia Kellam, Schenectady, N.Y.	87	86	90	263
72.	(2) Kathryn Salley, Columbia, S.C.	85	93	86	264
	(2) Nora Jensen, Orinda, Calif.	90	85	89	264
	(2) Barbar McGhie, East Haddam, Conn.	86	88	90	264
	(2) Clarice Sewell, Pasadena, Texas	88	85	91	264
76.	(1) Anne Teel, Capistrano Beach, Calif.	93	86	86	265
	(3) Elizabeth Wren, Williamsburg, Va.	89	88	88	265
	(1) Marie Winks, Forest, Va.	87	89	89	265
	(1) Mary Conarro, Warren, Pa.	90	84	91	265
80.	(3) Marjorie Chadsey, Greenwich, Conn.	88	92	86	266
	(4) Janet Beardsley, Centerville, Ohio	85	89	92	266
82.	(4) Mary Melnyk, Brunswick, Ga.	90	92	85	267
	(1) Margaret Shotton, Virginia Beach, Va.	93	88	86	267
	(1) Susan Byrne, Toledo, Ohio	86	91	90	267
85.	(3) Anne Johnston, Asheville, N.C.	91	90	87	268
	(1) Judith Evans, Boca Raton, Fla.	90	87	91	268
	(4) Ann Gregory, Gary, Ind.	88	88	92	268
88.	(2) Ann Richmond, Toronto, Ontario, Canada	90	92	87	269
	(2) Juanita Jones, Amarillo, Texas	85	93	91	269
90.	(3) Erma Keyes, Coatesville, Pa.	89	94	87	270
	(4) Beryl Miller, Hilton Head Island, S.C.	92	90	88	270
	(1) Linda Ellis, Hilton Head, S.C.	93	88	89	270
	(4) Ruth Miller, Palcentia, Calif.	87	90	93	270
94.	(3) Jean Hitchcock, Hingham, Mass.	92	92	87	271
	(4) Josephine Marchant, Greenville, S.C.	90	96	85	271
	(1) Fran Babbitt, Carlsbad, N.M.	92	90	89	271
97.	(1) Natalie Pacileo, Erie, Pa.	100	88	84	272
	(2) Sheila Hopkins, Lake Wylie, S.C.	92	93	87	272
99.	(1) Patsy Kavanagh, Pittsford, N.Y.	88	94	92	274
	(2) Phyllis Carlson, St. Paul, Minn.	90	90	94	274
101.	(2) Margery Crook, Eugene, Ore.	91	93	91	275
	(2) Walton Horton, Beaufort, S.C.	89	93	93	275
	(3) Sherry Barrett, St. Simons Island, Ga.	91	87	97	275
104.	(3) Mary Helen Rawls, Suffolk, Va.	90	93	93	276
105.	(2) Joan Ruvane, Durham, N.C.	89	92	96	277
106.	(1) Joan King, Jupiter, Fla.	100	90	88	278
107.	(1) Joan Shapiro, St. Paul, Minn.	96	93	90	279
	(3) Constance Lewis, Fairfield, Conn.	90	93	96	279
109.	(3) Mary Lou Crowder, Columbia, S.C.	97	93	90	280
	(1) Donna Bodtker, Portland, Ore.	95	93	92	280
	(2) Daisy Trobaugh, Columbia, S.C.	89	95	96	280
	(2) Mildred Ball, Highland Mills, N.Y.	96	88	96	280
113.	(2) Barbara Seale, Jasper, Texas	97	94	91	282
	(4) Elizabeth Williams, Lake Oswego, Ore.	95	92	95	282
115.	(3) Doris Malkiel, Stowe, Vt.	100	88	96	284
116.	(2) Ruth Allen, Jackson, Miss.	96	99	98	293
117.	(1) Nancy Spears, Orlando, Fla.	98	101	96	295
	(1) Marietta Guettermann, Breisgau, West Germany	80	84		WD
	(2) Doris Bryant, Santee, S.C.	88	96		WD
	(1) Charlotte Wood, Houston, Texas				WD

1989
TWENTY-EIGHTH SENIOR WOMEN'S AMATEUR CHAMPIONSHIP

October 18-20
The Tournament Players Course, The Woodlands, Texas
Yardage—5,717. Par 72.
119 entries, 105 starters

(1) ages 50-54
(2) ages 55-59
(3) ages 60-64
(4) ages 65 and above

					Score
1.	(1) Anne Sander, Seattle, Wash.	75	74	75	224
2.	(3) Alice Dye, Delray Beach, Fla.	75	83	75	233
3.	(2) Betty Probasco, Lookout Mt., Tenn.	73	86	76	235
	(1) Kathy Mankowski, Dallas, Tex.	81	79	75	235
	(2) Marlene Streit, Stouffville, Canada	83	79	73	235
6.	(3) Lois Hodge, Los Altos, Calif.	82	81	80	243
	(2) Mary Ann Morrison, Dubois, Wy.	81	84	78	243
8.	(1) Betty Cole, Edmonton, Canada	85	79	80	244
	(1) Phyllis Preuss, Colo. Sprgs, Col.	83	82	79	244
10.	(1) Dede Hoffman, Naples, Fla.	87	80	79	246
11.	(3) Mildred Stanley, Escondido, Calif.	79	88	81	248
	(1) Barbara McIntire, Colo. Sprgs, Col.	86	82	80	248
12.	(1) Merium Leeke, Montague, Mich.	80	85	84	249
	(2) Louise Wilson, Louisville, Ky.	77	88	84	249
14.	(4) Dorothy Porter, Cinnaminson, N.J.	80	85	85	250
	(1) Diane Dill, Pasadena, Tex.	87	83	80	250
16.	(1) Judy Bell, Colo. Springs, Colo.	87	84	81	252
	(1) Kathleen Graham, Winter Pk., Fla.	81	92	79	252
	(1) Donna Cunning, Phoenix, Ariz.	87	82	83	252
19.	(2) Janice Calin, St. Paul, Minn.	86	84	83	253
20.	(3) Mary Lou Scarf, Tulsa, Okla.	86	84	84	254
	(2) Beverly Baetge, Richmond, Tex.	84	86	84	254
	(3) Ceil MacLaurin, Savannah, Ga.	83	84	87	254
23.	(1) Karen Oldham, Stowe, Ohio	80	86	90	256
24.	(1) Ruth Parker, Phoenix, Ariz.	90	84	83	257
	(2) Barbara Young, Westport, Ct.	83	87	87	257
	(1) Levon Edwards, Lake Quivira, Kan.	85	85	87	257
27.	(2) Carol Barrett, Palm Desert, Calif.	91	88	79	258
28.	(3) Pauline Whitacre, Canton, Ohio	89	86	84	259
	(1) Nancy Coile, Montgomery, Tex.	90	79	90	259
30.	(2) Liz Culver, Seattle, Wash.	87	91	82	260
	(1) Carol Ellis, Minneapolis, Minn.	86	88	86	260
	(2) Roberta Brown, Tampa, Fla.	88	89	83	260
	(1) Susan Rennie, Venice, Calif.	87	91	82	260
	(1) Sandra Fullmer, Glenview, Ill.	94	83	83	260
35.	(3) Anita Weiner, Houston, Tex.	83	93	85	261
36.	(1) Carol Falk, Portland, Ore.	91	83	88	262
	(1) Emily Brown, Orange Park, Fla.	87	91	84	262
38.	(1) Peggy Brass, Orlando, Fla.	86	93	84	263
	(2) Juanita Jones, Amarillo, Tex.	85	84	94	263
40.	(2) Edena Ihlanfeldt, Seattle, Wash.	90	88	86	264
41.	(1) Hisae Ozeki, Tokyo, Japan	93	86	86	265
	(1) Elena Larralde, Santa Maria, Mexico	86	89	90	265
42.	(1) Prudence Smart, New Britain, Ct.	86	89	91	266
	(3) Kat Salley, Columbia, S.C.	92	87	87	266
	(1) Virginia Dillon, Far Hills, N.J.	87	91	88	266
45.	( ) Betty Dunn, Kingwood, Tex.	93	87	87	267
	(4) Phyllis Germain, St. George, Utah	91	88	88	267
47.	(3) Janice Vining, Toronto, Canada	90	91	87	268
	(3) Margarita Lillard, Terrace, Ohio	90	98	90	268
	(3) Rita Houston, Green Bay, Wis.	92	89	87	268
50.	(1) Eleanor Seibert, Isl. Hgts., N.J.	89	94	86	269
	(1) Pat Harrop-Schumacher, Sequim, Wa.	91	88	90	269
	(1) Heather Colhoun, Don Mills, Can.	87	93	89	269
53.	(3) Polly Riley, Ft. Worth, Tex.	84	96	90	270
54.	(2) Phyllis Carlson, St. Paul, Minn.	93	88	90	271
	(1) Margarite Conover, Houston, Tex.	92	94	85	271
56.	(2) Joanne Brown, Salem, Ore.	91	88	93	272
	(1) Donna Bodtker, Portland, Ore.	92	92	88	272
58.	(4) Virginia Jarvis, Winfield, Kan.	94	88	91	273
	(1) Rowena Vance, Gautier, Miss.	86	93	84	273
	(1) Dottie Blue, Northville, Mich.	90	93	90	273
	(2) Nora Jensen, Orinda, Calif.	91	90	92	273
	(2) Donna Wilwerding, Conroe, Tex.	97	87	89	273
	(3) Lenora Lang, Fort Myers, Fla.	95	90	88	273
64.	(2) Ann Richmond, Toronto, Can.	93	92	89	274
65.	(2) Marian Parks, Plymouth, Mass.	90	94	92	276
	(4) Ann Gregory, Gary, Ind.	94	89	93	276
	(2) Sheila Hopkins, Lake Wylie, S.C.	100	90	86	276

1989
TWENTY-EIGHTH SENIOR WOMEN'S AMATEUR CHAMPIONSHIP
Continued

68.	(3) Mary Westhoven, San Antonio, Tex.	96	93	88	277
	(3) Walton Horton, Beaufort, S.C.	89	89	99	277
	(2) Clarice Sewell, Pasadena, Tex.	98	91	88	277
	(4) Janet Blair, Dallas, Tex.	91	94	92	277
72.	(3) Anne Johnston, Ashville, N.C.	93	89	96	278
	(1) Janice Torrance, Weirton, W.V.	94	92	92	278
74.	(1) Ann Beard, Essex Fells, N.J.	95	89	95	279
	(1) Jean Danen, Richardson, Tex.	97	88	94	279
	(1) Betty Von Rump, St. Louis, Mo.	93	94	92	279
	(2) Judy Litman, Encinitas, Calif.	89	99	91	279
78.	(4) Fran Martell, Weatherford, Tex.	93	90	98	281
	(2) Gail Dils, Vancouver, Wash.	95	90	96	281
80.	(2) Sue Leach, Austin, Tex.	96	92	94	282
81.	(2) Margery Crook, Eugene, Ore.	94	94	95	283
	(4) Lee Sliger, Yuma, Ariz.	90	95	98	283
83.	(1) Helen Wall, Richardson, Tex.	97	96	91	284
84.	(1) Alma Matthes, St. Louis, Mo.	100	98	87	285
	(4) Ruth Thompson, Whittier, Calif.	100	91	94	285
86.	(4) Marion Senteno, Roswell, N.M.	99	93	95	287
	(1) Mary Rotan, Leesville, S.C.	95	94	98	287
88.	(3) Nancy MacMillan, Austin, Tex.	99	96	93	288
89.	(3) Ruth Antman, Vista, Calif.	92	100	97	289
	(1) Jacqie Galbraith, Vista, Calif.	98	98	93	289
91.	(4) Ruthe Hawkins, Austin, Tex.	94	100	96	290
92.	(3) Imo Greenwood, Alice, Tex.	98	99	96	293
	(4) Barbara Fox, St. Joseph, Mo.	94	101	98	293
94.	(4) Ruth Hume, Oceanside, Calif.	95	101	98	294
	(2) Pat Gainer, Austin, Tex.	101	100	93	294
	(3) Glenna Nelson, Waelder, Tex.	94	101	99	294
97.	(1) Cindy Edgerle, Grand Haven, Mich.	103	97	100	300
98.	(4) Ruth Miller, Placentia, Calif.	107	96	98	301
99.	(2) Barbara Young, Conroe, Tex.	96	103	104	303
	(1) Barbara White, Rainsville, Ala.	106	108	107	321
	(4) Alberta Bower, Charleston, S.C.	DQ			
	(3) Alice Sampson, Kingwood, Mo.	94	94	WD	
	(1) Linda Ellis, Hilton Head, S.C.	94	95	WD	
	(2) Jane Hawkins, Richmond, Va.	89	90	WD	
	(3) Natalie Gamble, Grosse Pt., Mich.	91	WD		

1990
TWENTY-NINTH SENIOR WOMEN'S AMATEUR CHAMPIONSHIP

September 19-21
Del Rio Golf and Country Club, Modesto, California
Yardage—5,986. Par 72.
133 entries, 117 starters

(1) ages 50-54
(2) ages 55-59
(3) ages 60-64
(4) ages 65 and above

					Score
1.	(1) Anne Sander, Seattle, Wash.	80	74	71	225 (72)
2.	(2) Marlene Streit, Stouffville, Ontario, Canada	72	77	76	225 (78)
3.	(2) Mary Ann Morrison, Dubois, Wy.	76	77	73	226
4.	(2) Barbara McIntire, Colorado Springs, Colo.	79	75	75	229
5.	(3) Mildred Stanley, Escondido, Calif.	77	75	78	230
6.	(4) Dorothy Porter, Cinnaminson, N.J.	81	75	75	231
	(1) Phyllis Preuss, Colorado Springs, Colo.	78	77	76	231
8.	(3) Alice Dye, Delray Beach, Fla.	78	77	77	232
9.	(3) Lois Hodge, Los Altos, Calif.	78	81	75	234
10.	(1) Jane Moffat, Toronto, Ontario, Canada	80	79	76	235
	(3) Betty Probasco, Lookout Mountain, Tenn.	75	77	83	235
	(4) Alberta Bower, Charleston, S.C.	77	78	80	235
13.	(2) Harriet Hart, New London, N.H.	83	74	79	236
14.	(1) Helen Oakes, Deerfield Beach, Fla.	81	77	79	237
15.	(3) Frances Stearns, Poughkeepsie, N.Y.	78	82	79	239
16.	(2) Marie Kuhn, North Hollywood, Calif.	83	78	79	240
17.	(1) Pat Harrop-Schumacher, Sequim, Wash.	80	84	77	241
18.	(3) Ceil Maaclaurin, Savannah, Ga.	80	78	84	242
19.	(1) Kathy Mankowski, Dallas, Texas	80	83	81	244
	(4) Phyllis Germain, St. George, Utah	82	81	81	244
	(1) Ruth Parker, Phoenix, Ariz.	82	78	84	244
22.	(2) Helen Brandon, San Jose, Calif.	83	84	78	245
	(1) Carol Falk, Portland, Ore.	86	79	80	245
24.	(1) Fumie Mock, San Diego, Calif.	83	83	80	246
	(2) Beverly Vanstrum, Dellwood, Minn.	80	84	82	246
26.	(1) Carole Holland, Kent, Wash.	86	80	81	247
	(2) Marlene Miller, Lake Bluff, Ill.	87	81	79	247
	(2) Carol Ley, Milbrae, Calif.	83	80	84	247
29.	(1) Hisae Ozeki, Tokyo, Japan	87	81	80	248
30.	(1) Ev Griggs, Los Alamos, N.M.	86	82	82	250
31.	(3) Charlotte Balick, Wilmington, Del.	90	77	84	251
	(1) Mary Schmitz, Oakland, Calif.	87	81	83	251
33.	(2) Pat Harbottle, Tacoma, Wash.	91	81	80	252
	(1) Claire Knipe, Alamo, Calif.	82	86	84	252
	(1) Carol Ellis, Minneapolis, Minn.	86	84	82	252
36.	(3) Nancy Goodwin, Stanford, Calif.	81	79	83	253
37.	(2) Donna Cunning, Phoenix, Ariz.	88	86	80	254
	(1) Robin Perdomo, San Dimas, Calif.	83	83	88	254
	(3) Rita Houston, Green Bay, Wis.	86	86	82	254
	(1) Alice Ney, San Jose, Calif.	83	80	91	254
	(3) Janice Vining, Toronto, Ontario, Canada	89	83	82	254
	(2) Gail Dils, Vancouver, Wash.	80	91	83	254
	(4) Marge Callahan, South Pasadena, Calif.	82	85	87	254
44.	(2) Liz Culver, Seattle, Wash.	84	88	83	255
45.	(1) Beverly Prichard, Modesto, Calif.	89	86	81	256
	(1) Anne Bailey, Prince Frederick, Md.	83	91	82	256
	(2) Joanne Brown, Salem, Ore.	88	87	81	256
	(1) Judy Bell, Colorado Springs, Colo.	91	82	83	256
	(2) Barbara Cameron, Corvallis, Ore.	85	86	85	256
	(4) Ruth Miller, Placentia, Calif.	87	85	84	256
	(4) Phyllis LaSorella, Pebble Beach, Calif.	87	86	83	256
52.	(3) Polly Riley, Fort Worth, Texas	81	92	84	257
	(1) Susan Rennie, Venice, Calif.	84	85	88	257
	(4) Peggy Deluchi, Lodi, Calif.	83	87	87	257
	(3) Kathryn Salley, Columbia, S.C.	84	85	88	257
	(2) Barbara McGhie, East Haddam, Conn.	86	82	89	257
57.	(1) Dottie Blue, Northville, Mich.	86	87	85	258
	(2) Jody Gumlia, Edina, Minn.	85	87	86	258
59.	(4) Ruth Thompson, Whittier, Calif.	89	87	83	259
	(2) Rita Dodge-Wannebo, Davis, Calif.	91	79	89	259
61.	(3) Barbara Wilson, Pleasanton, Calif.	89	88	83	260
	(3) Dona Holmes, Vancouver, Wash.	91	83	86	260
	(2) Virginia Dennehy, Palo Alto, Calif.	83	89	88	260
64.	(2) Gail Beauchamp, Sun City West, Ariz.	88	91	82	261
	(3) Shirley Teutsch, Eugene, Ore.	87	85	89	261
66.	(1) Anne Teel, Capistrano Beach, Calif.	85	93	84	262
	(3) Aldora Lucchesi, Modesto, Calif.	89	88	85	262

1990
TWENTY-NINTH SENIOR WOMEN'S AMATEUR CHAMPIONSHIP
Continued

68.	(1) Peggy Young, Concord, Calif.	86	90	87	263
	(4) Daisy McCoy, Modesto, Calif.	87	89	87	263
	(4) Jan Nichols, LaQuinta, Calif.	88	91	84	263
71.	(2) Bernice Glueck, Alamo, Calif.	85	92	87	264
	(2) Jan Bailey, Auburn, Calif.	88	88	88	264
	(3) Jane Anderson, San Luis Obispo, Calif.	85	86	93	264
74.	(2) Ann Richmond, Toronto, Ontario, Canada	87	91	87	265
	(3) Marg Lillard, Terrace Park, Ohio	92	84	89	265
76.	(2) Leila Hill, Los Altos, Calif.	88	88	90	266
	(2) Margery Crook, Eugene, Ore.	86	91	89	266
78.	(2) Phyllis Carlson, St. Paul, Minn.	96	86	85	267
79.	(1) Glena Wirtanen, Phoenix, Md.	88	94	86	268
	(2) Marie Lilliedoll, Davis, Calif.	92	86	90	268
81.	(3) Barbara Landry, Bridge City, Texas	88	94	87	269
82.	(2) Ann Guidera, Redlands, Calif.	91	95	84	270
	(1) LaJuana Clancy, New Baltimore, Mich.	91	90	89	270
	(2) Judy Isaac, Novato, Calif.	95	88	87	270
	(4) Virginia Jarvis, Winfield, Kan.	90	91	89	270
	(2) Nora Jensen, Orinda, Calif.	90	90	90	270
	(2) Clancy Todd, Bend, Ore.	88	90	92	270
	(2) Roseanne Minasian, Sherman Oaks, Calif.	90	87	93	270
89.	(3) Clarice Sewell, Pasadena, Texas	94	90	87	271
	(3) Shirley Durham, Rochester, N.Y.	89	94	88	271
	(1) Sheri Erskine, San Ramon, Calif.	99	89	83	271
	(3) Shirley Wherry, Modesto, Calif.	89	94	88	271
	(3) Jean Marshall, Canby, Ore.	92	92	87	271
	(2) Patricia Feiling, North Highlands, Calif.	87	87	97	271
95.	(4) Janet Beardsley, Centerville, Ohio	92	90	90	272
	(1) Marilyn Willey, San Jose, Calif.	88	91	93	272
	(4) Marion Senteno, Roswell, N.M.	89	90	93	272
98.	(2) Annette Reynolds, Yuba City, Calif.	95	89	89	273
	(2) Natalie Pacileo, Erie, Pa.	94	88	91	273
	(2) Donna Bodtker, Portland, Ore.	91	90	92	273
	(2) Joan Ruvane, Durham, N.C.	94	86	93	273
102.	(3) Lynn Polan, Cincinnati, Ohio	93	89	92	274
	(3) Ella Mae Record, San Jacinto, Calif.	89	91	94	274
	(4) Mary Gandsey, Templeton, Calif.	85	93	96	274
105.	(1) Joan Sheering, Carson City, Nev.	93	94	89	276
	(1) Cindy Edgerle, Grand Haven, Mich.	95	89	92	276
	(4) Jada Gay, The Dalles, Ore.	90	91	95	276
108.	(2) Catherine Swanson, Torrance, Calif.	90	93	95	278
109.	(4) Barbara Mills, San Francisco, Calif.	92	95	92	279
	(3) Betty Zaiger, Modesto, Calif.	91	98	90	279
111.	(2) Patricia Najarian, Alamo, Calif.	93	90	97	280
112.	(4) Kathryn Anhalt, Manitowoc, Wis.	92	100	94	286
113.	(4) Camilla Dittrich, Ormond Beach, Fla.	95	101	91	287
114.	(2) Shelah Clapp, Indianapolis, Ind.	93	97	99	289
115.	(1) Evelyn Burris, Modesto, Calif.	97	94	99	290
116.	(1) Barbara Fay Boddie, Shreveport, La.	97	101	95	293
117.	(4) Barbara Fox, St. Louis, Mo.	107	99	94	300

SENIOR OPEN CHAMPIONSHIP

FRANCIS OUIMET TROPHY

Presented in 1980 by

The Country Club, Brookline, Massachusetts, and
GOLFERS OF MASSACHUSETTS

HISTORY

1981—Arnold Palmer, 51, of Latrobe, Pennsylvania, won the Senior Open Championship at the Oakland Hills Country Club in Birmingham, Michigan. Although it was the second Senior Open, it was the first at the lowered age format of 50 and older. Palmer became only the second golfer to win three different USGA Championships. Palmer joins JoAnne Gunderson Carner who won the Girls' Junior once, the Women's Amateur five times and the Women's Open twice. Palmer had won his first, the 1954 Amateur Championship, just 19 miles down the road at the Country Club of Detroit. The second was his memorable come-from-behind victory in the 1960 Open Championship at Cherry Hills Country Club in Englewood, Colorado. The first round leader was former PGA Champion Lionel Hebert with a score of 70. Three players were home with 71s—Jim Ferree and two former Masters winners Art Wall, Jr., and Bob Goalby. Palmer and Stone were in a group at 72 which included Sam Snead, a former British Open, PGA and Masters Champion. Casper, the two-time Open Champion and a former Masters winner, was at 73. On the second day, Goalby posted a second consecutive 71 for a 142 total, one stroke ahead of Wall, Stone and George Bayer. Casper's 72 left him at 145, three off the pace, and Palmer stumbled to a 76 which left him at 148, six behind Goalby. Hebert, the first-round leader posted a 77 and fell out of contention. Before a large Saturday crowd, Palmer recorded a 68, the Championship's first under par round. It gained him a tie for the 54-hole lead with Casper and Wall at 216. Casper had a fine 71 and Wall, a 73. Stone posted a 74 and was one stroke back at 217. At one point in the fourth round when Wall and Stone finished the 14th hole and Palmer and Casper the 13th, all four players were tied at seven over par for the Championship. Wall lost a stroke to par on each of the last three holes to finish 10 over. Stone three-putted the 17th and 18th to finish nine over. Casper bogied the 14th and 15th, but parred the final three holes to finish also nine over. Palmer bogied the 16th when he overshot the green and parred the 17th. Standing on the 18th tee, Palmer had a one stroke lead over Casper, his playing companion and Stone, who had finished ahead of him. Palmer pulled his second shot to the 18th green and missed a 10-foot putt for par. Casper two-putted from 25 feet for a par. Palmer, Casper and Stone were deadlocked at 289, nine over par, setting the stage for a playoff on the fifth day. In the playoff, Stone birdied the second hole and eagled the fifth hole, holing a 7-iron from 170 yards out. At this point he was three under par and five strokes ahead of Palmer. When Palmer three-putted the sixth, he trailed Stone by six strokes. Casper, who had one bogey and the rest pars, was four strokes behind Stone. From the seventh hole on, Palmer had four birdies, one bogey and the rest pars. When Stone bogeyed the seventh and ninth holes and Palmer birdied the eighth and ninth, Stone's lead was reduced from six strokes to two. At the 12th hole, Palmer birdied from 10 feet and drew even with Stone, who bogeyed. At the 13th, a par-3, Stone regained the lead when Palmer three-putted, but Palmer drew even again with a par at the 14th. Casper, playing steady golf throughout, was just one stroke behind Palmer and Stone after 14 holes, but an 8 on the par-4 16th ended his chances. Palmer went on to birdie the 15th with a 40-foot putt after bouncing a low 3-iron shot onto the green. He then parred his way home from there while Stone was making three successive bogeys. Palmer finished with an even par 70 to Stone's 74 and Casper's 77. Forty-four professionals and six amateurs made the 36-hole cut at 154, 14 over par. Glenn Johnson was the low amateur with a 301 total. A total of $150,000 in prize money was awarded, an increase from $100,000 for the 1980 Championship. The USGA received 743 entries, up from 631 the first year.

1982—Miller Barber, 51, of Sherman, Texas, shot 65 in the fourth round and won the Senior Open Championship, played at the Portland Golf Club, in Portland, Oregon. The first-round leaders were a pair of club pros, Ken Towns, from Graeagle, California, and Joe Jimenez, of Jefferson City, Missouri, with even-par 71s. Barber was one back at 72, along with former Masters winner Bob Goalby, Freddie Haas, and Art Silvestrone. Former U.S. Open Champion Gene Littler took the 36-hole lead at 142. Goalby was one behind at 143, along with Gay Brewer, former Masters winner. Dan Sikes was at 144, along with defending champion Arnold Palmer. Towns remained in contention with 145, but Jimenez played his way out of the picture with 78, for 149. Sikes posted a 72 on Saturday to take the 54-hole lead at 216. One back was Barber, who fired the day's lowest round, 71; Goalby, who slipped to 74; Palmer, who posted 73; and Towns, who carded 72. Littler shot 76 and was next, at 218, along with Brewer, who could only manage 75. The final round belonged to Barber. His 65 was the lowest round of the week by three strokes. His score for 72 holes was 282, the only score under par. Littler shot 68 and tied for second, with Sikes, who had 70, at 286. Goalby had 72 and finished at 289, followed by Brewer and Palmer, at 291. Palmer trailed Barber by three strokes after making a birdie on the 13th hole, but Barber birdied the 14th and 16th to pick up six strokes on Palmer, who bogeyed the 14th and 15th and double-bogeyed the 16th. Towns finished seventh at 292 after a 75, followed by Charles Sifford, who used a final-round 69 to finish at 293. Barber's 282 established a new Championship record. Roberto DeVicenzo set the previous mark of 285 in the first Senior Open, at Winged Foot Golf Club (East Course), in 1980. Barber's final-round 65 also set by three shots a Championship record for lowest 18-hole score. In addition, another Championship record was set as seven sub-par rounds were recorded. Forty-six professionals and four amateurs made the 36-hole cut at 154, 12 over par. A total of $150,033 in prize money was awarded. The USGA received 665 entries, down from 743 the year before, but up from 631 the first year.

1983—Billy Casper, 52, of Mapleton, Utah, holed a 10-foot putt for a birdie on the first extra hole of a playoff round against Rod Funseth to win the U.S. Senior Open Championship, his third USGA title. Casper, the 1959 and 1966 U.S. Open Champion, shot 288, four over par, on rounds of 73-69-73-73. Funseth shot 73-71-74-70-288. Each shot 75 in the scheduled 18-hole playoff, and Casper then birdied the extra hole. The Championship was played at the Hazeltine National Golf Club, in Chaska, Minnesota. Three players tied for the lead at the end of the first round, with 70, one under par. They were Jack Harden, 70; John Cook, a Minnesota club professional; and Richard King, who played the first nine in 30, a record. Roberto De Vicenzo, the first Senior Open Champion, in 1980, was among a group of eight players at 71. Defending Champion Miller Barber, Casper, Funseth, and Arnold Palmer, the 1981 Senior Open Champion, were at 73. De Vicenzo moved into the 36-hole lead, at 141, by shooting 70 in the second round. One stroke behind, at 142, were Casper, who had 69, the lowest round of the Championship; Miller Barber and Dan Sikes, Jr., each with 70; and Guy Wolstenholme, with his second consecutive 71. Funseth's 71 left him at 144, two strokes behind. Gusty winds caused high scores in the third round. Casper took the lead with a 73 that gave him a 54-hole score of 215, two over par, and a three-stroke lead over De Vicenzo, who struggled to a 77; Jerry Barber, with 73; and Funseth, with 74. Miller Barber, Wolstenholme, and Sikes all shot 78 to fall five strokes behind Casper. In the fourth round, Casper played the first nine in even par while Funseth lost one stroke. With nine holes to play, Casper led Funseth by four strokes. Miller Barber and Wolstenholme were five back. Funseth birdied the 10th and 11th holes to move two strokes closer, and when Casper bogeyed the 12th, Funseth was only one behind. He drew even when Casper bogeyed the 14th. Miller Barber, meanwhile, birdied three holes on the closing nine, but he lost a stroke at the 18th and shot 70, for a 290 finish, one stroke ahead of Wolstenholme, who had another 71. Funseth took the lead with a birdie at the 17th. Playing just ahead of Casper, Funseth drove into a fairway bunker on the 18th hole and bogeyed. Tied with Funseth at that point, Casper drove from the 18th tee into the rough, missed the green with a 7-iron, but chipped within two feet and holed the putt to set up the playoff. Casper, who had lost a playoff for the 1981 Senior Open to Palmer, fell three strokes behind after four holes, but by the end of nine, he had made up all three strokes. He was one stroke ahead going to the last hole, but bogeyed, causing extra holes. On the extra hole, Casper drove 280 yards, hit his 8-iron to within 10 feet of the hole, and holed the winning putt. Despite the overall high scoring, the field recorded 12 under-par rounds, the most for any Senior Open. Fifty-three professionals and nine amateurs made the 36-hole cut, at 155, 13 over par. A total of $173,280 in prize money was awarded, including $30,566 to Casper. The USGA accepted a record 756 entries.

1984—Miller Barber, 53, of Sherman, Texas, became the first man to win the Senior Open championship twice. He shot 286 and won by two strokes over Arnold Palmer, at the Oak Hill Country Club, in Rochester, New York. Barber won previously in 1982. Bob Goalby held the first-round lead with 70, a figure that only two players bettered in the remainder of the championship. One was Palmer, with 68 in the second round, the lowest of the championship, with 142, he led Goalby by two strokes after 36 holes, and Barber was three strokes behind, at 145. After eight holes of the third round, Goalby had a three-stroke advantage on Palmer, but Palmer played the final 10 holes one under par and regained his two-stroke lead. Barber shot 70, which placed him just one stroke behind Palmer. Goalby faltered in the fourth round, and Palmer and Barber swapped the lead. Palmer led by two strokes after the fourth hole, but his approach to the fifth fell into a pond and Barber caught him with a birdie. Barber went ahead for good at the seventh with a par to Palmer's bogey, and Palmer fell three behind with bogeys at the 11th and 12th holes. Palmer birdied the 14th to draw within two strokes, but as he attempted to tap in a short putt for bogey on the 15th after missing from eight feet, Palmer scuffed the ground and missed the ball. No one but Palmer had seen it, but he called a penalty on himself. Barber then missed a short putt of his own for a par. Barber then led by three strokes. Dale Morey and Fordie Pitts, Jr., were low amateurs at 305. The USGA accepted a record 861 entries, an increase of 105 over 1983.

1985—Miller Barber, 54, of Sherman, Texas, won his second consecutive Senior Open Championship and his third in five tries. Barber's three-under-par 285 beat 1980 champion Roberto De Vicenzo by four strokes at Edgewood Tahoe Golf Course in Stateline, Nevada. Barber's other wins in the Senior Open came in 1982 and 1984. The first-round lead was held by Walter Zembriski of Orlando, Florida, who set a Senior Open first-round record with 68. Peter Thomson of Australia and Barber were the only other golfers to shoot rounds below par on the first day. Thomson posted a 70. Barber recorded a 71. Zembriski shot 73 in the second round, giving him a 141 total, one stroke better than De Vicenzo, who had a second-round 68. Barber posted an even-par 72 and was two strokes off the pace of Zembriski. Barber gained the lead in the third round, posting his second round of 71 for the Championship. Zembriski opened his round with five pars then managed only one birdie to six bogeys for the rest of the day and finished with a 78. De Vicenzo held onto second place, but his 75 left him three strokes behind Barber. The defending champion sealed his victory early on the final day as he birdied three of the first four holes on his way to another round of 71 and the victory. De Vicenzo shot a final-round 72 to secure second place, two strokes ahead of Gay Brewer. William Hyndman, III, the 1973 and 1983 Senior Amateur champion, was low amateur at 303. The USGA received a record 1,029 entries for the Championship.

1986—Dale Douglass, 50, of Boulder, Colorado, won the Senior Open Championship in his first year of eligibility. His 72-hole total of five-under-par 279 was a record for the championship. Gary Player finished second, one stroke behind Douglass. Harold Henning was two strokes off the pace in third. Douglass led throughout the week. He birdied five consecutive holes—the sixth through 10th—in the first round. His opening-round 66 placed him two strokes ahead of Lee Elder and three ahead of Jim Ferree, James Hatfield and Ken Still. Douglass built his lead to three strokes after a second-round 72. Still and Ferree also posted 72s to remain three strokes off the pace. A third-round 68 gave Douglass a 54-hole total of 206, seven under par. Gary Player shot 66 to move into second place at 210. Henning and Ferree were tied for third at 212. Douglass played erratically early in the fourth round, alternating birdies and bogeys and losing one stroke to par. Player parred the first seven holes before birdieing the eighth to pull to within two strokes. Another birdie at the par-4 11th cut Douglass' lead to one. The margin remained one stroke until the 15th, where Douglass saved par from the front greenside bunker while Player three-putted from fifteen feet for bogey. Player bogeyed the 16th as well to fall three strokes behind. A Player birdie on the 17th and a Douglass bogey on 18 reduced the final margin to one stroke. Robert Hoff of Rochester, New York, shot 299 to earn low-amateur honors. The USGA accepted a record 1,225 entries for the championship.

1987—Gary Player, 51, shot rounds of 69-68-67-66—270 to win the Senior Open at Brooklawn Country Club in Fairfield, Connecticut. Player's record total of 270 was nine strokes better than the previous record of 279 set by Dale Douglass in 1986. Player became the third golfer, along with Arnold Palmer and Billy Casper, to win the U.S. Open and the Senior Open. Player won the U.S. Open in 1965. Gordon Jones, who posted seven birdies during an eight-hole stretch, and Peter Thomson shared the opening-round lead at 66, five under par. John Brodie was one stroke behind at 67. Four golfers—Gene Borek, Larry Mowry, Chi Chi Rodriguez and Doug Sanders—were two strokes behind at 68. Rodriguez's second 68 gave him the 36-hole lead by one stroke over Brodie and Player, who stood at 137. Arnold Palmer was two strokes behind Rodriguez after shooting rounds of 69-69—138. Sixty-three players, including 10 amateurs, survived the 36-hole cut at 149. Player caught Rodriguez when he birdied the 17th hole of the third round, and he took a two-stroke advantage when Rodriguez bogeyed the 18th. Player's 54-hole total of 204 was five better than Bob Charles and Don Massengale, who shared third place at 209. Player recorded four birdies in the first eight holes of the final round, extending his lead to four strokes, and he never looked back on his way to a final round 66. Doug Sanders posted a 65 to finish in second place, six strokes behind Player and one stroke ahead of Rodriguez, who shot 71. The six-stroke margin of victory is the largest in Senior Open history. Dennis Iden, a reinstated amateur from Seal Beach, California, was the low amateur at eight-over-par 292. The USGA accepted a record 1,277 entries for the championship.

1988—Gary Player, 52, became the second man to win successive Senior Opens when he defeated Bob Charles by two strokes in an 18-hole playoff at Medinah (Illinois) Country Club. Miller Barber won the 1984 and 1985 Senior Open Championships in addition to his 1982 title. Player shot 74-70-71-73—288 to force a playoff with Charles, who had rounds of 75-70-70-73—288. Billy Casper, the 1983 Senior Open champion, and Walt Zembriski posted rounds of three-under-par 69 to share the first-round lead. Harold Henning was one stroke behind. Casper shot a 70, one under par, in the second round to take a four-stroke lead at four-under par 140. Zembriski was close behind Casper until the par-3 17th hole where he put two balls in Lake Kadijah on his way to a 7. He finished his round in 75 for an even-par 36-hole total of 144. Henning and Lou Graham, who had won the 1975 U.S. Open at Medinah, moved ahead of Zembriski. They were tied for second at 143. After the third round, Player and Casper shared the lead at one-under-par 215. Casper shot 76 in the third round and was tied with Graham, one stroke behind at even par. By the 14th hole of the final round, Charles had a three-stroke lead over Player, but Charles bogeyed the next three holes to Player's par and the two again were tied. Both men parred the 18th, forcing the playoff. Player took a two-stroke lead at the third hole of the playoff round when he tapped in a short birdie putt after Charles' bogey. Charles bogeyed the fourth to fall three strokes behind. Player birdied the seventh to extend his lead to four strokes. Charles managed to birdie three holes on the second nine, but Player played the back in two under par. He won the playoff 68-70. Robert Housen was the low amateur with rounds of 77-76-75-74—302. The USGA accepted 1,662 entries for the championship.

1989—Orville Moody charged into the lead with an eight-under-par 64 in the third round, and became only the fourth man to win both the U.S. Open and the U.S. Senior Open. Moody had won the U.S. Open in 1969. Moody won the Senior Open by two strokes over Frank Beard, shooting 279 at Laurel Valley Golf Club, in Ligonier, Pennsylvania. Beard shot 281. With rounds of 72 and 73, Moody, age 55, had fallen six strokes behind the leaders after two days of play. He took the lead near the end of the third round, and won by shooting 70 in the fourth round, helped by an eagle 3 on the sixth hole. He joins Arnold Palmer, Gary Player, and Billy Casper as winners of both. There were 14 rounds shot in the 60s, but except for Moody's 64, none drew as much attention as the 69 by amateur Frank Boydston in the first round. As Boydston fell behind on succeeding days, Jim McMurtrey became low amateur with a 72-hole total of 300.

1990—Lee Trevino combined first and last rounds of 67 and won by two strokes over Jack Nicklaus, at the Ridgewood Country Club, in Paramus, New Jersey. Trevino shot 275, 13 under par, and Nicklaus shot 277. Gary Player, Mike Hill and Chi Chi Rodriguez tied for third place, at 281. Hill and Rodriguez shot final rounds in the 60s, and Player shot 73. With rounds of 67-68, Trevino held a one-stroke advantage over Jim Dent after 36 holes, but he surrendered the lead to Nicklaus after the third round. Nicklaus shot 67, and led by a stroke, with 207. Trevino rebounded from his third round of 73 and promptly birdied the second, third, and sixth holes of his final round to regain the lead. Nicklaus made a move on the final nine, with birdies the 11th, 13th, 15th, and 16th, but a bogey at the 17th dropped him two strokes behind. Player's second round of 65 was the lowest score. He began the round with seven consecutive birdies—a record for the Senior Open.

SENIOR OPEN CHAMPIONSHIP

DATE	WINNER, RUNNER-UP	SCORE	SITE	ENTRY
1981 (July)	Arnold Palmer	289-70	Oakland Hills C.C.,	743
	Bob Stone	289-74	Birmingham, Mich.	
	Billy Casper	289-77		
1982 (July)	Miller Barber	282	Portland G.C.,	665
	Gene Littler	286	Portland, Ore.	
	Dan Sikes, Jr.	286		
1983 (July)	Billy Casper	†288-75-3	Hazeltine National G.C.,	756
	Ron Funseth	†288-75-4	Chaska, Minn.	
1984 (June-July)	Miller Barber	286	Oak Hill C.C.,	861
	Arnold Palmer	288	Rochester, N.Y.	
1985 (June)	Miller Barber	285	Edgewood Tahoe G.C.,	1,029
	Roberto De Vincenzo	289	Stateline, Nev.	
1986 (June)	Dale Douglass	279	Scioto C.C.,	1,225
	Gary Player	280	Columbus, Ohio	
1987 (July)	Gary Player	270	Brooklawn C.C.,	1,277
	Doug Sanders	276	Fairfield, Conn.	
1988 (Aug.)	Gary Player	228-68	Medinach C.C.,	1,662
	Bob Charles	288-70	Medinah, Ill.	
1989 (June-July)	Orville Moody	279	Laurel Valley G.C.,	1,762
	Frank Beard	282	Ligonier, Pa.	
1990 (June-July)	Lee Trevino	275	Ridgewood C.C.,	‡1,890
	Jack Nicklaus	277	Paramus, N.J.	

‡Record entry
†Sudden-death playoff

1981
SECOND SENIOR OPEN CHAMPIONSHIP

Oakland Hills Country Club (South Course), Birmingham, Michigan, July 9-12
Yardage—6,798. Par 70. †743 Entries, 150 Qualifiers, 150 Starters.

						Score	Money Prize
1	+Arnold Palmer, Laurel Valley G.C., Ligonier, Pa.	72	76	68	73	289	$26,000.00
	+Bob Stone, Crackerneck G.C., Independence, Mo.	72	71	74	72	289	9,586.00
	+Billy Casper, Springville, Utah	73	72	71	73	289	9,586.00
4	Art Wall, Sonoita, Ariz.	71	72	73	74	290	6,736.00
5	Gene Littler, Rancho Santa Fe, Calif.	75	71	75	71	292	6,136.00
6	Miller Barber, Woodlawn C.C., Sherman, Texas	74	71	74	74	293	5,636.00
7	Bob Goalby, Belleville, Ill.	71	71	76	76	294	5,136.00
8	Mike Souchak, Innisbrook, Tarpon Springs, Fla.	75	74	78	69	296	4,036.00
	Stan Thirsk, Kansas City C.C., Mission Hills, Kans.	73	77	75	71	296	4,036.00
	Michael Fetchick, Dix Hills, N.Y.	76	73	75	72	296	4,036.00
	Lionel Hebert, LaFayette, La.	70	77	74	75	296	4,036.00
12	Mac Main, Longwood College G.C., Farmville, Va.	78	75	71	74	298	3,136.00
13	Jim Ferree, Westmoreland C.C., Export, Pa.	71	78	79	72	300	2,569.34
	Billy Maxwell, Hyde Park G.C., Jacksonville, Fla.	76	75	75	74	300	2,569.33
	George Bayer, Detroit G.C., Detroit, Mich.	73	70	77	80	300	2,569.33
16	Dow Finsterwald, Broadmoor G.C., Colorado Springs, Colo.	81	73	74	73	301	1,856.00
	a-Glenn Johnson, Grosse Ile G.&C.C., Grosse Ile, Mich.	77	77	72	75	301	Medal
	Sam Snead, Homestead G.&T.C., Hot Springs, Va.	72	77	76	76	301	1,856.00
	Doug Higgins, Diamond Oaks C.C., Fort Worth, Texas	74	78	73	76	301	1,856.00
	Dick Sarta, Preakness Hills C.C., Wayne, N.J.	73	75	75	78	301	1,856.00
	Dan Sikes, Hidden Hills C.C., Jacksonville, Fla.	79	74	70	78	301	1,856.00
22	Stan Dudas, Mays Landing C.C., McKee City, N.J.	75	79	73	75	302	1,436.00
	Dean Lind, Sacramento, Calif.	76	74	76	76	302	1,436.00
	Howie Johnson, Chaparral C.C., Palm Desert, Calif.	76	75	74	77	302	1,436.00
	Freddie Haas, Metairie, La.	75	76	73	78	302	1,436.00
	Gardner Dickinson, Frenchman's Crk. G.C., Frenchman's Crk., Fla.	72	76	72	82	302	1,436.00
27	Bill Ogden, North Shore C.C., Glenview, Ill.	79	75	76	73	303	1,286.00
28	Doug Ford, Sherbrooke C.C., Lake Worth, Fla.	77	73	78	76	304	1,211.00
	Milon Marusic, Algonquin G.C., Glendale, Mo.	77	73	76	78	304	1,211.00
	Gordon E. Jones, Bay Hill C., Orlando, Fla.	74	78	74	78	304	1,211.00
	a-James G. Jackson, Algonquin G.C., Glendale, Mo.	73	79	73	79	304	Medal
32	Al Mengert, Oakland Hills C.C., Birmingham, Mich.	75	75	79	76	305	1,136.00
	Joe Cheves, Mimosa Hills G.&C.C., Morganton, N.C.	75	74	77	79	305	1,136.00
	Tom Nieporte, Winged Foot G.C., Mamaroneck, N.Y.	72	76	74	83	305	1,136.00
35	a-William C. Campbell, Guyan G.&C.C., Huntington, W.V.	72	79	77	78	306	Medal
36	a-Allan Sussel, Squires G.C., Ambler, Pa.	77	75	77	78	307	Medal
37	Ted Kroll, Boca Raton, Fla.	75	78	77	79	309	1,086.00
38	a-Joe Simpson, Stardust C.C., San Diego, Calif.	78	75	82	75	310	Medal
	Joe Jimenez, Jefferson City C.C., Jefferson City, Mo.	76	77	78	79	310	1,037.67
	Joseph Sodd, Olympic Hills G.C., Eden Prairie, Minn.	74	80	75	81	310	1,037.67
	Charles Owens, Tampa, Fla.	78	71	78	83	310	1,037.66
42	a-Leo Kubiak, Ironwood C.C., Palm Desert, Calif.	73	77	75	86	311	Medal
43	George L. Thomas, Elcona C.C., Elkhart, Ind.	77	77	72	86	312	996.00
44	Murry Jacobs, Lew F. Galbraith G.C., Berkeley, Calif.	72	78	79	84	313	976.00
45	Bob Duden, Glendoveer G.C., Portland, Ore.	76	78	83	77	314	946.00
	George Butler, Roger Park, Tampa, Fla.	79	75	78	82	314	946.00
47	B.G. Halbert, Onion Creek C., Austin, Texas	75	79	81	81	316	921.00
	Richard Lotz, Tower Tee, Affton, Mo.	77	75	81	83	316	921.00
49	Ray Montgomery, La Gorce C.C., Miami Beach, Fla.	75	78	80	84	317	906.00

+Playoff, July 13, 1981, Arnold Palmer 70, Bob Stone 74, Billy Casper 77.
a-Amateur
†Record Entry

Money prizes were divided among the 58 professionals who did not make the cut. The amount involved is $17,700.00. Accordingly, 131,702.00 was divided equally among the 49 professionals for a total of $149,102.00.

1982
THIRD SENIOR OPEN CHAMPIONSHIP

Portland Golf Club, Portland, Oregon, July 8-11.
Yardage — 6,439. Par 71. 665 Entries, 150 Qualifiers, 150 Starters.

						Score	Money Prize
1	Miller Barber, Woodlawn C.C., Sherman, Texas	72	74	71	65	282	$28,648.00
2	Gene Littler, Rancho Santa Fe G.C., Rancho Santa Fe, Calif.	73	69	76	68	286	12,519.50
	Dan Sikes, Jr., Hidden Hills G.C., Jacksonville, Fla.	75	69	72	70	286	12,519.50
4	Bob Goalby, Belleville, Ill.	72	71	74	72	289	6,532.00
5	Gay Brewer, Desert Horizons C.C., Indian Wells, Calif.	73	70	75	73	291	4,813.00
	Arnold Palmer, Laurel Valley G.C., Ligonier, Pa.	73	71	73	74	291	4,813.00
7	Ken Towns, Graeagle Meadows G.C., Graeagle, Calif.	71	74	72	75	292	3,942.00
8	Charles Sifford, Sleepy Hollow G.C., Brecksville, Ohio	76	71	77	69	293	3,572.00
9	Jack Fleck, Hardscrabble C.C., Ft. Smith, Ark.	73	72	75	74	294	3,282.00
10	Bob Gajda, Forest Lake C.C., Bloomfield Hills, Mich.	75	74	72	74	295	2,890.00
	Howie Johnson, Chaparral C.C., Palm Desert, Calif.	74	73	72	76	295	2,890.00
12	Art Wall, Jr., Sonoita, Ariz.	75	74	74	74	297	2,608.00
13	Billy Casper, Springville, Utah	77	76	72	73	298	2,409.00
	Joe Jimenez, Jefferson City C.C., Jefferson City, Mo.	71	78	72	77	298	2,409.00
15	Bob Rosburg, Silverado C.C., Napa, Calif.	74	74	74	77	299	2,223.00
16	Art Silvestrone, Bay Hill Club, Orlando, Fla.	72	77	80	71	300	2,058.00
	Joseph Sodd, Interlachen C.C., Edina, Minn.	77	74	74	75	300	2,058.00
18	Doug Higgins, Diamond Oaks C.C., Ft. Worth, Texas	81	73	74	73	301	1,865.50
	Peter Thomson, Malvern, Victoria, Australia	74	77	74	76	301	1,865.50
20	Billy Maxwell, Hyde Park G. & C.C., Jacksonville, Fla.	78	73	78	73	302	1,714.50
	Don Fairfield, Eldorado C.C., Indian Wells, Calif.	76	76	76	74	302	1,714.50
22	Dean Lind, Sacramento, Calif.	77	76	78	72	303	1,468.00
	John Langford, Inwood C.C., Inwood, N.Y.	78	76	77	72	303	1,468.00
	Stan Thirsk, Kansas City C.C., Mission Hills, Kan.	78	73	76	76	303	1,468.00
	Michael Fetchick, Dix Hills, N.Y.	78	74	75	76	303	1,468.00
	Tom Nieporte, Winged Foot G.C., Mamaroneck, N.Y.	73	79	74	77	303	1,468.00
	Robert Erickson, Deer Run G.C., Casselberry, Fla.	78	75	72	78	303	1,468.00
	Robert Stone, Crackerneck G.C., Independence, Mo.	77	74	73	79	303	1,468.00
29	Lionel Hebert, Lafayette, La.	76	77	80	71	304	1,249.00
	Mac Main, Longwood College G.C., Farmville, Va.	73	76	82	73	304	1,249.00
	Denis Hutchinson, South Africa	78	72	80	74	304	1,249.00
32	Fred Hawkins, Bristol, Wis.	75	78	79	73	305	1,146.00
	George Bayer, Detroit G.C., Detroit, Mich.	75	76	77	77	305	1,146.00
34	Jerry Barber, Griffith Park G.C., Los Angeles, Calif.	73	80	77	76	306	1,043.00
	John Zontek, The Olympic C., San Francisco, Calif.	73	80	77	76	306	1,043.00
	George Thomas, Elcona C.C., Elkhart, Ind.	77	76	77	76	306	1,043.00
37	Hampton Auld, Edgewood C.C., Sissonville, W. Va.	76	78	79	74	307	960.00
38	Donald Hoenig, Raceway G.C., Thompson, Conn.	77	77	77	77	308	919.00
39	Everett Vinzant, Overland Park G.C., Overland Park, Kans.	78	74	82	75	309	864.34
	Fred Wampler, French Lick Springs G. & T.C., French Lick, Ind.	78	76	78	77	309	864.33
	Jack Webb, Wakonda C., Des Moines, Iowa	79	75	77	78	309	864.33
42	a-John Harbottle, Tacoma C. & G.C., Tacoma, Wash.	79	72	80	79	310	Medal
43	Freddie Haas, Belle Terre C.C., La Place, La.	72	76	77	86	311	809.00
44	a-Ted Richards, Jr., Bel Air C.C., Los Angeles, Calif.	74	80	81	77	312	Medal
	a-Howard Slocum, Oswego Lake C.C., Lake Oswego, Ore.	75	79	77	81	312	Medal
	Tommy Williams, White Barn G.C., Pleasant View, Utah	77	73	84	78	312	768.00
	Stan Jawor, Southgate, Mich.	74	75	81	82	312	768.00
48	Dick Sarta, Preakness Hills C.C., Wayne, N.J.	79	75	76	83	313	727.00
49	a-Arthur Ellis, North Shore C.C., Glenview, Ill.	73	78	86	77	314	Medal
50	Chico Miartuz, Bayshore G.C., Miami, Fla.	74	77	82	82	315	699.00

a-Amateur

1983
FOURTH SENIOR OPEN CHAMPIONSHIP

Hazeltine National Golf Club, Chaska, Minnesota, July 21-25
Yardage—6,625. Par 71. †756 Entries, 150 Qualifiers, 150 Starters

						Score	Money Prize
† 1	Billy Casper, Mapleton, Utah	73	69	73	73	288	$30,566.00
†	Rod Funseth, Silverado C.C., Napa, Calif.	73	71	74	70	288	17,466.00
3	Miller Barber, Continental C.C., Wildwood, Fla.	72	70	78	70	290	10,525.00
4	Guy Wolstenholme, Cuyahoga Falls, Ohio	71	71	78	71	291	7,642.00
5	Peter Thomson, Victoria G.C., Melbourne, Australia	71	75	75	71	292	6,033.00
6	Roberto De Vicenzo, Ranelagh G.C., Argentina	71	70	77	75	293	5,229.00
7	Jerry Barber, Griffith Park G. Course, Los Angeles, Calif.	71	74	73	76	294	4,612.00
	Gay Brewer, Palm Springs, Calif.	76	71	74	74	295	4,178.00
9	Charles Sifford, Sleepy Hollow G.C., Brecksville, Ohio	73	72	74	77	296	3,840.00
10	Art Silvestrone, Winter Park Pines, Winter Park, Fla.	75	75	75	72	297	3,518.00
11	Arnold Palmer, Laurel Valley G.C., Ligonier, Pa.	73	79	75	71	298	3,148.00
	Gardner Dickinson, Frenchman's Cr.G.C., Frenchman's Cr., Fla.	72	76	77	73	298	3,148.00
13	Charles Green, Seabee G.C., Port Hueneme, Calif.	75	77	77	70	299	2,818.00
	Howard Johnson, Mission Hills C.C., Rancho Mirage, Calif.	78	76	74	71	299	2,818.00
15	Robert Stone, Crackerneck G. Course, Independence, Mo.	71	78	72	79	300	2,356.60
	Gene Littler, Rancho Santa Fe G.C., Rancho Santa Fe, Calif.	75	78	73	74	300	2,356.60
	Denis Hutchinson, Kewsington G.C., South Africa	74	78	73	75	300	2,356.60
	Paul Thomas, Zanesville C.C., Zanesville, Ohio	75	78	71	76	300	2,356.60
	Dan Sikes, Jr., Hidden Hill C.C., Jacksonville, Fla.	72	70	78	80	300	2,356.60
	a-Robert Rawlins, Las Colinas C.C., Irvine, Texas	71	76	76	78	300	Medal
21	Fred Hawkins, Sun N Lake C.C., Sebring, Fla.	76	77	78	70	301	2,006.00
	Freddie Haas, Belle Terre C.C., La Place, La.	74	73	76	78	301	2,006.00
23	George Thomas, Elcona C.C., Elkhart, Ind.	79	76	74	73	302	1,877.00
	John Cook, Minnetonka, Minn.	70	74	78	80	302	1,877.00
25	Joe Jimenez, Jefferson City C.C., Jefferson City, Mo.	74	78	78	73	303	1,717.00
	Billy Maxwell, Hyde Park G.C., Jacksonville, Fla.	78	72	79	74	303	1,717.00
	Doug Ford, Sherbrooke G.C., Lake Worth, Fla.	76	77	74	76	303	1,717.00
28	James Shaw, Eberhart G.C., Mishawaka, Ind.	74	79	78	73	304	1,534.00
	a-Allan Sussel, Squires G.C., Ambler, Pa.	77	76	76	75	304	Medal
	Lionel Hebert, Lafayette, La.	71	74	83	76	304	1,534.00
	Ed Causey, Grenelefe G. & T.C., Grenelefe, Fla.	74	78	76	76	304	1,534.00
	Robert Crowley, Pine Brook C.C., Weston, Mass.	76	72	79	77	304	1,534.00
33	Mike Fetchick, Dix Hills, N.Y.	80	73	77	75	305	1,389.50
	a-Richard Evans, Knollwood C., Lake Forest, Ill.	71	77	81	76	305	Medal
	Ken Towns, Graeagle Meadows G.C., Graeagle, Calif.	77	72	80	76	305	1,389.50
	a-E.R. Updegraff, Tucson C.C., Tucson, Ariz.	81	70	76	78	305	Medal
37	Robert Erickson, Casselberry, Fla.	75	78	81	72	306	1,295.00
	Bob Goetz, Preston Trail G.C., Dallas, Texas	78	75	76	77	306	1,295.00
39	Stan Thirsk, Kansas City C.C., Mission Hills, Kans.	73	79	82	73	307	1,198.00
	Roger Floyd, Bentwinds G. & C.C., Fuquay-Varina, N.C.	82	73	77	75	307	1,198.00
41	Dean Lind, Sacramento, Calif.	74	77	84	73	308	1,125.00
42	Jim Cochran, Crescent C.C., Crescent, Mo.	75	77	84	73	309	1,077.00
43	David Cupit, Rivermont G. & C.C., Alpharetta, Ga.	73	79	80	78	310	1,009.00
	James Hatfield, Elk River C.C., Noel, Mo.	76	76	80	78	310	1,009.00
	Frank Freer, Plymouth, Minn.	73	80	77	80	310	1,009.00
46	a-John Owens, Idle Hour C.C., Lexington, Ky.	76	79	79	77	311	Medal
47	Don Bergman, St. Andrews G.C., Cedar Rapids, Iowa	80	75	77	80	312	928.50
	Bob Gajda, Forest Lake C.C., Bloomfield Hills, Mich.	76	78	75	83	312	928.50
49	Dayton Olson, Meadowbrook G.C., Hopkins, Minn.	79	76	83	75	313	880.00
50	Milon Marusic, Algonquin G.C., Glendale, Mo.	76	76	86	76	314	815.67
	Jack Harden, Surf 'N Turf, Del Mar, Calif.	70	80	87	77	314	815.66
	Roland Stafford, Kass Inn, Margaretville, N.Y.	79	75	79	81	314	815.66
53	John Langford, Inwood C.C., Inwood, N.Y.	79	75	86	76	316	700.34
	John Kalinka, Bayview G. Center, Kaneohe, Hawaii	74	81	83	78	316	700.33
	Pete Hessemer, Memorial Park G. Course, Houston, Texas	78	76	83	79	316	700.33
	a-Richard Stearns, Tantallon, Tantallon, Md.	79	73	82	82	316	Medal
	a-John Harbottle, Tacoma C.& G.C., Tacoma, Wash.	81	74	79	82	316	Medal
58	a-Louis Raganella, Lake Lorraine G. & T.C., Shalimar, Fla.	77	78	80	84	319	Medal
	a-Loyal Chapman, Minneapolis G.C., Minneapolis, Minn.	74	79	81	85	319	Medal
60	Ralph Bond, Lyndhurst G. Course, Cleveland, Ohio	79	76	86	79	320	629.00
61	Richard King, Frenchman's Cr. G.C., N. Palm Beach, Fla.	70	80	83	103	336	595.00

†Playoff, July 25, 1983, Billy Casper 75-3, Rod Funseth 75-4.
a-Amateur
†Record Entry

1984
FIFTH SENIOR OPEN CHAMPIONSHIP

Oak Hill Country Club (East Course), Rochester, New York, June 28 - July 1
Yardage—6,636. Par 70. +861 Entries, 150 Qualifiers, 150 Starters

						Score	Prize Money
1	Miller Barber, Woodlawn C.C., Sherman, Texas	74	71	70	71	286	$36,448.00
2	Arnold Palmer, Laurel Valley G.C., Ligonier, Pa.	74	68	72	74	288	20,322.00
3	Gay Brewer, Palm Springs, Calif.	75	72	74	70	291	12,481.00
4	Bob Goalby, St. Clair C.C., Belleville, Ill.	70	74	72	76	292	9,040.00
5	Bob Stone, Crackerneck, Independence, Mo.	75	71	75	73	294	7,140.00
6	Peter Thomson, R. & A., St. Andrews, Scotland	75	73	73	74	295	6,185.00
7	Jim Feree, Westmoreland C.C., Export, Pa.	74	75	74	73	296	5,454.00
8	Rod Funseth, Plum Creek, Castle Rock, Colo.	77	75	71	74	297	4,940.00
9	Kel Nagle, Sydney, Australia	77	74	73	74	298	4,542.00
10	Al Mengert, Oakland Hills C.C., Birmingham, Mich	75	79	72	74	300	3,869.00
	Jack Fleck, Pines G. & H.C., Magazine, Ark.	79	75	69	77	300	3,869.00
	Paul Harney, Paul Harney G.C., E. Falmouth, Mass.	77	73	71	79	300	3,869.00
13	Jerry Barber, Griffith Park G.C., Los Angeles, Calif.	75	73	75	78	301	3,418.00
14	Billy Casper, Mapleton, Utah	77	74	76	75	302	3,083.00
	Charles Sifford, Sleepy Hollow G.C., Brecksville, Ohio	78	71	80	73	302	3,083.00
	Bill Johnston, Orange Tree C.C., Scottsdale, Ariz.	75	74	76	77	302	3,083.00
17	Orville Moody, Sulphur Spgs. G.C., Sulphur Springs, Texas	74	80	76	73	303	2,645.00
	Pat Schwab, Schwab's Pine Lks. G.C., Jacksonville, Fla.	81	74	73	75	303	2,645.00
	Ken Towns, Graeagle Meadows G.C., Graeagle, Calif.	77	78	71	77	303	2,645.00
20	John Kalinka, Bayview C.C., Kaneohe, Hawaii	82	70	78	74	304	2,334.00
	Hulen Coker, Cottonwood C.C., El Cajon, Calif.	75	79	77	73	304	2,334.00
	Kyle Burton, The Vintage Club, Indian Wells, Calif.	75	73	75	81	304	2,334.00
23	a-Dale Morey, Emerywood C.C., High Point, N.C.	71	79	79	76	305	Medal
	a-Fordie Pitts, Jr., Wollaston G.C., Milton, Mass.	78	72	78	77	305	Medal
	Doug Ford, Tuckahoe, N.Y.	75	77	77	76	305	2,143.00
	Mike Kelly, Nanango C.C., Nanangoaus, Australia	77	74	74	80	305	2,143.00
27	a-Bill Hyndman, III, Huntingdon Vly. C.C., Huntingdon Vly, Pa.	78	76	78	74	306	Medal
	Freddie Haas, Belle Terre G. & C.C., La Place, La.	78	78	75	75	306	1,962.00
	Paul Thomas, Zanesville C.C., Zanesville, Ohio	75	72	82	77	306	1,962.00
	Lionel Hebert, Lafayette, La.	74	74	77	81	306	1,962.00
31	Howie Johnson, Mission Hills C.C., Rancho Mirage, Calif.	78	74	73	82	307	1,842.00
32	Donald Hoenig, Raceway G.C., Thompson, Conn.	80	74	81	73	308	1,757.00
	a-William C. Campbell, Guyan G. & C.C., Huntington, W. Va.	76	79	78	75	308	Medal
	Adolph Popp, Harbor Muni. G.C., Melbourne, Fla.	84	73	75	76	308	1,757.00
	a-Robert Eaton, Greeley C.C., Greeley, Colo.	73	79	74	82	308	Medal
36	Stan Thirsk, Kanas City C.C., Mission Hills, Kans.	82	73	80	74	309	1,615.34
	Art Silvestrone, Sweetwater C.C., Longwood, Fla.	80	77	74	78	309	1,615.33
	Charles Green, Seabee G.C., Port Hueneme, Calif.	81	76	73	79	309	1,615.33
39	Fred Hawkins, Sun N Lake G. & C.C., Sebring, Fla.	85	70	83	72	310	1,315.25
	Roberto De Vicenzo, Ranelagh G.C., Buenos Aires, Argentina	80	77	77	76	310	1,315.25
	Jim Hatfield, Indian Creek G.C., Anderson, Mo.	78	79	76	77	310	1,315.25
	a-Pursie Pipes, Indian Creek C.C., Miami Beach, Fla.	77	78	77	78	310	Medal
	Jim Barber, Jeffersonville Elks, Jeffersonville, Ind.	82	73	77	78	310	1,315.25
	Ken Mast, Seven Rivers, Crystal River, Fla.	77	78	77	78	310	1,315.25
	Doug Higgins, Diamond Oaks C.C., Ft. Worth, Texas	81	75	76	78	310	1,315.25
	a-Bob Hoff, Oak Hill C.C. Rochester, N.Y.	77	76	78	79	310	Medal
	Dick Sarta, Preakness Hills C.C., Wayne, N.J.	75	75	80	80	310	1,315.25
	Chuck Scally, Scally's G.C., Coraopolis, Pa.	76	75	78	81	310	1,315.25
49	George Kallish, Jr., Forest Preserve Nat., Oak Forest, Ill.	79	76	80	76	311	1,117.00
50	Pete Hessemer, Memorial Park G.C., Houston, Texas	77	75	82	78	312	1,059.50
	Joe Moresco, The Woodmere Club, Woodmere, N.Y.	76	75	80	81	312	1,059.50
52	Bob Erickson, Sabal Point C.C., Longwood, Fla.	81	76	79	77	313	983.50
	Auggie Navarro, Sim Park G.C., Wichita, Kans.	78	79	78	78	313	983.50
54	a-Alton Duhon, Griffith Park, Los Angeles, Calif.	81	76	80	77	314	Medal
	George Reynolds, Minneapolis, Minn.	77	80	77	80	314	927.00
56	Doug Sanders, Houston, Texas	81	76	77	81	315	876.00
57	a-Ron Moore, Cherry Hills C.C., Englewood, Colo	81	72	83	80	316	Medal
	a-Dean Sheetz, Myers Park C.C., Charlotte, N.C.	73	81	80	82	316	Medal
59	Joe Jiminez, Jefferson City C.C., Jefferson City, Mo.	79	76	83	79	317	784.00
	Jim Cowan, Escondido, Calif.	80	75	80	82	317	784.00
	Gaylon Simon, Blossom Trail G.C., Benton Harbor, Mich.	80	76	78	83	317	784.00
	a-Keith Compton, Oak Hill C.C., San Antonio, Texas	80	75	78	84	317	Medal
63	Babe Lichardus, East Orange G.C., Short Hills, N.J.	76	81	84	78	319	681.50
	a-Jim Unruh, Tulsa C.C., Tulsa, Okla.	78	76	86	79	319	Medal
	Stan Dudas, Mays Landing C.C., McKee City, N.J.	80	76	79	84	319	681.50
66	a-Robert Rawlins, Las Colinas C.C., Irving, Texas	80	77	86	78	321	Medal

a-Amateur

+Record Entry

1985
SIXTH SENIOR OPEN CHAMPIONSHIP

Edgewod Tahoe Golf Course, Stateline, Nevada, June 27-30
Yardage—7,055. Par 72. +1,029 Entries, 150 Qualifiers, 150 Starters

						Score	Prize Money
1	Miller Barber, Woodlawn C.C., Sherman, Texas	71	72	71	71	285	$40,199.00
2	Roberto De Vicenzo, Tarzana, Calif.	74	68	75	72	289	22,835.00
3	Gay Brewer, La Quinta H.&G.C., La Quinta, Calif.	73	71	76	71	291	13,937.00
4	Peter Thomson, Victoria G.C., Australia	70	77	74	73	294	8,976.00
	Walter Zembriski, Orlando, Fla.	68	73	78	75	294	8,976.00
6	Harold Henning, S. Africa	75	73	75	72	295	6,852.00
7	Jack Fleck, Magazine, Ark.	76	77	74	70	297	6,054.00
8	Lee Elder, Washington, D.C.	75	73	75	75	298	5,051.34
	James King, Palm-Aire, Pompano Beach, Fla.	72	78	75	73	298	5,051.33
	Gene Littler, Rancho Santa Fe G.C., Rancho Santa Fe, Calif.	75	76	74	73	298	5,051.33
11	Orville Moody, Sulphur Springs C.C., Sulphur Springs, Texas	75	78	76	71	300	4,028.34
	Billy Casper, Gleneagles C.C., Boca Raton, Fla.	73	74	77	76	300	4,028.33
	Arnold Palmer, Laurel Valley G.C., Ligonier, Pa.	72	76	76	76	300	4,028.33
14	Ben Smith, Woodland Hills, Nacogdoches, Texas	72	78	75	76	301	3,510.50
	Jim Ferree, Westmoreland C.C., Export, Pa.	75	77	72	77	301	3,510.50
16	Charles Sifford, Sleepy Hollow G.C., Brecksville, Ohio	74	74	82	72	302	3,158.50
	Gordon Jones, Atlantis C.C., Atlantis, Fla.	74	73	78	77	302	3,158.50
18	Ken Still, Brookdale G.C., Tacoma, Wash.	73	83	74	73	303	2,867.00
	Dean Lind, Wilmette G.C., Wilmette, Ill.	75	77	76	75	303	2,867.00
	a-William Hyndman, III, Huntingdon Vly. C.C., Hunt. Vly, Pa.	73	74	80	76	303	MEDAL
21	Tommy Bolt, Tarpon Woods C.C., Palm Harbor, Fla.	73	76	78	77	304	2,677.00
22	Doug Higgins, Diamond Oaks C.C., Ft. Worth, Texas	76	79	79	71	305	2,551.50
	a-John Richardson, El Niguel C.C., Laguna Niguel, Calif.	79	74	79	73	305	MEDAL
	Howie Johnson, Skyline Woods C.C., Omaha, Neb.	77	80	72	76	305	2,551.50
25	William Collins, G.&R.C. Eastpointe, Palm Beach Gardens, Fla.	80	77	76	73	306	2,297.00
	Jesse Whittenton, Monterey C.C., Palm Desert, Calif.	78	75	77	76	306	2,297.00
	Adolph Popp, Harbor City Muni., Melbourne, Fla.	77	76	76	77	306	2,297.00
	Michael Fetchick, Dix Hills, N.Y.	77	76	75	78	306	2,297.00
29	Kel Nagle, Ponte Vedra, Fla.	74	76	83	74	307	2,077.50
	Robert Stone, Crackerneck C.C., Independence, Mo.	73	75	83	76	307	2,077.50
31	Stan Thirsk, Kansas City C.C., Shawnee Mission, Kan.	75	80	79	74	308	1,762.38
	Ray Montgomery, Fort Pierce, Fla.	77	80	77	74	308	1,762.38
	George Bellino, Tippecanoe C.C., Canfield, Ohio	73	81	77	77	308	1,762.38
	Bob Goalby, Gleneagles C.C., Belleville, Ill.	79	75	76	78	308	1,762.38
	Pat Schwab, Pine Lakes C.C., Jacksonville, Fla.	75	81	73	79	308	1,762.37
	Dick King, Singletree C.C., Vail, Colo.	79	68	81	80	308	1,762.37
	Don Bergman, St. Andrews G.C., Cedar Rapids, Iowa	78	73	77	80	308	1,762.37
	Bill Ezinicki, International G.C., Bolton, Mass.	79	76	73	80	308	1,762.37
39	Ken Towns, Graeagle Meadows, Graeagle, Calif.	78	80	78	73	309	1,446.50
	Rick Jetter, Haggin Oaks G.C., Sacramento, Calif.	76	76	82	75	309	1,446.50
	a-Amos Jones, Cherokee C.C., Atlanta, Ga.	74	78	77	80	309	MEDAL
	a-Frank Schmidt, Muirfield Village C.C., Dublin, Ohio	76	81	72	80	309	MEDAL
43	Dow Finsterwald, Broadmoor G.C., Colorado Springs, Colo.	79	76	79	76	310	1,346.50
	Roland Stafford, Kass Inn, Margaretville, N.Y.	78	77	75	80	310	1,346.50
45	Pete Hessemer, Memorial Park G.C., Houston, Texas	74	77	84	76	311	1,240.34
	Billy Maxwell, Hyde Park G.&C.C., Jacksonville, Fla.	78	78	78	77	311	1,240.33
	Casmere Jawor, Hampton G.C., Rochester, Mich.	83	73	74	81	311	1,240.33
48	Fred Hawkins, Sun N Lake C.C., Sebring, Fla.	79	78	78	77	312	1,113.34
	Jerry Barber, Griffith Park G.C., Los Angeles, Calif.	79	78	77	78	312	1,113.33
	Jackie Cummings, Indian Hills G.C., Tuscaloosa, Ala.	75	77	81	79	312	1,113.33
	George Bayer, Palm Desert, Calif.	76	76	80	80	312	1,113.33
52	Bob McCallister, Lake Shastina C.C., Weed, Calif.	79	79	77	78	313	1,001.00
	Walker Inman, Jr., Scioto C.C., Columbus, Ohio	76	81	77	79	313	1,001.00
54	a-Alton Duhon, Griffith Park G.C., Los Angeles, Calif.	73	80	87	74	314	MEDAL
	a-Robert Rawlins, Las Colinas C.C., Irving, Texas	76	80	78	80	314	MEDAL
56	Al Balding, Sun N Lake C.C., Sebring, Fla.	77	75	84	79	315	893.00
	Bill Bisdorf, Twilight G.C., Denver, Colo.	81	73	81	80	315	893.00
58	Dan Morgan, Continental G.C., Scottsdale, Ariz.	74	84	78	80	316	826.00
59	a-Edgar Bradley, Kenwood C.C., Cincinnati, Ohio	80	76	83	78	317	MEDAL
	Roy Beattie, Sylvania C.C., Sylvania, Ohio	77	77	82	81	317	781.00
61	Richard Lotz, Tower Tee G. Inc., Afton, Mo.	78	77	85	80	320	711.50
	Palmer Lawrence, Waialae C.C., Honolulu, Hawaii	77	78	84	81	320	711.50

a-Amateur
+Record Entry

1986
SEVENTH SENIOR OPEN CHAMPIONSHIP

Scioto Country Club, Columbus, Ohio, June 26-29
Yardage—6,709. Par 71. +1,225 Entries, 150 Starters

						Score	Prize Money
1	Dale Douglass, Arizona Biltmore Resort, Phoenix, Ariz.	66	72	68	73	279	$42,500.00
2	Gary Player, Johannesburg, South Africa	71	73	66	70	280	22,000.00
3	Harold Henning, Tournament Players Club, Jacksonville, Fla.	70	72	70	69	281	15,592.00
4	Bruce Crampton, Dallas, Texas	70	72	73	68	283	10,165.00
	Peter Thomson, Victoria G.C., Victoria, Australia	71	73	70	69	283	10,165.00
6	Jim Ferree, Long Cove Club, Hilton Head Island, S.C.	69	72	71	72	284	7,778.00
7	Miller Barber, Sherman, Texas	72	72	73	68	285	6,934.00
8	Gene Littler, Rancho Santa Fe G.C., Rancho Santa Fe, Calif.	72	76	69	69	286	6,336.00
9	Orville Moody, Sulphur Springs C.C, Sulphur Springs, Texas	73	75	71	68	287	5,765.00
10	Billy Casper, Gleneagles C.C., Delray Beach, Fla.	71	76	71	70	288	4,759.60
	Bob Charles, Christchurch C.C., New Zealand	72	75	70	71	288	4,759.60
	Bob Toski, St. Andrews C.C., Boca Raton, Fla.	70	73	73	72	288	4,759.50
	Jack Fleck, Los Alamitos C.C., Los Alamitos, Calif.	71	74	71	72	288	4,759.60
	Chi Chi Rodriguez, Dorado Beach, Dorado, Puerto Rico	74	72	70	72	288	4,759.60
15	Lee Elder, Washington, D.C.	68	75	74	73	290	4,060.00
16	Walker Inman, Jr., Scioto C.C., Columbus, Ohio	75	67	77	72	291	3,786.00
	Doug Sanders, Houston, Texas	73	73	73	72	291	3,786.00
18	Albert Chandler, Columbia, Mo.	78	70	71	73	292	3,392.00
	James King, Palm Aire C.C., Pompano Beach, Fla.	71	79	69	73	292	3,392.00
	Ken Still, Tacoma, Wash.	69	72	76	75	292	3,392.00
21	Buck Adams, C.C. of N. Carolina, Pinehurst, N.C.	70	74	76	73	293	3,045.00
	Quinton Gray, Oak Tree G.C., Edmond, Okla,	73	73	73	74	293	3,045.00
	Chuck Workman, Bethpage G.C., Farmingdale, N.Y.	70	72	73	78	293	3,045.00
24	Charles Sifford, Sleepy Hollow G.C., Brecksville, Ohio	72	75	72	75	294	2,842.00
25	Bob Bruno, Rye G.C., Rye, N.Y.	72	78	75	70	295	2,602.20
	Arnold Palmer, Laurel Valley G.C., Ligonier, Pa.	78	74	73	70	295	2,602.20
	Gay Brewer, Gleneagles C.C., Delray Beach, Fla.	72	72	78	73	295	2,602.20
	Art Silverstrone, Winter Pines, G.C., Winter Park, Fla.	72	75	73	75	295	2,602.20
	Joe Campbell, Purdue Univ. G.C., W. Lafayette, Ind.	73	72	74	76	295	2,602.20
30	Joe Jimenez, Jefferson City C.C., Jefferson City, Mo.	73	76	77	70	296	2,289.00
	Art Wall, Sonoita, Ariz.	75	76	72	73	296	2,289.00
	Howie Johnson, Skyline Woods C.C., Omaha, Neb	75	77	71	73	296	2,289.00
	Ken Mast, Citrus Hills C.C., Citrus Hills, Fla.	75	73	73	75	296	2,289.00
34	Billy Maxwell, Hyde Park G.C., Jacksonville, Fla.	73	76	73	75	297	2,158.00
35	El Collins, Reid Park G.C., Springfield, Ohio	72	78	75	73	298	2,079.00
	Stan Dudas, Mays Landing C.C., McKee City, N.J.	74	76	73	75	298	2,079.00
37	Jerry Barber, Griffith Park G.C., Los Angeles, Calif.	73	79	75	72	299	2,001.00
	a-Robert Hoff, Oak Hill C.C., Rochester, N.Y.	76	75	71	77	299	Medal
39	a-John Cain, Brae Burn C.C., Houston, Texas	75	76	76	73	300	Medal
	Hulen Coker, Cottonwood C.C., El Cajon, Calif.	71	77	77	75	300	1,922.00
	Gordon Jones, Atlantis C.C., Atlantis, Fla.	73	73	75	79	300	1,922.00
42	Bobby Nichols, Fiddlesticks C.C., Ft. Myers, Fla.	71	79	76	75	301	1,688.58
	Ralph Montoya, Dinsmore G.C., Staatsburg, N.Y.	78	75	73	75	301	1,688.57
	Chuck Green, Seabee G.C., Port Hueneme, Calif.	75	78	73	75	301	1,688.57
	Al Balding, Sun N Lake, Sebring, Fla.	76	76	73	76	301	1,688.57
	a-Bob Lowry, Huntsville, C.C. Huntsville, Ala.	75	77	73	76	301	Medal
	George Lanning, Tacoma, Wash.	75	73	76	77	301	1,688.57
	Dean Lind, Wilmette G.C., Wilmette, Ill.	75	73	76	77	301	1,688.57
	Bob Goalby, Gleneagles C.C., Delray Beach, Fla.	78	75	71	77	301	1,688.57
50	James Hatfield, Dawn Hills G.&C.C., Siloan Springs, Ark.	69	77	79	77	302	1,455.00
	Dick Plummer, Camargo Club, Cincinnati, Ohio	74	74	76	78	302	1,455.00
52	a-John Harbottle, Tacoma C.&.G.C., Tacoma, Wash.	73	80	77	73	303	Medal
	a-Morris Beecroft, James River C.C., Newport News, Va.	75	76	76	76	303	Medal
	Walter Zembriski, Cannongate G.C., Orlando, Fla.	76	75	75	77	303	1,377.00
55	Bill Ezinicki, International G.C., Bolton, Mass.	76	76	78	75	305	1,300.00
	Dow Finsterwald, The Broadmoor G.C., Colorado Sprgs., Colo.	77	75	76	77	305	1,300.00
57	Dick Sarta, Preakness Hills C.C., Wayne, N.J.	75	76	78	77	306	1,196.00
	Gordon Waldespuhl, Twin Oaks G.C., Covington, Ky.	71	76	77	82	306	1,196.00
59	M.C. Fitts, Indian Hills C.C., Tuscaloosa, Ala.	74	79	79	76	308	1,143.00
	Jack Webb, Des Moines G.&C.C., W. Des Moines, Iowa	76	77	76	79	308	1,143.00
	a-John Woodward, Palmetto G.C., Aiken, S.C.	74	79	76	79	308	Medal
62	George Clark, Midland C.C., Midland, Texas	75	77	76	82	310	1,121.00
63	Myron Hap Rose, Sherwood Forest, Sanger, Calif.	75	78	84	77	314	1,106.00
64	Allen Cross, Salem, Ore.	77	76	81	83	317	1,093.00
65	a-Clifford Taylor, Spring Lake C.C., Spring Lake, Mich.	78	75	84	81	318	Medal

a-Amateur
+Record Entry

1987
EIGHTH SENIOR OPEN CHAMPIONSHIP

Brooklawn Country Club, Fairfield, Connecticut, July 9-12
Yardage—6,599. Par 71. +1,277 Entries, 150 Starters.

						Score	Money Prize
1	Gary Player, Alaqua,*Orlando, Fla.	69	68	67	66	270	$47,000.00
2	Doug Sanders, Houston, Texas	68	71	72	65	276	24,000.00
3	Chi Chi Rodriguez, Miami, Fla.	68	68	70	71	277	17,164.00
4	Orville Moody, Sulphur Springs C.C., Sulphur Springs, Texas	72	72	66	69	279	12,525.00
5	Don Massengale, Del Lago, Montgomery, Texas	69	70	70	71	280	9,855.00
6	Robert Brue, Ozaukee C.C., Mequon, Wis.	70	70	70	71	281	8,097.50
	Dale Douglass, Phoeniz, Ariz.	71	71	68	71	281	8,097.50
8	Harold Henning, Palm Beach Gardens, Fla.	72	69	70	71	282	6,660.50
	Gene Borek, Metropolis C.C., White Plains, N.Y.	68	76	67	71	282	6,660.50
10	Larry Mowry, Metropolitan C., Decatur, Ga.	68	72	72	71	283	5,524.34
	Peter Thomson, Austin, Texas	66	73	72	72	283	5,524.33
	Walter Zembriski, Cannongate G.C., Orlando, Fla.	70	70	71	72	283	5,524.33
13	Miller Barber, Preston Trails C.C., Dallas, Texas	70	73	68	73	284	4,927.00
14	Gordon Jones, Alliance, Ohio	66	75	73	71	285	4,376.00
	Arnold Palmer, Laurel Valley G.C., Ligonier, Pa.	69	69	74	73	285	4,376.00
	John Brodie, La Quinta Hotel G.C., La Quinta, Calif.	67	70	74	74	285	4,376.00
	Bob Charles, Christchurch, New Zealand	73	68	68	76	285	4,376.00
18	Fred Hawkins, Sebring G.C., Sebring, Fla.	70	71	75	70	286	3,896.00
19	John Frillman, Happy Hollow Club, Omaha, Neb.	71	75	73	68	287	3,531.25
	Tommy Aaron, Stouffer Pine Isle Resort, Buford, Ga.	71	73	74	69	287	3,531.25
	Butch Baird, Miami Beach, Fla.	70	73	72	72	287	3,531.25
	Bobby Nichols, Fiddlesticks C.C., Ft. Myers, Fla.	69	70	74	74	287	3,531.25
23	Bob Duden, Glendover G.C., Portland, Ore.	74	74	71	69	288	3,182.50
	Charles Jones, Del Mar, Calif.	69	72	74	73	288	3,182.50
25	Dick Hendrickson, Radley Run C.C., West Chester, Pa.	71	73	74	71	289	2,865.00
	Bob Bruno, Rye G.C., Rye, N.Y.	75	70	73	71	289	2,865.00
	Billy Maxwell, Jacksonville, Fla.	76	71	71	71	289	2,865.00
	J.C. Goosie, Bloomingdale C.C., Brandon, Fla.	72	71	74	72	289	2,865.00
	Dave Hill, Horton, Mich.	71	74	71	73	289	2,865.00
30	Gay Brewer, Gleneagles C.C., Delray Beach, Fla.	72	72	76	70	290	2,491.00
	Jack Fleck, Los Alamitos C.C., Los Alamitos, Calif.	77	68	73	72	290	2,491.00
	Ken Towns, Graeagle Meadows G.C., Graeagle, Calif.	74	74	70	72	290	2,491.00
	Robert Rawlins, Las Colinas C.C., Irving, Texas	74	67	75	74	290	2,491.00
	Joe Campbell, Purdue G.C., West Lafayette, Ind.	70	76	70	74	290	2,491.00
35	Jerry Barber, La Canada, Calif.	69	77	74	71	291	2,145.58
	Bruce Crampton, Dallas, Texas	70	73	76	72	291	2,145.57
	George Lanning, Oakbrook G. & C.C., Tacoma, Wash.	72	71	75	73	291	2,145.57
	James King, Palm Aire C.C., Pompano Beach, Fla.	74	72	72	73	291	2,145.57
	Billy Casper, Gleneagles C.C., Delray Beach, Fla.	75	72	70	74	291	2,145.57
	Walker Inman, Jr., Scioto C.C., Columbus, Ohio	69	73	73	76	291	2,145.57
	Kenneth Still, Canterwood G. & C.C., Gig Harbor, Wash.	74	74	67	76	291	2,145.57
42	a-Dennis Iden, Old Ranch C.C., Seal Beach, Calif.	73	75	75	69	292	Medal
	Bob Toski, Boca Raton, Fla.	70	79	71	72	292	1,917.00
44	Joseph Lopez, Golden Hills G. & T.C., Ocala, Fla.	73	74	69	77	293	1,860.00
45	Casmere Jawor, Hampton G.C., Rochester Hills, Mich.	72	75	74	73	294	1,774.50
	Albert Chandler, Palm Beach Gardens, Fla.	74	73	72	75	294	1,774.50
47	Luther Godwin, Westwood Hills C.C., Poplar Bluff, Mo.	73	73	77	72	295	1,689.00
	Joe Jimenez, Jefferson City C.C., Jefferson City, Mo.	76	73	70	76	295	1,689.00
49	ar-Robert Moyers, Shenvalee G.C., New Market, Va.	77	72	75	72	296	—
	Donald Hoenig, Raceway G.C., Thompson, Conn.	72	76	74	74	296	1,632.00
51	Gene Thompson, Woodbridge G.L., Kings Mountain, N.C.	72	75	75	75	297	1,517.00
	Paul Messner, C.C. of Beloit, Beloit, Wis.	74	73	75	75	297	1,517.00
	Kel Nagle, Ponte Vedra, Fla.	76	73	72	76	297	1,517.00
54	a-James Frost, Broadmoor G.C., Seattle, Wash.	72	75	73	79	299	Medal
	Miguel Salla, El Rignon, Bogata, Columbia	74	73	73	79	299	1,401.00
56	a-Fordie Pitts, Wollaston G.C., Milton, Mass.	78	71	75	76	300	Medal
	a-Allan Sussell, JDM C.C., Palm Beach Gardens, Fla.	75	72	75	78	300	Medal
58	a-Bo Williams, Golden Hills G. & T.C., Ocala, Fla.	71	72	77	81	301	Medal
	Arthur Leon, Las Colinas C.C., Irving, Texas	71	77	78	75	301	Medal
60	Stan Jawor, Harbour Club G.C., Bellville, Mich.	72	75	80	77	304	1,344.00
61	a-Alton Duhon, Griffith Park, Los Angeles, Calif.	73	76	71	82	308	Medal
	Eddie Leonard, Chandler Park G.C., Detroit, Mich.	74	71	81	82	308	1,287.00
	a-William Hyndman, III, Huntingdon Valley C.C., Huntingdon Valley, Pa.	72	72				WD

a-Amateur
ar-Applicant for Reinstatement
†Record Entry

1988
NINTH SENIOR OPEN CHAMPIONSHIP

Medinah Country Club, Medinah, Illinois, August 4-7
Yardage—6,936. Par 72. +1,662 Entries, 150 Starters.

						Score	Money Prize
1	†Gary Player, Alaqua, Orlando, Fla.	74	70	71	73	288	$65,000.00
	†Bob Charles, Christchurch, New Zealand	75	70	70	73	288	32,500.00
3	Bruce Crampton, Dallas, Texas	73	74	70	72	289	21,285.00
4	Orville Moody, Sulphur Springs C.C., Sulphur Springs, Texas	72	73	72	73	290	13,877.50
	Peter Thomson, Austin, Texas	72	73	72	73	290	13,877.50
6	Chi Chi Rodriguez, Dorado Sands, Puerto Rico	73	76	75	67	291	10,042.00
	Harold Henning, Palm Beach Gardens, Fla.	70	73	76	72	291	10,042.00
8	Al Geiberger, Palm Desert, Calif.	73	71	77	71	292	8,259.50
	Lou Graham, Nashville, Tenn.	72	71	73	76	292	8,259.50
10	Butch Baird, Miami Beach, Fla.	73	75	73	73	294	7,060.50
	Billy Casper, Gleneagles C.C., Delray Beach, Fla.	69	71	76	78	294	7,060.50
12	Don Bies, PGA West, La Quinta, Calif.	77	71	76	71	295	6,121.67
	Gene Borek, Metropolis C.C., White Plains, N.Y.	73	75	75	72	295	6,121.67
	Gene Littler, Rancho Santa Fe G.C., Rancho Santa Fe, Calif.	73	72	76	74	295	6,121.66
15	Dave Hill, Jackson, Mich.	73	74	75	74	296	5,293.00
	J.C. Goosie, Bloomingdale C.C., Brandon, Fla.	75	72	74	75	296	5,293.00
	Walt Zembriski, Orlando, Fla.	69	75	74	78	296	5,293.00
18	Charles Coody, Abilene, Texas	76	74	74	73	297	4,831.00
19	Doug Dalziel, Grassy Hill C.C., Orange, Conn.	72	73	80	73	298	4,618.00
20	Dale Douglass, Phoenix, Ariz.	80	73	72	74	299	4,370.50
	Homero Blancas, Tucson, Ariz.	78	74	70	77	299	4,370.50
22	Bob Brue, Ozaukee C.C., Mequon, Wis.	76	78	72	75	301	4,016.34
	Paul Moran, Shackamaxon C.C., Scotch Plains, N.J.	83	70	73	75	301	4,016.33
	Arnold Palmer, Laurel Valley G.C., Ligonier, Pa.	75	74	75	77	301	4,016.33
25	a-Robert Housen, Manasquan River G.C., Brielle, N.J.	77	76	75	74	302	Medal
	Don Massengale, Conroe, Texas	77	74	76	75	302	3,712.50
	Ken Still, Canterwood G. & C.C., Gig Harbor, Wash.	78	74	74	76	302	3,712.50
28	Gay Brewer, Gleneagles C.C., Delray Beach, Fla.	75	79	78	71	303	3,392.00
	Dean Sheetz, Charlotte, N.C.	75	77	76	75	303	3,392.00
	Dick Hendrickson, Radley Run C.C., West Chester, Pa.	77	74	75	77	303	3,392.00
	Jim Ferree, Long Cove Club, Hilton Head Island, S.C.	75	75	73	80	303	3,392.00
32	John Frillman, Happy Hollow Club, Omaha, Neb.	77	78	74	75	304	3,016.60
	Tommy Aaron, Stouffer Pineisle G.C., Buford, Ga.	75	78	76	75	304	3,016.60
	Bobby Nichols, Fiddlesticks C.C., Fort Myers, Fla.	78	75	75	76	304	3,016.60
	Gordon Jones, La Quinta C.C., La Quinta, Calif.	77	76	75	76	304	3,016.60
	Jim King, Palm Aire C.C., Pompano Beach, Fla.	76	79	72	77	304	3,016.60
	a-Richard Sucher, Ozaukee C.C., Mequon, Wis.	75	77	74	78	304	Medal
38	Earl Puckett, Twin Orchard C.C., Long Grove, Ill.	78	75	79	73	305	2,766.50
	Bob Goalby, Belleville, Ill.	73	78	75	79	305	2,766.50
40	Billy Maxwell, Hyde Park G.C., Jacksonville, Fla.	74	72	80	80	306	2,660.00
41	a-Dick Siderowf, Century C.C., Purchase, N.Y.	76	74	80	77	307	Medal
	a-John Harbottle, Tacoma G. & C.C., Tacoma, Wash.	79	76	74	78	307	Medal
43	a-Robert Wylie, Calgary G. & C.C., Calgary, Canada	77	76	79	76	308	Medal
	a-John Paul Cain, Brae Burn C.C., Houston, Texas	78	74	78	78	308	Medal
	Larry Mowry, Atlanta, Ga.	77	79	70	82	308	2,589.00
46	Jay Hyon, Monterey Park G.C., Monterey Park, Calif.	76	79	78	76	309	2,518.00
47	Al Chandler, Palm Beach Gardens, Fla.	75	75	78	82	310	2,447.00
48	Robert Rawlins, Bent Tree C.C., Dallas, Texas	77	78	80	76	311	2,306.00
	Dick Plummer, Camargo Club, Cincinnati, Ohio	77	78	78	78	311	2,306.00
	Robert Boldt, Boundary Oak, Walnut Creek, Calif.	76	78	79	78	311	2,306.00
51	a-Jim Keim, Kahkwa C.C., Erie, Pa	74	82	79	78	313	Medal
	Paul Thomas, Zanesville C.C., Zanesville, Ohio	78	75	80	80	313	2,164.00
53	Kel Nagle, Ponte Vedra, Fla.	79	76	80	79	314	2,094.00
54	Linden Meade, Riverview C.C., Madison, W.Va.	74	82	82	77	315	1,987.50
	Dean Lind, Wilmitte G.C., Wilmette, Ill.	73	79	80	83	315	1,987.50
56	Don Hoenig, Raceway G.C., Thompson, Conn.	79	77	83	77	316	1,881.00
	a-Jackie Cummings, Indian Hills C.C., Tuscaloosa, Ala.	76	80	80	80	316	Medal
58	a-Bud Bradley, Wilshire C.C., Los Angeles, Calif.	76	80	80	81	317	Medal
59	Jack O'Keefe, Rancho Maria G.C., Santa Maria, Calif.	75	75	86	82	318	1,810.00
60	a-Marshall Trammell, Belle Meade C.C., Nashville, Tenn.	82	74	80	83	319	Medal
61	Dick McNeill, Doral Park, Miami, Fla.	74	77	79	91	321	1,740.00

† Playoff, August 8, Player 68, Charles 70
\+ Record Entry
a-Amateur

1989
TENTH SENIOR OPEN CHAMPIONSHIP

Laurel Valley Golf Club, Ligonier, Pennsylvania, June 29-July 2
Yardage—6,691. Par 72. Record 1,762 Entries, 150 Starters.

						Score	Money Prize
1	Orville Moody, Sulphur Springs C.C., Sulphur Springs, Texas	72	73	64	70	279	$80,000.00
2	Frank Beard, Palm Desert, Calif.	70	69	70	72	281	40,000.00
3	Dale Douglass, Phoenix, Ariz.	71	70	76	67	284	22,267.00
	Jim Dent, Tampa, Fla.	71	73	70	70	284	22,267.00
5	Charles Coody, Abilene, Texas	72	72	71	70	285	13,812.00
	Bobby Nichols, Fiddlesticks C.C., Fort Myers, Fla.	70	70	74	71	285	13,812.00
7	Al Geiberger, Palm Desert, Calif.	68	72	76	70	286	10.955.00
	Harold Henning, Palm Beach Gardens, Fla.	69	74	71	72	286	10,955.00
9	Bob Charles, Christchurch, New Zealand	73	74	73	67	287	8,594.00
	Jimmy Powell, La Quinta, Calif.	74	71	73	69	287	8,594.00
	Gary Player, Alaqua, Orlando, Fla.	72	73	73	69	287	8,594.00
	Bruce Crampton, Dallas, Texas	72	72	69	74	287	8,594.00
13	Larry Mowry, Atlanta, Ga.	71	73	73	71	288	7,391.00
14	Mike Hill, Brooklyn, Mich.	72	72	73	72	289	7,046.00
15	Don Bies, PGA West, La Quinta, Calif.	74	66	77	73	290	6,553.00
	Butch Baird, Miami Beach, Fla.	73	72	69	76	290	6,553.00
17	Terry Dill, Camden, S.C.	70	76	72	74	292	6,101.00
18	Chi Chi Rodriguez, Dorado Sands, Puerto Rico	75	72	75	72	294	5,715.00
	Dave Hill, Jackson, Mich.	70	72	73	79	294	5,715.00
20	Lou Graham, Nashville, Tenn.	77	74	75	69	295	5,373.00
21	Ben Smith, Orlando, Fla.	74	74	77	71	296	5,028.00
	Peter Thomson, Austin, Texas	74	74	76	72	296	5,028.00
	Rives McBee, Irving, Texas	73	71	78	74	296	5,028.00
24	Al Kelley, Orlando, Fla.	77	74	72	74	297	4,692.00
25	Al Chandler, Palm Beach Gardens, Fla.	76	76	74	73	299	4,426.00
	Don Massengale, Conroe, Texas	74	74	74	77	299	4,426.00
	Doug Dalziel, Grassy Hill C.C., Orange, Conn.	73	73	72	81	299	4,426.00
28	Dick Hendrickson, Radley Run C.C., West Chester, Pa.	72	74	82	72	300	4,103.00
	a-Jim McMurtrey, Danville, Calif.	73	77	77	73	300	
	Agim Bardha, Birmingham, Mich.	80	72	73	75	300	4,103.00
31	Dick Rhyan, Sarasota, Fla.	75	79	76	71	301	3,866.00
	Robert Rawlins, Bent Tree C.C., Dallas, Texas	76	68	78	79	301	3,866.00
33	Mike Joyce, Huntington, N.Y.	78	75	72	77	302	3,693.00
	Jim Cochran, Crescent, Mo.	73	74	77	78	302	3,693.00
35	Bob Brue, Ozaukee C.C., Mequon, Wis.	76	75	82	70	303	3,519.00
	Jim O'Hern, Louisville, Ky.	76	76	76	75	303	3,519.00
37	Jack Fleck, Magazine, Ark.	77	73	79	75	304	3,347.00
	Miller Barber, Sherman, Texas	75	79	74	76	304	3,347.00
39	a-Quinton Gray, Longboat Key, Fla.	76	80	78	71	305	
	a-Charlie Ebner, Kingsville, Md.	77	76	79	73	305	
	Carl Lohren, Glen Cove, N.Y.	76	80	76	73	305	3,175.00
	a-Ron Eulenfel, Peachtree City, Ga.	74	77	79	75	305	
	a-Frank Boydston, Phonix, Ariz.	69	76	78	82	305	
44	J.C. Goosie, Bloomingdale C.C., Brandon, Fla.	77	74	83	72	306	2,960.00
	Dudley Wyson, McKinney, Texas	73	79	77	77	306	2,960.00
	Gene Borek, Metropolis C.C., White Plains, N.Y.	78	77	74	77	306	2,960.00
47	Chuck Mehok, Phoenix, Ariz.	76	78	74	80	308	2,789.00
	a-Bo Williams, Ocala, Fla.	76	79	77	78	310	
	Bob Boldt, Walnut Creek, Calif.	78	75	77	80	310	2,661.00
	Tom Shaw, Plantation, Fla.	74	76	78	82	310	2,661.00
	a-Curtis Wagner, Peachtree City, Ga.	75	76	76	83	310	
52	Dave Ragan, Sarasota, Fla.	80	75	79	77	311	2,532.00
53	Charlie Lee, Los Angeles, Calif.	76	76	83	77	312	2,361.00
	Arnold Palmer, Laurel Valley, G.C. Ligonier, Pa.	76	77	82	77	312	2,361.00
	Ronald Weber, Eugene Ore.	77	76	77	82	312	2,361.00
56	Joe Campbell, West Lafayette, Ind.	78	78	80	78	314	2,147.00
	Joe Carr, Spencer, Mass.	80	74	80	80	314	2,147.00
58	a-Richard Sucher, Mequon, Wis.	79	76	81	79	315	
	a-Dave Finley, Sparks, Nev.	76	76	83	80	315	
	Dow Finsterwald, Colorado Springs, Colo.	73	81	81	80	315	1,976.00
	Bobby Greenwood, Cookeville, Tenn.	79	77	79	80	315	1,976.00
62	Donald Fox, Loveland, Colo.	78	78	83	77	316	1,902.00
63	a-Bob Lowry, Huntsville, Ala.	76	79	84	82	321	
	Ab Justice, Oklahoma City, Okla.	78	78	80	85	321	1,872.00
65	Joe Little, Pueblo, Colo.	80	76	80	89	325	1,850.00

a=amateur

1990
ELEVENTH SENIOR OPEN CHAMPIONSHIP

Ridgewood Country Club, Paramus, New Jersey, June 28-July 1
Yardage—6,697. Par 72. Record 1,890 Entries, 156 Starters.

						Score	Money Prize
1	Lee Trevino, Richardson, Tex.	67	68	73	67	275	90,000.00
2	Jack Nicklaus, Dublin, Ohio	71	69	67	70	277	45,000.00
3	Chi Chi Rodriguez, Akron, Ohio	73	74	68	66	281	20,881.33
	Gary Player, South Africa	75	65	68	73	281	20,881.33
	Mike Hill, Brooklyn, Mich.	72	67	73	69	281	20,881.33
6	Harold Henning, Lake Worth, Fla.	71	67	75	69	282	12,828.00
	Charles Coody, Abilene, Tex.	68	73	72	69	282	12,828.00
8	Don Bies, Seattle, Wash.	75	69	67	72	283	10,550.00
	Miller Barber, Sherman, Tex.	75	68	67	73	283	10,550.00
10	Jim Dent, Tampa, Fla.	68	68	72	76	284	9,292.00
11	Terry Dill, Irving, Tex.	71	73	73	68	285	8,480.00
	Orville Moody, Sulpher Springs, Tex.	75	69	69	72	285	8,480.00
13	Walter Zembriski, Orlando, Fla.	68	73	73	72	286	7,623.00
	George Archer, Gilroy, Calif.	70	72	72	72	286	7,623.00
15	Rocky Thompson, Plano, Tex.	72	73	74	68	287	6,614.00
	John Paul Cain, Houston, Tex.	68	71	76	72	287	6,614.00
	Dave Hill, Jackson, Mich.	73	69	73	72	287	6,614.00
	Bob Charles, New Zealand	73	71	69	74	287	6,614.00
19	Jack Rule, Jr., Englewood, Colo.	74	71	69	74	288	5,899.00
20	Jim Ferree, Hilton Head Island, S.C.	74	70	74	71	289	5,492.00
	Joe Jimenez, Jefferson City, Mo.	74	74	69	72	289	5,492.00
	Lou Graham, Nashville, Tenn.	70	73	72	74	289	5,492.00
23	Ken Still, Fircrest, Wash.	68	75	75	72	290	4,964.33
	Dick Hendrickson, West Chester, Pa.	73	71	74	72	290	4,964.33
	Al Kelley, Orlando, Fla.	73	73	71	73	290	4,964.33
26	Larry Mowrey, Atlanta, Ga.	72	74	71	74	291	4,674.00
27	Doug Sanders, Houston, Tex.	74	74	77	68	293	4,333.25
	Dewitt Weaver, Jr., Helen, Ga.	72	75	74	72	293	4,333.25
	John Brodie, La Quinta, Calif.	73	73	74	73	293	4,333.25
	Jim Albus, Locust Valley, N.Y.	70	72	76	75	293	4,333.25
31	Lynn Rosely, Quincy, Ill.	73	75	77	69	294	3,945.00
	Rives McBee, Irving, Tex.	73	74	74	73	294	3,945.00
	Bob Betley, Fish Haven, Idaho	75	72	74	73	294	3,945.00
	a-Gary Cowen, Ontario, Canada	73	71	74	76	294	Medal
35	Don Massengale, Conroe, Tex.	74	72	76	73	295	3,716.50
	Frank Beard, Palm Desert, Calif.	77	70	74	74	295	3,716.50
37	Art Wall, Sonita, Ariz.	73	72	77	74	296	3,443.50
	Paul Moran, Griffin, Ga.	74	73	74	75	296	3,443.50
	Al Geiberger, Solvang, Calif.	77	68	75	76	296	3,443.50
	Babe Hiskey, Galena Park, Tex.	69	75	73	79	296	3,443.50
41	Gay Brewer, Mission Hills, Kan.	72	76	77	72	297	3,081.50
	Jack Fleck, Magazine, Ark.	73	73	78	73	297	3,081.50
	Chick Evans, Kingston, N.Y.	69	75	77	76	297	3,081.50
	Derey Simon, Las Vegas, Nev.	75	70	75	77	297	3,081.50
45	a-Robert Cornett, Tampa, Fla.	76	71	79	72	298	
	Jimmy Powell, La Quinta, Calif.	74	72	79	73	298	2,855.00
47	Charles Jones, San Diego, Calif.	74	75	78	72	299	2,719.50
	Bobby Breen, Ontario, Canada	75	74	74	76	299	2,719.50
49	Dean Sheetz, Charlotte, N.C.	74	73	78	75	300	2,584.00
	a-Vance Maxom, Fort Lauderdale, Fla.	71	72	78	79	300	
51	Lee Elder, Washington, D.C.	77	70	77	77	301	2,448.50
	Art Proctor, Edmond, Okla.	76	71	76	78	301	2,448.50
53	Chuck Mehok, Phoenix, Ariz.	75	72	79	76	302	2,313.00
	a-Paul Erhardt, Wilmington, Del.	72	76	78	76	302	
55	Craig Shankland, Flager Beach, Fla.	70	74	77	82	303	2,222.00
56	John David McSwain, Fairfield, Calif.	72	77	79	76	304	2,087.00
	Robert Pfister, Havertown, Pa.	78	71	76	79	304	2,087.00
58	a-Richard Evenson, Noblesville, Ind.	71	76	80	79	306	
	Marshall Strauss, Dekalb, Ill.	74	74	76	82	306	2,009.00
60	Jim Ohern, Palm Beach Gardens, Fla.	73	75	81	78	307	1,977.00
61	Bob Boldt, Walnut Creek, Calif.	76	73	74		DQ	500.00

a-Amateur

Prize money of approximately $500,000 awarded to professionals.

MID-AMATEUR CHAMPIONSHIP

Robert T. Jones, Jr, Memorial Mid-Amateur Trophy
Presented in October 1981, by
Atlanta Athletic Club and the Georgia State Golf Association

HISTORY

1981—Jim Holtgrieve, 33, of Des Peres, Missouri, won the inaugural Mid-Amateur Championship at the Bellerive Country Club in nearby St. Louis. He defeated fellow Walker Cupper Bob Lewis, Jr., 37, of Warren, Ohio in the final, 2 up. Holtgrieve, who has his own business representing a number of manufacturers, was a member of both the 1979 and 1981 U.S. Walker Cup teams and of the 1980 U.S. World Amateur team. Lewis, who is an executive in a steel tubing business owned by his family, was also a member of the 1981 U.S. Walker Cup team. Lewis also is a former professional golfer who regained his amateur status in 1978. Medalist honors were shared by Jay Sigel, of Berwyn, Pennsylvania, and Jay Rustman, of Roselle, Illinois. Both players had 36-hole scores of 145, one over par, to lead the 64 players who advanced to match play. Sigel, 37, an insurance executive, was a member of the 1977, 1979 and 1981 U.S. Walker Cup teams and of the 1978 and 1980 U.S. World Amateur teams. Sigel lost in the quarterfinals while Rustman was eliminated in the second round. Holtgrieve and Lewis tied for third in the qualifying with scores of 146. Holtgrieve advanced to the final by defeating Tom Reed, of Broomfield, Colorado, 5 and 4; Tom Evans of Lake Bluff, Illinois, 3 and 1; Randy Nichols of Connersville, Indiana, 6 and 5; Kent Frandsen of Lebanon, Indiana, 4 and 3; and Bob Housen of Brielle, New Jersey, 4 and 3. In the other bracket, Lewis eliminated two-time Amateur Champion Gary Cowan of Kitchener, Ontario, Canada, 4 and 3; Jim Beltz of Southfield, Michigan, 6 and 5; John Ruby of Stratford, Connecticut, 3 and 1; Bill Malley of Hayward, California, 2 and 1; and Gordon Brewer of Huntingdon Valley, Pennsylvania, 5 and 4. In the 18-hole final, Lewis kept up his steady play through the first nine holes. He was one under par and 1 up. Both he and Holtgrieve scored pars on the first three holes of the second nine, and then the match turned. Lewis had not made a bogey through the 14 holes of his morning semifinal match and 12 holes of the afternoon final. At the 13th, a par 3, Lewis missed the green, chipped 10 feet past and missed the putt for his first bogey of the day. The match was even. Both players made pars at the 14th and bogeys at the 15th, so the match remained even. Holtgrieve went ahead on the 16th, another par 3, where he got down in two after his tee shot left him 70 feet away. Lewis three-putted from 50 feet. They halved the 17th in par 5s. At the long par-4 18th, Holtgrieve followed a long drive with a 7-iron shot which stopped 10 feet from the hole. He holed the putt for a birdie to end the match. The starting field included three former Amateur Champions: Cowan (1966, 1971), Marvin Giles III (1972) and Fred Ridley (1975). It took a 36-hole score of 158 to reach the match play portion of the Championship. The USGA accepted 1,638 entries from golfers with handicaps of five strokes or less.

1982—William Hoffer, 33, of Elgin, Illinois, won the Mid-Amateur Championship, played at the Knollwood Club, in Lake Forest, Illinois. He defeated Jeffrey Ellis, 30, of Oak Harbor, Washington, 3 and 2, in the final match. Hoffer, vice-president of sales for his family's plastics business, drove the 100-mile round-trip each day from Elgin to Knollwood Club. This was the second consecutive year that the champion won in his home state. In 1981, Jim Holtgrieve, of St. Louis, Missouri, won at the Bellerive Country Club, in St. Louis. The starting field of 150 included three members of the United States Team that had won the World Amateur Team Championship, at Lausanne, Switzerland, in September. They were Jay Sigel, who established a Mid-Amateur qualifying record with scores of 71-66—137; Bob Lewis, Jr., who was the Mid-Amateur runner-up in 1981; and Holtgrieve. Sigel and Holtgrieve both lost in the quarterfinals. Sigel, despite a round of 71 that included 17 pars and one bogey, lost to Barry Terjesen, an Akron, Ohio, lawyer, 1 up. Holtgrieve lost, 1 up, to David Oglesby, an insurance company systems analyst, from Jacksonville, Florida. Lewis lost in the second round to Bill Harvey on the 19th hole. In the 18-hole final, Hoffer and Ellis halved the first two holes with pars, although Ellis had to roll in a delicate 10-footer on the second for his. Ellis took his only lead at the third with a routine par. Ellis three-putted the par-3 fourth hole to allow Hoffer to square the match. Hoffer went 1 up at the sixth hole with a par 4 as Ellis struggled to a double-bogey 6. Ellis came right back at the seventh with a par 3 while Hoffer took 3 to get down from the right fringe of the green. Hoffer took the lead for good with a par at the eighth hole. Hoffer was again 1 up. On the ninth hole, a long par-4 guarded by a lake on the left, Ellis hooked his tee shot, ending up in the grass a few inches from the water and inside the boundary of the hazard. As he planned his second shot, Ellis reached over and picked up a leaf near his ball, violating Rule 33-1, which prohibits a player from moving loose impediments within a hazard. The penalty was loss of hole, and Ellis was 2 down. The match ended on the 16th. Surprisingly, there were no birdies in the match. It took a 36-hole score of 155 to reach the match-play portion of the Championship. Although only two years old, the Mid-Amateur has established itself as a popular national competition, as evidenced by the 1,779 entries received this year.

MID-AMATEUR CHAMPIONSHIP

1983—Jay Sigel, 39, of Berwyn, Pennsylvania, became the first golfer in 53 years to win two USGA Championships in the same year when he won the Mid-Amateur Championship, at the Cherry Hills Country Club, In Englewood, Colorado. Sigel defeated Randy Sonnier, of The Woodlands, Texas, 1 up, in the final. Only Bob Jones, in 1930, and Charles Evans, Jr., in 1916, won two USGA competitions in the same year, each winning the Open and Amateur Championships. Just 32 days earlier, before he won the Mid-Amateur, Sigel had won his second consecutive Amateur Championship, at the North Shore Country Club, in Glenview, Illinois. Sonnier and Larry Stubblefield, of Kailua, Hawaii, were co-medalists, at 139, three under par. In his first match, Sigel defeated Frank Brame, of Alexandria, Louisiana, 3 and 1. After that, he disposed of Steve Rogers, of Bowling Green, Kentucky, 7 and 6, and Stubblefield, 2 and 1, to enter the quarterfinals for the third consecutive year. His opponent was Bob Lewis, Jr., of Warren, Ohio, one of his U.S. Walker Cup and World Amateur teammates. Their match went 24 holes, tying the Mid-Amateur record. Sigel holed a 35-foot putt on the sixth extra hole. That afternoon, Sigel defeated Craig Scheibert, of Middletown, Ohio, 4 and 3, in a semifinal match. Bill Hoffer, of Elgin, Illinois, the defending Champion, lost in the second round to Mark Boyajian, of Belleville, Illinois, 4 and 3. Jim Holtgrieve, of St. Louis, Missouri, who won the inaugural Mid-Amateur, in 1981, lost to Lewis in the third round, 2 and 1. It is worth noting that Boyajian played the first nine holes of his first qualifying round in 29. This is believed to be the lowest nine-hole score ever shot in a USGA competition. He shot 67 for the round, 140 for the two days of qualifying, and eventually lost in the quarterfinals to Scheibert, on the 19th hole. In an unusual championship final, the first 10 holes were halved, seven of them with pars and three with bogeys. Sigel broke the impasse by winning the 11th, a 577-yard par 5, by hitting a 2-iron to within four feet of the hole. Sonnier, who still was not on the green with his fourth shot, conceded the eagle. They halved all but two of the remaining holes, with Sigel's three-footer at the 18th deciding the issue after Sonnier had missed from 10 feet. The Mid-Amateur attracted a record 2,186 entries.

1984—Michael Podolak, 30, of Fargo, North Dakota, defeated Bob Lewis, Jr., of Warren, Ohio, 5 and 4, in the final match, at the Atlanta Athletic Club in Atlanta, Georgia. Podolak, a reinstated amateur, was appearing in his sixth USGA competition and third Mid-Amateur, and he never before qualified for match play. Before reaching the final he defeated Chad Williams on the 19th hole, Dick Siderowf on the 20th hole, and David Jacobsen on the 19th hole. Lewis, the third reinstated amateur among the four semifinalists, won five matches without reaching the 18th hole. Podolak won three of the first six holes of the final and remained 3 up after the first nine holes. The pattern continued on the 10th hole. Podolak won with a birdie to yet another Lewis bogey, and Podolak went 5 up at the 12th. Lewis won the 13th, but Podolak holed a curving 20-foot birdie on the 14th hole to end the match. The USGA accepted a record 2,243 entries.

1985—Jay Sigel, 42, of Berwyn, Pennsylvania, defeated O. Gordon Brewer of Huntingdon Valley, Pennsylvania, 3 and 2, at The Vintage Club in Indian Wells, California. Sigel had now won four USGA Championships in the last four years: the 1982 and 1983 Amateur and the 1983 and 1985 Mid-Amateur. Dennis Saunders of Mesa, Arizona, was the medalist with a 137 but was defeated in the first round of match play by Seth Knight of Atlanta, Georgia, 4 and 2. Knight then faced Sigel and was four up with five holes to play. Sigel played the next five holes in five under par, however, to force the match to extra holes, then birdied the 19th hole to win. Sigel reached the final by defeating Mark Davis, of Mesa, Arizona, 3 and 2. Brewer was taken to 21 holes by Larry Seligmann of Houston, Texas, in the second round, but had little trouble after that. He downed Mike Haney of Glendale, California, 1 up, to reach the final. In the final, Sigel won the first hole with a birdie and the second with a par to go 2 up, but Brewer won the fourth and sixth with birdies to square the match. Sigel regained his two-hole advantage by winning the eighth and ninth holes. The two men exchanged birdies on the 10th and 11th holes and Sigel retained a lead he never relinquished for the rest of the match, eventually closing out Brewer with a five-foot par putt on the 16th hole. The USGA accepted a record 2,577 entries for the Championship.

1986—Bill Loeffler, 30, of Littleton, Colorado, defeated Charles Pinkard of Rockmart, Georgia, 4 and 3, at Annandale in Madison, Mississippi. Loeffler is the youngest man ever to win the Mid-Amateur. At 30 years and two months of age, he was two months younger than Michael Podolak was when he won the championship in 1984. Larry Clark of Kennesaw, Georgia, won the qualifying medal with a 36-hole total of four-under-par 140. Clark advanced to the third round before being eliminated by James Savage of Fort Worth, Texas, 1 up. Loeffler played the 18th hole only once in match play. That occurred in his quarterfinal meeting with George Zahringer of New York. Zahringer won three of the first four holes with birdies to take an early lead, but Loeffler fought back with three birdies of his own to square the match before the turn. Loeffler finally won 2 up. He defeated Randy Sonnier 3 and 2 in the semifinals. Pinkard twice had to play extra holes on his way to the final. He edged James Stahl of Cincinnati on the 19th hole in the quarterfinals and was extended to the second extra hole before ousting Bob Young of Atlanta in the semifinal round. Loeffler never trailed in the final. He won the third hole with a par, but bogeyed the par-5 fifth, squaring the match. Loeffler took the lead for good when Pinkard three-putted at the eighth. He went 2 up when Pinkard found a greenside bunker on the 11th, and 3 up when Pinkard declared his ball unplayable on the 12th. Loeffler closed out the match with a par on the par-3 15th to another Pinkard bogey. The USGA accepted 2,511 entries for the championship.

1987—Jay Sigel, 43, of Berwyn, Pennsylvania, defeated David Lind of Chicago on the 20th hole to win his fifth USGA championship, this time at Brook Hollow Golf Club in Dallas. He also won the U.S. Amateur in 1982 and 1983 and the Mid-Amateur in 1983 and 1985. Only Bob Jones, who won nine championships; JoAnne Carner, eight; and Glenna Collett Vare, Hollis Stacy and Jack Nicklaus, six apiece; have won more USGA titles. Randy Sonnier of The Woodlands, Texas, runner-up to Sigel in the 1983 championship, earned the qualifying medal at one-under-par 139. In the first qualifying round, Don Bliss of St. Louis, who started at the 10th tee, scored holes-in-one on the 10th and eighth holes. He is the first player to score two holes-in-one in the same round in a USGA championship. Sonnier advanced to the semifinal before losing to Sigel, 4 and 2. Lind eliminated Dean Overturf of Dallas, 1 up, in the other semifinal match. Sigel took a 1-up lead after four holes of the final but Lind won three of the next seven to take a two-hole advantage with seven to play. Sigel cut into Lind's lead with a winning par at the 14th, then drew even with a birdie at the 15th. Halves at the 16th, 17th and 18th sent the Mid-Amateur to extra holes for the first time. Sigel won with a par at the 20th hole. The USGA accepted a record 2,630 entries for the championship.

1988—David Eger, 36, a reinstated amateur from Ponte Vedra Beach, Florida, defeated Scott Mayne of Warwick, Bermuda, 2 and 1, in the final at Prairie Dunes Country Club in Hutchinson, Kansas. Three-time Mid-Amateur champion Jay Sigel of Berwyn, Pennsylvania; 1983 runner-up Randy Sonnier of The Woodlands, Texas; and John Harris of Edina, Minnesota, shared the qualifying medal at even-par 140. Sigel and Sonnier were eliminated in the second round. Harris advanced to the third round before losing. After defeating Bill Holstead of Wichita Falls, Texas, 1 up in his opening match, Eger defeated his next three opponents without playing the 15th hole. In the semifinals, Eger was extended to the 18th hole for the second time. He eliminated Shawn Baker of Brattleboro, Vermont, 1 up. Mayne twice won matches on the 18th green on his way to the final and, in the quarterfinal round, defeated Richard Stuntz of Lawrence, Kansas, in 23 holes. Mayne then scored a 2-and-1 victory over Craig Steinberg of Van Nuys, California, to reach the final. Eger birdied the first hole of the final to go 1 up and was 2 up after another birdie at the third. The next three holes were halved with pars before Mayne birdied the seventh. Mayne squared the match when Eger three-putted the 10th hole for a bogey. The next four holes were halved, then Eger regained the lead when he birdied the 15th. Another birdie on 16 gave him a two-hole lead, and he closed out the match at the 17th with his third consecutive birdie. The USGA accepted 2,492 entries for the championship.

1989—James Taylor, age 30, of Palm Beach Gardens, Florida, won three consecutive holes on the final nine and defeated William Hadden, of North Haven, Connecticut, by 4 and 3 in the U.S. Mid-Amateur Championship, at Crooked Stick Golf Club, in Carmel, Indiana. Taylor took the lead for good with a birdie on the par 5 5th hole. He birdied again, on the par 5 ninth hole and was 2 up before Hadden birdied the 10th, closing the gap. Taylor reasserted himself by winning the 12th, 13th, and 14th holes to go 4 up with only four holes still to play. And when the two halved the par 5 15th, the match was over. On his way to the final, Taylor defeated David Eger, of Ponte Vedra, Florida, the 1988 champion, by 2 and 1.

1990—Jim Stuart, of Macon, Georgia, clung to a narrow lead through the final eight holes and defeated Mark Sollenberger, of Scottsdale, Arizona, 1 up, at Troon Golf and Country Club, in Scottsdale. Stuart took a lasting lead with a birdie 4 on 11th hole of the afternoon round. He increased his lead to 2 up three holes later, but Sollenberger birdied the next to last hole to bring Stuart's lead back to 1 up. Each man parred the final hole. One of three Georgians in the semifinals, Stuart had only one easy match leading to the final; he was extended to the 17th hole on all but one. One of those he defeated was James Taylor, of Palm Beach Gardens, Florida, the defending champion, 1 up, in the third round. Stuart shot 84 in the first round of stroke play qualifying, but he came back with 71 and reached match play by two strokes. Thirteen shots better was Mitch Voges, of Simi Valley, California, the medalist, at 141. Two former champions, Jay Sigel, of Collegeville, Pennsylvania, (1983, 1985 and 1987) and David Eger, of Ponte Verde Beach, Florida, (1988) also advanced to match play, but they were eliminated before the semifinal round.

MID-AMATEUR CHAMPIONSHIP

DATE	WINNER, RUNNER-UP	SCORE	SITE	ENTRY
1981 (Oct.)	Jim Holtgrieve d. Bob Lewis, Jr.	2 up	Bellerive C.C., St. Louis, Mo. Co-Medalists—145: Jay Rustman Jay Sigel	1,638
1982 (Sept.)	William Hoffer d. Jeffrey B. Ellis	3 & 2	Knollwood Club, Lake Forest, Ill. Medalist—‡ 137: Jay Sigel	1,779
1983 (Oct.)	Jay Sigel d. Randy Sonnier	1 up	Cherry Hills C.C., Englewood, Colo. Co-Medalists—139: Lawrence Stubblefield Randy Sonnier	2,186
1984 (Sept.-Oct.)	Mike Podolak d. Bob Lewis, Jr.	5 & 4	Atlanta Athletic Club, Atlanta, Ga. Co-Medalists—146: Bob Lewis, Jr. Danny Yates	2,243
1985 (Nov.)	Jay Sigel d. O. Gordon Brewer, Jr.	3 & 2	The Vintage Club, Indian Wells, Calif. Medalist—‡137: Dennis Saunders	2,563
1986 (Oct.)	Bill Loeffler d. Charles Pinkard	4 & 3	Annandale, Madison, Miss. Medalist—140: Larry Clark	2,511
1987 (Oct.)	Jay Sigel d. David Lind	1 up, 20 holes	Brook Hollow G.C., Dallas, Texas Medalist—139: Randy Sonnier	2,630
1988 (Oct.)	David Eger d. Scott Mayne	2 & 1	Prairie Dunes C.C., Hutchinson, Kan. Co-Medalists—140: Jay Sigel Randy Sonnier John Harris	2,492
1989 (Sept.-Oct.)	Jim Taylor d. Bill Hadden	4 & 3	Crooked Stick G.C., Carmel, Ind. Medalist—135: Sean Knapp	3,007
1990 (Oct.)	Jim Stuart d. Mark Sollenberger	1 up	Troon G. & C.C., Scottsdale, Ariz. Medalist—141: Mitch Voges	*3,397

*Record entry
‡Record qualifying score, 36 holes.

1981
FIRST MID-AMATEUR CHAMPIONSHIP

Bellerive Country Club, St. Louis, Missouri, October 10-15
Yardage—7,090. Par 72. 1,638 Entries, 150 Starters, 64 Qualifiers.

Qualifying Score	1st Round (18 Holes)	2nd Round (18 Holes)	3rd Round (18 Holes)	4th Round (18 Holes)	Semi-Finals (18 Holes)	Final (18 Holes)	
*145	Jay Rustman, Roselle, Ill.	Rustman, 1 up					
154	Brian Gaddy, Pasadena, Calif.		Moore, 2 and 1				
151	Kent Moore, Littleton, Colo.	Moore, 1 up, 19 holes					
155	Chris Young, Jacksonville, Fla.						
150	Jimmy Wittenberg, Memphis, Tenn.	Mehok, 5 and 3		Brewer, 1 up			
155	Charles Mehok, Phoenix, Ariz.		Brewer, 5 and 4				
153	Gordon Brewer, Huntingdon Valley, Pa.	Brewer, 5 and 3			Brewer, 4 and 3		
157	Bill Bahn, St. Louis, Mo.						
148	Mark Sollenberger, Scottsdale, Ariz.	Sollenberger, 1 up					
155	John Jennison, Mount Vernon, N.Y.		Yates, 1 up, 19 holes				
152	Fred Ridley, Tampa, Fla.	Yates, 3 and 2					
156	Danny Yates, Atlanta, Ga.			Yates, 6 and 5			
151	John Grace, Forth Worth, Texas	Hollowell, 1 up					
155	Bruce Hollowell, Springfield, Mo.		Hollowell, 3 and 2				
153	Dobbs Long, Albany, Ga.	Long, 4 and 2					
158	Tom Flory, Annapolis, Md.					Lewis, 5 and 4	
146	Bob Lewis, Warren, Ohio	Lewis, 4 and 3					
155	Gary Cowan, Kitchener, Ont., Canada		Lewis, 6 and 5				
151	Jack Marin, Durham, N.C.	Beltz, 1 up, 19 holes					
156	Jim Beltz, Southfield, Mich.						
150	John Ruby, Stratford, Conn.	Ruby, 1 up, 20 holes		Lewis, 3 and 1			
155	David Jacobsen, Portland, Ore.						
153	James Stahl, Cincinnati, Ohio	Siderowf, 2 and 1	Ruby, 2 and 1				
157	Dick Siderowf, Westport, Conn.				Lewis, 2 and 1		
148	Roger Null, Ladue, Mo.	Malley, 3 and 1					
155	Bill Malley, Hayward, Calif.		Malley, 4 and 3				
153	Daniel Noonan, Somersworth, N.H.	Noonan, 1 up, 20 holes					
157	William Brown, Atlanta, Ga.			Malley, 2 and 1			
151	Jeff Burda, Turlock, Calif.	Marucci, 1 up					
155	George Marucci, Wayne, Pa.		Marucci, 5 and 4				
154	George Zahringer, New York, N.Y.	Zahringer, 1 up, 20 holes					
158	David Montgomery, Dallas, Texas						Jim Holtgrieve, 2 up
*145	Jay Sigel, Berwyn, Pa.	Sigel, 4 and 3					
152	Tom Studor, Plainfield, Ill.		Sigel, 2 and 1				
151	Bill Boles, Wilson, N.C.	Boles, 1 up					
156	Tom Amendola, Erie, Pa.						
150	Jeff Ellis, Oak Harbor, Wash.	Ellis, 3 and 2		Sigel, 2 up			
155	Larry Mattox, Columbia, S.C.		Ellis, 4 and 3				
153	William Charpek, Red Bank, N.J.	French, 1 up, 21 holes					
157	John French, Lathrup Village, Mich.				Housen, 1 up, 19 holes		
148	Robert Housen, Brielle, N.J.	Housen, 1 up, 20 holes					
155	Frank Brame, Alexandria, La.		Housen, 2 and 1				
152	Ben Dowdey, Birmingham, Ala.	Smith, 2 and 1					
157	James Smith, Clarksville, Ind.						
151	Richard Evans, Northbrook, Ill.	Mason, 4 and 3		Housen, 3 and 1			
155	Robert Mason, Kirkwood, Mo.		King, 3 and 2				
154	David King, Beltsville, Md.	King, 3 and 2				Holtgrieve, 4 and 3	
158	Bruce Chalas, Dover, Mass.						
146	Jim Holtgrieve, Des Peres, Mo.	Holtgrieve, 5 and 4					
155	Tom Reed, Broomfield, Colo.		Holtgrieve, 3 and 1				
152	Charles Harrison, Marietta, Ga.	Evans, 5 and 4					
156	Tom Evans, Lake Bluff, Ill.						
150	John Paul Cain, Houston, Texas	Nichols, 2 and 1		Holtgrieve, 6 and 5			
155	Randy Nichols, Connersville, Ind.		Nichols, 1 up				
153	Mitch Voges, Northridge, Calif.	Voges, 3 and 2					
157	Glenn Apple, Medina, Ohio				Holtgrieve, 3 and 2		
148	Kent Frandsen, Lebanon, Ind.	Frandsen, 4 and 3					
155	Henry Delozier, Chevy Chase, Md.		Frandsen, 2 and 1				
153	Jack Veghte, Clearwater, Fla.	Veghte, 2 up					
157	Roger Brown, Arkansas City, Kans.			Frandsen, 4 and 3			
151	Tom Hornbuckle, Ruidoso, N.M.	Buchwald, 2 and 1					
155	Lawrence Buchwald, Roswell, Ga.		Young, 5 and 4				
154	Robert Young, Atlanta, Ga.	Young, 5 and 4					
158	Doug Miller, Lakeville, Minn.						

*Co-Medalists

1982
SECOND MID-AMATEUR CHAMPIONSHIP

Knollwood Club, Lake Forest, Illinois, September 25-30.
Yardage — 6,834. Par 70. 1,779 Entries, 150 Starters, 64 Qualifiers.

Qualifying Score	1st Round (18 Holes)	2nd Round (18 Holes)	3rd Round (18 Holes)	4th Round (18 Holes)	Semifinals (18 Holes)	Final (18 Holes)
*137	Jay Sigel, Berwyn, Pa.	Sigel,				
150	Mark Sollenberger, Scottsdale, Ariz.	3 and 2	Sigel,			
147	Randy Reifers, Dublin, Ohio	Studer,	4 and 2			
153	Tom Studer, Plainfield, Ill.	1 up		Sigel,		
145	David Lind, Chicago, Ill.	Lind,		4 and 3		
151	John O'Neal, Carmel, Ind.	1 up	Lind,			
149	William D. Ploeger, Columbus, Ga.	Ploeger,	4 and 3			
154	William K. Myers, Scottsdale, Ariz.	1 up			Terjesen,	
144	Danny Yates, Atlanta, Ga.	Yates,			1 up	
151	Robert G. Housen, Brielle, N.J.	4 and 2	Terjesen,			
148	Barry Terjesen, Akron, Ohio	Terjesen,	2 and 1			
154	Donnell J. Smith, III, Vancouver, Wash.	2 and 1		Terjesen,		
146	Wesley G. Mohr, Jr., Houston, Texas	Mohr,		3 and 2		
153	Tom Maupin, Cleveland, Tenn.	5 and 3	C. Young,			
150	Chris Young, Jacksonville, Fla.	C. Young,	3 and 2			
154	Jerome A. Freeland, St. Louis, Mo.	5 and 3				Hoffer,
143	Lloyd Hughes, Dallas, Texas	Blick,				2 up
150	Jan P. Blick, Cadillac, Mich.	1 up, 19 holes	R. Young,			
147	Robert E. Young, Jr., Atlanta, Ga.	R. Young,	2 and 1			
154	David Apperson, Memphis, Tenn.	2 and 1		R. Young,		
146	James Montiegel, Rochester, Mich.	Gee,		3 and 2		
152	Greg Gee, Lockport, Ill.	1 up	Brewer,			
149	Jerry Dee Nelson, Burket, Ind.	Brewer,	6 and 5			
154	O. G. Brewer, Jr., Huntingdon Valley, Pa.	1 up, 20 holes			Hoffer,	
144	William Hoffer, Elgin, Ill.	Hoffer,			2 and 1	
151	Fordie H. Pitts, Jr., Scituate, Mass.	4 and 2	Hoffer,			
148	H. King Oehmig, Jackson, Miss.	Oehmig,	1 up, 20 holes			
154	Robert Fazio, Bedford Heights, Ohio	2 up		Hoffer,		
147	Frank C. Ford, III, Marietta, Ga.	Ford,		1 up		
153	Gregory W. Shelton, Cleveland, Ohio	5 and 4	Ford,			
150	Bruce C. Hollowell, Springfield, Mo.	Hollowell,	1 up, 20 holes			
155	David S. Narveson, Houston, Texas	2 and 1				
143	Paul Erhardt, Wilmington, Del.	Erhardt,				
150	John R. Johnson, Rochester, Mich.	3 and 2	Erhardt,			
147	David K. Brookreson, Dresher, Pa.	Brookreson,	2 and 1			
153	Ted Lyford, Redlands, Calif.	5 and 3		Erhardt,		
145	Bill Malley, Hayward, Calif.	Stahl,		1 up		
151	James E. Stahl, Jr., Cincinnati, Ohio	1 up, 24 holes	Gelatka,			
149	Ron Gelatka, Lynwood, Ill.	Gelatka,	1 up			
154	Mike Zichy, Edmonton, Alberta, Canada	1 up			Ellis,	
144	Bob Lewis, Jr., Warren, Ohio	Lewis,			3 and 2	
151	Ronald Henry, Jr., Fairfield, Conn.	6 and 5	Harvey,			
148	David K. DeWulf, Clarkston, Mich.	Harvey,	1 up, 19 holes			
154	Bill Harvey, Greensboro, N.C.	3 and 1		Ellis,		
146	J. Franklin Rose, Topeka, Kans.	Rose,		2 and 1		
153	Donald J. Sayet, Coral Gables, Fla.	8 and 6	Ellis,			
150	Jeffrey B. Ellis, Oak Harbor, Wash.	Ellis,	2 and 1			
155	Robert R. Mason, St. Louis, Mo.	3 and 2				Ellis,
144	Jim Holtgrieve, St. Louis, Mo.	Holtgrieve,				3 and 2
151	Donald C. Allen, Rochester, N.Y.	2 and 1	Holtgrieve,			
148	Raymond Warobick, Brookfield, Wis.	Warobick,	3 and 1			
154	James R. Fankhauser, Vienna, W. Va.	3 and 2		Holtgrieve,		
146	Don Shevorski, Yorba Linda, Calif.	Shevorski,		3 and 1		
152	M. C. McDonald, Lafayette, La.	3 and 2	Blooston,			
150	Richard E. Evans, Northbrook, Ill.	Blooston,	3 and 2			
154	Richard Blooston, Edina, Minn.	3 and 1			Oglesby,	
145	Kent Frandsen, Lebanon, Ind.	Murphy,			1 up	
151	Paul Murphy, Newton, Mass.	2 and 1	Oglesby,			
148	Robert Fairchild, Lakewood, Ohio	Oglesby,	4 and 3			
154	David Oglesby, Jacksonville, Fla.	3 and 2		Oglesby,		
147	Robert Kouwe, Tampa, Fla.	Kouwe,		4 and 3		
153	Marc Trout, Ft. Worth, Texas	1 up, 20 holes	Kouwe,			
150	William B. Boles, Jr., Wilson, N.C.	Boles,	1 up			
155	Patrick M. Neary, New Canaan, Conn.	2 up				

William Hoffer, 3 and 2

*Medalist

1983
THIRD MID-AMATEUR CHAMPIONSHIP

Cherry Hills Country Club, Englewood, Colorado, October 1-6
Yardage — 7,103 (7,082). Par 71. †2,186 Entries, 150 Starters, 64 Qualifiers

Qualifying Score	1st Round (18 Holes)	2nd Round (18 Holes)	3rd Round (18 Holes)	4th Round (18 Holes)	Semifinals (18 Holes)	Final (18 Holes)	
*139	Lawrence Stubblefield, Kailua, Hawaii	Stubblefield, 3 and 1					
149	John Harris, Edina, Minn.		Stubblefield, 3 and 1				
147	Roger Brown, Arkansas City, Kans.	Henrickson, 2 and 1					
151	Mark Henrickson, Grand Blanc, Mich.			Sigel, 2 and 1			
145	Steve Rogers, Bowling Green, Ky.	Rogers, 4 and 3					
151	George Janzen, El Paso, Texas		Sigel, 7 and 6				
148	Jay Sigel, Berwyn, Pa.	Sigel, 3 and 1					
152	Frank Brame, Alexandria, La.				Sigel, 1 up, 24 holes		
143	Jim Holtgrieve, St. Louis, Mo.	Holtgrieve, 2 and 1					
150	Scott Radcliffe, Lakewood, Colo.		Holtgrieve, 3 and 2				
148	James Kirkebo, Tacoma, Wash.	Kirkebo, 3 and 2					
152	Robert Wansker, Charlotte, N.C.			Lewis, 2 and 1			
146	Bob Lewis, Warren, Ohio	Lewis, 1 up					
151	Jack Shamblin, S. Charleston, W. Va.		Lewis, 3 and 2				
148	Alton Duhon, Los Angeles, Calif.	Woulfe, 1 up, 19 holes					
153	Richard Woulfe, Ft. Lauderdale, Fla.					Sigel, 2 and 1	
140	Mark Boyajian, Belleville, Ill.	Boyajian, 2 and 1					
149	Robert Blomberg, Alameda, Calif.		Boyajian, 4 and 3				
147	William Hoffer, Elgin, Ill.	Hoffer, 1 up					
152	Don Brown, Addison, Texas			Boyajian, 2 and 1			
145	James Joseph, Homewood, Ill.	O'Neal, 1 up					
151	John O'Neal, Carmel, Ind.		Sucher, 4 and 3				
148	Richard Sucher, Mequon, Wis.	Sucher, 1 up, 19 holes					
153	Thomas Evans, Lake Bluff, Ill.				Scheibert, 1 up, 19 holes		
144	Craig Scheibert, Middletown, Ohio	Scheibert, 2 up					
150	J. Frank Boydston, Phoenix, Ariz.		Scheibert, 5 and 4				
148	Bruce Zulaica, Alameda, Calif.	Zulaica, 2 and 1					
152	Joey Ferrari, Stockton, Calif.			Scheibert, 1 up, 19 holes			
146	Carlton Blewett, Roswell, N.M.	Terjesen, 1 up, 20 holes					
151	Barry Terjesen, Akron, Ohio		Williams, 1 up				
149	Warren MacGregor, Santa Maria, Calif.	Williams, 3 and 2					
153	Chad Williams, Plainview, Texas						Jay Sigel, 1 up
*139	Randy Sonnier, Woodlands, Texas	Sonnier, 1 up					
149	William Argabrite, Kingsport, Tenn.		Sonnier, 3 and 2				
147	Danny Yates, Atlanta, Ga.	Yates, 5 and 3					
152	Michael Rose, Wyncote, Pa.			Sonnier, 4 and 3			
145	John Grace, Ft. Worth, Texas	Grace, 6 and 5					
151	William Barnes, Kingsport, Tenn.		Grace, 5 and 4				
148	Earl Stewart, Dallas, Texas	Stewart, 2 up					
152	Victor Gavalas, Tallahasse, Fla.				Sonnier, 5 and 4		
144	David Huske, Glen Ellyn, Ill.	Dills, 2 and 1					
150	Joey Dills, Tulsa, Okla.		Frandsen, 2 and 1				
148	Fred Silver, Lewiston, N.Y.	Frandsen, 2 up					
152	Kent Frandsen, Lebanon, Ind.			Marucci, 4 and 2			
146	George Marucci, Ardmore, Pa.	Marucci, 3 and 2					
151	Rick TenBroeck, Chicago, Ill.		Marucci, 6 and 4				
149	John Vardaman, Washington, D.C.	Thames, 2 up					
153	Woody Thames, Dallas, Texas					Sonnier, 2 and 1	
143	Paul Erhardt III, Wilmington, Del.	Nichols, 2 and 1					
149	Randy Nichols, Connersville, Ind.		Nichols, 4 and 2				
148	C. Paul Brown, Grand Junction, Colo.	Brown, 1 up					
152	Robert Kouwe, Tampa, Fla.			Nichols, 5 and 3			
145	Marshall Marraccini, McKeesport, Pa.	Belden, 2 and 1					
151	Daniel Belden, Canton, Ohio		Womack, 3 and 2				
148	John McMorrow, Bloomington, Minn.	Womack, 2 and 1					
153	Ray Womack, Burlington, N.C.				Nichols, 4 and 3		
144	David Jacobsen, Portland, Ore.	Jacobsen, 1 up					
150	John McKey, Palm Beach, Fla.		Jacobsen, 2 up				
148	Ricardo Ronderos, Redondo Beach, Calif.	Ronderos, 3 and 2					
152	J.M. Jones, III, Sugarland, Texas			Jacobsen, 2 up			
146	Robert Young, Atlanta, Ga.	Young, 1 up, 20 holes					
151	Charles Murphy, Albany, N.Y.		Ellis, 5 and 4				
149	Jeffrey Ellis, Oak Harbor, Wash.	Ellis, 2 up					
153	Chris Nordling, Aurora, Colo.						

*Co-Medalist

†Record Entry

1984
FOURTH MID-AMATEUR CHAMPIONSHIP

Atlanta Athletic Club (Highlands Course), Atlanta, Georgia, September 29-October 4.
Yardage—6,933. Par 71. +2,243 Entries, 150 Starters, 64 Qualifiers

Qualifying Score	1st Round (18 Holes)	2nd Round (18 Holes)	3rd Round (18 Holes)	4th Round (18 Holes)	Semifinals (18 Holes)	Final (18 Holes)
*146	Danny Yates, Atlanta, Ga.	Yates, 5 and 4				
155	Craig Scheibert, Middletown, Ohio		Holtgrieve, 7 and 6			
153	Jim Holtgrieve, St. Louis, Mo.	Holtgrieve, 2 up				
156	Larry Sock, Lincoln, Neb.			Siderowf, 1 up, 20 holes		
149	Bill Morrison, Portland, Ore.	Siderowf, 3 and 2				
156	Dick Siderowf, Westport, Conn.		Siderowf, 6 and 5			
154	Arthur Butler, Glendora, Calif.	Butler, by default				
157	Don Erickson, Dubois, Pa.				Podolak, 1 up, 20 holes	
148	Douglas Clark, Concord, N.C.	Clark, 1 up, 19 holes				
155	Mayo Fitzhugh, Fairfax, Va.		Podolak, 4 and 2			
153	Chad Williams, Breaux Bridge, La.	Podolak, 1 up, 19 holes				
157	Michael Podolak, Fargo, N.C.			Podolak, 3 and 1		
152	Martin West, Rockville, Md.	West, 2 and 1				
156	Philip Pleat, Manchester, N.H.		West, 2 and 1			
154	Jay Sigel, Berwyn, Pa.	Sigel, 6 and 4				
158	Bruce Hollowell, Springfield, Mass.					Podolak, 1 up, 19 holes
147	Ron Gaiser, Birmingham, Ala.	Gaiser, 3 and 2				
155	James Kirkebo, Tacoma, Wash.		Steinbert, 2 and 1			
153	Craig Steinbert, Studio City, Calif.	Steinbert, 7 and 5				
156	Douglas Perry, Goleta, Calif.			Ridley, 4 and 3		
150	Fred Ridley, Tampa, Fla.	Ridley, 1 up				
156	Wayne Huff, Abilene, Texas		Ridley, 4 and 2			
154	Fred Silver, Lewiston, N.Y.	Silver, 4 and 3				
158	Doug Fischesser, Connersville, Ind.				Jacobsen, 4 and 2	
148	David Jacobsen, Portland, Ore.	Jacobsen, 1 up				
155	Seth Knight, Atlanta, Ga.		Jacobsen, 1 up, 22 holes			
153	Roger Brown, Arkansas City, Kan.	Brown, 3 and 2				
157	Bruce Fitzpatrick, Miami, Fla.			Jacobsen, 3 and 2		
152	Spencer Sappington, St. Louis, Mo.	Sappington, 1 up, 19 holes				
156	Thomas Francis, Boone, N.C.		Giroso, 4 and 3			
155	Blaise Giroso, Wilmington, Del.	Giroso, 2 and 1				
158	Ted Warner, Sterling, Colo.					
*146	Bob Lewis, Warren, Ohio	Lewis, 3 and 1				
155	David Brookreson, Huntington Valley, Pa.		Lewis, 4 and 3			
153	Robert Rawlins, Dallas, Texas	Marraccini, 2 and 1				
156	Marshall Marraccini, McKeesport, Pa.			Lewis 3 and 2		
149	Gary Jarmon, Norman, Okla.	Logan, 3 and 2				
156	Howard Logan, Shelbyville, Ky.		Logan, 2 up			
154	Walter Driver, Atlanta, Ga.	Driver, 2 up				
158	John Bracken, Scottsdale, Ariz.				Lewis, 5 and 4	
148	Robert Young, Atlanta, Ga.	Young, 4 and 3				
155	Robert Baker, Little Rock, Ark.		Young, 1 up, 19 holes			
153	Larry White, Chattanooga, Tenn.	White, 4 and 2				
157	Jeffrey Thomas, S. Plainfield, N.J.			Young, 1 up, 19 holes		
152	Tom Studer, Plainfield, Ill.	Grace, 3 and 1				
156	John Grace, Fort Worth, Texas		Bardha, 1 up, 19 holes			
155	John Pallin, Little Rock, Ark.	Bardha, 3 and 2				
158	Agim Bardha, Birmingham, Mich.					Lewis, 3 and 2
148	William Ploeger, Columbus, Ga.	Ploeger, 2 up				
155	Charles Weil, Encino, Calif.		Sonnier, 3 and 2			
153	Randy Sonnier, Woodlands, Texas	Sonnier, 3 and 2				
156	Frank Brame, Alexandria, La.			Brewer, 1 up, 20 holes		
152	Alan Doyle, LaGrange, Ga.	Holbrook, 2 up				
156	William Holbrook, Rome, Ga.		Brewer, 5 and 4			
154	Gordon Brewer, Huntington Valley, Pa.	Brewer, 2 up				
158	Robert Moyers, New Market, Va.				Brewer, 1 up, 19 holes	
149	Bill Hoffer, Elgin, Ill.	Hoffer, 4 and 2				
155	John Morgan, Birmingham, Mich.		Hoffer, 3 and 2			
154	Roy Schultheiss, Bay City, Mich.	Evans, 5 and 3				
157	Thomas Evans, Lake Bluff, Ill.			Hoffer, 2 and 1		
153	Tom Hamilton, Pleasantville, N.Y.	Hamilton, 2 up				
156	John Baldwin, New York, N.Y.		Smith, 4 and 3			
155	Charles Smith, Delaware, Ohio	Smith, 3 and 2				
158	John Parsons, Avon Park, Fla.					

Michael Podolak, 5 and 4

*Co-medalists
+ Record Entry

1985
FIFTH MID-AMATEUR CHAMPIONSHIP

The Vintage Club (Mountain Course), Indian Wells, California, November 9-14
Yardage—6,907. Par 72. +2,577 Entries, 150 Starters, 64 Qualifiers

Qualifying Score	1st Round (18 Holes)	2nd Round (18 Holes)	3rd Round (18 Holes)	4th Round (18 Holes)	Semifinals (18 Holes)	Final (18 Holes)
*137	Dennis Saunders, Mesa, Ariz.	Knight, 4 and 2	Sigel, 1 up, 19 holes	Sigel, 5 and 3	Sigel, 1 up	Sigel, 3 and 2
154	Seth Knight, Atlanta, Ga.					
150	Ron Gelatka, S. Holland, Ill.	Sigel, 1 up, 19 holes				
150	Jay Sigel, Berwyn, Pa.					
147	Brad Griffin, Rutland, Vt.	Griffin, 1 up, 19 holes	Griffin, 3 and 1			
152	Bob Lewis, Warren, Ohio					
147	Brian Lindley, Costa Mesa, Calif.	Riordan, 4 and 3				
152	Joseph Riordan, Flagstaff, Ariz.					
144	Bill Viele, Hemet, Calif.	Gallagher, 3 and 2	Gallagher, 1 up	Duncan, 1 up		
153	Denny Gallagher, Cincinnati, Ohio					
149	Robert Young, Atlanta, Ga.	Young, 2 and 1				
151	Chuck Cordell, Pinehurst, N.C.					
144	Randy Sonnier, Woodlands, Texas	Lee, 1 up, 19 holes	Duncan, 2 and 1			
153	William Lee, New Haven, Conn.					
149	Roscoe Staples, St. Augustine, Fla.	Duncan, 2 and 1				
151	Patrick Duncan, Rancho Santa Fe, Calif.					
140	Bill Holstead, Wichita Falls, Texas	Gee, 1 up, 19 holes	Davis, 4 and 3	Davis, 2 up	Davis, 3 and 2	
154	Greg Gee, Lockport, Ill.					
149	Anthony Cullinane, Chevy Chase, Md.	Davis, 5 and 4				
150	Mark Davis, Mesa, Ariz.					
147	John Gaffney, Williamsville, N.Y.	Gaffney, 2 up	Ridley, 4 and 3			
152	Jeffrey Thomas, S. Plainfield, N.J.					
148	Fred Ridley, Tampa, Fla.	Ridley, 2 and 1				
151	Michael Sanger, Stevenson, Md.					
142	Thomas McGraw, Westminster, Colo.	deLozier, 2 and 1	deLozier, 2 and 1	Stubblefield, 1 up, 19 holes		
154	Henri deLozier, Chevy Chase, Md.					
149	Roger Brown, Arkansas City, Kan.	Brown, 5 and 4				
151	Scott Masingill, Payett, Idaho					
146	Lawrence Stubblefield, Kailua, Hawaii	Stubblefield, 1 up	Stubblefield, 3 and 2			
152	Rick Ten Broeck, Chicago, Ill.					
148	Robert Pomerantz, Des Moines, Iowa	McCool, 2 and 1				
151	Robin McCool, Bethlehem, Pa.					
140	Agim Bardha, Birmingham, Mich.	Bardha, 3 and 2	Godwin, 1 up	Godwin, 1 up	Haney, 5 and 4	Brewer, 1 up
154	Guy Gordon, Los Gatos, Calif.					
150	Luther Godwin, Poplar Bluff, Mo.	Godwin, 1 up, 20 holes				
150	Jim Knoll, Sunnyvale, Calif.					
147	Steve Bogan, Placentia, Calif.	Bogan, 5 and 4	Bogan, 1 up, 19 holes			
152	Barry Terjesen, Akron, Ohio					
147	Bill Loeffler, Littleton, Colo.	Loeffler, 3 and 2				
152	Doug Clark, Concord, N.C.					
144	Bruce Robertson, San Mateo, Calif.	Robertson, 7 and 5	Rose, 1 up, 20 holes	Haney, 3 and 2		
153	Gordon Norwood, Houston, Texas					
149	J. Franklin Rose, Omaha, Neb.	Rose, 2 up				
151	Robert Timpson, Glendale, Calif.					
144	David Sheff, Irvine, Calif.	Sheff, 3 and 2	Haney, 1 up, 19 holes			
153	Carl Richardson, Salinas, Calif.					
149	Mike Haney, Glendale, Calif.	Haney, 6 and 5				
151	Bev Hargraves, Helena, Ark.					
140	Marshall Marraccini, McKeesport, Pa.	Jacobsen, 3 and 1	Jacobsen, 1 up, 20 holes	Brewer, 3 and 2	Brewer, 6 and 5	
154	David Jacobsen, Portland, Ore.					
150	Greg Reynolds, Grand Blanc, Mich.	Hamer, 1 up 19 holes				
150	John Hamer, Boulder, Colo.					
147	Gordon Brewer, Huntington Valley, Pa.	Brewer, 2 and 1	Brewer, 1 up, 21 holes			
152	Danny Yates, Atlanta, Ga.					
148	Larry Seligmann, Houston, Texas	Seligmann, 5 and 3				
152	John Antonini, Wilmington, Del.					
144	Wyn Norwood, Little Rock, Ark.	W. Norwood, 3 and 2	W. Norwood, 1 up, 20 holes	Alexander, 6 and 5		
154	Marshall Gleason, Foster City, Calif.					
149	Rick Lutz, Oklahoma City, Okla.	Verble, 4 and 3				
151	David Verble, San Antonio, Texas					
145	Michael Podolak, Fargo, N.D.	Alexander, 4 and 3	Alexander, 5 and 4			
153	John Alexander, Black Butte, Ore.					
148	Dick Siderowf, Westport, Conn.	Siderowf, 2 and 1				
151	Al Norris, Carmel, Calif.					

Jay Sigel, 3 and 2

*Medalist
+Record Entry

1986
SIXTH MID-AMATEUR CHAMPIONSHIP

Annandale, Madison, Mississippi, October 4-9
Yardage—6,912. Par 72. 2,511 Entries, 150 Starters, 64 Qualifiers

Qualifying Score	1st Round (18 Holes)	2nd Round (18 Holes)	3rd Round (18 Holes)	4th Round (18 Holes)	Semifinals (18 Holes)	Final (18 Holes)
*140	Larry Clark, Kennesaw, Ga.	Clark,				
154	Larry Seligmann, Houston, Texas	1 up	Clark,			
150	John Esterbrook, Rutland, Vt.	Esterbrook,	4 and 3			
150	Bob Stuart, Bronxville, N.Y.	1 up, 19 holes		Savage,		
148	Mike Podolak, Fargo, N.D.	Savage,		1 up		
152	James Savage, Fort Worth, Texas	3 and 1	Savage,			
148	Frank Magee, Phoenixville, Pa.	Benson,	3 and 2			
152	John Benson, Punxsutawney, Pa.	3 and 2			Pinkard,	
145	Roderick Mayne, Warwick, Bermuda	Mayne,			3 and 1	
153	Charles Lamb, Phoenix, Ariz.	4 and 2	Stahl,			
149	James Stahl, Cincinnati, Ohio	Stahl,	3 and 1			
151	Mark Burden, Atlanta, Ga.	5 and 4		Pinkard,		
145	Barry Turjesen, Akron, Ohio	Turjeson,		1 up, 19 holes		
153	Buddy Marucci, Villanova, Pa.	1 up	Pinkard,			
149	Bill Pelham, Houston, Texas	Pinkard,	5 and 4			
151	Charles Pinkard, Rockmart, Ga.	1 up				Pinkard,
143	Bob Young, Atlanta, Ga.	Young,				1 up, 19 holes
153	Jack Larkin, Atlanta, Ga.	2 and 1	Young,			
150	Phil Kenny, Glenview, Ill.	Kenny,	2 and 1			
151	Davis Driver, Irving, Texas	1 up, 20 holes		Young,		
147	Jon Buchman, San Diego, Calif.	Schnurbusch,		4 and 5		
153	Craig Schnurbusch, Farmington, Mo.	3 and 1	McClung,			
148	Jimmy Riddle, Madisonville, Ky.	McClung,	1 up			
152	Mike McClung, Dallas, Texas	2 and 1			Young,	
144	Randy Reifers, Dublin, Ohio	Reifers,			1 up, 19 holes	
153	Everett Dobson, Edmond, Okla.	3 and 1	Simson,			
150	Joel Hirsch, Chicago, Ill.	Simson,	1 up, 19 holes			
151	Paul Simson, Raleigh, N.C.	1 up, 19 holes		Simson,		
146	Bill Hadden, Hamden, Conn.	Hadden,		3 and 2		
153	Mark Infalt, Palm Harbor, Fla.	1 up, 25 holes	Alexander,			
149	Buddy Alexander, Baton Rouge, La.	Alexander,	1 up			
152	Ted Lyford, Redlands, Calif.	2 and 1				
142	Dennis Saunders, Mesa, Ariz.	Saunders,				
154	Chip Stewart, Dallas, Texas	2 and 1	Harwell,			
150	Wesley Paxson, Jacksonville, Fla.	Harwell,	5 and 4			
151	Barry Harwell, Peachtree City, Ga.	1 up		Sonnier,		
147	Randy Sonnier, Woodlands, Texas	Sonnier,		3 and 2		
152	Mike Bakula, Fresno, Calif.	4 and 3	Sonnier,			
148	Larry White, Chattanooga, Tenn.	White,	5 and 4			
152	Bob Fairchild, Lakewood, Ohio	3 and 2			Sonnier,	
144	Tom McKnight, Galax, Va.	McKnight,			3 and 2	
153	Kent Frandsen, Lebanon, Ind.	1 up, 19 holes	McKnight,			
150	Michael Hughett, Owasso, Okla.	Hughett,	1 up			
151	Martin West, Rockville, Md.	2 and 1		Duncan,		
146	Pat Duncan, Rancho Santa Fe, Calif.	Duncan,		1 up, 20 holes		
153	Greg Davis, Portland, Ore.	1 up, 19 holes	Duncan,			
149	Johnny Stevens, Wichita, Kan.	Stevens,	5 and 3			
151	John Pigg, Austin, Texas	2 up				Loeffler,
142	Agim Bardha, Birmingham, Mich.	Bardha,				3 and 2
153	Gunnar Bennett, Chicago, Ill.	3 and 2	Spillier,			
150	Kent Moore, Littleton, Colo.	Spillier,	3 and 2			
151	Lindsey Spillier, Baton Rouge, La.	7 and 6		Zahringer,		
147	George Zahringer, New York, N.Y.	Zahringer,		3 and 2		
152	Paul Staples, Fairburn, Ga.	1 up, 20 holes	Zahringer,			
148	Lloyd Hughes, Dallas, Texas	M. Davis,	5 and 4			
152	Mark Davis, Mesa, Ariz.	3 and 2			Leoffler,	
144	Mike Taylor, Meridian, Miss.	Taylor,			2 up	
153	Luther Godwin, Poplar Bluff, Mo.	2 and 1	Loeffler,			
150	Bill Loeffler, Littleton, Colo.	Loeffler,	3 and 2			
151	Steve Thomas, Fort Washington, Md.	5 and 4		Loeffler,		
146	Jay Sigel, Berwyn, Pa.	Brown,		2 and 1		
153	Roger Brown, Arkansas City, Kan.	1 up	Holtgrieve,			
149	Jim Holtgrieve, St. Louis, Mo.	Holtgrieve,	4 and 3			
151	John Parsons, Palm Beach Gardens, Fla.	4 and 3				

Bill Loeffler, 4 and 3

*Medalist

1987
SEVENTH MID-AMATEUR CHAMPIONSHIP

Brook Hollow Golf Club, Dallas, Texas, October 3-8
Yardage—6,677. Par 70. +2,630 Entries, 150 Starters, 64 Qualifiers

Qualifying Score	1st Round (18 Holes)	2nd Round (18 Holes)	3rd Round (18 Holes)	4th Round (18 Holes)	Semifinals (18 Holes)	Final (18 Holes)	
*139	Randy Sonnier, Woodlands, Texas	Sonnier, 4 and 3					
153	Richard Bryson, Akron, Ohio		Sonnier, 2 and 1				
151	Bill Hoffer, Elgin, Ill.	Pinkard, 2 and 1					
151	Charles Pinkard, Rockmart, Ga.			Sonnier, 5 and 3			
148	John Grace, Fort Worth, Texas	Baldwin, 2 and 1					
152	John Baldwin, New York, N.Y.		Hirsch, 1 up, 19 holes				
149	Martin Smith, El Paso, Texas	Hirsch, 2 and 1					
152	Joel Hirsch, Chicago, Ill.				Sonnier, 1 up, 19 holes		
146	Danny Yates, Atlanta, Ga.	Yates, 3 and 1					
152	Gary Vanier, Pleasant Hill, Calif.		Yates, 5 and 4				
150	William Spangler, Lincoln, Neb.	Ellis, 6 and 5					
151	Richard Ellis, Plano, Texas			Yates, 2 and 1			
146	John Harris, Edina, Minn.	Harris, 6 and 4					
152	Arnold Salinas, Dallas, Texas		Ball, 3 and 2				
150	Mark Sollenberger, Phoenix, Ariz.	Ball, 1 up, 19 holes					
151	Michael Ball, Rockville, Md.					Sigel, 4 and 2	
144	Jay Sigel, Berwyn, Pa.	Sigel, 1 up					
153	Stephen Holden, Pine Bluff, Ark.		Sigel, 4 and 3				
150	Lloyd Hughes, Dallas, Texas	Savage, 1 up					
151	James Savage, Fort Worth, Texas			Sigel, 2 and 1			
148	Larry Seligmann, Houston, Texas	Kelley, 5 and 4					
152	Tom Kelley, Fort Wayne, Ind.		Kelley, 5 and 4				
149	Mark Miller, Antioch, Calif.	Williamson, 3 and 1					
152	Dale Williamson, Chadron, Neb.				Sigel, 5 and 4		
144	David Eger, Ponte Vedra Beach, Fla.	Nichols, 5 and 3					
153	Randy Nichols, Connersville, Ind.		Nichols, 1 up				
150	Gerald Norquist, Eugene, Ore.	Strawn, 1 up					
151	David Strawn, Charlotte, N.C.			Holstead, 2 and 1			
148	Bill Holstead, Wichita Falls, Texas	Holstead, 2 and 1					
152	Scott Stegner, Plano, Texas		Holstead, 1 up				
149	Paul Hindsley, Glenview, Ill.	Hindsley, 3 and 1					
152	Seth Knight, III, Atlanta, Ga.						Jay Sigel, 1 up, 20 holes
143	Robert Young, Atlanta, Ga.	Keene, 2 and 1					
153	Richard Keene, Eastridge, Tenn.		Keene, 2 and 1				
151	Tom Knapp, North Palm Beach, Fla.	Knapp, 2 and 1					
151	Douglas Farr, Monroe, La.			Lind, 6 and 5			
148	Kent Frandsen, Lebanon, Ind.	Frandsen, 3 and 1					
152	Paul Erhardt, III, Wilmington, Del.		Lind, 7 and 6				
149	David Lind, Chicago, Ill.	Lind, 2 and 1					
152	Mitch Voges, Simi Valley, Calif.				Lind, 6 and 5		
146	Mike Podolak, Fargo, N.D.	Podolak, 2 and 1					
152	Robert Fairchild, Lakewood, Ohio		Steinberg, 3 and 2				
150	Craig Steinberg, Van Nuys, Calif.	Steinberg, 4 and 3					
151	Mark Davis, Mesa, Ariz.			Steinberg, 1 up			
147	Patrick Duncan, Rancho Sante Fe, Calif.	Lipari, 4 and 3					
152	John Lipari, Miami, Fla.		Marucci, 1 up, 19 holes				
150	Colin Bork, Brookings, S.D.	Marucci, 4 and 2					
151	George Marucci, Jr., Villanova, Pa.					Lind, 1 up	
144	Paul Simson, Raleigh, N.C.	Overturf, 3 and 2					
153	Dean Overturf, Dallas, Texas		Overturf, 1 up				
151	Jimmy Adams, Beaumont, Texas	Adams, 2 and 1					
151	Frank Vines, Birmingham, Ala.			Overturf, 2 up			
148	Ron Henry, Fairfield, Conn.	Henry, 6 and 5					
152	Fred Rowland, Overland Park, Kan.		Henry, 5 and 4				
149	Thomas Musselman, Lexington, Ky.	Merhib, 2 and 1					
152	Joe Merhib, Oklahoma City, Okla.				Overturf, 3 and 2		
146	George Zahringer, III, New York, N.Y.	Zahringer, 4 and 3					
153	Bill Pelham, Houston, Texas		Zahringer, 3 and 1				
150	Donald Bliss, Chesterfield, Mo.	Larson, by default					
151	Todd Larson, Columbus, Ohio			Zahringer, 3 and 2			
147	Bill Loeffler, Littleton, Colo.	Loeffler, 1 up					
152	Schley Purvis, Brandon, Miss.		Loeffler, 5 and 3				
149	Henri Delozier, Chevy Chase, Md.	Martin, 2 and 1					
152	James Martin, Dallas, Texas						

+ Record Entry
* Medalist

1988
EIGHTH MID-AMATEUR CHAMPIONSHIP

Prairie Dunes Country Club, Hutchinson, Kansas, October 1-6
Yardage—6,615. Par 70. 2,492 Entries, 150 Starters, 64 Qualifiers

Qualifying Score	1st Round (18 Holes)	2nd Round (18 Holes)	3rd Round (18 Holes)	4th Round (18 Holes)	Semifinals (18 Holes)	Final (18 Holes)	
*140	Jay Sigel, Berwyn, Pa.	Sigel, 2 and 1					
153	Larry Stubblefield, Kailua, Hawaii		Marraccini, 1 up				
148	Marshall Marraccini, McKeesport, Pa.	Marraccini, 6 and 5					
148	Dennis McMaster, Pleasanton, Calif.			S. Baker, 4 and 3			
146	Shawn Baker, Brattleboro, Vt.	S. Baker, 1 up					
151	Curtis Wagner, Peachtree City, Ga.		S. Baker, 1 up				
146	Steve Creekmore, Fort Smith, Ark.	Creekmore, 4 and 3					
150	David Ojala, Houston, Texas				S. Baker, 4 and 3		
143	Robert Baker, Little Rock, Ark.	DeWitt, 2 and 1					
152	Rick DeWitt, Arvada, Colo.		DeWitt, 1 up, 19 holes				
147	William McGuinness, Woodbury, N.J.	McGuinness, 6 and 5					
149	Rick Ten Broeck, Chicago, Ill.			DeWitt, 1 up			
144	Robert Sedorcek, Kansas City, Kan.	Sedorcek, 7 and 6					
152	John Price, Chantilly, Va.		Sedorcek, 4 and 2				
147	Mark Gilmartin, Reno, Nev.	Gilmartin, 1 up					
149	Fred Silver, Lewiston, N.Y.					Eger, 1 up	
142	Doug Farr, Lafayette, La.	Farr, 3 and 2					
152	James Camione, Upland, Calif.		Farr, 3 and 2				
148	Stephen Sharpe, Greensboro, N.C.	Reynolds, 6 and 5					
149	Greg Reynolds, Grand Blanc, Mich.			Holtgrieve, 3 and 2			
146	David Dougherty, LaGrange, Ga.	Dougherty, 3 and 2					
151	Paul Melson, Plantation, Fla.		Holtgrieve, 5 and 4				
147	Jim Holtgrieve, St. Louis, Mo.	Holtgrieve, 3 and 2					
150	Robb Pomerantz, Des Moines, Iowa				Eger, 5 and 4		
142	Mike Podolak, Hickson, N.D.	Podolak, 5 and 4					
152	William Jenks, Boston, Mass.		Waitulavich, 2 and 1				
148	Jon Lundgren, Bloomington, Minn.	Waitulavich, 5 and 4					
149	Jerry Waitulavich, Chesterfield, Mo.			Eger, 5 and 4			
145	David Eger, Ponte Vedra Beach, Fla.	Eger, 1 up					
151	Bill Holstead, Wichita Falls, Texas		Eger, 7 and 6				
147	David Lind, Chicago, Ill.	Lind, 2 and 1					
150	Mark Davis, Mesa, Ariz.						David Eger, 2 and 1
*140	John Harris, Edina, Minn.	Harris, 2 up					
152	Jerry Brown, Kennewick, Wash.		Harris, 1 up				
148	Dennis Saunders, Phoenix, Ariz.	Saunders, 6 and 4					
149	Adrian Druzgala, Jessup, Md.			Steinberg, 4 and 2			
146	Paul Simson, Raleigh, N.C.	Hirsch, 3 and 1					
151	Barry Hirsch, Tenafly, N.J.		Steinberg, 2 and 1				
146	George Glickley, Chicago, Ill.	Steinberg, 4 and 2					
150	Craig Steinberg, Van Nuys, Calif.				Steinberg, 4 and 2		
143	Henry Cagigal, Fort Worth, Texas	Cagigal, 5 and 4					
152	Herb Jensen, Carmichael, Calif.		Jones, 1 up, 19 holes				
147	John Jones, New Kensington, Pa.	Jones, 5 and 4					
149	Don Lizak, Levittown, N.Y.			Jones, 2 and 1			
145	Bob Lewis, Warren, Ohio	Lewis, 3 and 2					
152	Gregory Marshall, Portland, Ore.		Lewis, 2 up				
147	Dean Overturf, Dallas, Texas	Overturf, 1 up					
149	Mike Taylor, Meridian, Miss.					Mayne, 2 and 1	
*140	Randy Sonnier, The Woodlands, Texas	Sonnier, 6 and 5					
152	Ron Kilby, McAllen, Texas		Stuntz, 3 and 2				
148	David Smith, Longwood, Fla.	Stuntz, 1 up, 20 holes					
149	Richard Stuntz, Lawrence, Kan.			Stuntz, 2 up			
146	Michael Goodes, Reidsville, N.C.	Goodes, 5 and 4					
151	John Grace, Fort Worth, Texas		Zahringer, 5 and 3				
147	Tab Hudson, Jasper, Ala.	Zahringer, 1 up					
150	George Zahringer, III, New York, N.Y.				Mayne, 1 up, 23 holes		
143	Scott Mayne, Warwick, Bermuda	Mayne, 1 up					
152	George Marucci, Clementon, N.J.		Mayne, 6 and 5				
148	Alan Peters, Milwaukee, Wis.	Wyatt, 1 up, 21 holes					
149	Paul Wyatt, Highland Park, Ill.			Mayne, 1 up			
145	Wesley Mohr, Houston, Texas	Richart, 2 and 1					
151	Willard Richart, Ann Arbor, Mich.		Richart, 1 up				
147	Todd Shore, Boca Raton, Fla.	Shore, 4 and 2					
150	Todd Barker, Talorsville, Utah						

* Co-Medalists

1989
NINTH U.S. MID-AMATEUR CHAMPIONSHIP

Crooked Stick Golf Club, Carmel, Indiana, September 30-October 5
Yardage—6,827. Par 72. Record 3,007 Entries, 150 Starters, 64 Qualifiers

Qualifying Score	1st Round (18 Holes)	2nd Round (18 Holes)	3rd Round (18 Holes)	4th Round (18 Holes)	Semifinals (18 Holes)	Final (36 Holes)	
*135	Sean Knapp, Oakmont, Pa.	Knapp, 4 and 2					
153	Jim Goostree, Tuscaloosa, Ala.		Knapp, 20 holes				
150	Javier Sanchez, Redwood City, Calif.	Sanchez, 4 and 3					
150	Barry Terjesen, Akron, Ohio			Knapp, 2 and 1			
147	Bob Lewis, Jr., Warren, Ohio	Fischesser, 3 and 2					
151	Doug Fischesser, Connersville, Ind.		Baker, 1 up				
147	Todd Schaefer, Grand Forks, N.D.	Baker, 5 and 4					
151	Shawn Baker, Brattleboro, Vt.				Hadden, 2 and 1		
145	William Hadden, North Haven, Ct.	Hadden, 2 up					
153	Jeff Rhodes, Seattle, Wash.		Hadden, 6 and 5				
148	Harcourt Kemp, Louisville, Ky.	Kemp, 5 and 4					
151	Richard Stuntz, Lawrence, Kan.			Hadden, 19 holes			
145	Bill Pelham, Kirkland, Wash.	Camaione, 2 and 1					
152	James Camaione, Upland, Calif.		McGraw, 3 and 1				
148	Tom McGraw, Westminster, Colo.	McGraw, 21 holes					
151	Randy Sonnier, Woodlands, Texas					Hadden, 1 up	
143	Ron Richard, Fort Smith, Ark.	Richard, 2 and 1					
153	Jimmy Clagett, Dripping Springs, Texas		Richard, 2 and 1				
149	Jeff Kiley, New York, N.Y.	Stahl, 4 and 2					
150	James Stahl, Jr., Cincinnati, Ohio			Richard, 4 and 3			
146	Rick DeWitt, Arvada, Colo.	DeWitt, 2 and 1					
152	Steve Gill, Coppell, Texas		Burris, 1 up				
148	Craig Anderson, Fallbrook, Calif.	Burris, 3 and 2					
151	Jack Burris, High Point, N.C.				Yates, 2 and 1		
143	Kevin King, Hilton Head, S.C.	King, 3 and 2					
153	Dave Sheff, La Canadaa, Calif.		Alexander, 1 up				
149	Don Erickson, Dubois, Pa.	Alexander, 6 and 5					
150	Stewart Alexander, Gainsville, Fla.			Yates, 1 up			
146	Walton Ashwander, Hartselle, Ala.	Ashwande, 2 and 1					
152	Douglas Logan, Shelbyville, Ky.		Yates, 20 holes				
148	Danny Yates, Atlanta, Ga.	Yates, 3 and 2					
151	Jay Sigel, Berwyn, Pa.						James Taylor, 4 and 3
138	Mike Nixon, Nashville, Tenn.	Williamson, 1 up					
153	Sam Williamson, Ventura, Calif.		Long, 7 and 6				
150	David McCampbell, Marshall, Inc.	Long, 2 up					
150	Clayton Long, Albany, Ga.			Holtgrieve, 4 and 2			
146	Jim Holtgrieve, St. Louis, Mo.	Holtgrieve, 2 and 1					
152	Dee Sanders, Columbia, Mo.		Holtgrieve, 4 and 2				
147	Richard Keene, Chattanooga, Tenn.	Kelley, 2 and 1					
151	Tom Kelley, Fort Wayne, Ind.				Nick, 1 up		
145	George Zahringer, New York, N.Y.	Zahringer, 3 and 2					
153	Gordon Brewer, Huntingdon, Valley, Pa.		Zahringer, 3 and 2				
149	Tom McKnight, Galex, Va.	McKnight, 5 and 3					
150	Joel Hirsch, Chicago, Ill.			Nick, 1 up			
145	Joel Nick, Okmulgee, Okl.	Nick, 7 and 6					
152	Frank Rose, Omaha, Neb.		Nick, 4 and 3				
148	Paul Hindsley, Glenview, Ill.	Harris, 6 and 4					
151	John Harris, Edina, Minn.					Taylor, 2 and 1	
142	James Taylor, Palm Beach Gardens, Fla.	Taylor, 3 and 2					
153	Philip Pleat, Nashua, N.H.		Taylor, 7 and 6				
150	Mark Hendrickson, Grand Blanc, Mi.	Holland, 19 holes					
150	Richard Holland, Washington, D.C.			Taylor, 7 and 6			
146	Mike Podolak, Oxbow, N.D.	Culligan, 19 holes					
152	Tom Culligan, San Mateo, Calif.		Brewer, 2 and 1				
147	Ronald Brewer, Leawood, Kan.	Brewer, 2 up					
151	Bob Gibbons, Dallas, Texas				Taylor, 2 and 1		
144	Kirk Lombardi, Rockville, Md.	Goodes, 1 up					
153	Mike Goodes, Reidsville, N.C.		Goodes, 4 and 3				
149	Craig Steinberg, Van Nuys, Calif.	Chapman, 19 holes					
150	Jimmy Chapman, Irving, Texas			Eger, 2 and 1			
145	David Eger, Ponte Vedra Beach, Fla.	Eger, 3 and 2					
152	Gene Ryzewicz, Westport, Ct.		Eger, 3 and 2				
148	John Lindholm, Flint, Mich.	Lindholm, 4 and 2					
151	Alan Peters, Milwaukee, Wis.						

*Medalist

1990
TENTH U.S. MID-AMATEUR CHAMPIONSHIP

Troon Golf and Country Club, Scottsdale, Arizona, October 6-11
Yardage—6,799. Par 72. Record 3,397 Entries, 150 Starters, 64 Qualifiers

Qualifying Score	1st Round (18 Holes)	2nd Round (18 Holes)	3rd Round (18 Holes)	4th Round (18 Holes)	Semifinals (18 Holes)	Final (36 Holes)	
*141	Mitch Voges, Simi Valley, Calif.	Baldwin,					
157	John Baldwin, New York, N.Y.	2 and 1	Taylor,				
153	Robin McCool, Bethlehem, Pa.	Taylor,	5 and 4				
153	James Taylor, Palm Beach Gardens, Fla.	5 and 4		Stuart,			
150	Chris Dalrymple, Pinehurst, N.C.	Dalrymple,		1 up			
155	Mack Woodfin, Ingram, Texas	3 and 1	Stuart,				
151	Scott Thomas, St. Louis, Mo.	Stuart,	2 and 1				
155	Jim Stuart, Macon, Ga.	2 and 1			Stuart,		
148	William Bradfford, Broken Arrow, Okla.	Brafford,			5 and 4		
156	Michael Caprio, Meriden, Conn.	2 up	Lefebre,				
152	Michael Lefebre, West Palm Beach, Fla.	Lefebre,	3 and 1				
155	James Mason, Chesterfield, Mo.	5 and 3		Morgan,			
148	Robert Fairchild, Lakewood, Ohio	Jones,		20 holes			
156	John Jones, New Kensington, Pa.	5 and 4	Morgan,				
152	John Morgan, West Bloomfield, Mich.	Morgan,	19 holes				
155	Jay Pierson, Shreveport, La.	2 and 1				Stuart,	
145	Allen Doyle, La Grange, Ga.	Doyle,				2 up	
157	Cliff David, Suison, Calif.	4 and 3	Doyle,				
153	Kim Mansfield, Beldon, Miss.	Hier,	1 up				
154	Bruce Hier, Essex Junction, Vt.	3 and 1		Yates,			
149	Tom Studer, Joliet, Ill.	Studer,		2 and 1			
156	John O'Neal, Carmel, Ind.	4 and 3	Yates,				
151	Danny Yates, Atlanta, Ga.	Yates,	2 up				
155	Mark Small, Flossmoor, Ill.	5 and 3			Yates,		
146	Paul Simon, Raleigh, N.C.	Martin,			2 and 1		
156	Michael Martin, Springfield, Mass..	1 up	Martin,				
152	Michael Matthews, Oakton, Va.	Matthews,	2 and 1				
154	Joe Nick, Okmulkee, Okla.	1 up		Hadden,			
149	William Hadden, North Haven, Conn.	Hadden,		3 and 2			
156	David Ojala, Kingwood, Texas	4 and 3	Hadden,				
151	Ronald Richard, Fort Smith, Ark.	Richard,	6 and 4				Stuart, 1 up
155	Bob Clark, Santa Ana, Calif.	4 and 3					
142	Jay Sigel, Collegeville, Pa.	Sigel,					
157	Robert Rodriguez, St. Paul, Minn.	3 and 2	Sigel,				
153	Marshall Marraccini, Elizabeth, Pa.	Barkley,	4 and 3				
153	Mike Barkley, Clearwater, Fla.	2 up		Sigel,			
150	Frank Vines, Birmingham, Ala.	Vines,		4 and 3			
155	Tim Gamso, Dallas, Texas	3 and 2	Eger,				
151	David Eger, Ponte Verde Beach, Fla.	Eger,	1 up				
155	Joel Hirsch, Chicago, Ill.	1 up			Long,		
147	Paul Hindsley, Glenview, Ill.	Hindsley,			4 and 3		
156	Mike Hoyle, Arlington, Texas	19 holes	Long,				
152	Mark Matthews, Carmel, Ind.	Long,	3 and 2				
155	Clayton Long, Albany, Ga.	2 and 1		Long,			
148	Michael Evans, Monterey, Calif.	Evans,		3 and 2			
156	Jim Hulme, Fallon, Nev.	6 and 5	Tucker,				
151	Tommy Brennan, Metairie, La.	Tucker,	3 and 2				
155	James Tucker, Portland, Ore.	19 holes				Sollenbeger,	
143	Mark Sollenberger, Scottsdale, Ariz.	Sollenberger,				3 and 2	
157	David Brookreson, Huntingdon Valley, Pa.	1 up	Sollenberger,				
153	Dan Belden, Canton, Ohio	Inaba,	1 up				
154	Daryl Inaba, Honolulu, Hawaii	3 and 1		Sollenberger,			
150	Kemp Richardson, Laguna Niguel, Calif.	Knapp,		1 up			
155	Sean Knapp, Oakmont, Pa.	1 up	Fox,				
151	Jay Fox, Conway, Ariz.	Fox,	5 and 4				
155	Scott Fitzgerald, Dallas, Tex.	2 and 1			Sollenberger,		
146	Rick DeWitt, Arvada, Colo.	DeWitt,			2 and 1		
156	Gordon Brewer, Huntington Valley, Pa.	8 and 7	Scheultheiss,				
152	Worth Banner, Virginia Beach, Va.	Schultheiss,	1 up				
155	Roy Schultheiss, Bay City, Mich.	26 holes		Mortell,			
149	Les Peterson, San Ramon, Calif.	Peterson,		2 and 1			
156	Bill McGuinness, Woodbury, N.J.	1 up	Mortell,				
151	Sandy Galbraith, Fountain Valley, Calif.	Mortell,	2 and 1				
155	Michael Mortell, Oak Park, Ill.	2 up					

*Medalist

WOMEN'S MID-AMATEUR CHAMPIONSHIP

WOMEN'S MID-AMATEUR CHAMPIONSHIP TROPHY

Presented in October, 1987, by

MRS. HENRI PRUNARET

Chairman, Women's Committee 1959-1963

HISTORY

1987—Cindy Scholefield, 27, of Malibu, California defeated Pat Cornett of Corte Madera, California, 6 and 5, to win the first Women's Mid-Amateur Championship at Southern Hills Country Club in Tulsa, Oklahoma. Anne Sander, who had won the U.S. Senior Women's Amateur and reached the quarterfinals of the U.S. Women's Amateur earlier in the year, was the medalist at 157. She was defeated in the first round by Pat Milton, a semifinalist at the Women's Amateur, 1 up. Scholefield and Cornett advanced through the match-play draw with ease. Scholefield was extended to the 16th hole only once on her way to the final. She ousted Marilyn Horn of Mesa, Arizona, 4 and 2, in the semifinals. Cornett's one tense match occurred in the quarterfinals where she downed Lida Kinnicutt of Bloomfield, Connecticut, 3 and 2. She defeated Charlotte Wood of Beaumont, Texas, 5 and 3, to earn her spot in the final. Scholefield birdied the first, third and sixth holes of final, eventually taking a four-hole lead at the turn. The 10th was halved, then Scholefield won the 11th and 12th with pars to go 6 up. The 13th was halved, giving Scholefield the championship. The USGA accepted 320 entries for the championship.

1988—Martha Lang, 35, of Geneva, Illinois, defeated Mary Hanyak of Boynton Beach, Florida, 4 and 3, in the final played at Amelia Island (Florida) Plantation. Lang, as Martha Jones, was medalist in the 1969 Girls' Junior Championship. For the second consecutive year, Anne Sander of Seattle, Washington, earned the qualifying medal. She shot rounds of 74-74—148, four strokes better than Pat Cornett-Iker of Corte Madera, California, who placed second. Sander lost to Linda Olsen of Granada Hills, California, in the second round. Lang defeated Helen Kirkland of Colorado Springs, Colorado, 2 and 1 in the first round. After two relatively easy matches in the second and third rounds, she was extended to the 19th hole before she eliminated Cornett-Iker. Lang defeated Pam Holcombe of Quincy, Illinois, 1 up, to reach the final. Hanyak's first serious challenge came in the third round when she defeated Sharon Keil of Sylvania, Ohio, in 20 holes. She then ousted Olsen and Liz Rogers of Virginia Beach, Virginia, by 2-and-1 margins. Hanyak played the opening nine of the final in 46 to Lang's 36 and was four holes behind. She was not able to recover from that deficit and Lang won 4 and 3. The USGA accepted a record 347 entries for the championship.

1989—Robin Weiss saved par by holing a 12-foot putt on the fourth extra hole and won the Women's Mid-Amateur Championship, defeating Page Marsh-Lea at the Hills of Lakeway, in Austin, Texas. A 36-year-old resident of Palm Beach Gardens, Florida, Miss Weiss had fallen three holes down to Mrs. Marsh-Lea after seven holes. Miss Weiss fought back, pulled even on the 12th, and went ahead for the first time by birdieing the 16th, her third birdie in eight holes. Mrs. Marsh-Lea sent the match to extra holes by birdieing the 18th from 30 feet. This was the first Women's Mid-Amateur final that went to extra holes. They halved the first three extra holes with pars, but then Miss Weiss saved her par after driving into a fairway bunker on the fourth and won the match when Mrs. Marsha-Lea bunkered her approach and bogied. In her third appearance in the Mid-Amateur, Miss Weiss won five other matches to reach the final, including a one-hole victory over Anne Sander in 19 holes in the third round. Mrs. Sander shot 71, and Miss Weiss 72. Mrs. Marsh-Lea, 26, had played a near-perfect round until faltering with a couple of bogeys on the par 3s on the second nine.

1990—Carol Semple Thompson, 41, returned to her home area of western Pennsylvania and defeated Page Marsh-Lea, 3 and 1 in the final, at the Allegheny Country Club, where she had learned the game. Mrs. Thompson won her victory on the merit of her excellent final nine. She had fallen 2 down to 27-year-old Mrs. Marsh-Lea after eight holes, but she rallied to win five of the final nine holes. She began her comeback with birdies on the ninth, 10th, and 12th holes. The Women's Mid-Amateur is the latest in a long string of accomplishments for Mrs. Thompson, whose record includes the 1973 U.S. Women's Amateur, the 1974 British Women's Championship, and playing on six Curtis Cup teams, and three U.S. Women's World Amateur teams. This was the second consecutive year Mrs. Marsh-Lea had lost in the final. She lost in 22 holes to Robin Weiss in 1989. Mrs. Thompson was extended to the 18th hole only once in her first three matches, but she needed a miraculous finish to overtake Anne Sander in her semifinal match. Mrs. Thompson fell two holes behind through 12, but recovered and won four of the final six holes, winning 2 up.

WOMEN'S MID-AMATEUR CHAMPIONSHIP

DATE	WINNER, RUNNER-UP	SCORE	SITE	ENTRY
1987 (Oct.)	Miss Cindy Scholefield d. Dr. Pat Cornett	6 & 5	Southern Hills C.C., Tulsa, Okla. Medalist—157: Mrs. Anne Q. Sander	320
1988 (Oct.)	Mrs. Martha Lang d. Miss Mary Hanyak	4 & 3	Amelia Island Plantation, Amelia Island, Fla. Medalist—†148: Mrs. Anne Q. Sander	346
1989 (Oct.)	Miss Robin Weiss d. Mrs. Page Marsh Lea	1 up, 22 holes	The Hills of Lakeway G.C., Austin, Tex. Medalist—150: Mrs. Carol Semple Thompson	289
1990 (Sept.-Oct.)	Mrs. Carol Semple Thompson d. Mrs. Page Marsh Lea	3 & 1	Allegheny C.C., Sewickley, Pa. Medalist—149: Ms. Sally Krueger	*354

†Record Qualifying Score
*Record Entry

1987
FIRST U.S. WOMEN'S MID-AMATEUR CHAMPIONSHIP

Southern Hills Country CLub, Tulsa, Okla., October 10-15
Yardage—6,037. Par 72. 320 Entries, 135 Starters, 64 Qualifiers

Qualifying Score	1st Round (18 Holes)	2nd Round (18 Holes)	3rd Round (18 Holes)	4th Round (18 Holes)	Semifinals (18 Holes)	Final (18 Holes)
*157	Anne Sander, Seattle, Wash	Milton, 1 up				
177	Pat Milton, Munroe Falls, Ohio		Oliver, 2 up			
171	Judith Oliver, Sewickley, Pa.	Oliver, 3 and 2				
171	Peggy Hogan, Carpenteria, Calif.			Wood, 3 and 2		
166	Jean Crawford, Colorado Springs, Colo.	Wood, 3 and 2				
173	Charlotte Wood, Beaumont, Texas		Wood, 3 and 2			
166	Sue Ewart, Seal Beach, Calif.	Ewart, 2 up				
173	Stephanie Brower, Ocean Ridge, Calif.				Wood, 3 and 1	
163	Cindy Mah-Lyford, Stratton Mountain, Vt.	Smith, 2 and 1				
175	Lancy Smith, Snyder, N.Y.		Smith, 4 and 3			
169	Susan Marchese, Omaha, Neb.	Marchese, 2 up				
173	Lynda Wimberly, Winter Park, Fla.			Lee, 1 up		
164	Robin Weiss, Palm Beach, Fla.	Weiss, 6 and 5				
175	Nancy Koustas, Dearborn, Mich.		Lee, 2 up			
169	Mary Jane Anderson, Pontiac, Mich.	Lee, 1 up, 24 holes				
173	Tanna Lee, Fort Smith, Ark.					Cornett, 5 and 3
160	Pat Cornett, Corte Madera, Calif.	Cornett, 5 and 3				
176	Tracy Hart, Beavercreek, Ohio		Cornett, 8 and 7			
171	Tamara Bowman, Orlando, Fla.	Bowman, 6 and 5				
172	Shana Radford, Memphis, Tenn.			Cornett, 3 and 2		
165	Elizabeth Haines, Gladwyne, Pa.	Haines, 4 and 2				
174	Carol Ellis, Minneapolis, Minn.		MacMaster, 1 up			
167	Alecia MacMaster, Williston, N.D.	MacMaster, 4 and 2				
173	Debbie McClung, Horseshoe Bay, Texas				Cornett, 3 and 2	
160	Lida Kinnicutt, Bloomfield, Conn.	Kinnicutt, 1 up				
176	Susan Kennedy, Muskogee, Okla.		Kinnicutt, 6 and 5			
170	Diana Schwab, Kettering, Ohio	Schwab, 2 and 1				
172	Connie Shorb, York, Pa.			Kinnicutt, 6 and 5		
165	Nancy Fitzgerald, Carmel, Ind.	Fitzgerald, 2 up				
174	Joan Garety, Rockford, Mich.		Fitzgerald, 2 and 1			
167	Marianne Towersey, Santa Ana, Calif.	Towersey, 1 up, 20 holes				
173	Janice Calin, Edina, Minn.					
159	Leslie Shannon, Miami, Fla.	Shannon, 2 and 1				
176	Frances English, Indianapolis, Ind.		Olsen, 2 and 1			
171	Margaret Brass, Orlando, Fla.	Olsen, 1 up				
172	Linda Chen Olsen, Granada Hills, Calif.			Olsen, 1 up		
166	Carole Semple Thompson, Sewickley, Pa.	C. Thompson, 3 and 2				
173	Louise Wilson, Louisville, Ky.		C. Thompson, 1 up			
167	Brenda Seymour, Chantilly, Va.	Seymour, 3 and 1				
173	Anne Marie Tobin, Peabody, Mass.				Scholefield, 6 and 5	
162	Phyllis Preuss, Colorado Springs, Colo.	Wolf, 1 up, 19 holes				
175	Susan Wolf, Syosset, N.Y.		Wolf, 1 up, 19 holes			
169	Mary Cushing, Carmel, Calif.	Cushing, 3 and 2				
172	Barbara McIntire, Colorado Springs, Colo.			Scholefield, 4 and 3		
164	Cindy Scholefield, Malibu, Calif.	Scholefield, 8 and 6				
174	Millie Stanley, Escondido, Calif.		Scholefield, 7 and 5			
168	Dede Hoffman, Naples, Fla.	Hoffman, 5 and 4				
173	Linda Fuller, Issaquah, Wash.					Scholefield, 4 and 2
160	Pamela Holcombe, Quincy, Ill.	Holcombe, 3 and 2				
176	Sharon Keil, Sylvania, Ohio		R. Thompson, 1 up, 19 holes			
171	Rosemary Thompson, Albuquerque, N.M.	R. Thompson, 1 up				
172	Reggie Hawes, Rye, N.Y.			R. Thompson, 4 and 3		
166	Toni Wiesner, Fort Worth, Texas	Wiesner, 6 and 5				
174	Sharon Clark, Sugar Land, Texas		Wiesner, 2 up			
167	Helen Kirkland, Colorado Springs, Colo.	Kirkland, 5 and 3				
173	Lucille Ray, Rock Hill, S.C.				Horn, 2 and 1	
161	Suzy Ellison, Columbia, S.C.	Young, 2 up				
176	Robin Young, Los Angeles, Calif.		Hewitt, 2 and 1			
170	Marcia Dolan, Danbury, Conn.	Hewitt, 4 and 3				
172	Kathy Hewitt, Dallas, Texas			Horn, 5 and 4		
165	Kathleen Gook, Tempe, Ariz.	Anderson, 1 up, 19 holes				
174	Margo Anderson, Austin, Texas		Horn, 1 up			
167	Marilyn Horn, Mesa, Ariz.	Horn, 4 and 2				
173	JoAnn Lindsay, Edina, Minn.					

Cindy Scholefield, 7 and 6

+ Record Entry

* Medalist

1988
SECOND U.S. WOMEN'S MID-AMATEUR CHAMPIONSHIP

Amelia Island Plantation, Amelia Island, Florida, October 8-13
Yardage—5,970. Par 72. +346 Entries, 130 Starters, 64 Qualifiers

Qualifying Score	1st Round (18 Holes)	2nd Round (18 Holes)	3rd Round (18 Holes)	4th Round (18 Holes)	Semifinals (18 Holes)	Final (18 Holes)
*148	Anne Sander, Seattle, Wash.	Sander,				
168	Ann Probert, New Vernon, N.J.	7 and 5	Olsen,			
162	Margaret Brass, Orlando, Fla.	Olsen,	2 and 1			
163	Linda Olsen, Granada Hills, Calif.	4 and 3		Olsen,		
159	Connie Shorb, York, Pa.	Shorb,		1 up		
166	Marilyn Horn-Hardy, Houston, Texas	1 up, 19 holes	McCloskey,			
159	Tanna Lee, Fort Smith Ark.	McCloskey,	1 up			
166	Pam McCloskey, Boca Raton, Fla.	1 up			Hanyak,	
156	Frances English, Plainfield, Ind.	Hawes,			2 and 1	
167	Reggie Hawes, Rye, N.Y.	3 and 1	Hanyak,			
162	Mary Hanyak, Boynton Beach, Fla.	Hanyak,	5 and 4			
164	Lee Ann Vogel, West Gilgo Beach, N.Y.	3 and 2		Hanyak,		
156	Janice Albert, Bryn Mawr, Pa.	Avant,		1 up, 20 holes		
167	Kathy Avant, Tucson, Ariz.	4 and 3	Keil,			
162	Barbara Young, Wesport, Conn.	Keil,	5 and 4			Hanyak,
164	Sharon Keil, Sylvania, Ohio	1 up, 19 holes				2 and 1
155	Martha Leach, Savannah, Ga.	Leach,				
167	Toni Wiesner, Ft. Worth, Texas	3 and 2	Rogers,			
162	Liz Rogers, Virginia Beach, Va.	Rogers,	1 up	Rogers,		
163	Anne Marie Tobin, Peabody, Mass.	2 up		3 and 2		
158	Carol Semple Thompson, Sewickley, Pa.	C. Thompson,				
166	Judy Oliver, Sewickley, Pa.	4 and 3	C. Thompson,			
160	Ann Swanson, Bellevue, Wash.	Swanson,	4 and 3		Rogers	
164	Sarah Koeppel, New York, N.Y.	1 up			1 up, 21 holes	
155	Phyllis Preuss, Colorado Springs, Colo.	Preuss,				
167	Carol Falk, Portland, Ore.	5 and 4	Preuss,			
162	Mildred Stanley, Escondido, Calif.	Stanley,	3 and 2	Preuss,		
164	Marion Maney, Dedham, Mass.	1 up		2 up		
158	Andrea Dornin, Miami Springs, Fla.	Dornin,				
166	Rosemary Thompson, Albuquerque, N.M.	2 and 1	Dornin,			
161	Bobbie Beattie, Pompano Beach, Fla.	Cushing,	2 and 1			
164	Mary Cushing, Carmel, Calif.	7 and 5				
152	Pat Cornett-Iker, Corte Madera, Calif.	Cornett-Iker,				
168	Nancy Fitzgerald, Carmel, Ind.	3 and 1	Cornett-Iker,			
162	Lois Hodge, Los Altos, Calif.	Hodge,	7 and 6	Cornett-Iker,		
163	Robin Weiss, Palm Beach, Fla.	3 and 2		5 and 3		
159	Lida Kinnicutt, Bloomfield, Conn.	Kinnicutt,				
166	Elizabeth Haines, Gladwyne, Pa.	1 up	Mankowski,			
159	Kathy Mankowski, Dallas, Texas	Mankowski,	2 and 1		Lang,	
165	Sybil Whitman, Livingston, N.J.	1 up			1 up, 19 holes	
155	Leslie Shannon, Miami, Fla.	Roche,				
167	Laurie Roche, Hamden, Conn.	4 and 3	Roche,			
162	Lancy Smith, Snyder, N.Y.	Smith,	1 up, 20 holes			
164	Deborah Baronofsky, San Diego, Calif.	6 and 4		Lang,		
157	Helen Kirkland, Colorado Springs, Colo.	Lang,		4 and 3		
167	Martha Lang, Geneva, Ill.	2 and 1	Lang,			Lang,
161	Barbara McIntire, Colorado Springs, Colo.	McIntire,	4 and 3			1 up
164	Mary Jane Delcamp, Pontiac, Mich.	1 up				
155	Sue Ewart, Seal Beach, Calif.	Ewart,				
168	Pat Milton, Munroe Falls, Ohio	1 up	Brandvold,			
162	Cindy Brandvold, Jacksonville, Fla.	Brandvold,	3 and 2	Holcombe,		
163	Eleanor Walker, Norcross, Ga.	5 and 3		1 up		
159	Pam Holcombe, Quincy Ill.	Holcombe,				
166	Lynne Cowan, Aptos, Calif.	1 up	Holcombe,			
159	Louise Kepley, Cincinnati, Ohio	Giovainni,	1 up		Holcombe,	
164	Judy Giovainni, Akron, Ohio	1 up			2 up	
155	Martha Kirouac, Norcross, Ga.	Kirouac,				
167	Ann Kerwick, Rochester, N.Y.	3 and 1	Kirouac,			
162	Anita Harsch, West Burlington, Iowa	Harsch,	4 and 3	Hoffman,		
164	Lucille Ray, Rock Hill, S.C.	4 and 3		4 and 3		
158	Dede Hoffman, Naples, Fla.	Hoffman,				
166	Margo Anderson, Austin, Minn.	5 and 4	Hoffman,			
161	Vickie Layton, Greensboro, N.C.	Brower,	3 and 2			
164	Stephanie Brower, Ocean Ridge, Fla.	2 and 1				

Martha Lang, 4 and 3

† Record Entry

*Medalist

1989
THIRD U.S. WOMEN'S MID-AMATEUR CHAMPIONSHIP

The Hills of Lakeway, Lakeway, Texas, October 7-12
Yardage—5,988. Par 72. 289 Entries, 132 Starters, 64 Qualifiers

Qualifying Score	1st Round (18 Holes)	2nd Round (18 Holes)	3rd Round (18 Holes)	4th Round (18 Holes)	Semifinals (18 Holes)	Final (18 Holes)
* 150	Carol Thompson, Sewickley, Pa.	Thompson, 5 and 4				
168	Sue Joy-Sobota, Madison, Wis.		Thompson, 2 and 1			
163	Claudine Rubin, Los Angeles, Calif.	Rubin, 4 and 3				
163	Susan Campbell, Kalamazoo, Mich.			McCloskey, 1 up		
159	Pam McCloskey, Boca Raton, Fla.	McCloskey, 2 and 1				
164	Nancy Fitzgerald, Carmel, Ind.		McCloskey, 1 up			
164	Mary Ann Morrison, Dubois, Wy.	Morrison, 5 and 3				
159	Marilyn Hardy, Houston, Texas				Krueger, 2 up	
166	Suzy Ellison, Columbia, S.C.	Ellison, 1 up (19)				
156	Kathy Kahan, Longwood, Fla.		Krueger, 3 and 1			
160	Sally Krueger, San Francisco, Calif.	Krueger, 6 and 4				
164	Linda Pearson, Glendale, Calif.			Krueger, 4 and 2		
156	Lancy Smith, Snyder, N.Y.	Smith, 4 and 3				
166	Frances English, Plainfield, Ind.		Smith, 1 up			
164	Ann Swanson, Bellevue, Wash.	Swanson, 4 and 3				
160	Dana Harrity, Rye Beach, N.Y.					Marsh-Lea, 4 and 2
152	Susan Marchese, Omaha, Neb.	Marchese, 1 up				
167	Katherine Schaeffer, Ft. Myers, Fla.		Preuss, 2 and 1			
163	Phyllis Preuss, Colorado Springs, Col.	Preuss, 3 and 1				
162	Leslie Shannon, Ft. Lauderdale, Fla.			Marsh-Lea, 4 and 2		
158	Page Marsh-Lea, Williamsburg, Va.	Marsh-Lea, 4 and 2				
165	Debbie McClung, Horseshoe Bay, Texas		Marsh-Lea, 3 and 2			
164	Andrea Dornin, Miami Springs, Fla.	Dornin, 1 up (21)				
159	Mildred Stanley, Escondido, Calif.				Marsh-Lea, 3 and 2	
155	Teri Melanson, W. Hollywood, Calif.	Melanson, 1 up (19)				
166	Shena Bassett, San Antonio, Texas		Melanson, 4 and 3			
164	Vicki Layton, Greensboro, N.C.	Layton, 1 up				
162	Mary Cushing, Carmel, Calif.			Kirkland, 4 and 2		
165	Helen Kirkland, Colorado Springs, Col.	Kirkland, 2 up				
157	Natalie Gallagan, West Newton, Mass.		Kirkland, 1 up (19)			
159	Harriet Hart, Ponte Vedra, Fla.	Hart, 5 and 4				
164	Reggie Hawes, Purchase, N.Y.					
151	Toni Wiesner, Fort Worth, Texas	Wiesner, 4 and 2				
168	Judy Giovainni, Akron, Ohio		Burke, 5 and 3			
163	Robin Burke, Houston, Texas	Burke, 2 up				
163	Cynthia Powell, Lexington, Ky.			Budke, 2 up		
164	Mary Budke, S. Pasadena, Calif.	Budke, 2 up				
159	Martha Kirouac, Norcross, Ga.		Budke, 5 and 4			
159	Carolyn Creekmore, Dallas, Texas	Creekmore, 5 and 4				
164	Pat Milton, Monroe Falls, Ohio				Budke, 5 and 4	
166	Lisa Kartheiser, Pt. Washington, Wis.	Kartheiser, 1 up				
156	Martha Lang, Geneva, Ill.		Kartheiser, 1 up			
161	Barbara Berkmeyer, Frontenac, Mo.	Berkmeyer, 2 and 1				
164	Paula Eger, Tucson, Ariz.			Lee, 1 up		
156	Tanya Lee, Fort Smith, Ark.	Lee, 3 and 1				
166	Kieko Hamazaki, Westchester, Ill.		Lee, 1 up			
160	Lida Kinnicutt, Bloomfield, Ct.	Kinnicutt, 3 and 2				
164	Jaon Higgins, Claremont, Calif.					Weiss, 2 and 1
151	Pat Cornett-Iker, Corde Madera, Cal.	Cornett-Iker, 4 and 3				
167	Keiki Dawn Izumi, Kaneohe, Hi.		Cornett-Iker, 1 up			
163	Regina George, Port St. Lucie, Fla.	George, 1 up				
163	Liz Rogers, Virginia Beach, Va.			Holcombe, 1 up		
165	Ann Laney, Kentfield, Calif.	Laney, 5 and 4				
158	Connie Shurb, York, Pa.		Holcombe, 7 and 6			
159	Pam Holcombe, Quincy, Ill.	Holcombe, 1 up				
164	Diane Thompson, Ormond Beach, Fla.				Weiss, 4 and 3	
155	Robin Weiss, Palm Beach, Fla.	Weiss, 8 and 6				
166	Sue Ewart, Seal Beach, Calif.		Weiss, 4 and 3			
164	Mary Schmidt, Houston, Texas	Schmidt, 3 and 2				
161	Barbara McIntire, Colorado Springs, Col.			Weiss, 1 up (19)		
157	Anne Sander, Seattle, Wash.	Sander, 1 up				
166	Lynne Cowan, Aptos, Calif.		Sander, 4 and 3			
164	Taffy Brower, Ocean Ridge, Fla.	Brower, 2 and 1				
160	Elizabeth Haines, Gladwyne, Pa.					

Robin Weiss, 1 up (22)

*Medalist

1990
FOURTH U.S. WOMEN'S MID-AMATEUR CHAMPIONSHIP

Allegheny Country Club, Sewickley, Pennsylvania, September 29-October 4
Yardage—5,982. Par 72. Record 354 Entries, 135 Starters, 64 Qualifiers

Qualifying Score	1st Round (18 Holes)	2nd Round (18 Holes)	3rd Round (18 Holes)	4th Round (18 Holes)	Semifinals (18 Holes)	Final (18 Holes)	
* 149	Sally V. Krueger, San Francisco, Calif.	Krueger,					
165	Barbara Pagana, Selinsgrove, Pa.	5 and 4	Krueger,				
160	Connie Shorb, York, Pa.	Layton,	2 and 1				
160	Vicki Layton, Greensboro, N.C.	4 and 3		Weiss,			
157	Robin Weiss, Palm Beach, Fla.	Weiss,		4 and 3			
163	Marcia Morell, McCook, Neb.	8 and 6	Weiss,				
157	Pam Holcombe, Quincy, Ill.	Crawford,	4 and 2				
162	Jean Crawford, Rye, N.Y.	2 and 1			Weiss,		
154	Patty Moore, Charlotte, N.C.	Moore,			3 and 2		
164	Judy Giovainni, Akron, Ohio	1 up	Tobin,				
159	Anne Marie Tobin, Peabody, Mass.	Tobin,	3 and 2				
161	Teri Melanson, West Hollywood, Calif.	3 and 1		Tobin,			
155	Debbie Smither, Sarasota, Fla.	Smither,		4 and 3			
164	Cathy Carter, Jefferson City, Mo.	5 and 4	Smither,				
159	Wendy Goode, Palm City, Fla.	Leach,	5 and 4				
161	Martha Leach, Austin, Texas	2 and 1				Marsh Lea,	
151	Susan Marchese, Omaha, Neb.	Marchese,				2 up	
165	Marilyn Hardy, Houston, Tex.	6 and 5	Marchese,				
160	Toni Weisner, Fort Worth, Texas	Weisner,	3 and 2				
161	Lee Kaney, Fort Valley, Ga.	1 up		Marchese,			
157	Lancy Smith, Snyder, N.Y.	Hodge,		3 and 2			
163	Lois Hodge, Los Altos, Calif.	1 up	Thompson,				
158	Pat Milton, Munroe Falls, Ohio	Thompson,	2 up				
162	Diane Thompson, Ormond Beach, Fla.	4 and 3					
153	Leslie Shannon, Fort Lauderdale, Fla.	Shannon,			Marsh Lea,		
165	Sue Ewart, Seal Beach, Calif.	20 holes	Shannon,		2 and 1		
160	Anita Harsch, West Burlington, Iowa	Preuss,	4 and 3				
161	Phyllis Preuss, Colorado Springs, Colo.	2 and 1		Marsh Lea,			
156	Page Marsh Lea, Jamestown, N.C.	Marsh Lea,		2 and 1			
163	Linda Chen Olson, Granada Hills, Calif.	3 and 1	Marsh Lea,				
158	Judy Oliver, Sewickley, Pa.	Oliver,	2 up				
162	Amy Bubon, Westminster, Calif.	4 and 3					Thompson, 3 and 1
* 149	Carol Semple Thompson, Sewickley, Pa.	Thompson,					
165	Frances English, Plainfield, Ind.	3 and 2	Thompson,				
160	Ann Swanson, Bellevue, Wash.	Swanson,	3 and 1				
161	Marcia Fisher, Gladston, Ore.	5 and 4		Thompson,			
157	Joan Garety, Rockford, Mich.	Bierman,		7 and 6			
163	Mary Ann Bierman, Chagrin Falls, Ohio	5 and 4	Bierman,				
157	Martha Lang, Geneva, Ill.	Brower,	5 and 4				
162	Taffy Brower, Ocean Ridge, Fla.	4 and 3			Thompson,		
154	Natalie Galligan, West Newton, Mass.	Hjalmquist,			5 and 4		
165	Jennifer Hjalmquist, East Amherst, N.Y.	3 and 1	Hjalmquist,				
159	Nancy Fitzgerald, Carmel, Ind.	Fitzgerald,	20 holes				
161	Judith Bailey, New Orleans, La.	2 and 1		Hjalmquist,			
155	Andrea Dornin, Margate, Fla.	Dorin,		20 holes			
164	Jane Caruso, Cincinnati, Ohio	3 and 2	Fitzgerald,				
159	Jane Fitzgerald, Kensington, Md.	Fitzgerald,	2 up				
162	Mildred Stanley, Escondido, Calif.	4 and 3				Thompson,	
150	Dana Harrity, Rye Beach, N.H.	Harrity,				2 up	
165	Heather Hughes, Palo Alto, Calif.	1 up	Sander,				
160	Anne Sander, Seattle, Wash.	Sander,	3 and 1				
161	Carol Davis, Garrett Park, Md.	4 and 2		Sander,			
157	Marion McInerney, Dedham, Mass.	McInerney,		3 and 2			
163	Diana Schwab, Kettering, Ohio	5 and 4	McInerney,				
158	Pat Cornett-Iker, Corte Madera, Calif.	Cornett-Iker,	2 and 1				
162	Elizabeth Haines, Gladwyne, Pa.	3 and 2			Sander,		
153	Natalie Easterly, Richmond, Va.	Pearson,			6 and 5		
165	Linda Pearson, Glendale, Calif.	1 up	Lakowske,				
160	Helen Kirkland, Colorado Springs, Colo.	Lakowske,	5 and 4				
161	Rise Lakowske, Corvalis, Ore.	1 up		Lakowske,			
156	Marlene Streit, Ontario, Canada	Streit,		1 up			
164	Cathy Schaefer, Fort Myers, Fla..	3 and 1	Streit,				
159	Mary Budke, South Pasadena, Calif.	Eger,	3 and 1				
162	Paula Eger, Tuscon, Ariz.	2 and 1					

*Co-medalists

WALKER CUP MATCH

UNITED STATES GOLF ASSOCIATION

INTERNATIONAL CHALLENGE TROPHY

Presented in May, 1921, by

GEORGE H. WALKER

President of the United States Golf Association, 1920

HISTORY

1981—The United States won its fifth consecutive Walker Cup Match dating back to 1973. It was the U.S. team's 25th victory in the series, which began in 1922. Great Britain and Ireland have won only twice and one Match ended in a tie. The United States won 15-9 at the Cypress Point Club in Pebble Beach, California. Despite the American dominance of the series, the individual matches are usually very close and this year's matches exemplified just that point. Of the 24 individual matches, nine reached at least the 17th hole. Of those nine, the United States won five and Great Britain won four. The United States took a quick 3-1 lead during the first morning's foursomes matches. The Jim Holtgrieve-Frank Fuhrer III, Bob Lewis, Jr.-Dick von Tacky and Ron Commans-Corey Pavin teams gave the United States its first three points. The surprising losers were defending U.S. Amateur Champion Hal Sutton and three-time Walker Cupper Jay Sigel. They were defeated by the teenage pair of Philip Walton, 19, and Ronan Rafferty, 17, who was the youngest player in Walker Cup history. Walton and Rafferty won 4 and 2 after trailing by three holes early in the match. The United States also won five of the first afternoon's eight singles matches. That gave the United States an 8-4 lead midway through the competition. In singles, Sutton came back against Rafferty, 3 and 1; Joe Rassett and Jodie Mudd, both of whom had been on the sidelines during the morning action, came through with identical 1 up victories, Pavin won 4 and 3, while Sigel, the 1979 British Amateur Champion, downed Peter McEvoy, a two-time British Amateur Champion, 4 and 2. Great Britain and Ireland came back strong the next day taking three of the four foursomes matches. The most impressive of their three victories was a 6 and 4 decision by Walton and Rafferty over the Holtgrieve-Fuhrer combination. Rassett and Mudd won the only American point with a 5 and 4 triumph over Ian Hutcheon and Geoffrey Godwin. The United States lead was then only 9-7 with eight afternoon singles matches remaining. For Great Britain and Ireland to win the Walker Cup Match, they would have to win 5½ of the eight remaining points. Instead, the United States saved its best for last winning five matches, tying two and losing only one. Sigel, Mudd and Rassett played unbeatable golf to lead the way. Mudd was six under par on the front nine en route to a 7 and 5 victory over Colin Dalgleish. Sigel was 4 under as he ousted Paul Way, 6 and 5. Rassett was 4 under and won 4 and 3 against Peter Deeble. Holtgrieve and Fuhrer also won their matches. Commans and Pavin halved theirs. The lone British victor was Roger Chapman who was 5 under par after nine holes, but still had to hold on for a tense 1 up victory over Sutton. All 10 Americans contributed to their winning total of 15 points. James R. Gabrielsen, a member of the 1971 U.S. Walker Cup team and a member of the USGA Executive Committee, was the captain of the United States team. Rodney Foster, a member of five British Walker Cup teams, was making his second consecutive appearance as the captain of the Great Britain and Ireland team.

1983—The United States broke an 8-8 deadlock with five singles victories on the final afternoon to win its 26th victory in 29 Walker Cup Matches. The Americans, headed by Captain Jay Sigel, rolled to a 13½-10½ victory, at the Royal Liverpool Golf Club, in Hoylake, England. It was the sixth consecutive victory for the United States, dating back to 1973. The U.S. leads the series 26-2-1. Each side won two foursomes matches on the first morning of play. Willie Wood and Brad Faxon, of the United States, teamed for a 3 and 1 decision over Stephen Keppler and Arthur Pierse, of Great Britain and Ireland, while Bob Lewis, Jr., and Jim Holtgrieve, of the U.S., topped Malcolm Lewis and Martin Thompson, 7 and 6. For Great Britain and Ireland, George Macgregor and Philip Walton turned back Sigel and Rick Fehr, 3 and 2, while Lindsay Mann and Andrew Oldcorn were equally impressive in defeating Bill Hoffer and David Tentis, 5 and 4. In the afternoon, the U.S. won four singles matches and halved another to hold a 6½-5½ advantage by the day's end. Fehr, Faxon, Lewis, and Holtgrieve were the winners for the American side, while Wood settled for the half. Fehr defeated Keppler, 1 up; Faxon defeated David Carrick, 3 and 1; Lewis defeated Pierse, 3 and 1; and Holtgrieve defeated Mann, 6 and 5. Walton, an Irishman, who attended Oklahoma State University, scored an impressive triumph over Sigel, 1 up; Philip Parkin, an Englishman who attended Texas A&M, defeated Nathaniel Crosby, 6 and 4; and Oldcorn defeated Billy Tuten, 4 and 3. Wood and Macgregor halved. The British and Irish side dominated the second day's foursomes, winning two and halving one of the four matches. As some 10,000 spectators looked on, the British and Irish took an early lead in five of the final afternoon's singles matches. They were even in two others and trailed in only one. Within five holes, the Americans turned the day and were leading in six matches. In a battle of two Oklahoma State University teammates, Walton defeated Wood, 2 and 1, making six birdies in the process. When Lewis finished off Keppler, 6 and 5, the U.S. was assured of at least a tie. Tentis halved with Mann to clinch the U.S. victory. The final two matches were split with Oldcorn winning over Holtgrieve, 3 and 2, and Sigel regaining his form by defeating Carrick, 3 and 1. Oldcorn, a 22-year-old Englishman, was the first player from Great Britain and Ireland ever to win four points in one Match since the format was expanded in 1963. All 10 American players contributed to their winning total, led by Lewis and Faxon, with three points apiece. Charles W. Green, from Dumbarton, Scotland, was Captain for Great Britain and Ireland. Sigel, a four-time Walker Cupper, was the first golfer to serve in the dual role of player and Captain for the United States since Charles Coe, in 1959.

1985—The United States broke a 6-6 deadlock with three foursomes victories on the final morning and held on for a 13-11 victory. The win gives the United States a 27-2-1 advantage in the series, which began in 1922. Great Britain and Ireland gained a 2½-1½ advantage on the first morning of play. John Hawksworth and Garth McGimpsey of Great Britain and Ireland scored a 4 and 3 victory over Duffy Waldorf and Sam Randolph while Peter Baker and Peter McEvoy downed Randy Sonnier and Jerry Haas, 6 and 5. The only U.S. victory of the morning came when 1984 U.S. Amateur champion Scott Verplank and U.S. Team Captain Jay Sigel defeated Colin Montgomerie and George Macgregor, 1 up. Americans Davis Love III, and Mike Podolak earned a half in their match with Cecil Bloice and Sandy Stephen. The U.S. side evened the match in the afternoon by winning four singles matches and halving one. Verplank, Randolph, Sigel and Waldorf were winners for the American side while Sonnier earned a half. Verplank defeated McGimpsey, 2 and 1; Randolph defeated Paul Mayo, 5 and 4; Sigel defeated Montgomerie, 5 and 4; and Waldorf defeated David Gilford, 4 and 2. McEvoy gave Great Britain and Ireland its first singles victory, defeating Bob Lewis, Jr., 2 and 1; Macgregor defeated Clark Burroughs, 2 up; and Stephen defeated Haas, 4 and 2. Hawksworth and Sonnier halved their match. The American side dominated the second day's foursomes, earning 3½ points in the four matches to take a 9½-6½ advantage. Randolph and Haas defeated Hawksworth and McGimpsey, 3 and 2; Lewis and Burroughs defeated Baker and McEvoy, 2 and 1; Podolak and Love defeated Bloice and Stephen, 3 and 2. Mayo and Montgomerie earned Great Britain and Ireland its only half of the morning against Verplank and Sigel. The British and Irish side made a strong recovery in the afternoon as it won three of the first five matches. Hawksworth defeated Sigel, 4 and 3; Macgregor defeated Burroughs, 3 and 2; and Baker defeated Sonnier, 5 and 4. Love gave the U.S. its first singles victory of the day, defeating McEvoy, 5 and 3, while Randolph earned a half in his match with McGimpsey. The Americans clinched the victory when Verplank downed Montgomerie, 1 up, and Lewis defeated Bloice, 4 and 2. Stephen earned Great Britain and Ireland's final point, defeating Waldorf, 2 and 1. All 10 Americans contributed to the Team's winning total. Verplank earned 3½ points and Love, Randolph and Sigel contributed 2½ points each. Hawksworth and Stephen each earned 2½ points for Great Britain and Ireland.

1987—The United States defeated Great Britain and Ireland, 16½-7½, in the 31st Walker Cup Match played at Sunningdale Golf Club, Berkshire, England. It was the 28th win for the United States against two losses and one tie in a series which dates back to 1922. It was the most lopsided victory for the U.S. on British soil in history and the largest overall since 1961, when the United States earned an 11-1 victory. The U.S. swept the first-day foursomes matches, led by Buddy Alexander and Bill Mayfair's decisive 5-and-4 victory over Colin Montgomerie and Graeme Shaw in the first match of the morning. Bob Lewis and Bill Loeffler were three down after five holes of their match with George Macgregor and Jeremy Robinson, but captured the next five holes and won the match 2 and 1. Billy Andrade, Brian Montgomery, Jay Sigel, Lewis and Mayfair won singles matches on the first day. Montgomery, Shaw and David Curry gained GB&I's first points with opening-day singles victories. The U.S. held a 9-3 lead after the first day. The U.S. handily won the first three foursomes matches of the second day and were within one point of clinching the Match as the afternoon singles began. Alexander defeated Curry, 5 and 4, to earn the U.S. its 13th point and the Match. Lewis, Mayfair and Sigel also won their second-day singles matches. Jim Sorenson halved his match with Shaw to make the final tally 16½-7½. Loeffler earned four points for the U.S. during the Match, while Mayfair was undefeated in his three matches. Sigel also earned three points. Curry and Shaw were the leading scorers for GB&I, earning two points apiece.

1989—Great Britain and Ireland defeated the United States, 12½-11½, in a hard-fought match at the Peachtree Golf Club, in Atlanta. The Match was the first Britain and Ireland had ever won in the United States, and only its third in the series. This was one of the closest of all the Walker Cup Matches. Great Britain and Ireland went ahead from the start, winning two of the four foursomes matches the first morning and halving another, then four of the eight afternoon singles while halving two others. Leading 7½-4½ after the first day's matches, the British and Irish opened the lead to 11-5 by winning three of the four foursomes the next day. Needing seven points in the afternoon's singles, the

WALKER CUP MATCH

United States nearly saved the match, winning five matches and halving the other three. All three halved matches went to the 18th hole. Two holes down with two to play, Andrew Hare, of Great Britain and Ireland, won both from Doug Martin, and Eoghan O'Connell, also of Great Britain and Ireland, won the 17th hole when Phil Mickelson three-putted and halved his match, assuring Britain and Ireland at least a tie. The outcome was decided by the last match. Jay Sigel, of the United States, stood two holes up on Jim Milligan with three holes to play, but Milligan birdied the 16th, chipped into the cup from behind the 17th green, winning the hole with a par 4 and pulling even with Sigel, then halved the 18th, giving the visitors the half point they needed to win.

WALKER CUP MATCH

DATE	WINNER, RUNNER-UP	SCORE	SITE
1981	United States	15	Cypress Point Club,
	Great Britain & Ireland	9	Pebble Beach, Calif.
1983	United States	13½	Royal Liverpool G.C.,
	Great Britain & Ireland	10½	Hoylake, Merseyside, England
1985	United States	13	Pine Valley G.C.,
	Great Britain & Ireland	11	Pine Valley, N.J.
1987	United States	16½	Sunningdale G.C.,
	Great Britain & Ireland	7½	Berkshire, England
1989	Great Britain & Ireland	12½	Peachtree G.C.,
	United States	11½	Atlanta, Ga.

1981
TWENTY-EIGHTH INTERNATIONAL MATCH FOR THE WALKER CUP

Cypress Point Club, Pebble Beach, California
August 28-29

August 28
FOURSOMES

Great Britain and Ireland	Points	United States	Points
Philip Walton and Ronan Rafferty (4 and 2)	1	Hal Sutton and Jay Sigel	0
Roger Chapman and Peter McEvoy	0	Jim Holtgrieve and Frank Fuhrer, III (1 up)	1
Peter Deeble and Ian Hutcheon	0	Bob Lewis and Dick von Tacky (2 and 1)	1
Duncan Evans and Paul Way	0	Ron Commans and Corey Pavin (5 and 4)	1
Total	1	Total	3

SINGLES

Great Britain and Ireland	Points	United States	Points
Ronan Rafferty	0	Hal Sutton (3 and 1)	1
Colin Dalgleish	0	Joe Rassett (1 up)	1
Philip Walton (1 up)	1	Ron Commans	0
Roger Chapman (2 and 1)	1	Bob Lewis	0
Geoffrey Godwin	0	Jodie Mudd (1 up)	1
Ian Hutcheon	0	Corey Pavin (4 and 3)	1
Paul Way (3 and 1)	1	Dick von Tacky	0
Peter McEvoy	0	Jay Sigel (4 and 2)	1
Total	3	Total	5
Friday's Total	4	Friday's Total	8

August 29
FOURSOMES

Great Britain and Ireland	Points	United States	Points
Roger Chapman and Paul Way (1 up)	1	Hal Sutton and Jay Sigel	0
Philip Walton and Ronan Rafferty (6 and 4)	1	Jim Holtgrieve and Frank Fuhrer, III	0
Duncan Evans and Colin Dalgleish (3 and 2)	1	Bob Lewis and Dick von Tacky	0
Ian Hutcheon and Geoffrey Godwin	0	Joe Rassett and Jodie Mudd (5 and 4)	1
Total	3	Total	1

SINGLES

Great Britain and Ireland	Points	United States	Points
Roger Chapman (1 up)	1	Hal Sutton	0
Ronan Rafferty	0	Jim Holtgrieve (2 and 1)	1
Philip Walton	0	Frank Fuhrer, III (4 and 2)	1
Paul Way	0	Jay Sigel (6 and 5)	1
Colin Dalgleish	0	Jodie Mudd (7 and 5)	1
Geoffrey Godwin (halved)	½	Ron Commans (halved)	½
Peter Deeble	0	Joe Rassett (4 and 3)	1
Duncan Evans (halved)	½	Corey Pavin (halved)	½
Total	2	Total	6
Saturday's Total	5	Saturday's Total	7
Grand Total—Great Britain and Ireland	9	Grand Total—United States	15
Captain—Rodney Foster		Captain—James R. Gabrielsen	

1983
TWENTY-NINTH INTERNATIONAL MATCH FOR THE WALKER CUP

Royal Liverpool Golf Club, Hoylake, Merseyside, England
May 25-26

MAY 25
FOURSOMES

Great Britain and Ireland	Points	United States	Points
George MacGregor and Philip Walton (3 and 2)	1	Jay Sigel and Rick Fehr	0
Stephen Keppler and Arthur Pierse	0	Willie Wood and Brad Faxon (3 and 1)	1
Malcolm Lewis and Martin Thompson	0	Bob Lewis, Jr. and Jim Holtgrieve (7 and 6)	1
Lindsay Mann and Andrew Oldcorn (5 and 4)	1	William Hoffer and David Tentis	0
Total	2	Total	2

SINGLES

Great Britain and Ireland	Points	United States	Points
Philip Walton (1 up)	1	Jay Sigel	0
Stephen Keppler	0	Rick Fehr (1 up)	1
George MacGregor (halved)	½	Willie Wood (halved)	½
David Carrick	0	Brad Faxon (3 and 1)	1
Andrew Oldcorn (4 and 3)	1	Billy Tuten	0
Andrew Parkin (6 and 4)	1	Nathaniel Crosby	0
Arthur Pierse	0	Bob Lewis, Jr. (3 and 1)	1
Lindsay Mann	0	Jim Holtgrieve (6 and 5)	1
Total	3½	Total	4½
Wednesday's Total	5½	Wednesday's Total	6½

MAY 26
FOURSOMES

Great Britain and Ireland	Points	United States	Points
George MacGregor and Philip Walton	0	Nathaniel Crosby and William Hoffer (2 up)	1
Andrew Parkin and Martin Thompson (1 up)	1	Brad Faxon and Willie Wood	0
Lindsay Mann and Andrew Oldcorn (1 up)	1	Bob Lewis, Jr. and Jim Holtgrieve	0
Stephen Keppler and Arthur Pierse (halved)	½	Jay Sigel and Rick Fehr (halved)	½
Total	2½	Total	1½

SINGLES

Great Britain and Ireland	Points	United States	Points
Philip Walton (2 and 1)	1	Willie Wood	0
Andrew Parkin	0	Brad Faxon (3 and 2)	1
George MacGregor	0	Rick Fehr (2 and 1)	1
Martin Thompson	0	Billy Tuten (3 and 2)	1
Lindsay Mann (halved)	½	David Tentis (halved)	½
Stephen Keppler	0	Bob Lewis, Jr. (6 and 5)	1
Andrew Oldcorn (3 and 2)	1	Jim Holtgrieve	0
David Carrick	0	Jay Sigel (3 and 1)	1
Total	2½	Total	5½
Thursday's Total	5	Thursday's Total	7
Grand Total—Great Britain and Ireland	10½	Grand Total—United States	13½
Captain—Charles Wilson Green		Captain—Jay Sigel	

1985
THIRTIETH INTERNATIONAL MATCH FOR THE WALKER CUP

Pine Valley Golf Club, Pine Valley, New Jersey
August 21-22

AUGUST 21
FOURSOMES

Great Britain and Ireland	Points	United States	Points
Colin Montgomerie and George Macgregor	0	Scott Verplank and Jay Sigel (1 up)	1
John Hawksworth and Garth McGimpsey (4 and 3)	1	Duffy Waldorf and Sam Randolph	0
Peter Baker and Peter McEvoy (6 and 5)	1	Randy Sonnier and Jerry Haas	0
Cecil Bloice and Sandy Stephen (halved)	½	Mike Podolak and Davis Love, III (halved)	½
Total	2½	Total	1½

SINGLES

Great Britain and Ireland	Points	United States	Points
Garth McGimpsey	0	Scott Verplank (2 and 1)	1
Paul Mayo	0	Sam Randolph (5 and 4)	1
John Hawksworth (halved)	½	Randy Sonnier (halved)	½
Colin Montgomerie	0	Jay Sigel (5 and 4)	1
Peter McEvoy (2 and 1)	1	Bob Lewis	0
George Macgregor (2 up)	1	Clark Burroughs	0
David Gilford	0	Duffy Waldorf (4 and 2)	1
Sandy Stephen (2 and 1)	1	Jerry Haas	0
Total	3½	Total	4½
Wednesday's Total	6	Wednesday's Total	6

AUGUST 22
FOURSOMES

Great Britain and Ireland	Points	United States	Points
Paul Mayo and Colin Montgomerie (halved)	½	Scott Verplank and Jay Sigel (halved)	½
John Hawksworth and Garth McGimpsey	0	Sam Randolph and Jerry Haas (3 and 2)	1
Peter Baker and Peter McEvoy	0	Bob Lewis and Clark Burroughs (2 and 1)	1
Cecil Bloice and Sandy Stephen	0	Mike Podolak and Davis Love, III (3 and 2)	1
Total	½	Total	3½

SINGLES

Great Britain and Ireland	Points	United States	Points
Garth McGimpsey (halved)	½	Sam Randolph (halved)	½
Colin Montgomerie	0	Scott Verplank (1 up)	1
John Hawksworth (4 and 3)	1	Jay Sigel	0
Peter McEvoy	0	Davis Love, III (5 and 3)	1
Peter Baker (5 and 4)	1	Randy Sonnier	0
George Macgregor (3 and 2)	1	Clark Burroughs	0
Cecil Bloice	0	Bob Lewis (4 and 2)	1
Sandy Stephen (2 and 1)	1	Duffy Waldorf	0
Total	4½	Total	3½
Thursday's Total	5	Thursday's Total	7
Grand Total—Great Britain and Ireland	11	Grand Total—United States	13
Captain—Charles Wilson Green		Captain—Jay Sigel	

1987
THIRTY-FIRST INTERNATIONAL MATCH FOR THE WALKER CUP

Sunningdale Golf Club, Berkshire, England
May 27-28

MAY 27
FOURSOMES

Great Britain and Ireland	Points	United States	Points
Colin Montgomerie and Graeme Shaw	0	Buddy Alexander and Bill Mayfair (5 and 4)	1
David Curry and Paul Mayo	0	Chris Kite and Len Mattiace (2 and 1)	1
George Macgregor and Jeremy Robinson	0	Bob Lewis, Jr. and Bill Loeffler (2 and 1)	1
John McHenry and Paul Girvan	0	Jay Sigel and Bill Andrade (3 and 2)	1
Total	0	Total	4

SINGLES

Great Britain and Ireland	Points	United States	Points
David Curry (2 up)	1	Buddy Alexander	0
Jeremy Robinson	0	Bill Andrade (7 and 5)	1
Colin Montgomerie (3 and 2)	1	Jim Sorenson	0
John McHenry	0	Brian Montgomery (1 up)	1
Robert Eggo	0	Jay Sigel (3 and 2)	1
Paul Girvan	0	Bob Lewis, Jr. (3 and 2)	1
David Carrick	0	Bill Mayfair (2 up)	1
Graeme Shaw (1 up)	1	Chris Kite	0
Total	3	Total	5
Wednesday's Total	3	Wednesday's Total	9

MAY 28
FOURSOMES

Great Britain and Ireland	Points	United States	Points
David Curry and David Carrick	0	Bob Lewis, Jr. and Bill Loeffler (4 and 3)	1
Colin Montgomerie and Graeme Shaw	0	Chris Kite and Len Mattiace (5 and 3)	1
Paul Mayo and George Macgregor	0	Jim Sorenson and Brian Montgomery (4 and 3)	1
John McHenry and Jeremy Robinson (4 and 2)	1	Jay Sigel and Bill Andrade	0
Total	1	Total	3

SINGLES

Great Britain and Ireland	Points	United States	Points
David Curry	0	Buddy Alexander (5 and 4)	1
Colin Montgomerie (4 and 2)	1	Bill Andrade	0
John McHenry (3 and 2)	1	Bill Loeffler	0
Graeme Shaw (halved)	½	Jim Sorenson (halved)	½
Jeremy Robinson (1up)	1	Len Mattiace	0
David Carrick	0	Bob Lewis, Jr. (3 and 2)	1
Robert Eggo	0	Bill Mayfair (3 and 2)	1
Paul Girvan	0	Jay Sigel (6 and 5)	1
Total	3½	Total	4½
Thursday's Total	4½	Thursday's Total	7½
Grand Total—Great Britain and Ireland	7½	Grand Total—United States	16½
Captain—Geoffrey Marks		Captain—Fred Ridley	

1989
THE THIRTY-SECOND WALKER CUP MATCH
Peachtree Golf Club, Atlanta, Ga.
August 16-17, 1989

AUGUST 16
FOURSOMES

Great Britain and Ireland	Points	United States	Points
Russell Claydon and Darren Prosser	0	Robert Gamez and Doug Martin (3 and 2)	1
Peter McEvoy and Eoghan O'Connell (6 and 5)	1	Greg Lesher and Jay Sigel	0
Stephen Dodd and Garth McGimpsey (halved)	½	Danny Yates and Phil Mickelson (halved)	½
Jim Milligan and Andrew Hare (2 and 1)	1	David Eger and Kevin Johnson	0
Total	2½	Total	1½

SINGLES

Great Britain and Ireland	Points	United States	Points
Jim Milligan	0	Robert Gamez (7 and 6)	1
Russell Claydon (5 and 4)	1	Doug Martin	0
Eoghan O'Connell (5 and 4)	1	Ralph Howe	0
Stephen Dodd (halved)	½	Eric Meeks (halved)	½
Garth McGimpsey	0	Phil Mickelson (4 and 2)	1
Peter McEvoy (2 and 1)	1	Danny Yates	0
Craig Cassells (1 up)	1	Greg Lesher	0
Neil Roderick (halved)	½	Jay Sigel (halved)	½
Total	5	Total	3
Total August 16	7½	Total August 16	4½

AUGUST 17
FOURSOMES

Great Britain and Ireland	Points	United States	Points
Peter McEvoy and Eoghan O'Connell (halved)	½	Robert Gamez and Doug Martin (halved)	½
Russell Claydon and Craig Cassells (3 and 2)	1	Jay Sigel and Greg Lesher	0
Jim Milligan and Andrew Hare (2 and 1)	1	David Eger and Kevin Johnson	0
Garth McGimpsey and Stephen Dodd (2 and 1)	1	Phil Mickelson and Danny Yates	0
Total	3½	Total	½

SINGLES

Great Britain and Ireland	Points	United States	Points
Stephen Dodd	0	Robert Gamez (1 up)	1
Andrew Hare (halved)	½	Doug Martin (halved)	½
Russell Claydon	0	Greg Lesher (3 and 2)	1
Peter McEvoy	0	Danny Yates (4 and 3)	1
Eoghan O'Connell (halved)	½	Phil Mickelson (halved)	½
Neil Roderick	0	David Eger (4 and 2)	1
Craig Cassells	0	Kevin Johnson (4 and 3)	1
Jim Milligan (halved)	½	Jay Sigel (halved)	½
Total	1½	Total	6½
Total August 17	5	Total August 17	7
Grand Total—Great Britain and Ireland	12½	Grand Total—United States	11½
Captain—Goeffrey Marks		Captain—Fred Ridley	

CURTIS CUP MATCH

WOMEN'S INTERNATIONAL CUP

Presented in May, 1932, by

MISS HARRIOT S. CURTIS	and	MISS MARGARET CURTIS
Women's Amateur Champion		Women's Amateur Champion
1906		1907-1911-1912

HISTORY

1982—On the 50th anniversary of the first international match for the Curtis Cup, the United States defeated Great Britain and Ireland, 14½-3½, at the Denver Country Club, in Denver, Colorado. The victory was the 18th for the United States, and the 12th in succession. The score was the largest winning margin in the history of the competition. Formal competition between the United States and Great Britain and Ireland began in 1932, when a group of eight American women golfers went to Wentworth, England. As part of the anniversary ceremonies, every former player and captain from both sides was invited to a reunion at Denver. Forty-seven attended, including four members of the original 1932 teams—Glenna Collett Vare, Maureen Orcutt, and Dorothy Higbie from the American side, and Enid Wilson from the British side. The United States dominated the 1982 Match from the beginning. U.S. Amateur Champion Juli Inkster and four-time Curtis-Cupper Carol Semple opened the first day's foursomes with a 5-and-4 victory over Mary McKenna and Belle Robertson. Amy Benz and Cathy Hanlon, college teammates at Southern Methodist University, won, 2 and 1, over Gillian Stewart and Jane Connachan. British Women's Amateur Champion Kitrina Douglas and 17-year-old Janet Soulsby, the youngest competitor on either side, gave their team some hope by halving their foursomes match with Kathy Baker and four-time Curtis-Cupper Lancy Smith. At the end of the first day's foursomes, the United States led, 2½-½. In the singles, the United States won five and lost only one, to increase its lead to 7½-1½. Mrs. Inkster, Miss Baker, Miss Benz, Miss Hanlon, and Mari McDougall each won a match for the United States. Miss Soulsby won the only British point with a 2-up victory over three-time Curtis-Cupper Judith Oliver. The United States won the first hole in every match of the first day—the three foursomes and all six singles. The second day began with the United States needing only two more points to retain the Cup. Mrs. Inkster and Miss Semple opened the foursomes with a 3-and-2 victory over Miss Connachan and Wilma Aitken. Miss Baker and Miss Smith supplied the clinching point with a 1-up decision over Miss Douglas and Miss Soulsby when Miss Baker holed a delicate six-foot birdie putt at the final green. Miss McKenna, playing in a record-tying seventh Curtis Cup Match, and Mrs. Robertson, in her sixth Match, edged the American tandem of Miss Benz and Miss Hanlon, 1 up, to close the foursomes portion of the competition. In the final afternoon's singles, the United States again won five of six singles matches. Mrs. Inkster was the leading point winner with four of a possible four. All eight Americans contributed at least one point to the victory. Mrs. Scott L. Probasco, of Lookout Mountain, Tennessee, was the Captain of the U.S. Team. Mrs. Probasco had been selected to compete in the 1956 Curtis Cup Match, but had to decline because of the impending birth of a child. Mrs. Maire O'Donnell, of Donegal, Ireland, was the Captain of Great Britain and Ireland.

1984—The United States defeated Great Britain and Ireland, 9½-8½, at the Honourable Company of Edinburgh Golfers, Muirfield, Scotland. The victory was the 13th straight for the United States and its 19th victory in the 23-match series. The competition was as close as the score; only a missed four-foot putt on the final green on the final day by Penny Grice kept Great Britain and Ireland from a 9-9 tie. Ironically, the first victory for Great Britain and Ireland came at Muirfield, in 1952. The United States led, 5-4, the first day with 1½ points in the three foursomes matches and 3½ in the six singles. The teams were still one point apart after the foursomes matches the second day, and the outcome wasn't settled until the final hole of the fourth singles match of the afternoon, between Penny Grice, for Great Britain and Ireland, and Dana Howe, of the United States. Miss Grice had a 12-foot putt for a birdie on the 17th hole. Had she made the putt she would have evened the match. She missed, though, and Miss Howe earned a half by holing an 11-foot putt for a par and remained 1 up. With another chance to pull even on 18, Miss Grice missed from four feet, and Miss Howe won, 1 up, giving the United States the victory. Miss Phyllis (Tish) Preuss served as Captain of the United States team. Mrs. Diane Bailey was Captain for Great Britain and Ireland.

1986—Great Britain and Ireland won the Curtis Cup for the first time in 30 years, defeating the United States, 13-5, at Prairie Dunes Country Club in Hutchinson, Kansas. The win broke a 13-match winning streak for the United States and was the first win for Great Britain and Ireland on American soil in the series. The United States has won 19 matches in the series to three for Great Britain and

Ireland. There have been two ties. The visitors gained early control of the 1986 match and the Americans never threatened. Great Britain and Ireland won all three foursome matches on the first day. Lillian Behan and Jill Thornhill downed Kandi Kessler and Cindy Schreyer, 7 and 6; Patricia Johnson and Karen Davies defeated Danielle Ammaccapane and Dottie Mochrie, 2 and 1; and Belle Robertson and Mary McKenna edged Kim Gardner and Kathleen McCarthy, 1 up. Great Britain and Ireland won the first three singles matches in the afternoon. The Americans earned their first points when Kessler defeated Vicki Thomas, 3 and 2, and Schreyer edged Claire Hourihane, 2 and 1. Mochrie halved her match with Davies to make the score 6½-2½ in favor of the British and Irish after the first day. Great Britain and Ireland won two foursomes matches on the second day and halved the third to build its lead to 9-3. Behan and Thornhill defeated Shannon and Kim Williams, 5 and 3, and Johnson and Davies edged Ammaccapane and Mochrie, 1 up. Americans Gardner and McCarthy halved their match against Robertson and McKenna. Great Britain and Ireland clinched the victory when Johnson defeated McCarthy, 5 and 3. The only victory for the Americans in the second day's singles came when Gardner edged Behan, 1 up. Johnson won four points for Great Britain and Ireland in the Match while Robertson scored 3½. Gardner and Kessler each earned 1½ points to lead the United States side. Diane Bailey served as Captain for Great Britain and Ireland. Judy Bell was Captain for the United States.

1988—Great Britain and Ireland won its second consecutive Curtis Cup Match, defeating the United States, 11-7, at Royal St. George's Golf Club in Sandwich, England. It marked the first time the British and Irish had won consecutive matches in the 57-year-old series. The United States has won 19 matches to four for Great Britain and Ireland. Two matches have been halved. As it had in 1986, Great Britain and Ireland led after the first day's foursomes and were not challenged thereafter. The British and Irish won two matches and halved a third to lead 2½-½. Linda Bayman and Julie Wade downed Tracy Kerdyk and Kathleen Scrivner, 2 and 1; and Susan Shapcott and Karen Davies defeated Cindy Scholefield and Carol Semple Thompson, 5 and 4. Leslie Shannon and Caroline Keggi earned the first half for the United States in their match against Jill Thornhill and Vicki Thomas. The Great Britain and Ireland team extended its lead to 6-3 in the afternoon as Wade, Thomas and Shirley Lawson won their matches. Thompson scored the first victory for the Americans, 1 up over Shapcott; Pearl Sinn defeated Davies, 4 and 3. The United States posted its only foursomes victory on the second morning when Kerdyk and Scrivner defeated Bayman and Wade, 1-up. Great Britain/ Ireland won the other two morning matches to stretch its lead to 8-4. Three singles wins on the final afternoon were enough to clinch the victory for Great Britain and Ireland. Shapcott downed Keggi, 3 and 2; Bayman edged Sinn, 1 up; and Thomas defeated Pat Cornett, 5 and 3. Kerdyk, Scrivner and Thompson earned victories for the United States. Thomas won three matches and halved one for Great Britain and Ireland; Shapcott won three and lost one. Kerdyk led the United States, earning 2½ points; Scrivner and Thompson won two points for the United States.

1990—The United States defeated Great Britain and Ireland, 14-4, in the Curtis Cup Match, at Somerset Hills Country Club, in Bernardsville, New Jersey. The United States regained the Cup after losing in the two previous matches. The Americans led 6-3 after the first day's foursomes and singles matches, and then won all six singles matches on the second day. The match stood 8-4 in favor of the United States after foursomes on the second day, prior to singles play. First-time American players Brandie Burton, Katie Peterson, and Robin Weiss, and eight-time Curtis Cup player Anne Sander went undefeated in their matches. The most interesting pairing had Sander, the oldest player, at age 52, teamed with Vicki Goetze, the youngest player, at 17. They won their foursomes matches each day, by scores of 4 and 3, and 3 and 1.

CURTIS CUP MATCH

DATE	WINNER, RUNNER-UP	SCORE	SITE
1982	United States	14½	Denver C.C.,
	Great Britain & Ireland	3½	Denver, Colo.
1984	United States	9½	Honourable Company of
	Great Britain & Ireland	8½	Edinburgh Golfers,
			Muirfield, Gullane, Scotland
1986	Great Britain & Ireland	13	Praire Dunes C.C.,
	United States	5	Hutchinson, Kan.
1988	Great Britain & Ireland	11	Royal St. George's G.C.,
	United States	7	Sandwich, England
1990	United States	14	Somerset Hills C.C.,
	Great Britain & Ireland	4	Bernardsville, N.J.

1982
TWENTY-SECOND INTERNATIONAL MATCH FOR THE CURTIS CUP

Denver Country Club, Denver, Colorado.
August 5-6.

August 5
FOURSOMES

Great Britain and Ireland	Points	United States	Points
Mrs. Belle Robertson and Miss Mary McKenna ...	0	Mrs. Juli Inkster and Miss Carol Semple (5 and 4)	1
Miss Kitrina Douglas and Miss Janet Soulsby (halved)	½	Miss Kathy Baker and Miss Lancy Smith (halved) .	½
Miss Gillian Stewart and Miss Jane Connachan ..	0	Miss Amy Benz and Miss Cathy Hanlon (2 and 1)	1
Total	½	Total	2½

SINGLES

Great Britain and Ireland	Points	United States	Points
Miss Kitrina Douglas	0	Mrs. Juli Inkster (7 and 6)	1
Mrs. Belle Robertson	0	Miss Kathy Baker (7 and 6)	1
Miss Mary McKenna	0	Miss Amy Benz (2 and 1)	1
Miss Jane Connachan	0	Miss Cathy Hanlon (5 and 4)	1
Miss Wilma Aitken	0	Miss Mari McDougall (3 and 2)	1
Miss Janet Soulsby (2 up)	1	Mrs. Judy Oliver	0
Total	1	Total	5
Total August 5	1½	Total August 5	7½

August 6
FOURSOMES

Great Britain and Ireland	Points	United States	Points
Miss Jane Connachan and Miss Wilma Aitken ...	0	Mrs. Juli Inkster and Miss Carol Semple (3 and 2)	1
Miss Kitrina Douglas and Miss Janet Soulsby	0	Miss Kathy Baker and Miss Lancy Smith (1 up) ...	1
Miss Mary McKenna and Mrs. Belle Robertson (1 up)	1	Miss Amy Benz and Miss Cathy Hanlon	0
Total	1	Total	2

SINGLES

Great Britain and Ireland	Points	United States	Points
Miss Kitrina Douglas	0	Mrs. Juli Inkster (7 and 6)	1
Miss Gillian Stewart	0	Miss Kathy Baker (4 and 3)	1
Miss Mary McKenna	0	Miss Carol Semple (1 up)	1
Mrs. Belle Robertson (5 and 3)	1	Miss Lancy Smith	0
Miss Janet Soulsby	0	Miss Mari McDougall (2 and 1)	1
Miss Vicki Thomas	0	Mrs. Judy Oliver (5 and 4)	1
Total	1	Total	5
Total August 6	2	Total August 6	7
Grand Total Great Britain and Ireland	3½	Grand Total United States	14½

Non-playing Captain — Mrs. Maire O'Donnell

Non-playing Captain — Mrs. Scott L. Probasco

1984
TWENTY-THIRD INTERNATIONAL MATCH FOR THE CURTIS CUP

Honourable Company of Edinburgh Golfers, Muirfield, Gullane, Scotland

June 8-9

JUNE 8
FOURSOMES

Great Britain and Ireland	Points	United States	Points
Miss Claire Waite and Miss Beverly New (2 up)	1	Miss Joanne Pacillo and Mrs. Anne Sander	0
Mrs. Jill Thornhill and Miss Penny Grice (halved)	½	Miss Lancy Smith and Miss Jody Rosenthal (halved)	½
Miss Mary McKenna and Miss Laura Davies	0	Miss Mary Anne Widman and Miss Heather Farr (1 up)	1
Total	1½	Total	1½

SINGLES

Great Britain and Ireland	Points	United States	Points
Mrs. Jill Thornhill (halved)	½	Miss Joanne Pacillo (halved)	½
Miss Claire Waite	0	Miss Penny Hammel (4 and 2)	1
Miss Claire Hourihane	0	Miss Jody Rosenthal (3 and 1)	1
Miss Vicki Thomas (2 and 1)	1	Miss Dana Howe	0
Miss Penny Grice (2 up)	1	Mrs. Anne Sander	0
Miss Beverly New	0	Miss Mary Anne Widman (4 and 3)	1
Total	2½	Total	3½
Total June 8	4	Total June 8	5½

JUNE 9
FOURSOMES

Great Britain and Ireland	Points	United States	Points
Miss Claire Waite and Miss Beverly New	0	Miss Lancy Smith and Miss Jody Rosenthal (3 and 1)	1
Mrs. Jill Thornhill and Miss Penny Grice (2 and 1)	1	Miss Mary Anne Widman and Miss Heather Farr	0
Miss Vicki Thomas and Claire Hourihane (halved)	½	Miss Dana Howe and Miss Penny Hammel (halved)	½
Total	1½	Total	1½

SINGLES

Great Britain and Ireland	Points	United States	Points
Mrs. Jill Thornhill	0	Miss Joanne Pacillo (3 and 2)	1
Miss Laura Davies (1 up)	1	Mrs. Anne Sander	0
Miss Claire Waite (5 and 4)	1	Miss Lancy Smith	0
Miss Penny Grice	0	Miss Dana Howe (1 up)	1
Miss Beverly New	0	Miss Heather Farr (6 and 5)	1
Miss Claire Hourihane (2 and 1)	1	Miss Penny Hammel	0
Total	3	Total	3
Total June 9	4½	Total June 9	4½
Grand Total—Great Britain and Ireland	8½	Grand Total—United States	9½
Captain—Mrs. Diane Bailey		Captain—Miss Phyllis Preuss	

1986
TWENTY-FOURTH INTERNATIONAL MATCH FOR THE CURTIS CUP

Prairie Dunes Country Club, Hutchinson, Kansas
August 1-2

AUGUST 1
FOURSOMES

Great Britain and Ireland	Points	United States	Points
Miss Lillian Behan and Mrs. Jill Thornhill (7 and 6)	1	Miss Kandi Kessler and Miss Cindy Schreyer	0
Miss Patricia Johnson and Miss Karen Davies (2 and 1)	1	Miss Danielle Ammaccapane and Mrs. Dottie Mochrie	0
Mrs. Belle Robertson and Miss Mary McKenna (1 up)	1	Miss Kim Gardner and Miss Kathleen McCarthy	0
Total	3	Total	0

SINGLES

Great Britain and Ireland	Points	United States	Points
Mrs. Jill Thornhill (4 and 3)	1	Miss Kim Williams	0
Miss Patricia Johnson (1 up)	1	Mrs. Leslie Shannon	0
Miss Lillian Behan (4 and 3)	1	Miss Danielle Ammaccapane	0
Mrs. Vicki Thomas	0	Miss Kandi Kessler (3 and 2)	1
Miss Claire Hourihane	0	Miss Cindy Schreyer (2 and 1)	1
Miss Karen Davies (halved)	½	Mrs. Dottie Mochrie (halved)	½
Total	3½	Total	2½
Total August 1	6½	Total August 1	2½

AUGUST 2
FOURSOMES

Great Britain and Ireland	Points	United States	Points
Miss Lillian Behan and Mrs. Jill Thornhill (5 and 3)	1	Mrs. Leslie Shannon and Miss Kim Williams	0
Miss Patricia Johnson and Miss Karen Davies (1 up)	1	Miss Danielle Ammaccapane and Mrs. Dottie Mochrie	0
Mrs. Belle Robertson and Miss Mary McKenna (halved)	½	Miss Kim Gardner and Miss Kathleen McCarthy (halved)	½
Total	2½	Total	½

SINGLES

Great Britain and Ireland	Points	United States	Points
Mrs. Jill Thornhill (halved)	½	Mrs. Leslie Shannon (halved)	½
Miss Patricia Johnson (5 and 3)	1	Miss Kathleen McCarthy	0
Miss Lillian Behan	0	Miss Kim Gardner (1 up)	1
Mrs. Vicki Thomas (4 and 3)	1	Miss Kim Williams	0
Miss Claire Hourihane (5 and 3)	1	Miss Cindy Schreyer	0
Miss Karen Davies (halved)	½	Miss Kandi Kessler (halved)	½
Total	4	Total	2
Total August 2	6½	Total August 2	2½
Grand Total—Great Britain and Ireland	13	Grand Total—United States	5
Captain—Diane Bailey		Captain—Judy Bell	

1988
TWENTY-FIFTH INTERNATIONAL MATCH FOR THE CURTIS CUP

Royal St. George's Golf Club, Sandwich, England
June 10-11

JUNE 10
FOURSOMES

Great Britain and Ireland	Points	United States	Points
Mrs. Linda Bayman and Miss Julie Wade (2 and 1)	1	Miss Tracy Kerdyk and Mrs. Kathleen Scrivner	0
Miss Susan Shapcott and Miss Karen Davies (5 and 4)	1	Miss Cindy Scholefield and Mrs. Carol Semple Thompson	0
Mrs. Jill Thornhill and Mrs. Vicki Thomas (halved)	½	Mrs. Leslie Shannon and Miss Caroline Keggi (halved)	½
Total	2½	Total	½

SINGLES

Great Britain and Ireland	Points	United States	Points
Mrs. Linda Bayman (halved)	½	Miss Tracy Kerdyk (halved)	½
Miss Julie Wade (2 up)	1	Miss Cindy Scholefield	0
Miss Susan Shapcott	0	Mrs. Carol Semple Thompson (1 up)	1
Miss Shirley Lawson (1 up)	1	Mrs. Pat Cornett-Iker	0
Miss Karen Davies	0	Miss Pearl Sinn (4 and 3)	1
Mrs. Vicki Thomas (3 and 2)	1	Mrs. Leslie Shannon	0
Total	3½	Total	2½
Total June 10	6	Total June 10	3

JUNE 11
FOURSOMES

Great Britain and Ireland	Points	United States	Points
Mrs. Linda Bayman and Miss Julie Wade	0	Miss Tracy Kerdyk and Mrs. Kathleen Scrivner (1 up)	1
Miss Karen Davies and Miss Susan Shapcott (2 up)	1	Mrs. Leslie Shannon and Miss Caroline Keggi	0
Mrs. Jill Thornhill and Mrs. Vicki Thomas (6 and 5)	1	Miss Cindy Scholefield and Mrs. Carol Semple Thompson	0
Total	2	Total	1

SINGLES

Great Britain and Ireland	Points	United States	Points
Miss Julie Wade	0	Miss Tracy Kerdyk (2 and 1)	1
Miss Susan Shapcott (3 and 2)	1	Miss Caroline Keggi	0
Mrs. Linda Bayman (1 up)	1	Miss Pearl Sinn	0
Miss Shirley Lawson	0	Mrs. Kathleen Scrivner (4 and 3)	1
Mrs. Vicki Thomas (5 and 3)	1	Mrs. Pat Cornett-Iker	0
Mrs. Jill Thornhill	0	Mrs. Carol Semple Thompson (3 and 2)	1
Total	3	Total	3
Total June 11	5	Total June 11	4
Grand Total—Great Britain and Ireland	11	Grand Total—United States	7
Captain—Diane Bailey		Captain—Judy Bell	

1990
THE TWENTY-SIXTH CURTIS CUP MATCH
Somerset Hills Country Club, Bernardsville, New Jersey
July 28-29, 1990

JULY 28
FOURSOMES

Great Britain and Ireland	Points	United States	Points
Miss Catriona Lambert and Miss Helen Dobson	0	Miss Vicki Goetze and Mrs. Anne Sander (4 and 3)	1
Mrs. Julie Hall and Miss Kathryn Imrie (2 and 1)	1	Miss Karen Noble and Miss Margaret Platt	0
Miss Elaine Farquharson and Miss Helen Wadsworth	0	Miss Robin Weiss and Mrs. Carol Semple Thompson (3 and 1)	1
Total	1	Total	2

SINGLES

Great Britain and Ireland	Points	United States	Points
Mrs. Julie Hall (2 and 1)	1	Miss Vicki Goetze	0
Miss Kathryn Imrie	0	Miss Katie Peterson (3 and 2)	1
Miss Linzi Fletcher	0	Miss Robin Weiss (4 and 3)	1
Miss Elaine Farquharson	0	Miss Brandie Burton (3 and 1)	1
Miss Catriona Lambert	0	Miss Karen Noble (1 up)	1
Mrs. Vicki Thomas (1 up)	1	Mrs. Carol Semple Thompson	0
Total	2	Total	4
Total July 28	3	Total July 28	6

JULY 29
FOURSOMES

Great Britain and Ireland	Points	United States	Points
Miss Kathryn Imrie and Mrs. Julie Hall	0	Miss Vicki Goetze and Mrs. Anne Sander (3 and 1)	1
Miss Elaine Farquharson and Miss Helen Wadsworth	0	Miss Brandie Burton and Miss Katie Peterson (5 and 4)	1
Miss Helen Dobson and Miss Catriona Lambert (1 up)	1	Miss Karen Noble and Miss Margaret Platt	0
Total	1	Total	2

SINGLES

Great Britain and Ireland	Points	United States	Points
Miss Helen Dobson	0	Miss Vicki Goetze (4 and 3)	1
Miss Catriona Lambert	0	Miss Brandie Burton (4 and 3)	1
Miss Kathryn Imrie	0	Miss Katie Peterson (1 up)	1
Mrs. Julie Hall	0	Miss Karen Noble (2 up)	1
Miss Elaine Farquharson	0	Miss Robin Weiss (2 and 1)	1
Mrs. Vicki Thomas	0	Mrs. Carol Semple Thompson (3 and 1)	1
Total	0	Total	6
Total July 29	1	Total July 29	8
Grand Total—Great Britain and Ireland	4	Grand Total—United States	14

Captain—Mrs. Jill Thornhill

Captain—Mrs. Leslie Shannon

WORLD AMATEUR TEAM CHAMPIONSHIP

THE EISENHOWER TROPHY

Presented in October, 1958
by American Friends of Golf
through The United States Golf Association
and The Royal and Ancient Golf Club
of St. Andrews, Scotland

HISTORY

1982—The United States led every round and won the World Amateur Team Championship for the third consecutive time and for the ninth time in 13 attempts. The Championship was played at the Lausanne Golf Club, in Lausanne, Switzerland. The United States retained the Eisenhower Trophy with a score of 859, seven strokes ahead of Japan and Sweden, which tied for second place, at 866. France was fourth, at 874, followed by the Republic of China (Taiwan), 878; South Africa, 879; New Zealand, 881; Great Britain and Ireland and Germany, tied at 882; and Switzerland, 884. The United States led by two strokes after the first day on scores of 69 by Jay Sigel, 70 by Jim Holtgrieve, and 73 by Nathaniel Crosby, for a total of 212. Japan was second, at 214. Rounding out the top five were Spain, at 217; Norway, at 218; and the Philippines, at 219. In the second round, the United States slipped to a 215 but held on to its two-stroke lead over Japan, which also had 215. Sigel shot another 69. He was backed up by 73s from Holtgrieve and Lewis. The United States had 427 to Japan's 429. Sweden moved into third place, at 435, and those three teams remained in the same positions throughout the competition. In the third round, the United States increased its lead to four strokes despite a shaky 221. What saved the United States was that other teams were having problems also. Holtgrieve led the United States with 71, while teammates Sigel and Lewis added rounds of 73 and 77, respectively. Japan held on to second place, at 652, just one stroke ahead of Sweden, at 653. The United States shot 211 in the last round, the lowest daily team score of the week. Crosby, who had posted 81 the previous day, shot four-under-par 68, best of the Americans that day. Lewis closed with a 70, including a homeward nine of 33. Holtgrieve, the only American whose score counted each day, shot 73. While individual scores are not officially recognized, the low score came from Luis Carbonetti, of Argentina, which finished 14th. Carbonetti shot rounds of 69-69-74-72—284. Sigel, the U.S. Amateur Champion, shot 285. Holtgrieve and Krister Kinell, of Sweden, each had 287. The Captain of the United States Team was Frank D. Tatum, Jr., of San Francisco, California, a past President of the USGA. The Championship drew 32 team entries, short of the record 39 entries received for the 1980 event at Pinehurst, North Carolina.

1984—Japan used a strong second round to take the lead and continued on to win a seven-stroke victory, at the Royal Hong Kong Golf Club. The United States, which had won nine of 13 previous competitions, and the previous three in succession, led after the first round, with 209. Scott Verplonk, U.S. Amateur champion, shot 69, and Randy Sonnier and Jay Sigel each had 70. That gave the United States a four-stroke advantage over Great Britain and Ireland, with Argentina third, at 214, and Japan tied for fifth, with Malaysia, at 215. In the second round, the Japanese moved in front to stay as Tetsuo Sakata and Kazuhiko Kato shot 72 and Noriaki Kimura added 70. That gave Japan a four-stroke advantage over Great Britain and Ireland, at 433, and a five-stroke lead over New Zealand. The United States, meanwhile, stumbled to a 234 team total, its worst ever. Its best score was 77, by Verplank. Great Britain and Ireland made a serious move on the third day and cut the Japanese lead to one stroke. The United States was fifth, at 661, 10 strokes behind Japan. In the final round, the Japanese shot another 219, led by Sakata's 72, to win by seven strokes. The United States made a belated rally with a final-round 216, with Sonnier matching the day's low round of 69, and placed second. The Philippines was third, at 879, Great Britain and Ireland fourth, at 880, and Canada fifth, with 882. Luis Carbonetti, of Argentina, and Sakata each had 286, the lowest individual totals. Sonnier was third, with 289. Japan thus became the first Asian team and the first non-English-speaking nation to win the Eisenhower Trophy. The championship drew 38 entries, one short of the record 39 entries received for the 1980 event, at Pinehurst, North Carolina. Will F. Nicholson, Jr., of Denver, Colorado, served as Captain of the United States team.

1986—Canada erased a three-stroke deficit in the final round and won its first World Amateur Team Championship at Lagunita Country Club in Caracas, Venezuela. The Canadians' final-round 208, two-under-par, gave them a four-round total of 838. The United States, which had led after each of the first three rounds, finished second with 841. China finished third with 849 and Sweden fourth with 858. The United States forged a four-stroke lead after the first round with Billy Andrade leading off with a 68 and Buddy Alexander and Jay Sigel contributing rounds of 70 and 66, respectively, later in the day. Bob Lewis, Jr., the fourth member of the U.S. team, shot 71. The Americans' total of 204 was four better than second-place Canada. Brent Franklin shot 68 to lead Canada. The U.S. maintained its four-stroke lead after the second round. Lewis' 69 led the U.S. to a 210 total. The Canadians picked up a stroke in the third round with a 212 total for the day. Mark Brewer, who attends Miami (Ohio) University, led Canada in the third round with a 69. China moved into third place after 54 holes, eight strokes behind the United States. In the final round, Lewis led off for the U.S. with a 72 to Canadian Jack Kay's 76, seemingly securing the United States' hold on the lead. Sigel and Warren Sye of Canada followed with 71s. Brewer and Franklin, the final two Canadians, played the first nine under par, and it was clear that Kay's 76 would not be used for Canada's score. Brewer finished with a round of 69, picking up two strokes on Alexander. The U.S. needed Andrade to play Franklin even to win the championship. Franklin went out in 34, four strokes better than Andrade and, although he had lost a stroke to the American at the 12th, he finished with a round of 68 to Andrade's 73. Eduardo Herrera of Colombia and Brigham Young University shot 75-67-68-65—275 to post the low individual total of the championship. His fourth-round 65 set a record for the championship. The championship drew 39 entries, tying the record set in 1980 at Pinehurst (North Carolina) Country Club.

1988—Great Britain and Ireland took the lead after the second round and went on to win the 16th World Amateur Team Championship at Ullna Golf Club in Stockholm, Sweden. It was the third title for GB&I, which also won in 1964 and 1976. Sweden held a five-stroke lead after the first round. Frederik Lindgren led Sweden with a three-under-par 69. Anders Haglund and John Lindberg shot 72 and 73, respectively, to give the hosts a first-day total of 214. The United States, with Jay Sigel posting a 71, Danny Yates 72 and Eric Meeks 76, was second at 219. Great Britain and Ireland was in third place, one stroke behind the U.S. Great Britain and Ireland moved into first place on the second day. Peter McEvoy shot one-under-par 71 to go with Garth McGimpsey's 72 and Eoghan O'Connell's 75. The GB&I two-day total of 438 was three strokes better than that of the United States, which was led by Kevin Johnson and Meeks, who each shot 73. Yates added a 76. Sweden shot 229 and was five strokes behind GB&I. With McEvoy shooting a third-round 70, Great Britain and Ireland extended its lead to six strokes over the United States. O'Connell added a 72 and McGimpsey and Jim Milligan each shot two-under-par 70, the lowest score by an American during the championship. In the final round Great Britain and Ireland faltered for the first time. McEvoy shot another 71, but McGimpsey and Milligan shot 78 and 79, respectively, for a total of 882; but the U.S. could not capitalize. Yates' 73 and 77s by Meeks and Sigel left the U.S. at 887, five strokes behind. Australia was third at 895, two ahead of Sweden. McEvoy was low individual, finishing at four-under-par 284. David Ecob of Australia was second at 290, one stroke ahead of Yates. Thirty-nine countries were represented at the championship.

1990—Sweden became the second non-English speaking nation to win the championship shooting a total score of 879 and finishing 13 strokes ahead of New Zealand and the United States at the Christchurch Golf Club, in Christchurch, New Zealand. Japan, the 1984 champion, had been the only other non-English-speaking winner. Sweden led every round, and was never less than seven strokes ahead, its margin over Argentina, Korea, and New Zealand after the first round. The Swedes increased their lead to 14 strokes over Argentina after the second round, and to 16 over the United States after three. Led by a 70 by Mathias Gronberg, 72 by Klas Eriksson, and 73 by Gabriel Hjerstedt, Sweden shot 215 in the first round, and then Gronberg shot 67 in the second, while Hjerstedt shot 71. With Phil Mickelson, its Amateur Champion, opening with two rounds of 78, the United States trailed Sweden throughout the championship. The Americans fell 12 strokes behind after the first round, and trailed by 22 after the second. Sweden cooled off slightly in the third round, when Gronberg slipped to 77 and Eriksson to 78, but Hjerstedt's 74 kept them ahead. The Americans made up six strokes, climbing into second place behind Mickelson's 72, 75 by David Eger, and 76 by Allen Doyle. The United States had closed within nine strokes late in the round, but a strong wind blew in from the Pacific Ocean, the Americans lost seven strokes over the last few holes, and never threatened again. The Americans picked up three more strokes on Sweden in the last round, but they were too far behind to catch up, and were nearly passed by New Zealand. Mickelson, the last American on the course, holed a 40-foot putt on the last green to save a share of second place. Although neither an award nor official recognition is given the low individual scorer, since this is a team competition, Gronberg shot 70-67-77-72—286, and Hjerstedt 73-71-74-74—292, the two lowest 72-hole scores. Michael Long, of New Zealand, shot 294.

Year	Team	Score	Site
1982	United States	859	Lausanne G.C.,
	Japan	866	Lausanne,
	Sweden	866	Switzerland
1984	Japan	870	Royal Hong Kong G.C.,
	United States	877	Fanling, Hong Kong
	Philippines	879	
1986	Canada	838	Lagunita C.C.,
	United States	841	Caracas, Venezuela
	China	849	
1988	Great Britain-Ireland	882	Ullna G.C.,
	United States	887	Stockholm, Sweden
	Australia	895	
1990	Sweden	879	Christchurch G.C.,
	United States	892	Christchurch,
	New Zealand	892	New Zealand

1982
THIRTEENTH WORLD AMATEUR TEAM CHAMPIONSHIP
FOR THE EISENHOWER TROPHY

Lausanne Golf Club, Lausanne, Switzerland, September 15-18.
Yardage — 6,890. Par 72. 30 Team Entries.

*Team Captain	1st Round	2nd Round	3rd Round	4th Round	72-Hole Score
United States Grand Total		427	648		859
Nathaniel Crosby	73	75	81	68	297
Jim Holtgrieve	70	73	71	73	287
Bob Lewis	74	73	77	70	294
Jay Sigel	69	69	73	74	285
Total best 3, daily	212	215	221	211	
*Frank D. Tatum, Jr.					
Japan Grand Total		429	652		866
Tetsuo Sakata	72	72	75	76	295
Kazuhiko Kato	71	72	75	72	290
Masayuki Naito	75	71	74	73	293
Kiyotaka Oie	71	73	74	69	287
Total best 3, daily	214	215	223	214	
*Yoshio Hachiuma					
Sweden Grand Total		435	653		866
Per Andersson	77	76	74	74	301
Krister Kinell	72	70	75	70	287
Magnus Persson	76	71	72	73	292
Ove Sellberg	73	73	72	70	288
Total best 3, daily	221	214	218	213	
* J. Blomqvist					
France Grand Total		439	657		875
Marc Pendaries	74	78	74	72	298
Alexis Godillot	72	72	75	75	294
Jean-Louis Schneider	75	71	78	74	298
Philippe Ploujoux	80	75	69	71	295
Total best 3, daily	221	218	218	217	
*J. L. Dupont					
Republic of China Grand Total		437	659		878
Yuan Ching-chi	79	67	76	69	291
Li Wen-sheng	70	76	77	78	301
Lai Chen-jen	NR	77	73	73	223
Lin Chi-hsiang	76	69	73	77	295
Total best 3, daily	225	212	222	219	
*Lu Wei-hsiang					
South Africa Grand Total		442	662		879
Derek James	75	77	79	70	301
Neil James	73	74	75	76	298
Duncan Lindsay-Smith	76	72	72	71	291
David Suddards	74	74	73	76	297
Total best 3, daily	222	220	220	217	
*G. Bunting					
New Zealand Grand Total		440	665		881
Phillip Aickin	72	74	74	68	288
Michael Barltrop	73	72	75	73	293
Colin Taylor	76	77	78	78	309
Greg Turner	78	73	76	75	302
Total best 3, daily	221	219	225	216	
*B. Forrest					
Great Britain & Ireland Grand Total		440	658		882
George MacGregor	76	74	72	74	296
Andrew S. Oldcorn	74	74	75	78	301
Arthur D. Pierse	77	71	71	80	299
Philip Walton	71	77	75	72	295
Total best 3, daily	221	219	218	224	
*R. Foster					
Germany Grand Total		444	660		882
Thomas Hübner	80	79	75	80	314
Haans G. Reiter	73	72	76	72	293
Frank Schlig	74	75	70	78	297
Ulrich Schulte	73	77	71	72	293
Total best 3, daily	220	224	216	222	
*H. Lampert					
Switzerland Grand Total		445	663		884
Johnny Storjohann	76	77	76	72	301
Markus Frank	73	70	72	73	288
Carlo Rampone	72	78	87	77	314
Michael Buchter	75	78	70	76	299
Total best 3, daily	220	225	218	221	
*J. Pesko					

1982
THIRTEENTH WORLD AMATEUR TEAM CHAMPIONSHIP
FOR THE EISENHOWER TROPHY
Continued

		1st Round	2nd Round	3rd Round	4th Round	72-Hole Score
Spain	Grand Total		445	663		884
Alfonso Vidaor Ameztoy		81	75	71	74	301
Alejo Olle Bertrand		73	75	76	76	300
José M. Olazabal Manterola		72	75	76	73	296
Ramon Taya Munoz		72	80	77	77	306
Total best 3, daily		217	225	223	223	
*S. Fisas						
Italy	Grand Total		441	668		889
Mauro Bianco		73	71	80	70	294
Emanuele Bolognesi		80	72	75	71	298
Andrea Canessa		76	74	78	81	309
Lorenzo Silva		76	73	74	80	303
Total best 3, daily		225	216	227	221	
*P. Cora						
Philippines	Grand Total		444	667		890
Francisco Minoza		70	75	71	75	291
Guillermo Ababa		72	77	75	74	298
Joelito Saban		79	76	78	85	318
David Hernandez		77	74	77	74	302
Total best 3, daily		219	225	223	223	
*E. Javier						
Argentina	Grand Total		443	667		893
Luis G. Carbonetti		69	69	74	72	284
Miguel A. Prado		82	78	81	77	318
Fernando C. Chiesa		75	74	74	77	300
Roberto B. Benito		78	78	76	78	310
Total best 3, daily		222	221	224	226	
*Ivar Broström						
Denmark	Grand Total		460	676		897
Steen Tinning		77	78	70	71	296
Anders Sørensen		80	75	72	77	304
Jakob Rasmussen		80	77	74	73	304
Erik Groth Andersen		73	83	87	77	320
Total best 3, daily		230	230	216	221	
*Ole Pfeiffer						
Belgium	Grand Total		449	680		904
Michel Eaton		74	76	75	82	307
Thierry Goossens		71	75	78	71	295
Patrick Bonnelance		78	75	78	78	309
Benoit Dumont		78	78	88	75	319
Total best 3, daily		223	226	231	224	
*J. Bigwood						
Mexico	Grand Total		459	690		911
Ignacio de Leon		75	72	72	78	297
Feleciano Esparza		77	78	84	73	312
Carlos Pelaez		77	81	78	73	309
José Martinez		76	82	81	75	314
Total best 3, daily		228	231	231	221	
*E. Lanes						
Chile	Grand Total		454	687		912
*Felipe Taverne		77	71	75	72	295
Juan-Pablo Velasco		74	80	80	75	309
Francisco Cortes		81	77	78	78	314
Sebastian Aninat		78	77	80	81	316
Total best 3, daily		229	225	233	225	
Korea	Grand Total		456	692		915
Kim Ki Sup		72	77	77	74	300
Lee Jong Min		81	79	80	76	316
Kim Sung Ho		80	72	80	73	305
Kim Yung Hoon		76	79	79	77	311
Total best 3, daily		228	228	236	223	
*Limb Young Sun						
Norway	Grand Total		456	683		915
Eric Bjerkholt		71	79	75	76	301
Tore Sviland		71	78	73	81	303
Erik Doennestad		79	81	80	78	318
Lars E. Underthun		76	81	79	78	314
Total best 3, daily		218	238	227	232	
*Theo Holm						

1982
THIRTEENTH WORLD AMATEUR TEAM CHAMPIONSHIP FOR THE EISENHOWER TROPHY
Continued

		1st Round	2nd Round	3rd Round	4th Round	72-Hole Score
Austria	Grand Total		464	685		917
Klaus Nierlich		78	76	70	73	297
Christian Czerny		74	83	79	81	317
Fritz Porstendorfer		85	81	73	78	317
Max Lamberg		77	78	78	83	316
Total best 3, daily		229	235	221	232	
*Lambert Stolz						
Netherlands	Grand Total		461	689		920
Toby Rijks		75	85	74	78	312
Joost Hage		76	82	76	77	311
Victor Swane		78	78	78	79	313
Bart Nolte		76	74	79	76	305
Total best 3, daily		227	234	228	231	
*A. F. Knappert						
Brazil	Grand Total		459	695		924
Carlos Dluhosh		79	80	76	77	312
Roberto Gomez		74	80	80	76	310
Marcelo Stallone		74	76	82	76	308
Rafael Gonzales		NR	76	80	77	233
Total best 3, daily		227	232	236	229	
*S. Marvin						
Finland	Grand Total		460	699		937
Markku Louhio		83	77	80	79	319
Timo Sipponen		74	71	81	78	304
Patrik Hallama		77	78	78	81	314
Lassi-Pekka Tilander		87	83	91	83	344
Total best 3, daily		234	226	239	238	
*J. Huhtanen						
Venezuela	Grand Total		471	706		937
Ernesto Amengual		77	82	77	82	318
Carlos Whaite		80	79	80	88	327
Carlos Plaza		79	75	78	79	311
Vicente Amengual, Jr.		Disq.	81	83	70	234
Total best 3, daily		236	235	235	231	
*F. Alcantara						
Iceland	Grand Total		482	718		960
Ragnar Olafsson		82	75	81	82	320
Sigurdur Petursson		83	87	78	80	328
Sveinn Sigurbergsson		84	82	85	80	331
Björgvin Thorsteinsson		87	76	77	82	322
Total best 3, daily		249	233	236	242	
*L. Kjartan Palsson						
Hong Kong	Grand Total		483	732		971
Don M. Innes		78	77	81	80	316
Cam R. Gribben		83	80	84	80	327
Don Clegg		85	83	84	91	343
A. Clement-Brown		88	80	86	79	333
Total best 3, daily		246	237	249	239	
*H. de Lacy Staunton						
Bermuda	Grand Total		493	734		976
Hav Trott		80	81	78	78	317
Twilton Smith		84	88	79	82	333
Devent Smith		94	87	86	82	349
J. J. Madeiros		77	84	84	83	328
Total best 3, daily		241	252	241	242	
*J. Trott						
Guatemala	Grand Total		503	746		990
Arturo Casellas		83	91	81	78	333
Mario Ruiz		88	86	93	89	356
Gustavo Staebler		79	84	80	80	323
*Lewis Newbill		90	83	82	86	341
Total best 3, daily		250	253	243	244	
Greece	Grand Total		522	776		1025
George Nikitaides		83	88	86	83	340
Bassili Aronis		80	100	88	87	355
Paul Baillas		91	88	82	83	344
George Manuelides		92	92	86	83	353
Total best 3, daily		254	268	254	249	
*A. Manuelides						

1984
FOURTEENTH WORLD AMATEUR TEAM CHAMPIONSHIP FOR THE EISENHOWER TROPHY

Royal Hong Kong Golf Club, Fanling, Hong Kong, October 30-November 2
Yardage—6,757. Par 72. 38 Team Entries.

*Team Captain		1st Round	2nd Round	3rd Round	4th Round	72-Hole Score
Japan	Grand Total	215	429	651		870
Kazuhiko Kato		73	72	75	73	293
Noriaki Kimura		82	70	75	74	301
Kiyotaka Oie		74	81	73	77	305
Testuo Sakata		68	72	74	72	286
Total best 3 daily		215	214	222	219	
*Ginjiro Nakabe						
United States	Grand Total	209	443	661		877
John Inman		75	80	74	74	303
Jay Sigel		70	79	76	77	302
Randy Sonnier		70	78	72	69	289
Scott Verplank		69	77	72	73	291
Total best 3 daily		209	234	218	216	
*Will F. Nicholson, Jr.						
Philippines	Grand Total	219	437	659		879
Guillermo Ababa		72	76	75	78	301
Fernando Antolin		77	70	75	73	295
Robert Pactolerin		72	79	72	69	292
Carito Villaroman		75	72	75	78	300
Total best 3 daily		219	218	222	220	
*Simplicio C. Taguiam						
Great Britain & Ireland	Grand Total	213	433	652		880
David Gilford		68	77	75	78	298
Peter McEvoy		77	69	75	78	296
Garth McGimpsey		70	75	80	75	300
Colin Montgomerie		75	76	72	75	298
Total best 3 daily		213	220	219	228	
*Charlie W. Green						
Canada	Grand Total	218	447	668		882
Danny Mijovic		74	80	75	75	301
Ward Stouffer		71	73	72	80	296
Bill Swartz		79	79	74	72	304
Bob Wylie		73	77	75	70	295
Total best 3 daily		218	229	221	214	
*William A. Farlinger						
New Zealand	Grand Total	217	434	658		883
Michael Barltrop		79	70	73	76	298
Terry Cochrane		75	70	78	76	299
Greg Turner		67	77	74	73	291
John Williamson		75	78	77	77	307
Total best 3 daily		217	217	224	225	
*J. Barry Forrest						
France	Grand Total	221	447	663		885
Emmanuel Dussart		71	78	70	71	290
Alexis Godillot		74	74	73	80	301
Francois Illouz		77	81	73	73	304
Philippe Ploujoux		76	74	77	78	305
Total best 3 daily		221	226	216	222	
*Herve Freyssineau						
Sweden	Grand Total	224	443	663		889
Mikael Hogberg		79	71	75	74	299
John Lindberg		73	82	74	79	308
Jesper Parnevik		77	76	75	75	303
Carl M. Stromberg		74	72	71	77	294
Total best 3 daily		224	219	220	226	
*Rolf Wirhed						
Argentina	Grand Total	214	444	666		892
Luis G. Carbonetti		68	74	70	74	286
Fernando J. Chiesa		73	80	74	77	304
Jorge A. Nicolosi		80	81	78	75	314
Jaime Nougues		73	76	79	78	306
Total best 3 daily		214	230	222	226	
*Ivar Brostrom						

1984
FOURTEENTH WORLD AMATEUR TEAM CHAMPIONSHIP
FOR THE EISENHOWER TROPHY
Continued

		1st Round	2nd Round	3rd Round	4th Round	72-Hole Score
Italy	Grand Total	221	450	671		894
Alberto Binaghi		75	76	73	76	300
Emanuele Bolognesi		74	76	75	74	299
Silvio Grappasonni		72	77	73	73	295
Enrico Nistri		79	78	75	76	308
Total best 3 daily		221	229	221	223	
*Lorenzo Silva						
Spain	Grand Total	218	446	666		895
Jose L. De Bernado		72	79	73	75	299
Luis Gabardo		76	75	72	80	303
Jose Maria Olazabal		71	80	76	77	304
Eduardo De La Riva		75	74	75	77	301
Total best 3 daily		218	228	220	229	
*Santiago Fisas						
Greece	Grand Total	221	450	674		899
Craigen Pappas		73	78	75	74	300
Sean Pappas		75	74	71	74	294
George Vafiadis		79	77	78	77	311
Stefan Vafiadis		73	81	87	84	325
Total best 3 daily		221	229	224	225	
*Mike Kyranis						
Malaysia	Grand Total	215	441	671		900
Ravichanthiran		74	79	75	76	304
P. Segaran		72	75	81	78	306
Suffian Tan		69	72	79	77	297
Saad Yusof		75	79	76	76	306
Total best 3 daily		215	226	230	229	
*N.S. Choong						
Chile	Grand Total	221	444	669		900
Michael Geyger		75	78	78	85	316
Roy S. Mackenzie		75	72	69	76	292
Felipe Taverne		74	80	78	72	304
Juan Pablo Velasco		72	73	79	83	307
Total best 3 daily		221	223	225	231	
*Juan Armando Soruco						
Denmark	Grand Total	225	451	681		906
Rolf Nissen		73	73	77	72	295
Jacob Rasmussen		77	74	78	77	306
Soren Rolner		76	79	82	82	319
Steen Tinning		76	79	75	76	306
Total best 3 daily		225	226	230	225	
*Ole Pfeiffer						
Korea	Grand Total	229	450	679		906
Bum Soo Cho		79	78	78	78	313
Suck Jong Kim		83	75	79	75	312
Sung Ho Kim		76	74	77	85	312
Yu Hyun Kwak		74	72	74	74	294
Total best 3 daily		229	221	229	227	
*Young Sun Limb						
Netherlands	Grand Total	227	449	676		909
Bart Nolte		72	71	75	72	290
Rik Ruts		78	80	80	80	318
Daan Slooter		77	76	77	81	311
Siemon Vegter		78	75	75	85	313
Total best 3 daily		227	222	227	233	
*A.F. Knappert						
Germany	Grand Total	229	457	684		911
Thomas Dekorsy		78	78	78	77	311
Thomas Huebner		73	74	74	77	298
Hans-Gunter Reiter		79	81	76	73	309
Ulrich Schulte		78	76	77	77	308
Total best 3 daily		229	228	227	227	
*Hans Lampert						
Australia	Grand Total	229	460	686		913
Neil Crafter		79	75	79	73	306
Tony Dight		75	82	77	79	313
Gerard Power		75	77	72	77	301
David Smith		80	79	77	77	313
Total best 3 daily		229	231	226	227	
*Michael Fitchett						

1984
FOURTEENTH WORLD AMATEUR TEAM CHAMPIONSHIP
FOR THE EISENHOWER TROPHY
Continued

		1st Round	2nd Round	3rd Round	4th Round	72-Hole Score
Hong Kong	Grand Total	232	459	692		920
Dominique Boulet		75	75	77	79	306
Cam Gribben		80	83	84	77	304
Don Innes		77	77	76	77	307
Shui Wing Tang		83	75	80	74	312
Total best 3 daily		232	227	233	228	
*D. Clegg						
Venezuela	Grand Total	236	468	690		922
Vicente E. Amengual		72	78	75	78	303
Carlos Larrain		DQ	76	73	75	—
Luis R. Soto		79	78	74	85	316
Carlos A. Whaite		85	81	78	79	323
Total best 3 daily		236	232	222	232	
*Freddy C. Alcantara						
Switzerland	Grand Total	226	460	688		924
Michael Buchter		78	79	79	83	313
Markus Frank		74	79	79	78	310
Thomas Gottstein		74	76	75	75	300
Erwin Vonlanthen		79	82	74	93	328
Total best 3 daily		226	234	228	236	
*Jurg Pesko						
Indonesia	Grand Total	228	460	692		925
Mat Ani		82	82	81	81	326
Buari		82	73	77	76	308
Jubilant A. Harmidy		73	77	79	81	310
Sudjiono		73	84	76	76	309
Total best 3 daily		228	232	232	233	
*Haroen Harmidy						
India	Grand Total	228	467	691		926
Karan Atwal		76	83	75	84	318
Rajeev Mohta		77	78	76	83	314
Ranjit Handa		78	81	75	75	309
Alan Singh		75	80	74	77	306
Total best 3 daily		228	239	224	235	
*A.S. Malik						
Austria	Grand Total	228	458	690		928
Christian Czerny		81	78	79	79	317
Manfred Dollhaeubl		85	80	81	84	330
Max Lamberg		77	79	78	78	312
Klaus Nierlich		70	73	75	81	299
Total best 3 daily		228	230	232	238	
*Lambert Stolz						
Mexico	Grand Total	232	463	695		931
Guillermo Escalera		DQ	79	81	79	—
Jorge Perez Leon		76	77	76	80	309
Paul Muller		80	75	75	78	308
Miguel E. Quijano		76	79	82	79	316
Total best 3 daily		232	231	232	236	
*J. Pria						
Zimbabwe	Grand Total	232	471	699		933
Terry Bowes		76	79	75	78	308
Terry Cairns		80	78	79	83	320
Glen James		83	86	74	77	320
Anderson Rusike		76	82	80	79	317
Total best 3 daily		232	239	228	234	
*J. Clark						
Thailand	Grand Total	227	461	694		933
Pasda Buranasiri		80	80	85	82	327
Boonchoo Ruengkij		75	77	74	80	306
Thaworn Wiratchant		77	85	86	80	328
Yu-Pan Boonthan		75	77	74	79	305
Total 3 best daily		227	234	233	239	
*Somchai Hiranprueck						
Fiji	Grand Total	236	467	700		936
Mahmood Buksh		77	85	73	77	312
Vilikesa Kalou		77	75	83	77	312
Shiu Sami Naidu		82	77	78	82	319
Dharam Prakash		86	79	82	85	332
Total best 3 daily		236	231	233	236	
*Timothy M. Marsden						

1984
FOURTEENTH WORLD AMATEUR TEAM CHAMPIONSHIP
FOR THE EISENHOWER TROPHY
Continued

		1st Round	2nd Round	3rd Round	4th Round	72-Hole Score
Brazil	Grand Total	227	465	706		937
Antonio C. Barcellos		73	81	78	75	307
Roberto Gomes		84	78	81	78	321
Milton Tanigaki		79	83	85	82	329
Jean P. Van Tilburg		75	79	82	78	314
Total best 3 daily		227	238	241	231	
*Luiz Nardy						
Bermuda	Grand Total	236	471	704		939
Scott Mayne		83	77	78	80	318
Denton Outerbridge		78	82	82	83	325
Hav Trott		75	76	73	74	298
Noel Van Putten		84	86	87	81	338
Total best 3 daily		236	235	233	235	
*Jack Wahl						
Belgium	Grand Total	232	462	702		940
Patrick Bonnelance		80	80	82	81	323
Christophe Bosmans		76	80	81	78	315
Olivier Buysse		79	76	85	86	326
Thierry Goossens		77	74	77	79	307
Total best 3 daily		232	230	240	238	
*John Bigwood						
Pakistan	Grand Total	232	463	698		942
Mehmood Aziz		88	77	82	83	330
Taimur Hassan		75	79	78	80	312
Faisal Qureshi		79	75	75	81	310
Waqar Saigol		78	87	86	84	335
Total best 3 daily		232	231	235	244	
*R. Azim						
Norway	Grand Total	242	481	707		943
Tom Fredriksen		80	78	77	81	316
Per Haugsrud		84	82	74	76	316
Gard Midtvage		87	81	75	79	322
Ragnvald Risan		78	80	80	84	322
Total best 3 daily		242	239	226	236	
*Dag Opedal						
Trinidad & Tobago	Grand Total	232	471	710		951
Christopher Ammon		78	84	79	86	327
Robert Charlett		78	77	82	78	315
*Cliff Hinds		84	78	80	81	323
Christophe Richards		76	84	80	82	322
Total best 3 daily		232	239	239	241	
Singapore	Grand Total	236	477	709		954
A. Chelliah		82	79	84	82	327
Daniel Lim		79	83	77	80	319
*Douglas Ooi		86	84	79	86	335
Ee Kiat Poh		75	79	76	83	313
Total best 3 daily		236	241	232	245	
Papua New Guinea	Grand Total	234	482	716		964
Greg Fennell		82	84	80	82	328
John Keating		88	86	89	83	346
John Stuart		78	82	76	89	325
John Wilkinson		74	82	78	83	317
Total best 3 daily		234	248	234	248	
*John Daley						
Bahamas	Grand Total	248	495	742		990
Jim Duncombe		81	80	84	87	332
*Fred Higgs		90	94	97	WD	—
Harcourt Poitier		86	88	83	88	345
Zorro Stubbs		81	79	80	73	313
Total best 3 daily		248	247	247	248	

1986
FIFTEENTH WORLD AMATEUR TEAM CHAMPIONSHIP
FOR THE EISENHOWER TROPHY

Lagunita Country Club, Caracas, Venezuela, October 22-25.
Yardage—6,782. Par 70. 39 Team Entries.

*Team Captain		1st Round	2nd Round	3rd Round	4th Round	72-Hole Score
Canada	Grand Total		418	630		838
Mark Brewer		70	69	69	69	277
Brent Franklin		68	74	72	68	282
Jack Kay, Jr.		70	71	72	76	289
Warren Sye		73	70	71	71	285
Total best 3, daily		208	210	212	208	
*Doug Brewer						
United States	Grand Total		414	627		841
Buddy Alexander		70	71	71	71	283
Bill Andrade		68	71	76	73	288
Bob Lewis		71	69	72	72	284
Jay Sigel		66	70	70	71	277
Total best 3, daily		204	210	213	214	
*William C. Campbell						
China	Grand Total		423	635		849
Lin Chie-Hsiang		73	71	70	69	283
Lin Chin-Cheng		71	70	73	73	287
Hsieh Chin-Sheng		71	67	69	72	279
Cheng Yun-Mao		75	80	79	75	313
Total best 3, daily		215	208	212	214	
*Lu Wei Hsiang						
Sweden	Grand Total		431	647		858
Christian Hardin		70	73	71	72	286
Jesper Parnevik		74	70	77	70	291
J. Rystrom		73	71	71	69	284
C. Stromberg		77	73	74	72	296
Total best 3, daily		217	214	216	211	
*Rolf Wirhed						
Australia	Grand Total		441	652		859
Bradley King		75	76	74	76	301
Peter O'Malley		74	74	75	66	289
Raymond Picker		72	79	67	74	292
Stephen Taylor		70	75	70	67	282
Total best 3, daily		216	225	211	207	
*Bruce Nairn						
Germany	Grand Total		435	647		867
Hans G. Reiter		72	76	73	73	294
Ekkehart Schieffer		74	71	70	78	293
Sven Struever		74	70	74	69	287
Ralf Thielemann		72	76	69	79	296
Total best 3, daily		218	217	212	220	
*Christian Strenger						
New Zealand	Grand Total		431	649		868
P. Aicken		69	75	74	73	291
M. Barltrop		73	68	71	75	287
G. Goldfinch		78	DQ	73	71	—
B. Paterson		72	74	76	76	298
Total best 3, daily		214	217	218	219	
*G.M. Wardell						
Colombia	Grand Total		442	654		870
Fernando Arriola		84	80	74	80	318
Fabio Bernal		72	75	77	78	302
Alberto Evers		79	74	70	73	296
*Eduardo Herrera		75	67	68	65	275
Total best 3, daily		226	216	212	216	
France	Grand Total		438	651		870
*Alexis Godillot		73	74	77	73	297
Laurent LaSalle		74	75	71	74	294
Jean F. Remesy		82	74	74	72	302
Jean Van De Velde		73	70	68	74	285
Total best 3, daily		220	218	213	219	

1986
FIFTEENTH WORLD AMATEUR TEAM CHAMPIONSHIP
FOR THE EISENHOWER TROPHY
Continued

		1st Round	2nd Round	3rd Round	4th Round	72-Hole Score
Spain	Grand Total		439	659		873
Luis Cabarda		72	73	73	74	292
Eduardo De La Riva		76	71	76	73	296
Borja Queipo De Llano		75	72	71	68	286
Roman Taya		80	73	78	73	304
Total best 3, daily		223	216	220	214	
*Santiago Frisas						
Brazil	Grand Total		433	655		878
Erik Anderson		73	71	73	75	292
Antonio Barcellos		73	72	78	73	296
Roberto Gomez		73	71	71	75	290
Aldo Wolf		82	82	78	85	327
Total best 3, daily		219	214	222	223	
*Seymour Marvin						
Great Britain & Ireland	Grand Total		436	660		880
David Curry		77	73	75	72	297
Peter McEvoy		74	77	75	75	301
Garth McGimpsey		76	74	75	74	299
Colin Montgomerie		69	70	74	74	287
Total best 3, daily		219	217	224	220	
*Charles W. Green						
Venezuela	Grand Total		432	654		881
Francisco Alvarado		71	74	76	77	298
Vicente Amengual		76	73	75	75	299
Carlos Larrain		72	73	82	75	302
Enrique Lavie		74	69	71	77	291
Total best 3, daily		217	215	222	227	
*Carlos Plaza						
Japan	Grand Total		440	660		883
Yoshihiro Ito		71	77	77	76	301
Ryoken Kawagishi		75	68	73	75	291
Takahiro Nakagawa		77	75	74	75	301
Tetsuo Sakata		76	75	73	73	297
Total best 3, daily		222	218	220	223	
*Gingiro Nakabe						
Denmark	Grand Total		440	657		883
Peter Digebjerg		76	73	73	76	298
Leif Nyholm		77	78	80	78	313
Jan F. Pedersen		71	72	68	79	290
Jacob Rasmussen		73	75	76	72	296
Total best 3, daily		220	220	217	226	
*Helge Ejrnaes						
Chile	Grand Total		436	657		885
Sebastian Aninat		74	71	76	75	296
Francisco Cories		79	82	76	76	313
Roy Mackenzie		73	68	73	77	291
*Felipe Taverne		75	75	72	77	299
Total best 3, daily		222	214	221	228	
Italy	Grand Total		440	658		887
Alberto Binaghi		69	71	72	74	286
Luigi Figari		77	77	78	81	313
Enrico Nistri		78	72	72	74	296
Alessandro Rogato		78	73	74	82	307
Total best 3, daily		224	216	218	229	
*Piero Cora						
Mexico	Grand Total		442	668		891
Jorge Couglan		75	DQ	DQ	DQ	—
Bjorn Kauffman		82	76	77	76	311
Roberto Lebrija		70	73	72	75	290
Alberto Valenzuela		77	71	77	72	297
Total best 3, daily		222	220	226	223	
*Ignacio Velasco						

1986
FIFTEENTH WORLD AMATEUR TEAM CHAMPIONSHIP
FOR THE EISENHOWER TROPHY
Continued

		1st Round	2nd Round	3rd Round	4th Round	72-Hole Score
Greece	Grand Total		455	674		897
Ryno Bougus		78	78	77	81	314
George Nikitaidis		83	80	80	77	320
Craigen Pappas		74	78	66	74	292
Sean Pappas		74	73	76	72	295
Total best 3, daily		226	229	219	223	
*Mike Kyranis						
Netherlands	Grand Total		450	674		900
Stephane Lovey		73	83	76	78	310
Bart Nolte		75	73	76	72	296
Joost Steenkamer		74	75	72	77	298
Constant Van Waesberghe		78	80	78	77	313
Total best 3, daily		222	228	224	226	
*Robin Van Erven Dorens						
Finland	Grand Total		449	673		900
Anssi Kankkonen		76	74	76	73	299
Mikael Piltz		83	74	77	78	312
Juha Selin		75	74	73	79	301
Rikn Soravuo		76	77	75	76	304
Total best 3, daily		227	222	224	227	
*Lassi Tilander						
Switzerland	Grand Total		451	680		903
Frank Markus		71	77	77	72	297
Thomas Gottstein		73	72	74	74	293
Pascal Jaquet		85	75	78	77	315
Pierre-Alain Rey		84	76	81	84	325
Total best 3, daily		228	223	229	223	
*John Storjohann						
Trinidad & Tobago	Grand Total		456	688		907
Stephen Ames		77	69	77	68	291
Robert Charlett		80	85	82	78	325
Barry Ferdinand		83	86	79	77	325
*Christopher Harries		72	73	76	74	295
Total best 3, daily		229	227	232	219	
Korea	Grand Total		452	679		908
Kwang Soo Choi		77	78	75	77	307
Jong Il Kim		75	77	77	78	307
Jong Pil Kim		75	78	79	74	306
Jin Keun Oh		76	71	75	80	302
Total best 3, daily		226	226	227	229	
*Yuen Dong Yoo						
Argentina	Grand Total		445	679		908
Fernando J. Chiesa		72	74	77	78	301
Fernando Curuchet		76	81	88	77	322
Ricardo O. Marzorati		74	78	80	74	306
Federico D. McNeill		81	71	77	84	313
Total best 3, daily		222	223	234	229	
*Ivan F. Brostrom						
Paraguay	Grand Total		466	693		919
Juan Boardlage		86	81	81	75	323
Raul Fretes		72	78	73	77	300
*Richard Kent		82	81	84	83	330
Jorge Murdoch		76	77	73	74	300
Total best 3, daily		230	236	227	226	
Zimbabwe	Grand Total		455	684		922
Terry Bowes		73	75	76	76	300
Terry Cairns		72	80	76	85	313
John Curtis		81	86	84	84	335
Geoff Guy		77	78	77	78	310
Total best 3, daily		222	233	229	238	
*Lionel Johnson						

1988
SIXTEENTH WORLD AMATEUR TEAM CHAMPIONSHIP
FOR THE EISENHOWER TROPHY

Ullna Country Club, Stockholm, Sweden, September 15-18
Yardage—6,842. Par 72. 39 Team Entries.

*Team Captain		1st Round	2nd Round	3rd Round	4th Round	72-Hole Score
Gr. Britain/Ireland	Grand Total	220	438	654		882
Peter McEvoy		72	71	70	71	284
Garth McGimpsey		(76)	72	74	78	300
Jim Milligan		75	(80)	(74)	79	308
Eoghan O'Connell		73	75	72	(80)	300
Total best 3		220	218	216	228	
*Geoffrey Marks						
United States	Grand Total	219	441	460		887
Kevin Johnson		(77)	73	76	(78)	304
Eric Meeks		76	73	73	77	299
Jay Sigel		71	(78)	(78)	77	304
Danny Yates		72	76	70	73	291
Total best 3		219	222	219	227	
*James R. Hand						
Australia	Grand Total	226	457	473		895
David Ecob		70	71	75	74	290
Bradley Hughes		80	80	(78)	(77)	315
Lester Peterson		(85)	(84)	69	76	314
Shane Robinson		76	80	72	72	300
Total best 3		226	231	216	222	
*John Westacott						
Sweden	Grand Total	214	443	669		897
Anders Haglund		72	(85)	(78)	(78)	313
Christian Hardin		(75)	77	74	77	303
John Lindberg		73	75	74	75	297
Fredrik Lindgren		69	77	78	76	300
Total best 3		214	229	226	228	
*Rolf Wirhed						
France	Grand Total	225	455	682		899
Patrice Barquez		77	73	72	(76)	298
Christian Cevaer		73	79	(81)	74	307
Francois Illouz		(81)	78	77	72	308
Thomas Levet		75	(80)	78	71	304
Total best 3		225	230	227	217	
*Sven Boinet						
Denmark	Grand Total	230	448	678		906
Jan Andersen		(82)	(80)	75	76	313
Soren Bjorn		78	71	(84)	74	307
Christian Post		78	74	78	78	308
Henrik Simonsen		74	73	77	(79)	303
Total best 3		230	218	230	228	
*Herbert Fredriksen						
Spain	Grand Total	226	457	686		914
Jesus Arruti		73	72	79	73	297
Jose-Manuel Arruti		(83)	(88)	75	80	326
Yago Beamonte		76	77	75	75	303
Borja Queipo De Llano		77	82	(80)	(85)	324
Total best 3		226	231	229	228	
*Santiago Fisas						
Canada	Grand Total	229	453	678		915
Graham Cooke		(79)	(78)	76	78	311
Peter Major		78	71	72	(82)	303
Doug Roxburgh		78	75	77	78	308
Warren Sye		73	78	(78)	81	310
Total best 3		229	224	225	237	
*Harold Brownstein						
Japan	Grand Total	225	454	683		915
Ryoken Kawagishi		73	75	74	(83)	305
Ken Kusumoto		77	73	77	73	300
Kiyotaka Oie		(83)	(81)	(81)	79	324
Kiyoshi Okura		75	81	78	80	314
Total best 3		225	229	229	232	
*Tetsuo Sakata						

1988
SIXTEENTH WORLD AMATEUR TEAM CHAMPIONSHIP
FOR THE EISENHOWER TROPHY
Continued

*Team Captain		1st Round	2nd Round	3rd Round	4th Round	72-Hole Score
New Zealand	Grand Total	226	463	683		916
Phillip Aicken		77	81	75	(83)	316
Elliott Boult		(79)	(83)	69	78	309
Owen Kendall		74	77	(79)	80	310
Philip Tataurangi		75	79	76	75	305
Total best 3		226	237	220	233	
*Roger Brennand						
Chile	Grand Total	232	458	691		920
Michi Geyger		75	(82)	78	(80)	315
Mike Grasty		79	75	(79)	78	311
Roy McKenzie		(82)	76	78	76	312
Felipe Taverne		78	75	77	75	305
Total best 3		232	226	233	229	
*Mario Capez						
Switzerland	Grand Total	230	468	688		923
Andre Bossert		74	80	75	(83)	312
Markus Frank		76	79	71	75	301
Thomas Gottstein		(81)	(81)	(78)	82	322
Paolo Quirici		80	79	74	78	311
Total best 3		230	238	220	235	
*Martin Kessler						
Brazil	Grand Total	227	461	690		925
Erik Anderson		71	75	76	80	302
Antonio Cha. Barcellos		79	81	76	75	311
Roberto Gomez		(83)	78	(80)	80	321
Colin Woods		77	(86)	77	(84)	324
Total best 3		227	234	229	235	
*Seymour Marvin						
Finland	Grand Total	230	464	697		925
Mikael Piltz		73	81	74	75	303
Vuha Selin		79	(85)	81	80	325
Riku Soravuo		(80)	75	78	73	306
Erkki Valimaa		78	78	(82)	(82)	320
Total best 3		230	234	233	228	
*Veli-Matti Valimaa						
Argentina	Grand Total	234	474	701		926
Fernando Chiesa		73	78	76	75	302
Federico Macneill		(84)	82	76	74	316
Jaime Nougues		78	(88)	(77)	76	319
Julio Rivas		83	80	75	(81)	319
Total best 3		234	240	227	225	
*Eduardo Lorenzutti						
Republic of China	Grand Total	227	465	695		933
Jung-Hsin Chen		79	80	75	(88)	322
Hudh-Jen Huang		(80)	80	78	77	315
Ken-Chi Lin		77	78	77	79	311
Wen-Teh Lui		71	(85)	(79)	82	317
Total best 3		227	238	230	238	
*Wei-Hsiang Lu						
Germany	Grand Total	228	465	691		936
Friedrich Kotter		76	80	(83)	84	323
Jan-Erik Schapmann		(80)	80	80	83	323
Sven Struver		78	(81)	74	(85)	318
Ulrich Zilg		74	77	72	78	301
Total best 3		228	237	226	245	
*Christoph Stadler						
Greece	Grand Total	236	467	701		937
Ryno Bougas		(81)	(79)	(84)	79	323
George Nikitaides		79	78	82	79	318
Deane Pappas		80	74	79	(82)	315
Sean Pappas		77	79	73	78	307
Total best 3		236	231	234	236	
*Mike Kyranis						
Bermuda	Grand Total	231	469	695		939
Scott Mayne		73	76	72	81	302
Anthony Mocklow		74	80	76	80	310
David Purcell		84	(85)	78	83	330
J.R. Robinson		(85)	82	(86)	(90)	343
Total best 3		231	238	226	244	
*Jack Wahl						

1988
SIXTEENTH WORLD AMATEUR TEAM CHAMPIONSHIP
FOR THE EISENHOWER TROPHY
Continued

*Team Captain		1st Round	2nd Round	3rd Round	4th Round	72-Hole Score
India	Grand Total	231	466	704		944
Amandeep Johl		79	78	78	(83)	318
Rajeev Mohta		75	79	80	78	312
C. Milkha Singh		77	78	80	81	316
*Lakshman Singh		(85)	(81)	(85)	81	332
Total best 3		231	235	238	240	
Netherlands	Grand Total	238	477	706		948
Eelco Bouma		83	(88)	(79)	76	326
Stephan Lovey		80	83	74	84	321
Constant Smits van Waesberghe		(84)	76	76	(87)	323
Joost Steenkamer		75	80	79	82	316
Total best 3		238	239	229	242	
*Robin Van Erven Dorens						
Norway	Grand Total	238	479	711		950
Tom Fredriksen		78	78	79	81	316
Thomas Nilsen		82	(84)	75	78	319
Oyvind Rojahn		(84)	81	78	(82)	325
Tore Christ. Sviland		78	82	(82)	80	322
Total best 3		238	241	232	239	
*Knut Sanne						
Italy	Grand Total	234	468	706		951
Mario Aragnetti		78	79	80	82	319
Marco de Rossi		(82)	(80)	80	80	322
Enrico Nistri		80	77	78	(83)	318
Marcello Santi		76	78	(81)	83	318
Total best 3		234	234	238	245	
*Piero Cora						
Pakistan	Grand Total	241	485	717		956
Taimur Hassan		78	78	74	79	309
Faisal Qureshi		88	85	79	82	334
Waqar Saigol		(89)	(86)	(82)	(90)	347
Mohammed Sajid		75	81	79	78	313
Total best 3		241	244	232	239	
*M.M. Hashim Khan						
Belgium	Grand Total	229	475	711		957
Christophe Bosmans		78	80	(82)	84	324
Christophe Descampe		75	77	79	75	306
Bruno Dupont		(85)	(89)	80	(88)	342
Alain Eaton		76	89	77	87	329
Total best 3		229	246	236	246	
*Philippe Relecom						
Austria	Grand Total	234	479	712		959
Max Baltl		77	(89)	81	80	327
Marcus Brier		79	76	77	81	313
Alexander Mueller		(81)	83	75	86	325
Andreas Pallauf		78	86	(85)	(89)	338
Total best 3		234	245	233	247	
*Lambert Stoltz						
Venezuela	Grand Total	235	481	716		960
Luis Soto		82	(97)	75	82	336
Carlos Larrain		74	77	78	78	307
Henrique Lavie		79	83	(90)	(85)	337
Emilio Miartus		(88)	86	82	84	340
Total best 3		235	246	235	244	
*Carlos Hellmund						
Colombia	Grand Total	233	481	722		962
Fabio Bernal		77	(87)	82	80	326
Alberto Evers		77	84	76	79	316
Gustavo Giraldo		79	84	(83)	81	327
Felipe Harker		(82)	80	83	(83)	328
Total best 3		233	248	241	240	
*Juan Gufierrez						
Hong Kong	Grand Total	239	489	725		965
Dominique Boulet		74	(86)	76	76	312
Ian Hindhaugh		(87)	86	79	(85)	337
Richard Kan		86	83	(82)	80	331
Tang Man Kee		79	81	81	84	325
Total best 3		239	250	236	240	
*Tony Clement-Brown						

1988
SIXTEENTH WORLD AMATEUR TEAM CHAMPIONSHIP FOR THE EISENHOWER TROPHY
Continued

Philippines	Grand Total	240	480	726		968
Cesar Ababa		77	80	85	85	327
Danilo Cabajar-Zarate		( )	81	84	78	
Nestor Plana		84	(87)	(87)	79	337
Carito Villaroman		79	79	77	(91)	326
Total best 3		240	240	246	242	
*Tony Clement-Brown						
Portugal	Grand Total	243	491	730		972
Daniel P. da Silva		80	83	77	76	316
Ricardo J. J. da Silva		(88)	82	(97)	83	350
Carlos M. A. dos Santos		80	(85)	79	(90)	334
Jose Oliveir Granja		83	83	83	83	332
Total best 3		243	248	239	242	
*Joao Mendonca						
Mexico	Grand Total	237	487	723		973
Jorge Guadiano		(90)	82	(83)	(89)	344
Roberto Lebrija		81	83	75	82	321
Federico Ortiz		80	(85)	80	80	325
Viviano Villarreal		76	85	81	88	330
Total best 3		237	250	236	250	
*Miguel Angel Ortiz						
Singapore	Grand Total	244	495	729		978
M. Balraj		82	85	76	81	324
Samson Gimson		79	79	79	83	320
Kevin Lee		(83)	(90)	79	85	337
Douglas Ooi		83	87	(86)	(93)	349
Total best 3		244	251	234	249	
*Gerald Loong						
Ivory Coast	Grand Total	253	495	747		994
Djoman Doudjon		87	(86)	87	78	338
Hyacinthe Gnabe		(89)	83	89	87	348
Marcel Soumahoro		82	79	76	82	319
Siaka Kone		84	80	(92)	(88)	344
Total best 3		253	242	252	247	
*Coulou Konan						
Czechoslovakia	Grand Total	254	513	753		1006
Jan Juhaniak		84	87	75	(95)	341
Petr Mruzek		85	85	(84)	84	338
Miroslav Nemec		(88)	87	82	83	340
Jiri Zavazal		85	(89)	83	86	343
Total best 3		254	259	240	253	
*Hanus Goldscheider						
Zimbabwe	Grand Total	254	506	756		1014
Terry Bowes		78	83	84	84	329
Ross Dennett		88	88	83	(91)	350
Gerald McLaughlin		(90)	(91)	(90)	87	358
Anderson Rusike		88	81	83	87	339
Total best 3		254	252	250	258	
*Richard Meech						
Costa Rica	Grand Total	251	503	758		1030
*Tomas Duenas		(112)	( )	( )	( )	
Manuel Jiminez		82	83	87	92	344
Charlie Perez		85	85	88	89	347
Jan Ruge		84	84	80	91	339
Total best 3		251	252	255	272	
El Salvador	Grand Total	281	574	852		1132
*Guillermo Aceto		(110)	(110)	102	98	420
Jorge Casaus		104	91	83	90	368
Victor Henriquez		86	99	93	92	370
Carlos Iraheta		91	103	(103)	(105)	402
Total best 3		281	293	278	280	
Iceland	Grand Total	244	249		DISQUALIFIED	
Hilmar Bjorgvinsson		81	(97)	(DQ)	(DQ)	
Bjorn Knutsson		(90)	81	(DQ)	(DQ)	
Sveinn Sigurbergsson		80	86	81	(DQ)	
Sigurdur Sigurdsson		83	82	87	(DQ)	
Total best 3						
*Johann Benediktsson						

1990
SEVENTEENTH WORLD AMATEUR TEAM CHAMPIONSHIP FOR THE EISENHOWER TROPHY

Christchurch Golf Club, Christchurch, New Zealand, October 25-28
Yardage—7,002. Par 72. 33 Team Entries.

*Team Captain

		1st Round	2nd Round	3rd Round	4th Round	72-Hole Score
Sweden	Grand Total	215	427	656		879
Mathias Gronberg		70	67	77	72	286
Gabriel Hjertstedt		73	71	74	74	292
Klas Eriksson		72	74	78	77	301
Per Nyman		(77)	(78)	(82)	(80)	317
Total best 3		215	212	229	223	
*Arne Anderson						
New Zealand	Grand Total	222	444	674		892
Michael Long		71	71	79	73	294
Brent Paterson		76	76	74	(75)	301
Steven Alker		75	(77)	77	73	302
Grant Moorhead		(76)	75	(82)	72	305
Total best 3		222	222	230	218	
*Roger Brennand						
United States	Grand Total	227	449	672		892
Phil Mickelson		(78)	78	72	71	299
David Duval		77	69	(77)	76	299
David Eger		74	(80)	75	73	302
Allen Doyle		76	75	76	(76)	303
Total best 3		227	222	223	220	
*William J. Williams, Jr.						
Canada	Grand Total	224	446	673		903
Doug Roxburgh		76	73	75	77	301
Warren Sye		73	(78)	76	77	304
Craig Marseilles		(79)	73	76	(78)	306
Jeff Cannon		75	76	(86)	76	313
Total best 3		224	222	227	230	
*Robert G. Long						
France	Grand Total	228	449	680		903
Oliver Edmond		75	72	74	75	296
Francois Illouz		77	(78)	78	72	305
Christian Cevaer		76	73	79	(79)	307
Christophe Pottier		(77)	76	(79)	76	308
Total best 3		228	221	231	223	
*Sven Boinet						
Japan	Grand Total	228	452	684		903
Shigeki Maruyama		72	75	75	72	294
Kiyotaka Oie		80	72	(81)	71	304
Yasunobu Kuramoto		76	(78)	80	76	310
Noriaki Kimura		(81)	77	77	(79)	314
Total best 3		228	224	232	219	
*Tetsuo Sakata						
Italy	Grand Total	227	458	688		906
Massimo Scarpa		76	76	76	70	298
Massimo Florioli		74	78	76	71	299
Marcello Santi		77	77	78	77	309
Enrico Nistri		(77)	(81)	(86)	(78)	322
Total best 3		227	231	230	218	
*Stefano Cimatti						
Australia	Grand Total	224	452	684		908
Robert Allenby		73	74	78	77	302
Chris Gray		73	78	79	73	303
Lester Petersen		(82)	76	75	(78)	311
John Wade		78	(78)	(84)	74	314
Total best 3		224	228	232	224	
*John Westacott						
Great Britain/Ireland	Grand Total	228	454	680		910
Jim Milligan		77	75	79	74	305
Ricky Willison		77	74	(79)	79	309
Andrew Coltart		(77)	(87)	73	77	314
Gary Evans		74	77	74	(93)	318
Total best 3		228	226	226	230	
*Geoffrey Marks						

1990
SEVENTEENTH WORLD AMATEUR TEAM CHAMPIONSHIP
FOR THE EISENHOWER TROPHY
Continued

*Team Captain

		1st Round	2nd Round	3rd Round	4th Round	72-Hole Score
Spain	Grand Total	234	462	692		911
Diego Borrego		78	74	74	(79)	305
Alfonso Vidaor		78	(79)	77	73	307
Tomas Munoz		(79)	78	79	72	308
Eduardo de la Riva		78	76	(82)	74	310
Total best 3		234	228	230	219	
*Santiago Fisas						
Argentina	Grand Total	222	441	674		915
Ronaldo Damm		73	73	74	(83)	303
Diego Ventureira		(78)	74	78	78	308
Fernando Chiesa		74	72	81	81	308
Martin Lonardi		75	(85)	(87)	82	329
Total best 3		222	219	233	241	
*Eduardo R. Lorenzutti						
Netherlands	Grand Total	228	452	692		920
Michael Vogel		75	73	76	77	301
Stephanie Lovey		76	73	80	73	302
Rolf Muntz		77	78	84	(79)	318
Rik Ruts		(85)	(79)	(88)	78	330
Total best 3		228	224	240	228	
*Robin Van Erven Dorens						
Denmark	Grand Total	240	411	703		924
Jakob Greisen		75	80	78	74	307
Henrik Simonsen		80	76	79	72	307
Jan Andersen		85	75	75	75	310
Bjorn Norgaard		(86)	(81)	(81)	(78)	326
Total best 3		240	231	232	221	
*Helge Ejrnaes						
Germany	Grand Total	241	460	697		924
Jan Schapmann		78	73	77	75	303
Ekkehart Schieffer		81	73	(87)	74	315
Hans-Gunter Reiter		82	(77)	78	78	315
Rainer Mund		(87)	73	82	(81)	323
Total best 3		241	219	237	227	
*Kai Flint						
Norway	Grand Total	231	452	692		924
Oyvind Rojahn		78	74	80	74	306
Thomas Neilsen		75	71	78	(83)	307
Knut Ekjord		78	76	(85)	77	316
Bjorn Hage		(82)	(78)	82	81	323
Total best 3		231	221	240	232	
*Chris Selbekk						
Finland	Grand Total	236	460	694		925
Erkki Valimaa		74	74	80	73	301
Anssi Kankkonen		79	74	80	82	315
Juha Selin		83	76	74	(83)	316
Petri Pulkkinen		(84)	(81)	(89)	76	330
Total best 3		236	224	234	231	
*Lassi Tilander						
Korea	Grand Total	222	455	694		927
Joo Hwan Ahn		74	79	79	76	308
Ik Je Chang		(79)	77	76	78	310
Jin Kun Oh		74	77	(86)	79	316
Hye Sik Min		74	(85)	84	(79)	322
Total best 3		222	233	239	233	
*Duk Mo Kim						
Switzerland	Grand Total	227	463	702		928
Thomas Gottstein		77	(81)	80	72	310
Kouroche Achtari		75	79	79	79	312
Markus Frank		75	77	(81)	(81)	314
Christophe Bovet		(87)	80	80	75	322
Total best 3		227	236	239	226	
*Martin Kessler						

1990
SEVENTEENTH WORLD AMATEUR TEAM CHAMPIONSHIP
FOR THE EISENHOWER TROPHY
Continued

*Team Captain

		1st Round	2nd Round	3rd Round	4th Round	72-Hole Score
Mexico	Grand Total	236	468	705		936
Roberto Lebrija		72	73	78	75	298
Federico Ortiz		82	82	75	77	316
Alejandro Munoz		(84)	77	(87)	79	327
Miguel Quijano		82	(84)	84	(83)	333
Total best 3		236	232	237	231	
*Tomas Lehman						
Malaysia	Grand Total	234	466	707		939
Wong Hung Nung		(80)	76	79	76	311
P. Gunasagaran		77	(82)	78	78	315
John Eu		79	75	84	78	316
Saad Yusuf		78	81	(85)	(78)	322
Total best 3		234	232	241	232	
*David M.H. Lee						
Philippines	Grand Total	231	466	700		939
Francis Gaston		78	73	77	(82)	310
Danilo Cabajar		74	78	(81)	81	314
Vince Lauron		79	84	78	81	322
Felix Casas		(80)	(87)	79	77	323
Total best 3		231	235	234	239	
*Rodolfo H. Samson						
Austria	Grand Total	237	479	710		940
Fritz Poppmeier		81	80	73	76	310
Alexander Peterskovsky		75	84	78	75	312
Markus Brier		81	78	80	79	318
Rudi Sailer		(85)	(85)	(80)	(79)	329
Total best 3		237	242	231	230	
*Lambert Stolz						
Belgium	Grand Total	238	470	710		943
Amaury D'Ogimont		78	78	79	77	312
Christophe Bosmans		77	76	(86)	80	319
Emanuel Janssens		83	78	85	76	322
Dany Vanbegin		(83)	(85)	76	(82)	326
Total best 3		238	232	240	233	
*Roger Rabaey						
Hong Kong	Grand Total	235	468	711		944
Scott Rowe		81	76	80	76	313
Ian Hindhaugh		75	75	(83)	(84)	317
David Tonroe		79	(85)	82	78	324
Derek Fung		(82)	82	81	79	324
Total best 3		235	233	243	233	
*Dr. Brian Choa						
China	Grand Total	238	477	722		957
Wei-tze Yeh		73	77	82	78	310
Tse-peng Chang		82	78	81	77	318
Chi-huang Tsai		83	84	82	(81)	330
Tze-lang Huang		(85)	(84)	(84)	80	333
Total best 3		238	239	245	235	
*Ching-ming Ho						
Singapore	Grand Total	241	484	723		958
Dino Kwek		80	81	77	79	317
John Pang		80	(88)	76	79	323
Kevin Lee		81	79	86	(79)	325
Douglas Ooi		(82)	83	(86)	77	328
Total best 3		241	243	239	235	
*Douglas Ooi						
Bermuda	Grand Total	242	489	725		960
Scott Mayne		75	83	78	77	313
Robert Vallis		(88)	83	76	75	322
Jack Wahl		84	81	82	83	330
Dave Purcell		83	(84)	(87)	(88)	332
Total best 3		242	247	236	235	
*Brendan J. Ingham						

1990
SEVENTEENTH WORLD AMATEUR TEAM CHAMPIONSHIP
FOR THE EISENHOWER TROPHY
Continued

*Team Captain

		1st Round	2nd Round	3rd Round	4th Round	72-Hole Score
Ivory Coast	Grand Total	240	479	723		962
Marcel Soumahoro		76	81	77	75	309
Bertin Djedji		80	77	86	81	324
Siaka Kone		84	81	81	83	329
Alain Danho		(84)	(82)	(87)	(88)	341
Total best 3		240	239	244	239	
*Konan Coulou						
Brazil	Grand Total	245	481	720		966
Aldo Wolf		NR	NR	NR	NR	par
Rafael Gonzalez		85	79	78	76	318
Patrick Caussin		77	74	83	86	320
Wagner Rocumback		83	83	78	84	328
Total best 3		245	236	239	246	
*Patrick Caussin						
Zimbabwe	Grand Total	239	487	728		969
Craig Singleton		77	80	76	77	310
Anderson Rusike		80	84	(86)	82	332
Ross Dennett		82	84	84	82	332
Michael Dardagan		(82)	(86)	81	(86)	335
Total best 3		239	248	241	241	
*Paddy Francomb						
Fiji	Grand Total	246	497	756		999
Mahmood Buksh		83	86	81	80	330
Indra Warjan		83	83	89	79	334
Dharam Prakash		80	82	89	84	335
Jale Raman		(85)	(88)	(94)	(93)	360
Total best 3		246	251	259	243	
*Reg J. Woodman						
Puerto Rico	Grand Total	253	509	783		1031
Elvin Gonzales		80	90	88	80	338
Luis Juncos		85	(90)	90	79	344
Elvin Cordova		88	80	96	89	353
Andres Subira		(95)	86	(100)	(91)	372
Total best 3		253	256	274	248	
*Tito Santiago						
Guatemala	Grand Total	263	526	786		1055
Oscar Castillo		82	83	84	84	333
Gerardo Berger		83	91	(100)	91	365
Francisco Escobar		(99)	89	85	94	367
Rolando Vasquez		98	(107)	91	(97)	393
Total best 3		263	263	260	269	
*Arturo Herrera						

WOMEN'S WORLD AMATEUR TEAM CHAMPIONSHIP

THE ESPIRITO SANTO TROPHY

Presented in October 1964
by Mrs. Espirito Santo Silva of Portugal

HISTORY

1982—The United States set one record and tied another as it retained the Espirito Santo Trophy for the Women's World Amateur Team Championship, at the Geneva Golf Club, in Geneva, Switzerland. It was the eighth American victory in 10 events. The United States led every round in winning by 17 strokes, tying the largest margin of victory, set by the United States in 1976. The United States also set a record team score of 579 for the four days of competition, breaking the long-standing record of 580, set by the United States in 1966. Juli Inkster and Kathy Baker combined to give the United States a first-round total of 148, on scores of 73 and 75, respectively. It gave them a five-stroke lead over Switzerland, with 153. Spain was third, with 154. The next day, Miss Baker and Amy Benz shot 72s, giving the United States 144 for the day and 292 for the two rounds. Sweden moved into second place with 297. Great Britain and Ireland was third at 299. Tied for fourth at 300 were Switzerland and Spain. The third round ended with the United States once again leading by five strokes. Mrs. Inkster came in with 71 and Miss Benz with 75, for 146 and a 54-hole total of 438 against 443 for Great Britain and Ireland. The United States had its best showing in the final round. Mrs. Inkster shot 70 and Miss Baker added a 71 for a daily score of 141 and a four-day record of 579. New Zealand moved into second place with a final round of 143 behind 70 by Liz Douglas and 73 by Janice Arnold. It gave New Zealand a 72-hole score of 596. Great Britain and Ireland fell into third place with 598. While no official recognition is given to individual performances, it should be noted that Mrs. Inkster had rounds of 73-76-71-70—290 for the lowest 72-hole total. The Captain of the United States Team was Mrs. DeWitt L. Alexandre, of Far Hills, New Jersey, a past Chairman of the USGA Women's Committee. The Championship drew 26 team entries, only two fewer than played in the 1980 competition at Pinehurst, North Carolina.

1984—The United States led all four rounds and retained the Espirito Santo Trophy at the Royal Hong Kong Golf Club, in Fanling, Hong Kong. The United States won by 12 strokes with a four-round total of 585. France was second, at 597, and Great Britain and Ireland third, at 600. Heather Farr and Jody Rosenthal combined to give the United States a first-round score of 145 and a two-stroke advantage over Spain, with Miss Farr scoring 72 and Miss Rosenthal 73. The next day Deb Richard scored 75 and Miss Rosenthal added a 78 for 153, giving the United States a three-stroke advantage over Spain, with 301. Miss Richard then scored 70 and Miss Rosenthal 71 on the third day to give the United States a round of 141, five-under par, and an 11-stroke advantage over France. With Miss Farr scoring a 71 and Miss Richard adding 75, the United States added an additional stroke to its lead at the end of four rounds. While no official recognition is given to individual performance, it should be noted that Miss Richard was the low individual, at 295, on rounds of 75-75-70-75. Miss Farr was a stroke behind, at 72-80-73-71—296, and Miss Rosenthal was third at 73-78-71-76—298, a total matched by Great Britain and Ireland's Claire Waite, who returned 72-78-73-75. Valerie Pamard had France's low individual score, with 300, on rounds of 76-73-76-75. Miss Richard and Janice Arnold, of New Zealand, shared the low round for the competition; each shot 70 in the third round. The Captain of the United States team was Mrs. Dorothy Porter, the 1949 Women's Amateur Champion and four times the Senior Women's Amateur Champion. The Championship drew 22 team entries.

1986—Spain, on the strength of a third-round 139, five under par, won its first Women's World Amateur Team Championship at Lagunita Country Club in Caracas, Venezuela. Spain became the third country other than the United States to win the championship. The U.S. has won the championship nine times. France, Australia and now Spain each have won one championship. Great Britain and Ireland, which had won the Curtis Cup earlier in the year, took a four-stroke lead after the first round. Jill Thornhill shot 71 and Patricia Johnson shot 72 for a 143 total. Trailing in second place was Australia with France, Japan, Spain and Switzerland tied for third, five strokes behind GB&I. The United States shot 151 with Leslie Shannon posting a 74 and Kay Cockerill, a 77. Valerie Pamard shot 70 and Marie de Lorenzi-Taya added a 72 to give France a one-stroke lead after the second round. Great Britain and Ireland shot 148 and fell into second place. Japan was three strokes off the lead in third place. Spain was fourth four strokes back. The U.S., on the strength of Cockerill's 70, moved into fifth place, six strokes off the lead. Maria Orueta (69) and Macarena Campomanes (70) led Spain's move to the lead in the third round. The team score of 139 was the best of the week for any team and moved Spain two strokes ahead of France. Great Britain and Ireland was third, four strokes back. The United States, with rounds of 72 from Shannon and Cockerill, remained in fifth place. Campomanes shot 72 to open the fourth round for Spain, but Mary Navarro had to settle for 75, giving Spain a total of 580. De Lorenzi-Taya shot 68, the best ever in the fourth round, to give France a shot at the lead, but neither Cecilia Mourgue d'Algue nor Valerie Pamard were able to break 80, and the French had to settle for second place. The United States posted the best team score of the day at 144 and took third place at 584. De Lorenzi-Taya recorded the lowest individual score of the championship with a four-under-par 284. Cockerill recovered from her opening-round 77 to finish at 293. A record 29 teams competed in the championship, one more than competed in 1980 at Pinehurst (North Carolina) Country Club.

1988—The United States withstood a late rally by host Sweden and won the 13th Women's World Amateur Team Championship at Drottningholm Country Club in Stockholm. It was the 10th win for the United States in the series. France, Australia and Spain have each won the championship once. Sweden took a one-stroke lead after the first round. Eva Dahllof shot two-under-par 71 and Helen Alfreddson and Helene Albertsson each shot 75 for a 146 total. A 71 by Carol Semple Thompson and 76 by Pearl Sinn left the United States one stroke behind at 147, tied with Italy which was led by Stefania Croce's 71. Great Britain and Ireland were in fourth place, three strokes behind Sweden. Sinn posted a second-round 71 and Anne Sander shot even-par 73 to lift the United States into the lead after 36 holes. The U.S. total of 291 led Sweden by one stroke. Alfredsson and Andersson each shot second-round 73s for Sweden. Italy, thanks to an even-par 73 by Croce, was in third place at 300. Great Britain and Ireland, Switzerland and West Germany were tied for fourth at 304. The United States extended its lead to six strokes after the third round. Sinn led the U.S. with a 73; Thompson added a 75, giving the U.S. a three-round total of 439. Sweden's third round 153 left it just one stroke ahead of third-place Italy. The Italians again were led by Croce, whose 71 was the best round of the day. Great Britain remained in fourth place, 13 strokes off the lead. Sweden took a run at the United States in the fourth round. Thompson's 72 and Sinn's 76 on the final day gave the United States a total of 587. Dahllof shot a final-round 68, but 75s by Alfredsson and Andersson left Sweden at 588, one stroke out of the lead. Great Britain, led by Linda Bayman's 73, moved into third place at 600. Italy, Switzerland and Japan tied for fourth at 603. Japan's Michiko Hattori shot 67 in the fourth round, the lowest round in the championship's history. Thompson and Croce finished tied for low individual in the championship at one-over-par 293. Dahllof, Hattori, Evelyn Orley of Switzerland and Martina Koch of West Germany posted 295 totals. Teams representing 27 countries competed in the championship.

1990—The United States led every round and won its 11th Women's Championship, with a score of 585 at the Russley Golf Club, in Christchurch, New Zealand. The Americans won by 12 strokes over New Zealand, with 597. Great Britain and Ireland placed third, with 605. The Americans opened with 148, behind 74s by both Vicki Goetze, who one-putted seven of the first 13 greens, and Pat Hurst, the respective 1989 and 1990 U.S. Women's Amateur Champions. They led by two strokes over Denmark and Germany after 18 holes, by eight strokes over Great Britain and Ireland after 36, and by seven over New Zealand after 54, before pulling away in the last round. With Miss Hurst shooting 71 and Karen Noble 72, the United States shot a team total of 143, the best of the day by three strokes, and a 36-hole score of 291, eight strokes better than the 299 of Great Britain, built around a second round score of 146 behind 72 by Claire Hourihane and 74 by Vicki Thomas. A 74 by Miss Goetze and 79 by Miss Noble cost the United States one stroke of its lead in the third round, but by then New Zealand had climbed into second place. Jan Higgins had shot rounds of 74, 72, and 74 and led the New Zealand climb. The United States simply overpowered the field in the last round. Both Miss Goetze and Miss Hurst birdied the first two holes, and when New Zealand posted two bogeys, the United States had pulled ahead by 11 strokes. Vicki Goetze finished the round with 67, six strokes under Russley's par of 73, and Miss Hurst added 74, giving the United States 141 for the day, the best team score of the competition (Japan also shot 141 behind 70 by Aki Takamura and 71 by Michiko Hattori). With Annette Stott shooting 74 and 18-year-old Lisa Aldridge 72, New Zealand had 146 for the day, dropping five strokes to the United States. Miss Goetze, who had turned 18 during the championship, shot 291 for the 72 holes, matching Miss Higgins, of New Zealand. Although no official recognition is given individual scores, since this is a team competition, their performances merit mention nevertheless.

Year	Team	Score	Site
1982	United States	579	Geneva G.C.,
	New Zealand	596	Geneva, Switzerland
	Gr. Britain-Ireland	598	
1984	United States	585	Royal Hong Kong G.C.,
	France	597	Fanling, Hong Kong
	Gr. Britain-Ireland	600	
1986	Spain	580	Lagunita C.C.,
	France	583	Caracas, Venezuela
	United States	584	
1988	United States	587	Drottningholm G.C.,
	Sweden	588	Stockholm, Sweden
	Gr. Britain-Ireland	600	
1990	United States	585	Russley G.C.,
	New Zealand	597	Christchurch,
	Gr. Britain-Ireland	605	New Zealand

1982
TENTH WOMEN'S WORLD AMATEUR TEAM CHAMPIONSHIP FOR THE ESPIRITO SANTO TROPHY

Geneva Golf Club, Geneva, Switzerland, September 8-11.
Yardage — 6,070. Par 72. 26 Team Entries.

*Team Captain		1st Round	2nd Round	3rd Round	4th Round	72-Hole Score
United States	Grand Total	148	292	438		579
Kathy Baker		75	72	77	71	295
Amy Benz		79	72	75	74	300
Juli Inkster		73	76	71	70	290
Total best 2		148	144	146	141	
*Mrs. DeWitt Alexandre						
New Zealand	Grand Total	155	304	453		596
Janice Arnold		77	77	74	73	301
Liz Douglas		82	72	75	70	299
Brenda Rhodes		78	80	75	77	310
Total best 2		155	149	149	143	
*A. C. Fraser						
Great Britain & Ireland	Grand Total	155	299	443		598
Jane Connachan		78	70	72	81	301
Belle Robertson		77	74	72	75	298
Gillian Stewart		80	77	77	80	314
Total best 2		155	144	144	155	
*Ann Irvin						
Sweden	Grand Total	156	297	449		600
Hillewi Hagstrom		79	71	81	78	309
Liselotte Neumann		79	70	79	78	306
Liv Wollin		77	75	73	73	298
Total best 2		156	141	152	151	
*Barbro Montgomery						
Switzerland	Grand Total	153	300	450		601
Marie-Christine De Werra		82	75	78	73	308
Régine Lautens		77	72	72	78	299
Priscilla Staible		76	78	81	81	311
Total best 2		153	147	150	151	
*Monica Wieland						
Spain	Grand Total	154	300	447		601
Marta Figueras-Dotti		73	74	73	74	294
Cristina Marsans		—	77	75	83	235
Carmen Maestre		81	72	74	80	307
Total best 2		154	146	147	154	
*Emma Villacieros						
France	Grand Total	156	301	452		602
Eliane Berthet		78	74	74	81	307
Marie-Laure De Lorenzi-Taya		78	71	78	75	302
Cécilia Morgue D'Algue		84	83	77	75	319
Total best 2		156	145	151	150	
*Odile Semelaigne						
Brazil	Grand Total	158	313	462		613
Maria Alicia Gonzales		79	80	84	78	321
Isabelle Lopes		83	77	74	76	310
Betty Nickhorn		79	78	75	75	307
Total best 2		158	155	149	151	
*Yolanda Figueiredo						
Republic of China	Grand Total	160	312	465		614
Chen Li-Ying		79	83	75	72	309
Cheng Mei-Chi		81	75	78	77	311
Chen Yueh-Ying		84	77	78	79	318
Total best 2		160	152	153	149	
*Pearl C.G.						
Italy	Grand Total	158	316	465		616
Emanuela Braito		84	84	74	85	327
Marina Buscani		83	77	75	75	310
Federica Dassu		75	81	75	76	307
Total best 2		158	158	149	151	
*Lunella Rivetti						

1982
TENTH WOMEN'S WORLD AMATEUR TEAM CHAMPIONSHIP FOR THE ESPIRITO SANTO TROPHY
Continued

		1st Round	2nd Round	3rd Round	4th Round	72-Hole Score
Japan	Grand Total	156	311	464		618
Hiromi Kobayashi		79	80	84	78	321
Toshie Matsubara		77	75	77	81	310
Kimiko Yoshizawa		79	80	76	76	311
Total best 2		156	155	153	154	
*Shoko Masuda						
Denmark	Grand Total	165	317	470		623
*Merette Meiland		82	79	77	77	315
Lisa Eliasen		83	78	80	77	318
Anette Petersen		87	74	76	76	313
Total best 2		165	152	153	153	
Belgium	Grand Total	164	315	471		627
Francoise Bonnelance		81	77	78	80	316
Isabelle Declercq		86	74	78	78	316
Aline Van Der Haegen		83	83	81	78	325
Total best 2		164	151	156	156	
*Louise van den Bergue						
South Africa	Grand Total	163	321	475		638
Rae Hast		80	78	75	76	309
Laurette Maritz		85	81	79	83	328
Sheree Muirhead		83	80	81	77	321
Total best 2		163	158	154	153	
*Daniel Faith						
Netherlands	Grand Total	165	320	478		630
Alice Janmaat		83	78	77	75	313
Lisebeth Koopman		82	83	81	77	323
Marischka Zegger		83	77	82	79	321
Total best 2		165	155	158	152	
*Anneke Tuyt						
Germany	Grand Total	165	322	484		639
Susana Knodler		85	79	81	79	324
Elizabeth Peter		83	86	83	76	328
Ines Umsen		82	78	81	79	320
Total best 2		165	157	162	155	
*Dr. Barbara Rosner						
Argentina	Grand Total	161	320	477		639
Amanda De Felizia		83	89	78	84	334
Susana B. Garmendia		78	80	79	82	319
Maria E. Noguerol		84	79	81	80	324
Total best 2		161	159	157	162	
*Ivar Brostrom						
Norway	Grand Total	165	329	482		641
Reidun Dirdal		87	82	81	85	335
Ana Doennestad		84	83	72	74	313
Cathrine Schroeder		81	82	81	85	329
Total best 2		165	164	153	159	
*Elsa Gioertz						
Mexico	Grand Total	169	325	488		646
Liz Chahin		87	78	82	79	326
Carolina Fernandez		93	82	92	85	352
Adriana Ramirez		82	78	81	79	320
Total best 2		169	156	163	158	
*Nancy Besquin						
Chile	Grand Total	172	330	490		659
Marita Barrillas		86	81	85	83	335
Andrea Boettiger		86	85	83	86	340
Ana Maria Cambiaso		89	77	77	88	331
Total best 2		172	158	160	169	
*Gabriela Gacitua						

1982
TENTH WOMEN'S WORLD AMATEUR TEAM CHAMPIONSHIP
FOR THE ESPIRITO SANTO TROPHY
Continued

		1st Round	2nd Round	3rd Round	4th Round	72-Hole Score
Austria	Grand Total	161	336	497		668
Doris Derntl		82	88	81	88	339
Martina Franz		79	88	80	83	330
Alexandra Kotschwar		88	87	88	91	354
Total best 2		161	175	161	171	
*Monica Stolz						
Bermuda	Grand Total	180	357	528		698
*Ginette Spinucci		90	91	91	92	364
Judithanne Astwood		90	86	83	82	341
Nathalie Davis		98	99	88	96	381
Total best 2		180	177	171	174	
Finland	Grand Total	175	349	524		698
Varpu Hakulinen		92	96	89	92	369
Arja Sipronen		83	87	86	82	338
Pirjo Sipronen		97	87	93	96	373
Total best 2		175	174	175	174	
*Marja Hasila						
Indonesia	Grand Total	181	349	522		698
Ida Makasutji		91	88	88	94	361
Wani Tobing		91	84	86	94	355
Rien Tobing		90	84	87	82	343
Total best 2		181	168	173	176	
*Ciska Piay						
Iceland	Grand Total	184	374	560		744
Johanna Ingolfsdottir		98	96	90	92	376
Thordis Geirsdottir		91	100	109	87	Disq
Asgedur Sverrisdottir		93	94	96	92	375
Total best 2		184	190	186	184	
*Kristin Palsdottir						
Portugal	Grand Total	182	352	535		
Teresa Matta		97	90	97	88	372
Graca Medina		85	80	86	95	Disq.
Total best 2		182	170	183		
*Leonor Matta						

1984
ELEVENTH WOMEN'S WORLD AMATEUR TEAM CHAMPIONSHIP FOR THE ESPIRITO SANTO TROPHY

Royal Hong Kong Golf Club, Fanling, Hong Kong, October 30-November 2.
Yardage—5,983. Par 73. 22 Team Entries.

*Team Captain		1st Round	2nd Round	3rd Round	4th Round	72-Hole Score
United States	Grand Total	145	298	439		585
Heather Farr		72	80	73	71	296
Debra Richard		75	75	70	75	295
Jody Rosenthal		73	78	71	76	298
Total best 2		145	153	141	146	
*Dorothy Porter						
France	Grand Total	153	301	450		597
*Cécilia Mourgue D'Algue		82	79	73	72	306
Corine Soules		77	75	79	76	307
Valérie Pamard		76	73	76	75	300
Total best 2		153	148	149	147	
Great Britain & Ireland	Grand Total	149	304	453		600
Penny Grice		77	77	76	73	303
Gillian Stewart		80	81	77	74	312
Claire Waite		72	78	73	75	298
Total best 2		149	155	149	147	
*Jill Thornhill						
Japan	Grand Total	151	303	457		607
Yoshiko Ito		76	78	79	78	311
Michiko Hattori		81	74	77	74	306
Yoshie Takahashi		75	79	77	76	307
Total best 2		151	152	154	150	
*Hisae Ozeki						
Brazil	Grand Total	155	306	459		610
Elizabeth Nickhorn		75	75	75	75	300
Isabel Lopes		85	76	82	79	322
Maria Gonzales		80	81	78	76	315
Total best 2		155	151	153	151	
*Dora Nardy						
Spain	Grand Total	147	301	463		612
Carmen Maestre		80	80	81	79	320
Maria Orieta		74	76	82	76	320
Mary Navarro		73	78	81	73	305
Total best 2		147	154	162	149	
*Emma de Garcia-Ogaro						
Sweden	Grand Total	152	313	461		614
Viveca Hoff		74	82	78	80	314
Liselotte Neumann		78	85	71	79	313
Ann Oxenstierna		78	79	77	74	308
Total best 2		152	161	148	153	
*Barbro Montgomery						
Germany	Grand Total	156	310	468		617
Ursula Beer		81	78	80	78	317
Martina Koch		76	76	84	71	307
Stephanie Lampert		80	80	78	78	316
Total best 2		156	154	158	149	
*Barbara Rosner						
New Zealand	Grand Total	161	317	463		617
Janice Arnold		82	82	70	76	310
Brenda Ormsby		81	78	77	78	314
Debbie Smith		80	78	76	79	313
Total best 2		161	156	146	154	
*Barbara Nichol						
Australia	Grand Total	154	306	463		617
Louise Briers		78	76	80	76	310
Edwina Kennedy		76	82	88	91	337
Sandra McCaw		79	76	77	78	310
Total best 2		154	152	157	154	
*Pauline Sanderson						
Denmark	Grand Total	152	306	465		619
Anette Peitersen		78	79	83	77	317
Tina Pors		81	80	80	77	318
Lotta Schmidt		74	75	79	77	305
Total best 2		152	154	159	154	
*Helge Ejrnaes						

1984
ELEVENTH WOMEN'S WORLD AMATEUR TEAM CHAMPIONSHIP FOR THE ESPIRITO SANTO TROPHY
Continued

		1st Round	2nd Round	3rd Round	4th Round	72-Hole Score
Italy	Grand Total	157	311	473		620
Emanuella Braito		81	78	81	78	318
Marina Buscaini		78	76	81	75	310
Elena Girardi		79	81	83	72	315
Total best 2		157	154	162	147	
*Lunella Rivetti						
Switzerland	Grand Total	159	313	470		623
Regine Lautens		77	76	78	77	308
Eveline Orley		82	78	80	76	316
Jackie Orley		84	85	79	79	327
Total best 2		159	154	157	153	
*Claudia Rorholt						
Canada	Grand Total	157	310	468		627
*Marlene Streit		81	77	82	78	318
Patty Grant		77	76	76	81	310
Ann Lavis		80	84	82	83	329
Total best 2		157	153	158	159	
Venezuela	Grand Total	153	320	476		634
Maria Larrazabal		84	83	82	86	335
Yubiri Cortez		80	88	87	83	338
Graciela Quintana		73	84	74	75	306
Total best 2		153	167	156	158	
*Jesus Acosta						
Belgium	Grand Total	159	323	477		639
Aline van der Haegen		77	79	77	78	311
Agathe Verlegh		82	85	77	84	328
Jean-Louise Philippart de Foy		86	90	85	85	346
Total best 2		159	164	154	162	
*Louise van den Berghe						
Netherlands	Grand Total	161	323	487		649
Alice Janmaat		83	77	82	77	319
Marjan de Boer		82	88	85	85	337
Marischka Zegger		79	85	84	85	333
Total best 2		161	162	164	162	
*Nora Pont						
Thailand	Grand Total	168	333	495		655
Napasri Buranasiri		86	88	83	86	343
Prasertsri Krupanich		89	91	82	83	345
Rika Dila		82	77	80	77	316
Total best 2		168	165	162	160	
*Mayuree Kridakara Na Ayudhaya						
Norway	Grand Total	169	338	504		669
*Cathrine Schrøder		86	83	83	87	339
Elin Malde		83	86	83	78	330
Jannicke Nielsen		86	88	86	88	348
Total best 2		169	169	166	165	
Hong Kong	Grand Total	163	336	513		674
Greta Hobbs		87	89	89	82	347
Peggy Kwoh		76	87	88	80	331
Nanette Mann		90	86	89	81	346
Total best 2		163	173	177	161	
*Betty Hindhaugh						
Indonesia	Grand Total	178	347	515		684
Bas Tobing		93	85	83	83	344
Rien Tobing		88	84	85	88	345
Widjil Purnomo		90	92	90	86	358
Total best 2		178	169	168	169	
*Ciska Piay						
Singapore	Grand Total	174	344	515		684
*Jeannette Sim		101	105	94	100	400
Rosie Goh		87	85	93	86	351
Kee Bee Khim		87	85	78	83	333
Total best 2		174	170	171	169	

1986
TWELFTH WOMEN'S WORLD AMATEUR TEAM CHAMPIONSHIP FOR THE ESPIRITO SANTO TROPHY

Held at Lagunita Country Club, Caracas, Venezuela, October 14-17.
Yardage—6,007. Par 72. 27 Team Entries.

*Team Captain		1st Round	2nd Round	3rd Round	4th Round	72-Hole Score
Spain	Grand Total		294	433		580
Macarena Campomanes		76	74	70	72	292
Mary Carmen Navarro		73	78	73	75	299
Maria Orueta		75	72	69	83	299
Total best 2		148	146	139	147	
*Emma De Garcia Ogara						
France	Grand Total		290	435		583
Maria-Laure de Lorenzi Taya		72	72	72	68	284
*Cecilia Mourgue d'Algue		82	75	74	80	311
Valerie Pamard		76	70	73	82	301
Total best 2		148	142	145	148	
United States	Grand Total		296	440		584
Kay D. Cockerill		81	70	72	70	293
Kathleen McCarthy		77	81	76	79	313
Leslie Shannon		74	75	72	74	295
Total best 2		151	145	144	144	
*Mrs. E. Smith Jackson						
Great Britain & Ireland	Grand Total		291	437		585
Claire Hourihane		73	75	79	77	304
Patricia Johnson		72	73	74	72	291
Jill Thornhill		71	77	72	76	296
Total best 2		143	148	146	148	
*Mary McKenna						
Japan	Grand Total		293	438		586
Aiko Hashimoto		76	75	74	76	301
Michiko Hattori		75	70	71	72	288
Hiromi Kobayashi		73	75	81	79	308
Total best 2		148	145	145	148	
*Hisae Ozeki						
Venezuela	Grand Total		300	450		599
Yubiri Cortez		80	77	76	77	310
Maria Eugenia Larrazabal		74	79	83	75	311
Graciela Quintana		77	72	74	74	297
Total best 2		151	149	150	149	
*Felix Martinez						
Sweden	Grand Total		301	448		600
Helen Alfredsson		79	78	73	77	307
Eva Dahllof		73	76	75	75	299
Sofia Gronberg		79	73	74	78	304
Total best 2		152	149	147	152	
*Barbro Montgomery						
Switzerland	Grand Total		305	457		603
Regine Lautens		72	77	73	69	291
Evelyn Orley		76	80	79	77	312
Jackie Orley		80	86	82	82	338
Total best 2		148	157	152	146	
*Claudia Rorholt						
Germany	Grand Total		312	461		608
Susanne Knoedler		80	80	81	75	316
Martina Koch		74	82	71	74	301
Stephanie Lampert		78	80	78	73	309
Total best 2		152	160	149	147	
*Barbara Rosner						
Australia	Grand Total		304	458		610
Louise M. Briers		76	80	77	78	311
Edwina E. Kennedy		80	77	80	76	313
Sandra McCaw		71	80	77	76	304
Total best 2		147	157	154	152	
*P.E. Sanderson						
China	Grand Total		305	456		610
Yeh Wei-Fing		73	76	76	74	299
Li Wen-Lin		81	77	75	82	315
Chen Yueh-Shuang		80	76	81	80	317
Total best 2		153	152	151	154	
*Lu Chang Shu-Wo						

1986
TWELFTH WOMEN'S WORLD AMATEUR TEAM CHAMPIONSHIP
FOR THE ESPIRITO SANTO TROPHY
Continued

		1st Round	2nd Round	3rd Round	4th Round	72-Hole Score
Denmark	Grand Total		309	461		611
Merete Meiland		78	82	76	76	312
Annika Ostberg		75	77	76	74	302
Anette Peitersen		78	79	77	80	314
Total best 2		153	156	152	150	
*Lise Juul						
Peru	Grand Total		306	454		613
Marisa Alzamora		78	82	79	83	322
Alicia Dibos		72	74	74	76	296
Maria Julia Raffo		85	84	74	85	328
Total best 2		150	156	148	159	
*Maria Arias						
New Zealand	Grand Total		317	467		617
Karrien Duckworth		83	80	77	78	318
Marnie McGuire		85	79	75	78	317
Brenda Ormsby		81	74	75	72	302
Total best 2		164	153	150	150	
*M. Sargent						
Italy	Grand Total		308	469		623
Emanuela Braito Minetti		84	79	85	80	328
Stefania Croce		73	76	76	75	300
Stefania Scarpa		80	82	85	79	326
Total best 2		153	155	161	154	
*Laura Benazzo						
Brazil	Grand Total		309	463		623
Maria Alice Gonzalez		81	73	79	80	313
Elizabeth Nickhorn		78	77	75	80	310
Cristina Schmitt		82	84	79	80	325
Total best 2		159	150	154	160	
*Dora Nardy						
Belgium	Grand Total		313	466		624
Isabelle Declercq		81	77	77	82	317
Aline Van Der Haegen		84	76	76	84	320
Agathe Verlegh		81	75	79	76	311
Total best 2		162	151	153	158	
*Louise van den Berghe						
Canada	Grand Total		317	474		629
Gail Anderson		77	78	80	75	310
Judy Medlicott		82	86	77	80	325
Marilyn O'Conner		81	81	80	86	328
Total best 2		158	159	157	155	
*Ahlin Walker						
Mexico	Grand Total		320	478		630
Carolina Fernandez		83	75	83	75	316
Ana Luisa Hernandez		86	84	85	78	333
Adriana Ramirez		84	78	75	77	314
Total best 2		167	153	158	152	
*Elena Llanes						
Argentina	Grand Total		316	477		636
Maria Marta Abramoff		83	83	81	80	327
Maria Eugenia Noguerol		79	81	86	81	327
Nora Ventureira		78	78	80	79	315
Total best 2		157	159	161	159	
*Ivar Brostrom						
Colombia	Grand Total		317	469		636
Susie Faccini		76	79	75	83	313
Adriana Gomez		78	84	78	84	324
Claudia Penuela		79	85	77	84	325
Total best 2		154	163	152	167	
*Lucia De Gomez						
Austria	Grand Total		333	488		645
Alexandra Kotschwar		90	89	85	87	351
Daniela Rauch		86	77	78	82	323
Ike Wieser		87	83	77	75	322
Total best 2		173	160	155	157	
*Mrs. Waltraud Neuwirth						

1986
TWELFTH WOMEN'S WORLD AMATEUR TEAM CHAMPIONSHIP
FOR THE ESPIRITO SANTO TROPHY
Continued

		1st Round	2nd Round	3rd Round	4th Round	72-Hole Score
Hong Kong	Grand Total		336	496		658
Fiona E. Cameron		90	87	89	88	354
Nan Croockewet		82	81	78	86	327
Marianne Gerber		87	86	82	76	331
Total best 2		169	167	160	162	
*Elizabeth A. Hindhaugh						
Bermuda	Grand Total		336	504		669
Judithanne Astwood-Outerbridge		88	89	87	85	349
Diana Diel		90	90	86	93	359
Janice Trott		77	82	82	80	321
Total best 2		165	171	168	165	
*Jean Mylrea						
Costa Rica	Grand Total		333	508		681
Silvia P. Perez		88	89	89	90	356
*Silvia Siemon		78	78	88	83	327
Hilda Steinvorth		89	97	87	93	366
Total best 2		166	167	175	173	
Dominican Republic	Grand Total		349	521		682
*Brenda Corrie		75	81	79	72	307
Silvia Dowling		DQ	DQ	93	95	—
Pamela Gagnon		89	104	97	90	380
Total best 2		164	185	172	162	
Zimbabwe	Grand Total		342	513		691
E. Midgley		90	94	96	92	372
Karen Ryan		82	89	88	89	348
Linda M. Turnbull		85	86	83	89	343
Total best 2		167	175	171	178	
*Dorothy M. Mavros						

1988
THIRTEENTH WOMEN'S WORLD AMATEUR TEAM CHAMPIONSHIP FOR THE ESPIRITO SANTO TROPHY

Drottningholm Country Club, Stockholm, Sweden, September 8-11
Yardage—6,007. Par 72. 27 Team Entries.

*Team Captain		1st Round	2nd Round	3rd Round	4th Round	72-Hole Score
United States	Grand Total	147	291	439		587
Anne Sander		(80)	73	(81)	(80)	314
Pearl Sinn		76	71	73	76	296
Carol Thompson		71	(75)	75	72	293
Total best 2		147	144	148	148	
*Judy Bell						
Sweden	Grand Total	146	292	445		588
Helen Alfredsson		(75)	73	77	(75)	300
Helene Andersson		75	73	76	75	299
Eva Dahllof		71	(74)	(82)	68	295
Total best 2		146	146	153	143	
*Anders Werthen						
Great Britain/Ireland	Grand Total	149	304	452		600
Lindi Bayman		76	(79)	74	73	302
Susan Shapcott		(77)	78	74	(77)	306
Julie Wade		73	77	(78)	75	303
Total best 2		149	155	148	148	
*Jill Thornhill						
Italy	Grand Total	147	300	446		603
Marina Buscaini		76	(81)	(78)	79	314
Isabella Calogero		(80)	80	75	(82)	317
Stefania Croce		71	73	71	78	293
Total best 2		147	153	146	157	
*Lunella Rivetti						
Switzerland	Grand Total	153	304	458		603
Irene Dubs		76	(81)	(81)	(79)	317
Evelyn Orley		77	72	76	70	295
Marie Chris. De Werra		(85)	79	78	75	317
Total best 2		153	151	154	145	
*Claudia Rorholt						
Japan	Grand Total	157	309	460		603
Michiko Hattori		76	(78)	74	67	295
Chie Kihara		(82)	77	77	76	312
Asako Kita		81	75	(79)	(79)	314
Total best 2		157	152	151	143	
*Machiko Yamada						
Germany	Grand Total	150	304	464		606
Ursula Beer		78	76	84	73	311
Martina Fischer		(83)	(78)	(87)	(79)	327
Martina Koch		72	78	76	69	295
Total best 2		150	154	160	142	
*Barbara Rosner						
Netherlands	Grand Total	157	305	462		611
Mette Hageman		79	72	80	76	307
Barbara Van Strien		(84)	(83)	(81)	(90)	338
Dagmar De Vries		78	76	77	73	304
Total best 2		157	148	157	149	
*Anne-Elise Eschauzier						
New Zealand	Grand Total	154	309	459		613
Jan Cooke		77	77	75	77	306
Liz Douglas		(81)	(78)	75	77	311
Ingrid Van Steenbergen		77	78	(83)	(81)	319
Total best 2		154	155	150	154	
*Alison Bojesen-Trepka						
France	Grand Total	156	306	462		613
Delphine Bourson		80	75	77	76	308
Caroline Bourtayre		(83)	(82)	(81)	(81)	327
Valerie Pamard		76	75	79	75	305
Total best 2		156	150	156	151	
*Cecilia Mourgue d'Algue						

1988
THIRTEENTH WOMEN'S WORLD AMATEUR TEAM CHAMPIONSHIP FOR THE ESPIRITO SANTO TROPHY
Continued

*Team Captain		1st Round	2nd Round	3rd Round	4th Round	72-Hole Score
Australia	Grand Total	152	307	463		614
Louise Briers		77	(79)	78	76	310
Elizabeth Cavill		(82)	78	(80)	(77)	317
Nicole Lowien		75	77	78	75	305
Total best 2		152	155	156	151	
*G.E. Johnston						
Spain	Grand Total	152	306	459		620
Macarena Campomanes		76	78	79	(85)	318
Mary Carmen Navarro		76	76	(86)	79	317
Maria Orueta		(82)	(80)	74	82	318
Total best 2		152	154	153	161	
*Emma de Garcia-Ogara						
Canada	Grand Total	157	308	468		620
Audrey Bendick		77	76	79	75	307
Joye McAvoy		80	(78)	(82)	(82)	322
Terrill Samuel		(82)	75	81	77	315
Total best 2		157	151	160	152	
*Heather Alexander						
Denmark	Grand Total	156	309	469		620
Maren Binau		(82)	79	79	(81)	321
Mette Brandt-Andersen		75	74	81	73	303
Pernille Carlson		81	(80)	(84)	78	323
Total best 2		156	153	160	151	
*Lise Juul						
Brazil	Grand Total	154	308	465		621
Luciana Benvenutti		(83)	81	79	(80)	323
Elisabeth Nickhorn		77	73	(80)	76	306
Cristina Schmitt		77	(88)	78	80	323
Total best 2		154	154	157	156	
*Dora Cailby Nardy						
Republic of China	Grand Total	162	316	472		621
Liao Yueh-Hsiu		80	75	80	76	311
Tai Yu-Chuan		82	(89)	76	(77)	324
Tseng Hsiu-Feng		(84)	79	(88)	73	324
Total best 2		162	154	156	149	
*C.C. Hsu Niu Pearl						
Belgium	Grand Total	159	311	474		626
Sylvie Clausset		(85)	81	(86)	(90)	342
Isabelle Declercq		82	(82)	83	80	327
Aline van der Haeghen		77	71	80	72	300
Total best 2		159	152	163	152	
*Louise van den Berghe						
Mexico	Grand Total	161	314	473		630
Adriana Garcia		81	77	81	80	319
*Ana Luisa Hernandez		80	(86)	78	(81)	325
Florencia Rolz		(88)	76	(82)	77	323
Total best 2		161	153	159	157	
Argentina	Grand Total	158	318	476		631
Dolores Nava		78	(85)	79	80	322
Maria Noguerol		(81)	83	79	75	318
Nora Ventureira		80	77	(81)	(81)	319
Total best 2		158	160	158	155	
*Arturo Bengolea						
Colombia	Grand Total	156	321	484		641
Rocio Fonseca		79	(87)	78	78	322
Adriana Gomez		77	83	(86)	(81)	327
Sibile Suarez		(81)	82	85	79	327
Total best 2		156	165	163	157	
*Juan Gutierrez						
Norway	Grand Total	166	331	492		651
Anette Bech		(88)	82	(90)	82	342
Vibeke Stensrud		85	83	80	77	325
Elizabeth Vinter		81	(84)	81	(83)	329
Total best 2		166	165	161	159	
*John Edgar Nilsen						

1988
THIRTEENTH WOMEN'S WORLD AMATEUR TEAM CHAMPIONSHIP FOR THE ESPIRITO SANTO TROPHY
Continued

*Team Captain		1st Round	2nd Round	3rd Round	4th Round	72-Hole Score
Finland	Grand Total	173	332	497		654
Outi Eriksson		84	81	84	80	329
Sanna Kahiluoto		89	78	81	77	325
Marika Soravuo		(90)	(86)	(88)	(81)	345
Total best 2		173	159	165	157	
*Liisa Ahokas						
Chile	Grand Total	166	331	494		660
Ana Maria Cambiaso		82	82	(88)	86	338
Isabel Santa Maria		84	(85)	82	(90)	341
*Beatriz Steeger		(90)	83	81	80	334
Total best 2		166	165	163	166	
Venezuela	Grand Total	162	334	501		665
Maria Larrazabal		(88)	88	83	81	340
Graciela De Plaza		78	(90)	84	83	335
Angeles De Perez		84	84	(89)	(88)	345
Total best 2		162	172	167	164	
*Luis Plaza						
Iceland	Grand Total	163	329	495		667
Steinum Saemundsdottir		78	(91)	(86)	(87)	342
Karen Saevarsdottir		85	85	85	86	341
Asgerdur Sverrisdottir		(94)	81	81	86	342
Total best 2		163	166	166	172	
*Kristin Palsdottir						
Bermuda	Grand Total	173	347	510		677
J. Astwood-Outerbridge		(87)	89	81	85	342
Madeline Joell		86	(90)	82	(90)	348
Shirley Wildi		87	85	(86)	82	340
Total best 2		173	174	163	167	
*Jean Mylrea						
Portugal	Grand Total	170	339	513		681
*Teresa Abecassis		85	84	(89)	84	342
Graca Medina		85	(85)	86	84	340
Patricia Roquette		(86)	85	88	(87)	346
Total best 2		170	169	174	168	

1990
FOURTEENTH WOMEN'S WORLD AMATEUR TEAM CHAMPIONSHIP FOR THE ESPIRITO SANTO TROPHY

Russley Golf Club, Christchurch, New Zealand, October 18-21
Yardage—6,134. Par 73. 26 Team Entries.

*Team Captain

		1st Round	2nd Round	3rd Round	4th Round	72-Hole Score
United States	Grand Total	148	291	444		585
Vicki Goetze		74	(76)	74	67	291
Pat Hurst		74	71	(81)	74	300
Karen Noble		(77)	72	79	(77)	305
Total best 2		148	143	153	141	
*Katherine Graham						
New Zealand	Grand Total	152	301	451		597
Jan Higgins		74	72	74	(75)	295
Annette Stott		78	77	(82)	74	311
Lisa Aldridge		(88)	(80)	76	72	316
Total best 2		152	149	150	146	
*Peg Sargent						
Great Britain/Ireland	Grand Total	153	299	454		605
Claire Hourihane		79	72	79	74	304
Julie Hall		74	(77)	76	(79)	306
Vicki Thomas		(79)	74	(79)	77	309
Total best 2		153	146	155	151	
*Mary McKenna						
Japan	Grand Total	156	312	466		607
Michiko Hattori		79	78	78	71	306
Aki Takamura		77	78	(82)	70	307
Miki Saito		(80)	(80)	76	(80)	316
Total best 2		156	156	154	141	
*Machiko Yamada						
Australia	Grand Total	155	306	456		609
Louis Briers		78	76	73	78	305
Sarah Gautrey		(78)	75	(83)	75	311
Wendy Doolan		77	(82)	77	(86)	322
Total best 2		155	151	150	153	
*Pauline E. Sanderson						
France	Grand Total	155	304	460		611
Delphine Bourson		75	78	79	73	305
Sandrine Mendiburu		80	71	77	78	306
Kristel Mourgue-D'Algue		(81)	(80)	(80)	(80)	321
Total best 2		155	149	156	151	
*Cecilia Mourgue-D'Algue						
Germany	Grand Total	150	301	452		611
Martina Koch		77	73	75	(81)	306
Martina Fischer		(77)	78	76	79	310
Anette Jansen		73	(83)	(76)	80	312
Total best 2		150	151	151	159	
*Barbara Rosner						
Korea	Grand Total	159	313	463		611
Jae Sook Won		77	77	72	69	295
Jong Im Lee		82	(79)	78	79	318
Seung Mi Yeom		(85)	77	(78)	(81)	321
Total best 2		159	154	150	148	
*Wah Joong Yoon						
Sweden	Grand Total	160	308	463		614
Annika Sorenstam		78	71	77	74	300
Jennifer Allmark		82	77	(81)	77	317
Asa Gottmo		(83)	(83)	78	(79)	323
Total best 2		160	148	155	151	
*Pia Nilsson						
Spain	Grand Total	159	308	461		616
Esther Valera		78	74	76	75	303
Estefania Knuth		(83)	75	77	80	315
Carmen Floran		81	(79)	(80)	(80)	320
Total best 2		159	149	153	155	
*Vicky Pertierra						
Argentina	Grand Total	157	312	464		617
Maria Olivero		78	76	74	77	305
Maria Noguerol		79	(80)	(80)	76	315
Maria White		(82)	79	78	(79)	318
Total best 2		157	155	152	153	
*Maria Engenia Noguerol						

1990
FOURTEENTH WOMEN'S WORLD AMATEUR TEAM CHAMPIONSHIP
FOR THE ESPIRITO SANTO TROPHY
Continued

*Team Captain

		1st Round	2nd Round	3rd Round	4th Round	72-Hole Score
China	Grand Total	156	307	464		617
Yu-chen Huang		(79)	76	75	(79)	309
Pay-fen Lien		78	75	82	78	313
Hui-fan Huang		78	(83)	(85)	75	321
Total best 2		156	151	157	153	
*June Huang						
Denmark	Grand Total	150	305	463		619
Pernille Carlson		74	78	81	78	311
Anne Larson		(86)	77	77	78	318
Jane Kragh		76	(83)	(84)	(81)	324
Total best 2		150	155	158	156	
*Lise Juul						
Canada	Grand Total	157	312	464		620
Mary Ann Lapointe		(82)	76	77	74	309
Eve Lyne Biron		78	79	75	(83)	315
Terrill Samuel		79	(360)	NR	82	521
Total best 2		157	155	152	156	
*Heather Alexander						
Italy	Grand Total	153	306	469		622
Caterina Quintarelli		76	78	82	76	302
Silvia Cavalleri		77	(79)	(83)	77	316
Anna Nistri		(86)	75	81	(81)	323
Total best 2		153	153	163	153	
*Laura Benazzo						
Netherlands	Grand Total	158	313	471		622
Mette Hageman		75	76	78	73	302
Dagmar de Vries		(85)	79	80	78	322
Susan Huygen		83	(82)	(80)	(83)	328
Total best 2		158	155	158	151	
*Annelies E. Eschauzier						
Belgium	Grand Total	160	315	474		623
Catherine Pons		80	78	81	75	314
Aline van der Haegen		80	(82)	78	(76)	316
Sylvie Clausset		(84)	77	(86)	74	321
Total best 2		160	155	159	149	
*Maguy Reyers						
Philippines	Grand Total	157	310	473		627
Mary Grace Estuesta		77	79	83	74	313
Jamille Jose		80	74	80	80	314
Yvette de Leon		(87)	(82)	(83)	(84)	336
Total best 2		157	153	163	154	
*Wigberto Claveilla, Jr.						
Brazil	Grand Total	153	316	476		631
*Elisabeth Nickhorn		74	82	79	78	313
Cristina Schmitt		79	81	81	77	318
Beatriz Santin		(91)	(88)	(92)	(92)	363
Total best 2		153	163	160	155	
Switzerland	Grand Total	163	320	479		635
Jackie Orley		83	76	77	76	312
Sophie Ducrey		80	81	82	80	323
Priscilla Moore		(83)	(81)	(85)	(87)	336
Total best 2		163	157	159	156	
*Claudia Roerholt						
Austria	Grand Total	161	321	481		641
Ike Wieser		78	80	81	80	319
Katharine Poppmeier		(84)	80	79	80	323
Natascha Fink		83	(82)	(84)	(82)	331
Total best 2		161	160	160	160	
*Waltraud M. Neuwirth						
Mexico	Grand Total	166	323	480		641
Vinny Riviello		81	(83)	76	80	320
Roxana Lemus		85	80	81	(83)	329
Erika Diaz		(88)	77	(84)	81	330
Total best 2		166	157	157	161	
*Mary Bejarano						

1990
FOURTEENTH WOMEN'S WORLD AMATEUR TEAM CHAMPIONSHIP
FOR THE ESPIRITO SANTO TROPHY
Continued

*Team Captain

		1st Round	2nd Round	3rd Round	4th Round	72-Hole Score
Norway	Grand Total	167	327	485		644
Anna Donnestad		82	79	79	82	322
Vibeke Stensrud		85	81	79	77	322
Catherine Hoyer		(87)	(83)	(82)	(83)	335
Total best 2		167	160	158	159	
*John Edgar Nilsen						
Bermuda	Grand Total	172	329	493		654
Kim Marshall		85	81	87	82	335
Madeline Joell		(91)	76	(89)	79	335
Shirley Wildi		87	(89)	77	(84)	337
Total best 2		172	157	164	161	
*Edward Marshall						
Hong Kong	Grand Total	167	336	503		669
Sue Tonroe		85	84	(88)	84	341
Joann Hardeick		82	(96)	82	82	342
Victoria Scott		(85)	85	85	(88)	343
Total best 2		167	169	167	166	
*Indra Townsend						
Fiji	Grand Total	175	355	535		711
Sai Tuivanuavou		86	87	89	(89)	351
Kiji North		(92)	93	(94)	88	367
Lyndall Fisher		89	(102)	91	88	370
Total best 2		175	180	180	176	
*Rose Sue